WORLD LITERATURE

REVISED EDITION

ANNOTATED TEACHER'S EDITION

WORLD

LITERATURE

ANNOTATED TEACHER'S EDITION

REVISED EDITION

HOLT, RINEHART AND WINSTON
Harcourt Brace & Company

Austin • New York • Orlando • Atlanta • San Francisco • Boston • Dallas • Toronto • London

Cover: Paul Gauguin, *Ancestors of Tehemana,* 1893, oil on canvas, 76.3 × 54.3 cm.
Gift of Mr. and Mrs. Charles Deering McCormick, © 1998 The Art Institute of Chicago.

Acknowledgments: See pages T5–T6 and T16, which are extensions of the copyright page.

Printed in the United States of America

ISBN 0-03-051518-1

2 3 4 5 6 7 8   048   02 01 00 99

Acknowledgments

For permission to reprint copyrighted material, grateful acknowledgment is made to the following sources:

Addison Wesley Longman Ltd.: From "Krina" and from "The Lion's Awakening" from *Sundiata: An Epic of Old Mali* by D. T. Niane, translated by G. D. Pickett. Copyright © 1965 by Addison Wesley Longman Ltd.

Applause Theatre Books, 1841 Broadway, New York, NY 10023: From *The Life of the Drama* by Eric Bentley. Copyright © 1964 by Eric Bentley.

The Asia Society: From "Thoughts of Hanoi" by Nguyen Thi Vinh, translated by Nguyen Ngoc Bich. Copyright © 1975 by The Asia Society.

Associated University Presses: From "A Mother to Her First-Born" (Retitled: "Song of a Mother to Her Firstborn") from *Imitation. Translations from Poems of the Didinga & Lango Tribes* by J. H. Driberg. Copyright 1932 by The Golden Cockerel Press, London.

Cambridge University Press: From Ecclesiastes 9, from 1 Corinthians 13:13, from 2 Corinthians 2:4, from Galatians 3:1, from Isaiah 6:1, from John 10:11–14, and John 14:6, from Numbers 23:9, from Proverbs 15:1, Proverbs 14, and Proverbs 15:19 from *The New English Bible,* edited by William Safire. Copyright © 1961, 1970 by Oxford University Press and Cambridge University Press.

Columbia University Press: Quotation by Dogen from *Sources of Japanese Tradition* by William Theodore de Bary. Copyright © 1958 by Columbia University Press. Quotation by Ki no Tsurayuki from *The Pleasures of Japanese Literature* by Donald Keene. Copyright © 1988 by Columbia University Press. Quotation by Pan Ku from *Ssu-ma Ch'ien, Grand Historian of China,* translated by Burton Watson. Copyright © 1958 by Columbia University Press.

Farrar, Straus & Giroux: From "Russia 1812" by Victor Hugo from *Imitations,* translated by Robert Lowell. Copyright © 1961 by Robert Lowell; copyright renewed © 1986, 1987, 1989 by Caroline Lowell, Harriet Lowell, and Sheridan Lowell. From "Names of the Islands" from *Collected Poems 1948–1984* by Derek Walcott. Copyright © 1986 by Derek Walcott.

Grove Press, Inc.: From "Song 103" and from "Song 130" from *The Book of Songs,* translated by Arthur Waley. Copyright 1937 by Arthur Waley.

Harcourt Brace & Company: From "Sonnet" by Pierre de Ronsard from *Western Literature II: The Middle Ages, Renaissance, Enlightenment* by Robert Hollander and Bartlett Giamatti. Copyright © 1971 by Harcourt Brace & Company.

David Higham Associates Ltd.: From *Goethe's Faust, Parts I and II,* translated by Louis Mac-Neice. Copyright 1951, 1954 by Frederick Louis MacNeice; copyright renewed © 19— by Hedli MacNeice.

Indiana University Press: From "Laments on the War Dead" by Yehuda Amichai from *Israeli Poetry,* selected and translated by Warren Bargad and Stanley F. Chyet. Copyright © 1986 by Indiana University Press. Quotation by Li Po and quotation by Tu Fu from *An Introduction to Chinese Literature* by Liu Wu-chi. Copyright © 1966 by Liu Wu-chi.

Alfred A. Knopf, Inc.: From "Hard Roads in Shu" from *The Jade Mountain: A Chinese Anthology* by Li Po, translated by Witter Bynner. Copyright 1929 and renewed © 1957 by Alfred A. Knopf, Inc.

New Directions Publishing Corporation: From "Peonies" from *Complete Poems of Li Ch'ing-chao,* translated and edited by Kenneth Rexroth and Ling Chung. Copyright © 1979 by Kenneth Rexroth and Ling Chung.

Oxford University Press, Inc.: From "The Prodigal Son" and from "The Sower" from *The New English Bible,* edited by William Safire. Copyright © 1961, 1970 by Oxford University Press and Cambridge University Press.

Penguin Books Ltd.: "In the temple of Suma" from *The Narrow Road to the Deep North and Other Stories* by Matsuo Bashō, translated by Nobuyuki Yuasa (Penguin Classics, 1966). Copyright © 1966 by Nobuyuki Yuasa. From "The Exordium," from "The Cessation," from "Daylight," from "Comfort," from "Night," and excerpt from *The Koran,* translated by N. J.

(continued on page T16)

T6

A Chronological Survey
Of World Literature

ACKNOWLEDGMENTS
(Continued from page T6)

Yoruba quotation from *A Kì Í: Yorùbá Proscriptive and Prescriptive Proverbs* by Oyekan Owomoyela. Published by University Press of America, 1988.

From *The Experimental Novel and Other Essays* by Émile Zola, translated by Belle M. Sherman. Published by Haskell House, 1964.

From *Pushkin: Death of a Poet* by Wallace N. Vickery. Published by Indiana University Press, 1968.

CONTENTS: AN ORGANIZATION BY THEMES

TABLE OF FINE ART

INTEGRATING THE LANGUAGE ARTS

		Writing About Literature		
Selection	**Literary Elements**	**Creative Writing Response**	**Critical Writing Response**	**Language and Vocabulary/Speaking and Listening**
UNIT INTRODUCTION: WORLD MYTHS AND FOLKTALES page 2	Myths Folktales			
INTRODUCTION: TALES ABOUT BEGINNINGS page 8	Origin myths Archetype			
How the World Was Made, retold by Alice Marriott and Carol K. Rachlin page 11	Origin myth Characterization	Writing a Poem Based on a Myth	Making Inferences	Native American Words in the English Language
The Wooden People, from the **Popol Vuh**, translated by Dennis Tedlock page 18	Plot Climax Description	Narrating a Series of Events		Imagery
Coyote and the Origin of Death, retold by Richard Erdoes and Alfonso Ortiz page 23	Motivation Plot Inference	Writing a Television Script	Comparing and Contrasting Two Folktales	
INTRODUCTION: THE HERO AND THE QUEST page 26	Mythic hero Folktale hero Quest			
Theseus, retold by Robert Graves page 29	Characterization Character traits Theme	Extending the Story		Using Dialogue
Osiris and Isis, retold by Padraic Colum page 35	Point of view	Writing from a Different Point of View	Evaluating a Statement of Theme	
Green Willow, retold by Paul Jordan-Smith page 41	Conflict Mood Setting Crisis (turning point)	Writing a New Ending		Transitional Expressions: Time Order Summary
The White Snake, translated by Jack Zipes page 47	Fairy tale Moral lesson Suspense	Writing a Fairy Tale	Comparing Heroes	
BEHIND THE SCENES: THE BROTHERS GRIMM page 52	Romanticism			

UNIT 1: WORLD MYTHS AND FOLKTALES

UNIT 1: WORLD MYTHS AND FOLKTALES (CONTINUED)

Selection	Literary Elements	Writing About Literature		Language and Vocabulary/Speaking and Listening
		Creative Writing Response	Critical Writing Response	
LANGUAGE AND CULTURE: THE HERO AND THE QUEST: ALIVE AND WELL page 54	Heroic quest			

LANGUAGE SKILLS: USING TRANSITIONS FOR COMPARISON AND CONTRAST page 56				Transitions
				  Linking expressions;
				  Connectives

CRITICAL THINKING AND WRITING: DISCOVERING CONNECTIONS IN LITERATURE page 58	Subject Character Plot Imagery Theme		An Informative Essay Using Classification to Develop the Main Idea	

UNIT 2: THE AFRICAN LITERARY TRADITION

Selection	Literary Elements	Creative Writing Response	Critical Writing Response	Language and Vocabulary/Speaking and Listening
UNIT INTRODUCTION: AFRICAN LITERATURE page 64	Proverbs Praise songs Hymns Instructions Autobiographies Sacred (ritual) dramas Pastoral poetry Griots			
The Great Hymn to the Aten, translated by Miriam Lichtheim page 73	Epithet Hymn Apostrophe Point of view (second person) Repetition Parallelism	Writing a Hymn to the Sun		
BEHIND THE SCENES: DAILY LIFE IN ANCIENT EGYPT page 78				
New Kingdom Love Lyrics, translated by William Kelley Simpson page 81	Lyric poems Speaker Tone Metaphor	Writing as a Different Speaker	Comparing Love Poems	Clichés
THE ART OF TRANS-LATION: EGYPTIAN HIEROGLYPHICS page 83				Hieroglyphics Hieratic Demotic

Selection	Literary Elements	Writing About Literature		Language and Vocabulary/Speaking and Listening
		Creative Writing Response	Critical Writing Response	
African Proverbs page 85	Proverb Metaphor Alliteration Parallelism Rhyme Morals	Dramatizing a Proverb Creating Your Own Proverbs		
ELEMENTS OF LITERATURE: FEATURES OF AFRICAN ORAL LITERATURE page 88	Repetition Parallel structure Refrains			Repeat-and-vary technique Tonal assonance Call-and-response format
Song of a Mother to Her Firstborn, translated by Jack H. Driberg page 90	Cradle song Figurative language Similes Metaphors Imagery	Composing a Chant	Making and Supporting a Generalization	
African Dilemma Tales, retold by A.W. Cardinall page 95	Dilemma tales Folktales	Writing a Dilemma Tale	Analyzing Dilemma Tales	
Talk, retold by Harold Courlander page 98	Irony Situational irony Dialogue Indirect characterization Title		Identifying a Main Idea	
INTRODUCTION: FROM **SUNDIATA: AN EPIC OF OLD MALI** page 102	Epic Oral epics Primary epics Legend Griots			
From **Sundiata: An Epic of Old Mali**, translated by G.D. Pickett; retold by D.T. Niane page 105	Epic Metaphors Conflict Character Themes Context Appositive	Recording an Oral History	Explicating the Theme	Telling the Story of an Unlikely Hero Context Clues
LANGUAGE AND CULTURE: AFRICAN AMERICAN STORYTELLERS page 118				
LANGUAGE SKILLS: USING QUOTATIONS EFFECTIVELY page 120				Punctuating Brief Quotations Integrating Brief Quotations

UNIT 2: THE AFRICAN LITERARY TRADITION (CONTINUED)

Selection	Literary Elements	Writing About Literature		Language and Vocabulary/Speaking and Listening
		Creative Writing Response	Critical Writing Response	
CRITICAL THINKING AND WRITING: A PERSONAL RESPONSE TO LITERATURE page 122	Imagery Figurative Language Irony Repetition and Parallel Structure Onomatopoeia Dialogue		Developing a Generalization	

UNIT 3: THE ANCIENT MIDDLE EAST

Selection	Literary Elements	Creative Writing Response	Critical Writing Response	Language and Vocabulary/Speaking and Listening
UNIT INTRODUCTION: THE LITERATURE OF ANCIENT MESOPOTAMIA page 128				Cuneiform
INTRODUCTION: THE EPIC OF GILGAMESH page 136	Epic Archetype			
From the **Epic of Gilgamesh**, translated by N.K. Sandars page 139	Epic hero Motivations Myth Irony	Creating a New Episode of the Epic		Defending a Position
THE ART OF TRANSLATION: COMPARING TRANSLATIONS OF *GILGAMESH* page 153	Prose Verse			
INTRODUCTION: HEBREW LITERATURE page 154	Hebrew Bible Old Testament			
INTRODUCTION: THE HEBREW BIBLE page 160	Narrative Genres Psalm Torah Pentateuch Tanakh			
In the Beginning, from Genesis, King James Bible page 163	Repetition Metaphor Point of View Theme	Writing from the First-Person Point of View	Establishing a Theme	
BEHIND THE SCENES: THE KING JAMES BIBLE page 169	King James Bible Translation			

| Selection | Literary Elements | Writing About Literature | | Language and Vocabulary/Speaking and Listening |
		Creative Writing Response	Critical Writing Response	
Noah and the Flood, from Genesis, Jewish Publication Society of America page 171	Theme Character	Writing and Acting Out a Dramatic Sketch	Comparing and Contrasting Accounts of the Flood	
The Book of Ruth, King James Bible page 178	Short story Characters Setting Plot Theme Irony	Writing a Letter	Analyzing Characterization	
SEEING CONNECTIONS: BIBLICAL ALLUSIONS page 185	Literary allusion			
Psalms 23, 104, and 137, from the Book of Psalms, King James Bible page 187	Parallelism Imagery Mood		Comparing Translations of the Twenty-third Psalm	
ELEMENTS OF LITERATURE: PARALLELISM page 195	Parallelism Structural parallelism Restatement Antithesis			
INTRODUCTION: THE NEW TESTAMENT page 196	Gospels Epistle			
The Prodigal Son, The Sower, The Talents, New English Bible page 199	Parable Allegory Moral	Updating a Parable		
LANGUAGE AND CULTURE: DECIPHERING ANCIENT TEXTS page 204				Translation Cuneiform
LANGUAGE SKILLS: VARYING SENTENCE BEGINNINGS AND AVOIDING DANGLING MODIFIERS page 206				Introductory elements Dangling modifier
CRITICAL THINKING AND WRITING: WRITING AN AUTOBIOGRAPHICAL NARRATIVE page 208	Autobiography		A Narrative Essay Analyzing Causes and Effects	

INTEGRATING THE LANGUAGE ARTS

UNIT 4: GREEK AND ROMAN LITERATURES

Selection	Literary Elements	Writing About Literature		Language and Vocabulary/Speaking and Listening
		Creative Writing Response	Critical Writing Response	
UNIT INTRODUCTION: GREEK LITERATURE page 214	Epics Lyric poetry Tragedy Comedy			
INTRODUCTION: THE ILIAD page 224	Rhapsodes Conventions Invocation *In medias res* Flashbacks Epic (Homeric) similes Metrical structure Stock epithets			
From the **Iliad**, from Book 1, translated by Robert Fitzgerald page 229	Foreshadowing Flashback Character			
From the **Iliad**, from Books 22 and 24, translated by Robert Fitzgerald, page 246	Climax Epic simile Theme	Writing a Screenplay	Comparing and Contrasting Heroes	
THE ART OF TRANSLATION: A RECENT TRANSLATION OF HOMER'S *ILIAD* page 278	Images Epic simile			
Lyric poems, Sappho, translated by Mary Barnard page 281	Lyric poetry Imagery Personification	Writing a Lyric	Comparing Lyric Poetry	
Funeral Speech of Pericles, from **History of the Peloponnesian War**, Thucydides, translated by Benjamin Jowett page 286	Rhetoric Persuasion Argument		Comparing Democracies	Antithesis
From the **Apology**, from the **Dialogues**, Plato, translated by Benjamin Jowett page 295	Monologue Analogy Verbal irony Tone	Judging Socrates	Understanding Analogies	
INTRODUCTION: *OEDIPUS REX* page 302	Tragedy Tragic flaw Prologue *Parodos* Dialogue Choral odes *Exodos*			

UNIT 4: GREEK AND ROMAN LITERATURES (CONTINUED)

Selection	Literary Elements	Writing About Literature		Language and Vocabulary/Speaking and Listening
		Creative Writing Response	Critical Writing Response	
Oedipus Rex, Part 1, Sophocles, translated by Dudley Fitts and Robert Fitzgerald page 307	Dramatic irony		Analyzing Form	
Oedipus Rex, Part 2, Sophocles, translated by Dudley Fitts and Robert Fitzgerald page 342	Irony Climax Suspense Plot Tragedy	Extending the Myth	Analyzing Oedipus as a Tragic Hero	Figures of Speech Simile Metaphor Personification
A CRITICAL COMMENT: THEMES IN *OEDIPUS REX* page 367	Theme			
ELEMENTS OF LITERATURE: TRAGEDY AND THE TRAGIC HERO page 371	Tragedy Tragic hero Protagonist Catharsis			
INTRODUCTION: ROMAN LITERATURE page 372	Comedies Oratory			
INTRODUCTION: THE AENEID page 380	Epic model			
From the **Aeneid**, from **Book 2: The Fall of Troy**, Virgil, translated by Robert Fitzgerald page 383	*In medias res* Conflict Epic similes		Comparing Heroes	Analyzing an Epic Simile
A CRITICAL COMMENT: THEMES AND IMAGES IN BOOK 2 OF THE *AENEID* page 406	Theme Image Conflict			
Lyric Poems, Catullus, translated by Reney Myers, Robert J. Ormsby, and Peter Whigham page 411	Hyperbole Tone	Writing a Dramatic Scene	Comparing Lyric Poems	
The Golden Mean, Horace, translated by William Cowper; **Carpe Diem**, Horace, translated by Thomas Hawkins page 416	Ode Maxim Tone Metaphors Allusion	Writing an Advice Column	Comparing Poetic Themes	Latin Word Roots

UNIT 4: GREEK AND ROMAN LITERATURES (CONTINUED)

Selection	Literary Elements	Writing About Literature		Language and Vocabulary/Speaking and Listening
		Creative Writing Response	Critical Writing Response	
PRIMARY SOURCES: HORACE AND *THE ART OF POETRY* page 419	Treatise on writing poetry			
From **Metamorphoses**, Ovid, translated by Rolfe Humphries page 422	Allegory	Writing a Myth	Comparing Allegorical Interpretations of Myths	
The Burning of Rome, from **The Annals**, Tacitus, translated by George Gilbert Ramsay page 430	Style	Rewriting an Account		Exploring Connotations Connotations Denotations Loaded Language
LANGUAGE AND CULTURE: CLASSICAL ALLUSIONS IN MODERN ENGLISH page 436				Eponym
LANGUAGE SKILLS: MAINTAINING SUBJECT-VERB AGREEMENT page 438				Subject-verb agreement
CRITICAL THINKING AND WRITING: CREATING AN EPIC ADVENTURE page 440	Epic conventions Foreshadowing Flashback Epic similes Stock epithets Setting Conflict Character Theme	Writing a Brief Epic Adventure		

UNIT 5: INDIAN LITERATURE

Selection	Literary Elements	Writing About Literature		Language and Vocabulary/Speaking and Listening
UNIT INTRODUCTION: INDIAN LITERATURE page 446	Sanskrit literature Epic			Sanskrit Dravidian
Night, from the **Rig Veda**, translated by Wendy Doniger O'Flaherty page 456	Hymn Personification Simile	Writing a Description	Comparing and Contrasting Two Hymns	Apostrophe

UNIT 5: INDIAN LITERATURE (CONTINUED)

Selection	Literary Elements	Writing About Literature		Language and Vocabulary/Speaking and Listening
		Creative Writing Response	Critical Writing Response	
INTRODUCTION: THE MAHABHARATA page 458	Conflict Epic			
Hundred Questions, from the **Mahabharata**, translated by R.K. Narayan page 461	Theme Epic hero Setting Mood	Creating Riddles	Analyzing Theme	
Philosophy and Spiritual Discipline, from the **Bhagavad-Gita**, translated by Barbara Stoler Miller page 469	Paradox Parallelism Didactic verse	Writing a Rebuttal	Examining Paradox	
SEEING CONNECTIONS: THE *BHAGAVAD-GITA*'S INFLUENCE ON TRANSCEN-DENTALISM page 477	Transcendentalism			
Right-Mind and Wrong-Mind, from the **Panchatantra**, translated by Arthur William Ryder page 480	Epigram Fable Moral	Writing a Fable		
Rama and Ravana in Battle, from the **Ramayana**, translated by R. K. Narayan page 486	Epic External conflict Internal conflict Suspense	Writing a Sequel	Comparing Aspects of Two Indian Epics	
BEHIND THE SCENES: THE TALES BEHIND INDIA'S EPICS page 495				
LANGUAGE AND CULTURE: A GOD WITH UNIVERSAL APPEAL page 496	Trickster			
LANGUAGE SKILLS: AVOIDING SENTENCE FRAGMENTS AND RUN-ON SENTENCES page 498				Subject Verb Sentence fragment Independent clauses Run-on sentences

UNIT 5: INDIAN LITERATURE (CONTINUED)

Selection	Literary Elements	Writing About Literature		Language and Vocabulary/Speaking and Listening
		Creative Writing Response	**Critical Writing Response**	
CRITICAL THINKING AND WRITING: WRITING TO PERSUADE page 500			Writing a Persuasive Letter That Develops an Argument with Specific Reasons and Evidence	

UNIT 6: CHINESE AND JAPANESE LITERATURES

Selection	Literary Elements	Creative Writing Response	Critical Writing Response	Language and Vocabulary/Speaking and Listening
UNIT INTRODUCTION: THE LITERATURE OF CHINA page 506	Poetry Prose			Chinese characters
INTRODUCTION: THE BOOK OF SONGS page 512	Ballad			
From **The Book of Songs**, translated by Arthur Waley page 515	Repetition Refrain	Composing a Rap Song	Comparing and Contrasting Two Folk Songs	
Poems of Li Po, translated by Arthur Cooper page 520	Alliteration Mood Imagery Parallelism	Writing a Poem in Letter Form		Planning and Performing a Choral Reading
THE ART OF TRANSLATION: TRANSLATING CHINESE POETRY page 523	Translation			
Poems of Tu Fu, translated by Arthur Cooper and Kenneth Rexroth page 528	Mood Lament Tone Setting Theme Imagery Details		Comparing and Contrasting Two Poems	
Peonies, Li Ch'ing-chao, translated by Kenneth Rexroth and Ling Chung page 534	Personification Mood	Writing Song Lyrics	Analyzing the Poem's Effect	Ambiguity
From the **Analects**, Confucius, translated by Arthur Waley page 538	Maxim	Writing Maxims	Comparing and Contrasting Maxims	

UNIT 6: CHINESE AND JAPANESE LITERATURES (CONTINUED)

Selection	Literary Elements	Writing About Literature		Language and Vocabulary/Speaking and Listening
		Creative Writing Response	Critical Writing Response	
From the **Tao Te Ching**, Lao-tzu, translated by Stephen Mitchell page 543	Maxims Paradox	Creating a Dialogue	Comparing and Contrasting Two Passages	
Taoist Anecdotes, translated by Moss Roberts page 548	Anecdote		Comparing Views	Telling an Anecdote
Nieh Cheng, from **Records of the Historian**, Ssu-ma Ch'ien, translated by Burton Watson page 553	Tone Irony			Enacting a Courtroom Trial
INTRODUCTION: THE LITERATURE OF JAPAN page 558	Tanka Haiku Noh			
INTRODUCTION: TANKA POETRY page 564	Tanka			
Tanka Poems, translated by Geoffrey Bownas and Anthony Thwaite page 569	Assonance	Coauthoring a Tanka	Comparing Two Translations	
INTRODUCTION: HAIKU page 572	Haiku			
Haiku, translated by Harold G. Henderson, Peter Beilenson, and Harry Behn page 576	Imagery Tone	Writing a Haiku		
PRIMARY SOURCES: A GLIMPSE INTO A POET'S LIFE page 578				
From **The Pillow Book**, Sei Shōnagon, translated by Ivan Morris page 581	Wit	Creating a List	Writing a Character Sketch	The Active Voice
BEHIND THE SCENES: LADY MURASAKI'S TRIUMPH page 588	Novel			

UNIT 6: CHINESE AND JAPANESE LITERATURES (CONTINUED)

Selection	Literary Elements	Writing About Literature		Language and Vocabulary/Speaking and Listening
		Creative Writing Response	Critical Writing Response	
Zen Parables, translated by Paul Reps page 591	Parable Moral Symbol Paradox	Writing a Parable		Acting Out a Parable
INTRODUCTION: NOH PLAYS page 596	Noh			
Atsumori, Seami Motokiyo, translated by Arthur Waley page 600	Flat characters Round characters Conflict		Comparing Dramatic Forms	Oxymorons
PRIMARY SOURCES: FROM *THE TALE OF THE HEIKE*: "THE DEATH OF ATSUMORI" page 610	Japanese medieval epic			
LANGUAGE AND CULTURE: SENRYU: JAPAN'S COMIC VERSES page 612	Haiku Senryu			
LANGUAGE SKILLS: MAINTAINING PRONOUN-ANTECEDENT AGREEMENT page 614				Antecedents Pronoun Collective nouns
CRITICAL THINKING AND WRITING: ANALYZING IMAGERY page 616	Images Similes Metaphors Personification		Writing an Informative Essay Using Techniques of Literary Analysis	

UNIT 7: PERSIAN AND ARABIC LITERATURES

Selection	Literary Elements	Creative Writing Response	Critical Writing Response	Language
UNIT INTRODUCTION: PERSIAN AND ARABIC LITERATURES page 622	Rubá'i Ghazal			Persian Arabic
On Her Brother, al-Khansa, translated by Willis Barnstone page 631	Elegy Figures of Speech	Writing an Elegy		

UNIT 7: PERSIAN AND ARABIC LITERATURES (CONTINUED)

Selection	Literary Elements	Writing About Literature		Language and Vocabulary/Speaking and Listening
		Creative Writing Response	Critical Writing Response	
From the **Koran**, translated by N.J. Dawood page 635	Antithesis Sermon	Composing and Delivering a Sermon		
From **The Third Voyage of Sindbad the Sailor**, from **The Thousand and One Nights**, translated by N.J. Dawood page 640	Frame story Plot Conflict Complications Rising action Climax Resolution First-person point of view	Creating a Folktale	Analyzing the Narrator as a Character	
BEHIND THE SCENES: A THOUSAND AND ONE NIGHTS OF INSPIRATION page 645	Fantasy			
INTRODUCTION: THE *SHAHNAME*: THE EPIC OF PERSIA page 646	Couplet			
From **The Tragedy of Sohráb and Rostám**, from the **Shahname**, Ferdowsi, translated by Jerome W. Clinton page 649	Irony Dramatic irony First-person point of view	Writing a Diary Entry		Creating a News Report
From the **Rubáiyát**, Omar Khayyám, translated by Edward FitzGerald page 656	Rubá'i Rubáiyát Quatrain *Carpe Diem*	Writing a Rubá'i	Interpreting a Poet's Philosophy	
THE ART OF TRANSLATION: TWO TRANSLATIONS OF THE *RUBÁIYÁT* page 660	Imagery "Free translation" Literal translation			
Unmarked Boxes, Rumi, translated by John Moyne and Coleman Barks page 663	Analogy	Writing a Poem	Analyzing the Poem's Meaning	
Anecdotes and Sayings of Saadi, Saadi, translated by Idries Shah page 667	Anecdote Aphorism Moral Parable	Writing a Saying	Comparing a Sufi Saying and a Zen Parable	

UNIT 7: PERSIAN AND ARABIC LITERATURES (CONTINUED)

Selection	Literary Elements	Writing About Literature		Language and Vocabulary/Speaking and Listening
		Creative Writing Response	Critical Writing Response	
LANGUAGE AND CULTURE: WHERE THE MULLA GOES, LAUGHTER FOLLOWS page 672				Humor Folklore
LANGUAGE SKILLS: MAINTAINING VERB TENSE CONSISTENCY page 674				Verb tense sequence
CRITICAL THINKING AND WRITING: OBSERVING AND ANALYZING A PROCESS page 676	Description		Writing an Informative Essay Using Description and Process Analysis	

UNIT 8: THE MIDDLE AGES

Selection	Literary Elements	Creative Writing Response	Critical Writing Response	Language and Vocabulary/Speaking and Listening
UNIT INTRODUCTION: THE MIDDLE AGES page 682	Chronicles Epics Trouvères Ballads Romances Arthurian romances *Lais*			Vernacular
From the **Song of Roland**, translated by Frederick Goldin page 694	*Chansons de geste* Epic Epic hero Repetition Climax		Comparing Epic Heroes	Conducting an Interview
SEEING CONNECTIONS: *POEM OF THE CID*: SPAIN'S NATIONAL EPIC page 703	Epics			
Thor and Loki in Giantland, from the **Prose Edda**, Snorri Sturluson, translated by Jean I. Young page 706	Understatement Verbal irony Motif Characterization Myth	Writing a Humorous Episode		Norse Contributions to English
BEHIND THE SCENES: NORSE MYTHOLOGY AND MODERN FANTASY WRITERS page 714	Myths Sagas			

UNIT 8: THE MIDDLE AGES (CONTINUED)

Selection	Literary Elements	Writing About Literature		Language and Vocabulary/Speaking and Listening
		Creative Writing Response	Critical Writing Response	
Chevrefoil, Marie de France, translated by Robert Hanning and Joan Ferrante page 717	Metaphor Extended metaphor Conflict	Writing a Scene from a Larger Story	Analyzing a Story's Appeal	
The Grail, from **Perceval**, Chrétien de Troyes, translated by Ruth Harwood Cline page 722	Arthurian romance Description	Continuing the Narrative		Dramatizing a Scene
INTRODUCTION: THE NIBELUNGENLIED page 730	Epic Narrative poem Stanzas Couplets			
How Siegfried Was Slain, from the **Nibelunglied**, translated by A.T. Hatto page 733	Conflict Foreshadowing Foil	Writing a Persuasive Letter	Analyzing a Foil	
INTRODUCTION: THE DIVINE COMEDY page 742	Cantos Tercets Terza rima Epic			
From the **Inferno**, from the **Divine Comedy**, Dante Alighieri, translated by John Ciardi page 747	Vernacular Terza rima Symbol	Inventing a Board Game	Making a Literary Judgment	
THE ELEMENTS OF LITERATURE: ALLEGORY page 771	Allegory			
The Wife of Bath's Tale, from **The Canterbury Tales**, Geoffrey Chaucer, translated by Nevill Coghill page 774	Dynamic characters Static characters Moral			Interviewing to Find an Answer Comparing Middle English and Modern English
LANGUAGE AND CULTURE: DRAMA IN THE MIDDLE AGES page 786	Miracle plays Mystery plays Morality plays			
LANGUAGE SKILLS: CHOOSING EFFECTIVE DICTION page 788				Concrete nouns and verbs Abstract nouns and verbs

UNIT 8: THE MIDDLE AGES (CONTINUED)

| Selection | Literary Elements | Writing About Literature | | Language and Vocabulary/Speaking and Listening |
		Creative Writing Response	Critical Writing Response	
CRITICAL THINKING AND WRITING: WRITING A CHARACTER SKETCH page 790	Dialogue Setting Description	Writing a Description of a Medieval Character in a Modern Setting		

UNIT 9: FROM THE RENAISSANCE TO THE ENLIGHTENMENT

Selection	Literary Elements	Creative Writing Response	Critical Writing Response	Language and Vocabulary/Speaking and Listening
UNIT INTRODUCTION: RENAISSANCE LITERATURE page 796	Humanism Neoclassicism Metaphysical poets			
INTRODUCTION: THE SONNET IN THE RENAISSANCE page 804	Petrarchan sonnet Shakespearean sonnet Octave Sestet Volta Quatrain Couplet Meter Iambic pentameter			
Sonnet 61, Francesco Petrarch, translated by Joseph Auslander page 808 **To Hélène**, Pierre de Ronsard, translated by Robert Hollander page 809 **Sonnets 29 and 64**, William Shakespeare page 810	Sequence Meter Rhyme scheme Figures of speech Similes Metaphors Personification Oxymoron	Writing a Poem	Comparing and Contrasting Love Poems	
ELEMENTS OF LITERATURE: ENJAMBMENT page 812	Enjambment			
The Tale of the Falcon, from the **Decameron**, Giovanni Boccaccio, translated by Mark Musa and Peter Bondanella page 815	Frame story Situational irony	Exchanging Letters		A Storytelling Session

Selection	Literary Elements	Writing About Literature		Language and Vocabulary/Speaking and Listening
		Creative Writing Response	Critical Writing Response	
From **Don Quixote**, Miguel de Cervantes, translated by Samuel Putnam page 823	Courtly romances Parody Foil Epic heroes	Writing a Parody	Interpreting a Poem	
ELEMENTS OF LITERATURE: SATIRE page 838	Satire Exaggeration Verbal irony Incongruity Parody			
INTRODUCTION: THE ELIZABETHAN THEATER page 840	Stagecraft			
The Tempest, William Shakespeare **Act 1** page 845	Tragicomedies Dramatic structure Exposition (basic situation) Rising action Climax (turning point) Falling action Resolution Setting Character Imagery Theme			
Act 2 page 868	Rising action Complications Plot			
Act 3 page 890	Symbolism Climax (turning point)			
Act 4 page 905	Tone Mood Falling action Turning point			
Act 5 page 917	Resolution Epilogue Iambic pentameter Iamb End-stopped lines Enjambment Run-on lines Blank verse	Writing a Synopsis	Contrasting Characters Editing Shakespeare	Staging an Episode of the Play Blank Verse
A CRITICAL COMMENT: *THE TEMPEST* AND SHAKE-SPEARE'S VISION OF THE WORLD page 929	A critical reading of *The Tempest* as a product of Renaissance thought			

UNIT 9: FROM THE RENAISSANCE TO THE ENLIGHTENMENT (CONTINUED)

Selection	Literary Elements	Writing About Literature		Language and Vocabulary/Speaking and Listening
		Creative Writing Response	Critical Writing Response	
BEHIND THE SCENES: SHAKESPEARE AROUND THE WORLD page 933	Comedy Tragedy			
INTRODUCTION: LITERATURE OF THE ENLIGHTENMENT page 934	Rationalism Satire			
From **Fables**, Jean de La Fontaine, translated by Elizur Wright, Jr. page 942	Beast fable Epigrams Quatrain Moral	Writing a Fable		
From **Candide**, Voltaire, translated by Richard Aldington page 947	Satire	Writing a Satire	Analyzing an Author's Use of Humor	
ELEMENTS OF LITERATURE: THE UTOPIA AS A LITERARY GENRE page 963	Utopia Dystopia			
BEHIND THE SCENES: DRAMA IN THE ENLIGHTENMENT page 964	High comedy Commedia dell'arte Restoration drama			
LANGUAGE AND CULTURE: THE PRINT REVOLUTION: WHO *REALLY* INVENTED PRINTING? page 966				Gothic script Censorship
LANGUAGE SKILLS: USING ACTIVE AND PASSIVE VOICES EFFECTIVELY page 968				Voice
CRITICAL THINKING AND WRITING: RESOLVING A CONTROVERSY page 970			Writing an Informative Essay Developing a Problem and Proposing a Solution	

UNIT 10: THE NINETEENTH CENTURY: ROMANTICISM TO REALISM

Selection	Literary Elements	Writing About Literature		Language and Vocabulary/Speaking and Listening
		Creative Writing Response	Critical Writing Response	
UNIT INTRODUCTION: THE NINETEENTH CENTURY page 976	Romanticism Realism Naturalism Symbolism			
From **Faust**, **Part I**, Johann Wolfgang von Goethe, translated by Louis MacNeice page 988	Genre Drama Sturm und Drang Epic Novel Short Story Lyric Poetry Tone Tragedy Character	Writing a Speech for a Character Writing a Skit	Evaluating a Character's Actions	
The World Is Too Much with Us, William Wordsworth page 1004	Sonnet Petrarchan or Italian sonnet Iambic pentameter Octave Sestet Theme	Writing a Dialogue	Analyzing the Sonnet Form	
I Have Visited Again, Alexander Pushkin, translated by D.M. Thomas page 1008	Setting Mood Personification	Writing a Poem	Comparing Two Poems	
The Lorelei, Heinrich Heine, translated by Louis Untermeyer page 1013	Imagery Mood Tone	Writing About a Legend	Comparing Two Poems	
Russia 1812, from **The Expiation**, Victor Hugo, translated by Robert Lowell page 1017	Imagery Metaphor Irony	Writing a Newspaper Account	Comparing Poets' Views	
Invitation to the Voyage, Charles Baudelaire, translated by Richard Wilbur page 1023	Refrain Mood Images	Describing an Imaginary Land	Comparing Translations	
SEEING CONNECTIONS: THE FRENCH CONNECTION: CHARLES BAUDELAIRE AND EDGAR ALLAN POE page 1026	Symbolism			

| Selection | Literary Elements | Writing About Literature | | Language and Vocabulary/Speaking and Listening |
		Creative Writing Response	Critical Writing Response	
The Sky Is Just Beyond the Roof, Paul Verlaine, translated by Bergen Applegate page 1029 **The Sleeper of the Valley**, Arthur Rimbaud, translated by Ludwig Lewisohn page 1030	Imagery Symbols Repetition First-person point of view Mood Irony Diction	Writing a Poem	Analyzing Diction	
The Jewels, Guy de Maupassant, translated by Roger Colet page 1034	Plot Exposition Complications Climax Resolution Conflict Irony	Writing a Character Sketch	Supporting an Opinion	
A CRITICAL COMMENT: THE SHORT STORY IN THE NINETEENTH CENTURY page 1042	Realism Naturalism			
How Much Land Does a Man Need?, Leo Tolstoy, translated by Louise and Aylmer Maude page 1045	Parable Allegory Theme Resolution Conflict Foreshadow Tone	Writing an Allegory	Comparing and Contrasting Characters in Two Works	
A Problem, Anton Chekhov, translated by Constance Garnett page 1062	Plot Tone Irony Mood	Entering the Story Imagining a Character's Future		
A Doll's House, Henrik Ibsen, translated by Michael Meyer **Act 1** page 1071	Characterization Indirect characterization	Adopting a Character's Point of View		
Act 2 page 1093	Foreshadowing Symbol		Interpreting Symbolism	
Act 3 page 1109	Metaphor Extended metaphor	Writing a Fourth Act Analyzing a Character	Interpreting a Passage Identifying Themes	
A CRITICAL COMMENT: THE REALISTIC STAGE page 1127	Conflicts Realism Dialogue Characterization Stage directions			

UNIT 10: THE NINETEENTH CENTURY: ROMANTICISM TO REALISM (CONTINUED)

Selection	Literary Elements	Writing About Literature		Language and Vocabulary/Speaking and Listening
		Creative Writing Response	Critical Writing Response	
LANGUAGE AND CULTURE: THE GOTHIC NOVEL page 1128	Genre Gothic novel			
LANGUAGE SKILLS: KEEPING PRONOUN REFERENCE CLEAR page 1130				Pronoun Antecedent
CRITICAL THINKING AND WRITING: WRITING A LITERARY REVIEW page 1132	Diction Themes Figurative language Assonance Sound devices Style Tone Rhyme Meter Alliteration		Writing a Review Based on Objective Criteria	

UNIT 11: THE TWENTIETH CENTURY

UNIT INTRODUCTION: THE TWENTIETH CENTURY page 1138	Modernism Existentialism Magical realism Stream of consciousness Theater of the absurd Science fiction Latin American Boom Négritude			
Black Cat, Rainer Maria Rilke, translated by Stephen Mitchell page 1150 **The Swan**, Rainer Maria Rilke, translated by Robert Bly page 1151	Figurative language Simile Metaphor Extended metaphor	Writing a "Thing Poem" About an Animal Writing from Another Point of View		German and English
PRIMARY SOURCES: RILKE'S *LETTERS TO A YOUNG POET* page 1153				

Selection	Literary Elements	Writing About Literature		Language and Vocabulary/Speaking and Listening
		Creative Writing Response	Critical Writing Response	
The Metamorphosis, Franz Kafka, translated by Stanley Corngold page 1156	Surrealism Symbol Irony Allegory Climax Third-person point of view Motif	Writing from a Different Point of View Describing Another Metamorphosis	Analyzing a Character Responding to a Critic	Adjectives from People's Names
THE ART OF TRANSLATION: TWO TRANSLATIONS OF *THE METAMOR-PHOSIS* page 1194				Idioms
The Rat Trap, Selma Lagerlöf, translated by Florence and Naboth Hedin page 1198	Point of view Omniscient point of view Symbol Folktale	Writing a Different Conclusion	Comparing and Contrasting Characters	
Eveline, James Joyce page 1209	Epiphany Stream of consciousness Internal conflict External conflict Foreshadowing	Capturing Your Own Stream of Consciousness	Writing About an Epiphany	
The Ring, Isak Dinesen page 1216	Static character Dynamic character Protagonist Theme Symbolism Irony	Writing a Dialogue	Analyzing a Dynamic Character	Words from Place Names
Lot's Wife, Anna Akhmatova, translated by Richard Wilbur page 1225	Acmeism Stanzas Rhyme scheme Quatrains	Writing a Rhymed Stanza		
BEHIND THE SCENES: PASTERNAK'S TRIBUTE TO AKHMATOVA page 1227				
The Guitar, Federico García Lorca, translated by Rachel Benson and Robert O'Brien page 1230	Free verse Meter Rhyme scheme Imagery Alliteration Repetition Assonance Onomatopoeia Diction Rhythm		Comparing Translations	

| Selection | Literary Elements | Writing About Literature | | Language and Vocabulary/Speaking and Listening |
		Creative Writing Response	Critical Writing Response	
From **Night**, Elie Wiesel, translated by Stella Rodway page 1234	Autobiography Repetition	Narrating a Dramatic Event Writing a Script	Writing About a Title	
PRIMARY SOURCES: ELIE WIESEL ACCEPTS THE NOBEL PEACE PRIZE page 1242				
The Guest, Albert Camus, translated by Justin O'Brien page 1246	Existentialism	Continuing the Story	Writing About Existentialism	
The Enchanted Garden, Italo Calvino, translated by Archibald Colquhoun and Peggy Wright page 1259	Atmosphere Setting Descriptive details Symbolism Imagery	Creating an Atmosphere	Writing About Style	
Freedom to Breathe, A Journey Along the Oka, Alexander Solzhenitsyn, translated by Michael Glenny page 1266	Prose poetry Imagery Setting Figures of speech Simile Personification Symbolism Theme	Writing a Prose Poem Using Imagery	Analyzing the Poem's Theme	
Song of a Citizen, Czeslaw Milosz page 1272	Dramatic monologue Setting Imagery Allusion	Writing a Dramatic Monologue	Responding to a Writer's Questions	
Sonnets 49 and 71, Pablo Neruda, translated by Stephen Tapscott page 1277	Figures of speech Metaphor Personification Imagery Petrarchan sonnet	Creating a Love Collage	Comparing and Contrasting Sonnets	
Borges and Myself, Jorge Luis Borges, translated by N.T. di Giovanni and Jorge Luis Borges page 1282	First-person point of view Narrator	Letting a "Double" Speak		
SEEING CONNECTIONS: THE DIVIDED SELF page 1284	Modernism			

UNIT 11: THE TWENTIETH CENTURY (CONTINUED)

Selection	Literary Elements	Writing About Literature		Language and Vocabulary/Speaking and Listening
		Creative Writing Response	Critical Writing Response	
Wind and Water and Stone, Octavio Paz, translated by Mark Strand page 1287	Personification	Personifying Nature		
The Handsomest Drowned Man in the World, Gabriel García Márquez, translated by Gregory Rabassa page 1291	Myth Metamorphosis Allusions Magic realism Setting Theme Third-person point of view	Changing the Premise	Analyzing Magic Realism	
The Night Face Up, Julio Cortázar, translated by Paul Blackburn page 1300	Suspense Setting Details Simile Sensory details		Interpreting the Story	
And of Clay Are We Created, Isabel Allende, translated by Margaret Sayers Peden page 1310	Irony Situational irony Point of view Theme Metaphor Allusion	Writing a Scene	Comparing Fact and Fiction	
A Walk to the Jetty, from **Annie John**, Jamaica Kincaid page 1322	Internal conflict Character Metaphor	Describing a Place	Analyzing an Internal Conflict	
SEEING CONNECTIONS: *TALES OF THE ISLANDS* BY DEREK WALCOTT page 1329	Epigraph			
And We Shall Be Steeped, Léopold Sédar Senghor, translated by John Reed and Clive Wake page 1332	Négritude Imagery Alliteration Assonance	Writing About Heritage	Writing About Négritude	
Life Is Sweet at Kumansenu, Abioseh Nicol page 1336	Theme Foreshadowing		Writing About Foreshadowing	African Languages and English
Marriage Is a Private Affair, Chinua Achebe, page 1345	Verbal irony Conflict Subject Theme	Writing a Sequel	Analyzing a Conflict	

UNIT 11: THE TWENTIETH CENTURY (CONTINUED)

Selection	Literary Elements	Writing About Literature		Language and Vocabulary/Speaking and Listening
		Creative Writing Response	Critical Writing Response	
The Train from Rhodesia, Nadine Gordimer page 1353	Conflict External conflict Setting Personification Symbol	Writing an Interior Monologue	Analyzing Details	
In the Shadow of War, Ben Okri page 1360	Atmosphere Setting Character Symbol	Writing from a Different Perspective	Evaluating an Opinion	
From **Kaffir Boy**, Mark Mathabane page 1367	Autobiography	Writing an Autobiographical Episode	Writing About an Author's Purpose	
Half a Day, Naguib Mahfouz, translated by Denys Johnson-Davies page 1379	Theme Foreshadowing	Writing About a Childhood Memory	Comparing Themes in Two Stories	Arabic and English
From **Laments on the War Dead**, Yehuda Amichai, translated by Warren Bargad and Stanley F. Chyet page 1385	Repetition Incremental repetition Extended simile Elegy	Writing an Elegy	Writing About an Extended Simile	Hebrew and English
By Any Other Name, Santha Rama Rau page 1389	Essay Formal essay Informal (personal) essay	Writing a Personal Essay	Analyzing an Essay's Purpose	
The Silver Fifty-Sen Pieces, Yasunari Kawabata, translated by Lane Dunlop and J. Martin Holman page 1397	Theme Character Symbol	Describing a Special Object	Exploring a Theme	East Asian and Pacific Languages
Cranes, Hwang Sun-won, translated by Peter H. Lee page 1404	Conflict Internal conflict External conflict Flashbacks Symbolism	Writing About a Moment of Decision	Writing About Conflict	
Thoughts of Hanoi, Nguyen Thi Vinh, translated by Nguyen Ngoc Bich page 1411	Lyric poem Speaker Paradox	Writing a Poem	Comparing Viewpoints	
Love Must Not Be Forgotten, Zhang Jie, translated by Gladys Yang page 1416	Flashback	Writing a Diary Entry		Wade-Giles and Pinyin Transliterations

UNIT 11: THE TWENTIETH CENTURY (CONTINUED)

Selection	Literary Elements	Writing About Literature		Language and Vocabulary/Speaking and Listening
		Creative Writing Response	Critical Writing Response	
LANGUAGE AND CULTURE: CONSCIENCE AND CONTROVERSY page 1428				Censorship
LANGUAGE SKILLS: VARYING SENTENCES page 1430				Simple sentence Independent clause Compound sentence Complex sentence Dependent (subordinate) clause Compound-complex sentence
CRITICAL THINKING AND WRITING: IDENTIFYING A THEME page 1432	Theme		Writing an Informative Essay Identifying the Theme of a Story	

PROGRAM DESCRIPTION

FEATURES OF THE *WORLD LITERATURE* PUPIL'S EDITION

The Pupil's Edition of *World Literature* presents a chronological survey of world literature, integrating literature with writing, vocabulary, language, and speaking/listening activities. The Pupil's Edition includes a number of features that will enable students to approach world literature with greater confidence and a sense of active participation in the reading process.

UNIT FEATURES

Unit Openers clearly and succinctly present the Place, Time, and Literary Significance of the literature contained in the unit, providing students with an at-a-glance context for the works they are about to read.

Time Lines visually convey the important literary and cultural/historical events relevant to the culture or time period being covered in the unit.

Unit Introductions provide a concise background to the literature in the unit, providing students with a necessary context for a full appreciation of the literature to be covered in the unit. Side-margin quotations from famous authors and texts, as well as summary statements, highlight and amplify material covered in the introduction. Most artwork is captioned to provide further information or to pose critical-thinking questions. Maps are included where applicable to give students a sense of place and culture.

END-OF-UNIT FEATURES

Language and Culture is a motivational "just for fun" feature that explores some interesting aspect of language, literature, or culture not covered elsewhere in the unit.

Language Skills features enable students to integrate grammar, usage, and mechanics with literature and composition. This special feature directly prepares students for the culminating end-of-unit writing assignment.

Critical Thinking and Writing leads students through the steps of the writing process toward the successful completion of a major creative or critical writing assignment.

SELECTIONS

SEF/Art Resource, New York

Selection Introductions precede major works that require the students to have more in-depth knowledge of the work before they start to read.

An **Author Biography** page precedes each selection by a known author, providing students with interesting and pertinent biographical information that will inform their reading of the work.

A **Reader's Guide** precedes every selection, giving students adequate prereading information, motivation, and a purpose for reading. A brief Background section provides students with necessary information that will help them to approach the selection with a knowledge and awareness of cultural or historical meanings that inform the work. In the case of selections that are excerpts from longer works, Background serves to bring students "up to date" on what has been occurring in the narrative thus far. A Writer's or Oral Response activity serves as a useful prereading exercise to focus students' attention on the literary work and activate their own anticipatory responses to issues that are addressed in the literature they are about to read. A Literary Focus enables students to review or learn about for the first time a salient element of literature in the literary work: irony, plot, characterization, theme, and so on.

A **Headnote** precedes each selection, setting a purpose for reading.

Critical Thinking Questions accompany many of the works of art used to illustrate each selection, engaging the students in a dialogue between art and text.

A **First Thoughts** reader response question immediately follows each selection, eliciting the students' first and most immediate reaction to the selection they have just read.

Identifying Facts questions tap students' basic comprehension of the selection.

Interpreting Meanings offers interpretive and analytical discussion questions that explore the students' deepest understanding of the selection.

An **Applying Meanings** question combines reader response strategies with higher-level interpretation and analytic skills, asking students to form reasoned judgments about the literary work or to find real-world applications for key concepts they have discovered in their reading.

Creative Writing Response assignments give students the opportunity to use the literary selection as a springboard for imaginative assignments, such as writing a sequel to a selection, composing a haiku, writing a biography of a character, or transforming a scene into a screenplay.

Critical Writing Response assignments provide opportunities for analysis, comparison and contrast, and other higher-level thinking skills writing exercises. Students may be asked to compare a new piece of literature to one they have just read; defend their point of view; compare or contrast translations, themes, or characters; or analyze the use of a particular literary element in a selection.

Speaking and Listening activities invite students to deliver speeches, record passages from selections, dramatize scenes, and engage in a diversity of speaking and listening activities.

Language and Vocabulary activities suggested by the selections help students to increase their vocabularies and appreciate various aspects of language, from etymologies to word analogies.

SPECIAL FEATURES

Throughout the *World Literature* Pupil's Edition are a diversity of motivational features that extend and amplify material treated in the text.

■ **Behind the Scenes** features provide students with interesting information that will extend their knowledge of authors' lives, fascinating aspects of a culture, facts about the origins of literary works, information about various genres and literary movements only touched upon in the text, and so on.

■ **Seeing Connections** features serve to point out the often fascinating connections that can be made between one time period and another, between the literature of one culture and another, or the influences and literary "cross-pollinations" that exist between one work of literature and another.

■ **The Art of Translation** gives students an appreciation of the translator's craft, showing the various triumphs and pitfalls involved in translating from one language to another.

■ **Elements of Literature** highlights and expands instruction on particularly important or challenging literary terms, such as parallelism, allegory, and tragedy.

■ **Primary Sources** gives students added insight into a writer's life and times or provides information about the origin of a literary work.

■ **A Critical Comment** follows several of the more challenging literary works, summarizing for students some of the main points about the selection, such as its dominant themes or images.

END-OF-BOOK FEATURES

Glossary

The backmatter of the *World Literature* Pupil's Edition contains many important resources that you and your students will want to refer to often.

■ **Writing About Literature** is a concise handbook of important general information that students need in order to succeed when they are composing essays or writing on test questions about literature: recognizing key verbs in essay questions; how to write and revise an essay; and how to document sources in a research paper.

■ **Grammar, Usage, and Mechanics: A Reference Guide** serves as a mini-handbook to various common usage and mechanics problems that students face as they write about literature.

■ **A Handbook of Literary Terms** is a reference guide to the important literary terms that students will encounter throughout the text.

■ The **Glossary** provides definitions for hundreds of high-utility vocabulary words the students will encounter in the literary works in the book.

■ The **Index of Skills** is an important reference that will point you and your students to the literary, language and vocabulary, speaking and listening, composition, and critical thinking skills taught throughout the book.

■ The **Index of Authors and Titles** is a thorough list of every author, translator, and selection that appears in the Pupil's Edition.

FEATURES OF THE *WORLD LITERATURE* ANNOTATED TEACHER'S EDITION

The annotations in this text have been prepared to help you plan your lessons and your class discussions and to help you to evaluate student achievement. The following types of annotations are featured in the Annotated Teacher's Edition:

UNIT OPENERS AND TIME LINES

Humanities Connection. Annotations are provided for the unit opener artwork on the map spread that opens each unit. These annotations are specifically labeled, and they identify and provide additional cultural and historical background to the illustrative elements included on the map border.

Discussing the Time Line. Notes labeled Literary, Cultural, or Historical Background help you to direct the students' attention to important events noted on the Time Line spread.

UNIT INTRODUCTIONS

Unit Objectives. This feature lists three or four general objectives that pertain to the unit as a whole.

Teacher's Resources. This boxed feature gives you a quick overview of the various supplementary materials, such as Unit Introduction and Unit Review Tests, that are available to accompany the unit as a whole.

Teaching the Unit. This annotation provides an overview of the unit and gives specific teaching suggestions that will help to make the unit relevant and lively for the students. The note also addresses concepts or specific selections that students may find problematic, giving specific suggestions on how to present challenging or unfamiliar material effectively.

Making Connections. This annotation ties the literature of the unit to that of other times and places, stressing the comparative aspects of the study of world literature. It shows how the literature of the culture or time period has been influenced by the literature of other times and places, and ties the literature of the culture to later literary, historical, or cultural developments.

Reading Check. Five or ten brief, factual recall questions accompany every unit introduction, enabling you to quickly assess student comprehension of important points covered in the unit introduction.

For Further Study. Here you will find lists of relevant books, articles, and even films and videos that you and your students can use to extend your knowledge and appreciation of the culture or time period covered in the unit. Additional suggestions for further reading can be found in the Teaching Notes booklet that accompanies this program.

---

1 HISTORICAL BACKGROUND
Settlers of the Nile Valley:
Archaeological evidence shows that the early settlers of Egypt had established farms along the Nile by 4000 B.C. Two features made the Nile Valley an ideal place for an advanced culture to develop. First, the valley was fairly safe from attack. Second, the flooding of the Nile, resulting from heavy rains and melting snow in the mountains of present-day Ethiopia, occurred at the same time each year so that Egyptians could plan their planting and harvesting around the flood periods. Thus life in the Nile Valley was ordered and secure.

page 64

IN ADDITION TO GENERAL ANNOTATIONS GIVEN IN THE UNIT INTRODUCTIONS, SEVERAL SPECIFIC TYPES OF SIDE COLUMN ANNOTATIONS ARE PROVIDED:

Responding to the Quotation. Quotations by famous people or from major texts of the culture or period appear in the margins throughout unit introductions. Annotations are provided to supply background information to the quotations. In addition, the annotation ends with a question directed to the students, eliciting their response to the quotation. ▶

◀ **Cultural, Literary, and Historical Background.** Each of these annotations expands upon information given in the text and is followed by a subhead that quickly identifies the subject under discussion.

---

2 RESPONDING TO THE QUOTATION
The Maxims of Ptahhotpe dates from the Old Kingdom and is an early example of the instruction genre of Egyptian literature, offering rules for daily conduct. An emphasis on the importance of truth and justice recurs throughout the literature of the ancient Egyptians.
❓ *Which modern maxims or rules stress the value of truth?* (Most religious codes call for truthfulness; students may suggest such sayings as "The truth shall make you free.")

page 64

Teaching Tip. In this note you will find activities and helpful hints that will enable you to convey some of the more challenging material in the unit to students who find particular concepts difficult to grasp. ▶

Other side column annotations in the unit introductions, such as **Humanities Connections**, **Reader's Response**, **Cultural Diversity**, and **Writing to Learn**, also appear with individual selections and are described on the pages that follow.

THE SELECTIONS

Each selection will have numbered annotations that correspond to bracketed material from the text, as well as some unnumbered annotations that provide more general information to specific parts of the selection. Most selections are divided into several parts: the author biography page, the Reader's Guide page, and the selection (with apparatus) itself. The annotations provided for each selection allow you to adapt your lectures or discussions to classes of varying abilities. The following annotations are provided for each part of the selection:

TEACHING TIP

To help students understand why some African languages remained unwritten, remind them that the African oral tradition was highly developed, with bards, messengers, and oral historians trained to memorize the equivalent of multiple volumes of literature and factual data. Africa's remarkable oral tradition filled many of the needs that writing filled for other cultures. So that students can appreciate the skills required to maintain an oral tradition, assign them to memorize and recite one-page excerpts of their choice from this unit. You might want to have them present their recitations as African oral performances traditionally are presented, with props, gestures, and audience participation in the form of help when the performer stumbles.

page 69

AUTHOR BIOGRAPHY PAGE

◀ **More About the Author.** Here you will find intriguing supplementary information about the author. This annotation may include "literary gossip" of interest to the students and/or quotes from or about the author.

About the Translator. This note provides brief biographical information about the translator of the selection. ▶

MORE ABOUT THE AUTHOR

Saadi was middle-aged when he returned to Shiraz, the capital of the southern Persian province of Fars, and began writing. He was unusually versatile, composing in both Arabic and Persian (Farsi), and producing numerous lyrics and odes as well as *The Orchard* (epic verse) and *The Rose Garden* (primarily prose).

Saadi himself explained that the idea for *The Rose Garden* came to him in the springtime, after a period of dissatisfaction with his life. He saw a friend carrying a basket of roses, chided the friend for valuing something so transitory, and then found himself saying, "I am able to form a book of roses, which . . . will flourish forever." The friend challenged him to do so, and in a few days Saadi had the first two chapters "written out in my notebook, in a style that may be useful to orators and improve the skill of letter-writers." The rest of the book was finished before the summer ended. "I abridged the work," explained Saadi, "that it might not be thought tedious. . . . My design was to give advice, and I have spoken accordingly."

page 665

ABOUT THE TRANSLATOR

Jerome W. Clinton (1937–) teaches Near Eastern Studies at Princeton University. Of "The Tragedy of Sohráb and Rostám," he says, "What I like about teaching it is that, although it seems different at first—the names are unfamiliar, it's set in the East—the further you go into it, the more real and familiar and human it becomes."

page 647

READER'S GUIDE PAGE

Prereading Focus. This annotation provides additional information to supplement the Background, Writer's (or Oral) Response, and/or the Literary Focus on the Reader's Guide page.

■ **Background:** Where necessary, this annotation extends information given in the Background section.

SELECTION PAGES: TOP MARGIN TEACHING FEATURES

In the top margins of each individual selection, various recurring features appear to help you create a consistent lesson cycle for teaching each selection. These top margin features include:

Objectives. For every selection, specific, measurable objectives are provided. The first objective focuses on the genre or the selection as a whole; the second objective relates to the Literary Focus on the Reader's Guide page; and the third objective focuses on the end-of-selection writing assignments. An occasional fourth or fifth objective will focus on Language and Vocabulary skills or Speaking and Listening activities provided at the end of a selection.

Themes in World Literature. This boxed feature lists other selections in other parts of the book that share a thematic relationship to the selection students are about to read. This feature uses the same thematic categories that may be found in the Contents: An Organization by Themes in this Annotated Teacher's Edition.

Vocabulary in Context. This boxed list consists of five or ten high-utility vocabulary words chosen from the selection, and it is presented as a preview at the beginning of the selection. You may use the Vocabulary in Context box to preteach important vocabulary words. In the selection itself, these vocabulary words are underlined on the reduced pupil's page and defined in a side-margin note, enabling you to teach the vocabulary in context. These same words appear in the student's glossary, as well as on accompanying Vocabulary Activity Worksheets and Vocabulary Tests that appear in the *World Literature* Core Components Binder.

Integrating the Language Arts. This recurring feature gives you more options for integrating the study of literature and language. A specific grammar, usage, mechanics, or other language arts activity (indicated by a subhead) is presented with instruction and exercises, enabling you to integrate the skills into the teaching of the selection. ▼

INTEGRATING THE LANGUAGE ARTS: GRAMMAR

Placement of Adverbs

Adverbs—words that modify verbs, adjectives, or other adverbs—can often be placed in more than one position within a sentence. This flexibility allows the writer to consciously position adverbs for emphasis or rhythmic effect. Examples:

<u>Again</u> they firmly hitched their steeds . . .
(Compare with: *They firmly hitched their steeds <u>again</u>*)
He <u>swiftly</u> drew a dagger from his belt
(Compare with: *Swiftly he drew . . .* or *He drew a dagger <u>swiftly</u> . . .*)

Speaking and Listening. On the board, write this sentence from lines 76–77: ". . . For now / It does no good to slay yourself with grief." Ask volunteers to say the sentence aloud, moving the adverb *now* to other positions where it will make sense. Have others listen for changes in meaning, emphasis, or rhythm. ■

page 649

Reading Check. Five or ten brief factual recall questions are provided with most prose selections and longer narrative poems. These quick-check questions can help you to determine whether everyone in class has read the selection, and they can also help you to briefly recap the major events in the selection. You might want to use these questions as brief quizzes before the students approach the questions that follow the selection, which call for higher-level thinking skills.

Reteaching. This feature presents various creative activities (usually involving music, drama, art, and speaking and listening skills) that will help students review all or part of a selection. The Reteaching activity is especially helpful with students who find the material challenging and who would benefit from participating in a creative activity that helps them understand the main points of a selection they have read.

Extension and Enrichment. This note appears at the end of every selection. It suggests ways that you can carry the lesson beyond the book with creative projects or with further writing assignments, including research projects.

Closure. To close your lesson—and to review for students the main thrust of the instruction—you need to provide closure. Every selection ends with a suggested closure activity that helps you to tie up the lesson and perhaps preview the next selection. The activities are often oral, and the entire closing procedure should take only from five to ten minutes.

NOTE TO TEACHERS

ABRIDGED, ADAPTED, AND EXCERPTED LITERARY WORKS USED IN THIS TEXT

The following selection includes minor abridgments. This selection contains material deemed sensitive for use in a high school classroom. This material could be deleted without compromising the integrity of the original work. Deletions are indicated by ellipses (. . .).

A Doll's House (derogatory racial reference)

The following selection was abridged due to the presence of lengthy and obscure digressions, the absence of which in no way compromises the integrity of the original work.

"The Great Hymn to the Aten"

The following selections are abridgments of book-length works that cannot be included in their entirety. The featured excerpts were chosen with an eye to the literary, cultural, and historical elements that characterize the work as a whole. Intervening episodes are summarized in bridging passages where applicable and necessary for comprehension of the work as a whole.

from *Sundiata*
from the *Epic of Gilgamesh*
from Books 1, 22, and 24 of the *Iliad*
from Book 2 of the *Aeneid*
Lais 110, 130–134, 168–171, 173, 174, and 176 from the *Song of Roland*
Cantos 1, 3, 5, 33, and 34 from the *Inferno,* from the *Divine Comedy*
from *Don Quixote*
from *Candide*
from *Faust, Part I*

The following selections are episodes from far larger works. Excerpts were chosen on the basis of key literary elements and salient cultural and historical characteristics contained therein.

"The Wooden People," from the *Popol Vuh*
Funeral Speech of Pericles from *History of the Peloponnesian War*
The *Apology* from the *Dialogues*
"The Creation" and "The Four Ages" from *Metamorphoses*
"Night" from the *Rig Veda*
"Hundred Questions" from the *Mahabharata*
"Philosophy and Spiritual Discipline" from the *Bhagavad-Gita*
"Rama and Ravana in Battle" from the *Ramayana*
"Right-Mind and Wrong-Mind" from the *Panchatantra*
"Nieh Cheng" from *Records of the Historian*
"In Spring It Is Dawn," from "Hateful Things," "Things That Cannot Be Compared," "Embarrassing Things," "Masahiro Really Is a Laughing Stock," and "Pleasing Things" from *The Pillow Book*
From "The Third Voyage of Sindbad the Sailor," from *The Thousand and One Nights*
From "The Tragedy of Sohráb and Rostám," from the *Shahname*
"The Exordium," "The Cessation," "Daylight," and "Comfort" from the Koran
"Thor and Loki in Giantland" from the *Prose Edda*
"How Siegfried Was Slain" from the *Nibelungenlied*
"The Grail" from *Perceval*
"The Wife of Bath's Tale" from *The Canterbury Tales*
"The Tale of the Falcon" from the *Decameron*
"A Walk to the Jetty" from *Annie John*
from *Night*
from *Kaffir Boy*
from *Laments on the War Dead*
from *Love Must Not Be Forgotten*

Special titles or minor abridgments to existing titles were given to the following selections for their use in the anthology:

"The Wooden People"
"Song of a Mother to Her Firstborn"
"Thor and Loki in Giantland"
"The Tale of the Falcon"
"The Lorelei"
"Invitation to the Voyage"

WORLD LITERATURE

REVISED EDITION

HOLT, RINEHART AND WINSTON
Harcourt Brace & Company

Austin • New York • Orlando • Atlanta • San Francisco • Boston • Dallas • Toronto • London

ACKNOWLEDGMENTS

Field Test Participants

We wish to thank the following people, who participated in field testing of prepublication materials.

Patricia L. Ely
Reading Senior High School
Reading, Pennsylvania

Carol H. Farthing
Bangor High School
Bangor, Maine

Art Garbosky
Corona del Sol High School
Tempe, Arizona

Delmas E. Hare
Westlake High School
Atlanta, Georgia

Leslie M. Moore
Jenks High School
Jenks, Oklahoma

Fred B. Myers
Katella High School
Anaheim, California

Wendell Schwartz
Adlai E. Stevenson
  High School
Prairie View, Illinois

Marian S. Sheidy
Wheaton Central High School
Wheaton, Illinois

Sandra R. Walter
Boston Latin High School
Boston, Massachusetts

John R. Williamson
Johnson Central Senior High School
Paintsville, Kentucky

WRITERS

Susan Wittig Albert has a Ph.D. in English from the University of California, Berkeley. She has taught at the University of Texas at Austin, Southwest Texas State University, and Tulane University. She is the author of *Stylistic and Narrative Structures in Middle English Verse Romances.*

Richard Cohen is the author of three novels, including *Say You Want Me*, which was nominated for the Pulitzer Prize. He has taught creative writing at the University of Wisconsin, Madison.

Rose Sallberg Kam received her M.A. in English from California State University, Sacramento, and taught English at the secondary level for seventeen years. She has been a freelance writer of educational materials since 1983. She is currently writing a book on biblical women.

David Adams Leeming is a professor of English and Comparative Literature at the University of Connecticut, Storrs. For several years, he taught English at Robert College in Istanbul, Turkey. He is the author of *Mythology: The Voyage of the Hero; Flights: Readings in Magic, Mysticism, Fantasy, and Myth; Mythology;* and *The World of Myth.*

Thomas Monsell has taught secondary English, including Shakespearean drama, for twenty years. He has directed many school productions of Shakespeare's plays and has acted in and directed stock and community theaters.

Carroll Moulton has a Ph.D. from Yale University and has taught Classical Studies at Princeton University and Duke University. He is the author of *Similes in the Homeric Poems* and the translator of Menander's *Dyskolos.* He has been writing and editing educational materials for nearly fifteen years.

Susanna Nied received her M.A. from San Diego State University. She teaches comparative literature at the university level and is the translator of several modern Scandinavian literary works.

Eileen Hillary Oshinsky has been a freelance writer and anthologist for more than fifteen years. She specializes in American, British, and World literatures as well as in grammar and composition.

REVIEWERS AND CONSULTANTS

James Aune
St. Olaf College
Northfield, Minnesota

Abena P. A. Busia
Rutgers University
New Brunswick, New Jersey

Joan M. Crimmins
Bunnell High School
Stratford, Connecticut

Betty Sue Flowers
University of Texas at Austin
Austin, Texas

Robert Fox
Southern Illinois University
Carbondale, Illinois

Nancy Gardner
Mooresville High School
Mooresville, North Carolina

James D. Garrison
University of Texas at Austin
Austin, Texas

Margaret Garrison
Peninsula High School
Gig Harbor, Washington

Donald Gray
University of Indiana
Bloomington, Indiana

Julie H. Hiebert
University of Texas at Austin
Austin, Texas

Gerald B. Kinneavy
University of Colorado
Boulder, Colorado

David Adams Leeming
University of Connecticut
Storrs, Connecticut

Dore J. Levy
Brown University
Providence, Rhode Island

Dan McLeod
San Diego State University
San Diego, California

Barbara Stoler Miller
Barnard College
New York, New York

Richard Murphy
University of Texas at Tyler
Tyler, Texas

Frank Occhiogrosso
Drew University
Madison, New Jersey

Fernando Operé
University of Virginia
Charlottesville, Virginia

Gretchen Polnac
Reagan High School
Austin, Texas

John R. Williamson
Johnson Central Senior
   High School
Paintsville, Kentucky

ACKNOWLEDGMENTS

For permission to reprint copyrighted material, grateful acknowledgment is made to the following sources:

Addison Wesley Longman Ltd.: From "Krina" and from "The Lion's Awakening" from *Sundiata: An Epic of Old Mali* by D. T. Niane, translated by G. D. Pickett. Copyright © 1965 by Addison Wesley Longman Ltd.

The American-Scandinavian Foundation: From *The Life of Ibsen*, Vol. II, by Halvdan Koht. Copyright 1931 by The American-Scandinavian Foundation.

The Asia Society: "Thoughts of Hanoi" by Nguyen Thi Vinh, translated by Nguyen Ngoc Bich. Copyright © 1975 by The Asia Society.

Associated University Presses: "A Mother to Her Firstborn" (Retitled: "Song of a Mother to Her Firstborn") from *Initiation: Translations from Poems of the Didinga & Lango Tribes* by J. H. Driberg. Copyright 1932 by The Golden Cockerel Press, London.

Bantam Books, a division of Bantam Doubleday Dell Publishing Group, Inc.: From "The Second Teaching: Philosophy and Spiritual Decline" from *The Bhagavad-Gita*, translated by Barbara Stoler Miller. Translation copyright © 1986 by Barbara Stoler Miller. "The White Snake" from *The Complete Fairy Tales of the Brothers Grimm*, Vol. 1, translated by Jack Zipes. Translation copyright © 1987 by Jack Zipes.

Robert Bly: "The Guitar" by Federico García Lorca from *Lorca and Jiménez: Selected Poems,* chosen and translated by Robert Bly. Copyright © 1973 by Robert Bly. Published by Beacon Press, Boston, 1973.

Georges Borchardt, Inc. on behalf of Stanley Corngold: The Metamorphosis by Franz Kafka, edited and translated by Stanley Corngold. Copyright © 1972 by Stanley Corngold.

Cambridge University Press: "The Talents" and excerpts from Isaiah 62:1, John 14:6, Numbers 23:9, Proverbs 15:1, 15:4, 15:19 from *The New English Bible*, edited by William Safire. Copyright © 1961, 1970 by Oxford University Press and Cambridge University Press.

Carcanet Press Limited: "Theseus: An Ancient Myth" from *Greek Gods and Heroes* by Robert Graves. Copyright © 1960 by Robert Graves.

John Cech: "The Storytelling Stone," retold by John Cech from *Parabola, The Magazine of Myth and Tradition,* vol. IV, no. 4, 1979. Copyright © 1979 by John Cech.

China Books & Periodicals, Inc.: "Love Must Not Be Forgotten" and from "Biographical Note—My Boat" by Zhang Jie, translated by Gladys Yang from *Love Must Not Be Forgotten,* edited by Gladys Yang. Copyright © 1986 by China Books.

Public Administrator of the County of New York, as administratrix of the estate of Padraic Colum: "Osiris and Isis" from *Orpheus: Myths of the World* by Padraic Colum. Copyright 1930 by Padraic Colum.

Columbia University Press: From "Kamo Marbuchi: Kokuiko," translated by Heinrich Dumoulin, and quotation by Fujiwara no Teika, translated by Ryusaku Tsunoda from *Sources of Japanese Tradition,* compiled by Ryusaku Tsunoda, William Theodore de Bary, and Donald Keene. Copyright © 1958 by Columbia University Press. From *The Pillow Book of Sei Shōnagon,* translated by Ivan Morris. Copyright © 1991 by Ivan Morris. From "Introduction" from *The Columbia Book of Chinese Poetry,* translated and edited by Burton Watson. Copyright © 1984 by Columbia University Press. "Nieh Cheng" from *Records of the Historian: Chapters from the Shih chi of Ssu-ma Ch'ien,* translated by Burton Watson. Copyright © 1958, 1961, 1962, 1969 by Columbia University Press.

Doubleday, a division of Bantam Doubleday Dell Publishing Group, Inc.: "Marriage Is a Private Affair" from *Girls at War and Other Stories* by Chinua Achebe. Copyright © 1972, 1973 by Chinua Achebe. "Psalm 23" from *The Anchor Bible* by Mitchell Dahood. Translation, Introduction and Notes copyright © 1966 by Doubleday, a division of Bantam Doubleday Dell Publishing Group, Inc. From *The Iliad* by Homer, translated by Robert Fitzgerald. Copyright © 1974 by Robert Fitzgerald. "Old pond" and transliteration of "Old pond" by Bashō, comment by Harold Henderson, "A morning-glory vine" by Kobayashi Issa, "On top of skeletons" by Onitsura, and "If to the moon" by Sokan from *An Introduction to Haiku,* translated by Harold G. Henderson. Copyright © 1958 by Harold G. Henderson. "Half a Day" from *The Time and the Place and Other Stories* by Naguib Mahfouz, translated by Denys Johnson-Davies. Copyright © 1991 by the American University in Cairo Press. Six senryū from *The Country of Eight Islands,* edited and translated by Hiroaki Sato and Burton Watson. Copyright © 1981 by Hiroaki Sato and Burton Watson.

Dutton Signet, a division of Penguin Books USA Inc.: "Borges and Myself" from *The Aleph and Other Stories* by Jorge Luís Borges, translated by Norman Thomas di Giovanni. Translation copyright © 1968, 1969, 1970 by Emecé Editores, S.A., and Norman Thomas di Giovanni. "Saadi of Shiraz," edited by Idries Shah, from *The Way of the Sufi* by Idries Shah. Copyright © 1968 by Idries Shah.

Ecco Press: "Song of a Citizen" from *The Collected*

(continued on page 1500)

The following annotations are for the artwork surrounding the map, starting in the upper right-hand corner and moving in a counterclockwise direction.

Fanciful German Snake: This snake is based on a woodcut from Konrad Gesner's *Curious Woodcuts of Fanciful and Real Beasts*, printed in the 1500s. Scenes from folklore were popular subjects of woodblock printing in Germany in the 1400s and 1500s. Since one woodblock could produce thousands of prints, the process made art available to the common people for the first time in history.

Theseus Battling the Minotaur: This artwork is based on the scenes painted on an Attic amphora. An amphora is a type of ancient Greek vase or jar. Beginning about 700 B.C., painted vases were among the most highly developed art forms of ancient Greece. In Attica, a region that included Athens, vases depicting human figures in scenes from mythology and everyday life became popular.

Mayan Figure with God: This scene was originally carved on stone at Copan around A.D. 250–600. Copan, in what is now western Honduras, was a center of Mayan culture. Mayan artists carved symbols and mythological figures on steles, large, rectangular stone slabs which were erected to commemorate astronomical, religious, or civic events.

ASIA

AUSTRALIA

WORLD MYTHS AND FOLKTALES

▼ **Literary Significance** ▼

Myths and folktales are the world's oldest stories. People have told myths and folktales since language was created, keeping them alive and vital through the centuries by word of mouth.

Myths are stories about beginnings. They probably originally had a religious purpose, for they attempt to explain mysteries that people regard as sacred: how the world was created, why people must eventually die, why the world is imperfect.

Folktales are stories told by the common people. Most folktales are told for entertainment, although they may also teach values. Legends, tall tales, fables, and fairy tales are all forms of the folktale.

Myths and folktales are important in every world culture. A society without stories about its beginnings, its heroes, and its deepest values is like a person without a name, a family without roots.

Japanese Woman: From the seventeenth century to the nineteenth century, Japanese *surimono* (literally, "printed things") began to emphasize the world of earthly pleasures. For the aristocracy, artists produced painted screens and scrolls; for the less wealthy, they made woodblock prints depicting beautiful women, animals, and landscapes. In Japanese folklore, the love of a beautiful woman was considered a temptation from the hero's true path, as in "Green Willow" (pp. 40–45).

Pueblo Pottery: This polychrome jar was created about three hundred years ago by an artist of the Tewa, one of the Pueblo people of the American Southwest. Early Pueblo pottery featured black decorations on a white background. This pattern gave way to polychrome, or multicolored, decorations with symbolic scenes.

Gods of Ancient Egypt: Osiris, the supreme god of ancient Egypt, and his heroic wife, Isis, were often represented in Egyptian tombs and temples. In the "twisted" perspective of Egyptian art, the chest was presented frontally and the face, arms, and legs in profile. The face of Osiris, if painted, was always black or green, the colors associated with death and renewal, respectively.

Leopard Derived from African Sculpture: Traditional African sculpture was designed to capture the power of the spirit world or to pay tribute to kings. In Nigeria the leopard was regarded as a symbol of the power of kings. ■

1

OBJECTIVES

1. To compare and contrast the purposes and elements of myths and folktales
2. To analyze origin myths and tales of heroic quests from different cultures
3. To recognize common archetypes in the oral traditions of different cultures
4. To interpret and respond to myths and folktales both orally and in writing

TEACHER'S RESOURCES: 1
- Unit Introduction Test
- Word Analogies
- Unit Review Test
- Critical Thinking and Writing

1 RESPONDING TO THE QUOTATION

Willa Cather's great novels of the American frontier—*My Antonia, O Pioneers!*, and *Death Comes for the Archbishop*—deal with the timeless themes of people's relationship with nature and the unchanging rhythms of human life. Cather's statement can be seen as an informal definition of the term *archetype* (see p. 9), the recurring patterns in the human imagination which myths and other stories embody.

❓ *Think of book or movie plots that follow these archetypal story-lines: two brothers or sisters compete jealously for a parent's favor* (Possible responses: the story of Cain and Abel in the Bible, the movies *East of Eden* and *The Godfather*); *true love is thwarted by the lovers' warring families* (Possible responses: *Romeo and Juliet, West Side Story*, the legend of the Hatfields and the McCoys).

2 HISTORICAL BACKGROUND

Iroquois: The Seneca were one of the Five Nations of the Iroquois league that lived in the woodlands of New York State. The other four nations were the Cayuga, Onondaga, Oneida, and Mohawk.

3 CULTURAL BACKGROUND

Orenda: Most Native American cultures believed in an invisible spiritual force that flowed through the world and empowered nature as well as people. The Iroquois called this power *orenda*.

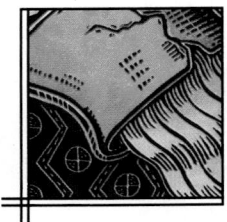

WORLD MYTHS AND FOLKTALES

> 1 " There are only two or three human stories, and they go on repeating themselves as fiercely as if they had never happened before. "
>
> — *Willa Cather*

Myths and folktales are the world's oldest stories, passed on by word of mouth from generation to generation. Stories have always been important to people. The following story, "The Storytelling Stone," comes from the oral tradition of the Seneca Indians of North America. It explains, perhaps better than any book on mythology ever could, how stories came to be, and why people both value and need them. 2

In another time before this one, there was a boy who hunted every day in the forest. Once, late in the afternoon, he stopped beside a large rock and sat down near it to fix his bow and make new points on his arrows.

A man's voice spoke to him. "I will tell you a story," it said.

The boy was startled and a little afraid, but he searched all around the stone to find the source of the voice. It could only be the rock, he thought. It must have orenda, *the magic power the old men talk about. So he spoke to it. "What did you say you wanted to tell me?"* 3

"They are called stories; they are traditions. But first you must give me a present for telling it to you."

"Will this partridge do?" asked the boy, placing one of the birds he had hunted that day on the stone.

"Come back in the evening," the stone said, "and you will hear a legend about the world that was."

In the evening the boy sat on the stone again. The voice told him of the people who lived in the sky above, the "first people," the ones with great magic. Among them lived an old woman who dreamed that the large tree with the white blossoms that stood in the center of her village should be dug up by its roots. When she told her people about this, they followed the dream's instructions, uprooting the tree.

■ **Writer's/Oral Response:** This note provides suggestions for motivating students or helps to clarify their thinking about the oral or written prereading response activity. At times, the annotation for a Writer's Response will tie in with a creative or critical writing activity given at the end of the selection.

■ **Literary Focus:** When necessary, this annotation gives further information—often with specific examples—about the literary element being focused upon in the selection. ▼

PREREADING FOCUS

Background: Students should keep in mind that to grasp the principles of Taoism, one cannot use reason. In fact, students of the Tao say that you cannot "grasp" Taoism at all. Instead, you "receive" the mysterious and poetic vision of Tao. If you are truly open, the Tao makes you one with all things.

Aspects of Taoism have been adopted by Confucianism, which in turn influenced Taoist thinking. Both philosophies grew out of a quest for integrity during times of political chaos. Taoism, however, being mystical, has attracted followers who also embrace superstition and cult lore, inviting scorn from the Chinese intelligentsia. Nevertheless, the *Tao Te Ching* is widely regarded as one of the "most provocative and inspired works in all Chinese literature."

Writer's Response: After students have generated several clusters, have them consider what each cluster says about water. Then ask, "What qualities of action and thought can water be used to symbolize?"

Literary Focus: In using paradox, Lao-tzu did not try to appeal to reason, but to spark in the reader a new, poetic view of life. The *Tao Te Ching* is characterized by symbols of paradox—such as water, which is both powerful and weak—as well as by the juxtaposition of seemingly opposite ideas in parallel structure.

page 542

SELECTION PAGES: SIDE MARGIN FEATURES AND ANNOTATIONS

Several types of notes and annotations are presented throughout a selection in the side margins. The nature of each annotation is indicated by a boldface head. Some notes suggest ways to guide the students' reading of a selection, while other notes provide ideas for extension and enrichment. The majority of annotations highlight a literary element or a critical reading or thinking technique. Passages to which annotations or questions refer are bracketed on the reduced student pages and referenced with a numeral for ease of teacher use. Critical thinking questions eliciting student response are always signaled by a question mark icon. Suggested responses to all annotation questions, with the exception of those that are purely reader response and therefore entirely subjective, are provided in the margin text.

Teacher's Resources. This recurring boxed feature occurs at the beginning of every selection to provide you with a quick checklist of supplementary materials—tests, worksheets, and the like—available to help you teach the selection.

◀ **Literary Element.** This frequently occurring annotation includes a subheading (Characterization, Irony, Imagery, and so on) indicating the literary element being addressed in the bracketed passage.

◀ **Guided Reading.** This annotation identifies lower-level reading comprehension skills being addressed in a bracketed passage. It is designated by such subheads as Identifying Details, Sequencing, Finding the Main Idea, Identifying Characteristics, and Supporting Details.

Higher-level Thinking Skills. These frequently occurring annotations are designated with a specific heading that identifies the reading/critical thinking skill being focused upon in the bracketed passage: Inferring, Making Judgments, Evaluating, Interpreting, Synthesizing, Analyzing, Speculating, Predicting, and so on. ▶

---

6 LITERARY ELEMENT

Foreshadowing: The episode of Laocoon, which became famous in painting and sculpture, is another example of Virgil's use of foreshadowing. What do you think will happen if the Trojans fail to heed Laocoon's warnings? (Possible response: The Trojans will haul the horse inside the city, and the hidden Greek troops will escape and destroy Troy.)

page 384

---

4 GUIDED READING

Sequencing: What sequence of events leads Monna Giovanna's son to covet Federigo's falcon? (When his father dies, he and his mother retire to the country for a year. They live very near Federigo's farm, and the boy goes hunting with Federigo.)

page 816

---

34 EVALUATING

How do you assess the courage and skill of the Trojans and the Greeks in the battle so far? (Possible response: The courage and skill of the warriors seem even.) Whose side does Virgil seem to favor? (Possible response: Virgil has emotionally weighted the narrative so the audience will sympathize with the Trojans rather than with the Greeks, who are often accused of treachery and guile.)

page 394

11 *LEP:* Students may have difficulty understanding lines 73–74. Explain that Ganelon doesn't want the king to believe that Roland is in battle and needs help. Therefore, Ganelon tries to mislead the king by saying that since he respects the king, he will not contradict what Charlemagne thinks about Roland's situation, but if anyone else had spoken the same words, Ganelon would have told that person that he was a liar. ∎

page 697

3 CULTURAL DIVERSITY

Although most medieval marriages were arranged by families for their own financial and social advantage and were not based on romantic love, many couples did establish a strong bond. Women could inherit land and titles, and many widows were able to exercise considerable power.

❓ *To what extent has the power of women today to manage and inherit property increased? (Have students support their opinions.)*

page 816

Social Studies: Virgil portrays Aeneas as a hero with many different, conflicting emotions. Write a psychological profile of Aeneas, basing your conclusions on his actions and thoughts. Discuss the relative importance in the hero's emotional makeup of such feelings as love, anger, loyalty, revenge, sympathy, and pride.

page 406

Comparing Literature. This annotation asks students to make a significant connection between a description, theme, plot device, character, image, or episode in the selection and that in another selection in the text. This kind of cross-referencing occurs not only between selections in the same unit but also between selections in different units. ▶

◀ **Meeting Individual Needs.** This note generally focuses upon idioms, dialect, and other features of the literature that students might have particular trouble with. Other notes challenge more advanced students or present ideas for getting information across to the various learning modalities. In some cases, suggestions for cooperative learning activities are provided. Several different subheads, including LEP (Limited English Proficiency), ESL (English as a Second Language), Cooperative Learning, Advanced Students, Visual Learners, Auditory Learners, Kinesthetic Learners, and others will appear under this heading to designate the application of the annotation.

Reader's Response. These notes tap students' immediate, gut-level responses to either a specific bracketed passage or to entire sections of a selection. At times they solicit student interaction with the text, asking students to make predictions or volunteer opinions about what they think should happen next. ▶

◀ **Cultural Diversity.** This annotation brings up a point of cultural interest that sheds light on an aspect of the selection. This annotation often concludes with a critical thinking question that asks students to make connections between their own culture or time period and the culture or time period that is represented by the selection. At times this annotation includes a suggestion for further research.

Humanities Connection. These notes suggest ways to help students appreciate the wealth of fine art reproduced on the student textbook pages. Humanities Connections may suggest ways to help students see connections between visual art and the literature they are reading. They often provide further information about the artist or the work of art. Many Humanities Connections end with a critical thinking question. ▶

◀ **Writing to Learn.** This note provides cross-curricular learning activities for students. The writing assignment uses information in the text itself as a springboard for exploration in another discipline, such as science, social studies, music, or art.

Answer Annotations. All questions that follow selections are answered in the Annotated Teacher's Edition. In addition, suggested responses to writing and speaking/listening activities are given.

Sohráb and Rostám realize one another's identity at almost the same moment. Have students compare their realization to Oedipus's realization that he has killed his father in *Oedipus Rex*, pp. 302–371.

❓ *How are the circumstances different?* (Oedipus's father dies without recognizing him. Oedipus realizes gradually, and others guess the truth first.)

page 651

8 READER'S RESPONSE

How do you feel toward Rostám at this point? How have your feelings toward him changed as his character has been revealed during the course of the selection? (Answers will vary, but students should see that his character deepens and becomes rounder.)

page 652

Once jailed for a political caricature of King Louis Philippe, and considered in his lifetime only an effective cartoonist and print maker, Honoré Daumier (dōm′yā′) is today also remembered as a skilled sculptor and powerful painter. Daumier carried over to his painting the bold simplicity of the print medium. As in this hallucinatory and ghostlike *Don Quixote*, many of his canvases center on an image done in broad, obvious strokes of black and white.

❓ *How do the sharp angles of Don Quixote's emaciated horse enhance the hallucinatory mood?* (Possible response: the skeletal appearance of the horse suggests a struggle for survival and perhaps death.) ∎

page 828

TEACHING WORLD MYTHS AND FOLKTALES

To help students start thinking about the myth-making process, tell them that myths are stories that answer people's most basic questions about the mysteries of life. Remind students that human curiosity begins in early childhood. Have students compile a list of questions they asked about the world when they were little or have heard young children ask. Students may come up with questions such as "Why is the sky blue?"; "Where do people go when they die?"; "Why does the ocean have tides?" and "What makes the stars shine?"

Point out that many questions about the universe have been answered by science, but many important ones remain. Have students give examples of questions they have about life, such as "Why do bad things happen to good people?"; "What is really important in life?"; and "Do I control my own destiny?" Tell them that to answer these questions, people in ancient times turned to myths and folktales.

From this discussion, elicit from students some characteristics of myths. Myths are stories that explain sacred mysteries about life and nature and reflect the religious beliefs of a culture. They often illuminate the basis or purpose of religious beliefs and rituals. The myths of a culture reveal that culture's particular values. More importantly, they reflect univer-

© David Muench 1996

4 *The stone has long been a symbol of strength and unity in the beliefs of many cultures, and it is often associated with foundations and with the origins of life.*
❓ *Do any of these symbolic meanings come into play in this tale?*

5 They were frightened and angry over the hole it left and threw the old woman into it. She fell to earth, and the earth, which was completely under water then, had to be brought up from the depths by the animals and put upon the turtle's back and patted by the beavers' tails and allowed to grow before it could receive her who had fallen from the sky.

When he finished the tale, he noticed the boy had dozed off and so he said, "You must tell me if you become sleepy, and we can rest. If you sleep you will not hear. It is better that you come back tomorrow evening, and I will tell

6 you more. Remember to bring my present."

Next day the boy hunted and in the evening returned to the rock with a string of birds. This time he did not miss a word. He came the next evening and the one after that.

"Where do you disappear to at night?" his friend asked him one day when they were out hunting together.

"I go to hear stories," he replied.

"What are they?"

"I don't know how to tell you about them, but come with me tonight and you will hear for yourself."

7 So he brought his friend to the stone, and its voice filled their ears with the tales of Genonsgwa and the stone coats, the Flying Heads, and the Porcupine people until the boys were sleepy and the stone sent them home to their beds.

Museum of American Indians, New York

4 TEACHING TIP
Have students collect quotations, song lyrics, nursery rhymes, folktales, proverbs, and advertisements that mention rocks and stones. Discuss examples that convey the archetypal associations described in the caption.

5 LITERARY BACKGROUND
Archetypes: Many tales of origin feature this "earth diver" motif, in which the earth is formed from mud brought up from underwater (see "How the World Was Made," p. 10). Tales of a "fall" from a perfect world are also common, although the fall is usually not as literal as this one.

6 CULTURAL DIVERSITY
Reciprocity is important in many religions. For every gift humans take from the universe, they are expected to give something back.
❓ *How could the ancient concept of reciprocity help solve some twentieth-century problems?* (Possible response: Replenishment and protection of the natural resources we use would help solve environmental problems.)

7 CULTURAL BACKGROUND
The stories told by the stone explain the origin of important Seneca rituals and beliefs. For example, the Flying Heads were evil spirits who hid in the forest and brought disease. To counteract their power, Iroquois peoples had False Face societies of masked men who performed healing ceremonies.

Introduction   **3**

sal human concerns about life and death, fate and free will, the origin of evil, and the search for meaning in a puzzling world. Myths often feature archetypal plots, characters, and themes—that is, recurring patterns found in myths all over the world. Joseph Campbell has pointed out similarities between the myth of Theseus (p. 29) and that of the medieval French knight Tristan, whose story is partially told in "Chevrefoil" (p. 717). Many myths recount the adventures of a hero with mysterious origins who sets out on a dangerous quest. By meeting the challenges of the quest, mythic heroes discover their true selves and share their wisdom with society.

Unlike myths, folktales focus on the struggles of everyday people, rather than on extraordinary heroes or gods and goddesses. Folktales are told for entertainment rather than for religious purposes, but often they also teach a moral lesson. In one type of folktale, the fairy tale, an ordinary person is helped by magical forces to overcome great obstacles and find a way to live "happily ever after."

Finally, to help students feel a sense of connection with the oral tradition, remind them that, in addition to asking questions, young children will frequently say, "Tell me a story." Even adults love to hear a good story that is not only entertaining

---

HUMANITIES CONNECTION

The storyteller dolls convey a value of Pueblo culture—the importance of stories—in a vivid way.

❓ *How do Americans reveal that they still value storytelling?* (Possible responses: by having professional storytellers at schools and libraries, and by reading to children) ■

8 CULTURAL BACKGROUND

Iroquois Gods: "The Master of Life" was the Sky God of the Iroquois. He represented order, truthfulness, and rationality. His twin brother Flint, who ruled the night and regions below this world, represented irrationality and deviousness. The Iroquois believed that people had qualities of both and had to keep these qualities in balance. The Iroquois regarded corn, beans, and squash, their three basic foods, as "the three sisters." In the spring, Iroquois women sang and danced in rituals so that the three sisters would grow.

9 CULTURAL DIVERSITY

In many cultures sacred stories could be told only by and to certain people, in certain places, and at certain sacred times of the year.

❓ *Why would a culture want to control who had power to tell and hear stories?* (Possible response: Leaders sought to ensure the continuation of the culture, their own power, and the purity of the stories by restricting knowledge of them.)

Lawrence Migdale

The Pueblo Indians create storyteller dolls which depict grandparent figures telling children stories of their ancestors and tales of the past.

Soon the whole village was buzzing with the news of the stone and the tales. The boys led the tribe to the place where the stone stood. The people carried fresh game with them which they left for the stone. They marveled over the things called tales that fell from its mouth. No one had ever heard about "The Master of Life" and "He Who Is Our Grandfather," or his enemy "He Who Is Clad in Ice." They did not know about such things as the songs of the corn or the prayer for the harvest, and the wisest among them knew then that they had known nothing until the stone had begun to speak. It took four years for the stone to tell all the tales, but the nights passed quickly.

The rock called the boy one evening after the others had left and said to him, "One day you will become old and be unable to hunt. These tales will help you in your old age. Tell the legends to others, but make sure that they give you something in return for them." And after it had told the boy the last story, the stone was silent and never spoke again.

The boy grew up and grew old. He did not forget the legends, and he told them to anyone who came to his lodge to listen. Many traveled from faraway tribes to hear the stories from the old man who had learned them from the stone when he was a boy. They gladly gave him tobacco,

but also sheds light on the meaning of life. Encourage students to think of "true" stories they have heard about amazing coincidences, proud or selfish people who got what they deserved in the end, people who were saved from a fatal accident by chance or a last-minute decision, and so on. You may wish to introduce "The Storytelling Stone" by pointing out that people love stories so much that some cultures even have a story about the origin of stories. To capture the full flavor of the oral roots of storytelling, you may wish to read "The Storytelling Stone" aloud to students.

Tell students that myths and folktales form the foundation of world literature because all written literature can be traced back, directly or indirectly, to the mythic impulse to tell meaningful stories. Lead students to see that the same oral tradition from which the myths arose eventually produced the great epics of the ancient world. These long poems, usually composed orally and later written down, celebrate the quest of human heroes and their

---

10 *meat, and pelts, for he knew the stories of their beginnings, too, and could tell them as well as the ones about his own tribe. There were few nights when his lodge did not have a crowd of listeners, enthralled and intent, catching the tales to take home with them to their own hearths.*

11 *That is the way stories came to be and why there are many stories in the world where none had been before. The people from the other world before ours, the ones who had the strong and wonderful magic that the stone told about, are the ones we cannot stop telling stories about, even today.*

—Retold by John Cech

"The Storytelling Stone" explains many of the most important things we need to know about myths and folktales. They tell about the beginnings of things. They include marvelous or supernatural events and tell of the deeds and adventures of gods and goddesses, heroes and heroines.

> Myths and folktales remain vital to modern readers because they reveal common truths, patterns, and themes that are familiar to all ages and cultures.

They explain the origins of various rituals that people follow. They are passed down from generation to generation by word of mouth. Most important of all, however, they explain the human experience. They tell us, in poetic, imaginative terms, the most important things that we can communicate to one another: who we are, where we came from, and what we believe in. As mythologist Joseph Campbell once pointed out, myths and folktales are in some ways even "truer" than history.

What Is a Myth?

A **myth** is an anonymous, traditional story that explains a belief, a custom, or a mysterious natural phenomenon. The word *myth* comes from the Greek word *muthos*, which simply means "story."

> 66 The study of mythology might be compared to the investigation of a sealed box. We do not know which is top or bottom, who sent it or why. 99
> —Mary Barnard

12

Lawrence Migdale

To help students appreciate the oral tradition, have them create and tell an "origin myth" having to do with how a family tradition came to be or how a community landmark got its name.

Origin Myths: Tales of more than one creation are common in some cultures. In the mythology of the Senecas and the sacred texts of the Hindus, for example, earlier creations are seen as superior to later ones. However, in the Mayan myths of the *Popol Vuh* (see p. 17), the gods first create defective people but keep on trying until they "get it right."

Comparing people's curiosity about life's mysteries to curiosity about the contents of a sealed box is a metaphor found in myths and folktales. For example, in an African folktale about Anansi the Spider, Anansi opens a box of stories, the stories fly out, and he is able to collect only a few of them. In the Greek myth about Pandora, the woman is so curious that she opens a mysterious box and sets loose all the troubles of the world.

? *Why is Barnard's comparison of mythology to a mysterious sealed box appropriate?* (Possible response: We usually cannot determine with certainty the origin and meaning of a myth.)

interactions with the gods. In Unit 3, students will read an excerpt from the great epic of ancient Mesopotamia, the *Epic of Gilgamesh* (p. 139) while in Unit 4 they will read selections from a Greek epic, the *Iliad* (p. 224), and a Roman epic, the *Aeneid* (p. 383). Unit 5 features sections of the great Indian epics the *Mahabharata* (p. 461) and the *Ramayana* (p. 486). Aspects of archetypal quest stories can also be found in the Hebrew Bible (p. 160), the Christian New Testament (p. 196), and the great book of Islam, the Koran (p. 635).

The Middle Ages produced the *Song of Roland* (p. 694) and *Perceval* (p. 722), Christian epics featuring chivalric knights as heroes, as well as the Germanic saga of the *Nibelungenlied* (p. 733).

During the Renaissance, Cervantes parodied the quests of chivalric heroes in *Don Quixote* (p. 823) and the age of Enlightenment inspired *Candide* (p. 947), Voltaire's satire of the hero's quest.

Joseph Campbell believed that societies without myths decline because they have no cultural ethos or heroic models to give direction or inspiration. Gabriel García Márquez's modern fable "The Handsomest Drowned Man in the World" (p. 1291) affirms Campbell's belief that myths give meaning to existence.

---

13 READER'S RESPONSE
Do you think people in our culture feel the need for similar explanations? If so, how do people today meet these needs? (Answers will vary.)

14 RESPONDING TO THE QUOTATION
Help students to see the similarities between myth and poetry by pointing out that both use similes, metaphors, personification, and symbols to make the world come alive and to help us experience life in a deep, meaningful way. To make this point, you might read aloud the twentieth-century poem "Wind and Water and Stone" by Octavio Paz (p. 1287). Have students describe how the poet makes nature come alive. Point out the personification in both the poem and the myth "The Storytelling Stone." Ask how well the poem fulfills Campbell's description of the effects of myth.

■ HUMANITIES CONNECTION ■

Joseph Campbell has referred to the Lascaux Cave as a "Stone Age cathedral of hunting magic." The paintings were created c. 15,000 B.C., but were not discovered until 1940. It is believed that within these cavernous sanctuaries early humans conducted rituals to increase the supply of animals and ensure the success of the hunt. ■

Museum of American Indians, New York

14

❝ Essentially, mythologies are enormous poems that are renditions of insights, giving some sense of the marvel, the miracle and wonder of life. ❞
—*Joseph Campbell*

CHINESE HORSE, from the Cave of Lascaux, Montignac, France. *These ancient cave paintings helped people to create a sense of order and belonging in the universe. Myths serve a similar function.*

Myths had specific purposes in their cultures. In every culture, however, the main functions of myths were:

1. To explain the creation of the world and the universe
2. To explain the human condition: how and why people were created, why they are flawed, why there is suffering in the world, why people must eventually die, and what happens to people after death
3. To explain natural phenomena, such as the setting of the sun and the phases of the moon
4. To explain the nature of gods and goddesses and how these deities and human beings interact
5. To explain the meanings behind religious rituals, customs, and beliefs
6. To explain historical events
7. To teach moral lessons

13

Myths were created out of a human need to make sense of the universe and explain how the world and its human inhabitants came to be.

Along with rituals, cave and rock paintings, songs, and prayers, myths were the means through which human beings in ancient times tried to find order and pattern in life. Myths helped people to feel a sense of harmony with a world that could be both beautiful and dangerous.

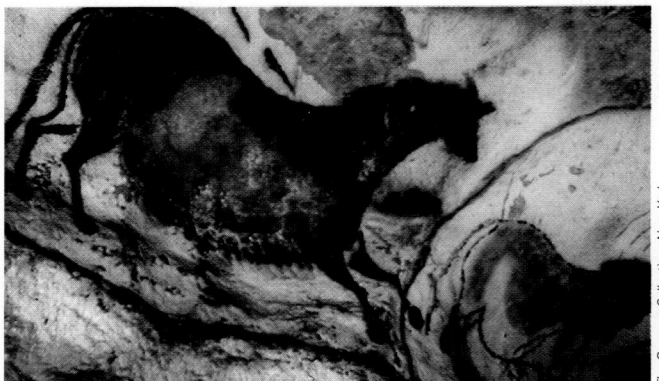

The Granger Collection, New York

READING CHECK
1. According to the Seneca Indians, stories were stolen from the gods. T F (F)
2. Myths are often stories about beginnings. T F (T)
3. Folktales usually focus on gods and goddesses. T F (F)
4. Both myths and folktales were originally passed down orally. T F (T)
5. Both myths and folktales teach moral values. T F (T)

FOR FURTHER STUDY
Nonfiction
Joseph Campbell's *The Hero with a Thousand Faces* is the classic study of the hero archetype.

Fiction
American Indian Myths and Legends, edited by Richard Erdoes and Alfonso Ortiz, includes tales from many Native American cultures. Jane Yolen's *Favorite Folktales from Around the World* includes trickster

and hero archetypes. Robin McKinley's *Beauty* retells the folktale "Beauty and the Beast."

Film and Video
Videocassettes of the PBS series *Joseph Campbell: The Power of Myth*, hosted by Bill Moyers, are available in many public libraries. Films based on heroic quests include *Star Wars*, *Raiders of the Lost Ark*, and *The Dark Crystal*. ■

The Differences Between Myths and Folktales

15 As myths were told and retold over generations, they transformed. Not only their specific details, but also the purposes they served in their cultures, changed. One of the storytelling forms that arose from the myth was the folktale.

A **folktale** is a story that is created by the "folk"—the common people—and passed along orally from generation to generation. Folktales include legends, fables, tall tales, fairy tales, and ghost stories. Folktales differ from myths in several important ways:

16
1. Folktales, unlike myths, are secular, or nonreligious.
2. Folktales were created as much for their entertainment value as for the teaching of social or moral values.
3. Folktales feature magic, transformations, and enchantments, just as myths do. But although folktales may sometimes include gods or goddesses as characters, they are usually not central actors in the story.
4. Folktale heroes tend to be common, everyday folk who don't have special powers, unlike the heroes of myths, who are the superhuman offspring of gods or goddesses and human parents.
5. Folktales are not associated with religious rituals.

Folktales are entertaining stories
about ordinary people
who survive by luck, by using their
wits, and by relying on their own
natural goodness.

The most important difference between a myth and a folktale concerns the purposes of each storytelling form. Myths are a direct expression of a culture's religious beliefs; folktales are not. But both myths and folktales explain important truths about life. They address our deepest needs and engage our sense of wonder. They are the stories of the human family.

The Granger Collection, New York

Title page to the first edition of Grimm's Kinder- und Hausmärchen (Fairy Tales), 1815–1821.

15 READER'S RESPONSE
Do you know any oral stories or jokes that have changed with the passage of time? Have you ever told a story that later came back to you in a different form? Explain.

16 TEACHING TIP
Have students recount legends, fables, tall tales, fairy tales, and ghost stories they know. Ask the class how well each story fits the five characteristics listed here.

HUMANITIES CONNECTION

The Brothers Grimm (see pp. 52–53) collected German folktales in the area of Kassel, Germany early in the nineteenth century. Their published collections became world famous and helped found the modern scholarly study of folklore.
How does the illustration compare with the Pueblo storyteller doll on p. 4? (Both show an old woman storyteller surrounded by children.) *Do the stories we hear as children have more influence on us than the ones we hear later in life? Why or why not?* (Possible response: The stories we hear as children have a greater impact because as children we are more imaginative and open to possibilities, while as adults we have more fixed beliefs about the way things are.) ■

1 COMPARING LITERATURE

The ideas of a "fall" from a Golden Age and a great flood appear in Roman literature in "The Four Ages" of Ovid's *Metamorphoses* (pp. 420–427). In the Golden Age described by Ovid, people were good and freely gathered the fruits of the earth. In the Age of Silver, the gods created extreme weather; people had to build shelters and farm. In the Age of Bronze, people invented weapons. Finally, in the Iron Age, there was war. The Greek myths of Hesiod and the classic myths of India also cite four ages.

2 READER'S RESPONSE

The Swiss psychologist Carl Jung (1875–1961) developed the concept of archetypes. He saw archetypes as attributes of a collective unconscious, a mental storehouse of images shared by all people in all times and cultures regardless of differences in individual experience. Jung believed that these universal archetypes were expressed in dreams, fantasies, and myths. He felt that becoming aware of these images in the collective unconscious could help individuals achieve a sense of wholeness and well-being. *Do you think the similarities of images and story structures that appear in myths from diverse times and places prove the existence of universal archetypes in the human mind? What other explanations might there be for these similarities?* (Possible response: The stories could have spread as a result of contact among cultures.)

Introduction

Tales About Beginnings

Probably the very first stories human beings told were **origin myths**—stories that explain how things came to be. Just as individual families have stories of where they came from, so do people all over the world have stories about their beginnings. Many of the great questions people had about their lives were answered by their origin myths: How was the world created? Why do people die? Is there life after death? Why is evil allowed to exist in the world? How did various animals, plants, and geographical features come to be?

◆

origin myths: *stories that explain how things came to be.*

Most cultures have myths that explain how the universe was created. Many cultures also have stories about the end of a society, an era, or even of the world itself. Sometimes the end comes in the form of a great flood that cleanses the earth of evil and sets the stage for a new beginning. And many cultures have stories about a long-ago "Golden Age"—a time when the world enjoyed perfect peace, happiness, and prosperity. But this Golden Age is lost when evil, sickness, and death come into the world.

The Roles of Gods and Goddesses

Gods and goddesses are nearly always associated with origin myths. It is usually a god or goddess who forms the earth and the life on it.

Like human beings, gods and goddesses form family groups, or **pantheons**. Often, a culture's pantheon is ruled by a powerful "father" god and a "mother" goddess. There are usually offspring and other relatives. These other gods and goddesses are often associated with various aspects of life, from abstract values such as wisdom, fertility, love, and justice, to concrete forces of nature such as the wind, the sea, the moon, and earthquakes.

The Staying Power of Mythic Patterns

The more myths you read, the more you'll notice that certain themes, characters, and images keep recurring. These recurring patterns are called **archetypes**. They serve as basic models to which specific cultural details are added.

Archetypes are so powerful that they simply change a bit over time and reappear in different forms in other types of literature. Thus, the archetype of the

THE PEACEABLE KINGDOM, EDWARD HICKS.
The "peaceable kingdom" is a popular vision of a Golden Age.
What human hopes and yearnings do you think the idea of a peaceable kingdom symbolizes?

Art Resource, New York

lost Golden Age might appear today in a novel about a woman who remembers a happy childhood in her old home town but returns to it in middle age only to find that everything has changed and that the joy and innocence of that earlier time cannot be recaptured. The

◆

archetype (är'kə·tīp'): *a pattern or model that serves as the basis for different, but related, versions of a character, plot, or theme.*

myth of a great flood might appear today in the form of a science-fiction novel about the end of the world in which a war, disease, or alien invasion destroys almost everything, but leaves possibilities open for the world's rebirth.

The Purpose of Origin Myths

Origin myths gave the people who told them a sense of their place in the universe. Such myths told people who they were, where they came from, and what their destiny would be. The stories we tell today serve much the same purpose. All stories are outgrowths of myths; all stories ultimately deal with the *hows* and *whys* of human existence.

3

OBJECTIVES

1. *To infer Cheyenne values from a creation myth*
2. *To determine the purpose of origin myths*
3. *To write a poem based on a myth and an inferential essay about the Cheyenne view of nature*
4. *To identify the origin of English words borrowed from Native American languages*

THEMES IN WORLD LITERATURE

Beginnings and Endings
"In the Beginning," from *Genesis*, pp. 162–168
From *Metamorphoses*, pp. 420–427

The Uses and Abuses of Power
"The Wooden People," from the Popol Vuh, pp. 17–21
"The Burning of Rome" from the *Annals*, pp. 429–435 ▪

PREREADING FOCUS

Background: The earth-diver is a motif, or recurring element, in the creation myths of cultures other than the Cheyenne. In some myths, the earth-diver figure later becomes an opponent of the creator god and brings evil into the world. Another recurring element is creation brought about by the uttering of words by the creator god. The birth of the world from a cosmic egg, the mating of the earth and sky, and the slaying of a monster whose body becomes the world are other motifs common to the creation myths of many cultures.

Oral Response: Ask students for words or phrases that come to mind when they think of women or femininity. Make a list of these words on the chalkboard, and then ask students how some of the terms might be applied to the earth. You may end the discussion by noting that many environmentalists have revived the ancient Greek idea of the earth as Gaia—a living entity that must be respected if life is to flourish on the planet.

ABOUT THE RETELLERS

Alice Marriott (1910–   ) and Carol K. Rachlin (1919–   ) are anthropologists. For many years they have specialized in collecting stories from Native Americans. This myth was told to them by Mary Little Bear Inkanish, a Cheyenne, in 1960.

Reader's Guide

HOW THE WORLD WAS MADE

Background

The Cheyenne, a Native American people, have inhabited the North American continent for centuries. During the seventeenth century, the Cheyenne migrated from the Great Lakes region to the central plains. Their life on the plains was firmly linked with nature in general—and with the buffalo in particular. They came to depend upon the buffalo for their livelihood, and they made use of virtually every part of the animal: its flesh, its hide, and even its bones. Many Cheyenne religious rituals, such as the Sun Dance, were designed to ensure the abundance of buffalo.

This Cheyenne myth is in many ways a "typical" creation story. It contains several common **motifs**, or recurring story features. Of special interest is the "earth-diver" motif. In this motif, a god sends a bird or animal to the depths of the ocean to bring back a bit of soil from which the entire earth can be created. This motif occurs among a variety of Native American peoples, but it occurs in remote parts of the world as well, such as Siberia. The turtle, too, is a recurring figure in the mythologies of many lands, from North America to China and India.

Oral Response

Many cultures view the earth as a female figure. The ancient Greeks, for example, personified the earth as a goddess called Gaia. The ancient Sumerians worshiped Ki, or Urash, the earth goddess. Today we often speak of "Mother Earth" and "the Earth Mother." As a class, discuss the feminine qualities of the earth. You may wish to record the class's ideas in the form of a word cluster on the chalkboard.

Literary Focus

An **origin myth** is a story that explains how something began. Origin myths provide explanations for mysteries that early peoples wanted to understand: why there are seasons, why we have day and night, why the moon has phases. Virtually every culture has an origin myth that explains the greatest mystery of all: the creation of the world.

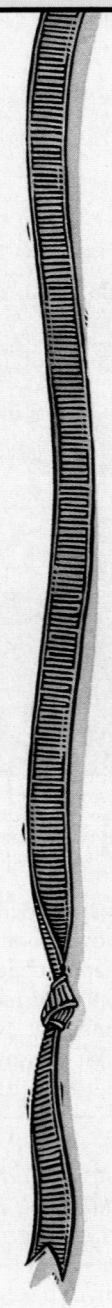

HOW THE WORLD WAS MADE

A Cheyenne Myth

retold by

ALICE MARRIOTT AND CAROL K. RACHLIN

❚ *Do any of the details in this Cheyenne creation myth remind you of other stories you are familiar with?*

In the beginning there was nothing, and Maheo, the All Spirit, lived in the void. He looked around him, but there was nothing to see. He listened, but there was nothing to hear. There was only Maheo, alone in nothingness.

Because of the greatness of his Power, Maheo was not lonesome. His being was a Universe. But as he moved through the endless time of nothingness, it seemed to Maheo that his Power should be put to use. What good is Power, Maheo asked himself, if it is not used to make a world and people to live in it?

With his Power, Maheo created a great water, like a lake, but salty. Out of this salty water, Maheo knew, he could bring all life that ever was to be. The lake itself was life, if Maheo so commanded it. In the darkness of nothingness, Maheo could feel the coolness of the water and taste on his lips the tang of the salt.

"There should be water beings," Maheo told his Power. And so it was. First the fish, swimming in the deep water, and then the mussels and snails and crawfish, lying on the sand and mud Maheo had formed so his lake should have a bottom.

Let us also create something that lives on the water, Maheo thought to his Power.

And so it was. For now there were snow geese, and mallards and teal and coots and terns and loons living and swimming about on the water's surface. Maheo could hear the splashing of their feet and the flapping of their wings in the darkness.

I should like to see the things that have been created, Maheo decided.

And, again, so it was. Light began to grow and spread, first white and bleached in the east, then golden and strong till it filled the middle of the sky and extended all around the horizon. Maheo watched the light, and he saw the birds and fishes, and the shellfish lying on the bottom of the lake as the light showed them to him.

How beautiful it all is, Maheo thought in his heart.

Then the snow goose paddled over to where she thought Maheo was, in the space above the lake. "I do not see You, but I know that You exist," the goose began. "I do not know where You are, but I know You must be everywhere. Listen to me, Maheo. This is good water that You have made, on which we live. But birds are not like fish. Sometimes

TEACHER'S RESOURCES
✔ Review and Response Worksheet
✔ Selection Test
✔ Language Skills Worksheet

1 GUIDED READING

Recognizing Cause and Effect: According to the myth, what caused the Cheyenne god to create the world? (He wanted to put his power to good use.)

2 INFERRING

Why does the teller focus only on images of taste and touch here, rather than on any of the other senses? (There was no light yet, so Maheo couldn't see; there were no creatures yet, so there wasn't anything to hear.)

3 COMPARING LITERATURE

Many students will recognize similarities between this passage and the creation of light in Chapter 1 of the Book of Genesis (pp. 163–165). Ask students to compare and contrast the tone of these two versions of the creation of light.

Nouns of Direct Address

When addressing a person in written discourse, set off the person's name with commas. Here are examples from "How the World Was Made":

Beginning of sentence: "Little brother, no man can do more than his best."
Middle of sentence: "Try, little brother, and see what you can do."
End of sentence: "Listen to me, Maheo."

1. **Reading and Speaking.** Have students identify and read aloud other sentences from the myth that contain nouns of direct address. Ask them to explain how the commas helped them in their reading.

HUMANITIES CONNECTION

Most shields of Cheyenne warriors were sacred objects. They were painted with images of creatures such as eagles, owls, or bears, whose powers the warrior hoped to possess. Actual body parts of such creatures were sometimes attached.

What "warriors" or athletes of today identify themselves with wild animals whose powers they hope to share? (Possible response: members of teams such as the Chicago Bears or Detroit Lions.) ■

4 PREDICTING

How do you think Maheo will respond to the birds' additional request? Will he get impatient with them? (Answers will vary.)

CULTURAL DIVERSITY

Many Native American groups viewed the elements and creatures of nature as "natural peoples," rather than as "things."

How might someone who perceived creatures as "peoples" treat them differently than someone who saw them as things? (Possible response: They might respect the creatures more and not abuse or carelessly destroy them.)

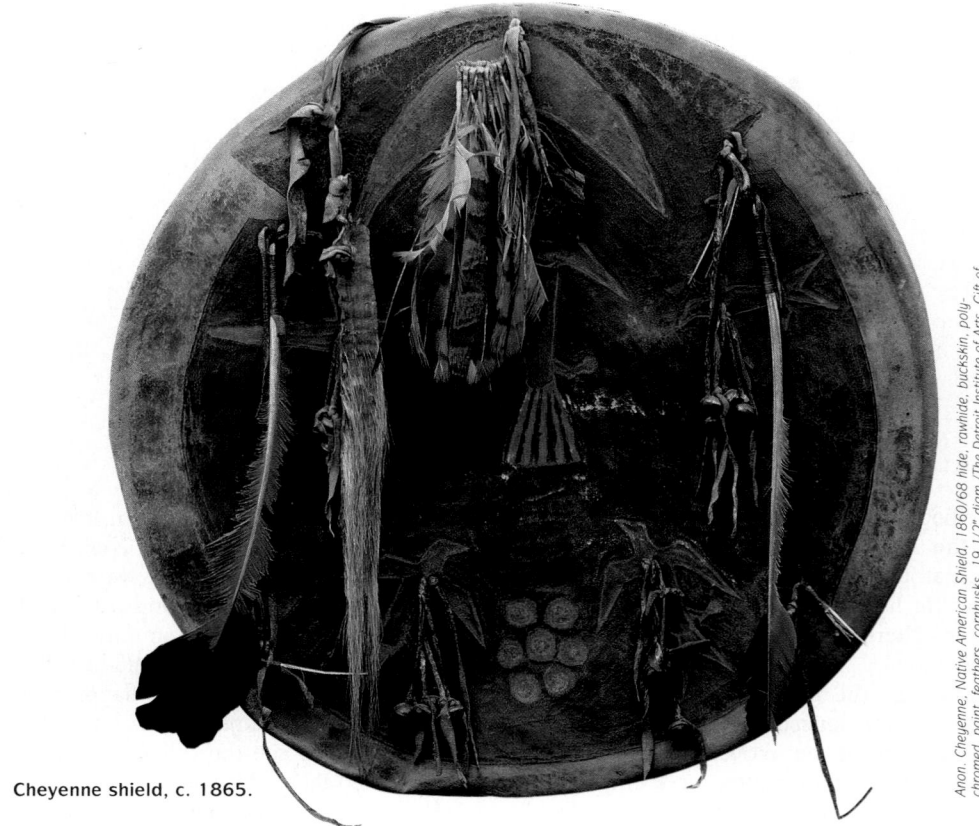

Cheyenne shield, c. 1865.

Anon. Cheyenne. Native American Shield, 1860/68 hide, rawhide, buckskin, polychromed, paint, feathers, cornhusks. 19 1/2" diam./The Detroit Institute of Arts, Gift of Detroit Scientific Association.

we get tired swimming. Sometimes we would like to get out of the water."

"Then fly," said Maheo, and he waved his arms, and all the water birds flew, skittering along the surface of the lake until they had speed enough to rise in the air. The skies were darkened with them.

"How beautiful their wings are in the light," Maheo said to his Power, as the birds wheeled and turned, and became living patterns against the sky.

The loon was the first to drop back to the surface of the lake. "Maheo," he said, looking around, for he knew that Maheo was all about him, "You have made us sky and light

to fly in, and You have made us water to swim in. It sounds ungrateful to want something else, yet still we do. When we are tired of swimming and tired of flying, we should like a dry solid place where we could walk and rest. Give us a place to build our nests, please, Maheo."

"So be it," answered Maheo, "but to make such a place I must have your help, all of you. By myself, I have made four things: the water, the light, the sky air, and the peoples of the water. Now I must have help if I am to create more, for my Power will only let me make four things by myself."

"Tell us how we can help You," said all

4

5

5 the water peoples. "We are ready to do what You say."

Maheo stretched out his hand and beckoned. "Let the biggest and the swiftest try to find land first," he said, and the snow goose came to him.

6 "I am ready to try," the snow goose said, and she drove herself along the water until the white wake behind her grew and grew to a sharp white point that drove her up into the air as the feathers drive an arrow. She flew high into the sky, until she was only a dark spot against the clearness of the light. Then the goose turned, and down she plunged, faster than any arrow, and dived into the water. She pierced the surface with her beak as if it were the point of a spear.

The snow goose was gone a long time. Maheo counted to four four hundred times before she rose to the surface of the water and lay there floating, her beak half open as she gasped for air.

"What have you brought us?" Maheo asked her, and the snow goose sighed sadly, and answered, "Nothing. I brought nothing back."

Then the loon tried, and after him, the mallard. Each in turn rose until he was a speck against the light, and turned and dived with the speed of a flashing arrow into the water. And each in turn rose wearily, and wearily answered, "Nothing," when Maheo asked him what he had brought.

At last there came the little coot, paddling across the surface of the water very quietly, dipping his head sometimes to catch a tiny fish, and shaking the water beads from his scalp lock whenever he rose.

"Maheo," the little coot said softly, "when I put my head beneath the water, it seems to me that I see something there, far below. Perhaps I can swim down to it—I don't know. I can't fly or dive like my sisters and

brothers. All I can do is swim, but I will swim down the best I know how, and go as deep as I can. May I try, please, Maheo?"

7 "Little brother," said Maheo, "no man can do more than his best, and I have asked for the help of all the water peoples. Certainly you shall try. Perhaps swimming will be better than diving, after all. Try, little brother, and see what you can do."

"Hah-ho!" the little coot said. "Thank you, Maheo," and he put his head under the water and swam down and down and down and down, until he was out of sight.

An American coot.
❓ *Why is it significant that such a humble creature plays such a large role in the creation of the world?*

Robert J. Ashworth/Shostal Associates/SuperStock International, Inc.

8 The coot was gone a long, long, long, long time. Then Maheo and the other birds could see a little dark spot beneath the water's surface, slowly rising toward them. It seemed as if they would never see the coot himself, but at last the spot began to have a shape. Still it rose and rose, and at last

---

5 **COMPARING LITERATURE**

❓ *How do the animals in this myth contrast with Coyote in "Coyote and the Origin of Death" on pp. 22–25?* (These animals are innocent and helpful while Coyote is deceitful and uncooperative.)

6 **LITERARY ELEMENT**

Similes: How do the comparisons made here reflect the culture from which the myth comes? (The bird's flying and diving are compared to the flying of an arrow and the piercing of a spear, two important weapons of the Cheyenne.) To what animals or objects in your own culture might you compare the bird's actions? (Answers will vary.)

7 **CULTURAL DIVERSITY**

In Cheyenne society, youngsters were encouraged to prove themselves by learning and practicing adult skills at an early age. They were enthusiastically rewarded for their efforts on behalf of the family and the tribe.

❓ *How does Maheo encourage the little coot in his undertaking?* (He points out the coot's strength—swimming ability—and emphasizes that the effort is more important than the outcome.)

8 **LITERARY ELEMENT**

Repetition: Why do you think the retellers left in four *long*'s instead of just one? (Possible responses: The repetition captures the flavor of a story told orally; it creates suspense and reinforces the idea of time passing.)

How the World Was Made   **13**

9 LITERARY ELEMENT

Theme: A myth reflects the values and attitudes of the culture from which it originated. What Cheyenne values are affirmed by the coot's act and the reward he receives? (Possible responses: courage, ingenuity, and community spirit)

10 READER'S RESPONSE

Do you find Maheo's predicament with the mud amusing? How does it affect your impression of him?

INFERRING

In what ways are the coot and the turtle unlikely heroes? (One is small and weak; the other is old and slow.) What does their success suggest about the Cheyennes' social attitudes? (Possible response: It suggests they felt that everyone, no matter how weak or small, had a part to play in community life.)

LITERARY ELEMENT

Repetition: What repeated phrase emphasizes that this myth is giving explanations for the origins of the Earth and its inhabitants? ("And so it was, and so it is.")

11 ANALYZING AND SPECULATING

In what sense is Maheo's comparison illogical? (He hasn't created woman yet, so logically he couldn't compare Earth to a woman at this point.) How do you think the original teller would respond to someone who raised this objection? How important is "logic" in myths? (Answers will vary.)

Maheo and the water peoples could surely see who it was. The little coot was swimming up from the bottom of the salty lake.

When the coot reached the surface, he stretched his closed beak upward into the light, but he did not open it.

"Give me what you have brought," Maheo said, and the coot let his beak fall open, so a little ball of mud could fall from his tongue into Maheo's hand, for when Maheo wanted to, he could become like a man.

9 "Go, little brother," Maheo said. "Thank you, and may what you have brought always protect you."

And so it was and so it is, for the coot's flesh still tastes of mud, and neither man nor animal will eat a coot unless there is nothing else to eat.

10 Maheo rolled the ball of mud between the palms of his hands, and it began to grow larger, until there was almost too much mud for Maheo to hold. He looked around for a place to put the mud, but there was nothing but water or air anywhere around him.

"Come and help me again, water peoples," Maheo called. "I must put this mud somewhere. One of you must let me place it on his back."

All the fish and all the other water creatures came swimming to Maheo, and he tried to find the right one to carry the mud. The mussels and snails and crawfish were too small, although they all had solid backs, and they lived too deep in the water for the mud to rest on them. The fish were too narrow, and their back fins stuck up

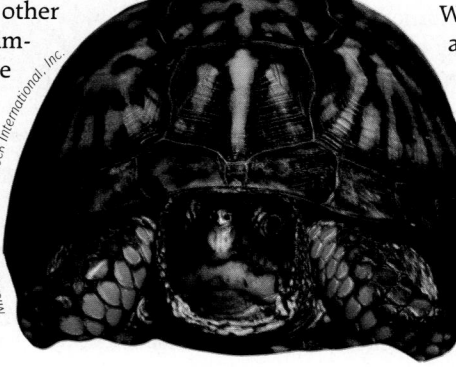

The box turtle.
Cheyenne culture is firmly linked with nature. How is this demonstrated in the myth?

Michael Cerone/SuperStock International, Inc.

through the mud and cut it to pieces. Finally only one water person was left.

"Grandmother Turtle," Maheo asked, "do you think that you can help me?"

"I'm very old and very slow, but I will try," the turtle answered. She swam over to Maheo, and he piled the mud on her rounded back, until he had made a hill. Under Maheo's hands, the hill grew and spread and flattened out, until the Grandmother Turtle was hidden from sight.

"So be it," Maheo said once again. "Let the earth be known as our Grandmother, and let the Grandmother who carries the earth be the only being who is at home beneath the water, or within the earth, or above the ground; the only one who can go anywhere by swimming or by walking as she chooses."

And so it was, and so it is. Grandmother Turtle and all her descendants must walk very slowly, for they carry the whole weight of the whole world and all its peoples on their backs.

Now there was earth as well as water, but the earth was barren. And Maheo said to his Power, "Our Grandmother Earth is like a woman; she should be fruitful. Let her begin to bear life. Help me, my Power." **11**

When Maheo said that, trees and grass sprang up to become the Grandmother's hair. The flowers became her bright ornaments, and the fruits and the seeds were the gifts that the earth offered back to Maheo.

The birds came to rest on her hands when they were tired, and the fish came close to her sides. Maheo looked at the Earth

READING CHECK

1. What is the first thing Maheo creates? (a great salty lake)
2. Why does Maheo decide to create the Earth? (The birds want a resting place.) How does the coot help? (by bringing up mud from the bottom of the lake)
3. According to the myth, why do turtles walk so slowly? (They are carrying the world on their backs.)

4. Why does Maheo decide to create people? (to show his love for Grandmother Earth and to keep the Earth company)
5. Why does Maheo create the buffalo? (to provide people with an animal that could take the place of all the others)

RETEACHING

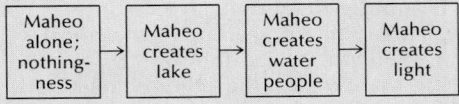

Maheo alone; nothing-ness → Maheo creates lake → Maheo creates water people → Maheo creates light

These boxes represent one series of events from the myth. Students can use them to draw a comic strip version of a sequence in the myth, with interactive characters and dialogue balloons.

Woman and he thought she was very beautiful; the most beautiful thing he had made so far.

She should not be alone, Maheo thought. Let me give her something of myself, so she will know that I am near her and that I love her.

Maheo reached into his right side, and pulled out a rib bone. He breathed on the bone, and laid it softly on the bosom of the Earth Woman. The bone moved and stirred, stood upright and walked. The first man had come to be.

"He is alone with the Grandmother Earth as I once was alone with the void," said Maheo. "It is not good for anyone to be alone." So Maheo fashioned a human woman from his left rib, and set her with the man. Then there were two persons on the Grandmother Earth, her children and Maheo's. They were happy together, and Maheo was happy as he watched them.

After a year, in the springtime, the first child was born. As the years passed, there were other children. They went their ways, and founded many tribes.

From time to time, after that, Maheo realized that his people walking on the earth had certain needs. At those times, Maheo, with the help of his Power, created animals to feed and care for the people. He gave them deer for clothing and food, porcupines to make their ornaments, the swift antelopes on the open plains, and the prairie dogs that burrowed in the earth.

At last Maheo thought to his Power, Why, one animal can take the place of all the others put together, and then he made the buffalo.

Maheo is still with us. He is everywhere, watching all his people, and all the creation he has made. Maheo is all good and all life; he is the creator, the guardian, and the teacher. We are all here because of Maheo.

First Thoughts

An **image** is a picture created by words. What was your favorite image in this myth?

Identifying Facts

1. Why does Maheo need the animals' help in order to complete the creation?
2. What is Grandmother Turtle's role in the creation?
3. Why does Maheo decide to create a human being? Describe how the first people are created.
4. What is the last thing Maheo creates?

Interpreting Meanings

1. An **origin myth** explains the beginnings of things. What beginnings, or origins, does this myth explain?
2. How would you **characterize** Maheo? What is his attitude toward his creations, including the earth and its inhabitants? Give three specific examples from the myth to support your views.
3. In this myth, all of the animals work together to help Maheo create the world. What does this suggest about the Cheyennes' view of nature?
4. How is the earth compared to a woman

1. Dramatic Reading. Have volunteers plan a dramatic reading of this short, lively myth. Assign the roles of narrator, Maheo, and the other characters. Before the reading, have the group discuss the personal traits of each character and of the narrator, and what tone of voice each should have. Have students practice their parts before presenting the myth to the class.

2. Research Project. Interested students may research another Native American creation myth, retell it orally for the class, and point out similarities to and differences from the Cheyenne myth.

Ask students to discuss the relationship between humans and animals portrayed in this myth. How does this view compare with contemporary attitudes toward the natural world? ■

Interpreting Meanings

1. water, water creatures, birds, light (sky), the earth, trees and plants, men and women, the land animals
2. Maheo cares for the earth and its creatures. *Examples:* giving birds power to fly; creating the earth as a resting place; creating animals to meet people's needs
3. They view nature as a whole in which all parts cooperate.
4. Maheo says, "Our Grandmother Earth is like a woman; she should be fruitful. Let her begin to bear life." Then trees and plants adorn her.

Applying Meanings
Answers will vary.

Creative Writing Response
Writing a Poem Based on a Myth. Poems should focus on one section of the myth and may contain original imagery.

Critical Writing Response
Making Inferences. Essays should focus on the Cheyennes' view of the interrelatedness of all things.

Language and Vocabulary
1. small mammal; Algonquian
2. cone-shaped dwelling; Algonquian **3.** earth-walled Native American shelter; Navaho
4. small wolf; Nahuatl **5.** long sled; Algonquian **6.** large animal in deer family; Algonquian
7. edible nut; Algonquian **8.** corn with the hull removed; Algonquian **9.** small striped squirrel; Algonquian **10.** marshy river; Choctaw ■

---

in this myth? Find the **descriptive language** that characterizes the earth as feminine.

Applying Meanings
Think about Maheo's question, "What good is Power . . . if it is not used to make a world and people to live in it?" What do *you* think is the proper use of power? Explain your thoughts.

Creative Writing Response
Writing a Poem Based on a Myth. "How the World Was Made" is full of vivid **imagery**, or language that appeals to the senses of sight, hearing, smell, taste, and touch. Try writing your favorite part of this myth in the form of a poem, using some of the same imagery that occurs in the prose version. Your poem does not have to rhyme. If you wish, you may change the emphasis of the poem, telling the creation story from the point of view of one of the animals, such as Grandmother Turtle. Exchange your first-draft poem with a classmate for revision ideas. Then read your completed poem aloud to the class.

Critical Writing Response
Making Inferences. Myths and folktales represent a culture's traditions, values, and attitudes. Although this myth does not directly tell you about the Cheyenne people, you can make **inferences**, or educated guesses, about some of their attitudes and basic values concerning nature. How do you think the Cheyenne felt about nature and their relationship to it? Using the following chart as a starting point, write a two- or three-paragraph essay about the Cheyenne view of nature as illustrated by the myth.

Evidence	Example from Myth	Inference
Maheo's reactions to his creations		
The role of animals in the creation of the world		

In the conclusion of your essay, describe how the Cheyenne view of nature is similar to or different from the view of nature held in your own time and culture.

Language and Vocabulary

Native American Words in the English Language

When European settlers first began colonizing North America, they found many places and things that they had no English names for. Native American languages supplied these names, and many American English words are direct "loans" from Native American languages. Below is a list of just a few of these words. Use a dictionary to find the words' contemporary meanings and the Native American language from which each word was borrowed.

1. raccoon   **6.** moose
2. wigwam   **7.** pecan
3. hogan   **8.** hominy
4. coyote   **9.** chipmunk
5. toboggan   **10.** bayou

OBJECTIVES
1. To infer the Mayan worldview from a creation myth
2. To recognize the climax of the myth
3. To narrate an imaginative series of events
4. To analyze the effects of imagery

Reader's Guide

THE WOODEN PEOPLE: *from the* POPOL VUH

Background

Popol Vuh (pō'pəl vu'), or The Book of Counsel, is the Quiché (kē·chā') Mayan book of creation. Called the Mayan Bible by poet Carlos Fuentes, the Popol Vuh is one of the most important sources of pre-Columbian myth in Central America.

The Quiché Mayans settled in the highlands of Guatemala in about the ninth century A.D. Their great work, the Popol Vuh, tells the story of their origins and destiny. The Quiché Mayans believed that the Popol Vuh was a gift from the gods that could help people to see beyond the obvious and to become aware of mysteries and secrets that would otherwise be beyond the range of human insight.

The Quiché Mayan creation myth that follows, "The Wooden People," comes from the first part of the Popol Vuh. This episode is the third creation story in a sequence of four. At this point in the mythic cycle, the gods have failed in two attempts to create suitable human beings. The first two attempts resulted in the creation of the animal kingdom and a being made of mud that disintegrated almost as soon as it was formed. Now the gods have made beings out of a more substantial material: wood. These wooden people, or manikins, become the world's first people.

Writer's Response

"The Wooden People" includes an account of a devastating flood. Before you read this myth, write your ideas about why a flood might have been seen by early people as both a destructive and a creative force. In what ways can a flood be "cleansing"?

Literary Focus

A **plot** is the series of connected events that make up a story. The most suspenseful or exciting point in a plot is the **climax**. In the climax, something happens to resolve the story's central conflict. The climax brings about a change in the situation presented in the story or results in a change in the main character or characters. As you read "The Wooden People," determine what the climax of the story is.

PREREADING FOCUS

Background: For generations the stories in the *Popol Vuh* were passed down orally and perhaps through books of picture writing. Then, in the 1500s, after the Spanish conquest, an unknown Quiché author wrote down the stories in his own language. This text was later shown to a trusted Spanish missionary in the early 1700s. Father Ximénez spent years translating it into Spanish, but his work lay undiscovered for over a century until two European travelers found it in a library in Guatemala in the 1850s and had it published. The work was not translated into English until 1950.

Writer's Response: Ask students to describe flood stories or incidents from TV, movies, or real life. Then draw a chart on the board listing characteristics of floods:

Flood	
Destructive	Creative

Brainstorm words that describe the destructiveness of floods and words that convey their cleansing powers. Ask students to use these words in their written responses.

ABOUT THE TRANSLATOR

Dennis Tedlock is a professor of religion and anthropology who specializes in Native American cultures. He worked on his translation of *Popol Vuh: The Mayan Book of the Dawn of Life* for over nine years and was awarded the PEN Translation Award in 1986.

Active Voice and Passive Voice

When verbs are in the active voice, the subject is the doer of the action. When they are in the passive voice, the subject is the receiver of the action. A verb in the passive voice is made up of a form of the verb *to be*, plus a past participle of another verb. Here are examples:

Active Voice: They *came* into being, they *multiplied*, they *had* daughters, they *had* sons, these manikins, woodcarvings.

Passive Voice: They *were pounded* down to the bones and tendons, smashed and pulverized even to the bones.

1. **Reading and Speaking.** Have students identify three verbs in the myth in the active voice and three in the passive. Then have them change the active voice verbs to passive ones and the passive verbs to active ones.

TEACHER'S RESOURCES
- ☞ Review and Response Worksheet
- ☞ Selection Test
- ☞ Language Skills Worksheet

HUMANITIES CONNECTION

The Mayans created sculpture for their burials and other rituals, as well as to mark important events and special days in their calendar. ∎

1 INFERRING

What faults or failings do these details about the wooden people hint at? (Possible responses: selfishness, ingratitude, thoughtlessness, pride)

CULTURAL DIVERSITY

Because the Mayans believed that history repeats itself, they expected present creations to be destroyed as past creations had been.

❓ *How does our view of time differ from that of the Mayans?* (Westerners see time as linear rather than cyclical.)

2 LITERARY ELEMENT

Climax: Note how early in the story the fate of the wooden people becomes clear. What holds our interest after we learn they will be destroyed? (Possible response: We want to know how and by whom their destruction will take place.)

THE WOODEN PEOPLE
from the Popol Vuh
A Quiché Mayan Myth
translated by
DENNIS TEDLOCK

‡ *Pay special attention to the behavior of the manikins—the wooden people. In what ways are they like us?*

Mayan statuette.
Instituto Nacional de Antropología e Historia

This was the peopling of the face of the earth:

They came into being, they multiplied, they had daughters, they had sons, these manikins, woodcarvings. But there was nothing in their hearts and nothing in their minds, no memory of their mason and builder. They just went and walked wherever they wanted. Now they did not remember the Heart of Sky.[1]

And so they fell, just an experiment and just a cutout for humankind. They were talking at first but their faces were dry. They were not yet developed in the legs and arms. They had no blood, no lymph. They had no sweat, no fat. Their complexions were dry, their faces were crusty. They flailed their legs and arms, their bodies were deformed.

And so they accomplished nothing before the Maker, Modeler[2] who gave them birth, gave them heart. They became the first numerous people here on the face of the earth.

Again there comes a humiliation, destruction, and demolition. The manikins, woodcarvings were killed when the Heart of Sky devised a flood for them. A great flood was made; it came down on the heads of the manikins, woodcarvings.

The man's body was carved from the wood of the coral tree by the Maker, Modeler. And as for the woman, the Maker, Modeler needed the pith of reeds for the woman's body. They were not competent, nor did they speak before the builder and sculptor who made them and brought them forth, and so they were killed, done in by a flood:

---

1. **Heart of Sky:** the father god of the Quiché Mayans.

2. **Maker, Modeler:** the Quiché Mayan god of creation.

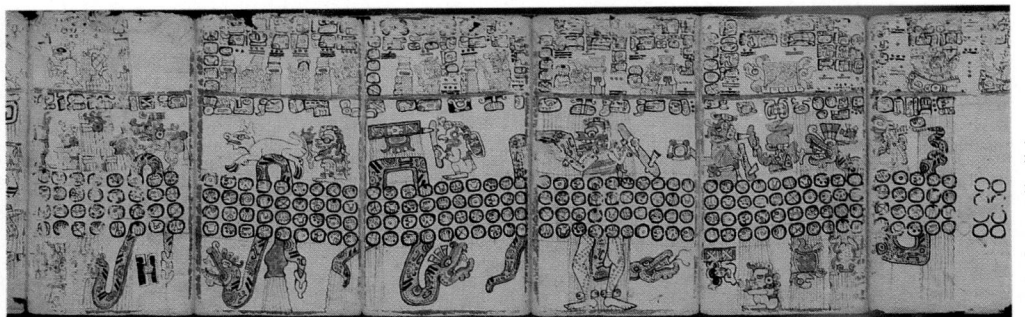

Fragment of the Madrid codex, Mayan. *The Quiché Mayans recorded the myth of the wooden people in the* Popol Vuh, *or* Book of Counsel.

❓ *What counsel, or advice, does this myth give?*

Scala/Art Resource, New York

There came a rain of resin from the sky.

There came the one named Gouger of Faces: he gouged out their eyeballs.

There came Sudden Bloodletter: he snapped off their heads.

There came Crunching Jaguar: he ate their flesh.

There came Tearing Jaguar: he tore them open.

They were pounded down to the bones and tendons, smashed and pulverized even to the bones. Their faces were smashed because they were incompetent before their mother and their father, the Heart of Sky, named Hurricane. The earth was blackened because of this; the black rainstorm began, rain all day and rain all night. Into their houses came the animals, small and great. Their faces were crushed by things of wood and stone. Everything spoke: their water jars, their tortilla griddles, their plates, their cooking pots, their dogs, their grinding stones, each and every thing crushed their faces. Their dogs and turkeys told them:

"You caused us pain, you ate us, but now it is *you* whom *we* shall eat." And this is the grinding stone:

"We were undone because of you.

Every day, every day,
in the dark, in the dawn, forever,
r-r-rip, r-r-rip,
r-r-rub, r-r-rub,
right in our faces, because of you.

This was the service we gave you at first, when you were still people, but today you will learn of our power. We shall pound and we shall grind your flesh," their grinding stones told them.

And this is what their dogs said, when they spoke in their turn:

"Why is it you can't seem to give us our food? We just watch and you just keep us down, and you throw us around. You keep a stick ready when you eat, just so you can hit us. We don't talk, so we've received nothing from you. How could you not have known? You *did* know that we were wasting away there, behind you.

"So, this very day you will taste the teeth in our mouths. We shall eat you," their dogs told them, and their faces were crushed.

And then their tortilla griddles and cooking pots spoke to them in turn:

1. What is in the hearts and minds of the wooden people? (nothing) Whom did they forget? (They forgot their creator.)
2. How are the wooden people destroyed? (by a flood and by attacks from ferocious animals)
3. Why do the wooden people's household objects and animals turn against them? (They feel they have been thoughtlessly abused by them.)

4. What happens when the manikins try to escape? (Houses collapse; trees throw them off; caves slam shut.)
5. According to the myth, why do monkeys look like people? (They are left-over wooden people.)

Have students work in small groups to dramatize a part of the myth or the entire myth. Encourage them to use masks, costumes, and props and to incorporate the dialogue found in the selection, such as the lines spoken by the grinding stone, the dogs, and the tortilla griddle. For the manikins' lines, students may use the work they completed in the Writing to Learn activity.

MEETING INDIVIDUAL NEEDS

5 ESL: Students may not be familiar with the expression *helter-skelter*, which means "in a confused, disorderly way." Encourage them to share a similar expression in their native language. ∎

6 COMPARING LITERATURE

Remind students that the Cheyenne myth "How the World Was Made" (pp. 8–16) included explanations for the characteristics of the turtle and the coot. Invite students from different cultural backgrounds to share stories or myths that explain the origin of monkeys or other animals.

PREDICTING

Remind students that this selection is the third Mayan creation story in a sequence of four. Have students predict what kind of people will be created in the fourth episode, providing a basis for their predictions.

WRITING TO LEARN

Point out to students that the wooden people do not speak in the myth. Have them consider what they might say if they could speak for themselves. Then have students create dialogue in which the wooden people either beg the Heart of Sky for their lives or respond to the complaints of their household objects and animals. ∎

"Pain! That's all you've done for us. Our mouths are sooty, our faces are sooty. By setting us on the fire all the time, you burn us. Since *we* felt no pain, *you* try it. We shall burn you," all their cooking pots said, crushing their faces.

5 The stones, their hearthstones were shooting out, coming right out of the fire, going for their heads, causing them pain. Now they run for it, helter-skelter.

They want to climb up on the houses, but they fall as the houses collapse.

They want to climb the trees; they're thrown off by the trees.

They want to get inside caves, but the caves slam shut in their faces.

6 Such was the scattering of the human work, the human design. The people were ground down, overthrown. The mouths and faces of all of them were destroyed and crushed. And it used to be said that the monkeys in the forests today are a sign of this. They were left as a sign because wood alone was used for their flesh by the builder and sculptor.

THE BONAMPOK FRESCO CYCLE, Mayan.
❓ *What non-human objects come to life in this myth? What do they do to the people?*

SEF/Art Resource, New York

So this is why monkeys look like people: they are a sign of a previous human work, human design—mere manikins, mere woodcarvings.

> ### First Thoughts
> What is the most exciting or dramatic part of this myth to you?

Identifying Facts

1. **Describe** the wooden people. In what ways are they just a "cutout," or preliminary design, for human beings? In what ways are they like us?
2. Why does the god Heart of Sky punish the wooden people? How does he punish them?
3. What origin does this myth explain?

Interpreting Meanings

1. What do you consider the **climax**, or point of greatest suspense, in this story? Does the climax occur in a brief moment, or does it take up a longer portion of the story? Explain.
2. The word *competent* means "having the right qualities or abilities to fulfill a function." In what way were the wooden people "not competent"—that is, unable to act as the Mayan gods expected?
3. The gods in the Popol Vuh tried to create humans three times, and three

1. Reacting to a Quote. The Native American Black Elk once said of a myth, "Whether it happened or not I do not know; but if you think about it you can see that it is true." Have students write an essay explaining how the quote applies to the insights the *Popol Vuh* expresses about the shortcomings of human nature.

2. Comparing Translations. Interested students can compare Dennis Tedlock's translation of this episode from the *Popol Vuh* with the original English translation by Adrián Recinos (University of Oklahoma Press, 1950) or the more recent translation by Ralph Nelson (Houghton Mifflin, 1976). Have students explain which translation they prefer, discussing specific passages from each work.

Ask students to discuss ways in which the Mayan myth can be taken as a warning, or cautionary tale, to human beings about proper ways to behave. Use the discussion as a springboard for comparison and contrast of views of human nature as represented in this myth and other myths with which the students are familiar. ■

---

times they failed. What does this tell you about the way the Quiché Mayans viewed their gods?

Applying Meanings

How do the wooden people fail the gods? How might this myth have served to teach the Quiché Mayan people proper behavior?

Creative Writing Response

Narrating a Series of Events. One of the most amazing incidents in this myth is the revenge of the pots, pans, and tortilla griddles against the wooden people. Write a one- or two-paragraph narrative in which you describe an inanimate object or objects coming to life and interacting with people. For example, what might your television say about your viewing habits? Tell *what* happens, *where* it happens, *when* it happens, and *who* is involved. Include vivid **imagery** to bring the fantastic situation to life for your readers. What is the **climax** of your narrative?

Language and Vocabulary

Imagery

Imagery is language that appeals to the senses. Most images in literature are visual—that is, they create pictures in the reader's mind by appealing to the sense of sight. But imagery can also appeal to the

senses of hearing, touch, taste, or smell. In fact, an effective image may appeal to several senses at once.

Dennis Tedlock's translation of the Popol Vuh is full of powerful imagery. Reread these passages from "The Wooden People." Then make a list of which sense each passage appeals to: sight, hearing, taste, touch, smell, or a combination of several.

1. "They were talking at first but their faces were dry. They were not yet developed in the legs and arms. They had no blood, no lymph. They had no sweat, no fat. Their complexions were dry, their faces were crusty."

2. "They were pounded down to the bones and tendons, smashed and pulverized even to the bones."

3. "The earth was blackened because of this; the black rainstorm began, rain all day and rain all night."

4. "Everything spoke: their water jars, their tortilla griddles, their plates, their cooking pots, their dogs, their grinding stones, each and every thing crushed their faces."

5. " 'Our mouths are sooty, our faces are sooty. By setting us on the fire all the time, you burn us.' "

Find other examples of imagery in this myth. How would you describe the overall effect of the imagery?

First Thoughts
Answers will vary.

Identifying Facts
1. Unlike us, they have dry faces; no blood, sweat, fat, or lymph; unformed limbs. Like us, they are thoughtless and ungrateful.
2. He punishes them for not remembering their creators and not being "competent." He destroys them with a flood and with attacks from other creatures.
3. the origin of monkeys

Interpreting Meanings
1. The climax is the flood; it takes up much of the story.
2. They couldn't think or love or even speak; they had no memory of their creators.
3. They saw their gods as "builders" or "sculptors" who made mistakes but tried to improve their creations.

Applying Meanings
The wooden people give no thought to anything—not even to their creators. The myth tells how bad human behavior is punished.

Creative Writing Response
Narrating a Series of Events.
Students can begin by listing events in chronological order. Entertaining dialogue could bring life to their narratives.

Language and Vocabulary
1. sight, touch 2. sight, sound, touch 3. sight, sound 4. sight, sound 5. sight, taste, touch Other examples will vary. ■

OBJECTIVES

1. *To interpret a Plains Indian (Caddo) tale*
2. *To analyze the motivation of a trickster character*
3. *To write a television script about a trickster figure and to compare and contrast two folktales about the origin of death*

PREREADING FOCUS

Background: The trickster archetype survives today in the festivals that celebrate disorder, such as Halloween, Mardi Gras, and April Fool's Day. Many societies have such festivals in which the rules of correct behavior are temporarily suspended. These festivals not only allow expression of the trickster in all of us, but also reinforce the rules we agree to live by for the rest of the year.

Writer's Response: Animals selected to represent tricksters in a particular literature were usually those considered intelligent or crafty by the local people. Those animals least likely to represent tricksters were large, lumbering animals such as elephants or buffaloes. Traditional tricksters have included the coyote, rabbit, raven, and bluejay in North America; the fox in Europe; the spider or tortoise in Africa; and the monkey in Asia.

ABOUT THE STORYTELLERS

Richard Erdoes (1912–) began writing the life story of a Sioux medicine man while on a photography assignment on a reservation. Since then, Erdoes has written many books on Native American culture.

Alfonso Ortiz (1939–) is a professor of anthropology at the University of New Mexico. He has written and edited several books on Native Americans.

Reader's Guide

COYOTE AND THE ORIGIN OF DEATH

Background

Almost every culture has a story that explains the origin of death. In myths and folktales from different parts of the world, death comes into the world in a variety of ways. Sometimes death enters the world because people disobey the gods; sometimes there is a kind of gamble involved in which people must decide between two alternatives, and the one they unintentionally choose is death. In some stories, death comes into the world through the actions of a **trickster,** a universal figure in world myths and folktales, especially those from Africa and North America.

Tricksters are ambivalent figures who tend to leave trouble and chaos behind wherever they go. They rebel against any kind of authority or social convention. Tricksters are not necessarily evil. In fact, they often possess positive traits, such as cleverness, curiosity, and creativity. Many tricksters are simply mischievous, much like children are before they "know better." Others are less innocent in their intentions. The trickster archetype survives today in the form of comedians, clowns, and heroes of popular culture such as Bugs Bunny and the teenage film character Ferris Bueller.

The following myth comes from the Native American Caddo people. Coyote plays the role of the trickster in Caddo tales.

Writer's Response

In myths and folktales, tricksters are often animals. Note at least three animals that you think could be cast as tricksters, and three that probably wouldn't be cast as tricksters. Briefly explain your choices.

Literary Focus

Storytellers and writers usually try to provide a character's **motivation**—the reasons for a character's actions. A character's motivations set the **plot,** or sequence of events in a story, into motion. Try to figure out Coyote's motivation for doing what he does. Is the motivation stated, or do we have to **infer** it from the text?

Adverb Clauses

An adverb clause is a subordinate clause that tells *how, when, where,* or *why.* It usually begins with a subordinate conjunction, such as *when, before, since, until, although, as,* or *unless.* When the clause begins a sentence, it is followed by a comma. Here are some examples:

When the spirit came, they would restore it to life.

Ever since Coyote closed the door, the spirits of the dead have wandered over the earth trying to find some place to go, *until at last they discovered the road to the spirit land.*

Writing/Speaking/Listening. Have students rewrite the story of Coyote and the whirlwind in their own words. Encourage them to use sentences with adverb clauses, using commas where needed. Afterward, have students read their stories aloud, and ask the class to identify the adverb clauses. ∎

COYOTE AND THE ORIGIN OF DEATH
A Caddo Myth
retold by
RICHARD ERDOES AND ALFONSO ORTIZ

Why does Coyote want to make certain that people stay dead forever?

In the beginning of this world, there was no such thing as death. Everybody continued to live until there were so many people that the earth had no room for any more. The chiefs held a council to determine what to do. One man rose and said he thought it would be a good plan to have the people die and be gone for a little while, and then return.

1 As soon as he sat down, Coyote jumped up and said he thought people ought to die forever. He pointed out that this little world is not large enough to hold all of the people, and that if the people who died came back to life, there would not be food enough for all.

2 All the other men objected. They said that they did not want their friends and relatives to die and be gone forever, for then they would grieve and worry and there would be no happiness in the world. Everyone except Coyote decided to have people die and be gone for a little while, and then come back to life again.

The medicine men built a large grass house facing the east. When they had completed it, they called the men of the tribe together and told them that people who died

Smithsonian Institution, Cat. # 378577

Carved wooden figure, Caddo.

would be restored to life in the medicine house. The chief medicine man explained that they would sing a song calling the spirit of the dead to the grass house. When the **3**

READING CHECK

1. Who thinks the dead should stay dead forever? (Coyote)
2. Who wants the dead to come back to life after a little while? (everyone else)
3. Why do the medicine men build a medicine house? (to attract the spirits of the dead and bring them back to life)

4. What does Coyote do when the whirlwind comes near the grass house? (shuts the door)
5. Why is Coyote always starving? (No one will feed him because of what he did.)

4 COMPARING LITERATURE

Students might find it interesting to read about Isis's attempts to bring her husband, Osiris, back to life in "Osiris and Isis" (pp. 34–39) and to compare Egyptian and Native American ideas about death.

5 LITERARY ELEMENT

Character's Motivation: Why did Coyote close the door of the grass house? (He did not want the spirits of the dead to be restored to life.)

6 READER'S RESPONSE

What do you think Coyote was afraid of? Do you think the people treated him fairly?

WRITING TO LEARN

Have students write either a WANTED poster or a certificate of merit for Coyote, based on their assessment of his behavior and its effects on society. ∎

ANSWERS
First Thoughts
Possible responses: He is not evil because he did what was necessary for life to continue, or he is evil because he betrayed people's wishes.

Identifying Facts
1. The world is not large enough and there is not enough food for everyone to live forever.
2. When the spirit of a dead person returns, he shuts the door to keep it out.

spirit came, they would restore it to life. All the people were glad, because they were anxious for the dead to come and live with them again.

4 When the first man died, the medicine men assembled in the grass house and sang. In about ten days a whirlwind blew from the west and circled about the grass house.

5 Coyote saw it, and as the whirlwind was about to enter the house, he closed the door. The spirit of the whirlwind, finding the door closed, whirled on by. In this way Coyote made death eternal, and from that time on, people grieved over their dead and were unhappy.

Now whenever anyone meets a whirlwind or hears the wind whistle, he says: "Someone is wandering about." Ever since Coyote closed the door, the spirits of the dead have wandered over the earth trying to find some place to go, until at last they discovered the road to the spirit land.

6 Coyote ran away and never came back, for when he saw what he had done, he was afraid. Ever after that, he has run from one place to another, always looking back first over one shoulder and then over the other to see if anyone is pursuing him. And ever since then he has been starving, for no one will give him anything to eat.

The North American coyote.
❓ *What qualities of the coyote does this story explain?*

Tim Fitzharris/ALLSTOCK

First Thoughts
Do you think that Coyote is an evil character? Why or why not?

Identifying Facts
1. What reasons does Coyote give for urging that people stay dead forever?
2. Describe the trick Coyote uses to prevent the dead from coming back to life.

3. What effect does Coyote's action have on society? What traits of the coyote does this tale explain?

Interpreting Meanings
1. Is Coyote selfish or wise? Explain. What do you think was his **motivation** for doing what he did?

1. Comparing Tricksters. Have students find tales about the Native American trickster Raven, the African trickster Anansi the Spider, and the African American trickster Br'er Rabbit. Have them analyze and compare the tricksters' characters, motivations, and effects on the people around them. Some students might enjoy role-playing the tricksters as the rest of the class interviews them.

2. Researching the Origin of Death Tales. Have students form small groups to research myths or folktales that explain the origin of death. You may wish to have each group find one tale from a culture of their choice and share it with the class.

Have students discuss how this myth reflects people's mixed feelings about death. How do people today view death? Can these mixed feelings about death ever be resolved? ■

---

2. In many myths and folktales, tricksters bring about sweeping changes in society, sometimes bringing order out of disorder. Why do you think the trickster is seen as an agent of change? How is this trickster quality brought out in this story?

3. Why do you think that the Caddo and many other Native American peoples chose the coyote to represent the trickster figure rather than some other animal?

Applying Meanings

If you had been at the council described at the beginning of this story, how would you have voted? Why?

Creative Writing Response

Writing a Television Script. Imagine the coyote of this tale as a cartoon character, like Wile E. Coyote, the troublemaker in the "Roadrunner" cartoons. Adapt this myth into a television script for a cartoon. You may need to give names to some of the characters, such as the chiefs and medicine men. Be sure to include teleplay (television script) directions in parentheses to describe the actions of the characters.

If you like to draw, you might try illustrating a few scenes from your cartoon adaptation.

Critical Writing Response

Comparing and Contrasting Two Myths. Read the following African tale from the Khoikhoi people called "The Origin of Death." As you read, think about elements it shares with the Caddo tale. Think about the differences. Then write a two- or three-paragraph essay in which you compare and contrast the two stories.

The Origin Of Death
A Khoikhoi Myth

retold by
Paul Radin

The Moon, it is said, once sent an insect to men, saying, "Go to men and tell them, 'As I die, and dying live; so you shall also die, and dying live.'"

The insect started with the message, but, while on his way, was overtaken by the hare, who asked, "On what errand are you bound?"

The insect answered, "I am sent by the Moon to men, to tell them that as she dies and dying lives, so shall they also die and dying live."

The hare said, "As you are an awkward runner, let me go." With these words he ran off, and when he reached men, he said, "I am sent by the Moon to tell you, 'As I die and dying perish, in the same manner you also shall die and come wholly to an end.'"

The hare then returned to the Moon and told her what he had said to men. The Moon reproached him angrily, saying, "Do you dare tell the people a thing which I have not said?"

With these words the Moon took up a piece of wood and struck the hare on the nose. Since that day the hare's nose has been split, but men believe what Hare had told them.

Use a chart like the one below to organize your thoughts about the two stories.

	Khoikhoi	Caddo
1. Characterization of animal responsible for bringing death into the world		
2. Condition of world before deception		
3. Condition of world after deception		
4. Lesson of story		

---

3. People die to give others room to live, but the permanent absence of the dead causes grief. The tale explains the coyote's constant running with its head turned and its difficulty finding enough to eat.

Interpreting Meanings

1. Possible responses: wise, because his motivation was to make sure the living could survive; or selfish, because he was mainly concerned about his own comfort

2. Possible response: The trickster's creative rebelliousness is necessary for innovation. Here Coyote thinks for himself, disobeys the elders, and brings about a drastic change.

3. Possible response: Coyotes possess traits, such as slyness, cunning, and a troublemaking nature, that suggest trickster qualities.

Applying Meanings
Answers will vary.

Creative Writing Response
Writing a Television Script. Scripts should be in play form with dialogue and teleplay directions.

Critical Writing Response
Comparing and Contrasting Two Myths. Essays should discuss specific similarities and differences. Students may use the subject-by-subject or feature-by-feature pattern. ■

1 CULTURAL DIVERSITY

Some heroes are known for their physical prowess, but others demonstrate strength by resisting action. For example, Sidhartha Gautama (a religious philosopher who lived in India in the sixth century B.C. and came to be known as the Buddha, or enlightened one) sat quietly as he was tempted by appeals to his sense of duty, his fears, and his desire for physical pleasure. By resisting, he found inner peace.

2 READER'S RESPONSE

Folktale heroes usually triumph over obstacles in their own lives and win personal happiness. Mythic heroes more often triumph over cosmic forces and bring about the regeneration of their society or the entire world. *Do you prefer tales of superheroes or of ordinary people who overcome great odds?*

COMPARING LITERATURE

Elements of the archetypal hero's quest appear not only in traditional oral myths and folktales but also in original works. For example, the seventeenth-century Spanish novel *Don Quixote* (pp. 821–837) satirizes the hero's idealistic quest by creating a comic hero who naively sets off on a bony old horse to right the wrongs of the world. On the darker side, the twentieth-century short story *The Metamorphosis* (pp. 1154–1194) describes its hero's descent into the psychological netherworld of alienation and loss of identity.

 Introduction

The Hero and the Quest

© Lucasfilm Ltd.

The heroic quest is a recurring archetype in American popular culture, as are heroes like Indiana Jones.
❓ *How is the heroic quest pattern played out in films like* Raiders of the Lost Ark?

Tales of the hero and the heroic quest occur in nearly every world culture. If we look closely at hero tales from all over the world and compare them, we find what the Irish novelist James Joyce and the American mythologist Joseph Campbell called the *monomyth*—literally, "the one story." This monomyth, or archetypal heroic quest story, has remarkably the same structure from culture to culture. It is as if each hero wears the particular "costume" of his or her culture, but is really the same hero underneath, facing the same kinds of challenges. Today, film heroes Luke Skywalker and Indiana Jones serve as modern versions of the quest hero.

The Nature of the Quest Hero

A **mythic hero** can be male or female. This hero usually has a remarkable birth or childhood. He or she is often the offspring of a god and a human being, and so possesses qualities of both immortals and mortals. Heroes may be born under unusual circumstances. Sometimes they are unaware of their origins and are raised by foster parents. The hero often shows early signs of being special, possessing either superhuman strength or supernatural powers.

The **folktale hero**, on the other hand, is often a very ordinary person, a stepchild or a neglected youngest child who is scoffed at by parents or older brothers

1

2

and sisters. Although the folktale hero may not have superhuman abilities, he or she might be out of the ordinary in other ways. Many such heroes, for example, are exceptionally kind, clever, or resourceful.

Both mythic and folktale heroes are called to participate in an adventure or forced to face a series of challenges or tests. They may at first refuse to face their challenges, but they suffer greatly for their refusal. Eventually, they are forced by circumstances to accept their role and overcome the obstacles placed before them.

The Hero's Quest

A **quest** is a journey taken in search of something of value. The prize that is sought may be a specific person, such as a beautiful princess; an abstract concept, such as truth or the meaning of life; or a concrete object, such as a treasure or a magical charm. Sometimes the hero is simply searching for his or her "roots," such as a parent he or she has never known.

◆

quest: *a journey taken in search of a person or object of great value.*

Mythic heroes are often aided on their quests by loyal friends or by god or goddess benefactors. Folktale heroes are often helped by people, animals, or magical beings who are repaying them for good deeds done earlier. The quest itself does not always go smoothly. The hero may be tempted to leave the "true path" by succumbing to some temptation, such as a beautiful woman or the lure of an easier lifestyle. Sometimes a character flaw in the hero—usually overwhelming pride or impatience—causes him or her to falter on the quest.

The quest may involve a descent into the underworld or to some other dark and frightening place, such as an enchanted cave or forest, that ordinary human beings dare not enter. This is the ultimate stage of the hero's journey—"to boldly go where no one has gone before," as the prologue to *Star Trek* proclaims. Sometimes, the hero's final adventure may even involve the greatest sacrifice of all: giving up his or her life for others. If the hero survives the journey to the underworld, he or she returns to society, often with something to share: new knowledge, a renewed commitment, or greater compassion and wisdom. The hero may be rewarded by entering into a royal marriage and living "happily ever after."

What the Quest Means to Us

Perhaps the heroic quest tale is so universal because the challenges that the quest hero faces are symbolic of the challenges that each of us must face in life. "Killing monsters" may symbolize the individual fighting against social injustices or against inner conflicts that prevent happiness. The journey to the underworld might symbolize facing unpleasant realities, such as the existence of death, or looking inside ourselves to ask and answer tough questions.

As long as people feel the need to tell stories about the human journey, they will tell the enduring story of the hero and the quest.

3 CULTURAL DIVERSITY
A hero who becomes a sacrificial victim for his society is called a *scapegoat*. Middle Eastern mythology is full of such figures, reflecting the idea that just as something of value must be planted in the earth before new crops can grow, so something of value must be offered to the gods before a society's sins can be washed away. Later, the word *scapegoat* was applied to anyone forced to bear the blame for the crimes of others.
❓ *Can you think of an example of a modern scapegoat?* (Possible response: Poor people receiving public assistance are often blamed for the general ills of a failing economy.)

4 CULTURAL DIVERSITY
Rites of passage are traditional components of the hero's quest. In rites of passage, an individual is expected to go through certain ritualized trials of intellectual or physical power before he or she is recognized as a full member of adult society. For example, Jewish children mark their passage into adulthood with bar mitzvah (boys') and bas mitzvah (girls') ceremonies. Christian children undergo the sacrament of confirmation. In many Asian and African societies, children prove their readiness for adulthood through ritual tests and ceremonies.
❓ *In what other ways does our society mark or celebrate the passage into adulthood?* (Possible responses: graduation ceremonies, college and job entrance exams)

OBJECTIVES

1. *To interpret a Greek myth about the hero's quest*
2. *To recognize methods of characterization used in the myth*
3. *To write a sequel extending the story of the hero*
4. *To write correctly punctuated dialogue between two characters*

PREREADING FOCUS

Background: The ancient Greeks believed their gods resided on Mount Olympus, which was thought to be the highest mountain in the world. The gods of Olympus lived in a hierarchical society with Zeus ruling over all the lesser gods. Though the gods had bodies and could be wounded, they always healed and remained eternally young. Individual gods had their favorites among humans and were often unfriendly to the favorites of other gods. Each Greek city-state claimed a specific god as its patron.

Literary Focus: The composers of myths had more important purposes than creating interesting, true-to-life characters. They wanted instead to dramatize truths about the origins of life and the nature of gods and humans. For this reason, characters in myths, both human and divine, tend to have rather obvious traits and are characterized or described directly more often than are the characters in modern short stories.

ABOUT THE RETELLER

Robert Graves (1895–1985) was a noted British author, translator, literary critic, and mythologist. He wrote many volumes of poetry, many nonfiction works, and several novels, including *I, Claudius*, about an emperor of ancient Rome.

Reader's Guide ■

THESEUS

Background

The story of Theseus, from ancient Greece, fits the general pattern of the hero and the quest in several ways. Theseus is secretly fathered by a king; he shows great strength as a boy; he kills a monster, wins a princess, and gains a kingdom; and he descends into the underworld.

The Greeks saw their gods as powerful beings who nevertheless had much in common with human beings, though on a grander scale. The Greek gods and goddesses could be generous and merciful, but they could also be petty and unfair. The ancient Greeks thought that their gods and goddesses played an active role in humans' lives.

Though all Greeks shared the same religion and language, their country was a group of separate, independent city-states. Among these were Athens, in central Greece, and Corinth, to the south. The island nation of Crete lay to the southeast. These three places form the setting of Theseus' story.

Writer's Response

Who is your favorite hero? Think of a superhuman character from books, television, or movies who appeals to you. Write a paragraph describing this hero and exploring what it is about him, her, or it that you admire.

Literary Focus

Characterization is the process by which an author reveals a character's personality. A writer can reveal character in the following ways:

1. By describing the character's appearance
2. By recording what the character says
3. By revealing the character's innermost thoughts and feelings
4. By showing the character's actions
5. By showing how other characters act toward the character
6. By telling us directly what the character is like: kind, untrustworthy, and so on

The first five methods are examples of **indirect characterization**. The last method is called **direct characterization**.

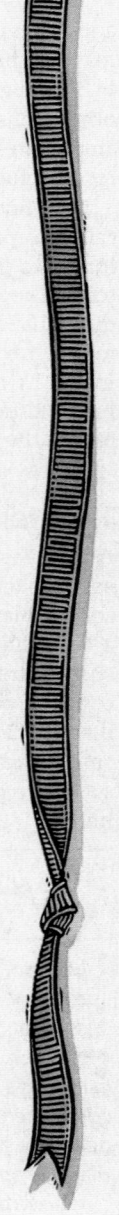

THESEUS
An Ancient Greek Myth
retold by
ROBERT GRAVES

When you come to the end of the third paragraph, identify the task that Theseus' mother gives him. Do you predict that Theseus will succeed or fail in his quest?

Temple of Apollo, overlooking the Aegean Sea on the Greek island of Naxos.

SEF/Art Resource, New York

On a visit to Corinth, King Aegeus of Athens secretly married the Princess Aethra. She had grown tired of waiting for Bellerophon,[1] whose wife she should have been, to come home from Lydia. After a few pleasant days with Aethra, Aegeus told her: "I am afraid I must leave now, my dear. It will be safest, in case you have a son, to pretend that his father is the God Poseidon.[2] My eldest nephew might kill you if he knew of our marriage. He expects to be the next King of Athens. Goodbye!"

Once back, Aegeus never left Athens again.

Aethra had a son whom she named Theseus, and on his fourteenth birthday she asked him: "Can you move that huge rock?" Theseus, a remarkably strong boy, lifted the rock and tossed it away. Hidden underneath, he found a sword with a golden snake pattern inlaid on the blade, and a pair of sandals. "Those were left there by your father," Aethra said. "He is Aegeus, King of Athens. Take them to him and say that you found them under this rock. But mind, not a word to his nephews, who will be furious if they discover that you are the true heir to the throne of Athens. Because of them I have pretended all these years that Poseidon, not Aegeus, was your father."

Theseus went by the coast road to Athens. First he met a giant named Sinis, who had the horrible habit of bending two pine trees down towards each other, tying some poor

---

1. **Bellerophon** (bə·ler'ə·fän'): The Greek hero Bellerophon rode the winged horse Pegasus and killed a fire-breathing monster called the Chimera.

2. **Poseidon** (pō·sī'dən): One of the Olympians, the twelve major Greek gods and goddesses. Poseidon, called Neptune by the Romans, was the god of the sea and of horses.

4 SYNTHESIZING

What do you think the adjective *Procrustean* means? (ruthlessly determined to make everyone conform to the same standard)

5 GUIDED READING

Identifying Details: What detail noticed by King Aegeus saves Theseus from Medea? (He notices the snake pattern on Theseus' sword, so he knows Theseus is his son and needs protection from Medea.)

6 GUIDED READING

Sequencing: What sequence of events led to the annual sacrifice of Athenian boys and girls to the Minotaur? (Androgeus, the Cretan king's son, won all the athletic events in Athens one year, so Aegeus's jealous nephews murdered him. Androgeus's father, King Minos, complained to the gods, and the gods ordered the sacrifice.)

7 LITERARY ELEMENT

Characterization: What do Theseus' words in response to being sent to Crete show about him? (He is brave, bold, loyal, and eager to correct injustice.) What kind of characterization is this? (indirect)

8 LITERARY ELEMENT

Characterization: What do Ariadne's actions suggest about her character? (She is brave, intelligent, assertive, and determined.)

traveler to their tops by his arms, and then suddenly letting go. The trees would fly upright and tear him in two. Theseus wrestled with Sinis, threw him senseless on the ground, and then treated him as he had treated others.

Next, Theseus faced and killed a monstrous wild sow, with tusks larger and sharper than sickles. Then he fought Procrustes, a wicked innkeeper who lived beside the main road and kept only one bed in his inn. If travelers were too short for the bed, Procrustes would lengthen them with an instrument of torture called "the rack"; if they were too tall, he would chop off their feet; and if they were the right size, he would smother them with a blanket. Theseus beat Procrustes, tied him to the bed, and cut off both his feet; but, finding him still too tall, cut off his head as well. He wrapped the dead body in a blanket and flung it into the sea.

King Aegeus had recently been married again: to a witch named Medea. Theseus did not know about this marriage, yet on his arrival at Athens, Medea knew by magic who he was; and decided to poison him—putting wolfbane[3] in a cup of wine. She wanted one of her own sons to be the next King. Luckily Aegeus noticed the snake pattern on Theseus' sword, guessed that the wine had been poisoned, and hastily knocked the cup from Medea's hand. The poison burned a large hole through the floor, and Medea escaped in a magic cloud. Then Aegeus sent a chariot to fetch Aethra from Corinth, and announced: "Theseus is my son and heir." The next day, Aegeus's nephews ambushed Theseus on his way to a temple; but he fought and killed them all.

Now, it had happened some years before that King Minos's son, Androgeus of Crete, visited Athens and there won all the competitions in the Athletic Games—running, jumping, boxing, wrestling, and throwing the discus. Aegeus's jealous nephews accused him of a plot to seize the throne, and murdered him. When Minos complained about this to the Olympians, they gave orders that Aegeus must send seven boys and seven girls from Athens every ninth year to be devoured by the Cretan Minotaur. The Minotaur was a monster—half bull, half man—which Minos kept in the middle of the Labyrinth, or maze, built for him by Daedalus. The Minotaur knew every twist and turn in the Labyrinth, and would chase his victims into some blind alley where he had them at his mercy.

So now the Athenians, angry with Theseus for killing his cousins, chose him as one of the seven boys sent to be eaten that year. Theseus thanked them, saying that he was glad of a chance to free his country of this horrid tribute. The ship in which the victims sailed carried black sails, for mourning, but Theseus took white sails along, too. "If I kill the Minotaur, I shall hoist these white sails. If the Minotaur kills me, let the black ones be hoisted."

Theseus prayed to the Goddess Aphrodite.[4] She listened to him and told her son Eros[5] to make Ariadne, Minos's daughter, fall in love with Theseus. That same night, she came to Theseus' prison, drugged the guards, unlocked the door of his cell with a key stolen from Minos's belt, and asked Theseus: "If I help you to kill the Minotaur, will you marry me?"

---

3. **wolfbane**, or wolfsbane: a poisonous plant of the buttercup family, with hoodlike yellow flowers.

4. **Aphrodite** (af'rə·dīt'ē): the Greek goddess of love and beauty, called Venus by the Romans.

5. **Eros** (er'äs'): the god of love, called Cupid by the Romans.

"With pleasure," he answered, kissing her hand.

Ariadne led the boys quietly from the prison. She showed them a magic ball of thread, given her by Daedalus before he left Crete. One need only tie the loose end of the thread to the Labyrinth door, and the ball would roll by itself through all the twisting paths until it reached the clear space in the middle. "The Minotaur lives there," Ariadne said. "He sleeps for exactly one hour in the twenty-four, at midnight; but then he sleeps sound."

Theseus' six companions kept guard at the entrance, while Ariadne tied the thread to the Labyrinth door. Theseus entered, ran his hand along the thread in the darkness and came upon the sleeping Minotaur just after midnight. As the moon rose, he cut off the monster's head with a razor-sharp sword lent him by Ariadne, then followed the thread back to the entrance where his friends stood anxiously waiting. Meanwhile, Ariadne had freed the seven girls, too, and all together they stole down to the harbor. Theseus and his friends, having first bored holes in the sides of Minos's ships, climbed aboard their own, pushed her off, and sailed for Athens. The Cretan ships which gave chase soon filled and sank; so Theseus got safely away, with the Minotaur's head and Ariadne.

Theseus beached his ship on the island of Naxos; he needed food and water. While Ariadne lay resting on the beach, the God Dionysus[6] suddenly appeared to Theseus. "I want to marry this woman myself," he said. "If you take her from me, I will destroy Athens by sending all its people mad."

Theseus dared not offend Dionysus and, since he had no great love for Ariadne anyway, he left her asleep and set sail. Ariadne wept with rage on waking, to find herself deserted; but Dionysus soon walked up, introduced himself, and offered her a large cup of wine. Ariadne drank it all, felt better at once, and decided that it would be far more glorious to marry a god than a mortal. Dionysus' wedding present to her was the splendid jeweled coronet which is now the constellation called "The Northern Crown." She bore several children to Dionysus, and eventually returned to Crete as Queen.

In the excitement, Theseus had quite forgotten to change the sails, and King Aegeus, watching anxiously from a cliff at Athens, saw the black sail appear instead of the white. Overcome by grief, he jumped into the sea and drowned. Theseus then became King of Athens and made peace with the Cretans.

A few years later, the Amazons, a fierce race of fighting women from Asia, invaded Greece and attacked Athens. Since Theseus listened to the Goddess Athene's[7] advice, he managed to defeat them; but never afterwards stopped boasting about his courage.

One day his friend Peirithous said to him: "I am in love with a beautiful woman. Will you help me to marry her?"

"By all means," Theseus answered. "Am I not the bravest king alive? Look what I did to the Amazons! Look what I did to the Minotaur! Who is the woman?"

"Persephone, Demeter's[8] daughter," Peirithous answered.

---

7. **Athene** (ə·thē′nē), also called Athena (-nə): the Greek goddess of wisdom, warfare, and crafts.

8. **Demeter** (di·mēt′ər): the Greek goddess of fruits, grains, and fertility; her daughter Persephone was abducted against her will by Hades, ruler of the underworld.

6. **Dionysus** (dī′ə·nī′səs): the Greek god of wine and celebration, called Bacchus by the Romans.

9 MAKING JUDGMENTS
How much credit do you think Ariadne deserves for Theseus' success in the Labyrinth? Why do you think so? (Answers will vary.)

■ **MEETING INDIVIDUAL NEEDS**

10 ESL: Students may not recognize these usages of the words *stole* and *bored*. Point out that *stole* is the past tense of *steal*, and ask how someone who had just stolen something might move (sneakily, quietly). Explain that *bored* is the past participle of the verb *bore*, and have students guess its meaning from the context. ■

11 COMPARING LITERATURE/ CULTURAL DIVERSITY
The Greek gods often acted with little concern for the suffering of humans.
❓ *In what sense do the Greek gods resemble the tricksters of other myths?* (They take action that affects human lives, but have no regard for human feelings.) *Why do you think the Greeks were drawn to the idea of unconcerned or impulsive gods?* (Possible response: This idea helps explain the unfairness of life.)

12 READER'S RESPONSE
Did you blame Theseus for King Aegeus's death? Why or why not? What lesson do you think the storyteller wished to get across by having events take this turn? (the consequences of carelessness)

READING CHECK

1. Who is Theseus' father? (King Aegeus of Athens)
2. What does Medea do when Theseus arrives in Athens? (tries to poison him)
3. What magic gift does Ariadne give Theseus? (a ball of thread to help him find the Minotaur and then find his way out of the Labyrinth)

4. What does Theseus boast about after defeating the Amazons? (his courage)
5. How does Hades trap Theseus? (by tricking him into sitting on a magic bench)

RETEACHING

Have the class create a board game based on the myth. First ask students to make a list of the places and people Theseus encounters in his journey from his birthplace to his return to Athens as king. Students can make sequential pictures of this journey on the gameboard, then use the list to write instructions on cards. For example: "Medea recognizes you. Move back two spaces."

13 INFERRING MOTIVATION

Why does Theseus let his friend talk him into the adventure in the underworld? (He wants to live up to his boast.)

HUMANITIES CONNECTION

In his poetry and art, William Blake was concerned with the conflict between good and evil, reality and the imagination. He favored fantastical subjects from mythology and his own imagination over realistic subjects from nature. *Why do you think the fantastical creatures from mythology have such a hold on people's imaginations?* (Answers will vary.) ■

14 LITERARY ELEMENT

Imagery: What senses does Graves appeal to in order to help us imagine the fate of Theseus at the end of the story? (*sound:* "roared for laughter"; *sight:* "ghostly spotted snakes"; *touch:* "whipped," "stung," "gnawed")

15 LITERARY ELEMENT

Theme: How does Hades' taunt reflect the underlying message of the myth? (Possible response: Excessive pride leads one to foolish behavior.)

WRITING TO LEARN

Imagine that you are one of the gods in the myth. Write a speech telling the other gods your opinion of Theseus. ■

Tate Gallery, London/Art Resource, New York

CERBERUS, WILLIAM BLAKE (1715–1827).

"Oh! Are you serious? Persephone is already married to King Hades, God of the Dead!"

"I know, but she hates Hades and wants children. She can have no living children by the God of the Dead."

"It seems rather a risky adventure," said Theseus, turning pale.

"Are you not the bravest king alive?"

"I am."

"Let us go, then!"

They buckled on their swords and descended to Tartarus[9] by the side entrance. Having given the dog Cerberus[10] three cakes dipped in poppy juice, to send him asleep, Peirithous rapped at the palace gate and entered.

Hades asked in surprise: "Who are you mortals, and what do you want?"

Theseus told him: "I am Theseus, the bravest king alive. This is my friend Peirithous,

who thinks that Queen Persephone is far too good for you. He wants to marry her himself."

Hades grinned at them. Nobody had ever seen him grin before. "Well," he said, "it is true that Persephone is not exactly happy with me. I might even let her go, if you promise to treat her kindly. Shall we talk the matter over quietly? Please, sit down on that comfortable bench!"

Theseus and Peirithous sat down, but the bench Hades had offered them was a magic one. They became attached to it, so that they could never escape without tearing away part of themselves. Hades stood and roared for laughter, while the Furies[11] whipped the two friends; and ghostly spotted snakes stung them; and Cerberus, waking from his drugged sleep, gnawed at their fingers and toes.

"My poor fools," chuckled Hades, "you are here for always!"

---

9. **Tartarus** (tär'tə·rəs): the Greek underworld, ruled by Hades.
10. **Cerberus** (sur'bər·əs): a hideous three-headed dog that guards the gate of Tartarus.

11. **Furies:** three female spirits who punish wrong-doers; the Furies have hair made of snakes.

1. **Role-Playing an Interview.** Have pairs of students role-play an interview between a news reporter and either Theseus or Ariadne after the escape from the Labyrinth. Each reporter should make up a list of questions in advance. Students role-playing Theseus or Ariadne should express the traits of their character in their answers. Invite pairs to present their interviews to the class.

2. **Creating a Poster.** Students might enjoy creating an illustrated poster of the gods mentioned in the myth: Poseidon, Aphrodite, Eros, Dionysus, Demeter, Persephone, and Hades. Posters should include sketches of how each god was usually represented, plus captions giving information about each one.

Have students discuss what factors led to Theseus' success in the Labyrinth. To what degree was his victory based on his own courage and skill? To what degree did he depend on others? What are some of his heroic qualities that are still valued today? ■

First Thoughts

Do you like Theseus? Does he fit your image of what a hero should be?

Identifying Facts

1. How does the young Theseus first prove his strength?
2. What is the Minotaur? What is his role in the story?
3. What finally happens to King Aegeus?
4. Why does Theseus journey to the underworld? What happens to him there?

Interpreting Meanings

1. List at least four **character traits**, or qualities, that Theseus shows in this story. Give examples of each. Then explain whether **direct** or **indirect characterization** is used to describe each trait.
2. Many mythic heroes, especially those in Greek and Roman mythology, develop excessive pride, or **hubris** (hy$\overline{oo}$'bris). This pride results in the hero's downfall at the hands of the gods. At which point in the story does Theseus show the first signs of excessive pride? What is the result of his pride?
3. List at least three events or aspects of the story that seemed funny to you. What do the humorous touches add to the story?
4. One possible statement of the **theme** of this story can be found in this saying from the Book of Proverbs in the Hebrew Bible: "Pride goeth before destruction, and an haughty spirit before a fall." In other words, pride and overconfidence can lead to failure. Do you agree that this is the theme of the story of Theseus, or can you think of another statement of theme that better fits this story?

Applying Meanings

Based on what you have learned about Theseus' character in this myth, do you think that he has learned anything by the end of this story? Use details from the story to support your answer.

Creative Writing Response

Extending the Story. In this version of the myth, Theseus' quest seems to end in Tartarus. In other versions of the story, however, Theseus is rescued by another Greek hero, Herakles (Hercules). Imagine that Theseus has been saved from the underworld. Write a brief story in which Theseus, newly released from his captivity, faces a new challenge. How does Theseus react to the challenge? Is he the same hero he was before the descent into the underworld, or has he somehow changed? Be sure to include **indirect characterization** (the character's own words and actions, and others' responses to the character) in your story to reveal how Theseus has or has not changed.

Language and Vocabulary

Using Dialogue

Author Robert Graves often uses **dialogue**, or quoted conversation between characters, as he retells the myth of Theseus. When you use dialogue, begin a new paragraph each time the speaker changes. Study the following example:

"It seems a rather risky adventure," said Theseus, turning pale.

"Are you not the bravest king alive?"

"I am."

Write several lines of dialogue between two real or imagined characters. Use correct indentation and punctuation. You may refer to the grammar handbook at the back of this book to review punctuation.

First Thoughts
Answers will vary.

Identifying Facts
1. by moving a big rock
2. a monster that is half bull and half man. Theseus must find and kill it in the Labyrinth.
3. He drowns himself.
4. to bring back Persephone for his friend. He becomes trapped on a magic bench.

Interpreting Meanings
1. Possible responses: physical strength (direct); courage, boastful pride, respect for the gods (all indirect)
2. when Peirithous asks for help. He is trapped in the underworld.
3. Possible responses: the sunken Cretan ships, Ariadne's sudden preference for Dionysus, Hades' trick; comic relief
4. Many students will agree with the stated theme. Others might make statements such as "Trust your own instincts. Be wary."

Applying Meanings
Possible response: Theseus has learned little. He shows no insight and seems unaware of the character faults that led to his downfall.

Creative Writing Response
Extending the Story. Stories should relate a challenge and use indirect characterization.

Language and Vocabulary
Using Dialogue. Students should use punctuation correctly. ■

OBJECTIVES

1. *To interpret an Egyptian myth about death, rebirth, and the power of love*
2. *To analyze the point of view of the myth*
3. *To rewrite the myth from a different point of view and to evaluate theme statements*

THEMES IN WORLD LITERATURE

Life and Loss

From the *Aeneid*, pp. 380–408
"The Handsomest Drowned Man in the World," pp. 1289–1297

The Power and Pain of Love

New Kingdom Love Lyrics, pp. 80–82
"Peonies," pp. 532–535
Sonnet 49 and Sonnet 71, pp. 1275–1279

Nature of Evil

Inferno from the *Divine Comedy*, pp. 741–770
From *Faust*, Part 1, pp. 986–1001

Transformations

"Green Willow," pp. 40–45
From *Metamorphoses*, pp. 420–427
"The Night Face Up," pp. 1298–1307 ■

PREREADING FOCUS

Background: In ancient Egypt, the king, or pharaoh, was considered a god, and periodically was expected to undergo a symbolic "death" and "resurrection," which recalled the death and rebirth of the god-king Osiris. The fertility of the land was seen as directly linked to the health of the pharaoh.

Writer's Response: Female heroes such as Helen of Troy, Daphne, and Antigone usually have more passive roles than their male counterparts. More information about female heroes can be found in collections such as *Clever Gretchen and Other Forgotten Folktales* by Alison Lurie (Crowell, 1980) and Jane Yolen's *Favorite Folktales from Around the World* (Pantheon, 1986), which includes both male and female heroes in a section entitled "Heroes Likely and Unlikely."

Literary Focus: Since myths express the collective understanding of an entire culture, they are usually told from an omniscient point of view, in which all things, past, present, and future, are known to the storyteller. The omniscient narrator also has access to the thoughts and feelings of every character.

ABOUT THE STORYTELLER

Padraic Colum [pă·drā'·ək cō' lōōm] (1881–1972), a noted reteller of myths, was born in Ireland. Though his works include poetry, plays, and novels, he is most famous for children's books.

Reader's Guide ■

OSIRIS AND ISIS

Background

The myth of Osiris and Isis, from ancient Egypt, tells the story of a god who dies and is brought back to life. Myths about dying gods were common in the ancient world and probably developed out of the sacrificial rites practiced by some ancient cultures. At the root of these ancient rites lies the notion that someone or something must die or be otherwise transformed before society can be renewed.

The ancient Egyptians associated Osiris' body with the Nile, the river that they depended on for their livelihood. They also believed that Osiris sat in judgment of the dead at the gates of the underworld. According to tradition, Osiris' attendants weighed the hearts of the dead against a feather. Only those whose hearts were lighter than the feather—that is, those who had led good lives—were granted the privilege of eternal life.

A key player in the myth of Osiris is his wife and sister, the goddess Isis. Like her Sumerian and Greek goddess counterparts Inanna and Demeter, Isis demonstrates persistence, strength, intelligence, and compassion. She uses these qualities to restore order to the world, serving as midwife in a new creation.

Writer's Response

Isis is one of the great female figures in mythology. Before you read, write a list of some other famous heroic female figures that you can think of. Describe their accomplishments. Are the roles of these female heroes different from the roles assigned to the men?

Literary Focus

Point of view is the vantage point from which a writer tells a story. In the **first-person point of view**, the narrator is a character in the story and we are limited to knowing only what that character sees and knows. In the **third-person limited point of view**, we can gain great insight into one character, but we can't know the inner workings of the other characters' minds except through inference. In the **omniscient**, or "all-knowing," **point of view**, we get a "god's-eye" view of every character and every event, even the past and the future.

OSIRIS AND ISIS
An Ancient Egyptian Myth

retold by

PADRAIC COLUM

The myth of Osiris and Isis has been called one of the world's oldest and greatest love stories. As you read, consider how Isis' quest to save her husband reveals her deep love for him.

When Osiris reigned death was not in the land. Arms were not in men's hands; there were not any wars. From end to end of the land music sounded; men and women spoke so sweetly and out of such depth of feeling that all they said was <u>oratory</u> and poetry.

Osiris taught men and women wisdom and he taught them all the arts. He it was who first planted the vine; he it was who showed men how and when to sow grain, how to plant and tend the fruit-trees; he caused them to rejoice in the flowers also. Osiris made laws for men so that they were able to live together in harmony; he gave them knowledge of the Gods, and he showed them how the Gods might be honored.

And this was what he taught them concerning the Gods: In the beginning was the formless <u>abyss</u>, Nuu. From Nuu came Re, the Sun. Re was the first and he was the most divine of all beings. Re created all forms. From his thought came Shu and Tefenet, the Upper and the Lower Air. From Shu and Tefenet came Qeb and Nut, the Earth and the Sky. The Earth and the Sky had been separated, the one from the other, but once they had been joined together. From the eye of Re, made out of the essence that is in that eye, came the first man and the first woman.

And from Qeb, the Father, and Nut, the Mother, Osiris was born. When he was born a voice came into the world, crying, "Behold, the Lord of all things is born!"

And with Osiris was born Isis, his sister. Afterwards was born Thout, the Wise One. Then there was born Nephthys. And, last, there was born Seth. And Seth tore a hole in his mother's side—Seth the Violent One. Now Osiris and Isis loved each other as husband and wife, and together they reigned over the land. Thout was with them, and he taught men the arts of writing and of <u>reckoning</u>. Nephthys went with Seth and was his wife, and Seth's <u>abode</u> was in the desert.

Seth, in his desert, was angered against Osiris, for everywhere green things that Seth hated were growing over the land—vine, and grain, and the flowers. Many times Seth tried to destroy his brother Osiris, but always his plots were baffled by the watchful care of Isis. One day he took the measurement of Osiris' body—he took the measurement from his shadow—and he made a chest that was the exact size of Osiris.

Soon, at the time before the season of drought, Seth gave a banquet, and to that banquet he invited all the children of Earth

Osiris was often depicted as a mummy to show that he was the ruler of the dead. Sometimes, however, he was depicted with green skin to show his association with fertility and resurrection, and sometimes with black skin to show his association with the underworld.

? *What other figures from legend and mythology have qualities or play roles similar to those of Osiris? (Possible responses: Pluto, Hel, the phoenix)* ■

diversified (də·vur′sə·fīd′): varied

resplendent (ri·splen′dənt): dazzling

soldered (säd′ərd): joined with melted metal alloy

3 PREDICTING

What clues enable you to predict Osiris' fate? (Students may mention Seth's building a chest to fit Osiris' body and his offer to give the chest to whomever fits into it most perfectly.)

4 LEP: Students may not recognize that *bore* here is the past tense of the verb *to bear* and means "carried." ■

and the Sky. To that banquet came Thout, the Wise One, and Nephthys, the wife of Seth, and Seth himself, and Isis, and Osiris. And where they sat at banquet they could see the chest that Seth had made—the chest made of fragrant and <u>diversified</u> woods. All admired that chest. Then Seth, as though he would have them enter into a game, told all of them that he would give the chest to the one whose body fitted most closely in it. The children of Qeb and Nut went and laid themselves in the chest that Seth had made: Seth went and laid himself in it, Nephthys went and laid herself in it, Thout went and

The Granger Collection, New York

Osiris enthroned in the domain of the Dead, 19th dynasty. *The ancient Egyptians worshiped Osiris as the ruler of the dead.*
? *In the beginning of this myth, what is Osiris' role on earth?*

laid himself in it, Isis went and laid herself in it. All were short; none, laid in the chest, but left a space above his or her head.

Then Osiris took the crown off his head and laid himself in the chest. His form filled it in its length and its breadth. Isis and Nephthys and Thout stood above where he lay, looking down upon Osiris, so <u>resplendent</u> of face, so perfect of limb, and congratulating him upon coming into possession of the splendid chest that Seth had made. Seth was not beside the chest then. He shouted, and his attendants to the number of seventy-two came into the banqueting hall. They placed the heavy cover upon the chest; they hammered nails into it; they <u>soldered</u> it all over with melted lead. Nor could Isis, nor Thout, nor Nephthys break through the circle that Seth's attendants made around the chest. And they, having nailed the cover down, and having soldered it, took up the sealed chest, and, with Seth going before them, they ran with it out of the hall.

Isis and Nephthys and Thout ran after those who bore the chest. But the night was dark, and these three children of Qeb and Nut were separated, one from the other, and from Seth and his crew. And these came to where the river was, and they flung the sealed chest into the river. Isis, and Thout, and Nephthys, following the tracks that Seth and his crew had made, came to the riverbank when it was daylight, but by that time the current of the river had brought the chest out into the sea.

Isis followed along the bank of the river, lamenting for Osiris. She came to the sea, and she crossed over it, but she did not know where to go to seek for the body of Osiris. She wandered through the world, and where she went bands of children went with her, and they helped her in her search.

The chest that held the body of Osiris had

drifted in the sea. A flood had cast it upon the land. It had lain in a thicket of young trees. A tree, growing, had lifted it up. The branches of the tree wrapped themselves around it; the bark of the tree spread itself around it; at last the tree grew there, covering the chest with its bark.

5 The land in which this happened was Byblos. The king and queen of the city, Melquart and Astarte, heard of the wonderful tree, the branches and bark of which gave forth a fragrance. The king had the tree cut down; its branches were trimmed off, and the tree was set up as a column in the king's house. And then Isis, coming to Byblos, was told of the wonderful tree that grew by the sea. She was told of it by a band of children who came to her. She came to the place; she found that the tree had been cut down and that its trunk was now set up as a column in the king's house.

She knew from what she heard about the wonderful fragrance that was in the trunk and branches of the tree that the chest she was seeking was within it. She stayed beside where the tree had been. Many who came to that place saw the queenly figure that, day and night, stood near where the wonderful tree had been. But none who came near was spoken to by her. Then the queen, having heard about the stranger who stood there, came to her. When she came near, Isis put her hand upon her head, and thereupon a fragrance went from Isis and filled the body of the queen.

6 The queen would have this majestical stranger go with her to her house. Isis went. She nursed the queen's child in the hall in which stood the column that had closed in it the chest which she sought.

She nourished the queen's child by placing her finger in its mouth. At night she would strip wood from the column that had grown as a tree, and throw the wood upon the fire. And in this fire she would lay the queen's child. The fire did not injure it at all; it burned softly around the child. Then Isis, in the form of a swallow, would fly around the column, lamenting.

One night the queen came into the hall where her child was being nursed. She saw no nurse there; she saw her child lying in the fire. She snatched the child up, crying out. Then Isis spoke to the queen from the column on which, in the form of a swallow, she perched. She told the queen that the child would have gained immortality had it been suffered to lie for a night and another night longer within the fire made from the wood of the column. Now it would be long-lived, but not immortal. And she revealed her own <u>divinity</u> to the queen, and claimed the column that had been made from the wonderful tree. 7

The king had the column taken down; it was split open, and the chest which Isis had sought for so long and with so many <u>lamentations</u> was within it. Isis wrapped the chest in linen, and it was carried for her out of the king's house. And then a ship was given to her, and on that ship, Isis, never stirring from beside the chest, sailed back to Egypt.

And coming into Egypt she opened the chest, and took the body of her lord and husband out of it. She breathed into his mouth, and, with the motion of her wings (for Isis, being divine, could assume wings), she brought life back to Osiris. And there, away from men and from all the children of Qeb and Nut, Osiris and Isis lived together.

But one night Seth, as he was hunting gazelles by moonlight, came upon Osiris and Isis sleeping. Fiercely he fell upon his brother; he tore his body into fourteen pieces. Then, taking the pieces that were the

5 GUIDED READING
Sequencing: What sequence of events leads to Osiris' presence in a column in the king's house? (A flood casts Osiris' chest upon the land amid young trees; a tree grows around the chest; the tree emits such a lovely fragrance that the king has it cut down and set up as a column in his house.)

6 LITERARY ELEMENT
Characterization: What qualities does Isis display by going home with the queen and taking care of her child? (determination, love for Osiris, humility, a capacity for nurturing)

7 LITERARY ELEMENT
Irony: What unintended result does the queen's attempt to save her child have? (She prevents her child from attaining immortality.)

> ■ **divinity** (də·vin′ə·tē): quality of being a god
> **lamentations** (lam′ən·tā′shənz): cries of grief

READING CHECK

1. Who tries to destroy Osiris? (his brother Seth)
2. How is Osiris killed the first time? (Seth lures Osiris into a chest which Seth then seals and throws into the ocean.)
3. How is Osiris killed the second time? (Seth tears his body into pieces and scatters them.)

4. What comes into the world with Osiris' death? (death, war, drought)
5. Who overcomes Seth in battle? (Horus, son of Osiris and Isis)

RETEACHING

Have pairs of students create and role-play a dialogue that might have occurred between Isis and Osiris after Isis brought him back to life the first time. What would Osiris remember about what had happened to him? What would he want to know? What would Isis tell him? How would they speak? As students consider these ideas, they will reconstruct the story's plot and the qualities of its main characters.

HUMANITIES CONNECTION

In art, each ancient Egyptian god was depicted in different attitudes and roles. Students might enjoy researching books of ancient Egyptian art and collecting various representations of Isis, Osiris, and the other gods mentioned in this myth. ■

meted (mēt′əd): distributed

8 GUIDED READING

Identifying Details: What becomes of Osiris after his second death? (He goes to live in the underworld.) What is his new role? (He judges men and women, conferring immortality when justly deserved.)

9 LITERARY ELEMENT

Resolution: Ancient Egyptians saw life as an ongoing conflict between contending opposites which had to be kept in balance. How does the resolution of this myth reflect the Egyptian view of life? (Isis and Horus allow the evil Seth to continue to live, albeit with diminished power and strength.)

WRITING TO LEARN

Write a further adventure of Horus in which he confronts his enemy Seth once again. Remember that the Egyptians did not expect to see evil totally and finally defeated, as it often is in many of the heroic myths from other cultures. ■

body of Osiris, he scattered them over the land.

Death had come into the land from the time Osiris had been closed in the chest through the cunning of Seth; war was in the land; men always had arms in their hands. No longer did music sound, no longer did men and women talk sweetly and out of the depths of their feelings. Less and less did grain, and fruit trees, and the vine flourish. The green places everywhere were giving way to the desert. Seth was triumphant; Thout and Nephthys cowered before him.

And all the beauty and all the abundance that had come from Re would be destroyed if the pieces that had been the body of Osiris were not brought together once more. So Isis sought for them, and Nephthys, her sister, helped her in her seeking. Isis, in a boat that was made of reeds, floated over the marshes, seeking for the pieces. One, and then another, and then another was found. At last she had all the pieces of his torn

body. She laid them together on a floating island, and reformed them. And as the body of Osiris was formed once more, the wars that men were waging died down; peace came; grain, and the vine, and fruit trees grew once more.

And a voice came to Isis and told her that Osiris lived again, but that he lived in the Underworld where he was now the Judge of the Dead, and that through the justice that he meted out, men and women had life immortal. And a child of Osiris was born to Isis; Horus he was named. Nephthys and the wise Thout guarded him on the floating island where he was born. Horus grew up, and he strove against the evil power of Seth. In battle he overcame him, and in bonds he brought the evil Seth, the destroyer of his father, before Isis, his mother. Isis would not have Seth slain; still he lives, but now he is of the lesser Gods, and his power for evil is not so great as it was in the time before Horus grew to be the avenger of his father.

8

9

Isis, from the sarcophagus of Ramses III, 20th dynasty. *Isis was the most popular and beloved Egyptian goddess. Among other things, she was regarded as a protector of children.*
❓ *What protective qualities does Isis demonstrate in this myth?*

Giraudon/Art Resource, New York

1. Writing a Song in Honor of Isis.
Some students might enjoy collaborating on a song in honor of Isis. In their song they may want to praise her actions or express her love for Osiris. Have them consider what kind of melody and rhythm would be suitable for their song and whether their singer, pair of singers, or chorus would need instrumental accompaniment.

2. Research Project. Students might be interested in researching ancient Egyptian views of death and the afterlife, the construction and contents of ancient Egyptian tombs and pyramids, or the development of the mummification process. Have them present oral reports on their findings using photographs, drawings, and other visual aids.

CLOSURE

The introduction to this myth refers to Isis as a "midwife in a new creation." A midwife is a person who assists at a birth. In what ways is Isis a midwife to new life in this myth? ■

First Thoughts

Which **metamorphosis**, or transformation, strikes you as the most important one in this myth?

Identifying Facts

1. At the beginning of this myth, what is life like under Osiris' reign?
2. Why does Seth want to destroy Osiris?
3. Describe the actions Isis takes to save Osiris after each of his "deaths."

Interpreting Meanings

1. From what **point of view** is "Osiris and Isis" told? What are the advantages of telling the myth from this point of view? Can you see any disadvantages?
2. What explanation does this myth give for the introduction of death and evil into the world?
3. According to this myth, how did Osiris' "death" change the world? How is the natural balance finally restored?

Applying Meanings

In this myth we learn that Isis allowed the troublemaking Seth to be spared. Why do you suppose she did this? How would you have acted if you had been in Isis' place?

Creative Writing Response

Writing from a Different Point of View.
Rewrite your favorite portion of this narrative from the point of view of one of the following characters: Osiris, Isis, or Seth. Let the character speak in the first person, using the pronoun *I*. Be sure that the character reveals only what he or she could possibly know. For example, if you tell the story from Isis' point of view, you can only reveal her thoughts and feelings; you cannot know Osiris' thoughts while he is locked in the chest or Seth's thoughts as he is plotting his revenge.

Critical Writing Response

Evaluating a Statement of Theme. Below are some general statements of the **theme**, or central idea, of the myth "Osiris and Isis." In one or two paragraphs, discuss which, if any, of the statements of theme listed below best express what you think is the story's main theme. If you find all of the statements inadequate, form your own statement of the major theme and defend it.

1. True love can overcome any obstacle.
2. In order for society to experience renewal, the old must give way to the new.
3. Without evil, no one would appreciate the goodness in life.
4. Change and transformation are necessary aspects of life.

ANSWERS

First Thoughts
Answers will vary.

Identifying Facts
1. perfectly harmonious
2. He hates all the growing things Osiris produces.
3. *First time:* She finds his body and restores it by breathing into him and beating her wings. *Second:* She rejoins the pieces of his body.

Interpreting Meanings
1. omniscient. *Advantage:* We know everything that happens and everyone's thoughts. *Disadvantage:* No character is explored from the inside.
2. One god is evil; his hatred of his brother brings death into the world.
3. It brought death, war, and destruction of crops. Balance is restored when Isis puts Osiris' body back together.

Applying Meanings
Answers will vary.

Creative Writing Response
Writing from a Different Point of View. Narratives should use the pronoun *I*, and be limited to one character's thoughts. They should not refer to events that the narrator could not know about.

Critical Writing Response
Evaluating a Statement of Theme. Evaluations and students' own theme statements should be supported by examples from the myth. ■

OBJECTIVES

1. *To evaluate the decisions made by the hero of a Japanese folktale*
2. *To distinguish between the hero's internal and external conflicts*
3. *To rewrite the end of the tale, including new conflicts*
4. *To write a summary of the tale using transitional expressions that show time order*

THEMES IN WORLD LITERATURE

The Quest and the Perilous Journey
"Theseus," pp. 28–33
"The Grail" from *Perceval*, pp. 720–729
From *Don Quixote*, pp. 821–837

The Power and Pain of Love
"Osiris and Isis," pp. 34–39
Sonnet 29, p. 810
"Love Must Not Be Forgotten,"
pp. 1414–1427

Choices in Life
"The Quarrel" from the *Iliad*,
pp. 228–245
From *Faust*, Part I, pp. 986–1001 ■

PREREADING FOCUS

Background: Originally drawn from Japan's aristocratic families, samurai warriors enjoyed a high social status. In turn, they swore to live by a strict code of behavior known as *bushido*, or the way of the warrior. Under this code, samurai warriors were expected to value courage, self-discipline, and personal honor even more than their own lives. Absolute loyalty and unquestioning obedience to one's *daimyo* were at the heart of the samurai ethic.

Literary Focus: In myths and folktales, the hero's external conflicts are often symbols of internal conflicts that people commonly face in their lives. For example, a hero's confrontation with a dragon or some other monster may represent an internal struggle with fear or self-doubt. In this story, Tomotada's choice between Green Willow and his daimyo mirrors an internal struggle between personal fulfillment and loyalty to duty.

ABOUT THE RETELLER

Paul Jordan-Smith is an American storyteller, writer, and editor living in Los Angeles. He performs as a storyteller and has published retellings of various myths and legends, as well as articles on mythology. He is an editor for *Parabola: The Magazine of Myth and Tradition*.

Reader's Guide

GREEN WILLOW

Background

Tomotada, the hero of this Japanese folktale, is a *samurai* (sam'ə·rī'), or warrior. During Japan's long feudal period (1200–1867), towns grew up around the castles of *daimyos* (dī'myōs'), feudal princes or lords. Each town was ruled by its daimyo, and each daimyo had many samurai at his command, much as feudal lords in England had knights. In this story, the Lord of Noto, Tomotada's prince, sends the samurai hero on an unspecified quest to the lord of the city of Kyoto.

One of the challenges of a questing hero is to resist distractions. In Tomotada's case, the distraction is a young woman named Green Willow. The tale "Green Willow" illustrates a particularly Japanese conflict. In Japanese culture, nature is valued, and the willow tree is especially admired because of its suppleness and grace, qualities important in Japanese tradition. Thus it is not only a particular woman, but also nature itself, that lures the hero away from the duties of his quest. Tomotada's conflict, then, shows a clash between the responsibilities of a samurai and the appeal of nature, a clash that appears often in Japanese folklore.

Writer's Response

Write a paragraph about a time when you chose to do something pleasant (perhaps watch television, go out with friends, or buy a treat) rather than complete a chore such as studying for a test or cleaning your room. Did you later regret your "distraction," or did you feel it was worth it?

Literary Focus

Conflict is a struggle or clash between opposing characters, forces, or emotions. In an **external conflict**, a character struggles against some outside force: another character, society, or a force of nature. An **internal conflict**, on the other hand, is a struggle between opposing desires or needs within a character's own mind. See if you can identify whether the conflicts Tomotada faces in this story are external, internal, or both.

GREEN WILLOW
A Japanese Folktale
retold by
PAUL JORDAN-SMITH

Read to the part of the story where Tomotada decides to ask to marry Green Willow (see page 43). Do you predict that Tomotada's decision will have a postive or negative effect on his life?

The Granger Collection, New York

Mounted Samurai cleaning his sword, 16th–17th century.

In the era of Bummei there lived a young samurai, Tomotada, in the service of the daimyo of Noto. He was a native of Echizen, but had been accepted at a young age into the palace of the Lord of Noto, where he proved himself a good soldier and a good scholar as well, and enjoyed the favor of his prince. Handsome and <u>amiable</u>, he was admired also by his fellow samurai.

One day, the Lord of Noto called for Tomotada and sent him on a special quest to the Lord of Kyoto. Being ordered to pass through Echizen, Tomotada asked and was granted permission to visit his widowed mother. And so he set out on his mission.

Winter had already come; the countryside was covered with snow, and though his horse was among the most powerful in the Lord of Noto's stable, the young man was forced to proceed slowly. On the second day of his journey, he found himself in mountain districts where settlements were few and far between. His anxiety was increased by the onslaught of a heavy snowstorm, and his horse was showing signs of extreme fatigue. In the very moment of his despair, however, Tomotada caught sight of a cottage among the willows on a nearby hill. Reaching the

TEACHER'S RESOURCES
- Review and Response Worksheet
- Selection Test
- Vocabulary Activity Worksheet
- Vocabulary Test

amiable (ā'mē·ə·bəl): friendly; good-natured

HUMANITIES CONNECTION

Though warriors, samurai were also devoted to learning, poetry, and calligraphy.
❓ *Do you see a contradiction between a life of war and a love of poetry? Do you think the two values can coexist in one person? (Answers will vary.)* ■

1 CULTURAL DIVERSITY
Tomotada's asking permission of his lord to visit his mother is an example of the complete obedience expected of a samurai. It also suggests how a samurai's competing loyalties might cause personal conflict.
❓ *What competing loyalties between personal and public life do people face today?* (Possible response: conflicting commitments to work and family)

2 LITERARY ELEMENT
External Conflict: What outside force does Tomotada struggle with? (nature)

3 INFERRING

Judging from the way the old
man addresses Tomotada,
what can you infer about their
relative social positions? (Tomotada is of high status; the
family, low status.)

MEETING INDIVIDUAL NEEDS

4 LEP: Students may find the
phrase "her clothes were still
of homespun" difficult to understand. Tell them that *homespun* refers to cloth made from
yarn that people spun at
home. This material was usually plain, rough, and loosely
woven. ■

5 CULTURAL DIVERSITY

Improvising linked verses,
called *renga*, was a popular
pastime or social entertainment among samurai, peas-
ants, and merchants in medieval Japan. One person would
begin a poem, and someone
else in the room would be
challenged to complete it. The
linked verses in this story take
on a serious purpose as Tomotada and Green Willow use
them to express their love.
? *Is poetry, verse, or other
wordplay an important part
of social life or romantic love
in your family's background?*
(Answers will vary.)

dwelling, he knocked loudly on the storm
doors which had been closed against the
wind. Presently the doors opened, and an
old woman appeared, who cried out with
compassion at the sight of the noble Tomotada, "Ah, how pitiful! Traveling in such
weather, and alone! Come in, young sir,
come in!"

"What a relief to find a welcome in these
lonely passes," thought Tomotada, as he led
his horse to a shed behind the cottage. After
seeing that his horse was well sheltered and
fed, Tomotada entered the cottage, where
he beheld the old woman and her husband,
and a young girl as well, warming themselves by a fire of bamboo splints. The old
couple respectfully requested that he be
seated, and proceeded to warm some rice
wine and prepare food for the warrior. The
young girl, in the meantime, disappeared behind a screen, but not before Tomotada had
observed with astonishment that she was
extremely beautiful, though dressed in the
meanest attire. He wondered how such a
beautiful creature could be living in such a
lonely and humble place. His thoughts, however, were interrupted by the old man, who
had begun to speak.

"Honored Sir," he began. "The next village
is far from here and the road is unfit for
travel. Unless your quest is of such importance that it cannot be delayed, I would
advise you not to force yourself and your
horse beyond your powers of endurance.
Our hovel is perhaps unworthy of your presence, and we have no comforts to offer;
nevertheless, please honor us by staying under this miserable roof."

Tomotada was touched by the old man's
words—and secretly, he was glad of the
chance afforded him to see more of the
young girl. Before long, a simple meal was
set before him, and the girl herself came
from behind the screen to serve the wine.
She had changed her dress, and though her
clothes were still of homespun, her long
loose hair was neatly combed and smoothed.
As she bent to fill his cup, Tomotada was
amazed to see that she was even more beautiful than he had at first thought: she was
the most beautiful creature he had ever seen.
She moved with a grace that captivated him,
and he could not take his eyes from her. The
old man spoke apologetically, saying, "Please
forgive the clumsy service of our daughter,
Green Willow. She has been raised alone in
these mountains and is only a poor, ignorant
girl." But Tomotada protested that he considered himself lucky indeed to be served by
so lovely a maiden. He saw that his admiring
gaze made her blush, and he left his wine
and food untasted before him. Suddenly
struck by inspiration, he addressed her in a
poem.

> As I rode through the winter
> I found a flower and thought,
> "Here I shall spend the day."
> But why does the blush of dawn
>   appear
> When the dark of night is still around
>   us?

Without a moment's hesitation, the girl
replied:

> If my sleeve hides the faint color of
>   dawn,
> Perhaps when morning has truly come
> My lord will remain.

Then Tomotada knew that the girl had accepted his admiration, and he was all the
more taken by the art of her verse and the
feelings it expressed. "Seize the luck that has
brought you here!" he thought to himself,
and he resolved to ask the old couple to give

MAN AND WOMAN BY A HEDGE, HARUNOBO, 1725–1770.
❓ *What is the ideal of feminine beauty according to this folktale?*

him the hand of their daughter in marriage. Alas for the Lord of Noto's quest!

The old couple were astonished by the request of Tomotada, and they bowed themselves low in gratitude. After some moments of hesitation, the father spoke: "Honored master, you are a person of too high a degree for us to consider refusing the honor your request brings. Indeed our gratitude is unmeasurable. But this daughter of ours is merely a country girl, of no breeding and manners, certainly not fit to become the wife of a noble samurai such as yourself. But since you find the girl to your liking, and have condescended to overlook her peasant origins, please accept her as a gift, a humble handmaid. Deign, O Lord, to regard her henceforth as yours, and act towards her as you will."

Now a samurai was not allowed to marry without the consent of his lord, and Tomotada could not expect permission until his quest was finished. When morning came, Tomotada resumed his journey, but his heart grew more apprehensive with every footfall of his horse. Green Willow rode behind her lord, saying not a word, and gradually the progress of the young man slowed to a halt. He could not tear his thoughts from the girl, and did not know whether he should bring her to Kyoto. He was afraid, moreover, that the Lord of Noto would not give him permission to marry a peasant girl, and afraid also that his daimyo might be likewise captivated by her beauty and take her for himself. And so he resolved to hide with her in the mountains, to settle there and become himself a simple farmer. Alas for the Lord of Noto's quest!

For five happy years, Tomotada and Green Willow dwelt together in the mountains, and not a day passed that did not bring them both joy and delight in each other and their life together. Forgotten was the time before Green Willow had come into his life. But one day, while talking with her husband about some household matter, Green Willow uttered a loud cry of pain, and became very white and still. "What is it, my wife?" cried Tomotada as he took her in his arms. "Forgive me, my lord, for crying out so rudely, but the pain was so sudden . . . My dear husband, hold me to you and listen—do not let me go! Our union has been filled with great joy, and I have known with you a happiness that cannot bear description. But now it is at an end: I must beg of you to accept it."

"Ah!" cried Tomotada, "It cannot be so. What wild fancies are these? You are only a

SuperStock International, Inc.

READING CHECK

1. Who sends Tomotada on a quest? (his daimyo, the Lord of Noto)
2. Where does Tomotada stop during a snowstorm? (in a humble cottage in the mountains)
3. Who is Green Willow? (the beautiful daughter of his poor hosts)
4. Why does Tomotada give up his quest? (to live with Green Willow)
5. What happens to Green Willow in the end? (She dies.) Why? (She has the soul of a tree, and the tree is cut down.)

RETEACHING

Have students work in groups to expand the final dialogue between the elderly Tomotada and the itinerant monk. Have them consider: How would Tomotada tell his own story? Would the monk realize the old man's true identity? If he did, what additional questions might the monk ask Tomotada? What emotions might Tomotada express about his experiences? Have a pair from each group present the dialogue to the class.

9 SYNTHESIZING

In Japanese art and literature, the beauty of nature is often portrayed as fragile and short-lived. Why was this emphasis on the brevity of life especially strong in medieval Japan? (Samurai warriors had to be ready to sacrifice their lives.)

> ■■ reverie (rev'ər·ē): dreamy
> ■ imagining; daydreaming

10 INTERPRETING

Shintoism, the native and still dominant religion of Japan, is based on the worship of *kami*, or gods believed to manifest themselves in natural objects. Shrines are built where kami are believed to dwell. How do these details help explain Tomotada's actions after the death of Green Willow? (Possible response: Tomotada acts according to Shinto beliefs.)

11 LITERARY ELEMENT

Repetition: How many times has "Alas for the Lord of Noto's quest!" been repeated in the tale so far? (three times) What effect does the repetition have? (Possible responses: It emphasizes the difficulties of pursuing a quest and the transitory nature of all human emotions and endeavors.)

WRITING TO LEARN

Social Studies: Imagine that you are the Lord of Noto or one of Tomotada's fellow samurai. Write a letter expressing your opinion of Tomotada's conduct, based on samurai ethics. ■

little unwell, my darling. Lie down and rest, and the pain shall pass."

"No, my dearest, it cannot be. I am dying —I do not imagine it. It is needless to hide from you the truth any longer, my husband. I am not a human being. The soul of a tree is my soul, the heart of a tree my heart, the sap of a willow is my life. And some one, at this most cruel of moments, has cut down my tree—even now its branches have fallen to the ground. And this is why I must die! I have not even the strength left to weep, nor the time . . . "

With another cry of pain, Green Willow turned her head and tried to hide her face behind her sleeve. In the same moment, her form seemed to fold in upon itself, and before Tomotada's astonished and grief-stricken eyes, her robes crumpled in the air and fell empty to the ground.

Many years after this, an itinerant[1] monk came through the mountain passes on his way to Echizen. He stopped for water beside a stream, on the banks of which stood the stumps of three willow trees—two old and one young. Nearby, a rude stone memorial had been set up, which showed evidence of regular care unusual in such a remote place. He inquired about it from an old priest who lived in the neighborhood and was told the story of Green Willow.

"And what of Tomotada?" asked the mendicant,[2] when the priest had finished his tale. But the old man had fallen into a <u>reverie</u> and gazed at the shrine, oblivious of his guest.

"Alas for the Lord of Noto's quest!" the old man sighed to himself and fell silent.

The air grew chill as the evening drew on. At length, the old priest shook himself from his dreams.

"Forgive me!" he told his guest. "As age creeps upon me, I sometimes find myself lost in the memories of a young samurai."

The Granger Collection, New York

EIGHT STALLIONS (detail), LANG SHIH-NING, Ch'ing Dynasty.
❓ *How does this folktale illustrate the Japanese regard for the beauties and value of nature?*

---

1. **itinerant** (ī·tin'ər·ənt): traveling from place to place.
2. **mendicant** (men'di·kənt): a monk or priest who lives mostly on charitable contributions.

1. Making a Puppet Theater. Students skilled in art and needlework may enjoy creating puppets and a puppet theater for this tale. Have them research the medieval Japanese countryside and the clothing the samurai and peasants wore. They could also research the traditional Japanese art of *bunraku*, in which performers combine storytelling, musical accompaniment, and puppetry.

2. Composing Linked Verse. Students who enjoy poetry may try their hand at improvising linked verse. Have students work with partners. The first should begin by composing several lines of verse and reciting them. The second must continue the verse, building on its content and theme. Themes, such as loyalty, romantic love, and nature's beauty, may be drawn from the story.

Have students summarize Tomotada's conflicting desires. Then ask how Tomotada resolves his conflict. What choice does he make? What are the consequences of his choice? What does the ending suggest about the values that were most important in medieval Japanese culture? ■

First Thoughts

What is your *first* reaction to this folktale? What feelings or emotions did you experience as you read it?

Identifying Facts

1. Why does Tomotada stop at the cottage among the willows? Whom does he meet there?
2. Why doesn't Tomotada take Green Willow with him on his mission?
3. What does Tomotada learn about Green Willow as she is dying? What has caused her death?

Interpreting Meanings

1. In a word or phrase, sum up the **mood** created in the first half of the story. How does the **setting**—the time of year, the area, the weather, the cottage— contribute to the mood?
2. What qualities in Green Willow attract the samurai and distract him from his quest?
3. What is Tomotada's main **conflict** in this story? Is this conflict **external**, **internal**, or both?
4. The **crisis**, or **turning point**, is the point at which the main character makes a decision or commits an action that will affect the entire outcome of the story. What is the crisis in this story?
5. Who is the old priest at the end of the story? How do you know?

Applying Meanings

What do you think Tomotada should have done after Green Willow's death? Why do you say so?

Creative Writing Response

Writing a New Ending. Rewrite the second half of the tale so that Tomotada continues his quest and reaches Kyoto. Does he take Green Willow with him or leave her behind? Does the Lord of Noto allow Tomotada to marry Green Willow, or does the lord try to marry her himself? What new conflicts does Tomotada face? In your new ending, include an explanation of what Tomotada gains or loses by fulfilling the Lord of Noto's quest.

Language and Vocabulary

Transitional Expressions: Time Order

Words and phrases that link ideas, paragraphs, or sentences are known as **transitional expressions**. Some transitional expressions show the passage of time. Stories would be monotonous if the storyteller kept repeating, "and then . . . and then . . . and then. . . ." Instead, a good storyteller chooses from a variety of phrases that reflect time passages of varying lengths. In "Green Willow," such phrases as "Winter had already come," "For five happy years," and "Many years after this" give the reader a sense of the passing of time in the story.

Among the most common transitional words expressing the passing of time are: *after, as soon as, at first, during, earlier, later, finally, first, last, formerly, meanwhile, moments later, next, since, soon, then, until,* and *when.*

Write a one-paragraph **summary** of "Green Willow." In your summary, use transitions to express what happens first, next, and last in the story so that your reader can easily follow the sequence of events.

OBJECTIVES

1. *To interpret the hero's quest in a German fairy tale*
2. *To identify and analyze typical features of a fairy tale*
3. *To write an original fairy tale with typical fairy-tale features, and to compare ideals of heroism in a German fairy tale and a Greek myth*

THEMES IN WORLD LITERATURE

The Quest and the Perilous Journey
"Theseus," pp. 28–33
From the *Iliad*, pp. 224–277
"The Grail" from *Perceval*, pp. 720–729
From *Don Quixote*, pp. 821–837

The Wisdom of the World
"Right-Mind and Wrong-Mind" from the *Panchatantra*, pp. 478–483
Zen Parables, pp. 589–595
La Fontaine's *Fables*, pp. 940–944 ∎

PREREADING FOCUS

Background: Child psychologist Bruno Bettelheim believed that fairy tales benefit children's psychological and moral development. In *The Uses of Enchantment*, he disagrees with those who criticize fairy tales as too violent or too unrealistic in their inevitable happy endings. According to Bettelheim, "Fairy tales intimate that a rewarding, good life is within one's reach despite adversity—but only if one does not shy away from the hazardous struggles without which one can never achieve identity."

Literary Focus: Inspired by the Grimms, scholars started collecting folktales from around the world. As they did, they began to recognize and classify common elements of folktales and fairy tales. One of the first to make such a classification was the Finnish folklorist Antti Aarne, who developed an index of fairy-tale types, such as the Enchanted Husband, Supernatural Tasks, Supernatural Helpers, and Magic Objects. Using such indexes, folklorists catalog tales of various types and note similarities and differences among tales from various cultures.

ABOUT THE TRANSLATOR

Jack Zipes is a professor of German and a storyteller in schools. He has developed fairy-tale plays for children's theater and is the editor of *Don't Bet on the Prince: Contemporary Feminist Fairy Tales in North America and England.*

Reader's Guide

THE WHITE SNAKE

Background

This story comes from the Grimm brothers' famous collection of German fairy tales, collected and assembled during the nineteenth century. The tale is set several centuries earlier, however, in medieval times, when each German town had its own lord and castle.

The hero of the tale, who is never named, is the poor but trusted servant of a king. The hero sets out on a journey to see the world. It is not until he is well into his journey that he discovers what his goal is. He also discovers that three apparently trivial incidents early in his travels were really tests. His performance in these "practice tests" helps him to succeed at later, harder trials that he must pass to reach his goal.

The servant's story fits a questing hero archetype found in folklore everywhere. In this archetype, the boy or girl hero must be tested before he or she can make a royal marriage and "live happily ever after." The trials in these tales may test courage, wit, or spiritual or physical strength. The test **motif,** or pattern, suggests that by undergoing trials, the hero can gain maturity, and that in passing the tests he or she will emerge a stronger person.

Writer's Response

Write about a test in which you performed especially well. The test may have been academic, or it may have been a challenging situation in your life. What was responsible for your success? Did your view of yourself change as a result of your performance?

Literary Focus

The **fairy tale** is a particular kind of folktale that features supernatural elements such as spirits, talking animals, and magic. Good-hearted common people who triumph over evil are usually the heroes of fairy tales. Things and events in fairy tales often come in three's: three characters, three trials, three attempts to reach a goal. Many fairy tales point out a **moral lesson**—a message about how people ought to behave.

THE WHITE SNAKE
Jakob and Wilhelm Grimm
translated by
JACK ZIPES

The white snake is mentioned in the first paragraph, but it does not appear again in the fairy tale. As you read, decide what makes the white snake important enough to give the tale its title.

A long time ago there lived a king who was famous throughout the entire country for his wisdom. Nothing remained hidden from him, and it seemed as if he could obtain news of the most secret things through the air. However, he had one strange custom. Every day at noon, after the table was cleared of food and nobody else was present, a trusted servant had to bring him one more dish. This dish was always covered, and the servant himself did not know what was in it, nor did anyone else, for the king did not take the cover from the dish and eat until he was all alone. The king continued this custom for quite some time, until one day the servant, while removing the dish, was overcome by curiosity. He took it into his room, and after he had carefully locked the door, he lifted the cover and found a white snake lying inside. Once he laid eyes on it, though, he had an irresistible desire to taste it. So he cut off a little piece and put it in his mouth. No sooner did his tongue touch it than he heard a strange whispering of exquisite voices outside his window. He went over to it to listen and noticed some sparrows talking to one another, telling what they had seen in the fields and forest. Tasting the snake had given him the power to understand the language of animals.

Now, it so happened that on this very day the queen lost her most beautiful ring, and the trusted servant was suspected of committing the theft because he had access to everything. The king summoned the servant and with harsh words threatened him, saying that if he was not able to name the

Asp woodcut, c. 1555.
Dover Publications

TEACHER'S RESOURCES
- ✔ Review and Response Worksheet
- ✔ Selection Test
- ✔ Language Skills Worksheet

1 LITERARY ELEMENT
Setting: Why do you think fairy tales almost always take place "a long time ago"? (Possible response: to make their miraculous events seem more plausible)

2 INFERRING
On the basis of what happens to the servant when he tastes the secret dish, what do you conclude is the source of the king's wisdom? (the magic power to understand the language of animals, which the king derives from eating the snake)

HUMANITIES CONNECTION

In the mythology and folklore of many cultures, snakes are associated with supernatural powers. In some cultures, the serpent represents God, eternity, healing, or wisdom; in others, it signifies evil, trickery, or the devil.
? *What do snakes represent for people today?* (Possible response: Many people still have irrational fears of snakes. Others have a more scientific view of the role of snakes in an ecosystem.) ∎

Using the Past Perfect Tense

The past perfect tense of a verb is used to show that one past action was completed before another past action began. To form the past perfect, use the helping verb *had* plus the past participle of the main verb.

Here are examples from the tale: "But when the first rays of the sun fell on the garden, he saw ten sacks all filled to the top. . . . The ant king *had come* during the night with thousands of ants, and the grateful insects *had picked up* the millet seeds. . . ."

1. **Writing.** Have students complete the following sentences by adding verbs in the past perfect tense: Three fish came to help the servant because earlier he _____.
Because the servant _____ the ravens, they brought him an apple from the Tree of Life.

3 LEP: Explain the expressions "It was to no avail" and "he was given a curt dismissal." The first expression means "It was no use"; the second, "he was rudely sent away." ■

4 GUIDED READING

Cause and Effect: How does the servant's new magic power help save his life? (He can overhear a duck complaining of having swallowed a ring.)

5 COMPARING LITERATURE

Have students compare the initial goal of this fairy-tale hero with the goals of Theseus (pp. 28–33), Isis (pp. 34–39), and Tomotada (pp. 40–45). (The servant's goal is vague—to see the world—in contrast to the other heroes' more specific goals.) Have students also compare the heroes in terms of their status. (Theseus, a king; Isis, a goddess; Tomotada, a samurai; servant, a common person)

6 LITERARY ELEMENT

Characterization: What character traits does the servant display by putting the fish back in the water? (kindheartedness, compassion)

7 LITERARY ELEMENT

Fairy-Tale Features: A repeated line such as "We'll remember this, and one day we'll repay you" is a common feature of fairy tales. What other fairy-tale features does this tale have? (talking animals, a good-hearted common person, three trials)

48 World Myths and Folktales

3 guilty person by morning, he himself would be considered the thief and would be executed. It was to no avail that the servant protested his innocence, for he was given a curt dismissal.

Distressed and afraid, he went down into the courtyard and tried to think of a way out of his predicament. Some ducks were peacefully sitting and resting by a running brook, preening themselves and chatting in a confidential tone. The servant stopped and listened to them as they told each other where they had been waddling about all morning and what good pickings they had found. But one of the ducks was irritable 4 and said, "There's something heavy in my stomach. I was eating too fast and swallowed a ring that was lying under the king's window."

Right away the servant grabbed the duck by its neck, carried it into the kitchen, and said to the cook, "This one's well-fed. It's time you killed it!"

"All right," said the cook, weighing it in his hands. "It certainly hasn't been shy about stuffing itself. Besides, it's been waiting long enough for its roasting."

So he cut off the duck's neck, and when it was being cleaned, the queen's ring was found in its stomach. Now the servant could easily prove his innocence, and since the king wanted to make amends for having wronged his servant, he granted him a favor and promised him whatever royal post of honor he desired. The servant declined all of this. His only request was for a horse and 5 some travel money, for he had a desire to travel about for a while and see the world.

When his wish had been granted, he set out on his way, and one day, as he was passing a pond, he noticed three fish trapped in the reeds and gasping for water. Though it is said that fish cannot talk, he heard them crying in distress and wailing that they had to die so miserably. Since he felt sorry for them, he got down from his horse and put 6 the three trapped fish back into the water. They wriggled for joy, stuck their heads out of the water, and cried out to him, "We'll remember you for saving our lives, and one day we'll repay you."

He rode on, and a while later it seemed to him that he heard a voice in the sand at his feet. He listened and heard an ant king complaining, "If only people with their clumsy beasts would keep away from us! That stupid horse is mercilessly trampling my people to death with his heavy hooves!"

The servant turned his horse onto a side path, and the ant king cried out to him, "We'll remember this, and one day we'll repay you."

The servant's path led into a forest, and there he saw a father and mother raven standing near their nest and pushing their young ones out of the nest.

"Get out! You're nothing but freeloaders!" they were exclaiming. "We can't find enough food to feed you anymore, and now you're big enough to feed yourselves."

The poor young birds lay on the ground, flapped their wings, and began crying, "We're just helpless children! How are we supposed to feed ourselves when we can't fly? All we can do is stay here and starve."

Then the kind young man dismounted, killed his horse with his sword, and left it for the young ravens to feed on. They hopped over to the horse, ate their fill, and 7 cried out, "We'll remember this, and one day we'll repay you."

Now the servant had to use his own legs. After he had walked a long way, he reached a big city where there was a great deal of noise and a large crowd in the streets. A man on horseback rode by and announced

Gift at the Request of Miss Ellen T. Bullard, Courtesy Museum of Fine Arts, Boston

SAINT EUSTACE, DÜRER, 1500–1502.
Many folktales and fables feature the motif of a person being aided by an animal that he or she had earlier done a kindness for.
❓ *What lesson about helpfulness and generosity do you think such stories teach?*

HUMANITIES CONNECTION

Considered the greatest German artist of the Renaissance, painter and printmaker Albrecht Dürer (1471–1528) was the son of a goldsmith. It was in his father's workshop that he learned the techniques he would later apply to his beautiful engravings, such as this one of Saint Eustace.

An engraving is made by cutting a design into a copper plate with a sharp instrument. Then ink is applied to the plate, and the design is printed onto paper. *Saint Eustace*, one of Dürer's largest engravings, was inspired by a legend about a soldier named Eustace who, on a hunt, saw a deer with a glowing crucifix between its antlers. According to legend, this miraculous vision convinced Eustace to convert to Christianity.

❓ *In what sense is this picture realistic?* (The animals, the man, and their setting are drawn in realistic detail.) *In what sense is it fanciful?* (It shows the miraculous apparition of a crucifix.) *How do fairy tales combine these two elements?* (Fairy tales mix magical and commonplace events.) ∎

WRITING TO LEARN

Rewrite this fairy tale as a play suitable for an audience of six- to ten-year-olds. Include all the typical fairy-tale elements and be sure to create suspense by emphasizing the dangers of the tests the hero must face. ∎

The White Snake   **49**

1. What power does the servant attain after tasting the white snake? (power to understand the language of animals)
2. Where is the queen's ring found? (inside a duck)
3. What three kinds of creatures does the servant help? (fish, ants, ravens)

4. What are the three impossible tasks the servant has to perform? (retrieving a ring from the sea, picking up millet scattered in the grass, bringing an apple from the Tree of Life)
5. What happens to the princess when she eats the apple? (She falls in love with the servant.)

RETEACHING

Have students compile a list of humorous *do*'s and *don't*'s for fairy-tale heroes, based on the story. To get them started, help them review what the servant did right at various testing points in the story and how the outcome might have differed if he had acted unwisely. Possible *do*'s and *don't*'s include the following: If at first a princess rejects you, try, try again. Never ignore the complaints of ants.

8 COMPARING LITERATURE

Can you recall other fairy tales or folktales in which the hero had to pass a test before he or she could marry the princess or prince? (Possible responses: Cinderella, Sleeping Beauty)

9 LITERARY ELEMENT

Suspense: How does the storyteller create tension or curiosity as soon as the servant arrives in the new kingdom? (The servant is given a very difficult task that might cost him his life.)

10 PREDICTING

Can you predict how the servant's predicament will be resolved? (Attentive readers will anticipate that the fish will retrieve the ring.)

11 READER'S RESPONSE

Do you think virtue is usually rewarded in real life?

HUMANITIES CONNECTION

Walter Crane (1845–1915), the son of an artist, began illustrating his favorite poems while still a boy. One of these early illustrations won Crane the notice of a famous critic and an apprenticeship to an engraver. During his career, Crane made colorful illustrations for over forty children's books. His books are known for their decorative borders and hand-lettered text.
What story details does Crane include in the border of this illustration? (the white snake, the three fish, the three ravens) ■

50   World Myths and Folktales

8 that the king's daughter was looking for a husband, but whoever declared himself a suitor would have to perform a difficult task, and if he did not complete it successfully, he would forfeit his life. Many men had already tried and had risked their lives in vain. When the young man saw the princess, he was so dazzled by her great beauty that he forgot all about the danger, went before the king, and declared himself a suitor. He was promptly led to the sea, and a gold ring was thrown into it before his eyes. The king told him **9** that he was to fetch the ring from the depths of the sea, and he added, "If you come up without it, you'll be continually pushed back down until you perish in the waves."

Everyone felt sorry for the handsome young man and left him alone by the sea. He was standing on the **10** shore thinking about what to do when he suddenly saw three fish swimming toward him. They were none other than the three fish whose lives he had saved. The one in the middle held a shell in its mouth, which it set down on the beach at the feet of the young man, who picked it up. When he opened the shell, he found the gold ring, and bursting with joy, he brought it to the king expecting that he would receive the promised reward. But **11** when the proud king's daughter discovered that he was not her equal in birth, she scorned him and demanded that he first perform another task. She went down into the garden, and she herself scattered ten sacks full of millet in the grass.

"He must pick them all up before the sun rises tomorrow," she said.

"And not a single grain may be missing."

The young man sat down in the garden and tried to think of a way to accomplish the task, but nothing occurred to him, and he sat there quite sadly, expecting to be led to his death at the break of dawn. But when the first rays of the sun fell on the garden, he saw ten sacks all filled to the top and

Illustration by Walter Crane for an 1886 edition of *Household Stories from the Collection of the Brothers Grimm.* Many tales from the folk tradition end "happily ever after." *Why might such stories give people hope?*

The Granger Collection, New York

1. Reacting to an Issue. Bruno Bettelheim believed in teaching children that if they persevere, they will succeed. Other critics and psychologists feel that fairy tales lead children to expect unrealistic happy endings. Ask students to discuss the ways that fairy tales affected their thinking as children. Did the tales contribute to a sense of disillusionment as they matured? Would they read these tales to their own children?

2. Illustrating a Fairy Tale. Students who like to draw may want to illustrate this or another tale for a children's picture book. Suggest that they study the illustrations of Walter Crane or Albrecht Dürer before they begin and that they consider whether to emphasize the realistic or the fantastic elements of the tale in their own pictures.

Ask students to think about the relationship between the hero of this tale and the white snake. Suggest that they contrast the king's use of the snake with that of the servant. Do students think the connection between servant and snake is strong enough to have entitled the story "The White Snake"? If students find this title inappropriate, ask them to suggest alternative titles and to explain their choices. ■

---

standing side by side. Not a single grain was missing. The ant king had come during the night with thousands and thousands of ants, and the grateful insects had picked up the millet seeds with great diligence and gathered them into the sacks. The princess herself went down to the garden and was amazed to see that the young man had accomplished the task. But her proud heart could not be tamed, and she said, "Even if he has accomplished the first two tasks, he shall not become my husband until he has brought me an apple from the Tree of Life."

The young man did not know where the Tree of Life was. Therefore, he set out with the intention of going as far as his legs could carry him, even though he had no hope of finding it. One evening, after he had traveled through three kingdoms and reached a forest, he sat down beneath a tree and wanted to sleep. But he heard a noise in the tree, and a golden apple fell into his hand. At the same time three ravens flew down to him, landed on his knees, and said, "We're the three young ravens whom you saved from starvation. When we grew up, we heard you were looking for the golden apple. So we flew across the sea to the end of the world, where the Tree of Life is standing, and we've fetched the apple."

Now the young man was full of joy and started on his way home. He brought the golden apple to the beautiful princess, who no longer had any excuses to make. They divided the apple of life and ate it together, and her heart filled with love for him. In time they reached a ripe old age in peace and happiness.

First Thoughts

Does this fairy tale remind you of any other fairy tales you have heard? Name some of the characters and events in this tale that are familiar to you from other tales. How is this story different from the other tales?

Identifying Facts

1. How does the hero prove his innocence to the king?
2. What does the hero do for the animals he encounters on his journey?
3. How is the hero able to pass the "impossible" tests of the princess?

Interpreting Meanings

1. **Suspense** is the feeling of uncertainty and curiosity about what will happen next in a story. List three places in this story where the suspense builds. How is the situation resolved and the suspense relieved in each instance?

2. The young man in this fairy tale is an honest, good-hearted person, a "trusted servant." Yet, he gives in to temptation and discovers the king's secret, gaining the ability that only the king had before. How do you explain this seeming contradiction?

3. **Fairy tales** often teach a **moral lesson**—a lesson about how people ought to behave. What lesson or lessons do you think this fairy tale teaches? Name some other fairy tales you know and discuss the lessons they teach.

Applying Meanings

Fairy tales are simple tales without much character development. Their "happily ever after" endings may seem unrealistic to modern readers. Yet, fairy tales are still popular today. Why do you think this is so? What satisfactions do they give to readers?

---

12 LITERARY ELEMENT

Moral: What moral values are exemplified by this hero, who has to prove himself several times before he is rewarded? (perseverance, patience)

13 COMPARING LITERATURE

In the mythologies of many cultures, a Tree of Life exists in a sacred place where the supernatural and human worlds meet and heroes encounter the mysteries of life and death, good and evil.

? *Can you think of another story in which the fruit of trees has extraordinary powers?* (Possible response: the Garden of Eden story from Genesis)

ANSWERS

First Thoughts

Possible responses: Sleeping Beauty, The Princess and the Pea, Cinderella, The Frog Prince. The enamored hero, the princess, and the three tests may be familiar.

Identifying Facts

1. He finds the duck that swallowed the ring.
2. He saves their lives.
3. He gets help from the animals he helped.

Interpreting Meanings

1. Possible responses: servant takes the king's dish—sees the snake; servant is accused of stealing—proves his innocence; servant faces each of the three tasks—performs each with animals' help.
2. Possible response: The servant uses his knowledge only to do good.
■→

3. Possible response: Kindness and perseverance are rewarded. Other tales and morals will vary.

Applying Meanings
Possible response: They give hope that with virtue and hard work, life's obstacles can be overcome.

Creative Writing Response
Writing a Fairy Tale. Tales should include typical features, teach morals, and be imaginative.

Critical Writing Response
Comparing Heroes. Essays should point out similarities and differences, give supporting details, and use block or point-by-point organization. ■

1 LITERARY BACKGROUND
German Folklore: As story collectors, the Grimms were inspired by nineteenth-century Romantic writers Johann Wolfgang von Goethe (p. 986) and Heinrich Heine (p. 1011), who based their works on German folklore. Goethe's poem "The Erl-King" is about the king of the goblins, who according to legend stalks victims in Germany's Black Forest. Goethe's play *Faust* (pp. 986–1001) concerns a proud man who barters his soul to Mephistopheles in exchange for an understanding of all human experience. Heine's poem "The Lorelei" (pp. 1011–1014) describes a beautiful female spirit who sits atop a rocky cliff overlooking the Rhine River, luring sailors to their destruction.

Creative Writing Response
Writing a Fairy Tale. Write a short original fairy tale. It may be humorous or serious, set in an imaginary time and place or set in contemporary times. Be sure to include as many features of the fairy tale as you can: a common person as the hero or heroine; supernatural elements; the triumph of good over evil; and a "happily ever after" ending. Try to make something in your fairy tale happen in three's: three characters or three similar incidents, for example. What moral lesson will your tale teach?

Critical Writing Response
Comparing Heroes. In a three- to five-paragraph essay, compare the ideal of heroism shown in "The White Snake" to the ideal of heroism shown in "Theseus." How are the heroes of each story alike and different? Do you think the two notions of heroism demonstrated in each story are more similar than different? Use specific details from both selections to support your statements.

BEHIND THE SCENES

The Brothers Grimm

In Germany, one book has sold more copies than any other book except the Bible. The book is called *Kinder- und Hausmärchen*—literally, *Children's and Household Tales*. In English, the book is known as *Grimms' Fairy Tales*.

The Brothers Grimm were Jakob and Wilhelm. Born in Hanau, Germany, in the late–eighteenth century, they were the eldest sons of a poor widow. The two brothers were close and shared a love of learning, but because they were not members of the upper class, they had to work hard to obtain their educations.

The first half of the nineteenth century was an era of enormous social change in Germany and throughout Europe. The growing middle and working classes in Germany were increasingly unhappy with the government, which was oppressive and disunified. The nineteenth century was also

the era of a European and American literary movement called **Romanticism**. Romantics believed in the values of passion and imagination. They rejected a slavish devotion to logic and reason. They were discontented with a society that had become urban and industrial. For artistic themes, they often turned to the folklore and the natural environment of the "common" people whose lifestyle they admired and idealized.

It was in this climate that the Grimms began to collect German folklore. They saw in it an opportunity to uncover the roots of the German heritage. They believed that folklore contained basic truths about the origins of civilization and that it recorded the only "true" laws and customs of the German people. They hoped that, by publishing the folklore of Germany before the oral tradition was lost, they could provide

1

2

The Granger Collection, New York

Jakob and Wilhelm Grimm.

2 German readers with a sense of national pride and purpose that was lacking in the chaotic social and political climate of the early nineteenth century.

The Grimms gathered stories from their middle-class neighbors, mostly educated women who had been told the stories by their nursemaids and servants. The brothers were determined to present the tales in as close to their original form as possible. But within their lifetimes, they revised their collection several times, hoping to appeal to an audience of middle-class Germans and their children. They added references to Christianity and the Protes-

tant work ethic. They also removed many of the gruesome elements that the middle-class Germans might not have wanted their children to read. This practice of "cleaning up" the tales continues to this day, for, as sanitized as they were, the Grimms' first edition of fairy tales is still far more graphic than twentieth-century retellings of the tales. Contrast, for example, the endings of the Walt Disney movie versions of *Snow White and the Seven Dwarfs* and *Cinderella* with the Grimms' versions. According to the Brothers Grimm, the wicked queen in "Snow White" must dance to her death in slippers of molten lead, and pigeons peck out the eyes of Cinderella's evil step-sisters. The Disney versions leave out these grisly details.

Psychologists, educators, folklorists, and literary critics have kept up a lively debate about the Grimm brothers' contributions to folklore preservation. Some argue that the edited tales have been totally altered from their original form and purpose, so that they do not accurately reflect the oral tradition that the Grimms were supposedly trying to preserve. Others credit the Grimms with creating a new genre, the *Buchmärchen,* or "book tale," a mixture of oral and literary traditions. The Grimms certainly added their own values to the tales. But they also preserved the spirit of social justice and collective pride that they felt all Germans, and perhaps all people everywhere, should claim as a part of their heritage.

2 HISTORICAL BACKGROUND
German Nationalism: In nineteenth-century Germany, as elsewhere in Europe, increased pride in ethnic heritage fueled the rise of nationalism, a yearning for national independence and unity. The German states were under French rule after Napoleon conquered them in 1806. In 1871, the Germans established a unified, independent country. *What political effects are nationalism and ethnic pride having in today's world?* (Possible responses: secessionist movements based on nationality or religion: ethnic voting blocs)

3 MAKING JUDGMENTS
According to the traditional Protestant work ethic, hard work and material success in this world were signs that a person was one of those selected by God for salvation after death. Do you think a work ethic plays a significant role in today's American society? (Possible response: People still work hard but do so for rewards in this life rather than the next.)

4 READER'S RESPONSE
Do you think fairy tales should be "cleaned up" before they are told to children, or told in their original versions with all the grisly details included? Students might be interested in holding a debate on the issue. ■

To motivate students to synthesize elements of the heroic
quest, rent a videocassette of
an episode from the old *Star
Trek* series, or ask fans of the
new series to tape an episode
for the class. As students
watch, have them note elements typical of the heroic
quests they have read in the
unit. After viewing the episode, students may compare
notes and compile a list of elements of the heroic quest
found in *Star Trek*.

1 COMPARING LITERATURE

❓ *In what way is Theseus*
(pp. 28–33) like the heroes
of Star Trek, *who "boldly go*
where no one has gone be-
fore"? (Theseus goes to the
underworld and challenges a
god, just as the *Star Trek*
heroes travel into space to
challenge unknown forces.)

LANGUAGE
— AND —
CULTURE

THE HERO AND THE QUEST: ALIVE AND WELL

Which of the following heroes was *not* featured in the unit you
have just read?
a) the Greek hero Theseus
b) a Japanese samurai warrior
c) the Egyptian goddess Isis
d) Captain Picard of the starship *Enterprise*

1

If you answered *d*, you're right—but Captain Picard would not be
out of place in such heroic company. The captain and crew of *Star
Trek* have quite a bit in common with the heroes and heroines in
the myths and folktales you have just read. They are the twentieth-century descendants of the archetypal heroes of old, undertaking twentieth-century equivalents of the heroic quest.

Updating the Archetypes

There are some differences between the heroes and quests of old
and their contemporary versions, to be sure. These differences
reflect the fact that popular entertainment today is more self-
conscious than tales from the oral tradition, incorporating

Kobal Collection/SuperStock International, Inc.

The popular film Star Wars *and its sequels project the heroic
quest archetype into another galaxy.*
❓ *Why do you think the quest story has endured for
thousands of years?*

specifically contemporary concerns. For example, instead of relying on superhuman powers or the intervention of gods and goddesses, the captain and crew of the starship *Enterprise* rely on futuristic technology, scientific knowledge, and a sophisticated understanding of diverse alien cultures in order to succeed on their various quests. In this way, although the *Star Trek* adventures contain echoes of the heroic quest story, they are unmistakably a product of the twentieth century. They reflect our enthusiasm about technology and echo ongoing modern debates about the morality of interfering in the development of other cultures and using force to solve conflicts.

2

A Heroic Quest to the Stars   5

3 In recent years, perhaps the most successful testament to the enduring popularity of mythic and folktale archetypes appeared in the form of George Lucas's *Star Wars* trilogy, three of the most successful and beloved films of all time. Luke Skywalker, the hero of the trilogy, is cast in the mold of the archetypal folktale hero. Born a simple farm boy and raised by foster parents, Luke is kept from knowing his true heritage, which he slowly learns as he is swept up in a galactic adventure. He rescues a princess and defeats a superior enemy, using only his inherent goodness and intuition—the power of "the Force." During his adventures he is aided by a variety of friends and teachers who enable him to succeed on his quest. Like many heroes, Luke has flaws: impatience, pride, and impulsiveness. While training with his teacher, Yoda, he descends into an "underworld" and has a vision that

4

gives him important clues to the seriousness of his quest. He is reluctant to face his destiny. But like Theseus in this unit, he is ultimately reunited with his true father—in this case, the evil Darth Vader. Only after many battles and hardships is Luke able to redeem his father and mature into the Jedi knight he is meant to be, becoming a hero of his culture.

An Appetite for Adventure

People of all ages are as fascinated by the hero and the quest today as they were thousands of years ago. Modern audiences stand in long lines at movie theaters to thrill to adventures that echo the heroic quest archetype: *Raiders of the Lost Ark, Back to the Future, The Dark Crystal, Aliens, Dances with Wolves, Willow.* They buy and collect comic books featuring such heroes as Spiderman, Wonder Woman, the Fantastic Four, and Batman. For over twenty-five years they have watched science-fiction adventures such as *Star Trek* and *Dr. Who* on television. And they have eagerly devoured the quest fantasy novels of J.R.R. Tolkien, Marion Zimmer Bradley, Anne McCaffrey, and a host of other science-fiction and fantasy writers.

Our modern heroes may look very different from their ancient counterparts, use different means to achieve their goals, and participate in different kinds of quests, but they are still heroic adventurers with sometimes superhuman abilities who embark on exciting journeys. They visit exotic places, meet strange beings, and battle awesome foes along the way, living out our fantasies and keeping alive the adventure-loving child within each of us.

WRITING TO LEARN

2 Write your own heroic quest story based on one of the themes mentioned here. ■

3 TEACHING TIP
In "The Hero's Adventure," an episode in the video series *Joseph Campbell: The Power of Myth* with Bill Moyers, Moyers and Campbell discuss at length the mythological archetypes embodied in the *Star Wars* films. You may want to view this episode in class or read portions of the transcript published in book form. Ask students whether understanding the mythological underpinnings of the films increases or takes away from their appreciation of them.

4 COMPARING LITERATURE
George Lucas, who created the *Star Wars* movies, was inspired by the Hindu theology of India. Students who admire the films may want to read some of the classics of Hindu literature in Unit 5 and report to the class on how the movies reflect Hindu concepts of *Atman, Brahman,* and *dharma.*

WRITING TO LEARN

5 Read a heroic fantasy novel by one of the writers mentioned here and then write an essay comparing the hero of the novel with either the hero of one of the films mentioned or the hero of one of the stories in the unit. ■

Language Skills

USING TRANSITIONS FOR COMPARISON AND CONTRAST

Transitions, also called **linking expressions** and **connectives**, are words and phrases that show the relationships between ideas. You can use transitions to link ideas within a sentence, within a paragraph, or within a longer piece of writing. Transitions help your reader to follow your train of thought. Notice how the italicized transitions improve the following paragraph, which compares two tales.

> *Although* "Green Willow" and "The White Snake" come from opposite sides of the world, the tales are similar in several ways. *Both* stories are set in feudal societies, and *both* feature heroes who face several trials. *In addition, both* tales deal with the importance of perseverance.

Transitions clarify the connections between ideas. *Although* alerts readers to a contrast between the ideas in the first part of a sentence and the ideas in the second part. *Both* and *in addition* link ideas that are alike. Note that transitions often are placed at the beginnings of clauses. Sometimes transitions serve to join sentences.

Transitions for Comparison and/or Contrast

Transitions can be grouped according to their uses. When you write about similarities and/or differences between ideas, you will find transitions from the groups below especially helpful.

Transitions that link similar ideas

again	furthermore
also	in addition
and	likewise
besides	moreover
both	similarly
each of	too

Transitions that contrast or limit ideas

although	instead
and yet	neither . . . nor
but	nevertheless
conversely	on the other hand
however	still
in spite of	yet

Exercise 1: Using Transitions for Comparison and/or Contrast

The numbered sentences in the paragraph below are followed by transitions in parentheses. Insert the transitions into the sentences to clarify similarities or differences between ideas.

The god Maheo and the goddess Isis have many traits in common. For example, Maheo uses his power to create the natural world. **1)** Isis uses her power to restore the dead Osiris to life (on the other hand). **2)** Both are creators of life (yet). **3,4)** The deities are persis-

tent and caring (moreover, both). Maheo does not give up while struggling to create land.   **5)** He does his best to provide for his creatures (in addition).
6) Isis does not give up while searching for Osiris' body, and she does her best to shield Osiris from Seth's evil deeds (similarly). Maheo is the creator and preserver of the world.   **7)** Isis is a restorer and preserver (likewise).
8) Maheo and Isis do have differences; on the whole, both are kind and nurturing deities (however).

Transitions for Other Connections

Transitions can do more than indicate similarities and differences. Study the following groups of transitions.

Transitions that indicate time or position

above	meanwhile
afterward	nearby
before	next
eventually	opposite to
first (second, etc.)	

Transitions that indicate purpose, cause, or effect

as	since
because	so, so that
consequently	then
for	therefore
just as . . . so	

Transitions that indicate a summary, a conclusion, or an example

as a result	in other words
for example	on the whole
for instance	overall
in conclusion	therefore
in fact	thus

Exercise 2: Choosing Transitions

For each numbered sentence, choose an appropriate transition from the list specified in parentheses. Then insert the transition into the sentence. Join sentences if necessary when you are adding transitions.

Myths about death show how cultural attitudes can differ.

1. In a Khoikhoi myth, people are not originally supposed to die (transition indicating an example). The moon wants people to know this.

2. Hare, who carries the message, changes it (transition indicating contrast).

3. Death is brought into the world (transition indicating effect). Hare is punished for his actions. This myth stresses the unfairness of death.

4. In a Caddo myth, death is not inevitable (transition linking similar ideas). A medicine man wants to let the wandering souls of the dead come into a grass house.

5. They will be able to return to life (transition indicating purpose).

6. Coyote does not want the earth crowded (transition indicating contrast).

7. He secretly bars the door (transition indicating purpose).

8. Coyote is punished (transition linking similar ideas). This myth demonstrates a belief that death serves a purpose.

9. Cultural attitudes toward death may differ (transition indicating summary).

10. Death is never accepted without question or protest (transition indicating contrast).

TEACHING TIP
To facilitate students' understanding of Exercise 2, suggest that they write the sentences in paragraph form rather than as a list of numbered items. Explain that when a numbered item contains two or more sentences, students need not try to use transitions to join these sentences.

ANSWERS TO EXERCISE 2: CHOOSING TRANSITIONS
Answers will vary. Here are possible responses.
Myths about death show how cultural attitudes can differ. 1) In a Khoikhoi myth, **for example**, people are not originally supposed to die. The moon wants people to know this. 2) **However**, Hare, who carries the message, changes it. 3) **Consequently**, death is brought into the world. Hare is punished for his actions. This myth stresses the unfairness of death. 4,5) **Similarly**, in a Caddo myth, death is not inevitable. A medicine man wants to let the wandering souls of the dead come into his tent **so that** they will be able to return to life. 6) **But** Coyote does not want the earth crowded. 7) **Therefore**, he secretly bars the door. 8) Coyote is punished, **too**. This myth demonstrates a belief that death serves a purpose. 9,10) **On the whole**, cultural attitudes toward death may differ, **but** death is never accepted without question or protest.

Background: Guide students in a discussion that will give them practice in identifying literary elements. On the chalkboard, write headings for the five types of similarities discussed in the text: *Subjects, Characters, Plots, Imagery,* and *Themes.* Then ask questions like the following: "How would you state the subject of 'Theseus'? of 'The Wooden People'?" and "What are some important images in 'Green Willow'? in 'Osiris and Isis'?" Elicit a variety of answers, and discuss the answers, reinforcing students' understanding of the literary element to which each heading refers. Prompt, if necessary, with definitions of terms: "Imagery evokes things that we can experience through our senses, such as sights, sounds, scents, tastes, and textures."

Next, have students brainstorm specifics from the unit selections to list under each heading. Begin the brainstorming for each heading with a statement like this one: "Give me a quick summary of each plot you remember from Unit 1," or "Give me the names of all the characters you remember from Unit 1, with an adjective to describe each." Write, or have a student volunteer to write, each suggestion in the appropriate category on the chalkboard. Students can use the resulting lists as idea banks for their essays.

Critical
Thinking
and
Writing

DISCOVERING CONNECTIONS IN LITERATURE

What characteristics do your close friends have in common? What similar features do your favorite singing groups share? Whenever you compare two or more items, you can discover new relationships among people, places, events, or ideas you've always thought of as different.

Writing Assignment

Write an informative essay identifying and discussing connections, or similarities, between any two of the unit selections. Assume that your audience is familiar with the literature and wants to know more. In this essay, you'll use classification to develop your main idea.

Background

In this unit, you have read myths and folktales from a variety of cultures. Because these traditional narratives reflect basic questions about the world and the individual's place in it, many similarities link the tales. Here are some of the kinds of connections you can find:

- **Similar Subjects.** On the simplest level, two stories may deal with the same subject. You may have two stories about the origins of life, about bravery, or about death.

- **Similar Characters.** Similar characters may pop up in stories from dissimilar cultures. You may recognize such archetypes as the brave hero, the wise prophet, or the selfish trickster.
- **Similar Plots.** Throughout the world's literature, some plots occur again and again—with different characters and settings. For example, an average person receives unexpected rewards for acts of kindness, or a hero sacrifices something for the good of society.
- **Similar Imagery.** You may discover works that share strong images—for example, images of water, storms, mountains, forests, valleys, or animals.
- **Similar Themes.** Two different stories may convey similar insights about life or human nature.

Prewriting

Focused Reading and Questioning. To find common elements among works in this unit, answer the following questions:

1. Which works deal with the **subject** of loyalty to others and/or love for others?
2. In which works does the main **character** go on a quest?
3. In which works does the **plot** trace how something originates or how the world changes after a catastrophe?

4. Which works include **imagery** of a peaceful, fertile world?
5. Which works explore **themes** of love and marriage, or the loss of love?

Use one of these questions as the basis for your writing, or ask a question of your own.

Using Classification. One way to develop a main idea is to classify information. From your answers to the questions above, choose two works that have at least two elements in common. Then develop material for your essay by using a chart like the following one.

	Selection 1	Selection 2
Subject		
Main characters		
Minor characters		
Plot summary		
Imagery		
Theme		

Synthesize the charted information into a **thesis statement**, a sentence stating one main idea about the similarities in the two works.

Writing

Use the following plan as you draft your essay.

1. **Introductory Paragraph.** Cite the titles of the two works you'll examine, and identify the cultures they come from. Place your thesis statement at the end of this paragraph.

2. **Body Paragraphs.** Choose an order for presenting your ideas. Either discuss all the charted elements in the first work and then compare the second work to it (AABB order), or take each element separately and show the similarities in both works (ABAB order). In either case, use transitions to connect your points of comparison (see page 56). To illustrate the similarities, present specific details from each work.

3. **Concluding Paragraph.** Summarize the similarities you've discovered. In your final sentence, make an observation about how the similarities between the two works might be meaningful.

Evaluating and Revising

Use the following questions to evaluate and revise your draft.

1. Does your first paragraph include a thesis statement as well as the titles of the two works you've chosen?

2. In the body paragraphs, have you discussed at least two similarities between the works, including specifics to support your points?

3. Have you used transitions to clarify links between the ideas in your sentences and paragraphs?

4. Have you checked paragraph organization and sentence structure?

Proofreading and Publishing

Proofread to eliminate errors in grammar and mechanics, and make a final copy of your essay. Meet with a group of classmates, exchange papers, and discuss the connections that group members have discovered.

Prewriting: Remind students that classification involves both determining categories and grouping subjects under categories. The focused reading questions suggest predetermined categories. However, students who develop their own questions also need to develop categories for classifying their ideas about similarities among the literary works in the unit.

Writing: Tell students that, in a brief essay, introductions and conclusions may also be brief. Each may contain as few as two sentences. The introduction, for example, may contain one sentence identifying the literary works being compared and a second sentence stating the thesis. Similarly, the conclusion need not restate the thesis. Rather, it may sum up, in two or more sentences, the writer's thoughts about the importance of the ideas developed in the essay.

Evaluating and Revising: Refer students to "Using Transitions for Comparison and Contrast," pp. 56–57. There they will find a list of transitions that are useful when writing about similarities, along with examples and usage tips.

Proofreading and Publishing: Interested students may want to submit their essays to the school literary magazine or use their essays to start a literary magazine. ■

The following annotations are for the artwork surrounding the map, starting in the upper right hand corner, and moving in a counterclockwise direction.

Nefertiti: This painted limestone bust from the ruins of Tel-el-Amarna shows the legendary beauty of Nefertiti, the wife of the New Kingdom pharaoh and poet Akhenaten. Nefertiti wears a headdress decorated with an inlay of semiprecious stones. Because Akhenaten had instituted a new, naturalistic style, called the Amarna style, in painting and sculpture, we can be fairly certain that this sculpture portrays Nefertiti as she really looked. Representations of the pharaoh from the same ruins portray him realistically as well, including his physical imperfections.

Nebamun and His Wife: This detail is from a mural decorating the tomb of Nebamun, who was a nobleman in the New Kingdom era. The mural shows Nebamun hunting birds, with a throwing stick in his left hand and several captured birds in his right. His wife stands behind him, with a cone that may contain incense on her head. Several similar murals exist, all showing Egyptian noble families fishing and hunting among the lotuses and papyrus plants of the Nile.

Knephren: An Old Kingdom pharaoh of the fourth dynasty, Knephren was the son of Cheops and the builder of one of the great pyramids at Giza.

AFRICAN KINGDOMS AND EMPIRES

c. 2700 B.C.–A.D. 1800

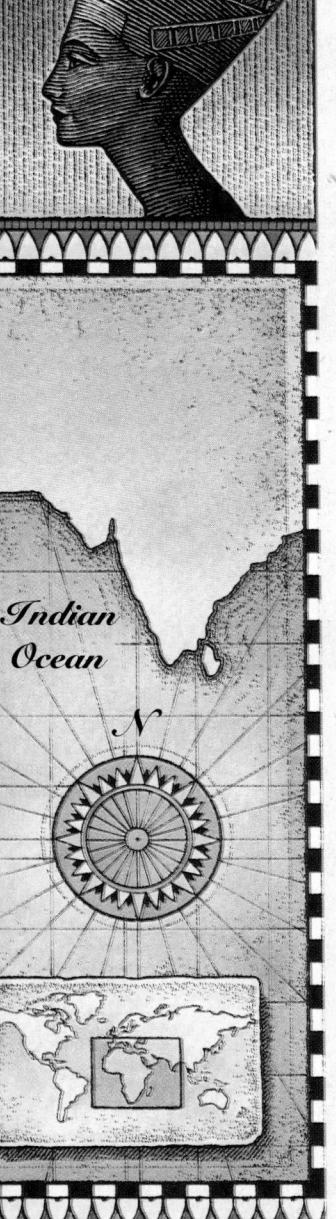

Indian
Ocean

N

UNIT 2

THE AFRICAN LITERARY TRADITION

▼ **Time** ▼

2700 B.C.–present

▼ **Place** ▼

Africa

▼ **Literary Significance** ▼

Africa's literary tradition begins in ancient Egypt. There, for the first time, people used paper and ink to record their thoughts and feelings. Ancient Egyptian literature is mainly a religious literature, but the Egyptians also wrote love poems and entertaining tales.

Although the written word has existed throughout Africa for centuries, the spoken word has remained the dominant form of creative expression in most African communities. For centuries, Africa's oral literature—its proverbs, chants, fables, folktales, and epics—has represented an ongoing creative process in which each reteller injects age-old themes with a fresh perspective.

Mosque of ibn Tulun: Built in A.D. 779, this is the oldest mosque in Cairo, Egypt.

Olokun: This sculpture from the Yoruba people of Nigeria shows the deity Olokun, ruler of the sea and of the marshes where the sea comes in, wearing a ceremonial neck circlet. There is some disagreement among various Yoruba groups over whether Olokun is male or female. Ife, where the sculpture was found, is said to have been the first Yoruba city and was in existence by the tenth century.

Ugandan Landscape: This scene of acacia trees and thatched huts was typical of large parts of equatorial Africa, including present-day Uganda.

Dogon Sculpture: The Dogon people of Mali carve wooden statues such as this one, with sharp, helmetlike profiles, as representations of ancestors. The sculptures are used for ancestor worship and other religious rituals. The zigzag decorative patterns are said to represent the route taken by the creator god when the world was being formed. ■

DISCUSSING THE TIME LINE

Explain that around 3500 B.C., two separate countries began to emerge in the Nile Valley: the kingdoms of Lower Egypt (the delta area, where the Nile flows into the Mediterranean) and Upper Egypt (the part of the Nile Valley extending from modern Cairo south to Aswan). The two lands were united in 3100 B.C.

The period between 3100 B.C. and 2700 B.C., known as the early dynastic period in ancient Egypt, saw the country consolidated and strengthened. By the reign of Cheops, the pharaoh who built the Sphinx and the first of the three great pyramids at Giza, around 2500 B.C., Egypt had entered into the time of prosperity and cultural expansion known as the Old Kingdom.

LITERARY BACKGROUND

Pyramid Texts: These Old Kingdom prayers and incantations were inscribed only on royal tombs, and were intended to resurrect the pharaohs and help them ascend into the sky to join the gods. From these evolved the Middle Kingdom *Coffin Texts*, spells and formulae inscribed on the coffins of nobles, reflecting the Middle Kingdom notion that nobles, as well as kings, could gain eternal life. By the time of the New Kingdom, the texts had expanded into the Book of the Dead, and eternal life was considered within reach of all who lived morally.

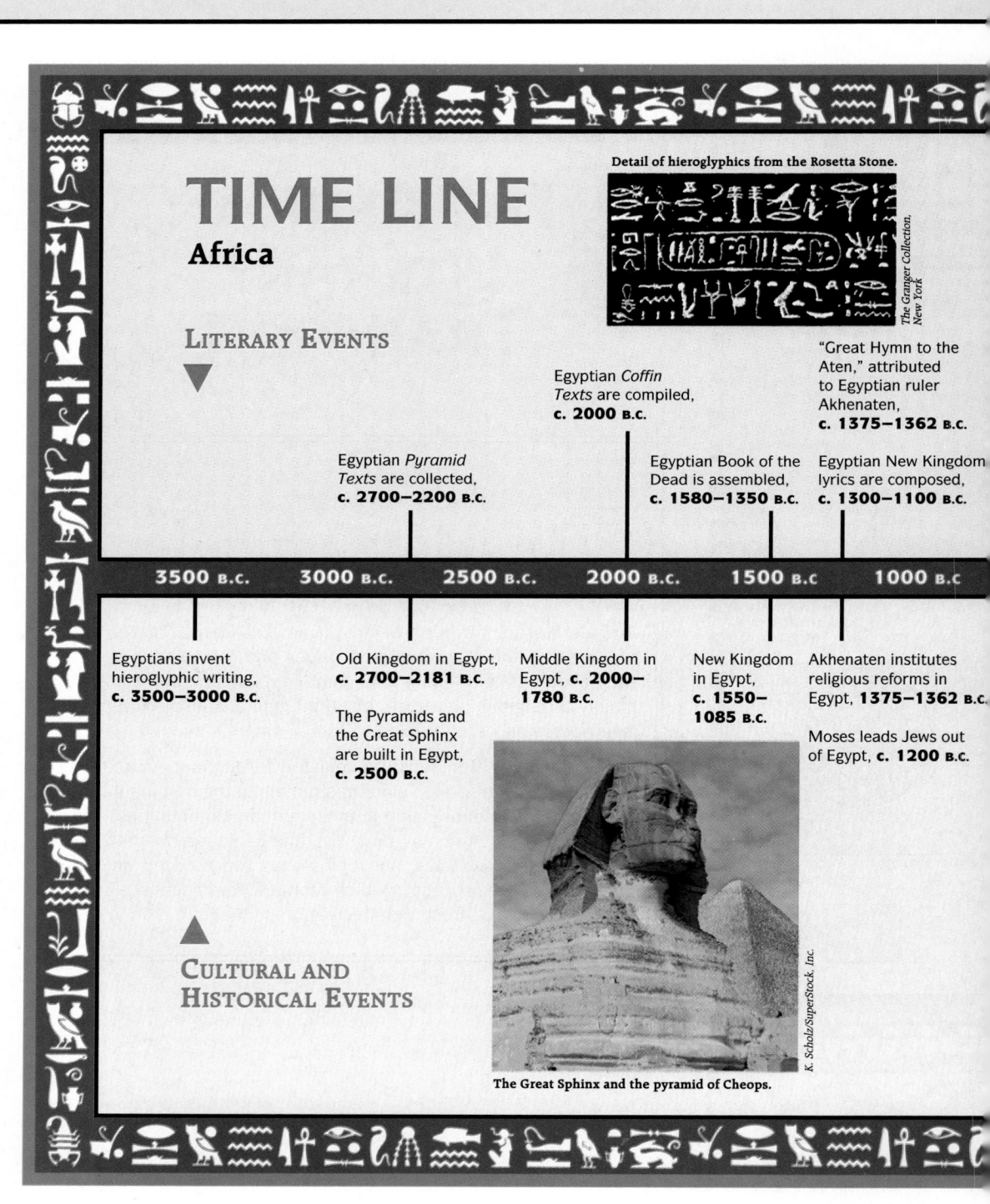

TIME LINE
Africa

Detail of hieroglyphics from the Rosetta Stone.

The Granger Collection, New York.

LITERARY EVENTS ▼

Egyptian *Pyramid Texts* are collected, **c. 2700–2200 B.C.**

Egyptian *Coffin Texts* are compiled, **c. 2000 B.C.**

Egyptian Book of the Dead is assembled, **c. 1580–1350 B.C.**

"Great Hymn to the Aten," attributed to Egyptian ruler Akhenaten, **c. 1375–1362 B.C.**

Egyptian New Kingdom lyrics are composed, **c. 1300–1100 B.C.**

3500 B.C.	3000 B.C.	2500 B.C.	2000 B.C.	1500 B.C.	1000 B.C.

Egyptians invent hieroglyphic writing, **c. 3500–3000 B.C.**

Old Kingdom in Egypt, **c. 2700–2181 B.C.**

The Pyramids and the Great Sphinx are built in Egypt, **c. 2500 B.C.**

Middle Kingdom in Egypt, **c. 2000–1780 B.C.**

New Kingdom in Egypt, **c. 1550–1085 B.C.**

Akhenaten institutes religious reforms in Egypt, **1375–1362 B.C.**

Moses leads Jews out of Egypt, **c. 1200 B.C.**

▲ CULTURAL AND HISTORICAL EVENTS

The Great Sphinx and the pyramid of Cheops.

K. Scholz/SuperStock, Inc.

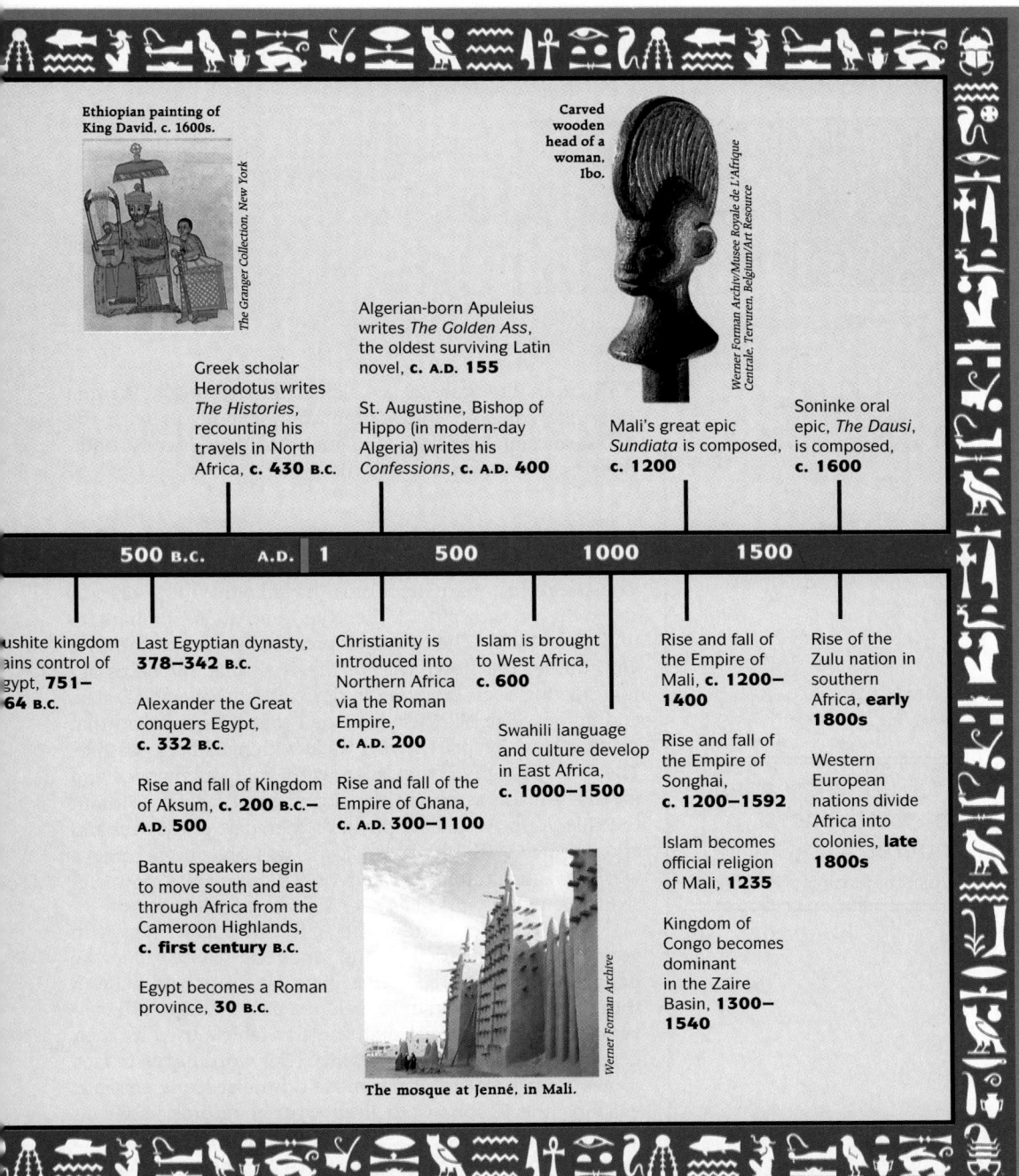

Ethiopian painting of
King David, c. 1600s.

The Granger Collection, New York

Carved
wooden
head of a
woman,
Ibo.

Werner Forman Archive/Musee Royale de L'Afrique Centrale, Tervuren, Belgium/Art Resource

Algerian-born Apuleius
writes *The Golden Ass*,
the oldest surviving Latin
novel, **c. A.D. 155**

Greek scholar
Herodotus writes
The Histories,
recounting his
travels in North
Africa, **c. 430 B.C.**

St. Augustine, Bishop of
Hippo (in modern-day
Algeria) writes his
Confessions, **c. A.D. 400**

Mali's great epic
Sundiata is composed,
c. 1200

Soninke oral
epic, *The Dausi*,
is composed,
c. 1600

| 500 B.C. | A.D. 1 | 500 | 1000 | 1500 |

[Ku]shite kingdom
[g]ains control of
[E]gypt, 751–
[6]64 B.C.

Last Egyptian dynasty,
378–342 B.C.

Alexander the Great
conquers Egypt,
c. 332 B.C.

Rise and fall of Kingdom
of Aksum, **c. 200 B.C.–
A.D. 500**

Bantu speakers begin
to move south and east
through Africa from the
Cameroon Highlands,
c. first century B.C.

Egypt becomes a Roman
province, **30 B.C.**

Christianity is
introduced into
Northern Africa
via the Roman
Empire,
c. A.D. 200

Rise and fall of the
Empire of Ghana,
c. A.D. 300–1100

Islam is brought
to West Africa,
c. 600

Swahili language
and culture develop
in East Africa,
c. 1000–1500

Rise and fall of
the Empire of
Mali, **c. 1200–
1400**

Rise and fall of
the Empire of
Songhai,
c. 1200–1592

Islam becomes
official religion
of Mali, **1235**

Kingdom of
Congo becomes
dominant
in the Zaire
Basin, **1300–
1540**

Rise of the
Zulu nation in
southern
Africa, **early
1800s**

Western
European
nations divide
Africa into
colonies, **late
1800s**

Werner Forman Archive

The mosque at Jenné, in Mali.

The border of this Time Line depicts Egyptian hieroglyphics, a form of
picture writing in which symbols represent words, syllables, or sounds.

Time Line   63

CULTURAL BACKGROUND

Kushite Kingdom: Kush, or
Nubia, with its archaeological
treasures, was flooded when
the Aswan Dam was built during the 1960s to create Lake
Nasser, a major water resource
for modern Egypt. However,
international teams of scientists and engineers managed to
preserve ancient temples at
Abu Simbel and Philae.

LITERARY BACKGROUND

Apuleius: Lucius Apuleius was
born in a Roman colony in
northern Africa. His *The Golden
Ass*, also called *Metamorphoses* or *The Transformations*, follows one character
through a series of adventures
involving gods, humans, and
magical changes. Written in
eleven volumes, *The Golden
Ass* is the only Latin novel that
survives in its entirety.

LITERARY BACKGROUND

St. Augustine: *The Confessions* of St. Augustine (A.D.
354–430) has profoundly influenced Western religious
thought. Augustine was born
in Roman north Africa. Shortly
after being appointed bishop,
he wrote the autobiographical
Confessions, in which he describes his wild youth and his
conversion and simultaneously
examines the basic tenets of
Christianity. His findings form
the philosophic foundation on
which Thomas Aquinas and
other religious thinkers later
built.

OBJECTIVES

1. To gain an overview of the traditional literatures of the African continent, including ancient Egyptian literature, and to identify literary and cultural contributions of principal African civilizations
2. To recognize the function and importance of the oral tradition in African literature from antiquity through modern times
3. To interpret and respond to African literature both orally and in writing

TEACHER'S RESOURCES: 2
- Unit Introduction Test
- Word Analogies
- Unit Review Test
- Critical Thinking and Writing

1 HISTORICAL BACKGROUND

Settlers of the Nile Valley:
Archaeological evidence shows that the early settlers of Egypt had established farms along the Nile by 4000 B.C. Two features made the Nile Valley an ideal place for an advanced culture to develop. First, the valley was fairly safe from attack. Second, the flooding of the Nile, resulting from heavy rains and melting snow in the mountains of present-day Ethiopia, occurred at the same time each year so that Egyptians could plan their planting and harvesting around the flood periods. Thus life in the Nile Valley was ordered and secure.

2 RESPONDING TO THE QUOTATION

The Maxims of Ptahhotpe dates from the Old Kingdom and is an early example of the instruction genre of Egyptian literature, offering rules for daily conduct. An emphasis on the importance of truth and justice recurs throughout the literature of the ancient Egyptians.

❓ *Which modern maxims or rules stress the value of truth?* (Most religious codes call for truthfulness; students may suggest such sayings as ''The truth shall make you free.'')

AFRICAN LITERATURE

2
> ❝ Truth is great and its effectiveness endures. ❞
> —*from* The Maxims of Ptahhotpe

A frican literature is as old as the pyramids. Written literature on the African continent began with the ancient Egyptians, and many of their literary traditions have counterparts in African literature today.

The "Gift of the Nile"

The Greek historian Herodotus (hə·räd′ə·təs) (485–425 B.C.) called Egypt the "gift of the Nile," and it is not hard to understand why. The Nile itself provided settlers with water and, during the flood season, the fertilizing silt necessary for growing such crops as barley, wheat, vegetables, flax, and grapes. The Nile also provided the transportation that made ancient Egypt's thriving trade with neighbors possible. The Nile brought boats laden with gold, hardwood, and metals—all the resources that Egypt itself lacked. Without the Nile, Egypt would simply have been part of the vast and arid Sahara. With the Nile, Egypt was able to become a wealthy agricultural land and one of the most powerful civilizations the world has ever known.

1

The Nile provided another gift that enabled Egypt to grow into a remarkable and enduring civilization: the **papyrus** (pə·pī′rəs) reeds that grew along its banks. From these reeds the Egyptians developed paper, a far more convenient writing material than the clay tablets used by their neighbors in ancient Mesopotamia. (Our word *paper*, in fact, comes from *papyrus*.) Paper made centralized rule possible, enabling the Egyptians to keep written records, issue instructions, write histories, compute taxes, survey land, and carry out the other practical tasks of a complex society. In addition, ideas and literature could be shared far and wide and handed down to future generations.

Honest, direct, and unpretentious, traditional African works spring from literatures that are full of life. From ancient hymn to modern humor, the selections grow in vividness as students realize the functions they served in the lives of the people who composed them. Point out to students at the outset that unlike many modern books, traditional African works were not created for large, unspecific audiences. Rather, each was composed for an individual or a small group the author knew well, and each was intended for immediate use, most likely being recited as it was composed. For this reason, the voices of the anonymous authors come through clearly, bringing an immediacy and a personal quality to the literature and doing much to bridge the expanses of time and distance that separate us from them. For the same reason, students will benefit from hearing each selection presented orally and reading it aloud themselves.

The unit opens with two selections from the hieroglyphic literature of ancient Egypt. The first, "The Great Hymn to the Aten," may daunt students with its length and its formal language. Yet in Miriam Lichtheim's clear translation, the pharaoh's worshipful, trusting tone is touching, and parts of the hymn, resembling

Twenty-seven Centuries of Civilization

3 Under thirty-one **dynasties**, or successive ruling families, Egyptian civilization flourished for more than twenty-seven centuries. Its greatest years are divided into three main eras:

The Old Kingdom—from about 2700 to 2200 B.C. The great pyramids were built during this period.

The Middle Kingdom—from about 2000 to 1800 B.C. This period was characterized by Egypt's expanding economy and political power.

The New Kingdom—from about 1600 to 1100 B.C. Egypt was at the peak of its political power during this period. Its vast empire reached north to Syria, east to the Euphrates (yōo·frāt'ēz) River, and south to the East African kingdoms of Nubia and Kush.

A Highly Organized Society

4 The organization of Egyptian society resembled the shape of its pyramids. A single, powerful ruler, the **pharaoh**, was the pinnacle of the social pyramid. Priests and scribes formed the next level of the pyramid. Then came the upper class, consisting of merchants, doctors, engineers, lawyers, and other professionals. Forming the bottom of the pyramidic structure was the largest class: the workers, peasants, and slaves.

The pharaoh was not only a political leader but also a spiritual leader, representing the earthly incarnation of the god Horus (hō'rəs), son of Osiris (ō·sī'ris). It was the pharaoh's destiny to go and live with the gods after death, and in the afterlife to become identified with Osiris, god of the underworld. To ease the pharaoh's journey to the afterlife, the Egyptians built magnificent pyramids, which contained the pharaoh's mummified body and earthly possessions.

The Egyptian Pantheon

Religion was inseparable from everyday life in ancient Egypt. Because the Egyptians believed that their ruler, the pharaoh,

The Granger Collection, New York

Statue of the falcon-headed god Horus, protecting the pharaoh, Ramses II. *The Egyptians believed that the pharaoh was the earthly incarnation of Horus.*

lists of the things the pharaoh likes best about life, are likely to appeal to students as well: the sight of fields and flocks in the morning sun, the Nile bustling with river traffic, the rain drenching distant hills and towns. Point out to students that the pharaoh composed this hymn in the belief that his god was listening and would be pleased.

The second Egyptian selection, a set of two brief love lyrics, will speak more directly to students, especially if they have read the *Behind the Scenes* feature, "Daily Life in Ancient Egypt," that precedes the poems. You might ask students if they have ever been at parties with live music, and explain that these lyrics were probably composed to be sung at such a party in an ancient Egyptian home.

The unit's selections from the African oral tradition begin with a group of proverbs from various cultures. Many are fresh and humorous, such as the Zulu "Do not speak of a rhinoceros if there is no tree nearby," and students will enjoy their lightness as well as their wisdom. The next selection, "Song of a Mother to Her Firstborn," contrasts sharply with the lightness of the proverbs, for it is a powerful evocation of the emotion of parental love. This oral poem's arresting language and vivid, unusual imagery will quickly draw students in. Help them to

5 RESPONDING TO THE QUOTATION

The Book of the Dead was a series of spells for resurrecting one's soul after death, following the magical rituals that the goddess Isis was said to have used to resurrect her husband, Osiris, after the evil Seth had killed and dismembered him. Each copy of the book was buried with its owner. Scribes mass-produced the Book of the Dead on papyrus scrolls, so that anyone could buy a scroll, get his or her name inserted in the blanks, and have a ready-made instruction manual for the afterlife. The negative confession was one of several that the soul recited while being judged by Osiris. If the soul was found worthy, it was granted eternal life; if not, it was eaten by a monster.

❓ *How does the moral code implied by this quotation resemble modern moral codes?* (Students' responses should be supported by real-life examples.)

Dallas Museum of Art, Gift of Elsa von Seggern

Thoth, the Egyptian god of learning.

> ❝ I have not done iniquity. . . . I have not robbed with violence. . . . I have not stolen. . . . I have done no murder; I have done no harm. . . . I have not defrauded the offerings. . . . ❞
>
> —*Negative Confession from the Egyptian Book of the Dead*

5

was a god, service to the ruler was the same as religious worship. Yet the ancient Egyptians recognized and worshiped many other gods and goddesses besides the earthly one. These divine beings—numbering somewhere between eighty and eighty-nine—had different forms and represented different powers. Probably the most important group of gods was the *ennead* (en′ē·ad′), the nine creation gods. These were Atum, the creator; his children Shu and Tefnut; their children Geb and Nut; and Osiris, his wife/sister Isis, his brother Seth, and Seth's wife/sister Nephthys.

The Cult of the Dead

A fascination with death pervaded Egyptian culture. This "cult of the dead" largely dictated Egyptian morality and ethics. Starting in the Old Kingdom, the Egyptians wrote many works dedicated to the quest for life after death. These works contained magical spells for the protection of the dead, burial rites, and other funerary texts. The New Kingdom saw the ultimate expression of Egyptian funerary literature: the Book of the Dead, a kind of "traveler's guide" to the afterlife containing everything the deceased needed to have and know after death.

Religious literature did not stop with the Book of the Dead. Virtually everything the Egyptians wrote was in some way tied to their religious beliefs, written either to instruct people in morality or to praise the gods.

> **Much of ancient Egyptian literature served to aid or instruct people in attaining the afterlife.**

Strictly religious texts included **praise songs** and **hymns**. The most famous of these, "The Great Hymn to the Aten," is the earliest known praise song (see page 73). Other popular genres, or forms of literature, in ancient Egypt included **instructions**, sets of moral teachings often presented in the form of proverbs, and **autobiographies**, a form of secular literature intended to teach lessons in morality. Although the Egyptians told stories for entertainment, such as "The Tale of the Shipwrecked Sailor" and "King Cheops and

see the similarities in the form and theme of this poem and those of the much older "The Great Hymn to the Aten." Each work contains elements of praise poetry.

Narratives in the African oral tradition are represented by the unit's three final selections: two short dilemma tales; a brief, humorous, Ashanti tale titled "Talk"; and a lengthier excerpt from *Sundiata*, the oral epic of Old Mali. The dilemma tales represent an interesting sub-genre of the folk tale, combining elements of the riddle and the moral tale and acting as a catalyst for group discussion. The humorous tale, "Talk," is contemporary in tone, funny and entertaining from the start, and filled with references to the rich Ashanti cultural heritage. This engaging tale may inspire some students to research Ashanti history and culture and report on them to the class. The *Sundiata* excerpt is neither as humorous nor as readily accessible as "Talk," but it offers a quirky, satisfying story and an intriguing view of an ancient culture. Guide students through the material that precedes the selection, and have them read the list of characters aloud after you to familiarize them with the unusual names. You might let students take turns reading the selection aloud in class, stopping at each heading to discuss the events of the preceding section.

the Magician," even these narratives were not without religious content. Finally, the Egyptians wrote **sacred** or **ritual dramas**—plays used in religious ceremonies.

During the New Kingdom, when the social structure and morality of the Egyptian culture had become less rigid, secular poetry was written. Much of this poetry was **pastoral**—that is, it portrayed everyday life in idyllic terms. Even today, the New Kingdom pastoral poetry delivers a fresh and honest view of romantic love.

The Granger Collection, New York

Osiris (left) and Atum. *Osiris was the father of Horus, and the Egyptians believed that the pharaoh became Osiris after death.*

The Rise of Africa's Great Civilizations

By the close of the New Kingdom (about 1000 B.C.), Egypt had lost much of its status as a world power. Internally divided and supported by weak rulers, Egypt fell into decline. But ancient Egypt was not the only civilization in Africa. As Egyptian power was waning, the kingdom of Kush, at the southern end of the Nile River, was gaining strength and prominence. For centuries the Egyptians had struggled to contain the Kushites' power. Between 751 and 664 B.C., Kushite kings succeeded in conquering and ruling

The influence of Egypt's traditional literatures on other cultures may have begun with "The Great Hymn to the Aten." The sequence and content of lines in the ancient Egyptian hymn are remarkably similar to those in the later Hebrew Psalm 104 (p. 188), and many critics have concluded that the psalm is based on the hymn.

New Kingdom love poems, dating from the period between 1550 B.C. and 1100 B.C., provide some of the world's earliest examples of lyrics written in the pastoral vein. Pastoral poetry was also popular in ancient Persia (see the *Rubáiyát*, pp. 654–659) and, later, in Europe during the sixteenth and seventeenth centuries (see The Sonnet, pp. 806–812).

Have students look at the map on p. 60 (or a more detailed map of Egypt and the Near East) to see how easily commercial and artistic exchanges could occur between the ancient Egyptians and their Arabic and Semitic neighbors across the Mediterranean and Red seas. The interchanges in this region led to a linguistic link between ancient Egypt and ancient Mesopotamia and Assyria. Egyptian is part of the Semitic language group that includes Arabic, Hebrew, and Phoenician. Akkadian, a Semitic dialect, was understood from Babylon to Egypt.

Major events occurred in Egypt around the same time as they occurred in Meso-

6 CULTURAL BACKGROUND

The Fasa: Ancestors of the Soninke people, the Fasa were an aristocratic group who emerged in the Fezzan area (now southern Libya) around 600 B.C. Over the course of several centuries, their complex, chivalric culture spread south and westward, and their troubadours created songs immortalizing the loves and battles of the Fasa heroes. Their legendary city, Wagadou, was said to vanish and reappear periodically.

7 HISTORICAL BACKGROUND

Old Zimbabwe: The mysterious, high-walled ruins of Old Zimbabwe, inhabited between A.D. 900 and 1400, are the only remaining traces of a major African civilization. Fragments of Chinese porcelain found in the ruins confirm that overland trade routes through the Sudan desert linked Zimbabwe with China and other eastern lands.

HUMANITIES CONNECTION

The Mbala, also called the Bambala, are a Bantu-speaking people whose traditional homeland is in western Zaire. The drummer's slightly shortened limbs, realistic facial features, placid expression, and closed eyes are characteristic of sculptures by groups along the lower Congo River—the area of the fifteenth-century kingdoms of Congo and Loango. Most of these sculptures had religious or ritual functions. ■

Marc & Evelyne Bernheim/Woodfin Camp & Associates, Paul & Ruth Tishman Collection

Statue of a drummer, from the Mbala people of the Congo.

Egypt. The Kushite kingdom continued to flourish long after Egypt's demise, and its capital city Meroë thrived as a major producer of iron well into the second century A.D.

In addition to Kush, smaller civilizations also existed around the edges of the Sahara, which was less extensive than it is today. These groups farmed and raised livestock in the fertile grasslands surrounding the desert. Among these were the Fasa of the northern Sudan, whose deeds are recalled today by the Soninke oral epic, *The Dausi.* ⎤ 6

In the third century A.D., a rich kingdom in eastern Africa called Aksum (äk'soom') arose in what is now Ethiopia. Aksum thrived at the center of a trade route that extended as far west as Rome and as far east as India. The culture fell into decline in the sixth century A.D., but not before it developed its own writing system, called Ethiopic script. This writing system developed into several modern scripts still used in Ethiopia today.

> **As the Egyptian civilization in the north of Africa fell into decline, new civilizations to the east, west, and south began to rise.**

Drought drove many migrants south and west. In western Africa, a series of great civilizations arose. The first of these, the kingdom of Old Ghana, was in place by A.D. 300. It was succeeded by the empires of Old Mali and Songhai, among others. The legendary city of Timbuktu was a center of trade and culture in both the Mali and Songhai empires.

New cultures sprang up throughout the South, including the Luba and Malawi (mä'lä·wē) empires in central Africa, the two Congo kingdoms, the Swahili (swä·hē'lē) culture of eastern Africa, the kingdom of Old Zimbabwe (zim·bä'bwā'), and the Zulu nation near the southern tip of the continent. ⎤ 7

The period between A.D. 300 and A.D. 1600 marked Africa's long Golden Age. During this time, sculpture, music, metalwork, textiles, and oral literature flourished. African oral literature, like the literature of the ancient Egyptians, includes praise poems, love poems, tales, ritual dramas, and moral instructions distilled into the form of proverbs and fables. It also includes epics and more specific kinds of

potamia. For example, writing began in Sumer about 3300 B.C. and in Egypt about 200 years later. Bring students' attention to the dates on the time line (pp. 62–63) and point out that the first two-thirds of the time line is exclusively Egyptian. Most of the great empires in the rest of Africa did not arise until some 3,000 years after the Egyptian Old Kingdom.

Oral literature from other parts of Africa also left its mark on distant cultures. For example, the Africans who came to the Caribbean and the United States as slaves brought their oral literature with them. Thus the Ashanti trickster figure, an admirably devious spider called Anansi, survives in Caribbean tales as Aunt Nancy, sly as ever despite the name change. In the same way, the Yoruba trickster Ijapa, a tortoise, became Brer Terrapin in the American South, a wise but malicious creature who often teams up with Brer Rabbit. Brer Rabbit himself is a version of the widely known hare, a trickster called by several names among the many Bantu-speaking peoples who occupy central and southern Africa.

Animal fables are used among African groups to entertain; to teach moral lessons, language use, and values to the young; and to comment indirectly on sticky social issues among adults. In the American South, animal tales kept all

The Granger Collection, New York

Timbuktu. *In the fifteenth century, Timbuktu—a center of trade and learning—was one of several bustling cities that dotted the kingdoms of West Africa.*

poems and narratives. From Africa's Golden Age came several oral epics, including the Mali epic *Sundiata* (see pages 102–117).

Foreign Influences in Africa

During the fourth century A.D., the Roman Empire had proclaimed Christianity as its state religion and taken control of the entire northern coast of Africa, including Egypt. This early Christian influence spread east to Aksum, eventually leading to the foundation of the Ethiopian Orthodox Church, still one of the largest religious groups in Ethiopia.

Around A.D. 700, Islam, the religion of the followers of Mohammed, was introduced into Africa. With Islam, the Arabic writing system was introduced as well. By 1235, Islam was the state religion of Old Mali. Somali and other eastern African nations were also largely Muslim.

Much later, near the close of Africa's Golden Age, Christianity and colonialism came hand in hand to sub-Saharan Africa. Ultimately, in the late 1800s, several European pow-

8

❝ . . . the singing that comes from your heart will echo in the ear of your son and live on in your people. **❞**

—*from* The Dausi, Soninke (Sudan)

TEACHING TIP
To help students understand why some African languages remained unwritten, remind them that the African oral tradition was highly developed, with bards, messengers, and oral historians trained to memorize the equivalent of multiple volumes of literature and factual data. Africa's remarkable oral tradition filled many of the needs that writing filled for other cultures. So that students can appreciate the skills required to maintain an oral tradition, assign them to memorize and recite one-page excerpts of their choice from this unit. You might want to have them present their recitations as African oral performances traditionally are presented, with props, gestures, and audience participation in the form of help when the performer stumbles.

8 HISTORICAL BACKGROUND
Islam: African groups that embraced Islam were exposed to and influenced by the literary traditions of the ancient Near East, just as the Arabs who brought Islam to Africa were influenced by African themes and philosophies. Critic Harold Courlander points out that African groups were "adept at receiving ideas, taking their most attractive and compatible features, and remolding them into something truly African in character, just as one tribe borrowed from another without any sense of indignity but rather with a sense of enrichment."

these functions, with the added twist that they also provided a safe way for enslaved Africans to make statements about their situations. A slave who could not call a master stupid or lazy could safely tell tales about stupid, lazy Bre'r Bear, perhaps including an anecdote in which the bear, native to America, was outwitted by clever Bre'r Rabbit, an African figure. Harold Courlander's 1967 novel *The African* details many of the ways in which the trans-planted Africans tried to maintain their cultures in America.

Africa's traditional visual arts and music have also influenced other cultures. The stylized African religious sculptures, with their angular limbs and exaggerated facial features, led Picasso, Cézanne, Braque, Matisse, Léger, and other modern European painters toward cubism. African music, with its antiphonal harmonies and syncopated rhythmic combinations, gave rise to jazz, to Jamaican reggae, and to contemporary zydeco. Paul Simon's *Graceland*, produced during the late 1980s, offers a sampling of today's African musical styles. In many ways, then, traditional literatures and cultures of Africa have influenced other world cultures over the centuries, and their influence continues today.

9 LITERARY BACKGROUND

Orature: The highly original works of Ugandan author Okot p'Bitek (1931–1982) combine the traditions of oral poetry with the form of the Western novel, which was introduced by European colonists. His novel-poems, *Song of Lawino* and *Song of Ocol*, are narrated by a man and a woman whose marriage mirrors a conflict between African cultures and Western values. Both works are masterfully translated into English from Lwo, the Acholi language, by the author.

10 RESPONDING TO THE QUOTATION

Chinweizu is a contemporary Nigerian author, scholar, and critic who examines the ironic fact that many Africans are taught to value European literary forms above traditional African forms.

❓ *In what way does literature "nurture" people?* (Possible response: Literature can transmit values that help to sustain a people's identity.)

CULTURAL DIVERSITY

Keepers of African oral literature differ from culture to culture. Some are primarily ceremonial singers; others are historians, lawyers, storytellers, or government speakers; many combine roles. Among the Hausa of Niger, those well-versed in oral traditions are called *malamai* and are also scribes. Among the Shangaan of southern Africa, only elderly women may serve as *Garingani*, official storytellers and historians.

10

> 66 What kind of people we become depends crucially on the stories we are nurtured on. . . . 99
>
> —*Chinweizu, Nigeria*

ers created colonized "countries." Social and political chaos reigned as traditional African nations were either split apart by European colonizers or joined with incompatible neighbors.

In the mid-1900s, a move toward independence gained force, and a rebirth of traditional cultures came with it. Literature written in African languages, rather than in English, French, or other European languages, gained popularity. This vital literature is clearly stamped with the tradition of African oral literature, or **orature**, as it has been called.

9

Kal Mueller/Woodfin Camp & Associates

A priest outside an Ethiopian Orthodox church. *Aksum, in modern-day Ethiopia, was a Christian kingdom by the sixth century* A.D.

Griots: Africa's Living Libraries

Traditionally, the keepers of oral literature in West Africa have been the **griots** (grē'ōz). In Africa today, a griot may be a professional storyteller, singer, or entertainer. In the past, though, the griot's role included all of these functions and more. Griots were skilled at creating and transmitting the many forms of African oral literature. Many also memorized their nations' histories and laws. Rather than consulting books or libraries, people in the kingdoms of Africa

1. Which geographic feature contributed most to the development of Egypt's culture? (the Nile)
2. Name one religious function of Egyptian literature. (moral advice, praise of gods)
3. In which part of Africa did the empires of Old Ghana, Mali, and Songhai arise? (the west)
4. Name two major foreign influences on African cultures. (Christianity, Islam, colonialism)
5. What was the traditional function of griots in western Africa? (keepers of oral literature)

FOR FURTHER STUDY
Nonfiction
A Treasury of African Folklore, edited by Harold Courlander, places African civilizations in a historical context and provides cultural notes on the extensive variety of oral literature it presents.

Fiction
Things Fall Apart, by Chinua Achebe, shows the role oral literature plays in a modern Nigerian village during political upheavals. ■

consulted griots. Elsewhere on the African continent, bards, storytellers, town criers, and oral historians also preserved and continued the oral tradition.

> As storytellers, tutors to nobility, and living records of a culture's laws and customs, the griots were indispensable to African civilizations.

The literary forms of Africa are many and varied. Yet they share certain features. Striking images of nature, poignant insights into the human condition, and subtle ironies allow these works to speak clearly to modern readers, thus transcending barriers of time and culture.

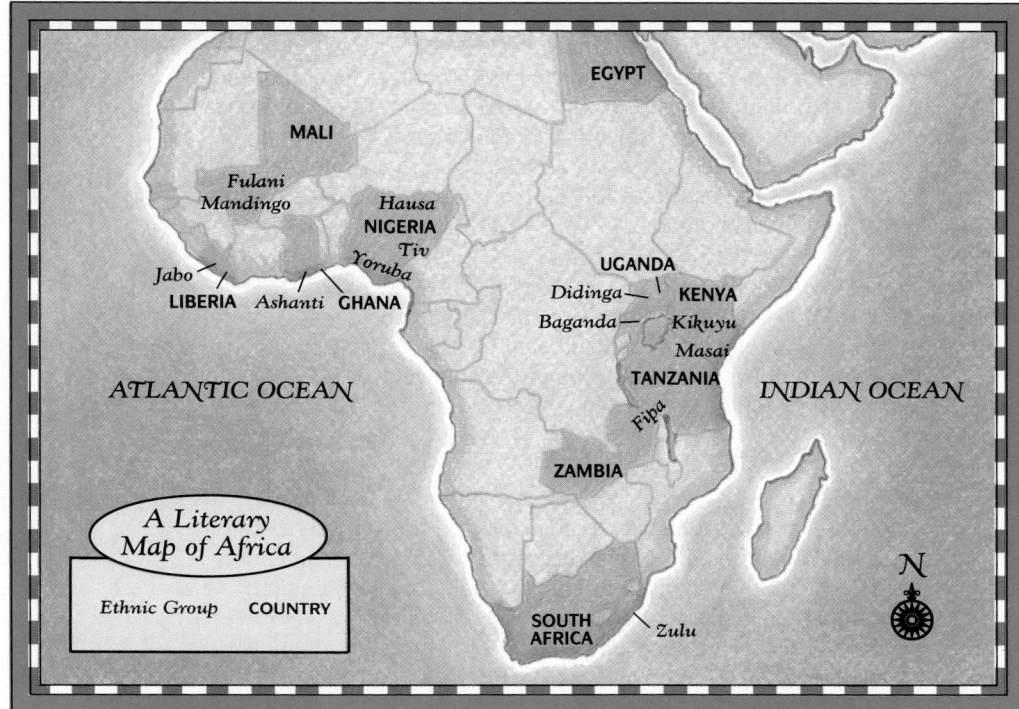

A Literary Map of Africa

Ethnic Group   COUNTRY

EGYPT
MALI
Fulani
Mandingo   Hausa
                NIGERIA
                Tiv
                Yoruba
Jabo   UGANDA
LIBERIA Ashanti GHANA   Didinga — KENYA
                           Baganda — Kikuyu
                                      Masai
                           TANZANIA
ATLANTIC OCEAN   Fipa   INDIAN OCEAN
ZAMBIA

SOUTH
AFRICA — Zulu

N

WRITING TO LEARN

Social Studies: Imagine yourselves scooped up by a time machine and taken to different time periods in various parts of Africa. Choose the time period and the part of Africa where you will land. After landing, make friends with people your own age and learn what their daily lives are like. Record your experiences in letters home, which you will send by time machine. Research the African civilizations of your chosen places and times in order to gather as many details as possible for your letters. After you finish, share your letters with other class members and discuss your "experiences." ■

TEACHING TIP

Tell students to be alert as they read the varied but related works in this unit for similarities in theme and philosophy. Explain that certain attitudes, such as an acceptance of cultural variety and an understanding of the interrelatedness of things in the natural world, have characterized many of the literatures of Africa since ancient times. This "unity within disunity" results from long-established trade and migration routes throughout the continental interior, which permitted communication and awareness of other cultures, even among groups that seemed physically isolated. ■

OBJECTIVES

1. To recognize the importance of praise songs in ancient Egyptian literature and to analyze a praise song
2. To identify and understand literary epithets
3. To write a modern praise song

PREREADING FOCUS

Background: "The Great Hymn to the Aten" reflects Akhenaten's concern with culture and religion and his break with the worship of Amen and other gods. Amen was the city god of Thebes, and when Thebes became the capital of Egypt, all Egyptians worshiped Amen as part of their allegiance to their capital city. Akhenaten changed his name from Amenhotep (which means "Amen is satisfied") and left Thebes. He founded a new capital at Tell el-Amarna that was sacred to Aten.

He also took a strong interest in the visual arts, encouraging innovative architecture, painting, and sculpture. Earlier rulers had been portrayed in idealized form and ritually correct poses, but Akhenaten had artists depict him more realistically, with his oddly elongated face and pot belly. Akhenaten's eye for visual detail is also evident in the imagery of "The Great Hymn to the Aten."

Literary Focus: **Epithet** comes from the Greek *epitithenai*, meaning "to place upon." Epithets were also used in the Greek epic poems, such as the *Odyssey* and the *Iliad*, to stress specific qualities of the characters and to add music to the lines.

ABOUT THE TRANSLATOR

Miriam Lichtheim (1914–) is acclaimed for her translations of Egyptian inscriptions and papyrus scrolls and for her analysis of the writing styles of the various dynasties.

Reader's Guide

THE GREAT HYMN TO THE ATEN

Background

"The Great Hymn to the Aten" is the longest of several New Kingdom **hymns,** or **praise songs,** to the sun god Aten. This hymn was found on the wall of a tomb built for a royal scribe named Ay and his wife. It was intended to assure their safety in the afterlife.

The Egyptians had worshiped the sun—along with a host of other gods and goddesses—since the Old Kingdom. But during the Amarna period of the New Kingdom, the pharaoh Amenhotep IV, who later took the name Akhenaten (a name meaning "he who serves the Aten"), declared that the sun god, Aten, was the one true god. Thus, Egypt was introduced to **monotheism,** or a doctrine of belief in one god.

Akhenaten (ä'ke·nät''n), who ruled from 1379 B.C. to 1362 B.C., was an unusual ruler. Under his reign, conservative, tradition-bound Egypt experienced a revolution that affected every aspect of life. Akhenaten was a talented poet, and this hymn, as well as several others, has been attributed to him. But Akhenaten's break with tradition must have seemed too risky for New Kingdom Egyptians, who for centuries had counted on the help of all the gods to keep them safe and happy after death. As soon as their radical pharaoh died, the people returned to worshiping their old gods.

Writer's Response

Imagine that an organization has commissioned you to write a "praise song" to the sun as part of its campaign to make people more aware of their environment. What features of the sun will you praise? Create a cluster of words and phrases that describe the sun's attributes, or qualities.

Literary Focus

An **epithet** is a descriptive name, adjective, phrase, or title that is used to describe a quality or characteristic of a person, place, or thing. We use epithets when we refer to "America the Beautiful," "Richard the Lionhearted," "Paris, the City of Lights," or "New Jersey, the Garden State." In "The Great Hymn to the Aten," epithets are used to show respect and honor for the attributes, or qualities, of the sun god.

Prepositional Phrases

A prepositional phrase contains a preposition, its object, and words modifying the object.

Adverb phrase:
You fill every land <u>with your beauty.</u>

Adjective phrase:
O living Aten, creator <u>of life!</u>

Prepositional phrases occurring at the ends of lines are part of the parallel structure, or pattern of repeating grammatical elements, that marks the poem.

1. **Reading and Speaking.** Ask students to locate other adverb and adjective phrases in stanzas 1 and 2.
2. **Writing and Sharing.** Ask each student

to write a sentence that describes the sun and that ends with a prepositional phrase. Then have students work in groups, or as a class, to put their lines together to form a poem about the sun. Evaluate the effectiveness of ending each line with a prepositional phrase. ■

THE GREAT HYMN TO THE ATEN

translated by

MIRIAM LICHTHEIM

❖ *Note the specific words and phrases that are used to praise Aten. What kind of god is Aten? What is the speaker's attitude toward the god?*

Splendid you rise in heaven's lightland,°
O living Aten, creator of life!
When you have dawned in eastern lightland,
You fill every land with your beauty.
5　You are beauteous, great, radiant,
High over every land;
Your rays embrace the lands,
To the limit of all that you made.
Being Re,° you reach their limits,
10　You bend them ⟨for⟩ the son whom you love;
Though you are far, your rays are on earth,
Though one sees you, your strides are unseen.

When you set in western lightland,
Earth is in darkness as if in death;
15　One sleeps in chambers, heads covered,
One eye does not see another.
Were they robbed of their goods,
That are under their heads,
People would not remark it.
20　Every lion comes from its den,
All the serpents bite;
Darkness hovers, earth is silent,
As their maker rests in lightland.

Earth brightens when you dawn in lightland,
25　When you shine as Aten of daytime;
As you dispel the dark,

1. **lightland:** the sky.

9. **Re** (rā): another name for the sun god.

TEACHER'S RESOURCES
✔ Review and Response Worksheet

MEETING INDIVIDUAL NEEDS

Students daunted by the length of the poem can gain a sense of its structure by noting the focus of each stanza. (The first deals with the rising sun; the second with the setting sun; the third with the rising sun again; the fourth through seventh with the sun god as creator and protector.) ■

1 LITERARY ELEMENT

Sound Devices: The original poem has a complex meter, but the translation has neither rhyme nor meter. In the first stanza, what sound devices add a rhythmic quality? (repetition, parallelism) Which words and word variants are repeated in the first stanza? (you/your, lightland/land, living/life, beauty/beauteous, radiant/rays/ Re, limit/limits, sees/unseen)

2 LITERARY ELEMENT

Imagery: What specific nature imagery is found in the second stanza? (sunset, darkness, lions emerging from dens, snakes biting) What does this imagery illustrate? (the bleakness and danger of night)

CULTURAL DIVERSITY

During the New Kingdom period, Upper (southern) Egypt stretched along the Nile from Thebes to Nubia. Lower (northern) Egypt followed the Nile's course through Memphis, Giza, and the fertile delta where the river empties into the Mediterranean. In Akhenaten's time, the Nile was a thoroughfare for trade and travelers, connecting all the cities of the Two Lands.

❓ *How did a river play a similar part in unifying the United States?* (The Mississippi linked the North and South, serving as a major trade route.)

3 LITERARY ELEMENT

Figurative Language: What kind of figure of speech is used in describing the Two Lands as "awake" and standing "on their feet" in line 29? (personification) How does this use of figurative language affect the tone of the poem? (It contributes to an attitude of reverence or awe.)

■ HUMANITIES CONNECTION

Tapestry weaving was practiced in ancient Egypt as early as 1483 B.C., perhaps learned through contact with Mesopotamian cultures. Tapestry fragments found in the tomb of Thutmose IV (1350 B.C.) contain hieroglyphic figures.

❓ *Which images in Ali Selim's modern tapestry echo those in the ancient hymn?* (shining sun, flying birds, growing trees and plants) See also the art on p. 76. ■

As you cast your rays,
The Two Lands° are in festivity.
Awake they stand on their feet,
30   You have roused them;
Bodies cleansed, clothed,
Their arms adore your appearance.
The entire land sets out to work,
All beasts browse on their herbs;
35   Trees, herbs are sprouting,
Birds fly from their nests,
Their wings greeting your *ka.*°
All flocks frisk on their feet,
All that fly up and alight,
40   They live when you dawn for them.
Ships fare north, fare south as well,
Roads lie open when you rise;
The fish in the river dart before you,
Your rays are in the midst of the sea. . . .

3 ⌐

28. **The Two Lands:** Upper and Lower Egypt.

37. *ka:* life force.

HYMN TO AKHENATEN (DETAIL), ALI SELIM.
❓ *Do the images in this modern tapestry match the mood of the ancient poem? Why or why not?*

74

45 How many are your deeds,
    Though hidden from sight,
    O Sole God beside whom there is none!
    You made the earth as you wished, you alone,
    All peoples, herds, and flocks;
50 All upon earth that walk on legs,
    All on high that fly on wings,
    The lands of Khor and Kush,°
    The land of Egypt.
    You set every man in his place,
55 You supply their needs;
    Everyone has his food,
    His lifetime is counted.
    Their tongues differ in speech,
    Their characters likewise;
60 Their skins are distinct,
    For you distinguished the peoples.

52. **Khor and Kush**: Syria and Nubia.

4   You made Hapy in *dat*,°
    You bring him when you will,
    To nourish the people,
65 For you made them for yourself.
    Lord of all who toils for them,
    Lord of all lands who shines for them,
    Aten of daytime, great in glory!
    All distant lands, you make them live,
70 You made a heavenly Hapy descend for them;
    He makes waves on the mountains like the sea,
    To drench their fields and their towns.
    How excellent are your ways, O Lord of eternity!
    A Hapy from heaven for foreign peoples,
75 And all lands' creatures that walk on legs,
    For Egypt the Hapy who comes from *dat*.

62. **Hapy in *dat***: Hapy is the river Nile; *dat* is the underworld. Ancient Egyptians thought that the Nile came from a river in the underworld.

5   Your rays nurse all fields,
    When you shine they live, they grow for you;
    You made the seasons to foster all that you
        made,
80 Winter to cool them, heat that they taste you.
    You made the far sky to shine therein,
    To behold all that you made;
    You alone, shining in your form of living Aten,
    Risen, radiant, distant, near.

CULTURAL DIVERSITY

Isolated by the desert and the sea, the Egyptians held insular and intolerant views of others for centuries. However, when the line of pharaohs preceding Akhenaten embarked on foreign conquests, they increased Egyptians' contact with other peoples. Akhenaten's hymn underscores his own more tolerant, inclusive concept of Aten's people.

❓ Can nations today remain isolated? Why or why not?

4 INTERPRETING

"Hapy in *dat*" (line 62) refers to the river Nile and its source, the underworld. What might "a heavenly Hapy" for distant lands (lines 69–70) refer to? (rain. Other lands had significant seasonal rainfall; Egypt did not.) How might the heavenly Hapy make "waves on the mountains" (line 71)? (Water floods down mountainsides during a rainstorm.)

5 GUIDED READING

Identifying Details: Which details in the sixth stanza show what Aten does for his people? (His warmth makes their fields grow; he provides cool relief in winter and lets people "taste" him in summer.)

COMPARING LITERATURE

Students may compare "The Great Hymn to the Aten" with Psalm 104 from the Hebrew Bible (pp. 188–191).

❓ What is similar about their use of epithets, their speakers' attitudes, their descriptions of the creators' relationships to the earth?

READING CHECK

1. Who is Aten? (the sun god, creator of all things)
2. Who is the speaker in the poem? (a devout worshiper of the sun god, probably Akhenaten himself)
3. Why is sunrise significant to the speaker in the poem? (It marks the daily return of the god.)
4. List three things that Aten causes to happen, according to the speaker. (Possible responses: He wakens all living things every day, makes crops grow, gives people their distinct features, creates the seasons, sends the water supply, creates everything that exists.)
5. Whom does Aten hold in special favor? (the pharaoh, Akhenaten, and his queen, Nefertiti)

RETEACHING

Explain that in Egyptian wall painting the sun is variously represented by an obelisk, a sacred scarab beetle, a cobra, or a disk with vertical rays emanating from it. Have students review "The Great Hymn to the Aten" and decide how they would depict or represent Aten. Encourage them to work in pairs to create an illustration of the god as he is portrayed in one or more stanzas of the poem.

WRITING TO LEARN

Social Studies: Imagine that you are a well-off farmer during the reign of Akhenaten. Write a dialogue with a visitor from a foreign land who wants to know what you see and do during a typical day and night. Base your dialogue on details from "The Great Hymn to the Aten." You may also consult the unit introduction, the *Reader's Guide*, and *Behind the Scenes*, pp. 64–71, 72, and 78–79. ∎

MEETING INDIVIDUAL NEEDS

6 ESL: Explain that the long string of phrases starting with "your son who came from your body" (line 97) and ending with "Akhenaten, great in his lifetime" (line 101), represents various titles of praise for Akhenaten. Similarly, lines 102–103 contain the various names of Queen Nefertiti. ∎

6 INTERPRETING

In lines 89–103, the speaker addresses Aten as the giver of eternal life. How does the speaker present the relationship between Akhenaten and the sun god? (Aten rouses the people for the sake of the King and calls Akhenaten "the son of Aten.")

PRAYER TO THE SUN (DETAIL), ALI SELIM.

Werner Forman Archive/Ramses Wissa Wassef School/Art Resource, New York

85 You made millions of forms from yourself alone,
    Towns, villages, fields, the river's course;
    All eyes observe you upon them,
    For you are the Aten of daytime on high. . . .

    ⟨Those on⟩ earth come from your hand as you
        made them,
90 When you have dawned they live,
    When you set they die;
    You yourself are lifetime, one lives by you.
    All eyes are on ⟨your⟩ beauty until you set,
    All labor ceases when you rest in the west;
95 When you rise you stir [everyone] for the King,
    Every leg is on the move since you founded the
        earth.
    You rouse them for your son who came from
        your body,
    The King who lives by Maat,° the Lord of the
        Two Lands,
    Neferkheprure, Sole-one-of-Re,
100 The Son of Re who lives by Maat, the Lord of
        crowns,
    Akhenaten, great in his lifetime;
    ⟨And⟩ the great Queen whom he loves, the Lady
        of the Two Lands,
    Nefer-nefru-Aten Nefertiti,° living forever.

98. **Maat:** The personification of truth, order, and moral law. The ancient Egyptians believed that only those who had followed Maat in life would achieve immortality.

103. **Nefertiti** (nef'ər·tē'tē): Akhenaten's wife, renowned for her beauty.

1. Using Epithets and Apostrophe. Have students work in groups to create hymns of praise to other elements or forces in the natural world, such as the oceans, air, moon, trees, plants, animals, or the planet Earth. Each hymn should contain appropriate epithets and apostrophes. Students may wish to set their hymns to music, illustrate them, and/or perform them.

2. Research Project. Scholars speculate that Akhenaten's religious reforms were politically motivated. Over the centuries, the priesthood and noble families had become powerful in the Egyptian government. By creating a new religion and by moving the capital, Akhenaten was able to appoint new priests and nobles, wresting power from the old orders. Students can investigate and evaluate this theory.

CLOSURE

How do you feel about Aten as he is described in this poem? (Encourage all responses.) Does he seem stern, indifferent, judgmental? How can you tell? (Aten is described as benevolent and attentive: he gives everyone a place, sees that everyone's needs are met, makes sure that people's "lifetimes are counted," toils and shines for his people. He made people and is pleased with them. The speaker seems to feel secure in his god's care.) ■

First Thoughts

Did the speaker's feelings about the sun seem strange to you, or could you understand and sympathize with them?

Identifying Facts

1. The speaker describes the sun's rising as a joyous occasion. How is the setting of the sun described?
2. Reread lines 45–88. Make a list of the things that Aten creates or makes possible.
3. A **hymn** is a song of praise. What attributes, or characteristics, of Aten does the speaker praise?

Interpreting Meanings

1. **Apostrophe** is a figure of speech in which a writer addresses some thing, concept, or absent person. Apostrophes are written in the **second person**, using the pronouns *you* and *yours*. Find three examples of apostrophe in "The Great Hymn to the Aten." How does the use of apostrophe convey respect to Aten?
2. An **epithet** is a brief descriptive name, title, or adjective that qualifies a person, place, or thing. An epithet appears in the second line of the hymn: "living Aten, creator of life!" Find two or three other epithets in the hymn. To what characteristics of Aten do they refer? What do they tell you about the relationship between Aten and his people?

3. This **hymn**, like other hymns and praise songs, was probably composed to be recited. What aspects of the poem make it particularly suitable for oral presentation? In your response, consider such features of the poem as **repetition**, **parallelism**, and the use of **apostrophe**. Read the poem aloud to hear its other oral characteristics.

Applying Meanings

"The Great Hymn to the Aten" is a celebration of an aspect of nature. Name some of the ways that people today celebrate or praise nature. How is our attitude toward nature similar to or different from the ancient Egyptians'?

Creative Writing Response

Writing a Hymn to the Sun. Refer to the cluster you made in your Writer's Response. In verse or prose, write a hymn in which you praise the sun's attributes and its contributions to life on earth. Remember that you are writing at the request of an environmental group and that your audience will be contemporary Americans, not ancient Egyptians. Don't hesitate to incorporate aspects of modern life in your hymn. Try to use several powerful **epithets**—descriptive words and phrases—in your hymn. If you wish, you may use **apostrophe** in your hymn, but be sure to maintain a consistent **second-person point of view**, addressing your subject, the sun, as *you*.

ANSWERS

First Thoughts
Answers will vary.

Identifying Facts
1. as dark, bleak, dangerous
2. Possible responses: the earth, all people and animals, the Nile, rain, growing crops, the seasons, the sky, towns, fields, life and death
3. Possible responses: beauty, creativity, benevolence, power

Interpreting Meanings
1. Possible responses: "Splendid you rise . . . O living Aten"; "O Sole God . . . you made the earth"; "How excellent are your ways, O Lord of Eternity!" They praise Aten's qualities.
2. Possible responses: "O Sole God beside whom there is none!" (supremacy); "Lord of all who toils for them," (benevolence); "the Aten of daytime on high" (beauty and omnipotence). Aten is loving and is loved by his people.
3. Possible responses: parallelism, repetition, alliteration, apostrophe, epithets, cadence

Applying Meanings
Modern celebrations: seasonal holidays, popular songs, TV specials. *Similar attitudes:* enjoyment, admiration. *Different:* We do not overtly worship nature.

Creative Writing Response
Writing a Hymn to the Sun. Hymns should convey a contemporary understanding of the sun's effect on the environment. ■

New Kingdom Women: While certain upper-class Egyptian males received formal education and entered the professions, upper-class females were generally fated to household management. Nevertheless, it was not unusual for women of the New Kingdom to receive a certain amount of priestly training and to perform limited temple duties. Women often functioned as chanters of hymns and incantations. In order to perform this duty, the women had to be able to read and had to be initiated into the secret rites of the gods. At least one woman is known to have become a full-fledged priest.

There was also a female pharaoh, Queen Hatshepsut, during the New Kingdom period. She ascended the throne after the death of her husband, Tuthmosis II. Apparently she or her reign was controversial, for her successor obliterated her name from all statues and monuments.

❓ *How do modern women's opportunities for religious service compare with those of New Kingdom women?* (Few of the major world religions permit women to be full-fledged members of the clergy, although there are some notable exceptions. However, most religions do permit women to play secondary roles in religious worship and teaching.) *Which modern countries have elected female politicians?* (the United Kingdom, Israel, Nicaragua, Iceland, India, and Pakistan, among others)

BEHIND THE SCENES

Daily Life in Ancient Egypt

Imagine yourself a New Kingdom Egyptian teenager, a member of the privileged upper classes. Your father, a high-ranking government worker, is wealthy. You live on an estate on the outskirts of Thebes, a center of government that lies on the banks of the Nile. Your colorfully decorated home has two stories plus a roof patio, a walled garden, and twenty rooms, counting guest rooms, toilets and baths, servants' quarters, and a shrine for daily worship. You may have a lotus pool filled with fish, and there is probably at least one pampered cat who shares your estate.

You wake up each morning in your slanted wooden bed, the head higher than the foot, with a brightly painted board at the lower end to keep you from sliding off. You don't use a pillow; instead, your head is supported by a wooden stand, made to measure for you and attached to the bedframe. You dress in a white linen kilt; over this, you wear a short-sleeved robe, also of white linen. These fashions have not changed much over the years; in fact, your ancestors hundreds of years earlier probably wore similar garb. Whether you are male or female, you don jewelry: a head circlet, bracelets, anklets, and a necklace made of silver and semiprecious blue and red stones. You rub yourself with oil and use a black cosmetic, *kohl* (kōl), as eye makeup. Finally, you don a heavy wig, both for the sake of appearance and for protection from the sun. Then you hurry, barefoot, to join your family at the shrine just inside the gates of your home.

In the shrine, busts of your ancestors, as well as statues of gods and goddesses, line the walls. Among them are a likeness of Bast, the goddess of joy and love; a statue of Hathor, the cow-headed goddess of music, dance, and maternal love; and the statue of a local god, Bes, a lion-headed dwarf who wards off evil spirits. You and your family offer food and incense to the deities in the shrine as the busts of your ancestors look on from their honored positions in the holy place.

Afterwards, your family eats breakfast, older boys and men in one area, women and children in another. Sitting on cushions, people help themselves to plates of fruit, breads and cakes, and cheese or cold, spiced meat, eating with their fingers. After eating, your father goes to work. The younger children, wearing few or no clothes, run off to play with their balls, dolls, and toy animals. If you are a girl, you and your mother begin your daily tasks, working with your father's steward to supervise the buying, cooking, brewing, weaving, and other details of managing a large household. If you are a boy, you probably help oversee the crops and livestock raised on your parents' land.

At some point during the day, you join your brothers and sisters for a religion lesson from your mother. She tells you the story of Osiris and Isis, then explains that, centuries before, people believed that only the pharaoh and his family could have eternal life. Now, however, Egyptians believe that anyone can enter the afterlife by living virtuously and by having the correct rituals performed after death.

Your brother is preparing to enter your father's profession. As is customary, one of the sons in an Egyptian family is chosen to follow in his father's footsteps. Like the apprentices of all government workers, whether tax collectors, judges, administrators, or high officials, your brother began scribal training at the age of five. By copying words and texts and taking dictation, he has learned to read and write both hieroglyphics and cuneiform (see pages 83 and 204), for dealing with other countries. Now, at sixteen, he is almost ready to "graduate" and begin work in the branch of civil service he has chosen.

Your brother's best friend plans on entering the profession of his father, a priest. His training, however, will not even begin until he turns seventeen. Then he will be required to shave his head and enter a temple school, learning to read and write hieroglyphics and to perform the ritual chants, dramas, and activities associated with the worship of the gods.

Unlike your brother and his friend, you haven't had any formal schooling. But, if you are male, you are learning all you need to know to run an estate: mathematics for accounting, geometry for resurveying your family's land after the Nile's annual floodwaters subside, and natural sciences for plant and animal husbandry.

Your life is not all work, however. In your free time, you can choose from many recreational activities: board games, hunting, wrestling, dancing, swimming, and other sports. You enjoy life in this world, even though you spend a great deal of time preparing yourself for the next world. Your family is very important to you, and it is in the home that you learn the beliefs and values that will govern your adult life as an upper-class Egyptian. Although you may not realize it, you are one of the most privileged people alive in the ancient world, a member of a mighty civilization that will thrive, all told, for almost three thousand years.

Scala/Art Resource, New York

Egyptian Book of the Dead papyrus. *This scene shows the domestic tasks that must be carried out even in the afterlife.*

WRITING TO LEARN

Social Studies: Imagine that you are a Theban teenager who has grown up with the traditional Egyptian polytheistic religion. Recently, however, Akhenaten has come to power and instituted major religious reforms. He has also moved the capital from Thebes to a new site 400 miles north along the Nile. How are these changes affecting your daily life? How do you feel about them? Write a letter in which you share your experiences, thoughts, and feelings with an old friend you have grown up with. Incorporate specifics from *Behind the Scenes* on p. 78 and from the *Reader's Guide* material on p. 72. For more details, reread the unit introduction. Read your letter to the class. ■

HUMANITIES CONNECTION

Many religions associate the afterlife with rest and peace. The Egyptians, on the other hand, believed you performed the same tasks whether alive or dead.

❓ *Which concept do you prefer?* (Answers will vary.) ■

OBJECTIVES

1. *To recognize the characteristics of lyric poetry and to interpret two New Kingdom love lyrics*
2. *To differentiate between the speaker and the author of the poem*
3. *To write a love lyric with a speaker very different from the student writer and to compare New Kingdom love lyrics with a nineteenth-century American love poem*
4. *To identify and rework clichés*

PREREADING FOCUS

Background: A lyric poem expresses the speaker's personal feelings. In "The Voice of the Wild Goose," the speaker likens his or her state to that of a trapped wild bird.

This first lyric uses simple, clear imagery drawn from everyday life in Egypt, where waterfowl abounded in the reedy marshlands bordering the Nile. Snaring wild geese was a common activity in ancient Egypt, practiced for sport and crop protection.

Literary Focus: When the speaker of a poem is obviously very different from the author, readers should consider why the author has chosen this particular voice. Egyptian scholars have theorized that the wealthy and sophisticated courtier–poets of the New Kingdom may have adopted the voice of young peasants because they idealized youthful feelings and a simple, rural lifestyle, as many urban Americans do today.

ABOUT THE TRANSLATOR

William Kelly Simpson (1928–) was curator of Egyptian Art at New York's Metropolitan Museum of Art and at Boston's Museum of Fine Arts. He has taught at the American University in Cairo, has written about Egyptian history, and has translated literature and records that shed light on ancient Egyptian life and culture.

Reader's Guide

NEW KINGDOM LOVE LYRICS

Background

Lyric poems do not tell a story but instead, like songs, create a vivid, expressive testament to a speaker's thoughts or emotional state. Lyric poetry was already being composed in ancient Egypt during the Middle Kingdom period. However, love lyrics—a specific type of lyric poetry—come to us only from the New Kingdom. Most scholars think that these New Kingdom love poems were, in fact, written to be sung, perhaps accompanied by a harp or a set of reed pipes.

In both of the following poems, the speaker is someone quite different from the poet. Although the language in the poems is fresh and simple, conveying the heartfelt language of young lovers, the lyrics' complex figures of speech and careful meter suggest that the poets were highly skilled and well educated, probably wealthy male members of the pharaoh's court.

Oral Response

Think of some love songs you have heard. As a class, brainstorm a list of common characteristics of popular love songs: the feelings they address, the figures of speech they use, the situations they describe. What qualities do these songs emphasize? What emotions do they celebrate? Write these characteristics on the chalkboard. What common features did you discover?

Literary Focus

The **speaker** of a poem is the voice that addresses us. The speaker expresses emotions or ideas that may or may not be those of the poet. It is helpful to think of the speaker as a character who may be very different from the poet: a different age, race, or gender, for example. Readers should not assume that the speaker and the poet are one and the same.

NEW KINGDOM LOVE LYRICS

translated by
WILLIAM KELLY SIMPSON

As you read, note how these ancient poems express themes that are common to the love poetry of all ages and cultures. Could these poems have been written in modern times?

The Voice of the Wild Goose

The voice of the wild goose,
caught by the bait, cries out.
Love of you holds me back,
and I can't loosen it at all.

5   I shall set aside my nets.
But what can I tell my mother
to whom I return every day
when I am laden with catch?

I did not set my traps today;
10   love of you has thus entrapped me.

Ray Richardson/Animals Animals

Most Beautiful Youth Who Ever Happened

Most beautiful youth who ever happened,
I want to take your house as housekeeper;
we are arm in arm,
and love of you goes round and round.

5   I say to my heart within me in prayer:
if far away from me is my lover tonight,
then I am like someone already in the grave.
Are you not indeed well-being and life?

Joy has come to me through your well-being,
10   my heart seeks you out.

1

2

ANSWERS

First Thoughts
Answers will vary.

Identifying Facts
1. returns to his/her mother with the geese caught. Today he/she has caught none.
2. to "take your house as housekeeper"

Interpreting Meanings
1. Possible response: The speakers seem intensely in love, aware of love's pain.
2. *First poem:* overwhelmed *Second poem:* full of longing
3. Answers will vary. Possible response: Love involves commitment, a permanent tie.

Applying Meanings
Possible responses: *First poem:* Love brings a loss of freedom. *Second poem:* Absence from the loved one is painful. Answers will vary.

Creative Writing Response
Writing as a Different Speaker. For their speaker, students can choose a living person whose speech they can hear before they write.

Critical Writing Response
Comparing Love Poems. Before writing, students can form small groups to discuss similarities and differences.

Language and Vocabulary
1. wearing . . . sleeve 2. loser; game of love 3. broke my heart; love . . . clutches 4. heart pounds; palms sweat. Revisions will vary. ■

First Thoughts
How would you describe the feelings of the speakers? Did you identify with them at all?

Identifying Facts
1. What does the speaker in the first poem do every day? Why is this day different?
2. What does the speaker in the second poem want to do?

Interpreting Meanings
1. How would you describe the speakers in these poems?
2. What is the speaker's **tone**, or attitude, toward love in each poem?
3. In "The Voice of the Wild Goose," love serves as a kind of trap. How is this **metaphor**, or comparison, appropriate? How does the metaphor comment on the notion of "true love"?

Applying Meanings
Each poem mentions a negative aspect of love. State these aspects in a few words. In your experience, do you think negative aspects are inevitable consequences of love? Why or why not?

Creative Writing Response
Writing as a Different Speaker. Try writing a love poem or love letter in which you create a speaker who is quite different from yourself. You might wish to write as a historical or literary figure, or even as a popular media figure such as an actor, a football player, or a politician. Let your imagination run wild, and be sure that your poem or letter is a convincing expression of the feelings of someone who is very different from you.

Critical Writing Response
Comparing Love Poems. Emily Dickinson was a reclusive American poet (1830–1886) whose poems expressed tremendous feelings of love and desire, often using strikingly original images and metaphors. Compare the following poem by Dickinson to the two Egyptian love poems you have read. In two or three paragraphs, explain the similarities and differences you see in these poems. Consider the speaker in each, the emotions that are expressed, and the imagery.

> It's All I Have to Bring Today—
> Emily Dickinson
>
> It's all I have to bring today—
> This, and my heart beside—
> This, and my heart, and all the fields—
> And all the meadows wide—
> Be sure you count—should I forget
> Some one the sum could tell—
> This, and my heart, and all the Bees
> Which in the Clover dwell.

Language and Vocabulary

Clichés

Clichés (klē-shāz') are words or phrases, often figures of speech, that have been used so often that they have become lifeless and almost meaningless. "Love makes the world go round," "The language of love," and "Love is blind" are only a few of the dozens of clichés associated with the topic of love.

See if you can identify the clichés in the following sentences. Then, challenge yourself by rewriting them, removing all clichés and replacing them with original language.

1. I've been wearing my heart on my sleeve ever since you first looked at me.
2. I'm just a loser at the game of love.
3. Even though she broke my heart, love still has me in its clutches.
4. My heart pounds and my palms sweat every time I see him.

THE ART OF TRANSLATION

Egyptian Hieroglyphics

The ancient Egyptians were among the earliest civilizations to create a written language and literature. They called their writing "the words of the god" and believed that it was invented by Thoth, god of wisdom and patron of scribes. Only the Sumerians, who lived in what is now Iraq, developed a writing system as early—probably between 4000 and 3000 B.C. The literature of the Old Kingdom period, including the *Pyramid Texts* and the *Instructions of Wisdom*, dates from the middle of the third millenium B.C.

The Granger Collection, New York

The Rosetta Stone

Hieroglyphics (hī′ər·ō′glif′iks) are a form of written language in which pictures represent ideas. Hieroglyphic writing was beautiful and ornamental, and it was often painted or carved into wood or stone, although the Egyptians did much of their writing on papyrus scrolls, using pen and ink. Over time, hieroglyphic symbols began to represent syllables and sounds, rather than ideas. In addition, two simplified, cursive forms of hieroglyphics evolved: **hieratic** (hī′ər·at′ik) and **demotic** (dē·mät′ik).

Around the fourth century A.D., when alphabetical writing began to replace hieroglyphics in Egypt, the knowledge needed to unlock the meaning of hieroglyphics was lost. By the Middle Ages, scholars took little interest in hieroglyphics and believed that they represented a mystical code intelligible only to ancient Egyptian priests. This was far from the truth. The hieroglyphic writings translated so far record everything from laundry lists to love poems.

Interest in hieroglyphics revived somewhat during the Renaissance, and a number of European scholars made it their lives' work to translate the cryptic writing. But none could make the mysteriously beautiful pictures "talk." Hieroglyphics would have kept their stony silence had not an officer in Napoleon's army discovered the Rosetta Stone near Rashid, Egypt, in 1799. This famous stone records a decree of King Ptolemy V (circa 196 B.C.) in three different scripts: one in hieroglyphics, one in demotic script, and one in Greek. By comparing the three texts, a French scholar, Jean François Champollion (shän·pô·lyōn′), was able to break the "code" of hieroglyphic writing in 1822. Because of Champollion's work, hieroglyphics can now be understood relatively easily with help from a hieroglyphic dictionary. But because hieroglyphics represent only consonants, without vowel sounds, scholars today are not sure how to pronounce the ancient Egyptian tongue.

1. *To recognize the function and importance of proverbs in the oral literature of Africa*
2. *To state and explain proverbs and to identify the literary elements they incorporate*
3. *To write a fable that dramatizes a proverb and to write a modern proverb*

PREREADING FOCUS

Background: Though proverbs reflect the values and experience of a culture, they can be misunderstood if taken too literally. Interpreting proverbs requires a realistic understanding of the culture they represent. For example, the Yoruba of Nigeria say, "One who is about to be barbecued does not anoint himself with oil and sit by the fire." However, a reader would be wrong to conclude that the Yoruba are in the habit of barbecuing people. On the contrary, the proverb is typical of Yoruba fondness for exaggeration and slapstick; it makes its cautionary point by using imagery just as outlandish and comical to the Yoruba as it is to us.

Literary Focus: Metaphor is a figure of speech in which a comparison is made without the use of the words *like* or *as*.
   Alliteration is a sound device in which the same initial consonant or vowel sound is used repeatedly.
   Parallelism is the repetition of sentences or sentence elements that are similar in structure or meaning.

Reader's Guide

AFRICAN PROVERBS

Background

In the oral literatures of the various peoples of Africa, proverbs are much more than quaint old sayings. Instead, they represent a poetic form that uses few words but achieves great depth of meaning. In cultures that have no written literature, proverbs function as the distilled essence of a people's values and knowledge. They are used to settle legal disputes, resolve ethical problems, and teach children the philosophy of their people. Because proverbs often contain puns, rhymes, and clever allusions, they also provide entertainment. Speakers who know and use such proverbs have power within the community; their eloquence makes others want to listen to them, and their ability to apply the proverbs to appropriate circumstances demonstrates an understanding of social and political realities. More than one modern African leader has turned to the wisdom of proverbs in order to make decisions and to gain popular support and respect.

   Proverbs are memorable not only because they are so brief (usually no more than a sentence) but also because, like poetry, they compress sometimes complicated ideas into a few thoughtfully crafted words. And unlike many other forms of literature, they can be easily translated into another language.

Oral Response

As a class, brainstorm as many English proverbs as you can: "It's no use crying over spilled milk," "A penny saved is a penny earned," and so on. Write the proverbs on the chalkboard. Then choose a proverb that is particularly meaningful to you and tell how you have experienced the truth of that proverb in your everyday life.

Literary Focus

A **proverb** is a short saying that expresses a common truth or experience, usually about human failings and the ways that people interact with one another. Proverbs often incorporate such literary elements as **metaphor** ("An ounce of prevention is worth a pound of cure"), **alliteration** ("He who laughs last laughs best"), **parallelism** ("Where there's a will, there's a way"), and **rhyme** ("When the cat's away, the mice will play").

Parallel Structure

The creators of oral literature often make use of balanced or parallel sentence elements. These balanced words, phrases, and clauses are often connected by coordinating conjunctions or linking verbs.

Phrases: The polite lie is better than the forceful truth.

Clauses: Words are easy, but real friendship is difficult.

Parallel structure makes proverbs and other oral literature easy to remember, and emphasizes key words and phrases.

1. **Reading.** Ask students to identify parallel elements in proverbs.

2. **Speaking and Listening.** Ask students to recite American proverbs containing balanced elements, while classmates listen for the elements. ∎

AFRICAN PROVERBS

The proverbs of several African groups are presented in this selection. The proverbs are listed by ethnic group, with the name of the country of origin in parentheses. Sometimes two groups have proverbs whose meaning is the same, but whose wording and imagery are different. Look for examples of these as you read. Do any of these proverbs remind you of proverbs you already know? What is specifically African about them?

Jabo (Liberia)

One does not embrace the leopard.

1 [It is not only giants that do great things.

If you have nothing you are anxious to please.

The man who listens is the one who understands.

Marc & Evelyne Bernheim/Woodfin Camp & Associates

Ashanti gold weight illustrating the proverb, "The bird's relation is the one he sits next to."

Ashanti (Ghana)

2 [One bird in your hand is better than ten birds in the sky.

When a nation is about to come to ruin, the cause begins in the homes of its people.

What is bad luck for one man is good luck for another.

No one knows the story of tomorrow's dawn.

When you do not know how to dance, then you say, "The drum is not sounding sweetly."

If one finger tries to pick up something from the ground, it cannot.

Yoruba (Nigeria)

One who asks never loses his way.

A person who has only one set of clothing does not play in the rain.

However large the ear, it cannot hear seven speeches at once.

He whom one loves never does anything wrong.

A delicious stew does not last long in the pot.

A river does not flow so far that it forgets its source.

The path does not close on a man with a machete.[1]

---

1. **machete** (mə·shet′ē): a large, curved knifelike instrument used as a weapon and for cutting through bushes or underbrush.

TEACHER'S RESOURCES

✔ Review and Response Worksheet
✔ Language Skills Worksheet

1 **COMPARING LITERATURE**

The second Jabo proverb reflects the idea that ordinary people can be more powerful and heroic than they realize.

❓ *How does "The White Snake," pp. 46–52, illustrate this same theme? (Its hero is a humble servant who overcomes great obstacles and wins a princess.)*

2 **CULTURAL DIVERSITY**

The proverb "A bird in the hand is worth two in the bush" has a message similar to that of the first Ashanti proverb.

❓ *Can you think of other proverbs from your background that have meanings similar to any of the Ashanti sayings? ("One man's meat is another man's poison" is similar to the third proverb.)*

MEETING INDIVIDUAL NEEDS

ESL: Encourage ESL students to recite proverbs from their first languages. Invite them to translate these proverbs into English, explain their meanings, and relate them to similar African proverbs. ∎

1. What is a proverb? (a short saying that expresses a common truth or experience)
2. What are some of the uses of Africa's proverbs? (settling legal disputes, resolving ethical problems, instructing children, providing entertainment)
3. List three animals named in the proverbs. (Possible responses: leopard, bird, snail, dog, weasel, zebra, lion, elephant, rhinoceros, cock, snake)
4. Name three African countries represented in the selection. (Possible responses: Nigeria, Liberia, Ghana, Uganda, Kenya, Tanzania, South Africa, Zululand)
5. According to the Baganda proverb, what finishes the argument? (silence)

3 INTERPRETING AND EVALUATING

What idea is implied in the Baganda proverb "A tree does not fall on one who is not there"? (Possible response: Trouble doesn't come to those who don't invite it.) Does your experience bear out this observation? (Answers will vary.)

■ HUMANITIES CONNECTION

In Yoruba art, conical or elongated heads indicate individuality and power. These shapes signify the *ase*, the powerful generating force that animates the Yoruba world. In most sculptures, the body was often geometrically shaped, and figures were usually seated. ■

Baganda (Uganda)

Those who love each other need only a small place.

Loose teeth are better than no teeth.

One who refuses you beans saves you from indigestion.

The man who has not carried loads himself does not know how heavy they are.

3 ⎡ A tree does not fall on one who is not there.

Wherever the snail goes, there also goes the shell.

Where there are no dogs, the weasels play.

Words are easy, but real friendship is difficult.

Silence finishes the argument.

Masai (Tanzania/Kenya)

Best of all advisors is the one who says what you would say.

The polite lie is better than the forceful truth.

The zebra does not despise its stripes.

Don't fight a lion with a stick.

The elephant is not burdened by its own tusks.

The eye with hatred in it can bore through stone.

There is no hill that never ends.

Yoruba fetish. *A fetish is an object believed to have magical powers.*

Marc & Evelyne Bernheim/Woodfin Camp & Associates

Zulu (Zululand, South Africa)

Do not speak of a rhinoceros if there is no tree nearby.

Even when there is no cock, day dawns.

One does not follow a snake into its hole.

One gets drowned even in shallow water.

The house of the talkative person lets in rain.

No snake ever forgot its hole.

Magic takes time.

1. Illustrating Proverbs. Have students make posters illustrating their favorite African proverbs. Students can begin with a brainstorming exercise to get ideas for visual presentations. Then have them create original art or find or take photographs that capture the essence of the proverbs they have chosen. Invite them to display their work and share their thoughts about it.

2. Research Project. Interested students might wish to research any of the cultures represented in the selection, reporting to the class on their way of life—especially on any aspect of their culture or environment that is expressed in the proverbs.

Ask students what they can infer from the proverbs about the African cultures from which they sprang. What does the imagery suggest about climate, culture, topography, plant and animal life, vocations, and so on? Then ask students which proverbs apply to their own lives. Use their answers as a springboard to discuss both the uniqueness and the universality of the African proverbs. ■

First Thoughts

Which of these proverbs would you most like to remember and use in your everyday life? Which ones did you have difficulty understanding?

Interpreting Meanings

1. Which Masai proverb tells you that the Masai value courtesy and diplomacy?
2. Which Baganda proverb is similar to the American expression "When the cat's away, the mice will play"?
3. The Yoruban "A river does not flow so far that it forgets its source" has much the same meaning as the Zulu "No snake ever forgot its hole." Locate another example of proverbs from different groups that have a similar meaning. Explain the meaning.

Applying Meanings

Decide which of the African proverbs you liked best. Did you prefer the humorous ones, the direct ones, or the political ones? Compare them with the proverbs you thought of in the Oral Response. Explain how your choices reflect your own values, principles, and sense of humor.

Creative Writing Response

1. **Dramatizing a Proverb.** Proverbs are similar to **morals**—the brief statements that appear at the end of many fables. A moral directly states the lesson the fable has taught. Choose a favorite African proverb and imagine that it is attached to the end of a fable. With a partner or a small group, write the fable that would dramatize the meaning of the proverb you have selected. Then act out the fable and have the class guess what the proverb is.

2. **Creating Your Own Proverbs.** Proverbs have stood the test of time because they address general truths. Is there some common truth of modern life that has not, as far as you know, been made the subject of a proverb? Think of an example and create a proverb that addresses it. Don't hesitate to use modern language or slang. If you can't think of a new topic, try updating or modernizing a well-known proverb.

The tonal qualities of African languages are what have allowed Africans to communicate over several miles via "talking drums." These large, conical drums can produce various tones, depending on where the player places his hands on the drumhead. Learning to play the drums requires special training; their combination of tones and rhythms mimics speech closely enough that master drummers can communicate phrases and sentences.

? *What rhythm and tone patterns have meaning in our culture?* (Possible responses: the first few bars of the William Tell Overture, the opening notes from the old *Dragnet* series, cheers and chants at sporting events) ■

ELEMENTS OF LITERATURE

Features of African Oral Literature

African orature, like other oral literature, is distinguished by its use of **repetition** and **parallel structure**. These techniques involve the repetition of words, phrases, lines, and sentence structures throughout a poem or tale. Such repetitions probably serve foremost as memory aids for griots and other storytellers. But repetition has other uses as well. It creates rhythm, builds suspense, and adds emphasis to parts of a poem or narrative. Repeated lines, or **refrains**, often mark places where an audience can join in the oral performance.

Another feature of African oral literature is the **repeat-and-vary** technique, in which lines or phrases are repeated with slight variations—sometimes just by changing a single word. In addition, African oral poems employ the sound device of **tonal assonance**. Most of the languages of Africa, like many Asian languages, are **tonal**; that is, the tones in which syllables are spoken determine the meanings of words. For example, in a Bantu language spoken in Cameroon, one word can mean "payment" if spoken in a high tone, and "crossroads" if spoken in a low tone. Though English is not tonal, we can get some idea of tonality if we think of the way we say "Uh, huh" for "Yes," "Uh, uh" for "No," and "Uh, oh" as a warning. In fact, linguists believe that these three expressions may have come to America with the African slave trade.

The tradition of African orature involves much more than the delivery of memorized words. Presentations of oral literature almost always include spirited audience participation. In certain types of oral poetry, such as chants, the listeners join in the chorus or chime in at other key points, underscoring lines and phrases with feeling. In addition, songs and tales sometimes use the **call-and-response** format, in which the leader calls out a line or phrase and the audience responds with an answering line or phrase, becoming performers themselves. Audiences listening to oral tales participate freely in singing the songs and shouting the proverbs that accompany the tales, as well as providing cheers, catcalls, and advice to the performer. This kind of audience involvement can even alter the form and content of a tale. In ways not immediately apparent to readers, then, Africa's orature is truly a living, dynamic literature.

Werner Forman Archive/Art Resource, New York

Musicians of the court of Temi of Ede (Nigeria) use talking drums to announce the arrival of a dignitary.

OBJECTIVES

1. To recognize and analyze the African cradle song as a type of oral poetry
2. To identify and interpret similes and metaphors
3. To compose a modern chant or song and to write an essay supporting a generalization

THEMES IN WORLD LITERATURE

Generations
"The Parable of the Prodigal Son," pp. 199–200
"Letter to His Two Small Children," pp. 520–521

The Power and Pain of Love
"Osiris and Isis," pp. 34–39
Sonnet 29, p. 810 ■

Reader's Guide

SONG OF A MOTHER TO HER FIRSTBORN

Background

This **cradle song** represents an important type of oral poetry. For centuries, African women have created poems like this to be chanted or sung. While the tender words and lulling repetitions express the mother's love, they also entertain and soothe the baby.

In the Didinga and Lango cultures of Uganda, as in many others, children are seen as a kind of immortality for the parents. The naming of a child involves a ceremony—mentioned in this poem—which does not occur until a certain number of days after the birth. The poem also mentions the traditions of a neighboring group, who believe that their gods will try to harm a child if it seems valuable. This neighboring group gives children names like "Worthless One" in order to trick the gods into sparing the child. But the mother who sings this poem reassures her baby that the gods of his own people are kind and wish him well. She refers, as well, to the positive changes the baby has made in her life and in his father's life, and she predicts that the baby will one day become a father in his turn and a great leader. In these ways, the poem places the new baby firmly within his family and within the social and religious traditions of his people.

Writer's Response

What do you think children need to know? In a paragraph, summarize what you would tell your children if you were a parent. Explain why it would be important to communicate those things.

Literary Focus

The narrator in this poem uses **figurative language** to show her love for her child. As you read, look for **similes** (indirect comparisons using the words *as* or *like*: *free as a bird*) and **metaphors** (direct comparisons made without the use of the words *as* or *like*: *time is money*).

PREREADING FOCUS

Background: Most African cradle songs are simple and informal, like American lullabies. This one, however, has some of the features of a praise song: formal language; apostrophes, in which the subject of the poem is addressed directly ("Speak to me," "O son," "And how shall we name you?"); epithets, or descriptive names ("child of my heart," "little one," "little warrior"); and an almost worshipful list of the new baby's attributes.

It is unclear whether this cradle song comes from the Didinga or Lango culture. However, the song refers to specific Lango customs involving naming (lines 17–42).

Literary Focus: Remind students that similes and metaphors compare two things that are seemingly different. Effective figurative language is original and surprising, allowing readers to see things in a fresh, new way. Similes and metaphors emphasize a feeling or idea and make an abstract concept vivid and concrete.

ABOUT THE TRANSLATOR

Jack H. Driberg (1888–1946), a British government officer and amateur anthropologist, lived first with the Lango people and then with the Didinga when their homelands were under British rule. His works are among the definitive references on both groups.

CULTURAL DIVERSITY

The Lango people inhabit the hot, marshy lowlands of Uganda, northeast of Lake Kyoga, near the Sudanese border. During the 1920s, when this song was recorded, the Lango lived by farming, herding, and occasional hunting. The Didinga, a small group centered northeast of the Sudanese border, were also herders. Both groups prized Brahma cattle, and both wielded spears and shields in periodic skirmishes.

❓ *Which details in the first ten lines reflect these cultures?* (mention of a calf, a warrior, a spear)

1 LITERARY ELEMENT

Simile: When might a calf be wet and shining? (Newborn calves' coats are glossy with amniotic fluid.) The mother likens her baby's eyes to a bull-calf because of its potential strength and its ability to bring wealth by siring more calves.

SONG OF A MOTHER TO HER FIRSTBORN

A Didinga or Lango Cradle Song (Uganda)

translated by

JACK H. DRIBERG

Have you ever seen a newborn baby? Many people find babies, with their small, puckered faces, far from beautiful. After reading to line 33, stop and notice how the speaker in this poem has described her baby's appearance. What does her choice of words tell you about her and her response to her child?

Speak to me, child of my heart.
Speak to me with your eyes, your round laughing
    eyes,

1 ⌈   Wet and shining as Lupeyo's bull-calf.

Speak to me little one,
5   Clutching my breast with your hand,
So strong and firm for all its littleness.
It will be the hand of a warrior, my son,
A hand that will gladden your father.
See how eagerly it fastens on me:
10   It thinks already of a spear.
O son, you will have a warrior's name and be a
    leader of men.
And your sons, and your sons' sons, will
    remember you long after you have slipped into
    darkness.
But I, I shall always remember your hand
    clutching me so.
I shall recall how you lay in my arms,
15   And looked at me so, and so,
And how your tiny hands played with my bosom.
And when they name you great warrior, then will
    my eyes be wet with remembering.

Ugandan women walking to work in the fields.

Robert Harding Picture Library

And how shall we name you, little warrior?
See, let us play at naming.
20 It will not be a name of despisal, for you are my
     firstborn.
Not as Nawal's son is named will you be named.
Our gods will be kinder to you than theirs.
Must we call you "Insolence" or "Worthless One"?
Shall you be named, like a child of ill fortune,
     after the dung of cattle?
25 Our gods need no cheating, my child:
They wish you no ill.
They have washed your body and clothed it with
     beauty.
They have set a fire in your eyes.
And the little puckering ridges of your brows—
30 Are they not the seal of their fingerprints when
     they fashioned you?
They have given you beauty and strength, child of
     my heart,
And wisdom is already shining in your eyes,
And laughter.
So how shall we name you, little one?
35 Are you your father's father, or his brother, or yet
     another?

---

insolence (in'sə·ləns): bold disrespect

2 CULTURAL DIVERSITY
A child born to a Lango mother who had lost several infants was named "Cattle Dung" to repel the malevolent spirits thought to be responsible for the babies' deaths.
? *If our society followed the Lango tradition, what might you have been named?* (Possible responses: Cockroach Bait, Garbage Dump)

3 LITERARY ELEMENT
Metaphor: What ideas are conveyed by the metaphor "[the gods] have set a fire in your eyes"? (Possible response: The eyes glow with energy, warmth, intelligence.)

4 GUIDED READING
Finding the Main Idea: Who are the "they" who have "fashioned" the baby and given him beauty and strength? (the gods) How would you sum up the main idea expressed in lines 27–33? (Possible response: The gods favor the baby.)

5 CULTURAL DIVERSITY
A first son was usually named for his father's father. But, depending on the portents at the naming ceremony, he might instead be named after an uncle or other relative.
? *How do people in your family choose names for babies?* (Answers will vary.)

READING CHECK

1. Who is the poem's speaker? (a mother)
2. How does the mother feel toward her baby? (loving, proud)
3. What is the baby's name? (He hasn't yet been named.)
4. What is "glowing like the eyes of a leopard in a thicket"? (the baby's eyes)
5. Whose soul does the mother say is "safe" in the child's "keeping"? (his father's soul)

RETEACHING

To reteach "Song of a Mother to Her Firstborn," suggest that students create sculptures, drawings, or magazine-photo collages representing the mother and her baby. Encourage them to reread the poem carefully for clues about the facial expressions and positions of the two characters. Guide students in deciding which meaningful objects might be portrayed with the mother and baby.

MEETING INDIVIDUAL NEEDS

6 ESL: Lines 36–38 indicate a belief that the spirit of one of the father's ancestors has been reborn in the newborn son. Ask your students if they, their families, or anyone they know hold similar beliefs. ■

7 INFERRING
What rituals does the mother expect her son to perform after his father dies? (tend his shrine, offer sacrifices, pray regularly) What do her expectations imply about the kind of person she hopes her son will be? (Possible responses: devout, dutiful, loving, respectful)

> **quickens** (kwik'ənz): becomes revived
>
> **oblation** (ə·blā'shən, äb·lā'-): an offering in a religious ceremony; in this case, in remembrance of an ancestor
>
> **loins** (loinz): the hips and lower abdomen, often regarded as the seat of strength and procreative power
>
> **redemption** (ri·demp'shən): a deliverance from sin and its penalties

8 COMPARING LITERATURE
Gilgamesh calls Enkidu his shield and spear, just as the mother here calls her child. Suggest that students read Gilgamesh's lament for Enkidu, from the *Epic of Gilgamesh* (pp. 136–152), comparing the uses of metaphor in both works.

6
Whose spirit is it that is in you, little warrior?
Whose spear-hand tightens round my breast?
Who lives in you and quickens to life, like last
    year's melon seed?
Are you silent, then?
40 But your eyes are thinking, thinking, and glowing
    like the eyes of a leopard in a thicket.
Well, let be.
At the day of the naming you will tell us.

O my child, now indeed I am happy.
Now indeed I am a wife—
45 No more a bride, but a Mother-of-one.
Be splendid and magnificent, child of desire.
Be proud as I am proud.
Be happy as I am happy.
Be loved as now I am loved.
50 Child, child, child, love I have had from my man.
But now, only now, have I the fullness of love.
Now, only now, am I his wife and the mother of
    his firstborn.
His soul is safe in your keeping, my child, and it
    was I, I, I who have made you.
Therefore am I loved.
55 Therefore am I happy.
Therefore am I a wife.
Therefore have I great honor.

7
You will tend his shrine when he is gone.
With sacrifice and oblation you will recall his
    name year by year.
60 He will live in your prayers, my child,
And there will be no more death for him, but
    everlasting life springing from your loins.
8
You are his shield and his spear, his hope and
    redemption from the dead.
Through you he will be reborn, as the saplings in
    the Spring.
And I, I am the mother of his firstborn.
65 Sleep, child of beauty and courage and fulfillment,
    sleep.
I am content.

Ugandan woman working in the field.
? *What kind of life does the mother in this poem want for her child?*

Robert Harding Picture Library

Choral Reading. Encourage students to script a choral reading of the poem. Help them to decide at which points new readers should take over, which lines should be read by a single person and which by a group, and how the various lines should be delivered. Arrange for them to present their choral reading, perhaps to another English class.

Ask how the birth of a first child changes the lives of contemporary mothers and fathers; elicit a variety of answers based on people students know. Next, ask what traditions Americans follow to introduce a baby to society. If necessary, prompt by mentioning birth announcements, baby showers, religious ceremonies, and so on.

Then lead a discussion in which students identify the feelings expressed in the poem and compare them to feelings expressed by modern Americans. ∎

First Thoughts

As you read this poem, you probably formed mental images of both the baby and the mother. How did you visualize them in your mind?

Identifying Facts

1. What have the gods done for the baby?
2. What does the mother finally decide about the baby's name?
3. How has the baby brought "great honor" to his mother?

Interpreting Meanings

1. Much of the **imagery** in this poem centers on the baby's eyes. How are they described throughout the poem? What does this imagery tell you about the mother's feelings for her baby?
2. In lines 29–30, to what are the baby's wrinkled brows compared? What kind of **figure of speech** is used in this comparison?
3. List all the things to which the child is compared. What characteristics and strengths do these things suggest?
4. How will the child fulfill his father's immortality?

Applying Meanings

Think about the hopes that parents today have for their children and for their children's future positions in society. How do you think these hopes are like those expressed in the poem? How are they different?

Creative Writing Response

Composing a Chant. Reread the paragraph you wrote for the Writer's Response on page 89, about what you would like to tell your children. Compose a song or chant, perhaps similar in form to "Song of a Mother to Her Firstborn," in which you restate some of the ideas from your paragraph. In your chant, use **metaphors** and **similes** to create vivid images and to make your meaning clear.

Critical Writing Response

Making and Supporting a Generalization. Based on the evidence in this poem, what can you generalize about the roles of men and women in the Didinga and Lango cultures, and the expectations that are held for their lives? Consider especially the mother's hopes and expectations for her son and the effect that his birth will have on her own life. In a three-paragraph essay, support your generalization with at least three examples from the poem. In your final paragraph, explain the limitations of making such generalizations about an entire culture based on only one poem. You may use a chart like the one below to organize your essay.

	Generalized Role	Lines in Poem that Support Generalization
Male		
Female		

First Thoughts
Answers will vary.

Identifying Facts
1. made him beautiful, set a fire in his eyes, set their seal on him, given him strength
2. that the baby will reveal it on the day of his naming
3. She has won her husband's favor by bearing his first child.

Interpreting Meanings
1. laughing, wet as a bull-calf, filled with fire, shining with wisdom, thinking, glowing like a leopard's. She is delighted, proud, and reverent.
2. *Comparison:* to fingerprints the gods left on him. *Figure of speech:* metaphor
3. a bull-calf, a warrior, the gods' creation, a leopard, a shield, a spear. prosperity, strength, holiness, protection
4. continue the father's line and keep his memory alive

Applying Meanings
Possible responses: Parents today also hope their children will be successful and carry on the family heritage. Many try to avoid burdening children with parental expectations.

Creative Writing Response
Composing a Chant. Chants should focus on one or two central messages.

Critical Writing Response
Making and Supporting a Generalization. Have students consider what the poem suggests about the difference in how men and women in this society achieve success. ∎

OBJECTIVES

1. *To analyze two short African folktales*
2. *To identify the characteristics of a dilemma tale*
3. *To write a contemporary dilemma tale for an American audience*
4. *To write an essay analyzing the effective use of realistic and fantastic elements in dilemma tales*

PREREADING FOCUS

Background: Literature that emphasizes moral behavior is not unique to African dilemma tales. From the fables of Aesop to the contemporary American "moral fiction" argued for by the late novelist John Gardner, the creators of imaginary worlds have often felt that their deepest purpose was to stimulate thought about the best way to live. What makes dilemma tales unique, however, is that they directly ask the audience to participate in this process by making a choice among characters. The classic short story "The Lady, or the Tiger?" by Frank R. Stockton, which many students may have read, might be considered a nineteenth-century American dilemma tale, for, as well as being entertaining and asking for the reader's involvement, it raises questions about the nature of justice and love.

Writer's Response: Students who cannot immediately think of examples may wish to review favorite fictional characters from their past—TV characters, comic book heroes, even particular toys based on fictional characters—that may have inspired "let's pretend" games. Encourage students to use techniques of personal writing, such as anecdote and reflection, in their freewrite.

ABOUT THE RETELLER

Allan W. Cardinall was a folklorist best known for his collection, *Tales Told in Togoland*.

Reader's Guide

AFRICAN DILEMMA TALES

Background

Some types of African folktales are moral tales, intended for listeners to discuss and debate. A particularly important kind of African moral tale is the **dilemma tale**, or **enigma tale**, an open-ended story that concludes with a question that asks the audience to choose from among several alternatives. By encouraging animated discussion, a dilemma tale invites its audience to think about right and wrong behavior and about how to best live within society.

Although they are not unique to Africa, dilemma tales appear more frequently in various African oral traditions than in the storytelling traditions of most other cultures. Dilemma tales are among the most interactive of all types of oral literature, for they are incomplete without a judgment from the audience. As the anthropologist William Bascom noted, "Even when they have standard answers, dilemma tales generally evoke spirited discussions, and they train those who participate in the skills of debate and argumentation."

African dilemma tales are almost always about human characters and frequently about family and community relationships. These stories often present life-or-death situations, and though the events may be fantastic or supernatural, the underlying message usually is relevant to the problems of real life.

Writer's Response

From soap operas that friends argue about to novels that readers ponder privately, fiction can stir emotions and cause us to reflect on life. What can you learn about yourself and about life from works of fiction and their characters? Freewrite your thoughts.

Literary Focus

A typical **dilemma tale** may have a climax, but instead of a true resolution, the tale ends with a stock question, such as "Who is most deserving?" or "Who behaved best?" Thus, the dilemma tale has the characteristics of both a folktale and a riddle. Unlike riddles, though, most dilemma tales do not have a set answer. Sometimes the audience comes to the conclusion that there is no completely satisfactory answer, no clear-cut "best" or "bravest."

Compound Sentences

A compound sentence is a sentence that contains two or more independent clauses—clauses that could stand alone as separate sentences—and no subordinate clauses. When independent clauses are combined into a compound sentence, they are separated by a comma followed by a coordinating conjunction such as *and, or,* or *but: There was no answer,* and *the chief told the people to climb up and see what was the matter.*

1. **Reading and Speaking.** Ask students to identify three compound sentences in each of the dilemma tales. Have them recite the sentences aloud, identifying the independent clauses in each.

2. **Writing.** Have students write a one-paragraph summary of either of the tales, using at least two compound sentences in their retelling. ∎

WONDROUS POWERS: MIRROR, SANDALS, AND A MEDICINE BAG
A Togo Dilemma Tale (Togo)

retold by

A. W. CARDINALL

As you read these stories, think about how their lack of a single "correct" resolution might inspire discussion among the members of an audience. How would you answer the questions that end these tales?

An old man had three children, all boys. When they had grown up to manhood, he called them together and told them that now he was very old and no longer able to provide, even for himself. He ordered them to go out and bring him food and clothing.

The three brothers set out, and after a very long while they came to a large river. As they had gone on together for such a time, they decided that once they got across they would separate. The eldest told the youngest to take the middle road, and the second to go to the right, while he himself would go to the left. Then, in a year's time, they would come back to the same spot.

So they parted, and at the end of a year, as agreed, they found their way back to the riverside. The eldest asked the youngest what he had gotten during his travels, and the boy replied: "I have nothing but a mirror, but it has wonderful power. If you look into it, you can see all over the country, no matter how far away." When asked, in turn, what he had gotten, the second brother replied:

"Only a pair of sandals that are so full of power, that if one puts them on one can walk at once to any place in the country in one step." Then, the eldest himself said: "I, too, have obtained but little, a small calabash[1] of medicine, that is all. But let us look into the mirror and see how father fares."

The youngest produced his mirror, and they all looked into it and saw that their father was already dead and that even the funeral custom was finished. Then the elder said: "Let us hasten home and see what we can do." So the second brought out his sandals, and all three placed their feet inside them and, immediately, they were borne to their father's grave. Then the eldest shook the medicine out of his bag, and poured it over the grave. At once their father arose, as if nothing had been the matter with him. Now which of these three sons has performed the best?

---

1. **calabash** (kalʹə·bashʹ): a container made from a hollowed-out gourd.

TEACHER'S RESOURCES

✔ Review and Response Worksheet

1 INTERPRETING

Considering that the father is asking for immediate necessities like food and clothing, why do you suppose the sons take a whole year before they return to him? (Possible responses: The father's request is a literary device that gives the sons a motive for their journey; the sons, being young, become so involved in their travels that they forget the goal of their quest; the term *year* is simply a folkloric device to suggest a long but finite time.)

2 LITERARY ELEMENT

Folktale Motifs: What familiar folktale motifs did you find in this tale? (Possible responses: the motif of the number three [three sons, three roads, three magical objects]; the quest and the perilous journey; magical objects; restoring the dead to life)

1. At the beginning of "Wondrous Powers," what does the old man tell his sons to do? (go and bring him food and clothing)
2. What do the sons decide to do? (They travel separately for a year and reunite at their starting point.)
3. What do the sons learn with the help of magic objects? (Their father has died.)
4. In "The Five Helpers," how does the chief's daughter respond to most marriage offers? (She refuses them.)
5. From where do the five helpers rescue the chief's daughter? (from the python's stomach; from the lake)

Ask students to present their favorite of the two tales orally. One or more members of a small group should retell the tale in their own words. The rest of the group should discuss the dilemma. One member of the group might take notes on the ideas expressed.

3 COMPARING LITERATURE

The motif of a beautiful but proud young woman who spurns her suitors is common in folktales from all world cultures. Call students' attention to a similar motif in "The White Snake" (p. 47), and ask them to think of other examples. What might be the moral point of such a motif? (Possible response: Dissatisfaction with the ordinary and everyday can lead to tragedy.)

HUMANITIES CONNECTION

Togo, formerly French Togoland, is a small nation (at its widest point, only about 90 miles) in the western portion of Africa. Togo became an independent republic in 1960. These batik fabrics come from a textile mill in Lomé, the capital of Togo. A port town that boasts Togo's only university, Lomé serves as the main point of departure for Togo's export trade. ■

4 COMPARING LITERATURE

A character who emerges after being swallowed by a huge creature is found in the Old Testament story of Jonah; a character restored to life is found in the New Testament story of Lazarus. How do you explain these parallels? (Possible responses: Certain story motifs may be universal in the human experience; biblical motifs may have been imported into African folktales through the influence of Christian missionaries.)

THE FIVE HELPERS
A Grumshi Dilemma Tale (Togo)

retold by

A. W. CARDINALL

There was once a beautiful girl, the daughter of a chief. She was finer to look upon than any other girl that men could see. But there was no one whom she would agree to marry.

Men came from all countries, but she would not have them. And all the land heard the news of this girl, that though she was of marriageable age, she would take no one.

There was also a snake, a large python who dwelt in a vast lake nearby the river. When he heard about this girl, he decided that he would marry her. So he changed himself into a man and came to the village.

As soon as the maiden saw the young man she was delighted, and said she would marry him at once. Everyone was pleased, and that night they took the young man and the girl on to the roof of the house, for the houses in that village had flat roofs, and there they left them.

Now during the night, the snake licked the girl all over and swallowed her, and changing again into his snake form, he made off to the great lake.

Next morning people came to the house and called to the girl and her man to come down. There was no answer, and the chief told the people to climb up and see what was the matter. This they did, and reported that both the girl and the man were missing.

The chief was very angry, and at once ordered all the people to follow the girl and her lover. But they could find no tracks. So they called for a man who could smell every-thing. He at once smelled the trail of the girl and followed it down to the great water. There he could go no further. The people, urged on by the anger of the chief, then called on a man famous through all the country for his thirst. They told him to drink up

Samples of fabric from Togo's batik industry in a market in Lomé.

Betty Press/Woodfin Camp & Associates

1. **Planning a Film Version.** Ask students to imagine that they are directors planning to make a short film of one of the dilemma tales. Have them discuss the following questions: Should the film be live-action or animated? Should it be a comedy or a drama? What special effects would be needed? Who would star in it, either as on-screen performers or as cartoon voices? Suggest that students sketch scenes that demonstrate their visualization of the film.

2. **Researching Folktale Variants.** Like other kinds of folktales, dilemma tales often exist in variant versions. Have interested students research examples of other dilemma tales, keeping an eye out for different versions of these two dilemma tales.

CLOSURE

Invite students to compare and contrast the two tales. Which one did they prefer, and why? What other folktales did the dilemma tales remind them of? Since the audience's answers are an integral part of a dilemma tale, you might list suggested answers to the dilemmas on the chalkboard and take a poll of students' preferences. Then contrast the dilemma tales with the subsequent selection, "Talk," which is more comic in tone. ∎

---

the lake. This he did. But still there was no sign of the man or the girl. Then the people called a man famous for his capacity for work and told him to take out all the mud from the lake. This he did, and thereby revealed a hole. But it was so deep that no one could reach the bottom. Then they remembered that there was a man with an arm that could stretch over all the Dagomba Island.

They told him to put his arm in the hole and pull. Out came the great python, which was immediately killed. And when they had cut open its stomach, they found the girl inside, but she was dead. Then the people remembered a man who had the power of medicine, and was able to raise the dead. He came at once and restored the girl to life. Now which of those five men did best?

4

> ## First Thoughts

How do you feel about stories that ask you to supply part of the ending? Explain.

Identifying Facts

1. Describe the powers of the mirror, the sandals, and the medicine bag.
2. In "The Five Helpers," what is the role of the python?
3. In "The Five Helpers," what does each of the five helpers do?

Interpreting Meanings

1. In what ways are these **dilemma tales** similar to other folktales you have read? In what ways are they different?
2. **Folktales** entertain, but they also often teach values. Give two examples of each purpose in these **dilemma tales**.
3. What was your answer to the question posed at the end of each dilemma tale? Support your response with specific evidence from each tale.
4. What do you think is the value of debating a question to which there may be no correct answer?
5. In what ways do you think your responses to these tales would be different if you were in a village in Togo, hearing them as oral-literature performances and participating in the discussions they prompted?

Applying Meanings

These tales are products of a specific culture. What meaning or importance do you think they can have for people in other cultures? In what ways do they speak to you and to the concerns of your life?

Creative Writing Response

Writing a Dilemma Tale. Write your own dilemma tale, using situations that are recognizable to a contemporary American audience. If you wish, include supernatural or exaggerated fairy-tale-like elements. Be sure to conclude with an open-ended question that the entire class can discuss.

Critical Writing Response

Analyzing Dilemma Tales. In a brief essay, analyze how dilemma tales effectively employ both realistic and fantastic elements. Identify at least three examples of characters, events, or details in these tales that are realistic, and three examples of things that are fantastic—that could not be found in real life. Then explain whether or not you think the blend of realistic and fantastic elements detracts from or enhances the potential moral messages of these tales. Would the tales be more or less effective if they were completely realistic? Use specific examples from the tales you have just read.

PREREADING FOCUS

Background: The characters in
this tale exemplify common
occupations of the Ashanti—
farming, fishing, and weaving.
Like many oral tales, it combines such realistic elements
with fantasy elements, like
talking objects and animals.

Oral tales in African literature fall into overlapping categories. Among them are myths
and religious stories; tales using animal characters to make
social statements; problem
tales, which have open endings so that listeners can discuss the values and ethical
questions posed; morality
tales, which convey a message
or moral; and tales that simply
entertain, touching on universal themes. "Talk," with its galloping action, skillful characterization, and ironic absurd-
ities, is entertainment at its
best.

Literary Focus: Situational
irony in fiction often expresses
a profound truth: even though
people want to believe that life
is reasonable and they are in
control, chance and the unexpected can interfere at any
time. Because situational irony
reflects a truth that everyone
has experienced, it can easily
move readers to laughter (or
sometimes to tears).

ABOUT THE TRANSLATOR

Harold Courlander (1908–1996)
was an American anthropologist, author, and collector of
oral literature.

TALK
An Ashanti Tale (Ghana)
retold by
HAROLD COURLANDER

Reader's Guide

Background The following tale comes
from the Ashanti, whose traditional
homeland is the dense and hilly forest
beyond the city of Kumasi in south-
central Ghana. There the Ashanti cleared
the jungle for small farms, fished the rivers, hunted, and pursued their skills in
weaving, metalworking, and other arts.
Ghana was colonized by the British in the
mid-nineteenth century and exploited for
its gold and other natural resources. But
the Ashanti, protected in their geographical stronghold, were able to maintain
their ancient culture. Ghana regained its
independence in 1960. Today Ashanti
people live in all parts of the country.

Writer's Response Imagine that some inanimate object you use often, such as this
textbook or your pen, could talk. What
might it tell you? Write several lines of
dialogue between yourself and the
object.

Literary Focus **Irony** is the contrast between expectation and reality. In **situational irony**, what happens is very
different from what we expect to happen.
Ironic contrast can be very humorous, as
this African tale shows.

TALK

*The first sentence in this tale establishes the setting as real
and specific, leading the reader to expect a realistic story.
What happens to your expectations in the second sentence?*

A farmer went out to his field one morning
to dig up some yams. While he was digging,
one of the yams said to him: "Well, at last
you're here. You never weeded me, but now
you come around with your digging stick. Go
away and leave me alone!"

The farmer turned around and looked at
his cow in amazement. The cow was chewing her cud and looking at him.

"Did you say something?" he asked.

The cow kept on chewing and said nothing, but the man's dog spoke up.

Punctuating Dialogue

Dialogue is enclosed in quotation marks. Indentation is used whenever a different character begins to speak. Examples:

"Is that all?" the man with the fish trap asked. "Is that so frightening?"

"Well," the man's fish trap said, "did he take it off the stone?"

When a speaker tag interrupts a direct quotation, commas are used to separate the quotation.

1. **Reading.** Have students locate places in the tale where different characters begin to speak.
2. **Writing.** Read aloud a brief excerpt from "Talk" that includes dialogue.

Ask students to write down the dialogue, using correct punctuation. Afterward, allow students to check their punctuation against the original text. ■

1

"It wasn't the cow who spoke to you," the dog said. "It was the yam. The yam says leave him alone."

The man became angry, because his dog had never talked before, and he didn't like his tone besides. So he took his knife and cut a branch from a palm tree to whip his dog. Just then the palm tree said, "Put that branch down!"

The man was getting very upset about the way things were going, and he started to throw the palm branch away, but the palm branch said, "Man, put me down softly!"

He put the branch down gently on a stone, and the stone said, "Hey, take that thing off me!"

This was enough, and the frightened farmer started to run for his village. On the way he met a fisherman going the other way with a fish trap on his head.

"What's the hurry?" the fisherman asked.

"My yam said, 'Leave me alone!' Then the dog said, 'Listen to what the yam says!' When I went to whip the dog with a palm branch the tree said, 'Put that branch down!' Then the palm branch said, 'Do it softly!' Then the stone said, 'Take that thing off me!' "

"Is that all?" the man with the fish trap asked. "Is that so frightening?"

"Well," the man's fish trap said, "did he take it off the stone?"

"Wah!" the fisherman shouted. He threw the fish trap on the ground and began to run with the farmer, and on the trail they met a weaver with a bundle of cloth on his head.

"Where are you going in such a rush?" he asked them.

"My yam said, 'Leave me alone!' " the farmer said. "The dog said, 'Listen to what the yam says!' The tree said, 'Put that branch down!' The branch said, 'Do it softly!' And the stone said, 'Take that thing off me!' "

"And then," the fisherman continued, "the fish trap said, 'Did he take it off?' "

"That's nothing to get excited about," the weaver said, "no reason at all."

"Oh, yes it is," his bundle of cloth said. "If it happened to you you'd run too!"

"Wah!" the weaver shouted. He threw his bundle on the trail and started running with the other men.

They came panting to the ford in the river and found a man bathing.

Gold insignia worn by the Ashanti king's high servants.

CULTURAL DIVERSITY

The tellers of oral tales usually acted out the roles by singing, dancing, and using props. The audience cheered, screamed, and gasped at appropriate places, or shouted criticisms.

❓ *At what events do American audiences participate in similar ways?* (Possible responses: sports events, live TV shows, melodramas)

1 LITERARY ELEMENT

Irony: How do the farmer's responses to the talking objects and animals add to the situational irony? (His responses to these fantastic events are realistic: first he is amazed and then angry at the insolence of the yam and the dog.)

HUMANITIES CONNECTION

This insignia shows the intricate artistry of Ashanti goldsmiths.

❓ *How does repetition figure both in this design and in the story?* (It plays a prominent part in building aesthetic expectations.) ■

READING CHECK

1. Why does the farmer go to his field? (to dig yams)

2. What does the dog say to the farmer? (that the yam spoke, saying to leave it alone)

3. Why does the fisherman start running? (His fish trap starts talking too.)

4. Why does the man in the river join the others? (The river speaks to him.)

5. What happens after the chief dismisses the men? (His stool talks to him.)

RETEACHING

Divide students into two groups. Have one group act out the tale; encourage them to choose props, gestures, tones of voice, and actions appropriate for each character and object. Have the second group be a participating audience, cheering and shouting warnings, advice, and comments. Then let groups trade roles to give the tale a second interpretation. Have students decide which group's techniques were most effective, and why.

HUMANITIES CONNECTION

This gold mask portrays an Ashanti chief. It was made to be buried with him when he died. Part of a royal treasure, the mask was removed by the British in 1873–74.

❓ *From this mask and the tale, what can you infer about the role of a chief in Ashanti society?* (Possible response: He was an important, imposing figure who settled disputes.) ■

2 LITERARY ELEMENT

Dramatic Irony: Dramatic irony occurs when readers know something that a character does not. How does the bather's initial question create dramatic irony? (It shows that he expects a realistic explanation for the men's running, but readers know that his expectations will be overturned.)

3 LITERARY ELEMENT

Indirect Characterization: What do the chief's words and actions reveal about his personality? (He is courteous but quick to judge; he has confidence in his perceptions and in his authority.)

4 READER'S RESPONSE

What do you expect the chief to do after his stool talks to him? If the story were to continue, how might events upset your expectations?

2 "Are you chasing a gazelle?" he asked them.

The first man said breathlessly: "My yam talked at me, and it said, 'Leave me alone!' And my dog said, 'Listen to your yam!' And when I cut myself a branch the tree said, 'Put that branch down!' And the branch said, 'Do it softly!' And the stone said, 'Take that thing off me!' "

The fisherman panted, "And my trap said, 'Did he?' "

The weaver wheezed, "And my bundle of cloth said, 'You'd run too!' "

"Is that why you're running?" the man in the river asked.

"Well, wouldn't you run if you were in their position?" the river said.

The man jumped out of the water and began to run with the others. They ran down the main street of the village to the house of the chief. The chief's servants brought his stool out, and he came and sat on it to listen to their complaints. The men began to recite their troubles.

"I went out to my garden to dig yams," the farmer said, waving his arms. "Then everything began to talk! My yam said, 'Leave me alone!' My dog said, 'Pay attention to your yam!' The tree said, 'Put that branch down!' The branch said, 'Do it softly!' And the stone said, 'Take it off me!' "

"And my fish trap said, 'Well, did he take it off?' " the fisherman said.

"And my cloth said, 'You'd run too!' " the weaver said.

"And the river said the same," the bather said hoarsely, his eyes bulging.

Ashanti mask.
❓ *How does the repetition in this story increase the humor?*

The Wallace Collection

The chief listened to them patiently, but he couldn't refrain from scowling.

"Now this is really a wild story," he said at last. "You'd better all go back to your work before I punish you for disturbing the peace." 3

So the men went away, and the chief shook his head and mumbled to himself, "Nonsense like that upsets the community."

"Fantastic, isn't it?" his stool said. "Imagine, a talking yam!" 4

Group Project. Assign students to work in small groups to create cartoon strips or brief skits in which they have a dialogue with a familiar object. Have them base their work on the dialogues they began in the *Writer's Response* section of the *Reader's Guide* page. Encourage them to use situational irony and to share their work with the class.

Ask students to discuss the use of irony in the tale. How are the reader's expectations repeatedly set up and then overturned? Challenge students to decide which character learns something and what he learns, and then to formulate a statement of the tale's theme. Guide them to see that the humor results from a strong theme and careful crafting. ■

First Thoughts

A "punch line" is the final line of a joke. Usually, the punch line is surprising and contains the point of the joke. Did the final line of this story act as a punch line for you?

Identifying Facts

1. What are the yam's reasons for speaking to the farmer?
2. Why does the farmer begin to run?
3. Who joins the farmer as he runs?
4. How does the chief settle the matter?

Interpreting Meanings

1. The storyteller uses **dialogue** as a means of **indirect characterization**. What do the farmer's words reveal about his personality? Name one of the farmer's strengths and one of his weaknesses.
2. This story is based on **situational irony**. What is the first ironic occurrence in the story? What is the main effect of the story's irony?
3. Explain why the story's **title** is, or is not, appropriate. Does it accurately sum up what the story is about, or would you have given the story another title?

Applying Meanings

Did you find that this story became funnier to you as it went along? What would the effect have been if the joke had been shorter?

Critical Writing Response

Identifying a Main Idea. Many folktales from Africa—as well as from other parts of the world—warn about the dangers of talking too much or saying foolish things. Read "The Talking Skull" and, in two or three well-developed paragraphs, compare and contrast it to "Talk." Consider the two stories in terms of action and plot, situational irony, and surprise endings. Does "The Talking Skull" end with a punch line? Does it have a moral? Does "Talk" have a moral, or is it simply an entertaining story?

The Talking Skull
A Nigerian Folktale
translated by
Leo Frobenius and Douglas G. Fox

A hunter goes into the bush. He finds an old human skull. The hunter says: "What brought you here?" The skull answers: "Talking brought me here." The hunter runs off. He runs to the king. He tells the king: "I found a dry human skull in the bush. It asks you how its father and mother are."

The king says: "Never since my mother bore me have I heard that a dead skull can speak." The king summons the Alkali, the Saba, and the Degi, and asks them if they have ever heard the like. None of the wise men has heard the like and they decide to send a guard out with the hunter into the bush to find out if his story is true, and, if so, to learn the reason for it. The guard accompany the hunter into the bush with the order to kill him on the spot should he have lied. The guard and the hunter come to the skull. The hunter addresses the skull: "Skull, speak." The skull is silent. The hunter asks as before: "What brought you here?" The skull does not answer. The whole day long the hunter begs the skull to speak, but it does not answer. In the evening the guard tell the hunter to make the skull speak, and when he cannot they kill him in accordance with the king's command. When the guard are gone the skull opens its jaws and asks the dead hunter's head: "What brought you here?" The dead hunter's head replies: "Talking brought me here!"

First Thoughts
Answers will vary.

Identifying Facts
1. The farmer has neglected it; now it wants him to leave it alone.
2. Even a stone talks to him.
3. a fisherman, a weaver, and a man bathing in the river
4. He rebukes the men and sends them back to work.

Interpreting Meanings
1. Possible responses: *strength:* politeness; *weakness:* impulsiveness
2. *First ironic occurrence:* The yam talks. *Main effect of irony:* humor
3. Possible response: A more specific title might be more accurate but would spoil the ironic surprises.

Applying Meanings
Eliminating repetition would eliminate the buildup of suspense that adds to the humor.

Critical Writing Response
Identifying a Main Idea. Each essay should contain a thesis sentence that makes a point about the two tales' similarities and differences. Organization may be either block or point-by-point. Specifics from the tales, focusing on plot, irony, endings, and possible themes or morals, should support the thesis. Students should use transitions appropriate for comparison and contrast. ■

1 **CULTURAL BACKGROUND**
Old Mali: Many of the Mandingo living today can still
trace their family histories back
to Old Mali during Sundiata's
reign. In fact, Musa Traoré, the
president of Mali since 1969,
claims descent from one of
Sundiata's generals.

2 **CULTURAL BACKGROUND**
Orature: Oral performances
of *Sundiata* are given wherever
the Mandingo language is spoken. The Mandingo people are
now widely scattered throughout West Africa (in Senegal,
Gambia, Mali, Guinea, Upper
Volta, Ivory Coast, and Mauri-
tania), but they speak a common language. During the
1960s and 1970s, researchers
recorded several oral versions
of *Sundiata* in Gambia and
Mali. Each time, the epic was
recited to musical accompaniment on a guitar, a *kora* (a
harp-lute with 21 strings), or a
balo (a standing wooden xylophone with 18 keys). In one
performance, the griot's accompanist also intoned "Indeed," "True," or "Amen, oh
my Lord," at the end of each
line of the epic.

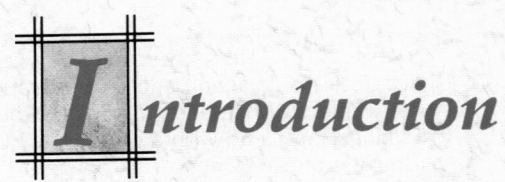

*I*ntroduction

from Sundiata: An Epic of Old Mali

*"I teach kings the history of their ancestors . . . for the world is
old, but the future springs from the past."*

—Djeli Mamoudou Kouyaté, *Sundiata*

1   These words of the griot who narrates the Mali epic *Sundiata*
(sōōn·dyä'tə) could also apply to the
epic itself. An **epic**, or long narrative
poem, is like a bridge from the past to
the future. Epic tales of vanished heroes—partly human, partly superhuman,
who embody the highest values of a society—do more than entertain. They
also carry a culture's history, values, and
traditions forward to future generations.

The Oral Epic

2   Most ancient epics began as **oral epics**,
also known as **primary epics**. Researchers in all parts of the world—from Eastern Europe to Africa—have found oral
epics that have yet to be recorded in
writing. From listening to these performances, they have learned that an oral
epic includes much more than words.
Traditional repetitions, gestures, sound
effects, songs, and proverbs play an
important role in the "live" performance of epics. An oral epic, in fact, is
an exciting blend of narrative, poetry,
and drama.

It is usually not until long after its
form is more-or-less fixed that an epic is
written down. As it is written and translated into foreign languages, the epic
undergoes another kind of change. Many

---

legend: *a story about extraordinary
deeds, based to some extent on fact.*

---

elements of oral epics do not carry over
well into writing. Repetition, for example, enlivens an oral performance, but
tends to deaden written works. Translators find it difficult to carry over the
original poetic elements such as rhyme
and meter into foreign languages. But
the narrative, or storytelling, elements of
epics *do* carry over into writing, and
they survive translation easily.

The African Epic Tradition

The African literary tradition boasts of
several oral epics. Among them are *The
Dausi*, from the Soninke of Sudan; *Mon-
zon and the King of Kore*, from the
Bambara of western Africa; the epic of

Askia the Great, medieval ruler of the Songhai empire in western Africa; and the epic of Shaka Zulu, eighteenth-century founder of the Zulu empire of southern Africa. Some African epics have been lost over time. Others survive as fragments. A few African epics have even provided the inspiration for modern African novels. To date, however, the best-preserved, best known African epic is *Sundiata*, from the Mandingo people of western Africa. This epic is known to several peoples of West Africa and exists in several versions. Like other African epics, *Sundiata* has been preserved and passed on by **griots**, Africa's oral historians and "living libraries."

Sundiata: Fact and Legend

Like most of the world's epics, *Sundiata* is a fascinating blend of fact and legend. Sundiata Keita, the story's hero, really existed. He was a powerful leader who, in 1235, defeated the Sosso nation of western Africa and reestablished the Mandingo Empire of Old Mali. Under Sundiata, Mali expanded from the Atlantic coast to the northern border of present-day Nigeria, including the lands today called Guinea, Gambia, Senegal, Mali, and western Niger. Arts and trade flourished during his reign, and the empire he founded lasted more than 250 years. Sundiata's empire

Marc & Evelyne Bernheim/Woodfin Camp & Associates

Ceremonial mask from Mali.

finally fell to the Songhai, under Askia the Great, in 1493.

But *Sundiata* is not a historical document. Rather, the story of Sundiata, over time, became transmuted into **legend**—a story about extraordinary deeds that has been passed on from one generation to the next. Like all legends, the story of Sundiata is based to some extent on fact, but it is fact that has become greatly embellished over time. Supernatural powers are attributed to Sundiata, and he is involved in a mighty conflict between good and evil.

Sundiata in Written Form

The epic of Sundiata was first recorded in Guinea during the 1950s, when it was told by the griot Djeli Mamoudou Kouyaté (djä'lēmä'moo-doo koo-yä'tā) to folklorist D. T. Niane. No one knows how many centuries old this version of the epic is. Niane edited the epic as he heard it and translated it from Mandingo into French. His version was later translated into English. Because the epic is now "twice removed" from its original source, it has lost many of the features of the original language: its meter, assonance, and alliteration. However, it still contains some of the original songs, repetition, and proverbs that accompanied the oral performance.

3

OBJECTIVES

1. *To analyze an oral epic from Old Mali*
2. *To identify the characteristics of the epic*
3. *To record an oral history and write an essay explaining the theme of the epic*
4. *To distinguish four types of context clues that help determine word meaning*
5. *To recount orally the life story of a disadvantaged hero and to consider why such stories are popular*

THEMES IN WORLD LITERATURE

What Is a Hero?
From the *Epic of Gilgamesh*, pp. 136–152
From the *Iliad*, pp. 224–277
From the *Aeneid*, pp. 379–408
"Philosophy and Spiritual Discipline" from the *Bhagavad-Gita*, pp. 467–476

Triumph and Defeat
From the *Ramayana*, pp. 484–494
"The Tragedy of Sohráb and Rostám" from the *Shahname*, pp. 646–653
"How Siegfried Was Slain" from the *Nibelungenlied*, pp. 730–740 ∎

PREREADING FOCUS

Background: Besides conveying cultural values and traditions, an epic often illustrates a culture's religious beliefs. Explain to students that Mali has been a Muslim nation for seven centuries and that *Sundiata* reflects this monotheistic tradition. Some epics, like the *Iliad* and the *Epic of Gilgamesh*, reflect pantheistic religions in which there are many gods contending for power. These epics include a large cast of gods and goddesses whose actions affect the lives of the human characters. Other epics, like *Sundiata* and the *Song of Roland*, are rooted in monotheism. In these epics, such forces as fate, destiny, prophecy, and sorcery are important elements in the unfolding of events. They are seen as signs of the divine plan that humans cannot alter.

Literary Focus: One function of an epic like *Sundiata* is to reaffirm social alliances among families or clans. Thus the epic specifies Sundiata's family background, as well as the family backgrounds of his griot and other personal helpers. Similarly, the epic endorses political alliances. It names many armies that came to Sundiata's aid and kings who formally submitted to Sundiata's rule. The recitation of the names and deeds of these groups strengthens historical bonds while contributing to the elevated, ritualistic tone of the epic.

Reader's Guide

from SUNDIATA: AN EPIC OF OLD MALI

Background

The hero Sundiata, like other epic heroes, has an unusual childhood and shows signs of greatness even in these early years. As he grows up, he endures many trials. He undertakes a long journey into exile and back before emerging as a leader of his people, one who embodies many of his culture's highest values. The supernatural plays a major role in the epic: Sundiata, as well as his mother, sister, and enemies, all possess supernatural powers. His story is told in a formal, elevated style, and the "stage" on which the action takes place is broad. The events of the epic, including its many detailed battle scenes, have a wide-ranging significance. All these aspects of *Sundiata* reflect patterns common to epics throughout the world.

However, the setting and characters in *Sundiata* also reveal the unique history and traditions of the culture from which the epic sprang. Mali in the thirteenth century was a powerful kingdom, enriched by alliances with many neighboring nations. Its civilization was complex and wealthy, its leaders well educated. But its king, Sundiata's father, died when Sundiata was still a child, leaving Mali vulnerable. An invasion by enemies, the Sossos, is the event that tests Sundiata's heroism.

Writer's Response

Whom do you consider heroic? Think of a man, woman, or fictional character whom you consider a hero. In a paragraph, describe your hero, explaining which qualities make him or her heroic.

Literary Focus

An **epic** is a long narrative work that relates the deeds of a larger-than-life hero who embodies the values of his or her society. Epics blend history, legend, and myth and are often told orally for generations before finally being written down.

from SUNDIATA
An Epic of Old Mali

D. T. Niane
translated by
G. D. PICKETT

These excerpts from Sundiata show the hero in his first childhood triumph and end with his great triumph in adulthood. As you read, note Sundiata's qualities as a leader and hero to his people.

CHARACTERS IN THE EPIC

Maghan Sundiata: the hero of the epic. He is also called "Mari Djata" and "Sogolon Djata."

King Maghan Kon Fatta: Sundiata's father, the king of Mali.

Sogolon Kedjou: Sundiata's mother.

Balla Fasséké: Sundiata's griot.

Sassouma Bérété: the queen mother; the first wife of the king.

Dankaran Touman: Sassouma Bérété's son. He is King Maghan Kon Fatta's successor and Sundiata's half brother.

Soumaoro Kanté: the sorcerer-king of Sosso; Sundiata's nemesis.

from The Lion's Awakening

Maghan Sundiata, also called Mari Djata, is the son of King Maghan Kon Fatta of Mali and his second wife, Sogolon Kedjou. A mysterious hunter has predicted that the boy will one day be a mightier leader than Alexander the Great, the legendary Greek conqueror. Few people believe this prophecy, however, because Mari Djata is already seven years old and has still not learned how to walk. He seems an unlikely candidate for emperor.

King Maghan Kon Fatta dies and his first wife, Sassouma Bérété, makes her own son the king. Always jealous of Mari Djata and his mother, she banishes them to the backyard of the palace, forcing them to live a life of poverty.

Sogolon Kedjou and her children lived on the queen mother's leftovers, but she kept a little garden in the open ground behind the village. It was there that she passed her brightest moments looking after her onions and gnougous.[1] One day she happened to be short of condiments and went to the queen mother to beg a little baobab[2] leaf.

---

1. **gnougous:** root vegetables.
2. **baobab** (bā'ō·bab'): a tropical tree whose leaves are used as a cooking herb.

Point of View

Point of view refers to the vantage point from which a narrator tells a story. A first-person point of view reveals the thoughts of only one character, who uses the pronoun *I*. An omniscient point of view, on the other hand, reveals the thoughts of more than one character.

Sundiata is told from an omniscient point of view, thus allowing the development of various characters. Examples: (Sundiata's mother) "She had never imagined . . ." (people in general) "The words of Doua . . . came back to men's minds . . ." (Sundiata) "These words . . . left Djata worried . . ."

1. **Reading.** Have students identify other lines in the epic that reveal the thoughts of a character.
2. **Writing.** Direct students to recount a brief episode from the epic as a character telling it in the first person. Have them discuss the effect of this change on the episode. ■

1 READER'S RESPONSE

Can you understand why Sundiata's mother reacts so strongly to Sassouma's insult? Do you think that her response is justified? How might the values of her culture have influenced her reaction? (Possible response: A mother's status depends on the position of her son in society.)

affront (ə·frunt′): intentional insult

2 LITERARY ELEMENT

Diction: The diction in this part of the epic is informal. In the oral epic, the elevated tone is created by songs and long lists of praise names, whereas the diction of the narrative is close to that of everyday speech. *What informal language or slang do Sundiata and his mother use in their conversation?* ("Shut up," "But what then?" "Cheer up," "It's too much") *How does this diction make you feel about Sundiata and his mother?* (Possible response: They are not so different from people today.)

3 INFERRING

Sundiata's response to his mother, even when she hits him with a stick, is concerned and deferential. Considering that Sundiata embodies the values of the Mandingo culture, what might his response imply about the way the Mandingo people believed parents should be treated? (Possible response: It suggests that respect for parents was a strong Mandingo value.)

Comstock, Inc./Boyd Norton

Baobab landscape.
What role does the baobab tree play in the conflict between Sassouma and Mari Djata (Sundiata)?

"Look you," said the malicious Sassouma, "I have a calabash[3] full. Help yourself, you poor woman. As for me, my son knew how to walk at seven and it was he who went and picked these baobab leaves. Take them then, since your son is unequal to mine." Then she laughed derisively with that fierce laughter which cuts through your flesh and penetrates right to the bone.

Sogolon Kedjou was dumbfounded. She had never imagined that hate could be so strong in a human being. With a lump in her throat she left Sassouma's. Outside her hut Mari Djata, sitting on his useless legs, was blandly eating out of a calabash. Unable to contain herself any longer, Sogolon burst into sobs and seizing a piece of wood, hit her son.

"Oh son of misfortune, will you never walk? Through your fault I have just suffered the greatest affront of my life! What have I done, God, for you to punish me in this way?"

Mari Djata seized the piece of wood and, looking at his mother, said, "Mother, what's the matter?"

"Shut up, nothing can ever wash me clean of this insult."

"But what then?"

"Sassouma has just humiliated me over a matter of a baobab leaf. At your age her own son could walk and used to bring his mother baobab leaves."

"Cheer up, Mother, cheer up."

"No. It's too much. I can't."

"Very well then, I am going to walk today," said Mari Djata. "Go and tell my father's smiths to make me the heaviest possible iron rod. Mother, do you want just the leaves

---

3. **calabash:** a hollowed-out gourd used as a bowl.

3 of the baobab or would you rather I brought you the whole tree?"

"Ah, my son, to wipe out this insult I want the tree and its roots at my feet outside my hut."

4 Balla Fasséké, who was present, ran to the master smith, Farakourou, to order an iron rod.

Sogolon had sat down in front of her hut. She was weeping softly and holding her head between her two hands. Mari Djata went calmly back to his calabash of rice and began eating again as if nothing had happened. From time to time he looked up discreetly at his mother who was murmuring in a low voice, "I want the whole tree, in front of my hut, the whole tree."

5 All of a sudden a voice burst into laughter behind the hut. It was the wicked Sassouma telling one of her serving women about the scene of humiliation and she was laughing loudly so that Sogolon could hear. Sogolon fled into the hut and hid her face under the blankets so as not to have before her eyes this heedless boy, who was more preoccupied with eating than with anything else. With her head buried in the bedclothes Sogolon wept and her body shook violently. Her daughter, Sogolon Djamarou, had come and sat down beside her and she said, "Mother, Mother, don't cry. Why are you crying?"

Mari Djata had finished eating and, dragging himself along on his legs, he came and sat under the wall of the hut for the sun was scorching. What was he thinking about? He alone knew.

The royal forges were situated outside the walls and over a hundred smiths worked there. The bows, spears, arrows and shields of Niani's warriors came from there. When
6 Balla Fasséké came to order the iron rod, Farakourou said to him, "The great day has arrived then?"

"Yes. Today is a day like any other, but it will see what no other day has seen."

The master of the forges, Farakourou, was the son of the old Nounfaïri, and he was a soothsayer like his father. In his workshops there was an enormous iron bar wrought by his father Nounfaïri. Everybody wondered what this bar was destined to be used for. Farakourou called six of his apprentices and told them to carry the iron bar to Sogolon's house.

When the smiths put the gigantic iron bar down in front of the hut the noise was so frightening that Sogolon, who was lying down, jumped up with a start. Then Balla Fasséké,[4] son of Gnankouman Doua, spoke.

"Here is the great day, Mari Djata. I am speaking to you, Maghan, son of Sogolon. The waters of the Niger can efface the stain from the body, but they cannot wipe out an insult. Arise, young lion, roar, and may the bush know that from henceforth it has a master."

The apprentice smiths were still there, Sogolon had come out and everyone was watching Mari Djata. He crept on all fours and came to the iron bar. Supporting himself on his knees and one hand, with the other hand he picked up the iron bar without any effort and stood it up vertically. Now he was resting on nothing but his knees and held the bar with both his hands. A deathly silence had gripped all those present. Sogolon Djata closed his eyes, held tight, the muscles in his arms tensed. With a violent jerk he

6

---

4. **Balla Fasséké:** Before he died, the king had named Balla Fasséké as Mari Djata's griot. As griots traditionally served kings, this apppointment indicated Maghan Kon Fatta's faith in the prophecy that Sundiata would one day become king. Here, Balla Fasséké is playing the role of the town crier for Sundiata.

MEETING INDIVIDUAL NEEDS

4 LEP: If students are confused about the role of Balla Fasséké, remind them that he is Sundiata's griot. (Balla's father, Doua, was the griot of Sundiata's father.) Balla Fasséké functions not only as a bard but also as an attendant and tutor to Sundiata. ■

5 GUIDED READING
Identifying Characteristics: Which of Sassouma's characteristics lead the narrator to describe her as "wicked"? (She is discourteous and vindictive.) How are these traits revealed? (She humiliates Sundiata's mother, mocks her, and gossips about her.)

6 CULTURAL DIVERSITY
In the Mandingo culture, as in other West African cultures, both blacksmiths and griots were thought to have occult powers. Thus the "master of the forges" is a soothsayer "like his father." Similarly, the narrator mentions that the griot is the "son of Gnankouman Doua" in order to emphasize that Balla Fasséké has prophetic powers like those of his father, who prophesied Sundiata's greatness.
? What dialogue reveals the prescience, or foreknowledge, of the blacksmith and the griot? (When the griot asks him for an iron rod, the blacksmith says, "The great day has arrived then?" The griot affirms that it has.)

efface (ə·fās'): rub out, as from a surface

Traditionally, when the griot narrating the epic sang songs, he was joined by his accompanist, by apprentices attending the performance, or by certain members of the audience.

7 LITERARY ELEMENT

Epic Characteristics: Epithets, or praise names, are found in many epics. Here they occur in the griot's songs about Sundiata. In the first song, the epithet *Simbon* means "lion." Where is this epithet used again? (in the line "The lion has walked") Which characteristics might the "lion" epithet emphasize? (power, royalty, ruthlessness)

HUMANITIES CONNECTION

These headdresses representing antelopes were worn by dancers during sowing and harvest feasts. The dancers attempted to imitate the leaps of antelopes.

? *In the third song, how does the griot's mention of fleeing antelopes intensify the image of Sundiata as a lion?* (Possible response: It suggests threat, terror.) ▪

threw his weight on to it and his knees left the ground. Sogolon Kedjou was all eyes and watched her son's legs which were trembling as though from an electric shock. Djata was sweating and the sweat ran from his brow. In a great effort he straightened up and was on his feet at one go—but the great bar of iron was twisted and had taken the form of a bow!

Then Balla Fasséké sang out the "Hymn to the Bow," striking up with his powerful voice:

"Take your bow, Simbon,
Take your bow and let us go.
Take your bow, Sogolon Djata."

When Sogolon saw her son standing she stood dumb for a moment, then suddenly she sang these words of thanks to God who had given her son the use of his legs:

"Oh day, what a beautiful day,
Oh day, day of joy;
Allah[5] Almighty, you never created
a finer day.
So my son is going to walk!"

Standing in the position of a soldier at ease, Sogolon Djata, supported by his enormous rod, was sweating great beads of sweat. Balla Fasséké's song had alerted the whole palace and people came running from all over to see what had happened, and each stood bewildered before Sogolon's son. The queen mother had rushed there and when she saw Mari Djata standing up she trembled from head to foot. After recovering his breath Sogolon's son dropped the bar and the crowd stood to one side. His first steps were those of a giant. Balla Fasséké fell into step and pointing his finger at Djata, he cried:

"Room, room, make room!
The lion has walked;   ☐ 7
Hide antelopes,
Get out of his way."

Behind Niani there was a young baobab tree and it was there that the children of the town came to pick leaves for their mothers. With all his might the son of Sogolon tore up the tree and put it on his shoulders and went back to his mother. He threw the tree in front of the hut and said, "Mother, here are some baobab leaves for you. From henceforth it will be outside your hut that the women of Niani will come to stock up."

Ceremonial headdresses from Mali.

5. **Allah:** the Muslim name for God.

Sogolon Djata walked. From that day forward the queen mother had no more peace of mind. But what can one do against destiny? Nothing. Man, under the influence of certain illusions, thinks he can alter the course which God has mapped out, but everything he does falls into a higher order which he barely understands. That is why Sassouma's efforts were vain against Sogolon's son, everything she did lay in the child's destiny. Scorned the day before and the object of public ridicule, now Sogolon's son was as popular as he had been despised. The multitude loves and fears strength. All Niani talked of nothing but Djata; the mothers urged their sons to become hunting companions of Djata and to share his games, as if they wanted their offspring to profit from the nascent glory of the buffalo-woman's son. The words of Doua on the name-giving day[6] came back to men's minds and Sogolon was now surrounded with much respect; in conversation people were fond of contrasting Sogolon's modesty with the pride and malice of Sassouma Bérété. It was because the former had been an exemplary wife and mother that God had granted strength to her son's legs for, it was said, the more a wife loves and respects her husband and the more she suffers for her child, the more valorous will the child be one day. Each is the child of his mother; the child is worth no more than the mother is worth. It was not astonishing that the king Dankaran Touman was so colorless, for his mother had never shown the slightest respect to her husband and never, in the presence of the late king, did she show that humility which every wife should show before her husband.

---

6. **The words . . . name-giving day:** Doua, King Maghan's griot, had repeated the hunter's prophecy at the infant Sundiata's ceremonial naming.

People recalled her scenes of jealousy and the spiteful remarks she circulated about her co-wife and her child. And people would conclude gravely, "Nobody knows God's mystery. The snake has no legs yet it is as swift as any other animal that has four."

While still a child, Sundiata becomes a great hunter. He becomes friends with Manding Bory, the son of his father's third wife. When an attempt to kill Sundiata fails, Sassouma and her son Dankaran Touman drive Sundiata into exile. The hero and his family find refuge in the kingdom of Mema.

As Sundiata grows to manhood, the evil Soumaoro Kanté, sorcerer-king of a neighboring kingdom, gains power and conquers many nations. When Sundiata hears that Soumaoro has invaded Mali, he decides to challenge the sorcerer-king and gain control of his rightful kingdom. Sundiata thus makes his way to Sosso, Soumaoro's capital city, to meet Soumaoro face to face. Sundiata fights and wins several battles along the way and becomes a popular leader. Many new soldiers gladly join his ranks.

from Krina

Sundiata went and pitched camp at Dayala in the valley of the Niger. Now it was he who was blocking Soumaoro's road to the south. Up till that time, Sundiata and Soumaoro had fought each other without a declaration of war. One does not wage war without saying why it is being waged. Those fighting should make a declaration of their grievances to begin with. Just as a sorcerer ought not to attack someone without taking him to task for some evil deed, so a king should not wage war without saying why he is taking up arms.

Soumaoro advanced as far as Krina, near the village of Dayala on the Niger and

Metaphor: Soumaoro uses several metaphors to describe himself. What does Sundiata do with each metaphor? (He extends each to describe how he will best Soumaoro.) What traits of Sundiata are revealed in this exchange? (Possible responses: quick wit, resourcefulness, determination)

11 **CULTURAL DIVERSITY**

"Skin" refers to the animal skin that each person traditionally sat on in his home or that a king sat on in his palace.
❓ *How might you express the idea that "there is not room for two kings on the same skin" in your everyday language?* (Possible response: A country can have only one leader.)

12 **LITERARY ELEMENT**

Foreshadowing: The verbal battle foreshadows the prowess Sundiata and Soumaoro will show in the physical battle to come. Are the two men equal in verbal skill? (Answers will vary.) Which verbal skills does each reveal? (Both are articulate. Soumaoro shows originality; Sundiata shows cleverness.) Who has the last word in the verbal battle? (Sundiata)

decided to assert his rights before joining battle. Soumaoro knew that Sundiata also was a sorcerer, so, instead of sending an embassy, he committed his words to one of his owls. The night bird came and perched on the roof of Djata's tent and spoke. The son of Sogolon in his turn sent his owl to Soumaoro. Here is the dialogue of the sorcerer-kings:

"Stop, young man. Henceforth I am the king of Mali. If you want peace, return to where you came from," said Soumaoro.

"I am coming back, Soumaoro, to recapture my kingdom. If you want peace you will make amends to my allies and return to Sosso where you are the king."

"I am king of Mali by force of arms. My rights have been established by conquest."

"Then I will take Mali from you by force of arms and chase you from my kingdom."

"Know, then, that I am the wild yam of the rocks;[7] nothing will make me leave Mali."

10
"Know, also that I have in my camp seven master smiths who will shatter the rocks. Then, yam, I will eat you."

"I am the poisonous mushroom that makes the fearless vomit."

"As for me, I am the ravenous cock, the poison does not matter to me."

"Behave yourself, little boy, or you will burn your foot, for I am the red-hot cinder."

"But me, I am the rain that extinguishes the cinder; I am the boisterous torrent that will carry you off."

"I am the mighty silk-cotton tree that looks from on high on the tops of other trees."

"And I, I am the strangling creeper that

climbs to the top of the forest giant." ⌐ 10
"Enough of this argument. You shall not have Mali."

"Know that there is not room for two kings ⌐
on the same skin, Soumaoro; you will let me | 11
have your place." ⌐

"Very well, since you want war I will wage war against you, but I would have you know that I have killed nine kings whose heads adorn my room. What a pity, indeed, that your head should take its place beside those of your fellow madcaps."

"Prepare yourself, Soumaoro, for it will be long before the calamity that is going to crash down upon you and yours comes to an end."

12

Balla Fasséké, Sundiata's griot, and Nana Triban, Sundiata's half-sister, have been imprisoned in Soumaoro's palace, but they finally escape. They join Sundiata on the eve of the battle of Krina. Fakoli Koroma, Soumaoro's nephew, also arrives at the camp. Because Soumaoro kidnapped his

Statue of ancestral couple from Mali.

---

7. . . . **the wild yam of the rocks:** When the vines of these yams grow in boulder-strewn areas, their underground tubers anchor them among the rocks and make them very difficult to uproot.

wife, Fakoli has vowed revenge. Nana Triban and Fakoli pledge their loyalty to Sundiata, and Nana Triban tells Sundiata that the way to insure Soumaoro's defeat is to touch him with a cock's spur. On the morning of the battle, Sundiata and Manding Bory, his half brother, devise a plan to strip Soumaoro of his power.

13

"Brother," said Manding Bory, "have you got the bow ready?"

"Yes," replied Sundiata. "Look."

He unhooked his bow from the wall, along with the deadly arrow. It was not an iron arrow at all, but was made of wood and pointed with the spur of a white cock. The cock's spur was the Tana of Soumaoro,[8] the secret which Nana Triban had managed to draw out of the king of Sosso.

"Brother," said Nana Triban, "Soumaoro now knows that I have fled from Sosso. Try to get near him for he will avoid you the whole battle long."

These words of Nana Triban left Djata worried, but Balla Fasséké, who had just come into the tent, said to Sundiata that the

soothsayer had seen the end of Soumaoro in a dream.

The sun had risen on the other side of the river and already lit the whole plain. Sundiata's troops <u>deployed</u> from the edge of the river across the plain, but Soumaoro's army was so big that other sofas[9] remaining in Krina had ascended the <u>ramparts</u> to see the battle. Soumaoro was already distinguishable in the distance by his tall headdress, and the wings of his enormous army brushed the river on one side and the hills on the other. As at Neguéboria,[10] Sundiata did not deploy all his forces. The bowmen of Wagadou[11] and the Djallonkés stood at the rear ready to spill out on the left towards the hills as the battle spread. Fakoli Koroma and Kamandjan[12] were in the front line with Sundiata and his cavalry.

14

With his powerful voice Sundiata cried "*An gnewa*."[13] The order was repeated from tribe to tribe and the army started off. Soumaoro stood on the right with his cavalry.

Djata and his cavalry charged with great dash but they were stopped by the horsemen of Diaghan and a struggle to the death began. Tabon Wana[14] and the archers of Wagadou stretched out their lines towards the hills and the battle spread over the entire plain, while

---

8. **the Tana of Soumaoro:** The cock's spur (the spiny projection on the leg of a rooster) is Soumaoro's Tana, that is, the taboo, or prohibition, imposed on him by his ancestors. In breaking this taboo, Soumaoro will incur the wrath of his ancestors, who will then withdraw the magic powers that have made him invincible.
9. **sofas:** warriors.
10. **Neguéboria:** an earlier battle fought and won by Sundiata.
11. **Wagadou:** a name for Old Ghana.
12. **Kamandjan:** king of Sibi; one of Sundiata's childhood friends.
13. *An gnewa:* Forward.
14. **Tabon Wana:** king of Tabon; also called Fran Kamara.

13 GUIDED READING

Identifying Details: Which details show the role that family unity plays in Sundiata's defeat of Soumaoro? (Sundiata's half sister reveals the sorcerer's weakness; she and Sundiata's brother both help the hero devise a successful plan.)

HUMANITIES CONNECTION

Figures like these were believed to embody a family's spirit. They were passed down through generations; some were used in burial rituals.

❓ *How do the sculptures suggest family unity?* (They are similar in posture and appearance, and one figure has its arm around the other.) ∎

14 LITERARY ELEMENT

Setting: Setting can contribute to the mood, or emotional atmosphere, of a narrative. The griot describes a detailed setting for the battle of Krina. What is the setting for the battle? (The sun is rising; the armies, including horsemen and archers, are massed on a vast plain, between a river and surrounding hills, in the morning light.) What mood does the setting convey? (high spirits, pride, optimism)

---

deployed (dē·ploid'): stationed in accordance with a plan

ramparts (ram'pärts'): embankments of earth, usually surrounded by parapets, encircling a castle or fort for defense against attack

Epic Characteristics: The action in many epics is episodic, consisting of repeated sets of complications and their resolutions. What complication is announced by the statement "The battle was not yet won"? (Soumaoro is defeating Fakoli's outnumbered troops, who are fighting for Sundiata.) How is this complication later resolved? (Sundiata wounds Soumaoro and is then able to win the battle.)

rout: overwhelming defeat

WRITING TO LEARN

Social Studies: Note details about tactics and equipment used in the battles of Krina and Sosso by the warriors of Old Mali. You might research the subject further in an encyclopedia under *Mandingo*, *Mandinke*, or *Mali*. Then use your information to write a first-person narrative of the battle of Krina or Sosso from the viewpoint of one of the warriors. ■

an unrelenting sun climbed in the sky. The horses of Mema were extremely agile, and they reared forward with their forehooves raised and swooped down on the horsemen of Diaghan, who rolled on the ground trampled under the horses' hooves. Presently the men of Diaghan gave ground and fell back towards the rear. The enemy center was broken.

It was then that Manding Bory galloped up to announce to Sundiata that Soumaoro, having thrown in all his reserve, had swept down on Fakoli and his smiths. Obviously Soumaoro was bent on punishing his nephew. Already overwhelmed by the numbers, Fakoli's men were beginning to give ground. The battle was not yet won.

His eyes red with anger, Sundiata pulled his cavalry over to the left in the direction of the hills where Fakoli was valiantly enduring his uncle's blows. But wherever the son of the buffalo passed, death rejoiced. Sundiata's presence restored the balance momentarily, but Soumaoro's sofas were too numerous all the same. Sogolon's son looked for Soumaoro and caught sight of him in the middle of the fray. Sundiata

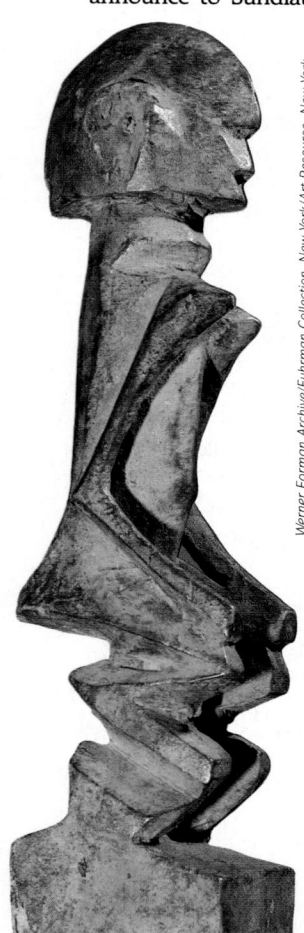

Werner Forman Archive/Fuhrman Collection, New York/Art Resource, New York

15

struck out right and left and the Sossos scrambled out of his way. The king of Sosso, who did not want Sundiata to get near him, retreated far behind his men, but Sundiata followed him with his eyes. He stopped and bent his bow. The arrow flew and grazed Soumaoro on the shoulder. The cock's spur no more than scratched him, but the effect was immediate and Soumaoro felt his powers leave him. His eyes met Sundiata's. Now trembling like a man in the grip of a fever, the vanquished Soumaoro looked up towards the sun. A great black bird flew over above the fray and he understood. It was a bird of misfortune.

"The bird of Krina," he muttered.

The king of Sosso let out a great cry and, turning his horse's head, he took to flight. The Sossos saw the king and fled in their turn. It was a <u>rout</u>. Death hovered over the great plain and blood poured out of a thousand wounds. Who can tell how many Sossos perished at Krina? The rout was complete and Sundiata then dashed off in pursuit of Soumaoro.

Werner Forman Archive/Dallas Museum of Fine Art/Art Resource, New York

Sundiata and Fakoli pursue Soumaoro, who has fled with his son Sosso Balla. They succeed in capturing Sosso Balla, but Soumaoro escapes into a cave. He is never heard from again. Sundiata heads for the nearby village of Koulikoro, where he waits for his army.

The victory of Krina was dazzling. The remains of Soumaoro's army went to shut themselves up in Sosso. But the empire of Sosso was done for. From everywhere around kings sent their submission to Sundiata. The king of Guidimakhan sent a richly furnished embassy to Djata and at the same time gave his daughter in marriage to the victor. Embassies flocked to Koulikoro, but when Djata had been joined by all the army he marched on Sosso. Soumaoro's **16** city, Sosso, the <u>impregnable</u> city, the city of smiths skilled in wielding the spear.

In the absence of the king and his son, Noumounkeba, a tribal chief, directed the defense of the city. He had quickly amassed all that he could find in the way of provisions from the surrounding countryside.

Sosso was a magnificent city. In the open plain her triple rampart with awe-inspiring towers reached into the sky. The city <u>comprised</u> a hundred and eighty-eight fortresses and the palace of Soumaoro loomed above the whole city like a gigantic tower.

16 Sosso had but one gate; colossal and made of iron, the work of the sons of fire. Noumounkeba hoped to tie Sundiata down outside of Sosso, for he had enough provisions to hold out for a year.

The sun was beginning to set when Sogolon Djata appeared before Sosso the

Magnificent. From the top of a hill, Djata and his general staff gazed upon the fearsome city of the sorcerer-king. The army encamped in the plain opposite the great gate of the city and fires were lit in the camp. Djata resolved to take Sosso in the course of a morning. He fed his men a double ration and the tam-tams[15] beat all night to stir up the victors of Krina. **17**

At daybreak the towers of the ramparts were black with sofas. Others were positioned on the ramparts themselves. They were the archers. The Mandingoes[16] were masters in the art of storming a town. In the front line Sundiata placed the sofas of Mali, while those who held the ladders were in the second line protected by the shields of the spearmen. The main body of the army was to attack the city gate. When all was ready, Djata gave the order to attack. The drums resounded, the horns blared and like a tide the Mandingo front line moved off, giving mighty shouts. With their shields raised above their heads the Mandingoes advanced up to the foot of the wall, then the Sossos began to rain large

Werner Forman Archive/Fuhrman Collection, New York/Art Resource, New York

Werner Forman Archive/Dallas Museum of Fine Art/Art Resource, New York

15. **tam-tams:** small drums.
16. **Mandingoes:** the inhabitants of Old Mali.

HUMANITIES CONNECTION

Stylized sculptures like these, some with headdresses, chin ornaments, and armbands, may have been shrine figures representing ancestors.

? *What emotions might be indicated in the postures of the four figures?* (Answers will vary.) ∎

impregnable (im·preg'nə·bəl): not capable of being captured or entered by force

comprised (kəm·prīzd'): consisted of

16 INFERRING

What descriptions of Sosso emphasize its links with iron-working? ("the city of smiths skilled in wielding the spear"; the iron gate that was "the work of the sons of fire") Since smiths were believed to have occult powers, what might these descriptions imply about the city? (Possible response: It has supernatural protection.)

17 CONTRASTING

How is Sundiata's attitude before the battle of Sosso different from his attitude before the battle of Krina? (He shows no worry or uncertainty; he is enthusiastic, confident, and decisive.) What might account for the differences? (Possible responses: Soumaoro is gone; many more kings have allied with Sundiata; Sundiata knows that he is coming into his own.)

Sundiata **113**

READING CHECK

1. How old is Sundiata when he first walks? (seven)
2. How do the villagers treat Sundiata after he begins walking? (They admire him and flock around him.)
3. Who is Soumaoro? (the sorcerer-king of Sosso)

4. What happens at Krina in the valley of the Niger? (a battle between the rival forces of Sundiata and Soumaoro)
5. What does Sundiata do to the city of Sosso? (razes it and burns it to the ground)

RETEACHING

To reteach *Sundiata*, divide students into three groups. Have each group script and then act out one portion of the narrative. The first group will dramatize the events from "The Lion's Awakening," the second, the events of the battle of Krina, and the third, the destruction of Sosso. Encourage students to decide which values each of the main characters reveals and how the characters' words and actions can best convey these values.

LITERARY ELEMENT

Imagery: In the description of the attack on Sosso, what details appeal to the sense of hearing? (at the start—p. 113—the drums, horns, shouts; then the stones falling, the screams and pleas of women and children, the flapping of owls on the ground) What detail appeals to the sense of smell? (smoke)

implored (im·plôrd'): begged earnestly for

ANALYZING

The details of imagery and action used to describe the attack on Sosso and its aftermath slow and draw out the narrative. Why might the narrator want to do this? (to emphasize the importance of this episode) Which plot element does the destruction of Sosso correspond to? (the climax)

HUMANITIES CONNECTION

In a society with an oral tradition, a stool is an important piece of furniture because storytellers need them for long recitations. This particular stool contains the image of a tree.

❓ *Which trees are named in the epic?* (baobab, silk-cotton, bourein) *How is each linked to a significant event?* (The baobab inspires Sundiata to walk; the silk-cotton is Soumaoro's image of himself before Krina; the bourein is a reminder of Sundiata's victory.) ∎

stones down on the assailants. From the rear, the bowmen of Wagadou shot arrows at the ramparts. The attack spread and the town was assaulted at all points. Sundiata had a murderous reserve; they were the bowmen whom the king of the Bobos had sent shortly before Krina. The archers of Bobo are the best in the world. On one knee the archers fired flaming arrows over the ramparts. Within the walls the thatched huts took fire and the smoke swirled up. The ladders stood against the curtain wall and the first Mandingo sofas were already at the top. Seized by panic through seeing the town on fire, the Sossos hesitated a moment. The huge tower surmounting the gate surrendered, for Fakoli's smiths had made themselves masters of it. They got into the city where the screams of women and children brought the Sossos' panic to a head. They opened the gates to the main body of the army.

Then began the massacre. Women and children in the midst of fleeing Sossos <u>implored</u> mercy of the victors. Djata and his cavalry were now in front of the awesome tower palace of Soumaoro. Noumounkeba, conscious that he was lost, came out to fight. With his sword held aloft he bore down on Djata, but the latter dodged him and, catching hold of the Sosso's braced arm, forced him to his knees whilst the sword dropped to the ground. He did not kill him but delivered him into the hands of Manding Bory.

Soumaoro's palace was now at Sundiata's mercy. While everywhere the Sossos were begging for quarter,[17] Sundiata, preceded by Balla Fasséké, entered Soumaoro's tower. The griot knew every nook and cranny of the palace from his captivity and he led Sundiata to Soumaoro's magic chamber.

When Balla Fasséké opened the door to the room it was found to have changed its appearance since Soumaoro had been touched by the fatal arrow. The inmates of the chamber had lost their power. The snake in the pitcher was in the throes of death, the owls from the perch were flapping pitifully about on the ground. Everything was dying in the sorcerer's abode. It was all up with the power of Soumaoro. Sundiata had all Soumaoro's fetishes[18] taken down and before the palace were gathered together all Soumaoro's wives, all princesses taken from their families by force. The prisoners, their hands tied behind their backs, were already herded together. Just as he had wished, Sundiata had taken

Stool used in religious ceremonies, from Mali. The base and seat represent the earth and sky, connected by a central tree. Images of nature play an important role in Sundiata.
❓ *How does the narrator use nature imagery to describe the downfall of Sosso?*

Werner Forman Archive/Dallas Museum of Fine Art/Art Resource, New York

---

17. **quarter:** mercy.

18. **fetishes:** objects believed to have magical powers.

1. Creating a New Episode. Have students create new episodes for the epic. They may have Sundiata meet and share an adventure with another epic hero or with a modern hero from either film or real life. Students could work cooperatively to plan and write their episodes. Those with artistic talent could furnish illustrations, and those with musical talent could compose songs to accompany the episode.

2. Research Project. Encourage interested students to read the entire text of D. T. Niane's *Sundiata: An Epic of Old Mali* (Longman, 1965) and report on it to the class. Ask them to pay special attention to the character traits of Sundiata and his friends and enemies and to the values they reveal.

Many epic heroes experience great physical or emotional pain as well as great triumphs. Often, epic heroes change and grow because of their suffering. Ask students to decide what pain Sundiata endures and how it affects him. Then guide students in exploring similarities between Sundiata's exploits and the trials every young person goes through—facing daunting odds, battling for control and respect—to reach maturity. ■

Sosso in the course of a morning. When everything was outside of the town and all that there was to take had been taken out, Sundiata gave the order to complete its destruction. The last houses were set fire to and prisoners were employed in the razing of the walls. Thus, as Djata intended, Sosso was destroyed to its very foundations.

Yes, Sosso was razed to the ground. It has disappeared, the proud city of Soumaoro. A ghastly wilderness extends over the places where kings came and humbled themselves before the sorcerer-king. All traces of the houses have vanished and of Soumaoro's seven-story palace there remains nothing more. A field of desolation, Sosso is now a spot where guinea fowl and young partridges come to take their dust baths.

Many years have rolled by and many times the moon has traversed the heaven since these places lost their inhabitants. The bourein,[19] the tree of desolation, spreads out its thorny undergrowth and insolently grows in Soumaoro's capital. Sosso the Proud is nothing but a memory in the mouths of griots. The hyenas come to wail there at night, the hare and the hind come and feed on the site of the palace of Soumaoro, the king who wore robes of human skin.

Sosso vanished from the earth and it was Sundiata, the son of the buffalo, who gave these places over to solitude. After the destruction of Soumaoro's capital the world knew no other master but Sundiata.

---

19. **bourein:** a dwarf shrub.

First Thoughts

Which episode from this epic stands out most clearly in your mind? Why? Did any portion of the epic remind you of any other stories you have read?

Identifying Facts

1. How are Mari Djata (Sundiata) and his family mistreated after his father dies?
2. How does Mari Djata avenge his mother's humiliation at the hands of Sassouma?
3. Why do Sundiata and Soumaoro have a "dialogue" at the beginning of "Krina"? What **metaphors** do they use to describe themselves?
4. What is the outcome of the **conflict** between Sundiata and Soumaoro?

5. What does Sosso look like before the battle of Krina? What does it look like afterward?

Interpreting Meanings

1. The incident in which Mari Djata (Sundiata) begins to walk reveals a great deal about his **character**. From that incident, what can you infer about Sundiata's sense of justice? What does the incident reveal about his physical strength and determination?
2. Three brief songs occur in "The Lion's Awakening." What events do these songs accompany? What purpose do you think these songs serve in the narrative?

---

razing (rāz'iŋ): tearing down completely

First Thoughts
Answers will vary.

Identifying Facts
1. Sundiata is denied his rightful throne; they are forced to live in poverty and are mocked.
2. He pulls up a whole baobab tree and brings it to her.
3. They must say why they are waging war. Soumaoro says he is a wild yam of the rocks, a poisonous mushroom, a red-hot cinder, a silk-cotton tree; Sundiata says he will eat the yam, is a rooster who will eat the mushroom, rain that will put out the cinder, a creeper that will strangle the tree.
4. Soumaoro is defeated.
5. *Before:* magnificent, 188 fortresses topped by a palace, all surrounded by a triple rampart covered with archers, an iron gate and high towers dark with warriors. *After:* a dusty, desolate wilderness, with no traces of buildings, where only birds and scavenging animals come and thorn trees grow

Interpreting Meanings
1. It is so strong that it motivates him to do what seems impossible. His strength and determination are superhuman.
2. *Events:* Sundiata bends the iron bar and stands; his mother sees him stand; Sundiata walks. The songs slow

the narrative, heightening suspense, and underscore the significance of the events.

3. Possible response: It might have unified and inspired the army.

4. In the chamber, the sorcerer's magic animals are dying, implying that his power has been destroyed, too.

5. Possible responses: as a warning to potential enemies; to display his power; to oppose the forces of evil, which Soumaoro's city represents

6. Possible responses: *Honored values:* determination, respect for parents, justice, forthrightness, physical strength, verbal skill. *Despicable behavior:* underhandedness, discourtesy, taking unfair advantage of others

Applying Meanings

Answers will vary. Some students may feel that the modern media, by showing the reality of war, discourage its glorification. Others may feel that media attention, positive or negative, is in itself a kind of glorification.

Creative Writing Response
Recording an Oral History.
Oral histories should give the time and place of the interview, a brief background of the person interviewed, and verbatim questions and answers. Students will need to use a tape recorder.

---

3. An exchange of boasts before battle, like Sundiata's and Soumaoro's dialogue, occurs frequently in epics. Scholars think that *Sundiata* was often performed for the Mandingo army before battles. What effect do you think the boastful exchange might have had on such an audience?

4. How does Soumaoro's secret chamber look after he is wounded by Sundiata's arrow? What does the room's appearance imply about the sorcerer's fate?

5. Why do you think Sundiata chose to completely destroy the city of Sosso rather than make it a part of his kingdom?

6. An **epic**, with its blend of history and legend, reflects a society's values. Based on your reading of these excerpts from *Sundiata*, what values do you think were honored by the Mandingo culture? Can you tell what kinds of behaviors they found despicable?

Applying Meanings

Sundiata, like many epics, glorifies war. War is depicted in the epic as colorful, even spectacular. Explain how modern views of war are similar to those expressed in *Sundiata* and how they differ. Consider the media of modern culture, such as television, literature, and movies. Which changes might be responsible for the differences?

Creative Writing Response

Recording an Oral History.   Begin an oral history of your own family, school, or community. Interview someone about a historical event, large or small, that that person witnessed. Perhaps the person you interview will remember details about a famous leader or other celebrity. Or perhaps he or she participated in a war or some large group effort, or witnessed a natural disaster. Ask the person to recall details about

---

the event. Write up your interview, and share it with the class.

Critical Writing Response

Explicating the Theme.   An epic, like any longer piece of literature, may contain several **themes**, or messages, that give central insights into human life. In a sentence, state one or more of the themes that you see in *Sundiata*. One of the following questions, or some questions of your own, may lead you to some possible statements of theme from the epic:

1. How much control do people have over fate?

2. Does strength alone constitute power, or must strength be combined with virtue?

3. What makes a just, strong leader?

4. What are the duties of a leader to his or her country or community?

5. What is a true "national hero"?

From the answer to the question, formulate a statement of the theme that you believe is a central theme of *Sundiata*. Then, in a three- or four-paragraph essay, explain how the epic illustrates that theme. Use specific details from the epic to support your statements.

Speaking and Listening

Telling the Story of an Unlikely Hero.
Sundiata has an unpromising start in life. He is serious, seldom speaks, doesn't play with other children, and, at the age of seven, still hasn't learned to walk. Do you think it is likely that a child who starts out like Sundiata could become a great leader? Think of another hero of history, myth, or folklore who was at first considered insignificant, or even "backward," but who went on to do great things. (Remember that a hero can be either male or female.) Briefly recount the hero's story to the class. End your story with your own

opinions about why people all over the world like stories about people who overcome hardship and triumph in the end.

Language and Vocabulary

Context Clues

You can often guess the meaning of an unfamiliar word by examining its **context**—the other words, phrases, and sentences that surround it. There are several main types of context clues:

1. **Synonyms**—The sentence may contain a word or phrase that is similar in meaning to the word you do not know.
2. **Antonyms**—The sentence may contain a word or phrase that means the opposite of the word you do not know.
3. **Definitions**—The sentence may contain a direct definition of the word.
4. **Restatements**—The word's meaning may be clarified by a restatement that

is signaled by dashes, parentheses, or even a phrase such as *that is* or *in other words*. Sometimes the meaning of a word is revealed by an **appositive**—a restatement set off by commas.

In the following sentences, words from *Sundiata* are shown in italics. (In the text, these words are footnoted.) What type of context clue can help you to determine the meaning of each italicized word?

1. The hungry child looked inside the *calabash* carefully, checking the hollowed-out gourd bowl for remnants of food.
2. The *sofas* stood outside the castle walls, ready with their bows to face the enemy warriors' attack.
3. The *gnougous,* a root vegetable, was a common part of the diet of the people of Old Mali.
4. The *baobab* is a tropical tree with edible fruit and leaves that can be used as an herb for cooking.

Arrange for a storyteller to perform for the class (you might consult a librarian for the names of local storytellers, or you might recruit a drama teacher or an experienced student). Have students read the story beforehand, and elicit students' reactions after the performance: Which elements or events stood out more in the spoken story than in the written version? What did the storyteller add, omit, or change? Which version is easier to recall? Finally, encourage students to select and prepare their own stories to tell to the class. Explain that the stories may come from any sources and that students may use appropriate props and costumes. Set aside a class session for the storytelling. Afterward, allow time for audience response and questions.

1 CULTURAL DIVERSITY

Many African groups open and close stories with idioms or formulaic sayings. The Hausa of Niger end with "There it is. Off with the rat's head." The Shangaan of southern Africa begin with "I am Narrator, daughter of Narrator!" to which listeners reply, "Narrator!" When the tale has ended, the narrator says, "I spit! I throw a branch to close the gate [against evil spirits]!"

Which idiomatic or formulaic beginnings or endings occur in the stories you know? (Students may suggest "Once upon a time" or "That's all, folks!")

LANGUAGE
— AND —
CULTURE

AFRICAN AMERICAN STORYTELLERS

"Hey, ever'body. I'm Brother Blue, a street cat callin' you. Come close. . . ." So begins a tale by Brother Blue, really Dr. Hugh Morgan Hill, African American storyteller. Blue performs at hospitals and prisons, preschools and libraries. But just as often, he simply stands on the Boston sidewalks, wearing his bright clothes and a knit cap decorated with ribbons, flowers, and balloons, telling stories to passers-by. He chants his tales in a blend of rap and poetry, moving to the beat as he talks.

Brother Blue has been performing for almost fifty years. He grew up poor, the only black child in a white school. He was below average as a student, and he had a severe stammer. But somehow he discovered that when he told a story, recited poetry, or sang, his stammering stopped. When he began telling stories to his classmates and at school assemblies, he didn't know that he was stepping into a tradition thousands of years old.

Encouraged by a caring teacher, Blue overcame his academic difficulties. He went on to graduate from both Harvard and Yale, where he studied drama, theology, and the oral tradition. In 1972, he launched Brother Blue's Soul Theater, a forum for his unique blend of storytelling, chanting, singing, dancing, and acting. He had realized by then that oral literature was his calling.

The African American Storytelling Tradition

Brother Blue, like all storytellers, gets his tales from many sources. Some come from his own experiences or from his imagination; some come from books or from other storytellers. Some, however, are stories he heard as a child, tales from the African American tradition. Traditional African American stories show many links to the oral tradition of Africa. For example, most African groups tell animal tales. In many African animal tales, a hare appears as a trickster figure. When African slaves were brought to America, the hare became Brer Rabbit. He was joined by Brer Fox, Brer Bear, Brer Possum, and others based on animals native to the North American continent. Among the peoples of Africa, animal tales had been used to dramatize, in a tactful way, personality quirks and social issues affecting the community. In fact, the Ewe (ā'wā') people of Togo have a saying: "Because I tell tales about animals, I have never been named in a libel suit."

1

Jason Lauré

Dogon griot.
? How has the role of the griot been transported to African American culture?

An American Griot

Some modern storytellers work to strengthen the connections between African and African American storytelling traditions. One of these storytellers is Mary Carter Smith, who has been called an urban American griot. Born in Alabama, she worked for thirty-one years as a teacher and a librarian in inner-city Baltimore. She shared with her students the stories and songs she had learned as a child in the South, and she began writing her own poetry as well. Eventually, Smith began performing her tales and songs at other schools and colleges. Today she travels widely throughout America, dressed in flowing robes and scarves made from African textiles, telling tales.

Entertainment—and More

2   Because it lets performers and listeners work together, storytelling has been called a "co-creative" process; between the words of the storyteller and the imagination of the audience, the story comes alive. The satisfaction of this shared effort is one of the main reasons that storytelling entertains.

In sharing enjoyment, of course, other benefits occur. Among the peoples of Africa, storytelling provides a chance to communicate social rules and values and an indirect way to resolve community conflicts. In the African American tradition, too, storytelling has served as a means of passing on values and making social comments. Modern African American storytellers also notice other positive effects. Brother Blue explains, "When you're there in the streets, you meet the street people. The people who are suffering, dying, lost, some going mad, some drunk. . . . You know, you can sober up a man with a story. Stories are healing." Mary Carter Smith offers a similar viewpoint. She sees her stories as tearing down walls between people and building bridges of understanding. "I have committed myself," she explains, ". . . to truth, freedom, justice, and peace for all peoples, black or white, young or old, free or in bondage. My stories are my message."

African American storyteller Mary Carter Smith.

Language Skills

USING QUOTATIONS EFFECTIVELY

To avoid confusing your readers, punctuate quotations correctly, and work them smoothly into your writing. Punctuation shows your readers which words you have written and which you have **quoted**—taken directly from sources. Note how a lack of proper punctuation causes confusion.

CONFUSING

My experience bears out what the griot knew: that growth is not always easy, and it is not as quick as you would like it.

CLEAR

My experience bears out what the griot knew: that "growth is not always easy. . . ." and "[it] is not as quick as you would like it."

In the second sentence, quotation marks tell the reader which words come from a literary work. Ellipses (. . .) show where material has been omitted from the quotation, and brackets ([ ]) show where a word has been added.

Punctuating Brief Quotations

Notice how the boldface commas, quotation marks, upper- and lower-case letters, and other marks are used in the examples that follow.

QUOTING A SENTENCE

The poet tries to flatter the sun god when he writes, **"Y**ou made the earth as you wished, you alone.**"**

QUOTING A FRAGMENT

An Ashanti proverb states that the cause of a country's ruin **"b**egins in the homes of its people.**"**

QUOTING A QUOTATION

Like the chief in the Ashanti tale, my cousin Jarrel said, **" 'N**ow this is really a wild story.**' "**

SHOWING OMISSIONS (USING ELLIPSES)

According to a Yoruban poem, the god Ogun **"k**ills **. . .** the owner of stolen goods.**"**

SHOWING INSERTIONS (USING BRACKETS)

The man grew angry not with the yam, but with the dog, because he didn't like **"[**the dog's**]** tone.**"**

QUOTING LINES OF POETRY

The Egyptians' tolerance of cultural differences is reflected in the lines, **"**Their tongues differ in speech, **/** Their characters likewise; **/** Their skins are distinct, **/** For you distinguished the peoples.**"**

(For over three lines of poetry or prose, separate the quotation from the text and indent each line ten spaces from the left margin.)

Exercise 1: Punctuating Brief Quotations

Use part or all of each quotation in a sentence. Use correct punctuation.

1. "The snake has no legs yet it is as swift as any other animal that has four." (*Sundiata*)

2. "One who asks never loses his way."
   (Yoruba proverb)
3. "Though you are far, your rays are on
   earth, / Though one sees you, your
   strides are unseen." ("The Great Hymn
   to the Aten")
4. "Do not speak of a rhinoceros if there
   is no tree nearby." (Zulu proverb)

Integrating Brief Quotations

When you are using brief quotations, you
must **integrate** them—work them
smoothly into your sentences and show
their relevance to your ideas.

DISJOINTED

Like a knife, the Yoruban god Ogun is
useful but dangerous. "Ogun's laughter
is no joke." He is bloodthirsty.

INTEGRATED

Like a knife, the Yoruban god Ogun is
useful but dangerous. *Ironically, even*
"Ogun's laughter is no joke," *for* he is
bloodthirsty even when he is happy.

In the second passage, an introductory
phrase and a subordinate clause work the
quotation smoothly into the writing. They
also show how the writer has interpreted
the quotation.

Methods for Inserting Brief Quotations

You can place quotations in various positions in your sentences. Study these
examples.

Final Position
For several reasons, "Ogun's laughter is
no joke."

Beginning Position
"Ogun's laughter is no joke"; instead, it
inspires fear.

Middle Position
Just as "Ogun's laughter is no joke," so
is his justice almost unjust.

Interrupted
"Ogun's laughter," warns the singer, "is
no joke."

Exercise 2: Integrating Quotations

Choose four quotations from works in this
unit, and use a different method for inserting each into a sentence you write. Use
correct punctuation.

TEACHING TIP

After students have read "Integrating Brief Quotations," pair
them and let them work cooperatively to choose a single
African proverb and integrate
it into a sentence or a brief
paragraph.

Then have them read "Methods for Inserting Brief Quotations." Let them choose another proverb and practice
incorporating it into a sentence in four different ways.

ANSWERS TO EXERCISE 2: INTEGRATING QUOTATIONS

Answers will vary. Here are
possible responses.
1. The mother shows deep
love when she tells her child
that the gods made **"the little
puckering ridges of your brows."**
2. **"Many years have rolled by,"**
intones the griot, alluding to
the age of the epic.
3. When Balla Fasséké sings,
"The lion has walked," he is referring to the young Sundiata.
4. **"O son,"** the mother predicts proudly, **"you will . . . be
a leader of men."**

Background: Lead students in a discussion that will make them more aware of their personal responses to the literature they have read in Unit 2. Begin by asking which image, of all the images they encountered in the unit selections, stands out most in their minds. Accept a variety of answers, and elicit responses to the imagery that are as specific as students can make them. Point out the abundance of images drawn from the daily lives of the authors of the selections, and discuss differences between the authors' daily lives and those of the students.

Next, ask which lines or selections students found humorous, and have them share their responses with the rest of the class. Finally, challenge students to recall or locate examples of onomatopoeia and dialogue ("Talk" contains examples of both). Encourage them to discuss how these elements affected their enjoyment of the works. You might close the discussion by clustering on the chalkboard, as students dictate, the range of their responses to the selections in the unit.

Prewriting: Encourage students to fill out a chart like that in the text. Remind them that they need to locate several examples from the selection to illustrate ideas relating to their general response. You may want to help students by filling out a sample chart on the blackboard.

Critical Thinking and Writing

A PERSONAL RESPONSE TO LITERATURE

"I think I know what this poet's talking about—I've had days like that." "I'm not sure I get the point of the story." "That character's a lot like my crazy cousin." All these comments reflect personal connections between readers and literary works. By exploring your personal responses to what you read, you can discover new depths, both in literature and in yourself.

Writing Assignment

Write an essay expressing your feelings about one of the works in this unit. You might explain how some aspect of the work relates to your own life. You might explore your thoughts or feelings about some aspect of the work. Or you might trace your reading process, recalling your initial responses to the work and recounting how your responses changed as you reread the work and thought about it or discussed it. Assume that your audience is familiar with the literature and is curious about your opinion. In this essay, you'll develop and support a generalization.

Background

In this unit, you've found examples of ancient written literature as well as timeless oral literature. Each selection speaks to readers in a unique way, and each

reader brings to the literature a unique set of responses. For your essay, consider the range of your personal responses. As you read, you may have felt amusement or boredom, sorrow or delight, puzzlement or deep understanding. Consider, too, the range of elements that evoked your responses. Works in this unit rely especially upon:

- **Imagery** drawn from daily life, in which words evoke for readers the sights, sounds, smells, tastes, and textures familiar to the writer
- **Figurative language**, in which a striking comparison can deepen readers' insights
- **Irony**, in which readers' expectations are reversed, creating surprise or humor
- **Repetition** and **parallel structure**, in which words, phrases, or sentence structures recur, creating patterns that underscore ideas
- **Onomatopoeia** and **dialogue**, in which sound effects and speech patterns communicate subtleties of emotion

Prewriting

Focused Reading and Questioning. To generate ideas, first choose the work that you liked most (or least) in this unit. Then freewrite answers to these questions.

FOR FURTHER HELP

Refer students to *Grammar, Usage, and Mechanics: A Reference Guide* at the back of their textbooks for detailed information that will help them write, revise, and proofread their essays.

1. Did you like or dislike the selection? Why?

2. Which image or idea from the work is most memorable to you? Why?

3. In what ways does the work relate to your own experience?

4. What was the author trying to accomplish?

5. What questions do you have about the work?

Developing a Generalization. Look over your freewriting and group responses that can be connected. Choose the set of responses you'd like to write about. Next, draft a **generalization**, a broad statement covering the responses in the set. Fill in a chart like the one below to be sure you have enough specific material to support your generalization.

Generali-zation	Support 1	Support 2	Support 3
	Example	Example	Example
	Example	Example	Example

Writing

Use the following plan as you draft your essay.

1. **Introductory Paragraph.** Catch your readers' interest by quoting, from the work you have chosen, a line or phrase that is especially relevant to your response. Explain how the quotation relates to your response. Then use your generalization as a thesis statement. Be sure to cite the title of the work you have chosen and specify the culture from which it comes.

2. **Body Paragraphs.** Referring to your chart, present the material that supports your generalization. From your freewriting, draw examples that will help you express your response. Use quotations from the work, as well. If you are tracing your response process, arrange paragraphs chronologically. Otherwise, move from your simplest response to your most complicated, or from your least powerful point to your most powerful.

3. **Concluding Paragraph.** Restate your generalization in new terms. Leave readers with a strong impression of your main response.

Evaluating and Revising

Use these questions to evaluate and revise your essay.

1. Does your introduction catch your readers' attention and clearly state your general response?

2. Is your generalization valid? Does it cover all the specifics you've cited?

3. Have you explained your generalization with enough specifics (including examples and quotations)?

4. Do your paragraphs follow a logical order?

5. Have you worked your quotations smoothly into your sentences?

Proofreading and Publishing

Proofread to eliminate errors in grammar and mechanics. Then make a final copy of your essay. Organize the response essays into a class literary journal for everyone to read.

Writing: Remind students that a thesis statement is usually expressed in a single, declarative sentence. The thesis should both set forth and limit the topic of the essay. Offer the following examples of appropriate thesis statements for essays expressing personal responses to literature.

- *The imagery in* Sundiata *is at least as compelling as the imagery in my favorite action-adventure movie.*
- *The punchline is not the only part of "Talk" that appeals to my sense of humor; the style in which the tale is recounted kept me chuckling from the first line to the last.*

Evaluating and Revising: Remind students to be sure that all material taken directly from the selection is enclosed within quotation marks. Refer them to the *Language Skills* feature entitled "Using Quotations Effectively," pp. 120–121, for details on incorporating quoted material smoothly and punctuating it correctly.

Proofreading and Publishing: Explain that a literary journal is a written compilation of responses evoked by literary works. By keeping a class literary journal and browsing through it as the semester progresses, students will be able to track their responses to literature and share ideas and experiences with one another. ∎

HUMANITIES CONNECTION

The following annotations are for the artwork surrounding the map, starting in the upper right-hand corner and moving in a counterclockwise direction.

Lion of Babylon: This lion was part of a glazed brick panel (c. 575 B.C.). Because mud and clay were readily available, bricks were popular building materials in Mesopotamia, and the Sumerians learned how to make bricks in molds very early in their culture. The Babylonians, who came to power after the Sumerians, often decorated walls with glazed brickwork of many colors.

Sumerians with Livestock: In this detail from the *Royal Standard of Ur* (c. 2500 B.C.), commoners are shown bringing gifts of livestock and fish to the gods. Sheep, goats, oxen, donkeys, and dogs were domesticated by the Sumerians. See p. 131 for a fuller view of the *Royal Standard of Ur*, an important relic of the Sumerian culture.

Scorpion Man: This scene is from an inlay on a harp (c. 2600 B.C.) The Scorpion Man, who appears in the *Epic of Gilgamesh*, was a common Mesopotamian motif. Here he is shown with a gazelle. You may wish to have students name other half-human, half-animal creatures they are familiar with, such as the minotaur and satyr of ancient Greece or the fabled mermaid.

124

UNIT 3

THE ANCIENT MIDDLE EAST

▼ **Time** ▼
c. 3000 B.C.–A.D. 100

▼ **Place** ▼
The Ancient Middle East

▼ **Literary Significance** ▼

Mesopotamian Literature: Sumerian and Babylonian literature consists of hymns, laments, dirges, proverbs, essays, rules of conduct, fables, myths, and epic tales. The most famous surviving work from the ancient cultures of Mesopotamia is a long narrative poem about a king named Gilgamesh, which may be the world's oldest epic.

Hebrew Literature: The Hebrew Bible, known to Christians as the Old Testament, is both the great sacred text of the Hebrews and the chronicle of their history. It contains examples of many diverse literary forms, from psalms, or sacred hymns, to historical narratives and proverbs.

Tree of Knowledge: Taken from the archbishop of Salzburg's missal (1481) this illustration of Adam's and Eve's temptation in the Garden of Eden (p. 165) exemplifies the enduring influence of Hebrew literature on European culture. ❓ *What do you know about the Tree of Knowledge from the account of the Fall in the Hebrew Bible?* (Possible response: Adam's and Eve's breaking of God's prohibition against eating from the tree led to their expulsion from Eden.)

Harpist: In Mesopotamia, as in ancient Greece and medieval Ireland, the harp was a major musical instrument used by bards while singing legends.

Exiled Israelites: This artwork is from a bas-relief depicting the Assyrian king Sennacherib driving the Israelites out of Israel in 701 B.C. Sennacherib is also known for destroying the city of Babylon and conquering the Phoenician cities of Sidon and Tyre. He proceeded toward Egypt until some mysterious reversal, perhaps a plague, made his army suddenly turn and go back.

Noah's Ark: This illustration of Noah's Ark was taken from the first book ever printed on a printing press, the *Gutenberg Bible* (c. 1456). From the time of the earliest civilization of the Sumerians, floods from the Euphrates River were an ever-present danger. The story of the flood appears in the *Epic of Gilgamesh* (p. 145), as well as in *Genesis* (p. 171). ■

125

Events similar to those shown here were occurring in Egypt, as outlined on the Time Line of Africa (pp. 62–63). Students may note, for example, what was happening in the Middle East at the time of the building of the pyramids or of Akhenaten's rule. Later, when they study Greek and Roman literature, students will notice that certain events have been recorded occurring on all three time lines (the conquests of Alexander the Great, Roman rule, the beginning of Christianity). Seeing these connections will help students appreciate the intricate relationship between the ancient Mediterranean and the Middle East. City-states, kingdoms, and empires fought one another, each achieving dominance for a time and then relinquishing it. Virtually all the major cultures in the area influenced one another through conquest, trade, and intellectual contact.

CULTURAL BACKGROUND

Writing: Literacy may have begun with the Sumerians' inscription of cuneiform on clay tablets. If so, how long has the human race been literate? (about 5,500 years) Picture-writing at first, cuneiform in time became stylized symbols that stood for sounds. What were some of the early writings of the Ancient Middle East? (Hammurabi's Code, the *Epic of Gilgamesh*, the Torah, the Book of Ruth, Psalms, the Hebrew Bible, the New Testament) What was the time period during which the Hebrew Bible was written? (c. 1010–300 B.C.)

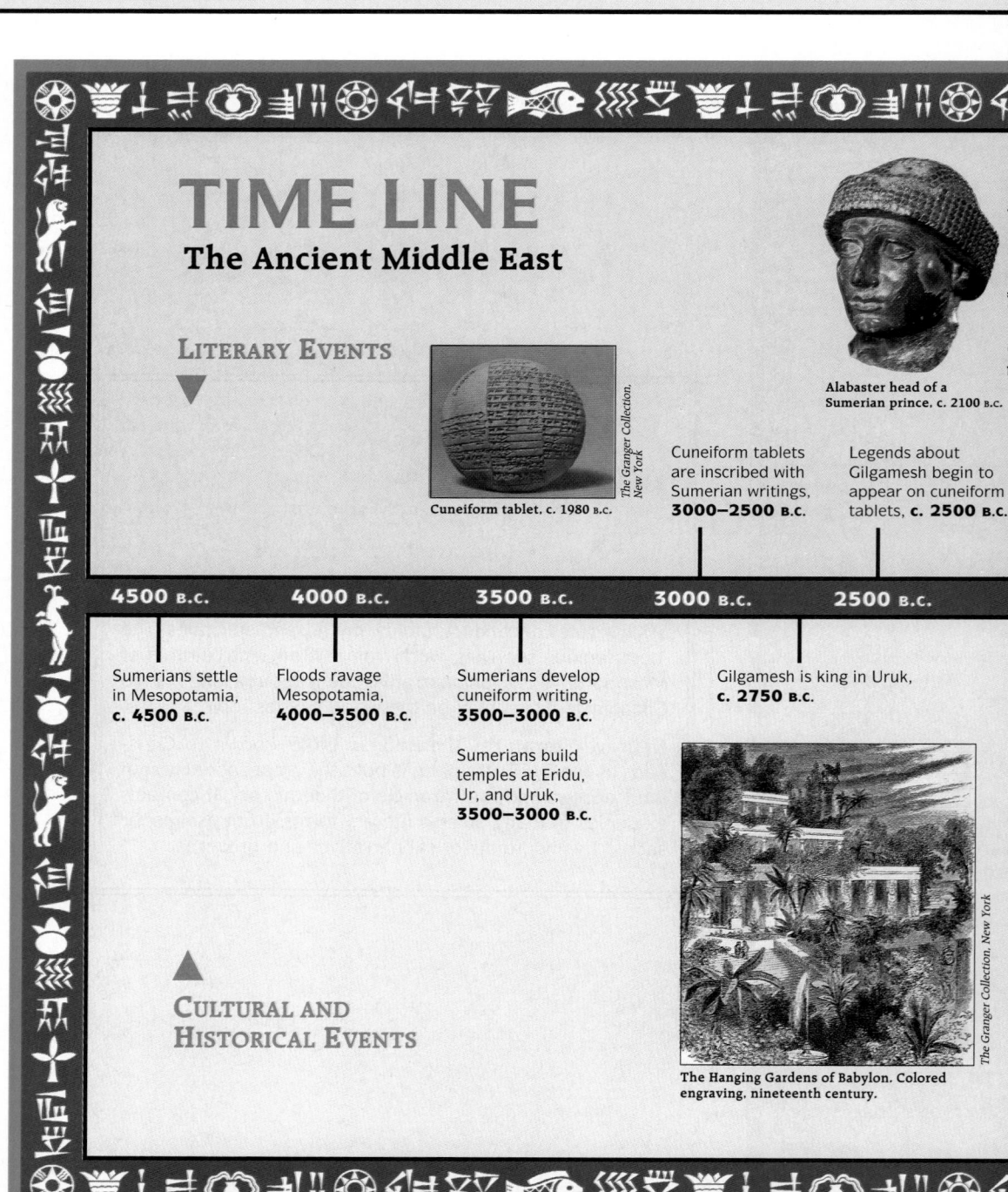

TIME LINE
The Ancient Middle East

▼ **LITERARY EVENTS**

Cuneiform tablet. c. 1980 B.C.
The Granger Collection, New York

Alabaster head of a Sumerian prince. c. 2100 B.C.
The Granger Collection, New York

Cuneiform tablets are inscribed with Sumerian writings, **3000–2500 B.C.**

Legends about Gilgamesh begin to appear on cuneiform tablets, **c. 2500 B.C.**

4500 B.C.	4000 B.C.	3500 B.C.	3000 B.C.	2500 B.C.

Sumerians settle in Mesopotamia, **c. 4500 B.C.**

Floods ravage Mesopotamia, **4000–3500 B.C.**

Sumerians develop cuneiform writing, **3500–3000 B.C.**

Sumerians build temples at Eridu, Ur, and Uruk, **3500–3000 B.C.**

Gilgamesh is king in Uruk, **c. 2750 B.C.**

▲ **CULTURAL AND HISTORICAL EVENTS**

The Hanging Gardens of Babylon. Colored engraving. nineteenth century.
The Granger Collection, New York

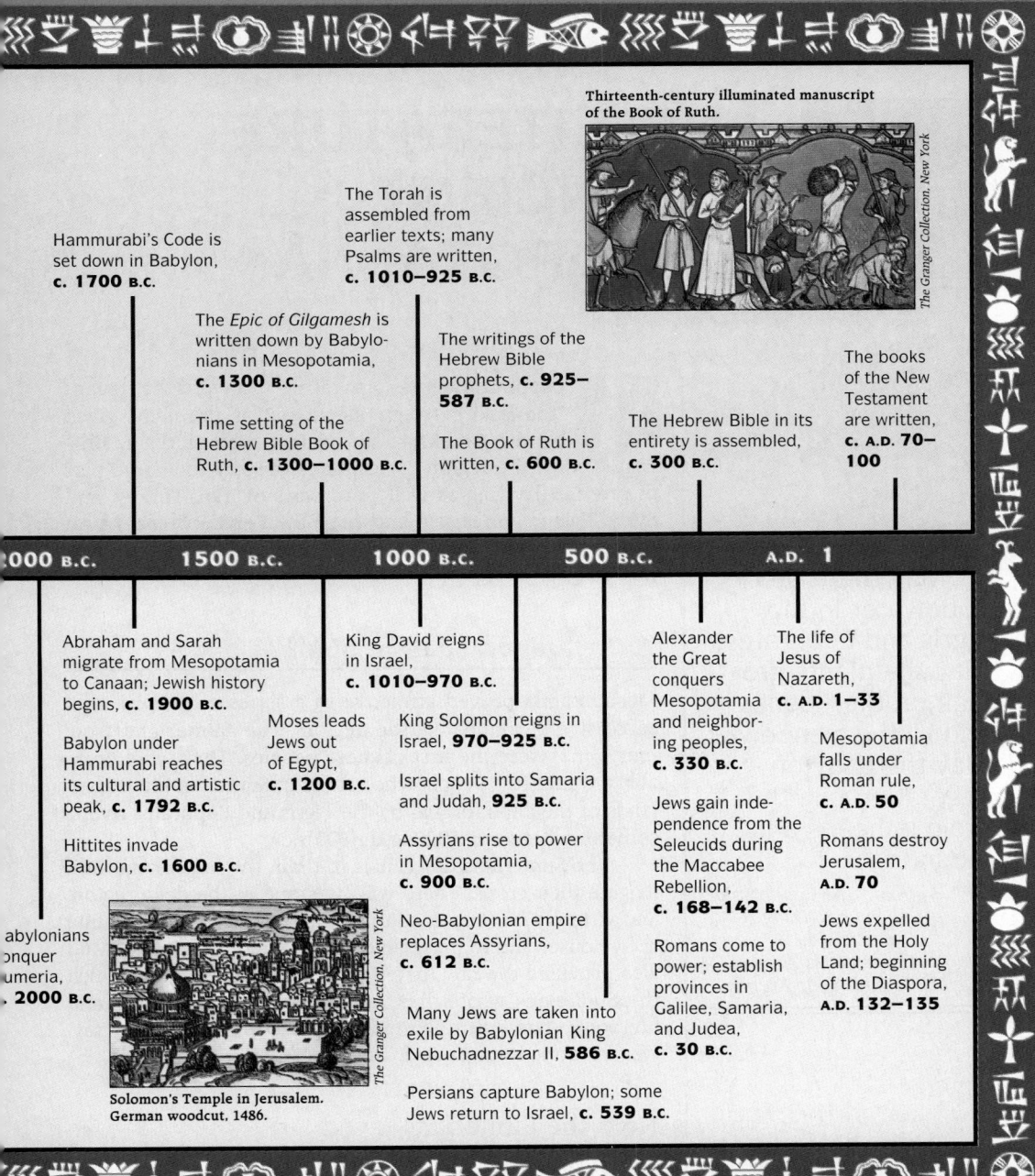

Thirteenth-century illuminated manuscript of the Book of Ruth.

The Granger Collection, New York

Hammurabi's Code is set down in Babylon, **c. 1700 B.C.**

The *Epic of Gilgamesh* is written down by Babylonians in Mesopotamia, **c. 1300 B.C.**

Time setting of the Hebrew Bible Book of Ruth, **c. 1300–1000 B.C.**

The Torah is assembled from earlier texts; many Psalms are written, **c. 1010–925 B.C.**

The writings of the Hebrew Bible prophets, **c. 925–587 B.C.**

The Book of Ruth is written, **c. 600 B.C.**

The Hebrew Bible in its entirety is assembled, **c. 300 B.C.**

The books of the New Testament are written, **c. A.D. 70–100**

2000 B.C.	1500 B.C.	1000 B.C.	500 B.C.	A.D. 1

Abraham and Sarah migrate from Mesopotamia to Canaan; Jewish history begins, **c. 1900 B.C.**

Babylon under Hammurabi reaches its cultural and artistic peak, **c. 1792 B.C.**

Hittites invade Babylon, **c. 1600 B.C.**

abylonians onquer umeria, **, 2000 B.C.**

Moses leads Jews out of Egypt, **c. 1200 B.C.**

King David reigns in Israel, **c. 1010–970 B.C.**

King Solomon reigns in Israel, **970–925 B.C.**

Israel splits into Samaria and Judah, **925 B.C.**

Assyrians rise to power in Mesopotamia, **c. 900 B.C.**

Neo-Babylonian empire replaces Assyrians, **c. 612 B.C.**

Many Jews are taken into exile by Babylonian King Nebuchadnezzar II, **586 B.C.**

Persians capture Babylon; some Jews return to Israel, **c. 539 B.C.**

Alexander the Great conquers Mesopotamia and neighboring peoples, **c. 330 B.C.**

Jews gain independence from the Seleucids during the Maccabee Rebellion, **c. 168–142 B.C.**

Romans come to power; establish provinces in Galilee, Samaria, and Judea, **c. 30 B.C.**

The life of Jesus of Nazareth, **c. A.D. 1–33**

Mesopotamia falls under Roman rule, **c. A.D. 50**

Romans destroy Jerusalem, **A.D. 70**

Jews expelled from the Holy Land; beginning of the Diaspora, **A.D. 132–135**

Solomon's Temple in Jerusalem. German woodcut, 1486.

The Granger Collection, New York

HISTORICAL BACKGROUND

Predecessors: In the crucial prehistoric period called the Neolithic Age (several thousand years before the period of this time line), some important events in the development of the human race occurred in this region. About 9000 B.C., people living in the foothills of the Zagros Mountains (northeast of Mesopotamia) were among the world's first cultivators of grain and domesticators of sheep. Before 7000 B.C., Jericho, perhaps the world's first city, was built in what is today Israel. Irrigation, division of labor, and organized worship were other innovations of the age. It was a period of migrations, during which farmers and shepherds from the north and later Semitic nomads from Syria and Arabia entered Mesopotamia. These people paved the way for the impressive Sumerian civilization, with its city-states, massive architecture, and creation of cuneiform in the 3000s B.C.

CULTURAL BACKGROUND

The Hanging Gardens of Babylon: In the sixth century B.C., the Babylonian king Nebuchadnezzar II built one of the Seven Wonders of the World, the famous Hanging Gardens of Babylon. These gardens appeared to float above the rooftops of the palace. They were, in fact, terraced gardens lined with lead and irrigated by water pumped from the Euphrates River. What problems must the architect have dealt with in designing these gardens? (Possible response: the weight of soil, seepage of water into the rooms below)

This time line border depicts images derived from Sumerian cuneiform. Invented around 3500 B.C., cuneiform is considered the world's oldest system of writing.

OBJECTIVES
1. *To gain an overview of Mesopotamian culture, philosophy, and history*
2. *To read excerpts from a Mesopotamian epic and to determine the epic's themes and the characteristics of its hero*
3. *To respond to Mesopotamian literature and culture both orally and in writing*

TEACHER'S RESOURCES: 3

✔ Unit Introduction Test
✔ Word Analogies
✔ Unit Review Test
✔ Critical Thinking and Writing

1 GEOGRAPHICAL BACKGROUND

Tigris and Euphrates: The Euphrates River is 1,800 miles long, and the Tigris is 1,150. Tributaries and mountain passes form links to neighboring regions such as Persia (Iran) and Asia Minor (Turkey). Within the land area of Mesopotamia itself, climate and soil vary greatly. In the northwest, the soil is rocky, but there is enough rain for the cultivation of olive trees; farther south, on the alluvial plain, irrigation becomes necessary, and dates are the major crop. Marshes and lakes dominate the landscape at the lower ends of the rivers.

2 RESPONDING TO THE QUOTATION

According to a Sumerian myth, the goddess Inanna, the queen of heaven, charmed a god into giving her the arts of civilization, which she presented to the Sumerians. Inanna's courtship of Dumuzi, the shepherd-god, ended in her preferring Enkimdu, the farmer-god.

❓ *What cultural change might be reflected in a myth in which a goddess prefers a farmer-god to a shepherd-god?* (the adoption of agriculture by people who had been shepherds) *In what ways did the rivers make the Sumerian civilization possible?* (Possible response: By supplying water for irrigation in the hot, dry climate, and by depositing silt that led to fertile soil, the rivers provided arable land.)

THE LITERATURE OF ANCIENT MESOPOTAMIA

Mesopotamia (mes′ə·pə·tā′mē·ə), a word that means "the land between the rivers," is the name given by the Greeks to an ancient area of the Middle East. Today, the region corresponds roughly to a large part of present-day Iraq as well as to parts of Iran, Turkey, and Syria. This region is also known as the **Fertile Crescent**, an agriculturally rich land watered by the **Tigris** and **Euphrates** (yoo·frāt′ēz) rivers.

1

> ❝ May there be floodwater in the Tigris and Euphrates,/ May the plants grow high on their banks and fill the meadows,/ May the Lady of Vegetation pile the grain in heaps and mounds. ❞
>
> —from "The Courtship of Inanna and Dumuzi" translated by Diane Wolkstein and Samuel Noah Kramer

2

A Civilization Built on Mud

Mesopotamia proved attractive to a series of peoples who successively dominated the region. The **Sumerians** (soo·mer′ē·ənz) were the first of these peoples. They were probably a wandering people who settled in Sumer, in the marshlands of the delta formed by the Tigris and Euphrates rivers, sometime between 5000 and 4000 B.C.

The Sumerians dug canals to drain the marshlands and irrigate their crops. There was no stone in the delta region, and virtually no timber, so the Sumerians used mud to build their houses and to make an excellent grade of pottery. Mud also provided the raw material for the clay tablets on which the Sumerians wrote their laws, financial transactions, and literature. The entire Sumerian civilization, one might say, was fashioned out of river mud.

How the Sumerians Lived

The Sumerians made their living mainly by growing crops, such as wheat and barley, and by raising cattle, goats, and sheep. They developed a reputation as successful merchants

Of all the cultures discussed in this textbook, that of Mesopotamia may seem the most remote to your students at first. Assure students, however, that the many ancient cuneiform tablets that have survived reveal the Sumerians of Mesopotamia as a people much like ourselves. They valued humor, beauty, courage, and self-discipline, and made remarkable achievements in science and commerce. The cultural base for this society, as for our own, was the school, which they called the *edubba*. Due to extensive archaeological findings, scholars know much more about the edubba than they do about later Greek and Roman schools. Unlike in our culture, however, only a small fraction of Mesopotamian youngsters went to school—those who were to become scribes. Students who attended the edubba were often the sons of high officials or of successful scribes. To illustrate to your students that the experiences of those ancient students were not much different from their own, ask two students to read the following snippet of conversation between a father and his truant son, taken from an ancient cuneiform tablet:

"Where did you go?"

"I did not go anywhere."

"Why do you idle about? Go to school. . . . Don't stand about in the public square or wander about the boulevard. . . ."

The Granger Collection, New York

Sumerian bronze lintel. *This lintel—the top part of a doorframe—was mounted over the main entrance of a temple, c. 2500 B.C.*

and traders, and they were known for their beautiful stonework, metalwork, and sculpture. They had many goods to trade with their neighbors on the Persian Gulf.

> The Sumerians achieved a high level of culture. With farming and trade as their economic base, they were able to turn their energies to artistic accomplishments.

3 The Sumerians lived in **city-states**, each consisting of a large town or city and its surrounding lands. These city-states were walled for protection against invaders. Archaeological finds show that the city-states were laid out around
4 great pyramidlike temples called **ziggurats** (zig′oo·ratz′). The ziggurats were six or seven stories high, layered rather like a wedding cake, and probably brightly decorated, with each story, or layer, painted a different color. In each city, the ziggurat was presided over by a priest-king, whom the people regarded as the earthly representative of the local god. Some of the ancient ziggurats are still standing in Iraq today.

Albright-Knox Art Gallery, Buffalo, New York, Charles Clifton Fund, 1937

Female Worshiper, Sumerian. Early Dynasty III, c. 2800–2550 B.C.

The Sumerians depicted animals and human beings in sculptures and wall reliefs of bronze or stone. These materials had to be imported from hundreds of miles away.

? *How would you characterize the sculpture of the Sumerians based on this example?* (Possible response: detailed, realistic) ■

3 HISTORICAL BACKGROUND

City-State: The independent city-state was a recurring institution in the ancient world. It may have first emerged in Sumer, where each city-state had its own written code of law, assembly of citizens, king, and chief god. *What are some advantages and disadvantages of city-states?* (Possible response: advantage—unity within a small, self-contained community; disadvantage— lack of resource-sharing and mutual defense with neighbors in the region)

4 CULTURAL BACKGROUND

Ziggurats and Pyramids: Mesopotamian ziggurats differed from Egyptian pyramids. The pyramids were royal tombs made of stone with networks of rooms within. Ziggurats were solid clay structures, which functioned only as foundations for temples. The triangular pyramids ended in an apex; ziggurats were flat-topped and had exterior steps for worshipers to climb to reach the temples above.

Also read aloud this Mesopotamian eulogy from a student about a teacher who "guided my hand on the clay, showed me how to behave properly, opened my mouth with words, uttered good counsel, focused my eyes on the rules that guide the man of achievement."

Tell your students that the Sumerians invented true writing, and have students look at a sample of cuneiform writing on p. 153. Explain that this highly sophisticated form of writing required years of practice to master. For the scribes-in-training, school days lasted from sunrise to sundown, with six days off per lunar month. The students were all males, though a few records refer to a woman scribe and a woman doctor; they may have been privately educated. Ask your students to speculate about the curriculum stressed in this school for scribes. Then tell them that language, grammar, and writing were most important, but law, medicine, arithmetic, and geometry were also studied. The Sumerians not only had a practical need for mathematics to perform their commercial and architectural calculations, but they also engaged in theoretical mathematics. At first, cuneiform tablets were used solely for commercial record-keeping, but within a few generations, some of the world's earliest literature was being written in cuneiform. The

5

> ❝ No matter where the Sumerians came from, and whatever type of culture they brought with them, this much is certain: their arrival led to an extraordinary ethnic and cultural fusion with the native population that brought about a major creative spurt for the history of civilization. ❞
>
> —*Samuel Noah Kramer*

Scala/Art Resource, New York

Statue of a woman, Sumerian.

In fact, during the Persian Gulf Conflict in 1991, allied pilots were instructed not to bomb these ancient structures. The Iraqi Air Force, knowing that allied bombers would be reluctant to bomb anywhere near these sites, parked their own jets under the protective shadow of these ancient archaeological treasures.

The largest Sumerian city-states, such as Ur, Uruk, and Lagash, had populations in the tens of thousands. Many of the city-states were within sight of one another. Yet, the Sumerians seem never to have developed a central, unifying government. Because of this lack of a unifying political force, the city-states often competed against one another for land and precious resources.

Sumerian Society and Cultural Achievements

Sumerian society was based on a strict, three-level class system. At the top of the social ladder were the nobles, who mainly consisted of the priests and government officials. Below them were the members of the Sumerian "middle class," the merchants and artisans, as well as professional people such as doctors. At the bottom of the Sumerian social structure were the peasants—most of whom were farmers—and the slaves.

The Sumerians achieved a high level of culture. They had an advanced knowledge of architecture, as their ziggurats and other buildings show. Their knowledge of science and mathematics enabled them to develop a mathematical system based on a unit of sixty. They also created a remarkably precise twelve-month calendar based on cycles of the moon.

Sumerian Cuneiform: "Wedge-Writing"

Of all their innovations, the development of one of the world's first systems of writing was probably the Sumerians' chief cultural achievement. They wrote on clay tablets using a type of writing that we call **cuneiform** (kyo͞o·nē′ə·fôrm′), from the Latin word *cuneus*, meaning "wedge." Cuneiform was a system of wedge-shaped markings made with a pointed stick, or **stylus**.

6

literature of Mesopotamia is both personal and philosophical. Inform students that the Sumerians kept journals and wrote love poetry as well as letters of complaint. They were also concerned with questions of justice: Mesopotamia may have been the first civilization to uphold the rights of the oppressed individual. The Sumerians questioned the unfairness of the world in philosophical works that were precursors of the biblical Book of Job. They lived in an unpredictable environment. The Tigris and Euphrates rivers that gave life to the fertile valleys would also flood their banks from time to time, destroying crops and property. As a result, the Sumerians tended to view life as uncertain and fraught with difficulties. To them, life seemed beyond human control and full of pain as well as pleasure. In the *Epic of Gilgamesh* (p. 136), the poet grapples with the biggest question of all: the mystery of death. The answer proposed is strangely similar to the one expressed thousands of years later, in the twelfth century Persian poem, the *Rubáiyát* of Omar Khayyám (p. 654).

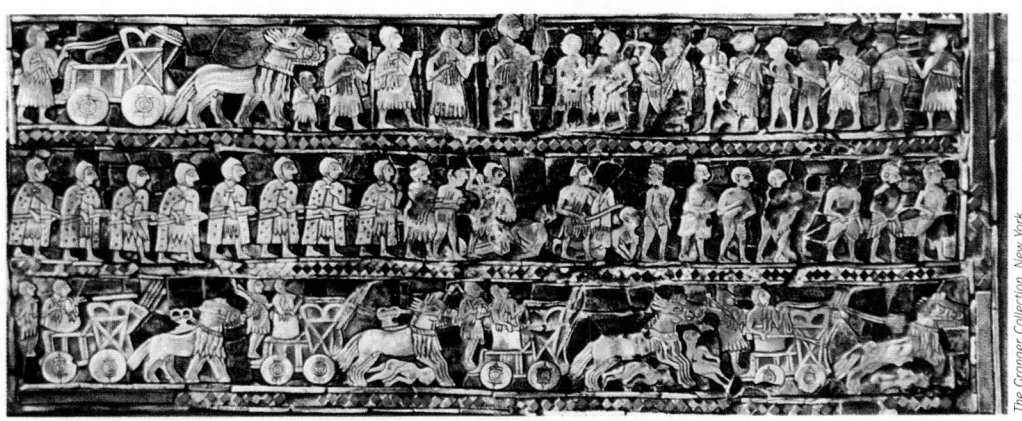

The Granger Collection, New York

THE ROYAL STANDARD OF UR, c. 2500 B.C. *This portion of the standard depicts a military victory.*

Tens of thousands of clay tablets have been excavated since the end of the last century, and many more tablets may still be awaiting discovery. The majority of tablets

> The Sumerians developed one of the world's first writing systems, called *cuneiform*, a system of wedge-shaped markings.

contain financial transactions and other examples of practical record keeping. But thousands more of the tablets contain imaginative literature, including myths, epics, hymns, laments, proverbs, and fables.

Waves of Invaders

Perhaps because the Sumerians failed to form a unified government of all their city-states, they were vulnerable to invaders. A succession of different peoples dominated Mesopotamia after the Sumerians. First came the **Akkadians** (ə·kā'dē·ənz), a Semitic people. Under their king, **Sargon**, the Akkadians established a great empire that lasted nearly a century. Thanks mostly to a famous Sumerian ruler named **Gudea**, Sumerian culture managed to rebound for a short

7

MAKING CONNECTIONS

Mesopotamian influence on modern Western civilizations is more pervasive than most people realize. This influence has come to us largely through the ancient Hebrew civilization, which absorbed much of Mesopotamian culture. Students familiar with the Hebrew Bible will perceive this connection readily. They may experience a shock of recognition at learning, for instance, that in the Mesopotamian lunar calendar, the day of the full moon was a day of rest, called *sapatty*. The Hebrews took the concept a step further when they decreed a day of rest every seven days, the *shabbat*. The phonic similarity to the English word *sabbath* will be obvious. An important segment of Western history began when Abraham and his followers set out for Canaan. Abraham was born as Abram, a resident of Ur, a major Mesopotamian city. Both before and after Abraham, the history of the Hebrews was intertwined with that of the Mesopotamians. For example, many students will be familiar with the biblical story of Noah and the Flood (p. 170). Earlier Mesopotamian mythology also contained stories of a great flood that washed away most of humanity. Such stories seem connected to the geohistorical fact that the Euphrates, like the Nile, did indeed flood regularly. Archaeologists have found evidence of several destructive floods in

The Granger Collection, New York

Sumerian bronze of a harnessed chariot, c. 3000–2000 B.C. Disunity among the various city-states left the Sumerians vulnerable to invasion by neighboring peoples.
? **How did elements of Sumerian culture survive in spite of the arrival of successive waves of invaders?**

Inscribed relief of Assurbanipal.

time after the Akkadian empire ended. But then a second wave of Semitic invaders arrived on the scene. These newcomers established a magnificent new capital city on the banks of the Euphrates River and called it **Babylon**, meaning "gate of the gods."

The Rise of Babylon

The Babylonians, as the builders of Babylon came to be called, suppressed the Sumerians politically, removing all their power. By 2000 B.C. the Sumerians no longer existed as an independent people. But the Babylonians recognized the value of Sumerian culture and adopted it as their own. They adapted the Sumerian cuneiform script to their own Semitic language and translated many of the Sumerian writings, including the fragmented story of a great king called Gilgamesh, who searched the world for the secret of eternal life. The Babylonians continued to use Sumerian as a literary language, much as Europeans used Latin during the Middle Ages.

In addition to the *Epic of Gilgamesh*, the literature of Babylon included creation myths, hymns, and stories of the

the region at periods prior to these written accounts.

From the Hebrew Bible, we have also received largely negative views of the Babylonians, Assyrians, and Hittites, all enemies of the Hebrew people. These same peoples, however, produced magnificent architectural monuments, beautiful artifacts and sculpture, and a tradition of learning and law. The Babylonians were the great astronomers of the ancient world, having identified and named some twenty-five stars. The Mesopotamian system of counting in units of sixty is still used in our system of timekeeping and of measuring the circle. The Mesopotamians' geometry and observations of nature enabled them to construct great pyramid-like structures and to turn mud and marsh into irrigated agricultural land. (A fascinating parallel exists between the step pyramids and base-sixty mathematics of the Mesopotamians and those of the later Mayans.) In addition, the Mesopotamians used herbal remedies in their medical practice.

Law is another area in which we owe a great deal to Mesopotamian culture. Hammurabi's Code was a major influence on Mosaic law. It is easy to criticize the harshness of Hammurabi's Code since some of the punishments prescribed are stricter than in earlier Sumerian law. How-

---

Great Flood. The Babylonian style was known for its use of parallelism (see page 195), which resulted in a balanced literary structure similar to the Hebrew, or biblical, style.

In about 1792 B.C., under the reign of **Hammurabi** (hä′moo·rä′bē), the sixth Babylonian ruler, Babylon reached the peak of its glory, becoming the religious and cultural center of western Asia. Today, Hammurabi is most famous for creating a set of laws known as the **Code of Hammurabi**, a collection of 282 laws that regulated every aspect of Babylonian life, from building codes to marriage and divorce. The Code of Hammurabi was highly detailed and harshly punitive. It was based on the unyielding concept of "an eye for an eye, a tooth for a tooth."

The Great Library of Nineveh

In about 1600 B.C., the **Hittites**, a warlike group of conquerors from Asia Minor, invaded Mesopotamia and looted Babylon. Although they did not hold on to Babylon permanently, the Hittites left behind their laws, which were less drastic than the Code of Hammurabi. After the Hittites, Babylon suffered invasion after invasion by mountain peoples looking for a better life in the rich Tigris-Euphrates Valley. Then, in about 900 B.C., the **Assyrians** (ə·sir′ē·ənz) came into Mesopotamia.

The Assyrians were fiercely warlike and feared throughout the ancient world. However, like many conquerors

THE DRAGON OF MARDUK from the Ishtar Gate, Babylonian.

Founders Society Purchase, Detroit Institute of Arts

❝ I will proclaim to the world the deeds of Gilgamesh. This was the man to whom all things were known; this was the king who knew the countries of the world. He was wise, he saw mysteries and knew secret things. . . . **❞**

—from the Epic of Gilgamesh, translated by N. K. Sandars

---

8 HISTORICAL BACKGROUND

Hammurabi's Code: The famous Code was not the first of its kind, but it was the most extensive and specified the most severe punishments. Perjury, adultery, sorcery, and receiving stolen goods were capital offenses. Most of the laws, however, regulated commerce, land tenure, and marriage and family life. There were also provisions to help victims of floods and robbery. Women were treated fairly by the standards of the time.

■ HUMANITIES CONNECTION

The Ishtar Gate was a ceremonial gate to the city of Babylon, made of colored glazed tiles and dedicated to the goddess Ishtar. A walled, 80-foot-wide avenue paved with limestone and pink marble led up to the gate. The avenue was used for processions in honor of the god Marduk, the Babylonian creator god.

❓ *Compare and contrast the Mesopotamian dragon to dragons in other cultures. (Possible response: Dragons of the Middle Ages appeared to be more monstrous and fiery.)* ■

ever, Hammurabi also took action to protect widows, orphans, mistreated slaves, and private citizens who had been cheated by the rich and powerful. Establishing a uniform standard was in itself a constructive innovation that has lasted.

Mesopotamian cuneiform writing influenced the Phoenician syllabic alphabet and, through the Phoenician, the Greek and Hebrew alphabets. Commerce was a major vehicle for cross-cultural contacts.

Because Mesopotamia imported wood, stone, and metal, and paid for it by exporting wool, grain, and dates, trade networks were established that helped turn the diverse cultures of the ancient world into an interactive system.

READING CHECK

1. Who were the first known people to settle in Mesopotamia? (the Sumerians)
2. What was the system of writing developed by the Sumerians? (cuneiform)
3. In what great city did Nebuchadnezzar build his Hanging Gardens? (Babylon)
4. What is Hammurabi known for? (a code of law)
5. What great city did the Assyrians create? (Nineveh)

9 HISTORICAL BACKGROUND

Assurbanipal: This least modest of monarchs called himself "King of the Universe" and claimed to have been reared by the gods. A priest, scholar, and fearsome soldier, he spent his spare time hunting lions with a spear, ringed by armed soldiers. The ruins of Nineveh contain beautifully carved alabaster wall reliefs illustrating Assurbanipal's feats, with words of praise that he wrote himself, with the aid of scribes.

HUMANITIES CONNECTION

The Mesopotamians were musical innovators who used their knowledge of mathematics to create a geometric progression of notes. Their major instruments were the lyre, harp, drums, pipes, and trumpets. Many ornately carved lyres have been found in the royal cemetery of Ur.

❓ *What connection might there be between the scenes on this lyre and the music that the lyre's players created?* (Possible response: Bards may have sung of mythological subjects.) ∎

The University Museum, University of Pennsylvania, #T4-109

Front of a lyre, Mesopotamian. *This ornately decorated lyre features mythological figures, including the epic hero Gilgamesh (top).*

throughout history, they appreciated the accomplishments of the culture they had conquered, and they preserved its richness. The Assyrians built their capital, **Nineveh** (nin′ə·və), on the banks of the Tigris, about 230 miles north

> The Babylonians and Hittites left their cultural imprint on the civilization established by the Sumerians. But it was the brutal and warlike Assyrians who ultimately preserved the Mesopotamian literary legacy.

of present-day Baghdad. There, by decree of **King Assurbanipal**, they created a magnificent library in which they carefully stored and preserved the clay tablets containing Sumerian and Babylonian literature. Archaeologists uncovered the remains of this library in the ruins of Nineveh. Tablets containing the priceless remains of Sumerian/Babylonian writings were excavated from these ruins in the middle of the eighteenth century. In fact, it was through the ruins of the Assyrian civilization that archaeologists got their very first glimpse of Mesopotamia's rich and ancient past.

The Rebirth and Final Fall of Babylon

In 612 B.C. the Assyrians' combined enemies, led by the **Chaldeans** (kal·dē′ənz), overthrew them. After the Chaldeans took control of Mesopotamia, Babylon rose once again to enjoy a period of further glory. The Chaldean ruler **Nebuchadnezzar** (neb′yə·kəd·nez′ər) rebuilt the city, creating spectacular palaces and temples of glazed multicolored bricks. Under Nebuchadnezzar's reign, Babylon became known for its Hanging Gardens, one of the Seven Wonders of the World recognized by the ancient Greeks. (According to legend, the king built the huge tiered "mountain"—really a ziggurat—that supported the hanging gardens as a gift to his wife, Amytis, who longed for her wooded and mountainous homeland.) Babylon was also known for a great ziggurat that some historians have identified as the "Tower

9

FOR FURTHER STUDY

Nonfiction

Eminent authority Samuel Noah Kramer has written several books, including *The Sumerians* and *Cradle of Civilization*, the latter a well-illustrated entry in the Time-Life *Great Ages of Man* series. H. W. F. Saggs' *Everyday Life in Babylonia and Assyria* has similarly stood the test of thirty years.

Fiction

John Gardner's 1972 novel *The Sunlight Dialogues*, though set in twentieth-century America, uses the *Epic of Gilgamesh* as a major leitmotif.

Film

Michael Woods' *Legacy* television series on PBS contains an excellent segment on the Sumerian culture and shows the ruin of a ziggurat. ■

of Babel," mentioned in the Hebrew Bible as the tower built by the survivors of the Great Flood. ("Babel" was the Hebrew name for Babylon.) Nebuchadnezzar was the king who destroyed Jerusalem and kept the Jews captive in Babylon for seventy years.

Babylon, which once flourished on the site of the modern-day Iraqi city of al Hillah, fell to **Cyrus the Great** of Persia in 539 B.C. It remained a center of trade and culture for several centuries, until a new port was dug at a more favorable site on the Euphrates. After that, Babylon, the last of the great ancient Mesopotamian empires, fell into ruins.

> “ The Pyramids first, which in Egypt were laid;/Next Babylon's Garden, for Amytis made. . . . ”
>
> —from "Seven Wonders of the Ancient World," Anonymous

10

Robert Harding Picture Library

THE TOWER OF BABEL. *From a fifteenth-century illuminated manuscript. The legend of the tower may have been inspired by the architectural wonders of ancient Babylon.*

10 RESPONDING TO THE QUOTATION

❓ *If you were asked to draw up a list of seven wonders of the modern world, what would they be?* (Possible response: computers, spacecraft, artificial hearts, television, biogenetic laboratories, worldwide telephone communication systems)

HUMANITIES CONNECTION

In the Hebrew Bible, God punishes the overreaching ambition of the builders of the Tower of Babel by making the workers speak in a bewildering confusion of languages.

❓ *How does this story reflect the actual ethnic history of the city?* (Babylon, built by Semitic invaders, was also home at various times to Sumerians, Assyrians, Chaldeans, Jews, and Persians.) ■

TEACHING TIP

Invite students to draw up a written code of laws for present-day American high schools. In discussion, compare and contrast the spirit of the student-drawn codes with that of Hammurabi.

WRITING TO LEARN

Social Studies: Imagine you are a scribe from any era of Mesopotamian history. Write a paragraph that will go on a wall relief, describing the wonders of your society. Then, write a note to a friend describing a social problem. ■

The *Epic of Gilgamesh* was one of the most influential pieces of literature of the ancient world. Some scholars speculate that Enkidu and Gilgamesh served as prototypes for Hercules, the Greek slayer of monsters, and that their friendship served as a model for that of Achilles and Patroclus in the *Iliad*.

Obvious parallels exist between *Gilgamesh* and the Hebrew Bible, which share the same cultural and geographical roots. The description of the Garden of Eden in Genesis (pp. 165–166) reads much like that of the "garden of the gods" in *Gilgamesh* (p. 143); and the flood accounts of *Gilgamesh* and Genesis ("Noah and the Flood," pp. 171–175) parallel each other in many details. Even some of the values expressed in the *Epic of Gilgamesh* are echoed in late Hebrew writing. For example, in *Gilgamesh*, Siduri advises the weary Gilgamesh that, since death is the lot of all human beings, he should feast, dance, and make his wife happy while he can (p. 144). The Hebrew poet of Ecclesiastes (c. 250 B.C.) writes: ". . . one and the same fate befalls every man. . . . [The dead] are utterly forgotten. . . . Go to it then, eat your food and enjoy it, and drink your wine with a cheerful heart. . . . Enjoy life with a woman you love all the days of your allotted span here under the sun, . . . for that is your lot" (Ecclesiastes 9).

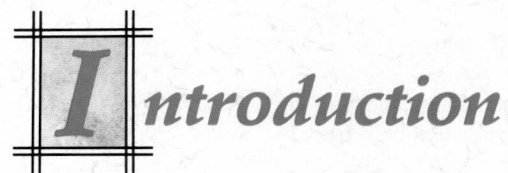

Introduction

The Epic of Gilgamesh

Written 4,000 years ago, the *Epic of Gilgamesh* is at least a thousand years older than the Greek epics the *Iliad* and the *Odyssey*, as well as most of the books of the Hebrew Bible. This tale of a superhuman Sumerian king was popular in ancient times throughout the Middle East. Today, its story of the king's painful search for everlasting life still touches readers deeply. Yet the epic lay forgotten for almost 2,500 years, until an amateur archaeologist stumbled upon it in 1839.

The Story of King Gilgamesh

Like most epics, the *Epic of Gilgamesh* is based on at least some grains of fact. Many scholars believe that Gilgamesh was an actual king who reigned over the city-state of Uruk, in Sumer, sometime between 2700 and 2500 B.C. Gradually, over the centuries, King Gilgamesh became a legendary figure of mythic proportions, rather like King Arthur in the European Middle Ages. Tales of Gilgamesh's exploits grew and were probably recited in verse for centuries before being recorded in writing. The earliest written fragments date from about 2000 B.C. Later, the tale was repeated and reworked by writers from the Sumerian, Babylonian, and Assyrian cultures. Some scholars believe that the epic was finally put into its most complete form by a scribe in 1300 B.C.

◆

epic: *a long narrative that recounts the deeds of a larger-than-life hero who embodies the values of a particular society.*

The Gilgamesh of the epic is a superhuman hero, two parts god and one part human. He thus possesses both supernatural powers and human weaknesses, and in many ways it is his human weaknesses that make him so interesting to us and to the ancient peoples who eagerly listened to and learned from his exploits. He is the leader of his people and the builder of a great city, yet he suffers from excessive pride. In fact, it is because he rejects the love of Ishtar, the goddess of love and war, and insults the gods that he suffers the death of his dear friend, Enkidu. Refusing to accept death, "the common lot of man," Gilgamesh embarks on a quest for immortality. With superhuman strength, courage, and persistence, he confronts obstacles along the way, but he must ultimately accept human limitations.

Giraudon/Art Resource, New York

Relief of Gilgamesh from the Temple of Sargon II, eighth century B.C.

Versions of the Epic

The selections from *Gilgamesh* presented here are based on twelve clay tablets of cuneiform script. These tablets were among 25,000 discovered in modern Iraq, at Nineveh, in the buried ruins of the library of King Assurbanipal of Assyria (669–626 B.C.). Nineveh was razed by Persian invaders in 612 B.C., and the original tablets were broken and marred. But the recent discovery of older versions of the epic has helped scholars to clarify many parts of the story that once were missing or vague.

Versions of the *Epic of Gilgamesh* have now been found at sites almost as far north as the Black Sea and as far south as Jerusalem, and from the Mediterranean coast eastward to the Persian Gulf. The epic was so widely known that many scholars believe it served as an **archetype**, or model, for hero myths that would appear later in Greece, India, and Persia.

The *Epic of Gilgamesh* reveals a great deal about the ancient Mesopotamians' sometimes pessimistic views of existence. But it also shows us the sensitivity and humanity of these ancient peoples, who are not unlike us in their joys, sorrows, and strivings.

The British Museum

Statue of the Sumerian king Gudea of Lagash, 2200 B.C.

HUMANITIES CONNECTION

In this relief, Gilgamesh is accompanied by a lion, a symbol of his strength. The lion has signified strength, courage, and status in many cultures. The figure of a lion helps to support the British Royal Arms. Gustavus Adolphus, the Swedish warrior-king of the seventeenth century, was known as "the lion of the North." Amenhotep III of ancient Egypt and Saint Louis of the Seventh Crusade hunted the lion to prove their bravery.

❓ *Where in this epic are lions featured in a demonstration of Gilgamesh's strength?* (He fends off lions in the mountain passes. See p. 142.) ∎

HUMANITIES CONNECTION

Gudea, the pious king of Sumeria who reigned around 2130 B.C., was dedicated to building temples to the gods of his city. In these temples Gudea put statues of himself and his family, and the statues prayed perpetually to the gods. One might suppose that the gods favored Gudea, as his reign was peaceful and prosperous, in contrast to the chaos reigning in neighboring areas. This statue was carved in diorite, a costly, very hard, black stone imported from India.

❓ *What can you deduce about King Gudea's character from the features and pose of this statue?* (Possible response: Gudea was a serene, powerful man.) ∎

OBJECTIVES

1. *To analyze episodes from a Mesopotamian epic*
2. *To recognize and analyze the qualities of an epic hero*
3. *To write a new episode for the epic*
4. *To defend a position in a debate concerning the value of reading an ancient epic*

THEMES IN WORLD LITERATURE

The Quest and the Perilous Journey

"Theseus," pp. 28–33
"Osiris and Isis," pp. 34–39
"Noah and the Flood" from *Genesis*, pp. 170–176
"The Grail" from *Perceval*, pp. 720–729

The Search for Meaning

"Philosophy and Spiritual Discipline" from the *Bhagavad-Gita*, pp. 467–476
Inferno from the *Divine Comedy*, pp. 741–770
From *Faust*, Part I, pp. 986–1001 ∎

PREREADING FOCUS

Writer's Response: Students should be familiar with the Spanish explorer Ponce de Leon's futile search for a legendary Fountain of Youth. Discuss the positive and negative effects of the quest: it gave impetus to exploration of the New World, but also generated greed and inhumane treatment of Native Americans. Ask the class if the quests for eternal life that students write about brought similar mixed results.

Literary Focus: People of every era have sought heroes, and those heroes show remarkable similarities from ancient to modern times. Ask the class to brainstorm a list of heroes from literature, the entertainment media, and real life. (Heroes from literature might include King Arthur, Roland, and Beowulf. *Star Trek* characters, Indiana Jones, and Wonder Woman might be among the entertainment media heroes cited. Real-life heroes might range from explorers and astronauts to historical or sports figures.) Have students discuss these questions: Which heroes embark on a quest of some kind? Are any of the quests similar? Why are some heroes easier to relate to than others? If people in a future generation were to find a movie or book about your favorite hero, what might they conclude about the beliefs and values of the culture that produced him or her?

Reader's Guide

from the EPIC OF GILGAMESH

Background

Though the Sumerian and Babylonian civilizations were advanced for their time and offered their citizens certain comforts and pleasures, the people were powerless against ever-present threats of devastating floods, severe droughts, and belligerent neighbors who sought "the good life" in the Tigris and Euphrates Valley. It is no wonder, then, that the religious beliefs of the ancient Mesopotamians were somewhat pessimistic. The people worshiped a pantheon, or family, of unpredictable gods and goddesses who could bring about misfortune as well as favor. Regardless of one's status or how one lived one's life, there was no joyful afterlife to look forward to. The end of life offered no consolation, only emptiness.

These beliefs are evident in the epic, as the hero Gilgamesh, in spite of his great powers, suffers a life-changing loss. When the person who means the most to him dies, the proud Gilgamesh must come to terms with the reality that he will not live forever. And because, in the Sumerian view, death offers only emptiness, Gilgamesh rebels against it, and sets off on a quest to attain immortality.

Writer's Response

The search for everlasting life is a common theme in world literature. Think of stories you have read or films you have seen that deal with this theme. What is the usual outcome of people's search for immortality? What do you think is the point of such stories?

Literary Focus

Gilgamesh is the earliest known **epic hero**, and he may have been the model for many later epic heroes, including Homer's Odysseus. All epic heroes are superior human beings. All have supernatural strength and spiritual powers, and all are mighty leaders of their people. But most of them, like Gilgamesh, are of mixed divine and human birth, and thus possess human weaknesses. We admire these heroes for their divine, superhuman qualities. At the same time, we sympathize with them because their weaknesses and difficulties remind us of our own. If even they must accept human limitations, what of us?

from the EPIC OF GILGAMESH

translated by

N. K. SANDARS

Read to the end of the first paragraph of the section entitled "The Search for Everlasting Life." What is Gilgamesh's motivation for seeking out Utnapishtim? Do you predict that Gilgamesh will succeed or fail in his quest?

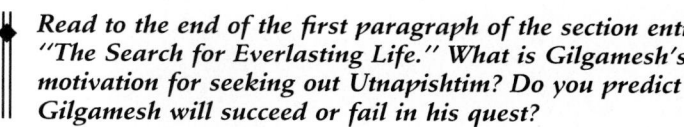

CHARACTERS IN THE EPIC

Anu (ā'nōō): the god of the heavens; the father-god.

Ea (ā'ə): the god of wisdom; usually a friend to humans.

Enkidu (en'kē·dōō): Gilgamesh's friend; a wild man whom the gods created out of clay.

Enlil (en·lil'): the god of the air, the wind, and the earth.

Gilgamesh (gēl'gə·mesh', or gil'gə·mesh'): the king of Uruk and the epic's hero.

Ishtar (ish'tär): the goddess of love and war; the queen of heaven.

Ninurta (nə·nʉr'tə): the god of war and of irrigation.

Shamash (shä'mäsh): a god associated with the sun and human laws.

Siduri (sə·doo'rē): goddess of wine and brewing.

Urshanabi (ʉr'shə·nä·bē): the ferryman who travels daily across the sea of death to the home of Utnapishtim.

Utnapishtim (oot·nə·pēsh'təm): the survivor of a flood sent by the gods to destroy humanity; the gods granted him eternal life.

The epic opens with an introduction to Gilgamesh, king of the city-state of Uruk. Gilgamesh, who is two-thirds god and one-third man, is handsome, courageous, and powerful. But he is also arrogant, and he continually oversteps his bounds as a ruler. His people, upset over the liberties Gilgamesh takes with them, pray to the gods for relief. In response, the gods send a match for Gilgamesh: the wild man Enkidu, reared by wild animals and unfamiliar with civilization. When the two men meet, they engage in a fierce wrestling match, which Gilgamesh wins. But the two men become close friends,

---

1 LITERARY BACKGROUND

Gilgamesh may have rebuffed the goddess of love's overtures because she had previously turned some men who had loved her into beasts.

2 CULTURAL DIVERSITY

The ancient Mesopotamians believed that their many deities possessed supernatural powers but also resembled human beings. Their gods lived in temples built for them by humans, conceived children with human beings, served as landlords of fields cultivated by humans, and went to battle with human armies. The gods also rewarded the virtuous and punished wrongdoers, but reward and punishment came in this world.

❓ *How is the behavior of Ishtar and the other deities mentioned in the summary like that of human beings? (When they feel insulted, they react angrily.)*

■ **somber** (säm'bər): dark and gloomy

MEETING INDIVIDUAL NEEDS

3 *Visual Learners:* Showing pictures of the characters may benefit visual learners. Ask a talented student volunteer to draw an illustration of the man-bird or of Enkidu with his arms turned into wings and to share it with the class. ∎

Oriental Institute, University of Chicago

Winged, human-headed bull that once flanked the entrance to the throne room of King Sargon II's palace, 721–705 B.C.
❓ *How is the Sumerian underworld described in Enkidu's dream?*

1
2

and Enkidu, now civilized, joins Gilgamesh on a series of adventures. First they destroy Humbaba, the demon who guards the great Cedar Forest, and then they level the forest. When they dare to criticize the goddess Ishtar, who makes romantic overtures to Gilgamesh, she sends the Bull of Heaven to ravage the land as punishment. Gilgamesh and Enkidu destroy the bull. The gods cannot tolerate such disrespect, and they decree that one of the heroes must die. In this section of the epic, Enkidu has fallen mortally ill.

The Death of Enkidu

As Enkidu slept alone in his sickness, in bitterness of spirit he poured out his heart to his friend. "It was I who cut down the cedar, I who leveled the forest, I who slew Humbaba and now see what has become of me. Listen, my friend, this is the dream I dreamed last night. The heavens roared, and earth rumbled back an answer; between them stood I before an awful being, the somber-faced man-bird; he had directed on me his purpose. His was a vampire face, his foot was a lion's foot, his hand was an eagle's talon. He fell on me and his claws were in my hair, he held me fast and I smothered; then he transformed me so that my arms became wings covered with feathers. He turned his stare towards me, and he led me away to the palace of Irkalla,[1] the Queen of Darkness, to the house from which none who enters ever returns, down the road from which there is no coming back.

3

---

1. **Irkalla** (ir·kä'lə): also called Ereshkigal; goddess of the underworld.

"There is the house whose people sit in darkness; dust is their food and clay their meat. They are clothed like birds with wings for covering, they see no light, they sit in darkness. I entered the house of dust and I saw the kings of the earth, their crowns put away forever; rulers and princes, all those who once wore kingly crowns and ruled the world in the days of old. They who had stood in the place of the gods like Anu and Enlil, stood now like servants to fetch baked meats in the house of dust, to carry cooked meat and cold water from the water skin. In the house of dust which I entered were high priests and acolytes,[2] priests of the incantation and of ecstasy; there were servers of the temple, and there was Etana, that king of Kish whom the eagle carried to heaven in the days of old. I saw also Samuqan, god of cattle, and there was Ereshkigal, the Queen of the Underworld; and Belit-Sheri squatted in front of her, she who is recorder of the gods and keeps the book of death. She held a tablet from which she read. She raised her head, she saw me and spoke: 'Who has brought this one here?' Then I awoke like a man drained of blood who wanders alone in a waste of rushes; like one whom the bailiff has seized and his heart pounds with terror."

Gilgamesh had peeled off his clothes, he listened to his words and wept quick tears, Gilgamesh listened and his tears flowed. He opened his mouth and spoke to Enkidu: "Who is there in strong-walled Uruk who has wisdom like this? Strange things have been spoken, why does your heart speak strangely? The dream was marvelous but the terror was great; we must treasure the dream whatever the terror; for the dream has shown that misery comes at last to the healthy man, the end of life is sorrow." And

2. **acolytes** (ak'ə-līts'): priests' assistants.

Gilgamesh lamented, "Now I will pray to the great gods, for my friend had an ominous dream."

This day on which Enkidu dreamed came to an end and he lay stricken with sickness. One whole day he lay on his bed and his suffering increased. He said to Gilgamesh, the friend on whose account he had left the wilderness, "Once I ran for you, for the water of life, and I now have nothing." A second day he lay on his bed and Gilgamesh watched over him but the sickness increased. A third day he lay on his bed, he called out to Gilgamesh, rousing him up. Now he was weak and his eyes were blind with weeping. Ten days he lay and his suffering increased, eleven and twelve days he lay on his bed of pain. Then he called to Gilgamesh, "My friend, the great goddess cursed me and I must die in shame. I shall not die like a man fallen in battle; I feared to fall, but happy is the man who falls in the battle, for I must die in shame." And Gilgamesh wept over Enkidu. . . .

Gilgamesh laments Enkidu's death for seven days and nights. Finally, he has the people of Uruk fashion a magnificent statue of Enkidu as a memorial. Then the grieving Gilgamesh leaves Uruk.

5

The Search for Everlasting Life

Bitterly Gilgamesh wept for his friend Enkidu; he wandered over the wilderness as a hunter, he roamed over the plains; in his bitterness he cried, "How can I rest, how can I be at peace? Despair is in my heart. What my brother is now, that shall I be when I am dead. Because I am afraid of death I will go as best I can to find Utnapishtim whom

6

incantation (in'kan·tā' shən): words chanted to evoke supernatural effects

ominous (äm'ə·nəs): serving as an evil omen

4 CULTURAL DIVERSITY
The existence described in Enkidu's dream is a shadowy half-life awarded to those who were honorably buried. Food and drink were placed at their graves to prevent their hungry spirits from wandering this world.

❓ *How does this view of life after death contrast with the views of other traditions, such as that of Islam or Christianity?* (Possible response: In Christianity and Islam there is the hope of a joyful afterlife.)

WRITING TO LEARN

5 Art History: Write the instructions Gilgamesh might have given the artisans who made Enkidu's statue. They should include the size of the statue, the pose, and materials to be used. Check the story and encyclopedias for materials used in Mesopotamian sculpture. ∎

6 GUIDED READING
Finding the Main Idea: Read the entire first paragraph of "The Search for Everlasting Life." Why does Gilgamesh plan to seek out Utnapishtim? (He is afraid of death.) What does Utnapishtim possess that Gilgamesh desires? (He is the only human being who has been granted everlasting life.)

7 LITERARY ELEMENT

Epic Characteristics: Note that Gilgamesh here sets out on the long and perilous journey that characterizes the epics of many cultures.

8 CULTURAL DIVERSITY

The "M" of early alphabets seems to have been based on the twin peaks of mountains perceived as breasts of the ancient deity, the Great Mother. One such Mesopotamian goddess was Ninhursag of ancient Sumer, who, it was believed, gave birth to the world. Mashu was a later goddess of Mesopotamia, whose "paps" are here described as reaching down to the underworld. It was believed that she gave birth daily to the sun. Similarly, a goddess of ancient India was Chomo-Lung-Ma, Mother of the Universe. Her mountain is now called Mount Everest.

9 GUIDED READING

Sequencing: What animals does Gilgamesh encounter first on his journey, and how does he react? (He encounters lions, and he kills them.) What creatures does he meet next, and why does he react differently? (He meets the Scorpions who guard the gate to Mashu. Since their glance is fatal and they are gods, he addresses them with civility instead of attacking them.)

---

they call the Faraway, for he has entered the assembly of the gods." So Gilgamesh traveled over the wilderness, he wandered over the grasslands, a long journey, in search of Utnapishtim, whom the gods took after the deluge; and they set him to live in the land of Dilmun,[3] in the garden of the sun; and to him alone of men they gave everlasting life.

At night when he came to the mountain passes Gilgamesh prayed: "In these mountain passes long ago I saw lions, I was afraid and I lifted my eyes to the moon; I prayed and my prayers went up to the gods, so now, O moon god Sin,[4] protect me." When he had prayed he lay down to sleep, until he was woken from out of a dream. He saw the lions round him glorying in life; then he took his axe in his hand, he drew his sword from his belt, and he fell upon them like an arrow from the string, and struck and destroyed and scattered them.

So at length Gilgamesh came to Mashu,[5] the great mountains about which he had heard many things, which guard the rising and the setting sun. Its twin peaks are as high as the wall of heaven and its paps reach down to the underworld. At its gate the Scorpions stand guard, half man and half dragon; their glory is terrifying, their stare strikes death into men, their shimmering halo sweeps the mountains that guard the rising sun. When Gilgamesh saw them he shielded his eyes for the length of a moment only; then he took courage and approached. When they saw him so undismayed the Man-Scorpion called to his mate, "This one who comes to us now is flesh of the gods."

---

3. **Dilmun:** the land beyond the seas (the Persian Gulf); the paradise of the Sumerians.
4. **Sin:** father of Shamash, the sun god, and Ishtar, the goddess of love; son of Enlil, the chief god.
5. **Mashu:** in the Lebanon ranges.

The mate of the Man-Scorpion answered, "Two thirds is god but one third is man."

Then he called to the man Gilgamesh, he called to the child of the gods: "Why have you come so great a journey; for what have you traveled so far, crossing the dangerous waters; tell me the reason for your coming?" Gilgamesh answered, "For Enkidu; I loved him dearly, together we endured all kinds of hardships; on his account I have come, for the common lot of man has taken him. I have wept for him day and night, I would not give up his body for burial, I thought my friend would come back because of my weeping. Since he went, my life is nothing; that is why I have traveled here in search of Utnapishtim my father; for men say he has entered the assembly of the gods, and has found everlasting life. I have a desire to question him concerning the living and the dead." The Man-Scorpion opened his mouth and said, speaking to Gilgamesh, "No man born of woman has done what you have asked, no mortal man has gone into the mountain; the length of it is twelve leagues of darkness; in it there is no light, but the heart is oppressed with darkness. From the rising of the sun to the setting of the sun there is no light." Gilgamesh said, "Although I should go in sorrow and in pain, with sighing and with weeping, still I must go. Open the gate of the mountain." And the Man-Scorpion said, "Go, Gilgamesh, I permit you to pass through the mountain of Mashu and through the high ranges; may your feet carry you safely home. The gate of the mountain is open."

Gilgamesh successfully makes his way through the twelve leagues of darkness. When he comes out on the other side of Mashu, he is greeted with an astounding sight.

**Copper statue of a Sumerian goddess,
c. 2100–2000 B.C.**

There was the garden of the gods; all round him stood bushes bearing gems. Seeing it he went down at once, for there was fruit of carnelian with the vine hanging from it, beautiful to look at; lapis lazuli leaves hung thick with fruit, sweet to see. For thorns and thistles there were hematite and rare stones, agate, and pearls from out of the edge of the sea. While Gilgamesh walked in the garden by the edge of the sea Shamash saw him, and he saw that he was dressed in the skins of animals and ate their flesh. He was distressed, and he spoke and said, "No mortal man has gone this way before, nor will, as long as the winds drive over the sea." And to Gilgamesh he said,

10

"You will never find the life for which you are searching." Gilgamesh said to glorious Shamash, "Now that I have toiled and strayed so far over the wilderness, am I to sleep, and let the earth cover my head forever? Let my eyes see the sun until they are dazzled with looking. Although I am no better than a dead man, still let me see the light of the sun."

Beside the sea she lives, the woman of the vine, the maker of wine; Siduri sits in the garden at the edge of the sea, with the golden bowl and the golden vats that the gods gave her. She is covered with a veil; and where she sits she sees Gilgamesh coming towards her, wearing skins, the flesh of the gods in his body, but despair in his heart, and his face like the face of one who has made a long journey. She looked, and as she scanned the distance she said in her own heart, "Surely this is some felon; where is he going now?" And she barred her gate against him with the cross-bar and shot home the bolt. But Gilgamesh, hearing the sound of the bolt, threw up his head and lodged his foot in the gate; he called to her, "Young woman, maker of wine, why do you bolt your door; what did you see that made you bar your gate? I will break in your door and burst in your gate, for I am Gilgamesh who seized and killed the Bull of Heaven, I killed the watchman of the cedar forest, I overthrew Humbaba who lived in the forest, and I killed the lions in the passes of the mountain."

11

Then Siduri said to him, "If you are that Gilgamesh who seized and killed the Bull of Heaven, who killed the watchman of the cedar forest, who overthrew Humbaba that lived in the forest, and killed the lions in the passes of the mountain, why are your cheeks so starved and why is your face so drawn? Why is despair in your heart and your face

The Sumerian goddesses were feared and respected for their life-giving and death-dealing powers. Ishtar, the primary deity of the Near East for over 3,000 years, was the goddess of love and fertility, and also of war. Many of her attributes were later identified with Artemis, Aphrodite, and other Greek goddesses.
? *How is Ishtar like Artemis and Aphrodite?* (Possible responses: Artemis is a cunning hunter, but feminine; Aphrodite, the goddess of love, can be wrathful.) *Siduri is the Sumerian wine goddess. Who is the Greek wine god?* (Dionysus) ■

10 COMPARING LITERATURE
Compare the description of the garden of the gods in this epic with the description of the Garden of Eden in Genesis on pp. 165–166.
? *What is similar about the two gardens?* (Semiprecious stones abound in both.) *Who lives in these gardens?* (only the gods in the Mesopotamian epic; Adam and Eve, at least for a while, in Genesis)

11 LITERARY ELEMENT
Situational Irony: What is ironic about the behavior of Gilgamesh and Siduri toward each other, in light of who they are? (Siduri is a goddess, but she shows her fear of him by barring her gate. Gilgamesh is part human, but he speaks aggressively to the goddess and even sticks his foot in her gate.)

In the ancient Middle East, the bull was a common symbol of strength and virility. It was often used to signify a powerful male deity, such as Canaan's Baal, Assyria's Shedu, and Mesopotamia's Marduk.

The head of the bull depicted on this page is made of wood overlaid with gold leaf. The bull's eyes are lapis lazuli, a blue, semiprecious stone. The head decorates a lyre, a stringed musical instrument similar to a harp.

? *Why might Sumerian artisans decorate a lyre in this way?* (They admired strength and virility and wanted to associate music not only with cultural heroes such as Gilgamesh but also with their god Marduk.) ■

▣ **allotted** (ə·lät′əd): distributed as a share

12 READER'S RESPONSE

Do you agree with Siduri's advice to Gilgamesh? Explain your answer. (Possible responses: Yes, the best way to cope with the certainty of death is by living life to the fullest; or no, Siduri's advice ignores the spiritual dimension of human destiny.)

like the face of one who has made a long journey? Yes, why is your face burned from heat and cold, and why do you come here wandering over the pastures in search of the wind?"

Gilgamesh answered her, "And why should not my cheeks be starved and my face drawn? Despair is in my heart and my face is the face of one who has made a long journey, it was burned with heat and with cold. Why should I not wander over the pastures in search of the wind? My friend, my younger brother, he who hunted the wild ass of the wilderness and the panther of the plains, my friend, my younger brother who seized and killed the Bull of Heaven and overthrew Humbaba in the cedar forest, my friend who was very dear to me and who endured dangers beside me, Enkidu my brother, whom I loved, the end of mortality has overtaken him. I wept for him seven days and nights till the worm fastened on him. Because of my brother I am afraid of death, because of my brother I stray through the wilderness and cannot rest. But now, young woman, maker of wine, since I have seen your face do not let me see the face of death which I dread so much."

She answered, "Gilgamesh, where are you hurrying to? You will never find that life for which you are looking. When the gods created man they <u>allotted</u> to him death, but life they retained in their own keeping. As for you Gilgamesh, fill your belly with good things; day and night, night and day, dance and be merry, feast and rejoice. Let your clothes be fresh, bathe yourself in water, cherish the little child that holds your hand, and make your wife happy in your embrace; for this too is the lot of man."

But Gilgamesh said to Siduri, the young woman, "How can I be silent, how can I rest, when Enkidu whom I love is dust, and I too

The University Museum, University of Pennsylvania, #T4-278

Lyre with bull's head, Sumerian, c. 2500 B.C.
? *What role did the Bull of Heaven play in the events leading to Gilgamesh's quest?*

shall die and be laid in the earth. You live by the seashore and look into the heart of it; young woman, tell me now, which is the way to Utnapishtim, the son of Ubara-Tutu? What directions are there for the passage; give me, oh, give me directions. I will cross the Ocean if it is possible; if it is not I will wander still farther in the wilderness."

Siduri sends Gilgamesh into the woods to find Urshanabi, the ferryman, who is building a boat. In anger and ignorance, Gilgamesh smashes some sacred stones that Urshanabi is fashioning into a prow to protect his boat. Gilgamesh then builds another boat, and Urshanabi guides him across the ocean and over the waters of death.

12

So Urshanabi the ferryman brought Gilgamesh to Utnapishtim, whom they call the Faraway, who lives in Dilmun at the place of the sun's transit, eastward of the mountain. To him alone of men the gods had given everlasting life.

Now Utnapishtim, where he lay at ease, looked into the distance and he said in his heart, musing to himself, "Why does the boat sail here without tackle and mast; why are the sacred stones destroyed, and why does the master not sail the boat? That man who comes is none of mine; where I look I see a man whose body is covered with skins of beasts. Who is this who walks up the shore behind Urshanabi, for surely he is no man of mine?" So Utnapishtim looked at him and said, "What is your name, you who come here wearing the skins of beasts, with your cheeks starved and your face drawn? Where are you hurrying to now? For what reason have you made this great journey, crossing the seas whose passage is difficult? Tell me the reason for your coming."

He replied, "Gilgamesh is my name. I am from Uruk, from the house of Anu." Then Utnapishtim said to him, "If you are Gilgamesh, why are your cheeks so starved and your face drawn? Why is despair in your heart and your face like the face burned with heat and cold; and why do you come here, wandering over the wilderness in search of the wind?"

Gilgamesh explains his quest and asks Utnapishtim for the secret of eternal life. The old man's reply is not what Gilgamesh expects.

Utnapishtim said, "There is no permanence. Do we build a house to stand forever, do we seal a contract to hold for all time? Do brothers divide an inheritance to keep forever, does the flood time of rivers endure? It is only the nymph of the dragonfly who sheds her larva and sees the sun in his glory. From the days of old there is no permanence. The sleeping and the dead, how alike they are, they are like a painted death. What is there between the master and the servant when both have fulfilled their doom? When the Anunnaki,[6] the judges, come together, and Mammetun the mother of destinies, together they decree the fates of men. Life and death they allot but the day of death they do not disclose."

Then Gilgamesh said to Utnapishtim the Faraway, "I look at you now, Utnapishtim, and your appearance is no different from mine; there is nothing strange in your features. I thought I should find you like a hero prepared for battle, but you lie here taking your ease on your back. Tell me truly, how was it that you came to enter the company of the gods and to possess everlasting life?" Utnapishtim said to Gilgamesh, "I will reveal to you a mystery, I will tell you a secret of the gods."

The Story of the Flood

"You know the city Shurrupak,[7] it stands on the banks of Euphrates? That city grew old and the gods that were in it were old. There was Anu, lord of the firmament, their father, and warrior Enlil their counselor, Ninurta the helper, and Ennugi watcher over canals; and with them also was Ea. In those days the world teemed, the people multiplied, the world bellowed like a wild bull, and the great god was aroused by the clamor. Enlil heard

---

6. **Anunnaki** (ä·nōō·nä′kē): underworld gods who serve Ereshkigal by judging the dead.
7. **Shurrupak** (shə·roop′ak): the ancient city of Sumer.

13 LITERARY ELEMENT

Epic Hero: How is Gilgamesh's humanity, rather than his superhuman qualities, emphasized in his meeting with Utnapishtim? (He is roughly clothed in animal skins, drawn and hungry, and weary from the hardships of travel and the uncertainty of reaching his goal.)

14 LITERARY ELEMENT

Symbolism: A dragonfly lives the first part of its life underwater as a thick-bodied, wingless brown form called a nymph. At maturity, it climbs up a plant stem into the sunlight for the first time. Its dull exterior peels off to reveal an irridescent body and wings with which it soars through the skies. *How does Utnapishtim use the dragonfly's life as a symbolic contrast to mankind's?* (Mankind's earthly life is like the nymph's, but unlike the mature dragonfly, mankind will not ultimately soar to the sun, that is, abide with the gods.)

15 PREDICTING

In the last line of "The Search for Everlasting Life," Utnapishtim offers to tell Gilgamesh "a secret of the gods." The secret is not revealed for several more pages. What do you imagine the secret will be? (Many will predict that Utnapishtim will reveal a secret to possessing immortality.)

16 COMPARING LITERATURE

Compare this description of worldly clamor with Genesis 11:1–9 from the Hebrew Bible.

? *Although the Bible story has a more detailed plot, in what way is its plot similar to the passage from* Gilgamesh? (The "babel" of the people annoys the deities in both.)

17 COMPARING LITERATURE

Read the first three paragraphs of "Noah and the Flood" (p. 171) alongside Utnapishtim's explanation for God's anger and for his own salvation.

? *How do the two accounts differ?* (Possible responses: In the story of Noah, God plans to destroy humans and animals because of mankind's wickedness; in *Gilgamesh*, Enlil plans to destroy humans and animals because the people's clamor is keeping the gods awake. In "Noah," God speaks directly to the patriarch and gives him instructions. Here, Ea, the god of wisdom, warns Utnapishtim through a dream.)

HUMANITIES CONNECTION

In this statuary, note the stiff, formal poses of the figures and their careful arrangement into a pyramid-shaped composition.

? *How do these details reinforce the characterization of the Sumerian gods?* (Possible response: The supplicating poses and the composition make the gods seem more formidable.) ∎

---

16 the clamor and he said to the gods in council, 'The uproar of mankind is intolerable and sleep is no longer possible by reason of the babel.' So the gods agreed to exterminate mankind. Enlil did this, but Ea because of his oath warned me in a dream. He whispered their words to my house of reeds, 'Reed-house, reed-house! Wall, O wall, hearken reed-house, wall reflect; O man of Shurrupak, son of Ubara-Tutu; **17** tear down your house and build a boat, abandon possessions and look for life, despise worldly goods and save your soul alive. Tear down your house, I say, and build a boat. These are the measurements of the bark as you shall build her: let her beam equal her length, let her deck be roofed like the vault that covers the abyss; then take up into the boat the seed of all living creatures."

"When I had understood I said to my lord, 'Behold, what you have commanded I will honor and perform, but how shall I answer the people, the city, the elders?' Then Ea opened his mouth and said to me, his servant, 'Tell them this: I have learned that Enlil is wrathful against me, I dare no longer walk in his land nor live in his city; I will go down to the Gulf to dwell with Ea my lord. But on you he will rain down abundance, rare fish and shy wildfowl, a rich harvest-tide. In the evening the rider of the storm will bring you wheat in torrents.'

"In the first light of dawn all my household gathered round me, the children brought pitch and the men whatever was necessary. On the fifth day I laid the keel and the ribs, then I made fast the planking. The ground-space was one acre, each side of the deck measured one hundred and twenty cubits, making a square. I built six decks below, seven in all, I divided them into nine sections with bulkheads between. I drove in wedges where needed, I saw to the punt-poles, and laid in supplies. The carriers

Courtesy of The Oriental Institute of the University of Chicago

Sumerian votive statues. *These statues, whose eyes are wide with awe of the gods, were installed in temples to worship in place of their human counterparts.*
? *Based on Utnapishtim's story, how would you characterize the Sumerian gods?*

brought oil in baskets, I poured pitch into the furnace and asphalt and oil; more oil was consumed in caulking, and more again the master of the boat took into his stores. I slaughtered bullocks for the people and every day I killed sheep. I gave the shipwrights wine to drink as though it were river water, raw wine and red wine and oil and white wine. There was feasting then as there is at the time of the New Year's festival; I myself anointed my head. On the seventh day the boat was complete.

"Then was the launching full of difficulty; there was shifting of ballast above and below till two thirds was submerged. I loaded into her all that I had of gold and of living things, my family, my kin, the beast of the field both wild and tame, and all the craftsmen. I sent them on board, for the time that Shamash had ordained was already fulfilled when he said, 'In the evening, when the rider of the storm sends down the destroying rain, enter the boat and batten her down.' The time was fulfilled, the evening came, the rider of the storm sent down the rain. I looked out at the weather and it was terrible, so I too boarded the boat and battened her down. All was now complete, the battening and the caulking; so I handed the tiller to Puzur-Amurri the steersman, with the navigation and the care of the whole boat.

"With the first light of dawn a black cloud came from the horizon; it thundered within where Adad, lord of the storm was riding. In front over hill and plain Shullat and Hanish, heralds of the storm, led on. Then the gods of the abyss rose up; Nergal[8] pulled out the dams of the nether waters, Ninurta the warlord threw down the dikes, and the seven judges of hell, the Annunaki, raised their torches, lighting the land with their livid flame. A stupor of despair went up to heaven when the god of the storm turned daylight to darkness, when he smashed the land like a cup. One whole day the tempest raged, gathering fury as it went, it poured over the people like the tides of battle; a man could not see his brother nor the people be seen from heaven. Even the gods were terrified at the flood, they fled to the highest heaven, the firmament of Anu; they crouched against the walls, cowering like curs. Then Ishtar the sweet-voiced Queen of Heaven cried out like a woman in travail: 'Alas the days of old are turned to dust because I commanded evil; why did I command this evil in the council of all the gods? I commanded wars to destroy the people, but are they not my people, for I brought them forth? Now like the spawn of fish they float in the ocean.' The great gods of heaven and of hell wept, they covered their mouths.

"For six days and six nights the winds blew, torrent and tempest and flood overwhelmed the world, tempest and flood raged together like warring hosts. When the seventh day dawned the storm from the south subsided, the sea grew calm, the flood was stilled; I looked at the face of the world and there was silence, all mankind was turned to clay. The surface of the sea stretched as flat as a rooftop; I opened a hatch and the light fell on my face. Then I bowed low, I sat down and I wept, the tears streamed down my face, for on every side was the waste of water. I looked for land in vain, but fourteen leagues distant there appeared a mountain, and there the boat grounded; on the mountain of Nisir[9] the boat held fast, she held fast and did not budge. One day she held, and a second day on the mountain

---

8. **Nergal:** god of plagues of the underworld.

9. **Nisir:** sometimes identified with Ararat.

Compare the events that follow the storm with those that follow the storm in "Noah and the Flood," pp. 173–174.

❓ *What similarities do you find?* (mountain landing, sending out of birds, offerings to deities) *What differences do you find in the reactions of the deities and in the endings of the stories?* (Noah's God is pleased with Noah and promises never again to flood the earth. Enlil is angry that anyone survived but ultimately grants everlasting life to Utnapishtim and his wife.)

▨ **consigned** (kən·sīnd′): handed over

transgression (trans·gresh′ən): breaking of a law

pestilence (pes′tə·ləns): a deadly epidemic disease

21 LITERARY ELEMENT

Characterization: Is Ea telling the truth when he denies revealing the gods' plan? If you are not sure, reread the first paragraph on p. 146. (Ea is hiding the truth by playing on words. He did warn Utnapishtim but did so in a dream.)

---

of Nisir she held fast and did not budge. A third day, and a fourth day she held fast on the mountain and did not budge; a fifth day and a sixth day she held fast on the mountain. When the seventh day dawned I loosed a dove and let her go. She flew away, but finding no resting-place she returned. Then I loosed a swallow, and she flew away but finding no resting-place she returned. I loosed a raven, she saw that the waters had retreated, she ate, she flew around, she cawed, and she did not come back. Then I threw everything open to the four winds, I made a sacrifice and poured out a libation on the mountain top. Seven and again seven cauldrons I set up on their stands, I heaped up wood and cane and cedar and myrtle. When the gods smelled the sweet savor, they gathered like flies over the sacrifice. Then, at last, Ishtar also came, she lifted her necklace with the jewels of heaven that once Anu had made to please her. 'O you gods here present, by the lapis lazuli round my neck I shall remember these days as I remember the jewels of my throat; these last days I shall not forget. Let all the gods gather round the sacrifice, except Enlil. He shall not approach this offering, for without reflection he brought the flood; he consigned my people to destruction.'

"When Enlil had come, when he saw the boat, he was wroth[10] and swelled with anger at the gods, the host of heaven, 'Has any of these mortals escaped? Not one was to have survived the destruction.' Then the god of the wells and canals Ninurta opened his mouth and said to the warrior Enlil, 'Who is there of the gods that can devise without Ea? It is Ea alone who knows all things.' Then Ea opened his mouth and spoke to warrior Enlil, 'Wisest of gods, hero Enlil, how

---

10. **wroth** (rôth): (British) angry.

---

could you so senselessly bring down the flood?

Lay upon the sinner his sin,
Lay upon the transgressor his transgression,
Punish him a little when he breaks loose,
Do not drive him too hard or he perishes;
Would that a lion had ravaged mankind
Rather than the flood,
Would that a wolf had ravaged mankind
Rather than the flood,
Would that famine had wasted the world
Rather than the flood,
Would that pestilence had wasted mankind
Rather than the flood.

It was not I that revealed the secret of the gods; the wise man learned it in a dream. Now take your counsel what shall be done with him.'

"Then Enlil went up into the boat, he took me by the hand and my wife and made us enter the boat and kneel down on either side, he standing between us. He touched our foreheads to bless us saying, 'In time past Utnapishtim was a mortal man; henceforth he and his wife shall live in the distance at the mouth of the rivers.' Thus it was that the gods took me and placed me here to live in the distance, at the mouth of the rivers."

The Return

Utnapishtim said, "As for you, Gilgamesh, who will assemble the gods for your sake, so that you may find that life for which you are searching? But if you wish, come and put it to the test: only prevail against sleep for six days and seven nights." But while Gilgamesh sat there resting on his haunches, a mist of sleep like soft wool teased from the fleece drifted over him, and Utnapishtim said to his wife, "Look at him now, the

Courtesy of The Oriental Institute of the University of Chicago

Seated couple, Sumerian.

strong man who would have everlasting life, even now the mists of sleep are drifting over him." His wife replied, "Touch the man to wake him, so that he may return to his own land in peace, going back through the gate by which he came." Utnapishtim said to his wife, "All men are deceivers, even you he will attempt to deceive; therefore bake loaves of bread, each day one loaf, and put it beside his head; and make a mark on the wall to number the days he has slept."

So she baked loaves of bread, each day one loaf, and put it beside his head, and she marked on the wall the days that he slept; and there came a day when the first loaf was hard, the second loaf was like leather, the third was soggy, the crust of the fourth had mold, the fifth was mildewed, the sixth was fresh, and the seventh was still on the embers. Then Utnapishtim touched him and he woke. Gilgamesh said to Utnapishtim the Faraway, "I hardly slept when you touched

and roused me." But Utnapishtim said, "Count these loaves and learn how many days you slept, for your first is hard, your second like leather, your third is soggy, the crust of your fourth has mold, your fifth is mildewed, your sixth is fresh and your seventh was still over the glowing embers when I touched and woke you." Gilgamesh said, "What shall I do, O Utnapishtim, where shall I go? Already the thief in the night has hold of my limbs, death inhabits my room; wherever my foot rests, there I find death."

Then Utnapishtim spoke to Urshanabi the ferryman: "Woe to you Urshanabi, now and forevermore you have become hateful to this harborage; it is not for you, nor for you are the crossings of this sea. Go now, banished from the shore. But this man before whom you walked, bringing him here, whose body is covered with foulness and the grace of whose limbs has been spoiled by wild skins, take him to the washing-place. There he shall wash his long hair clean as snow in the water, he shall throw off his skins and let the sea carry them away, and the beauty of his body shall be shown, the fillet[11] on his forehead shall be renewed, and he shall be given clothes to cover his nakedness. Till he reaches his own city and his journey is accomplished, these clothes will show no sign of age, they will wear like a new garment." So Urshanabi took Gilgamesh and led him to the washing-place, he washed his long hair as clean as snow in the water, he threw off his skins, which the sea carried away, and showed the beauty of his body. He renewed the fillet on his forehead, and to cover his nakedness gave him clothes which would show no sign of age, but would wear like a new garment till he reached his own city, and his journey was accomplished.

11. **fillet** (fil'it): a narrow headband.

22

23

HUMANITIES CONNECTION

Only fragments remain of the large wooden statues of ancient Mesopotamia, covered with copper or gold and adorned with lapis lazuli. But small statues up to 28 inches high have survived.

? *Would you describe these figures as "stodgy," as one art critic has, or do they make a different impression on you?* ■

22 INTERPRETING

What is Utnapishtim's purpose in having his wife bake a loaf of bread each day that Gilgamesh sleeps? (He must be able to prove, through the condition of each loaf, that Gilgamesh has slept for seven days.) What is his purpose in proving to Gilgamesh that he has had a prolonged sleep? (If Gilgamesh cannot resist sleep, how can he expect to escape death?)

23 LITERARY ELEMENT

Symbolism: Symbols are characters, events, or objects that stand for something beyond themselves. What might Gilgamesh's ritual bath, hair washing, and donning of new clothes symbolize? (These actions suggest renewal. The rituals may symbolize his new acceptance of Enkidu's death and of his own mortality.) Who had already advised Gilgamesh to revive his spirit by bathing and donning fresh clothes? (Siduri)

Identifying Details: Utna-pishtim's wife reminds him of the secret he mentioned to Gilgamesh before he began the story of the flood. What is the secret? (There is an underwater plant that can restore a man's lost youth if he succeeds in seizing it.)

■ **sluices** (sloōs′əz): gates to regulate the flow of water in artificial channels

---

HUMANITIES CONNECTION

The stone in many parts of Mesopotamia was not suitable for building, but it was used extensively for relief sculptures like this. The most common subjects of these reliefs are scenes of banquets, the hunt, and warfare. The battles pictured on Sumerian monuments were generally caused by squabbles between neighboring cities about water rights for crop irrigation, or by raids of tribes from the mountains of Persia or from the desert to the west.

This is part of an Assyrian relief giving a detailed record of warfare. The Assyrian reliefs bear many stylistic similarities to the wall paintings and bas reliefs of ancient Egypt. ■

Relief of King Assurbanipal's armed guard, Assyrian, c. 800 B.C.

Western Asiatic Collection/The British Museum

24

Then Gilgamesh and Urshanabi launched the boat on to the water and boarded it, and they made ready to sail away; but the wife of Utnapishtim the Faraway said to him, "Gilgamesh came here wearied out, he is worn out; what will you give him to carry him back to his own country?" So Utnapishtim spoke, and Gilgamesh took a pole and brought the boat in to the bank. "Gilgamesh, you came here a man wearied out, you have worn yourself out; what shall I give you to carry you back to your own country? Gilgamesh, I shall reveal a secret thing, it is a mystery of the gods that I am telling you. There is a plant that grows under the water, it has a prickle like a thorn, like a rose; it will wound your hands, but if you succeed in taking it, then your hands will hold that which restores his lost youth to a man."

When Gilgamesh heard this he opened the sluices so that a sweet-water current might carry him out to the deepest channel; he tied heavy stones to his feet and they dragged him down to the water-bed. There he saw the plant growing; although it pricked him he took it in his hands; then he cut the heavy stones from his feet, and the sea carried him and threw him on to the shore. Gilgamesh said to Urshanabi the ferryman, "Come here, and see this marvelous plant. By its virtue a man may win back all his former strength. I will take it to Uruk of the strong walls; there I will give it to the old men to eat. Its name shall be 'The Old Men Are Young Again'; and at last I shall eat it myself and have back all my lost youth." So Gilgamesh returned by the gate through which he had come, Gilgamesh and Urshanabi went together. They traveled their twenty leagues and then they broke their fast; after thirty leagues they stopped for the night.

Gilgamesh saw a well of cool water and he went down and bathed; but deep in the pool there was lying a serpent, and the serpent

READING CHECK

1. On his quest, what does Gilgamesh seek? (the secret of everlasting life)
2. What advice do the gods give Gilgamesh? (to abandon his quest)
3. Why did the gods once flood the earth? (People were too noisy.)
4. Who escaped the flood? (Utnapishtim)
5. What great gift was granted to Utnapishtim? (everlasting life)
6. Whom does Utnapishtim blame for Gilgamesh's visit? (Urshanabi)
7. How is the clothing given to Gilgamesh unusual? (It will not show wear.)
8. What is the power of the plant Gilgamesh retrieves? (It restores youth.)
9. What prevents Gilgamesh from taking the plant home? (A serpent steals it.)
10. On returning to Uruk, what does Gilgamesh do? (writes about his journey)

RETEACHING
Have students write an imaginary one-paragraph announcement prepared by a court official on Gilgamesh's return. The proclamation could summarize the nature of Gilgamesh's quest, what happened on the journey, and Gilgamesh's reactions to his experience. The announcement could also promise the full story to come, in a twelve-tablet saga. Invite students to role-play the court writer and read their announcements to the class.

25 sensed the sweetness of the flower. It rose out of the water and snatched it away, and immediately it sloughed its skin and returned to the well. Then Gilgamesh sat down and wept, the tears ran down his face, and he took the hand of Urshanabi; "O Urshanabi, was it for this that I toiled with my hands, is it for this I have wrung out my heart's blood? For myself I have gained nothing; not I, but the beast of the earth has joy of it now. **26** Already the stream has carried it twenty leagues back to the channels where I found it. I found a sign and now I have lost it. Let us leave the boat on the bank and go."

After twenty leagues they broke their fast, after thirty leagues they stopped for the night; in three days they had walked as much as a journey of a month and fifteen days. When the journey was accomplished they arrived at Uruk, the strong-walled city. Gilgamesh spoke to him, to Urshanabi the ferryman, "Urshanabi, climb up on to the wall of Uruk, inspect its foundation terrace, and examine well the brick work; see if it is not of burnt bricks; and did not the seven wise men lay these foundations? One third of the whole is city, one third is garden, and one third is field, with the precinct of the goddess Ishtar. These parts and the precinct are all Uruk."

This too was the work of Gilgamesh, the king, who knew the countries of the world. He was wise, he saw mysteries and knew secret things, he brought us a tale of the days before the flood. He went a long journey, was weary, worn out with labor, and returning engraved on a stone the whole story.

25 GUIDED READING
Identifying Details: In the ancient Middle East snakes were believed to be immortal because they periodically shed their skins and seemed to begin life anew. How does the story explain the origins of the serpent's supposed gift of immortality? (The serpent stole from Gilgamesh the magic plant that restored lost youth.)

 sloughed (sluft): discarded

26 READER'S RESPONSE
Were you surprised that Gilgamesh did not pursue the plant after it floated away? How could you explain his behavior? (Some students will be surprised that Gilgamesh would meekly allow the snake to steal the plant. Others will see his acquiescence as appropriate for the new Gilgamesh, who has accepted his inevitable death.)

ANSWERS
First Thoughts
Possible response: He has accepted death as inevitable.

Identifying Facts
1. to learn the secret of immortality from him
2. Humans kept them awake. They are terrified.
3. It restores lost youth. He wants to feed it to the old men of Uruk and himself.
4. The serpent snatches the plant; the plant floats away. Gilgamesh weeps bitterly, but continues his journey home.

> **First Thoughts**
What do you think Gilgamesh has learned by the end of the epic?

Identifying Facts
1. Why does Gilgamesh want to find Utnapishtim?
2. According to the story of the flood, why do the gods decide to destroy humanity? How do the gods react when they see the effects of the flood?
3. What extraordinary power does Utnapishtim claim the magical plant possesses? What does Gilgamesh want to do with the plant?
4. What happens to the plant, and what is Gilgamesh's reaction to this event?

Interpreting Meanings
1. According to Enkidu's dream, what is the underworld like? Why is this dream important for an understanding of Gilgamesh's **motivations** in seeking immortality?
2. What pleasures does Siduri tell Gilgamesh to content himself with? Why do you think Gilgamesh is unwilling to take Siduri's advice at this point in his journey?
3. Summarize Utnapishtim's response to Gilgamesh when Gilgamesh asks him for the secret of eternal life. Do you think Utnapishtim's argument is convincing? In what ways is Utnapishtim not what Gilgamesh expected?
4. Some scholars believe that the story of the flood was originally a separate **myth** that was later woven into the story of Gilgamesh. Do you think that the flood story interrupts the narrative, or does it add something to the meaning of the story? Explain.

1. **Planning a Mini-series.** Have students plan a television mini-series based on the epic. Divide the class into groups. Ask each group to create a narrative description of everything that will occur on screen during a specific episode. Individuals within each group should be responsible for dialogue, setting, lighting, costumes, and special effect specifications. Allow students to sketch the sets and costumes if they prefer.

2. **Researching Guardian Figures in Literature.** Suggest students research guardian figures in mythology or literature and write an essay comparing and contrasting them to the Scorpions that try to deter Gilgamesh. Possible choices include the Minotaur in the labyrinth of Crete, Cerberus in Virgil's *Aeneid*, the gorgon Medusa of Greek mythology, and the Cherubim at the east of Eden (see Genesis, p. 167).

Review with students the human and superhuman attributes of Gilgamesh revealed in these episodes. Then ask them to consider whether Gilgamesh failed, succeeded, or was only partially successful in his quest. (Answers will vary.) Was Gilgamesh changed as a result of his experiences? (Gilgamesh becomes less arrogant and takes renewed joy in his earthly life.) Was he more or less of a hero upon his return? (Answers will vary.) ∎

Interpreting Meanings

1. It is a place of misery. The prospect of death is horrifying.
2. Siduri urges him to enjoy his present life. Doing so would render his efforts up to this point meaningless.
3. He argues that the same death is allotted to all humans. Answers will vary. He leads a lazy, unheroic life.
4. Possible response: It interrupts the flow, but reveals much about the gods and the precariousness of human life.
5. Gilgamesh really believes he slept only an instant. The sleep was not natural.
6. A snake so easily achieves what Gilgamesh has struggled so hard for. It teaches him to accept the limits imposed upon humankind.
7. Personal sorrow motivates him. He wants to offer the plant to the old men of Uruk. He brings a better understanding of the human condition.

Applying Meanings

Answers will vary. Many will feel that the ancient Sumerians believed in enjoying life while they could.

Creative Writing Response
Creating a New Episode of the Epic.
Evaluate the consistency of Gilgamesh's character as seen in his love for Enkidu and his persistence through trials.

Speaking and Listening
Defending a Position.
Evaluate debates for cogency of arguments and appropriateness of examples. ∎

5. Utnapishtim asks his wife to bake a loaf of bread to mark each day that Gilgamesh sleeps, because "all men are deceivers." Is Gilgamesh deliberately deceiving Utnapishtim by claiming that he hardly slept? Is it possible that Gilgamesh himself has been somehow deceived? Explain.

6. **Irony** is the contrast between what is expected to happen and what actually does happen. Explain what is ironic about what happens to the plant of eternal youth. What does this irony teach Gilgamesh?

7. An **epic hero** always in some way represents the highest values of his or her culture and acts with his or her people in mind. In what ways is Gilgamesh's quest selfish? In what ways is he undertaking his quest not only for himself, but for all the people of Uruk? What does he ultimately bring back to his people?

Applying Meanings
Some people feel that an awareness of the inevitability of death makes people more aware that life is precious and that they should make the most of time. Other people feel that knowing life must eventually come to an end makes it impossible to fully enjoy life's pleasures. What do you think about this issue? How do you think the ancient Sumerians felt about it, based on the epic you have just read?

Creative Writing Response
Creating a New Episode of the Epic. What if, after he had lost the magic flower, Gilgamesh had tried to retrieve it again, and succeeded? How will Gilgamesh use the plant? Will he share it with others? Will he try to bring Enkidu back to life? Will he discover that eternal youth has its drawbacks? Write an account of Gilgamesh's retrieval of the plant and its results. Show both the actions and the feelings of Gilgamesh. If you wish, you may continue your episode into a new ending for the epic.

Speaking and Listening
Defending a Position. Imagine that you are one of the following students who has just finished reading the *Epic of Gilgamesh*.

Student #1: That was the stupidest story I've ever read. Gilgamesh obviously had the brain of a flea, or he would never have gone off on such a wild-goose chase in the first place. Everyone knows there's no such thing as immortality. It's a totally unrealistic story and a waste of time. I want to read something that I can relate to my life.

Student #2: Well, most myths and epics are unrealistic. I mean, no one literally goes out and fights monsters or descends to the underworld. But I think the story rings true in some way. It's like Gilgamesh had to find out that people aren't meant to live forever, just so that he could make peace with Enkidu's death and accept his own mortality. I really sympathized with his situation.

Which student's views are most similar to your own? Pair off with a classmate who holds the opposite view and, in front of the class, defend the position of Student #1 or #2. Use specific examples from the epic to defend your position.

THE ART OF TRANSLATION

Comparing Translations of Gilgamesh

The original *Epic of Gilgamesh* was presented in verse rather than prose. Several fine verse translations of the epic are available. Some are direct translations from cuneiform tablets. One of the most successful versions of the epic, however, is Herbert Mason's very personal translation. Mason was a student at Harvard when he was first introduced to the epic. Because Mason had suffered a deep loss—the death of his father—when he was a child, he sympathized strongly with Gilgamesh's grief over the loss of Enkidu and with Gilgamesh's quest. Mason created a new retelling of the Gilgamesh epic, freely reshaping material from several sources.

Compare the following passage from the Mason translation with the same passage from the Sandars prose translation you have just read (see page 142). Then discuss the differences you see between the two versions.

When he arrived at the mountains of Mashu,
Whose peaks reach to the shores of
    Heaven
And whose roots descend to Hell, he saw
The Scorpion people who guard its gate,
Whose knowledge is awesome, but whose
    glance is death.

When he saw them, his face turned ashen
    with dismay,
But he bowed down to them, the only way
    to shield himself
Against effusions of their gaze.
The Scorpion man then recognized
In Gilgamesh the flesh of gods and told his
    wife:
This one is two-thirds god, one-third man
And can survive our view, then spoke to
    him:
Why have you come this route to us?
The way is arduous and long
And no one goes beyond.

I have come to see my father,
Utnapishtim,
Who was allowed to go beyond.
I want to ask him about life and death,
To end my loss. My friend has died.
I want to bring him back to life.

—*translated by Herbert Mason, 1971*

Sumerian cuneiform tablet.

The Granger Collection, New York

OBJECTIVES

1. *To analyze the literature of the ancient Hebrews, including Old Testament narratives and psalms and New Testament parables*
2. *To examine the influence of ancient Hebrew ideas and writings on Western civilization*
3. *To respond orally and in writing to Hebrew literature*

TEACHER'S RESOURCES: 3
☑ Unit Introduction Test

1 HISTORICAL BACKGROUND

Abraham and Sarah: Genesis 11 and 12 report the path by which Abraham and Sarah journeyed to Canaan. Following a well-established trade route that connected Africa, Europe, and Asia, they traveled along the Fertile Crescent for approximately 1,000 miles. They first moved north along the Euphrates River to Haran. After living there for an indeterminate time, they migrated to Canaan. In terms of today's Middle East, they traveled from southern Iraq to northern Syria to southern Israel. (See map and map inset on p. 158.)

HUMANITIES CONNECTION

The illumination draws upon Exodus 31–34, in which God gives Moses on Mount Sinai two stone tablets containing the Ten Commandments. Upon descending from the mountain, Moses discovers the Israelites worshiping a golden calf. Creating and worshiping such an image were expressly forbidden by Jewish law. Angry, Moses casts down the tablets of the law and breaks them. Despite his disappointment with the people, Moses intercedes for them with God, and in Exodus 34, God replaces the tablets and renews his covenant with Israel.

❓ *Why do you think the Hebrew people reverted to the worship of idols?* (Possible response: Habits and beliefs persist, especially in times of stress or hardship.) ∎

HEBREW LITERATURE

The Granger Collection, New York

Moses holding the Ten Commandments, from a fourteenth-century illuminated manuscript.

For much of their history, the Hebrews were wanderers. Instead of building great monuments or far-reaching empires like the Egyptians and many of their neighbors in Mesopotamia, the Hebrews, or Jews, forged a rich cultural life based on their religious beliefs. These beliefs are given form in the **Hebrew Bible**, known to Christians as the **Old Testament**. In a way, the Hebrew Bible is the great "monument" left behind by the ancient Hebrews, for it is the record of their spiritual, literary, and historical experience.

The Early Hebrew Patriarchs

Hebrew history begins in Mesopotamia with **Abraham**, the first Hebrew patriarch, or "founding father." According to the Hebrew Bible, Abraham and his wife Sarah left the Babylonian city of Ur and crossed the Jordan River to the land of **Canaan**, the part of the Fertile Crescent that lay between the Jordan River and the Mediterranean Sea. The descendants of Abraham and Sarah came to be called *Hebrews*, which means "people from across the river."

The Hebrews lived in Canaan for four generations under the Hebrew patriarchs: Abraham, his son Isaac, and his grandson Jacob. Jacob, who was later named Israel, lent his name to the Hebrews, who came to be called the **Israelites**. The Book of Genesis in the Hebrew Bible tells the story of Joseph, Jacob's favorite son, who was betrayed and sent into slavery in Egypt by his eleven jealous brothers. Joseph won the favor of the pharaoh in Egypt by predicting a famine, thus enabling Egypt to store grain in preparation for a severe drought to come. When the famine struck, Egypt was well prepared, but Canaan was caught unaware. Joseph saved the Israelites from starvation by bringing them into Egypt.

First, make sure students understand that the study of the Bible in this unit will be from a literary, cultural, and historical standpoint, not a religious one. Even students whose training has been strictly secular may be familiar with some of the characters, stories, psalms, parables, and proverbs from Hebrew literature. Invite students to share their knowledge with the class. Then point out that the Mesopotamian and ancient Hebrew cultures thrived during the same time and in the same region of the world. Yet while most Americans know little of the culture of Mesopotamia, Hebrew writings, beliefs, and ideas have had a powerful, direct influence on our civilization. Review the fact that the Assyrians and Babylonians of Mesopotamia were conquerors of the Hebrews, who occupied a small and remote corner of the Fertile Crescent. Tell students that the long history of the Hebrew people began with a nomadic life in the desert, followed by enslavement in Egypt, intertribal warfare, brief independence, and long periods of domination by Babylonians, Greeks, and Romans. Finally, the Hebrew people were dispersed throughout the world; yet they and their culture outlasted the rise and fall of several empires. Their history well illustrates the saying, "The pen is mightier than the sword."

The Granger Collection, New York

The Egyptians drowning in the Red Sea. *Colored engraving after Gustave Doré.*

❓ *What aspect of early Hebrew history does this engraving depict?*

Captivity and the Flight from Egypt

In Egypt, the Israelites organized themselves into twelve tribes. But years after Joseph had led the Israelites to salvation in Egypt, a new Egyptian pharaoh enslaved them. Various historical sources indicate that around 1200 B.C. a leader named **Moses** led the Hebrews on an *exodus,* or "going forth," to freedom across an arm of the Red Sea and into the Sinai Desert. In the Hebrew Bible, the **Book of Exodus** tells how God aided Moses in this daring escape from slavery in Egypt.

The Book of Exodus also relates an event that has become central to the Hebrew faith. While traveling through the desert toward Canaan, called "the Promised Land," Moses received from God the **Ten Commandments,** a code of ethics, or moral conduct. God promised to lead the Hebrews to the Promised Land on the condition that they obey these Commandments. The Ten Commandments laid the foundation for what has come to be known as **Mosaic law.**

Moses died during the difficult years in the Sinai desert. But one of his followers, **Joshua,** eventually led the Israelites back into Canaan.

> 66 He that is slow to anger is better than the mighty; and he that ruleth his spirit than he that taketh a city. 99
>
> —*Proverbs 16:32*
> *King James Bible*

2

HUMANITIES CONNECTION

This engraving, made in the style of noted French illustrator Gustave Doré (1832–1883), depicts Exodus 14:22–27, in which Yahweh opens a dry path through the Red Sea for the Israelites but drowns the pursuing Egyptian army. Scholars believe that the Book of Exodus condenses into one event several incidents in which the Hebrews emigrated from Egypt.

The Exodus narrative has had a tremendous impact through the ages. Michelangelo's statue of Moses, for example, is a monument to the hero of Exodus. In more recent times, the narrative has inspired such creative works as the spiritual "Go Down, Moses" and Cecil B. DeMille's 1956 film *The Ten Commandments.*

❓ *Why do you think that Exodus has had such a powerful hold?* (Possible response: It taps a universal longing to escape from bondage, whether physical or spiritual.) ■

2 RESPONDING TO THE QUOTATION

❓ *How would you restate this quotation from the Hebrew Bible in contemporary English?* (Possible response: A person who can control his or her temper has more strength of character than a person who can subdue a city by force or fear.) *Do you think the moral insight expressed in the quotation from Proverbs has relevance in today's world? Discuss by giving examples.* ■

Explain that the Hebrew literature in this unit is from both the Hebrew Bible and the New Testament (see pp. 196–197). Then invite students to discover in the narratives from Genesis (pp. 162–176) and in the New Testament parables brief stories that offer profound insights into questions of human identity and the meaning of life. In the Book of Ruth (p. 177), students will encounter a story, written over two thousand years ago, that seems modern in its detail, character, and theme. Likewise the Psalms (p. 186) maintain their emotional power even in translation. As students read the selections from the Hebrew Bible, they should look for archetypes or recurring motifs that they have encountered in the religious literature of other cultures. For example, the Book of Genesis (pp. 162–176) includes accounts of the creation of the world, the origin of evil and death, and the destruction of the world in a flood. Invite comparison with selections from Unit 1 and with the *Epic of Gilgamesh* (p. 138). Also, the New Testament parables could be compared with the Taoist Anecdotes (p. 546) and the Zen Parables (p. 589) from Unit 6.

The Hebrews left few physical remains in the form of architecture or artifacts; in fact, their religion, strictly interpreted, forbade such artistic expressions. Their lasting "monuments," however, are a book, a tradition, and a way of life.

3 HISTORICAL BACKGROUND

Judges: The Judges were charismatic religious and military leaders like Deborah, Gideon, and Samson who settled disputes among the Hebrew people. During the period of the Judges (between c. 1400 and 1100 B.C.), the Israelites were primarily herders and farmers, united solely by their worship of Yahweh. The central motif of the Book of Judges is the importance for the Israelites of keeping their covenant with Yahweh. When they fail to do so, they are inevitably conquered or enslaved by foreign powers, and Yahweh must raise up a hero to save them.

HUMANITIES CONNECTION

In his short life, the Renaissance artist Raphael, or Raffaello Sanzio, produced a large number of incomparably beautiful paintings, frescoes, and tapestries. Pope Julius II commissioned him, at age 25, to organize a Vatican workshop from which emerged a fresco cycle on Old Testament subjects. As in the painting *The Giving of the Tablets of the Law,* the frescoes reverberate with energy and power.

❓ *Ask students to compare details in Raphael's painting with the events recounted in Exodus 24:12–13, 31:18, 32:1–35, and 34:1–11.* ∎

The Promised Land

When the Israelites arrived in Canaan, it was already inhabited by other peoples, among them the Canaanites and the Philistines. The Israelites struggled to make a place for themselves over the next two hundred years. Their task was difficult because of disagreements among the twelve tribes of Israel. This period in Hebrew history is recounted in the book called **Judges**, because judges were the only unifying political and military power within the twelve tribes.

Eventually, around 1020 B.C., a Hebrew leader named **Saul** succeeded in unifying the twelve tribes, becoming the first king of Israel. The Israelites flourished under his rule

THE GIVING OF THE TABLETS OF THE LAW, RAPHAEL (1483–1520).
❓ *In exchange for following his commandments, what did God promise Moses and his followers?*

Scala/Art Resource, New York

Art can be used to help students gauge the influence of ancient Hebrew civilization. Have students flip through the art in this subunit and notice how much is European and American. Raphael, Poussin, Rubens, Gustave Doré, Edward Hicks, and Lucas Cranach are major artists who chose biblical subjects for their work. You can extend this activity by bringing in a copy of an art history textbook, such as Janssen's *History of Art*, and examining the subjects of European works of art, particularly from the Middle Ages and the Renaissance.

Remind students that Christianity was an offshoot of Judaism and that it has had an incalculable influence on European and American values. The ethics of the Ten Commandments, the Hebrew virtues of righteousness, charity, and justice, and the Christian precepts of humility, mercy, and forgiveness have impressed the modern Western mind in ways that go beyond denomination or doctrine. The investigation of the problem of evil in the Book of Job remains a touchstone for philosophers. It was from the biblical prophets that Western civilization inherited the idea of the individual who is called on to "speak truth to power"—an injunction that inspired leaders like John Adams, Henry David Thoreau, Harriet Tubman, and Martin Luther King, Jr.

---

and became the most powerful group of people in Canaan. However, the Hebrews were never able to gain complete and lasting control over the Philistines, who inhabited the coastal area of Canaan. (The Romans, in fact, called Canaan Palestine, after the Philistines.)

An Interlude of Peace and Stability

For almost one hundred years, the Hebrews enjoyed an era of prosperity and stability. Saul's successor, **King David**, who reigned from 1010 to 970 B.C., was able to break the Philistine's control of coastal lands and capture the city of the Jebusites (jeb′yə·sīts). Under David, this small hill town was transformed into the Hebrew capital city of **Jerusalem**. David's son **Solomon**, who reigned until about 925 B.C., launched many ambitious projects to beautify Jerusalem. His greatest contribution was the construction of the magnificent **Temple of Jerusalem**, a central place of worship which became an important symbol of the Hebrews' spiritual unity. Today, all that remains of this once-splendid structure is its western wall, now known as the Wailing Wall because of the many tearful prayers said there over the centuries by people mourning the Temple's destruction.

Conflict and Division

After Solomon's death, Israel again entered a period of political and economic turmoil. Internal conflicts drove the twelve tribes apart. To the south, the tribes of Benjamin and Judah founded **Judah**, or Judea, from which the word *Jew*,

> With Solomon's death, disagreements among the twelve tribes split the Hebrew kingdom in two: Israel to the north and Judah to the south.

used interchangeably with the word *Hebrew*, comes. Judah contained the city of Jerusalem. To the north, the remaining ten tribes founded **Israel**, later called Samaria. Although the twelve tribes had split politically into two kingdoms, they continued to think of themselves as one people spiritually.

> 66 In those days there was no king in Israel; every man did that which was right in his own eyes. 99
> —*Judges 21:25*

4

The Youthful David, Andrea del Castagno (1423–57).

LITERARY/HISTORICAL BACKGROUND

From Monarchy to Exile: The period of monarchy, which lasted about four centuries, is described in 1 and 2 Samuel, 1 and 2 Kings, and the books of the Hebrew Bible written by various prophets between 1000 and 400 B.C. A selective, idealized retelling also occurs in 1 and 2 Chronicles written as late as 250 B.C.

The Books of 1 and 2 Samuel narrate the lives of the prophet Samuel, King Saul, and King David. Included are tales of heroism, such as David's killing of the Philistine giant, Goliath, and tales of passion, such as David's desire for Bathsheba.

The Books of Kings move from the time of Solomon, a period of peace and prosperity, to that of the Babylonian Exile (see p. 158).

The Books of the Prophets Amos and Hosea recount events in the northern kingdom of Israel prior to invasion by Assyria in 722 B.C. The Books of Micah, Zephaniah, and Jeremiah cover events in Judah until the Babylonian conquest of 586 B.C. The Book of Isaiah spans the Assyrian conquest to the Babylonians, and the Book of Ezekiel chronicles the Babylonian Exile.

4 RESPONDING TO THE QUOTATION
This points to the need for a common set of laws.
❓ *What would society be like without government?* (Possible response: dangerous, disorderly)

Introduction **157**

Hebrew influence has been particularly strong in the development of Western ideas of justice. If the Hebrews can be called the people of the book, they can also justly be called the people of the law. The ideal of a society based on laws rather than on personal power has endured, and the Ten Commandments are still considered a pithy summary of personal obligations to one's God, self, and others.

Biblical stories, such as those in this unit, have remained a fertile source of inspiration for writers over the centuries; in fact, biblical themes and imagery can be traced through much of European and American literature. For example, biblical knowledge is central to understanding Dante's epic poem, the *Divine Comedy* (p. 741), and such writers as Shakespeare and Chaucer, although their subjects are secular, draw heavily on the Bible for their use of language and imagery. The Bible is even a source of themes and motifs for modern writers. One example is Anna Akhmatova's poem "Lot's Wife" (p. 1223). Ask students to read "Seeing Connections: Biblical Allusions" (p. 185), and explain that this feature will help them understand the pervasiveness of biblical allusions. Finally, suggest that as students read the biblical selections in the unit, they consider the impact that these ancient writings have had on their own lives.

5 RESPONDING TO THE QUOTATION

Psalm 137 expresses the Hebrew psalmist's feelings during the Babylonian Captivity.

❓ *What emotion is the psalmist expressing?* (grief) How do you think this quotation from the Bible affected Westerners' views of the Babylonian civilization through the ages? (Possible response: It created negative feelings.)

GEOGRAPHIC BACKGROUND

Canaan: As the map shows, Canaan extended no more than 200 miles from north to south. It offered little in the way of mineral resources but provided a varied climate and a beautiful landscape. In the north lay fertile plains, small hills, and valleys; in central Canaan, beaches and mountains; and in the south, mostly desert. Some grazing was possible, and figs, olives, grapes, and grain were grown in the fertile Jordan River Valley.

Canaan was a natural highway for trade, for it was situated where the cultures of Africa, Asia, and Europe met. Such a geographic setting predisposed the Hebrews to be herders and farmers and, later, merchants and artisans.

❓ *How did Canaan's terrain and its location at the crossroads of the known world enhance the Hebrews' literary traditions?* (In their travels in search of pastures and trade, the Hebrews continually told their own story and refined their written tradition, creating the literary monument of the Bible.)

5
> ❝By the rivers of Babylon, there we sat down, yea, we wept when we remembered Zion . . . ❞
>
> —*Psalm 137:1*

Mesopotamian Invaders

Although Israel was larger and wealthier than Judah, its internal weaknesses made it vulnerable to attack from invaders. In 722 B.C., the Assyrian rulers of Mesopotamia conquered Israel. The ten tribes of Israel scattered, and they were gradually absorbed into the surrounding cultures. Hebrew tradition refers to these groups as the "Ten Lost Tribes."

In 586 B.C., after the Chaldeans had supplanted the Assyrians as the dominant power in Mesopotamia, the Chaldean king **Nebuchadnezzar** conquered Israel's stronger neighbor, Judah. He destroyed the Temple of Jerusalem and took many Hebrews into slavery in Babylon. Thus began one of the most bitter periods in Hebrew history, the **Babylonian Exile**.

Despite their separation from their homeland, the exiled Hebrews remembered their culture and kept it alive.

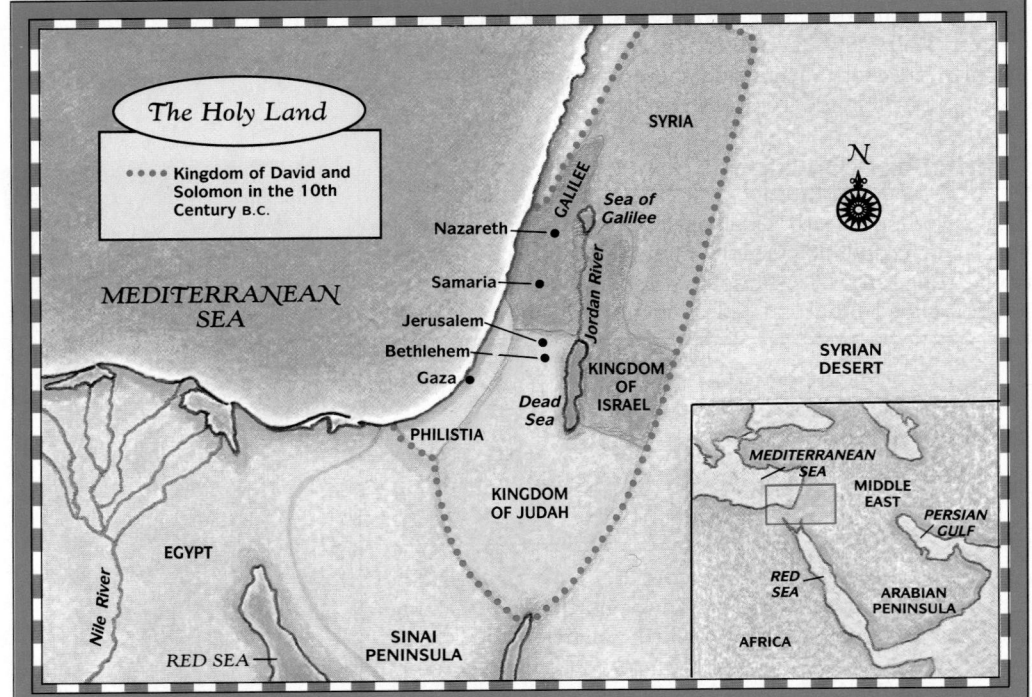

The Holy Land

•••• Kingdom of David and Solomon in the 10th Century B.C.

SYRIA
GALILEE
Sea of Galilee
Nazareth
Samaria
Jerusalem
Bethlehem
Gaza
MEDITERRANEAN SEA
Jordan River
Dead Sea
KINGDOM OF ISRAEL
PHILISTIA
KINGDOM OF JUDAH
SYRIAN DESERT
EGYPT
Nile River
RED SEA
SINAI PENINSULA

N

MEDITERRANEAN SEA
MIDDLE EAST
PERSIAN GULF
RED SEA
ARABIAN PENINSULA
AFRICA

READING CHECK

1. What are the two major divisions of the Bible? (the Hebrew Bible and the New Testament)
2. Who was the "founding father" of the Jews? (Abraham)
3. What journey does the Book of Exodus describe? (the flight of the Jews from Egypt)
4. What is meant by monotheism? (worship of one god)
5. What is a covenant? (a binding agreement)

FOR FURTHER STUDY

Nonfiction
Michael Grant's *The History of Ancient Israel* (Scribner, 1984) is a fact-filled and readable account. Northrop Frye's *The Great Code* (Harcourt Brace Jovanovich, 1982) and Harold Bloom's *The Book of J* (Grove Weidenfeld, 1990) presents eminent critics' views of the Bible as literature.

Fiction
Thomas Mann's *Joseph and His Brothers* (Knopf, 1934) charts the development of Joseph's character.

Film
Films set in biblical times include *The Ten Commandments*, John Huston's *The Bible*, and Zeffirelli's *Jesus of Nazareth*. ∎

When the Persian leader **Cyrus the Great** conquered Babylon and freed the Hebrew slaves in 539 B.C., many Hebrews returned to Jerusalem to rebuild the temple and reestablish their society. Some Hebrews, however, stayed in Babylon. Thus were sown the first seeds of the *Diaspora* (dī·as′pə·rə)—literally, the "scattering"—that would come to characterize the state of the Hebrew nation.

For almost eight hundred years, the tiny kingdom of Judah withstood conquest, slavery, and domination at home by a series of foreign rulers.

Although Cyrus allowed the Hebrews to return to Jerusalem, he did not grant them independence. Instead, for the next three-and-a-half centuries the Hebrews lived under the domination of a series of foreign rulers, including Alexander the Great of Macedonia. None of these rulers seriously threatened the Hebrews until 167 B.C., when the Seleucid king, Antiochus (an·tī′ə·kəs) IV, tried, ultimately unsuccessfully, to suppress Judaism.

6

The Hebrew Identity: A Covenant with God

7

The experience of living in a state of exile left the Hebrews vulnerable in many ways, but also provided inspiration for remarkable cultural creativity and spiritual unity. Since ancient times, the Hebrew people have focused on their God, **Yahweh**, as their source of unity. Unlike most of their neighbors in the Middle East, the Hebrews were **monotheists**—that is, they worshiped one god. They viewed Yahweh as a guiding entity who was always with them and rejected the notion that a human king could also be divine.

Yahweh differed from other gods in many ways, but especially in establishing with his people a special agreement, or **covenant**. The terms of this covenant meant that he would always guide Hebrew history, protecting his people if they fulfilled his law. Thus, even when the Hebrew people lost their homeland, they found a sense of belonging in their ongoing relationship with Yahweh.

> " Now therefore, if ye will obey my voice indeed, and keep my covenant, then ye shall be a peculiar treasure unto me above all people. . . . "
> —*Exodus 19:5*

8

6 HISTORICAL BACKGROUND
When the Seleucid Greek King Antiochus IV of Syria tried to suppress Judaism, the Hebrews, led by the Maccabee family, began a twenty-five-year revolt that resulted in a brief period of independence in 142 B.C. The Hebrew Bible ends with the story of this successful rebellion, which is commemorated in the Jewish festival of Hanukkah.

7 LITERARY BACKGROUND
During the centuries of exile and domination by foreign powers (c. 700–200 B.C.), the Hebrew people collected and edited their literary works and wrote many new ones, including the Book of Jonah and the Song of Songs. In sum, they fashioned the Law, the Prophets, and the Writings into the Hebrew Bible, a "monument" that has outlasted the architectural wonders of Mesopotamia.

8 RESPONDING TO THE QUOTATION
In this quotation, the speaker is the Hebrew God, Yahweh.
? *What is the significance of the quotation to the Hebrew people?* (God designates the Hebrews as His chosen people.)

WRITING TO LEARN

Invite students to choose a character from the Hebrew Bible and write a paragraph describing that person realistically in his or her historical context. ∎

*I*ntroduction

The Hebrew Bible

For good reason, the Hebrews have often been referred to as the "people of the book." The "book" is the Hebrew Bible, the great document of Jewish historical, literary, and spiritual experience.

The History of the Hebrew Bible

The Hebrew Bible tells the history of the Jewish people and presents the basic laws and teachings of their faith. The contents of the Hebrew Bible existed first in oral tradition. Then, over a period of centuries lasting from approximately 1000 to 100 B.C., the various parts of the Hebrew Bible were written and assembled. The Hebrew Bible was mostly written in Hebrew and Aramaic, another Semitic language that had replaced Hebrew as the language spoken by the Jews in about 400 B.C.

What Is the Hebrew Bible?

The Hebrew Bible is not one book, but many. In fact, the very name "Bible" comes from *biblia*, the plural of the Greek word *biblion*, "a book." The Hebrew Bible consists of twenty-four separate books, beginning with the Book of Genesis and ending with Chronicles. Christians refer to the Hebrew Bible as the Old Testament and accept it as sacred, but unlike the Jews they accept a second book of sacred writings, the New Testament (see page 196), as part of their Bible as well.

The Books of the Hebrew Bible

The Jewish people call their Bible **Tanakh**, an acronym formed from the first letters of the Hebrew words for the three categories of books contained in it: **Torah** (Law), **Nevi'im** (Prophets), and **Ketuvim** (Writings).

The Torah, or Law, is the first and oldest part of the Hebrew Bible. Sometimes called the Five Books of Moses—for, according to tradition, Moses wrote them—the Torah consists of five books that contain the earliest historical narratives of the Jewish people: Genesis, Exodus,

narrative: *a kind of writing that tells a story or relates an event.*

Leviticus, Numbers, and Deuteronomy. It also contains the basic tenets, or beliefs, and laws of Jewish faith, with detailed instructions on worship practices and conduct for daily life. The Torah is also known by the Greek word *Pentateuch,* meaning "five scroll jars," referring to the fact that at one time the five scrolls on which the Torah was written were kept in jars. The Torah is held in such reverence by Jewish people that no copy of it, no matter how old or worn, is ever destroyed. In cases of serious damage, it must be given a full funeral and buried as a beloved member of the family.

Nevi'im, or Prophets, contains the powerful words of the prophets: Isaiah, Jeremiah, and Ezekiel, among others. The prophets were not "fortunetellers" but social and spiritual reformers who were believed to be divinely inspired. The prophets called on the people of Israel to repent and lead purer lives, in keeping with God's covenant. These books also include the historical narratives of Joshua, the Judges, and the succession of Hebrew rulers that began with Saul, David, and Solomon.

Finally, Ketuvim, or Writings, consists of a rich variety of **genres**, or types, of literature, from Psalms and Proverbs to the Song of Songs (or Song of Solomon), Ecclesiastes, the Book of Job, and the Book of Ruth. The Book of Psalms contains lyrical hymns of praise that overflow with poignant emotions and imagery.

◆

psalm (säm): *a sacred song or hymn.*

The Book of Ruth is a tender work about compassion, loyalty, and tolerance that is sometimes described as a "short story." And the Book of Job features a dramatic dialogue between God and a man named Job, in which the question

The Jewish Museum, New York/Art Resource, New York

Torah ark curtain, late eighteenth century.

of human suffering is deeply and movingly probed.

The Themes of the Hebrew Bible

The Hebrew Bible is concerned above all with exploring the Hebrews' developing relationship with God. In the Hebrew Bible, God, or Yahweh, makes promises to people, but he also makes constant demands of them. Human beings are often tested, and they do not always pass their tests. They make mistakes and suffer the consequences of their actions. But they also experience the mercy of God and the constant promise of spiritual renewal, for the power to fulfill the covenant with God is within the power of each individual.

3

3 CULTURAL BACKGROUND
Yahweh: The Hebrew relationship with God developed over many centuries. At first the Hebrews worshiped a tribal god whom they called the God of their ancestors—the God of Abraham, Isaac, and Jacob. By the time of King David (c. 1000 B.C.), this ancestral God had become identified with the God of Moses, *Yahweh*—a name based on the verb "to be," usually understood as meaning the one who is before all things and who causes them to be.

The laws given to Moses by Yahweh focused the Jewish people on serving God by living righteous lives. National identity was fostered by the performance of ritual sacrifice in the Temple of Jerusalem. When the Assyrians forced many Jews into exile in 722 B.C. and the Chaldeans destroyed the Temple in 586 B.C. (see p. 158), it was the Hebrew Bible that sustained the Jews as a people.

LITERARY BACKGROUND
The Hebrew Bible is one of the seminal documents of western civilization. Its influence on Jews, Christians, and even Muslims is untold. Even today, thousands of years since the days of Moses, it is probably the most quoted book in western literature.

OBJECTIVES

1. *To analyze the events and themes of three Genesis narratives*
2. *To recognize the use of repetition to achieve rhythm and suspense*
3. *To write a first-person narrative in the persona of Adam, Eve, or the serpent and an analysis of the theme of moral struggle*

PREREADING FOCUS

Background: Scholars believe that the Book of Genesis combines three major accounts. The first and earliest, called the "J" document, depicts a God who plants, walks in the garden, speaks, breathes, and experiences human emotions. The second document, called "P," takes a more priestly tone and concentrates on God's divinity, his omnipotence (exercised through his voice alone), and the establishment of Jewish rituals. The third source, labeled "E," introduces angels and dreams as means by which God communicates with humanity. None of "E" is present in the passages from Genesis in the text. Ask students to look for passages from the "J" and "P" documents.

Writer's Response: If students do not volunteer any details about Adam and Eve, show them a painting of the temptation scene in the Garden of Eden and have them pick out such symbols as the apple, the snake, or the fig leaves. Be sure to point out, however, that Genesis does not actually mention an apple but only an indeterminate "fruit." Since apples were not native to ancient Palestine, scholars speculate that the author may have envisioned an apricot or some kind of citrus fruit. Over the years, the "fruit" of Eden was depicted as an apple, especially in western art, probably because apples recur as symbols of life in the myths of many western cultures.

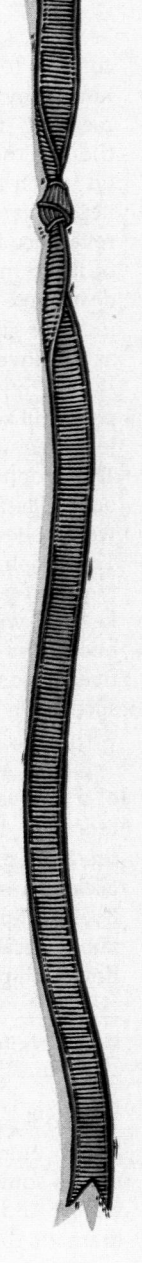

Reader's Guide

IN THE BEGINNING
from Genesis

Background

The Book of Genesis is the first of the Five Books of Moses, or the Torah. Genesis reflects the Hebrew people's beliefs about the origins of things, and it contains the core teachings of Jewish belief. Genesis begins with the birth of the universe and goes on to explain the emergence of evil, the cause of the Great Flood, the origin of languages, and the development of God's covenant with the Hebrew people.

Most scholars today believe that Genesis is actually a composite of separate narratives by different writers collected over a period of several hundred years. This may explain why Genesis contains two accounts of the creation of human beings. The first narrative tells us that God created the universe in six days and that man and woman were created at the same time. The second story, set in the Garden of Eden, tells us that Adam was created first and that Eve was created from his rib. Taken together, the two creation stories give us a fuller picture of the Hebrews' concept of God and humanity's relationship with God. We also come to understand their answers to some of the questions that concern all humankind: how and why people were created, why there is pain and conflict on earth, and why there is death.

Writer's Response

What do you already know, or think you know, about the story of creation in Genesis? Jot down some of the details you remember about Adam and Eve and the story of creation. As you read, see if you have remembered those details correctly, or if there are any details that you have forgotten. Does anything in the story of creation surprise you?

Literary Focus

Repetition—the repeating of words, phrases, or even entire sentences or passages—is an important feature of the Hebrew, or biblical, style. Repetition can serve several functions in a work of literature. It can create rhythm and build suspense and dramatic intensity. It can also help to emphasize important words and ideas.

IN THE BEGINNING
from Genesis
King James Bible

The Greek word genesis means "coming into being" or "originating." What beginnings, or origins, do these portions of the Book of Genesis explain?

The Creation

In the beginning God created the heaven and the earth. And the earth was without form, and void; and darkness was upon the face of the deep. And the Spirit of God moved upon the face of the waters.[1]

And God said "Let there be light": and there was light. And God saw the light, that it was good: and God divided the light from the darkness. And God called the light Day, and the darkness he called Night. And the evening and the morning were the first day.

And God said, "Let there be a firmament[2] in the midst of the waters, and let it divide the waters from the waters." And God made the firmament, and divided the waters which were under the firmament from the waters which were above the firmament: and it was so. And God called the firmament Heaven. And the evening and the morning were the second day.

And God said, "Let the waters under the heaven be gathered together unto one place, and let the dry land appear": and it was so.

And God called the dry land Earth; and the gathering together of the waters he called Seas: and God saw that it was good. And God said, "Let the earth bring forth grass, the herb[3] yielding seed, and the fruit tree yielding fruit after his[4] kind, whose seed is in itself, upon the earth": and it was so. And the earth brought forth grass, and herb yielding seed after his kind, and the tree yielding fruit, whose seed was in itself, after his kind: And God saw that it was good. And the evening and the morning were the third day.

And God said, "Let there be lights in the firmament of the heaven to divide the day from the night; and let them be for signs, and for seasons, and for days, and years. And let them be for lights in the firmament of the heaven to give light upon the earth": and it was so. And God made two great lights; the greater light to rule the day, and the lesser light to rule the night: he made the stars also. And God set them in the firmament of

---

1. **waters:** According to Hebrew belief, only water existed before the creation began.
2. **firmament:** the sky, seen as an arch or a vault.
3. **herb:** vegetation.
4. **his:** its (*Its*, the neuter form of the pronoun, did not come into common use until late in the seventeenth century, after the King James Bible was published).

Erastus Salisbury Field (1805–1900) was an American painter born in Leverett, Massachusetts. His subjects included scenes from American history, mythology, and the Bible. *The Garden of Eden* and *Historical Monument of the American Republic* are two of his best-known works. ∎

MEETING INDIVIDUAL NEEDS

Visual and Kinesthetic Learners: Have students make a "creation calendar" illustrating on a calendar square what God created each day of the week, ending with God resting on the seventh day. Suggest that students start with a wavy horizontal line to represent the waters covering the formless earth.

ESL: Explain to students that the verb ending *-th* is an archaic form for indicating present tense. It is equivalent to the present-day use of *-s* at the end of certain verbs, such as has and moves (ha*th* and move*th*). Remind them also that the masculine possessive pronoun *his* is used here instead of the more modern use of the neuter pronoun *its*. ∎

dominion (də·min′yən): power to rule

SuperStock International, Inc.

THE GARDEN OF EDEN, ERASTUS S. FIELD (1805–1900).
How does this painting compare with your own image of the Garden of Eden?

the heaven to give light upon the earth, and to rule over the day and over the night, and to divide the light from the darkness: and God saw that it was good. And the evening and the morning were the fourth day.

And God said, "Let the waters bring forth abundantly the moving creature[5] that hath life, and fowl that may fly above the earth in the open firmament of heaven." And God created great whales, and every living creature that moveth, which the waters brought forth abundantly, after their kind,[6] and every winged fowl after his kind: and God saw that it was good. And God blessed them, saying, "Be fruitful, and multiply, and fill the waters in the seas, and let fowl multiply in

the earth." And the evening and the morning were the fifth day.

And God said, "Let the earth bring forth the living creature after his kind, cattle, and creeping thing, and beast of the earth after his kind": and it was so. And God made the beast of the earth after his kind, and cattle after their kind, and every thing that creepeth upon the earth after his kind: and God saw that it was good.

And God said, "Let us make man in our image, after our likeness: and let them have dominion over the fish of the sea, and over the fowl of the air, and over the cattle, and over all the earth, and over every creeping thing that creepeth upon the earth." So God created man in his own image, in the image of God created he him; male and female created he them. And God blessed them, and

---

5. **creature:** an old plural form without the *s*.
6. **their kind:** their nature.

God said unto them, "Be fruitful, and multiply, and replenish the earth, and subdue it: and have dominion over the fish of the sea, and over the fowl of the air, and over every living thing that moveth upon the earth."

And God said, "Behold, I have given you every herb bearing seed, which is upon the face of all the earth, and every tree, in the which is the fruit of a tree yielding seed; to you it shall be for meat.[7] And to every beast of the earth, and to every fowl of the air, and to every thing that creepeth upon the earth, wherein there is life, I have given every green herb for meat": and it was so. And God saw every thing he had made, and, behold, it was very good. And the evening and the morning were the sixth day.

Thus the heavens and the earth were finished, and all the host[8] of them. And on the seventh day God ended his work which he had made; and he rested on the seventh day from all his work which he had made. And God blessed the seventh day, and sanctified it: because that in it he had rested from all his work which God created and made.

The Garden of Eden

These are the generations of the heavens and of the earth when they were created, in the day that the Lord God made the earth and the heavens, and every plant of the field before it was in the earth, and every herb of the field before it grew: for the Lord God had not caused it to rain upon the earth, and there was not a man to till the ground. But there went up a mist from the earth, and watered the whole face of the ground. And

the Lord God formed man of the dust of the ground, and breathed into his nostrils the breath of life; and man became a living soul.

And the Lord God planted a garden eastward in Eden; and there he put the man whom he had formed. And out of the ground made the Lord God to grow every tree that is pleasant to the sight, and good for food; the tree of life also in the midst of the garden, and the tree of knowledge of good and evil. And a river went out of Eden to water the garden; and from thence it was parted, and became into four heads. The name of the first is Pison: that is it which compasseth the whole land of Havilah,[9] where there is gold; and the gold of that land is good: there is bdellium[10] and the onyx stone. And the name of the second river is Gihon: the same is it that compasseth the whole land of Ethiopia. And the name of the third river is Hiddekel:[11] that is it which goeth toward the east of Assyria. And the fourth river is Euphrates.[12] And the Lord God took the man, and put him into the garden of Eden to dress it and to keep it. And the Lord God commanded the man, saying, "Of every tree of the garden thou mayest freely eat. But of the tree of the knowledge of good and evil, thou shalt not eat of it: for in the day that thou eatest thereof thou shalt surely die."

And the Lord God said, "It is not good that the man should be alone; I will make him an help meet[13] for him." And out of the

---

7. **meat:** In the King James Bible, meat simply means food in general. Animal meat is called flesh.

8. **host:** multitude.

9. **Pison** (pē'sən) . . . **Havilah** (hav'ə·lə): land rich in gold, perhaps located in Arabia.

10. **bdellium** (del'ē·əm): a kind of jewel—either a crystal, a pearl, or a deep-red gem such as a garnet.

11. **Gihon** (gē'hän) . . . **Hiddekel** (hid'ə·kəl): *Hiddekel* is the biblical name for the Tigris River.

12. **Euphrates** (yoo·frāt'ēz): longest river in western Asia.

13. **help meet:** helpful companion; often a spouse.

---

replenish (ri·plen'ish): make full

subdue (səb·dōō'): bring land under cultivation

GUIDED READING

Contrasting: There are two accounts of creation in Genesis. One appears here under the title "The Creation," and the other, under "The Garden of Eden." What are the most striking differences between the two accounts? (Possible response: The second account does not divide creation into an orderly seven-day sequence. Instead, it describes the Garden of Eden in detail and dramatizes the creation of Adam and of Eve from Adam's rib.)

WRITING TO LEARN

Geography: The author of Genesis provides specific information about the location of the Garden of Eden by naming the rivers that originate there (see p. 165). Build on this information by consulting atlases and encyclopedias. Then write a factual description of the location, terrain, climate, vegetation, wildlife, and minerals in the area identified by the Genesis author. ∎

3 CULTURAL DIVERSITY

Hebrews associated the serpent with the false gods of their neighbors in the Middle East. In many of these religions, the serpent supposedly possessed secret knowledge and often represented goddesses with powers over life and death.

❓ *What do people today associate with snakes and serpents? Are they still influenced by the role of the serpent in Genesis? What other influences may shape their associations?* (Many people associate snakes with danger because certain species are poisonous. Those who feel snakes are categorically evil are probably influenced by Genesis.)

HUMANITIES CONNECTION

Lucas Cranach the Elder (1472–1553) was a German painter and engraver whose works included numerous biblical paintings, several depicting the Fall of Adam and Eve. The stag had symbolic significance for medieval artists and writers. It was believed to seek out and devour or trample serpents (symbols of evil). Its horns were also thought to have healing properties. Because of these supposed attributes, artists found the stag an apt symbol for Christ.

❓ *Why might Cranach have put a stag in this painting?* (to link the Old Testament story of the Fall with the New Testament stories of Christ as the redeemer) ∎

---

ground the Lord God formed every beast of the field, and every fowl of the air; and brought them unto Adam to see what he would call them: and whatsoever Adam called every living creature, that was the name thereof. And Adam gave names to all cattle, and to the fowl of the air, and to every beast of the field; but for Adam there was not found an help meet for him. And the Lord God caused a deep sleep to fall upon Adam, and he slept: and he took one of his ribs, and closed up the flesh instead thereof; and the rib, which the Lord God had taken from man, made he a woman, and brought her unto the man. And Adam said, "This is now bone of my bones, and flesh of my flesh: she shall be called Woman, because she was taken out of Man." Therefore shall a man leave his father and his mother, and shall cleave unto his wife: and they shall be one flesh.

The Fall

And they were both naked, the man and his wife, and were not ashamed.

3 ⌈ Now the serpent[14] was more subtil[15] than any beast of the field which the Lord God had made. And he said unto the woman, ⌊ "Yea, hath God said, 'Ye shall not eat of every tree of the garden'?" And the woman said unto the serpent, "We may eat of the fruit of the trees of the garden. But of the fruit of the tree which is in the midst of the garden, God hath said, 'Ye shall not eat of it, neither shall ye touch it, lest ye die.'" And the serpent said unto the woman, "Ye shall not surely die. For God doth know that in

---

14. **the serpent:** traditionally understood to be, or to be possessed by, Satan; formerly the angel Lucifer, Satan was cast out of heaven because he set himself up as God's enemy.

15. **subtil:** subtle, meaning here crafty or sly.

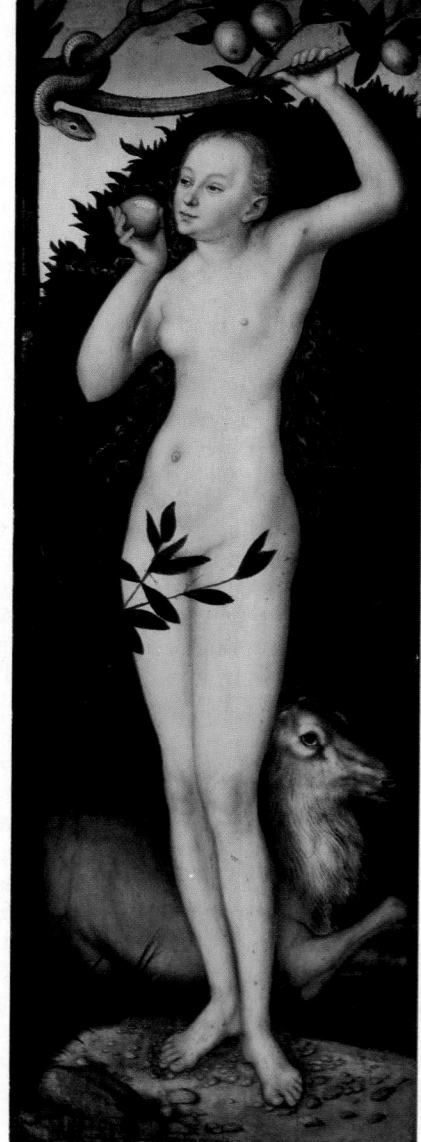

Lucas Cranach the Elder, German, 1472–1553, Eve, oil on panel, c. 1530, 107.6 × 36.4 cm, Charles H. and Mary F.S. Worcester Collection, The Art Institute of Chicago

EVE, LUCAS CRANACH THE ELDER, c. 1530. Eve's temptation has been a popular subject in European art for centuries.

READING CHECK

1. What does God do on the seventh day of creation? (God rests.)
2. In the first creation account, how does God make men and women? (in his own image)
3. In the second account, how does God create Adam and Eve? (Adam from dust and Eve from one of Adam's ribs)

4. What does the serpent promise Eve if she eats the fruit? (that she will be like a god, knowing good and evil)
5. What new feelings do Adam and Eve experience after they eat the fruit? (self-consciousness and guilt)

RETEACHING

Have students work together to act out the three Genesis narratives, devising props and costumes to represent the elements and the first humans and animals. They may use the dialogue from Genesis as their script and hold auditions for the main roles of God, Adam, Eve, and the serpent. After several rehearsals and class performances, students may wish to videotape a polished performance.

the day ye eat thereof, then your eyes shall be opened, and ye shall be as gods, knowing good and evil." And when the woman saw that the tree was good for food, and that it was pleasant to the eyes, and a tree to be desired to make one wise, she took of the fruit thereof, and did eat, and gave also unto her husband with her; and he did eat. And the eyes of them both were opened, and they knew that they were naked; and they sewed fig leaves together, and made themselves aprons. And they heard the voice of the Lord God walking in the garden in the cool of the day: and Adam and his wife hid themselves from the presence of the Lord God amongst the trees of the garden. And the Lord God called unto Adam, and said unto him, "Where art thou?" And he said, "I heard thy voice in the garden, and I was afraid, because I was naked; and I hid myself." And he said, "Who told thee that thou wast naked? Hast thou eaten of the tree, whereof I commanded thee that thou shouldest not eat?" And the man said, "The woman whom thou gavest to be with me, she gave me of the tree, and I did eat." And the Lord God said unto the woman, "What is this that thou hast done?" And the woman said, "The serpent beguiled me, and I did eat." And the Lord God said unto the serpent, "Because thou hast done this, thou art cursed above all cattle,[16] and above every beast of the field; upon thy belly shalt thou go, and dust shalt thou eat all the days of thy life. And I will put enmity between thee and the woman, and thy seed and her seed; it shall bruise thy head, and thou shalt bruise his heel." Unto the woman he said, "I will

greatly multiply thy sorrow and thy conception;[17] in sorrow thou shalt bring forth children; and thy desire shall be to thy husband, and he shall rule over thee." And unto Adam he said, "Because thou hast hearkened unto[18] the voice of thy wife, and hast eaten of the tree, of which I commanded thee, saying, Thou shalt not eat of it: cursed is the ground for thy sake; in sorrow shalt thou eat of it all the days of thy life; thorns also and thistles shall it bring forth to thee; and thou shalt eat the herb of the field; in the sweat of thy face shalt thou eat bread, till thou return unto the ground: for out of it wast thou taken, for dust thou art, and unto dust shalt thou return." And Adam called his wife's name Eve; because she was the mother of all living. Unto Adam also and to his wife did the Lord God make coats of skins, and clothed them.

And the Lord God said, "Behold, the man[19] is become as one of us, to know good and evil: and now, lest he put forth his hand, and take also of the tree of life,[20] and eat, and live for ever": therefore the Lord God sent him forth from the garden of Eden, to till the ground from whence he was taken. So he drove out the man; and he placed at the east of the garden of Eden, Cherubims[21] and a flaming sword which turned every way, to keep the way of[22] the tree of life.

---

16. **cattle:** a general term for all animals.
17. **conception:** childbearing pains.
18. **hearkened unto:** listened to and obeyed.
19. **man:** man and woman.
20. **tree of life:** a second tree in Eden, apparently a source of immortality.
21. **Cherubims** (cher′yoo·bimz′): warrior angels who act as guardian spirits and support the throne of God.
22. **keep the way of:** prevent access to.

4

---

beguiled (bē·gīld′): deceived

enmity (en′mə·tē): hostility

4 GUIDED READING

Identifying Details: Hebrews believed that the speaker of a blessing or curse could not call back or undo the utterance. In the next-to-last paragraph, what curses does God place on the serpent and the earth? (The serpent will always crawl on its belly and be despised by humanity; the earth will produce thorns and thistles.) How will Adam and Eve's lives change? (Adam will sweat in the fields; Eve will suffer in childbirth; they will experience death.)

INTERPRETING

How does God's attitude toward his creations change in the course of these three narratives? (Initially, God is proud of the goodness of his creations, of humans especially. In the final paragraphs, God is disappointed with and angry at Adam and Eve.)

CULTURAL DIVERSITY

How would you describe the relationship of human beings to nature as presented in the Genesis account? (Humans are presented as masters whose role is to subdue nature for the good of humans.) Do other cultures see this relationship differently? Give examples. (Students may point to the Native American belief in humanity's harmony with nature as evidenced in "How the World Was Made," pp. 10–16.)

EXTENSION AND ENRICHMENT

Acting as Critics. Have students research the literary or artistic use of the creation, Eden, or Fall story in a single work, for example, James Weldon Johnson's poem "The Creation"; John Milton's epic *Paradise Lost*; Mark Twain's short story "The Diary of Adam and Eve"; Gerard Manley Hopkins's poem "God's Grandeur"; William Blake's painting "Adam Naming the Beasts"; Jacopo da Ponte Bassano's painting "The Earthly Paradise"; Michelangelo's fresco "The Creation of Adam"; or the song of Gary Puckett and the Union Gap called "Let's Give Adam and Eve Another Chance."

Students should report orally in the "thumbs up" and "thumbs down" manner of television movie critics, providing examples and cogent reasons for approving or not approving the artist's reworking of the Genesis material.

CLOSURE

The Greek word *genesis* means "coming into being" or "originating." These Genesis stories give the answers of the Hebrew people to some basic questions about the universe and human experience. For example, Genesis answers the question of how the universe came into being. Ask students, What are some other questions that these stories answer? (Possible responses: origin of plants, animals, human beings, pain, suffering, death) ■

ANSWERS

First Thoughts
Answers will vary.

Identifying Facts
1. dominion over the earth
2. out of dust. as a partner for the man. out of Adam's rib
3. become self-conscious
4. Adam must toil. Eve will suffer in childbirth. The serpent will eat dust, crawl on its belly, and be hated by humanity.
5. evil, sorrow, pain, death

Interpreting Meanings
1. They establish rhythm and create suspense. God can create things merely by speaking.
2. It implies that he now has power over them.
3. Answers will vary. They will both suffer and die, and they are both driven from Eden.
4. Answers will vary. The second story is more dramatic and explains human pain and death. A male-dominated society would prefer the second; it upholds men's primacy.

Applying Meanings
Possible "kinds of temptations": cheating, drugs, mixed messages on sexual behavior. Answers will vary.

Creative Writing Response
Writing from the First-Person Point of View. Evaluate for use of details from Genesis and for imaginative fleshing out of the character.

Critical Writing Response
Establishing a Theme. Essays should focus on the moral conflicts within Eve, between Eve and the serpent, and between humanity and God. ■

168 The Ancient Middle East

First Thoughts
The story of creation answers many questions about the human condition, but it also raises some tantalizing questions. What questions does the account of the creation leave you with?

Identifying Facts
1. What responsibilities or privileges does God give to humans in the first account of creation?
2. In the second creation account, how is man created? Why is woman created, and how does God create her?
3. In "The Fall," how do Adam and Eve change after they eat the forbidden fruit?
4. How does God punish Adam, Eve, and the serpent?
5. What problems that still plague humanity are explained in "The Fall"?

Interpreting Meanings
1. **Repetition** occurs in the first account of the creation with the phrases "God said . . . and it was so" and "God saw that it was good." Why do you think these phrases are repeated so often? How do they help to characterize God?
2. In "The Garden of Eden," how does Adam's naming of the birds and the beasts assert his "dominion," or authority?
3. Does God seem to consider Adam and Eve equally guilty, or does he punish one of them more than the other? Explain your answer.
4. In the first creation account, God approves of all his creations. Men and women seem to be created equal, and no mention is made of the Fall. Why do you think that people tend to forget this story, and focus instead on Eve's creation from Adam's rib and the subsequent temptation and Fall?

Applying Meanings
Artists often use the story of the Fall as a **metaphor** for a person's loss of innocence, or for passing from childhood into adulthood. What kinds of temptations does the world present to people your age today? Who or what could be cast in the role of the serpent? If you were Adam or Eve, would you accept or reject the fruit the serpent urged you to take? Explain.

Creative Writing Response
Writing from the First-Person Point of View. Absent from the creation stories of Genesis are personal details—glimpses into the psychology of the characters. Rewrite the account of the Fall from the **first-person point of view** of Adam, Eve, or the serpent, using the pronoun *I*. Reveal as much about the character of your narrator as possible, describing the setting and interactions with the other characters in a way you believe he, she, or it would describe them.

Critical Writing Response
Establishing a Theme. Many scholars say that the moral struggle of men and women is a central **theme** of the Hebrew Bible. The first book of the Hebrew Bible plays a critical role in "setting the stage" for that theme. Find examples from the accounts from Genesis that you have just read—episodes, conflicts, characterization—that anticipate or illustrate this theme. Then write a three-paragraph essay showing how your examples support this theme. You might want to use a chart like the one below to organize your evidence.

Creation	The Garden of Eden	The Fall

BEHIND THE SCENES

The King James Bible

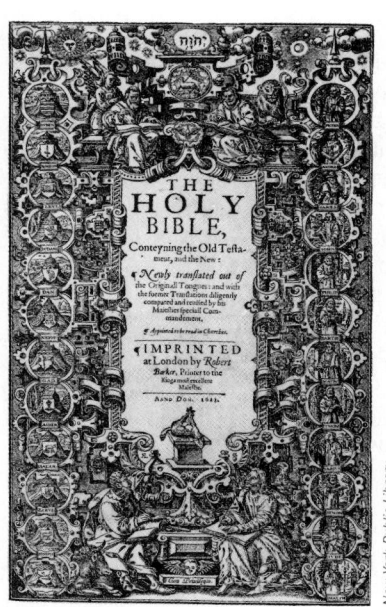

Frontispiece to the King James Bible, (1611). *Engraving.*

The King James Bible, published in 1611, is a product of Renaissance England. In 1604, the newly crowned English king, King James, called a conference of clergymen and scholars to discuss a new English translation of the Bible. Several translations of the Bible already existed, but during the Renaissance people began to be more aware of history and more sensitive to the idea that translations could be inaccurate. King James decided to gather to-

gether a group of some of the finest scholars and clergymen in England and commission them to assemble the most faithful translation of the Bible ever published. This translation, he decided, would draw upon the best Hebrew and Greek texts available, and it would leave out the interpretive—and generally inaccurate and biased—comments so common in English translations of the time.

Seven years later, fifty-four scholars and a team of bishops published their results. Their work has come to be known as the King James Bible, also known as the Authorized Version (after the Anglican Church that approved it), and the English Bible.

Modern English literature—especially the literature of the seventeenth through the nineteenth centuries—would be very different had the King James Bible not existed. In fact, the English language itself owes the popularization of many everyday expressions to the King James Bible: "loving kindness," "tender mercy," and "the wisdom of Solomon."

Even in its own day, however, the language of the King James Bible was considered old-fashioned. For example, even though by 1611 the English were beginning to use the pronoun *you,* the King James Bible continued to use the archaic form, *thou.* But in spite of its archaic-sounding language, many believe that the King James Bible ranks with the works of Shakespeare as a model of the English language at its most expressive and poetic.

CULTURAL DIVERSITY

The scholars who translated the King James Bible were divided into six groups of eight or more members. Two groups met at Oxford, two at Cambridge, and two at Westminster. Each group was assigned sections of the Bible to translate, and a committee of six edited the groups' drafts. Using a basic vocabulary of only 8,000 words, all groups worked toward homogeneity of diction and a graceful style. (In contrast, Shakespeare used 30,000 words, and a literate adult is said to recognize 15,000 or more words.) In this way, the translators achieved their goal: to make the Bible more accessible to every reader of English.

One of the key translators was a scholar named John Bois, who reportedly had read the entire Bible in Hebrew by the time he was six. Through Bois's diary, kept during his committee work, modern scholars have learned of the challenges the translators faced in trying to achieve an accurate but poetic rendition of the scriptures. To their credit, the committee members reviewed their work and substituted a variety of synonyms for the translation of a single Hebrew or Greek word in order to achieve richness without sacrificing uniformity of style. The translators and their editors succeeded so well that the King James Bible has been described as the only literary masterpiece ever created by a committee. ■

Reader's Guide

NOAH AND THE FLOOD
from Genesis

Background

The Hebrew story of Noah and the Flood preserves the memory of a terrifying deluge that occurred in Mesopotamia some time in the distant past. By the time the Book of Genesis was assembled, Hebrew storytellers knew many different versions of the ancient story. Instead of discarding any version, the people who assembled the various accounts in Genesis combined the different stories into one long narrative.

Even with various story strands braided into one story, however, the basic ideas are clear: God sends the flood to punish humanity for wickedness, but he saves one good man and his family. God then invites this family into a special pact, or **covenant**, in which God promises never again to destroy the entire earth. God makes the rainbow a symbol of this promise.

Like the creation stories of Genesis, the story of Noah explains beginnings. For example, it explains the appearance of rainbows after a storm. It also explains the development of the covenant, the ongoing pact between the Hebrews and God.

Writer's Response

The story of Noah and the Flood is so famous that most people know something about it, even if they have not read it. List all the features of the story that you are already familiar with. After you have read the story, check your list. Were all of your items accurate?

Literary Focus

Theme is the central idea or insight of a work of literature. Most themes are **implied**—that is, a reader must determine the theme based on details given in the story. A theme is usually the view of a particular writer, but in the Hebrew Bible, themes are expressive of the Hebrew people's deepest beliefs and concerns. The story of Noah and the Flood is the first occurrence in the Hebrew Bible of what is perhaps the most important theme in the Book of Genesis: the theme of the covenant, of the solemn promise that God makes with humankind, binding God and his creation together for eternity.

Imperative Sentences

On the basis of their purpose, sentences are categorized as declarative, interrogative, exclamatory, or imperative. An imperative sentence gives an order or makes a request. The subject of an imperative sentence is not expressed but is understood to be "you."

In this narrative, lines attributed to God are often imperative: "Be fertile and increase, and fill the earth."

1. **Reading and Speaking.** On each of the first three pages of the narrative, ask students to identify the sentences in which God expresses commands.

2. **Speaking.** God's commands are detailed and specific. Discuss with students what these commands suggest about the relative status of Noah and of God. (God's commands allow no room for discussion, interpretation, or adaptation; God expects Noah to obey without question.) ■

NOAH AND THE FLOOD
from Genesis
Jewish Publication Society of America

As you read, note any details that help to characterize God and Noah. What kind of person is Noah? What is God's attitude toward his creation before and after the Flood?

1 The Lord saw how great was man's wickedness on earth, and how every plan devised by his mind was nothing but evil all the time. And the Lord regretted that He had made man on earth, and His heart was saddened. The Lord said, "I will blot out from the earth the men whom I created—men together with beasts, creeping things, and birds of the sky; for I regret that I made them." But Noah found favor with the Lord.

This is the line of Noah. Noah was a righteous man; he was blameless in his age; Noah walked with God. Noah begot three sons: Shem, Ham, and Japheth.

1 The earth became corrupt before God; the earth was filled with lawlessness. When God saw how corrupt the earth was, for all flesh had corrupted its ways on earth, God said to Noah, "I have decided to put an end to all flesh, for the earth is filled with lawlessness because of them: I am about to destroy them with the earth. Make yourself an ark of gopher wood;[1] make it an ark with compartments, and cover it inside and out with pitch.[2] This is how you shall make it: the

2 length of the ark shall be three hundred cubits,[3] its width fifty cubits, and its height thirty cubits. Make an opening for daylight in the ark, and terminate it within a cubit of the top. Put the entrance to the ark in its side; make it with bottom, second, and third decks.

"For My part, I am about to bring the Flood waters upon the earth to destroy all flesh under the sky in which there is breath of life; everything on earth shall perish. But I will establish My covenant with you, and you shall enter the ark, with your sons, your wife, and your sons' wives. And of all that lives, of all flesh, you shall take two of each into the ark to keep alive with you; they shall be male and female. From birds of every kind, cattle of every kind, every kind of creeping thing on earth, two of each shall come to you to stay alive. For your part, take of everything that is eaten and store it away, to serve as food for you and for them." Noah did so; just as God commanded him, so he did.

Then the Lord said to Noah, "Go into the ark, with all your household, for you alone have I found righteous before Me in this

1. **gopher wood:** an unidentified type of wood.
2. **pitch:** a gummy, tar-like substance used for waterproofing.

3. **cubit** (kyōō'bit): a measure of 17 to 22 inches.

TEACHER'S RESOURCES

- Review and Response Worksheet
- Selection Test
- Vocabulary Activity Worksheet
- Vocabulary Test

1 **LITERARY ELEMENT**

Repetition: Ancient Hebrew writers often repeated slightly different versions of the same story from the oral tradition instead of combining them into a single version. Which ideas are repeated in the first and third paragraphs? (wickedness of humanity, God's decision to destroy human beings) What idea does the first paragraph contain that is not mentioned in the third paragraph? (God's feeling of sadness)

terminate (tʉr'mə·nāt'): end, finish

covenant (kuv'ə·nənt): a binding and solemn agreement

WRITING TO LEARN

2 *Mathematics:* Write a word problem for a math workbook using the information on the dimensions of the ark given in "Noah and the Flood," including the footnote about cubits. Make it clear whether you want the answer in inches or feet. (A cubit was originally the length of an arm from the tip of the middle finger to the elbow.) ■

3 CULTURAL DIVERSITY

In Hebrew literature, and in many other ancient cultures, some numbers carry symbolic value as well as literal meaning. The number 2, for example, suggests "the including of opposites"; 3—"completeness"; 7—"perfection" or "completeness"; 40—"many" or "a long time."

❓ *Do we still think of numbers in nonliteral or symbolic ways?* (Students may mention "lucky" numbers and expressions such as "one in a million.")

COMPARING LITERATURE

Ancient stories of floods that caused mass destruction are common in many cultures besides those of the ancient Sumerians and Hebrews. For example, the Chinese, Greek, Navajo, and pre-Incan Tiahuanaco cultures all have their own flood myths. Have your students research these and other flood stories, report their findings, and discuss similarities and differences among the various stories.

HUMANITIES CONNECTION

American painter Edward Hicks (1780–1849) is best known for his many versions of the allegorical *Peaceable Kingdom*, which features animals such as the lion and lamb serenely coexisting.

❓ *How does the painting by Edward Hicks compare with the way you imagine the animals boarding the ark?* (Answers will vary.) ■

3

generation. Of every clean[4] animal you shall take seven pairs, males and their mates, and of every animal which is not clean, two, a male and its mate; of the birds of the sky also, seven pairs, male and female, to keep seed alive upon all the earth. For in seven days' time I will make it rain upon the earth,

4. **clean:** The Hebrews made a distinction between animals that were clean—that is, fit for eating and free from ceremonial defilement—and those that were unclean.

forty days and forty nights, and I will blot out from the earth all existence that I created." And Noah did just as the Lord commanded him.

Noah was six hundred years old when the Flood came, waters upon the earth. Noah, with his sons, his wife, and his sons' wives, went into the ark because of the waters of the Flood. Of the clean animals, of the animals that are not clean, of the birds, and of everything that creeps on the ground, two

3

NOAH'S ARK, EDWARD HICKS, 1846.

Philadelphia Museum of Art: Bequest of Lisa Norris Elkins

of each, male and female, came to Noah into the ark, as God had commanded Noah. And on the seventh day the waters of the Flood came upon the earth.

In the six hundredth year of Noah's life, in the second month, on the seventeenth day of the month, on that day

All the fountains of the great deep burst apart,

And the floodgates of the sky broke open.

The rain fell on the earth forty days and forty nights. That same day Noah and Noah's sons, Shem, Ham, and Japheth, went into the ark, with Noah's wife and the three wives of his sons—they and all beasts of every kind, all cattle of every kind, all creatures of every kind that creep on the earth, and all birds of every kind, every bird, every winged thing. They came to Noah into the ark, two each of all flesh in which there was breath of life. Thus they that entered comprised male and female of all flesh, as God had commanded him. And the Lord shut him in.

The Flood continued forty days on the earth, and the waters increased and raised the ark so that it rose above the earth. The waters swelled and increased greatly upon the earth, and the ark drifted upon the waters. When the waters had swelled much more upon the earth, all the highest mountains everywhere under the sky were covered. Fifteen cubits higher did the waters swell, as the mountains were covered. And all flesh that stirred on earth perished—birds, cattle, beasts, and all the things that swarmed upon the earth, and all mankind. All in whose nostrils was the merest breath of life, all that was on dry land, died. All existence on earth was blotted out—man, cattle, creeping things, and birds of the sky; they were blotted out from the earth. Only Noah was left, and those with him in the ark.

And when the waters had swelled on the earth one hundred and fifty days, God remembered Noah and all the beasts and all the cattle that were with him in the ark, and God caused a wind to blow across the earth, and the waters subsided. The fountains of the deep and the floodgates of the sky were stopped up, and the rain from the sky was held back; the waters then receded steadily from the earth. At the end of one hundred and fifty days the waters diminished, so that in the seventh month, on the seventeenth day of the month, the ark came to rest on the mountains of Ararat.[5] The waters went on diminishing until the tenth month; in the tenth month, on the first of the month, the tops of the mountains became visible.

At the end of forty days, Noah opened the window of the ark that he had made and sent out the raven; it went to and fro until the waters had dried up from the earth. Then he sent out the dove to see whether the waters had decreased from the surface of the ground. But the dove could not find a resting place for its foot, and returned to him to the ark, for there was water over all the earth. So putting out his hand, he took it into the ark with him. He waited another seven days, and again sent out the dove from the ark. The dove came back to him toward evening, and there in its bill was a plucked-off olive leaf! Then Noah knew that the waters had decreased on the earth. He waited still another seven days and sent the dove forth; and it did not return to him any more.

In the six hundred and first year, in the first month, on the first of the month, the waters began to dry from the earth; and when Noah removed the covering of the ark, he saw that the surface of the ground was

---

5. **Ararat** (ar'ə·rat'): the highest mountain in Turkey.

4 CULTURAL DIVERSITY

The ancient Hebrews thought of the earth as a plate of land supported by pillars that stood in an abyss of water. Springs allowed some of the water from under the earth to reach the surface. The Hebrews pictured the sky as a dome that contained lights (sun, moon, stars) and windows. The windows, or gates, held back great stores of water above the sky.

? *How has the way we visualize the earth changed through the centuries?* (Medieval people imagined a flat earth; today we envision a spherical, blue earth moving through space in a solar system that is only a tiny part of a vast universe of galaxies.)

subsided (səb·sīd'id): sank to a lower level

5 LITERARY ELEMENT

Repetition: The writer recounts two versions of Noah's release of birds. In the first account, what kind of bird does Noah send out? (a raven) How does the second version of the story, contained in the same paragraph, differ? (He sends out a dove three times. The second time it returns with an olive branch.)

5 LITERARY ELEMENT

Symbol: What symbolic significance do the dove and the olive branch often have in art and literature? (They symbolize peace—in this case, God's renewed peace with humanity.)

In the Hebrew culture, a hero was an ordinary person chosen by God to perform an extraordinary task. A hero like Noah or Deborah (in the Book of Judges) possessed no special powers; instead, he or she relied on God. Ask students from religious traditions other than the Judeo-Christian to cite the qualities of their own heroes.

> **reckoning** (rek′ən·iŋ): a settlement of rewards or penalties
>
> **abound** (ə·bound′): be plentiful, exist in large numbers or amounts

drying. And in the second month, on the twenty-seventh day of the month, the earth was dry.

God spoke to Noah, saying, "Come out of the ark, together with your wife, your sons, and your sons' wives. Bring out with you every living thing of all flesh that is with you: birds, animals, and everything that creeps on earth; and let them swarm on the earth and be fertile and increase on earth." So Noah came out, together with his sons, his wife, and his sons' wives. Every animal, every creeping thing, and every bird, everything that stirs on earth came out of the ark by families.

Then Noah built an altar to the Lord and, taking of every clean animal and of every clean bird, he offered burnt offerings on the altar. The Lord smelled the pleasing odor, and the Lord said to Himself: "Never again will I doom the earth because of man, since the devisings of man's mind are evil from his youth; nor will I ever again destroy every living being, as I have done.

> So long as the earth endures,
> Seedtime and harvest,
> Cold and heat,
> Summer and winter,
> Day and night
> Shall not cease."

God blessed Noah and his sons, and said to them, "Be fertile and increase, and fill the earth. The fear and the dread of you shall be upon all the beasts of the earth and upon all the birds of the sky—everything with which the earth is astir—and upon all the fish of the sea; they are given into your hand. Every creature that lives shall be yours to eat; as with the green grasses, I give you all these. You must not, however, eat flesh with its life-blood in it. But for your own life-blood I will require a reckoning: I will re-

quire it of every beast; of man, too, will I require a reckoning for human life, of every man for that of his fellow man!

> Whoever sheds the blood of man,
> By man shall his blood be shed;
> For in His image
> Did God make man.

Be fertile, then, and increase; abound on the earth and increase on it."

And God said to Noah and to his sons with him, "I now establish My covenant with you and your offspring to come, and with every living thing that is with you—birds, cattle, and every wild beast as well—all that have come out of the ark, every living thing on earth. I will maintain My covenant with you: never again shall all flesh be cut off by the waters of a flood, and never again shall there be a flood to destroy the earth."

God further said, "This is the sign that I set for the covenant between Me and you, and every living creature with you, for all ages to come. I have set My bow[6] in the clouds, and it shall serve as a sign of the covenant between Me and the earth. When I bring clouds over the earth, and the bow appears in the clouds, I will remember My covenant between Me and you and every living creature among all flesh, so that the waters shall never again become a flood to destroy all flesh. When the bow is in the clouds, I will see it and remember the everlasting covenant between God and all living creatures, all flesh that is on earth. That," God said to Noah, "shall be the sign of the covenant that I have established between Me and all flesh that is on earth."

The sons of Noah who came out of the ark were Shem, Ham, and Japheth—Ham

---

6. **bow** (bō): rainbow.

READING CHECK

1. What sets Noah apart from the rest of humanity, in God's eyes? (Only Noah is "righteous.")
2. How does the story account for the re-birth of animals and people on the earth? (Noah's family and pairs of animals escape on the ark.)
3. What makes Noah decide that the waters have receded? (The dove that he sent forth does not return.)

4. What promise will God remember whenever he sees the rainbow? (never again to flood the earth)
5. Why does Noah bless two of his sons? (They treat him with respect even when he is drunk.)

RETEACHING

Divide students into groups. Ask each group to create an illustrated storybook on Noah and the Flood for kindergarten children. Direct students to reexamine the narrative to decide how much detail to include in their version and which episodes they wish to illustrate. Suggest that they make their illustrations simple but colorful and dramatic. Have volunteers organize a reading for young children.

being the father of Canaan. These three were the sons of Noah, and from these the whole world branched out.

Noah, the tiller of the soil, was the first to plant a vineyard. He drank of the wine and became drunk, and he uncovered himself within his tent. Ham, the father of Canaan, saw his father's nakedness and told his two brothers outside. But Shem and Japheth took a cloth, placed it against both their backs and, walking backwards, they covered their father's nakedness; their faces were turned the other way, so that they did not see their father's nakedness. When Noah woke up from his wine and learned what his youngest son had done to him, he said,

"Cursed be Canaan;
The lowest of slaves
Shall he be to his brothers."
And he said,
"Blessed be the Lord,
The God of Shem;
Let Canaan be a slave to them.
May God enlarge Japheth,
And let him dwell in the tents of Shem;
And let Canaan be a slave to them."

Noah lived after the Flood 350 years. And all the days of Noah came to 950 years; then he died.

6 COMPARING AND CONTRASTING

What attitude toward Noah is shown by the actions of Shem and Japheth? (respect) In contrast, what is the attitude shown by Ham? (disrespect, contempt)

HUMANITIES CONNECTION

As an adherent of the Classical school, the French painter Nicolas Poussin (poo·san'), 1594–1665, attempted to imitate the balance and unity of Greek and Roman art. He is noted for his biblical and mythological subjects.

❓ Does Poussin's painting contain any unexpected elements that were not part of the biblical account of the Flood? (The painting shows the anguish of those excluded from the ark.) ■

THE FLOOD, NICOLAS POUSSIN, 1664.
❓ Why do you think "Noah and the Flood" is one of the most popular stories from the Bible?

Scala/Art Resource, New York

Creating a Poster. Imagine Noah as a cruise director in a world where animals speak and act like human beings. Seeing no sign of a coming flood, none of the animals wants to leave home. What kind of poster might Noah develop in order to persuade the animals to board the ark?

Create an imaginative poster for "Noah's Cruise" in which you emphasize the fantastic experience that awaits the traveler. As you plan your poster, consider these questions: What kind of emotional appeal will Noah use? Will he try to scare the animals or appeal to their desire to be the "first" to do something exciting? How will he "sell" them on the fine qualities of his boat? Will he mention the limited space available? How will he state his own qualifications to be captain?

Ask students to discuss the covenant theme of "Noah and the Flood." What prohibition is included in the covenant God establishes with humanity through Noah? (Murder is forbidden.) Who is included in God's covenant? (God states that the covenant is with "every living thing.") Why is this agreement important? (It reveals God's love for his whole creation.) ■

ANSWERS

First Thoughts
Answers will vary.

Identifying Facts
1. God regrets having created them. Noah is righteous.
2. to learn whether the flood has subsided. The water has receded below the treetops.
3. He offers sacrifices.

Interpreting Meanings
1. The survivors will repopulate the earth.
2. Noah shows faith and obedience by building the ark and offering sacrifices. He shows weakness and bad temper by his drunkenness and rebuke of Ham.
3. God promises never again to destroy his creatures, whom he loves.
4. In the creation story, God delights in the goodness of his creation. In the flood story, the wickedness of humanity angers God. Portrayals of God will vary, but have students support their opinions.

Applying Meanings
Answers will vary. Define *redeeming* as "valuable" or "worth saving."

Creative Writing Response
Writing and Acting Out a Dramatic Sketch. Characters should react as believable human beings.

Critical Writing Response
Comparing and Contrasting Accounts of the Flood. Students should cite examples of how the two flood narratives and the two cultures are alike and different. ■

> ## First Thoughts
How did you feel when you read about the destruction of all living things except for the creatures on the ark?

Identifying Facts
1. Why does God destroy the earth with a flood? Why are Noah and his family spared?
2. Why does Noah send a dove out of the ark? What does the return of the dove with an olive branch tell Noah?
3. What is the first thing Noah does after the ark is unloaded?

Interpreting Meanings
1. Water can symbolize rebirth as well as destruction. How are both destruction and rebirth involved in the flood story?
2. What clues can you find in the story of the Flood that show the virtuous side of Noah's **character**? What can you infer about Noah's personality from the final section of the story?
3. Paraphrase the **theme** of God's covenant with all living things. What does the making of this covenant tell you about God's attitude toward his creation?
4. Compare the story of Noah to the story of creation. Is God characterized the same way in both stories? Is he portrayed as more forgiving or more vengeful in the story of Noah than in the story of Adam and Eve?

Applying Meanings
According to the story of Noah, God is discouraged by the corruption and wickedness of his creation. Do you think that the best way to fix a mistake is usually to obliterate it and start over? Or do you believe that there is something redeeming about everything that is created?

Creative Writing Response
Writing and Acting Out a Dramatic Sketch. Stories in the Hebrew Bible often do not include the background and details that we have come to associate with modern narratives. How do you suppose Noah's neighbors reacted to his building of the ark? With a partner or small group, write a short dramatic sketch, one to two pages long, in which Noah explains to his neighbors why he is building an enormous ark. How do his neighbors respond to his project? Are they understanding, alarmed, or mocking? How does Noah deal with his neighbors' reactions? As a group, present your sketch to the class.

Critical Writing Response
Comparing and Contrasting Accounts of the Flood. The story of the flood in the *Epic of Gilgamesh* (see page 145) is strikingly similar to the story of "Noah and the Flood." In each story a man is warned of a flood and is saved from destruction by building an ark for himself, his family, and a number of animals. Think of other ways that the two flood stories resemble each other, and ways in which they are different. What do you think these two cultures—Mesopotamian and Hebrew—have in common? What differences exist between the cultures? Write a two- to three-paragraph essay in which you explore these questions. You might want to use a diagram like the one below to plan your essay.

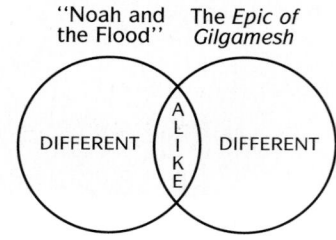

"Noah and the Flood"   The *Epic of Gilgamesh*

DIFFERENT   ALIKE   DIFFERENT

OBJECTIVES

1. *To recognize the literary merits of a biblical narrative*
2. *To analyze the Book of Ruth in terms of the elements of a short story: characterization, setting, plot, and theme*
3. *To write a letter in the persona of Ruth and an essay analyzing methods of characterization*

THEMES IN WORLD LITERATURE

Choices in Life

"The Garden of Eden" from *Genesis,* pp. 165–166
"The Parable of the Prodigal Son," pp. 199–200
"Lot's Wife," pp. 1223–1226

The Individual and Society

A Doll's House, pp. 1069–1126
"The Guest," pp. 1244–1257

Life and Loss

"On Her Brother," pp. 630–632
From "The Tragedy of Sohráb and Rostám" from the *Shahname,* pp. 646–653
"And of Clay Are We Created," pp. 1308–1319 ■

Reader's Guide

THE BOOK OF RUTH

Background

The story of Ruth is set about 1100 B.C., approximately the same time that the Trojan War was taking place in Asia Minor. But it was probably not written down until nearly seven hundred years later, when the Hebrew people returned to Israel after their seventy-year captivity in Babylon. This was a time of turmoil when Hebrew leaders perceived foreign customs as a threat to the identity of the Jewish people.

Ruth was a woman from Moab (mō'ab'), a kingdom east of the Dead Sea. The religion of Moab involved the worship of idols—a practice the Hebrews condemned. Ruth married a Jewish man, Mahlon, but was soon left widowed and childless. In 1100 B.C., a woman who had no husband or son could expect to experience dire poverty. Fortunately, the ancient Israelites practiced a custom called "levirate" (lev'ə·rit) marriage (from *levir,* meaning "husband's brother"). According to this custom, a close male relative of the dead husband, such as a brother, was obliged to marry the widow if the husband had left no son. The firstborn son of this second marriage would be raised in the dead husband's name and would be considered his legal heir. Despite being an outsider, Ruth went to Israel with her mother-in-law Naomi and ultimately married Boaz (bō'az'), a relative of her husband's.

Oral Response

Most of us have felt like outsiders at one time or another. Hold a class discussion in which each of you describes an experience in which you felt as if you "didn't belong." What was the cause of this feeling? Who or what helped you overcome this feeling? Or does something—society or yourself—still need to change in order for you to stop feeling this way?

Literary Focus

The Book of Ruth is sometimes called the first **short story** ever written. Unlike the poetry of the Book of Psalms or the narratives in the Book of Genesis, the Book of Ruth contains developed **characters**, a specific **setting**, a definite **plot**, or course of events, and an underlying **theme** about loyalty and acceptance.

PREREADING FOCUS

Background: The unknown author stresses that Ruth is a woman of Moab, an outsider (once in Chapter 1, four times in Chapter 2, twice in Chapter 4). This repetition reflects the racial and religious exclusivism that often prevailed in Jerusalem after the Hebrews returned from exile in Babylon. One psalmist of that era, for example, derides Moab as Yahweh's "washbowl" (Psalm 108:9). Ezra, a Jewish leader of the time, expresses horror when some Jews "pollute" the blood of Israel by marrying Moabites and other foreigners (Ezra 9:1–4).

Previous Hebrew experiences with Moabites had alternated between periods of cooperation and periods of conflict. Genesis acknowledges the distant kinship of Moabites and Jews (e.g., Genesis 19:37), yet Deuteronomy 23:3 forbids citizenship to people of Moabite descent "to the tenth generation."

Oral Response: You might extend students' grasp of the outsider theme by asking them to discuss parallels between Ruth's experience and that of some individuals today, such as refugees or illegal immigrants. Mention that Ruth had no status or rights as an individual in her new country: she was of the "wrong" race (a despised Moabite), the "wrong" gender (a woman in a male-dominated world), and the "wrong" class (one of the poor).

VOCABULARY IN CONTEXT

The words listed below will appear in the side margin at the point of instruction:

1. sojourn
2. tarry
3. entreat
4. afflicted
5. kindred
6. sheaves
7. nativity
8. recompense
9. sufficed
10. reproach

INTEGRATING THE LANGUAGE ARTS: GRAMMAR

Archaic Diction and Word Order

Archaic diction and word order are words and word patterns that were commonly used in the past but have fallen into disuse. Contemporary readers should use context clues to figure out word meanings, or consult an unabridged dictionary.

1. **Listening/Speaking.** Ask students to express these archaic words in contemporary English:
   1. ye, thee, thou (you)
   2. hath, grieveth (has, grieves)
   3. doest, goest (do, go)
   4. say unto (say to)
   5. nay (no)

TEACHER'S RESOURCES

- ✔ Review and Response Worksheet
- ✔ Selection Test
- ✔ Vocabulary Activity Worksheet
- ✔ Vocabulary Test
- ✔ Language Skills Worksheet

1 LITERARY ELEMENT

Setting: What can you infer about the time and place of the story from the opening sentences? (The story takes place before the Hebrews had kings, in the time of the judges. It probably occurs in Bethlehem or Moab or both. Explain that this era was about 1250–1000 B.C. Hebrew judges settled disputes, led armies, and acted as religious leaders.

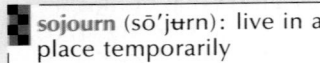

sojourn (sō'jŭrn): live in a place temporarily
tarry (tar'ē): delay or linger

MEETING INDIVIDUAL NEEDS

ESL: For those who are finding the archaic English of the King James Bible a stumbling block, provide or suggest more modern translations, such as the New International Bible or the Good News Bible. Also, since some ESL students are themselves newcomers, invite them to compare and contrast their experiences with those of Ruth in her new home in Judah. ■

THE BOOK OF RUTH

King James Bible

The Book of Ruth is an entertaining story, but it is also a lesson about devotion, tolerance, and compassion. Pay attention to the message of the story of Ruth, and note the rewards received by characters who express devotion.

Chapter 1

1 Now it came to pass in the days when the judges ruled that there was a famine in the land. And a certain man of Bethlehem-Judah[1] went to sojourn in the country of Moab,[2] he, and his wife, and his two sons.

And the name of the man was Elimelech, and the name of his wife Naomi, and the names of his two sons Mahlon and Chilion, Ephrathites[3] of Bethlehem-Judah. And they came into the country of Moab and continued there.

And Elimelech, Naomi's husband, died; and she was left, and her two sons.

And they took them wives of the women of Moab; the name of the one was Orpah, and the name of the other Ruth: and they dwelled there about ten years.

And Mahlon and Chilion died also, both of them; and the woman was left of her two sons and her husband.

Then she arose with her daughters-in-law, that she might return from the country of Moab: for she had heard in the country of Moab how that the Lord had visited his people in giving the bread.

Wherefore she went forth out of the place where she was, and her two daughters-in-law with her; and they went on the way to return unto the land of Judah.

And Naomi said unto her two daughters-in-law, "Go, return each to her mother's house: the Lord deal kindly with you, as ye have dealt with the dead and with me. The Lord grant you that ye may find rest, each of you in the house of her husband." Then she kissed them; and they lifted up their voice and wept.

And they said unto her, "Surely we will return with thee unto thy people."

And Naomi said, "Turn again, my daughters: why will ye go with me? Are there yet any more sons in my womb, that they may be your husbands?

"Turn again, my daughters, go your way; for I am too old to have a husband. If I should say I have hope, if I should have a husband also tonight and should also bear sons, would ye tarry for them till they were

---

1. **Bethlehem-Judah:** that is, Bethlehem in Judah; Judah was a region in southern Palestine that eventually became a kingdom rivaling Israel to the north.
2. **Moab:** a kingdom of the Dead Sea, in what is today called Jordan.
3. **Ephrathites** (ef'rə·thīts): natives of Bethlehem, once known as Ephrath; members of the clan of Ephrah.

Ashmolean Museum, Oxford

RUTH AND NAOMI, WILLEM DROST. *Ruth's famous quote, "Wither thou goest, I will go," is often used in wedding ceremonies.*

❓ *What quality in Ruth does this speech demonstrate?*

grown? Would ye stay for them from having husbands? Nay, my daughters; for it grieveth me much for your sakes that the hand of the Lord is gone out against me."

2 [And they lifted up their voice and wept again: and Orpah kissed her mother-in-law, but Ruth clave unto[4] her.

And she said, "Behold, thy sister-in-law is gone back unto her people and unto her gods: Return thou after thy sister-in-law."

3 [And Ruth said, "<u>Entreat</u> me not to leave thee or to return from following after thee:

for whither thou goest, I will go; and where thou lodgest, I will lodge: thy people shall be my people, and thy God my God: where thou diest, will I die, and there will I be buried: the Lord do so to me, and more also, if ought[5] but death part thee and me."] 3

When she saw that she was steadfastly minded to go with her, then she left speaking unto her.

So they two went until they came to Bethlehem. And it came to pass, when they were come to Bethlehem, that all the city was moved about them, and they said, "Is this Naomi?" And she said unto them, "Call me not Naomi, call me Mara:[6] for the Almighty hath dealt very bitterly with me. I went out full, and the Lord hath brought me home again empty: Why then call ye me Naomi, seeing the Lord hath testified against me, and the Almighty hath <u>afflicted</u> me?"

So Naomi returned, and Ruth the Moabitess, her daughter-in-law, with her, which returned out of the country of Moab: and they came to Bethlehem in the beginning of barley harvest.] 4

Chapter 2

And Naomi had a kinsman of her husband's, a mighty man of wealth, of the family of Elimelech; and his name was Boaz.

And Ruth the Moabitess said unto Naomi, "Let me now go to the field and glean ears of corn after him in whose sight I shall find grace."[7] And she said unto her, "Go, my daughter."

---

5. **ought** (archaic): aught, meaning "anything."
6. **Naomi . . . Mara:** Naomi means "pleasantness" or "my pleasant one," in Hebrew, and Mara means "bitterness" or "the bitter one."
7. **glean. . . grace:** According to biblical law, the poor were entitled to glean in the fields—that is, to gather the bits of grain left or dropped by the reapers. The corners of the fields were also left for the poor to reap.

---

4. **clave unto:** clung to; was faithful to (archaic form of *cleaved*).

LITERARY ELEMENT
Exposition: Note that in Chapter 1 the setting, the main characters, and their situation are laid out for the reader. What problem do Naomi and her daughters-in-law face? (They are all widows without husbands or sons to provide for them.)

2 LITERARY ELEMENT
Characterization: Chapter 1 has introduced three women—Naomi, Orpah, and Ruth. How is Naomi similar to a pioneer or an immigrant? (She is willing to leave her home in search of a better life.) What does Orpah's decision to stay behind reveal about her character? (Orpah is cautious and more secure with what is familiar.)

3 LITERARY ELEMENT
Characterization: What do Ruth's words to Naomi reveal about Ruth's character? (Above all, Ruth is loyal and devoted to those she loves.)

4 PREDICTING
Before you go on to Chapter 2, stop to consider the life that awaits Naomi and Ruth in Judah. How do you think they will support themselves? What dangers might they face? (Answers will vary.)

■ **entreat** (en·trēt'): make an earnest appeal; plead
afflicted (ə·flikt'əd): caused pain or suffering to

5 LITERARY ELEMENT

Characterization: How does Boaz exceed the demands of custom or justice? (See footnote 7 on p. 179. Boaz is not required to protect Ruth or give her water, only to let her glean.) What qualities of character do Boaz's words reveal about him? (kindness, generosity, protectiveness)

HUMANITIES CONNECTION

The French painter Paul-Gustave Doré (1832–1883) illustrated more than 90 books. ❓ *Which figures in Doré's work represent Ruth and Boaz? How does his depiction of gleaning compare with the scene you imagined?* ∎

COMPARING LITERATURE

Ask students to compare Ruth to other female figures in the Hebrew Bible, such as Eve or Esther. ❓ *What qualities do they have in common? How do they differ?*

And she went, and came, and gleaned in the field after the reapers: and her hap[8] was to light on a part of the field belonging unto Boaz, who was of the kindred of Elimelech.

And, behold, Boaz came from Bethlehem and said unto the reapers, "The Lord be with you." And they answered him, "The Lord bless thee."

Then said Boaz unto his servant that was set over the reapers, "Whose damsel is this?"

And the servant that was set over the reapers answered and said, "It is the Moabitish damsel that came back with Naomi out of the country of Moab. And she said, 'I pray you, let me glean and gather after the reapers among the sheaves': so she came, and hath continued even from the morning until now, that she tarried a little in the house."

5 · Then said Boaz unto Ruth, "Hearest thou not, my daughter? Go not to glean in another field, neither go from hence, but abide here fast by my maidens. Let thine eyes be on the field that they do reap, and go thou after them. Have I not charged the young men that they shall not touch thee? And when thou art athirst, go unto the vessels, and drink of that which the young men have drawn."

Then she fell on her face and bowed herself to the ground and said unto him, "Why have I found grace in thine eyes, that thou shouldest take knowledge of me, seeing I am a stranger?"

And Boaz answered and said unto her, "It hath fully been showed me all that thou hast done unto thy mother-in-law since the death of thine husband: and how thou hast left thy father and thy mother, and the land of thy nativity and art come unto a people which

thou knewest not heretofore. The Lord recompense thy work, and a full reward be given thee of the Lord God of Israel, under whose wings thou art come to trust."

Then she said, "Let me find favor in thy sight, my lord; for that thou hast comforted me, and for that thou hast spoken friendly unto thine handmaid, though I be not like unto one of thine handmaidens."

And Boaz said unto her, "At mealtime come thou hither, and eat of the bread, and dip thy morsel in the vinegar." And she sat beside the reapers: and he reached her

Dover Publications

RUTH AND BOAZ, GUSTAVE DORÉ.

---

8. **hap:** luck.

parched corn, and she did eat, and was sufficed, and left.

And when she was risen up to glean, Boaz
commanded his young men, saying, "Let her
glean even among the sheaves, and reproach
her not. And let fall also some of the handfuls on purpose for her, and leave them, that
she may glean them, and rebuke her not."

6 So she gleaned in the field until even, and
beat out that she had gleaned: and it was
about an ephah⁹ of barley.

7 And she took it up and went into the city:
and her mother-in-law saw what she had
gleaned: and she brought forth and gave to
her what she had reserved after she was
sufficed.

And her mother-in-law said unto her,
"Where hast thou gleaned today? and where
wroughtest thou? Blessed be he that did take
knowledge of thee." And she showed her
mother-in-law with whom she had wrought,
and said, "The man's name with whom I
wrought today is Boaz."

And Naomi said unto her daughter-in-law,
"Blessed be he of the Lord, who hath not left
off his kindness to the living and to the dead."
And Naomi said unto her, "The man is near
of kin unto us, one of our next kinsmen."

And Ruth the Moabitess said, "He said
unto me also, 'Thou shalt keep fast by my
young men, until they have ended all my
harvest.'"

And Naomi said unto Ruth her daughter-
in-law, "It is good, my daughter, that thou
go out with his maidens, that they meet thee
not in any other field."

So she kept fast by the maidens of Boaz
to glean unto the end of barley harvest and
of wheat harvest; and dwelt with her
mother-in-law.

Chapter 3

Then Naomi her mother-in-law said unto
her, "My daughter, shall I not seek rest for
thee,¹⁰ that it may be well with thee? And
now is not Boaz of our kindred, with whose
maidens thou wast? Behold, he winnoweth
barley tonight in the threshing floor. Wash
thyself therefore, and anoint thee, and put
thy raiment upon thee, and get thee down
to the floor: but make not thyself known
unto the man, until he shall have done eating
and drinking. And it shall be, when he lieth
down, that thou shalt mark the place where
he shall lie, and thou shalt go in and uncover
his feet and lay thee down; and he will tell
thee what thou shalt do."

And she said unto her, "All that thou say-
est unto me I will do."

And she went down unto the floor and
did according to all that her mother-in-law
bade her.

And when Boaz had eaten and drunk and
his heart was merry, he went to lie down at
the end of the heap of corn: and she came
softly and uncovered his feet and laid her
down.

And it came to pass at midnight, that the
man was afraid and turned himself: and, behold, a woman lay at his feet.

And he said, "Who art thou?" And she
answered, "I am Ruth thine handmaid:
Spread therefore thy skirt¹¹ over thine handmaid; for thou art a near kinsman."

And he said, "Blessed be thou of the Lord,
my daughter: for thou hast showed more
kindness in the latter end than at the beginning, inasmuch as thou followedst not young

---

9. **ephah** (ē′fə): a little more than a bushel.

10. **seek rest for thee:** that is, seek a husband; Naomi is trying to fulfill the responsibility of a parent for arranging the marriage of a child.

11. **Spread therefore thy skirt:** a formal act of betrothal.

■ **sufficed** (sə·fīst′): filled up;
satisfied

reproach (ri·prōch′):
criticize

6 GUIDED READING
Interpreting Details: An
ephah (a little more than a
bushel) was an unusually large
amount of grain for anyone to
glean by *even* (evening). How
do you account for Ruth's having gathered so much? (Boaz's
workers followed his instructions to leave extra grain for
her and to let her glean even
among uncut rows.)

7 GUIDED READING
Finding the Main Idea: The
archaic language and confusing pronoun references in
these two paragraphs may puzzle some students. Read aloud
these paragraphs from a translation in modern English. Then
ask students, What did Ruth
take to Naomi? (the barley she
had gleaned, and a portion of
her own food that she had
saved for Naomi) What is another, more contemporary
word for *wrought?* (worked)

8 INFERRING
Remember that Ruth is not familiar with Hebrew customs.
From her readiness to follow
Naomi's mysterious instructions, what can you infer about
the relationship between Ruth
and Naomi? (They trust each
other completely.)

Theme: Why does Boaz consider Ruth virtuous? (She does not seek a young man but follows the customs of her mother-in-law's people.) How is Boaz a virtuous man? (He does not marry Ruth until he is sure no nearer kinsman has priority over him.)

10 CULTURAL DIVERSITY

The levirate laws of ancient Israel were designed primarily to preserve a man's family line and keep his property within the clan. A man could refuse to honor the laws if they endangered the handing down of his own name and property. While the laws had the desirable effect of rescuing a sonless widow from poverty, they reflect a socio-economic structure in which women had no property rights. Students might investigate marriage customs and property rights, particularly with regard to widows, in various countries today, including those in the Middle East. In parts of Iraq, for example, it is still common for a man to marry his brother's widow.

11 CULTURAL DIVERSITY

In ancient Israel, putting one's foot or sandal on property indicated one had taken possession of it. By giving his sandal to Boaz, the kinsman is transferring his right to the purchase of the property.

❓ *How is ownership and right of ownership established in America today?* (through deeds drawn up and notarized in the presence of witnesses)

182   The Ancient Middle East

9

men,[12] whether poor or rich. And now, my daughter, fear not; I will do to thee all that thou requirest: for all the city of my people doth know that thou art a virtuous woman. And now it is true that I am thy near kinsman: howbeit, there is a kinsman nearer than I. Tarry this night, and it shall be in the morning that if he will perform unto thee the part of a kinsman, well; let him do the kinsman's part: but if he will not do the part of a kinsman to thee, then will I do the part of a kinsman to thee, as the Lord liveth: lie down until the morning."

And she lay at his feet until the morning: and she rose up before one could know another. And he said, "Let it not be known that a woman came into the floor."

Also he said, "Bring the veil that thou hast upon thee, and hold it." And when she held it, he measured six measures of barley and laid it on her: and she went into the city.

And when she came to her mother-in-law, she said, "Who art thou, my daughter?" And she told her all that the man had done to her.

And she said, "These six measures of barley gave he me; for he said to me, 'Go not empty unto thy mother-in-law.'"

Then said she, "Sit still, my daughter, until thou know how the matter will fall: for the man will not be in rest until he have finished the thing this day."

Chapter 4

Then went Boaz up to the gate and sat him down there and, behold, the kinsman of whom Boaz spake came by; unto whom he said, "Ho, such a one! turn aside, sit down here." And he turned aside and sat down.

And he took ten men of the elders of the city and said, "Sit ye down here." And they sat down.

And he said unto the kinsman, "Naomi, that is come again out of the country of Moab, selleth a parcel of land, which was our brother Elimelech's. And I thought to advertise thee, saying, Buy it before the inhabitants and before the elders of my people. If thou wilt redeem it, redeem it: but if thou wilt not redeem it, then tell me, that I may know: for there is none to redeem it beside thee; and I am after thee." And he said, "I will redeem it."

Then said Boaz, "What day thou buyest the field of the hand of Naomi, thou must buy it also of Ruth the Moabitess, the wife of the dead, to raise up the name of the dead upon his inheritance."

And the kinsman said, "I cannot redeem it for myself, lest I mar mine own inheritance:[13] Redeem thou my right to thyself; for I cannot redeem it."

10

Now this was the manner in former time in Israel concerning redeeming and concerning changing, for to confirm all things; a man plucked off his shoe, and gave it to his neighbor: and this was a testimony in Israel.

Therefore the kinsman said unto Boaz, "Buy it for thee." So he drew off his shoe.

11

And Boaz said unto the elders and unto all the people, "Ye are witnesses this day, that I have bought all that was Elimelech's, and all that was Chilion's and Mahlon's, of the hand of Naomi. Moreover, Ruth the

---

12. **thou followedst not young men:** Boaz, who is eighty years old, is praising Ruth for her willingness to fulfill the levirate marriage obligation by marrying him even though he is old.

13. **lest I mar mine own inheritance:** in other words, by spending money on property that will go to the son legally regarded as Mahlon's, rather than his own.

READING CHECK

1. Why does Naomi decide to leave Moab? (She is a poor widow without sons to support her.)
2. What is Ruth's relationship to Naomi? (her daughter-in-law)
3. To where do Naomi and Ruth travel? (Bethlehem in Judah, Naomi's birthplace)

4. According to Jewish law, who is expected to marry a widow? (a close relative of the dead husband)
5. Who marries Ruth? (Boaz)

RETEACHING

Have students work separately or together as a class to construct a flow chart representing the sequence of important events in the plot. Begin with Ruth's marriage to Naomi's son and end with the birth of Obed. At least eight key events should be included. Students may also want to construct a family tree so they can see the relationships among the characters and their descendants.

The Pierpont Morgan Library, New York; M.638, f.17v

RUTH AND BOAZ WITH THE REAPERS, *French miniature, c. 1250.*

Moabitess, the wife of Mahlon, have I purchased to be my wife, to raise up the name of the dead upon his inheritance, that the name of the dead be not cut off from among his brethren and from the gate of his place: Ye are witnesses this day."

And all the people that were in the gate and the elders said, "We are witnesses. The Lord make the woman that is come into thine house like Rachel and like Leah,[14]

which two did build the house of Israel: and do thou worthily in Ephrath, and be famous in Bethlehem. And let thy house be like the house of Pharez, whom Tamar bare unto Judah,[15] of the seed which the Lord shall give thee of this young woman."

So Boaz took Ruth, and she was his wife: and when he went in unto her, the Lord gave her conception, and she bare a son.

And the women said unto Naomi, "Blessed be the Lord, which hath not left thee this day without a kinsman, that his name may be famous in Israel. And he shall be unto thee a restorer of thy life and a nourisher of thine old age: for thy daughter-in-law, which loveth thee, which is better to thee than seven sons, hath born him."

And Naomi took the child and laid it in her bosom and became nurse unto it.

And the women her neighbors gave it a name, saying, "There is a son born to Naomi";[16] and they called his name Obed: He is the father of Jesse, the father of David.

Now these are the generations of Pharez: Pharez begat Hezron, and Hezron begat Ram, and Ram begat Amminadab, and Amminadab begat Nahshon, and Nahshon begat Salmon, and Salmon begat Boaz, and Boaz begat Obed, and Obed begat Jesse, and Jesse begat David.

12

---

15. **Pharez . . . Judah:** Judah was the fourth son of Jacob and Leah. After his daughter-in-law Tamar had twice been left a childless widow after two of his sons died, she tricked Judah into becoming the father of her twin sons, Pharez and Zarah.

16. **son born to Naomi:** not literally, but rather a son in the sense of a legal heir to both her dead husband and dead sons; some biblical scholars suggest that the child may have been legally regarded as Naomi's.

---

14. **like Rachel and like Leah:** two sisters who were Jacob's wives, their sons were among the twelve sons of Jacob who founded the twelve tribes of Israel.

WRITING TO LEARN

Social Studies: Suppose that the Book of Ruth were the only piece of ancient Hebrew literature available to us. Studying it carefully, what could you deduce about the society's customs in the areas of farming, public welfare or charity, or marriage? Choose *one* of these areas, and write a brief essay about the values and customs of ancient Israel as they are suggested in the Book of Ruth. Support your conclusions with details from the story. ∎

HUMANITIES CONNECTION

The medieval scribes decorated the initial letters of books or chapters of their manuscripts with biblical or other devotional images. These rich, full-color drawings were called illuminations. In the thirteenth century, Paris was the birthplace of new ideas in Bible ornamentation. Text and pictures were closely integrated, and the stylized figures often resembled those of stained-glass windows. ∎

12 LITERARY ELEMENT

Climax and Resolution: How are the economic and social problems of Naomi and Ruth resolved? (by Ruth's marriage to Boaz) How are Ruth and Naomi rewarded? (They are looked after in their old age and are honored as the forebears of King David, the greatest king of Israel.)

Creating a "News Scroll." Divide students into several groups. Ask each group to create an edition of the *Bethlehem Herald*, an imaginary "news scroll" that periodically reports major events in the village. Scrolls might include obituaries for Elimelech and his sons, news articles about the return of Naomi with Ruth to Bethlehem, the engagement of Boaz and Ruth, and a birth announcement for Obed. Other reports might cover crop production and prices for barley and other grains grown in the region (students would research the currency used at that time), locations where the poor can glean grain, jobs available for farm laborers, and livestock for sale. Individual articles can be taped end to end and wound on dowels to form a scroll.

CLOSURE

Ask students to imagine that the *Bethlehem Herald* has named Ruth "Woman of the Year." Invite students to consider what qualities she displays that the Jewish community values. Then ask the class to write the lead for the article about Ruth, explaining why she merits the honor. ■

ANSWERS

First Thoughts
Answers will vary.

Identifying Facts
1. Naomi argues that she can give them no more sons as husbands.
2. Ruth gleans grain.
3. Boaz notices Ruth's hard work. He also has heard of her devotion to Naomi.
4. The other is a closer kinsman.

Interpreting Meanings
1. Details cited should be appropriate to the virtue listed.
2. Answers will vary. The marriage is based on mutual respect and duty to family.
3. that the greatest Hebrew king is partly of Moabite blood
4. The Genesis stories possess flat characters and an episodic narrative structure. The Book of Ruth has *developed characters* (Ruth, Naomi, Boaz); a *setting* in time, place, and sociocultural conditions; a *plot* with exposition, rising action, climax, and resolution; and a *theme* about love and loyalty.

Applying Meanings
Answers will vary.

Creative Writing Response
Writing a Letter. Letters should reflect Ruth's character and her experiences in Judah. She might hope for a son.

Critical Writing Response
Analyzing Characterization. Essays should give examples of all methods of characterization *except* description of Ruth's appearance and dress, which does not occur. ■

184   The Ancient Middle East

> ## First Thoughts
How did you feel about the conclusion of the Book of Ruth? Did you find it satisfying and appropriate, or did you expect a different ending?

Identifying Facts
1. How does Naomi try to persuade Ruth and Orpah not to follow her?
2. How do Ruth and Naomi manage to survive in Bethlehem?
3. How does Ruth come to the attention of Boaz? Why does he admire her?
4. Why does Boaz first ask another relative to "redeem" the property and wife of Elimelech?

Interpreting Meanings
1. Ruth's decision to forsake her people and follow Naomi is celebrated as a shining example of selfless devotion. Her virtue is best expressed in the famous line, "Whither thou goest, I will go." Go back to the story and list the details that emphasize each of the following values: hospitality, courtesy, modesty, acceptance, and respect for custom and tradition.
2. The relationship between Ruth and Boaz is sometimes spoken of as a "love story." Do you think this is a good way to describe it? If so, what attitudes toward love and marriage does their relationship represent?
3. **Irony** is the contrast between what is expected and what actually takes place. At the end of the story, it is said that David, the greatest king of Israel, will be descended from Ruth. What is **ironic** about this detail?
4. The Book of Ruth is often called a **short story**. Discuss the specific differences between the story of Ruth and the stories you have read from the Book of Genesis. Consider the elements that make the Book of Ruth a short story: **character development**, **setting**, **plot**, and **theme**.

Applying Meanings
After her husband's death, Ruth has the opportunity to stay in her homeland and live with her own family, yet she decides to go with Naomi to Israel. Have you ever willingly or unwillingly found yourself an outsider in a strange or foreign place or among people you didn't know well? Describe your situation, how you felt about it, and the choices you made.

Creative Writing Response
Writing a Letter. Imagine that you are Ruth and that a day or two has passed since you married Boaz. Write a letter to your sister-in-law, Orpah. Summarize for her the experiences you have had since you and Naomi left Moab. Tell Orpah what you have found difficult and what you have enjoyed. Be sure to share your hopes for the future.

Critical Writing Response
Analyzing Characterization. Ruth is a strong, complex **character**. Characters can be drawn in several different ways. A writer can reveal a character directly by telling what he or she is like. On the other hand, a writer can sketch a character indirectly by describing the character's appearance and dress, letting the character speak to others, revealing the character's thoughts and feelings, showing how the character affects other people, and showing the character's actions. Write a two- to three-paragraph essay exploring the characterization of Ruth in the Book of Ruth. Provide examples of **direct** and **indirect characterization** from the story.

SEEING CONNECTIONS

Biblical Allusions

A **literary allusion** is a reference made in one work of literature to another work of literature. Such an allusion is only effective when the reader recognizes the reference and sees how the two works are associated. Literature abounds with allusions to the Bible. John Keats, an English poet, found inspiration in the story of Ruth. In his "Ode to a Nightingale" (1819), he speaks of the immortality of the poetic melody in the bird's song:

Thou wast not born for death, immortal
   Bird!
   No hungry generations tread thee down;
The voice I hear this passing night was
   heard
   In ancient days by emperor and clown:
Perhaps the selfsame song that found a path
   Through the sad heart of Ruth, when,
      sick for home,
1   She stood in tears amid the alien corn;
      The same that ofttimes hath
   Charmed magic casements, opening on
      the foam
      Of perilous seas, in faery lands forlorn.

Keats expects his readers to recognize the biblical allusion and to associate it with a specific context. Explain Keats's allusion to the story of Ruth. Is the allusion accurate, or has Keats taken liberties with Ruth's story? Is the allusion effective?
2
   Frequently, the titles of books, plays,

songs, and movies contain biblical allusions. In the following list, each title is a phrase (or paraphrase) from the King James version of the Hebrew Bible. Look in a copy of a King James Bible for the context of the following titles. Read the original passage and identify the person, place, thing, event, or phrase used in each of the following titles.

1. *Adam's Rib,* a movie by James Cukor (Genesis 2:21)
2. *East of Eden,* a novel by John Steinbeck (Genesis 3:24)
3. "Adam Raised a Cain," a song by Bruce Springsteen (Genesis 4:1)
4. *Exodus,* a novel by Leon Uris (Book of Exodus)
5. *Absalom! Absalom!,* a novel by William Faulkner (2 Samuel 19:4)   3
6. *By the Skin of Our Teeth,* a play by Thornton Wilder (Job 19:20)
7. *The Sun Also Rises,* a novel by Ernest Hemingway (Ecclesiastes 1:5)
8. *Song of Solomon,* a novel by Toni Morrison (Song of Solomon)

See if you can locate other works whose titles are allusions to the Hebrew Bible.
   What other biblical persons, places, or events could be used as allusions in current films you have seen or in stories, novels, and plays with which you are familiar?

OBJECTIVES

1. *To recognize the emotional quality of three Hebrew psalms*
2. *To analyze the effects of parallelism*
3. *To write an essay comparing two translations of Psalm 23*

PREREADING FOCUS

Background: For centuries, the Book of Psalms has been the chief source of hymns for Jews and Christians. Martin Luther called the Book of Psalms "the immortal song book of the human heart," and it has been translated more than any other book of the Jewish Tanakh (the Christian Old Testament). In fact, the first book published in the American colonies was the [Massachusetts] *Bay Psalm Book* of 1640.

Although individual psalms emphasize different human emotions and responses to life's joys and hardships, the psalms in general are based on these beliefs: (1) God is sovereign over heaven, earth, and human history, (2) God's most wonderful creation is humanity, (3) God has given nature to human beings for their sustenance and pleasure, (4) Faith sustains the human spirit, and (5) Justice will ultimately triumph.

David, the author of some of the psalms, was the great-grandson of Ruth (see The Book of Ruth, p. 177). While still a shepherd boy, David killed the giant Goliath, a Philistine leader who terrorized the Israelites. Later, David, a talented harpist, soothed the troubled spirit of King Saul with his music and song. Despite David's service, Saul feared his popularity and tried to kill him. Saul's son Jonathan, a friend of David, warned him of Saul's plots. After Saul and Jonathan were slain in battle, David became king of Judah.

Reader's Guide

PSALMS 23, 104, AND 137
from the Book of Psalms

Background

The Book of Psalms contains 150 poems. The poems were combined into a single collection around the fourth century B.C. or even later, and the book now appears in the section of the Hebrew Bible called Writings. Nearly half the psalms carry the title "Song of David," but this does not mean that every poem was composed personally by King David, who lived around 1000 B.C. Some psalms were performed in sacred rituals long before David ruled, and others, such as Psalm 137, were composed after his reign.

The Greek word *psalmos*, which means "a plucking of strings," tells us that the poems were sung to musical accompaniment. The Hebrew title *Tehillim* means "songs of praise." Many psalms, like Psalm 104, sing praise to God. But adoration is not the only emotion the psalms express. They are lyric poems, and, like other lyric poems, they range in emotion from bitter anger to joyous exultation. The Book of Psalms features laments, personal meditations, and even battle songs. Much of the Hebrew Bible is devoted to the narration of the ancient history of the Hebrews, but the psalms' emphasis on personal responses to God makes them unique.

Writer's Response

What are some songs you especially like? From the lyrics of one or more songs, write down a few lines or phrases that mean a great deal to you. How do they express or arouse your feelings?

Literary Focus

Parallelism is the repetition of words, grammatically similar phrases, or ideas. Rather than relying on poetic devices like rhyme and meter, the psalms use parallelism to create a sense of balance and order and to show the relationship between similar ideas.

PSALM 23

King James Bible

The Twenty-third Psalm is probably the most often recited of all the psalms. It compares God to a shepherd who loves his flock and to a host who lavishes hospitality on his guests. People often find comfort in this psalm. Which lines do you find especially comforting?

The Lord is my shepherd;
I shall not want.[1]

He maketh me to lie down in green pastures:
He leadeth me beside the still waters.

5 He restoreth my soul:
He leadeth me in the paths of righteousness for
    his name's sake.

Yea, though I walk through the valley of the
    shadow of death, I will fear no evil: for thou art
    with me;
Thy rod and thy staff they comfort me.

Thou preparest a table before me in the presence
    of mine enemies:
10 Thou anointest my head with oil;[2] my cup
    runneth over.

Surely goodness and mercy shall follow me all the
    days of my life:
And I will dwell in the house of the Lord for ever.

Scala/Art Resource, New York

THE GOOD SHEPHERD.
Marble statue, fourth century.

---

1. **want:** lack the necessities of life.
2. **anointest . . . oil:** It was a Jewish custom to show respect or hospitality toward a man by pouring oil on his head, since his hair and beard might be dusty from the roads or fields.

INTEGRATING THE LANGUAGE ARTS: SPEAKING

Rhythm and Sound Effects

Since the psalms were meant to be sung or chanted, they are rich in rhythm and sound effects. Rhythm is created by the repetition of words, especially at the beginning of sentences. Note the repetition of the word *Who* at the beginning of lines 4–9 of Psalm 104. Alliteration is the repetition of initial consonant sounds, as in line 8 of Psalm 104: "Who walketh upon the *wings* of the *wind*."

1. **Reading and Speaking.** Ask students to read Psalm 104 silently, looking for other examples of words repeated at the beginnings of lines. Then have volunteers read their examples aloud.

2. **Speaking and Listening.** Ask a student to read Psalm 137 aloud to the class. Have the others listen for repetition of initial consonant sounds and jot down examples. Students can share their lists of alliterated words and discuss the effects of alliteration on the rhythm of the psalm. ■

2 LITERARY ELEMENT

Metaphor: What words suggest that the universe is God's house? (curtains, [ceiling] beams, foundations)

■ **ministers** (min'is·tərz): people or things that serve as the agent of some power

rebuke (ri·byook'): scolding, reprimand

PSALM 104

King James Bible

❙ *As you read the following psalm, imagine the scenes the psalmist creates in words. What can you see? What can you hear? What specific details appeal to the senses of smell and taste and touch?*

Bless the Lord, O my soul.
O Lord my God, thou art very great;
Thou art clothed with honor and majesty:

Who coverest thyself with light as with a garment:
5 Who stretchest out the heavens like a curtain:

Who layeth the beams of his chambers in the
    waters:
Who maketh the clouds his chariot:
Who walketh upon the wings of the wind:

Who maketh his angels spirits;
10 His ministers a flaming fire:

Who laid the foundations of the earth,
That it should not be removed for ever.

Thou coveredst it with the deep as with a garment:
The waters stood above the mountains.

15 At thy rebuke they fled;
At the voice of thy thunder they hasted away.

They go up by the mountains;
They go down by the valleys unto the place which
    thou hast founded for them.

Thou hast set a bound that they may not pass
    over;
20 That they turn not again to cover the earth.

3

He sendeth the springs into the valleys,
Which run among the hills.

They give drink to every beast of the field:
The wild asses quench their thirst.

25 By them shall the fowls of the heaven have their
habitation,
Which sing among the branches.

© David Muench 1996

3 LITERARY ELEMENT

Personification: In what ways do the waters of the earth act as if they were human? (They flee when scolded, have limits set for them by God, and give drink to the beasts.)

MEETING INDIVIDUAL NEEDS

Auditory Learners: Psalm 104 is a good choice for an antiphonal reading—two individuals or groups reciting alternate passages. The stanza breaks are appropriate points for alternation of speakers. Because of the archaic word endings, individuals or groups should rehearse their reading before presenting it to the class. ■

COMPARING LITERATURE

Psalm 104 echoes many of the thoughts and images of "The Great Hymn to the Aten" (pp. 72–77). See how many similarities students can find between the two praise songs. Also, have students reread the historical background of the Jews (pp. 154–159), particularly the section entitled "Captivity and the Flight from Egypt," and the background accompanying "The Great Hymn to the Aten." Discuss the possibility that the Egyptian hymn influenced the Hebrew psalm. Such a discussion could lead to the generalization that religions often influence one another and that cultures in general rarely develop in isolation from other cultures.

HUMANITIES CONNECTION

David is known as much for his musical ability as for his prowess in war. When he is introduced in 1 Samuel 16, it is primarily as a young man whose music brings relief to the melancholy King Saul. David's renown as poet and singer became so great that tradition ascribed to him the entire Book of Psalms, although the poems were actually collected over a period of centuries. ∎

He watereth the hills from his chambers:
The earth is satisfied with the fruit of thy works.

He causeth the grass to grow for the cattle,
30   And herb for the service of man:
That he may bring forth food out of the earth;

And wine that maketh glad the heart of man,
And oil to make his face to shine,
And bread which strengtheneth man's heart.

35   The trees of the Lord are full of sap;
The cedars of Lebanon, which he hath planted;

Where the birds make their nests:
As for the stork, the fir trees are her house.

The high hills are a refuge for the wild goats;
40   And the rocks for the conies.[1]

He appointed the moon for seasons:
The sun knoweth his going down.

Thou makest darkness, and it is night:
Wherein all the beasts of the forest do creep
   forth.

45   The young lions roar after their prey,
And seek their meat from God.

The sun ariseth, they gather themselves together,
And lay them down in their dens.

Man goeth forth unto his work
50   And to his labor until the evening.

O Lord, how manifold are thy works!
In wisdom hast thou made them all:
The earth is full of thy riches.

The young David with pipe, bell, and harp. *From a thirteenth-century illuminated manuscript.*

---

1. **conies:** probably rabbits.

So is this great and wide sea,
55   Wherein are things creeping innumerable, both
      small and great beasts.

There go the ships:
There is that leviathan,² whom thou hast made to
      play therein.

These wait all upon thee;
That thou mayest give them their meat in due
      season.

60   That thou givest them they gather:
    Thou openest thine hand, they are filled with
      good.

Thou hidest thy face, they are troubled:
Thou takest away their breath, they die, and
      return to their dust.

Thou sendest forth thy spirit, they are created:
65   And thou renewest the face of the earth.

The glory of the Lord shall endure for ever:
The Lord shall rejoice in his works.

He looketh on the earth, and it trembleth:
He toucheth the hills, and they smoke.

70   I will sing unto the Lord as long as I live:
    I will sing praise to my God while I have my
      being.

My meditation of him shall be sweet:
I will be glad in the Lord.

Let the sinners be consumed out of the earth,
75   And let the wicked be no more.
    Bless thou the Lord, O my soul.
    Praise ye the Lord.

On what kinds of images does this psalm focus? What is the overall effect of the imagery?

---

2. **leviathan** (lə·vī′ə·thən): probably a whale.

ANALYZING
Why does the author describe in such detail the behavior of animals, man, and the natural elements? (These descriptions emphasize an order on earth and in heaven ordained by God.)

4 LITERARY ELEMENT
Parallelism: How do lines 68–69 illustrate parallel sentence patterns? (They begin with the same subject, followed by an active verb, and both are compound sentences, showing a cause-and-effect relationship.)

meditation (med′ə·tā′shən): solemn reflection on sacred matters as a devotional act

consumed (kən·sōōmd′): destroyed; done away with

5 INTERPRETING
The psalmist refers directly to himself only in lines 1–2 and in lines 70–77. What personal emotions do these lines express? (They present the psalmist's worshipful and grateful response to a generous God who has given human beings the wonders of creation.)

Geography: Read the Introduction to Unit 3 (pp. 128–135) for additional information about the Babylonian exile (586–539 B.C.). Consult a historical atlas that shows the location of ancient settlements. Then locate ancient Jerusalem and Babylon. (Jerusalem still exists, in today's state of Israel. Babylon was located south of today's Baghdad in Iraq, roughly in the area of today's Hilla on the Euphrates River.) After using a topographical map to determine the nature of the terrain between Jerusalem and Babylon, write a description of what it would have been like for the Hebrews to travel that route by foot in the psalmist's time. ■

6 INTERPRETING

How does the psalmist's choice of consequences if he should forget Jerusalem dramatize the intensity of his feelings? (For a lover of music, losing the ability to play and sing would be a very great deprivation.)

PSALM 137
King James Bible

The following psalm expresses the sorrow of the Jews during their exile in Babylon after King Nebuchadnezzar destroyed Jerusalem. The opening verses immediately capture the Hebrews' emotional pain. At what point does the psalmist's extreme sorrow turn to a bitterness that causes him to start cursing his captors?

By the rivers of Babylon, there we sat down,
Yea, we wept, when we remembered Zion.[1]

We hanged our harps upon the willows in the
    midst thereof.

For there they that carried us away captive
    required of us a song;
5   And they that wasted us required of us mirth,
    saying, Sing us one of the songs of Zion.

How shall we sing the Lord's song in a strange
    land?

6   If I forget thee, O Jerusalem, let my right hand
    forget her cunning.

If I do not remember thee, let my tongue cleave
    to the roof of my mouth;
If I prefer not Jerusalem above my chief joy.

10 Remember, O Lord, the children of Edom[2] in the
    day of Jerusalem;

---

1. **Zion** (zī'ən): the Jewish homeland; also, the hill in Jerusalem on which the temple was built.
2. **Edom** (ē'dəm): a country south of the Dead Sea.

READING CHECK

1. In Psalm 23, which of the following words best describes the speaker's attitude toward the Lord: fearful, confident, confused? (confident)
2. According to Psalm 104, why did the waters flee? (God rebuked them.)
3. What does man do every day, according to Psalm 104? (goes to work)
4. What musical instruments hang on a willow tree in Psalm 137? (harps)
5. What city does the author of Psalm 137 vow never to forget? (Jerusalem)

RETEACHING

Have students imagine they are roving photographers who have been assigned to illustrate these psalms. They must produce at least two pictures that capture the key ideas or feelings of each psalm. Ask students to explain what images they would choose to reflect specific passages or the overall feeling expressed by each psalm.

Who said, Raze it, raze it, even to the foundation
   thereof.

O daughter of Babylon, who art to be destroyed;
Happy shall he be, that rewardeth thee as thou
   hast served us.

Happy shall he be, that taketh and dasheth thy
   little ones against the stones.

HISTORICAL BACKGROUND

Point out that except for a brief period of independence beginning in 142 B.C., the Jewish people had no independent homeland from the beginning of the Babylonian exile (586 B.C.) until the creation of Israel in 1948. In light of this history, have students discuss the likely significance of Psalm 137 to the Jewish people.

HUMANITIES CONNECTION

Peter Paul Rubens (1577–1640), a Flemish painter, is best remembered for his portraits, landscapes, and dramatic depictions of biblical and mythological events.
❷ *What feature of Rubens's painting identifies the subject as David?* (the harp. David played the harp as a youth to soothe King Saul and might have played it in later life as an accompaniment to his poems and songs.) ∎

SuperStock International, Inc.

KING DAVID, PETER PAUL RUBENS (1577–1640).

Psalms   **193**

Choosing Music: Frederick Douglass (1817?–1895) wrote eloquently of the spirituals created and sung in the American South around the time of the Civil War. These "wild notes," he wrote, mostly "told a tale of grief and sorrow." Although we do not know exactly how the Hebrews sang their psalms, we can imagine the pain and longing of the first part of Psalm 137 as somehow matching the pain in the refrain, "Let my people go," from the spiritual, "Go Down, Moses."

Ask students to work in groups to locate spirituals and other music that convey emotions similar to those of the psalms. Each group should present a recorded or live rendition of one piece of music, together with a brief oral explanation of why they consider the piece representative of psalmlike emotion.

Ask students to create either an appropriate title or an appropriate refrain for each of the three psalms. (For example, Psalm 104 might be titled "The Wonders of Creation" or be given the refrain, "All God's works are wonderful.") ■

ANSWERS

First Thoughts
Answers will vary.

Identifying Facts
1. The Lord provides food, water, and guidance through danger.
2. God is the mighty creator and generous provider. The psalmist gratefully rejoices in God's goodness to him.
3. to sing one of their own songs. They bitterly refuse.

Interpreting Meanings
1. Possible response: the consolation that God will see us through all hardship and be with us forever
2. *Sight:* sun, moon, darkness. *Sound:* lions' roar. *Smell:* sap, smoking hills. *Touch:* sap. *Taste:* wine, bread. The images help the listener understand God's presence through creation.
3. Line 7 marks the change from a tone of sorrow to one of anger. The last line shocks the reader with its depth of bitterness.
4. Possible responses: Psalm 23, lines 3–4; Psalm 104, lines 9–10 and 29–30; Psalm 137, lines 4–5 and 7–8. General effect is emphasis and balance.

Applying Meanings
Answers will vary.

Critical Writing Response
Comparing Translations of the Twenty-third Psalm.
Check essays for overall flow and coherence and for concrete details that support choices. ■

First Thoughts
Which of the psalms did you find most moving and memorable? Why?

Identifying Facts
1. According to the Twenty-third Psalm, how is the Lord like a shepherd?
2. How is God portrayed in Psalm 104?
3. In Psalm 137, what have the Babylonians asked the exiled Hebrews to do? How do the Hebrews respond?

Interpreting Meanings
1. The Twenty-third Psalm is often read at funeral services as a consolation to mourners, and people recite it to give themselves courage and hope in troubled times. What kind of consolation might this psalm offer people? Do you find it consoling?
2. Find at least one example of **imagery** in Psalm 104 that appeals to each of the five senses. What is the effect of the imagery?
3. At what point in Psalm 137 does the **mood**, or emotional atmosphere, change sharply? How would you describe the mood of the psalm before the shift? How would you describe it after? What is the emotional effect of the final line of Psalm 137?
4. Each of the psalms contains many examples of **parallelism**, or parallel structure—places where actual words and phrases are repeated, or an idea is restated in slightly different words. Find at least one example of parallelism in each of the psalms you have read. Then describe the effect of this use of parallelism.

Applying Meanings
Think of contemporary poems or song lyrics—even sung advertisements or political speeches—that use parallelism or other forms of repetition. What is the purpose and effect of the parallelism in each case?

Critical Writing Response
Comparing Translations of the Twenty-third Psalm. The following version of the Twenty-third Psalm is from the Psalms of the Anchor Bible, published in 1965. The Anchor Bible is designed to convey the meaning of the original Hebrew to contemporary readers. Read this version, and compare it to the King James translation you have just read. Which version do you find more literal? More beautiful? Which version do you like better? Which details of vocabulary or figurative language affect your conclusions? Present your answers to these questions in a two- or three-paragraph essay.

Psalm 23
The Anchor Bible Translation (1965)

Yahweh is my shepherd,
  I shall not lack.
In green meadows he will make me lie down;
Near tranquil waters will he guide me,
5 to refresh my being.
He will lead me into luxuriant pastures,
  as befits his name.
Even though I should walk
  in the midst of total darkness,
10 I shall fear no danger
  since you are with me.
Your rod and your staff—
  behold, they will lead me.
You prepare my table before me,
15 in front of my adversaries.
You generously anoint my head with oil,
  my cup overflows.
Surely goodness and kindness will attend me
  all the days of my life;
20 And I shall dwell in the house of Yahweh
  for days without end.

ELEMENTS OF LITERATURE

Parallelism

Parallelism, or **parallel structure**, is the repetition of words, phrases, or sentences that have the same grammatical structure or that restate a similiar idea. Parallelism is used frequently in literature that is meant to be read aloud, such as poetry and speeches. The technique of parallelism occurs often in the Hebrew, or biblical, style. It is especially striking in the Book of Psalms. The psalms do not rely on rhyme, meter, or other obvious poetic devices. Instead, they use the rhythm created by parallel structure to unify ideas, emphasize images, and heighten the emotional effect of the words.

Parallelism often occurs in the repetition of a word or an entire sentence pattern. This is called **structural parallelism**, and it can be seen in the following example:

> If I forget thee, O Jerusalem, let my
> right hand forget her cunning.
> If I do not remember thee, let my
> tongue cleave to the roof of my
> mouth.
>
> (Psalm 137:7–8)

Parallelism can also take the form of a **restatement** of an entire idea in different words. This restatement can occur in a single line or in successive lines:

> Lord, my heart is not haughty,
> nor mine eyes lofty;
> neither do I exercise myself in great
> matters,
> or in things too high for me.
>
> (Psalm 131:1)

Note that the lines above do not rely on repeated words or sentence patterns, but instead on the restatement of ideas. By presenting two versions of the same idea, the psalmist adds a layer of meaning to the psalm. In addition, the repetition creates emotional intensity.

Another form of parallelism involves **antithesis** (an·tith'ə·sis), or contrast. In antithesis, ideas are tied together because they are complementary, or opposite, rather than similar, as in the following example:

> Weeping may endure for a night,
> but joy cometh in the morning.
>
> (Psalm 30:5)

Read each of the psalms in this unit aloud. Listen for examples of parallelism. Does the parallelism occur in the repetition of words or sentence structure, in the restatement of ideas, or in the use of contrasting ideas? What is the effect of the parallelism in each case?

1 CULTURAL BACKGROUND

Many of the symbols and metaphors of the New Testament derived or evolved from the Hebrew Bible. Christian writers view the sacrifice of the Passover lamb from Exodus as a symbolic prelude to the sacrificial death of Jesus, the "Lamb of God." They also recall the Adam of Genesis as having brought sin into the world, while Jesus, the "new Adam," brings salvation. Overall, New Testament writers present Jesus Christ as the embodiment of a new covenant (testament) between God and humanity.

2 LITERARY BACKGROUND

Gospels: The synoptic Gospels differ because each writer stresses the aspects of Jesus most understandable to his audience. Mark, addressing a non-Jewish audience, emphasizes the humanity of a Jesus who must touch people to heal them. Matthew, writing for Jewish followers, repeatedly cites Hebrew scriptures to show Jesus as a teacher, a "new Moses." Luke, addressing the cosmopolitan Christians of Rome, shows that Jesus embraced all kinds of people—men and women, upper and lower classes, even social outcasts and foreigners.

John's Gospel differs from all three synoptics because it proclaims a Jesus who is God's own Son. This Jesus speaks in metaphors appropriate to so transcendent a being: "I am the way, the truth, and the life" (John 14:6).

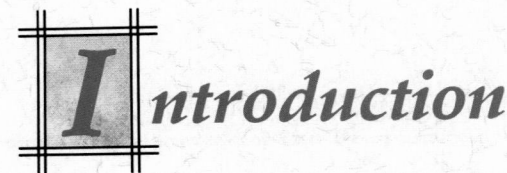

Introduction

The New Testament

The Christian Bible includes both the Hebrew Bible and the New Testament. Like the Hebrew Bible, the New Testament is a collection of books: twenty-seven books written within the relatively short time span of the first two centuries A.D. Because Greek was the most commonly spoken language around the Mediterranean at that time, the New Testament was written in everyday Greek. But because the writers of the New Testament were Hebrews, they wrote from the perspective of the Hebrew culture and tradition.

Christ, meaning "the anointed one," implies divinity, and Jesus' followers believe that he is the divine son of God. According to Christian belief, God established a new covenant, or testament, with humanity by sending his only son to die for people's sins. Thus, Christians see the New Testament as a continuation of the Hebrew covenant with God.

◆

Gospels: *the teachings of Jesus and the Apostles, which appear as the first four books of the New Testament.*

The Four Gospels

The Hebrew Bible opens with the Five Books of Moses, which explain the origins of the Hebrew people and their beliefs. Similarly, the New Testament opens with four Gospels, which explain the origins and key beliefs of Christianity. The word *Gospel* comes from the Old English word *godspel* or "good news," a direct translation of *euangelion,* the Greek name for these books. The "good news" of the Gospels is that of the life and message of Jesus Christ, a wandering Jewish teacher who attracted a great deal of attention during the era of Roman rule in Jerusalem. The word

The four Gospels are attributed to Matthew, Mark, Luke, and John, but scholars do not know the exact identity of these writers. Mark's Gospel was the first one written. Matthew and Luke based their Gospels partly on Mark's work. As a result, these three Gospels parallel each other closely enough to be called the synoptic (si·näp′tik) gospels. The word *synoptic* comes from the Greek word *syn,* meaning "same," and *optic,* meaning "vision." Even the synoptic Gospels, however, differ somewhat from one another, for each writer wrote for a different audience and emphasized different aspects of Christ's life and works.

Illumination from the Irish *Book of Kells*, eighth century. *Medieval art often uses the symbols of the angel, the lion, the bull, and the eagle to represent the four evangelists, Matthew, Mark, Luke, and John, respectively.*

The Other Books of the New Testament

After the Gospels, the other books of the New Testament are, in order, the Acts of the Apostles, the Epistles, and Revelation. The Acts of the Apostles, written by Luke, continues Luke's gospel. It covers events from about A.D. 30 to A.D. 50 and features the deeds of the missionary Paul. Paul, originally named Saul, was a dogged persecutor of Christians who converted to Christian-

ity—and changed his name—after receiving a vision. Paul contributed to the next section of the New Testament, the Epistles. Epistles are letters written to various people and communities to spread the teachings of Christ. Paul wrote seven of the Epistles, and scholars believe that his disciples wrote another seven in his name. These epistles explain the Gospels in more detail, especially as they apply to concrete problems faced by early Christians.

3

◆

epistle (ē·pis'əl): *(1) a long, formal letter giving instruction to the recipient; (2) a letter in the New Testament written by a follower of Christ to spread the word of Christianity.*

The final book of the New Testament, Revelation, was written in about A.D. 95, probably by a prophet identified by some scholars as John of Patmos. The name *Revelation* is a direct translation of the Greek word *apokalypsis*, "apocalypse" (ə·päk'ə·lips'). The apocalypse, a popular form of literature, was full of symbols and visions, and Revelation, like other apocalyptic literature of its time, vividly recounts the age-old struggle between good and evil and the ultimate triumph of good. Through the writer's choice of symbols, Revelation also brings the Bible full circle. It unites the Hebrew Bible with the New Testament through the use of images associated with the creation accounts of Genesis: "a new heaven and a new earth" and a new "tree of life" (Revelation 21:1 and 22:2).

3 LITERARY BACKGROUND

Epistles: The adaptation of the letter for religious purposes is unique to the writers of the New Testament. The epistles of Paul, in particular, vary widely in style and mood. Paul scolds one community severely: "You stupid Galatians!" (Galatians 3:1). He reveals deep feeling: "That letter . . . how many tears I shed as I wrote it!" (2 Corinthians 2:4). And he rises to lyric poetry: ". . . three things . . . last forever: faith, hope, and love; but the greatest of them all is love" (1 Corinthians 13:13).

OBJECTIVES
1. *To recognize the characteristics of biblical parables*
2. *To analyze literal and symbolic levels of meaning in three parables*
3. *To rewrite a biblical parable in a contemporary context*

PREREADING FOCUS

Background: Presented here are three of the best known parables of Jesus. "The Prodigal Son" appears in Luke as one of three parables about lost things—in this case, a lost son. Jesus tells the story in response to criticism of his willingness to welcome sinners among his followers.

"The Sower" appears in Mark 4:3–8, Matthew 13:1–23, and Luke 8:4–15. Mark's version (the earliest) is presented here. Use of the story by three writers reflects the concern of early Christians about public response to the message of Jesus.

"The Talents" appears in Luke 19:12–27 and Matthew 25:14–30. Matthew's version, used here, is one of several parables about the need to use one's time and abilities wisely.

ABOUT THE TRANSLATION

A bestseller when introduced in 1970, the New English Bible has been praised as a clear, accurate, literary version of the original Hebrew Old Testament and Greek New Testament texts. By removing instances of archaic English, the NEB has made the biblical texts more accessible to millions of contemporary readers. Because the English language and biblical scholarship continue to develop, however, a revision of the NEB has already appeared—the Revised English Bible of 1989.

Reader's Guide ∎

THE PRODIGAL SON, THE SOWER, THE TALENTS

Background

A **parable** is a short narrative that teaches a moral, or lesson about life. It is like a fable, except that its characters are humans rather than animals. The message of the parable does not need to be directly stated, for it can usually be inferred, or guessed from the text itself.

The New Testament contains about forty parables, and they occur in all four Gospels. They are attributed to Jesus, who, like other Jewish teachers, used them to make his messages clear. The parables tend to be down-to-earth and easy to grasp on a literal level, involving ordinary events that people of Jesus' time could relate to: a shepherd searching for a sheep that has strayed from the flock; bridesmaids who are asleep and unprepared when the bridal party arrives; a poor woman who loses a coin. The underlying messages of the parables concern deep truths such as conduct in life and moral laws.

Oral Response

One of the most famous and often-quoted parables in the New Testament is "The Good Samaritan." It is about a traveler who is robbed, beaten, and left to die on a road between Jericho and Jerusalem. Two "upstanding citizens" ignore the victim, but a Samaritan—a member of a despised ethnic and religious minority—tends the man's wounds and pays an innkeeper to take care of him until he is well. How would you state the moral of this parable?

Literary Focus

The word **parable** comes from a Greek word meaning "comparison" or "analogy." Parables convey morals, or lessons about life, through the use of **allegory**—a story with an underlying message that can be understood on both a literal and a symbolic level. Because symbols can be interpreted in more than one way, even a brief allegory can yield more than one meaning. All the New Testament parables use characters, objects, and events to symbolize, or stand for, abstract concepts.

THE PRODIGAL SON

New English Bible

The word __prodigal__ usually means "recklessly extravagant" or "wasteful," but it can also imply great generosity. As you read the parable, try to determine to which son the word applies. Could the word prodigal *apply to the father as well?*

Scala/Art Resource, New York

THE RETURN OF THE PRODIGAL SON, REMBRANDT (1609–1669).

Again he[1] said: "There was once a man who had two sons; and the younger said to his father, 'Father, give me my share of the property.' So he divided his estate between them.[2] A few days later the younger son

turned the whole of his share into cash and left home for a distant country, where he squandered it in reckless living. He had spent it all, when a severe famine fell upon that country and he began to feel the pinch. So he went and attached himself to one of the local landowners, who sent him on to his farm to mind the pigs.[3] He would have been glad to fill his belly with the pods that the pigs were eating; and no one gave him anything. Then he came to his senses and said, 'How many of my father's paid servants have more food than they can eat, and here am I, starving to death! I will set off and go to my father, and say to him, "Father, I have sinned, against God and against you; I am no longer fit to be called your son; treat me as one of your paid servants."' So he set out for his father's house. But while he was still a long way off his father saw him, and his heart went out to him. He ran to meet him, flung his arms round him, and kissed him. The son said, 'Father, I have sinned, against God and against you; I am no longer fit to be called your son.' But the father said to his servants, 'Quick! fetch a robe, my best one, and put it on him; put a ring on his finger

---

1. Jesus
2. **So he divided his estate between them:** The younger son's share would be one third.

3. **mind the pigs:** Because the Jews considered pigs to be unclean animals, tending pigs was considered degrading work.

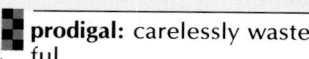

Pronouns and Their Antecedents

Antecedent means "going before." The antecedent of a pronoun is the noun to which a pronoun refers. In these sentences from "The Sower," *sower* is the antecedent of *he*: "A *sower* went out to sow. And it happened that as *he* sowed. . . ."

1. **Listening and Speaking.** Read aloud "The Prodigal Son," through "Father, I have sinned." As you read, replace *he, them,* and *him* with their antecedents—"the father," "the sons," "the younger son," "my father." Ask students to tell what happens to the flow of the story.

2. **Reading and Writing.** Ask students to read the last paragraph of "The Prodigal Son" and to write down each pronoun and its antecedent. Are all the antecedents clear? (No, the antecedent for "But he was angry" is ambiguous.) ■

---

3 CULTURAL DIVERSITY

Among the Jews in biblical times, the killing of a fatted calf represented lavish hospitality. Such a gesture was usually reserved for visitors, not family members, as in Genesis 18:3–8, when Abraham serves a meal to three passing strangers. (They turn out to be angels in disguise.)

? *For whom might people "kill the fatted calf" today?* (Possible responses: a boss or good friend)

retorted (ri·tôrt'əd): replied sharply

4 LITERARY ELEMENT

Symbolism: In allegory, characters, events, and objects work together as symbols that can be interpreted in many ways. On an allegorical level, who might the father, the elder son, and the younger son represent? (God, people who live righteously, sinners)

COMPARING LITERATURE

"The Prodigal Son" and The Book of Ruth (pp. 177–184) both tell stories about a person who leaves home and endures hardship, but who receives genuine hospitality and love in the end. The two characters are very different, however. Ask students to list three ways the characters are alike and three ways they are different.

---

3 and shoes on his feet. Bring the fatted calf and kill it, and let us have a feast to celebrate the day. For this son of mine was dead and has come back to life; he was lost and is found.' And the festivities began.

"Now the elder son was out on the farm; and on his way back, as he approached the house, he heard music and dancing. He called one of the servants and asked what it meant. The servant told him, 'Your brother has come home, and your father has killed the fatted calf because he has him back safe and sound.' But he was angry and refused to go in. His father came out and pleaded with him; but he retorted, 'You know how I have slaved for you all these years; I never once disobeyed your orders; and you never gave me so much as a kid, for a feast with my friends. But now that this son of yours turns up, after running through your money with his women, you kill the fatted calf for him.' 'My boy,' said the father, 'you are always with me, and everything I have is yours. How could we help celebrating this happy day? Your brother here was dead and has come back to life, was lost and is found.'" **4**

Luke 15:12–30

THE SOWER
New English Bible

In Jesus' time, farmers planted their fields by hand. With sacks of seed hung around their necks, they walked along, scattering the seed in wide arcs. How does this practice help to explain the situation described in the parable?

On another occasion he[1] began to teach by the lake-side. The crowd that gathered round him was so large that he had to get into a boat on the lake, and there he sat, with the whole crowd on the beach right down to the water's edge. And he taught them many things by parables.

As he taught he said:

"Listen! A sower went out to sow. And it happened that as he sowed, some seed fell along the footpath; and the birds came and ate it up. Some seed fell on rocky ground, where it had little soil, and it sprouted quickly because it had no depth of earth; but when the sun rose the young corn was scorched, and as it had no proper root it

1. **he:** Jesus.

withered away. Some seed fell among thistles; but the thistles shot up and choked the
corn, and it yielded no crop. And some of
the seed fell into good soil, where it came
up and grew, and bore fruit; and the yield
was thirtyfold, sixtyfold, even a hundredfold." He added, "If you have ears to hear,
then hear."

When he was alone, the Twelve[2] and
others who were round him questioned him
about the parables. He replied, "To you the
secret of the kingdom of God has been given;
but to those who are outside everything
comes by way of parables, so that (as Scripture says) they may look and look, but see
nothing; they may hear and hear, but understand nothing; otherwise they might turn
to God and be forgiven."

So he said, "You do not understand this
parable? How then are you to understand
any parable? The sower sows the word.[3]
Those along the footpath are people in
whom the word is sown, but no sooner have
they heard it than Satan[4] comes and carries
off the word which has been sown in them.
It is the same with those who receive the
seed on rocky ground; as soon as they hear
the word, they accept it with joy, but it
strikes no root in them; they have no stay-
ing-power; then, when there is trouble or
persecution on account of the word, they fall
away at once. Others again receive the seed

Gift of Quincy Adams Shaw through Quincy A. Shaw, Jr., and Mrs. Marian
Shaw Haughton. Courtesy of the Museum of Fine Arts, Boston.

THE SOWER, JEAN FRANÇOIS MILLET (1814–1875).
? *In this parable, who or what does the sower
represent?*

among thistles; they hear the word, but
worldly cares and the false glamour[5] of
wealth and all kinds of evil desire come in
and choke the word, and it proves barren.
And there are those who receive the seed in
good soil; they hear the word and welcome
it; and they bear fruit thirtyfold, sixtyfold,
or a hundredfold."

Mark 4:1–20

---

2. **the Twelve:** the twelve disciples of Jesus; also
called the Apostles.
3. **the word:** the word of God; the Gospels.
4. **Satan:** the devil.

5. **glamour:** (British) glamor.

5 LITERARY ELEMENT

Symbolism: Jesus explains that
the seed symbolizes "the
word," his teachings. Who
might the sower represent?
(himself and his disciples)
What kind of people are those
(a) along the footpath, (b) on
rocky ground, (c) among thistles, and (d) in good soil? (Possible responses: those who (a)
ignore the teachings, (b) abandon the teachings during difficult times, (c) are distracted by
worldly goods, and (d) nurture
God's word and see it flourish)

HUMANITIES CONNECTION

Although French artist Jean
François Millet (1814–1875)
painted classical and religious
subjects, he specialized in depicting peasants at work. Millet's *The Sower*, like his *The
Gleaners*, demonstrates how
little the farming of his day
had changed from that of biblical times.
? *Do you feel Millet's work
has any religious overtones?*
(Answers will vary.) ∎

SYNTHESIZING

How could this parable apply
to situations other than the
spreading of Christian doctrine? (The parable suggests
that regardless of how good a
"seed" [idea] is, it will not
flourish [spread] under adverse
conditions. The "sower" could
be any artist, teacher, philosopher, or political leader seeking to "plant" new ideas,
which some will reject and
some will embrace.)

READING CHECK

1. What is the purpose of a parable? (to teach a moral)
2. In "The Prodigal Son," how does the younger son use his inheritance? (He wastes it in reckless living.)
3. In "The Prodigal Son," which character is the most generous and loving? (the father)

4. What happens to most of the seed in the parable of "The Sower"? (It does not bear fruit.)
5. In "The Talents," what does the third man do with his master's money? (He buries it.)

RETEACHING

Some bumper stickers or posters, like parables, communicate a moral value in a concise and easy-to-understand way. This bumper sticker protests the amassing of nuclear weapons: YOU CAN'T HUG YOUR CHILD WITH NUCLEAR ARMS. Have students write a bumper sticker or caption for a poster that captures the message of each parable. Encourage clever wordplay, but limit students to twelve words per message.

---

capacity (kə·pas'i·tē): ability

forfeit (fôr'fit): lose

6 INTERPRETING

If the bags of money are understood to represent the talents or abilities given to different people, why is the master angry with the servant who has only one bag? (because the servant did nothing with the gifts he was given—neither he nor anyone else benefited from them)

7 READER'S RESPONSE

On the literal level of the story, do you think the master's reaction to the third servant is fair? Why or why not? (Answers will vary.)

CULTURAL DIVERSITY

The message of "The Talents" reinforces the widely held American value of developing individual potential to the fullest, as expressed in the Army's recruiting slogan, "Be all that you can be."

❓ *What other expressions of this value are common today?* (Possible responses: "Don't hide your light under a bushel"; "Realize your potential")

THE TALENTS
New English Bible

This parable is called "The Talents" because earlier translations used the name of a valuable gold coin, the talent, instead of the phrase "bags of gold." What does the word talent usually mean today? How does the parable apply to both meanings of talent?

"It is like a man going abroad, who called his servants and put his capital in their hands; to one he gave five bags of gold, to another two, to another one, each according to his capacity. Then he left the country. The man who had the five bags went at once and employed them in business, and made a profit of five bags, and the man who had the two bags made two. But the man who had been given one bag of gold went off and dug a hole in the ground, and hid his master's money. A long time afterwards their master returned, and proceeded to settle accounts with them. The man who had been given the five bags of gold came and produced the five he had made: 'Master,' he said, 'you left five bags with me; look, I have made five more.' 'Well done, my good and trusty servant!' said the master. 'You have proved trustworthy in a small way; I will now put you in charge of something big. Come and share your master's delight.'[1] The man with the two bags then came and said, 'Master, you left two bags with me; look, I have made two more.' 'Well done, my good and trusty servant!' said the master. 'You have proved trustworthy in a small way; I will now put

The Granger Collection, New York

you in charge of something big. Come and share your master's delight.' Then the man who had been given one bag came and said, 'Master, I knew you to be a hard man: you reap where you have not sown, you gather where you have not scattered; so I was afraid, and I went and hid your gold in the ground. Here it is—you have what belongs to you.' 'You lazy rascal!' said the master. 'You knew that I reap where I have not sown, and gather where I have not scattered? Then you ought to have put my money on deposit, and on my return I should have got it back with interest. Take the bag of gold from him, and give it to the one with the ten bags. For the man who has will always be given more, till he has enough and to spare; and the man who has not will forfeit even what he has. Fling the useless servant out into the dark, the place of wailing and grinding of teeth!'"

6

7

---

1. **share your master's delight:** enjoy the same prosperity as the master.

Matthew 25:14–31

1. Holding a Press Conference. Divide the class into four role-playing groups: Group 1 will portray characters from "The Prodigal Son"; Group 2, characters from "The Talents"; Groups 3 and 4, reporters who will interview Groups 1 and 2. Actors should prepare by identifying key qualities of their characters, and reporters should plan questions that probe the feelings and motivations of the characters.

2. Reading Other Parables. Suggest that students read three of the following New Testament parables and explain the lesson of each in a sentence or two: "The Mustard Seed" (Matthew 13:31–32); "The Two Builders" (Luke 6:46–49); "The Lost Sheep" and "The Lost Coin" (Luke 15:4–10); "The Unjust Steward" (Luke 16:1–13); or "The Father and the Persistent Friend" (Luke 11:5–13).

CLOSURE

Because they deal with perennial human problems and failings, the best parables teach lessons that apply in any time period or place. Ask students to consider: What lesson might the parable of "The Prodigal Son" offer a teenage runaway of today? How might the lessons of "The Sower" and "The Talents" apply to other problems today's young people face? ∎

First Thoughts

Which of the parables could you most easily apply to your own life?

Identifying Facts

1. In "The Prodigal Son," why does the younger son want to return home? What is his father's reaction to his return? What is his brother's reaction?
2. In what four places do the seeds land in "The Sower"? What happens to the seeds in each location?
3. In "The Talents," what does each servant do with the gold he receives? Why is the master angry with the third servant?

Interpreting Meanings

1. What did you think of the father's reaction to his son's return in "The Prodigal Son"? On an **allegorical** level, what might this **parable** be saying about God's love for sinners?
2. In "The Sower," some seeds fall among thistles, which Jesus identifies as "worldly cares and the false glamour of wealth and all kinds of evil desire." What are some of the "thistles" in today's world?
3. In "The Talents," the third servant simply hides his gold rather than risk investing it. On an allegorical level, what has he done? If the master symbolizes God, what does this parable say about what God expects people to do with their "talents"?
4. Choose one of the three **parables**, and state its **moral**, or lesson, in a sentence. Then think of a situation in your everyday life to which the parable could apply.

Applying Meanings

At different times in your life, have you been—or could you be—the younger son who returns, the older son who feels cheated, or the father who forgives in "The Prodigal Son"? Discuss how a person could identify with each of these characters at different times in his or her life. In what ways is this parable universal—that is, applicable to both Christians and non-Christians alike?

Creative Writing Response

Updating a Parable. Take any one of the three parables, and rewrite it using language, situations, and references that a modern reader would understand. To plan your updated parable, make a chart that shows the details of the original parable and the allegorical meaning of those details. Then decide how you will change the details in your parable. The allegorical meaning should remain the same. You might want to use a chart similar to the following example—for "The Prodigal Son"—to plan your parable.

Original Details (characters, places, things)	Allegorical Meaning	Updated Details (characters, places, things)
the father	forgiveness; God	school principal
the younger son	recklessness; sinner	high-school student who ditches classes
the older son	obedience; faithful follower who is jealous	honors student who never misses a day of class

ANSWERS

First Thoughts
Answers will vary.

Identifying Facts
1. The younger son wants to escape hunger and poverty. His father welcomes him with joy. His brother is jealous.
2. beside the path (birds eat them), on rocky ground (they wither), among thistles (they are choked), and in good soil (they bear fruit).
3. The first two men invest the money profitably; the third man buries it. He did not invest the money or deposit it in a bank.

Interpreting Meanings
1. Possible responses: The father is forgiving to the point of foolishness. God's love is boundless.
2. Answers will vary.
3. He has "buried" his abilities. Talents must be used.
4. Possible responses: "The Prodigal Son": One should forgive others their mistakes; "The Sower": Ideas will die in a hostile environment; "The Talents": One should use talents and gifts wisely, not bury them.

Applying Meanings
Answers will vary. The parable deals with basic human emotions and conflicts.

Creative Writing Response
Updating a Parable. Evaluate the parables for retention of the moral of the story and for use of a coherent set of contemporary details. ∎

LANGUAGE
— AND —
CULTURE

DECIPHERING ANCIENT TEXTS

T he study of ancient literatures is part art, part science, and part adventure. While not all archaeologists are cast in the mold of an Indiana Jones, many do risk life and limb—facing treacherous weather, dangerous terrain, and hostile governments—in their efforts to recover ancient writings. No less taxing are scholars' efforts to understand the meaning of the long-lost texts. Ancient scripts can be as baffling as codes or ciphers. In fact, linguists often do employ the principles of modern cryptography, or the art of writing and deciphering codes, to "break the code" of ancient texts.

Once "decoded," ancient texts must be translated into modern language. The translator tries to preserve both the spirit and the form of the ancient language. Occasionally, the translator must reconstruct parts of the text that are unreadable, never recovered, or simply too obscure to understand. To recreate missing text, the translator needs a thorough understanding of the historical and cultural context in which the work was written. Sometimes so much of an ancient text has been lost that any attempts to reconstruct it would be futile.

The Discovery of Sumerian Cuneiform

Cuneiform is a system of writing based on the precise arrangement of wedge-shaped markings. Our knowledge of the long-extinct Sumerian culture comes from clay tablets inscribed in cuneiform between 3500 B.C. and 2000 B.C. But until excavation of Sumerian cuneiform tablets began in the mid-nineteenth century, there had been no knowledge of the Sumerian culture for thousands of years.

Sumerian, a non-Semitic language, has little in common with other ancient languages of Mesopotamia and the surrounding regions. But Babylonian and Assyrian conquerers of Sumer adopted the Sumerian script and language as their own literary language. The *Epic of Gilgamesh* that appears in this unit is in fact a Babylonian version of earlier Sumerian epics. Babylonian scribes recorded many of their own texts twice: once in Sumerian and once in Akkadian, the Babylonians' own language. Linguists found the earlier, solely Sumerian texts difficult, if not impossible, to translate. They were able to decipher the meaning of Sumerian cuneiform only when they compared it to corresponding Akkadian texts. In addition, because archaeologists usually found the cuneiform tablets in fragments, like the pieces of a jigsaw puzzle, they had few complete texts to work from.

Cuneiform in "Triplicate"

Fortunately for translators, the diligent Sumerian and Babylonian scribes tended to copy texts several times. Scholars were able to reconstruct many broken tablets from multiple copies. Scholars were also aided by an important feature of Sumerian literary style: the repetition of key passages. For example, in one narrative, a messenger is sent with a message, and the message is recorded both as he receives it and as he delivers it. Modern readers would find this kind of repetition tiresome and boring, but thanks to this stylistic tendency, a missing fragment from a passage of text could be filled in when the same passage was repeated later on.

Still, neither the Sumerians' taste for repetition nor the Babylonians' careful copying could completely prevent the ravages of time. Many cuneiform tablets have been lost—either disintegrated or buried under four thousand years' accumulation of soil.

The Dead Sea Scrolls

Unlike the long-lost Sumerian texts, the languages of the Bible have been "alive" continuously for about 2000 years. The text that we call the Hebrew Bible was first passed on orally, then written down in Hebrew, Aramaic, and Greek. Questions about biblical texts are caused not so much by missing or undecipherable material as by conflicting interpretations.

An exciting archaeological advance in biblical interpretation occurred in 1947, however, when an Israeli shepherd, out looking for his herd, stumbled upon some ancient scrolls in a cave near the Dead Sea. Many more

scrolls were eventually found in the same area. Some of the scrolls dated from 200 B.C. The Dead Sea Scrolls, as they have been named, probably belonged to a Jewish sect called the Essenes.

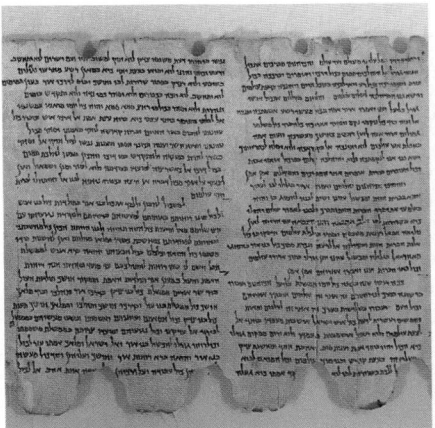

DEAD SEA SCROLL: THE MANUAL OF DISCIPLINE, COLUMN 2–4.

These scrolls, which contain most of the contents of the Hebrew Bible, represent the oldest written fragments of the Bible ever discovered. They demonstrate that there existed a unified Hebrew Bible by A.D. 70. Surprisingly, the first translations released show that later versions of the Hebrew Bible (those in circulation from antiquity until now) were fairly faithful transcriptions of the earliest sources. It was not until late in 1991 that the Huntington Library in California, amid much controversy, released the complete Dead Sea Scrolls to the public. Thus, the mystery behind the scrolls is still unfolding.

HISTORICAL BACKGROUND

The Dead Sea Scrolls: The discovery of the Dead Sea Scrolls near the ruins of Qumran east of Jerusalem was one of the most exciting in archaeological history. A Bedouin shepherd, noticing the opening to a cave, idly tossed in a stone and was surprised to hear it hit pottery. He crawled into the cave and found eight jars containing bundles of parchment. Before anyone had an inkling of their importance, they were brought to the Bedouin marketplace in Bethlehem and sold to an antique dealer. The dealer showed the find to an archaeology professor at Hebrew University, who quickly recognized the scrolls as ancient documents. This discovery triggered an excited search by the Bedouin, who succeeded in finding more documents in nearby caves.

The Dead Sea Scrolls are probably the remains of the extensive library of an ascetic Jewish sect called the Essenes. It is thought that the Essenes hid their library in the caves of Qumran when they were invaded by the Romans, some time around A.D. 68.

When the scrolls were first discovered, an international team of seven scholars was granted control of the manuscripts. For forty-four years this group denied other researchers access to the documents, but now, in what the New York Times calls "the scholarly equivalent of breaking down the Berlin Wall," the scrolls are available to everyone.

Language Skills

VARYING SENTENCE BEGINNINGS AND AVOIDING DANGLING MODIFIERS

Caught up in the flow of writing a narrative, you may find yourself composing sentence after sentence with the same basic structure. One way to correct this tendency is to use introductory elements to achieve sentence variety and to add information. An **introductory element**—any word, phrase, or clause that comes before the subject of a sentence—lets you vary sentence rhythms. In addition, it offers a concise way to include facts and details. Compare the examples below.

MONOTONOUS

Boaz is impressed by Ruth's beauty, loyalty, and dignity. He makes generous offers. He also takes practical steps to clear the way for their marriage. Boaz guards her reputation with these steps, which demonstrate his love.

IMPROVED

Impressed by Ruth's beauty, loyalty, and dignity, Boaz makes generous offers. He also takes practical steps to clear the way for their marriage. *By guarding her reputation with these steps,* he demonstrates his love.

Notice how the introductory elements, italicized in the second passage, allow the writer to vary and condense sentences without losing important details.

Types of Introductory Elements

In the following examples, each introductory element is followed directly by the subject of the sentence.

Adjectives
Simple and rhythmic, the psalms express intense emotions.

Adverb
Frequently, psalms employ parallel structure and contrast.

Prepositional Phrase
In the parable, one servant hides his master's money.

Present Participial Phrase
Begging forgiveness, the prodigal son returns to his father.

Past Participial Phrase
Reared among animals, Enkidu is shaggy-haired and wild.

Appositive Phrase
A very human hero, Gilgamesh suffers from excessive pride.

Adverbial Clause
Although they are simple stories, parables convey complex thoughts.

Exercise 1: Using Introductory Elements

Restructure each of the following sentences, making the italicized portion an introductory element. Be sure that the subject of the sentence comes directly after each introductory element.

1. Gilgamesh constructs a magnificent wall *around Uruk*. (prepositional phrase)
2. Gilgamesh and Enkidu insult the gods *shamelessly*. (adverb)
3. Gilgamesh seeks immortality *because he hopes to avoid his friend's fate*. (adverbial clause)
4. Utnapishtim, *warming to his tale*, tells the story of the flood. (present participial phrase)
5. Gilgamesh, *a wiser person now*, returns to his tasks in Uruk. (appositive phrase)

Dangling Modifiers

A **dangling modifier**—an introductory element that does not refer clearly to the word it modifies—can be either amusing or confusing. To correct a dangling modifier in your writing, reword the sentence so that the introductory element appears as close as possible to the word it modifies.

DANGLING MODIFIERS

Tempted by the serpent, the apple is irresistible to Eve. (Is the apple tempted by the serpent?)

Handsome and brave, everyone's admiration focuses on Gilgamesh. (Is admiration handsome and brave?)

CORRECTED SENTENCES

Tempted by the serpent, Eve finds the apple irresistible.

Handsome and brave, Gilgamesh attracts everyone's admiration.

Notice that correcting the sentence can involve choosing new words to convey the same meaning.

An introductory element cannot modify the possessive form of a noun or a possessive adjective.

DANGLING MODIFIER

Tamed by civilization, Enkidu's friendship with Gilgamesh costs him his life. ("Enkidu's friendship" was not tamed.)

CORRECTED SENTENCE

Tamed by civilization, Enkidu loses his life because of his friendship with Gilgamesh.

Exercise 2: Correcting Dangling Modifiers

Reword the sentences below to correct each dangling modifier. Try to avoid changing the introductory elements.

1. Ashamed and guilty, God punishes Adam and Eve.
2. Growing in the once-fruitful ground, Adam and Eve now find thorns and thistles.
3. With their bleak mud and shadows, Sumerians expected no joy in the caves of the afterlife.
4. By treating the goddess disrespectfully, Enkidu's doom is sealed.
5. Like Noah, Utnapishtim's boat is built according to divine specifications.
6. Taught to act unselfishly, biblical parables show how ordinary people can achieve extraordinary things.
7. Admiring epic heroes for their superhuman abilities, their human failings also help us to empathize with them.

Background: Use the following role-playing activity to help students begin thinking about the kinds of incidents, large and small, that can affect people's lives. Group students in fours, and assign each group member a character: Gilgamesh, Ruth, Noah, or Eve. Have each student, in character, tell other group members about two or three of the most meaningful events in his or her life. (Allow students to use their imaginations as well as details from the unit selections to fill out their incidents.)

Afterward, let one member of each group summarize for the class the events that each character recounted. Lead a discussion of the variations in the narratives of each group. Help students to see that even events which seem minor at the time can have far-reaching impacts.

Prewriting: Before students begin freewriting, show them a model of a narrative that is rich in sensory details, such as Enkidu's description of his descent to the underworld in the *Epic of Gilgamesh* (pp. 140–141). Let students discuss the ways in which the excerpt appeals to each of the senses. (*touch/feeling:* feathers, pounding heart, smothering embrace of the "awful being"; *taste:* food of clay and dust; *sound:* roaring and rumbling of heavens and earth, cold voice of the goddess; *sight:* darkness, kings clothed as birds)

Critical Thinking and Writing

WRITING AN AUTOBIOGRAPHICAL NARRATIVE

Now that you've read the *Epic of Gilgamesh* and several biblical tales and parables, it's your turn to be a storyteller. By delving into ancient literature, you have found reflections of a variety of human experiences: the loss of a loved one, failure to reach a goal, and leaving one's home for new surroundings, among others. You can find similar reflections by narrating incidents, either large or small, from your own life.

Writing Assignment

In a narrative essay, tell the story of an incident in your life: a success or failure, a realization about yourself, a special time with a friend. Bring the event to life for your audience, and show how it has affected you. Assume that you are writing for teen and adult readers of a general-interest magazine. For this assignment, you will analyze causes and effects.

Background

Characters in this unit respond to their experiences in realistic ways. Some, like Gilgamesh, gain insight from adversity. Others, like Adam and Eve, the prodigal son, and the lazy servant, suffer because of their actions. Still others, like Noah and Ruth, are rewarded for their choices. Think of your experiences, large and small. Which have most affected your attitudes, feelings, and behavior?

Prewriting

Recalling an Incident. The incident you choose needn't be dramatic; simple, everyday events can also have lasting effects. Think of two or three different experiences that changed you or brought new discoveries about yourself, about another person, or about life in general. Choose the incident most meaningful to you. Then freewrite about it, focusing on sensory details (sights, sounds, scents, tastes, and textures) and on your thoughts and feelings during the incident.

Analyzing Causes and Effects. Reflect on causes and effects of your incident, and fill out a diagram based on the one below. Decide which effects have, in turn, created further effects.

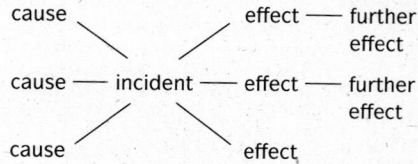

Next, sum up in one or two sentences the significance your experience had for you.

Writing

Follow these guidelines for drafting a narrative.

1. **Introductory Paragraph.** Draw readers in immediately by beginning with action. Your freewriting may provide strong, sensory verbs that will be useful here. Go on to work in any background information (about setting or characters, for example) that readers will need to understand the incident. End the paragraph with a reference to the significance this incident has for you.

2. **Body Paragraphs.** Again, pull the most vivid details out of your freewriting, and bring your narrative to life by showing rather than telling. Well-chosen details describing sights, sounds, textures, and so on can convey your experiences more effectively than whole paragraphs of explanation could.

   Organize your narrative chronologically, beginning with the causes of the incident, then recounting the incident, and finally showing its effects on you. Or, if appropriate, use flashback: begin with the effects, and then move backward in time to show how and why they occurred. In either case, refer to your cause-and-effect diagram as you write, so that you can include details showing not only what happened, but also why it happened and what resulted from it. Use transitions (see page 56) to keep both the time order and

the cause-and-effect relationships clear.

3. **Concluding Paragraph.** Your conclusion should communicate your reflections about the incident. Leave readers with a definite idea of how this incident affected your life.

Evaluating and Revising

Use these questions to evaluate and revise your draft.

1. Does your introductory paragraph show action and refer to the significance of the incident?
2. Do you use enough specific, sensory details? Are all details relevant to your focus?
3. Have you recounted the incident from beginning to end in a clear and logical way?
4. Have you shown causes and results of the incident? Have you clearly stated its significance and its effect on your life?
5. Are your sentences varied in structure and grammatically correct?

Proofreading and Publishing

Proofread your work, correcting errors in spelling and mechanics, and make a final copy. With your teacher's guidance, select a local or national periodical that features personal-experience articles, and submit your essay for publication.

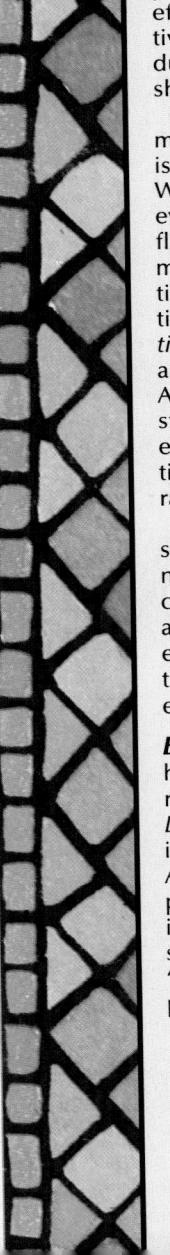

Writing: As students begin their drafts, explain that narratives, whether fictional or nonfictional, are based on elements of setting, character, plot/conflict, and theme. Three effective ways to start a narrative are to set the scene, introduce a main character, or show a conflict.

Remind students that, in the main body of a narrative, time is the controlling factor. Whether students recount events chronologically or use flashbacks, they will need to make the order of events in time clear to readers. Transitions such as *first, next, by that time, beforehand, afterward,* and *meanwhile* can help. Another useful technique is to start a new paragraph whenever a significant amount of time has passed in the narrative.

You might want to emphasize that the conclusions of narratives do not necessarily call for summaries. Rather, an autobiographical narrative can end with comments showing the impact that the recounted event has had on the writer.

Evaluating and Revising: For help in achieving sentence variety, students can turn to the *Language Skills* feature "Varying Sentence Beginnings and Avoiding Dangling Modifiers," pp. 206–207. They can also find information about varying basic sentence structure in "Varying Sentences" on pp. 1430–1431. ■

The following annotations are for the artwork surrounding the map, starting in the upper right-hand corner and moving in a counterclockwise direction.

Greek Woman: This detail from a mural shows the simplicity and idealization typical of Greek art.

? *How does the portrait of the Greek woman at the upper right contrast with that of the Roman princess at the lower left?* (Possible response: The Roman bust is less idealized.)

Armed Fighters of Ancient Greece: By the sixth century B.C., bronze was readily available for armor. Armed spearmen called hoplites, each wearing armor that weighed about 80 pounds and fighting on foot, became the backbone of the Greek armies. As this detail from the Oinochoe Chigi vase shows, hoplites painted their cities' symbols on their shields. Athens' symbol was the owl.

Sculpted Bust of Homer: This is not a likeness of the poet, since not even the classical Greeks knew Homer's true identity. Tradition pictures him as a blind old wanderer reciting his poems, but many scholars believe his epics were developed through many generations of oral storytellers.

? *What do you think the sculptor conveys about Homer?* (Possible responses: maturity, wisdom)

Atlantic Ocean

BRITAIN

GAUL

Alps

Pyrenees Mountains

Rubicon R.

Tiber R.

IBERIA

Black Sea

MACEDONIA

Byzantium

MAGNA GRAECIA

ITALY

Rome

ASIA MINOR

SICILY

Delphi

Thebes

Troy

Carthage

Corinth

Athens

GREECE

Sparta

CYPRUS

PELOPONNESUS

Mediterranean Sea

CRETE

PALE

Alexandria

NORTH AFRICA

Memphis

Jer

EGYPT

SAHARA

Nile River

Thebes

ANCIENT GREECE AND ROME

☐ Ancient Greece
☐ Roman Empire, c. A.D. 120

UNIT 4

GREEK AND ROMAN LITERATURES

▼ **Time** ▼
800 B.C.—A.D. 200

▼ **Place** ▼
The Ancient Mediterranean

▼ **Literary Significance** ▼

Ancient Greece: The literature of ancient Greece includes the Homeric epics the *Iliad* and the *Odyssey,* lyric poetry, drama, philosophical works, and histories. The fourth and fifth centuries B.C. are considered the classical period of ancient Greece, a period in which Greece, especially the city-state of Athens, made outstanding cultural and political achievements. After Athens's decline, Alexander the Great conquered many lands, spreading Greek cultural influences—including political, literary, and philosophical traditions—throughout much of the Mediterranean, western Asia, and North Africa.

Ancient Rome: After the death of Alexander the Great, the Romans continued to spread and preserve the legacy of Greek civilization. Eventually, however, the Romans developed a rich culture of their own. Among the treasures of the Roman literary legacy are the *Aeneid*—an epic describing the legend of the founding of Rome—lyric poetry, high comedy, oratory, and history. The Roman Empire steadily expanded its territory through military conquest until its decline in the fifth century A.D.

Public Amphitheater at Athens: This huge amphitheater accommodated thousands of spectators. It was used by both the Greeks and the Romans for dramatic competitions and performances.
❓ *What kinds of public gathering places in our society accommodate as many people?* (Possible responses: sports stadiums, convention centers)

Bust of Roman Princess: Roman sculptors were noted for their originality in creating realistic individual portraits. This is one area of the arts in which the Romans surpassed the Greeks.

Roman Aqueduct: This aqueduct, 882 feet long, was built by the Romans over the river Gard at Nimes, France, about two thousand years ago. Aqueducts conducted the water supply of the Roman Empire, and portions of this extensive system still stand in France, Italy, Spain, and Tunisia, attesting to the skill of the Roman engineers.

Emperor Augustus: The first and greatest Roman emperor, Augustus ruled Rome from 27 B.C. to A.D.14. He established an era of peace and prosperity, encouraged learning, and patronized the arts.
❓ *What words derived from the Latin word Augustus are used in modern English?* (the month of *August;* the adjective *august,* meaning "majestic") ■

Invite students to examine the Time Line to work out the chronological relationship between Greece and Rome. Point out that for the most part, the left side of the Time Line deals with Greece and the right side with Rome. Explain that although the founding of Rome coincided with the emergence of the Greek city-states, Rome did not become a force in world affairs until after the decline of Alexander the Great's empire.

Invite students to analyze how literary creation was influenced by political events. For example, Homer's epics, which set forth elements of the Greek religion, were written during an era of recovery from a dark age. Lead students to see that the century of greatest Greek political influence (the fifth century B.C.) was also the century of greatest achievements in drama and historical writing. In contrast, Greek philosophy flourished during the fourth century, after Athens had suffered plague and military losses, perhaps a time of disillusionment and reevaluation.

Roman literature flourished during Rome's period of greatest political strength because Emperor Augustus gathered around him a group of writers, including Virgil, who strove to write works expressing Roman pride.

Students may turn to Time Lines for Africa and the Middle East (pp. 62–63, 126–127) to see how events in nearby civilizations fit into the pattern of Greek and Roman development.

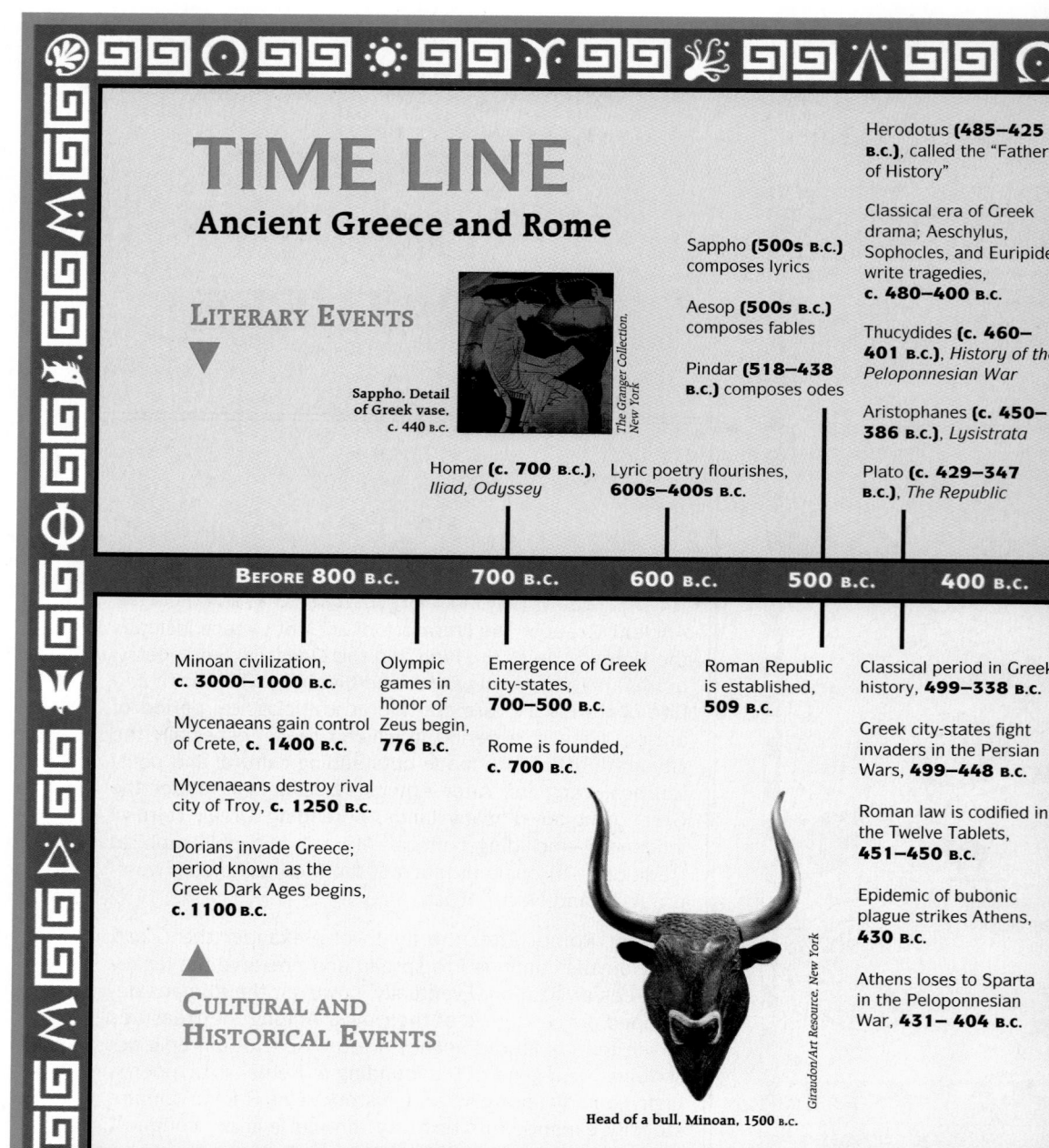

TIME LINE
Ancient Greece and Rome

LITERARY EVENTS

Sappho. Detail of Greek vase, c. 440 B.C.

The Granger Collection, New York

Sappho **(500s B.C.)** composes lyrics

Aesop **(500s B.C.)** composes fables

Pindar **(518–438 B.C.)** composes odes

Herodotus **(485–425 B.C.)**, called the "Father of History"

Classical era of Greek drama; Aeschylus, Sophocles, and Euripides write tragedies, **c. 480–400 B.C.**

Thucydides **(c. 460–401 B.C.)**, *History of the Peloponnesian War*

Aristophanes **(c. 450–386 B.C.)**, *Lysistrata*

Plato **(c. 429–347 B.C.)**, *The Republic*

Homer **(c. 700 B.C.)**, *Iliad, Odyssey*

Lyric poetry flourishes, **600s–400s B.C.**

| BEFORE 800 B.C. | 700 B.C. | 600 B.C. | 500 B.C. | 400 B.C. |

Minoan civilization, **c. 3000–1000 B.C.**

Mycenaeans gain control of Crete, **c. 1400 B.C.**

Mycenaeans destroy rival city of Troy, **c. 1250 B.C.**

Dorians invade Greece; period known as the Greek Dark Ages begins, **c. 1100 B.C.**

Olympic games in honor of Zeus begin, **776 B.C.**

Emergence of Greek city-states, **700–500 B.C.**

Rome is founded, **c. 700 B.C.**

Roman Republic is established, **509 B.C.**

Classical period in Greek history, **499–338 B.C.**

Greek city-states fight invaders in the Persian Wars, **499–448 B.C.**

Roman law is codified in the Twelve Tablets, **451–450 B.C.**

Epidemic of bubonic plague strikes Athens, **430 B.C.**

Athens loses to Sparta in the Peloponnesian War, **431– 404 B.C.**

CULTURAL AND HISTORICAL EVENTS

Head of a bull, Minoan, 1500 B.C.

Giraudon/Art Resource, New York

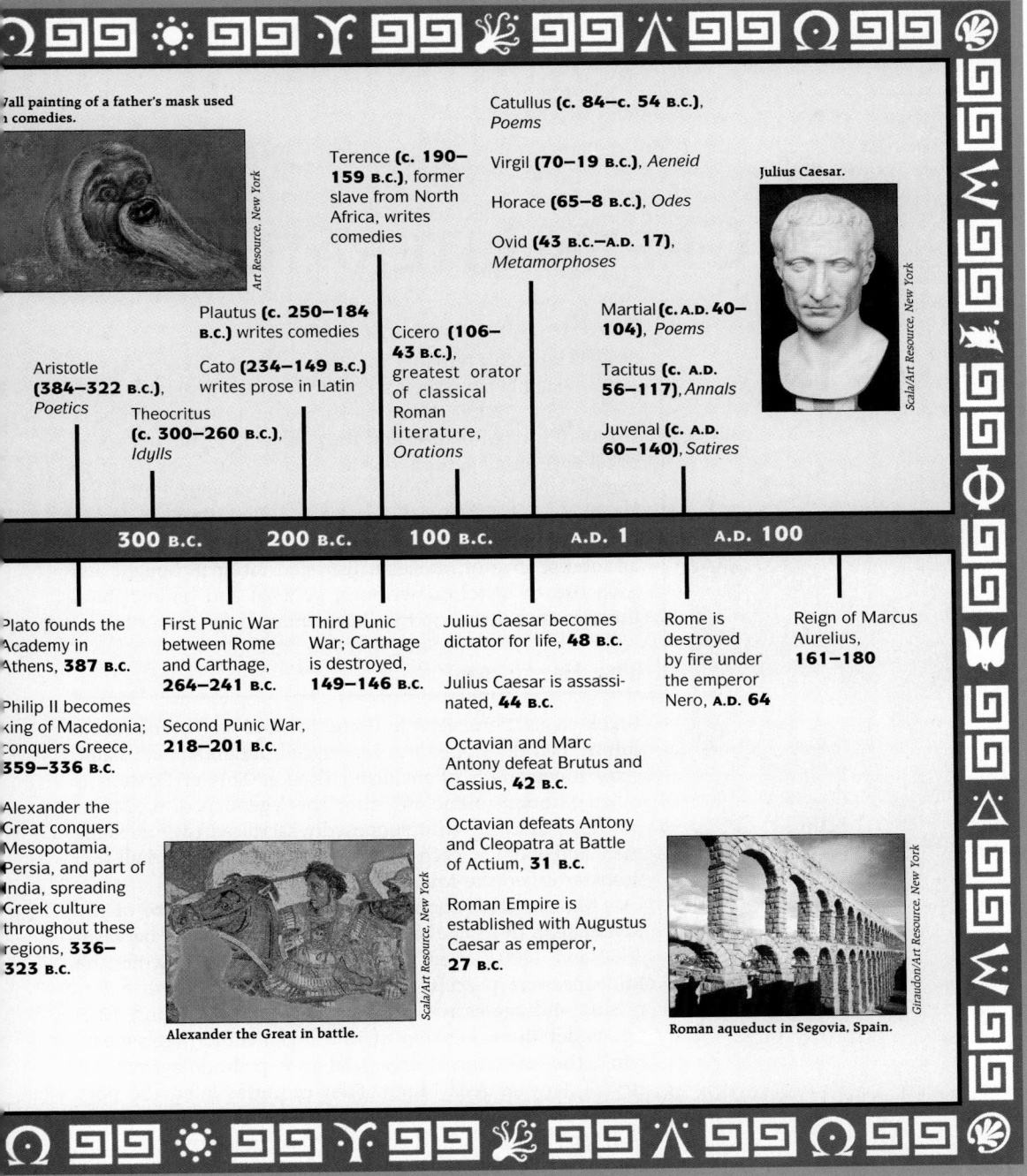

Wall painting of a father's mask used in comedies.

Art Resource, New York

Catullus **(c. 84–c. 54 B.C.)**, *Poems*

Terence **(c. 190–159 B.C.)**, former slave from North Africa, writes comedies

Virgil **(70–19 B.C.)**, *Aeneid*

Horace **(65–8 B.C.)**, *Odes*

Ovid **(43 B.C.–A.D. 17)**, *Metamorphoses*

Plautus **(c. 250–184 B.C.)** writes comedies

Cato **(234–149 B.C.)** writes prose in Latin

Aristotle **(384–322 B.C.)**, *Poetics*

Theocritus **(c. 300–260 B.C.)**, *Idylls*

Cicero **(106–43 B.C.)**, greatest orator of classical Roman literature, *Orations*

Martial **(c. A.D. 40–104)**, *Poems*

Tacitus **(c. A.D. 56–117)**, *Annals*

Juvenal **(c. A.D. 60–140)**, *Satires*

Julius Caesar.

Scala/Art Resource, New York

| 300 B.C. | 200 B.C. | 100 B.C. | A.D. 1 | A.D. 100 |

Plato founds the Academy in Athens, **387 B.C.**

Philip II becomes king of Macedonia; conquers Greece, **359–336 B.C.**

Alexander the Great conquers Mesopotamia, Persia, and part of India, spreading Greek culture throughout these regions, **336–323 B.C.**

First Punic War between Rome and Carthage, **264–241 B.C.**

Second Punic War, **218–201 B.C.**

Third Punic War; Carthage is destroyed, **149–146 B.C.**

Julius Caesar becomes dictator for life, **48 B.C.**

Julius Caesar is assassinated, **44 B.C.**

Octavian and Marc Antony defeat Brutus and Cassius, **42 B.C.**

Octavian defeats Antony and Cleopatra at Battle of Actium, **31 B.C.**

Roman Empire is established with Augustus Caesar as emperor, **27 B.C.**

Rome is destroyed by fire under the emperor Nero, **A.D. 64**

Reign of Marcus Aurelius, **161–180**

Alexander the Great in battle.

Scala/Art Resource, New York

Roman aqueduct in Segovia, Spain.

Giraudon/Art Resource, New York

This time line border is decorated with images found on ancient Greek pottery.

HISTORICAL BACKGROUND

Greek City-States: Greece was divided into many small city-states. To fight Persia, their common enemy, the city-states banded together; nevertheless, ancient Greece never became a unified state. Despite a common language, religion, and literature, and similar customs, the city-states maintained their independence.

CULTURAL BACKGROUND

Head of a Bull, Minoan: The Greeks were influenced by the earlier Minoan and Mycenaean civilization. In the 1900s, a great Minoan palace was discovered and excavated by archaeologists. Paintings on the palace walls depict acrobats vaulting over the backs of bulls. A maze of rooms that resembles a labyrinth was discovered in the palace. According to ancient Greek mythology, the Minoans had a dreaded monster, half man, half bull, called the Minotaur, who lived in the labyrinth. This creature demanded a yearly tribute from Athens of seven youths and seven maidens. The legendary Athenian hero Theseus killed the Minotaur. Students might wish to review the myth of Theseus on page 29 of this text.

HISTORICAL BACKGROUND

Octavian: The great-nephew and heir of Julius Caesar, Octavian had the name Augustus conferred on him by the Roman Senate when he was the emperor.

1 HISTORICAL BACKGROUND

Protagoras: Protagoras was the first person to describe himself as a *sophist*—an itinerant professional teacher. For forty years, he traveled through Greece, giving public lectures and private tutorials. He considered the kinds of ultimate questions on the nature of human existence that were to become the basis of Western philosophical inquiry.

HUMANITIES CONNECTION

The Athenian soldier wore, beneath his cloak, tough body armor, made from leather boiled in wax and shaped to fit his torso exactly. His helmet, unlike that of the Spartan soldier, was topped by a brightly colored crest of horsehair or feathers.
❓ *Why do you think the helmets of the Spartans did not feature crests?* (Possible response: The Spartan sense of aesthetics valued simplicity rather than decoration.) ∎

2 HISTORICAL BACKGROUND

Mycenaeans: In contrast to the unfortified Minoan palace at Knossos, the Mycenaean rulers lived in fortresses. They traded throughout the eastern Mediterranean, and routinely plundered neighboring cities. The Mycenaean civilization rose and fell during an unstable period when the entire Aegean world was affected by the fall of the Hittite Empire, centered in Asia Minor.

GREEK LITERATURE

Lee Boltin Picture Library

Draped warrior, bronze, 6th century B.C.

he achievements of the ancient Greeks flowed mainly from their ability to wonder, to ask the question, "Why?" The Greeks sought to know the basic truths of human nature, and they believed in the pursuit of excellence in all aspects of life. "Man is the measure of all things," declared the philosopher and teacher Protagoras (prō·tag′ə·rəs) (c. 485–410 B.C.). The Greeks' efforts to understand themselves and the peoples around them produced an intense love of intellectualism and rational thought and gave rise to historical writings, political and philosophical theories, and literature that have endured for centuries.

1

The Heroic Age

Greek civilization began in Crete. By 2000 B.C., a remarkable culture had developed on this rugged, mountainous island, sixty miles south of mainland Greece. This civilization is called **Minoan** (mi·nō′ən), after the legendary King Minos (mī′näs′) of Crete, who supposedly sacrificed twelve young men and women each year to feed a half-man, half-bull monster called the Minotaur.

Minoan civilization directly influenced the rise of the **Mycenaean** (mī′sə·nē′ən) culture which flourished between 1500 and 1200 B.C. on the Greek mainland. But while the Minoans were peaceful, the Mycenaeans were both enterprising and aggressive. Scholars believe that around 1250 B.C., under the leadership of King Agamemnon (ag′ə·mem′ nän′), the Mycenaeans organized an expedition against the city of Troy in Asia Minor. Four centuries later, the poet Homer immortalized the heroes of this "Trojan War" in the *Iliad*, one of the earliest epics in Western literature. To the Greeks of Homer's time, the Mycenaean era was known as the **Heroic Age**.

2

The Greek influence on philosophy, science, art, architecture, politics, and literature is a legacy that twentieth-century Americans continue to enjoy. To begin a class discussion of this legacy, ask students to brainstorm a list of possible reasons why ancient Greece has been such an inspiration to Western civilization. Next, suggest that students find photographs of the Greek countryside or consult an atlas to discover the topography of the region. Explain that the rugged terrain of the Attic peninsula encouraged self-contained, local communities. Even small villages could be largely self-sufficient because townspeople could find, within walking distance, meadows for planting crops, pastureland for grazing livestock, forests for hunting game, and the sea for catching fish.

Individual communities were known for olives, wine, marble, pottery—or even religious shrines, such as Apollo's oracle at Delphi—that drew traders and travelers from around the Greek world.

Local self-sufficiency made the city-state the natural unit of ancient Greek government. These city-states were small but very independent. Because of the limited size of the government, the pattern of life in a Greek city-state was such that public and private interests often coincided. The army, for example, was more like a group

Photo Nimatallah/Art Resource, New York

Fresco of Knossos. *The fresco depicts the ritual of bull-jumping practiced by Minoan youths, both male and female. The figure of the bull was worshiped as a symbol of strength and fertility.*

The Dark Age in Greece

Less than fifty years after the Trojan War, Mycenaean culture began a mysterious decline. This decline accelerated when a wave of invaders called the **Dorians** (dôr′ē·ənz) swept across the Greek peninsula in 1100 B.C. The Dorians burned the Mycenaean palace centers, and Greek culture entered a so-called **Dark Age** that lasted several centuries. During the Dark Age, writing apparently fell out of use, and there is no record of cultural development during this long period.

The Epic Age

The earliest surviving works of Greek poetry are the **epics** the *Iliad* and the *Odyssey* by Homer (see page 224). Around 750 B.C., shortly after Homer composed his epics, the Greeks developed a script for their language, based on a system borrowed from the Phoenicians. This system became what we know as the alphabet, named for its two initial letters, *alpha* and *beta.* Whether its purpose was to aid commercial dealings or, as one theory holds, to record Homer's epics for posterity, the Greek invention of the alphabet opened the door to a remarkable age of literary achievement.

66 Our way is to consider each separate thing alone by itself; the Greeks always saw things as parts of a whole, and this habit of mind is stamped upon everything they did. 99

—*Edith Hamilton*

3

HUMANITIES CONNECTION

The palace at Knossos, whose complex four-acre design made the Greeks think of it as a labyrinth, was excavated by British archaeologist Sir Arthur Evans in 1900. Many of its rooms and wall paintings have been reconstructed, including a famous fresco of swimming dolphins in the queen's room. On the whole, Minoan art gives the impression of a people who found joy in life: one of their major religious relics is a dance-floor.

❓ *How do you think the Minoan bull-jumpers felt?* (Possible responses: afraid; elated by the challenge) ■

3 RESPONDING TO THE QUOTATION
Edith Hamilton was an eminent classical scholar who spent her career studying Greek literature and civilization.

❓ *Do you accept her opinion about how people today see the world? For example, do Americans view their role as citizens as a fundamental part of their identity?* (Possible response: No, most Americans view their various roles such as worker, citizen, husband, or wife as separate domains governed by different values and rules.)

of citizens defending their own neighborhood than a professional military organization. Citizens listened to and participated in political discussions on a daily basis at the *agora*, or marketplace, and the theater was both a religious celebration and a free public event. Thus, the typical citizen of a Greek city-state was intimately involved in the public life of his community. In fact, the citizen who did not participate in public life was scorned. The English word *idiot* comes from the Greek *idiotes*, meaning "a private person." Thus, the political and cultural milieu encouraged ancient Greeks to pursue excellence in many walks of life. For instance, Pericles (494–429 B.C.) was a model soldier, statesman, orator, and patron of the arts.

The Greeks made important contributions to the history of Western writing in the forms of the epic, lyric poetry, prose, and drama. Before introducing the epic—in this case the excerpt from the *Iliad*—be sure students understand the Greek concept of *arete*, the highest level of excellence to which a warrior hero could aspire. Arete is a combination of courage, pride, and nobility; the hero's primary concern is his untarnished reputation and his personal honor. Explain that this concept, which may seem foreign to many high school students, resembles a type of high-minded *machismo*. Achilles' arete,

4 CULTURAL DIVERSITY

A *culture* is the collective customs of a group of people while a *nation* is a political and geographical entity with a single government. Thus a nation may contain many cultures; a culture may be spread over several nations or may be one part of a nation of many cultures.)

? *With what culture or cultures do you identify?* (Answers will vary.)

The Rise of the City-States

Between 700 and 500 B.C., Greek life became more organized and institutional. Small, fragmented settlements banded together to form communities. Soon a number of **city-states** emerged. The typical city-state, called a *polis* (from which the word *politics* is derived) was ruled by a king.

Delphi, Athenian temple to Apollo. *Apollo was one of the Greek gods worshiped universally in ancient Greece and its territories.*

Tzovaras/Art Resource, New York

In this period of city-states, the Greeks still did not think of themselves as a single nation. However, they did feel some common cultural bonds. They called themselves **Hellenes** (hel'ēnz'), believing themselves direct descendants of Hellen, the son of Deucalion (doo·kāl'ē·ən), who, according to a Greek myth, was the sole survivor of a great flood and thus the ancestor of all Greeks. This cultural identity set the Greeks apart from their "barbarian" neighbors, and

> Although the Greeks did not think of themselves as a unified nation, they forged a cultural identity based on shared athletic contests, religious worship, and a belief in their mythological origins.

4

the resulting sense of unity found expression in various social and religious institutions. A regular series of athletic contests brought the main Greek city-states in contact with one another and fostered a sense of Greek identity. The most important games were those held at Olympia every

his concern about his status among the Athenian warriors, leads to the tragedies and triumphs of the Trojan War, as described by Homer in the *Iliad*.

Sappho is one of the most accessible writers of the period. On the other hand, students may need help with the complex prose of Thucydides and Plato. Although prose was written in earlier societies, it was the Greeks who first used it as an analytical tool to explore the serious issues of their time. In most other cultures, prose was used mainly for business matters. Point out that Thucydides was the first to introduce shrewd political analysis into an objective account of a historical event. As an approach to reading his "Funeral Speech of Pericles," encourage students to separate the political analysis and patriotic rhetoric from the historical facts.

Before students read the excerpt from Plato's *Apology*, pique their interest in Socrates by describing him as a paunchy, ugly stonecutter who believed that when the Delphic oracle pronounced him the wisest man in the Greek world, it was because he appreciated his own ignorance. Socrates held that in order to truly learn, it was necessary to recognize one's own ignorance. Encourage students to keep Socrates' stance in mind as they read his speech to the jurors who have condemned him.

four years in honor of the god Zeus. A number of religious shrines, chief among them that of the god Apollo (ə·päl'ō) at Delphi (del'fī), were universal centers of worship.

Greek Gods and Goddesses

We have our first glimpses of Greek religion in the epics of Homer, since the gods play important roles in both the *Iliad* and the *Odyssey.* The ancient Greeks saw their gods as being very human. In fact, they often possessed the worst traits of humans: jealousy, irrational anger, and pettiness. There

⌐ 5

The Gods and Goddesses of Ancient Greece

Greek Name	Roman Name	Area of Activity or Power
Kronos (krō'nəs) also Cronus	Saturn	Head of the Titans; agriculture; father of Zeus
Zeus (zoōs)	Jupiter	King of the gods; ruler of the sky; weather; upholder of oaths; hospitality
Hera (hir'ə)	Juno	Wife of Zeus and queen of the gods; upholder of marriage
Poseidon (pō·sī'dən)	Neptune	Brother of Zeus; ruler of the sea; horses; earthquakes
Hades (hā'dēz')	Pluto	Brother of Zeus; ruler of the underworld
Demeter (di·mēt'ər)	Ceres (sir'ēz')	Goddess of the earth; corn and crops
Persephone (pər·sef'ə·nē)	Proserpina (prō·sʉr'pē'nə)	Daughter of Demeter and wife of Hades; queen of the underworld
Ares (er'rēz')	Mars	God of war
Apollo (ə·päl'ō)	Apollo	Prophecy; light; youth; music; archery; both healing and plague; the sun; poetry
Athena (ə·thē'nə)	Minerva	Wisdom; warfare; crafts
Artemis (är'tə·mis)	Diana	Hunting and wild animals; childbirth; the moon
Hephaestus (hē·fes'təs)	Vulcan	Fire; smelting; crafts; blacksmith for the gods
Hermes (hʉr'mēz')	Mercury	Messenger of the gods; travelers; trickery; theft; commerce; science
Aphrodite (af'rə·dīt'ē)	Venus	Love; beauty; pleasure
Eros (er'äs')	Cupid	Love
Dionysus (dī'ə·nī'səs)	Bacchus (bak'əs)	Liberation; wine; music; theater; fertility

5 CULTURAL BACKGROUND
Greek religion was even more complicated than the chart of gods and goddesses indicates, since the role of the deities and the style of worshiping them varied from place to place. Though all the gods and goddesses on the chart were worshiped throughout Greece, certain deities were sacred or special to individual cities or regions. For instance, while Athena represented wisdom, she was given special prominence in Athens as the protector of the city. The residents of Argos, on the other hand, worshiped Hera as their protector. In addition to these major gods, there were multitudes of minor deities, such as nymphs and nayads, who inhabited streams and mountains. Smaller communities and families often had minor protective deities whom they worshiped at home. There were also officially suppressed mystery cults whose rituals were carried out in private. *What advantages do you think the ancient Greeks derived from having such a large pantheon of gods?* (Possible response: They could choose to worship the god who seemed appropriate to the particular circumstance.)

READER'S RESPONSE
What problems might develop in the worship of deities whose behavior so resembled that of human beings? (Possible response: In time, worshipers might lose respect for deities who seemed no better than themselves.)

Finally, to motivate students to tackle Sophocles' tragedy, *Oedipus Rex*, pose an imaginary situation in which a teenager unwittingly commits a crime. Ask students to debate the teenager's guilt or innocence. Is ignorance a good excuse? Are we always responsible for our own actions?

MAKING CONNECTIONS

Without the influence of ancient Greece, our philosophical ideas, political institutions, art, literature, and even our language would be vastly different. You may wish to begin by pointing out how much our language owes to Greek. To get students' attention, ask them if they listen to compact discs. Explain that the word *disc* comes from the Greek *discos*, meaning a round, flat object originally used in athletic contests. Then tell students that the names of many areas of study or bodies of knowledge, such as psychology, biology, and zoology, are derived from Greek roots. In addition, Greek prefixes and suffixes are used to form hundreds of common English words. Write this partial list on the chalkboard, and ask students to give examples of English words containing each affix: *a-*, without; *anti-*, against; *hyper-*, over; *hypo-*, under; *sym-*, together; *-ist*, someone who does; *-ish*, to do; *-ize*,

6 RESPONDING TO THE QUOTATION

Remind students that Greek epics were originally sung.

? *How does Homer make his role as bard seem very important?* (Possible response: by likening a singer to the gods) *How does the role of poetry in Homer's culture differ from its role in ours?* (Possible response: In Homer's culture it was not a matter of private appreciation but a civic and religious function.)

HUMANITIES CONNECTION

King Darius of Persia invaded Greece in 490 B.C., and was defeated at the battle of Marathon, which took place not far from Athens. This relief of a Greek enemy is from the early period of Greek sculpture, more than a century before the "high classical" period. The figure and face are less realistic than those of the later classical period.

? *How does this wall relief compare and contrast with Egyptian and ancient Middle Eastern sculptures illustrated in this book?* ■

6

> **❝** Surely indeed it is a good thing to listen to a singer/ Such as this one before us, who is like the gods in his singing. **❞**
> —*Homer, from the* Odyssey

SEF/Art Resource, New York

Relief of a soldier of Darius, 518–460 B.C.

were two fundamental differences that distinguished the gods from humanity. First, gods and goddesses were ageless and immortal. Second, they were immensely more powerful than human beings. But the gods were not puppet masters who controlled human beings. Rather, the Greeks believed that everyone had his or her own destiny, or fate. A god could help you or hinder you, depending on your relationship with the god, your own character and talents, and the trouble you took to give the god proper respect through rituals of prayer and offerings.

The Lyric Age

From about the seventh to the fifth centuries B.C., **lyric poetry** began to flourish among the Greeks. Unlike the epic, this new poetry did not recount heroic deeds of men and gods. Instead, lyric poetry used relatively few lines to express the personal emotions of a single speaker. Only a small fraction of this poetry has survived. The odes of **Pindar** (pin'dər) (518–438 B.C.) celebrated the victors in the major athletic contests, while the lyrics of **Sappho** (saf'ō) (early sixth century B.C.) comprise some of the finest and most honest love poems ever written (see page 279).

Sparta and Athens

Despite their cultural bonds, bitter rivalries often occurred between the Greek city-states. By the start of the fifth century B.C., two rival states—**Sparta** and **Athens**—had emerged

> By the early fifth century B.C., Athens and Sparta were the two chief city-states. Sparta was noted for its discipline and conservatism. Athens experimented with political democracy and became a brilliant center of ancient Greek culture.

from these conflicts as the most powerful in Greece. Sparta owed its prominence to an extremely militaristic and conservative culture, where, according to popular legends, all

to cause to be; -ous, marked by. You might have students look up the meanings of the following Greek roots and give examples of their use in English words: *arch*, ancient, chief; *auto*, self; *biblio*, book; *chrom*, color; *demo*, people; *geo*, earth; *gram* and *graph*, writing; *hydro*, water; *micro*, small; *mono*, one; *neo*, new.

While the Greeks were not the first scientists (they learned much of their geometry from Egypt and their astronomy from the Chaldeans), they pursued knowledge of the natural world with a fervor. You might want to mention some of their achievements to students and ask them to do further research on one of these topics. For example, the geometric principles laid down by Euclid are still the basis of such practical pursuits as surveying. Doctors in training still take the oath that Hippocrates, the "father of medicine," gave to his students. Physicists today still owe a debt to Democritus, a scientific philosopher of the fifth century, who was the first to propose that all matter was composed of atoms. In philosophy, Socrates remains a model of intellectual inquiry and personal integrity, and teachers continue to use the Socratic method of questioning in schools today. Socrates' famous pupil Plato envisioned a realm of ideal forms that were superior to the world we see,

LEONIDES AT THERMOPYLES, JACQUES-LOUIS DAVID (1748–1825). *Leonides was a Spartan ruler during the Persian Wars who made a heroic but unsuccessful stand against the Persians at the Battle of Thermopylae, 480 B.C.*

Kavaler/Art Resource, New York

HUMANITIES CONNECTION

The neoclassical French painter David was one of a number of late eighteenth-century artists who tried to revive ancient Greek and Roman values in the face of the collapse of the French monarchy and the chaos of the revolution.

? *What ancient values does the painting express?* (Possible responses: courage; harmony of form; architectural balance) ■

7 LITERARY BACKGROUND

Persian Wars: Herodotus (c. 485–425 B.C.) wrote *The History of the Persian Wars*. It is considered the first book of history in the Western tradition, as well as the earliest example of Greek prose literature.

8 RESPONDING TO THE QUOTATION

? *What are our major sources of knowledge about Greek religion?* (Possible response: literature, such as Homer's two epics, and myths) *What does the absence of official documents and scriptures suggest about Greek religion?* (Possible response: It was not based on written documents and textual analysis as revealed religions such as Islam and Christianity are. It depended more on the relationship of the individual to the gods than on church hierarchy.)

boys and girls underwent years of rigorous physical training, and frail infants were left on mountaintops to die.

Athens emerged as a power to be reckoned with when the city played a leading role in the **Persian Wars**, which began in 499 B.C. and ended in 448 B.C. The Persian emperor Darius launched these wars when the Greek cities in Asia Minor revolted against Persian rule. At one point, the Persians entered Athens and nearly destroyed the city, but the Athenians finally defeated the Persian invaders.

Pericles and the Golden Age of Athens

Athens was the main beneficiary of the Persian Wars in Greece. The important victories of the Athenians at Marathon (490 B.C.) and Salamis (480 B.C.) marked the beginning of the great age of Athens, in which Athens took its place

> **"** Ritual and myth are the two forms in which Greek religion presents itself to the historian. . . . There are no founding figures and no documents of revelation, no organizations of priests and no monastic orders. **"**
>
> —*Walter Burkert*

7

8

which is just a reflection of these forms. This philosophy later fascinated many thinkers such as the Christian theologian St. Augustine (354–430). Finally, the starting point of any philosophical study in science, government, or metaphysics during the Middle Ages and the Renaissance began with Plato's star pupil Aristotle. He is considered the father of modern logic and, in his *Poetics*, the first to develop a systematic criticism of art and literature.

The Christian philosopher St. Thomas Aquinas (1224–1274) developed his Scholastic philosophy from Aristotelian thought by dividing the realm of reason and the realm of faith.

The Greek epics, still read and admired today, have inspired many subsequent works. For instance, the Victorian author Alfred, Lord Tennyson wrote a number of poems modeled on episodes from Homer's *Odyssey*. The modern Irish writer

James Joyce also based the structure of his masterpiece *Ulysses* on the *Odyssey*. In addition, the *Iliad* has inspired such plays as William Shakespeare's *Troilus and Cressida* and Jean Baptiste Racine's *Andromache*.

The Greeks also invented tragedy, and with the exception of Shakespeare, no dramatist has surpassed Aeschylus, Sophocles, and Euripides in that genre. Sophocles' *Oedipus Rex*, in particular, not only

---

HUMANITIES CONNECTION

The Parthenon was one of several magnificent buildings of the Acropolis, the fortified hill just outside Athens. The architect of the Parthenon was Ictinus; the chief sculptor was Phidias. Money for building the Parthenon was extracted from the peoples Athens conquered. Its purpose was to glorify Athenian power after the victory against Persia. Many of the friezes (sculptured bands around a building) were brought to the British Museum in 1801–1804 by Lord Elgin and are known as the Elgin Marbles.

❓ *How does this frieze compare with the wall relief on p. 218?* (Possible response: Despite similar styles, the later frieze shows the human figure more realistically.) ∎

9 RESPONDING TO THE QUOTATION

❓ *Which American would you choose as the representative of our age, and why?* (Possible response: Martin Luther King, Jr., for his belief in equality within a multicultural, democratic society and in nonviolence as a means of change)

10 HISTORICAL BACKGROUND

Pericles: Athenian government was not designed for one-man rule, but Pericles achieved a dominating influence, largely because of his oratorical skill. Officially, he was one of ten generals, or *strategoi*, who guided Athens' military affairs.

The Bridgeman Art Library/Art Resource, New York

Parthenon frieze. *The Parthenon was a temple dedicated to the goddess Athena, built between 447 and 432* B.C.

9

❝ Sophocles' *Oedipus* is not only the greatest creation of a major poet and the classic representative figure of his age: he is also one of the long series of tragic protagonists who stand as symbols of human aspiration and despair.... ❞

—*Bernard Knox*

as the wartime leader of all the city-states and the chief naval power of Greece. Despite the power that Athens had acquired as a result of the wars, at home the Athenians established a **democratic government**, or rule by the people (or free adult males, at least—women and slaves could not vote), rather than a dictatorship. Athenian democracy was one of the earliest democratic governments, and it had a tremendous influence on the formation of both the Roman Republic and American democracy.

Starting in the late 460s B.C., during the height of the Athenian "Golden Age," the great general and statesman **Pericles** (per′i·klēz′) (c. 494–429 B.C.) guided the fortunes of Athens for over three decades. Pericles was a skillful politician who steered a middle course between extremist views in the democratic assembly. He was also a patron of literature, philosophy, and the arts. It was Pericles who organized the campaign to build Athens's most famous temple, the Parthenon, dedicated to the city's patron goddess, Athena.

10

affected the thinking of Sigmund Freud, the founder of Freudian psychology, but also influenced playwrights such as Eugene O'Neill.

Even in ruin, Greek architecture, sculpture, and painted pottery greatly influenced later Western art. Ask students to compare photographs of Greek architecture with the wide porticos and massive columns of many public buildings in Washington D.C. and state capitals throughout the United States. Even the modern artist Pablo Picasso acknowledged his indebtedness to the styles and subjects of Minoan wall paintings. Volunteers may want to find reproductions of works by Picasso that show this Minoan influence.

Finally, review with students the immeasurable influence of Greek democracy on American political institutions. Although Athens was only a limited democracy, it introduced the idea to the world and realized it for its male citizens. Not only our form of government, but our values of free speech, freedom of assembly, and freedom of inquiry owe much to the ideals of ancient Greece. The Jeffersonian ideal of a small, self-sufficient community of farmers, soldiers, and scholars strongly resembles the model of the Greek city-state. Interested students may want to further investigate the influence of Greek political thought on the founding fathers.

The Rise of Greek Drama

Three of the greatest authors of **tragedy** in the history of Western literature—**Aeschylus** (es'ki·ləs), **Sophocles** (säf'ə-klēz'), and **Euripides** (yoo·rip'ə·dēz')—all lived during the intellectual ferment of Athens in the fifth century B.C. Their plays posed profound questions about the limits of knowledge, individual free will, moral responsibility, and human suffering.

> The Age of Pericles, or the Golden Age of Athens, fostered the rise of Greek drama. Playwrights such as Aeschylus, Sophocles, and Euripides were encouraged to explore and question in their works the wide range of human emotions.

11 Sophocles (c. 496–406 B.C.) was the most admired playwright of his day and the winner of over twenty prizes for his dramas. As a general and a friend of the statesman Pericles, he was involved in many of the great events of his time. He explores the issues of pride, loyalty, and personal responsibility in works such as *Oedipus Rex* (see page 302) and *Antigone.*

12 In addition to tragedy, the Athenian stage was also the site for the production of great **comedies.** One of the best-loved authors of comedy in ancient Greece was **Aristophanes** (ar'i·stäf'ə·nēz') (c. 450–c. 386 B.C.). Aristophanes' comedies used farce and satire to deal with such serious issues as education and war.

The Historians: Herodotus and Thucydides

During the fifth and fourth centuries B.C., the Greek search for knowledge also resulted in the flourishing of historical writings. **Herodotus** (hə·räd'ə·təs) (c. 485–c. 425 B.C.) is considered—in the West, at least—the first historian. He not only wrote a chronicle of the Persian Wars but also reported on many foreign lands and customs of peoples he met in

SEF/Art Resource, New York

Bust of Aeschylus. *Aeschylus (525–456 B.C.) was the first great Greek playwright. His tragedies expanded dramatic form and considered the conflict of individual will and the greater forces of the world. Only seven of his eighty plays survive.*

11 LITERARY BACKGROUND
Sophocles and Euripides: Sophocles, who lived during a more troubled period in Athens than Aeschylus, dramatized his melancholy view of the inevitability of fate. The third great Athenian tragedian, Euripides, is the most modern in temperament, the most realistic in his characterizations, and the most critical of Greek society. Euripides also created the most complex and interesting female characters.

12 LITERARY BACKGROUND
Aristophanes: Aristophanes savagely ridiculed some of the most important Athenians of his day, including Socrates and Euripides. In 426 B.C. he was brought before the Council for slandering Athenian officials. In three of his plays, most notably *Lysistrata,* the women take over Athens, to its great benefit.

READING CHECK

1. What was the unit of ancient Greek government? (the city-state, or *polis*)
2. What civilization flourished on Crete around 2000 B.C.? (Minoan)
3. Who were the major Greek philosophers? (Socrates, Plato, Aristotle)
4. What were the two most important Greek city-states? (Sparta and Athens)
5. Who was the king of the gods? (Zeus)

FOR FURTHER STUDY

Nonfiction
Edith Hamilton's *The Greek Way* and *Mythology* have introduced students to classical culture for fifty years. Robert Graves' two-volume *The Greek Myths* makes more extensive connections among mythologies. H. D. F. Kitto's lively paperback survey *The Greeks* has sold over 1.5 million copies and I. F. Stone's *The Trial of Socrates* is a thought-provoking view of ancient Greek ideals.

Fiction
Mary Renault's novels, such as *The King Must Die* and *The Bull from the Sea*, provide a fascinating reconstruction of early Greek civilizations. Works of literature by English authors, which are set during the Trojan War, include Chaucer's *Troilus and Cressida* and Shakespeare's play of the same name. Marion Zimmer Bradley's *The Firebrand* (1987) retells the story of the Trojan War, blending history with myth.

13 LITERARY BACKGROUND

Herodotus and Thucydides:
Herodotus's work is read today chiefly for its entertaining anecdotes and its insights into the Greek view of the world. Herodotus traveled more widely than any Greek before him, and so his work is the predecessor of modern travel writing and anthropological observation. Thucydides' history contains a brief account of his own failure as the general in charge of an Athenian fleet that arrived too late to help his colleagues against Sparta.

HUMANITIES CONNECTION

Aristotle has been described as bald and spindly, with a taste for luxurious apparel, jewelry, and elegant dinners. This bust, like many Greek sculptures, seems idealized and may have been done by someone who had never seen Aristotle.

? *What kind of character is represented in this bust?* (Possible response: a wise, dignified one) ■

14 CULTURAL BACKGROUND

Socrates: Socrates said that his wisdom lay only in admitting his ignorance. In his own day, he was esteemed by his followers for his integrity, indifference to wealth, and cheerful endurance of hardship. Like Aeschylus, Socrates was a patriot, proud of his combat service in the Athenian army, even though he was eventually condemned for crimes against the welfare of the state.

Scala/Art Resource, New York

Bronze bust of Aristotle. Aristotle was founder of a school called the Lyceum, and he served as teacher to Alexander the Great.

his travels. **Thucydides** (thoo·sid'i·dēz') (c. 460–401 B.C.) analyzed the Athenian rise to power and the conflict with Sparta in his *History of the Peloponnesian War* (see page 284). Unlike Herodotus, who filled his narrative with colorful character sketches and interesting digressions, Thucydides' work stressed rigorous research and objective reporting. Like Herodotus, however, Thucydides also conceived his role as that of a moral teacher. In this respect, the Greek historians resembled the philosophers and the playwrights.

The Great Greek Philosophers: Socrates, Plato, and Aristotle ■

The Golden Age of Greek history also saw the emergence of great philosophical thinkers and writers. According to tradition, the Greek philosopher **Socrates** (säk'rə·tēz') (469–399 B.C.) once asked a young Athenian boy whether he thought a great deal. The boy modestly replied no, but at least, he said, he had wondered a great deal. The response Socrates gave the boy has become proverbial: "Wisdom," he replied, "begins in wonder." Socrates called himself a "philosopher," a Greek word meaning "lover of wisdom."

> The Greek philosophers' efforts to ask questions, record ideas, devise methods, and teach moral principles have had an enormous and lasting impact on Western culture.

Socrates' pupil **Plato** (plā'tō) (c. 429–c. 347 B.C.) preserved his mentor's method of questioning in a series of dialogues, or conversations, in which the "character" Socrates would pose and answer philosophical questions. Plato's writings examined such concepts as freedom of conscience, the nature of reality, the existence of the soul, ideal government, and how to lead a virtuous and happy life.

Plato's greatest pupil was **Aristotle** (ar'is·tät'l) (384–322 B.C.), who studied in Athens and later became tutor to the young Alexander the Great. Aristotle wrote numerous treatises on such subjects as logic, ethics, political theory, rhetoric, and biology. In the *Poetics*, one of his most influential works, he set forth the principles of Greek tragic drama (see page 371). Aristotle's systematic inquiry into numerous branches of knowledge had an enormous impact on the development of Western philosophy. Even modern students of philosophy and literature must acquaint themselves with the works of Plato and Aristotle.

The Decline of Athens

The increasing resentment toward and envy of Athenian expansion led to clashes and then to full-scale war between Athens and its chief rival, Sparta. The **Peloponnesian War**, which involved other city-states on each side, lasted from 431 to 404 B.C. Sparta was victorious, and Athens spiraled into a decline from which it never recovered.

In the middle of the fourth century B.C., the kingdom of Macedon, ruled first by Philip and then by his son **Alexander the Great**, emerged as the most powerful state in the Greek-speaking world. Alexander, in particular, conquered lands from Egypt to India. By the time of Alexander's death in 323 B.C., Greek language and culture had spread throughout the Mediterranean, North Africa, and western Asia. This continuation of Greek culture by Alexander, and later by the Romans who would conquer the Macedonians in 197 B.C., is called the **Hellenistic Age** because it emulated, or imitated, the Hellenic Age, the age of the Greeks. The Romans would be greatly responsible for the preservation and spread of Greek knowledge in the West.

> ❝ The absence of romance in my history will, I fear, detract somewhat from its interest; but if it be judged useful by those inquirers who desire an exact knowledge of the past as an aid to the interpretation of the future, which in the course of human things must resemble if it does not reflect it, I shall be content. ❞
>
> —*Thucydides*

Scala/Art Resource, New York

Battle of Alexander, mosaic.
Alexander the Great was responsible for the revival of the waning Greek culture, spreading it far beyond the reaches of the original Greek territories.

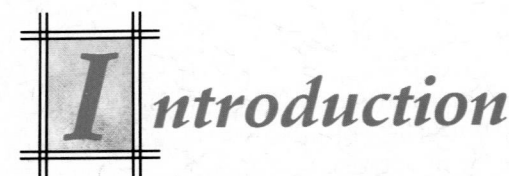

*I*ntroduction

The Iliad

Europe's first, and most enduring, literary epics, the *Iliad* (il′ē-əd) and the *Odyssey* (äd′i·sē), were composed sometime between 900 and 700 B.C. We know little about Homer, the author of these epics. Homer was probably a native of the Greek district of Ionia on the western coast of Asia Minor. The name *Homer* means "hostage," indicating that the poet may have been a slave or descended from slaves. Tradition says Homer was blind, a detail probably based more on convention than on fact:

Bust of Homer.

SEF/Art Resource, New York

In Greek culture, physical blindness was often a metaphor for profound insight.

Homer belonged to a class of bards called **rhapsodes**. Like the griots of African oral tradition (see page 70), the rhapsodes played a vitally important role in Greek society, serving as both oral historians and entertainers.

The written versions of the epics became a staple of Greek education during the Athenian Golden Age, from the sixth to the fourth centuries B.C. The *Iliad* and the *Odyssey* were the "Bibles" of Greek civilization: they gave coherence to a chaotic pantheon of gods and goddesses, and their heroes embodied the ideal of *arete* (ä·re′tā), or excellence, for which the ancient Greeks strived.

The Legend of the Trojan War

Both the *Iliad* and the *Odyssey* tell stories about the heroes and events of the Trojan War. According to oral tradition, the war began with a beauty contest. Three goddesses—Aphrodite, Athena, and Hera—decided to compete for a golden apple that was inscribed "To the Fairest." The gods, smart enough not to get involved in a potentially hazardous situation, chose a mortal man to judge who was the most beautiful goddess. Paris, a young and handsome but naive prince of Troy, was selected. He was offered bribes by each goddess in turn. The bribe he accepted was Aphrodite's, for she offered him the most appealing gift: marriage with the world's most beautiful woman, Helen, the wife of King Menelaus of Greece. Paris took Helen from Menelaus, and the two sailed for Troy. As a result of the abduction of Helen, the various Greek chieftains, bound by oaths of loyalty, banded together under the leadership of Menelaus's brother, Agamemnon, and attacked Troy. The war party laid seige to Troy, beginning a conflict that would drag on for ten years, until the Greeks, thanks to the wiles of the clever hero Odysseus, finally succeeded in sacking Troy and recapturing Helen.

The Conventions of the Homeric Epics

Certain features of Homer's work were so widely imitated in later written epics, such as Virgil's *Aeneid* (see page 380) and Milton's *Paradise Lost*, that they became recognizable characteristics, or **conventions**, of the epic genre. Yet the origins of many of these conventions lie in the oral tradition that gave birth to the *Iliad* and the *Odyssey*. The oral poets used formulas that allowed them to rapidly summarize past events or quickly sketch characters in the epic. Following are some of the epic conventions that occur in the *Iliad*:

1. Invocation. The *Iliad* begins with an **invocation**, or formal plea for aid, to

Scala/Art Resource, New York

PARNASSUS, RAPHAEL (1483–1520).
Detail. *The medieval poet Dante, an admirer of Homer, stands to the right of the Greek bard.*

the Muse Calliope (kə·lī′ə·pē′), one of the nine goddesses who presided over the arts and sciences. The Greeks believed that this "immortal one" spoke through mortal epic poets:

> Anger be now your song, immortal one,
> Achilles' anger, doomed and ruinous,
> that caused the Achaeans loss on bitter loss
> and crowded brave souls into the undergloom. . . .

The invocation also serves to state the epic's subject and theme.

2. *In medias res.* The epic plunges us into the middle of the action—that is, *in medias res* (in mā′dē·äs′ res′), a Latin term meaning "into the midst of things." **Flashbacks** are then used to inform the

3 HISTORICAL BACKGROUND
The Greek historian Thucydides (pp. 284–292) reports a different reason for the Greek expedition to Troy: a naked attempt to plunder a rich overseas kingdom. Do you think Thucydides or Homer is correct, or are both right? (Answers will vary.)

HUMANITIES CONNECTION

In a life nearly as short as that of Alexander the Great, Raphael (Raffaello Sanzio, 1483–1520) became the master painter of the Italian High Renaissance. *Parnassus* shows poets of the ages gathered around Apollo and the Muses. ■

4 LITERARY BACKGROUND
Invocations: For purposes of comparison, here is the invocation in the *Odyssey*:

> Sing in me, Muse, and
>   through me tell the story
> of that man skilled in all
>   ways of contending,
> the wanderer, harried for
>   years on end,
> after he plundered the
>   stronghold
> on the proud height of Troy.
> (*Odyssey*, Book 1, lines 1–5, translated by Robert Fitzgerald)

What similarities do you notice between the invocation to the Muse in the Iliad *and the invocation to the Muse in the* Odyssey? (Possible response: The Muse is addressed directly and asked to sing through the poet but is not called by name.)

Nearly 13 by 16 feet in size, the *Apotheosis of Homer* hangs in the Louvre in Paris. Ingres (aŋ'grə, 1780–1867) was a French painter who studied in Italy and served as director of the Académie de France in Rome. Some of his most famous paintings depict classical themes in a restrained, balanced, neoclassic style.

? *In this painting, what details show that Homer is revered as godlike?* (An angel is about to crown him with a laurel wreath; people offer gifts; he is enthroned.) ∎

5 LITERARY BACKGROUND

Achilles: In his speeches in the *Iliad*, Achilles uses more epic similes than any other character: eight full-length comparisons. Achilles' language also contains a high proportion of nonformulaic expressions. In fact, in Book 9, Homer presents Achilles as a "singer of tales." *Why might an oral poet depict a hero as a "singer of tales"?* (The Greeks regarded the gift of storytelling highly.)

6 LITERARY BACKGROUND

Meter: We can get a rough idea of the Greek hexameter from the famous first line of Henry Wadsworth Longfellow's *Evangeline*:

This ĭs thĕ fórĕst prímĕvăl,
thĕ múrmŭrĭng pínes ănd
thĕ hémlŏcks

In this example, each of the first five feet is a dactyl.

APOTHEOSIS OF HOMER, JEAN-AUGUSTE-DOMINIQUE INGRES, 1827.
? Apotheosis *means exaltation or deification. Why do you think Homer was represented in this way centuries after his death?*

Giraudon/Art Resource, New York

audience of events that took place before the narrative's current time setting.

3. Epic similes. One of the most striking features of the language of the *Iliad* is Homer's use of extended, elaborate comparisons called **epic** or **Homeric similes**. Some epic similes are developed over many lines. These similes compare heroic events to simple, everyday events—events that Homer's audience could easily understand. For example, when, in Book 9, Achilles feels all his heroic deeds have gone unrewarded, he says "A bird will give her fledglings every scrap/she comes by, and go hungry, foraging./That is the case with me." Homer's listeners would have been familiar with the image of the bird; this simile would help them to understand the epic hero's feelings.

4. Metrical Structure. The *Iliad* was originally composed in dactylic hexameter, a meter consisting of six stressed syllables per line. This meter probably closely imitated the speech patterns of the Greeks during Homer's time. But the meter is also formulaic, or fixed and conventional. The use of a conventional,

5

6

predictable metrical structure would have given the rhapsodes a standard pattern to follow, thereby aiding memorization of lines and passages.

5. Stock epithets. Another figure of speech that occurs frequently in the *Iliad* is the **stock epithet**, a descriptive adjective or phrase that is repeatedly used with—or in place of—a noun or proper name. Thus, the audience repeatedly hears of "Andromache of the ivory-white arms" and "the pale-gold goddess Aphrodite." The repetition of these epithets helped the audience to follow the narrative and also helped the rhapsode as he improvised the poem in performance.

The Characters of the *Iliad*

The Greeks

Achilles (ə·kil′ēz′): the son of a mortal king, Peleus, and the sea-goddess Thetis, king of the Myrmidons, Achilles is the mightiest of the Greek warriors.

Agamemnon (ag′ə·mem′nän): king of Mycenae and commander of the Greek forces. He is Menelaus's older brother.

Ajax (ā′jaks′): one of the strongest Greek warriors.

Calchas (kal′kəs): a seer or prophet who counsels the Greeks.

Clytemnestra (klī′təm·nes′trə): Agamemnon's wife; Helen's sister.

Helen (hel′ən): the wife of Menelaus, whose abduction by Paris is the cause of the legendary war.

Menelaus (men′ə·lā′əs): king of Sparta; husband of Helen.

Nestor (nes′tər): king of Pylos. The oldest of the Greek leaders at Troy, he serves as a counselor.

Odysseus (ō·dis′ē·əs): a wily, middle-aged Greek warrior. He is the protagonist of Homer's *Odyssey.*

Patroclus (pə·trō′kləs): Greek warrior and dearest friend of Achilles.

The Trojans

Andromache (an·dräm′ə·kē): faithful wife of Hector.

Astyanax (as·tī′ə·naks′): youngest son of Hector and Andromache.

Briseis (brī′si·əs): a girl captured from the Trojans by Achilles as a prize of war.

Chryseis (kri′si·əs): a girl captured by Agamemnon during the plunder of Chrysa. Her father, Chryses, is a priest of the god Apollo.

Hector (hek′tər): the son of King Priam and Queen Hecuba and commander of the Trojan forces.

Hecuba (hek′yōō·bə): the queen of Troy; Priam's wife.

Paris (par′is): son of King Priam and Queen Hecuba. He is also known as Alexandros.

Priam (prī′əm): the king of Troy; the father of Hector and Paris.

Gods and Goddesses

Aphrodite (af′rə·dīt′ē): the goddess of love. She sides with the Trojans during the war.

Apollo (ə·päl′ō): the god of poetry, music, and prophecy; he also sides with the Trojans. He is often referred to only as the son of Zeus and Leto, the daughter of Titans.

Athena (ə·thē′nə): the goddess of wisdom; she takes the Greeks' side in the conflict.

Hera (hir′ə): wife of Zeus; enemy of the Trojans.

Hermes (hur′mēz′): messenger of the gods, also called the Wayfinder.

Thetis (thēt′is): a sea-goddess; mother of Achilles.

Zeus (zyōōs): the father-god; he remains more or less neutral throughout the conflict.

ABOUT THE TRANSLATOR

Robert Fitzgerald (1910–1985) won acclaim both for his original poetry and his translations of ancient Greek and Roman classics. Fitzgerald started his career as a journalist for the *New York Herald Tribune* and *Time* magazine. He held academic positions at a number of colleges and universities, including Princeton, Mt. Holyoke, and Harvard, where he served as the Boylston Professor of Rhetoric. As Fitzgerald delighted in pointing out, one perquisite of this professorship (endowed in the eighteenth century) was the privilege of pasturing a cow in Harvard Yard!

Fitzgerald's collections of poetry include *A Wreath for the Sea* (1943), *In the Rose of Time* (1956), and *Spring Shade* (1972). In the 1930s, he started a long and productive collaboration with the poet Dudley Fitts in translating ancient Greek tragedy. Their work includes a powerful version of Sophocles' *Oedipus Rex* (1949) (pp. 302–371). In 1961, Fitzgerald's translation of Homer's *Odyssey* won the Bollingen Award. His renderings of Homer's *Iliad* (1974) and Virgil's *Aeneid* (1980) were eagerly anticipated and highly praised as major literary events.

OBJECTIVES

1. *To recognize the conventions of an ancient Greek epic and to analyze parts of an epic*
2. *To identify and interpret foreshadowing and flashback*
3. *To write a screenplay and an essay of comparison and contrast*

THEMES IN WORLD LITERATURE

Choices in Life

From the *Epic of Gilgamesh*, pp. 136–152
From *Candide*, pp. 945–962

What Is a Hero?

From the *Ramayana*, pp. 484–494
From the *Song of Roland*, pp. 692–702

Triumph and Defeat

From *Sundiata: An Epic of Old Mali*, pp. 102–117
"The Fall of Troy" from the *Aeneid*, pp. 379–406
From "The Tragedy of Sohráb and Rostám" from the *Shahname*, pp. 646–653 ■

PREREADING FOCUS

Background: Before students begin to read the *Iliad*, you may want to discuss Homer's concept of fate. Homer portrays the gods as knowing the future and as intervening in human affairs, but still he allows his human characters to exercise choice and free will. The human characters are not puppets of destiny or divine whim. For example, in the epic, Achilles must choose between a long life with no glory and great glory at the price of a premature death. Homer's gods know the outcome in advance, but Achilles is still free to make the choice.

Writer's Response: As a prewriting activity, have students discuss these questions. In what areas is personal excellence important to you—in living up to your code of ethics, in maintaining an image, in your family life or friendships, in your studies, in sports or other activities? In what areas would an ideal of excellence improve our society? In education? technology? human relationships? government? environmental concerns?

Literary Focus: Homer's audiences, knowing the general plot of the *Iliad*, would have enjoyed his use of foreshadowing to hint at future events. Flashbacks were useful for providing information outside the scope of the main narrative.

Reader's Guide

from the ILIAD

Background

As the *Iliad* begins, the war between the Greeks and the Trojans has been a stalemate for nearly ten years. The Greek forces face a crisis: A deadly plague has swept through their army. On the tenth day of the plague, the hero Achilles calls an assembly of the entire army to discuss the crisis. This meeting leads to the great quarrel between Achilles and Agamemnon that opens the epic.

As you read the *Iliad*, keep in mind the following facts about the beliefs held by the Greeks of Homer's time:

1. A warrior's material possessions—the spoils of war won in combat—were a direct measure of his honor and prestige in the community. The loss of these possessions was equivalent to being publicly shamed, the worst insult a hero could suffer.
2. The Greeks believed that their gods and goddesses played an active role in the affairs of human beings. Although people are the actual combatants in the war, the gods take sides in the conflict and have a profound effect on its outcome.
3. Respect for the dead was considered a sacred duty, for an unburied corpse was considered an offense to the gods. The soul of a person whose body was not buried was doomed to wander the earth forever.

Writer's Response

The Greek warriors strove to achieve *arete*, or personal honor and excellence. What does personal excellence mean to you? How can an ideal of excellence help to make a better society? Can the pursuit of excellence actually harm a society? Freewrite your ideas.

Literary Focus

Foreshadowing is the use of clues to hint at what is going to happen later in a plot. Foreshadowing arouses the reader's curiosity and increases suspense. A **flashback** is a scene that interrupts the present action of a plot to narrate the events of an earlier time. Watch for foreshadowing and flashbacks throughout the *Iliad*.

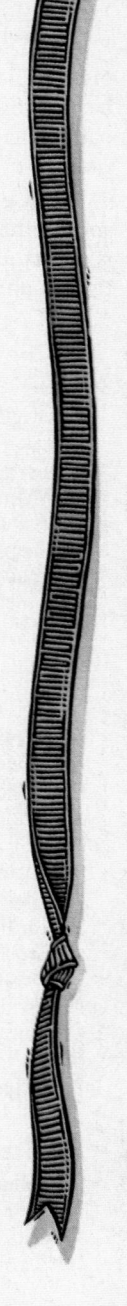

TEACHER'S RESOURCES
- Review and Response Worksheet
- Selection Test
- Vocabulary Activity Worksheet
- Vocabulary Test
- Language Skills Worksheet

from the ILIAD
from Book 1
Homer
translated by
ROBERT FITZGERALD

Notice how Homer characterizes Agamemnon and Achilles, the two central figures in Book 1. What do you think of these two men? How do you think Homer wants you to view them?

BOOK 1: The Quarrel

Anger be now your song, immortal one,
Achilles' anger, doomed and ruinous,
that caused the Achaeans° loss on bitter loss
and crowded brave souls into the undergloom,
5   leaving so many dead men—carrion
for dogs and birds; and the will of Zeus was done.
Begin it when the two men first contending
broke with one another—

                  the Lord Marshal
Agamemnon, Atreus' son, and Prince Achilles.

10   Among the gods, who brought this quarrel on?
The son of Zeus by Leto.° Agamemnon
angered him, so he made a burning wind
of plague rise in the army: rank and file
sickened and died for the ill their chief had done
15   in despising a man of prayer.
This priest, Chryses, had come down to the ships
with gifts, no end of ransom for his daughter;
on a golden staff he carried the god's white bands
and sued for grace from the men of all Achaea
20   the two Atridae° most of all:

                         "O captains
Menelaus and Agamemnon, and you other
Achaeans under arms!
The gods who hold Olympus, may they grant you

3. **Achaeans** (ə·kē'ənz): one of the names used in the *Iliad* for the Greeks.

11. **The son . . . Leto** (lē'tō): Apollo.

20. **Atridae** (ə·trī'dē): Agamemnon and Menelaus are the sons of Atreus (ā'trē·əs), the king of Mycenae. At the time of the Trojan War, and in Homer's own day, Greece was not a unified country but an amalgam of diverse kingdoms. The *Atridae* refers to one of many families of kings.

1 LITERARY ELEMENT
Invocation: The first nine lines of the *Iliad* are the invocation to the Muse. Where does Homer refer to this spirit in the passage? (in the phrase "immortal one" in line 1) What kind of assistance might Homer need at the beginning of a long tale? (aid with memory, stamina) What words in Homer's invocation reveal his central theme? ("anger," "doomed," "ruinous")

2 CULTURAL DIVERSITY
In ancient Greece, the god Apollo was associated with music, archery, light, and the lyre. The Greeks worshiped Apollo as a god who could send both plague and healing. There are many parallels in other cultures: The Hindu goddess Shitala in India, for example, may both inflict and avert smallpox.

3 LITERARY ELEMENT
Flashback: In line 16, the poet begins an extended flashback (lasting through line 65) that explains how Agamemnon's insult to the priest Chryses caused the plague. In line 16, what verb tense does the poet use to indicate a flashback? (past perfect tense—*had come*)

4 LITERARY ELEMENT

Characterization: What do lines 29–30 suggest about Agamemnon's character? (that he is willful, selfish, and potentially violent)

5 LITERARY ELEMENT

Imagery: Which of the senses does this description of Chryses most appeal to? (sight and hearing) What is unusual about the description of the sea? (It is described as "clamorous" and "whispering" in the same line. Homer may have compressed two auditory images of the surf by referring in the same line to an angry sea and to the calmer waves on the seashore. With "whispering," he may also be suggesting that the sea is secretly speaking to Chryses.)

6 SPECULATING

Who calls the meeting to discuss the plight of the Greeks? (Achilles) Who, as commander-in-chief, would normally convene such a meeting? (Agamemnon) Why do you suppose Agamemnon did not take the initiative, and how do you think he will feel about Achilles' assuming that responsibility? (Possible response: He probably did not call a meeting because he guessed he might be responsible for the plague, and he probably will resent Achilles' action.)

plunder of Priam's town and a fair wind home,
25 but let me have my daughter back for ransom
as you <u>revere</u> Apollo, son of Zeus!"

Then all the soldiers murmured their <u>assent</u>:
"Behave well to the priest. And take the ransom!"

4 But Agamemnon would not. It went against his desire,
30 and brutally he ordered the man away:

"Let me not find you here by the long ships
loitering this time or returning later,
old man; if I do,
the staff and ribbons of the god will fail you.
35 Give up the girl? I swear she will grow old
at home in Argos, far from her own country,
working my loom and visiting my bed.
Leave me in peace and go, while you can, in safety."

5 So harsh he was, the old man feared and obeyed him,
40 in silence trailing away
by the shore of the tumbling clamorous whispering sea,
and he prayed and prayed again, as he withdrew,
to the god whom silken-braided Leto bore:

"O hear me, master of the silver bow,
45 protector of Tenedos and the holy towns,
Apollo, Sminthian,° if to your liking
ever in any grove I roofed a shrine
or burnt thighbones in fat upon your altar—
bullock or goat flesh—let my wish come true:
50 your arrows on the Danaans° for my tears!"

Now when he heard this prayer, Phoebus Apollo
walked with storm in his heart from Olympus's crest,
quiver and bow at his back, and the bundled arrows
clanged on the sky behind as he rocked in his anger,
55 descending like night itself. Apart from the ships
he halted and let fly, and the bowstring slammed
as the silver bow sprang, rolling in thunder away.
Pack animals were his target first, and dogs,
but soldiers, too, soon felt transfixing pain
60 from his hard shots, and pyres burned night and day.
Nine days the arrows of the god came down
broadside upon the army. On the tenth,

6 Achilles called all ranks to assembly. Hera,

46. **Sminthian** (smin'thē·ən): epithet for Apollo, probably in reference to his role as destroyer of mice; the Greek for *mouse* is *sminthos*.

50. **Danaans** (dān'ənz): one of the names for the Greeks.

7 │ whose arms are white as ivory, moved him to it,
65 │ as she took pity on Danaans dying.
│ All being mustered, all in place and quiet,
│ Achilles, fast in battle as a lion,
│ rose and said:

8 │   "Agamemnon, now, I take it,
│ the siege is broken, we are going to sail,
70 │ and even so may not leave death behind:
│ if war spares anyone, disease will take him . . .
│ We might, though, ask some priest or some diviner,
│ even some fellow good at dreams—for dreams
│ come down from Zeus as well—

Fresco of the *Iliad*,
showing the Greek
gods, by Sabatelli. *Many
of the gods are painted
here with clues to their
identities. Zeus and Hera, for
instance, are seated in their
thrones at the top of the painting.*
Can you identify Ares, the god of
war, or Aphrodite, the goddess of love?

7 LITERARY ELEMENT

Epithet: In line 64, the phrase "whose arms are white as ivory" is a stock epithet associated with the goddess Hera. (It is also associated with Andromache.) What is the stock epithet used for Agamemnon in line 9? ("Atreus' son")

8 GUIDED READING

Finding the Main Idea: What plan of action for ending the plague does Achilles propose? (consulting a seer to find out why Apollo is angry) Point out that soothsayers who interpreted dreams and omens, such as the flight of birds, were highly regarded in Greek society.

HUMANITIES CONNECTION

Italian frescoes were made by applying paint directly to damp lime plaster. The lime bound the paint to the wall. A large fresco consisted of many small sections, each painted in a day and carefully joined to make the seams inconspicuous. The artist first prepared a sectioned cartoon, or drawing, of the entire work. Then he applied the outline of each day's section to the wall through perforations in the cartoon. Since fine gradations of color tend to deteriorate on a lime-based surface, frescoes are generally boldly colored without much gradation. ■

from the Iliad, Book 1   **231**

9 HISTORICAL BACKGROUND

Line 83 refers to an incident that Homer's audiences would have known: the becalming of the Greek ships at the port city of Aulis, when the expedition was on its way to Troy. On that occasion, Calchas had favorably interpreted an omen; as a result, the wind picked up, and the army was able to resume the journey.

10 PREDICTING

Calchas pointedly refuses to name the man he fears. Whom do you think Calchas is afraid of? (Agamemnon) Why? (perhaps because he knows the warrior will punish anyone who accuses him)

formidable (fôr′mə·də·bəl): causing fear or dread

11 LITERARY ELEMENT

Imagery: What image is used for anger in line 94? (burning in the belly) Look back at lines 12 and 60. How is the imagery in these lines related to that in line 94? (In line 12, "burning" describes the wind of plague made by the angry Apollo; in line 60, "burned" refers to pyres on which plague victims are cremated.) What effect is created by linking these images? (Possible response: The anger of "a great man" is associated with the plague.)

75 why all this anger of the god Apollo?

8
Has he some quarrel with us for a failure
in vows or hecatombs?° Would mutton burned
or smoking goat flesh make him lift the plague?"

80 Putting the question, down he sat. And Calchas,
Calchas Thestorides, came forward, wisest
by far of all who scanned the flight of birds.

9
He knew what was, what had been, what would be,
Calchas, who brought Achaean's ships to Ilion°
by the diviner's gift Apollo gave him.

85 Now for their benefit he said:

"Achilles,
dear to Zeus, it is on me you call
to tell you why the Archer God° is angry.
Well, I can tell you. Are you listening? Swear
by heaven that you will back me and defend me,

10
90 because I fear my answer will enrage
a man with power in Argos, one whose word
Achaean troops obey.

A great man in his rage is formidable

11
for underlings: though he may keep it down,
he cherishes the burning in his belly
95 until a reckoning day. Think well
if you will save me."

Said Achilles:

"Courage.
Tell what you know, what you have light to know.
I swear by Apollo, the lord god to whom
100 you pray when you uncover truth,
never while I draw breath, while I have eyes to see,
shall any man upon this beachhead dare
lay hands on you—not one of all the army,
not Agamemnon, if it is he you mean,
105 though he is first in rank of all Achaeans."

The diviner then took heart and said:

"No failure
in hecatombs or vows is held against us.
It is the man of prayer whom Agamemnon
treated with contempt: he kept his daughter,
110 spurned his gifts: for that man's sake the Archer

77. **hecatombs** (hek′ə·tōmz′): sacrifices to the gods; originally a hecatomb consisted of a hundred oxen.

83. **Ilion** (il′ē·ən): another name for Troy; the founder of Troy was Ilus, who named the city for his father, Tros.

87. **the Archer God:** Apollo.

Greek vase.

visited grief upon us and will again.
Relieve the Danaans of this plague he will not
until the girl who turns the eyes of men°
shall be restored to her own father—freely,
115 with no demand for ransom—and until
we offer up a hecatomb at Chryse.
Then only can we calm him and persuade him."

He finished and sat down. The son of Atreus,
ruler of the great plain, Agamemnon,
120 rose, furious. Round his heart resentment
welled, and his eyes shone out like licking fire.
Then, with a long and boding look at Calchas,
he growled at him:

                      "You visionary of hell,
never have I had fair play in your forecasts.
125 Calamity is all you care about, or see,
no happy portents; and you bring to pass
nothing agreeable. Here you stand again
before the army, giving it out as oracle
the Archer made them suffer because of me,
130 because I would not take the gifts
and let the girl Chryseis go; I'd have her
mine, at home. Yes, if you like, I rate her
higher than Clytemnestra, my own wife!
She loses nothing by comparison
135 in beauty or womanhood, in mind or skill.

For all of that, I am willing now to yield her
if it is best; I want the army saved
and not destroyed. You must prepare, however,
a prize of honor for me, and at once,
140 that I may not be left without my portion—
I, of all Argives.° It is not fitting so.
While every man of you looks on, my girl
goes elsewhere."

Prince Achilles answered him:

145 "Lord Marshal, most insatiate of men,
how can the army make you a new gift?
Where is our store of booty? Can you see it?
Everything plundered from the towns has been
distributed; should troops turn all that in?
150 Just let the girl go, in the god's name, now;

113. the girl . . . of men: He is referring to Chryseis.

Plate of Apollo crowned with myrtle. *Myrtle is a small, wild evergreen that the ancient Greeks considered sacred to the goddess Aphrodite.*

141. Argives (är′gīvz′): Greeks from Argos, in the northeastern part of the Peloponnesus.

12 GUIDED READING
Identifying Details: What two conditions does Calchas say must be fulfilled before Apollo will release the Greeks from the plague? (Agamemnon must restore Chryseis to her father without ransom, and the Greeks must sacrifice to the god at Chryse.)

13 LITERARY ELEMENT
Simile: In line 121, how does the poet continue using the imagery of "fire" and "burning" for anger? (by describing the angry Agamemnon's eyes as "like licking fire")

HUMANITIES CONNECTION

The fine quality of Greek ceramic ware demonstrates the Greek concern with beauty in every aspect of life. Potters and painters transformed items designed for the most prosaic uses into splendid artwork.
? *Can you think of examples of everyday items from other cultures that were crafted so carefully as to become works of art?* (Possible responses: patchwork quilts, duck decoys, Shaker furniture) ∎

14 READER'S RESPONSE
How do you feel about what Agamemnon says in lines 132–135? (Possible response: anger at his treating women as objects to be used and rated) Point out that in Greek culture such attitudes were accepted; women were considered spoils of war.

15 LEP: Be sure students follow the punctuation of this passage as they read. Point out that the phrase "gives us leave" means "allows us." ■

16 GUIDED READING

Sequencing: According to Agamemnon, what event will take place before he decides whose prize he will claim as a substitute for Chryseis? (the return of Chryseis to her father in Chryse)

17 LITERARY ELEMENT

Flashback: In a brief flashback, Achilles remembers his peaceful life before the war. What details contribute to this description and contrast with the present? (cattle, horses, black farmland, shadowy hills, foaming seas) How do these memories heighten Achilles' rage? (He realizes what he has left behind to help Agamemnon's cause.)

HUMANITIES CONNECTION

Ajax is described in the *Iliad* as a warrior of colossal stature, second only to Achilles in courage and strength but comparatively slow-witted and overly proud.

? *Can you think of contemporary figures who are often depicted with characteristics similar to those of Ajax?* (Possible responses: bodybuilders, TV wrestlers) ■

15 we'll make it up to you, twice over, three
times over, on that day Zeus gives us leave
to plunder Troy behind her rings of stone."

Agamemnon answered:

"Not that way
155 will I be gulled, brave as you are, Achilles.
Take me in, would you? Try to get around me?
What do you really ask? That you may keep
your own winnings, I am to give up mine
and sit here wanting her? Oh, no:
160 the army will award a prize to me
and make sure that it measures up, or if
they do not, I will take a girl myself,
your own, or Ajax's, or Odysseus' prize!
Take her, yes, to keep. The man I visit
165 may choke with rage; well, let him.
But this, I say, we can decide on later.

16 Look to it now, we launch on the great sea
a well-found ship, and get her manned with oarsmen,
load her with sacrificial beasts and put aboard
170 Chryseis in her loveliness. My deputy,
Ajax, Idomeneus,° or Prince Odysseus,
or you, Achilles, fearsome as you are,
will make the hecatomb and quiet the Archer."
Achilles frowned and looked at him, then said:

175 "You thick-skinned, shameless, greedy fool!
Can any Achaean care for you, or obey you,
after this on marches or in battle?
As for myself, when I came here to fight,
I had no quarrel with Troy or Trojan spearmen:
17 180 they never stole my cattle or my horses,
never in the black farmland of Phthia°
ravaged my crops. How many miles there are
of shadowy hills between, and foaming seas!
No, no, we joined for you, you insolent boor,
185 to please you, fighting for your brother's sake
and yours, to get revenge upon the Trojans.
You overlook this, dogface, or don't care,
and now in the end you threaten to take my girl,
a prize I sweated for, and soldiers gave me!

190 Never have I had plunder like your own

Scala/Art Resource, New York

Detail of a vase handle depicting Ajax.

171. **Idomeneus** (ī·däm′i·nōōs′, -nyōōs′): king of Crete and leader of the Cretan forces against Troy.

181. **Phthia** (thī′ə): Achilles' home in northern Greece.

from any Trojan stronghold battered down
by the Achaeans. I have seen more action
hand to hand in those assaults than you have,
but when the time for sharing comes, the greater
195   share is always yours. Worn out with battle
I carry off some trifle to my ships.
Well, this time I make sail for home.
Better to take now to my ships. Why linger,
cheated of winnings, to make wealth for you?"

200   To this the high commander made reply:

"Desert, if that's the way the wind blows. Will I
beg you to stay on my account? I will not.
Others will honor me, and Zeus who views
the wide world most of all.

                        No officer

205   is hateful to my sight as you are, none
given like you to <u>faction</u>, as to battle—
rugged you are, I grant, by some god's favor.
Sail, then, in your ships, and lord it over
your own battalion of Myrmidons.° I do not
210   give a curse for you, or for your anger.
But here is warning for you:

              Chryseis

being required of me by Phoebus Apollo,
she will be sent back in a ship of mine,
manned by my people. That done, I myself
215   will call for Briseis at your hut, and take her,
flower of young girls that she is, your prize,
to show you here and now who is the stronger
and make the next man sick at heart—if any
think of claiming equal place with me."

220   A pain like grief weighed on the son of Peleus,°
and in his shaggy chest this way and that
the passion of his heart ran: should he draw
longsword from hip, stand off the rest, and kill
in single combat the great son of Atreus,
225   or hold his rage in check and give it time?
And as this tumult swayed him, as he slid
the big blade slowly from the sheath, Athena
came to him from the sky. The white-armed goddess,
Hera, sent her, being fond of both,

Lee Boltin Picture Library

Marble bust of Zeus, c. 131 B.C.

209.   **Myrmidons** (mur′mə-dänz′):
warriors from Thessaly, in
northern Greece; followers of
Achilles.

220.   **son of Peleus:** Achilles.

■ **faction** (fak′shən): dissen-
sion

18 PREDICTING
Agamemnon now threatens
Achilles even more explicitly.
How do you think Achilles will
react if Agamemnon carries
out this threat to confiscate
the girl Briseis, who is Achilles'
prize? (Accept reasonable responses: He may try to kill
Agamemnon or defend Briseis;
he may yield but seek revenge
for the insult to his honor.)
What do you think of a commander who treats his best
warrior with such disdain? (Answers will vary.)

19 LITERARY ELEMENT
Conflict: In lines 222–225,
what internal conflict does Homer portray? (Achilles wonders
whether to kill Agamemnon
with his sword or to restrain
his rage.)

HUMANITIES CONNECTION

The bust of Zeus is a copy of a
lost fourth century B.C. Greek
original.
❓ *In comparing the bust of
Zeus with that of Aristotle,
shown on p. 222, what details
seem to distinguish a god from
a man?* (Possible response: A
god has greater nobility of
face, stylized hair and beard,
and lacks emotional
expression) ■

How do you know that this conversation between Achilles and Athena is not overheard but is private? (Since we know that Athena is "visible to no one except Achilles," lines 231–232, we can infer that the dialogue is private.) What does Athena's presence reveal about the Greek view of the role of the gods in human affairs? (The gods feel free to advise their favorites.) How might a modern reader interpret the appearance of the goddess? (as a symbol of an aspect of Achilles' character or conscience)

HUMANITIES CONNECTION

The frescoes, portraits, and etchings of the Venetian artist Tiepolo (tye′pō·lō) display the technique of chiaroscuro (interplay of light and dark) and express an underlying melancholy. His skill at creating illusionary effects makes it difficult to distinguish real architectural features, such as doors, from painted ones in his frescoes. Other works by Tiepolo appear on pp. 242 and 385. ■

230　concerned for both men. And Athena, stepping
　　　up behind him, visible to no one
　　　except Achilles, gripped his red-gold hair.

　　　Startled, he made a half turn, and he knew her
　　　upon the instant for Athena: terribly
235　her gray eyes blazed at him. And speaking softly
　　　but rapidly aside to her he said:

　　　"What now, O daughter of the god of heaven
　　　who bears the stormcloud,° why are you here? To see
　　　the wolfishness of Agamemnon?
240　Well, I give you my word: this time, and soon,
　　　he pays for his behavior with his blood."

　　　The gray-eyed goddess Athena said to him:

20 | "It was to check this killing rage I came
　　　from heaven, if you will listen. Hera sent me,
245　being fond of both of you, concerned for both.
　　　Enough: break off this combat, stay your hand
　　　upon the sword hilt. Let him have a lashing

237–238. **god . . . who bears the stormcloud:** Zeus.

Giraudon/Art Resource, New York

ATHENA RESTRAINING THE ANGER OF ACHILLES IN BATTLE WITH AGAMEMNON.
GIOVANNI BATTISTA TIEPOLO (1696–1770).
❓ *Why has Hera sent Athena? What is Athena's promise to Achilles?*

with words, instead: tell him how things will be.
Here is my promise, and it will be kept:

21 250 winnings three times as rich, in due season,
you shall have in requital for his arrogance.
But hold your hand. Obey."

The great runner,
Achilles, answered:

"Nothing for it, goddess,
but when you two immortals speak, a man

22 255 complies, though his heart burst. Just as well.
Honor the gods' will, they may honor ours."
On this he stayed his massive hand
upon the silver pommel,° and the blade
of his great weapon slid back in the scabbard.

258. **pommel:** the knob on the end of the hilt of a sword or dagger.

260 The man had done her bidding. Off to Olympus,
gaining the air, she went to join the rest,
the powers of heaven in the home of Zeus.

But now the son of Peleus turned on Agamemnon
and lashed out at him, letting his anger ride
265 in execration:

"Sack of wine,

23 you with your cur's eyes and your antelope heart!
You've never had the kidney to buckle on
armor among the troops, or make a sortie
with picked men—oh, no; that way death might lie.
270 Safer, by god, in the middle of the army—
is it not?—to commandeer the prize
of any man who stands up to you! Leech!
Commander to trash! If not, I swear,
you never could abuse one soldier more!

275 But here is what I say: my oath upon it
by this great staff: look: leaf or shoot
it cannot sprout again, once lopped away
from the log it left behind in the timbered hills;
it cannot flower, peeled of bark and leaves;
280 instead, Achaean officers in council
take it in hand by turns, when they observe
by the will of Zeus due order in debate:

24 let this be what I swear by then: I swear
a day will come when every Achaean soldier
285 will groan to have Achilles back. That day
you shall no more prevail on me than this

21 LITERARY ELEMENT
Foreshadowing: This passage foreshadows two major scenes later in the *Iliad*: the offer by Agamemnon of compensation to Achilles, in Book 9, and the eventual payment of the compensation, in Book 19.

22 GUIDED READING
Cause and Effect: What reason does Achilles give for obeying Athena? (If mortals obey the gods, the gods may show favor in return.)

execration (ek′si·krā′shən): the act of speaking abusively of someone or something

23 LITERARY ELEMENT
Imagery: What examples of animal imagery can you identify in lines 266–272? ("cur's eyes," "antelope heart," "leech") What human traits are those animal images meant to suggest? (The trait of cowardice is suggested by *cur*, which means "an inferior dog" or "a cowardly person," and by the swift-running *antelope*; taking advantage of others is suggested by *leech*, "a blood-sucking parasite.")

from the *Iliad*, Book 1

24

dry wood shall flourish—driven though you are,
and though a thousand men perish before
the killer, Hector. You will eat your heart out,
290 raging with remorse for this dishonor
done by you to the bravest of Achaeans."

25

He hurled the staff, studded with golden nails,
before him on the ground. Then down he sat,
and fury filled Agamemnon, looking across at him.
295 But for the sake of both men Nestor arose,
the Pylians'° orator, eloquent and clear;
argument sweeter than honey rolled from his tongue.
By now he had outlived two generations
of mortal men, his own and the one after,
300 in Pylos land, and still ruled in the third.
In kind reproof he said:

"A black day, this.
Bitter distress comes this way to Achaea.
How happy Priam and Priam's sons would be,
and all the Trojans—wild with joy—if they
305 got wind of all these fighting words between you,
foremost in council as you are, foremost
in battle. Give me your attention. Both
are younger men than I, and in my time
men who were even greater have I known
310 and none of them disdained me. Men like those
I have not seen again, nor shall: Peirithous,
the Lord Marshal Dryas, Caereus, Exadius,
Polyphemus, Theseus°—Aegeus's son,
a man like the immortal gods. I speak
315 of champions among men of earth, who fought
with champions, with wild things of the mountains,
great centaurs° whom they broke and overpowered.

26

Among these men I say I had my place
when I sailed out of Pylos, my far country,
320 because they called for me. I fought
for my own hand among them. Not one man
alive now upon earth could stand against them.
And I repeat: they listened to my reasoning,
took my advice. Well, then, you take it too.
325 It is far better so.

Lord Agamemnon,
do not deprive him of the girl, <u>renounce</u> her.

296. **Pylians** (pīl'ē·ənz): people from Pylos (pī'los), a town in the Peloponnesus.

311–313. **Peirithous . . . Theseus:** heroes of Nestor's generation.

317. **centaurs:** legendary creatures, half-man and half-horse.

Mycenaean death mask, once
thought to be the mask of
Agamemnon.
? *What is Agamemnon's
attitude toward Achilles?*

Scala/Art Resource, New York

HUMANITIES CONNECTION

The making of death masks
was a respected skill in early
Greece, Egypt, and Rome. A
mold was created by applying
a coating of plaster of paris or
wax and allowing it to harden.
From the mold, a mask could
be made of another material.
Egyptians favored thin gold
plate. ■

prowess (prou′is): bravery
relent (ri·lent′): yield, let
up

27 LITERARY ELEMENT
Metaphor: Homer uses two
metaphors in line 335. To what
is Achilles compared? (a ''sea
wall'' for the Achaeans) To
what is war compared? (the
dangerous ''black waves'' of a
stormy ocean) Whose position
in the quarrel do these metaphors support? (Possible response: They emphasize
Achilles' critical role as protector of the Greek army.)

28 ANALYZING
Agamemnon hints that
Achilles' real ambition is to
supplant him as the Greek
leader. Can you find any direct, independent support up
to this point for Agamemnon's
statement? (no) Based on your
analysis, what conclusion
might you draw about Aga-
memnon? (He seems paranoid
and defensive about his authority and position.)

The army had allotted her to him.
Achilles, for your part, do not defy
your King and Captain. No ones vies in honor
330 with him who holds authority from Zeus.
You have more <u>prowess</u>, for a goddess bore you;
his power over men surpasses yours.

But, Agamemnon, let your anger cool.
I beg you to <u>relent</u>, knowing Achilles
27 335 a sea wall for Achaeans in the black waves of war.''

Lord Agamemnon answered:

"All you say

is fairly said, sir, but this man's ambition,
remember, is to lead, to lord it over
28 everyone, hold power over everyone,
340 give orders to the rest of us! Well, one
will never take his orders! If the gods
who live forever made a spearman of him,
have they put insults on his lips as well?''

from the Iliad, Book 1   **239**

Achilles interrupted:

"What a poltroon,°   344. **poltroon** (päl·trōōn′): coward.

345 how lily-livered I should be called, if I
knuckled under to all you do or say!
Give your commands to someone else, not me!
And one more thing I have to tell you: think it
over: this time, for the girl, I will not
350 wrangle in arms with you or anyone,
though I am robbed of what was given me;
but as for any other thing I have
alongside my black ship, you shall not take it
against my will. Try it. Hear this, everyone:
355 that instant your hot blood blackens my spear!"

They quarreled in this way, face to face, and then
broke off the assembly by the ships. Achilles
made his way to his squadron and his quarters,
Patroclus by his side, with his companions.

360 Agamemnon proceeded to launch a ship,
assigned her twenty oarsmen, loaded beasts
for sacrifice to the god, then set aboard
Chryseis in her loveliness. The versatile
Odysseus took the deck, and, all oars manned,
365 they pulled out on the drenching ways of sea.
The troops meanwhile were ordered to police camp
and did so, throwing refuse in the water;
then to Apollo by the barren surf
they carried out full-tally hecatombs,
370 and the savor curled in crooked smoke toward heaven.

That was the day's work in the army.

          Agamemnon
had kept his threat in mind, and now he acted,
calling Eurybates and Talthybios,
his aides and criers:

          "Go along," he said,
375 "both of you, to the quarters of Achilles
and take his charming Briseis by the hand
to bring to me. And if he balks at giving her
I shall be there myself with men-at-arms
in force to take her—all the more gall for him."

380 So, ominously, he sent them on their way,
and they who had no stomach for it went

29

30 ⌐

A scene of sacrifice.

along the waste sea shingle° toward the ships
and shelters of the Myrmidons. Not far
from his black ship and hut they found the prince
385 in the open, seated. And seeing these two come
was cheerless to Achilles. Shamefast, pale
with fear of him, they stood without a word;
but he knew what they felt and called out:

                              "Peace to you,
criers and couriers of Zeus and men!
390 Come forward. Not one thing have I against you:
Agamemnon is the man who sent you
for Briseis. Here then, my lord Patroclus,
bring out the girl and give her to these men.
And let them both bear witness before the gods
395 who live in bliss, as before men who die,
including this harsh king, if ever hereafter
a need for me arises to keep the rest
from black defeat and ruin.

                              Lost in folly,
the man cannot think back or think ahead
400 how to come through a battle by the ships."
Patroclus did the bidding of his friend,
led from the hut Briseis in her beauty
and gave her to them. Back along the ships
they took their way, and the girl went, <u>loath</u> to go.
405 Leaving his friends in haste, Achilles wept,
and sat apart by the gray wave, scanning the endless sea.
Often he spread his hands in prayer to his mother:°

"As my life came from you, though it is brief,
honor at least from Zeus who storms in heaven
410 I call my due. He gives me precious little.
See how the lord of the great plains, Agamemnon,
humiliated me! He has my prize,
by his own whim, for himself."

                              Eyes wet with tears,
he spoke, and her ladyship his mother heard him
415 in green deeps where she lolled near her old father.
Gliding she rose and broke like mist from the inshore
gray sea face, to sit down softly before him,
her son in tears; and fondling him she said:

---

382. **shingle:** beach covered with large, coarse gravel.

407. **mother:** the goddess Thetis (thē′tis), a daughter of Nereus, the old man of the sea.

---

from the Iliad, Book 1   **241**

34 LITERARY ELEMENT

Flashback: This flashback alludes to a cattle raid on the town of Thebe, which is ruled by Eetion. Achilles recalls that it was in this raid that Chryseis was captured by the Greeks. Throughout the *Iliad*, however, we learn that this particular raid was especially significant because Eetion was the father of Andromache, the wife of Troy's chief defender, Hector, son of Priam. Homer will gradually reveal that Achilles killed Eetion in battle, along with Andromache's seven brothers.

Fresco of Agamemnon carrying away Briseis, by Giovanni Battista Tiepolo.
How is Briseis important to the plot of the Iliad?

"Child, why do you weep? What grief is this?
420 Out with it, tell me, both of us should know."
Achilles, fast in battle as a lion,
groaned and said:

               "Why tell you what you know?
We sailed out raiding, and we took by storm
that ancient town of Eetion° called Thebe,
425 plundered the place, brought slaves and spoils away.
At the division, later,
they chose a young girl, Chryseis, for the king.
Then Chryses, priest of the Archer God, Apollo,
came to the beachhead we Achaeans hold,
430 bringing no end of ransom for his daughter;

424. **Eetion** (ē·ē′tē·än): king of Thebe (thē′bē), a city near Troy.

SEF/Art Resource, New York

he had the god's white bands on a golden staff
and sued for grace from the army of Achaea,
mostly the two Atridae, corps commanders.
All of our soldiers murmured in assent:
435 'Behave well to the priest. And take the ransom!'
But Agamemnon would not. It went against his desire,
and brutally he ordered the man away.
So the old man withdrew in grief and anger.
Apollo cared for him: he heard his prayer
440 and let black bolts of plague fly on the Argives.

One by one our men came down with it
and died hard as the god's shots raked the army
broadside. But our priest divined the cause
and told us what the god meant by the plague.

445 I said, 'Appease the god!' but Agamemnon
could not contain his rage; he threatened me,
and what he threatened is now done—
one girl the Achaeans are embarking now
for Chryse beach with gifts for Lord Apollo;
450 the other, just now, from my hut—the criers
came and took her, Briseus' girl, my prize,
given by the army.

               If you can, stand by me:
go to Olympus, pray to Zeus, if ever
by word or deed you served him—
455 and so you did, I often heard you tell it
in Father's house: that time when you alone
of all the gods shielded the son of Cronus°
from peril and disgrace—when other gods,
Pallas Athena, Hera, and Poseidon,
460 wished him in irons, wished to keep him bound,
you had the will to free him of that bondage,
and called up to Olympus in all haste
Aegaeon, whom the gods call Briareus,°
the giant with a hundred arms, more powerful
465 than the sea-god, his father. Down he sat
by the son of Cronus, glorying in that place.
For fear of him the blissful gods forbore
to manacle Zeus.

               Remind him of these things,
cling to his knees and tell him your good pleasure

457. **son of Cronus:** Zeus; Cronus ruled over the Titans until his son, Zeus, dethroned him and became ruler over the Olympians.

463. **Briareus** (brī·är'ē·əs): a giant who helped Zeus and the Olympians overcome the Titans.

35 LITERARY ELEMENT
Epic Characteristics: In lines 422–452, Achilles summarizes what has already happened and what the Homeric audience already knows. This kind of summary—which involves verbatim, formulaic repetition—is a convention of Homeric epic. Why might such a summary be a useful device for an oral poet? (It allows the poet to entertain his audience with slight variations of earlier material while he thinks about the new directions of his narrative.)

appease (ə·pēz'): pacify by giving in to the demands of

36 LITERARY ELEMENT
Flashback: This flashback recalls a mythical event on Olympus quite different from the legends that surrounded the Trojan War (some of which have been shown to have a historical basis). How did Thetis come to Zeus's aid? (She summoned the hundred-armed giant, Briareus, to defend Zeus against the aggression of the other gods.)

37 CULTURAL DIVERSITY
Clinging to a person's knees was the standard sign of supplication in ancient Greek religion and ritual. One of Zeus's attributes was "god of suppliants," so it is likely that Thetis's plea will meet with success, especially since she has done Zeus an important favor.
What signs of supplication are you aware of in other cultures? (Answers will vary.)

38 **LITERARY ELEMENT**

Foreshadowing: What does Thetis predict about Achilles' life in lines 477–482? (that he will die young) How might he have avoided this fate? (by being "serene upon this beachhead" and not quarreling with Agamemnon)

39 **GUIDED READING**

Finding the Main Idea: What does Thetis promise Achilles that she will do? (intervene with Zeus on Achilles' behalf)

HUMANITIES CONNECTION

Over 20,000 pieces of ceramic ware have survived from ancient Greek times. The pottery had many household purposes, including storage of oil and honey. It is notable for its variety of shapes, such as this handled vase. At first, vases were decorated with geometric designs or simple objects. Later artists focused on narrative scenes drawn from daily life and mythology. ■

470 if he will take the Trojan side
and roll the Achaeans back to the water's edge,
back on the ships with slaughter! All the troops
may savor what their king has won for them,
and he may know his madness, what he lost
475 when he dishonored me, peerless among Achaeans."

Her eyes filled, and a tear fell as she answered:

"Alas, my child, why did I rear you, doomed
the day I bore you? Ah, could you only be
serene upon this beachhead through the siege,
480 your life runs out so soon.
Oh early death! Oh broken heart! No destiny
so cruel! And I bore you to this evil!

But what you wish I will propose
To Zeus, lord of the lightning, going up
485 myself into the snow-glare of Olympus
with hope for his consent.

                Be quiet now
beside the long ships, keep your anger bright
against the army, quit the war.

                      Last night
Zeus made a journey to the shore of Ocean
490 to feast among the Sunburned,° and the gods
accompanied him. In twelve days he will come
back to Olympus. Then I shall be there
to cross his bronze doorsill and take his knees.
I trust I'll move him."

                    Thetis left her son
495 still burning for the softly belted girl
whom they had wrested from him. . . .

38

39

Scala/Art Resource, New York

Vase depicting Thetis bringing armor to Achilles.
What is the relation of Thetis to Achilles? Why would she bring him his armor?

490. **the Sunburned:** Ethiopians.

Fresco from the isle of Crete.

Photo Nimatallah/Art Resource, New York

READING CHECK

1. Why does Apollo punish the Greeks by sending the plague? (Agamemnon has dishonored Apollo's priest by refusing to surrender Chryseis.)
2. Who prevents Achilles from trying to kill Agamemnon? (the goddess Athena)
3. Once he has given up Chryseis, whose prize does Agamemnon claim as a substitute? (Achilles' prize, Briseis)
4. To whom does Achilles pray, and what does he ask for? (to Thetis, his mother; for her to intervene on his behalf with Zeus)
5. What does Thetis prophesy about her son? (that Achilles will die young)

First Thoughts

Which character do you think was more in the right, Agamemnon or Achilles? Explain.

Identifying Facts

1. What crisis in the Greek camp confronts the leaders at the opening of the epic? How does this crisis lead to a conflict between Achilles and Agamemnon?
2. What action does Agamemnon take to appease Apollo? What does he take from Achilles?
3. What oath does Achilles swear? Why does he withdraw from the battle?
4. What does Thetis promise to do for her son Achilles?

Interpreting Meanings

1. What impression do you form of Agamemnon's **character** from his own words and actions and the reactions of Calchas and Achilles?

2. What ominous, or threatening, images can you identify in the first fifteen lines of Book 1 of the *Iliad*? What future events do these images **foreshadow**?
3. In the scene between Achilles and his mother Thetis, there is a **flashback** to an earlier time when Thetis helped to defend Zeus. What purpose does this flashback serve?
4. What role do the gods and goddesses play in Book 1? Are they aloof observers, fair intermediaries, or meddling nuisances? Describe the roles played by Apollo, Athena, and Thetis in this book of the *Iliad*.

Applying Meanings

Do you think that Achilles is justified in his wrath against Agamemnon and his subsequent withdrawal from battle? Imagine that Achilles is a modern-day military officer. Would a modern general be justified in withdrawing from combat if his personal honor were at stake? If so, under what circumstances?

Parthenon frieze (477–432 B.C.). *This frieze depicts Ares, the god of war, at right, and Dionysus, the god of agriculture and wine, facing Demeter, the goddess of fertility.*

The Bridgeman Art Library/Art Resource, New York

ANSWERS

First Thoughts
Answers will vary.

Identifying Facts
1. plague; Achilles becomes angry when Agamemnon refuses to give up the girl Chryseis to end the plague.
2. He agrees to restore Chryseis to her father. He takes Briseis away from Achilles.
3. to withdraw from battle; because of his anger at Agamemnon
4. to intervene with Zeus

Interpreting Meanings
1. Possible responses: He is arrogant, selfish, and violent. He is more concerned with his position than with his troops.
2. Possible responses: the crowd of dead souls (line 4), carrion for dogs and birds (lines 5–6), burning wind of plague (lines 12–13), sickness and death (lines 13–14); images foreshadow death and ruin
3. The flashback shows that Zeus is indebted to Thetis and that her plea to Zeus on Achilles' behalf will probably be successful.
4. Possible response: Deities are intermediaries, with Apollo sending the plague, Athena restraining Achilles from killing Agamemnon, and Thetis agreeing to intervene on her son's behalf with Zeus.

Applying Meanings
Answers will vary.

TEACHER'S RESOURCES

- ✔ Review and Response Worksheet
- ✔ Selection Test
- ✔ Vocabulary Activity Worksheet
- ✔ Vocabulary Test
- ✔ Language Skills Worksheet

1 LITERARY BACKGROUND

In Book 16, when Patroclus persuades Achilles to permit him to rejoin the battle, Achilles insists that his friend borrow and wear Achilles' own armor. After Hector slays Patroclus, the Trojan hero succeeds in stripping Patroclus's body of this armor—although the body itself is reclaimed by the Greeks. In Book 18, the gods themselves provide Achilles with new armor for his return to battle, while Hector puts on the armor that had belonged to Achilles. *In the confrontation between Hector and Achilles that is coming in Book 22, what effect do you think the sight of the enemy wearing his own armor might have on Achilles?* (It might further enrage him.)

from the ILIAD
from Books 22 and 24
Homer
translated by
ROBERT FITZGERALD

Based on what you have learned about Achilles in the epic thus far, how do you predict he will behave toward his enemy, the Trojan hero Hector, when the two men finally meet in battle?

Without Achilles' help, the Greeks are at a serious disadvantage against the Trojans, who are led by their great warrior Hector, the son of the Trojan king, Priam. In Book 6, we glimpse Hector's humanity as he shares a loving moment with his wife Andromache and his son Astyanax. Book 6 also reveals to us Hector's pride, for we learn that although he believes Troy is doomed, honor will not allow him to surrender.

Hector returns to battle, fighting fiercely for the Trojans. As fear grows in the Greek camp, Agamemnon admits that he has wronged Achilles. He sends a delegation of ambassadors to offer amends and to ask Achilles and his comrades to return to battle. Achilles' immense pride is revealed as he stubbornly refuses to accept Agamemnon's gifts. He tells the delegates that he has decided to return to his kingdom and live out his life in comfort, forgoing the honor of dying a hero's death in battle.

When the Trojans break through the Greek defenses, Achilles' best friend Patroclus pleads with the hero to permit him to rejoin the fighting. Achilles reluctantly agrees (Books 11–15). As the battle rages, the god Apollo strikes Patroclus from his horse, giving Hector the opportunity to slay the warrior and strip the corpse of its armor.

On hearing of Patroclus's death, Achilles is overcome with grief and rage. Vowing to avenge his friend, he finally returns to the battle, mercilessly slaying the Trojan forces (Books 19–21). As Book 22 opens, the exhausted Trojans take refuge behind the high walls of the city. One Trojan remains outside the walls: Hector.

1

Fresco from the isle of Crete.

BOOK 22: The Death of Hector

Once in the town, those who had fled like deer
wiped off their sweat and drank their thirst away,
leaning against the cool stone of the ramparts.°
Meanwhile Achaeans with bright shields aslant
5 came up the plain and nearer. As for Hector,
fatal destiny pinned him where he stood
before the Scaean Gates, outside the city.

Now Achilles heard Apollo calling
back to him:

          "Why run so hard, Achilles
10 mortal as you are, after a god?
Can you not comprehend it? I am immortal.
You are so hot to catch me, you no longer
think of finishing off the men you routed.
They are all in the town by now, packed in
15 while you were being diverted here. And yet
you cannot kill me; I am no man's quarry."

Achilles bit his lip and said:

"Archer of heaven, deadliest
of immortal gods, you put me off the track,
20 turning me from the wall this way. A hundred
might have sunk their teeth into the dust
before one man took cover in Ilion!
You saved my enemies with ease and stole
my glory, having no punishment to fear.
25 I'd take it out of you, if I had the power."

Then toward the town with might and main he ran,
magnificent, like a racing chariot horse
that holds its form at full stretch on the plain.
So light-footed Achilles held the pace.
30 And aging Priam was the first to see him
sparkling on the plain, bright as that star
in autumn rising, whose unclouded rays
shine out amid a throng of stars at dusk—
the one they call Orion's° dog, most brilliant,
35 yes, but baleful as a sign: it brings
great fever to frail men. So pure and bright
the bronze gear blazed upon him as he ran.
The old man gave a cry. With both his hands

3. **ramparts:** defensive embankments surrounding a town.

Statue of Apollo.

34. **Orion:** a constellation named after a hunter who was loved and accidentally killed by the goddess Artemis.

2 LITERARY ELEMENT
Foreshadowing: Apollo has assumed the shape of Agenor, Hector's half-brother, to lure Achilles away from the gates of Troy, enabling the Trojans to retreat. Apollo's deception of Achilles foreshadows Athena's deception of Hector (lines 270–271). How does this scene prove that even the greatest heroes are no match for the gods? (The gods are immortal beings with supernatural powers.)

3 LITERARY ELEMENT
Epic Simile: Achilles is compared to a star in the constellation named for a hunter. What earlier imagery uses hunting comparisons? (line 1, soldiers are likened to fleeing deer; line 16, Apollo says he is "no man's quarry.") Who is Achilles' real quarry? (Hector) How does this comparison of Achilles to a star in Orion affect your reaction to the hero? (Possible response: He seems glorious but remote, cold, and inhuman.)

HUMANITIES CONNECTION

Revered as the patron of music, archery, prophecy, and poetry, Apollo represented the virtues most esteemed by the ancient Greeks. Even today *Apollonian* means "serene, disciplined, and well-balanced." ❓ *What details of the statue suggest that Apollo was the Greek ideal of male youth?* (Possible responses: beauty, nobility, grace) ■

4 LITERARY ELEMENT

Irony: In verbal irony, a speaker means the opposite of what he or she appears to be saying. Explain Priam's verbal irony in lines 48–49. (Priam is using "dear" in two senses: "precious" and "expensive." By "dear to me," he means that Achilles has exacted a great price from Priam: his sons.) How do you know how Priam really feels about Achilles? (In lines 50–51, he wishes that Achilles were dead and eaten.)

5 LITERARY ELEMENT

Irony: Dramatic irony occurs when the audience knows something that a character does not. Priam is ignorant of the fate of his sons Polydorus and Lycaon. The audience knows, from Books 20 and 21, that Achilles has slain them.

6 COMPARING LITERATURE

Compare Priam's vivid premonition of the circumstances of his own death, in lines 78–84, with Virgil's graphic description of the old king's slaughter in Book 2 of the *Aeneid* (lines 351–460, pp. 395–398.)

❓ *How has Virgil drawn on this passage in the* Iliad? (Priam is stabbed in his home as he cowers by an altar.)

thrown up on high he struck his head, then shouted,
40 groaning, appealing to his dear son. Unmoved,
Lord Hector stood in the gateway, resolute
to fight Achilles.
                                    Stretching out his hands,
old Priam said, imploring him:
                                    "No, Hector!
Cut off as you are, alone, dear son,
45 don't try to hold your ground against this man,
or soon you'll meet the shock of doom, borne down
by the son of Peleus. He is more powerful
by far than you, and pitiless. Ah, were he
but dear to the gods as he is dear to me!
50 Wild dogs and kites would eat him where he lay
within the hour, and ease me of my torment.
Many tall sons he killed, bereaving me,
or sold them to far islands. Even now
I cannot see two sons of mine, Lycaon°
55 and Polydorus,° among the Trojans massed
inside the town. A queen, Laothoe,
conceived and bore them. If they are alive
amid the Achaean host, I'll ransom them
with bronze and gold: both I have, piled at home,
60 rich treasures that old Altes, the renowned,
gave for his daughter's dowry. If they died,
if they went under to the homes of Death,
sorrow has come to me and to their mother.
But to our townsmen all this pain is brief,
65 unless you too go down before Achilles.
Come inside the wall, child; here you may
fight on to save our Trojan men and women.
Do not resign the glory to Achilles,
losing your own dear life! Take pity, too,
70 on me and my hard fate, while I live still.
Upon the threshold of my age, in misery,
the son of Cronus° will destroy my life
after the evil days I shall have seen—
my sons brought down, my daughters dragged away,
75 bedchambers ravaged, and small children hurled
to earth in the atrocity of war,
as my sons' wives are taken by Achaeans'
ruinous hands. And at the end, I too—
when someone with a sword-cut or a spear

54. **Lycaon** (lī·kā′än)
55. **Polydorus** (pôl·i·dō′rəs)

72. **son of Cronus:** Zeus.

6

80 has had my life—I shall be torn apart
on my own doorstep by the hounds
I trained as watchdogs, fed from my own table.
These will lap my blood with ravenous hearts
and lie in the entranceway.

Everything done
85 to a young man killed in war becomes his glory,
once he is riven° by the whetted bronze:
dead though he be, it is all fair, whatever
happens then. But when an old man falls,
and dogs disfigure his gray head and cheek
90 and genitals, that is most harrowing
of all that men in their hard lives endure."

86. **riven:** split or torn apart.

The old man wrenched at his gray hair and pulled out
hanks of it in both hands, but moved
Lord Hector not at all. The young man's mother
95 wailed from the tower across, above the portal,
streaming tears, and loosening her robe
with one hand, held her breast out in the other,
saying:

"Hector, my child, be moved by this,
and pity me, if ever I unbound
100 a quieting breast for you. Think of these things,
dear child; defend yourself against the killer
this side of the wall, not hand to hand.
He has no pity. If he brings you down,
I shall no longer be allowed to mourn you

8

105 laid out on your bed, dear branch in flower,
born of me! And neither will your lady,
so endowed with gifts. Far from us both,
dogs will devour you by the Argive ships."

With tears and cries the two implored their son,
110 and made their prayers again, but could not shake him.
Hector stood firm, as huge Achilles neared.
The way a serpent, fed on poisonous herbs,
coiled at his lair upon a mountainside,
with all his length of hate awaits a man

9

115 and eyes him evilly: so Hector, grim
and narrow-eyed, refused to yield. He leaned
his brilliant shield against a spur of wall
and in his brave heart bitterly reflected:
"Here I am badly caught. If I take cover,

HECTOR TAKING LEAVE FROM
ANDROMACHE, ANGELICA KAUFFMANN
(1741–1807).

Tate Gallery, London/Art Resource, New York

7 **INTERPRETING**
Why does the death of young
warriors distress Priam less
than the death of old people?
(because, according to the
Homeric code, young heroes
have honor, while the old have
only shame)

8 **LITERARY ELEMENT**
Foreshadowing: What does
Hecuba say will happen if Hector chooses to fight Achilles?
(Dogs will devour Hector by
the Argive ships.) What mood
does this forecast create? (a
mood of foreboding)

9 **COMPARING LITERATURE**
*In lines 112–116, to what is
Hector compared?* (a poi-
sonous serpent who is about
to strike a man) In the *Aeneid*,
Virgil uses a similar epic simile
for Pyrrhus, the son of
Achilles, just before Pyrrhus
slays Priam (see lines 353–358
on p. 395). *Which simile portrays its hero in the worst light?*
(Virgil portrays Pyrrhus as merciless, while Hector is seen
here as a brave hero who refuses to yield to a superior
enemy.)

HUMANITIES CONNECTION

The Swiss painter Maria Anna
Angelica Kauffmann worked
mainly in London and Rome.
She became especially well
known for her mythological
and historical subjects in the
restrained neoclassical style. ■

10 LITERARY ELEMENT

Epic Characteristic: Hector's speech (lines 119–156) illustrates another epic convention: a scene of deliberation in which a hero weighs his alternatives, in this case, to withdraw into the walled town, to negotiate with Achilles, or to fight. How does Hector's predicament—he is caught between his desire to retreat and his fear of the townspeople's taunts—make him seem more human? (Accept reasonable responses. Most students will have experienced a similar situation when they were torn between fear of mockery and fear of danger.)

Scala/Art Resource, New York

Stone etching of a battle of the Trojan War.
❓ *Why does Hector refuse to back down? How does he talk himself into facing Achilles?*

```
120  slipping inside the gate and wall, the first
     to accuse me for it will be Polydamas,°
     he who told me I should lead the Trojans
     back to the city on that cursed night
     Achilles joined the battle. No, I would not,
125  would not, wiser though it would have been.
     Now troops have perished for my foolish pride,
     I am ashamed to face townsmen and women.
     Someone inferior to me may say:
     'He kept his pride and lost his men, this Hector!'
130  So it will go. Better, when that time comes,
     that I appear as he who killed Achilles
     man to man, or else that I went down
     fighting him to the end before the city.
     Suppose, though, that I lay my shield and helm
135  aside, and prop my spear against the wall,
     and go to meet the noble Prince Achilles,
     promising Helen, promising with her
     all treasures that Alexandros° brought home
     by ship to Troy—the first cause of our quarrel—
```

10

121. **Polydamas** (pō·lid′ə·məs): a Trojan leader.

138. **Alexandros:** another name for Paris. *Alexandros* means "champion."

140 that he may give these things to the Atridae?
Then I might add, apart from these, a portion
of all the secret wealth the city owns.
Yes, later I might take our counselors' oath
to hide no stores, but share and share alike
145 to halve all wealth our lovely city holds,
all that is here within the walls. Ah, no,
why even put the question to myself?
I must not go before him and receive
no quarter, no respect! Aye, then and there
150 he'll kill me, unprotected as I am,
my gear laid by, defenseless as a woman.
No chance, now, for charms from oak or stone
in parley with him—charms a girl and boy
might use when they enchant each other talking!
155 Better we duel, now at once, and see
to whom the Olympian awards the glory."

These were his shifts of mood. Now close at hand
Achilles like the implacable god of war
came on with blowing crest, hefting the dreaded
160 beam of Pelian ash° on his right shoulder.
Bronze light played around him, like the glare
of a great fire or the great sun rising,
and Hector, as he watched, began to tremble.
Then he could hold his ground no more. He ran,
165 leaving the gate behind him, with Achilles
hard on his heels, sure of his own speed.
When that most lightning-like of birds, a hawk
bred on a mountain, swoops upon a dove,
the quarry dips in terror, but the hunter,
170 screaming, dips behind and gains upon it,
passionate for prey. Just so, Achilles
murderously cleft the air, as Hector
ran with flashing knees along the wall.
They passed the lookout point, the wild fig tree
175 with wind in all its leaves, then veered away
along the curving wagon road, and came
to where the double fountains well, the source
of eddying Scamander.° One hot spring
flows out, and from the water fumes arise
180 as though from fire burning; but the other
even in summer gushes chill as hail

160. **Pelian** (pēl′ē·ən) **ash:** wood cut from trees on Mount Pelion, one of the highest mountains in Greece.

178. **Scamander** (skə·man′dər): river of Troy.

MEETING INDIVIDUAL NEEDS

11 *LEP:* You may want to explain that "parley" in line 153 means "conference" or "talk" and that "Olympian" in line 156 is a reference to Zeus. ■

implacable (im·plā′kə·bəl): cannot be pacified

12 LITERARY ELEMENT
Epic Simile: Notice that this epic simile presents a double comparison. To what is Achilles compared? (a hawk) To what is Hector compared? (a dove) Why are the details of the simile appropriate? (The hawk, a swift hunter, pursues the terror-stricken dove just as Achilles, who is said to be "murderous," runs after the fleeing Hector.)

13 LITERARY ELEMENT

Suspense: In lines 177–186, Homer departs from the main narrative and then circles back to resume it. The fountains, easy to visualize, evoke the "days of peace" and offer a poignant contrast to the violence of the chase scene. How does the digression also build suspense? (by forcing the audience to wait for the outcome of the chase)

14 ANALYZING

The simile in lines 193–198 compares Achilles and Hector to racing chariot-teams. How does this comparison make the scene more vivid? (Possible response: The comparison emphasizes the race's serious intent and its dizzying speed. In addition, it brings to mind the athletic games held as part of the funeral rites for the dead. The gods gaze on Hector's and Achilles' race to the death as if they were at a game or spectacle.)

15 CULTURAL DIVERSITY

Zeus's suggestion that Hector be allowed to escape his fate underlines the ancient Greeks' tendency to portray their gods as deities with human traits. Even Zeus, who ideally should be impartial, could show favoritism.

? *In which other ancient cultures are the gods portrayed as having human qualities?* (Possible responses: ancient Egypt, ancient India)

or snow or crystal ice frozen on water.
13 Near these fountains are wide washing pools
of smooth-laid stone, where Trojan wives and daughters
185 laundered their smooth linen in the days
of peace before the Achaeans came. Past these
the two men ran, pursuer and pursued,
and he who fled was noble, he behind
a greater man by far. They ran full speed,
190 and not for bull's hide or a ritual beast
or any prize that men compete for: no,
but for the life of Hector, tamer of horses.
14 Just as when chariot-teams around a course
go wheeling swiftly, for the prize is great,
195 a tripod° or a woman, in the games
held for a dead man, so three times these two
at full speed made their course round Priam's town,
as all the gods looked on. And now the father
of gods and men° turned to the rest and said:

200 "How sad that this beloved man is hunted
around the wall before my eyes! My heart
is touched for Hector; he has burned thigh flesh
of oxen for me often, high on Ida,°
at other times on the high point of Troy.
205 Now Prince Achilles with devouring stride
is pressing him around the town of Priam.
15 Come, gods, put your minds on it, consider
whether we may deliver him from death
or see him, noble as he is, brought down
210 by Peleus' son, Achilles."

                                            Gray-eyed Athena
said to him:

                                    "Father of the blinding bolt,
the dark stormcloud, what words are these? The man
is mortal, and his doom fixed, long ago.
Would you release him from his painful death?
215 Then do so, but not all of us will praise you."

Zeus who gathers cloud replied:

                                      "Take heart,
my dear and honored child. I am not bent
on my suggestion, and I would indulge you.
Act as your thought inclines, refrain no longer."

195. **tripod:** a bronze altar used in sacrifices.

198–199. **father of gods and men:** Zeus.

203. **Ida:** Mount Ida, in Phrygia, the source of many rivers, including the Scamander.

220 So he encouraged her in her desire,
and down she swept from ridges of Olympus.
Great Achilles, hard on Hector's heels,
kept after him, the way a hound will harry
a deer's fawn he has startled from its bed
225 to chase through gorge and open glade, and when
the quarry goes to earth under a bush
he holds the scent and quarters till he finds it;
so with Hector: he could not shake off
the great runner, Achilles. Every time
230 he tried to spring hard for the Dardan gates°
under the towers, hoping men could help him,
sending missiles down, Achilles loomed
to cut him off and turn him toward the plain,
as he himself ran always near the city.
235 As in a dream a man chasing another
cannot catch him, nor can he in flight
escape from his pursuer, so Achilles
could not by his swiftness overtake him,
nor could Hector pull away. How could he
240 run so long from death, had not Apollo
for the last time, the very last, come near
to give him stamina and speed?

                                    Achilles
shook his head at the rest of the Achaeans,
allowing none to shoot or cast at Hector—
245 none to forestall him, and to win the honor.
But when, for the fourth time, they reached the springs,
the Father poised his golden scales.

                                  He placed
two shapes of death, death prone and cold, upon them,
one of Achilles, one of the horseman, Hector,
250 and held the midpoint, pulling upward. Down
sank Hector's fatal day, the pan went down
toward undergloom, and Phoebus Apollo left him.
Then came Athena, gray-eyed, to the son
of Peleus, falling in with him, and near him,
255 saying swiftly:

                      "Now at last I think
the two of us, Achilles loved by Zeus,
shall bring Achaeans triumph at the ships
by killing Hector—unappeased
though he was ever in his thirst for war.

230. **Dardan gates:** gates of Troy; Dardania, a city built near the foot of Mount Ida, became part of Troy.

Bust of Athena.

Lee Boltin Picture Library

16 **LITERARY ELEMENT**
Epic Simile: Look back at the epic similes that describe Achilles' pursuit of Hector, at lines 167, 193, and 223. How is the content of this epic simile different from those earlier comparisons? (The earlier similes featured animals: hawk, dove, racehorses drawing a chariot, hound, and fawn. This simile features two human runners in a dream.) How would you describe the emotional effect of this comparison? (Possible response: The effect is nightmarish and unreal, for the simile suggests that the chase may continue indefinitely.)

 stamina (stam′ə·nə): endurance

17 **LITERARY ELEMENT**
Plot: Why might Zeus's weighing of the fates of Achilles and Hector be regarded as the climax of the chase scene? (When Hector's fate sinks down in the scales and Apollo leaves him, his doom is sealed.)

HUMANITIES CONNECTION

Athena was primarily the goddess of wisdom and of civilized life. When she assisted warriors, it was usually in defense of civilized values. She was said to have sprung from the head of Zeus fully grown and clad for battle. ∎

18 PREDICTING

Deiphobus is Hector's favorite brother. He has played an important role in the fighting in Book 13. Why do you think Athena has taken his form? (Possible response: to fool Hector into fighting Achilles)

19 ANALYZING

In lines 284–285, how does Athena shrewdly use details to add credibility to her impersonation? (By mentioning the pleas of Priam and Hecuba, she reminds Hector of his parents' entreaty that he not oppose Achilles. Because these details ring true, Hector has no reason to suspect a trap.)

20 GUIDED READING

Identifying Details: What phrase in lines 289–292 clearly shows that Athena is setting a trap to deceive Hector? ("by guile" in line 292)

21 EVALUATING

How do you assess Hector's heroism so far in Book 22? (Hector's flight from Achilles diminishes his status as a hero. His firm stand here helps to restore his heroic stature. Hector's fear before a superior, god-like opponent is only human.)

▌ HUMANITIES CONNECTION ▐

The actual vase uses the "red-figure" technique of pottery painting that began to replace the "black-figure" style about 500 B.C. In the red-figure style, a black glaze was applied over the background, leaving space for a detailed painting in the reddish-orange clay. ■

254 Greek and Roman Literatures

260 There is no way he may escape us now,
not though Apollo, lord of distances,
should suffer all indignity for him
before his father Zeus who bears the stormcloud,
rolling back and forth and begging for him.
265 Now you can halt and take your breath, while I
persuade him into combat face to face."

These were Athena's orders. He complied,
relieved, and leaning hard upon the spearshaft
armed with its head of bronze. She left him there
18 270 and overtook Lord Hector—but she seemed
Deiphobus° in form and resonant voice,
appearing at his shoulder, saying swiftly:
"Ai! Dear brother, how he runs, Achilles,
harrying you around the town of Priam!
275 Come, we'll stand and take him on."

To this,

great Hector in his shimmering helm replied:

"Deiphobus, you were the closest to me
in the old days, of all my brothers, sons
of Hecuba and Priam. Now I can say
280 I honor you still more
because you dared this foray for my sake,
seeing me run. The rest stay under cover."

Again the gray-eyed goddess spoke:

19 "Dear brother, how your father and gentle mother
285 begged and begged me to remain! So did
the soldiers round me, all undone by fear.
But in my heart I ached for you.
Now let us fight him, and fight hard.
No holding back. We'll see if this Achilles
20 290 conquers both, to take our armor seaward,
or if he can be brought down by your spear."

This way, by guile, Athena led him on.
And when at last the two men faced each other,
Hector was the first to speak. He said:

21 295 "I will no longer fear you as before,
son of Peleus, though I ran from you
round Priam's town three times and could not face you.
Now my soul would have me stand and fight,

271. **Deiphobus** (de·if'ō·bəs): one of Hector's brothers.

Alinari/Art Resource, New York

Vase depicting Achilles.

whether I kill you or am killed. So come,
300 we'll summon gods here as our witnesses,
none higher, arbiters° of a pact: I swear
that, terrible as you are,

22 I'll not insult your corpse should Zeus allow me
victory in the end, your life as prize.
305 Once I have your gear, I'll give your body
back to Achaeans. Grant me, too, this grace."

But swift Achilles frowned at him and said:

"Hector, I'll have no talk of pacts with you,
forever unforgiven as you are.
23 310 As between men and lions there are none,
no concord between wolves and sheep, but all
hold one another hateful through and through,
so there can be no courtesy between us,
no sworn truce, till one of us is down
315 and glutting with his blood the wargod Ares.
Summon up what skills you have. By god,
you'd better be a spearman and a fighter!
Now there is no way out. Pallas Athena
will have the upper hand of you. The weapon
320 belongs to me. You'll pay the reckoning
in full for all the pain my men have borne,
who met death by your spear."

                                        He twirled and cast
24 his shaft with its long shadow. Splendid Hector,
keeping his eye upon the point, eluded it
325 by ducking at the instant of the cast,
so shaft and bronze shank passed him overhead
and punched into the earth. But unperceived
by Hector, Pallas Athena plucked it out
and gave it back to Achilles. Hector said:

25 330 "A clean miss. Godlike as you are,
you have not yet known doom for me from Zeus.
You thought you had, by heaven. Then you turned
into a word-thrower, hoping to make me lose
my fighting heart and head in fear of you.
335 You cannot plant your spear between my shoulders
while I am running. If you have the gift,
just put it through my chest as I come forward.
Now it's for you to dodge my own. Would god
you'd give the whole shaft lodging in your body!

301. **arbiters:** judges.

 eluded (ē·lōōd′əd): evaded

22 GUIDED READING
Finding the Main Idea: What does Hector promise in lines 303–306, and what does he ask of Achilles? (to treat Achilles' corpse with respect if he is the victor; he asks the same of Achilles)

23 LITERARY ELEMENT
Epic Simile: To what pairs of creatures does Achilles compare himself and Hector in the epic simile that begins at line 310? (to men and lions and to wolves and sheep) What is Achilles' basic point in this simile? (that he and Hector are such bitter enemies that there can be no reconciliation between them) How do you respond to Achilles' refusal to make a pact with Hector? (Answers will vary.)

24 LITERARY ELEMENT
Epithet: The phrase "shaft with its long shadow," line 323, is a stock epithet for spears in Homer. What other epithets have you noticed in the *Iliad*? (Possible responses: "grayeyed Athena," "father of the stormclouds" for Zeus)

25 LITERARY ELEMENT
Irony: Why is the beginning of Hector's speech, lines 330–331, dramatically ironic? (Hector knows only that Achilles' spear thrust has missed. He does not know that Zeus has weighed his fate and his scale has sunk or that Athena has magically restored Achilles' spear to him.)

HUMANITIES CONNECTION

Rubens is noted for his excellent use of light in paintings done in the extravagant Baroque style. Born in Westphalia, a German province bordering on the Netherlands, he settled in Antwerp, Belgium, in 1609. He was called to Paris in 1622 to decorate the Luxembourg Palace for Marie de Médici, wife of Henry IV of France. Between 1621 and 1630, he served as a diplomat for the Hapsburg royal house. Rubens painted landscapes and portraits but is especially remembered for his historical and sacred subjects.
? *How does Rubens achieve a sense of action in this battle scene?* (The swirling robes and rounded forms, especially the shields, create a whirlwind effect.) ∎

26 INFERRING

Hector realizes that he has been tricked by a divinity when Deiphobus disappears. How might he know that it is specifically Athena who has tricked him? (from Achilles' reference in lines 318–319)

Giraudon/Art Resource, New York

HECTOR KILLED BY ACHILLES, PETER PAUL RUBENS (1577–1640).
? *How do Hector and Achilles differ as heroes? With which hero do you most identify? Why?*

340 War for the Trojans would be eased
if you were blotted out, bane° that you are."

341. **bane:** the cause of distress, death, or ruin.

With this he twirled his long spearshaft and cast it,
hitting his enemy mid-shield, but off
and away the spear rebounded. Furious
345 that he had lost it, made his throw for nothing,
Hector stood <u>bemused</u>. He had no other.
Then he gave a great shout to Deiphobus
to ask for a long spear. But there was no one
near him, not a soul. Now in his heart
350 the Trojan realized the truth and said:

26

"This is the end. The gods are calling deathward.
I had thought
a good soldier, Deiphobus, was with me.
He is inside the walls. Athena tricked me.
355 Death is near, and black, not at a distance,
not to be evaded. Long ago
this hour must have been to Zeus's liking
and to the liking of his archer son.°
They have been well disposed before, but now

358. **archer son:** Apollo.

27

360 the appointed time's upon me. Still, I would not
die without delivering a stroke,
or die ingloriously, but in some action
memorable to men in days to come."

With this he drew the whetted blade that hung
365 upon his left flank, ponderous and long,
collecting all his might the way an eagle
narrows himself to dive through shady cloud
and strike a lamb or cowering hare: so Hector
lanced ahead and swung his whetted blade.
370 Achilles with wild fury in his heart
pulled in upon his chest his beautiful shield—
his helmet with four burnished metal ridges
nodding above it, and the golden crest
Hephaestus° locked there tossing in the wind,

28

375 Conspicuous as the evening star that comes,
amid the first in heaven, at fall of night,
and stands most lovely in the west, so shone
in sunlight the fine-pointed spear
Achilles poised in his right hand, with deadly
380 aim at Hector, at the skin where most
it lay exposed. But nearly all was covered

29

by the bronze gear he took from slain Patroclus,
showing only, where his collarbones
divided neck and shoulders, the bare throat
385 where the destruction of a life is quickest.
Here, then, as the Trojan charged, Achilles
drove his point straight through the tender neck,
but did not cut the windpipe, leaving Hector
able to speak and to respond. He fell
390 aside into the dust. And Prince Achilles
now exulted:

30

"Hector, had you thought
that you could kill Patroclus and be safe?
Nothing to dread from me; I was not there.
All childishness. Though distant then, Patroclus's
395 comrade in arms was greater far than he—
and it is I who had been left behind
that day beside the deep-sea ships who now
have made your knees give way. The dogs and kites
will rip your body. His will lie in honor
400 when the Achaeans give him funeral."

374. **Hephaestus** (hē·fes'təs): the
blacksmith of the gods, who
forged new arms for Achilles
after Patroclus, wearing
Achilles' armor, was slain by
Hector.

27 CULTURAL BACKGROUND
Note the hero's wish not to
die without glory or fame. In
Homer, the *kleos*, or glory of
heroes, is the only defense
against death.

28 LITERARY ELEMENT
Epic Simile: What simile em-
bellishes the battle scene? (the
comparison of Achilles' spear
to the evening star) What earlier comparison does the simile echo? (the comparison of
Achilles to an evening star in
lines 31–37) What effect do
these comparisons of Achilles
and his weapons to the stars
create? (Achilles himself seems
like a force of nature; his
victory over Hector seems
inevitable.)

29 LITERARY ELEMENT
Theme: How does the mention of the armor worn by
Hector point up the theme of
revenge? (When Achilles sees
his own armor that he had lent
to Patroclus and that Hector
had stripped from Patroclus's
dead body, he can hardly fail
to remember that Hector killed
his best friend. This detail
therefore reinforces the theme
of anger and revenge.)

30 LITERARY ELEMENT
Epic Convention: It is an epic
convention for the victor to
make a "vaunting speech"
over the body of a defeated
warrior. Students can find examples in some of the "battle
books" of the unexcerpted
Iliad (Books 5, 11, 13, 16).

31 ANALYZING
Why does Hector beg to have his body returned to his parents? (Proper burial rites were extremely important to the ancient Greeks. They believed that a person whose corpse was not given proper rites could never attain peace.)

32 LITERARY ELEMENT
Foreshadowing: At the close of Book 16, the dying Patroclus predicts to Hector that Achilles will take revenge on Hector and slay him. How do Hector's words in lines 426–429 contain a parallel example of foreshadowing? (Like Patroclus, the defeated Hector warns his slayer of his own imminent death.)

33 LITERARY BACKGROUND
Homer alludes to the death of Achilles several times in the *Iliad*, as he does here and in lines 426–429, but the event takes place after the end of the epic. According to legend, the archer god, Apollo, aids Paris in shooting Achilles in the heel. Achilles' mother, the sea goddess Thetis, had protected him when he was an infant by dipping him in the magic waters of the river Styx. She had, however, held the boy by the heel, so this part of his body remained vulnerable. *Explain the expression ''Achilles' heel.''* (Refer students to pages 436–437 for more information on this and other classical eponyms.)

Hector, barely whispering, replied:

> "I beg you by your soul and by your parents,
> do not let the dogs feed on me
> in your encampment by the ships. Accept
405 the bronze and gold my father will provide
> as gifts, my father and her ladyship
> my mother. Let them have my body back,
> so that our men and women may accord me
> decency of fire when I am dead."

410 Achilles the great runner scowled and said:

> "Beg me no beggary by soul or parents,
> whining dog! Would god my passion drove me
> to slaughter you and eat you raw, you've caused
> such agony to me! No man exists
415 who could defend you from the carrion pack—
> not if they spread for me ten times your ransom,
> twenty times, and promise more as well;
> aye, not if Priam, son of Dardanus,
> tells them to buy you for your weight in gold!
420 You'll have no bed of death, nor will you be
> laid out and mourned by her who gave you birth.
> Dogs and birds will have you, every scrap."

Then at the point of death Lord Hector said:

> "I see you now for what you are. No chance
425 to win you over. Iron in your breast
> your heart is. Think a bit, though: this may be
> a thing the gods in anger hold against you
> on that day when Paris and Apollo
> destroy you at the Gates,° great as you are."

430 Even as he spoke, the end came, and death hid him;
spirit from body fluttered to undergloom,
bewailing fate that made him leave his youth
and manhood in the world. And as he died
Achilles spoke again. He said:

435 "Die, make an end. I shall accept my own
whenever Zeus and the other gods desire."
At this he pulled his spearhead from the body,
laying it aside, and stripped
the bloodstained shield and cuirass° from his shoulders.
440 Other Achaeans hastened round to see

428–429. **Paris . . . Gates:** Achilles is later slain by Paris, who shoots an arrow into Achilles' heel, the only part of his body that is vulnerable.

439. **cuirass** (kwi·ras'): armor protecting the breast and back.

Hector's fine body and his comely face,
and no one came who did not stab the body.
Glancing at one another they would say:

"Now Hector has turned vulnerable, softer
445 than when he put the torches to the ships!"

And he who said this would inflict a wound.
When the great master of pursuit, Achilles,
had the body stripped, he stood among them,
saying swiftly:

                              "Friends, my lords and captains
450 of Argives, now that the gods at last have let me
bring to earth this man who wrought
havoc among us—more than all the rest—
come, we'll offer battle around the city,
to learn the intentions of the Trojans now.
455 Will they give up their strongpoint° at this loss?   455. **strongpoint:** Troy.
Can they fight on, though Hector's dead?

                                        But wait:

why do I ponder, why take up these questions?
Down by the ships Patroclus's body lies
unwept, unburied. I shall not forget him

The funeral of Patroclus.
? *What effect does Patroclus's death have on
the events of the Trojan War?*

Alinari/Art Resource, New York

34 INTERPRETING
How do the details in lines
440–445 help to increase sympathy for Hector? (Possible response: Hector is praised for
his fine body and handsome
face; by contrast, the Greeks
who stab and insult him when
he is dead seem petty, heartless, and vengeful.)

MEETING INDIVIDUAL NEEDS

35 LEP: You may wish to define "wrought havoc" (caused
ruin and destruction) and to
point out that the idiom "offer
battle" means "make war." ∎

36 GUIDED READING
Finding the Main Idea: What
does Achilles suddenly remember in lines 458–459? (that
Patroclus's body is still
unburied)

HUMANITIES CONNECTION

This detail is from a krater
(krā'tər), a jar or bowl with a
large round body and a wide
mouth, used for aerating wine
or mixing it with water. Greek
artists often painted scenes on
the bottom and the inside of a
krater, as well as on the outside. The ceremonial funeral of
Patroclus is described in Book
23 of the *Iliad*, as mentioned in
the summary at the top of
p. 264. ∎

from the Iliad, Book 22   **259**

37 READER'S RESPONSE
How does this passage make you feel about Achilles? About Hector? (Possible responses: shock and disgust toward Achilles, pity for Hector)

38 COMPARING LITERATURE
The final destruction of Troy is narrated in detail by Virgil's epic hero, Aeneas, in Book 2 of the *Aeneid* (see pp. 402–406).
 What connection does this hint about Troy's coming doom establish between the death of Hector and the fate of the city of Troy? (Now that Hector, who was Troy's best warrior, is dead, the city's fate is sealed.)

> **defiled** (dē·fīld'): made filthy
>
> **scourge** (skʉrj): a cause of serious trouble or affliction
>
> **destitute** (des'tə·tōōt'): abandoned

39 LITERARY ELEMENT
Imagery: What metaphor does Priam use for Achilles here? (a scourge) What imagery does Priam use for his own dead sons? (flowers cut away in their youth)

HUMANITIES CONNECTION

In the "black-figure" style of pottery painting, silhouetted black figures were painted directly on the reddish-orange clay, and other designs were cut into the background.

460 while I can keep my feet among the living.
     If in the dead world they forget the dead,
     I say there, too, I shall remember him,
     my friend. Men of Achaea, lift a song!
     Down to the ships we go, and take this body,
465 our glory. We have beaten Hector down,
     to whom as to a god the Trojans prayed."

     Indeed, he had in mind for Hector's body
     outrage and shame. Behind both feet he pierced
     the tendons, heel to ankle. Rawhide cords
470 he drew through both and lashed them to his chariot,
     letting the man's head trail. Stepping aboard,
     bearing the great trophy of the arms,°
     he shook the reins, and whipped the team ahead
     into a willing run. A dustcloud rose
475 above the furrowing body; the dark tresses
     flowed behind, and the head so princely once
     lay back in dust. Zeus gave him to his enemies
     to be defiled in his own fatherland.
     So his whole head was blackened. Looking down,
480 his mother tore her braids, threw off her veil,
     and wailed, heartbroken to behold her son.
     Piteously his father groaned, and round him
     lamentation spread throughout the town,
     most like the clamor to be heard if Ilion's
485 towers, top to bottom, seethed in flames.
     They barely stayed the old man, mad with grief,
     from passing through the gates. Then in the mire
     he rolled, and begged them all, each man by name:
     "Relent, friends. It is hard; but let me go
490 out of the city to the Achaean ships.
     I'll make my plea to that demonic heart.
     He may feel shame before his peers, or pity
     my old age. His father, too, is old.
     Peleus, who brought him up to be a scourge
495 to Trojans, cruel to all, but most to me,
     so many of my sons in flower of youth
     he cut away. And, though I grieve, I cannot
     mourn them all as much as I do one,
     for whom my grief will take me to the grave—
500 and that is Hector. Why could he not have died
     where I might hold him? In our weeping, then,
     his mother, now so destitute, and I

472. **great trophy of the arms:** Hector's armor.

Dallas Museum of Art, Munger Fund

Black-figured panel amphora depicting dueling figures.

might have had surfeit° and relief of tears."

These were the words of Priam as he wept,
505 and all his people groaned. Then in her turn
Hecuba led the women in lamentation:

"Child, I am lost now. Can I bear my life
after the death of suffering your death?
You were my pride in all my nights and days,
510 pride of the city, pillar to the Trojans
and Trojan women. Everyone looked to you
as though you were a god, and rightly so.
You were their greatest glory while you lived.
Now your doom and death have come upon you."

515 These were her mournful words. But Hector's lady
still knew nothing; no one came to tell her
of Hector's stand outside the gates. She wove
upon her loom, deep in the lofty house,
a double purple web with rose design.
520 Calling her maids in waiting,
she ordered a big caldron on a tripod
set on the hearthfire, to provide a bath
for Hector when he came home from the fight.
Poor wife, how far removed from baths he was
525 she could not know, as at Achilles' hands
Athena brought him down.

                              Then from the tower
she heard a wailing and a distant moan.
Her knees shook, and she let her shuttle° fall,
and called out to her maids again:

                              "Come here.
530 Two must follow me, to see this action.
I heard my husband's queenly mother cry.
I feel my heart rise, throbbing in my throat.
My knees are like stone under me. Some blow
is coming home to Priam's sons and daughters.
535 Ah, could it never reach my ears! I die
of dread that Achilles may have cut off Hector,
blocked my bold husband from the city wall,
to drive him down the plain alone! By now
he may have ended Hector's deathly pride.
540 He never kept his place amid the chariots
but drove ahead. He would not be outdone
by anyone in courage."

503. **surfeit:** an excess of.

528. **shuttle:** as used here, an instrument that carries thread back and forth; used in the craft of weaving.

from the Iliad, Book 22   **261**

42 EVALUATING

Why do you think Homer had Andromache learn of her husband's death by seeing his body being dragged by Achilles' chariot? (It is the most dramatic way for her to learn the news, and her response reinforces the audience's sense of shock at Achilles' wrathful revenge.)

43 LITERARY ELEMENT

Flashback: What flashback do the details in line 553 about Andromache's band and veil introduce? (her wedding day) What does this flashback add to the narrative? (This brief vignette of her wedding day adds to the pathos and sympathy for Andromache, who has just been widowed.)

44 LITERARY BACKGROUND

Andromache's allusions in lines 555 and 565 to her father, Eetion, would have reminded Homer's audience that Achilles slew Eetion, as well as Andromache's seven brothers, and sacked their city. At that time, Achilles showed that he was capable of mercy, for he buried Eetion's body with proper funeral rites.

45 LITERARY BACKGROUND

Andromache's vivid predictions about the fate of her fatherless son may appeal to the audience's pity, but they are also ironic. After the sack of Troy, the victorious Greeks fear that Hector's son will one day take revenge, and so they throw him to his death from the city walls.

Saying this, she ran

42
545 like a madwoman through the megaron,°
her heart convulsed. Her maids kept at her side.
On reaching the great tower and the soldiers,
Andromache stood gazing from the wall
and saw him being dragged before the city.
Chariot horses at a brutal gallop
pulled the torn body toward the decked ships.

550 Blackness of night covered her eyes; she fell
backward swooning, sighing out her life,
and let her shining headdress fall, her hood

43
and diadem,° her plaited band and veil
that Aphrodite once had given her,
555 on that day when, from Eetion's house,
for a thousand bridal gifts, Lord Hector led her.

Now, at her side, kinswomen of her lord
supported her among them, dazed and faint
to the point of death. But when she breathed again
560 and her stunned heart recovered, in a burst
of sobbing she called out among the women:

"Hector! Here is my desolation. Both
had this in store from birth—from yours in Troy
in Priam's palace, mine by wooded Placus

44 565 at Thebe in the home of Eetion,
my father, who took care of me in childhood,
a man cursed by fate, a fated daughter.
How I could wish I never had been born!
Now under earth's roof to the house of Death
570 you go your way and leave me here, bereft,
lonely, in anguish without end. The child
we wretches had is still in infancy;
you cannot be a pillar to him, Hector,
now you are dead, nor he to you. And should
575 this boy escape the misery of the war,
there will be toil and sorrow for him later,
as when strangers move his boundary stones.

45
The day that orphans him will leave him lonely,
downcast in everything, cheeks wet with tears,
580 in hunger going to his father's friends
to tug at one man's cloak, another's chiton.°
Some will be kindly: one may lift a cup
to wet his lips at least, though not his throat;
but from the board some child with living parents

543. **megaron** (meg'ə·rän): the central hall of the house.

553. **diadem:** ornamental headband.

Albright-Knox Art Gallery, Buffalo, New York. Charles W. Goodyear Fund, 1933. Attributed to the "Athena Master"; Panathenaic Athena and two Heiropoioi, c. 500–485 B.C. White-ground terra cotta, 11¾" × 4⅛" × 2⅝".

Vase showing a black-figured Lekythos, c. 500–485 B.C. *This vase is attributed to the "Athena Master," an unknown Greek sculptor thought to be responsible for many surviving renderings of Athena.*

581. **chiton** (kī'tən): a tunic.

Greek coins, or drachmas (dräk´ mas),
depicting Aphrodite, c. 4th century B.C.

Lee Boltin Picture Library

HUMANITIES CONNECTION

Because ancient coins were struck by hand, they showed many individual variations. Common materials used include gold, silver, nickel, bronze, copper, and a combination of metals. Additional examples of ancient coins appear on pp. 375 and 376. ■

46 PREDICTING

Do you think Andromache is correct in assuming that Hector's body will never be given a proper burial? Explain your answer. (Possible responses: Yes, Achilles appears to be heartless and vengeful; no, the allusion in annotation 44 may foreshadow Achilles' decision to relent and ransom the body of Hector to Priam.)

585 gives him a push, a slap, with biting words:
  'Outside, you there! Your father is not with us
  here at our feast!' And the boy Astyanax
  will run to his forlorn mother. Once he fed
  on marrow only and the fat of lamb,
590 high on his father's knees. And when sleep came
  to end his play, he slept in a nurse's arms,
  brimful of happiness, in a soft bed.
  But now he'll know sad days and many of them,
  missing his father. 'Lord of the lower town'
595 the Trojans call him. They know, you alone,
  Lord Hector, kept their gates and their long walls.
  Beside the beaked ships now, far from your kin,
  the blowflies' maggots in a swarm will eat you
  naked, after the dogs have had their fill.
600 Ah, there are folded garments in your chambers,
  delicate and fine, of women's weaving.
  These, by heaven, I'll burn to the last thread
  in blazing fire! They are no good to you,
  they cannot cover you in death. So let them
605 go, let them be burnt as an offering
  from Trojans and their women in your honor."

  Thus she mourned, and the women wailed in answer.

46

47 CULTURAL BACKGROUND
In Greek mythology, Hermes was the messenger of the gods. He also escorted the souls of the dead to the underworld—a shadowy land where spirits were believed to remain after death. Given Hermes' mythological associations, why would the epithet "the Wayfinder" in line 3 be appropriate for him? (because as both a messenger and an escort he was responsible for finding the route or passage) What "way" did he "find" to allow Priam to enter the Greek camp? (He put the sentries to sleep and had the gates unbarred.)

48 LITERARY ELEMENT
Setting: What details contribute to the mysterious, somewhat ominous setting at the beginning of Book 24? (night, sentries at supper fire, "mist of slumber," magic unbarring of the gates, the emphasis on Achilles' nearly superhuman strength)

MEETING INDIVIDUAL NEEDS

49 LEP: To help students understand Hermes' speech (lines 21–30), read it aloud as students follow along in their texts. Then encourage partners to make sense of difficult passages by reading to each other. Stress the need to follow punctuation markings for pauses and run-on lines. ■

BOOK 24: Priam and Achilles

After he slays Hector in Book 22, Achilles prepares for Patroclus's ceremonial funeral. When the Greeks burn Patroclus's body, they also hold elaborate athletic contests, a custom in funeral services for distinguished men (Book 23).

As Book 24 opens, Achilles is still so enraged at Hector's killing of Patroclus that he refuses to give up Hector's body for burial. This is a particularly offensive form of revenge, for both the Greeks and Trojans believed that certain funeral rites were necessary before the soul of a dead person could find rest. Achilles' shameful treatment of Hector's body offends Zeus, and he finally orders Achilles to give up the body to Priam. The aged king, bowed with grief and bearing a rich ransom to exchange for his son's corpse, is escorted to the Greek camp by the god Hermes, who is disguised as a young man.

Greek vase depicting Achilles and Ajax playing dice.

Scala/Art Resource, New York

47

                          Now night had fallen,
bringing the sentries to their supper fire,
but the glimmering god Hermes, the Wayfinder,
showered a mist of slumber on them all.
5 As quick as thought, he had the gates unbarred
and open to let the wagon enter, bearing
the old king and the ransom.

                                Going seaward
they came to the lofty quarters of Achilles,
a lodge the Myrmidons built for their lord
10 of pine trees cut and trimmed, and shaggy thatch
from mowings in deep meadows. Posts were driven
round the wide courtyard in a palisade,
whose gate one crossbar held, one beam of pine.
It took three men to slam this home, and three

48

15 to draw the bolt again—but great Achilles
worked his entryway alone with ease.
And now Hermes, who lights the way for mortals,
opened for Priam, took him safely in
with all his rich gifts for the son of Peleus.

49

20 Then the god dropped the reins, and stepping down
he said:

                        "I am no mortal wagoner,
but Hermes, sir. My father° sent me here
to be your guide amid the Achaean men.

22. **father:** Zeus.

Now that is done, I'm off to heaven again
25 and will not visit Achilles. That would be
to compromise an immortal's dignity—
to be received with guests of mortal station.
Go take his knees, and make your supplication:
invoke his father, his mother, and his child;
30 pray that his heart be touched, that he be reconciled."

Now Hermes turned, departing for Olympus,
and Priam vaulted down. He left Idaeus°
to hold the teams in check, while he went forward
into the lodge. He found Achilles, dear
35 to Zeus, there in his chair, with officers
at ease across the room. Only Automedon°
and Alcimus° were busy near Achilles,
for he had just now made an end of dinner,
eating and drinking, and the laden boards
40 lay near him still upon the trestles.

                                          Priam,
the great king of Troy, passed by the others,
knelt down, took in his arms Achilles' knees,
and kissed the hands of wrath that killed his sons.

When, taken with mad Folly in his own land,
45 a man does murder and in exile finds
refuge in some rich house, then all who see him
stand in awe.
So these men stood.

                                    Achilles
gazed in wonder at the splendid king,
50 and his companions marveled too, all silent,
with glances to and fro. Now Priam prayed
to the man before him:

                              "Remember your own father,
Achilles, in your godlike youth: his years
like mine are many, and he stands upon
55 the fearful doorstep of old age. He, too,
is hard pressed, it may be, by those around him,
there being no one able to defend him
from bane of war and ruin. Ah, but he
may nonetheless hear news of you alive,
60 and so with glad heart hope through all his days
for sight of his dear son, come back from Troy,
while I have deathly fortune.

32. **Idaeus** (ī'dē'əs): the herald of the Trojans.

36. **Automedon** (ô·täm'ə·dän): Achilles' charioteer.
37. **Alcimus** (al·sī'məs): son of Ares, the god of war.

Alinari/Art Resource, New York

Vase with detail of Hermes.
Hermes—the messenger god as well as the god of travelers—is identified by the staff he carries and the wings on his feet.

50 CULTURAL BACKGROUND
By clasping another's knees, a suppliant visibly signaled weakness and need. This gesture, however, also conferred rights on the suppliant, since the Greeks believed it was an offense against Zeus to injure suppliants. Where else in the epic is there a reference to this practice? (Achilles asks his mother, Thetis, to grasp the knees of Zeus, Book 1, line 469, p. 243.)

51 GUIDED READING
Identifying Details: Which details in lines 41–43 show that Priam begs for Achilles' mercy? (Priam kneels, clasps Achilles' knees, and kisses the hands of the man who slew his sons.)

52 SUMMARIZING
In his speech in lines 52–63, what comparisons and contrasts does Priam point out between himself and Peleus, Achilles' father? (*Comparisons:* They are both old and defenseless. *Contrasts:* Peleus may yet live to welcome his son back from Troy, whereas most of Priam's sons have been killed.) What is the dramatic irony of lines 60–61? (The audience knows that Peleus's hope is vain, since Achilles is destined to die young at Troy.)

HUMANITIES CONNECTION

? *In this illustration, which item of Hermes' apparel suggests his service as a messenger of the gods?* (Possible response: winged sandals) ■

53 LITERARY ELEMENT
Characterization: What can you infer about Priam's character from lines 78–79? (Priam's love for his son is greater than his concern for his own life and greater than any wish for revenge upon Achilles.)

■ **evocation** (ēv·ō·kā′shən): drawing forth of a mental image

54 INTERPRETING
In line 86, what knowledge of his own destiny may cause Achilles to weep for his father? (knowing that he will die at Troy and thus bereave his father)

55 LITERARY ELEMENT
Resolution: Achilles' tears and his pity for Priam are an important turning point, marking the beginning of the resolution of the plot. What may be Homer's underlying theme in this scene of reconciliation? (Possible response: Human beings must transcend feelings of revenge and rage in order to recover their true humanity by sympathizing with others.)

HUMANITIES CONNECTION

❓ *How does this figure suggest the age and grief of Priam?* (The posture, hair, beard, and staff suggest age; the hand to the face suggests tears.) ■

52
                                             Noble sons
   I fathered here, but scarce one man is left me.
   Fifty I had when the Achaeans came,
65 nineteen out of a single belly, others
   born of attendant women. Most are gone.
   Raging Ares cut their knees from under them.
   And he who stood alone among them all,
   their champion, and Troy's, ten days ago
70 you killed him, fighting for his land, my prince,
   Hector.
                          It is for him that I have come
   among these ships, to beg him back from you,
   and I bring ransom without stint.°
                                        Achilles,

   be reverent toward the great gods! And take
75 pity on me, remember your own father.
   Think me more pitiful by far, since I
   have brought myself to do what no man else
53 has done before—to lift to my lips the hand
   of one who killed my son."

                                Now in Achilles
80 the evocation of his father stirred
   new longing, and an ache of grief. He lifted
   the old man's hand and gently put him by.
   Then both were overborne as they remembered:
   the old king huddled at Achilles' feet
85 wept, and wept for Hector, killer of men,
54 while great Achilles wept for his own father
   as for Patroclus once again; and sobbing
   filled the room.
                          But when Achilles' heart
   had known the luxury of tears, and pain
55 90 within his breast and bones had passed away,
   he stood then, raised the old king up, in pity
   for his gray head and graybeard cheek, and spoke
   in a warm rush of words:

                                "Ah, sad and old!
   Trouble and pain you've borne, and bear, aplenty.
95 Only a great will could have brought you here
   among the Achaean ships, and here alone
   before the eyes of one who stripped your sons,

73. **without stint:** unlimited, unrestricted.

Alinari/Art Resource, New Yo...

Detail of vase depicting Priam.

your many sons, in battle. Iron must be
the heart within you. Come, then, and sit down.
100 We'll probe our wounds no more but let them rest,
though grief lies heavy on us. Tears heal nothing,
drying so stiff and cold. This is the way
the gods ordained the destiny of men,
to bear such burdens in our lives, while they
105 feel no affliction. At the door of Zeus
are those two urns° of good and evil gifts
that he may choose for us; and one for whom
the lightning's joyous king dips in both urns
will have by turns bad luck and good. But one
110 to whom he sends all evil—that man goes
contemptible by the will of Zeus; ravenous
hunger drives him over the wondrous earth,
unresting, without honor from gods or men.
Mixed fortune came to Peleus. Shining gifts
115 at the gods' hands he had from birth: felicity,
wealth overflowing, rule of the Myrmidons,
a bride immortal at his mortal side.
But then Zeus gave afflictions too—no family
of powerful sons grew up for him at home,
120 but one child, of all seasons and of none.
Can I stand by him in his age? Far from my country
I sit at Troy to grieve you and your children.
You, too, sir, in time past were fortunate,
we hear men say. From Macar's isle of Lesbos
125 northward, and south of Phrygia and the Straits,°
no one had wealth like yours, or sons like yours.
Then gods out of the sky sent you this bitterness:
the years of siege, the battles and the losses.
Endure it, then. And do not mourn forever
130 for your dead son. There is no remedy.
You will not make him stand again. Rather
await some new misfortune to be suffered."

The old king in his majesty replied:

"Never give me a chair, my lord, while Hector
135 lies in your camp uncared for. Yield him to me
now. Allow me sight of him. Accept
the many gifts I bring. May they reward you,
and may you see your home again.
You spared my life at once and let me live."

106. **urns:** vases with feet or
pedestals.

125. **the Straits:** the Dardanelles,
narrow waterway between
the Aegean Sea and the Sea
of Marmara.

56 CULTURAL BACKGROUND
The Greeks believed their divinities were immortal and felt no burdens or afflictions. How does this belief heighten the poignancy of the scene? (The allusion to the gods' carefree state magnifies the human tragedy of the war.)

 felicity (fə·lis′i·tē): happiness

57 INTERPRETING
How does Achilles apply the parable of the two urns to Peleus? (Peleus's fortunes mixed great happiness and great sorrow.)

58 EVALUATING
From Achilles' parable about the two urns, what seems to be his philosophy of life? (that one's fortune, good, bad, or mixed, is determined by Zeus and must be accepted) What do you think of this philosophy? (Answers will vary. Many students will agree with Achilles; others may argue that his philosophy is too fatalistic.)

Scala/Art Resource, New York

Menelaus and the dead Patroclus.
❓ *Based on events in the* Iliad, *what can you infer about the Greek warrior code? What values were Greek warriors willing to die for? What actions did they consider dishonorable?*

140 Achilles, the great runner, frowned and eyed him
under his brows:

                "Do not vex me, sir," he said.
"I have intended, in my own good time,
to yield up Hector to you. She who bore me,°
the daughter of the Ancient of the sea,
145 has come with word to me from Zeus. I know
in your case, too—though you say nothing, Priam—
that some god guided you to the shipways here.
No strong man in his best days could make entry
into this camp. How could he pass the guard,
150 or force our gateway?

                    Therefore, *let me be.*
Sting my sore heart again, and even here,
under my own roof, suppliant though you are,
I may not spare you, sir, but trample on
the express command of Zeus!"

143. **She who bore me:** Thetis.

59

When he heard this,

155 the old man feared him and obeyed with silence.

Now like a lion at one bound Achilles
left the room. Close at his back the officers
Automedon and Alcimus went out—
comrades in arms whom he esteemed the most
160 after the dead Patroclus. They unharnessed
mules and horses, led the old king's crier
to a low bench and sat him down.
Then from the polished wagon
they took the piled-up price of Hector's body.
165 One chiton and two capes they left aside
as dress and shrouding for the homeward journey.
Then, calling to the women slaves, Achilles
ordered the body bathed and rubbed with oil—
but lifted, too, and placed apart, where Priam
170 could not see his son—for seeing Hector
he might in his great pain give way to rage,
and fury then might rise up in Achilles
to slay the old king, flouting Zeus's word.
So after bathing and anointing Hector
175 they drew the shirt and beautiful shrouding over him.
Then with his own hands lifting him, Achilles
laid him upon a couch, and with his two
companions aiding, placed him in the wagon.
Now a bitter groan burst from Achilles,
180 who stood and prayed to his own dead friend:

"Patroclus,

do not be angry with me, if somehow
even in the world of Death you learn of this—
that I released Prince Hector to his father.
The gifts he gave were not unworthy. Aye,
185 and you shall have your share, this time as well."

The Prince Achilles turned back to his quarters.
He took again the splendid chair that stood
against the farther wall, then looked at Priam
and made his declaration:

"As you wished, sir,

190 the body of your son is now set free.
He lies in state. At the first sight of Dawn
you shall take charge of him yourself and see him.
Now let us think of supper. We are told

---

60 LITERARY ELEMENT
Simile: This brief simile echoes other comparisons of Achilles to a lion: for example, Book 1, line 421, p. 242. How does this simile strengthen the idea that Achilles is to be feared? (The simile points up his savage force, great strength, swiftness, and dangerousness.)

61 LITERARY ELEMENT
Characterization: Why is Achilles careful not to let Priam see the body of Hector at this point? (Priam might become angry and provoke Achilles, who might in turn kill the old king in fury.) What light do these precautions shed on Achilles' character? (He knows his own nature well enough to guard against his anger.)

 flouting (flout'iŋ): mocking or scoffing at

62 LITERARY ELEMENT
Conflict: What internal conflict do lines 179–185 reveal in Achilles? (his wish to obey Zeus by ransoming Hector's body versus his grief for his friend Patroclus) How does Achilles try to resolve this conflict? (by asking Patroclus to forgive him and by promising him a share in the ransom)

63 COMPARING LITERATURE

Ancient Greek and Roman mythology contains many tales of the gods' cruel punishment of mortals who are bold enough to boast of their equality or superiority. Many of these tales were collected in *Metamorphoses* by the Roman poet Ovid (see pp. 420–427). For example, Athena punishes the weaver Arachne, who had boasted of her craftsmanship at the loom, by turning her into a spider. Apollo, jealous of the musician Marsyas for his skill in flute-playing, has him flayed alive. Interested students might read these stories, as well as Ovid's account of the myth of Niobe in Book 6 of *Metamorphoses*.

64 ANALYZING

The narrative resumes after the digression on Niobe, with line 213 ("Like her we'll think of supper") echoing line 193 ("Now let us think of supper"). How does Achilles apply the tale of Niobe to the present situation between himself and Priam? (Like Niobe, Achilles and Priam have suffered great grief, but they must go on living.)

broods (broōodz): contemplates in a troubled way

63

that even Niobe in her extremity
195   took thought for bread—though all her brood had perished,
her six young girls and six tall sons. Apollo,
making his silver longbow whip and sing,
shot the lads down, and Artemis with raining
arrows killed the daughters—all this after
200   Niobe had compared herself with Leto,
the smooth-cheeked goddess.
                              She has borne two children,
Niobe said, How many have I borne!
But soon those two destroyed the twelve.
                                          Besides,
nine days the dead lay stark, no one could bury them,
205   for Zeus had turned all folk of theirs to stone.
The gods made graves for them on the tenth day,
and then at last, being weak and spent with weeping,
Niobe thought of food. Among the rocks
of Sipylus' lonely mountainside, where nymphs
210   who race Achelous's° river go to rest,
she, too, long turned to stone, somewhere broods on
the gall immortal gods gave her to drink.°

64

Like her we'll think of supper, noble sir.
Weep for your son again when you have borne him
215   back to Troy; there he'll be mourned indeed."
In one swift movement now Achilles caught
and slaughtered a white lamb. His officers
flayed it, skillful in their butchering
to dress the flesh; they cut bits for the skewers,
220   roasted, and drew them off, done to a turn.
Automedon dealt loaves into the baskets
on the great board; Achilles served the meat.
Then all their hands went out upon the supper.
When thirst and appetite were turned away,
225   Priam, the heir of Dardanos, gazed long
in wonder at Achilles' form and scale—
so like the gods in aspect. And Achilles
in his turn gazed in wonder upon Priam,
royal in visage° as in speech. Both men
230   in contemplation found rest for their eyes,
till the old hero, Priam, broke the silence:

"Make a bed ready for me, son of Thetis,
and let us know the luxury of sleep.

210. **Achelous** (ə·kel′ō·əs): a river god.

194–212. **Niobe** (nī′ō·bə′) . . . **drink:** a woman whose children were killed by the goddess Artemis and the god Apollo because she boasted of her superiority to their mother, Leto; Niobe was then turned into a pillar of stone, from which her tears are still said to flow. This pillar of stone is on a mountain called Sipylus (si′pil·əs) in Asia Minor.

229. **visage:** face, expression.

From that hour when my son died at your hands
235 till now, my eyelids have not closed in slumber
over my eyes, but groaning where I sat
I tasted pain and grief a thousandfold,
or lay down rolling in my courtyard mire.
Here for the first time I have swallowed bread
240 and made myself drink wine.
                        Before, I could not."

Achilles ordered men and serving women
to make a bed outside, in the covered forecourt,
with purple rugs piled up and sheets outspread
and coverings of fleeces laid on top.
245 The girls went out with torches in their hands
and soon deftly made up a double bed.
Then Achilles, defiant of Agamemnon,
told his guest:

                        "Dear venerable sir,
you'll sleep outside tonight, in case an Achaean
250 officer turns up, one of those men
who are forever taking counsel with me—
as well they may. If one should see you here
as the dark night runs on, he would report it
to the Lord Marshal Agamemnon. Then
255 return of the body would only be delayed.
Now tell me this, and give me a straight answer:
How many days do you require
for the funeral of Prince Hector?—I should know
how long to wait, and hold the Achaean army."

260 Old Priam in his majesty replied:

"If you would have me carry out the burial,
Achilles, here is the way to do me grace.
As we are penned in the town, but must bring wood
from the distant hills, the Trojans are afraid.
265 We should have mourning for nine days in hall,
then on the tenth conduct his funeral
and feast the troops and commons;
on the eleventh we should make his tomb,
and on the twelfth give battle, if we must."

270 Achilles said:

                        "As you command, old Priam,

from the Iliad, Book 24 271

65 LITERARY ELEMENT
Theme: Priam, like Achilles, has denied himself human sustenance because of his grief. How might their dining together stress the theme of reconciliation and healing? (Sharing a meal shows the two men transcending their rage and grief and displaying sympathy for each other.)

deftly (deft'lē): in a skilled, sure manner

66 PREDICTING
In lines 252–255, do you think Achilles is justified in implying that Agamemnon might cause trouble, or does this remark simply reflect Achilles' resentment of Agamemnon? (Answers will vary.)

Michel Colombe (c. 1430–c. 1512) was a French sculptor especially noted for the tomb he designed for Duke Francis II of Brittany and his wife, Marguerite, in the cathedral at Nantes.

? *What is striking about this depiction of a scene from the* Iliad? (The characters and setting are medieval; no attempt is made to re-create an ancient Greek setting.) ■

67 LITERARY ELEMENT

Symbol: A symbol is a person, place, thing, or event that stands for itself and for something beyond itself as well. What might the action in these two lines symbolize? (Achilles' action seems to be a sealing of his promise. It may also symbolize reconciliation between former enemies and the healing of intense grief on both sides.)

■ allay (a·lā′): put to rest

68 LITERARY BACKGROUND

Agamemnon restored Briseis to Achilles in Book 19, along with many other gifts, as compensation for the Greek leader's insults to Achilles in the quarrel of Book 1.

Giraudon/Art Resource, New York

PRIAM BEFORE HECTOR'S TOMB IN THE TEMPLE OF APOLLO, **from the studio of Colombe, c. 1500.** *This scene is a medieval rendering of the story of Troy.*

the thing is done. I shall suspend the war
for those eleven days that you require."
67 He took the old man's right hand by the wrist
and held it, to <u>allay</u> his fear.

Now crier
275 and king with hearts brimful retired to rest
in the sheltered forecourt, while Achilles slept
deep in his palisaded lodge. Beside him,
68 lovely in her youth, Briseis° lay.
And other gods and soldiers all night long,
280 by slumber quieted, slept on. But slumber
would not come to Hermes the Good Companion,
as he considered how to ease the way
for Priam from the camp, to send him through
unseen by the formidable gatekeepers.
285 Then Hermes came to Priam's pillow, saying:

278. **Briseis:** In order to appease Achilles, Agamemnon had had Briseis returned to him.

"Sir, no thought of danger shakes your rest,
as you sleep on, being great Achilles' guest,
amid men fierce as hunters in a ring.
You triumphed in a costly ransoming,
290 but three times costlier your own would be
to your surviving sons—a monarch's fee—
if this should come to Agamemnon's ear
and all the Achaean host should learn that you are here."

The old king started up in fright, and woke
295 his herald. Hermes yoked the mules and horses,
took the reins, then inland like the wind
he drove through all the encampment, seen by no one.
When they reached Xanthus,° eddying and running
god-begotten river, at the ford,
300 Hermes departed for Olympus. Dawn
spread out her yellow robe on all the earth,
as they drove on toward Troy, with groans and sighs,
and the mule-team pulled the wagon and the body.
And no one saw them, not a man or woman,
305 before Cassandra.° Tall as the pale-gold
goddess Aphrodite, she had climbed
the citadel of Pergamus° at dawn.
Now looking down she saw her father come
in his war-car, and saw the crier there,
310 and saw Lord Hector on his bed of death
upon the mulecart. The girl wailed and cried
to all the city:

                           "Oh, look down, look down,
go to your windows, men of Troy, and women,
see Lord Hector now! Remember joy
315 at seeing him return alive from battle,
exalting all our city and our land!"

Now, at the sight of Hector, all gave way
to loss and longing, and all crowded down
to meet the escort and body near the gates,
320 till no one in the town was left at home.
There Hector's lady and his gentle mother
tore their hair for him, flinging themselves
upon the wagon to embrace his person
while the crowd groaned. All that long day
325 until the sun went down they might have mourned
in tears before the gateway. But old Priam

298. **Xanthus** (zan´thəs): also called *Scamander*.

305. **Cassandra** (kə·san´drə): a daughter of Priam and Hecuba; in Greek mythology, Apollo gives her the gift of prophecy, but when she rejects his advances, he decrees that no one will believe her predictions. She figures more prominently in other versions of the Trojan War legend, such as in Euripides' drama *The Trojan Women*.
307. **Pergamus** (pur´gə·məs): the citadel, or fortress, of Troy.

69 LITERARY BACKGROUND

In the Homeric epics, divinities frequently appear to mortals in dreams. Sometimes, as in this passage, the god appears to warn a mortal to take specific action. Why does Hermes advise Priam to leave the Greek camp secretly? (to avoid being captured by the Greek troops and held for ransom) How were Hermes' words foreshadowed by Achilles'? (In lines 252–255, Achilles warns that if Agamemnon were to learn of Priam's presence in the camp, the return of Hector's body would be delayed.)

70 COMPARING LITERATURE

The Trojan princess Cassandra plays a minor role in the *Iliad*, yet she is a fascinating figure. For her portrayal by Virgil in the *Aeneid*, see Book 2, line 131 (p. 388) and line 292 (p. 392). After the Trojan War, Agamemnon brings Cassandra back to his palace at Mycenae as a concubine. They are murdered by Agamemnon's wife, Clytemnestra, and her lover, Aegisthus. These postwar strands of the legend are dramatized by Aeschylus in his tragedy *Agamemnon*.

MEETING INDIVIDUAL NEEDS

71 *LEP:* You may wish to explain that in line 321 "Hector's lady" refers to his wife, Andromache; his "gentle mother" is Hecuba. ■

73 **Literary Element**
Foreshadowing: This is Andromache's second long speech foreshadowing misery for herself and her son. When did she make a similar speech? (in Book 22, when she realized that Achilles had slain Hector; see lines 562–606 on pp. 262–263) What new details about the fate of her son does Andromache add in this speech? (She predicts that an angry Greek soldier may hurl the child to his death from a tower of the city as revenge for a relative slain by Hector.)

spoke to them from his chariot:

"Make way,
let the mules pass. You'll have your fill of weeping
later, when I've brought the body home."

330 They parted then, and made way for the wagon,
allowing Priam to reach the famous hall.
They laid the body of Hector in his bed,

72   and brought in minstrels, men to lead the dirge.°   333. **dirge:** funeral hymn.
While these wailed out, the women answered, moaning.

335 Andromache of the ivory-white arms
held in her lap between her hands
the head of Hector who had killed so many.
Now she lamented:

"You've been torn from life,
my husband, in young manhood, and you leave me

340 empty in our hall. The boy's a child
whom you and I, poor souls, conceived; I doubt
he'll come to manhood. Long before, great Troy
will go down plundered, citadel and all,
now that you are lost, who guarded it

345 and kept it, and preserved its wives and children.
They will be shipped off in the murmuring hulls
one day, and I along with all the rest.

73   You, my little one, either you come with me
to do some grinding labor, some base toil

350 for a harsh master, or an Achaean soldier
will grip you by the arm and hurl you down
from a tower° here to a miserable death—   351–352. **hurl you down from a tower:** Indeed, after the fall
out of his anger for a brother, a father,   of Troy, Astyanax *was* thrown
or even a son that Hector killed. Achaeans   by the Greek conquerors
from the walls of the city.

355 in hundreds mouthed black dust under his blows.
He was no moderate man in war, your father,
and that is why they mourn him through the city.
Hector, you gave your parents grief and pain
but left me loneliest, and heartbroken.

360 You could not open your strong arms to me
from your deathbed, or say a thoughtful word,
for me to cherish all my life long
as I weep for you night and day."

Her voice broke,
and a wail came from the women. Hecuba

365 lifted her lamenting voice among them:

"Hector, dearest of sons to me, in life
you had the favor of the immortal gods,
and they have cared for you in death as well.
Achilles captured other sons of mine
370 in other years, and sold them overseas
to Samos, Imbros, and the smoky island,
Lemnos.° That was not his way with you.
After he took your life, cutting you down
with his sharp-bladed spear, he trussed and dragged you
375 many times round the barrow° of his friend,
Patroclus, whom you killed—though not by this
could that friend live again. But now I find you
fresh as pale dew, seeming newly dead,
like one to whom Apollo of the silver bow
380 had given easy death with his mild arrows."

Hecuba sobbed again, and the wails redoubled.
Then it was Helen's turn to make lament:

"Dear Hector, dearest brother to me by far!
My husband is Alexandros,
385 who brought me here to Troy—God, that I might
have died sooner! This is the twentieth year
since I left home, and left my fatherland.
But never did I have an evil word
or gesture from you. No—and when some other
390 brother-in-law or sister would revile me,
or if my mother-in-law spoke to me bitterly—
but Priam never did, being as mild
as my own father—you would bring her round
with your kind heart and gentle speech. Therefore
395 I weep for you and for myself as well,
given this fate, this grief. In all wide Troy
no one is left who will befriend me, none;
they all shudder at me."

                                    Helen wept,
and a moan came from the people, hearing her.
400 Then Priam, the old king, commanded them:

"Trojans, bring firewood to the edge of town.
No need to fear an ambush of the Argives.
When he dismissed me from the camp, Achilles
told me clearly they will not harass us,
405 not until dawn comes for the twelfth day."

371–372. **Samos** (sā'mäs), **Imbros** (im'bräs) . . . **Lemnos** (lem'näs): islands in the Aegean Sea.

375. **barrow:** a mound of earth and stones built over a grave.

74 GUIDED READING
Finding the Main Idea: According to Hecuba, what favor have the gods shown to the body of Hector? (They have restored the mangled body to good condition.)

redoubled (rē·dub'əld): became twice as great

revile (ri·vīl'): use abusive language about

75 ANALYZING
Consider the position of Helen of Troy as the woman whose elopement with (or kidnapping by) the Trojan prince Paris served as the immediate cause of the Trojan War. Why would many members of Priam's family treat Helen badly? (because her marriage to Paris had brought war and suffering to Troy)

1. Why is Achilles angry at Apollo at the opening of Book 22? (Apollo has tricked him by using a disguise.)
2. Who urges Hector not to fight? (Priam and Hecuba)
3. Which divinity aids Achilles? (Athena)
4. How does Achilles defile Hector's corpse? (He drags it behind his chariot.)
5. Who learns last of Hector's fate? (his wife)

6. Why does Priam journey to Achilles' tent? (to ransom his son's body)
7. In Achilles' story, what do the urns contain? (good and evil gifts)
8. What does Hermes advise Priam to do? (leave the Greek camp secretly)
9. Who first sees Priam returning? (Cassandra)
10. Why does Andromache think her son may be killed? (to avenge a Greek)

RETEACHING

To reteach Homer's *Iliad*, divide students into pairs. Ask each pair of students to choose from the selection a speech of 15–30 lines that they think is especially moving or eloquent. Have partners rehearse and critique each other's oral interpretations of their speeches, and then have them perform the speeches for the class.

---

shrouding (shroud'iŋ): hiding, covering

quarter (kwôrt'ər): district or neighborhood

WRITING TO LEARN

Social Studies: Using what you have learned from the *Iliad* about the structure and values of the Homeric world, write some letters home from the point of view of a common soldier in Achilles' troops, the Myrmidons. Your letters might describe and comment on the quarrel between Achilles and Agamemnon, Achilles' grief at the death of Patroclus, the news that Achilles has slain Hector, or the reconciliation of Priam and Achilles in Book 24. ■

ANSWERS
First Thoughts
Answers will vary.

Identifying Facts
1. to withdraw from battle
2. to take cover and to negotiate
3. by impersonating Deiphobus. Hector is fated to die.
4. not to dishonor his body. Achilles spurns his plea.
5. to ransom the body to Priam

Then yoking mules and oxen to their wagons
the people thronged before the city gates.
Nine days they labored, bringing countless loads
of firewood to the town. When Dawn that lights
410 the world of mortals came for the tenth day,
they carried greathearted Hector out at last,
and all in tears placed his dead body high
upon its pyre, then cast a torch below.
When the young Dawn with finger tips of rose
415 made heaven bright, the Trojan people massed
about Prince Hector's ritual fire.
All being gathered and assembled, first
they quenched the smoking pyre with tawny wine
wherever flames had licked their way, then friends
420 and brothers picked his white bones from the char
in sorrow, while the tears rolled down their cheeks.
In a golden urn they put the bones,
shrouding the urn with veiling of soft purple.
Then in a grave dug deep they placed it
425 and heaped it with great stones. The men were quick
to raise the death-mound, while in every quarter
lookouts were posted to ensure against
an Achaean surprise attack. When they had finished
raising the barrow, they returned to Ilion,
430 where all sat down to banquet in his honor
in the hall of Priam king. So they performed
the funeral rites of Hector, tamer of horses.

Helen and Priam. *The abduction of the Greek Helen by the Trojan Paris eventually led to the deaths of his brother Hector and his father Priam by the vengeful Greek forces.*

First Thoughts
How did you feel about Achilles' behavior toward Hector and Priam in these two books?

Identifying Facts
1. What advice do Priam and Hecuba give to Hector as he stands outside the walls of the city?
2. In lines 119–156 of Book 22, what courses of action does Hector consider and reject before fighting Achilles?
3. How does Athena deceive Hector? Why is Zeus unable to save Hector?
4. What is Hector's dying request, and how does Achilles respond to it?
5. What does Achilles agree to do to allow Hector a proper burial?

Interpreting Meanings
1. The meeting of Hector and Achilles in Book 22 is the dramatic **climax** of the *Iliad.* At this climactic confrontation, Hector trembles and then runs away. How does Homer prepare you for Hector's flight by his revelation of the Trojan's thoughts and by his description of Achilles' advance? Does Hector's action

1. Discussing Theme. Homer's concern is the interrelationship between *moira*, or fate, and a person's character. Ask students: Do you feel that Hector was doomed by his noble character, by fate, or by both? (By choosing to confront Achilles, Hector contributes to his own death. On the other hand, "gray-eyed Athena" says that Hector's doom was "fixed long ago.")

2. Research Project. Invite students to explore how Homer's *Iliad* has been translated through the ages. Encourage them to read excerpts from other great translations of Homer into English, such as the versions by George Chapman, Alexander Pope, and Richmond Lattimore. Have students present their comparative analyses of these translations in an oral report, in which they read and compare translations aloud.

CLOSURE

During World War II, the French critic Simone Weil wrote a famous essay on the *Iliad*, referring to Homer's epic as "the poem of might." Ask the class, "Do you agree that this is an appropriate subtitle for the *Iliad*? Can you suggest a subtitle that would be more suitable?" Use the discussion as a springboard into what the *Iliad* may mean to us today. ■

---

diminish your respect for him, or could you sympathize with his reaction? Explain your response.

2. An **epic simile** is an extended simile in which an event of epic proportions is compared to something from everyday life that would be familiar to the audience. Reread the description in Book 22 of the duel between Achilles and Hector, and identify all the epic similes Homer uses to describe their final clash.

3. What new aspects of Achilles' character are revealed by the scene with Priam in Book 24? How would your perception of Achilles have been affected if the *Iliad* had ended with Hector's death in Book 22?

4. Consider the role of the Olympian gods and goddesses in the *Iliad* as a whole. List at least three incidents in the epic in which the Olympians direct or influence events. Do you think the mortal characters in the epic are puppets manipulated by the Olympians, or do they exercise freedom of choice or action? Give reasons for your answer.

5. Some critics see the central **theme** of the *Iliad* as concerned with the idea that people must exercise generosity with one another—that if people behaved with reason, they might be able to live together in peace and harmony. Which portions of the epic support this view of the theme? Do you agree that it is a central theme of the work? Why or why not?

Applying Meanings

The *Iliad* is primarily a war epic. In your view, is the *Iliad* a condemnation of the brutality of war, a celebration of the heroism that war can inspire, or an evenly developed examination of both of these aspects? Justify your answer.

Creative Writing Response

Writing a Screenplay. One of the most enjoyable aspects of the *Iliad* is its vivid portrayal of character and action. Select one of the scenes you have read from Homer's *Iliad*, and write a screenplay for a film version of the scene. Your script should include not only dialogue but also notes on costumes, casting choices, and special effects that you think would contribute to an effective film version of the scene. Experiment with different settings in place and time. For example, you might set your film during World War II, the Vietnam War, or even imagine a similar conflict between aliens on another planet.

Critical Writing Response

Comparing and Contrasting Heroes. Consider Achilles and Hector as ideals of the hero in ancient Greece. What special qualities does each hero exhibit? In what ways do they mirror one another? Are their limitations and weaknesses the same, or are they different? Is one more "human" than the other? Write a brief essay in which you compare and contrast Achilles and Hector as heroes. Cite evidence from the epic to support your findings. You may use a chart like the one below to organize your ideas.

	Achilles	Hector
Similarities		
Differences		
Strengths		
Weaknesses		

Interpreting Meanings

1. Possible response: Hector wavers, but Achilles advances steadily. Answers will vary.
2. Achilles like a racehorse (Book 22, line 27) and like a star (line 31); Achilles and Hector like hawk and dove (lines 167–168); the runners like chariot-teams (line 193); Achilles and Hector like hound and fawn (lines 223–224); the chase like a pursuit in a dream (line 235); the opponents like men and lions or wolves and sheep (lines 310–311); Hector and Achilles like eagle and lamb (lines 366–368); Achilles' spear like a star (line 375)
3. magnanimity and compassion. Achilles would have seemed totally dominated by revenge.
4. Possible responses: Apollo's plague, Thetis's intervention with Zeus, Apollo and Athena on the battlefield, Hermes in Book 24. Answers will vary.
5. Answers will vary.

Applying Meanings
Answers will vary.

Creative Writing Response
Writing a Screenplay. Students may include sound effects and music.

Critical Writing Response
Comparing and Contrasting Heroes. Essays might focus on the two heroes as portrayed in Book 22. ■

THE ART OF TRANSLATION

A Recent Translation of Homer's Iliad

There are many English translations of Homer's Iliad, *both in prose and in verse. Below is an excerpt from Book 22 of Robert Fagles's recent translation of the* Iliad. *Read the lines of verse below; then, on page 251, reread lines 157 through 173 of the Fitzgerald translation.*

                So he wavered,
waiting there, but Achilles was closing on
  him now
like the god of war, the fighter's helmet
  flashing,
over his right shoulder shaking the Pelian
  ash spear,
that terror, and the bronze around his
  body flared
like a raging fire of the rising, blazing sun.
Hector looked up, saw him, started to
  tremble,
nerve gone, he could hold his ground no
  longer,
he left the gates behind and away he fled
  in fear—
and Achilles went for him, fast, sure of his
  speed

as the wild mountain hawk, the quickest
  thing on wings,
launching smoothly, swooping down on a
  cringing dove
and the dove flits out from under, the
  hawk screaming
over the quarry, plunging over and over,
  his fury
driving him down to break and tear his
  kill—
so Achilles flew at him, breakneck on in
  fury
with Hector fleeing along the walls of Troy,
fast as his legs would go.

What different images does each translator emphasize in showing Hector's fear, Achilles' wrath and determination, and the speed with which Hector flees? What are the differences in the way each translator handles the epic simile that compares Achilles' pursuit of Hector to a hawk hunting its prey? Which version do you prefer? Why?

Sappho
Early Sixth Century B.C.

Lee Boltin Picture Library

Sappho (saf′ō) was born on the Greek island of Lesbos toward the end of the seventh century B.C. She wrote nine books of lyric verse—more than five hundred poems—but only a few fragments survive. Nevertheless, she is still considered a supreme Greek lyric poet of this period. In fact, Plato admiringly dubbed her "the tenth Muse":

Some say nine Muses—but count again.
Behold the tenth: Sappho of Lesbos.

This remark is fitting because the Muses, or spirits of poetic inspiration, like Sappho, were women, and because few Greek poets, male or female, achieved Sappho's stature.

Most scholars believe that Sappho was an educated woman who at some point in her life was exiled to Sicily. She may have returned to Lesbos to become the head of a group of priestesses who worshiped Aphrodite. We know that Sappho married and had a daughter, Cleis (klā′əs). Sappho's love for her daughter is the subject of some of her most moving lyric poems. According to one legend, Sappho killed herself for the love of a ferryman by throwing herself from a cliff. Another source, however, suggests that she died of old age in her bed, tended by her daughter.

Sappho composed most of her poems in a style called *monody*—that is, the poems were meant to be sung by a single voice, rather than by a chorus. Although it is clear that Sappho wrote for public occasions such as marriage ceremonies, most of her verse is intensely private and personal. In most of the poems that survive, Sappho speaks to the women who were her companions and friends.

Sappho's poetry exists today in fragmentary form. Many of these fragments were found on papyrus strips carelessly thrown away or wadded up into the mummified bodies of crocodiles. In many cases, all that remains of an original poem is two or three lines. In addition, the poems were copied, recopied, and translated by many different people over the centuries. Nevertheless, the genius of Sappho's poetic expression shines brightly in a handful of glittering fragments.

MORE ABOUT THE AUTHOR
According to a biography of Sappho that was compiled in medieval times, the poet's parents were wealthy aristocrats named Scamandronymus and Cleis. Sappho apparently named her own beloved daughter for her mother. In her lyric "Don't Ask Me What to Wear" (p. 282), she links the three generations of her family. In another lyric, "Tonight I've Watched" (p. 282), Sappho laments the passing of her youth, suggesting that she may have lived well into middle age. After her death, her poetry was read and admired throughout the ancient world, especially by the Roman poets Catullus, Ovid, and Horace. Unfortunately, by the Middle Ages, her work had fallen out of favor and the Church ordered all her manuscripts burned. It was not until the late 1800s that fragments of her poems turned up stuffed into mummified crocodiles at an archaeological dig in Egypt.

ABOUT THE TRANSLATOR
Mary Barnard, born in Vancouver, Washington, is the author of *A Few Poems* (1952) and *The Mythmakers* (1967), as well as a contributor to *Five Young American Poets* (1940). She has done social work and has also served as the curator of the poetry collection at the Lockwood Memorial Library of Buffalo, New York. Barnard received the Levinson Award of *Poetry* magazine in 1935. Her *Sappho: A New Translation* was published by the University of California Press in 1958.

OBJECTIVES

1. *To recognize the characteristics of Greek lyric poetry in the work of Sappho*
2. *To identify and analyze the use of imagery in lyric poetry*
3. *To write a brief lyric poem and to write an essay comparing a twentieth-century poem with the lyrics of Sappho*

PREREADING FOCUS

Background: Emotional intensity was common to all Greek lyric poetry. It is because of this emotional content that lyric poems are usually written in the first person, where the speaker, "I," tells of his or her feelings. In composing their lyrics, Sappho and the other Greek poets used a wide variety of meters, whose complex rhythms cannot be accurately conveyed in an English translation. Some of the Roman poets—notably Catullus (see pp. 409–413) and Horace (see pp. 414–418)—however, adapted Greek lyric meters for their verse in Latin. Horace composed his ode "The Golden Mean," for example, in the Sapphic meter—a measure named especially for Sappho because she used it with such frequency and skill.

Writer's Response: Before writing, students should be encouraged to visualize each of the people they care about most. This may help them focus their feelings and think of words that express these feelings vividly and concretely.

Literary Focus: Remind students that sensory imagery appeals to one or more of the five senses: sight, hearing, taste, touch, and smell. Imagery often plays a part in figures of speech, such as similes, metaphors, and personification. Ask students to watch for how Sappho uses such figures of speech in her lyrics.

Reader's Guide

SAPPHO'S LYRIC POEMS

Background

Greek lyric verse resulted from a move away from the epic tradition to a poetry that expressed more intimate and personal themes. The word *lyric* is derived from *lyre*, the stringed instrument on which poets, including Sappho, accompanied themselves. These poet/singers addressed a variety of themes and topics. Some other prominent masters of Greek lyric poetry included Archilochus (är·kil'ə·kəs), Alcaeus (al·sē'əs), Simonides (sī·män'ə·dēz'), and Pindar, all of whom flourished from the seventh to the fifth centuries B.C.

The speaker of a lyric poem is not always the poet but a **persona**, or character whose voice and concerns do not necessarily reflect those of the poet. For example, the speaker in "Don't Ask Me What to Wear" may be Sappho herself speaking to her daughter Cleis, but the speaker in "To an Army Wife, in Sardis" is clearly an army officer stationed far from home.

Writer's Response

Lyric poets often write to express their feelings about the people closest to them. Think about the people you care most about, and jot down one or two words that express your feelings about each person.

Literary Focus

The power of **lyric poetry** lies in its immediacy and its ability to quickly and fully describe a strong emotion. This is done through the first-person speaker, the "I" telling the poem, and through the use of sensory **imagery**—that is, images that appeal to the senses and trigger memories and emotional responses. For instance, the purple ribbon in "Don't Ask Me What to Wear" evokes for the speaker memories of her mother and of her youth. The reader is invited to share the speaker's wistfulness, if not her memories.

LYRIC POEMS
Sappho
translated by
MARY BARNARD

❚❚ *As you read the following lyrics, note how the poet uses*
❚❚ *simple words and strong, vivid images.*

You Are the Herdsman of Evening

1

You are the herdsman of evening

Hesperus,[1] you herd
homeward whatever
Dawn's light dispersed

You herd sheep—herd
goats—herd children
home to their mothers

Sleep, Darling

Sleep, darling

2

I have a small
daughter called
Cleis,[2] who is

like a golden
flower

    I wouldn't
take all Croesus'[3]
kingdom with love
thrown in, for her

PARNASSUS, RAPHAEL (1483–1520). *Detail depicting Sappho.*

We Drink Your Health

We drink your health

Lucky bridegroom!
Now the wedding you
asked for is over

5

and your wife is the
girl you asked for;
she's a bride who is

---

1. **Hesperus** (hes′pər·əs): the evening star.
2. **Cleis** (klā′əs)
3. **Croesus** (krē′səs): Lydian king famous for his great wealth.

1 LITERARY ELEMENT
Personification: What human ability does the poet give the evening star? (the ability to lead or tend a herd) What image does this create? (Possible response: children being watched over as they return home)

2 LITERARY ELEMENT
Simile: To what is the daughter compared, and what does this suggest about her? (to "a golden flower"; that she has blonde hair and is as sweet, pretty, and fragile as a flower) What other image in the poem might echo the golden color as it points up Cleis's value? ("Croesus' kingdom" suggests gold and reveals her value.)

HUMANITIES CONNECTION

This detail from Raphael's *Parnassus* shows Sappho holding a lyre in her right hand. In her upraised left hand she holds a scroll identifying her as a poet. ❓ *Why is a lyre as appropriate as a scroll to represent the poet Sappho?* (Greek poets accompanied themselves on the lyre.) ■

To reteach these lyrics, divide the class into small groups of three or four students. Instruct each group to select one of Sappho's poems to illustrate. Tell students that their illustrations can be either realistic or abstract; that is, they can draw a scene described in the lyric, or they can evoke the emotion that the lyric conveys through an abstract or expressionistic design.

MEETING INDIVIDUAL NEEDS

3 LEP: Tell students that the second stanza of "To an Army Wife, in Sardis" can be thought of as the answer to a question: What do people maintain is the finest sight on dark earth? (whatever one loves) ■

4 LITERARY ELEMENT

Allusion: Sappho assumes that her audience is familiar with the legend of Helen of Troy. "The flower of the world's manhood" refers to the Trojan prince Paris, who ran away with Helen. What is the purpose of the allusion? (to underscore the importance of love and to draw certain parallels between Helen, who abandoned her first husband, Agamemnon, and Anactoria, who has left Lesbos for Sardis)

5 LITERARY ELEMENT

Imagery: What emotions does the speaker express in lines 5–8 of "Tonight I've Watched"? (Possible responses: loneliness, regret for fleeting youth) What images make these emotions vivid and concrete? (the half-gone night, the speaker in bed alone)

6 LITERARY ELEMENT

Imagery: How do you think the speaker feels about her daughter in this last lyric? (Possible responses: tender, loving, admiring) What image most strongly conveys the speaker's admiration? ("hair . . . yellower than torchlight")

charming to look at,
with eyes as soft as
10 honey, and a face

that Love has lighted
with his own beauty.
Aphrodite has surely

outdone herself in
15 doing honor to you!

To an Army Wife, in Sardis

To an army wife, in Sardis:[4]

Some say a cavalry corps,
some infantry, some, again,
will maintain that the swift oars

3

5 of our fleet are the finest
sight on dark earth; but I say
that whatever one loves, is.

This is easily proved: did
not Helen—she who had scanned
10 the flower of the world's manhood—

4

choose as first among men one
who laid Troy's honor in ruin?
Warped to his will, forgetting

love due her own blood, her own
15 child, she wandered far with him.
So Anactoria, although you

being far away forget us,
the dear sound of your footstep
and light glancing in your eyes

20 would move me more than glitter
of Lydian horse or armored
tread of mainland infantry

You May Forget But

You may forget but

Let me tell you
this: someone in
some future time
will think of us

Tonight I've Watched

Tonight I've watched

The moon and then
the Pleiades[5]
go down

5

The night is now
half-gone; youth
goes; I am

in bed alone

Don't Ask Me What to Wear

Don't ask me what to wear

I have no embroidered
headband from Sardis to
give you, Cleis, such as
5 I wore
    and my mother
always said that in her
day a purple ribbon
looped in the hair was thought
to be high style indeed

6

10 but we were dark:
        a girl
whose hair is yellower than
torchlight should wear no
headdress but fresh flowers

---

4. **Sardis** (sär'dis): capital of the ancient kingdom of Lydia; of strategic importance in the ancient world.

5. **Pleiades** (plē'ə·dēz'): a star cluster in the constellation Taurus.

1. **Creating a Song.** Remind students that Sappho accompanied her lyrics with the music of the lyre. Encourage students to find out all they can about this ancient instrument. How was the lyre played? Would a singer such as Sappho strum or pluck the instrument as she sang? Have students work in small groups to set one of Sappho's poems to music.

2. **Tracing Influences.** Interested students may wish to trace Sappho's influence on the Roman poet Catullus. One common thread the two poets share is their commitment to the theme of love. Another link is the name *Lesbia* that Catullus gives to his beloved. This name was probably inspired by Sappho's birthplace, Lesbos, off the coast of Asia Minor.

CLOSURE

Ask students to discuss how simple words and strong, vivid images are generally more effective than complex, abstract language for expressing powerful emotions. Have them choose examples for the discussion by selecting two or three of their favorite images from the lyric poems by Sappho. Students may also wish to contribute relevant examples from their favorite modern poets or songwriters. ■

First Thoughts

Which of the seven poems that you read was your favorite? Why?

Identifying Facts

1. In "You Are the Herdsman of Evening," what is the function of Hesperus, the evening star? What is the function of "Dawn's light"?
2. What is the occasion of the poem "We Drink Your Health"? Whom does the speaker address?
3. What prediction does the speaker make in "You May Forget But"?
4. In "Don't Ask Me What to Wear," why does the speaker not give Cleis the ribbon she wants?

Interpreting Meanings

1. What **personification**, or treatment of an inanimate object as human, is developed in "You Are the Herdsman of Evening"? How is this comparison extended throughout the poem?
2. In "Sleep, Darling," what **image** does the speaker use to show how valuable her daughter is? How is that image similar to the one in "To an Army Wife, in Sardis"?
3. How do you imagine the speaker in "You May Forget But"? For what do you think he or she will be remembered?
4. Which of the poems seems most lyrical to you, that is, which one speaks the most intensely and eloquently of an emotion? Explain.

Applying Meanings

Were you able to relate to Sappho's poems? Have you ever had feelings similar to those expressed by the speakers in these poems? Explain why you think it is —or is not—possible to identify with these poems from ancient Greece.

Creative Writing Response

Writing a Lyric. Look again at the list of people and feelings you made in the Writer's Response on page 280. Then write a brief lyric poem about your feelings for one of those people. Remember to use the first-person singular—the pronoun "I"— and to include images that help convey how you feel about your subject.

Critical Writing Response

Comparing Lyric Poetry. The American poet H. D. (Hilda Doolittle, 1886–1961), who was at the center of the Imagist movement of the early twentieth century, was influenced by the stark imagery and symbolism of ancient Greek poetry. Read H. D.'s poem "Moonrise," and compare it to the poems of Sappho that you have read. Consider both poets' use of the first-person speaker, the kind of emotion that is expressed, and the images used to express these emotions. You might want to make a chart like the one below.

	Sappho	**H. D.**
Speaker		
Emotions		
Images		

Moonrise
H. D.

Will you glimmer on the sea?
will you fling your spear-head
on the shore?
what note shall we pitch?
we have a song,
on the bank we share our arrows;
the loosed string tells our note:

O flight,
bring her swiftly to our song.
She is great,
we measure her by the pine trees.

Greek and Roman Literatures

MORE ABOUT THE AUTHOR

Thucydides believed that the writing of an accurate history was a task of great importance because of its value to future generations. The Greek word for *history* is *historia*, meaning "search" or "inquiry," and Thucydides dedicated much of his life to a painstaking search for reliable information about the Peloponnesian War. He has asserted that he employed "the most severe and detailed tests possible" to check the accuracy of his sources. His conclusions, he boasts, are rigorous and reliable, and "will not be disturbed either by the lays of a poet displaying the exaggeration of his craft, or by the compositions of the chroniclers that are attractive at truth's expense."

ABOUT THE TRANSLATOR

Benjamin Jowett (1817–1893) was so brilliant at Greek and Latin that Balliol College, Oxford, elected him to a fellowship (or teaching post) while he was still an undergraduate. He rose to become a professor of Greek and then vice-chancellor of the university. Devoted to his students, Jowett was respected for his New Testament scholarship as well as for his translations of Plato and Thucydides.

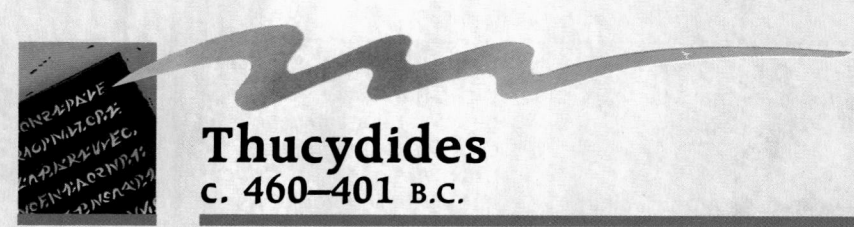

Thucydides
c. 460–401 B.C.

Scala/Art Resource, New York

As a young man, Thucydides (thoo·sid′ i·dēz′) enjoyed wealth and privilege, and he went on to become a leading participant in the brilliant flowering of culture during the later fifth century B.C. in Athens. He had a bright future ahead of him as a military officer and a statesman. All that changed, however, during the Peloponnesian War between Athens and Sparta, which broke out in 431 B.C.

The war, which involved nearly every Greek city-state, lasted twenty-seven years, ending with the bitter defeat of Athens. The conflict was personally catastrophic for Thucydides. In 424 B.C. he was placed in charge of a fleet in the northern Aegean Sea. His failure to relieve the town of Amphipolis, which was under siege by the Spartans, cost him his post. He was sentenced to twenty years of exile from Athens.

Even before his exile, Thucydides had conceived the idea of writing a history of the Peloponnesian War. Now it became his all-consuming passion. By seeking out information from *both* Athenians and Spartans and keeping his narrative focused on his chosen topic, he set standards for himself that have defined the historian's craft down to the present day.

Thucydides viewed human beings as caught up in endless, predictable conflicts of self-interest. An accurate chronicle of the war, he believed, could provide invaluable lessons for future conduct. Time has proved him correct: even now, one of the basic texts at the U. S. Naval War College in Newport, Rhode Island, is Thucydides' *History of the Peloponnesian War.*

In his description of warfare, Thucydides turned away from the vision of heroic glory presented in earlier Greek works such as Homer's *Iliad.* For Thucydides, warfare was brutal and destructive—in his own phrase, "a violent teacher." Thucydides' *History* is filled with a sense of tragic destiny not far removed from that of his contemporary, the dramatist Sophocles (see page 301). In fact, some critics read the *History* as a kind of tragic drama of the pride and fall of Athens.

OBJECTIVES

1. To recognize the characteristics of ancient historical writing and the importance of Thucydides
2. To identify and discuss methods of persuasion
3. To write an essay analyzing ways in which American democracy reflects Athenian ideals
4. To identify and evaluate antithesis

THEMES IN WORLD LITERATURE

Conflict of Cultures and Values
From the *Bhagavad-Gita*, pp. 467–476
"By Any Other Name," pp. 1387–1394

The Individual and Society
From *Don Quixote*, pp. 821–837
A Doll's House, pp. 1069–1126
The Metamorphosis, pp. 1154–1195 ■

VOCABULARY IN CONTEXT

The words listed below will appear in the side margin at the point of instruction:

1. obscurity
2. reprobation
3. adversaries
4. impediment
5. requiting

6. sepulchers
7. commiserate
8. vicissitudes
9. emulate
10. arduous

Reader's Guide

FUNERAL SPEECH OF PERICLES
from History of the Peloponnesian War

Background

The greatest Athenian statesman of Thucydides' day was Pericles (per′i·klēz′). The occasion for the famous speech reproduced here was the annual public funeral for the Athenian war dead of the previous year—in this instance, the first year of the Peloponnesian War (431–430 B.C.). In Thucydides' day, **rhetoric**—the use of language, especially oratory, for persuasion—was considered the highest form of prose. It was common practice for historians to present history through the "speeches" of famous figures. These speeches were a valued means of showing a particular viewpoint. Thus, Pericles' speech embodies not only Pericles' opinions, but the views of patriotic Athenians in general. Of course, Thucydides was not able to capture Pericles' address word for word, but no historian put this practice of recording speeches to better use than Thucydides.

Oral Response

In part of his speech, Pericles describes the Athenian form of government. Ancient Athens is often called the "cradle" of democracy. What are some of the characteristic features of a democracy? As a class, discuss what the word **democracy** means to you.

Literary Focus

Persuasion is a kind of writing that tries to convince the reader or listener to think or act in a certain way. Examples of persuasion include political speeches, newspaper editorials, and advertisements, as well as many essays and longer works of literature. Persuasion often appeals to the emotions as, for example, in advertisements that promise consumers greater attractiveness or increased popularity. The kind of persuasive writing that appeals primarily to reason rather than to emotion is called **argument**.

PREREADING FOCUS

Background: The highest elected official in Athens, Pericles (c. 495–429 B.C.) was a personal friend of many of Athens' leading cultural figures, including the tragedian Sophocles (see p. 301). During Pericles' term of office, he oversaw the most extensive building program in Athenian history, with the Parthenon, the renowned temple of Athena, as its centerpiece. From 443 B.C. to his death, Pericles had no significant political opposition.

Shortly after he delivered this funeral oration in 430 B.C., a terrible plague broke out in Athens. A year later, Pericles died of the plague. Thucydides, who was infected by the disease but survived, graphically describes it in his *History of the Peloponnesian War*. In Thucydides' opinion, with Pericles' death, Athens lost the only leader who could have steered the city successfully through the turmoil of the Peloponnesian War.

Oral Response: You may want to point out that *democracy* comes from two Greek words: *dēmos*, meaning "people," and *kratos*, meaning "strength, power." *Democracy* can be literally translated as "people power."

Literary Focus: Remind students that persuasive appeals to emotion are perfectly legitimate as long as they avoid deliberately deceptive and misleading techniques or appeals to hatred or violence.

FUNERAL SPEECH OF PERICLES
from History of the Peloponnesian War
Thucydides
translated by
BENJAMIN JOWETT

◆ *Some of the more difficult passages in this selection have been paraphrased within the text. As you read, try to identify the goal of Pericles' persuasion in this speech. How does he want his listeners to think about their city?*

"Most of those who have spoken here before me have commended the lawgiver who added this oration to our other funeral customs; it seemed to them a worthy thing that such an honor should be given at their burial to the dead who have fallen on the field of battle. But I should have preferred that, when men's deeds have been brave, they should be honored in deed only, and with such an honor as this public funeral, which you are now witnessing. Then the reputation of many would not have been imperiled on the eloquence or want of eloquence of one, and their virtues believed or not as he spoke well or ill. For it is difficult to say neither too little nor too much; and even moderation is apt not to give the impression of truthfulness. The friend of the dead who knows the facts is likely to think that the words of the speaker fall short of his knowledge and of his wishes; another who is not so well informed, when he hears of anything which surpasses his own powers, will be envious and will suspect exaggeration. Mankind are tolerant of the praises of others so long as each hearer thinks that he can do as well or nearly as well himself, but, when the speaker rises above him, jealousy is aroused and he begins to be incredulous. However, since our ancestors have set the seal of their approval upon the practice, I must obey, and to the utmost of my power shall endeavor to satisfy the wishes and beliefs of all who hear me.

"I will speak first of our ancestors, for it is right and seemly that now, when we are lamenting the dead, a tribute should be paid to their memory. There has never been a time when they did not inhabit this land, which by their valor they have

The law which enjoins this oration has been often praised. But I should prefer to praise the brave by deeds only, not to imperil their reputation on the skill of an orator. Still, our ancestors approved the practice, and I must obey.

I will first commemorate our predecessors, who gave us freedom and empire. And before praising the dead, I will describe how Athens has won her greatness.

handed down from generation to generation, and we have received from them a free state. But if they were worthy of praise, still more were our fathers, who added to their inheritance, and after many a struggle transmitted to us their sons this great empire. And we ourselves assembled here today, who are still most of us in the vigor of life, have carried the work of improvement further, and have richly endowed our city with all things, so that she is sufficient for herself both in peace and war. Of the military exploits by which our various possessions were acquired, or of the energy with which we or our fathers drove back the tide of war, Hellenic or barbarian, I will not speak; for the tale would be long and is familiar to you. But before I praise the dead, I should like to point out by what principles of action we rose to power, and under what institutions and through what manner of life our empire became great. For I conceive that such thoughts are not unsuited to the occasion, and that this numerous assembly of citizens and strangers may profitably listen to them.

"Our form of government does not enter into rivalry with the institutions of others. We do not copy our neighbors, but are an example to them. It is true that we are called a democracy, for the administration is in the hands of the many and not of the few. But while the law secures equal justice to all alike in their private disputes, the claim of excellence is also recognized; and when a citizen is in any way distinguished, he is preferred to the public service, not as a matter of privilege, but as the reward of merit. Neither is poverty a bar, but a man may benefit his country whatever be the obscu-

Our government is a democracy, but we honor men of merit, whether rich or poor. Our public life is free from exclusiveness, our private from suspicion; yet we revere alike the injunctions of law and custom.

rity of his condition. There is no exclusiveness in our public life, and in our private intercourse we are not suspicious of one another, nor angry with our neighbor if he does what he likes; we do not put on sour looks at him which, though harmless, are not pleasant. While we are thus unconstrained in our private intercourse, a spirit of reverence pervades our public acts; we are prevented from doing wrong by respect for the authorities and for the laws, having an especial regard to those which are ordained for the protection of the injured as well as to those unwritten laws which bring upon the transgressor of them the reprobation of the general sentiment.

"And we have not forgotten to provide for our weary spirits many relaxations from toil; we have regular games and sacrifices throughout the year; our homes are beautiful and elegant; and the delight which we daily feel in all these things helps to banish melancholy. Because of the greatness of our city the fruits of the whole earth flow in upon us; so that we enjoy the goods of other countries as freely as of our own.

We find relaxation in our amusements, and in our homes; and the whole world contributes to our enjoyment.

"Then, again, our military training is in many respects superior to that of our adversaries. Our city is thrown open to the world, and we never expel a foreigner or prevent him from seeing or learning anything of which the secret if revealed to an enemy might profit him. We rely not upon management or trickery, but upon our own hearts and hands. And in the matter of education, whereas they from early youth are always undergoing laborious exercises which are to make them brave, we live at ease, and yet are equally ready to face

In war we singly are a match for the Peloponnesians united; though we have no secrets and undergo no laborious training.

4 ANALYZING
Why does Pericles begin his speech by praising his Athenian ancestors? (He wants to emphasize the long tradition of Athenian patriotism.)

5 LITERARY ELEMENT
Persuasive Techniques: How does Pericles attempt to win over his Athenian audience? (by appealing to their civic pride in stating that Athenians do not copy their neighbors)

6 SYNTHESIZING
What advantages does Pericles single out in the democracy of Athens? (equal justice for all; promotion on the basis of merit rather than privilege; no prejudice against the poor) Why do you think Pericles is praising Athenian democracy? (Possible response: to establish that the dead have perished for a good cause)

obscurity (əb·sky$\overline{oo}$r′ə·tē): inconspicuousness; lack of fame

reprobation (rep′rə·bā′shən): disapproval

adversaries (ad′vər·ser′ēz): enemies

7 CULTURAL DIVERSITY
Athenian sea power was the basis of the city's imperial status and its network of trade relations, stretching from Sicily in the West to Phoenicia and Egypt in the East.
What other states have grown powerful because of sea power? (Possible responses: Spain, Portugal, Holland, England)

Identifying Cause and Effect:
According to Pericles, why have the Spartans never felt the "united strength" of Athens? (because much effort goes to maintaining the Athenian navy, and the land forces are stationed in many different areas)

9 LITERARY ELEMENT

Persuasive Techniques: Does Pericles' statement about the enemy appeal primarily to reason or to emotion? (Possible response: primarily to emotions of pride and patriotism) What has Pericles said that makes this statement reasonable and believable? (that Athenian forces have been fragmented and have not yet acted as a unified whole)

10 READER'S RESPONSE

Do you agree with Pericles' opinion about participation in public affairs? (Possible responses: Yes, a citizen in a democracy has a duty to participate in public affairs; no, people have the right to choose not to participate.)

■ **impediment** (im·ped'ə·mənt): hindrance

requiting (ri·kwīt'iŋ): repaying

11 LITERARY ELEMENT

Metaphor: To what does Pericles compare Athens? (to the school of Hellas, or the Greeks) What does this metaphor mean? (Athens is a model city; all other Greek cities can learn from the Athenian way of life.)

288 Greek and Roman Literatures

---

the perils which they face. And here is the proof. The Lacedaemonians[1] come into Attica[2] not by themselves, but with their whole confederacy following; we go alone into a neighbor's country; and although our opponents are fighting for their homes and we on a foreign soil, we have seldom any difficulty in overcoming them. Our enemies have never yet felt our united strength; the care of a navy divides our attention, and on land we are obliged to send our own citizens everywhere. But they, if they meet and defeat a part of our army, are as proud as if they had routed us all, and when defeated they pretend to have been vanquished by us all.

"If then we prefer to meet danger with a light heart but without laborious training, and with a courage which is gained by habit and not enforced by law, are we not greatly the gainers? Since we do not anticipate the pain, although, when the hour comes, we can be as brave as those who never allow themselves to rest; and thus too our city is equally admirable in peace and in war. For we are lovers of the beautiful, yet simple in our tastes, and we cultivate the mind without loss of manliness. Wealth we employ, not for talk and ostentation, but when there is a real use for it. To avow poverty with us is no disgrace; the true disgrace is in doing nothing to avoid it. An Athenian citizen does not neglect the state because he takes care of his own household; and even those of us

We are not enervated by culture or vulgarized by wealth. We are all interested in public affairs, believing that nothing is lost by free discussion. Our goodness to others springs not from interest, but from the generous confidence of freedom.

who are engaged in business have a very fair idea of politics. We alone regard a man who takes no interest in public affairs, not as a harmless, but as a useless character; and if few of us are originators, we are all sound judges of a policy. The great <u>impediment</u> to action is, in our opinion, not discussion, but the want of that knowledge which is gained by discussion preparatory to action. For we have a peculiar power of thinking before we act and of acting too, whereas other men are courageous from ignorance but hesitate upon reflection. And they are surely to be esteemed the bravest spirits who, having the clearest sense both of the pains and pleasures of life, do not on that account shrink from danger. In doing good, again, we are unlike others; we make our friends by conferring, not by receiving favors. Now he who confers a favor is the firmer friend, because he would fain by kindness keep alive the memory of an obligation; but the recipient is colder in his feelings, because he knows that in <u>requiting</u> another's generosity he will not be winning gratitude but only paying a debt. We alone do good to our neighbors not upon a calculation of interest, but in the confidence of freedom and in a frank and fearless spirit. To sum up: I say that Athens is the school of Hellas,[3] and that the individual Athenian in his own person seems to have the power of adapting himself to the most varied forms of action with the utmost versatility and grace. This is no passing and idle word, but truth and fact; and the assertion is verified

In fine,[4] Athens is the school of Hellas. She alone in the hour of trial rises above her reputation. Her citizens need no poet to sing their praises: for every land bears witness to their valor.

---

1. **Lacedaemonians** (las'ə·di·mō'nē·ənz): Spartans.
2. **Attica** (at'i·kə): the region of Greece surrounding Athens.
3. **Hellas** (hel'əs): Greece; *Hellenes* (hel'ēnz') are Greeks.
4. **In fine** (fīn): in conclusion.

The Acropolis in Athens. *The Athenian Acropolis was the religious center of Athens; the Parthenon, or temple to Athena, was built there.*

Scala/Art Resource, New York

by the position to which these qualities have raised the state. For in the hour of trial Athens alone among her contemporaries is superior to the report of her. No enemy who comes against her is indignant at the reverses which he sustains at the hands of such a city; no subject complains that his masters are unworthy of him. And we shall assuredly not be without witnesses; there are mighty monuments of our power which will make us the wonder of this and of succeeding ages; we shall not need the praises of Homer or of any other panegyrist[5] whose poetry may please for the moment, although

his representation of the facts will not bear the light of day. For we have compelled every land and every sea to open a path for our valor, and have everywhere planted eternal memorials of our friendship and of our enmity. Such is the city for whose sake these men nobly fought and died; they could not bear the thought that she might be taken from them; and every one of us who survive should gladly toil on her behalf.

"I have dwelt upon the greatness of Athens because I want to show you that we are contending for a higher prize than those who enjoy none of these privileges, and to establish by manifest proof the merit of these men

The praise of the city is the praise of these men, for they made her great. Good and bad, rich and poor alike, preferred death to dishonor.

---

5. **panegyrist** (pan'ə·jir'ist, -jī'rist): someone who gives a formal speech or written tribute of great praise.

Thucydides   **289**

2

12

13

14 ANALYZING

What moral virtues or social values does Pericles seem to regard as the most important of all? (patriotism and courage) What argument does he use to support his opinion of the worthiest action? (Possible response: Courage in the service of the state is so important that it makes up for any private actions of an individual that have harmed the state.)

15 LITERARY ELEMENT

Antithesis: What two ideas does Pericles sharply contrast in this description of fallen heroes? (running away versus standing firm) What transition words reinforce this use of antithesis? (*rather than, but*)

sepulchers (sep'əl·kərz): graves; tombs

16 LITERARY ELEMENT

Metaphor: To what does Pericles compare the graves of famous men? (to the whole earth) Explain the metaphor. (Possible response: Famous men enjoy praises throughout the world after their deaths, and so they can be said to be "buried" everywhere.)

whom I am now commemorating. Their loftiest praise has been already spoken. For in magnifying the city I have magnified them, and men like them whose virtues made her glorious. And of how few Hellenes can it be said as of them, that their deeds when weighed in the balance have been found equal to their fame! Methinks that a death such as theirs has been gives the true measure of a man's worth; it may be the first revelation of his virtues, but is at any rate their final seal. For even those who come short in other ways may justly plead the valor with which they have fought for their country; they have blotted out the evil with the good, and have benefited the state more by their public services than they have injured her by their private actions. None of these men were enervated by wealth or hesitated to resign the pleasures of life; none of them put off the evil day in the hope, natural to poverty, that a man, though poor, may one day become rich. But, deeming that the punishment of their enemies was sweeter than any of these things, and that they could fall in no nobler cause, they determined at the hazard of their lives to be honorably avenged, and to leave the rest. They resigned to hope their unknown chance of happiness; but in the face of death they resolved to rely upon themselves alone. And when the moment came they were minded to resist and suffer, rather than to fly and save their lives; they ran away from the word of dishonor, but on the battlefield their feet stood fast, and in an instant, at the height of their fortune, they passed away from the scene, not of their fear, but of their glory.

"Such was the end of these men; they were worthy of Athens, and the living need not desire to have a more he- *Contemplate and love Athens, and you will know how to value them. They were united in their deaths, but their glory is separate* roic spirit, although they may pray for a less fatal issue. The value of such a spirit is not to be expressed in words. Anyone can discourse to you forever about the advantages of a brave defense, *and single. Their sepulcher is the remembrance of them in the hearts of men. Follow their example without fear: it is the prosperous, not the unfortunate, who should be reckless.* which you know already. But instead of listening to him I would have you day by day fix your eyes upon the greatness of Athens, until you become filled with the love of her; and when you are impressed by the spectacle of her glory, reflect that this empire has been acquired by men who knew their duty and had the courage to do it, who in the hour of conflict had the fear of dishonor always present to them, and who, if ever they failed in an enterprise, would not allow their virtues to be lost to their country, but freely gave their lives to her as the fairest offering which they could present at her feast. The sacrifice which they collectively made was individually repaid to them; for they received again each one for himself a praise which grows not old, and the noblest of all sepulchers—I speak not of that in which their remains are laid, but of that in which their glory survives, and is proclaimed always and on every fitting occasion both in word and deed. For the whole earth is the sepulcher of famous men; not only are they commemorated by columns and inscriptions in their own country, but in foreign lands there dwells also an unwritten memorial of them, graven not on stone but in the hearts of men. Make them your examples, and, esteeming courage to be freedom and freedom to be happiness, do not weigh too nicely the perils of war. The unfortunate who has no hope of a change for the better has less reason to throw away his life than the prosperous who, if he survives, is always

READING CHECK

1. Of whom does Pericles say he will speak first? (the ancestors)
2. What form of government does Athens have? (democracy)
3. How do the Athenians regard someone who takes no interest in public affairs? (as useless)

4. Besides columns and inscriptions, where else is the fame of the dead memorialized? (in the hearts of men)
5. What benefit will the children of the dead heroes receive? (being maintained at public expense until they grow up)

RETEACHING

Chart the progression of Pericles' argument:

(1) praising the deeds of Athenian ancestors
(2) praising Athenian democracy
(3) equating praise of Athens with praise of the fallen heroes
(4) urging others to emulate the brave deeds of the dead
(5) consoling the bereaved

liable to a change for the worse, and to whom any accidental fall makes the most serious difference. To a man of spirit, cowardice and disaster coming together are far more bitter than death striking him unperceived at a time when he is full of courage and animated by the general hope.

"Wherefore I do not now commiserate the parents of the dead who stand here; I would rather comfort them. You know that your life has been passed amid manifold vicissitudes; and that they may be deemed fortunate who have gained most honor, whether an honorable death like theirs, or an honorable sorrow like yours, and whose days have been so ordered that the term of their happiness is likewise the term of their life. I know how hard it is to make you feel this, when the good fortune of others will too often remind you of the gladness which once lightened your hearts. And sorrow is felt at the want of those blessings, not which a man never knew, but which were a part of his life before they were taken from him. Some of you are of an age at which they may hope to have other children, and they ought to bear their sorrow better; not only will the children who may hereafter be born make them forget their own lost ones, but the city will be doubly a gainer. She will not be left desolate, and she will be safer. For a man's counsel cannot have equal weight or worth, when he alone has no children to risk in the general danger. To those of you who have passed their prime, I say: Congratulate yourselves that you have been happy during the greater part of your days; remember that your life of

The parents of the dead are to be comforted rather than pitied. Some of them may yet have children who will lighten their sorrow and serve the state; while others should remember how large their share of happiness has been, and be consoled by the glory of those who are gone.

sorrow will not last long, and be comforted by the glory of those who are gone. For the love of honor alone is ever young, and not riches, as some say, but honor is the delight of men when they are old and useless.

"To you who are the sons and brothers of the departed, I see that the struggle to emulate them will be an arduous one. For all men praise the dead, and, however preeminent your virtue may be, hardly will you be thought, I do not say to equal, but even to approach them. The living have their rivals and detractors, but when a man is out of the way, the honor and good will which he receives is unalloyed. And, if I am to speak of womanly virtues to those of you who will henceforth be widows, let me sum them up in one short admonition: To a woman not to show more weakness than is natural to her sex is a great glory, and not to be talked about for good or for evil among men.

Sons and brothers will find their example hard to imitate, for men are jealous of the living, but envy follows not the dead. Let the widows restrain their natural weakness, and avoid both praise and blame.

"I have paid the required tribute, in obedience to the law, making use of such fitting words as I had. The tribute of deeds has been paid in part; for the dead have been honorably interred, and it remains only that their children should be maintained at the public charge until they are grown up: this is the solid prize with which, as with a garland, Athens crowns her sons living and dead, after a struggle like theirs. For where the rewards of virtue are greatest, there the noblest citizens are enlisted in the service of the state. And now, when you have duly lamented, everyone his own dead, you may depart."

So have I paid a due tribute of words to the dead. The city will pay them in deeds, as by this funeral, so too by the maintenance of their children.

17

18

19

▣ **commiserate** (kə·miz′ər·āt′): feel pity or sympathy for

vicissitudes ⟨vi·sis′ə·tōodz′⟩: unpredictable changes in fortune

emulate (em′yōo·lāt): imitate in order to equal or surpass

arduous (är′jōo·əs): difficult

---

17 LITERARY ELEMENT
Antithesis: What sharp contrast does Pericles make between the living and the dead? (He says that the living have rivals and detractors but that the dead are honored and viewed only with good will.)

18 INFERRING
Given Pericles' words to and about women, what can you infer about official Athenian attitudes toward women? (Athenian society was patriarchal; women were treated as second-class citizens.)

19 CULTURAL BACKGROUND
The words *prize* and *garland* evoke an association with the athletic contests of ancient Greece such as the Olympic Games. The prizes for victors in these games were garlands of olive leaves.

■ **WRITING TO LEARN** ■

Social Studies: Imagine that you are among the Athenians who heard Pericles' speech. Write him a letter explaining why you agree or disagree with him and telling how his appeal to patriotism affected you emotionally. ■

1. Reacting to a Quote. The historian Donald Kagan has written: "Pericles' Funeral Oration was delivered during a war that was clearly going to continue for some time. Thus its chief purpose, even more important than praising the dead, was to explain why they had been right to risk their lives and why the living should be willing to do likewise." Have students evaluate this analysis of purpose.

2. Research Project. Some students may wish to research the background and political career of Pericles. Encourage them to read about Pericles in encyclopedias or other reference books and to read Pericles' other speeches in Thucydides' *History of the Peloponnesian War* (to be found in Chapter I.139 and II.60). Students can present their findings in a written or an oral report.

CLOSURE

Have methods of political persuasion changed very much from the time of ancient Greece to the present? Ask students who think methods have changed to explain to the class how they think people in power today attempt to persuade the public. Ask students who think persuasive methods have remained much the same to provide modern parallels to the methods of persuasion that Pericles uses in this speech. ■

ANSWERS

First Thoughts
Possible response: patriotism

Identifying Facts
1. rule by the many and not by the few.
2. Spartan training starts earlier and is more laborious. The Athenians can still win battles with only part of their army.
3. Their children have gained honor. not to show weakness, not to be talked about

Interpreting Meanings
1. by stressing the difficulty of his task; by praising ancestors
2. to inspire a love of the city. to make sacrifices in war
3. Possible responses: *reason*: the reputation of the dead should not depend on the eloquence of an orator. *emotion*: "the greatness of Athens" (p. 289)
4. Possible response: Words to women are condescending.
5. patriotism, sacrifice, courage, civic service, individual merit

Applying Meanings
Answers will vary.

Critical Writing Response
Comparing Democracies. *Valued by both:* rule by the many, justice for all, dying for one's country. *Not valued by ancient Greeks:* gender equality

Language and Vocabulary
1. Possible responses: p. 290: "not of their fear, but their glory"; "collectively made . . . individually repaid"; "not on stone but in the hearts of men"
2. Possible response: Pointed contrasts are memorable. ■

First Thoughts
Which single emotion in his listeners do you think Pericles wanted to appeal to most in this speech? Explain your answer.

Identifying Facts
1. When Pericles speaks about the Athenian form of government, how does he define a democracy?
2. How does Pericles contrast the Athenians' military training with the training of the Spartans? What proof does he offer of the Athenians' superiority?
3. Why does Pericles feel that the parents of the dead should not be pitied? What advice does he offer the widows who mourn their dead?

Interpreting Meanings
1. Explain how Pericles gains the sympathetic attention of his listeners in the introduction to his speech.
2. Pericles' funeral oration is an outstanding example of the rhetorical art of **persuasion**. What do you think is Pericles' purpose in praising Athens and Athenian democracy? What is he trying to persuade his listeners to do or believe?
3. Identify at least one example of **argument**, or persuasion that appeals to reason. Then identify a part of the speech that seems designed to appeal primarily to emotion.
4. Athens in Pericles' day was a man's world as far as public life was concerned. How do Pericles' words to the women of Athens reflect this situation?
5. Briefly summarize the values praised by Pericles in the funeral oration.

Applying Meanings
Imagine that the United States is at war, and that the President delivers a speech similar to that of Pericles' funeral oration.

Would such a speech repel or inspire you? Why or why not? Explain your answer.

Critical Writing Response
Comparing Democracies. Many of the claims made by Pericles sound remarkably similar to descriptions of the American democratic system given in speeches by political leaders today. In a brief essay, analyze the ways in which American democracy reflects the ancient Greek ideal of democracy. What ideals were held in high esteem by the Greeks? In what ways does American democracy diverge from these ideals? Completing a chart like the one below may help you to plan your essay.

Ideals	Athens	U.S.A.
Freedom of speech		
Promotion on merit		

Language and Vocabulary

Antithesis

Antithesis (an·tith'ə·sis) is the use of language to express sharply contrasting ideas in parallel phrases or structures. The saying "Whoever is not with us is against us" is an example of antithesis. Pericles often uses this device to make his speech more pointed and effective, as in these examples:

> We do not copy our neighbors, but are an example to them.

> We rely not upon management or trickery, but upon our own hearts and hands.

1. What other examples of antithesis can you find in Pericles' speech? List at least three examples.
2. Why do you think that antithesis—the juxtaposition of directly contrasting ideas—is such an effective device of persuasion?

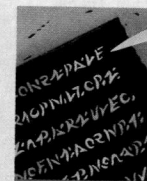

Plato
c. 429–c. 347 B.C.

SEF/Art Resource, New York

Plato was the preeminent philosopher of the Golden Age. As a young student of rhetoric from an aristocratic family, Plato's destiny was sealed when he met Socrates (469–399 B.C.). The older man was a teacher whose unorthodox style and uncompromising pursuit of the truth appealed to many prominent young men of Plato's time.

Most of what we know about Socrates comes from Plato's works, for the older philosopher left no writings of his own. Socrates was an eccentric. Pretending to be ignorant, he wandered the streets of Athens, a shabby and unkempt figure who questioned people about concepts such as virtue, truth, and wisdom. He never preached or offered his own solutions, but he would demonstrate by his ceaseless questioning that no argument was infallible. The tech-nique of questioning that he developed is known as the **Socratic method**.

Socrates' pointed criticism of official authorities earned him a reputation as a public nuisance. The controversy over his teaching methods and his belief that an "unexamined life is not worth living" led to a vicious persecution. In 399 B.C., he was tried and executed on false charges of corrupting the minds of his young students.

Plato recorded much of Socrates' philosophy and many of his speeches in his *Dialogues*. Nearly all of Plato's thirty-four philosophical works are written in the form of such **dialogues**, in which two or more characters debate with the principal speaker and challenger, Socrates. Plato used the dialogues as a vehicle to present a comprehensive philosophical system known as **Platonism**. According to the Platonic system, ideas are the only reality, and people should rely on reason, not on their senses, to comprehend the world.

In 387 B.C., Plato founded a school called the Academy, a center of philosophical learning. He wrote a number of famous works, including *The Republic*, which sets forth in brilliant detail his theory of an ideal state ruled by philosopher-kings. When he was sixty years old, during a sea voyage, Plato's ship was raided by pirates, and he was sold as a slave to a former student, who helped him return to Athens. Plato never left the city again.

OBJECTIVES
1. *To analyze and discuss Socrates' defense of his philosophy*
2. *To identify and explain analogy*
3. *To write an essay from a judge's point of view and to construct and explain a set of analogies*

VOCABULARY IN CONTEXT
The words listed below will appear in the side margin at the point of instruction:
1. procured
2. acquittal
3. censuring
4. intimation
5. reprove

PREREADING FOCUS

Background: Athens at the time of Socrates' trial (399 B.C.) was a far less tolerant place than it had been at the time of Pericles' funeral speech, just over thirty years earlier. Having lost the Peloponnesian War in 404 B.C., Athens suffered a reign of terror under the so-called "Thirty Tyrants"—absolutists who summarily executed citizens who favored democracy. One of the most savage of these despots was Critias, an aristocrat who was a cousin of Plato and a former student of Socrates. Soon after democracy was restored in 403 B.C., Critias was killed. Socrates had never cooperated with the tyrants; but in the backlash that ensued after their overthrow, he may have been condemned as a result of "guilt by association" with Critias and his friends. The judges sentenced Socrates to die by drinking a potion made from poisonous hemlock.

Writer's Response: You may want to spark students' thinking by mentioning such well-known figures in American history as Nathan Hale, Abraham Lincoln, and Dr. Martin Luther King, Jr.

Literary Focus: You may wish to point out that analogies serve as the basis for many figures of speech, such as similes and metaphors.

Reader's Guide

from the APOLOGY
from the Dialogues

Background

The term *apology* did not have the same meaning for the Greeks as it does for modern readers. Socrates' apology at his trial was not an expression of regret or shame; it was a defense of his philosophy and way of life as well as a bitingly sarcastic attack on his judges. At the conclusion of Socrates' speech, the jury of 501 Athenian citizens voted, found him guilty, and condemned him to death by poison.

Although the *Apology* is among Plato's *Dialogues*, it is itself a **monologue**, or a speech given at length by one person. In Socrates' case, the monologue was his opportunity to explain himself and to honor the letter of the law. He even went so far as to suggest ironically that his services to Athens merited a pension. At this point, the jury reconfirmed the death penalty by an even larger majority. The selection that follows includes Socrates' final address to the court.

Writer's Response

In this speech to the court, Socrates refuses to compromise his loyalty to the pursuit of truth, even at the cost of his life. How do you feel about people who refuse to compromise their beliefs? Are some beliefs worth dying for? Freewrite your answers for a few minutes.

Literary Focus

An **analogy** is a comparison of two things to show that they are alike in certain respects. We use analogies to show how something unfamiliar is like something well known or widely experienced. One famous example of analogy is Benjamin Franklin's *Epitaph on Himself*:

The body of Benjamin Franklin, Printer (like the cover of an old book, its contents torn out and stripped of its lettering and gilding), lies here, food for worms; but the work shall not be lost, for it will (as he believed) appear once more in a new and more elegant edition, revised and corrected by the Author.

Socrates uses several analogies in the *Apology* to make his points clearer to his listeners and to strengthen his arguments.

from the APOLOGY
from the Dialogues
Plato

translated by
BENJAMIN JOWETT

As you read the following speech, try to determine why Socrates has been so highly admired throughout the ages as both a philosopher and a teacher.

SCHOOL OF ATHENS, RAPHAEL. *Plato, the older figure in the center (left) stands next to Aristotle. Socrates, in the upper left, debates with the youth of Athens.*

Scala/Art Resource, New York

HUMANITIES CONNECTION

Like Raphael's *Parnassus* (pp. 225 and 281), *The School of Athens* (1510–1511) is a fresco painted on a wall in the Vatican Palace in Rome. In it, Plato, holding his book *Timaeus*, points toward heaven as the source of ideas. Aristotle, holding his *Ethics*, indicates Earth as the object of all study. Socrates, at the upper left, seems to be debating philosophical principles with the youth of Athens. At the lower left Pythagoras, observed by students, delineates a proposition. The philosopher Heraclitus is lost in thought in the center foreground. In the upper right, Euclid bends over a slate balanced on his knee. Raphael drew unmistakable parallels between the classical past and his own era by using Leonardo da Vinci as his model for Plato, the architect Bramante for Euclid, and Michelangelo for Heraclitus. ∎

procured (prō·kyo͞ord'): secured; brought about by effort

acquittal (ə·kwit'əl): act of clearing a person of charges of wrongdoing

censuring (sen'shər·iŋ): expressing strong disapproval of

1 GUIDED READING

Interpreting Cause and Effect:
What does Socrates imply has been one of the causes of his conviction? (his refusal to behave in a remorseful, humble manner)

2 LITERARY ELEMENT

Analogy: To what does Socrates compare his legal situation? (to that of a soldier at war) What is similar about the two situations? (In both cases, there are ways of escaping death, some of which are not honorable.)

3 LITERARY ELEMENT

Analogy: According to Socrates' comparison, who is the faster runner? (unrighteousness) Who is the slower runner? (death)

4 SYNTHESIZING

How might you restate Socrates' teaching so that it becomes a guide for citizens of a modern democracy? (Possible response: You cannot escape the consequences of your actions by silencing your accuser. The best policy is to face up to your responsibilities and make amends for any wrongdoing.)

Not much time will be gained, O Athenians, in return for the evil name which you will get from the detractors of the city, who will say that you killed Socrates, a wise man; for they will call me wise, even although I am not wise, when they want to reproach you. If you had waited a little while, your desire would have been fulfilled in the course of nature. For I am far advanced in years, as you may perceive, and not far from death. I am speaking now not to all of you, but only to those who have condemned me to death. And I have another thing to say to them: You think that I was convicted because I had no words of the sort which would have procured my acquittal—I mean, if I had thought fit to leave nothing undone or unsaid. Not so; the deficiency which led to my conviction was not of words—certainly not. But I had not the boldness or impudence or inclination to address you as you would have liked me to do, weeping and wailing and lamenting, and saying and doing many things which you have been accustomed to hear from others, and which, as I maintain, are unworthy of me. I thought at the time that I ought not to do anything common or mean when in danger; nor do I now repent of the style of my defense; I would rather die having spoken after my manner, than speak in your manner and live. For neither in war nor yet at law ought I or any man to use every way of escaping death. Often in battle there can be no doubt that if a man will throw away his arms, and fall on his knees before his pursuers, he may escape death; and in other dangers there are other ways of escaping death, if a man is willing to say and do anything. The difficulty, my friends, is not to avoid death, but to avoid unrighteousness; for that runs faster than death. I am old and move slowly, and the slower runner has overtaken me, and my accusers are keen and quick, and the faster runner, who is unrighteousness, has overtaken them. And now I depart hence condemned by you to suffer the penalty of death—they too go their ways condemned by the truth to suffer the penalty of villainy and wrong; and I must abide by my award—let them abide by theirs. I suppose that these things may be regarded as fated—and I think that they are well.

And now, O men who have condemned me, I would fain prophesy to you; for I am about to die, and in the hour of death men are gifted with prophetic power. And I prophesy to you who are my murderers, that immediately after my departure punishment far heavier than you have inflicted on me will surely await you. Me you have killed because you wanted to escape the accuser, and not to give an account of your lives. But that will not be as you suppose: far otherwise. For I say that there will be more accusers of you than there are now; accusers whom hitherto I have restrained: and as they are younger they will be more inconsiderate with you, and you will be more offended at them. If you think that by killing men you can prevent some one from censuring your evil lives, you are mistaken; that is not a way of escape which is either possible or honorable; the easiest and the noblest way is not to be disabling others, but to be improving yourselves. This is the prophecy which I utter before my departure to the judges who have condemned me.

Friends, who would have acquitted me, I would like also to talk with you about the thing which has come to pass, while the magistrates are busy, and before I go to the place at which I must die. Stay then a little, for we may as well talk with one another while there is time. You are my friends, and I should like to show you the meaning of this event which has happened to me. O my

Scala/Art Resource, New York

Bust of Socrates.

judges—for you I may truly call judges—I should like to tell you of a wonderful circumstance. Hitherto the divine faculty of which the internal oracle[1] is the source has constantly been in the habit of opposing me even about trifles, if I was going to make a slip or error in any matter; and now as you see there has come upon me that which may be thought, and is generally believed to be, the last and worst evil. But the oracle made no sign of opposition, either when I was leaving my house in the morning, or when I was on my way to the court, or while I was speaking, at anything which I was going to say; and yet I have often been stopped in the middle of a speech, but now in nothing I either said or did touching the matter in hand has the oracle opposed me. What do I take to be the explanation of this silence? I will tell you. It is an <u>intimation</u> that what

has happened to me is a good, and that those of us who think that death is an evil are in error. For the customary sign would surely have opposed me had I been going to evil and not to good.

Let us reflect in another way, and we shall see that there is great reason to hope that death is a good; for one of two things—either death is a state of nothingness and utter unconsciousness, or, as men say, there is a change and migration of the soul from this world to another. Now, if you suppose that there is no consciousness, but a sleep like the sleep of him who is undisturbed even by dreams, death will be an unspeakable gain. For if a person were to select the night in which his sleep was undisturbed even by dreams, and were to compare with this the other days and nights of his life, and then were to tell us how many days and nights he had passed in the course of his life better and more pleasantly than this one, I think that any man, I will not say a private man, but even the great king will not find many such days or nights, when compared with the others. Now, if death be of such a nature, I say that to die is gain; for eternity is then only a single night. But if death is the journey to another place, and there, as men say, all the dead abide, what good, O my friends and judges, can be greater than this? If, indeed, when the pilgrim arrives in the world below, he is delivered from the professors of justice in this world, and finds the true judges who are said to give judgment there, Minos and Rhadamanthus and Aeacus and Triptolemus,[2] and other sons of

---

1. **oracle:** Socrates believed that he was constantly guided by a divine inner voice which warned him against evil acts and wrong choices.

2. **Minos** (mī'näs): king of Crete. **Rhadamanthus** (rad'ə·man'thəs): brother of Minos. **Aeacus** (ē'ə·kəs): according to one legend, the father of Achilles. **Triptolemus** (trip·tōl'ə·məs): priest of Demeter; after death, all were made judges in Hades, the world of the dead.

8 LITERARY ELEMENT

8 LITERARY ELEMENT

Allusion: An allusion is a reference to a person, event, place, statement, or thing from history or literature. Socrates' allusions to Palamedes and Ajax set up an implied analogy that links his own situation with theirs. *What does Socrates share with these legendary heroes?* (Possible response: They were all victims of injustice.)

HISTORICAL BACKGROUND

Plato consistently portrays Socrates as a seeker of truth and wisdom. Socrates denies that he is wise, stressing instead that his goal is to learn from the wisdom of others. Ironically, he usually finds that other people rarely think through their premises or the dangers of their views. How might Socrates' dedication to the search for wisdom make him a hero in the Greek tradition? (Like the ancient epic heroes, he pursues his goal with determination and bravely faces death for his beliefs.)

Scala/Art Resource, New York

Roman mosaic of the School of Plato.

God who were righteous in their own life, that pilgrimage will be worth making. What would not a man give if he might converse with Orpheus and Musaeus and Hesiod[3] and Homer? Nay, if this be true, let me die again and again. I myself, too, shall have a wonderful interest in there meeting and conversing with Palamedes,[4] and Ajax[5] the son

8

---

3. **Orpheus** (ôr'fē·əs): a famous musician and poet of Greek mythology. **Musaeus** (mōō·zē'əs): Greek poet who lived around 1400 B.C. **Hesiod** (hē'sē·əd): Greek poet of the eighth century B.C.

4. **Palamedes** (pal'ə·mē'dēz): a Greek hero who fought in the Trojan War; he was accused of treachery and stoned to death.

5. **Ajax:** a Greek hero in the Trojan War; feeling that the armor of Achilles was unjustly awarded to Odysseus and not to himself, Ajax went mad.

READING CHECK

1. What does Socrates say he refused to do at his trial? (to gain acquittal by weeping and wailing)
2. Why, according to Socrates, did his enemies condemn him to death? (to escape accusation and avoid giving an account of their lives)
3. What conclusion does Socrates draw from the silence of his "oracle" about his trial? (that his death is a good)

4. To what two things does Socrates compare death? (sleep and a journey to another place)
5. For what two reasons may Socrates' sons deserve to be reproved in the future? (for preferring riches or anything else to virtue or for being pretentious)

RETEACHING

Have students imagine that they can ask Socrates one question about the major subjects he deals with in his speech: his own conduct, his prophecies to his judges, and the nature of death. Have each student write a question on a slip of paper. Then divide students into groups of five or six. Each group should hold a panel discussion with one student playing the role of Socrates and others addressing questions to him or her.

8 of Telamon, and any other ancient hero who has suffered death through an unjust judgment; and there will be no small pleasure, as I think, in comparing my own sufferings with theirs. Above all, I shall then be able to continue my search into true and false knowledge; as in this world, so also in the next; and I shall find out who is wise, and who pretends to be wise, and is not. What would not a man give, O judges, to be able to examine the leader of the great Trojan expedition; or Odysseus[6] or Sisyphus,[7] or numberless others, men and women too! What infinite delight would there be in conversing with them and asking them questions! In another world they do not put a man to death for asking questions: assuredly not. For besides being happier than we are, they will be immortal, if what is said is true.

9 Wherefore, O judges, be of good cheer about death, and know of a certainty, that no evil can happen to a good man, either in life or after death. He and his are not neglected by the gods; nor has my own approaching end happened by mere chance. But I see clearly that the time had arrived when it was better for me to die and be released from trouble; wherefore the oracle gave no sign. For which reason, also, I am not angry with my condemners, or with my accusers; they have done me no harm, although they did not mean to do me any good; and for this I may gently blame them.

Still, I have a favor to ask of them. When my sons are grown up, I would ask you, O my friends, to punish them; and I would have you trouble them, as I have troubled you, if they seem to care about riches, or anything, more than about virtue; or if they pretend to be something when they are really nothing—then reprove them, as I have reproved you, for not caring about that for which they ought to care, and thinking that they are something when they are really nothing. And if you do this, both I and my sons will have received justice at your hands.

The hour of departure has arrived, and we go our ways—I to die, and you to live. Which is better God only knows.

9

10

---

6. **Odysseus** (ō·dis′ē·əs): cleverest of the Greek warriors; hero of Homer's *Odyssey*.
7. **Sisyphus** (sis′ə·fəs): After his death, Sisyphus was punished in Hades by eternally having to roll up a hill a huge stone that always rolled down just as it got to the top.

> ## First Thoughts
> Do you think Socrates acts heroically, or is his decision to die for his beliefs foolish? Explain.
>
> ### Identifying Facts
> 1. What prophecy does Socrates make in the opening of his speech to those who voted to condemn him?

2. When he addresses those friends who voted to acquit him, how does Socrates explain the silence of his internal oracle?
3. Why does Socrates say he is not angry with his condemners and accusers? For what does he gently blame them?
4. Why does Socrates say he is not afraid of death?
5. At the conclusion of his speech, what favor does Socrates ask of his judges?

9 GUIDED READING

Finding the Main Idea: Why, according to Socrates, should the judges be cheerful about death? (because nothing evil can happen to a good man)

■ **reprove** (ri·prōōv′): express disapproval of

10 COMPARING LITERATURE

In the *Epic of Gilgamesh*, composed about 1500 years before Socrates' time, the hero seeks immortality. How does Gilgamesh differ from Socrates in his attitude toward death? (Gilgamesh is less calm about the inevitability of death.) Why do you suppose this is so? (Socrates is mainly concerned about the moral life; he also holds out the possibility of a pleasant afterlife.)

WRITING TO LEARN

Social Studies: Imagine that you were among the supporters of Socrates who witnessed his speech in his own defense. Write a letter to a friend in which you recount your impressions of that day. Try to re-create the scene vividly, summarize Socrates' major points, and give your personal reactions. ■

ANSWERS

First Thoughts
Answers will vary.

Identifying Facts
1. They will suffer a far more severe punishment soon.
2. as meaning that death for him now is a good thing

1. **Staging a Trial.** Suggest that students stage the trial of Socrates. Have them first break up into small groups to research the trial (which appears earlier in the *Apology*) and brainstorm lines for the accusers, supporters, and jury. After they stage the trial, allow several students to take turns role-playing Socrates, each reading a part of his speech. Urge students to practice their gestures, demeanor, and delivery.

2. **Research Project.** Although Socrates was one of the most influential figures in the history of Western philosophy, we do not have a word written by him. We learn of him through the words of Plato. Invite students to research the "Socratic method" of oral dialogue and question-and-answer and its use in education today. Ask students to report their findings and to teach something to the class using the Socratic method.

CLOSURE

Ask students to go back over the selection and pick out passages where Socrates seems to be teaching, even as he faces the death penalty. Then have students use these passages as a point of departure for a discussion on whether or not they think Socrates would be respected today and in what forum—television, pulpit, university, and so on. Urge students to support their opinions with reasons. ■

---

3. They have done him no harm; they did not intend to do good.
4. No evil can happen to a good man; there is reason to believe that death is a good.
5. to reprove his sons if they prefer anything to virtue or behave pretentiously

Interpreting Meanings
1. unrighteousness to a swift runner, death to a slower runner. It shows that unrighteousness can easily overtake the unwary.
2. death as sleep and as a journey to the abode of the dead
3. The people in that other world are already dead.
4. Possible responses: solemn, serene, assured, gently ironic
5. Socrates believed that virtue ultimately overcomes all evil.

Applying Meanings
Answers will vary.

Creative Writing Response
Judging Socrates. Essays should refer to Socrates' defense of his actions and to his words about death.

Critical Writing Response
Understanding Analogies. Students may rephrase Socrates' words from the *Apology* in analogy form. Example: "Socrates: death:: his supporters: life" (rephrasing of last two sentences, p. 299). ■

Interpreting Meanings
1. Toward the end of the first paragraph, Socrates uses the **analogy** of two runners to argue that pleading for his life would be dishonorable. Explain what is being compared in this analogy. How does this comparison help to strengthen Socrates' argument?
2. What **analogies** does Socrates draw when he argues that it is reasonable to hope that death is a good thing?
3. Socrates was renowned for his use of sarcasm, or **verbal irony**: saying one thing but meaning another. Given the circumstances, what is ironic about his remark at the end of his speech that "in another world they do not put a man to death for asking questions"?
4. What adjective would you use to describe Socrates' **tone** in this speech?
5. Socrates was an observer of the best and the worst in human nature, and he also experienced bitter injustice in his own life. Yet he says that "no evil can happen to a good man, either in life or after death" (see page 299). How do you explain this apparent contradiction?

Applying Meanings
How do you think a man like Socrates would be regarded today? Would you enjoy him as one of your own teachers? What do you think you could learn from him? Explain.

Creative Writing Response
Judging Socrates. Imagine that you are one of the judges who voted against Socrates and that you have just heard his final speech. How do you feel now? Are you likely to change your vote in his favor? Write a three-paragraph essay in which you explain why you were or were not persuaded by Socrates' speech. You may want to refer to the notes you took in Writer's Response (see page 294).

Then, as a class, take a vote. Will you allow Socrates to live, or is he still condemned to die?

Critical Writing Response
Understanding Analogies. On one level, an **analogy** is a simple comparison of two unlike things, but analogies can be more complicated. Not only are unlike things compared to one another, but the relationship between two things or ideas can in turn be compared to the relationship between two other things or ideas. The typical construction of this kind of analogy is: "*a* is to *b* as *c* is to *d*," often written in this form: "a:b::c:d." For example:

1. Socrates is to Plato as a teacher is to a student. (Socrates:Plato::teacher: student)
2. A speech is to an orator as a poem is to a poet. (speech:orator::poem:poet)
3. A microscope is to a biologist as a hammer is to a carpenter. (microscope:biologist::hammer:carpenter)

In the first analogy, the comparison of teacher to student actually describes the relationship between Socrates and Plato. In the second analogy, the first part of each comparison is something made by each of the second parts: orators make speeches and poets make poems. Finally, in the third analogy, the first part of each comparison is a tool used by the second: biologists use microscopes and carpenters use hammers.

Try to construct at least two analogies of your own. For example, you could begin with "Inexperience is to youth as. . . ." Then, in a few sentences, explain the relationship between the parts of your analogies.

Sophocles
c. 496–406 B.C.

Lee Boltin Picture Library

The tragedies of Sophocles probe the depth of human suffering and despair as profoundly as the works of any writer in world literature. The playwright himself, in contrast to the misery he portrayed in his works, lived a long, comfortable, and happy life. He grew up in a well-to-do family in Athens, enjoyed a carefree childhood and education, and eventually became a distinguished public official as well as an outstanding dramatist.

Sophocles first achieved recognition in the theater at the age of twenty-eight, when he defeated Aeschylus—another great Greek playwright—in an annual dramatic competition. He went on to win twenty-four first prizes over the next six decades—the best record of any Greek playwright. He produced 123 plays, of which only seven survive today.

The artistic fulfillment of Sophocles' long life reflects the spirit of the age in which he lived. The first half of the fifth century B.C. in Athens was a time of political expansion and social optimism, following the great victories of the Greeks over the invading Persians at Marathon (490 B.C.) and Salamis (480 B.C.). In the second half of the century, the Athenians experienced tremendous intellectual and cultural developments. This was the brilliant era of the statesman Pericles, the historians Herodotus and Thucydides, and the philosopher Socrates. It was the age that raised the majestic temple called the Parthenon on the Acropolis high above the city and developed democracy as a political system. The age of Sophocles was indeed a time when anything seemed possible through human effort and reason.

Toward the end of Sophocles' life, however, this expansive spirit began to dwindle, largely because of the costly investment of Athenian lives and resources in the long Peloponnesian War (431–404 B.C.). This conflict pitted Athens and her allies against the rival city of Sparta and various other allied city-states for twenty-seven years. Perhaps this is one of the reasons that Sophocles' surviving plays—most of which were written after 440 B.C.—are so deeply troubling. They depict characters caught up in unsolvable dilemmas that test their faith in divine and human justice.

MORE ABOUT THE AUTHOR
Sophocles lived through most of Athens' Golden Age. The playwright's love for Athens began in his youth, when he was chosen to lead one of the city's victory celebrations after the defeat of the Persians at the battle of Salamis in 480 B.C. An actor as well as a playwright, he also held high elective offices in Athens, once as imperial treasurer and twice as general. He was friendly with the leading figures of his time, including the political ruler Pericles and the historian Herodotus. In 430 B.C. Sophocles lived through a plague like the one that sweeps through the city of Thebes in *Oedipus Rex*. The plague killed Pericles, as well as thousands of others. Sophocles' own death did not occur until years later, when he was ninety years old.

ABOUT THE TRANSLATORS
Dudley Fitts (1903–1968), a celebrated poet, critic, and translator, also taught English for many years at the well-known Choate School and Phillips Academy, Andover. He published several volumes of his own verse and achieved high acclaim as a translator of Greek tragedy and comedy.

Robert Fitzgerald. See the *Iliad*, page 227.

1 LITERARY BACKGROUND

Tragedy: The word *tragedy* is derived from the Greek words *tragos* ("goat") and *ode* ("song"). *Tragedy* may have originally referred to a type of song or pantomime performed in goat costumes at the religious festivals of Dionysus. In these performances, men were dressed in goatskins to play satyrs attending the god.

2 HISTORICAL BACKGROUND

The close connection between drama and civic life in Athens is illustrated by the claim that Sophocles' *Antigone* (produced in 442 B.C.) was so popular that the playwright was elected general—the highest public office a citizen could hold—the following year. What importance do dramatists have in today's society? How are they honored?

3 HISTORICAL BACKGROUND

As far as we know, ancient Greek tragedies never used more than three actors. The chorus in Sophocles' day was made up of fifteen dancer-singers. It was the responsibility of the playwright-director to train the chorus.

Introduction

Oedipus Rex

Oedipus Rex is considered one of the world's greatest tragedies. A **tragedy** is a serious drama featuring a noble, dignified main character—often a member of royalty—who strives to achieve something and is ultimately defeated. The defeat of the hero may appear to be brought about by forces beyond his or her control, and the outcome, or fate, seems almost predetermined. But often the main character's downfall is brought about by his or her own character flaw or weakness—the **tragic flaw.** In spite of defeat and even death, however, the tragic hero is ennobled by his or her newly gained self-knowledge and wisdom.

The Greek Theater

The second half of the fifth century B.C. was the golden age of Greek drama, especially of tragedy, which grew out of religious ritual drama. In Athens, the dramatic festivals and contests were the center of cultural life. The annual festival in honor of the god Dionysus, called the Dionysia, was a four-day extravaganza held in March or April, during which fifteen thousand spectators witnessed a variety of plays in the open-air Theater of Dionysus. Tragedies were usually presented in trilogies, or cycles of three linked plays, together with comedies or other forms of lighter drama. The dramatic festival was so important to civic life that the city magistrates selected the playwrights for each annual competition, and wealthy citizens with political ambitions subsidized the production fees. Judges ranked the competing playwrights and awarded prizes to the winners.

The Theater of Dionysus was carved out of a stone hillside and resembled a semicircle with steeply rising tiers of seats. At the bottom was the rounded **orchestra**, or performance area, where the chorus sang and danced. Behind the orchestra was an open, practically bare stage, where the actors spoke their lines from behind huge masks. These masks were often decorated to suggest character types familiar to the audience: for example, a king, a messenger, a prophet, a queen, or a nurse. All the roles in Greek plays were performed by male actors. By switching masks, one actor could play a number of roles—both male and female—in a single play.

Roberto Valladares/The Image Bank

Theater of Dionysus.
How is this ancient Greek theater like or unlike the theater today? How do you think the Greeks might have compensated for a lack of amplified sound and artificial lighting?

The Oedipus Trilogy

Oedipus Rex is one of Sophocles' three "Theban plays"—three tragedies about King Oedipus (ed′i·pəs) of Thebes and his family. Sophocles did not write these three plays to be performed at a single festival, as was a common practice in his day. Instead, he composed them over a 36-year period—actually beginning with the tragedy *Antigone*, the third and last part of the story, which was first performed in 442 B.C. This play, which takes place after the death of Oedipus, dramatizes a fateful struggle between Oedipus's daughter Antigone and his successor as the ruler of Thebes, King Creon. In *Antigone*, Sophocles explored a timeless conflict: the clash between individual conscience and established authority, or the law of the state.

The middle part of the story—the death and redemption of Oedipus in exile and old age—became the subject of Sophocles' last tragedy, *Oedipus at Colonus*. This play, produced in 406 B.C., was written when the playwright was nearing the age of ninety. Remarkably, the play does not reflect any decline in Sophocles' poetic powers.

4 LITERARY BACKGROUND
Sophocles was credited with being an innovator in several respects. He increased the chorus from twelve to fifteen performers, added a third actor, and was the first playwright to discard the Greek custom of writing trilogies and instead wrote single plays.

5 LITERARY BACKGROUND
Another traditional but unverifiable story claims that Sophocles' son attempted to have his father judged incompetent because of the playwright's advanced age. Sophocles (aged 90) defended himself by reading aloud to the court one of the choral odes he had composed for *Oedipus at Colonus*. He asked the judges if his poetry sounded like that of a mentally incompetent or defective person. Needless to say, the court ruled in the playwright's favor.

Oedipus's name also contains a pun on the Greek verb "I know" (*oida*). Oedipus's knowledge is an important theme in *Oedipus Rex:* He knows how to solve the riddle of the Sphinx, but does not know enough about himself to avert the tragedy that befalls him.

The Sphinx: A famous mythical animal, the Sphinx probably originated in Egypt, where the Great Sphinx can be seen to this day at the foot of the Pyramids of Giza, just outside Cairo. This lion-headed figure, sometimes male and sometimes female, was known also to the ancient Syrians, Phoenicians, and Mycenaean Greeks.

HUMANITIES CONNECTION

This detail from a Greek drinking cup shows Oedipus confronting the Sphinx. Mortified at Oedipus's success in solving her riddle, the Sphinx killed herself.

❓ *To what kind of person would you apply the term* Sphinx? (someone who is mysterious and hard to figure out) ∎

The Story of Oedipus

Oedipus Rex—chronologically the first part of the Theban trilogy—was actually written second. The tale of King Oedipus would have been familiar to the Greek audience of the time. Oedipus is the ill-fated king of Thebes whose mysterious past catches up with him and wreaks havoc on himself and his family. Oedipus won the hand of Queen Jocasta after the death of her husband, King Laius, by solving a riddle posed by the Sphinx, a monster that was terrorizing the city of Thebes.

Oedipus had been traveling to Thebes from Corinth, having run away from his home there because of a divine prediction that he would someday murder his father and marry his mother. Oedipus did not know that he was not the child of the king and queen of Corinth, but was in fact the child of Jocasta and Laius of Thebes. They, too, had heard the prophecy when he was born and had made arrangements for a shepherd to leave the infant, with its ankles pinned together, on the side of a mountain to die. The shepherd, however, took pity on the child and gave him to a Corinthian messenger, who in turn brought him to the king and queen of Corinth. They named him Oedipus, which means "swollen foot," and raised him as their son. Years later, as Oedipus traveled to Thebes, he unknowingly met King Laius, his real father, on the road and killed him, thus setting the prophecy into motion.

Oedipus earned his reputation of deliverer of the Thebans by solving the riddle of the Sphinx and saving the city of Thebes from disaster. The Sphinx was a monster in the shape of a lion with the wings of an eagle and the head of a woman. It lay waiting outside the city and would challenge passersby to solve the riddle: "What walks on four legs in the morning, on two legs at noon, and on three legs in the evening?" If they could not answer, they were killed immediately. Until Oedipus, no one had the answer to the riddle—"Man"—and the city was suffering. After solving the riddle of the Sphinx, Oedipus marries Jocasta, has four children with her, and rules with her and Creon, her brother, for twenty years.

As the play begins, the city of Thebes is suffering again, this time from a terrible plague. Creon reports from the oracle, or priestess, of Apollo that the plague will not end until the murderer of King Laius is found and punished. Oedipus commits himself to locating the

Detail of Oedipus and the Sphinx.

Scala/Art Resource, New York

murderer and suffers terrible consequences as he discovers the truth about
himself and his identity.

The Structure and Themes of the Play

Because the story of Oedipus was well
known to the fifth-century B.C. audience,
Sophocles was able to focus his play on
the discovery of deeds committed before
the action of the play begins. All the violence takes place offstage, and what the
audience sees are the responses of those
who must live with the truth or perish.

The play maintains a tight dramatic
framework. All the action takes place in
a single location and involves a small
number of characters interacting with
the central figure Oedipus, who remains
on stage for nearly the entire play. In
addition, the Chorus, which serves simply as a nameless onlooker and commentator in other Greek tragedies, is
turned by Sophocles into a collective "actor" within the drama itself.

The play consists almost entirely of
dramatic dialogue. But in this work what
is left unsaid is often more powerful
than what is explicitly expressed. Practically every line contains a possible double meaning or an ambiguity. This verbal
irony serves to reinforce the dramatic
irony of the play, as the main characters
and even the Chorus only gradually
come to grips with what is evident to
the audience at the very start. The
razor-sharp irony in *Oedipus Rex* is one
of the elements that has given the play
its power to spellbind audiences for
thousands of years—and has also made
updated versions of the story popular

**Roman mosaic of actors preparing for a
performance with masks.**

Scala/Art Resource, New York

from Roman times to the present day.

The themes, or underlying messages,
of *Oedipus Rex* are crucial to the play's
long-lasting appeal. Audiences for generations have recognized and been affected
by the issues that lead to Oedipus's
downfall. The themes explored include:

1. The quest for identity
2. The nature of innocence and guilt
3. The nature of moral responsibility
4. Human will versus fate
5. The abuse of power

The structure of most Greek tragedies
presents a tight, formal arrangement of
parts. These parts include the **prologue**
(opening scene), the ***parodos*** (the first of
the Chorus's lyric songs or choral odes),
a regular alternation of scenes in **dialogue** and **choral odes**, and, finally, the
exodos (concluding scene). These terms
have been retained in this translation of
Oedipus Rex.

8 LITERARY BACKGROUND
The legend of Oedipus
stretches back to a time many
centuries before Sophocles.
Homer's version of the story,
given briefly in Book 11 of the
Odyssey, lines 271–280, alludes
to the parricide and incest of
Oedipus and to the suicide of
Jocasta (whom Homer calls
Epikaste).

HUMANITIES CONNECTION

The masks used in Greek
drama were constructed to
portray a fixed emotion, such
as grief or rage, and contained
metallic mouthpieces designed
to enhance the resonance of
the actor's voice. The use of
masks was preserved in the
Roman theater and passed on
into early Italian theater and
the miracle plays of the Middle
Ages.
*For what occasions do we
wear masks today?* (Possible
responses: Halloween, Mardi
Gras, carnivals or other costume or masquerade parties) ■

9 LITERARY BACKGROUND
Most stage productions of
Oedipus Rex last less than an
hour and a half—significantly
shorter, for example, than a
Shakespeare play. *Macbeth*, a
relatively short Shakespeare
tragedy, lasts about twice as
long as *Oedipus Rex.*

OBJECTIVES

1. *To analyze* Oedipus Rex *and to recognize the conventions of ancient Greek tragedy*
2. *To identify and interpret dramatic irony*
3. *To write an essay analyzing the form of the play, a sequel extending the plot, and an essay analyzing Oedipus as a tragic hero*
4. *To identify and analyze figures of speech*

THEMES IN WORLD LITERATURE

The Search for Meaning

From "The Tragedy of Sohráb and Rostám" from the *Shahname*, pp. 646–653
From *Faust*, Part I, pp. 986–1001
"The Jewels," pp. 1032–1041

What Is a Hero?

"Theseus," pp. 28–33
From the *Aeneid*, pp. 379–406
From the *Nibelungenlied*, pp. 730–740 ▪

VOCABULARY IN CONTEXT

The words listed below will appear in the side margin at the point of instruction:

1. supplication	6. disdain
2. compunction	7. void
3. expedient	8. venerate
4. decrepit	9. primal
5. incarnate	10. engendered

PREREADING FOCUS

Background: The original title of Sophocles' play was simply *Oedipus*. Only later was the Greek word *tyrannos* (meaning "non-hereditary king" rather than "tyrant" in the modern sense) or the Latin word *rex* (meaning "king") appended to the title. We do not know the exact year in which the play was first performed. From the references to the plague, we can infer that the first performance occurred shortly after the outbreak of the plague in Athens in 430 B.C. Curiously enough, this most famous of Greek tragedies won only second prize for Sophocles at its premier dramatic festival.

Literary Focus: You may wish to review the various types of irony and provide examples of each. Dramatic irony results from a discrepancy in knowledge. Point out that verbal irony also involves a discrepancy or pointed contrast— between what is said on the surface and what is really meant. In situational irony, there is a contrast between what is expected to happen and what actually occurs.

Reader's Guide

OEDIPUS REX

Background

During the early years of the Peloponnesian War, when *Oedipus Rex* was first produced, Athens was suffering from both political instability and a devastating plague that was taking its toll on the population. Thus, Sophocles opens his play with a situation that the Athenians could readily identify with: The city of Thebes is beset by a terrible plague, and there is no end in sight. According to the oracle of Apollo, the plague will continue until the murderer of King Laius, still living in Thebes, is caught and punished for his crime. Oedipus, casting himself in the role of savior of Thebes, as he did once before with the deadly Sphinx, vows to do everything in his power to apprehend the murderer and save his people. Little does he realize that his vow will relentlessly lead him to an encounter with himself and his darkest secrets.

Writer's Response

The ancient Greeks cited the myth of Oedipus as a striking example of how human fortunes can suffer unexpected drastic reversals—how even good and noble people can suffer at the hands of fate or the will of the gods. Can you think of other examples from literature or real life in which people suddenly experience a sharp reversal of fortune? What were the circumstances? Were the people involved responsible for what happened, or were they innocent victims? How do people explain and cope with such tragedies? Freewrite your answer.

Literary Focus

Irony is the difference between what is expected to happen and what actually happens. **Dramatic irony** occurs when the reader or audience knows something important that a character in a story or drama does not know. The fundamental irony in *Oedipus Rex* stems from the fact that the audience knows King Oedipus's true identity, while he is unaware of it. Sophocles ingeniously creates numerous variations on this central irony throughout the play, increasing the audience's suspense and heightening their pity and horror.

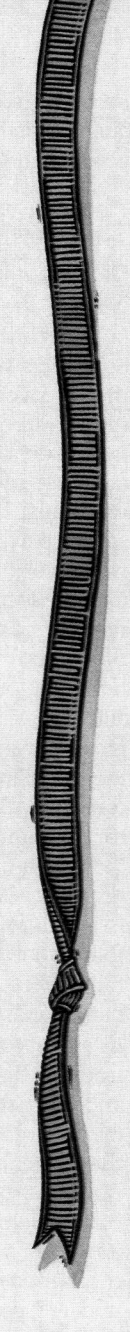

OEDIPUS REX
Part 1
Sophocles
translated by
DUDLEY FITTS AND ROBERT FITZGERALD

The action of **Oedipus Rex** may be described as a search for the truth. As you read, pay attention to the role each character plays in either fulfilling or further complicating this search.

CHARACTERS

Oedipus (ed'i·pəs, ē'di-), King of Thebes

A Priest

Creon (krē'än'), brother of Jocasta

Teiresias (tī·rē'sē·əs), a blind seer

Jocasta (jō·kas'tə), wife of Oedipus and widow of Laius (lā'yəs), former King of Thebes

Messenger, from Corinth

Shepherd of Laius

Second Messenger, from the palace

Chorus of Theban Elders

Choragos (kə·rā'gəs), the leader of the Chorus

Antigone (an·tig'ə·nē) and **Ismene** (is·mē'nē), daughters of Oedipus and Jocasta

Suppliants

Page

Servants and Attendants

SCENE

Before the palace of OEDIPUS, *King of Thebes. A central door and two lateral doors open onto a platform which runs the length of the facade. On the platform, right and left, are altars; and three steps lead down into the "orchestra," or chorus-ground. At the beginning of the action these steps are crowded by suppliants who have brought branches and chaplets of olive leaves and who lie in various attitudes of despair.* OEDIPUS *enters.*

LITERARY BACKGROUND
Sophocles' audience would have been familiar with the Oedipus legend. The playwright had already produced his *Antigone*, which was based on a later phase of the legend. In addition, Sophocles' predecessor Aeschylus (525–456 B.C.) had produced a trilogy of plays on the same theme about thirty-five years before *Oedipus Rex*.

1 CULTURAL DIVERSITY
The Theater of Dionysus at Athens was one of the largest in the ancient Mediterranean world. The entire Globe Theater of Elizabethan times could have fit into the orchestra. The ancient Athenian spectators, therefore, sat quite far away from the chorus and even farther away from the actors, who had to project their voices a long distance.

❓ *What has been lost and gained in the modern theatrical world through the use of microphones and other devices?* (The natural strength of an actor's voice is less important now; in a modern theater it is much easier to make the performance audible to every member of the audience.)

Performing Choral Odes

Greek tragedies alternate between dialogue spoken by the characters on stage and lyric odes sung in unison by members of the Chorus as they dance to musical accompaniment in the orchestra. In the odes of *Oedipus Rex*, the Chorus comments on the action by expressing the Theban people's thoughts and emotions. The choral odes may also include flashbacks, related incidents from other Greek myths, or foreshadowings. The language of choral lyrics tends to be highly metaphorical; thus, the odes are often more difficult to understand than the dialogue.

Reading and Speaking. Divide students into groups of five or six. Then have each group choose a different choral ode from *Oedipus Rex*. After students are confident that they have a good grasp of the ode's meaning and have practiced reciting in unison, have each group present its ode to the class. ∎

---

supplication (sup′lə·kā′shən): a humble prayer or request

2 LITERARY ELEMENT

Characterization: Playwrights must use indirect methods of characterization to reveal the personalities of their characters. What do Oedipus's words to the Thebans in lines 13–15 reveal about his character? (Possible response: He is concerned, sympathetic, and eager to help his subjects.)

Billy Rose Theatre Collection, New York Public Library for the Performing Arts

═ PROLOGUE ═

Oedipus.

My children, generations of the living
In the line of Cadmus,° nursed at his ancient hearth:
Why have you strewn yourselves before these altars
In supplication, with your boughs and garlands?
5   The breath of incense rises from the city
With a sound of prayer and lamentation.

                     Children,
I would not have you speak through messengers,
And therefore I have come myself to hear you—
I, Oedipus, who bear the famous name.

10   (*to a* PRIEST) You, there, since you are eldest in the
      company,
Speak for them all, tell me what preys upon you,
Whether you come in dread, or crave some blessing:
Tell me, and never doubt that I will help you
In every way I can; I should be heartless

2. **Cadmus** (kad′məs): in Greek mythology, a prince who killed a dragon and sowed its teeth, which turned into an army of men who fought one another; with the five survivors of the battle, Cadmus founded Thebes.

6 ❓ Try to visualize the despairing postures of the suppliants as Oedipus addresses the people. Together with the details of the incense and the sounds of lamentation, what mood does the scene suggest at the opening of the play?

9 ❓ Do you think Oedipus is boasting here? Or is he merely being objective about his own status as the King of Thebes?

2 ⌐15   Were I not moved to find you suppliant here.

Priest.

     Great Oedipus, O powerful King of Thebes!
     You see how all the ages of our people
3   Cling to your altar steps: here are boys
     Who can barely stand alone, and here are priests
  20   By weight of age, as I am a priest of God.
     And young men chosen from those yet unmarried;
     As for the others, all that multitude,
     They wait with olive chaplets in the squares,
     At the two shrines of Pallas, and where Apollo
  25   Speaks in the glowing embers.
                   Your own eyes
4   Must tell you: Thebes is tossed on a murdering sea
     And cannot lift her head from the death surge.
     A rust consumes the buds and fruits of the earth;
     The herds are sick; children die unborn,
  30   And labor is vain. The god of plague and pyre
     Raids like detestable lightning through the city,
     And all the house of Cadmus is laid waste,
5   All emptied, and all darkened: Death alone
     Battens upon the misery of Thebes.

  35   You are not one of the immortal gods, we know;
     Yet we have come to you to make our prayer
     As to the man surest in mortal ways
     And wisest in the ways of God. You saved us
     From the Sphinx, that flinty singer,° and the tribute
  40   We paid to her so long; yet you were never
     Better informed than we, nor could we teach you:
     It was some god breathed in you to set us free.

6   Therefore, O mighty King, we turn to you:
     Find us our safety, find us a remedy,
  45   Whether by counsel of the gods or men.
     A king of wisdom tested in the past
     Can act in a time of troubles, and act well.
     Noblest of men, restore
     Life to your city! Think how all men call you
  50   Liberator for your triumph long ago;
     Ah, when your years of kingship are remembered,
     Let them not say *We rose, but later fell*—
     Keep the State from going down in the storm!
     Once, years ago, with happy augury,

22 ❓ What gestures might the Priest make as he says these lines?

39. **Sphinx . . . singer:** The Sphinx was a winged monster that killed anyone who could not answer her riddle: "What walks on four legs in the morning, two legs at noon, and three legs in the evening?" Oedipus gave the correct answer: "A man crawls as an infant, walks erect as a man, and uses a staff in old age." The Sphinx then killed herself.

42 ❓ What qualities or personality traits in Oedipus does the Priest single out as the ruler's special virtues?

53 ❓ What familiar metaphor for a state or kingdom is suggested by this line? How does the Priest refer again to this metaphor in line 58?

ANSWER TO MARGIN QUESTION

Line 60. Oedipus's referring to the Thebans as children suggests that he sees himself in a fatherly role, looking after his subjects. Dramatic irony lies in the fact that Oedipus is himself a child of a ruler of Thebes. Though he does not know this about his ancestry, the listening audience does.

7 LITERARY ELEMENT

Irony: What does Oedipus mean by this reference to his "sickness" in lines 62–63? (He is distressed and anguished because of his subjects' suffering.) What dramatic irony do you see in his words? (The audience knows, though Oedipus does not, that he really is "sicker" than anyone because of his hidden past.)

8 GUIDED READING

Finding the Main Idea: What does Oedipus say he has already done to bring relief to the city? (He says he has sent Creon to Delphi to learn from the oracle how Oedipus can save the city.)

9 DRAMATIC ELEMENT

Stage Directions: Scholars believe that Sophocles did not use stage directions. Entrances and exits are, therefore, often commented on by the characters on stage or by the chorus. You may wish to remind students that tragic actors wore masks. Creon's mask might not have conveyed the expression he was meant to have at that moment, so Sophocles describes it in line 83.

---

55 You brought us fortune; be the same again!
No man questions your power to rule the land:
But rule over men, not over a dead city!
Ships are only hulls, citadels are nothing,
When no life moves in the empty passageways.

Oedipus.
60 Poor children! You may be sure I know
All that you longed for in your coming here.
I know that you are deathly sick; and yet,
Sick as you are, not one is as sick as I.
Each of you suffers in himself alone
65 His anguish, not another's; but my spirit
Groans for the city, for myself, for you.

I was not sleeping, you are not waking me.
No, I have been in tears for a long while
And in my restless thought walked many ways.
70 In all my search, I found one helpful course,
And that I have taken: I have sent Creon,
Son of Menoeceus,° brother of the Queen,
To Delphi, Apollo's place of revelation,°
To learn there, if he can,
75 What act or pledge of mine may save the city.
I have counted the days, and now, this very day,
I am troubled, for he has overstayed his time.
What is he doing? He has been gone too long.
Yet whenever he comes back, I should do ill
80 To scant whatever duty God reveals.

Priest.
It is a timely promise. At this instant
They tell me Creon is here.

Oedipus.   O Lord Apollo!
May his news be fair as his face is radiant!

Priest.
It could not be otherwise: he is crowned with bay,
85 The chaplet is thick with berries.

Oedipus.   We shall soon know;
He is near enough to hear us now.

[*Enter* CREON.]
                                        O Prince:

Brother: son of Menoeceus:
What answer do you bring us from the god?

60 **?** Notice how Oedipus repeatedly refers to the Thebans as "children." What does this suggest about the way he regards them?

72. **Menoeceus** (me·nē′sus)
73. **Delphi** (del′fī) . . . **revelation:** Delphi was the seat of the most famous oracle of the god Apollo.

Line 90. The actor could deliver Creon's lines with forthrightness and confidence, with great optimism, with the paternal tone of someone giving advice, with condescension, or with pomposity and self-importance.

Line 95. Oedipus's words suggest an unselfish attitude, a feeling of sympathy for the people and trust in them. Creon's words suggest an attitude of caution, reserve, and self-protection, a feeling of separation from the people.

Line 109. The audience knows, though Oedipus does not, that Oedipus *did* see Laius, at the crossroads where Oedipus met the former king and killed him in an altercation.

10

Creon.
A strong one. I can tell you, great afflictions

90 Will turn out well, if they are taken well.

Oedipus.
What was the oracle? These vague words
Leave me still hanging between hope and fear.

Creon.
Is it your pleasure to hear me with all these
Gathered around us? I am prepared to speak,

95 But should we not go in?

Oedipus.   Let them all hear it.
It is for them I suffer, more than for myself.

Creon.
Then I will tell you what I heard at Delphi.
In plain words
The god commands us to expel from the land of Thebes

11

100 An old defilement we are sheltering.
It is a deathly thing, beyond cure;
We must not let it feed upon us longer.

Oedipus.
What defilement? How shall we rid ourselves of it?

Creon.
By exile or death, blood for blood. It was

105 Murder that brought the plague-wind on the city.

Oedipus.
Murder of whom? Surely the god has named him?

Creon.
My lord: long ago Laius was our king,
Before you came to govern us.

Oedipus.   I know;
I learned of him from others; I never saw him.

Creon.

110 He was murdered; and Apollo commands us now
To take revenge upon whoever killed him.

12

Oedipus.
Upon whom? Where are they? Where shall we
find a clue
To solve that crime, after so many years?

Creon.
Here in this land, he said.
                             If we make enquiry,

90 ❓ In what different ways could the actor playing Creon deliver these lines?

95 ❓ These two short speeches about where to hold their discussion suggest a contrast between Oedipus's and Creon's attitudes toward the people. What is this contrast?

109 ❓ What is dramatically ironic about Oedipus's line here?

10 CULTURAL BACKGROUND
In ancient Greece there were many oracles, people through whom the gods were believed to speak. The oracle of Apollo at Delphi was famous throughout the Greek world. Many people considered the oracles infallible.

11 LITERARY ELEMENT
Metaphor: In lines 101–102, Creon's words compare the "old defilement" to something terrible (possibly the plague) that the Thebans are sheltering. How would you paraphrase that metaphor? (Possible response: A fatal cancer or some other disease "feeds" upon the people in Thebes by devouring their flesh.)

12 LITERARY ELEMENT
Flashback: Since Sophocles' tragedy dramatizes Oedipus's discovery of his terrible past deeds, the play contains many flashbacks. What information does Creon give Oedipus (and the audience) about the past? (He says that Laius, the previous king of Thebes, was murdered. Apollo now commands revenge on whoever killed him.)

Line 127. Possible responses: Oedipus's possible slip might suggest that his unconscious mind is remembering the occurrence when he alone killed a regal man on the highway. In his unconscious, Oedipus may have begun to recognize that it was he who killed Laius.

Line 143. Oedipus's speculation suggests that the ancient Greek kingship was sometimes obtained through violence and that the king was often in danger of being assassinated.

13 LITERARY ELEMENT

Plot: Many readers have compared Sophocles' play to a detective story. Oedipus is portrayed as a master detective who "tracks down" the murderer of Laius and eventually finds it is himself. How does Oedipus start to assemble clues in lines 116–117? (He asks where Laius was murdered.)

14 LITERARY ELEMENT

Suspense: How is suspense created by this information about an eyewitness to the murder? (Possible response: We wonder who the witness may turn out to be and whether and when the witness may reveal more facts about the murder.)

> compunction (kəm·pungk'shən): remorse; feeling of guilty uneasiness

115   We may touch things that otherwise escape us.

Oedipus.
   Tell me: Was Laius murdered in his house,
   Or in the fields, or in some foreign country?

Creon.
   He said he planned to make a pilgrimage.
   He did not come home again.

Oedipus.   And was there no one,
120   No witness, no companion, to tell what happened?

Creon.
   They were all killed but one, and he got away
   So frightened that he could remember one thing only.

Oedipus.
   What was that one thing? One may be the key
   To everything, if we resolve to use it.

Creon.
125   He said that a band of highwaymen attacked them,
   Outnumbered them, and overwhelmed the King.

Oedipus.
   Strange, that a highwayman should be so daring—
   Unless some faction here bribed him to do it.

Creon.
   We thought of that. But after Laius' death
130   New troubles arose and we had no avenger.

Oedipus.
   What troubles could prevent your hunting down
     the killers?

Creon.
   The riddling Sphinx's song
   Made us deaf to all mysteries but her own.

Oedipus.
   Then once more I must bring what is dark to light.
135   It is most fitting that Apollo shows,
   As you do, this compunction for the dead.
   You shall see how I stand by you, as I should,
   To avenge the city and the city's god,
   And not as though it were for some distant friend,
140   But for my own sake, to be rid of evil.
   Whoever killed King Laius might—who knows?—
   Decide at any moment to kill me as well.
   By avenging the murdered king I protect myself.

127 ❓ Notice how Oedipus refers to a single "highwayman" in this line, whereas Creon had just mentioned a "band of highwaymen" in the plural in line 125. Do you think this is just a casual change from the plural to the singular? What might this slip on Oedipus's part (if it is a slip) suggest? Explain.

143 ❓ These lines are dramatically ironic, since the audience knows that Oedipus himself is the murderer. In addition to the dramatic irony, what does Oedipus's speculation about his own danger suggest about the nature of ancient Greek kingship?

Come, then, my children: leave the altar steps,
145　Lift up your olive boughs!
                              One of you go
　　And summon the people of Cadmus to gather here.
　　I will do all that I can; you may tell them that.

                              [*Exit a* PAGE.]
　　So, with the help of God,
　　We shall be saved—or else indeed we are lost.

Priest.
150　Let us rise, children. It was for this we came,
　　And now the King has promised it himself.
　　Phoebus° has sent us an oracle; may he descend
　　Himself to save us and drive out the plague.

　　[*Exeunt* OEDIPUS *and* CREON *into the palace by
　　the central door. The* PRIEST *and the* SUPPLIANTS
　　disperse right and left. After a short pause the CHO-
　　RUS *enters the orchestra.*]

═ PARADOS° ═══════════════

Strophe 1

Chorus.
　　What is God singing in his profound
155　Delphi of gold and shadow?
　　What oracle for Thebes, the sunwhipped city?

　　Fear unjoints me, the roots of my heart tremble.

　　Now I remember, O Healer,° your power, and wonder:
　　Will you send doom like a sudden cloud, or
　　　　weave it
160　Like nightfall of the past?

　　Speak, speak to us, issue of holy sound:
　　Dearest to our expectancy: be tender!

Antistrophe 1

　　Let me pray to Athena, the immortal daughter of Zeus,
　　And to Artemis her sister
165　Who keeps her famous throne in the market ring,
　　And to Apollo, bowman at the far butts of heaven—

152. **Phoebus** (fē′bəs): a name for Apollo as sun god; here, alluding to him as the god of prophecy.

Parados (par′ə·dōs′): the entrance song of the Chorus. Song and speech alternate throughout the play. In this choral song, the *strophe* (strō′fē) was sung as the Chorus turned from one side of the orchestra to the other. The *antistrophe* (an·tis′trə·fē) was sung while the Chorus moved in a direction opposite from that of the strophe.

158. **Healer:** Apollo, the god of medicine.

Line 170. They are alluding to Oedipus's saving the people of Thebes by solving the riddle of the Sphinx.

Line 187. In the first strophe and antistrophe, the mood is of awe, supplication, and hope. In the second strophe and antistrophe, by contrast, the mood is dark and despairing. Images that focus on death and decay include barren land, infertile women, ephemeral lives that last only until a bird takes wing or a spark dies, a plague that burns, dead children who lie unmourned, and "old gray women by every path" who flock to the altars where they wail to Apollo.

Line 196. The Chorus associates archery with Apollo. The Chorus imagines Apollo both as a destroyer who can demolish the enemy of Thebes and as a healer who can save Thebes from the plague.

---

19 LITERARY ELEMENT

Imagery: The Parados contains imagery of fire and burning to refer to the plague. Why are the gods likened to "three streams"? (because water is cooling and puts out fire) In line 30, there is a reference to "plague and pyre." What do you think the fire imagery means? (Possible responses: The fires may be the burning of a high fever from disease, the burning of dead bodies on a pyre, and a fiery, all-consuming grief.)

20 LITERARY ELEMENT

Imagery: Images of infertility recur throughout the play. In lines 28–29, how does the Priest also make use of agricultural imagery to stress the city's plight? (rust consuming buds and fruits, sick herds)

21 LITERARY BACKGROUND

The description of the plague in Thebes would have had a tremendous impact on Sophocles' audience. First, the audience would have recalled the actual plague in Athens that broke out in the year 430 and is described in Book 2 of Thucydides' *History of the Peloponnesian War.* Second, the audience would have been reminded of the opening scenes of Homer's *Iliad*, in which Apollo sends a plague to punish the Greek army for the arrogance of Agamemnon (see p. 229).

19
O gods, descend! Like three streams leap against
The fires of our grief, the fires of darkness;
Be swift to bring us rest!

170
As in the old time from the brilliant house
Of air you stepped to save us, come again!

Strophe 2

Now our afflictions have no end,
Now all our stricken host lies down
And no man fights off death with his mind;

20   175
The noble plowland bears no grain,
And groaning mothers cannot bear—
See, how our lives like birds take wing,
Like sparks that fly when a fire soars,
To the shore of the god of evening.

Antistrophe 2

180
The plague burns on, it is pitiless,
Though pallid children laden with death
Lie unwept in the stony ways,

And old gray women by every path
Flock to the strand about the altars

21   185
There to strike their breasts and cry
Worship of Phoebus in wailing prayers:
Be kind, God's golden child!

Strophe 3

There are no swords in this attack by fire,
No shields, but we are ringed with cries.
190
Send the besieger plunging from our homes
Into the vast sea room of the Atlantic
Or into the waves that foam eastward of Thrace°—

For the day ravages what the night spares—

Destroy our enemy, lord of the thunder!
195
Let him be riven by lightning from heaven!

Antistrophe 3

Phoebus Apollo, stretch the sun's bowstring,
That golden cord, until it sing for us,

---

170 ? The Chorus says that Apollo saved the city of Thebes once before. To what previous crisis do you think they are alluding?

187 ? How does the mood of Strophe 2 and Antistrophe 2 contrast with the mood of the first strophe and antistrophe? What images in the second pair of stanzas focus on death and decay?

192. **Thrace** (thrās): a region lying between the Aegean Sea, the Danube River, and the Black Sea.

196 ? What physical activity does the Chorus associate with Apollo? In the Chorus's imagination, is Apollo primarily a healer or a destroyer? Or is he both at once? Explain.

Flashing arrows in heaven!

                                  Artemis, Huntress,

Race with flaring lights upon our mountains!

200   O scarlet god, O golden-banded brow,

        O Theban Bacchus in a storm of Maenads,°

[*Enter* OEDIPUS, *center.*]

        Whirl upon Death, that all the Undying hate!

        Come with blinding torches, come in joy!

201. **Theban Bacchus** (bak′əs): Bacchus, also known as Dionysus, was the god of revelry and of brutality. He came to Thebes accompanied by women who sang and danced wildly. When Pentheus, the king of Thebes, mocked the god and his followers, he was punished by being torn limb from limb. **Maenads** (mē′nadz): priestesses of Bacchus.

22

New York Public Library/Stratford Festival, Ontario, Canada

23 LITERARY ELEMENT

Imagery: Oedipus's imagery in line 209 is part of a repeated cluster of "hunting" and "tracking" images. Why might this cluster of images strike the audience as ironic? (Oedipus is "hunting" a quarry who turns out to be himself.)

24 GUIDED READING

Identifying Details: What does Oedipus declare will happen to the murderer of Laius? (He will live an evil, wretched existence.)

CULTURAL BACKGROUND

Oedipus's words about punishing the murderer would have been terrifying for an ancient Greek audience. Exile from the protection of a household and a city-state and exclusion from all religious rites would have meant a life of misery on a par with death. Ironically, this is to be Oedipus's own fate at the end of the play.

= SCENE 1 =

Oedipus.

Is this your prayer? It may be answered. Come,
205   Listen to me, act as the crisis demands,
And you shall have relief from all these evils.

Until now I was a stranger to this tale,
As I had been a stranger to the crime.
Could I track down the murderer without a clue?
23   210   But now, friends,
As one who became a citizen after the murder,
I make this proclamation to all Thebans:
If any man knows by whose hand Laius, son
        of Labdacus,
Met his death, I direct that man to tell me everything.
215   No matter what he fears for having so long withheld it.
Let it stand as promised that no further trouble
Will come to him, but he may leave the land
        in safety.

Moreover: If anyone knows the murderer to
        be foreign,
Let him not keep silent: he shall have his
        reward from me.
220   However, if he does conceal it; if any man
Fearing for his friend or for himself disobeys this edict,
Hear what I propose to do:

I solemnly forbid the people of this country,
Where power and throne are mine, ever to
        receive that man
225   Or speak to him, no matter who he is, or let him
Join in sacrifice, lustration,° or in prayer.
I decree that he be driven from every house,
Being, as he is, corruption itself to us: the Delphic
Voice of Zeus has pronounced this revelation.
230   Thus I associate myself with the oracle
And take the side of the murdered king.

As for the criminal, I pray to God—
Whether it be a lurking thief, or one of a number—
I pray that that man's life be consumed in evil
        and wretchedness.
24   235   And as for me, this curse applies no less

207 ❓ What is unintentionally ironic about Oedipus's statement here?

226. **lustration** (lus·trā'shən): purification through ritual.

235 ❓ How does Sophocles deepen the irony of Oedipus's curse in these lines?

Line 235. Sophocles deepens the irony by having Oedipus say that his curse applies even if the culprit is his guest. This makes it evident to the audience that Oedipus's curse must apply to Oedipus himself, since he is the actual culprit.

Line 251. Possible response: The actor's tone might be earnest, expressing honesty and openness and a concern for the fate of Laius. His tone would also express some anger on behalf of the dead king.

If it should turn out that the culprit is my guest here,
Sharing my hearth.
          You have heard the penalty.
I lay it on you now to attend to this
For my sake, for Apollo's, for the sick
240 Sterile city that heaven has abandoned.
Suppose the oracle had given you no command:
Should this defilement go uncleansed forever?
You should have found the murderer: your king,
A noble king, had been destroyed!
               Now I,
245 Having the power that he held before me,
Having his bed, begetting children there
Upon his wife, as he would have, had he lived—
Their son would have been my children's brother,
If Laius had had luck in fatherhood!
250 (But surely ill luck rushed upon his reign)—
I say I take the son's part, just as though
I were his son, to press the fight for him
And see it won! I'll find the hand that brought
Death to Labdacus' and Polydorus' child,°
255 Heir of Cadmus' and Agenor's line.°
And as for those who fail me,
May the gods deny them the fruit of the earth,
Fruit of the womb, and may they rot utterly!
Let them be wretched as we are wretched, and
     worse!
260 For you, for loyal Thebans, and for all
Who find my actions right, I pray the favor
Of justice, and of all the immortal gods.

Choragos.
Since I am under oath, my lord, I swear
I did not do the murder, I cannot name
265 The murderer. Might not the oracle
That has ordained the search tell where to find him?

Oedipus.
An honest question. But no man in the world
Can make the gods do more than the gods will.

Choragos.
There is one last expedient—

Oedipus.
                  Tell me what it is.
270 Though it seem slight, you must not hold it back.

251 ❓ The irony in this long speech now reaches an almost unbearable intensity. What tone of voice might an actor playing Oedipus use for these lines?

254. **Labdacus** (lab′də·kəs): king of Thebes and father of Laius. **Polydorus' child:** Polydorus (päl·i·dō′rəs) was the grandfather of Laius.

255. **Agenor's** (ə·jē′nôr) **line:** Agenor, father of Cadmus, the founder of Thebes.

25 LITERARY ELEMENT
Imagery: What images do Oedipus's references to "sick," "sterile," "defilement," and "uncleansed" in lines 239–242 suggest? (images of disease and infertility)

26 LITERARY ELEMENT
Irony: Oedipus stresses his marriage to Jocasta, Laius's widow, and the children of this marriage. What is especially ironic about lines 248–249? (Possible response: Oedipus does not realize that, as the son of Laius and Jocasta, he is really the hypothetical "son" he speaks of in line 248, and thus the "brother" of his own children. He fails to see that Laius's bad "luck in fatherhood" came from having had a child.)

27 LITERARY BACKGROUND
The leader of the Chorus, the Choragos, speaks for the first time in lines 263–266. This spokesman represents the ordinary citizen of legendary Thebes, and perhaps of ancient Athens as well. He and the Chorus have an important role, as commentators on the action and, to some degree, as participants.

expedient (ek·spē′dē·ənt): a thing useful to achieving an end

28 LITERARY BACKGROUND

Teiresias, the old blind prophet, was regarded as a holy man of Thebes who knew more about the will of the gods than anyone else. He played a role in several of the Greek myths. For example, after Oedipus's exile and death, when Creon was ruler of Thebes, Teiresias prophesied the death of Creon's son Menoeceus.

Sophocles' audience would have been familiar with a number of ancient legends about Teiresias. It was said, for example, that he was blinded by Athena, whom he had seen naked while she was bathing. Another legend related that he saw snakes procreating, struck them with a stick, and was changed into a woman. He then was changed back into a man when the same thing happened again. A third legend related that Zeus and Hera asked Teiresias to resolve their dispute as to which sex derived more pleasure from making love. When Teiresias answered that it was the female, Hera grew angry and blinded him. To make up for this injury, Zeus gave Teiresias the power of prophecy and rewarded him with long life.

Choragos.
  A lord clairvoyant° to the lord Apollo,
  As we all know, is the skilled Teiresias.
  One might learn much about this from him, Oedipus.
Oedipus.
  I am not wasting time:
275 Creon spoke of this, and I have sent for him—
  Twice, in fact; it is strange that he is not here.
Choragos.
  The other matter—that old report—seems useless.
Oedipus.
  Tell me. I am interested in all reports.
Choragos.
  The King was said to have been killed by highwaymen.
Oedipus.
280 I know. But we have no witnesses to that.
Choragos.
  If the killer can feel a particle of dread,
  Your curse will bring him out of hiding!
Oedipus.   No.
  The man who dared that act will fear no curse.

  [*Enter the blind seer* TEIRESIAS, *led by a* PAGE.]

Choragos.
  But there is one man who may detect the criminal.
285 This is Teiresias, this is the holy prophet
  In whom, alone of all men, truth was born.
Oedipus.
  Teiresias: seer: student of mysteries,
  Of all that's taught and all that no man tells,
  Secrets of Heaven and secrets of the earth:
290 Blind though you are, you know the city lies
  Sick with plague; and from this plague, my lord,
  We find that you alone can guard or save us.

  Possibly you did not hear the messengers?
  Apollo, when we sent to him,
295 Sent us back word that this great pestilence
  Would lift, but only if we established clearly
  The identity of those who murdered Laius.
  They must be killed or exiled.
                                        Can you use
  Birdflight or any art of divination°

28

271. **clairvoyant** (kler·voi′ənt): capable of perceiving through intuition things that cannot be seen.

276. Compare Oedipus's statement here with lines 76-80. How does this passage resemble his earlier speech?

Billy Rose Theatre Collection, New York Public Library for the Performing Arts

299. **Birdflight . . . divination:** The flight of birds was observed by prophets and used in interpreting the future.

300   To purify yourself, and Thebes, and me
        From this contagion? We are in your hands.
        There is no fairer duty
        Than that of helping others in distress.

Teiresias.
        How dreadful knowledge of the truth can be
305   When there's no help in truth! I knew this well,
        But made myself forget. I should not have come.

Oedipus.
        What is troubling you? Why are your eyes so cold?

Teiresias.
        Let me go home. Bear your own fate, and I'll
        Bear mine. It is better so: trust what I say.

Oedipus.
310   What you say is ungracious and unhelpful
        To your native country. Do not refuse to speak.

Teiresias.
        When it comes to speech, your own is neither temperate
        Nor opportune. I wish to be more prudent.

Oedipus.
        In God's name, we all beg you—

Teiresias.   You are all ignorant.
315   No; I will never tell you what I know.
        Now it is my misery; then, it would be yours.

Oedipus.
        What! You do know something, and will not tell us?
        You would betray us all and wreck the State?

Teiresias.
        I do not intend to torture myself, or you.
320   Why persist in asking? You will not persuade me.

Oedipus.
        What a wicked old man you are! You'd try a stone's
        Patience! Out with it! Have you no feeling at all?

321   Is Oedipus's annoyed reaction here understandable, in your opinion? Or is Oedipus prematurely angry with Teiresias?

Teiresias.
        You call me unfeeling. If you could only see
        The nature of your own feelings . . .

Oedipus.   Why,
325   Who would not feel as I do? Who could endure
        Your arrogance toward the city?

Teiresias.   What does it matter!

29 EVALUATING
What do you think Teiresias means in lines 304–305? (Possible response: Knowledge of the truth can be a heavy burden when that knowledge cannot improve a situation.) Do you agree with Teiresias' statement? Why or why not? (Answers will vary.)

30 INTERPRETING
What has Oedipus inferred about Teiresias? (Teiresias has some important knowledge, yet is determined to be silent. To Oedipus, his silence amounts to treason.) Are these inferences justified? (Possible response: Teiresias himself has alluded that he possesses important knowledge. Oedipus's determination to get the information that his subjects' lives depend on is understandable; however, he seems rash in assuming that Teiresias has no good reasons for being silent.)

31 LITERARY ELEMENT
Dialogue: The play contains many instances in which one character misses the true point of what another is saying. What does Teiresias really mean by "the nature of your own feelings" in line 324? (the true nature of Oedipus's marriage, in which he loves his mother as his wife) How does Oedipus interpret the reference to his feelings? (to mean that he has no real concern for his subjects)

32 INTERPRETING

In line 327, Teiresias speaks as if fate will force out the truth. Do you think Sophocles portrays Oedipus as a puppet of fate or as a man with free will? (Possible response: Oedipus's actions were predestined from infancy, but it is still Oedipus's choice whether to pursue the identity of the murderer.)

33 CULTURAL BACKGROUND

The word *pollution* has a specific meaning in ancient Greek religion. Serious crimes like murder were thought literally to "pollute" the entire community until the criminal was punished or expelled.

34 CULTURAL BACKGROUND

Help students to understand Teiresias' accusation in a political context. In ancient Greece, a ruler who had not inherited his kingdom would be extremely sensitive to a charge that he had usurped the throne by violence. Oedipus, who believes that he has gained the throne of Thebes through peaceful means, is appropriately outraged by the prophet's charge. If Oedipus allows the charge to stick, he may reasonably fear assassination, rebellion, or civil war.

HUMANITIES CONNECTION

❓ *Compare the scene depicted on the Greek vase on page 320 with that of the Roman mosaic on page 305. What differences or similarities strike you?* ■

32 ☐   Whether I speak or not, it is bound to come.

Oedipus.
    Then, if "it" is bound to come, you are bound to
        tell me.

Teiresias.
    No, I will not go on. Rage as you please.

Oedipus.
330   Rage? Why not!
                  And I'll tell you what I think:
    You planned it, you had it done, you all but
    Killed him with your own hands: if you had eyes,
    I'd say the crime was yours, and yours alone.

Teiresias.
    So? I charge you, then,
335   Abide by the proclamation you have made:
    From this day forth
    Never speak again to these men or to me;
    You yourself are the pollution of this country.

33 ☐

Oedipus.
    You dare say that! Can you possibly think you have
340   Some way of going free, after such insolence?

Teiresias.
    I have gone free. It is the truth sustains me.

Oedipus.
    Who taught you shamelessness? It was not your craft.

Teiresias.
    You did. You made me speak. I did not want to.

Oedipus.
    Speak what? Let me hear it again more clearly.

Teiresias.
345   Was it not clear before? Are you tempting me?

Oedipus.
    I did not understand it. Say it again.

Teiresias.
    I say that you are the murderer whom you seek.

34

Oedipus.
    Now twice you have spat out infamy. You'll pay
        for it!

Teiresias.
    Would you care for more? Do you wish to be
    really angry?

331 ❓ How do you react to Oedipus's accusation in these lines?

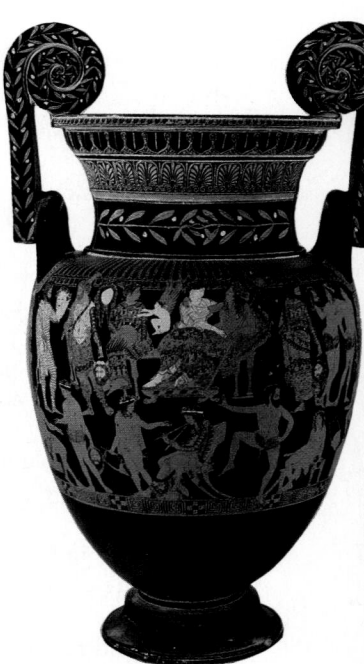

Greek vase showing preparations for a play.

ANSWER TO MARGIN QUESTION

Line 364. The mention of Apollo may remind Oedipus that it was from Creon that he first learned of Teiresias. It was Creon who first told Oedipus that Teiresias had an intuitive understanding of Apollo and might be able to shed light on Laius's fate.

Oedipus.
350   Say what you will. Whatever you say is worthless.

Teiresias.
    I say you live in hideous shame with those
    Most dear to you. You cannot see the evil.

Oedipus.
    It seems you can go on mouthing like this forever.

Teiresias.
    I can, if there is power in truth.

Oedipus.   There is:
355   But not for you, not for you,
    You sightless, witless, senseless, mad old man!

Teiresias.
    You are the madman. There is no one here
    Who will not curse you soon, as you curse me.

Oedipus.
    You child of endless night! You cannot hurt me
360   Or any other man who sees the sun.

Teiresias.
    True: it is not from me your fate will come.
    That lies within Apollo's competence,
    As it is his concern.

Oedipus.   Tell me:
    Are you speaking for Creon, or for yourself?

Teiresias.
365   Creon is no threat. You weave your own doom.

Oedipus.
    Wealth, power, craft of statesmanship!
    Kingly position, everywhere admired!
    What savage envy is stored up against these,
    If Creon, whom I trusted, Creon my friend,
370   For this great office which the city once
    Put in my hands unsought—if for this power
    Creon desires in secret to destroy me!

    He has bought this <u>decrepit</u> fortuneteller, this
    Collector of dirty pennies, this prophet fraud—
375   Why, he is no more clairvoyant than I am!
                                    Tell us:
    Has your mystic mummery° ever approached the
        truth?
    When that hellcat the Sphinx was performing here,

364 ❓ Why should Oedipus
    suddenly connect Creon
with Teiresias here? Look
back to see if line 275 gives
you a clue.

376. **mummery:** pretentious or
hypocritical rites.

Line 383. In saying that he "knows nothing," Oedipus is being deliberately ironic since it was he alone who knew enough to solve the riddle of the Sphinx. The unintentional irony, however, is in the audience's awareness that Oedipus does "know nothing" about the crimes he has committed while Teiresias has full knowledge of these terrible deeds.

Line 391. Possible response: Yes, the Chorus is right, since Oedipus's anger does not seem to accomplish anything toward purging Thebes of the plague.

---

38 GUIDED READING

Finding the Main Idea: According to Teiresias, in what sense is Oedipus the one who is "blind"? (Possible response: He does not see his true situation.)

39 LITERARY ELEMENT

Metaphor: To what does Teiresias compare the "curse" of Oedipus's parents? (to a "double lash" that will "whip" Oedipus out of the land)

40 LITERARY ELEMENT

Setting: This is the first mention of Mount Cithaeron. Located in the region of Thebes, Cithaeron will gradually acquire great importance in this play as an off-stage "setting." According to the side note, what happened on Mount Cithaeron? (Oedipus was left there as an infant to die.)

What help were you to these people?
Her magic was not for the first man who came along:
380   It demanded a real exorcist. Your birds—
What good were they? or the gods, for the matter of that?
But I came by,
Oedipus, the simple man, who knows nothing—
I thought it out for myself, no birds helped me!
385   And this is the man you think you can destroy,
That you may be close to Creon when he's king!
Well, you and your friend Creon, it seems to me,
Will suffer most. If you were not an old man,
You would have paid already for your plot.

Choragos.
390   We cannot see that his words or yours
Have been spoken except in anger, Oedipus,
And of anger we have no need. How can God's will
Be accomplished best? That is what most
        concerns us.

Teiresias.
You are a king. But where argument's concerned
395   I am your man, as much a king as you.
I am not your servant, but Apollo's.
I have no need of Creon to speak for me.

Listen to me. You mock my blindness, do you?
But I say that you, with both your eyes, are blind:
400   You cannot see the wretchedness of your life,
Nor in whose house you live, no, nor with whom.
Who are your father and mother? Can you tell me?
You do not even know the blind wrongs
That you have done them, on earth and in the
        world below.
405   But the double lash of your parents' curse will whip you
Out of this land some day, with only night
Upon your precious eyes.
Your cries then—where will they not be heard?
What fastness of Cithaeron° will not echo them?
410   And that bridal-descant° of yours—you'll know it
        then,
The song they sang when you came here to Thebes
And found your misguided berthing.
All this, and more, that you cannot guess at now,
Will bring you to yourself among your children.

383 ❓ This line furnishes a complex illustration of Sophoclean irony. As he mocks Teiresias, Oedipus tries deliberately to be ironic when he says he is a "simple man, who knows nothing." Explain how this line contains another, unintentional level of dramatic irony.

391 ❓ Choragos speaks for the entire Chorus. Do you agree with the Chorus's reaction to Oedipus here?

409. **Cithaeron** (si·thē′rän): a mountain in Boeotia (bē·ō′shə), where Oedipus as an infant was left to die.
410. **descant** (des′kant′): melody.

41   415
> Be angry, then. Curse Creon. Curse my words.
> I tell you, no man that walks upon the earth
> Shall be rooted out more horribly than you.

Oedipus.
> Am I to bear this from him?—Damnation
> Take you! Out of this place! Out of my sight!

Teiresias.
420
> I would not have come at all if you had not asked me.

Oedipus.
> Could I have told that you'd talk nonsense, that
> You'd come here to make a fool of yourself, and of me?

42   **Teiresias.**
> A fool? Your parents thought me sane enough.

Oedipus.
> My parents again!—Wait: who were my parents?

Teiresias.
425
> This day will give you a father, and break your heart.

Oedipus.
> Your infantile riddles! Your damned abracadabra!

Teiresias.
> You were a great man once at solving riddles.

Oedipus.
> Mock me with that if you like; you will find it true.

Teiresias.
> It was true enough. It brought about your ruin.

Oedipus.
430
> But if it saved this town?

Teiresias (*to the* PAGE).   Boy, give me your hand.

Oedipus.
> Yes, boy; lead him away.
>
>   —While you are here
> We can do nothing. Go; leave us in peace.

Teiresias.
> I will go when I have said what I have to say.
> How can you hurt me? And I tell you again:
435
> The man you have been looking for all this time,
> The damned man, the murderer of Laius,
> That man is in Thebes. To your mind he is foreign-born,
> But it will soon be shown that he is a Theban,
> A revelation that will fail to please.
>
>   A blind man,

427 ⓘ Explain Teiresias' mocking irony in this line. To what achievement of Oedipus does the prophet refer?

41 LITERARY ELEMENT

Foreshadowing: Teiresias' prediction in lines 415–417, that no man will be "rooted out more horribly" than Oedipus, will later be borne out. What earlier curse had Oedipus uttered? (a solemn curse on the murderer) What do Teiresias' predictions now suggest about Oedipus's curse? (The curse will backfire, since Oedipus is the murderer.)

42 LITERARY ELEMENT

Dialogue: Sophocles often uses subtle cues to develop the dialogue of the play. For example, Teiresias' mention of Oedipus's parents in line 423 suddenly causes Oedipus to shift gears and ask the prophet who his parents really were. *Who does Oedipus believe are his parents?* (King Polybus and Queen Merope of Corinth)

Line 446. Possible responses: When Teiresias speaks of Oedipus, the blind man might gesture in the direction of Oedipus. When he speaks of Oedipus's fate, he might point to his own eyes and tap with his cane. When he says "Enough," he might gesture with a sweep of his hand, palm outward.

Line 455. The Chorus alludes to the god Apollo.

Line 467. By "a wilder thing," the Chorus means Teiresias' stating that Oedipus is the murderer and prophesying a terrible fate for him. The "old man skilled at hearing Fate" is Teiresias.

---

43 INTERPRETING

What facts will the audience, who knows the truth about Oedipus's past, understand from Teiresias' words in lines 442–445? (Oedipus is both father and brother to his own children, is both son and husband to Jocasta, and has murdered his own father.)

MEETING INDIVIDUAL NEEDS

44 *LEP:* Be sure students understand that the "Delphic stone of prophecies" in line 449 refers to Apollo's oracle at Delphi. Point out that in line 450, "ancient regicide" alludes to the murder of King Laius, and that in line 451, "a still bloody hand" refers to the fact that Laius' murderer still has not been caught and punished. ∎

45 CULTURAL BACKGROUND

In Greek religion, the Furies were terrifying spirits believed to avenge the shedding of blood, especially within a family or clan.

---

440   Who has his eyes now; a penniless man, who is
        rich now;

And he will go tapping the strange earth with his staff

43 To the children with whom he lives now he will be

Brother and father—the very same; to her

Who bore him, son and husband—the very same

445   Who came to his father's bed, wet with his father's
        blood.

Enough. Go think that over.

If later you find error in what I have said,

You may say that I have no skill in prophecy.

[*Exit* TEIRESIAS, *led by his* PAGE. OEDIPUS
goes into the palace.]

446 ❓ What gestures might Teiresias make as he says these lines?

═ ODE° 1 ═

Strophe 1

Chorus.

44 450   The Delphic stone of prophecies

Remembers ancient regicide

And a still bloody hand.

That killer's hour of flight has come.

He must be stronger than riderless

Coursers of untiring wind,

455   For the son of Zeus armed with his father's thunder

45 Leaps in lightning after him;

And the Furies° follow him, the sad Furies.

Ode: a song chanted by the Chorus. An ode separates one scene from the next.

455 ❓ To whom does the Chorus allude when they mention "the son of Zeus"? (The "Delphic stone" in line 449 and "Holy Parnassus' peak of snow" in line 458 are clues.)

457. **Furies:** avenging spirits.

Antistrophe 1

Holy Parnassus'° peak of snow

Flashes and blinds that secret man,

460   That all shall hunt him down:

Though he may roam the forest shade

Like a bull gone wild from pasture

To rage through glooms of stone.

Doom comes down on him; flight will not avail him;

465   For the world's heart calls him desolate,

And the immortal Furies follow, forever follow.

458. **Parnassus** (pär·nas'əs): the mountain where Apollo's oracle was located.

467 ❓ What does the Chorus mean by a "wilder thing" in this line? Who is the "old man skilled at hearing Fate" who has appeared in the previous scene?

Strophe 2

But now a wilder thing is heard

Billy Rose Theatre Collection, New York Public Library for the Performing Arts

46 LITERARY ELEMENT
Conflict: In lines 469–475, the Chorus refers to both an external conflict and an internal conflict. What possible external conflict does the Chorus mention but reject? (a conflict between the royal house of Thebes and the "son of Polybus," or Oedipus) Of what internal conflict in their own minds is the Chorus beginning to be aware? (a conflict between their belief in the oracle and their loyalty to Oedipus)

47 GUIDED READING
Finding the Main Idea: How would you state the main idea of the Chorus in lines 476–480? (Possible response: Only the gods have perfect wisdom; human beings, even diviners, are fallible.)

From the old man skilled at hearing Fate in the
    wingbeat of a bird.
Bewildered as a blown bird, my soul hovers and
    cannot find
470 Foothold in this debate, or any reason or rest of mind.
But no man ever brought—none can bring
Proof of strife between Thebes' royal house,
Labdacus' line, and the son of Polybus;
And never until now has any man brought word
475 Of Laius' dark death staining Oedipus the King.

Antistrophe 2

Divine Zeus and Apollo hold
Perfect intelligence alone of all tales ever told;
And well though this diviner works, he works in
    his own night;
No man can judge that rough unknown or trust in
    second sight,

Oedipus Rex, Ode 1   **325**

Line 484. The Chorus, who represent the common people, saw Oedipus as courageous and heroic when he stood up to the Sphinx and saved the Thebans. They find it impossible to believe that he could be Laius's murderer.

Line 486. Creon refers to Oedipus's accusations that he and Teiresias have plotted to overthrow Oedipus by accusing him of Laius's murder.

Line 503. Opinions will vary. Possible response: The Chorus wants to play peacemaker, as they dislike conflict. Earlier, the Choragos had said to Oedipus "of anger we have no need."

48 GUIDED READING

Identifying Details: Creon's lines as he enters make clear that there has been a small lapse of time between the end of the last scene and the beginning of this one—enough for a witness to report Oedipus's accusations to Creon. What relation is Creon to Oedipus? (his brother-in-law, and also his uncle)

49 LITERARY ELEMENT

Characterization: In lines 497–504, Sophocles indirectly characterizes both the Choragos and Creon through the dialogue. How would you characterize the Choragos from his words? (Possible response: He is cautious and willing to give Oedipus the benefit of the doubt.) What do Creon's questions imply about his personality? (Possible response: He insists on knowing the facts.)

480
For wisdom changes hands among the wise.
Shall I believe my great lord criminal
At a raging word that a blind old man let fall?
I saw him, when the carrion woman° faced him of old,
Prove his heroic mind! These evil words are lies.

483. **carrion woman:** the Sphinx.

484 ❓ Why does the Chorus refuse to believe Teiresias' accusations against Oedipus?

SCENE 2

Creon.

485
Men of Thebes:
I am told that heavy accusations
Have been brought against me by King Oedipus.

I am not the kind of man to bear this tamely.

486 ❓ What are the accusations to which Creon refers here?

If in these present difficulties
490
He holds me accountable for any harm to him
Through anything I have said or done—why, then,
I do not value life in this dishonor.
It is not as though this rumor touched upon
Some private indiscretion. The matter is grave.
495
The fact is that I am being called disloyal
To the State, to my fellow citizens, to my friends.

Choragos.
He may have spoken in anger, not from his mind.

Creon.
But did you not hear him say I was the one
Who seduced the old prophet into lying?

Choragos.
500
The thing was said; I do not know how seriously.

Creon.
But you were watching him! Were his eyes steady?
Did he look like a man in his right mind?

Choragos. I do not know,
I cannot judge the behavior of great men.
But here is the King himself.

[*Enter* OEDIPUS.]

Oedipus. So you dared come back.
505
Why? How brazen of you to come to my house,

503 ❓ Is the Chorus noncommittal here because they want to play the peacemaker, or are they "passing the buck," in your opinion?

50   You murderer!

                          Do you think I do not know

51   That you plotted to kill me, plotted to steal my throne?

Tell me, in God's name: am I a coward, a fool,

That you should dream you could accomplish this?

510   A fool who could not see your slippery game?

A coward, not to fight back when I saw it?

You are the fool, Creon, are you not? hoping

Without support or friends to get a throne?

Thrones may be won or bought: you could do neither.

Creon.

515   Now listen to me. You have talked; let me talk, too.

You cannot judge unless you know the facts.

Oedipus.

You speak well: there is one fact; but I find it hard

To learn from the deadliest enemy I have.

Creon.

That above all I must dispute with you.

Oedipus.

520   That above all I will not hear you deny.

Creon.

52   If you think there is anything good in being stubborn

Against all reason, then I say you are wrong.

Oedipus.

If you think a man can sin against his own kind

And not be punished for it, I say you are mad.

Creon.

525   I agree. But tell me: what have I done to you?

Oedipus.

You advised me to send for that wizard, did you not?

Creon.

I did. I should do it again.

Oedipus.   Very well. Now tell me:

How long has it been since Laius—

Creon.   What of Laius?

53

Oedipus.

Since he vanished in that onset by the road?

Creon.

530   It was long ago, a long time.

Oedipus.   And this prophet,

Was he practicing here then?

50 LITERARY ELEMENT

Irony: What is ironic about Oedipus's calling Creon a murderer? (Oedipus himself is a murderer.)

51 LITERARY ELEMENT

Characterization: What character traits do Oedipus's questions in lines 506–511 suggest? (Possible responses: He is somewhat paranoid and inclined to anger; he is proud of his intelligence and his courage; he is quick to fight back when he feels threatened.)

52 LITERARY ELEMENT

Repetition: What words are repeated in lines 519–524? ("That above all" and "If you think") How is the repetition created, and what is the effect? (Oedipus creates the repetition by echoing Creon's statements. By echoing Creon, Oedipus matches his statements with equally strong ones, and mocks him as well.)

53 ANALYZING

Why does Oedipus ask Creon these particular questions? (to pin down the time of the murder; to establish a connection between the prophet Teiresias and the murder)

ANSWER TO MARGIN QUESTION

Line 537. Possible responses: quiet and rational, self-righteous and indignant, or somewhat sarcastic (to imply that Oedipus has unwisely spoken out before he knows the facts)

54 EVALUATING

What is Oedipus's reason for alleging that Teiresias must have conspired with Creon? (He says Teiresias would not otherwise have accused Oedipus of the murder of Laius.) Is this reasoning logical, in your opinion? (Possible response: It is not logical because Teiresias could have accused him for many other reasons.)

55 LITERARY ELEMENT

Dialogue: In lines 544–549, the usual pattern in the question-and-answer dialogue of the play is reversed: Creon asks the questions, and Oedipus answers them. What may be Creon's objective as he puts these questions to the king? (to prove his innocence)

Creon.   He was; and with honor, as now.
Oedipus.
Did he speak of me at that time?
Creon.   He never did;
At least, not when I was present.
Oedipus.   But . . . the inquiry?
I suppose you held one?
Creon.   We did, but we learned nothing.
Oedipus.
535   Why did the prophet not speak against me then?
Creon.
I do not know; and I am the kind of man
Who holds his tongue when he has no facts to go on.
Oedipus.
There's one fact that you know, and you could tell it.
Creon.
What fact is that? If I know it, you shall have it.
Oedipus.
540   If he were not involved with you, he could not say
That it was I who murdered Laius.
Creon.
If he says that, you are the one that knows it!—
But now it is my turn to question you.
Oedipus.
Put your questions. I am no murderer.
Creon.
545   First, then: You married my sister?
Oedipus.   I married your sister.
Creon.
And you rule the kingdom equally with her?
Oedipus.
Everything that she wants she has from me.
Creon.
And I am the third, equal to both of you?
Oedipus.
That is why I call you a bad friend.
Creon.
550   No. Reason it out, as I have done.
Think of this first: Would any sane man prefer
Power, with all a king's anxieties,

537 ❓ What tone of voice might the actor playing Creon use for this line?

ANSWERS TO MARGIN QUESTIONS
Line 560. Possible response: Creon's reasoning is faulty. He does not have the same rights and powers as the king, since all of his rights, power, and influence depend on the king.
Line 582. It takes time to prove the goodness of a just man, while condemnation is easy, quick, and often rash.
Line 587. Oedipus is addressing the Choragos.

To that same power and the grace of sleep?
Certainly not I.

555 I have never longed for the king's power—only his rights.
Would any wise man differ from me in this?
As matters stand, I have my way in everything
With your consent, and no responsibilities.
If I were king, I should be a slave to policy.

560 How could I desire a scepter more
Than what is now mine—untroubled influence?
No, I have not gone mad; I need no honors,
Except those with the perquisites I have now.
I am welcome everywhere; every man salutes me,

565 And those who want your favor seek my ear,
Since I know how to manage what they ask.
Should I exchange this ease for that anxiety?
Besides, no sober mind is treasonable.
I hate anarchy

570 And never would deal with any man who likes it.

Test what I have said. Go to the priestess
At Delphi, ask if I quoted her correctly.
And as for this other thing: if I am found
Guilty of treason with Teiresias,

575 Then sentence me to death! You have my word
It is a sentence I should cast my vote for—
But not without evidence!
                        You do wrong
When you take good men for bad, bad men for good.
A true friend thrown aside—why, life itself

580 Is not more precious!
                        In time you will know this well:
For time, and time alone, will show the just man,
Though scoundrels are discovered in a day.

Choragos.
    This is well said, and a prudent man would ponder it.
    Judgments too quickly formed are dangerous.

Oedipus.
585   But is he not quick in his duplicity?
    And shall I not be quick to parry him?
    Would you have me stand still, hold my peace, and let
    This man win everything, through my inaction?

560 **?** What do you think of Creon's reasoning in these lines? Is his argument convincing, or is it sophistic—that is, fair-seeming, but logically faulty?

582 **?** Explain the contrast that Creon draws between just men and scoundrels in these lines.

587 **?** Whom does Oedipus address in these lines?

56 PARAPHRASING
Creon uses a form of argument that was popularized by the late fifth-century sophists, or professional teachers, in Athens: the so-called "argument from likelihood." State Creon's basic point in your own words. (Possible response: Since Creon already enjoys power as the king's second-in-command, it would be unlikely for him to envy the king's position, which also carries the burdens of responsibility.)

57 ANALYZING
What second argument does Creon add here in his defense? (No "sober mind" would plot treason; he hates anarchy, as would any reasonable man, and would never deal with plotters.)

58 LITERARY ELEMENT
Characterization: What do you think these lines show about Creon's character? (Possible responses: He values friendship; he is not afraid to point out Oedipus's errors to him.)

incarnate (in·kär′nit): appearing as a recognizable, living example; personified

59 PREDICTING

Will Jocasta be able to resolve this quarrel? (Possible responses: Yes, because she may have information about the murder that others do not. No, because this is more than a family squabble.)

60 LITERARY ELEMENT

Personification: How does Jocasta personify the city of Thebes in line 603? (She speaks as if the city were a person with a fatal disease.)

Creon.
    And you want—what is it, then? To banish me?

Oedipus.
590   No, not exile. It is your death I want,
    So that all the world may see what treason means.

Creon.
    You will persist, then? You will not believe me?

Oedipus.
    How can I believe you?

Creon.   Then you are a fool.

Oedipus.
    To save myself?

Creon.   In justice, think of me.

Oedipus.
595   You are evil incarnate.

Creon.   But suppose that you are wrong?

Oedipus.
    Still I must rule.

Creon.   But not if you rule badly.

Oedipus.
    O city, city!

Creon.   It is my city, too!

Choragos.
    Now my lords, be still. I see the Queen,
    Jocasta, coming from her palace chambers;
600   And it is time she came, for the sake of you both.
    This dreadful quarrel can be resolved through her.

[*Enter* JOCASTA.]

Jocasta.
    Poor foolish men, what wicked din is this?
    With Thebes sick to death, is it not shameful
    That you should rake some private quarrel up?
605   (*to* OEDIPUS) Come into the house.
                  —And you, Creon, go now:
    Let us have no more of this tumult over nothing.

Creon.
    Nothing? No, sister: what your husband plans for me
    Is one of two great evils: exile or death.

Oedipus.
    He is right.

596 ❓ Why do you think Oedipus says that he *must* rule? Is it the tyrant in him, or a belief in fate?

                              Why, woman, I have caught him squarely
610   Plotting against my life.
Creon.   No! Let me die
          Accursed if ever I have wished you harm!

Jocasta.
          Ah, believe it, Oedipus!
          In the name of the gods, respect this oath of his
          For my sake, for the sake of these people here!

Strophe 1

Choragos.
615   Open your mind to her, my lord. Be ruled by her,
              I beg you!
Oedipus.
          What would you have me do?

Choragos.
          Respect Creon's word. He has never spoken like a fool,
          And now he has sworn an oath.
Oedipus.   You know what you ask?
Choragos.   I do.
Oedipus.   Speak on, then.
Choragos.
          A friend so sworn should not be baited so,
620   In blind malice, and without final proof.
Oedipus.
          You are aware, I hope, that what you say
          Means death for me, or exile at the least.

Strophe 2

Choragos.
          No, I swear by Helios,° first in Heaven!
              May I die friendless and accursed,
625   The worst of deaths, if ever I meant that!
              It is the withering fields
                  That hurt my sick heart:
              Must we bear all these ills,
                  And now your bad blood as well?
Oedipus.
630   Then let him go. And let me die, if I must,
          Or be driven by him in shame from the land of
              Thebes.

623. **Helios** (hē′lē·äs′): one of the Titans; sun god often confused with Apollo. He was associated with the truth.

61 LITERARY ELEMENT
Characterization: What do Jocasta's pleas in lines 612–614 reveal about her character? (Possible responses: She has absolute trust in her brother; she desires harmony; she is sympathetic with the people's plight; she is confident enough to challenge Oedipus.)

62 LITERARY BACKGROUND
Between lines 615 and 654, Sophocles uses a hybrid of spoken dialogue and choral lyric, involving both the Choragos and the actors. This dramatic form usually occurs in Greek tragedy at points of heightened emotion or tension.

63 GUIDED READING
Identifying Cause and Effect: What two reasons does the Choragos give Oedipus for respecting Creon's word? (Creon has never spoken unwisely. Moreover, he has sworn an oath that he is telling the truth.)

64 LITERARY ELEMENT
Tone: How would you describe the tone of lines 623–629? (highly emotional, almost desperate) What are some of the charged words and phrases that contribute to this tone? (Possible responses: "I swear by Helios," "May I die friendless and accursed," "worst of deaths," "hurt my sick heart," "bad blood")

65 **EVALUATING**
Based on the portrait of Oedipus so far in the play, how valid is Creon's judgment of Oedipus's nature in line 636? (Possible response: Creon's judgment may be accurate, since Oedipus's sharp intellect and volatile emotions seem to make life difficult for him.)

66 **LITERARY ELEMENT**
Characterization: Sophocles portrays Jocasta as influential with her husband, with Creon, and with the Thebans. What do these questions imply about her character? (She is intelligent, active, and involved with matters of state.)

67 **LITERARY ELEMENT**
Extended Metaphor: What extended comparison does the Choragos make in lines 651–654? (The state is like a ship, with Oedipus as the helmsman.) Where has this comparison appeared earlier in the play? (in lines 26–27, 53, 58)

It is your unhappiness, and not his talk,
That touches me.
                    As for him—
Wherever he goes, hatred will follow him.
Creon.
    Ugly in yielding, as you were ugly in rage!   635
    Natures like yours chiefly torment themselves.
Oedipus.
    Can you not go? Can you not leave me?
Creon.   I can.
    You do not know me; but the city knows me,
    And in its eyes I am just, if not in yours.

                            [*Exit* CREON.]

                    Antistrophe 1
Choragos.
    Lady Jocasta, did you not ask the King to go to   640
        his chambers?
Jocasta.
    First tell me what has happened.
Choragos.
    There was suspicion without evidence; yet it rankled
    As even false charges will.
Jocasta.   On both sides?
Choragos.   On both.
Jocasta.   But what was said?
Choragos.
    Oh let it rest, let it be done with!
    Have we not suffered enough?   645
Oedipus.
    You see to what your decency has brought you:
    You have made difficulties where my heart saw none.

                    Antistrophe 2
Choragos.
    Oedipus, it is not once only I have told you—
    You must know I should count myself unwise
    To the point of madness, should I now forsake you—   650
        You, under whose hand,
            In the storm of another time,

632 **?** Why does Oedipus yield to the Chorus's request not to punish Creon?

New York Public Library/Stratford Festival/Photo by: Don McKague

68 INFERRING
What do Oedipus's words in lines 657–659 imply about his feelings for Jocasta? (Possible response: He respects her opinion and confides in her.)

67
> Our dear land sailed out free.
> But now stand fast at the helm!

Jocasta.
655 In God's name, Oedipus, inform your wife as well:
Why are you so set in this hard anger?

68
Oedipus.
> I will tell you, for none of these men deserves
> My confidence as you do. It is Creon's work,
> His treachery, his plotting against me.

Jocasta.
660 Go on, if you can make this clear to me.

Oedipus.
He charges me with the murder of Laius.

661 ❓ Think carefully: Has Creon in fact charged Oedipus with the murder of Laius?

69 LITERARY ELEMENT

Flashback: This scene includes two extensive flashbacks, the first by Jocasta (lines 669–681) and the second by Oedipus (lines 730–772). What new information do we learn in lines 669–673? (An oracle told Laius he would be killed by his own son.) What is Jocasta's purpose in giving Oedipus this information? (to prove that oracles are not to be trusted)

70 CULTURAL BACKGROUND

The ancient custom of "exposing" unwanted children enabled the Greeks to avoid the "pollution" associated with outright murder. They placed such infants out in the open and let nature take its course. In line 677, Jocasta reports an especially cruel expedient: piercing the baby's ankles to make sure it could not crawl to safety. (The play eventually reveals that Oedipus, whose name means "swollen foot," was this baby.)

71 LITERARY ELEMENT

Irony: What is ironic about Jocasta's "proof" that oracles are unreliable? (Her words, far from being comforting to Oedipus, disturb him even more as he begins to understand how Teiresias' words may be true.)

72 LITERARY ELEMENT

Suspense: What detail of Jocasta's flashback does Oedipus focus on? (the place where three roads meet) How does this detail heighten suspense? (It awakens Oedipus's memory and thus begins to establish a link between him and the murder of Laius.)

Jocasta.
Has he some knowledge? Or does he speak from
hearsay?

Oedipus.
He would not commit himself to such a charge,
But he has brought in that damnable soothsayer
665   To tell his story.

Jocasta.   Set your mind at rest.
If it is a question of soothsayers, I tell you
That you will find no man whose craft gives knowledge
Of the unknowable.

Here is my proof:

69
670   An oracle was reported to Laius once
(I will not say from Phoebus himself, but from
His appointed ministers, at any rate)
That his doom would be death at the hands of his
own son—
His son, born of his flesh and of mine!

70
Now, you remember the story: Laius was killed
675   By marauding strangers where three highways meet;
But his child had not been three days in this world
Before the King had pierced the baby's ankles
And left him to die on a lonely mountainside.

Thus, Apollo never caused that child
680   To kill his father, and it was not Laius' fate
To die at the hands of his son, as he had feared.
This is what prophets and prophecies are worth!
Have no dread of them.
                         It is God himself
Who can show us what he wills, in his own way.

71
Oedipus.
685   How strange a shadowy memory crossed my mind,
Just now while you were speaking; it chilled my heart.

Jocasta.
What do you mean? What memory do you speak of?

72
Oedipus.
If I understand you, Laius was killed
At a place where three roads meet.

Jocasta.   So it was said;
690   We have no later story.

ANSWERS TO MARGIN QUESTIONS

Line 692. Students' drawings should show a single road that divides into a fork. The single road might be labeled *Theban Way*, with one fork pointing toward *Delphi* and the other fork, toward *Daulis*.

Line 695. Oedipus's tone might change suddenly to one of distress, agitation, or horror.

Line 703. Oedipus may begin to suspect that he himself murdered Laius.

73

Oedipus.   Where did it happen?

Jocasta.
Phocis,° it is called: at a place where the Theban Way
Divides into the roads toward Delphi and Daulis.°

Oedipus.
When?

Jocasta.   We had the news not long before you came
And proved the right to your succession here.

Oedipus.
695   Ah, what net has God been weaving for me?

Jocasta.
Oedipus! Why does this trouble you?

Oedipus.   Do not ask me yet.
First, tell me how Laius looked, and tell me
How old he was.

Jocasta.   He was tall, his hair just touched
With white, his form was not unlike your own.

74

Oedipus.
700   I think that I myself may be accursed
By my own ignorant edict.

Jocasta.   You speak strangely.
It makes me tremble to look at you, my King.

Oedipus.
I am not sure that the blind man cannot see.
But I should know better if you were to tell me—

Jocasta.
705   Anything—though I dread to hear you ask it.

Oedipus.
Was the King lightly escorted, or did he ride
With a large company, as a ruler should?

Jocasta.
There were five men with him in all: one was a herald,
And a single chariot, which he was driving.

Oedipus.
710   Alas, that makes it plain enough!
                   But who—
Who told you how it happened?

Jocasta.   A household servant,
The only one to escape.

Oedipus.   And is he still

75

691. **Phocis** (fō'sis): country in which Mount Parnassus was located.

692. **Daulis** (dô'lis): in Phocis, east of Delphi.

692 ❓ Try to visualize the place where the "three roads" meet, and then draw a diagram.

695 ❓ What sudden change of tone might Oedipus use in this line?

703 ❓ As Oedipus starts to question Jocasta more carefully, what might he begin to suspect?

Line 720. Jocasta behaved graciously toward the lone witness, willingly granting his request.

Line 729. Possible response: Oedipus feels he can be open with Jocasta. He trusts her and wants to confide in her.

76 SPECULATING

Jocasta does not comment on why the eyewitness might have wished to be sent away to a remote area. Why do you think he made this request? (Possible responses: He recognized Oedipus, who had just become the new king, as Laius's murderer. He may have been afraid Oedipus would recognize him as the witness to the crime, or he may have been unwilling to live under the rule of a murderer.)

77 GUIDED READING

Identifying Cause and Effect: What reason does Oedipus give for wishing to question the shepherd? (Oedipus says he has made decisions hastily and now wants to determine the facts.)

78 LITERARY ELEMENT

Flashback: In these lines, Oedipus begins a lengthy flashback that continues until line 772. Where does Oedipus say he grew up? (Corinth) What led him to question his parents about his birth? (A drunken man charged that Oedipus was not the true son of Polybus.)

79 ANALYZING

Why do you think Polybus and Merope lied? (Possible response: to protect Oedipus and prevent him from learning that he was adopted)

76

A servant of ours?

Jocasta.   No; for when he came back at last
715 And found you enthroned in the place of the dead king,
He came to me, touched my hand with his, and begged
That I would send him away to the frontier district
Where only the shepherds go—
As far away from the city as I could send him.
I granted his prayer; for although the man was a
    slave,
720 He had earned more than this favor at my hands.

Oedipus.
Can he be called back quickly?

Jocasta.   Easily.
But why?

77

Oedipus.   I have taken too much upon myself
Without inquiry; therefore I wish to consult him.

Jocasta.
Then he shall come.
                    But am I not one also
725 To whom you might confide these fears of yours?

Oedipus.
That is your right; it will not be denied you,
Now least of all; for I have reached a pitch
Of wild foreboding. Is there anyone
To whom I should sooner speak?

78

730 Polybus° of Corinth is my father.
My mother is a Dorian: Merope.°
I grew up chief among the men of Corinth
Until a strange thing happened—
Not worth my passion, it may be, but strange.

735 At a feast, a drunken man maundering in his cups°
Cries out that I am not my father's son!

I contained myself that night, though I felt anger
And a sinking heart. The next day I visited
My father and mother, and questioned them.
    They stormed,

79

740 Calling it all the slanderous rant of a fool;
And this relieved me. Yet the suspicion
Remained always aching in my mind;
I knew there was talk; I could not rest;
And finally, saying nothing to my parents,

720 ? How did Jocasta behave toward the lone witness to the attack on her husband?

729 ? How would you describe Oedipus's feelings toward Jocasta?

730. **Polybus** (päl'i·bəs): king of Corinth.

731. **Merope** (mer'ə·pē): The Dorians were descended from Dorus, a son of Apollo.

735. **maundering** (môn'dər·ing) **in his cups:** talking aimlessly while under the influence of wine.

ANSWER TO MARGIN QUESTION

Line 773. Possible responses: Oedipus may not yet be emotionally ready to accept that he has killed Laius, so he cannot say what he is thinking—that the stranger and Laius were one and the same. Or, with the word *kin*, he may be trying to cushion the blow for Jocasta.

745   I went to the shrine at Delphi.
The god dismissed my question without reply;
He spoke of other things.
                    Some were clear,
Full of wretchedness, dreadful, unbearable:
750   As, that I should lie with my own mother, breed
Children from whom all men would turn their eyes;
And that I should be my father's murderer.

I heard all this, and fled. And from that day
Corinth to me was only in the stars
755   Descending in that quarter of the sky,
As I wandered farther and farther on my way
To a land where I should never see the evil
Sung by the oracle. And I came to this country
Where, so you say, King Laius was killed.

I will tell you all that happened there, my lady.

760   There were three highways
Coming together at a place I passed;
And there a herald came towards me, and a chariot
Drawn by horses, with a man such as you describe

Seated in it. The groom leading the horses
765   Forced me off the road at his lord's command;
But as this charioteer lurched over towards me
I struck him in my rage. The old man saw me
And brought his double goad down upon my head
As I came abreast.
                    He was paid back, and more!
770   Swinging my club in this right hand I knocked him
Out of his car, and he rolled on the ground.
                    I killed him.

I killed them all.
Now if that stranger and Laius were—kin,
Where is a man more miserable than I?
775   More hated by the gods? Citizen and alien alike
Must never shelter me or speak to me—
I must be shunned by all.
                    And I myself
Pronounced this malediction upon myself!

Think of it: I have touched you with these hands,
780   These hands that killed your husband. What defilement!

New York Public Library/Stratford Festival/Peter Smith & Company

773 ❓ Why do you think Oedipus hesitates before the word *kin* in this line?

80 GUIDED READING
Identifying Cause and Effect: Why does Oedipus say he fled from Corinth? (to prevent the oracle's predictions from coming true)

81 EVALUATING
Assuming that Oedipus's account of the death of Laius (lines 760–772) is reasonably objective, do you think he was morally to blame for the outcome? Take into account the dangerous conditions of travel in ancient times, and also consider who provoked this violent encounter. Would you judge Oedipus's action to be murder, self-defense, justifiable homicide, or something else? (Answers will vary. Most students will agree that Oedipus was provoked. Some may argue that his reaction was disproportionately violent and that he thus bears some degree of guilt.)

Line 785. Oedipus does not yet suspect that he is Laius's son, and that the prophecy that he would kill his father was true.

Line 803. The issue of plural vs. singular assailants was hinted at in lines 125–127, when Creon told Oedipus that Laius was attacked by "a band of highwaymen" and Oedipus responded by speaking of a daring "highwayman."

82 COMPARING LITERATURE

A number of Sophocles' dramas deal with the theme of undeserved or disproportionate human suffering. The gods in his plays often seem indifferent to human misery. Shakespeare's King Lear sums up this world view in a memorable simile: "As flies to wanton boys are we to the gods; they kill us for their sport."

83 PREDICTING

The Choragos intervenes with subdued optimism, claiming that the shepherd may be a source of hope for Oedipus. Yet, remember the ironic reversal when Jocasta intended to comfort Oedipus by telling him of the oracle's prophecy and instead disturbed him more. Given that outcome, what do you think may happen when the shepherd tells his tale? (Possible response: His words may, ironically, amount to the conclusive proof of Oedipus's guilt.)

84 LITERARY ELEMENT

Irony: Again, Jocasta intends her words to be comforting— but they are full of dramatic irony. What ironic prediction of the oracle is brought to the audience's attention here? (The murderer would be the son of Laius and Jocasta.)

Am I all evil, then? It must be so,
Since I must flee from Thebes, yet never again
See my own countrymen, my own country,
For fear of joining my mother in marriage
785   And killing Polybus, my father.
                              Ah,
82 [If I was created so, born to this fate,
Who could deny the savagery of God?

Oh holy majesty of heavenly powers!
May I never see that day! Never!
790   Rather let me vanish from the race of men
Than know the abomination destined me!

Choragos.
83 [We too, my lord, have felt dismay at this.
But there is hope: you have yet to hear the shepherd.

Oedipus.
Indeed, I fear no other hope is left me.

Jocasta.
795   What do you hope from him when he comes?
Oedipus.   This much:
If his account of the murder tallies with yours,
Then I am cleared.
Jocasta.   What was it that I said
Of such importance?
Oedipus.   Why, "marauders," you said,
Killed the King, according to this man's story.
800   If he maintains that still, if there were several,
Clearly the guilt is not mine: I was alone.
But if he says one man, single-handed, did it,
Then the evidence all points to me.

Jocasta.
You may be sure that he said there were several;
805   And can he call back that story now? He cannot.
The whole city heard it as plainly as I.
But suppose he alters some detail of it:
He cannot ever show that Laius' death
Fulfilled the oracle: for Apollo said
84 [
810   My child was doomed to kill him; and my child—
Poor baby!—it was my child that died first.

No. From now on, where oracles are concerned,
I would not waste a second thought on any.

---

785 ❓ Oedipus now suspects that he has unwittingly cursed himself as the true murderer of Laius. However, given the fact that he still calls Polybus of Corinth his father in this line, what dreadful truth does he *not* yet suspect?

803 ❓ Jocasta referred to "marauding strangers" in the plural at line 675, and Oedipus now distinguishes between plural and singular. Where was the issue of plural vs. singular assailants hinted at earlier in the play?

ANSWER TO MARGIN QUESTION

Line 817. In this context, *cross* means "go against," "thwart or interfere with."

Oedipus.

You may be right.

But come: let someone go

815 For the shepherd at once. This matter must be settled.

Jocasta.

I will send for him.

I would not wish to cross you in anything,

And surely not in this.—Let us go in.

[*Exeunt into the palace.*]

817 ❓ What does the word *cross* mean in this line?

═ **ODE 2** ═══════════════

Strophe 1

Chorus.

Let me be reverent in the ways of right,

820 Lowly the paths I journey on;

Let all my words and actions keep

The laws of the pure universe

From highest Heaven handed down.

For Heaven is their bright nurse,

825 Those generations of the realms of light;

Ah, never of mortal kind were they begot,

Nor are they slaves of memory, lost in sleep:

Their Father is greater than Time, and ages not.

Antistrophe 1

The tyrant is a child of Pride

830 Who drinks from his great sickening cup

Recklessness and vanity,

Until from his high crest headlong

He plummets to the dust of hope.

That strong man is not strong.

835 But let no fair ambition be denied;

May God protect the wrestler for the State

In government, in comely policy,

Who will fear God, and on His ordinance° wait.

838. **ordinance** (ôrd''n·əns): decree or command.

Strophe 2

Haughtiness and the high hand of <u>disdain</u>

840 Tempt and outrage God's holy law;

And any mortal who dares hold

Line 844. The Chorus predicts that the haughty man will be caught up in "a net of pain," and that "the crackling blast of heaven" will blow "on his head, and on his desperate heart." Thus, the Chorus predicts that the gods will punish the haughty man severely.

Line 856. The Chorus insists that the actions and prophecies they have heard about will be found to form a consistent pattern and will be understood.

88 EVALUATING

Compared with Ode 1 (lines 449–484), do the sympathies of the Chorus seem to have shifted? If so, how? (Possible response: In Ode 1, the Chorus refused to criticize Oedipus; now, they seem critical in lines 861–864 of their master's dismissal of the Delphic oracle.)

New York Public Library/Stratford Festival/Peter Smith & Company

No immortal Power in awe
Will be caught up in a net of pain:
The price for which his levity is sold.
845 Let each man take due earnings, then,
And keep his hands from holy things,
And from blasphemy stand apart—
Else the crackling blast of heaven
Blows on his head, and on his desperate heart;
850 Though fools will honor impious men,
In their cities no tragic poet sings.

844 ❓ What fate does the Chorus predict for the haughty man?

Antistrophe 2

Shall we lose faith in Delphi's obscurities,
We who have heard the world's core
Discredited, and the sacred wood
855 Of Zeus at Elis° praised no more?
The deeds and the strange prophecies
Must make a pattern yet to be understood.
Zeus, if indeed you are lord of all,
Throned in light over night and day,
860 Mirror this in your endless mind:
Our masters call the oracle
Words on the wind, and the Delphic vision blind!
Their hearts no longer know Apollo,
And reverence for the gods has died away.

855. Elis (ē′lis): city in the Peloponnesus.

856 ❓ What does the Chorus insist will happen?

READING CHECK

1. What does the Priest beg Oedipus to do? (save the city)
2. Whom has Oedipus sent to Delphi? (Creon)
3. What is Teiresias' profession? (prophet)
4. Why is Oedipus at first very angry with Teiresias? (The seer refuses to tell what he knows.)
5. Why is Creon so upset when he enters in Scene 2? (Oedipus has charged him with treason.)
6. Which two characters intervene in Oedipus's quarrel with Creon? (Jocasta and the Choragos)
7. Where does Jocasta say Laius was killed? (at a place where three roads meet)
8. How did Polybus and Merope respond to Oedipus's questions about his parentage? (They said the drunken man's charge was slander and that Oedipus was their son.)
9. Who forced Oedipus off the road? (Laius's groom)
10. At the end of Scene 2, whom is Oedipus determined to question? (the shepherd)

First Thoughts

How did you react to Oedipus in the first scenes of the play? Does he strike you as a proud tyrant, as a sympathetic ruler, or as something in between? Explain your answer.

Identifying Facts

1. What conflict or problem do the people of the city of Thebes face as the play opens?
2. According to Ode 1, which god will inevitably punish the murderer of Laius? What misgiving disturbs the Chorus's confidence in this ode, and how do they deal with this misgiving?
3. What argument does Jocasta use to persuade Oedipus to ignore the soothsayers or oracles? In the course of her argument, what minor detail motivates Oedipus to pursue a new line of investigation?
4. Explain why Oedipus left Corinth. What chance remark caused him to question Polybus and Merope? What was he afraid of?

Interpreting Meanings

1. In line 35, the Priest says that the Thebans know that Oedipus is not "one of the immortal gods." How *do* the Thebans regard Oedipus? What reasons do they have for their opinion of him?
2. When Oedipus questions Creon about the murder of Laius, what **dramatic irony** does the playwright begin to develop?
3. It is significant that the seer, or prophet, Teiresias, is blind. Explain how this is ironic. Also, explain the irony of Oedipus's angry and arrogant response to the prophet.
4. In the course of Ode 1, the Chorus expresses both confident optimism and nervous apprehension. How is the Chorus's indecision a comment on the basic conflict of the play so far? What possible resolutions to the conflict can you predict?
5. What personality trait in Oedipus's character do you think drives him on to insist at lines 814–815 that the shepherd be summoned? If you were Oedipus, would you let well enough alone at this point, or would you insist on probing further to get at the truth?
6. In Ode 2, the Chorus comments harshly on those who defy prophecy. What in the previous scene is the Chorus responding to? What does this say about where the Chorus stands in the play—in other words, whose side is the Chorus on? Explain your answer.

Applying Meanings

Oedipus's hot-tempered reactions to Teiresias and Creon in Scenes 1 and 2 contrast strongly with his sympathy and compassion for the people of Thebes in the Prologue. Sophocles portrays Oedipus as a complex ruler with many conflicting character traits. Do you think a complex personality is likely to prove an advantage or a liability for a leader? Explain your answer.

Critical Writing Response

Analyzing Form. Each scene in *Oedipus Rex* is followed by an ode, performed by the Chorus. Reread the Parodos (the Chorus's entrance scene), Ode 1, and Ode 2. What seems to be the function of each ode in response to the preceding scene? Is the function similar in each ode? Explain your answer in a one- to two-page essay.

ANSWERS

First Thoughts
Answers will vary.

Identifying Facts
1. A plague ravages the city.
2. Apollo. A possible link between Oedipus and Laius's death; they reject this connection
3. that the oracles falsely prophesied the murder of Laius by his son. The murder occurred where three roads meet.
4. to prevent the fulfillment of a prediction that he would slay his father and marry his mother. That he wasn't their true son. The oracle's prediction

Interpreting Meanings
1. as a noble man of wisdom. He solved the Sphinx's riddle.
2. the audience knowing that Oedipus himself is the murderer
3. Only the blind Teiresias "sees" the truth. Oedipus's anger and arrogance emphasize his blindness to the truth.
4. The Chorus reflects the conflict of Oedipus's great knowledge vs. his ignorance of the terrible truth about his own past. Predictions will vary.
5. Possible responses: a desire to know the truth, persistence. Answers will vary.
6. Jocasta's skepticism about oracles. Answers will vary.

Applying Meanings
Answers will vary.

Critical Writing Response
Analyzing Form. Partners might reread and discuss the odes together before writing.

Line 871. The new prophecies are those of Teiresias, who has said that Oedipus murdered Laius, and that the murderer of Laius will be blind, penniless, and husband to his mother. The old prophecies are those of the oracle at Delphi, who at first said that Laius's own child would murder him, and later said that Oedipus would kill his father and lie with his mother. Jocasta thinks that all the prophecies are false because she believes that her son by Laius died in infancy. She wants Oedipus to see that since the old prophecies could not be true, the new prophecies are also untrue.

Line 878. She and the others are compared to "helpless sailors," and Oedipus to a "helmsman."

1 ANALYZING

Based on her comments in the previous scene, in lines 666–684, some readers have inferred that Jocasta is dangerously critical of traditional religion. As Scene 3 opens, however, she is about to sacrifice to the gods. Do you think Jocasta is irreligious, or can you resolve this apparent conflict about her character? (Possible response: She is skeptical of prophecies and oracles, but she still honors the tradition of sacrifice—or at least turns to religion when she feels she is on shaky ground.)

2 LITERARY ELEMENT

Simile: To what earlier figures of speech in the play does this simile relate? (In lines 26–27, 53, and 58, Thebes is compared to a ship; in lines 651–654, the land is compared to a ship and Oedipus to a helmsman.) How do these similes link the fates of Thebes and Oedipus? (Possible response: They imply that the well-being of the city depends on the well-being of its king.)

OEDIPUS REX
Part 2
Sophocles
translated by
DUDLEY FITTS AND ROBERT FITZGERALD

As you read, look for the turning point, the moment at which Oedipus and others begin to suspect the truth of the situation. Watch how the various characters respond to or cover up their growing doubts.

SCENE 3

[*Enter* JOCASTA.]

Jocasta.

1   865
Princes of Thebes, it has occurred to me
To visit the altars of the gods, bearing
These branches as a suppliant, and this incense.
Our King is not himself: his noble soul
Is overwrought with fantasies of dread,

870
Else he would consider
The new prophecies in the light of the old.
He will listen to any voice that speaks disaster,
And my advice goes for nothing.

[*She approaches the altar, right.*]

                To you, then, Apollo,
Lycian° lord, since you are nearest, I turn in prayer.

875
Receive these offerings, and grant us deliverance
From defilement. Our hearts are heavy with fear
When we see our leader distracted, as helpless sailors

2
Are terrified by the confusion of their helmsman.

[*Enter* MESSENGER.]

Messenger.
Friends, no doubt you can direct me:

880
Where shall I find the house of Oedipus,
Or, better still, where is the King himself?

871 ❓ What does Jocasta mean by "the new prophecies in the light of the old"? Explain what the new prophecies are. What were the old ones? What does Jocasta think of these prophecies?

874. **Lycian** (lish′ē-ən): One of Apollo's names is Lycius, which has been explained variously as "wolf-god," "god of light," and "god of Lycia."

878 ❓ Explain Jocasta's simile here. Who is being compared to whom?

Choragos.
It is this very place, stranger; he is inside.
This is his wife and mother of his children.

Messenger.
I wish her happiness in a happy house,
885   Blest in all the fulfillment of her marriage.

Jocasta.
I wish as much for you: your courtesy
Deserves a like good fortune. But now, tell me:
Why have you come? What have you to say to us?

Messenger.
Good news, my lady, for your house and your
    husband.

Jocasta.
890   What news? Who sent you here?

Messenger.   I am from Corinth.
The news I bring ought to mean joy for you,
Though it may be you will find some grief in it.

Jocasta.
What is it? How can it touch us in both ways?

Messenger.
The word is that the people of the Isthmus°
895   Intend to call Oedipus to be their king.

Jocasta.
But old King Polybus—is he not reigning still?

Messenger.
No. Death holds him in his sepulcher.

Jocasta.
What are you saying? Polybus is dead?

Messenger.
If I am not telling the truth, may I die myself.

Jocasta.
900   (*to a* MAIDSERVANT) Go in, go quickly; tell this
    to your master.

O riddlers of God's will, where are you now!
This was the man whom Oedipus, long ago,
Feared so, fled so, in dread of destroying him—
But it was another fate by which he died.

[*Enter* OEPIDUS, *center.*]

894. **Isthmus:** Corinth is located on a narrow strip of land connecting the Peloponnesus with eastern Greece.

901 ❓ What tone of voice might Jocasta use here?

3 LITERARY ELEMENT
Irony: What dramatic irony do you see in the fact that the Corinthian Messenger goes out of his way to specify happiness in the "fulfillment of her marriage"? (Possible response: The audience knows that Jocasta's home and marriage will not be happy or blessed because of her incest.)

4 LITERARY ELEMENT
Paradox: What is apparently contradictory about the Messenger's description of his news in lines 891–892? (He says he brings good news that might cause some grief.)

5 INFERRING
What conclusion does Jocasta draw from the Corinthian Messenger's news? (She infers that, since Polybus has died, the prophecy that Oedipus would kill his father has to be false.)

6 INTERPRETING

In line 912, Oedipus first reacts to the Messenger's news by asking if Polybus was the victim of treason. What earlier episode in the play has prepared us for this reaction? (Oedipus's earlier charging of Creon with treason)

7 LITERARY ELEMENT

Irony: What is the dramatic irony of Oedipus's joyful outburst in lines 915–920? (The audience knows that Oedipus has no real cause for joy, since Polybus was not really his father.)

8 GUIDED READING

Identifying Details: In line 927, Oedipus recalls the second half of the Delphic prophecy. Where did Oedipus summarize this prophecy earlier in the play? (In lines 745–751, when Oedipus told Jocasta of the "dreadful, unbearable" things he had heard from the oracle at Delphi, he told her of the prophecy that he should lie with his own mother.)

Oedipus.

905   Dearest Jocasta, why have you sent for me?

Jocasta.

   Listen to what this man says, and then tell me
   What has become of the solemn prophecies.

Oedipus.

   Who is this man? What is his news for me?

Jocasta.

   He has come from Corinth to announce your
      father's death!

Oedipus.

910   Is it true, stranger? Tell me in your own words.

Messenger.

   I cannot say it more clearly: the King is dead.

Oedipus.

6   Was it by treason? Or by an attack of illness?

Messenger.

   A little thing brings old men to their rest.

Oedipus.

   It was sickness, then?

Messenger.   Yes, and his many years.

Oedipus.

915   Ah!

7   Why should a man respect the Pythian hearth,° or
   Give heed to the birds that jangle above his head?
   They prophesied that I should kill Polybus,
   Kill my own father; but he is dead and buried,
920   And I am here—I never touched him, never,
   Unless he died of grief for my departure,
   And thus, in a sense, through me. No. Polybus
   Has packed the oracles off with him underground.
   They are empty words.

Jocasta.   Had I not told you so?

Oedipus.

925   You had; it was my faint heart that betrayed me.

Jocasta.

   From now on never think of those things again.

Oedipus.

8   And yet—must I not fear my mother's bed?

Jocasta.

   Why should anyone in this world be afraid,

916. **Pythian** (pith′ē·ən) **hearth:** Delphi was also known as Pythia. The priestess of Apollo was called Pythia.

ANSWER TO MARGIN QUESTION

Line 939. Possible response: He might be listening carefully to Oedipus's and Jocasta's conversation, while trying not to appear nosy or disrespectful.

930 Since Fate rules us and nothing can be foreseen?
A man should live only for the present day.

Have no more fear of sleeping with your mother:
How many men, in dreams, have lain with their
    mothers!
No reasonable man is troubled by such things.

Oedipus.
That is true; only—
935 If only my mother were not still alive!
But she is alive. I cannot help my dread.

Jocasta.
Yet this news of your father's death is wonderful.

Oedipus.
Wonderful. But I fear the living woman.

Messenger.
Tell me, who is this woman that you fear?

Oedipus.
940 It is Merope, man; wife of King Polybus.

Messenger.
Merope? Why should you be afraid of her?

Oedipus.
An oracle of the gods, a dreadful saying.

Messenger.
Can you tell me about it or are you sworn to silence?

Oedipus.
I can tell you, and I will.
945 Apollo said through his prophet that I was the man
Who should marry his own mother, shed his
    father's blood
With his own hands. And so, for all these years
I have kept clear of Corinth, and no harm has come—
Though it would have been sweet to see my
    parents again.

Messenger.
950 And is this the fear that drove you out of Corinth?

Oedipus.
Would you have me kill my father?

Messenger.   As for that
You must be reassured by the news I gave you.

Oedipus.
If you could reassure me, I would reward you.

939 ❓ The Corinthian Messenger, who has been listening to the dialogue between Oedipus and Jocasta since line 915, now joins in for a crucial exchange that moves Oedipus several steps further toward the truth. How might the actor playing the messenger behave in the interval between lines 915 and 939?

9 Advanced Learners: Selected students may be interested in researching Sigmund Freud's theory of the "Oedipus complex." In *The Interpretation of Dreams*, Freud gave his opinion that Jocasta's speech in lines 931–933 was "the key to the tragedy." Freud based his psychoanalytical theory on this secret Oedipal desire that Jocasta refers to. ■

10 LITERARY ELEMENT
Characterization: What does line 949, added almost as an afterthought, reveal about Oedipus's feelings for the land he considers "home" and for his parents? (Oedipus is fond of and loyal to the country he considers his homeland, and he loves his parents.) What emotional effect might this line have on the audience? (Possible response: The line may move the audience because of its poignancy and irony.)

11 LITERARY ELEMENT

Suspense: How does Sophocles construct the dialogue in this passage to build suspense? (He has the Messenger delay his critical revelation.)

12 LITERARY ELEMENT

Tone: What tone of voice do you think the actors playing the Messenger and Oedipus might use for their dialogue in lines 963–966? (Possible response: The Messenger might use a triumphant and somewhat complacent, know-it-all tone; Oedipus might use an incredulous tone.)

13 LITERARY ELEMENT

Irony: What dramatic irony do you see in Oedipus's declaration that the Messenger is "nothing" to him? (Possible response: In a literal sense the statement is correct, since the Messenger has no blood relationship with Oedipus. We will later learn, however, that the Messenger played a vital role in Oedipus's fate, since it was he who gave the infant Oedipus to King Polybus.)

14 GUIDED READING

Identifying Cause and Effect: According to the Messenger, why did Polybus eagerly adopt Oedipus? (He had no children.)

Messenger.
I had that in mind, I will confess: I thought
955 I could count on you when you returned to Corinth.
Oedipus.
No: I will never go near my parents again.
Messenger.
Ah, son, you still do not know what you are doing—
Oedipus.
What do you mean? In the name of God tell me!
Messenger.
—If these are your reasons for not going home.
Oedipus.
960 I tell you, I fear the oracle may come true.
Messenger.
And guilt may come upon you through your parents?
Oedipus.
That is the dread that is always in my heart.

Messenger.
Can you not see that all your fears are groundless?
Oedipus.
How can you say that? They are my parents, surely?
Messenger.
965 Polybus was not your father.
Oedipus.   Not my father?
Messenger.
No more your father than the man speaking to you.
Oedipus.
But you are nothing to me!
Messenger.   Neither was he.
Oedipus.
Then why did he call me son?
Messenger.   I will tell you:
Long ago he had you from my hands, as a gift.
Oedipus.
970 Then how could he love me so, if I was not his?
Messenger.
He had no children, and his heart turned to you.
Oedipus.
What of you? Did you buy me? Did you find me
   by chance?

967 ❓ What do you imagine is Oedipus's emotional state at this point: one of growing relief, confusion, or despair?

ANSWER TO MARGIN QUESTION

Line 980. The meaning of the name would be ironically appropriate because the story stems from Oedipus's ignorance of who he really is. The meaning of the name would be appropriate without irony, however, in discussing Oedipus's knowledge or wisdom in solving the riddle of the Sphinx.

Messenger.
I came upon you in the crooked pass of Cithaeron.

Oedipus.
And what were you doing there?

Messenger.   Tending my flocks.

Oedipus.
975   A wandering shepherd?

Messenger.   But your savior, son, that day.

Oedipus.
From what did you save me?

Messenger.   Your ankles should tell you that.

Oedipus.
Ah, stranger, why do you speak of that childhood
      pain?

Messenger.
I cut the bonds that tied your ankles together.

Oedipus.
I have had the mark as long as I can remember.

Messenger.
980   That was why you were given the name you bear.

Oedipus.
God! Was it my father or my mother who did it?
Tell me!

Messenger. I do not know. The man who gave you
      to me
Can tell you better than I.

Oedipus.
It was not you that found me, but another?

Messenger.
985   It was another shepherd gave you to me.

Oedipus.
Who was he? Can you tell me who he was?

Messenger.
I think he was said to be one of Laius' people.

Oedipus.
You mean the Laius who was king here years ago?

Messenger.
Yes; King Laius; and the man was one of his herdsmen.

Oedipus.
990   Is he still alive? Can I see him?

980 ❓ This line refers to the derivation of the name *Oedipus* from words meaning "swollen" and "foot." The first part of Oedipus's name, however, may also be related to a Greek word meaning "to know." Why would this etymology also be ironically appropriate?

15 LITERARY ELEMENT

Irony: What situational irony does the exchange in line 975 emphasize? (Possible response: A lowly, wandering shepherd turns out to be a king's savior, but in saving Oedipus the shepherd condemns him to fulfill the prophecy.) In the original Greek, when the Messenger addresses Oedipus as "son," he uses the same word that Oedipus used in line 1 for the "children" who were his subjects. Why would the Greek audience have found this ironic? (because it reverses Oedipus's role)

16 CULTURAL BACKGROUND

Since many factual details about the production of ancient Greek tragedy are not known, we cannot say for certain if the actor playing Oedipus walked with a limp—or drew attention in some other way to the mutilation of his feet when he was an infant. In ancient Greek legends, kings were usually presented as physically perfect. Oedipus's infirmity would have marked him as an exception.

17 PREDICTING

Given lines 984–987, what decision regarding the shepherd would you expect Oedipus to make? (Possible response: He will want to summon and question the shepherd.)

Line 999. Possible response: Jocasta's expressions might show interest and reassurance at first; but beginning with line 967, her expressions might change from apprehension to fear to shock and horror. She might put her hands to her face, wring her hands, or put her hand out to stop the Messenger from talking.

Line 1014. Oedipus assumes that Jocasta fears he is of lowly birth, unequal to her royal lineage. This is ironic because what Jocasta actually fears is that Oedipus will learn he is her own son.

LITERARY ELEMENT

Plot: In Part 1, at the beginning of Scene 2, who was attempting to relieve Oedipus's anxiety? (Jocasta) Who attempts to do the same thing in Scene 3? (the Messenger) What is the ironic result in each case? (an additional complication of the mystery and an increase in Oedipus's anxiety and dread)

18 GUIDED READING

Identifying Details: In lines 995–997, the Choragos says that the shepherd whom Oedipus now wants to interview and the shepherd whom Jocasta mentioned earlier may be one and the same. What did Jocasta say earlier about this shepherd? (He was the eyewitness who escaped when Laius was murdered.)

19 INFERRING

In the dialogue in lines 1000–1005, Jocasta pleads with Oedipus not to pursue his investigation. What does her sudden attempt to dissuade him imply about her own knowledge at this point in the play? (She has concluded that he murdered Laius, and also that he is her son by Laius.) How do you think she has figured out the truth? (Jocasta knows the truth once she realizes that the shepherd she gave her baby to did not leave him to die, but gave him to the Messenger, who in turn gave him to King Polybus and Queen Merope.)

Messenger.   These men here
    Know best about such things.

Oedipus.   Does anyone here
    Know this shepherd that he is talking about?
    Have you seen him in the fields, or in the town?
    If you have, tell me. It is time things were made plain.

18 | 995 **Choragos.**
    I think the man he means is that same shepherd
    You have already asked to see. Jocasta perhaps
    Could tell you something.

Oedipus.   Do you know anything
    About him, Lady? Is he the man we have
        summoned?
    Is that the man this shepherd means?

19 | 1000 **Jocasta.**   Why think of him?
    Forget this herdsman. Forget it all.
    This talk is a waste of time.

Oedipus.   How can you say that,
    When the clues to my true birth are in my hands?

Jocasta.
    For God's love, let us have no more questioning!
    Is your life nothing to you?
1005 My own is pain enough for me to bear.

Oedipus.
    You need not worry. Suppose my mother a slave,
    And born of slaves: no baseness can touch you.

Jocasta.
    Listen to me, I beg you: do not do this thing!

Oedipus.
    I will not listen; the truth must be made known.

Jocasta.
1010 Everything that I say is for your own good!

Oedipus.   My own good
    Snaps my patience, then; I want none of it.

Jocasta.
    You are fatally wrong! May you never learn who you are!

Oedipus.
    Go, one of you, and bring the shepherd here.
    Let us leave this woman to brag of her royal name.

Jocasta.
1015 Ah, miserable!

999 ❓ Now it is Jocasta's turn to rejoin the dialogue after a long silence since line 937. Between lines 938 and 999, what gestures or facial expressions might Jocasta use to register her reactions to the revelations of the Corinthian Messenger?

1014 ❓ What does Oedipus assume about Jocasta in this bitter remark? Why is this assumption ironic?

New York Public Library/Stratford Festival/Peter Smith & Company

20 PREDICTING
The Choragos suggests that he fears for Jocasta. What do you think she intends to do? Explain your answer. (Answers will vary but should take into account Jocasta's extreme agitation in lines 1003–1005, 1008, 1010, 1012, and 1015–1017.)

21 EVALUATING
Oedipus's speeches in this part of the play leave no doubt that he is determined to pursue the clues to his true identity, no matter what the cost. Do you admire his thirst for the truth or do you think he is behaving without thinking? (Answers will vary.)

22 CULTURAL BACKGROUND
The ancient Greeks considered *Tychē*, or "luck," a minor goddess. The concept of *tychē* also included the ideas of "fortune" (good or bad) and "coincidence." Oedipus is a "child of coincidence"—even more than he knows—because his two horrible crimes involve a number of unfortunate coincidences.)

That is the only word I have for you now.
That is the only word I can ever have.

[*Exit into the palace.*]

Choragos.
Why has she left us, Oedipus? Why has she gone
In such a passion of sorrow? I fear this silence:
1020   Something dreadful may come of it.

Oedipus.   Let it come!
However base my birth, I must know about it.
The Queen, like a woman, is perhaps ashamed
To think of my low origin. But I
Am a child of Luck; I cannot be dishonored.
1025   Luck is my mother; the passing months, my
         brothers,
Have seen me rich and poor.
                          If this is so,
How could I wish that I were someone else?
How could I not be glad to know my birth?

1025 ❓ What metaphors does Oedipus use in these lines for his parentage and family relationships?

Oedipus Rex, Scene 3   **349**

23 LITERARY ELEMENT

Setting: In lines 1031–1034, what vivid details contribute to the Chorus's description of Mount Cithaeron? (the torches, the full moon, the dance, the singing choir) What mood do these details help establish? (Possible response: a joyful, festive mood)

24 CULTURAL DIVERSITY

The notion that Oedipus might have been the son of a deity reflects many Greek legends in which the heroes had one immortal parent.

❓ *Can you name one such Greek hero?* (Possible responses: Achilles, son of Peleus and the nymph Thetis; Aeneas, son of Anchises and the goddess Venus; Hercules, son of Alcmene and the god Zeus)

25 SYNTHESIZING

Sophocles creates both ambiguity and irony by having Oedipus say he does not "know the man" who enters, at the start of Scene 4, because at some level Oedipus does seem to recognize the Shepherd. On what two prior occasions has Oedipus seen this man? (when he was rescued from death as an infant on the mountainside, and when he killed Laius on the road)

═ ODE 3 ═

Strophe

Chorus.

If ever the coming time were known
1030 To my heart's pondering,
Cithaeron, now by Heaven I see the torches
At the festival of the next full moon,
And see the dance, and hear the choir sing
A grace to your gentle shade:
1035 Mountain where Oedipus was found,
O mountain guard of a noble race!
May the god who heals us lend his aid,
And let that glory come to pass
For our king's cradling-ground.

Antistrophe

1040 Of the nymphs that flower beyond the years,
Who bore you, royal child,
To Pan° of the hills or the timberline Apollo,
Cold in delight where the upland clears,
Or Hermes for whom Cyllene's° heights are piled?
1045 Or flushed as evening cloud,
Great Dionysus, roamer of mountains,
He—was it he who found you there,
And caught you up in his own proud
Arms from the sweet god-ravisher°
1050 Who laughed by the Muses' fountains?°

1042. **Pan:** son of Hermes; part goat, part man; associated with woodlands, forests, and mountains. Shepherds loved the music he played on his reed pipes.

1044. **Cyllene** (sə·lē′nē): the mountain where Hermes was born.

1045. ❓ What fantasy does the Chorus briefly indulge about Oedipus's infancy in these lines? How does the mood of the ode deepen the irony of the play at this point?

1049. **god-ravisher:** the presumed mother of Oedipus.

1050. **Muses' fountains:** The Muses were born at a spring on the slopes of Mount Olympus.

═ SCENE 4 ═

Oedipus.

Sirs: though I do not know the man,
I think I see him coming, this shepherd we want:
He is old, like our friend here, and the men
Bringing him seem to be servants of my house.
1055 But you can tell, if you have ever seen him.

[*Enter* SHEPHERD *escorted by servants.*]

Choragos.

I know him, he was Laius' man. You can trust him.

Oedipus.
  Tell me first, you from Corinth: is this the shepherd
  We were discussing?

Messenger.   This is the very man.

Oedipus.
  (*to* SHEPHERD) Come here. No, look at me. You
    must answer

1060   Everything I ask.—You belonged to Laius?

Shepherd.
  Yes: born his slave, brought up in his house.

Oedipus.
  Tell me: what kind of work did you do for him?

Shepherd.
  I was a shepherd of his, most of my life.

Oedipus.
  Where mainly did you go for pasturage?

Shepherd.
1065   Sometimes Cithaeron, sometimes the hills nearby.

Oedipus.
  Do you remember ever seeing this man out there?

Shepherd.
  What would he be doing there? This man?

Oedipus.
  This man standing here. Have you ever seen him
    before?

Shepherd.
  No. At least, not to my recollection.

Messenger.
1070   And that is not strange, my lord. But I'll refresh
  His memory: he must remember when we two
  Spent three whole seasons together, March to
    September,
  On Cithaeron or thereabouts. He had two flocks;
  I had one. Each autumn I'd drive mine home
1075   And he would go back with his to Laius' sheepfold.—
  Is this not true, just as I have described it?

Shepherd.
  True, yes; but it was all so long ago.

Messenger.
  Well, then: do you remember, back in those days,
  That you gave me a baby boy to bring up as my own?

1059 ❓ How would Oedipus indicate his reaction to a movement or gesture by the Shepherd as he speaks this line? What tone of voice might Oedipus use?

Bust of Bacchus, god of wine and vegetation, c. 131–115. *Bacchus is the Roman version of the Greek god Dionysus.*

Lee Boltin Picture Library

26 LITERARY ELEMENT
Dialogue: Here begins the culminating interrogation by Oedipus. Which characters has he already cross-examined in his effort to solve the mystery of Laius's murder and of his own identity? (Creon, Teiresias, Jocasta, and the Messenger)

27 LITERARY ELEMENT
Suspense: Suspense builds with the Shepherd's reluctance to answer questions. How does the Shepherd evade Oedipus's questions in lines 1067 and 1069? (He turns aside the first question with two of his own, and he answers the second with the vague phrase "'not to my recollection.") What impression of the Shepherd do these evasions create? (Possible response: He is frightened and guilty; he is hiding something.)

HUMANITIES CONNECTION

Bacchus was the name the Romans used for the Greek god Dionysus. From his beginnings as a god of vegetation, he came to be worshiped as the god of wine, who initiated frenzied, celebratory rites. Dionysus also became associated with poetry and music, and it was from early choral odes performed in his honor that dramatic tragedy developed.
❓ *How might mystic elements related to regeneration and resurrection have come to be associated with Dionysus?* (Vegetation dies in winter and is reborn in spring.) ∎

Line 1082. Possible response: The Shepherd is trying to hide the fact that he took the infant Oedipus and gave him to King Polybus. The Shepherd, who was a witness when Laius was murdered, realizes that Oedipus is the son of Laius and that Oedipus murdered his father.

Line 1090. Teiresias has called him "wretched"; Jocasta has called him "miserable."

---

28 LITERARY ELEMENT

Dialogue: At especially tense points in the drama, Sophocles uses what the Greeks called *stichomythia*, or rapid-fire dialogue, in which the characters speak only one line each. Why does he use such dialogue in this scene? (Possible response: because he is building up to the climax in which Oedipus learns the truth about his birth)

29 LITERARY ELEMENT

Characterization: Oedipus threatens to torture the old Shepherd. What does this reveal about his character? (Possible response: He can be relentless and cruel.)

30 INTERPRETING

What is the dilemma the Shepherd expresses in line 1094? (If he fails to speak, he will die; if he speaks, he may not be able to live.)

31 SPECULATING

What may be the Shepherd's motives in his desperate attempt to evade Oedipus's questions? (Possible responses: pity for Oedipus, fear for his own safety)

Shepherd.

1080   What if I did? What are you trying to say?

Messenger.

King Oedipus was once that little child.

Shepherd.

Damn you, hold your tongue!

Oedipus.   No more of that!

It is your tongue needs watching, not this man's.

Shepherd.

My King, my Master, what is it I have done wrong?

Oedipus.

1085   You have not answered his question about the boy.

Shepherd.

He does not know . . . He is only making
        trouble . . .

Oedipus.

Come, speak plainly, or it will go hard with you.

Shepherd.

In God's name, do not torture an old man!

Oedipus.

Come here, one of you; bind his arms behind him.

Shepherd.

1090   Unhappy king! What more do you wish to learn?

Oedipus.

Did you give this man the child he speaks of?

Shepherd.   I did.

And I would to God I had died that very day.

Oedipus.

You will die now unless you speak the truth.

Shepherd.

Yet if I speak the truth, I am worse than dead.

Oedipus.

1095   Very well; since you insist upon delaying—

Shepherd.

No! I have told you already that I gave him the boy.

Oedipus.

Where did you get him? From your house? From
        somewhere else?

Shepherd.

Not from mine, no. A man gave him to me.

1082 ❓ Why do you think the Shepherd bursts in so angrily here?

1090 ❓ Who else in the play so far has called Oedipus "unhappy" because of his desire to learn more?

352   Greek and Roman Literatures

ANSWER TO MARGIN QUESTION

Line 1110. Jocasta. He may call her "unspeakable" because of her unmotherly actions (giving the baby to the Shepherd, who is to let him die). On a subconscious level, Oedipus may use the term because he cannot bring himself to call his wife his mother.

Oedipus.
Is that man here? Do you know whose slave he was?

Shepherd.
For God's love, my King, do not ask me any more!

Oedipus.
You are a dead man if I have to ask you again.

Shepherd.
Then . . . Then the child was from the palace of Laius.

Oedipus.
A slave child? or a child of his own line?

Shepherd.
Ah, I am on the brink of dreadful speech!

Oedipus.
And I of dreadful hearing. Yet I must hear.

Shepherd.
If you must be told, then . . .
They said it was Laius' child;
But it is your wife who can tell you about that.

Oedipus.
My wife!—Did she give it to you?

Shepherd.   My lord, she did.

Oedipus.
Do you know why?

Shepherd.   I was told to get rid of it.

Oedipus.
An unspeakable mother!

Shepherd.   There had been prophecies . . .

Oedipus.
Tell me.

Shepherd. It was said that the boy would kill his
own father.

Oedipus.
Then why did you give him over to this old man?

Shepherd.
I pitied the baby, my King,
And I thought that this man would take him far
away
To his own country.
He saved him—but for what a fate!
For if you are what this man says you are,
No man living is more wretched than Oedipus.

1100

1105

1110

1115

1110 ❓ Who is the "mother"?
Explain why you think
Oedipus uses the adjective
"unspeakable" to describe
her here.

32

33

34

32 READER'S RESPONSE
How do you react to the Shepherd's plea and to Oedipus's threat in lines 1100–1101? With whom do you sympathize? (Answers will vary.)

33 PREDICTING
At the climactic moment of the play, what do you think the Shepherd will tell Oedipus? (Possible response: Oedipus is really the son of Laius, and thus his father's murderer, and both the son and the husband of Jocasta.) How do you think Oedipus will react? (Possible response: with despair and possibly violence)

34 GUIDED READING
Identifying Cause and Effect: According to the Shepherd, in line 1113, what motive did he have for giving the abandoned baby to the Corinthian? (pity)

35 LITERARY BACKGROUND
Oedipus's outburst beginning at line 1118 marks his recognition of the truth at last. This is the point in a Greek tragedy that Aristotle described as *anagnorisis*, or the moment of recognition. In the *Poetics*, Aristotle says that tragedies like *Oedipus Rex* are especially effective since the moment of recognition occurs simultaneously with the reversal of the hero's fortunes from good to bad.

36 LITERARY ELEMENT
Theme: One of Sophocles' themes is the struggle of human beings to uncover their true identity or nature. What terrifying past deeds does Oedipus have to accept as his own, in lines 1122–1123? (killing his father and marrying his mother)

Oedipus.

35
> Ah God!
> It was true!
> > All the prophecies!
> > > —Now,

1120
> O Light, may I look on you for the last time!
> I, Oedipus,

36
> Oedipus, damned in his birth, in his marriage damned,
> Damned in the blood he shed with his own hand!

[*He rushes into the palace.*]

1123 **?** What do you predict Oedipus will do as he rushes offstage after this speech?

New York Public Library/Stratford Festival/Central Casting Agency

■ void: *n.* an empty space;
vacuum; *adj.* containing
nothing; empty

═══ ODE 4 ═══

Strophe 1

Chorus.
    Alas for the seed of men.

1125 What measure shall I give these generations
    That breathe on the void and are void
    And exist and do not exist?

37
1130
    Who bears more weight of joy
    Than mass of sunlight shifting in images,
    Or who shall make his thought stay on
    That down time drifts away?

    Your splendor is all fallen.

    O naked brow of wrath and tears,
    O change of Oedipus!
1135 I who saw your days call no man blest—
38 [Your great days like ghosts gone.

Antistrophe 1

    That mind was a strong bow.

39
    Deep, how deep you drew it then, hard archer,
    At a dim fearful range,
1140 And brought dear glory down!

    You overcame the stranger—
    The virgin with her hooking lion claws°—
    And though death sang, stood like a tower
    To make pale Thebes take heart.

1145 Fortress against our sorrow!

    True king, giver of laws,
    Majestic Oedipus!
    No prince in Thebes had ever such renown,
    No prince won such grace of power.

Strophe 2

40
1150 And now of all men ever known
    Most pitiful is this man's story:
    His fortunes are most changed, his state
    Fallen to a low slave's
    Ground under bitter fate.

1138 ❓ Who is the "archer"
    addressed by the Chorus
in these lines?

1142. **virgin . . . claws:** The Sphinx
    was depicted as having the
    paws of a lion.

37 GUIDED READING
Finding the Main Idea: What
seems to be the Chorus's main
idea in lines 1128–1131? (Possible response: Human joy and
thought are doomed to vanish.)

38 LITERARY ELEMENT
Simile: To what does the
Chorus compare Oedipus's
"great days," in line 1136?
(ghosts) What abstract idea
about Oedipus's good fortune
does this simile emphasize?
(Possible response: His good
fortune is insubstantial and
fleeting.)

39 LITERARY BACKGROUND
One of Apollo's attributes is
his patronage of archery. In
the description of the plague
at the beginning of the *Iliad*,
for example, Homer likens
Apollo to an archer who uses
his weapon, the bow, to unleash a deadly stream of arrows on the Greek army
(see p. 230).

40 READER'S RESPONSE
Here Oedipus's fortunes are
completely reversed. What
does the Chorus say is to
blame? (bitter fate) Do you
agree? (Answers will vary.)

Line 1183. The distinction is between evil that is done consciously and evil done unconsciously. The distinction is important in the action of the play, as Oedipus was not consciously aware that he had killed his father and taken his mother as his wife. The intentional evil that the Second Messenger refers to is Jocasta's suicide.

41 LITERARY ELEMENT

Theme: One of Sophocles' themes is the importance of learning the truth before it is too late to avert disaster. In what play about young lovers does Shakespeare use this theme? (*Romeo and Juliet*)

MEETING INDIVIDUAL NEEDS

42 *LEP:* Help students paraphrase lines 1163–1167. For example: "All actions are revealed and judged in time. Even though the incest was committed in ignorance, the dreadful deed has now been exposed and judged." ∎

43 LITERARY ELEMENT

Imagery: What images do the members of the Chorus use to describe their ignorance of the dreadful truth about Oedipus? (blindness, sleep) What do they mean by "ease of breath" and "the false years"? (living without fear; the years when they did not know the truth about Oedipus)

venerate (ven′ər·āt′): look upon with great respect; revere

44 LITERARY ELEMENT

Diction: The formal diction of the Second Messenger may seem stilted, but it is a convention of Greek tragedy that messengers use highly formal language. How does this speech compare with the opening statements of the Messenger in lines 879–895? (Both use formal diction.)

1155   O Oedipus, most royal one!
       The great door that expelled you to the light
       Gave at night—ah, gave night to your glory:
       As to the father, to the fathering son.

41   All understood too late.

1160   How could that queen whom Laius won,
       The garden that he harrowed at his height,
       Be silent when that act was done?

Antistrophe 2

       But all eyes fail before time's eye,
       All actions come to justice there.
42 1165 Though never willed, though far down the deep past,
       Your bed, your dread sirings,
       Are brought to book at last.
       Child by Laius doomed to die,
       Then doomed to lose that fortunate little death,
1170   Would God you never took breath in this air
       That with my wailing lips I take to cry:

       For I weep the world's outcast.

       I was blind, and now I can tell why:
43   Asleep, for you had given ease of breath
1175   To Thebes, while the false years went by.

═ EXODOS° ═

[Enter, from the palace, SECOND MESSENGER.]

Second Messenger.
       Elders of Thebes, most honored in this land,
       What horrors are yours to see and hear, what weight
       Of sorrow to be endured, if, true to your birth,
       You venerate the line of Labdacus!
44 1180 I think neither Istros nor Phasis,° those great rivers,
       Could purify this place of the corruption
       It shelters now, or soon must bring to light—
       Evil not done unconsciously, but willed.

       The greatest griefs are those we cause ourselves.
Choragos.
1185   Surely, friend, we have grief enough already;
       What new sorrow do you mean?

Exodos (eks′ə·dəs): the final scene.

1180. **Istros** (is′trəs) **nor Phasis** (fā′sis)

1183 ❓ What distinction does the Second Messenger draw in this line? How is this contrast important to the action of the play as a whole?

Second Messenger. The Queen is dead.

Choragos.
    Jocasta? Dead? But at whose hand?

Second Messenger. Her own.
    The full horror of what happened you cannot know,
    For you did not see it; but I, who did, will tell you
1190   As clearly as I can how she met her death.

    When she had left us,
    In passionate silence, passing through the court,
    She ran to her apartment in the house,
    Her hair clutched by the fingers of both hands.
1195   She closed the doors behind her; then, by that bed
    Where long ago the fatal son was conceived—
    That son who should bring about his father's death—
    We heard her call upon Laius, dead so many years,
    And heard her wail for the double fruit of her
        marriage,
1200   A husband by her husband, children by her child.

    Exactly how she died I do not know:
    For Oedipus burst in moaning and would not let us
    Keep vigil to the end: it was by him
    As he stormed about the room that our eyes
        were caught.
1205   From one to another of us he went, begging a sword,
    Cursing the wife who was not his wife, the mother
    Whose womb had carried his own children and
        himself.
    I do not know: it was none of us aided him,
    But surely one of the gods was in control!
1210   For with a dreadful cry
    He hurled his weight, as though wrenched out of
        himself,
    At the twin doors: the bolts gave, and he rushed in.
    And there we saw her hanging, her body swaying
    From the cruel cord she had noosed about her neck.
1215   A great sob broke from him, heartbreaking to hear,
    As he loosed the rope and lowered her to the
        ground.

    I would blot out from my mind what happened next!
    For the King ripped from her gown the golden
        brooches

1200 **?** Explain what the Messenger means by this apparently contradictory line.

45 READER'S RESPONSE
Did you anticipate Jocasta's suicide, or did it come as a surprise to you?

46 GUIDED READING
Sequencing: Reread the Messenger's account in lines 1191–1200. Then describe Jocasta's actions in their correct sequence. (She ran to her apartment while clutching her hair, closed the doors, called upon Laius while she was near her marriage bed, and bewailed Oedipus.)

47 EVALUATING
On the basis of lines 1202–1209, some critics have suggested that Oedipus may have intended either to kill Jocasta or to commit suicide. Do you believe that either of these actions would be consistent with the character of Oedipus as presented in the play? Explain. (Possible response: Oedipus seems devoted to Jocasta. However, he has harshly and wrongly judged those who seemed to cross him, so it is conceivable that he might harm her. There is little evidence to suggest that he would commit suicide.)

48 INTERPRETING
Why is it appropriate that Jocasta killed herself behind bolted doors? (Possible response: Throughout the play, she wished to keep problems private. She urged Creon and Oedipus to bring their quarrel inside the house, urged Oedipus not to pursue the search for his identity, and ran to her own apartments when the truth was revealed.)

ANSWER TO MARGIN QUESTION

Line 1246. Possible response: The Chorargos and Messenger may be conferring in hushed tones at one side of the stage, while glancing anxiously toward the other side of the stage. Oedipus may enter from this side, stretching out one arm and stumbling. His clothes are spattered with blood, and his eye sockets are empty.

49 LITERARY ELEMENT

Symbolism: In addition to its literal significance as a self-punishing act, what symbolic meaning does Oedipus's self-blinding have in terms of the play's leading themes? (Possible response: Because Oedipus did not "see" the truth while he had eyes, his self-blinding may symbolize the limitations of human knowledge or "vision" in general.)

50 LITERARY ELEMENT

Simile: What comparison does the Messenger use that enables the audience to visualize the streaming of Oedipus's blood? (red hail) Point out that hail often symbolizes destruction. For instance, in Exodus 9 from the Hebrew Bible, God sends hail as a plague on the evil pharaoh and his people.

49

That were her ornament, and raised them, and
        plunged them down
1220   Straight into his own eyeballs, crying, "No more,
No more shall you look on the misery about me,
The horrors of my own doing! Too long you
        have known
The faces of those whom I should never have seen,
Too long been blind to those for whom I was
        searching!
1225   From this hour, go in darkness!" And as he spoke,
He struck at his eyes—not once, but many times;
And the blood spattered his beard,

50

Bursting from his ruined sockets like red hail.

So from the unhappiness of two this evil has sprung,
1230   A curse on the man and woman alike. The old
Happiness of the house of Labdacus
Was happiness enough: where is it today?
It is all wailing and ruin, disgrace, death—all
The misery of mankind that has a name—
1235   And it is wholly and forever theirs.

Choragos.
Is he in agony still? Is there no rest for him?

Second Messenger.
He is calling for someone to lead him to the gates
So that all the children of Cadmus may look upon
His father's murderer, his mother's—no,
1240   I cannot say it!
                    And then he will leave Thebes,
Self-exiled, in order that the curse
Which he himself pronounced may depart from
        the house.
He is weak, and there is none to lead him,
So terrible is his suffering.
                            But you will see:
1245   Look, the doors are opening; in a moment
You will see a thing that would crush a heart
        of stone.

[*The central door is opened;* OEDIPUS, *blinded, is led in.*]

51

Choragos.
Dreadful indeed for men to see.

1246 Stage direction: Describe the way you visualize the stage action and the entrance of Oedipus here.

ANSWERS TO MARGIN QUESTIONS
Lines 1259–1263. Possible response: with great sadness, despair, and horror
Line 1271. Possible responses: Oedipus's self-blinding might be viewed as a demonstration of his great remorse, or as an act of fury against himself for his blindness to the truth about his identity.

Never have my own eyes
Looked on a sight so full of fear.

1250   Oedipus!
What madness came upon you, what daemon°
Leaped on your life with heavier
Punishment than a mortal man can bear?
No: I cannot even
1255   Look at you, poor ruined one.
And I would speak, question, ponder,
If I were able. No.
You make me shudder.

Oedipus.
God.   God.
1260   Is there a sorrow greater?
Where shall I find harbor in this world?
My voice is hurled far on a dark wind.
What has God done to me?

Choragos.
Too terrible to think of, or to see.

Strophe 1

Oedipus.
1265   O cloud of night,
Never to be turned away: night coming on,
I cannot tell how: night like a shroud!

My fair winds brought me here
                    O God. Again
The pain of the spikes where I had sight,
1270   The flooding pain
Of memory, never to be gouged out.

Choragos.
This is not strange.
You suffer it all twice over, remorse in pain,
Pain in remorse.

Antistrophe 1

Oedipus.
1275   Ah dear friend
Are you faithful even yet, you alone?
Are you still standing near me, will you stay
    here,

1251. **daemon** (dē′mən): evil spirit.

1259–1263 ❓ How would you read these lines?

1271 ❓ Do you read Oedipus's act of self-blinding as a punishment, an attempt to "shut out" the truth, or something else?

51 INTERPRETING
In lines 1247–1249, what words and phrases does the Choragos use that continue to draw our attention to the hero's self-blinding? (Possible responses: "to see," "my own eyes," "a sight so full of fear") How does he echo these phrases in lines 1254–1255? (He says he "cannot even/Look" at Oedipus.)

52 INTERPRETING
What does the Choragos mean when he says to Oedipus that "You suffer it all twice over"? (Possible response: Oedipus suffers painful remorse from the memory of his terrible deeds. He also suffers pain because of his eyes. This pain reminds him of his crimes, which leads to remorse.)

53 LITERARY ELEMENT
Tone: What tone of voice do you think the actor playing Oedipus should use to deliver lines 1275–1281? (Possible responses: pathetic, grateful, affectionate, pleading, self-pitying)

ANSWER TO MARGIN QUESTION

Line 1290. Apollo brought Oedipus's bitter fate upon him, but Oedipus willfully blinded himself.

54 INTERPRETING

What do Oedipus's words in lines 1285–1288 suggest about the questions of moral responsibility, fate, and free will raised in *Oedipus Rex*? (Possible response: Both the will of the gods and the will of Oedipus are involved in his fate.)

55 LITERARY ELEMENT

Foreshadowing: These words, in lines 1295–1296, foreshadow an event at the end of the play. What event might that be? (Oedipus's exile from Thebes)

56 INTERPRETING

The phrase *my darlings* in line 1305 translates a word in the original Greek which literally means "dear ones" or "my own ones" in the sense of close family relations. To whom is Oedipus specifically referring? (to Jocasta and their children)

53

Patient, to care for the blind?
                                    The blind man!
1280 Yet even blind I know who it is attends me,
By the voice's tone—
Though my new darkness hide the comforter.

Choragos.
Oh fearful act!
What god was it drove you to rake black
Night across your eyes?

Strophe 2

Oedipus.
54 1285 Apollo. Apollo. Dear
Children, the god was Apollo.
He brought my sick, sick fate upon me.
But the blinding hand was my own!
How could I bear to see
1290 When all my sight was horror everywhere?

Choragos.
Everywhere; that is true.

Oedipus.
And now what is left?
Images? Love? A greeting even,
Sweet to the senses? Is there anything?
55 1295 Ah, no, friends: lead me away.
Lead me away from Thebes.
                                    Lead the great wreck
And hell of Oedipus, whom the gods hate.

Choragos.
Your fate is clear, you are not blind to that.
Would God you had never found it out!

Antistrophe 2

Oedipus.
1300 Death take the man who unbound
My feet on that hillside
And delivered me from death to life! What life?
If only I had died,
This weight of monstrous doom
56 1305 Could not have dragged me and my darlings down.

Choragos.
I would have wished the same.

1290 ❓ According to Oedipus, who is responsible for his blindness?

ANSWERS TO MARGIN QUESTIONS
Line 1328. The malediction is the curse that Oedipus declared against the murderer of King Laius, praying that the criminal's life "be consumed in evil and wretchedness" (lines 232–234).

Line 1334. Possible response: He might place his hands over his ears.

Oedipus.
Oh never to have come here
With my father's blood upon me! Never
To have been the man they call his mother's
    husband!
1310   Oh accursed! Oh child of evil,
To have entered that wretched bed—
                     the selfsame one!
More primal than sin itself, this fell to me.

Choragos.
I do not know how I can answer you.
You were better dead than alive and blind.

Oedipus.
1315   Do not counsel me any more. This punishment
That I have laid upon myself is just.
If I had eyes,
I do not know how I could bear the sight
Of my father, when I came to the house of Death,
1320   Or my mother: for I have sinned against them both
So vilely that I could not make my peace
By strangling my own life.
                Or do you think my children,
Born as they were born, would be sweet to my
    eyes?
Ah never, never! Nor this town with its high walls,
1325   Nor the holy images of the gods.
                For I,
Thrice miserable!—Oedipus, noblest of all the line
Of Cadmus, have condemned myself to enjoy
These things no more, by my own malediction
Expelling that man whom the gods declared
1330   To be a defilement in the house of Laius.
After exposing the rankness of my own guilt,
How could I look men frankly in the eyes?
No, I swear it,
If I could have stifled my hearing at its source,
1335   I would have done it and made all this body
A tight cell of misery, blank to light and sound:
So I should have been safe in a dark agony
Beyond all recollection.
              Ah Cithaeron!
Why did you shelter me? When I was cast upon
    you,

57

58

1328 **?** What is the "malediction" to which Oedipus refers in this line?

1334 **?** What gesture might Oedipus make as he speaks these lines?

■ primal (prī′məl): original

57 LITERARY BACKGROUND
Many Greeks believed that after death they would meet the souls of those who had died before them in a shadowy place called the "underworld." In Plato's *Apology*, for example, Socrates looks forward to meeting and questioning the shades of some of the great epic heroes after his death (see pp. 297–299).

58 INTERPRETING
Why does Oedipus consider it fitting for him to be the victim of his own curse? (After the terrible deeds he has committed, he cannot face others without shame.)

New York Public Library/Stratford Festival/Peter Smith & Company

1340   Why did I not die? Then I should never
Have shown the world my execrable birth.

59
Ah Polybus! Corinth, city that I believed
The ancient seat of my ancestors: how fair
I seemed, your child! And all the while this evil
1345   Was cancerous within me!
                                        For I am sick
In my daily life, sick in my origin.

60
O three roads, dark ravine, woodland and way
Where three roads met: you, drinking my father's
        blood,
My own blood, spilled by my own hand: can you
        remember
1350   The unspeakable things I did there, and the things
I went on from there to do?
                                        O marriage, marriage!
The act that engendered me, and again the act
Performed by the son in the same bed—
                                        Ah, the net
Of incest, mingling fathers, brothers, sons,

Line 1366. Possible response: because Oedipus had falsely accused Creon of plotting to become the ruler of Thebes

Line 1371. Possible response: Creon is not mocking when he refers to Oedipus as "this pollution." In keeping with the religion of his day, Creon believes that Oedipus is contaminated and must be hidden from the gods and from other people. His words in lines 1375–1376 seem gentle and may indicate a concern for Oedipus.

61 CULTURAL BACKGROUND

Oedipus's statement in line 1360, "You need not fear to touch me," refers to the ancient Greek belief that the taint of moral "pollution" could be physically transmitted—exactly like a contagious disease. Oedipus challenges conventional wisdom when he asserts in line 1361 that *his* pollution is so grave and unique that it cannot be "catching."

62 CULTURAL BACKGROUND

Creon's comments about Helios, the sun god, in lines 1370–1374 make sense if we interpret them in the context of ancient Greek religious ideas. Just as Oedipus feels that he is too polluted to look upon the light of the sun or on other people—and has therefore blinded himself—Creon believes that Oedipus is too polluted to be seen by the holy sun god and must therefore be hidden.

MEETING INDIVIDUAL NEEDS

63 *LEP:* You may want to explain that the formal, archaic phrase "since your courtesy/Ignores my dark expectation" means something like "since your polite behavior was not at all what I expected." You might also inform students that *execrable*, in line 1379, means "horrible" or "detestable." ∎

1355   With brides, wives, mothers: the last evil
That can be known by men: no tongue can say
How evil!
        No. For the love of God, conceal me
Somewhere far from Thebes; or kill me; or hurl
    me
Into the sea, away from men's eyes forever.

61 ⌐1360   Come, lead me. You need not fear to touch me.
Of all men, I alone can bear this guilt.

[*Enter* CREON.]

Choragos.
   We are not the ones to decide; but Creon here
May fitly judge of what you ask. He only
Is left to protect the city in your place.

Oedipus.
1365   Alas, how can I speak to him? What right have I
To beg his courtesy whom I have deeply wronged?

1366 ❓ Explain why Oedipus feels that he can hardly face speaking to Creon.

Creon.
   I have not come to mock you, Oedipus,
Or to reproach you, either.
   (*to* ATTENDANTS)   —You, standing there:
If you have lost all respect for man's dignity,

62 ⌐1370   At least respect the flame of Lord Helios:
Do not allow this pollution to show itself
Openly here, an affront to the earth
And Heaven's rain and the light of day. No, take
   him
Into the house as quickly as you can.
   └1375   For it is proper
That only the close kindred see his grief.

1371 ❓ Do you think that Creon's comment about Oedipus as an example of "pollution" contradicts his earlier statement that he has not come to "mock" or "reproach" Oedipus? Or can you reconcile these two statements? Explain.

Oedipus.
63 ⌐   I pray you in God's name, since your courtesy
Ignores my dark expectation, visiting
   └ With mercy this man of all men most execrable:
1380   Give me what I ask—for your good, not for mine.

Creon.
   And what is it that you would have me do?

Oedipus.
   Drive me out of this country as quickly as may be
To a place where no human voice can ever greet me.

64 LITERARY ELEMENT

Characterization: Given what you already know about Creon, how does his statement in lines 1384–1385 fit his character? (Possible response: It reflects his habitual caution and unwillingness to act before he knows all the facts.)

65 INTERPRETING

In lines 1394–1396, why do you think that Oedipus does not refer to Jocasta by name but only indirectly as "the woman in there" and as "your sister"? (Possible response: He may shrink from naming her directly because he is so appalled at the knowledge of his incest.)

66 LITERARY ELEMENT

Setting: Why is it appropriate that Oedipus wants to die on Mount Cithaeron? (As the site of his exposure as an infant, it seems to be the place fated for his death.)

67 LITERARY BACKGROUND

Oedipus has two sons, Eteocles and Polyneices, and two daughters, Antigone and Ismene. These children would have been known to Sophocles' audience since they figured as characters in a number of tragedies, including Aeschylus' *Seven Against Thebes* and Sophocles' *Antigone*.

64

Creon.
　　I should have done that before now—only,
1385　God's will had not been wholly revealed to me.
Oedipus.
　　But his command is plain: the parricide°
　　Must be destroyed. I am that evil man.
Creon.
　　That is the sense of it, yes; but as things are,
　　We had best discover clearly what is to be done.
Oedipus.
1390　You would learn more about a man like me?
Creon.
　　You are ready now to listen to the god.
Oedipus.
　　I will listen. But it is to you
　　That I must turn for help. I beg you, hear me.

65
1395　The woman in there—
　　Give her whatever funeral you think proper:
　　She is your sister.
　　　　　　　　—But let me go, Creon!

66
　　Let me purge my father's Thebes of the pollution
　　Of my living here, and go out to the wild hills,
1400　To Cithaeron, that has won such fame with me,
　　The tomb my mother and father appointed for me,
　　And let me die there, as they willed I should.
　　And yet I know
　　Death will not ever come to me through sickness
　　Or in any natural way: I have been preserved
1405　For some unthinkable fate. But let that be.

67
　　As for my sons, you need not care for them.
　　They are men, they will find some way to live.
　　But my poor daughters, who have shared my table,
　　Who never before have been parted from their
　　　　father—
1410　Take care of them, Creon; do this for me.
　　And will you let me touch them with my hands
　　A last time, and let us weep together?
　　Be kind, my lord,
　　Great prince, be kind!
　　　　　　　　Could I but touch them,

1386. **parricide** (par′ə·sīd′): one who murders his or her parent.

Line 1416. Possible response: At first have Antigone and Ismene seem frightened of Oedipus because they are seeing him blinded and powerless for the first time. Then have them run to him and have Oedipus touch them with great affection, while they show their love for him. The tenderness between father and daughters should be touching to the audience.

Line 1440. Antigone and Ismene were conceived and born as the result of incest between Jocasta and Oedipus. Because of the taboo against incest and the possibility that as children of incest they or their children may be in some way malformed, Antigone and Ismene will always be stigmatized.

1415   They would be mine again, as when I had my eyes.

[*Enter* ANTIGONE *and* ISMENE, *attended.*]
        Ah, God!
        Is it my dearest children I hear weeping?
        Has Creon pitied me and sent my daughters?

Creon.
        Yes, Oedipus: I knew that they were dear to you
1420   In the old days, and know you must love them still.

Oedipus.
        May God bless you for this—and be a friendlier
        Guardian to you than he has been to me!

        Children, where are you?
        Come quickly to my hands: they are your
            brother's—
1425   Hands that have brought your father's once clear
            eyes
        To this way of seeing—
                            Ah dearest ones,
        I had neither sight nor knowledge then, your father
        By the woman who was the source of his own life!
        And I weep for you—having no strength to see
            you—,
1430   I weep for you when I think of the bitterness
        That men will visit upon you all your lives.
        What homes, what festivals can you attend
        Without being forced to depart again in tears?
        And when you come to marriageable age,
1435   Where is the man, my daughters, who would dare
        Risk the bane that lies on all my children?
        Is there any evil wanting? Your father killed
        His father; sowed the womb of her who bore him;
        Engendered you at the fount of his own existence!
1440   That is what they will say of you.
                            Then, whom
        Can you ever marry? There are no bridegrooms
            for you,
        And your lives must wither away in sterile
            dreaming.

        O Creon, son of Menoeceus!
        You are the only father my daughters have,

1416 ❓ Antigone and Ismene have no lines. How could you best make use of their presence on the stage?

1440 ❓ Why is Oedipus convinced that his daughters' futures will be all suffering? Why must they pay for his sins?

68 LITERARY ELEMENT
Characterization: What do Creon's words in lines 1419–1420 reveal about his character? (He is capable of kindness, consideration, affection, and generosity; he respects the power of love.)

69 LITERARY BACKGROUND
Oedipus's predictions about his daughters foreshadow the fact that they will remain unmarried. The tragic destiny of Antigone, in particular, was familiar from Sophocles' earlier tragedy *Antigone*. When she disobeyed Creon's edict by burying her brother Polyneices, who had been killed as he led an attack against Thebes, Creon sentenced Antigone to death.

■ **engendered** (en·jen'dərd): begot

Line 1462. In his malediction, Oedipus had cursed the murderer of Laius and had said that anyone having knowledge of the crime who did not come forward should be exiled from Thebes. Now it is Oedipus's wish to be exiled himself, as he himself is the murderer.

Line 1466. Possible responses: solemn, stern, commanding

Line 1475. Possible response: Human beings should never count their lives happy before they die, since bad fortune can strike at any time.

70 LITERARY BACKGROUND

Oedipus's moving plea to Creon to protect his daughters would have reminded Greek audiences of the intense conflict between Creon (who represents the laws of the state) and the heroine Antigone (who represents the higher "unwritten laws" of the gods) in Sophocles' *Antigone*. Creon won that struggle, but at tremendous cost: the death of Antigone and the suicides of his son Haemon and his wife, Eurydice.

71 EVALUATING

The falling action (denouement) of the play occurs in lines 1456–1466, as Creon gently but firmly ushers Oedipus inside the palace. Is this scene psychologically realistic and convincing, in your view? (Answers will vary.)

1445 Since we, their parents, are both of us gone
    forever.

70

They are your own blood: you will not let them
Fall into beggary and loneliness;
You will keep them from the miseries that are mine!
Take pity on them; see, they are only children,
1450 Friendless except for you. Promise me this,
Great Prince, and give me your hand in token of it.

[CREON *clasps his right hand.*]

Children:
I could say much, if you could understand me,
But as it is, I have only this prayer for you:
1455 Live where you can, be as happy as you can—
Happier, please God, than God has made your
    father!

Creon.
Enough. You have wept enough. Now go within.

Oedipus.
I must; but it is hard.

Creon.   Time eases all things.

Oedipus.
But you must promise—

Creon.   Say what you desire.

Oedipus.
1460 Send me from Thebes!

Creon.   God grant that I may!

71

Oedipus.
But since God hates me . . .

Creon.   No, he will grant your wish.

Oedipus.
You promise?

Creon.   I cannot speak beyond my knowledge.

Oedipus.
Then lead me in.

Creon.   Come now, and leave your children.

Oedipus.
No! Do not take them from me!

Creon.   Think no longer
1465 That you are in command here, but rather think

1462 Explain the irony of this line, given all that has gone before in the play.

1. What news about King Polybus does the Messenger from Corinth bring? (The king is dead.)
2. What does Oedipus then learn about his own parentage? (He is not Polybus's son.)
3. Who gave the infant Oedipus to the Messenger? (a shepherd)
4. What does Oedipus use to blind himself? (brooches from Jocasta's gown)
5. Where does Oedipus beg Creon to send him? (to exile on Mount Cithaeron)

RETEACHING

To reteach *Oedipus Rex*, divide the class into groups of three students each to prepare oral readings of the play. Ask each group to select a different scene or choral ode. Groups working on a scene need to choose and interpret roles or parts; groups presenting odes need to practice reading the lyric aloud in unison. After taking time for rehearsals, encourage students to present a dramatic reading of their portion of the tragedy to the class.

71

How, when you were, you served your own
    destruction.

[*Exeunt into the house all but the* CHORUS; *the* CHORAGOS *chants directly to the audience:*]
Choragos.
    Men of Thebes: look upon Oedipus.

72

1470

This is the king who solved the famous riddle
And towered up, most powerful of men.
No mortal eyes but looked on him with envy,
Yet in the end ruin swept over him.

Let every man in mankind's frailty
Consider his last day; and let none
Presume on his good fortune until he find

1475

Life, at his death, a memory without pain.

1466 ❓ What tone of voice might Creon use for this line?

1475 ❓ What moral lesson does the Chorus draw from the action of the play?

72 **LITERARY ELEMENT**

Irony: In lines 1468–1471, how does the Choragos sum up a central irony of the play? (The history of Oedipus is ironic because he began as the envy of all and ended alone, ruined, and in pain.)

WRITING TO LEARN

Psychology: Sigmund Freud thought that the Oedipus myth expressed certain psychological conflicts in the unconscious mind. Based on what you know about myths from various cultures, do you think that myths can reflect certain universal human emotions and conflicts that transcend national and cultural boundaries? Write a brief paper explaining your opinion. Remember to support your views with reasons and examples from several myths. ∎

A CRITICAL COMMENT

Themes in Oedipus Rex

Many readers have wondered about the theme or message that Sophocles intended to convey in *Oedipus Rex*. Some critics say that the play is nothing more than an ingenious detective story, in which the detective himself turns out to be the hated culprit. Others assume that the play must mask hidden references to Sophocles' own time, so that Oedipus's pride and downfall mirror the figure of the Athenian statesman Pericles, or perhaps the fortunes of Athens itself. While each of these theories may represent part of the truth, many readers have recognized that the implications of the tragedy go far beyond its structure as a detective story or its relevance to real life in the playwright's own time.

One of the main questions of the drama has to do with the degree of guilt to be assigned to the fallen king. In one view, Oedipus must be held fully responsible for his actions. Even if his monumental crimes were committed unintentionally, critics say, Oedipus might have avoided them through greater vigilance. Others insist that the very process of discovery shows the great king's tragic flaw: his own self-confidence and pride as revealed in his arrogant treatment of Teiresias and Creon. The actual Greek title of the play is, in fact, *Oedipus Tyrannos* (the title *Oedipus Rex* is Latin for "Oedipus the King"). The term *tyrant* in ancient Greek refers more to a powerful, self-made ruler than to an evil despot, and Oedipus, as portrayed by Sophocles, does

1. Responding to a Critical Opinion. The critic Robert D. Murray, Jr., wrote that the riddle of the Sphinx was "close to the heart" of *Oedipus Rex*: "Oedipus reenacts the riddle; as infant on the slopes of Kithaeron, as the kind and intelligent king at the beginning of the tragedy, as the faltering blind man at the end." Have students respond to Murray's evaluation of the importance of the riddle to the tragedy.

2. Research Project. Students can report on the many parallels to the Oedipus story in myth and folklore from other cultures. Two sources will be especially helpful: *Oedipus: A Folklore Casebook* edited by L. Edmunds and A. Dundes (Garland Publishing, 1984) and *Oedipus: The Ancient Legend and Its Later Analogues* by L. Edmunds (Johns Hopkins University Press, 1985).

Ask students to review the five themes listed in the *Introduction* to the play (pp. 302–305). Then ask them to consider which of these themes they think is most important or central to Sophocles' conception of the Oedipus story. Have students hold a roundtable discussion to exchange and support their opinions. ∎

ANSWERS

First Thoughts
Answers will vary.

Identifying Facts
1. King Polybus is dead. Oedipus is not Polybus's son.
2. He received the son of Laius from Jocasta and gave the infant to the Corinthian Messenger.
3. Oedipus has fallen from an extremely high position to an extremely low one. He is compared to a low slave ground under bitter fate.
4. Jocasta has hung herself and Oedipus has blinded himself.

Interpreting Meanings
1. The Messenger expects Oedipus to find joy in the new kingship but sadness over the death of Polybus; instead, ironically, Oedipus is joyful to hear of Polybus's death, but disturbed to learn he is not Polybus's son.
2. Oedipus is her son. details about the infant's ankles, where and by whom he was rescued
3. These lines come just before the revelation of the terrible truth about Oedipus's past.
4. No. Possible response: compassionate but aware of Oedipus's flaws
5. Possible response: Yes. We want to know Oedipus's reaction to his fate.

not seem to be particularly tyrannical. Still, the flaw of pride in Oedipus cannot be lightly dismissed.

On the other hand, we also see from numerous touches of characterization in the play that Oedipus is basically a sincere ruler, a good man, and a loving father. We are therefore forced to consider even larger questions of divine justice and the individual's place in the world. Are human beings creatures of free will, or are their actions, for good or ill, determined by forces beyond their control? In interpreting this play, it is difficult to say exactly where Sophocles stands on this issue. Certainly we can hear the faith and reverence for the gods reflected in most of the choral odes. On the other hand, Sophocles also

carefully removes any direct divine intervention from the action of the play itself. Moreover, he allows Oedipus and Jocasta to serve occasionally as spokespersons for the religious skepticism that was in the air in Athens during the later fifth century B.C. At several points in the play, Oedipus defines himself as "a child of luck," also suggesting a denial of the power of the gods.

In the final moments of the drama, this issue emerges in a new light. Throughout the play, the idea that the individual is a completely self-sufficient creature is undermined by irony and doubt. But in the end, it is Oedipus's self-knowledge, in fulfillment of the injunction to "know thyself," that gives him the strength to face the truth and to go out to meet his fate.

First Thoughts
How did you react to the end of the tragedy? What emotions did you experience?

Identifying Facts
1. What news does the Corinthian Messenger announce? After this announcement, what does the Messenger reveal about Oedipus's true parentage?
2. After Oedipus threatens him with torture, what crucial facts does the Shepherd disclose?
3. According to the Chorus in lines 1150–1154, how have Oedipus's fortunes changed? What comparison do they use for their king in these lines?
4. Summarize the news announced by the Second Messenger. What actions by Oedipus and Jocasta does he describe?

Interpreting Meanings
1. In lines 891–892, the Corinthian Messenger indicates that his news may contain both joy and grief. Explain how this

comment turns out to be a classic example of **irony** as the scene progresses.
2. In line 1000, what conclusion has Jocasta evidently reached? What information supplied by the Messenger has enabled her to reach this conclusion?
3. Explain how lines 1104–1105 might be regarded as the **climax**, or turning point, of the play.
4. In lines 1320–1322, Oedipus says that he has sinned so vilely against both his parents that he could not bear to see them even in the house of Death. Yet we know that Oedipus acted in ignorance. By most modern standards, would Oedipus be judged guilty? Judging from his portrayal of Oedipus's reaction to the discovery of his deeds, how do you think Sophocles felt about Oedipus's crimes?
5. In your opinion, does Sophocles succeed in maintaining **suspense** in the play right up to the end? Explain your answer.

Applying Meanings

Consider the closing speech made by the Chorus in lines 1467–1475. They speak sadly of Oedipus's pride and stature and pronounce:

> and let none
> Presume on his good fortune until he find
> Life, at his death, a memory without pain.

What do you think this means? Do you think it is possible to live a life that will be a "memory without pain"?

The Play as a Whole
Interpreting Meanings

1. Do you think that Oedipus is an admirable character, or do you think that he is significantly flawed? If he is admirable, what are some of the positive qualities you admire in him? If he is flawed, what are some of his negative traits?

2. Sophocles' play raises some very difficult questions regarding guilt and responsibility for unintentional crimes. Can you think of any other examples of unforgivable acts committed in ways that make the assignment of responsibility almost impossible?

3. The **plot** of *Oedipus Rex* builds with irresistible force to a climax when Oedipus discovers the truth about his identity and his past actions. Why do you think that the play does not end with the revelation of the truth and Oedipus's self-blinding? What is the dramatic function of the final meeting between Oedipus and Creon?

4. Compare the first song of the Chorus in the Parodos with its lament in Ode 4. How has the attitude of the Chorus changed in the course of the drama? Do you think the Chorus reflects the point of view of the author, the audience, or

any of the characters? Explain the reasons for your answer.

5. In Greek drama the most violent actions, such as Jocasta's suicide and Oedipus's self-blinding, customarily occurred offstage and were reported by messengers. How might this treatment of violence differ in a modern version of the play for the stage or the screen? Could one argue that the secondhand reporting of violence might, in fact, produce a more chilling impression on an audience than an actual presentation of the violent actions themselves?

6. Based on your reading of *Oedipus Rex*, can you understand why the experience of an audience observing the suffering of a character in a **tragedy** may be, in fact, uplifting and exhilarating?

Creative Writing Response

Extending the Myth. At the end of *Oedipus Rex*, several issues are left unresolved. Will Creon agree to exile Oedipus from Thebes? What will happen to Oedipus's children? Will the plague be lifted from the city of Thebes? What special fate is reserved for the hero himself (see lines 1403–1405)? Using either prose narrative or dramatic dialogue, write a short sequel to *Oedipus Rex*. Then compare the plot of your sequel with the plot line of Sophocles' play, *Oedipus at Colonus*.

Critical Writing Response

Analyzing Oedipus as a Tragic Hero. Consider the character of Oedipus in the light of Aristotle's theory of tragedy as this theory is explained on page 371. Do you agree that Oedipus's misfortune is brought about by "some error of judgment or frailty," or do you have a different interpretation? Write a three- to four-paragraph essay in which you analyze Oedipus as a tragic hero. Use evidence from the play to support your ideas.

Language and Vocabulary

1. *Metaphors:* plague compared to a murdering sea, Thebes to a ship. *Personification:* a sea that murders and Thebes lifting her head
2. *Similes:* doom compared to a cloud and to nightfall. *Metaphor:* healer may weave doom like a cloth or web
3. *Similes:* lives compared to birds or sparks of fire
4. *Metaphor and personification:* parents' curse compared to lash. *Metaphor:* night compared to blindness
5. *Simile:* murderer compared to wild bull
6. *Metaphors:* Oedipus compared to ship's captain, Thebes to ship, Sphinx's killings to storm at sea
7. *Metaphor:* destiny compared to net
8. *Personification:* haughtiness and disdain given human qualities
9. *Personification:* luck compared to a mother and the months compared to brothers
10. *Simile:* Oedipus's past days of glory compared to ghosts

Language and Vocabulary

Figures of Speech

A **figure of speech** is a word or phrase that describes one thing in terms of another and is not meant to be understood on a literal level. The most common figures of speech are:

1. The **simile**, which compares one thing to another with the use of connective words such as *like* or *as*
2. The **metaphor**, which makes a comparison between two seemingly unlike things without using any connective words
3. **Personification**, in which a nonhuman thing or quality is referred to as if it were human

Sophocles' play abounds with figurative language. Identify the figures of speech in the passages below as **similes**, **metaphors**, or **personification**. Then explain what things are being compared or personified in each passage. Some passages may contain more than one figure of speech.

1. **Priest.** Your own eyes
   Must tell you: Thebes is tossed on a murdering sea
   And cannot lift her head from the death surge (lines 25–27)
2. **Chorus.** Now I remember, O Healer, your power, and wonder:
   Will you send doom like a sudden cloud, or weave it
   Like nightfall of the past? (lines 158–160)
3. **Chorus.** See, how our lives like birds take wing,
   Like sparks that fly when a fire soars,
   To the shore of the god of evening. (lines 177–179)
4. **Teiresias.** But the double lash of your parents' curse will whip you
   Out of this land some day, with only night
   Upon your precious eyes. (lines 405–407)
5. **Chorus.** Holy Parnassus' peak of snow
   Flashes and blinds that secret man,
   That all shall hunt him down:
   Though he may roam the forest shade
   Like a bull gone wild from pasture
   To rage through glooms of stone. (lines 458–463)
6. **Choragos.** Oedipus, it is not once only
   I have told you—
   You must know I should count myself unwise
   To the point of madness, should I now forsake you—
   You, under whose hand,
   In the storm of another time,
   Our dear land sailed out free.
   But now stand fast at the helm! (lines 648–654)
7. **Oedipus.** Ah, what net has God been weaving for me? (line 695)
8. **Chorus.** Haughtiness and the high hand of disdain
   Tempt and outrage God's holy law. (lines 839–840)
9. **Oedipus.** Luck is my mother; the passing months, my brothers,
   Have seen me rich and poor. (lines 1025–1026)
10. **Chorus.** I who saw your days call no man blest—
    Your great days like ghosts gone. (lines 1135–1136)

11. **Oedipus.** O cloud of night,
    Never to be turned away: night coming on,
    I cannot tell how: night like a shroud!
    (lines 1265–1267)
12. **Oedipus.** O three roads, dark ravine,
    woodland and way
    Where three roads met: you, drinking
    my father's blood,

My own blood, spilled by my own
    hand: can you remember
The unspeakable things I did there,
    and the things
I went on from there to do? (lines
    1347–1351)

11. *Metaphor:* blindness compared to a cloud of night. *Simile:* night compared to a shroud
12. *Personification:* three roads, ravine, and woodland compared to drinkers of blood ∎

ELEMENTS OF LITERATURE

Tragedy and the Tragic Hero

The Greek philosopher Aristotle (384–322 B.C.) pays special attention to tragedy in his treatise *The Poetics*. He explains that tragic dramas should be tightly unified constructions based on a single action and featuring a single protagonist, or hero. Tragedies generally deal with characters who are neither exceptionally virtuous nor exceptionally evil. According to Aristotle, the hero should have "a character between these two extremes—that of a man [or a woman] who is not preeminently good and just, yet whose misfortune is brought about not by vice or depravity, but by some error of judgment or frailty." This weakness is known as *hamartia* (hä′mär·tē′ə), which is often translated as "tragic flaw." Typically, this flaw takes the form of excessive pride or arrogance, called *hubris* (hyoo′bris).

As a tragedy unfolds, according to Aristotle, the tragic hero goes through one or more reversals of fortune leading up to a final recognition of a truth that has remained hidden from him. In the process he experiences profound suffering. Aristotle supplements his theory by observing that as the members of an audience witness this deep suffering, their emotions of pity and fear lead them to experience a feeling of *catharsis* (kə·thär′sis), or purgation, that leaves them with a new sense of self-awareness and renewal. Paradoxically, then, the experience of watching a tragedy and being purged of upsetting emotions brings a kind of pleasure to the spectator.

In his analysis of tragedy in *The Poetics*, Aristotle cites Sophocles' play *Oedipus Rex* several times as a supreme example of tragic drama. Were you moved to pity and fear by this tale of Oedipus's suffering? Did you also feel a final sense of renewal through the experience?

1 LITERARY BACKGROUND
Greek Terms: In ancient Greek the literal meanings of these famous terms are quite different from the definitions usually given them. The word *hamartia* literally means "a missing of the mark"—as happens, for example, when an archer shoots an arrow and misses the target. The word *hubris* literally means physical violence or assault—it was the name of a crime under Athenian law. ∎

OBJECTIVES

1. To gain an overview of ancient Roman literature and civilization
2. To analyze a Roman epic, lyric poetry, and historical prose
3. To interpret and respond to Roman literature both orally and in writing

TEACHER'S RESOURCES: 4
✔ Unit Introduction Test

1 RESPONDING TO THE QUOTATION

Invite students to brainstorm associations with the word *Rome*. Possible responses include Ben Hur, Pontius Pilate, gladiators, military strength, togas, and chariot races.

❓ *How might Bourne's statement about Rome apply to our own civilization?* (Answers will vary.)

2 HISTORICAL BACKGROUND

Aeneas: According to legend, Aeneas founded the dynasty of Latium in Italy. Among his ancestors were twin brothers, Romulus and Remus, who were raised by a she-wolf after their wicked uncle abandoned them. One of the brothers, Romulus, was the legendary founder of Rome.

3 HISTORICAL BACKGROUND

Oligarchy: The Roman Republic was dominated by an oligarchy of patricians; that is, a few wealthy families monopolized most high government offices. Although these patricians had originally valued *pietas* (duty), *gravitas* (dignity), and *fides* (loyalty), class conflict developed and eventually grew violent. The civil conflicts led to a series of reforms such as limiting terms of office and establishing a second legislative house. But the oligarchies' abuses became so widespread that the common people and soldiers were willing to trade allegiance to a dictator such as Julius Caesar in exchange for limitations on the power of the patricians.

ROMAN LITERATURE

66 One of the great strengths of their empire was their willingness . . . to borrow and to adapt freely from others whatever they found useful. This made possible the transmission of religions, ideas, and ideals from older cultures, and it helped them construct . . . a respectable literature, an efficient military machine, a formidable bureaucracy, and the world's greatest legal system. **99**

—*Frank C. Bourne*

After the death of Alexander the Great in 323 B.C., the center of power in the Mediterranean world gradually shifted westward to Rome. With this shift, the legacy of Greek civilization also passed into Roman hands. When the Romans emerged as the undisputed masters of a vast empire, they began to produce literary and artistic works that could rival those of their Greek teachers.

The Founding of Rome

The Romans' own ideas about their origins appear in legends about the founding of the city. One such legend was the basis for the *Aeneid* (ē·nē′id), the national epic of Rome written by the poet Virgil (vur′jəl) (70–19 B.C.). According to the epic, when the Greeks sacked Troy, the hero Aeneas fled from the flaming ruins of the city, carrying his aged father on his back and leading his young son by the hand. Together with his followers, Aeneas established a colony of the Trojan people on Italian soil (see page 380).

In reality, the founding of Rome was less dramatic. The city of Rome began in the year 753 B.C. as an agricultural settlement on the east bank of the river Tiber in the region known as Latium.

In the late sixth century B.C., the Romans set up a republican government, that is, a government in which voters elect representatives to make political decisions for them. This republican form of government lasted nearly five centuries and was looked to as a model by the framers of the U.S. Constitution in the eighteenth century.

The Romans were a practical people. They valued order, thrift, ambition, and loyalty. Three Latin words sum up traditional Roman values: *pietas* (pē′ā·täs), or religious observance; *gravitas* (grav′i·täs′), or seriousness of conduct and purpose; and *fides* (fē′dās), or patriotism and loyalty.

Historians who ponder the rise and fall of the Roman Empire often ask to what extent the United States is a modern-day Rome. Begin a class discussion by pointing out several points of similarity. Like ancient Rome, modern America owes much of its intellectual heritage to earlier civilizations. Like Rome, modern America has superseded many of its predecessors economically and technologically but has not, in the eyes of some, surpassed them in culture or refinement. Like Rome, American society is a vast, heterogeneous civilization, influenced by many foreign cultures. In recent times, as in ancient Rome, the values of our society seem in flux and the disparity between wealth and poverty, power and powerlessness, is fostering discontent.

Differences between Rome and the United States are also apparent. Unlike the leaders of imperial Rome, our leaders succeed one another in an orderly process dictated by the ballot box. Our nation, unlike the Roman Empire, is not too unwieldy to protect. Interested students may wish to research such topics as the history of slavery or the influence of religion in Rome, to further compare and contrast the two cultures.

Whether or not students see parallels between America and Rome, it is important that they appreciate the extent of the

Scala/Art Resource, New York

THE FORUM, GIUSEPPE BECCHETTI (1724–1794). *Watercolor.*

The Republic and Roman Expansion ■

4 By 270 B.C., all Italy south of the river Rubicon was in Roman hands. During the centuries that followed, the Romans conquered Spain and waged three costly and lengthy conflicts,

> **The Romans steadily expanded their territory through military conquest, first in Italy and then overseas in Spain, North Africa, and Greece.**

5 known as the **Punic** (pyoō'nik) **Wars**, with their rival city Carthage, situated across the Mediterranean in North Africa (see the map on page 381). During these wars, a daring attack by the Carthaginian general Hannibal, who led a troop

Introduction   **373**

historical and cultural debt Rome owes to ancient Greece. The Roman Empire eventually included most of the lands conquered by Alexander the Great. Young Roman men went to Athens to study, and Roman generals brought Greek libraries back to their Roman estates. The Romans, however, were superior to the Greeks as administrators and engineers. By linking their conquered lands with a system of roads that ran from Britain to the Eu-

phrates River in modern Iraq, the Romans were able to prolong their Empire.

Ask students to note how Greek literary models were the inspiration for Roman writers. Virgil's *Aeneid* (p. 379) is patterned on Homer's epics. The histories of Tacitus (p. 428) were modeled on Thucydides (p. 284). Catullus's lyric poetry (p. 409) follows in the tradition of Sappho (p. 279), and Roman rhetoricians such as Cicero were indebted to Greek orators such

as Demosthenes (384–322 B.C.). Except for the art of letter writing, the Romans borrowed their forms, style, and subject matter from the Greeks. Roman writers were as talented as their Greek counterparts, but Rome's literary glory was brief. To illustrate this fact, have students examine the dates of the Roman authors, noting that the birth date of the oldest author, Catullus, is only 201 years before the death date of the youngest, Tacitus. Also

---

6 HISTORICAL BACKGROUND

Carthage: The Greek historian Polybius (c. 205–c. 125 B.C.) witnessed the razing of Carthage. He described the Romans burning the city, plowing the ground and sowing it with salt, and pronouncing a curse on anyone who tried to restore it. From this victory Rome gained fifty thousand slaves and a province containing much grain-producing land.

7 RESPONDING TO THE QUOTATION

❓ *What personal qualities might Caesar's statement suggest?* (Possible responses: pride, arrogance, ruthlessness)

8 HISTORICAL BACKGROUND

Julius Caesar: One of the best-educated men of his time, Caesar was a distinguished writer whose *Commentaries* on his military campaigns are still read by students of Latin. As an orator he was considered second only to Cicero. His military skill ranks with Hannibal's, and he was also a superb politician. Unfortunately, his solution to the Republic's problems was personal dictatorship.

HUMANITIES CONNECTION

❓ *In what ways does H. F. Fuger's neoclassical painting seem realistic, and in what ways unrealistic?* (Possible response: The figures' expressions and clothing seem realistic, but the poses are artificial.) *How would you characterize the emotional tone of the scene?* (Possible response: intense, dramatic) ∎

374 Greek and Roman Literatures

7
❝ *Veni, vidi, vici* — I came, I saw, I conquered. ❞

—*Julius Caesar*

ASSASSINATION OF CAESAR, H. F. FUGER.

Photo Nimatallah/Art Resource, New York

---

of African elephants across Spain and the Alps, nearly brought the terrified Romans to their knees. In 146 B.C., however, the Romans finally prevailed and reduced Carthage to ruins. In the same year, the Romans assured their conquest of Greece with a decisive victory over the city of Corinth.

6

Julius Caesar and the Breakdown of the Republic

As Roman armies pushed farther from home, full-time professional troops replaced citizen soldiers. These men were loyal primarily to their personal commander, rather than to the state. Far from home, an army commander could make major decisions entirely on his own and could acquire enormous personal wealth. By far the most successful of these army commanders was **Julius Caesar** (102–44 B.C.).

8

ask students to look for the clash between the ideals and realities of Roman life in the literature they read. For example, in Catullus's writing, students will find the feelings and experiences of real Romans; in Virgil, by contrast, they will find an idealized portrayal of the founder of the Roman state.

The influence of ancient Rome on Western civilization has been more direct than that of Greece; therefore it will probably be easier for your students to identify.

To illustrate the enormous impact of the Latin language on English, ask students to glance through the etymologies on a page or two of an unabridged dictionary. Approximately half the words in the English language can be traced back to Latin. Whereas the Greek influence on English

has been predominant in specific fields such as science and philosophy, the Latin influence is far more pervasive. For instance, in the preceding sentence, the word *philosophy* comes from Greek, but *influence, predominantly, specific, science,* and *specialties* all have Latin roots.

Many English words that come from Latin are abstract and polysyllabic because they entered English via Norman French when the Normans conquered England in

---

In a power struggle for the control of Rome, Caesar was the victor in 48 B.C. He became dictator for life—but he did not grow old in office. On March 15 (the "Ides of March" in the Roman calendar) in 44 B.C., a conspiracy of senators who disliked Caesar's reforms and feared his power assassinated him in the senate house. The assassins, however, had underestimated Caesar's great popularity with the people, and angry crowds forced the leaders of the conspiracy, Brutus and Cassius, to flee from Rome. Two years later, in 42 B.C., the conspirators lost a decisive battle to Mark Antony and **Octavian**, Caesar's great-nephew, as well as his adopted son and heir. The victors, however, soon became enemies, and more years of civil war ensued. Antony withdrew to the East, where he joined forces with Queen Cleopatra of Egypt. Octavian defeated them at the battle of Actium in 31 B.C. Antony and Cleopatra committed suicide, leaving Octavian, at the age of thirty-two, the undisputed leader of the Roman world.

Early Latin Literature

Early Roman writings were highly dependent in style and content on Greek literary models. But by the middle of the third century B.C., the Romans accepted the challenge of producing a national literature. Roman literary genius first

> Roman literature flowered first in the genres of comedy and oratory, and then in lyric and philosophical poetry.

flourished in drama, specifically witty **comedies** about human follies and misadventures. The popular playwright **Plautus** (plôt′əs) (c. 250–184 B.C.) established the outlines of Roman comedy in his raucous farces. His successor **Terence** (c. 190–c. 159 B.C.), a freed black slave from North Africa, produced polished comedies that appealed to the sophisticated urban elite.

A second literary genre in which the Romans excelled was **oratory**, or speech. From the earliest days, legal disputes and political debates were intense and required a logical and sophisticated speaking style. It was natural, then, for the

Roman coins, c. 60–44 B.C.
These coins depict figures such as Julius Caesar, Venus, Mark Antony, an elephant, and trophies.

Lee Boltin Picture Library

9

1066. These words were used originally for official government and church business, while the common people continued to use their own Anglo-Saxon words. Often when there are two words with the same meaning in English, one short and earthy and one longer and more refined, such as *dead* and *deceased*, the former is likely to come from Anglo-Saxon and the latter from Latin. Ask students to make lists of such pairs and read their Anglo-Saxon words aloud and have others provide the Latin equivalents.

After the fall of Rome, the Latin language did not die. It remained the written language of educated Europeans for well over a thousand years. Latin learning made the Renaissance possible, both as a direct source of Roman thought and an indirect source of Greek thought. Latin was the international language of scholars, clergymen, and diplomats. Works of clas-sical philosophy and Christian theology were preserved in Latin throughout the medieval period. Often, these were works originally written in Greek or Hebrew and later translated into Latin. Thus Christianity was profoundly influenced by the Roman civilization in which it arose.

Be sure students understand that Rome had a more direct influence on Europe than did Greece, because Rome physically conquered much of the continent, while

10 LITERARY BACKGROUND

Cicero: Cicero's surviving body of work includes fifty-eight speeches, seven works on the art of oratory, and nearly twenty volumes of philosophy. Scholars of the Renaissance saw Cicero as a champion of individualism, and writers of the eighteenth century often imitated his distinct style. Cicero, however, downplayed his work, saying he borrowed most of his ideas from the Greeks. He commented, "just copies, and all the easier to write; I supply nothing but words, and I have plenty of those."

11 RESPONDING TO THE QUOTATION

Encourage students to express their image of the struggling emperor in either a satirical cartoon or prose sketch. Students should have fun depicting the lone emperor emerging above tons of red tape produced by the bureaucrats.

HUMANITIES CONNECTION

❓ *What do the bust and coins suggest about the attitude of the Romans toward Augustus?* (Possible response: They revered him.) *What similarity to our own culture do you see in the symbols?* (Possible response: We also create statuaries, such as the Lincoln Memorial, to honor leaders.) ∎

> **❝** [The emperor] Theodosius I [A.D. 379–395] struggled powerfully with the problems of his day, so far as one man was able. But it is hardly too much to say that, while he reigned, the empire was ruled by ten thousand clerks. **❞**
>
> —*Ramsay MacMullen*

Bust of Augustus surrounded by the coins of his reign (63 B.C.–A.D. 14). *These coins depict the emperor's zodiac sign, his grandsons, and the Roman conquest of Egypt.*

Romans to adapt Greek rhetorical styles and practices to their own needs. **Cicero** (sis'ə·rō) (106–43 B.C.), an orator of the late Roman republic, was a master of rhetoric as well as the author of distinguished philosophical essays.

Poetry was also a favorite literary form in the last years of the Republic. Many Roman poets, like **Lucretius** (loo·krē'shəs) (c. 96–55 B.C.), wrote philosophical poems, while **Catullus** (kə·tul'əs) (c. 84–54 B.C.) wrote intensely personal lyric verse (see page 409).

Roman Religion and Philosophy

The earliest Roman gods and goddesses were local deities associated with the earth, the rain, the harvest, and other phenomena related to farming. As the modest village of Rome expanded its boundaries and incorporated new territories and larger populations, these rural deities rose in status and became organized into a state cult. This "official" religion revolved around major gods such as Jupiter, the principal god of heaven, and Mars, the god of war. The Roman pantheon gradually assimilated many of the Greek gods and goddesses, changing their names but keeping their essential attributes (see the chart on page 217).

After about 150 B.C., various philosophical schools competed with religious movements in the search for ways to live in the world. The **Epicureans** (ep'i·kyoo'rē·ənz), for example, held that the object of life was to seek pleasure, avoid pain, and value true friendship. The **Stoics** (stō'iks) disagreed, arguing that the goal of the wise individual was to seek tranquility through moderation in all things.

Augustus and the Early Empire

After he had defeated Antony and Cleopatra in 31 B.C., Julius Caesar's adopted son and heir Octavian took control of the Roman Empire. Octavian carefully maintained the forms of republican rule, but he steadily directed all power into his own hands. The Roman Republic formally became an empire in 27 B.C., when Octavian was given the name *Augustus* (meaning "of good omen") and the title *imperator* ("emperor"). Augustus spent much of his vast wealth rebuilding the city of Rome. In a popular phrase, he "found Rome brick, and left it marble." During his long reign (27 B.C.–A.D. 14)

Greece did not. Ask students to research examples of Roman architecture from Britain to the Black Sea and bring to class illustrations of Roman arches, aqueducts, roads, walls, and buildings. Explain that the paths of many modern European highways follow old Roman roads. Dozens of modern European cities—Bath in England, Marseilles in France, Vienna in Austria—were originally Roman forts, ports, or resorts.

Make sure that students also understand Rome's influence on law and government. The Roman code of law became the basis for later European law, and many of the institutions of the Roman republic were adapted by framers of the United States government. The words *republic* and *senate* themselves originated in Rome. The founders of the United States looked to republican Rome as the model for a government based on elected representation with powers divided among branches of government. In the constitutional debates of 1787, Hamilton's model of a centralized republic defeated Jefferson's plan for a decentralized federation of states.

---

12 peace returned at last to the Roman world. Roman propaganda of the age celebrated Augustus as the heroic restorer of a Golden Age, and even during his lifetime cults sprang up dedicated to his worship as a god.

The reign of Augustus marked the transition from republic to empire in Rome.

During the **Age of Augustus**, Rome essentially became a *monarchy*, meaning that the emperor ruled for life and chose his successor, usually from his own family. The cruelty and incompetence of Augustus's successors—Tiberius, Caligula, Claudius, and Nero—were amply detailed by Roman historians. One outstanding example is the account of Nero's behavior during the great fire of Rome in A.D. 64 by Cornelius **Tacitus** (tas'i·təs), a historian who revealed ironic and sometimes extreme disgust for imperial rule (see page 428).

By contrast with Augustus's immediate successors, a line of capable rulers upheld order and prosperity throughout the empire in the second century A.D. At the start of this period, the Roman Empire reached its greatest geographical extent, stretching from Spain and Britain in the west to the borders of Persia in the east.

> **66** When that the poor have cried, Caesar hath wept; / Ambition should be made of sterner stuff: / Yet Brutus says he was ambitious; / And Brutus is an honorable man. **99**
>
> —*from* Julius Caesar, William Shakespeare

13

Scala/Art Resource, New York

The Roman Forum today.

12 READER'S RESPONSE
How do you respond to the idea of Romans worshiping their emperor? (Answers will vary.) Are there any circumstances in which rule by an emperor would be preferable to a democratic government? (Answers will vary.)

13 RESPONDING TO THE QUOTATION
The quotation is from Mark Antony's funeral oration in Act 3, Scene 2, in which he undermines Brutus's "honorable" character by arousing the crowd's emotions. Remind students that Mark Antony is reacting to Caesar's brutal murder by Brutus and others (see pp. 374–375). For his characterization of Caesar, Shakespeare relied largely on Plutarch's *Lives*.
? *What is your impression of Julius Caesar?* (Answers will vary. Encourage students to read some of Caesar's own writing before forming a final opinion.)

HUMANITIES CONNECTION

The Forum provided a central open space, surrounded by arcades, temples, and state buildings. Fountains, colonnades, arches, and statues adorned the area.
? *How have later city planners used the concept of the forum?* (Possible response: Town squares and inner courtyards of public buildings provide contained open space for large gatherings.) ∎

1. What North African city was Rome's greatest rival? (Carthage)
2. What form of government did Rome have before becoming an empire? (republican, or representative)
3. Whose assassination in 44 B.C. led to a civil war in Rome? (Julius Caesar's)
4. Who was the first emperor of Rome? (Augustus)
5. What principle of living did the Stoics stress? (moderation)

FOR FURTHER STUDY

Nonfiction

Edith Hamilton's *The Roman Way* and Donald R. Dudley's *The Civilization of Rome* are popular starting points. Michael Vickers's *The Roman World* has good photographs of Roman ruins.

Fiction

Robert Graves's *I, Claudius* and *Claudius, the God* and Gore Vidal's *Julian* are fine novels about Roman emperors.

Film

Movies set in Rome include *Spartacus* and *Ben-Hur*. The 1953 MGM film of Shakespeare's *Julius Caesar* stars Marlon Brando and James Mason. ■

14 RESPONDING TO THE QUOTATION

Actium was the site, in 31 B.C., of Octavian's (Augustus') victory over Antony and Cleopatra, after which the Roman Republic became an empire.

❓ *What is Tacitus' tone as he discusses Actium?* (Possible responses: ironic, nostalgic, bitter) *How do you respond to older people's discussions of wars and other events that occurred before you were born?* (Answers will vary.)

LITERARY BACKGROUND

The later history of Rome, not covered in this introduction, is the subject of a sublime work of eighteenth-century English prose, Edward Gibbons's multi-volume *Decline and Fall of the Roman Empire*. Abridged editions are available; encourage students interested in history to read at least parts of this great work.

TEACHING TIP

Divide students into teams of "Greeks" and "Romans." Ask each group to collect data that would support a claim for the superiority of their designated civilization. Have the "Greeks" and the "Romans" select three or four representatives from their teams to present their cases in a class debate.

WRITING TO LEARN

Write a piece of historical fiction or drama set in Rome, containing accurate historical information and believable characters and conflicts. ■

14

> ❝At home all was tranquil, and there were magistrates with the same titles; there was a younger generation, sprung up since the victory of Actium, and even many of the older men had been born during the civil wars. How few were left who had seen the republic! ❞
>
> —*Tacitus*

Latin Literature of the Empire

After he consolidated his power in the late first century B.C., Augustus gathered around his court the most gifted writers to celebrate the achievements of their age. Chief among them was the poet **Virgil**. His epic, the *Aeneid*, depicts the story of Aeneas's legendary founding of Rome. Virgil deliberately wove the emperor Augustus into the epic by linking him through family lines to Aeneas (see page 380). In this way, Virgil gave Rome a national epic that connected history to contemporary life. Other writers who enjoyed the patronage of Augustus were the historian **Livy** (59 B.C.–A.D. 17), who devoted forty years of his life to writing a massive chronicle of events from the founding of Rome to his own times, and the poets **Horace** (65–8 B.C.) and **Ovid** (43 B.C.–A.D. 17) (see pages 414 and 420).

The Later Empire: Rome's Decline and Fall

During the late second and third centuries A.D., the Roman Empire began its slow decay. Poor supervision of the empire resulted in corruption and inefficiency. The military began to dominate the process of finding new rulers.

In the late third century A.D., the emperor Diocletian (ruled 284–305) tried to solve the problem of governing the enormous Roman Empire by dividing it into two administrative units. Rome remained the capital of the western region, while the eastern part was ruled from Byzantium. In the fourth century, Byzantium became Constantinople (modern Istanbul in Turkey) in honor of the emperor Constantine (ruled 306–337). This ruler's conversion to Christianity and his efforts to install the Christian religion throughout the empire had far-reaching effects on the history of medieval Europe. Latin became the language of the Western church and remained the principal language of rulers, scholars, scientists, and the clergy throughout the Middle Ages.

During the later fourth and fifth centuries, a weakened Rome became increasingly vulnerable to the invasions of tribes such as the Germans, the Visigoths, and the Huns. The date usually given for the fall of Rome is A.D. 476, when it was overrun by the forces of the German chief, Odoacer. The eastern empire continued to exist until 1453, when the Ottoman Turks besieged and conquered Constantinople.

Virgil
70–19 B.C.

Alinari/Art Resource, New York

Publius Vergilius Maro, known as Virgil (vʉr'jəl), lived most of his life under the shadow of political turmoil. During his youth and early adult years, various political factions struggled for control of Rome in a series of bloody civil wars. Only when Virgil was nearly forty did Julius Caesar's great-nephew Octavian finally restore order by becoming Rome's sole ruler. The reign of Octavian, who used the honorary title *Augustus* (meaning "revered one"), ushered in one of the longest eras of peace and order in the history of Rome. It was during this time that Virgil composed his epic history of the founding of Rome.

Born near the northern town of Mantua, Virgil had deep roots in the Italian countryside. His father was a farmer who found the means to provide Virgil with a good education. This was the first opportunity for the shy young Virgil to experience the sophisticated life of the city. In Rome, like youths of nobler birth, Virgil studied widely in Greek law, philosophy, and literature. He tried life in the court system but found it too nerve-racking. With the outbreak of another war, Virgil retired to his country home. There he began to write pastoral poetry, or poetry that idealizes rural life.

During the war, the land owned by Virgil's family was confiscated. It was returned later through the influence of Octavian's minister of propaganda, who had taken an interest in Virgil's work. With the publication of the pastoral *Eclogues*, Virgil's reputation was fully established, and he turned away from the pastoral form to write the epic story of Aeneas, called the *Aeneid.* He worked slowly and methodically on the *Aeneid* during the last ten years of his life. In a letter, he complained that the project was driving him "almost out of his mind." When the poem was nearly complete, Virgil became ill during a voyage to Greece. With his dying breath he begged his friends to burn the manuscript, for he was not satisfied with it. Fortunately, the emperor Augustus, who recognized the value of Virgil's poem both as literature and as favorable propaganda for his own rule, refused to comply with the poet's last wish and preserved the *Aeneid* for future generations.

MORE ABOUT THE AUTHOR
Before he started work on the *Aeneid*, Virgil produced two collections of poetry that reflect his rural background. His *Eclogues*, completed about 37 B.C., are ten relatively brief poems in the pastoral genre. A *pastoral* is a type of poem that depicts rustic life in idyllic, idealized terms. From about 37 to 30 B.C., Virgil composed his *Georgics*, a set of four longer poems on farming and agriculture. In both the *Eclogues* and the *Georgics*, Virgil interweaves rustic settings, charming vignettes of the Italian countryside, and lessons on animal husbandry with serious themes, such as war and peace, death and rebirth, the beauty of nature, and the human need for love.

ABOUT THE TRANSLATOR
Robert Fitzgerald. See the *Iliad*, page 227.

1 CULTURAL BACKGROUND

The tragic love affair of Dido and Aeneas, recounted by Virgil in Book 4 of the *Aeneid*, has inspired many other artists through the centuries. For example, two musical masterpieces inspired by the *Aeneid* are the operas *Dido and Aeneas* by Henry Purcell (1689) and *Les Troyens* (The Trojans) by Hector Berlioz (1859).

2 LITERARY ELEMENT

Epic Convention: Aeneas's journey to the underworld in Book 6 is the turning point of the epic. Midway between his exile from the ruins of Troy and his conquests in Italy, Aeneas's prophetic vision of Roman glory confirms him in his mission. This episode in the *Aeneid* was influenced by Book 11 of Homer's *Odyssey*. A hero's journey to the underworld (or some other dangerous destination) is an ingredient of epic poetry. *What other epic narratives feature a dangerous journey or a visit to the land of the dead?* (Possible response: the *Epic of Gilgamesh*)

Introduction

The Aeneid

At an early point in his career, Virgil resolved to devote his poetic powers to composing a great national epic of Rome that would put recent Roman achievements on a par with those of the Greeks. In writing a long epic about the wanderings of a refugee from Troy, Virgil consciously imitated Homer (see page 224). The first six books of the *Aeneid* contain many episodes and scenes inspired by Homer's *Odyssey*, while the last six books are roughly modeled on scenes from the *Iliad.* On one level, the story of Aeneas is not so different from that of Odysseus, who, returning from the Trojan wars, traveled far and met with much adventure.

The Story of Aeneas

Aeneas's travels begin when he goes into exile after the fall and burning of Troy. The ghost of his dead wife, Creusa, has told him to sail to Italy, where he will found an empire. Over the following six years, Aeneas travels by sea, often blown off course. At one point he lands in Carthage, where he meets Queen Dido. They fall in love and plan to marry, but the gods push Aeneas on towards Italy. As he sails from Carthage, Dido curses him and dramatically

commits suicide out of grief at his departure. In Cumae, Aeneas consults the priestess Sibyl who takes him to the underworld, where he meets the ghost of his father, Anchises. There Aeneas receives a fuller prophecy of the founding of Rome. He sees a long line of Roman leaders who will descend from him. The line culminates with Augustus, Virgil's own patron. The concluding books of the *Aeneid* describe Aeneas's arrival in Italy and the conquests and battles he undergoes in order to establish a settlement for his people and to begin the Roman culture.

A New Kind of Epic Hero

Virgil, being thoroughly Roman, could not help but transform everything he borrowed from his Greek epic model. Most importantly, he refashioned the characterization of the Homeric heroes, adjusting them to fit a concept of the ideal Roman character. It is significant, for example, that the first time Virgil presents his hero in Book 1, Aeneas is weeping in frustration and envying the dead who fell at Troy. Virgil's Aeneas is no machine-like, larger-than-life warrior like Homer's Achilles; he is complex and enigmatic. He is courageous and valiant,

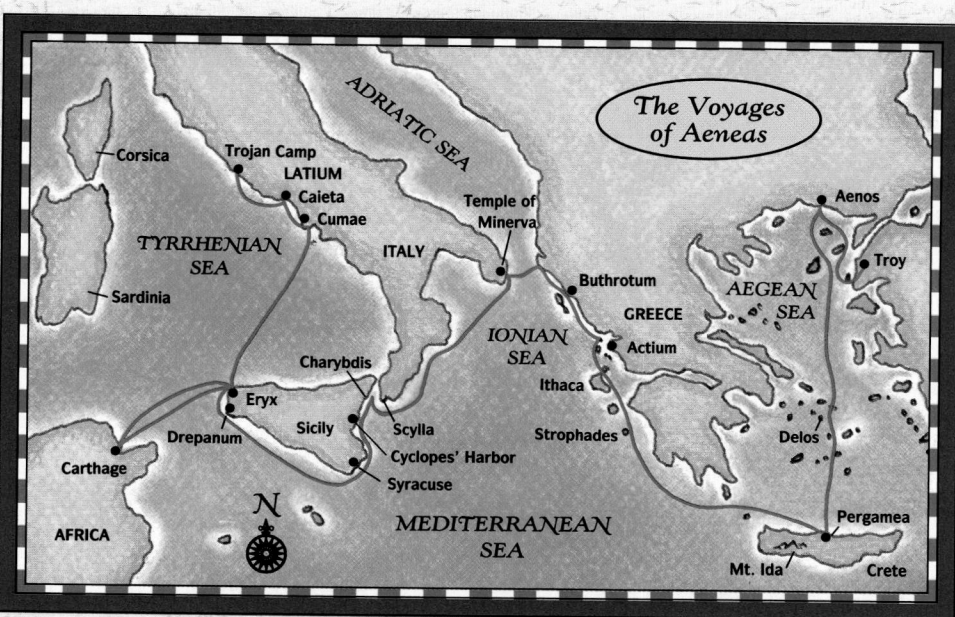

The Voyages of Aeneas

[Map labels: Corsica, Trojan Camp, LATIUM, Caieta, Cumae, Temple of Minerva, TYRRHENIAN SEA, ITALY, Sardinia, ADRIATIC SEA, Aenos, Troy, Buthrotum, AEGEAN SEA, GREECE, Actium, IONIAN SEA, Ithaca, Charybdis, Eryx, Scylla, Strophades, Delos, Drepanum, Sicily, Cyclopes' Harbor, Syracuse, Carthage, AFRICA, MEDITERRANEAN SEA, Pergamea, Mt. Ida, Crete, N]

3 READER'S RESPONSE
Would you prefer to read about a complex hero who has inner conflicts or about a super-hero whose conflicts are all with outer forces? Explain. (Possible responses: a complex hero, because the reader can identify with his or her problems; a superhero, because there is more action and excitement)

4 LITERARY BACKGROUND
Virgil was so revered and so popular in the Middle Ages that lines from his poems were used to predict the future. People opened a manuscript of the *Aeneid* and put their fingers on a line at random. They then "interpreted" this line as either a prophecy or as a guide to important decisions or future conduct.

but also deeply sensitive and often divided by the conflict between duty and passion. The *Aeneid* marks the passing of an older heroic ideal and its replacement with a more complex hero sharply constricted by adverse fate and human limitations. Virgil repeatedly stresses that Aeneas's greatness involves his ability to sacrifice his own will for the public good. Aeneas achieves great things, but he is also acutely aware that no achievement is possible without pain and loss.

Virgil's Influence

Virgil is a classical writer who has had a great influence on Western literature not only because of the quality of his work, but also because of the time in which he lived and the values he admired. The Age of Augustus, which the poet celebrated, was one of the high points of Roman civilization. Virgil created his epic of Rome shortly before the birth of Christ and the founding of the Christian religion, whose history would be affected by the Roman Empire for the next four centuries. One reason for Virgil's remarkable impact on later literature was his appeal to Christian authors and educators during the early centuries and later in the Middle Ages. Christianity condemned many pagan authors as unsuitable reading, but the moral virtues of duty, moderation, and piety that Virgil emphasized made him acceptable to Christians, and his poems were used as school texts. Literary critics eventually recognized Virgil's poetry as the fullest development of classical epic and pastoral poetry. The *Aeneid* became a model that inspired the works of Dante Alighieri (see page 741), Edmund Spenser, and John Milton, among others.

OBJECTIVES

1. To recognize the place of Virgil in Roman literature and to distinguish the characteristics of the ancient Roman epic
2. To identify and interpret external and internal conflict
3. To write an essay comparing and contrasting Aeneas with another epic hero
4. To analyze an epic simile

PREREADING FOCUS

Background: As Odysseus is the "singer" of his own heroic adventures, so Aeneas is the "teller" of his own exploits. The tones of the two extended flashbacks, however, are quite different. Homer emphasizes Odysseus' role as an admired and revered hero who delights in recounting the many wonders he has seen. Virgil, on the other hand, stresses the painful emotions that Aeneas's memories arouse in him. The Roman hero takes little pleasure in his account. In fact, just before this excerpt from Book 2 begins, Aeneas says that the memory of these events causes him to "shudder" and to "shrink again in grief."

Writer's Response: You may want to hold a brief brainstorming session before students freewrite their ideas.

Literary Focus: You may wish to explain that internal conflict often occurs when a character must struggle with his or her conscience or choose between two compelling courses of action. Encourage students to give some examples of both internal and external conflicts from their reading and from everyday life.

Reader's Guide

from the AENEID
from Book 2, The Fall of Troy

Background

Like Homer before him, Virgil chose to begin his long tale not at the beginning, but at a point in the thick of the story: *in medias res,* literally "in the middle of things." Book 1 opens with Aeneas's shipwreck at Carthage on the shores of North Africa and with his fateful encounter with the tragic queen Dido. Books 2 and 3 provide an extended flashback in which Aeneas recounts his earlier suffering and adventures, just as Odysseus does in Books 9-12 of the *Odyssey.* (Odysseus is called by his Roman name, Ulysses, in the *Aeneid.*)

At the start of Book 2, a great banquet is in progress, at which Dido asks Aeneas to describe his experiences during the fall of Troy. The banquet hall at Carthage is hushed as Aeneas summons the inner strength to recount in this lengthy flashback the "unspeakable" suffering of his people during the siege of the Greeks. Aeneas will speak firsthand of the infamous Trojan horse, the death of King Priam, and his encounters with Helen of Troy, his mother (the goddess Venus), and the ghost of his wife, Creusa.

Writer's Response

Do you think the lives of great leaders show a mixture of triumph and tragedy, achievements and setbacks? Think of one or two great leaders, either living or dead, whom you admire. Freewrite on the theme of triumph and tragedy in the lives of these leaders.

Literary Focus

Conflict is a struggle or clash between opposing characters, forces, or emotions. In an **external conflict**, a character struggles against some outside force: another character, society as a whole, or some natural force. For example, during much of Book 2, Aeneas must fight the invading Greeks. An **internal conflict**, on the other hand, is a struggle between opposing needs, desires, or emotions within a single character. In Book 2, Virgil depicts Aeneas as suffering from internal conflicts at several points in the narrative. One example is his desire to destroy Helen despite Venus's warning to him.

from the AENEID
from Book 2: The Fall of Troy
Virgil
translated by
ROBERT FITZGERALD

 As you read, note how Virgil uses many of the elements of the Homeric epic, such as elaborate similes, epithets—or repeated, concise descriptions—and dramatic speeches.

CHARACTERS IN THE AENEID

Aeneas (i·nē'əs): ancestor of the Roman rulers; son of the goddess Venus and Anchises, the king of Dardanus.

Anchises (an·kī'sēz'): father of Aeneas; king of Dardanus; ally of Priam—the king of Troy.

Ascanius (as·kā'nē·əs): son of Aeneas and Creusa, also called Iulus.

Creusa (krē·yoō'sə): Priam's daughter; wife of Aeneas; first to tell him to journey to Italy.

Dido (dī'dō): queen of Carthage; lover of Aeneas who kills herself when he leaves her for Italy.

The Sibyl (sib'əl): the priestess of Apollo who leads Aeneas through the underworld.

"Knowing their strength broken in warfare, turned
Back by the fates, and years—so many years—
Already slipped away, the Danaan° captains
By the divine handicraft of Pallas° built
5   A horse of timber, tall as a hill,
And sheathed its ribs with planking of cut pine.
This they gave out to be an offering
For a safe return by sea, and the word went round.

3. **Danaan** (dān'ə·ən): a name for the Greeks.

4. **Pallas** (pal'əs): a name for the goddess Athena, here called Minerva.

1 LITERARY BACKGROUND
Virgil also imitated Homer with such epic elements as extended battle scenes and the opening invocation to the Muse. You may wish to tell students before Book 1 was *Arma virumque cano,* "I sing of arms and the man." (More than two thousand years later, George Bernard Shaw borrowed Virgil's image for the title of his play *Arms and the Man.*)

2 COMPARING LITERATURE
Aeneas plays a secondary role in Homer's *Iliad.* His most important appearances are in the battle scenes of Book 5 (where the god Apollo rescues Aeneas from the attack of the Greek champion Diomedes) and Book 20 (where Aeneas is again rescued, this time from Achilles, by the divine intervention of Poseidon).

3 GUIDED READING
Identifying Facts: This is the famous "Trojan horse," a byword for strategic cunning or for treachery, depending on the point of view. What false rumor did the Greeks start about the horse? (that it was a sacrificial offering)

Foreshadowing: How does this description of the island foreshadow events to come? (The anchorage is described as "treacherous," much as the Greeks are in their plans to conceal men in a horse. Also, the reference to Priam's reign being over sets an ominous tone.)

MEETING INDIVIDUAL NEEDS

5 LEP: Be sure students realize that the meaning of line 19 is "So [we assumed] that Teucer's town [Troy] was freed. . . ." Lead students to see that "We thought they'd gone" (line 17) provides the clue to line 19's meaning. ■

6 LITERARY ELEMENT

Foreshadowing: The episode of Laocoon, which became famous in painting and sculpture, is another example of Virgil's use of foreshadowing. What do you think will happen if the Trojans fail to heed Laocoon's warnings? (Possible response: The Trojans will haul the horse inside the city, and the hidden Greek troops will escape and destroy Troy.)

384   Greek and Roman Literatures

But on the sly they shut inside a company
10 Chosen from their picked soldiery by lot,
Crowding the vaulted caverns in the dark—
The horse's belly—with men fully armed.
Offshore there's a long island, Tenedos,°
Famous and rich while Priam's kingdom lasted,
15 A treacherous anchorage now, and nothing more.
They crossed to this and hid their ships behind it
On the bare shore beyond. We thought they'd gone,
Sailing home to Mycenae° before the wind,
So Teucer's town° is freed of her long anguish,
20 Gates thrown wide! And out we go in joy
To see the Dorian° campsites, all deserted,
The beach they left behind. Here the Dolopians°
Pitched their tents, here cruel Achilles lodged,
There lay the ships, and there, formed up in ranks,
25 They came inland to fight us. Of our men
One group stood marveling, gaping up to see
The dire gift of the cold unbedded goddess,°
The sheer mass of the horse.
                          Thymoetes° shouts
It should be hauled inside the walls and moored
30 High on the citadel—whether by treason
Or just because Troy's fate went that way now.
Capys° opposed him; so did the wiser heads:
'Into the sea with it,' they said, 'or burn it,
Build up a bonfire under it,
35 This trick of the Greeks, a gift no one can trust,
Or cut it open, search the hollow belly!'

Contrary notions pulled the crowd apart.
Next thing we knew, in front of everyone,
Laocoon with a great company
40 Came furiously running from the Height,
And still far off cried out: 'O my poor people,
Men of Troy, what madness has come over you?
Can you believe the enemy truly gone?
A gift from the Danaans, and no ruse?
45 Is that Ulysses'° way, as you have known him?
Achaeans° must be hiding in this timber,
Or it was built to butt against our walls,
Peer over them into our houses, pelt
The city from the sky. Some crookedness

13. **Tenedos** (ten′ə·däs): an island sacred to Apollo.

18. **Mycenae** (mī·sē′nē): capital of the kingdom ruled by Agamemnon.
19. **Teucer's town:** Teucer (tū′sər) was a former king of Troy.
21. **Dorian** (dôr′ē·ən): one of the peoples of Greece.
22. **Dolopians** (dōl·ō′pē·ənz): people from Thessaly.

27. **cold . . . goddess:** Minerva.

28. **Thymoetes** (thī·mō′tēz)

32. **Capys** (ka′pəs): Aeneas's comrade.

45. **Ulysses** (yoo·lis′ēz): the Roman name for the Greek hero Odysseus.
46. **Achaeans** (ə·kē′ənz): a name for the Greeks.

7   50   Is in this thing. Have no faith in the horse!
Whatever it is, even when Greeks bring gifts
I fear them, gifts and all.'
                 He broke off then

8   And rifled his big spear with all his might
Against the horse's flank, the curve of belly.
55   It stuck there trembling, and the rounded hull
Reverberated groaning at the blow.
If the gods' will had not been sinister,
If our own minds had not been crazed,
He would have made us foul that Argive° den

9   60   With bloody steel, and Troy would stand today—
O citadel of Priam, towering still!
But now look: hillmen, shepherds of Dardania,°
Raising a shout, dragged in before the king
An unknown fellow° with hands tied behind—
65   This all as he himself had planned,
Volunteering, letting them come across him,
So he could open Troy to the Achaeans.

59. **Argive** (är'gīv): a name for the Greeks.

62. **Dardania** (där·dā'nē·ə): Troy. The founder of the city was Dardanus.

64. **unknown fellow:** Sinon.

7 GUIDED READING
Finding the Main Idea: Summarize Laocoon's advice to the Trojans. (Possible response: Do not trust the Greeks or their gifts, and be especially suspicious of the horse.)

8 LITERARY ELEMENT
Imagery: How does Virgil help you visualize this scene? (through details that appeal to the senses of sight, hearing, and touch; through such concrete verbs and adjectives as *rifled* and *reverberated*, *trembling* and *groaning*)

9 LITERARY ELEMENT
Tone: At line 61, how does the phrase "O citadel of Priam" affect the emotional tone of the narrative? (Possible response: It charges the narrative with even greater emotion by suggesting Aeneas's personal attachment to his ruined city.)

HUMANITIES CONNECTION

❓ How does Tiepolo's imaginative painting differ from your own ideas of the "horse of timber, tall as a hill" described on the preceding pages? (Answers will vary.) ∎

THE PROCESSION OF THE TROJAN HORSE INTO TROY, GIOVANNI BATTISTA TIEPOLO.

The Granger Collection, New York

from the Aeneid, Book 2   **385**

This portrayal of Sinon as a deceitful "double agent" may strike a universal chord since personalities of his sort seem to exist in all times and places. *Can you think of any modern parallels to Sinon?* (Possible responses: cold-war spies, international terrorists)

■ undulating (un'dyoo·lāt'iŋ): moving in a wavelike manner

11 LITERARY ELEMENT
Imagery: The vividness of this description of the snakes makes it easy to visualize their approach. To what senses do the details in lines 82–91 appeal? (sight, touch, hearing) Where does Virgil mention blood in the description? (lines 86 and 90) What emotions may these references to blood prompt? (fear, horror)

12 PREDICTING
The snakes were sent by Athena, the Greek goddess of war, to kill Laocoon and his sons. How do you think the ghastly destruction of Laocoon and his sons may affect the Trojans and their decision about the horse? (Possible response: The fate of Laocoon may persuade the Trojans that he was divinely punished for not respecting the gift horse, and, consequently, they may decide to bring the horse inside the city.)

---

10 ⎡ Sure of himself this man was, braced for it
        Either way, to work his trick or die.
70   From every quarter Trojans run to see him,
        Ring the prisoner round, and make a game
        Of jeering at him. Be instructed now
        In Greek deceptive arts: one barefaced deed
        Can tell you of them all.

The spy Sinon puts on a convincing performance to persuade the Trojans that he has escaped from the Greeks after being betrayed and condemned to death. Having gained the Trojans' confidence, he easily makes them believe that the Greeks have abandoned the siege of the city, leaving the strange wooden horse behind to appease the angry gods.

75   And now another sign, more fearful still,
        Broke on our blind miserable people,
        Filling us all with dread. Laocoon,
        Acting as Neptune's priest that day by lot,
        Was on the point of putting to the knife
80   A massive bull before the appointed altar,
        When ah—look there!
        From Tenedos, on the calm sea, twin snakes—
        I shiver to recall it—endlessly
        Coiling, uncoiling, swam abreast for shore,
85   Their underbellies showing as their crests
        Reared red as blood above the swell; behind
11 They glided with great underlying backs.
        Now came the sound of thrashed seawater foaming;
        Now they were on dry land, and we could see
90   Their burning eyes, fiery and suffused with blood,
        Their tongues a-flicker out of hissing maws.
        We scattered, pale with fright. But straight ahead
        They slid until they reached Laocoon.
        Each snake enveloped one of his two boys,
95   Twining about and feeding on the body.
        Next they ensnared the man as he ran up
12 With weapons; coils like cables looped and bound him
        Twice round the middle; twice about his throat
        They whipped their back-scales, and their heads
            towered,
100   While with both hands he fought to break the knots,

Laocoon and his two sons battle the twin snakes.
❓ *How do the snakes serve as an omen to the Trojans?*

Photo Nimatallah/Art Resource, New York

Laöcoon and His Sons is a celebrated marble sculpture, dating from the Hellenistic period, now housed in the Vatican Museum.
❓ *Which line on p. 386 does the sculpture illustrate especially well?* (Possible response: line 100, ". . . with both hands he fought. . . .") ■

13 LITERARY ELEMENT
Simile: Just before the snakes appeared in the sea, Laocoon was about to sacrifice a bull. To what is Laocoon now compared? (to a bull that escapes from a sacrificial altar) What may the associations with sacrifice and Roman religious ritual imply about Laocoon's fate? (Possible response: that he, not the bull, is the victim who must be ritually "sacrificed" so that Troy's destined destruction can take its course)

14 CULTURAL DIVERSITY
Roman religion laid great emphasis on animal sacrifice, proper ritual, and the interpretation of omens and auguries. Laocoon's death is regarded by the crowd as an omen or portent.
❓ *What conclusion about Laocoon's previous actions does the crowd draw from his death?* (Possible response: They regard his death as a divine punishment for his sin of profaning the horse with his spear thrust.)

> Drenched in slime, his headbands black with venom,
> Sending to heaven his appalling cries
> Like a slashed bull escaping from an altar,
> The fumbled axe shrugged off. The pair of snakes
> 105   Now flowed away and made for the highest shrines,
> The citadel of pitiless Minerva,
> Where coiling they took cover at her feet
> Under the rondure° of her shield. New terrors
> Ran in the shaken crowd: the word went round
> 110   Laocoon had paid, and rightfully,
> For profanation of the sacred hulk
> With his offending spear hurled at its flank.
> 'The offering must be hauled to its true home,'
> They clamored. 'Votive prayers to the goddess
> 115   Must be said there!'
>   So we breached the walls
> And laid the city open. Everyone

108. **rondure** (rän'dyŏŏr'): circle.

Pitched in to get the figure underpinned
With rollers, hempen lines around the neck.
Deadly, pregnant with enemies, the horse
120 Crawled upward to the breach. And boys and girls
Sang hymns around the towrope as for joy
They touched it. Rolling on, it cast a shadow
Over the city's heart. O Fatherland,
O Ilium,° home of gods! Defensive wall
125 Renowned in war for Dardanus's people!
There on the very threshold of the breach
It jarred to a halt four times, four times the arms
In the belly thrown together made a sound—
Yet on we strove unmindful, deaf and blind,
130 To place the monster on our blessed height.
Then, even then, Cassandra's lips unsealed
The doom to come: lips by a god's command
Never believed or heeded by the Trojans.
So pitiably we, for whom that day
135 Would be the last, made all our temples green
With leafy festal boughs throughout the city.

As heaven turned, Night from the Ocean stream
Came on, profound in gloom on earth and sky
And Myrmidons° in hiding. In their homes
140 The Teucrians lay silent, wearied out,
And sleep enfolded them. The Argive fleet,
Drawn up in line abreast, left Tenedos
Through the aloof moon's friendly stillnesses
And made for the familiar shore. Flame signals
145 Shone from the command ship. Sinon, favored
By what the gods unjustly had decreed,
Stole out to tap the pine walls and set free
The Danaans in the belly. Opened wide,
The horse emitted men; gladly they dropped
150 Out of the cavern, captains first, Thessandrus,
Sthenelus and the man of iron, Ulysses;
Hand over hand upon the rope, Acamas, Thoas,
Neoptolemus and Prince Machaon,°
Menelaus and then the master builder,
155 Epeos,° who designed the horse decoy.
Into the darkened city, buried deep
In sleep and wine, they made their way,
Cut the few sentries down,

124. **Ilium** (il′ē·əm): another name for Troy.

139. **Myrmidons** (mur′mə·dänz′): followers of Achilles.

150–153. **Thessandrus** (thə·san′drəs); **Sthenelus** (sthen′ə·ləs); **Acamas** (ak′ə·məs); **Thoas** (thō′əs); **Machaon** (ma·kā′on)

155. **Epeos** (e·pē′əs).

Wall carving of a Roman ship and its warriors.

Scala/Art Resource, New York

HUMANITIES CONNECTION

In Roman times, a warship was about 100 feet long. For maneuverability, it had a mast and sail but depended in combat on its banks of oars. It is no surprise that Horace described a man willing to embark on the high seas in such a vessel as needing a wrapping of oak and three-ply bronze around his heart. Yet as uncomfortable, crowded, and primitive as sea travel was, it was considered the safest, cheapest, and most comfortable way to travel to the farflung regions of the empire. ■

19 COMPARING LITERATURE

Virgil's description of Hector is clearly indebted to Homer's account in Book 22 of the *Iliad* (see pp. 259–260).

? *How did Achilles defile Hector's corpse?* (He tied it to his chariot and dragged it around the walls of Troy.)

Let in their fellow soldiers at the gate,
160 And joined their combat companies as planned.

That time of night it was when the first sleep,
Gift of the gods, begins for ill mankind,
Arriving gradually, delicious rest.
In sleep, in dream, Hector appeared to me,
165 Gaunt with sorrow, streaming tears, all torn—
As by the violent car on his death day—
And black with bloody dust,
His puffed-out feet cut by the rawhide thongs.
Ah god, the look of him! How changed
170 From that proud Hector who returned to Troy
Wearing Achilles' armor, or that one
Who pitched the torches on Danaan ships;
His beard all filth, his hair matted with blood,
Showing the wounds, the many wounds, received
175 Outside his father's city walls. I seemed
Myself to weep and call upon the man
In grieving speech, brought from the depth of me:

19

20 LEP: Explain to students that "Dardania," in line 178, is another name for Troy. Explain that the metaphor describes Hector as the "light" of Troy because Hector was Troy's best defender. ■

21 LITERARY BACKGROUND
It may seem odd to students that Aeneas does not know the details of Hector's death. It may be Virgil's intent to emphasize the mysterious nature of the dream by having Aeneas remember only that Hector has disappeared from the Trojan ranks.

22 LITERARY ELEMENT
Foreshadowing: What events does the appearance of Hector foreshadow in lines 189–198? (the fall of Troy, Aeneas's caretaking of Troy's household gods, and Aeneas's founding of Rome)

23 LITERARY ELEMENT
Epic Simile: How does the simile in lines 207–213 paint a graphic picture of the effects of war? (by comparing war to forces of fire and flood that destroy pastoral peace) What does comparing Aeneas to a shepherd say about his role? (Possible response: He is a leader, responsible for the survival of his followers.)

20
'Light of Dardania, best hope of Troy,
What kept you from us for so long, and where?
180 From what far place, O Hector, have you come,
Long, long awaited? After so many deaths
Of friends and brothers, after a world of pain
For all our folk and all our town, at last,
Boneweary, we behold you! What has happened
21 185 To ravage your serene face? Why these wounds?'

He wasted no reply on my poor questions
But heaved a great sigh from his chest and said:
'Ai! Give up and go, child of the goddess,°
Save yourself, out of these flames. The enemy
190 Holds the city walls, and from her height
Troy falls in ruin. Fatherland and Priam
Have their due; if by one hand our towers
Could be defended, by this hand, my own,
22 They would have been. Her holy things, her gods
195 Of hearth and household° Troy commends to you.
Accept them as companions of your days;
Go find for them the great walls that one day
You'll dedicate, when you have roamed the sea.'

As he said this, he brought out from the sanctuary
200 Chaplets and Vesta, Lady of the Hearth,
With her eternal fire.
                          While I dreamed,
The turmoil rose, with anguish, in the city.
More and more, although Anchises' house
Lay in seclusion, muffled among trees,
205 The din at the grim onset grew; and now
I shook off sleep, I climbed to the roof top
To cup my ears and listen. And the sound
Was like the sound a grassfire makes in grain,
Whipped by a Southwind, or a torrent foaming
23 210 Out of a mountainside to strew in ruin
Fields, happy crops, the yield of plowing teams,
Or woodlands borne off in the flood; in wonder
The shepherd listens on a rocky peak.
I knew then what our trust had won for us,
215 Knew the Danaan fraud: Deiphobus'°
Great house in flames, already caving in
Under the overpowering god of fire;
Ucalegon's° already caught nearby;

188. **child of the goddess:** Aeneas is the son of Venus.

194–195. **gods . . . household:** Romans had household and domestic gods called Lares (lā′rēz) and Penates (pē·nā′tēz′).

HRW Photo By Barbar

Temple of Vesta in Rome. *Vesta was the goddess of the hearth and home.*

215. **Deiphobus** (dē′ə·fō′bəs)

218. **Ucalegon** (yōō·kal′ə·gän)

The glare lighting the straits beyond Sigeum;°
220 The cries of men, the wild calls of the trumpets.

To arm was my first maddened impulse—not
That anyone had a fighting chance in arms;
Only I burned to gather up some force
For combat, and to man some high redoubt.°
225 So fury drove me, and it came to me
That meeting death was beautiful in arms.
Then here, eluding the Achaean spears,
Came Panthus, Othrys'° son, priest of Apollo,
Carrying holy things, our conquered gods,
230 And pulling a small grandchild along: he ran
Despairing to my doorway.
                              'Where's the crux,
Panthus,' I said. 'What strongpoint shall we hold?'
Before I could say more, he groaned and answered:
'The last day for Dardania has come,
235 The hour not to be fought off any longer.
Trojans we have been; Ilium has been;
The glory of the Teucrians is no more;
Black Jupiter has passed it on to Argos.°
Greeks are the masters in our burning city.
240 Tall as a cliff, set in the heart of town,
Their horse pours out armed men. The conqueror,
Gloating Sinon, brews new conflagrations.
Troops hold the gates—as many thousand men
As ever came from great Mycenae; others
245 Block the lanes with crossed spears; glittering
In a combat line, swordblades are drawn for slaughter.
Even the first guards at the gates can barely
Offer battle, or blindly make a stand,'

Impelled by these words, by the powers of heaven,
250 Into the flames I go, into the fight,
Where the harsh Fury, and the din and shouting,
Skyward rising, calls. Crossing my path
In moonlight, five fell in with me, companions:
Ripheus, and Epytus, a great soldier,
255 Hypanis, Dymas, cleaving to my side
With young Coroebus, Mygdon's° son. It happened
That in those very days this man had come
To Troy, aflame with passion for Cassandra,

219. **Sigeum** (si·jē′əm)

224. **redoubt** (ri·dout′): defense.

228. **Panthus** (pan′thəs); **Othrys**
(ôth′ris)

238. **Argos** (är′gôs, -gəs): a town
in the Peloponnesus.

254–256. **Ripheus** (rif′ōōs); **Epytus**
(e′pi·təs); **Hypanis** (hī′pan·əs);
Dymas (dī′məs); **Mygdon**
(mig′dän)

27 LITERARY ELEMENT

Foreshadowing: What hint does Virgil give in lines 260–261? (He hints that Coroebus will suffer because he ignored Cassandra's prophecies.)

28 READER'S RESPONSE

How would you rate Aeneas as a military commander? (Possible responses: high marks for his last-ditch stand; criticism for his foolhardiness)

> **predatory** (pred′ə·tôr′ē): living by hunting and feeding on other animals

29 LITERARY ELEMENT

Epic Simile: To what does Virgil compare Aeneas and his companions? (to predatory wolves) How does the comparison contribute to your understanding of the soldiers? (The comparison reveals that the soldiers are desperate and that they are fighting for their own and their children's survival.)

30 LITERARY ELEMENT

Epigram: An epigram is a brief, memorable statement. Virgil was widely quoted because of short, pithy statements like the one in lines 290–291. How would you paraphrase it? (Possible response: When the gods are feeling willful, no one can count on their support.) How would you paraphrase the epigram in line 271? (Possible response: The only sure hope for the defeated is no hope.)

Bringing to Priam and the Phrygians°

260 A son-in-law's right hand. Unlucky one,
To have been deaf to what his bride foretold!
Now when I saw them grouped, on edge for battle,
I took it all in and said briefly,

'Soldiers,

Brave as you are to no end, if you crave

265 To face the last fight with me, and no doubt of it,
How matters stand for us each one can see.
The gods by whom this kingdom stood are gone,
Gone from the shrines and altars. You defend
A city lost in flames. Come, let us die,

270 We'll make a rush into the thick of it.
The conquered have one safety: hope for none.'

The desperate odds doubled their fighting spirit:
From that time on, like predatory wolves
In fog and darkness, when a savage hunger

275 Drives them blindly on, and cubs in lairs
Lie waiting with dry famished jaws—just so
Through arrow flights and enemies we ran
Toward our sure death, straight for the city's heart,
Cavernous black night over and around us.

280 Who can describe the havoc of that night
Or tell the deaths, or tally wounds with tears?
The ancient city falls, after dominion
Many long years. In windrows° on the streets,
In homes, on solemn porches of the gods,

285 Dead bodies lie. And not alone the Trojans
Pay the price with their heart's blood; at times
Manhood returns to fire even the conquered
And Danaan conquerors fall. Grief everywhere,
Everywhere terror, and all shapes of death.

Aeneas and his small band of friends overcome a detachment of Greek soldiers and put on their armor and insignia. Thus disguised, they are able to cut down a number of the invaders.

When gods are contrary

290 They stand by no one. Here before us came
Cassandra, Priam's virgin daughter, dragged
By her long hair out of Minerva's shrine,
Lifting her brilliant eyes in vain to heaven—

259. Phrygians (frij′ē·ənz): people of Phrygia, a country in Asia Minor where Troy was located.

Wall carving of a soldier in armor.

Scala/Art Resource, New York

283. windrows: rows of hay or grain that have been raked together.

295   Her eyes alone, as her white hands were bound.
      Coroebus, infuriated, could not bear it,
      But plunged into the midst to find his death.
      We all went after him, our swords at play,
      But here, here first, from the temple gable's height,
300   We met a hail of missiles from our friends,
      Pitiful execution, by their error,
      Who thought us Greek from our Greek plumes and
          shields.
      Then with a groan of anger, seeing the virgin
      Wrested from them, Danaans from all sides
305   Rallied and attacked us: fiery Ajax,
      Atreus'° sons, Dolopians in a mass—
      As, when a cyclone breaks, conflicting winds
      Will come together, Westwind, Southwind, Eastwind
      Riding high out of the Dawnland; forests
310   Bend and roar, and raging all in spume
      Nereus with his trident churns the deep.
      Then some whom we had taken by surprise
      Under cover of night throughout the city
      And driven off, came back again: they knew
315   Our shields and arms for liars now, our speech
      Alien to their own. They overwhelmed us.

306. **Atreus** (ā′trē·əs): father of Agamemnon and Menelaus.

One by one the remaining Trojan warriors are killed in a hail of missiles from their own side. Aeneas is drawn by the cry of battle to Priam's castle, where a great massacre is about to take place.

                           Mars gone berserk, Danaans
      In a rush to scale the roof; the gate besieged
      By a tortoise shell of overlapping shields.
320   Ladders clung to the wall, and men strove upward
      Before the very doorposts, on the rungs,
      Left hand putting the shield up, and the right
      Reaching for the cornice. The defenders
      Wrenched out upperworks and rooftiles: these
325   For missiles, as they saw the end, preparing
      To fight back even on the edge of death.
      And gilded beams, ancestral ornaments,
      They rolled down on the heads below. In hall

31 LITERARY ELEMENT
Irony: Situational irony refers to a development that is the opposite of what is expected or appropriate. How does the Trojan trick backfire? (Possible response: Aeneas and his men are attacked by Trojan troops, who think they are the enemy because they have disguised themselves in Greek armor.) What is the modern term for the unintentional killing of soldiers by their own forces? (friendly fire)

32 LITERARY ELEMENT
Epic Simile: To what are the battling Trojans and Greeks compared in this simile? (to conflicting winds) Which details describe land and sea? (the bending and roaring forests and the raging and churning ocean)

MEETING INDIVIDUAL NEEDS

33 *LEP:* You may need to help some students with the details in lines 317–326. Be sure students understand that Mars is the god of war and that the mention of him, in line 317, is metaphorical. The "tortoise shell" (line 319) was the name of an infantry formation in the Roman Army. The "cornice" (line 323) and the "upperworks" (line 324) are architectural details of the palace roof. ∎

34 EVALUATING

How do you assess the courage and skill of the Trojans and the Greeks in the battle so far? (Possible response: The courage and skill of the warriors seem even.) Whose side does Virgil seem to favor? (Possible response: Virgil has emotionally weighted the narrative so the audience will sympathize with the Trojans rather than with the Greeks, who are often accused of treachery and guile.)

> **respite** (res′pit): a period of temporary relief or rest
> **futile** (fyoot′l): useless

35 LITERARY ELEMENT

Flashback: How does Virgil use a brief flashback to create a contrast with the main narrative? (The description of family visits and the palace halls in the days of peace contrasts with the destruction and chaos in the narrative.)

HUMANITIES CONNECTION

"Attic" refers to Attica, the province of ancient Greece in which Athens became the first Greek "city-state."

❓ How might the three mini-scenes depicted on the cup have served a storyteller as a pictorial guide to the story of Troy? (Cassandra's prophecy of the Fall of Troy was ignored; the Trojan people were destroyed; and Andromache was taken captive and Astyanax killed.) ∎

Others with swords drawn held the entrance way,
330 Packed there, waiting. Now we plucked up heart
To help the royal house, to give our men
A respite, and to add our strength to theirs,
Though all were beaten. And we had for entrance
A rear door, secret, giving on a passage
335 Between the palace halls; in other days
Andromache,° poor lady, often used it,
Going alone to see her husband's parents
Or taking Astyanax° to his grandfather.
I climbed high on the roof, where hopeless men
340 Were picking up and throwing futile missiles.
Here was a tower like a promontory
Rising toward the stars above the roof:
All Troy, the Danaan ships, the Achaean camp,
Were visible from this. Now close beside it
345 With crowbars, where the flooring made loose joints,
We pried it from its bed and pushed it over.
Down with a rending crash in sudden ruin

Lauros-Giraudon/Art Resource, New York

Attic cup, c. 5th century. *This vase depicts Cassandra, a wounded Trojan, and Andromache protecting her son Astynax.*

Wide over the Danaan lines it fell;
But fresh troops moved up, and the rain of stones
350 With every kind of missile never ceased.

Just at the outer doors of the vestibule
Sprang Pyrrhus, all in bronze and glittering,
As a serpent, hidden swollen underground
By a cold winter, writhes into the light,
355 On vile grass fed, his old skin cast away,
Renewed and glossy, rolling slippery coils,
With lifted underbelly rearing sunward
And triple tongue a-flicker. Close beside him
Giant Periphas and Automedon,°
360 His armorbearer, once Achilles' driver,
Besieged the place with all the young of Scyros,°
Hurling their torches at the palace roof.
Pyrrhus shouldering forward with an axe
Broke down the stony threshold, forced apart
365 Hinges and brazen doorjambs, and chopped through
One panel of the door, splitting the oak,
To make a window, a great breach. And there
Before their eyes the inner halls lay open,
The courts of Priam and the ancient kings,
370 With men-at-arms ranked in the vestibule.
From the interior came sounds of weeping,
Pitiful commotion, wails of women
High-pitched, rising in the formal chambers
To ring against the silent golden stars;
375 And, through the palace, mothers wild with fright
Ran to and fro or clung to doors and kissed them.
Pyrrhus with his father's brawn stormed on,
No bolts or bars or men availed to stop him:
Under his battering the double doors
380 Were torn out of their sockets and fell inward.
Sheer force cleared the way: the Greeks broke through
Into the vestibule, cut down the guards,
And made the wide hall seethe with men-at-arms—
A tumult greater than when dikes are burst
385 And a foaming river, swirling out in flood,
Whelms every parapet and races on
Through fields and over all the lowland plains,
Bearing off pens and cattle. I myself
Saw Neoptolemus furious with blood

359. **Periphas** (pᵘr′ə·fəs); **Automedon** (ô·tä′mə·dən)

361. **Scyros** (sī′rəs): an island in
the Aegean Sea.

36 LITERARY BACKGROUND
At this point in the Trojan legend, Achilles has already met
his death at the hands of Paris,
who treacherously slew him
with an arrow to the heel. Pyrrhus, who is also called Neoptolemus, is the son of Achilles.
He is portrayed favorably by
Greek authors, including the
tragedian Sophocles. Virgil,
however, in the scene of
Priam's death, presents Pyrrhus as a ruthless serpent.

36 LITERARY ELEMENT
Epic Simile: What details in
the epic simile in lines 352–358
suggest danger and violence?
(Possible responses: "swollen
underground," "writhes," "on
vile grass fed," "rolling slippery coils," "triple tongue a-
flicker")

37 PREDICTING
Based on Virgil's description of
Pyrrhus so far, what role do
you think he will play in Troy's
ruin? (Possible response: Pyrrhus may slaughter some of
the royal family in the palace,
perhaps even Troy's King
Priam himself.)

38 LITERARY ELEMENT
Epic Simile: How are the
Greeks in the palace like a
river when the dike has burst?
(Like the flooding river, the
Greeks are an overwhelming
and unstoppable force that de-
stroys everything in its path.)

39 LITERARY BACKGROUND
According to the legends of
the Trojan War, Priam also
fathered fifty sons, some by
Hecuba and some by various
other wives and concubines.

40 LITERARY ELEMENT
Imagery: What details in lines
405–411 help create a graphic,
vivid picture of the scene? (the
central court, big altar, old and
leaning laurel tree, the household gods in the tree's shade,
white doves huddling together
in a black storm)

consecrated (kän′si·krāt′əd):
set apart as holy

390   In the entrance way, and saw the two Atridae;°
       Hecuba I saw, and her hundred daughters,
       Priam before the altars, with his blood
       Drenching the fires that he himself had blessed.
       Those fifty bridal chambers, hope of a line
395   So flourishing; those doorways high and proud,
       Adorned with takings of barbaric gold,
       Were all brought low: fire had them, or the Greeks.
       What was the fate of Priam, you may ask.
       Seeing his city captive, seeing his own
400   Royal portals rent apart, his enemies
       In the inner rooms, the old man uselessly
       Put on his shoulders, shaking with old age,
       Armor unused for years, belted a sword on,
       And made for the massed enemy to die.

405   Under the open sky in a central court
       Stood a big altar; near it, a laurel tree
       Of great age, leaning over, in deep shade
       Embowered the Penates.° At this altar
       Hecuba and her daughters, like white doves
410   Blown down in a black storm, clung together,
       Enfolding holy images in their arms.
       Now, seeing Priam in a young man's gear,
       She called out:
                        'My poor husband, what mad thought
       Drove you to buckle on these weapons?
415   Where are you trying to go? The time is past
       For help like this, for this kind of defending,
       Even if my own Hector could be here.
       Come to me now: the altar will protect us,
       Or else you'll die with us.'
                                    She drew him close,
420   Heavy with years, and made a place for him
       To rest on the <u>consecrated</u> stone.
                                    Now see
       Polites, one of Priam's sons, escaped
       From Pyrrhus' butchery and on the run
       Through enemies and spears, down colonnades,
425   Through empty courtyards, wounded. Close behind
       Comes Pyrrhus burning for the death-stroke: has him,
       Catches him now, and lunges with the spear.
       The boy has reached his parents, and before them
       Goes down, pouring out his life with blood.

390. **Atridae** (ə·trī′dē): Agamemnon
     and Menelaus.

408. **Penates** (pē·nā′tēz′): Roman
     household gods.

<blockquote>
430   Now Priam, in the very midst of death,
    Would neither hold his peace nor spare his anger.

    'For what you've done, for what you've dared,' he said,
    'If there is care in heaven for atrocity,
    May the gods render fitting thanks, reward you
435   As you deserve. You forced me to look on
    At the destruction of my son: defiled
    A father's eyes with death. That great Achilles
    You claim to be the son of—and you lie—
    Was not like you to Priam, his enemy;
440   To me who threw myself upon his mercy
    He showed compunction, gave me back for burial
    The bloodless corpse of Hector, and returned me
    To my own realm.'

              The old man threw his spear
    With feeble impact; blocked by the ringing bronze,
445   It hung there harmless from the jutting boss.°
    Then Pyrrhus answered:

              'You'll report the news
    To Pelides,° my father; don't forget
    My sad behavior, the degeneracy
    Of Neoptolemus. Now die.'
</blockquote>

445. **boss:** here, an architectural protuberance.

447. **Pelides** (pē′li·dēz): Achilles, son of Peleus.

41 COMPARING LITERATURE

Priam's reference in lines 436–443 to his ransoming of Hector's body from Pyrrhus's father, the great hero Achilles, would have been familiar to Virgil's audience from the episode in Book 24 of the *Iliad* (see p. 264).

❓ *How does Priam contrast Achilles with Pyrrhus?* (He says Pyrrhus is unworthy of his father because Achilles showed Priam mercy.)

42 LITERARY ELEMENT

Irony: Verbal irony refers to speech that conveys one meaning but really means the opposite. What is ironic in Pyrrhus's last words to Priam? (Pyrrhus does not mean that he is "degenerate," but he applies this term to himself in order to mock the helpless Priam.) The irony recoils again, since Virgil does indeed intend his audience to regard Pyrrhus as "degenerate."

Bowl depicting soldiers in battle.

Alinari/Art Resource, New York

43 Cultural Background

Both the Greeks and the Romans regarded altars as places of sanctuary sacred to the gods. Thus Pyrrhus's dragging of Priam to the altar and his slaughter of him there would have been especially shocking to Virgil's audience.

44 Historical Background

The details in lines 459–460 would have reminded Virgil's Roman audience of the fate of Gnaeus Pompey, the principal rival of Julius Caesar, who was stabbed to death in 48 B.C. Virgil's ability to allude subtly in his epic to events from Roman history helped him achieve popularity.

45 Literary Element

Conflict: How does Aeneas express his feelings about the horrors he has witnessed? (He shakes from head to foot.) What are some of the internal conflicts that may be going through his mind at this point in the narrative? (Possible responses: fear for his father and his wife; pity for King Priam; concern about his house; apprehension about his son, Iulus; dismay that all his men have disappeared and that he is alone; despair that Troy has been defeated)

43

> With this,
> 450 To the altar step itself he dragged him trembling,
> Slipping in the pooled blood of his son,
> And took him by the hair with his left hand.
> The sword flashed in his right; up to the hilt
> He thrust it in his body.

That was the end
455 Of Priam's age, the doom that took him off,
With Troy in flames before his eyes, his towers
Headlong fallen—he that in other days
Had ruled in pride so many lands and peoples,
The power of Asia.

44

On the distant shore
460 The vast trunk headless lies without a name.

45

For the first time that night, inhuman shuddering
Took me, head to foot. I stood unmanned,
And my dear father's image came to mind
As our king, just his age, mortally wounded,
465 Gasped his life away before my eyes.
Creusa came to mind, too, left alone;
The house plundered; danger to little Iulus.
I looked around to take stock of my men,
But all had left me, utterly played out,
470 Giving their beaten bodies to the fire
Or plunging from the roof.

It came to this,
That I stood there alone. And then I saw
Lurking beyond the doorsill of the Vesta,
In hiding, silent, in that place reserved,
475 The daughter of Tyndareus.° Glare of fires
Lighted my steps this way and that, my eyes
Glancing over the whole scene, everywhere.
That woman, terrified of the Trojans' hate
For the city overthrown, terrified too
480 Of Danaan vengeance, her abandoned husband's
Anger after years—Helen, that Fury
Both to her own homeland and Troy, had gone
To earth, a hated thing, before the altars.
Now fires blazed up in my own spirit—
485 A passion to avenge my fallen town
And punish Helen's whorishness.

46

'Shall this one

475. **daughter of Tyndareus** (tin·der′ē·əs): Helen.

Look untouched on Sparta and Mycenae
After her triumph, going like a queen,
And see her home and husband, kin and children,
490 With Trojan girls for escort, Phrygian slaves?
Must Priam perish by the sword for this?
Troy burn, for this? Dardania's littoral°
Be soaked in blood, so many times, for this?
Not by my leave. I know
495 No glory comes of punishing a woman,
The feat can bring no honor. Still, I'll be
Approved for snuffing out a monstrous life,
For a just sentence carried out. My heart
Will teem with joy in this avenging fire,
500 And the ashes of my kin will be appeased.'

So ran my thoughts. I turned wildly upon her,
But at that moment, clear, before my eyes—
Never before so clear—in a pure light
Stepping before me, radiant through the night,
505 My loving mother came: immortal, tall,

492. **littoral** (lit'ə·rəl): here, shore-line.

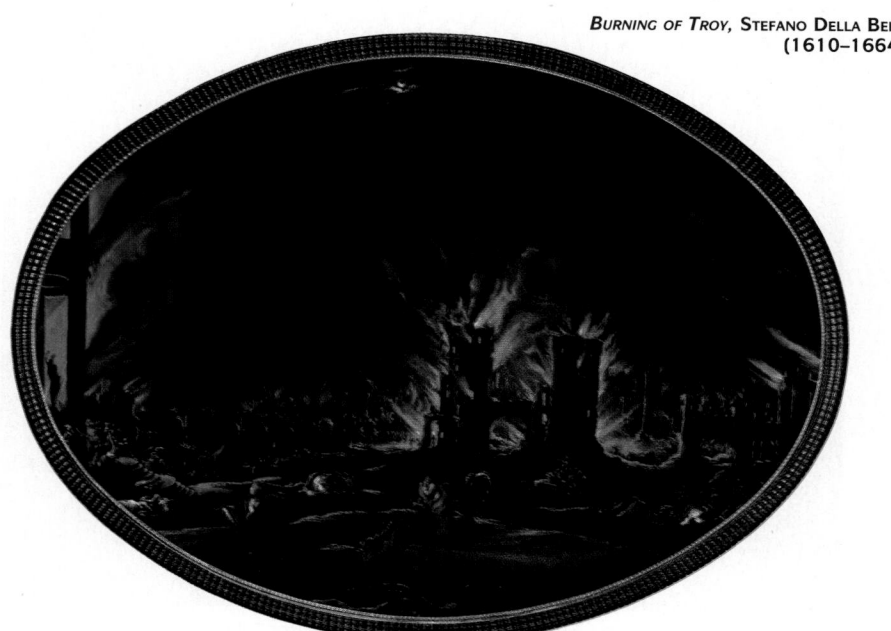

BURNING OF TROY, STEFANO DELLA BELLA (1610–1664).

Scala/Art Resource, New York

from the Aeneid, Book 2   **399**

48 COMPARING LITERATURE

In the words of Venus, in lines 509–511, Virgil points to some of the major themes in the epic: Aeneas must undergo great suffering; he must restrain the "fury" in his nature that causes him to lose control and forget his destiny; and he must think of others rather than himself.

? *How do these characteristics of Aeneas as a hero contrast with the Homeric ideal of heroism, as exemplified by Achilles?* (Possible response: Although the Homeric hero suffers to win glory, he is less subject to restraint than is Aeneas, and he is not asked to sacrifice himself for others.)

▨ **goad** (gōd): urge into action

49 GUIDED READING

Cause and Effect: Venus denies that Helen is responsible for the fall of Troy. What does Venus say is the real cause of Troy's defeat? ("the will of the gods")

HUMANITIES CONNECTION ▪

This painting is one of the best-known works of Baron Pierre-Narcisse Guérin (gā·raŋ', 1774–1833), a French master who taught the famed Romantic painters, Théodore Géricault and Eugène Delacroix. Like his students, Guérin was known for his brilliant use of color.

? *Does the mood of the painting reflect the mood of the story Aeneas is telling?* ▪

And lovely as the lords of heaven know her.
Catching me by the hand, she held me back,
Then with her rose-red mouth reproved me:
                                                            'Son,

Why let such suffering <u>goad</u> you on to fury
510 Past control? Where is your thoughtfulness
For me, for us? Will you not first revisit
The place you left your father, worn and old,
Or find out if your wife, Creusa, lives,
And the young boy, Ascanius—all these
515 Cut off by Greek troops foraging everywhere?
Had I not cared for them, fire would by now
Have taken them, their blood glutted the sword.
You must not hold the woman of Laconia,°
That hated face, the cause of this, nor Paris.
520 The harsh will of the gods it is, the gods,
That overthrows the splendor of this place
And brings Troy from her height into the dust.

518. **woman of Laconia** (lə·kō′nē·ə): Helen.

AENEAS RECOUNTING TO DIDO THE FALL OF TROY, BARON PIERRE-NARCISSE GUÉRIN (1774–1833).

Scala/Art Resource, New York

Look over there: I'll tear away the cloud
That curtains you, and films your mortal sight,
525 The fog around you.—Have no fear of doing
Your mother's will, or balk at obeying her.—
Look: where you see high masonry thrown down,
Stone torn from stone, with billowing smoke and dust,
Neptune is shaking from their beds the walls
530 That his great trident pried up, undermining,
Toppling the whole city down. And look:
Juno in all her savagery holds
The Scaean Gates,° and raging in steel armor
Calls her allied army from the ships.
535 Up on the citadel—turn, look—Pallas Tritonia°
Couched in a stormcloud, lightening, with her
    Gorgon!°
The Father° himself empowers the Danaans,
Urges assaulting gods on the defenders.
Away, child; put an end to toiling so.
540 I shall be near, to see you safely home.'

She hid herself in the deep gloom of night,
And now the dire forms appeared to me
Of great immortals, enemies of Troy.
I knew the end then: Ilium was going down
545 In fire, the Troy of Neptune going down,
As in high mountains when the countrymen
Have notched an ancient ash, then make their axes
Ring with might and main, chopping away
To fell the tree—ever on the point of falling,
550 Shaken through all its foliage, and the treetop
Nodding; bit by bit the strokes prevail
Until it gives a final groan at last
And crashes down in ruin from the height.

Now I descended where the goddess guided,
555 Clear of the flames, and clear of enemies,
For both retired; so gained my father's door,
My ancient home.

*Arriving home, Aeneas finds his father, Anchises,
resolved to die in the carnage of Troy. Unable to
convince him to flee, he swears, despite his wife's
piteous pleas, that he will join his father in death.
Then he sees an omen that changes his mind.*

533. **Scaean** (skē′ən) **Gates:** the
northwest entry to Troy.

535. **Pallas Tritonia** (trə·tō′nē·ə): a
name for Minerva; she was
supposed to have been born
near Lake Tritonis in Libya.

536. **Gorgon** (gôr′gən): Medusa, a
terrifying monster slain by
Perseus; her head was given
to the goddess Minerva, who
carried it upon her father's
shield.

537. **Father:** Jupiter.

■ **undermining** (un′dər·mīn′iŋ):
weakening the foundations
of

50 COMPARING LITERATURE
In Greek and Roman mythology, it is useless for mortals to strive against the gods, as Venus points out to Aeneas. The same point is made by a god at the beginning of Book 22 of the *Iliad* (see p. 247). Apollo warns Achilles to stop pursuing him, since even the greatest mortal hero is no match for the strength of a divinity.

51 LITERARY ELEMENT
Epic Simile: What is being compared in the epic simile in lines 546–553? (Troy is being compared to an ancient ash tree that is felled by woodsmen in the mountains.) How does the downfall of the tree help you visualize the fate of Troy? (Like the tree notched by the woodsmen, Troy has been marked for felling by the gods. Troy, like the great tree, is shaken to its roots by incessant, inescapable blows that finally topple it.)

52 SPECULATING
From this summary, what kinds of conflicts do you think Aeneas experienced in the intervening passages? (Possible response: Aeneas probably felt pulled in a number of different directions, experiencing external conflicts with his father and his wife, feeling torn between his duties as son and as husband.)

from the Aeneid, Book 2   **401**

53 HISTORICAL BACKGROUND

Aeneas's son is known by two names in the epic: Ascanius and Iulus. The second name alludes to the family name of Julius Caesar and his great-nephew and heir, Augustus. The Julian family invested much energy in propagandizing its "direct descent" from the founders of Rome. Virgil, whose patron was the emperor Augustus himself, seems to have consented to this fiction.

omnipotent (äm·nip′ə·tənt): all-powerful

54 INFERRING

Thunder and shooting stars or meteors were thought to be portents sent by Jupiter who, as king of the gods and lord of the sky, was believed to control celestial phenomena. What conclusion does Anchises draw from these omens? (that the gods approve the family's flight from Troy)

55 CULTURAL BACKGROUND

Aeneas's special concern for his father exemplifies the Roman virtue of *pietas*, or "loyalty," "fidelity." What does Aeneas's comment about his wife in line 593 imply about Roman society? (Possible responses: either that women were not considered equal to men or that women were to be kept at a safe distance from danger)

She went on, and her wailing filled the house,
But then a sudden portent came, a marvel:

53 560 Amid his parents' hands and their sad faces
A point on Iulus' head seemed to cast light,
A tongue of flame that touched but did not burn him,
Licking his fine hair, playing round his temples.
We, in panic, beat at the flaming hair
565 And put the sacred fire out with water;
Father Anchises lifted his eyes to heaven
And lifted up his hands, his voice, in joy:

'Omnipotent Jupiter, if prayers affect you,
Look down upon us, that is all I ask,
570 If by devotion to the gods we earn it,
Grant us a new sign, and confirm this portent!'
The old man barely finished when it thundered
A loud crack on the left. Out of the sky
Through depths of night a star fell trailing flame
575 And glided on, turning the night to day.
We watched it pass above the roof and go
To hide its glare, its trace, in Ida's° wood;
But still, behind, the luminous furrow shone
And wide zones fumed with sulphur.

54

                                Now indeed
580 My father, overcome, addressed the gods,
And rose in worship of the blessed star.

'Now, now, no more delay. I'll follow you.
Where you conduct me, there I'll be.
                                Gods of my fathers,
Preserve this house, preserve my grandson. Yours
585 This portent was. Troy's life is in your power.
I yield. I go as your companion, son.'
Then he was still. We heard the blazing town
Crackle more loudly, felt the scorching heat.

55 590 'Then come, dear father. Arms around my neck:
I'll take you on my shoulders, no great weight.
Whatever happens, both will face one danger,
Find one safety. Iulus will come with me,
My wife at a good interval behind.
Servants, give your attention to what I say.
595 At the gate inland there's a funeral mound
And an old shrine of Ceres the Bereft;°

577. **Ida** (ī′də): a mountain near Troy, the setting for the Judgment of Paris.

596. **Ceres the Bereft:** the mother of Proserpina (prō·sʉr′pi·nə), who was fated to spend part of the year in the underworld.

Near it an ancient cypress, kept alive
For many years by our fathers' piety.
By various routes we'll come to that one place.
600   Father, carry our hearthgods, our Penates.
It would be wrong for me to handle them—
Just come from such hard fighting, bloody work—
Until I wash myself in running water.'

When I had said this, over my breadth of shoulder
605   And bent neck, I spread out a lion skin
For tawny cloak and stooped to take his weight.
Then little Iulus put his hand in mine
And came with shorter steps beside his father.
My wife fell in behind. Through shadowed places
610   On we went, and I, lately unmoved
By any spears thrown, and squads of Greeks,
Felt terror now at every eddy of wind,
Alarm at every sound, alert and worried
Alike for my companion and my burden.
615   I had got near the gate, and now I thought
We had made it all the way, when suddenly
A noise of running feet came near at hand,
And peering through the gloom ahead, my father
Cried out:
                'Run, boy; here they come; I see
620   Flame light on shields, bronze shining.'
                                        I took fright,
And some unfriendly power, I know not what,
Stole all my addled wits—for as I turned
Aside from the known way, entering a maze
Of pathless places on the run—
                                        Alas,
625   Creusa, taken from us by grim fate, did she
Linger, or stray, or sink in weariness?
There is no telling. Never would she be
Restored to us. Never did I look back
Or think to look for her, lost as she was,
630   Until we reached the funeral mound and shrine
Of venerable Ceres. Here at last
All came together, but she was not there;
She alone failed her friends, her child, her husband.
Out of my mind, whom did I not accuse,
635   What man or god? What crueler loss had I

Scala/Art Resource, New York

AENEAS AND ANCHISES, GIOVANNI
LORENZO BERNINI (1598–1680).
*Anchises holds a statue of the
penates, or gods who protected
household supplies in individual
homes.*

56 HISTORICAL BACKGROUND
The scene Virgil describes in
the lines depicting Aeneas, his
father, and his son was also
shown on Roman coins issued
by Augustus. The coins served
as a visible advertisement of
the emperor's family ties to
the earliest (and therefore the
most revered) Romans.

57 GUIDED READING
Cause and Effect: What explanation does Aeneas give in
lines 620–627 for his separation
from his wife? (As the result of
his father's alarm, he becomes
bewildered, strays from the
main route, and then discovers
that she has been lost. Aeneas
blames the loss on "grim
fate.")

HUMANITIES CONNECTION

Bernini (1598–1680) was an Italian sculptor, architect, and
painter, and the creator of the
exuberant Baroque style in
sculpture. His creative combinations of architecture and
sculpture include the tombs of
Pope Urban VIII and Pope
Alexander VII, the piazza and
colonnade of St. Peter's in
Rome, and the elaborate, pil-
lared baldachin over the main
altar of St. Peter's. A preco-
cious talent who attracted
powerful patrons, Bernini was
the dominant influence on European sculpture for more
than a century.

? *What lines from p. 402 are
reflected in Bernini's statue?*
(lines 589–592) ∎

Note how the artist has used the limbs of the figures to convey the sensation of flight. Creusa's swirling robes mirror the swirls of smoke and flame from the burning city in the background.

❓ *During a catastrophe such as the burning of Troy, how could one member of a family perish while others escaped?* (as a result of panic, terror, and confusion) ∎

58 LITERARY ELEMENT

Epic Hero: What is Aeneas described as doing in lines 641–647? (running desperately back into the city to search for his wife) How does this description affect your impression of Aeneas as an epic hero? (Answers may vary. Some may argue that Aeneas bravely risks his life on the chance that he can rescue Creusa; others may argue that Aeneas, however brave, is shown in an unheroic, almost desperate light as the result of his own carelessness.)

Alinari/Art Resource, New York

THE BURNING OF TROY, SIENA. *The figure in the center of the painting is Creusa, or her ghost.*
❓ *How is Creusa significant to Aeneas's adventures?*

Beheld, that night the city fell? Ascanius,
My father, and the Teucrian Penates,
I left in my friends' charge, and hid them well
In a hollow valley.
           I turned back alone
640 Into the city, cinching my bright harness.
Nothing for it but to run the risks
Again, go back again, comb all of Troy,
And put my life in danger as before:
First by the town wall, then the gate, all gloom,
645 Through which I had come out—and so on backward,
Tracing my own footsteps through the night;
And everywhere my heart misgave me: even

58

Stillness had its terror. Then to our house,
Thinking she might, just might, have wandered there.
650 Danaans had got in and filled the place,
And at that instant fire they had set,
Consuming it, went roofward in a blast;
Flames leaped and seethed in heat to the night sky.
I pressed on, to see Priam's hall and tower.
655 In the bare colonnades of Juno's shrine
Two chosen guards, Phoenix° and hard Ulysses,
Kept watch over the plunder. Piled up here
Were treasures of old Troy from every quarter,
Torn out of burning temples: altar tables,
660 Robes, and golden bowls. Drawn up around them,
Boys and frightened mothers stood in line.
I even dared to call out in the night;
I filled the streets with calling; in my grief
Time after time I groaned and called Creusa,
665 Frantic, in endless quest from door to door.
Then to my vision her sad wraith° appeared—
Creusa's ghost, larger than life, before me.
Chilled to the marrow, I could feel the hair
On my head rise, the voice clot in my throat;
670 But she spoke out to ease me of my fear:

'What's to be gained by giving way to grief
So madly, my sweet husband? Nothing here
Has come to pass except as heaven willed.
You may not take Creusa with you now;
675 It was not so ordained, nor does the lord
Of high Olympus give you leave. For you
Long exile waits, and long sea miles to plow.
You shall make landfall on Hesperia°
Where Lydian Tiber° flows, with gentle pace,
680 Between rich farmlands, and the years will bear
Glad peace, a kingdom, and a queen for you.
Dismiss these tears for your beloved Creusa.
I shall not see the proud homelands of Myrmidons
Or of Dolopians, or go to serve
685 Greek ladies, Dardan lady that I am
And daughter-in-law of Venus the divine.
No: the great mother of the gods detains me
Here on these shores. Farewell now; cherish still
Your son and mine.'

656. **Phoenix** (fē′niks)

666. **wraith** (rāth): ghost.

678. **Hesperia** (hes·pir′ē·ə): name given to Italy by Aeneas.

679. **Lydian** (lid′ē·ən) **Tiber:** The Etruscans were supposed to have come from Lydia, a region in Asia Minor.

59 VISUALIZING
After reading these lines, close your eyes and try to visualize the scene Virgil has described through Aeneas's eyes. What details of the description do you recall most vividly? (Answers will vary.)

60 INFERRING
How does Virgil let the reader know the fate of Creusa? (by having her wraith, or ghost, appear. The reader then realizes that Creusa is dead.)

61 LITERARY ELEMENT
Theme: How does Creusa's comment summing up the fall of Troy recall Venus's words to Aeneas in lines 520–522? (Both stress that Troy has fallen because of the gods' will.)

62 LITERARY ELEMENT
Foreshadowing: What does Creusa predict for Aeneas's future? (a long exile and sea journey, landing near the Tiber, peace at last, a kingdom, a new queen)

READING CHECK

1. Who warns the Trojans of treachery? (Laocoon)
2. What does Hector advise Aeneas to do? (to flee Troy)
3. Whose warnings about Troy's doom are ignored? (Cassandra's)
4. What does Pyrrhus do to Polites? (kills him in front of his father, Priam)
5. Who prevents Aeneas from killing Helen? (Venus)

6. What omens persuade Anchises to flee? (thunder and a shooting star)
7. Where does Aeneas order the members of his household to meet? (at a cypress tree near the shrine of Ceres)
8. What does Aeneas do when he finds that Creusa is missing? (rushes back into Troy to find her)
9. What does Creusa's ghost tell Aeneas he will find? (peace, a kingdom, and a queen)

10. Where does Aeneas head as dawn breaks and he and his father leave Troy for good? (for the mountain range)

> **tenuous** (ten'yoo·əs): insubstantial; flimsy

63 LITERARY ELEMENT

Mood: Virgil repeats lines 691–695 in Book 6, when Aeneas tries to embrace the ghost of his father, Anchises, in the underworld. What mood or atmosphere do these lines help create? (Possible responses: sadness, frustration, grief)

WRITING TO LEARN

Social Studies: Virgil portrays Aeneas as a hero with many different, conflicting emotions. Write a psychological profile of Aeneas, basing your conclusions on his actions and thoughts. Discuss the relative importance in the hero's emotional makeup of such feelings as love, anger, loyalty, revenge, sympathy, and pride.

With this she left me weeping,
690 Wishing that I could say so many things,
And faded on the <u>tenuous</u> air. Three times
I tried to put my arms around her neck,
Three times enfolded nothing, as the wraith
Slipped through my fingers, bodiless as wind,
695 Or like a flitting dream.
So in the end
As night waned I rejoined my company.
And there to my astonishment I found
New refugees in a great crowd: men and women
Gathered for exile, young—pitiful people
700 Coming from every quarter, minds made up,
With their belongings, for whatever lands
I'd lead them to by sea.
The morning star
Now rose on Ida's ridges, bringing day.
Greeks had secured the city gates. No help
705 Or hope of help existed.
So I resigned myself, picked up my father,
And turned my face toward the mountain range."

A CRITICAL COMMENT

Themes and Images in Book 2 of the Aeneid

The full force of Virgil's narrative lies not in its focus on descriptive details, but rather in the personal response of Aeneas to the advancing tragedy. Aeneas's thirst for revenge comes into conflict with his duties as a survivor and with the pronouncements of fate. These conflicts recur throughout the *Aeneid*, constituting central themes of the epic.

At the beginning of the enemy attack, the sleeping Aeneas has a vision of the slain Trojan hero Hector, who urges him to escape the holocaust and save the sacred treasures of the city. However, it is only when Aeneas climbs to the roof of his house and sees the fires engulfing the homes of his friends that he grasps the full magnitude of the Greek assault. His first reaction is blind rage: he can think only of throwing himself into the flames or giving himself over to revenge to quench his own fury.

In what follows, Virgil repeatedly emphasizes the idea of wasted valor. First the young Coroebus throws away his life in a failed attempt to save his beloved Cassandra. Then, in the ensuing fight, Aeneas's small band of warriors are cut down by the missiles of their own countrymen. Finally, Aeneas returns to the palace of Priam and witnesses in helpless outrage the brutal killing of the feeble, broken king.

At this point, Aeneas's thoughts turn to his own family, and he begins to accept the awesome responsibility of the survivor as something greater than his overpowering desire for revenge. Virgil here emphasizes another central theme of his epic: the problem of fate and free will. On his way back to save his family, Aeneas comes face to face with Helen—the cause, from his point of view, of the entire war. He is about to vent his fury on her when his mother Venus stays his hand. Venus gives Aeneas a powerful display of the divine forces orchestrating the destruction of Troy—forces that are far beyond any factors of human guilt and retribution.

The debate over individual responsibility is resumed when Aeneas returns to his family. This time it is his father Anchises who nearly melts Aeneas's own resolve, until he is swayed by a startling portent: the image of flickering flames around the head of his own son, followed by a meteor

pointing the way to safety. Aeneas is now ready to shoulder the burden of his past and future destiny as he sets off, carrying his father on his back and leading his young son by the hand.

As we begin to understand as early as Book 2, the power of "destiny" or "fate" is not simply a matter of resignation by Aeneas to the rule of unseen powers. Instead, destiny calls forth even greater force of will and commitment on the part of the hero. This is precisely the idea of self-mastery that is expressed by the epithet *pius* (variously translated as "pious," "responsible," "dutiful," "conscientious") attached to the name of Aeneas throughout the poem. This heroic quality occasionally gives Aeneas the strength to overcome external enemies, but more often it puts him into conflict with himself. Aeneas's internal conflicts set up some of the emotional high points of the poem. These conflicts come into focus as the hero gives himself over to indulgence of his love for Dido in Book 4, his weariness in Book 5, and his obsessive revenge in Book 12.

Many of the themes and images developed in Book 2 reverberate throughout the whole epic. For example, the shared tragedy of fathers and sons is a pattern that repeatedly unfolds in Books 9 to 12. The sense of the awesome power of fate recurs with particular force in the prophetic vision in the underworld in Book 6, and again in the pageant of Roman history engraved on Aeneas's divine shield in Book 8.

1 LITERARY ELEMENT
Plot: On the surface, Virgil's plot structure may seem simple and straightforward. There are, however, many fascinating connections among the details of different episodes in Book 2. For example, the fact that the Trojans' disguise backfires disastrously in lines 299–302 ironically echoes and inverts the Greeks' success at treachery and disguise in the trick of the horse.

2 CULTURAL DIVERSITY
A major undercurrent of Book 2 is the theme of Aeneas's guilt at surviving the ruin of Troy. In his reckless fury, Aeneas seems almost determined to perish rather than bear the pain of living on after Troy's fall. Virgil's psychological insight is echoed in modern times in the accounts of feelings of guilt by survivors of the Holocaust of World War II and of the atomic bombings of Hiroshima and Nagasaki.

ANSWERS
First Thoughts
Answers will vary.

Identifying Facts
1. The Greeks proclaim the horse an offering for a safe voyage home, their ships are hidden, the Trojans believe Sinon. as an omen that the horse must be accepted
2. Priam is killed by Pyrrhus. Venus intervenes for Helen.
3. light around Iulus's head, thunder, a shooting star
4. when he reaches the meeting place, the shrine of Ceres. He will travel, found a kingdom, get a new wife.

1. Evaluating a Critical Opinion. In a famous essay, the poet and critic T. S. Eliot wrote that Virgil's epic hero embodied the values of duty, hard work, and obedience to destiny but that Aeneas was flawed because of his inability to love others. Have students hold a discussion to assess the validity of Eliot's view of Aeneas.

2. Research Project. The poet Virgil is a major character in Dante's the *Divine Comedy*, where he serves as Dante's guide to the underworld in *Inferno* (see pp. 741–770). Encourage students to find out why Dante may have chosen Virgil for this role and to identify some details that Dante uses in his epic to describe Virgil. Have students report their results to the class.

CLOSURE

Ask students to compare and contrast their general impressions of Homer's *Iliad* and Virgil's *Aeneid*. Which epic do they think is more heroic? Which epic, in their opinion, speaks more forcefully and vividly to modern readers? With which epic hero, Achilles or Aeneas, can students more readily identify or sympathize? Ask students to support their choices with reasons and examples. ■

Interpreting Meanings

1. his willingness to shoulder responsibility, to sacrifice for others, and to master his emotions. his fury and confusion
2. impulse for revenge on Helen (turned aside by Venus) and indecision about whether to remain in Troy or flee. (He flees because of omens.)
3. Cassandra, who predicted Troy's downfall, is taken by the Greeks; Hecuba witnesses Priam's murder; Venus guides Aeneas, stops revenge on Helen; Creusa's ghost tells Aeneas to leave Troy.
4. soldiers like wolves (line 273), the battle like winds (line 307), Pyrrhus like a serpent (line 351), fall of Troy like the fall of an ash tree (line 546).

Applying Meanings
Answers will vary.

Critical Writing Response
Comparing Heroes. Essays might also explain how the heroes embody cultural values.

Language and Vocabulary
Analyzing an Epic Simile.
1. Climax focuses on the wolves' desperate need, which is compared to the soldiers' last-ditch defense of Troy.
2. Possible responses: blindness of adult wolves in fog and darkness, cubs' famished jaws ■

▶ First Thoughts
How did you react to the violence in Aeneas's account of the fall of Troy?

Identifying Facts
1. Why do the Trojans assume that the Greeks have sailed for home? How do they interpret the death of Laocoon?
2. What is Priam's fate? How is Helen saved from Aeneas's fury?
3. What signs convince Aeneas and Anchises that they must leave Troy?
4. At what point does Aeneas realize that his wife is gone? What is Creusa's parting message to Aeneas?

Interpreting Meanings
1. What strengths make Aeneas a leader of his people? What weaknesses does Virgil reveal in his epic hero?
2. The narrative in Book 2 clearly portrays Aeneas's **external conflicts** with the Greeks. He experiences **internal conflict** when he witnesses Priam's death. Find at least two other examples of internal conflict. What is the outcome of each conflict?
3. Although the title character of Virgil's epic is a man, the poem is deeply concerned with female characters. How do Cassandra, Hecuba, Venus, and Creusa play important roles in the poem?
4. Like Homer, Virgil uses **epic similes**, or extended comparisons in which epic events are likened to ordinary events in order to make them more accessible or interesting to the reader. Identify two examples of epic similes and explain what makes them vivid and exciting.

Applying Meanings
How do you rate Aeneas as a leader? If you were a Trojan refugee, would you follow him? Why or why not?

Critical Writing Response
Comparing Heroes. In a three- to four-paragraph essay, compare and contrast Aeneas with one of the heroes you have read about in this book or with a modern hero from television or film. Consider:
1. The nature of their quests
2. The use of their intelligence, physical strength, or special powers
3. Their acceptance of aid from others
4. Their loyalties
5. Their attitudes toward violence

Language and Vocabulary

Analyzing an Epic Simile

Reread lines 273–279 from Book 2, in which Aeneas describes his companions' and his own desperation as they rush to make a final stand against the Greeks. Then compare these lines with the following paraphrase:

> From that time on, while black night enveloped us, we ran straight for the heart of the city, toward our certain death, moving through flights of arrows and enemy troops, in the same way that preying wolves run in fog and darkness when they are driven recklessly on by fierce hunger and their starving cubs lie waiting in lairs.

This paraphrase conveys the meaning of the passage from the epic, but not its emotional impact.
1. How does Virgil organize the elements of the comparison so that his simile builds to a climax?
2. Which images are particularly effective in communicating the desperate emotional state of Aeneas and his small band of Trojans?

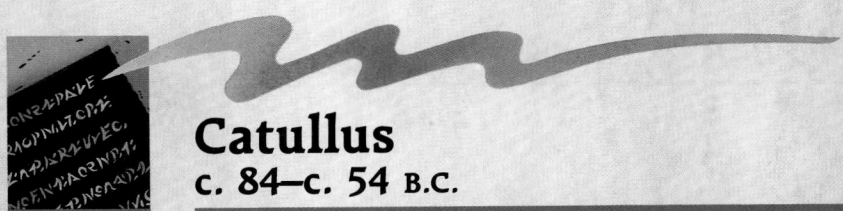

Catullus
c. 84–c. 54 B.C.

The Granger Collection, New York

Quintus Catulus Orator et Poeta

After 60 B.C., the maneuverings for power by Julius Caesar and his principal rival, Pompey, threatened to bring an end to the Roman Republic and to drag Rome into civil war. Most writers at this time were chiefly concerned with politics and public debate. One voice, the personal, lyric voice of Gaius Valerius Catullus (kə·tul′əs), stood out among them. Catullus turned away from the models of the Roman epics, which focused on war and politics. Instead, he found inspiration in the lyric poetry of the ancient Greeks, particularly the love lyrics of Sappho. Despite the personal nature of his poetry, Catullus won many admirers, including Julius Caesar himself. Ironically, Catullus's only attempt at public satire was a number of poems that showed his opposition to the ambitions of Julius Caesar. Fortunately, the Roman leader seemed not to take the satires to heart.

As a young man, Catullus left the home of his prosperous family in Verona and headed for Rome. He soon joined the fashionable social and literary circles of the capital. His love affair with a wealthy Roman woman named Clodia (klō′dē·ə) is the subject of a long series of poems that explore the range of his feelings for her. Around 57 B.C., when he was disillusioned with love, Catullus left Rome to travel and to visit the tomb of his brother who had recently died. During his travels, he wrote much about his feelings of love and loss.

Catullus occupies an important place in the history of Latin poetry, not only for the excellence of his lyrics, but also for his experimentation with form. He popularized the use of the elegiac couplet—a pair of lines consisting of a hexameter (six metrical feet) and a pentameter (five metrical feet). This meter later became standard for an entire genre of Latin poetry called the "love elegy."

Centuries later, Catullus became one of the most popular of the Roman poets rediscovered in the Renaissance. Leading European writers such as the Italian Petrarch (see page 806) and the English Ben Jonson imitated the lyrics of Catullus. Since the era of the Renaissance, Catullus's short "book" of 116 poems has been universally admired for its passion, sophistication, and charm.

MORE ABOUT THE AUTHOR
Catullus was part of a circle called the new or neoteric poets in the last century of the Roman Republic. These poets sharply rejected traditional forms and styles. In this respect, they may be compared to the Pléiade in sixteenth-century France or the modernist writers in Britain and America just before and after World War I. The Roman neoteric writers spurned the grand forms of epic and tragedy, turning instead to genres like the love elegy, the hymn, and the epyllion (a kind of mini-epic). Catullus and his friends much admired the Greek poets of the Hellenistic Age who were centered in Alexandria or wrote in the Alexandrian (a learned and graceful) style.

ABOUT THE TRANSLATOR
In addition to his highly praised translation of the poems of Catullus, Peter Whigham has published a collection of poetry entitled *Things Common, Properly*. He edited (with J. P. Sullivan) a collection of works by the Roman writer Martial, *Epigrams of Martial Englished by Divers Hands* (1987), and wrote *Do's and Don'ts of Translation* (1982).

PREREADING FOCUS

Background: If scholars are correct, "Lesbia" was Clodia, Catullus's mistress. Clodia was the wife of Quintus Metellus Celer, a high-ranking noble who was elected consul (Rome's highest office under the republic) in 60 B.C. After Metellus's death in 59 B.C., Catullus was supplanted temporarily in Lesbia's affections by Marcus Caelius Rufus, a politician whose stormy career included a celebrated lawsuit in which he was defended by the Roman orator Cicero.

Catullus's own poetry shows that Lesbia was both passionate and fickle. Other portraits, notably Cicero's description in his speech *Pro Caelio* and his references to her in his letters, were unflattering to the point of insult. In fact, Cicero calls her the Medea of the Palatine and a two-bit Clytemnestra. This name-calling indicates that Clodia was as evil as Medea and Clytemnestra, women from Greek mythology who murdered husbands, sons, and brothers.

Oral Response: Spark students' memories and thoughts by mentioning some possible types of intense relationships: with boyfriends, girlfriends, siblings, parents, coaches, teachers, or close friends.

Literary Focus: Remind students that we all tend to use hyperbole in daily conversation. Point out, however, that overuse of this figure of speech results in a loss of the desired effect.

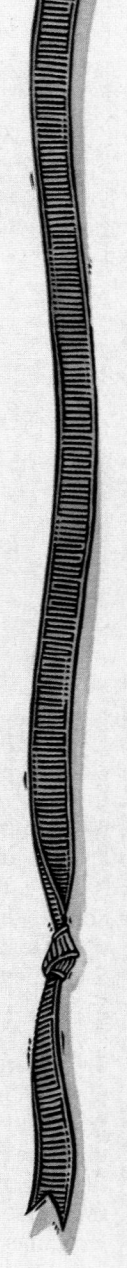

Reader's Guide

LYRIC POEMS OF CATULLUS

Background

A large number of Catullus's poems are addressed to a Roman woman named Clodia with whom he had a passionate affair. She was ten years older than the poet and was married to a prominent Roman politician. Her brother, Publius Clodius, was a notorious troublemaker in Roman politics and the bitter enemy of the famous orator, Cicero. Clodia herself seems to have been both beautiful and faithless.

In his poems, Catullus calls Clodia by the name Lesbia, a reference to the great Greek lyric poet Sappho (see page 279), who lived on the island of Lesbos and whose love poetry Catullus admired. Catullus's poems to and about Lesbia cover a range of emotions—from hope at the beginning of their relationship to anger and disillusionment at the end. At its best, his poetry is direct and intensely emotional.

Oral Response

Have you ever been in a relationship where you have felt difficult, strong emotions for another person? For instance, have you ever had a friend or a relative whom you loved one day and were angry with the next? In your journal, make a list of all the feelings you had for this person. Were these feelings confusing or contradictory? How did you express and resolve these feelings?

Literary Focus

Hyperbole is a figure of speech that uses exaggeration or overstatement for emphasis, often for comic effect. For example, when a friend tells you that she heard a joke so funny that she nearly died of laughter, she is demonstrating hyperbole. You believe the joke was very funny, but you know your friend could not have died from it.

LYRIC POEMS
Catullus
translated by

RENEY MYERS, ROBERT J. ORMSBY, AND PETER WHIGHAM

┃ *As you read, make a list of the range of emotions expressed in*
┃ *each lyric poem. Do you think that Catullus is accurately*
┃ *describing the variety and changeability of human emotion?*

Wretched Catullus, Leave off Playing the Fool

Wretched Catullus, leave off playing the fool:
Give up as lost what is forever past.
But once, bright, golden suns beamed down
    and cast
A happiness on you when she would rule
5 Your steps and lead you into joyous play.
How much you loved her! More than any man
Can ever love. With her, what joy began!
That sunny world seemed yours in every way.
Yet now she does not want you, and alas,
10 You must not chase her nor live wretchedly,
Thus make your heart as hard as it can be.
So goodbye, baby! Catullus now will pass
You up, won't need you, nor will entertain
A thought of you nor seek your company.
15 Oh wicked thing, I'm tough as I can be!
Now who'll invite you? Where will you obtain
Praise of your beauty? Who'll make sorrows
    blisses?
Who'll love you now? Or bite your lips in kisses?
Not Catullus! He's determined to abstain.

—*translated by Reney Myers and*
  Robert J. Ormsby

Roman depiction of Spring as a woman picking flowers.

Scala/Art Resource, New York

3 LITERARY ELEMENT

Hyperbole: How does the speaker use hyperbole, or overstatement, in the opening lines of "Lesbia Says She'ld Rather Marry Me"? (Possible response: He says that Lesbia prefers him to Jupiter, the king of the gods.)

4 INTERPRETING

What does Catullus state in the last two lines about women's ability to keep their promises? (Possible response: Women do not keep their promises, especially when they make them to their lovers "in desire.")

5 LITERARY ELEMENT

Rhetorical Question: A rhetorical question is one to which the speaker expects no answer because the answer is obvious or because the question is posed for emphasis or to make a point. What answers would you give to the two rhetorical questions in the closing lines of "If Ever Anyone Anywhere"? (Possible responses: no one; nothing)

6 LITERARY ELEMENT

Paradox: A paradox is an apparently contradictory statement that is actually true. What is paradoxical about the first line of "I Hate and I Love"? (Possible response: Catullus says that he both hates and loves at the same time.) How might the paradox be explained? (Possible response: The poet experiences rapidly shifting, conflicting emotions about his love affair.)

Lesbia Says She'ld Rather Marry Me

Lesbia says she'ld rather marry me
than anyone,
            though Jupiter himself came asking
or so she says,
            but what a woman tells her lover in desire
should be written out on air & running water.

—translated by Peter Whigham

If Ever Anyone Anywhere

If ever anyone anywhere, Lesbia, is looking
            for what he knows will not happen
and then unexpectedly it happens
            the soul is astonished,
as we are now in each other,
            an event dearer than gold,
for you have restored yourself, Lesbia, desired
restored yourself, longed for, unlooked for,
            brought yourself back
to me. White day in the calendar!
            Who happier than I?
What more can life offer
than the longed for unlooked for event
    when it happens?

—translated by Peter Whigham

I Hate and I Love

I hate and I love. And if you ask me how,
I do not know: I only feel it, and I'm torn in two.

—translated by Peter Whigham

Roman fresco of a poet or scribe.

1. Creating Song Titles. It is possible that ancient Italian folk songs might have influenced Catullus's decision to use clear, powerful words in his love lyrics. Tell students to assume that each poem has been set to music as a popular song. Then have them choose a title for each song that will send it to the top of pop music charts.

2. Research Project. One of Catullus's most famous lyric poems is "Let Us Live, My Lesbia, and Let Us Love." Have students locate and read a translation of this poem. Then ask them to compare the translation to Ben Jonson's adaptation of Catullus's poem "Come, My Celia, Let Us Prove" in his play *Volpone* (1606).

Ask students to reexamine the question posed in the headnote on p. 411. What emotions does Catullus express most often in his poems? Does he conspicuously avoid treating certain emotions? If so, which emotions are they? ■

First Thoughts

In which of these poems does Catullus seem to be happiest? In which does he seem most miserable?

Identifying Facts

1. "Wretched Catullus, Leave off Playing the Fool" is divided into two sections. What advice does Catullus give himself in the first eleven lines? Whom does he address in lines 12–19, and what does he say?

2. In "Lesbia Says She'ld Rather Marry Me," what attitude does Catullus express toward women in general?

3. What is the "unlooked for event" that the poet celebrates in "If Ever Anyone Anywhere"?

Interpreting Meanings

1. What does the last line of "Lesbia Says She'ld Rather Marry Me" imply about Lesbia's sincerity? How would you describe the **tone**, or attitude, of the speaker of this poem? Is it bitter, accepting, or indifferent? Explain.

2. "I Hate and I Love" is a brief statement of ambivalence, or the feeling of two strong, contradictory emotions at once. How is the speaker's tone in this poem different from that in "Lesbia Says She'ld Rather Marry Me"?

3. What examples of **hyperbole**, or deliberate overstatement, can you find in Catullus's poetry? What effect does the hyperbole have in each case?

4. Describe the contrast between the first part (lines 1–11) and the second part (lines 12–19) of "Wretched Catullus, Leave Off Playing the Fool." Is the speaker's "toughness" in the second part convincing? Give reasons for your answer.

Applying Meanings

One critic has suggested that the Romans may have considered Catullus's poetry frivolous or trivial. How do you feel about Catullus's poetry? Do you think it is frivolous? Or do you think the expression of personal feelings is a valid and important use of literature? Explain.

Creative Writing Response

Writing a Dramatic Scene. Catullus's lyrics give readers many insights into his own personality, as well as that of his beloved Lesbia. Using these hints as a point of departure for characterization and dialogue, write a short dramatic scene that involves Catullus and Lesbia. Feel free to use one of the situations implied by the poems (for example, a quarrel or a reconciliation), or create a dramatic situation of your own. Try to include at least one example of **hyperbole**, or deliberate exaggeration, in your scene.

Critical Writing Response

Comparing Lyric Poems. In a brief essay, compare and contrast one of Catullus's love lyrics with a lyric written by Sappho (see page 279). In your essay, be sure to include a discussion of how the speaker in each poem conveys emotion through imagery, figures of speech, and the careful control of tone.

ANSWERS

First Thoughts
Possible responses: happiest in "If Ever Anyone Anywhere"; most miserable in "Wretched Catullus, Leave Off Playing the Fool" or "I Hate and I Love"

Identifying Facts
1. to harden his heart and forget Lesbia. addresses Lesbia, saying he will abandon her and implying she will miss him
2. distrusting, maybe cynical
3. an unexpected reconciliation

Interpreting Meanings
1. she is insincere. bitter, suspicious, disillusioned
2. The tone in "I Hate and I Love" is more honest and anguished and less cynical.
3. Possible responses: mention of Jupiter ("Lesbia Says She'ld Rather Marry Me"), speaker "torn in two" ("I Hate and I Love"), an event "dearer than gold" ("If Ever Anyone Anywhere"). All add emphasis, drama, and intensity.
4. tender nostalgia versus sharp reproach. Answers on "toughness" will vary.

Applying Meanings
Answers will vary.

Creative Writing Response
Writing a Dramatic Scene.
Students might use hyperbole in dialogue to reveal the lovers' personalities.

Critical Writing Response
Comparing Lyric Poems. Essays should clearly identify the poems and the speakers. ■

Horace
65–8 B.C.

Scala/Art Resource, New York

As a young man, Horace made the mistake of fighting with Brutus on the losing side of the civil war that followed Julius Caesar's assassination in 44 B.C. Though his small landholdings were confiscated after the war, Horace proved to be a survivor. He started to write poetry in order to make a place for himself in Roman society. His poetic gifts, combined with a sense of humor that prevented him from taking himself too seriously, made Horace a favorite of the rich literary patrons who surrounded the new emperor Augustus. Horace remained at the center of sophisticated Roman literary society for the rest of his comfortable life.

Horace tended to moralize, and some critics feel that his poetry is not very profound. His poems are known more for their style than for their substance. He wrote on a wide variety of subjects, both light and serious. He is best known for his humorous *Satires*, his poetic *Epistles* (letters in verse to various friends), and his *Epodes* (lyric lampoons). His work about the poet's craft, *The Art of Poetry*, had a profound effect on poets and critics during the Age of Rationalism in the seventeenth and eighteenth centuries in Europe.

Quintus Horatius Flaccus, better known as Horace, lived during the Augustan Age, one of the most creative periods of Roman civilization. Horace, who was to become one of the greatest of Roman poets, had humble beginnings as the child of a father who was a freed slave. Nevertheless, his father was determined to give his son a first-rate education. Thus, as a boy, Horace was sent to study rhetoric and philosophy both in Rome and in Athens, Greece—a great privilege usually reserved only for the sons of the wealthiest upper classes.

OBJECTIVES

1. *To distinguish the characteristics of Horatian odes*
2. *To identify and evaluate the poet's tone*
3. *To use Horatian philosophy in an advice column and to write an essay comparing and contrasting the themes of two odes*
4. *To identify Latin word roots*

THEMES IN WORLD LITERATURE

The Wisdom of the World
"Right-Mind and Wrong-Mind" from the *Panchatantra*, pp. 478–483
From the *Analects* of Confucius, pp. 536–540
La Fontaine's *Fables*, pp. 940–944

Choices in Life
From "Candide," pp. 945–962
"Eveline," pp. 1207–1213 ■

VOCABULARY IN CONTEXT
The words listed below will appear in the side margin at the point of instruction:

1. adverse
2. timorously
3. eminence
4. magnanimity
5. protracted

Reader's Guide

THE GOLDEN MEAN AND CARPE DIEM

Background

Horace's greatest literary achievement may be his collection called *Odes*. An **ode** is a complex, songlike poem devoted to a serious subject. Before Horace, the typical ode was written for ceremonial or public occasions. Horace perfected a more personal and reflective type of ode.

"The Golden Mean" and "Carpe Diem," both from the *Odes*, express messages that can be put in the form of **maxims**, or short sayings. A "mean" is a middle position between two extremes. The idea of a harmonious "golden mean" occurs throughout classical Greek and Roman literature. Indeed, the motto said to have been inscribed on the ancient temple of Apollo at Delphi in Greece was *mēden agan*—"Nothing to excess." The concept of the golden mean also appears in other cultures: in the *Analects* of Confucius, in the Indian *Panchatantra*, and in the comedies of the French dramatist Molière. *Carpe diem* means "Seize the day," or "Enjoy life fully while you can." This is another philosophy of life that appears commonly throughout world literature.

Writer's Response

Before you read these poems, think about these two maxims: "Nothing to excess" and "Seize the day." Do you agree, for example, that people should avoid extremes, or do you believe that it's impossible to have too much of a good thing? Do you believe in "seizing the day," or do you think that it's wiser to put off enjoyment today in order to assure greater rewards in the future? How does the way you live your life reflect either of these maxims? Briefly freewrite your response.

Literary Focus

Tone is the attitude a writer takes toward the reader, a subject, or a character. It is conveyed through the writer's choice of words and details. A tone can be described as satirical, tender, comic, awed, ironic, passionate, wistful, melancholy, or by any of a number of other adjectives. As you read "The Golden Mean" and "Carpe Diem," pay attention to the tone of each. Does Horace seem to approve of living by "the golden mean"? Does he believe in "seizing the day"?

PREREADING FOCUS

Background: An ode is one of the freest forms of lyric verse. In ancient Greece and Rome, odes were composed on an immense variety of subjects and themes. Horace's *Odes* reflect the influence of several Greek lyric poets, notably Pindar (518–438 B.C.), who wrote victory odes for the winners of the Olympic Games, and Callimachus (305–240 B.C.), who composed odes and hymns in the graceful "Alexandrian" style. Horace's poems, however, are uniquely Roman in subject matter and style. They are marked by elaborate wordplay and well-balanced structural arrangements.

Writer's Response: You might want to spark students' responses by writing a few familiar proverbs with similar themes on the chalkboard: for example, "Moderation in all things" for "The Golden Mean" or "Eat, drink, and be merry, for tomorrow we die" for "Carpe Diem."

Literary Focus: To make the literary concept of tone more accessible, you may want to suggest the analogy of the tone—or general emotional feeling—of a piece of music.

Stanza Form

A stanza is a group of consecutive lines in a poem that form a single unit. A stanza in poetry often expresses a single thought, just as a paragraph in prose often expresses a single idea. Stanzas vary greatly in their number of lines, the length of their lines, and in their rhyme schemes (if any). "The Golden Mean" illustrates a six-line stanza called a sestet. "Carpe Diem" is written in couplets, or pairs of consecutive, rhyming lines.

Reading and Speaking. Have students work in pairs and alternate reading the sestets and couplets of the two poems. Students should jot down the rhyme scheme of the sestet (*aabccb*). Then have students discuss whether a single main idea can be identified in each sestet of "The Golden Mean" and in each couplet of "Carpe Diem." ∎

TEACHER'S RESOURCES

✔ Review and Response Worksheet
✔ Vocabulary Activity Worksheet
✔ Vocabulary Test

adverse (ad·vʉrs'): unfavorable; harmful

timorously (tim'ər·es·lē): fearfully; timidly

eminence (em'i·nəns): loftiness; greatness

1 LITERARY ELEMENT

Theme: The second stanza states Horace's theme or moral insight in "The Golden Mean." How would you paraphrase this theme in your own words? (Possible response: People will be happier if they avoid extremes.)

2 INFERRING

What conclusion does Horace want readers to draw from the description of tall trees and a lofty tower in lines 13–15? (Possible response: The proudest and most powerful people may suffer the steepest, cruelest falls.)

3 INTERPRETING

What is Horace's main point about the philosopher in the fourth stanza? (Possible response: In good times, he rejoices only moderately; in adversity, he maintains hope for better times.)

THE GOLDEN MEAN
Horace
translated by
WILLIAM COWPER

❦ *As you read this poem, try to decide what Horace's ideal of a "golden mean" is.*

Receive, dear friend, the truths I teach;
So shalt thou live beyond the reach
  Of adverse fortune's power;
Not always tempt the distant deep,
5 Nor always timorously creep
  Along the treacherous shore.

1
He that holds fast the golden mean,
And lives contentedly between
  The little and the great,
10 Feels not the wants that pinch the poor,
Nor plagues that haunt the rich man's door,
  Embittering all his state.

2
The tallest pines feel the most power
Of winter blasts; the loftiest tower
15 Comes heaviest to the ground;
The bolts that spare the mountain's side,
His cloud-capped eminence divide,
  And spread the ruin round.

3
The well-informed philosopher
20 Rejoices with a wholesome fear
  And hopes, in spite of pain;
If winter bellows from the north,
Soon the sweet spring comes dancing forth,
  And nature laughs again.

25 What if thine heaven be overcast,
The dark appearance will not last;
  Expect a brighter sky.
The God that strings the silver bow,°

The Metropolitan Museum of Art, Rogers Fund, 1903 (03.14.5)

Roman wall painting, mid-first century B.C.

28. **God . . . bow:** Apollo, who was god of music and poetry and who played a golden lyre. In his destructive aspect, Apollo used the bow to slay his enemies.

To reteach these odes, have students try to think of other familiar proverbs that have similar or related themes to "The Golden Mean" or "Carpe Diem" or both. For example, "Don't throw out the baby with the bathwater" expresses a view related to "The Golden Mean." "Strike while the iron is hot" is similar to "Carpe Diem." As an alternative, students might enjoy making up their own proverbs that express or oppose Horace's views.

Awakes sometimes the Muses° too,
30   And lays his arrows by.

If hindrances obstruct thy way,
Thy <u>magnanimity</u> display,
And let thy strength be seen;
But Oh! if fortune fill thy sail
35   With more than a propitious° gale,
Take half thy canvas in.

4

29. **Muses:** nine goddesses who presided over the arts.

35. **propitious** (prō·pish′əs): favorable.

magnanimity (mag′nə·nim′ə·tē): the quality of being noble or generous

protracted (prō·trakt′id): drawn out; lengthened

4 LITERARY ELEMENT
Tone: How does the exclamation "Oh!" in line 34 affect Horace's tone in the final stanza? (Possible response: adds a note of urgency)

5 LITERARY ELEMENT
Imagery: What vivid word picture does Horace use to describe winter in lines 5–6? (the rough waves of the sea dashing against rocks)

6 LITERARY ELEMENT
Personification: How is time personified in line 9? (It is given the human quality of envy.)

Scala/Art Resource, New York

CARPE DIEM
Horace
translated by
THOMAS HAWKINS

Carpe diem is a recurring theme throughout world literature. Is Horace's idea of carpe diem *best expressed by the saying "Eat, drink, and be merry," or is Horace expressing a deeper view of the theme?*

Strive not, Leuconoe,° to know what end
The gods above to me or thee will send;
Nor with astrologers consult at all,
That thou mayst better know what can befall;
5   Whether thou liv'st more winters, or thy last
Be this, which Tyrrhen waves° 'gainst rocks do
cast.
Be wise! Drink free, and in so short a space
Do not <u>protracted</u> hopes of life embrace;
Whilst we are talking, envious time doth slide;
10   This day's thine own; the next may be denied.

5

6

1. **Leuconoe** (lyo͞o·kō′nō·ē): an intimate friend of the poet.

6. **Tyrrhen** (tir′ēn) **waves:** a reference to the Tyrrhenian Sea, a part of the Mediterranean, southwest of Italy.

1. Evaluating an Opinion. Some critics have pointed out that Horace is a difficult poet for young people to enjoy and that his lyrics are more appealing to older readers. Have students write a paragraph or two in which they agree or disagree with this opinion. Students should be sure to give reasons that support their evaluations.

2. Research Project. Some students may be interested in researching the enormous influence Horace has had on English literature, especially during the eighteenth century. Encourage such students to research Horace's influence on the poetry of Alexander Pope (1688–1744), considered by many the finest English poet of his time. Students can summarize their findings in an oral report to the class.

CLOSURE

Ask students to make believe that they can use a time machine to interview anyone in history. Would Horace be an interesting subject to interview? Why or why not? Have students discuss the questions they might ask Horace. Then have groups of students role-play an interview with Horace and perhaps Gaius Maecenas. ■

ANSWERS
First Thoughts
Answers will vary.

Identifying Facts
1. This person feels neither the wants of the poor nor the plagues of the rich.
2. try to know the future

Interpreting Meanings
1. Possible responses: future dangers compared to ocean deeps and treacherous shore; danger also in behaving rashly or timidly; wants of the poor said to "pinch"; plagues said to "haunt" the rich
2. by illustrating that life offers affliction and good fortune
3. Possible response: serene and moderate. Avoid emotional extremes.

Applying Meanings
Answers will vary.

Creative Writing Response
Writing an Advice Column.
Answers should include a summary of the reader's problem as well as an adaptation of Horatian philosophy.

Critical Writing Response
Comparing Poetic Themes. Essays should note that the first poem might seem to conflict with the second.

Language and Vocabulary
1. fortuna—chance, fate
2. timor—fear
3. contentus—contain
4. e—out + mineo—stand
5. ob—against + struo—pile up
6. magnus—great + anima—soul
7. pro—for + petere—rushing forward
8. ad—toward + verto—turn ■

▷ First Thoughts
What were the strongest impressions you had after reading these poems? Did you agree or disagree with their messages?

Identifying Facts
1. According to the second stanza of "The Golden Mean," what advantage is gained by someone who "holds fast the golden mean"?
2. In lines 1–6 of "Carpe Diem," what does the speaker advise Leuconoe *not* to do?

Interpreting Meanings
1. What **metaphors** does Horace use to present the idea of moderation in the first two stanzas of "The Golden Mean"?
2. Line 28 of "The Golden Mean" is an **allusion**, or reference, to the god Apollo, the patron of musicians, poets, and healers whom the Greeks and Romans viewed as an embodiment of beauty and reason. But Apollo could also be cruel and unforgiving. How does this allusion add to the meaning of the poem?
3. Describe the **tone** of the last four lines of "Carpe Diem." Would you say that it is enthusiastic and high-spirited, urging Leuconoe to go out and have a good time? Or is it thoughtful and even melancholy, urging Leuconoe to make the best use of time and not take life for granted? Explain.

Applying Meanings
Is Horace's advice in these poems valuable as a practical guide to life today, or are there some situations in which you would reject the speaker's philosophy? Explain your answer.

Creative Writing Response
Writing an Advice Column. Imagine that you are a writer of a newspaper advice column. Adopt the philosophy that Horace promotes in either "The Golden Mean" or "Carpe Diem" in one of your responses to a reader needing personal advice. For example, perhaps your reader wants to quit high school and travel around the country. You might advise him or her to follow a philosophy of moderation instead. Your advice to a shy and timid person who is afraid of taking risks might be quite different, however. In your response, summarize the reader's problem, give your advice, and explain why you think the philosophy of either "The Golden Mean" or "Carpe Diem" offers the best approach to dealing with the reader's problem.

Critical Writing Response
Comparing Poetic Themes. In a two- or three-paragraph essay, compare and contrast the themes of "The Golden Mean" and "Carpe Diem." Do you see any potential conflicts between the philosophies expressed in each poem? How do you think Horace would have resolved any apparent conflict?

Language and Vocabulary
Latin Word Roots

Many words in Modern English have Latin roots. Use a good dictionary to identify the **etymology**, or word origin, of the following words from "The Golden Mean." In addition to tracing the Latin word roots, identify any prefixes and suffixes that you discover.
1. fortune
2. timorously
3. contentedly
4. eminence
5. obstruct
6. magnanimity
7. propitious
8. adverse

PRIMARY SOURCES

Horace and The Art of Poetry

PARNASSUS, RAPHAEL.

? *Do you agree with Horace that the poet's aim should be "to blend in one the delightful and the useful"?*

Scala/Art Resource,
New York

Horace's The Art of Poetry *was published in 13 B.C., when the author was in his early fifties. It was probably the last work that he wrote. Although his ideas were directed mainly to writers of dramatic poetry, much of his advice is useful for any writer—and can even speak to us today. Read the following excerpts from his brief work. If you were giving advice to writers today, which of these quotations would you find useful? Which quotations do you think give good advice for your own writing?*

1 You writers, choose a subject that is within your powers, and ponder long what your shoulders can and cannot bear. He who makes every effort to select his theme aright will be at no loss for choice of words or lucid arrangement.

The secret of all good writing is sound judgment. . . . I shall bid the clever imitator to look to life and morals for his real model, and draw thence language true to life. **2**

The poet's aim is either to profit or to please, or to blend in one the delightful and the useful. Whatever the lesson you would convey, be brief, that your hearers may catch quickly what is said and faithfully retain it. Every superfluous word is spilled from the too-full memory. **3**

A kind and sensible critic will censure verses when they are weak, condemn them when they are rough; ugly lines he will score in black, will lop off pretentious ornaments, force you to clear up your obscurities, criticize a doubtful phrase, and mark what needs a change. . . .

1 LITERARY BACKGROUND
Decorum: One of Horace's key concepts in *The Art of Poetry* is the idea of decorum, or what is fitting or appropriate. Horace emphasizes that a writer's subject should be suitable to his or her abilities. He extends the idea of decorum to virtually all aspects of writing, including the length of a work, the proportions of its separate parts, and the author's choice of words and images.

2 CULTURAL BACKGROUND
Art as Imitation: The idea of art as "imitation" (or "mimesis" in Greek) was extremely influential in ancient Greece and Rome. The origins of the theory that poetry is an imitation of life or reality can be traced to Plato's *Republic*.

3 LITERARY BACKGROUND
The idea that poetry and, more broadly, literature in general should be a blend of the delightful and the useful is another key Horatian concept. In the eighteenth century in England, Samuel Johnson echoed Horace when he wrote in his *Preface to Shakespeare* (1765) that the aim of poetry is "to instruct by pleasing."

HUMANITIES CONNECTION

In *Parnassus,* Raphael (1483–1520), one of the foremost painters of the Italian High Renaissance, pictures nine great classical poets and nine of his contemporaries. Also included are the nine Muses, whose poses were copied from Roman sarcophagi. ∎

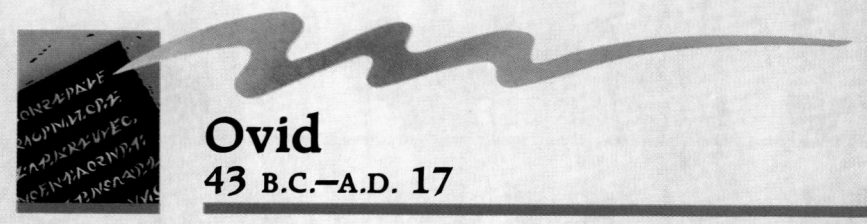

Ovid
43 B.C.–A.D. 17

MORE ABOUT THE AUTHOR

Ovid wrote poetry in a great variety of genres. Besides the *Ars Amatoria* and the *Remedia Amoris*—in which the poet posed as a wise counselor (or, in Latin, a *praeceptor amoris*, literally an "instructor in love")—Ovid's love poetry included the *Amores* ("Loves") and the *Heroides* ("Heroines"). The *Heroides* were fictitious love letters written by legendary noble ladies to absent husbands or lovers. Ovid also recorded the sadness of his miserable life of exile in the *Tristia*, verse letters to friends in Rome. Perhaps his most unusual poems were the *Halieutica*, a catalog of fishes, and *Nux*, a lament by a nut tree over the stones thrown at it by careless wayfarers.

ABOUT THE TRANSLATOR

Rolfe Humphries (1894–1969) taught Latin and English at Hunter College in New York and Amherst College in Amherst, Massachusetts. He published several volumes of his own verse, as well as translations of Virgil, Ovid, Juvenal, Lucretius, and the Spanish poet Federico García Lorca.

L ike his older contemporary, Horace, Publius Ovidius Naso, better known as Ovid (äv′id), thrived in Rome's high society. But unlike Horace, who moved in a circle that enjoyed the approval of the emperor Augustus, Ovid was attracted to Rome's more freewheeling fast set, a clique that included the emperor's unruly granddaughter, Julia. Ovid's poetry—much of which celebrated women—was considered witty and elegant, but not very serious. However, it caused the emperor Augustus a great deal of outrage, for Augustus, whose own rise to power was accomplished with much underhandedness and bloodshed, decided late in life that Rome was becoming dangerously immoral. He worried that Ovid's poetry encouraged infidelity in married women. Worse, he feared that his own granddaughter, Julia, had fallen under Ovid's influence.

In an effort to fend off Rome's decline—and a family scandal—the emperor accused Ovid of irreverence toward the state and sent him into exile. Ovid, whose only true crime may have been the possession of knowledge about Julia's promiscuous behavior, was forced to leave Rome for a remote town on the Black Sea. The Latin poet and lover of the Latin language lived out his life among foreigners.

Among Ovid's most famous surviving works are his daring *Ars Amatoria* ("The Art of Love"), a poem that graphically outlines the techniques of amorous conquest, and its tongue-in-cheek sequel, *Remedia Amoris* ("The Cures of Love"). These works reinforced the impression of Ovid as a spokesman for decadence and pleasure-seeking. In spite of this reputation, however, Ovid's works present a balanced view of both the creative and the destructive forces of human passion. These two sides of Ovid's literary concern also underlie his greatest poetic masterpiece, *Metamorphoses* (met′ə·môr′fə·sēz′). Ovid's popularity experienced a revival during the Middle Ages, when he enjoyed the reputation of a wise professor of love. His teachings contributed to the medieval concept of courtly love.

OBJECTIVES
1. To understand and interpret excerpts from an ancient Roman narrative poem
2. To identify and interpret allegory
3. To write a myth of cultural change and an essay contrasting the allegorical interpretations of Ovid's narratives

Reader's Guide

from METAMORPHOSES

Background

In *Metamorphoses,* Ovid uses the same verse form, the dactylic hexameter, employed by Homer and Virgil. The dactylic hexameter, a meter consisting of six stressed syllables per line, was traditional for Greek and Roman epics, suggesting that Ovid intended his huge collection of tales to be read as a grand epic. Unlike the epics of Homer and Virgil, however, *Metamorphoses* does not feature a central epic hero. Instead, it presents the whole range of Roman mythology—roughly two hundred poems in all—woven together in a continuous narrative sequence from the creation of the world down to the assassination of Julius Caesar.

Metamorphoses, which means "transformations," had a tremendous influence on later European literature, providing countless source-stories for writers such as Chaucer (see page 772), Boccaccio (see page 813), and Shakespeare (see page 839). Many still regard *Metamorphoses* as a model of tight narrative structure. In fact, Ovid's brief verse narratives about the transformations—seldom longer than two or three pages each—resemble short stories. Each narrative moves swiftly to establish the characters, the setting, and a central conflict, which then, more often than not, leads directly to the metamorphosis that is the heart of the story.

Writer's Response

Metamorphosis, or transformation, serves as the unifying theme of Ovid's work. Briefly describe the stages of your own life in terms of a series of metamorphoses.

Literary Focus

An **allegory** is a poem or story in which characters, settings, or events stand for other people or events, or for abstract qualities or ideas. For example, some readers have interpreted the myth of the Four Ages as an allegory for the general decline of civilization from a state of innocence to a state of strife and discord.

PREREADING FOCUS

Background: It must have been difficult for Ovid to structure so many disparate tales into a unified work. One unifying device Ovid uses in *Metamorphoses* is the hexameter verse form, while another is the general theme of transformation. Ovid also frequently uses the technique of the frame and the inset, or the tale within a tale, to tie the myths together. Finally, he creates thematic unity by grouping together tales with similar themes. An example of this technique occurs in Book 6 of *Metamorphoses*, in which the first three tales (Arachne, Niobe, and Marsyas) all concern the horrible fate of mortals who imprudently dared to boast of their equality with the gods.

Writer's Response: You may want to offer one or two suggestions of metamorphoses as springboards: for example, the child's transformation from crawling to walking or from baby talk to adult speech.

Literary Focus: You may want to point out that allegories are usually highly structured networks of symbols, in which each character, event, or detail has at least two levels of meaning.

1 COMPARING LITERATURE
Homer and Virgil began their great epic poems by invoking the Muse. Ovid echoes this convention with his statement of purpose in lines 1–4, when he calls on the gods to help him.

❓ *Why would a poet ask the help of a Muse or of the gods to tell a story?* (Possible response: to indicate that the narrative is inspired and important)

■ **inert** (in·ʉrt'): remaining in a fixed position; unchanging

discordant (dis·kôrd''nt): conflicting; unharmonious

2 CULTURAL DIVERSITY
A theory of tiny, invisible elements that could not be split (the literal meaning of the Greek word *a-tomon*) was developed by the Greek philosopher Democritus (late fifth century B.C.). The Greek philosopher Epicurus (342–271 B.C.) incorporated the theory into his philosophy, which held that the universe consisted of atoms and the void and that the goal of humans should be the enjoyment of moderate pleasures.

from METAMORPHOSES
Ovid
translated by
ROLFE HUMPHRIES

 As you read the following selections, think about how they illustrate Ovid's central theme of transformation.

1
My intention is to tell of bodies changed
To different forms; the gods, who made the changes,
Will help me—or I hope so—with a poem
That runs from the world's beginning to our own days.

The Creation

5 Before the ocean was, or earth, or heaven,
Nature was all alike, a shapelessness,
Chaos, so-called, all rude and lumpy matter,
Nothing but bulk, <u>inert</u>, in whose confusion
2 <u>Discordant</u> atoms warred: there was no sun
10 To light the universe; there was no moon
With slender silver crescents filling slowly;
No earth hung balanced in surrounding air;
No sea reached far along the fringe of shore.
Land, to be sure, there was, and air, and ocean,
15 But land on which no man could stand, and water
No man could swim in, air no man could breathe,
Air without light, substance forever changing,
Forever at war: within a single body
Heat fought with cold, wet fought with dry, the hard
20 Fought with the soft, things having weight contended
With weightless things.
        Till God, or kindlier Nature,

Participles and Participial Phrases

Participles are verb forms that function like adjectives. A participial phrase consists of a participle together with any modifiers or complements. Present participles end in *-ing*, such as "surrounding air." Past participles of regular verbs end in *-d* or *-ed*, such as "of bodies changed." Some verbs, however, have irregular past participle forms, such as "<u>burnt</u> air." Poets sometimes invert the word order of participial phrases. For example, the participial phrase in line 11 of "The Creation" would read this way in normal word order: "filling slowly with slender silver crescents."

Writing and Sharing. Ask students to write a letter from Ovid to the emperor Augustus that protests his exile from Rome (see p. 420). Tell students to use at least four participial phrases. Partners can read each other's letters and underline the phrases. ■

3

  Settled all argument, and separated
  Heaven from earth, water from land, our air
  From the high stratosphere, a liberation
25 So things evolved, and out of blind confusion
  Found each its place, bound in eternal order.

4

  The force of fire, that weightless element,
  Leaped up and claimed the highest place in
      heaven;
  Below it, air; and under them the earth
30 Sank with its grosser portions; and the water,
  Lowest of all, held up, held in, the land.

5

  Whatever god it was, who out of chaos
  Brought order to the universe, and gave it
  Division, subdivision, he molded earth,
35 In the beginning, into a great globe,
  Even on every side, and <u>bade</u> the waters
  To spread and rise, under the rushing winds,
  Surrounding earth; he added ponds and marshes,
  He banked the river-channels, and the waters
40 Feed earth or run to sea, and that great flood

Giraudon/Art Resource, New York

CELESTIAL ATLAS: SOUTHERN HEMISPHERE, GÈRARD VALK AND PIETER SCHENK, 1708

3 GUIDED READING

Cause and Effect: What two alternative causes does Ovid give for the separation of heaven from earth? ("God," "kindlier Nature")

4 CULTURAL DIVERSITY

Many of the Greek pre-Socratic philosophers of the sixth and fifth centuries B.C. developed theories about the primal substance(s) of the universe. Thales, for example, thought that all things were basically made of water, while Heraclitus theorized that everything was made of fire. Later philosophers recognized four basic elements: fire, air, water, and earth. Ovid reflects this theory of the four elements in lines 27–31.

❓ *What are some modern scientific theories about the basic elements of the universe?* (Answers will vary.)

■ bade (bad): commanded

5 COMPARING LITERATURE

The Book of Genesis (see pp. 162–168) presents a strikingly similar account of the creation that is described here in lines 32–80. In both accounts, God first makes the heavens and the earth and then creates the oceans, the features of the land, the animals, and finally human beings.

torrid (tôr'id): subject to intense heat, especially from the sun

sage (sāj): a wise person

Meeting Individual Needs

6 *LEP:* Be sure your students understand that in lines 48–50 Ovid excludes two of the earth's climatic regions ("torrid" and polar) as too hot and too cold, respectively, for human habitation. The opinion Ovid expresses here, of course, reflects ancient and limited concepts of geography and climate. ■

7 Literary Element

Personification: How does Ovid personify the winds in lines 57–59? (as quarreling brothers)

8 Guided Reading

Cause and Effect: According to lines 72–74, what was the reason for the creation of human beings? (because a "sage" or "ruler" was needed)

Washes on shores, not banks. He made the plains
Spread wide, the valleys settle, and the forest
Be dressed in leaves; he made the rocky
  mountains
Rise to full height, and as the vault of Heaven
Has two zones, left and right, and one between
  them
Hotter than these, the Lord of all Creation
Marked on the earth the same design and pattern.
The torrid zone too hot for men to live in,
6 The north and south too cold, but in the middle
Varying climate, temperature and season.
Above all things the air, lighter than earth,
Lighter than water, heavier than fire,
Towers and spreads; there mist and cloud
  assemble,
And fearful thunder and lightning and cold winds,
But these, by the Creator's order, held
No general dominion; even as it is,
These brothers brawl and quarrel; though
7   each one
Has his own quarter, still, they come near tearing
The universe apart. Eurus is monarch
Of the lands of dawn, the realms of Araby,
The Persian ridges under the rays of morning.
Zephyrus holds the west that glows at sunset,
Boreas, who makes men shiver, holds the north,
Warm Auster governs in the misty southland,
And over them all presides the weightless ether,
Pure without taint of earth.
                    These boundaries given,
Behold, the stars, long hidden under darkness,
Broke through and shone, all over the spangled
  heaven,
Their home forever, and the gods lived there,
And shining fish were given the waves for
  dwelling
And beasts the earth, and birds the moving air.

But something else was needed, a finer being,
8 More capable of mind, a sage, a ruler,
So Man was born, it may be, in God's image,
Or Earth, perhaps, so newly separated

From the old fire of Heaven, still retained
Some seed of the celestial force which fashioned
Gods out of living clay and running water.
All other animals look downward; Man,
80 Alone, erect, can raise his face toward Heaven.

The Four Ages

The Golden Age was first, a time that cherished
Of its own will, justice and right; no law,
No punishment, was called for; fearfulness
Was quite unknown, and the bronze tablets held
85 No legal threatening; no suppliant throng
Studied a judge's face; there were no judges,
There did not need to be. Trees had not yet
Been cut and hollowed, to visit other shores.
Men were content at home, and had no towns
90 With moats and walls around them; and no
      trumpets
Blared out alarums; things like swords and
      helmets
Had not been heard of. No one needed soldiers.
People were unaggressive, and unanxious;
The years went by in peace. And Earth,
      untroubled,
95 Unharried by hoe or plowshare, brought forth all
That men had need for, and those men were
      happy,
Gathering berries from the mountainsides,
Cherries, or blackcaps, and the edible acorns.
Spring was forever, with a west wind blowing
100 Softly across the flowers no man had planted,
And Earth, unplowed, brought forth rich grain;
      the field,
Unfallowed, whitened with wheat, and there were
      rivers
Of milk, and rivers of honey, and golden nectar
Dripped from the dark-green oak-trees.

                          After Saturn°
105 Was driven to the shadowy land of death,
And the world was under Jove, the Age of Silver
Came in, lower than gold, better than bronze.
Jove made the springtime shorter, added winter,

**Medieval manuscript page of
Metamorphoses depicting
Jupiter's revolt against Saturn.**

104. **Saturn:** the Roman god of
the seasonal cycle, loosely
associated with Cronus the
Titan, who was overthrown
by his son Zeus (Jove, or Jupiter).

9 LITERARY ELEMENT
Allegory: What abstract quality
of human beings might the detail about Man's ability to
"raise his face toward Heaven"
stand for allegorically? (Possible responses: human
pride, nobility, or spiritual
aspirations)

10 GUIDED READING
Finding the Main Idea: Explain Ovid's main idea in lines
81–87 in your own words. (Possible response: At first, no
laws were needed because
people were naturally just.)

11 LITERARY ELEMENT
Imagery: To what senses do
the images in lines 97–104 appeal? (Possible responses:
touch, sight, smell, and taste)

■ **unfallowed** (un·fal′ōd):
land cultivated instead of
left idle

HUMANITIES CONNECTION

The earliest known illustrated
manuscripts come from an-
cient Egypt, and manuscript illumination reached its height
in the Middle Ages. Little survives of ancient Greek illumination, although epic poetry
and scientific treatises are said
to have contained illustrations.
❓ *How does the illustration
on this page give life to the
footnote on lines 104–105
about Saturn?* (It shows Jupiter's successful military
overthrow.) ■

Ovid   **425**

READING CHECK

1. What existed before the creation? (chaos)
2. How many quarreling winds does Ovid mention? (four)
3. Who is the only animal that can look upward? (man)
4. In which of the Four Ages did Jove create the four seasons? (the Age of Silver)
5. In which age did Justice flee from the earth? (the Iron Age)

RETEACHING

To reteach Ovid's *Metamorphoses*, divide the class into small groups and invite each group to select one of the scenes described in the selections. Have students work together to illustrate this scene with a drawing, a painting, or a collage. When students have completed their work, invite them to share their illustrations with the class.

12 SPECULATING

Ovid gives very few details about the Age of Bronze. Based on what you have read about the other ages, what specific details would you choose to describe life in this age? (Possible response: There was hostility among people, but there was still a sense of justice and morality.)

13 LITERARY ELEMENT

Personification: What words in lines 134–135 show that Ovid is personifying "iron" and "gold" by giving them human qualities? ("guilt" and "guilty")

> ▪ **revel** (rev′əl): to make merry; celebrate
>
> **brandished** (bran′disht): handled in an exultant manner
>
> **dire** (dīr): arousing terror or distress
>
> **piety** (pī′ə·tē): devotion to religious duties

MEETING INDIVIDUAL NEEDS

14 LEP: Be sure that students recognize that Piety (line 142) and Justice (line 143) are personifications of abstract qualities. ▪

Summer, and autumn, the seasons as we know
    them.
110 That was the first time when the burnt air glowed
White-hot, or icicles hung down in winter.
And men built houses for themselves; the caverns,
The woodland thickets, and the bark-bound
    shelters
No longer served; and the seeds of grain were
    planted
115 In the long furrows, and the oxen struggled
Groaning and laboring under the heavy yoke.

12 ⎡ Then came the Age of Bronze, and dispositions
     Took on aggressive instincts, quick to arm,
     Yet not entirely evil. And last of all
120 The Iron Age succeeded, whose base vein
Let loose all evil: modesty and truth
And righteousness fled earth, and in their place
Came trickery and slyness, plotting, swindling,
Violence and the damned desire of having.
125 Men spread their sails to winds unknown to
    sailors,
The pines came down their mountainsides,
    to <u>revel</u>
And leap in the deep waters, and the ground,
Free, once, to everyone, like air and sunshine,
Was stepped off by surveyors. The rich earth,
130 Good giver of all the bounty of the harvest,
Was asked for more; they dug into her vitals,
Pried out the wealth a kinder lord had hidden
In Stygian shadow,° all that precious metal,

13 ⎣ 135 The root of evil. They found the guilt of iron,
     And gold, more guilty still. And War came forth
That uses both to fight with; bloody hands
<u>Brandished</u> the clashing weapons. Men lived on
    plunder.
Guest was not safe from host, nor brother from
    brother,
A man would kill his wife, a wife her husband,
140 Stepmothers, <u>dire</u> and dreadful, stirred their brews

14 ⎡ With poisonous aconite, and sons would hustle
     Fathers to death, and <u>Piety</u> lay vanquished,
     And the maiden Justice, last of all immortals,
     Fled from the bloody earth.

Giraudon/Art Resource, New York

The god Mars, or a fighting warrior. Etruscan statue, 5th century B.C.

133. **Stygian** (stij′ē·ən) **shadow:** the netherworld, through which the River Styx is said to flow.

EXTENSION AND ENRICHMENT

1. **Reacting to a Quote.** The translator Rolfe Humphries wrote: "There are . . . times when Ovid is bored, and shows it. . . . But presently . . . it [his writing] brightens again, and here is the old insight back, the fun, the delight. . . ." Have students evaluate Humphries' judgment of Ovid. Suggest that they find passages elsewhere in *Metamorphoses* that might bore a reader and others that "brighten again."

2. **Research Project.** Some of your students may be interested in the enormous influence Ovid had on European writers during the Middle Ages and the Renaissance. Encourage these students to research the impact of Ovid's *Metamorphoses* or of his other works on medieval and Renaissance Europe. Invite students to report their findings to the class.

CLOSURE

Remind students that Ovid was a poet of remarkable talent who seems to have been able to write charming verse about almost any subject. Ask students what subjects they think Ovid would choose for his poetry if he were writing today. Have them hold a discussion to suggest and explore some interesting topics for a contemporary Ovid. ∎

First Thoughts

How did you visualize the Golden Age as described by Ovid?

Identifying Facts

1. What was nature like before the creation? After the creation, what warring pairs of elements continued to threaten to "tear the universe apart"?
2. According to "The Creation," how do human beings differ from the animals?
3. Identify the Four Ages. What are the characteristics of each age?

Interpreting Meanings

1. Ovid's poetic treatment of the process of creation bears a number of striking similarities to the biblical account in the Book of Genesis (see page 163). What are some of these similarities?
2. An **allegory** is a work in which characters, setting, or events stand for more general ideas. How can "The Four Ages" be read as an allegory for the decline of humanity from a state of innocence? Find three or four examples from the text that contribute to this allegorical interpretation. Decide whether the last age, the Age of Iron, can be read as an allegory for our own day.
3. During the Golden Age, only one of the four seasons exists. What is this season, and why is it appropriate?
4. What, if anything, motivates each of the stages of decline in "The Four Ages"? Does a human action precede each stage of degeneration, or is the decline beyond human control? Discuss.

Applying Meanings

Allegories about the decline of civilization accept as a premise that there was once a Golden Age—that civilization was indeed once nearer to paradise than it is now. Do you believe that this premise is true? Do you think that there literally was a time when life on earth was peaceful and harmonious? Argue your opinion.

Creative Writing Response

Writing a Myth. Make up your own brief myth that explains the development of American culture from some point in the past to the present. Where your myth begins is up to you: You could, for example, choose to begin thousands of years before the arrival of Columbus, the Pilgrims' landing at Plymouth Rock in 1620, or the American Revolution of 1776. Like Ovid, you may want to designate a certain number of "ages" or "stages" for your myth. For each age, give a few notable characteristics or events, or provide a description that helps to distinguish that era from the others.

Critical Writing Response

Comparing Allegorical Interpretations of Myths. The characters, settings, and events in an **allegory** may stand for other people or events, or for abstract qualities or ideas. In a brief essay, discuss how "The Creation" and "The Four Ages" might be interpreted as contrasting allegorical stories. How does "The Creation" suggest an optimistic point of view about the inevitability of progress? How does "The Four Ages" suggest a pessimistic viewpoint about the inevitability of decline? In your essay, be sure to support your points with specific references to the stories. A chart like the one below might help you to organize your ideas.

	Creation	Four Ages
Characterization of humans		
Characterization of gods		

Ovid   **427**

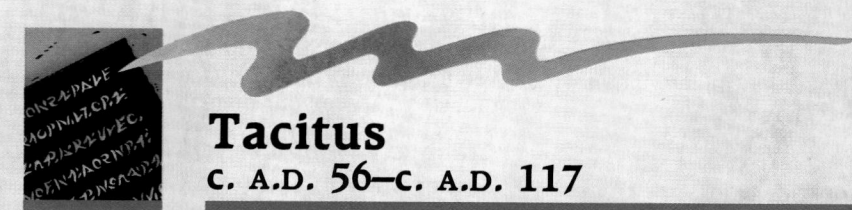

Tacitus
c. A.D. 56–c. A.D. 117

The Bettmann Archive

If Cornelius Tacitus (tas′i·təs) had lived in
another age, he might have become a
great statesman. He was an exceptionally
skilled orator, and he served Rome in a variety of public offices. He spent a good part
of his life, however, under the tyrannical rule
of unusually cruel and corrupt emperors. He
grew up, for example, during the reign of
Nero (nir′ō), who ruled A.D. 54–68, and spent
most of his adult years under the reign of
the sadistic Domitian (də·mish′ən), who
ruled A.D. 81–96.

Tacitus' firsthand observations of the injustice and cruelty of the Roman emperors
of his time drove him to take up the pen.
Nearly all of Tacitus' writing shows a spirit
of defiance. His first published work, *Agri-
cola*, was a defense of his father-in-law, a
public official who had been treated unjustly.

Tacitus is best known for his two historical works, of which only fragments have
survived. The *Annals* depicts the troubled
reigns of Tiberius, Caligula, Claudius, and
Nero, which took place between the years
A.D. 14 and A.D. 68. The *Histories* continues
the chronicle up to the death of Domitian in
A.D. 96. Tacitus also wrote an important treatise on rhetoric, or the art of persuasive
speaking, called *Dialogues of the Orators*.

Modern readers expect histories to be
complete, accurate, and "objective," that is,
written without directly revealing the writer's bias or point of view. Objective writing
allows the reader to form his or her own
opinions and conclusions. The notion of objective historical writing dates back to the
earliest Greek historians, particularly Thucydides. But Tacitus seems to have felt differently. He often allowed his emotions and
personal convictions to appear in his narrative. His contempt for the emperors' abuses
of power and for those Romans who hypo-
critically flattered the rulers is also clear.

Tacitus thought history should be used for
moral purposes: He believed that the evil
deeds of powerful people should not be forgotten after their deaths; he also believed
that good deeds should be recorded and
praised. Whether or not Tacitus exaggerated
or distorted details to suit his own purposes,
as some of his critics have claimed, he contributed perhaps more than any other source
to the shaping of our picture of the early
Roman Empire.

OBJECTIVES
1. *To identify the characteristics of a sample of Roman historical writing*
2. *To analyze and evaluate Tacitus' writing style*
3. *To rewrite Tacitus' account, changing the overall tone from negative to positive*
4. *To recognize and distinguish between the connotations of words*

THEMES IN WORLD LITERATURE

The Uses and Abuses of Power
"The Wooden People" from the Popol Vuh, pp. 17–21
The Tempest, pp. 839–932

The Nature of Evil
"Black Cat," p. 1150
"The Rat Trap," pp. 1196–1206 ∎

VOCABULARY IN CONTEXT
The words listed below will appear in the side margin at the point of instruction:
1. calamitous
2. tortuous
3. inextricable
4. conducive
5. propitiate
6. bounty
7. atoning
8. iniquity
9. avowal
10. slaking

Reader's Guide

THE BURNING OF ROME

Background

This selection, which describes a disastrous fire that swept through Rome in A.D. 64, is drawn from Book XV of Tacitus' *Annals*. It offers a fine example of the historian's preoccupation with moral bankruptcy and general ruin. Nero, whose actions lie at the center of Tacitus' account, became emperor of Rome in A.D. 54 at the age of seventeen. Although the young ruler and his advisers initiated some enlightened programs during his first five years in power, the emperor became steadily more vain, corrupt, and violent. In addition to revealing Tacitus' bitterness and disgust toward Nero's irresponsibility during the crisis of the fire, this account also records for the first time the reaction of first-century pagan Rome toward the new religion of Christianity.

Writer's Response

Why would it be important for a historian to distinguish between fact and opinion? Is it even possible to write objectively about history? Freewrite your answer.

Literary Focus

Style is the way a writer expresses his or her thoughts through language. All writers have some idea about how they can best convey their ideas. As a result, they make decisions about which words to use, how long or short the sentences and paragraphs should be, and what images and figures of speech are appropriate and fitting. Style is often viewed separately from content, but often the style is what makes the content memorable.

PREREADING FOCUS

Background: One of Tacitus' most shocking narratives is his account in Book 14 of the *Annals* of Nero's arrangements for the murder of his mother, Agrippina, in A.D. 59. When a bizarre plan involving a ship-wreck failed, Nero dispatched his freedman Anicetus to assassinate Agrippina. Tacitus writes:

> The assassins closed in round her couch, and the captain of the trireme [ship] first struck her head violently with a club. Then, as the centurion bared his sword for the fatal deed, presenting her person, she exclaimed, "Smite my womb," and with many wounds she was slain. . . . Many years before, Agrippina had anticipated this end for herself and had spurned the thought. For when she consulted the astrologers about Nero, they replied that he would be emperor and kill his mother. "Let him kill her," she said, "provided he is emperor." (*Annals* 14.8–9)

Writer's Response: As a springboard for class discussion, you may wish to invite students to discuss controversial films about historical subjects, such as Oliver Stone's *JFK* (1991).

Literary Focus: You may want to suggest to students that an author's style is a very important component of his or her *tone*, or attitude toward the subject.

THE BURNING OF ROME
from The Annals
Tacitus
translated by
GEORGE GILBERT RAMSAY

◆ *As you read, note how effectively Tacitus suits his style to his subject. Notice his choice of language and the way he forms his sentences in his description of a traumatic time in Roman history.*

Bust of Nero, emperor of Rome.

Lee Boltin Picture Library

And now came a calamitous fire—whether it was accidental or purposely contrived by the Emperor remains uncertain for on this point authorities are divided—more violent and destructive than any that ever befell our city. It began in that part of the Circus[1] which adjoins the Palatine and Caelian hills.[2] Breaking out in shops full of inflammable merchandise, it took hold and gathered strength at once; and being fanned by the wind soon embraced the entire length of the Circus, where there were no mansions with protective walls, no temple-enclosures, nor anything else to arrest its course. Furiously the destroying flames swept on, first over the level ground, then up the heights, then again plunging into the hollows, with a rapidity which outstripped all efforts to cope with them, the ancient city lending itself to their progress by its narrow tortuous streets and its misshapen blocks of buildings. The

---
1. **Circus:** Circus Maximus, a great arena used for chariot races.
2. **Palatine** (pal′ə·tīn′) **and Caelian** (sē′lē·ən) **hills:** two of the seven hills of ancient Rome.

shrieks of panic-stricken women; the weakness of the aged, and the helplessness of the young; the efforts of some to save themselves, of others to help their neighbors; the hurrying of those who dragged their sick along, the lingering of those who waited for them—all made up a scene of <u>inextricable</u> confusion.

Many persons, while looking behind them, were enveloped from the front or from the side; or having escaped to the nearest place of safety, found this, too, in possession of the flames, and even places which they had thought beyond their reach in the same plight with the rest. At last, not knowing where to turn, or what to avoid, they poured into the roads or threw themselves down in the fields: some having lost their all, not having even food for the day; others, though with means of escape open to them, preferred to perish for love of the dear ones whom they could not save. And none dared to check the flames; for there were many who threatened and forced back those who would extinguish them, while others openly flung in torches, saying that *they had their orders;*—whether it really was so, or only that they wanted to plunder undisturbed.

At this moment Nero was at Antium.[3] He did not return to the city until the flames were approaching the mansion which he had built to connect the Palatine with the Gardens of Maecenas;[4] nor could they be stopped until the whole Palatine, including the palace and everything around it, had been consumed. Nero assigned the Campus Martius[5] and the Agrippa[6] monuments for the relief of the fugitive and houseless multitude. He threw open his own gardens also, and put up temporary buildings for the accommodation of the destitute; he brought up provisions from Ostia and the neighboring towns; and he reduced the price of corn to three sesterces[7] the peck. But popular as these measures were, they aroused no gratitude; for a rumor had got abroad that at the moment when the city was in flames Nero had mounted upon a stage in his own house, and by way of likening modern calamities to ancient, had sung the tale of the sack of Troy.

Not until the sixth day was the fire got under, at the foot of the Esquiline hill,[8] by demolishing a vast extent of buildings, so as to present nothing but the ground, and as it were the open sky, to its continued fury. But scarcely had the alarm subsided, or the populace recovered from their despair, when it burst out again in the more open parts of the city; and though here the loss of life was less, the destruction of temples and porticoes of pleasance was still more complete. And the scandal attending this new fire was the greater that it broke out in property owned by Tigellinus,[9] in the Aemilian[10]

---

3. **Antium** (ant′i·əm): a seaside town about thirty-two miles south of Rome, and Nero's birthplace; it is now called Anzio.
4. **Gardens of Maecenas** (mī·sē′nəs): a luxurious pleasure palace built by Maecenas, an intimate supporter of the Emperor Augustus and an important patron of literary men, including Horace and Virgil.
5. **Campus Martius** (mär·shəs): the Field of Mars, an area of central Rome, originally the site of a temple of Mars; it was later expanded to include a great many buildings, including baths, temples, and gardens constructed for Agrippa around 25 B.C.
6. **Agrippa** (ə·grip′ə): Marcus Vipsanius Agrippa (63–12 B.C.), a Roman military leader.
7. **sesterces** (ses·tûr′sēz): silver pieces, each worth about five cents.
8. **Esquiline** (es′kwə·līn′) **hill:** one of the seven hills of ancient Rome.
9. **Tigellinus** (tĭj′ə·lī′nəs): Nero's worthless friend, who joined and encouraged the emperor in his cruelties and debaucheries.
10. **Aemilian** (i·mē′li·ən)

3 LITERARY ELEMENT
Parallel Structure: How does the use of parallel structure here contribute to the mood of this scene? (The linking of opposites—the aged and the young, the hurrying and the lingering, and so on—through parallel structure contributes to the atmosphere of chaos and confusion.)

■ **inextricable** (in·eks′·tri·kə·bəl): relating to something from which one cannot get disentangled

4 EVALUATING
Tacitus states that the authorities may have deliberately encouraged the fire to spread. How strong is the evidence Tacitus offers in support of this theory? (His evidence is weak and not specific. He does not give names, and his one report of what was said is vague.)

5 COMPARING LITERATURE
The burning of Troy is the subject of the second book of Virgil's epic, the *Aeneid* (see pp. 383–406). The story that "Nero fiddled while Rome burned," which Tacitus describes as a "rumor," may or may not be true.

6 CULTURAL DIVERSITY

Tacitus had ample basis for his view that Nero suffered from megalomania, or insane egotism. The emperor, whose enthusiasm for Greek culture and for his own artistic abilities was boundless, founded a series of athletic games at Rome that were called the Neronia. During a visit to Greece in A.D. 67, Nero competed in the Olympic Games and had himself awarded well over a thousand prizes.

❓ *Can you think of examples of contemporary figures whose power or prominence led to excess or loss of good judgment?* (Possible responses: Saddam Hussein; Ferdinand and Imelda Marcos)

7 HISTORICAL BACKGROUND

Servius Tullius was the sixth of the seven kings of early Rome and ruled in the mid-sixth century B.C. Evander was a legendary king before the founding of Rome, who furnished important support for Aeneas after that hero's landing in Italy (see pp. 383–406).

■ HUMANITIES CONNECTION

Brewer's Dictionary of Phrase and Fable defines "fiddling while Rome burns" as "trifling during an emergency or crisis." As Tacitus reports the original rumor, Nero mounted a stage in his own house and sang the tale of the sack of Troy. ■

THE EMPEROR PLAYING HIS LYRE WHILE ROME BURNED, nineteenth-century engraving.
❓ *Why do you think the subject of Nero and the burning of Rome would be interesting to modern audiences and modern artists?*

6 quarter; the general belief being that Nero had the ambition to build a new city to be called after his own name. For of the fourteen regions into which Rome was divided only four remained intact. Three were burnt to the ground; in the other seven, nothing remained save a few fragments of ruined and half-burnt houses.

To count up the number of mansions, of tenements, and of temples that were destroyed would be no easy matter. Among the oldest of the sacred buildings burnt was **7** that dedicated by Servius Tullius to the Moon, and the Great Altar and fane[11] raised by Evander to the Present Hercules. The temple vowed by Romulus[12] to Jupiter, the Stayer of Flight; the Royal Palace of Numa;[13] the Temple of Vesta,[14] with the Household Gods[15] of the Roman people, were all destroyed; added to these were the treasures won in numerous battles, and masterpieces of Greek art, as well as ancient and genuine monuments of Roman genius which were remembered by the older generation amid all the splendor of the restored city, and which could never be replaced. Some noted that the nineteenth of July, the day on which the fire began, was also the day on which the Senonian Gauls[16] had taken and burnt the

---

11. **fane** (fān): sanctuary or temple.
12. **Romulus** (räm'yoo·ləs): the legendary founder of Rome.

13. **Numa:** Numa Pompilius (noo'mə päm·pil'i·əs): second king of Rome; he succeeded Romulus.
14. **Vesta** (ves'tə): goddess of the hearth.
15. **Household Gods:** the Lares (lā'rez') and Penates (pē·nā'tēz'), minor deities that presided over family and home.
16. **Senonian Gauls** (sə·nō'ni·ən gôlz): barbarians from northern Italy who captured and burned Rome about 390 B.C.

city; others were so curious in their calculations as to discover that the two burnings were separated from one another by exactly the same number of years, of months, and of days.

Nero profited by the ruin of his country to erect a palace in which the marvels were not to be gold and jewels, the usual and common-place objects of luxury, so much as lawns and lakes and mock-wildernesses, with woods on one side and open glades and vistas on the other. His engineers and masters-of-works were Severus and Celer; men who had the ingenuity and the impudence to fool away the resources of the Empire in the attempt to provide by Art what Nature had pronounced impossible.

For these men undertook to dig a navigable canal, along the rocky shore and over the hills, all the way from Lake Avernus to the mouths of the Tiber.[17] There was no other water for supplying such a canal than that of the Pontine marshes;[18] and even if practicable, the labor would have been prodigious, and no object served. But Nero had a thirst for the incredible, and traces of his vain attempt to excavate the heights adjoining Lake Avernus are to be seen to this day.

The parts of the city unoccupied by Nero's palace were not built over without divisions, or indiscriminately, as after the Gallic fire, but in blocks of regular dimensions, with broad streets between. A limit was placed to the height of houses; open spaces were left; and colonnades were added to protect the fronts of tenements, Nero undertaking to build these at his own cost, and to hand over the building sites, cleared of rubbish, to the proprietors. He offered premiums also, in proportion to the rank and means of owners, on condition of mansions or tenements being completed within a given time; and he assigned the marshes at Ostia for the reception of the rubbish, which was taken down the Tiber in the same vessels which had brought up the corn. Certain parts of the houses were to be built without beams, and of solid stone, Gabian or Alban, those stones being impervious to fire. Then as water had often been improperly intercepted by individuals, inspectors were appointed to secure a more abundant supply, and over a larger area, for public use; owners were required to keep appliances for quenching fire in some open place; party walls were forbidden, and every house had to be enclosed within walls of its own.

These useful provisions added greatly to the appearance of the new city; and yet there were not wanting persons who thought that the plan of the old city was more conducive to health, as the narrow streets and high roofs were a protection against the rays of the sun, which now beat down with double fierceness upon broad and shadeless thoroughfares.

Such were the measures suggested by human counsels; after which means were taken to propitiate the Gods. The Sibylline books[19] were consulted, and prayers were offered, as prescribed by them, to Vulcan, to Ceres, and to Proserpine. Juno[20] was supplicated by

---

17. **Lake Avernus** (ə·vur′nəs): a small lake near Cumae, in the center of an extinct volcano; **Tiber:** The Tiber River runs through Rome.
18. **Pontine** (pän′tēn) **marshes:** a swampy region between Rome and Naples.
19. **Sibylline** (sib′ə·līn′) **books:** nine ancient books, supposedly written by the Sybil, or prophetess; these books reveal the destiny of Rome.
20. **Vulcan** (vul′kən): god of fire and metalworking; **Ceres** (sir′ēz): goddess of grain and harvest; **Proserpine** (prō·sur′pi·nə): wife of Pluto, king of Hades; **Juno** (jōō′nō): queen of the gods and goddess of marriage.

Tacitus   **433**

READING CHECK

1. Where was Nero when the fire broke out? (outside Rome at Antium)
2. How many days did the fire last? (six)
3. When a second fire broke out, what did the people believe about Nero? (that he set it)

4. How does Tacitus say that Nero profited from the fire? (He built a luxurious new palace and park.)
5. What spectacle involving Christians occurred in Nero's gardens? (burning Christians alive)

RETEACHING

To reteach this excerpt from Tacitus, ask students to list some of the ways in which the historian creates an unfavorable picture of the emperor Nero. Then have student volunteers prepare a skit, dramatizing the behavior of the villainous Nero and his friends at Nero's seaside home while Rome burned.

■ **bounty** (boun'tē): reward; generosity

atoning (ə·tōn'iŋ): making amends for

iniquity (i·nik'wi·tē): wickedness

avowal (ə·vou'əl): an open acknowledgment or declaration

slaking (slāk'iŋ): satisfying

10 GUIDED READING

Identifying Cause and Effect:
According to Tacitus, what was Nero's secret reason for using the Christians as scapegoats? (to end the suspicion that Nero himself had ordered the burning of Rome)

11 LITERARY ELEMENT

Understatement: How does Tacitus' use of understatement emphasize the horror of the burning of the Christians? (Possible response: He calls attention to the horror by matter-of-factly commenting that the burning of human beings served "the purpose of lamps when daylight failed.")

the matrons, in the Capitol first, and afterwards at the nearest point upon the sea, from which water was drawn to sprinkle the temple and image of the Goddess; banquets to the Goddesses and all-night festivals were celebrated by married women.

But neither human aid, nor imperial bounty, nor atoning-offerings to the Gods, could remove the sinister suspicion that the fire had been brought about by Nero's order. To put an end therefore to this rumor, he shifted the charge onto others, and inflicted the most cruel tortures upon a body of men detested for their abominations, and popularly known by the name of Christians. This name came from one Christus, who was put to death in the reign of Tiberius by the Procurator Pontius Pilate; but though checked for the time, the detestable superstition broke out again, not in Judaea only, where the mischief began, but even in Rome, where every horrible and shameful iniquity, from every quarter of the world, pours in and finds a welcome.

First those who acknowledged themselves of this persuasion were arrested; and upon their testimony a vast number were condemned, not so much on the charge of incendiarism as for their hatred of the human race. Their death was turned into a diversion. They were clothed in the skins of wild beasts, and torn to pieces by dogs; they were fastened to crosses, or set up to be burned, so as to serve the purpose of lamps when daylight failed. Nero gave up his own gardens for this spectacle; he provided also Circensian games,[21] during which he mingled with the populace, or took his stand upon a chariot, in the garb of a charioteer. But guilty as these men were and worthy of direst punishment, the fact that they were being sacrificed for no public good, but only to glut the cruelty of one man, aroused a feeling of pity on their behalf.

Meanwhile Italy was ransacked for contributions. The provinces and allied peoples were rifled, as well as the states which are called 'free.' Even the Gods had to submit to being plundered. The temples in the city were despoiled, and emptied of the gold consecrated at triumphs, or vowed by past generations of Romans in times of panic or prosperity. As for Asia and Achaia,[22] not offerings only, but the very images of the Gods were carried off by Acratus and Secundus Carrinas, who were sent out to those provinces for the purpose. The former was a freedman ready for any kind of villainy; the latter was a man whose lips were tinged with Greek learning, but who had no real culture in his heart.

We are told that Seneca[23] craved leave to withdraw to a remote country retreat to avoid the odium of such sacrilege; on this being denied him, he pretended to be suffering from some muscular ailment, and shut himself up in his own chamber. Other accounts say that Nero ordered poison to be administered to him by one of his own freedmen, called Cleonicus; but that Seneca escaped the trap, either by the man's avowal, or by his own precaution in adopting a simple diet of natural fruits, and slaking his thirst from running water.

---

21. **Circensian** (sûr·ken'si·ən) **games:** games held in the Circus, or arena.

22. **Asia and Achaia** (ə·kā'ə): Asia Minor and Greece.
23. **Seneca** (sen'i·kə): Nero's minister of state, a Stoic philosopher; he retired from office in A.D. 62. He was forced to commit suicide as the result of a court intrigue in A.D. 65.

1. **Evaluating a Historian's Purpose.** Tacitus writes: "My purpose is not to relate at length every motion [in the Senate], but only such as were conspicuous for excellence or notorious for infamy. This I regard as history's highest function, to let no worthy action be uncommemorated, and to hold out the reprobation of posterity as a terror to evil words and deeds." (*Annals* 3.65). Ask students to debate this view.

2. **Research Project.** Tacitus' *Annals* also offers memorable portraits of the emperors Tiberius (ruled A.D. 14–37) in Books 1–6 and of Claudius (ruled A.D. 41–54) in Books 11–12. Interested students may research Tacitus' accounts of these rulers and summarize their findings in an oral report.

CLOSURE

Are students impressed with or skeptical of Tacitus' method of recording history and of describing events? Ask them to discuss their responses to Tacitus as a writer and a historian. Is Tacitus interesting to read? Why or why not? Is he reliable as a source of information about the past? ■

First Thoughts

Do you think this is an eyewitness report of the burning of Rome, rather than a secondhand account of the disaster?

Identifying Facts

1. According to Tacitus, why was nothing done to stop the burning of Rome?
2. When a second fire broke out in the open parts of the city, what rumor about the emperor was circulated? What steps did Nero take to squelch this rumor?
3. How did Nero pay for the rebuilding of Rome?

Interpreting Meanings

1. Locate the details that describe Nero. What impression do these details create of the emperor? Which details might have led another historian to a different conclusion?
2. Consider Tacitus' description of the first outbreak of the fire in Rome in the first paragraph (see page 430). Judging from his use of language, his tone, and his images, how would you describe his **style**? For example, is it concise, impassioned, or detached? Support your answer with examples from the selection.
3. Tacitus' famous passage about the Christians is one of the earliest historical references to Christianity by a non-Christian writer. How does Tacitus show that he is prejudiced against the Christians? On what grounds does he express anger about their persecution?

Applying Meanings

If you were the editor in chief of a major daily newspaper, and Tacitus put in an application for a job as a reporter, would you give him the job? Why or why not?

Creative Writing Response

Rewriting an Account. You are one of the historical "authorities" whom Tacitus mentions on page 430. You believe the fire at Rome was accidental, and that Nero did his best to relieve the people's hardship and to rebuild the city. Write a short account of the fire, changing the tone toward the emperor from negative to positive.

Language and Vocabulary

Exploring Connotations

The **connotations** of words—as distinct from their literal meanings or **denotations**—are their associations or emotional overtones. Tacitus uses words whose connotations seem calculated to have an emotional impact on the reader. Such a style, of course, influences the reader indirectly. By using **loaded language**, language that appeals to readers' emotions, Tacitus reveals his own prejudices.

Reread the following passages. Then explain how the connotations of the italicized words or phrases differ from those of the words or phrases given in parentheses.

1. "But Nero had *a thirst for the incredible,* and traces of his *vain* attempt to excavate the heights adjoining Lake Avernus are to be seen to this day." (a taste for the unusual; unsuccessful)
2. "To put an end therefore to this rumor, he shifted the charge on to others; and inflicted the most cruel tortures upon a body of men detested for their *abominations,* and popularly known by the name of Christians." (crimes)
3. " . . . but though checked for the time, the *detestable superstition* broke out again, not in Judaea only, where the *mischief* began, but even in Rome. . . ." (religious belief; trouble)

LANGUAGE
—AND—
CULTURE

CLASSICAL ALLUSIONS IN MODERN ENGLISH

An **eponym** (ep′ə·nim′) is a person—either mythical or real—from whose name the name of a nation, idea, or term has been derived. Classical Greek and Roman myth and literature have lent English dozens of eponymous expressions. See how many of the following expressions you know.

Achilles' Heel

According to Homer's *Iliad*, the hero Achilles was fated to win great glory but to die an early death. Achilles' mother, the sea nymph Thetis, tried to forestall her son's destiny when he was still an infant by dipping every part of his body in the waters of the Styx, a river in the underworld. The magic waters were supposed to protect Achilles against all wounds in battle. However, Thetis forgot to immerse one part of her son's body: the heel by which she held him. Years later, the Trojan prince Paris slew Achilles with an arrow that pierced him—you guessed it—in the heel. Nowadays, "Achilles' heel" is used to refer to any vulnerable point in a plan or in a person's character.

Midas Touch

The Greeks told several legends about Midas, who ruled the kingdom of Phrygia (frij′ē·ə) in Asia Minor (now Turkey). In the most famous story, the god Dionysus granted Midas one wish. Midas wished that everything he touched would turn to gold. Dionysus took him literally, and Midas became the original "Goldfinger" and an instant billionaire. Unfortunately, the king's food, wine, and even his daughter were also transformed into gold as soon as he touched them. Today, the expression "Midas touch" applies to anyone who easily acquires riches.

Pandora's Box

Hesiod (hē′sē·əd), a poet who was roughly contemporary with Homer, tells the story of Zeus's creation of the first woman, Pandora. Before he sent Pandora to live on earth, Zeus gave her a mysterious box, instructing her never to open it. Once on earth, however, Pandora's curiosity got the better of her. When she opened the box, war, plague, and famine escaped and took up permanent residence in the world. Only hope remained inside the box, as a consolation prize to mortals. The expression "opening a

PANDORA, DANTE GABRIEL ROSSETTI, 1869.
How would you describe Pandora's expression in Rossetti's painting? Is it fitting to her mythological role?

Pandora's box" now refers to an action likely to lead to unforeseen—and unpleasant—consequences.

Pyrrhic Victory

In 279 B.C., King Pyrrhus (pir'əs) fought the Romans for control of his territories in northwestern Greece. Pyrrhus hoped to panic the Romans by sending a herd of trained battle elephants charging against them, but his strategy failed. The Romans fought back fiercely, and Pyrrhus's army suffered heavy losses. Although Pyrrhus was technically victorious, he is said to have remarked after the battle that another such victory would ruin him. A "Pyrrhic (pir'ik) victory" still refers to any victory that is too costly to be worthwhile.

Scylla and Charybdis

During his ten-year return voyage home from Troy in Homer's *Odyssey,* the hero Odysseus had to navigate a perilous strait. The six-headed monster Scylla (sil'ə) guarded the strait on one side. To the other side was a churning whirlpool, Charybdis (kə·rib'dis). If Odysseus sailed too near, Charybdis would suck his ship down into the abyss. Odysseus chose to sail near the Scylla, who promptly reached down from her rocky perch on a cliff into Odysseus' ship, seizing and eating six men, one for each of her ghastly jaws. Even now, "to be caught between Scylla and Charybdis" is to be forced to choose between two unattractive options. It's the classical equivalent of being caught between a rock and a hard place.

Siren's Song

This expression also comes from the *Odyssey,* where the sirens were seductive sea nymphs, each one part bird and part woman. They sang so beautifully that all the sailors who passed near their rock longed to hear them. Those who yielded to this temptation, however, were drawn toward the Sirens' island and died on its rocky coast. The curious—and wily—Odysseus managed to have his cake and eat it, too. He ordered his men to plug their ears with beeswax and to lash him to the mast so that he could listen to the Sirens' song. Nowadays, a "siren song" refers to any irresistible attraction. The danger associated with the ancient sirens is reflected in another meaning of the word *siren* that surfaced in the nineteenth century: a loud signal meant as an alert or a warning, as in a police or ambulance siren.

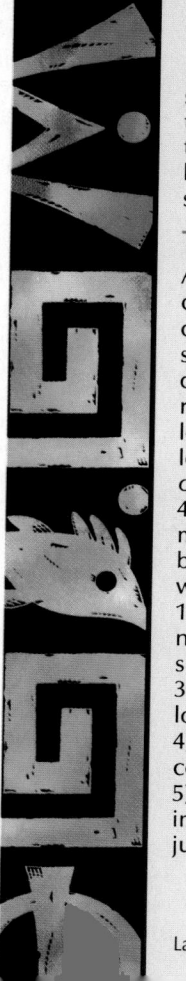

HUMANITIES CONNECTION

Dante Gabriel Rossetti (1828–1882) was a leader of the Pre-Raphaelite Brotherhood, a group of English artists who rebelled against their era's formal rules of painting. Instead of painting the England of their time, they concentrated on mystical and exotic subjects from the Middle Ages and antiquity.

Do you think this portrait of Pandora expresses a view of humanity that the ancient Greeks would have shared? Why or why not? (Possible response: Yes, because it portrays the human figure realistically and expresses such human emotions as sadness, shame, and rebellion.) ∎

TEACHING TIP

Ask students to research the classical sources of the italicized words in the following sentences: 1) For years the dictator inflicted *Draconian* rule on the people. 2) Napoleon met his *nemesis* at Waterloo. 3) The beauty queen's *narcissism* alienated her friends. 4) His *protean* personality makes his testimony unreliable. 5) The smell of the food was *tantalizing.* (Answers: 1) from Draco, a harsh Athenian lawmaker; 2) from Nemesis, goddess of vengeance; 3) from Narcissus, who fell in love with his own reflection; 4) from Proteus, a sea god who could change his shape; 5) from Tantalus, who was kept in the underworld with food just beyond his reach)

Linking Verbs: Remind students that linking verbs include the various tense forms of *be, seem,* and *become* and the intransitive forms of *feel, look, smell, sound, taste.* In a sentence, the meaning of a linking verb is completed by the subject complement, a word that identifies, describes, or qualifies the subject. Here are examples:

       S   LV   COMPLEMENT
<u>Horace</u> <u>became</u> **famous** for his
    odes.
       S   LV   COMPLEMENT
<u>Aeneas</u> <u>was</u> the **leader** of a band
    of Trojan refugees.

Indefinite Pronoun Subjects:
You might want to explain that very few indefinite pronouns (*all, any, half, most, none,* and *some*) may take either a singular or a plural verb. For these pronouns, the context of the sentence determines the number of the verb. Here are examples:

Lyric poetry can have many effects; <u>some</u> <u>is</u> even humorous. (Meaning: Some of the poetry is even humorous.)

The poems of Catullus are of varying lengths; <u>some</u> <u>are</u> only two lines long. (Meaning: Some poems are only two lines long.)

Language Skills

MAINTAINING SUBJECT-VERB AGREEMENT

As you enrich your writing with details of character and action, your sentences grow more complex. Making verbs agree with subjects in sentences can be tricky, even for experienced writers. Yet errors in **subject–verb agreement** distract readers and reduce your credibility. By learning to double-check certain constructions, you can keep your writing credible and clear.

Subject-Verb Agreement

Make each verb agree in number with its subject. In many English sentences and clauses, the subject comes right before the verb. Subject-verb agreement is easy then: a singular verb for a singular subject (A Greek fights a Trojan.), a plural verb for a plural subject (Greeks fight the Trojans.). However, variations on the standard sentence pattern can increase agreement problems. Study the following five types.

Problems in Subject-Verb Agreement

1. Intervening Words
INCORRECT
   The tone of Sappho's verses remind me of Amy Lowell's poetry.
CORRECT
   The *tone* of Sappho's verses *reminds* me of Amy Lowell's poetry.

Even if other nouns come between subject and verb, a verb still must agree with its subject.

2. Compound Subjects
INCORRECT
   In the end, Achilles or Hector have to die.
CORRECT
   In the end, Achilles or Hector *has* to die.

Most compound subjects take a plural verb: Achilles and Hector *have* great strength. But compound subjects joined by *or* or *nor* take a singular verb.

3. Linking Verbs
INCORRECT
   The best selection were two odes by Horace.
CORRECT
   The best *selection was* two odes by Horace.

A linking verb must agree with its subject, not with the complement (the complement in this case is "two odes"). This is true even if the subject is singular and the complement plural.

4. Indefinite Pronouns
INCORRECT
   Despite the two men's boasting, neither help the victim.
CORRECT
   Despite the two men's boasting, *neither helps* the victim.

The indefinite pronouns listed below always take singular verbs.

anyone	nobody
everyone	somebody
no one	each
someone	either
anybody	neither
everybody	

5. Adjective Clauses

INCORRECT

Tacitus is among the many historians who loves to digress.

Oedipus is the only one of all the travelers who answer the riddle correctly.

CORRECT

Tacitus is among the many *historians* who *love* to digress.

Oedipus is the only *one* of all the travelers who *answers* the riddle correctly.

In clauses with relative pronouns (*who, which,* or *that*) as subjects, the verb may be either singular or plural. It should agree with the relative pronoun's antecedent (*historians* and *one* in the above examples).

Exercise 1: Subject-Verb Agreement

Choose the correct verb form.

1. Only a slim volume of Sappho's poems (survive, survives) today.
2. Patroclus, respecting Achilles' feelings, (justify, justifies) his hero's actions.
3. Careful reporting and perceptive political analysis (mark, marks) Thucydides' *History of the Peloponnesian War.*
4. Neither Jocasta nor Oedipus (realize, realizes) that they are related.
5. A horrific sight in the underworld (was, were) the three snarling mouths of Cerberus.
6. Plato's *Dialogues* are many and varied, but each (teach, teaches) an aspect of Plato's philosophy.
7. Achilles is typical of many epic heroes who knowingly (face, faces) death rather than live without glory.
8. The writings of Tacitus, which (is, are) rich in historical detail and gossip, make fascinating reading.
9. (Is/Are) Herodotus or Thucydides considered the "father of Greek history"?
10. Anyone who (read, reads) the *Aeneid* finds Aeneas a complex hero.

Exercise 2: Revising for Subject-Verb Agreement

Scan a story or an essay you have written, underlining the following kinds of sentences:

1. those in which words intervene between subject and verb
2. those with compound subjects
3. those with linking verbs and complements
4. those containing indefinite pronouns
5. those containing relative clauses

Check your sentences for subject-verb agreement, and correct any such errors that you find.

Background: Tell students that heroes can be either female or male. You might refer them to "Osiris and Isis," p. 34, and The Book of Ruth, p. 177, for examples of female heroes.

Ask students to explain how Achilles, Aeneas, and Oedipus fit the conventions of epic heroes. Note that the excerpt from the *Aeneid* in the text does not contain details about the childhood of Aeneas, and the excerpts from the *Iliad* provide only a brief mention of Achilles' childhood. Ask volunteers to skim the selections to find out what the selections do reveal about the lineage, childhood, personal qualities, and journeys of each hero. Write students' responses on the chalkboard under appropriate headings.

After students have seen how the epic conventions apply to heroes they have read about, let them work as a class to list new details under each heading that could describe a modern American hero. Then tell students that, if they wish, they may make this hero the star of the epic adventures they will write.

Prewriting: Remind students before they brainstorm that heroes' characters and accomplishments should reflect the values of their societies or cultures.

Critical Thinking and Writing

CREATING AN EPIC ADVENTURE

Today's heroes are usually people like us, fallible but capable of courageous acts. Heroes of Greek and Roman antiquity, however, are far larger than life, superhuman in bravery and prowess. Which kind of hero makes a more appealing role model?

Writing Assignment

Write a brief adventure featuring a hero of your own invention. Your audience is fourth- and fifth-graders, and you want to offer them a new way of looking at the world, as well as to entertain them. In this assignment, you will use the literary elements that you have become familiar with: setting, characters, plot, and theme.

Background

Though they represent different time periods and cultures, the tales of Achilles, Oedipus, and Aeneas share a number of **epic conventions**. Consider the following points as you invent your hero. (You don't have to pattern your hero after the Greek or Roman models, however.)

- **Lineage.** The hero is the offspring of a mortal and a deity. (Oedipus, the exception, is of royal birth.) Heroes have divine powers but human weaknesses.
- **Childhood.** The hero shows early signs of unusual wisdom, strength, or courage.

- **Character.** Heroes are virtuous, determined, passionate, valiant, and noble. Their strength of character lets them endure pain and loss to achieve their goals.
- **Journeys.** The hero goes on a quest, endures trials, and emerges as a leader. Heroes are helped and hindered by gods and goddesses.

Prewriting

Brainstorming. Brainstorm background information about a hero. Decide which time period and place the hero comes from, what his or her society values, and what the hero hopes to accomplish. Also, consider the epic conventions listed above.

Planning. Drawing on the material you have brainstormed, plan a single adventure featuring your hero. Use a story map like the one on the following page.

Writing

1. **Introductory Paragraphs.** You might begin by showing the hero involved in an action or a dialogue that initiates the **conflict.** However you choose to begin, capture your readers' attention and provide enough detail to get them involved in the story.

2. **Body Paragraphs.** Include events that advance the plot, reveal char-

FOR FURTHER HELP

Refer students to *Grammar, Usage, and Mechanics: A Reference Guide* at the back of their textbooks for detailed information that will help them write, revise, and proofread their essays.

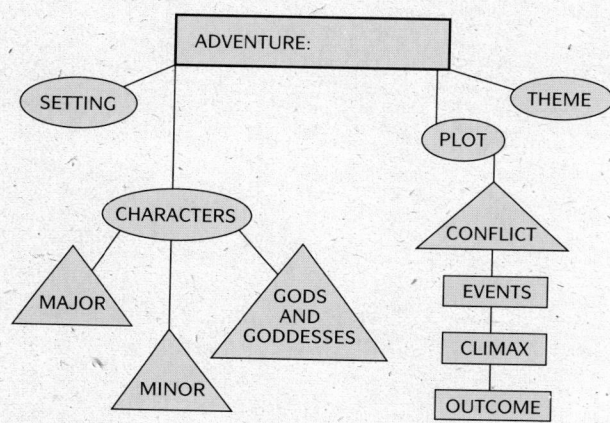

acter, and underscore the conflict or the theme. You might experiment with the use of **foreshadowing** to hint at the climax to come, or with the use of **flashback** to fill in background information.

Combine dialogue, description, and action to bring your adventure to life. Use **epic similes** (extended, grandiose comparisons) and **stock epithets** (descriptive phrases that take the place of names) to create special effects.

3. **Concluding Paragraph.** By the end of your adventure, the conflict should be resolved. The theme of your adventure should emerge from the whole story, but emphasize it now by your choice of details for the ending.

Evaluating and Revising

Use these questions to evaluate and revise your draft.

1. Does the **setting** help readers to picture the action and grasp the mood? Do vivid details bring the setting to life?

2. Does a **conflict** set the chain of events in motion? Is the order of events clear? Does the action have a plausible climax and resolution?

3. Are the **characters'** personalities revealed through the use of dialogue and other indirect forms of characterization?

4. Have you provided enough clues for your readers to grasp the **theme**— the central idea you want your story to convey?

5. Are your sentences varied and grammatically correct?

Proofreading and Publishing

Proofread to eliminate errors in mechanics, and make a final copy of your adventure. Work with your classmates to present your adventures to elementary-school students.

Writing: Encourage students to refer to their story maps as they write. Explain, however, that such maps need not be followed slavishly. If students writing a first draft want to explore an area not indicated by their story maps, they should feel free to do so. Later, during the revision phase, they can integrate the various parts of their drafts into a smooth whole.

Evaluating and Revising: Peer readers can be especially helpful as students evaluate their stories. Readers might note which parts seem most vivid, which seem unnecessary, and which need more detail. For pointers on highlighting vivid details, refer students to ''Choosing Effective Diction,'' pp. 788–789.

Proofreading and Publishing: You might have students pay special attention to subject-verb agreement as they proofread, following the guidelines in the *Language Skills* feature on pp. 438–439.

Have students begin planning their presentations by deciding which parts of their stories will appeal most to younger students and how they can emphasize those parts in their readings. Remind students that sound effects and simple props are effective in Reader's Theater, and let them choose those most appropriate to their stories. ∎

The following annotations are for the artwork surrounding the map, starting in the upper right-hand corner and moving in a counterclockwise direction.

Buddha: This detail from a sandstone sculpture of the fourth century reflects the preoccupation with the spiritual that characterizes Indian art. The plethora of figures of the Buddha praying, contemplating, or teaching attests to the profound influence of Buddhism on religious thought throughout India and Asia (see p. 451).

Illustration from the Mahabharata: The *Mahabharata* is a great heroic epic of India. Like the Greek epics, it was passed down orally for centuries from one generation to the next before being written down. This detail, showing birds with fantastically embellished feathers, is from a lavishly illustrated seventeenth-century manuscript of the *Mahabharata*.

Indra: This artwork is from a wood carving of Indra, the chief of the Vedic gods, who was known for slaying the demon of drought.

❓ *What does the carving suggest about Indra?* (Possible response: great power; strength; determination)

ANCIENT INDIA

About A.D. 450

☐ Gupta Empire

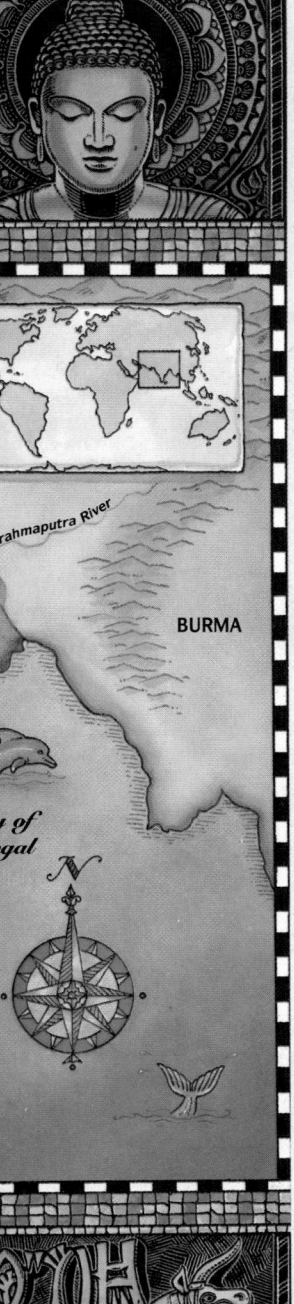

BURMA

Brahmaputra River

INDIAN LITERATURE

▼ **Time** ▼

2500 B.C.—A.D. 1500

▼ **Place** ▼

India

▼ **Literary Significance** ▼

India boasts a rich, diverse, and long-lasting literary tradition. Most Westerners are surprised to discover that the Indian literary tradition contains more texts than the ancient Greek and Roman traditions combined.

The earliest Indian literature has survived from the Aryan migrations that occurred around 1500 B.C. The literature of this period is called Vedic literature, after the Vedas, collections of sacred hymns.

In the sixth century B.C., Indian literature entered its classical period, which lasted until about A.D. 1000. The literature of this period, which includes epics, court poems, and dramas, was written in Sanskrit, an elite language known for its formality and richness of expression.

Both the Vedic and classical literatures reflect the beliefs of India's dominant religion, Hinduism. Such central Hindu concepts as *dharma*, *karma*, and reincarnation feature prominently in the literature of the classical period. This literature includes the Indian epics the *Mahabharata* and the *Ramayana*, as well as the less lofty but thoroughly entertaining beast fables represented in the *Panchatantra* and other collections.

Krishna with Flute: Krishna is one of the incarnations of the Hindu god Vishnu. It is said that as a youth Krishna played his flute and danced with milkmaids by moonlight. Hindus regard this story of playful love as a metaphor for the human soul's relationship with the divine.

Elephant: This detail from a miniature (c. 1620) focuses on the elephant, revered in India for its energy and power. The gods Krishna and Shiva sometimes appear as elephants.

Shiva: This artwork is based on a bronze statue of Shiva cast in the tenth or eleventh century. In his terrible aspect, Shiva is the god of destruction. Here he appears in another of his forms, as Lord of the Cosmic Dance. He is shown with four hands that hold symbolic objects. In blending masculine and feminine qualities, the features of Shiva are meant to suggest the oneness of all creation.

Cow from a Stone Seal: This carving from an Indus Valley civilization dates back to the dawn of Indian history (c. 2500–1500 B.C.). According to one Indian creation myth, the universe was formed when the primordial Sea of Milk, from the great Goddess-Cow, curdled. Use of animals in Indian art reflects the belief that all life is sacred. ■

The Time Line focuses on India from about 2500 B.C. to A.D. 1500, ending at the point when Europeans first entered the country. Students should note that all of the time since then—A.D. 1500 to 2000—would add only one small column to the Time Line. India has such a long history that the two centuries of British colonialism, which began in the second half of the eighteenth century, represent little more than an interruption in Indian culture.

Students may relate events in previous units with events shown on this Time Line. For example, by 2500 B.C., systems of writing were well developed in both Egypt and Mesopotamia. About 2000 B.C., the ancestors of the Hebrews began their trek from Mesopotamia to Canaan, the Sumerian authors of the *Epic of Gilgamesh* were conquered by the Babylonians, and the Egyptians had already collected the literary works called the *Pyramid Texts* and the *Coffin Texts*. In about 1000 B.C., when the Indians were writing down the earliest hymns of the *Rig Veda*, the Hebrews under King David were recording psalms, proverbs, and stories of their origins.

As they study the Time Lines, students will note overlaps in the histories of the ancient cultures. How did people of different cultures encounter one another's ideas? (through travelers on the trade routes; through war and conquest)

TIME LINE
India

LITERARY EVENTS
▼

Bronze female dancer from the Indus Valley civilization, c. 2500 B.C.

The Granger Collection, New York

Later Vedas, Upanishads, and Brahmanas are comp[...]
c. 900–c. 500 B.C.

Earliest hymns from the *Rig Veda* are written down, **c. 1000 B.C.**

Vedic period, **1500–500 B.C.**

2500 B.C.	2000 B.C.	1500 B.C.	1000 B.C.

Indus Valley civilization in northwest India reaches its height, **c. 2500 B.C.**

Invasions of Indo-European-speaking nomads coincide with decay of Indus Valley civilization, **c. 1500 B.C.**

Hinduism develops; groups move across India and develop stable kingdoms, **c. 1500–c. 500 B.C.**

▲
CULTURAL AND HISTORICAL EVENTS

Krishna *(center)*, an important Hindu god.

The Granger Collection, New York

Lions from the column of Ashoka, 240 B.C.

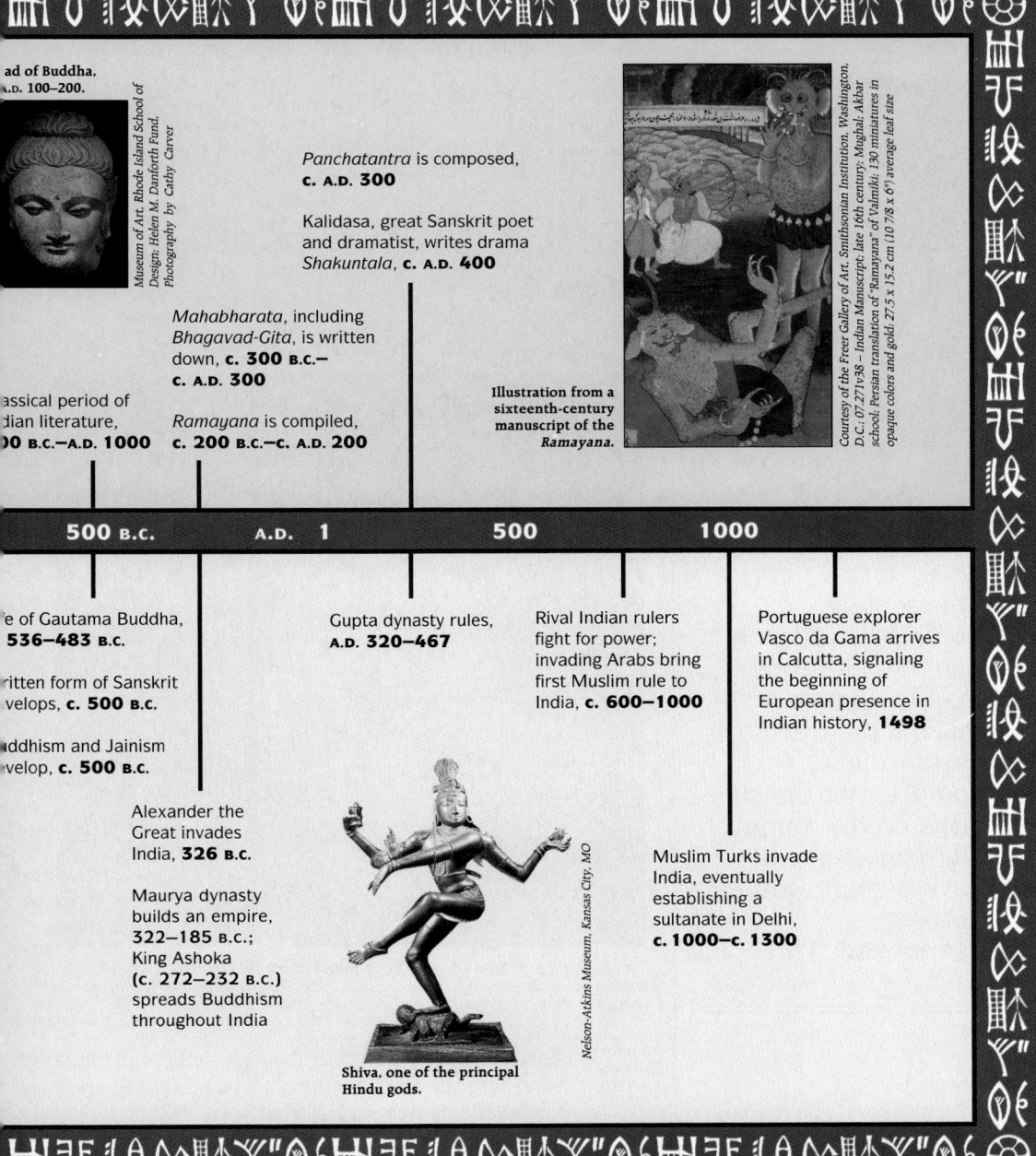

Head of Buddha,
A.D. 100–200.

Museum of Art, Rhode Island School of Design; Helen M. Danforth Fund. Photography by Cathy Carver

Panchatantra is composed,
c. A.D. 300

Kalidasa, great Sanskrit poet
and dramatist, writes drama
Shakuntala, **c. A.D. 400**

Mahabharata, including
Bhagavad-Gita, is written
down, **c. 300 B.C.–
c. A.D. 300**

Classical period of
Indian literature,
00 B.C.–A.D. 1000

Ramayana is compiled,
c. 200 B.C.–c. A.D. 200

Illustration from a
sixteenth-century
manuscript of the
Ramayana.

Courtesy of the Freer Gallery of Art, Smithsonian Institution, Washington, D.C.: 07.271v38 – Indian Manuscript; late 16th century; Mughal; Akbar school; Persian translation of 'Ramayana' of Valmiki; 130 miniatures in opaque colors and gold; 27.5 x 15.2 cm (10 7/8 x 6") average leaf size

| **500 B.C.** | **A.D. 1** | **500** | **1000** |

Life of Gautama Buddha,
536–483 B.C.

Written form of Sanskrit
develops, **c. 500 B.C.**

Buddhism and Jainism
develop, **c. 500 B.C.**

Gupta dynasty rules,
A.D. 320–467

Rival Indian rulers
fight for power;
invading Arabs bring
first Muslim rule to
India, **c. 600–1000**

Portuguese explorer
Vasco da Gama arrives
in Calcutta, signaling
the beginning of
European presence in
Indian history, **1498**

Alexander the
Great invades
India, **326 B.C.**

Maurya dynasty
builds an empire,
322–185 B.C.;
King Ashoka
(c. 272–232 B.C.)
spreads Buddhism
throughout India

Muslim Turks invade
India, eventually
establishing a
sultanate in Delhi,
c. 1000–c. 1300

Nelson-Atkins Museum, Kansas City, MO

**Shiva, one of the principal
Hindu gods.**

This time line border shows characters from the still-undeciphered Indus Valley
script, developed in ancient India between 2500 and 1500 B.C.

Time Line **445**

CULTURAL BACKGROUND
Indus Valley Script: Notice
the ancient script in the border
that surrounds the Time Line.
How do these characters resemble early Egyptian hieroglyphic and Sumerian cuneiform writing? (All are based on
pictures; in this border, a man,
wheel, and fish can be distinguished.)

CULTURAL BACKGROUND
Hinduism: Hindus believe that
at death the soul passes into
another body, either human or
animal. Because of this belief,
Hindus avoid killing any living
creature. What aspects of life
would such a practice influence? (Possible response:
food—not eating meat or fish;
agriculture—not killing pests
harmful to crops; health and
quality of life—not killing such
pests as mosquitoes and ro-
dents; aggression—warfare not
an option)

CULTURAL BACKGROUND
Age of Thinkers: During the
500s and 400s B.C., many great
thinkers arose in ancient civilizations. In India, Buddha appeared; in Israel, the prophet
Isaiah; in Greece, the philosophers Socrates and Plato; in
China, the philosopher Confucius; and in Persia, the religious leader Zoroaster. Thinkers like these addressed
fundamental questions about
the cosmos, humanity, and
government. How is their influence felt today? (They for-
mulated principles of behavior
that people still try to follow.)

OBJECTIVES

1. *To gain an overview of classical Indian literature*
2. *To appreciate the Hindu concepts of dharma, karma, the caste system, and reincarnation, and their influence on Indian culture*
3. *To understand the elements of the Indian epic and the epic hero*
4. *To interpret and respond to Indian literature both orally and in writing*

TEACHER'S RESOURCES: 5

✔ Unit Introduction Test
✔ Word Analogies
✔ Unit Review Test
✔ Critical Thinking and Writing

1 RESPONDING TO THE QUOTATION

As Twain intimates, India is a land of contradictions—a land of beauty and squalor, extravagance and asceticism, intense spirituality and sporadic violence. Nature has endowed India with a terrain that ranges from the Himalayas to fertile plains, lush coastal regions, tropical jungles, and deserts. The birthplace of four major world religions—Hinduism, Buddhism, Jainism, and Sikhism—India also boasts a thriving Muslim community.

❓ *What do you think is most extraordinary about India?*

■ HUMANITIES CONNECTION

According to myth, the warrior god Indra sprang full-grown from his mother's side and immediately rescued his people, who were suffering the effects of a drought. By releasing the cloud-cattle from captivity, he brought life-giving rains.

❓ *Indra's symbol is the thunderbolt. Why is this appropriate?* (Possible response: It suggests great power and is associated with rainstorms.) ■

2 HISTORICAL BACKGROUND

Indus Valley: The valley of the Indus River, in present-day Pakistan, was the cradle of Indian civilization. The people who lived there before the Aryan invasion were literate, cultured city-builders whose art included stone seals like those of Sumer.

INDIAN LITERATURE

SEF/Art Resource, New York

Indra, the Vedic god of war, accompanied by the celestial nymphs, fresco from the Ajanta Caves, c. A.D. 580. *The Hindus eventually incorporated Indra into their own pantheon as a sky god.*

1

❝ So far as I am able to judge, nothing has been left undone, either by man or Nature, to make India the most extraordinary country that the sun visits on his round. Nothing seems to have been forgotten, nothing overlooked. ❞

—*Mark Twain*

Scholars are not sure who the first settlers of India were, but they do know that an advanced civilization flourished in northern India between 2500 and 1500 B.C. This was the so-called **Indus Valley** civilization, whose remaining artifacts—undiscovered by archaeologists until the early nineteenth century—show some interesting similarities to the art of later Hindu (hin'do͞o') culture in India.

2

To spark students' interest, tell them that the ancient epics of India still keep millions of people entertained today. Explain that people in India eagerly watch films of these epics in televised installments, much as people in our culture watch a TV miniseries. Challenge students, as they read these spicy tales of adventure and intrigue, to look for those qualities that mesmerize Indian viewers.

Before students begin to read, you may find it helpful to give them an overview of the Hindu theology that underlies the selections. Explain that Hinduism is a religion with 330 million gods, yet at its center is the vision of a single god, Brahma, the World Soul, the unifying principle of the cosmos, the sum of all that ever was or ever will be. A Hindu believer sets out to find Atman, the essential inner self. After dedicating the whole of life to this task, a devout Hindu then seeks a way to merge Atman with Brahma, the World Soul.

For the Hindu, this quest for unity with the World Soul may take many lifetimes. The doctrines of *samsara, karma, nirvana,* and *yoga* suggest the difficulty of the task. *Samsara,* a Sanskrit word that means "passing through intensely," translates as "reincarnation." Once born into the world, an individual soul does not die but inhabits the bodies of increasingly complex creatures, until it is born into a hu-

---

3

Around 1500 B.C., a wave of migrations into India began that would continue into the seventeenth century A.D. The earliest known migrants called themselves **Aryans** (ar'ē·ənz). They were a group of nomadic, or wandering, warriors and herders. Many scholars believe that the Aryans, like other Indo-European peoples, probably originated in central Asia. Although the Aryans were not city-builders like their predecessors in the Indus Valley, they brought with them a well-developed language and literature, as well as a set of religious beliefs.

The Vedic Period in India

The first literary period in India is known as the **Vedic** period, lasting from 1500 B.C. to approximately 500 B.C. This period is named for the **Vedas** (vā'dəz), a set of hymns that formed the cornerstone of the Aryan culture. Hindus still consider the Vedas to be the most sacred of all literature, for they believe that these sacred hymns were revealed to humans directly by the gods. The oldest existing Vedic hymns are collected in the *Rig Veda* (rig' vā'də), featuring poems of praise to the beauty of the earth and the wonder of existence. (The word *veda* and our word *video* both come from the Indo-European root *weid-*, meaning "to see" or "to know.") For centuries, the Vedas were transmitted orally by priests who had memorized every syllable. Even after a system for writing literature had been introduced in the sixth century B.C., the Vedas were still passed on orally by priests.

4

The Classical Period: The Legacy of Sanskrit

After the Vedic period ended, and until about A.D. 1000, Indian literature entered its **classical** period. The main literary language of northern India during this period was **Sanskrit** (san'skrit'), an Indo-European language. Most languages of northern India tend, like Sanskrit itself, to belong to the Indo-European family of languages. The main languages of southern India, by contrast, come from an independent family of languages with ancient roots in the Indian subcontinent: the **Dravidian** (drə·vid'ē·ən) languages, such as Tamil (tam'əl) and Kannada (kä'nə·də). But even the "higher,"

Statue of a man recovered from the ruins of Mohenjo-Daro, a center of the Indus Valley civilization.

Pakistan Government, Department of Archaeology

Introduction   **447**

man body. With the human incarnation comes self-consciousness and moral responsibility. *Karma*, or action, is the way a human soul strives to escape the endless cycle of death and rebirth. If the goal of each believer is freedom from continuous reincarnation, then good karma in the present life is of supreme importance. If a person has led a good life, the soul moves upward toward God; if a person has done evil, the soul may pass back into the body of an animal. Good karma leads finally to *nirvana*, the liberation from suffering that follows release from reincarnation and union with Brahma.

Another key Hindu concept to present is *yoga*. Yoga is a training or discipline for reaching union with God. According to Hindu teaching, there are four such paths: knowledge, love, work, and spiritual meditation. Each yoga has its own methods and discipline.

As Hindus see the human soul traveling through a succession of reincarnations, they also see history as a succession of cycles. The three gods of the Hindu trinity, Shiva, Brahma, and Vishnu, work together to keep these cycles in motion. As each cycle draws to a close, Shiva destroys the old world and Brahma creates a new one. During a cycle, Vishnu occasionally comes to earth in the form of a human being to offer the world help. For

---

5 HISTORICAL BACKGROUND

Sanskrit: Early in the seventeenth century, European traders began to establish outposts in India. It was this contact that brought India's ancient language and literature to the attention of the Western world. Englishman Charles Wilkins (1749–1836) was one of the first to learn Sanskrit, and in 1784 he published the *Bhagavad-Gita* in English, the first direct translation of a Sanskrit work. Although Sanskrit is now a dead language, it is still recognized in the Indian constitution as an "official language" because of its association with the classical literature and religion of India.

6 RESPONDING TO THE QUOTATION

❓ *What is implied in Gandhi's quotation about the function of religious texts like the* Bhagavad-Gita? (One of their functions is to strengthen and console those who suffer sorrow or doubt.)

Ram Rahman Photography

Sanskrit inscriptions on the interior walls of a dome, India.

6 ❝ When doubts haunt me, when disappointments stare me in the face, and I see not one ray of light on the horizon, I turn to the *Bhagavad-Gita*, and find a verse to comfort me; and I immediately begin to smile in the midst of overwhelming sorrow. ❞

—*Mahatma Gandhi*

or elite, forms of the Dravidian languages often borrowed the cultural concerns and vocabularies of Sanskrit texts.

One of the most fascinating facts about Sanskrit is that by 600 B.C. it had become a "frozen" literary language. In other words, over long periods of time written Sanskrit barely changed to reflect evolutions in everyday speech, and it remained much the same in its grammar and syntax for centuries. An analogy to this situation would be if we today spoke contemporary English but wrote everything in Old English, the language used in Anglo-Saxon literary works such as *Beowulf.*

> By 600 B.C., Sanskrit had become a fixed and frozen literary language that would change very little over the centuries to come.

5

Sanskrit, which means "perfect speech," is one of the most important legacies of India's ancient literary tradition. It is considered a sacred language, the language spoken by the gods and goddesses. As such, Sanskrit was seen as the only appropriate form of expression for the noblest literary works—epics, court poems, and dramas, among others. Although India claims more than fourteen major languages and hundreds of regional dialects, Sanskrit has given an amazing cohesiveness to Indian literature over the past 3500 years. Poets, novelists, and dramatists, writing in various Indian languages, have drawn much of their inspiration from the classical tradition represented by Sanskrit texts, which are known for their beauty and intellectual subtlety.

Literature During the Classical Period

Like the ancient Greeks, the Indians had two great epics— the **Mahabharata** (mə·hä′bä′rə·tə) and the **Ramayana** (rä·mä′yə·nə). These works had been part of India's oral tradition for centuries, but they were finally written down in a more-or-less fixed form during the classical period. Poetry and drama reached a high point during this period. Beast fables were also immensely popular and often used by religious teachers to illustrate moral points. During the

example, Krishna, the charioteer in the *Bhagavad-Gita*, and Rama, the great warrior prince in the *Ramayana*, are both incarnations (or avatars) of Vishnu.

To demonstrate India's intense spirituality, show or describe the scene in "India: Empire of the Spirit," a segment of the PBS *Legacy* series (1991), in which ten to fifteen million people converge on the banks of the Ganges at an annual festival. Point out that many of these people have spent their life savings to make the pilgrimage. Students can appreciate the fervor that animates such believers if they imagine a crowd gathering from all over the United States to attend a world-class rock concert. The Hindus' presence on the Ganges is a sign of their lifelong search for spiritual union.

Point out to students that the selections in this unit deal with the ultimate questions: Who am I? What is the meaning of life? Who is God and how does humanity relate to God? How shall we conduct our lives? How can we achieve happiness? Students may wish, as they read, to compare and contrast their own principles and beliefs with those of the Hindu faith. Urge them to bear in mind that, though the texts they are reading are ancient, they are the heritage of a living religion that is widely practiced in India today.

classical period, many beast fables from the oral tradition were finally put together in collections, the most famous of which was the **Panchatantra**, a world classic that has appeared in some two hundred versions in many different languages.

Hinduism: The Key to Indian Culture

It is tempting for a Westerner to stereotype all of India's literature as essentially religious or mythological, whereas in fact India boasts a wide array of literary types, from the love and war poems of the classical Tamil tradition to the deeply personal lyric poems of such women poets as Mira Bai. Nevertheless, it is impossible to understand the Indian literary tradition—which claims more texts than the ancient Greek and Latin traditions combined—without speaking of the religion that claims the majority of India's 900 million people as followers: **Hinduism**.

Hinduism evolved from the beliefs of the ancient Aryans of the Vedic period. More than a religion, Hinduism is a way of life, with a seemingly endless variety of beliefs, rituals, and gods. It has no single written doctrine or set of rules, and no single prophet or religious leader, such as Jesus Christ or Mohammed. Its pantheon, or assembly of gods and goddesses, consists of (by some counts) 330 million different deities. Nevertheless, three particular deities stand out in the Hindu pantheon: Brahma (brä′mə) the Creator, Vishnu (vish′n$\overline{oo}$) the Protector, and Shiva (shē′və) the Destroyer.

Despite the enormous number of different cults and sects in Hinduism, many Hindus believe that all the gods—and indeed, everything in the universe—are aspects of a single essence, or immortal spirit. This belief in the ultimate oneness of existence serves as a counterweight to the diversity of India's enormous population and its many different classes of people and methods of worship.

The earliest texts of Hinduism are the Vedic hymns and an entire body of sacred prose literature, including the **Upanishads** ($\overline{oo}$·pan′i·shadz′), that serve as commentaries on, or philosophical extensions of, the hymns. The two great Hindu epics, the *Mahabharata* and the *Ramayana*, vividly illustrate the lessons of Hinduism, focusing on the Hindu concepts of *dharma*, *karma*, and reincarnation.

HUMANITIES CONNECTION

❓ *How does the picture of "The Godly Pair" suggest the Hindu idea that all of creation is interconnected? (Possible response: Riding on a bird suggests an interdependence between humans and animals.)* ∎

State Museum, East Berlin

THE GODLY PAIR (KRISHNA AND RAHDA) ON THE BIRD GARUDA

Henry David Thoreau (1817–1862), the author of *Walden*, testified that his mind had been shaped by two works, Emerson's essay on nature and the *Bhagavad-Gita*. Arthur Schopenhauer, a famous German thinker, based his philosophy on Hindu ideas. He wrote, "In the whole world there is no study so beneficial and so elevating. It has been the solace of my life and it will be the solace of my death."

In our own century there has developed in the West a widespread appreciation of Indian philosophy and religion. Inspired by the *Bhagavad-Gita*, Thoreau wrote "Civil Disobedience." This famous essay in turn inspired Mohandas K. Gandhi, who applied its principles of nonviolent protest in his fight for Indian independence from British colonial rule. Gandhi's protest in turn inspired Martin Luther King, Jr., as he led a nonviolent struggle for the civil rights of African-Americans. At the root of these great movements is the ancient Hindu way to wisdom enshrined in the *Bhagavad-Gita*—the book Gandhi called "the book *par excellence* for the knowledge of Truth."

Following Emerson and Thoreau, many writers have been influenced by Indian thinking. Rudyard Kipling (1865–1936), who was born in India of English parents, described life there with a romantic view of British imperialism. His poem "Gunga

---

7 CULTURAL DIVERSITY

Dharma: The word *dharma* is derived from a Sanskrit root that means "to hold together." It is similar in meaning to the word *religion*, which is based on the Latin roots *re-* and *ligare*, "to tie back or bind together."

❓ *How can the Hindu dharma be compared to the Greek concept of fate?* (*Dharma* and *moira* (the Greek word for fate) are extremely complex concepts. A simple, but incomplete answer to the question would be that the Greeks believed that we have no power over fate, while Hindus believe that we can choose to fulfill our dharma or not.)

TEACHING TIP

To help students understand the caste system, ask them to imagine that all young people in the United States had to do the jobs that were done by their parents and grandparents. Elicit the pros and cons of a society organized in this manner.

Courtesy of the Arthur M. Sackler Museum Harvard University, Cambridge, Massachusetts Private Collection

A SCRIBE, c. 1625.

Lessons of Indian Literature: Following One's Dharma

Dharma (där'mə) comes from a Sanskrit verb meaning "to hold." The closest word in English that begins to define dharma is "religion." Dharma is also close in meaning to such concepts as duty, righteousness, ethics, morality, law, and order.

According to Hindu belief, every individual is born with a unique dharma, which unfolds throughout a lifetime according to the individual's choices. Most of the lessons of dharma—what to do or not to do in a given situation—must be determined by the individual on a moment-by-moment basis. There are times when even the most righteous person, such as the god Krishna in the *Mahabharata*, must lie or act in other seemingly unrighteous ways in order to act in accordance with his or her dharma. Ultimately, dharma requires that a person fulfill the duties of his or her station in life, however lofty or humble it might be.

The Caste System in India

A person's dharma depends upon his or her **caste** (kast), or social standing. In Indian tradition, people are not created equal. Rather, they are categorized at birth into one of four groups, or ranks of society. Hindu religious law uses the word **varna** (vur'nə), meaning "color" or "rank," to refer to the order of the various castes in society. The origin of the varnas goes back at least to the *Rig Veda*. One Vedic hymn speaks of the four varnas resulting from the sacrifice of the primal man, called Purusa. His body was divided into the fourfold varna system: from his head came the *Brahmans* (brä'mənz), the scholars, priests, and teachers; from his torso came the *Kshatriyas* (kə·shat'rē·yəz), the rulers and warriors; from his thighs came the *Vaisyas* (vīs'yəz), the merchants, farmers, and artisans; and from his feet came the *Sudras* (soo'drəz), those who clean up after all the others and do much of life's unpleasant work.

The caste system is also a key element of Indian literature. In the *Bhagavad-Gita* (bug'ə·vəd gē'tä), part of the *Mahabharata*, the god Krishna (krish'nə) continually appeals to the warrior Arjuna's sense of his varna. As a warrior, it is Arjuna's dharma to fight. If he does not fight as a warrior

Din" and his collection of children's stories, *The Jungle Book*, are widely known. E. M. Forster (1879–1970) wrote one of the best novels of this century, *A Passage to India* (1924), on the conflict between the Western and the Indian ways of life. T. S. Eliot concluded his famous poem, "The Waste Land" (1922), with a Hindu benediction: *Shantih, shantih, shantih*, meaning "Peace, peace, peace." In the same year Hermann Hesse, a German writer, pub-

lished his novel *Siddhartha*, based on the life of Gautama, the founder of Buddhism, who lived about 2500 years ago. Even the Beatles, exhausted by Beatlemania, went to India in search of peace and enlightenment. The songs in their album *Magical Mystery Tour* reflect the influence of what they found there.

Many other Westerners have traveled to India or found a *guru* (master or teacher) here in the West. Americans have prac-

ticed yoga or meditation less as a religious exercise than as a discipline for self-improvement. An Indian guru named Maharishi Mahesh Yogi popularized a form of yoga called Transcendental Meditation in the United States during the 1960s and '70s. Words like *karma* and *nirvana* have entered the common vocabulary, and many people find reincarnation a helpful way to understand what happens to the soul after death.

---

should, he will violate his dharma, harming not only himself, but also his family, his society, and ultimately the world order. Arjuna knows all this. The question that baffles Arjuna, and other epic heroes and heroines, is not what dharma is supposed to be, but how it can be successfully carried out with the greatest happiness and least hardship.

The caste system in India finds its origins in the Vedic hymns of the ancient Aryans.

Karma and Reincarnation

Hindus also believe in the concepts of karma and reincarnation. **Karma** (kär'mə) is a Sanskrit word meaning "action." **Reincarnation**, also known as the "transmigration of souls," is a process in which one's soul is reborn in another body. One's actions, or karma, in this life influence one's rebirth and future life. For example, good karma in this life leads to rebirth in a higher form and social position. When a soul is sufficiently purified, it is united with Brahman, the ultimate spiritual reality.

Buddhism—The Search for Spiritual Peace

Great religious and political ferment marked the close of the Vedic Age. It was during this time that a major religion, **Buddhism** (bood'iz'əm), came into being. Buddhism was founded by **Siddharta Gautama** (sid·där'tə gout'ə·mə) (563–483 B.C.), a young prince who renounced his life of wealth and ease in order to discover the key to spiritual peace. ("Buddha" means "Enlightened One," a title given to Siddharta by his followers.) As a result of intense spiritual contemplation, he came to believe that life was suffering, that the cause of suffering was a wrongheaded desire for individual fulfillment, and that the path to mastering this desire was a life of honesty, nonviolence, willpower, continual self-examination, and profound meditation. In contrast to the social stratification of the Hindu caste system, Buddhism insists that all people are potentially equal.

8

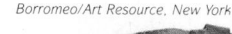
Borromeo/Art Resource, New York

Statue of Buddha, second century A.D., Indian. *Buddhism was born in India but found its greatest following in Southeast Asia.*

8 HISTORICAL BACKGROUND

Buddha: When Siddharta was twenty-nine he made a complete break with his way of life. Leaving his house in the middle of the night, he dressed himself in rags, shaved his head, and began six years of wandering in search of the meaning of life.

First he studied yoga and philosophy. Then he tried asceticism, meditating and fasting to the point of exhaustion. Still searching, he sat down beneath a fig tree one evening and in forty-nine days of meditation achieved his Great Awakening. From then until his death at age eighty, Siddharta traveled about India teaching, preaching, and training the monks who had flocked to him. After his death Buddhism became a separate religion that swept over the Far East.

Hinduism has also influenced a little-known Western mystical tradition known as Theosophy ("Divine Wisdom"). The French novelist Honoré de Balzac, the Swedish playwright August Strindberg, and the Irish poet William Butler Yeats all had their spiritual ideas colored by Hinduism through Theosophy.

Joseph Campbell, a scholar of mythology and comparative religion, has become a *guru* to many modern Americans

through his books and taped interviews. Among Campbell's disciples is George Lucas, whose popular *Star Wars* movies are shaped by Hindu mythology. Luke Skywalker's inner journey to find the Force (Atman) within himself and unite it with the Universal Force (Brahma) is pure Hinduism, and so are the discussions of duty and honor (dharma). It seems astonishing to find such ancient ideas animating a popular film about the far future.

This influence across the millennia should not, however, really surprise us. Though there are Hindus who fear and hate other religions—it was a Hindu fanatic who killed Gandhi because he preached tolerance of Islam—in principle, Hinduism accepts the truth of all world religions. This philosophical openness is a two-way street that allows Indian ideas to make their way into our own world.

9 HISTORICAL BACKGROUND

Ashoka: One of the greatest of kings in ancient times, Ashoka unified much of northern India. Later he sickened of war and turned to Buddhism, establishing monasteries and sending missionaries abroad in search of converts. He professed Mahayana Buddhism, the version that understands the Buddha not as a saint but as a savior. Mahayana Buddhism opens the possibility of enlightenment to the ordinary lay person; Hinayana Buddhism, on the other hand, confines this possibility to the monks who can practice their religion full time. It is Mahayana Buddhism that has become the religion of most of the Far East.

TEACHING TIP

Interested students might enjoy researching the differences between Mahayana Buddhism and Hinayana (also called Theravada) Buddhism. After beginning with the encyclopedia, students might turn to the classic study by Huston Smith, *The Religions of Man* (1958). Students may also be interested in researching Zen, the variety of Buddhism that took root in Japan and has attracted much attention in the Western world.

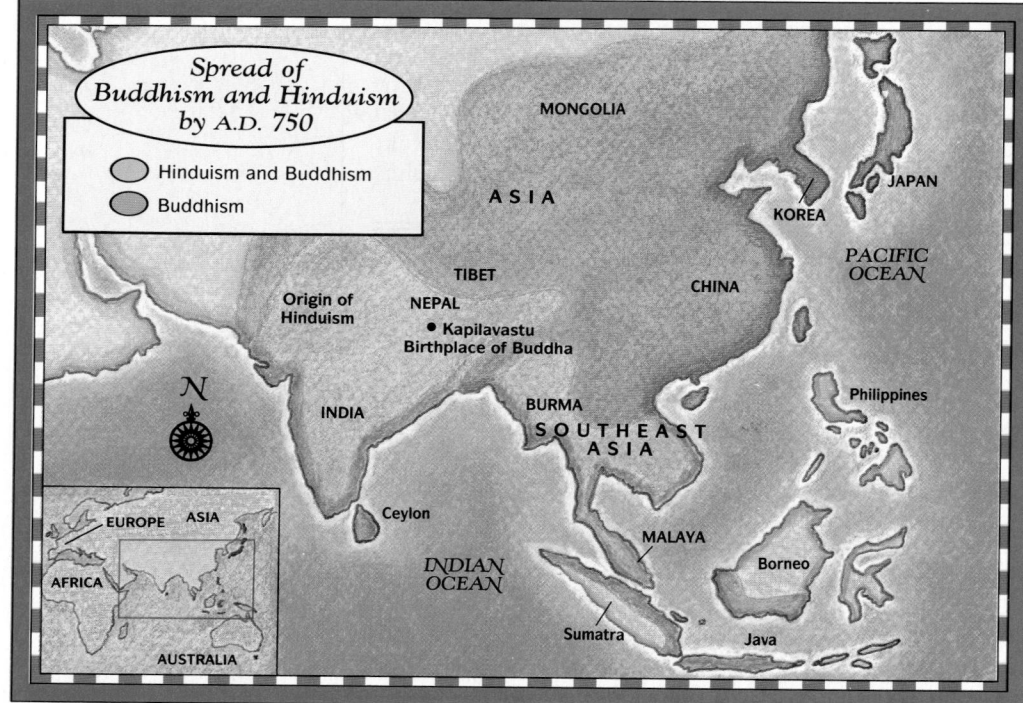

Spread of Buddhism and Hinduism by A.D. 750

Ashoka, the "Righteous" Emperor

The **Maurya empire** (322–230 B.C.) was the first Indian empire; through warfare and iron-fisted rule, it claimed at its height most of northern India. Yet its greatest ruler, **Ashoka** (d. 232 B.C.), preached goodness, nonviolence, and "righteousness." He also promoted Buddhism, closely monitoring the ethics of his officials' behavior, encouraging vegetarianism, and outlawing hunting for sport. Most significantly, he made Buddhism a religion of missionaries, sending teachers as far away as Southeast Asia, where Buddhism still thrives.

After Ashoka's death in 232 B.C., Buddhism fell into decline, and by the end of the first century A.D. it had nearly disappeared in India. But Buddhism's effect on Hinduism has never been erased. Many Hindus practice some degree of vegetarianism, and the contemplative life preached by Buddha remains a key aspect of Hinduism.

The Gupta Empire

The next great political power in India was the **Gupta dynasty**, which controlled most of northern India from A.D. 320 to 467. Under the Guptas, Hinduism reached a full flowering, and a fertile ground was provided for the expression of Hindu culture through the arts. During this time, Hindu sculpture flourished, and the classical period of Indian literature reached its height.

10

> ### Hinduism reached a full flowering during the Gupta empire (A.D. 320–467).

Unity Through Diversity

11

Indian culture may be characterized as a struggle to achieve unity in the face of enormous diversity. In many ways, it has been the geography of India—the land itself—that has ultimately unified India's multitude of languages, customs, and beliefs. Certainly Indian politics have only periodically achieved this unity. Indian literature, especially classical Sanskrit literature, has fared better. For it is in the classical literature of India—the epics, dramas, poems, and tales—that we see, again and again, expressions of the Hindu belief in the connection between all living things and their oneness in the divine unity.

ASVATTHAMAN SHOOTS AN ARROW OF FIRE AT THE PANDAVAS. *Illustration from the* Razm-nama.

Free Library of Philadelphia, Rare Book Department, John Frederick Lewis Collection. Photo by Joan Broderick

> **"OM. This eternal Word is all: what was, what is and what shall be, and what beyond is in eternity. All is OM. "**
> —*from* Mandukya Upanishad

12

HRW Photo by Richard Weiss

Detail of the Meenakshi Temple wall, India.

10 HISTORICAL BACKGROUND
Gupta Empire: The period of the Gupta Empire is often called the "Golden Age" of Hinduism. Science, literature, music, painting—the arts of peace—flourished during this time. Buddhism was still the state religion, as established centuries earlier by Ashoka, but Hinduism was reviving and absorbing the best elements of Buddhism. Buddhism later disappeared from India.

11 CULTURAL DIVERSITY
❓ *What is the cause of diversity in the United States?* (Immigration has brought together peoples of many different languages, races, religions, and backgrounds.) *What is the source of our unity?* (Answers will vary. Possible response: belief in democratic ideals)

12 RESPONDING TO THE QUOTATION
The word *om* indicates assent or affirmation. For devout Hindus, its utterance over and over during prayer is a means of affirming one's acceptance of the universe. A close analogy in Western religion is *amen*, a word of Hebrew origin meaning "truly" or "so be it." At the end of a prayer it signifies the congregation's assent or approval. The quotation suggests that all religion, all doctrine, all gods, can be reduced to a one-syllable word meaning "yes."
❓ *Do you think it is possible for one word to embody the essence of sacred teachings? Explain.* (Answers will vary.) ■

The Aryan nomads who created this yakshi, or nature spirit, showed the forces of nature as attributes of a human being.

? *What force of nature is emphasized in this work of art?* (The strong female features of the yakshi emphasize fertility, the source of life, and abundance.) ■

1 CULTURAL BACKGROUND

The *Rig Veda* is considered the most important of the four most sacred books of Hinduism, known as *Vedas*. The remaining Vedas—the *Yajur Veda*, the *Sama Veda*, and the *Atharva Veda*—deal with instructions for priests, ritual formulas, and magical spells.

COMPARING LITERATURE

Unlike other sacred scriptures, such as the Bible, the *Rig Veda* provides little information about historical events. It contains no dates, names of rulers, or descriptions of wars and alliances. However, the *Rig Veda* does help to explain how religion and society evolved in India between 1500 and approximately 700 B.C.

2 CULTURAL BACKGROUND

The Vedic hymns reveal the ancient Aryans as a highly spiritual and imaginative people. Most of the hymns praise the natural world and the wonder of existence. In many of them, such as "Night," the events and forces of nature are addressed as gods and goddesses.

The Rig Veda
c. 1000 B.C.

The Cleveland Museum of Art. Purchase, John L. Severance Fund, 71.15

A yakshi, Indian, c. A.D. 150.

The *Rig Veda* (rig' vā'də) is a collection of more than one thousand hymns that have come to be revered as the sacred texts of the Hindu religion. The original hymns are in an archaic form of Sanskrit, an ancient Indo-European language brought to India by the Aryans, who migrated from the west around 1500 B.C.

The *Rig Veda*, which has come to mean "hymns of supreme sacred knowledge," began as part of sacred rituals in the lives of the Aryan people. Because the Hindus regarded the *Rig Veda* as being divinely inspired, or "heard" directly from the gods, they thought it only fitting that later generations also "hear" the hymns. Thus, even

after Sanskrit became a written language, the hymns were transmitted orally by Vedic priests.

Generations of Hindu priests, or *brahmans* (brä'mənz), learned the hymns according to a strict method of memorization. Today, we can appreciate how effective this method was by comparing written versions of the *Rig Veda* made by different scribes: The hymns appear in practically the same words in each manuscript.

The Vedas reveal a great deal about early Indo-European civilizations. We know that the Aryans who came to India were nomads, people with no permanent home. According to the Vedic hymns, the Aryans eventually settled down and became farmers who raised crops and livestock, built simple huts, wore woven wool clothing, made iron tools, and developed communities. The hymns also tell us that the Aryan settlers had their share of social problems, including drunkenness, gambling, and fighting. But most of all, the hymns reveal that the Aryans were a highly poetic people who worshiped the forces of nature.

The Aryans laid the foundation for a powerful religious faith: Hinduism. Hindu worship today generally departs a great deal from the rituals outlined in the ancient texts. On occasions such as weddings and funerals, however, brahman priests in modern India still solemnly chant hymns from the Vedas.

1

2

OBJECTIVES
1. *To analyze a hymn from the* Rig Veda
2. *To identify the characteristics and purposes of a hymn*
3. *To write a descriptive paragraph about night and a short essay comparing and contrasting two hymns*
4. *To recognize the use and purpose of apostrophe*

Reader's Guide

NIGHT
from the Rig Veda

Background

The *Rig Veda* contains not only the oldest Vedic hymns but also the most lyrical ones. In their beauty and simplicity, these hymns have been compared to the psalms of the Hebrew Bible.

In the Vedic literature, a god or goddess was assigned to nearly every aspect of nature: For example, the god Surya was associated with the sun, while the god Agni was associated with fire. The hymns were songs of praise for the beauty and wonders of nature. They were also prayers used to seek protection and cooperation from the forces of nature. "Night," like many of the hymns, reveals that the ancient nomads who sang these songs both loved and feared the natural world around them.

"Night" is the only hymn in the ten books of the *Rig Veda* that is dedicated to Ratri (rä'trē), the goddess of night. Night was thought to be a sister of Dawn, a bright goddess. Instead of being depicted as simply dark, Night is also described as a bright deity whose eyes, the stars, drive away the darkness.

Writer's Response

In everyday life and in many literary works, night is often associated with danger or evil. The ancient Aryans, however, believed that night also had some beneficial and beautiful aspects. What qualities do you associate with night? Freewrite your response.

Literary Focus

A **hymn** is a lyric poem, or song, that is addressed to a divine being. Through hymns, people praise the power and wisdom of their deities. Hymns are also often a way of asking for divine help or mercy. Usually intended to be sung during ceremonies or religious worship, most hymns are formal and dignified in tone. The hymn "Night" achieves two purposes: It sings the praises of the goddess and enlists her help in protecting the singer's community.

PREREADING FOCUS

Background: Although the hymns of the *Rig Veda* are dedicated to individual gods, the Aryans did not believe that the various gods had ultimate control over the universe. Instead, they believed in a supreme unifying force called *rita*, a pervasive cosmic order regulating all existence. The Aryans saw evidence of *rita* in the order of nature—in the regular movement of the heavenly bodies and in the dependable rising and setting of the sun, for example. As part of nature, human beings also had to conform to the rules of nature. Actions such as lying or drunkenness were considered dangerous challenges to the cosmic order.

Literary Focus: Hymns have a number of characteristics that make them particularly suitable for oral presentation. Many address a god directly, thus creating an intimate intensity with deep emotional resonance for the singer and the audience. Many hymns also use repetition and parallelism (both within verses and between verses). These devices make the hymns easy to remember by giving them cadence and by emphasizing important ideas.

ABOUT THE TRANSLATOR

Dr. Wendy Doniger O'Flaherty is an expert on South Asian studies and the history of religion. She has published books about Hindu mythology and has translated and interpreted many classical Sanskrit works.

NIGHT
from the Rig Veda
translated by
WENDY DONIGER O'FLAHERTY

❚ *As you read this hymn, make a list of the qualities that are attributed to the goddess of night. Why do you think that the night is seen as feminine?*

1   1 The goddess Night has drawn near, looking about on many sides with her eyes. She has put on all her glories.

    2 The immortal goddess has filled the wide space, the depths and the heights. She stems the tide of darkness with her light.

    3 The goddess has drawn near, pushing aside her sister the twilight. Darkness, too, will give way.

2   4 As you came near to us today, we turned homeward to rest, as birds go to their home in a tree.

    5 People who live in villages have gone home to rest, and animals with feet, and animals with wings, even the ever-searching hawks.

    6 Ward off the she-wolf and the wolf; ward off the thief. O night full of waves, be easy for us to cross over.

    7 Darkness—palpable, black, and painted—has come upon me. O Dawn, banish it like a debt.

    8 I have driven this hymn to you as the herdsman drives cows. Choose and accept it, O Night, daughter of the sky, like a song of praise to a conqueror.

The Cleveland Museum of Art, Edward L. Whittemore Fund, 32.118

LADY WAITING, Indian, c. 1800.
❓ *Does this painting strike you as a good illustration for the hymn? Why or why not?*

Research Project. Students may be interested in finding out more about other important gods of the Hindu religion who are presented in the *Rig Veda*. Besides the goddess Night and the gods mentioned on p. 456, students might research the characteristics and roles played by such deities as Vishnu; Rudra (later called Shiva); Varuna, a god of the sky; Indra; and the Maruts, or storm gods. Encourage students to read relevant sections of the *Rig Veda* and consult reference sources on the Hindu religion.

CLOSURE

Have students return to the headnote that precedes the hymn. Ask them what characteristics are attributed to the night and what feelings about night the poem evokes. On the chalkboard, record their answers in a word web with "Night" written in the center. Finally, have students speculate on why night is personified as feminine. ■

First Thoughts

What image in this poem struck you as the most powerful or memorable? Why?

Identifying Facts

1. Find the verse in which Night is spoken of in terms not of darkness but of light.
2. In verse 6, what request does the speaker make of Night?
3. In the last verse of this hymn, what offering does the speaker ask Night to "choose and accept"?

Interpreting Meanings

1. What positive or beneficial qualities of night are suggested in this **hymn**?
2. **Personification** is a figure of speech in which a nonhuman thing is talked about as though it were human. In this hymn, Night is referred to as "she," as if it were alive. What other details personify Night?
3. A **simile** is a figure of speech that makes a comparison between two unlike things using a word such as *like, as,* or *than.* Find at least three similes in this hymn. Explain what is being compared in each.

Applying Meanings

Although this hymn is set in an ancient world very different from ours, many of its details seem timeless. Which details mean the most to you? Which would probably not mean much to a modern reader?

Creative Writing Response

Writing a Description. Review your freewriting about the qualities you associate with night. Then use the associations as the basis for a paragraph in which you vividly describe night. You may imitate the form of the hymn and address your description to night as if it were a living being or deity.

Critical Writing Response

Comparing and Contrasting Two Hymns. In a two- or three-paragraph essay, compare and contrast the hymn "Night" from the *Rig Veda* to the New Kingdom Egyptian hymn "The Great Hymn to the Aten" (see page 73). In your essay, you may wish to consider the following points of each hymn:

1. The **subject**
2. The **purpose** (to praise the deity; to ask for divine help or mercy)
3. The **imagery** and **figures of speech** (**apostrophe, epithets, similes, metaphors**)
4. The **tone** (dignified, informal)

Explore any other points of similarity or difference that you can find in the two hymns. In your concluding paragraph, speculate on the similarities and differences between the New Kingdom Egyptians' and the ancient Aryans' views of their deities as revealed in their hymns.

Language and Vocabulary

Apostrophe

Apostrophe is a figure of speech in which a speaker directly addresses an absent or dead person, an abstract quality, or something nonhuman as if it were present. This technique is typically employed in hymns that address a divine being.

1. Which lines of the hymn contain examples of apostrophe? Who is addressed?
2. Apostrophe can serve as a way to "get a handle on" cosmic forces beyond our control. Addressing such forces directly seems to make them more approachable, as in the nursery rhyme, "Rain, rain, go away!" Can you name two more examples?

ANSWERS

First Thoughts
Answers will vary.

Identifying Facts
1. verse 2 (Night "stems the tide of darkness with her light")
2. a request for protection
3. the hymn itself

Interpreting Meanings
1. She prevents total darkness, and encourages rest.
2. Night is a "goddess" and a "daughter"; she has eyes; she can ward off wolves.
3. *Comparisons:* villagers going home to birds roosting (verse 4); darkness to debt (verse 7); the hymn to a song praising a conquerer (verse 8).

Applying Meanings
Answers will vary. Meaningful details might include the desire for protection at night. References to herdsmen may mean little to modern readers.

Creative Writing Response
Writing a Description. Descriptions should be vivid and have an overall mood.

Critical Writing Response
Comparing and Contrasting Two Hymns. Essays should cite specific similarities and differences in the hymns' styles and in the deities.

Language and Vocabulary
Apostrophe. 1. Night is addressed in verses 4 and 8; dawn, in verse 7. **2.** Possible responses: "Star light, star bright . . ."; "Twinkle, twinkle, little star . . ." ■

1 LITERARY BACKGROUND

The *Mahabharata*, consisting of nearly 100,000 stanzas in eighteen books, is about eight times the length of Homer's *Iliad* and *Odyssey* combined. In addition to the eighteen books considered to be the original *Mahabharata*, there is a final book, the *Harivamsa*, or "Dynasty of Hari," which is thought to be a later addition.

2 CULTURAL BACKGROUND

Vyasa: How could one person have managed to write a work of the *Mahabharata*'s enormous length? According to legend, Vyasa, the "compiler," had special help.

Supposedly, the epic came to Vyasa in a vision. Ganesha, a popular Indian diety with an elephant head, then agreed to transcribe it on the condition that Vyasa dictate the lines to him without pause. Vyasa agreed but he added his own condition that Ganesha must understand the meaning of every word before writing it down. Thus, whenever Vyasa found Ganesha outpacing him, Vyasa dictated particularly difficult passages that forced Ganesha to slow down and ponder. These dense passages can be found interspersed throughout the epic.

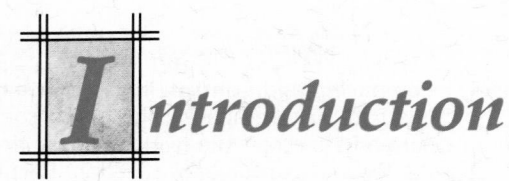

Introduction

The Mahabharata

The *Mahabharata* (mə·hä′bä′rə·tə), which may well be the longest poem ever composed in any language, is one of the two great epics of ancient India. Hundreds of millions of people regard this ancient poem as a rich source of religious, philosophical, and practical wisdom.

The Scope of the Epic

The word *Mahabharata* means "great story of Bharata's descendants." The epic poem tells about two rival families descended from a legendary king named Bharata: the Kauravas (kou′rä·vəz) and the Pandavas (pän′də·vəz). The main story takes up less than half the poem.

◆

conflict: *a struggle or clash between opposing characters, forces, or emotions.*

The remainder of this vast narrative is composed of independent texts and digressions, or asides, into other subjects. The most famous of these digressions is the religious and philosophical dialogue known as the *Bhagavad-Gita* (bug′ə·vəd gē′tä) (see page 467).

Historians believe that some of the events and settings depicted in the epic have a basis in fact, referring to events that took place as long ago as 1000 B.C. For example, the epic's central battle between the rival families may reflect a historical struggle for control of lands bordering the upper Ganges and Yamuna rivers, near what is now the city of Delhi, the capital of modern India.

The Author of the *Mahabharata*

The *Mahabharata* in its present form was composed sometime between the fourth century B.C. and the fourth century A.D. According to tradition, the author of the epic was a sage named Vyasa, meaning "compiler" or "arranger." Whether Vyasa actually existed or not, the name is appropriate, for the epic is a collection of works gathered from many sources. The work is probably the result of many hands.

A Struggle for Power

The central conflict of the epic is the rivalry between two families, or sets of cousins, over the kingdom of Kurukshe-tra (koo·roo·kshā′trə). Both sets of cousins are partly divine—that is, they were fathered by gods. The quarrel between the two families is ignited by Duryo-dhana (do͞or·yō′də·nə), the eldest of the Kaurava branch of the family.

After his father gives a piece of the Kaurava kingdom to his cousins the Pandavas, Duryodhana, whose name means "Mr. Dirty Fighter," becomes jealous. On the advice of his uncle, a gambler, Duryodhana challenges Yudhistira (yo͞o·dē′stē·rə), the eldest of the Pandava brothers, to a game of chance using loaded dice. At a climactic moment early in the epic, Yudhistira blindly stakes all of the Pandavas' worldly goods on the game. By the end of the game, he has lost not only his wealth but also his freedom and that of his brothers and their wife. Duryodhana then sentences the Pandavas to twelve years of exile in the forest. A final provision of the sentence is that, after the final year of exile, the Pandavas must leave the forest and live for a year in disguise, undetected by anyone. If they can fulfill this condition, they can regain all that they lost.

The Pandavas are accompanied in exile by their common wife, a woman of breathtaking beauty and inner strength named Draupadi (drou′pə·dē). Won by the warrior Arjuna (är′jo͞o·nə) in a contest, Draupadi lives with each Pandava brother in turn—an arrangement resulting from an order of the Pandavas' mother that all the brothers should share in whatever good comes to one.

When the Pandavas return from exile and demand their rightful share of the kingdom, the Kauravas refuse. The Pandavas feel they have no choice but to go to war with their cousins. Although they emerge victors from the great epic battles of the *Mahabharata*, the cost of the Pandavas' victory is immense destruction and suffering.

The Continuing Appeal of the *Mahabharata*

The *Mahabharata* is both a popular entertainment and a treasure trove of wisdom and philosophy. As a testament to its popularity, the *Mahabharata* has been translated into nearly all the languages of India, and it has also been absorbed

Scene from *The Mahabharata*, a film by Peter Brook.

into the various cultural traditions of Southeast Asia. Such popular entertainments as Indian folk theater and Indonesian shadow-puppet theater have taken their plot elements from episodes of the *Mahabharata*. A highly rated Indian television series based on the epic has drawn millions of hooked viewers. An internationally acclaimed stage and film adaptation by English director Peter Brook has proven appealing to American and European audiences. Even today, the *Mahabharata* speaks to a large and diverse audience.

CULTURAL BACKGROUND

The Fifth Veda: Although the *Mahabharata* is called the fifth Veda, the Vedas are considered to be divine revelation, while the *Mahabharata* is regarded as a work of human origin. According to Hindu thinking, an original "Golden Age," referred to in Sanskrit as the "Best Throw of the Dice," has been succeeded by declining "throws" through several eons, during which the creative spirit has deteriorated. Thus the four Vedas, revealed during the earlier era, are regarded as perfect and complete, while the later *Mahabharata* is viewed as imperfect.

OBJECTIVES
1. *To recognize the characteristics of the Mahabharata, a classic Indian epic*
2. *To infer the theme of this episode*
3. *To write sets of riddles and answers, as well as an essay analyzing the episode's theme*

PREREADING FOCUS

Background: In Hindu thought, *dharma* is both a person's preordained path and the universal order of the cosmos. To understand the concept of dharma, Westerners must not confuse it with their own ideas of virtue or right action. Right or wrong actions can only be judged in relation to a person's dharma, his or her fated course in life determined at birth by social caste. For example, when the noble Yudhistira dies later in the *Mahabharata*, he is punished because he had cursed the gods for calling him to war. Such a protest against his preordained dharma as a warrior offended the gods. On the other hand, Yudhistira's vain cousin, whose greed had brought on the war, feasts happily in the company of the gods after his death, for he fulfilled his dharma by going to war without complaint.

Literary Focus: Students may have difficulty distinguishing between a **moral**, a lesson in right and wrong behavior, and a **theme**, the central, underlying idea of the selection as a whole. To help students discover the theme, encourage them to look for details that suggest a general view of life or human nature rather than a specific prescription for correct conduct in a particular situation.

Reader's Guide

HUNDRED QUESTIONS
from the Mahabharata

Background

The episode "Hundred Questions" comes from Book 2 of the *Mahabharata*, near the end of the Pandava brothers' twelve-year exile in the forest. At first glance, this episode seems a far cry from sacred matters. Yet the *Mahabharata* is an important text of the Hindu religion.

The Hindu concept of *dharma* (där′mə), or sacred duty, is central to the *Mahabharata*. In Hinduism, each person has prescribed responsibilities and duties that make up his or her dharma. By performing these duties, each individual contributes to a universal order. Thus, a devout Hindu servant will try to be as loyal as possible, and a devout leader will strive to embody the highest qualities of leadership: wisdom, humility, and respect for his or her parents and the gods. Thus, heroism in the *Mahabharata*, unlike heroism depicted in many other world epics, depends less on physical prowess or great cleverness and more on the proper fulfillment of dharma.

In this episode, Yudhistira, the eldest Pandava brother, must respond to a series of questions that test his character and challenge him to fulfill his dharma.

Writer's Response

Two of the questions that Yudhistira must answer in this episode are "Who is really happy?" and "What is the greatest wonder of the world?" Freewrite your own answers to both these questions. As you read the selection, compare your answers to those the hero gives.

Literary Focus

The **theme** is the central idea of a work of literature. A theme is not the same as the subject of a work. The theme is the idea the writer wishes to convey *about* the subject. For example, in the poem "Carpe Diem" (see page 417), Horace's *subject* is the passage of time, but his *theme* is that we must make the most of each moment.

While the themes of some works are directly stated, most themes are implied. It is up to the reader to piece together all the clues the writer has provided about the work's underlying meaning.

HUNDRED QUESTIONS
from the Mahabharata
translated by
R. K. NARAYAN

Read to the end of the paragraph that begins "He wept and lamented aloud," on page 463. Do you predict that Yudhistira will suffer the same fate as his brothers?

ABOUT THE TRANSLATOR
R. K. Narayan was born and educated in southern India. In addition to translations of the *Mahabharata* and the *Ramayana*, he has written numerous novels, essays, and short stories. He lives in India.

pilgrimage (pil'grim·ij): a long journey

CULTURAL DIVERSITY
If you have students with Indian backgrounds, encourage them to share what they know of the importance of the *Mahabharata* in modern Indian life.

Yudhistira (right), in a scene from *The Mahabharata*, a film by Peter Brook.

G. Abegg/Sygma Photo News

THE FIVE PANDAVA BROTHERS

Yudhistira (yōō·dē'stē·rə): the eldest and most capable brother.

Bhima (bē'mə): second son of Pandu.

Arjuna (är'jōō·nə): the third son and greatest warrior of the epic.

Nakula (nä'kōō·lə): one of the twins born to Madri, second wife of Pandu.

Sahadeva (sä·hä·dā'və): the other twin born to Madri.

The Pandavas were in a hopeful mood when they came back to their original starting point, Dwaitavana,[1] after their prolonged pilgrimage. Dwaitavana was rich in fruits and roots, and the Pandavas lived on sparse diets, performing austerities[2] and practicing rigid vows.

They managed to live, on the whole, a

---

1. **Dwaitavana** (dwä·ta'və·nə): a place in the forest.
2. **austerities** (ô·ster'ə·tēz): practices of self-denial and self-discipline.

Complex Sentences

A clause is a group of words that contains a subject and a predicate. Independent clauses express a complete thought and can stand alone as sentences. Subordinate clauses do not express a complete thought and are used as nouns or modifiers. Complex sentences are made up of one independent clause and one or more subordinate clauses. Here is an example from "Hundred Questions":

Complex Sentence: He had no time even to consider what to say (independent clause), as the questions came in a continuous stream (subordinate clause).

1. Reading and Speaking. Ask students to identify three examples of complex sentences in the selection. Have students share the sentences with the class and discuss which clauses are independent and subordinate.

---

1 CULTURAL DIVERSITY

Indian society was based on a system of hereditary classes, or castes. The *brahmins*, the highest caste, were the priests. The *kshatriyas*, the second caste, were soldiers and rulers charged with protecting and defending others. Yudhistira and his brothers are members of this second caste.

❓ *Can you think of other cultures that had similar warrior classes?* (Possible responses: the *samurai* of medieval Japan; the knights of medieval Europe)

2 INFERRING

Why do you think Nakula immediately obeys Yudhistira's commands? (As the eldest and most capable, Yudhistira is recognized as the leader.)

3 LITERARY ELEMENT

Characterization: What do Arjuna's and Bhima's actions after they hear the voice and see their brothers' bodies reveal about their characters? (They are aggressive and foolhardy.) What are all four brothers primarily concerned with? (satisfying their thirst, regardless of the consequences)

tranquil life—until one day a brahmin[3] arrived in a state of great agitation. He had lost a churning staff and two faggots[4] of a special kind, with which he produced the fire needed for his religious activities. All his hours were normally spent in the performance of rites. But that day, he wailed, "A deer of extraordinary size, with its antlers spreading out like the branches of a tree, dashed in unexpectedly, lowered its head, and stuck the staff and the faggots in its horns, turned round, and vanished before I could understand what was happening. I want your help to recover those articles of prayer, for without them I will not be able to perform my daily rites. You can see its hoof marks on the ground and follow them."

1 As a *kshatriya*,[5] Yudhistira felt it his duty to help the brahmin, so with his brothers, he set out to chase the deer. They followed its hoof marks and eventually spotted it, after a long chase. But when they shot their arrows, the deer sprang away, tempted them to follow it here and there, and suddenly vanished without a trace. They were by this time drawn far into the forest and, feeling fatigued and thirsty, they sat under a tree to rest.

2 Yudhistira told his youngest brother, Nakula, "Climb this tree and look for any sign of water nearby."

Presently, Nakula cried from the top of the tree, "I see some green patches and also hear the cries of cranes . . . must be a water source." He came down and proceeded towards a crystal-clear pond, sapphire-like, reflecting the sky. He fell down on his knees and splashed the water on his face. As he did this, a loud voice, which seemed to come from a crane standing in the water, cried, "Stop! This pond is mine. Don't touch it until you answer my questions. After answering, drink or take away as much water as you like." Nakula's thirst was so searing that he could not wait. He bent down and, cupping his palms, raised the water to his lips. He immediately collapsed, and lay, to all purposes, dead.

After a while, Yudhistira sent his brother, Sahadeva, to see what was delaying Nakula's return. He too rushed forward eagerly at the sight of the blue pond, heard the warning, tasted the water, and fell dead.

Arjuna followed. On hearing the voice, he lifted his bow, shot an arrow in the direction of the voice, and approached the water's edge. The voice said, "Don't be foolhardy. Answer me first before you touch the water."

Arjuna, surveying with shock and sadness the bodies of his younger brothers, replied, "When you are silenced with my arrows, you will cease to question. . . ." Driven to desperation with thirst and enraged at the spectacle of his dead brothers, he sent a rain of arrows in all directions. As the voice continued to warn, "Don't touch," he stooped and took the water to his lips and fell dead.

3 Next came Bhima. He saw his brothers lying dead, and swung his mace and cried back when he heard the voice, "O evil power, whoever you may be, I will put an end to you presently, but let me first get rid of this deadly thirst. . . ." Turning a deaf ear to the warning, he took the water in the cup of his palm and with the first sip fell dead, the mace rolling away at his side.

Yudhistira himself presently arrived, passing through the forest where no human being had set foot before except his brothers. He was struck by the beauty of the

---

3. **brahmin** (brä'min): person of the highest, priestly caste; also, **brahman**.
4. **faggots:** bundles of sticks.
5. ***kshatriya*** (kə·shat'rē·yə): person of the warrior caste.

2. **Writing and Sharing.** Ask students to write a complex sentence related to the story, using the words "that," "when," "who," "because," "after," "before," or "as" to begin the subordinate clause. ∎

Yudhistira's brothers Arjuna, Bhima, Nakula, and Sahadeva, and their wife Draupadi. From *The Mahabharata*, a film by Peter Brook.
? *What happens to Yudhistira's brothers when they drink from the lake?*

surroundings—enormous woods, resonant with the cry of birds, the occasional grunt of a bear, or the light tread of a deer on dry leaves—and then he came upon the magnificent lake, looking as if made by heavenly hands. There on its bank he saw his brothers.

He wept and lamented aloud. Both the poignancy and the mystery of it tormented him. He saw Arjuna's bow and Bhima's mace lying on the ground, and reflected, "Where is your promise to split Duryodhana's thigh?[6]

What was the meaning of the gods' statement at Arjuna's birth that no one could vanquish him?" How was he to explain this calamity to Kunthi?[7]

A little later he said to himself, "This is no ordinary death. I see no marks of injury on any of them. What is behind it all?" Could it be that Duryodhana had pursued them, and had his agents at work? He observed the dead faces; they bore no discoloration or sign of decay. He realized that his brothers could not have been killed by mortals, and concluded that there must be some higher power responsible. Resolving not to act hastily, he considered all the possibilities, and stepped into the lake to perform the rites for the dead.

The voice now said, "Don't act rashly; answer my questions first and then drink and take away as much water as you like. If you disregard me, you will be the fifth corpse here. I am responsible for the deaths of all these brothers of yours; this lake is mine and whoever ignores my voice will die. Take care!"

Yudhistira said humbly, "What god are you to have vanquished these invincible brothers of mine, gifted and endowed with <u>inordinate</u> strength and courage? Your feat is great and I bow to you in homage, but please explain who you are and why you have slain these innocent slakers of thirst? I do not understand your purpose, my mind is agitated and curious. Please tell me who you are."

At this request he saw an immense figure materializing beside the lake, towering over the surroundings. "I am a yaksha.[8] These brothers of yours, though warned, tried to force their way in and have paid for it with

---

6. **Duryodhana's thigh:** a promise made by Bhima at the end of the game of dice after the Pandavas had lost everything to their cousins.

7. **Kunthi** (ko͞on′tē): the mother of Yudhistira, Arjuna, and Bhima.

8. **yaksha** (yak′shə): forest divinity or nature spirit.

4 GUIDED READING

Contrasting: How is Yudhistira different from his brothers? (Possible response: On the way to the lake, Yudhistira, unlike his brothers, is struck by the beauty of his surroundings. Also, he weeps at the sight of the bodies and prepares to perform the proper rites for the dead before satisfying his own thirst.) How does Yudhistira show himself to be rational rather than rash? (He examines the bodies and concludes that the deaths were caused by supernatural agents.)

5 PREDICTING

What character traits has Yudhistira shown thus far? (caution, respect, intelligence) Based on these traits, how do you predict Yudhistira will react to the voice? (Possible response: He will heed the warning.)

■ **inordinate** (in·ôr′də·nit): excessive

6 SPECULATING

What do you suppose the *yaksha* is trying to learn about Yudhistira through the first two questions? (Possible response: The yaksha may be testing to see if Yudhistira will acknowledge the ultimate importance of Brahma and dharma in the workings of the universe.)

■ **HUMANITIES CONNECTION**

This image is from the wall of a temple in Khajuraho, one of the most important temple sites in India. The image celebrates Tantrism, a form of Hinduism in which the union of male and female is sometimes thought to symbolize a union between humanity and divinity.

❓ *How do humanity and divinity seem to be unified in "Hundred Questions"?* (Possible response: The gods seem to pervade the realm of human existence. The yaksha shows this not only by preventing the brothers from drinking, but also by judging Yudhistira's answers. Moreover, Yudhistira's answers refer to deities such as Brahma, "Mother," and "Father," who regulate the natural workings of the earth.) ■

---

their lives. If you wish to live, don't drink this water before you answer my questions."

Yudhistira answered humbly, "O yaksha, I will not covet what is yours. I will not touch this water without your sanction, in spite of my thirst. I will answer your questions as well as I can."

The yaksha asked, "What makes the sun rise? . . . What causes him to set?"

6 Yudhistira answered, "The Creator Brahma[9] makes the sun rise, and his dharma[10] causes the sun to set. . . ."

Yudhistira had to stand a grueling test. He had no time even to consider what to say, as the questions came in a continuous stream. Yudhistira was afraid to delay an answer or plead ignorance. Some of the questions sounded fatuous, some of them profound, some obscure but packed with layers of significance. Yudhistira was constantly afraid that he might upset the yaksha and provoke him to commit further damage, although one part of his mind reflected, "What worse fate can befall us?"

Without giving him time to think, the questions came, sometimes four at a time in one breath. Their range was unlimited, and they jumped from one topic to another.

"What is important for those who sow? What is important for those who seek prosperity?" Before Yudhistira could complete his sentence with "Rain," he also had to be answering the next question with "Offspring. . . ."

The yaksha went on to ask, "What is weightier than the earth?"

"Mother."[11]

"Higher than the heavens?"

Detail from the wall of an Indian temple.

HRW Photo by Richard Weiss

"Father."[12]

"Faster than the wind?"

"Mind."

"What sleeps with eyes open?"

"Fish."

"What remains immobile after being born?"

"Egg."

"Who is the friend of the exile?"

"The companion on the way."

---

9. **Brahma** (brä'mə): a Hindu creator god.
10. **dharma** (där'mə): rule or law.
11. **Mother:** possibly because "mother Earth" personified is thought to live deep inside the earth.
12. **Father:** possibly because "Father" is conceived of here as a sky-god.

1. Why are Yudhistira and his brothers so tired and thirsty? (They have been following the trail of an elusive deer.)
2. What does the voice tell the brothers that they must do before drinking any water? (answer questions)
3. What happens to the four brothers when they disobey the voice? (They fall dead.)

4. Why does Yudhistira choose Nakula as the brother to be revived? (so both of his father's wives will have one son alive)
5. What gift does the yaksha give Yudhistira to help him during his last year of exile? (the power to remain unrecognized)

RETEACHING
Have students create questions they would like to ask the yaksha. Remind students that the questions should lead the yaksha to reveal truths about life or to offer guidance for developing a strong moral character. Invite students to take turns role-playing the yaksha and answering their classmates' questions.

"Who is the friend of one about to die?"

"The charity done in one's lifetime."

"Who is that friend you could count on as God given?"

"A wife."

"What is one's highest duty?"

"To refrain from injury."

To another series of questions on renunciation, Yudhistira gave the answers: "Pride, if renounced, makes one agreeable; anger, if renounced, brings no regret; desire, if renounced, will make one rich; avarice, if renounced, brings one happiness. True tranquility is of the heart. . . . Mercy may be defined as wishing happiness to all creatures. . . . Ignorance is not knowing one's duties. . . . Wickedness consists in speaking ill of others."

"Who is a true brahmin? By birth or study or conduct?"

"Not by birth, but by knowledge of the scriptures and right conduct. A brahmin born to the caste, even if he has mastered the Vedas,[13] must be viewed as of the lowest caste if his heart is impure."

There were a hundred or more questions in all. Yudhistira felt faint from thirst, grief, and suspense, and could only whisper his replies. Finally, the yaksha said, "Answer four more questions, and you may find your brothers—at least one of them—revived. . . . Who is really happy?"

"One who has scanty means but is free from debt; he is truly a happy man."

"What is the greatest wonder?"

"Day after day and hour after hour, people die and corpses are carried along, yet the onlookers never realize that they are also to die one day, but think they will live for ever. This is the greatest wonder of the world."

"What is the Path?"

"The Path is what the great ones have trod. When one looks for it, one will not find it by study of scriptures or arguments, which are contradictory and conflicting."

> 7

At the end of these answers, the yaksha said, "From among these brothers of yours, you may choose one to revive."

Yudhistira said, "If I have only a single choice, let my young brother, Nakula, rise."

The yaksha said, "He is after all your stepbrother. I'd have thought you'd want Arjuna or Bhima, who must be dear to you."

"Yes, they are," replied Yudhistira. "But I have had two mothers. If only two in our family are to survive, let both the mothers have one of their sons alive. Let Nakula also live, in fairness to the memory of my other mother Madri."[14]

The yaksha said, "You have indeed pleased me with your humility and the judiciousness of your answers. Now let all your brothers rise up and join you."

> 8

The yaksha thereafter revived all his brothers and also conferred on Yudhistira the following boon: "Wherever you may go henceforth, with your brothers and wife, you will have the blessing of being unrecognized." The yaksha was none other than Yama,[15] the God of Justice, and father of Yudhistira, who had come to test Yudhistira's strength of mind and also to bless him with the power to remain incognito—a special boon in view of the conditions laid down for the last year of exile.[16]

> 9

---

13. **Vedas** (vā′dəz): sacred collection of Hindu wisdom.

14. **Madri** (mä′drē): The twins Nakula and Sahadeva were born to Madri, second wife of Pandu. Madri was thus the "other mother" of the three elder brothers.

15. **Yama** (yä′mə): In most versions of the epic, the father of Yudhistira is Dharma ("right" or "law" personified), and Yama is the god of death.

16. **conditions . . . exile:** The Pandavas had agreed to spend the last year of their exile outside the forest and in disguise.

READER'S RESPONSE
Think about Yudhistira's replies to the yaksha's questions. Which of his answers would be most useful in your own life?

WRITING TO LEARN
Social Studies: Based on information given in the episode, list some of the duties and qualities expected of members of two Indian castes in the time of the *Mahabharata*: the brahmins and the kshatriyas. Make inferences from the behavior of the brahmin and of Yudhistira and his brothers. ■

7 INTERPRETING
What is meant by "the Path"? (Possible responses: the right way to live, one's dharma)

8 LITERARY ELEMENT
Theme: Yudhistira's character is the focus of most of this episode. Since he is rewarded for his behavior, what would you say is the theme of this episode? (Possible response: True heroes have qualities such as humility, respect for others, caution, persistence, and wisdom.)

judiciousness (jōō·dish′əs·nis): sound judgment

MEETING INDIVIDUAL NEEDS

9 *LEP:* Explain that *incognito* means "with true identity concealed or disguised." ■

1. Riddles in Literature. Invite students to explore riddles in ancient literature, such as the *100 Riddles of Symphosius*, the Bible (the Book of Judges), *The Thousand and One Nights*, or the Anglo-Saxon *Exeter Book*; or in modern literature, such as *The Hobbit*. Students could each select riddles from these or other sources and ask a partner to answer them.

2. Creating a Setting. Ask students to draw or paint an appropriate setting for this episode. Have them return to the text and find descriptions of the scene, such as a "magnificent lake" made "by heavenly hands" and "a deer of extraordinary size, with its antlers spreading out like the branches of a tree." Encourage students to capture the magical, otherworldly atmosphere.

CLOSURE

Review the concept of dharma explained on p. 460, and have students discuss ways in which Yudhistira and his brothers do and do not act in accord with their duty in life. Explain that Arjuna, Yudhistira's brother, is further challenged to fulfill his dharma in the next selection (pp. 467–476), a later episode from the *Mahabharata.* ■

ANSWERS

First Thoughts
Answers will vary.

Identifying Facts
1. They sought a deer that had stolen a brahmin's ritual churning staff and sticks.
2. He obediently answers. Possible questions and answers: What is weightier than the earth? (Mother) Who is the friend of the exile? (the companion on the way)
3. Yama, God of justice and father of Yudhistira; to test Yudhistira. By reviving his brothers and bestowing the blessing of being unrecognized

Interpreting Meanings
1. He is humble, respectful.
2. Possible response: his ingenuity, wisdom, and patience. He is quick-witted and wise.
3. a pond of heavenly beauty. The otherworldly beauty creates a mysterious mood.
4. Possible response: Humility and respect are rewarded. *Evidence:* Yudhistira shows respect for the yaksha and for his own stepmother.

Applying Meanings
Answers will vary.

Creative Writing Response
Creating Riddles. Riddles should display paradoxes, puns, or personification.

Critical Writing Response
Analyzing Theme. Essays should refer to the differences between Yudhistira and his brothers, Yudhistira's answers, and the brothers' resurrection. However, be sure students give a single theme statement. ■

First Thoughts
What did you think of Yudhistira's answers? Which ones did you agree or disagree with most?

Identifying Facts
1. Explain how the Pandava brothers came to find themselves, tired and thirsty, deep in the forest.
2. How does Yudhistira respond when the yaksha questions him? List two of the yaksha's questions and Yudhistira's responses.
3. What is the real identity of the yaksha, and why has he come to the lake? How does the yaksha reward Yudhistira for his correct answers?

Interpreting Meanings
1. How does Yudhistira's character differ from the characters of his four brothers?
2. An **epic hero** must often endure a test or trial of his physical strength or of his ethical values. What qualities in Yudhistira do you think are being tested in the question-and-answer challenge? How and why does Yudhistira succeed in this challenge?
3. Describe the **setting** of this episode. (See especially the fifth and tenth paragraphs.) How does the setting contribute to the **mood** of the episode?
4. What **theme**, or message, about human behavior does this episode from the *Mahabharata* suggest? Support your answer with evidence from the selection.

Applying Meanings
In one of his answers, Yudhistira tells the yaksha what the greatest wonder of the world is. Do you agree with his answer? If not, what do you consider the greatest wonder?

Creative Writing Response
Creating Riddles. Some of the questions that the yaksha asks Yudhistira are **riddles**, in that some twist of logic must be unraveled to answer them. For example, one part of a question seems to contradict another: "What remains immobile after being born?" (Answer: "Egg.") Work with a partner to create your own sets of riddles and answers. Then pose your riddles to the class, and see how other students respond.

Critical Writing Response
Analyzing Theme. In a three-paragraph essay, identify and analyze the **theme**, or underlying meaning, of this episode in the epic. Pay special attention to these aspects of the story: the contrast between Yudhistira and his brothers; Yudhistira's answers to the yaksha's questions; and the resurrection of the brothers from death to life as a result of Yudhistira's correct answers. Completing a chart like the one below may help you to organize the material for your essay.

Yudhistira's traits	Brothers' traits
Caution	Foolhardiness

Questions	Answers
What is highest duty?	Refrain from injury.

The Bhagavad-Gita
c. 300 B.C.–c. A.D. 300

Philadelphia Museum of Art: Purchase: Edith H. Bell Fund

ARJUNA AND HIS CHARIOTEER, LORD KRISHNA.

If you ask any devout Hindu what passage in the *Mahabharata* is the most sacred, the answer will probably be the *Bhagavad-Gita* (bug′ə·vəd gē′tä), literally, "Song of the Lord." The *Gita*, as it is affectionately known, is an episode that interrupts the epic *Mahabharata* (see page 458). By the beginning of Book 6 of the main epic, the five Pandava brothers have returned from exile and are seeking to regain their share of the kingdom. The leader of the Kauravas, Duryodhana, decides to destroy his cousins, the Pandavas, whom he regards as dangerous rivals. The armies of each side then mass for battle.

The *Gita* episode consists of a dialogue between the Pandava brother Arjuna and his charioteer, Krishna, just before the great battle begins. The hero Arjuna sits weeping because he does not want to spill the blood of his relatives, the Kauravas. Krishna urges Arjuna to forget his doubts and to fight.

Krishna plays a double role in the epic. He is at once Arjuna's human brother-in-law and, unbeknownst to the hero, the embodiment of Vishnu (vish′nōo), one of the most important gods in the Hindu pantheon.

The *Bhagavad-Gita* is divided into eighteen sections, or "teachings." The poem is a fine example of **didactic verse**, or poetry meant to convey a philosophy. The *Gita* deals with the nature of the body and the soul, the relationship of human beings to the divine, and the ways the individual can attain "the pure calm of infinity." The *Gita* has been called the bedside book of every pious Hindu. Many Hindus believe that they will attain instant salvation if they hear the *Gita* recited just before they die.

The teachings of this ancient poem also played a major role in shaping the philosophy of Mahatma Gandhi (1869–1948), the charismatic leader who guided India to independence from Britain in 1947. Gandhi called the *Gita* his "spiritual dictionary," a book that taught him to free himself of money, property, and ambition.

Gandhi's philosophy of nonviolent protest profoundly influenced Dr. Martin Luther King, Jr., when he led the Civil Rights movement in the 1960s. The teachings of the ancient *Bhagavad-Gita* have thus indirectly but critically affected modern American society.

HUMANITIES CONNECTION

? What surrounds the regal figures of Arjuna and Krishna? (armies massed for war) Point out to students that, like most epics, the *Mahabharata* is concerned with war. ■

1 LITERARY BACKGROUND

In the episodes that follow the dialogue between Arjuna and Krishna, Arjuna goes to war against his cousins and achieves the status of an epic hero. Eventually most of the Kauravas are killed in battle, but in a sneak attack by night, the survivors slay all of the Pandavas and their allies except for the five brothers.

2 CULTURAL BACKGROUND

The Krishna of the *Bhagavad-Gita* reveals a strong shift in Hindu religious thinking. Unlike earlier gods, who were viewed as impersonal forces, Krishna is portrayed as a loving deity who will help humanity and who wants to receive love in return. By the fourth century A.D., this new view of Krishna had given rise to a new form of worship, an intense kind of personal devotion to individual gods, such as Vishnu and Shiva.

CULTURAL BACKGROUND

The *Gita* provides an overview of the religious thought of India through history and has been translated into more languages than any other Hindu scripture.

OBJECTIVES

1. *To recognize the importance of the Bhagavad-Gita in Hindu culture*
2. *To recognize and understand paradox*
3. *To write a rebuttal of Krishna's arguments and an essay examining the paradoxes in the dialogue between Krishna and Arjuna*

PREREADING FOCUS

Background: The concept of reincarnation, which is central to Hindu thought, underlies Krishna's arguments as he encourages Arjuna to fulfill his *dharma*, or sacred duty. Hindus believe that souls experience a cycle of death and rebirth as they seek eventual absorption into a universal spirit. The concept can be understood more easily by comparing the body to a suit of clothes in which the soul resides. At death, one set of "clothing" is exchanged for another as the soul continues its spiritual journey. To advance the soul in this cycle of death and rebirth, a person must act in accord with his or her dharma.

Literary Focus: Paradoxes are attention-getting devices. Their seeming illogic forces readers to think about complex emotions and ideas. "Parting is such sweet sorrow" is an example of a paradox from Shakespeare's *Romeo and Juliet*, and "waging the peace" is a modern example of a paradoxical expression.

ABOUT THE TRANSLATOR

Barbara Stoler Miller (1940–1993) was a professor and department chairperson of Oriental studies at Barnard College. Fluent in French, Spanish, Hindi, Sanskrit, Pali, and Prakrit, she translated many works of poetry and fiction and wrote widely about Indian culture and literature.

Reader's Guide

PHILOSOPHY AND SPIRITUAL DISCIPLINE
from the Bhagavad-Gita

Background

In this selection from the *Bhagavad-Gita*, Krishna urges the warrior-hero Arjuna to fulfill his *dharma,* or "sacred duty," by waging battle. Krishna argues that since it is the fate of every soul to be reincarnated after death—that is, to assume another bodily form—Arjuna need not feel guilty about killing his enemies. The wise warrior should fulfill his dharma as a faithful Hindu and not care about pleasure or pain, profit or loss, success or failure. The narrator who reports this conversation between Krishna and Arjuna is Sanjaya, an attendant to Arjuna's blind uncle, King Dhritarashtra.

Oral Response

Recall one or two specific examples from your own experience, or that of someone you know, when fulfilling a duty created an internal conflict. A diagram like the following may help you explain to the class the source of the conflict in these situations:

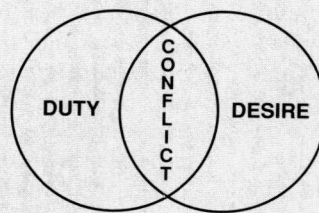

Literary Focus

A **paradox** is an apparent contradiction that is actually true. For example, in this selection Krishna states a paradox when he tells Arjuna, "Our bodies are known to end,/but the embodied self is enduring,/indestructible and immeasurable. . . ." How can something be "embodied" and still live forever? In Hindu beliefs, the "embodied self" is the spirit that inhabits the living body. The spirit endures; the physical body does not. As you read Krishna's words in the *Bhagavad-Gita*, you will find many such paradoxes.

PHILOSOPHY AND SPIRITUAL DISCIPLINE
from the Bhagavad-Gita
translated by
BARBARA STOLER MILLER

❖ *As you read the dialogue below, try to identify the different arguments Krishna uses to persuade Arjuna. How effective is each argument, in your opinion?*

PRINCIPAL CHARACTERS IN THE *BHAGAVAD-GITA*

Sanjaya (sän·jī′ä): attendant to King Dhritarashtra.

Arjuna (är′jōō·nə): the third of the five Pandava brothers.

Krishna (krish′nə): Arjuna's charioteer, who is really a god.

Bhishma (bēsh′mə): great-uncle to the Pandava brothers.

Drona (drō′nə): Arjuna's teacher in archery.

Dhritarashtra (drē·tə·räsh′trə): Arjuna's uncle and father of the Pandavas' enemies, the Kauravas.

Sanjaya

1   Arjuna sat dejected,
    filled with pity,
    his sad eyes blurred by tears.
    Krishna gave him counsel.

Lord Krishna

2   Why this cowardice
    in time of crisis, Arjuna?

The coward is ignoble, shameful,
foreign to the ways of heaven.

3   Don't yield to impotence!
    It is unnatural in you!
    Banish this petty weakness from your heart.
    Rise to the fight, Arjuna!

2

Arjuna

4   Krishna, how can I fight
    against Bhishma and Drona
    with arrows
    when they deserve my worship?

5   It is better in this world
    to beg for scraps of food
    than to eat meals
    smeared with the blood
    of elders I killed
    at the height of their power
    while their goals
    were still desires.

6   We don't know which weight
    is worse to bear—
    our conquering them
    or their conquering us.

1 EVALUATING
Among the gods in the Hindu pantheon, Krishna has long been extremely popular. As the god of fire, lightning, storms, the heavens, and the sun, he maintains the order of nature and protects the world from destruction. Krishna is usually regarded as the eighth incarnation of Vishnu, and he often descends to earth to protect the world from demons. In the *Bhagavad-Gita*, Krishna provides divine guidance and comfort. Yet along with his supernatural powers, he has endearing human frailties. (For more information about Krishna, see pp. 496–497.)
❓ *What personality traits is Krishna showing here?* (Possible responses: concern for Arjuna's welfare, moral superiority, the ability to command)

2 GUIDED READING
Finding the Main Idea: In stanzas 4 and 5, what reason does Arjuna give for not wanting to fight? (He does not want to kill his elders, especially those whom he admires.)

Arjuna and Krishna, from Peter Brook's film version of the *Mahabharata*.
❓ *What is Krishna's true identity?*

We will not want to live
if we kill
the sons of Dhritarashtra
assembled before us.

3 ⌐ 7 The flaw of pity
blights my very being;
conflicting sacred duties
4 ⌐   confound my reason.
I ask you to tell me
decisively—Which is better?
I am your pupil.
Teach me what I seek!

8 I see nothing
that could drive away
the grief

that withers my senses;
even if I won kingdoms
of unrivaled wealth
on earth
and sovereignty over gods.

Sanjaya

9 Arjuna told this
to Krishna—then saying,
"I shall not fight,"
5 ⌐   he fell silent.

10 Mocking him gently,
Krishna gave this counsel
as Arjuna sat dejected,
between the two armies.

Lord Krishna

11 You grieve for those beyond grief,
and you speak words of insight;
but learned men do not grieve
for the dead or the living.

12 Never have I not existed,
nor you, nor these kings;
and never in the future
shall we cease to exist.

13 Just as the embodied self
enters childhood, youth, and old age,
so does it enter another body;
this does not confound a steadfast man.

14 Contacts with matter make us feel
heat and cold, pleasure and pain.
Arjuna, you must learn to endure
fleeting things—they come and go!

15 When these cannot torment a man,
when suffering and joy are equal
for him and he has courage,
he is fit for immortality.

16 Nothing of nonbeing comes to be,
nor does being cease to exist;
the boundary between these two
is seen by men who see reality.

17 Indestructible is the presence
that pervades all this;
no one can destroy
this unchanging reality.

18 Our bodies are known to end,
but the embodied self is enduring,
indestructible, and immeasurable;
therefore, Arjuna, fight the battle!

19 He who thinks this self a killer
and he who thinks it killed,

both fail to understand;
it does not kill, nor is it killed.

20 It is not born,
it does not die;
having been,
it will never not be;
unborn, enduring,
constant, and primordial,
it is not killed
when the body is killed.

21 Arjuna, when a man knows the self
to be indestructible, enduring, unborn,
unchanging, how does he kill
or cause anyone to kill?

22 As a man discards
worn-out clothes
to put on new
and different ones,
so the embodied self
discards
its worn-out bodies
to take on other new ones.

23 Weapons do not cut it,
fire does not burn it,
waters do not wet it,
wind does not wither it.

24 It cannot be cut or burned;
it cannot be wet or withered;
it is enduring, all-pervasive,
fixed, immovable, and timeless.

25 It is called unmanifest,
inconceivable, and immutable;
since you know that to be so,
you should not grieve!

26 If you think of its birth
and death as ever-recurring,

from the Bhagavad-Gita   **471**

8 CULTURAL DIVERSITY

Help students recognize that in stanzas 31–38, Krishna shifts the emphasis to Arjuna's duty, or dharma, as a warrior. In Hindu philosophy, the greatest personal responsibility is to fulfill the role one was created to play in the divinely ordained cosmic order.

9 SYNTHESIZING

According to Hindu belief, what impact will Arjuna's deci-sion have on his soul? (As a member of the caste of war-riors and rulers, Arjuna would violate his dharma by failing to go to war, thereby destroying his soul's chances of advancing on the spiritual path.)

10 CULTURAL DIVERSITY

Explain that in stanza 39 Krishna again shifts focus. In stanzas 39–52, he discusses spiritual discipline and an "in-ner core of resolve" which will help one escape from the "bondage of action." Krishna is talking about the importance of fulfilling one's dharma with-out worrying about the out-come of one's actions.

472   Indian Literature

then too, Great Warrior,
you have no cause to grieve!

27   Death is certain for anyone born,
and birth is certain for the dead;
since the cycle is inevitable,
you have no cause to grieve!

28   Creatures are unmanifest in origin,
manifest in the midst of life,
and unmanifest again in the end.
Since this is so, why do you lament?

29   Rarely someone
sees it,
rarely another
speaks it,
rarely anyone
hears it—
even hearing it,
no one really knows it.

30   The self embodied in the body
of every being is indestructible;
you have no cause to grieve
for all these creatures, Arjuna!

8   [31   Look to your own duty;
do not tremble before it;
nothing is better for a warrior
than a battle of sacred duty.

32   The doors of heaven open
for warriors who rejoice
to have a battle like this
thrust on them by chance.

9   [33   If you fail to wage this war
of sacred duty,
you will abandon your own duty
and fame only to gain evil.

34   People will tell
of your undying shame,
and for a man of honor
shame is worse than death.

35   The great chariot warriors will think
you deserted in fear of battle;
you will be despised
by those who held you in esteem.

36   Your enemies will slander you,
scorning your skill
in so many unspeakable ways—
could any suffering be worse?

37   If you are killed, you win heaven;
if you triumph, you enjoy the earth;
therefore, Arjuna, stand up
and resolve to fight the battle!

38   Impartial to joy and suffering,
gain and loss, victory and defeat,
arm yourself for the battle,
lest you fall into evil.

10   [39   Understanding is defined in terms of
philosophy;
now hear it in spiritual discipline.
Armed with this understanding, Arjuna,
you will escape the bondage of action.

40   No effort in this world
is lost or wasted;
a fragment of sacred duty
saves you from great fear.

41   This understanding is unique
in its inner core of resolve;
diffuse and pointless are the ways
irresolute men understand.

11   [42   Undiscerning men who delight
in the tenets of ritual lore

utter florid speech, proclaiming,
"There is nothing else!"

43   Driven by desire, they strive after
         heaven
      and contrive to win powers and
         delights,
      but their intricate ritual language
      bears only the fruit of action in rebirth.

44   Obsessed with powers and delights,
      their reason lost in words,
      they do not find in contemplation
      this understanding of inner resolve.

45   Arjuna, the realm of sacred lore
      is nature—beyond its triad of qualities,
      dualities, and mundane rewards,
      be forever lucid, alive to your self.

46   For the discerning priest,
      all of sacred lore
      has no more value than a well
      when water flows everywhere.

47   Be intent on action,
      not on the fruits of action;
      avoid attraction to the fruits
      and attachment to inaction!

48   Perform actions, firm in discipline,
      relinquishing attachment;
      be impartial to failure and success—
      this equanimity is called discipline.

49   Arjuna, action is far inferior
      to the discipline of understanding;
      so seek refuge in understanding—pitiful
      are men drawn by fruits of action.

50   Disciplined by understanding,
      one abandons both good and evil deeds;

Dallas Museum of Art, gift of Mrs. John Leddy Jones

Vishnu with attendants, Indian, c. 1026. *The Hindu god Vishnu has many incarnations, one of whom is Krishna.*

so arm yourself for discipline—
discipline is skill in actions.

51   Wise men disciplined by understanding
      relinquish the fruit born of action;
      freed from these bonds of rebirth,
      they reach a place beyond decay.

MEETING INDIVIDUAL NEEDS

11 ***Advanced Students:*** Ask students with a knowledge of, or background in, Eastern philosophies or religions to explain Krishna's preference for "contemplation" over "ritual lore" in stanzas 42–45. (Possible response: Inner understanding derived from meditation leads to the ultimate end of the cycle of rebirths.) ∎

mundane (mun'dān'): of the world, especially as distinguished from heavenly
lucid (lōō'sid): rational; clear-thinking
equanimity (ek'wə·nim'ə·tē): evenness of mind

HUMANITIES CONNECTION

Krishna is one of the most popular incarnations of Vishnu, a god who is thought to have ten classical avatars, or incarnations.
❓ *Why do you suppose Vishnu takes so many different physical forms?* (Vishnu is thought to be the preserver and protector of the world; his various incarnations allow him to return to earth at critical periods to help humanity.) ∎

from the Bhagavad-Gita   **473**

1. What is *dharma?* (a person's divinely ordained sacred duty)
2. Why does Arjuna hesitate to fight?
   (He does not want to harm his own
   relatives.)
3. According to Krishna, why is death unimportant? (Only the body dies, not the
   soul.)

4. According to Krishna, what will people
   do if Arjuna does not fight? (slander
   him)
5. According to Krishna, what results from
   giving up all desires? (peace)

RETEACHING

Organize students into small groups. Have
each student select three or four stanzas
that he or she finds particularly difficult to
understand. Have students in each group
take turns acting as Krishna and explaining
the meaning of the stanzas. As students
take the part of Krishna, encourage them
to use the surrounding context and the
introductory material on p. 467 to figure
out the meaning of each stanza.

INTERPRETING

In other translations, spiritual
discipline, whose attainment is
discussed in stanzas 39–52, is
translated as "yoga." In Hindu
thought, yoga is the path of
action taken without care for
results (called "attraction to
the fruits" in stanza 47). Yoga
frees the will so that it can devote itself to self-realization.
*How else might the terms
"spiritual discipline" and
"yoga" be explained?* (Possible
responses: renunciation of
worldly values, concentration
on the process rather than the
goal, meditation)

12 GUIDED READING

Finding the Main Idea: What
does Krishna say is necessary
to attain spiritual discipline? (a
turning from sacred lore to
contemplation)

MEETING INDIVIDUAL NEEDS

13 ***LEP:*** Encourage students
to make a list of the ways a
person can gain sure insight,
by looking at the "when"
clauses in stanzas 55–61. ∎

sensuous (sen'shoo·əs):
bringing pleasure to the
senses

MEETING INDIVIDUAL NEEDS

14 ***Visual Learners:*** Have students make a flow chart show-
ing the chain of events that
leads to ruin, described in
stanzas 62 and 63. ∎

474   Indian Literature

---

52 When your understanding passes
     beyond
the swamp of delusion,
you will be indifferent to all
that is heard in sacred lore.

12 53 When your understanding turns
from sacred lore to stand fixed,
immovable in contemplation,
then you will reach discipline.

Arjuna

54 Krishna, what defines a man
deep in contemplation whose insight
and thought are sure? How would he
     speak?
How would he sit? How would he
     move?

Lord Krishna

13 55 When he gives up desires in his mind,
is content with the self within himself,
then he is said to be a man
whose insight is sure, Arjuna.

56 When suffering does not disturb his
     mind,
when his craving for pleasures has
     vanished,
when attraction, fear, and anger are
     gone,
he is called a sage whose thought is
     sure.

57 When he shows no preference
in fortune or misfortune
and neither exults nor hates,
his insight is sure.

58 When, like a tortoise retracting
its limbs, he withdraws his senses
completely from sensuous objects,
his insight is sure.

59 Sensuous objects fade
when the embodied self abstains from
     food;
the taste lingers, but it too fades
in the vision of higher truth.

60 Even when a man of wisdom
tries to control them, Arjuna,
the bewildering senses
attack his mind with violence.

61 Controlling them all,
with discipline he should focus on me;
when his senses are under control,
his insight is sure.

14 62 Brooding about sensuous objects
makes attachment to them grow;
from attachment desire arises,
from desire anger is born.

63 From anger comes confusion;
from confusion memory lapses;
from broken memory understanding is
     lost;
from loss of understanding, he is
     ruined.

64 But a man of inner strength
whose senses experience objects
without attraction and hatred,
in self-control, finds serenity.

65 In serenity, all his sorrows
dissolve;
his reason becomes serene,
his understanding sure.

66 Without discipline,
he has no understanding or inner
     power;
without inner power, he has no peace;
and without peace where is joy?

1. Writing About Reincarnation. In Hindu thought, reincarnation is governed by *karma*—a law which provides that good actions have positive results while evil actions have bad ones in this life or in subsequent lives. Starting from this premise, have students write stories in which a character is reincarnated on the basis of behavior in a past life.

2. Research Project. Both Mahatma Gandhi and Motilal Nehru (father of Jawaharlal Nehru, the first prime minister of independent India) saw the *Bhagavad-Gita* as an important source for their views on nonviolence. Have students research one of these Indian leaders and write a report summarizing his importance in Indian history and the impact the *Bhagavad-Gita* had on his political philosophy.

CLOSURE

Remind students that Krishna stressed the importance of reincarnation, sacred duty, spiritual discipline, and the attainment of pure insight in trying to convince Arjuna to go to battle. Ask students which of his arguments they would find most convincing if they were faced with the prospect of going into battle. Encourage them to explain their choices and to consider any other arguments that would influence them in their decision. ■

Arjuna with his bow, from Peter Brook's film version of the *Mahabharata*.

67 If his mind submits to the play
of the senses,
they drive away insight,
as wind drives a ship on water.

15
68 So, Great Warrior, when withdrawal
of the senses
from sense objects is complete,
discernment is firm.

69 When it is night for all creatures,
a master of restraint is awake;
when they are awake, it is night
for the sage who sees reality.

16
70 As the mountainous depths
of the ocean
are unmoved when waters
rush into it,
so the man unmoved
when desires enter him
attains a peace that eludes
the man of many desires.

71 When he renounces all desires
and acts without craving,
possessiveness,
or individuality, he finds peace.

72 This is the place of the infinite spirit;
achieving it, one is freed from delusion;
abiding in it even at the time of death,
one finds the pure calm of infinity.

---

15 LITERARY ELEMENT
Paradox: Explain the paradox in stanza 68 in your own words. (Possible response: Only when you are able to pull your senses away from objects can you fully understand the world around you.)

16 LITERARY ELEMENT
Analogy: Explain the analogy used in stanza 70. (Possible response: A person who has learned to renounce all desires is like the depths of the ocean, which remain unmoved when other waters rush in.) How does the image of motionless ocean depths reinforce Krishna's point? (The image suggests infinity and peace.)

ANSWERS
First Thoughts
Answers will vary.

Identifying Facts
1. Since the embodied self is indestructible, Arjuna will not destroy his enemies even if he kills them. Both allies and enemies will call Arjuna a coward and a deserter.
2. He advises Arjuna to be indifferent to success and failure. Arjuna should be intent on action, not on its results.

First Thoughts
Do you agree with Krishna's teachings concerning worldly success? Why or why not?

Identifying Facts
1. In stanzas 30–31, what argument does Krishna use to persuade Arjuna to fight? According to Krishna in stanzas 33–36, what are the dangers to Arjuna's reputation if he fails to fight?

2. In stanzas 47–48, what outlook toward failure and success does Krishna recommend to Arjuna? On what should Arjuna be "intent"? On what should he *not* be intent?

■→

from the Bhagavad-Gita   **475**

3. His insight is driven away. He finds peace.

Interpreting Meanings
1. He is loyal, respectful of his elders, and reluctant to inflict injury. These values make the thought of fulfilling his duty as a warrior as painful as the thought of not fulfilling it.
2. The parallel phrases all begin with the adverb "rarely" and then continue with an indefinite pronoun subject, a transitive verb, and the direct object "it."
3. They establish the concept of the inner self that cannot kill or be killed.
4. Answers will vary.

Applying Meanings
Answers will vary. Many students may see the wisdom in renouncing "cravings and possessiveness"; however, students may also point out that the positive value of individuality is deeply rooted in the American psyche.

Creative Writing Response
Writing a Rebuttal. Rebuttals should be in the form of a speech addressed to Arjuna. They should persuade Arjuna not to fight by refuting each of Krishna's principal arguments.

Critical Writing Response
Examining Paradox. Essays should discuss at least two examples of paradox from the poem, and evaluate Krishna's success in resolving the paradoxes in his arguments. ∎

3. In stanza 67, what does Krishna say happens to a man who gives in to his senses? In stanza 71, what does Krishna say happens when a man gives up all desires?

Interpreting Meanings
1. From stanzas 4–8, what can you infer about Arjuna's values? How have these values contributed to his dilemma? Give specific examples to support your points.
2. The technique of **parallelism** is the repetition of words or phrases that have the same grammatical structure. For example, the four lines of stanza 23 illustrate a parallel arrangement of words in each line. How does the poet use parallelism in stanza 29?
3. In "Hundred Questions," the hero Yudhistira, Arjuna's brother, says that one's highest duty is to refrain from injury (see page 465). In the *Bhagavad-Gita,* however, Krishna tells Arjuna that it is his sacred duty to fight. How do stanzas 18–21 help to resolve this **paradox**, or apparent contradiction?
4. What do you think is the most important teaching, or lesson, in Krishna's advice to Arjuna? Possible answers might include the importance of self-control, the need to do one's duty, the importance of living in the present, the importance of knowing oneself, and the need to protect one's reputation. Briefly explain your choice.

Applying Meanings
The *Bhagavad-Gita* states that someone who "renounces all desires and acts without craving, possessiveness, or individuality" will achieve inner peace. Do you believe this? How relevant is this advice in today's world? Explain the reasons for your answer.

Creative Writing Response
Writing a Rebuttal. Imagine that you are in the Pandavas' camp and you have an opportunity to talk to Arjuna after Krishna finishes. Write a brief impassioned speech in which you rebut, or maintain a point of view opposite to, Krishna's argument that Arjuna should fight his cousins. In your argument, you might mention the love you have for your own family and the fear you and your comrades have of dying a futile death. If you wish, you may act out the speech with classmates.

Critical Writing Response
Examining Paradox. Santha Rama Rau, a contemporary Indian writer, has said that the *Bhagavad-Gita* is "full of philosophical and moral paradox. It can, for instance, be interpreted as pacifist doctrine or as a call to war." The nature of paradox is that it reveals a kind of truth, although it seems at first to be self-contradictory and untrue. In a brief essay, examine the element of paradox in the dialogue between Krishna and Arjuna. Does Krishna resolve the seeming contradictions of his argument? If so, how? Some of the main topics of Krishna's paradoxical arguments you may want to consider include the following: the nature of duty, the purposes of action, the role of reincarnation in the universe, and the consequences of desire. In your essay, be sure to refer to specific passages in the poem.

SEEING CONNECTIONS

The Bhagavad-Gita's Influence on Transcendentalism

The philosophy of Transcendentalism flourished in New England between 1830 and 1860. American writers Ralph Waldo Emerson (1803–1882) and Henry David Thoreau (1817–1862) were the leaders of the Transcendentalist movement. Transcendentalists taught that the most profound realities go beyond, or *transcend*, everyday human experience. They believed human beings needed to look beyond surfaces to a deeper reality, and that in this way they could find signs of God everywhere, in nature and in individuals.

The *Bhagavad-Gita* in New England

When the Sanskrit classics of ancient India started to appear in English translation in the first half of the nineteenth century, the Transcendentalists eagerly pored over the Indian texts. Thoreau was profoundly impressed by the *Bhagavad-Gita* and the Indian tradition. As he wrote in *Walden*—his most famous work—"The pure Walden water mingled with the sacred water of the Ganges [India's most sacred river]."

Cosmic Unity

The Transcendentalists were especially attracted to the concept in the *Gita* of an eternal, cosmic unity called *brahman*, similar to Emerson's concept of the "Over-Soul." According to the *Gita*, the *atman*, or individual soul, of every human being merges again with the *brahman* of the universe.

In 1857, Emerson published "Brahma," a poem that expressed many Transcendentalist ideas. The poem's speaker, Brahma, is the embodiment of a universal, creative force.

> If the red slayer thinks he slays,
>   Or if the slain think he is slain,
> They know not well the subtle ways
>   I keep, and pass, and turn again.
>
> Far or forgot to me is near;
>   Shadow and sunlight are the same;
> The vanished gods to me appear;
>   And one to me are shame and fame.
>
> They reckon ill who leave me out;
>   When me they fly, I am the wings;
> I am the doubter and the doubt,
>   And I the hymn the Brahman sings.
>
> The strong gods pine for my abode,
>   And pine in vain the sacred Seven;
> But thou, meek lover of the good!
>   Find me, and turn thy back on
>   heaven.

The words "sacred Seven" in the last stanza refer to the greatest Hindu saints. Note how the first stanza in the selection above strikingly resembles stanza 19 from the *Bhagavad-Gita* (see page 471).

1 LITERARY BACKGROUND
Stanza 45 of the *Bhagavad-Gita* passage calls nature "the realm of sacred lore" through which one finds the self. Embracing this philosophy, Thoreau lived simply for two years in a cabin on Walden Pond, Massachusetts, closely observing nature and contemplating the meaning of life. In *Walden* (1854), the book Thoreau wrote about his experience, the transparent water of the pond serves as the central symbol for the immutable soul, Krishna's "embodied self." Thoreau, like Krishna, saw worldly possessions as enslaving and distracting.

Ironically, Thoreau himself later had a great impact on Indian culture: Mahatma Gandhi was inspired by Thoreau's essay "Civil Disobedience" to lead a nonviolent movement for Indian independence from British rule.

2 LITERARY ELEMENT
Paradox: Emerson conceived of the "Over-Soul" as a universal spirit that includes everyone. What do the paradoxes in the second and third stanzas suggest about the qualities of the Over-Soul? (Possible response: Though opposites exist in earthly life, their inner essences return to the same greater whole.) ■

This illustration is from an Arabic version of the *Panchatantra*. Although the artist has maintained the lush natural setting typical of Indian art, the translator probably made some minor changes in the tales.

❓ *As the fables were absorbed into different cultures, how do you think they might have changed?* (Each culture might have defined the five aspects of *niti*, especially "resolute action," differently. Also, the names of animals and the settings might change.) ∎

1 CULTURAL BACKGROUND

The Hindu storytellers of the *Panchatantra* intended to create a textbook for learning "worldly wisdom," which Hindus regarded as one of the three objects of human desire. (*Dharma*, or "duty," and *kama*, or "love," are the other two objects of desire.) This interest in worldly wisdom is evident in the morals of the *Panchatantra* fables, which glorify shrewdness and practicality. This shift in classical Indian literature from spiritual to practical concerns may have resulted from the intensity of the struggle for political power in India at the time the fables were developed.

The Panchatantra
C. A.D. 300

The Metropolitan Museum of Art. The Nasli Heeramaneck Collection, Gift of Alice Heeramaneck. 1981. (1981.373)

Illustration from an Arabic version of the *Panchatantra*.

The *Panchatantra* (pun'chə·tän'trə) began in ancient India as a tool for teaching statecraft to young princes. The anonymous work consists of a series of fables, or brief stories that teach practical lessons about life. The stories are contained within a larger outer story, a narrative framework that gives the tales a thematic unity.

In the outer story, called the "frame," a brahman priest named Vishnusharman (vish'nōō·shär'mən) tries to teach the art of rulership to two rather dimwitted young princes. The lessons take the form of a series of fables, presented in five sections: how one loses friends, how one wins friends, how one should handle international relations, how one may lose profits and possessions, and how hasty actions can have harmful consequences.

The central theme that runs through the *Panchatantra* is the idea of *niti* (ni'tē), which means "worldly wisdom." A person needs five things in order to achieve *niti:* physical security, freedom from want, resolute action, good friends, and the use of intelligence. A person with *niti* is the sort of person who can get the better of evil or unscrupulous rivals or plotters by turning the tables on them.

The *Panchatantra* is among the most well-known collections of fables in the world. It was translated into Persian as early as the sixth century A.D. During the Middle Ages, it was translated into Arabic, Greek, Hebrew, Latin, German, and Italian. The classical Indian fables have influenced works as diverse as *The Thousand and One Nights* (see page 638), Geoffrey Chaucer's *Canterbury Tales* (see page 772), and Giovanni Boccaccio's *Decameron* (see page 813). All three of these works, like the *Panchatantra*, rely on a frame story to establish overall unity.

OBJECTIVES
1. To identify the origin, purpose, and central theme of the stories in the Panchatantra
2. To identify the characteristics of a fable
3. To write an original fable about a behavior that is destructive to friendship

VOCABULARY IN CONTEXT
The words listed below will appear in the side margin at the point of instruction:

1. residue   4. reflected
2. vulnerable   5. discern
3. dictum

Reader's Guide

RIGHT-MIND AND WRONG-MIND
from the Panchatantra

Background

The fable "Right-Mind and Wrong-Mind" and the second fable it contains, "A Remedy Worse Than the Disease," illustrate two of the main literary elements of the *Panchatantra*. One of these is the use of the story-within-a-story device to emphasize different aspects of the lesson being taught by the main fable. In this case, "A Remedy Worse Than the Disease" casts light on the lesson being taught by "Right-Mind and Wrong-Mind." Another prominent literary element of the *Panchatantra* is an intermingling of prose and **epigrams**—brief, clever verses that often contain a moral. Epigrams are effective devices for summarizing the message of the story line. The frequent use of epigrams gives the *Panchatantra* much of its special flavor and appeal.

This selection is taken from "The Loss of Friends," the first section of the *Panchatantra*. Like many of the fables in the section, "Right-Mind and Wrong-Mind" shows how greed and malice can destroy a friendship.

Oral Response

If you wanted to teach a friend a moral or practical lesson about life, do you think it would be more effective to use the direct method of a lecture or the indirect method of telling a fable? Discuss the reasons for your opinion with the rest of the class.

Literary Focus

A **fable** is a brief story in prose or verse that teaches a moral or a practical lesson about life. The characters in most fables are animals that behave and speak like human beings. Occasionally, however, the characters—whether humans or humanlike animals—represent abstract qualities. The following selection features both types of characters. The young man named Right-Mind, for example, is not so much a fully developed character as he is a symbol of the quality of virtue. The heron, on the other hand, is more like a real person, since he is neither all good nor all bad.

PREREADING FOCUS

Background: The importance of friendship is at the heart of the *Panchatantra*. The larger framework of the first section, "The Loss of Friends," is the story of the bull Lively and the lion Rusty. They meet each other in the forest and become friends. However, a jackal, feeling left out, tells both the bull and the lion that his friend is plotting against him. A battle ensues, in which Lively is killed and the jackal enjoys the results of his maneuverings. Within this framework there are thirty-four stories, most of them told by two jackals, Victor and Cheek. In this case, Cheek tells the fable "Right-Mind and Wrong-Mind" to Victor.

Literary Focus: The most famous fables are those by Aesop, who lived around 600 B.C. However, those by the seventeenth-century French writer La Fontaine are almost as popular (see *Fables*, pp. 940–944). Fables in which animals are the main characters are called "beast fables," and the tales of the *Panchatantra* are often referred to in this way.

ABOUT THE TRANSLATOR
Arthur W. Ryder's translation of the *Panchatantra* was one of the earliest English translations made directly from the Sanskrit. Educated at Harvard University and the University of Leipzig, Ryder not only translated Sanskrit works into English, but also composed original poetry in Sanskrit.

Compound and Compound–Complex Sentences

Compound sentences contain two or more independent clauses but no subordinate clauses. Compound–complex sentences contain two or more independent clauses and one or more subordinate clauses.

Compound Sentences: ". . . Wrong-Mind disdained the paternal warning, and during the night he hid his father out of sight in the hole in the tree." (two independent clauses)

Compound–Complex Sentence: He debated the matter with Wrong-Mind, and they decided to go home, since their object was attained. (two independent clauses and one subordinate clause)

Writing. Have students combine pairs of simple sentences and pairs of simple and complex sentences from the selection to form compound or compound–complex sentences. ■

TEACHER'S RESOURCES

🖙 Review and Response Worksheet
🖙 Selection Test
🖙 Vocabulary Activity Worksheet
🖙 Vocabulary Test
🖙 Language Skills Worksheet

1 LITERARY ELEMENT

Characterization: What do the names "Right-Mind" and "'Wrong-Mind" suggest about how well-rounded or multidimensional these characters are? (Possible response: These characters are one-dimensional and represent particular abstract qualities.)

MEETING INDIVIDUAL NEEDS

2 Explain to students that "as a consequence of favoring fortune" means "as the result of good luck." Fortune is favoring the two merchants. ■

3 PREDICTING

What do you think may happen to the money? (Possible response: Wrong-Mind's name implies that he will misuse the money in some way.)

4 EVALUATING

Is Wrong-Mind's plan a good test of virtue or friendship? Why or why not? (Answers will vary.)

■ **residue** (rez′ə·doō′): leftover portion; remainder

vulnerable (vul′nər·ə·bəl): sensitive to influence; temptable

---

RIGHT-MIND AND WRONG-MIND
from the Panchatantra
translated by
ARTHUR WILLIAM RYDER

> As you read, pay attention to the **epigrams**—*short verses that present a moral*—that appear throughout the tale. Do you think these epigrams unnecessarily interrupt the story, or do they serve a useful purpose?

1 In a certain city lived two friends, sons of merchants, and their names were Right-Mind and Wrong-Mind. These two traveled to another country far away in order to earn money. There the one named Right-Mind, **2** as a consequence of favoring fortune, found a pot containing a thousand dinars,[1] which had been hidden long before by a holy man. He debated the matter with Wrong-Mind, and they decided to go home, since their **3** object was attained. So they returned together.

When they drew near their native city, Right-Mind said: "My good friend, a half of this falls to your share. Pray take it, so that, now that we are at home, we may cut a brilliant figure before our friends and those less friendly."

But Wrong-Mind, with a sneaking thought of his own advantage, said to the other: "My good friend, so long as we two hold this treasure in common, so long will our virtuous friendship suffer no interruption. Let us each take a hundred dinars, and go to our homes after burying the remainder. The decrease or increase of this treasure will serve **4** as a test of our virtue."

Now Right-Mind, in the nobility of his nature, did not comprehend the hidden duplicity of his friend, and agreed to the proposal. Each then took a certain sum of money. They carefully hid the <u>residue</u> in the ground, and made their entrance into the city.

Before long, Wrong-Mind exhausted his preliminary portion because he practiced the vice of unwise expenditure and because his predetermined fate offered <u>vulnerable</u> points. He therefore made a second division with Right-Mind, each taking a second hundred. Within a year this, too, had slipped in the same way through Wrong-Mind's fingers. As a result, his thoughts took this form: "Suppose I divide another two hundred with him, then what is the good of the remainder, a paltry four hundred, even if I steal it? I

---

1. **dinars** (di·närz′): A dinar was originally a Roman coin (*decenarium*). This currency of varying values was used in many parts of the Mediterranean and the Middle East.

think I prefer to steal a round six hundred."
After this meditation, he went alone, removed the treasure, and leveled the ground.

A mere month later, he took the initiative,
going to Right-Mind and saying: "My good
friend, let us divide the rest of the money
equally." So he and Right-Mind visited the
spot and began to dig. When the excavation
failed to reveal any treasure, that impudent
Wrong-Mind first of all smote his own head
with the empty pot, then shouted: "What

*Cincinnati Art Museum, Museum Purchase with funds
given by Mrs. Herbert Marcus, 1976.28*

**Page from the dictionary of Sāhāngīr, Mughal,
17th century.**
*Why do you think fables have been
used as teaching tools?*

became of that good lucre?[2] Surely, Right-
Mind, you must have stolen it. Give me my
half. If you don't, I will bring you into court."

"Be silent, villain!" said the other. "My
name is Right-Mind. Such thefts are not in
my line. You know the verse:

> A man right-minded sees but trash,
> Mere clods of earth, in others' cash;
> A mother in his neighbor's wife;
> In all that lives, his own dear life."

So together they carried their dispute to
court and related the theft of the money.
And when the magistrates learned the facts,
they decreed an ordeal[3] for each. But Wrong-
Mind said: "Come! This judgment is not
proper. For the legal <u>dictum</u> runs:

> Best evidence is written word;
> Next, witnesses who saw and heard;
> Then only let ordeals prevail
> When witnesses completely fail.

In the present case, I have a witness, the
goddess of the wood. She will reveal to you
which one of us is guilty, which not guilty."
And they replied: "You are quite right, sir.
For there is a further saying:

> To meanest witnesses, ordeals
> Should never be preferred;
> Of course much less, if you possess
> A forest goddess' word.

Now we also feel a great interest in the case.
You two must accompany us tomorrow
morning to that part of the forest." With this
they accepted bail from each and sent them
home.

Then Wrong-Mind went home and asked
his father's help. "Father dear," said he, "the

2. **lucre** (loo'kər): riches; money.
3. **ordeal:** here, a form of trial in which guilt or innocence was determined by subjecting the accused
to painful or dangerous tests.

5 ANALYZING
How would you summarize the
ethical ideas behind Right-
Mind's epigram? (Possible response: The righteous person
does not covet the belongings
of others and respects all living
things as he respects himself.)

dictum (dik'təm): a formal
pronouncement or state-
ment

6 GUIDED READING
Sequencing: According to
Wrong-Mind's epigram, in
what order should evidence be
relied on? (The best evidence
is written statements; next is
oral statements by witnesses,
followed by ordeals—grueling
tests given to accused persons
to determine their innocence
or guilt.)

MEETING INDIVIDUAL NEEDS

7 ESL: Explain that *meanest*,
in this context, means "poorest" or "of low caste," not
"most cruel." Invite students
to help paraphrase the epigram. (Even if the witnesses
are of low caste, their testimony is preferred over ordeals—even more so, if the
witness is a forest goddess.) ■

READING CHECK

1. What did Right-Mind find in the far-off country? (a thousand dinars)
2. What did Wrong-Mind want his father to do for him? (impersonate a goddess and testify falsely against Right-Mind)
3. Who told the story "A Remedy Worse Than the Disease"? (Wrong-Mind's father)
4. In the story-within-the-story, what animal did the heron want the mongoose to kill? (a snake)
5. What was Wrong-Mind's punishment for stealing and trying to lay the blame on Right-Mind? (He was hanged.)

RETEACHING

Ask different students to choose and dramatize an incident from either the frame story or "A Remedy Worse Than the Disease." Encourage students to create their own dialogue as they act out their incidents. After each dramatization, encourage the audience to describe what has happened and what the action reveals about the character(s) involved.

8 PREDICTING

Who will fail to weigh the "good and bad" of a given scheme in the main story? (Wrong-Mind and to a lesser extent his father, who complies with Wrong-Mind's request.)

9 LITERARY ELEMENT

Characterization: The leading characters in the *Panchatantra* are animals who are fairly static and one-dimensional. The monkey is generally foolish, for example; the jackal, crafty and greedy, and the lion, strong but dull-witted. *What characteristic is associated with the heron?* (stupidity) *the crab?* (craftiness)

> reflected (ri·flekt'id): thought seriously; pondered

COMPARING LITERATURE

Some scholars believe that stories from the *Panchatantra* had made their way to Greece by 600 B.C. There they may have influenced Aesop in the construction of his own collection of beast fables. Compare one of the animal characters in the *Panchatantra* with a character from one of Aesop's fables. *In which fable does the animal character behave more like a human being?*

HUMANITIES CONNECTION

The Tree symbolizes the creative force. Bulls, monkey-spirits, and a five-headed *naga*, a serpent spirit, surround the trunk of the Tree. ∎

dinars are in my hand. They only require one little word from you. This very night I am going to hide you out of sight in a hole in the mimosa tree that grows near the spot where I dug out the treasure before. In the morning you must be my witness in the presence of the magistrates."

"Oh, my son," said the father, "we are both lost. This is no kind of scheme. There is wisdom in the old story:

8

> The good and bad of given schemes
>   Wise thought must first reveal:
> The stupid heron saw his chicks
>   Provide a mongoose meal."

"How was that?" asked Wrong-Mind. And his father told the story of

A Remedy Worse Than the Disease

A flock of herons once had their nests on a fig tree in a part of a forest. In a hole in the tree lived a black snake who made a practice of eating the heron chicks before their wings sprouted.

At last one heron, in utter woe at seeing the young ones eaten by a snake, went to the shore of the pond, shed a flood of tears, and stood with downcast face. And a crab who noticed him in this attitude, said: "Uncle, why are you so tearful today?" "My good friend," said the heron, "what am I to do? Fate is against me. My babies and the youngsters belonging to my relatives have been eaten by a snake that lives in a hole in the fig tree. Grieved at their grief, I weep. Tell me, is there any possible device for killing him?"

9

On hearing this, the crab reflected: "After all, he is a natural-born enemy of my race. I will give him such advice—a kind of true lie—that other herons may also perish. For the proverb says:

Tree of life, Indian, c. 1600–1700.
What is the meaning of the title, "A Remedy Worse Than the Disease"?

> Let your speech like butter be;
> Steel your heart remorselessly;
> Stir an enemy to action
> That destroys him with his faction."

And he said aloud: "Uncle, conditions being as they are, scatter bits of fish all the way from the mongoose burrow to the snake's hole. The mongoose will follow that trail and will destroy the villainous snake."

When this had been done, the mongoose followed the bits of fish, killed the villainous snake, and also ate at his leisure all the herons who made their home in the tree.

"And that is why I say:

> The good and bad of given schemes, . . .

and the rest of it."

But Wrong-Mind disdained the paternal warning, and during the night he hid his

1. Reading Additional Fables. Interested students might read additional stories from the *Panchatantra* and report on them to the class. Encourage students to discuss the qualities the main characters in these fables show and the practical morals the stories teach.

2. Interviewing a Character. Students might enjoy acting out an interview with either Right-Mind's or Wrong-Mind's father about the events of the fable. Some students could act as interviewers, others as the person being interviewed. Have the interviewer prepare a series of questions aimed at bringing out motivations and reactions to what occurred. Have pairs of students act out their interviews.

CLOSURE

Ask the class, "If you were a king ruling a country, what moral or lesson, other than those illustrated in this fable, would you want to remember to help you rule wisely? Can you express your moral in an epigram?" ■

---

father out of sight in the hole in the tree. When morning came, the scamp took a bath, put on clean garments, and followed Right-Mind and the magistrates to the mimosa tree, where he cried in piercing tones:

"Earth, heaven, and death, the feeling mind,
Sun, moon, and water, fire and wind,
Both twilights, justice, day and night
Discern man's conduct, wrong or right.

O blessed goddess of the wood, which of us two is the thief? Speak."

Then Wrong-Mind's father spoke from his hole in the mimosa: "Gentlemen, Right-Mind took that money." And when all the king's men heard this statement, their eyes blossomed with astonishment, and they searched their minds to discover the appropriate legal penalty for stealing money, in order to visit it on Right-Mind.

Meanwhile, Right-Mind heaped inflammable matter about the hole in the mimosa and set fire to it. As the mimosa burned, Wrong-Mind's father issued from the hole with a pitiful wail, his body scorched and his eyes popping out. And they all asked: "Why, sir! What does this mean?"

"It is all Wrong-Mind's doing," he replied. Whereupon the king's men hanged Wrong-Mind to a branch of the mimosa, while they commended Right-Mind and caused him satisfaction by conferring upon him the king's favor and other things.

> ■ **discern** (di·zurn′): recognize (the difference); make out clearly

WRITING TO LEARN

Science: Select an animal, do research to find out its natural enemy, and write one or two paragraphs reporting your findings. ■

ANSWERS

First Thoughts
Answers will vary.

Identifying Facts
1. He says it will test their virtue. He then steals the money.
2. He wants his father to pretend to be a goddess and falsely accuse Right-Mind.
3. He sets fire to the tree, forcing Wrong-Mind's father to come out.

Interpreting Meanings
1. Possible answers: Be on guard against advice from unreliable sources. Consider all the consequences of any plan.
2. Characters act hastily, depend on advice from untrustworthy sources, and fail to consider all consequences.
3. Most students will probably choose "The good and bad of given schemes . . ."

Applying Meanings
Answers will vary.

Creative Writing Response
Writing a Fable. Fables should illustrate a behavior that could cause a person to lose a friend, and should have a clear moral. ■

First Thoughts

Did you feel that Right-Mind was doing the right thing by setting the fire? Did his action surprise you?

Identifying Facts

1. Why does Wrong-Mind want Right-Mind to bury most of the treasure? What does Wrong-Mind then do on his own?
2. Why does Wrong-Mind want to hide his father in the mimosa tree?
3. How does Right-Mind expose Wrong-Mind's scheme?

Interpreting Meanings

1. What lessons about rulership can be learned from "Right-Mind and Wrong-Mind"?
2. How does the second **fable**, "A Remedy Worse Than the Disease," shed light on, or reinforce, the **moral** of "Right-Mind and Wrong-Mind"?
3. An **epigram** is a brief, clever, and usually memorable statement. Which of the four-line epigrammatic verses in each fable best sums up the story's **moral**?

Applying Meanings

Do you think "Right-Mind and Wrong-Mind" has any relevance to modern readers? How might the moral of the fable be applied today to such fields as business and law?

Creative Writing Response

Writing a Fable. "Right-Mind and Wrong-Mind" is taken from the first part of the *Panchatantra*, which features tales under the heading "Loss of Friends." Make a list of the behaviors that could cause a person to lose a friend. Choose one behavior in particular that you think is the most destructive to friendship. Then think of a brief fable of your own that would illustrate that behavior and its effects. You may create characters who represent specific traits. Try to write at least one **epigram** to include in your tale.

COMPARING LITERATURE

The *Ramayana* resembles the Babylonian, Greek, and Roman epics in many aspects of its structure, characterization, and theme. For example, the *Ramayana* centers on a single hero with a remarkable dual nature as half god, half man. We may compare him to Gilgamesh, to Achilles in Homer's *Iliad*, and to Aeneas in Virgil's *Aeneid*. Other elements in the *Ramayana* that parallel the *Epic of Gilgamesh* and the Greek and Roman epics are its central quest pattern of separation and return, its use of a secondary warrior as a foil to the main hero, and its balance between large-scale battle scenes and scenes of an intimate, romantic nature.

❓ *What details do you recall from the* Epic of Gilgamesh *and the Greek and Roman epics that remind you of elements in the summary of the* Ramayana? *(Possible responses: the wandering of Odysseus and Gilgamesh, the friendship of Achilles and Patroclus)*

ABOUT THE TRANSLATOR

R. K. Narayan has translated the *Mahabharata* as well as the *Ramayana*. Born in 1907 in South India, he is often considered India's leading novelist. Through his characters, Narayan has examined Hinduism in the modern world. Narayan's novel *The Guide* (1958) won India's highest literary award, and in 1964, Prime Minister Nehru awarded him the Padma Bhushan, an annual award for distinguished service.

The Ramayana
c. 200 B.C.–C. A.D. 200

Courtesy of The Arthur M. Sackler Museum, Harvard University, Cambridge, Massachusetts, Private Collection

TWO SPIES DISGUISED AS MONKEYS APPROACH THE ARMY OF RAMA.

The *Ramayana* (rä·mä′yə·nə) is one of India's great Hindu epics. The main character Rama (rä′mə) is, like Krishna, an incarnation of the Hindu god Vishnu (vish′nōō). Rama and his wife Sita (sē′tə) are semidivine figures, but their story in the epic is a moving, human tale of love and jealousy, loss and recovery, separation and return.

The *Ramayana* is a long poem of some 25,000 couplets. As in the case of the *Mahabharata*, the authorship of the *Ramayana* is attributed to a shadowy figure, the poet-sage Valmiki (väl·mē′kē), who composed the epic in Sanskrit.

The main plot of the epic begins with Prince Rama, who, having won his bride Sita through a miraculous trial of strength, is ready to inherit his rightful throne. Rama, however, is banished from his father's kingdom as the result of an evil court intrigue, and for many years he wanders in exile, accompanied by Sita and by his loyal brother Lakshmana (läk′shmə·nə).

In the first half of the epic, Sita is abducted by the fierce Ravana (rä′və·nə), the many-headed king of the demons, and brought to Ravana's island fortress, the kingdom of Lanka. During their quest to rescue Sita, Rama and Lakshmana ally themselves with the monkey-king Hanuman (hän′oo·män′). Rama finally conquers Ravana, wins back his bride, and returns in triumph to his kingdom.

During her captivity, Sita has proved to be as faithful as she is beautiful and wise. But despite the fact that Sita has passed through an ordeal of fire to prove her purity, Rama harbors lingering doubts about her fidelity. These doubts lead, in the end, to Sita's tragic despair and departure from the earth to assume her place as a goddess.

The image of Sita as a flesh-and-blood woman of saintly devotion and great physical endurance reflects the ideal portrait of many classic Indian heroines. Similarly, the loving description of the lush forests, cool hermitages, and other holy places gives us insight into the "geography" of Indian consciousness. The *Ramayana*, like all national epics, holds up a mirror to a rich and complex culture.

OBJECTIVES

1. To recognize the place of the Ramayana in Hindu culture and to understand the main elements of its plot
2. To recognize the characteristics of the epic
3. To write a sequel to Rama's victory and an essay comparing aspects of the Rama-yana and the Bhagavad-Gita

THEMES IN WORLD LITERATURE

War and Peace

From the *Iliad*, pp. 224–277
From the *History of the Peloponnesian War*, pp. 284–292
From the *Annals*, pp. 428–435

What Is a Hero?

From the *Epic of Gilgamesh*, pp. 136–152
From the *Song of Roland*, pp. 692–702 ∎

Reader's Guide

RAMA AND RAVANA IN BATTLE

from the Ramayana

Background

The following selection, which describes the climax of the titanic battles between Rama and Ravana, is drawn from Book 6 of the *Ramayana*. R. K. Narayan's retelling of the narrative is based on a medieval version of the *Ramayana* by the south Indian poet Kamban. Kamban, who drew upon the Sanskrit original of Valmiki, composed his version of the epic in the Tamil language. In this climactic episode, the magic weapons and supernatural powers make for an exciting sequence. More important, however, is the sense we get of a blurring of reality and illusion, and of a conflict that goes beyond the simple opposition between good and evil.

Writer's Response

Thousands of years before such films as *Star Wars*, the struggle between good and evil in the *Ramayana* was imagined as a battle unfolding on a cosmic scale, involving fantastic weapons that could destroy the whole universe. Freewrite for a few minutes your ideas for a science-fiction film that would present an epic struggle between good and evil.

Literary Focus

An **epic** is a long narrative poem that relates the great deeds of a larger-than-life hero who embodies the values of a particular society. Most epics include elements of myth, legend, folklore, and history. The tone is serious and the language grand. Most epic heroes undertake quests to achieve something of tremendous value to themselves or their society.

PREREADING FOCUS

Background: The story of Rama has been retold in different languages and different regions throughout India for centuries. The poets who wrote later versions transformed many details and, in keeping with their times, turned Rama into more than a warrior hero. In the original first and last books, Rama was a warrior whose divinity was merely suggested; later writers, including the medieval poet Kamban, saw him as a god. In Kamban's version of the *Ramayana*, Rama is both a mortal created by the gods to fight Ravana and an incarnation of the god Vishnu.

Literary Focus: Scholars have long debated the origin of epics. One theory is that the earliest epics were formed from the scattered works of various unknown poets who drew from oral accounts of history and legend. A second theory holds that the raw material for epics may have arisen in this way, but that a single person had to later shape the episodes into a unified narrative. Epics with a strong central theme and consistent style are called "literary epics" and are usually considered to have been the work of a single author. Epics whose authorship is uncertain or collective are called "folk epics." The *Ramayana* is a literary epic.

RAMA AND RAVANA IN BATTLE
from the Ramayana
translated by
R. K. NARAYAN

As you read this account of the final confrontation between the epic hero Rama and his enemy Ravana, try to identify the values and character traits that make Rama an ideal epic hero.

Every moment, news came to Ravana of fresh disasters in his camp. One by one, most of his commanders were lost. No one who went forth with battle cries was heard of again. Cries and shouts and the wailings of the widows of warriors came over the chants and songs of triumph that his courtiers arranged to keep up at a loud pitch in his assembly hall. Ravana became restless and abruptly left the hall and went up on a tower, from which he could obtain a full view of the city. He surveyed the scene below but could not stand it. One who had spent a lifetime in destruction now found the gory spectacle intolerable. Groans and wailings reached his ears with deadly clarity; and he noticed how the monkey hordes[1] reveled in their bloody handiwork. This was too much for him. He felt a terrific rage rising within him, mixed with some admiration for Rama's valor. He told himself, "The time has come for me to act by myself again."

He hurried down the steps of the tower, returned to his chamber, and prepared himself for the battle. He had a ritual bath and performed special prayers to gain the benediction of Shiva;[2] donned his battle dress, matchless armor, armlets, and crowns. He had on a protective armor for every inch of his body. He girt his swordbelt and attached to his body his accouterments[3] for protection and decoration.

When he emerged from his chamber, his heroic appearance was breathtaking. He summoned his chariot, which could be drawn by horses or move on its own if the horses were hurt or killed. People stood aside when he came out of the palace and entered his chariot. "This is my resolve," he said to himself: "Either that woman Sita, or my wife Mandodari,[4] will soon have cause to cry and roll in the dust in grief. Surely, before this day is done, one of them will be a widow."

---

1. **monkey hordes:** a tribe of spirits aiding Rama in his battle with Ravana.

2. **Shiva** (shē'və): a god of destructive forces; originally a storm god; he carries a trident.
3. **accouterments** (ə·kōōt'ər·mənts): a soldier's equipment, not including clothes or arms.
4. **Mandodari** (mən·dō'də·rē)

Auditory Image

An auditory image is a word or phrase that appeals to the sense of hearing. Vivid auditory images can be created through use of specific nouns and adjectives and through action verbs. Here are examples of auditory images from the *Ramayana*:

Groans and *wailings* reached his ears with deadly clarity. . .

Ravana *blew* his conch, and its *shrill* challenge *reverberated* through space.

Reading and Speaking. Ask students to find five more sentences in the selection containing vivid auditory images. Have students read aloud their examples. Invite volunteers to identify the nouns, adjectives, and adverbs that build an auditory image. ■

Courtesy of the Freer Gallery of Art, Smithsonian Institution, Washington, D.C., 07.271.259v—Indian manuscript, late 16th century. Mughal; Akbar school; Persian translation of "Ramayana" of Valmiki; 150 miniatures in opaque colors and gold. 27.5 × 15.2 cm. (10 7/8 × 6") average leaf size

RAVANA WITH CHARIOT. Ravana is typically portrayed as having numerous heads and arms.

The gods in heaven noticed Ravana's determined move and felt that Rama would need all the support they could muster. They requested Indra[5] to send down his special chariot for Rama's use. When the chariot appeared at his camp, Rama was deeply impressed with the magnitude and brilliance of the vehicle. "How has this come to be here?" he asked.

"Sir," the charioteer answered, "my name is Matali.[6] I have the honor of being the charioteer of Indra. Brahma, the four-faced god and creator of the Universe, and Shiva, whose power has emboldened Ravana now to challenge you, have commanded me to bring it here for your use. It can fly swifter than air over all obstacles, over any mountain, sea, or sky, and will help you to emerge victorious in this battle."

Rama reflected aloud, "It may be that the rakshasas[7] have created this illusion for me. It may be a trap. I don't know how to view it." Whereupon Matali spoke convincingly to dispel the doubt in Rama's mind. Rama, still hesitant, though partially convinced, looked at Hanuman[8] and Lakshmana[9] and asked, "What do you think of it?" Both answered, "We feel no doubt that this chariot is Indra's; it is not an illusory creation."

Rama fastened his sword, slung two quivers full of rare arrows over his shoulders, and climbed into the chariot.

The beat of war drums, the challenging cries of soldiers, the trumpets, and the rolling chariots speeding along to confront each other, created a deafening mixture of noise. While Ravana had instructed his charioteer to speed ahead, Rama very gently ordered his chariot-driver, "Ravana is in a rage; let him perform all the antics he desires and

---

5. **Indra** (in'drə): important Hindu god appearing in various forms; sometimes considered the god of war, sometimes the chief of all the minor gods.

6. **Matali** (mə·təl·ē')

7. **rakshasas** (räk'shə·səz): malevolent spirits capable of assuming various shapes.

8. **Hanuman** (hän'oo·män'): a form of the name Hanumat; he is a monkey-king and the principal ally of Rama in his war with Ravana.

9. **Lakshmana** (läk'shmə·nə): half brother of Rama; known as the embodiment of loyalty.

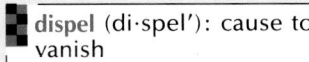

HUMANITIES CONNECTION

Ravana is the embodiment of evil and is shown to be extremely powerful. Artists traditionally portray him with twenty arms and ten heads. *What do students think these multiple body parts signify?* (In Indian culture, multiple body parts signify extra power. In western art forms, a supernatural hero, such as Superman, is shown as a mortal man but with a large, muscular torso. In Indian art, supernatural beings have normal-sized bodies and extra body parts.) ■

3 GUIDED READING

Identifying Details: Throughout the *Ramayana*, the gods aid Rama with magical devices and gifts. What do the gods decide to give Rama? (the god Indra's chariot) What are the special powers of their gift? (The chariot can fly swiftly over all obstacles.)

4 LITERARY ELEMENT

Foreshadowing: How does Rama's suspicion of the gift chariot foreshadow the type of weapons that will be used in the impending battle? (Rama's suspicion that the chariot is an illusion created by his enemies implies that the heroes will use supernatural rather than ordinary weapons in the battle; in fact, Ravana's "Maya" (p. 490) is a weapon of illusion.)

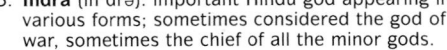

dispel (di·spel'): cause to vanish

5 **LITERARY ELEMENT**
Characterization: What can we learn about Rama's character from what he says to his charioteer? (Possible response: He is clever, careful, and a good strategist.)

■ **grappling** (grap' liŋ): struggling in hand-to-hand combat

6 **ANALYZING**
Why does Ravana insist that only he should confront Rama? (Possible response: It is a matter of honor and pride to Ravana. He wants to kill Rama by himself or not at all.)

■ **HUMANITIES CONNECTION**

Rama is one of the incarnations of Vishnu.
? *What is the significance of showing Rama in counsel with Shiva and Brahma?* (Since Rama is the avatar of Vishnu, the illustration shows the three great divinities conferring together. Vishnu is the protector and preserver of the world; Shiva is the destroyer; and Brahma is the creator.) ■

7 **ANALYZING**
Why would Rama be interested in saving Ravana? (Possible response: Although Ravana acts wickedly, Rama senses that he has good in him and has simply embraced the wrong ideal.)

5 exhaust himself. Until then be calm; we don't have to hurry forward. Move slowly and calmly, and you must strictly follow my instructions; I will tell you when to drive faster."

Ravana's assistant and one of his staunchest supporters, Mahodara[10]—the giant among giants in his physical appearance—begged Ravana, "Let me not be a mere spectator when you confront Rama. Let me have the honor of grappling with him. Permit me to attack Rama."

6 "Rama is my sole concern," Ravana replied. "If you wish to engage yourself in a fight, you may fight his brother Lakshmana."

Noticing Mahodara's purpose, Rama steered his chariot across his path in order to prevent Mahodara from reaching Lakshmana. Whereupon Mahodara ordered his chariot-driver, "Now dash straight ahead, directly into Rama's chariot."

The charioteer, more practical-minded, advised him, "I would not go near Rama. Let us keep away." But Mahodara, obstinate and intoxicated with war fever, made straight for Rama. He wanted to have the honor of a direct encounter with Rama himself in spite of Ravana's advice; and for this honor he paid a heavy price, as it was a moment's work for Rama to destroy him, and leave him lifeless and shapeless on the field. Noticing this, Ravana's anger mounted further. He commanded his driver, "You will not slacken now. Go." Many ominous signs were seen now—his bow strings suddenly snapped; the mountains shook; thunders rumbled in the skies; tears flowed from the horses' eyes; elephants with decorated foreheads moved along dejectedly. Ravana, noticing them, hesitated only for a second, saying, "I don't care. This mere mortal Rama

10. **Mahodara** (mə·hō′də·rə)

National Gallery of Canada, Ottawa, Gift of Max Tanenbaum, Toronto, 1979

RAMA IN COUNSEL WITH SHIVA AND BRAHMA, Indian, c. 1610.
? *What do Shiva and Brahma send to help Rama?*

is of no account, and these omens do not concern me at all." Meanwhile, Rama paused for a moment to consider his next step; and suddenly turned towards the armies supporting Ravana, which stretched away to the horizon, and destroyed them. He felt that this might be one way of saving Ravana. With his armies gone, it was possible that Ravana might have a change of heart. But it had only the effect of spurring Ravana on; he plunged forward and kept coming nearer Rama and his own doom.

Rama's army cleared and made way for Ravana's chariot, unable to stand the force

7

of his approach. Ravana blew his conch[11] and its shrill challenge reverberated through space. Following it another conch, called "Panchajanya,"[12] which belonged to Maha-vishnu[13] (Rama's original form before his present incarnation), sounded of its own ac-cord in answer to the challenge, agitating the universe with its vibrations. And then Matali picked up another conch, which was Indra's, and blew it. This was the signal in-dicating the commencement of the actual battle. Presently Ravana sent a shower of arrows on Rama; and Rama's followers, un-able to bear the sight of his body being stud-ded with arrows, averted their heads. Then the chariot horses of Ravana and Rama glared at each other in hostility, and the flags topping the chariots—Ravana's ensign of the Veena[14] and Rama's with the whole universe on it—clashed, and one heard the stringing and twanging of bowstrings on both sides, overpowering in volume all other sound. Then followed a shower of arrows from Ra-ma's own bow. Ravana stood gazing at the chariot sent by Indra and swore, "These gods, instead of supporting me, have gone to the support of this petty human being. I will teach them a lesson. He is not fit to be killed with my arrows but I shall seize him and his chariot together and fling them into high heaven and dash them to destruction." Despite his oath, he still strung his bow and sent a shower of arrows at Rama, raining in thousands, but they were all invariably shat-tered and neutralized by the arrows from Rama's bow, which met arrow for arrow. Ultimately Ravana, instead of using one bow,

used ten with his twenty arms, multiplying his attack tenfold; but Rama stood unhurt.

Ravana suddenly realized that he should change his tactics and ordered his charioteer to fly the chariot up in the skies. From there he attacked and destroyed a great many of the monkey army supporting Rama. Rama ordered Matali, "Go up in the air. Our young soldiers are being attacked from the sky. Follow Ravana, and don't slacken."

There followed an aerial pursuit at dizzy-ing speed across the dome of the sky and rim of the earth. Ravana's arrows came down like rain; he was bent upon destroying everything in the world. But Rama's arrows diverted, broke, or neutralized Ravana's. Terror-stricken, the gods watched this pursuit. Presently Ravana's arrows struck Rama's horses and pierced the heart of Ma-tali himself. The charioteer fell. Rama paused for a while in grief, undecided as to his next step. Then he recovered and resumed his offensive. At that moment the divine eagle Garuda[15] was seen perched on Rama's flag-post, and the gods who were watching felt that this could be an auspicious sign.

After circling the globe several times, the dueling chariots returned, and the fight con-tinued over Lanka.[16] It was impossible to be very clear about the location of the battle-ground as the fight occurred here, there, and everywhere. Rama's arrows pierced Ravana's armor and made him wince. Ravana was so insensible to pain and impervious to attack that for him to wince was a good sign, and the gods hoped that this was a turn for the better. But at this moment, Ravana suddenly changed his tactics. Instead of merely shoot-ing his arrows, which were powerful in

---

11. **conch** (känch): a shell used as a trumpet.
12. **Panchajanya** (pän·chə·jän′yə)
13. **Mahavishnu** (mə·hä·vish′nōō)
14. **ensign of the Veena**: banner with the image of an ancient stringed instrument.

15. **Garuda** (gə·rōō′də)
16. **Lanka** (läng′kə): Ravana's kingdom.

---

contemptuously (kən·temp′ chōō·əs·lē): scornfully; disdainfully; as if looking down on someone as mean or unworthy

intermittently (in′ tər·mit′ nt·lē): with intervals of stops and starts

enterprise (ent′ ər·prīz′): undertaking

11 ANALYZING
Since both Ravana and Rama are calling on supernatural powers rather than relying on their own strength, on what does the success of their efforts now depend? (Possible response: the ingenuity with which they select asthras and the power of those asthras)

12 SPECULATING
How do you think Rama feels when he sees armies that he thought were dead rise and fight? (Possible responses: shock; fright) What do you think he will do? (Possible response: call upon supernatural resources of his own)

13 LITERARY ELEMENT
Characterization: Rama uses a weapon called "wisdom" or "perception," while Ravana uses weapons that create darkness and destruction. What does their choice of asthras suggest about the two characters? (Possible response: Rama makes use of positive forces while Ravana is drawn to negative ones.)

themselves, he also invoked several supernatural forces to create strange effects: he was adept in the use of various asthras[17] which could be made dynamic with special incantations. At this point, the fight became one of attack with supernatural powers, and parrying of such an attack with other supernatural powers.

Ravana realized that the mere aiming of shafts with ten or twenty of his arms would be of no avail because the mortal whom he had so contemptuously thought of destroying with a slight effort was proving formidable, and his arrows were beginning to pierce and cause pain. Among the asthras sent by Ravana was one called "Danda,"[18] a special gift from Shiva, capable of pursuing and pulverizing its target. When it came flaming along, the gods were struck with fear. But Rama's arrow neutralized it.

11 Now Ravana said to himself, "These are all petty weapons. I should really get down to proper business." And he invoked the one called "Maya"[19]—a weapon which created illusions and confused the enemy.

12 With proper incantations and worship, he sent off this weapon and it created an illusion of reviving all the armies and its leaders—Kumbakarna[20] and Indrajit[21] and the others—and bringing them back to the battlefield. Presently Rama found all those who, he thought, were no more, coming on with battle cries and surrounding him. Every man in the enemy's army was again up in arms. They seemed to fall on Rama with victorious cries. This was very confusing and

---

17. **asthras** (ä′strəs): weapons endowed with supernatural powers.
18. **Danda** (dän′də)
19. **Maya** (mä′yä′)
20. **Kumbakarna** (kum·bə·kär′nə)
21. **Indrajit** (in·drə·jit′)

Rama asked Matali, whom he had by now revived, "What is happening now? How are all these coming back? They were dead." Matali explained, "In your original identity you are the creator of illusions in this universe. Please know that Ravana has created phantoms to confuse you. If you make up your mind, you can dispel them immediately." Matali's explanation was a great help. Rama at once invoked a weapon called "Gnana"[22]— which means "wisdom" or "perception." This was a very rare weapon, and he sent it forth. And all the terrifying armies who seemed to have come on in such a great mass suddenly evaporated into thin air.

Ravana then shot an asthra called "Thama,"[23] whose nature was to create total darkness in all the worlds. The arrows came with heads exposing frightening eyes and fangs, and fiery tongues. End to end the earth was enveloped in total darkness and the whole of creation was paralyzed. This asthra also created a deluge of rain on one side, a rain of stones on the other, a hailstorm showering down intermittently, and a tornado sweeping the earth. Ravana was sure that this would arrest Rama's enterprise. But Rama was able to meet it with what was named "Shivasthra."[24] He understood the nature of the phenomenon and the cause of it and chose the appropriate asthra for counteracting it.

Ravana now shot off what he considered his deadliest weapon—a trident endowed with extraordinary destructive power, once gifted to Ravana by the gods. When it started on its journey there was real panic all round. It came on flaming toward Rama, its speed

13

---

22. **Gnana** (gnä′nə)
23. **Thama** (tä′mə)
24. **Shivasthra** (shi·vä′strə)

or course unaffected by the arrows he flung at it.

When Rama noticed his arrows falling down ineffectively while the trident sailed towards him, for a moment he lost heart. When it came quite near, he uttered a certain mantra[25] from the depth of his being and while he was breathing out that incantation,

---

25. **mantra** (man'trə): a formula believed to have magical power; used in incantation.

Courtesy of the Freer Gallery of Art, Smithsonian Institution, Washington, D.C.: 07.271.37R – Indian Manuscript: late 16th century; Mughal; Akbar school; Persian translation of "Ramayana" of Valmiki; 130 miniatures in opaque colors and gold; 27.5 × 15.2 cm. (10 7/8 × 6") average leaf size

RAMA IS PRESENTED WITH THE CELESTIAL WEAPONS.
❓ *How are these weapons, or asthras, special?*

---

an esoteric syllable in perfect timing, the trident collapsed. Ravana, who had been so certain of vanquishing Rama with his trident, was astonished to see it fall down within an inch of him, and for a minute wondered if his adversary might not after all be a divine being although he looked like a mortal. Ravana thought to himself, "This is, perhaps, the highest God. Who could he be? Not Shiva, for Shiva is my supporter; he could not be Brahma,[26] who is four faced; could not be Vishnu, because of my immunity from the weapons of the whole trinity. Perhaps this man is the primordial being, the cause behind the whole universe. But whoever he may be, I will not stop my fight until I defeat and crush him or at least take him prisoner."

With this resolve, Ravana next sent a weapon which issued forth monstrous serpents vomiting fire and venom, with enormous fangs and red eyes. They came darting in from all directions.

Rama now selected an asthra called "Garuda" (which meant "eagle"). Very soon thousands of eagles were aloft, and they picked off the serpents with their claws and beaks and destroyed them. Seeing this also fail, Ravana's anger was roused to a mad pitch and he blindly emptied a quiverful of arrows in Rama's direction. Rama's arrows met them half way and turned them round so that they went back and their sharp points embedded themselves in Ravana's own chest.

Ravana was weakening in spirit. He realized that he was at the end of his resources. All his learning and equipment in weaponry were of no avail and he had practically come to the end of his special gifts of destruction. While he was going down thus, Rama's own

---

26. **Brahma** (brä'mə): the god of creation.

14 CULTURAL DIVERSITY

In Hinduism, Mahavishnu, the Supreme God, divides himself into a trinity. In this trinity, Brahma is the creator; he is responsible for such things as the renewal of the earth each spring. Shiva is the destroyer; he destroys creation in the sense that age destroys youth. Vishnu is the preserver in the sense that he preserves life in such things as seeds.
❓ *In terms of a trinity, how is Hinduism like Christianity? How is it different?* (Possible response: Both sets of religious beliefs have a trinity of divine beings, but the attributes of the members of the trinity are different.)

15 READER'S RESPONSE

Of all the asthras mentioned so far, which do you find most frightening? Why? (Answers will vary.)

? *What gods or mythological monsters from other cultures resemble Ravana in having multiple body parts?*

17 LITERARY ELEMENT

Epic Characteristics: What heroic quality does Rama show by refusing to attack Ravana while he is in a faint? (Possible response: respect for honorable warfare or fair play)

18 COMPARING LITERATURE

Ravana is vulnerable only in one place, his heart.

? *What other epic heroes can you think of who are vulnerable in only one place?* (Possible responses: Achilles, from the *Illiad* (pp. 224–277), is vulnerable only in his heel; Siegfried, from the *Niebelungenlied* (pp. 730–740), is vulnerable at a small point on his back.)

---

invoked (in·vōkt′): called on a supernatural power for help

---

19 LITERARY ELEMENT

Characterization: What does Ravana's failure to strengthen his heart, while developing other parts of his body, imply about his values? (Possible response: He cared most about acquiring power and ignored spiritual things, following his own desires rather than the will of God.)

16 spirit was soaring up. The combatants were now near enough to grapple with each other and Rama realized that this was the best moment to cut off Ravana's heads.[27] He sent a crescent-shaped arrow which sliced off one of Ravana's heads and flung it far into the sea, and this process continued; but every time a head was cut off, Ravana had the benediction of having another one grown in its place. Rama's crescent-shaped weapon was continuously busy as Ravana's heads kept cropping up. Rama lopped off his arms but they grew again and every lopped-off arm hit Matali and the chariot and tried to cause destruction by itself, and the tongue in a new head wagged, uttered challenges, and cursed Rama. On the cast-off heads of Ravana devils and minor demons, who had all along been in terror of Ravana and had obeyed and pleased him, executed a dance of death and feasted on the flesh.

Ravana was now desperate. Rama's arrows embedded themselves in a hundred places on his body and weakened him. Presently he collapsed in a faint on the floor of his chariot. Noticing his state, his charioteer pulled back and drew the chariot aside. Matali whispered to Rama, "This is the time to finish off that demon. He is in a faint. Go on. Go on."

17 But Rama put away his bow and said, "It is not fair warfare to attack a man who is in a faint. I will wait. Let him recover," and waited.

When Ravana revived, he was angry with his charioteer for withdrawing and took out his sword, crying, "You have disgraced me. Those who look on will think I have retreated." But his charioteer explained how Rama suspended the fight and forebore to attack when he was in a faint. Somehow, Ravana appreciated his explanation and patted his back and resumed his attacks. Having exhausted his special weapons, in desperation Ravana began to throw on Rama all sorts of things such as staves,[28] cast-iron balls, heavy rocks, and oddments he could lay hands on. None of them touched Rama, but glanced off and fell ineffectually. Rama went on shooting his arrows. There seemed to be no end of this struggle in sight.

Now Rama had to pause to consider what final measure he should take to bring this campaign to an end. After much thought, he decided to use "Brahmasthra,"[29] a weapon specially designed by the Creator Brahma on a former occasion, when he had to provide one for Shiva to destroy Tripura,[30] the old monster who assumed the forms of flying mountains and settled down on habitations and cities, seeking to destroy the world. The Brahmasthra was a special gift to be used only when all other means had failed. Now **18** Rama, with prayers and worship, invoked its fullest power and sent it in Ravana's direction, aiming at his heart rather than his head; Ravana being vulnerable at heart. While he had prayed for indestructibility of his several **19** heads and arms, he had forgotten to strengthen his heart, where the Brahmasthra entered and ended his career.

Rama watched him fall headlong from his chariot face down onto the earth, and that was the end of the great campaign. Now one noticed Ravana's face aglow with a new quality. Rama's arrows had burnt off the layers of dross, the anger, conceit, cruelty, lust, and egotism which had encrusted his real self, and now his personality came through in its **20**

---

27. **Ravana's heads:** Ravana is a demon-king usually depicted with ten heads and ten pairs of arms.

28. **staves:** staffs.
29. **Brahmasthra** (brä·mä′strə)
30. **Tripura** (trip′oo·rə)

READING CHECK

1. Who is thought to be the original author of the *Ramayana*? (Valmiki)
2. Why are Rama and Ravana fighting? (Ravana abducted Rama's wife, Sita.)
3. Where does Ravana live? (on the island of Lanka)
4. What animals make up a large part of Rama's army? (monkeys)
5. What vehicle do the gods send down for Rama's use in battle? (a chariot)
6. What are the magical weapons used by Rama and Ravana called? (asthras)
7. What happens when Rama cuts off Ravana's head? (another grows)
8. In what part of his body is Ravana vulnerable? (his heart)
9. What god provides the weapon that finally kills Ravana? (Brahma)
10. Why is Rama concerned when he sees a scar on Ravana's back? (He thinks he has killed a retreating enemy.)

20 pristine form—of one who was devout and capable of tremendous attainments.[31] His constant meditation on Rama, although as an adversary, now seemed to bear fruit, as his face shone with serenity and peace. Rama noticed it from his chariot above and commanded Matali, "Set me down on the ground." When the chariot descended and came to rest on its wheels, Rama got down and commanded Matali, "I am grateful for your services to me. You may now take the chariot back to Indra."

Surrounded by his brother Lakshmana and Hanuman and all his other war chiefs, Rama approached Ravana's body, and stood gazing on it. He noted his crowns and jewelry scattered piecemeal on the ground. The decorations and the extraordinary workmanship of the armor on his chest were blood covered. Rama sighed as if to say, **21** "What might he not have achieved but for the evil stirring within him!"

At this moment, as they readjusted Ravana's blood-stained body, Rama noticed to his great shock a scar on Ravana's back and said with a smile, "Perhaps this is not an episode of glory for me, as I seem to have killed an enemy who was turning his back and retreating. Perhaps I was wrong in shooting the Brahmasthra into him." He looked so concerned at this supposed lapse on his part that Vibishana,[32] Ravana's brother, came forward to explain. "What you have achieved is unique. I say so although it meant the death of my brother."

"But I have attacked a man who had turned his back," Rama said. "See that scar."

Vibishana explained, "It is an old scar. In ancient days, when he paraded his strength around the globe, once he tried to attack the

---

31. **attainments:** accomplishments.
32. **Vibishana** (vi′bē·shä′nə)

Courtesy of the Freer Gallery of Art, Smithsonian Institution, Washington, D.C. 07, 271-270 – Indian Manuscript; late 16th century; Mughal: Akbar school; Persian translation of "Ramayana" of Valmiki; 130 miniatures in opaque colors and gold; 27.5 × 15.2 cm. (10 7/8 × 6") average leaf size

THE DEATH OF RAVANA.

divine elephants that guard the four directions. When he tried to catch them, he was gored in the back by one of the tuskers and that is the scar you see now; it is not a fresh one though fresh blood is flowing on it."

Rama accepted the explanation. "Honor him and cherish his memory so that his spirit may go to heaven, where he has his place. And now I will leave you to attend **22** to his funeral arrangements, befitting his grandeur."

pristine (pris′tēn′): unspoiled; uncorrupted

20 LITERARY ELEMENT
Characterization: What do the changes in Ravana after his defeat by Rama suggest about him? (Possible response: He was a being of great strength and potential who took the wrong path in one lifetime, doing evil rather than good.)

21 LITERARY ELEMENT
Epic Characteristics: What does Rama's sighed response to the sight of Ravana's body suggest about the ideas of his culture? (Possible response: Indian culture of the time believed that a person would come to a sad and pitiable end if he could not overcome the evil within his soul.)

22 LITERARY ELEMENT
Characterization: What qualities does Rama show by his request that the dead Ravana be honored? (Possible responses: respect for a worthy adversary; duty to the gods through honoring the dead)

WRITING TO LEARN

Social Studies: Use encyclopedias and other resources to find out what instruments, weapons, and vehicles were actually used in India during the time the *Ramayana* was composed. Pretend to be a soldier in this era, and write a letter home about one of your battles, using the information you have gathered. ■

from the Ramayana **493**

1. Creating Magical Weapons. Students who are interested in science fiction or who have found the magical weapons described in the *Ramayana* particularly interesting may enjoy designing magical weapons of their own. Have students draw pictures of their weapons and then write short essays describing how the weapons work, what their effects are, and how opposing forces can fight against them.

2. Researching Hanuman. Hanuman, the monkey king, is one of the *Ramayana's* best-loved characters and is even worshiped in some regions of India today. Tell students that Hanuman is depicted with a red face; he is also able to fly and change sizes. Then ask students to find out more about this sacred monkey.

CLOSURE

Ask students to compare and contrast Rama and Ravana. What warrior qualities do they share? How are they different? Encourage students to speculate on what might have happened at the end of this episode if Ravana had defeated Rama. Would Ravana have treated Rama with the same kind of respect? What would the world of the *Ramayana* be like if Ravana were free to roam through it unchallenged? ■

ANSWERS

First Thoughts
Answers will vary.

Identifying Facts
1. Either he or Rama will die.
2. a special chariot. He suspects it is a trap; the charioteer, Hanuman, and Lakshmana.
3. Instead of attacking Lakshmana, he attacks Rama; Rama kills him.
4. bows and arrows; weapons that, among other things, chase and pulverize targets; a trident; a crescent-shaped arrow; "staves, cast-iron balls, heavy rocks, and oddments." He is killed by Brahmasthra, which Rama aims at his heart.

Interpreting Meanings
1. They show Ravana at war with Rama; his rage is mixed with admiration.
2. Possible response: by making it unclear which weapons will prevail
3. They create and supply weapons.
4. valor, fairness, strength, resourcefulness; Rama won't kill Ravana while he is down, worries he has shot him in the back, and asks that his memory be honored.

Applying Meanings
Answers will vary.

Creative Writing Response
Writing a Sequel. Sequels should show Sita's love and Rama's suspicion.

Critical Writing Response
Comparing Aspects of Two Indian Epics. Essays should contain relevant details. ■

First Thoughts
Does this episode from the *Ramayana* call to mind any scenes from other epics you have read?

Identifying Facts
1. At the beginning of this episode, what does Ravana resolve after he has put on his armor and summoned his chariot?
2. What support do the gods give Rama? What doubts does Rama have about the chariot, and who reassures him?
3. How does Mahodara disobey Ravana's orders, and what is the result of this disobedience?
4. What kinds of weapons are used in the battle between Rama and Ravana? How is Ravana finally killed?

Interpreting Meanings
1. How do the details in the first paragraph establish the main **external conflict** of this episode? Which details show Ravana's **internal conflict**?
2. **Suspense** is the uncertainty or anxiety we feel about what is going to happen next in a story. How does the author of the *Ramayana* create suspense in this episode?
3. What role is played by the gods in the *Ramayana*?
4. What values does Rama, the hero of this national **epic**, embody? How does Rama's treatment of the defeated Ravana emphasize these values?

Applying Meanings
Rama is portrayed as extremely cautious when he uses his ultimate weapon, the "Brahmasthra," to defeat Ravana. This weapon is not described in the text; it is simply said to be "a special gift to be used only when all other means had failed." How do you envision this weapon?

Creative Writing Response
Writing a Sequel. Rama's victory over Ravana in the epic is followed by his rescue of Sita, who had been abducted and imprisoned by the demon. Using clues from the introduction to this selection (see page 484) and from the characterization of Rama, write your own version of the reunion between the hero and his wife.

Critical Writing Response
Comparing Aspects of Two Indian Epics. The *Bhagavad-Gita* (see page 467) and the *Ramayana* represent very different kinds of epic narratives, but the selections you have read express some common views of the nature of human struggle and death. In an essay, consider how aspects of Krishna's teaching to Arjuna are similar to the treatment of Rama's final confrontation with Ravana. Before you begin writing, list details from both selections in a chart like the following one.

	Arjuna	Rama
How do the gods help each hero?		
What is the hero's "sacred duty" in each epic?		
What moments of doubt does each hero have?		
What is the importance of self-control and self-discipline for each hero?		

BEHIND THE SCENES

The Tales Behind India's Epics

Who *are* the two shadowy figures who created the *Ramayana* and the *Mahabharata*? No one knows. But, as you may expect, there are stories about each.

According to tradition, the sage Valmiki wrote the *Ramayana* after being inspired by a god and a bird. Valmiki had been listening to Narada, the messenger god, tell the tale of Rama's life. Later, bathing in the Ganges and pondering all he had heard, Valmiki noticed two herons soaring and diving along the banks of the river. Suddenly a hunter shot one of the pair. The other heron cried out in grief. Valmiki, filled with pity, cursed the hunter and was surprised to find that his angry words emerged as poetry. Then the god Brahma appeared. He explained that the poetry was a gift; Valmiki must use it to write the story of Rama's life. Valmiki was eager to obey, and the *Ramayana* was the result.

The story of the *Mahabharata*'s origin, like the *Mahabharata* itself, is longer. The tale behind this epic begins with an unwise king, a wise man, and a snake. It ends with a time-warp twist worthy of modern science fiction.

King Pariksit, a descendant of the family whose final victory the *Mahabharata* recounts, was hunting deer when he offended a meditating wise man. The wise man's son cursed Pariksit, dooming the king to die within seven days from the poison of Taksaka, a huge, black cobra. The wise man, horrified, warned the king but could not avert the curse. King Pariksit built himself

Vyasa *(right)* dictating the story of the *Mahabharata* to the god Ganesha *(center)*.

G. Abegg/Sygma Photo News

a tower, set guards around its base, and climbed aloft, armed with doctors, priests, and magical remedies. But the wily Taksaka transformed himself into a basket of fruit and, changing several of his helpers into messengers, had himself delivered to King Pariksit. Pariksit died before anyone could intervene.

Pariksit's son, Janamejaya, then ascended the throne. He began a campaign to burn all snakes, hoping to destroy Taksaka. However, a sage begged the young king to have pity on the serpent, and Janamejaya spared Taksaka. It was then that Vyasa appeared. This wise man was a reincarnation of Janamejaya's ancestor, one of the heroic Pandavas who had participated in the battles with the Kauravas. Janamejaya begged Vyasa to tell the whole story of the struggle. Vyasa complied, and the *Mahabharata* was born.

LITERARY BACKGROUND
Most scholars now believe that the *Ramayana* actually had one author, named Valmiki, and that the name Vyasa is merely symbolic or honorific. As evidence, scholars point out that Vyasa is the name given as the author of eighteen major *Puranas* (books of religious stories and ideas) and of four Vedas. In addition, they point out that the *Ramayana* is a work with sophisticated literary qualities: It is unified; it has a clear beginning, middle, and end, and one central hero. The *Mahabharata*, on the other hand, lacks the unity that is expected when a work is composed by one gifted poet. ■

1 CULTURAL BACKGROUND

In Hinduism, Vishnu is one of the three aspects of the supreme spirit, Brahma. He is known as the preserver; Brahma is the creator and Shiva is the destroyer. Vishnu has had nine incarnations, or *avatars*. These include Rama, the hero of the epic *Ramayana*; the Buddha; and Krishna. Vishnu's next avatar, Kalki, is to come in the form of a winged horse. The notion of successive incarnations enabled Hinduism to keep up with the evolving beliefs and interests of its followers.

2 CULTURAL BACKGROUND

Another story tells how Krishna subdues a hundred-headed cobra. Krishna, the master of all musical arts, jumps on the cobra's heads and dances the serpent almost to death. Just as the snake is about to die, its wives intercede, begging Krishna for mercy. He takes away the cobra's poison and spares its life.

■ HUMANITIES CONNECTION

Mythology has run riot with Krishna's life story.

? *What might be the story behind this painting?* (Answers will vary.) *How does this portrayal of Krishna make you feel about him?* (Possible response: He is set apart from others in the painting, emphasizing his special qualities.) ■

LANGUAGE —AND— CULTURE

A GOD WITH UNIVERSAL APPEAL

Who's super-strong, irresistibly attractive, and blue? If you guessed the Hindu god Krishna, the Highest Soul, the Infinite One, you're right. As an incarnation of the blue-skinned Vishnu, Krishna is usually shown with skin of the same hue. Krishna uses his superhuman strength to fight demons and monsters, and his powers, combined with his good looks and high spirits, endear him to men as well as women of all ages.

1

2

The Metropolitan Museum of Art. Purchase, Edward C. Moore, Jr. Gift, 1928 (28.63.1)

KRISHNA LIFTS MOUNT GOUARDHAN.
? *What are Krishna's special characteristics?*

Krishna, Mischief-Maker

According to legend, Krishna was secretly placed in the care of a cowherd and his wife immediately after birth. This trick was necessary to protect the baby from a demon, Kamsa, who was bent on destroying him. So Krishna grew up in a rural village, playing in the mud and pulling cows' tails like the other boys, his identity disguised. As he grew older, he was known throughout the village as a mischief-maker, often pilfering food or breaking things and then lying about it. Yet his beauty was so great that his parents, and everyone else in the village, saw his pranks as charming and loved him for them.

One story tells of Krishna's being reproved by his mother for eating dirt. Lying, he denies the accusation, inviting her to look into his mouth and see for herself. When she looks into his mouth, she sees "the whole universe in all its variety, with all the forms of life and time and nature and action and hopes, and her own village, and herself." She realizes that her son is a god. She instantly forgets all she has seen, but she is filled with even greater love for the boy.

A Very Human God

Krishna was a latecomer to the Hindu pantheon. He appeared when emphasis was shifting away from the worship of the raw forces of nature (fire or storms, for example) toward the worship of human qualities. The young Krishna's very human faults, and his parents' and neighbors' tolerant, even delighted, response to them, underscore this shift.

Some of Krishna's dealings with monsters illustrate another aspect of the Krishna cult: the idea that vengeance should be tempered with mercy. Legend has it that Krishna was still a baby when he killed his first monster. She was an ogress sent to destroy Krishna. She had transformed herself into a beautiful, godlike woman, but had smeared herself with poison. She visited the baby's hut and held him to her poisoned breast to kill him. Using his superhuman strength, Krishna killed her instead. Then, mercifully, he wiped out her sins, so that her soul reached "the heaven of the good."

Krishna's charming personality and good looks made him irresistible to women. When Krishna played his flute at night, any woman who heard it was compelled to join him. In Hindu religious thought, the women's attraction to Krishna symbolized the soul's longing for holiness. The fact that even married women left their homes to follow Krishna's flute signified that Krishna's worshipers were expected to leave their worldly concerns and follow the ways of the god.

As the cult of Krishna spread, it sometimes conflicted with the worship of the older gods. One tale reflecting this conflict describes how the resentful Agni, god of fire, started a brushfire to kill Krishna and the other cowherds. Krishna calmly sucked the fire into his mouth, extinguishing it. In the same way, the cult of Krishna extinguished the cults of many of the older gods.

Krishna has been portrayed in many ways in Hindu art and literature. Whether he appears as a plump baby or a mighty slayer of monsters, as a simple cowherd or a dazzling prince, he is above all a god who loves humanity. And, for many centuries, this charming, blue-skinned trickster god has been devoutly loved in return.

3 CULTURAL BACKGROUND

Many tales tell of conflicts between Krishna and the demon Kamsa. In one story, Kamsa invites Krishna to a festival of games. During the games, Kamsa expects one of his wrestlers to kill Krishna; instead, Krishna defeats his opponent. Soon afterward, Krishna grabs Kamsa by the hair and throws him to the ground, killing him.

CULTURAL DIVERSITY

According to some stories, Krishna's father, a king, is warned that his son will kill him. He tries to avert this fate by imprisoning Krishna. When Krishna escapes, the King orders all the male infants in his realm to be put to death. Krishna finds safe haven with a peasant. In some accounts, Krishna is vulnerable only in his heel.

❓ *What stories from other cultures are similar to these?* (Possible responses: Greek stories about Oedipus, Perseus, and Achilles; the biblical account of King Herod's ordering all male infants slain)

4 READER'S RESPONSE

Think about Krishna's personality. What do you like about him? (Possible responses: his mercy, his charm) What traits, if any, do you dislike? (Possible response: his mischievousness)

Explain that a word ending
with -ing is part of a verb only
when preceded by a form of to
be. Compare the following:
COMPLETE SENTENCE: The
authors of the hymns **were
praising** the earth's beauty.
FRAGMENT: praising the
earth's beauty in song and
story

ANSWERS TO EXERCISE 1:
CORRECTING SENTENCE
FRAGMENTS

Answers will vary. Here are
possible responses.
1. Indra, sending a chariot for
Rama, **offers support**.
2. **Hymns and epics** are part of
the literature of India.
3. When his brothers drink
from the lake, **they appear to
die**.
4. The *Mahabharata* **tells** of the
war between the sons of royal
brothers.
5. The *Panchatantra* **is** a compilation of Hindu legend and
thought.
6. As a result of Yudhistira's
answers, **his brothers come
back to life**.
7. Krishna, who serves as Arjuna's trusted charioteer, **persuades him to fight**.
8. **People of unknown ancestry**
lived and farmed in the Indus
Valley thousands of years ago.
9. The Vedic period in
India **marked an early literary
flowering**.
10. The poets writing in
Sanskrit **considered it a sacred
language**.

Language Skills

AVOIDING SENTENCE FRAGMENTS AND RUN-ON SENTENCES

Sentence Fragments

Unclear sentences make your writing hard
to follow. Sentence fragments leave readers hanging, missing half the substance of
your thought. Run-on sentences leave
readers struggling to sort out too many
piled-up concepts.

Each sentence must contain a **subject**
and a **verb** and express a complete
thought. A **sentence fragment** is a phrase
or a dependent clause used as an independent sentence. To correct it, add the missing parts to make a complete sentence.

SENTENCE FRAGMENT (No verb)
Hymns praising the earth's beauty.

(Note that a word ending in -ing, by itself,
is not a verb.)

COMPLETE SENTENCE (Verb phrase added)
Hymns praising the earth's beauty *make
up* the *Rig Veda*.

SENTENCE FRAGMENT (No subject)
Receive the attention of poets.

COMPLETE SENTENCE (Subject added)
Natural wonders receive the attention of
poets.

SENTENCE FRAGMENT (No verb or subject)
All the wonders of creation.

COMPLETE SENTENCE (Subject and verb
added)
The Vedic hymns celebrate all the wonders of creation.

SENTENCE FRAGMENT (Subordinate clause)
Because the hymns were a way to ask
for divine help and mercy.

COMPLETE SENTENCE (Joined to independent clause)
Because the hymns were a way to ask
for divine help and mercy, *they were
viewed as religious poems*.

Notice how the italicized words complete
each thought. In informal writing, you may
use fragments on purpose for emphasis or
tone. Unintentional fragments, however,
weaken your writing.

Exercise 1: Correcting Sentence Fragments

Correct each fragment, using the most appropriate method.
1. Indra, sending a chariot for Rama.
2. Are part of the literature of India.
3. When his brothers drink from the lake.
4. The war between the sons of royal
brothers.
5. A compilation of Hindu legend and
thought.
6. As a result of Yudhistira's answers.
7. Krishna, who serves as Arjuna's
trusted charioteer.
8. Lived and farmed in the Indus Valley
thousands of years ago.
9. The Vedic period in India.
10. The poets writing in Sanskrit.

Run-on Sentences

Independent clauses—word groups that contain subjects and verbs and express complete thoughts—cannot be joined indiscriminately. They must be joined with an appropriate connector or punctuation mark. Incorrectly joined, two or more independent clauses create a **run-on sentence**.

RUN-ON SENTENCES

No punctuation

Krishna reminds Arjuna that it is his sacred duty to wage battle he urges him to rise above the pain and suffering of war.

Comma splice

Krishna reminds Arjuna that it is his sacred duty to wage battle, he urges him to rise above the pain and suffering of war.

(A comma alone is not enough to join two independent clauses.)

METHODS FOR CORRECTING RUN-ON SENTENCES

1. **Use a semicolon.** Krishna reminds Arjuna that it is his sacred duty to wage battle; he urges him to rise above the pain and suffering of war.

2. **Use a comma and coordinating conjunction.** Krishna reminds Arjuna that it is his sacred duty to wage battle, *and* he urges him to rise above the pain and suffering of war.

3. **Subordinate one clause.** Krishna reminds Arjuna that it is his sacred duty to wage battle, *though he urges him to rise above the pain and suffering of war.*

Subordinating one clause can give it less weight or emphasis in the sentence. Note that conjunctive adverbs—words like *however, in addition, furthermore, then, next*—cannot be used to subordinate a clause unless they are correctly punctuated.

RUN-ON SENTENCE

Krishna reminds Arjuna that it is his sacred duty to wage battle, *however* he urges him to rise above the pain and suffering of war.

CORRECTED SENTENCE

Krishna reminds Arjuna that it is his sacred duty to wage battle; *however,* he urges him to rise above the pain and suffering of war.

A conjunctive adverb between two independent clauses must be preceded by a semicolon.

Exercise 2: Correcting Run-on Sentences

Correct each run-on sentence in all three of the ways illustrated above.

1. In the *Panchatantra*, a story contained within another story emphasizes different aspects of a lesson being taught, the lesson is emphasized by the use of epigrams.

2. Much of the *Ramayana* concerns Rama's attempts to win back his wife Sita, then he banishes her because he fears she has been unfaithful.

3. Ralph Waldo Emerson's poem "Brahma" echoes the philosophy and even the wording of the *Bhagavad-Gita* this is not surprising since he was fascinated by ancient Indian literature.

ANSWERS TO EXERCISE 2: CORRECTING RUN-ON SENTENCES

1. **(a)** In the *Panchatantra*, a story contained within another story emphasizes different aspects of a lesson being taught; the lesson is emphasized by the use of epigrams. **(b)** In the *Panchatantra*, a story contained within another story emphasizes different aspects of a lesson being taught, **and** the lesson is emphasized. . . . **(c)** In the *Panchatantra*, **when a story contained within another story emphasizes different aspects of a lesson being taught,** the lesson is emphasized by the use of epigrams.

2. **(a)** Much of the *Ramayana* concerns Rama's attempts to win back his wife Sita; then he banishes her because he fears she has been unfaithful. **(b)** Much of the *Ramayana* concerns Rama's attempts to win back his wife Sita, **whom he then banishes**. . . . **(c)** Much of the *Ramayana* concerns Rama's attempts to win back his wife Sita, **but** then he banishes her. . . .

3. **(a)** Ralph Waldo Emerson's poem "Brahma" echoes the philosophy . . . of the *Bhagavad-Gita*; this is not surprising since he was fascinated by ancient Indian literature. **(b)** Ralph Waldo Emerson's poem "Brahma" echoes the philosophy . . . of the *Bhagavad-Gita*, **and** this is not surprising since. . . . **(c)** Ralph Waldo Emerson's poem "Brahma" echoes the philosophy . . . of the *Bhagavad-Gita*, **which is not surprising since.** . . .

Background: To help students find subjects for their letters, let them do a brief, focused freewriting exercise in answer to the question, "What is one thing that you would like to talk a member of your family into doing?" Next, have a second freewriting session on the question, "What one thing would you like to talk the school principal into doing?" Finally, have them freewrite in answer to the question, "What is one thing that you would like to talk the President (or another world leader) into doing?"

Instruct students to read over the results of their free-writing, underlining ideas that seem especially important to them. These can serve as sources of ideas for the letters they will write in this assignment.

Prewriting: Explain that persuasion is most effective when the writer can establish some common ground, an area of shared concern, with the audience. In order to establish this common ground, it is helpful to have an idea of the audience's interests and of their knowledge, opinions, and arguments about the issue. Suggest that students answer questions 1, 2, 4, and 5 about their audience first; the answers to these questions may help them find the best answer to question 3.

Critical Thinking and Writing

WRITING TO PERSUADE

What's the best way to talk you into doing something? Does coaxing work better than coercion? Is logic more convincing than manipulation? Whether you want to convert others to your viewpoint or encourage them to act in support of a cause, persuasive techniques will help you to build plausible and convincing arguments.

Writing Assignment

Write a letter about a national, local, school, or personal issue that you consider important. Your audience is a friend or group of friends whose position differs from yours, and your purpose is to persuade your audience to accept your viewpoint or to take action. In this assignment, you will develop an argument with specific reasons and evidence.

Background

In this unit you have encountered several kinds of persuasion. In the *Bhagavad-Gita,* Krishna uses argument and counter-argument to urge Arjuna into battle. The fables of the *Panchatantra* rely on analogies to convince readers to accept certain morals. In these selections, as in all effective persuasion, opinions are directly or indirectly justified and evidence is presented. As you choose your topic and plan your letter, think about the kinds of persuasion that will be most compelling.

Prewriting

Analyzing Your Audience. Answer these questions in detail about the friends you hope to convince.

1. What do they already know about the issue?
2. How and why is their opinion different from yours?
3. What concerns do they share with you?
4. What will make it difficult to persuade them?
5. What will be their strongest counter-argument?

Generating Evidence and Organizing Support

In one sentence, sum up the opinion you hope to convince your audience of or the action you want your audience to take. Beneath that sentence, list the reasons for your opinion. Next, begin generating facts and examples that can support your reasons; brainstorm for evidence based on your personal experience and observation. Then research books, periodicals, and media presentations, filling in the gaps in your knowledge with expert testimony.

FOR FURTHER HELP

Refer students to *Grammar, Usage, and Mechanics: A Reference Guide* at the back of their textbooks for detailed information that will help them write, revise, and proofread their essays.

Finally, familiarize yourself with opposing points of view and the reasons people hold those points of view, and look for evidence that disproves their reasons.

To organize your material, complete a chart like the one below. Use your brainstorming material, your research notes, and your answers to the audience analysis questions.

	My Position	Opponent's Position
Reason A		
Evidence		
Reason B		
Evidence		
Reason C		
Evidence		

Writing

Use these steps to draft your letter.

1. **Introductory Paragraph.** Follow the standard conventions for beginning a letter. Then introduce your topic with a question, a quotation, or an unusual fact. Explain key terms if necessary. End with your position statement, the sentence that sums up your opinion.

2. **Body Paragraphs.** Treat your points in order of importance (least important first). Explain each point, supported by facts and examples, in a separate paragraph. In each paragraph, you may also cite opposing views and counter them. Or you may cover all opposing views in one paragraph. In either case, use the kinds of persuasion that will be most effective for your audience: direct, logical argument; emotional appeals; or argument by analogy. Use transitions to link ideas.

3. **Concluding Paragraph.** Restate your opinion and briefly sum up your main points. End with a strong call to action, whether literal action or the acceptance of a new viewpoint. Add an appropriate closing and signature.

Evaluating and Revising

Use these questions to evaluate and revise your letter.

1. Does your introduction catch readers' attention and state your position clearly?
2. Have you provided enough reasons, facts, and examples?
3. Have you dealt fairly with opposing views?
4. Are your main points and support logically organized?
5. Have you used effective persuasive techniques and transitions?
6. Have you followed standard letter form?

Proofreading and Publishing

Proofread to eliminate errors in grammar and mechanics, and make a final copy of your letter. As your teacher directs, exchange letters with classmates. Use discussion or role-playing to explore each letter's effectiveness.

Writing: After students have used personal knowledge inventories and research to marshall and organize evidence on the prewriting chart, have them evaluate and revise their position statements. Position statements serve the same functions as thesis statements in expository writing, so they should be based on the facts of the issue.

Evaluating and Revising: As students evaluate their persuasive techniques, remind them that appeals to emotion (such as the use of loaded words) can be useful. However, point out that the most effective persuasion is sparing in the use of emotional appeals, relying instead on careful reasoning and solid evidence.

Proofreading and Publishing: Before students proofread, explain that persuasive writers sometimes use sentence fragments for effect; one sees fragments often in newspaper and magazine advertisements, for example. However, inadvertent fragments undermine a writer's credibility, as do run-on sentences. Refer students to the guidelines in the *Language Skills* feature on pp. 498–499 to identify and correct unintentional fragments and run-ons. ■

The following annotations are for the artwork surrounding the map, starting in the upper right-hand corner and moving in a counterclockwise direction.

Portrait of the Emperor Wen-Ti: This portrait is by Yen Li-pen (d. 673), a T'ang dynasty painter and imperial official who specialized in commemorative portraits of great figures from China's past dynasties. He is known for his attention to realistic details and his talent for capturing his subjects' character. His portrait of Sui Emperor Wen-Ti endows the leader with great dignity.

Chinese Dragon: Unlike the dragons of Western mythology, dragons in most Asian cultures are considered benevolent, protective spirits. In China, they are associated with water, which is life-giving, though it can also cause destruction through storms and floods. Dragons became the symbol of the Chinese emperors, who were viewed as divinely chosen protectors of the people.

Detail from Handscroll: Famous for his intricately detailed studies of nature, Ch'ien Hsüan (1235–1290) worked during the Mongol invasion of China. Unlike other great artists of the time, he refused his services to the new Mongol rulers. Some critics note a sense of melancholy in his work, which may have been a reaction to political events.

CHINA AND JAPAN

☐ Chinese Empire, c. 1775
☐ Japan, c. 1850

UNIT 6

CHINESE AND JAPANESE LITERATURES

▼ **Time** ▼
2000 B.C.–A.D. 1900

▼ **Place** ▼
China and Japan

▼ **Literary Significance** ▼

China: Perhaps no other world culture has produced as much superb poetry as China, which reveres poetry as the highest art form. Influenced by Confucianism, Taoism, and Buddhism, Chinese poetry often focuses on the contemplation of nature and the search for harmony. China also boasts a strong tradition of philosophical and historical prose writings. Chinese storytelling grew from an oral tradition to a written tradition of moral tales, supernatural tales, and, by the eighteenth century, the novel.

Japan: The earliest Japanese writings were written in Chinese, but between the fifth and eighth centuries A.D., the Japanese adapted the Chinese system of writing to fit their own language. Japanese poetry is distinguished by such forms as the **tanka** and the **haiku**. The prose tradition in Japan reached a height during the Heian Period (794–1185), when diaries, journals, and other forms of narrative were given a high polish by aristocrats, many of them women. By the eleventh century, a Japanese writer, Lady Murasaki, had composed the world's first novel, *The Tale of Genji.* Japanese literature is also known for its unique dramatic forms, particularly the subtle and mysterious Noh plays.

The Great Buddha of Kamakura, Japan: In Mahayana Buddhism, the principal form of Buddhism in China, Korea, and Japan, large sculptures of the Buddha were often placed in temples. The Buddha figures were made of bronze, wood, or clay and then gilded or colored. The Daibutsu (literally, "great Buddha") of Kamakura is over fifty feet high. It was cast in bronze in 1252 and conveys the Buddhist spirit of peaceful contemplation. In 1495, it survived a tidal wave that destroyed the temple and town where it was located.

Japanese Woodblock Print: Hokusai (1760–1849) is one of the best-known Japanese artists who created woodblock prints for the urban population of Edo (Tokyo). Hokusai is said to have created over 30,000 designs and is admired for the sense of spirit and freedom in his work.

Samurai: During Japan's long feudal period (1200–1867), samurai warriors came to represent values of courage, loyalty, and self-discipline. These values were codified as *Bushido,* or "the way of the warrior," and they continue to have a powerful hold on the Japanese imagination.

Japanese Woman: In his multi-color, woodblock prints of women, Utamaro (1753–1806) developed his own distinctive ideal of female beauty. Many of his prints appeared as illustrations in books of Japanese legends. ■

DISCUSSING THE TIME LINE

Point out the early dates for the development of writing in China (c. 1500–1122 B.C.) and for the compilation of China's first anthology of classic poetry, *The Book of Songs*, (1000–600 B.C.). Have students compare these dates with those we have for the earliest written literature of the Middle East, Greece and Rome, and India (see Time Lines on pp. 126, 212, and 444).

Next, have students notice that all the literary events on the B.C. side of the time line are Chinese works, and ask why they think this is so. (Japan did not have a written language then.)

Have students identify the schools of thought that have influenced Chinese and Japanese cultures (Confucianism, Taoism, and Buddhism) and tell which two great thinkers were contemporaries and when they lived. (Confucius and Lao-tzu both lived around 500 B.C.) Ask how much later Buddhism arrived in China. (about 300 years later) Ask what cultural sharing occurred between the countries and when it occurred. (Chinese writings were introduced in Japan in A.D. 400–500, and Japan began to adopt Chinese culture around A.D. 600.) Point out that China's "Golden Age" overlapped with the flowering of Japanese culture in the Heian period.

Finally, encourage students to relate Genghis Khan's conquests of China and Persia (Time Line on p. 621), as well as events from A.D. 500–1800, to events occurring in the same time frame in Europe (Time Lines on pp. 680 and 794).

504

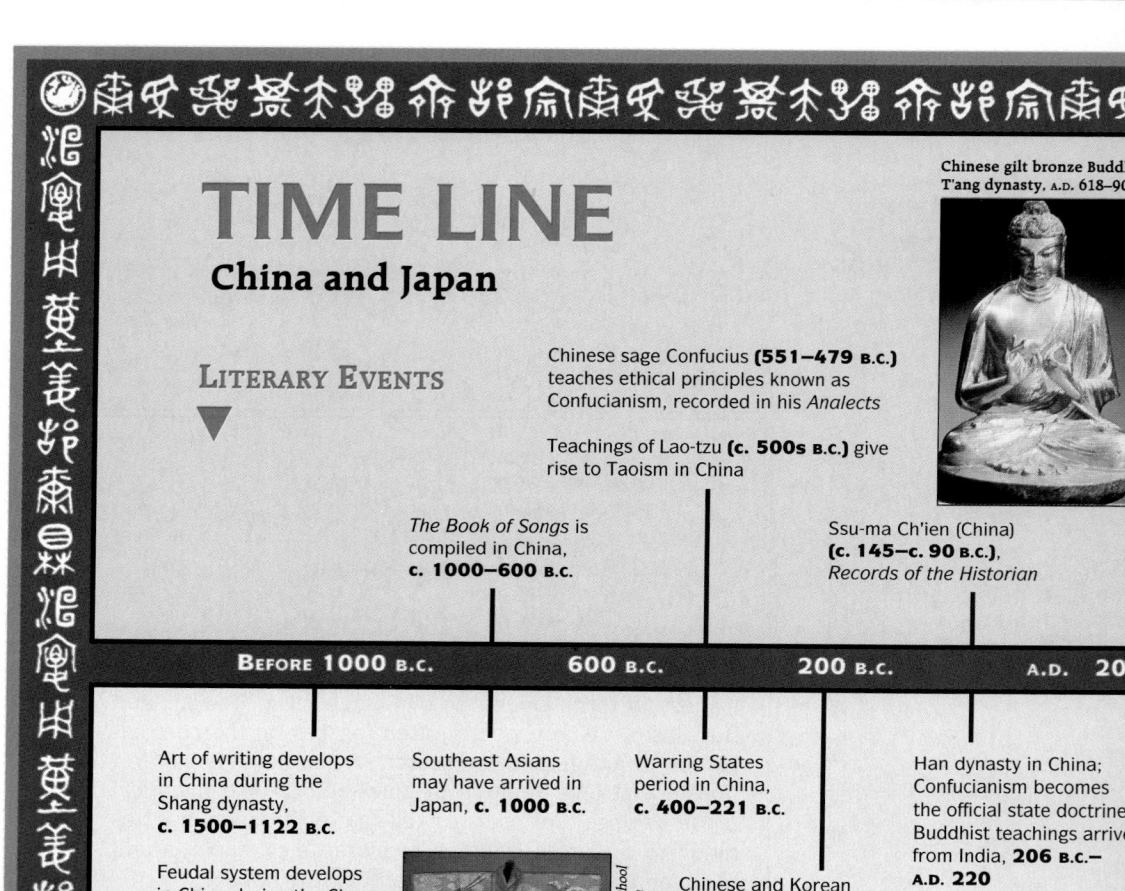

TIME LINE
China and Japan

LITERARY EVENTS

Chinese gilt bronze Buddh[a]
T'ang dynasty, A.D. 618–90[7]

Chinese sage Confucius **(551–479 B.C.)** teaches ethical principles known as Confucianism, recorded in his *Analects*

Teachings of Lao-tzu **(c. 500s B.C.)** give rise to Taoism in China

The Book of Songs is compiled in China, **c. 1000–600 B.C.**

Ssu-ma Ch'ien (China) **(c. 145–c. 90 B.C.)**, *Records of the Historian*

BEFORE 1000 B.C.	600 B.C.	200 B.C.	A.D. 20[0]

Art of writing develops in China during the Shang dynasty, **c. 1500–1122 B.C.**

Southeast Asians may have arrived in Japan, **c. 1000 B.C.**

Warring States period in China, **c. 400–221 B.C.**

Han dynasty in China; Confucianism becomes the official state doctrine; Buddhist teachings arrive from India, **206 B.C.– A.D. 220**

Feudal system develops in China during the Chou dynasty; the Hundred Schools period sees a profusion of teachers and philosophers, **1122–256 B.C.**

Chinese and Korean immigrants introduce rice paddy agriculture into Japan, **c. 250 B.C.– A.D. 250**

Ch'in dynasty unifies China; Great Wall is built, **221–207 B.C.**

Museum of Art, Rhode Island School of Design. Gift of Lucy T. Aldrich

Japanese Noh robe.

CULTURAL AND HISTORICAL EVENTS

The Great Wall of China.

Sei Shōnagon (Japan) **(late 900s–early 1000s)**, *The Pillow Book*

Murasaki Shikibu (Japan) **(c. 978–c. 1026)**, *The Tale of Genji*

Man'yoshu, an anthology of poetry, and the *Kojiki*, chronicles of the legendary origins of Japan, are compiled, **c. 700**

Li Po **(701–762)** and Tu Fu **(712–770)** (China) compose poetry

The aristocrats of Japan's Heian court compose tanka, **c. 800–1200**

Kokinshu, Imperial anthology of Japanese poetry, **905**

Li Ch'ing-chao (China) **(1084–1151)** composes poetry

The Tale of Heike, Japanese epic, **c. 1225**

Yoshida Kenko (Japan) **(c. 1283–c. 1352)**, *Essays in Idleness*

Development of Noh drama in Japan, **c. 1338–1568**; Seami Motokiyo **(c. 1363–1442)** writes *Atsumori* and other dramas

Matsuo Bashō **(1644–1694)**, and Uejima Onitsura **(1660–1738)** are among the earliest poets to write haiku

Ts'ao Hsueh-ch'in **(c. 1700–1764)** writes *Dream of the Red Chamber*, one of China's most famous novels

Taniguchi Buson **(1715–1783)** and Kobayashi Issa **(1762–1826)** write haiku

600	**1000**	**1400**	**1800**

Japanese Prince Shotoku encourages the adoption of Chinese culture, **593–622**

Sung dynasty in China sees the development of Neo-Confucianism, **960–1279**

The shogun becomes the supreme power in Japan, **1192**

Boxer Rebellion ignites revolutionary spark in China, **1900**

...ato clan emerges as dominant political force ...apan, **c. A.D. 400**

T'ang dynasty, called China's "Golden Age," **618–907**

Zen sect of Buddhism develops in Japan, **c. 1200s**

Portuguese merchants and Christianity reach Japan, **1540s**

...dhism and Chinese ...ings are introduced to ...an, **400s–500s**

Japan's Heian era witnesses a cultural flowering and the rise of feudalism, **c. 794–1185**

Mongol leader Genghis Khan conquers China; his grandson Kubla Khan establishes the Yuan dynasty, **1279–1368**

Shogun closes Japan to foreigners, **1639**

Ch'ing (Manchu) dynasty in China, **1644–1911**

Treaty of Nanking gives Britain control of Hong Kong, signaling the rise of Western imperialism in China, **1842**

Period of civil war and turmoil in Japan, **1338–1568**

Commodore Perry ends Japanese isolationist policy, **1853**

Ming dynasty in China, **1368–1644**

Meiji Restoration; Japan begins industrialization, **1868**

Japanese shrine, Hiroshima.

Travelpix/FPG International

This time line border features a form of Chinese writing known as "seal style," which had developed by the third century B.C. and is still in use today.

Time Line **505**

HISTORICAL BACKGROUND

Great Wall: Parts of the Great Wall, constructed mainly in the third century B.C., still stand—remnants of a barrier that wound 1,500 miles over mountain and plain. The wall was built in an effort to keep out the barbarian invaders from the north.

HISTORICAL BACKGROUND

Shogun: The shogun was the chief military commander. He appointed military governors (*shugo*) in the provinces and land stewards (*jito*) on private estates. Military rule began in the eleventh century, when the samurai, or warriors, first seized power. They set up a feudal system that resembled the medieval system in Europe.

HISTORICAL BACKGROUND

Far East Isolation: When did Europeans begin to intrude in the Far East? (In the 1540s Portuguese merchants reached Japan.) What was the result? (By the 1630s, Japan was closed to foreigners). When did Japan's isolation end and who brought this about? (in 1853; Commodore Perry) Westerners also intruded in China. The Boxers were Chinese rebels who called for all foreigners to leave China. When they began to kill Westerners, Western soldiers put down the rebellion in 1900, killing many Chinese and destroying much of Beijing in the process.

OBJECTIVES

1. *To evaluate the contributions of Confucianism, Taoism, and Buddhism to Chinese literature*
2. *To analyze the structure, imagery, and themes of Chinese poetry and the main ideas of Chinese maxims, anecdotes, and biography*
3. *To interpret and respond to Chinese literature both orally and in writing*

TEACHER'S RESOURCES: 6
- Unit Introduction Test
- Word Analogies
- Unit Review Test
- Critical Thinking and Writing

1 RESPONDING TO THE QUOTATION

Confucius was a great Chinese teacher. In the quotation he is contrasting knowledge and understanding. As a down-to-earth example of his maxim, have students imagine someone who has memorized baseball statistics without understanding the game. Why would that person's learning be "labor lost"? Then have them imagine someone who is judging a baseball player without knowing the facts about the player's past performance. Why would that person's thoughts be "perilous"? Students may suggest other real-life situations to which Confucius' maxim might apply.

HUMANITIES CONNECTION

The Shang dynasty marked the first appearance of bronze in China. Shang artists also produced marble sculpture, jade figurines, and pottery. When we see Shang bronzes in museums today, they are encrusted with blue and green oxides, the product of centuries of burial in the earth.
❷ *How does the design of this vessel combine practicality and beauty?* (Possible response: The sides of the vessel are in the form of birds.) ∎

2 TEACHING TIP

To reinforce the antiquity of Chinese culture, have students note on the time line (pp. 504–505) the year of the United States founding (1787).

THE LITERATURE OF CHINA

> 1 ❝ Learning without thought is labor lost; thought without learning is perilous. ❞
> —*from* The Confucian Analects

Ritual wine vessel, Shang dynasty, c. 1200–c. 1000 B.C.

Courtesy of The Arthur M. Sackler Museum, Harvard University-

Chinese civilization as a distinct and continuous culture has existed for nearly four thousand years—longer than any other world culture. The art of writing, using a unique "alphabet" of over three thousand characters, developed in the second millennium B.C. (2000–1000) in China, and with it came the beginning of a literary tradition that continues to this day. The nature of Chinese literature reflects the political and social history of China and the impact of powerful religions that came from within and outside the country. 2

TEACHING CHINESE LITERATURE

Like the literature of India, Chinese literature has a tradition that goes back thousands of years and has often been inspired by philosophical questions about the meaning of life, how to live ethically in society, and how to live in spiritual harmony with the natural order of the universe. In China the dominant philosophical and religious ideas have come from Confucianism, Taoism, and Buddhism.

To motivate students to begin considering these belief systems and their potential impact on a culture, write the following maxims of Confucius and Lao-tzu, the founder of Taoism, on the board:

Never do to others what you would not like them to do to you. —Confucius

Do you want to improve the world? I don't think it can be done. —Lao-tzu

Moderation in all things. —Confucius

He who knows he has enough is rich. —Lao-tzu

Have students discuss which sayings appeal to them and which remind them of sayings from other traditions with which they are familiar. Tell them that Confucianism deals primarily with social morality and that its ideas were the basis for educating Chinese government officials for over two thousand years. Taoism is a more mystical philosophy that focuses on

Chinese History: Dynastic Rule

3 The political profile of China over the centuries is one of periods of stability, enforced by a strong central authority, followed by struggles between warring local princes and rival families trying to wrest control from the ruling family.

The **Shang** (shäng) **dynasty**, which came to power in China around the year 1766 B.C. and continued until 1122 B.C., is the first period of family rule about which there is historical evidence. It was during the Shang reign that the **4** unique system of Chinese writing began to develop. Unlike our modest alphabet of twenty-six letters representing a limited number of sounds, the thousands of Chinese characters represent complete words or units of meaning.

The **Chou** (jō) **dynasty** overthrew the Shang and held power until about 256 B.C.—the longest dynastic rule in Chinese history. The Chou established a structure of imperial rule that became the model of government for China until the early twentieth century. The emperor, usually the oldest son of the ruling family, controlled a vast territory by

Chinese jade, large dark green mountain, 19th century.

Art Resource, New York

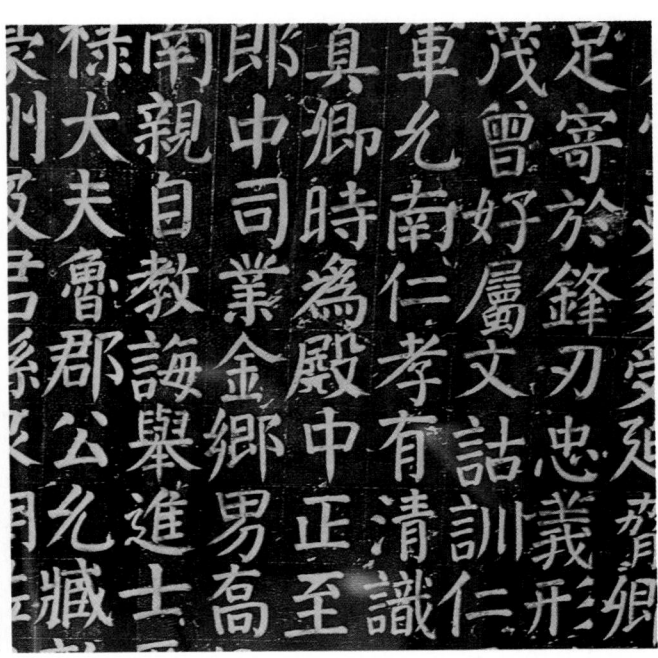

Sample of Chinese calligraphy.

Shostal Associates/SuperStock International

3 CULTURAL DIVERSITY

According to the Confucian doctrine of "Heaven's Mandate," rulers were divinely appointed, but lost divine favor when they began to rule unwisely. The Chinese therefore believed that citizens had a right and duty to rebel against bad leaders, an idea that promoted revolution.

? *How would you compare modern American ideas about order, stability, authority, and rebellion to those held by the Chinese?* (Possible response: Americans do not give their leaders as much power as Chinese leaders have had, and Americans can eliminate unpopular leaders through democratic processes.)

4 CULTURAL BACKGROUND

Chinese Characters: Chinese writing has been a great unifying force in Chinese history. Although China's people speak many different dialects, they can all read each other's writing because words with the same meaning, although pronounced differently in different dialects, are written with the same characters.

HUMANITIES CONNECTION

The Chinese prized jade and excelled at carving this tough stone into works of beauty. Highly skilled craftsmen learned their trade through long apprenticeships, starting in childhood. ∎

the individual's relationship with nature and on the importance of stillness and inaction in achieving peace of mind. Although some of the ideas of the two philosophies seem contradictory to Westerners, the Chinese consider them complementary.

Taoism and Buddhism played an important part in the development of Chinese poetry, the most revered form of literature in the culture. Both traditions emphasize contemplation and heightened awareness of nature as a means to discover truth, a focus that has consistently dominated Chinese poetry.

For centuries, Chinese leaders were chosen for their knowledge of Confucian texts and traditional poems, as well as for their ability to compose poetry of their own. Perhaps no culture has placed a greater value on learning and literary tradition than China.

Fiction and drama developed late in Chinese history, and although some novels became popular, fiction was not considered a respectable art form until the twentieth century. Traditionally, biographies and histories that taught moral lessons were also admired.

The Granger Collection, New York

Chinese glazed earthenware tomb figure of a lion, T'ang dynasty, early eighth century A.D.

creating a network of local government officials whose advancement depended on their loyalty to the imperial family.

In 221 B.C., the **Ch'in dynasty** overpowered the Chou. (Some believe the name *China* was derived from *Ch'in.*) The Ch'in rulers connected and fortified their empire by building roads and completing a long wall across their northern border, the famous Great Wall of China.

The Han (hän), T'ang (täng), and Sung (sōōng) dynasties that followed were periods of expansion and greater contact with the outside world. Literature, the arts, technology, and trade flourished; yet each dynasty, eventually weakened by corruption and infighting, was succeeded in turn by a more vigorous force.

Outside Influences

The **Mongols**, a warlike, semi-nomadic people from northeastern Asia, conquered imperial China in the late twelfth century A.D. Mongol rule was overthrown and Chinese rule restored in 1368 with the accession of the **Ming dynasty**. The Ming and later dynasties sought to reassert Chinese culture by limiting contact with foreign influences.

Despite centuries of Chinese efforts to limit outside influence, the expanding nations of nineteenth-century Europe (Great Britain, France, Germany, and Russia) forced the imperial Chinese authority to grant them large areas of China that they could run for their economic advantage.

Twentieth-century China has seen civil war and the installation of a harsh Communist regime. But even the last four decades of Communist rule have run true to the age-old pattern of Chinese political history. There have been alternating periods of stability and unrest, revolutionary fervor followed by greater ideological flexibility, and periodic demands for more democracy brutally crushed by a totalitarian central government.

Chinese Religion and Philosophy

Chinese literature, and indeed all of Chinese culture, has been profoundly influenced by three great schools of thought, all originating in the sixth and fifth centuries B.C.: the philosophies of **Confucianism** and **Taoism**, and the religion of **Buddhism**.

MAKING CONNECTIONS

Chinese literature and culture had a profound impact on Japanese and other cultures of the Far East. Some scholars have compared its influence to that of ancient Greek culture on the Western world. In fact, Japan had no written language—and hence, no written literature—until it adopted Chinese characters, using them to represent the Japanese equivalents of Chinese words.

Chinese ideas began to arrive in Japan around the fifth century A.D. By A.D. 700 Japanese scholars began using Chinese characters to record Japanese myths and legends. The cultural flowering of Japan's Heian period soon followed.

From the Middle Ages, the Western world was eager to trade with China. China's tea, silk, jade, and art made valuable cargoes even when carried by caravans over mountains and desert. Chinese textiles, woven with exquisite designs, were prized in the West. In 1516, the Portuguese opened the sea trade to China. Europeans imported Chinese porcelain, which became so fashionable among the wealthy that "china mania" ensued. Rulers vied to discover the secret of making true porcelain.

In the late sixteenth century, Jesuit missionaries first made Chinese literature and philosophy available to the West. To gain the respect of Chinese rulers, the mis-

Denman Waldo Ross Collection, Courtesy of the Museum of Fine Arts, Boston

THE THIRTEEN EMPERORS (detail), ATTRIBUTED TO YEN LI-PEN (d. A.D. 673), T'ang dynasty, Silk handscroll.

Confucius (551–479 B.C.) was the first great Chinese teacher, and since his time, the profession of teaching has commanded great respect in China. His teaching emphasized ethical values such as honesty, loyalty, respect for elders, love of learning, and moral restraint. Confucius did not write down any of his teachings, but after his death they were compiled by his disciples in books now called the ***Analects*** (see page 538).

> The sixth and fifth centuries B.C. gave rise to three belief systems that have influenced Chinese culture: Confucianism, Taoism, and Buddhism.

The next great teacher to influence Chinese thinking was **Lao-tzu** (lou′dzə′), sometimes spelled Lao-tze. He was born around 570 B.C., but little is known of his personal life and background. However, the values expressed in his book

sionaries studied Chinese literature and admired the Confucian education of Chinese government officials. Their translations and interpretations of Confucian works won admiration in Europe—so much that Confucius was called "the patron saint of the Enlightenment."

In the twentieth century, ancient Chinese poetry influenced British and American poets. Ezra Pound admired the ability of ancient Chinese poets, such as Li Po, to convey intense emotions with concrete images. Pound's translation of these poems in his volume *Cathay* has been hailed as the harbinger of a new, modern American poetry based on ancient Chinese sources. Other Imagists included Amy Lowell, Hilda Doolittle (H.D.), and William Carlos Williams. The contemporary American poets Kenneth Rexroth and Gary Snyder have also been influenced by Chinese poetry.

HUMANITIES CONNECTION

Like Chinese poetry, Chinese art often contemplates the beauty of nature. With delicate brush strokes, this artist has captured an impression of nature.

❓ *In what ways is a painting like a poem?* (Possible responses: Both create a picture, a poem with words, a painting with lines and colors; both express feelings; both have balance and rhythm.) ∎

10 CULTURAL DIVERSITY

According to historian Will Durant, the Chinese civil service system combined the best aspects of democracy and aristocracy, as everyone was eligible to compete for government service, but only the brightest and best-trained were chosen.

❓ *Do you think this ancient Chinese system of choosing leaders is superior to our own?* (Possible response: yes, our election system, relying heavily on money and connections, invites corruption)

11 RESPONDING TO THE QUOTATION

The "human" quality of Chinese poetry may be due to the importance of the folk tradition. In *The Book of Songs* (p. 512), the most revered book in Chinese literature, many folk songs express basic human feelings in unromantic images. Have students compare symbolic or romantic poetry in this book with the Chinese poetry in this unit.

The Granger Collection, New York

PEACOCK AND APRICOT BLOSSOMS, LÜ CHI, **Ming Dynasty.**

11

> ❝ Chinese poetry is of all poetry I know the most human and the least symbolic or romantic. ❞
> —*Goldsworthy Lowes Dickinson*

Tao Te Ching (see page 543) have deeply affected Chinese thought and expression. Above all, the Taoist (dou'ist) philosophy reveres nature as the great teacher and urges people to seek wisdom by contemplating the simplicity and power of natural forces.

Confucianism and Taoism were enriched by the arrival of a third powerful system of belief, Buddhism (see page 451), imported from India during the Han dynasty. Buddhist thought stresses the importance of ridding oneself of earthly desires and of seeking ultimate peace and enlightenment through detachment. With its stress on living ethically and its de-emphasis on material concerns, Buddhism appealed to both Confucians and Taoists.

The Balance of Opposites

Unlike Western religions, Chinese religions are based on the perception of life as a process of continual change in which opposing forces, such as heaven and earth or light and dark, balance one another. These opposites are symbolized by the *yin* and the *yang*. *Yin*, the passive and feminine force, counterbalances *yang*, the active and masculine force, and each contains a "seed" of the other, as represented in the traditional *yin-yang* symbol.

Chinese Literature

In terms of sheer volume, Chinese literature dwarfs all other literatures of the world. It has been estimated that more than half of all the books ever written have been Chinese. Moreover, literature and learning have been among the highest cultural values. Indeed, for centuries the main avenue to power and prestige for ambitious young men in China was passing the imperial examinations. These exams for entrance into the imperial bureaucracy tested a candidate's knowledge of the classic Chinese texts and his ability to compose poetry.

Chinese Poetry

To the Chinese, poetry has always been an exercise for the mind and the spirit rather than a purely literary pursuit. In keeping with Confucian, Taoist, and Buddhist thought,

FOR FURTHER STUDY

Nonfiction
Founders of Faith, by Carrithers, et al, summarizes the teachings of the Buddha, Confucius, Jesus, and Mohammed.
Bright Moon, Perching Bird, translated by J. P. Seaton and James Cryer, contains over 75 poems by the T'ang masters Li Po and Tu Fu.

Fiction
The eighteenth-century Chinese novel *Dream of the Red Chamber*, by Tsao Hsueh-chin, translated by Wang Chi-chen, is available in paperback. Pearl Buck's *Imperial Woman* describes life in the Forbidden City of the Ch'ing dynasty as it tells the story of the last empress of China.

Films
Bernard Bertolucci's stunning film *The Last Emperor*, which also chronicles the last days of the Ch'ing dynasty, is available on videocassette. "China: The Mandate of Heaven," part of the PBS series *Legacy*, provides a sweeping overview of Chinese civilization, and is available on videocassette. ■

Chinese poetry often involves the contemplation of nature and the search for harmony between the inner and outer worlds. Chinese poetry is almost exclusively lyrical. Its essence is the exploration of passing feelings and impressions.

> The Chinese have traditionally valued poetry above all genres, seeing it as a vehicle for spiritual attainment and the cultivation of wisdom.

The Book of Songs, or *Shih Ching* (see page 512), first compiled in the sixth century B.C., is the oldest collection of Chinese poetry and has been revered and studied for centuries as a model of poetic expression and moral insight. Chinese lyrical poetry reached its height, however, during the T'ang dynasty (A.D. 618–907). Inspired by scenes of natural beauty, T'ang poets such as **Li Po** and **Tu Fu** wrote about the fragile blossoms in spring, the falling of leaves in autumn, or the changing shape of the moon.

Chinese Prose and Drama

Although the Chinese have traditionally revered poetry above all other literary forms and have viewed fiction and drama as lesser art forms, Chinese prose has a long and distinguished history. Chinese writers have always admired their ancient prose literature for its style, particularly the clear, unadorned expression of the Confucian *Analects* and the biographical writings of the great historian **Ssu-ma Ch'ien** (see page 551).

Chinese storytelling began with oral folktales and Buddhist parables, but over the centuries, a tradition of written narrative developed, including cycles of heroic adventures, tales of the supernatural, and monumental family chronicles, such as the immensely popular eighteenth-century novel, *Dream of the Red Chamber*.

Sophisticated stage art emerged late in China, around the eleventh or twelfth century. It developed from popular entertainment or court performances into a full-length dramatic medium. Today, Chinese drama is famous for its gorgeous costumes, raucous music, and lively acrobatics.

> " The [Chinese] poem is the voice of the poet not self-consciously addressing posterity or the world at large, but speaking quietly to a few close friends, or perhaps simply musing to himself. "
> —Burton Watson

12

The Granger Collection, New York

NARCISSUS AND PLUM, CH'IU YING. Ming dynasty.

12 RESPONDING TO THE QUOTATION
Burton Watson is a highly respected scholar, translator, and compiler of Chinese literature. Invite students to tell how they respond to poems that speak in a quiet, intimate voice. Encourage students to explain their responses by referring to specific poems.

13 LITERARY BACKGROUND
Lyric Poetry: Review the definition of a lyric (a songlike poem that expresses emotion). Explain that lyric poetry is found in every literature of the world and is often contrasted with narrative poetry, which tells a story.

14 LITERARY BACKGROUND
Development of Fiction: Chinese fiction based on the spoken colloquial language did not begin to develop until after the growth of cities and the education of the merchant class during the Sung and Yuan dynasties (960–1368). Although fiction was read by all classes of Chinese society, it did not become a completely respectable form until the twentieth century. *Dream of the Red Chamber*, a novel about the decline of an aristocratic family, is admired for its psychological insights and vivid characterizations. Today, many Chinese novelists base their works on Western rather than traditional Chinese models. Have students note Western literary influences on Zhang Jie's "Love Must Not Be Forgotten" (p. 1416). ■

13

4

During the T'ang dynasty, artists began to specialize. Chou Fang established the genre of portraits of noblewomen. By placing the five women in this scroll at subtly varied angles, Chou Fang achieved an effect of quiet harmony that matches the music they are playing. The background—two trees and a rock—is more detailed than had been customary before Chou Fang's time. The colors, which have faded over time, were originally very rich. The musical instrument is a *ch'in*, resembling a zither.

? *What do you think artists gain or lose when they specialize?* (Possible response: They become highly skilled within their limits but don't explore and grow beyond them.) ■

1 CULTURAL DIVERSITY

Chinese Poetry: In the opinion of many scholars, Chinese poetry is straightforward, the most human and down-to-earth poetry ever written. Among early Chinese poets, many of whom were exiles, the themes of love and longing for family and the homeland prevailed.

? *How would you characterize poetry written in the twentieth century?* (Possible response: A large portion is symbolic.)

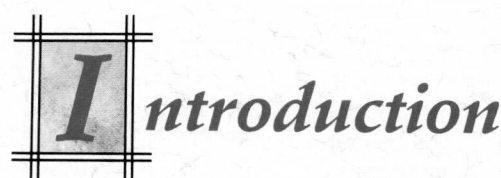

*I*ntroduction

The Book of Songs

TUNING THE LUTE AND DRINKING TEA, **attributed to** CHOU FANG **(fl.** A.D. 780–810).** *Artists of the T'ang dynasty, such as Chou Fang, set the standard for Chinese figure composition.*

The Nelson-Atkins Museum of Art, Kansas City, Missouri

The *Book of Songs* is a collection of 305 of the earliest recorded poems in Chinese history. First compiled in the sixth century B.C., these poems were actually meant to be sung, although their melodies have long been lost. Regarded as the foundation of Chinese literature, *The Book of Songs* provides a lyrical record of the people who lived in northern China and the feudal states surrounding the Yellow River during the early centuries of the Chou (jō) dynasty (1122–249 B.C.). It is fitting that the Chinese word for poetry, *shih* (shə), is rooted in the *Songs'* Chinese title *Shih Ching* (shə jing).

A Record of the Chinese Past

The Book of Songs includes court songs that entertained the aristocracy, story songs that recounted Chou dynasty legends, and hymns that were sung in the temples, accompanied by dance. Many of the poems are brief folk songs or ballads.

◆

ballad: *a simple, traditional song, particularly one that tells a romantic or sentimental story.*

In the *Songs,* unknown singers created images of people farming and hunting, courting and marrying, performing rituals, and fighting in battles. We hear

1

OBJECTIVES
1. To recognize some distinctive features of classical Chinese lyric poetry
2. To understand the purpose of repetition
3. To compose a rap song and to compare and contrast folk songs from two different cultures

2 their happiness as they describe a well-to-do lover or celebrate the planting season and hear their bitterness and suffering as they complain of a rejecting lover or the hardships of war.

Traditional Interpretations of the *Songs*

By the seventh century B.C., the *Songs* had already achieved a legendary status in the Chou dynasty. They were well known in the feudal courts and were often performed as court entertainment. Because the *Songs* were so familiar, scholars began quoting lines or verses out of context, and often inaccurately, applying them to new situations. Interpreters wrote commentaries that cast new light on the poems' social and political significance. Eventually, many songs acquired interpretations probably never intended by the ancient singers.

Around 500 B.C., the Chinese philosopher and teacher Confucius (see page 536) reinterpreted many of the *Songs* to make them into models of his moral teachings, although there is no evidence to support the legend that he himself compiled the *Songs*. However, Confucius did have strong feelings about the importance of the poems. He felt that the *Songs* described a wide range of emotion and experience and that to not study them would be like closing one's eyes to the world.

3

A Revered Place in Chinese History

The Book of Songs became one of the "Five Classics" of Confucianism—texts that embodied Confucian ideals in the five areas of metaphysics, politics, history, society, and poetry. As an expression of the Confucian poetic vision, the *Book of Songs* became part of the basic educational curriculum in China when Confucianism was adopted as the official state doctrine during the Han dynasty (206 B.C.–A.D. 220). Each poem was accompanied by an official interpretation that explained the poem's relationship to the moral and social fabric of the period in which it was written. Until recent times, Chinese schoolchildren studied *The Book of Songs* as both poetry and moral lessons and were required to memorize all 305 songs.

4

Today, however, scholars are laying aside such traditional interpretations to see *The Book of Songs* simply as a classic work of literature that expresses a people's humanity. In the *Songs*, the people of Chou still sing to us across time, revealing the inner and outer worlds they lived in and, in the process, establishing the strong lyrical tradition that has shaped Chinese poetry.

Standing warrior, T'ang dynasty.

The Art Institute of Chicago, Chinese Armored guardian, earthenware with polychrome pigments and gilding, Tang dynasty, 1st half 8th century, ht: 96.5 cm, Gift of Russell Tyson, 1943.1139. 3/4 view. Photograph by Bob Hashimoto.

2 CULTURAL BACKGROUND

Nature: The importance of nature imagery in Chinese literature is foreshadowed in the myths surrounding the origin of the Chinese script. One story, dating back to the first century B.C., tells how the legendary Yellow Emperor ordered the recording of China's history. For that prodigious undertaking, the court historian invented Chinese characters, according to legend, by imitating footprints that birds and animals made in the sand.

3 LITERARY BACKGROUND

Confucius: Ssu-ma Ch'ien (145–86 B.C.?), the greatest Chinese historian, maintains that Confucius personally sang all the *Songs* and played the melodies on a stringed instrument. In what way would our knowledge of the tunes of these songs enhance our appreciation of these ancient poems? (Possible response: Knowing the tunes would help us to hear the lyricism of the poems.)

4 CULTURAL DIVERSITY

In China, being able to recognize an allusion to *The Book of Songs* in conversation and to respond intelligently were traditionally considered marks of a cultivated mind. Likewise, ignorance on that score carried the stigma of being "culturally illiterate"—a humiliating setback for one aspiring to refinement and social standing in a culture that reveres knowledge.

❓ *What are the prerequisites for being "culturally literate" today?* (Answers will vary.)

Interrogative and Exclamatory Sentences

An interrogative sentence poses a question and ends with a question mark (?). An exclamatory sentence conveys strong feeling and ends with an exclamation point (!). Word order also distinguishes interrogative and exclamatory sentences from declarative sentences (sentences that make statements). Examples: *That is true. Is that true? How true that is!*

Note these examples from Song 130:

Are we buffaloes, are we tigers
That our home should be these desolate wilds?
Alas for us soldiers,

Alas for us soldiers,
Neither by day nor night can we rest!

These sentences can be made declarative *without* altering meaning:

We are [not] buffaloes, we are [not] tigers; our home should [not] be these desolate wilds. We soldiers, neither by day nor night, can rest.

PREREADING FOCUS

Background: Tradition holds that the first emperor of the Chou dynasty dispatched emissaries to the feudal principalities to bring back songs of the common people because the emperor wanted to gain insight into his subjects' lives. *The Book of Songs* was culled from the thousands collected. The songs express practical and heartfelt concerns with poignant simplicity. The predominant theme of *The Book of Songs*, according to Confucius, is "to keep the heart right."

Oral Response: Ask students: When you miss friends or family, how do you express your feelings? Do you phone? Send a letter? Write in a journal? Do you sometimes make up a poem or a song to express your longing?

Literary Focus: In the Chinese songs, the refrain is both unifying and dynamic. In "O Oriole, Yellow Bird," for example, each repetition introduces new images. First, the bird lights on "corn" and "millet," then on "mulberries" and "sorghum," then on "oaks" and "wine-millet." The effect may be likened to a *montage*, or verbal motion picture, of a restless bird flitting about with no secure place to settle. At the same time, the refrain builds a "composite image" of a captive bride longing to take flight, like the oriole she is addressing.

Reader's Guide

from The Book of Songs

Background

The two selections from *The Book of Songs* come from a collection of 160 folk songs attributed to the feudal states of the Chou empire. Among the earliest of the *Songs*, these folk songs have apparently been revised and refined since they were written centuries ago.

Like many selections in *The Book of Songs*, these folk songs tend to have strong, regular rhythms that echo the gongs, drums, bronze bells, and stone chimes of early Chinese music. These compact lyrics also feature repeated words and phrases, although there are often subtle changes in the repetition. The folk songs are best known, however, for their direct outpourings of human feeling, especially on the themes of separation, hardship, and love.

According to Chinese tradition, Song 103 expresses the feelings of a young princess of the state of Wei (wā). Long ago she was separated from her family by an unhappy marriage to the Lord of Hsü (shoo), the ruler of a small, nearby state. When she tried to return to her people, the men of Hsü detained her against her will. Song 130 probably expresses the lament of a Chinese peasant, one who represents the common man forced to take up arms for a war lord. *The Book of Songs* contains some of history's earliest antiwar songs.

Oral Response

The speakers in both of these poems are far from home. How have you felt when you have been separated from your home, family, and friends? Discuss your experiences with the class.

Literary Focus

Repetition is a literary device that consists of repeated sounds, words, phrases, or other elements in prose and poetry. Writers use repetition to unify a work, build rhythm, and add emphasis to particular feelings and ideas. In folk songs and ballads, repetition often appears in the form of a recurring word or group of words called a **refrain**. For example, the refrain "For I'm weary with hunting, and fain would lie down" appears at the end of several stanzas in the Scottish ballad "Lord Randall." Like many refrains, this one also repeats with a slight variation: "For I'm sick at the heart, and fain would lie down."

from The Book of Songs

translated by
ARTHUR WALEY

❖ *As you read, notice how repeated words and phrases emphasize the speakers' concerns. What feelings are conveyed by this repetition?*

1 ⌷

O Oriole, Yellow Bird
103

O oriole, yellow bird,
Do not settle on the corn,
Do not peck at my millet.°
The people of this land
5   Are not minded to nurture me.
I must go back, go home
To my own land and kin.

2 ⌷

O oriole, yellow bird,
Do not settle on the mulberries,
10   Do not peck my sorghum.°
With the people of this land
One can make no covenant.
I must go back, go home
To where my brothers are.

3 ⌊

15   O oriole, yellow bird
Do not settle on the oaks,
Do not peck my wine-millet.
With the people of this land
One can come to no understanding.
20   I must go back, go home
To where my own men° are.

3. **millet** (mil'it): in Asia, a cereal grass with small grain used for food.

10. **sorghum** (sôr'gəm): a tropical grass grown for its food products, such as syrup or grain.

21. **men:** here, the speaker's adult kinsmen, such as her father and uncles.

TEACHER'S RESOURCES
↙ Review and Response Worksheet

ABOUT THE TRANSLATOR
Arthur Waley (1889–1966) has played a leading role in making Asian literature accessible to Western readers. Best known of his many translations are *A Hundred and Seventy Chinese Poems* and his masterpiece *The Tale of Genji.*

1 READER'S RESPONSE
The title identifies the song by restating the first line and introducing a recurring image. What does the title lead you to expect? (Possible response: praise to an oriole)

2 HISTORICAL BACKGROUND
Silkworms live on mulberry leaves. Thus mulberry trees, frequently mentioned in Chinese literature, have long been vital to China's culture and economy. Raising silkworms has been a thriving enterprise in China since 1400 B.C.

3 LITERARY ELEMENT
Repetition: In what ways is stanza three linked to the first two stanzas? (Possible responses: The syntax, nature imagery, and first-line refrain follow a similar pattern; the speaker's emotion and desire remain the same.)

To reteach the poems from *The Book of Songs*, have students create a diary or journal entry that could have served as a basis or an inspiration for one of the songs. Encourage students to try to imagine how the speaker might have expressed his or her experience in prose in a diary. Students might also want to include pen-and-ink drawings as diarists sometimes do to enhance their memory. Point out that the introductory material (pp. 512–513) can help them estimate dates for their imaginary diary entries.

MEETING INDIVIDUAL NEEDS

4 ESL: Explain that the word *bounds* refers to the boundaries, or borders, of the kingdom. ■

5 LITERARY ELEMENT

Rhythm: In the first two lines of stanza four, the use of simple, one-syllable words alters the poem's rhythm. How would you describe this change? (slower, less lyrical) How does the rhythm reflect what the speaker is doing? (Possible response: Like the weary soldier, the rhythm plods along.)

5 INTERPRETING

Stanza four breaks the pattern of questions and exclamations in the preceding stanzas. What does the shift to declarative sentences suggest about the speaker's outlook? (Possible response: He is resigned to his sad lot in life.)

HUMANITIES CONNECTION

Wall paintings from the T'ang dynasty were frescoes: colors were applied to wet plaster, which was then allowed to harden, so that the painting became part of the wall.
❓ *How does this wall painting resemble and differ from* The Book of Songs *in its treatment of the subject?* (Possible response: The first-person poems are more subjective in feeling; the wall painting is more objective.) ■

What Plant Is Not Faded?
130

What plant is not faded?
What day do we not march?
What man is not taken
To defend the four bounds?

5   What plant is not wilting?
What man is not taken from his wife?
Alas for us soldiers,
Treated as though we were not fellow-men!

Are we buffaloes, are we tigers
10 That our home should be these desolate wilds?
Alas for us soldiers,
Neither by day nor night can we rest!

The fox bumps and drags
Through the tall, thick grass.
15 Inch by inch move our barrows
As we push them along the track.

Wall painting, T'ang dynasty, c. A.D. 618–906.
❓ *What feelings does the speaker in Song 130 express about the life of a soldier?*

K. Scholz/SuperStock, Inc.

1. Setting the Songs to Music. Encourage students to find or compose simple folk tunes whose melodies and rhythms capture the spirit of one of these poems. Have them work in small groups to present a musical performance of a song to the class or to produce an audiotape or video. Also, give students the option to choose another poem from the Waley translation of *The Book of Songs* (Houghton Mifflin, 1937).

2. Research Project. History buffs may enjoy doing an in-depth study of an aspect of ancient Chinese culture suggested by one of the songs—such as marriage customs, family life, gender roles, or feudal wars and politics. Students can begin their research with an encyclopedia article and then go on to more specialized sources, such as books or journal articles.

CLOSURE

Return with students to the comment in the *Introduction* on p. 513: "scholars . . . [now] see *The Book of Songs* simply as a classic work of literature that expresses a people's humanity." Ask students to what extent they think Song 103 and Song 130 bear out that view. Lead students to discuss aspects of these two ancient songs that relate to their own experience. ∎

First Thoughts

What kinds of emotions do these ancient Chinese poems express?

Identifying Facts

1. To whom is Song 103 addressed? What are the speaker's three complaints about "the people of this land"?
2. What great desire does the speaker of Song 103 express?
3. Point out three lines in Song 130 that state the speaker's concerns.

Interpreting Meanings

1. In Song 103, why does the speaker tell the oriole of her desire to go home?
2. The first four sentences of Song 130 are all questions. What is the significance of the speaker's many questions? What feelings do they evoke?
3. Choose an example of **repetition** in each poem. What emotion is expressed by the repeated phrase?

Applying Meanings

In what ways do these poems remind you of songs you know? Could they be set to music and still be relevant today?

Creative Writing Response

Composing a Rap Song. Like these poems from *The Book of Songs*, rap music is a direct expression of feelings. Rap also uses strong, repetitive rhythms and, often, a refrain. With a partner or small group, compose a two- to three-verse rap song that expresses your feelings about love, war, or some other subject. Include a refrain that echoes your main idea. Be ready to perform your rap song for the class.

Critical Writing Response

Comparing and Contrasting Two Folk Songs. In a two- to three-paragraph essay, compare and contrast Song 130 ("What Plant Is Not Faded?") with the classic folk song "Where Have All the Flowers Gone?" by Pete Seeger, below.

> Where Have All the Flowers Gone?
> Pete Seeger
>
> Where have all the flowers gone,
>   Long time passing?
> Where have all the flowers gone,
>   Long time ago.
> Where have all the flowers gone?
> The girls have picked them every one.
> When will they ever learn?
> When will they ever learn?
>
> Where have all the young men gone,
>   Long time passing?
> Where have all the young men gone,
>   Long time ago.
> Where have all the young men gone?
> Gone for soldiers every one.
> When will they ever learn?
> When will they ever learn?
>
> Where have all the soldiers gone,
>   Long time passing?
> Where have all the soldiers gone,
>   Long time ago.
> Where have all the soldiers gone?
> Gone to graveyards every one.
> When will they ever learn?
> When will they ever learn?
>
> Where have all the graveyards gone,
>   Long time passing?
> Where have all the graveyards gone,
>   Long time ago.
> Where have all the graveyards gone?
> Gone to flowers every one.
> When will they ever learn?
> When will they ever learn?

ANSWERS

First Thoughts

Possible responses: homesickness, loneliness, rejection, alienation, resentment

Identifying Facts

1. Oriole, or Yellow Bird. no nurturing, no covenant or agreement, no understanding
2. to go home
3. lines 6, 8, and 12

Interpreting Meanings

1. Possible response: The oriole may be the only creature to which she can confide her thoughts; it emphasizes her loneliness.
2. Possible responses: The implied answer to each question is *none*. The repetition evokes feelings of weariness without hope of relief.
3. Possible responses: In Song 103, the repeated phrase "Do not settle" mirrors feelings of rejection. In Song 130, the refrain "What man is not taken" conveys hopelessness.

Applying Meanings

Most will agree that aside from dated images, the songs are still relevant.

Creative Writing Response

Composing a Rap Song. Songs should contain repetitive rhythms and a refrain. Imagery should depict a current situation, but emotion should arise from basic human nature.

Critical Writing Response

Comparing and Contrasting Two Folk Songs. Essays should argue the points using either a point-by-point or a block organizational pattern. ∎

At fifteen, Li Po (lē bō) wrote his first poem, a *fu*—a prose-poem. His subject was *Ming-t'ang*, the Hall of Light (mentioned in "Peonies," p. 534). While ambition to win favor at the imperial court inspired his fu, shortly after composing it, Li Po retreated to the mountains to live as a recluse. Reflecting on his life as a hermit, Li Po wrote, "I kept thousands of rare birds who came and ate out of my hand when I called to them, without any trace of fear or suspicion." (from *The Poetry and Career of Li Po*) His rapport with birds earned him fame as a "person of unusual capacity" and an invitation to the capital—the Civil Service screened recruits by noting their effect on birds, who were thought to befriend only the worthy.

In time, Li Po rejoined society, accepting the Emperor's summons to return to court. As an aspiring statesman, Li Po proposed his plans for expanding the dynasty's power, but he was ignored. Although unsuccessful in politics, Li Po was celebrated as a poet. He was even considered a Banished Immortal—one whose disorderly conduct in Heaven earned him a return to Earth.

ABOUT THE TRANSLATOR

Arthur Cooper (1937–) became interested in Icelandic verse while still a boy. While on a tour of duty in Hong Kong and Singapore for the British Civil Service his interests in world literature expanded to include Japanese and Chinese poetry.

Li Po
A.D. 701–762

New York Public Library Picture Collection

Chinese poet Li Po (lē bō) lived during the T'ang (täng) dynasty (618–907), an age of great prosperity and cultural achievement. Two of China's greatest poets, Li Po and his friend Tu Fu (dōō fōō), wrote during this golden age of poetry. These two poets of contrasting dispositions and styles embody the highest poetic achievements of the T'ang dynasty. Tu Fu, a melancholy wanderer, wrote innovative poetry known for its elegance, realism, and social consciousness. Li Po, a free-spirited vagabond, wrote traditional lyric poetry characterized by its sense of playfulness, fantasy, and grace.

Although Li Po was probably born in central Asia, he grew up in the province of Szechwan (se'chwän') in southwestern China. He was a well-educated youth from a good family who chose to forego the test for imperial service taken by many young men of the upper classes. Instead, the young Li Po lived as a hermit and served as a wandering knight, a sword-wielding avenger of wrongs against women and children. At the age of twenty-five he became a vagabond who wandered for most of his days.

As he traveled throughout China, Li Po wrote poetry and made many friends of government officials, fellow poets, and even hermits. He also married four times and fathered several children, although he never seems to have settled down in a home of his own.

Li Po's travels in China served to spread his fame as a poet. Even the emperor admired him. In fact, Li Po abandoned his nomadic life for a time to serve the emperor as an imperial court poet. There Li Po delighted in a life of unaccustomed luxuries.

Some time afterward, Li Po entered into the service of a rebel prince. When the prince's bid for power failed, however, Li Po was imprisoned and then banished, a sentence that was revoked just as he was on his way to exile. Three years later, the poet died suddenly. An appropriately romantic Chinese legend tells that he drowned one night as he leaned from his boat to embrace the watery reflection of the moon.

OBJECTIVES

1. To analyze the form and content of Li Po's poems
2. To understand the use of alliteration
3. To write a poem in letter form
4. To plan and perform a choral reading

Reader's Guide

POEMS OF LI PO

Background

Like most of his contemporaries, Li Po wrote in a wide range of poetic forms, of which the brief verse "Quiet Night Thoughts" and the longer "Letter to His Two Small Children" are two examples. Many of his masterpieces are "old style" verses that imitate the rhythms and flow of rambling folk songs. According to Chinese critics, however, Li Po was at his best in concise four-line poems with five to seven words per line. His poem *Yeh-ssu* (ye sə), translated here as "Quiet Night Thoughts," is a masterpiece of this form. It has been memorized by virtually all Chinese schoolchildren for centuries. The English translation provided here has eight lines, twice as many as the original, in order to accommodate the rhythms of English verse.

A lifelong observer of nature, Li Po created vivid images of China's best-known mountains and streams, often recalled in a mood of solitude. "Quiet Night Thoughts" and "A Letter to His Two Small Children," though different in form, both resonate with images of nature and the thoughts and emotions of the solitary poet. Traditional Chinese poets like Li Po were often inspired by watching the moon, visiting the mountains, or viewing spring blossoms. By writing poems they completed their experiences.

Writer's Response

Imagine yourself far away from home, like Li Po, dreaming of the people and places left behind. Using specific word pictures, write a few phrases describing the sights and sounds you would miss most.

Literary Focus

Alliteration is the repetition of consonant sounds in words that appear close together. Alliteration usually occurs at the beginning of words, as in *broken bottle*. But alliteration may also occur within words, as in *He was always wide-awake*. Poets may use alliteration to give their poems greater unity, to achieve special rhythmic and musical effects, or to emphasize particular words. Alliteration is a commonly used sound device in traditional Chinese poetry.

PREREADING FOCUS

Background: Li Po took respite from heartache in taverns, love, and, most significantly, nature. His poetry reflects the restlessness of the ever-traveling poet, who was drawn again and again to the healing refuge of mountains and rivers. "Letter to His Two Small Children" was written near the Yangtze River where several years later, according to legend, Li Po drowned. Po-ch'in, the cherished son addressed in the letter-poem, was affectionately called Bright Moon Slave by his poet father.

Literary Focus: Sound devices such as alliteration, rhyme, and shifting intonation (integral to the Chinese language) are essential to the music of Chinese poetry. Translators also make use of alliteration in an attempt to maintain some of the musical quality of the original. Have students note the power generated by the repetition of the sound *s* in this line from Li Po:

   And *s*end through ten thou-
   *s*and valleys a thunder of
   *s*pinning *s*tones.

Encourage students to note how alliteration also enhances meaning in the poems that follow.

QUIET NIGHT THOUGHTS
Li Po
translated by
ARTHUR COOPER

 What is the central image in this poem?

P. Van Rhijn/SuperStock, Inc.

1 ⌐   Before my bed
     there is bright moonlight
       So that it seems
2 ⌐   like frost on the ground:

5   Lifting my head
     I watch the bright moon,
       Lowering my head
     I dream that I'm home.

LETTER TO HIS TWO SMALL CHILDREN
Li Po
translated by
ARTHUR COOPER

 What mood and experience do the poet's images create?

Here in Wu° Land mulberry leaves are green,
Silkworms in Wu have now had three sleeps:

My family, left in Eastern Lu,
Oh, to sow now Turtle-shaded fields,

1. **Wu** (wo͞o): a river in central
   China.

RETEACHING

To reteach "Letter to His Two Small Children," have students work in pairs to write a letter from P'ing-yang and Po-ch'in to their father, in response to the poem. Encourage students to refer to the poem for ideas on what would be meaningful or comforting to the children's father, as well as for clues on how to address the envelope.

5   Do the Spring things I can never join,
    Sailing Yangtze° always on my own—

    Let the South Wind blow you back my heart,
    Fly and land it in the Tavern court
    Where, to the East, there are sprays and leaves
10 Of one peach tree, sweeping the blue mist;

    This is the tree I myself put in
    When I left you, nearly three years past;
    A peach tree now, level with the eaves,
    And I sailing cannot yet turn home!

15 Pretty daughter, P'ing-yang is your name,
    Breaking blossom, there beside my tree,
    Breaking blossom, you cannot see me
    And your tears flow like the running stream;

    And little son, Po-ch'in you are called,
20 Your big sister's shoulder you must reach
    When you come there underneath my peach,
    Oh, to pat and pet you too, my child!

    I dreamt like this till my wits went wild,
    By such yearning daily burned within;
25 So tore some silk, wrote this distant pang
    From me to you living at Wen Yang . . .

6. **Yangtze** (yangk'sē): the longest river in China, flowing from Tibet to the East China Sea.

The Cleveland Museum of Art, John L. Severance Fund, 54.582

POET WANDERING IN THE MOONLIGHT, TU CHIN.
? What does the growth of a peach tree measure in this poem?

3 LITERARY ELEMENT
Simile: To what does the poet compare his daughter's tears? (the running stream) What impression of his daughter's sadness does this comparison create? (Possible response: It is deep and unending.)

4 LITERARY ELEMENT
Alliteration: Have students identify the alliteration in line 23. (wits went wild) How would you explain its effect? (Possible response: The repeated *w* sound accentuates words that convey the pain of yearning.)

COMPARING LITERATURE
? What theme do Song 103 and Song 130 from The Book of Songs (pp. 512–517) and these poems by Li Po share? (yearning for home) In what way do the poems vary the theme? (Possible response: In the poems from *The Book of Songs*, the young bride and the soldier are away from home against their will while the speakers in Li Po's poems may have chosen to leave.)

HUMANITIES CONNECTION

Tu Chin (active 1465–1487) was considered a conservative painter at the time of the Ming Dynasty. In this painting, he shows a poet contemplating nature—one of the common motifs of Chinese landscape painting. Note how the pale poet, and even paler rock, indicate the effect of moonlight. ∎

1. **Transforming Prose into Poetry.** Students who keep a diary or have written an essay of special personal significance can use the ideas and feelings in their prose pieces as the basis for an eight-line poem, modeled on Li Po's "Quiet Night Thoughts." Students should imitate Li Po's concise yet complete form and make use of some of the poetic devices that contribute to the poem's effectiveness.

2. **Charting a Literary Map.** Have interested students work in small groups to create a "literary map" of China. The biographical notes on Li Po on p. 518 and "Letter to His Two Small Children" give the names of some important regions, rivers, and mountains to include on the map, as do other introductions to selections in this unit.

Ask students to return to the poems and point out examples of images drawn from nature and discuss how they are used to accentuate the central feeling, or message, of each poem. ■

ANSWERS

First Thoughts
Answers will vary.

Identifying Facts
1. (1) frost; (2) green, Spring, sprays, blossom
2. dreams of home
3. b/m, w/t

Interpreting Meanings
1. Possible response: Images of the moon, its cold light, the speaker's movements and activities—*lifting, lowering, watch, dream*—and the word *home* convey a pensive or wistful mood.
2. Parallel lines are *Lifting . . . / Lowering . . .* and *I watch . . . / I dream. . . .* The contrasting ideas are appreciation for the moon and longing for home.
3. Possible response: Images of *one peach tree, breaking blossom*, and a *South Wind* blowing back his heart accent solitude. Emotions may include sadness and yearning.
4. "Quiet Night Thoughts"; enhances its mood of solitude.

Applying Meanings
Accept all reasonable answers.

Creative Writing Response
Writing a Poem in Letter Form. The imagery and alliteration should contribute to a general mood.

Speaking and Listening
Planning and Performing a Choral Reading. At the outset, students should decide what feelings they want to evoke in the audience. ■

First Thoughts
What dominant feelings do these two poems evoke? Which images communicate these feelings most effectively?

Identifying Facts
1. What word or words suggesting a season does Li Po use in each poem?
2. What dreams does Li Po describe in his poems?
3. Which repeated consonants create **alliteration** in the lines, "Before my bed/ there is bright moonlight" and "I dreamt like this till my wits went wild"?

Interpreting Meanings
1. What is the overall **mood**, or feeling, of "Quiet Night Thoughts"? How does the poet use **imagery**, or word pictures, to convey that mood?
2. Like many Chinese poets, Li Po uses a form of **parallelism** in which pairs of lines follow the same basic sentence structure. Point out the parallelism in the last four lines of "Quiet Night Thoughts." What two ideas are contrasted in these two parallel pairs of lines?
3. How does the poet use images of nature to emphasize his solitude in "Letter to His Two Small Children"? What emotions are evoked in this poem?
4. In which of Li Po's two poems is **alliteration** used more frequently? How do these repeated consonants add to the poem's effect?

Applying Meanings
The poems' speakers chose to express their feelings by using images of nature and the seasons. If you felt as lonely as the speakers, what season would you use to express your emotions? Why?

Creative Writing Response
Writing a Poem in Letter Form. Imagine that you are far away and thinking of family members or friends and how much you miss them. As Li Po did, write a letter in the form of a poem that expresses your feelings. To help convey your emotion, use at least two **images**, or word-pictures, that suggest the appropriate seasons or aspects of nature. For example, a flock of migrating birds might convey the idea of yearning to head home. Try to use the sound device of **alliteration** in some of your lines.

Speaking and Listening
Planning and Performing a Choral Reading. With a partner or a small group, prepare and perform a choral reading of either "Quiet Night Thoughts" or "Letter to His Two Small Children." You might want to accompany your reading with a recording of appropriate Chinese music or the live sounds of a flute and drums, if class musicians are available. Use the following list as a guide to prepare and perform your reading for the class.

1. Decide which lines will be read by each solo, or single, voice and which lines might be read by a chorus. For example, "Quiet Night Thoughts" could be read by two solo voices reading alternating pairs of lines.
2. Make a copy of the poem and mark the reading parts you've decided upon.
3. For your part, underline the words you particularly want to stress and note the punctuation where you will pause or stop.
4. Practice your choral reading before performing it for the class.

THE ART OF TRANSLATION

Translating Chinese Poetry

Many masterpieces of world literature would be unavailable to us if it were not for **translation**, the rendering of spoken or written words from one language into another. Literary translators practice a complex art. To begin with, they must be able to understand the meaning, structure, and style of the original work. Then they must convey these elements artfully in a second language, striking a balance between the two extremes of upholding form over content or content over form.

The best translators are often themselves writers, such as the poets Witter Bynner and Ezra Pound, who produced different translations of the same poem by Li Po. Such poetic translations may begin with a "word-for-word" rendering like the following literal translation of another classical Chinese verse. In the classical Chinese language, each character usually stands for a single syllable that also represents a one-syllable Chinese word.

月 耀 如 晴 雪

Moon rays like pure snow

梅 花 似 照 晃

Plum flowers resemble bright stars

可 憐 金 鏡 轉

Can admire gold disc turn

庭 上 玉 芳 馨

Garden high above jewel weeds fragrant

Here is Ezra Pound's more graceful rendering of the moon poem, based on the literal translation you have just read:

> The moon's snow falls on the plum tree;
> Its boughs are full of bright stars.
> We can admire the bright turning disc;
> The garden high above there, casts its
>   pearls to our weeds.

Classical Chinese poetry is open to wide-ranging interpretations because of the unique grammatical structure of the Chinese language. In classical Chinese, there are no indications of pronoun gender, verb tenses, or noun number. Connecting words and even the subjects of sentences are often omitted. Translators must therefore rely on clues given in the poem's context and imagery.

Two very different translations of the same Li Po poem appear on the following pages. In preparing his translation of the Li Po poem that appears on page 524, Pound worked from an English prose translation of a Japanese version. Bynner, for his translation on page 525, worked from the original Chinese poem. In both versions of the poem, a young woman whose marriage was undoubtedly arranged by her parents describes how her feelings toward her husband blossomed into love.

ABOUT TRANSLATION

The absence of verb tense and noun number in Chinese, says translator Burton Watson, is not as perplexing for the translator as the modern reader of English might expect. In Watson's view, T'ang poetry invites the reader to fill in the landscape, permitting context to imply what grammar does not reveal. Other critics view the verb without tense as an advantage because it does not fix an image in time, but rather suggests its true ongoing nature, like a flowing river.

ABOUT THE TRANSLATORS

Ezra Pound (1885–1972) led the early twentieth-century Imagist school of poetry in its rebellion against what he referred to in *A Glossary of Literary Terms* as the "blurry, messy . . . sentimentalistic" poetry of the Romantic and Victorian periods. The Imagists' poetry, influenced by the Japanese haiku (see pp. 572–577), is characterized by clear images whose relationship or meaning is suggested rather than explained.

Born in Idaho, Pound chose to leave the U.S. and live in turn in London, Paris, and Italy, where he became a major influence on the new poets on both sides of the Atlantic in the 1920s and 1930s.

Witter Bynner (1881–1968) grew up in Boston and attended Harvard University. He traveled in China, where he was drawn to the philosophy of Lao-tzu (see p. 541) and later wrote a commentary called *The Way of Life According to Laotzu*.

The River Merchant's Wife: A Letter
Li Po
translated by
Ezra Pound

1 ⌈While my hair was still cut straight across my forehead
 I played about the front gate, pulling flowers.
 You came by on bamboo stilts, playing horse,
 You walked about my seat, playing with blue plums.
 And we went on living in the village of Chokan:
 Two small people, without dislike or suspicion.

At fourteen I married My Lord you.
 I never laughed, being bashful.
 Lowering my head, I looked at the wall.
 Called to, a thousand times, I never looked back.

At fifteen I stopped scowling,
 I desired my dust to be mingled with yours
 Forever and forever and forever.
 Why should I climb the look out?

At sixteen you departed,
 You went into far Ku-to-yen, by the river of swirling eddies,
 And you have been gone five months.
 The monkeys make sorrowful noise overhead.

2 ⌈You dragged your feet when you went out.
 By the gate now, the moss is grown, the different mosses,
3 Too deep to clear them away!
 The leaves fall early this autumn, in wind.
 The paired butterflies are already yellow with August
 Over the grass in the West garden;
4 ⌈They hurt me. I grow older.
 If you are coming down through the narrows of the river Kiang,
 Please let me know beforehand,
 And I will come out to meet you
                    As far as Cho-fu Sa.

THE NORTH SEA (left section), CHOU CH'EN (c. 1455–c. 1537).

The Nelson-Atkins Museum of Art, Kansas City, Missouri

A Song of Ch'ang-Kan
Li Po
translated by
Witter Bynner

My hair had hardly covered my forehead.
I was picking flowers, playing by my door,
When you, my lover, on a bamboo horse,
Came trotting in circles and throwing green plums.
We lived near together on a lane in Ch'ang-kan,
Both of us young and happy-hearted.
. . . At fourteen I became your wife,
So bashful that I dared not smile,
And I lowered my head toward a dark corner
And would not turn to your thousand calls;
But at fifteen I straightened my brows and laughed,
Learning that no dust could ever seal our love,
That even unto death I would await you by my post
And would never lose heart in the tower of silent watching.
. . . Then when I was sixteen, you left on a long journey
Through the Gorges of Ch'ü-t'ang, of rock and whirling water.
And then came the fifth month, more than I could bear,
And I tried to hear the monkeys in your lofty far-off sky.
Your footprints by our door, where I had watched you go,
Were hidden, every one of them, under green moss,
Hidden under moss too deep to sweep away.
And the first autumn wind added fallen leaves.
And now, in the eighth month, the yellowing butterflies
Hover, two by two, in our west-garden grasses. . . .
And because of all this, my heart is breaking
And I fear for my bright cheeks, lest they fade.
. . . Oh, at last, when you return through the three Pa districts,
Send me a message home ahead!

Eighteenth-century Chinese print from a series depicting women's occupations.

SEF/Art Resource, New York

1. Pound calls Li Po's poem a letter and includes its "writer" in the title. Bynner calls the poem a "song." How do these different titles affect your reading of each poem?
2. What are the main differences in imagery in each poem?
3. Which translator's version of the poem do you prefer? Why?

Tu Fu
A.D. 712–770

SuperStock International

T u Fu (doo foo) was born into a noble family of scholar-officials. As a youth, he was confident of securing one of the imperial appointments that was the dream of every young aristocrat in the T'ang (täng) dynasty. So it was a bitter blow when, at the age of twenty-four, he failed the writing examinations in prose and poetry that were the means of gaining imperial positions.

Having failed the tests, Tu Fu spent most of his days wandering and moving in and out of minor government positions throughout the empire. Although he passed the imperial examinations much later in life, he did so without distinction. His failure kept him from realizing his youthful dream of becoming an advisor to the emperor.

Tu Fu's family connections and modest wealth nonetheless assured him of relative comfort until 755, when a violent rebellion ended the T'ang dynasty's days of glory. After that, Tu Fu was often on the road, searching for a way to make a living. In 757, while Tu Fu was away seeking work, his young son died, possibly from starvation or a plague. During the remaining years of his life, Tu Fu lived in hardship and poor health. He died in 770 on a houseboat on a river near Hangchow.

The uncertain course of Tu Fu's life is reflected in his poetry, which is often marked by bitterness and melancholy. As a young man, he wrote mainly about the beauty of nature and his own sorrows. But as he grew older, Tu Fu's poems turned to more humanitarian themes. He became sensitive to people's sufferings and was the first Chinese poet to write at length about current social concerns. After the bloody rebellion of 755, he wrote many poems condemning the folly of war—a common theme in Chinese poetry.

Although Tu Fu was neither well known nor especially well regarded as a poet during his own lifetime, he wrote in an elegant style that influenced later Chinese poets for centuries after his death. His poetry is even more polished than that of Li Po (lē bō), the friend and fellow poet with whom he is often linked. To the Chinese, "Li Po is the people's poet, Tu Fu is the poets' poet."

OBJECTIVES

1. *To analyze several poems by Tu Fu, a classical Chinese poet of the T'ang dynasty*
2. *To identify mood in poetry*
3. *To compare and contrast poems from two different centuries and cultures*

VOCABULARY IN CONTEXT

The words listed below will appear in the side margin at the point of instruction:

1. grizzled
2. sequence
3. courtiers
4. pathos
5. imperceptibly

Reader's Guide

POEMS OF TU FU

Background

Perhaps the most respected of all the ancient Chinese poets, Tu Fu focused on the affairs of the world and the sufferings of his people. In stating his goal as a poet, Tu Fu once said, "If my words aren't startling, death itself has no rest."

Like many Chinese poets of his time, Tu Fu wrote in a variety of forms, but he was unequaled in his mastery of the difficult eight-line classical verse form called the *lü-shih* (lyoo'shə), meaning "regulated verse." This demanding form, somewhat like the Western poetic form the *sonnet* (see page 804), was considered a showcase for a Chinese poet's classical technique.

The poems included here represent the poet's realistic and sometimes ironic outlook on life. As you read these poems, notice the vivid images and the concrete details that are a hallmark of Tu Fu's poetry.

Writer's Response

Tu Fu often wrote poems about the social concerns of his time. List five pressing social concerns that might inspire a contemporary Tu Fu to write poetry today.

Literary Focus

Mood is the overall feeling or atmosphere of a work of literature. A poem's mood might be cheerful or gloomy, defiant or accepting. Writers usually establish a mood by using descriptive details and evocative language—words that call up particular images or feelings. In the traditional Chinese poetry of Tu Fu's time, a single mood usually characterized each poem. But Tu Fu broke new ground by including shifting moods within a single poem.

PREREADING FOCUS

Background: While Tu Fu perfected the Chinese counterpart of the sonnet, exemplified in "Night Thoughts Afloat," his genius lay in making poetic form serve his larger thematic purpose. For example, the poem "For Wei Pa, in Retirement" is highly structured in Chinese, beginning and ending in couplets that describe separation. In addition, each poetic unit of meaning in the first half of the poem is part of a symmetrical balance, with its counterpart in the second half; yet the whole narrative maintains a natural, conversational flow.

Writer's Response: Have students brainstorm a list of contemporary social issues and then discuss how they would prioritize the issues on their list. Have them consider how a poet might address some of these concerns.

Literary Focus: The changing moods in Tu Fu's poems reflect his effort to awaken readers to social injustice as well as his changing personal fortunes. Critic Burton Watson remarked on how Tu Fu's condensed language gives his work a purposeful ambiguity, which challenges even the best translators.

Economy of Expression in Poetry
Economy of expression refers to precise word choice and a cutting away of all excess verbiage. Have students reread stanza three of "Night Thoughts Afloat." What details about the speaker's life and feelings are revealed by a mere thirteen words? What words have been left out that would probably be used in ordinary speech? Encourage a discussion of how Tu Fu conveys so much meaning with so few words.

1. **Reading and Speaking.** Have students rewrite stanza three or another stanza of "Night Thoughts Afloat" as a prose paragraph. Invite them to read their paragraphs aloud and to share their observations on how their prose versions compare with Tu Fu's economic use of language.

2. **Listening and Writing.** Have pairs of students share pieces of their own narrative or descriptive writing, reading aloud to each other. Ask them to

---

1 CULTURAL DIVERSITY
The term *Pa*—meaning "eight" and signifying the eighth born in a family—is an informal and intimate form of address. When a Chinese official was said to be "in retirement," it usually meant that he was in disfavor at court and was currently out of employment.

❓ *What euphemisms do we use today to indicate that someone has been fired?* (Possible responses: "early retirement," "restructuring of the workforce")

grizzled (griz'əld): gray, especially in reference to hair

sequence (sē'kwens): the following of one thing after another

2 LITERARY ELEMENT
Mood: How would you describe the shifts in mood occurring in lines 4–8? (Possible response: Enthusiasm and delight at their reunion shift to reflective sadness on the passage of time and finally to shock in the face of death.)

1

FOR WEI PA, IN RETIREMENT

Tu Fu

translated by

ARTHUR COOPER

In this poem, Tu Fu seems to celebrate a friend's retirement. What are Tu Fu's feelings about being retired from the world's affairs?

Our livelong days we never meeting
Move as do stars in other clusters,
Yet this evening ("And what an evening!")
We're sharing this lamp and candlelight;
5 But youth and strength, how briefly it lasts
For both our heads have become grizzled
And half of those we ask about, ghosts,
Till cries of shock pierce our very breasts:
How could we know twenty years would pass
10 Before I came again to your house?
Though in those days you were unmarried
Suddenly sons and daughters troop in,
"Greet merrily Papa's Companion,"
Ask from what parts it is that I come?
15 But such exchange remains unfinished:
You chase them off to get out the wine
"And in night rain pull up spring onions"
To be steamed fresh with yellow millet . . .
Now (with your "Come, we can meet seldom")
20 You've charged my glass ten times in sequence:
Ten times and still I'm not quite tipsy
But filled with sense of old acquaintance;
For tomorrow the hills divide us,
Both out of sight in the world's affairs!

2
2

ENJOYING FRESH AIR IN A MOUNTAIN RETREAT, SHENG MOU (c. 1330–1369).

The Nelson-Atkins Museum of Art, Kansas City, Missouri

listen for and then discuss each
other's key images and ideas. Encourage them to transform their narrative or descriptive prose into
poems, using Tu Fu's poetry as a
model for precision and economy of
expression. ■

NIGHT THOUGHTS AFLOAT
Tu Fu
translated by
ARTHUR COOPER

*As you read this poem, jot down two possible meanings for
the word drifting in line 13.*

By bent grasses
in a gentle wind
  Under straight mast
I'm alone tonight,

5 And the stars hang
above the broad plain
  But moon's afloat
in this Great River:

    Oh, where's my name
10 among the poets?
  Official rank?
"Retired for ill health."

    Drifting, drifting,
what am I more than
15   A single gull
between sky and earth?

THE NORTH SEA (right section), CHOU CH'EN (c. 1455–1537).
The goal of much of Chinese painting is to capture spirit through form.
❓ **What spirit does this painting seem to express? Do you think it
suits the spirit of the poem?**

The Nelson-Atkins Museum of Art, Kansas City, Missouri

MEETING INDIVIDUAL NEEDS

3 Visual Learners: Invite students to quick-sketch the setting, using the imagery in the
first two stanzas as a guide.
Remind students to keep in
mind where the speaker has
placed himself in the setting—
in a boat on the Yangzte, or
"Great River." ■

4 LITERARY ELEMENT
Mood: In which line do you
notice a significant shift in
mood? (line 9: "Oh, where's
my name") How would you
describe the emotion ex-
pressed in that line? (Possible
responses: regret, disappointment, despair)

HUMANITIES CONNECTION

Have students recall the left
section of *The North Sea*,
which they recently encountered on p. 524.
❓ *Do you think the two sections of the painting fit together well? Why or why not?*
(Answers will vary.)
  Chou Ch'en is remembered
for landscapes but even more
for his figure paintings, which
featured people from the
lower classes. Those works,
which offended the aristocracy
of the day, are seen by some
critics as political protests—
very rare phenomena in China
at that time. ■

RETEACHING

To reteach Tu Fu's poetry, have students use words and ideas from each poem in other forms of creative expression. For example, students can:

- perform a skit based on the story told in "For Wei Pa, in Retirement"
- illustrate "Night Thoughts Afloat" on a four-panel storyboard—one panel for each stanza
- write lyrics for a folk song using images and ideas from "Jade Flower Palace"

5 LITERARY ELEMENT

Mood: How would you describe the mood the setting creates? (Possible response: desolate, melancholy, fearful) What images convey the mood? (moaning wind, scurrying rats, broken tiles, ruins)

6 VISUALIZING

What does the image "green ghost fires" in line 6 suggest to your imagination? (Possible response: tufts of grass growing where fires formerly warmed the vacant rooms)

> **courtiers** (kôrt′ē·ərz): attendants in a royal court
>
> **pathos** (pā′thäs′) the quality that stirs feelings of pity, sorrow, or compassion
>
> **imperceptibly** (im′pər·sep′tə·blē): in a way not easily sensed or realized

7 LITERARY ELEMENT

Word Choice/Theme: Name some words the poet uses to create "pathos." (broken, shattered, scatters, crumbled) What main idea might be suggested by these words? (Possible responses: the futility of human striving, the transience of human grandeur)

COMPARING LITERATURE

How does the theme and mood of "Jade Flower Palace" compare with Shakespeare's Sonnet 64, p. 810? (Possible responses: The two poems share themes of wonder, loss, and decay, and a pensive mood and sense of pathos.)

JADE FLOWER PALACE
Tu Fu
translated by
KENNETH REXROTH

❖ *What does this poem reveal about Tu Fu's perspective on imperial wealth and power?*

The stream swirls. The wind moans in
The pines. Gray rats scurry over
Broken tiles. What prince, long ago,
Built this palace, standing in
5   Ruins beside the cliffs? There are
Green ghost fires in the black rooms.
The shattered pavements are all
Washed away. Ten thousand organ
Pipes whistle and roar. The storm
10   Scatters the red autumn leaves.

His dancing girls are yellow dust.
Their painted cheeks have crumbled
Away. His gold chariots
And courtiers are gone. Only
15   A stone horse is left of his
Glory. I sit on the grass and
Start a poem, but the pathos of
It overcomes me. The future
Slips imperceptibly away.
20   Who can say what the years will bring?

WHILING AWAY THE SUMMER, LIU KUAN-TAO (c. 1279–1300).
❓ *How does this poem contrast the past and the present?*

The Nelson-Atkins Museum of Art, Kansas City, Missouri

1. Imitating Tu Fu's Poetry. Invite students to imitate the form of one of Tu Fu's poems, substituting their own words and images for his. Aspects of form they might imitate include line length, number of stanzas, use of repetition, parallel words and sentences, and shifting moods. The choices of images and moods, however, should reflect the students' own outlooks and experience.

2. Role-playing the Poets. While Tu Fu held Li Po in awe, Li Po had doubts about his friend's radical poetic innovations. Have students role-play the two poets debating the appropriate subjects and form for poetry. To prepare, students can reread the biographical and background notes in this book and consult other books on the poets, such as *Li Po and Tu Fu* by Arthur Cooper (Penguin Books, 1974).

CLOSURE

Ask students to return to each poem and find words and phrases that contribute significantly to its predominant mood. Have students make some generalizations about Tu Fu's views on human life. Then ask: Do you share his views, or do you see life differently? ■

First Thoughts

What concerns seem to preoccupy Tu Fu?

Identifying Facts

1. Describe the **setting** (time and place) of "For Wei Pa, in Retirement." What specific **details** bring the setting to life?
2. To what does Tu Fu compare himself in "Night Thoughts Afloat"?
3. What did Tu Fu try to do after he had looked at the Jade Flower Palace? Why did he fail?

Interpreting Meanings

1. Tu Fu's poem "For Wei Pa, in Retirement" is both a celebration and a kind of **lament**, or expression of sorrow. What experiences does the poem celebrate? What experiences does it mourn?
2. The first two stanzas of "Night Thoughts Afloat" describe a scene and the last two express the poet's feelings. What is the **mood** of the first two stanzas? Of the last two?
3. In Tu Fu's time, a poem was expected to represent only one **mood, tone,** and **setting.** Tu Fu broke with tradition and often shifted moods, tones, and images within a poem. Find at least two shifts in any of Tu Fu's poems. How do these shifts affect your reading of each poem?

Applying Meanings

Which of Tu Fu's poems has the most meaning for you in terms of your own personal experience? Why?

Critical Writing Response

Comparing and Contrasting Two Poems. Tu Fu's poem "Jade Flower Palace" is similar in **theme** to the following poem, "Ozymandias," by Percy Bysshe Shelley, a nineteenth-century English Romantic poet.

Ozymandias
Percy Bysshe Shelley

I met a traveler from an antique land
Who said—"Two vast and trunkless legs of
    stone
Stand in the desert. . . . Near them, on the
    sand,
Half sunk a shattered visage lies, whose
    frown,
And wrinkled lip, and sneer of cold com-
    mand,
Tell that its sculptor well those passions
    read
Which yet survive, stamped on these lifeless
    things,
The hand that mocked them and the heart
    that fed;
And on the pedestal these words appear:
'My name is Ozymandias, king of kings:
Look on my works, ye Mighty, and despair!'
Nothing beside remains. Round the decay
Of that colossal wreck, boundless and bare
The lone and level sands stretch far away."

In two or three paragraphs, compare and contrast "Jade Flower Palace" and "Ozymandias." Consider the similarities and differences in **mood, tone,** and **setting** between the two poems. How do the poets use **imagery** and concrete **details**? In the final paragraph, state which poem you prefer and why. You may organize your ideas in a chart like the one below.

	Jade Flower Palace	Ozymandias
Setting (concrete details)		
Mood and tone		
Images in poem		
Theme		

First Thoughts

Possible responses: changes that come with age and passing time; questions about his standing at court

Identifying Facts

1. the home of Wei Pa, evening. Wine, spring onions steamed with yellow millet, candlelight, sons and daughters, the process of growing tipsy.
2. a single gull
3. He started to write but was overcome by pathos.

Interpreting Meanings

1. The poem celebrates reunion and friendship. It mourns the end of youth, strength, the death of old friends, and another separation.
2. Possible responses: peace, appreciation, and awe. Anguish and sorrow
3. In each poem, students can locate shifts in mood, tone, or setting. They should note when a shift disarms the reader or reveals something about a poem's theme.

Applying Meanings

Answers will vary.

Critical Writing Response

Comparing and Contrasting Two Poems. As a group, students can brainstorm criteria for evaluating poetry to guide and support their preferences. ■

Li Ch'ing-chao
C. A.D. 1084–1151

Art Resource, New York

After years of bitter political conflict, Li Ch'ing-chao's husband held his last imperial post in the walled city of Nanking (nän'king'). Here Li Ch'ing-chao often climbed the city walls to view the far-off landscape, even in snowstorms. Afterward, she would write a poem and challenge her husband to create a rhyming verse.

Of the six volumes of lyric poetry Li Ch'ing-chao wrote, only about fifty poems survive. Yet this sampling reveals remarkable skill and versatility—especially praiseworthy because it defies a Chinese proverb generally accepted in her time, "A woman's virtue lies in her ignorance."

ABOUT THE TRANSLATORS

Kenneth Rexroth. See Poems of Tu Fu on page 526.

Ling O. Chung, a poet and scholar from Taiwan, received her doctorate at the University of Wisconsin. Together, she and Rexroth translated *The Orchid Boat: Women Poets of China* and *Li Ch'ing-chao: The Complete Poems*.

For hundreds of years, many women in China have excelled at composing classical poetry. But no one is the equal of Li Ch'ing-chao (lē ching jou), long regarded as China's greatest woman poet of any period. A gifted and versatile writer, Li Ch'ing-chao was also one of the most liberated women of her day.

Li Ch'ing-chao grew up in a literary-minded family of noted scholars and officials. Her mother wrote poetry and her father belonged to a powerful literary circle. Because of her father's position as an imperial scholar-officer, Li Ch'ing-chao was brought up in court society and was trained in the arts and classical literature. This was an unusual upbringing for a woman of the Sung dynasty.

When Li Ch'ing-chao was seventeen, she competed with a friend of her father's in writing poetry. She also dared to criticize the friend's views in her poems. In doing so, she violated the Confucian code of conduct for aristocratic women. But instead of being punished for her immodesty, Li Ch'ing-chao gained admiration for her talents.

At the age of eighteen, Li Ch'ing-chao married the son of a powerful minister from an illustrious family. It was a happy marriage in which Li Ch'ing-chao and her husband wrote poems to each other and shared common interests in literature and the arts. Over time, they amassed one of the largest art collections in China. In 1129, Li Ching-chao's whole world collapsed when her husband died, possibly of typhoid, just before the imperial capital was invaded by barbarians from the north. During the next few years, Li Ch'ing-chao fled for her life, following the Sung court's retreat south of the Yangtze (yangk'sē) River.

In her later years as a widow, Li Ch'ing-chao remained a target of court intrigue. She lost many of her precious possessions and lived the last years of her life in misery.

Only about fifty poems remain of the six volumes of lyric poetry Li Ch'ing-chao wrote in her lifetime. Many of her poems celebrate her happy marriage or express her loneliness when her husband was away. The aim of her poetry, she said, was to capture a single moment in time.

OBJECTIVES

1. *To recognize the characteristics of the tz'u, or "lyric meter," a popular form of classical Chinese poetry*
2. *To identify and evaluate personification*
3. *To write song lyrics and analyze a poem's effect*
4. *To recognize ambiguity and understand its purpose*

THEMES IN WORLD LITERATURE

The Seasons of a Human Life
"For Wei Pa, in Retirement,"
 p. 528
To Hélène, p. 809

Life and Loss
"Green Willow," pp. 40–45
From the *Epic of Gilgamesh*,
 pp. 136–152 ∎

Reader's Guide

PEONIES

Background

Li Ch'ing-chao composed many poems in the *tz'u* (tsə), or "lyric meter" form, which requires that the poet supply words to pre-established musical patterns. Chinese poets, in fact, never say that they "write a tz'u." Instead, they "fill in a tz'u," keeping to the precise patterns of well-known Chinese songs.

Originally, the tz'u were lyrics written to songs from Central Asia sung by popular musical entertainers. Later, the elite poets of China wrote tz'u by following the songs' different metrical patterns, including the number and length of lines and specific rhyme schemes. Along with the title of their tz'u, Chinese poets often included the original tune title to indicate the metrical pattern they followed. Later tz'u were usually not intended to be sung.

Li Ch'ing-chao is regarded as the greatest writer of tz'u poetry from any period. Her poem "Peonies" reflects the special poetic qualities of ambiguity, delicacy, and indirectness that distinguish tz'u from other forms of Chinese verse.

Writer's Response

Peonies (pē'ə·nēz) are large, fragrant flowers that have been a favorite in Chinese gardens for centuries. The Chinese view the peony as a symbol of female beauty and love, as well as a sign of spring. It is the queen of flowers, and it is often used as a symbol of the emperor's favorite lady.

Write the name of your favorite flower or plant in the center of a sheet of paper. Around the name, make a word cluster of whatever images the flower or plant brings to your mind: its color, scent, the time of year you associate with it, and so on.

Literary Focus

Personification is a figure of speech in which a nonhuman thing or quality is described as if it were human. The phrase "Mother Earth," for example, personifies our home planet by associating it with the nurturing human qualities of motherhood. In traditional Chinese poetry, poets often personify elements in nature, such as the wind, clouds, and flowers.

PREREADING FOCUS

Background: The *tz'u* form reached its peak during the late T'ang and Sung dynasties, but it has continued to be a vital poetic medium in China to the present day.

Li Ch'ing-chao's poetry reflects the characteristic pathos of tz'u, a quality that evokes a sense of sorrow, pity, or sympathy. A typical tz'u, "Peonies" speaks of a beautiful woman and of romantic love. It "fills in" the pattern of the old tune, "I Celebrate the Clear Slow Dawn."

Literary Focus: Personification is a form of metaphor, the identification of two seemingly unlike elements. For example, the Chinese traditionally identified natural objects such as flowers with certain human characteristics. Chrysanthemums, for instance, which bloom in the withering chill of fall, were considered the "poet's flower," signifying the strength, pride, solitude, and "nobility of soul" essential to creating fine verse. Encourage students to note instances in "Peonies" where human attributes are ascribed to the flowers of the title.

PEONIES
Li Ch'ing-chao
translated by
KENNETH REXROTH AND LING CHUNG

Li Ch'ing-chao's poems are complex in feeling. As you read this poem, note places where the mood shifts subtly.

You open the low curtains of the women's quarter
   in the palace.
And carefully the carved railings guard you.
You stand alone in the middle of the balcony in
   the end of Spring.
Your flowerlike face is clear and bright as flowing water.
Gentle, modest, your natural innocence is apparent to all.
All flowers have withered except you.
In the morning breeze, in glittering dew,
You make your morning toilet
And become still more splendid and bewitching.
The wind envies you as you laugh at the moon.
The God of Spring falls in love with you forever.
Over the east side of the city the sun rises
And shines on the ponds and the gardens
And teahouses of the courtesans in the south side.
The perfumed carriages run home.
The banquet tables are cleared of scattered flowers
   and silks.
Who will succeed you when you have become
   perfumed dust?
The Palace of Brilliant Light° was not more beautiful,
As the sun rises through the branches of your
   blossoms.
I pledge my love to you in a gold cup.
As the painted candles gutter and die,
I for one do not welcome the yellow twilight.

The Granger Collection, New York

18. **Palace of Brilliant Light:** an allusion to the emperor's palace, whose golden staircases and inlaid-pearl walls glowed in the dark with a brilliant light.

1. Transforming Poetry into Dance. Students interested in expressive movement can create a dance inspired by "Peonies." Encourage them to express the ideas, images, and moods of the poem in movements with or without musical accompaniment. Invite students to dance for the class in a live performance or to make a video. If possible, have students create costumes and sets to enhance the performance.

2. Research Project. Students may be intrigued by Li Ch'ing-chao's career and marriage—atypical for women of her time and culture. Encourage students to find out more about her and the traditions she challenged, tracing changes in the roles of Chinese women from ancient to recent times.

CLOSURE

Ask students to reflect on the comment that Li Ch'ing-chao's poems are complex in feeling. Ask students how accurately that statement applies to "Peonies." What range of feelings does "Peonies" suggest? Students can compare it to "A Song of Ch'ang-Kan" (p. 525) or Song 103 (p. 515). Ask students: Do you find "Peonies" more emotionally complex than the other two song-poems? Encourage students to share their observations. ■

First Thoughts

Which image in this poem struck you as being the most vivid and memorable? Why?

Identifying Facts

1. What do the opening lines of the poem tell you about the place and time of year in which the poem is set?
2. How is twilight described in "Peonies"? What words express the speaker's feelings about that time?

Interpreting Meanings

1. What does the **personification** of the peonies reveal about the poet's feelings toward nature?
2. What **mood** is suggested in the first and middle parts of "Peonies"? What contrasting mood is expressed in the last part of the poem? Which particular lines express the subtle change in mood?
3. Is "Peonies" simply a celebration of a very beautiful woman, or does it express other concerns? Before you answer, consider the meaning implied in lines 6 and 17.

Applying Meanings

In this poem springtime evokes somber thoughts as well as feelings of delight. Why might spring be regarded as a melancholy as well as a happy season?

Creative Writing Response

Writing Song Lyrics. "Peonies" was originally composed to fit a popular melody. Choose a song that you like, and write new lyrics for it. Write about any subject, but make sure that the words you write fit the rhythmic pattern and the rhyme scheme of the song you have selected. You may want to record your song or perform it for the class when you have finished.

Critical Writing Response

Analyzing the Poem's Effect. In a two-paragraph essay, identify how "Peonies" affected you and why it had that effect. Use your answers to the following questions to stimulate prewriting ideas.

1. What were my feelings about the poem? Did it intrigue, bore, puzzle, or move me?
2. How did the poem's imagery affect me? Were the images colorful? interesting? confusing?
3. From its name, what did I expect the poem to be about? How did my expectations affect my response?

Language and Vocabulary

Ambiguity

Ambiguity is the expression of an idea in language that suggests more than one meaning. Poet Li Ch'ing-chao uses ambiguity in "Peonies" when she says, "I for one do not welcome the yellow twilight." Is the poet referring to the time just after sunset or to any developing darkness? Or does she intend "twilight" to mean a gradual period of decline in her youth and beauty? The poet's ambiguity deliberately leads us into different streams of thought, all of which make sense in the context of the poem.

Answer the following questions to analyze the poet's use of ambiguity in "Peonies."

1. Identify the lines that suggest the poet is addressing a flower in this poem. Which lines suggest that she is addressing a woman?
2. Toward the end of the poem, the speaker says, "I pledge my love to you in a gold cup." Who might "I" be if "you" refers to a woman? If "you" refers to a flower?

ANSWERS

First Thoughts
Answers will vary.

Identifying Facts
1. The place is a palace; the time is late spring.
2. as "painted candles." "I . . . do not welcome the yellow twilight."

Interpreting Meanings
1. Possible response: Nature is a beautiful but fragile being, to be appreciated while she lasts.
2. Possible responses: admiring praise, then a sense of loss. ". . . tables are cleared of scattered flowers . . ."
3. Possible response: The poem speaks of aging and loss of beauty, even for those who achieve glory.

Applying Meanings
Answers will vary.

Creative Writing Response
Writing Song Lyrics. Encourage students to analyze the lyrics that they are replacing to discover the patterns of rhythm and rhyme they will want to reproduce.

Critical Writing Response
Analyzing the Poem's Effect. Essays should focus on one dominant impression, citing specific images, words, and sounds that create an effect.

Language and Vocabulary
1. *Flower:* lines 6–7 and 17–19. *Woman:* lines 1–5 and 8–16. Line 20 is ambiguous
2. Possible response: a lover. the poet ■

Confucius was born in eastern China in the state of Lu in c. 551 B.C. China's revered scholar must have been full of curiosity even as a boy, for one historical account notes that at fifteen, during a visit to the Grand Temple of Lu, he inquired about everything.

One day, according to legend, Confucius heard the heartbroken wails of a woman crying by the roadside. To find out what was the matter, he sent one of his disciples, who discovered that the woman's uncle and husband had recently been killed by a ferocious tiger, and now her son had met the same cruel fate. When the disciple asked why she had not moved to a safer place, she replied, "But the officials here are not oppressive." Confucius, a tireless reformer, then cried out, "You hear that, my children! An oppressive official is more to be feared than a dangerous tiger."

Confucius believed it his mission to restore morality to government in an era of rampant corruption and violence. To that end, he trained an estimated three thousand students for public office. Ironically, Confucius did not himself achieve lasting political prominence, nor was he highly esteemed as a teacher in his lifetime. Yet his impact on government in China is still felt today, nearly twenty-five hundred years later.

ABOUT THE TRANSLATOR
Arthur Waley. See *The Book of Songs* on page 515.

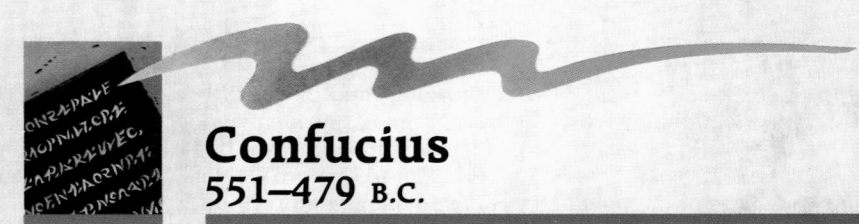

Confucius
551–479 B.C.

The Granger Collection, New York

His family name was K'ung, and he is known in Chinese history by the title K'ung-fu-tzu (koon′fōo·dzə′), which means Master K'ung. In the West he is known as Confucius (kən·fyōo′shəs).

Confucius grew up in a poor family of possibly noble heritage. He lived an ordinary life that was marked by an extraordinary love for learning. When he married at the age of nineteen, Confucius had already distinguished himself as a young scholar. By the time he died in 479 B.C. at the age of seventy-three, this largely self-educated man had become the most learned teacher in China.

Confucius was the first person in recorded Chinese history to believe in education for all and to regard teaching as a life's work. He gave private lessons to young men, train-ing them in the moral character he saw as proper and necessary to the ruling classes. But he longed for a more public position in government that would allow him to reform society according to the ancient "Way of Goodness," a traditional code of personal ethics and honor which contemporary rulers had discarded in favor of personal gain. For a decade or more, Confucius traveled from state to state seeking a ruler who would put this traditional moral code into practice. But his notions were out of step with the rulers' ways of oppression and violence. Finally, at the age of sixty-seven, Confucius returned home to teach a small band of followers in the practice of the Way.

Confucius left no writings. The only written record of his teachings was put together by his followers long after his death. This record of conversations with Confucius, the Master, is known in English as the *Analects*, which means "selected sayings," or "selections from a group of works." The *Analects* is divided into twenty books. Only six or seven of them may be Confucius' actual teachings. The other books were probably added by later disciples of the Confucian school. Generations after Confucius' death, Confucian thought took hold in China and profoundly influenced all of East Asia, including Japan and Korea. In traditional China, the *Analects* was essential reading for every educated person for more than two thousand years.

OBJECTIVES
1. *To understand representative teachings of Confucius in the form of maxims*
2. *To recognize and interpret maxims*
3. *To write original maxims and to compare and contrast the maxims of Confucius and Benjamin Franklin*

VOCABULARY IN CONTEXT

The words listed below will appear in the side margin at the point of instruction:

1. docile   4. intent
2. dictates   5. dispense
3. filial

Reader's Guide

from the ANALECTS

Background

The sayings in the *Analects* range from brief statements to more extended dialogues between Confucius and his students. The sayings express ideas based on Chinese traditions as well as on the ways of the Chinese kings Confucius admired. Confucius declared that he was not really a creator but instead a transmitter of ideas, a man who was not born with special wisdom, but only a love for past tradition. He believed that studying ancient teachings enabled people to join the continuous chain of minds from the past to their own time.

In the *Analects*, Confucius, called "the Master," speaks about the inherent goodness people should cultivate within themselves. The true self of every person—marked by unselfishness, courage, and honor—is a reflection of *chung-yung*, usually translated as "the Golden Mean," an ideal of universal moral and social harmony. The *Analects* instructs the individual on how to achieve "moderation in all things" through moral education, the building of a harmonious family life, and the development of virtues such as loyalty, obedience, and a sense of justice.

Throughout the *Analects*, Confucius also emphasizes "filial piety," the carrying out of basic obligations to one's living parents or dead ancestors. In addition, the *Analects* stresses Confucius' concern with social and religious rituals. To Confucius, a person's inner virtues can be fully realized only through concrete acts of "ritual propriety," proper behavior toward other human beings.

Writer's Response

Confucius believed that all people could develop good moral character. List five qualities that you admire in people you know. How do these qualities reflect good moral character?

Literary Focus

A **maxim** is a brief, direct statement that expresses a basic rule of human conduct or a general truth about human behavior, as in the statement: "Success is getting what you want; happiness is wanting what you get." Familiar proverbs such as "The early bird catches the worm" are also maxims. A maxim provides a simple and direct way to capture a profound, complex truth about human conduct and behavior.

PREREADING FOCUS

Background: In China, a Buddhist or Taoist can be—and usually is, by virtue of being Chinese—a "Confucianist." Confucianism goes beyond being a philosophy or doctrine that one samples, adopts, or dismisses in favor of another. Rather, it pervades Chinese culture, having shaped the language, thinking, and character of the people.

While Confucius was given to reverent contemplation, he did not seek endorsement from divine authority. He was idealistic, but also practical, social, and earthly. To counteract superstition, he appealed to rational thought; to overcome cruelty, he called for compassion. Thus the *Analects*, neither sectarian nor partisan, belongs to the literary and cultural heritage of China.

Literary Focus: The *Analects* is a collection of instructive verses, of which several are maxims. Thus Confucius' maxims share many characteristics with poetry, such as precise word choice, repetitions and parallelisms, and rhythmic patterns conducive to orature. Like poetry, maxims compress or pack profound meaning into a few words that provoke thought. Often easy to memorize but challenging to interpret, Confucius' maxims have been taught as the "basics" of education throughout Asia for eight centuries.

Commas with Introductory Elements

A comma sets off an introductory word, phrase, or clause in a sentence. The pause indicated affects emphasis, meaning, and readability.

Yu, shall I teach you what knowledge is?

At thirty, I had planted my feet firm upon the ground.

If there is no feeling of respect, wherein lies the difference?

1. **Reading and Speaking.** Have students look in the *Analects* for commas used to set off introductory elements. Encourage students to read each sample sentence aloud and discuss the effect of the comma.

2. **Writing and Listening.** Ask students to write one or two original sentences with an introductory element that calls for a comma. Have them read their sentences aloud while other students listen to determine the effect created by the comma. ■

TEACHER'S RESOURCES

- ✔ Review and Response Worksheet
- ✔ Vocabulary Activity Worksheet
- ✔ Vocabulary Test

1 LITERARY ELEMENT

Maxim: Using the first maxim as a model, determine what qualities make a maxim an effective teaching device. (Possible responses: Fewer words convey a more powerful message; a simile makes a memorable visual impression; one can quickly memorize it and let its meaning unfold.)

CULTURAL DIVERSITY

The *Analects* grew out of Confucius' conviction that Chinese government and society could survive only by putting into practice the morality and virtues of previous generations. In the United States, we too are guided by the wisdom of our ancestors. We look to the Constitution, as well as traditional values, for answers. Yet we also tend to be "futurists," seeking new solutions for social ills, such as crime, poverty, and injustice.

? *To solve such serious problems in our society, do you think we should emphasize practicing the wisdom of our nation's founders or finding new solutions? (Answers will vary.)*

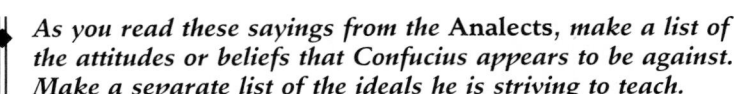

from the ANALECTS
Confucius
translated by
ARTHUR WALEY

As you read these sayings from the Analects, *make a list of the attitudes or beliefs that Confucius appears to be against. Make a separate list of the ideals he is striving to teach.*

Portrait of Confucius, seventeenth century.

Bridgeman Art Library/SuperStock, Inc.

1   The Master said, "He who rules by moral force is like the polestar,[1] which remains in its place while all the lesser stars do homage to it." (II, 1)

The Master said, "If out of the three hundred *Songs*[2] I had to take one phrase to cover all my teaching, I would say 'Let there be no evil in your thoughts.' " (II, 2)

---

1. **polestar:** the North Star, toward which the earth's axis points; also, a directing principle.

2. ***Songs:*** The Book of Songs.

READING CHECK

1. Which phrase best describes the purpose of the *Analects*: moral instruction, literary model, or wholesome entertainment? (moral instruction)
2. In his reference to *The Book of Songs*, what did Confucius urge people to dismiss from their thoughts? (evil)
3. In accordance with filial piety, what is the most important thing for children to give their parents: food and shelter, respect, or a proper burial? (respect)

4. What did Confucius *not* identify as a sign of knowledge: knowing the Chinese classics, recognizing what you do not know, or recognizing what you do know? (knowing the Chinese classics)
5. Which adversity did Confucius consider the most detrimental to people: insufficient food, a poorly equipped military, or mistrust of leaders? (mistrust of leaders)

RETEACHING

To reteach the *Analects*, have students form a "publishing team" to produce an illustrated "big book" version of the *Analects* suitable for reading to elementary-school children. While putting the maxims into language more accessible to young readers, students should remain true to the style and spirit of Confucius.

2

The Master said, "At fifteen I set my heart upon learning. At thirty, I had planted my feet firm upon the ground. At forty, I no longer suffered from perplexities. At fifty, I knew what were the biddings of Heaven. At sixty, I heard them with <u>docile</u> ear. At seventy, I could follow the <u>dictates</u> of my own heart; for what I desired no longer overstepped the boundaries of right." (II, 4)

Tzu-yu[3] asked about the treatment of parents. The Master said, " 'Filial sons nowadays are people who see to it that their parents get enough to eat. But even dogs and horses are cared for to that extent. If there is no feeling of respect, wherein lies the difference?" (II, 7)

The Master said, "Yu,[4] shall I teach you what knowledge is? When you know a thing, to recognize that you know it, and when you do not know a thing, to recognize that you do not know it. That is knowledge." (II, 17)

The Master said, "He who seeks only coarse food to eat, water to drink, and bent arm for pillow, will without looking for it find happiness to boot. Any thought of accepting wealth and rank by means that I know to be wrong is as remote from me as the clouds that float above." (VII, 15)

The Duke of She[5] asked Tzu-lu[6] about Master K'ung (Confucius). Tzu-lu did not reply. The Master said, "Why did you not say 'This is the character of the man: so <u>intent</u> upon enlightening the eager that he forgets his hunger, and so happy in doing so that he forgets the bitterness of his lot and does not realize that old age is at hand.' That is what he is." (VII, 18)

Tzu-kung[7] asked about government. The Master said, "Sufficient food, sufficient weapons, and the confidence of the common people." Tzu-kung said, "Suppose you had no choice but to <u>dispense</u> with one of these three, which would you forgo?" The Master said, "Weapons." Tzu-kung said, "Suppose you were forced to dispense with one of the two that were left, which would you forgo?" The Master said, "Food. For from of old, death has been the lot of all men; but a people that no longer trusts its rulers is lost indeed." (XII, 7)

Someone said, "What about the saying 'Meet resentment with inner power'?" The Master said, "In that case, how is one to meet inner power? Rather, meet resentment with upright dealing and meet inner power with inner power." (XIV, 36)

The Master said, "A gentleman is distressed by his own lack of capacity; he is never distressed at the failure of others to recognize his merits." (XV, 18)

Tzu-kung asked saying, "Is there any single saying that one can act upon all day and every day?" The Master said, "Perhaps the saying about consideration: 'Never do to others what you would not like them to do to you.'" (XV, 23)

4

docile (däs'əl): easily managed or disciplined
dictates (dik'tāts'): guiding principles; demands made by authority
filial (fil'ē·əl): pertaining to one's children
intent (in·tent'): firmly fixed or directed
dispense (di·spens'): to do away with

2 GUIDED READING
Sequencing: How has Confucius organized the order of sentences in maxim II, 4? (chronologically) What might be the purpose of stressing the chronology? (Possible response: to show how wisdom increases with age)

3 INTERPRETING
What does maxim VII, 15 say about the relationship between happiness and wordly success? (Possible responses: Happiness does not depend on money and status; being corrupt in order to succeed is not worthwhile.)

4 MAKING JUDGMENTS
Explain why you do or do not agree that having trust in leaders is more important than having sufficient food. (Accept answers that students can support.)

---

3. **Tzu-yu** (dzə yō): one of Confucius' principal disciples, often credited with sayings of his own.
4. **Yu** (yō): a disciple of humble birth.
5. **Duke of She** (shu): an adventurer and self-styled nobleman, a contemporary of Confucius.
6. **Tzu-lu** (dzə loo): a disciple of Confucius, known for his outgoing personality.

---

7. **Tzu-kung** (dzə goong): a disciple of Confucius, who also served as a government official.

1. Designing a Board Game. Have students collaborate on creating a board game based on the *Analects*. For example, each player begins a winding path to a goal, such as the throne in the "Forbidden City." A player draws a card with a question about a Confucian maxim. The answer determines how far a marker advances or backs up or if it stays put. Creative obstacles and bonuses can be included.

2. Writing a Political Platform. Challenge students to decide on a political office for which Confucius might campaign, and to write a platform for him. To expand their understanding of Confucius' ideas for government ethics and reform, students might refer to *Sources of Chinese Tradition*, compiled by William Theodore de Bary, Wing-tsit Chan, and Burton Watson (Columbia University Press, 1960).

CLOSURE

Encourage students to share their lists from *Writer's Response* of the ideals that Confucius endeavored to teach. Ask: Which, if any, of his maxims do you consider particularly relevant to American society today? Use students' ideas to prompt comparison and contrast between the teachings of the *Analects* and those of the *Tao Te Ching*, featured in the next selection. ■

ANSWERS

First Thoughts
Answers will vary.

Identifying Facts
1. "Never do to others what you would not like them to do to you."
2. They lack respect for their parents.

Interpreting Meanings
1. Possible response: Confucius taught that right actions (e.g., caring for parents) must be accompanied by a proper spiritual state (e.g., genuine respect for parents).
2. "Never do to others what you would not like them to do to you." The Golden Rule emphasizes what to do to others; Confucius' maxim emphasizes what *not* to do.
3. Possible translation: Righteous people are upset when they do not meet their own goals, not when others fail to praise them. Answers will vary.

Applying Meanings
Possible response: They express universal truths and are practical rules of conduct.

Creative Writing Response
Writing Maxims. Students can use elements of Confucian style such as parallelism, word choice, and conciseness.

Critical Writing Response
Comparing and Contrasting Maxims. Views expressed should be supported with references to specific maxims. ■

First Thoughts
Which of the statements in the *Analects* do you find most meaningful? Why? Which would you find the most difficult to put into action in your own life?

Identifying Facts
1. According to the Master, Confucius, what simple rule of conduct summarizes his teaching?
2. To the Master's way of thinking, what is wrong with the "filial sons" of the day?

Interpreting Meanings
1. In Book II, Analect 7, Confucius speaks of filial piety (honoring one's parents) as more than just a form of good behavior. Why do you think he emphasizes such conduct in his teachings?
2. Which of the Master's sayings is most like the Bible's Golden Rule: "Do unto others as you would have them do unto you"? What is the main difference between Confucius' saying and the Golden Rule?
3. One of the **maxims** in the *Analects* states: "A gentleman is distressed by his own lack of capacity; he is never distressed at the failure of others to recognize his merits." Translate this maxim into your own words. Do you agree or disagree with it? Why?

Applying Meanings
Many people still quote traditional sayings that state rules of conduct, such as "Look before you leap" and "A penny saved is a penny earned." Why do you think such **maxims** have stood the test of time?

Creative Writing Response
Writing Maxims. Think of one or more rules of conduct and one or more general truths about human experience that you feel are important. Then write these rules or simple truths in the form of maxims, such as: "The more things you own, the more they own you." Take your favorite maxim and design it as a bumper sticker.

Critical Writing Response
Comparing and Contrasting Maxims. In America, one of the most popular writers of often-quoted maxims was none other than Benjamin Franklin, the great inventor, diplomat, and politician. Franklin wrote humorous but wise maxims. Many of them were taken from proverbs in other languages, folk sayings, and the words of other writers. Here is a sampling of Franklin's wit and wisdom:

> If a man empties his purse into his head, no man can take it away from him. An investment in knowledge always pays the best interest.
>
> Glass, china, and reputation are easily cracked and never well mended.
>
> He that composes himself is wiser than he that composes books.
>
> 'Tis hard for an empty bag to stand upright.
>
> Nothing brings more pain than too much pleasure; nothing more bondage than too much liberty.
>
> None preaches better than the ant, and she says nothing.

Compare Franklin's maxims to those you have just read by Confucius. What are the similarities and differences in the two writers' views, as expressed in their maxims? Do you think that the two men would agree with each other, or would they have grounds for dispute? Do both of them seem to follow the idea of a Golden Mean—that is, of moderation in all things? Write your ideas in a paragraph or two. Be sure to support your views with specific examples from each writer's works.

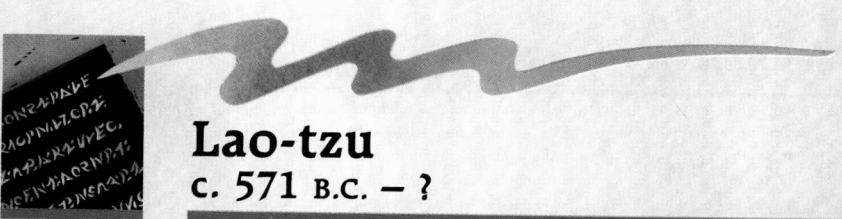

Lao-tzu
c. 571 B.C. – ?

New York Public Library Picture Collection

According to Chinese legend, Lao-tzu (lou'dzə') had a miraculous birth: He was born as an old, bearded, white-haired man, who was thereafter called "The Old Philosopher" or "The Old Boy" and lived to the age of 160. As the legend suggests, Lao-tzu, the reputed founder of the Chinese philosophy of Taoism (dou'iz'əm), is a shadowy figure, more of a legend than a historical reality.

In his biography of Lao-tzu, China's Grand Historian Ssu-ma Ch'ien (sə mä chen) recounts a legendary meeting between Lao-tzu and the much younger philosopher Confu-

cius, who supposedly came seeking Lao-tzu's advice about rituals. Instead, Lao-tzu counseled Confucius to rid himself of excessive enthusiasm, arrogance, and other traits that Lao-tzu said were of no use to Confucius' "true person."

Whether or not this meeting between Confucius and Lao-tzu actually occurred, it does serve to highlight the differences between their two contrasting schools of thought. Broadly defined, Taoism consists of the joyful acceptance of life and a willingness to yield to the natural world, becoming one with it. Confucianism, on the other hand, emphasized the individual's responsibility to act purposefully and sensibly, always consciously carrying out prescribed duties to family and society. Both philosophies, however, are rooted in ancient Chinese tradition, and the Chinese people see them as complementary, rather than opposing, views.

In defining the essence of his philosophy, Lao-tzu said, "He who knows does not speak. He who speaks does not know." Chinese poet Po Chü-i (bō jü ē) underscored the irony of this statement when he wrote:

"He who talks doesn't know,
he who knows doesn't talk":
that is what Lao-tzu told us,
in a book of five thousand words.
If he was the one who knew,
how could he have been such
    a blabbermouth?

MORE ABOUT THE AUTHOR

Even though the philosophy associated with Lao-tzu is one of the most influential in China, we know only the barest facts about Lao-tzu's life. He was born into a noble family and served as Keeper of the Imperial Archives at the Chou (jō) dynasty's capital in Luoyang (lə·wō'yäng'). After retiring in middle age, he disappeared from sight. What little else we know about him is told us by his biographer, China's Grand Historian, Ssu-ma Ch'ien. (See p. 551.)

Those who seek to understand Taoism find that it can be as elusive and mysterious as its founder. Confucius was so struck by Lao-tzu's wisdom that he told his disciples, "I know a bird can fly; I know a fish can swim; I know animals can run. . . . But the dragon is beyond my knowledge; it ascends into heaven on the clouds and the wind. Today I have seen Lao-tzu, and he is like the dragon!"

ABOUT THE TRANSLATOR

Stephen Mitchell (1943–) was born in Brooklyn and studied comparative literature at Amherst and Yale. His poems appear in *The New Yorker* and literary journals. His translations include the poetry of Rainer Maria Rilke and Yehuda Amichai, as well as the *Tao Te Ching*, the Book of Job, and *The Gospel According to Jesus*.

OBJECTIVES

1. *To recognize characteristics of the Tao Te Ching and to understand its outlook on life*
2. *To recognize and interpret paradox*
3. *To create a dialogue and to compare and contrast passages from the Tao Te Ching and a biblical poem.*

PREREADING FOCUS

Background: Students should keep in mind that to grasp the principles of Taoism, one cannot use reason. In fact, students of the Tao say that you cannot "grasp" Taoism at all. Instead, you "receive" the mysterious and poetic vision of Tao. If you are truly open, the Tao makes you one with all things.

   Aspects of Taoism have been adopted by Confucianism, which in turn influenced Taoist thinking. Both philosophies grew out of a quest for integrity during times of political chaos. Taoism, however, being mystical, has attracted followers who also embrace superstition and cult lore, inviting scorn from the Chinese intelligentsia. Nevertheless, the *Tao Te Ching* is widely regarded as one of the most thought-provoking and inspired works of Chinese literature.

Writer's Response: After students have generated several clusters, have them consider what each cluster says about water. Then ask, "What qualities of action and thought can water be used to symbolize?"

Literary Focus: In using paradox, Lao-tzu did not try to appeal to reason, but to spark in the reader a new, poetic view of life. The *Tao Te Ching* is characterized by symbols of paradox—such as water, which is both powerful and weak—as well as by the juxtaposition of seemingly opposite ideas in parallel structure.

Reader's Guide ■

from the TAO TE CHING

Background

The *Tao Te Ching* (dou deh jing) is a brief collection of sayings and poetry that teach the nature of Taoism. According to the Grand Historian Ssu-ma Ch'ien, Lao-tzu wrote the *Tao Te Ching* when, fed up with the decay he saw in government, he retired from his work as an archivist. The result of his retirement was the *Tao Te Ching*, or "Classic of the Way of Power," which, among other things, was intended to provide guidance for rulers who wished to govern according to *Tao*, or the Way. After the Bible, the *Tao Te Ching* has been the most translated book in history.

   These passages from the *Tao Te Ching*, like those in the Confucian *Analects*, often teach through **maxims**, or brief sayings about life, and use parallel language and other repetitive devices to unify the text and enhance oral reading and memorization. The heart of the *Tao Te Ching*, however, is the presence of a central figure called "the Master." According to the translator of this version, "the Master" is a man or woman "whose life is in perfect harmony with the way things are" and who has become one with "the Tao, the Truth, the Life." Although traditional translations refer to the Master as *he*, the translator here often uses *she*, for "the Master" could mean anyone—including you.

Writer's Response

According to Lao-tzu, water symbolizes, or stands for, a model of Tao. Write the word *water* in the center of a piece of paper. Around it, create clusters of words and phrases that describe water's essential qualities and benefits to the world.

Literary Focus

A **paradox** is an apparently contradictory phrase or statement that is actually true. For example, in the New Testament, Saint Paul uses a paradox when he declares, "For when I am weak, then I am strong" (2 Corinthians). The statement challenges us to find an underlying truth that resolves the apparent contradiction. Saint Paul means that when he is weak in worldly terms, he is strong in his spirit. Lao-tzu uses paradoxes to focus attention on important points in his text. Reconciling these paradoxes is a key to understanding Taoist philosophy.

from the TAO TE CHING

Lao-tzu

translated by

STEPHEN MITCHELL

As you read these passages about Taoism, jot down the phrases or lines that have the greatest meaning for you. Also jot down the lines you find the most mysterious or puzzling.

2

When people see some things as beautiful,
other things become ugly.
When people see some things as good,
other things become bad.

Being and non-being create each other.
Difficult and easy support each other.
Long and short define each other.
High and low depend on each other.
Before and after follow each other.

Therefore the Master
acts without doing anything
and teaches without saying anything.
Things arise and she lets them come;
things disappear and she lets them go.
She has but doesn't possess,
acts but doesn't expect.
When her work is done, she forgets it.
That is why it lasts forever.

1

Founders Society Purchase, General Membership and Donations Fund, The Detroit Institute of Arts

EARLY AUTUMN, CH'IEN HSUAN.
How might the teachings of the first four lines of Passage 2 be applied to the viewing of this painting? How do you feel about the painting?

TEACHER'S RESOURCES
📖 Review and Response Worksheet

1 LITERARY ELEMENT

Paradox: How are the Master's teaching methods described here contradictory? (Possible response: "Acting" and "teaching" seem to contradict "not doing" and "without saying.") How does the line "Before and after follow each other" help to explain the paradox? (Possible response: Enlightenment follows Truth as "before" follows "after.")

HUMANITIES CONNECTION

Ch'ien Hsuan (1235–1290) was a highly traditional Yüan artist best known as a painter of birds, flowers, and animals. Here he depicts the vibrant life of a pond.
With what aspects of Taoist thought do you think the painter would be sympathetic? (Accept reasonable responses: quietude, acceptance of fate, respect for nature) ■

READING CHECK

1. What segment of the population did Lao-tzu have especially in mind when he wrote the *Tao Te Ching*? (those who rule)

2. Is a "Master" a man or woman who can best be described as: a talented teacher; a person in harmony with life; a wise leader? (a person in harmony with life)

3. Does the *Tao Te Ching* say that your work should give you enjoyment, benefit humanity, or challenge your intellect? (give you enjoyment)

4. Do people who try to "improve the world," tend to live longer, cause ruin, or safeguard nature? (cause ruin)

5. According to the Tao, does the teacher teach by asking questions or without saying anything? (without saying anything)

8

The supreme good is like water,
which nourishes all things without trying to.
It is content with the low places that people disdain.
Thus it is like the Tao.

In dwelling, live close to the ground.
In thinking, keep to the simple.
In conflict, be fair and generous.
In governing, don't try to control.
In work, do what you enjoy.
In family life, be completely present.

When you are content to be simply yourself
and don't compare or compete,
everybody will respect you.

29

Do you want to improve the world?
I don't think it can be done.

The world is sacred.
It can't be improved.
If you tamper with it, you'll ruin it.
If you treat it like an object, you'll lose it.

There is a time for being ahead,
a time for being behind;
a time for being in motion,
a time for being at rest;
a time for being vigorous,
a time for being exhausted;
a time for being safe,
a time for being in danger.

The Master sees things as they are,
without trying to control them.
She lets them go their own way,
and resides at the center of the circle.

MOUNTAINS, STREAMS, AND AUTUMN-TINTED TREES,
WANG HUI (1632–1717), Ch'ing dynasty.

The Granger Collection, New York

1. **Playing "More Tao Than Thou."** Have students write statements from the Taoist passages on slips of paper. Mix up the slips in a sack and invite students to take turns drawing statements. After each draw, the player's task is to provide a real-life example that supports the Taoist thought. The same example cannot be used twice. Players who cannot provide an example drop out until only one is left.

2. **Reading** *The Tao of Physics.* Students who are intrigued by the Taoist point of view may be challenged to form a book group to read and discuss *The Tao of Physics* by Fritjof Capra (Shambhala, Berkeley, Calif., 1975). Encourage the book group members to share their findings and discussion highlights with the class.

CLOSURE

Invite students to share their thoughts on which lines from the Taoist passages they find particularly meaningful or relevant and which ones they find puzzling. Encourage students to discuss possible ways to interpret the mysterious lines. You may want to use students' ideas to prompt comparison and contrast beween Taoism and Confucianism. ■

First Thoughts

In what circumstances might Taoism be helpful as an approach to life? In what circumstances might it be ineffective as an approach to life?

Identifying Facts

1. In passage 2, what is the Master's approach to acting and teaching? What happens when she forgets her work?

2. In passage 8, in what two ways is water like the Tao? What must one do to gain people's respect?

3. In passage 29, what will happen if you mistreat the world? How does the Master act toward the world?

Interpreting Meanings

1. In passage 2, point out one **paradox**, or apparent contradiction, that actually makes sense. What does Lao-tzu mean in these lines?

2. In passage 29, what does Lao-tzu mean when he says the world cannot be improved? How does the rest of this passage support this idea?

3. What is the message of passage 8? Do you agree or disagree with it? Why or why not?

Applying Meanings

Confucian thought is most often directed to social situations and conduct in everyday life, while Taoist thought applies to a broad relationship between people and nature. Suppose that you had to choose either Confucianism or Taoism as a guide to life. Which philosophy would you feel more comfortable living by? Why?

Creative Writing Response

Creating a Dialogue. Create an imaginary dialogue between a modern high-school student and Lao-tzu in which the philosopher tries to answer a question the student has raised. Focus your dialogue on a concrete problem with a friendship, schoolwork, or a career choice that a modern student might actually face. Be sure that your answer is in harmony with Lao-tzu's beliefs.

Critical Writing Response

Comparing and Contrasting Two Passages. Lines 7–14 of passage 29 from the *Tao Te Ching* are similar in theme and form to the biblical poem "To Every Thing There Is a Season" from Chapter 3 of Ecclesiastes. In a two- or three-paragraph essay, compare and contrast "There is a time for being ahead . . ." with "To Every Thing There Is a Season." In your essay, consider similarities and differences in style, language, and theme or message.

To Every Thing There Is a Season
King James Bible

To every thing there is a season,
And a time to every purpose under the heaven:
A time to be born, and a time to die;
A time to plant, and a time to pluck up that which is planted;
A time to kill, and a time to heal;
A time to break down, and a time to build up;
A time to weep, and a time to laugh;
A time to mourn, and a time to dance;
A time to cast away stones, and a time to gather stones together;
A time to embrace, and a time to refrain from embracing;
A time to get, and a time to lose;
A time to keep, and a time to cast away;
A time to rend, and a time to sew;
A time to keep silence, and a time to speak;
A time to love, and a time to hate;
A time of war, and a time of peace.

—Ecclesiastes 3:1–8

Chuang Tzu's vision of Taoism is considered more far-reaching and complete than that expressed in Lao-tzu's *Tao Te Ching*, the original work of Taoist thought (see pp. 543–544). In Chuang Tzu's vision, all life is one with the Tao, or the Way, which has no beginning or end, no right or wrong. The true Taoist, according to Chuang Tzu, is the moral man who follows his own heart, remaining free from the bonds of obligation and tradition and the need to alter the course of the world.

Lieh Tzu renounced the world and lived as a hermit sage. Legend holds that he dispensed with walking and "rode the wind," a poetic description of his spiritual journey. From the Taoist point of view, however, happiness is not absolute until the rider and the wind are one.

Lui An was a skillful writer of verse as well as a devoted Taoist. The *Huainan-Tzu* reflects his guidance and dedication to bringing unity to the various and often conflicting interpretations of Taoist teachings.

ABOUT THE TRANSLATOR

Moss Roberts has written extensively on Chinese philosophy and philology—the study of language used in literature. Other work includes his acclaimed translation of the classic *Three Kingdoms*, China's first novel, written in the fourteenth century by Lo Kuan-chung.

Taoist Writers
Fourth through Second Centuries B.C.

Landscape (left half), Ming dynasty.

Shostal Associates/SuperStock International

Chuang Tzu (fourth century B.C.)

The Chinese philosopher Chuang Tzu (jwäng dzə) was the most important early interpreter of the philosophy of Taoism (dou'iz'əm). Very little is known of Chuang Tzu's life except that he served as a minor court official.

What we do know about Chuang Tzu comes mainly from the fictional stories about him in the final chapters of *Chuang Tzu*, a book of stories that contains his teachings, although it was written by others. In these stories, Chuang Tzu appears as a quirky character who cares little for either public approval or material possessions.

Content to live humbly, this wise man wears patched clothing and shabby shoes tied on with string. In one tale, Chuang Tzu even insists to his protesting disciples that they should not bury him when he dies. He wants nature as his only coffin and the heavenly bodies as his only jewels.

Lieh Tzu (fourth century B.C.)

Some scholars doubt that Lieh Tzu (lē'ə dzə) ever existed. Much of the *Lieh Tzu*, the book that bears his name, has been shown to be a forgery. Nevertheless, most experts believe that there was a real Lieh Tzu, a Taoist teacher who had many philosophical differences with his forebears Lao-tzu and Chuang Tzu. Lieh Tzu argued that a sequence of causes predetermines everything that happens, including one's choice of action. Since no one can change the unchangeable Way, or Tao, people should pursue their own self-interests.

Lui An (172–122 B.C.)

Lui An (lə än) was not only a Taoist scholar but the grandson of the founder of the Han dynasty (206 B.C.–A.D. 221). Lui An's royal title was the Prince of Haui-nan (hwī nan). The prince surrounded himself with a circle of philosophers, and under his patronage they produced a collection of essays on metaphysics, cosmology, politics, and conduct. Lui An took his own life after organizing a failed coup against his cousin, the emperor.

OBJECTIVES

1. *To interpret some Taoist Anecdotes*
2. *To recognize elements of anecdotes and to understand how they convey messages*
3. *To make comparisons between personal views and those expressed in an anecdote*
4. *To tell an anecdote about a personal experience and to summarize its meaning with an original maxim*

THEMES IN WORLD LITERATURE

The Wisdom of the World
From the *Analects* of Confucius, pp. 536–540
Zen Parables pp. 589–595
La Fontaine's *Fables*, pp. 940–944

Choices in Life
Parables from the New Testament, pp. 196–203

Atsumori, pp. 598–611
"The Tale of the Falcon," from the *Decameron*, pp. 813–820 ■

Reader's Guide

TAOIST ANECDOTES

Background

Chinese philosophers, whether followers of Taoism or Confucianism, have long used **anecdotes**, or brief stories, to convey indirectly the teachings of their philosophy. These anecdotes are the works of three Taoist philosophers. The stories are intended to impart the spiritual teachings of Taoism, with its focus on oneness with the world and the unchangeable nature of the Way.

These anecdotes often reflect different approaches to Taoist philosophy. Chuang Tzu, for example, tends to point directly to the Tao, or the Way, at work in the universe, while Lieh Tzu emphasizes the folly of those who don't see beyond the obvious to the underlying patterns that Taoists believe govern all action. But the anecdotes also have much in common. To make their philosophical points easier to accept, the philosophers convey their ideas in a single, colorful incident intended to amuse their readers. The anecdotes often use witty dialogue and light-hearted humor to "sugar coat" the philosophical point of their tales.

Writer's Response

Many of these ancient Chinese anecdotes can be boiled down to a **maxim**, a saying that states a truth about human experience or a rule for human conduct, such as "You can't tell a book by its cover" or "All is fair in love and war." Make a list of other popular maxims that could be illustrated in brief stories.

Literary Focus

An **anecdote** is a brief story that focuses on a single interesting incident or event, often an event that reveals the character of an important person. The writer of an anecdote surrounds this incident with just enough details to make the point of the anecdote clear and vivid for readers. Many anecdotes, like the ones you are about to read, are witty as well as instructive.

PREREADING FOCUS

Background: The writings attributed to Chuang Tzu and his disciples broke tradition with the Taoism of Lao-tzu, which concerned itself with ways to interact with a troubled world. Chuang Tzu shifted the focus to the inner journey, liberating the mind and spirit from the restrictions of personal prejudice and limited awareness. Rather than contending with the evils of society, his followers rose above them and withdrew from public life. Chuang Tzu's vision, once characterized by the historian Ssu-ma Ch'ien as essentially an egotistical one which had little practical use in dealing with problems of governing, has continued to influence the Chinese mind.

Literary Focus: In a sense, the anecdote serves as a metaphor, giving readers a concrete and familiar vehicle by which to gain insight into the mystical Taoist vision. Chuang Tzu, in particular, made extensive use of anecdotes. His are characterized by humor as well as poetic imagery, as found in "Wagging My Tail in the Mud."

TAOIST ANECDOTES

translated by

MOSS ROBERTS

As you read these different anecdotes, try to discover the Taoist "point" that is hidden in each story.

Wagging My Tail in the Mud

The hermit poet Chuang Tzu was angling[1] in the River Pu. The king of Ch'u sent two noblemen to invite Chuang to come before him. "We were hoping you would take on certain affairs of state," they said. Holding his pole steady and without looking at them, Chuang Tzu said, "I hear Ch'u has a sacred tortoise that has been dead three thousand years, and the king has it enshrined in a cushioned box in the ancestral hall. Do you think the tortoise would be happier wagging its tail in the mud than having his shell honored?" "Of course," replied the two noblemen. "Then begone," said Chuang Tzu. "I mean to keep wagging my tail in the mud."

—*Chuang Tzu*

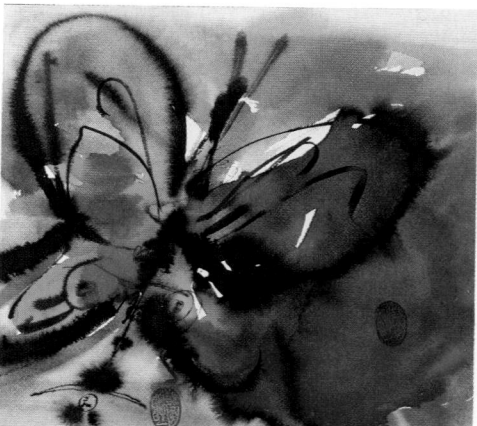

BUTTERFLY, DIANE ONG.

D. Ong/SuperStock, Inc.

The Butterfly

Chuang Tzu said, "Once upon a time I dreamed myself a butterfly, floating like petals in the air, happy to be doing as I pleased, no longer aware of myself! But soon enough I awoke and then, frantically clutching myself, Chuang Tzu was I! I wonder: Was Chuang Tzu dreaming himself the butterfly, or was the butterfly dreaming itself Chuang Tzu? Of course, if you take Chuang Tzu and the butterfly together, then there's a difference between them. But that difference is only due to their changing material forms."

—*Chuang Tzu*

Gold, Gold

Many, many years ago there was a man of the land of Ch'i who had a great passion for gold. One day at the crack of dawn he went to the market—straight to the gold dealers'

---

1. **angling:** fishing.

READING CHECK

1. Why did Taoist philosophers put profound messages into amusing anecdotal form? (to make them clear and vivid)
2. Did the sacred tortoise shell enshrined in a box represent honor and respect or the end of happiness to Chuang Tzu? (end of happiness)
3. What kept the gold thief from noticing the people around? (passion for gold)

4. Does "The Missing Axe" show that suspicion affects perception, young thieves can change their ways, or material possessions have no value? (Suspicion affects perception.)
5. Which point does "The Lost Horse" *not* make: a blessing may actually become a disaster; a disaster may be a blessing in disguise; something of value never changes? (Something of value never changes.)

RETEACHING

To reteach the *Taoist Anecdotes*, divide the class into small groups to discuss the Taoist messages conveyed by the anecdotes. Have each group rewrite the teachings as brief statements or maxims for "Taoist Fortune Cookies." Students might like to share their work by inserting the Taoist fortunes into real cookies. Participants can read their fortunes aloud and discuss their relevance to their own lives.

Giraudon/Art Resource, New York

Horseman, late Han dynasty.

stalls, where he snatched some gold and ran. The market guards soon caught him. "With so many people around, how did you expect to get away with it?" a guard asked.

3 "When I took it," he replied, "I saw only the gold, not the people."

—*Lieh Tzu*

The Missing Axe

A man whose axe was missing suspected his neighbor's son. The boy walked like a thief, looked like a thief, and spoke like a thief. But the man found his axe while he was 4 digging in the valley, and the next time he saw his neighbor's son, the boy walked, looked, and spoke like any other child.

—*Lieh Tzu*

The Lost Horse

A man who lived on the northern frontier of China was skilled in interpreting events.

One day for no reason, his horse ran away to the nomads across the border. Everyone tried to console him, but his father said, "What makes you so sure this isn't a blessing?" Some months later his horse returned, bringing a splendid nomad stallion. Everyone congratulated him, but his father said, "What makes you so sure this isn't a disaster?" Their household was richer by a fine horse, which the son loved to ride. One day he fell and broke his hip. Everyone tried to console him, but his father said, "What makes you so sure this isn't a blessing?" 5

A year later the nomads came in force across the border, and every able-bodied man took his bow and went into battle. The Chinese frontiersmen lost nine of every ten men. Only because the son was lame did the father and son survive to take care of each other. Truly, blessing turns to disaster, and disaster to blessing: the changes have no end, nor can the mystery be fathomed. 6

—*Lui An*

HUMANITIES CONNECTION

In early China, horses were highly valued as a symbol of wealth, especially by soldiers and noblemen. Numerous figures of horses, sculpted from stone, bronze, or terra-cotta, were found in ancient tombs. **?** *How has the sculpture linked the horse and the rider?* (Possible response: The position of the rider's hands suggests he is holding the horse's bridle.) ∎

3 READER'S RESPONSE
Have you ever let your passion blind you to obvious consequences and acted irrationally?

4 LITERARY ELEMENT
Anecdote: What does this story say about human nature? (Possible response: Blaming others is a strong temptation and can distort our perception.)

5 GUIDED READING
Sequencing: What pattern does the sequence of events in this anecdote follow? (disaster—blessing—disaster—blessing) What aspect of human life does the pattern reinforce? (Possible response: Alternating outcomes illustrate that human perception is limited and only change itself is certain.)

MEETING INDIVIDUAL NEEDS

6 ESL: Explain that *fathomed* means "probed in order to understand." The concept derives from the seafaring term *fathom*, a unit of six feet used to measure the depth of water. ∎

1. Creating a Mural. Students can create a mural depicting each of the anecdotes. The art may be done in the style of Chinese painting and drawing, using the several illustrations shown in this unit as models. Or students might choose to update and "Americanize" the art, to show that Taoism is a philosophy that transcends time and culture.

2. Creating a Taoist Sitcom. Challenge students to teach a lesson using one of the Taoist anecdotes by putting it into the form of a modern television sitcom. Students can build on a show that exists, or create an original production, and present it to the class.

CLOSURE

Briefly discuss the effectiveness of using anecdotes as a medium for teaching Taoism to ordinary folks. Then ask students what means the ancient sages could use if they were living in the United States today. To prompt discussion, you might suggest some possibilities—serial road signs, lyrics for rap or rock music, and comic strips, for example. ∎

ANSWERS

First Thoughts
Answers will vary.

Identifying Facts
1. He chooses happiness over fame, wealth, and glory.
2. finding his axe
3. Passion for gold blinds him to his surroundings.
4. It is good luck, making him unfit for battle.

Interpreting Meanings
1. Possible response: Chuang Tzu has the inner strength to resist fame and fortune. Chuang Tzu knows and accepts his own nature.
2. Possible response: One must look beyond the surface and resist the temptation to label events as "good" or "bad."
3. Possible responses: Greed prevents people from seeing reality clearly; suspicions or preconceptions can prevent you from seeing people as they are; both illustrate the limitations of human perception.
4. Possible response: to illustrate that differences between creatures and humans is a matter of form, not essence

Applying Meanings
Answers will vary.

Critical Writing Response
Comparing Views. The essays can use original anecdotes, or variations of a Taoist anecdote, to illustrate differences.

Speaking and Listening
Telling an Anecdote. The point of the anecdotes should apply to life in general. ∎

First Thoughts

Which of these anecdotes contained a message that you could apply to your own life?

Identifying Facts

1. How does Chuang Tzu defy society's expectations in "Wagging My Tail in the Mud"?
2. In Lieh Tzu's tale "The Missing Axe," what causes a man to change his views of his neighbor's son?
3. In "Gold, Gold," why does the thief attempt a robbery in broad daylight?
4. In "The Lost Horse," is the frontiersman's broken hip good luck or a disaster? Why?

Interpreting Meanings

1. What does "Wagging My Tail in the Mud" reveal about Chuang Tzu's character? How does the tale reflect Taoist beliefs concerning oneness with nature and the need to be true to oneself?
2. What does Lui An's tale "The Lost Horse" teach about how people tend to interpret the events of their lives?
3. Many **anecdotes** can be reduced to a simple observation about human nature. Sum up the points of "Gold, Gold" and "The Missing Axe," each in a single sentence. In what way are the points of these two anecdotes similar?
4. What is Chuang Tzu's purpose in comparing himself to a tortoise in "Wagging My Tail in the Mud"? In imagining himself a butterfly in "The Butterfly"?

Applying Meanings

Of the five anecdotes told here, choose one or two that seem to mirror most closely your own observations about human nature. What human strengths or weaknesses do these anecdotes praise or criticize?

Critical Writing Response

Comparing Views. Some of the anecdotes you have just read might express attitudes toward life that you find surprising, baffling, or in conflict with your own views and beliefs. Choose one anecdote that expresses a view quite different from your own. Then write two or three well-developed paragraphs explaining the difference between the way you would be likely to approach a particular situation and the way the philosopher to whom the anecdote is attributed would approach it. What are the advantages of your attitude? What truth and value do you find in the view expressed in the anecdote?

Speaking and Listening

Telling an Anecdote. Everyone has a story to tell—something humorous, strange, frightening, important, or silly that has happened to them. Think of an anecdote from your own life that you would be willing to share with the rest of the class. It could be a story about something funny that you did when you were younger, an adventure you had one summer vacation, or an embarrassing incident at a family get-together. Be sure that your anecdote makes a point, even if it is a general point such as "Truth is stranger than fiction." Present your anecdote to the class orally. End your anecdote with a maxim that tells what point the anecdote is making.

Ssu-ma Ch'ien
c. 145–90 B.C.

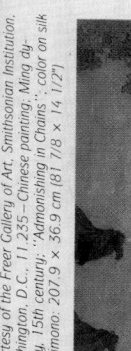

CH'EN YUAN ADMONISHING LIU TSUNG, Ming dynasty, artist unknown.

S su-ma Ch'ien (sə mä chen) was the greatest of China's "Grand Historians." The son of the court historian to the Han (hän) dynasty, he succeeded his father in that important position. Ssu-ma Ch'ien then dedicated himself to completing the first history of China, a project his father had begun. This sweeping historical record would cover the whole world known to him—that is, the Han empire and the surrounding areas of East and Central Asia. It would extend from the dawn of Chinese history to the dramatic events of his own day: the founding of the first central university, the expansion of the empire into Central Asia, and the creation of overland trade routes, like the great Silk Road, that for the first time joined China with the European world.

But a personal tragedy interrupted Ssu-ma Ch'ien's work on this monumental project. He incurred the wrath of the reigning ruler, Emperor Wu, by defending a disgraced general accused of treason. As a result, Ssu-ma Ch'ien was imprisoned and condemned to the cruel punishment of castration for his crime.

According to Chinese custom, a gentleman sentenced to such a humiliating punishment was expected to commit suicide and die unscarred. However, Ssu-ma Ch'ien, by submitting to the mutilation, chose a life of bitterness and shame instead. As he explained years later in a letter to a friend, "If I concealed my feelings and clung to life, . . . it was because I could not bear to leave unfinished my deeply cherished project, because I rejected the idea of dying without leaving to posterity my literary work. . . . When it finally becomes known in the world, I shall have paid the debt of my shame; nor will I regret a thousand deaths."

After eighteen years of work, Ssu-ma Ch'ien fulfilled his dream. He completed the *Records of the Historian* a few years before he died at the age of fifty-five. In this historic chronicle, Ch'ien covers almost three thousand years of Chinese history in more than half a million written characters painstakingly etched onto bamboo tablets. Considered a masterpiece of historical writing, the *Records* established a structure for all the dynastic histories of China to come.

MORE ABOUT THE AUTHOR

Ssu-ma Ch'ien organized the 130 chapters of the *Records* into five major sections: annals of the imperial rulers, hereditary houses of the feudal lords, chronological tables, treatises on various topics, and biographies. It is the last and longest part, the biographies, that has ensured Ssu-ma Ch'ien's lasting fame as a writer. In these chapters, he translates history into the stories of individual lives. Through his stories of memorable men and women, the Grand Historian gives the vast sweep of Chinese history a human face.

ABOUT THE TRANSLATOR

Burton Watson, who has lived in Japan since 1973, was introduced to Asian culture at the end of World War II in Yokohama while a sailor in the United States Navy. Watson, a former professor at Columbia University and Kyoto University, is now recognized as one of the world's leading translators of Chinese and Japanese literature.

HUMANITIES CONNECTION

Liu Tsung was a nomadic leader who ruled part of northern China from 310 to 318, during a period when various nomadic and settled groups fought for power, producing a chaotic succession of rulers. Liu captured and destroyed the Chinese capital of Loyang but soon lost power, lacking the charisma to keep followers. ■

OBJECTIVES

1. *To recognize the characteristics of historical biography as found in "Nieh Cheng"*
2. *To determine the tone of "Nieh Cheng" and analyze how it is achieved*
3. *To enact a courtroom trial of the subject of the biography*

THEMES IN WORLD LITERATURE

The Power and Pain of Love
From the *Epic of Gilgamesh*, pp. 136–152
A Doll's House, pp. 1069–1126

Triumph and Defeat
From the *Ramayana*, pp. 484–494
From *Don Quixote*, pp. 821–837 ∎

VOCABULARY IN CONTEXT

The words listed below will appear in the side margin at the point of instruction:

1. retaliation
2. valor
3. etiquette
4. apprehension
5. profound

PREREADING FOCUS

Background: Ssu-ma Ch'ien's earlier circumstances fostered his role as China's premier historian. As a young man he had traveled extensively, visiting China's intellectual centers and exploring places of historic significance. As a part of Emperor Wu's court, Ssu-ma Ch'ien had witnessed history in the making. As Duke Grand Astrologer, the designated observer of the heavens and the calendar, he had had access to the imperial library, where all historical archives were kept. While the *Records of the Historian* is largely a compilation of documents that Ssu-ma Ch'ien copied, the biographies are his original work. Pan Ku, Ssu-ma Ch'ien's critic and biographer, wrote, "His [Ssu-ma Ch'ien's] writing is direct and his facts sound. He does not falsify what is beautiful, nor does he conceal what is evil. Therefore his may be termed a 'true record.'"

Writer's Response: Students can exchange their verbal portraits with partners and draw the assassin the other has described.

Literary Focus: Ssu-ma Ch'ien has been criticized for allowing his tone to betray his biases. In "Nieh Cheng," for example, along with the vivid details and lively dialogue, which breathe life into the ancient story, is the editorial slant of a writer who sympathizes with the plight of his subject.

Reader's Guide

NIEH CHENG
from Records of the Historian

Background

The story of Nieh Cheng (nye jung) is taken from a section of Ssu-ma Ch'ien's biographies devoted to "assassin-retainers," wandering avengers of injustice who were an ancient tradition in China. Although the assassins' vengeful acts were strictly illegal, they were, paradoxically, also considered honorable, especially if they were undertaken on behalf of women and children who had been victims of wrongdoing. According to the Confucian code of conduct, revenge against wrongdoings was a duty, and, like many Chinese customs of the time, this duty far outweighed the rules of law.

In choosing to immortalize such subjects as assassin-retainers, Ssu-ma Ch'ien is recognizing the value of human beings who hold a low station in life. The assassins he wrote about are worthy men, he explains, even though "some succeeded in carrying out their duty and some did not. But it is perfectly clear that they had all determined upon the deed. They were not false to their intentions. Is it not right, then, that their names should be handed down to later ages?" Given this outlook, it is not surprising that many of Ssu-ma Ch'ien's biographies memorialize individuals whose defiant spirits struggled against hopeless odds to uphold a personal ideal or principle, as Ssu-ma Ch'ien himself did.

Writer's Response

What do you predict a hired assassin will be like? Think of images you know from movies and TV. Then write a brief description to convey your impressions of a paid assassin.

Literary Focus

Tone is the attitude a writer takes toward the reader, a subject, or a character. Like a speaker's tone of voice, a writer's tone may be described as lighthearted, melancholy, serious, ironic, or as reflecting any number of other emotions. Tone is conveyed through the writer's choice of words and details. The tone of the historian Ssu-ma Ch'ien's writings reveals his views of the people whose lives he recorded.

NIEH CHENG
from Records of the Historian
Ssu-ma Ch'ien
translated by
BURTON WATSON

As you read this biography, ask yourself why Nieh Cheng chose to act as he did. Do you agree with the choices he made? Could he have avoided his fate?

Chinese sword. *The introduction of the iron sword into China enabled the Ch'in dynasty to unify the numerous, smaller Chinese states in 221 B.C.*

Scala/Art Resource

Nieh Cheng

Some forty years later there was the affair of Nieh Cheng in Chih.[1] Nieh Cheng was from the village of Deep Well in Chih. He killed a man and, in order to escape retaliation, went with his mother and elder sister to the state of Ch'i,[2] where he made a living as a butcher. Some time later Yen Chung-tzu of P'u-yang,[3] an official in the service of Marquis Ai of Han, had a falling-out with Han Hsia-lei,[4] the prime minister of Han. Fearful that he might be put to death, Yen Chung-tzu fled from the state and traveled about to other states searching for someone who would be willing to get back at Hsia-lei for him.

When he arrived in Ch'i, someone told him that Nieh Cheng was a man of valor and daring who, fleeing from his enemies, was hiding out among the butchers. Yen Chung-tzu went to his door and requested an interview, but was several times turned away. He then prepared a gift of wine which he asked to be allowed to offer in the presence of Nieh Cheng's mother. When the drinking was well underway, Yen Chung-tzu brought forth a hundred taels[5] of yellow gold which he laid before Nieh Cheng's mother with wishes for a long life. Nieh Cheng was astounded at such generosity and firmly re-

1. **Nieh Cheng** (nye jung) **in Chih** (jər)
2. **Ch'i** (chē)
3. **Yen Chung-tzu** (yen joong dzə) **of P'u-yang** (pōō yang)
4. **Han Hsia-lei** (hän shä lā)
5. **tael** (tāl): a monetary unit roughly equivalent to 1 1/3 ounces of silver.

TEACHER'S RESOURCES

- Review and Response Worksheet
- Selection Test
- Vocabulary Activity Worksheet
- Vocabulary Test

retaliation (ri·tal′ē·ā′shən): an injury or evil done to get even
valor (val′ər): bravery

HUMANITIES CONNECTION

What materials did iron supersede? (bronze, stone, wood) *How might this new technology have affected the arts?* (Accept reasonable responses: Depending on the region, it might or might not have replaced other materials in architecture and sculpture.) ■

1 LITERARY ELEMENT

Tone: How would you describe the author's attitude toward Nieh Cheng in paragraph 2—neutral or biased? Explain. (Possible response: Neutral. Ssu-ma Ch'ien reports that someone regards Nieh Cheng as a man of valor, which is not necessarily his own view.)

fused the gift. When Yen Chung-tzu just as firmly pressed it on him, Nieh Cheng repeated his refusal, saying, "I am fortunate enough to have my old mother with me. Though our family is poor and I am living in a strange land and earning my way as a dog butcher,[6] I am still able, come morning and evening, to find some sweet or tasty morsel with which to nourish her. She has everything she needs for her care and comfort—I could not be so bold as to accept your gift."

Yen Chung-tzu asked the others present all to withdraw and spoke to Nieh Cheng in private. "I have an enemy," he said, "and I have already traveled about to a great many states. When I reached Ch'i, however, I was privileged to learn that you, sir, are a man of extremely high principles. Therefore I have presented these hundred taels of gold, hoping that you may use them to purchase some trifling gift of food for your honored parent and that I may have the pleasure of your friendship. How would I dare hope for anything more?"

Nieh Cheng replied, "I have been content to humble my will and shame my body, living as a butcher here by the marketplace and well, only because I am fortunate enough to have my old mother to take care of. While she lives, I dare not promise my services to any man!"

Yen Chung-tzu continued every effort to persuade him, but to the end Nieh Cheng was unwilling to accept the gift. Yen Chung-tzu nevertheless did all that etiquette demands of a proper guest before taking his leave.

Some time later Nieh Cheng's mother died

and, when she had been buried and the mourning period was over, Nieh Cheng said to himself, "Ah! I am a man of the marketplace and well, swinging a knife and working as a butcher, while Yen Chung-tzu is chief minister to one of the feudal lords. And yet he did not consider it too far to come a thousand miles, driving far out of his way just to make friends with me. I treated him very shabbily indeed! I have accomplished no great deeds for which I might be praised, yet Yen Chung-tzu presented a hundred taels of gold to my mother with wishes for her continued good health. Though I did not accept it, it is clear that he did so simply because he has a profound appreciation of my worth. Now a worthy gentleman, burning with anger and indignation, has offered friendship and trust to a poor and insignificant man. Can I bear to remain silent and let it end there? Earlier, when he made his request of me, I refused only because my mother was still alive. Now that her years have come to a close, I shall offer my services to one who truly understands me!"

Thereupon he journeyed west to P'u-yang in Wey[7] and went to see Yen Chung-tzu. "The reason I would not agree earlier," he said, "was simply that my mother was still alive. Now, unfortunately, the years Heaven gave her have come to a close. Who is this enemy that you wish to take revenge on? I request permission to undertake the task!"

Yen Chung-tzu then related to him the whole story. "My enemy is Han Hsia-lei, the prime minister of Han. He is also the younger uncle of the ruler of Han. His clan is numerous and powerful and there are many armed guards stationed wherever he happens to be.

---

6. **dog butcher:** Dog meat was considered acceptable to eat in China during this time.

7. **Wey** (wā)

Courtesy of the Freer Gallery of Art, Smithsonian Institution, Washington, D.C., 57.14 –
Chinese painting; Yuan dynasty; by Ch'ien Hsuan; "Yang Kuei-fei Mounting a Horse"; ink
and color on paper: 29.5 × 117.0 cm. (11 1/2 × 46 1/8")

YANG KUEI-FEI MOUNTING A HORSE (detail), CH'IEN HSUAN. *In Chinese
painting, the line is the basic element of the painting, in contrast to
light and shadow, which serve as the foundations for much of
Western art.*

I had hoped to send someone to stab him
to death, but so far no one has been able to
accomplish it. Now if you are so kind as not
to reject my plea for help, I hope you will
allow me to give you additional carriages and
men to assist you in the job."

But Nieh Cheng said, "Han and Wey are
near neighbors. Now if one is going to murder the prime minister of another state, and
the prime minister also happens to be a close
relative of the ruler, then the circumstances
make it unwise to send a large party of men.
If you try to use a lot of men, then there are
bound to be differences of opinion on how
best to proceed; if there are differences of
opinion, then word of the undertaking will
leak out; and if word leaks out, then the
whole state of Han will be up in arms against
you! What could be more dangerous?"

Nieh Cheng therefore declined to accept
any carriages or attendants, but instead took
leave and set off alone, disguising his sword
as a walking stick, until he reached Han.
When he arrived, the Han prime minister
Hsia-lei happened to be seated in his office,
guarded and attended by a large body of men
bearing lances and other weapons. Nieh
Cheng walked straight in, ascended the
steps, and stabbed Hsia-lei to death. Those
about the prime minister were thrown into
great confusion, and Nieh Cheng, shouting
loudly, attacked and killed thirty or forty of
them. Then he flayed the skin of his face,
gouged out his eyes, and, butchering himself
as he had once done animals, spilled out his
bowels and in this way died.

The ruler of Han had his corpse taken and
exposed in the marketplace, offering to re-

1. Did Ssu-ma Ch'ien view the assassins he wrote about as national heroes, worthy men of principle, or examples of corruption? (worthy men of principle)

2. What prompts Nieh Cheng to escape with his mother and sister to a small, distant village? (He killed a man.)

3. Why does Nieh Cheng refuse to serve Yen Chung-tzu when he is offered gold? (He wants to care for his mother.)

4. Does Nieh Cheng mutilate his own face to punish himself, blot out his identity, or grieve for his mother's death? (blot out his identity)

5. Why does Nieh Cheng's sister Jung come to identify his body in spite of threat of execution? (so that his name will not be lost forever)

RETEACHING

Have students role-play "live, on-site" TV news reports. One "broadcast" can cover the assassination of Han Hsia-lei and Nieh Cheng's suicide; another can cover Jung's death in the marketplace. Students who play reporters can interview several witnesses—as well as people who know the family—to get reactions, opinions, and details. Encourage participants to stay within the spirit and actual details of the story.

---

apprehension (ap′rē·hen′shən): dread

profound (prō·found′): deeply felt

7 GUIDED READING

Sequencing: What time words begin these paragraphs? (*meanwhile, then*) Why are words related to the chronology or sequence particularly important in a biography? (Possible response: As a historical record, a biography should present events accurately.)

8 ANALYZING

What moral conflict does Jung's bold response to her brother's death reveal? (submission to the rule of law versus loyalty to personal ideals, or duty) What moral lesson does Ssu-ma Ch'ien draw in this story? (Possible response: There can be honor in defying law to uphold personal ideals.)

9 LITERARY ELEMENT

Tone: How does the tone in the last paragraph vary, if at all, from elsewhere in the biography? (Possible response: It's overt. Here, Ssu-ma Ch'ien makes a personal observation about Nieh Cheng's decisions rather than reporting someone else's view.)

ward anyone who could identify him, but no one knew who he was. The ruler then hung up the reward, promising to give a thousand pieces of gold to anyone who could say who it was that had killed Prime Minister Hsia-lei. A long time passed but no one came forward with the answer.

Meanwhile Nieh Cheng's elder sister Jung[8] heard that someone had stabbed and killed the prime minister of Han, but that the blame could not be fixed since no one knew the culprit's name. His corpse had been exposed in the marketplace with a reward of a thousand pieces of gold hanging above it, she was told. Filled with apprehension, she said, "Could it be my younger brother? Ah— Yen Chung-tzu certainly knew what he was capable of!"

Then she set off at once and went to the marketplace of Han, where she found that the dead man was indeed Nieh Cheng. Throwing herself down beside the corpse, she wept in profound sorrow, crying, "This man is called Nieh Cheng from the village of Deep Well in Chih!"

The people passing back and forth through the market all said to her, "This man has committed an act of violence and treachery against the prime minister of our state and our king has posted a reward of a thousand gold pieces for anyone who can discover his name—have you not heard? How dare you come here and admit that you were acquainted with him?"

Jung replied, "Yes, I have heard. But Cheng was willing to accept shame and disgrace, throwing away his future and making a living in the marketplace, because our mother was still in good health and I was not yet married. After our mother had ended her years and departed from the world, and I had found a husband, then Yen Chung-tzu, recognizing my brother's worth, lifted him up from hardship and disgrace and became his friend, treating him with kindness and generosity. So there was nothing he could do. A gentleman will always be willing to die for someone who recognizes his true worth. And now, because I am still alive, he has inflicted this terrible mutilation upon himself so as to wipe out all trace of his identity. But how could I, out of fear that I might be put to death, allow so worthy a brother's name to be lost forever?"

Having astounded the people of the marketplace with these words, she cried three times in a loud voice to Heaven and then died of grief and anguish by the dead man's side. When the inhabitants of Chin, Ch'u, Ch'i, and Wey heard of this, they all said, "Cheng was not the only able one—his sister too proved herself a woman of valor!"

If Cheng had in fact known that his sister would be unwilling to stand by in silence but, heedless of the threat of execution and public exposure, would make her way a thousand miles over the steep passes, determined to spread his fame abroad, so that sister and brother would both end as criminals in the marketplace of Han, then he would surely never have agreed to undertake such a mission for Yen Chung-tzu. And as for Yen Chung-tzu, it can certainly be said that he knew how to recognize a man's ability and win others to his service.

---

8. **Jung** (roong)

1. Writing a Libretto. Students interested in music and theater can convert dramatic scenes from "Nieh Cheng" into text for arias, modeled on the style of Italian opera. Setting the words to music is an option music buffs might explore. Puccini's *Turandot*, a tragedy set in ancient China, may provide inspiration for students' dramatization.

2. Comparing Biographies. Students can write an essay comparing and contrasting this biography by Nieh Cheng with that of one or more Americans who exemplified such values as courage, sacrifice, and achievement. Possible subjects may be folk heroes and legendary figures such as Paul Revere, Davy Crockett, Frederick Douglass, and John Brown.

CLOSURE

Draw a continuum on the board. At one end, write *noble*; at the other end write *foolish*. Then ask students to trace the decisions Nieh Cheng made that led to his fate. Discuss as a class where each decision should go on the continuum. When the continuum is completed, ask, "Do you think Nieh Cheng was mostly a hero or a fool? Why?" ▪

First Thoughts

How did you feel about what Nieh Cheng did? How did you feel about what his sister did? In your opinion, were their actions moral?

Identifying Facts

1. Why is Yen Chung-tzu searching for an assassin?
2. Why does Nieh Cheng refuse Yen Chung-tzu's request at first? Why does he later have a change of heart?
3. After he assassinates the prime minister, why does Nieh Cheng mutilate and kill himself?
4. Why do the people finally declare Cheng's sister to be "a woman of valor"?

Interpreting Meanings

1. In this biography of Nieh Cheng, what seems to be the author's attitude toward his subject? For example, is the author's **tone** admiring, scornful, pitying, disinterested, respectful, or severe? Give examples from the text to support your view.
2. Was Yen Chung-tzu's cause necessarily a noble one? How do you account for Nieh Cheng's decision to lay down his life for a man he hardly knew?

3. **Irony** refers to a contrast between what is expected and what actually happens. Think about Cheng's reasons for killing himself as he did. In what way is his sister's behavior ironic?

Applying Meanings

Would you do anything for someone who alone seemed to recognize your inner worth? Why or why not?

Speaking and Listening

Enacting a Courtroom Trial. Imagine that Nieh Cheng has not committed suicide but has decided to stand trial instead. As directed by your teacher, stage Nieh Cheng's courtroom trial using the ancient details of his story but trying him according to twentieth-century American views of justice. Choose members of the class to be the judge, jury, defendant (Cheng), defense attorney, prosecuting attorney, and witnesses for both sides. Include Cheng's sister Jung, imagining that she, too, is alive. Have a student record the proceedings on videotape, if possible, or make a sound recording of the trial. Play back the proceedings later and critique your performances.

ANSWERS

First Thoughts
Answers will vary.

Identifying Facts
1. Yen Chung-tzu fears Han Hsia-lei will have him put to death if he doesn't have him killed first.
2. Nieh Cheng wants only to care for his mother. After she dies, he decides to serve Yen Chung-tzu, who he feels recognizes his true worth.
3. Nieh Cheng wants to destroy his identity so as not to endanger or shame his sister.
4. She proves herself to be as brave and honorable as her brother.

Interpreting Meanings
1. Possible response: Ssu-ma Ch'ien does not praise or condemn Nieh Cheng's actions, but he shows respect and sympathy for him. Cheng is portrayed as a person of solid virtues—loyal to his family and responsible for his actions. Ssu-ma Ch'ien's tone is respectful, admiring, and approving.
2. Accept all reasonable responses that students can support.
3. Nieh Cheng killed himself to protect his sister, but she came forward to memorialize his name.

Applying Meanings
Answers will vary.

Speaking and Listening
Enacting a Courtroom Trial.
All participants in the trial should adhere to the actual details of the biography. ▪

OBJECTIVES

1. **To gain an understanding of Japanese literature and of the historical and cultural influences on its development**
2. **To interpret examples of Japanese poetry, prose, and drama**
3. **To respond to Japanese literature both orally and in writing, and to apply an understanding of its elements in creative writing projects**

TEACHER'S RESOURCES: 6
☑ Unit Introduction Test

1 RESPONDING TO THE QUOTATION

Beginning in the seventh century, Japanese rulers sent promising young people to study in China—at that time the richest, most technologically advanced country in the world. The knowledge of writing, art, science, philosophy, law, and architecture that these scholars took back to Japan greatly influenced its early development.

❓ *Why might Donald Keene refer to Chinese writing as "wholly unsuitable"?* (Chinese characters cannot convey the verb endings that indicate tense and level of respect in Japanese.)

■ HUMANITIES CONNECTION ■

As part of the blending of Shintoism and Buddhism in Japan, the major Shinto gods, such as the god of war, were considered special Japanese manifestations of the highest Buddhist deities. During the eighth and ninth centuries, sculptors and priests devoted themselves to carving deities in wood, using deep, bold lines. The gracefully curved, loose-hanging garments characterized much of the wood sculpture of this period.

❓ *Why do you think the sculptors used wood rather than other materials?* (Possible response: It was readily available and easy to carve.) ■

THE LITERATURE OF JAPAN

1 ❝ It was in fact the widespread adoption of Chinese culture, including the wholly unsuitable Chinese method of writing, which was to determine the course of Japanese literature over the centuries. ❞

—*Donald Keene*

Hachiman, the Shinto god of war, in the guise of a Buddhist monk. Late Heian period, ninth century A.D. *When Buddhism was introduced into Japan, Shintoism was temporarily pushed into the background. However, the two religions eventually became intermingled.*

Although early Japan borrowed much from Chinese culture, including the Chinese system of writing, Japanese culture evolved its own character and style over time. The distinctiveness of Japanese culture grew out of the unique social arrangements and world view developed by a people who, living on a starkly beautiful chain of mountainous islands, were largely isolated from their neighbors.

Although many of the selections in this unit were written centuries ago, the literature of Japan may seem remarkably fresh to your students. Whether a haiku poet evokes the beauty of a pear tree in the moonlight, or a sophisticated lady-in-waiting in the tenth century imperial court pokes fun at a clumsy courtier, a great deal of Japanese literature speaks with simplicity and eloquence.

The unit opens with two classical forms of poetry—the tanka and haiku. For its literary foundation, the English-speaking world looks to the themes and conflicts dramatized by Shakespeare or developed by nineteenth-century novelists. In Japan, however, it is the classical poetry—brief, lyrical, and personal—that has inspired most forms of literary expression over the centuries.

As students read and discuss the poetry selections, help them to see that the brevity of the poems creates a paradoxical quality of timelessness and immediacy. Japanese poetic forms are simply too short to permit abstractions or reflections. Every word must count toward communicating a single moment of insight. Without elaborate descriptions or figures of speech, classical Japanese poets created images so concentrated and complete in themselves that readers could grasp a timeless truth in very few words.

Early Japan

Japan's early political structure was based on clan, or family, divisions. Each clan developed a well-defined hierarchy of classes, with aristocrats, warriors, and priests at the top and peasants and workers at the bottom. Without any central authority, the clans constantly fought one another. Finally, in the fourth century A.D., one family group, the **Yamato**, grew powerful enough to subdue the others.

The Yamato admired Chinese culture, political organization, and philosophy and took steps to introduce these Chinese forms to Japan. The Yamato prince **Shotoku** (shô·tô·kōo) actually imposed the Chinese imperial system on Japan, creating an emperor, an imperial bureaucracy, and a grand capital city. In Japan, however, the emperor for the most part remained a figurehead.

The Feudal Era: Warlords and Samurai

In the eighth century A.D. ambitious aristocrats began to assemble huge private estates in the countryside, beyond the reach of the imperial authority. These local landowning lords surrounded themselves with professional warriors, called **samurai** (sam'ə·rī'). The samurai lived by a very strict code of behavior, somewhat like the chivalric code of the knights of medieval Europe but based more on absolute loyalty to one's overlord and on concepts of personal honor than on religious ideals.

> The Yamato clan in the fourth century A.D. introduced Chinese culture, political structures, and ideas into Japanese society.

In the latter part of the twelfth century, a strongman named Yoritomo seized effective control of the empire and had himself declared **shogun**, or "general." Over the next five centuries, a series of shoguns ruled Japan, but none could ever completely control the feuding warlords, who kept the country in a state of constant warfare.

The Granger Collection, New York

Samurai suit of armor, c. 1515.

2 CULTURAL BACKGROUND

Samurai: Although the samurai were ruthless warriors, they respected the social and aesthetic traditions of the emperor's court. They were expected to appreciate and compose poetry and to enjoy theater. As an elite social class, the samurai demanded works of art to represent their culture and honor their success. Therefore, in spite of a state of almost constant warfare during most of the fourteenth through the seventeenth centuries, the arts flourished.

HUMANITIES CONNECTION

During the fourteenth and fifteenth centuries, as feudalism strengthened its hold on Japan, armorers rose in importance and vied to produce work unsurpassed in practical usefulness and artistic beauty. The construction of Japanese armor—tiny scales of iron laced in rows with silk cords—produced a far lighter and more flexible protection than that worn by European knights. The silk and leather cords and gold and silver plating and inlaying in Japanese armor often resulted in artistically brilliant creations.

? *Why might beauty in armor be important?* (Possible response: Beautiful armor conferred status and prestige on a samurai warlord.) ∎

The *Pillow Book* also has a timeless quality. Sei Shōnagon's remarks about human nature seem as contemporary as those of any modern writer. Cultural historians continue to study *The Pillow Book* for clues about social life at the ancient Heian court, but Shōnagon's witty observations of the embarrassments, annoyances, and pleasures of everyday life can hold the interest of the most casual reader.

The figures in Japanese history most familiar to students may be the shoguns and samurai of the feudal era. As far as Japanese literature is concerned, many students may be familiar with haiku poetry. You might point out that the samurai code of behavior and the aesthetic principles underlying haiku were both influenced by Zen Buddhism. Zen, as discussed in the text, demanded a mental discipline and an austerity that appealed to the samurai.

Other qualities associated with Zen—such as harmony with nature, simplicity, asymmetry, and emptiness—had a tremendous influence on the painting, architecture, poetry, music, and drama of Japan. Another Zen characteristic, an appreciation for the suggested rather than the directly stated, is evident in the Zen parables, in haiku, and in Noh drama, which often depends on moments of silence to communicate meaning.

HUMANITIES CONNECTION

During the Tokugawa shogunate, woodblock prints became enormously popular. Merchants and artisans enjoyed decorating their homes with art that reflected the lives they led. Once scorned by the Japanese upper classes, woodblock prints of the Tokugawa era are now considered among the world's great artistic achievements.

? *Why might Suzuki's work remind viewers of the lyrical quality of a Japanese poem?* (Possible response: because of its grace, beauty, and emotion) ■

3 HISTORICAL BACKGROUND

Opening to the West: Because of its isolation, Japan never placed much importance on its military strength. The arrival of Commodore Perry's huge steamships—the first signs of modern military power the Japanese had ever seen—deeply shocked the Japanese. Japan's subsequent desire to modernize, therefore, was based not on admiration of Western civilization, but on the fear that Japan would not survive the imperial appetites of the West.

The Granger Collection, New York

YOUNG WOMAN ATTENDED BY A MAID,
SUZUKI HARUNOBU, C. 1766.
Woodblock print.

The Downfall of Feudalism

Finally, in the late 1500s, a powerful shogun crushed the warring feudal lords and the **Tokugawa shogunate**, or shogun-ruled regime, controlled all of Japan from a new capital at Edo, later called Tokyo. At about this time, the Western world was seeking contact with Japan. These contacts alarmed the shogunate, which feared revolt at home or invasion from abroad. By 1630, Japan was a closed society: all foreigners were expelled, Japanese Christians were persecuted, and foreign travel was forbidden under penalty of death.

Opening to the West

This government-imposed isolation continued for two centuries. Then, in 1853, Commodore Matthew Perry of the United States Navy steamed into Tokyo Bay with demands that Japan open its doors to the West. Treaties were negotiated and Japan began to trade with the Western powers. As feared, outside influences did cause changes in Japan. The shogunate was ended in 1868, and Japan, under a new and more powerful emperor, rapidly acquired the latest technological knowledge, introduced universal education, and created an impressive industrial economy.

3

Shintoism and Buddhism

Shintoism, the ancient religion of Japan, reveres indwelling divine spirits called *kami*, found in natural places and objects. Later, divinity was ascribed to revered ancestors and

> The native Japanese Shinto religion, which regarded both nature and dead ancestors as divine, easily accommodated the arrival of new religions such as Buddhism.

finally to the emperor himself. The native Shinto tradition easily accommodated the various strains of Buddhism that

MAKING CONNECTIONS

Japan's history is marked by long periods of isolation from the rest of Asia and from Europe. This isolation gave Japan the chance to transform the cultural elements it borrowed from other countries into a highly distinctive culture of its own. When Japan opened its doors in the mid-1800s, Europeans and Americans were struck by the sophistication, subtlety, and beauty of an advanced country that had developed along lines so different from their own.

Japanese prints and paintings had a strong influence on modern European art. The woodblock prints of landscapes and society people (so common in Japan they were sometimes used as wrapping paper) were eagerly collected by Europeans. The influence of these Japanese prints can be seen in the Impressionist and Post-impressionist paintings of Manet, Monet, Degas, and Van Gogh, as well as in the work of the American artist James MacNeil

Whistler.

The simplicity of Japanese art and design had a strong influence on Western architecture as well. Architects in the United States in the early twentieth century turned away from the elaborate Victorian styles of the previous century to design simpler buildings with uncluttered interiors.

Japanese literature has influenced English and American writers of the twentieth

Statue of Japan's first Shogun, Minamoto Yorimoto, thirteenth century.

Tokyo National Museum, Kodansha International

had been adopted by the Japanese from the Chinese and the Koreans, beginning in the fifth and sixth centuries A.D.

Although Buddhism originated in India, it was elaborated by many Chinese monks and scholars and developed into a series of schools or sects quite distinct from its Indian counterparts. Although all schools of Buddhism sought the attainment of spiritual freedom and inner tranquility, the various sects stressed different paths to this goal. **Zen Buddhism**, for example, emphasized the importance of meditation, concentration, and self-discipline as the way to enlightenment.

Japanese Literature: Pride in Poetry

Although originally inspired by Chinese models and preceded by a long oral tradition, Japanese written literature came into its own after the fifth century A.D., when the Japanese adapted the Chinese system of writing to the needs of their own language.

> **❝** Japanese poetry has as its subject the human heart. It may seem to be of no practical use and just as well left uncomposed, but when one knows poetry well, one understands also without explanation the reasons governing order and disorder in the world. **❞**
> —*Kamo Mabuchi (1697–1769)*

4

4 RESPONDING TO THE QUOTATION

Modern readers do not usually associate poetry with practicality, but in many cultures poetry traditionally served practical purposes. Greeks and Romans wrote treatises in verse about farming, astronomy, and philosophy. Many early Japanese poets accepted the traditional Chinese view that poetry was useful in promoting good government.

❓ *What is the primary purpose of poetry today?* (Possible response: primarily to give pleasure, both emotional and intellectual)

5 CULTURAL BACKGROUND

System of Writing: In Chinese writing, each character has a meaning of its own. When the Japanese began to employ Chinese characters, they used them to represent specific sounds without regard to their meaning. Eventually, Japan developed a writing system that includes two phonetic Japanese scripts and about two thousand Chinese characters. As a result Japanese is considered the most complex written language in the world today.

century. For example, many Western poets and playwrights, including William Butler Yeats, George Bernard Shaw, Ezra Pound, Jean Genêt, and Bertold Brecht, showed a deep interest in Noh drama.

Through Zen Buddhism, Japan's influence on the world has extended far beyond its impact on artistic and literary styles. The teachings of Zen have given a new approach to many twentieth-century philosophers, psychologists, and theologi-ans. Various forms of meditation popular in the West have their roots in Zen, although release from tension rather than spiritual enlightenment is sometimes the primary goal of Western practitioners. Judo, a popular sport in Europe and the United States as well as in Japan, requires a mental discipline and a reliance on the "wisdom of the body" that reflect Zen attitudes.

Now, Japan's economic strength as well as its traditional culture is making its mark on the world. Japan's ability, since 1945, to achieve tremendous influence and strength without resorting to military power might serve as an inspiration to countries looking for ways to prosper in peace.

HUMANITIES CONNECTION

Kitagawa Utamaro, a wood-block artist of the late 1700s, is best known for his sensuous portrayal of women. In his later work, he departed from the tradition of depicting idealized women, portraying instead a wide range of women with different temperaments and from various walks of life, sometimes revealing the subject's emotions or state of mind.

6 RESPONDING TO THE QUOTATION

Although some have departed from the classical forms, modern Japanese poets are expected to be familiar with the conventions of classical poetry.

❓ *How might reading the works of the masters teach the art of writing?* (Possible response: The masters' works are models of style and form.)

6

❝There are no teachers of Japanese poetry. But they who take the old poems as their teachers, steep their minds in the old style, and learn their words from the masters of former time—who of them will fail to write poetry?❞

—*Fujiwara no Teika (1162–1241)*

M. Howell/SuperStock, Inc.

PORTRAIT OF A WOMAN, KITAGAWA UTAMARO, late eighteenth century. *Kitagawa's rich and sensuous composition influenced European artists such as Toulouse-Lautrec.*

As in China, composing poetry has always been a highly respected activity in Japan. From the beginnings of imperial government to the present day, poetry writing has been encouraged by official competition and rewarded by publication in collections, or anthologies. Beginning with the five-line **tanka** form in the eighth century A.D., Japanese poetry has been known for its brief lyrical bursts of feeling and the

READING CHECK

1. What country greatly influenced the early development of Japan? (China)
2. Who ruled Japan during the feudal era? (military rulers, or shoguns)
3. During what time period was Japan closed to foreigners? (1630–1853)
4. What is the native religion of Japan? (Shintoism)
5. How have poets been treated in Japan? (with respect)

FOR FURTHER STUDY

Nonfiction

Seventy-seven Keys to the Civilization of Japan includes essays on Japanese culture, religion, and history. Donald Keene's *The Pleasures of Japanese Literature* is a brief introduction to Japanese aesthetic traditions and literature. *The Way of Zen*, by Alan Watts, is a good introduction for the Westerner.

Fiction

Some Prefer Nettles, by Junichirō Tanizaki, is a novel dealing with the conflict between East and West. Other well-known Japanese novelists include Yukio Mishima and Kōbō Abe.

Film

Japanese films of interest include *Ran*, *Rashōmon*, *The Seven Samurai*, *MacArthur's Children*, and *The Makioka Sisters*. ■

extreme compression of its verse. The culmination of the Japanese poets' tendency to compress meaning into a few

---

Early Japanese literature was influenced by Chinese models, but after the fifth century A.D., literature in Japan developed its own distinctive style.

---

words came in the seventeenth century with the development of the **haiku** (hī'kōō) form.

Japanese Prose

The greatest flowering of classical Japanese prose occurred during the **Heian** (hā'än) **period** (A.D. 794–1185), when a leisurely life at court made it possible for well-educated women to chronicle the hothouse atmosphere in which they lived. In the long and detailed *Tale of Genji*, considered by many scholars to be the world's first true novel, the aristocrat **Lady Murasaki Shikibu** traces the life of a gifted and charming prince. Her accomplishment led her to become as highly regarded in Japan as William Shakespeare (see page 839) is in English-speaking countries. Another tenth-century court lady, **Sei Shōnagon**, also immortalized the Heian age by writing witty and revealing journal entries about court life in *The Pillow Book*.

Japanese Drama

The most distinctive form of Japanese drama is called **Noh** (nō), which literally means "talent" or "skill." The purpose of Noh dramas is the invocation of a moment of wisdom or truth in the tradition of Zen Buddhism. **Kabuki** (kä·bōō'kē) is another form of Japanese drama. The Kabuki drama appeals to a more general audience than Noh drama and makes use of stock characters and stylized situations, but the acting is broadly melodramatic and the emotions portrayed are easily understood. Colorful costumes and lively music and dance also please Kabuki audiences.

Courtesy of the Freer Gallery of Art, Smithsonian Institution, Washington, D.C.

UKIYOE SCHOOL, KATSUKAWA SHUNSHO (1726–1792).

> **"** . . . Nō [Noh] does not make a frontal attack on the emotions. It creeps at the subject warily. **"**
>
> —Arthur Waley

7 HISTORICAL BACKGROUND

Heian Period: While the peasants in the rest of Japan struggled, life at the Heian court was characterized by great elegance and elaborate social conventions. The exact shade of paper on which a letter was written, for example, carried great social significance. Clothing was similarly elaborate—men wore black lacquered headgear and women as many as twelve silk robes of different colors. The literature of this period is among the most treasured in Japan.

8 CULTURAL DIVERSITY

Japanese Drama: Noh and Kabuki drama were developed for distinctly different audiences. Noh plays, filled with quotations from poetry and complicated wordplay, were written for the educated people of the shogun's court.
Can you think of two different levels of entertainment or artistic expression in your own culture? (Possible response: television soap operas and serious dramas) ■

9 RESPONDING TO THE QUOTATION

Arthur Waley was a famous translator of Chinese and Japanese literature. In this quotation, he describes a characteristic of Noh drama that distinguishes it from the more easily understood Kabuki drama. Have students describe works of literature, plays, or movies that affected them in similar ways.

1 CULTURAL DIVERSITY

Japanese Aesthetics: The uneven number of lines and syllables in the tanka illustrate the Japanese appreciation for irregularity. This differs greatly from the traditional Chinese and Western preference for symmetry. The Japanese value irregular patterns in artistic forms ranging from poetry, painting, and calligraphy to architecture, ceramics, and music.

❓ *Can you think of examples of how this Japanese appreciation for irregularity has influenced modern Western art forms?* (Possible responses: Japanese influence on modern poets such as T. S. Eliot and Ezra Pound and modern artists like Monet and Matisse)

2 LITERARY BACKGROUND

When educated poets wanted to say more than the restrictive tanka form permitted, they often wrote long poems in Chinese.

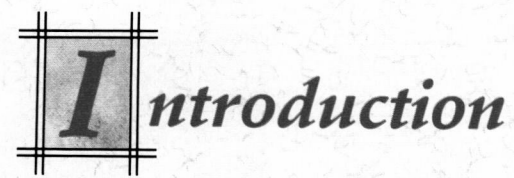

Introduction

Tanka Poetry

The **tanka** (täng'kə) may be the most beloved form of Japanese poetry. Invented more than a thousand years ago, tanka are still being composed by Japanese poets. Even today, the Emperor of Japan holds an annual tanka-writing competition to celebrate the New Year.

Tanka Form

Tanka, meaning "short songs," are brief and lyrical poems. The traditional tanka consists of exactly thirty-one syllables divided among five lines. Three of the poem's lines have seven syllables, and the other two have five syllables. Within this rigid form the

1

2

◆

tanka (täng'kə): *a traditional form of Japanese poetry consisting of thirty-one syllables divided among five lines.*

great tanka poets managed to compress an entire world of beauty and emotion. Eventually, tanka provided the inspiration for an even more condensed poetic form—the **haiku**, a three-line poem of seventeen syllables (see page 572).

Poem cards by Shinsai Ga, c. 1805. *In the Japanese tradition, poetry and illustration are often combined in cards like these.*

The Origin of Tanka

The earliest known tanka appeared in a collection of poems that was written in the eighth century A.D. Called the *Man-yōshū* (män·yō'shōō), or *Collection of Ten Thousand Leaves*, this anthology, which features a variety of poetic forms, is still widely quoted and praised.

At the time that the *Manyōshū*

appeared, Japanese poets were just beginning to break away from the powerful influence of Chinese literary tradition. In early times, Japanese was exclusively a spoken language; there was no system for writing it down. The earliest Japanese poets wrote in Chinese. Between the fifth and the eighth centuries, a system for writing Japanese was developed, adapting Chinese characters to describe Japanese sounds. These phonetic characters came to be known as *kana* (kä'nä), meaning "borrowed names."

By the time the *Manyōshū* was compiled, Japanese poets had begun to appreciate the lyrical power of their own language. Historically, the Japanese view the *Manyōshū* as the beginning of a written literature that they could call entirely their own. Many of the tanka in the Manyōshū describe nature, the impermanence of life, solitude, and love—themes that are echoed in modern tanka.

Tanka and Medieval Court Life

Tanka continued to thrive throughout the medieval period. During the Heian (hā'än) period (A.D. 794–1185), writing tanka was a common ritual of court life. A prince would dash off a tanka and send it to his loved one, who would reply with her own poem. Aristocrats amused themselves by playing a game in which one person would invent the first three lines of a tanka and another would finish it.

In 905 a second great anthology featuring tanka verse, the *Kokinshū* (kō·kēn'shoō), appeared. The poems in the *Kokinshū*, numbering more than a thousand, are subtle and sophisticated. Many rely on repetition of a sound to create an emotional effect. In a poem by Ki nō Tomonori (kē nō tō·mō·nō'rē), for example, the consonant *h* is repeated to reinforce the poem's tranquil mood:

Hisakata no	This perfectly still
Hikari nodokeki	Spring day bathed in the soft light
Haru no hi ni	From the spread-out sky,
Shizu kokoro naku	Why do the cherry blossoms
Hana no chiruramu	So restlessly scatter down?

Ki nō Tsurayuki (kē nō tsoō·rä·yoō'kē), one of the editors of the *Kokinshū*, summarized the essence of Japanese tanka in his preface:

Poetry has its seeds in man's heart. . . . Man's activities are various and whatever they see or hear touches their hearts and is expressed in poetry. When we hear the notes of the nightingale among the blossoms, when we hear the frog in the water, we know that every living being is capable of song. Poetry, without effort, can move heaven and earth, can touch the gods and spirits . . . it turns the hearts of man and woman to each other and it soothes the soul of the fierce warrior.

Though his comments were written over a thousand years ago, they still hold true for much of Japanese verse.

3
4

3 LITERARY BACKGROUND

Themes in Japanese Poetry: In the preface to the *Kokinshū*, Ki Tsurayuki presented some of the circumstances and situations that prompted poets to seek solace through tanka:

". . . when they saw the blossoms fall on a spring morning, or heard the leaves fall of an autumn evening; . . . or when they were startled into realizing the brevity of life on noticing dew on the grass or foam on the water; or when, having fallen in the world, they have become estranged from those they loved."

These themes of impermanence, love, loneliness, and nostalgia continued to dominate Japanese poetry for many centuries.

4 CULTURAL BACKGROUND

Tanka as Love Letters: During the Heian period, tanka played a key role in courtship. Lovers wrote tanka in calligraphy and sent them to each other on beautiful paper, often with special seasonal flowers. Both the paper and the calligraphy were meant to highlight the content of the tanka. Even the messengers carrying the poems were carefully dressed to complement the expressions of love. In addition to using beautiful papers, lovers also sent poems inscribed on paintings and lacquerwork or sewn on kimonos.

Tanka Poets
Seventh through Twelfth Centuries A.D.

Spencer Museum of Art, The University of Kansas, William Bridges Thayer Memorial

THE POETESS ONO KOMACHI, early 1820s.

The poets who wrote tanka centuries ago are still widely read in Japan. In fact, their poems are so familiar that they are the basis of a popular "poem-card" game traditionally played in Japan at the New Year. In this game, one player reads the first half of a poem from the thirteenth-century anthology, *The Verses of a Hundred Poets.* The other players must then choose the correct ending to the poem from among the hundred cards spread on the floor. Yet ironically, very few facts are known about these early masters whose words have become so deeply ingrained in Japanese culture.

Princess Nukada
(seventh century A.D.)

One of the earliest composers of tanka, the Princess Nukada (nōō·kä′dä) was a favorite at the court of two emperors and was the most accomplished female poet of her time. We know little else about her, however. The only clues we have to her character are her poems, which are delicate and passionate. Some of them, including the one reproduced here, were written for her elder sister, the Princess Kagami (kä·gä′mē).

Oshikochi Mitsune
(late ninth century A.D.)

Oshikochi Mitsune (ō′shē·kō′chē mē·tsōō′nä) was among the greatest poets of the early Heian era. He was one of the editors of the *Kokinshū*, and some of his verses appear in that anthology. Many of his poems are melancholy, but they are never sentimental.

Ki Tsurayuki (A.D. 884–946)

Another editor of the *Kokinshū*, Ki Tsurayuki (kē′ tsōō·rä·yōō′kē), was a high court official as well as an accomplished writer and calligrapher. In addition to his fine tanka poems, he also wrote a travel diary that interwove poetry with prose. At the time, most cultured Japanese men chose to write prose in Chinese. Generally, only women and those men who could not afford a classical education wrote in Japanese. Be-

Courtesy of the Freer Gallery of Art, Smithsonian Institution, Washington, D.C. 70.22.—Japanese Painting, Edo Period, 19th century; Rimpa School; by Sakai Hoitsu "The Thirty-six Poets"; ink and colors on paper 150.90 × 163.0 cm [59 1/2 × 64 1/8"]

THE THIRTY-SIX MASTER POETS, SAKAI HOITSU, Edo period. *Although the "master poets" depicted here are all men, much of the best Japanese poetry was composed by women. Men tended to use the Chinese system of writing, which did not lend itself to poetic composition in Japanese.*

cause Ki Tsurayuki preferred to write in Japanese, and did not want to invite ridicule, he wrote his diary under a woman's name.

Ono Komachi (mid-tenth century A.D.)

Of all the poets whose tanka appeared in the *Kokinshū*, Ono Komachi (ō′nō kō·mä′chē) is perhaps the most revered. Her great physical beauty and the emotional power of her verse made her a celebrated figure in her time. More than three centuries after her death, Kan'ami Kiyotsugu, a Noh dramatist, wrote a play about Ono Komachi, whom he described as:

The brightest flower long ago
Her dark brows arched
Her face bright-powdered always
When cedar-scented halls could scarce
    contain
Her damask robes.

Saigyo (A.D. 1118–1190)

Among the most accomplished twelfth-century tanka poets was Saigyo (sä′ē·gyō), who abandoned his position as a royal bodyguard at the age of twenty-three to become a priest. His tanka were written during his years of wanderings through the Japanese countryside.

Ono Komachi was the subject of many popular legends, due primarily to the great intensity and passion of her poems.

Saigyo, one of the three best-loved poets in Japan, is especially well known for his poems about war, autumn, and cherry blossoms. His life as a priest allowed him the freedom to travel and to write over 2,000 tanka.

ABOUT THE TRANSLATORS

Anthony Thwaite, born in Great Britain in 1930, has served as a visiting lecturer at Tokyo University in Japan. With Geoffrey Bownas, he edited and translated the *Penguin Book of Japanese Verse*.

HUMANITIES CONNECTION

In Japanese art, male portraiture, *otoko-e*, was characterized by bold, energetic lines created by forceful brush strokes.

❓ *What do you think the poets are doing in this informal gathering?* (Possible response: they are waiting for a poetry contest to begin.) ∎

Tanka   **567**

OBJECTIVES

1. To analyze the characteristics of Japanese tanka poetry and to interpret tanka
2. To identify the use and effect of assonance in the tanka
3. To write an original tanka and a brief essay comparing and contrasting two tanka translations

PREREADING FOCUS

Background: The importance of suggestion, or indirect or incomplete expression, is evident throughout Japanese poetry. To appreciate the many levels of meaning in this poetry requires that readers use their imaginations fully. Just as a Japanese brush painting of a branch allows the viewer to imagine the entire tree, a description of a fallen plum blossom in Japanese poetry often allows the reader to imagine the blossom in bud, in bloom, and then floating to the ground.

Writer's Response: Poets evoke feelings by choosing images that trigger the reader's power of association. Ask students to brainstorm the scenes and activities that they associate with loneliness or quiet reflection.

Literary Focus: Assonance is important in tanka because of the nature of the Japanese language and the brevity of the form. Because metered verse is not possible in the Japanese language and rhyme is too easy to achieve, Japanese poetic forms are based on syllable and line counts. Therefore, the use of assonance, with the implied meanings evoked by different vowel sounds, helps poets say and suggest as much as possible within the challenging confines of the tanka form.

Reader's Guide

TANKA POEMS

Background

The tanka you are about to read were composed by five different poets over a period of more than five centuries, yet they share similar forms and techniques. All are brief, all evoke strong images and emotions, and all are subtle and indirect. The themes of the poems reflect each author's age, social position, and philosophy. In the art of tanka, what the poet does *not* say is often just as important as what he or she *does* say. It is up to the reader to make the connections between what is stated directly and what is implied.

In certain ways, the translations you are about to read differ notably from the original poems. Only one of the translated poems follows the traditional tanka form of thirty-one syllables. Nor do the translated poems have the same rhythm and cadence as the originals. Yet in other respects the translated poems are faithful to traditional Japanese style. None of the lines in the translated poems rhyme, for instance, which is in keeping with classical tanka tradition.

Writer's Response

Many tanka poems describe a scene that evokes a sense of loneliness or quiet reflection. Imagine that you were going to take a photograph to convey a similar mood. Freewrite for five minutes, describing in detail what you would include in your photograph.

Literary Focus

Assonance is the repetition of similar vowel sounds in words that are close together. For example, listen to the assonance in this line: "The br*ee*ze stirred the gr*ee*n l*ea*ves." The Japanese language lends itself to assonance, for Japanese has fewer vowel sounds than English. Thus, it is easy to create words or phrases that repeat the same vowel sound. In classical tanka, assonance was used to create certain moods or ideas. The vowel sound *a*, for instance, was linked with the idea of brilliance or clarity. The vowel sound *o*, on the other hand, evoked a sense of gloominess or obscurity, as in the phrase *oboro-zuki*, which means "pale, clouded moon." In the tanka translated in the Introduction (see page 565), the vowel sounds *a* or *o* occur in all except three of the original Japanese words.

Using Personification

Personification is a form of comparison in which non-human things are assigned human qualities. In poetry, personification can bring descriptions to life and suggest feelings that a poet does not want to express directly. Here are examples from the tanka:

My blind / Stirred at the touch / Of the autumn breeze.

The poet is suggesting that the blind responds to the breeze just as a person responds to the touch of another person. The blind stirs when the breeze touches it.

Reading and Speaking. Ask students to locate two places in the tanka where feelings are stated directly. Then have students invent examples of personification that convey the same feelings. Compare the examples of personification with the direct statements, and discuss the different effects that each creates. ∎

TANKA POEMS

translated by

GEOFFREY BOWNAS AND ANTHONY THWAITE

> Each of these five poems contains at least one example of assonance—similar vowel sounds. As you read, look for the words in each poem that are linked by assonance.

I Waited and I

1,2

I waited and I
Yearned for you.
My blind
Stirred at the touch
Of the autumn breeze.

—*Princess Nukada*

The End of My Journey

3

The end of my journey
Was still far off,
But in the tree-shade
Of the summer mountain
4 I stood, my mind floating.

—*Oshikochi Mitsune*

Now, I Cannot Tell

Now, I cannot tell
What my old friend is thinking:
But the petals of the plum
In this place I used to know
Keep their old fragrance.

—*Ki Tsurayuki*

The Granger Collection, New York

PLUM GARDEN, ANDŌ HIROSHIGE (1797–1858).
Andō Hiroshige is noted for the lyrical vision of his paintings.
❓ *What mood does* Plum Garden *evoke?*

TEACHER'S RESOURCES
✔ Review and Response Worksheet
✔ Selection Test

1 LITERARY ELEMENT

Theme: Yearning, especially unfulfilled yearning, is a common theme throughout the poetry of the Heian Age. What emotion inspires one person to yearn for another? (love)

2 LITERARY ELEMENT

Assonance: Which words have the same vowel sound in this tanka? (*I, I, my, blind*) What effect does the repeated vowel sound have? (Possible response: The speaker *I* is indirectly linked to the blind, the central image of the poem.)

3 COMPARING LITERATURE

Often important changes take place within a character as she or he travels from place to place. The *Epic of Gilgamesh* is one example.

❓ *Name other poems or stories that describe a journey.* (Possible responses: the *Iliad*, the *Divine Comedy*, the Old Testament)

4 READER'S RESPONSE

What do you think someone in the midst of a long journey might stop and think about? (Possible responses: a loved one far away, a happy memory, the meaning of life)

5 LITERARY ELEMENT

Simile: To what does the speaker compare her body? (a reed severed at the roots) What feeling does the simile suggest? (Possible responses: helplessness, passivity)

6 LITERARY ELEMENT

Implied Theme: What does the speaker suggest about change? (Possible response: Change, in its very ceaselessness, embodies permanence.)

ANSWERS

First Thoughts

Answers will vary. Moods created might include yearning, contentment, sorrow, loneliness, and tranquility.

Identifying Facts

1. autumn breeze; tree-shade of summer mountain; petals of the plum; severed reed; moon shining
2. Possible answers: "Now, I Cannot Tell"—*old, know, old;* "How Helpless My Heart!"—*stream, reed*

Interpreting Meanings

1. Possible response: The speaker is waiting to be touched by the person she yearns for, just as the breeze touches the blind.
2. Possible responses: contemplation, daydreaming. Most will find it pleasant.
3. Possible response: His friend's thoughts may stay the same, like the fragrance of the blossoms. Many will find the comparison comforting.
4. Possible response: the person the speaker loves; passive; *severed, drift*

How Helpless My Heart!

How helpless my heart!
Were the stream to tempt,
My body, like a reed
5   Severed at the roots,
Would drift along, I think.

—*Ono Komachi*

Every Single Thing

Every single thing
Changes and is changing
6   Always in this world.
Yet with the same light
The moon goes on shining.

—*Priest Saigyo*

Tanka poet Ki Tsurayuki.

▷ **First Thoughts**

Which image in these tanka was most memorable for you? Did the image create a distinctive mood?

Identifying Facts

1. List one **image** of nature used in each tanka to help convey its theme.
2. Point out examples of **assonance**, or similar vowel sounds, in two different poems.

Interpreting Meanings

1. In Princess Nukada's poem, what is the relationship between the idea of waiting and the autumn breeze stirring the blind?
2. In the poem by Oshikochi Mitsune, what state of mind is suggested by the phrase "my mind floating"? Does it seem to be a pleasant or unpleasant state of mind?
3. In Ki Tsurayuki's poem, what parallel does the speaker seem to be drawing

between his old friend and the scent of the plum blossoms? Does the speaker draw comfort from this comparison, or does it make him sad?

4. In the poem by Ono Komachi, what might the stream symbolize? Is the speaker's attitude toward the stream active or passive? Point out specific words in the poem to support your answer.
5. What views of permanence and change are expressed in the poem by Priest Saigyo through the image of the moon? Explain how the use of **assonance** in the poem links the ideas of permanence and change.

Applying Meanings

Reread the five poems. If you were asked to make a generalization about the subjects and themes of tanka poetry based on these five poems, what would your conclusion be? What do tanka poems say about the relationship between people and

Creating a Tanka Anthology. Ask students to go to the library and read through selections of tanka. Have each student select three tanka that they find particularly moving. (Some students may prefer to use their own tanka.) Then ask them to copy each tanka onto a sheet of paper using a stylized handwriting of their own invention. Have students share their tanka by holding a class poetry reading. Encourage them to respond to the tanka by describing memories, dreams, or ideas that the poems bring to mind. Finally, have students gather the tanka sheets together and form a class anthology of tanka poetry.

Encourage students to talk about the way the tanka poets use images of nature to convey the inevitability of change. Ask students to discuss the feelings the tanka poets associate with change. Then have students share their own feelings about change and compare and contrast them with those expressed in the tanka poetry. ■

---

nature, for example? What is their attitude toward the idea of time and change?

Creative Writing Response

Coauthoring a Tanka. Play the traditional Japanese game of writing a tanka with a partner (see page 566). On a 3″ x 5″ note card, write the first three lines of a tanka. Then exchange your card with a partner, who will write the last two lines on another card. Identify the two ''halves'' of the tanka by writing the same number on the back of each card. Then spread all the cards tanka-side up on a table or on the floor and let students decide which ''halves'' go together. Remember that the tanka should have thirty-one syllables— three lines of seven syllables each and two lines of five syllables each. You might look back at your description of the imaginary photograph (see page 568) for ideas of tanka to write.

Critical Writing Response

Comparing Two Translations. Reread Ono Komachi's tanka on page 570. Then read the following translation of the same poem:

> **So Lonely Am I**
> Ono Komachi
> translated by
> Donald Keene
>
> So lonely am I
> My body is a floating weed
> Severed at the roots.
> Were there water to entice me
> I would follow it, I think.

Write a two-paragraph essay comparing and contrasting the two translations. Consider the following points:

- Which translation seems more romantic or sentimental? Cite details to support your answer.
- In which translation does the speaker seem more helpless? Point out words in each poem that create an impression of passiveness or free choice.
- How does the translation affect the **theme** of the poem?

5. Possible response: While everything in the world changes, the moon continues shining; it is permanent even though it too continually changes. The repetition of vowel sounds and the shifting vowel sounds illustrate the way that change and permanence coexist in nature.

Applying Meanings

Possible responses: nature, love, and change. People and nature are closely intertwined; nature can mirror and soothe the lives of people existing within it. Time and change are accepted, but often with sadness and regret.

Creative Writing Response
Coauthoring a Tanka. Tanka should follow the proper syllable and line counts and include assonance. Images should be drawn from nature to highlight the feelings or themes expressed.

Critical Writing Response
Comparing Two Translations. Students should present their comparison-and-contrast essays, discussing the theme, mood, and effectiveness of the two translations. References should be made to specific words or techniques used in each translation. ■

RIVER LANDSCAPE WITH FIREFLIES (DETAIL)

The Nelson-Atkins Museum of Art, Kansas City, Missouri (Nelson Fund) 74-12/1,2

1 LITERARY BACKGROUND

The haiku has its roots in other Japanese literary forms, particularly the tanka (see pp. 564–571) and the *haikai*, or linked-verse poem. Originally, the three-line haiku served as the opening stanza in a haikai, but as time passed, haiku were composed as independent poems.

2 CULTURAL DIVERSITY

One example of the influence of the Japanese haiku on Western literature is Ezra Pound's well-known poem "In a Station of the Metro."
❓ *Do you know any other poems that might have been influenced by Japanese haiku?* (Answers will vary.)

3 LITERARY ELEMENT

Imagery: Though compressed in form, an effective haiku can evoke a range of sensory and emotional responses. The best haiku poems link two or more images in an unexpected way to create a distinct atmosphere or mood. These images are not limited to the visual; they can also describe a sound, scent, or touch.

4 ABOUT TRANSLATION

In the traditional haiku, two images, one suggesting time-lessness and the other suggesting change, are usually divided by a *kireji* or "cutting word." While translations may vary in the interpretations of particular words, most translators try to maintain the essential tension that the cutting word creates within the poem.

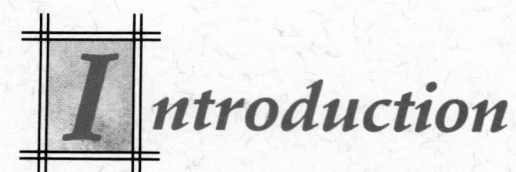

Introduction

Haiku

A **haiku** (hī′kōō) is a brief, unrhymed poem three lines long. In Japanese, the first and last lines have five syllables each and the middle line has seven. This strict, condensed form challenges poets to convey their feelings and observations in a few vivid images.

The History of Haiku

1 Examples of short verses similar to haiku have been found in thirteenth- or fourteenth-century Japanese literature. However, the art of haiku was not perfected until later in the seventeenth century, when the greatest of the classical haiku poets, Bashō (ba′shō), lived. When English authors such as John Milton were composing vast and intricate poems, Bashō and his pupils were writing strikingly pure, compressed verses

2 only a few words long. In the centuries since Bashō, the haiku form has been adopted by poets the world over. The haiku's emphasis on familiar images from nature, presented in compact form, has given the form a lasting appeal.

The Art of Haiku

Unlike many Western poets, the classical haiku masters do not present sensory

images with similes, metaphors, or other figures of speech. Rather, haiku poets simply present unadorned images, and the reader must make an imaginative leap to understand the connection between them. 3

haiku (hī′kōō): *a brief, unrhymed, three-line poem in which the first and third lines have five syllables each and the middle line has seven.*

The Japanese language differs greatly from English. For example, it has no articles and rarely uses pronouns. To accommodate these differences, the English translators of the haiku in this section have made some changes. In some cases, the translators have chosen to make the English haiku rhyme, though this is not in keeping with Japanese tradition. In other cases, the poems do not have exactly seventeen syllables, or the syllables are not divided among the three lines of the poem according to the classical formula.

Japanese haiku, even in their original form, leave much unsaid, compounding the challenges of translation. As a result, one haiku may have numerous translations with subtle differences. Consider, 4 for example, the following well-known haiku by Bashō:

Furu-ike ya
   kawazu tobi-komu
     mizu-no-oto

Harold G. Henderson's literal translation of this haiku reads:

Old pond:
   frog jump-in
     water-sound.

Harry Behn's translation retains the seventeen-syllable structure of the original Japanese:

An old silent pond . . .
A frog jumps into the pond,
   splash! Silence again.

A looser translation by Asatarō Miyamori captures the image and abandons the three-line form:

The ancient pond!
A frog plunged—splash!

The Lasting Appeal of Haiku

Some haiku contain allusions to Zen philosophy and Japanese history and customs. These references might be lost on non-Japanese readers. Yet most haiku can be understood and appreciated by readers from any culture. Consider this early haiku:

If to the moon
   one puts a handle—what
     a splendid fan!

     —Sokan (1465–1553)
       —*translated by Harold G. Henderson*

THE CAP FOR THE COMING OF AGE CEREMONY,
RYŪRYŪKYO SHINSAI, 1800s.
Spencer Museum of Art, The University of Kansas, William Bridges Thayer Memorial

In a few words, the author manages to create a vivid picture of the full moon seen behind the branch of a tree.

A more subtle comparison of images appears in the following haiku, composed almost two centuries after Sokan's:

On top of skeletons
   they put a gala dress, and then—
     the flower-viewing!

     —Onitsura (1660–1738)
       —*translated by Harold G. Henderson*

The poem alludes to a Japanese tradition that signals the beginning of spring. Families dress in their finest clothes and walk through the cherry orchards to see the cherry trees covered in the first blossoms of the year. Yet both the fashionable people and the cherry trees have only temporarily disguised their "skeletons." Onitsura's haiku may have reminded his audience of the Buddhist teaching that what is beautiful today may wither and die tomorrow.

5 **LITERARY ELEMENT**
Symbol: Change and permanence are suggested in two ways in Bashō's famous haiku. On one level, the old pond represents permanence, while the frog's movement represents change. On another level, the frog itself reveals both qualities: The frog was traditionally used in Japanese poetry to represent permanence, but Bashō describes it in a way that represents change. *What other polarities or opposites might this haiku suggest?* (Possible responses: silence/noise; old/young; stasis/movement)

6 **INTERPRETING**
What feeling does Sokan create by linking the images of two dissimilar objects, the full moon and the fan? (Possible response: restful coolness)

7 **CULTURAL BACKGROUND**
Cherry Blossoms: Images of cherry blossoms have been used in numerous tanka and haiku. The Japanese appreciate cherry blossoms because of their perishable beauty. Unlike other blossoms, which can remain flowering for a month, the cherry blossoms fall to the ground after a few days. The Japanese plant cherry trees everywhere just to enjoy the three-day bloom.

Haiku Poets
Seventeenth through Nineteenth Centuries

At the age of twenty-eight, Matsuo Bashō traveled to the city of Edo, where he won a minor government post and devoted all of his spare time to composing and teaching poetry. Unlike many poets of his time, who supported themselves by reading and correcting the poems of others, Bashō lived with the help of gifts from his students and by selling his calligraphy.

By the age of nineteen, Uejima Onitsura was already a prolific writer. About 700 of his thousands of haiku have survived. Considered one of the most important poets between the times of Bashō and Buson, Onitsura eventually gave up poetry entirely at the age of seventy-three, and became a Buddhist priest.

Taniguchi Buson, also known as Yosa Buson, left his home in Settsu to study poetry in Edo. After declaring his independence from the established schools of poetry, he settled in the city of Kyoto. In addition to being considered one of the greatest poets of his time, Buson was recognized as one of the finest painters of eighteenth-century Japan.

Kobayashi Issa focused his haiku on personal experiences as well as on the lives of vulnerable animals and people, especially the young. In addition to haiku, Issa wrote haikai, memoirs, and other poetic collections.

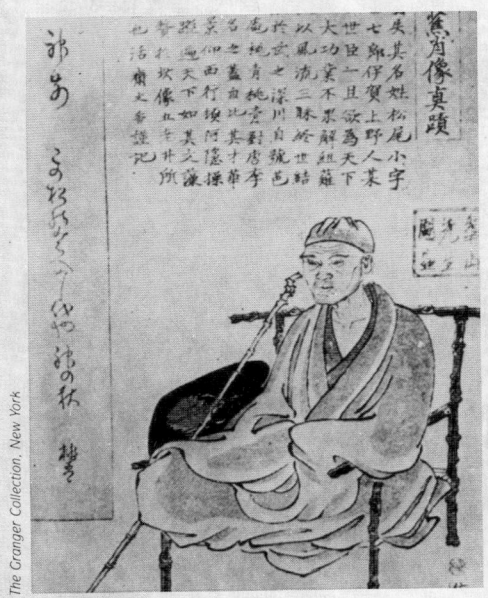

MATSUO BASHŌ, WATANAHE KWASAN.

The Granger Collection, New York

Matsuo Bashō (1644–1694)

The son of a samurai, Matsuo Bashō spent his youth in the service of a local lord. He began writing verses when he was nine and soon showed remarkable promise. Before he was thirty, he had won acclaim as a poet and had started his own poetry school.

Two things shaped Bashō's poetry: his devotion to Zen Buddhism and his travels. In 1684, at the age of forty, Bashō set out on the first of his many journeys through Japan. Traveling alone, Bashō endured great discomforts and loneliness. Yet some of his best haiku were composed on these lonely journeys.

Uejima Onitsura (1660–1738)

One of Bashō's greatest admirers was Uejima Onitsura (ō·nēt·sōō′ra). Like Bashō, Onitsura came from a samurai background and began writing poetry at an early age. Though Onitsura admired Bashō, he did not imitate Bashō's style. His poems are more joyful and exuberant than Bashō's and somewhat less philosophical.

Taniguchi Buson (1715–1783)

Taniguchi Buson (bōō′sän′), a younger contemporary of Onitsura, soon established his own poetic style. His haiku are generally regarded as second only to Bashō's. Buson was an accomplished painter, and his poems reflect his fascination with light and color.

Kobayashi Issa (1762–1826)

Kobayashi Issa (ē′sä′) is one of the most beloved of Japan's haiku masters. His life was extraordinarily sad. His mother died when he was an infant, and his relations with his stepmother were so poor that his father sent him away from home to study when he was only fourteen. His first wife bore him five children, but all of them died in infancy before his wife succumbed to an illness. Possibly because of these many sorrows, Issa's verses are taut with emotion, though they are rarely sentimental.

OBJECTIVES

1. *To analyze the qualities and elements of haiku and interpret poems*
2. *To analyze the use of imagery in haiku*
3. *To write a haiku that reveals the beauty in an ordinary object or event*

Reader's Guide

HAIKU

Background

The six poems that follow were written by four different poets over a span of two centuries. In spite of this, the poems have a great deal in common. All adhere to haiku's strict form. Each poem combines two or more images in vivid and sometimes surprising ways. However, all the poems vary greatly in mood. Some are philosophical or somber, while others are romantic or fanciful.

The first three selections are by Bashō. In all three poems, Bashō finds beauty in seemingly insignificant or ordinary objects or events. This insight is inspired by the Buddhist belief that, through contemplation, a person can find significance in even the humblest of things. In most haiku, the meaning is present in the images themselves. The haiku master stands back from the images he creates and allows his readers to draw their own conclusions.

Writer's Response

Many haiku describe subtle signs of the changing seasons and the emotions that these changes arouse. Which season of the year makes you the most happy? Which signs—sights, sounds, odors—tell you that that season is approaching? Freewrite for five minutes about the approach of your favorite season.

Literary Focus

Imagery is language that appeals to the senses—sight, hearing, smell, touch, and taste. The imagery a writer selects helps readers imagine a scene and respond emotionally to it. For example, a writer might describe an ocean as "a crashing gray tide" to build a feeling of fear or as "rippling blue waves" to suggest tranquility. Haiku poets rarely state an emotion; instead, they challenge the reader to extract the meaning of the poem by looking closely at the images.

1 LITERARY ELEMENT

Imagery: What two images are juxtaposed in each of Bashō's poems? (Possible responses: (1) a crow on a withered branch, autumn nightfall; (2) no bells ringing, spring dusk; (3) no rice, a flower in a gourd) What feeling does each pair of images evoke? (Possible responses: (1) old age; (2) boredom; (3) hope)

2 LITERARY ELEMENT

Personification: What human quality is assigned to natural objects in this poem? (The stones "compose songs.") What does the use of personification suggest about the poet's view of nature? (Possible response: Nature mirrors human life.)

3 INTERPRETING

To what senses does the image of the pear blossoms appeal? (sight, smell) What mood, or atmosphere, does this image create when linked with the image of the woman? (Possible responses: romance, beauty, solitude)

HAIKU
translated by
HAROLD G. HENDERSON, PETER BEILENSON, AND HARRY BEHN

❖ *As you read the following haiku, decide how the images in each shape your emotional response.*

Matsuo Bashō

1

On a withered branch
   A crow has settled—
      autumn nightfall.

A village where they ring
   no bells!—Oh, what *do* they do
      at dusk in spring?

No rice?—In that hour
   we put into the gourd
      a maiden-flower.
            —*translated by Harold G. Henderson*

Uejima Onitsura

2

Even stones in streams
   of mountain water compose
      songs to wild cherries.
            —*translated by Peter Beilenson and Harry Behn*

Taniguchi Buson

3

Blossoms on the pear;
   and a woman in the moonlight
      reads a letter there. . . .
            —*translated by Harold G. Henderson*

Kobayashi Issa

A morning-glory vine
   all blossoming, has thatched
      this hut of mine.
            —*translated by Harold G. Henderson*

MORNING GLORIES, IKEGAMI SHŪBO.
❓ *How has a vine "thatched" the speaker's hut in Issa's poem?*

The University of Michigan Museum of Art, Gift of Mr. and Mrs. Frederic R. Smith, Acc. no. 1973/2.89

Comparing a Modern Poem to a Haiku.
Have students find and read poems by American and British Imagist poets from the early twentieth century, such as Hilda Doolittle, Richard Aldington, and William Carlos Williams. Then ask students to choose one Imagist poem they find especially moving, and compare it to a haiku by Bashō, Onitsura, Buson, or Issa. Invite volunteers to share their findings in an oral report to the class.

Ask students to think about why the Japanese haiku poets placed such importance on nature imagery. Were they uninterested in the human world? What relationship do they see between the human and natural worlds? ■

First Thoughts

Which haiku made you feel most joyful? Which one is the saddest?

Identifying Facts

1. Images of nature are central to traditional Japanese haiku. List the elements of nature mentioned in the haiku that you have just read.
2. What seasons do the images in these haiku suggest?

Interpreting Meanings

1. Does nature seem to be a positive or a negative force in the haiku? Give examples to support your opinion.
2. In many haiku, the poet surprises and delights the reader by showing a relationship between two dissimilar things. In Bashō's first haiku, what relationship does he establish between the image in the third line and the image in the first two lines?
3. **Tone** is the attitude a writer takes toward the reader, a subject, or a character. What is the tone of Onitsura's haiku? What makes you say so?
4. What **imagery** occurs in Buson's haiku?
5. What two things are contrasted in Issa's poem? What might each of these two things symbolize or stand for?

Applying Meanings

In Issa's poem, nature transforms something plain into something beautiful. What experiences have you had in which nature transformed something ugly into something delightful—for example, raindrops transforming a spider's web into shimmering lace or flowers growing in a junkyard?

Creative Writing Response

Writing a Haiku. Reread Bashō's haiku "On a Withered Branch." According to translator and critic Harold G. Henderson, at the time Bashō wrote this famous poem, he was "consciously looking for the poetic beauty to be found in things not in themselves particularly beautiful." Look through the haiku you have just read. Which other haiku seem to find beauty in ordinary things? How does the poet manage to make these ordinary things seem beautiful and meaningful?

Try writing your own haiku about an everyday object or event that might not seem very beautiful or interesting: a tin can lying on a sidewalk, a moss-covered rock, the reflection of light on an old brick wall, or an insect skittering across a log. Jot down a list of possible images and some descriptions that occur to you. Then compose a haiku based on your favorite image. Remember that a haiku is unrhymed and three lines long. The first and last lines should have five syllables each, and the middle line should have seven. Revise your haiku until it is as simple and compressed as you can possibly make it. Then read it aloud to the class.

PRIMARY SOURCES

A Glimpse into a Poet's Life

1   *Matsuo Bashō is still the most beloved Japanese poet, admired for mixing sorrow and humor in his haiku. A wanderer who gave up the comforts of home, Bashō led an active life, but in his later years he was more and more drawn to solitude. This excerpt from his biographical work "Prose Poem on the Unreal Dwelling" gives us a firsthand insight into Bashō's love of both solitude and nature.*

2   My body, now close to fifty years of age, has become an old tree that bears bitter peaches, a snail which has lost its shell, a bagworm separated from its bag; it drifts with the winds and clouds that know no destination. Morning and night I have eaten traveler's fare, and have held out for alms a pilgrim's wallet. On my last journey 3 my face was burnt by the sun of Matsushima, and I wetted my sleeve at the holy mountain. I longed to go as far as that shore where the puffins cry and the Thousand Islands of the Ainu can be seen in the distance, but my companion drew me back, telling how dangerous so long a journey would be with my sickness. I yielded. Then I bruised my heels along the rough coast of the northern sea, where each step in the sand dunes is painful. This year I roamed by the shores of the lake in quest of a place to stay, a single stalk of reed where the floating nest of the grebe might be borne to rest by the current. This is my Unreal Dwelling, and it stands by the

mountain called Kokubu. An ancient shrine is near, which so purifies my senses that I feel cleansed of the dust of the world. . . .

The man who used to live here had most refined tastes, and did not clutter up the hut even with objects of art. Apart from the household shrine there is just the little alcove for hanging nightclothes. Once, when he heard that the High Priest of Mount Kora was in the capital, he asked him for a plaque to decorate the alcove. The priest nonchalantly took his brush in hand and wrote the words "Unreal Dwelling." On the back he inscribed his name to serve as a memento to later people who might see it.

In this hut where I live as a hermit, as a passing traveler, there is no need to accumulate household possessions. All I have is a broadbrimmed hat of nettle wood and a rush raincoat, which I hang on a post above my pillow. During the day the old gentleman who looks after the shrine or villagers from the foot of the mountain come here and pass the day in stories of a kind to which I am unaccustomed, how boars are grubbing up the rice seedlings, or about rabbits infesting the bean fields. Or when, as very rarely happens, visitors come from afar, we sit calmly at night, the moonlight our companion, arguing with our shadows.

—*translated by Donald Keene*

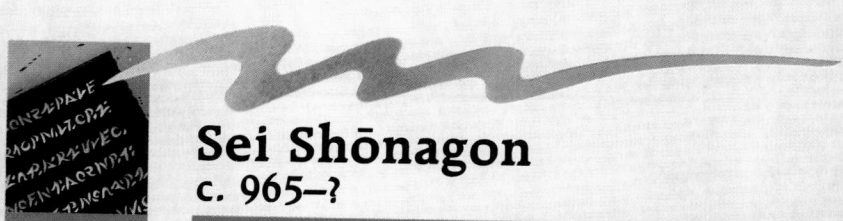

Sei Shōnagon
c. 965–?

Heibonsha Ltd.

Some of the liveliest female voices in Japanese literature are nearly a thousand years old. One of the most vital belongs to Sei Shōnagon (sā'ē shō'nä·gōn'), who served as a lady-in-waiting to the Empress Sadako (sä'dä·kō) in the late tenth century.

We know very little about Shōnagon's life. She was born around 965 into the Kiyowara (kē·yō·wä'rä) clan. Her father, a minor government official, had earned a modest reputation as a poet. Sometime around 990, Shōnagon went to Kyoto, where she served in the royal court for about ten years. What became of her after she left the court remains a mystery.

The little knowledge we have of Shōnagon's life comes from her writings. During her ten years in Kyoto, Shōnagon jotted down various ideas and impressions and tucked the papers away in her room. Part diary, part random notes, these writings came to be known as the *Notes of the Pillow*. In Shōnagon's day, "pillows" were made of wood, and some had drawers in which letters or journals could be stored. Men and women at court may have amused themselves by scribbling their thoughts in a notebook in the evenings and hiding the notes in these "pillow books."

Lady Shōnagon wrote prose so clear and expressive that it is still held up as a model to Japanese schoolchildren. It is therefore hard to imagine that she did not intend *The Pillow Book* to be published. Nevertheless, she claimed to be dismayed after her book was discovered:

> I wrote these notes at home, when I had a good deal of time to myself and thought no one would notice what I was doing. Everything that I have seen and felt is included. Since much of it might appear malicious and even harmful to people, I was careful to keep my book hidden. But now it has become public, which is the last thing I expected. . . .

Some scholars claim that this passage was added long after Shōnagon died. Despite centuries of exhaustive research, many mysteries surround Shōnagon's life and her manuscript. Shōnagon probably would have enjoyed that irony.

MORE ABOUT THE AUTHOR

Near the end of *The Pillow Book*, Shōnagon reveals how her book came to be circulated around court without her permission. One day, a captain of the Left Guards visited her and spotted the book lying on a straw mat:

> "I [Shōnagon] snatched at the book and made a desperate effort to get it back; but the Captain instantly took it off with him and did not return it until much later."

Though the Captain's behavior may have deserved inclusion on Shōnagon's list of "Hateful Things," modern readers and historians are grateful that he brought the book to light.

Most of what is known about Shōnagon is derived from *The Pillow Book* itself. The name "Shōnagon" is actually a court name meaning "Minor Counselor." Her real name may have been Nagiko. Records suggest Shōnagon was married twice to government officials and bore two children. While the date and circumstances of her death are not known, legends persist that she became a Buddhist nun or died in lonely poverty.

ABOUT THE TRANSLATOR

Ivan Morris wrote widely on Japanese literature and served as chairman of the Department of East Asian Languages and Cultures at Columbia University.

OBJECTIVES

1. To recognize Sei Shōnagon's contribution to Japanese literature and understand what a pillow book is
2. To recognize and understand wit
3. To write a personal list and a character sketch, and to differentiate the active from the passive voice

THEMES IN WORLD LITERATURE

The Individual and Society
The Book of Ruth, pp. 177–184
A Doll's House, pp. 1070–1126

People and Nature
"Quiet Night Thoughts," p. 520
Haiku Poetry, pp. 572–577
"The World Is Too Much with Us,"
    pp. 1002–1005 ■

PREREADING FOCUS

Background: During the Heian period, the aristocrats numbered about ten thousand people, out of a total of four million. The aristocracy was divided into a complex system of ranks—four of princes and thirty of ordinary aristocrats. Members of the lower aristocracy, from which Shōnagon sprang, maneuvered obsessively to become accepted at court, often through marriage.

Women at court often recorded their impressions in diaries. These journals are now considered the earliest examples of the discursive essay in Japan and possibly the origin of the modern first-person, "I-novel."

Literary Focus: Arthur Waley, another translator of *The Pillow Book*, wrote that wit "evaporates in the process of explanation." Wit appeals to the intellect, which delights in deft turn of phrase that produces a shock of comic surprise. While wit is rapid and sharp, humor is slow, evolving through series of amusing details. Wit is always verbal, while humor may arise from either words or actions. For instance, Shōnagon's scathing remark that Masahiro's elegant clothes only inspire the thought that it's "a shame someone else isn't wearing these things" is witty. On the other hand, the scene in which Masahiro bumbles with the lamp is humorous.

Reader's Guide ■

from THE PILLOW BOOK

Background

In Japan, forms of personal writing such as the diary have been a major literary genre for centuries. *The Pillow Book* represents a unique form of the diary genre. More a collection of inspired jottings than a diary, Shōnagon's masterpiece contains vivid sketches of people and places, sly anecdotes and witticisms, snatches of poetry, and 164 lists. Every phrase is stamped with Shōnagon's personality. She was quick to praise an elegant turn of phrase or a beautiful kimono, but, like all aristocrats of her time, she seldom took notice of ordinary working people. When she did it was usually to note their rough and—to her—unseemly ways.

The Pillow Book provides a vivid picture of court life during the Heian (hā'än) period (794–1185). Through Shōnagon we learn that the Japanese calendar dictated everything from coronations to cutting toenails; that royal cats had a higher rank than some governors; and that musicians were forbidden to walk in the emperor's presence. Aristocratic women let their long straight hair sweep down past their ankles, colored their teeth black, and wore clothes dyed to match the colors of the seasons. They spent most of their lives behind decorative screens even though they, like Shōnagon, were often highly educated, talented, and influential.

Oral Response

According to Lady Shōnagon, *The Pillow Book* was intended to be a private journal, yet it was discovered and eventually printed. The last words of *The Pillow Book* state Shōnagon's views of this breach of privacy: "Whatever people may think of my book, I still regret that it ever came to light." How would you react if someone read and made public a letter or diary that you had intended to be private? Discuss the topic of personal writing and privacy.

Literary Focus

Wit is a quality of speech or writing that combines verbal cleverness with keen perception, especially of contradictory elements. Lady Shōnagon's writing sparkles with clever word play, puns, sharp observations, and descriptions of humorous situations.

from THE PILLOW BOOK

Sei Shōnagon

translated by

IVAN MORRIS

Nothing, it seems, escaped Sei Shōnagon's sharp eye—or her sharp wit. As you read these excerpts from The Pillow Book, *pay attention not only to what Shōnagon reveals about her society, but also to what she reveals about herself.*

RIVER LANDSCAPE WITH FIREFLIES (detail).
❓ *What specific details does Sei Shōnagon use to describe each of the four seasons?*

In Spring It Is the Dawn

In spring it is the dawn that is most beautiful. As the light creeps over the hills, their outlines are dyed a faint red and <u>wisps</u> of purplish cloud trail over them.

In summer the nights. Not only when the moon shines, but on dark nights too, as the fireflies flit to and fro, and even when it rains, how beautiful it is!

In autumn the evenings, when the glittering sun sinks close to the edge of the hills and the crows fly back to their nests in threes and fours and twos; more charming still is a file[1] of wild geese, like specks in the distant sky. When the sun has set, one's heart is moved by the sound of the wind and the hum of the insects.

1. **file** (fīl): a single line or row.

TEACHER'S RESOURCES

- ✔ Review and Response Worksheet
- ✔ Selection Test
- ✔ Vocabulary Activity Worksheet
- ✔ Vocabulary Test
- ✔ Language Skills Worksheet

HUMANITIES CONNECTION

Shiokawa created the impression of fireflies among reeds with just a few brush strokes. ❓ *What does this artistic style have in common with the descriptions in Shōnagon's work and in Japanese haiku?* (They all simplify. Haiku poetry evokes scenes with a few choice words; Shōnagon's prose also implies much that is left out. Japanese art often depicts scenes with only a few exquisitely executed lines.) ■

1 LITERARY ELEMENT

Imagery: Which of the five senses do Shōnagon's nature descriptions most appeal to? (the sense of sight) What do her descriptions suggest about her? (Like many Japanese writers of the period, she was a careful observer of nature.)

■ **wisps:** thin strands

Direct and Indirect Quotations

In direct quotations, quotation marks enclose a speaker's exact words. In indirect quotations, no quotation marks appear since the sentence is conveying the general content rather than the exact words of the speaker. Here are examples from *The Pillow Book*:

Direct Quotation: "Send two servants," he said.

Indirect Quotation: He said to send two servants.

1. **Writing and Sharing.** Ask students to write a direct quotation that would be appropriate for incorporating into one of the other entries in *The Pillow Book*. Have students read their quotations aloud in their contexts and explain how they affect the entry.

---

2 CULTURAL BACKGROUND

In ancient Asia pine soot was mixed with glue to form inksticks, called *sumi*, which could be carried more easily than liquid. The sticks were rubbed against a stone to produce a powder which was mixed with water to form ink. Shōnagon, somewhat of a perfectionist, would not want a hair in the ink spoiling her calligraphy.

3 GUIDED READING

Comparing/Contrasting: How does the visit of the exorcist seem similar to, and different from, an appointment with the doctor? (Accept reasonable responses: The family's anxiety and the exorcist's lateness seem very modern. Modern doctors, however, rarely make house calls.)

4 CULTURAL DIVERSITY

In Heian mansions, curtains, screens, or sliding doors made of thick paper divided the large rooms into areas for different activities. These thin partitions enabled one to overhear conversations taking place nearby, doubtless adding spice to Heian gossip.

❓ *How do modern housing arrangements sometimes present similar problems?* (Privacy is sometimes difficult to find.)

◼ **insignificant** (in'sig·nif'i· kənt): unimportant

In winter the early mornings. It is beautiful indeed when snow has fallen during the night, but splendid too when the ground is white with frost; or even when there is no snow or frost, but it is simply very cold and the attendants hurry from room to room stirring up the fires and bringing charcoal, how well this fits the season's mood! But as noon approaches and the cold wears off, no one bothers to keep the braziers[2] alight, and soon nothing remains but piles of white ashes.

from Hateful Things

One is in a hurry to leave, but one's visitor keeps chattering away. If it is someone of no importance, one can get rid of him by saying, "You must tell me all about it next time"; but, should it be the sort of visitor whose presence commands one's best behavior, the situation is hateful indeed.

2 ⌈ One finds that a hair has got caught in the stone on which one is rubbing one's inkstick, or again that gravel is lodged in the inkstick, making a nasty, grating sound.

3 ⌈ Someone has suddenly fallen ill and one summons the exorcist.[3] Since he is not at home, one has to send messengers to look for him. After one has had a long fretful wait, the exorcist finally arrives, and with a sigh of relief one asks him to start his incantations. But perhaps he has been exorcizing too many evil spirits recently; for hardly has he installed himself and begun praying when his voice becomes drowsy. Oh, how hateful!

---

2. **braziers** (brā'zhərz): metal pans or bowls used to hold burning coals or charcoal.
3. **exorcist** (eks'ôr·sist): a person who drives away an evil spirit or spirits through ritual prayers or incantations.

A man who has nothing in particular to recommend him discusses all sorts of subjects at random as though he knew everything.

Things That Cannot Be Compared

Summer and winter. Night and day. Rain and sunshine. Youth and age. A person's laughter and his anger. Black and white. Love and hatred. The little indigo plant[4] and the great philodendron. Rain and mist.

When one has stopped loving somebody, one feels that he has become someone else, even though he is still the same person.

In a garden full of evergreens the crows are all asleep. Then, towards the middle of the night, the crows in one of the trees suddenly wake up in a great flurry and start flapping about. Their unrest spreads to the other trees, and soon all the birds have been startled from their sleep and are cawing in alarm. How different from the same crows in daytime!

Embarrassing Things

While entertaining a visitor, one hears some servants chatting without any restraint in one of the back rooms. It is embarrassing to know that one's visitor can overhear. But how to stop them?

A man whom one loves gets drunk and keeps repeating himself.

To have spoken about someone not knowing that he could overhear. This is embarrassing even if it be a servant or some other completely insignificant person.

---

4. **indigo** (in'di·gō') **plant**: a plant that yields a deep blue dye. Dyeing was an important art form of the aristocratic women of the Heian period.

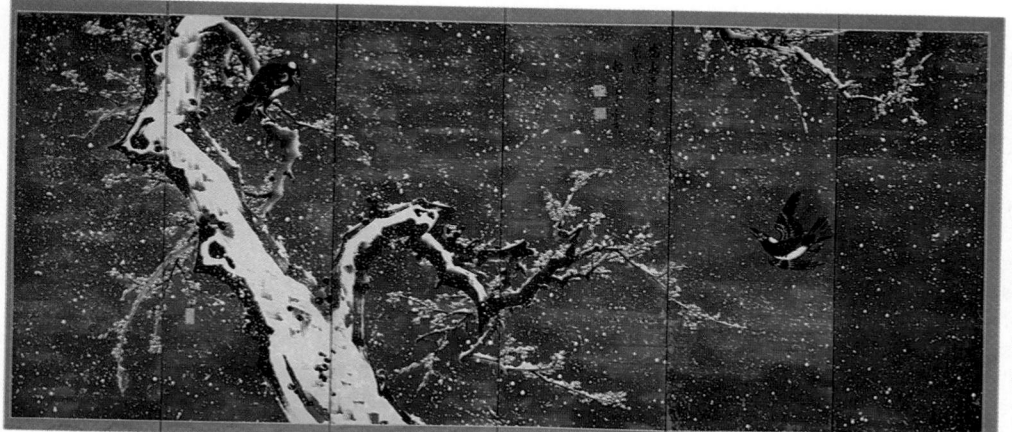

Crows and Plum Tree, and Rabbits and Pine Trees in Snow. (Detail) Katsu Jagyoku, Shin'enkan Collection, Los Angeles County Museum of Art

RABBITS AND CROWS IN THE NIGHT SNOW (one half of a screen), DAGYOKU SANJIN (1733–1778).

What imagery does Sei Shōnagon use to contrast crows at night with crows during the day?

To hear one's servants making merry. This is equally annoying if one is on a journey and staying in cramped quarters or at home and hears the servants in a neighboring room.

Parents, convinced that their ugly child is adorable, pet him and repeat the things he has said, imitating his voice.

An ignoramus[5] who in the presence of some learned person puts on a knowing air and converses about men of old.

A man recites his own poems (not especially good ones) and tells one about the praise they have received—most embarrassing.

Lying awake at night, one says something to one's companion, who simply goes on sleeping.

In the presence of a skilled musician, someone plays a zither[6] just for his own pleasure and without tuning it.

A son-in-law who has long since stopped visiting his wife runs into his father-in-law in a public place.

Masahiro Really Is a Laughing-Stock

Masahiro really is a laughing-stock. I wonder what it is like for his parents and friends. If people see him with a decent-looking servant, they always call for the fellow and laughingly ask how he can wait upon such a master and what he thinks of him. There are skilled dyers and weavers in Masahiro's household, and when it comes to dress, whether it be the color of his under-robe or

5. **ignoramus** (ig'nə·rā'məs): an ignorant and stupid person.

6. **zither** (zith'ər): an inaccurate translation. The instrument being referred to here is really a *koto*, a Japanese instrument with thirteen strings.

Sei Shōnagon   **583**

the style of his cloak, he is more elegant than most men; yet the only effect of his elegance is to make people say, "What a shame someone else isn't wearing these things!"

And how strangely he expresses himself! Once, when he was due to report for night duty at the Palace, he ordered that the clothes and other things he would need should be brought from his house. "Send *two* servants," he said. One man came and said that he could easily carry everything. "You're an odd fellow," said Masahiro. "How can one man bring the things of two people? After all, can you put two measures in a one-measure jar?" No one had the slightest idea what he meant; but there was loud laughter.

On another occasion a messenger brought Masahiro a letter from someone, asking for an immediate reply. "You hateful fellow!" said Masahiro. "Has someone been putting peas on the stove?[7] And who's stolen the ink and brush I had in this residence? Very odd! I could understand people taking rice or wine . . ." And again everyone laughed.

When the Empress Dowager was ill, Masahiro was sent from the Palace to inquire after her. When he came back, people asked which of her gentlemen-in-waiting had been present. He named a few people, four or five in all. "Was no one else there?" "Well, there were some others," replied Masahiro, "but they had all left." It is amazing that we could still laugh at him—so accustomed were we to hearing his foolishness.

One day when I was alone he came up to me and said, "My dear lady, I have something I must tell you at once—something that I've just heard." "And what may that be?" I asked. He approached my curtain.[8] "I heard someone who instead of saying, 'Bring your body closer,' used the phrase 'Bring up your five parts.'"[9] And again I burst into laughter.

On the middle night during the period of official appointments Masahiro was responsible for filling the lamps with oil. He rested his foot on the cloth under the pedestal of one of the lamps, and since the cloth happened to have been freshly oiled, his foot stuck to it. As soon as he started to walk off, the lamp fell over and, as he hurried along with the cloth stuck to his foot, the lamp dragged after him, making a terrible clatter.

One day when he thought he was alone in the Table Room, neither of the First Secretaries having reported for duty, Masahiro took a dish of beans that was lying there and went behind the Little Screen.[10] Suddenly someone pulled aside the screen—and there was Masahiro, stealthily munching away at the beans. Everyone who saw him was convulsed with laughter.[11]

---

7. **peas on the stove:** In Shōnagon's time, the image of peas popping in a stove was used to describe people in a hurry, but Masahiro's use of the expression is peculiar.

8. **curtain:** Masahiro is speaking to Shōnagon through a curtain. In feudal Japan, women of high society spent much of their time behind wooden screens hung with heavy curtains. The screens protected the women from being seen by men and strangers.

9. **five parts:** a Buddhist term referring to the knees, elbows, and head. When a person bowed and touched all "five parts" to the ground, it implied utmost respect.

10. **Little Screen:** In the royal palace in Kyoto, this separated the Imperial Dining Room from the Imperial Washing Room. It had a cat painted on one side, and birds and bamboo on the other.

11. **saw him . . . laughter:** Eating was a private business in Heian Japan—most aristocrats ate alone. Thus, Masahiro's behavior would seem strange and ludicrous to Shōnagon and other court members—almost like being caught without his clothes on.

Pleasing Things

Finding a large number of tales that one has not read before. Or acquiring the second volume of a tale whose first volume one has enjoyed. But often it is a disappointment.

Someone has torn up a letter and thrown it away. Picking up the pieces, one finds that many of them can be fitted together.

One has had an upsetting dream and wonders what it can mean. In great anxiety one consults a dream-interpreter, who informs one that it has no special significance.

A person of quality is holding forth about something in the past or about a recent event that is being widely discussed. Several people are gathered round him, but it is oneself that he keeps looking at as he talks.

A person who is very dear to one has fallen ill. One is miserably worried about him even if he lives in the capital and far more so if he is in some remote part of the country. What a pleasure to be told that he has recovered!

I am most pleased when I hear someone I love being praised or being mentioned approvingly by an important person.

A poem that someone has composed for a special occasion or written to another person in reply is widely praised and copied by people in their notebooks. Though this is something that has never yet happened to me, I can imagine how pleasing it must be.

A person with whom one is not especially <u>intimate</u> refers to an old poem or story that is unfamiliar. Then one hears it being mentioned by someone else and one has the pleasure of recognizing it. Still later, when one comes across it in a book, one thinks, "Ah, this is it!" and feels delighted with the person who first brought it up.

I feel very pleased when I have acquired some Michinoku paper, or some white, decorated paper, or even plain paper if it is nice and white.

A person in whose company one feels awkward asks one to supply the opening or

Crows and Plum Tree, and Rabbits and Pine Trees in Snow. (Detail) Katsu Jagyoku, Shin'enkan Collection, Los Angeles County Museum of Art

RABBITS AND CROWS IN THE NIGHT SNOW (one half of a screen), DAGYOKU SANJIN (1733–1778).

9 LITERARY ELEMENT

Characterization: Based on the passages about the "person of quality," the ill friend, and the person being praised, do you think Shōnagon was unselfish and loving or vain and selfish? Support your answer. (Accept reasonable responses.)

10 CULTURAL DIVERSITY

All Heian aristocrats were expected to be able to write poetry as well as to recognize and use allusions to Japanese and Chinese literature. Poetry-writing contests were a frequent recreation, and verse was the standard form of messages between friends or lovers. The writer's calligraphy, or handwriting, and the kind and color of paper used revealed the sender's character.
❓ *How important are letter- and poetry-writing today?* (Answers will vary.) ∎

HUMANITIES CONNECTION

Japanese painting was often done on screens, with each panel showing a discrete scene. This work in the "black and white" school of painting relies on contrast between light and dark rather than brilliant color for its effect.
❓ *How does the artist achieve the mottling of the tree bark?* (Possible response: by splashing dark splotches of ink against white paper) ∎

intimate (in'tə·mət): closely acquainted

1. In what period of Japanese history did Sei Shōnagon write *The Pillow Book*? (Heian)
2. Which of the following does Shōnagon not discuss in this selection: pleasing things, hateful things, terrifying things, or embarrassing things? (terrifying things)
3. Does Shōnagon prefer people of high rank or ordinary people? (people of high rank)

4. What piece of furniture usually separated males from females in medieval Japanese mansions? (a screen or curtain)
5. Does Shōnagon love, respect, pity, fear, or ridicule Masahiro? (ridicule)

RETEACHING
To reteach *The Pillow Book*, divide students into small groups. Ask each group to dramatize one amusing incident from "Masahiro Really Is a Laughing-Stock." Encourage students to use costumes and props and to incorporate the dialogue found in the selection. Call attention to how the punctuation signals pauses and how voice inflections can add humor to the various scenes.

---

11 INTERPRETING

What does Shōnagon's pleasure over "taking in" someone, "especially . . . a man" suggest about herself and her culture? (Possible responses: Some students may see the remark as vindictive: Shōnagon gloats because women in Heian culture were considered "inferior," an attitude she probably resented. Others may feel the remark reflects traditional male/female rivalry and could have been made in any culture.)

ANSWERS

First Thoughts
Answers will vary.

Identifying Facts
1. Possible responses: fireflies flitting to and fro and birds flying at sunset
2. Possible responses: his use of two servants, his secretly eating beans, and his getting the lamp stuck on his foot
3. Possible responses: when they talk loudly or make merry when she has a guest

Interpreting Meanings
1. She loves finding a new story, a good sequel, a lost book, and fine writing paper.
2. People of high rank dazzle Shōnagon. She gloats when a person of quality or the Empress notices her.
3. Possible responses: Shōnagon's remarks about parents' blindness to their children's flaws, talking to a sleeping companion, and unexpectedly meeting with the father of an estranged wife are witty.

586 Chinese and Japanese Literatures

---

closing line of a poem. If one happens to recall it, one is very pleased. Yet often on such occasions one completely forgets something that one would normally know.

I look for an object that I need at once, and I find it. Or again, there is a book that I must see immediately; I turn everything upside down, and there it is. What a joy!

When one is competing in an object match[12] (it does not matter what kind), how can one help being pleased at winning?

I greatly enjoy taking in someone who is pleased with himself and who has a self-confident look, especially if he is a man. It is amusing to observe him as he alertly waits for my next repartee;[13] but it is also interesting if he tries to put me off my guard by

---

12. **object match:** a kind of game in which teams of players competed to solve riddles about objects, such as flowers, seashells, birds, insects, and fans.
13. **repartee** (rep'ər·tē'): a quick, witty reply.

---

adopting an air of calm indifference as if there were not a thought in his head.

I realize that it is very sinful of me, but I cannot help being pleased when someone I dislike has a bad experience.

It is a great pleasure when the ornamental comb that one has ordered turns out to be pretty.

I am more pleased when something nice happens to a person I love than when it happens to myself.

Entering the Empress's room and finding that ladies-in-waiting are crowded round her in a tight group, I go next to a pillar which is some distance from where she is sitting. What a delight it is when Her Majesty summons me to her side so that all the others have to make way!

First Thoughts
Is Lady Shōnagon the sort of person you would like to have as a friend? Why or why not?

Identifying Facts
1. Point out two passages from "Things That Cannot Be Compared" and "In Spring It Is the Dawn" that highlight the beauty of the natural world. Which images are especially striking?
2. What three actions does Shōnagon offer as proof that Masahiro "really is a laughing-stock"?
3. In "Embarrassing Things," what conduct does Shōnagon find embarrassing in servants?

Interpreting Meanings
1. In "Pleasing Things," what role do reading and writing seem to play in Shōnagon's life? Cite at least four examples to support your view.
2. What is Shōnagon's attitude toward people of very high rank? Give two examples to support your opinion.
3. Give three examples of Shōnagon's **wit**, or verbal cleverness. In each example, identify what the wit reveals about Shōnagon's insightfulness, playfulness, or even spitefulness.
4. What are two positive and two negative aspects of human nature implied in "Pleasing Things" and "Hateful Things"?

1. **Creating a Pillow Book.** Compile a class pillow book, including responses to the seasons, amusing incidents, character sketches, and students' personal lists. Students with artistic talent might contribute illustrations or copy the manuscript in calligraphy. If possible, have students examine *The Pillow Book Scroll*, a fourteenth-century work depicting many of Shōnagon's incidents.

2. **Research Project.** Perhaps one of your students was fascinated by the references to music in Heian culture. Encourage such students to pursue these or other special interests. Reports might focus on government, family life, clothing, architecture, technology, the calendar, agriculture, or trade. Students might refer to *The World of the Shining Prince*, a study of Heian Japan by Ivan Morris.

Lady Murasaki, whose life and work are discussed on page 588, rather haughtily noted in her diary that Sei Shōnagon indulged herself in *The Pillow Book*, giving free rein to her emotional whims and sampling every interesting thing that came along. Ask the class whether they agree with Lady Murasaki's assessment. Do they find *The Pillow Book* to be the undisciplined musings of a frivolous person, or a serious, well-observed memoir? ■

---

5. Which contrasts in "Things That Cannot Be Compared" are most obvious? Why? Which contrasts might be the least obvious to observers? Why?

Applying Meanings

For centuries, people in many different cultures have used journals and other forms of private writing to express thoughts and beliefs that they may not have been able to convey in any other way. What do you think are the values of keeping a journal or some other form of private writing? What could a person learn by keeping some form of diary or journal?

Creative Writing Response

Creating a List. *The Pillow Book* is full of Shōnagon's lists of everything from "Different Ways of Speaking" and "Things That Fall from the Sky" to "Depressing Things" and "Things That Should Be Large." Create your own list of things, people, or situations that are connected in some way. For example, you could write a list of habits that annoy you, jobs you'd never want to take, things that look better in the dark, or situations that make you squirm. Write spontaneously and lightheartedly, as Shōnagon did. Try to make some of your entries witty and clever by using sarcasm, humor, or wordplay. Don't be afraid to show your personality and opinions in your writing.

Critical Writing Response

Writing a Character Sketch. *The Pillow Book* reveals as much about Lady Shōnagon as it does about Japanese court life. Write a two- or three-paragraph essay describing what kind of person you think Shōnagon was, based on inferences you have drawn from the excerpts you have read. Be sure to support your assessment of her character with specific examples from *The Pillow Book*.

Language and Vocabulary

The Active Voice

A sentence may be written in either the **active** or the **passive** voice. In a sentence written in the active voice, the subject performs the action, as in "Masahiro filled the lamps." In a sentence written in the passive voice, the subject receives the action of the verb, as in "The lamps were filled by Masahiro."

Most writers prefer the active voice because it is more direct than the passive voice. It emphasizes the role of the person or thing performing the action. It is also usually more concise than the passive voice.

Rewrite the following sentences in the active voice:
1. A light was seen by them in the distance.
2. Anna was told by the music teacher that she had great talent.
3. The ground is covered by fallen snow.
4. The letter was snatched from her hand by Thomas.
5. The blueberry pie had been eaten by the dog.

---

4. *Positive aspects:* People are pleased when an ill loved one has recovered or when something nice happens to a loved one. *Negative aspects:* People are pleased when unpleasant things happen to people they dislike. Unqualified people often pretend to be authorities.
5. Contrasts between elements of nature are most obvious because one can perceive them. The contrast between the beloved person before and after one has stopped loving him is least obvious, because it is an emotional change.

Applying Meanings
Possible responses: to record one's observations, to clarify one's thoughts and feelings, and to explore the meaning of one's experience

Creative Writing Response
Creating a List. Lists should include items linked by a similar effect on the writer.

Critical Writing Response
Writing a Character Sketch. Essays might show that Shōnagon is intelligent, snobbish, witty, and sensitive to beauty.

Language and Vocabulary
1. They saw a light in the distance. 2. The music teacher told Anna that she had great talent. 3. The snow fell and covered the ground. 4. Thomas snatched the letter from her hand. 5. The dog ate the blueberry pie. ■

LITERARY BACKGROUND

Lady Murasaki: Not much is known about Lady Murasaki, despite the fact that her extensive diary has survived. It remains unclear, for example, what her real name was. "Shikibu," an official title, was held at one point by her father, and her friends started calling her "Murasaki," which means "purple," after one of the main characters in her masterpiece.

Lady Murasaki's date of birth is also unknown. From her diary it can be determined, however, that in 998 or 999 she was married to a distant kinsman and that he died in an epidemic just a few years later. She was a widow when she received her court appointment, and, like Sei Shōnagon, author of *The Pillow Book*, she remained in the service of the Empress for many years.

At the Imperial Court, rivalries between courtesans flourished. For instance, in her diary, Murasaki, who was fluent in Chinese, took pleasure in noting that Shōnagon wrote badly in that language:

> She thought herself so clever, and littered her writings with Chinese characters, but if you examined them closely, they left a great deal to be desired.

The intrigues of feudal court life make up much of *The Tale of Genji*. By the time Murasaki finished her masterpiece about Prince Genji, it spanned fifty-four huge chapters, covering roughly three-quarters of a century in its narrative. ■

BEHIND THE SCENES

Lady Murasaki's Triumph

Sei Shōnagon's contemporary and rival was Lady Murasaki Shikibu (moo′rä·sä′kē shē′kē·boo′), one of the most celebrated writers of the Heian era. Murasaki wrote what is widely regarded as the world's first true novel, *The Tale of Genji*. The sprawling epic recounts the adventures of Genji, the handsome, sensitive, and talented young son of a Japanese emperor. The genius of the tale lies in the author's deep insight into human emotions and motivations. Lady Murasaki's novel is one of the earliest examples of psychological realism ever written. Her achievement is all the more remarkable considering that, at the time she lived, very little prose was written in Japan, as poetry was the favored form.

By all accounts, Lady Murasaki was an extraordinary woman, far more educated than most upper-class men of her generation. Her father, a minor government official and member of a powerful clan, lamented the fact that his brilliant child seemed destined to waste her talents because she was not born a man. He need not have worried. When Murasaki was in her late twenties, she was appointed to serve in the royal court of the reigning emperor. While at court, her skills blossomed in the presence of a brilliant circle of painters, dancers, and poets, many of them women. Murasaki's observations of Heian court intrigues feature prominently in *Genji*, the most vivid prose work to come from medieval Japan.

SuperStock International

THE LADY FUJITSUBO WATCHING PRINCE GENJI DEPARTING IN THE MOONLIGHT, ANDŌ HIROSHIGE (1797–1858) AND U. TOYOKUNI (1769–1825).

Zen Parables

Zen Monk, Japan.

Zen is difficult to describe. It is a sect of Buddhism, but it is less a religion than a form of Buddhist meditative practice. It has no holy book, no ornate church, no complicated ritual. Zen monks do not preach sermons about right and wrong behavior. Zen focuses on the inner self, rather than on the outer self that acts in the world. Yet for eight hundred years, Zen has exerted a strong appeal to Japanese warriors as well as monks, to politicians as well as artists. Today, it is practiced by businesspeople who use its principles to relieve stress and focus their minds on essential priorities.

The Philosophy of Zen

The object of Zen is to free the mind from everyday, conventional logic through medi-tation. Followers of Zen believe that medi-tation empties the mind and suppresses the ego, leading to a clearer understanding of one's own nature. According to one legend, Bodhidharma, a famous Zen monk, gazed at a blank wall for nine years before achieving inner enlightenment.

Monks and Warriors

Originating in India and spreading to China, Zen Buddhism was introduced to Japan in 1191. Zen monasteries were soon founded in Kamakura and Kyoto. During the Kama-kura period (1185–1333), the samurai, the warriors who served the aristocracy, were attracted to Zen by its discipline and sim-plicity. They applied Zen principles to mar-tial arts such as archery and fencing.

Virtually every aspect of Japanese culture was influenced by Zen. Because Zen monks drank bitter green tea in order to stay awake during meditation, tea drinking grew into a lengthy and symbol-laden ritual. The arts also felt the impact of Zen, as manifested in the stylized formality of the Noh drama (see page 596) and the conciseness of haiku po-etry (see page 572). Nearly every art form of classical Japan—painting, poetry, dance, ar-chitecture, drama, and gardening—has been influenced by Zen, with its emphasis on sim-plicity, self-discipline, and meditation. Even the expressions of everyday speech in Japan draw from this austere religion.

1 HISTORICAL BACKGROUND

Buddhism was first introduced in Japan in the sixth century when the king of Paekche in Korea sent a picture of the Buddha and his sacred writ-ings, explaining that they rep-resented a doctrine that would lead to a complete apprecia-tion of the loftiest wisdom. The Japanese government at that time soon declared Bud-dhism the official religion of Japan, and many different Buddhist sects have developed over the centuries. When Zen was introduced in 1191, Japan was ruled by the Minamoto (mē·nä·mō′tō) clan, a powerful military aristocracy that ruled from Kamakura (kä′mä·koo′rä), near modern Tokyo.

2 CULTURAL BACKGROUND

The study of Zen Buddhism continues in Japan today. In a serene temple near Yokohama, you will find a row of black-clad men with shaved heads sitting cross-legged on straw mats, staring intently at a wall and learning *zazen*, the art of meditation. In order to be-come a Zen Buddhist monk, a novice must maintain this pos-ture for several hours a day, with only a few short breaks for exercise, meals, and chores. When the novices be-gin to doze, attendants keep them alert by rapping them with a flat wooden "awaken-ing" stick. Even school chil-dren engage in weekly half-hour instruction in *zazen*.

OBJECTIVES

1. *To recognize the characteristics of Zen parables*
2. *To analyze the elements of a Zen parable*
3. *To write a parable containing a paradox*
4. *To act out a parable*

PREREADING FOCUS

Background: Many conversations between the great Zen master, Dogen (1200–1253), and his students were recorded by his pupil, Ejo. In one conversation, Dogen explains enlightenment:

> Our attainment of enlightenment is something like the reflection of the moon in water. The moon does not get wet, nor is the water cleft apart. Though the light of the moon is vast and immense, it finds a home in water only a foot long and an inch wide. The whole moon and the whole sky find room enough in a single dewdrop, a single drop of water. And just as the moon does not cleave the water apart, so enlightenment does not tear man apart.

You may wish to have students spend five minutes freewriting their responses to this passage.

Oral Response: Ask students to state the lessons that their parables or fables offer. You might also have them relate personal experiences that illustrate the wisdom of the lessons. If some students are unfamiliar with the parables or fables mentioned, arrange a storytelling session in which students can share their favorites.

Reader's Guide

ZEN PARABLES

Background

Zen parables are deceptively simple stories originally used to teach aspiring monks about Buddhism. The relationship between a Zen monk and his teacher is an extraordinary one. Instead of imparting facts in a clear and logical way, the Zen master first tries to confuse his students, to force them to abandon all preconceived notions of what knowledge is. This technique prepares them to understand the parables.

To intimidate his students, the master may assume a fierce expression and a cold demeanor. He may ask a pupil a question and then interrupt the pupil halfway through his answer. He may pose what appear to be ridiculous questions, such as "What did your face look like before you were born?" Or he may command students to perform seemingly impossible tasks: "Pull a bird out of your sleeve." (An advanced student might respond by folding a sheet of paper into the shape of a bird.) The master might answer a serious question with an absurd response. If the pupil asks, "What is the nature of the Buddha?" his master might reply, "Pass me that fan!" or "Pork dumpling!"

A Zen master behaves this way in part to make a student wary of language. Words, according to Zen, are dangerous, for they can prevent people from experiencing the world directly.

Oral Response

As a class, compile a list of stories that you are familiar with that teach a lesson—perhaps parables from the Bible or fables. How did you determine their messages? Do any have similar messages?

Literary Focus

A **parable** is a brief allegorical story that teaches a moral, or lesson about life. Parables are a form of didactic literature. The most famous parables in Western literature are those told by Jesus in the New Testament (see page 198). Jesus presented moral lessons in short tales about events in everyday life—for example, a stray sheep or a spendthrift son. Many Zen stories, like the biblical parables, are also deceptively simple tales that contain profound truths.

ZEN PARABLES

translated by

PAUL REPS

TEACHER'S RESOURCES

- ✔ Review and Response Worksheet
- ✔ Selection Test
- ✔ Vocabulary Activity Worksheet
- ✔ Vocabulary Test
- ✔ Language Skills Worksheet

In addition to their entertainment value, each of these Zen parables contains a moral lesson. After each story, see if you can write the moral in a sentence or two.

Art Resource, New York

Painting of a Zen monk, Japanese.

Muddy Road

Tanzan and Ekido[1] were once traveling together down a muddy road. A heavy rain was still falling.

Coming around a bend, they met a lovely girl in a silk kimono[2] and sash, unable to cross the intersection.

"Come on, girl," said Tanzan at once. Lifting her in his arms, he carried her over the mud.

Ekido did not speak again until that night when they reached a lodging temple. Then he no longer could restrain himself. "We monks don't go near females," he told Tanzan, "especially not young and lovely ones. It is dangerous. Why did you do that?"

"I left the girl there," said Tanzan. "Are you still carrying her?"

A Parable

Buddha told a parable in a sutra:[3]

A man traveling across a field encountered a tiger. He fled, the tiger after him. Coming to a precipice, he caught hold of the root of

---

1. **Tanzan** (tän'zän') **and Ekido** (e·kē'dō)
2. **kimono:** a wide-sleeved robe, fastened with a sash; part of the traditional costume for men and women in Japan.
3. **sutra** (soo'trə): one of a collection of stories that describe the teachings of the Buddha.

ABOUT THE COMPILER

The five Zen parables included here were first written down by a Zen master named Muju (moo·joo) during the thirteenth century, but they may be much older. Muju's most famous collection of parables is called *Shasekishu,* or *Sand and Pebbles.* For most of his life, he lived in a small temple near the modern city of Nagoya. Muju is especially known for his funny parables about ordinary situations.

CULTURAL BACKGROUND

Zen means "meditation" or "concentration." The study of Zen is meant to lead to inner tranquility and enlightenment, but there is no one final or ultimate goal. Zen is not a path leading toward one revelation or insight; rather, Zen represents a process of continual awakening.

 precipice (pres'i·pis): a steep cliff

HUMANITIES CONNECTION

Ryuanji Temple is one of the many Buddhist temples in Kyoto, Japan. The placement of the rocks and the carefully raked sand and pebbles are said to calm the viewer and promote a meditative state. ■

COMPARING LITERATURE

As with tanka and haiku, readers must draw their own lessons or meanings from the Zen parables. While some of the morals seem obvious, many of the parables have more than one level of meaning. Have students compare and contrast the lessons of the Zen parables with the parables from the New Testament (pp. 199–202).

❓ *Which parables do you find easier to understand? Why?*

1 INTERPRETING

What is surprising about the man's eating the strawberry at the end of the parable? (Possible response: He seems to have forgotten his dangerous situation.) What moral does this parable illustrate? (Possible responses: We appreciate sensual pleasures more when it appears we may lose them, or we must live so fully in the moment that we can appreciate small things even in the face of death.)

Ryoanji Temple's rock garden. *The Japanese rock garden, carefully created out of rock and sand, is an expression of the Zen concept of God.*

Shostal Associates/SuperStock International

a wild vine and swung himself down over the edge. The tiger sniffed at him from above. Trembling, the man looked down to where, far below, another tiger was waiting to eat him. Only the vine sustained him.

Two mice, one white and one black, little by little started to gnaw away the vine. The man saw a luscious strawberry near him. Grasping the vine with one hand, he plucked the strawberry with the other. How sweet it tasted!

Publishing the Sutras

Tetsugen,[4] a devotee of Zen in Japan, decided to publish the sutras, which at that time were available only in Chinese. The books were to be printed with wood blocks in an edition of seven thousand copies, a tremendous undertaking.

Tetsugen began by traveling and collecting donations for this purpose. A few sympathizers would give him a hundred pieces of gold, but most of the time he received only small coins. He thanked each donor with equal gratitude. After ten years Tetsugen had enough money to begin his task.

It happened that at that time the Uji River[5] overflowed. Famine followed. Tetsugen took the funds he had collected for the books and spent them to save others from starvation. Then he began again his work of collecting.

Several years afterwards an epidemic spread over the country. Tetsugen again gave away what he had collected, to help his people.

For a third time he started his work, and after twenty years his wish was fulfilled. The printing blocks which produced the first edi-

---

4. **Tetsugen** (tet·sŏo′gen)

5. **Uji** (ŏo′jē′) **River**: a minor river near Kyoto on the Japanese island of Honshu.

tion of sutras can be seen today in the Obaku[6] monastery in Kyoto.

The Japanese tell their children that Tetsugen made three sets of sutras, and that the first two invisible sets surpass even the last.

The Thief Who Became a Disciple

One evening as Shichiri Kojun[7] was reciting sutras a thief with a sharp sword entered, demanding either his money or his life.

Shichiri told him: "Do not disturb me. You can find the money in that drawer." Then he resumed his recitation.

A little while afterwards he stopped and called: "Don't take it all. I need some to pay taxes with tomorrow."

The intruder gathered up most of the money and started to leave. "Thank a person when you receive a gift," Shichiri added. The man thanked him and made off.

A few days afterwards the fellow was caught and confessed, among others, the offense against Shichiri. When Shichiri was called as a witness he said: "This man is no thief, at least as far as I am concerned. I gave him the money and he thanked me for it."

After he had finished his prison term, the man went to Shichiri and became his disciple.

The Taste of Banzo's Sword

Matajuro Yagyu[8] was the son of a famous swordsman. His father, believing that his son's work was too mediocre to anticipate mastership, disowned him.

So Matajuro went to Mount Futara[9] and there found the famous swordsman Banzo.[10] But Banzo confirmed the father's judgment. "You wish to learn swordsmanship under my guidance?" asked Banzo. "You cannot fulfill the requirements."

"But if I work hard, how many years will it take me to become a master?" persisted the youth.

"The rest of your life," replied Banzo.

"I cannot wait that long," explained Matajuro. "I am willing to pass through any hardship if only you will teach me. If I become your devoted servant, how long might it be?"

"Oh, maybe ten years," Banzo relented.

"My father is getting old, and soon I must take care of him," continued Matajuro. "If I work far more intensively, how long would it take me?"

"Oh, maybe thirty years," said Banzo.

"Why is that?" asked Matajuro. "First you say ten and now thirty years. I will undergo any hardship to master this art in the shortest time!"

"Well," said Banzo, "in that case you will have to remain with me for seventy years. A man in such a hurry as you are to get results seldom learns quickly."

"Very well," declared the youth, understanding at last that he was being rebuked for impatience, "I agree."

Matajuro was told never to speak of fencing and never to touch a sword. He cooked for his master, washed the dishes, made his bed, cleaned the yard, cared for the garden, all without a word of swordsmanship.

Three years passed. Still Matajuro labored on. Thinking of his future, he was sad. He

---

6. **Obaku** (ō·bä′kōō)
7. **Shichiri Kojun** (shē·chē′rē kō′jun)
8. **Matajuro Yagyu** (mä·tä·jōō′rō yäg′ū)
9. **Mount Futara** (fōō·ta′ra)
10. **Banzo** (bän′zō)

1. What happens when Ekido and Tanzan meet a girl in a rainstorm? (Tanzan carries the girl over the muddy road.)
2. How do the mice pose a danger in "A Parable"? (They gnaw at the vine to which the man is clinging.)
3. In "Publishing the Sutras," why does Tetsugen travel through the country? (to collect donations to print the sutras)
4. Whose disciple does the thief become in "The Thief Who Became a Disciple"? (Shichiri's)
5. What does Matajuro do for his master Banzo for three years? (acts as his servant)

7 INTERPRETING

What might an aspiring samurai learn from this parable? (Possible responses: The student must be completely humble. Defense, not offense, is the crucial skill in swordsmanship, and it can be achieved only through patience, alertness, and concentration.)

HUMANITIES CONNECTION

Of all the woodblock artists of the eighteenth and nineteenth centuries, Hiroshige is probably the best loved in Japan and the best known in the West.

The names of the most famous Japanese swordmakers are as well known in Japan as the names of famous painters, poets, and historic figures. Scholars divide sword blades into two classes. Those produced before 1660 are designated *koto*, or old swords; those made after that time are referred to as *shinto*, or new swords. The skills and precise calculations that went into tempering sword blades were priceless professional secrets handed down from father to son or from master to pupil. ■

had not even begun to learn the art to which he had devoted his life.

But one day Banzo crept up behind him and gave him a terrific blow with a wooden sword.

The following day, when Matajuro was cooking rice, Banzo again sprang upon him unexpectedly.

After that, day and night, Matajuro had to defend himself from unexpected thrusts. Not a moment passed in any day that he did not have to think of the taste of Banzo's sword.

He learned so rapidly he brought smiles to the face of his master. Matajuro became the greatest swordsman in the land.

SWORDSMAN AND SPEARMAN FIGHTING, ANDŌ HIROSHIGE (1797–1858).
Do you agree with Banzo's observation that someone in a hurry to learn will not *learn quickly*?

Victoria & Albert Museum, London/Art Resource, New York

1. Creating an Anthology of Modern Parables. Ask pairs of students to select a story from a newspaper that could be used to teach a lesson or moral. Then ask them to write a parable, using events and characters from the newspaper article to make their moral point. Have students share their completed parables by first reading them aloud to the class and then collecting the parables into a class anthology.

2. Research Project. Today, books with titles like *The Zen of Seeing, Zen to Go, Zen Flesh, Zen Bones,* and even *Zen and the Art of Motorcycle Maintenance* fill the shelves of American bookstores. Some students may wish to report to the class on recent literature that applies Zen teachings to contemporary American life. Students can also test the usefulness of Zen in their own daily lives, and report their conclusions.

CLOSURE

Have students discuss parables that have a useful lesson they can apply to their own lives. In addition, invite students from different cultural backgrounds to share parables from their own cultures with their classmates. Have students discuss the lesson of each parable and how it might apply to their present lives. Then lead the class to compare and contrast the values represented by the parables they have shared. ■

First Thoughts
Would you prefer these parables to have explicitly stated meanings or morals? Why or why not?

Identifying Facts
1. Who are Tanzan and Ekido? For what does Ekido criticize Tanzan in "Muddy Road"?
2. Name all the dangers that the man in "A Parable" faces.
3. What events slow the monk Tetsugen's attempts to publish a Japanese edition of the sutras in "Publishing the Sutras"?
4. In "The Thief Who Became a Disciple," what does Shichiri testify in court?
5. In "The Taste of Banzo's Sword," why does Matajuro become sad working with the master, Banzo?

Interpreting Meanings
1. In "Muddy Road," what does Tanzan mean when he asks Ekido if he is still carrying the girl?
2. In "A Parable," what might the precipice, the tigers, and the mice **symbolize**, or stand for? What is the significance of the man eating the strawberry? What lesson about life do you think this **parable** teaches?
3. According to "Publishing the Sutras," the Japanese tell their children that Tetsugen's two "invisible" editions of the sutras were superior to the actual books. What point do you think this statement makes?
4. Why do you think the thief becomes the disciple of Shichiri Kojun? What values does this **parable** teach?
5. Describe Banzo's unconventional teaching methods. What do you think he is teaching Matajuro about the art of swordsmanship?

Applying Meanings
Each of the parables you have just read teaches a lesson about life. Which parable seems most relevant to a situation in your own life? Explain. Do you disagree with the lessons taught by any of these parables?

Creative Writing Response
Writing a Parable. Many Zen parables contain a **paradox**, an apparent contradiction that is actually true. For instance, the notion that the best way to reform a thief is to thank him for stealing is a paradox. Think for a few minutes about how a seeming contradiction can ultimately prove true, keeping in mind some of the Zen parables you have read. Then write a brief parable of your own about one of the following paradoxical situations:
1. A person who becomes rich by giving something away
2. A competition that is won through losing
3. An enemy who becomes a friend when he or she is trusted
4. A dangerous situation that changes when a person stops feeling fear
5. A difficult task that becomes easy when a person stops trying hard

Speaking and Listening
Acting Out a Parable. Many Zen parables express universal truths. Pair off with another student and choose a Zen parable that you have read and enjoyed. See if you can adapt it to a modern setting and situation without losing the moral. For instance, you could adapt "The Taste of Banzo's Sword" by making Banzo a baseball coach who teaches his students by throwing balls at them when they least expect it. Then, with your partner, create a script in which you enact the parable. Perform your parable for the rest of the class.

ANSWERS

First Thoughts
Answers will vary.

Identifying Facts
1. monks; for carrying the girl
2. tigers, precipice, mice
3. a famine and an epidemic
4. The money was a gift for which he was thanked.
5. He regrets not studying swordsmanship.

Interpreting Meanings
1. Tanzan wonders if Ekido is still thinking about the girl.
2. challenges or dangers of life. Giving in to desires or savoring life's pleasures. We appreciate things we are about to lose, or we are too easily distracted by sensual pleasures.
3. Actions are greater than words; helping people comes before study.
4. Shichiri's lesson lets him see himself in a new way. Treat people with respect; material things do not matter.
5. Banzo refuses to teach for years and then attacks Matajuro unawares. The student must be humble and alert.

Applying Meanings
Students should analyze events from their own lives.

Creative Writing Response
Writing a Parable. Students should use plausible details to illustrate the paradox.

Speaking and Listening
Acting Out a Parable. Encourage students to choose a parable that is especially meaningful to them. ■

*I*ntroduction

Noh Plays

Noh (nō) is the great dramatic art of medieval Japan. In Japanese, Noh is written with a Chinese character,

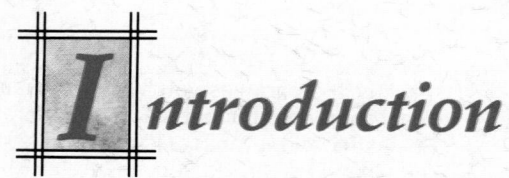

which signifies "talent." Indeed, the actors who perform Noh plays must be talented mimes and dancers as well as skilled interpreters of character. They must also be able to convey a mood or feeling in a single word or gesture. The power of Noh, with its emphasis on the spiritual, lies in its ability to convey emotions subtly and create a mood of otherworldly silence.

The Noh Tradition

Noh was developed in fourteenth-century Japan, at about the same time that the Italian poet Dante Alighieri was writing *The Divine Comedy* (see page 742). Like Dante's poems, Noh plays have religious sources. They are strongly influenced by Zen, the meditative Buddhist religion.

◆

Noh (nō): *a classic Japanese dramatic form that incorporates music, dance, and mime.*

By the mid-fourteenth century, Noh had become popular with the Japanese royalty. Under the patronage of powerful shoguns and samurai, Noh texts became increasingly complex. They were embroidered with so many historical and literary allusions that they became almost unintelligible to common folk. Yet the best Noh plays, particularly those composed by the actor, critic, and playwright Seami Motokiyo (zā·ä'mē mō·tō·kē'yō), strike deep chords and are still performed today.

The Granger Collection, New York

Japanese Noh mask, c. 1400s. *The wearing of masks is traditional in Japanese Noh drama.*

Noh robe. *Artisans had to innovate to produce the elaborate cloth used for Noh robes.*

Masks, Flutes, and Drums

Noh plays are formal and stylized. They are performed on a small stage, about eighteen by eighteen feet. The stage is bare, save for a symbolic pine tree and pillars. Musicians and a chorus flank the main stage. The actors are few, and they are always male. Most of them wear heavy robes and hand-painted wooden masks that represent a particular character or emotion: a vengeful ghost, a holy man, a beautiful girl, a warrior, a wrathful serpent-woman. The masks muffle the voices of the actors, giving them an unreal, otherworldly quality. The chorus consists of eight or ten singers who never take part in the action of the play. Instead, they echo a principal actor's words or speak for him as he dances or mimes an action.

Priests and Ghosts

Each Noh drama involves two principal actors. The first is a restless ghost, or spirit, called the *shite* (shtā), who has assumed the form of an ordinary person. The second actor is a bystander, or *waki* (wä′kē′), who is often a wandering priest. The *waki* poses some questions to the spirit, who is typically plagued by disturbing memories of passion or injustice from his or her past life. The *waki's* questions inspire the *shite* to unburden his soul and reveal his true identity. One of the most common themes in Noh drama involves the *shite's* release from the suffering he or she is feeling in death.

A Stylized Dramatic Form

Noh plays were traditionally staged in groups of five, with the first performance beginning in the morning and the last ending long after dark.

Unlike most Western plays, Noh dramas have sketchy plots, the characters are flat and one-dimensional, and time and space are treated in an unrealistic way. A span of several years may be distilled into one motion of a fan, or a single moment of joy or pain may be expressed in a lengthy dance. Noh thrives on such contradictions. Indeed, some of the most acclaimed moments in Noh plays are those in which nothing happens at all. The most difficult role in Noh drama is that of a *shite* who sits—masked, silent, and motionless—for an hour and a half. Somehow the actor must convey his emotions through the sheer force of his will.

Seami's twenty-one treatises on Noh drama were extremely important in the development of Noh, and they have been equally important in contemporary scholars' understanding of Noh. In one essay about the art of Noh, Seami defined the perfect actor as "he who can win certain praise alike in palaces, temples, or villages, or even at festivals held in the shrines of the remotest provinces. . . ."

ABOUT THE TRANSLATOR

Arthur Waley. See *The Book of Songs*.

HUMANITIES CONNECTION

Makers of Noh masks sought to express the essential quality of each character in a Noh drama—whether humble, fierce, noble, or tragic. Although the masks were carved to represent types, the great skill of the sculptor, combined with the performer's acting techniques, resulted in masks that seemed to change facial expressions, depending on the way light struck them. ■

Seami Motokiyo
c. 1363–1443

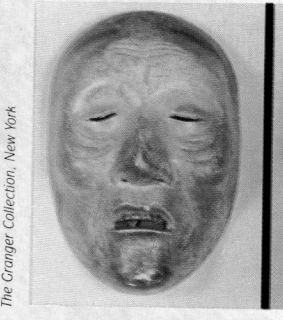
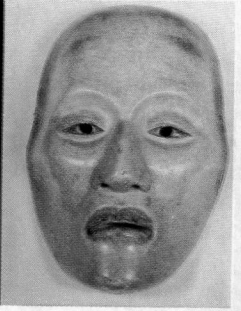

The Granger Collection, New York

Two Japanese Noh masks. *Noh masks, which represent certain emotions or supernatural qualities, are often masterpieces of sculpture.*

Seami Motokiyo had acting in his blood, for his father Kanami (kä'nä·mē'), a priest, was one of the finest performers of his day. At the time of Seami's birth in 1363, Noh was still an unrefined art—more chants and dances than true drama. Under the patronage of the shogun Ashikaga Yoshimitsu (äsh·ē·kä'gä yō·shē·mē'tsoō), this began to change. Ashikaga, a Zen convert and passionate devotee of the arts, brought various performers, including Seami's father, to live at his palace in Kyoto. He was particularly fond of young Seami and personally supervised the boy's education.

Seami's training in Noh began very early, probably around the time he was seven years old. Five years later, he was performing at court. At the age of twenty, not long after his father's death, he took over his father's acting school and began to write plays. At least two dozen of the best Noh dramas are attributed to Seami.

We know very little of Seami's personal life. Some say he became a Zen priest late in life; others say he had two sons, both of them actors. After Ashikaga's death in 1408, Seami lost favor at court and was eventually exiled for a period of time in 1434. According to legend, this brilliant and versatile figure of Noh drama died alone at the age of eighty-one in a Buddhist temple near Kyoto.

Seami was the main theorist and a noted critic of Noh drama in his time. In fact, many of the scant details we know of Seami's life come from the treatises on the Noh theater he wrote for his students. By all accounts, Seami, like his father, was a brilliant actor. His performances were said to have been graceful, restrained, and mysterious. He strove to invest his students with the same qualities, encouraging them to act purely for the fun of it in the beginning of their training at the age of six or seven, then work hard for the next fifteen or twenty years to achieve mastery of three basic roles: the warrior, the woman, and the old man. Like the practice of Zen, mastery of Noh was a lifelong task requiring immense discipline.

OBJECTIVES

1. *To recognize the characteristics of Japanese Noh drama*
2. *To identify the qualities of flat and round characters and analyze their differences*
3. *To compare aspects of Noh drama with those of Western drama*
4. *To recognize an oxymoron and create original oxymorons*

THEMES IN WORLD LITERATURE

Life and Loss
From ''The Tragedy of Sohráb and Rostám'' from the *Shahname*, pp. 646–653
''How Siegfried Was Slain'' from the *Nibelungenlied*, pp. 730–740

War and Peace
''The Fall of Troy'' from the *Aeneid*, pp. 379–408
''Funeral Speech of Pericles,'' pp. 284–292
From the *Song of Roland*, pp. 692–702 ∎

Reader's Guide

ATSUMORI

Background

Atsumori (ä·tsōō·mō′rē) is one of Seami's most famous plays. It is drawn from an episode of *The Tale of the Heike* (hā′kə), a medieval Japanese epic based on historical fact that tells the story of the rise and fall of the Taira family, otherwise known as the Heike. The epic describes how the Taira are vanquished by a rival clan, the Minamoto (or Genji) family, the same Genji family of Lady Murasaki's *The Tale of Genji* (see page 588).

The Heike suffered one of their most terrible defeats at a place by the sea called Ichi no tani. The play takes place many years after this battle. A priest named Rensei, who was once a warrior with the Genji clan, has decided to return to the scene of the battle to pray for a sixteen-year-old named Atsumori, whom he killed on the beach that terrible day. Rensei had taken pity on Atsumori and had almost refrained from killing him. He realized, though, that if he did not kill the boy, his fellow warriors would. He explained to Atsumori that he must kill him, and promised to pray for his soul.

When Rensei reaches Ichi no tani years later, he meets two peasants who are returning home from their fields. It is dusk, and one of them is playing a flute. This reminds the priest of Atsumori, who was carrying a flute when he died. Rensei soon makes an astonishing discovery about one of the peasants.

Writer's Response

Rensei regrets his slaying of Atsumori so much that he spends the rest of his life trying to atone for his deed. Think of a time in your life when you regretted something you did. How did you try to make up for it?

Literary Focus

The characters in *Atsumori* are **flat**—that is, they possess only one or two visible traits. **Flat characters** contrast with **round characters**, who, like real people, gradually reveal complex, often conflicting qualities. Flat characters do not seem realistic to us, and yet in some cases a writer may have a good reason for creating them. Some one-dimensional characters, for instance, may function as symbols of emotions or universal human qualities, such as repentance, anger, or wisdom.

PREREADING FOCUS

Background: The set, costumes, masks, and acting style all contribute to the symbolic quality of the Noh drama. The movements of the actors are suggestive, not realistic as in most Western drama. If an actor hits his knee with one hand, he means to show excitement. If he takes three steps forward, he wants to indicate that his travels have come to an end.

In Seami's early writings, he placed value on realistic representation, or *monamare*. However, as his dramatic theories developed, he moved farther and farther away from the idea of theater as imitation. Instead he pursued the concept of *yugen*, or beauty, and that idea became the ultimate goal of Noh drama.

Writer's Response: You might encourage responses by assuring students that their examples will remain private.

CULTURAL DIVERSITY
Noh plays frequently quote and make allusions to classical Japanese poetry. Because of the knowledge of poetic tradition required of an audience, the Noh was most appreciated by the aristocracy until the sixteenth century, when drama was written to appeal to the less educated population.

? *Do you think that audiences today must be highly educated to appreciate theater in the United States?*

COMPARING LITERATURE
Scholars have compared Noh drama to giant haiku. In the original Japanese, Noh plays are written in alternating lines of five and seven syllables.

? *What other characteristics do Noh and haiku share?* (Possible responses: simplicity, evocativeness, strict structure)

1 DRAMATIC ELEMENT
Cast of Characters: How many major characters are there? (two) Who might be the *waki*? (Priest Rensei) Who might be the *shite*? (a young reaper/ghost of Atsumori)

ATSUMORI
Seami Motokiyo
translated by
ARTHUR WALEY

‖ *As you read this play, pay attention to the techniques of the Noh drama that were described in the introduction. Try to imagine what effect these techniques would have on the audience watching the play.*

Fenollosa–Weld Collection, Courtesy of Museum of Fine Arts, Boston

NIGHT ATTACK ON THE SANJO PALACE, c. 1250, artist unknown.

1

PERSONS

The Priest Rensei (ren'sā), formerly the warrior Kumagai of the Genji clan

A Young Reaper, who turns out to be the ghost of

Atsumori (ä·tsōō·mō'rē), a young warrior of the (Taira) Heike clan

His Companion

Chorus

Inverted Word Order

Dramatists use inverted word order for two reasons. Like the Noh mask, costumes, and acting style, it can help create a formal or stylized tone in a play. This tone can distance an audience from a drama, calling attention to the play as art rather than a replication of real life.

Writers also invert word order to emphasize particular words, thoughts, or observations through sentence structure. Examples from *Atsumori*:

. . . this I have done because of my grief . . . Happy am I, for though you know not my name, . . .

Speaking and Listening. Have pairs of students locate three examples of inverted word order in the Noh play. Have them rewrite the sentences to sound like ordinary speech. Finally, have them read the original and rewritten sentences aloud to each other and compare their effects. ■

Priest.

2

Life is a lying dream, he only wakes
Who casts the world aside.

I am Kumagai no Naozane, a man of the country of
Musashi. I have left my home and call myself the
priest Rensei; this I have done because of my grief
at the death of Atsumori, who fell in battle by my
hand. Hence it comes that I am dressed in priestly
guise.

And now I am going down to Ichi no tani[1] to pray
for the salvation of Atsumori's soul.

[*He walks slowly across the stage, singing a song descriptive of his journey.*]

3

I have come so fast that here I am already at Ichi no
tani, in the country of Tsu.

Truly the past returns to my mind as though it were
a thing of today.

But listen! I hear the sound of a flute coming from a
knoll of rising ground. I will wait here till the
flute-player passes, and ask him to tell me the
story of this place.

Reapers (*together*).

4

To the music of the reaper's flute
No song is sung
But the sighing of wind in the fields.

Young Reaper.

They that were reaping,
Reaping on that hill,
Walk now through the fields
Homeward, for it is dusk.

Reapers (*together*).

Short is the way that leads
From the sea of Suma back to my home.
This little journey, up to the hill
And down to the shore again, and up to the hill—
This is my life, and the sum of hateful tasks.
If one should ask me
I too would answer
That on the shore of Suma

---

2 INTERPRETING

What do you think the Priest means by the remark, "Life is a lying dream, he only wakes / Who casts the world aside"? (Possible response: What appears real is unreal; one can understand the truth only by transcending "reality.")

3 LITERARY ELEMENT

Setting: What do you notice about the treatment of time and place in this play? (Possible answer: It is stylized, unrealistic; it is established by the two lines spoken by the central character, without change of scenery.)

■ **guise** (gīz): manner of dress

knoll (nōl): small hill

4 LITERARY ELEMENT

Mood: What feeling is suggested by the lines "To the music of the reaper's flute / No song is sung / But the sighing of wind in the fields"? (Possible responses: sadness, regret, loneliness)

---

1. **Ichi no tani** (ē'chē nō tä'nē): the location of a battle lost by the Taira (Heike) clan, of which Atsumori was a member.

estranged (e·strānjd'): kept apart or away

5 LITERARY ELEMENT

Characterization: What can you learn about the Young Reaper from what he says? (Possible response: He seems to be well educated; he chides the Priest for his ignorance of "poets' verses" and for his attitude toward those "below" him.)

6 LITERARY ELEMENT

Characterization: In what way is the character of Rensei developed as he speaks to the reapers? (Possible response: He is agreeable, thoughtful.) Does he seem to be a flat character or a round character? (Students' opinions should be supported by specific references to the text.)

I live in sadness.
Yet if any guessed my name,
Then might I too have friends.
But now from my deep misery
Even those that were dearest
Are grown estranged. Here must I dwell abandoned
To one thought's anguish:
That I must dwell here.[2]

Priest.

Hey, you reapers! I have a question to ask you.

Young Reaper.

Is it to us you are speaking? What do you wish to
know?

Priest.

Was it one of you who was playing on the flute just
now?

Young Reaper.

Yes, it was we who were playing.

Priest.

It was a pleasant sound, and all the pleasanter because one does not look for such music from men
of your condition.

Young Reaper.

Unlooked for from men of our condition, you say!
Have you not read:
"Do not envy what is above you
Nor despise what is below you"?
5   Moreover the songs of woodmen and the flute-
playing of herdsmen,
Flute-playing even of reapers and songs of wood-
fellers
Through poets' verses are known to all the world.
Wonder not to hear among us
The sound of a bamboo flute.

Priest.

6   You are right. Indeed it is as you have told me.
Songs of woodmen and flute-playing of herdsmen . . .

---

2. The reapers are speaking as one person. It is common in Noh
theater for a chorus to speak a leading character's lines, often
while the lead character is dancing.

Reaper.
Flute-playing of reapers . . .

Priest.
Songs of wood-fellers . . .

Reapers.
Guide us on our passage through this sad world.

Priest.
Song . . .

Reaper.
And dance . . .

Priest.
And the flute . . .

Reaper.
And music of many instruments . . .

Chorus.
These are the pastimes that each chooses to his taste.
Of floating bamboo wood
Many are the famous flutes that have been made;
Little Branch and Cicada Cage,
And as for the reaper's flute,
Its name is Green Leaf;
On the shore of Sumiyoshi
The Korean flute they play.
And here on the shore of Suma
On Stick of the Salt-kilns[3]
The fishers blow their tune.

Priest.
How strange it is! The other reapers
have all gone home, but you alone
stay loitering here. How is that?

Reaper.
How is it, you ask? I am seeking for a
prayer in the voice of the evening waves. Perhaps
you will pray the Ten Prayers for me?

Priest.
I can easily pray the Ten Prayers for you, if you will
tell me who you are.

The Granger Collection, New York

Scene from a Noh play performance.

---

3. **Little Branch**, **Cicada Cage**, **Green Leaf**, and **Stick of the Salt-kilns** are all names of flutes; a cicada is a type of insect.

---

10 LITERARY ELEMENT

Plot: Why do you think Rensei is happy to hear that the Reaper is a member of Atsumori's family? (Possible response: He knows he has reached his destination and can begin praying for the salvation of Atsumori's soul.)

11 LITERARY ELEMENT

Chorus: For which character does the chorus speak here? (the Reaper) In what way does the chorus contribute to the "flatness" of the character? (Possible response: Because the Reaper's thoughts and feelings are removed from him, his character does not seem "round"; instead, the character takes on a symbolic quality.)

interlude (in'tər·lo͞od'): any performance between the acts of a play

12 DRAMATIC ELEMENT

Costumes: The *shite*, or central character, often appears in two separate costumes in a Noh play. The first costume is a disguise and the second reveals his true identity. *How does Rensei react to the ghostly warrior?* (He thinks he is dreaming of Atsumori.)

12 CULTURAL DIVERSITY

Ghostly encounters often appear in theater of many different ages and cultures. ? *Can you name any stories or plays from your background that feature ghosts?* (Answers will vary.)

Reaper.
To tell you the truth—I am one of the family of Lord Atsumori.

10 **Priest.**
One of Atsumori's family? How glad I am!
Then the priest joined his hands (*he kneels down*) and prayed:

Namu Amidabu.[4]

Praise to Amida Buddha![5]
"If I attain to Buddhahood,
In the whole world and its ten spheres
Of all that dwell here none shall call on my name
And be rejected or cast aside."

11 **Chorus.**
"Oh, reject me not!
One cry suffices for salvation,
Yet day and night
Your prayers will rise for me.
Happy am I, for though you know not my name,
Yet for my soul's deliverance
At dawn and dusk henceforward I know that you will pray."
So he spoke. Then vanished and was seen no more.

[*Here follows the Interlude between the two Acts, in which a recitation concerning* ATSUMORI*'s death takes place. These interludes are subject to variation and are not considered part of the literary text of the play.*]

Priest.
Since this is so, I will perfom all night the rites of prayer for the dead, and calling upon Amida's name will pray again for the salvation of Atsumori.

12 [*The ghost of* ATSUMORI *appears, dressed as a young warrior.*]

Atsumori.
Would you know who I am

4. ***Namu Amidabu*** (nä'mo͞o ä'mə·dä'bo͞o): the prayer by which followers of the Amida Buddha obtained salvation.
5. **Amida Buddha** (ä'mē'dä bo͞o'də): an enlightened being worshiped by followers of a Buddhist sect in medieval Japan.

That like the watchmen at Suma Pass
Have wakened at the cry of sea birds roaming
Upon Awaji shore?
Listen, Rensei. I am Atsumori.

Priest.

How strange! All this while I have never stopped
beating my gong and performing the rites of the
Law.[6] I cannot for a moment have dozed, yet I
thought that Atsumori was standing before me.
Surely it was a dream.

Atsumori.

Why need it be a dream? It is to clear the karma[7]
of my waking life that I am come here in visible
form before you.

Priest.

Is it not written that one prayer will wipe away ten
thousand sins? Ceaselessly I have performed the
ritual of the Holy Name[8] that clears all sin away.
After such prayers, what evil can be left? Though
you should be sunk in sin as deep . . .

Atsumori.

As the sea by a rocky shore,
Yet should I be saved by prayer.

Priest.

And that my prayers should save you . . .

Atsumori.

This too must spring
From kindness of a former life.[9]

Priest.

Once enemies . . .

Atsumori.

But now . . .

3

Noh mask.
*How do you envision the speech and
movements of the characters?*

13 CULTURAL DIVERSITY
Traditionally, prayers were offered to free a tortured spirit
from his or her continued attachment to the earth. The attachment was often caused by
the spirit's painful or unrecon-
ciled death.
*How does this attitude to-
ward a warrior's death compare to Krishna's attitude in the
Bhagavad-Gita? (Possible response: Hindus are reconciled
to death through the belief in
reincarnation; Buddhists believe prayer will free the dead
from their attachment to the
earth.)*

---

6. **the rites of the Law:** the doctrines of Buddhism, or of a Buddhist
   sect.
7. **karma** (kär′mə): a person's actions, which Buddhists believe influence the fate of a person in this and future lives.
8. **the ritual of the Holy Name:** the recitation of the prayer "Namu
   Amidabu."
9. **From kindness of a former life:** Atsumori must have done Rensei some kindness in a former incarnation. This would account for
   Rensei's remorse.

Seami Motokiyo   **605**

14 INTERPRETING

What idea is suggested by the line: "Friends in Buddha's Law"? (Possible response: The two characters are united through Zen.)

15 DRAMATIC ELEMENT

Chorus: The chorus often takes on the voices of the other characters in a Noh play; it does not have an identity of its own. For which character does the chorus speak when it says "There is a saying . . ."? (Rensei)

16 LITERARY ELEMENT

Imagery: What two contrasting images from nature are used to describe Buddha's bidding? (flowers of spring, the moon drowned in autumn waves) What do the images suggest about Buddha? (Possible response: He helps people both in their hopefulness and in their despair.)

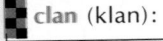

clan (klan): a tribal division

17 LITERARY ELEMENT

Simile: What simile is used to describe the Taira clan? ("Spread over the earth like the leafy branches of a great tree") What does it suggest? (Possible response: The clan has multiplied fruitfully)

18 LITERARY ELEMENT

Theme: The chorus often serves as a mouthpiece for a Noh dramatist's statement about life. What view is expressed here? (Possible answer: Human glory is fleeting; it is but a spark in darkness.)

Priest.
In truth may we be named . . .

14 **Atsumori.**
Friends in Buddha's Law.

15 **Chorus.**
There is a saying, "Put away from you a wicked
    friend; summon to your side a virtuous enemy."
For you it was said, and you have proven it true.
And now come tell with us the tale of your confes-
    sion, while the night is still dark.

16 **Chorus.**
He[10] bids the flowers of spring
Mount the treetop that men may raise their eyes
And walk on upward paths;
He bids the moon in autumn waves be drowned
In token that he visits laggard men
And leads them out from valleys of despair.

17 **Atsumori.**
Now the <u>clan</u> of Taira,[11] building wall to wall,
Spread over the earth like the leafy branches of a
    great tree:

18 **Chorus.**
Yet their prosperity lasted but for a day;
It was like the flower of the convolvulus.[12]
There was none to tell them
That glory flashes like sparks from flint-stone,
And after—darkness.
Oh wretched, the life of men!

Atsumori.
When they were on high they afflicted the humble;
When they were rich they were reckless in pride.
And so for twenty years and more
They ruled this land.
But truly a generation passes like the space of a
    dream.
The leaves of the autumn of Juyei[13]

---

10. **He:** Buddha.
11. **Taira** (tä·ē'rä): the clan of the Heike.
12. **convolvulus** (kən·väl'vyo͞o·ləs): a flower of the morning-glory family.
13. **Juyei** (jo͞o·yā'): The Taira evacuated the capital in the second year of Juyei, 1188.

The Granger Collection, New York

Japanese Noh actor. *Most Noh plays contain the "Three Roles" of the old person, the woman, and the warrior. To achieve* yugen, *a mark of high accomplishment in the arts, Seami says that the three roles must be acted beautifully.*

? *How does* Atsumori *deviate from the traditional three-role Noh drama?*

Were tossed by the four winds;
Scattered, scattered (like leaves too) floated their
ships.
And they, asleep on the heaving sea, not even in
dreams
Went back to home.
Caged birds longing for the clouds—
Wild geese were they rather, whose ranks are broken
As they fly to southward on their doubtful journey.
So days and months went by; spring came again
And for a little while
Here dwelt they on the shore of Suma
At the first valley.[14]
From the mountain behind us the winds blew down
Till the fields grew wintry again.
Our ships lay by the shore, where night and day
The sea gulls cried and salt waves washed on our
sleeves.
We slept with fishers in their huts
On pillows of sand.
We knew none but the people of Suma.
And when among the pine trees
The evening smoke was rising,
Brushwood, as they called it,
Brushwood we gathered
And spread for carpet.
Sorrowful we lived
On the wild shore of Suma,
Till the clan Taira and all its princes
Were but villagers of Suma.

Atsumori.

But on the night of the sixth day of the second
month
My father Tsunemori[15] gathered us together.
"Tomorrow," he said, "we shall fight our last fight.
Tonight is all that is left us."
We sang songs together, and danced.

Priest.

Yes, I remember; we in our siege-camp

---

14. **the first valley:** Ichi no tani.
15. **Tsunemori** (tsü′nə·mō′rē): one of the lords of the Taira clan.

Seami Motokiyo   **607**

19 LITERARY ELEMENT
Repetition: What effect does the repeated reference to sorrow and sadness create throughout the play? (Possible response: It serves as a constant reminder of the sad plight of Atsumori.)

20 LITERARY ELEMENT
Flashback: What earlier scene is brought to your mind when you read the Priest's reminiscence (which continues on p. 608)? (the Reapers playing their flutes in the beginning of the play) Why do you think Atsumori is associated with flute music throughout the play? (The Japanese felt the flute expressed the emotions of the soul.)

READING CHECK

1. For whose soul is Rensei going to pray, and why? (Atsumori's soul; he killed Atsumori in battle)
2. What does the Priest hear as he approaches the hill? (flute music)
3. Why does the Reaper ask the Priest to pray for him? (He is the ghost of Atsumori.)

4. When does Rensei think he is dreaming? (when Atsumori appears before him as a young warrior)
5. What does Atsumori realize at the end of the play? (that Rensei is not his enemy)

RETEACHING
Assign students rotating roles and have them act out the play. Encourage the class to use their knowledge of Noh drama to recreate the solemn mood and capture the tone that Seami intended. Suggest that students try to keep expressions frozen on their faces while they act, or create masks to wear. You might also ask members of the chorus to practice synchronizing their dialogue before performing it in front of others.

21 COMPARING LITERATURE

During Bashō's journeys, he traveled to Sumadera and was reminded of Atsumori's flute. He then wrote the following haiku:

In the temple of Suma,
Under the shade of a tree,
I thought I had heard
An ancient flute on the march.

? *What mood does Bashō's poem evoke for you?* (Possible responses: reflective, haunting) *Is the feeling suggested by the poem like or unlike the feeling suggested in the play, as Atsumori reminisces about his flute playing?* (Most students will see a parallel.)

22 LITERARY ELEMENT

Narration: According to the chorus's description of the battle scene, who has abandoned Atsumori? (his own clan)

23 MAKING JUDGMENTS

Here the chorus assumes the role of the narrator and finishes Atsumori's reminiscence. What effect, if any, does this have on the play? (Possible response: It adds to its stylized, otherworldly quality.)

23 COMPARING LITERATURE

Students may be interested in comparing this battle scene with those described in "Rama and Ravana in Battle" (pp. 486–493) and "The Fall of Troy" (pp. 383–406) from the *Aeneid*.

Heard the sound of music
Echoing from your tents that night;
There was the music of a flute . . .

21 **Atsumori.**
The bamboo flute! I wore it when I died.

Priest.
We heard the singing . . .

Atsumori.
Songs and ballads . . .

Priest.
Many voices

Atsumori.
Singing to one measure.

[ATSUMORI *dances.*]
First comes the royal boat.

22 **Chorus.**
The whole clan has put its boats to sea.
He[16] will not be left behind;
He runs to the shore.
But the royal boat and the soldiers' boats
Have sailed far away.

Atsumori.
What can he do?
He spurs his horse into the waves.
He is full of perplexity.
And then

23 **Chorus.**
He looks behind him and sees
That Kumagai pursues him;
He cannot escape.
Then Atsumori turns his horse
Knee-deep in the lashing waves,
And draws his sword.
Twice, three times he strikes; then, still saddled,
In close fight they twine; roll headlong together
Among the surf of the shore.
So Atsumori fell and was slain, but now the Wheel of Fate
Has turned and brought him back.

---

16. **He:** Atsumori; the passage is mimed throughout.

S. Engelmann/SuperStock, Inc.

Samurai warrior.

1. Role-playing a Ghostly Encounter.
Ghostly characters are an important feature of Noh plays, Shakespeare's plays, and others. Tell students to imagine and create a brief scene in which they encounter a ghost who reveals a crucial piece of information about their past or their future. Have students work in pairs to rehearse and present their dialogues to the class.

2. Creating a Musical Score. Music was important in Noh drama, as it is in movies today. With one or two other classmates, have students develop a musical score to accompany *Atsumori*. As students choose instruments, voices, and sounds, encourage them to create an atmosphere and to highlight events in the play.

Have students discuss the emotional impact of *Atsumori*. Encourage them to focus on the aspects that they felt were most effective, and to speculate on the kinds of influence Noh drama might have had on the development of modern theater. ■

[ATSUMORI *rises from the ground and advances toward the Priest with uplifted sword.*]

"There is my enemy," he cries, and would strike,
But the other is grown gentle
And calling on Buddha's name
Has obtained salvation for his foe;
So that they shall be reborn together
On one lotus[17] seat.
"No, Rensei is not my enemy.
Pray for me again, oh pray for me again."

24

---

17. **lotus** (lōt'əs): a water lily sacred to Buddhists.

First Thoughts
What dominant feeling did this play leave you with?

Identifying Facts
1. What discovery does Rensei make about the Young Reaper?
2. Read the final eight lines of the play, in which the chorus speaks with the voice of Atsumori. How does Atsumori feel about Rensei?

Interpreting Meanings
1. What is the essential **conflict** between Rensei and Atsumori? How do they bring this conflict to a resolution?
2. Both Rensei and Atsumori are **flat characters**. Nevertheless, the character of Rensei is more developed than that of Atsumori. What conflicting feelings does Rensei have that bring him to life as a character?
3. In the middle of the play, Atsumori makes a long speech comparing warriors to images from nature. Name some of these images, and explain what they reveal about Atsumori's view of war.

4. Very near the end of the play, Atsumori almost attacks Rensei, then changes his mind. He declares, "No, Rensei is not my enemy," and pleads, "Pray for me again, oh pray for me again." What impression of Atsumori's state of mind does this line create?
5. Do you think the music the reapers play on their flutes is happy or sad? Why? Support your conclusion with quotations from the play.

Applying Meanings
Think about the saying on page 606: "Put away from you a wicked friend: summon to your side a virtuous enemy." In the play, Rensei is the "virtuous enemy." Have you ever had someone or something you thought was an enemy do something good for you? How did you react?

Critical Writing Response
Comparing Dramatic Forms. Think of three aspects of a Noh drama—such as the unusual treatment of time and space—that are different from conventional plays performed in the West. Write a

---

24 LITERARY ELEMENT
Resolution: The conflict of a Noh play is resolved when its central character attains a moment of wisdom or truth in the Zen tradition. What is the nature of this truth in Atsumori's case? (Possible response: that Rensei is not his enemy and that they shall be "reborn together" through prayer)

ANSWERS
First Thoughts
Answers will vary.

Identifying Facts
1. He is Atsumori's ghost.
2. Possible response: forgiving

Interpreting Meanings
1. Rensei killed Atsumori. Rensei prays for Atsumori's salvation.
2. Possible response: He is sorry he killed Atsumori, yet he feels he had no choice.
3. Possible responses: He hates war. The tossed leaves suggest that the warriors had no control over their lives; the caged birds suggest that they wanted freedom, peace.
4. Vengeance turns to forgiveness in a flash of truth.
5. Possible response: sad. "To the music of the reaper's flute / No song is sung / But the sighing of wind in the fields" and "I live in sadness."

Applying Meanings
You might wish to keep students' experiences private.

➡

Seami Motokiyo   **609**

1 LITERARY BACKGROUND

Sources: Playwrights throughout the ages have "borrowed"
plots from other sources, such
as myths, folktales, historical
accounts, and other writers'
works. William Shakespeare,
for example, took many of the
plot ideas for his greatest
plays—*Hamlet, Romeo and Juliet, Macbeth*—from earlier
sources, which was a common
practice in his day. The same is
true throughout the history of
Japanese literature.

2 LITERARY BACKGROUND

Episodes from *The Tale of the
Heike* were recited by wandering minstrels who accompanied themselves on the *biwa*, a
Japanese lute. In addition to
this work, a more detailed historical account was written
about the Heike called *The
Rise and Fall of the Minamato
and Taira.* By the time of Seami
Motokiyo's birth in 1363, the
tale was known throughout the
empire.

three-paragraph essay explaining how
these aspects illustrate the ways in which
classical Japanese theater differs from our
own. To help you formulate your ideas, use
a chart like the one below. Part of the
chart has been filled in for you.

Dramatic Features	Japanese Noh Drama	Western Drama
Characterization	Characters are flat, showing only one or two traits	Main characters are usually round; secondary characters may be flat
Conflict		
Setting: time and space		
Other		

Language and Vocabulary

Oxymorons

An **oxymoron** is a figure of speech that
combines apparently contradictory or opposing ideas, as in the phrases "deafening
silence" and "living death." In *Atsumori*,
the chorus recites a saying that contains
two oxymorons: "Put away from you a
wicked friend; summon to your side a virtuous enemy." The oxymoronic phrases
"wicked friend" and "virtuous enemy" are
striking and powerful because they challenge our conventional ideas about friends
and enemies.

Many oxymorons challenge our conventional notions of a thing or idea. For
instance, the oxymoron "cruel kindness"
suggests that an apparent kindness may
actually be wounding.

What adjectives can be paired with the
following nouns to create oxymorons?

1. law **3.** dream **5.** loneliness
2. sorrow **4.** love **6.** duty

PRIMARY SOURCES

from The Tale of the Heike: *"The Death of Atsumori"*

1 *Many Noh plays were based on dance-
ballads or poems that would have been
familiar to the audiences of the time. The
Noh play* Atsumori *is based on an episode
from* The Tale of the Heike, *a Japanese
2 epic from the thirteenth century.*
  Unlike many medieval epics composed in

the West, The Tale of the Heike *does not
glorify war. Its tone is melancholy, and it
portrays glory as a mixed blessing. Here,
Kumagai Naozane, who later becomes the
priest Rensei, meets the young Atsumori on
the battlefield at Ichi no tani and reluctantly kills him.*

The Death of Atsumori

When the Heike were routed at Ichi no tani, and their nobles and courtiers were fleeing to the shore to escape in their ships, Kumagai Naozane came riding along a narrow path onto the beach, with the intention of intercepting one of their great captains. Just then his eye fell on a single horseman who was attempting to reach one of the ships in the offing. The horse he rode was dappled-gray, and its saddle glittered with gold mounting. Not doubting that he was one of the chief captains, Kumagai beckoned to him with his war fan, crying out: "Shameful! to show an enemy your back. Return! Return!"

The warrior turned his horse and rode back to the beach, where Kumagai at once engaged him in mortal combat. Quickly hurling him to the ground, he sprang upon him and tore off his helmet to cut off his head, when he beheld the face of a youth of sixteen or seventeen, delicately powdered and with blackened teeth, just about the age of his own son and with features of great beauty. "Who are you?" he asked. "Tell me your name, for I would spare your life."

"Nay, first say who you are," replied the young man.

"I am Kumagai Naozane of Musashi, a person of no particular importance."

"Then you have made a good capture," said the youth. "Take my head and show it to some of my side, and they will tell you who I am."

"Though he is one of their leaders," mused Kumagai, "if I slay him it will not turn victory into defeat, and if I spare him, it will not turn defeat into victory. When my son Kojirō was but slightly wounded at Ichi no tani this morning, did it not pain me? How this young man's father would grieve to hear that he had been killed! I will spare him."

Just then, looking behind him, he saw Doi and Kajiwara coming up with fifty horsemen. "Alas! look there," he exclaimed, the tears running down his face, "though I would spare your life, the whole countryside swarms with our men, and you cannot escape them. If you must die, let it be by my hand, and I will see that prayers are said for your rebirth in Paradise."

"Indeed it must be so," said the young warrior. "Cut off my head at once."

Kumagai was so overcome by compassion that he could scarcely wield his blade. His eyes swam and he hardly knew what he did, but there was no help for it; weeping bitterly he cut off the boy's head. "Alas!" he cried, "what life is so hard as that of a soldier? Only because I was born of a warrior family must I suffer this affliction! How lamentable it is to do such cruel deeds!" He pressed his face to the sleeve of his armor and wept bitterly. Then, wrapping up the head, he was stripping off the young man's armor when he discovered a flute in a brocade bag. "Ah," he exclaimed, "it was this youth and his friends who were amusing themselves with music within the walls this morning. Among all our men of the Eastern Provinces I doubt if there is any one of them who has brought a flute with him. How gentle the ways of these courtiers!"

When he brought the flute to the Commander, all who saw it were moved to tears; he discovered then that the youth was Atsumori, the youngest son of Tsunemori, aged sixteen years. From this time the mind of Kumagai was turned toward the religious life.

3 SPECULATING
Why do you think Kumagai baited Atsumori by yelling, "Shameful to show an enemy your back. Return! Return!"? (Possible response: to get him to fight) If Rensei knew the young warrior's true identity, do you think he would have called out the same words? (Answers will vary.)

4 INTERPRETING
With whom does Kumagai identify at this time? (Atsumori's father) How does his response point out war's senselessness? (Possible response: It highlights the fact that soldiers all have parents who would mourn their deaths.)

5 COMPARING LITERATURE
How does the depiction of Atsumori's death differ between the play and the tale? (Possible response: The characters are rounder in the tale, and the setting is described in much greater detail. Not as much is left up to the reader's imagination.)

6 LITERARY ELEMENT
Symbol: What do you think the flute symbolizes? (Possible responses: art, life, happiness, gentleness, youth, peace)

LITERARY ELEMENT
Characterization: In *The Tale of the Heike*, do Kumagai and Atsumori appear to be "round" or "flat" characters? Support your answer. (Possible response: They appear round because they seem realistic; their feelings and actions are described.)

Advanced Students: Challenge students to choose a haiku from those they have read in this unit and write a parody of it in the form of senryu. Invite them to share their finished work with the rest of the class. ■

1 COMPARING LITERATURE

In English, limericks are short witty poems that call attention to the different aspects of human nature. Like senryu, they are often playful and irreverent. Have students name and recite any funny limerick they may know. (Possible response: There was an Old Man of the Dee/Who was sadly annoyed by a Flea;/When he said, "I will scratch it,"/They gave him a hatchet,/Which grieved that Old Man of the Dee.")

2 CULTURAL DIVERSITY

This senryu describes an ordinary scene from Japanese life. **?** *Does this poem express an observation that one might make today, or is it dated?* (Possible response: It is timeless.)

3 LITERARY ELEMENT

Imagery: Haiku and senryu have little in common in tone and subject matter. What similarities do you notice in the use of imagery in the two forms? (Possible response: The images draw on the senses of sight, smell, and taste; often dissimilar images are juxtaposed; the reader has to draw on his or her own associations to complete the meaning.)

LANGUAGE
—AND—
CULTURE

SENRYU: JAPAN'S COMIC VERSES

After he's scolded   *Zen priest,*
His wife too much,   *Meditation finished,*   **1**
He cooks the rice.   *Looking for fleas.*

"Don't worry!" he says,
And then tells you something
That really gets you worried.

Do you notice anything funny about these "haiku"? Do they sound more like a comedian than like Bashō? Well, you're right: the poems above are not haiku but *senryu* (sen·rōō). Similar in form, senryu and haiku differ in tone and purpose. Most senryu are intended to be funny—some seem the poetic equivalent of cartoons—but they have a deeper purpose as well. These small verses focus on everyday events in order to point out the humor and irony inherent in the human condition.

2

Workmen eating lunch,   *First childbirth—*
With a side order   *Her husband feels like*
Of gripes.   *He did half the work.*

Off to work,
The burglar to his wife:
"Lock up tight when you go to bed!"

Both haiku and senryu contain seventeen Japanese syllables, usually grouped in a 5-7-5 pattern. However, a traditional haiku relies on nature imagery for part of its impact, and it must contain a word referring to a season of the year. Most haiku are serious, even mystical, in tone. Senryu, by contrast, need not include nature imagery or refer to the seasons. Instead, they emphasize the small but telling dramas played out in daily life. And the tone of senryu ranges from playful to irreverent to ribald:

3

Judging from the pictures,
Hell looks the more
Interesting place.

Home from work,   *One bite*
The bachelor sniffs   *And I'm doing a dance—*
At the leftover rice.   *Red peppers.*

SHOKI AND DEMON, YOSA
(TANIGUCHI) BUSON, 1777.

Christie, Manson & Woods International, Inc.

Senryu means "River Willow," which was the pen name of Karai Hachiemon (1718–1790), the poet who made senryu famous. Before Hachiemon's time, the verse form had been called *maekuzuke* (mā′ē·kōō·zōō′kē), and it had first appeared during the late 1600s. The tradition of Japanese humorous verse, from which senryu developed, is older still: humorous poetry has been a part of Japanese literature for over a thousand years.

Karai "Senryu" Hachiemon was trained as a writer of haiku. He had little success as a poet; he may have been a bit too down-to-earth for haiku. He did much better as an editor, publishing several popular collections of poems in the genre that came to bear his name. Many of the senryu in his collections are anonymous, though a number are thought to be the work of Hachiemon himself.

Some early senryu poke fun at more serious Japanese literature. One poet, Kenkabô, slyly ridicules Sei Shōnagon, tenth-century author of *The Pillow Book* (see page 579):

> *Sei Shōnagon*
> *Makes her dictionary*
> *A pillow.*

The implication here is that Shōnagon was too lazy to consult her dictionary and write proper Japanese; instead, she dozed at her writing, using her dictionary as a literal "pillow book."

One virtue of senryu is that, unlike much other classical literature, it never takes itself too seriously. As a result, it's doubtful that anyone, no matter how intimidated by poetry in general, has ever approached a senryu verse thinking, "This stuff is too deep for me." Modern senryu writers tackle modern subjects:

> *"Do take out your teeth*
> *Once more!"*
> *Begs the grandchild.*
> *—Shunu*

> *On a bicycle,*
> *Lifting up both legs,*
> *Through a puddle.*
> *—Shukei*

But the underlying tone, realistic and emphatically human, remains the same. Is it any wonder that this unpretentious verse form has stayed popular for almost three hundred years?

MAINTAINING PRONOUN-ANTECEDENT AGREEMENT

Making pronouns agree with **antecedents**—the words they refer to—can be a difficult challenge. However, a few basic rules can help you to keep your writing clear.

Pronoun-Antecedent Agreement

Choose pronouns that agree in number and gender with their **antecedents**. A **pronoun**—a word that stands for a noun or another pronoun—can be singular or plural, masculine or feminine. In general, singular nouns call for singular pronouns, and plural nouns call for plural pronouns. But be alert for problems in the four areas listed below.

1. Compound Antecedents
INCORRECT
Lao-tzu and Buddha explained *his* ideas.
CORRECT
Lao-tzu and Buddha explained *their* ideas.

Compound antecedents joined by *and* take a plural pronoun. Compound antecedents joined by *or* or *nor* take a singular pronoun.
INCORRECT
Did Sei Shōnagon or Murasaki Shikibu record *their* observations in *The Pillow Book*?
CORRECT
Did Sei Shōnagon or Murasaki Shikibu record *her* observations in *The Pillow Book*?

2. Indefinite Pronouns as Antecedents
INCORRECT
Among the Japanese empress's handmaidens, everyone had *their* own rank in the hierarchy.
CORRECT
Among the Japanese empress's handmaidens, everyone had *her* own rank in the hierarchy.

The following indefinite pronouns, used as antecedents, are singular.

anyone	nobody
everyone	somebody
no one	each
someone	either
anybody	neither
everybody	

Their gender depends on sentence context. If you are unsure, use *his or her,* or reword the sentence. The following indefinite pronouns can be singular or plural, depending on sentence sense.

any	enough
more	none
plenty	most
some	

INCORRECT

Of all Li Ch'ing-chao's poems, none took *their* theme from politics.

CORRECT

Of all Li Ch'ing-chao's poems, none took *its* theme from politics.

None is used here in the sense of "not one," so it needs a singular pronoun.

3. Abstract and Collective Nouns

INCORRECT

Bashō's imagery achieved *their* effects through a succession of vivid flashes.

CORRECT

Bashō's imagery achieved *its* effects through a succession of vivid flashes.

Some abstract nouns seem to name clusters of things: imagery, poetry. Still, they take singular pronouns. **Collective nouns** name groups: series, set, collection, group, majority, amount, number. These may take plural pronouns if your sentence refers to individual items within the group.

INCORRECT

These poets' works were rich in imagery, and a number reflected specifics from *its* authors' daily lives.

CORRECT

These poets' works were rich in imagery, and a number reflected specifics from *their* authors' daily lives.

Here *number* refers to several works being considered individually.

4. Titles

INCORRECT

Confucius' *Analects* conveyed *their* message in a way anyone could understand.

CORRECT

Confucius' *Analects* conveyed *its* message in a way anyone could understand.

The title of a literary work, even if it is plural, takes a singular pronoun.

Exercise: Making Pronouns Agree with Antecedents

Revise each sentence so that pronouns agree with their antecedents.

1. Each haiku poet can express their emotions simply and unpretentiously.
2. The *Analects* and the *Tao Te Ching* taught its lessons through maxims.
3. Everyone will probably have their own interpretation of "Gold, Gold."
4. Striking images used by Shōnagon include the series that may reflect their creator's malice.
5. Through poetry, either Li Ch'ing-chao or Princess Nukada will work their magic on the reader.
6. Lao-tzu and Ssu-ma Ch'ien did not write merely to entertain; instead, he wanted to convey serious points about life.
7. Though over a thousand years old, Li Po's "Quiet Night Thoughts" will never lose their place of honor in Chinese literature.
8. Tu Fu left behind a poetry collection that still can touch their readers today.
9. Li Ch'ing-chao wrote love poems for their readers.
10. Li Ch'ing-chao's artistry is evident in the poem "Peonies"; they contain complex imagery.

Background: Be sure students understand that imagery most often appeals to the sense of sight, but can also appeal to the senses of taste, touch, smell, and hearing. The images an author chooses, and the way they are presented, provide clues to the feelings the author wants to express and help to establish the *mood*, or emotional atmosphere, of the work. For example, in Unit 6, Sei Shōnagon (p. 579) establishes a mood of contentment with an image of crows flying to their nests on an autumn evening. Later, she uses an image of crows cawing and flapping in the middle of the night to establish a mood of irritation and displeasure.

Prewriting: In order to complete the prewriting chart, students must know how to identify the themes of the literary work(s) they have selected. Explain that a *theme* is a general insight that a work suggests (but usually does not state directly) about life or human nature. The title of a work occasionally offers a clue to the theme. One way to discover the theme of a prose work, and of some poems, is to consider what the main character or the narrator learns. One can explore the theme of a poem by trying to express in a sentence or two the poem's central insight.

Critical Thinking and Writing

ANALYZING IMAGERY

Has the sound of music or the sight of a child's toy ever transported you back to an earlier time in your life? Do the words *concert* and *storm* conjure up pictures in your mind? These **images**, or representations of sensory experiences, stimulate the imagination and engage the emotions. Whether they occur in real life or in literature, images call forth personal associations.

Writing Assignment

Choose a work from this unit and write an informative essay about it. In your essay, examine the ways in which the work's imagery contributes to its mood and theme. Assume that your audience has read the work and is interested in your interpretation. For this assignment, you will use techniques of literary analysis.

Background

In many cases, works in this unit are word paintings, celebrating nature or recreating the total experience of a moment in life. Some make imaginative comparisons using the following figures of speech.

- **Similes** are comparisons using the word *like* or *as*: ". . . bright moonlight . . . like frost on the ground."—Li Po, "Quiet Night Thoughts."

- **Metaphors** are comparisons without the word *like* or *as*: "His dancing girls are yellow dust."—Tu Fu, "Jade Flower Palace."
- **Personification** assigns human qualities to animals, objects, or ideas: "Were the stream to tempt, / My body. . . ."—Ono Komachi.

Notice such figures of speech as you choose a work and interpret its imagery.

Prewriting

Focused Reading. Choose a work (or several, if you are using tanka or haiku verses) and reread it at least twice—once aloud. To begin your analysis, complete a chart like this one.

Image	
Figure(s) of speech used to create image	
Emotions/ mood image produces	
Image's relation to theme	

Interpreting Imagery. Referring to your chart, answer the following questions to determine how the imagery functions in the poem as a whole.

1. What are the main images in this work?
2. How do the images relate to one another?
3. What emotions do the images convey?
4. Why might the author have chosen these particular images?
5. How would you state the theme of the work?
6. How do the images relate to the theme?

From your answers, synthesize one idea that you can explain in detail about the imagery in this work. Sum up your idea into a thesis sentence.

Writing

Use the following plan as you draft your essay.

1. **Introductory Paragraph.** Consider beginning with a personal response to this work, perhaps explaining why you have chosen it. Cite the title and the author. End with your thesis sentence.
2. **Body Paragraphs.** Each body paragraph should contain one point about the imagery, supported with explanations and quotations from the work. Arrange your points logically, perhaps from simplest to most complicated.

3. **Concluding Paragraph.** Restate your thesis in light of the points you've explained. Consider ending with another personal response to the work. Try to entice readers to revisit the work and make their own analysis.

Evaluating and Revising

Use these questions to evaluate and revise your essay.

1. Does the first paragraph catch readers' interest and state your thesis?
2. Do details and quotations support your points about the imagery? Are quotations well chosen and well integrated?
3. Are your ideas in a logical order?
4. Does your conclusion reinforce your thesis, leaving readers with something to think about?
5. Are your sentences varied and grammatically correct?

Proofreading and Publishing

Proofread carefully to eliminate errors in mechanics. Share your analysis with classmates who have selected the same work, and plan a panel discussion to explore the variations in your interpretations.

Writing: Before students begin drafting, clarify the goals of the assignment: to identify one or more images in a selection and then to offer an explanation of how the images relate to the selection's mood and/or theme. Remind students that the figurative language an author uses to express an image may reveal how the image relates to mood or theme. In order to illustrate their statements about imagery, students should refer to, or quote, specific lines or phrases from the literary works they have chosen.

Evaluating and Revising: For a review of how to integrate quotations smoothly and punctuate them correctly, refer students to "Using Quotations Effectively," pp. 120–121.

Proofreading and Publishing: Point out that when writers use titles of literary works, abstract nouns (such as *imagery* or *poetry*), or collective nouns (such as *group* or *type*), errors in pronoun-antecedent agreement become more frequent. Suggest that students focus on pronoun-antecedent agreement as they proofread, and refer them to "Maintaining Pronoun-Antecedent Agreement," pp. 614–615. ■

The following annotations are for the artwork surrounding the map, starting in the upper right-hand corner and moving in a counterclockwise direction.

Detail from Koran: Calligraphy was considered a high art in Islamic culture, and the line between decorative calligraphy and scrollwork such as the section of border shown here was somewhat blurred.

Musical Instruments: In Arab lands, book illustrations originated in scientific works. Artists were not distinct from calligraphers. When copying scientific works from Greek or Latin, calligraphers began adding illustrative diagrams. Eventually, as these became more elaborate, book illustration emerged as a discipline in its own right.

Bird with Blossoms: Most Islamic art consists of geometric and floral patterns, probably because injunctions in the Koran against image worship raised doubt about whether representation of any kind was permissible. Generally, pure abstraction was considered the safest form of art, with representation of plants, birds, and animals less safe, and human representation the least safe of all.

Persian Woman: This artwork is based on a detail from the *Kalila Wa Dimna*, a book of animal fables. Such fables were highly popular among both Arabs and Persians. Many illustrated versions of this book have been published.

Atlantic Ocean

EUROPE

SPAIN
• Cordova
• Granada

ITALY

MACEDONIA

GREECE

Black Sea

Mediterranean Sea

SYRIA
• Damascus

Baghdad

NORTH AFRICA

LIBYA

Cairo •
EGYPT

ARABIA
• Medina
• Mecca

Nile River

Red Sea

ISLAMIC EMPIRE
C. A.D. 900

SAHARA

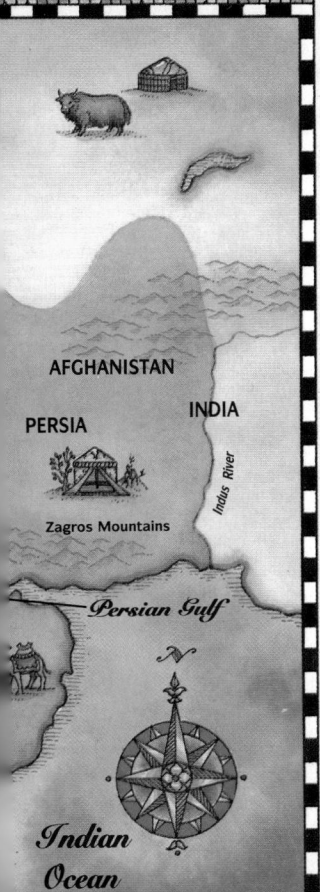

AFGHANISTAN

PERSIA   INDIA

Indus River

Zagros Mountains

Persian Gulf

Indian Ocean

UNIT 7

PERSIAN AND ARABIC LITERATURES

▼ **Time** ▼
(700 B.C.–A.D. 1400)

▼ **Place** ▼
The Middle East

▼ **Literary Significance** ▼

In A.D. 641, Arabs invaded the Persian Empire, which had flourished in the Middle East since about 700 B.C. The Arabs converted much of the Middle East to Islam, the religion founded by the prophet Mohammed. The Koran, which Muslims believe to be the direct word of Allah, or God, still inspires the millions of Muslims around the world. In addition to the Koran, Arabic writings include lyric poetry, philosophy, religion, history, and science. The Arabic work best known in the West is *The Thousand and One Nights*, a collection of fabulous tales from the Arab oral tradition.

Since the Islamic conquest in the seventh century, native Persian language and literary forms had been all but eclipsed by Arabic language and culture. But in the ninth century A.D., a renaissance of Persian culture began. The poet Ferdowsi completed a national epic of Persia (now Iran), the *Shahname*. Later, Omar Khayyám wrote the *Rubáiyát*, a famous collection of brief poems that evolved from traditional Persian poetic forms. This same period in Persian literature saw the rise of Sufism, a sect of Islam. The mystical works of Sufi writers and poets are still cherished by readers throughout the world.

Astrolabe: This device, perfected by Muslims as early as A.D. 1000, was used to calculate the distance to the sun and other celestial bodies. It was an indispensable instrument for navigation on the open seas.

Persian Delegation: This artwork is based on a frieze at Persepolis, the capital of the Persian Empire. This palatial city was burned down by Alexander the Great in 330 B.C. Friezes like this one emphasize the grandeur of the emperor by showing delegations paying him tribute.

Rostám: The one form of representational art that emerged from Islamic culture was book illustration. The book most frequently illustrated was the *Shahname*, or *Book of Kings* (p. 646). This vast epic features a cast of thousands, but the mightiest hero is Rostám. ∎

TEACHING TIP

Map: To appreciate the extent of the Islamic Empire at its height, students might compare this map to a contemporary one of Eurasia and list all the countries that now exist wholly or partly within the shaded area. Students might also find it interesting to compare the Islamic domain to the empires of the Persians, of Alexander, of the Romans, or of Genghis Khan, using maps in this book or in a historical atlas.

You may wish to point out to students that the Time Line for Persia and Arabia, spanning nine hundred years, covers the same period as that of the Middle Ages in Europe (Unit 8). Ask students to name any events they know of that were occurring during the period A.D. 500–1500. (Answers will vary. Students may refer to events in India, China, and Japan that they studied in earlier units.)

To help students make this Time Line more meaningful to them, encourage them to work in small groups to create a corresponding one on transparent tracing paper, using the same scale but listing events familiar to them from European (or other) history. These can be general events (for example, Viking Raids, 800–1000), historical figures (Charlemagne, 742–814), specific events (Battle of Hastings, 1066), or even legendary figures (Robin Hood, roughly 1200)—anything students find familiar that serves to frame the events of Islamic civilization.

LITERARY BACKGROUND

Page from Koran: Muslims regard the Koran itself—not just its "meaning" but the actual lines on the written page (not to mention the sounds of the recited verses)—as an incarnation of divine power. This is one reason a high regard developed for books as art objects and why great care was lavished on the production of beautiful editions of the Koran.

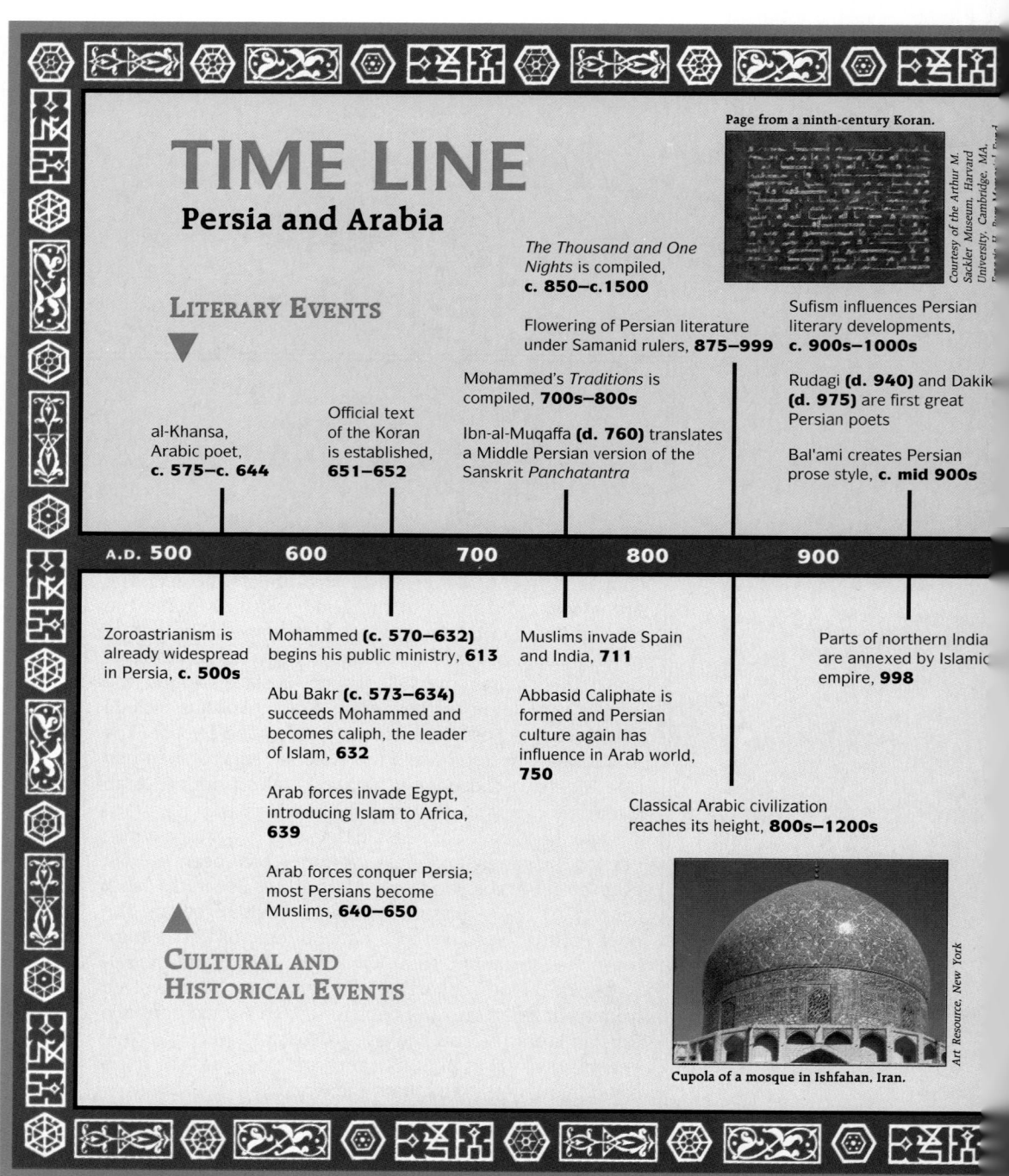

TIME LINE
Persia and Arabia

Page from a ninth-century Koran.

Courtesy of the Arthur M. Sackler Museum, Harvard University, Cambridge, MA.

LITERARY EVENTS

The Thousand and One Nights is compiled, **c. 850–c.1500**

Flowering of Persian literature under Samanid rulers, **875–999**

Sufism influences Persian literary developments, **c. 900s–1000s**

Mohammed's *Traditions* is compiled, **700s–800s**

Rudagi **(d. 940)** and Dakik **(d. 975)** are first great Persian poets

al-Khansa, Arabic poet, **c. 575–c. 644**

Official text of the Koran is established, **651–652**

Ibn-al-Muqaffa **(d. 760)** translates a Middle Persian version of the Sanskrit *Panchatantra*

Bal'ami creates Persian prose style, **c. mid 900s**

A.D. 500	600	700	800	900

Zoroastrianism is already widespread in Persia, **c. 500s**

Mohammed **(c. 570–632)** begins his public ministry, **613**

Muslims invade Spain and India, **711**

Parts of northern India are annexed by Islamic empire, **998**

Abu Bakr **(c. 573–634)** succeeds Mohammed and becomes caliph, the leader of Islam, **632**

Abbasid Caliphate is formed and Persian culture again has influence in Arab world, **750**

Arab forces invade Egypt, introducing Islam to Africa, **639**

Classical Arabic civilization reaches its height, **800s–1200s**

Arab forces conquer Persia; most Persians become Muslims, **640–650**

CULTURAL AND HISTORICAL EVENTS

Cupola of a mosque in Ishfahan, Iran.

Art Resource, New York

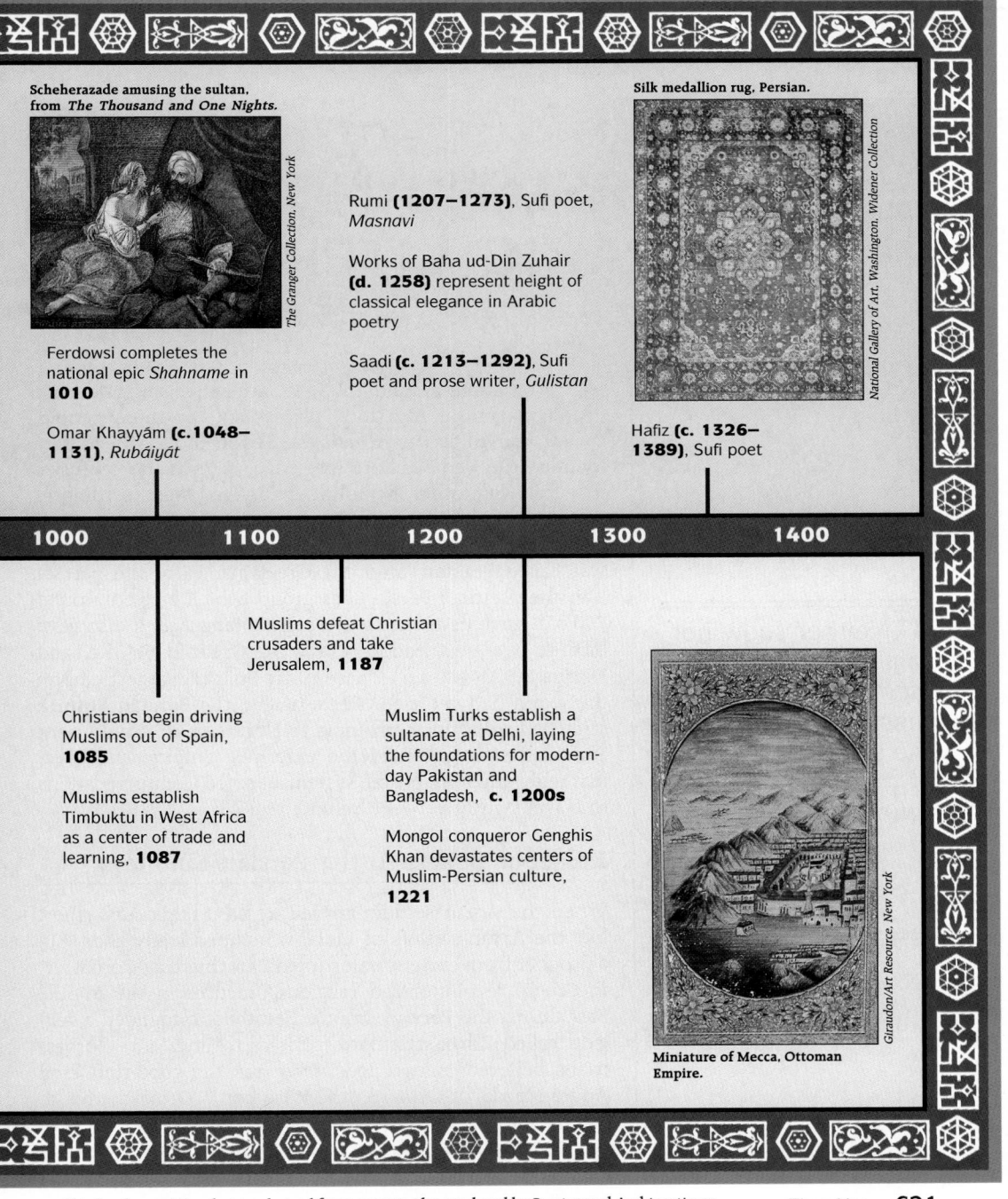

Scheherazade amusing the sultan. from *The Thousand and One Nights*.

The Granger Collection, New York

Silk medallion rug, Persian.

National Gallery of Art, Washington. Widener Collection

Rumi **(1207–1273)**, Sufi poet, *Masnavi*

Works of Baha ud-Din Zuhair **(d. 1258)** represent height of classical elegance in Arabic poetry

Saadi **(c. 1213–1292)**, Sufi poet and prose writer, *Gulistan*

Ferdowsi completes the national epic *Shahname* in **1010**

Omar Khayyám **(c.1048–1131)**, *Rubáiyát*

Hafiz **(c. 1326–1389)**, Sufi poet

1000	1100	1200	1300	1400

Muslims defeat Christian crusaders and take Jerusalem, **1187**

Christians begin driving Muslims out of Spain, **1085**

Muslims establish Timbuktu in West Africa as a center of trade and learning, **1087**

Muslim Turks establish a sultanate at Delhi, laying the foundations for modern-day Pakistan and Bangladesh, **c. 1200s**

Mongol conqueror Genghis Khan devastates centers of Muslim-Persian culture, **1221**

Giraudon/Art Resource, New York

Miniature of Mecca, Ottoman Empire.

This border contains designs derived from ceramic tiles produced by Persian and Arabic artisans. Such tiles were a basic element of decorative architecture throughout the Islamic world.

CULTURAL BACKGROUND

Cupola: Along with minarets, cupolas are distinctive features of mosque architecture throughout the Islamic world.

LITERARY BACKGROUND

Scheherazade: Scheherazade appeared first in a Persian book titled *Hazar Afsana*, or "A Thousand Stories." Her name may be a corruption of *Chihrazd*, which means "of noble race."

CULTURAL BACKGROUND

Silk Rug: Persian carpets are known for their quality and beauty. The development of the art of rug making reflects the interaction between Persia and the nomadic Turkomans, who have always prized richly decorated portable objects and remain perhaps the world's master rug makers today.

CULTURAL BACKGROUND

Miniature of Mecca: Islamic artists have always been fascinated with the challenges of miniaturization, and this is one example. Other examples include painted miniatures used to illustrate books, and miniaturized calligraphy—for example, long chapters of the Koran written on an egg or a whole verse on a grain of rice.

OBJECTIVES

1. *To gain an introduction to Persian (Farsi) and Arabic literatures*
2. *To recognize how Islam has shaped culture and literature in the Middle East*
3. *To identify the oral and written traditions in Persian and Arabic literatures*
4. *To interpret and respond to Persian and Arabic literatures both orally and in writing*

TEACHER'S RESOURCES: 7

- ✔ Unit Introduction Test
- ✔ Word Analogies
- ✔ Unit Review Test
- ✔ Critical Thinking and Writing

1 HISTORICAL BACKGROUND

Persian Policies: Contrary to their reputation as tyrants, the Persians were progressive for their time. They practiced the hitherto-unknown policy of allowing autonomy to conquered peoples instead of just enslaving them. This enabled the Persians to forge a heterogeneous empire larger than Egypt, Assyria, and Babylonia combined. Students might be interested in comparing the Persian system for holding together a multicultural empire with such later attempts as those of the British and Soviet empires.

2 RESPONDING TO THE QUOTATION

Today this quotation from the great Greek historian is often invoked in jest—perhaps because mail delivery strikes the modern ear as mundane and unheroic.

❓ *Why might the swift completion of postal rounds have impressed an observer in the ancient Persian Empire?* (Travel was by horse or horse-drawn cart; postal workers often had to move through dangerous territories where hostile or greedy local lords exercised absolute authority.)

PERSIAN AND ARABIC LITERATURES

> **"** Neither snow nor rain nor heat nor gloom of night stays these couriers from the swift completion of their appointed rounds. **"**
>
> —*Inscription on the New York City Post Office, adapted from a comment by Herodotus on the Persian postal system*

Sometime around 1500 B.C., a massive migration out of central Asia took place. Some of these people, known as the **Aryans**, settled in India, where they founded the Vedic culture (see page 447). In the centuries that followed, other Aryan groups moved west, settling in what is now the Middle Eastern country of Iran. (*Iran* comes from the word "Aryan.") One of these Aryan communities was called **Persian**, after the Greek name for the part of Iran they settled, Persis. This group, which arrived around 700 B.C., gave its name to the Persian language. It also gave birth to two great leaders: **Cyrus the Great** (d. 529 B.C.) and **Darius I** (520–486 B.C.). These rulers built the largest empire the world had yet seen. At its height, the **Persian Empire** stretched from northern India to North Africa. An efficient administration governed the extensive empire, and a remarkably modern postal system allowed communications to travel swiftly between remote regions.

Religious Beliefs in the Persian Empire

When the Aryan settlers arrived in the Middle East, they, like the Aryan settlers of India, worshiped many gods. But a prophet from eastern Iran named **Zarathustra** ("Zoroaster" in Greek) revolutionized religious practices in the Middle East during the Persian Empire. Zarathustra founded a religion called **Zoroastrianism** (zō'rō·as'trē·ən·iz'əm). Zoroastrians believed in two gods. One was the good and kind Ahura Mazda, or Ormazd, "the Wise Lord." Ormazd embodied the virtues of truth and law. His enemy was the evil god Ahriman. Zoroastrians believed that the good Ormazd and the evil Ahriman were engaged in an ongoing struggle, and that one day Ormazd would triumph. People who fol-

To help students approach Persian literature, you may wish to emphasize its roots in the oral tradition of storytelling. Stories told orally were meant to grip and move an audience by appealing to deeply felt cultural values. Thus, in a male-dominated culture that regarded the birth of a son as the greatest fortune, Ferdowsi's theme of a father killing his own son (see p. 649) is the ultimate tear-jerker.

Explain to students that Arabic literature has its roots in the oral traditions of the Bedouins. Point out how the poetry celebrates the warrior virtues of these tribal nomads (honor, strength, loyalty) as well as their tribal pride (see al-Khansa's lament, p. 631). Readers might also note how a sense of the physical environment pervades the Koran itself (see p. 633). The stark grandeur of Allah is reflected in the uncluttered immensity of the Arabian desert.

The Arabic oral tradition also included storytelling as a form of entertainment. Explain to students that these storytellers worked under much the same imperative as popular movie-makers: to grip and galvanize an audience. For example, witness in the Sindbad story (p. 640) the writer's use of shock and gore; this is a horror story in fanciful surroundings.

The main key to the Persian and Arabic literatures, however, is an understanding

Ahura Mazda, the chief god of Zoroastrianism, the religion of ancient Persia. *Ahura Mazda, a benevolent god, was usually represented as a winged figure.*

Erich Lessing/Magnum Photos, Inc.

Though they originated as two of many gods worshipped by the polytheistic early Medes and Persians, the good Ahura Mazda (Ormazd) and his evil twin Ahriman evolved into the only two divinities of Zoroastrianism. Many representations like this one of Ahura Mazda are found in the great palace at Persepolis (in what is now southwestern Iran). The technique of bas–relief seen here— sculptural projection raised slightly above the surrounding surface—may have been copied from the Assyrians, whom the Persians conquered and from whom they borrowed many artistic and architectural ideas. This winged representation of Ahura Mazda resembles the winged animal gods of the Assyrians.

3 LITERARY BACKGROUND
Zoroastrian Literature: The earliest surviving work of Persian literature is the *Avesta,* (the hymns of Zoroaster).

4 HISTORICAL BACKGROUND
The Seventh-Century Political Map: Islam arose near two superpowers. To the northeast, the Sassanids had restored the Persian Empire after many years in which the realm had been fragmented into local kingdoms ruled by Greeks or Turko-Mongol invaders. To the north was the Byzantine Empire, or Eastern Roman Empire, which survived the Western Empire by a thousand years.

lowed Ormazd during their lifetimes would live in paradise after death.

3   As the Persians conquered their neighbors, they spread the practice of Zoroastrianism. In 331 B.C., the Greek emperor **Alexander the Great** conquered the Persian Empire. But the Persians continued to fight fiercely, first with the Greeks, then with the Romans, to preserve their religious

> The mighty Persian Empire spread the practice of Zoroastrianism, which would influence the development of later religions throughout the Middle East and beyond.

and cultural practices. The struggle would continue until the seventh century A.D. At this time, another people, the **Arabs**, would sweep through the region with the force of a whirlwind, bringing with them a new religion—**Islam**.

The Birth of Islam

4   The Arabs were largely sheltered from world events on the Arabian peninsula, which they called "the Arab island." Although some Arabs lived in cities, most led a nomadic, or wandering, lifestyle. No central power dominated the peninsula. Some Arab rulers held power locally along stretches

of Islam. Students need to grasp that this religion is a political, social, and religious system woven into one inextricable whole. It is anchored by a canon of law called the *Sharia*, which regulates every aspect of conduct from eating, dress, and social relationships to criminal justice, inheritance, divorce, and finance. Most of the writers in this unit lived and worked within this Islamic world view. If students realize the detailed and comprehensive nature of the *Sharia*, it will be easier for them to understand how Sufism arose as a search for something more.

Sufis were not rebels against Islam, but believers who wanted the hidden fruit they were sure Islam contained—they wanted to "feel the feeling." Christmas rituals may provide a useful analogy. Giving gifts, singing carols, and so on can be either empty rituals or the vehicle for an inner experience sometimes called the "Christmas Spirit." Sufis, similarly, accepted the rituals of Islam but wanted to achieve the inner experience—a living understanding of the Islamic axiom that everything is relative except God, who is absolute. They tried to gain understanding by various paths—asceticism, solitude, meditation, chanting, dancing—but the goal was always the same inner experience. This "Experience," the heart of the Sufi revelation, is the point of reference

---

Muslims are required to face Mecca when they pray, which is why a mihrab is always built facing that city. The tilework on this mihrab typifies the floral and geometric abstraction that Islamic art has always favored over representation. The outer border contains a quotation from the Koran.

? *Why does Islamic art favor abstraction?* (Depicting living things is disrespectful to Allah, the sole creator.) ■

CULTURAL DIVERSITY

Islamic Tenets: Though Islam shares many ideas and values with the Judeo-Christian tradition, it also has distinctive features. Foremost among these are the so-called "five pillars," duties required of every Muslim: to testify daily that there is only one God and that Mohammed was his prophet; to perform ritual prayers five times a day; to give to charity; to fast during a certain month each year; and to make a pilgrimage to Mecca at least once.

? *How do you think the "five pillars" affect life in the Muslim world?* (Possible response: They promote a sense of unity among the people.)

5 READER'S RESPONSE

How does the information about Islam's attitude toward Jews and Christians fit in with what you already know or think about Islam? Does this information change your impression? How?

The Metropolitan Museum of Art, Harris Brisbane Dick Fund, 1939. (39.20)

A *mihrab* from the temple of Ishfahan in Iran. *The mihrab, a prayer niche that faces Islam's holy city of Mecca, is a feature of every mosque.*

of sea coast or interior desert passages, but the nomadic tribes lived in continual movement, following the lines of desert wells. Into the vast region of scattered tribes came a man who preached a faith called **Islam** that would unify the peninsula politically and spiritually.

The founder of Islam was a native Meccan named **Mohammed** (c. A.D. 570–632). In Mohammed's day, Mecca was a city plagued by poverty. The lot of the poor so upset Mohammed that he often retreated to the hills to seek spiritual peace through meditation. Muslims believe that during one of these retreats, Mohammed was visited by the angel Gabriel, who revealed to him the word of God. Mohammed continued to witness these revelations throughout his life. Later, Mohammed gained many followers, to whom he dictated the revelations of *Allah*, the one god. These revelations were later compiled into the holy book of Islam, the **Koran**, which means "recitation" (see page 633).

Many of the traditions familiar to Christians and Jews continue in Islam. For example, the Hebrew laws from the time of Moses are fundamental to the teachings of Islam. And, like Christians, **Muslims**—the followers of Islam—believe in the hierarchy of the angels and the day of judgment. Islam also teaches that God, all-powerful, acts through prophets and believers. Muslims are taught the traditions of the prophets, from Abraham to Jesus, and believe that Mohammed was the last in a long line of prophets. Although Islam rejects some of the key beliefs of Christianity, such as the concept of the Trinity, the Koran requires Muslims to respect the other believers of "the books," Jews and Christians. One of the main requirements of Islam is that believers submit their will to Allah. The word *Islam*, in fact, means "submission."

5

The Rise of the Islamic Empire ■

Islam, which stresses community and charity, held a strong appeal for Mecca's poor, and Mohammed quickly made scores of converts. However, after the first congregation of believers in Mecca, powerful men sought to silence Mohammed permanently. He narrowly escaped and fled north to Medina, where he officially founded his ministry in 613. Later, outside Medina, Mohammed's followers defeated

for much Persian poetry. It is a given that only Sufis can know what it is and that they cannot recreate it in writing. Non-Sufi readers of Sufi works can only have intimations or brief glimpses, and for the reader these glimpses raise intriguing questions: What is the nature of this mysterious Experience? How could the same Experience produce the impassioned ecstasy of Rumi (see p. 663) and the steady, sensible irony of Saadi (see p. 667)? What about Khayyám? Did he actually have the Experience? Sufi poets routinely used a lexicon of earthly pleasures—wine, music, love, and so on—to stand for aspects of their indescribable Experience. However, Khayyám could have been a failed Sufi, one who gained a living understanding of the first part of the revelation—"Everything is relative"—but never achieved the second part—"Except God, who is absolute." Because such questions arise with many Persian poets, Persian poetry is considered to be at once ambiguous and powerful.

---

6 Meccan forces, returning to Mecca in triumph. Thirty years after Mohammed's death, Arab armies, with the sword in one hand and the Koran in the other, swarmed across the Persian Empire as far east as Afghanistan and as far west as Spain. The influence of Islam proved lasting, and the word of Allah eventually spread to parts of Africa and the Far East. Today, Islam claims more than 800 million followers around the world.

The Abbasid Caliphate

8 Following Mohammed's death, Islamic political and spiritual leadership was placed in the hands of a *caliph* (kā'lif), or "successor." The seat of the caliph's power was the Caliphate. In A.D. 750, a powerful Muslim leader named Abbas and his followers, the **Abbasids**, founded a Caliphate in Baghdad (the capital of modern Iraq). Here, Arabic influences mixed freely with Persian traditions. This marriage of cultures produced splendid results. Although most Persians converted to Islam, Persian literary and governmental practices were maintained. Intellectual activity blossomed. Well before Europe opened its first university, the "House of Wisdom" had been established in Baghdad. The **Abbasid Caliphate** sparked a cultural explosion that swept across the empire. Classical Arabic civilization reached a peak between the ninth and thirteenth centuries. New stability and order allowed for developments in the sciences and the arts.

> The Abbasid Caliphate marked the cultural high point of the Islamic empire. Sciences and the arts flourished.

After Europe emerged from the Middle Ages, it received the fruit of the Arab cultural legacy. In addition to developing the Arabic system of numerals, the Arabs had made great strides in the sciences, especially algebra, chemistry, and astronomy. Arabic treatises on music theory and philosophy also influenced Europeans. Europe would also receive, via Arab libraries, the classical Greek and Roman works that fueled the European Renaissance.

7

> **"** Doubtless Mohammed had no idea of world conquest. He conceived it his duty to give all his fellow countrymen the chance of embracing Islam. If the summons was resisted by violence, then he must fight back. **"**
>
> —J. J. Saunders,
> History Today, *Vol. XI, No. 3*

The Koran has had little impact on literature outside the Islamic world, but Islam itself has become widespread, and is predominant today in the Middle East, North Africa, Indonesia, Bangladesh, Pakistan, and parts of Europe. The United States is home to Muslims with traditional beliefs, as well as to an order established in the 1930s that is now called the American Muslim Mission. Members of this order are sometimes called Black Muslims, though they reject the name themselves. Their practices are based mainly on traditional Muslim practices.

Medieval Islamic civilization kept the intellectual heritage of Greece and Rome alive during the Dark Ages of Europe. The works translated by the Arabs and Persians and the advances they made in fields such as astronomy, mathematics, and medicine fueled the European Renaissance of the fifteenth century. During the Dark Ages, Muslim influence seeped into Europe from Andalusia in southern Spain. Spanish culture still bears some of the traces of this—in the striking similarity, for example, between Andalusian and Arabian music. The lyric poetry of the Moors inspired later European troubadours, who in turn helped to engender the poetry of courtly love that subsequently influenced Dante and Petrarch. In the *Divine Comedy*, Dante employed a model drawn from

10 CULTURAL DIVERSITY

Oral Tradition: Among the pre-Islamic Bedouins, men called *rawi* specialized in memorizing and reciting poetry at festivals. Most rawi were poets themselves but would not recite their own poetry; instead, they memorized and recited each other's work. This ability to memorize thousands of lines emerged again later in the Islamic figure of the *hafiz*, or "memorizer," a person who could recite the whole Koran by heart. Traditionally, on a certain night of the month of fasting, in each community the hafiz publicly recites the whole Koran in one long sitting.

❓ *What special religious celebrations do you know of that include long readings from sacred texts?* (Answers will vary.)

HUMANITIES CONNECTION

The gold and lapis lazuli Islamic artists used in their paints gave their work a luminous quality reminiscent of the illuminated manuscripts of medieval Christian monks. This picture is unusual, however, because Muslim artists rarely painted religious scenes; and when they did they often left Mohammed's face blank.

❓ *How is medieval Islamic art different from medieval Christian art?* (In medieval Christian art, representations of Jesus were customary, and God the Father and the Holy Spirit were also sometimes depicted.) ∎

ASCENT OF THE PROPHET MOHAMMED TO HEAVEN, **Persian illustration.**

Arabic Literature

The Arabs have a long oral tradition in literature. One center of oral literature in pre-Islamic Arabia was Souk Ozak (sook' ō·zäk'), "Ozak market." Here, once a year, poets gathered to sing in bardic contests. The oral tradition is still alive in Arabic cities today. From the Arab proverbs, the most an-

10

The Bridgeman Art Library/Art Resource, New York

Islamic sources when he symbolized the ascension of the soul toward God with a journey through concentric cosmic rings.

From a purely literary standpoint, the most influential Arabic work has been *The Thousand and One Nights*. Tales from this masterpiece have found their way into the standard canon of children's stories throughout the Western world, and the spirit of the work has inspired many artists. Rimsky-Korsakov's orchestral work *Scheherazade* and the "Oriental" paintings of nineteenth-century French Romantics such as Delacroix are examples of works that attempted to capture a sense of that sumptuous world evoked in *The Thousand and One Nights*. The modern American author John Barth acknowledges his debt to *The Thousand and One Nights* as a model for his own elaborately structured plots.

As Christian Europe rose to power it forgot its intellectual debt to Islam. In the seventeenth century, however, Persian poetry burst into European consciousness with considerable force. The *Gulistan* of Saadi, the *Divan* of Hafiz, the poems of Omar Khayyám, and other works were translated into Latin, German, and French, captivating writers as varied as Goethe, Voltaire, Joseph Addison, and Benjamin Franklin. Voltaire honored his Persian sources with the literary pretense that his

---

cient of Arabic literature, to the Koran, the streets of Arab cities and towns buzz with the poetry of the Arabic tongue. While Christians traditionally use bells to call the faithful to worship, Muslims use the human voice. Throughout the day, Arabic communities echo with the various calls to communal prayer.

The Arabs have a long written tradition as well. The language of the Koran became the model of classical Arabic, which still unites Muslims worldwide in spite of numerous languages and local dialects. The study of the Koran led to the composition of the *Hadith*, "Traditions of the Prophet." The *Hadith* is a vast collection of sayings and actions attributed to Mohammed. Together, the Koran and the *Hadith* provided a sturdy foundation for the development of a thriving Arabic literary tradition.

Poetry was highly valued from the beginnings of Arabic literature. Poets were greatly respected among pre-Islamic Arabs, and they continued to be throughout the Islamic period. The Arabic word for poet is *sha'er*, literally, "he who knows." Not all poets were men, however. One type of verse, a lament for the deceased, was composed exclusively by women. In pre-Islamic Medina, early in the seventh century, a woman named **al-Khansa** wrote strikingly poignant verse about the deaths of her two brothers (see page 630).

In the classical era, many Arabic poets created sensual lyrics that stood in sharp contrast to the puritanical prose written by interpreters of the Koran. These love lyrics overflowed with courtly love conventions similar to those found in later medieval European poetry.

Much of Arabic prose dealt with interpretations of the Koran, but influential prose writers appeared in secular fields as well. The travel writings of Ibn Battuta gave birth to the modern science of sociology, and the Arab historical tradition became a model for European imitations. But Arabic prose writers also aimed at sheer, delightful entertainment: *The Thousand and One Nights*, composed in Baghdad from the ninth through the sixteenth centuries, still provides surprises to modern readers (see page 638). Perhaps the greatest gift of Arabic culture, however, was translation. The vast library of Alexandria, which housed myriad volumes of Greek and Roman literature in translation, inspired awe in Arabs and foreigners alike.

1

2

> **❝ O serene soul! Return to your Lord, joyful, and pleasing in His sight. Join My servants and enter My Paradise. ❞**
>
> —from the Koran, translated by N. J. Dawood

13

play *Zadig* had been translated from that language; and Goethe wrote his own version of Hafiz's poems, entitled the *Westostlicher Divan*.

British civil servants in India learned Persian (the court language of the Moghuls) and soon introduced Saadi, Hafiz, and other Persian poets to English households. The lushness of Persian imagery appealed to Romantic poets and emerged in the works of Victorians such as Tennyson and Matthew Arnold. The latter penned his own long narrative poetic version of the story of Sohráb and Rostám, based on the *Shahname*. The vogue for Persian poetry climaxed with FitzGerald's translation of the *Rubáiyát of Omar Khayyám*, which engendered the curious and widespread turn-of-the-century Omar Khayyám clubs.

In the twentieth century, the western audience for Persian poetry has dwindled somewhat, but Sufism as an idea continues to influence the works of poets such as Robert Bly. Among the many Eastern religions that found their way into North American life in the 1960s, one was a movement devoted to "Sufi dancing," supposedly inspired by Rumi and the Sufi order he founded.

14 RESPONDING TO THE QUOTATION

Byron was an archetypal Romantic poet—dashing, passionate, emotional.

❓ *What does his statement (taken almost word for word from Herodotus) make you think of the ancient Persians?* (Possible response: They were simple, noble, and heroic.)

HUMANITIES CONNECTION

Sultan Sayyid–'Ali was attached to the court of Humayun, the Moghul emperor of India. Muslim rulers of the time competed fiercely to attract the finest poets, artists, and thinkers to their courts. Humayun lured Sayyid–'Ali away from the Persian Shah Tamasp. In painting *Nomadic Encampment*, Sayyid-'Ali was probably attempting to please his patrons, for the Turko-Mongol Moghuls were fond of romanticizing their not-so-distant past as warrior nomads on the southern Siberian steppe.

❓ *What does the competition for poets, artists, and thinkers suggest about the Muslim rulers?* (Possible response: They were cultured, wanted culture to thrive in their courts, and were wealthy enough to support many artists and thinkers.) ∎

14

❝ The antique Persians taught three useful things—To draw the bow, to ride, and speak the truth. ❞

—George Noel Gordon, Lord Byron

NOMADIC ENCAMPMENT, MIR SAYYID-'ALI, c. 1540. *At first, the Arabic conquerors of the Middle East attempted to impose their culture throughout the empire.*
❓ *Did this project succeed? Why or why not?*

Persian Poetry

Classical Persian literature flourished under Arab occupation in Persia. Under the enormous momentum of its initial conquests, the Islamic empire made hundreds of thousands of converts, not only to Islam but also to the Arabic language. But eventually the cultures and languages of the conquered peoples made a comeback. Less well-controlled reaches of the empire produced their own ruling dynasties. In Iran, for example, the **Samanid dynasty** held considerable power from 875 to 999. Although it upheld Islamic law, this dynasty, a family of rulers descended from Persians, encouraged the use of Persian forms for artistic pursuits.

Courtesy of The Arthur M. Sackler Museum
Harvard University, Cambridge, Massachusetts, Gift of John Goelet

READING CHECK

1. What was the main religion of ancient Persia? (Zoroastrianism)
2. What beliefs do Muslims and Christians have in common? (life after death, a day of judgment, one god)
3. What is the *Hadith*? (a collection of Mohammed's sayings)
4. What happened to Persian literature during the Samanid period? (It flourished.)
5. What is the most important belief in Sufism? (A direct experience with Allah can be achieved through intuition.)

FOR FURTHER STUDY

Nonfiction
Islam by Alfred Guillaume is a readable overview of the religion and its history.
Fiction
The Dunyazadiad by John Barth is a twist on *The Thousand and One Nights*.
Films
The Home and the World by Satyajit Ray gives an inside view of Muslim culture. ■

The first great Persian poets and prose writers arose under Samanid patronage. **Dakiki** (d. 975) was the first important poet of this Persian revival. His work emphasized Persian history, including Zoroastrian ideas. Later, **Ferdowsi** (c. 940–1020) used Dakiki's material in the composition of the Persian epic **Shahname**, or *Book of Kings* (see page 646).

> Persian culture made a comeback under the Samanid dynasty. The use of the Persian language in poetry, initially suppressed by the Islamic empire, was revived.

The poet **Omar Khayyám** (c. 1048–1131) wrote in a traditional Persian form, the ***rubá'i***. The *rubá'i* was not considered "high art" by Khayyám's contemporaries; in fact, the poet was immortalized not by Persians but by the nineteenth-century translator Edward FitzGerald. FitzGerald's fabulously popular translation of the *Rubáiyát* (see page 654) has made Khayyám the most famous Persian poet in the West.

Some of the greatest works of Persian poetry were a product of **Sufism**, a sect of Islam that attracted many Persian followers. A mystical sect, Sufism teaches that a direct experience with Allah can be achieved through intuition. Sufis developed a popular poetic form called the *ghazal*, a type of ode. The Sufi poet **Hafiz** (1326–1389) was a master of this form. **Rumi** (1207–1273) wrote the *Masnavi*, a book of mystical poetry that crowns the literary masterpieces of Sufi poetry (see page 661).

Persian Prose

Most Persian prose works were produced in the fields of philosophy and history. Animal fables, however, were also a great favorite among Persian audiences. In fact, the *Panchatantra*, a collection of fables from ancient India (see page 478), came to the West by way of a Persian translation. The Sufis produced Persian prose works in the form of sayings, anecdotes, and didactic stories. The *Gulistan* of **Saadi** (see page 665), a thirteenth-century Sufi sage, stands as a masterpiece of Persian prose.

Courtesy of The Arthur M. Sackler Museum, Harvard University, Cambridge, Massachusetts, Gift of Stuart Cary Welch

Binder of the *Divan (Poetical Works)* of Hafiz. Hafiz was a fourteenth-century Sufi poet.

OBJECTIVES
1. *To analyze a pre-Islamic Arabic elegy to a fallen warrior*
2. *To identify the characteristics of an elegy*
3. *To write a modern elergy*

THEMES IN WORLD LITERATURE

Life and Loss
Poems of Tu Fu, pp. 526–531
"And of Clay Are We Created,"
pp. 1308–1319
From *Laments on the War Dead,*
pp. 1381–1384

The Power and Pain of Love
New Kingdom Love Lyrics, pp. 80–82
Poems by Sappho, pp. 279–283 ■

TEACHER'S RESOURCES
Review and Response
Worksheet

MORE ABOUT THE AUTHOR

As the daughter of a clan leader, al-Khansa lived a nomadic life in the desert northwest of Medina, much as Bedouins still do today. Though women in her culture generally had less power and fewer rights than men, al-Khansa was an unusually strong person, indignantly refusing to marry the man her family originally chose for her and firmly speaking her mind on many issues. She outlived three husbands and four sons, who died in battle. Her remaining son and daughter also became poets.

The works of al-Khansa, like all pre-Islamic poetry, were composed to be recited aloud. Pre-Islamic poetry is characterized by nature imagery, metaphor, and simile. Al-Khansa's consummate skill in the use of these elements comes through even in translation. Lost in translation, however, is her mastery of complex sound devices. In the original Arabic, her poems reveal elaborate metrical schemes, using variations on sixteen possible meters, and a rhyme scheme that maintains the same end-sound throughout each poem.

ABOUT THE TRANSLATOR

Willis Barnstone (1927–) teaches comparative literature at Indiana University and has published many volumes of poetry in translation. Barnstone believes that translators must be faithful not only to the language but also to the poetic quality of the original. Every good translator, he maintains, must think like a poet.

al-Khansa
c. A.D. 575–c. 644

FIGURE OF A WOMAN WRITING, TCHÉHEL SOLOUN, seventeenth century, Persian.

SEF/Art Resource, New York

Her full name was Tumadir bint Amr, but this Arabian poet is best known by her nickname, *Khansa,* which means "snub-nosed." Only a few facts about her have survived the centuries since she lived. She was born about A.D. 575 and belonged to the Sulyam tribe and the Sharid clan. She was married to a kinsman and bore six children. Around 630, when she was in her mid-fifties, her community accepted the then-new religion of Islam. She joined them and may even have been part of the delegation that went to Medina to offer its submission directly to Mohammed. The exact date of her death is unknown, but she lived into old age, dying around 644 or, as some reports assert, perhaps as late as 660.

Only a thousand or so lines of al-Khansa's poetry remain, but that fragment is enough to assure her place in Arabic literature. Her work is technically brilliant, emotionally rich, and highly eloquent. Among her poems is "On Her Brother," an elegy, or poem composed to lament one who is dead. Even in al-Khansa's day, the elegy was an ancient form. But she gave it a new degree of refinement. Her poem is richly textured with pride and sorrow that resonate through time. The poem conveys a sense of the characters of both the subject and the poet.

As a poet, al-Khansa enjoyed respect and high status in her community. Pre-Islamic clans such as hers felt themselves blessed when one of their members proved to have the poetic gift, because through poetry the memory of their accomplishments could endure beyond their lifetimes. A talented poet like al-Khansa thus helped to ensure the community's immortality. Her poems have not only kept her name and those of her brothers alive, but have also preserved the memory of her clan.

ON HER BROTHER

al-Khansa

translated by

WILLIS BARNSTONE

Reader's Guide

Background Although al-Khansa died a Muslim, her poetry belongs to the pre-Islamic era. Pre-Islamic Arab society in general did not believe in an afterlife; for them, the only possible immortality was an enduring reputation. Since the Arabs of al-Khansa's time had no tradition of historical writing, it was the poets who preserved the memory of esteemed community members and their deeds.

Writer's Response To the pre-Islamic Arabs, immortality meant being remembered by the living. Do you agree that this is a form of immortality? In what other ways can people be "immortalized"? Freewrite your ideas.

Literary Focus Usually, an **elegy** is a poem that memorializes the death of a person or laments something lost. Elegies may express sorrow over the passing of life and beauty, or they may be meditations on the nature of death. An elegy is usually formal in language and structure, and its tone is usually solemn or melancholy.

ON HER BROTHER

In this poem al-Khansa honors a brother lost in battle. What aspects of his character does she emphasize most?

My brother was not a camel driver,
a coward, shallow-hearted like a beast.

His sword glittered like a pool
under roaming night clouds.

5 He ran faster
than any of his men.

EXTENSION AND ENRICHMENT

Art Project. Divide students into groups, and have each group illustrate one scene mentioned in the poem, for example, the brother on horseback, raucous attackers overtaking him, and bereaved families visiting a grave. Illustrations may be drawings or photo montages. Encourage interested students to research Bedouin lifestyles for possible details. Have students arrange their illustrations in the order in which the images occur.

CLOSURE

Ask students which of their own qualities they would most like to be remembered for. Next, ask them to decide which aspects of her brother's character al-Khansa wanted remembered. Then guide students in evaluating the extent to which the poem achieves its purpose. Does it make the brother's character vivid and memorable to you? If so, which parts are most effective? If not, to whom might the poem appeal today? ∎

2 READER'S RESPONSE

Describe your reaction to the events of al-Khansa's brother's death. (Accept reasonable responses.)

MAKING JUDGMENTS

Is the purpose of al-Khansa's elegy to meditate on the nature of death, or to preserve the memory of her brother? (Possible response: to preserve the memory of her brother) Why do you think so? (Most of the imagery focuses on his personal characteristics.)

ANSWERS

First Thoughts

Possible responses: sad, angry, disillusioned, proud

Interpreting Meanings

1. *Metaphor:* he was not a camel driver. *Similes:* he was not cowardly and shallow-hearted like a beast; his sword glittered like a pool under night clouds; he was like a knight. *Comparison:* he ran faster than his men.
2. Possible responses: Lines 7–8 convey sorrow. The poem also expresses love and admiration (lines 3–6, 11–14) and anger (lines 1–2, 15–16).

Applying Meanings

Answers will vary.

Creative Writing Response

Writing an Elegy. Each elegy should contain descriptive details and be unified by a dominant impression. ∎

What good is life—even if he were
happy—since he ran out of time?

Each man whose family was happy in him
10   will visit his grave.

You saw a knight
on a horse running with its tail floating

in the wind, a brown warrior wrapped
in a coat of thin iron.

15   When they overtook him they shouted
like shepherds at daybreak.

Battle scene, Persian, c. 1530.
How do you think the speaker of the poem feels about war?

Courtesy of the Freer Gallery of Art, Smithsonian Institution, Washington, D.C., 54.4—Battle Scene. Persian painting. Attributed to Muhmud Musawwir. Safavid period. Tabriz school or Qazvin, 16th century. Color and gold on paper: 32.2 × 20.6 cm.

First Thoughts

What emotions are expressed in "On Her Brother"? Is the speaker sad, angry, or indifferent? What makes you say so?

Interpreting Meanings

1. What **figures of speech**, or comparisons, does al-Khansa use to make her opinion of her brother's worth clear?
2. Which lines in al-Khansa's **elegy** convey her sorrow? What feelings besides sorrow does she express? Explain.

Applying Meanings

What human needs do you think are met by a memorial such as an elegy?

Creative Writing Response

Writing an Elegy. Write a brief elegy in remembrance of someone who has died whose loss you keenly felt. You need not write about someone you knew personally; you might choose someone famous, like Martin Luther King, Jr. Use figures of speech and images that fittingly express your sadness.

The Koran
C. A.D. 651–652

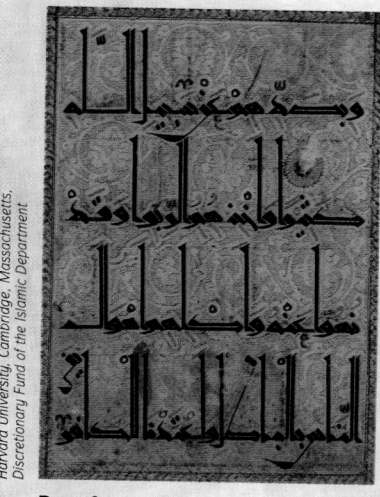

Page from a Koran, c. 1100.

To more than eight hundred million Muslims, the Koran (kə·ran′) is the word of Allah, the Arabic name for God. According to Muslim belief, the Koran comes from tablets kept in heaven, dictated by the angel Gabriel to the prophet Mohammed.

Mohammed was born into a prominent family in the Arabian city of Mecca around A.D. 570. Despite his family's social position, Mohammed's childhood was filled with hardship and sorrow. By the age of six he was an orphan. Nevertheless, by adulthood he had managed to become a worldly and successful merchant.

When he was about forty, this prosperous businessman, possibly troubled by civil unrest in Mecca, began to meditate at night in a hillside cave near his home. It was here that, according to Islamic belief, the angel Gabriel appeared to Mohammed and announced, "You are the messenger of God." Mohammed received numerous visions, or revelations, in the years that followed, and he dedicated his life to preaching the oneness of God and rejecting the beliefs that many Arabs followed in his day.

Mohammed recognized similarities between the messages he had received and the doctrines of Christianity and Judaism. However, more than these religions, Mohammed's preaching emphasized the power of divine judgment and the need for pious submission to the will of Allah. Hence, the name given to Mohammed's religion, *Islam*, means "submission." One who accepts Islam is a *Muslim*—"one who submits to God."

According to tradition, Mohammed could neither read nor write, so his followers memorized his utterances or jotted them down on whatever they could find—a leaf, a scrap of leather, a rock. After Mohammed died, his followers feared that his words would be lost forever if they did not gather all these versions and record them in a single authoritative Arabic text. Within twenty years, a group of scribes had accomplished this goal and had ordered the destruction of all other versions of Mohammed's revelations. They called this scripture the *Koran*, an Arabic word meaning "recitation," and decreed it the official scripture of Islam.

CULTURAL BACKGROUND
Contemporaries described Mohammed as a charismatic man whose personal charm drew others to him. Many of his later visionary experiences are said to have come to him without words. They were signaled by a ringing bell that only he could hear or by an unexplained physical sensation.

Many of Mecca's prosperous merchants reacted hostilely to Mohammed's teaching. In 622, a plot against his life forced the prophet to make his famous *Hegira* (emigration) from Mecca to Medina, another city in Arabia. Mohammed and his seventy followers began to attract attention by attacking hostile merchant caravans. By 624, Mohammed's followers numbered three hundred. They defeated an army of one thousand in a battle that came to be known as "The Miracle at Bedru." As a result of this victory, thousands converted to Islam. In 630, Mohammed returned triumphantly to Mecca and destroyed the idols worshiped in the Kaaba, then a pagan shrine. Since that time, Muslims have regarded the Kaaba as the most holy site of their religion and face in its direction five times a day to pray.

When Mohammed died in 632, Islam had already swept across Arabia, eventually reaching all of the Near East, North Africa, and much of South Asia.

ABOUT THE TRANSLATOR
N. J. Dawood. See *The Thousand and One Nights* on page 640.

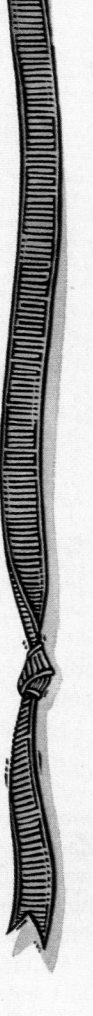

OBJECTIVES

1. *To understand the importance of the Koran in the Islamic religion and in Arabic literature*
2. *To identify antithesis and recognize its use*
3. *To write and deliver a modern sermon on morals or responsibility*

VOCABULARY IN CONTEXT

The words listed below will appear in the side margin at the point of instruction:

1. admonition
2. abhor
3. chide
4. renown
5. fervor

PREREADING FOCUS

Background: The Surahs, or chapters, of the Koran are arranged according to their length, with the longest at the beginning, rather than in the order in which they were revealed to Mohammed or according to their topic. "The Exordium" is an exception; although brief, it opens the Koran. The other three Surahs presented here appear near the end of the Koran. All three focus on beliefs about this world and the next that are central to Islamic theology, and each emphasizes the moral responsibilities of the individual.

Oral Response: Have students think of a time when they, or someone they know, faced a difficult decision and felt torn between what they felt was right and the popular or easy thing to do. Provide examples of the struggle between good and evil that can be seen in the events of everyday life.

Literary Focus: In the example of antithesis from Alexander Pope, humanity contrasts with divinity. The sentence can be seen as "balancing" a contrasting infinitive and an adjective on either side of the semicolon: "to err" and "human" on one side and "to forgive" and "divine" on the other. Words and phrases showing antithesis can also balance on either side of a coordinating conjunction or comma: "The two most powerful words in the world today are not guns and money, but wheat and oil."—Frederic Birmingham

Reader's Guide

from the KORAN

Background

Because of the Koran's divine authority, as well as the grace and power of its language, orthodox Muslims consider it perfect and unalterable. Consequently, when readers recite the Koran on public occasions, precise rules govern their tone and pronunciation. In addition, Muslims consider that translations can lead to distortion and can only approximate the words of Allah. Although the Koran appears in Turkish, Urdu, English, and many other languages, these translations are considered paraphrases and cannot be used for rituals or ceremonies.

Because of the Koran's importance in Islam, Muslim scholars have devoted their lives to the study of the text. This practice, known as *tafsir*, involves interpreting classical Arabic words and writing commentaries on various passages of the holy book. The purpose of *tafsir* is to ensure that Muslims understand Allah's revelation, but the scholars' work has served, as well, to confirm the Koran as the perfect model of Arabic grammar and diction.

The central theme of the Koran is that there is only one all-powerful God—Allah—who created the world. This God is merciful and compassionate, but he is also the God of Judgment Day. The proper response to Allah is to submit to his will, be generous to the poor, and lead an upright life. Every individual has a choice between following the good, which leads to an afterlife of eternal bliss, or giving in to evil, which leads to eternal damnation.

Oral Response

Discuss with your classmates the idea of an eternal struggle between good and evil. When have you been aware of such a struggle, either in your own life or in the world around you?

Literary Focus

Antithesis is a form of parallelism in which sharply contrasting ideas are expressed in grammatically balanced sentences. For example, the English poet Alexander Pope wrote "To err is human; to forgive, divine." The statement presents the antithesis between humans who err (sinners) and a divine God who forgives.

from the KORAN

translated by

N. J. DAWOOD

The Koran consists of 114 Surahs, or chapters. Notice that each of the following Surahs begins in the same way, with the line "In the name of Allah, the Compassionate, the Merciful." Why do you think this is done?

THE EXORDIUM

*IN THE NAME OF ALLAH
THE COMPASSIONATE
THE MERCIFUL*

*Praise be to Allah, Lord of the Creation,
The Compassionate, the Merciful,
King of Judgment-day!
You alone we worship, and to You alone
we pray for help.
Guide us to the straight path
The path of those whom You have favored,
Not of those who have incurred Your wrath,
Nor of those who have gone astray.*

1

THE CESSATION

*In the Name of Allah,
the Compassionate, the Merciful*

When the sun ceases to shine; when the stars fall down and the mountains are blown away; when camels big with young are left untended and the wild beasts are brought together; when the seas are set alight and men's souls are reunited; when the infant girl, buried alive, is asked for what crime she was slain; when the records of men's deeds

2

The Metropolitan Museum of Art, Rogers Fund, 1910 (10.218)

Koran stand from Turkestan, eighth to fourteenth century.

READING CHECK

1. What basic belief does Islam share with Judaism and Christianity? (a belief that there is one God, the same as that worshiped by Jews and Christians)
2. What role does the angel Gabriel play in the life of Mohammed? (The angel told Mohammed that he was Allah's special messenger.)
3. Who is addressed at the beginning of each chapter, or Surah? (Allah)

4. What scene is described in "The Cessation"? (the end of the world, Judgment Day)
5. According to the Koran, what follows every hardship? (ease)

RETEACHING

To reteach the Koran, divide students into four groups. Have each group script one of the Surahs for a choral reading. Allow time for planning and practice, and then have the groups perform their readings for the class. Afterward, ask the class to discuss how the choral reading affected their understanding or appreciation of the meaning and beauty of the text.

3 ANALYZING

Mohammed calls his message a warning and asks, "Whither then are you going?" What is the central message of the prophet in "The Cessation"? (The prophet warns that all people will have to answer for their deeds at the end of the world. Those who have the will to choose an upright life will be going to Paradise; those who do not will be going to Hell.)

4 LITERARY ELEMENT

Antithesis: Which ideas are contrasted in "Daylight"? (light of day, fall of night; life to come, present life; orphan, shelter; error, guidance; poverty, enrichment) How do these contrasting ideas emphasize Allah's mercy? (They show the many ways Allah cares for his people.)

COMPARING LITERATURE

"The Cessation," "Daylight," and "Comfort" offer advice on how to behave. Suggest that students compare this advice to that offered in the excerpt from the *Tao Te Ching*, pp. 541–550.

---

admonition (ad'mə·nish'ən): warning

abhor (ab·hôr'): draw back in hatred or disgust

chide (chīd): scold mildly

renown (ri·noun'): great fame

fervor (fûr'vər): zeal

PRAYER IN THE MOSQUE OF 'AMR, JEAN-LÉON GÉRÔME (1824–1904).
? *What attitude toward Allah do these selections urge?*

The Metropolitan Museum of Art,
Bequest of Catharine Lorillard Wolfe, 1887.
Catharine Lorillard Wolfe Collection (87.15.130)

are laid open and the heaven is stripped bare; when Hell burns fiercely and Paradise is brought near: then each soul shall know what it has done.

I swear by the turning planets and by the stars that rise and set; by the fall of night and the first breath of morning: this is the word of a gracious and mighty messenger, held in honor by the Lord of the Throne, obeyed in heaven, faithful to his trust.

No, your compatriot is not mad. He saw him[1] on the clear horizon. He does not grudge the secrets of the unseen; nor is this the utterance of an accursed devil.

Whither then are you going? ⌐ 3

This is an admonition to all men: to those among you that have the will to be upright. Yet you cannot will, except by the will of Allah, Lord of the Creation.

DAYLIGHT

In the Name of Allah,
the Compassionate, the Merciful

By the light of day, and by the fall of night, your Lord has not forsaken you, nor does He abhor you.

The life to come holds a richer prize for you than this present life. You shall be gratified with what your Lord will give you.

Did He not find you an orphan and give you shelter?

Did He not find you in error and guide you?

Did He not find you poor and enrich you?

Therefore do not wrong the orphan, nor chide away the beggar. But proclaim the goodness of your Lord.

4

COMFORT

In the Name of Allah,
the Compassionate, the Merciful

Have We[2] not lifted up your heart and relieved you of the burden which weighed down your back?

Have We not given you high renown?

Every hardship is followed by ease. Every hardship is followed by ease.

When your task is ended resume your toil, and seek your Lord with all fervor.

---

1. **He saw him:** a reference to the Prophet's vision of Gabriel.

2. **We:** Allah.

1. Mixed-media Presentation. Guide the class in creating a mixed-media presentation based on these Surahs of the Koran. Students should choose music that they think is appropriate for the tone and content of each Surah, then create videos or slide presentations to accompany the music, showing images that echo the message of the Surah. Consider arranging for other classes to view the presentation.

2. Research Project. Point out that in the seventh century A.D., Arabs had far greater knowledge of astronomy and other sciences than Europeans. For example, in "The Cessation," the phrase "the turning planets" reveals knowledge of each planet revolving around the sun and rotating on an axis. Assign students to research the extent and the sources of scientific knowledge in the Arab world at this time.

CLOSURE

Ask students how common it is for people to violate their personal codes of ethics and how people often feel when they do something they believe is wrong. Then ask them to speculate about why each Surah begins "In the name of Allah, the Compassionate, the Merciful." Guide them in seeing that the possibility of compassion and mercy is a central theme in the Koran, as in the literature of many other religions with strict codes of ethics. ■

First Thoughts

Do these excerpts from the Koran remind you of any other examples of sacred literature that you have read elsewhere in this book? Explain.

Identifying Facts

1. In "The Exordium," what does the speaker ask Allah to do?
2. What does "The Cessation" say souls will learn when the earth ends?
3. According to "Daylight," what three things should a person do to show gratitude for the Lord's goodness?
4. What reassuring words does "Comfort" offer?

Interpreting Meanings

1. In "The Exordium," Mohammed seeks guidance to "the path of those whom You have favored,/Not of those who have incurred Your wrath." The righteous, described in the first prepositional phrase, stand in **antithesis** to the sinful, described in the second prepositional phrase. Find and explain one or two other examples of antithesis in these excerpts from the Koran.
2. Many of the sentences in "Daylight" and "Comfort" are punctuated as questions. How does the use of questions reinforce the point being made in these passages?
3. Which of the images in these excerpts do you find most striking? What impact do you think these images are intended to have on readers?

Applying Meanings

In "The Cessation," Mohammed admonishes his followers to be "upright." In "Daylight," he instructs them not to "wrong the orphan, nor chide away the beggar." How might modern Muslims apply these teachings to decisions in their daily lives?

Creative Writing Response

Composing and Delivering a Sermon. Create a brief **sermon**—a speech that addresses morals or responsibility—to deliver to your classmates. Begin by choosing for your theme some moral lesson: the necessity for personal responsibility; the need to consider the rights of others; the importance of working cooperatively. Decide how you want to motivate your friends—through fear of punishment, hope for reward, an appeal to their sense of fairness, or some other means. Then write your sermon. You might want to practice delivering your sermon at home before presenting it to the class.

LITERARY BACKGROUND

The first translation of *The Thousand and One Nights* into a European language was Antoine Galland's 1704 French version, which led to an English translation in 1706. Since then, many Western authors, such as Alexander Pope and William Wordsworth, have been inspired by *The Thousand and One Nights*.

CULTURAL BACKGROUND

The frame story and a few of the episodes in *The Thousand and One Nights* came from a Persian storybook called *The Thousand Tales*, which was translated into Arabic around A.D. 850. Over the next several centuries, these tales became a part of the oral tradition. During the course of many retellings, the tales picked up more and more Arabic cultural elements. They also developed the action-packed plots and long, rambling sentences—punctuated by the storyteller's gestures and intonations—that mark Arabia's early oral literature.

COMPARING LITERATURE

Boccaccio's *Decameron* (pp. 813–820) and Chaucer's *The Canterbury Tales* (pp. 772–785) are also unified by frame stories. Each frame reflects its own time and culture. Boccaccio's tales are told by a group of house-bound people waiting out one of the epidemics of bubonic plague that swept medieval Europe. Chaucer's are told by a group of medieval Christians making an annual religious pilgrimage.

The Thousand and One Nights
c. 850–c. 1500

The Granger Collection, New York

**Frontispiece by Edmund Dulac from
Sinbad the Sailor and Other Stories.**

Ever since the writer Antoine Galland translated *The Thousand and One Nights*—or *The Arabian Nights' Entertainments*—into French in the early eighteenth century, this collection of tales has been the best-known and most widely read work of Arabic literature in the West. The often fantastic adventures of the characters Ali Baba, Aladdin, and Sindbad are known throughout the world today.

The Thousand and One Nights probably developed over several centuries. The original stories came from many oral and written sources, including such collections as the Indian *Panchatantra* (see page 478) and tales brought by travelers from China, India, and every part of the Middle East. Scholars have identified sources for many of the stories, but the true origins of many others remain unknown because they exist in more than one version and in more than one language.

The earliest references to *The Thousand and One Nights* appear in manuscripts from as early as the ninth century A.D. Kept alive by Arab storytellers throughout the Middle Ages, the collection grew and changed. By the mid-sixteenth century, the stories had been put into the form we know today by an unknown Egyptian compiler. The group of tales was first published in Arabic in 1548.

The tales in the collection are loosely held together by an element that was common in medieval literature—a **frame story**. In the frame story, a sultan, Shahriyar, is enraged at his wife's unfaithfulness and orders her executed. He then takes a new wife each day but has her killed at dawn the next day because he believes that no woman can ever be faithful. The supply of potential wives is running low when the sultan takes Scheherazade (shə·her′ə·zä′də) as his wife.

Scheherazade is a spellbinding storyteller. Each night, she entertains the sultan with a new tale but delays revealing the ending until the following night. The captivated sultan keeps postponing her execution in order to hear the stories. After one thousand and one nights of tales, he abandons his plans to kill Scheherazade, and the couple remains happily married.

OBJECTIVES

1. *To recognize the place of* The Thousand and One Nights *and of the tales of Sindbad in Arabic and world literature*
2. *To identify the basic pattern of plot development*
3. *To write a modern folktale and an analysis of the character of Sindbad as a first-person narrator*
4. *To infer meanings of words from context*

THEMES IN WORLD LITERATURE

The Quest and the Perilous Journey

"Theseus," pp. 28–33
"The Search for Everlasting Life" from the *Epic of Gilgamesh*, pp. 141–145
"Hundred Questions" from the *Mahabharata*, pp. 458–466

The Stirrings of the Imagination

The Tempest, pp. 844–932
"The Lorelei," pp. 1011–1014 ■

VOCABULARY IN CONTEXT

The words listed below will appear in the side margin at the point of instruction:

1. rent
2. disconsolately
3. spits
4. corpulent
5. ogre
6. approbation
7. martyr's
8. nimbly
9. stupendous
10. contrived

Reader's Guide

from THE THIRD VOYAGE OF SINDBAD THE SAILOR
from The Thousand and One Nights

Background

Sindbad, one of the heroes in *The Thousand and One Nights*, is a rich young man from Baghdad (now the capital of Iraq) who becomes a sea merchant after recklessly spending all of his wealth. Sindbad's marvelous adventures during the several voyages he makes to regain his fortune are the subject of this story cycle. The stories of Sindbad the Sailor are almost certainly Arabic in origin, but no one knows from which part of the Arab world they come. Some scholars believe that the tales originated in Baghdad. Others argue persuasively that the stories originated in Oman (a country on the southeast coast of the Arabian peninsula) and became associated with Baghdad only later.

Every seafaring culture—ancient Greece, medieval Arabia, and post-Renaissance Europe, to name a few—has produced imaginative literature about adventures at sea. In seafaring literature, the voyage becomes an opportunity to show courage and ambition, the shipwreck is a symbol of ultimate misfortune and loneliness, and the threatening monster represents the universal fear of the unknown.

Writer's Response

Even if you have never read a Sindbad story before, you might know something about Sindbad and his adventures or about other seafaring adventure stories such as *Treasure Island* or *Robinson Crusoe*. Write down some of the words, phrases, and images that you associate with such stories. What do you predict will be some of the features of the story you are about to read?

Literary Focus

Most **plots** follow the same basic pattern. They begin with a situation in which there is a **conflict**, or a problem, that the characters have to solve. As they try to solve the problem, the characters encounter a series of **complications** that usually make their problem worse. This part of the plot is called the **rising action**. The rising action builds to a high point, which is called the **climax**. After the climax comes the **resolution**, the part of the plot in which the problem is finally resolved.

PREREADING FOCUS

Background: The tale of Sindbad's third voyage takes up three of Scheherazade's 1,001 nights, and each of the tale's segments is filled with adventure and high fantasy. However, like many other fantasy adventures, the tale begins realistically. The first part of the voyage can be traced on a map: from Baghdad, which is situated between the Tigris and Euphrates rivers, Sindbad sails down the Tigris to Basrah, at the mouth of the Persian Gulf. He then proceeds through the gulf into "mid-ocean"—the Indian Ocean. Arab audiences would have been familiar with this route because ancient records reveal that even before the Christian era, Omani sailors plied the Indian Ocean, trading along the coasts of Africa and India. However, in the vast ocean, Sindbad's ship is blown off course. At that point, in the tradition of seafaring adventures from the *Odyssey* to *Robinson Crusoe*, Sindbad's story enters the realm of fantasy.

Literary Focus: Most of this selection from the Sindbad tales is devoted to rising action. The conflict is sketched by the captain's speech in the third paragraph. After this speech, complication after complication arises. The action reaches its climax in the last two paragraphs, when the men blind the giant and flee. The resolution takes up only the last few lines of the story.

from THE THIRD VOYAGE OF SINDBAD THE SAILOR
from The Thousand and One Nights
translated by
N. J. DAWOOD

Who is narrating this story? List everything you learn about the narrator in the first paragraph. Then read on to the end of the third paragraph. How do you predict the narrator will respond to the dangerous situation in which he finds himself?

The Metropolitan Museum of Art, Bequest of Edward C. Moore, 1891. The Edward C. Moore Collection

Astrolabe, Yemeni, 1296–1297. *Astrolabes, which calculate the altitudes of stars, were an invaluable tool to early navigators.*

Know, my friends, that for some time after my return I continued to lead a happy and tranquil life, but I soon grew weary of my idle existence in Baghdad and once again longed to roam the world in quest of profit and adventure. Unmindful of the dangers of ambition and worldly greed, I resolved to set out on another voyage. I provided myself with a great store of goods and, after taking them down the Tigris,[1] set sail from Basrah,[2] together with a band of honest merchants.

The voyage began prosperously. We called at many foreign ports, trading profitably with our merchandise. One day, however, whilst we were sailing in midocean, we heard the captain of our ship, who was on deck scanning the horizon, suddenly burst out in a loud lament. He beat himself about the face, tore his beard, and <u>rent</u> his clothes.

"We are lost!" he cried, as we crowded round him. "The treacherous wind has

1. **Tigris** (tī′gris): river in southwest Asia, flowing from Turkey through Iraq.
2. **Basrah** (bus′rə): port at the head of the Shatt-al-Arab Channel, where the Tigris and Euphrates rivers join.

driven us off our course towards that island which you see before you. It is the Isle of the Zughb, where dwell a race of dwarfs more akin to apes than men, from whom no voyager has ever escaped alive!"

Scarcely had he uttered these words when a multitude of apelike savages appeared on the beach and began to swim out towards the ship. In a few moments they were upon us, thick as a swarm of locusts. Barely four spans[3] in height, they were the ugliest of living creatures, with little gleaming yellow eyes and bodies thickly covered with black fur. And so numerous were they that we did not dare to provoke them or attempt to drive them away, lest they should set upon us and kill us to a man by force of numbers.

They scrambled up the masts, gnawing the cables with their teeth and biting them to shreds. Then they seized the helm and steered the vessel to their island. When the ship had run ashore, the dwarfs carried us one by one to the beach, and, promptly pushing off again, climbed on board and sailed away.

Disconsolately we set out to search for food and water, and by good fortune came upon some fruit trees and a running stream. Here we refreshed ourselves, and then wandered about the island until at length we saw far off among the trees a massive building, where we hoped to pass the night in safety. Drawing nearer, we found that it was a towering palace surrounded by a lofty wall, with a great ebony door which stood wide open. We entered the spacious courtyard, and to our surprise found it deserted. In one corner lay a great heap of bones, and on the far side we saw a broad bench, an open oven,

pots and pans of enormous size, and many iron spits for roasting.

Exhausted and sick at heart, we lay down in the courtyard and were soon overcome by sleep. At sunset we were awakened by a noise like thunder. The earth shook beneath our feet and we saw a colossal black giant approaching from the doorway. He was a fearsome sight—tall as a palm tree, with red eyes burning in his head like coals of fire; his mouth was a dark well, with lips that drooped like a camel's loosely over his chest, whilst his ears, like a pair of large round discs, hung back over his shoulders; his fangs were as long as the tusks of a boar and his nails were like the claws of a lion.

The sight of this monster struck terror to our hearts. We cowered motionless on the ground as we watched him stride across the yard and sit down on the bench. For a few moments he eyed us one by one in silence; then he rose and, reaching out towards me, lifted me up by the neck and began feeling my body as a butcher would a lamb. Finding me little more than skin and bone, however, he flung me to the ground and, picking up each of my companions in turn, pinched and prodded them and set them down until at last he came to the captain.

Now the captain was a corpulent fellow, tall and broad-shouldered. The giant seemed to like him well. He gripped him as a butcher grips a fatted ram and broke his neck under his foot. Then he thrust an iron spit through his body from mouth to backside and, lighting a great fire in the oven, carefully turned his victim round and round before it. When the flesh was finely roasted, the ogre tore the body to pieces with his fingernails as though it were a pullet, and devoured it limb by limb, gnawing the bones and flinging them against the wall. The monster then stretched himself out on the bench and soon

---

3. **spans:** A span was a measurement equal to nine inches, based on the distance between the extended thumb and little finger.

1 LITERARY ELEMENT

Plot: In the original version, the story of Sindbad's third voyage takes up the 298th, 299th, and 300th nights of Scheherazade's storytelling. The 298th night ends with the sailors seeing "far off among the trees a massive building, where we hoped to pass the night in safety."

❓ *Where on a plot diagram would this part of the story be charted?* (complication or rising action) *How might a listener be affected if the storyteller paused here?* (The listener would be left in suspense.)

2 LITERARY ELEMENT

Figurative Language: To which animals is the giant compared in metaphors and similes? (a camel, a boar, and a lion) Which characteristics of the giant are implied in these comparisons? (inhumanity, surliness, ferocity, menace)

fell fast asleep. His snores were as loud as the grunts and gurgles that issue from the throat of a slaughtered beast.

Thus he slept all night, and when morning came he rose and went out of the palace, leaving us half-crazed with terror.

As soon as we were certain that the monster had gone, we began lamenting our evil fortune. "Would that we had been drowned in the sea or killed by the apes!" we cried. "That would surely have been better than the foul death which now awaits us! But that which Allah has ordained must surely come to pass."

We left the palace to search for some hiding place, but could find no shelter in any part of the island, and had no choice but to return to the palace in the evening. Night came, and with it the black giant, announcing his approach by a noise like thunder. No sooner had he entered than he snatched up one of the merchants and prepared his supper in the same way as the night before. Then, stretching himself out to sleep, he snored the night away.

Next morning, when the giant had gone, we discussed our desperate plight.

"By Allah," cried one of the merchants, "let us rather throw ourselves into the sea than remain alive to be roasted and eaten!"

"Listen, my friends," said another. "We must kill this monster. For only by destroying him can we end his wick-

Illustration by Edmund Dulac from *Sinbad the Sailor and Other Stories*.

READING CHECK

1. Why does Sindbad go to sea again? (He grows bored with his easy life in Baghdad; he wants adventure and profit.)
2. Why is the Isle of the Zughb said to be dangerous? (Apelike killer dwarfs live there.)
3. What problem do the sailors encounter in the massive palace on the island? (a giant who roasts and eats people)

4. Why is Sindbad's life spared on the first night in the palace? (The giant finds him too thin and dines on the plump captain instead.)
5. What idea does Sindbad contribute to the sailors' plan of escape? (He suggests the building of a raft.)

RETEACHING

Have students rewrite this tale from the giant's point of view. Students can give their own explanations of his relationship with the apelike dwarfs, how he felt when he found the sailors asleep in his palace, and why he acted as he did. Encourage students to create plausible motivations. Remind them to retain all the events of the plot. The retelling should end with the giant's responses to the sailors' escape.

edness and save good Muslims from his barbarous cruelty."

This proposal was received with general approbation; so I rose in my turn and addressed the company. "If we are all agreed to kill this monster," I said, "let us first build a raft on which we can escape from this island as soon as we have sent his soul to damnation. Perchance our raft will take us to some other island, where we can board a ship bound for our country. If we are drowned, we shall at least escape roasting and die a martyr's death."

"By Allah," cried the others, "that is a wise plan."

Setting to work at once, we hauled several logs from the great pile of wood stacked beside the oven and carried them out of the palace. Then we fastened them together into a raft, which we left ready on the seashore.

In the evening the earth shook beneath our feet as the black giant burst in upon us, barking and snarling like a mad dog. Once more he seized upon the stoutest of my companions and prepared his meal. When he had eaten his fill, he stretched himself upon the bench as was his custom and soon fell fast asleep.

Noiselessly we now rose, took two of the great iron spits from the oven, and thrust them into the fire. As soon as they were red-hot we carried them over to the snoring monster and plunged their sharpened ends deep into his eyes, exerting our united weight from above to push them home. The giant gave a deafening shriek which filled our hearts with terror and cast us back on the ground many yards away. Totally blinded, he leapt up from the bench groping for us with outstretched hands, while we nimbly dodged his frantic clutches. In despair he felt his way to the ebony door and

THE COLOSSUS, FRANCISCO JOSÉ DE GOYA Y LUCIENTES. *Goya was one of the greatest painters of nineteenth-century Spain and, indeed, of Europe.*
Does Goya's Colossus match your own image of the giant in this tale? Why or why not?

staggered out of the yard, groaning in agonies of pain.

Without losing a moment we made off towards the beach. As soon as we reached the water we launched our raft and jumped aboard; but scarcely had we rowed a few yards when we saw the blind savage running towards us, guided by a foul hag of his own kind. On reaching the shore they stood howling threats and curses at us for a while, and then caught up massive boulders and hurled them at our raft with stupendous force. Missile followed missile until all my companions, save two, were drowned; but we three who escaped soon contrived to paddle beyond the range of their fury.

4 LITERARY ELEMENT

Plot: The 299th night ends with the sailors' plan to kill the giant and escape on a raft. At which point on a plot diagram would these events fall? (rising action, near the climax) Which subsequent events of the plot make up the climax? (the sailors' blinding the giant, escaping on the raft, and being stoned)

approbation (ap·rə·bā′ shən): approval

martyr's (mart′ərz): of a person who undergoes immense pain or suffering for a long time

nimbly (nim′blē): moving quickly or lightly

stupendous (stoo·pen′dəs): amazingly great

contrived (kən·trīvd′): managed

COMPARING LITERATURE

Have students compare and contrast the ogre in this tale with the Minotaur in "Theseus" (pp. 28–33), and the yaksha in the selection from the *Mahabharata* (pp. 458–466), noting how each calls forth the hero's individual strengths. (To outwit the Minotaur, Theseus needs foresight, cunning, the ability to accept others' help, and physical skill. In dealing with the yaksha, Yudhistira needs respect for others and metaphysical insight. Sindbad, in escaping the ogre, needs foresight, daring, and luck.) Point out that the heroes' qualities reflect cultural values.

from The Third Voyage of Sindbad the Sailor

Enacting a Melodrama: Present "The Third Voyage of Sindbad the Sailor" as a class melodrama. Call for a volunteer to serve as narrator and assign others the roles of Sindbad, his shipmates, the captain, the dwarfs, the giant, and the hag. Have the class work as a whole to script the tale, choose costumes and props, and design scenery.

The narrator can read the tale aloud as the others act it out. Encourage the audience to cheer, boo, gasp, and so on as the action rises, peaks, and falls.

CLOSURE

Lead a discussion about Sindbad as a hero. Point out that the swashbuckling, profit-hungry adventurer is a standard character type (an archetype). Even if audiences disapprove of some of his traits, he still generates excitement and wins admiration. Ask students to think of modern characters, real and fictional, who arouse this response. Then ask them to identify the universal human needs, desires, or experiences that explain their appeal. ■

ANSWERS

First Thoughts
Answers will vary.

Identifying Facts
1. Dwarfs force them ashore.
2. roasts and devours them
3. blind him with the spits
4. on a raft they have built

Interpreting Meanings
1. *Complications:* The boat is captured; the sailors are stranded. A giant eats several of them. *Climax:* Sailors blind the giant and escape on a raft. *Resolution:* Sindbad and two others escape.
2. Possible responses: The sailors are physically realistic. Their behavior is unconvincing when they allow the dwarfs to carry them ashore and when they return to the giant's home.
3. Possible responses: *Agree:* No character but Sindbad is developed, and some of the plotting is implausible. *Disagree:* The tale has cultural value and archetypal themes.
4. cleverness and courage. greed and a mercenary attitude

Applying Meanings
Critiques should identify weaknesses in the plot.

Creative Writing Response
Creating a Folktale. Students might choose a mundane experience, but invent fantastic characters and obstacles.

Critical Writing Response
Analyzing the Narrator as a Character. Students should support their analyses with specifics from the tale. ■

First Thoughts
What did you think of Sindbad as a hero? Does he rely more on strength or on intelligence? Did any of his actions surprise you?

Identifying Facts
1. How do Sindbad and his companions happen to land on the island?
2. What does the giant do to the captain and two other companions of Sindbad?
3. How do the sailors render the giant helpless to pursue them?
4. How do the survivors finally escape from the island?

Interpreting Meanings
1. What plot **complications** do Sindbad and his companions meet in this story? What is the story's **climax** and **resolution**?
2. Did you feel that Sindbad and his fellow sailors were realistic characters? Why or why not? Did their behavior ever seem unconvincing to you?
3. Some Arab scholars have dismissed *The Thousand and One Nights* as mere popular entertainment. They have argued that the tales are not great literature because the stories have crude and simplistic plots and no depth in characterization or theme. Do you agree with this assessment? Why or why not?
4. Which of Sindbad's qualities enable him to survive? Which of his qualities do not meet the heroic ideal?

Applying Meanings
If the storyteller Scheherazade had been telling this story to you, is there any point at which she would have lost your interest? Does the plot bog down at any point? Give Scheherazade a critique of her storytelling effort.

Creative Writing Response
Creating a Folktale. Imagine that you are a modern-day Scheherazade forced to tell intriguing stories night after night in order to save your life. What story would you tell that first night? Make up a brief folktale of your own about a modern hero who launches on an adventure and encounters many strange creatures. To help structure your tale, design a plot diagram like the one below, showing the different creatures your hero encounters. Be sure to include fantastic and imaginative details.

THE JOURNEY THROUGH FINAL EXAM WEEK

Monster 3: The Memory-Sweeper

Monster 2: The Note-Eater

Monster 1: The Party-Hopper

Final Grades

Critical Writing Response
Analyzing the Narrator as a Character. Sindbad's story is written from the **first-person point of view**. The character of a first-person narrator is revealed by what he or she says and does in the story, as well as by the way he or she reveals the actions of the other characters. Write an analysis of Sindbad's character. Cite specific details from the narrative to support your analysis.

BEHIND THE SCENES

A Thousand and One Nights of Inspiration

The stories in *The Thousand and One Nights*—especially the adventures of Sindbad, Ali Baba, Aladdin, and the enchanting storyteller, Scheherazade—have inspired many artists. An example is classical composer Rimsky-Korsakov's symphonic suite *Scheherazade,* which was produced by the noted Russian ballet master, Sergei Diaghilev, in 1910. It also became the score for an animated sequence in the film *Invitation to the Dance.*

The great French artist Henri Matisse (1869–1954) produced ''The Thousand and One Nights,'' a series of charming paper cutouts based on the tales. A number of other artists, including the Russian painter Marc Chagall (1889–1985), have also used the tales as a subject for their work.

Several classic swashbuckler movies of the 1930s and 1940s were loosely based on the adventures of the Arabian Nights heroes. These films include *The Thief of Baghdad* (1940) and *Sinbad the Sailor* (1947). Many more recent films, such as *The Seventh Voyage of Sinbad the Sailor* (1958) and *Sinbad and the Eye of the Tiger* (1977) have brought the fantastic elements of these tales to life with special effects technology.

Look around for examples of the influence of *The Thousand and One Nights* on the arts. You may find examples in advertisements, on the covers of recordings, in art books, and in popular novels. Find out what aspect of the Arabian Nights tales might have inspired the artist, what tales the work refers to, and what fantastic elements the work contains. You may wish to look up the original stories that inspired the modern work. Share your findings with the class. If you like, create your own story, poem, drawing, or other artwork inspired by *The Thousand and One Nights.*

HUMANITIES CONNECTION

The post-impressionist style of Henri Matisse (1869–1954) involves flowing contours, few interior details, and large, luminous patches of color. Many of his works have patterns that bring to mind textile designs from the Islamic world.

? *How does Matisse frame the images in this work?* (with a border design) *How is a framed set of images appropriate for an illustration of* The Thousand and One Nights? (The tales in the collection are also ''framed'' by the story of Scheherazade.) ■

The Carnegie Museum of Art, Pittsburgh; Acquired through the generosity of the Sarah Mellon Scaife family, 71.23 © 1998 Succession H. Matisse, Paris/Artists Rights Society (ARS), New York

From "The Thousand and One Nights," a collection of cut-paper illustrations by Henri Matisse.

As long ago as the sixth century B.C., Persians told tales celebrating their past kings and heroes, according to the Greek historian Herodotus. These oral tales, with others that accumulated over the centuries, provided the source material for the *Shahname*. One critic has compared the epic's place in Iranian culture to that of Homer's epics in the West: They depict a time before monotheism and serve as reminders of their cultures' roots in the ancient past. At the same time, the *Shahname*'s heroes illustrate many traits that are still valued in Iranian society today.

The *Shahname*'s influence on Persian literature has also been significant. Many generations of Persian writers have considered its narrative techniques definitive, and even today the epic is valued for its insights into human motivation.

The original work consists of couplets, sets of two lines whose end-rhymes are often feminine (ending in vowels) and whose sentence structures are often parallel. Jerome W. Clinton's translation into modern English uses blank verse rather than rhyme, but maintains the formal tone of the original.

HUMANITIES CONNECTION

The calligraphy in Persian manuscripts blends with the illustrations to reinforce the overall artistic effect. These manuscripts were copied and illuminated by hand. ∎

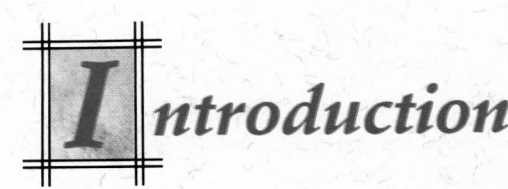

Introduction

The *Shahname:* The Epic of Persia

The *Shahname* (shä·nä·me'), or *Book of Kings,* is an epic poem of more than 60,000 **couplets**, or rhymed pairs of lines. Unlike the *Odyssey* or the *Aeneid,* the *Shahname* does not tell a single story or have a single hero. Instead, it is organized according to a

◆

couplet: *a consecutive pair of rhymed lines.*

loose chronological sequence of dynasties—some of them mythical, some historical—tracing the line of Persian kings back to the beginning of time.

The Contents of the *Shahname*

The *Shahname* begins with a description of the creation of the world. According to Persian mythology, in the thousand years after creation there arose a line of hero-kings, or *shahs,* who struggled against the forces of darkness to bring civilization to the Persian people.

A large part of the poem centers on the warfare between Iran and nearby Turan, an area of central Asia from which Turkish nomads repeatedly invaded Iran. The mythical hero in this centuries-long battle was Rostám

(rō·stam'), an Iranian warrior of supernatural strength and skill, who reappears periodically over a period of three hundred years to drive back the Turks.

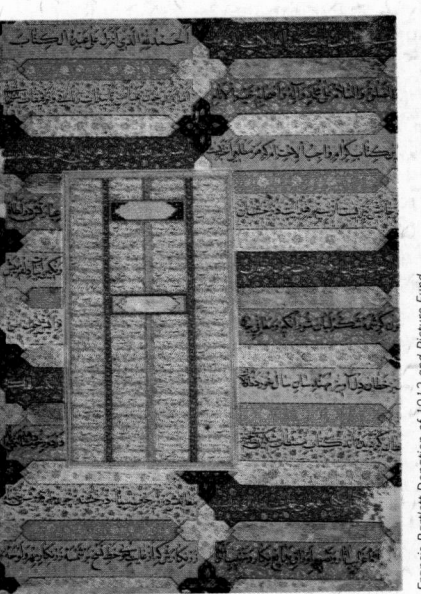

Page from a manuscript of the *Shahname.* *Different scripts are used in this ornately calligraphed manuscript, which shows Ferdowsi's text in the center rectangular area, surrounded by commentary in the margins.*
❓ *What does the ornateness of this manuscript page suggest about the importance of the Shahname to Persian culture?*

The Origin of the *Shahname*

Before the ninth century A.D., there was no lyric or epic poetry written in Persian, the native language of Iran. Only Arabic was used, for Arabs had ruled Iran since the Islamic conquest of A.D. 641. But when new rulers, the Samanids (sə·män·idz'), took over from the previous Arab rulership in Iran in A.D. 875, they encouraged the revival of Persian language and culture.

The Samanid rulers commissioned the court poet Dakiki to compile all the scattered stories of Iran's splendid past into a national epic. Dakiki never finished this monumental undertaking; he died after composing only a thousand lines.

The Poet Ferdowsi (c. 940–1020)

Dakiki's unfinished work was taken up by the poet Abol-Qasem Mansur ebn Ebrahim Hasan, known as Ferdowsi (fer·dō·sē'), meaning "Heavenly One." Ferdowsi labored over the epic for the next thirty-five years. He wrote his epic in the "pure" grammar and vocabulary of spoken Persian, avoiding all Arabic words and phrases that had flooded the Persian language.

By the time Ferdowsi finally finished the *Shahname*, the Samanid dynasty had been overthrown. But the new ruler, Mahmud (mä·mōod'), also encouraged the use of the Persian language and was an enthusiastic supporter of the arts. He offered to pay Ferdowsi fifty thousand gold pieces upon completion of the *Shahname*. But, for unknown reasons, Mahmud paid Ferdowsi less than half what the poet had been promised. Disgrun-

Detail of manuscript page depicting the poet Ferdowsi (left).

The Granger Collection, New York

tled, Ferdowsi supposedly gave his payment away to a bath attendant and a street vendor, thus openly displaying his contempt for Mahmud. Then he left Mahmud's court and made his way to the court of a Persian prince named Shareyar (shä'rē·yär), offering to dedicate the poem to him instead of Mahmud. The tactful prince persuaded Ferdowsi to leave the poem's dedication as it was— to Mahmud—and he paid Ferdowsi five times more than the poet had received from Mahmud.

The Legacy of the *Shahname*

Often considered the greatest of the Persian poets, Ferdowsi is credited with preserving the history of Persia and rescuing the Persian language from possible extinction. From his time to the present, no work of Persian literature has been more widely read and admired than the *Shahname*, and no work has done more to shape the Persians'—now the Iranians'—sense of their national identity.

MORE ABOUT THE AUTHOR

Toward the end of his life, Ferdowsi returned to his hometown of Tus, which lay in Mahmud's realm. According to one source, Mahmud regretted his treatment of Ferdowsi and tried to make amends by giving the poet a fortune in indigo, a valuable dye. But the monarch's change of heart came too late; the camels loaded with indigo arrived just as Ferdowsi's body was being carried out for burial.

Although he may have been discouraged by Mahmud's treatment, Ferdowsi, at the conclusion of the *Shahname*, shows great satisfaction and pride in his achievement:

And when this famous book
    shall reach its end,
Throughout the land my
    praises will be heard.
From that day on I shall not
    die, but live
For I'll have sown my words
    both far and wide.

ABOUT THE TRANSLATOR

Jerome W. Clinton (1937–   ) teaches Near Eastern Studies at Princeton University. Of "The Tragedy of Sohráb and Rostám," he says, "What I like about teaching it is that, although it seems different at first—the names are unfamiliar, it's set in the East—the further you go into it, the more real and familiar and human it becomes."

OBJECTIVES

1. To analyze an excerpt from a Persian epic, and to recognize the place of the Shahname in Persian literature
2. To identify the effects of dramatic irony
3. To write a diary entry in the character of Rostám
4. To compose and deliver a news report based on events in the epic

THEMES IN WORLD LITERATURE

Life and Loss

Oedipus Rex, pp. 302–371
"On Her Brother," pp. 630–632
"Freedom to Breathe," p. 1266

Triumph and Defeat

From Sundiata: An Epic of Old Mali, pp. 102–117
"Rama and Ravana in Battle" from the Ramayana, pp. 484–494 ■

PREREADING FOCUS

Background: "The Tragedy of Sohráb and Rostám" was the first part of the Shahname to attract attention in the West. Translated from Persian (Farsi) into English in 1814, it soon appeared in other European languages. In 1853, using a verse form that echoed contemporary translations of Homer, the British poet Matthew Arnold reached an even wider audience with his retelling of "Sohrab and Rustum."

Earlier portions of the Shahname present Sohráb and Rostám with many of the superhuman attributes common to epic heroes. Sohráb is a polo champion at age three, masters the bow and javelin at five, and at ten can beat any warrior in Turan in open combat. Rostám, besides being long-lived and an invincible warrior, is huge in stature. He can pull up a tree with one arm and eats a whole onager (a wild donkey), bones and all, as a snack. Both heroes also have tragic flaws: Sohráb is gullible and naive, and Rostám is proud to the point of arrogance.

Literary Focus: Dramatic irony and tragedy often go hand in hand. One definition of tragedy is "a literary work in which a noble hero is brought to ruin." The ruin can come about as a result of the workings of fate, or as a result of the hero's tragic flaw—a weakness or an error in judgment. In many literary works, including this one, the hero's tragic flaw is ironically apparent to the audience long before the hero himself realizes it.

Reader's Guide

from THE TRAGEDY OF SOHRÁB AND ROSTÁM
from the Shahname

Background

This selection from the Shahname tells of the battle between the Iranian hero Rostám (rō·stam') and Sohráb (sō·räb'), a young warrior from Turan. Sohráb is Rostám's son, the result of a single encounter some years before between Rostám and Tamine (ta·mē·ne'), a Turanian princess. Tamine has told Sohráb that the great Iranian hero Rostám is his real father. Under his armor, Sohráb wears the seal that Rostám had given to Tamine to bestow on their child as proof of his paternity. But because Tamine had told Rostám that his child was a daughter, Rostám does not know he has a son.

When the armies of Turan and Iran meet, Sohráb hopes to reveal himself to Rostám as his son by challenging the now aging warrior to hand-to-hand combat. Rostám agrees to fight, but out of pride he chooses to appear in unmarked armor and refuses to reveal his name.

Although Sohráb feels that the man he is to fight in one-on-one combat is Rostám, he cannot be entirely sure. For his part, Rostám suspects that the young Turanian favorite is his son, but he rejects the idea. At last father and son meet on the field of battle. Their first duel takes an entire day and ends in a draw when night falls. At dawn they meet again, and in this second encounter Sohráb is almost victorious, but Rostám tricks Sohráb into letting him go. After Rostám regains his strength, the two heroes meet again for a final encounter.

Writer's Response

What do you predict will be the outcome of this fateful meeting between father and son?

Literary Focus

Irony is the contrast between what is expected and what actually happens. **Dramatic irony** occurs when the audience knows something important about a situation that a character in the story does not know. In "The Tragedy of Sohráb and Rostám," dramatic irony is created when Rostám and Sohráb go into battle not knowing that they are father and son.

from THE TRAGEDY OF SOHRÁB AND ROSTÁM

from the Shahname

Ferdowsi

translated by

JEROME W. CLINTON

> *Pay attention to the animal imagery that is used to describe the two heroes as they battle. What do these comparisons to animals suggest about the Persians' views of their heroes?*

Again they firmly hitched their steeds, as ill-
Intentioned fate revolved above their heads.
Once more they grappled hand to hand. Each seized
The other's belt and sought to throw him down.
5 Whenever evil fortune shows its wrath,
It makes a block of granite soft as wax.
Sohráb had mighty arms, and yet it seemed
The skies above had bound them fast. He paused
In fear; Rostám stretched out his hands and seized
10 That warlike leopard by his chest and arms.
He bent that strong and youthful back, and with
A lion's speed, he threw him to the ground.
Sohráb had not the strength; his time had come.
Rostám knew well he'd not stay down for long.
15 He swiftly drew a dagger from his belt
And tore the breast of that stout-hearted youth.
He writhed upon the ground; groaned once aloud,
Then thought no more of good and ill. He told
Rostám, "This was the fate allotted me.
20 The heavens gave my key into your hand.
It's not your fault. It was this hunchback fate,
Who raised me up then quickly cast me down.
While boys my age still spent their time in games,

Star tile depicting the battle of Sohráb and Rostám. *Because the Shahname is vital to Persian culture, key scenes from the epic are often depicted in such decorative pieces as pottery and tiles.*

Walters Art Gallery, Baltimore

ANALYZING

What lines indicate the key role fate plays in the meeting of Sohráb and Rostám? ("fate revolved above their heads," "evil fortune shows its wrath," "his time had come," " 'This was the fate allotted me,' " " 'It was this hunchback fate,' " " 'Then Fate may thirst for yours as well' " [lines 2, 5, 13, 19, 21, 29]) What figure of speech is used in many of these references to fate? (personification)

1 INFERRING

What does Sohráb's dying speech (lines 19–40) reveal about his character? (Possible responses: He seems intelligent and philosophical in his assessment of fate and his own life. His threats of his father's revenge are spirited, revealing a strong sense of justice despite his weakened state.)

My neck and shoulders stretched up to the clouds.
25 My mother told me who my father was.
My love for him has ended in my death.
Whenever you should thirst for someone's blood,
And stain your silver dagger with his gore,
Then Fate may thirst for yours as well, and make
30 Each hair upon your trunk a sharpened blade.
Now should you, fishlike, plunge into the sea,
Or cloak yourself in darkness like the night,
Or like a star take refuge in the sky,
And sever from the earth your shining light,
35 Still when he learns that earth's my pillow now,
My father will avenge my death on you.
A hero from among this noble band
Will take this seal and show it to Rostám.
'Sohráb's been slain, and humbled to the earth,'
40 He'll say, 'This happened while he searched for
    you.' "
When he heard this, Rostám was near to faint.
The world around grew dark before his eyes.
And when Rostám regained his wits once more,
He asked Sohráb with sighs of grief and pain,
45 "What sign have you from him—Rostám? Oh, may
His name be lost to proud and noble men!"
"If you're Rostám," he said, "you slew me while
Some evil humor had confused your mind.
I tried in every way to draw you forth,
50 But not an atom of your love was stirred.
When first they beat the war drums at my door,
My mother came to me with bloody cheeks.°
Her soul was racked by grief to see me go.
She bound a seal upon my arm, and said,
55 'This is your father's gift, preserve it well.
A day will come when it will be of use.'
Alas, its day has come when mine has passed.
The son's abased before his father's eyes.
My mother with great wisdom thought to send
60 With me a worthy pahlaván° as guide.
The noble warrior's name was Zhende Razm,°
A man both wise in action and in speech.
He was to point my father out to me,
And ask for him among all groups of men.
65 But Zhende Razm, that worthy man, was slain.

2

3

4

Manuscript page from the *Shahname.*

New York Public Library Picture Collection

52. **bloody cheeks:** In Persian poetry, weeping bloody tears is the conventional image used to indicate intense grief.

60. **pahlaván** (pa·la·vän′): hero; warrior.
61. **Zhende Razm** (jən·də räzm′): the aged warrior whom Tamine had sent with Sohráb to identify Rostám. During a night reconnaissance he was killed by Rostám.

And at his death my star declined as well.
Now loose the binding of my coat of mail,
And look upon my naked, shining flesh."
When he unloosed his armor's ties and saw
70 That seal, he tore his clothes and wept.
"Oh, brave and noble youth, and praised among
All men, whom I have slain with my own hand!"
He wept a bloody stream and tore his hair;
His brow was dark with dust, tears filled his
  eyes.
75 Sohráb then said, "But this is even worse.
You must not fill your eyes with tears. For now
It does no good to slay yourself with grief.
What's happened here is what was meant to be."
  When the radiant sun had left the sky,
80 And Tahamtán° had not returned to camp,
Some twenty cavaliers rode off to see
How matters stood upon the field of war.
They saw two horses standing on the plain,
Both caked with dirt. Rostám was somewhere
  else.
85 Because they did not see his massive form
Upon the battlefield and mounted on
His steed, the heroes thought that he'd been
  slain.
The nobles all grew fearful and <u>perplexed</u>.
They sent a message swiftly to the shah,
90 "The throne of majesty has lost Rostám."
From end to end the army cried aloud,
And suddenly confusion filled the air.
Kavús° commanded that the horns and drums
Be sounded, and his marshal, Tus, approached.
95 Then Kavús spoke, "Be quick, and send a scout
From here to view the battlefield
And see how matters stand with bold Sohráb.
Must we lament the passing of Irán?
If by his hand the brave Rostám's been slain,
100 Who from Irán will dare approach this foe?
We now must strike a wide and general blow;
We dare not tarry long upon this field."
  And while a <u>tumult</u> rose within their camp,
Sohráb was speaking thus with Tahamtán,
105 "The situation of the Turks has changed

80. **Tahamtán** (ta·ham·tan'): an epithet for Rostám, meaning "huge body." Rostám was so large at birth that he had to be delivered by magic.

93. **Kavús** (ka·vōōs'): the shah of Iran.

COMPARING LITERATURE
Sohráb and Rostám realize one another's identity at almost the same moment. Have students compare their realization to Oedipus's realization that he has killed his father in *Oedipus Rex*, pp. 302–371.

? *How are the circumstances different?* (Oedipus's father dies without recognizing him. Oedipus realizes gradually, and others guess the truth first.)

5 LITERARY ELEMENT
Epithet: Why is Tahamtán, meaning "huge body," an appropriate epithet, or praise-name, for Rostám? (The hero was so large at birth that he had to be delivered by magic, and is so large as an adult that only one certain horse can carry him [see footnote line 115, p. 652].) What function might epithets such as this serve in epics? (Possible response: They relieve the monotony of hearing one name repeated, and highlight character traits.)

perplexed (pər·plekst'): uncertain

tumult (tōō'mult'): uproar

6 ANALYZING
Why does the shah believe that the Iranian army must "strike a wide and general blow" at the Turks if Rostám has been killed by Sohráb? (because if Sohráb has been able to defeat the powerful Rostám, no individual can stand against Sohráb)

1. What combat do Sohráb and Rostám engage in at the beginning of the selection? (They wrestle.)
2. What weapon does Rostám use to kill Sohráb? (a dagger)
3. What did Sohráb's mother give him that proved his identity? (a seal that she had received from Rostám)

4. Why do the Iranian cavaliers think Rostám has been killed? (They see two dirt-caked horses on the battlefield, but they don't see Rostám.)
5. Who says, "The evil I have done is quite enough," and when does he say it? (Rostám says it, in the last line of the selection, as he explains to the Iranians why he doesn't want to continue the war with the Turks.)

Have students write specifications for illustrations (or draw them) for each part of the selection. Tell them to decide how fate will be depicted, since it plays a major role in the selection. (Ferdowsi describes fate as revolving above the heroes' heads, and Sohráb calls it a hunchback.) Tell students to think about how the heroes' expressions, postures, and actions can reveal their characters.

7 GUIDED READING

Interpreting Dialogue: What is Sohráb asking of Rostám as the Iranian army makes its plans? (to spare the Turks)

8 READER'S RESPONSE

How do you feel toward Rostám at this point? How have your feelings toward him changed as his character has been revealed during the course of the selection? (Answers will vary, but students should see that his character deepens and becomes rounder.)

■ prostrate (präs'trāt): lying face down

HUMANITIES CONNECTION

The spike at the top of the helmet, like the ornamentation around the edges, served the practical purpose of deflecting blows to the wearer's head as well as the aesthetic purpose of beautifying the helmet and perhaps inspiring the wearer. Today, military personnel sometimes decorate their equipment with the names or pictures of heroes, religious figures, or mascots.
❓ *What purposes do you think these modern decorations serve?* (Accept reasonable responses.) ■

In every way, now that my days are done.
Be kind to them, and do not let the shah
Pursue this war or urge his army on.
It was for me the Turkish troops rose up,
110   And mounted this campaign against Irán.
I it was who promised victory, and I
Who strove in every way to give them hope.
They should not suffer now as they retreat.
Be generous with them, and let them go."
115   Rostám then mounted Rakhsh,° as swift as dust.
His eyes bled tears, his lips were chilled with sighs.
He wept as he approached the army's camp,
His heart was filled with pain at what he'd done.
When they first spied his face, the army of Irán
120   Fell prostrate to the earth in gratitude,
And loudly praised the Maker of the World,
That he'd returned alive and well from war.
But when they saw him thus, his chest and clothes
All torn, his body heavy and his face
125   Begrimed by dust, they asked him all at once,
"What does this mean? Why are you sad at heart?"
He told them of his strange and baffling deed,
Of how he'd slain the one he held most dear.
They all began to weep and mourn with him,
130   And filled the earth and sky with loud lament.

At last he told the nobles gathered there,
"It seems my heart is gone, my body too.
Do not pursue this battle with the Turks.
The evil I have done is quite enough."

115. **Rakhsh** (raksh): Rostám's horse. He is the only horse large and strong enough to carry Rostám. He is described in the epic as an elephant to indicate both his size and his warlike qualities.

Courtesy of The Arthur M. Sackler Museum, Harvard University, Cambridge, Massachusetts, Gift of John Goelet

Seventeenth-century Iranian helmet with chain mail.
This ornate steel helmet is inscribed with both hunting scenes and the names of heroes from the Shahname.
❓ *What lessons might Persian warriors have learned from the story of Sohráb and Rostám? Do you think they would have found the story inspiring, cautionary, or both?*

1. **Art Project.** Suggest that students plan and construct sculptures of Sohráb and Rostám. The sculptures may be either realistic or abstract, and of any size. Students should choose materials with some relevance to the characters of the two heroes. The positions of the figures should reveal as much as possible about the events and the tone of "The Tragedy of Sohráb and Rostám."

2. **Research Project.** Allow interested students to research the way Persians lived during the reign of Darius I, around 500 B.C. Have them share with the class their findings about the daily lives—the dress, implements, household furnishings, etc.—of the people who may have been the earliest audiences for oral versions of "The Tragedy of Sohráb and Rostám."

Invite students to summarize the values revealed in the selection. Prompt, if necessary, by asking how Sohráb responds when mortally wounded, and how Rostám reacts when emotionally devastated. Guide students in seeing that this epic places value on insight, transcendence, and compassion, as well as on the more conventional epic virtues of strength, courage, and determination. ■

First Thoughts

Would you change the outcome of this story if you could? How?

Identifying Facts

1. How does Rostám learn Sohráb's identity?
2. How does Rostám react to the discovery that he has killed his son?
3. Why doesn't Sohráb blame Rostám for his death?
4. What is Sohráb's dying wish? How does Rostám honor it?

Interpreting Meanings

1. Sohráb declares that what happens to him is the work of fate—in other words, it was meant to be and could not be avoided. Do you agree? What factors besides fate might have led to the outcome?
2. Readers are aware, as Rostám is not, that Sohráb is Rostám's son. How does this **dramatic irony** heighten the tragic aspect of this episode?
3. For which of the characters do you feel a greater sympathy—Sohráb or Rostám? Why?
4. How might the final outcome of the battle between Sohráb and Rostám make Sohráb's death seem less pointless?

Applying Meanings

Sometimes we reconsider a first reaction to a situation after we have looked at it more carefully. Look back at your response to "First Thoughts." Would you still change the outcome of the story? Why or why not?

Creative Writing Response

Writing a Diary Entry. How do you think Rostám's life changes after the death of his son? Does he enter into a depression from which he never recovers, gain wisdom and compassion from his experience, or become old and embittered? Does he approach life differently? Imagine that you are Rostám in old age, recording the events of your life in a diary. How did you feel after you learned that you had killed your own son? Did you feel that the entire tragic episode was senseless? Did you find any comfort as time went on? Write several paragraphs of Rostám's diary entry, using the **first-person point of view**.

Speaking and Listening

Creating a News Report. Imagine that you are a television war correspondent reporting on the duel between Sohráb and Rostám. Write a report to be delivered on the evening news after the death of Sohráb. Be sure to identify yourself and include background information about the war and the two heroes, along with a description of their final battle. Remember also to report on the peace that resulted from the duel. End with a brief comment offering perspective on the whole situation. Deliver your report to the class.

ANSWERS

First Thoughts
Answers will vary.

Identifying Facts
1. Sohráb shows him a seal that Rostám had given Sohráb's mother.
2. He weeps, laments, and tears his hair and clothes.
3. Sohráb blames fate.
4. that the Turks be left unharmed. Rostám halts the war.

Interpreting Meanings
1. Some students may say the battle between father and son was a coincidence. Others may point to tragic flaws in both heroes.
2. Possible response: Readers anticipate the heroes' sorrow.
3. Possible responses: Sohráb, because he must die; Rostám, because he must live with himself and his loss.
4. Sohráb's death saves the lives of many Turks and spares both Iran and Turan a war.

Applying Meanings
Some students may show new appreciation for the peace between Turan and Iran. Others may feel greater sympathy for the tragedy.

Creative Writing Response
Writing a Diary Entry. Students should touch on the aging Rostám's memories, and reveal feelings through diction and tone as well as by direct statement.

Speaking and Listening
Creating a News Report. Students can watch the televised news for tips on preparing and delivering their reports. ■

MORE ABOUT THE AUTHOR

Omar Khayyám was born in Nishapur (modern Neyshabur), then a major center of government and learning in the northeastern Persian province of Khorasan. He was strongly influenced by the writings of the philosopher and physician Ibn Sina, or Avicenna (980–1037), whose works contributed to the advance of Western medical knowledge. References to Khayyám's poetry appear in works by contemporaries, but Khayyám himself apparently considered his verses and epigrams minor in comparison to his scientific writings.

ABOUT THE TRANSLATOR

Edward FitzGerald (1809–1883) had been studying Persian for three years when a colleague found an ancient manuscript of Persian quatrains lying uncataloged in Oxford's Bodleian Library and gave him a transcription. Fascinated, FitzGerald began the translations that would occupy him for the next two decades. He freely adapted and rearranged the verses, creating his own interpretations. The resulting poems combine Khayyám's and FitzGerald's imagery, philosophy, and poetic skill. FitzGerald published other volumes of verse and translations, but none achieved the fame of the *Rubáiyát*.

Omar Khayyám
C. A.D. 1048–1131

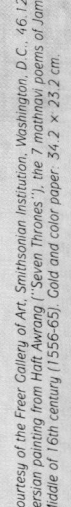

Courtesy of the Freer Gallery of Art, Smithsonian Institution, Washington, D.C., 46.12 – Persian painting from Haft Awrang ("Seven Thrones"), the 7 mathnavi poems of Jami, Middle of 16th century (1556–65). Gold and color paper: 34.2 × 23.2 cm.

TWO LOVERS LANDING ON THE ISLAND OF TERRESTRIAL BLISS, Persian, 1556–1565.

The poet Ghiyasoddin Abolfat'h Omar ebn Ebrahim is known as "Omar Khayyám" (kī·yäm'), which means "Omar, the tentmaker." Khayyám, however, was not a tentmaker, but a scholar whose knowledge extended to an amazing variety of disciplines. Not only was he thoroughly familiar with the works of Greek philosophers, but he also understood the sciences of his day, including medicine and astronomy. He was also an excellent mathematician.

While still in his twenties, he wrote a scholarly paper on algebra in which he showed how to solve a kind of problem no one had ever been able to solve before. Another paper, on elementary geometry, helped advance the knowledge of numbers. He was also one of a group of astronomers who revised the Islamic calendar. The calendar Khayyám and his colleagues produced was unmatched in accuracy until the Gregorian calendar was developed in the West almost five hundred years later.

Impressive as these achievements were, Westerners know of Omar Khayyám today not because of his work in science, but because he wrote a number of four-line verses of poetry, called *rubá'i* (roo·bä·ī'), a Persian poetic form. The poet behind the verses is a somewhat mysterious figure. It was not until the 1940s that researchers determined the dates of his birth and death. None of his poetry came to light until well after his death. And although hundreds of these four-line verses have been attributed to Omar Khayyám, scholars have so far been able to confirm his authorship of only a few of them.

In Persia, Omar Khayyám's verses enjoyed only modest popularity. But in the 1850s, an English poet and translator named Edward FitzGerald (1809–1883) was struck by the poetic beauty of the rubáiyát (the plural form of rubá'i) and began translating them into English. It was FitzGerald's translation that brought Khayyám worldwide fame as a poet over seven hundred years after he died.

OBJECTIVES

1. *To recognize the place of Omar Khayyám's verses in Persian literature and to analyze the themes of his work*
2. *To identify the characteristics of a rubá'i, or ancient Persian quatrain*
3. *To write a modern rubá'i and an essay interpreting a poet's philosophy*

THEMES IN WORLD LITERATURE

The Wisdom of the World
African Proverbs, pp. 84–87
"Carpe Diem," pp. 414–418
Zen Parables, pp. 589–595

The Search for Meaning
"The Search for Everlasting Life," from the *Epic of Gilgamesh*, pp. 136–152
"The Enchanted Garden," pp. 1258–1263 ■

VOCABULARY IN CONTEXT
The words listed below will appear in the side margin at the point of instruction:

1. destined
2. inverted
3. impotently
4. wax
5. wane

Reader's Guide

from the RUBÁIYÁT

Background

Omar Khayyám's birthplace, the region of Khorasan, or "the land of the sun," is now divided between Iran and Afghanistan. In the poet's day it lay at the crossroads of trade and travel between Asia and Europe and therefore was a bustling and cosmopolitan area. Merchants and travelers from all over the world passed through the region, enriching the native Persian culture with artistic and philosophical influences from China, India, and classical Greece.

But during Khayyám's lifetime, Khorasan was repeatedly attacked and then ruled by a Turkic people called the Seljuks (sel'jōōks'). The Seljuk Turks brought with them an authoritarian and religiously orthodox rule. Muslim orthodoxy prohibited wine and other sensual pleasures that Khayyám so clearly enjoyed. His verse, with its focus on the sweetness and pleasure of life, gently challenged the repression of the times.

Writer's Response

Omar Khayyám's *Rubáiyát* expresses that earthly life is good and to be enjoyed fully. The poet argues that it is foolish to postpone pleasure until another day because the opportunity may never repeat itself. You have met this *carpe diem* motif previously in the *Epic of Gilgamesh* and in the poems of Horace. Do you agree with this view of life? Jot down your reasons for agreeing or disagreeing.

Literary Focus

Rubá'i—rubáiyát (rōō'bī·yät') in the plural—is the Persian word for **quatrain**, or four-line verse. In English translation, the standard form for rubáiyát is that the first, second, and last lines rhyme. The third line usually does not rhyme with the other three. The rubá'i is an ancient literary form that Persian poets have used to express their thoughts on diverse subjects. Because a rubá'i is so short and its rhyme scheme so restrictive, it often makes use of metaphor or imagery to express its meaning.

PREREADING FOCUS

Background: The repressive rule of the Seljuks was not the only factor casting shadows over Khorasan in Omar Khayyám's time. There was also the constant threat of invasion by Mongol hordes. Whether because of these political uncertainties, or because of Persia's ancient Zoroastrian heritage, with its awareness of the strength of evil as well as good, the tone of some of Khayyám's verses reflects a resigned sorrow, mourning the impermanence of earthly pleasures.

In 1222, only ninety-one years after Khayyám's death, Mongols under Ghengis Khan overran the Seljuk Empire. They decimated Khorasan, razing Nishapur and other major cities and burning libraries and universities. Copies of Khayyám's *Algebra* were preserved in libraries in India, but his verses had not reached that far, and so the few copies made during his lifetime were lost. However, his poetry was popular enough to remain in the Persian oral tradition.

Literary Focus: The rubá'i, self-contained and suited to a variety of topics, has long been a popular verse form with both amateur and professional poets writing in Persian (Farsi), just as the haiku is for Japanese writers. The standard approach to writing a rubá'i is to use the first three lines to introduce the topic and the final line to comment on it. Often the last line contains a surprising statement or an ironic twist.

Past Participles

Formed from verbs, past participles can function as adjectives. The past participles of regular verbs end in *-ed*; the past participles of irregular verbs are the forms used with *have* to make the present perfect tense: *broken, caught.* Examples from the *Rubáiyát*:

Think, in this *battered* Caravanserai . . .
Among the Guests *Star-scattered* on the grass . . .

These participles allow the translator to express vivid action imagery with a minimum of words.

Reading. Have students locate three other past participles used as adjectives in the *Rubáiyát*. Ask them to determine which noun or pronoun each past participle modifies. ■

1 PREDICTING

FitzGerald reordered Khayyám's verses to suggest the progress of a day, from dawn to dark. With which images does verse 1 begin? (Night fades; the sun rises.) Which images do you predict the last verses will contain? (Possible response: nightfall, sunset)

2 LITERARY ELEMENT

Metaphor: What point does the last line of verse 7 make about the ideas introduced in the first three lines? (Life is too brief for regrets.) What metaphor makes the point memorable? (A human lifetime is compared to the brief flight of a bird already in the air.)

3 INTERPRETING

Some seek happiness in earthly glory; others, in a paradise after death. Where does Khayyám find happiness, according to verses 12 and 13? (in simple pleasures of the moment)

from the RUBÁIYÁT
Omar Khayyám
translated by
EDWARD FITZGERALD

Rubáiyát are often **epigrams**—*short, witty comments in verse form. Omar Khayyám wrote each rubá'i as a separate poem, but he repeats his major ideas. As you read, note the thoughts that are expressed most frequently in these poems.*

1

Wake! For the Sun, who scattered into flight
The Stars before him from the Field of Night,
  Drives Night along with them from Heav'n
    and strikes
The Sultán's Turret with a Shaft of Light.

7

Come, fill the Cup, and in the fire of Spring
Your Winter-garment of Repentance fling:
  The Bird of Time has but a little way
To flutter—and the Bird is on the Wing.

12

A Book of Verses underneath the Bough,
A Jug of Wine, a Loaf of Bread—and Thou
  Beside me singing in the Wilderness—
Oh, Wilderness were Paradise enow![1]

13

Some for the Glories of This World; and some
Sigh for the Prophet's[2] Paradise to come;
  Ah, take the Cash, and let the Credit go,
Nor heed the rumble of a distant Drum!

1. **enow** (ē·nou'): enough (archaic).

2. **Prophet's:** Mohammed's.

17

Think, in this battered Caravanserai[3]
Whose Portals are alternate Night and Day,
　How Sultán after Sultán with his Pomp
Abode his <u>destined</u> Hour, and went his way.

19

I sometimes think that never blows so red
The Rose as where some buried Caesar bled;
　That every Hyacinth[4] the Garden wears
Dropped in her Lap from some once lovely Head.

24

Ah, make the most of what we yet may spend,
Before we too into the Dust descend;
　Dust into Dust, and under Dust to lie
Sans[5] Wine, sans Song, sans Singer, and—sans End!

27

Myself when young did eagerly frequent
Doctor and Saint, and heard great argument
　About it and about: but evermore
Came out by the same door where in I went.

28

With them the seed of Wisdom did I sow,
And with mine own hand wrought to make it grow;
　And this was all the Harvest that I reaped—
"I came like Water, and like Wind I go."

71

The Moving Finger writes; and, having writ,
Moves on: nor all your Piety nor Wit
　Shall lure it back to cancel half a Line,
Nor all your Tears wash out a Word of it.

3. **Caravanserai** (kar'ə·van'sə·rī'): inns providing services for caravans.

4. **Hyacinth** (hī'ə·sinth'): In classical mythology, the hyacinth sprang up from the blood of Hyacinthus after he was accidentally killed by Apollo. In the *Odyssey*, locks of hair are compared to clusters of hyacinth.

5. **Sans** (sanz): without (French).

Giraudon/Art Resource, New York

Persian manuscript page. *Persian miniatures, or illuminated manuscript pages, are known for their ornate detail, jewel-like colors, and fantastic details of court and battle scenes, people in nature, and plants and animals.*

■ **destined** (des'tind): predetermined

4 COMPARING
How are the ideas in verses 17 and 19 similar? (Both note the impermanence of worldly power and glory.)

5 LITERARY ELEMENT
Tone: How do the last lines in verses 27 and 28 reveal the narrator's tone, or attitude? (The tongue-in-cheek humor of the last line in verse 27 hints at bitterness; the poignancy of the last line in verse 28 implies sorrow.) What evokes these feelings? (the uselessness of wisdom in the face of life's impermanence)

6 EVALUATING
To understand the subject of verse 71, readers can approach it as a riddle: What always moves forward and never moves backward? (time) How appropriate, or inappropriate, is a writing hand as a metaphor for time? (Most writing actually can be obliterated; however, as Khayyám's verses demonstrate, even writing that seems to have disappeared can persist in memory and tradition.)

■ **HUMANITIES CONNECTION**

Persian miniaturists began with detailed line drawings, then used gouache and sometimes gold or silver leaf to color them in.
❓ *How is the detail in this scene similar to the imagery in the poetry?* (Both are rich and striking.) ■

Omar Khayyám　　**657**

To reteach the *Rubáiyát*, instruct students to recast the verses as prose epigrams, using diction and imagery from modern America. Encourage them to use metaphors and similes as Omar Khayyám and FitzGerald did. Suggest they try to make a surprising comment or give an ironic twist to the last line of each epigram. For example:

72

Don't look to the sky to help you escape your pitiful destiny; it, like you, moves on a predetermined course.

7 LITERARY ELEMENT

Setting: Many of the rubáiyát are set in a garden or in the countryside. In Persian literature, a pastoral setting is often a metaphor for life, and the four seasons, metaphors for the stages of human life: springtime for youth, summer for adulthood, autumn for age, winter for death.

❓ *How are the seasons and elements of the garden used as metaphors in verse 96?* (A fading rose, vanishing spring, and lost nightingale are metaphors for the disappearance of youth.)

---

inverted (in·vʉrt′əd): turned upside down

impotently (im′pə·tənt·lē): powerlessly

wax (wax): gradually grow larger

wane (wān): gradually grow smaller

72

And that <u>inverted</u> Bowl they call the Sky,
Whereunder crawling cooped we live and die,
   Lift not your hands to *It* for help—for It
As <u>impotently</u> moves as you or I.

96

7

Yet Ah, that Spring should vanish with the Rose!
That Youth's sweet-scented manuscript should close!
   The Nightingale that in the branches sang,
Ah whence, and whither flown again, who knows!

99

Ah Love! could you and I with Him conspire
To grasp this sorry Scheme of Things entire,
   Would not we shatter it to bits—and then
Remold it nearer to the Heart's Desire!

100

Yon rising Moon that looks for us again—
How oft hereafter will she <u>wax</u> and <u>wane</u>;
   How oft hereafter rising look for us
Through this same Garden—and for *one* in vain!

101

And when like her, O Sákí,[6] you shall pass
Among the Guests Star-scattered on the Grass,
   And in your joyous errand reach the spot
Where I made One—turn down an empty Glass!

TAMÁM[7]

6. **Sákí** (sä′kē): wine-bearer (Persian).

7. **Tamám:** finished, complete (Persian).

1. Literary Dialogue. Have students plan and then stage meetings between Omar Khayyám and Edward FitzGerald or with other literary figures of their choice. They should plan topics of conversation based on the content of the *Rubáiyát* and the works with which the other figures are associated. Let students act out the roles for the rest of the class.

2. Research Project. Encourage interested students to compare Persian and modern art. Have them first examine Persian art from the eleventh and twelfth centuries and then locate examples of the work of various twentieth-century illustrators of the *Rubáiyát*, including Edmund Dulac and Elihu Vedder. Challenge students to consider whether the modern artists were influenced by the ancient Persians.

CLOSURE

Ask students to summarize the reasoning behind Khayyám's advice to live for the moment rather than to wait for the future. Then ask whether Khayyám's reasoning is convincing, and encourage them to back up their responses with facts and examples from their own lives. Finally, challenge students to decide how one might combine living for the present with planning and working for the future. ■

First Thoughts

What were your first reactions to Omar Khayyám's rubáiyát? Did any of them make a particular impression on you? If so, which ones?

Identifying Facts

1. In verse 12, what does the speaker say would be "Paradise enow" for him?
2. In verse 99, what does the speaker say that he and his love would do if they could?

Interpreting Meanings

1. Paraphrase verse 99. What ironic twist does the speaker give his thoughts? What other verses seem to you to express a similar idea?
2. The theme of *carpe diem* (seize the day) also appears in the Gilgamesh epic and in the poems of Horace. Does Omar Khayyám express the *carpe diem* idea in the same way as the *Epic of Gilgamesh* and the works of Horace, or do their attitudes differ?
3. Verse 24 is a particularly good example of a **rubá'i**, a four-line poem that expresses an idea in a brief, witty style, often with a twist at the end. What is the speaker in verse 24 saying about life and death? How does the ending of the poem provide a clever twist?
4. In verse 71, what is the "Moving Finger"? State the meaning of the verse in your own words. What does it imply about how one should live life?

Applying Meanings

Khayyám's *Rubáiyát* has been consistently in print since FitzGerald's translation in the 1850s. If you were a bookseller, would you order copies of the book to sell to your customers? Do you think there is an audience for the book today? Why or why not?

Creative Writing Response

Writing a Rubá'i. Imagine that you are a new Omar Khayyám, celebrating life in your own hometown in the 1990s. Using some of your favorite images and simple metaphors, write a four-line poem in praise of living each day fully. Try to follow the pattern of Omar Khayyám's rubáiyát, in which the first, second, and fourth lines rhyme.

Critical Writing Response

Interpreting a Poet's Philosophy. A hedonist makes pleasure-seeking a way of life. A pessimist expects the worst to happen. Omar Khayyám has been called both a hedonist and a pessimist. Do you think it is possible to be both at the same time? In an essay of three to four paragraphs, cite passages from the *Rubáiyát* that support your point of view. Organize your ideas by jotting down evidence on a chart like the following one.

Hedonist		Pessimist	
rubá'i #	ideas/ phrases	rubá'i #	ideas/ phrases

THE ART OF TRANSLATION

Two Translations of the **Rubáiyát**

Edward FitzGerald's translation of the *Rubáiyát of Omar Khayyám* has been called the most famous translation of a literary work into English. Other translations of Omar Khayyám's work have been made, but none has gained the popularity or fame of FitzGerald's, although most scholars agree that the other versions are more literally true to the original. The selections you have just read were taken from FitzGerald's fifth and final version of the *Rubáiyát*.

FitzGerald considered himself a "free translator" who focused on what he felt to be the meaning and spirit of the poetry, rather than on the literal meaning of the words. He wanted English readers to respond to the rubáiyát as he imagined the readers of the originals might have responded. Therefore, he used contemporary images that were more familiar to British readers to illustrate Omar Khayyám's ideas whenever the original imagery struck him as obscure.

Here is a translation by FitzGerald of a rubá'i:

> But helpless Pieces of the Game He plays
> Upon this Checker-board of Nights and Days;
> Hither and thither moves, and checks, and slays,
> And one by one back in the Closet lays.

This is a literal translation by A. J. Arberry of the same rubá'i:

> We are playthings, and heaven is the player—
> in very truth, not metaphorically: we play
> (our) little game on the board of existence,
> (then) we fall back one by one into the box of non-existence.

1. What images does FitzGerald use instead of Arberry's "playthings," "heaven," "little game on the board of existence," and "the box of non-existence"?

2. Do you prefer FitzGerald's verse translation or Arberry's literal translation? Explain your choice.

Illustration by Edmund Dulac from the *Rubáiyát of Omar Khayyám*. *In the late nineteenth and early twentieth centuries, the popularity of the* Rubáiyát *in English-speaking countries led publishers to create many beautifully illustrated versions of the work.*

OBJECTIVES

1. To recognize Rumi's place in Persian literature and to interpret a poem by Rumi
2. To identify and explain analogies used in poetry
3. To write a poem using imagery to illuminate a theme, and a paragraph explaining the meaning of a stanza

Rumi
A.D. 1207–1273

New York Public Library

Jalāl ad-Dīn Mohammed ebn Mohammed, known as Rumi (roo'mē), was born in Balkh, in the province of Khorasan, now divided between modern Afghanistan and Iran. His father was a famous teacher and mystic—one who believes that God's truth comes not through learning or through the senses, but through flashes of enlightenment.

Rumi grew up to practice Sufism (soo'fiz'əm), a mystical form of Islam. Sufis stress the importance of understanding God through personal intuition. By 1240, Rumi's fame as a Sufi teacher had spread throughout the region, and he had gathered about him a group of followers, or disciples.

The turning point in Rumi's life, however, was his relationship with the wandering holy man Shams ad-Dīn ("Sun of Religion"), whom he met in 1244. To Rumi, Shams seemed a nearly perfect example of beauty and truth, and the two mystics became inseparable. However, one night in 1247 Shams mysteriously disappeared. Researchers have recently established that the holy man was murdered and hurriedly buried close to a well that still exists in Konya. It is believed that followers of Rumi—perhaps with the consent of Rumi's own sons—committed the murder because they were jealous of Shams' relationship with their master. Assuming Shams had abandoned him, Rumi turned to poetry for consolation and wrote a collection of lyrics and odes, the Divan-i-Shams-i-Tabrizi. Rumi signed Shams' name to the poems in honor of his beloved friend and in keeping with the Sufi belief that he and Shams were one in spirit.

Rumi's prose work fills three volumes, but he is most famous for a volume of poetry entitled the Masnavi. This didactic epic of 26,000 couplets—pairs of rhyming lines—written in informal, colloquial language, defines Sufi teachings. Interspersed with the teachings are quotations from the Koran, stories of the life and teachings of Mohammed, legends of pre-Islamic poets and prophets, Arabic versions of Sanskrit beast fables, and Near Eastern folktales. It has been said that Rumi's Masnavi is for Persians "second in importance only to the Koran."

MORE ABOUT THE AUTHOR

When Rumi was a teenager, he left Balkh with his family, fleeing the Mongols who overran Khorasan between A.D. 1220 and 1222. Rumi's family wandered across Asia, finally settling at Qonia (modern Konya) in Turkey. Qonia, on the Anatolian plain, was a part of the Eastern Roman Empire, which the Arabs called Rum. It was from the name of his adopted home that Rumi took his pen name.

According to legend, one day Rumi heard the chiming hammer of a goldsmith and was inspired to begin a whirling dance. This dance was to become the principal ritual of one of the world's most enduring mystical orders, the Whirling Dervishes (dervish means "holy one"). In a trancelike state, Whirling Dervishes seek union with God by twirling in circles to the music of a flute or the beat of a drum. Tradition says that Rumi composed his poems as he whirled and danced, walked, or even bathed, and that a disciple copied them down. These unusual ways of finding inspiration produced some of the greatest poetry in Farsi, the Persian language.

Formal and Informal Language

Informal language is like everyday speech, using simple diction, contractions, and the pronouns *I*, *me*, and *you*. Formal language uses complex diction, avoids contractions, and prefers the use of *one*, *he*, *she*, and *it* to *I*, *me*, and *you*.

Informal language in the poem:
Don't grieve. Anything you lose comes round . . .
(Formal language: *One need not grieve, for anything that one loses returns . . .*)
Rumi uses informal language to create a bond with readers.

1. **Writing.** Have students rewrite in formal language the following lines from "Unmarked Boxes":
I don't want to make anyone fearful.
Hear what's behind what I say.
I'm only talking about them.

PREREADING FOCUS

Background: The Sufi of today still call Rumi "Our Master." His *Masnavi*, from which "Unmarked Boxes" is taken, has been a powerful influence both on Sufi thought and on Persian literature for over seven centuries. One critic explains that, in *Masnavi*, Rumi developed a new style of writing in Persian that uses language and images from everyday life. Rumi is also popular among Westerners because, unlike many Middle Eastern writers, he values feelings over intellect.

Oral Response: Encourage students to think of tangible losses and gains (such as belongings, pets, friends, homes), as well as intangible losses and gains (such as security or independence).

Literary Focus: Analogies are based on extended metaphors or similes, and they are often used in expository or persuasive prose. Rumi's use of analogy underscores the fact that his purpose is didactic as well as literary: that is, he intends to teach and enlighten, as well as to create a work of literary art.

Reader's Guide

UNMARKED BOXES

Background

The poet Rumi belonged to the branch of Islamic mysticism known as Sufism. Like mystics of other faiths, Sufis believe that knowledge and understanding of God come through personal experience of God, not through the senses or through study. The Sufis believe in the doctrine of *Vahdat-ol-Vojood*, or "the unity of all things." To Sufis, this means that all things profane (that is, impure or not holy) are, in fact, holy. Although this may sound contradictory, it is simply a way of saying that God is present in everything. For example, a rose, a profane object, may embody God's perfect beauty and therefore be sacred for what it represents. Sufi belief also suggests that all things and beings in the visible world are different only in form, for they are essentially one in God. Finally, the doctrine implies that God is at once present and absent—present because God resides in all beings, but absent because we do not directly perceive God through our five senses.

Oral Response

This poem begins with a statement of a comforting belief: "Don't grieve. Anything you lose comes round/ in another form." In other words, the things we think we lose—the carefree pleasures of early childhood, for example—are replaced by other pleasures, such as the privilege of getting a driver's license at age sixteen. What do you think of Rumi's idea? What things have you lost and gained throughout life?

Literary Focus

An **analogy** is a kind of comparison that explains something unfamiliar by describing it in terms of something familiar. For example, someone might draw an analogy between riding in a helicopter and an exciting fairground ride, such as a roller coaster. You might then understand that a helicopter lurches and dips, and you would know the feeling in your stomach that accompanies such a ride. Analogies can help to explain ideas and objects as well as experiences.

UNMARKED BOXES

Rumi

translated by

JOHN MOYNE AND COLEMAN BARKS

As you read Rumi's poem, note how he interprets the Sufi belief that all things are essentially one. According to this poem, what things and beings are manifestations, or physical evidence, of God?

1

Don't grieve. Anything you lose comes round
in another form. The child weaned from mother's milk
now drinks wine and honey mixed.

God's joy moves from unmarked box to unmarked box,
5   from cell to cell. As rainwater, down into
      flowerbed.
As roses, up from ground.
Now it looks like a plate of rice and fish,
now a cliff covered with vines,
now a horse being saddled.
10   It hides within these,
till one day it cracks them open.

2

Part of the self leaves the body when we sleep
and changes shape. You might say, "Last night
I was a cypress tree, a small bed of tulips,
15 a field of grapevines." Then the phantasm goes away.
You're back in the room.
I don't want to make anyone fearful.
Hear what's behind what I say.

3

Fa'ilatun fa'ilatun fa'ilatun fa'ilat.°
20 There's the light gold of wheat in the sun
and the gold of bread made from that wheat.
I have neither. I'm only talking about them,

as a town in the desert looks up
at stars on a clear night.

Courtesy of The Arthur M. Sackler Museum Harvard University, Cambridge, Massachusetts, Grace Nichols Strong, Francis H. Burr Memorial, and Friends of the Fogg Fund

MYSTICAL JOURNEY.
❓ *How do the swirling, dreamlike shapes in this drawing suggest the theme of Rumi's poem?*

19. **Fa'ilatun . . . fa'ilat:** This line is composed of phrases used to indicate various types of poetic "feet." It is the equivalent of "iamb, iamb, iamb, trochee."

Describing Natural Cycles. Rumi reveals the poetry in natural cycles, following the course of rainwater from clouds to earth to roses. Challenge students to use verbal or visual imagery in a similar way to illustrate other processes or cycles they have studied in science courses, such as photosynthesis, mitosis, or entropy. Encourage them to create poems or visual montages that reveal the natural processes.

Ask students: What speaks to you more powerfully in the poem—its imagery or its intellectual message? Encourage a variety of responses, eliciting reasons for each. Guide students to appreciate Rumi's interweaving of complex philosophical concepts and poetic imagery into a work that speaks to readers across several continents and seven centuries. ■

ANSWERS

First Thoughts
Answers will vary.

Identifying Facts
1. "Anything you lose comes around in another form."
2. a plate of rice and fish, a cliff covered with vines, a horse being saddled

Interpreting Meanings
1. ordinary things. God's joy is manifested everywhere.
2. Possible responses: rainwater bringing roses, rice and fish becoming nourishment. *Examples:* Rotting leaves provide soil for new plant life; wind and water make sandy beaches from rocky cliffs.
3. sleep with dreams, death
4. Analogies include: losing infant pleasures but gaining adult pleasures; rainwater returning as roses; a dreamer wakening, returning to reality; the gold of wheat returning as the golden crust of baked bread.

Applying Meanings
Possible response: Everything plays a part in nature's balance, which we must preserve.

Creative Writing Response
Writing a Poem. Images may be from childhood or the present.

Critical Writing Response
Analyzing the Poem's Meaning. *Ideas that might cause fear:* the self leaving the body, allusions to death. *Comforting thought:* Even in death, nothing is lost. ■

First Thoughts
Do you find Rumi's words comforting? Why or why not?

Identifying Facts
1. Why does the speaker say the reader should not grieve?
2. What, according to the speaker, does God's joy look like?

Interpreting Meanings
1. What does Rumi mean by "unmarked boxes"? Explain in your own words what the line "God's joy moves from unmarked box to unmarked box" means.
2. The first stanza suggests that nothing is ever lost; rather, things only change form. Which of the images in stanza 2 best express this idea? Can you think of other examples that illustrate the same idea?
3. In stanza 3, to what kind of sleep is Rumi referring? Explain your answer.
4. How has the poet used **analogy** to explain the idea that "anything you lose comes round in another form"? List the analogies the poet makes.

Applying Meanings
How does the idea that all things are in essence one relate to such modern-day concerns as ecology or recycling?

Creative Writing Response
Writing a Poem. Rumi points out the joy that can come from such everyday sights as a plate of rice and fish, a vine-covered cliff, or a horse being saddled. List some joyous moments that you have experienced. What **images** best capture your moments of joy? Use the images you've chosen and write a poem on the theme of recapturing the experience of joy. If you prefer, collect some favorite images from magazines and other sources and create a collage of "joyous moments."

Critical Writing Response
Analyzing the Poem's Meaning. In lines 17–18, the speaker says, "I don't want to make anyone fearful./Hear what's behind what I say." Why might the poet's words in this stanza make someone fearful? What comforting thought underlies the poet's words? Write a paragraph in which you explain the meaning of the third stanza.

Saadi
C. A.D. 1213–1292

New York Public Library

The poet Musharrif Oddin Muslih Oddin, known as Saadi (sä'dē), which means "fortunate" in Persian, spent much of his life as a wandering dervish, or holy man, moving from place to place, studying and practicing Sufi doctrine (see page 662). He had neither a home nor personal belongings, yet he somehow produced two of the great classics of Persian literature—the *Bustan* (*The Orchard*) and the *Gulistan* (*The Rose Garden*).

Scholars know only a few facts about Saadi's life. He was born in Shiraz, and his father died at an early age. He attended college at the Nizamiya Academy in Baghdad, where he received a classical Islamic education. A devout Sufi, he chose poverty and rootlessness as a way of life, wandering great distances. His books mention journeys to Central Asia and India, and it is believed that he made several religious pilgrimages to Mecca. On these journeys, he may have studied under the famous mystic Suhrawardi and met the poet Jalal al-Din Rumi, author of the *Masnavi* (see page 661).

During Saadi's lifetime, the Middle East was in almost constant turmoil. Mongol armies swept down from the plains to the east, and crusaders from Western Europe, intent on claiming the lands around Jerusalem for Christianity, made war on the Islamic peoples. On a journey to North Africa, Saadi was captured by crusaders and held in Tripoli (now part of Libya) where he was forced to labor as a ditch digger. According to one story, he married the daughter of the man who paid his ransom, but the marriage was unhappy. Eventually, Saadi abandoned his wife and made his way back to Shiraz, where he enjoyed the patronage of the royal ruler Sa'd bin Zangi (sä'd bēn zän·jē'), whose first name he adopted as his own.

Saadi's work is greatly beloved by the Iranian people, and his place in Persian literature is firmly established. His stories and sayings seem simple and use plain language, but they express Sufi wisdom in a way that has won admiration from scholars and general readers alike. Because his work had such wide appeal, Saadi ensured the continuation of Sufi beliefs.

MORE ABOUT THE AUTHOR

Saadi was middle-aged when he returned to Shiraz, the capital of the southern Persian province of Fars, and began writing. He was unusually versatile, composing in both Arabic and Persian (Farsi), and producing numerous lyrics and odes as well as *The Orchard* (epic verse) and *The Rose Garden* (primarily prose).

Saadi himself explained that the idea for *The Rose Garden* came to him in the springtime, after a period of dissatisfaction with his life. He saw a friend carrying a basket of roses, chided the friend for valuing something so transitory, and then found himself saying, "I am able to form a book of roses, which . . . will flourish forever." The friend challenged him to do so, and in a few days Saadi had the first two chapters "written out in my notebook, in a style that may be useful to orators and improve the skill of letter-writers." The rest of the book was finished before the summer ended. "I abridged the work," explained Saadi, "that it might not be thought tedious. . . . My design was to give advice, and I have spoken accordingly."

ABOUT THE TRANSLATOR

Idries Shah (1924–1996) was born in Simla, India, and lived in London. He was a businessman, scholar, author, and Sufi master who translated from many languages, including English, Arabic, Urdu, and Persian (Farsi).

PREREADING FOCUS

Background: Critics consider Saadi's simple yet elegant language a model of the finest Persian literary style. His work was the first Persian writing known in the West. (*The Rose Garden* was first translated in the mid-1600s and won an immediate audience.) As Sufism spread, Saadi's works were widely read and emulated in Turkey and India.

Though Saadi's writing is grounded in mysticism—his two masterpieces deal with Sufi beliefs and standards of behavior—he is a very down-to-earth mystic. His advice about behavior is based on common sense and practicality, and his tone is wryly human.

The *Gulistan*, or *The Rose Garden*, from which this selection is taken, is divided into eight chapters, such as "On Love and Youth" and "On the Effects of Education." Each contains tales that deal with human experience. Most of the anecdotes and aphorisms in this selection are excerpted from tales in the first two chapters, "On the Manners of Kings" and "On the Manners of Dervishes."

Literary Focus: An **anecdote** is a brief story that illustrates a point. An **aphorism** is a concise, sometimes witty, saying that expresses a principle, truth, or observation about life. Saadi uses anecdotes and aphorisms to express abstract ideas in concrete, comprehensible, and sometimes humorous ways.

Reader's Guide

ANECDOTES AND SAYINGS OF SAADI

Background

Saadi's writings are notable for two reasons: First, their simple, direct language has made them an ideal textbook for beginning students of Persian. Second, although they consist primarily of only simple sayings and stories, they are considered some of the finest expressions of Sufi beliefs.

For Sufis, Sufism is not only a religion or a philosophy, but a way of life. Sufis are not attached to belongings and places, and they are not driven by concerns of time, money, or achievement. They concentrate instead on the development of the human mind and on reaching a higher plane of understanding than can be achieved through the senses. The achievement of Sufi understanding may be likened to the process of a child growing to adulthood—just as a child attains the wisdom of adulthood slowly, a person attains Sufi knowledge through a gradual process of thought and practice. Thus, Sufi mystics withdrew from the material world and devoted themselves to living a stark, homeless existence. As they wandered, they begged for a living and meditated on God's love. It is in their writing that mystics such as Saadi reached out to share their thoughts with the world at large.

Oral Response

What familiar sayings do you know and use? Do you ever say "If the shoe fits, wear it" or "No pain, no gain"? Have you ever considered what these sayings really mean? Brainstorm a list of such sayings with your classmates and discuss their meanings.

Literary Focus

Much of literature can be understood on more than one level. On the surface a story or saying may convey its meaning directly. However, many "simple" pieces of literature have an underlying meaning, or subtext. An **anecdote**, for example, may serve to illustrate an idea about human behavior in general. In the same way, an **aphorism**, or saying, may have wider meaning than is at first apparent. "Don't cry over spilt milk" is about more than milk: it is about not regretting something from the past that cannot be changed.

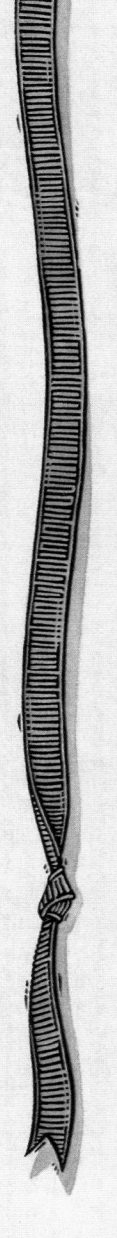

ANECDOTES AND SAYINGS OF SAADI

Saadi

translated by

IDRIES SHAH

*Saadi uses brief **anecdotes** and **aphorisms**, or sayings, to convey Sufi thinking on many subjects. As you read the anecdotes and sayings that follow, think about the underlying meanings that each might have.*

The Pearl

A raindrop, dripping from a cloud,
Was ashamed when it saw the sea.
"Who am I where there is a sea?" it said.
When it saw itself with the eye of humility,
A shell nurtured it in its embrace.

Learning

None learned the art of archery from me
Who did not make me, in the end, the target.

Conceit

He who has self-conceit in his head—
Do not imagine that he will ever hear the truth.

To Know One's Faults

In the eyes of the wise, the seeker of combat with an elephant is not really brave.

Brave is he who says nothing unbecoming in wrath.
A lout abused a man who patiently said:
"O you of bright prospects: I am worse even than you say.
I know all my faults, while you do not know them."

Fernando Bueno/The Image Bank

Pearls.
? *What point is Saadi making in his poetic anecdote, "The Pearl"?*

1 LITERARY ELEMENT
Anecdote: Summarize the story told in "The Pearl." (A raindrop falls from a cloud, sees the sea, feels humbled, and comes to rest in a sea-shell.) How does the anecdote illustrate the value of humility? (The raindrop's humility earns it the nurturing "embrace" of the shell, where it becomes a pearl, a thing of beauty.)

nurtured (nur′chərd): cared for, protected

lout: awkward, stupid person

2 LITERARY ELEMENT
Aphorism: What concrete nouns appear in "Learning"? (archery, target) What visual image does the aphorism create? (students of archery shooting arrows at their in-structor) To what abstract idea might this concrete image re-fer? (If students truly learn what a teacher has taught, they will ultimately challenge the teacher, making him or her a target of criticism.)

Subject–Verb Agreement

Even when words or phrases intervene between subject and verb, a verb must still agree in number with its subject, rather than with the nearest noun.

Examples from Anecdotes and Sayings of Saadi:

A <u>donkey</u> laden with books <u>is</u> neither an intellectual nor a wise man.

(The verb *is* agrees with *donkey*, the subject, not with *books*, the nearest noun.)

These <u>wearers</u> of the patchwork robe <u>are</u> as impassive as animals . . .

(The verb *are* agrees with *wearers*, the subject, not with *robe*, the nearest noun.)

Speaking and Listening. Have students identify the subject of each sentence and then choose the correct verb:

The Metropolitan Museum of Art, The Cora Timken Burnett Collection of Persian Miniatures and Other Persian Objects, Bequest of Cora Timken Burnett, 1956. (57.51.30)

A DERVISH. Dervishes are holy men who live by begging, often wandering from place to place. By denying themselves earthly comforts, they believe they can come closer to a spiritual reality.
? *What does Saadi's anecdote "The Thief and the Blanket" reveal about the dervishes' approach to life?*

Relative

A Lamp has no rays at all in the face of the sun;
And a high minaret[1] even in the foothills of a mountain
 looks low.

3

Information and Knowledge

However much you study, you cannot know without
 action.
A donkey laden with books is neither an intellectual
 nor a wise man.
Empty of essence, what learning has he—
 Whether upon him is firewood or book?

The Sick Man

Throughout the long night a man wept
At the bedside of a sick man.
When day dawned the visitor was dead—
And the patient was alive.

The Thief and the Blanket

A thief entered the house of a Sufi, and found nothing there. As he was leaving, the dervish[2] perceived his disappointment and threw him the blanket in which he was sleeping, so that he should not go away empty-handed.

The Destiny of a Wolf-cub

The destiny of a wolf-cub is to become a wolf, even if it is reared among the sons of men.

The Straight Path

I have never seen a man lost who was on a straight path.

---

1. **minaret** (min′ə·ret′): a tower attached to a mosque from which worshipers are called to prayer.
2. **dervish:** a member of any Muslim sect who lives a life of poverty and chastity. Some dervishes practice a whirling dance as a form of worship.

A Tree Freshly Rooted

A tree, freshly rooted, may be pulled up by one man on his own. Give it time, and it will not be moved, even with a crane.

The Dervish Under a Vow of Solitude

A dervish under a vow of solitude sat in a desert as a king passed with his retinue. Being in a special state of mind he took no notice, not even raising his head as the procession passed.

The king, emotionally overcome by his regal pretensions, was angry and said: "These wearers of the patchwork robe are as impassive as animals, possessing neither politeness nor due humility."

His vizier[3] approached the dervish, saying: "O dervish! The Sultan of the whole of the Earth has just passed by you. Why did you not pay the required homage?"

The dervish answered: "Let the Sultan look for homage from those who seek to benefit from his goodwill. Tell him, too, that kings are created for the protection of their subjects. Subjects are not created for the service of kings."

If You Cannot Stand a Sting

If you cannot stand a sting, do not put your finger in a scorpion's nest.

Ambition

Ten dervishes can sleep beneath one blanket; but two kings cannot reign in one land. A devoted man will eat half his bread, and give the other half to dervishes. A ruler may have a realm, but yet plot to overcome the world.

---

3. **vizier** (vi·zir'): a minister of state in the Ottoman Empire.

WHIRLING DERVISHES. *As part of their worship, one order of dervishes, known as whirling dervishes, dance until they reach a state of ecstasy in which they experience a direct communion with Allah.*

The Metropolitan Museum of Art, Rogers Fund, 1918 (17.81.4)

Saadi   **669**

1. List the different animals mentioned in the sayings. (elephants, wolves, donkeys, scorpions)
2. What happens to the thief who breaks into a dervish's house? (He finds nothing to steal, but the dervish gives him a blanket.)
3. What is the destiny of a wolf-cub raised among humans? (to become a wolf, regardless of upbringing)

4. What does Saadi say about people on straight paths? (They don't get lost.)
5. In "The Dervish in Hell," why was the king sent to heaven and the dervish to hell? (The king respected dervishes; the dervish gave up his principles by associating with kings.)

To reteach Anecdotes and Sayings of Saadi, instruct students to work in groups, using various media to create brief, modern stories that illustrate Saadi's anecdotes and aphorisms. Their stories may be in written form, accompanied by illustrations, or in the form of comic strips. Direct groups to begin by arriving at a consensus on the meaning of each anecdote or aphorism.

COMPARING LITERATURE

Have students compare and contrast the views in "Ambition" and "The Dervish in Hell" with those in the Taoist anecdote "Wagging My Tail in the Mud," p. 548.

❓ *What ideas about worldly power occur in all three anecdotes?* (Power corrupts or enslaves; seekers of truth must not compromise, even with kings.)

> **heedless** (hēd′lis): paying no attention

HUMANITIES CONNECTION

Persian miniatures often include several focuses of action.

❓ *What action do you see in this painting? What would you say is the main focus?* (Answers might include the game players in the foreground, the men in the middle ground, or the ornamental architecture itself.) ∎

The Dervish in Hell

One night a king dreamt that he saw a king in paradise and a dervish in hell.

The dreamer exclaimed: "What is the meaning of this? I should have thought that the positions would be reversed."

A voice answered: "The king is in heaven because he respected dervishes. The dervish is in hell because he compromised with kings."

Heedless Man

Whoever gives advice to a <u>heedless</u> man is himself in need of advice.

The Fool and the Donkey

A foolish man was raving at a donkey. It took no notice. A wiser man who was watching said: "Idiot! The donkey will never learn *your* language—better that you should observe silence and instead master the tongue of the donkey."

Saadi's Visit to an Indian Temple, seventeenth-century Persian miniature.
Courtesy of The Arthur M. Sackler Museum, Harvard University, Cambridge, Massachusetts. Gift of Philip Hofer in honor of Stuart Cary Welch

1. Dramatizing an Anecdote. Encourage students to work as a class to script several of Saadi's anecdotes as skits. Direct them to choose costumes such as patchwork robes and props such as crowns that will underscore the contrasts and ironies that Saadi uses to make his points. If possible, arrange for them to present their skits to another class.

2. Research Project. Students interested in history may want to learn more about events in Persia during the time when Saadi was writing (c. 1255–1290). Saadi describes it as a time of peace and prosperity after a period of political turmoil. Students might explore the development of architecture, painting, music, and literature during this time period.

Ask students which of the anecdotes and aphorisms could be seen as humorous. Many involve surprising twists or imagery that borders on slapstick: "The Thief and the Blanket," "The Sick Man," "The Dervish in Hell," and "The Fool and the Donkey." Point out parallels with other great thinkers, such as Confucius, and guide students to see that achieving humor and simplicity requires considerable skill and great depth of thought. ■

First Thoughts

Which of these sayings had the most meaning for you? Why?

Identifying Facts

1. According to "To Know One's Faults," who is brave in the eyes of the wise?

2. What is ironic, or unexpected, about the outcome of "The Sick Man"?

3. In "Heedless Man," what does a person need who gives advice to someone who does not listen?

Interpreting Meanings

1. Bearing in mind that a simple saying may have more than one level of interpretation, what do you think is the underlying meaning of "The Straight Path"?

2. What does "A Tree Freshly Rooted" imply about the advantages of allowing something to "take root"? When might pulling up something freshly rooted be advantageous?

3. In "Learning," what does the speaker suggest about the wisdom of teaching the art of archery? To what might this **aphorism**, or saying, apply besides archery?

4. In "Conceit," why will a person who is conceited "never hear the truth"? What advice does this **aphorism** imply?

5. In "Information and Knowledge," what does the speaker mean by "you cannot know without action"? How would you sum up the difference between "information" and "knowledge"?

6. What appears to be the **moral** of the **anecdote** "The Dervish in Hell"?

Applying Meanings

The Sufis use the sayings and anecdotes of Saadi and others as teaching tools, urging people to meditate upon the deeper meanings contained in them. Do you think that such sayings and anecdotes are effective teaching devices? What did you learn from them?

Creative Writing Response

Writing a Saying. Saadi's saying "If you cannot stand a sting, do not put your finger in a scorpion's nest" is analogous to the English expression, "If you can't stand the heat, stay out of the kitchen." Try creating two or three sayings of your own. Use Saadi's sayings, as well as sayings that you already know, as models.

Critical Writing Response

Comparing a Sufi Saying and a Zen Parable. Like Sufism, Zen (see page 589) is a system of belief that expresses complex ideas in simple ways. Read the Zen **parable** "The Thief Who Became a Disciple" (see page 593). Then compare and contrast that parable with "The Thief and the Blanket." Discuss how the two tales are alike and different on the surface, as well as how they are alike and different in underlying meaning.

First Thoughts
Answers will vary.

Identifying Facts
1. "he who says nothing unbecoming in wrath"
2. The visitor dies.
3. advice

Interpreting Meanings
1. Possible response: A person who is righteous is on a "straight path" and will never get lost because his or her inner moral bearings are sure.
2. Things allowed to "take root" gain strength. when it is rooted in something harmful
3. The wise teacher expects to be challenged by an apt student. the teaching of any subject
4. Conceited people are too full of themselves to admit other thoughts. Seekers of truth should beware their own conceit.
5. Study is not enough; application is crucial. Knowledge is information plus experience.
6. Respect for others and refusal to compromise one's principles are both important.

Applying Meanings
Answers will vary.

Creative Writing Response
Writing a Saying. Suggest that students draw ideas from modern life.

Critical Writing Response
Comparing a Sufi Saying and a Zen Parable. To organize their ideas, students might use a chart to list likenesses and differences. ■

1 CULTURAL BACKGROUND

Mulla: The title *mulla* refers to the most basic level of Muslim cleric. Unlike *ulema*, who advise the state or *muftis*, who use their deep scholarship to settle thorny religious issues, the mulla lives among the people, leads prayers, teaches children to read and write, gives advice about how to apply Islam in daily life, and presides over everyday ceremonies related to birth, circumcision, death, marriage, and the like. As a class, mullas sometimes have much power, but as individuals they are often quite humble, down-to-earth figures, living in the mosque and surviving on the charity of their community. Mullas are not priests, since Islam rejects the concept of priesthood. They are the practical face of the religion in daily life—respected, but hardly sacred.

2 CULTURAL BACKGROUND

Nasrudin's Tomb: The tomb itself is an embodiment of the typical Nasrudin joke: it has three stout walls and an impregnable door locked shut with an enormous padlock; but the fourth wall is missing, so that anyone can enter the tomb by the back way. Ask students how this indication of the Mulla's legendary humor might also be an allegory for some deep truth about life.

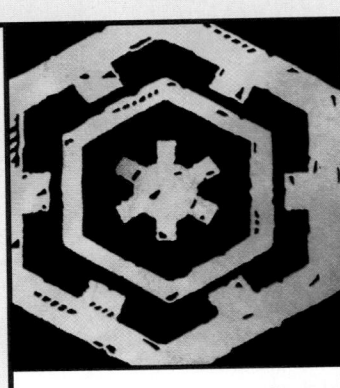

LANGUAGE
— AND —
CULTURE

WHERE THE MULLA GOES, LAUGHTER FOLLOWS

Heads up, everyone—here comes the Mulla Nasrudin (mul'ə näs·rä·dēn'), master philosopher and adviser to kings, wrapped in his patched cloak, plodding along on his small, gray donkey. As Nasrudin fans the world over know, wherever this unlikely wisdom figure goes, laughter is sure to follow.

> *Mulla made a business of riding his donkey across the border to the neighboring country daily, loading the panniers with straw. The border inspector, suspecting Mulla to be a smuggler, examined his panniers thoroughly every time but failed to find anything. Years later when Mulla retired, he happened to meet the old inspector.*
>
> *"Now that you have retired, Mulla, tell me whatever it was you smuggled so successfully."*
>
> *"Donkeys," answered Mulla.*

In one sense, no one yet has been able to catch Nasrudin. No one even knows whether he really lived, much less when or where. The tales of his exploits apparently originated in Persia. They may have been devised by the Sufis, who saw humor as a useful tool for bringing about enlightenment. Persian stories about the Mulla (the "Master") Nasrudin date from at least the thirteenth century, and, having traveled like Nasrudin himself, they are told today throughout the Near East. In Saudi Arabia, Nasrudin stories sometimes merge with jokes about an Arab prankster called Joha. In Turkey, Nasrudin has become the Hodja Nasr-ed-din, and the town of Eskishehir (Ak Shehir) is considered his birthplace. There, an annual Nasr-ed-din festival is held, while on a nearby hill the Hodja's "tomb" is shown off to tourists.

Stories originally told about Nasrudin appear, in altered form, in Europe as well. From Turkish folklore they slipped into Greek folklore, and from Greek into Italian. The tales also crop up in the written literature of several Western countries.

Nasrudin has crossed even the most rigid political boundaries at the most tension-filled times. During the 1960s, the Coral Gables High-Energy Physics Conference, in Florida, issued a report using Nasrudin tales to explain scientific concepts that would have been cumbersome, if not unintelligible, in ordinary prose. Around the same period, on the other side of the then-impenetrable Iron Curtain, the Soviet Union produced a film called *The Adventures of Nasrudin*, in which the Mulla repeatedly made fools of

1

2

Caricature portrait of a Mulla on a donkey.

Scala/Art Resource, New York

wealthy capitalists. And almost simultaneously, in Communist China, a book of Nasrudin tales was published as part of a series of folklore studies.

Mulla's watch stopped working. He opened it and found a dead fly inside the springs.

"No wonder it stopped working," said Mulla. "The poor operator is dead!"

Perhaps Nasrudin has remained so popular, and has cut across so many cultural boundaries, precisely because he is, beneath his turban, that most universal of human figures: a clown. Clowns have always been great teachers, because humor is an ideal vehicle for conveying knowledge and insights painlessly and pleasurably—a fact Sufis know well.

A friend visiting Mulla from another town brought him a duck for a gift. Mulla broiled the duck and shared it

with his friend. For a time Mulla kept having visitors who claimed they were friends of the friends of the friend who brought him the duck and asked him for a duck meal.

The last stranger who showed up claimed, "I am the friend of the friend of the friend of the friend of the friend who brought you the duck."

Inviting the stranger in, Mulla offered him a bowl of hot water.

"And what is this?" the guest inquired.

"This is the soup of the soup of the soup of the soup of the duck which my friend brought me as a gift," said Mulla.

Considering his seven centuries of popularity, his adaptability, and his continuing power to amuse, the odds are good that old Mulla Nasrudin will continue to amuse audiences the world over for a long time to come.

Translations of Mulla tales by Mehdi Nakosteen

3 COMPARING LITERATURE

Nasrudin belongs to that category of classic folk characters known as wise fools. Other examples might include Jack the Giant-Killer and Sholom Aleichem's fools of Chelm. Usually the wise fool is clearly an innocent, someone who leads a charmed existence. Nasrudin is distinctive because one cannot be certain whether he is really a fool—or is actually a sage. He hovers in some ambiguous zone between the two.

WRITING TO LEARN

Compare the Mulla as he appears in these stories with other comic figures you know. Is there any clown or comedian in contemporary life who resembles the Mulla? If so, in what way? ■

4 LITERARY BACKGROUND

Soup of the Soup: This may be an example of a Mulla Nasrudin tale that tells a joke on the surface but conveys a Sufi message underneath. Sufis often stress the gap between language and experience—the inadequacy of language, in short, to re-create the Sufi experience. Compared to the mystical experience itself, even the finest poem about it is soup of the soup of the soup of the duck.

Language Skills

MAINTAINING VERB TENSE CONSISTENCY

By writing, you can project your thoughts into the future; you can map out potential processes and make plans. The tenses of the verbs you use reflect the directions in which your thoughts move. Not only do verb tenses show whether you are dealing with the past, the present, or the future, they also show whether you are dealing with conjecture or fact. Unnecessary tense shifts, then, can distort your meaning.

Change verb tenses only to show changes in actual or relative time. In general, when you begin a passage using one tense, keep all verbs in that tense.

INCONSISTENT

Soon Sindbad *will grow* tired of idleness. Then he *sets* out to roam the world again.

CONSISTENT

Soon Sindbad *will grow* tired of idleness. Then he *will set* out to roam the world again.

In the corrected example, both verbs are in the future tense.

Using Correct Tense Sequences

Sometimes, of course, writers must change tenses to show changes in time. **Tense sequence**—the pattern of verb tenses in a sentence or a passage—usually follows common sense.

INCORRECT

Muslim scholars *consider The Thousand and One Nights* inferior literature, but the tales *delight* readers for centuries.

CORRECT

Muslim scholars *consider The Thousand and One Nights* inferior literature, but the tales *have delighted* readers for centuries.

The present perfect tense is used in the second part of the sentence to show that an action began in the past and continues into the present.

Exercise 1: Correcting Verb Tense Shifts

Correct the tense shift in each sentence.

1. At birth, Rostám was already so big that he has to be delivered by magic.
2. The *Shahname* recounts the life stories of several dynasties of kings; it was much more than a single story about a single hero.
3. When the giant thunders into the palace, he planned to roast and eat Sindbad and his companions.
4. Edward FitzGerald's translation of the *Rubáiyát* is not literally accurate; however, it preserved the spirit of Khayyám's poems.
5. FitzGerald's translation won great popularity within a few years after he has published it.

Special Problems with Tense Shifts

Some constructions create special verb tense problems. Study the examples below.

INCORRECT

Sohráb *would have escaped* death if he *would have recognized* Rostám sooner.

CORRECT

Sohráb *would have escaped* death if he *had recognized* Rostám sooner.

If the main clause in a sentence uses "would have," the dependent clause need only use "had."

Sentences expressing wishes that past events had turned out differently need not use "would" at all.

INCORRECT

Rostám *wished* that he *would have spared* his son's life.

CORRECT

Rostám *wished* that he *had spared* his son's life.

Exercise 2: Correcting Verb Tense Problems

Correct the tense shift, incorrect tense sequence, or other verb tense problem in each sentence.

1. Rostám repents his actions in killing Sohráb. He therefore ordered his army not to pursue war with the Turks.

2. The narrator in the *Rubáiyát* celebrated each moment and cautions readers not to waste time in useless regrets.

3. In his arrogance, the king wished that the dervish would have paid him homage.

4. Muslims believe that the Koran represents truths that the angel Gabriel revealed to Mohammed, and for centuries they consider it the word of God.

5. Al-Khansa would not be famous today if her brother would not have suffered an early and tragic death.

6. Saadi, who lived during the thirteenth century, writes, "The Destiny of a Wolf Cub," exploring the problem of nature versus nurture.

7. The work of Rumi is rich in mystical themes and images. It reflected the traditional Sufi way of viewing life.

8. The customs agents wished that they would have caught the Mulla.

9. Tales of the Mulla's exploits originated in the thirteenth century, and they continued to amuse readers ever since.

10. Mohammed founds Islam, and it remained a major religion today.

Background: Students might benefit from rereading Omar Khayyám's *Rubáiyát* and Rumi's "Unmarked Boxes" to find examples of unusual and memorable descriptions of "the good life." For Omar Khayyám, the ideal life involves living for the moment, enjoying the beauty of nature and the pleasure of friends' company. Khayyám describes, among other things, a sunrise, a nightingale's song, and a group of friends enjoying an evening party in a garden. For Rumi, a Sufi mystic, the ideal life is lived in harmony with "God's joy." Rumi finds this harmony in experiences that may seem trivial: eating a plate of rice and fish, saddling a horse, seeing a small desert town under the stars.

Prewriting: You may want to give students the option of writing either a humorous or a serious essay for this assignment.

Some students who choose to write a serious essay may not know yet what they would like to do in the future or how they define success. To help them gain an idea of their priorities, ask them to imagine that they have only one year left to live. Where, and with whom, would they want to spend the most time? Which activities would they concentrate on? What would they stop doing?

Critical Thinking and Writing

OBSERVING AND ANALYZING A PROCESS

Whose way of living appeals to you most? Poets and philosophers, religious leaders and everyday people have always tried to define "the good life." Omar Khayyám focuses on seizing the moment; Saadi and Rumi stress enlightenment; the Koran advocates charity and personal responsibility; and the tale of Sindbad shows the allure of a life of adventure. What approach represents your ideal life? How might you attain such a life?

Writing Assignment

In an informative essay, show what you think a good life is. Then trace the process by which you might achieve it. You may consider the general hallmarks of a fulfilling life, or you may concentrate on one aspect, perhaps an appealing location or a satisfying career. Describe your ideal lifestyle or an aspect of it, and detail the steps you imagine taking in order to reach it. In this essay you will use both description and process analysis.

Background

Much of the literature in this unit reflects a serious inquiry into the significance of life and the meaningful ways in which it can be led.

Review the selections and decide which works relate to your own concept of the good life. You may want to refer to these works as you plan and write your essay.

Prewriting

Focused Questioning. Write at least two sentences to answer each of the following questions as you reflect on your ideal life.

1. Whose lifestyle is especially appealing to you? What makes it so?
2. Which area would you most like to live in? Do you prefer the city or the country?
3. How do you define success? How could you achieve it? How important is it to you?
4. What is the difference between a job and a career? Which would you prefer?
5. How important are love and friendship? What kinds of friends make you happy? Do you foresee marriage and children?
6. What kind of old age will you have? How do you want to be remembered?

Now, choose the one or two questions that intrigue you most. Use them as the basis of a longer, focused freewriting.

Organizing Your Ideas. Review your freewriting and your answers to the preceding questions. Then, in a sentence, sum up your idea of a good life. Next, plan the chronology of your ideal life, constructing a time line like the one on page 677. Along

AGE	18 years old	25 years old	30 years old	40 years old	55 years old	68 years old	80 years old
EVENTS							

the time line, write each relevant event that you foresee, using an arrow to specify the event's place in a time period.

Writing

Use these guidelines to draft your essay.

1. **Introductory Paragraph.** You might open with song lyrics, a brief anecdote, or several lines of dialogue that reflect your main idea about a good life. Perhaps a line from a work in this unit would be relevant. Lead into a description of one day, or even one hour, in the life you consider good, using specifics from your freewriting and from your observations of others who lead lives you admire. Use concrete, sensory details to show actions, places, objects, and emotions. End the paragraph with a thesis statement summing up your ideal life and the direction that will lead you to it.

2. **Body Paragraphs.** Explain in detail the main steps for achieving your ideal lifestyle. Use chronological order to organize, referring to your time line for sequence. Your freewriting, and the thoughts and images it inspires, can be a source of specifics as you detail each step. Choose appropriate transitions (see page 56) to clarify the order of the events you foresee and the results you hope they will have.

3. **Concluding Paragraph.** You might conclude by offering a comment on the process you have traced, perhaps assessing its difficulties and its merits. Or you might project your thoughts even further into the future, reflecting on how you will feel, or what changes might occur, once you have attained the kind of life you hope for.

Evaluating and Revising

Use these questions to evaluate and revise your essay.

1. Does your first paragraph vividly describe the life you consider good?
2. Do your body paragraphs detail the steps that could lead to your ideal lifestyle?
3. Do transitions and chronological order make the process easy for readers to follow?
4. Does your conclusion reflect on the process you have traced or project your ideas further into the future?
5. Are your sentences varied in structure and grammatically correct?

Proofreading and Publishing

Proofread carefully, eliminating errors in mechanics, and make a final copy. Compile class essays into a *Book of the Future*, and devise a way to save it for class reunions after graduation.

Writing: Before students begin drafting, explain that in writing a process analysis, as in writing a narrative, time is the controlling factor. As they outline the process or steps by which they will attain their ideal lifestyles, students should focus on the order of events in time. However, they must also describe the effects each event will have. How will the steps they outline lead to the achievement of their goals? What will they experience when they attain their goals? To achieve these two purposes, they will need to use transitions showing chronological order, transitions showing causality, and vivid, descriptive details. (You might refer them to the lists of transitions in the *Language Skills* feature on pp. 56–57.)

Evaluating and Revising: Be sure students understand that their essays should contain specific, sensory details in order to describe for readers the life that they wish to attain. Yet the description need not be lengthy. One scene, or a brief moment in time, skillfully described, can evoke a range of other details in readers' minds.

Proofreading and Publishing: Students should also interview older acquaintances, asking how they envisioned their lives after high school and whether they achieved their goals. The class might find it interesting to compare their own responses with those of the older people. ▪

The following annotations are for the artwork surrounding the map, starting in the upper right-hand corner and moving in a counterclockwise direction.

The Wife of Bath: This detail is from the Ellesmere manuscript, which is generally thought to be the most reliable version of *The Canterbury Tales.* The Ellesmere manuscript is one of approximately ninety manuscripts that preserve Chaucer's work.

❓ *What can the reader surmise about the Wife of Bath from this illustration?* (Possible response: She is neither rich nor poor.)

The Battle of San Romano: The Florentine painter Paolo Uccello (c. 1397–1475) created this large panel painting for the Medici palace. Warfare was the characteristic method of settling land claims in the medieval world; thus many paintings depict knights defending the rights of their lords.

Section of a French Illuminated Manuscript: Until the late fourteenth century, parchment, not paper, was the material used to write upon. Made from the skin of sheep, goats, or other animals, parchment was relatively easy to ornament. Thus some of the best artwork of the Middle Ages, including beautiful illustrations and the elaboration of individual letters, can be found in manuscripts.

❓ *When do you think illumination became a "lost art"?* (when paper replaced parchment and books were printed, not copied)

EUROPE IN THE MIDDLE AGES
Fourteenth Century

NORWAY
SCOTLAND
IRELAND
Origins of Arthurian Legend
DENM
WALES
ENGLAND
Salisbury
Canterbury
(GERMA
Origins of Nibelungen
Origins of Chanson de Geste
Rhine River
Holy Roman Empire
BRITTANY
Seine River
Paris
Rheims
Danube
Chartres
Atlantic Ocean
FRANCE
Troubadors
Avignon
PORTUGAL
SPAIN
(ITA
Barcelona
Mediterranean Sea
Sic
Muslim States
N

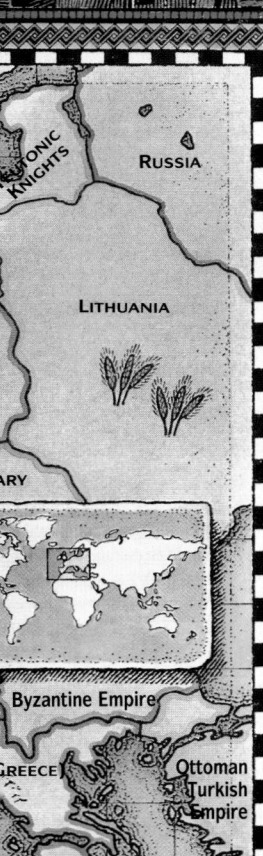

UNIT 8

THE MIDDLE AGES

▼ **Time** ▼
A.D. 500–1500

▼ **Place** ▼
Europe

▼ **Literary Significance** ▼

The European Middle Ages lies between the classical era and the Renaissance. After the downfall of the Roman Empire, the Frankish king Charlemagne encouraged learning and innovation. Still, most people could not read, and most literature was oral. The oral literature of pre-Christian Europe during this period includes the epics *Beowulf* and the *Nibelungenlied,* as well as the Icelandic sagas, all of which were eventually written down. Christian Europe produced its own heroic tales in the form of saints' lives and *chansons de geste*—tales of heroic deeds that were sung by traveling minstrels. Romances such as Chrétien de Troyes's *Perceval* expressed the ideals of chivalry and courtly love that developed during the Middle Ages. By the late Middle Ages, the authority of feudalism and the Church began to decay. More and more people, not only the clergy, could read and had access to written materials. Writers like Geoffrey Chaucer and Dante Alighieri, writing in vernacular, or native, languages, reflected the new spirit of the age.

The Last Judgment: Jan van Eyck, who lived in Flanders in the fifteenth century, is known as the creator of oil painting. This painting, tempera and oil on canvas, depicts a subject that was important to medieval society.
❓ *What does the skull stand for?* (death) *What view of an afterlife is illustrated?* (one that encompasses both heaven and hell)

Church Façade: This church in France dates from the twelfth century. At that time decorative sculpture became as important as the functional architecture of the church. Everything was decorated, including the façade.

A Knight and Lady: This picture illustrates a major literary genre of the medieval era—the romance. In the Middle Ages, marriages were arranged. Often a knight and the lady he wished to claim could spend only a few stolen minutes together because she belonged to another.

Stained-Glass Window: The technique that led to the production of stained glass began to be perfected during the tenth century. Stained glass became popular in churches during the eleventh century because of its light-giving qualities and its receptivity to changes in the strength and position of the sun. The stained-glass window depicted here is from the cathedral of Strasbourg and shows an emperor.
❓ *What can you infer about the relationship between church and state in the Middle Ages?* (It was a close relationship.)

Point out to students that the Middle Ages began about A.D. 300. You may ask them to identify the first historical events cited. (Christianity proclaimed the official religion about 330 and the division of the Roman Empire in 395)

Looking at the literary events above the line, students will see that before 900 the only works listed are sacred writings and *Beowulf*. Literature flourished, nevertheless. Can students explain how? (As in earlier times, in such places as Africa and Greece, it was transmitted orally from one generation to another.) Minstrels and troubadors traveled from village to village, embellishing their stories with music and other forms of entertainment. Moreover, many of the literary works of the later Middle Ages have a basis in the oral tradition. In *The Canterbury Tales,* for example, the pilgrims relate a host of stories that Chaucer had heard and made his own through his writing.

Explain that most historians date the end of the Middle Ages at about 1500. Ask students to note the last date and event on the Time Line. (1492; the Moors were driven out of Spain) What other event occurred in that year that transformed people's perceptions of the world and signaled the end of the medieval period? (Columbus reached the Americas, which led Europeans to begin exploiting a new continent.) What other events on the Time Line may indicate the end of an era? (weakening of feudal system, church divisions and reforms, the Black Death)

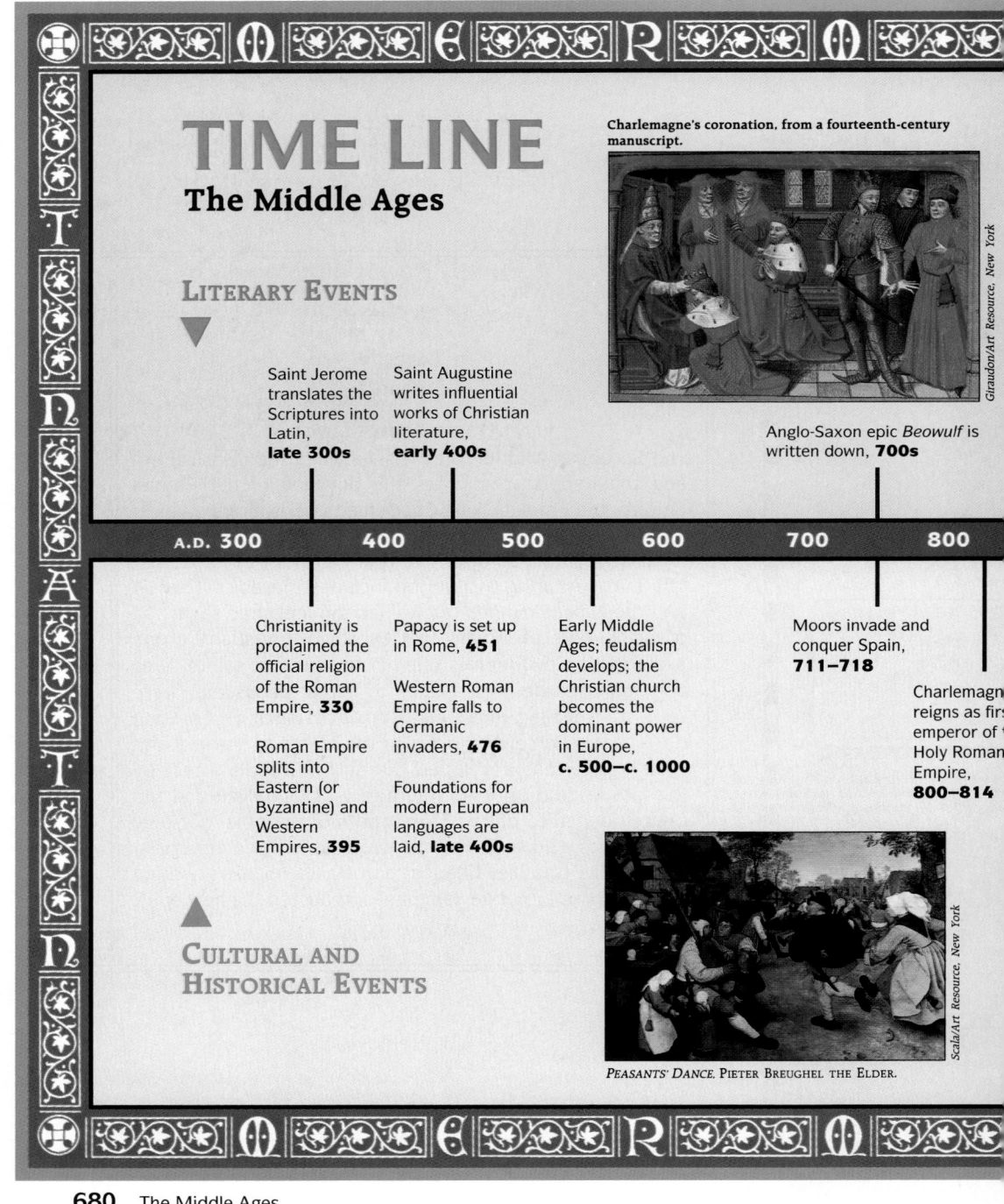

TIME LINE
The Middle Ages

LITERARY EVENTS

Charlemagne's coronation, from a fourteenth-century manuscript.

Giraudon/Art Resource, New York

Saint Jerome translates the Scriptures into Latin, **late 300s**

Saint Augustine writes influential works of Christian literature, **early 400s**

Anglo-Saxon epic *Beowulf* is written down, **700s**

| A.D. 300 | 400 | 500 | 600 | 700 | 800 |

Christianity is proclaimed the official religion of the Roman Empire, **330**

Roman Empire splits into Eastern (or Byzantine) and Western Empires, **395**

Papacy is set up in Rome, **451**

Western Roman Empire falls to Germanic invaders, **476**

Foundations for modern European languages are laid, **late 400s**

Early Middle Ages; feudalism develops; the Christian church becomes the dominant power in Europe, **c. 500–c. 1000**

Moors invade and conquer Spain, **711–718**

Charlemagne reigns as first emperor of the Holy Roman Empire, **800–814**

CULTURAL AND HISTORICAL EVENTS

PEASANTS' DANCE. PIETER BREUGHEL THE ELDER.

Scala/Art Resource, New York

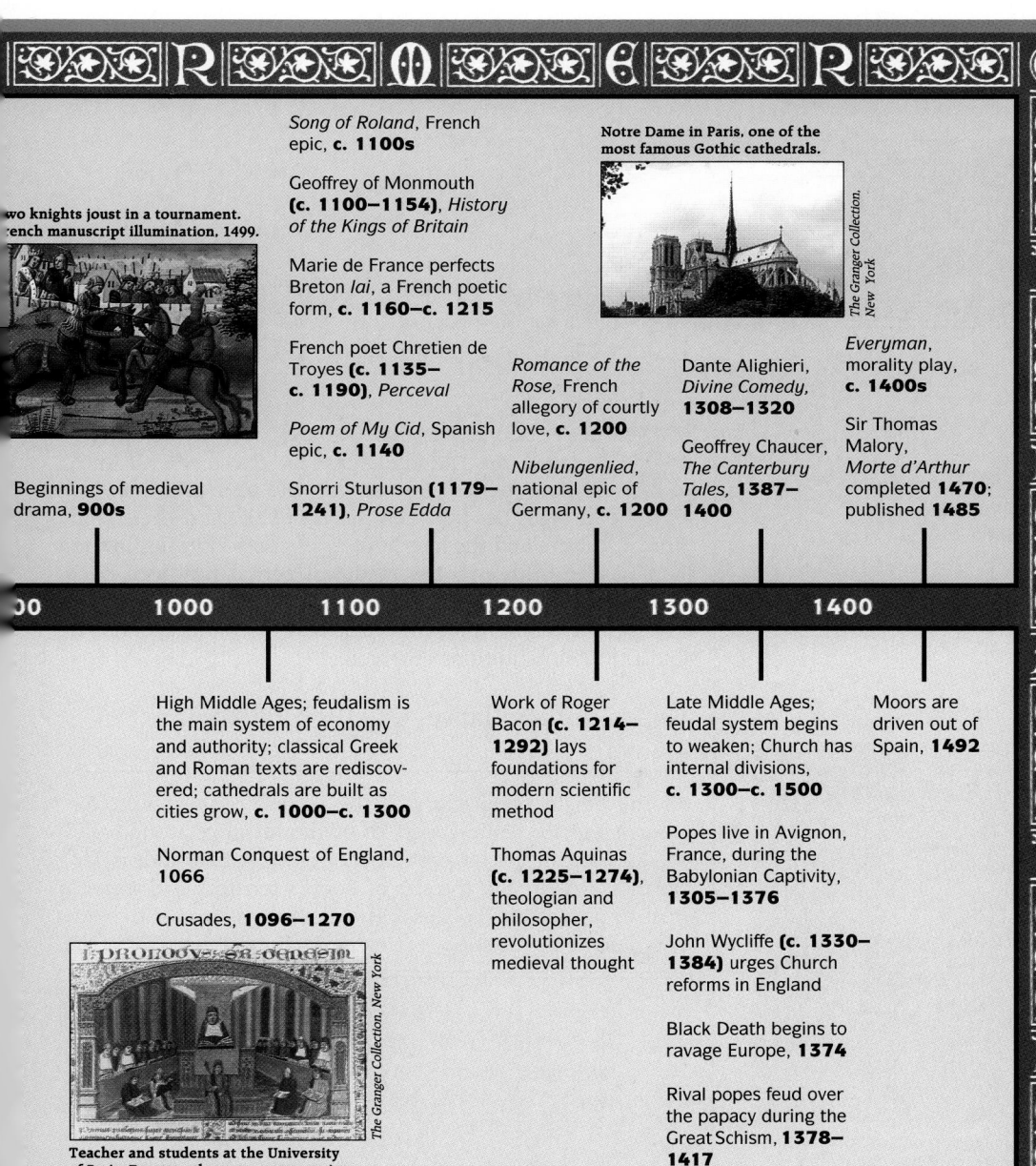

Song of Roland, French epic, **c. 1100s**

Geoffrey of Monmouth **(c. 1100–1154)**, *History of the Kings of Britain*

Marie de France perfects Breton *lai*, a French poetic form, **c. 1160–c. 1215**

French poet Chretien de Troyes **(c. 1135–c. 1190)**, *Perceval*

Poem of My Cid, Spanish epic, **c. 1140**

Snorri Sturluson **(1179–1241)**, *Prose Edda*

Romance of the Rose, French allegory of courtly love, **c. 1200**

Nibelungenlied, national epic of Germany, **c. 1200**

Dante Alighieri, *Divine Comedy*, **1308–1320**

Geoffrey Chaucer, *The Canterbury Tales*, **1387–1400**

Everyman, morality play, **c. 1400s**

Sir Thomas Malory, *Morte d'Arthur* completed **1470**; published **1485**

Notre Dame in Paris, one of the most famous Gothic cathedrals.

The Granger Collection, New York

wo knights joust in a tournament. rench manuscript illumination, 1499.

Beginnings of medieval drama, **900s**

| 00 | 1000 | 1100 | 1200 | 1300 | 1400 |

High Middle Ages; feudalism is the main system of economy and authority; classical Greek and Roman texts are rediscovered; cathedrals are built as cities grow, **c. 1000–c. 1300**

Norman Conquest of England, **1066**

Crusades, **1096–1270**

Work of Roger Bacon **(c. 1214–1292)** lays foundations for modern scientific method

Thomas Aquinas **(c. 1225–1274)**, theologian and philosopher, revolutionizes medieval thought

Late Middle Ages; feudal system begins to weaken; Church has internal divisions, **c. 1300–c. 1500**

Popes live in Avignon, France, during the Babylonian Captivity, **1305–1376**

John Wycliffe **(c. 1330–1384)** urges Church reforms in England

Black Death begins to ravage Europe, **1374**

Rival popes feud over the papacy during the Great Schism, **1378–1417**

Moors are driven out of Spain, **1492**

Teacher and students at the University of Paris. Fourteenth-century manuscript illumination.

The Granger Collection, New York

This border contains patterns and letters derived from illuminated manuscripts, which were created by Christian monks in monasteries throughout Europe.

Time Line **681**

HISTORICAL BACKGROUND

Feudalism: Feudalism was based on the control of land and on the rights and responsibilities that this control conferred. Serfs tilled the soil for the lords of the manor who protected them; the lords, in turn, protected the nobles from whom they had obtained the land; and the nobles protected the king, who owed his allegiance to God alone.

HISTORICAL BACKGROUND

Moors' Invasion: When the Moors invaded Spain, Europe was a Christian society. The Muslim invasion of a Christian country set the stage for many battles between Christians and Muslims.

CULTURAL BACKGROUND

Beowulf: This heroic epic contains some traces of the Christian ethos. Because it was written in Old English, it must be translated for modern readers.

CULTURAL BACKGROUND

Roger Bacon and Science: People sometimes overlook the fact that science was studied and practiced in the Middle Ages. One of Roger Bacon's major interests was the field of optics. He used mathematics and scientific methodology and experimentation to study optics. He succeeded in presenting an accurate description of the eye and the optic nerve.

OBJECTIVES

1. To relate feudalism, the Christian Church, courtly love, and the rise of the middle class to medieval literature
2. To distinguish the Icelandic, French, German, Italian, and English strands of medieval literature
3. To recognize the elements of the heroic epic and the romance
4. To interpret and respond to medieval literature both orally and in writing

TEACHER'S RESOURCES: 8

- ✔ Unit Introduction Test
- ✔ Word Analogies
- ✔ Unit Review Test
- ✔ Critical Thinking and Writing

HUMANITIES CONNECTION

The Book of Kells, dating from the late eighth to early ninth century, is an illuminated manuscript of the four Gospels from Ireland. Illumination is usually divided into two distinct styles: outline drawing and fully colored. In the fully colored style, the vellum was covered with a base to allow the burnished gold to adhere more firmly, and then the dyes, mixed with egg and gum and dissolved in water, were applied.

? *Why might monks have decorated medieval manuscripts instead of merely copying the texts? (Possible response: They wanted to associate beauty with the word of God.)* ∎

CULTURAL BACKGROUND

Dark Ages: At one time the term *Dark Ages* was used to describe the early Middle Ages, from about the fifth to the eleventh centuries. It is true that during the early Middle Ages, most Germanic peoples were illiterate, scholarly materials were monopolized by the Church, and European trade was stagnant. Modern scholars, however, generally agree that the term *Dark Ages* is a misnomer that arose when people knew little about the medieval period. The more researchers learn about the early medieval era, the more they recognize that the intellectual, artistic, literary, and scientific achievements of the period have been underestimated.

Illumination of the *Book of Kells,* a ninth-century manuscript created by Irish monks.

Trinity College Library, Dublin

THE MIDDLE AGES

The period between A.D. 500 and A.D. 1500 in Europe is called the "Middle Ages," or the *medieval* (mē′ dē·ē′vəl) period. In one way, the term is useful, for the Middle Ages lies between the era of classical Greek and Roman culture and the later rebirth of classical values in the Renaissance. Although the medieval period has been perceived as a static, or unchanging, interval in history, it was in fact a dynamic time in which new political, economic, and cultural institutions emerged.

Chaos and Collapse: The End of Roman Culture

At the height of its glory in the second century A.D., the Roman Empire commanded all of the territory around the Mediterranean, as far east as modern-day Iran and as far north as Britain. But the size of Rome's territory had a great deal to do with its collapse. The central government could not defend its frontiers or maintain contact with isolated

> When the Roman Empire collapsed under its own weight, it broke into two parts: the Byzantine Empire in the East and the fragmented Western Empire in Europe.

outposts. The Roman Empire thus broke into two large pieces, the Eastern, or Byzantine (biz′ən·tēn′), and the Western. The **Byzantine Empire**, with its seat of government at Constantinople (now Istanbul), ruled Egypt, the eastern Mediterranean, Asia Minor, and the Balkans. Throughout

TEACHING THE MIDDLE AGES

Students may have the preconceived notion that they are not going to like studying the literature of the Middle Ages. This attitude may stem from the belief that life was static in those days—that people worked in the fields from sunrise to sunset, day after day, with no prospect for their lives except the same tedious toil. Though this notion may contain a kernel of truth about the lives of serfs, the Middle Ages was actually an exciting time.

The literature of the period reflects the changes of the age—from the bloody wars waged by feudal kings (*Song of Roland*, *Prose Edda*, and the *Nibelungenlied*) through the gruesome and exotic campaigns of the Crusades to the emergence of courtly love ("Chevrefoil") and the rise of the middle class and the risk-taking mercantile society that it nurtured (*The Canterbury Tales*).

In order to entice students into the literature, you should try to re-create the flavor of medieval times as much as possible. You might want to plan a medieval feast in which students dress in appropriate costumes, prepare and eat foods in the medieval fashion (without forks), and listen to poets, jongleurs, and troubadours. You might also stage tumbling routines, limerick contests, and perhaps even a joust. If you are especially ambitious, students could perform a small skit based

---

the Middle Ages, classical knowledge and culture lost in the West were preserved by the Byzantine Empire.

The **Western Empire** did not fare as well. It fell to invading Germanic tribes who gradually conquered the Roman Empire in the early fifth century A.D. The Lombards controlled Italy, and the Anglo-Saxons dominated Britain. The Franks established a kingdom in northern France and became strong supporters of Christianity. All of these Germanic tribes contributed to the later development of the mainstays of medieval European culture: knighthood, the feudal system, and the code of chivalry.

The Age of Faith: The Christian Church as Undisputed Authority

In A.D. 330, the emperor **Constantine** proclaimed Christianity the official religion of the Roman Empire, and in 451, the Pope became the undisputed religious authority of the Church. When the Roman Empire fell apart, the Christian Church maintained and enlarged its authority. The key to its success was a strong organization that enabled it to assert its independence from princes and kings and to build a government of its own.

One way the Church exerted its authority was through its monopoly over knowledge. Because Latin was the language in which knowledge was preserved and transmitted, and because only the clergy could read and write Latin, the Church maintained a firm control over education.

The Church maintained strict control over knowledge and education throughout the Middle Ages.

Although the writings of the Church focused on religion and philosophy, monasteries—communities of monks and other clerics—often maintained **chronicles**, or records of events. Many chronicles were local, recording weather conditions, the state of crops, and day-to-day happenings. Other chronicles mingled legends and local fairy tales with reported facts. As time went on, the chronicles became more factual and detailed. Indeed, the best chroniclers of the later

> ❝ People of the Middle Ages existed under mental, moral, and physical circumstances so different from our own as to constitute almost a foreign civilization. ❞
>
> —A Distant Mirror, Barbara Tuchman

1

Art Carolingien IX-X, Statue Equestre de Charlemagne, Louvre, © Photo R.M.N.

Statue of Charlemagne on horseback, ninth century. *As both a warrior king and supporter of the arts and education, Charlemagne transformed medieval Europe.*

1 RESPONDING TO THE QUOTATION

Life in the Middle Ages was different from modern life in many respects. For example, in the early years of the Middle Ages, only the members of the clergy were educated, and Latin was the language of learning. Because the teachings of the Church were influential, people believed that this life was only a brief stopping place on the way to an eternal afterlife.

Daily life was hard for the majority of the people. Disease, famine, hard labor, and frequent warfare made a long life or comfortable existence practically impossible.

❓ *Based on these differences, do you agree that the Middle Ages was "almost a foreign civilization"?* (Possible responses: Yes, there were profound differences in world view. No, many people today are illiterate, religious, or poverty-stricken.)

HUMANITIES CONNECTION

Charlemagne preserved art by refuting the arguments of the iconoclasts and prohibiting their practice of destroying images. Although he allowed images to be made, he spoke out against the practice of worshiping them.

❓ *Why do you think the people of medieval times might have worshiped images?* (Possible response: In general, it is easier for people to understand and feel close to that which they can see and touch.) ■

on Ganelon's treachery in the *Song of Roland*. Films that take place in the Middle Ages are also helpful in building atmosphere. You might consider renting the following videocassettes: *Robin Hood, Prince of Thieves* (1991) starring Kevin Costner as Robin; *Becket* (1964) starring Richard Burton as Thomas à Becket; and *The Lion in Winter*, starring Peter O'Toole as Henry II and Katharine Hepburn as Eleanor of Aquitaine.

Although the selections within the unit appear in chronological order, you might want to sequence your presentation so that the most accessible come first. For instance, students might relate to the ribald humor and feminist concerns of "The Wife of Bath's Tale" more easily than to the concept of the Christian knight in the *Song of Roland*. After reading Chaucer, you might present the doomed lovers of "Chevrefoil" and finally move on to the

heroic epics. Before presenting the epics, hold a class discussion to probe students' opinions about famous acts of treachery in history. Often, when students understand that these epics are full of tales of envy, conspiracy, and deception, they appreciate them more.

It might be a good idea before reading the *Divine Comedy* to explain Dante's cosmology. Dante, like most of his contemporaries, saw the earth as the center

3

❝ [Charlemagne] made attempts at writing, too, and was accustomed to surround his pillows on his bed with tablets and notebooks for this purpose, so that when he had any spare time he would train his hand to form letters. But he met with little success in these efforts because he had started too late in life. ❞

—*from* Vita Karoli, *Einhard*

Scala/Art Resource, New York

OCTOBER, an illuminated detail from the Grimani Breviary, 16th century.

Middle Ages were the forerunners of modern-day historians and journalists. Their records are an invaluable aid to understanding the life of the era.

The Rise of Charlemagne

In 768, **Charlemagne** (shär'lə·mān') became king of the Franks, and in 800 he became the first emperor of the new Holy Roman Empire. Although he could not read or write, Charlemagne encouraged scholarship, education, innovation in architecture, and expansion into new territories. Charlemagne's reign opened a new era of learning, for he ordered

> In A.D. 800, Pope Leo III crowned Charlemagne as Holy Roman Emperor, and a new era of learning and expansion began in Europe.

classical Greek and Roman manuscripts to be collected, encouraged the development of a new system for writing Latin, and invited scholars to open schools. Charlemagne's splendid court was copied in other parts of Europe. The arts and architecture began to flourish, and many great cathedrals were raised to glorify God. Over the course of the next three hundred years, Charlemagne's heroic deeds became legendary. The story of his expedition against Muslims in Spain was written down as the *Song of Roland* (see page 692).

With Charlemagne's death in 814, his kingdom, which covered all of France and much of what is now Italy and eastern Europe, was split up among his three sons and invaded by Vikings. The legends and fierce deeds of the Vikings were chronicled in myths and sagas by the Icelandic poet **Snorri Sturluson** (see page 704), in the early eleventh century.

Feudalism: A System of Allegiance

After Charlemagne's death in 814, rule in Europe fell into the hands of numerous nobles. Powerful and independent, these aristocrats ruled local areas by a system called **feudalism** (fyōōd'l·iz'əm). Feudalism was an economic, social, and military system in which **vassals** (vas'əlz), or tenants, pledged their loyalty to a lord, exchanging work on his land

of the universe with the heavens revolving around it. The earth was divided into two hemispheres, one of land and one of water. Hell was an inverted cone under the land narrowing toward the center of the earth where God had imprisoned Satan. Rising out of the hemisphere of water on the opposite side of the earth was the Mount of Purgatory. The Garden of Eden was at its summit and beyond that the gateway to heaven. Once students grasp this world view, they will understand Dante's allegory better.

To appreciate not only the *Divine Comedy* but all the works of the Middle Ages, students must understand the role of the Church in medieval society. Because students come from a country where church and state are separate, they might not understand that the medieval Church was an integral part of the daily lives of everyone in society. Nearly everybody subscribed to the same spiritual and social ethics and accepted the Church as the wellspring and arbiter of intellectual life.

Another aspect of medieval life that students may find puzzling is that of feudalism. Explain that in a society that fought continual wars, physical security and protection from enemies were dominant concerns. Lead students to draw parallels between the hot wars of the Middle Ages and the recently ended cold war of the

Bibliotheque Nationale, Paris

or service in his military in return for his protection. Usually, the lord himself was vassal to a more powerful overlord, who in turn served as a vassal to a prince or king. Thus, the feudal system was like a pyramid. At the bottom were

Feudalism and the Church were the two great pillars of medieval society.

the **serfs**, or peasants, who worked their lord's land, had few rights, and were totally subject to the lord's will. At the top was the king, who recognized only God as his sovereign. Loyalty to one's lord and to one's peers was the vital element that held the feudal system together.

Epic Deeds of Heroes and Heroines

Warfare between feudal lords was commonplace, and medieval literature simultaneously reflected both ideals of valor and the desire for order and peace. Throughout the early Middle Ages, a rich tradition of stories was passed on by minstrels, who sang or chanted the fabulous deeds of earlier heroes. Many of these stories became **epics** that are still enjoyed today. The eighth-century Anglo-Saxon poem ***Beowulf***, for example, tells the story of Beowulf, a warrior who

TOLL BEING PAID ON BARRELS OF WINE, medieval painting, artist unknown.

Bibliotheque Nationale, Paris

SIEGE OF JERUSALEM, SEBASTIAN MAMEROT. *This illuminated manuscript depicts a battle scene from the Crusades.*

twentieth century. Ask them to consider in what ways the quest for security was an important theme in both eras. (Just as the maintenance of NATO and a nuclear arsenal seemed to provide a sense of security to most Americans, the feudal armies of the lord of the manor offered protection to all the vassals of the feudal lord.)

4 RESPONDING TO THE QUOTATION

This quotation is a good example of how the medieval mind worked. People believed that natural phenomena such as these were indications of God's displeasure.

❓ *How might people who had acquired a basic knowledge of science have explained the events of February 16?* (Because of the change of temperature in the upper atmosphere, a violent thunderstorm erupted. The storm was accompanied by a ball of lightning that took on the aspects of a fireball before it disappeared. An earthquake occurred when the earth shifted along a fault line. The fiery shape of a dragon was actually a cloud that had moved in front of and obscured the sun. The conjunction of these natural events and the assertion of a heretical challenge to the doctrines of the Church was purely coincidental.)

HUMANITIES CONNECTION

Raphael (1483–1520) is considered one of the major artists of the High Renaissance period. He painted *Saint George and the Dragon* while he was living in Florence.

❓ *What does the picture tell you about the Middle Ages?* (Possible responses: People believed that the saints had superhuman powers; they also viewed events allegorically, depicting Saint George and the dragon as symbols of the warring forces of good and evil.) ∎

4

> 66 On February 16 there were great claps of thunder and the intense heat of the sun scorched the earth, and in certain districts of the land an earthquake occurred, and the fiery shape of a dragon was seen in the air. In the same year, a wicked heresy arose. 99
>
> —*from the chronicle of the German town of Xanten, 838*

SAINT GEORGE AND THE DRAGON, **1504–06. RAPHAEL.** *St. George, the patron saint of England, was one of the Middle Ages' most popular saints. According to legend, he saved a king's daughter from being sacrificed to a dragon.*

braves the ferocious monster Grendel and kills a terrible dragon. The ***Nibelungenlied***, the national epic of Germany (see page 730), was composed in the early 1200s out of much older tales. It relates the heroic exploits of Siegfried, who has great magical powers. The Norse-Icelandic **sagas**

> **Heroism was an important theme of much of the literature of the early Middle Ages. Both the epic hero and the Christian saint opposed evil and stood for what was right.**

of Snorri Sturluson and others originated about this time as well. These were tales about historical kings, pre-Christian Norse deities, and legendary heroes. In general, the medieval epics glorify physical strength, courage, and loyalty, celebrating warriors who defeat evil and restore order.

Andrew Mellon Collection, National Gallery of Art, Washington, D.C.

The Church and the castle are the two most powerful symbols of the Middle Ages. At the height of the period, almost everyone in Europe professed allegiance to the Roman Church which, because of its extensive land ownership (estimated to be one third of western Europe), made its bishops seem not much better than feudal lords. Indeed, bishops put on armor and fought with the best of their lay brethren.

The precarious balance of power be-tween the Church and the state unwound over the issue of investiture. Especially in the Holy Roman Empire, the king believed that he had the right to appoint bishops; actually his government depended on it. Gregory VII, pope at this time, asserted his equally strong belief that he had the right to appoint bishops, with diastrous consequences for the Empire which, weakened, fell into chaos and was never reunited. The Protestant Reformation was given momentum as an indirect result of this struggle when small principalities (such as Luther's Saxony) asserted their right to protect Protestants in their lands, and thus broke away from the Empire.

These events in medieval Europe indi-rectly influenced the political develop-ment of the United States. The knowledge of the abuses that resulted from the en-tanglement of church and state led the Protestant leaders of the new nation to

---

A different approach to heroism evolved in the **saints' lives**, tales of the lives of the Christian saints, many of whom were women. The typical saint's life contained super-natural elements, showing saints miraculously healing peo-ple and animals, resisting evil (usually to the point of martyrdom), and being revived after death. In a sense, these stories were the Church's answer to pagan epics like the *Nibelungenlied*. The saints' miraculous deeds glorified the Christian virtues of piety and humble submission to God's will, just as the epics glorified the often militaristic values held dear by the Germanic groups such as the Anglo-Saxons and the Franks.

Medieval Oral Literature

It was not only the church that provided Christian Europe with entertainment during the Middle Ages. From the elev-enth to the fourteenth centuries, French poets called **trou-vères** (trōō·verz′) composed the popular *chansons de geste* ("songs of heroic deeds"). The Christian epic *Song of Roland* (see page 692) survives as a fine example of this form.

It is important for us today to realize that, as most people during the Middle Ages were illiterate, most litera-ture was presented orally, and sometimes visually, as in the case of drama. Common people in particular entertained themselves with folktales, beast fables, and ballads. **Ballads**, or narrative songs, have endured because they tell the kind of sensational stories that make the headlines in today's tabloids—stories about murder, love, and revenge.

The Romance and Courtly Love

In time, the rough realities of feudalism were refined by the code of chivalry. **Chivalry**, a term derived from the French word for knight, *chevalier*, was basically a military code of behavior. A knight was supposed to be fair to his opponents, loyal to his lord, and honorable in all things. He was also supposed to show Christian humility to his peers, kindness to those beneath him, and generosity to all. Of course, not all knights could live up to this code, or even tried to. Many were, after all, mercenary soldiers available to the highest bidder. But unquestionably, chivalry helped to civilize the competitive, often brutal world of the Middle Ages.

Giraudon/Art Resource, New York

JULY: WHEAT HARVEST AND SHEEPSHEARING, an illuminated detail from the Grimani Breviary, 16th century Italy.

❝ The only pests of London are the immoderate drinking of fools and the frequency of fires. **❞**
—*William FitzStephen*

5

WRITING TO LEARN

To learn more about the dragon and the unicorn, pre-pare a report on medieval bes-tiaries. These were collections of stories in which human qualities were ascribed to ani-mals in order to teach a lesson. ■

HUMANITIES CONNECTION

This detail from the Grimani Breviary illustrates the labors associated with the month of July. The harvesting of wheat was carried out in that month. The importance of this activity can be inferred from the num-ber of sculptures in Gothic ca-thedrals that feature people engaged in the process of har-vesting wheat. Such artwork also suggests the abundance of God's providence.

❓ *What details of this illustra-tion seem symbolic to you?* (Possible response: the wheat, the tree, the sheep) ■

5 RESPONDING TO THE QUOTATION

In the 1170s, FitzStephen wrote glowing accounts of London. Among other things, he spoke of a bracing climate, a Chris-tian and honorable citizenry, and strong fortifications.

❓ *How does the quotation on this page fit in with his overall assessment of London?* (Possible response: It is in ac-cordance with his general as-sessment, since fires and in-toxicated people are to be found in every city.)

enshrine in the Constitution and the Bill of Rights the doctrine of separation of church and state.

The literature of the Middle Ages has had a profound influence on literary history. Probably no other romance cycle has captured the imagination of so many people as have the tales of King Arthur and his knights of the Round Table. From the first literary treatment of King Arthur and his court, which is credited to Chrétien de Troyes, these stories have been told and retold right up to the present day. English versions include Thomas Malory's *Le Morte d'Arthur*, Edmund Spenser's *The Faerie Queene*, Alfred Lord Tennyson's *Idylls of the King*, E. A. Robinson's *Merlin* and *Lancelot*, and Mark Twain's satirical novel *A Connecticut Yankee in King Arthur's Court*.

Many musical adaptations of the Arthurian tales have also been composed and performed over the centuries. Foremost among them are Dryden's opera *King Arthur* (featuring music by Purcell) and several other operas composed by Richard Wagner: *Lohengrin*, *Tristan*, and *Parsifal*. The popular twentieth-century musical *Camelot* was based on T. H. White's rendering of the age-old legend, *The Once and Future King*.

In assessing the role of the *Divine Comedy* in literary history, be sure students

---

6 RESPONDING TO THE QUOTATION

The legends of King Arthur and his knights were recorded in the twelfth century when people apparently believed in the validity and vitality of the chivalric code. By the fourteenth century, that belief was dead. Many knights no longer fought in the Crusades to free the Holy Land. Instead, they fought for personal gain or to destroy heretics.

? *Do you think that the actual historical knights of the Middle Ages were ever like the knights of King Arthur's court? Why or why not?* (Possible response: No; King Arthur's knights were symbols of heroic ideals to which people aspired but seldom achieved.)

HUMANITIES CONNECTION

Pieter Breughel the Elder (c. 1525–1569), a sixteenth-century painter from Brussels, often depicted scenes from peasant life. His technique was minutely precise and his colors were usually vivid. In *The Wedding Dance* (1566), Breughel's portrayal of the individuals in the foreground emphasizes the rhythm of the dance.

? *Why might Breughel have been more interested in portraying peasant life than in depicting the aristocracy?* (Possible response: He might have believed that peasants deserved to be commemorated as much as did wealthy, powerful people.)

6

> 66 King Arthur's knights adventured for the right against dragons, enchanters, and wicked men, establishing order in a wild world. . . . In practice, they were themselves the oppressors, and by the 14th century the violence and lawlessness of men of the sword had become a major agency of disorder. 99
>
> —A Distant Mirror, Barbara Tuchman

The **romances** were the literary expression of chivalric ideals. These were long poems about knightly adventures that were recited by traveling poets. The stories were later written down, both in verse and in prose.

The **Arthurian romances** were among the most popular of the medieval romances. The stories of Arthur, a legendary Celtic king, and his knights of the Round Table spread first throughout England and Wales and then migrated to the Continent. **Chrétien de Troyes** (see page 720), who wrote in French in the late twelfth century, was one of the most famous of the medieval romance poets. His stories, especially those of Perceval and Lancelot, influenced later versions of the Arthurian legend.

The romance theme of courtly love made the heroic epics seem out of date.

Like epic heroes, the knights who served as heroes of the medieval romance were strong, courageous, and loyal. But they were also courtly lovers who were devoted to one special lady. This new element of **courtly love** served to distinguish the romances from the earlier epics. The knight's glorious deeds were not performed in the service of king or country, but on behalf of a beautiful, fair, and noble lady,

WEDDING DANCE, PIETER BREUGHEL, THE ELDER.
? *What kind of world does Breughel depict here? Does it seem very different from a modern family or community gathering?*

Giraudon/Art Resource, New York

appreciate that Dante deliberately set out to write a masterpiece as his idol Virgil had done in the *Aeneid*. Medieval literature abounded with works that depicted visions of the afterlife. Dante's particular vision was based on the theology of Thomas Aquinas. Dante's epic was later to inspire Milton's *Paradise Lost* and Longfellow's poem "Divina Commedia."

Finally, Chaucer as "father of English literature" has affected writers down to our own day. Like *The Canterbury Tales*, Edgar Lee Masters' *Spoon River Anthology* (1950) is an attempt in verse to tell the story of a place through the individual voices of its people.

British Museum

TILTING KNIGHTS: KING RICHARD AND SALADIN.
❓ *What place did knights hold in the system of feudalism? How did they figure in the literature of the time?*

who was above him in status and usually married—and therefore unattainable. Sometimes she was a person the knight had only glimpsed from a distance or heard about.

Praise for an unattainable courtly lady was already a popular theme in medieval poetry. During the eleventh century in southern France, poet-musicians called **troubadours** (trōō′bə·dôrz′)—from a French word meaning "to compose" or "to invent"—had begun to write light, graceful lyrics based on the theme of courtly love.

Also in France, the Breton *lais* (*lai* means "song") were influenced by the ideals of courtly love. The *lais* were short stories with supernatural or fairy-tale elements, written in verse and sung to the accompaniment of the lyre or the lute. A number of *lais* were collected in French by **Marie de France** (see page 715), who lived in the English court not long after the Normans of France had conquered England.

> " Woe to our day, since the pursuit of letters has perished from among us. "
>
> —History of the Franks, *Gregory of Tours*

7

THE FIRST KISS OF LANCELOT, illumination from a medieval manuscript. *Lancelot was one of King Arthur's knights.*

The Pierpont Morgan Library

HUMANITIES CONNECTION

Saladin was the sultan of Egypt and Syria in the late twelfth century. After the Franks had violated a peace treaty, Saladin conquered Jerusalem. The Third Crusade was directed against him. Though King Richard defeated Saladin's forces at Arsuf, he and his forces were unable to win back Jerusalem. ■

7 RESPONDING TO THE QUOTATION

With the collapse of the Roman Empire, learning became the province of church officials. From the late 500s, when Gregory of Tours wrote the *History of the Franks*, until the mid-700s, learning was a neglected art. In the late Middle Ages, the academic disciplines were divided into the *Trivium*—grammar, rhetoric, and dialectic—and the *Quadrivium*—arithmetic, geometry, astronomy, and music.
❓ *Why do you think that astronomy, rather than another branch of science, was singled out as a special field of study?* (Possible response: People have always been fascinated by objects in the heavens. The study of astronomy affirmed that abiding fascination.)

HUMANITIES CONNECTION

❓ *What does this illumination suggest about Lancelot and the courtly tradition?* (Possible response: By kissing the lady, Lancelot broke the tradition, because she was supposed to be unattainable.) ■

Introduction   **689**

1. What medieval leader is credited with bringing about a revival of learning? (Charlemagne)

2. What were the tiers of feudal society? (At the bottom were the serfs who tilled the lord's soil. The lord was the vassal of a more powerful overlord. That overlord was the vassal of a prince or a king. The prince or king owed allegiance only to God.)

3. What were the Crusades? ("holy wars" instituted to reclaim the land where Jesus had lived and died)

4. How did the language of literature change during the Middle Ages? (The vernacular replaced Latin.)

5. What distinguishes the heroic epic from the romance? (In a romance, brave or virtuous deeds are done for a fair lady rather than for king, tribe, or glory.)

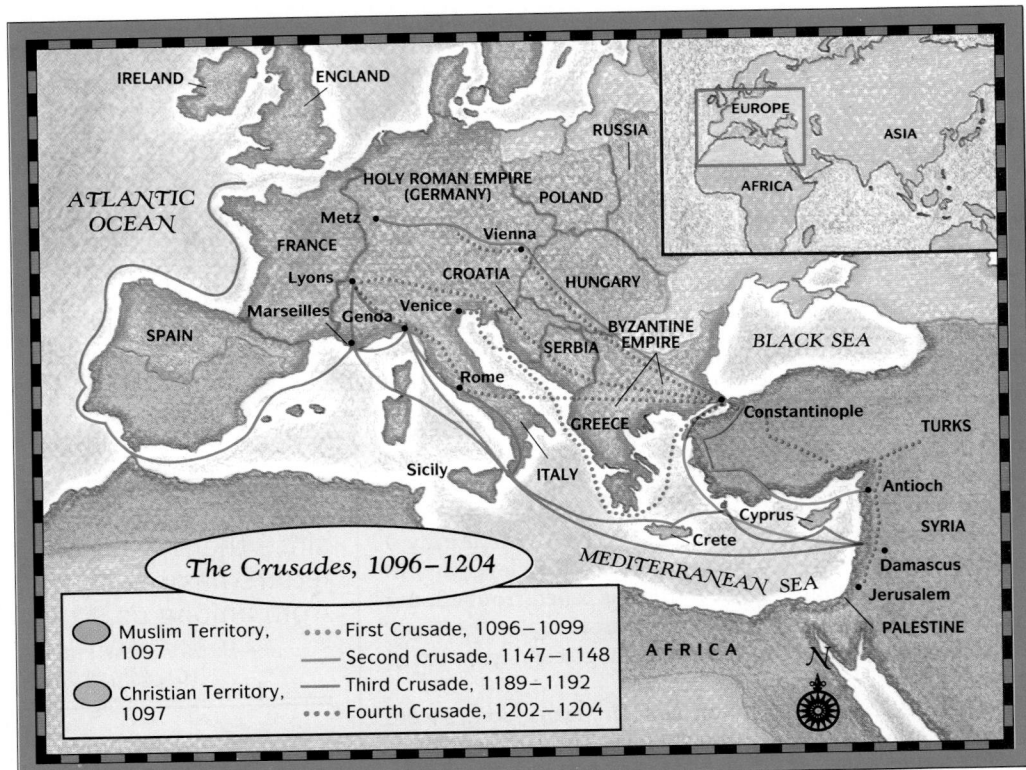

The Crusades, 1096–1204

Muslim Territory, 1097
Christian Territory, 1097

• • • • First Crusade, 1096–1099
—— Second Crusade, 1147–1148
—— Third Crusade, 1189–1192
• • • • Fourth Crusade, 1202–1204

The Late Middle Ages

The late Middle Ages, from about 1300 to about 1500, was a time of enormous upheaval that dealt severe blows to the two great medieval institutions, the feudal system and the Church. The **Crusades** (1096–1270), which were Christian attempts to forcefully regain the Holy Land from the Muslims, had cost many European lives but had also opened up trade routes to the East. These routes allowed an influx of new goods and ideas that enhanced the financial status of the merchant class and accelerated the development of towns and cities. Some cities founded universities, new centers of learning that opened doors for the middle class.

A dramatic climate change in the 1300s, later called the Little Ice Age, brought bitterly cold weather and reduced

FOR FURTHER STUDY

Nonfiction

Medieval Days and Ways by Gertrude Hartman describes early medieval times, the feudal system, the importance of the Church, and town life. *Life in a Medieval City* by Joseph and Frances Gies tells of home life in Troyes in 1250; describes events such as weddings and funerals; and depicts the environments of the governments, schools, theaters, and fairs.

Fiction

Some of Sir Walter Scott's novels depict the wars of the Middle Ages. *Ivanhoe* is set during the struggle between the Normans and the Saxons, and *The Talisman* recounts the conflict between Christians and Muslims. Horace Walpole's *The Castle of Otranto* contains all the elements of a medieval romance, including a prince, knights in armor, and the influence of supernatural forces.

Films

Becket, starring Peter O'Toole and Richard Burton, focuses on a conflict between castle and church—that of King Henry II of England and Thomas á Becket, the Archbishop of Canterbury. *The Lion in Winter*, starring Peter O'Toole and Katharine Hepburn, tells the story of King Henry II and Eleanor of Aquitaine and their conflict over the issue of royal succession. ■

crop yields. Soon after, the Black Death, or bubonic plague, wiped out entire European villages. As a result, there were few serfs to work the fields, and the serfs who remained demanded more freedoms. Technology created change, too, for the development of gunpowder meant that a cannon could decide the outcome of a feudal battle in a matter of hours. Thus the system of feudalism was gradually undermined as the Middle Ages came to a close.

The power of the Church was also being challenged. Charges of corruption and internal arguments, or **schisms** (siz'əmz), weakened the Church at its foundations. The Church's role as biblical interpreter was undermined, too, for another development of the late Middle Ages was that more people learned to read. With the growth of literacy came a new intellectual independence. And with the development of the printing press, critics and reformers were able to write, print, and circulate literary **satires** that ridiculed the Church's corrupt practices.

The most significant development in literature during the late Middle Ages, however, was the rise of the use of the **vernacular**, or regional, languages instead of Latin, the language of the educated elite throughout medieval times. This development signaled that great changes were taking place all over Europe: an emerging sense of nationalism, the increase of educated readers, the availability of printed material, and the recognition and acceptance of the value of

> The late Middle Ages was marked by the building of the great cathedrals, the opening of trade routes, and an increase in the number of people who could read and write in the vernacular languages.

such local oral literatures as stories and songs. The use of vernacular in works such as Wycliffe's translation of the Bible into English, Chaucer's *Canterbury Tales*, and Dante's *Divine Comedy* established the vernacular as acceptable in literature. The world was becoming more secular, and this change was more fittingly expressed in literature that used the languages of everyday people.

The Pierpont Morgan Library

First Lindan book cover, late eighth century.

8 LITERARY BACKGROUND

Vernacular: The English of Chaucer's *Canterbury Tales* is not the language of English speakers in the contemporary United States. Chaucer used the language that ordinary Londoners spoke in his time, a dialect now referred to as Middle English, specifically of the South East Midland type. If students were to read Chaucer in its original Middle English, they would probably be struck by the differences in spelling between Middle English and contemporary American English and by the fact that the final e that is silent in most of our contemporary English words is pronounced in Middle English as a separate syllable.

HUMANITIES CONNECTION

Ornate covers became popular during the Middle Ages. These highly decorative covers are emblematic of the beauty of the illuminated manuscripts they contained. The most impressive covers were made of gold embellished with both precious and semiprecious stones.

? *What kinds of manuscripts do you think were deemed worthy of such resplendent covers? Explain.* (Possible response: probably religious books, because the Church was the keeper of learning during the Middle Ages. The use of precious stones symbolizes the Church's respect for the value of the sacred word.) ■

The *Song of Roland* resembles earlier heroic epics in its emphasis on fierce warfare, personal betrayal, and destructive pride. However, two elements reflect medieval culture: the feudal code, which required the unswerving allegiance of vassals to their lords, and the emergence of Christianity as the motivation for many "holy wars."

1 HISTORICAL BACKGROUND

Charlemagne agreed to help Suleiman, the Moorish governor of Barcelona. Charlemagne was probably motivated in this strange alliance by the potential for gaining more territory (the Basque provinces).

2 CULTURAL BACKGROUND

One version of the epic identifies Roland as both the son and nephew of Charlemagne, as a result of Charlemagne's rumored incestuous relationship with his sister. Thus, the medieval audience could have interpreted Charlemagne's defeat and Roland's death as a form of divine retribution.

■ HUMANITIES CONNECTION

Charlemagne was crowned Holy Roman Emperor in 800 by Pope Leo III. He did much to advance learning and the arts, and he rebuilt many monasteries and founded new ones. ❓ *What kind of relationship must have existed between the Church and state at this time?* (a close one, because the pope crowned the emperor and the emperor built religious buildings) ■

The Song of Roland
c. 1100

STORIES OF THE EMPEROR: THE CORONATION OF CHARLEMAGNE.

Scala/Art Resource, New York

Generally considered the national epic of France, the *Song of Roland* is based on a historical event. The story dates back to the time of Charlemagne, the king of the Franks from A.D. 768 to 814.

In Charlemagne's time, Spain was ruled by Arab Muslims. Charlemagne agreed to help one of two Muslim rivals who were battling each other for control of Spain. But Charlemagne's campaign in Spain was a complete disaster, and in 778 his army was forced to retreat. As they crossed back into France, the rear guard of his army was overrun by the Basques (bäskz), a people who live in the Pyrenees Mountains that divide France and Spain. One of the commanders of Charlemagne's rear guard during this battle at Roncesvalles was a man named Roland.

By the eleventh century, Europe was in the midst of the Crusades, the "holy wars" in which Christians tried to reconquer Jerusalem and wrest it from the Muslims. Anti-Muslim feelings ran high in Europe. As the world had changed, so, too, did the story of Roland and the battle of Roncesvalles. From an account of a power struggle between two Arab Muslims in the eighth century, the story had evolved into a national epic about the religious conflict between Christians and Muslims in the eleventh century. The Basques were transformed into Arabs—referred to in the poem as "Saracens," "pagans," and "idol worshipers." Meanwhile, Roland, who had played only a minor role in history, became a legendary hero, a nephew of Charlemagne, and a model Christian knight.

OBJECTIVES

1. To recognize the characteristics of the chanson de geste, a French form of epic poetry
2. To identify and analyze the ideals of eleventh- and twelfth-century French society as represented in the epic
3. To compare and contrast epic heroes
4. To conduct an interview with a character from the epic

THEMES IN WORLD LITERATURE

Triumph and Defeat

From the *Iliad*, pp. 224–277
From the *Aeneid*, pp. 379–407
"Rama and Ravana in Battle" from the *Ramayana*, pp. 484–494

What Is a Hero?

From *Sundiata: An Epic of Old Mali*, pp. 102–117
From the *Nibelungenlied*, pp. 730–740 ∎

VOCABULARY IN CONTEXT

The words listed below will appear in the side margin at the point of instruction:

1. exulting   4. feigned
2. siege   5. fostered
3. peers

Reader's Guide

from the SONG OF ROLAND

Background

The *Song of Roland* is the earliest surviving example of the Old French *chansons de geste* (shän·sōnz′ də zhest′), or "songs of deeds," composed in the eleventh and twelfth centuries. These epic poems focus on the heroic deeds of Charlemagne and other feudal lords. The *Song of Roland* shares many characteristics with classical epic poems such as the *Iliad* and the *Aeneid*: long speeches, descriptions of battles, dreams, supernatural elements, and the repetition of key phrases.

As the selection begins, Roland, his noble friend Oliver, and their small force are trapped in a mountain pass in the Pyrenees Mountains. Their dire situation is a result of the treachery of Ganelon, Roland's stepfather, who is envious of Roland's reputation as a warrior and furious because Roland has recommended him for dangerous duty as Charlemagne's ambassador to the Saracen king Marsilion. Ganelon has encouraged King Marsilion to attack the rear guard of Charlemagne's army with an overwhelming force—400,000 Saracens against 20,000 Franks. He has also persuaded Charlemagne to place Roland in command of the rear guard, the portion of the army in greatest danger. In this translation of the *Song of Roland*, Charlemagne, which means "Charles the Great," is referred to simply as Charles.

Writer's Response

Roland, the hero of the *Song of Roland*, acts according to his concept of honor. What does *honor* mean to you? List three decisions you or people you know have made that you consider honorable.

Literary Focus

An **epic** is a long narrative poem that relates the great deeds of a larger-than-life figure. The **epic hero**, the main character of an epic, embodies the values of the particular society he represents. For example, a hero of the Indian epic *Mahabharata* (see page 458) exhibits the qualities of intelligence and thoughtfulness, while the Persian epic heroes Sohráb and Rostám (see page 646) are courageous and physically powerful. Roland, on the other hand, is the ultimate medieval European knight: a heroic fighter, a loyal follower of his king, a trusted friend, and a devout Christian.

PREREADING FOCUS

Background: The *chansons de geste* were passed down orally by *jongleurs*, travelling performers who not only told stories of the deeds of great heroes but also entertained the public with juggling, acrobatics, and instrumental music. The jongleurs depended for their livelihood on the generosity of their audience, and therefore were likely to tailor their stories to their audience's tastes. Since at the time only the clergy and the higher nobility could read and write, jongleurs were most likely illiterate. This did not interfere with their storytelling, however, as some jongleurs were able to recite *chansons* as long as 35,000 lines.

No one knows for certain when the *Song of Roland* was first written down, but most historians believe it must have been in the latter part of the eleventh century. There are no copies of the poem in its original form, but six subsequent versions have survived, three of them in French. The most famous, and probably the closest to the original, is called the Oxford version.

Writer's Response: To help students focus on the meaning of *honor*, encourage them to think of people who have responded to difficult situations in ways they admired or respected. Examples may be drawn from sports, politics, or ordinary life. An action that is admirable is usually also honorable.

from the SONG OF ROLAND

translated by
FREDERICK GOLDIN

As you read, pay attention to clues to Roland's character: what he says, what others say to him and about him, and what he does. In what ways is he a hero? Which of his character traits are most responsible for his downfall?

Maria Antoinette Evans Fund, Courtesy, Museum of Fine Arts, Boston

Olifant, carved ivory, c. A.D. 1100. *Roland does not sound his horn, olifant, until it is too late to save the French troops.*
❓ What would you have done in his position?

Roland's companion Oliver has seen the advancing Saracen army and knows that the small French rear guard is outnumbered. He begs Roland to blow on his horn, the olifant, in order to summon more troops from Charles's (Charlemagne's) army, but Roland refuses, saying that he will lose his reputation and bring shame on the French if he calls for help. He believes that he and the other French fighters are more than equal to the Saracens. Oliver continues to urge Roland to call for help, to no avail. Finally Roland, Oliver, Archbishop Turpin, and the other French fighters clash with the Saracens in the mountain pass. For a time, the French hold their own.

110

The battle is fearful and full of grief.
Oliver and Roland strike like good men,
the Archbishop, more than a thousand blows,
and the Twelve Peers° do not hang back, they strike!
5 the French fight side by side, all as one man.
The pagans die by hundreds, by thousands:
whoever does not flee finds no refuge from death,
like it or not, there he ends all his days.
And there the men of France lose their greatest arms;

4. **Twelve Peers:** noblemen chosen as Charles's select band of leaders.

10 they will not see their fathers, their kin again,
or Charlemagne, who looks for them in the
  passes.

2 Tremendous torment now comes forth in France,
a mighty whirlwind, tempests of wind and
  thunder,
rains and hailstones, great and immeasurable,
15 bolts of lightning hurtling and hurtling down:
it is, in truth, a trembling of the earth.
From Saint Michael-in-Peril° to the Saints,
from Besançon° to the port of Wissant,
there is no house whose veil of walls does not
  crumble.

3 20 A great darkness at noon falls on the land,
there is no light but when the heavens crack.
No man sees this who is not terrified,
and many say: "The Last Day! Judgment Day!
The end! The end of the world is upon us!"
25 They do not know, they do not speak the truth:
it is the worldwide grief for the death of Roland.

17. **Saint Michael-in-Peril**: a sanctuary on the coast of Normandy.
18. **Besançon** (bə·zän·sōn′): a city in east central France, part of the original kingdom of Burgundy.

Roland and the Twelve Peers fight fiercely against the Saracens, but they are greatly outnumbered. At last it becomes apparent even to Roland that the battle cannot be won, and he finally decides to use his magical horn, the olifant, to call Charlemagne's army for relief. But Oliver, angered that

Roland's pride had prevented him from blowing the horn earlier, when it could have done some good, stops Roland with harsh words, pointing out that it truly would be a disgrace to sound the horn now, when all hope has been lost.

130

4 And Roland says: "We are in a rough battle.
I'll sound the olifant, Charles will hear it."
Said Oliver: "No good vassal would do it.

5 30 When I urged it, friend, you did not think it right.
If Charles were here, we'd come out with no
  losses.
Those men down there—no blame can fall on
  them."

6 Oliver said: "Now by this beard of mine,
If I can see my noble sister, Aude,°
35 once more, you will never lie in her arms!"

34. **Aude** (ō′dā): Roland's betrothed.

from the Song of Roland 695

---

2 LITERARY ELEMENT
Imagery: How does the storm imagery in lines 12–16 reflect and foreshadow the events of the poem? (Possible response: It echoes the ferocity of the fighting and foreshadows the "worldwide grief" for the hero who is about to die.)

3 CULTURAL DIVERSITY
In line 20, the poet tells of "darkness at noon."
❓ *Within the Christian tradition, when did darkness at noon occur?* (Good Friday, the day Christ died)

4 LITERARY BACKGROUND
The sound of Roland's horn, which had belonged to his grandfather Charles the Hammer, reportedly made the earth shake and birds fall from the trees. However, only Roland was capable of making it emit such a sound.

5 ORAL INTERPRETATION
In line 30, Oliver addresses Roland as "friend." If you were saying Oliver's lines, what tone of voice would you use, and why? (Possible responses: sarcastic, sad, or angry. Oliver wants to emphasize that Roland did not heed his advice as a friend would have.)

MEETING INDIVIDUAL NEEDS

6 ESL: Point out that "Now by this beard of mine" is an idiomatic expression (one without a sensible literal meaning) that emphasizes Oliver's anger. It is used throughout the epic when a character makes a point strongly. ∎

7 INTERPRETING
To what relationship is Oliver referring when he uses the word "vassal" in line 38? (Roland's relationship with Charlemagne; Charlemagne is the king and Roland has pledged to serve him loyally, as vassals do their lords.)

8 GUIDED READING
Identifying Details: What virtues does Oliver value in a vassal? (good judgment, restraint) What faults does he find with Roland's behavior? (recklessness, impulsiveness)

9 CULTURAL BACKGROUND
Although Turpin the Archbishop is a clergyman, he fights for his king on the battlefield. In medieval times, the clergy did not restrict themselves to spiritual matters, but were involved in every aspect of society—politics, warfare, business, and education.

> **exulting** (eg·zult'iŋ): rejoicing greatly

10 CULTURAL DIVERSITY
Archbishop Turpin says that the King will make sure that they are buried "in the courts of churches." Medieval Christians believed that unless they were buried in consecrated ground, their souls would not be admitted to heaven.
❓ *What other cultures have valued proper burial?* (Possible response: The ancient Egyptians had very elaborate burial practices for their nobility; the ancient Greeks believed a spirit could not rest without a proper funeral.)

131

And Roland said: "Why are you angry at me?"
Oliver answers: "Companion, it is your doing.
7 — I will tell you what makes a vassal good:
   it is judgment, it is never madness;
8 — restraint is worth more than the raw nerve of
   a fool.
40 Frenchmen are dead because of your wildness.
And what service will Charles ever have from us?
If you had trusted me, my lord would be here,
we would have fought this battle through to the end,
Marsilion would be dead, or our prisoner.
45 Roland, your prowess—had we never seen it!
   And now, dear friend, we've seen the last of it.
No more aid from us now for Charlemagne,
a man without equal till Judgment Day,
you will die here, and your death will shame
   France.
We kept faith, you and I, we were companions;
   and everything we were will end today.
50 We part before evening, and it will be hard."

132

9 — Turpin the Archbishop hears their bitter words,
digs hard into his horse with golden spurs
and rides to them; begins to set them right:
"You, Lord Roland, and you, Lord Oliver,
55 I beg you in God's name do not quarrel.
To sound the horn could not help us now, true,
but still it is far better that you do it:
let the King come, he can avenge us then—
these men of Spain must not go home exulting!
60 Our French will come, they'll get down on their
   feet,
and find us here—we'll be dead, cut to pieces.
10 — They will lift us into coffins on the backs of
   mules,
and weep for us, in rage and pain and grief,
and bury us in the courts of churches;
65 and we will not be eaten by wolves or pigs or dogs."
Roland replies, "Lord, you have spoken well."

Giraudon/Art Resource, New York

CHARLEMAGNE, ALBRECHT DÜRER, early 16th century.
❓ *What role does Charlemagne—Charles the Great—play in this epic?*

133

Roland has put the olifant to his mouth,
he sets it well, sounds it with all his strength.
The hills are high, and that voice ranges far,
70 they heard it echo thirty great leagues away.
King Charles heard it, and all his faithful men.
And the King says: "Our men are in a battle."
And Ganelon disputed him and said:
"Had someone else said that, I'd call him liar!"

134

75 And now the mighty effort of Roland the Count:
he sounds his olifant; his pain is great,
and from his mouth the bright blood comes
    leaping out,
and the temple bursts in his forehead.
That horn, in Roland's hands, has a mighty voice:
80 King Charles hears it drawing through the passes.
Naimon° heard it, the Franks listen to it.
And the King said: "I hear Count Roland's horn;
he'd never sound it unless he had a battle."
Says Ganelon: "Now no more talk of battles!
85 You are old now, your hair is white as snow,
the things you say make you sound like a child.
You know Roland and that wild pride of his—
what a wonder God has suffered it so long!
Remember? he took Noples° without your
    command:
90 the Saracens rode out, to break the siege;
they fought with him, the great vassal Roland.
Afterwards he used the streams to wash the blood
from the meadows: so that nothing would show.
He blasts his horn all day to catch a rabbit,
95 he's strutting now before his peers and bragging—
who under heaven would dare meet him on the
    field?
So now: ride on! Why do you keep on stopping?
The Land of Fathers lies far ahead of us."

81. **Naimon:** a duke and adviser to Charlemagne.

89. **Noples:** in Spain.

15 The dying Oliver loses his sight and, mistaking Roland for a foe, strikes Roland with his sword. Keeping in mind the medieval emphasis on duty to God and king, compose Oliver's final speech to Roland. For what does Oliver ask Roland's forgiveness? What advice would Oliver offer Roland? ■

16 CULTURAL DIVERSITY
The swords of the heroes of medieval epics were considered so important that they were often given names and seen as personal allies. Roland's sword was called Durendal, and Oliver's sword, Halteclere.
❓ *What are some names given to modern weapons?* (Possible responses: Patriot missile, Stealth bomber, Trident submarine)

| **feigned** (fānd): pretended |

17 INTERPRETING
Why does the Saracen say he'll "carry this sword home to Arabia" in line 122? (Possible responses: He wants to show proof that Roland is dead. The sword would be a trophy for him.)

Roland sounds his horn again. Charles commands his army to ride to Roland's aid, but it is too late to save Roland and his peers, who have been defeated by the Saracens. Before he dies, Oliver asks forgiveness of Roland.

15 ⌈

168

Now Roland feels that death is very near.
100 His brain comes spilling out through his two ears;
prays to God for his peers: let them be called;
and for himself, to the angel Gabriel;
took the olifant: there must be no reproach!
took Durendal° his sword in his other hand,
105 and farther than a crossbow's farthest shot
he walks toward Spain, into a fallow land,
and climbs a hill: there beneath two fine trees
stand four great blocks of stone, all are of marble;
and he fell back, to earth, on the green grass,
110 has fainted there, for death is very near.

16 ⌈

104. **Durendal** (dü'ren·däl): Roland's unbreakable sword; said to be the sword that had belonged to the Trojan hero Hector.

169

High are the hills, and high, high are the trees;
there stand four blocks of stone, gleaming of marble.
Count Roland falls fainting on the green grass,
and is watched, all this time, by a Saracen:
115 who has <u>feigned</u> death and lies now with the others,
has smeared blood on his face and on his body;
and quickly now gets to his feet and runs—
a handsome man, strong, brave, and so crazed with pride
that he does something mad and dies for it:
120 laid hands on Roland, and on the arms of Roland,
and cried: "Conquered! Charles's nephew conquered!
I'll carry this sword home to Arabia!"
As he draws it, the Count begins to come round.

17 ⌈

170

125 Now Roland feels *someone taking his sword!*
opened his eyes, and had one word for him:
"I don't know you, you aren't one of ours";
grasps that olifant that he will never lose,
strikes on the helm beset with gems in gold,
130 shatters the steel, and the head, and the bones,
sent his two eyes flying out of his head,
dumped him over stretched out at his feet dead;
and said: "You nobody! how could you dare
lay hands on me—rightly or wrongly: how?
Who'll hear of this and not call you a fool?
135 Ah! the bell-mouth of the olifant is smashed,
the crystal and the gold fallen away."

171

Now Roland the Count feels his sight is gone;
gets on his feet, draws on his final strength,
the color on his face lost now for good.
140 Before him stands a rock; and on that dark rock
in rage and bitterness he strikes ten blows:
the steel blade grates, it will not break, it stands unmarked.
"Ah!" said the Count, "Blessed Mary, your help!

The Metropolitan Museum of Art, Cloisters Collection, Purchase 1962

French reliquary shrine, mid-fourteenth century. *A reliquary was an ornate case designed to contain religious relics, or physical remains of saints.*

HUMANITIES CONNECTION

Throughout the Middle Ages, pieces of Christ's True Cross (thought to be one upon which Christ was crucified) and the remains of saints were kept in reliquaries made of gilded silver or bronze and decorated with enameled religious scenes or precious jewels. The containers created with these valuable materials often took the shapes of sacred objects or even saints' body parts. Reliquaries were placed on church altars, carried in religious processions, or privately owned.

This reliquary shrine depicting the Virgin and Child (Paris, c. 1345) is believed to have been made to hold relics owned by Queen Elizabeth of Hungary. Made of gilded silver and translucent enamel with hinged wings on each side, it is in the form of a miniature altarpiece. ∎

18 COMPARING LITERATURE
Some students might want to compare the level of graphically violent description in lines 126–134 with examples of vivid violence in the Anglo-Saxon epic *Beowulf.* They might discuss the effect of these violent scenes on medieval and modern audiences.

19 INTERPRETING
Why does Roland strike ten blows on a rock in lines 140–141? (Possible response: Roland is infuriated with the Saracen. He knows he will die soon and wants to break Durendal rather than surrender it to an infidel.)

from the Song of Roland **699**

20 COMPARING LITERATURE
Roland has a magic horn and an unbreakable sword. What other heroes, ancient or modern, have possessions with supernatural, or magical, powers? (Possible responses: King Arthur's sword Excalibur, Thor's hammer Mjollnir)

21 CULTURAL BACKGROUND
During the Crusades (1096–1291), Christian knights often carried sacred relics with them on their campaigns against "the infidels," as they called all non-Christians. Relics, like those embedded in Roland's sword, included parts of the body or the clothing of a deceased saint, or parts of a sacred object, such as the cross of Christ. Such objects were believed to bring divine protection or miraculous cures and were therefore highly valued. It would have been considered a sacrilege for relics, such as those in Roland's sword, to fall into the hands of a nonbeliever. Ironically, his sword was said to have originally belonged to the Trojan pagan Hector!

Ah Durendal, good sword, your unlucky day,
145 for I am lost and cannot keep you in my care.
The battles I have won, fighting with you,
the mighty lands that holding you I conquered,
that Charles rules now, our King, whose beard
   is white!
Now you fall to another: it must not be
   a man who'd run before another man!
150 For a long while a good vassal held you:
there'll never be the like in France's holy land."

173

20
Roland the Count strikes down on a dark rock,
and the rock breaks, breaks more than I can tell,
and the blade grates, but Durendal will not break,
155 the sword leaped up, rebounded toward the sky.
The Count, when he sees that sword will not be
   broken,
softly, in his own presence, speaks the lament:
"Ah Durendal, beautiful, and most sacred,
the holy relics in this golden pommel!
21
160 Saint Peter's tooth and blood of Saint Basile,°
a lock of hair of my lord Saint Denis,°
and a fragment of blessed Mary's robe:
your power must not fall to the pagans,
you must be served by Christian warriors.
165 May no coward ever come to hold you!
It was with you I conquered those great lands
that Charles has in his keeping, whose beard is
   white,
the Emperor's lands, that make him rich and
   strong."

160. **Saint Basile** (ba·sēl'): fourth-century religious writer and monastery administrator; fought for orthodoxy within the Catholic Church.
161. **Saint Denis** (den'is): third-century apostle to the Gauls, who was martyred; patron saint of France.

174

Now Roland feels death coming over him,
170 death descending from his temples to his heart.
He came running underneath a pine tree
and there stretched out, face down, on the green
   grass,
lays beneath him his sword and the olifant.
He turned his head toward the Saracen hosts,

1. Before the battle, what does Oliver want Roland to do? (blow his horn so Charlemagne will come to their aid)
2. Why does Roland ignore Oliver's advice? (He is proud, reckless, and overconfident.)
3. Why does Archbishop Turpin urge Roland to call for help even after their defeat is certain? (so Charlemagne can avenge their deaths and bury them properly)
4. What does Ganelon advise Charles to do when they hear the horn? (ignore it and keep riding toward France)
5. What does Roland do with his sword before he dies? (He tries to destroy it to prevent its falling into the wrong hands.)

RETEACHING

Divide students into small groups. Ask them to imagine that each group is a team of war correspondents traveling with the French rear guard near Roncesvalles. They manage to escape from the bloody battle in time to file an eyewitness account of the defeat of Roland. Have each team create a front page news story, including an attention-getting headline and an exciting opening paragraph, covering the five W's—who, what, when, where, and why.

175   and this is why: with all his heart he wants
King Charles the Great and all his men to say,
he died, that noble Count, a conqueror;
makes confession, beats his breast often, so feebly,
offers his glove, for all his sins, to God.

176

180   Count Roland lay stretched out beneath a pine;
he turned his face toward the land of Spain,
began to remember many things now:
how many lands, brave man, he had conquered;
and he remembered: sweet France, the men of
    his line,
185   remembered Charles, his lord, who fostered him;
cannot keep, remembering, from weeping, sighing;
but would not be unmindful of himself:
he confesses his sins, prays God for mercy:
"Loyal Father, you who never failed us,
190   who resurrected Saint Lazarus° from the dead,
and saved your servant Daniel° from the lions:
now save the soul of me from every peril
for the sins I committed while I still lived."
Then he held out his right glove to his Lord:
195   Saint Gabriel° took the glove from his hand.
He held his head bowed down upon his arm,
he is gone, his two hands joined, to his end.
Then God sent him his angel Cherubim°
and Saint Michael,° angel of the sea's Peril;
200   and with these two there came Saint Gabriel:
they bear Count Roland's soul to Paradise.

190. **Saint Lazarus:** The story of this miracle appears in John 11:1–44.
191. **Daniel:** The story is told in Daniel 6:16–27.

195. **Saint Gabriel:** one of the seven archangels; messenger of good news.

198. **Cherubim** (cher'yoo·bim): one of the heavenly beings at God's throne.
199. **Saint Michael:** one of the archangels.

22 COMPARING LITERATURE
How does the death of Roland differ from the death of the heroes of the classical epics, such as Achilles? (Possible response: Roland begs God's forgiveness for his sins. He seems to bear more personal responsibility for his end than the classical heroes, who seemed to be merely living out their destiny.)

fostered (fôs'tərd): brought up with care

23 LITERARY ELEMENT
Symbol: What might the offering of the glove symbolize in lines 194–195? (Possible response: By offering his glove, Roland is surrendering his soul to God.)

CULTURAL BACKGROUND
The Church of medieval times did not approve of many of the popular heroic epics because they glorified men, making them seem to have powers rivaling those of God. The story of Roland was an exception, however, because of its Christian overtones. Later versions of the story became even more overtly Christian. One mid-twelfth century version was supposedly written by Archbishop Turpin himself, who, according to that version, did not die with Roland but recovered from his wounds.

1. Toot Your Own Horn—With Heraldry. Heraldry (the devising of insignia for armor) began to develop about the same time that the *Song of Roland* was written down. Students might enjoy learning more about the significance of the animals, objects, colors, and abstract designs used on medieval armor. Suggest they design their own shields on posterboard using medieval heraldic elements and then explain to the class the significance of those elements. Alternatively, students might research the styles of armor used by the Moorish or French armies during Charlemagne's day, and draw a poster showing a typical knight or soldier.

2. Research Project. Some students may be interested in Ganelon's betrayal of Roland. Encourage these students to read Stanzas 20–54 of the *Song of Roland* and then compare Ganelon to another notorious traitor, such as Judas Iscariot or Benedict Arnold. Their reports should also reveal what finally happens to Ganelon.

CLOSURE

Ask students to explain how the concept of honor played a role in Roland's downfall. Have them also compare Roland's idea of honor with Oliver's. ■

ANSWERS

First Thoughts
Answers will vary.

Identifying Facts
1. sound his horn for help. Oliver says it is too late.
2. that he is in battle
3. blowing the horn kills him.

Interpreting Meanings
1. Possible response: Roland seems more interested in personal honor, and Oliver with the honor of the group.
2. Roland is proud, glory-seeking, and impulsive. Oliver is more cautious and interested in the general good.
3. "death is very near" (creates suspense), "the steel blade grates . . . will not break" (emphasizes the sword's magical strength)
4. Possible responses: loyalty to a lord or king, loyalty to the Christian faith, courage
5. Possible response: As a warrior, he would have preferred a death by sword.

Applying Meanings
Possible response: He dies trying to save his men. Today, this would be a victory.

Critical Writing Response
Comparing Epic Heroes. Remind students that they are comparing not only two warriors but also two different sets of cultural values.

Speaking and Listening
Conducting an Interview. Questions and answers should show a knowledge of the character's view of events. ■

First Thoughts
Did Roland fit your idea of a hero? What did you admire about him? Which of his qualities did you *not* admire?

Identifying Facts
1. As the battle proceeds, it becomes clear that the Franks will be defeated. What does Roland want to do? How does Oliver respond?
2. What does Charles think the sound of Roland's horn means?
3. What finally happens to Roland?

Interpreting Meanings
1. The code of chivalry that Roland follows puts great emphasis on personal honor. How does the concern for honor influence the behavior of Roland? Of Oliver? How are the two men's responses similar and different?
2. What does Roland and Oliver's disagreement reveal about their characters?
3. **Repetition** is an important feature of the *chansons de geste*. Give at least two examples of repetition in this poem. In each case, why do you think repetition is used?
4. As an **epic hero**, Roland represents the values of his society. Based on your understanding of his character, list at least three of the values that this epic seems to celebrate.
5. In the **climax** of the selection, Roland dies not from a battle wound but from the bursting of his blood vessels when he blows the horn. Do you think Roland would have preferred this death to one from a Saracen sword? Why or why not?

Applying Meanings
Do you think that in this epic death is a defeat for the hero? Why or why not? If Roland were a contemporary war hero, do you think that his death would be mourned as a defeat or celebrated as a victory?

Critical Writing Response
Comparing Epic Heroes. Write a short essay comparing Roland and Achilles (see page 224) as epic heroes. In your discussion, consider the qualities each figure represents. What faults do they share? Consider, too, how the codes of honor of the two heroes differ. A chart like the following can help you to organize your ideas.

	Roland	Achilles
Codes of honor		
Positive character traits		
Negative character traits		
Conclusion		

Speaking and Listening
Conducting an Interview. Imagine that you are a television newscaster reporting on the Battle of Roncesvalles. Pair yourself with a classmate who will play the part of one of the main characters in the *Song of Roland*—Roland, Oliver, or Charles (Charlemagne). Together, decide what issues your interview will cover. Be sure to deal with the most important aspects of the battle, and be sure that the interviewer asks probing questions that reveal the character's motives and judgment. Then conduct your interview for the rest of the class.

SEEING CONNECTIONS

Poem of the Cid: *Spain's National Epic*

Glory, gore, and God provide the foundations for two of Europe's medieval epics: France's *Song of Roland* and Spain's *Poem of the Cid*. Christianity, in whose name countless Arabs' blood is shed, is a key element in both epics. But while *Song of Roland* is filled with mythic elements—Roland's ancestry is traced to the Trojan hero Hector and the Germanic god Wotan (Odin)—Spain's twelfth-century epic is remarkably free of mythic and supernatural elements and is instead characterized by gritty realism.

The Spanish epic's hero, Ruy Diaz de Bivar, better known as the Cid (thēd), begins his career as one of King Alfonso VI's tribute collectors—a sort of medieval collection agent. His humble origins make him vulnerable to the whims of the King and the counts from whom he collects tribute. When the Cid is unjustly exiled by the king for pressing one of the monarch's own vassal's too hard for tribute, the hero sets out to gain the king's pardon. But the Cid is clever enough to realize that the only way to gain King Alfonso's forgiveness is to leave him with no choice: he sets out to become as powerful as the king himself. The Cid and his followers set out to conquer the Moorish strongholds in Seville and Valencia. ("Moors" are the Spanish equivalent of the Saracens in *Song of Roland*—that is, Arabs.) Only when the king can no longer ignore the now fabulously wealthy Cid does he grant his "pardon."

The climactic moments of *Poem of the Cid* take place not in the battlefield but in the courtroom. The Cid petitions the king for justice after the hero's sons-in-law, the royal princes of Carrión, have dishonored his daughters, beating and abandoning them in the wilderness. Here we see the central issues of the epic—the tension between the aristocracy and the commoner—brought into focus. For the Cid, despite his heroism and enormous wealth, is still for all practical purposes a commoner. His triumph in court reinforces the ideals of medieval Spain, where honor is measured not by bloodlines but by heroism and by wealth *earned* in hard labor.

Poem of the Cid gives its audience a hero not from the classical tradition or even from a nation's royalty, but from the common folk—a hero not unlike themselves. Unlike Roland, who dies at the height of his glory, penitent for his overreaching pride, the Cid dies a wealthy old man, thankful to God for his good fortune but apologizing to no one—for the medieval audience, a deeply satisfying dream come true.

HISTORICAL BACKGROUND

Scholars do not know who wrote the *Poem of the Cid*, but the composer was probably a native of the Castilian area, close to lands occupied by the Moors. (The border area between the Spanish Christians and the Moors was constantly in dispute during the eleventh and twelfth centuries.)

The most widely accepted guess for the date of composition is about 1140. Like Roland, the Cid was based on a real person. As a matter of fact, at the time the poem is believed to have been written, the actual Cid had been dead for only forty years. Therefore, there would have been people alive who remembered him.

The Cid (which means "my lord") also was known as "the battler"—*campidoctor* in Latin and *el campeador* in Spanish. The hero earned these names because of his prowess on the battlefield.

CULTURAL DIVERSITY

Just as Roland became a source of pride for France, so the Cid became the national hero of Spain. Many legends evolved about the Cid, and as time passed, the tales became more fantastic. Probably the most successful later version of the Cid's career is that of the French playwright Pierre Corneille, whose play *The Cid* was first presented in 1636. In the 1950s, Hollywood released its own big-screen version of the legendary hero, starring Charlton Heston. ▪

MORE ABOUT THE AUTHOR

Snorri Sturluson's life was as full of adventure as the tales he recounts in his *Prose Edda*. As soon as he reached adulthood and achieved great wealth through a fortunate marriage, he plunged into the turbulent politics of his day. His ability and family connections brought him important positions in Iceland's government. His poetry made him a favorite of King Haakon, whom he attended in Norway for years.

Appointed the king's agent in Iceland, Snorri seems to have used his position more to enhance his own wealth and prestige than to advance the king's interests. At any rate, he and the king had a falling-out. In Norway he joined a conspiracy against Haakon. After sailing back to Iceland to protect his property against the king's allies, he was attacked in his house and killed by his own son-in-law.

Snorri's writings show him to be a great poet and historian, a scholar as well as a careful stylist. His biography suggests personal qualities of a very different sort; he was cunning, ambitious, and greedy. However, he left a priceless legacy in the *Prose Edda* and in his *Sagas of the Norwegian Kings*, a history of Norway's kings up to 1177. In addition, he built a magnificent stone house and a bath with running water from a nearby hot spring. This bath can still be seen in Reykjaholt, Iceland, where Snorri lived.

Snorri Sturluson
1179–1241

The Granger Collection, New York

One-eyed Norse god Odin astride Sleipnir, illumination from *Poetic Edda*, a 13th-century Icelandic manuscript.

Snorri Sturluson (snô′rē stur′lə·sən), whose name means "sharp-witted one," was a great poet and historian as well as a rich landowner, a learned lawyer, and the head of Iceland's most important clan. His books are classics of Icelandic literature and are important sources of mythological lore as well as historical information.

As a youth, Snorri developed a fine sense of the beauty of the Icelandic language. However, by the age of twenty, he also displayed an interest in acquiring property and political power. In 1199, he married an heiress and bought an estate near Reykjaholt, then the capital of Iceland. He was twice elected president of the legislative assembly and supreme court of Iceland, first serving

between 1215 and 1218. Snorri lived in harsh times and was constantly shifting his political position in order to hold on to his power. Eventually, his political intrigues aroused ill will, even within his own family, and led to his murder.

Despite his active and controversial political life, Snorri still found time to devote to literature, and it is the grandeur of his writing that makes him one of Iceland's national heroes. Around 1200, Snorri grew concerned with preserving the myths of his ancient Viking heritage. The result was the *Prose Edda*, which is both a handbook for the writing of Icelandic verse and a collection of Scandinavian myths.

The *Prose Edda* includes (in spite of its title) both poetry and mythology, the two most important elements of the Norse heritage. The work was designed to teach poets of Snorri's time the style of the ancient Viking poets, or *skalds.* As examples it presents ancient myths from both written and oral sources. The stories in the *Prose Edda* are among the best accounts we have of the pre-Christian mythology shared by many Norse peoples.

Interestingly enough, no one knows what the word *edda* means. It may possibly signify "great-grandmother" and appear in the title to show the ancient origin of the tales. Or, it may be derived either from *Oddi,* Snorri's birthplace, or from the original Norse word for "poetry."

OBJECTIVES

1. To recognize the humor of Norse myth and to identify the strengths and weaknesses of its heroic characters
2. To recognize and understand understatement and verbal irony and their effects
3. To write a humorous episode about a hero or heroine, god or goddess
4. To identify the Norse origins of common English words

THEMES IN WORLD LITERATURE

The Comic Vision
From *The Pillow Book*, pp. 578–587
From *Don Quixote*, pp. 821–837

Triumph and Defeat
From *Sundiata: An Epic of Old Mali*, pp. 102–117
From the *Song of Roland*, pp. 692–702 ■

VOCABULARY IN CONTEXT

The words listed below will appear in the side margin at the point of instruction.

1. compensation
2. reconciliation
3. din
4. arrogant
5. excel

Reader's Guide

THOR AND LOKI IN GIANTLAND
from the Prose Edda

Background

The tales in Snorri Sturluson's masterpiece, the *Prose Edda*, relate the adventures of the Norse gods, called the Aesir (a'sir'), along with the actions of heroes, giants, and demons. Frequently, no clear line separates the natural and supernatural. Magic and charms work as much for humans and other mortal creatures as they do for the gods, and humans sometimes triumph over the Aesir and other superhuman beings.

The following selection is from "The Deluding of Gylfi" in the first part of the *Prose Edda*. In this part, we are told that Gylfi was a king of the lands now called Sweden. As the narrative begins, Gylfi goes among the Aesir to find out about them and their heritage. The Aesir tell him a number of stories about life and death, the origins of the world, and the various gods. After being told that Thor was the greatest of all gods, Gylfi asks the Aesir whether Thor ever met a being with powers greater than his own. In answer to this question, the Aesir tell Gylfi the story that follows.

Writer's Response

In this myth, both Thor and the king of the giants use trickery to achieve their ends. Under what circumstances, if any, is it admirable to use trickery or deception in order to achieve a goal? Think of some characters from television, film, or books who use trickery, or underhanded means, to get what they want. Do these characters succeed? What do you think of these characters? Freewrite your ideas.

Literary Focus

Understatement is a figure of speech that consists of saying less than what is really meant, or saying something with less force than is appropriate. It is a form of **verbal irony**, in which a writer or speaker says one thing but really means the opposite, as when someone comes inside from sub-zero weather and says, "It's a bit chilly out there." Understatement often adds a light, comic flavor to writing.

PREREADING FOCUS

Background: The cosmos envisioned in the Norse myths has three levels. Asgard, the topmost, is the home of the gods. A flaming rainbow bridge called Bifrost connects Asgard with Midgard, the middle world, where both men and giants live. In the following selection, Thor and Loki travel over Bifrost into Midgard, where they are joined by Thjalfi and Roskva. They then travel eastward into Jotunheim, land of the giants, and make their way to Utgard, the stronghold of Utgard-Loki. The Midgard Serpent, Jormungand, completely encircles the Middle World with his body, holding his tail in his mouth. The third level is Niflheim, the world of the dead.

WRITER'S RESPONSE

Prior to writing, discuss the distinction between cunning and deceit. A detective—Sherlock Holmes or Lieutenant Columbo, for example—is cunning, not deceitful.

LITERARY FOCUS

The kind of understatement employed by Utgard-Loki in tricking Thor is called *litotes*. Litotes affirms something by negating its contrary. A good example is the narrator's description of the giant Skrymir: "And he was no pygmy." The understatements of Skrymir in response to Thor's mighty blows do not take the form of litotes, but they have a similar effect, adding to the humor of the story.

Concrete Details

Writers use concrete details to dramatize a story or to make a scene or action more realistic or impressive. In "Thor and Loki in Giantland," for example, Snorri tells us that when Thor gripped his hammer, "his knuckles went white," frightening the farmer and his family.

1. **Writing.** Ask students to create concrete details to describe the following three parts of the myth: the giant Skrymir, Utgarð-Loki's gigantic hall, and the old woman Elli.

2. **Writing/Listening.** Ask students to work in pairs to rewrite a paragraph from the myth, adding three or four concrete details to Snorri's narrative. Encourage students to read their expanded versions aloud. ■

1 INFERRING

What is suggested here about the powers of the hammer Mjollnir? (Possible response: If the hammer can reanimate the goats from bones and skins, it must have magical powers.) Tell students that Mjollnir represents the thunderbolt. Mjollnir has many marvelous qualities, including the ability to return to the thrower like a boomerang.

2 LITERARY ELEMENT

Characterization: Certain human expressions, such as a smile or a frown, seem to be almost universal in meaning. What does Thor's expression reveal about his emotions? (As in most cultures, his threatening scowl reveals anger.) Why is Thor upset? (Thor is angry at the laming of one of his goats.)

THOR AND LOKI IN GIANTLAND

from the Prose Edda

Snorri Sturluson

translated by

JEAN I. YOUNG

This myth humorously describes a contest of strength between Thor, the mightiest of gods, and Utgarð-Loki, king of the giants. As you read, decide whom you think deserves to win.

Gods	**Thor:** god of thunder and lightning; the mightiest god.	
	Loki (lō'kē): mischief-maker.	
Giants	**Skrymir** (skrē'mər): giant dwelling in the woods.	
	Utgarð-Loki (ōōt'gärth' lō'kē): king of the giants.	
	Logi **Hugi** **Elli**	members of Utgarð-Loki's household.
Humans	**Thjalfi** (thē·al'fē') and **Roskva** (rœsk'vä'): son and daughter of a farmer.	

"The beginning of the story is that Thor-the-charioteer was on a journey with his goats and in his chariot and with him the god Loki, when they came one evening to a farmer's where they got lodgings for the night. During the evening Thor took the goats and slaughtered them, then had them skinned and put into a caldron. When they were cooked, Thor and his companion sat down to supper and Thor invited the farmer and his wife and children to the meal. The farmer's son was called Thjalfi and his daughter, Roskva. Thor spread the skins out away from the fire, and told the farmer and his household to throw the bones onto the skins. Thjalfi, the farmer's son, took firm hold of a thighbone of one of the goats and split it with his knife, breaking it for the marrow. Thor stayed there that night, and just before daybreak got up and dressed, took the hammer Mjollnir,[1] raised it and consecrated the goatskins. Then the goats stood up. One of them was lame of a hind leg; Thor noticed that and declared that the farmer and his household had done something silly with the bones; he knew that a thighbone was broken. There is no need to make a long story about it; everyone can guess how terrified the farmer would be when he saw Thor letting his eyebrows sink down over his eyes—but when he saw what he did of the eyes he thought he would drop

---

1. **Mjollnir** (myəl'nər)

down dead for the look in them alone. Thor gripped the handle of his hammer so that his knuckles went white. Then the farmer and his whole household did what you might expect, screamed out and begged for mercy for themselves, offering in compensation everything they possessed. But when Thor saw their terror, his anger left him and he calmed down and took from them in reconciliation their children Thjalfi and Roskva. They became his bondservants and accompanied him ever afterwards.

"He left his goats behind him there and set off on an expedition eastwards to Giantland, traveling all the way to the sea and then away over the deep ocean. When he came to land he went ashore and with him Loki and Thjalfi and Roskva. They had not walked very long before they came upon a big wood, and they walked the whole day till dark. Thjalfi, who could run faster than anyone else, was carrying Thor's knapsack, but they were not very well off for food.

"When it got dark they made a search for somewhere to stay the night, and came across an enormous hall with a door opening at the end as broad as the hall was wide. There they sought night quarters for themselves. But at midnight there was a great earthquake; the ground went rocking under them and the building shook. Thor stood up and called to his companions, and they made a search and discovered in the middle of the hall a side-room to the right, and went up to it. Thor sat down in the doorway, but the others went further in from him; they were terrified, but Thor gripped the handle of his hammer and determined to defend himself. Then they heard a great din of muffled roaring. When day came, Thor went outside and saw a man lying a short way off in the wood and he was no pygmy. He was asleep and snoring loudly. Thor thought he understood

then what sort of noises they had been hearing in the night. He put on his belt of strength and his divine power increased, but at that moment the man woke up and sprang to his feet. And they saw that for once Thor was too startled to hit him with the hammer, and asked him what his name was. The man replied it was Skrymir; 'and there's no need for me to ask you yours,' he said, 'I know you are Asa-Thor.[2] Have you moved my glove?' He stretched out his hand and picked up the glove. Then Thor realized that that was what he had had as a sleeping-hall in the night, and the side-room was the thumb.

"Skrymir asked Thor if he would like to have his company and Thor said he would. Then Skrymir undid his provision bag and got ready to eat breakfast, but Thor and his companions had theirs in another place. Skrymir suggested that they should pool their provisions; Thor agreed to that, and Skrymir tied up all their provisions in one bag and put it on his own back. He went on ahead during the day, taking immense strides, and late in the evening found them a lodging for the night under a large oak. Then Skrymir told Thor he wished to lie down and go to sleep, 'but you take the provision bag and get your supper ready. The next minute Skrymir was asleep and snoring loudly. Thor took the provision bag intending to undo it, but, however incredible it may seem, it must be related that he was unable to get a single knot undone or strap-end moved so that it was tied less tightly than before. When he saw he was wasting his time he grew angry, gripped the hammer Mjollnir with both hands, stepped a pace forward to where Skrymir was lying and struck him on the head. Skrymir woke up

---

2. **Asa-Thor** (a'sä thôr)

3 CULTURAL BACKGROUND
As well as his magic hammer Mjollnir, Thor owned a pair of iron gloves and a belt of strength that enabled him to perform superhuman feats.

4 INTERPRETING
How do you think Thor feels when he realizes that they slept in the giant's glove? (Possible response: Thor is amazed and baffled, struck with wonder.)

5 LITERARY GENRE
Myth: Since Thor and his companions are so much smaller than the giant, how likely is it that they would be able to catch up with him when he was "taking immense strides"? (not likely at all) How does this improbability, as well as the exaggeration of Skrymir's size, reveal the kind of story this is? (By using exaggeration and by ignoring realistic probabilities, Snorri creates a myth that resembles a humorous tall tale.)

6 LITERARY ELEMENT
Characterization: What does Thor's reaction to being unable to open the bag reveal about his temperament? (Possible response: His reaction reveals his fiery temper. Like a child, Thor cannot tolerate frustration. His immediate impulse is to release his feelings in violence.)

Snorri Sturluson   **707**

708   The Middle Ages

---

7 and asked if a leaf had fallen on his head or if they had had supper and were ready for bed. Thor said they were just going to sleep, and they went under another oak tree. To tell you the truth they were much too frightened to sleep. At midnight Thor heard Skrymir snoring so that the wood resounded. Then Thor got up, went to him, lifted his hammer quickly and fiercely and struck him in the middle of his crown; he knew that the face of the hammer sank deep into his head. At that instant Skrymir woke up and asked: 'What's the matter now? Did an acorn fall on my head? What's happened to you, Thor?' Thor, however, retreated hastily, saying he had just woken up and that it was the middle of the night and still time to sleep. He reflected, however, that if he got an opportunity of hitting him a third blow Skrymir would never survive it, and he lay still, waiting for Skrymir to fall asleep [again].

8 "A little before daybreak he knew from what he was hearing that Skrymir had fallen asleep. He stood up and made for him, lifting the hammer with all his might and striking him on the temple that was turned up; the hammer sank in up to the handle. Skrymir, however, sat up rubbing his cheek and asking: 'Are there any birds up in the tree above me? When I was waking up I fancied that some droppings from the twigs fell onto my head. Are you awake, Thor? It's time to get up and dress. You haven't far to go now, however, to reach the stronghold called Utgarð.[3] I've heard you whispering amongst yourselves that I'm no small man, but if you get to Utgarð you'll see bigger men there. Now I'm going to give you some good advice. Don't behave in an arrogant manner; Utgarð-

---

3. **Utgarð** (ōōt′gärth): The letter ð ("edh" or "eth") represents a consonant sound like the *th* in *the*.

Loki's retainers won't put up with the bragging of such whippersnappers as you are. Your other course would be to go back and in my opinion it would be better for you to do that, but if you will go on, travel eastwards; my way lies north to those mountains you will be able to see now.'

9 "Skrymir took the provision bag and throwing it over his back turned abruptly away from them into the wood. It is not related that the Aesir expressed any desire to meet him again.

10 "Thor and his companions continued their way and walked on till midday. Then they saw a stronghold on a plain. They had to bend their necks right back before they could see over the top of it. They went up to the stronghold and there was a gate in the entrance and it was shut. Thor went up to the gate but could not get it opened. Then they tried their hardest to get inside the stronghold and [finally] did so by squeezing between the bars of the gate. After that they saw a huge hall and went up to it. The door was open and, entering, they saw a large number of men and most of them pretty big, sitting on two benches. Next they came before the king, Utgarð-Loki, and greeted him, but it was some time before he took any notice of them. He smiled contemptuously at them and remarked: 'News travels slowly from distant parts, or am I mistaken in thinking that this urchin is Thor-the-charioteer? You must be stronger than you look to me. At what arts do you and your companions think you excel? We don't allow anyone to stay with us who is not a past master of some craft or accomplishment.'

11 "Then the one who brought up the rear, Loki, said: 'I have an accomplishment which I am ready to try; there's no one here will eat faster than I can.' Utgarð-Loki replied: 'That's a feat if you can perform it and we'll

THOR'S FIGHT WITH THE GIANTS, MARTEN WINGE 1872.
❓ *How does this romanticized depiction of Thor compare to the way he is described in the selection?*

Marten Eskill WINGE: Thor's Fight with the Giants, 1872, Nationalmuseum, Stockholm

2   put it to the test.' He called over to the very end of the bench that the man called Logi[4] should take the floor in front of the company

3   and pit himself against Loki. Then a trencher was fetched and brought into the hall and filled with chopped-up meat. Loki sat down at one end and Logi at the other, and each of them ate as fast as he could. They met in the middle of the trencher and by then Loki had left only the bones of his meat, but Logi had eaten all his meat, bones, and trencher into the bargain, so everyone thought that Loki had lost the contest.

"Then Utgarð-Loki asked what the youngster there could do. Thjalfi said he would run a race against anyone Utgarð-Loki produced. Utgarð-Loki said that that was a good accomplishment; he reckoned he must be very good at running to perform this feat,

---

4. **Logi** (lōg´ē)

14 PREDICTING

Utgarð-Loki predicts that Thjalfi will lose the third foot-race. Do you agree with him? (Most students will agree.) What makes this a safe prediction? (Possible response: Thjalfi has already lost twice, the second time by a larger margin than the first time.)

HUMANITIES CONNECTION

? *How does this image of Thor compare and contrast with the one on p. 709? (This statue is stylized, while the painting presents Thor with a realistic looking human body.)* ■

15 CULTURAL BACKGROUND

The sconce-horn, made from a hollowed-out animal horn, held liquids for drinking in ancient Norse society. Retainers were the warriors who fought for the King, in exchange for his protection.

---

yet he agreed it should be tried forthwith. Utgarð-Loki got up and went outside then, and there along a level bit of ground was a good running track. Utgarð-Loki called to him a lad whose name was Hugi[5] and told him to run a race with Thjalfi. They ran the first race and Hugi was so far ahead that he turned back to meet Thjalfi at the end of it.

"Then Utgarð-Loki said: 'You will have to exert yourself a bit more, Thjalfi, if you are to win this contest and yet it's true that no men have [ever] come here who have struck me as being quicker on their feet than this.' Then they ran the second race, and this time when Hugi came to the end and turned round, Thjalfi was a long crossbow shot behind.

14 Utgarð-Loki said: 'I think Thjalfi is a good runner, but I don't believe he will win the contest now; we'll prove it, however, when they run the third race.' Then they ran yet another race. Hugi had reached the end and turned back, however, before Thjalfi had come halfway and everyone said that this sport had been put to the test.

"Then Utgarð-Loki asked Thor what accomplishment it would be he was going to display to them—and men after telling such great tales of his mighty deeds. Thor answered that he would like best to pit himself against someone in drinking. Utgarð-Loki said that that might well be and went into

BRONZE STATUETTE OF THOR HOLDING HIS HAMMER, Iceland, C. A.D. 1000.

Werner Forman Archive/National Museum, Iceland

the hall and calling his cupbearer bade him fetch the sconce-horn the retainers were accustomed to drink from. The cupbearer at once came forward with the horn and placed it in Thor's hands. Utgarð-Loki remarked:

'We consider it good drinking if this horn is drained at one drink, some men take two to empty it, but no one is such a wretched drinker that he can't finish it in three.' Thor looked at the horn. It did not strike him as being very big, although it was a bit on the long side, and he was very thirsty. He began drinking in great gulps and thought he would not need to bend to the horn more than once. When, however, his breath failed and he raised his head from it to see what progress had been made in the drinking, it seemed to him that it was only a little lower in the horn than before.

"Then Utgarð-Loki said: 'You drank well but not too much; I would never have believed it if I had been told that Asa-Thor couldn't take a bigger drink. However, I know you will empty it at the second draft.' Thor made no reply, put the horn to his mouth intending to take a bigger drink and strove at the drinking until he was out of breath; yet he saw that the end of the horn would not tilt up as much as he would have liked. When he took the horn from his mouth and looked into it, it seemed to him that he had made still less impression than before, although there was now enough space between the rim and the liquor to carry the horn without spilling.

---

5. **Hugi** (yōo′gē)

"Then Utgarð-Loki said: 'What about it, Thor? Aren't you leaving more for the one drink left over than will be quite convenient for you? It seems to me, if you are going to empty the horn at the third draft, that this will have to be the biggest. You won't be considered so great a man here amongst us as you are with the Aesir, you know, unless you can give a better account of yourself in other contests than it seems to me you will in this.' At that Thor grew angry, put the horn to his mouth and took a tremendously long drink as hard as he could; and when he looked at the horn, he had at any rate made a slight difference. He then gave up the horn and would drink no more.

"Utgarð-Loki remarked: 'It is evident that your strength is not as great as we had imagined. But do you want to make trial of any other feats? It is clear that you don't show to advantage in this one.' Thor answered: 'I can make trial of some feats yet; when I was at home with the Aesir, however, I'd have thought it strange for drinks like these to be called little—what sport are you proposing for me now?'

"Then Utgarð-Loki said: 'Youngsters here perform the feat—it's not thought much of— of lifting my cat up from the ground; I would never have suggested such a thing to Asa-Thor if I'd not seen that you aren't nearly as strong as I thought you were.' Thereupon a gray cat jumped forward onto the hall floor. It was rather a big one, but Thor went up to it, put his arm round under the middle of its belly, and lifted up. The cat arched its back as Thor raised his arm, and when he was stretching up as high as he could, the cat had to lift one of its paws [from the floor]; that was all Thor could do in that trial of skill.

"Then Utgarð-Loki said: 'This contest has gone as I expected; it's rather a big cat and Thor is a short little fellow compared with such big men as we have here.' At that Thor said: 'Call me little if you like, but let some-one come and wrestle with me now; now I am angry!' Utgarð-Loki looked along the bench and said: 'I don't see anyone here who wouldn't feel it beneath him to wrestle with you.' He added, however, 'Wait a bit, call my foster mother, the old woman Elli,[6] here, and let Thor wrestle with her if he wants to. She has brought down men who have struck me as being stronger-looking than Thor.'

"Thereupon an aged crone came into the hall and Utgarð-Loki said she was to come to grips with Asa-Thor. There is no need to make a long story of it. The wrestling went so that the harder Thor exerted himself the firmer she stood her ground. Then the old woman began trying holds and Thor lost his balance; there was a tremendous tussle, but it was not long before Thor fell onto one knee. Utgarð-Loki went up to them then and told them to stop wrestling, saying there was no need for Thor to offer to wrestle with any more of his retainers. By that time it was late in the evening. Utgarð-Loki showed Thor and his companions where to sit down and they stayed there the night and were shown great hospitality.

"As soon as dawn broke the next day Thor and his companions got up, dressed, and were ready to go away. Then Utgarð-Loki came to where they were and had a table set up for them. There was no lack of good cheer in the way of food and drink. When they had finished the meal, they set out on their journey and Utgarð-Loki accompanied them, going out of the stronghold with them. At their parting he addressed Thor, asking him how he thought his journey had turned out and whether he had ever met a man mightier than he [Utgarð-Loki] was.

6. **Elli** (el′ē)

---

16 LITERARY ELEMENT

Conflict: What is at stake in the contests set for Thor and his companions? (Thor's repu-tation as one who excels among the Aesir and among the giants)

17 GUIDED READING

Finding the Main Idea: How does the result here, after Thor's tremendous effort, compare with the effect of his hammer blows on Skrymir's head? (Possible response: In both cases his mighty efforts fail. Thor is bewildered; he cannot understand why his powers seem ineffectual.)

18 INTERPRETING

Why is Thor angry? (Possible response: He and his friends have lost every contest, and Utgarð-Loki is taunting him for not living up to his reputation.)

19 PREDICTING

Given the pattern of events so far, what prediction can you make about the wrestling match? (Thor will be defeated yet again.)

20 SPECULATING

After receiving Thor and his companions coolly, why do you think the giants now offer them hospitality? (Possible re-sponse: Perhaps the giants feel they can afford to treat them like guests now that the giants have proved their superiority.)

1. Why does Thor instruct the family to save the goats' bones by throwing them on the skins? (so he can revive the goats the next morning)

2. In actuality, what is the "hall" where the travelers spend the night? (Skrymir's glove)

3. What do Thor's three hammer blows on the head feel like to Skrymir? (a falling leaf, a falling acorn, bird droppings)

4. What contests does Thor face in Utgarđ-Loki's stronghold? (drinking, lifting the cat, and wrestling)

5. How did Utgarđ-Loki, using his magical powers, prevent Thor from draining the sconce-horn? (He put the other end of the horn in the sea.)

RETEACHING

To reteach "Thor and Loki in Giantland," invite the students to create comic strips with four or five panels depicting the most important events of the story. They might focus on the events in the farmer's house, the episode with Skrymir, or the contests with Utgarđ-Loki. They might work together in pairs, with one person doing the drawings and the other the words. Allow students to show and explain their strips when they are finished.

21 LITERARY ELEMENT

Plot: What surprising revelations occur in Utgarđ-Loki's speech? (He reveals to Thor that all of the "defeats" were deceptions created by magic spells.) What part of the plot does Utgarđ-Loki's speech represent? (the climax)

WRITING TO LEARN

Social Studies: Using the details given in the story, write a paragraph summarizing the customs and values of the society represented by the giants. Take into consideration references to reputation, accomplishments, animals, eating and drinking, and hospitality. ■

22 INTERPRETING

How does each of Thor's apparent defeats turns out to be an achievement that enhances his reputation? (Possible response: Although he could not drain the sconce-horn, he drank so much of the ocean that he created the ebb tide. Although he could not pick up the cat, he was really lifting the Miđgarđ Serpent almost to the sky. Although he could not defeat Elli, he was really wrestling with old age and only fell onto one knee.)

23 READER'S RESPONSE

Do you agree that this is an entertaining tale? Why or why not? (Possible response: The tale's ending is amusing. It shows Thor as the dupe of the clever giant, yet at the same time a doer of great deeds.)

Thor replied that he would not deny that he had been put to shame in their dealings with each other. 'I know besides that you'll dub me a nobody and I don't like that.'

21 ⌈ "Then Utgarđ-Loki said: 'I'm going to tell you the truth now that you've come out of ⌊ the stronghold—if I live and have any say in the matter, you are never going to come inside it again; upon my word you'd never have got in if I'd known you had so much strength; you nearly landed us in disaster. But I have deceived you with spells. The first time when I came across you in the wood I'd come to meet you, and when you were to undo the provision bag, I'd tied it up with iron wire and you didn't discover where to undo it. After that you hit me three blows with the hammer, the first of these was the least and yet if it had reached me it would have been my death. Where you saw a saddle-backed hill close to my stronghold and in it three square-shaped valleys and one very deep—they were the marks left by your hammer. I put the saddle-backed hill in front of your blows, but you didn't see that. The same thing goes for the contests in which you strove against my retainers. The first was what Loki did. He was very hungry and ate fast, but the man called Logi was "wild-fire" and he burned the trencher as quickly as he did the chopped meat. And when Thjalfi was running against the one called Hugi, that was my thought, and Thjalfi couldn't be expected to compete in speed with that. And when you were drinking from the horn and thought you were being slow, upon my word, I never would have believed such a miracle possible; the other end of the horn was in the sea but you didn't perceive that, and now when you come to the ocean you'll see how much you have made it shrink.' That is called the ebb tide

now. He continued: 'I thought it no less wonderful when you lifted up the cat and, to tell you the truth, everyone who saw it was terrified when you lifted one of its paws from the ground. That cat was not what it appeared to be; it was the Miđgarđ[7] Serpent that lies curled round the world and is scarcely long enough head to tail to encircle the earth. You stretched up so high that it wasn't far to the sky. It was a marvelous thing, too, that you held out so long in the wrestling match and only fell down onto one knee when you were struggling with Elli, because there never has been, nor ever will be anyone (if he grows old enough to become aged), who is not tripped up by old age. And now, as a matter of fact, we are going to part and it will be better for us both for you not to come to see me again. I shall go on defending my stronghold with some such magic or other so that you will not win any power over me.'

⌉ 22

"When Thor heard this speech he gripped his hammer and swung it aloft but, when he was going to strike, he saw no Utgarđ-Loki. Then he turned round to the stronghold with the idea of destroying it. He saw no stronghold there—[only] spacious and beautiful plains. He turned away and went on his journey until he came back to Thruđvangar.[8] To tell you the truth, however, it was then he resolved to see if he could contrive an encounter with the Miđgarđ Serpent, as he afterwards did. Now I don't think that anyone could tell you a better tale about this ⌉ 23 expedition of Thor's."

---

7. **Miđgarđ** (mith'gärth): the middle level of the Norse universe, inhabited by human beings, dwarfs, and giants.

8. **Thruđvangar** (thruth'vän·gər): Thor's realm in Asgard, world of the gods.

1. Pantomiming the Myth. Because "Thor and Loki in Giantland" is full of physical action, it is ideal for pantomiming. Students with acting experience could play the pantomime parts; others could create a narrative to accompany the mime. Allow students to rehearse and present their pantomime to the class.

2. Research Project. Students might read more about the exploits of Thor, such as his encounter with the Midgard Serpent mentioned at the end of the narrative. An excellent source, with lively versions of the stories of Snorri Sturluson, is *The Norse Myths*, retold by Kevin Crossley-Holland (New York: Pantheon, 1980).

CLOSURE

Review the headnote on p. 706. What are the giant's motives for using magic? Do his motives make him a more sympathetic character? Will Thor's losses really diminish his reputation? ■

First Thoughts

How do you feel about the giant's use of trickery? Would you react the way Thor does when he learns about it?

Identifying Facts

1. Why does Thor become angry with the farmer and his family? How does he punish them?
2. Why does Thor become angry with Skrymir? What happens when, in his anger, Thor strikes Skrymir with his hammer?
3. What contests do the visitors engage in? What are the results?
4. What does Utgard-Loki admit to Thor as Thor is about to depart?

Interpreting Meanings

1. How is **understatement** used in the description of Skrymir and in Skrymir's reaction to Thor's hammering on his head? What impact does this understatement have on the mood of the story? What other examples of understatement can you find in this story?
2. A **motif** is a word, character, object, image, metaphor, or idea that recurs in a work or in several works. The contest motif is central to this story. What is the importance of the contests here?
3. How is Thor **characterized** here? What do his actions and their results reveal about the Norse system of values?
4. A **myth** is a story about superhuman beings that may be used to explain events and actions in the real world. Myths are usually stories with much action but little description or character development. In what ways does the myth about Thor in Giantland reflect these characteristics?

Applying Meanings

This myth might be interpreted as a depiction of a contest between cleverness and physical strength. In any contest between cleverness and strength, which quality would you expect to win? Why?

Creative Writing Response

Writing a Humorous Episode. This myth presents a god, Thor, from an unusual perspective. Think of a god or goddess, hero or heroine, that you have read about. Imagine that character in a humorous situation that seems beneath his or her dignity. For example, imagine the Egyptian goddess Isis having trouble with her laundry, or the Roman hero Aeneas having difficulty explaining what he does for a living to his young son. Try to use **understatement** and other examples of **verbal irony** in your humorous episode.

Language and Vocabulary

Norse Contributions to English

In the fifth century, England was invaded by Anglo-Saxon tribes who spoke a Germanic language. Their language developed into Old English. Basic words such as *the, you, to,* and *be* date back to the original Anglo-Saxon language.

Centuries later, the Vikings invaded England. The language of these invaders was close enough to Old English to make communication possible, and Old English was soon enriched by words from Old Norse.

Norse contributions to English include many important, everyday terms. Use a dictionary with etymologies to find out the origins of these common words.

1. they
2. sky
3. egg
4. scare
5. wrong
6. dirt

ANSWERS
First Thoughts
Answers will vary.

Identifying Facts
1. Thjalfi breaks goat's bone; Thor takes the children as servants.
2. cannot open bag; nothing
3. Loki loses the eating contest; Thjalfi loses three footraces; Thor fails to drain the horn, to lift the cat off the floor, and to throw or pin Elli.
4. that Thor and his men's failures were really successes

Interpreting Meanings
1. Skrymir is "no pygmy"; reacts to Thor's blows by asking if a leaf, an acorn, or bird droppings have fallen on his head. These responses create humor. "You drank well but not too much" is an example.
2. They carry out the plot.
3. Thor is brave and powerful, but not very bright; valued cleverness as much as strength
4. It explains the square valleys, the ebb tide, and the power of wildfire and old age.

Applying Meanings
Answers will vary.

Creative Writing Response
Writing a Humorous Episode. The heroic character should be recognizable.

Language and Vocabulary
Norse Contributions to English. 1. Old Norse *their* 2. Old Norse *sky* 3. Old Norse *egg* 4. Old Norse *skjarr,* meaning "timid" 5. Old Norse *rangr,* meaning "awry" 6. Old Norse *drit.* ■

BEHIND THE SCENES

Norse Mythology and Modern Fantasy Writers

The British writers J.R.R. Tolkien (1892–1973) and C. S. Lewis (1898–1963) both developed an early interest in Norse mythology. As adults, both writers continued to pursue their fascination with the Norse myths, and both became famous for writing fantasies that featured mythical worlds.

1   As a boy, Tolkien was captivated by the old Icelandic tales. His favorite was the story of the Germanic hero Sigurd (Siegfried), who slays the dragon Fafnir. Tolkien became obsessed with dragons and other mythical creatures. This boyhood interest was reflected in his first novel, *The Hobbit,* which features the villainous dragon Smaug.

C. S. Lewis was a young boy when he came across these lines in a book of poems by Henry Wadsworth Longfellow:

2
> I heard a voice, that cried,
> "Balder the beautiful
>   Is dead, is dead!"

At the time, Lewis did not know that Balder was the Norse god of goodness and harmony. Nevertheless, the words gave him an extraordinary feeling: a vision of great cold expanses of northern sky filled his mind. Later, when he was fifteen, Lewis came across an illustration for a story about Siegfried, and he was hooked. He began reading everything he could about Norse mythology.

Much later, Tolkien and Lewis met at Oxford University in 1926. Tolkien, already a professor, decided to organize a club to read Icelandic sagas and myths. The club was called the Coalbiters, after the humorous Icelandic word *Kolbitar,* which means "those who sit close enough to the fire they could bite the hot coals." Lewis was invited to join.

The Coalbiters began by reading Snorri Snurluson's *Prose Edda* in the original Icelandic. The group then moved on to the *Elder Edda,* an ancient collection of Norse mythology. Out of their shared love for Norse mythology, Tolkien and Lewis developed a strong and lasting friendship.

For a while, Lewis wrote his own versions of existing Norse myths. Then he moved on to other writings, including his classic Narnia tales for children, as well as science-fiction tales focusing on moral problems.

3   Tolkien, too, decided to invent his own mythical universe. He created a complex realm of legend and heroes, complete with detailed maps and imaginary languages based on the old Norse and Anglo-Saxon languages. His book *The Hobbit* (1937) and his three-volume work *The Lord of the Rings* (1954–1956) chronicle the adventures of hobbits, small, humanlike creatures with furry feet. Elves, dwarfs, and goblins inhabit this magical world. Tolkien gave his characters names from the Norse myths: Gandalf, Thorin, Bombur, and Durin. In Tolkien's works, the grand heroics of the Norse myths are transformed to appeal to new generations of adults and children.

Marie de France
Twelfth Century

Osterreichische NationalBibliothek

Illumination of Tristan and Iseult.

An atmosphere of mystery will probably always surround Marie de France. She is considered one of the greatest writers of the Middle Ages, and yet all we know for certain about her is that her name appears in three separate works written in French between 1160 and 1215. The first, the *Lais*, is a group of narratives written in verse. The second is the *Fables*, a collection of fables translated from English into Old French. The third, *St. Patrick's Purgatory*, is a translation from Latin into French of the life of a saint.

The name "Marie de France" comes from a reference toward the end of the *Fables*. The writer of the *Fables* refers to herself by saying: "Marie is my name, I am of France." Scholars have concluded that Marie was of noble birth, since she was very well educated. In addition to her native French, she knew Latin and English and was familiar with the Greek and Roman classics as well as with contemporary French works.

Marie's *Lais* differed from much of the romantic literature of her day. First, she drew her inspiration from tales of Celtic origin—tales told by the peoples of Brittany, Ireland, Scotland, and Wales. Second, in an age dominated by lengthy romances, Marie's *lais* were brief, presenting an involved story about romantic passion in relatively few lines. Third, the typical literature of the Middle Ages, such as the *Song of Roland* (see page 692) and *Perceval* (see page 720), was dominated by masculine ideas about war, love, and chivalry and focused on the knight's responsibility to society. Although Marie's *lais* are set in chivalric society, she was primarily concerned with presenting the personal lives of both knights and their ladies.

Marie wrote during what is sometimes called the "Renaissance of the Twelfth Century." The educated classes, bored with the larger-than-life portraits of heroes and military events in the epics, wanted stories that were more personal. Marie de France provided for their needs with her stories about human misfortune, unhappy and restricting marriages, and heroes and heroines trapped by life's circumstances.

OBJECTIVES

1. To recognize the characteristics of a lai
2. To identify and analyze metaphors and extended metaphor
3. To write a representative scene from a longer story and an analysis of a story's appeal

PREREADING FOCUS

Background: Marie de France idealized love between partners who could not marry (usually because the woman was already married), as did other medieval authors who wrote in the courtly love tradition. Ironically, the illicit love of such pairs was portrayed as constant, devoted, and true, and was often described in religious terms. Although the literature of courtly love was promoted by the nobility, extramarital relationships had to be kept secret. In the Arthurian romances, composed about the same time as "Chevrefoil," the disclosure of the love between Sir Lancelot and King Arthur's wife, Guinevere, destroys Arthur's realm. (Like Tristan and Iseult, Lancelot and Guinevere fell in love when Lancelot was sent by Arthur to bring Guinevere to him so they could be married.)

Literary Focus: A metaphor is usually thought of as having two parts: *tenor* and *vehicle*. The tenor of a metaphor is the subject or idea of the comparison. The vehicle is the image by which the subject or idea is communicated. In the extended metaphor in "Chevrefoil," the tenor is the love of Tristan and Iseult, and the vehicle is the image of the union of the honeysuckle and the hazel tree.

Reader's Guide

CHEVREFOIL

Background

"Chevrefoil" (shev'rə·fwäl'), which means "honeysuckle," concerns the forbidden love of Tristan and Iseult (i·sōolt'). According to this famous Celtic story, Tristan goes to Ireland to bring Iseult, a beautiful princess, to Cornwall. There she is supposed to wed Tristan's uncle, King Mark. However, on the way to Cornwall, the pair accidentally drink a magic potion that makes them fall eternally in love. King Mark marries Iseult, but later, he discovers the love between Tristan and Iseult. Mark sends Tristan into exile. Many adventures befall the lovers from that time on, and eventually they die on the same day.

In "Chevrefoil," Marie de France focuses on a single moment in the story of Tristan and Iseult. Because the details of the entire narrative would have been familiar to her readers, Marie is free to concentrate on a scene that summarizes the sorrow and fatefulness of this famous love story.

Because medieval marriages were arranged by parents, romantic love was not a part of marriage. As a result, an elaborate system known as courtly love evolved in upper-class society. Typically, a young lover idealized a married woman of aristocratic background, suffering lovesickness when they were apart and longing to be united with her.

Oral Response

Think of all the love stories that you have read, seen on television or at the movies, or heard about. Discuss the features of these love stories. Are they happy or tragic? Do the lovers die or do they live "happily ever after"?

Literary Focus

A **metaphor** is a figure of speech that makes a direct comparison between two apparently unlike things without using such connective words as *like, as, than,* or *resembles.* An **extended metaphor** is a metaphor that is developed over several lines of writing or throughout an entire work. As you read the narrative verse, you will see that the union of the honeysuckle and the hazel tree is used as an extended metaphor for the love of Tristan and Iseult.

CHEVREFOIL

Marie de France

translated by

ROBERT HANNING AND JOAN FERRANTE

As you read the verse, try to decide what view of love Marie de France is expressing. What do you think her attitude is toward the lovers?

Honeysuckle (detail), engraving for Basilius Besler's *Florilegium*, Nuremberg, 1613.

1

I should like very much
to tell you the truth
about the *lai* men call *Chevrefoil*—
why it was composed and where it
came from.
5   Many have told and recited it to me
and I have found it in writing,
about Tristan and the queen
and their love that was so true,
that brought them much suffering
10   and caused them to die the same day.
King Mark was annoyed,
angry at his nephew Tristan;
he exiled Tristan from his land
because of the queen whom he loved.
15   Tristan returned to his own country,
South Wales, where he was born,
he stayed a whole year;
he couldn't come back.
Afterward he began to expose himself
20   to death and destruction.
Don't be surprised at this:
for one who loves very faithfully
is sad and troubled
when he cannot satisfy his desires.
25   Tristan was sad and worried,
so he set out from his land.
He traveled straight to Cornwall,
where the queen lived,

TEACHER'S RESOURCES
- ↙ Review and Response Worksheet
- ↙ Selection Test

LITERARY BACKGROUND

Tristan had been orphaned at an early age and was reared by King Mark, his mother's brother. Though Tristan serves his uncle loyally, Mark is unpredictable and jealous. On more than one occasion, Mark angrily sends Tristan away, only to summon him when he is needed in time of war.

Marie de France's "Chevrefoil" is not an excerpt from a longer work or a fragment from a lost manuscript. It is a complete work in 188 lines, based on the legend of Tristan and Iseult. Marie de France's readers would have been familiar with the story from oral tradition.

1 LITERARY ELEMENT

Narrative Technique: The first ten lines serve as a kind of prologue or summary introduction. Why might the author have chosen to write in the first person? (Possible response: to make the written word seem more like an oral story, as if she were talking directly to the reader) Why does she then switch to the third person? (Possible response: to appear to be telling the story in a more objective manner)

Since the union of the hazel
tree and the honeysuckle is a
metaphor for the love of the
unhappy couple, what might
Tristan's actions in lines 51–52
represent? (Possible response:
Tristan's cutting a hazel tree in
half suggests the painful and
permanent separation of the
lovers.)

3 **INFERRING**

What do Tristan and Iseult
seem to want in the present?
(merely the opportunity to see
and talk to each other) What
do they expect in the future?
(to die of separation)

MEETING INDIVIDUAL NEEDS

4 **ESL:** Be sure students realize that when the queen says
she wants "to dismount and
rest," she is merely creating a
pretext for stopping and going
into the woods to meet
Tristan. ■

SPECULATING

Why do you think Marie de
France never refers to Queen
Iseult by name? (Possible response: Her audience knew
that the queen was Iseult.
Also, the conventions of the
courtly love tradition emphasized the unattainability of the
lady and the need for discretion among aristocratic people.)

and entered the forest all alone—

30 he didn't want anyone to see him;
he came out only in the evening
when it was time to find shelter.
He took lodging that night,
with peasants, poor people.

35 He asked them for news
of the king—what he was doing.
They told him they had heard   **3**
that the barons had been summoned
     by ban.[1]
They were to come to Tintagel[2]

40 where the king wanted to hold his court;
at Pentecost[3] they would all be there,
there'd be much joy and pleasure,
and the queen would be there too.
Tristan heard and was very happy;

45 she would not be able to go there
without his seeing her pass.
The day the king set out,
Tristan also came to the woods
by the road he knew

2   50 their assembly must take.
     He cut a hazel tree in half,
     then he squared[4] it.
When he had prepared the wood,
he wrote his name on it with his knife.

55 If the queen noticed it—
and she should be on the watch for it,
for it had happened before
and she had noticed it then—
she'd know when she saw it,

60 that the piece of wood had come
     from her love.
This was the message of the writing
that he had sent to her:
he had been there a long time,

had waited and remained

65 to find out and to discover
how he could see her,
for he could not live without her.
With the two of them it was just
as it is with the honeysuckle

70 that attaches itself to the hazel tree:
when it has wound and attached
and worked itself around the trunk,
the two can survive together;
but if someone tries to separate them,

75 the hazel dies quickly
and the honeysuckle with it.
"Sweet love, so it is with us:
You cannot live without me, nor I
     without you."
The queen rode along;

80 she looked at the hillside
and saw the piece of wood; she knew
     what it was,
she recognized all the letters.
The knights who were accompanying her,
who were riding with her,   **4**

85 she ordered to stop:
she wanted to dismount and rest.
They obeyed her command.
She went far away from her people
and called her girl

90 Brenguein, who was loyal to her.
She went a short distance from the road;
and in the woods she found him
whom she loved more than any living thing.
They took great joy in each other.

95 He spoke to her as much as he desired,
she told him whatever she liked.
Then she assured him
that he would be reconciled with the king—
for it weighed on him

100 that he had sent Tristan away;
he'd done it because of the accusation.
Then she departed, she left her love,
but when it came to the separation,
they began to weep.

---

1. **ban:** official proclamation.
2. **Tintagel** (tin·ta′jəl): cape in northwest Cornwall
   where, according to legend, King Arthur was born.
3. **Pentecost** (pen′ti·kôst′): the seventh Sunday after
   Easter; Whitsunday.
4. **squared:** to cut to a square or rectangular shape.

1. Writing Song Lyrics. Ask students to think about a relationship between two things in nature that might express the bond between lovers. Suggest that students choose a melody they like and compose lyrics for a love song, identifying the bond between lovers with a natural phenomenon. Invite students to tape their songs and play them for the class.

2. Researching Other Versions. The story of Tristan and Iseult has fascinated and inspired many writers. Suggest that students research and read other versions of the story, such as Matthew Arnold's poem "Tristan and Iseult," a modern translation of Thomas Malory's account in *Le Morte D'Arthur*, or a synopsis of the plot of Richard Wagner's opera *Tristan und Isolde*.

To help students understand the essence of the medieval lai, pose this question: If you had to give the French title of this poem an English subtitle, what subtitle would you choose? Explain the reasons for your choice. ∎

105 Tristan went to Wales,
   to wait until his uncle sent for him.
   For the joy that he'd felt
   from his love when he saw her,
   by means of the stick he inscribed
110 as the queen had instructed,
   and in order to remember the words,

   Tristan, who played the harp well,
   composed a new *lai* about it.
   I shall name it briefly:
115 in English they call it *Goat's Leaf*
   the French call it *Chevrefoil*.
   I have given you the truth
   about the *lai* that I have told here.

First Thoughts

What do you think Tristan and Iseult ought to do? Should they renounce their love, or should they follow their hearts? Why?

Identifying Facts

1. What do we learn about Tristan and Iseult in the first twenty-four lines of the poem?
2. How does Tristan discover that the queen will be traveling through the forest?
3. How does Tristan let Iseult know that he wants to meet her?
4. What happens during the meeting between Tristan and Iseult?

Interpreting Meanings

1. In the forest, the lovers meet and speak briefly. What specific details does the poet include to convey their feelings for each other? How would you describe the quality of their relationship?
2. An **extended metaphor** creates a comparison over several lines of a poem or even throughout an entire poem. What is the meaning of the extended metaphor that compares Tristan and Iseult to the honeysuckle and the hazel tree?
3. A **conflict** is a struggle or clash between opposing characters, forces, or emotions. What is the main conflict in "Chevrefoil"?

Applying Meanings

In what ways might Tristan and Iseult behave differently in the modern world? In what ways have the constraints of society changed? Do similar constraints still exist?

Creative Writing Response

Writing a Scene from a Larger Story. "Chevrefoil" focuses on a single event in a much larger story. Think of a well-known story from a book, television, or film and write a brief scene that focuses tightly on the characters and a particular event from the story. You could, for example, write a scene featuring Beauty and the Beast from the fairy tale, or Robin Hood and Maid Marian from *Robin Hood*. The story need not be romantic, but it should, like "Chevrefoil," represent the story as a whole.

Critical Writing Response

Analyzing a Story's Appeal. Many writers throughout the centuries have retold or alluded to the story of the unhappy lovers Tristan and Iseult. Write a three-paragraph essay exploring why this tale of forbidden love has had such a lasting appeal. You might want to consider the comment by a character in Shakespeare's *A Midsummer Night's Dream* who says, "The course of true love never did run smooth." In your essay, mention other tragic love stories that you are familiar with.

First Thoughts
Answers will vary.

Identifying Facts
1. They are in love but suffering because they are separated. King Mark exiled Tristan for loving the queen, and Tristan has spent an unhappy and reckless year in South Wales. The lovers ultimately die on the same day.
2. from the peasants he was lodging with
3. He carves his name on wood from a hazel tree.
4. She assures him he will be reconciled with the king.

Interpreting Meanings
1. They were joyful, spoke freely, and wept when they parted. Possible responses: loving, understanding, mournful
2. They are so tightly bound by their love that both will die if they are separated.
3. the conflict between personal love and societal or religious constraints

Applying Meanings
Possible response: People today choose their own mates, and separation is possible when love dies.

Creative Writing Response
Writing a Scene. Stories should be cohesive and represent the larger story.

Critical Writing Response
Analyzing a Story's Appeal. Students may state that a story of forbidden love is dramatic because it presupposes conflicts with other loyalties. ∎

Chrétien de Troyes
c. 1135–c. 1190

Historians believe Chrétien de Troyes wrote *Perceval* between 1180 and 1190, though no definite date can be established. It was the last of five verse romances Chrétien wrote under the patronage of the nobles Marie de Champagne and Phillipe of Flanders.

By the mid-twelfth century, the verse romance had become more popular than the older *chanson de geste* among the aristocracy in France. In general, the new verse romances emphasized the adventures of knights motivated by romantic love, chivalric ideals, or religious devotion, rather than a desire for glory. Chrétien's romances about King Arthur's knights were among the most popular of the genre. They were consciously literary, composed to be read rather than sung or recited by *jongleurs*. However, some scholars believe that Chrétien himself was a traveling storyteller when he was young and that he may have added "de Troyes" to his name to identify his place of origin.

ABOUT THE TRANSLATOR

Ruth Harwood Cline (1946–   ) is an American translator of French works into English. In addition to translating *Perceval*, she has done a verse translation of Chrétien's *Yvain: or, the Knight with the Lion*.

Bibliotheque Nationale, Paris

King Arthur draws the sword from the stone, from a medieval French illumination.

C hrétien de Troyes (krā·tyan də trwà′) was one of the most famous French medieval court poets. We have little definite knowledge of Chrétien's life, but he probably was born at Troyes, a city in northeastern France, and trained for a position in the Church. His education most likely included study of the classics, since early in his career he wrote verse adaptations of works by the Roman poet Ovid (see page 420). However, he soon became so fascinated by Celtic stories of King Arthur and his knights that he created a new type of poetic narrative called the **Arthurian romance**.

Most of the Arthurian romances focus not on King Arthur but on particular knights of the Round Table and their loves and adventures. Chrétien's most influential work, *Perceval, or the Story of the Grail*, focuses on a new kind of medieval hero, a knight who is less interested in worldly glory than in such Christian values as penitence and charity. Rather than seeking the love of a lady, this hero's quest is for spiritual perfection, and he performs his great deeds for the love of God.

Chrétien's *Perceval* is the earliest known version of the legend of the Holy Grail, a cup or platter regarded as a holy object. The Grail is used to carry communion wafers, which are an important element in Christian ritual. In later Arthurian romances, the Grail is described as the cup from which Christ drank at the Last Supper, the same cup that is later used to collect drops of Christ's blood at the Crucifixion. Many knights of Arthur's Round Table try and fail to find this holy object, which can only be obtained by a person who is absolutely pure.

Chrétien de Troyes died before completing *Perceval*, so no one knows precisely how he intended to resolve the story. What we do know, however, is that Chrétien de Troyes, by uniting Celtic myth and legend with the Christian legend of the Grail, created a story filled with adventure, love, danger, humor, and spirituality that has lasted through the centuries.

OBJECTIVES

1. *To recognize the characteristics of a medieval verse romance*
2. *To recognize descriptive language that appeals to the senses*
3. *To write an ending for the Perceval romance*
4. *To write and perform a scene from the romance*

THEMES IN WORLD LITERATURE

The Quest and the Perilous Journey

From the *Epic of Gilgamesh*, pp. 136–153
From the *Aeneid*, pp. 379–408
Inferno from the *Divine Comedy*, pp. 741–770

The Search for Meaning

Atsumori, pp. 596–611
From *Night*, pp. 1232–1242 ∎

VOCABULARY IN CONTEXT

The words listed below will appear in the side margin at the point of instruction:

1. accord
2. misgiving
3. sheer
4. elated
5. forged
6. tempered
7. exasperated
8. juxtaposed
9. undeterred
10. inferred

Reader's Guide

THE GRAIL
from Perceval

Background

Although Perceval is the son of a great knight, his mother has kept him from knowing anything about knighthood because she does not want her son to die young as her husband and two other sons have done. However, as soon as Perceval meets five wandering knights, he gets a taste of adventure and instantly decides to desert his mother and become a knight himself.

Perceval reaches King Arthur's court, where his worth is immediately recognized. There he receives the armor and weapons of a knight. However, he is also ridiculed at the court because his manners are so crude. An older knight, Gornemant of Gohort, takes Perceval aside and advises him how to behave. Among other things, he advises Perceval not to talk too much, since his speech may reveal his lack of education. Perceval later defends a besieged castle and falls in love with its lady, Blancheflor. As the selection you are about to read opens, Perceval, overcome with regret for abandoning his mother, has just left Blancheflor's castle to find his mother. Along the way, Perceval meets a fisherman who invites him to another castle. There Perceval meets a mysterious, unidentified nobleman known as the Fisher King.

Writer's Response

Have you ever failed to do something and later regretted that you had not taken action? For example, have you ever wished that you had spoken up for something you believed in, or tried to talk to someone you wanted to get to know better? Freewrite about your experience.

Literary Focus

A **description** is a written passage that is intended to create, or re-create, a person, place, thing, event, or experience. Description shows us how something looks, sounds, smells, tastes, or feels. The sentence *It was a fancy room* does not offer much by way of description, but the sentence *The light of hundreds of candles reflected from the golden shields hanging on the walls* appeals to the reader's sense of sight. In the following selection, memorable descriptions help the reader recognize the special importance of two objects: a lance and a grail.

PREREADING FOCUS

Background: One of the interesting aspects of Chrétien's *Perceval* is that it has not one hero but two heroes—Perceval and Gauvain (Gawain)—both knights of King Arthur's Round Table. The characters of Perceval and Gauvain present a contrast: Perceval, forbidden by his mother to learn knightly ways, is an unrefined country lad, whereas Gauvain is the perfect knight, a model of refinement, courage, and courtesy. Both Perceval and Gauvain are determined to find the Holy Grail, but Perceval must first atone for his heartless treatment of his mother before he can undertake the quest.

Writer's Response: If students seem reluctant to write from personal experience, you might have them discuss appropriate examples from novels, short stories, or television shows. After sharing various fictional incidents, students may feel more comfortable writing about a personal experience.

Chrétien de Troyes   **721**

THE GRAIL
from Perceval
Chrétien de Troyes
translated by
RUTH HARWOOD CLINE

In this section of the romance, Perceval is referred to only as "the youth" or "the young man," because he does not yet know his true name, Perceval. When you reach line 73, stop and jot down a few words and phrases that describe what kind of person Perceval seems to be.

The youth began his journey from
the castle, and the daytime whole
he did not meet one living soul:
no creature from the wide earth's span,
5 no Christian woman, Christian man
who could direct him on his way.
The young man did not cease to pray
the sovereign father, God, Our Lord,
if He were willing, to <u>accord</u>
10 that he would find his mother still
alive and well. He reached a hill
and saw a river at its base.
So rapid was the current's pace,
so deep the water, that he dared
15 not enter it, and he declared,
"Oh God Almighty! It would seem,
if I could get across this stream,
I'd find my mother, if she's living."
He rode the bank with some <u>misgiving</u>
20 and reached a cliff, but at that place
the water met the cliff's <u>sheer</u> face
and kept the youth from going through.
A little boat came into view;
it headed down the river, floating
25 and carrying two men out boating.

The Antioch Chalice, fourth century A.D. *This is probably the oldest existing Christian chalice.*

The Metropolitan Museum of Art, Cloisters Collection Purchase 1950

The young knight halted there and waited.
He watched the way they navigated
and thought that they would pass the place
he waited by the cliff's sheer face.
30 They stayed in mid-stream, where they stopped
and took the anchor, which they dropped.
The man afore, a fisher, took
a fish to bait his line and hook;
in size the little fish he chose

35 was larger than a minnow grows.
The knight, completely at a loss,
not knowing how to get across,
first greeted them, then asked the pair,
"Please, gentlemen, nearby is there
40 a bridge to reach the other side?"
To which the fisherman replied,
"No, brother, for besides this boat,
the one in which we are afloat,
which can't bear five men's weight
    as charge,
45 there is no other boat as large
for twenty miles each way and more,
and you can't cross on horseback, for
there is no ferry, bridge, nor ford."
"Tell me," he answered, "by Our Lord,
50 where I may find a place to stay."
The fisherman said, "I should say
you'll need a roof tonight and more,
so I will lodge you at my door.
First find the place this rock is breached[1]
55 and ride uphill, until you've reached
the summit of the cliff," he said.
"Between the wood and river bed
you'll see, down in the valley wide,
the manor house where I reside."
60 The knight rode up the cliff until
he reached the summit of the hill.
He looked around him from that stand
but saw no more than sky and land.
He cried, "What have I come to see?
65 Stupidity and trickery!
May God dishonor and disgrace
the man who sent me to this place!
He had the long way round in mind,
when he told me that I would find
70 a manor when I reached the peak.
Oh, fisherman, why did you speak?
For if you said it out of spite,
you tricked me badly!" He caught sight

of a tower starting to appear
75 down in a valley he was near,
and as the tower came into view,
if people were to search, he knew,
as far as Beirut,[2] they would not
find any finer tower or spot.
80 The tower was dark gray stone, and square,
and flanked by lesser towers, a pair.
Before the tower the hall was laid;
before the hall was the arcade.[3]
On toward the tower the young man rode
85 in haste and called the man who showed
the way to him a worthy guide.
No longer saying he had lied,
he praised the fisherman, elated
to find his lodgings as he stated.
90 The youth went toward the gate and found
the drawbridge lowered to the ground.
He rode across the drawbridge span.
Four squires awaited the young man.
Two squires came up to help him doff
95 his arms and took his armor off.
The third squire led his horse away
to give him fodder, oats, and hay.
The fourth brought a silk cloak, new-made,
and led him to the hall's arcade,
100 which was so fine, you may be sure
you'd not find, even if you were
to search as far as Limoges,[4] one
as splendid in comparison.
The young man paused in the arcade,
105 until the castle's master made
two squires escort him to the hall.
The young man entered with them all
and found the hall was square inside;
it was as long as it was wide;
110 and in the center of its span

5

---

1. **the place this rock is breached:** an opening in the cliff wall.

2. **Beirut** (bā·ro͞ot´): capital of Lebanon; seaport on the Mediterranean.
3. **arcade** (är·kād´): passage with arched roof or line of arches.
4. **Limoges** (lē·mōzh´): city in west-central France.

3 CULTURAL DIVERSITY
The ethic of hospitality is a recurring theme in medieval literature as well as in the earlier heroic epics. The ideal host entertains the guest lavishly, even if the two are enemies. Mutual trust between guest and host is assumed once hospitality has been extended and accepted.

❓ *How has the practice of hospitality changed over time?* (Possible response: In the past people were probably more willing to open up their homes and share what they had with a stranger. Today people are more cautious or fearful.)

4 GUIDED READING
Finding the Main Idea: What does Perceval suspect has happened? (He thinks the fisherman has purposely misled him.)

MEETING INDIVIDUAL NEEDS

5 **LEP:** Students may find lines 86–89 confusing because many of the words do not have clear antecedents. You may want to clarify as follows:
the way to him (Perceval) a worthy guide.
No longer saying he (the fisherman) had lied,
he (Perceval) praised the fisherman, elated
to find his (the fisherman's) lodgings as he (the fisherman) stated. ■

elated (ē·lāt´əd): very happy

Chrétien de Troyes   **723**

6 Inferring

What can you infer about the nobleman from the details used to describe his clothing in lines 113–115? (Possible response: The sable and silk suggest wealth, and the dark colors suggest sadness.)

7 Literary Element

Exaggeration: What is the purpose of the exaggeration in lines 118–123? (to emphasize how large, light, and well heated the room is) What does this description suggest about the castle? (It must be immense or perhaps enchanted in some way.)

8 Comparing Literature

How is the sword described in lines 163–166 different from Roland's sword, Durendal, described in lines 140–142 of the *Song of Roland*? (This sword, though very strong, will break on one occasion, when the bearer's life is at stake, whereas Roland's sword did not break even when struck repeatedly against a rock.)

forged (fôrjd): made a metal object by heating and hammering

tempered (tem'pərd): strengthened by heating and sudden cooling

9 Cultural Diversity

In medieval culture, the number *three* was imbued with mystical qualities, growing out of Christian associations.

he saw a handsome nobleman[5]
with grayed hair, sitting on a bed.
The nobleman wore on his head
a mulberry-black sable cap
115 and wore a dark silk robe and wrap.
He leaned back in his weakened state
and let his elbow take his weight.
Between four columns, burning bright,
a fire of dry logs cast its light.
120 In order to enjoy its heat,
four hundred men could find a seat
around the outsized fire, and not
one man would take a chilly spot.
The solid fireplace columns could
125 support the massive chimney hood,
which was of bronze, built high
   and wide.
The squires, one squire on either side,
appeared before their lord foremost
and brought the youth before his host.
130 He saw the young man, whom he
   greeted.
"My friend," the nobleman entreated,
"don't think me rude not to arise;
I hope that you will realize
that I cannot do so with ease."
135 "Don't even mention it, sir, please,
I do not mind," replied the boy,
"may Heaven give me health and joy."
The lord rose higher on the bed,
as best he could, with pain, and said,
140 "My friend, come nearer, do not be
embarrassed or disturbed by me,
for I command you to come near.
Come to my side and sit down here."
The nobleman began to say,
145 "From where, sir, did you come today?"
He said, "This morning, sir, I came

from Belrepeire,[6] for that's its name."
"So help me God," the lord replied,
"you must have had a long day's ride:
150 to start before the light of morn
before the watchman blew his horn."
"Sir, I assure you, by that time
the morning bells had rung for prime,"[7]
the young man made the observation.
155 While they were still in conversation,
a squire entered through the door
and carried in a sword he wore
hung from his neck and which thereto
he gave the rich man, who withdrew
160 the sword halfway and checked the blade
to see where it was forged and made,
which had been written on the sword.
The blade was wrought, observed the lord
of such fine steel, it would not break
165 save with its bearer's life at stake
on one occasion, one alone,
a peril that was only known
to him who forged and tempered it.
The squire said, "Sir, if you permit,
170 your lovely blonde niece sent this gift,
and you will never see or lift
a sword that's lighter for its strength,
considering its breadth and length.
Please give the sword to whom you
   choose,
175 but if it goes to one who'll use
the sword that he is given well,
you'll greatly please the demoiselle.[8]
The forger of the sword you see
has never made more swords than
   three,
180 and he is going to die before

---

5. **a handsome nobleman:** The lord of the castle is generally known as the Fisher King, who suffers from a mysterious malady.

6. **Belrepeire** (bel·rə·pār'): the castle of Perceval's lady, Blancheflor; before meeting the Fisher King, Perceval defended Belrepeire, which was under seige.

7. **prime:** in the Catholic liturgy, the first hour of daylight.

8. **demoiselle** (dem'wä·zel'): damsel; young lady.

The Bridgeman Art Library

QUEST FOR THE HOLY GRAIL, **tapestry from design by Edward Burne-Jones, woven by Morris and Co., 19th century.**

he ever forges any more.
No sword will be quite like this sword."
Immediately the noble lord   **11**
bestowed it on the newcomer,
185 who realized that its hangings were
a treasure and of worth untold.
The pommel[9] of the sword was gold,
the best Arabian or Grecian;
the sheath's embroidery gold Venetian.
190 Upon the youth the castle's lord
bestowed the richly mounted sword
and said to him, "This sword, dear
   brother,
was destined for you and none other.
I wish it to be yours henceforth.
195 Gird on the sword and draw it forth."
He thanked the lord, and then the
   knight
made sure the belt was not too tight,
and girded on the sword, and took
the bare blade out for a brief look.
200 Then in the sheath it was replaced; **12**
it looked well hanging at his waist

and even better in his fist.
It seemed as if it would assist
the youth in any time of need
205 to do a brave and knightly deed.
Beside the brightly burning fire
the youth turned round and saw a squire,
who had his armor in his care,
among the squires standing there.
210 He told this squire to hold the sword
and took his seat beside the lord,
who honored him as best he might.
The candles cast as bright a light
as could be found in any manor.
215 They chatted in a casual manner.
Out of a room a squire came, clasping
a lance of purest white; while grasping
the center of the lance, the squire
walked through the hall between the fire
220 and two men sitting on the bed.
All saw him bear, with measured tread,
the pure white lance. From its white tip
a drop of crimson blood would drip
and run along the white shaft and
225 drip down upon the squire's hand,
and then another drop would flow.
The knight who came not long ago

9. **pommel** (pum′əl): knob on the hilt of a sword or dagger.

HUMANITIES CONNECTION

Tell students that according to medieval legend, when Jesus was crucified, Joseph of Arimathea caught his blood in a cup, or grail. He then brought the Holy Grail to England. King Arthur and his knights went on a quest to find the Holy Grail.
? *What tone, or mood, does this tapestry convey? What details of composition convey or contribute to this mood?* (Possible response: The strong vertical lines and the play of light and dark shadows create a somber mood.) ∎

10 EVALUATING

In light of the medieval code of hospitality, how has the Fisher King treated Perceval? (Possible response: He has been very hospitable, receiving Perceval warmly and giving him a gold-encrusted sword.)

11 PREDICTING

In light of the prophecy about the sword, what do you think will be Perceval's experience with it? (Answers will vary.)

12 LITERARY ELEMENT

Allusion: To what event in the Bible might the lance and the blood refer? (A lance was used to pierce the side of Christ on the cross.)

beheld this marvel, but preferred
not to inquire why it occurred,
230 for he recalled the admonition
the lord made part of his tuition,[10]
since he had taken pains to stress
the dangers of loquaciousness.[11]

13
The young man thought his questions might
235 make people think him impolite.
and that's why he did not inquire.
Two more squires entered, and each squire
held candelabra, wrought of fine
pure gold with niello[12] work design.

14
240 The squires with candelabra fair
were an extremely handsome pair.
At least ten lighted candles blazed
in every holder that they raised.
The squires were followed by a maiden
245 who bore a grail, with both hands laden.
The bearer was of noble mien,[13]
well dressed, and lovely, and serene,
and when she entered with the grail,
the candles suddenly grew pale,
250 the grail cast such a brilliant light,
as stars grow dimmer in the night
when sun or moonrise makes them fade.
A maiden after her conveyed
a silver platter past the bed.
255 The grail, which had been borne ahead,
was made of purest, finest gold
and set with gems; a manifold

16
display of jewels of every kind,
the costliest that one could find

260 in any place on land or sea,
the rarest jewels there could be,
let not the slightest doubt be cast.
The jewels in the grail surpassed
all other gems in radiance.
265 They went the same way as the lance:
they passed before the lord's bedside
to another room and went inside.
The young man saw the maids' procession
and did not dare to ask a question
270 about the grail or whom they served;
the wise lord's warning he observed,
for he had taken it to heart.

15
I fear he was not very smart;
I have heard warnings people give:
275 that one can be too talkative,
but also one can be too still.
But whether it was good or ill,
I do not know, he did not ask.
The squires who were assigned the task
280 of bringing in the water and
the cloths obeyed the lord's command.
The men who usually were assigned
performed these tasks before they dined.
They washed their hands in water, warmed,
285 and then two squires, so I'm informed,
brought in the ivory tabletop,
made of one piece: they had to stop
and hold it for a while before
the lord and youth, until two more

16
290 squires entered, each one with a trestle.[14]
The trestles had two very special,
rare properties, which they contained
since they were built, and which remained
in them forever: they were wrought
295 of ebony, a wood that's thought
to have two virtues: it will not
ignite and burn and will not rot;

---

10. **the lord made part of his tuition:** Perceval had been instructed by the knight Gornemant not to talk too much so that people will not realize how uneducated he is.
11. **loquaciousness** (lō·kwā'shəs·nis): talkativeness.
12. **niello** (nē·el'ō): a method of decorating with inlaid metals.
13. **mien** (mēn): appearance.

---

14. **trestle** (tres'əl): a frame used to support a tabletop.

Bibliothèque Nationale, Paris

King Arthur and his knights at the Round Table, from a medieval French illumination.

315　Again the grail passed by the bed,
　　and still the youth remained reserved
　　about the grail and whom they served.
　　He did not ask, because he had
　　been told so kindly it was bad
320　to talk too much, and he had taken
　　these words to heart. He was mistaken;
　　though he remembered, he was still
　　much longer than was suitable.
　　At every course, and in plain sight,
325　the grail was carried past the knight,
　　who did not ask whom they were
　　　　serving,
　　although he wished to know, observing
　　in silence that he ought to learn
　　about it prior to his return.
330　So he would ask: before he spoke
　　he'd wait until the morning broke,
　　and he would ask a squire to tell,
　　once he had told the lord farewell
　　and all the others in his train.
335　He put the matter off again
　　and turned his thoughts toward drink
　　　　and food.
　　They brought, and in no stingy mood,
　　the foods and different types of wine,
　　which were delicious, rich and fine.
340　The squires were able to provide
　　the lord and young knight at his side
　　with every course a count, king, queen,
　　and emperor eat by routine.
　　At dinner's end, the two men stayed
345　awake and talked, while squires made
　　the beds and brought them fruit:
　　　　they ate
　　the rarest fruits: the nutmeg, date,
　　fig, clove, and pomegranate red.
　　With Alexandrian gingerbread,
350　electuaries[16] at the end,
　　restoratives, a tonic blend,

17

18

these dangers cause no harm nor loss.
　　They laid the tabletop across
300　the trestles, and the cloth above.
　　What shall I say? To tell you of
　　the cloth is far beyond my scope.
　　No legate,[15] cardinal, or pope
　　has eaten from a whiter one.
305　The first course was of venison,
　　a peppered haunch, cooked in its fat,
　　accompanied by a clear wine that
　　was served in golden cups, a pleasant,
　　delicious drink. While they were present
310　a squire carved up the venison.
　　He set the peppered haunch upon
　　a silver platter, carved the meat,
　　and served the slices they would eat
　　by placing them on hunks of bread.

---

15. **legate** (leg'it): ambassador.

16. **electuaries** (ē·lek'chōo·er'ēz): medicinal pastes formed by combining honey or syrup with a drug.

HUMANITIES CONNECTION

One Arthurian legend suggests that the king chose a round table seating 1,600 knights so that they would not argue about who had the seats of honor. In another version, the table seats only twelve in imitation of the Last Supper. One empty place was reserved for the knight who would find the Holy Grail.

? *Which version would more likely be associated with this illustration?* (the latter) ■

17 GUIDED READING

Identifying Details: What is Perceval's plan of action? (He decides not to ask any questions now; but after he says good-bye to the lord, he will ask a squire the significance of all that he has seen.)

WRITING TO LEARN

Social Studies: Consider why the nutmeg, date, fig, clove, and pomegranate are referred to as the "rarest fruits." Think about the climate of France and the hardiness of these plants as you plan your answer. ■

18 LITERARY ELEMENT

Description: In lines 346–359, why are all the foods enumerated? (so the reader can "see" how sumptuous the feast is) What might this feast symbolize? (Possible response: God's sustaining love, as evidenced in the Last Supper of Christ with his disciples and in the Eucharistic feast)

Chrétien de Troyes

727

1. How does the fisherman help Perceval when they meet at the stream? (He tells Perceval that he can stay at his house.)

2. Why does Perceval get angry at the fisherman at first? (He does not see the castle and thinks he has been tricked.)

3. How does the Fisher King show hospitality to Perceval? (Perceval is treated to a great feast and given a sword.)

4. What happens when Perceval awakens the morning after the feast? (No one is around for him to question.)

5. What happens as Perceval leaves the castle grounds? (The drawbridge begins to close before he and his horse have cleared it.)

Encourage students to reread the following four scenes: (1) the description of the ailing Fisher King, (2) the procession with the sword, (3) the procession with the lance, and (4) the procession with the grail. After discussing possible interpretations, ask students how they would have reacted if they had been Perceval. Would they have questioned the Fisher King?

---

exasperated (eg·zas′pər·āt′ əd): very much annoyed

juxtaposed (juks′tə·pōzd′): placed side by side

undeterred (un·dē·tʉrd′): not kept from action

inferred (in·fʉrd′): concluded

CULTURAL DIVERSITY

The Arthurian romances combine Christian symbolism with magical elements similar to those found in fairy tales and folk tales.

? *What persons, events, or objects in "The Grail" appear to have magical properties?* (Possible responses: the sudden appearance of the castle, the nearly indestructible sword, the bleeding lance, the disappearance of the castle's occupants, the mysterious malady of the Fisher King) *What kinds of fictional works containing magical elements do people read and write today?* (Possible responses: science fiction stories and fantasy fiction, such as the *Narnia Chronicles* by C. S. Lewis and *The Lord of the Rings* trilogy by J. R. R. Tolkien)

MEETING INDIVIDUAL NEEDS

The strong rhyme and the rich imagery are very appealing to students with many different learning styles. Ask volunteers to read the poem aloud. Stop at intervals to develop a list on the chalkboard of people and things Perceval sees. After completing the poem, suggest that students select certain passages to illustrate. ■

and pliris archonticum[17]
for settling his stomachum.
Then various liqueurs were poured
355 for them to sample afterward:
straight piment,[18] which did not contain
sweet honey or a single grain
of pepper, wine of mulberries,
clear syrups, other delicacies.
360 The youth's astonishment persisted;
he did not know such things existed.
"Now, my dear friend," the great lord said,
"the time has come to go to bed.
I'll seek my room—don't think it queer—
365 and you will have your bed out here
and may lie down at any hour.
I do not have the slightest power
over my body anymore
and must be carried to my door."
370 Four nimble servants, strongly set,
came in and seized the coverlet
by its four corners (it was spread
beneath the lord, who lay in bed)
and carried him away to rest.
375 The others helped the youthful guest.
As he required, and when he chose,
they took his clothing off, and hose,[19]
and put him in a bed with white,
smooth linen sheets; he slept all night
380 at peace until the morning broke.
But when the youthful knight awoke,
he was the last to rise and found
that there was no one else around.
Exasperated and alone,
385 he had to get up on his own.
He made the best of it, arose,
and awkwardly drew on his hose

without a bit of help or aid.
He saw his armor had been laid
390 at night against the dais'[20] head
a little distance from his bed.
When he had armed himself at last,
he walked around the great hall past
the rooms and knocked at every door
395 which opened wide the night before,
but it was useless: juxtaposed,
the doors were tightly locked and closed.
He shouted, called, and knocked outside,
but no one opened or replied.
400 At last the young man ceased to call,
walked to the doorway of the hall,
which opened up, and passed through
   there,
and went on down the castle stair.
His horse was saddled in advance.
405 The young man saw his shield and lance
were leaned against the castle wall
upon the side that faced the hall.
He mounted, searched the castle whole,
but did not find one living soul,
410 one servant, or one squire around.
He hurried toward the gate and found
the men had let the drawbridge down,
so that the knight could leave the town
at any hour he wished to go.
415 His hosts had dropped the drawbridge so
the youth could cross it undeterred.
The squires were sent, the youth inferred,
out to the wood, where they were set
to checking every trap and net.
420 The drawbridge lay across the stream.
He would not wait and formed a scheme
of searching through the woods as well
to see if anyone could tell
about the lance, why it was bleeding,
425 about the grail, whom they were feeding,
and where they carried it in state.
The youth rode through the castle gate

---

17. **pliris archonticum** (plē′ris är·kon′tē·kəm): a kind of electuary.
18. **piment**: a drink usually made of wine flavored with honey and spices.
19. **hose**: tight-fitting, stockinglike outer garments worn by men during medieval times.
20. **dais** (dā′is): a raised platform.

1. Creating a Game. Suggest that students create a board game based on Perceval's quest for the grail. The game should provide obstacles and advancements to the questing players. For example, a "good deed" card would help a player advance to the goal. Encourage students to imitate familiar board games when creating instruction cards, the board itself, and the playing pieces.

2. Comparing Works. A number of writers developed their own versions of the Perceval story. These works include Thomas Malory's account in *Le Morte d'Arthur* (1485) and Alfred Lord Tennyson's versions in *Idylls of the King* (1869). Interested students might read one of these versions and prepare a report, comparing its treatment of "Perceval" and the grail with that of Chrétien.

CLOSURE

Ask students how the advice of Gornemant, a well-meaning older knight in King Arthur's court, proved a detriment to Perceval in his meeting with the Fisher King. What advice would students have given the young Perceval? ∎

and out upon the drawbridge plank.
Before he reached the other bank,
430 the young man started realizing
the forefeet of his horse were rising.
His horse made one great leap indeed.
Had he not jumped well, man and steed
would have been hurt. His rider swerved
435 to see what happened and observed
the drawbridge had been lifted high.
He shouted, hearing no reply.

"Whoever raised the bridge," said he,
"where are you? Come and talk to me!
440 Say something to me; come in view.
There's something I would ask of you,
some things I wanted to inquire,
some information I desire."
His words were wasted, vain and fond;[21]
445 no one was willing to respond.

21. **fond:** foolish.

First Thoughts

If you were Perceval, what would you have done to find out what you wanted to know?

Identifying Facts

1. What object does the Fisher King give Perceval at his castle? What special qualities does this object have?
2. At the feast, why does Perceval fail to ask about the unusual objects he has seen? Why is he unable to ask about them the next morning?

Interpreting Meanings

1. Why does the Fisher King give Perceval the sword? What does the gift suggest about Perceval's future?
2. What details of **description** let you know that the lance and the grail have special importance? What do you think the lance and grail symbolize?
3. In medieval tales, heroes often have to pass various kinds of tests on the path to knighthood. Does Perceval undergo a test in this episode? If so, what is the test, and do you think he passes it? Why or why not?

Applying Meanings

Like any youth venturing out into the world, Perceval is introduced to aspects of life that are strange to him. What new aspects of life have *you* encountered as you have matured? How would you advise someone like Perceval?

Creative Writing Response

Continuing the Narrative. After leaving the castle, Perceval learns that had he asked about the lance and grail, the Fisher King would have been healed. Perceval vows to find the lance and grail. Chrétien de Troyes died before he could describe Perceval's return to the castle. What do you think might have happened if Perceval had returned? Write your own ending to the story of Perceval's quest for the grail. Try to create an **atmosphere**—that is, overall mood or feeling—of mystery.

Speaking and Listening

Dramatizing a Scene. Turn the episode describing Perceval's evening in the Fisher King's castle into a short play. Prepare a brief script including the speeches of the various characters in the poem. You may want to rewrite the dialogue in your own words. Also include stage directions that describe the characters' actions and their surroundings. With other students, perform the scene for the class, using as many or as few props as you wish.

ANSWERS

First Thoughts
Answers will vary. He might have asked the servants who helped him prepare for bed.

Identifying Facts
1. a sword. It will break only when the owner's life is in danger.
2. An older knight has advised him not to speak. No one is present the next morning.

Interpreting Meanings
1. He recognizes Perceval as exceptional. It suggests Perceval will have many adventures as a knight.
2. The lance bleeds, and the golden grail casts a brilliant light, suggesting supernatural powers. Answers will vary.
3. Perceval undergoes a test of character rather than of physical prowess. He has to decide whether to act on his own initiative or heed the advice of others. The narrator questions the wisdom of his decision.

Applying Meanings
Answers will vary.

Creative Writing Response
Continuing the Narrative. The story endings should include mysterious events and descriptive language.

Speaking and Listening
Dramatizing a Scene. Scripts should convey the characters' central traits. ∎

1 CULTURAL DIVERSITY

The *Nibelungenlied* is considered the national epic of Germany, much as *Beowulf* is regarded as the national epic of the Anglo-Saxon culture, the *Song of Roland* of the French, and *The Cid* of the Iberian. However, unlike the heroes of the other epics, Siegfried dies before the tale is half over. Thus the revenge motif, rather than the adventures of a single hero, unites the various episodes of the narrative.

ABOUT THE TRANSLATOR

Arthur Thomas Hatto, a translator of a number of medieval German works, chose to do a prose, rather than a verse, translation of the *Nibelungenlied*. According to Hatto, the strophic meter of the original, which was probably chosen so that the lines could be chanted or sung, makes a readable verse translation into English very difficult.

Introduction

The Nibelungenlied

SIEGFRIED SLAYING THE DRAGON, nineteenth-century colored engraving.

1 | The *Nibelungenlied* (nē′bə·loōng′ən·lēt′), the national epic of Germany, is a gripping tale of love, revenge, and murder. The title literally means "song of the Nibelungs." In German myth and literature, the Nibelungs were an evil family that possessed an accursed treasure, which included a hoard of gold and a magic ring.

A Treasure and a Curse

The hero of the *Nibelungenlied* is Siegfried (sig′frēd), a prince who lives on the lower Rhine River in western Europe. As the epic opens, Siegfried has taken possession of the treasure of the Nibelungs. As a result, he is placed under a curse. Thus, from the start of the story, we know that although Siegfried will accomplish great things, he is ultimately doomed.

The treasure of the Nibelungs bestows magical powers as well as a curse, however. Along with the treasure, Siegfried also comes into possession of a cloak that makes its wearer invisible. Armed with these new powers, Siegfried kills a dragon and bathes in its blood. The blood hardens his skin, thereafter protecting him from all wounds. As he bathes, however, a linden leaf falls between his shoulders, so that the dragon's blood fails to touch one small spot. Thus, Siegfried is forever vulnerable in that one spot—just as the Greek hero Achilles was vulnerable in his heel.

The Epic's Structure

The *Nibelungenlied* was originally written as a long narrative poem divided into two parts. In the first half of the epic, Siegfried woos and weds the beautiful Princess Kriemhild (krēm'hilt'), the sister of King Gunther (gōōn'tər), king of Burgundy, an area of what is now southeast France. Gunther, in turn, woos a warrior princess of Iceland, Brunhild (brōōn'hilt'). However, he cannot win her without Siegfried's secret help.

By helping Gunther win Brunhild, Siegfried sows the seeds of his own downfall, for Brunhild later discovers that she has been tricked and has Siegfried killed. Kriemhild later takes her own revenge for Siegfried's death, but ultimately she, too, is killed.   2

Origins of the *Nibelungenlied*

The *Nibelungenlied* resembles the *Song of Roland*, the national epic of France (see page 692), in many ways. Like the *Song of Roland*, the *Nibelungenlied* consists of materials pieced together from many oral and written sources that were familiar to medieval audiences. The unknown author of the German epic transformed these materials into a single work. This anonymous author is thought to have lived somewhere near the Danube River in what is now Austria. Scholars generally agree that he composed the poem sometime between the years 1195 and 1205.

As with the plot of the *Song of Roland*, the story of the *Nibelungenlied* is based on real historical events. Again, however, the details of these events are sketchy. As the story unfolds, realism combines with elements of the supernatural. Indeed, the *Nibelungenlied* often has the feel of a German fairy tale, with all the elements of fantasy and horror associated with the tales collected much later by the Grimm brothers.   3

The Style of the Original Epic

The original *Nibelungenlied* was written in stanzas. Each stanza consists of four lines containing two pairs of rhymed couplets, a form that lends itself to oral presentation. The rhythmic verse of the *Nibelungenlied*, combined with the poem's simple and direct narrative style, produced an epic that has gripped the German artistic imagination for centuries.

2 LITERARY BACKGROUND

Although the first half of the epic centers on Siegfried, many critics point out that Kriemhild and Hagen, the vassal who kills Siegfried, actually dominate the story. Kriemhild is introduced in the second stanza as a "noble maiden" who was to cause the death of many warriors. In the second half of the epic, Kriemhild vows to avenge Siegfried's death, and she descends into treachery and violence to fulfill that vow. On the other hand, Hagen is portrayed more sympathetically.

The first part of the epic resembles a romance in its use of courtly love, the chivalric code, supernatural events, and vestiges of Christian values. The second part, with its emphasis on revenge and bloody battles, is more in the heroic tradition of the pagan epics.

3 HISTORICAL BACKGROUND

The plot of the *Nibelungenlied* imaginatively weaves together historical events and legendary material. It draws on events that took place during the fifth and sixth centuries. For example, in 437, Attila the Hun conquered the Burgundians, ruled by King Gundahari (Gunther here). Historians have identified King Etzel with Attila. (Kriemhild marries King Etzel in the second part of the *Nibelungenlied*.) Some aspects of the Siegfried–Brunhild story also resemble actual events that took place around A.D. 600, during the dynasty of the Frankish king Sigebert and his queen, Brunechild.

OBJECTIVES

1. To analyze a German epic poem
2. To recognize plot conflict and determine whether it is internal or external
3. To write a persuasive letter and to analyze a foil character

THEMES IN WORLD LITERATURE

What Is a Hero?
From the *Ramayana*, pp. 484–494
From the *Song of Roland*, pp. 692–702

Life and Loss
"On Her Brother," pp. 630–632
From *Laments on the War Dead*,
pp. 1383–1386 ■

VOCABULARY IN CONTEXT
The words listed below will appear in the side margin at the point of instruction:

1. instigation   6. repast
2. vent   7. thwarted
3. sinister   8. sumptuous
4. intrepid   9. perfidious
5. versatile   10. jeopardy

PREREADING FOCUS

Background: The two women, Kriemhild and Brunhild, argued over who was subservient to whom. Queen Brunhild maintained that all were subservient to King Gunther, her husband, and thus to her. Kriemhild disagreed and, out of spite, revealed the secret of Siegfried's deception of Brunhild many years before. No words from either Gunther or Siegfried could calm Brunhild, and Hagen assured her that he would find a way to avenge the insult.

After Siegfried had volunteered for a battle campaign with King Gunther, Hagen visited Kriemhild and offered to protect Siegfried in battle in any way he could. Believing Hagen to be sincere, Kriemhild told him of Siegfried's one vulnerable spot. She even sewed an identifying cross on Siegfried's tunic so that Hagen could deflect any injury aimed at that area of Siegfried's back.

Literary Focus: Conflict is a struggle between two opposing forces—often a *protagonist*, the hero of a story, and an *antagonist*, the one who opposes the hero. However, in some stories the conflict can be between a character and a force of nature, between a character and society, between a character and some internal force, or between a character and fate.

Reader's Guide

HOW SIEGFRIED WAS SLAIN
from the Nibelungenlied

Background

Before the events of the selection you are about to read, Siegfried had fallen in love with the famous beauty Kriemhild. He won her hand in marriage by doing "service" for her. As part of this service, he helped her brother, King Gunther, marry the powerful Queen Brunhild.

Brunhild had vowed that she would marry only the man who could beat her at hurling a spear, throwing a stone, and jumping. Using his cloak of invisibility, Siegfried stood beside Gunther and accomplished these feats for him. Years later, however, during an argument, Kriemhild reveals to Brunhild how Siegfried had tricked her. Brunhild vows revenge, and Gunther and his servant Hagen (Hä'gǝn) become her accomplices in a plot to kill Siegfried during a hunt.

As the selection begins, Siegfried is leaving the worried Kriemhild to take part in the hunt. Hagen, who deeply resents Siegfried's superiority over Gunther, has just tricked Kriemhild into revealing the secret of Siegfried's vulnerable spot.

Oral Response

The theme of betrayal runs through the *Nibelungenlied* and, in fact, through much of the literature of the medieval period. During the Middle Ages, loyalty was one of the supreme virtues and disloyalty one of the greatest wrongs. Discuss the issues of loyalty and betrayal for a few minutes. What do they mean to you? Do you think that most people today value loyalty and think that betrayal is a great wrong?

Literary Focus

A **conflict** is a struggle or clash between opposing characters, forces, or emotions. Usually conflicts are resolved by the end of a story. In an epic such as the *Nibelungenlied*, the plot is usually built around **external conflicts** between characters or forces, rather than an **internal conflict** taking place within a single individual.

Effective Use of Adjectives

An effective writer helps the reader visualize characters and events by choosing vivid and specific adjectives. For example, the writer of the *Nibelungenlied* describes "a fierce and monstrous buck." The adjectives *fierce* and *monstrous* help the reader form a vivid mental picture that the word *buck* alone would not do.

Writing and Speaking. Have students choose two or three examples from the selection in which adjectives are used to create a vivid picture. Then have students change the effect of the description by rewriting the sentences using different adjectives. Ask for volunteers to read their sentences aloud; ask other students to explain the mental picture each set of adjectives created in their minds. ■

HOW SIEGFRIED WAS SLAIN
from the Nibelungenlied
translated by
A. T. HATTO

❚ *Much of the action of the* **Nibelungenlied** *is based on trickery. As you read, note the ways that various characters deceive each other.*

CHARACTERS

Siegfried (sig'frēd): a prince of the lower Rhine.

Kriemhild (krēm'hilt'): Siegfried's wife and the sister of King Gunther.

Gunther (gōōn'tər): king of Burgundy.

Hagen (hä'gən): Gunther's chief vassal or subject.

The fearless warriors Gunther and Hagen treacherously proclaimed a hunt in the forest where they wished to chase the boar, the bear, and the bison—and what could be more daring? Siegfried rode with their party in magnificent style. They took all manner of food with them; and it was while drinking from a cool stream that the hero was to lose his life at the instigation of Brunhild, King Gunther's queen.

Bold Siegfried went to Kriemhild while his and his companions' hunting gear was being loaded onto the sumpters[1] in readiness to cross the Rhine, and she could not have been more afflicted. "God grant that I may see you well again, my lady," he said, kissing his dear wife, "and that your eyes may see me, too. Pass the time pleasantly with your relations who are so kind to you, since I cannot stay with you at home."

Kriemhild thought of what she had told Hagen, but she dared not mention it and began to lament that she had ever been born. "I dreamt last night—and an ill-omened dream it was—" said lord Siegfried's noble queen, weeping with unrestrained passion, "that two boars chased you over the heath and the flowers were dyed with blood! How can I help weeping so? I stand in great dread of some attempt against your life.— What if we have offended any men who have the power to vent their malice on us? Stay away, my lord, I urge you."

"I shall return in a few days time, my darling. I know of no people here who bear me any hatred. Your kinsmen without exception wish me well, nor have I deserved otherwise of them."

"It is not so, lord Siegfried. I fear you will come to grief. Last night I had a sinister dream of how two mountains fell upon you and hid you from my sight! I shall suffer cruelly if you go away and leave me." But he clasped the noble woman in his arms and after kissing and caressing her fair person

---

1. **sumpters:** pack horses.

TEACHER'S RESOURCES
- ✔ Vocabulary Activity Worksheet
- ✔ Vocabulary Test
- ✔ Review and Response Worksheet
- ✔ Selection Test

1 INTERPRETING
What is the effect of the use of the word *treacherously* in the first sentence? (It foreshadows trouble to come by suggesting that Gunther and Hagen have a hidden motive for organizing the hunt.)

instigation (in·stə·gā'shən): urging on to an evil act

vent: express or release

sinister (sin'is·tər): threatening harm or evil

2 GUIDED READING
Identifying Details: What had Kriemhild told Hagen that she dared not mention to Siegfried? (the location of his one vulnerable spot) How does she try to warn Siegfried? (by telling him about her ominous dreams of the two boars and the two mountains)

SuperStock International

King Conrad IV, from the Manness Scroll, a fourteenth-century German manuscript.

3 very tenderly, took his leave and went forthwith. Alas, she was never to see him alive again.

They rode away deep into the forest in pursuit of their sport. Gunther and his men were accompanied by numbers of brave knights, but Gernot and Giselher stayed at home. Ahead of the hunt many horses had crossed the Rhine laden with their bread, wine, meat, fish, and various other provisions such as a King of Gunther's wealth is bound to have with him.

The proud and intrepid hunters were told to set up their lodges on a spacious isle in the river on which they were to hunt, at the skirt of the greenwood over towards the spot where the game would have to break 4 cover. Siegfried, too, had arrived there, and

this was reported to the King. Thereupon the sportsmen everywhere manned their relays.

"Who is going to guide us through the forest to our quarry, brave warriors?" asked mighty Siegfried.

"Shall we split up before we start hunting here?" asked Hagen. "Then my lords and I could tell who are the best hunters on this foray into the woods. Let us share the huntsmen and hounds between us and each take the direction he likes—and then all honor to him that hunts best!" At this, the hunters quickly dispersed.

"I do not need any hounds," said lord Siegfried, "except for one tracker so well fleshed that he recognizes the tracks which the game leave through the wood: then we shall not fail to find our quarry." 5

An old huntsman took a good sleuthhound and quickly led the lord to where there was game in abundance. The party chased everything that was roused from its lair, as good hunting men still do today. Bold Siegfried of the Netherlands killed every beast that his hound started, for his hunter was so swift that nothing could elude him. Thus, versatile as he was, Siegfried outshone all the others in that hunt.

The very first kill was when he brought down a strong young tusker,[2] after which he soon chanced on an enormous lion. When his hound had roused it he laid a keen arrow to his bow and shot it so that it dropped in its tracks at the third bound. Siegfried's fellow huntsmen acclaimed him for this shot. Next, in swift succession, he killed a wisent, an elk, four mighty aurochs,[3] and a fierce and monstrous buck—so well mounted was 6

---

2. **tusker:** wild boar.
3. **wisent** (vē′zənt) . . . **aurochs** (ô′räks′): European terms for bison and wild oxen.

he that nothing, be it hart or hind, could evade him. His hound then came upon a great boar, and, as this turned to flee, the champion hunter at once blocked his path, bringing him to bay; and when in a trice the beast sprang at the hero in a fury, Siegfried slew him with his sword, a feat no other hunter could have performed with such ease. After the felling of this boar, the tracker was returned to his leash and Siegfried's splendid bag was made known to the Burgundians.

"If it is not asking too much, lord Siegfried," said his companions of the chase, "do leave some of the game alive for us. You are emptying the hills and woods for us today." At this the brave knight had to smile.

There now arose a great shouting of men and clamor of hounds on all sides, and the tumult grew so great that the hills and the forest re-echoed with it—the huntsmen had unleashed no fewer than four and twenty packs! Thus, many beasts had to lose their lives there, since each of these hunters was hoping to bring it about that *he* should be given the high honors of the chase. But when mighty Siegfried appeared beside the campfire there was no chance of that.

The hunt was over, yet not entirely so. Those who wished to go to the fire brought the hides of innumerable beasts, and game in plenty—what loads of it they carried back to the kitchen to the royal retainers! And now the noble King had it announced to those fine hunters that he wished to take his repast, and there was one great blast of the horn to tell them that he was back in camp.

At this, one of Siegfried's huntsmen said: "Sir, I have heard a horn blast telling us to return to our lodges.—I shall answer it." There was much blowing to summon the companions.

"Let us quit the forest, too," said lord Siegfried. His mount carried him at an even pace, and the others hastened away with him but with the noise of their going they started a savage bear, a very fierce beast.

"I shall give our party some good entertainment," he said over his shoulder. "Loose the hound, for I can see a bear which will have to come back to our lodges with us. It will not be able to save itself unless it runs very fast." The hound was unleashed, and the bear made off at speed. Siegfried meant to ride it down but soon found that his way was blocked and his intention thwarted, while the mighty beast fancied it would escape from its pursuer. But the proud knight leapt from his horse and started to chase it on foot, and the animal, quite off its guard, failed to elude him. And so he quickly caught and bound it, without having wounded it at all—nor could the beast use either claws or teeth on the man. Siegfried tied it to his saddle, mounted his horse, and in his high-spirited fashion led it to the campfire in order to amuse the good knights.

And in what magnificent style Siegfried rode! He bore a great spear, stout of shaft and broad of head; his handsome sword reached down to his spurs; and the fine horn which this lord carried was of the reddest gold. Nor have I ever heard tell of a better hunting outfit: he wore a surcoat of costly black silk and a splendid hat of sable, and you should have seen the gorgeous silken tassels on his quiver, which was covered in panther skin for the sake of its fragrant odor![4] He also bore a bow so strong that apart from Siegfried any who wished to span it would have had to use a rack. His hunting suit was all of otter skin, varied throughout its length with furs of other kinds from

---

4. **odor:** It was believed that the panther's hide gave off a pleasant scent that attracted other animals.

7 SPECULATING

In what tone of voice do you think Siegfried's companions spoke to him about leaving them some game? (Possible response: a joking tone, perhaps with a tinge of envy) What does this tone suggest to you about their relationship? (Possible response: an easy, casual, trusting relationship)

repast (ri·past'): a meal
thwarted (thwôrt'əd): hindered; blocked

8 COMPARING LITERATURE

Compare the use of horn blowing in this excerpt from the *Nibelungenlied* with the use of horn blowing in the *Song of Roland* (p. 694). (Here horns are used to summon everyone to a specific location, and there is no controversy over whether to blow them. In the *Song of Roland*, the horn was used to summon help when in trouble, which Roland was too proud to do until it was too late.)

MEETING INDIVIDUAL NEEDS

10 **Advanced Students:** Challenge students to write a description in verse of Siegfried's appearance on horseback or of the hunt itself. ∎

11 **LITERARY ELEMENT**
Humor: What details does the narrator include to convey an atmosphere of comic pandemonium? (Possible responses: fleeing cooks, flying caldrons, scattered food, lords leaping from their seats, yipping hounds) Student volunteers may enjoy dramatizing this scene in a broad slapstick style.

∎ sumptuous (sump'choo·əs): lavish

perfidious (pər·fid'ē·əs): treacherous

12 **LITERARY ELEMENT**
Tone: What is ironic and prophetic about the king's statement that Hagen wants the company to die of thirst? (The statement is an example of foreshadowing and of verbal irony since Siegfried will die in the course of satisfying his thirst.)

whose shining hair clasps of gold gleamed out on either side of this daring lord of the hunt. The handsome sword that he wore was Balmung,[5] a weapon so keen and with such excellent edges that it never failed to bite when swung against a helmet. No wonder this splendid hunter was proud and gay. And (since I am bound to tell you all) know that his quiver was full of good arrows with gold mountings and heads a span in width, so that any beast they pierced must inevitably soon die.

Thus the noble knight rode along, the very image of a hunting man. Gunther's attendants saw him coming and ran to meet him to take his horse—tied to whose saddle he led a mighty bear! On dismounting, he loosed the bonds from its muzzle and paws, whereupon all the hounds that saw it instantly gave tongue. The beast made for the forest and the people were seized with panic. Affrighted by the tumult, the bear strayed into the kitchen—and how the cooks scuttled from their fire at its approach! Many caldrons were sent flying and many fires were scattered, while heaps of good food lay among the ashes. Lords and retainers leapt from their seats, the bear became infuriated, and the King ordered all the hounds on their leashes to be loosed—and if all had ended well they would have had a jolly day! Bows and spears were no longer left idle, for the brave ones ran towards the bear, yet there were so many hounds in the way that none dared shoot. With the whole mountain thundering with peoples' cries the bear took to flight before the hounds and none could keep up with it but Siegfried, who ran it down and then dispatched it with his sword. The bear was later carried to the campfire, and all who had witnessed this feat declared that Siegfried was a very powerful man.

The proud companions were then summoned to table. There were a great many seated in that meadow. Piles of sumptuous dishes were set before the noble huntsmen, but the butlers who were to pour their wine were very slow to appear. Yet knights could not be better cared for than they and if only no treachery had been lurking in their minds those warriors would have been above reproach.

"Seeing that we are being treated to such a variety of dishes from the kitchen," said lord Siegfried, "I fail to understand why the butlers bring us no wine. Unless we hunters are better looked after, I'll not be a companion of the hunt. I thought I had deserved better attention."

"We shall be very glad to make amends to you for our present lack," answered the perfidious King from his table. "This is Hagen's fault—he wants us to die of thirst."

"My very dear lord," replied Hagen of Troneck, "I thought the day's hunting would be away in the Spessart[6] and so I sent the wine there. If we go without drink today I shall take good care that it does not happen again."

"Damn those fellows!" said lord Siegfried. "It was arranged that they were to bring along seven panniers[7] of spiced wine and mead[8] for me. Since that proved impossible, we should have been placed nearer the Rhine."

---

5. **Balmung** (bäl'mung): In medieval epics, weapons often have names.

6. **Spessart** (spes'ərt): a mountain range in southern Germany.

7. **panniers** (pan'yərz): a large basket for carrying loads on the back.

8. **mead** (mēd): an alcoholic drink made from honey and water, sometimes mixed with spices, fruit, or malt.

SuperStock International

Knight receives ring from one of his ladies, from the Manness Scroll.

"You brave and noble knights," said Hagen of Troneck, "I know a cool spring nearby—do not be offended!—let us go there."—A proposal which (as it turned out) was to bring many knights into jeopardy.

Siegfried was tormented by thirst and ordered the board to be removed all the sooner in his eagerness to go to that spring at the foot of the hills. And now the knights put their treacherous plot into execution.

Word was given for the game which Siegfried had killed to be conveyed back to Worms[9] on wagons, and all who saw it gave him great credit for it.

Hagen of Troneck broke his faith with Siegfried most grievously, for as they were leaving to go to the spreading lime tree he said: "I have often been told that no one can

keep up with Lady Kriemhild's lord when he cares to show his speed. I wish he would show it us now."

"You can easily put it to the test by racing me to the brook," replied gallant Siegfried of the Netherlands. "Then those who see it shall declare the winner."

"I accept your challenge," said Hagen.

"Then I will lie down in the grass at your feet, as a handicap," replied brave Siegfried, much to Gunther's satisfaction. "And I will tell you what more I shall do. I will carry all my equipment with me, my spear and my shield and all my hunting clothes." And he quickly strapped on his quiver and sword. The two men took off their outer clothing and stood there in their white vests. Then they ran through the clover like a pair of wild panthers. Siegfried appeared first at the brook. **13**

Gunther's magnificent guest who excelled so many men in all things quickly unstrapped his sword, took off his quiver, and after leaning his great spear against a branch of the lime, stood beside the rushing brook. Then he laid down his shield near the flowing water, and although he was very thirsty he most courteously refrained from drinking until the King had drunk. Gunther thanked him very ill for this. **14**

The stream was cool, sweet, and clear. Gunther stooped to its running waters and after drinking stood up and stepped aside. Siegfried in turn would have liked to do the same, but he paid for his good manners. For now Hagen carried Siegfried's sword and bow beyond his reach, ran back for the spear, and searched for the sign[10] on the **15**

---

9. **Worms** (vôrmz): a city on the Rhine.

10. **sign:** Kriemhild had unwittingly told Hagen that Siegfried was vulnerable in only one spot, between his shoulder blades. Hagen suggested that she sew a cross on Siegfried's clothing so that Hagen would know where to shield him in battle.

HUMANITIES CONNECTION

Lords and ladies enjoy a respite from a hunt or tournament under an elegant tent. Note the coat of arms on the horse's armor.

? *How do the colors of the illustration contribute to the gaiety of the mood?* (Possible response: the bold striping of the tent and the checked rug add life to the gathering.) ∎

jeopardy (jep'ər·dē): great danger

13 LITERARY ELEMENT
Simile: What does the comparison "they ran through the clover like a pair of wild panthers" suggest about the competition between Hagen and Siegfried? (Possible response: They have shed good sense or moral values with their clothing and are behaving more like instinctual animals than civilized men.)

14 COMPARING LITERATURE
What values of the feudal or chivalric code are upheld or ignored in the encounter between Siegfried and Gunther? (Siegfried behaves courteously and loyally toward his king, but the king does not intend to protect his vassal.)

15 GUIDED READING
Identifying Cause-and-Effect: How does Hagen kill Siegfried? (He takes away his other weapons and hurls Siegfried's own spear at his vulnerable spot.)

from the Nibelungenlied **737**

15 brave man's tunic. Then, as Siegfried bent over the brook and drank, Hagen hurled the spear at the cross, so that the hero's heart's blood leapt from the wound and splashed against Hagen's clothes. No warrior will ever do a darker deed. Leaving the spear fixed in Siegfried's heart, he fled in wild desperation, as he had never fled before from any man.

When lord Siegfried felt the great wound, maddened with rage he bounded back from the stream with the long shaft jutting from his heart. He was hoping to find either his bow or his sword, and, had he succeeded in doing so, Hagen would have had his pay. But **16** finding no sword, the gravely wounded man had nothing but his shield. Snatching this from the bank he ran at Hagen, and King Gunther's vassal was unable to elude him. Siegfried was wounded to death, yet he struck so powerfully that he sent many precious stones whirling from the shield as it smashed to pieces. Gunther's noble guest would dearly have loved to avenge himself. Hagen fell reeling under the weight of the blow and the riverside echoed loudly. Had Siegfried had his sword in his hand it would have been the end of Hagen, so enraged was the wounded man, as indeed he had good cause to be.

The hero's face had lost its color and he was no longer able to stand. His strength had ebbed away, for in the field of his bright countenance he now displayed Death's token. Soon many fair ladies would be weeping for him.

The lady Kriemhild's lord fell among the flowers, where you could see the blood surging from his wound. Then—and he had cause—he rebuked those who had plotted **17** his foul murder. "You vile cowards," he said as he lay dying. "What good has my service done me now that you have slain me? I was always loyal to you, but now I have paid for it. Alas, you have wronged your kinsmen so that all who are born in days to come will be dishonored by your deed. You have cooled your anger on me beyond all measure. You will be held in contempt and stand apart from all good warriors."

The knights all ran to where he lay wounded to death. It was a sad day for many of them. Those who were at all loyal-hearted mourned for him, and this, as a gay and valiant knight, he had well deserved.

The King of Burgundy too lamented Siegfried's death.

"There is no need for the doer of the deed to weep when the damage is done," said the dying man. "He should be held up to scorn. It would have been better left undone."

"I do not know what you are grieving for," said Hagen fiercely. "All our cares and sorrows are over and done with. We shall not find many who will dare oppose us now. I am glad I have put an end to his supremacy." **18**

"You may well exult," said Siegfried. "But had I known your murderous bent I should easily have guarded my life from you. I am sorry for none so much as my wife, the lady Kriemhild. May God have mercy on me for ever having got a son who in years to come will suffer the reproach that his kinsmen were murderers. If I had the strength I would have good reason to complain. But if you feel at all inclined to do a loyal deed for anyone, noble King," continued the mortally wounded man, "let me commend my dear sweetheart to your mercy. Let her profit from being your sister. By the virtue of all princes, stand by her loyally! No lady was ever more greatly wronged through her dear friend. As to my father and his vassals, they will have long to wait for me."

The flowers everywhere were drenched with blood. Siegfried was at grips with Death, yet not for long, since Death's sword **19**

READING CHECK

1. Why do Hagen and Gunther decide to kill Siegfried? (as revenge for the way he had tricked Brunhild)
2. What joke does Siegfried play on the feasting hunters? (He lets a bear loose in the camp.)
3. Who proposes a race to the stream? (Hagen)

4. Why is it necessary for Gunther, Hagen, and Siegfried to arrive at the stream first? (so the others cannot intervene in the murder of Siegfried)
5. Why is Siegfried not able to kill Hagen? (Hagen has hidden his sword.)

RETEACHING

Suggest that students write an obituary for Siegfried. In their obituary they should include not only the facts about Siegfried's character and achievements but also a description of the circumstances of his death.

19 | ever was too sharp. And now the warrior who had been so brave and gay could speak no more.

When those lords saw that the hero was dead they laid him on a shield that shone red with gold, and they plotted ways and means of concealing the fact that Hagen had done the deed. "A disaster has befallen us," many of them said. "You must all hush it up and declare with one voice that Siegfried rode off hunting alone and was killed by robbers as he was passing through the forest."

"I shall take him home," said Hagen of Troneck. "It is all one to me if the woman who made Brunhild so unhappy should come to know of it. It will trouble me very little, however much she weeps."

SPECULATING

Reread the speeches on the final page. What further conflicts between the various characters do you think will develop as the epic continues? (Possible responses: Kriemhild will seek revenge on Hagen; Gunther might turn against Hagen; the lords might take sides; Kriemhild will plot against Brunhild.)

THE DEATH OF SIEGFRIED, mural.

Archiv Für Kunst Und Geschichte, Berlin

1. Creating Dialogue. Ask groups of students to write a scene that might take place when Hagen returns with Siegfried's body. Have them create dialogue for Siegfried's hunting companions as well as for Kriemhild, Gunther, Hagen, and Brunhild. Invite groups to present their scene to the class. Encourage them to use props, costumes, and music to set an appropriate mood.

2. Comparing Versions. The German composer Richard Wagner (1813–1883) used the *Nibelungenlied* along with the *Prose Edda* as sources for his *Ring of the Nibelungs* opera cycle. Suggest that students read a synopsis of the *Ring* operas, or a translation of the Siegfried story in the *Prose Edda*. Then have them report orally on similarities and differences in the characters and plots of the different versions.

CLOSURE

Ask students to list the treacherous deeds that appear in this excerpt of the *Nibelungenlied* or are given in the background on page 732. Ask them to discuss why some of these deceptions might be considered more serious than others. In their discussion, students should consider what values were most important in Siegfried's society. ■

ANSWERS

First Thoughts
Answers will vary.

Identifying Facts
1. She has revealed Siegfried's vulnerable spot to Hagen and has had disturbing dreams.
2. uses one tracker yet kills many beasts; captures bear without wounding it
3. challenge him to a race
4. hurls a spear at Siegfried's vulnerable spot

Interpreting Meanings
1. The main conflict is between Siegfried and Hagen. Their conflict grew out of Siegfried's deception of Brunhild, which caused a conflict between Brunhild and Kriemhild.
2. Kriemhild hides what she told Hagen and tells Siegfried of her ominous dreams; the narrator says that Kriemhild never saw Siegfried alive again.
3. to appeal to medieval audiences; it shows his power, strength, and superiority.
4. He calls it a "dark deed."
5. Possible response: "Gunther's noble guest" and "magnificent"

Applying Meanings
Answers will vary.

Creative Writing Response
Writing a Persuasive Letter.
The opening should state the writer's position; the body should support it convincingly.

Critical Writing Response
Analyzing a Foil. Essays should focus on the differences between the characters. ■

▰ *First Thoughts*
Earlier in the epic, Siegfried had used his powers to trick Brunhild into marrying Gunther. Do you think he deserved to die for his earlier trickery? Why or why not?

Identifying Facts
1. Why is Kriemhild so concerned for Siegfried as he leaves for the hunt?
2. How does Siegfried show his skill as a hunter?
3. How do Hagen and Gunther manage to lure Siegfried alone to the stream?
4. How does Hagen kill Siegfried?

Interpreting Meanings
1. What is the main **conflict** in this section of the *Nibelungenlied*? Which characters are in opposition to each other, and what is the basis for their conflict?
2. **Foreshadowing** is the use of clues to hint at what is going to happen later in the plot. What clues are given at the beginning of the selection to suggest what will happen to Siegfried? How did these clues affect your reading of the story?
3. Why is the hunt described in such detail? What does it reveal about Siegfried?
4. What is the author's attitude toward Hagen and Gunther's murder of Siegfried? How can you tell?
5. Find two examples of details and language that make Siegfried seem especially heroic.

Applying Meanings
This selection describes Brunhild's dramatic and cruel revenge on Siegfried. What motivates people to seek revenge? Name some other stories you know that deal with the concept of revenge. Is revenge ever an appropriate response to injustice? Explain your answers.

Creative Writing Response
Writing a Persuasive Letter. Imagine that you have found out that Brunhild is plotting to have Siegfried killed. What arguments might you use to persuade her to change her plans? Write a three-paragraph persuasive letter to Brunhild. Tell her that you think she should change her mind, and give her three strong reasons for doing so. Conclude your letter with a strong, convincing appeal.

Critical Writing Response
Analyzing a Foil. A **foil** is a literary character who provides a contrast to another character. Authors often use foils to emphasize certain traits in their heroes, just as shadows make contrasting highlights all the more prominent. In this selection, Hagen provides a foil for Siegfried. Write an essay analyzing the contrast between the two characters. In particular, which of Siegfried's qualities are emphasized by the contrast to Hagen? Before writing, you might want to use a chart like the following to help you organize your thoughts.

	Siegfried	Hagen
Appearance		
Physical strength		
Courage		
Moral sense		
Personality		

Dante Alighieri
1265–1321

Dante Alighieri (dän′tā ä′lē·gyä′rē), was born in Florence to an old and moderately distinguished family. Little is known about his early life, but one event from his youth stands out. At the age of nine, Dante attended a May Day party at the home of a gentleman named Folco Portinari. There he met and fell in love with Portinari's daughter Beatrice, who was a year younger than he. He met Beatrice again nine years later, and it was at this meeting that she first spoke to him. Unfortunately, a misunderstanding developed between them, and before it could be mended, Beatrice died. Dante was heartbroken. Although he eventually married and had children, Beatrice's spirit dominated his emotional and religious life, as well as his literary work, for as long as he lived.

From an early age, Dante wrote poetry and associated himself with the literary people of Florence, but his life was not limited to the pursuit of the arts. His was a time of political turbulence, and Florence was torn by civil war three times during his residence there. He may have participated in the fighting at least once himself. Certainly he became deeply involved in the political life of the city and, as an elected official, sought to end Florence's civil strife, going so far on one occasion as to exile his best friend and some of his wife's relatives because of their part in the conflict. Dante was strongly opposed to the involvement of the Pope and the Church in political conflicts. He favored the renewal of a Roman empire to take care of worldly concerns so that the Church could focus solely on spiritual matters.

In 1301, while Dante was out of Florence on an official mission, the city was seized by his political enemies, and in his absence he was sentenced to die. He never returned to his beloved city but lived the rest of his life in exile. Where he lived and whether he saw his wife and children again after leaving Florence are not known. What is known is that he died in Ravenna, where he is buried, and that during his exile he completed his great poetic achievement, the *Divine Comedy*, which shows the influence of his political beliefs and experiences.

MORE ABOUT THE AUTHOR

Dante met Beatrice in 1274, when they were both children. After marrying another man, she died in 1290. Dante tells the story of his love for her in the *Vita Nuova* (New Life), a collection of poems connected by a prose narrative. The *Vita Nuova* ends with Dante's vow to write something about Beatrice that would resemble nothing ever written of any woman. The *Divine Comedy* fulfilled that vow.

Throughout Dante's lifetime, the stability of the Italian city-states was continually ruptured by violence between political factions. The Ghibellines (the old aristocracy) favored imperial authority in Italy, while the Guelphs (the lesser nobility and burghers) opposed it. By 1300, the Florentine Guelphs were themselves divided into two factions: the Blacks, who favored papal authority over Florence, and the Whites, who wanted independence from papal rule. When the Black Guelphs came into power in 1301, Dante, a White Guelph, was banished. Because Dante's wife's family were Black Guelphs, she was not banished with her husband.

ABOUT THE TRANSLATOR

John Ciardi (1916–1986) was an award-winning poet who served as poetry editor of the *Saturday Review* for many years and authored a famous textbook titled *How Does a Poem Mean?*

Holding a book to show that he is an author, Dante stands between his earthly world—cosmopolitan thirteenth-century Italy—and the visionary world through which he travels in the *Divine Comedy.* This painting depicts Dante as a pious man of letters, dominating the splendid Italian architecture on his left and calmly inviting the viewer to see the awesome secrets of the afterlife described in his work.

? *Whom do you think the naked man and woman crowning the structure in the background represent?* (Possible response: Adam and Eve, who were naked in the Garden of Eden at the height of their innocence, then came to know good and evil) ∎

Introduction

The Divine Comedy

DANTE'S WORLD, DOMENICO DI MICHELINO, 1465. Notice the artist's rendering of Dante's Hell, in the left foreground. Purgatory is in the background, and Heaven is to the right of Dante.

? *Does this depiction match your image of what Hell would be?*

1 The *Divine Comedy*, written between 1308 and 1321, tells of an imaginary journey that takes Dante through Hell, Purgatory, and Paradise. This journey is symbolic of the spiritual quest for salvation. It involves recognizing sin (the journey through Hell, or the *Inferno*), rejecting sin and awaiting redemption (the time in Purgatory), and finally achieving salvation through faith in divine revelation (seeing the light of God in Paradise).

2 During his journey, especially through Hell, Dante encounters historical figures from ancient Rome, characters from classical Greek mythology, and political enemies from his own era. Because of the range of people and experiences on which Dante reflects in the *Divine Comedy*, the work provides a portrait of almost every aspect of medieval human life.

Form, Number, and Symbol

3 Dante carefully constructed his epic poem in accord with a special scheme of numbers. The poem contains one hundred **cantos**, or "chapters," because the number one hundred was regarded in the Middle Ages as the perfect number. The work begins with an introductory canto, and it is then divided equally into three sections of thirty-three cantos each. The whole poem is composed in **tercets** (tur′ sits), three-line stanzas, and uses a rhyme scheme called **terza rima** (tert′sə rē′mə). In this rhyme scheme, the middle line of one tercet rhymes with the first and third lines of the next tercet, giving the poem a strong sense of unity.

The number three is important in the *Divine Comedy* because of its relation to the Christian Trinity, which is the union of three divine figures—Father, Son, and Holy Spirit—in one God. The poem is divided into three parts, with the first part, the *Inferno*, focusing on the power of God the Father, as evidenced in the punishments of the damned. The second part, *Purgatorio*, focuses on the wisdom of Christ the Son, and the hope for salvation that he offers to those awaiting final judgment. The third part, *Paradiso*, focuses on the love of the Holy Spirit. In addition, Dante's spiritual journey takes place over three days, beginning in Hell on Good Friday, the day of Christ's crucifixion, and ending symbolically in Paradise on Easter Sunday. Finally, the entire action of the poem takes place under the guidance of three ladies: the Virgin Mary, the mother of Christ who mediates between God and man; Saint Lucia, the patron saint of Dante and of all those without spiritual sight; and Beatrice, Dante's love, who appears to him toward the end of his journey through Purgatory and leads him into Paradise.

The Role of Virgil

For much of his journey through the *Inferno* and *Purgatorio*, Dante is guided not by a saint or an angel but by Virgil, the Roman poet who died nineteen years before the birth of Christ (see page 379). Virgil explains and instructs, and the clarity of his mind is constantly contrasted with Dante's own confusion.

Dante speaks of Virgil with reverence, as if he were talking about a divine figure, calling him "my true master and first author" and "the sole maker from

1 LITERARY BACKGROUND
The journey has long been a popular literary motif. Odysseus' journey from Troy back to Ithaca in the *Odyssey* (c. 800 B.C.) is probably the most famous journey in literature. In Virgil's *Aeneid* (c. 30 B.C.), Aeneas undertakes a journey that culminates in the founding of Rome. In contrast to the journeys in these heroic epics, Dante's journey is an allegorical or symbolic one, representing the progress of the soul toward redemption (see p. 771).

2 LITERARY BACKGROUND
Dante adds realism to his allegory by peopling Hell with his own contemporaries (who were easily recognizable to readers of his own time) as well as with famous sinners from legend and history.

3 CULTURAL BACKGROUND
In medieval times, certain numbers had symbolic significance. The number three, representing the Holy Trinity, was the most important symbolic number. By using threes to organize the *Divine Comedy*, Dante sought to endow his poem with the same firm structure he perceived in the cosmos which it represented. The number four was also meaningful, for there were four seasons, four points of the compass, four humors in the human body, and four elements (earth, air, fire, and water). Five acquired importance from the five wounds of Christ and the five joys of Mary. There were Seven Deadly Sins and seven liberal arts.

William Blake, a book illustrator and engraver by trade, created his color pictures through a process called "illuminated printing." First, Blake engraved a picture on a metal plate and made a print from it in black. Then he hand-colored the printed picture.

The *Inferno* tells us that Virgil cannot enter Paradise because he lived before the birth of Christ and therefore never had a chance to embrace His teachings. Instead, Virgil remains perpetually in Limbo, a state from which residents have no hope of emerging.

❓ *What about Virgil's remaining in Limbo could be seen as ironic?* (Possible responses: He is apparently not rewarded in the afterlife for his great achievements as a poet. The Roman gods whom he worshiped during his lifetime have no control over his ultimate fate.) ■

4 CULTURAL BACKGROUND

Dante is the first of the "Christian Humanists," men whose intellectual loyalties were divided between their religion and their interest in classical culture. Some Christian Humanists—Petrarch, for example—felt this divided loyalty as a conflict. Dante's use of Virgil as a guide suggests that he had little trouble integrating the two loyalties.

Tate Gallery, London/Art Resource, New York

INSCRIPTION OVER HELL'S GATE, WILLIAM BLAKE, early 19th century. *Blake (1757–1827) is best known to modern readers as an early Romantic poet, though he made his living as an engraver and artist. His poetry and his art both display his vivid imagination and unorthodox vision of the world.*
❓ *What do you think is the warning of the inscription?*

whom I drew the breath." Yet Dante's Christian beliefs require that Virgil, who had never been baptized, be consigned to the first circle of Hell, along with other "virtuous pagans" from the classical eras of Greece and Rome.

Dante's attitude toward Virgil reflects the split between his strict Christian beliefs and his sympathy for the emerging humanism of the Renaissance. The classical poets Homer, Horace, and Ovid, as well as the great philosophers and scientists of the pre-Christian age, are all in Hell, yet Dante feels honored when they call him one of their own. "I glory in the glory I have seen," he exults.

Virgil is the perfect guide for the early part of the journey because, for Dante, he is the ultimate symbol of what human reason can achieve without faith. Reason uses logic and fact to arrive at the truth. However, Dante saw reason as limited; it is only through faith that Dante can grasp the truth of Paradise.

Beatrice—Dante's Spiritual Guide

Beatrice is Dante's symbol of love and faith. She sends Virgil to guide Dante through Hell and Purgatory. It is she alone who can guide Dante toward salvation and Paradise.

The entire journey, blessed throughout by the love of Beatrice, is expected to turn Dante forever from error. It is a journey toward truth and grace, made possible by the love of the woman who first gave Dante a glimpse of spiritual perfection.

Style and Language

Dante's epic poem avoids the lofty language generally used in important works, especially literary epics and tragedies. This, along with the fact that the epic has a happy ending, was one of the reasons Dante called his poem a divine "comedy." Dante's language is sparse, direct, and idiomatic, much like the ordinary speech of his time. But the style of the *Divine Comedy* is so perfectly modulated that it is regarded as the finest poetry ever written in Italian. It was a stroke of genius to use everyday language, or the **vernacular**, in a poem of such encyclopedic proportions. The work ranges widely across all levels of imagination and reality. It deals with the mythological, the legendary, the historical, the political, the religious, and the intensely personal. Indeed, the *Divine Comedy* encompasses Dante's vision of God's judgment on every significant aspect of human life.

6

Eugène Delacroix, Dante et Virgile aux enfers, Louvre, © Photo R.M.N.

DANTE AND VIRGIL IN HELL, EUGÈNE DELACROIX, 1822.
? *How does the artist convey the tortures of Hell?*
How would you describe Dante's reaction to the horrors he sees?

OBJECTIVES

1. *To analyze the allegorical and realistic qualities of the Divine Comedy*
2. *To recognize the symbolic structure of the poem*
3. *To invent a board game and write a persuasive essay defending either fire or ice as more appropriate for Hell*

THEMES IN WORLD LITERATURE

Choices in Life

From the *Epic of Gilgamesh*, pp. 136–152
From *Faust*, Part I, pp. 986–1001

The Nature of Evil

From *Candide*, pp. 945–962
From *Night*, pp. 1232–1242 ■

VOCABULARY IN CONTEXT

The words listed below will appear in the side margin at the point of instruction:

1. glut
2. despicable
3. reprimand
4. flails
5. dalliance
6. infamy
7. avid
8. writhes
9. dexterously
10. clambered

PREREADING FOCUS

Background: Dante called his great work the *Commedia* (comedy). The adjective *divina* was not added to the title until 1555, but the adjective is appropriate to describe both Dante's subject and his work. Like the poetry of Homer, Virgil, and (later) Milton, the *Divine Comedy* is epic in scope. But Dante's great work is unique because the unifying thread is not the story but the storyteller, Dante himself. As Dante reveals the bewildering variety of human evils, the more hopeful realms of Purgatory, and the bright light of Paradise, he does more than tell a story; he creates an imaginatively complete moral universe.

Literary Focus: As their art and literature show, people of the Middle Ages viewed the material world as a symbol of an infinitely more important, though invisible, spiritual reality. The modern mind, on the other hand, tends to give more importance to and see more reality in the material world, valuing the symbolic as merely suggestive of mental or emotional states.

Reader's Guide

from the INFERNO
from the Divine Comedy

Background

The first section of the *Divine Comedy*, the *Inferno*, is the best known and most dramatic of the poem's three parts. The first canto finds Dante lost in the "dark wood" of worldliness and sin. In the following thirty-three cantos, Dante travels through the nine levels of Hell, or the Inferno, descending slowly away from God and into the bowels of the earth. At each level, Dante meets suffering souls tormented for eternity in ways that befit their sins. The condemned sinners include people from the ancient world as well as people from Dante's own time. Many of these sinners are Dante's bitter enemies, the clerics and politicians who banished him from his beloved Florence.

The "Dante" of the poem represents suffering humanity as well as the real-life Florentine poet, Dante Alighieri, who is trying to recover from a spiritual crisis. Dante's plight has been observed in heaven. Through the intercession of the Virgin Mary, Saint Lucia, and Beatrice, the spirit of Virgil has been summoned to help Dante begin the journey that can save him.

Translator John Ciardi precedes each canto with prose summaries and notes and follows the **terza rima** rhyme scheme used by Dante.

Oral Response

In your opinion, what are the greatest wrongs that people can commit? Murder? Betrayal? Revenge? Theft? Cheating? If punishments could be made to fit crimes, what would be the appropriate punishment for each of these wrongdoings? Discuss.

Literary Focus

A **symbol** is a person, place, thing, or event that stands both for itself and for something beyond itself. In the *Inferno*, for example, the structure of Hell is symbolic, since the worst sinners are placed at the lowest levels, farthest from God. As you read, look for other symbols. Note, for example, how people represent different kinds of sin, and how the punishments in the *Inferno* are symbolically appropriate to the sins being punished.

Making Allusions

An allusion in a literary work is a reference to something outside the text, from history, religion, myth, politics, science, or some other field of knowledge. Allusions add richness to the reading experience by drawing on knowledge shared by the writer and the reader. For example, in Canto 5, line 67, Dante refers to the story of Tristan and Iseult, assuming his readers will know this tale of unhappy love (see p. 757).

Writing and Sharing. Ask students to identify each of the allusions below, using a reference work. Have them share what they learn in an oral report.

a. "The evil seed of Adam in its Fall" (Canto 3, line 112)

b. "See Helen there,/from whom such ill arose." (Canto 5, lines 64–65)

c. "you modern Thebes! those tender lives you spilt" (Canto 33, line 88) ∎

from the INFERNO
from the Divine Comedy
Dante Alighieri
translated by
JOHN CIARDI

As you read, try making a map of where the different types of sinners have been placed in Hell. What does this arrangement of Hell reveal about Dante's system of morality?

New York Public Library Picture Collection

THE FOREST, GUSTAVE DORÉ. *The journey into a "dark wood" is a common motif in literature, symbolizing a confrontation with the unknown.*

TEACHER'S RESOURCES
- Review and Response Worksheet
- Selection Test

HUMANITIES CONNECTION

Gustave Doré (1832–1883) was a French painter, sculptor, and illustrator who achieved great popularity in his lifetime. Today he is best known for his illustrations of literary masterpieces, such as the *Divine Comedy*, the Bible, Tennyson's *Idylls of the King*, Cervantes' *Don Quixote*, the works of Balzac and Rabelais, Coleridge's "Rime of the Ancient Mariner," and Poe's "The Raven."

This picture might remind Dante's readers of not only the Dark Wood of Error but also the Wood of Suicides, one of the innermost circles of Hell, where people who have committed suicide become trees because they have voluntarily destroyed their human bodies. Point out to students that the detail linework and the resulting textural richness are characteristic of Doré's engravings. ∎

COMPARING LITERATURE

Ask students to read "The Rat Trap" (pp. 1196–1206) and compare Dante's description of the Dark Wood of Error to Selma Lagerlöf's forest.

CANTO 1

The Dark Wood of Error

1 Midway in his allotted threescore years and ten, Dante comes to himself with a start and realizes that he has strayed from the True Way into the Dark Wood of Error (Worldliness). As soon as he has realized his loss, Dante lifts his eyes and sees the first light of the sunrise (the Sun is the Symbol of Divine Illumination) lighting the shoulders of a little hill (The Mount of Joy). It is the Easter Season, the time of resurrection, and the sun is in its equinoctial rebirth. This juxtaposition of joyous symbols fills Dante with hope and he sets out at once to climb directly up the Mount of Joy, but almost immediately his way is blocked by the Three Beasts of Worldliness: *The Leopard of Malice and Fraud, The Lion of Violence and Ambition,* and *The She-Wolf of Incontinence.* These beasts, and especially the She-Wolf, drive him back despairing into the darkness of error.

But just as all seems lost, a figure appears to him. It is the shade of *Virgil,* Dante's symbol of *Human Reason.*

2 Virgil explains that he has been sent to lead Dante from error. There can, however, be no direct ascent past the beasts: the man who would escape them must go a longer and harder way. First he must descend through Hell (The Recognition of Sin), then he must ascend through Purgatory (The Renunciation of Sin), and only then may he reach the pinnacle of joy and come to the Light of God. Virgil offers to guide Dante, but only as far as Human Reason can go. Another guide (*Beatrice,* symbol of *Divine Love*) must take over for the final ascent, for Human Reason is self-limited. Dante submits himself joyously to Virgil's guidance and they move off.

3

Midway in our life's journey,[1] I went astray
  from the straight road and woke to find myself
3 alone in a dark wood. How shall I say

what wood that was! I never saw so drear,
  so rank, so arduous a wilderness!
6 Its very memory gives a shape to fear.

Death could scarce be more bitter than that place!
  But since it came to good, I will recount
9 all that I found revealed there by God's grace.

How I came to it I cannot rightly say,
  so drugged and loose with sleep had I become
12 when I first wandered there from the True Way.

But at the far end of that valley of evil
  whose maze had sapped my very heart with fear
15 I found myself before a little hill

and lifted up my eyes. Its shoulders glowed
  already with the sweet rays of that planet[2]
18 whose virtue leads men straight on every road,

and the shining strengthened me against the fright
  whose agony had wracked the lake of my heart
21 through all the terrors of that piteous night.

Just as a swimmer, who with his last breath
  flounders ashore from perilous seas, might turn
24 to memorize the wide water of his death—

---

1. **Midway . . . journey:** Dante sets the action in 1300, when he was thirty-five.

2. **planet:** the sun, which was thought to be a planet by Ptolemaic astronomers in ancient Greece.

so did I turn, my soul still fugitive
   from death's surviving image, to stare down
27 that pass that none had ever left alive.

And there I lay to rest from my heart's race
   till calm and breath returned to me. Then rose
30 and pushed up that dead slope at such a pace

each footfall rose above the last. And lo!
   almost at the beginning of the rise
33 I faced a spotted Leopard, all tremor and flow

and gaudy pelt. And it would not pass, but stood
   so blocking my every turn that time and again
36 I was on the verge of turning back to the wood.

This fell at the first widening of the dawn
   as the sun was climbing Aries with those stars
39 that rode with him to light the new creation.³

Thus the holy hour and the sweet season
   of commemoration did much to arm my fear
42 of that bright murderous beast with their good
   omen.

Yet not so much but what I shook with dread
   at sight of a great Lion that broke upon me
45 raging with hunger, its enormous head

held high as if to strike a mortal terror
   into the very air. And down his track,
48 a She-Wolf drove upon me, a starved horror

ravening and wasted beyond all belief.
   She seemed a rack for avarice, gaunt and
   craving.
51 Oh many the souls she has brought to endless
   grief!

She brought such heaviness upon my spirit
   at sight of her savagery and desperation,
54 I died from every hope of that high summit.

And like a miser—eager in acquisition
   but desperate in self-reproach when Fortune's
   wheel
57 turns to the hour of his loss—all tears and
   attrition

I wavered back; and still the beast pursued,
   forcing herself against me bit by bit
60 till I slid back into the sunless wood.

And as I fell to my soul's ruin, a presence
   gathered before me on the discolored air,
63 the figure of one who seemed hoarse from long
   silence.

At sight of him in that friendless waste I cried:
   "Have pity on me, whatever thing you are,
66 whether shade or living man." And it replied:

"Not man, though man I once was, and my blood
   was Lombard, both my parents Mantuan.
69 I was born, though late, *sub Julio*,⁴ and bred

in Rome under Augustus in the noon
   of the false and lying gods. I was a poet
72 and sang of old Anchises' noble son⁵

who came to Rome after the burning of Troy.
   But you—why do *you* return to these distresses
75 instead of climbing that shining Mount of Joy

which is the seat and first cause of man's bliss?"
   "And are you then that Virgil and that fountain
78 of purest speech?" My voice grew tremulous:

---

3. **This fell . . . creation:** Dante awakens in the Dark Wood just before dawn of Good Friday. His spiritual rebirth begins in the Easter season, the time of the Resurrection of Christ.

4. *sub Julio*: in the reign of Julius Caesar.
5. **Anchises'** (an·kī'sēz') **noble son:** Aeneas, hero of the *Aeneid*; according to legend he was the founder of Rome.

4 LITERARY ELEMENT

Descriptive Details: Despite the allegorical nature of the Leopard, the Lion, and the She-Wolf, Dante invites us to believe in them as real beasts. What descriptive words or phrases does he use to make the Leopard, the Lion, and the Wolf seem real? (The Leopard is ''all tremor and flow/and gaudy pelt." The Lion holds its enormous head high. The She-Wolf is ''a starved horror . . . gaunt and craving.")

5 LITERARY BACKGROUND

The allusion to Fortune's wheel in line 56 refers to the medieval belief that the turn of a mythical wheel determines people's fate, especially the rise to power and downfall of great people. The wheel of fortune is a recurring motif in the works of Chaucer (pp. 772–785) and in early Renaissance tragedies.

6 INTERPRETING

If the dark wood represents error and the She-Wolf represents incontinence (failure to restrain sexual appetite), what allegorical interpretation is intended when Dante is forced back into the wood by the beast? (Possible response: His inability to restrain his passions causes him to fall back into sin [error] and despair.)

7 INFERRING

Why does Virgil refer to the Roman divinities as ''false and lying gods'' (line 71)? (Virgil lived before Christ's birth. Now that he is dead, he has learned the truth as revealed by Christ.)

Dante Alighieri   **749**

8 SPECULATING

Given what Dante says about Virgil in lines 79–85, what role do you suppose Virgil's *Aeneid* played in Dante's education? (It seems likely that Dante studied the *Aeneid* closely as he learned Latin. Moreover, since he speaks of "apprenticeship," he probably modeled his own writing style on Virgil's.)

9 LITERARY ELEMENT

Symbolism: What details in lines 92–93 suggest that the She-Wolf is more symbolic than real? (Unlike a real beast, the She-Wolf does not get filled up as she devours her prey. Eating simply makes her hungrier.)

▨ **glut:** fullness, satisfaction

10 ALLEGORY

Who does Virgil predict will destroy the She-Wolf? (the Greyhound) In the allegory, who is the Greyhound who "shall be the resurrection and new day"? (Christ)

11 LITERARY BACKGROUND

Lines 105–116 summarize the whole of the *Divine Comedy*: the journey through Hell and Purgatory to Heaven, and Dante's meeting with Beatrice ("a worthier spirit").

12 SPECULATING

Why do you think Dante accepts Virgil's invitation to travel with him to the "sad halls of Hell"? (Possible response: He is willing to suffer to escape sinfulness and secure his own salvation.)

8

"Glory and light of poets! now may that zeal
  and love's apprenticeship that I poured out
81 on your heroic verses serve me well!

For you are my true master and first author,
  the sole maker from whom I drew the breath
84 of that sweet style whose measures have
  brought me honor.

See there, immortal sage, the beast I flee.
  For my soul's salvation, I beg you, guard me
  from her,
87 for she has struck a mortal tremor through me."

And he replied, seeing my soul in tears:
  "He must go by another way who would escape
90 this wilderness, for that mad beast that fleers

9

before you there, suffers no man to pass.
  She tracks down all, kills all, and knows no glut,
93 but, feeding, she grows hungrier than she was.

10

She mates with any beast, and will mate with
  more
  before the Greyhound comes to hunt her down.
96 He will not feed on lands nor loot, but honor

and love and wisdom will make straight his way.
  He will rise between Feltro and Feltro,[6] and
  in him
99 shall be the resurrection and new day

of that sad Italy for which Nisus died,
  and Turnus, and Euryalus, and the maid
  Camilla.[7]

11

102 He shall hunt her through every nation of sick
  pride

till she is driven back forever to Hell
  whence Envy first released her on the world.
105 Therefore, for your own good, I think it well

you follow me and I will be your guide
  and lead you forth through an eternal place.
108 There you shall see the ancient spirits tried

in endless pain, and hear their lamentation
  as each bemoans the second death of souls.[8]
111 Next you shall see upon a burning mountain[9]

souls in fire and yet content in fire,
  knowing that whensoever it may be
114 they yet will mount into the blessed choir.

To which, if it is still your wish to climb,
  a worthier spirit shall be sent to guide you.
117 With her shall I leave you, for the King of Time,

who reigns on high, forbids me to come there
  since, living, I rebelled against his law.
120 He rules the waters and the land and air

and there holds court, his city and his throne.
  Oh blessed are they he chooses!" And I to him:
123 "Poet, by that God to you unknown,

12

lead me this way. Beyond this present ill
  and worse to dread, lead me to Peter's gate
126 and be my guide through the sad halls of Hell."

And he then: "Follow." And he moved ahead
  in silence, and I followed where he led.

---

6. **Feltro and Feltro:** Can Grande della Scala (1290–1329) was an Italian leader born in Verona, which is situated between Feltre and Montefeltro.

7. **Nisus . . . Turnus . . . Euryalus . . . Camilla:** When Aeneas led the Trojans into Italy, these figures were killed in a war between the Trojans and the Latins.

8. **second death of souls:** damnation.

9. **burning mountain:** the mountain Purgatory.

CANTO 3

The Vestibule of Hell

The Opportunists

The Poets pass the Gate of Hell and are immediately assailed by cries of anguish. Dante sees the first of the souls in torment. They are *The Opportunists*, those souls who in life were neither for good nor evil but only for themselves. Mixed with them are those outcasts who took no sides in the Rebellion of the Angels. They are neither in Hell nor out of it. Eternally unclassified, they race round and round pursuing a wavering banner that runs forever before them through the dirty air; and as they run they are pursued by swarms of wasps and hornets, who sting them and produce a constant flow of blood and putrid matter which trickles down the bodies of the sinners and is feasted upon by loathsome worms and maggots who coat the ground.

The law of Dante's Hell is the law of symbolic retribution. As they sinned so are they punished. They took no sides, therefore they are given no place. As they pursued the ever-shifting illusion of their own advantage, changing their courses with every changing wind, so they pursue eternally an elusive, ever-shifting banner. As their sin was a darkness, so they move in darkness. As their own guilty conscience pursued them, so they are pursued by swarms of wasps and hornets. And as their actions were a moral filth, so they run eternally through the filth of worms and maggots which they themselves feed.

Dante recognizes several, among them *Pope Celestine V*, but without delaying to speak to any of these souls, the Poets move on to *Acheron*, the first of the rivers of Hell. Here the newly-arrived souls of the damned gather and wait for monstrous *Charon* to ferry them over to punishment. Charon recognizes Dante as a living man and angrily refuses him passage. Virgil forces Charon to serve them, but Dante swoons with terror, and does not reawaken until he is on the other side.

I AM THE WAY INTO THE CITY OF WOE.
I AM THE WAY TO A FORSAKEN PEOPLE.
3 I AM THE WAY INTO ETERNAL SORROW.

SACRED JUSTICE MOVED MY ARCHITECT.
I WAS RAISED HERE BY DIVINE OMNIPOTENCE,
6 PRIMORDIAL LOVE AND ULTIMATE INTELLECT.

ONLY THOSE ELEMENTS TIME CANNOT WEAR
WERE MADE BEFORE ME, AND BEYOND TIME I
  STAND.[10]
9 ABANDON ALL HOPE YE WHO ENTER HERE.[11]

These mysteries I read cut into stone
  above a gate. And turning I said: "Master,
12 what is the meaning of this harsh inscription?"

And he then as initiate to novice:[12]
  "Here must you put by all division of spirit
15 and gather your soul against all cowardice.

This is the place I told you to expect.
  Here you shall pass among the fallen people,
18 souls who have lost the good of intellect."

So saying, he put forth his hand to me,
  and with a gentle and encouraging smile
21 he led me through the gate of mystery.

---

10. **BEYOND TIME I STAND:** The punishment of sin is endless.

11. **YE WHO ENTER HERE:** the damned.

12. **as initiate to novice:** as one who has been instructed to one who has not.

Dante Alighieri   **751**

This picture shows Charon, the ferryman, loading condemned souls into his boat. It was his job to take sinners across the river Acheron into the place of punishment.

? *Which figure is that of Charon? How can we tell?* (Charon is the figure holding the oar. We can tell because he is beating the condemned.) ■

18 LITERARY ELEMENT

Imagery: Which of the five senses does Dante appeal to in his description of the hellish scene in lines 22–29? (hearing and sight) What feeling does the imagery evoke? (a feeling of confusion, tumult, and horror)

■ **despicable** (des′pi·kə·bəl): hateful, abominable

THE EMBARKATION OF THE SOULS, GUSTAVE DORÉ.
? *Who are the first souls that Dante sees? How does their punishment fit their crime?*

Here sighs and cries and wails coiled and recoiled
on the starless air, spilling my soul to tears.
24 A confusion of tongues and monstrous accents toiled

18

in pain and anger. Voices hoarse and shrill
and sounds of blows, all intermingled, raised
27 tumult and pandemonium that still

whirls on the air forever dirty with it
as if a whirlwind sucked at sand. And I,
30 holding my head in horror, cried: "Sweet Spirit,

what souls are these who run through this black haze?"
And he to me: "These are the nearly soulless
33 whose lives concluded neither blame nor praise.

They are mixed here with that despicable corps
of angels who were neither for God nor Satan,
36 but only for themselves. The High Creator

scourged them from Heaven for its perfect beauty,
and Hell will not receive them since the wicked
39 might feel some glory over them." And I:

"Master, what gnaws at them so hideously
their lamentation stuns the very air?"

19 ⌈ 42 "They have no hope of death," he answered me,

"and in their blind and unattaining state
their miserable lives have sunk so low
45 that they must envy every other fate.

No word of them survives their living season.
Mercy and Justice deny them even a name.
48 Let us not speak of them: look, and pass on."

I saw a banner there upon the mist.
Circling and circling, it seemed to scorn all
pause.
51 So it ran on, and still behind it pressed

a never-ending rout of souls in pain.
I had not thought death had undone so many
54 as passed before me in that mournful train.

And some I knew among them; last of all
I recognized the shadow of that soul
57 who, in his cowardice, made the Great Denial.[13]

At once I understood for certain: these
were of that retrograde and faithless crew
60 hateful to God and to His enemies.   21

⌈ These wretches never born and never dead
ran naked in a swarm of wasps and hornets
63 that goaded them the more the more they fled,

0 ⌊ and made their faces stream with bloody gouts
of pus and tears that dribbled to their feet
66 to be swallowed there by loathsome worms and
maggots.

Then looking onward I made out a throng
assembled on the beach of a wide river,
69 whereupon I turned to him: "Master, I long

to know what souls these are, and what strange
usage
makes them as eager to cross as they seem
to be
72 in this infected light." At which the Sage:

"All this shall be made known to you when we
stand
on the joyless beach of Acheron."[14] And I
75 cast down my eyes, sensing a reprimand

in what he said, and so walked at his side
in silence and ashamed until we came
78 through the dead cavern to that sunless tide.

⌈ There, steering toward us in an ancient ferry
came an old man[15] with a white bush of hair,
81 bellowing: "Woe to you depraved souls! Bury

here and forever all hope of Paradise:
I come to lead you to the other shore,
84 into eternal dark, into fire and ice.

And you who are living yet, I say begone
from these who are dead." But when he saw
me stand
87 against his violence he began again:

"By other windings and by other steerage
shall you cross to that other shore. Not here!
Not here!
⌊ 90 A lighter craft than mine must give you passage."

---

13. **I . . . Great Denial:** This reference is generally believed to be to Pope Celestine V. Fearing that his
own soul would be corrupted by worldliness, he
abdicated in favor of Pope Boniface VIII, who became a political enemy of Dante's and represented
the worst sort of evil secularization of the Church.

14. **Acheron** (ak'ər·än'): in Greek mythology, the river
of woe in the underworld; dead souls were ferried
across the river to Hades.

15. **an old man:** Charon (ker'ən); in Greek mythology,
the ferryman who carried the dead to Hades.

19 INFERRING
What does line 42 suggest
about the punishment suffered
by the souls of the uncom-
mitted? (It may be worse than
death, since they are unable to
die and escape their fate.)

20 READER'S RESPONSE
The wretches observed by
Dante in lines 34–35 and in
lines 61–66 are angels and human souls who sinned by not
taking sides in a conflict between good and evil. Do you
think those who refuse to
stand up for principle, who act
only for their own survival, deserve to suffer such a hideous
fate? (Answers will vary.)

  reprimand (rep'rə·mand):
rebuke or scolding

MEETING INDIVIDUAL NEEDS

**21 Auditory/Kinesthetic
Learners:** Selected students
may better appreciate the impact of Charon ferrying the
damned across into Hell by
dramatizing the scene using
the dialogue from the poem. ■

Dante Alighieri   **753**

22 LITERARY ELEMENT
Characterization: By what three means is Charon characterized in lines 94–99? (by his appearance; his behavior; and his effect on others)

MEETING INDIVIDUAL NEEDS

23 ESL: Charon's oar "whistles" because it is being swung through the air as Charon beats the stragglers. ■

flails (flālz): beats, strikes

24 LITERARY ELEMENT
Simile: To what does Dante compare the damned souls as they cast themselves from the shore? (to the dropping of leaves from the trees in autumn and to migrating birds)

25 CULTURAL BACKGROUND
Medieval Christian doctrine taught that those who die without confessing their sins and receiving the absolution of a priest are condemned to Hell. Because the church stands ready to forgive any repentant sinner, it is assumed that those who die in sin have chosen to do so. Therefore, in line 123, "they yearn for what they fear"—i.e., Hell.

26 GUIDED READING
Identifying Details: What is Dante's reaction to his first glimpse of Hell? (He faints.) What is the cause of this reaction? (Possible response: He is shocked and overwhelmed by what he has seen.)

And my Guide to him: "Charon, bite back your spleen:
this has been willed where what is willed must be,
93 and is not yours to ask what it may mean."

The steersman of that marsh of ruined souls,
who wore a wheel of flame around each eye,
96 stifled the rage that shook his woolly jowls.

But those unmanned and naked spirits there
turned pale with fear and their teeth began to chatter
99 at sound of his crude bellow. In despair

they blasphemed God, their parents, their time on earth,
the race of Adam, and the day and the hour
102 and the place and the seed the womb that gave them birth.

But all together they drew to that grim shore
where all must come who lose the fear of God.
105 Weeping and cursing they come for evermore,

and demon Charon with eyes like burning coals
herds them in, and with a whistling oar
108 flails on the stragglers to his wake of souls.

As leaves in autumn loosen and stream down
until the branch stands bare above its tatters
111 spread on the rustling ground, so one by one

the evil seed of Adam in its Fall
cast themselves, at his signal, from the shore

and streamed away like birds who hear their call.

So they are gone over that shadowy water,
and always before they reach the other shore
117 a new noise stirs on this, and new throngs gather.

"My son," the courteous Master said to me,
"all who die in the shadow of God's wrath
120 converge to this from every clime and country.

And all pass over eagerly, for here
Divine Justice transforms and spurs them so
123 their dread turns wish: they yearn for what they fear.[16]

No soul in Grace comes ever to this crossing;
therefore if Charon rages at your presence
126 you will understand the reason for his cursing."

When he had spoken, all the twilight country
shook so violently, the terror of it
129 bathes me with sweat even in memory:

the tear-soaked ground gave out a sigh of wind
that spewed itself in flame on a red sky,
132 and all my shattered senses left me. Blind,

like one whom sleep comes over in a swoon,
I stumbled into darkness and went down.

---

16. **Divine Justice . . . fear:** The damned have actually chosen Hell. They have free will and the power to sin or not to sin.

PAOLO AND FRANCESCA, GUSTAVE DORÉ. *In this canto, Dante meets two lovers whose passions have condemned them to eternal suffering.*
? *Do you think anyone deserves to suffer for loving too much?*

New York Public Library Picture Collection

TEACHER'S RESOURCES
✔ Review and Response Worksheet
✔ Selection Test

HUMANITIES CONNECTION

? *How does Doré use line to convey the "choir of anguish" of sinners caught in the whirlwind?* (Possible response: The ropelike swirl of twisted figures wrapped in trailing shrouds conveys the sinners' anguish.) ■

27 CULTURAL BACKGROUND
Limbo, according to medieval Christian theology, is a place on the outer edge of Hell for souls who are neither saved nor condemned. The souls of children who die before baptism reside in Limbo for eternity, as do the souls of righteous people who lived and died before the birth of Christ, such as Virgil. Limbo is not a place of punishment, except that souls confined there have no hope of seeing God.

28 GUIDED READING
Interpreting Details: Explain how Dante applies the law of symbolic retribution to those condemned for carnal sins. (Possible response: As in life, their judgment was "swept away" by stormy passions, so in death the carnal sinners are continually whirled around in a hellish storm.)

CANTO 5

Circle Two   *The Carnal*

The Poets leave Limbo and enter the *Second Circle.* Here begin the torments of Hell proper, and here, blocking the way, sits *Minos,* the dread and semi-bestial judge of the damned who assigns to each soul its eternal torment. He orders the Poets back; but Virgil silences him as he earlier silenced Charon, and the Poets move on.

They find themselves on a dark ledge swept by a great whirlwind, which spins within it the souls of the *Carnal,* those who betrayed reason to their appetites. Their sin was to abandon themselves to the tempest of their passions: so

they are swept forever in the tempest of Hell, forever denied the light of reason and of God. Virgil identifies many among them. *Semiramis* is there, and *Dido, Cleopatra, Helen, Achilles, Paris,* and *Tristan.* Dante sees *Paolo* and *Francesca* swept together, and in the name of love he calls to them to tell their sad story. They pause from their eternal flight to come to him, and Francesca tells their history while Paolo weeps at her side. Dante is so stricken by compassion at their tragic tale that he swoons once again.

Dante Alighieri   **755**

29 Students with artistic talent might enjoy making a cartoon drawing of a damned soul facing Minos, learning his or her fate from the number of coils around Minos's body. ■

30 LITERARY BACKGROUND
Minos's warning to Dante in line 20 echoes a famous passage in the New Testament: "Wide is the gate, and broad is the way, that leadeth to destruction, and many there be that go in thereat: Because strait is the gate, and narrow is the way, which leadeth unto life, and few there be that find it" (Matthew 7:13–14). Ask students to paraphrase what both Minos and Saint Matthew are saying.

31 LITERARY ELEMENT
Mood: What overall impression is created in lines 28–35, and what verbs are used to build that vivid impression? (The verbs "roaring," "wracked," "sweeps," "whirling," "battering," and "drives" build an impression of an overwhelming, unceasing, inescapable whirlwind.)

32 LITERARY ELEMENT
Simile: To what does Dante compare the condemned souls in lines 46–48? (to cranes crying harshly as they fly overhead)

So we went down to the second ledge[17] alone;
  a smaller circle of so much greater pain
3 the voice of the damned rose in a bestial moan.

29   There Minos[18] sits, grinning, grotesque, and hale.
  He examines each lost soul as it arrives
6 and delivers his verdict with his coiling tail.

That is to say, when the ill-fated soul
  appears before him it confesses all,
9 and that grim sorter of the dark and foul

decides which place in Hell shall be its end,
  then wraps his twitching tail about himself
12 one coil for each degree it must descend.   **31**

The soul descends and others take its place:
  each crowds in its turn to judgment, each confesses,
15 each hears its doom and falls away through space.

"O you who come into this camp of woe,"
  cried Minos when he saw me turn away
18 without awaiting his judgment, "watch where you go

once you have entered here, and to whom you turn!
30   Do not be misled by that wide and easy passage!"
21 And my Guide to him: "That is not your concern;

it is his fate to enter every door.
  This has been willed where what is willed must be,
24 and is not yours to question. Say no more."

Now the choir of anguish, like a wound,
  strikes through the tortured air. Now I have come
27 to Hell's full lamentation, sound beyond sound.

I came to a place stripped bare of every light
  and roaring on the naked dark like seas
30 wracked by a war of winds. Their hellish flight

of storm and counterstorm through time foregone,
  sweeps the souls of the damned before its charge.
33 Whirling and battering it drives them on,

and when they pass the ruined gap of Hell
  through which we had come, their shrieks begin anew.
36 There they blaspheme the power of God eternal.

And this, I learned, was the never ending flight
  of those who sinned in the flesh, the carnal and lusty
39 who betrayed reason to their appetite.

As the wings of wintering starlings bear them on
  in their great wheeling flights, just so the blast
42 wherries these evil souls through time foregone.

Here, there, up, down, they whirl and, whirling, strain
  with never a hope of hope to comfort them,
45 not of release, but even of less pain.

32   As cranes go over sounding their harsh cry,
  leaving the long streak of their flight in air,
48 so come these spirits, wailing as they fly.

And watching their shadows lashed by wind,

---

17. **second ledge:** In keeping with a concept borrowed from Aristotle, Dante places the sins of the flesh on the upper circles of Hell, where punishment is mildest; the sins of anger in the middle circles; and the sins resulting from an abuse of reason at the lowest circles, where the torment is greatest.
18. **Minos** (mī′näs′): the semibestial judge of the damned; Minos, the son of Europa and Zeus, is also one of the judges of Hades in classical Greek mythology.

I cried:
    "Master, what souls are these the very air
51 lashes with its black whips from side to side?"

                                                              35

    "The first of these whose history you would know,"
    he answered me, "was Empress of many tongues.
54 Mad sensuality corrupted her so

    that to hide the guilt of her debauchery
    she licensed all depravity alike,
57 and lust and law were one in her decree.

    She is Semiramis[19] of whom the tale is told
    how she married Ninus and succeeded him
60 to the throne of that wide land the Sultans hold.

    The other is Dido;[20] faithless to the ashes
    of Sichaeus, she killed herself for love.
63 The next whom the eternal tempest lashes

    is sense-drugged Cleopatra. See Helen there,
    from whom such ill arose. And great Achilles,[21]
66 who fought at last with love in the house of
        prayer.

    And Paris. And Tristan."[22] As they whirled above
    he pointed out more than a thousand shades
69 of those torn from the mortal life by love.

---

19. **Semiramis** (si·mir'ə·mis): a legendary queen of
    Assyria.
20. **Dido** (dī'dō): a legendary queen of Carthage who
    vowed to be true to her dead husband, Sichaeus,
    but broke her vow when she fell in love with
    Aeneas; after Aeneas abandoned her, Dido threw
    herself on a funeral pyre.
21. **Achilles:** the great Greek warrior who deserted his
    army in order to marry Polyxena (pō·lik'sē·nə), a
    Trojan princess; Achilles was killed by Paris, a Tro-
    jan warrior, when he went to the temple for the
    wedding.
22. **Tristan:** In medieval legend, Tristan fell in love
    with Iseult (i·soolt'), a young princess betrothed to
    his uncle, King Mark of Cornwall. Eventually, both
    lovers died on the same day (see page 716).

I stood there while my Teacher one by one
    named the great knights and ladies of dim time;
72 and I was swept by pity and confusion.

At last I spoke: "Poet, I should be glad
    to speak a word with those two[23] swept
        together
75 so lightly on the wind and still so sad."

And he to me: "Watch them. When next they
        pass,
    call to them in the name of love that drives
78 and damns them here. In that name they will
        pause."

Thus, as soon as the wind in its wild course
    brought them around, I called: "O wearied souls!
81 if none forbid it, pause and speak to us."

                                                              36

As mating doves that love calls to their nest
    glide through the air with motionless raised
        wings,
84 borne by the sweet desire that fills each breast—

Just so those spirits turned on the torn sky
    from the band where Dido whirls across the air;
87 such was the power of pity in my cry.

"O living creature, gracious, kind, and good,
    going this pilgrimage through the sick night,
90 visiting us who stained the earth with blood,

were the King of Time our friend, we would pray
        His peace
    on you who have pitied us. As long as the wind
93 will let us pause, ask of us what you please.

---

23. **those two:** Paolo (pä'ô·lô) and Francesca (frän·
    ches'kä); Francesca da Rimini, a niece of Dante's
    patron, had been murdered with her lover, Paolo
    Malatesta, by her husband, Giovanni (who was
    also Paolo's brother), when he found the lovers
    together.

MEETING INDIVIDUAL NEEDS

33 ESL: Explain that the "Empress of many tongues" is
Semiramis, the Assyrian queen
who ruled people who spoke
many different languages
(tongues). ■

34 COMPARING LITERATURE
The list of people presented in
lines 58–67 are figures from
legend and literature, most of
them pre-Christian, who were
known for sins of sexual
passion.
? What epic convention do
these lists resemble? (the
epic lists, or catalogs, of
heroes or vanquished enemies
in the *Iliad*, the *Odyssey*, and
the *Aeneid*)

35 GUIDED READING
Identifying Details: In lines
71–72, what emotions do the
"great knights and ladies" condemned for sins of love evoke
in Dante? (He feels pity and
confusion.) Whom does Dante
wish to speak to? (the condemned lovers, Paolo and
Francesca)

36 LITERARY ELEMENT
Simile: What simile does
Dante use to describe the
doomed lovers? (mating doves
called to their nest) What feeling for the lovers does such an
image evoke? (Possible response: sympathy, tenderness)

37 HISTORICAL BACKGROUND

In 1300, the supposed date of Dante's journey into the afterworld, the murderer of the lovers, Giovanni Malatesta, the husband of Francesca and brother of Paolo, was still living. The place reserved for him in Circle 9 of Hell is a place of far worse torment than that suffered by the adulterous lovers.

38 READER'S RESPONSE

Do you find Francesca's story, in lines 124–133, of how she and Paolo were led into sin believable? Could a legend or fictional story have the power described in this passage? (Answers will vary, but many students will agree that reading a love story together could bring closer two people who are already attracted to each other.)

■ **dalliance** (dal′ē·əns): flirting

---

39 INTERPRETING

Why does Dante faint? (Possible response: He is overcome by emotions of pity and horror at Paolo and Francesca's suffering.) What does Dante's feeling for the lovers suggest about his moral values? (Dante's sympathy for the lovers suggests that he considers failure to control one's passions as more understandable and far less evil than the deliberate desire to hurt others.)

The town where I was born lies by the shore
  where the Po descends into its ocean rest
96 with its attendant streams in one long murmur.

Love, which in gentlest hearts will soonest bloom
  seized my lover with passion for that sweet
  body
99 from which I was torn unshriven to my doom.

Love, which permits no loved one not to love,
  took me so strongly with delight in him
102 that we are one in Hell, as we were above.

37 Love led us to one death. In the depths of Hell
  Caina[24] waits for him who took our lives." **38**
105 This was the piteous tale they stopped to tell.

And when I had heard those world-offended
  lovers
  I bowed my head. At last the Poet spoke:
108 "What painful thoughts are these your lowered
  brow covers?"

When at length I answered, I began: "Alas!
  What sweetest thoughts, what green and young
  desire
111 led these two lovers to this sorry pass."

Then turning to those spirits once again,
  I said: "Francesca, what you suffer here
114 melts me to tears of pity and of pain.

But tell me: in the time of your sweet sighs
  by what appearances found love the way
117 to lure you to his perilous paradise?"

And she: "The double grief of a lost bliss
  is to recall its happy hour in pain.
120 Your Guide and Teacher knows the truth of this.

But if there is indeed a soul in Hell
  to ask of the beginning of our love
123 out of his pity, I will weep and tell:

On a day for dalliance we read the rhyme
  of Lancelot,[25] how love had mastered him.
126 We were alone with innocence and dim time.

Pause after pause that high old story drew
  our eyes together while we blushed and paled;
129 but it was one soft passage overthrew

our caution and our hearts. For when we read
  how her fond smile was kissed by such a lover,
132 he who is one with me alive and dead

breathed on my lips the tremor of his kiss.
  That book, and he who wrote it,[26] was a
  pander.
135 That day we read no further." As she said this,

the other spirit, who stood by her, wept
  so piteously, I felt my senses reel
138 and faint away with anguish. I was swept **39**

by such a swoon as death is, and I fell,
  as a corpse might fall, to the dead floor of Hell.

---

24. **Caina:** the level of Hell reserved for murderers of kin; named for Cain, the son of Adam and Eve, who slew his brother Abel.

25. **Lancelot:** In the medieval legends of King Arthur, Lancelot fell in love with Guinevere, Arthur's queen, and their love led to the downfall of the Knights of the Round Table.

26. **he who wrote it:** In an old French version of the romance of Lancelot, the character who urges on the secret lovers Lancelot and Guinevere is called Gallehaut. The Italian for *Gallehaut* is *Galeotto,* which is also the word for ''pander,'' that is, a go-between for lovers, one who urges on the passions between secret lovers. The book was thus a kind of ''pander'' between Paolo and Francesca.

First Thoughts

Describe Dante's emotional responses at several key points in the narrative thus far. Do you think your reactions would be similar to his? Explain.

Identifying Facts

1. What is Dante's state of mind at the beginning of the poem?
2. How does Virgil offer to help Dante? Why is Virgil himself unable to take Dante directly to the Light of God?
3. What is the sin of the first group of condemned souls that Dante meets?
4. Who is Charon? According to Virgil, why does Charon refuse to allow Dante to cross Acheron?
5. What is Minos's role in the second circle of Hell? How does he perform this duty?
6. What types of sinners does Dante see in the second circle? What is their eternal punishment?

Interpreting Meanings

1. In line 12 of the first canto, Dante says that he has wandered from the "True Way." If the Dark Wood of Error is a **symbol** of worldliness, what does the "True Way" represent? What might the three animals that try to force Dante back into the Dark Wood symbolize?

2. Dante is the author of the *Divine Comedy* as well as a character in it. How does Dante feel when he learns Virgil's identity in Canto 1? Why is Virgil important to Dante as a poet?
3. As Dante's guide, Virgil often explains things to him. In line 18 of Canto 3, Virgil tells Dante that the fallen people are those " 'who have lost the good of intellect.' " What does he mean?
4. The inscription on the gate of Hell tells the damned to abandon all hope. In what ways does hopelessness torment the spirits of the damned in Canto 3? Comment on lines 42–45 and 100–102.
5. In Canto 5, lines 82–87, Dante compares Paolo and Francesca to doves. Why do you suppose Dante uses such a sympathetic image for the lovers?
6. By including details about Paolo and Francesca's reading, what attitude do you think Dante is expressing toward courtly love poetry?

Applying Meanings

Dante believed that faith was the most important value in life. Next to faith, however, he saw reason as the highest human value. How do you define faith and reason? Which is more valued in today's world? Which do you think *should* be more highly valued? Explain your response.

This engraving of Count Ugolino chewing on Archbishop Ruggieri's head is macabre but also a bit ridiculous.

? *Ugolino and Ruggieri may have looked like upright men while they lived. How do they look now?* (Possible response: Compared with Dante and Virgil, who stand upright and dignified onshore, the two condemned men look pathetic.) ■

1 LITERARY ELEMENT

Organization: The geography of Dante's Hell is precisely worked out. Dante conceived the whole realm as a vast conical pit with its bottom at the center of the earth. He and Virgil descend through nine circles, each reserved for punishments of increasing severity. The nine circles are grouped in threes, corresponding to the three kinds of vice that Dante learned from Aristotle: incontinence (symbolized by the She-Wolf), violence (symbolized by the Lion), and fraud and malice (symbolized by the Leopard). The ninth circle, Cocytus, is reserved for sins of fraud and treachery. The lower three circles are further divided into several rounds, each devoted to a particular kind of sin.

UGOLINO AND THE ARCHBISHOP RUGGIERI, GUSTAVE DORÉ.

? *What purpose does Dante serve by telling the tales of various sinners to the world?*

New York Public Library Picture Collection

1 Dante and Virgil continue to descend deeper and deeper into Hell, encountering increasingly horrible sins and their corresponding punishments. Near the end of Canto 32, Dante, having reached the frigid ninth circle of Hell, encounters two souls squeezed into the same icy hole. One sinner is chewing on the head of the other. Dante asks the first soul why he is devouring the other, offering to tell the sinner's story to the world. In the following canto, Canto 33, Dante will learn the gruesome history of Count Ugolino and Bishop Ruggieri, both Dante's contemporaries in thirteenth-century Italy.

CANTO 33

Circle Nine: Cocytus
Round Two: Antenora
Round Three: Ptolomea

Compound Fraud
The Treacherous to Country
The Treacherous to Guests and Hosts

In reply to Dante's exhortation, the sinner who is gnawing his companion's head looks up, wipes his bloody mouth on his victim's hair, and tells his harrowing story. He is *Count Ugolino* and the wretch he gnaws is *Archbishop Ruggieri.* Both are in Antenora[1] for treason. In life they had once plotted together. Then Ruggieri betrayed his fellow-plotter and caused his death, by starvation, along with his four "sons." In the most pathetic and dramatic passage of the *Inferno,* Ugolino details how their prison was sealed and how his "sons"[2] dropped dead before him one by one, weeping for food. His terrible tale serves only to renew his grief and hatred, and he has hardly finished it before he begins to gnaw Ruggieri again with renewed fury. In the immutable Law of Hell, the killer-by-starvation becomes the food of his victim.

The Poets leave Ugolino and enter *Ptolomea,* so named for the Ptolomaeus of *Maccabees,* who murdered his father-in-law at a banquet. Here are punished those who were *Treacherous Against the Ties of Hospitality.* They lie with only half their faces above the ice and their tears freeze in their eye sockets, sealing them with little crystal visors. Thus even the comfort of tears is denied them. Here Dante finds *Friar Alberigo* and *Branca d'Oria,* and discovers the terrible power of Ptolomea: so great is its sin that the souls of the guilty fall to its torments even before they die, leaving their bodies still on earth, inhabited by Demons.

The sinner raised his mouth from his grim repast
   and wiped it on the hair of the bloody head
3 whose nape he had all but eaten away. At last

he began to speak: "You ask me to renew
   a grief so desperate that the very thought
6 of speaking of it tears my heart in two.

But if my words may be a seed that bears
   the fruit of infamy for him I gnaw,
9 I shall weep, but tell my story through my tears.

Who you may be, and by what powers you reach
   into this underworld, I cannot guess,
12 but you seem to me a Florentine by your speech.

I was Count Ugolino, I must explain;
   this reverend grace is the Archbishop Ruggieri:[3]
15 now I will tell you why I gnaw his brain.

That I, who trusted him, had to undergo
   imprisonment and death through his treachery,
18 you will know already. What you cannot know—

---

1. **Antenora:** part of the ninth circle set aside for traitors; named for Antenor, who, in some versions of the story of the Trojan War, betrayed Troy to the Greeks.
2. **"sons":** Actually, two of the four men bricked up with Ugolino were his grandsons; the younger one was fifteen.

3. **Ugolino . . . Ruggieri:** Count Ugolino and Archbishop Ruggieri were originally allies in political factions jockeying for power in the city of Pisa. In 1288, Ruggieri betrayed Ugolino and imprisoned him and his sons. The next year Ruggieri had the dungeon sealed and starved the prisoners to death.

2 LITERARY ELEMENT
Theme: This is another instance of Dante's view that the punishment should be equal to the crime. Do you share this belief in fitting retribution? (Answers will vary.)

3 GUIDED READING
Identifying Cause and Effect: What reason does the gnawing man give for his willingness to tell his painful story? (He wishes to harm the reputation of his enemy.)

infamy (in'fə·mē): a reputation for great wickedness

4 LITERARY ELEMENT
Tone: In what tone does Ugolino refer to his worst enemy in line 14? (His words "reverend grace" are ironic, since this brutal man deserves no reverence or respect.)

5 INTERPRETING

What foreboding does Ugolino
feel after his frightening
dream? (He is afraid that Ruggieri is about to betray him
and his sons and grandsons.)

6 ANALYZING

If Ugolino's sons are actually
grown men and the younger
grandson is fifteen, why might
Dante want the reader to think
of them as young boys? (Possible response: Making them
young, innocent, and helpless
heightens the pathos of their
situation and the inhumanity
of Ruggieri's crime.)

7 EVALUATING

What is your reaction to Ugolino's sons' offer to serve as
food for their father? What do
you think was Dante's purpose
in including such a detail?
(Possible response: to cause
revulsion against evil)

that is, the lingering inhumanity
  of the death I suffered—you shall hear in full:[4]
21 then judge for yourself if he has injured me.   **5**

A narrow window in that coop of stone
  now called the Tower of Hunger for my sake
24 (within which others yet must pace alone)

had shown me several waning moons already
  between its bars, when I slept the evil sleep
27 in which the veil of the future parted for me.

This beast[5] appeared as master of a hunt
  chasing the wolf and his whelps across the
    mountain
30 that hides Lucca from Pisa.[6] Out in front

of the starved and shrewd and avid pack he had
    placed
  Gualandi and Sismondi and Lanfranchi[7]   **6**
33 to point his prey. The father and sons had raced

a brief course only when they failed of breath
  and seemed to weaken; then I thought I saw
36 their flanks ripped open by the hounds' fierce
    teeth.

Before the dawn, the dream still in my head,
  I woke and heard my sons, who were there
    with me,
39 cry from their troubled sleep, asking for bread.

4. **you shall hear in full:** By 1300, supposedly the
   date when Dante began the *Divine Comedy,* everyone in adjacent cities would have known that Ruggieri had imprisoned his former ally. But because the
   dungeon was sealed, no one would have known exactly how he and the others met their deaths.
5. **This beast:** i.e., Ruggieri.
6. **the mountain that hides Lucca from Pisa:** Mount
   San Giuliano stands between the two cities.
7. **Gualandi . . . Lanfranchi:** Like Ugolino, these three
   were nobles of Pisa and friends of Archbishop
   Ruggieri.

You are cruelty itself if you can keep
  your tears back at the thought of what
    foreboding
42 stirred in my heart; and if you do not weep,

at what are you used to weeping?—The hour
    when food
  used to be brought, drew near. They were now
    awake,
45 and each was anxious from his dream's dark
    mood.

And from the base of that horrible tower I heard
  the sound of hammers nailing up the gates:
48 I stared at my sons' faces without a word.

I did not weep: I had turned stone inside.
  They wept. 'What ails you, Father, you look so
    strange,'
51 my little Anselm,[8] youngest of them, cried.   **6**

But I did not speak a word nor shed a tear:
  not all that day nor all that endless night,
54 until I saw another sun appear.

When a tiny ray leaked into that dark prison
  and I saw staring back from their four faces
57 the terror and the wasting of my own,

I bit my hands in helpless grief. And they,
  thinking I chewed myself for hunger, rose
60 suddenly together. I heard them say:

7

'Father, it would give us much less pain
  if you ate us: it was you who put upon us
63 this sorry flesh; now strip it off again.'

I calmed myself to spare them. Ah! hard earth,
  why did you not yawn open? All that day

8. **my little Anselm:** Anselm, Gaddo (line 67), Brigata,
   and Uguccione (line 89) were the sons and grandsons entombed with Ugolino.

66 and the next we sat in silence. On the fourth,

Gaddo, the eldest, fell before me and cried,
stretched at my feet upon that prison floor:
69 'Father, why don't you help me?' There he died.

And just as you see me, I saw them fall
one by one on the fifth day and the sixth.
72 Then, already blind, I began to crawl

from body to body shaking them frantically.
Two days I called their names, and they were
dead.
75 Then fasting overcame my grief and me."

His eyes narrowed to slits when he was done,
and he seized the skull again between his teeth
78 grinding it as a mastiff grinds a bone.

Ah, Pisa! foulest blemish on the land
where "si" sounds sweet and clear,[9] since those
nearby you
81 are slow to blast the ground on which you stand,

may Caprara and Gorgona[10] drift from place
and dam the flooding Arno[11] at its mouth
84 until it drowns the last of your foul race!

For if to Ugolino falls the censure
for having betrayed your castles, you for your
part
87 should not have put his sons to such a torture:

you modern Thebes![12] those tender lives you spilt—
Brigata, Uguccione, and the others

9   90 I mentioned earlier—were too young for guilt!

10   We passed on further,[13] where the frozen mine
entombs another crew in greater pain;
93 these wraiths are not bent over, but lie supine.

Their very weeping closes up their eyes;
and the grief that finds no outlet for its tears
96 turns inward to increase their agonies:

for the first tears that they shed knot instantly
in their eye-sockets, and as they freeze they
form
99 a crystal visor above the cavity.

11 And despite the fact that standing in that place
I had become as numb as any callus,
102 and all sensation had faded from my face,

somehow I felt a wind begin to blow,
whereat I said: "Master, what stirs this wind?
105 Is not all heat extinguished here below?"

And the Master said to me: "Soon you will be
where your own eyes will see the source and
cause
108 and give you their own answer to the
mystery."[14]

And one of those locked in that icy mall
cried out to us as we passed: "O souls so cruel
111 that you are sent to the last post of all,[15]

---

9. **the land . . . sweet and clear:** Italy; *si* is the Italian word for ''yes.''
10. **Caprara and Gorgona:** two islands near the mouth of the Arno River, possessions of Pisa.
11. **Arno:** river in Italy; Florence and Arezzo are located on its banks, and Pisa is located at its mouth.
12. **you modern Thebes:** Ancient Thebes was the scene of much violence and bloodshed.

13. **We passed on further:** Here Dante and Virgil pass into Ptolomea, the place of punishment for traitors against hospitality; named for Ptolomeus, who invited Simon Maccabeus, king of Judea, and his two sons to a banquet and then assassinated them in 135 B.C.
14. **their own answer to the mystery:** The answer to Dante's question about the source of the wind will be given in Canto 34.
15. **the last post of all:** This sinner thinks Virgil and Dante are condemned souls who are being sent to the very lowest part of the ninth circle because their crimes were worse than his.

8 READER'S RESPONSE
As horrible as Ugolino's revenge is, do you think it is justified, in view of Ruggieri's crime against him? If so, does that mean that revenge is justifiable in principle? (Answers will vary.)

9 GUIDED READING
Whom is Dante addressing in this passage? (the city of Pisa) How had Ugolino betrayed Pisa? (He had given up certain castles during a war with another city.) For what sin does Dante blame Pisa? (for allowing Ugolino's innocent children to die)

10 LITERARY ELEMENT
Metaphor: What metaphor is used for Hell in line 91, and why is it apt? (Hell is a ''frozen mine.'' The metaphor suggests the coldness and darkness of a world far from God's radiant warmth and light.)

11 INTERPRETING
Why has Dante become ''numb as any callus,'' in line 101? (from the cold) What symbolic significance might his numbness have? (Possible response: He is emotionally numbed after seeing so many horrors and hearing so many terrible stories. In addition, he is losing human feeling, growing cold, as he moves further away from God and closer to Satan.)

12 ESL: Some students may need to be told that "to take . . . in" is an idiom meaning to fool or deceive. ■

13 INTERPRETING
In lines 115–117, Dante promises to relieve Friar Alberigo's sufferings if he will identify himself and tell his story. Why, in lines 148–150, does he break his promise? (Possible response: To keep his promise would mean lightening the punishment of someone who richly deserves to suffer. Further, as Dante sees it, to break faith with someone capable of such a monstrous sin carries no shame.)

relieve me for a little from the pain
 of this hard veil; let my heart weep a while
114 before the weeping freeze my eyes again."

And I to him: "If you would have my service,
 tell me your name; then if I do not help you
117 may I descend to the last rim of the ice."

"I am Friar Alberigo," he answered therefore,
 "the same who called for the fruits from the bad
  garden.[16]
120 Here I am given dates for figs full store."

"What! Are you dead already?" I said to him.
 And he then: "How my body stands in the
  world
123 I do not know. So privileged is this rim

of Ptolomea, that often souls fall to it
 before dark Atropos has cut their thread.[17]
126 And that you may more willingly free my spirit

of this glaze of frozen tears that shrouds my face,
 I will tell you this: when a soul betrays as I did,
129 it falls from flesh, and a demon takes its place,

ruling the body till its time is spent.[18]
 The ruined soul rains down into this cistern.
132 So, I believe, there is still evident

In the world above, all that is fair and mortal
 of this black shade who winters here behind me.
135 If you have only recently crossed the portal

from that sweet world, you surely must have known
 his body: Branca D'Oria[19] is its name,
138 and many years have passed since he rained down."

12

"I think you are trying to take me in," I said,
 "Ser Branca D'Oria is a living man;
141 he eats, he drinks, he fills his clothes and his bed."

"Michel Zanche had not yet reached the ditch
 of the Black Talons," the frozen wraith replied,
144 "there where the sinners thicken in hot pitch,

when this one left his body to a devil,
 as did his nephew and second in treachery,
147 and plumbed like lead through space to this
  dead level.

13

But now reach out your hand, and let me cry."
 And I did not keep the promise I had made,
150 for to be rude to him was courtesy.

Ah, men of Genoa![20] souls of little worth,
 corrupted from all custom of righteousness,
153 why have you not been driven from the earth?

For there beside the blackest soul of all
 Romagna's evil plain,[21] lies one of yours
156 bathing his filthy soul in the eternal

glacier of Cocytus for his foul crime,
 while he seems yet alive in world and time!

---

16. **the fruits from the bad garden:** To avenge an insult, Friar Alberigo invited his brother Manfred and Manfred's son to dinner. At the signal, "Bring in the fruit," hired murderers killed them.

17. **before . . . thread:** According to Greek mythology, there were three Fates: Clotho spun the web of a person's life; Lachesis measured out its length; Atropos cut it at the moment of death.

18. **a demon . . . its time is spent:** Dante includes in Hell the souls of some who were still alive at the time of writing. He explains this by suggesting that certain sins are so grave that the sinners' spirits are immediately damned, while their bodies, animated by demons, live out a natural span of life.

19. **Branca D'Oria:** he invited his father-in-law, Michel Zanche, to a feast and then murdered him.
20. **men of Genoa:** Branca D'Oria was a Genoan.
21. **Romagna's evil plain:** a region of northeast Italy, formerly part of the Papal States.

THE JUDECCA, LUCIFER, GUSTAVE DORÉ.
? *How does this image of Satan compare with modern conceptions of the Devil?*
Do you find it surprising that the center of Hell is icy rather than fiery?

New York Public Library Picture Collection

CANTO 34

Ninth Circle: Cocytus
Round Four: Judecca
The Center

Compound Fraud
The Treacherous to Their Masters
Satan

"On march the banners of the King," Virgil begins as the Poets face the last depth. He is quoting a medieval hymn, and to it he adds the distortion and perversion of all that lies about him. "On march the banners of the King—of Hell." And there before them, in an infernal parody of Godhead, they see Satan in the distance, his great wings beating like a windmill. It is their beating that is the source of the icy wind of Cocytus, the exhalation of all evil.

All about him in the ice are strewn the sinners of the last round, *Judecca*, named for Judas Is-

cariot. These are the *Treacherous to Their Masters.* They lie completely sealed in the ice, twisted and distorted into every conceivable posture. It is impossible to speak to them, and the Poets move on to observe Satan.

He is fixed into the ice at the center to which flow all the rivers of guilt; and as he beats his great wings as if to escape, their icy wind only freezes him more surely into the polluted ice. In a grotesque parody of the Trinity, he has three faces, each a different color, and in each mouth he clamps a sinner whom he rips eternally with

HUMANITIES CONNECTION

This image depicts Virgil and Dante's first glimpse of Satan frozen in the ice, gnawing three sinners in his three mouths, his great bat-wings beating the freezing wind through hell.
? *What details form the landscape of Hell, and what impression do they build?* (Hell looks like a cold, gloomy place in the depths of the earth, as suggested by the stalactites, the rocky landscape, and the desolate, open expanse of the scene.) ∎

14 LITERARY BACKGROUND
The last circle is called Cocytus, after one of the rivers of the underworld in Greek mythology. Its name comes from a Greek word meaning "shrieking, wailing, or howling." Round Four, Judecca, is named after Judas Iscariot, the disciple who betrayed Jesus. *What does Dante consider the worst sin of all?* (treachery to those who deserve one's complete loyalty)

15 INTERPRETING
The icy wind Dante feels comes from the incessant beating of Satan's great wings. What allegorical meaning is suggested here? (Satan is the source of all evil, as well as of the sufferings of hell.)

Dante Alighieri **765**

his teeth. *Judas Iscariot* is in the central mouth: *Brutus* and *Cassius* in the mouths on either side.

Having seen all, the Poets now climb through the center, grappling hand over hand down the hairy flank of Satan himself—a last supremely symbolic action—and at last, when they have passed the center of all gravity, they emerge from Hell. A long climb from the earth's center to the Mount of Purgatory awaits them, and they push on without rest, ascending along the sides of the river Lethe, till they emerge once more to see the stars of Heaven, just before dawn on Easter Sunday.

"On march the banners of the King of Hell,"[22]
my Master said. "Toward us. Look straight ahead:
3 can you make him[23] out at the core of the frozen shell?"

Like a whirling windmill seen afar at twilight,
or when a mist has risen from the ground—
6 just such an engine rose upon my sight

stirring up such a wild and bitter wind
I cowered for shelter at my Master's back,
9 there being no other windbreak I could find.

16
I stood now where the souls of the last class
(with fear my verses tell it) were covered wholly;
12 they shone below the ice like straws in glass.

Some lie stretched out; others are fixed in place
upright, some on their heads, some on their soles;
15 another, like a bow, bends foot to face.

17
When we had gone so far across the ice
that it pleased my Guide to show me the foul creature
18 that once had worn the grace of Paradise,

he made me stop, and, stepping aside, he said:
"Now see the face of Dis![24] This is the place
21 where you must arm your soul against all dread."

Do not ask, Reader, how my blood ran cold
and my voice choked up with fear. I cannot write it:
24 this is a terror that cannot be told.

18
I did not die, and yet I lost life's breath:
imagine for yourself what I became,
27 deprived at once of both my life and death.

19
The Emperor of the Universe of Pain
jutted his upper chest above the ice;
30 and I am closer in size to the great mountain

the Titans[25] make around the central pit,
than they to his arms. Now, starting from this part,
33 imagine the whole that corresponds to it!

If he was once as beautiful as now
he is hideous, and still turned on his Maker,
36 well may he be the source of every woe!

---

22. **On march . . . Hell:** Virgil is deliberately distorting the words of a medieval hymn that was written to celebrate the Holy Cross.
23. **him:** Satan.
24. **Dis** (dis): Satan; in Greek mythology, the god of the underworld; also the realm of the dead.
25. **Titans** (tīt''nz): in Greek mythology, a family of gods that was overthrown by Zeus and the Olympians and confined to Tartarus, the region below Hades.

With what a sense of awe I saw his head
   towering above me! for it had three faces:
39 one was in front, and it was fiery red;

the other two, as weirdly wonderful,
   merged with it from the middle of each
   shoulder
42 to the point where all converged at the top of
   the skull;

the right was something between white and bile;
   the left was about the color one observes
45 on those who live along the banks of the Nile.

Under each head two wings rose terribly,
   their span proportioned to so gross a bird:
48 I never saw such sails upon the sea.

They were not feathers—their texture and their
   form
   were like a bat's wings—and he beat them so
51 that three winds blew from him in one great
   storm:

it is these winds that freeze all Cocytus.[26]
   He wept from his six eyes, and down three
   chins
54 the tears ran mixed with bloody froth and
   pus.[27]

In every mouth he worked a broken sinner
   between his rake-like teeth. Thus he kept three
57 in eternal pain at his eternal dinner.

For the one in front the biting seemed to play
   no part at all compared to the ripping: at times
60 the whole skin of his back was flayed away.

"That soul that suffers most," explained my Guide,
   "is Judas Iscariot,[28] he who kicks his legs
63 on the fiery chin and has his head inside.

Of the other two, who have their heads thrust
   forward,
   the one who dangles down from the black face
66 is Brutus:[29] note how he writhes without a
   word.

And there, with the huge and sinewy arms, is the
   soul
   of Cassius.[30]—But the night is coming on
69 and we must go, for we have seen the whole."

Then, as he bade, I clasped his neck, and he,
   watching for a moment when the wings
72 were opened wide, reached over dexterously

and seized the shaggy coat of the king demon;
   then grappling matted hair and frozen crusts
75 from one tuft to another, clambered down.

When we had reached the joint where the great
   thigh
   merges into the swelling of the haunch,
78 my Guide and Master, straining terribly,

turned his head to where his feet had been
   and began to grip the hair as if he were
   climbing;
81 so that I thought we moved toward Hell again.

"Hold fast!" my Guide said, and his breath came
   shrill
   with labor and exhaustion. "There is no way
84 but by such stairs to rise above such evil."

---

26. **Cocytus** (kō·sīt′əs): one of the six rivers of the underworld.
27. **bloody . . . pus:** the grisly result of chewing sinners.

28. **Judas Iscariot** (jōō′dəs is·ker′ē·ət): the disciple who betrayed Jesus Christ.
29. **Brutus:** one of the Roman conspirators who assassinated Julius Caesar.
30. **Cassius** (kas′ē·əs): Brutus's coconspirator.

Dante Alighieri   **767**

At last he climbed out through an opening
in the central rock, and he seated me on the
rim;
87   then joined me with a nimble backward spring.

I looked up, thinking to see Lucifer[31]
as I had left him, and I saw instead
90   his legs projecting high into the air.   **24**

Now let all those whose dull minds are still
vexed
by failure to understand what point it was
93   I had passed through, judge if I was perplexed.

"Get up. Up on your feet," my Master said.
"The sun already mounts to middle tierce,[32]
96   and a long road and hard climbing lie ahead."

It was no hall of state we had found there,
but a natural animal pit hollowed from rock
99   with a broken floor and a close and sunless air.   **25**

"Before I tear myself from the Abyss,"
I said when I had risen, "O my Master,
102   explain to me my error in all this:

where is the ice? and Lucifer—how has he
been turned from top to bottom: and how can
the sun
105   have gone from night to day so suddenly?"

23 And he to me: "You imagine you are still
on the other side of the center where I grasped
108   the shaggy flank of the Great Worm of Evil

which bores through the world—you *were* while I
climbed down,
but when I turned myself about, you passed
111   the point to which all gravities are drawn.

You are under the other hemisphere where you
stand;
the sky above us is the half opposed
114   to that which canopies the great dry land.

Under the midpoint of that other sky
the Man[33] who was born sinless and who lived
117   beyond all blemish, came to suffer and die.

You have your feet upon a little sphere
which forms the other face of the Judecca.[34]
120   There it is evening when it is morning here.

And this gross Fiend and Image of all Evil
who made a stairway for us with his hide
123   is pinched and prisoned in the ice-pack still.

On this side he plunged down from heaven's
height,
and the land that spread here once hid in the
sea
126   and fled North to our hemisphere for fright;

and it may be that moved by that same fear,
the one peak[35] that still rises on this side
129   fled upward leaving this great cavern here."

Down there, beginning at the further bound
of Beelzebub's[36] dim tomb, there is a space
132   not known by sight, but only by the sound

of a little stream[37] descending through the hollow
it has eroded from the massive stone
135   in its endlessly entwining lazy flow."

---

31. **Lucifer** (loo'sə·fər): Satan.
32. **middle tierce:** seven-thirty A.M.
33. **the Man:** Christ.
34. **Judecca:** the level of Hell named for Judas Iscariot, who betrayed Christ.
35. **one peak:** the Mount of Purgatory.
36. **Beelzebub's** (bē·el'zə·bub'): here, another name for Satan.
37. **a little stream:** Lethe (lē'thē); in classical mythology, the river of forgetfulness.

READING CHECK

1. Who leads Dante out of the Dark Wood of Error? (the shade of Virgil)
2. Who is Charon and what is his function? (A brutal ferryman from Greek mythology, who conveys the damned to their eternal fate.)
3. How many levels are there in Hell? (nine)
4. For what sins are Cleopatra, Achilles, and Tristan being punished? (sins of sexual passion)

5. What led Paolo and Francesca to give in to their desire for each other? (reading the tale of Lancelot and Guinevere)
6. What does Dante do after hearing the tale of Paolo and Francesca? (He faints.)
7. After having been starved to death, what grim food does Count Ugolino feed on in Hell? (the head and neck of Ruggieri, his murderer)

8. By whom is Friar Alberigo's still living, physical body occupied? (a demon)
9. What causes the icy wind in Hell? (Satan's incessantly beating wings)
10. Who does Satan chew on, and why? (Judas Iscariot, because he betrayed Christ)

THE POETS EMERGE FROM HELL, GUSTAVE DORÉ.

In feeling and atmosphere, how does this engraving by Doré differ from the others you have seen in this selection?

New York Public Library Picture Collection

HUMANITIES CONNECTION

This Doré engraving serves as a splendid "farewell" for the *Inferno*. The calm evening scene is spangled with natural light, a welcome sight to Dante as he emerges from Hell.

? *Compared to previous scenes in the Inferno, what is the mood of this scene?* (Possible responses: peaceful, hopeful) *Dante and Virgil look small standing on the high cliff overlooking the sea. What might this imply about Dante's feelings as he emerges from Hell?* (Possible responses: Dante might feel humbled by the experience, and might now view earthly life as a great, challenging opportunity to avoid eternal damnation.) ▪

26 LITERARY ELEMENT

Verse Form: How does Dante change his verse form at the end of each canto? (He moves from tercets to a couplet, two rhyming lines.) What is the effect of the change? (Possible response: It gives the canto a sense of completion.)

My Guide and I crossed over and began
  to mount that little known and lightless road
138 to ascend into the shining world again.

He first, I second, without thought of rest
  we climbed the dark until we reached the point
141 where a round opening brought in sight the
    blest

26   and beauteous shining of the Heavenly cars.
And we walked out once more beneath the
    Stars.**38**

---

38. **Stars:** Each of the three divisions of Dante's poem ends with the symbolism of heavenly stars. The time—just before dawn on Easter Sunday—is also symbolic of hope.

Dante Alighieri   **769**

The *Inferno* is rich in graphic description. Suggest that students create a wall mural depicting Hell's landscape and the characters that Dante and Virgil encounter on their journey. Divide the class into groups. Assign each group a section of the poem to illustrate in a specified area of the mural. Allow the class to decide where Virgil and Dante should be placed in the mural.

EXTENSION AND ENRICHMENT

Creating a Parody. Assign students to groups and ask them to invent appropriate punishments for sins that Dante did not consider. To create the effect of parody, groups should think of small sins, perhaps social transgressions such as throwing spitballs or being late to class. Groups should decide on a symbolic retribution and invent a narrative describing Dante's discovery of them in Hell.

CLOSURE

Many of the evil deeds Dante describes are still being done today, while some of our present evils are uniquely modern, such as drug-dealing. Ask students to think about other types of wrongdoing that seem to be new to our era. Then have them discuss what they think makes each action morally wrong. Guide students to a consideration of whether the grounds for moral condemnation have changed much since Dante's day. ■

ANSWERS

First Thoughts
Answers will vary.

Identifying Facts
1. the fraudulent and treacherous. betrayed guests, hosts, or their masters
2. vengeful. resumes his gnawing
3. those who betrayed their masters. frozen wholly in ice
4. He has three different-colored faces, six bat-wings, and a shaggy pelt. He is weeping and beating his wings as he chews on sinners.

Interpreting Meanings
1. Ruggieri's hunting dogs turn on his friends. He will turn on Ugolino and his sons.
2. Alberigo's crime was so heinous he was unworthy of Dante's mercy.
3. They betrayed their masters. Judas's master was Christ.
4. They are a symbolic parody of the Trinity.

Applying Meanings
Possible response: Sexual misconduct is still regarded by most people as the least serious sin, and violence as the most serious. Reasons will vary.

Creative Writing Response
Inventing a Board Game. Assess the creativeness of the idea and the clarity and correctness of the writing.

Critical Writing Response
Making a Literary Judgment. Students' positions should be stated clearly and supported with convincing arguments. ■

First Thoughts
Which images do you find the most striking in Cantos 33 and 34? Why?

Identifying Facts
1. According to Canto 33, what souls are punished in the ninth circle? What sins have they committed?
2. How does Ugolino's grim story make Ugolino himself feel? What does he then do to express his feelings?
3. According to Canto 34, what sinners are punished in the lowest, last circle? How are they punished?
4. According to Dante, what does Satan look like? What is Satan doing?

Interpreting Meanings
1. Describe Ugolino's evil dream (Canto 33, lines 28–36) and explain how it parts "the veil of the future" (line 27)— that is, forecasts coming events.
2. Why does Dante not keep his promise to Friar Alberigo?
3. Why does Dante regard Judas, Brutus, and Cassius as the worst sinners of all? How does Judas's sin differ from that of Brutus and Cassius?
4. In what way could Satan's three faces be explained as **symbols**?

Applying Meanings
By his placement of different sinners in Hell, Dante ranks human sins from the least to the most serious. What sins do people today regard as the least serious? As the most serious? Why do you think so?

Creative Writing Response
Inventing a Board Game. Imagine that you work for a company that manufactures board games. You want to convince the president of your company to manufacture an exciting board game that you have invented based on Dante's *Inferno*. The object of your board game is to journey successfully through Hell without getting caught there forever. Along the way there are helpers, such as Virgil and Beatrice, but there are also those who will try to prevent you from successfully completing your journey, such as Charon the ferryman, the monster Minos, and the various sinners who inhabit the Inferno. Decide on the rules of your game and what pieces it will consist of: figures, playing cards, and so on. Then write a detailed memo describing the game in terms that will convince the president of the company to manufacture it. If you wish, illustrate the various components of your board game.

Critical Writing Response
Making a Literary Judgment. Many readers are surprised to find that Dante describes the center of Hell as a frozen rather than fiery place. English Puritan writer John Milton in *Paradise Lost* pictures Hell as a gigantic furnace, as shown in the following lines from Book I:

> A dungeon horrible, on all sides round
> As one great furnace flamed, yet from those flames
> No light, but rather darkness visible
> Served only to discover sights of woe,
> Regions of sorrow, doleful shades, where peace
> And rest can never dwell, hope never comes
> That comes to all; but torture without end
> Still urges, and a fiery deluge, fed
> With everburning sulphur unconsumed. . . .

Think of the qualities of both fire and ice. In your opinion, which is better suited to symbolically describe the place farthest from God, the center of Hell? Write an essay of three paragraphs defending your position. Be sure to support your choice with at least three strong reasons.

ELEMENTS OF LITERATURE

Allegory

Dante wrote the *Divine Comedy* as an **allegory**, a narrative that takes place on both a literal and a figurative, or symbolic, level. Dante begins the poem with an age-old metaphor that is so common it has become a cliché: the description of life as a journey. When Dante says, "Midway in our life's journey," we can readily understand that he has reached middle age. From "I went astray," we understand that he is no longer acting as he thinks he should. A "dark wood" could be a state of mental confusion. In thinking further about the poem, we may even decide that the *I* in this passage has an allegorical, or symbolic, meaning, since the character of Dante could also be any one of us.

In an allegory, concrete details from the external world are used to represent inner mental states or spiritual truths. By choosing this form of expression, an author may be able to communicate ideas that would otherwise be difficult to explain. An author may also be able to make these truths highly dramatic. It would be one thing for Dante to say that he overcame the evil in his own heart. It is quite another thing for him to describe himself "grappling matted hair and frozen crusts" as he climbs on Satan's flank.

On a literal level in the *Divine Comedy*, the character of Dante travels through Hell, Purgatory, and Paradise before reaching God. On a symbolic level, however, his journey represents the progress of every individual soul toward God as well as the progress of people in their political and social lives toward peace on earth. Throughout the *Divine Comedy*, Dante mentions people, places, ideas, and events that are firmly rooted in his own time. But far from being an outdated work that makes sense only in the context of the Middle Ages, the *Divine Comedy* has great relevance to us today. By writing an allegory, Dante gives his narrative significance that goes far beyond the specifics of particular people and events.

Drawing by Weber © 1991, The New Yorker Magazine, Inc.

"Hon, what's an allegory?"

LITERARY ELEMENT
Allegory: Allegory always possess two levels of meaning: the literal and the symbolic. The literal level is the simple narrative. The symbolic level, the system of ideas linked to the literal action, is hidden beneath the surface and may become apparent only after close analysis. Allegories such as John Bunyan's *Pilgrim's Progress*, Jonathan Swift's *Gulliver's Travels*, and George Orwell's *Animal Farm* can be read literally and enjoyed by children. However, *Gulliver's Travels* and *Animal Farm* both serve as political allegories, while *Pilgrim's Progress*, like the *Divine Comedy*, is a religious allegory depicting the Christian's journey through life's temptations.

COMPARING LITERATURE
The allegory of the journey was particularly important in the medieval period, which was steeped in Christian values (see Introduction, p. 743). The allegorical journey also appears in many modern literary works, for example, Mark Twain's *Adventures of Huckleberry Finn*, Frank Baum's *The Wizard of Oz*, Robert Frost's "The Road Not Taken," and Francis Coppola's *Apocalypse Now*. Invite students to suggest and discuss other works, including hymns, popular songs, and films, that might be considered allegories. ■

Geoffrey Chaucer did not leave behind diaries or personal letters, so biographers have had to deduce the details of his life from his works and from impersonal sources such as account books. Some scholars have hypothesized that Chaucer himself went on a pilgrimage in the spring of 1387, the year that he is generally believed to have begun *The Canterbury Tales*. Since no reference to his wife, Philippa, can be found after that time, some speculate that he might have made a pilgrimage in hopes of finding a cure for his sick wife, who apparently died in spite of his efforts.

The journey to Canterbury is called the "frame" for the collection of tales told by the pilgrims, who represent a cross-section of medieval English types. They range from a chivalric knight to people of the middle social ranks, such as the Merchant, to members of religious orders, as well as to people from the lower end of the social scale, such as the Plowman. An innkeeper named Harry Bailly acts as judge of the pilgrims' tales, one of which he abruptly terminates because he deems it "illiterate stuff." Chaucer even includes himself as one of the pilgrims.

ABOUT THE TRANSLATOR

Nevill Coghill's lively translation of *The Canterbury Tales* into modern English won new readers for Chaucer and great critical acclaim for Coghill.

Geoffrey Chaucer
c. 1342–1400

The National Portrait Gallery, London

Generally considered the "Father of English poetry," Chaucer was a well-educated man who knew French and Latin and was familiar with contemporary as well as classical literature. But just as important as his reading was Chaucer's remarkably broad experience of life. In his teens he served as a page, or messenger boy, to royalty, and later he went on to hold important positions in the king's service as a customs officer, a justice of the peace, a clerk of the king's works in charge of maintenance and repairs, and a member of Parliament. These posts brought Chaucer into close contact with people from all walks of life and gave him a rich understanding of human beings and all their follies and frailties.

Chaucer began his most famous work, *The Canterbury Tales*, in 1387. His plan in writing the story was to present a group of men and women representing nearly every level of medieval English society as they traveled on a pilgrimage to Canterbury, a city in southeastern England that is the site of a shrine to the martyred twelfth-century archbishop, St. Thomas à Becket. Each pilgrim was to tell two stories on the way to Canterbury and two on the way home. Chaucer died before completing the whole plan, but he left behind an unforgettable collection of stories and characters.

Chaucer wrote in Middle English, an ancestor of the English spoken today. In choosing to write in English, the vernacular, Chaucer was taking a bold step. French was still the language of the English court, and most serious literature of Chaucer's time was written in either French or Latin. But Chaucer, like Dante, decided to use the everyday language of his countrymen rather than the language of the elite. He thus lent respectability to the English language.

OBJECTIVES

1. To recognize Geoffrey Chaucer's contribution to the development of literature in English and to appreciate the variety and unity in his collection of tales
2. To differentiate between a dynamic and a static character
3. To conduct interviews and provide a summary of results
4. To discover the Middle English precedents of Modern English words

THEMES IN WORLD LITERATURE

The Wisdom of the World
African Proverbs, pp. 84–87
"Hundred Questions" from the *Mahabharata*, pp. 460–466

The Quest and the Perilous Journey
"The Grail" from *Perceval*, pp. 720–729
From *Don Quixote*, pp. 821–837 ■

VOCABULARY IN CONTEXT
The words listed below will appear in the side margin at the point of instruction:

1. purged
2. petitioning
3. statutes
4. concede
5. extort
6. subtly
7. sovereignty
8. disperses
9. temporal
10. lineage

Reader's Guide

THE WIFE OF BATH'S TALE
from The Canterbury Tales

Background

"The Wife of Bath's Tale" is part of a section of *The Canterbury Tales* frequently called the "marriage group." Responding to each other's stories, a number of the pilgrims tell tales about marriages, both good and bad. Through their stories, they conduct a kind of debate about what roles men and women should (and do) play in marriage. The Wife of Bath, who has already outlived five husbands and may have joined the pilgrimage to look for a sixth, has strong opinions on this subject.

In the prologue to her tale, the Wife of Bath (Bath is a city in southwestern England) delivers a very candid autobiography. The unmarried life may be fine for other people, she contends, but not for her. She goes on to assert that marriage is happiest when the wife holds sway over the husband—at least in private. She offers as proof the story of her five marriages, and particularly the fifth, to a younger man named Johnny. Johnny made her miserable until they had a fight in which she pretended he had killed her. After that, he submitted to her, and the couple never quarreled again but lived happily as equals.

Having told the pilgrims her own life story, the Wife of Bath then proceeds to tell them the following tale, which supports her own conclusions about relationships between men and women.

Oral Response

The knight in "The Wife of Bath's Tale" must find the answer to the question "What is the thing that women most desire?" What do you think is the answer to this question? Discuss your ideas with your classmates.

Literary Focus

Some characters in fiction are **dynamic characters**—people who undergo real changes in the course of a story. The decisions these characters make, the things that they say, or simply their inner thoughts reflect these inner changes. **Static characters**, on the other hand, remain unchanged from the beginning of a story to the end. Most works of fiction contain characters of both kinds, but the central characters in lengthier works tend to be dynamic.

PREREADING FOCUS

Background: The group of marriage tales is the most cohesive series of tales within the larger collection. They appear one after the other in the narrative, interspersed with repartee among the pilgrims and references to one another's tales. "The Wife of Bath's Prologue and Tale," in which she argues for the sovereignty of women, begins the series. The Friar and the Summoner break in, argue, and then tell unflattering stories about each other. The Clerk then tells a tale about patient Griselda; the Merchant relates a story about an old man who is deceived by a young wife. The Squire tells a tale of romantic love, and the series ends with the Franklin's Tale, which stresses truth and loyalty in marriage.

"The Wife of Bath's Tale" draws on other medieval folk tales about old hags who are transformed into young women. In Chaucer's time no thought was given to "stealing" someone else's story because of the long tradition of oral storytelling.

Oral Response: Remind students that the "thing" that women most desire is not necessarily something tangible.

1 LITERARY ELEMENT

Allusion: The Wife of Bath begins by alluding to King Arthur, whom most of Chaucer's audience would know of from French or Latin literature or from storytellers. Why might the Wife of Bath begin her story with a reference to King Arthur? (Possible response: to alert her audience that her tale will be about a knight and the courtly tradition)

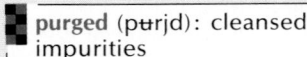
purged (pʉrjd): cleansed of impurities

2 LITERARY ELEMENT

Irony: Verbal irony occurs when a character says the opposite of what is meant. What verbal irony occurs in lines 22–26? (Although the narrator says that women are apparently safe now that there are no supernatural entities to threaten them, she implies that they still have the very real menace of human clerics.)

THE WIFE OF BATH'S TALE
from The Canterbury Tales
Geoffrey Chaucer
t r a n s l a t e d b y
NEVILL COGHILL

> *When you reach line 44 of "The Wife of Bath's Tale," make a prediction about what will happen to the knight. What fate do you think he deserves?*

1
When good King Arthur ruled in ancient days
(A king that every Briton loves to praise)
This was a land brim-full of fairy folk.
The Elf-Queen and her courtiers joined and broke
5 Their elfin dance on many a green mead,
Or so was the opinion once, I read,
Hundreds of years ago, in days of yore.
But no one now sees fairies any more.
For now the saintly charity and prayer
10 Of holy friars seem to have <u>purged</u> the air;
They search the countryside through field and stream
As thick as motes that speckle a sunbeam,
Blessing the halls, the chambers, kitchens, bowers,
Cities and boroughs, castles, courts and towers,
15 Thorpes,° barns and stables, outhouses and dairies,
And that's the reason why there are no fairies.
Wherever there was wont to walk an elf
Today there walks the holy friar himself
As evening falls or when the daylight springs,
20 Saying his matins° and his holy things,
Walking his limit round from town to town.

2
Women can now go safely up and down
By every bush or under every tree;
There is no other incubus° but he,
25 So there is really no one else to hurt you
And he will do no more than take your virtue.

Poverty, carrying a sack of wheat to the mill, arrives at a dangerous bridge; from a French manuscript, c. 1455–1460.

15. **Thorpes:** villages; hamlets.

20. **matins** (mat''nz): morning prayers.

24. **incubus** (in'kyōo·bəs): an evil spirit or demon that people believed descended on a sleeping woman and made her pregnant.

Now it so happened, I began to say,
Long, long ago in good King Arthur's day,
There was a knight who was a lusty liver.°
30 One day as he came riding from the river
He saw a maiden walking all forlorn
Ahead of him, alone as she was born.
And of that maiden, spite of all she said,
By very force he took her maidenhead.°
35   This act of violence made such a stir,
So much petitioning to the king for her,
That he condemned the knight to lose his head
By course of law. He was as good as dead
(It seems that then the statutes took that view)
40 But that the queen, and other ladies too,
Implored the king to exercise his grace
So ceaselessly, he gave the queen the case
And granted her his life, and she could choose
Whether to show him mercy or refuse.
45   The queen returned him thanks with all her
            might,
And then she sent a summons to the knight
At her convenience, and expressed her will:
"You stand, for such is the position still,
In no way certain of your life," said she,
50 "Yet you shall live if you can answer me:
What is the thing that women most desire?
Beware the axe and say as I require,
    "If you can't answer on the moment, though,
I will concede you this: you are to go
55 A twelvemonth and a day to seek and learn
Sufficient answer, then you shall return.
I shall take gages° from you to extort
Surrender of your body to the court."
    Sad was the knight and sorrowfully sighed,
60 But there! All other choices were denied,
And in the end he chose to go away
And to return after a year and day
Armed with such answer as there might be sent
To him by God. He took his leave and went.
65   He knocked at every house, searched every
            place,
Yes, anywhere that offered hope of grace.
What could it be that women wanted most?

29. **liver:** In medieval times, the liver, and not the heart, was believed to be the source of desires and emotions.

34. **maidenhead:** virginity.

The Knight, detail from the Ellesmere manuscript.

The Huntington Library, San Marino, California

57. **gages:** things pledged to ensure that an obligation will be fulfilled.

Geoffrey Chaucer   775

7 READER'S RESPONSE

Can you think of other answers to the knight's question not given here? Can you think of a more interesting question about male-female relationships? (Answers will vary.)

8 GUIDED READING

Finding the Main Idea: What criticism of women is the Wife of Bath making here? (She suggests they are hypocritical, wishing to do what they please but always to appear virtuous.) Do you agree with this criticism? (Answers will vary.)

MEETING INDIVIDUAL NEEDS

9 ESL: Be sure students understand that "not worth the handle of a rake" in line 95 means "not worth much of anything." ■

10 ANALYZING

For what purpose might the Wife of Bath have interrupted her own tale with that of King Midas? (to illustrate her point that women cannot keep secrets) What might Chaucer's purpose be in including the digression? (Possible responses: to present a more complete picture of the personality of the Wife of Bath; to build an awareness that digressions are typical of the Wife's narrative style.)

subtly (sut'lē): in a delicately skillful manner

But all the same he never touched a coast,
Country or town in which there seemed to be
70 Any two people willing to agree.
　　Some said that women wanted wealth and treasure,
"Honor," said some, some "Jollity and pleasure,"
Some "Gorgeous clothes" and others "Fun in bed,"
"To be oft widowed and remarried," said
75 Others again, and some that what most mattered
Was that we should be cossetted° and flattered.
That's very near the truth, it seems to me;
A man can win us best with flattery.
To dance attendance on us, make a fuss,
80 Ensnares us all, the best and worst of us.
　　Some say the things we most desire are these:
Freedom to do exactly as we please,
With no one to reprove our faults and lies,
Rather to have one call us good and wise.
85 Truly there's not a woman in ten score°
Who has a fault, and someone rubs the sore,
But she will kick if what he says is true;
You try it out and you will find so too.
However vicious we may be within
90 We like to be thought wise and void of sin.
Others assert we women find it sweet
When we are thought dependable, discreet
And secret, firm of purpose and controlled,
Never betraying things that we are told.
95 But that's not worth the handle of a rake;
Women conceal a thing? For Heaven's sake!
Remember Midas?° Will you hear the tale?
　　Among some other little things, now stale,
Ovid° relates that under his long hair
100 The unhappy Midas grew a splendid pair
Of ass's ears; as subtly as he might,
He kept his foul deformity from sight;
Save for his wife, there was not one that knew.
He loved her best, and trusted in her too.
105 He begged her not to tell a living creature
That he possessed so horrible a feature.
And she—she swore, were all the world to win,
She would not do such villainy and sin
As saddle her husband with so foul a name;

76. **cossetted** (käs'it·id): pampered; fondled.

85. **score:** twenty; "ten score" is two hundred.

97. **Midas** (mī'dəs): a mythical king who was given the power to turn everything he touched into gold.

99. **Ovid** (äv'id): the Roman poet (43 B.C.–C. A.D. 17); Ovid's *Metamorphoses*, a compilation of mythical tales, includes one version of the story of King Midas.

110 Besides to speak would be to share the shame.
Nevertheless she thought she would have died
Keeping this secret bottled up inside;
It seemed to swell her heart and she, no doubt,
Thought it was on the point of bursting out.

115 Fearing to speak of it to woman or man,
Down to a reedy marsh she quickly ran
And reached the sedge. Her heart was all on fire
And, as a bittern° bumbles in the mire,
She whispered to the water, near the ground,

120 "Betray me not, O water, with thy sound!
To thee alone I tell it: it appears
My husband has a pair of ass's ears!
Ah! My heart's well again, the secret's out!
I could no longer keep it, not a doubt."

125 And so you see, although we may hold fast
A little while, it must come out at last,
We can't keep secrets; as for Midas, well,
Read Ovid for his story;° he will tell.

This knight that I am telling you about

130 Perceived at last he never would find out
What it could be that women loved the best.
Faint was the soul within his sorrowful breast,
As home he went, he dared no longer stay;
His year was up and now it was the day.

135 As he rode home in a dejected mood
Suddenly, at the margin of a wood,
He saw a dance upon the leafy floor
Of four and twenty ladies, nay, and more.
Eagerly he approached, in hope to learn

140 Some words of wisdom ere he should return;
But lo! Before he came to where they were,
Dancers and dance all vanished into air!
There wasn't a living creature to be seen
Save one old woman crouched upon the green.

145 A fouler-looking creature I suppose
Could scarcely be imagined. She arose
And said, "Sir knight, there's no way on from
here.
Tell me what you are looking for, my dear,
For peradventure that were best for you;

150 We old, old women know a thing or two."
"Dear Mother," said the knight, "alack the day!

118. **bittern** (bit'ərn): a kind of wading bird.

128. **Ovid for his story:** In the original story of King Midas, it is Midas's barber, not his wife, who tells the secret of the ears to a hole in the ground. Reeds grow up in the hole and whisper the story whenever they are rustled by a breeze.

HUMANITIES CONNECTION

The handcrafted Kelmscott *Chaucer* is the crowning achievement of the Kelmscott Press, begun in 1891 by William Morris (1834–1896). Taking medieval calligraphy as his model, Morris created a new type font and designed elaborate borders for the pages. The Pre-Raphaelite painter Edward Burne-Jones drew nearly ninety illustrations, which were transferred to woodcuts and imprinted on the handmade paper with special dyes. The book took five years to complete. ■

MEETING INDIVIDUAL NEEDS

15 *LEP:* Students may need help in understanding that "pay your hire" in line 154 means that the knight promises to repay the woman for her help. ■

16 GUIDED READING

Paraphrasing: Ask students to state in their own words the agreement between the knight and the old crone. (Possible response: She will tell him the answer to the riddle, if he will swear to do whatever she says next.)

17 EVALUATING

Why is the word *crooned* in line 167 a better choice than the word *spoke*? (Possible responses: *Crooned* implies a certain intimacy as in the phrase "crooning a love song"; the use of *crooned* foreshadows what is to come.)

Pages from the *Kelmscott Chaucer*, a nineteenth-century masterpiece of bookmaking created by British artist and designer William Morris.

I am as good as dead if I can't say
What thing it is that women most desire;
If you could tell me I would pay your hire."

15

155 "Give me your hand," she said, "and swear to do
Whatever I shall next require of you
16 —If so to do should lie within your might—
And you shall know the answer before night."
"Upon my honor," he answered, "I agree."
160 "Then," said the crone, "I dare to guarantee
Your life is safe; I shall make good my claim.
Upon my life the queen will say the same.
Show me the very proudest of them all
In costly coverchief or jeweled caul°
165 That dare say no to what I have to teach.
Let us go forward without further speech."
17 And then she crooned her gospel in his ear
And told him to be glad and not to fear.
      They came to court. This knight, in full array,
170 Stood forth and said, "O Queen, I've kept my day
And kept my word and have my answer ready."
      There sat the noble matrons and the heady
Young girls, and widows too, that have the grace
Of wisdom, all assembled in that place,
175 And there the queen herself was throned to hear
And judge his answer. Then the knight drew near
And silence was commanded through the hall.

164. **coverchief or jeweled caul** (kôl): articles of headgear for women; the coverchief covered the head entirely. The caul was a small, netted cap, sometimes ornamented.

The queen gave order he should tell them all
What thing it was that women wanted most.
180 He stood not silent like a beast or post,
But gave his answer with the ringing word
Of a man's voice and the assembly heard:
    "My liege and lady, in general," said he,
"A woman wants the self-same sovereignty
185 Over her husband as over her lover,
And master him; he must not be above her.
That is your greatest wish, whether you kill
Or spare me; please yourself. I wait your will."
    In all the court not one that shook her head
190 Or contradicted what the knight had said;
Maid, wife, and widow cried, "He's saved his life!"
    And on the word up started the old wife,
The one the knight saw sitting on the green,
And cried, "Your mercy, sovereign lady queen!
195 Before the court disperses, do me right!
Twas I who taught this answer to the knight,
For which he swore, and pledged his honor to it,
That the first thing I asked of him he'd do it,
So far as it should lie within his might.
200 Before this court I ask you then, sir knight,
To keep your word and take me for your wife;
For well you know that I have saved your life.
If this be false, deny it on your sword!"
    "Alas," he said, "Old Lady, by the Lord
205 I know indeed that such was my behest,
But for God's love think of a new request,
Take all my goods, but leave my body free."
"A curse on us," she said, "If I agree!
I may be foul, I may be poor and old,
210 Yet will not choose to be, for all the gold
That's bedded in the earth or lies above,
Less than your wife, nay, than your very love!"
    "My love?" said he. "By heaven, my damnation!
Alas that any of my race and station
215 Should ever make so foul a misalliance!"
Yet in the end his pleading and defiance
All went for nothing, he was forced to wed.
He takes his ancient wife and goes to bed.
    Now peradventure some may well suspect
220 A lack of care in me since I neglect

The Wife of Bath, detail from the Ellesmere manuscript.

The Huntington Library, San Marino, California

■ sovereignty (säv'rən·tē): supreme authority

disperses (di·spʉr'səz): breaks up

HUMANITIES CONNECTION

In the Prologue the narrator describes the Wife of Bath as someone who is vain about her appearance. In addition, he states that she seems somewhat deaf.

❓ *What might the narrator be implying by that remark?* (Possible response: She likes to talk but does not like to listen.) ■

CULTURAL DIVERSITY

Medieval Christians commonly made pilgrimages to churches or shrines to seek favor with God. Construction of Canterbury Cathedral began in the eleventh century and continued over the next 400 years. Although Becket's splendid shrine is no longer there, grooves in its stone steps testify to the countless pilgrims who knelt before it.

❓ *In what other cultures do people make journeys for spiritual purposes similar to the medieval pilgrimages?* (Possible response: Followers of Islam make pilgrimages to Mecca.)

18 INFERRING

What are some of the objections the knight has to marrying the old woman? (She is ugly, old, poor, and not of noble birth.) On what basis does she insist they marry? (He swore to do whatever she asked if she saved his life.)

19 Advanced Students:
Some students may be interested in finding out more about the knights of King Arthur's court. Suggest they read *Sir Gawain and the Green Knight* (written by an unknown author at about the same time as *The Canterbury Tales*) and compare Sir Gawain's behavior with that of Chaucer's knight. ∎

20 READER'S RESPONSE
What do you think of the knight's reaction to the old woman? (Possible responses: The knight's feelings of revulsion are understandable; the knight is a shallow person, since he places too much value on appearance.)

21 CULTURAL BACKGROUND
The Christian Church in medieval times preached the teachings of Christ as found in the New Testament. The New Testament idea of love or gentleness was meant to supersede the Old Testament maxim of "an eye for an eye, a tooth for a tooth." The chivalric code of the medieval knights, however, was a curious mixture of the Christian ideal of protecting the weak and a love of fighting, adventure, and summary justice.

To tell of the rejoicings and display
Made at the feast upon their wedding-day.
I have but a short answer to let fall;
I say there was no joy or feast at all,
225 Nothing but heaviness of heart and sorrow.
He married her in private on the morrow
And all day long stayed hidden like an owl,
It was such torture that his wife looked foul.
      Great was the anguish churning in his head
230 When he and she were piloted to bed;
He wallowed back and forth in desperate style.
His ancient wife lay smiling all the while;
At last she said "Bless us! Is this, my dear,
How knights and wives get on together here?
19 235 Are these the laws of good King Arthur's house?
Are knights of his all so contemptuous?
I am your own beloved and your wife,
And I am she, indeed, that saved your life;
And certainly I never did you wrong.
240 Then why, this first of nights, so sad a song?
You're carrying on as if you were half-witted
Say, for God's love, what sin have I committed?
I'll put things right if you will tell me how."
      "Put right?" he cried. "That never can be now!
20 245 Nothing can ever be put right again!
You're old, and so abominably plain,
So poor to start with, so low-bred to follow;
It's little wonder if I twist and wallow!
God, that my heart would burst within my breast!"
250 "Is that," she said, "the cause of your unrest?"
"Yes, certainly," he said, "and can you wonder?"
"I could set right what you suppose a blunder,
That's if I cared to, in a day or two,
If I were shown more courtesy by you.
255 Just now," she said, "you spoke of gentle birth,
Such as descends from ancient wealth and worth.
If that's the claim you make for gentlemen
Such arrogance is hardly worth a hen.
Whoever loves to work for virtuous ends,
260 Public and private, and who most intends
To do what deeds of gentleness he can,
Take him to be the greatest gentleman.
21 Christ wills we take our gentleness from Him,

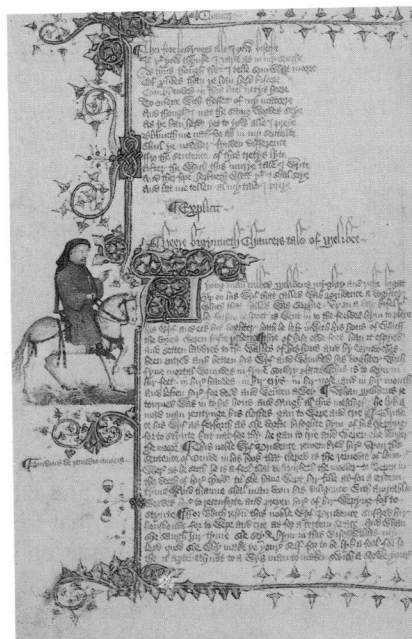

A page from the Ellesmere manuscript of Chaucer's *Canterbury Tales*.

Henry E. Huntington Library, San Marino, CA

Not from a wealth of ancestry long dim,
265 Though they bequeath their whole establishment
By which we claim to be of high descent.
Our fathers cannot make us a bequest
Of all those virtues that became them best
And earned for them the name of gentlemen,
270 But bade us follow them as best we can.
      "Thus the wise poet of the Florentines,
Dante by name, has written in these lines,
For such is the opinion Dante launches:
'Seldom arises by these slender branches
275 Prowess of men, for it is God, no less,
Wills us to claim of Him our gentleness.'
For of our parents nothing can we claim
Save temporal things, and these may hurt and
      maim.
      "But everyone knows this as well as I;
280 For if gentility were implanted by
The natural course of lineage down the line,
Public or private, could it cease to shine
In doing the fair work of gentle deed?
No vice or villainy could then bear seed.
285 "Take fire and carry it to the darkest house
Between this kingdom and the Caucasus,°
And shut the doors on it and leave it there,
It will burn on, and it will burn as fair
As if ten thousand men were there to see,
290 For fire will keep its nature and degree,
I can assure you, sir, until it dies.
      "But gentleness, as you will recognize,
Is not annexed in nature to possessions.
Men fail in living up to their professions;°
295 But fire never ceases to be fire.
God knows you'll often find, if you enquire,
Some lording full of villainy and shame.
If you would be esteemed for the mere name
Of having been by birth a gentleman
300 And stemming from some virtuous, noble clan,
And do not live yourself by gentle deed
Or take your father's noble code and creed,
You are no gentleman, though duke or earl.
Vice and bad manners are what make a churl.°
305   "Gentility is only the renown

286. **Caucasus** (kô′kə·səs): a mountain range between the Black Sea and the Caspian Sea; Chaucer uses the name simply to suggest somewhere far away.

294. **professions:** declarations of beliefs.

304. **churl** (churl): a rude, boorish person.

22 GUIDED READING
Finding the Main Idea: What point does the Wife of Bath emphasize by alluding to Dante? (Gentleness—in the sense of virtuous conduct—cannot be inherited or assumed because of one's possessions and social rank. Gentleness is bestowed by God on all those who will nurture it.)

23 HISTORICAL BACKGROUND
By the fourteenth century, feudalism had broken down in England. No longer was society made up of only three classes—the lords, the clergy, and the peasants. Some peasants had moved away from the manors and had become involved in occupations in the growing towns. The lords had to pay cash for services. Clearly, the Wife of Bath belonged to the emerging middle class. In lines 298–304, she expresses the view of her class that noble birth has little to do with the intrinsic worth of a person.

Geoffrey Chaucer   **781**

24 READER'S RESPONSE

Do you agree with the Wife of Bath's views about poverty in lines 337–348? (Answers will vary.) In the Middle Ages, many Christians embraced poverty as an outward expression of their inner piety.

For bounty that your fathers handed down,
Quite foreign to your person, not your own;
Gentility must come from God alone.
That we are gentle comes to us by grace
310 And by no means is it bequeathed with place.
　　"Reflect how noble (says Valerius°)
Was Tullius surnamed Hostilius,°
Who rose from poverty to nobleness.
And read Boethius, Seneca° no less,
315 Thus they express themselves and are agreed:
'Gentle is he that does a gentle deed.'
And therefore, my dear husband, I conclude
That even if my ancestors were rude,
Yet God on high—and so I hope He will—
320 Can grant me grace to live in virtue still,
A gentlewoman only when beginning
To live in virtue and to shrink from sinning.
　　"As for my poverty which you reprove,
Almighty God Himself in whom we move,
325 Believe and have our being, chose a life
Of poverty, and every man or wife
Nay, every child can see our Heavenly King
Would never stoop to choose a shameful thing.
No shame in poverty if the heart is gay,
330 As Seneca and all the learned say.
He who accepts his poverty unhurt
I'd say is rich although he lacked a shirt.
But truly poor are they who whine and fret
And covet what they cannot hope to get.
335 And he that, having nothing, covets not,
Is rich, though you may think he is a sot.°
　　"True poverty can find a song to sing.
Juvenal° says a pleasant little thing:
'The poor can dance and sing in the relief
340 Of having nothing that will tempt a thief.'
Though it be hateful, poverty is good,
A great incentive to a livelihood,
And a great help to our capacity
For wisdom, if accepted patiently.
345 Poverty is, though wanting in estate,
A kind of wealth that none calumniate.°
Poverty often, when the heart is lowly,
Brings one to God and teaches what is holy,

311. **Valerius** (və·lir′ē·əs): a first-century Roman writer who compiled anecdotes for the use of orators.

312. **Tullius** (tul′ē·əs) **surnamed Hostilius** (hos·til′ē·əs): a legendary king of Rome who was said to have risen from humble rustic origins to become ruler of his nation.

314. **Boethius** (bō·ē′thē·əs): a philosopher (c. 480–525); in his *Consolation of Philosophy,* Boethius argues that rank is no guarantee of honorable conduct from those whom society elevates. **Seneca** (sen′i·kə): a first-century philosopher and dramatist whose works were popular in the Middle Ages; Seneca was born in Spain and educated in Rome.

336. **sot:** fool.

338. **Juvenal** (jōō′və·n′l): a Roman satirist who wrote between A.D. 98 and 128.

346. **calumniate** (kə·lum′nē·āt′): make false statements about.

24

Gives knowledge of oneself and even lends
350 A glass by which to see one's truest friends.
And since it's no offense, let me be plain;
Do not rebuke my poverty again.

    "Lastly you taxed me, sir, with being old.
Yet even if you never had been told
355 By ancient books, you gentlemen engage
Yourselves in honor to respect old age.
To call an old man 'father' shows good breeding,
And this could be supported from my reading.
    "You say I'm old and fouler than a fen.°
360 You need not fear to be a cuckold,° then.
Filth and old age, I'm sure you will agree,
Are powerful wardens over chastity.
Nevertheless, well knowing your delights,
I shall fulfill your worldly appetites.
365   "You have two choices; which one will you try?
To have me old and ugly till I die,
But still a loyal, true, and humble wife
That never will displease you all her life,
Or would you rather I were young and pretty
370 And chance your arm what happens in a city
Where friends will visit you because of me,
Yes, and in other places too, maybe.
Which would you have? The choice is all your
        own."
        The knight thought long, and with a piteous
            groan
375 At last he said, with all the care in life,
"My lady and my love, my dearest wife,
I leave the matter to your wise decision.
You make the choice yourself, for the provision
Of what may be agreeable and rich
380 In honor to us both, I don't care which;
Whatever pleases you suffices me."

    "And have I won the mastery?" said she,
"Since I'm to choose and rule as I think fit?"
"Certainly, wife," he answered her, "that's it."
385 "Kiss me," she cried. "No quarrels! On my oath
And word of honor, you shall find me both,
That is, both fair and faithful as a wife;
May I go howling mad and take my life
Unless I prove to be as good and true

359. **fen:** a swamp.

360. **cuckold** (kuk'əld): a man whose
wife has committed adultery.

NOVEMBER, detail from the *Book of Hours* of Jean, Duc de Berry, French illuminated manuscript.

25 INFERRING

In line 353, the old woman states that the knight complained that she was old. Why might the Wife of Bath want to argue against such an objection? (Possible responses: She was probably quite old herself, yet her fifth husband was quite young.)

26 CULTURAL DIVERSITY

The choice the old woman offers the knight in lines 365–373 resembles similar choices in popular medieval folk tales involving a hag and a young man. In some versions, the knight must choose between the woman being beautiful by day and ugly by night, or ugly by day and beautiful by night. What values does Chaucer's old woman introduce into the equation in addition to physical attractiveness? (loyalty, peace of mind, devoted service)

27 LITERARY ELEMENT

Characterization: Compare the knight's words in lines 376–381 with his earlier views in lines 213–215 and 245–249. Is the knight a static or a dynamic character? Explain. (dynamic. He has changed from a shallow, arrogant man to a humbler, more mature man.)

1. What role does the queen play in the tale? (She sets the tale in motion by sending the knight out to answer her question.)

2. Why does the knight have difficulty finding the answer to the question? (Everyone he asks has a different answer.)

3. When does the knight meet the woman who gives him the answer? (the day before he is to be executed)

4. After the knight answers the question correctly at court, what does the old woman demand in return? (The knight must marry her.)

5. What choice does the woman give the knight after they are wed? (He can have her ugly but loyal, or beautiful but unfaithful.)

RETEACHING

Have students imagine that they are one of the pilgrims on the road to Canterbury. Today they met the Wife of Bath for the first time and listened to her tale. Night has fallen, and the pilgrims are writing their impressions of the day in their journals. Invite students to write a journal entry recording their impressions of the Wife of Bath, her beliefs, and her tale.

COMPARING LITERATURE

The Wife of Bath's narrative is an *exemplum*, a type of story that was very popular in the Middle Ages. An exemplum is a tale with a moral; its plot may come out of history or legend. In the case of the Wife of Bath, she gives her views on marriage in her Prologue and then illustrates them by means of her tale, the exemplum. Preachers in medieval times often made their points in the same way: the moral would be stated in the sermon and then would be illustrated by means of a tale or anecdote—the exemplum.

❓ *Can you think of other types of literature whose purpose is teaching a moral or lesson?* (fables, parables, Taoist or Zen anecdotes)

28 LITERARY ELEMENT

Irony: Why are lines 407–410 ironical? (The Wife appeals to Jesus, a proponent of forgiveness, "to cut short the lives" of husbands who won't be governed by their wives.) What is the effect of the irony? (humor)

390   As ever wife was since the world was new!
      And if tomorrow when the sun's above
      I seem less fair than any ladylove,
      Than any queen or empress east or west,
      Do with my life and death as you think best.
395   Cast up the curtain, husband. Look at me!"
          And when indeed the knight had looked to see,
      Lo, she was young and lovely, rich in charms.
      In ecstasy he caught her in his arms,
      His heart went bathing in a bath of blisses
400   And melted in a hundred thousand kisses,
      And she responded in the fullest measure
      With all that could delight or give him pleasure.
          So they lived ever after to the end
      In perfect bliss; and may Christ Jesus send
405   Us husbands meek and young and fresh in bed,
      And grace to overbid them when we wed.
      And—Jesu hear my prayer!—cut short the lives
      Of those who won't be governed by their wives;
      And all old, angry niggards of their pence,
410   God send them soon a very pestilence!

Pilgrims to Canterbury; detail of an English
illuminated manuscript, c. 1400.

The Granger Collection, New York

1. Interviewing the Wife of Bath. Suggest that interested students work in pairs to stage a mock talk-show interview with the Wife of Bath. Encourage the host to ask questions that deal with issues of male-female relations in the context of contemporary society. The Wife of Bath should remain in character when answering questions.

2. Writing an Analysis of the Narrator. Point out to students that in telling stories, narrators often reveal a great deal about their own characters. Suggest that students write a three-paragraph analysis of the Wife of Bath's character. Ask them what they can infer about her, based on the story she chooses to tell, the words she uses, and the details she includes. Remind students to give examples to support their generalizations.

Have students reread lines 376–381 on page 783 and discuss how these six lines summarize the theme of "The Wife of Bath's Tale." ▪

First Thoughts

Do you agree that married men should be "governed by their wives"? Why or why not?

Identifying Facts

1. Why does the knight need to find out what women most desire?
2. Where does the knight find the answer to the question? What is the answer he finds?
3. What objection does the knight make to the old woman as a wife? How does she respond?
4. How is the conflict between the knight and his wife resolved?

Interpreting Meanings

1. Reread lines 1–8 in the opening of the tale and lines 135–144 in the section just before the knight meets the old lady. Who do you think the lady *really* is?
2. Do you consider the knight and the lady to be **dynamic** or **static characters**? Explain your answer.
3. A **moral** is a lesson about life that a story teaches. What moral does the Wife of Bath want us to draw from her tale? How does she make this moral clear?
4. What examples of humor do you find in "The Wife of Bath's Tale"? What is the effect of the humor in this story?

Applying Meanings

Based on what you know about her views on marriage, do you believe the Wife of Bath would be happy in contemporary American society? Why or why not?

Speaking and Listening

Interviewing to Find an Answer. Interview at least ten classmates to find the answer to *this* question: "What is the thing that *men* most desire?" Be sure to explain that your question relates to what men want in marriage. Try to interview an equal number of males and females. Keep a record of the answers you get. Then write a one- or two-paragraph summary of what people say. Conclude by giving your own response.

Language and Vocabulary

Comparing Middle English and Modern English. Read the lines below from Chaucer's original Middle English version of *The Canterbury Tales*. (These lines are translated in lines 180–191 on page 779.) Then read the words in the list that follows. Write the Middle English words that were the ancestors of these modern English words. You may find it useful to read the lines aloud. Let context help you figure out which Middle English words preceded our modern English words.

This knyght ne stood nat stille, as dooth a best,
But to his questioun anon answerde,
With manly voys, that al the court it herde.
  "My lige lady, generally," quod he,
"Wommen desiren to have sovereyntee
As wel over hir housband as hir love
And for to been in maistrie hym above.
This is youre mooste desir, thogh ye me kille.
Dooth as yow list. I am here at youre wille."
  In al the court ne was ther wyf, ne mayde,
Ne wydwe that contraried that he sayde;
But seyden he was worthy han his lyf.

1. beast	6. widow
2. desire	7. you
3. husband	8. wife
4. most	9. voice
5. said	10. life

First Thoughts
Answers will vary.

Identifying Facts
1. If he doesn't, he will die.
2. from an old woman in the woods. Women want sovereignty over their husbands.
3. She is poor, old, ugly, and lowly. Virtue and goodness do not depend on noble birth.
4. He lets her decide whether she will be ugly and faithful or beautiful and unfaithful.

Interpreting Meanings
1. Elf-Queen
2. The knight is dynamic because he changes from a violator of women to a good husband. The old woman is static in terms of her character, but her appearance changes.
3. Marriage is happiest when the husband gives his wife sovereignty. She rewards the knight.
4. Possible response: the Wife's comments about friars. It makes it entertaining.

Applying Meanings
Answers will vary.

Speaking and Listening
Interviewing to Find an Answer. Students might like to interview people of different generations.

Language and Vocabulary
1. best	6. wydwe
2. desiren, desir	7. ye, yow
3. housband	8. wyf
4. mooste	9. voys
5. sayde, seyden	10. lyf ▪

Geoffrey Chaucer   **785**

1 CULTURAL BACKGROUND

Tropes: The short plays that were presented during church services were called tropes. They were not part of the liturgical service but were dramatic additions to it. The earliest tropes were created for two important religious celebrations—Easter and Christmas. The first Easter trope, for example, dramatized the announcement of the resurrection. As two or more Marys entered the tomb of Jesus to anoint his body, one or more angels greeted them and told them that "He has risen."

2 LITERARY BACKGROUND

Although medieval drama is divided into three types of plays, the distinction between mystery and miracle plays began to be made only in the eighteenth century. Originally the word *miracle* was used to refer to any medieval play. Students might enjoy reading one play of each type and comparing the differences for themselves.

DRAMA IN THE MIDDLE AGES

Shortly before Christmas of 1991, television viewers could have seen an American production of a medieval Spanish miracle play, *La Pastorela* (known in English as "The Shepherd's Play"). Visitors to Salzburg, Austria, are treated to an annual performance of *Everyman*, a morality play popular in Europe in the 1500s. These dramas belong to a centuries-old tradition, yet performances of these and other medieval plays are still well-attended by modern audiences.

The Roots of Medieval Drama

Medieval drama in France, England, and Germany, and to some extent in Italy and the Netherlands, developed from Catholic church services. Starting around the tenth century, priests and other clergy would act out short plays based on stories from the Bible, as well as stories about the lives of the saints.   1

As they grew in popularity, these religious plays caused some problems within the Church: church buildings became uncomfortably crowded as members of the congregation fought each other for space, and the audience's loud and sometimes rowdy approval of the plays shocked the clergy and disrupted church services. In 1210, upon the orders of the Pope, the plays moved out of the churches and into the streets and marketplaces.

The medieval religious plays were typically performed on carts or wagons called "pageants." In small towns, several separate stands arranged in a circle would be set up in the town square or another public place. The audience would watch the scene performed at one stand, and then move on to the next. In larger towns, whose public squares were too small to hold everyone who wanted to see the shows, the plays were moved around the town in a procession, from one public square to another. Often there were several levels to the makeshift stage. For instance, a rickety platform or balcony might indicate heaven. From a lower level or a trapdoor representing Hell, devils would dramatically spring out and dash into the frightened audience. Even in medieval times, producers knew the value of special effects.

Mysteries, Miracles, and Morality

Three kinds of religious plays were popular in the Middle Ages. The **miracle plays**, which dramatized the lives of the saints and the Virgin Mary, were performed on saints' days, while the **mystery plays**, whose subject was the mystery of Christ's redemption   2

Engraving by David Jee of one stage in a mystery play. In towns too large to hold many people in a single square, the stages were moved in a pageant throughout the town.

New York Public Library Picture Collection

of sinners, were performed on the same days as church festivals. Popular miracle plays in France included the stories of St. Nicholas and the Virgin Mary. In England, long cycles of mystery plays, usually beginning with the Creation, were produced.

Morality plays were a third popular form of medieval drama. *Everyman* is the most famous of the morality plays, which dealt with themes of right and wrong and the struggle between good and evil for man's soul. Other morality plays were produced in France, the Netherlands, and occasionally in Germany. The characters in morality plays are allegorical, abstract personifications such as Truth, Mercy, Good Deeds, and Everyman. These characters dramatized the content of

the religious sermons that were so familiar to medieval audiences.

Medieval Humor

Although religion was a serious affair to the people of the Middle Ages, it was rarely taken *too* seriously in medieval drama. In a play about the Flood, for example, Noah's shrill and stubborn wife refuses to board the ark, and is finally carried aboard, kicking and screaming. In a play about the birth of Jesus, the theft of a sheep leads to a rowdy, comic scene. Even the Devil is often portrayed as a comic character in the miracle plays.

In England, different guilds—that is, unions of tradesmen or artisans—took over from the Church the task of staging and performing the miracle and mystery plays. Each guild was assigned a play based on the expertise of its craftsmen. For example, the water carrier's guild usually performed the story of Noah and the Flood. In Europe, on the other hand, the plays were usually performed by troupes of trained actors.

The miracle, mystery, and morality plays of the Middle Ages continued to be popular in Europe until the Reformation, when Catholic church leaders began to clamp down on non-official interpretations of biblical events. Meanwhile, the great playwrights of the Renaissance—among them Italy's Ariosto, Spain's Lope de Vega, and England's Shakespeare—ushered in a new age of drama.

HUMANITIES CONNECTION

This engraving shows the stage of a mystery play and the area in front of the stage where some of the action took place. The stage was built up to enable the audience to see, and to facilitate the comings and goings of the actors.

❓ *What other unusual feature do you notice about the stage?* (Possible response: The stage appears to be open on all sides, allowing everyone in the audience to see.) ■

3 CULTURAL DIVERSITY

Everyman, the most famous of the morality plays, focuses on a subject that every person must face—death. The play was usually acted out on church steps to lend it moral authority; but wherever it was performed, an open sepulcher was nearby. In the beginning of the play, Everyman believes that he has many friends, including Beauty, Discretion, and Strength. He discovers during the course of his journey to Death, however, that only one friend—Good Deeds—remains with him to the end. Thus the audience learns that the road to salvation is paved with good deeds.

❓ *How, if at all, do contemporary writers teach moral lessons?* (Possible response: They teach lessons subtly by depicting the consequences of the behavior of ordinary people.)

Concrete Nouns and Verbs:
You might point out that concrete words refer to things that we can experience through the five senses: seeing, hearing, smelling, tasting, or touching/feeling. Have students think of examples of concrete nouns and verbs. (Prompt, if necessary, with verbs like *gallop*, *flutter*, and *sizzle*, and nouns like *motorcycle*, *slush*, and *cinnamon*). Write students' words on the chalkboard and ask which sense we associate with each word.

ANSWERS TO EXERCISE 1: CHOOSING CONCRETE NOUNS AND VERBS

1. row; fire and ice
2. Perceval; baits his hook
3. reddens; flowers
4. knight; begs for advice from
5. sound his horn; Charlemagne and his troops
6. carves his name; the trunk of a hazel tree

TEACHING TIP

Exact Nouns and Verbs: In general, the more exact a noun or verb, the greater its effectiveness in a sentence. For example, *fruit*, *apple*, and *pippin* are all concrete nouns, but *pippin* is most specific or exact and therefore most likely to add strength to a sentence. Challenge students to think of even more exact nouns and verbs to replace each of the following: *berry, sports car, computer, shoe* (nouns); *stand, speak, drink, build* (verbs).

Language Skills

CHOOSING EFFECTIVE DICTION

You can probably think of a string of adjectives to describe a medieval hero. But experienced writers know that too many modifiers weaken a sentence. In strong writing, nouns and verbs do most of the work. Two guidelines will help you choose nouns and verbs that invigorate your writing.

Concrete Nouns and Verbs

First, keep nouns and verbs as concrete as possible. **Concrete** nouns and verbs name physical things and show physical actions. **Abstract** nouns and verbs name intangible things and refer to intangible actions.

ABSTRACT

         N   V   N
The *hero observed* the *situation*.

CONCRETE

         N   V   N
Roland's *gaze swept* the *battlefield*.

To write the first sentence above is to create a gap; readers grope to connect the words with their meanings. To write the second is to create action and substance; readers can see Roland's eyes scanning the battlefield.

When you discuss abstractions, you may need abstract nouns or verbs. But concrete nouns and verbs can also express abstract meanings.

Exercise 1: Choosing Concrete Nouns and Verbs

Choose the more concrete words from each set in parentheses.

1. At the shore, Charon waits to (row/convey) Dante into a realm of (extremes/fire and ice).
2. (The youth/Perceval) watches as the Fisher King (baits his hook/proceeds with his task).
3. Blood (reddens/discolors) even the (vegetation/flowers) in the field where Siegfried dies.
4. The Wife of Bath tells of a (character/knight) who (gets involved with/begs for advice from) a hag.
5. Because he waits too long to (call/sound his horn) for (Charlemagne and his troops/help), Roland is killed.
6. Tristan (leaves a sign/carves his name) in (the trunk of a hazel tree/a secret place).

Exact Nouns and Verbs

Second, to avoid overusing modifiers, choose exact nouns and verbs. **Exact** nouns and verbs specify meaning. Vague nouns and verbs do not.

VAGUE

Thor's defiant *words* to the giant *were* loud and angry.

EXACT

Thor *thundered* his *challenge* to the giant.

Notice how replacing *were* with *thundered* wakes up the sentence. *Were*, along with the other forms of "to be," is among the least exact verbs in English. Notice, too, that choosing a more exact verb eliminates two modifiers; *thundered* implies loudness and anger. Similarly, choosing the more exact noun, *challenge,* eliminates the need for the adjective *defiant.* Study the lists of vague verbs and nouns.

Vague Verbs **Vague Nouns**

make	do	thing	situation
have	get	factor	aspect
move	be	type	phase
go	come	kind	area

Vague verbs and nouns are general; strong ones are specific. Sometimes, of course, you need the general words listed above. But in most cases, try to replace general words with specific ones.

VAGUE

Siegfried *goes* from *doing* a dangerous *thing* to *being* in a *situation* that *is* even worse.

EXACT

Siegfried courts danger when he lays aside his sword and shield; he risks even more when he bends to drink at the brook.

The italicized words empty the first sentence of meaning. Try to avoid all forms of vague verbs; *doing* and *being* do not act as verbs here, but they still dilute meaning. In the second sentence, exact nouns and verbs clarify meaning.

Exercise 2: Using Effective Diction

Review a piece of your own writing, underlining each noun and verb. Draw an arrow from each modifier to the noun or verb it modifies. Then follow these steps:

1. Circle all abstract nouns and verbs. Wherever possible, replace them with more concrete ones.
2. Circle all nouns and verbs listed above as weak. Wherever possible, replace them with more exact ones. Reword sentences as necessary.
3. Examine each modifier. Now that your nouns and verbs are more concrete and exact, delete unnecessary modifiers.

TEACHING TIP

Paring Unnecessary Words: Vague nouns and verbs attract other vague, unnecessary words, creating wordy sentences. Paring such sentences down to their essential core strengthens them. Elicit suggestions for eliminating the vague words from the following sentences.
1. If there is one thing the Wife of Bath loves, it is a good story. (The Wife of Bath loves a good story.)
2. Pride is a major factor that makes Roland do the type of thing that ultimately costs him his life. (Pride costs Roland his life.)
3. Loki's strength is in the area of getting creative ideas. (Loki's stength lies in creative thinking. *Or* Loki thinks creatively.)

ANSWERS TO EXERCISE 2: USING EFFECTIVE DICTION

In each sentence, nouns and verbs should be underlined. The more abstract and general nouns and verbs should also be circled, and sentences in which they occur should be reworded with more concrete, exact terms.

Peer Revision: After students finish Exercise 2, you might allow them to form small groups, exchange revised papers, comment on the strengths of the revisions, and offer suggestions for further revisions.

Background: Advise students that humor and even melodrama may have a place in this assignment. Medieval authors, from Snorri Sturluson to Geoffrey Chaucer, used both.

To help students choose characters to write about, begin by asking for a list of all the characters students remember from the unit. Then have each student choose a favorite. Tell students to imagine their characters sitting next to them in class. Suggest they spend a few minutes writing imaginary dialogues with their characters. A dialogue might include questions the student and character ask each other about subjects ranging from clothing and hairstyles to personal experiences.

Afterward, students might want to share their work. The dialogues should help students clarify their basic impressions of their characters; they can also provide ideas about the characters' responses to students' daily lives.

Prewriting: After students have reread the selections for details about their characters, remind them that the freewritings should not be mere knowledge inventories. Rather, they should include students' insights and intuitions, as well as factual details, about their characters.

Critical Thinking and Writing

WRITING A CHARACTER SKETCH

How would a medieval character fare in modern America? What might Roland, Thor, or the Wife of Bath make of a visit to a mall? In this unit, you have met memorable characters from another time. Now you can use observation and reasoning to bring them into your own world.

Writing Assignment

Write a description of a character from this unit, speculating about how the character might react in a modern setting. Assume that classmates are your audience. In this assignment, you will identify observations on which to base a reliable prediction.

Background

Choose a vivid character and scan the work in which the character appears, noting details about the character. Vivid characterization is often indirect. Look for the following means of indirect characterization:

▪ **Dialogue.** A character's speech patterns and word choices reveal background and motivations.

▪ **Actions.** A character's actions demonstrate likes and dislikes, strengths and weaknesses.

▪ **Other Characters.** The responses and comments of those who associate with a character shed light on his or her looks and personality.

▪ **Setting.** A character's surroundings illustrate his or her tastes and place in society.

▪ **Changes.** Changes in personality indicate the character's depth and potential.

Prewriting

Focused Questioning. To generate descriptive details, freewrite answers to these questions.

1. How does the character look and sound? How does he or she act?

2. What are the character's inner qualities? How would you feel around him or her? What are his or her strengths and weaknesses?

3. How have events or people in the character's life shaped him or her?

4. Which parts of your daily life would you most like to show to the character?

Read over your freewriting and list three or four of your character's most prominent traits. Then sum up the essence of your character in a single sentence. This dominant impression can guide your writing as a thesis would.

FOR FURTHER HELP

Refer students to *Grammar, Usage, and Mechanics: A Reference Guide* at the back of their textbooks for detailed information that will help them write, revise, and proofread their essays.

Observing and Predicting. Reliable predictions are based on careful observation. Formulate predictions about your character by using a chart like the one below. List prominent character traits. Cite observations—examples from the work that illustrate each trait. Then predict how each trait would cause the character to respond to the things that make up your daily life.

Traits	
Observations	
Predictions	

Writing

Use these guidelines as you draft your essay.

1. **Introductory Paragraph.** Set your character sketch in the present. Begin with an image of your character in action, in a setting from your daily life. You may choose a dramatic action that illustrates a prominent trait, or you may choose a subtle action that reveals general personality. Consulting your prewriting notes, state the relationship between this action and your dominant impression.

2. **Body Paragraphs.** Focus on two or more of your character's main traits, devoting a paragraph to each. Let your character's further reactions to the modern world reveal these traits. Experiment with dialogue and other indirect methods of characterization. Your prewriting

notes can provide specifics. Arrange your paragraphs in spatial order or time order.

3. **Concluding Paragraph.** You might conclude by summarizing the ways your character changes in the modern world. Or you might speculate about how the modern world will be changed by your character. In either case, tie your description once more to the dominant impression.

Evaluating and Revising

Use the following questions to revise your draft.

1. Does the introduction show the character in action? Does it state the dominant impression?

2. Is the character sketch set in the present? Does it use specific sensory details to show, rather than tell, what the character is like?

3. Do you tell enough about the character's past actions to justify your ideas of his or her reactions to a modern setting?

4. Does your conclusion leave readers with one clear impression?

5. Are your sentences varied and grammatically correct?

Proofreading and Publishing

Proofread your character sketch to eliminate errors in mechanics, and make a final copy. Work with classmates to dramatize your sketch. Act it out for your class or other classes.

Writing: As students draft, they might want to consider not only their characters' responses to a modern setting, but also how modern people would respond to the medieval characters. Point out that the interplay between a character and a new environment can create the kind of tension or humor that makes writing interesting and effective.

Evaluating and Revising: Before they evaluate their work, students might want to go back to the selection to ensure that the reactions they have created for their characters are in line with the characters' personalities. Then, as they revise, refer students to the *Language Skills* feature entitled "Choosing Effective Diction," pp. 788–789, to increase the impact of their descriptive and narrative passages.

Proofreading and Publishing: Students could work cooperatively, in groups of four or five, to dramatize the sketches they find most entertaining. Remind them that in a dramatized sketch, the setting, action, and dialogue must express indirectly the ideas that the narrator's voice states more directly in the prose piece. ■

The following annotations are for the artwork surrounding the map, starting in the upper right-hand corner and moving in a counterclockwise direction.

Shakespeare: This famous engraving by Martin Droeshout was printed in the first collected edition of Shakespeare's plays. Published after his death in 1623, the First Folio was edited by Shakespeare's friends John Heminge and Henry Condell. Because no manuscripts of Shakespeare's plays survive, the First Folio is the most important source for many of the plays.

Florence—Center of the Arts: This painting comes from a fifteenth-century *cassone* (a decorated wedding chest) painted in Florence by Francesco di Antonio. The elegance of the clothing reflects the affluence of the family who bought the chest. Florence's fame as a cultural center stemmed in part from its prominence as a center of commerce and banking. The gold florin, coined in Florence, became known all over Europe.

Printing Press: This artwork is based on a drawing made in 1511 by the German artist Albrecht Dürer. It shows a man at work in one of the printshops of Anton Koberger. In 1470, Koberger established the first printshop in Nuremberg.

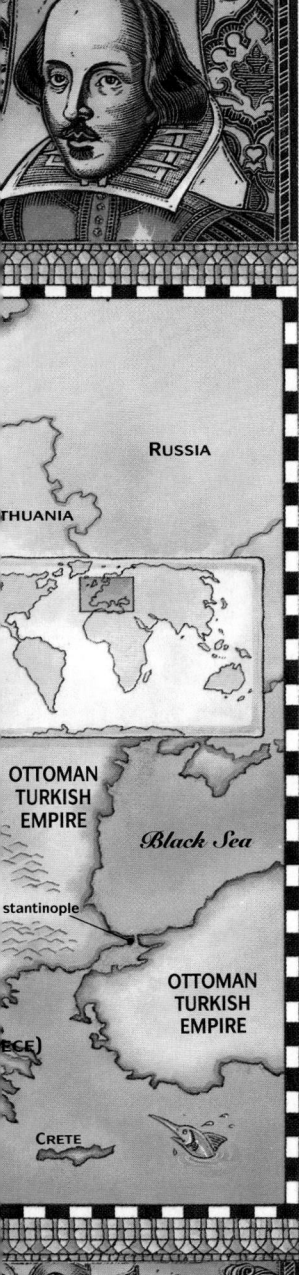

FROM THE RENAISSANCE TO THE ENLIGHTENMENT

▼ **Time** ▼
1300–1800

▼ **Place** ▼
Europe

▼ **Literary Significance** ▼

The Renaissance (1300–1650): The literature of the Renaissance reflected a renewed interest in human, rather than religious, affairs as well as a "rediscovery" of the Western classical tradition. During the Renaissance, new literary forms, among them the sonnet and short prose fiction, were created to give expression to timeless themes for an ever-growing audience.

The Enlightenment (1650–1800): The Enlightenment was an age that celebrated human reason and scorned human folly and excess. Literature of the time, mostly poetry, drama, and essays, was valued for its formal qualities: a regular meter, polished images, and verbal wit. Writers like Voltaire and La Fontaine turned to satire to comment on the hypocrisy and immorality of the overindulged upper classes of this period.

Renaissance Lady: This richly dressed lady appears in "The Nativity of the Virgin," a fresco painted by the Florentine artist Dominico Ghirlandaio (1449–1494). The fresco suggests that wealth and beauty, as well as piety, were prized by the Florentines.

Copernicus: Nicholas Copernicus was the Polish astronomer who revolutionized the medieval view of the universe by putting the sun, rather than the earth, at the center. The portrait that this illustration is based on appears in *The Life of N. Copernicus* (1654) by Pierre Gassendi.

Theater of the Enlightenment: These elegant ladies and gentlemen are lounging in an English theater during an intermission. The medieval theater served the purposes of the Church. By the eighteenth century, however, the theater had become a worldly art form intended primarily for the amusement of aristocratic and middle-class audiences. The etching, dated 1786, is by the English artist Thomas Rowlandson, who turned a keen satirical eye on the contemporary scene.

Spanish Armada: This detail is from *An Engagement Between the English Fleet and the Spanish Armada.* The heavily armed armada was sent by Philip II of Spain to reclaim Protestant England for the Roman Catholic faith. The faster, more agile English ships destroyed the Spanish fleet in 1588. The victory marked the emergence of England as a major naval power. ■

DISCUSSING THE TIME LINE

This Time Line spans 500 years, from 1300 to 1800. From the events listed, have students identify the major European countries of the Renaissance. (Italy, France, Germany, England, Spain) Ask: In which country and at what time did the Renaissance begin? (Italy, fourteenth century) When did the English Renaissance begin? (sixteenth century) Elicit from students the many different ways in which creativity was expressed—in invention (the printing press), in science (the work of Copernicus, Galileo, Newton), in exploration (Columbus, da Gama), in art (Leonardo), and in philosophy, music, architecture, government, and literature. An indication of the creative genius of the time is the fact that Shakespeare and Cervantes, each considered by many to be the greatest writer of his country, were contemporaries.

Students should notice when the Enlightenment began and what events signaled its start. (about 1675; advances in science and the world-power status of England, France, and Spain) Ask students to identify a new country that is named on the Time Line and the events for which it is cited. (the United States; writing of the Constitution) How might the flowering of the arts and sciences have helped to spark America's independence? (Possible responses: Artists expressed their individuality; science and the arts inspired questioning of authority and expression of bold new ideas.)

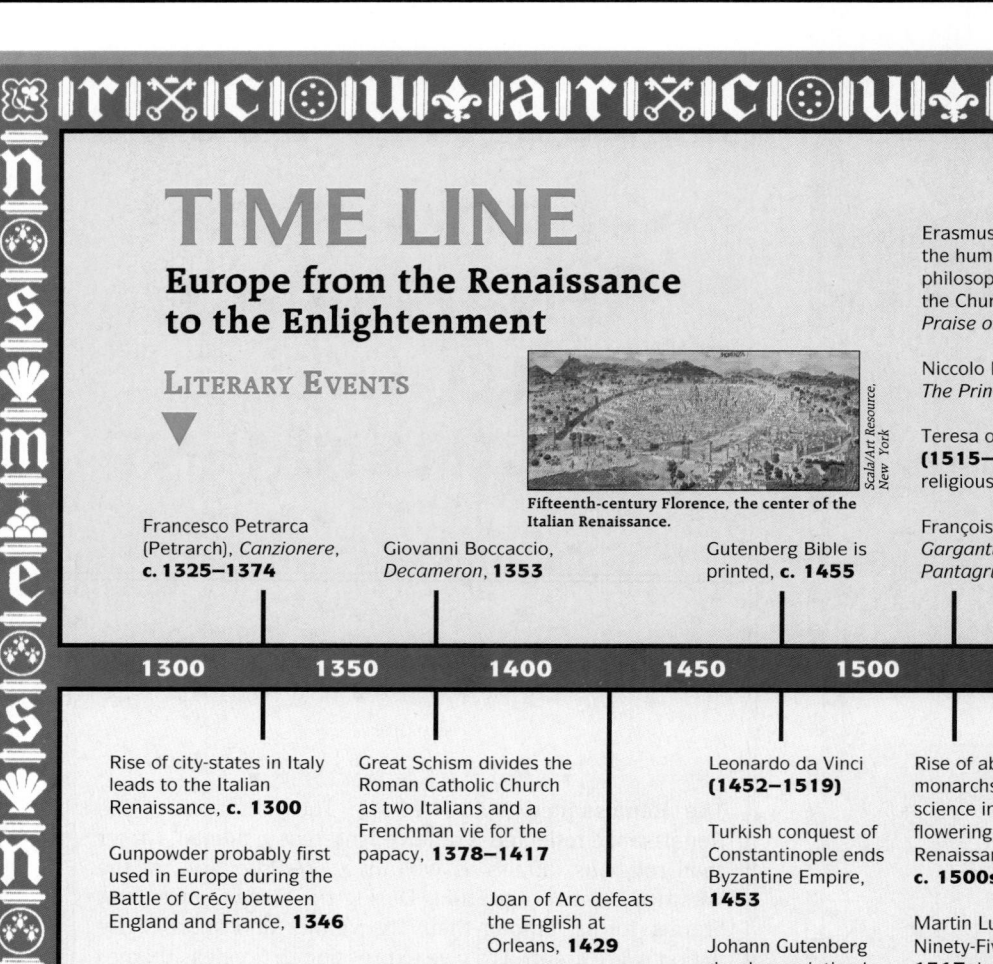

TIME LINE
Europe from the Renaissance to the Enlightenment

LITERARY EVENTS
▼

Fifteenth-century Florence, the center of the Italian Renaissance.

Scala/Art Resource, New York

Francesco Petrarca (Petrarch), *Canzionere*, **c. 1325–1374**

Giovanni Boccaccio, *Decameron*, **1353**

Gutenberg Bible is printed, **c. 1455**

Erasmus, leader of the humanist school of philosophy, satirizes the Church in *In Praise of Folly*, **1509**

Niccolo Machiavelli, *The Prince*, **1513**

Teresa of Avila, **(1515–1582)**, religious poet

François Rabelais, *Gargantua and Pantagruel*, **1532**

| 1300 | 1350 | 1400 | 1450 | 1500 |

Rise of city-states in Italy leads to the Italian Renaissance, **c. 1300**

Gunpowder probably first used in Europe during the Battle of Crécy between England and France, **1346**

Great Schism divides the Roman Catholic Church as two Italians and a Frenchman vie for the papacy, **1378–1417**

Joan of Arc defeats the English at Orleans, **1429**

Leonardo da Vinci **(1452–1519)**

Turkish conquest of Constantinople ends Byzantine Empire, **1453**

Johann Gutenberg develops printing by movable type, **c. 1454**

Columbus reaches the Americas, **1492**

Vasco da Gama rounds the Cape of Good Hope, **1497**

Rise of absolute monarchs and modern science in Europe; flowering of English Renaissance, **c. 1500s–1600s**

Martin Luther posts Ninety-Five Theses, **1517**; beginning of Protestant Reformation

Henry VIII breaks with Rome and becomes head of the Church of England, **1534**

Nicholas Copernicus demonstrates that the earth revolves around the sun, **1543**

▲
CULTURAL AND HISTORICAL EVENTS

MONA LISA. LEONARDO DA VINCI, 1503–1506.

Scala/Art Resource, New York

World map. c. 1545.

The Granger Collection, New York

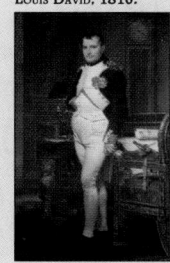

Portrait of Napoleon Bonaparte. JACQUES LOUIS DAVID, 1810.

National Gallery of Art, Washington D.C., Samuel H. Kress Collection

rre de Ronsard, *nnets pour Hélène*, 78

chel de Montaigne, *ays*, 1580–1588

mund Spenser, *The erie Queene*, 1590

Miguel de Cervantes, *Don Quixote*, 1605, 1615

Ben Jonson, *Volpone*, c. 1605

William Shakespeare, *The Tempest*, 1611

Blaise Pascal, *Pensées (Thoughts)*, 1662

Theaters reopen in England; Restoration comedies become popular, 1660

John Milton, *Paradise Lost*, 1665

Molière, *The Misanthrope*, 1666

Jean de la Fontaine, *Fables*, 1668–1694

The novel becomes popular in England, 1700s

Jonathan Swift, *Gulliver's Travels*, 1726

Alexander Pope, *An Essay on Man*, 1733

Samuel Richardson, *Clarissa*, 1747–1748

Voltaire, *Candide*, 1759

Richard Sheridan, *The Rivals* (1775)

1550	1600	1650	1700	1750	1800

gland defeats the anish Armada, gnaling England's sing power, 1588

Age of Absolute Monarchs; baroque style in visual arts, architecture, and music, c. 1600–1750

Thirty Years' War between German Catholics and Protestants, 1618–1648

Italian physicist Galileo is tried by the Inquisition for supporting Copernicus's view of the universe, 1633

René Descartes, *Discourse on Method* (1637), founds Cartesian school of rational philosophy

English Civil wars, 1642–1649

Age of Enlightenment; science makes rapid advances; England, France, and Spain become world powers, c. 1650–1800

Sir Isaac Newton describes the universe as a machine governed by absolute laws in *The Mathematical Principle of Natural Philosophy* (1687)

Restoration in England, 1660–1688

David Hume shapes modern metaphysics in *A Treatise of Human Nature*, 1739–1740

Neoclassicism in the arts and architecture, c. 1750–1850

Jean Jacques Rousseau influences late eighteenth-century political developments with *The Social Contract*, 1762

American Revolution, 1775–1783

U. S. Constitution is written, 1787; Bill of Rights is added, 1791

French Revolution, 1789–1799

Napoleon comes to power, 1799

ait of the French arch Louis XIV. NTHE RIGAUD, 1701.

This border is composed of family insignia. During the Renaissance, these insignia appeared on flags, coats of arms, and badges and played an important role in marriages and other public festivities.

Time Line 795

795

HISTORICAL BACKGROUND

Gunpowder Use in Europe: In ninth-century China gunpowder was used for fireworks. Its use in Europe in guns and cannons revolutionized warfare; no fort or castle could stand up to continual pounding by cannon balls.

HUMANITIES CONNECTION

The *Mona Lisa* is a portrait of the wife of a Florentine banker. Her serene mood and enigmatic smile have made Leonardo da Vinci's masterpiece one of the most famous portraits of all time. ∎

HISTORICAL BACKGROUND

Thirty Years' War: Fought over political as well as religious differences, the Thirty Years' War devastated central Europe. More than twenty-five percent of the population of Germany died; entire cities, villages, and farms were destroyed; and the arts, academia, industry, and trade slumped.

LITERARY BACKGROUND

Reopening of the Theaters in England: When the Puritans assumed power in 1642, they closed all the public theaters. When the monarchy was restored in 1660, the theater was reopened and different styles of production were introduced. Women appeared on the English stage for the first time, and new theaters were enclosed (as opposed to open-air) with proscenium stages.

OBJECTIVES

1. To gain an overview of major works of literature in Renaissance Europe and their authors
2. To recognize the spirit of the Renaissance and the Reformation
3. To analyze the elements of the Italian or Petrarchan sonnet and its variations in English
4. To interpret and respond to Renaissance literature both orally and in writing

TEACHER'S RESOURCES: 9
- Unit Introduction Test
- Word Analogies
- Unit Review Test
- Critical Thinking and Writing

1 RESPONDING TO THE QUOTATION

The bubonic plague, or "Black Death," began in 1347 in Constantinople, then spread to Europe. The bacterium that caused the disease originated in infected rats and was transmitted to humans by fleas. Highly contagious, the disease could be spread from one person to another by coughing or even talking. Today this disease can be cured with antibiotics, but then there was no treatment for it. Millions of people died of the disease. The last major outbreak of the plague occurred in London in 1664–1665.

❓ *According to the quotation, how did the plague influence European history?* (It weakened feudal society, setting the stage for the Renaissance.)

2 HISTORICAL BACKGROUND

Constantinople, once the capital of the Eastern Roman Empire, had a long tradition of culture and scholarship. When it fell to the Turks in 1453, many of its scholars fled westward to Italy, bringing ancient Greek and Latin manuscripts with them. This flood of previously unknown material stimulated new interest in classical culture. *Can you think of another example of an outburst of creativity fostered by the meeting of two cultures?* (Possible responses: the Sumerians' encounter with the native culture of Mesopotamia, the Romans' assimilation of Greek culture)

RENAISSANCE LITERATURE

> 1
>
> ❝ The entire structure of feudal society, which had been under stress for many years, was undermined by the plague. The upheaval . . . set the stage for the new world of Renaissance Europe and the Reformation. ❞
>
> —Charles L. Mee

The word *renaissance* means "rebirth." Historians use it to describe a period of change and growth, from roughly 1300–1650, during which Europeans began to discover anew the riches of the Greek and Roman classics. During this time, which marks the beginning of the modern world in Europe, people began to be stirred by the imagination, to thirst for knowledge, and to explore the scope of human potential as never before.

The Renaissance Begins in Italy

The Crusades had introduced new products into the economy of eleventh- and twelfth-century Europe. The rapidly increasing demand for exotic Eastern spices, cloth, and wood created new wealth for traders and merchants. Commercial centers prospered, especially the Italian city-states which were trade links to the Near East and Africa. Wealthy Italian merchant families used the riches they earned from trade to support the exploration of human thought and imagination. They became patrons of the arts, financing the work of writers, musicians, philosophers, and other artists and thinkers.

The Italian poet **Francesco Petrarch** (1304–1374), who was perhaps the first person to use the term "Renaissance" to describe the time in which he lived, was a key figure in the Italian Renaissance. Petrarch's deep interest in human individuality led him to become known as the first **humanist**. He and his contemporary, **Giovanni Boccaccio** (1313–1375), were among the first writers to use the **vernacular**, that is, the language spoken by the people (in this case, Italian), rather than the traditional language of literature, Latin. Boccaccio is best known for the **Decameron**, a collection of stories that shows his lively interest in men and

TEACHING RENAISSANCE LITERATURE

The variety of the literature in this unit reflects the vigor and inventiveness of the European Renaissance. In lyric poems, Petrarch, Ronsard, and Shakespeare used the sonnet form and rich figurative language. Writing in the Italian vernacular, Boccaccio created an entertaining tale about love and sacrifice. In *Don Quixote*, Cervantes humorously satirized the popular romances of his day. In *The Tempest*, Shakespeare combined sprightly fantasy with profound meditations on love, loyalty, and the imagination.

Point out to students that despite their status as classics, these works were originally written to entertain. These "classics" once served some of the same purposes as today's sitcoms and action films.

Two works in particular will appeal to students' love of adventure. In *Don Quixote*, the hero, with his short, fat squire Sancho Panza, sets out on a knightly quest to find maidens to rescue and monsters to kill. *The Tempest* begins with a tumultuous storm at sea and a shipwreck on an exotic island ruled by a master magician. Yet as fanciful as these plots and characters may be, Shakespeare and Cervantes also reflect the values of their own place and time. In *The Tempest*, Miranda extols a "brave new World," mirroring the optimistic outlook of the Renaissance. In addition, we can see in Prospero's magical

women as unique individuals. The stories are told by people trying to escape the outbreak of bubonic plague that struck Europe in the late 1340s, killing one third of Europe's population and undermining the stability of feudalism.

An Emphasis on the Individual

The humanists' interest in *human* values distinguishes them from medieval philosophers, whose thought was fundamentally centered around God and questions of religion. Humanists believed that people as individuals were the most important subject of study. Their intense curiosity led to the revival of the study of classical Greek and Roman art, literature, history, and philosophy. In doing so, the humanists broke away from the narrow emphasis on Christian theology that characterized medieval learning.

> Unlike medieval thinkers, who took a God-centered view of the universe, the humanists adopted a human-centered view.

The works of Renaissance artists clearly expressed the humanist belief that humankind is the measure of all things. In the 1300s, the Italian painter **Giotto** (jŏt'tō) developed a new style of painting that emphasized natural-looking forms instead of flat, stylized figures. The paintings and sculptures of **Michelangelo** demonstrate a fascination with the shape, substance, and power of the human body.

Perhaps the most imaginative and gifted humanist was **Leonardo da Vinci** (1452–1519), who embodied the qualities of the ultimate "Renaissance person"—someone with skills and interests in many areas. Almost everyone knows his famous paintings *Mona Lisa* and *The Last Supper*. In addition to being a great artist, however, Leonardo was also an inventor, an architect, a musician, and a scientist, with interests in meteorology and geology. He studied the moon's effect on the tides, theorized about the formation of fossils, initiated the science of hydraulics, and studied human anatomy. He also believed that humans were capable of flight and designed several flying devices.

> 66 The Renaissance's primary concern with the world of here and now stimulated experimentation rather than logic, observation rather than inherited precepts. 99
> —Renaissance Culture
> *Julian Mates and Eugene Cantelupe*

3

Scala/Art Resource, New York

Detail of a fifteenth-century map of Florence. *Florence was the seat of the Italian Renaissance.*

3 RESPONDING TO THE QUOTATION

One result of this shift of focus to the empirical was a renewed interest in science. Observation and experimentation, the bases of science, imply an openness to what the senses reveal. The medieval approach to truth was quite different, emphasizing an acceptance of divine revelation as interpreted by the Church.

❓ *How might the shift in focus from inherited precepts to experimentation and observation foster a "rebirth" of culture?* (Possible response: by valuing the individual's knowledge, insight, and creativity)

HUMANITIES CONNECTION

In the northern Italian city-state of Florence, the arts flourished during the Renaissance. The writers Dante and Boccaccio, the sculptor Donatello, and the painters Leonardo and Raphael all lived or worked in Florence at some point in their careers. Lorenzo de Medici (1449–1492), the greatest of the city's rulers, was a patron of the arts. Botticelli and Michaelangelo both worked under his patronage.

❓ *In what ways would an environment such as Renaissance Florence encourage artistic expression?* (Possible response: Support by a patron would free artists to devote time and energy to art and assure them that their work is valued; a community of artists would stimulate each other's creativity.) ∎

kingdom the embodiment of the Renaissance ideals of reason, order, and imagination. Cervantes' sympathetic portrayal of Don Quixote's misguided but well-intentioned idealism reflects the Renaissance belief in human striving and the perfectibility of man. Both Shakespeare and Cervantes also mirror their times by portraying a panoply of characters from all levels of society. In *Don Quixote*, Sancho Panza, a lowly man of the people, is a foil for Don Quixote, a minor aristocrat. In *The Tempest*, Shakespeare includes all ranks of society, from kings to servants, all of whose characteristics and concerns are realistically, and sometimes humorously, presented.

The sonnets and "The Tale of the Falcon," on the other hand, were not written to depict a large cast of characters but to celebrate the theme of romantic love. Petrarch, Ronsard, and Shakespeare wrote their sonnets out of the same strong personal attachments that students may experience in their own lives.

The best way to approach these classics is through oral performance. As students hear the sonnets read aloud, they will come to appreciate the subtle influence of the rhythm and rhyme and the broader effects of tone. As Boccaccio's frame device suggests, "The Tale of the Falcon" is a story meant to be told aloud. You may

HUMANITIES CONNECTION

An ornithopter is a heavier-than-air vehicle that is meant to fly by moving its wings like a bird. Although Leonardo da Vinci created many designs for such machines, he never built one that worked, nor has anyone else since his time. Leonardo did, however, design objects like submarines and parachutes that were to become commonplace in the modern world. Interested students may wish to research Leonardo's designs for mechanical devices; some were precursors of modern machines. ■

4 RESPONDING TO THE QUOTATION

Machiavelli based *The Prince* on the political career of Cesare Borgia (1476–1507), a powerful military prince. Borgia betrayed and murdered many enemies while consolidating his political position. The advice offered in the quotation is typical of Borgia's calculating behavior.

❓ *Would Machiavelli be a good advisor for a ruler?* (Possible response: While the advice might be effective, it would probably lead to a totalitarian regime in which the ruler would be feared and despised.)

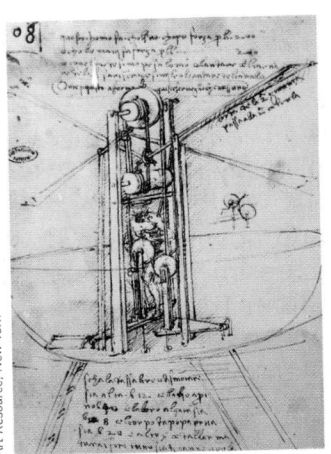

Art Resource, New York

MAN IN ORNITHOPTER, **LEONARDO DA VINCI.**

4

> 66 In taking a state the conqueror must arrange to commit all his cruelties at once, so as not to have to recur to them every day, and so as to be able to reassure people and win them over by benefiting them. Whoever acts otherwise . . . is always obliged to stand with knife in hand, and can never depend on his subjects . . . 99
>
> —The Prince, *Machiavelli*

A New Spirit of Inquiry

Leonardo da Vinci's meticulous habits of observation—all carefully recorded in his "mirror writings," notebooks which read backwards unless held to a mirror—were fundamental to his work. This method of inquiry was different from the medieval method of relying on outside authorities, especially those authorities approved by the Church. As scientists developed their skills of observation, they also questioned accepted authorities. **Nicolaus Copernicus** (1473–1543), a Polish astronomer who taught in Italy, challenged Ptolemy's second-century idea that the sun revolved around the earth. Copernicus argued that the earth rotated on an axis and revolved around the sun. His ideas frightened many religious people because they contradicted the Church's teaching that the earth was the hub of the universe and that humans

> ### The new science challenged traditional authority by insisting on the power of observation.

were the focus of God's attention. A century later, the Italian astronomer **Galileo** (1564–1642) used the newly-invented telescope to scan the skies. In 1630, Galileo wrote a book defending Copernicus's theory that the earth moved around the sun. The Church's Inquisitors—officials who examined supposed heretics—forced him to recant. But legend has it that as Galileo rose from his knees after his recantation, he whispered "But it does move!"

Like his counterparts in the sciences, one Italian statesman, **Niccolo Machiavelli** (1469–1527), embraced the new humanist spirit of inquiry and observation and turned it toward the political landscape of the Italian city-states. In *The Prince*, Machiavelli gave unusual advice. Whereas most writers advised rulers to be kind and generous, Machiavelli advised them to be calculating and coldblooded. He had observed the way power was actually gained and lost. Because he saw that conflict among the various city-states kept Italy in chaos, he argued that the state needed a powerful central authority to keep order. Machiavelli's name has come to be associated with the philosophy of **pragmatism**: the idea that the ends justify the means.

wish to point out that *Don Quixote* also was written more for the ear than the eye. Literacy was far from universal in Cervantes' time; it is likely that many people were able to appreciate this famous novel only by hearing sections of it read aloud.

In order to help students overcome the difficulties of Elizabethan English in *The Tempest*, allow them to read along while listening to an audiotape. The professional actors' interpretations will condition students to pause where punctuation occurs rather than at the end of lines, making it easier to grasp the gist of the characters' speeches. Once students have become accustomed to the sound of Shakespeare's verse, you can try improvisations of dramatic situations, prepared readings of selected scenes, and actual student performances.

A complementary teaching approach is to accent the theme of music in the play.

Many of Ariel's songs can be sung by students. You also might play some Renaissance madrigals, and then encourage students who play the flute or violin to improvise a musical accompaniment to a scene. If at all possible, make arrangements for students to attend a production of *The Tempest* after they have studied it.

Later events proved Machiavelli right in his argument for a strong central government. In 1527, Rome was sacked by a mercenary army led by the Duke of Bourbon. This event signaled the end of the Italian Renaissance. The further expansion of the Renaissance imagination occurred in northern Europe and England.

Voyages to New Worlds

The Turkish conquest of Constantinople in 1453 temporarily blocked the overland route to the East. The need for new trade routes led to great voyages of discovery and exploration. In 1492, the Italian explorer **Christopher Columbus**

Girandon/Art Resource, New York

Portrait of Nicolaus Copernicus, the father of modern astronomy.

The Bridgeman Art Library/Art Resource, New York

QUEEN ISABELLA AND COLUMBUS, HENRY NELSON O'NEIL (1817–1880).
? *What historical event precipitated the Age of Exploration?*

HUMANITIES CONNECTION

Nicolaus Copernicus, famous for replacing the idea of an earth-centered solar system with a sun-centered system, was a "Renaissance person." A physician who studied astronomy, he also held a degree in church law and was a good mathematician.
? *What aspect of the medieval world view was threatened by Copernicus's theory?* (that the earth and humanity held a central place in the divine scheme) ∎

TEACHING TIP

"The Age of Exploration" is a metaphor for the spirit of the Renaissance. Mariners explored the limits of the globe, Galileo explored the heavens, and Leonardo probed the secrets of nature. The medieval community lived in an enclosed, secure world; the Renaissance mentality pushed out into a wider, unknown world. Invite students to create a pair of emblems that illustrate the medieval and the Renaissance world views.

HUMANITIES CONNECTION

Christopher Columbus was not the only mariner of his time who dreamed of sailing west to reach the ports of India, China, and Japan, but he was the first to launch a full-scale expedition, backed by Queen Isabella of Spain.
? *What attitude does Columbus show toward Queen Isabella?* (Possible response: reverence, submission, gratitude) ∎

Introduction

The influence of the Renaissance on our world is so pervasive that it is hard to appreciate it fully. Lead students to understand that modern Western values in science, art, religion, psychology, exploration, and statecraft have their roots in Renaissance attitudes. Some of these attitudes are so basic that Westerners have no one word to sum them up. For example, most Western societies place great importance on achieving tangible goals and gaining the material means to live a happy life. This value is a legacy of Renaissance humanism.

It is a paradox that the Renaissance, which marks the start of modern history, began with a renewed appreciation of ancient Greek civilization. The Renaissance revived Greek ideals, recast them in new molds, and transmitted them to subsequent generations, ultimately shaping the modern Western consciousness. As an example of the impact of the Renaissance on modern times, you may wish to discuss the origins of opera with your students. This art form was invented in sixteenth-century Italy by classical humanists who thought they were re-creating the ancient Greek theater. In imitation of the Greeks, the creators of early opera used a chorus, music, and dance as part of their dramatic productions. In Florence in 1594, Jacopo Peri wrote the music for *Dafne*, a forerun-

5 RESPONDING TO THE QUOTATION

The quotation suggests Columbus's attitude toward the Native American people he found in the New World.

? *How would you characterize that attitude?* (Possible response: By taking these people by force to serve as translators, Columbus showed that he considered them inferior and uncivilized. Though they were intelligent enough to give him information, he considered them intellectually primitive.)

6 HISTORICAL BACKGROUND

Printing: A Florentine printer named Aldus Manutius decided to capitalize on the new market of humanist thinkers by bringing out elegant "pocket editions" of classical texts. By 1506, he had a list of 36 titles that spread the new learning throughout Europe.

7 HISTORICAL BACKGROUND

John Wycliffe: A religious thinker, Wycliffe was a forerunner of the Protestant Reformation. John Huss, a Czech reformer, was much influenced by Wycliffe; and Huss in turn influenced Martin Luther, whose protests against church corruption started the Protestant Reformation in 1517.

5

> **❝** As soon as I arrived in the Indies . . . I took by force some [natives] so that they might learn [Castilian] and give me information . . . I still have them with me, and they are still of the opinion that I come from the sky. . . . **❞**
> —*Christopher Columbus*

Plate with the figure of a gentleman. Florentine, late sixteenth century.

Nimatallah/Art Resource, New York

persuaded Ferdinand and Isabella, the rulers of Spain, that he could reach the East by sailing west across the Atlantic. Columbus failed to reach Asia; instead, he landed in the Americas. Spain's rapid conquest of the New World brought fabulous wealth and power. In 1497, Portugal commissioned **Vasco da Gama** to open an eastern route to Asia. Da Gama reached India in 1498, and within five years Indian merchandise was flowing into Portugal. In 1519, the Portuguese navigator **Ferdinand Magellan**—in search of a western trade route for Spain—sailed around South America and into a vast ocean that he called "Pacific."

The Rise of Printing: Fuel for New Thought

The imaginative fervor that had begun in Italy and spread throughout Europe was fueled by the technology of printing. Around 1455, **Johann Gutenberg** (c. 1400–c. 1468) produced Europe's first printed book, the Bible. But the new print technology met strong resistance from the Church. Through-

6

> **Humanism attempted to reform the Church and encourage people to make religious choices for themselves.**

out Europe, Church leaders imposed strong restrictions on the printing and sales of books, and more than one printer was burned at the stake as a heretic.

The Church had good reason to try to control printing technology. In northern Europe, humanism had taken the form of a widespread effort to reform the corrupt Church and to loosen its hold on people's minds. Humanist critics questioned the sale of indulgences—the practice of "forgiving" sins in exchange for money—and demanded that the wealthy Church practice the poverty it preached. Other humanists directly undermined the authority of the Church. **John Wycliffe** (c. 1329–1384), for example, translated the Bible into English and sent teachers, called "Poor Preachers," to read it in the churches. Wycliffe taught that people had a direct relationship to God and did not need priests to act as go-betweens. The Bible, he said, was the sole source of divine authority. The Church had Wycliffe executed in 1384

7

ner of modern opera. The glories of the modern operatic stage evolved from this beginning.

To illustrate the deep influence of Renaissance ideas on another of the arts, have students list all the words related to the theater that come from the Greek via the Italian Renaissance: *tragedy, comedy, orchestra, protagonist, antagonist, spectacle, spectator, critic, scene, proscenium, drama, poetry, music, lyric,* and *epic.*

In addition, point out that the Renaissance scholars rediscovered not only classical theater but also classical science. This development radically changed the modern world. During this period, astronomy developed from ancient astrology, and chemistry from alchemy. There is a direct line from Copernicus to Galileo to Kepler to Newton, whose theories underlie the orbiting of present-day satellites. Renaissance explorers like Columbus

helped to complete the global map. The impulse to explore the unknown that drove them still drives today's space programs, sending robot spacecraft swinging past the outer planets into the void or penetrating the murky, boiling atmosphere of Venus. In 1979–1981, the *Voyager* space probe took sharp, close-up photographs of volcanoes on Io, one of the moons of Jupiter that Galileo saw dimly through his telescope in 1610.

---

and—to drive its point home—removed his body from its grave and had it burned in 1415.

But reform could not be stopped. Humanists like **Desiderius Erasmus** (c. 1466–1536), a Dutch priest and scholar, exerted an enormous intellectual influence. Erasmus was a sharp critic of the Church and an effective advocate of reform. His scholarly study, and that of humanists such as **Sir Thomas More** in England, paved the way for the radical reforms of Martin Luther and John Calvin.

The Reformation: The Church Loses Power

The **Reformation** officially began in 1517 when the German monk **Martin Luther** (1483–1546) made public a list of complaints against Church practices. These complaints, called the **Ninety-five Theses**, brought Pope Leo's condemnation. The Pope ordered Luther to recant, but Luther refused, and the reform movement, called **Protestantism**, gathered force. Reformers appeared in Scandinavia, Scotland, Switzerland, and the Netherlands. The ideas of the

> The Reformation was fired by the idea that people did not need the Church to mediate between them and God.

most famous reformer, the French theologian **John Calvin** (1509–1564), were accepted in Switzerland and Scotland. In France, however, Protestant reforms were resisted, and the Church maintained its spiritual authority.

The active individualism that fired the Reformation in northern Europe energized art and literature as well. The Flemish brothers Jan and Hubert Van Eyck, the two Breughels, and the German artist Albrecht Dürer created paintings rich with realistic detail based on close observation of their settings and subjects. Artists were interested in movement—in people *doing* things.

Writers were also interested in showing people as active and dynamic. Authors increasingly wrote stories held together by carefully crafted plots, which in turn were determined by the actions and motivations of characters. In Spain, **Miguel de Cervantes** (1547–1616) wrote what many

Alinari/Art Resource, New York

MARTIN LUTHER, LUCAS CRANACH THE ELDER (1472–1553). *Luther's Ninety-five Theses sparked the Reformation and led to the development of Protestantism.*

Each of the works in this unit has influenced literary history. Petrarch's sonnet (p. 808) became a model for the sonnet during the Renaissance, influencing Ronsard in France (p. 809) and Shakespeare (p. 810) and Spenser in England. Other great English writers of sonnets followed: John Donne, John Milton, William Wordsworth, John Keats, and Gerard Manley Hopkins. Robert Frost is the outstanding American sonneteer.

Besides providing Renaissance dramatists and poets with some of their plots, the tales in Boccaccio's *Decameron* have served as models for short prose fiction for all of Europe. In the nineteenth and twentieth centuries, the short story, an outgrowth of the Renaissance tale, became a major genre all over the world.

Cervantes' hero Don Quixote has become a model in the popular imagination of the overly idealistic hero. The mournful knight has been depicted in art by French painter Honoré Daumier, in ballet by choreographer George Balanchine, and on Broadway in *Man of La Mancha*.

Shakespeare has had a greater impact on British and American English, literature, and drama than any other writer. His drama and poetry in translation have also succeeded in transcending the barriers of time, language, and culture throughout the world.

9 RESPONDING TO THE QUOTATION

Elizabeth I reigned in England from 1558 to 1603, one of the greatest periods of English power and prosperity. A Protestant, ruling as a woman in a man's world, Elizabeth maintained her power by artful promises of marriage, which she never kept. In 1559, she refused an offer of marriage from Philip II, the king of Spain, who wanted to reclaim England for Roman Catholicism. Her refusal resulted in Philip's launching of the Spanish Armada in 1588, but his great fleet was defeated off the south coast of England by storms and a powerful English navy.

? *In the quotation, Elizabeth is exhorting her troops before the battle. What spirit do her words suggest?* (Possible responses: courageous defiance, determination)

HUMANITIES CONNECTION

Reflecting the rise of individualism and private wealth, Renaissance aristocrats, merchants, clerics, statesmen, and other wealthy patrons would often commission portraits of themselves and their families.

? *What qualities of character does the painter give the gentleman in the portrait?* (Possible responses: strength, self-confidence, nobility) ∎

9

❝ I know I have the body but of a weak and feeble woman; but I have the heart and stomach of a king, and of a king of England too, and think foul scorn that Parma or Spain, or any prince of Europe, should dare to invade the borders of my realm; to which rather than any dishonor shall grow by me, I myself will take up arms. **❞**

—*Queen Elizabeth I, Speech to the Troops at Tilbury*

consider to be the first novel, about a would-be knight named Don Quixote.

To the poets, particularly French poets, the humanist spirit demanded the imitation of classical Greek and Roman forms. This imitation is called **neoclassicism**. **Pierre de Ronsard** (1524–1585) is famous for the French poems he modeled after classical poets, as well as for his sonnets.

England: From Reformation to Renaissance

In England, the Renaissance of culture would have to wait until the turmoil created by the English Reformation subsided. England's Reformation was very different from Europe's; it sprang largely from the political and personal motivations of one person, **King Henry VIII** (1491–1547). In 1533, Henry broke with the Roman Catholic Church when the Pope refused to recognize Henry's divorce and remarriage to Anne Boleyn, the mother of Elizabeth I. Henry had Parliament appoint him and his successors Supreme Head of the newly created Anglican Church, or the Church of England. After Henry died in 1547, his son Edward VI

PORTRAIT OF A GENTLEMAN, **Holland, 1611.**

Giraudon/Art Resource, New York

1. What impact did the Black Death of 1348 have on early Renaissance Europe? (It killed one third of the population.)

2. Why did the Church ban Galileo's theory that the earth moves around the sun? (The theory implied that humanity was not the center of God's universe.)

3. List the contributions of Christopher Columbus, Vasco da Gama, and Ferdinand Magellan. (opened the New World to Spain; established trade routes with India; discovered the Pacific)

4. What marked the beginning of the Reformation in Germany? (Luther's Ninety-five Theses)

5. When did the English navy defeat the Spanish Armada? (1588)

FOR FURTHER STUDY

Nonfiction
The Elizabethan Renaissance, by A. L. Rowse (Scribner, 1971), is a study in cultural history. Lacy Baldwin Smith's *The Horizon Book of the Elizabethan World* (American Heritage, 1967) is illustrated.

Films
Films are available of Robert Bolt's play about Sir Thomas More, *A Man for All Seasons* (1966), and *The Tempest* (1987) ■

National Trust Photographic Library/A. C. Cooper/Art Resource, New York

THE FAERIE QUEENE, WILLIAM BLAKE (1757–1827). *Blake's illustration was inspired by* The Faerie Queene, *a narrative poem by Edmund Spenser that was popular during the English Renaissance.*

supported Protestantism in England. Edward was followed in 1553 by his sister Mary, a Catholic. Her persecution of non-Catholics earned her the name Bloody Mary. When Mary's Anglican sister Elizabeth became queen five years later, England welcomed the peace she brought.

With Elizabeth's reign came an exuberant swelling of English pride. England defeated Spain's previously indomitable navy, the Armada, in 1588, and England emerged as a naval power. Trade and industry grew, and the economy expanded. In this atmosphere of buoyant optimism, the arts flourished. Nowhere was the spirit of the English Renaissance better expressed than in drama, and in particular in the plays of **William Shakespeare**. His comedies, such as *As You Like It* and *Twelfth Night* (1600), show both the endearing and the silly sides of human nature. His tragedies, such as *Hamlet* (1601) and *King Lear* (1605), triumphantly affirm the courage of the human spirit. *The Tempest* (1611), one of his last plays, celebrates the power of the imagination. Shakespeare's skill in language and characterization earned him a place with the greatest playwrights of all time.

The exuberance of the English Renaissance was muted after Elizabeth I died in 1603. The satiric plays of Ben Jonson (such as *Volpone* in 1605 and *The Alchemist* in 1610) were more sober than those of the Elizabethan period. With the works of **metaphysical poets** such as John Donne, poetry became less musical and more complex and intellectual. *Paradise Lost*, John Milton's epic poem which sets the biblical story of the Fall of Adam and Eve against the backdrop of the cosmic conflict between God and Satan, may be considered the last poem of the English Renaissance.

The Granger Collection, New York

JOHN MILTON, artist unknown. *One of England's most celebrated poets, Milton marked the turning point in literature between the Renaissance and the Enlightenment.*

HUMANITIES CONNECTION

The visionary poet William Blake is best known for writing, engraving, and painting two of his own books of poetry, *Songs of Innocence* and *Songs of Experience*. The latter contains his famous "The Tiger." Blake earned his living by illustrating and engraving the works of other writers. Regarded as a genius today, he died unrecognized by his peers. The Renaissance poet Edmund Spenser (15??–1599) was, however, considered by *his* contemporaries to be the greatest poet of his age. *The Faerie Queene* is his long allegorical poem dedicated to Queen Elizabeth. In the poem the queen's title, Gloriana, suggests the glory of her reign. The Red Cross Knight stands for St. George, England's patron saint. A gifted poet, Spenser invented a new nine-line stanza, now called Spenserian. Encourage students to find out more about the Spenserian stanza and determine why the form is suitable for a poem about heroic exploits. ■

TEACHING TIP
William Shakespeare, the great poet and playwright, once wrote, ". . . imagination bodies forth / the forms of things unknown. . . ." Discuss this quotation as a byword of the Renaissance. Challenge students who disagree to find another quotation or to create a saying to sum up the age. ■

COMPARING LITERATURE

The sonnet form has continued to challenge poets over the centuries. Even poets of the Romantic period, who celebrated freedom from rules, produced beautiful sonnets. William Wordsworth actually wrote a sonnet about the sonnet, in which he paid tribute to Shakespeare's achievements with the form:

"Scorn not the sonnet; Critic, you have frowned / Mindless of its just honors; with this key / Shakespeare unlocked his heart. . . . in his hand / The thing became a trumpet; whence he blew / Soul-animating strains—alas, too few!"

Students may enjoy reading Wordsworth's sonnet "The World Is Too Much with Us" (p. 1004) and determining whether it is a Petrarchan or Shakespearean sonnet.

SPECULATING

The sonnet form spread to countries throughout Europe, including Spain, Portugal, France, and Poland. What types of changes do you think poets writing in different languages might have made in the sonnet form? (Possible responses: changes in meter, rhyme scheme, imagery, stanzaic form)

READER'S RESPONSE

Do you suspect that the sonnet form is popular with poets today? Why or why not?

Introduction

The Sonnet in the Renaissance

The word *sonnet* is derived from the Italian word *sonetto*, meaning "little sound" or "song." A **sonnet** is a fourteen-line lyric poem. It is one of the most difficult forms for a poet to master because it must conform to strict patterns of rhythm and rhyme.

The Petrarchan Sonnet

In Italy, the sonnet form was perfected by Francesco Petrarca, known in English as Petrarch. The form he popularized is called the **Italian**, or **Petrarchan**, **sonnet**.

The Petrarchan sonnet has two parts: an eight-line section, called the **octave**, followed by a six-line section, called the **sestet**. The octave rhymes *abbaabba*, and the sestet rhymes *cdecde, cdcdcd, ccdeed,* or *cdcdee.* This form makes the Italian sonnet perfectly suited for a two-part statement: question/answer, problem/solution, or theme/comment. The transition between the two parts, called the **volta**, or turn, is usually found in the ninth line—the beginning of the sestet—as in Petrarch's Sonnet 42, below.

Sonnet 42
Petrarch
translated by Joseph Auslander

The spring returns, the spring wind softly blowing	*a*
Sprinkles the grass with gleam and glitter of showers,	*b*
Powdering pearl and diamond, dripping with flowers,	*b*
Dropping wet flowers, dancing the winters going;	*a*
The swallow twitters, the groves of midnight are glowing	*a* octave
With nightingale music and madness; the sweet fierce powers	*b*
Of love flame up through the earth; the seed-soul towers	*b*
And trembles; nature is filled to overflowing . . .	*a*
The spring returns, but there is no returning	*c* volta
Of spring for me. O heart with anguish burning!	*c*
She that unlocked all April in a breath	*d*
Returns not . . . And these meadows, blossoms, birds	*d* sestet
These lovely gentle girls—words, empty words	*e*
As bitter as the black estates of death!	*d*

The Shakespearean Sonnet

Petrarchan sonnets are difficult to write in English because of the demanding rhyme scheme. English poets, limited by their "rhyme-poor" language, soon created their own version, called the **English**, or **Shakespearean**, **sonnet**. Like the Petrarchan sonnet, the Shakespearean sonnet is fourteen lines long. However, instead of the octave-sestet arrangement, this sonnet form uses three four-line units, called **quatrains**, followed by a final **couplet**. The Shakespearean sonnet is written in a particular **meter**, or rhythmic pattern, called **iambic pentameter**, with each line consisting of five unstressed (‿) syllables alternating with five stressed (′) syllables. The typical rhyme scheme of the Shakespearean sonnet is *abab cdcd efef gg*. William Shakespeare's Sonnet 73, which describes old age, is an example:

THE MONTH OF APRIL, SIMON BENNICK (1483–1561). *Flemish, watercolor on parchment.*

Victoria & Albert Museum, London/Art Resource, New York

Sonnet 73
William Shakespeare

That time of year thou mayst in me behold   *a* ⎫
When yellow leaves, or none, or few, do hang   *b* ⎪
Upon those boughs which shake against the cold,   *a* ⎬ **quatrain**
Bare ruined choirs where late the sweet birds sang.   *b* ⎭

In me thou see'st the twilight of such day   *c* ⎫
As after sunset fadeth in the west;   *d* ⎪
Which by and by black night doth take away,   *c* ⎬ **quatrain**
Death's second self that seals up all in rest.   *d* ⎭

In me thou see'st the glowing of such fire   *e* ⎫
That on the ashes of his youth doth lie,   *f* ⎪
As the deathbed whereon it must expire,   *e* ⎬ **quatrain**
Consumed with that which it was nourished by.   *f* ⎭

This thou perceiv'st, which makes thy love more strong,   *g* ⎫ **couplet**
To love that well which thou must leave ere long.   *g* ⎭

Although Francesco Petrarch achieved fame as a poet, he suffered greatly as he tried to balance his worldly ambitions with his religious values. He saw his love for Laura and his desire for fame as two golden chains holding him back from the love of God. Petrarch took religious orders in 1330, but he was unable to commit himself to religious life. In 1341 he was crowned poet laureate in Rome.

Pierre de Ronsard seemed destined from a very young age for a career in diplomacy, serving as page in the Scottish court of King James V. But when Ronsard was sixteen, an illness left him partially deaf, cutting short his diplomatic career. Rejecting a life as a priest, he instead began studying the classics. In reading Greek and Latin poetry, he discovered his true vocation as a poet.

William Shakespeare is most famous today for his great plays, but in his own time writing poetry, rather than plays, was considered the path to lasting fame for a writer. Composed between 1592 and 1609, Shakespeare's sonnets are among the most beautiful poems in the English language. Because of the poems' passionate intensity, many literary detectives have presumed them to be autobiographical. Others maintain that even the sonnets are the work of Shakespeare the dramatist and that the speaker of the poems is not Shakespeare himself.

Renaissance Sonnet Writers

Giraudon/Art Resource, New York

FRANCESCO PETRARCH, artist unknown.

Francesco Petrarch, 1304–1374

The Italian poet Petrarch was a man of two worlds: the dying Middle Ages and the emerging Renaissance. Although Petrarch achieved great fame as a poet and scholar, he suffered considerably as he tried to balance his own worldly ambitions and desires with the religious values of medieval life.

Although Petrarch's love for a woman named Laura is legendary, a personal relationship never developed between them. He managed to see her only occasionally from a distance. She died of the plague in 1348. Laura's idealized image inspired the 317 sonnets contained in Petrarch's *Canzoniere* ("Song Book"). This first series of sonnets, written in Italian, set the fashion throughout the Renaissance for bittersweet love lyrics in various European languages.

Pierre de Ronsard, 1524–1585

With six other poets, Pierre de Ronsard (rōn·sàr') founded an influential group known as the *Pléiade*—a name derived from the seven stars of the constellation of the *Pléiades*. The *Pléiade* maintained that vernacular French was worthy of more than just popular *lais* and *ballades*. The group used the vernacular in their odes, elegies, and satires based on the works of classical Greek and Roman poets. Ronsard's four books of *Odes* (1550–1552), written in French and dedicated to the classical poets Pindar and Horace, were so successful that his own generation called him "the Prince of Poets."

William Shakespeare, 1564–1616

During the Renaissance, sonnets were frequently written in the form of a **sequence**, a collection of poems linked by a common theme. Shakespeare's sonnet sequence consists of 154 poems, probably written during his middle years. The entire sequence provides a rough outline of a mysterious story that has intrigued scholars for centuries. Most of the poems are addressed to a young nobleman whom the speaker admires. Some are concerned with a rival poet who has also written poems to this young man. The final sonnets in the series are addressed to a "dark lady" with whom both the speaker and the young man are in love. (For more information about Shakespeare's life and works, see page 839.)

OBJECTIVES

1. *To interpret four Renaissance sonnets on the theme of love*
2. *To analyze the meter, rhyme scheme, and figures of speech in Petrarchan and Shakespearean sonnets*
3. *To write a modern version of Shakespeare's Sonnet 29, and to compare and contrast two love poems from two different periods*

Reader's Guide

RENAISSANCE SONNETS

Background

The sonnet became popular during the Renaissance because people were writing more about worldly things: science, politics, geographic exploration, and romantic love. During the Middle Ages, most lyric poems had been written to praise God. But the sonnet of the Renaissance is secular, or nonreligious. The sonnet serves as an expression of a poet's intense personal feelings, whether they be feelings of romantic love or regret in old age. Sometimes both emotions manage to make their way into the sonnets. A major theme in Renaissance poetry was *carpe diem* (kär'pē dī'em), a Latin phrase meaning "seize the day"—that is, make the most of the present moment because life is short. *Carpe diem* implies that the best things in life, such as youth, love, and beauty, are only fleeting pleasures and need to be enjoyed while they can. The sonnets presented here reveal a bittersweet mixture of love and sadness typical of much Renaissance poetry.

Oral Response

Love has probably been the most written-about emotion of all. As a class, discuss contemporary views of love relationships. Do we tend to idealize love as many writers of the past did? Or is our view of love more "practical"? Consider what our culture conveys about love relationships (all types: romantic, familial, patriotic) through movies, television programs, popular songs, and romance novels.

Literary Focus

The sonnets of the Renaissance followed not only strict formal conventions of **meter** and **rhyme scheme**, but they used many stylistic conventions as well. For instance, the poet could not simply express his feelings outright, but had to disguise or camouflage them in **figures of speech**. Petrarchan and Shakespearean sonnets are characterized by certain recurring **similes**, used to describe the idealized beauty of a lady: "cheeks like roses," "eyes like stars," "teeth like pearls." The poets also use **metaphors** to draw comparisons of themselves to captive birds, wounded stags, or moths drawn to a flame. **Personification** occurs frequently, too. Love, for example, is often personified as Cupid.

PREREADING FOCUS

Background: The phrase *carpe diem* was first used by the Roman poet Horace (see p. 417) in his *Odes*. The idea was picked up by Renaissance poets who rediscovered classical authors. Two famous expressions of the theme can be found in works by the English poets Robert Herrick (1591–1674) and Andrew Marvell (1621–1678). Herrick's "To the Virgins" contains the famous lines

"Gather ye rosebuds while ye may, / Old Time is still a-flying; / And this same flower that smiles today, / Tomorrow will be dying."

Marvell's "To His Coy Mistress" includes the unforgettable lines

"But at my back I always hear / Time's wingèd Chariot hurrying near: / . . . / The Grave's a fine and private place, / But none, I think, do there embrace."

In contemporary times, the translated phrase *Seize the Day* was used as the title of a Saul Bellow novel.

Literary Focus: Point out that the similes and metaphors cited were original in their own time, but have since become clichés. Challenge students to think of their own original figures of speech to describe lovers and loved ones.

ABOUT THE TRANSLATOR
Joseph Auslander (1897–1965) was a poet, teacher, editor, and literary historian. Known as a translator of Petrarch and of the French fable writer La Fontaine, Auslander also taught at Harvard and Columbia universities and served as a poetry consultant to the Library of Congress.

1 COMPARING LITERATURE
Students might enjoy comparing the "sweet pain" of love experienced by Petrarch's speaker with the range of mixed feelings about love expressed in the works of the ancient Roman poet Catullus, pp. 409–413.

2 LITERARY ELEMENT
Sonnet Form/Rhyme Scheme: Where does the sestet of the sonnet begin? (line 9) What rhyme scheme does it have? (cdcdee)

3 READER'S RESPONSE
How did you react to the repetitions in the poem's last line? Did they seem a realistic expression of a person in love?

SONNET 61
Francesco Petrarch
translated by
JOSEPH AUSLANDER

In Sonnet 61 the poet blesses, or expresses grateful thanks for, all things connected with his first encounter with Laura. What is the most important word in this sonnet?

Victoria & Albert Museum, London/Art Resource, New York

APRIL: GATHERING FLOWERS, from the *Playfair Book of Hours*, French, late 1400s.

Blest be the day, and blest the month and year,
Season and hour and very moment blest,
The lovely land and place where first possessed
By two pure eyes I found me prisoner;
5 And blest the first sweet pain, the first most dear,
Which burned my heart when Love° came in as guest;
And blest the bow, the shafts which shook my breast,
And even the wounds which Love delivered there.
Blest be the words and voices which filled grove
10 And glen with echoes of my lady's name;
The sighs, the tears, the fierce despair of love;
And blest the sonnet-sources of my fame;
And blest that thought of thoughts which is her own,
Of her, her only, of herself alone!

6. **Love:** Cupid, the god of love, often depicted as a winged child with bow and arrow.

To Hélène
Pierre de Ronsard
translated by
Robert Hollander

One of Ronsard's most famous sonnets, "To Hélène" is part of a collection of love poems dedicated to a court lady who may have rejected the then-aging poet. What argument does Ronsard develop? How do you think the real Hélène would have responded to this argument?

When you are very old, in evening candlelight,
Moved closer to the coals and carding out your
   wool,[1]
You'll sing my songs and marvel that you were
   such a fool:
"O Ronsard did praise me when I was young and
   bright."

5   Then you'll have no handmaid to help you pass
   the night,
Spinning while your gossip leads her into lull,
Until you say my name and her rousèd eyes grow
   full
In wonder of your glory in what Ronsard did
   write.

When I am in the earth, poor ghost without his
   bones,
10   A sleeper in the shade of myrtle trees and stones,
Then you, beside the hearth, old and crouched
   and gray,
Will yearn for all that's lost, repenting your
   disdain.
Live it well, I pray you, today won't come again:
Gather up the roses before they fall away.

ARACHNE, **an illumination from a sixteenth-century French manuscript,** *The Lives of Famous Women.*

Giraudon/Art Resource, New York

---

1. **carding out your wool:** combing strands of wool
to untangle them before spinning threads.

ABOUT THE TRANSLATOR
Robert Hollander (1933–) has translated major literary works from French and Italian, compiled several anthologies, and written scholarly books on the works of Dante and Boccaccio.

HUMANITIES CONNECTION

Illuminations often depict women of all social classes carding, spinning, weaving, or sewing, because prior to the Industrial Revolution women *were* the textile industry. In this illumination, the lady's pose echoes the circular form of the spinning wheel as she bends over her work, and she appears wrapped up in her own thoughts. ■

4 MAKING JUDGMENTS
How would you characterize the speaker of this poem? Is he humble? conceited? ingratiating? self-mocking? (Possible response: His estimation of his own talents as a poet seems conceited, but he may also be self-mocking.)

5 LITERARY ELEMENT
Sonnet Form: Where does the *volva*, or abrupt turn of thought, occur in this Petrarchan sonnet? (line 9)

READER'S RESPONSE
In this poem, the speaker addresses his lady directly. If you were Hélène, would you find his arguments persuasive? Why or why not?

To reteach the sonnets, write the following excerpts on the board:

"Live it well, I pray you, today won't come again: / Gather up the roses before they fall away."

"Haply I think on thee, and then my state, / Like to the lark at break of day arising / From sullen earth, sings hymns at Heaven's gate."

"And blest the first sweet pain . . . /

Which burned my heart when Love came in as guest;"

"Ruin hath taught me thus to ruminate— / That Time will come and take my love away."

Have students identify from which poem each excerpt comes. Then have them discuss which view of love they found most true to life.

LITERARY ELEMENT

Archaic Words: Many words that were common in Shakespeare's time have become archaic today—that is, they have fallen out of use. What archaic words do you find in Sonnet 29? (*beweep, bootless, Haply*) Encourage students to use context to determine the meaning and provide modern substitutes for each word.

6 LITERARY ELEMENT

Meter/Rhyme Scheme: What is the rhyme scheme of the poem's first quatrain? (*abab*) How many beats are there in each line? (five)

7 LITERARY ELEMENT

Rhyme Scheme: Which lines of the poem are a rhyming couplet? (lines 13 and 14)

8 LITERARY ELEMENT

Personification: What abstract idea is personified, or given human characteristics, in Sonnet 64? (Time) What kinds of qualities are attributed to it? (destructive)

WRITING TO LEARN

Imagine you could travel back in time to visit one of the poets. What would you tell him about how attitudes toward love have changed or stayed the same since his time? Write your ideas as a dialogue with the poet. ■

SONNETS
William Shakespeare

❙❙ *What does the speaker complain about in each poem? Does the thought of love add to or relieve the complaint?*

Sonnet 29

6
When in disgrace with fortune and men's eyes
I all alone beweep my outcast state,°
And trouble deaf Heaven with my bootless° cries,
And look upon myself and curse my fate,
5 Wishing me like to one more rich in hope,
Featured like him,° like him with friends possessed,
Desiring this man's art and that man's scope,°
With what I most enjoy contented least—
Yet in these thoughts myself almost despising,
10 Haply I think on thee, and then my state,
Like to the lark at break of day arising
From sullen earth, sings hymns at Heaven's gate.

7
   For thy sweet love remembered such wealth brings
   That then I scorn to change my state with kings.

2. **state:** condition.

3. **bootless:** useless; futile.

6. **like him:** like another.
7. **scope:** breadth of knowledge.

Sonnet 64

8
When I have seen by Time's fell° hand defaced
The rich proud cost of outworn buried age;
When sometime lofty towers I see down-razed,
And brass eternal slave to mortal rage;°
5 When I have seen the hungry ocean gain
Advantage on the kingdom of the shore,
And the firm soil win of the watery main,
Increasing store with loss, and loss with store;
When I have seen such interchange of state,
10 Or state itself confounded to decay;
Ruin hath taught me thus to ruminate—
That Time will come and take my love away.
   This thought is as a death, which cannot choose
   But weep to have that which it fears to lose.

1. **fell:** cruel; deadly.

4. **And brass eternal slave to mortal rage:** Several interpretations are possible; brass is "a slave to mortal rage" because it can be melted into many forms, including weapons; it also becomes dented when thrown.

1. Setting a Sonnet to Music. The regular rhythm and rhyme of sonnets make them very songlike. In Ronsard's time, many of his poems were set to music, and Shakespeare's poems have also been sung. Have students listen to recordings of Renaissance lute or recorder music and choose a melody to which one of the poems could be set. Have them perform their musical setting of the poem for another class.

2. Listening to Love Lyrics. Students might enjoy comparing and contrasting views of love expressed in popular songs over the last twenty years. To inspire discussion, you might play a variety of selections that express views such as: love as perfect bliss, love as suffering, love as a game, love as an impossible dream, and so on.

Have students discuss whether they think love poetry or love songs give people unrealistic ideas about love or whether such works help people cope with the ups and downs of love. ■

First Thoughts

Was one poem more "realistic" to you than any other? Which one? Explain why.

Interpreting Meanings

1. What **metaphors**, or direct comparisons, does the speaker in Petrarch's Sonnet 61 use to describe his state of mind? Find two examples.

2. **Oxymoron** (äks′i·mō′rän′) is a figure of speech that states an apparent contradiction, such as "deafening silence" or "hateful love." Identify two oxymorons in Petrarch's Sonnet 61. What is the effect of these figures of speech?

3. In your own words, tell what advice Ronsard is giving to Hélène in the last two lines of "To Hélène." What can we conclude overall about the poet's feelings for her?

4. Find at least two **similes**, or comparisons, that Shakespeare uses in Sonnet 29 to describe the speaker's feelings about love.

5. What situation is the speaker in Shakespeare's Sonnet 64 contemplating? How would you summarize the speaker's views?

Applying Meanings

Suppose you were the recipient of any one of these sonnets. How would you respond? Would you be touched or would you laugh? Explain your reaction.

Creative Writing Response

Writing a Poem. In Sonnet 29, Shakespeare describes how he overcomes feelings of despair and failure by remembering his love. People today also experience temporary periods of depression when they feel their looks, possessions, friends, or accomplishments don't measure up. Write a modern version of Shakespeare's Sonnet 29, but instead of following the sonnet form write the poem entirely in couplets. To get ideas for your poem, consider these questions: What might people today envy in their neighbors? What might help a modern person feel more satisfied? You may wish to pattern your poem after the model below.

When I am feeling low and sad and blue
I sit alone and sigh and think of you.

And _____
And _____
Wanting _____
Wishing _____
Desiring _____
Contented least with _____
Yet _____
Suddenly _____
Then _____
Like _____
For remembering _____
That then I _____

Critical Writing Response

Comparing and Contrasting Love Poems. Read "When You Are Old," by the Irish poet W. B. Yeats (1865–1939), written in imitation of Ronsard's sonnet "To Hélène."

> When you are old and gray and full of sleep,
> And nodding by the fire, take down this book,
> And slowly read, and dream of the soft look
> Your eyes had once, and of their shadows
>   deep;
>
> How many loved your moments of glad grace,
> And loved your beauty with love false or
>   true;
> But one man loved the pilgrim soul in you,
> And loved the sorrows of your changing face.
>
> And bending down beside the glowing bars,
> Murmur, a little sadly, how Love fled
> And paced upon the mountains overhead
> And hid his face amid a crowd of stars.

First Thoughts
Answers will vary.

Interpreting Meanings
1. Possible responses: "found me prisoner," "the shafts which shook my breast," "the wounds which Love delivered"
2. Possible responses: "Sweet pain" and "fierce despair" suggest that love can involve both pleasure and pain.
3. Possible responses: to enjoy the pleasures of youth while she can. He seems determined to win her.
4. Possible responses: "like to the lark at break of day arising"; implied comparison of being as contented as a king
5. the fact that things are destroyed over time. He's afraid his love may be lost, so he takes little joy in it.

Applying Meanings
Reactions will vary.

Creative Writing Response
Writing a Poem. Poems should be written entirely in couplets, can follow the model, and should show a definite mood change.

Write four paragraphs comparing and contrasting Yeats's poem, "When You Are Old," with Ronsard's "To Hélène." Your essay should include answers to the following questions:

1. To whom is each poem addressed? In what way are these persons similar?

2. How does the speaker in each poem want the person addressed to think of him in the future?

3. What does each speaker want the person he is addressing to do?

4. In what ways are the speakers' intentions similar and different?

ELEMENTS OF LITERATURE

Enjambment

Enjambment, or run-on lines, refers to the spilling over of a thought from one line of verse to the next. The term is from a French word meaning "to straddle"—that is, the sentence or idea "straddles" two or more lines. Inexperienced readers tend to stop at the end of each line in a poem, usually at a rhyme, regardless of the punctuation. As a result, many poems when read aloud sound like nursery rhymes, and the rhyme interferes with the meaning of the lines. Readers with more experience know that if a thought continues for more than one line they should read through to the end of the thought and not stop simply because there is a rhyme.

Often enjambment is used to create suspense: the first part of the thought may lead up to something that the second part in the next line may or may not carry through. Also, enjambment takes the emphasis off the rhyme scheme. Otherwise the poem would become boring and sing-song, a mere repetition of sounds and a strict reproduction of form rather than the expression of a poet's complex thoughts and feelings.

Try to get a sense of the flow of the lines by reading aloud the sonnets of Petrarch, Ronsard, and Shakespeare. Pay attention to the punctuation and the enjambment. Enjambment works to make a poem more meaningful or more like a real person speaking his or her thoughts. Read a sonnet for a classmate and then have that person read the same sonnet to you. How are your readings different? Which interpretation sounds more natural? Why?

Giovanni Boccaccio
1313–1375

SEF/Art Resource, New York

Giovanni Boccaccio (bō·kä'chō) was born in the summer of 1313, perhaps in Florence or possibly in Certaldo, a small Tuscan town twenty miles outside the city. The illegitimate son of an unknown French-woman and a Florentine merchant banker, Boccaccio spent his boyhood with his father. At the age of fourteen, however, he was sent to Naples, where his father had arranged for him to be a clerk in one of his banks.

After finishing his apprenticeship at the bank, Boccaccio entered the University of Naples and earned a degree in law. But in 1340, Boccaccio's father suffered a financial setback, and he asked his son to return to Florence. There Boccaccio met Francesco Petrarch, the great Italian poet (see page 806),

who became a lifelong friend and literary advisor. And there, too, he experienced the most catastrophic event of his lifetime: in 1348, the Black Death struck Florence. During this plague three out of four people in Florence died a gruesome death, their bodies covered with black spots.

Boccaccio used the plague as the backdrop for his masterpiece, the *Decameron.* Written in Italian, instead of Latin, the *Decameron* is a collection of one hundred tales told by ten wealthy young Florentines, seven women and three men, who have retreated to a villa in the hills of Fiesole to escape the Black Death. Here, safe from the pestilence, they pass the time by telling each other stories. They stay ten days—the word *decameron* comes from the Greek words for "ten" and "day"—and on each day the group hears ten stories.

Completed about 1353, the *Decameron* established Boccaccio's literary reputation. Boccaccio, however, did not consider the *Decameron* to be his best work. In fact, he considered it trifling and, in later life, shifted his attention to writing scholarly works in Latin. He made great strides in the human-istic study of the ancient Greek and Roman classics. Nevertheless, it is the *Decameron* that has survived the test of time. William Shakespeare, John Milton, and many other writers in English and other languages have used Boccaccio's work as both a model and a source.

OBJECTIVES

1. To analyze the characters and theme of a Renaissance love story based on a medieval tale of courtly love
2. To recognize examples of situational irony
3. To write letters from the points of view of story characters
4. To participate in a storytelling session similar to that in the Decameron

THEMES IN WORLD LITERATURE

The Power and Pain of Love
Lyric Poems by Catullus, pp. 409–413
"Chevrefoil," pp. 715–719
"The Wife of Bath's Tale" from *The Canterbury Tales*, pp. 772–785
Sonnets, pp. 804–812

Choices in Life
A Doll's House, pp. 1069–1126
"The Guest," pp. 1244–1257 ■

VOCABULARY IN CONTEXT

The words listed below will appear in the side margin at the point of instruction:

1. legitimate
2. anguish
3. presumption
4. oblige
5. console

PREREADING FOCUS

Background: The frame story structure of the *Decameron* was very common in the Middle Ages. It was also used in Chaucer's *Canterbury Tales*, written at least thirty years after the *Decameron*. Many scholars believe, however, that Boccaccio's tales demonstrate more of a Renaissance spirit, as they show people striving to test their powers and virtues against the limitations of fortune. Other scholars cite Boccaccio's rational attitude toward religion and his down-to-earth feelings about love as signs of his Renaissance spirit.

Many tales from the *Decameron* influenced later writers. "Bernabo of Genoa" for example, inspired the plot of Shakespeare's play *Cymbeline*, and "Isabella," a supernatural tale of love and revenge, was adapted as a poem by Keats.

Writer's Response: Have students consider items that are valuable because of their craftsmanship or materials, as well as items that might seem "worthless" to other people but are valued for their association with important memories or with loved ones.

Reader's Guide ■

THE TALE OF THE FALCON
from the Decameron

Background

The *Decameron*, a masterpiece of Italian prose, presents the comic exploits and tragic foibles of a world of people. Many of these tales were adaptations of folktales, fables, and anecdotes that Boccaccio learned as a youth. Boccaccio places these tales in a **frame story**, a story that serves to bind together several different narratives. In Boccaccio's frame story, ten young Florentines entertain one another by telling tales while waiting out the plague. Each day one young Florentine youth is chosen king or queen for that day and is allowed to select a certain theme for the tales. As a result, there are many different types of stories: tales of adventure, tales of romantic exploits, tales of trickery, and stories of unhappy love affairs and courtly romance.

"The Tale of the Falcon," the ninth tale of the fifth day, features some of the stock themes of the medieval tale of courtly love: the handsome young man who loves a beautiful married lady; his despair over being refused; his gallant sacrifice; and his process of learning courtesy and, above all, humility before he can hope for success. However, Boccaccio's characters do not come from the chivalric order, and this otherwise formulaic story is invested with a surprising ironic twist.

Writer's Response

Have you ever had a prized possession, something you felt you could never give up? Write briefly about your reasons for valuing the possession, and what it would take to make you sacrifice it.

Literary Focus

Situational irony occurs when what actually happens in a story, novel, or drama is the opposite of what is expected or appropriate. For example, in Greek mythology, the story of greedy King Midas, whose touch turned everything to gold, is filled with situational irony. Midas soon discovers to his dismay that he turns food, drink, and even his beloved daughter to gold. Thus, far from making him happy as he expected, Midas's golden touch ironically makes him miserable. Situational irony always produces an unexpected turn of events.

THE TALE OF THE FALCON

from the Decameron

Giovanni Boccaccio

t r a n s l a t e d   b y

MARK MUSA AND PETER BONDANELLA

Read to the fourth paragraph, when Monna Giovanna's son asks for Federigo's falcon, believing that it will make him well. What do you predict will happen? Will the boy get his wish? Will Federigo part with his falcon? Read on to find out.

There was once in Florence a young man named Federigo,[1] the son of Messer Filippo Alberighi,[2] renowned above all other men in Tuscany for his prowess in arms and for his courtliness. As often happens to most gentlemen, he fell in love with a lady named Monna Giovanna, in her day considered to be one of the most beautiful and one of the most charming women that ever there was in Florence; and in order to win her love, he participated in jousts and tournaments, organized and gave feasts, and spent his money without restraint; but she, no less virtuous than beautiful, cared little for these things done on her behalf, nor did she care for the one who did them. Now, as Federigo was spending far beyond his means and was taking nothing in, as easily happens he lost his wealth and became poor, with nothing but his little farm to his name (from whose revenues he lived very meagerly) and one falcon which was among the best in the world.

1. **Federigo** (fed·ər·ē′gō)
2. **Messer Filippo Alberighi** (mes′ər fə·lē′pō al·bər·ē′gē): Messer is a title of address, similar to *sir*.

AUGUST, from *Tres Riches Heures du Duc du Berry*, a fifteenth-century French Book of Hours, or prayer book.

Giraudon/Art Resource, New York

HUMANITIES CONNECTION

The three Limbourg brothers worked for the Duke of Berry from 1411 to 1416, when he and they died of the plague. They produced the most elegant of all illuminated Books of Hours, the "Very Rich Hours," dated c. 1415. Instead of beginning with the traditional tiny illustrations of the signs of the zodiac and the labors associated with each month, they created twelve large calendar pages and positioned the astrological information in an overhead arch. ■

MEETING INDIVIDUAL NEEDS

1 LEP: Students may need help interpreting "prowess in arms." Explain that *prowess* means "skill" and that *arms* in this context refers to weapons. ■

2 LITERARY ELEMENT
Characterization: Why is Monna Giovanna considered virtuous? (She is unmoved by displays of wealth and courage.) How does Federigo behave extravagantly? (by spending all his money to impress Monna Giovanna)

More in love than ever, but knowing that he would never be able to live the way he wished to in the city, he went to live at Campi, where his farm was. There he passed his time hawking whenever he could, asked nothing of anyone, and endured his poverty patiently. Now, during the time that Federigo was reduced to dire need, it happened that the husband of Monna Giovanna fell ill, and realizing death was near, he made his last will: he was very rich, and he made his son, who was growing up, his heir, and, since he had loved Monna Giovanna very much, he made her his heir should his son die without a <u>legitimate</u> heir; and then he died.

Monna Giovanna was now a widow, and as is the custom among our women, she went to the country with her son to spend a year on one of her possessions very close by to Federigo's farm, and it happened that this young boy became friends with Federigo and began to enjoy birds and hunting dogs; and after he had seen Federigo's falcon fly many times, it pleased him so much that he very much wished it were his own, but he did not dare to ask for it, for he could see how dear it was to Federigo. And during this time, it happened that the young boy took ill, and his mother was much grieved, for he was her only child and she loved him enormously; she would spend the entire day by his side, never ceasing to comfort him, and often asking him if there was anything he desired, begging him to tell her what it might be, for if it were possible to obtain it, she would certainly do everything possible to get it. After the young boy had heard her make this offer many times, he said:

"Mother, if you can arrange for me to have Federigo's falcon, I think I would be well very soon."

When the lady heard this, she was taken aback for a moment, and she began to think what she should do. She knew that Federigo had loved her for a long while, in spite of the fact that he never received a single glance from her, and so, she said to herself:

"How can I send or go and ask for this falcon of his which is, as I have heard tell, the best that ever flew, and besides this, his only means of support? And how can I be so insensitive as to wish to take away from this gentleman the only pleasure which is left to him?"

And involved in these thoughts, knowing that she was certain to have the bird if she asked for it, but not knowing what to say to her son, she stood there without answering him. Finally the love she bore her son persuaded her that she should make him happy, and no matter what the consequences might be, she would not send for the bird, but rather go herself for it and bring it back to him; so she answered her son:

"My son, take comfort and think only of getting well, for I promise you that the first thing I shall do tomorrow morning is to go for it and bring it back to you."

The child was so happy that he showed some improvement that very day. The following morning, the lady, accompanied by another woman, as if going for a stroll, went to Federigo's modest house and asked for him. Since it was not the season for it, Federigo had not been hawking for some days and was in his orchard, attending to certain tasks; when he heard that Monna Giovanna was asking for him at the door, he was very surprised and happy to run there; as she saw him coming, she greeted him with feminine charm, and once Federigo had welcomed her courteously, she said:

"Greetings, Federigo!" Then she continued: "I have come to compensate you for the harm you have suffered on my account by loving me more than you needed to; and the

THE SEVENTH DAY OF THE DECAMERON, PAUL FALCONER POOLES (1807–1879).

The Bridgeman Art Library/Art Resource, New York

HUMANITIES CONNECTION

Notice the languid poses of the young people hiding from the plague.

? *How would you describe their mood? What are they doing at the moment Pooles catches them in the painting?* (Possible response: listening to a story) ∎

7 LITERARY ELEMENT

Theme/Courtly Love: How does Federigo's reaction reflect the medieval code of courtly love? (Possible response: The lover welcomes the suffering caused by his unattainable love because it ennobles him.)

8 PREDICTING

How do you predict Federigo will manage to have a meal prepared for Monna Giovanna? (Answers will vary.)

anguish (ang'gwish): great pain and suffering because of loss, worry, or grief

9 LITERARY ELEMENT

Situational Irony: Why is it ironic that Federigo can find nothing to feed Monna Giovanna? (In the past, he spent all his money feeding other people to impress her; now, when she finally comes to his house, he has nothing left.)

compensation is this: I, along with this companion of mine, intend to dine with you—a simple meal—this very day."

To this Federigo humbly replied: "Madonna,[3] I never remember having suffered any harm because of you; on the contrary: so much good have I received from you that if ever I have been worth anything, it has been because of your merit and the love I bore for you; and your generous visit is certainly so dear to me that I would spend all over again that which I spent in the past; but you have come to a poor host."

And having said this, he received her into his home humbly, and from there he led her into his garden, and since he had no one there to keep her company, he said:

"My lady, since there is no one else, this good woman here, the wife of this workman, will keep you company while I go to set the table."

Though he was very poor, Federigo, until now, had never before realized to what extent he had wasted his wealth; but this morning, the fact that he found nothing with which he could honor the lady for the love of whom he had once entertained countless men in the past gave him cause to reflect: in great anguish, he cursed himself and his fortune and, like a man beside himself, he started running here and there, but could find neither money nor a pawnable object. The hour was late and his desire to honor the gracious lady was great, but not wishing to turn for help to others (not even to his own workman), he set his eyes upon his good falcon, perched in a small room; and since he had nowhere else to turn, he took the bird, and finding it plump, he decided that it would be a worthy food for such a lady. So, without further thought, he wrung its neck and quickly gave it to his servant girl to pluck, prepare, and place on a spit to

---

3. **Madonna** (mə·dän'ə): a title for a woman, similar to *madam.*

Dramatic Irony: Dramatic irony occurs when readers know something that the characters do not. As Federigo and Monna Giovanna sit down to eat, what do we know that she does not? (that she is about to eat the falcon) What do we know that he does not? (that Monna Giovanna came to ask for the falcon for her son)

> **presumption** (pré·zump' shən): an overstepping of proper limits

11 COMPARING LITERATURE

Students might enjoy conducting a cross-cultural analysis of parent–child relationships, drawing on their reading of "Song of a Mother to Her Firstborn" (p. 90), "The Prodigal Son" (p. 199), and *Oedipus Rex* (p. 307).

MEETING INDIVIDUAL NEEDS

12 ESL: Help students acquiring English figure out the meaning of the colloquial expression "taken by," using the context of the sentence in the story. (Possible response: fascinated by) ■

WRITING TO LEARN

Social Studies: Imagine that you are Federigo's servant girl, who cooked the falcon for Monna Giovanna's visit. Write a dialogue between yourself and another servant in which you express your opinions about your master's great sacrifice and his ideas of love. ■

be roasted with care; and when he had set the table with the whitest of tablecloths (a few of which he still had left), he returned, with a cheerful face, to the lady in his garden, saying that the meal he was able to prepare for her was ready.

The lady and her companion rose, went to the table together with Federigo, who waited upon them with the greatest devotion, and they ate the good falcon without knowing what it was they were eating. And having left the table and spent some time in pleasant conversation, the lady thought it time now to say what she had come to say, and so she spoke these kind words to Federigo:

"Federigo, if you recall your past life and my virtue, which you perhaps mistook for harshness and cruelty, I do not doubt at all that you will be amazed by my presumption when you hear what my main reason for coming here is; but if you had children, through whom you might have experienced the power of parental love, it seems certain to me that you would, at least in part, forgive me. But, just as you have no child, I do have one, and I cannot escape the common laws of other mothers; the force of such laws compels me to follow them, against my own will and against good manners and duty, and to ask of you a gift which I know is most precious to you; and it is naturally so, since your extreme condition has left you no other delight, no other pleasure, no other consolation; and this gift is your falcon, which my son is so taken by that if I do not bring it to him, I fear his sickness will grow so much worse that I may lose him. And therefore I

Giraudon/Art Resource, New York

THE CONCERT, **French tapestry, late 1400s.**
❓ *Which of Monna Giovanna's qualities make her a "lady" according to the chivalric ideal?*

READING CHECK

1. How does Federigo lose his wealth? (by spending lavishly to impress Monna Giovanna)
2. What is Federigo's prized possession? (his falcon)
3. Who wishes to have the falcon? (Monna Giovanna's son)
4. Why does Federigo kill his falcon? (to serve it to Monna Giovanna for dinner)

5. Who does Monna Giovanna decide to marry in the end? (Federigo)

RETEACHING

To reteach "The Tale of the Falcon," have students play the *If Only* game. Have them find points in the plot where characters might have acted differently, and speculate on how the plot might have developed differently as a result. For example, "*If only* Federigo hadn't spent all his money, he never would have moved to the country and taken Monna Giovanna's son falconing."

beg you, not because of the love that you bear for me, which does not <u>oblige</u> you in the least, but because of your own nobleness, which you have shown to be greater than that of all others in practicing courtliness, that you be pleased to give it to me, so that I may say that I have saved the life of my son by means of this gift, and because of it I have placed him in your debt forever."

When he heard what the lady requested and knew that he could not oblige her since he had given her the falcon to eat, Federigo began to weep in her presence, for he could not utter a word in reply. The lady, at first, thought his tears were caused more by the sorrow of having to part with the good falcon than by anything else, and she was on the verge of telling him she no longer wished it, but she held back and waited for Federigo's reply after he stopped weeping. And he said:

"My lady, ever since it pleased God for me to place my love in you, I have felt that Fortune has been hostile to me in many things, and I have complained of her, but all this is nothing compared to what she has just done to me, and I must never be at peace with her again, thinking about how you have come here to my poor home where, while it was rich, you never deigned to come, and you requested a small gift, and Fortune worked to make it impossible for me to give it to you; and why this is so I shall tell you briefly. When I heard that you, out of your kindness, wished to dine with me, I considered it fitting and right, taking into account your excellence and your worthiness, that I should honor you, according to my possibilities, with a more precious food than that which I usually serve to other people; therefore, remembering the falcon that you requested and its value, I judged it a food worthy of you, and this very day you

had it roasted and served to you as best I could; but seeing now that you desired it in another way, my sorrow in not being able to serve you is so great that I shall never be able to <u>console</u> myself again."

And after he had said this, he laid the feathers, the feet, and the beak of the bird before her as proof. When the lady heard and saw this, she first reproached him for having killed such a falcon to serve as a meal to a woman; but then to herself she commended the greatness of his spirit, which no poverty was able or would be able to diminish; then, having lost all hope of getting the falcon and, perhaps because of this, of improving the health of her son as well, she thanked Federigo both for the honor paid to her and for his good will, and she left in grief, and returned to her son. To his mother's extreme sorrow, either because of his disappointment that he could not have the falcon, or because his illness must have necessarily led to it, the boy passed from this life only a few days later.

After the period of her mourning and bitterness had passed, the lady was repeatedly urged by her brothers to remarry, since she was very rich and was still young; and although she did not wish to do so, they became so insistent that she remembered the merits of Federigo and his last act of generosity—that is, to have killed such a falcon to do her honor—and she said to her brothers:

"I would prefer to remain a widow, if that would please you; but if you wish me to take a husband, you may rest assured that I shall take no man but Federigo degli Alberighi."

In answer to this, making fun of her, her brothers replied:

"You foolish woman, what are you saying? How can you want him; he hasn't a penny to his name?"

oblige (ə·blīj′): cause to do something by moral, legal, or physical force; do a favor

console (kən·sōl′): cause to feel less sad or disappointed

13 LITERARY ELEMENT
Climax: The story reaches a high point of tension after Monna Giovanna asks for the falcon. Why do you think Boccaccio has Monna Giovanna make a long speech about her reasons for asking for the bird, rather than having Federigo answer her request immediately? (Possible response: to heighten our suspense about how he will react)

14 CULTURAL BACKGROUND
Fortune, luck, or fate was often personified as a woman in ancient times, the Middle Ages, and the Renaissance. Often, Fortune was pictured as blind or blindfolded and sitting on an unstable globe. Fortune was also depicted as a woman turning a wheel. As the wheel turned, the lowly rose and the proud were brought down.

15 INTERPRETING
What qualities of Federigo did Monna Giovanna appreciate when she "commended the greatness of his spirit"? (his nobility and generosity)

16 READER'S RESPONSE
Were you surprised that Monna Giovanna decided to take Federigo as her husband in the end? Explain your response.

1. Researching the Sport of Falconry. Students may be interested in exploring further the history of falconry, especially the training of falcons, their importance in the Middle Ages and the Renaissance, and areas of the world where the sport continues today. Have students share their findings with the rest of the class.

2. Collecting Images of Fortune. Have students work in small groups to study art collections from the Middle Ages and the Renaissance, as well as ancient Greece and Rome, to find images representing Fortune, the Fates, or Nemesis. Have them display the images for the class and discuss how the idea of Fate evolved throughout Western history.

Have students compare and contrast the view of love expressed in this tale with the views expressed in the sonnets of Petrarch, Ronsard, and Shakespeare (pp. 804–812). ■

ANSWERS
First Thoughts
Answers will vary.

Identifying Facts
1. He participates in jousts, gives feasts, and spends money.
2. She reproaches him at first, then thanks him for his good will.
3. Federigo's act of generosity

Interpreting Meanings
1. when Federigo kills the falcon to feed Monna Giovanna; when she decides to marry him even though he is penniless because of his generous sacrifice for her
2. She respects and trusts his generosity and goodness.
3. *Romantic:* Federigo's patience, generosity, and lack of resentment toward Monna Giovanna; her gentleness and restraint; their living together "happily ever after" *Realistic:* consequences of squandering wealth; presence of death; cruelty of fate

Applying Meanings
Answers will vary.

Creative Writing Response
Exchanging Letters. Letters should be from the characters' points of view and should be written in a courtly style.

Speaking and Listening
A Storytelling Session. Storytellers should speak clearly and with expression. ■

To this she replied: "My brothers, I am well aware of what you say, but I would rather have a man who needs money than money that needs a man."

Her brothers, seeing that she was determined and knowing Federigo to be of noble birth, no matter how poor he was, accepted her wishes and gave her in marriage to him with all her riches; when he found himself the husband of such a great lady, whom he had loved so much and who was so wealthy besides, he managed his financial affairs with more prudence than in the past and lived with her happily the rest of his days.

First Thoughts
Do you think that Federigo was wise or foolish in making his sacrifice?

Identifying Facts
1. At first, what does Federigo do to win Monna Giovanna's love?
2. What does Monna Giovanna do when she learns what Federigo has made for supper?
3. When her brothers urge her to remarry, what does Monna Giovanna remember?

Interpreting Meanings
1. The unexpected visit of Monna Giovanna to Federigo after he has lost all his money is an example of **situational irony**, which occurs when what actually happens is the opposite of what is expected. Cite two other examples of situational irony in the story. How is the falcon central to these ironic events?
2. How does Federigo's sacrifice change Monna Giovanna's opinion of him? Why will she "take no man but Federigo"?
3. This story is a mixture of the romantic and the realistic. Which aspects of the story are romantic? Which are realistic?

Applying Meanings
"The Tale of the Falcon" focuses on a chivalric sacrifice to suggest that spiritual values are more important than money or possessions. Can you think of a modern work of film or literature that features a chivalric sacrifice? Do you think that such stories teach positive values, or are they "fairy tales" that promote unrealistic expectations?

Creative Writing Response
Exchanging Letters. Imagine that Monna Giovanna and Federigo exchange letters after Monna Giovanna's period of mourning is over. With a partner, write a letter from Monna Giovanna to Federigo, accepting his love and offering to marry him. Make sure that this letter explains why she "'would rather have a man who needs money than money that needs a man.'" What does she mean by "a man"? Then write Federigo's reply, keeping in mind his courtliness and longtime love for his lady.

Speaking and Listening
A Storytelling Session. The seven women and three men in the frame story of Boccaccio's *Decameron* tell stories while the Black Death rages around them. The stories they tell include folktales, fables, and anecdotes. Imagine that you and your classmates are isolated along with Boccaccio's storytellers. What story will you tell to entertain your companions and pass the time? Tell your story to the class. It can be a story you have made up yourself, a story you have read or heard, or even a lengthy joke. If you wish, record your storytelling session and critique one another's oral performance.

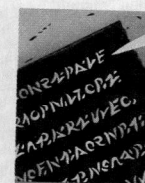

Miguel de Cervantes
1547–1616

The Granger Collection, New York

Miguel de Cervantes (sər·vän′tāz′), son of a wandering apothecary, or druggist, was born near Madrid, Spain, in 1547. In 1569, Cervantes, seeing no prospects at home, enlisted in the army, fought valiantly, and was wounded at the Battle of Lepanto in 1571. His left hand was crippled, earning him the nickname, "el manco de Lepanto"— "the one-handed man of Lepanto."

Cervantes hoped to be promoted to an army captain after the war, but his plans were later thwarted when he was captured by Barbary pirates and held as a slave for five years in Algeria. He returned to Spain in 1580, jobless, in debt, and without any hope of regaining his army career. Over the years he worked as a playwright, bureaucrat, and tax collector before finally landing in jail for failure to pay his debts, many of which had accrued as a result of his family scraping together the ransom money to buy his freedom from the pirates.

According to legend, it was while he was in jail that the idea for *Don Quixote* came to Cervantes. His hero, Don Quixote, is a poor, aging landowner who reads nothing but romantic tales of chivalry. As he teeters on the edge of insanity, the old man becomes convinced that he is a knight-errant, even though the age of knights is long past.

The Ingenious Gentleman Don Quixote of La Mancha was published in January of 1605, and immediately caused a sensation. Once the first edition sold out, pirated—illegally printed—copies began to appear. Six editions were issued in the first year, and translations into French and English appeared within ten years. It seemed that everyone in Spain, and soon everyone in Europe, was laughing at the droll adventures of the ridiculous knight, Don Quixote.

Cervantes, at the age of fifty-eight, was now a famous author, but he was still poor. As was common until the nineteenth century, authors were at the mercy of publishers and were seldom able to retain the copyrights on their books. Thus, *Don Quixote*'s publisher, not Cervantes, reaped the lion's share of the book's profits. Spain's greatest writer died in poverty on April 22, 1616. To his family Cervantes left only a little money and many debts. To the world he left a comic masterpiece that earned him the title of "father of the modern novel."

MORE ABOUT THE AUTHOR

Cervantes' life after his return to Spain was one of bitter disillusionment. He wrote:

> I returned home with riches and honors, intending to remain some days there in order to enjoy the society of my parents, who were both living, and of the friends who expected me. But that which men call fortune—for my part I know not what she is—envious of my tranquility, turning the wheel she is said to hold, threw me down from the summit on which I had been placed into the depths of misery wherein you see me now. . . .

Though *Don Quixote* was a very popular work, Cervantes never won the acceptance of the Spanish literary establishment of his day. His down-to-earth style and mocking tone did not fit with the elegant, authority-flattering conventions of Renaissance Spanish literature.

ABOUT THE TRANSLATOR

Samuel Putnam (1892–1950) was a journalist, translator, and author who wrote a critically acclaimed book about American expatriate writers in Paris. His translation of *Don Quixote* is considered one of his most distinguished achievements.

OBJECTIVES

1. *To analyze a great comic novel of the Spanish Renaissance and to contrast its two main characters*
2. *To analyze the techniques and effects of parody*
3. *To write a story about a modern comic hero, and to interpret and evaluate a contemporary poem containing an allusion to Don Quixote.*

THEMES IN WORLD LITERATURE

Satire and the Absurd
From *Candide*, pp. 945–962
The Metamorphosis, pp. 1154–1195

The Quest and the Perilous Journey
"Theseus," pp. 28–33
"The Grail" from *Perceval*, pp. 720–729 ■

VOCABULARY IN CONTEXT

The words listed below will appear in the side margin at the point of instruction:

1. conjectures	6. incongruous
2. infatuation	7. assailed
3. interminable	8. novice
4. affable	9. asininely
5. ingenuity	10. patriarch

PREREADING FOCUS

Background: Over the centuries, scholars and casual readers alike have debated the extent of Cervantes' intentions and achievements in *Don Quixote*. Early readers accepted at face value Cervantes' claim that the work was simply a parody of courtly romances. By the nineteenth century, however, critics of the Romantic era began to see Don Quixote as a tragic hero, "the immortal representative of all men of exalted imagination who carry the noblest enthusiasms to the point of folly." It is this interpretation that has inspired contemporary works such as the musical *Man of La Mancha*, for which the popular song "The Impossible Dream" was written.

Literary Focus: Parody was a popular literary form in Cervantes' time, but most parodies were inspired by an intense dislike of an author or a genre and were rather nasty in tone. Cervantes' parody, on the other hand, is an affectionate send-up of a genre for which he had a certain fondness. (Evidence suggests that Cervantes was an enthusiastic reader of courtly romances.)

In all parodies, readers are invited to laugh at the characters' expense and to feel superior to them. However, the genius of Cervantes' work lies in the fact that while we may laugh at Don Quixote, we are not always sure that our way of seeing the world is superior to his, and we come to share the author's affection for him.

Reader's Guide ■

from DON QUIXOTE

Background

Initially, Cervantes intended *Don Quixote* to lampoon tales of **chivalry** and **courtly romances**, stories from the medieval period about romantic love and knightly adventure, which were still eagerly devoured by the audience of Cervantes' time. In these stories, idealized knights fought villains, dragons, and monsters, and embarked on quests in honor of ladies to whom they had sworn their love. Such heroes stood for military values such as honor, courage, and loyalty, combined with Christian virtues such as piety, courtesy, and chastity.

Cervantes used the conventions of chivalric romances and satirized them at the same time. Don Quixote wears a cardboard visor on his helmet and mistakes windmills for giants. These actions, and others like them, suggest the discrepancy between the real world and the idealism portrayed in chivalric romances. Yet *Don Quixote* is much more than a parody of the romances of Cervantes' day. It touchingly develops two of literature's most enduring themes: the struggle of the idealist in a materialistic world and the interplay of fantasy and reality.

Writer's Response

Cervantes' novel resulted in a new word used to describe a person who is a well-intentioned, impractical, foolishly idealistic dreamer: *quixotic* (kwiks·ät'ik). What quixotic heroes in popular culture—films, comic strips, television, and books—can you think of? What traits do these heroes share? Do they succeed in their adventures?

Literary Focus

A literary **parody** is an imitation of another work of literature for amusement or instruction. A parody uses exaggeration or inappropriate subject matter to make something serious seem laughable. For example, in a serious chivalric romance a hero would be dubbed a knight by his lord, usually a king, and he would prepare for the ceremony during an all-night vigil in which he watched over his armor in a chapel. In *Don Quixote*, Don Quixote arranges to be dubbed a knight by the fat innkeeper of a rural inn that he mistakes for a castle, and he places his rusty armor in a horse-trough rather than on an altar. In the novel, many other uproarious scenes parody chivalric romances.

from DON QUIXOTE

Miguel de Cervantes

translated by
SAMUEL PUTNAM

As you read, note how often Don Quixote refers to chivalric romances he has read to explain or justify what he does or what happens to him.

Chapter 1

Which treats of the station in life and the pursuits of the famous gentleman, Don Quixote de la Mancha.

In a village of La Mancha,[1] the name of which I have no desire to recall, there lived not so long ago one of those gentlemen who always have a lance in the rack, an ancient buckler, a skinny nag, and a greyhound for the chase. A stew with more beef than mutton in it, chopped meat for his evening meal, scraps for a Saturday, lentils on Friday, and a young pigeon as a special delicacy for Sunday went to account for three quarters of his income. The rest of it he laid out on a broadcloth greatcoat and velvet stockings for feast days, with slippers to match, while the other days of the week he cut a figure in a suit of the finest homespun. Living with him were a housekeeper in her forties, a niece who was not yet twenty, and a lad of the field and marketplace who saddled his horse for him and wielded the pruning knife.

This gentleman of ours was close on to fifty, of a robust constitution but with little flesh on his bones and a face that was lean and gaunt. He was noted for his early rising, being very fond of the hunt. They will try to tell you that his surname was Quijada or Quesada[2]—there is some difference of opinion among those who have written on the subject—but according to the most likely conjectures we are to understand that it was really Quejana. But all this means very little so far as our story is concerned, providing that in the telling of it we do not depart one iota from the truth.

You may know, then, that the aforesaid gentleman, on those occasions when he was at leisure, which was most of the year around, was in the habit of reading books of chivalry with such pleasure and devotion as to lead him almost wholly to forget the life of a hunter and even the administration of his estate. So great was his curiosity and infatuation in this regard that he even sold many acres of tillable land in order to be able to buy and read the books that he loved,

---

1. **La Mancha:** a province of south-central Spain, a poor plateau land lying alongside the mountains called Sierra Morena; to Cervantes, La Mancha represented a poor, backward area in the middle of nowhere.

2. **Quijada** (kē·hä′dä) **or Quesada** (kā·sä′dä): distinguished Spanish family names.

DON QUIXOTE IN HIS STUDY, GEORGE CATTERMOLE (1800–1868).
What tone does the narrator adopt to report Don Quixote's obsession with romances?

Victoria & Albert Museum, London/Art Resource, New York

and he would carry home with him as many of them as he could obtain.

Of all those that he thus devoured, none pleased him so well as the ones that had been composed by the famous Feliciano de Silva,[3] whose lucid prose style and involved conceits were as precious to him as pearls; especially when he came to read those tales of love and amorous challenges that are to be met with in many places, such a passage as the following, for example: "The reason of the unreason that afflicts my reason, in such a manner weakens my reason that I with reason lament me of your comeliness." And he was similarly affected when his eyes fell upon such lines as these: "... the high heaven of your divinity divinely fortifies you with the stars and renders you deserving of that desert your greatness doth deserve."

The poor fellow used to lie awake nights in an effort to disentangle the meaning and make sense out of passages such as these, although Aristotle himself would not have been able to understand them, even if he had been resurrected for that sole purpose. He was not at ease in his mind over those wounds that Don Belianís gave and received;

---

3. **Feliciano de Silva:** a sixteenth-century writer of romances, including *Don Florisel de Niquea*, from which the following quotation is taken.

for no matter how great the surgeons who treated him, the poor fellow must have been left with his face and his entire body covered with marks and scars. Nevertheless, he was grateful to the author for closing the book with the promise of an <u>interminable</u> adventure to come; many a time he was tempted to take up his pen and literally finish the tale as had been promised, and he undoubtedly would have done so, and would have succeeded at it very well, if his thoughts had not been constantly occupied with other things of greater moment.

He often talked it over with the village curate, who was a learned man, a graduate of Sigüenza,[4] and they would hold long discussions as to who had been the better knight, Palmerin of England or Amadis of Gaul;[5] but Master Nicholas, the barber of the same village, was in the habit of saying that no one could come up to the Knight of Phoebus,[6] and that if anyone *could* compare with him it was Don Galaor, brother of Amadis of Gaul, for Galaor was ready for anything—he was none of your finical knights who went around whimpering as his brother did, and in point of valor he did not lag behind him.

In short, our gentleman became so immersed in his reading that he spent whole nights from sundown to sunup and his days from dawn to dusk in poring over his books, until, finally, from so little sleeping and so much reading, his brain dried up and he went completely out of his mind. He had filled his imagination with everything that he had read, with enchantments, knightly encounters, battles, challenges, wounds, with tales of love and its torments, and all sorts of impossible things, and as a result had come to believe that all these fictitious happenings were true; they were more real to him than anything else in the world. He would remark that the Cid[7] Ruy Díaz had been a very good knight, but there was no comparison between him and the Knight of the Flaming Sword, who with a single backward stroke had cut in half two fierce and monstrous giants. He preferred Bernardo del Carpio, who at Roncesvalles had slain Roland despite the charm[8] the latter bore, availing himself of the stratagem which Hercules employed when he strangled Antaeus,[9] the son of Earth, in his arms.

He had much good to say for Morgante[10] who, though he belonged to the haughty, overbearing race of giants, was of an <u>affable</u> disposition and well brought up. But, above all, he cherished an admiration for Rinaldo of Montalbán,[11] especially as he beheld him sallying forth from his castle to rob all those that crossed his path, or when he thought of him overseas stealing the image of Mohammed which, so the story has it, was all of gold. And he would have liked very well to have had his fill of kicking that traitor Galalón,[12] a privilege for which he would have given his housekeeper with his niece thrown into the bargain.

---

7. **Cid** (thēd): the subject of Spain's national epic.
8. **charm:** magic that made him invulnerable.
9. **Antaeus** (an·tē′əs): In Greek mythology, Antaeus could not be killed as long as he remained in contact with the earth. Hercules lifted him and then strangled him.
10. **Morgante:** a character in an Italian epic.
11. **Rinaldo of Montalbán:** one of Charlemagne's knights.
12. **Galalón:** Ganelon, who in the *Song of Roland* betrayed the French at the pass of Roncesvalles.

---

4. **Sigüenza:** a minor Spanish university with a poor reputation, hence an ironic reference.
5. **Palmerin of England or Amadis of Gaul:** famous heroes of chivalric romances.
6. **Phoebus:** Apollo, the sun god in Greek mythology; here used as a symbolic name.

interminable (in·tur′mi·nə·bəl): seemingly endless

affable (af′ə·bəl): easy to approach and talk to

6 LITERARY ELEMENT
Tone: What attitude does the narrator reveal toward de Silva's work by using the adjective "interminable"? (that the books seem endless because of their convoluted style and improbable plots) How does his attitude differ from Don Quixote's? (Don Quixote hates to see the books end and can't wait for sequels.)

MEETING INDIVIDUAL NEEDS

7 *LEP:* The phrase "of greater moment" means "of more importance." Ask students why the statement is an example of verbal irony, saying one thing and meaning another. (Possible response: Don Quixote really doesn't have anything important to do.) ■

8 EVALUATING
Do you consider Don Quixote genuinely insane or a noble victim of an overactive imagination? (Responses will vary.)

9 COMPARING LITERATURE
Students may enjoy reading the excerpt from the *Song of Roland* on p. 694. Have them compare and contrast Roland and Don Quixote as heroes.

At last, when his wits were gone beyond repair, he came to conceive the strangest idea that ever occurred to any madman in this world. It now appeared to him fitting and necessary, in order to win a greater amount of honor for himself and serve his country at the same time, to become a knight-errant and roam the world on horseback, in a suit of armor; he would go in quest of adventures, by way of putting into practice all that he had read in his books; he would right every manner of wrong, placing himself in situations of the greatest peril such as would redound to the eternal glory of his name. As a reward for his valor and the might of his arm, the poor fellow could already see himself crowned Emperor of Trebizond[13] at the very least; and so, carried away by the strange pleasure that he found in such thoughts as these, he at once set about putting his plan into effect.

The first thing he did was to burnish up some old pieces of armor, left him by his great-grandfather, which for ages had lain in a corner, moldering and forgotten. He polished and adjusted them as best he could, and then he noticed that one very important thing was lacking: there was no closed helmet, but only a morion,[14] or visorless headpiece, with turned-up brim of the kind foot soldiers wore. His ingenuity, however, enabled him to remedy this, and he proceeded to fashion out of cardboard a kind of half-helmet, which, when attached to the morion, gave the appearance of a whole one. True, when he went to see if it was strong enough to withstand a good slashing blow, he was somewhat disappointed; for when he drew his sword and gave it a couple of

Equestrian Portrait, Albrecht Dürer (1471–1528). Art Resource, New York

thrusts, he succeeded only in undoing a whole week's labor. The ease with which he had hewed it to bits disturbed him no little, and he decided to make it over. This time he placed a few strips of iron on the inside, and then, convinced that it was strong enough, refrained from putting it to any further test; instead, he adopted it then and there as the finest helmet ever made.

After this, he went out to have a look at his nag; and although the animal had more *cuartos*, or cracks, in its hoof than there are quarters in a real,[15] and more blemishes than

---

13. **Trebizond** (treb′i·zänd′): Greek empire that was an offshoot of the Byzantine Empire.
14. **morion** (mōr′ē·än′): a helmet with a curved peak, used in the sixteenth and seventeenth centuries.

15. **real** (rā·äl′): an old Spanish coin, something like a nickel; there were eight *cuartos* (meaning both "quarter" and "crack") in a real.

Gonela's steed[16] which *tantum pellis et ossa fuit*,[17] it nonetheless looked to its master like a far better horse than Alexander's Bucephalus or the Babieca[18] of the Cid. He spent all of four days in trying to think up a name for his mount; for—so he told himself—seeing that it belonged to so famous and worthy a knight, there was no reason why it should not have a name of equal renown. The kind of name he wanted was one that would at once indicate what the nag had been before it came to belong to a knight-errant and what its present status was; for it stood to reason that, when the master's worldly condition changed, his horse also ought to have a famous, high-sounding appellation, one suited to the new order of things and the new profession that it was to follow.

After he in his memory and imagination had made up, struck out, and discarded many names, now adding to and now subtracting from the list, he finally hit upon "Rocinante,"[19] a name that impressed him as being sonorous and at the same time indicative of what the steed had been when it was but a hack, whereas now it was nothing other than the first and foremost of all the hacks in the world.

Having found a name for his horse that pleased his fancy, he then desired to do as much for himself, and this required another week, and by the end of that period he had made up his mind that he was henceforth to be known as Don Quixote,[20] which, as has been stated, has led the authors of this veracious history to assume that his real name must undoubtedly have been Quijada, and not Quesada as others would have it. But remembering that the valiant Amadis was not content to call himself that and nothing more, but added the name of his kingdom and fatherland that he might make it famous also, and thus came to take the name Amadis of Gaul, so our good knight chose to add his place of origin and become "Don Quixote de la Mancha"; for by this means, as he saw it, he was making very plain his lineage and was conferring honor upon his country by taking its name as his own.[21]

And so, having polished up his armor and made the morion over into a closed helmet, and having given himself and his horse a name, he naturally found but one thing lacking still: he must seek out a lady of whom he could become enamored; for a knight-errant without a ladylove was like a tree without leaves or fruit, a body without a soul.

"If," he said to himself, "as a punishment for my sins or by a stroke of fortune I should come upon some giant hereabouts, a thing that very commonly happens to knights-errant, and if I should slay him in a hand-to-hand encounter or perhaps cut him in two, or, finally, if I should vanquish and subdue him, would it not be well to have someone to whom I may send him as a present, in order that he, if he is living, may

---

16. **Gonela's steed:** Gonela, the jester of the Duke of Ferrara, had a horse that was the butt of many jokes.

17. *tantum . . . fuit:* "was nothing but skin and bones" (Latin).

18. **Bucephalus** (byōō·sef′ə·ləs): war horse of Alexander the Great . . . **Babieca** (bä·bye′kə); Cid's champion horse.

19. **Rocinante** (rō′sē·nän′tä): coined from the word *rocin*, meaning "a nag" or "hack" and the word *ante*, meaning "before"; *Rocinante* therefore means "formerly a nag" and implies a grand new status.

20. **Quixote** (kē·hōt′ē): the name for a piece of armor that covers the thigh.

21. **name as his own:** If a man named Smith from Wichita called himself Lord Smythe of Kansas, the effect might be something like this.

13 **LITERARY ELEMENT**
Humor: A hack is an old, worn-out horse. Why is it funny to describe Rocinante as "the first and foremost of all the hacks in the world"? (Possible response: It isn't much of an honor to be the best in an undistinguished category; Rocinante is still an old, worn-out horse.)

14 **GUIDED READING**
Identifying Details: After Don Quixote renames his horse, what does he spend a whole week doing? (thinking of a new name for himself) Why is this detail humorous? (A week is a long time to spend on something so trivial. It suggests he had nothing better to do.)

15 **LITERARY ELEMENT**
Parody: How does Don Quixote's approach to love contrast ironically with that of the heroes of courtly romances? (Instead of being overwhelmed by feelings for a specific woman, he purposely sets out to find "a lady of whom he could become enamored," simply to follow the rules for courtly heroes.)

Once jailed for a political caricature of King Louis Philippe, and considered in his lifetime only an effective cartoonist and printmaker, Honoré Daumier (dōm'yā') is today also remembered as a skilled sculptor and powerful painter. Daumier carried over to his painting the bold simplicity of the print medium. As in this hallucinatory and ghostlike *Don Quixote*, many of his canvases center on an image done in broad, obvious strokes of black and white.

❓ *How do the sharp angles of Don Quixote's emaciated horse enhance the hallucinatory mood?* (Possible response: the skeletal appearance of the horse suggests a struggle for survival and perhaps death.) ∎

Giraudon/Art Resource, New York

DON QUIXOTE, HONORÉ DAUMIER (1808–1879).
❓ *Do you think that this and the following painting (page 831) succeed at capturing the atmosphere of the selection? Why or why not?*

come in, fall upon his knees in front of my sweet lady, and say in a humble and submissive tone of voice, 'I, lady, am the giant Caraculiambro, lord of the island Malindrania, who has been overcome in single combat by that knight who never can be praised enough, Don Quixote de la Mancha, the same who sent me to present myself before your Grace that your Highness may dispose of me as you see fit'?"

Oh, how our good knight reveled in this speech, and more than ever when he came to think of the name that he should give his lady! As the story goes, there was a very good-looking farm girl who lived nearby, with whom he had once been smitten, although it is generally believed that she never knew or suspected it. Her name was Aldonza Lorenzo, and it seemed to him that she was the one upon whom he should bestow the title of mistress of his thoughts. For her he wished a name that should not be incongruous with his own and that would convey the suggestion of a princess or a great lady; and accordingly, he resolved to call her "Dulcinea[22] del Toboso," she being a native of that place. A musical name to his ears, out of the ordinary and significant, like the others he had chosen for himself and his appurtenances.

from Chapter 2

Which treats of the first sally that the ingenious Don Quixote made from his native heath.

Having, then, made all these preparations, he did not wish to lose any time in putting his plan into effect, for he could not but blame himself for what the world was losing by his delay, so many were the wrongs that were to be righted, the grievances to be redressed, the abuses to be done away with, and the duties to be performed. Accordingly, without informing anyone of his intention and without letting anyone see him, he set out one morning before daybreak on one of those very hot days in July. Donning all his armor, mounting Rocinante, adjusting his ill-contrived helmet, bracing his shield on his arm, and taking up his lance, he sallied forth by the back gate of his stable yard into the open countryside. It was with great contentment and joy that he saw how easily he had made a beginning towards the fulfillment of his desire.

No sooner was he out on the plain, however, than a terrible thought assailed him, one that all but caused him to abandon the enterprise he had undertaken. This occurred when he suddenly remembered that he had never formally been dubbed a knight, and so, in accordance with the law of knighthood, was not permitted to bear arms against one who had a right to that title. And even if he had been, as a novice knight he would have had to wear white armor,[23] without any device on his shield, until he should have earned one by his exploits. These thoughts led him to waver in his purpose, but, madness prevailing over reason, he resolved to have himself knighted by the first person he met, as many others had done if what he had read in those books that he had at home was true. And so far as white armor was concerned, he would scour his own the first chance that offered until it shone whiter than any ermine. With this he became more tranquil and continued on his

---

22. **Dulcinea** (dul'sə·nē'ə) derived from the Spanish word *dulce,* meaning ''sweet.''

23. **white armor:** that is, armor without any insignia or signs of use. Here Don Quixote is taking the term literally.

Miguel de Cervantes 829

---

incongruous (in·käng'grōō·əs): inconsistent; lacking in harmony

assailed (ə·sāld'): attacked

novice (näv'is): beginner

16 LITERARY ELEMENT
Satire: Don Quixote spends a great deal of time and energy renaming himself, his ladylove, and his horse. What human folly might Cervantes be mocking with his main character's obsession with names? (Possible response: people's concern for form over substance)

17 LITERARY ELEMENT
Tone: What tone, or attitude, toward Don Quixote's mission does the narrator convey in the first paragraph of Chapter 2? (Possible responses: amused, sympathetic, mocking)

18 ANALYZING
Does Don Quixote's madness and imagination seem to be a source of distress or comfort to him? Give a specific example to support your answer. (Comfort; whenever a problem or sudden awareness of reality arises to disturb him, he thinks of an imaginative, if ridiculous, way of solving it to his own satisfaction. His solution to the problem of never having been knighted is a good example.)

19 way, letting his horse take whatever path it chose, for he believed that therein lay the very essence of adventures....

20 *Don Quixote gets himself "knighted" by a bewildered innkeeper, who marvels at such an extraordinary variety of madness, but he is finally tricked by his friends and brought home, where he is treated as a lunatic. His family deprives him of the dangerous books, and they hope that the madness will pass.*

from Chapter 7

Of the second sally of our good knight, Don Quixote de la Mancha.

... He remained at home very tranquilly for a couple of weeks, without giving sign of any desire to repeat his former madness. During that time he had the most pleasant conversations with his two old friends, the curate and the barber, on the point he had raised to the effect that what the world **21** needed most was knights-errant and a revival of chivalry. The curate would occasionally contradict him and again would give in, for it was only by means of this artifice that he could carry on a conversation with him at all.

In the meanwhile Don Quixote was bringing his powers of persuasion to bear upon a farmer who lived nearby, a good man—if this title may be applied to one who is poor—but with very few wits in his head. The short of it is, by pleas and promises, he got the hapless rustic to agree to ride forth with him and serve him as his squire. Among other things, Don Quixote told him that he ought to be more than willing to go, because no telling what adventure might oc-**22** cur which would win them an island, and then he (the farmer) would be left to be the governor of it. As a result of these and other similar assurances, Sancho Panza forsook his wife and children and consented to take upon himself the duties of squire to his neighbor.

Next, Don Quixote set out to raise some money, and by selling this thing and pawning that and getting the worst of the bargain always, he finally scraped together a reasonable amount. He also asked a friend of his for the loan of a buckler[24] and patched up his broken helmet as well as he could. He advised his squire, Sancho, of the day and hour when they were to take the road and told him to see to laying in a supply of those things that were most necessary, and, above all, not to forget the saddlebags. Sancho replied that he would see to all this and added that he was also thinking of taking along with him a very good ass that he had, as he was not much used to going on foot.

With regard to the ass, Don Quixote had to do a little thinking, trying to recall if any knight-errant had ever had a squire thus asininely mounted. He could not think of any, but nevertheless he decided to take Sancho with the intention of providing him with a nobler steed as soon as occasion offered; he had but to appropriate the horse of the first discourteous knight he met. Having furnished himself with shirts and all the other things that the innkeeper had recommended, he and Panza rode forth one night unseen by anyone and without taking leave of wife and children, housekeeper or niece. They went so far that by the time morning came they were safe from discovery had a hunt been started for them.

Mounted on his ass, Sancho Panza rode along like a patriarch, with saddlebags and flask, his mind set upon becoming governor

---

24. **buckler:** a small shield.

The Bridgeman Art Library/Art Resource, New York

SANCHO AND DON QUIXOTE, HONORÉ DAUMIER.

23 LITERARY ELEMENT

Humor: Why is Sancho's way of addressing Don Quixote as "Sir Knight-errant, your Grace" humorous? (Sancho addresses Don Quixote by a number of titles that show respect, although both Sancho and the reader know that Don Quixote really is not a knight.)

24 HISTORICAL BACKGROUND

The titles of *count* and *marquis* originated during the feudal age. Feudal society was based on a chain of mutual obligations between peasants, landed nobility, and kings. *Count* is the lowest title of European nobility. A *marquis* is the next highest title, followed by a *duke*. Such titles were usually hereditary.

25 COMPARING LITERATURE

Students may enjoy comparing and contrasting the optimism and idealism of characters in *Don Quixote* with those of characters in *Candide* (pp. 946–962).

26 LITERARY ELEMENT

Character Motivation: What is Sancho's motivation for calling Don Quixote "so illustrious a master"? (to stay in Don Quixote's good graces so he will get the title Don Quixote has promised) What does Sancho's willingness to believe Don Quixote's promises show about him? (Possible response: He is gullible.)

---

of that island that his master had promised him. Don Quixote determined to take the same route and road over the Campo de Montiel[25] that he had followed on his first journey; but he was not so uncomfortable this time, for it was early morning and the sun's rays fell upon them slantingly and accordingly did not tire them too much.

23 "Look, Sir Knight-errant," said Sancho, "your Grace should not forget that island you promised me; for no matter how big it is, I'll be able to govern it right enough."

"I would have you know, friend Sancho Panza," replied Don Quixote, "that among the knights-errant of old it was a very common custom to make their squires governors of the islands or the kingdoms that they won, and I am resolved that in my case so pleasing a usage shall not fall into desuetude.[26] I even mean to go them one better; for they very often, perhaps most of the time, waited until their squires were old men who had had their fill of serving their masters during bad days and worse nights, **24** whereupon they would give them the title of count, or marquis at most, of some valley or province more or less. But if you live and **25** I live, it well may be that within a week I shall win some kingdom with others dependent upon it, and it will be the easiest thing in the world to crown you king of one of them. You need not marvel at this, for all sorts of unforeseen things happen to knights like me, and I may readily be able to give you even more than I have promised."

"In that case," said Sancho Panza, "if by one of those miracles of which your Grace was speaking I should become king, I would certainly send for Juana Gutiérrez, my old

---

25. **Campo de Montiel** (käm′pō dā mōn·tyēl′): the site of a famous battle in 1369.
26. **desuetude** (des′wi·tōōd′): disuse.

---

lady, to come and be my queen, and the young ones could be infantes."[27]

"There is no doubt about it," Don Quixote assured him.

"Well, I doubt it," said Sancho, "for I think that even if God were to rain kingdoms upon the earth, no crown would sit well on the head of Mari Gutiérrez,[28] for I am telling you, sir, as a queen she is not worth two maravedis.[29] She would do better as a countess, God help her."

"Leave everything to God, Sancho," said Don Quixote, "and he will give you whatever is most fitting; but I trust you will not be so pusillanimous[30] as to be content with anything less than the title of viceroy."

26 "That I will not," said Sancho Panza, "especially seeing that I have in your Grace so illustrious a master who can give me all that is suitable to me and all that I can manage."

from Chapter 8

Of the good fortune which the valorous Don Quixote had in the terrifying and never-before-imagined adventure of the windmills, along with other events that deserve to be suitably recorded.

At this point they caught sight of thirty or forty windmills which were standing on the plain there, and no sooner had Don Quixote laid eyes upon them than he turned to his squire and said, "Fortune is guiding our affairs better than we could have wished; for you see there before you, friend Sancho

---

27. **infantes** (in·fan′tāz′): a term used to designate the children of a Spanish king.
28. **Mari Gutiérrez:** Sancho's wife, who appears under several names during the course of the story.
29. **maravedis** (mar′ə·vä′dēz): old Spanish coins of trifling value.
30. **pusillanimous** (pyōō′si·lan′ə·məs): timid.

From the Renaissance to the Enlightenment

Panza, some thirty or more lawless giants with whom I mean to do battle. I shall deprive them of their lives, and with the spoils from this encounter we shall begin to enrich ourselves; for this is righteous warfare, and it is a great service to God to remove so accursed a breed from the face of the earth."

"What giants?" said Sancho Panza.

"Those that you see there," replied his master, "those with the long arms, some of which are as much as two leagues in length."

"But look, your Grace, those are not giants but windmills, and what appear to be arms are their wings which, when whirled in the breeze, cause the millstone to go."

"It is plain to be seen," said Don Quixote, "that you have had little experience in this matter of adventures. If you are afraid, go off to one side and say your prayers while I am engaging them in fierce, unequal combat."

Saying this, he gave spurs to his steed Rocinante, without paying any heed to Sancho's warning that these were truly windmills and not giants that he was riding forth to attack. Nor even when he was close upon them did he perceive what they really were, but shouted at the top of his lungs, "Do not seek to flee, cowards and vile creatures that you are, for it is but a single knight with whom you have to deal!"

At that moment a little wind came up and the big wings began turning.

"Though you flourish as many arms as did

27
28
28

27 HISTORICAL BACKGROUND

According to the ideals of chivalry, knights fought to protect the weak and to serve God and society. In fact, they lived on what they could plunder from their enemy in "spoils," and their constant battles often harmed innocent bystanders.

28 GUIDED READING

Identifying Details: Who points out to Don Quixote that the giants are really windmills? (Sancho) How does Don Quixote respond to this attempt to bring him back to reality? (He claims Sancho has no experience in adventure and is afraid.)

HUMANITIES CONNECTION

Have students compare the illustrations on pp. 831, 833.
Which picture presents an actual event from Chapter 8? (Don Quixote and the Windmill) *Why do you think Torrome painted Sancho Panza and Don Quixote as such small figures in an empty expanse?* (Possible response: to heighten the futility of their efforts in fighting windmills) ■

DON QUIXOTE AND THE WINDMILL, FRANCISCO J. TORROME, c. 1900.

The Bridgeman Art Library/Art Resource, New York

Miguel de Cervantes   **833**

29 ANALYZING

How does Don Quixote use his knowlege of literature and mythology to help support his fantasy about the windmills? (He compares the so-called giants he is fighting to Briareus, a giant in Greek mythology who had a hundred arms.)

30 READER'S RESPONSE

Were you able to visualize Don Quixote's attack on the windmills? What was funniest about the episode?

31 INTERPRETING

What emotions do you think Sancho is feeling as he sees his master and his horse sprawled on the ground? (Possible responses: exasperation, concern for Don Quixote's welfare, disbelief)

32 LITERARY ELEMENT

Dialogue: What effect does Sancho's response to Don Quixote's first speech after his encounter with the windmills have on the reader? (Possible response: It deflates Don Quixote's grand ambitions by reminding us that he is really a decrepit, ridiculous old man who just experienced a humiliating defeat in his ''battle'' with the windmills.)

33 READER'S RESPONSE

Do you think Cervantes approves of the chivalric value of bearing pain stoically, or is he mocking it? How do you feel about such values?

29 the giant Briareus,"[31] said Don Quixote when he perceived this, "you still shall have to answer to me."

He thereupon commended himself with all his heart to his lady Dulcinea, beseeching her to succor him in this peril; and, being **30** well covered with his shield and with his lance at rest, he bore down upon them at a full gallop and fell upon the first mill that stood in his way, giving a thrust at the wing, which was whirling at such a speed that his lance was broken into bits and both horse and horseman went rolling over the plain, very much battered indeed. Sancho upon his donkey came hurrying to his master's assistance as fast as he could, but when he reached the spot, the knight was unable to move, so great was the shock with which he and Rocinante had hit the ground.

31 "God help us!" exclaimed Sancho, "did I not tell your Grace to look well, that those were nothing but windmills, a fact which no one could fail to see unless he had other mills of the same sort in his head?"

"Be quiet, friend Sancho," said Don Quixote. "Such are the fortunes of war, which more than any other are subject to constant change. What is more, when I come to think of it, I am sure that this must be the work of that magician Frestón, the one who robbed me of my study and my books, and who has thus changed the giants into windmills in order to deprive me of the glory of overcoming them, so great is the enmity that he bears me; but in the end his evil arts shall not prevail against this trusty sword of mine."

"May God's will be done," was Sancho Panza's response. And with the aid of his squire the knight was once more mounted on Rocinante, who stood there with one shoulder half out of joint. And so, speaking of the adventure that had just befallen them, they continued along the Puerto Lápice highway; for there, Don Quixote said, they could not fail to find many and varied adventures, this being a much-traveled thoroughfare. The only thing was, the knight was exceedingly downcast over the loss of his lance.

"I remember," he said to his squire, "having read of a Spanish knight by the name of Diego Pérez de Vargas, who, having broken his sword in battle, tore from an oak a heavy bough or branch and with it did such feats of valor that day, and pounded so many Moors, that he came to be known as Machuca,[32] and he and his descendants from that day forth have been called Vargas y Machuca. I tell you this because I, too, intend to provide myself with just such a bough as the one he wielded, and with it I propose to do such exploits that you shall deem yourself fortunate to have been found worthy to come with me and behold and witness things that are almost beyond belief."

"God's will be done," said Sancho. "I believe everything that your Grace says; but straighten yourself up in the saddle a little, for you seem to be slipping down on one side, owing, no doubt, to the shaking up that you received in your fall."

"Ah, that is the truth," replied Don Quixote, "and if I do not speak of my sufferings, it is for the reason that it is not permitted knights-errant to complain of any wound whatsoever, even though their bowels may be dropping out."

"If that is the way it is," said Sancho, "I have nothing more to say; but, God knows,

31. **Briareus** (brī·är′ē·əs): in Greek mythology, a giant with a hundred arms, who helped Zeus overthrow the Titans.

32. **Machuca** (mä·chōō′kä): literally, ''the pounder,'' the hero of an old ballad.

KNIGHTS JOUSTING, ALBRECHT DÜRER.

Art Resource, New York

34 LITERARY ELEMENT
Irony: Why is Don Quixote's response to Sancho's "simplicity" ironic? (Don Quixote laughs at Sancho as if Sancho were the ridiculous one, when in fact Sancho seems the more sensible of the two.)

35 LITERARY ELEMENT
Foil: What words would you use to describe Sancho? (down-to-earth, loyal only to his bodily needs such as food and drink, totally unconcerned with abstract principles) How would you describe Don Quixote? (ascetic, imaginative to the point of lunacy, meticulous in adhering to the "ordinances" of chivalry) How do Sancho and Don Quixote function as foils? (Possible response: The two characters as well as the contrasting values they represent are accentuated.)

HUMANITIES CONNECTION

Albrecht Dürer (1471–1528) drew so skillfully that he has been called "the German counterpart to Leonardo da Vinci."
What interested Dürer most in these sketches of jousting knights? (Possible response: the musculature of the horses in combat) ∎

it would suit me better if your Grace did complain when something hurts him. I can assure you that I mean to do so, over the least little thing that ails me—that is, unless the same rule applies to squires as well."

Don Quixote laughed long and heartily over Sancho's simplicity, telling him that he might complain as much as he liked and where and when he liked, whether he had good cause or not; for he had read nothing to the contrary in the ordinances[33] of chivalry. Sancho then called his master's attention to the fact that it was time to eat. The knight replied that he himself had no need of food at the moment, but his squire might eat whenever he chose. Having been granted this permission, Sancho seated himself as best he could upon his beast, and, taking out from his saddlebags the provisions that he had stored there, he rode along leisurely behind his master, munching his victuals and taking a good, hearty swig now and then at the leather flask in a manner that might well have caused the biggest-bellied tavernkeeper of Málaga to envy him. Between drafts he gave not so much as a thought to any promise that his master might have made him, nor did he look upon it as any hardship, but rather as good sport, to go in quest of adventures however hazardous they might be.

The short of the matter is, they spent the night under some trees, from one of which Don Quixote tore off a withered bough to

---

33. **ordinances** (ôrd''n·əns·əz): authoritative commands.

1. From what district of Spain does Don Quixote come? (la Mancha)
2. How old is Don Quixote? (close to fifty)
3. What does Don Quixote make out of cardboard? (a visor for his helmet)
4. In what condition is Don Quixote's horse? (old and worn out)

5. Why does Don Quixote rename his horse? (so it will have a name that suits the animal of a famous knight)
6. Who is Dulcinea? (a peasant girl whom Don Quixote has chosen to be his ladylove)
7. Who accompanies Don Quixote on his first sally? (no one)

8. What job does Don Quixote give Sancho Panza? (squire)
9. What does Don Quixote promise Sancho? (an island for Sancho to rule)
10. What are the "giants" that Don Quixote fights? (windmills)

---

36 SYNTHESIZING

What does the narrator say Don Quixote was used to nourishing himself on? (savorous memories) In what sense does Don Quixote live on memories? (Possible response: His memories of books he has read provide meaning and motivation for his life.)

WRITING TO LEARN

Imagine you had to spend a week with either Don Quixote or Sancho Panza. Which character would you choose and why? Write a brief essay giving reasons for your choice. ■

ANSWERS

First Thoughts
Answers will vary.

Identifying Facts
1. books of chivalry. He seems to have lost his mind, believing what he reads.
2. He polishes old armor, makes a cardboard visor for the helmet, renames his old nag, changes his own name, and chooses a ladylove and renames her.
3. because Don Quixote promises to make him governor of an island
4. He says that an evil magician changed the giants into windmills to deprive him of glory.
5. hunger, thirst, sleep

---

serve him as a lance, placing it in the lance head from which he had removed the broken one. He did not sleep all night long for thinking of his lady Dulcinea; for this was in accordance with what he had read in his books, of men of arms in the forest or desert places who kept a wakeful vigil, sustained by the memory of their ladies fair. Not so with Sancho, whose stomach was full, and not with chicory water.[34] He fell into a dreamless slumber, and had not his master called him, he would not have been awakened either by the rays of the sun in his face or by the many birds who greeted the coming of the new day with their merry song.

Upon arising, he had another go at the flask, finding it somewhat more flaccid than it had been the night before, a circumstance which grieved his heart, for he could not see that they were on the way to remedying the deficiency within any very short space of time. Don Quixote did not wish any breakfast; for, as has been said, he was in the habit of nourishing himself on savorous memories. They then set out once more along the road to Puerto Lápice, and around three in the afternoon they came in sight of the pass that bears that name.

36

---

34. **chicory water:** an inexpensive coffee substitute.

"There," said Don Quixote as his eyes fell upon it, "we may plunge our arms up to the elbow in what are known as adventures. But I must warn you that even though you see me in the greatest peril in the world, you are not to lay hand upon your sword to defend me, unless it be that those who attack me are rabble and men of low degree, in which case you may very well come to my aid; but if they be gentlemen, it is in no wise permitted by the laws of chivalry that you should assist me until you yourself shall have been dubbed a knight."

"Most certainly, sir," replied Sancho, "your Grace shall be very well obeyed in this; all the more so for the reason that I myself am of a peaceful disposition and not fond of meddling in the quarrels and feuds of others. However, when it comes to protecting my own person, I shall not take account of those laws of which you speak, seeing that all laws, human and divine, permit each one to defend himself whenever he is attacked."

"I am willing to grant you that," assented Don Quixote, "but in this matter of defending me against gentlemen you must restrain your natural impulses."

"I promise you I shall do so," said Sancho. "I will observe this precept as I would the Sabbath day." . . .

First Thoughts
Do you like Don Quixote? Did your attitudes toward him change as you read? Explain your answer.

Identifying Facts
1. What sorts of books does Don Quixote like to read, and what effect do these books have on his life?
2. What preparations does Don Quixote make before setting out on his quest?
3. Why does Sancho Panza become a squire to Don Quixote?
4. After being knocked down by the windmill, how does Don Quixote explain the fact that he has not killed a giant?
5. What natural human needs, which Don Quixote ignores, does Sancho Panza insist on satisfying for himself?

RETEACHING

To reteach this excerpt from *Don Quixote*, have students choose a piece of dialogue between Don Quixote and Sancho and draw a cartoon based on it. In the cartoon, have them draw two dialogue balloons for Sancho: one showing what he is saying to Don Quixote and the other showing what he is really thinking. Have the class discuss what the cartoons reveal about the two characters and their relationship.

EXTENSION AND ENRICHMENT

Comparing Don Quixote and Its Contemporary Adaptation. Have students listen to the soundtrack of the musical *Man of La Mancha* and compare the characters of Don Quixote and Sancho Panza as presented in the musical with the characters as presented in the novel. Have them pay special attention to the lyrics of the song "The Impossible Dream."

CLOSURE

Tell students that, according to a Spanish saying, the readers of the seventeenth century responded to *Don Quixote* with a laugh, the next century responded with a smile, and the nineteenth century responded with a tear. Have them discuss which of these reactions comes closest to their own response to the novel. In addition, have students speculate on why the work has continued to provide such varied responses over the centuries. ■

Interpreting Meanings

1. How are Don Quixote's helmet, horse, and mistress examples of **parody**?
2. A **foil** is a character who is used as a contrast to another character. Sancho Panza functions as a foil to Don Quixote. How does the behavior of the two men suggest that they are opposites? What traits in Don Quixote become more prominent because of the contrast between Quixote and Sancho?
3. What are Don Quixote's reasons for going on his quest? How are his reasons similar to those of **epic heroes**? How are they different?
4. An idealist, or romantic, views the world as he or she thinks it ought to be. A realist views the world as it is. Is Don Quixote an idealist or a realist? Which role does Sancho Panza fit?

Applying Meanings

Don Quixote's exploits have given us the term *quixotic* to describe any idealistically impractical project, whether great or small. The phrase "going off to fight windmills" suggests the same idea. Do you know anybody whose behavior could be described as "quixotic"? Have you ever "gone off to fight windmills"?

Creative Writing Response

Writing a Parody. Don Quixote is inspired to become a knight-errant by reading stories about heroic knights in shining armor. Imagine a modern character like Quixote fascinated by twentieth-century romances about heroes, perhaps in movies, comic books, or TV shows. Write a parody in which your character takes on the role of a modern hero and goes to places such as the supermarket or the video rental store in search of adventure.

Critical Writing Response

Interpreting a Poem. The following poem refers to the sentence in Chapter 2 which describes Quixote continuing on his way, "letting his horse take whatever path it chose, for he believed that therein lay the very essence of adventures."

Parable
Richard Wilbur

I read how Quixote in his random ride
   Came to a crossing once, and lest he lose
The purity of chance, would not decide
Whither to fare, but wished his horse to
   choose.
For glory lay wherever he might turn.
His head was light with pride, his horse's
   shoes
Were heavy, and he headed for the barn.

In the novel, Rocinante does not head for the barn. The fact that the nag *does* in the poem suggests a certain attitude toward Don Quixote and his quest. Explain that attitude in a short essay. Do you agree or disagree with the poet's view of Don Quixote's quest?

Interpreting Meanings

1. The visor on his helmet is made of cardboard; his horse is an old nag; his ladylove is a peasant girl.
2. Possible response: Don Quixote sees things as he wishes they were and lives through his imagination; Sancho sees things as they are and is more concerned with satisfying his bodily needs. his idealism and imagination
3. Possible response: to right wrongs, win glory, and serve his country. The reasons are similar, but epic heroes usually achieve these goals while Don Quixote has little chance of achieving them.
4. Don Quixote is an idealist; Sancho is a realist.

Applying Meanings
Answers will vary.

Creative Writing Response
Writing a Parody. Stories should parody popular contemporary genres and satirize the values they uphold.

Critical Writing Response
Interpreting a Poem. Essays should analyze and evaluate the tone of the speaker in Wilbur's poem. ■

Satire: The motive of satirical writers is often to inspire some improvement in human beings and their institutions. Satire was popular in ancient Greece and Rome. Two fundamental categories of satire are named for satirists of ancient Rome: *Horatian* satire is gentle and displays a certain sympathy for the people and things it mocks; *Juvenalian* satire, on the other hand, is bitterly angry and expresses contempt for the things it mocks.

Satiric tales often are episodic, with little plot structure, and feature characters who show little development, although they may experience a dramatic change of heart at the end of the tale, corresponding to the satirist's point of view. The characters and events of satires are often wildly improbable, requiring a considerable suspension of disbelief on the reader's part.

WRITING TO LEARN

Popular Culture: Read newspaper comic strips and editorial cartoons for a week, and then write an essay evaluating the importance of satire in them. Analyze satiric techniques used, and determine what aspects of modern life or human nature are most often satirized. ■

ELEMENTS OF LITERATURE

Satire

A **satire** is any work that ridicules human weakness, vice, or folly. Cervantes' original purpose in writing *Don Quixote* was to satirize romantic tales of chivalry that were popular in his day. Cervantes found these stories absurd because they portrayed a world that no longer existed and indeed never had existed in the falsely glowing colors in which it had been painted by storytellers. Eventually, Cervantes widened his satire to include the institutions of his day as well as all kinds of timeless human follies. In writing *Don Quixote*, Cervantes used many satiric techniques that are familiar to us today, such as **exaggeration**, **verbal irony** (saying one thing and meaning another), **incongruity** (deliberately pairing things that don't belong together), and **parody** (a humorous imitation of a work).

Throughout the novel, Cervantes parodies the chivalric romance, imitating it in an exaggerated way. Quixote tries to set himself up like the knights of old, but his armor is rusty, his horse is a nag, and his noble squire is a chubby peasant who does not particularly respect his master, much less feel like laying down his life for him.

Cervantes frequently uses exaggeration to ridicule the chivalric romance. The narrator tells us that Quixote read so many romances that "his brain dried up." Many passages from such tales are seen as so

tangled and confusing that "Aristotle himself would not have been able to understand them, even if he had been resurrected for that sole purpose." Wickedly, Cervantes quotes literally from a tale by a sixteenth-century writer whose language is so exaggerated that Cervantes does not need to embellish it further: "The reason of the unreason that afflicts my reason, in such a manner weakens my reason that I with reason lament me of your comeliness."

Cervantes' voice is often ironic—that is, he says one thing and means another. For example, the village curate is described as a "learned man, a graduate of Sigüenza," which was, in fact, a minor institution with a poor reputation. The comment pokes fun at people who show off their academic degrees. But underneath it all, Cervantes' satire is rooted in incongruity that arises from the clash between the romantic and the real. In this sense, the novel goes beyond its specific targets to universal human qualities. We can laugh at Quixote, but there is something of him in all of us. Like Quixote, who wished to live before his time, and like Cervantes himself, who wished to be a great military hero, we all have dreams that cannot come true. Yet we cannot relinquish these dreams without giving up an important part of ourselves.

William Shakespeare
1564–1616

AP/Wide World Photos

William Shakespeare, often called "the immortal bard," was, of course, as mortal as the rest of us. During his lifetime, he was known simply as a successful playwright. Because few people of his day considered him extraordinary, no one took pains to record the details of his life.

We know for certain that Shakespeare was born in Stratford-on-Avon, a market town on the river Avon about one hundred miles northwest of London. Shakespeare's father was a shopkeeper who was also active in town government. His mother, Mary Arden, was from one of the most prominent families of the area. Shakespeare probably attended the Stratford Grammar School. There he studied Latin, some Greek, the Bible, and the great Roman dramatists. Most scholars believe that Shakespeare went to London sometime between 1586 and 1588 to begin his apprenticeship as an actor. We do know that by 1592 he had become a successful actor and playwright.

Although Shakespeare spent most of his life in London, he also had a family in Stratford. In 1582, he married Anne Hathaway, who was 27. Together, they had a daughter, Susanna, and two years later, twins: Hamnet, who died in childhood, and Judith.

In 1594, Shakespeare joined the Lord Chamberlain's Men, a company of actors that became the King's Men in 1603. The company performed in a playhouse called simply "The Theater." Shakespeare wrote about two plays a year for this company, and by 1596, he was a moderately wealthy man, earning money as an actor, a playwright, and a shareholder in The Theater. In 1599, he financed a new theater on the south side of the Thames, the Globe. In 1612, Shakespeare retired to his comfortable home in Stratford. He had written 37 plays—comedies, histories, tragedies, and romances—and more than 150 poems. He died on April 23, 1616. The epitaph over his grave inside the church at Stratford warns those who may be tempted to move him to the graveyard outdoors:

> Good friend, for Jesus' sake forbear
> To dig the bones enclosèd here!
> Blest be the man that spares these stones,
> And curst be he that moves my bones.

Theater in Shakespeare's day was a popular medium undergoing rapid change. During Shakespeare's childhood, plays were often performed in the courtyards of inns and were subject to frequent interruptions. In 1574, the London Common Council passed a law requiring theater companies to be licensed because "great disorders and inconveniences have been found to ensue in this city by the inordinate haunting of great multitudes of people, specially youth, to plays. . . ." The Council's ruling proved a strong incentive for Londoners to build permanent public theaters, and thus led to the golden age of Elizabethan drama.

As royalty and the aristocracy took an increasing interest in drama, they constructed private theaters, roofed and equipped with torchieres for night performances. Shakespeare's company used a private theater, Blackfriars, as its winter quarters.

The Renaissance theater continued to thrive until 1642, when Puritans seized control of the government, closed or demolished the theaters, and severely punished actors caught performing. When Charles II regained the throne in 1660, one of his first acts was to re-establish acting companies. The populace, long deprived of dramatic entertainment, flocked to the theaters.

Introduction

The Elizabethan Theater

During the Elizabethan (ē·liz' ə·bē'thən) period in England (1558–1603, the years of Elizabeth I's reign), drama underwent a renaissance of its own. The Globe is the most famous of the Elizabethan theaters not only because it was owned by the company that Shakespeare belonged to but also because it is where Shakespeare's greatest plays were first performed. The Globe consisted of three parts: the building proper, the stage, and the backstage area. In *Henry V*, Shakespeare refers to

The Granger Collection, New York

The Globe theater, London. Drawing, c. 1600.

the theater building as "this wooden O." It was, in fact, a sixteen-sided polygon surrounding an open space about sixty-five feet in diameter. The building was three stories high and had tiers of seats built into the walls (or galleries). Most of the spectators, however, stood in the open courtyard area in the center. These "groundlings" paid a penny admission while those in the gallery paid another penny or so. The richest members of the audience could buy seats on the stage itself. The stage and the gallery seats were protected by a roof or awning, but the groundlings were subject to the whims of the unpredictable English weather. The theater could hold about three thousand people altogether.

The stage was a large platform about five feet off the ground. It projected about halfway into the open circle. Below the stage was an area used by musicians and sound effects men. At the back of the stage were dressing rooms, places for machinery, and a curtained inner stage with a second floor used for balcony scenes like that in *Romeo and Juliet* or to suggest the walls of a castle or the bridge of a ship. The front part of the stage had a trap door that was especially useful for burial scenes or for the entrances and exits of ghosts and other supernatural creatures.

Reconstruction of the second Globe theater in London. *On stage, one actor arises through a trap door. Elizabethan theaters were often equipped with pulleys and trap doors to allow the dramatic entrances and exits of ghosts, faeries, and the like.*

The Granger Collection, New York

Stagecraft: Sets, Costumes, Lighting

Much of what is accomplished in the modern theater through the technology of stagecraft was achieved in the Elizabethan theater almost entirely with language. Shakespeare's audiences needed to listen closely and use their imaginations to fill out what the actors' lines suggested. In *As You Like It*, for example, the character Rosalind creates a forest scene by announcing, "Well, this is the forest of Arden." In *Hamlet*, Shakespeare indicates that the night is over by having Horatio say, "But look, the morn in russet mantle clad/Walks o'er the dew of yon high eastward hill."

Because the audience could imagine such scenes, there was no need for elaborate scenery. And because there were no scene changes, the scenes flowed with no interruption—just as they flow today in movies or on television.

The stage itself was very lively. Characters were lowered from the heavens by cranes, and there were often elaborate processions, music and dancing, and sound effects, including gunpowder explosions. There were also beautiful banners or tapestries at the back of the stage. Because the plays were performed in the afternoons, there was no need for lighting. Characters carried torches or lanterns to indicate that certain scenes were occurring at night.

MORE ABOUT ACTORS

Shakespeare acted in his own plays and those of others. Apparently he was a solid actor but not a great one, playing some kingly roles but not the great ones (Lear or Richard III). These and other starring roles, such as Hamlet and Othello, were played by Richard Burbage, the most famous actor of Shakespeare's time. Traditionally Shakespeare is believed to have played the Ghost in *Hamlet*—a short but important role. Shakespeare probably did not appear in *The Tempest*; his last documented stage appearance was in 1603, in Ben Jonson's tragedy *Sejanus*.

HUMANITIES CONNECTION

Have students compare De Witt's drawing of the interior of the Swan Theater with the engraving of the second Globe theater on p. 841. Working back and forth between the illustrations, they should be able to identify various features: acting areas at the back of the main stage; galleries for musicians, actors, and viewers; "hell" beneath the main stage; and standing room for playgoers. ∎

The audience wanted excitement, humor, passion, and action—even gore. (*Titus Andronicus* is as gory as any *Friday the Thirteenth* horror movie.) They also appreciated puns and word games. *The Tempest* provides vigorous action, boisterous humor, and splendid poetry. All of Shakespeare's plays provide subtle poetry, deep philosophy, and scenes of both sensational violence and quiet, psychological conflict.

Kings and other rich or royal characters were often spectacularly costumed. Some costumes conveyed agreed-upon meanings: one theater manager's inventory included "a robe for to go invisible in." The manager-producer Philip Henslowe lists properties of the Globe theater that include chariots, fountains, dragons, beds, tents, thrones, and other fanciful props.

Drawing of the Swan theater, London, by Johannes De Witt, c. 1596.

Actors in Shakespeare's Time

Elizabethan actors *had* to be good, or the audience would quickly get out of hand. Today we go to the theater and sit quietly in darkness. The Elizabethan theater was a much livelier occasion—more like a rowdy party. The audience came early, talked with friends, met new people, walked about, and ate and drank before and during the performance. All sorts of shady characters mingled with the crowd—most notably, pimps and pickpockets. Because of all the distractions, the Elizabethan playwright had to write lively scenes, and the actors had to perform them with energy and verve—and sometimes, outright overblown acting—to hold the attention of some three thousand restless people, many of whom would just as soon go back to their talking, eating, and drinking.

In Shakespeare's time, the theater was considered a rather disreputable profession—certainly not a profession for women. Thus, all actors were men. All female parts were played by young boys who still had high-pitched voices. Because women's fashions consisted of long dresses, wigs, and heavy makeup, it was not difficult to transform a young boy into a beautiful woman.

The Tempest

The Tempest, the last of Shakespeare's romances or tragicomedies, is a far-fetched fantasy with love as a central concern. As with other romances of its

Detail from Cornelius Visscher's View of London, 1616.
The Globe theater is visible on the south bank of the Thames.

The Granger Collection, New York

MORE ABOUT *THE TEMPEST*

MORE ABOUT *THE TEMPEST*

With the possible exception of *Henry VIII*, *The Tempest* is Shakespeare's last complete play. He probably wrote it during the fall and winter of 1610–1611, for it was performed at court in the winter of 1611 for the marriage festivities of King James I's daughter to the Elector of Palantine of the Holy Roman Empire. This play is the culmination of Shakespeare's twenty years of writing for the theater, perfecting stagecraft, and exploring themes of love, betrayal, forgiveness, nature, and art. More specifically, *The Tempest* is the culmination of Shakespeare's work in the romance genre—*A Winter's Tale*, *Cymbeline*, and *Pericles*—and in tragicomedy—*Measure for Measure*, *All's Well That Ends Well*, and *Troilus and Cressida*.

The romances typically have episodic plots, often with magical occurrences, and exotic settings. Their endings reconcile not just individual lovers or enemies, but entire communities and lineages. The plays often explore the human spirit's capacity for endurance in times of adversity. They also affirm the natural goodness in humanity and the ultimate justice in Fate.

time, the surface action is a simple fairy tale, complete with good and bad characters, a pure, uncomplicated love, and many miraculous incidents, such as magic storms, charms that paralyze the evil characters and protect the good, and a play within a play featuring mythological deities. The play is rich in atmosphere and poetry, featuring characters that are somewhat symbolic and abstract.

Although the events and situations in *The Tempest* are improbable, the characters' emotions and responses to events are real. As a tragicomedy, it contains tragic elements in the form of malevolent characters and actions. Caliban plots to murder Prospero. Antonio and Sebastian plot against Alonso and Gonzalo. The play constantly reminds us that the world contains evil. Prospero's victory is won only by constant vigilance and an understanding of the evil within humanity. The malevolence is overcome and the play ends happily.

The Tempest has often been called a "summing up" play in which Shakespeare expresses "farewell to his art." Prospero, like Shakespeare, is the supreme creator of a unique universe, which he rules through the enormous power of his intellect and his imagination. At the end of the play, Prospero clears the stage—just as a tired Shakespeare might have done in the days of the Globe theater—and makes one last request of the audience: that they pause and think about the meaning of the drama.

OBJECTIVES

1. *To interpret a Shakespearean romance*
2. *To recognize dramatic structure in a play*
3. *To compose a short story, a prose narrative from the point of view of a character, and a diary entry*
4. *To write essays contrasting two characters, analyzing tragicomic form, and examining dramatic structure*
5. *To analyze examples of blank verse*
6. *To describe the staging of a scene*

THEMES IN WORLD LITERATURE

The Comic Vision
"Thor and Loki in Giantland," pp. 704–713
From *Don Quixote*, pp. 821–837

Nightmares, Dreams, and Visions
From *Candide*, pp. 945–962
"The Handsomest Drowned Man in the World," pp. 1289–1297
"The Night Face Up," pp. 1298–1307

The Uses and Abuses of Power
"Do You Want to Improve the World?," p. 544
From *Faust*, Part I, pp. 986–1001 ∎

PREREADING FOCUS

Background: Shakespeare took almost all his plots from existing sources, such as Ovid's *Metamorphoses* (pp. 420–427) or Raphael Holinshed's *Chronicles of England, Scotland, and Ireland*. The plot of *The Tempest* is one of his two original plots. (The other is that of *Love's Labors Lost*.) However, Shakespeare found inspiration for *The Tempest*'s characters and episodes in a variety of sources. The name Caliban, for example, is an anagram for the word *cannibal*, further linking *The Tempest* to Montaigne's essay "Of Cannibals." Prospero's great speech in Act 5, Scene 1, lines 33–57, was derived partly from a speech by Medea in Ovid's *Metamorphoses*. A 1567 translation reads: "Ye airs and winds, ye elves of hills, of brooks, of woods along,/ Of standing lakes, and of the night, approach ye everyone."

Writer's Response: To generate discussion of fantasy, mention such familiar classics as *The Chronicles of Narnia*, *The Lord of the Rings*, or *Peter Pan*, as well as science-fiction films such as *Star Wars*. Which of these contain elements of magic? How do these stories explore the uses and abuses of power in a fantasy setting? What do they reveal about human nature?

Reader's Guide ∎

THE TEMPEST

Background

William Shakespeare's earliest plays—among them *Romeo and Juliet, Henry IV, Hamlet,* and *As You Like It*—were either tragedies, comedies, or historical dramas. In the last few years of his career, Shakespeare began to write romantic, lyrical plays with elements of both tragedy and comedy: **tragicomedies**. Critics suggest different reasons for this shift in Shakespeare's later works, but it is most likely that he had said all he wanted to say with the tragedies and comedies and simply wanted to explore a different kind of expression. Audiences' preferences were changing as well; the utopian themes presented in romances and tragicomedies became increasingly popular during the Renaissance. *The Tempest* fit the bill. With its exotic portrayal of a distant land, it created an optimistic picture of human society.

There has been much speculation about the source of *The Tempest*. It is reasonable to assume that Shakespeare had access to a translation of French writer Montaigne's essay "Of Cannibals" when he was writing the play. In this essay, Montaigne argued that "primitive" societies may possess greater harmony and justice than "civilized" groups. A shipwreck on Bermuda in 1609, which caused much excitement in England, may also have sparked Shakespeare's imagination.

Writer's Response

The Tempest is often called a fantasy—a work that takes place in an unreal world and features incredible characters. How prevalent is fantasy in popular entertainment today—in movies, comics, television, and books? Do you prefer fantasy to other kinds of entertainment? Why or why not? Write a paragraph exploring these questions.

Literary Focus

Shakespeare's plays demonstrate a fairly consistent **dramatic structure**, or method of development. The five acts of *The Tempest* can be broken down, respectively, into **exposition**, where relevant background information is presented; **rising action**, where the plot accelerates and complications are introduced; the **climax**, or **turning point**, which is the point of greatest emotional intensity or suspense; **falling action**; and the **resolution**, where the play's conflicts are resolved.

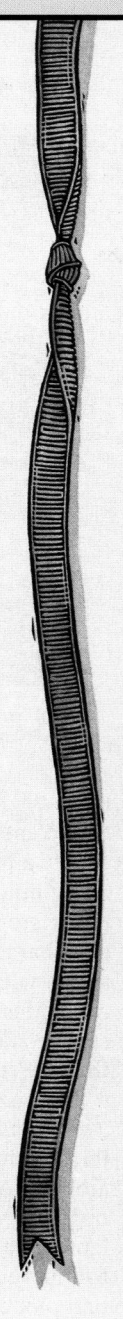

THE TEMPEST
Act 1
William Shakespeare

Act 1 presents the exposition, or basic situation, of the play. Who are the major characters, and what are their conflicts?

CHARACTERS

Alonso, King of Naples

Sebastian, brother to Alonso

Prospero, the rightful Duke of Milan

Antonio, brother to Prospero, the usurping Duke of Milan

Ferdinand, son to the King of Naples

Gonzalo, an honest old counselor

Adrian }
Francisco } lords

Caliban, a savage and deformed slave

Trinculo, a jester

Stephano, a drunken butler

Master of a ship

Boatswain

Mariners

Miranda, daughter to Prospero

Ariel, an airy spirit

Iris
Ceres } spirits
Juno

Nymphs

Reapers

Other Spirits, attendants to Prospero

Scene: a ship at sea; an uninhabited island

Summary of Act 1, Scene 1. *Alonso, King of Naples, is returning from his daughter's wedding to a foreign prince with his brother Sebastian and Antonio, the Duke of Milan. Their ship is overcome by a tremendous storm. As the scene ends, it seems certain that the ship will sink and that all lives will be lost.*

ANSWER TO MARGIN QUESTION

Lines 15–16. The boatswain is somewhat disrespectful toward the king.

1 EVALUATING

Do you think Gonzalo is exercising his authority properly in this scene? (Possible response: No, he is meddling in something he knows nothing about.) Do you think the boatswain is overstepping his authority? (Possible response: No; although he is somewhat rude, circumstances necessitate that he assert his authority to save the ship.)

ACT 1

Scene 1. *A ship at sea.*

[*A tempestuous noise of thunder and lightning heard. Enter a* SHIPMASTER *and a* BOATSWAIN.]

Master.
　Boatswain!

Boatswain.
　Here, master. What cheer?

Master.
　Good, speak to the mariners; fall to't yarely,° or we run ourselves aground! Bestir, bestir!　　　　　[*Exit.*]

> 3. **Good:** my good fellow; **yarely:** immediately, briskly.

[*Enter* MARINERS.]

Boatswain.
5　Heigh, my hearts! Cheerly, cheerly, my hearts! Yare, yare! Take in the topsail! Tend to the master's whistle! Blow till thou burst thy wind, if room enough!

[*Enter* ALONSO, SEBASTIAN, ANTONIO, FERDINAND, GONZALO, *and others.*]

Alonso.
　Good boatswain, have care. Where's the master? Play the men.°

> 9. **Play the men:** behave like men.

Boatswain.
10　I pray now, keep below.

Antonio.
　Where is the master, bos'n?

Boatswain.
　Do you not hear him? You mar our labor. Keep your cabins: you do assist the storm!

> How would you describe the boatswain's attitude toward the king?

Gonzalo.
　Nay, good, be patient.

Boatswain.
15　When the sea is. Hence! What cares these roarers for the name of king? To cabin! Silence! Trouble us not!

Gonzalo.
　Good, yet remember whom thou hast aboard.

Boatswain.
　None that I more love than myself. You are a counselor: if you can command these elements to silence and work
20　the peace of the present,° we will not hand a rope more; use your authority. If you cannot, give thanks you have lived so long, and make yourself ready in your

> 19–20. **work the peace of the present:** calm the storm.

1

cabin for the mischance of the hour, if it so hap.—
Cheerly, good hearts!—Out of our way, I say.   [*Exit.*]

Gonzalo.

25   I have great comfort from this fellow. Methinks he
hath no drowning mark upon him; his complexion is
perfect gallows.° Stand fast, good Fate, to his hanging!
Make the rope of his destiny our cable, for our own
doth little advantage. If he be not born to be hanged,
30   our case is miserable.   [*Exeunt.*]

[*Reenter* BOATSWAIN.]

Boatswain.

Down with the topmast! Yare! Lower, lower! Bring her
to try with the main course!° (*a cry within*) A plague
upon this howling! They are louder than the weather
or our office.°

[*Enter* SEBASTIAN, ANTONIO, *and* GONZALO.]

35   Yet again? What do you here? Shall we give o'er and
drown? Have you a mind to sink?

Sebastian.

A pox o' your throat, you bawling, blasphemous, in-
charitable dog!

Boatswain.

Work you then.

Antonio.

40   Hang, cur, hang, you whoreson, insolent noisemaker!
We are less afraid to be drowned than thou art.

Gonzalo.

I'll warrant him for drowning,° though the ship were
no stronger than a nutshell and as leaky as an un-
stanched wench.

Boatswain.

45   Lay her ahold, ahold! Set her two courses!° Off to sea
again! Lay her off!°

[*Enter* MARINERS, *wet.*]

Mariners.

All lost! To prayers, to prayers! All lost!   [*Exeunt.*]

Boatswain.

What, must our mouths be cold?°

Gonzalo.

The King and Prince at prayers! Let's assist them,
50   For our case is as theirs.

Sebastian.   I am out of patience.

25–27. Methinks . . . perfect gallows: an old proverb stated, "He that is born to be hanged shall never be drowned."

32. main course: mainsail; leaving only the mainsail set will, the boatswain hopes, keep the ship stable enough that it neither founders nor runs aground.

34. office: duty, which is, at this moment, yelling orders to the sailors.

? What impression are you forming of Sebastian and Gonzalo?

42. I'll warrant him for drowning: I will guarantee that he will not drown. Gonzalo still has the proverb in mind.

45. Set her two courses: Raise another sail.
46. Lay her off: turn away from shore; the ship is getting too close to shore.

48. cold: full of prayers; as opposed to warm and full of liquor, as the boatswain's mouth is.

---

2 INTERPRETING

Why does Gonzalo take "great comfort" from the boatswain? (Gonzalo says the boatswain looks as though he were born to be hanged, not drowned. His appearance is therefore a good omen for their own survival.) Why does he refer to the boatswain's fate as a "rope of . . . destiny"? (Possible response: The terms *rope* and *cable* are nautical; in classical mythology, humans were pictured hanging by threads that the Fates snipped when they saw fit.)

3 COMPARING AND CONTRASTING

How are the King and Prince reacting to the storm at sea? (praying for deliverance) What is the boatswain's reaction? (bold, capable, a little reckless)

4 EVALUATING

Clarify that "split" refers to the hull of the ship. Do you think Shakespeare's dramatization of the storm is realistic or fantastic? Support your answer with details. (Most students will agree that the storm is realistically portrayed.) What effect is created by opening the play in this way? (Possible response: The crisis draws the audience immediately into the story.)

HUMANITIES CONNECTION

Called "the Elder" to distinguish him from his son of the same name, Pieter Brueghel (broi'gəl) is considered the greatest Flemish painter of his century. His drawings and engravings range from landscapes and mountain scenes to biblical episodes, peasant scenes, and fantastic compositions similar to those of Hieronymus Bosch. Sometimes the ostensible subject comes in second to the scenic panorama, as in the case of two tiny legs sticking up from the sea in *Icarus Falling into the Sea*. *A Seastorm* demonstrates Brueghel's mastery of the bird's eye view.

? *How does the painting on this page suggest the frailty of a boat in a storm at sea?* (The boat looks lost amid the huge waves.) ∎

Antonio.
We are merely° cheated of our lives by drunkards.
This wide-chopped° rascal—would thou mightst lie drowning
The washing of ten tides!°

Gonzalo.   He'll be hanged yet,
Though every drop of water swear against it
55 And gape at wid'st to glut° him.

[*A confused noise within*]
                                        "Mercy on us—
We split, we split!—Farewell, my wife and children!—
Farewell, brother!—We split, we split, we split!"
                                        [*Exit* BOATSWAIN.]

Antonio.
Let's all sink with the King.

Sebastian.   Let's take leave of him.
                    [*Exeunt* ANTONIO *and* SEBASTIAN.]

Gonzalo.
60 Now would I give a thousand furlongs of sea for an acre of barren ground—long heath, brown furze, anything. The wills above be done, but I would fain die a dry death.   [*Exit.*]

51. **merely:** altogether; completely.
52. **wide-chopped:** big-mouthed; i.e., both overly talkative and full of liquor.
53. **The washing of ten tides:** Antonio refers to the way in which pirates were executed: They were hanged at the low-tide mark and left there through three high tides.
55. **glut:** swallow; take in.

? The storm has gotten so violent that even Gonzalo is ready to admit defeat. How would you indicate the increasing force of the tempest throughout Scene 1?

A SEASTORM, PIETER BREUGHEL THE ELDER (c. 1525–1569).

Saskia/Art Resource, New York

ANSWERS TO MARGIN QUESTIONS

Lines 1–13. Miranda shows empathy by saying she suffered with those on the ship, and compassion by describing how she would have liked to have saved them.

Lines 16–22. Possible response: His dominant role here is as father; in this scene, Prospero shows great paternal devotion as he discloses his and Miranda's identity and past.

Summary of Act 1, Scene 2. *Miranda questions her father Prospero about his motives for causing the tempest. Reassuring Miranda that all aboard the ship are safe, Prospero tells her that he is the former Duke of Milan, whose throne was taken from him by his scheming brother Antonio with the support of Alonso, King of Naples. He explains that they had been cast into the sea, where they floated until they reached this enchanted island. A wise old counselor, Gonzalo, had aided them with food, clothing, and books.*

Prospero puts Miranda to sleep, then questions Ariel, a spirit who is in bondage to him, about the storm. When Ariel begs for his freedom, Prospero reminds Ariel that he had released him from a cruel punishment imposed by Sycorax, the witch who had once ruled the island, and that Ariel's debt to Prospero for his deliverance has not been fully repaid. Prospero summons his slave Caliban, Sycorax's son. Caliban curses Prospero, whom he despises and fears.

Ariel brings Ferdinand, Prince of Naples, forth from the shipwreck. It is Prospero's wish that Miranda and Ferdinand will fall in love, but he first intends to test him to see if he is worthy of Miranda's love.

Scene 2. *The island. Before* PROSPERO's *cell.*

[*Enter* PROSPERO *and* MIRANDA.]

Miranda.
    If by your art, my dearest father, you have
    Put the wild waters in this roar, allay them.
    The sky, it seems, would pour down stinking pitch
    But that the sea, mounting to the welkin's° cheek,
5   Dashes the fire out. O, I have suffered
    With those that I saw suffer! A brave vessel
    (Who had no doubt some noble creature in her)
    Dashed all to pieces! O, the cry did knock
    Against my very heart! Poor souls, they perished!
10   Had I been any god of power, I would
    Have sunk the sea within the earth or ere
    It should the good ship so have swallowed and
    The fraughting souls° within her.

Prospero.   Be collected.
    No more amazement. Tell your piteous heart
15   There's no harm done.

Miranda.   O, woe the day!

Prospero.   No harm.
    I have done nothing but in care of thee,
    Of thee, my dear one, thee my daughter, who
    Art ignorant of what thou art, naught knowing
20   Of whence I am; nor that I am more better
    Than Prospero, master of a full poor cell,
    And thy no greater father.

4. **welkin's:** sky's.

? In what specific ways does Miranda show her compassionate nature in lines 1–13?

13. **fraughting souls:** the human beings the ship carried as freight.

? In this scene, Prospero appears in several of his different roles: magician, father, and duke. As the scene progresses, try to determine which role is dominant. What makes you say so?

8 LITERARY ELEMENT

Fantasy Characteristics: What does Prospero's statement about the storm lead you to believe about its origin or cause? (It was magically rather than naturally produced.) Point out to students that the fantasy element in the play is introduced in this scene. In Shakespeare's romances, violence is often suggested but no harm actually occurs. In this case, the storm is a fantasy or illusion created by Prospero.

9 LITERARY ELEMENT

Exposition: "The hour's now come" for Prospero to tell Miranda about the past. Whom else is he telling? (the audience) Why do you think Prospero removes his magic cloak at this point? (He is acting as a father, not a magician.)

Miranda.   More to know
Did never meddle with my thoughts.
Prospero.   'Tis time
I should inform thee farther. Lend thy hand
25 And pluck my magic garment from me. So,

[*Takes off his magic robe.*]

Lie there, my art.° Wipe thou thine eyes; have
   comfort.
The direful spectacle of the wrack,° which touched
The very virtue of compassion in thee,
I have with such provision° in mine art
30 So safely ordered that there is no soul—
No, not so much perdition° as an hair
Betid° to any creature in the vessel
Which thou heardst cry, which thou sawst sink. Sit
   down;
For thou must now know farther.
Miranda.   You have often
35 Begun to tell me what I am, but stopped
And left me to a bootless° inquisition,
Concluding, "Stay! Not yet."
Prospero.   The hour's now come;
The very minute bids thee ope thine ear.
Obey, and be attentive. Canst thou remember
40 A time before we came unto this cell?
I do not think thou canst, for then thou wast not
Out° three years old.
Miranda.   Certainly, sir, I can.
Prospero.
By what? By any other house or person?
Of anything the image tell me that
45 Hath kept with thy remembrance.
Miranda.   'Tis far off,
And rather like a dream than an assurance
That my remembrance warrants. Had I not
Four or five women once that tended me?
Prospero.
Thou hadst, and more, Miranda. But how is it
50 That this lives in thy mind? What seest thou else
In the dark backward and abysm of time?
If thou rememb'rest aught ere thou camest here,
How thou camest here thou mayst.
Miranda.   But that I do not.

26. **my art:** Prospero's cloak is the source of his powerful magic.
27. **wrack:** wreck.

29. **provision:** foreknowledge; foresight.

31. **perdition:** loss.
32. **Betid:** befallen; occurred.

36. **bootless:** useless; futile.

(?) Shakespeare never describes Prospero's "cell" (line 40) for us. What do you imagine it looks like?

42. **Out:** beyond.

Prospero.
    Twelve year since, Miranda, twelve year since,
55   Thy father was the Duke of Milan and
    A prince of power.
Miranda.   Sir, are not you my father?
Prospero.
    Thy mother was a piece of virtue, and
    She said thou wast my daughter; and thy father
    Was Duke of Milan; and his only heir
60   A princess—no worse issued.
Miranda.   O the heavens!
    What foul play had we that we came from thence?
    Or blessed was't we did?
Prospero.   Both, both, my girl!
    By foul play, as thou sayst, were we heaved thence,
    But blessedly holp° hither.
Miranda.   O, my heart bleeds
65   To think o' the teen° that I have turned you to,
    Which is from my remembrance! Please you, farther.
Prospero.
    My brother, and thy uncle, called Antonio—
    I pray thee mark me—that a brother should
    Be so perfidious!—he whom next thyself
70   Of all the world I loved, and to him put
    The manage of my state, as at that time
    Through all the seignories° it was the first,
    And Prospero the prime duke, being so reputed
    In dignity, and for the liberal arts
75   Without a parallel; those being all my study,
    The government I cast upon my brother
    And to my state grew stranger, being transported
    And rapt in secret studies—thy false uncle—
    Dost thou attend me?
Miranda.   Sir, most heedfully.
Prospero.
80   Being once perfected° how to grant suits,
    How to deny them, who t' advance, and who
    To trash for overtopping,° new-created
    The creatures that were mine, I say, or changed 'em,
    Or else new-formed 'em; having both the key
85   Of officer and office, set all hearts i' the state
    To what tune pleased his ear, that now he was
    The ivy which had hid my princely trunk
    And sucked my verdure out on't.° Thou attendst
      not!

64. **holp:** helped.

65. **teen:** sorrow.

72. **seignories:** states; dukedoms.

? Why did Prospero give over the management of the state to his brother, according to his speech in lines 67–79?

80. **Being once perfected:** once understanding.

82. **trash for overtopping:** inhibit the speed of one that is able to run ahead of the others (e.g., a dog in a pack).

88. **verdure:** power; **on't:** of it.

Lines 89–107. The reality was that Prospero was duke and Antonio executed commands in Prospero's name; Antonio's belief was that he himself ruled.

13 ANALYZING
What effect do you think Shakespeare was aiming for in Miranda's line "Your tale, sir, would cure deafness."? (Possible response: comic) What do you think Miranda's attitude is toward Prospero's story? (Possible response: She is interested in her past but bored by her father's long-windedness.)

14 LITERARY ELEMENT
Metaphor: What comparison does Shakespeare use to describe Antonio's delusion that he is the Duke of Milan? (He describes Antonio as acting a part in a play.) Remind students that Prospero, in causing the shipwreck, is staging another play for Antonio to take part in.

15 CULTURAL BACKGROUND
Explain that Renaissance Italy was made up of many city-states, each vying to control the others. Here, Antonio agrees to subjugate Milan to Naples if the King will help him seize the dukedom.

16 GUIDED READING
Finding the Main Idea: What does line 121 mean? (Good parents sometimes produce bad children.) Who in the play are specific examples of this truism? (Prospero and Antonio are good and bad sons, respectively, of the same parents.)

Miranda.
  O, good sir, I do.
Prospero.   I pray thee mark me.
90 I thus neglecting worldly ends, all dedicated
  To closeness, and the bettering of my mind
  With that which, but by being so retired,
  O'erprized all popular rate,° in my false brother
  Awaked an evil nature, and my trust,
95 Like a good parent, did beget of him
  A falsehood in its contrary as great
  As my trust was, which had indeed no limit,
  A confidence sans° bound. He being thus lorded,
  Not only with what my revenue yielded
100 But what my power might else exact, like one
  Who having unto truth, by telling of it,
  Made such a sinner of his memory
  To credit his own lie, he did believe
  He was indeed the Duke, out o' the substitution
105 And executing the outward face of royalty
  With all prerogative. Hence his ambition growing—
  Dost thou hear?

13 [**Miranda.**   Your tale, sir, would cure deafness.

Prospero.
  To have no screen between this part he played
14 [And him he played it for, he needs will be
110 Absolute Milan.° Me (poor man) my library
  Was dukedom large enough! Of temporal royalties°
  He thinks me now incapable; confederates°
  (So dry he was for sway°) with the King of Naples
  To give him annual tribute, do him homage,
15 [115 Subject his coronet to his° crown, and bend
  The dukedom yet unbowed (alas, poor Milan!)
  To most ignoble stooping.

Miranda.   O the heavens!
Prospero.
  Mark his condition, and the event; then tell me
  If this might be a brother.
Miranda.   I should sin
120 To think but nobly of my grandmother.
16 [Good wombs have borne bad sons.

Prospero.   Now the condition.
  This King of Naples, being an enemy
  To me inveterate, hearkens my brother's suit;
  Which was, that he, in lieu o' the premises,°
125 Of homage and I know not how much tribute,

92–93. **but by being so retired,/ O'erprized all popular rate:** It (the topic of Prospero's studies) would have been valued above all else if it had been widely known.

98. **sans:** without.

❓ Prospero's speech in lines 89–107 touches upon one of the key themes in Shakespeare's work: appearance vs. reality. How were appearances—and Antonio's beliefs—different from the reality of the situation, according to Prospero?

110. **Absolute Milan:** sole and legal Duke of Milan.
111. **temporal royalties:** worldly power (to rule).
112. **confederates:** unites in conspiracy.
113. **So dry he was for sway:** so thirsty was he for power.
115. **his coronet:** the Duke of Milan's crown; a coronet was worn by rulers of lower rank than a king. **his:** the King of Naples'.

124. **in lieu o' the premises:** in return for payments of money, according to an agreement.

Should presently extirpate me and mine
Out of the dukedom and confer fair Milan,
With all the honors, on my brother. Whereon,
A treacherous army levied, one midnight
130　　Fated to the purpose, did Antonio open
The gates of Milan; and, i' the dead of darkness,
The ministers for the purpose hurried thence
Me and thy crying self.

Miranda.　　　　　　　Alack, for pity!
I, not rememb'ring how I cried out then,
135　　Will cry it o'er again. It is a hint°
That wrings mine eyes to't.

135. **hint:** opportunity; occasion.

17 **LITERARY ELEMENT**
Dialogue: Note how the "gestic" dialogue reflects Miranda's emotion and demeanor. How might a contemporary playwright indicate that he intends a character to cry? (in a stage direction in brackets, separate from the rest of the dialogue)

HUMANITIES CONNECTION

❓ *In this photograph, which lines from Scene 2 might the actors be saying or reacting to? On what details do you base your opinion? (Answers will vary.)* ■

Zoe Dominic

Still from a 1975 production of *The Tempest* at the Wyndham Theater, London.

ANSWERS TO MARGIN QUESTIONS

Line 160. Prospero believes that divine providence brought him to the island.

Lines 169–170. These lines contain dramatic irony in that the audience knows that Gonzalo is already on the island, so Miranda will indeed see him.

18 LITERARY ELEMENT

Imagery: What kinds of images appear in lines 150–152? (images of sounds, such as crying, roaring, sighing) What is the effect of such imagery? (a distressing dramatic effect, reminiscent of the shipwreck in Scene 1)

Prospero.   Hear a little further,
And then I'll bring thee to the present business
Which now's upon's; without the which this story
Were most impertinent.

Miranda.   Wherefore did they not
140   That hour destroy us?

Prospero.   Well demanded, wench.
My tale provokes that question. Dear, they durst not,
So dear the love my people bore me; nor set
A mark so bloody on the business; but
With colors fairer painted their foul ends.
145   In few, they hurried us aboard a bark,
Bore us some leagues to sea; where they prepared
A rotten carcass of a butt, not rigged,
Nor tackle, sail, nor mast; the very rats
Instinctively have quit it. There they hoist us,
150   To cry to the sea, that roared to us; to sigh
To the winds, whose pity, sighing back again,
Did us but loving wrong.

Miranda.   Alack, what trouble
Was I then to you!

Prospero.   O, a cherubin
Thou wast that did preserve me! Thou didst smile,
155   Infused with a fortitude from heaven,
When I have decked the sea with drops full salt,
Under my burden groaned; which raised in me
An undergoing stomach,° to bear up
Against what should ensue.

Miranda.   How came we ashore?

Prospero.
160   By providence divine.
Some food we had, and some fresh water, that
A noble Neapolitan, Gonzalo,
Out of his charity, who being then appointed
Master of this design, did give us, with
165   Rich garments, linens, stuffs, and necessaries
Which since have steaded much. So, of his gentleness,
Knowing I loved my books, he furnished me
From mine own library with volumes that
I prize above my dukedom.

Miranda.   Would I might
170   But ever see that man!

Prospero.   Now I arise.
Sit still, and hear the last of our sea-sorrow.

158. **undergoing stomach:** courage to continue; the stomach was thought to be the seat of courage.

The forces that control human action are dramatized again and again in *The Tempest*. According to Prospero in line 160, what force brought him to the island?

Explain the irony of Miranda's lines (169–170). What type of irony is it?

Lines 186–189. Possible responses: Prospero might cast a spell using hypnotic techniques—a swinging pendulum and a slow, soothing voice. He might summon Ariel with an upraised hand or a beckoning motion.
Lines 190–194. Ariel mentions flying (air), swimming (water), and diving into fire.

Lines 196–207. Possible response: Ariel should move quickly and gracefully about the stage, pantomiming the actions he mentions.

Here in this island we arrived; and here
Have I, thy schoolmaster, made thee more profit
Than other princess can, that have more time
175 For vainer hours, and tutors not so careful.
Miranda.
Heavens thank you for't! And now I pray you,
　sir,—
For still 'tis beating in my mind,—your reason
For raising this sea-storm?
Prospero.　　　　　　　　Know thus far forth.°
By accident most strange, bountiful Fortune
180 (Now my dear lady)° hath mine enemies
Brought to this shore; and by my prescience°
I find my zenith doth depend upon
A most auspicious star, whose influence
If now I court not, but omit, my fortunes
185 Will ever after droop.° Here cease more questions.
Thou art inclined to sleep. 'Tis a good dullness,
And give it away. I know thou canst not choose.

[MIRANDA *sleeps.*]

Come away, servant, come! I am ready now.
Approach, my Ariel. Come!

[*Enter* ARIEL.]
Ariel.
190 All hail, great master! Grave sir, hail! I come
To answer thy best pleasure; be't to fly,
To swim, to dive into the fire, to ride
On the curled clouds. To thy strong bidding task°
Ariel and all his quality.°
Prospero.　　　　　　　Hast thou, spirit,
195 Performed to point the tempest that I bade thee?
Ariel.
To every article.
I boarded the King's ship. Now on the beak,
Now in the waist, the deck, in every cabin,
I flamed amazement.° Sometime I'd divide
200 And burn in many places; on the topmast,
The yards, and bowsprit would I flame distinctly,°
Then meet and join. Jove's lightnings, the <u>precursors</u>
O' the dreadful thunderclaps, more momentary
And sight-outrunning were not. The fire and cracks
205 Of sulphurous roaring the most mighty Neptune
Seem to besiege and make his bold waves tremble;
Yea, his dread trident shake.

19

20

21

178. **thus far forth:** this much further.
179–180. **Fortune (Now my dear lady):** Fortune, now being kind to me. Fortune is personified here as a woman.
181. **prescience:** foreknowledge.
182–185. **I find . . . will ever after droop:** I foresee that if I do not act now, while the stars of my horoscope are favorable, I will never have another chance to regain my rightful place.

? How would you stage Miranda's falling asleep and Prospero's summoning of Ariel?

? Elizabethans believed that all matter was composed of water, fire, air, and earth. How does Ariel's entrance speech (lines 190–194) relate to three of these elements?

193. **task:** give a task to.
194. **quality:** band of fellow spirits.

199. **flamed amazement:** frightened and amazed the men by appearing on the ship in the form of fire.
201. **distinctly:** simultaneously.

? How would you have Ariel perform lines 196–207?

19 PREDICTING
What does Prospero say his purpose is in creating the storm? (He hopes to change his fortune and regain the dukedom.) Given his former indifference toward ruling, what other motive do you think he might have? (Possible responses: to take revenge on his enemies; to find a better life for his daughter)

GUIDED READING
Sequencing: Ask students to place the following events in correct sequence on a time line: A storm strikes Antonio's ship, Prospero is Duke of Milan, Miranda and Prospero are set adrift, Prospero becomes overly absorbed in his studies, Gonzalo helps Prospero, Antonio plots against Prospero.

20 INFERRING
What does the dialogue between Prospero and Ariel reveal about their relationship? (Possible response: Ariel is under Prospero's power and takes orders directly from him.)

21 LITERARY ELEMENT
Theme: What form or shape does Ariel assume when he boards Antonio's ship? (He takes the form of fire and appears in more than one place at a time.)

▓ **precursors** (prē·kur'sərz): things that go before; forerunners

Humanities Connection

Agnolo (än′yō·lō) di Cosimo (dē·kōz′ē·mō), called Il Bronzino (ēl′ brän·zē′nō), was a Florentine painter of elegant, decorative portraits. Admiral Andrea Doria (1466–1560) fit the role of Neptune, god of the sea, by reason of his Mediterranean patrols against Turks and pirates with his own fleet of galleys.

? *In lines 204–207 on p. 855, Ariel describes Neptune. What details of the portrait on this page illustrate Ariel's words?* (Appearance of mightiness, holding a trident) ■

Meeting Individual Needs

22 ***ESL:*** Clarify that "mad" in this context means "insane," or "confused," not "angry." Ask students to paraphrase "Not a soul/But felt the fever of the mad" in modern English. ("There was no one who did not experience panic and confusion.") What does the line convey about the behavior of those on the ship? (They behaved in a frenzied manner, like mad people.) ■

23 **Speculating**
What might the fact that Ferdinand was the first to leap from the ship suggest about him? (Possible responses: he is cowardly; he is smart to jump free of a sinking ship; he is superstitious.)

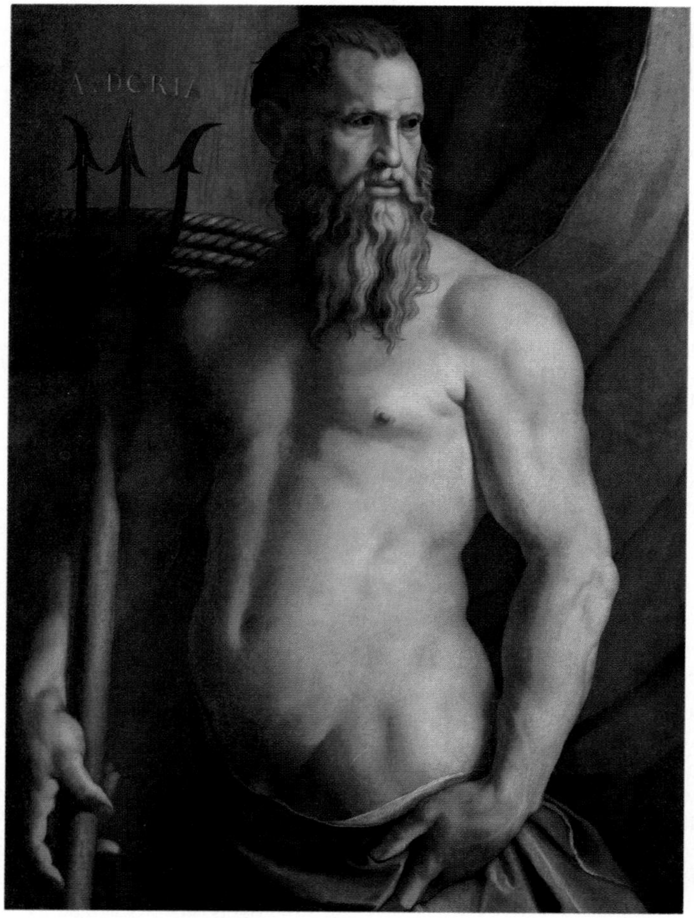

Scala/Art Resource, New York

Portrait of Andrea Doria as Neptune, Agnolo Bronzino (1503–1572). ***Andrea Doria was a celebrated sixteenth-century Italian admiral and statesman.***

Prospero. My brave spirit!
Who was so firm, so constant, that this coil°
Would not infect his reason?
Ariel. Not a soul
22 But felt a fever of the mad° and played
Some tricks of desperation. All but mariners
Plunged in the foaming brine and quit the vessel,
Then all afire with me. The King's son Ferdinand,
23 With hair up-staring (then like reeds, not hair),
Was the first man that leapt; cried "Hell is empty,
And all the devils are here!"

208. **coil:** commotion; confusion.

210. **of the mad:** of madness.

Prospero.   Why, that's my spirit!
But was not this nigh shore?
Ariel.   Close by, my master.
Prospero.
But are they, Ariel, safe?
Ariel.   Not a hair perished.
On their sustaining garments° not a blemish,
220   But fresher than before; and as thou badest me,
In troops I have dispersed them 'bout the isle.
The King's son have I landed by himself,
Whom I left cooling of the air with sighs
In an odd angle of the isle, and sitting,
225   His arms in this sad knot.
Prospero.   Of the King's ship
The mariners say° how thou hast disposed,
And all the rest o' the fleet.
Ariel.   Safely in harbor
Is the King's ship; in the deep nook where once
Thou calledst me up at midnight to fetch dew
230   From the still-vexed Bermoothes,° there she's hid;
The mariners all under hatches stowed,
Who, with a charm joined to their suff'red labor,
I have left asleep; and for the rest o' the fleet,
Which I dispersed, they all have met again,
235   And are upon the Mediterranean float°
Bound sadly home for Naples,
Supposing that they saw the King's ship wracked
And his great person perish.
Prospero.   Ariel, thy charge
Exactly is performed; but there's more work.
240   What is the time o' the day?
Ariel.   Past the mid season.
Prospero.
At least two glasses.° The time 'twixt six and now
Must by us both be spent most preciously.
Ariel.
Is there more toil? Since thou dost give me pains,
Let me remember thee what thou hast promised,
245   Which is not yet performed me.
Prospero.   How now? moody?
What is't thou canst demand?
Ariel.   My liberty.
Prospero.
Before the time be out? No more!

219. **sustaining garments:** their clothing, which kept them afloat.

225–226. **Of the King's ship/ The mariners say:** Of the King's ship and the mariners, say.

230. **still-vexed Bermoothes:** ever-stormy Bermudas.

235. **float:** sea.

241. **glasses:** turns of the hourglass; i.e., hours.

24 GUIDED READING
Identifying Details: What has become of the ship and its passengers and crew? (The ship and the sailors are in a safe harbor, and the passengers are scattered safely in different places on the island.)

25 LITERARY BACKGROUND
In *The Tempest,* Shakespeare preserved the classical unities of time, place, and action, something he had not done since one of his earliest plays, *The Comedy of Errors*. The play occurs on a single day and in a single setting, and all the action is under Prospero's control and aimed toward a single purpose. *Since the "mid season" (line 240) must mean noon, what time is it at this point? (2 o'clock) How many hours are left to accomplish Prospero's goal? (four)*

ANSWER TO MARGIN QUESTION

Lines 265–270. Prospero released Ariel from the cruel imprisonment of the witch Sycorax.

LITERARY ELEMENT

Exposition: How does the dialogue between Prospero and Ariel serve a similar purpose to the earlier dialogue between Prospero and Miranda? (Again, Shakespeare uses dialogue to give the audience additional information on events that took place earlier in the play.) In this case, the dialogue also enhances the characterizations by showing Ariel's impatience to be free and Prospero's irritation with him, and introduces more magical elements into the play.

> **malignant** (mə·lig′nənt): very evil

26 COMPARING AND CONTRASTING

What similarities and differences are there between Prospero and Sycorax? (Possible responses: They both were abandoned on the island with their children; they both have magical powers, although Sycorax seems truly evil while Prospero seems well-intentioned.)

Ariel.   I prithee,
Remember I have done thee worthy service,
Told thee no lies, made no mistakings, served
250 Without or grudge or grumblings. Thou didst promise
To bate° me a full year.
Prospero.   Dost thou forget
From what a torment I did free thee?
Ariel.   No.
Prospero.
Thou dost; and thinkst it much to tread the ooze
Of the salt deep,
255 To run upon the sharp wind of the North,
To do me business in the veins o' the earth
When it is baked with frost.
Ariel.   I do not, sir.
Prospero.
Thou liest, malignant thing! Hast thou forgot
The foul witch Sycorax, who with age and envy
260 Was grown into a hoop? Hast thou forgot her?
Ariel.
No, sir.
Prospero. Thou hast. Where was she born?
Speak! Tell me!
Ariel.
Sir, in Argier.°
Prospero.   O, was she so? I must
265 Once in a month recount what thou hast been,
Which thou forgetst. This damned witch Sycorax,
For mischiefs manifold, and sorceries terrible
To enter human hearing, from Argier
Thou knowst was banished. For one thing she did
270 They would not take her life. Is not this true?
Ariel.
Ay, sir.
Prospero.
This blue-eyed° hag was hither brought with child
And here was left by the sailors. Thou, my slave,
As thou reportst thyself, wast then her servant;
275 And, for thou wast a spirit too delicate
To act her earthy and abhorred commands,
Refusing her grand hests, she did confine thee,
By help of her more potent ministers,
And in her most unmitigable rage,
280 Into a cloven pine; within which rift

251. **bate:** abate; shorten (the length of Ariel's service).

264. **Argier:** Algiers.

"Once in a month," according to Prospero (line 265), Ariel must be reminded of his past suffering. What important information does this speech of Prospero's convey to the audience?

272. **blue-eyed:** eyes discolored blue, by circles or shadows.

ANSWERS TO MARGIN QUESTIONS

Line 287. Answers will vary.

Lines 302–303. Possible response: Ariel jumps, claps, and hugs Prospero to express his renewed enthusiasm.

Line 306. Prospero can be an impatient, scolding master, but he is also generous, fair, and forgiving. Answers will vary.

Imprisoned thou didst painfully remain
A dozen years; within which space she died
And left thee there; where thou didst vent thy
    groans
285 As fast as mill wheels strike. Then was this island
(Save for the son that she did litter here,
A freckled whelp, hag-born) not honored with
A human shape.

Ariel.   Yes, Caliban, her son.

Prospero.
Dull thing, I say so! he, that Caliban
290 Whom now I keep in service. Thou best knowst
What torment I did find thee in. Thy groans
Did make wolves howl and penetrate the breasts
Of ever-angry bears. It was a torment
To lay upon the damned, which Sycorax
295 Could not again undo. It was mine art,
When I arrived and heard thee, that made gape
The pine, and let thee out.

Ariel.   I thank thee, master.

Prospero.
If thou more murmurst, I will rend an oak
And peg thee in his knotty entrails till
Thou hast howled away twelve winters.

Ariel.   Pardon, master.
300 I will be correspondent to command°
And do my spriting gently.

Prospero.   Do so; and after two days
I will discharge thee.

Ariel.   That's my noble master!
What shall I do? Say what! What shall I do?

Prospero.
Go make thyself like a nymph o' the sea. Be subject
305 To no sight but thine and mine; invisible
To every eyeball else. Go take this shape
And hither come in't. Go! Hence with diligence!
                   [*Exit* ARIEL.]
Awake, dear heart, awake! Thou hast slept well.
Awake!

Miranda.
310 The strangeness of your story put
Heaviness in me.

Prospero.   Shake it off. Come on.
We'll visit Caliban, my slave, who never

? The way that Ariel says the name "Caliban" in line 287 may betray fear; the two characters are completely alien to each other—Caliban is of the earth, and Ariel is of the air. What famous actors would you choose to play each role?

300. **I will be correspondent to command:** I will obey your commands.

? How would you dramatize Ariel's shift in mood in lines 302–303?

? What have his interactions with Ariel revealed about Prospero's character? Do you like or dislike Prospero at this point in the play?

---

27 **ANALYZING**
What do you think Ariel is feeling when he says, "I thank thee, master." (Possible response: fear, a desire to please the person with complete power over him)

28 **GUIDED READING**
Identifying Details: Again, Prospero commands Ariel to change shape. What appearance is he to assume now? (a sea nymph's) What other extraordinary feat does Prospero demand of Ariel? (Ariel is to make himself invisible to everyone but Prospero.)

29 LITERARY ELEMENT

Characterization: Note the differences in the connotations of the words Prospero uses to refer to Caliban ("villain," "slave," "tortoise") and to Ariel ("apparition," "quaint"). How do these words highlight the contrast between the two slaves? (Possible response: Caliban seems to have no redeeming features while Ariel does.)

■ **apparition** (ap·ə·rish′ən): strange figure, like a ghost, that appears suddenly

30 CULTURAL DIVERSITY

The Tempest was written at a time when English settlers were first making their way to the New World, and when tales of its native peoples held Europe spellbound. Shakespeare had read the story of a shipwreck off Bermuda shortly before writing the play, and though Prospero's island is in the Mediterranean, its charmed atmosphere owes much to European visions of the New World.

❓ *How might the characterization of Caliban reflect Renaissance Europe's attitudes toward the natives of the New World?* (Possible response: Caliban is identified with the earth and is portrayed as ugly, insensitive, stubborn, and malicious—useful as a servant but undeserving of freedom or humane treatment.)

Yields us kind answer.

Miranda.   'Tis a villain, sir,
I do not love to look on.

Prospero.   But as 'tis,
We cannot miss° him. He does make our fire,
315   Fetch in our wood, and serves in offices
That profit us. What, ho! slave! Caliban!
Thou earth,° thou! Speak!

Caliban.
(*within*)   There's wood enough within.

Prospero.
Come forth, I say! There's other business for thee.
Come, thou tortoise! When?

[*Enter* ARIEL *like a water nymph.*]
320   Fine apparition! My quaint Ariel,
Hark in thine ear.

Ariel.   My lord, it shall be done.   [*Exit.*]

Prospero.
Thou poisonous slave, got by the Devil himself
Upon thy wicked dam, come forth!

[*Enter* CALIBAN.]

Caliban.
As wicked dew as e'er my mother brushed
325   With raven's feather from unwholesome fen°
Drop on you both! A southwest blow on ye
And blister you all o'er!

Prospero.
For this, be sure, tonight thou shalt have cramps,
Side-stitches that shall pen thy breath up; urchins°
330   Shall, for that vast of night that they may work,
All exercise on thee; thou shalt be pinched
As thick as honeycomb, each pinch more stinging
Than bees that made 'em.

Caliban.   I must eat my dinner.
This island's mine by Sycorax my mother,
335   Which thou takest from me. When thou camest first,
Thou strokedst me and made much of me; wouldst give me
Water with berries in't; and teach me how
To name the bigger light, and how the less,
That burn by day, and night; and then I loved thee
340   And showed thee all the qualities o' the isle,
The fresh springs, brine-pits, barren place and fertile.

314. **miss:** get by without.

317. **earth:** piece of the earth; i.e., dirt.

❓ An Elizabethan theater might have featured entrances through trapdoors in the floor of the stage or by pulleys suspended from the ceiling. Which entrance would be most appropriate for Ariel? for Caliban? Why?

325. **fen:** marshland; swamp.

329. **urchins:** goblins that assumed the form of hedgehogs.

❓ How is Prospero's treatment of Caliban similar to his treatment of Ariel? How is it different?

Zoe Dominic

31 INTERPRETING
How does Caliban feel about his experience with Prospero? (He loved and trusted Prospero at first and introduced him to all the features of the island. For his generosity, he received only abuse and was held captive.)

32 READER'S RESPONSE
Do you think Prospero's attitude toward Caliban is just, considering Caliban's behavior toward Miranda? Do you see parallels between Prospero and Caliban's relationship and that of the conquerors and conquered in the New World? (Answers will vary. Most should see strong parallels.)

    Cursed be I that did so! All the charms
    Of Sycorax—toads, beetles, bats light on you!
    For I am all the subjects that you have,
345 Which first was mine own king; and here you sty°
      me
    In this hard rock, whiles you do keep from me
    The rest o' the island.

Prospero.   Thou most lying slave,
    Whom stripes may move, not kindness! I have used
      thee
    (Filth as thou art) with humane care, and lodged
      thee
350 In mine own cell till thou didst seek to violate
    The honor of my child.

Caliban.
    O ho, O ho! Would't had been done!
    Thou didst prevent me; I had peopled else
    This isle with Calibans.

Miranda.   Abhorred slave,
355 Which any print of goodness wilt not take,
    Being capable of all ill! I pitied thee,
    Took pains to make thee speak, taught thee each
      hour
    One thing or other. When thou didst not, savage,
    Know thine own meaning, but wouldst gabble like
360 A thing most brutish, I endowed thy purposes

345. **sty:** to lodge, as in a pigpen.

? What is Caliban's reaction to Prospero's fatherly concern for Miranda (lines 352–354)?

ANSWER TO MARGIN QUESTION

Lines 354–365. Possible responses: The tone and content of this speech are akin to those of Prospero's previous speeches, and he is more believable in the role of Caliban's teacher than Miranda.

33 GUIDED READING

Identifying Cause and Effect:
What does Miranda see as the root cause of Caliban's offenses? (He comes from a "vile race"; his nature is inherently bad.) What conclusions does Miranda draw from this premise? (Caliban deserves to be confined and punished; he will not benefit from any attempts to educate him.)

34 LITERARY ELEMENT

Staging: Since Ariel is meant to be invisible to Ferdinand, how would you stage Ariel's entrance? (Possible response: He could appear behind a thin curtain or screen.)

33

With words that made them known. But thy vile
   race,
Though thou didst learn, had that in't which
   good natures
Could not abide to be with. Therefore wast thou
Deservedly confined into this rock, who hadst
365   Deserved more than a prison.

Caliban.
You taught me language, and my profit on't
Is, I know how to curse. The red plague rid you
For learning me your language!

Prospero.   Hag-seed, hence!
Fetch us in fuel; and be quick, thou'rt best,
370   To answer other business. Shrugst thou, malice?
If thou neglectst or dost unwillingly
What I command, I'll rack thee with old° cramps,
Fill all thy bones with aches, make thee roar
That beasts shall tremble at thy din.

Caliban.   No, pray thee.
375   (*aside*) I must obey. His art is of such pow'r
It would control my dam's god, Setebos,°
And make a vassal of him.

Prospero.   So, slave; hence!

[*Exit* CALIBAN.]

34 [*Enter* FERDINAND; *and* ARIEL, *invisible, playing
and singing.*]

[ARIEL's *song.*]
Come unto these yellow sands,
   And then take hands.
380   Curtsied when you have° and kissed,
   The wild waves whist,°
Foot it featly° here and there;
And, sweet sprites, the burden bear.
   Hark, hark!

385   [*Burden dispersedly.°*]   Bow, wow!
           The watchdogs bark.

[*Burden dispersedly.*]   Bow, wow!

Ariel.   Hark, hark! I hear
        The strain of strutting chanticleer
390   Cry, cock-a-diddle-dowe.

Ferdinand.
Where should this music be? I' the air, or the earth?

> ❓ Some directors and editors give this speech (lines 354–365) to Prospero, arguing that it is too strong for Miranda. Others argue that if she does not speak occasionally, she would not need to be included in this scene. Which position would you side with?

372. **old:** terrible.

376. **Setebos:** a god of the natives of South America, known to Europeans through travelogues.

380. **Curtsied when you have:** when you have curtsied.
381. **whist:** quiet.
382. **featly:** skillfully; gracefully.

385. **dispersedly:** from several different directions.

ANSWER TO MARGIN QUESTION

Lines 400–408. The song "Come unto these yellow sands" is merrily mocking; "Full fathom five" is mysterious and elegaic. The first might be performed up-tempo, the second slowly.

FERDINAND LURED BY ARIEL, SIR JOHN EVERETT MILLAIS (1826–1896).

The Bridgeman Art Library/Art Resource, New York

35 LITERARY ELEMENT

Imagery: How does the imagery of Ariel's song make death seem beautiful and magical rather than frightening? (It describes death as a "sea-change / Into something rich and strange." The imagery of pearls and coral creates a picture of beauty and peace.) How does this imagery reflect one of the play's major themes? (The imagery suggests transformation, or shape-changing.)

■ HUMANITIES CONNECTION

A child prodigy, Millais (mil·ā′) attended the Royal Academy Schools from ages eleven to seventeen. He was only nineteen when, with William Holman Hunt and Dante Gabriel Rossetti, he co-founded the Pre-Raphaelite Brotherhood. (See annotation on Rossetti's *Pandora*, Unit 4, p. 437.) Millais's most famous painting is the evocative and realistically rendered *Ophelia*, based on her drowning scene in Shakespeare's *Hamlet*.

❓ *How does Millais's Ariel compare with the Ariel you imagine?* (Answers will vary.) ■

It sounds no more; and sure it waits upon
Some god o' the island. Sitting on a bank,
Weeping again the King my father's wrack,
395   This music crept by me upon the waters,
Allaying both their fury and my passion
With its sweet air. Thence I have followed it,
Or it hath drawn me rather; but 'tis gone.
No, it begins again.

            [ARIEL's *song.*]
400   Full fathom five thy father lies;
            Of his bones are coral made;
        Those are pearls that were his eyes;
            Nothing of him that doth fade
        But doth suffer a sea-change
405   Into something rich and strange.
        Sea nymphs hourly ring his knell:

[*Burden.*]   Ding-dong.
        Hark! now I hear them—Ding-dong bell.

❓ Would this song have the same mood and tempo as Ariel's previous one (lines 378–384)? How would you perform each song?

The Tempest, Act 1, Scene 2   **863**

36 VISUALIZING

Are Prospero and Miranda visible to Ferdinand? (They are not invisible in the sense that Ariel is, but he does not see them yet. He is enchanted by the music, and probably separated from Prospero and Miranda by scenery or props.)

37 INTERPRETING

What confusion does Miranda express when she first sees Ferdinand? (She thinks he must be divine since he is fairer than anyone else she has ever seen.) Point out to students that the name Miranda comes from the Latin word *mirari*, to wonder. Why might this name be appropriate for the girl? (She has led a secluded life and is easily impressed by the world.)

38 LITERARY ELEMENT

Rising Action: What event is indicated by Ferdinand's line, "Most sure, the goddess/ On whom these airs attend!"? (He sees Miranda for the first time.) How does this speech echo Miranda's words upon seeing him for the first time? (He also thinks she is a divine being.)

Ferdinand.
The ditty does remember my drowned father.
410   This is no mortal business, nor no sound
That the earth owes.° I hear it now above me.

411. **owes:** owns; possesses.

Prospero.
The fringed curtains of thine eye advance°
And say what thou seest yond.

412. **advance:** draw back.

Miranda.   What is't? a spirit?
Lord, how it looks about! Believe me, sir,
415   It carries a brave form. But 'tis a spirit.

Prospero.
No, wench. It eats, and sleeps, and hath such senses
As we have, such. This gallant which thou seest
Was in the wrack; and, but he's something stained
With grief (that's beauty's canker), thou mightst call him
420   A goodly person. He hath lost his fellows
And strays about to find 'em.

Miranda.   I might call him
A thing divine, for nothing natural
I ever saw so noble.

Prospero (*aside*).   It goes on,° I see,
As my soul prompts it. Spirit, fine spirit! I'll free thee
425   Within two days for this.

? How would Miranda deliver lines 421–423? What can you gather about her emotional state at this moment?

423. **It goes on:** My plan progresses.

Ferdinand.   Most sure, the goddess
On whom these airs attend! Vouchsafe my pray'r
May know if you remain upon this island,
And that you will some good instruction give
How I may bear° me here. My prime request,
430   Which I do last pronounce, is (O you wonder!)
If you be maid or no?

429. **bear:** behave; conduct.

Miranda.   No wonder, sir,
But certainly a maid.

Ferdinand.   My language? Heavens!
I am the best° of them that speak this speech,
Were I but where 'tis spoken.

433. **the best:** the highest ranking; believing that his father is dead, Ferdinand considers himself to be king.

Prospero.   How? the best?
435   What wert thou if the King of Naples heard thee?

Ferdinand.
A single thing, as I am now, that wonders
To hear thee speak of Naples. He does hear me;
And that he does I weep. Myself am Naples,

ANSWER TO MARGIN QUESTION

Lines 457–460. Prospero is trying to place obstacles between Miranda and Ferdinand so that the lovers will not value each other too lightly.

Who with mine eyes, never since at ebb, beheld
440 The King, my father, wracked.

Miranda.   Alack, for mercy!
Ferdinand.
Yes, faith, and all his lords, the Duke of Milan
And his brave son being twain.

Prospero (*aside*).   The Duke of Milan
And his more braver daughter could control thee,°
If now 'twere fit to do't. At the first sight
445 They have changed eyes.° Delicate Ariel,
I'll set thee free for this!—A word, good sir.
I fear you have done yourself some wrong. A word!

Miranda.
Why speaks my father so ungently? This
Is the third man that e'er I saw; the first
450 That e'er I sighed for. Pity move my father
To be inclined my way!

Ferdinand.   O, if a virgin,
And your affection not gone forth, I'll make you
The Queen of Naples.

Prospero.   Soft, sir! one word more.
(*aside*) They are both in either's pow'rs. But this
swift business
455 I must uneasy make, lest too light winning
Make the prize light.—One word more! I charge
thee
That thou attend me. Thou dost here usurp
The name thou owest not, and hast put thyself
Upon this island as a spy, to win it
460 From me, the lord on't.

Ferdinand.   No, as I am a man!
Miranda.
There's nothing ill can dwell in such a temple.
If the ill spirit have so fair a house,
Good things will strive to dwell with't.

Prospero.   Follow me.—
Speak not you for him; he's a traitor.—Come!
465 I'll manacle thy neck and feet together;
Sea water shalt thou drink; thy food shall be
The fresh brook mussels, withered roots, and husks
Wherein the acorn cradled. Follow.

Ferdinand.   No.
I will resist such entertainment till
470 Mine enemy has more power.

---

443. **control thee:** inform you correctly; Prospero knows that all these men are alive and on the island.
445. **changed eyes:** exchanged loving glances.

? Why is Prospero accusing Ferdinand of being a spy in lines 457–460, knowing full well that he is not?

---

39 LITERARY ELEMENT
Characterization: What character trait of Miranda's, which we have already seen, is expressed in her line, "Alack, for mercy!"? (compassion) How do you think it will help advance the love theme in the play? (Her compassion for Ferdinand will help spark their love.)

40 GUIDED READING
Identifying Details: Who are the other two men Miranda has seen? (Prospero and Caliban)

usurp (yoo·zurp'): take unlawfully

41 INTERPRETING
What does "There's nothing ill can dwell in such a temple" mean? (A good-looking person such as Ferdinand could not possibly have a bad character.)

ANSWERS TO MARGIN QUESTIONS

Lines 479–485. Prospero is "acting." Student opinions of his behavior will vary.

Lines 497–499. Possible response: Prospero's "It works" suggests that he magically sparked the couple's love; however, it is also believable that bringing Miranda and Ferdinand together was all the magic that was needed.

42 COMPARING LITERATURE

The motif of the hero who must undergo a test or trial in order to win the hand of a ruler's or sorcerer's daughter is very common in myths and fairy tales. Invite students to discuss other works they know that contain this motif. (Possible response: "The White Snake," pp. 46–51)

advocate (ad′və·kit): a person who speaks on another's behalf

43 ANALYZING

Why does Prospero tell Miranda that, compared to most men, Ferdinand is a Caliban—an ugly monster? (Possible response: It is part of his testing of the couple's love.) How does Miranda meet the test? (She does well by declaring her satisfaction with Ferdinand regardless of whether others might be better looking.)

[*He draws, and is charmed from moving.*]

Miranda.   O dear father,
Make not too rash a trial of him, for
He's gentle, and not fearful.°

Prospero.   What, I say,
My foot my tutor?°—Put thy sword up, traitor!
Who makest a show but darest not strike, thy conscience
475   Is so possessed with guilt. Come, from thy ward!°
For I can here disarm thee with this stick
And make thy weapon drop.

Miranda.   Beseech you, father!

Prospero.
Hence! Hang not on my garments.

Miranda.   Sir, have pity.
I'll be his surety.

Prospero.   Silence! One word more
480   Shall make me chide thee, if not hate thee. What,
An advocate for an impostor! Hush!
Thou thinkst there is no more such shapes as he,
Having seen but him and Caliban. Foolish wench!
To the most of men this is a Caliban,
485   And they to him are angels.

Miranda.   My affections
Are then most humble. I have no ambition
To see a goodlier man.

Prospero.   Come on, obey!
Thy nerves° are in their infancy again
And have no vigor in them.

Ferdinand.   So they are.
490   My spirits, as in a dream, are all bound up.
My father's loss, the weakness which I feel,
The wrack of all my friends, nor this man's threats
To whom I am subdued, are but light to me,
Might I but through my prison once a day
495   Behold this maid. All corners else o' the earth
Let liberty make use of; space enough
Have I in such a prison.

Prospero (*aside*).   It works. (*to* FERDINAND)
Come on.—
Thou hast done well, fine Ariel! (*to* FERDINAND)
Follow me.—
500   (*to* ARIEL) Hark what thou else shalt do me.

472. He's gentle, and not fearful: He is a gentleman, not a coward.

473. My foot my tutor: My daughter presumes to tell me what to do.

475. ward: defensive stance.

Is Prospero really angry in lines 479–485, or is he "acting"? How do you feel about his behavior toward Miranda?

488. nerves: muscles.

In lines 497–499, Prospero is delighted that the "magic" of love has bloomed. Has he *caused* Miranda and Ferdinand to fall in love, or merely helped their romance along by throwing them together?

Miranda. Be of comfort.
My father's of a better nature, sir,
Than he appears by speech. This is unwonted
Which now came from him.
Prospero. Thou shalt be as free
As mountain winds; but then exactly do
505 All points of my command.
Ariel. To the syllable.
Prospero.
Come, follow —Speak not for him. [*Exeunt.*]

First Thoughts

What kind of person is Prospero? In your opinion, what is Prospero's primary ambition—Miranda's happiness, or revenge upon his enemies?

Identifying Facts

1. What is the **setting** of the play's first scene? What is the purpose of the voyage made by the king and his party?
2. Gonzalo believes that the ship's passengers will be saved. What reason does he give?
3. Who were Caliban's parents?
4. Who is Prospero's brother? What has he done to Prospero?
5. What does Prospero reveal to Miranda about his past and about how they came to the island?
6. Where and for how long had Ariel been imprisoned?
7. What happens when Miranda and Ferdinand meet?

Interpreting Meanings

1. Scene 1 presents the **exposition**, or **basic situation**, of the play, giving us a first glimpse of the **characters** of Gonzalo, Antonio, Sebastian, and Alonso. Compare and contrast these characters, listing everything you have learned about them thus far.

2. One critic has suggested that the play's dominant **image** is sound. Give examples of the use of sound **imagery** in Act 1. What effect does this imagery have?
3. What has been unique about Miranda's upbringing? How is she different from other young women?
4. What does Prospero's treatment of Ariel, Caliban, and Miranda reveal about his **character**?
5. Why does Prospero want Miranda and Ferdinand to fall in love?
6. **Theme** is the central idea or insight of a work of literature. One of the major themes of *The Tempest* is that of change or transformation. Give examples from Act 1 of this theme.

Applying Meanings

Important elements of fantasy are introduced in Act 1 of *The Tempest*. Refer to the paragraph you wrote in the Writer's Response (see page 844). Is Prospero's island like another world of fantasy you have seen in a movie or read or heard about? Do the characters of Ariel and Caliban remind you of other fantasy characters? Why do you think this fantasy world—invented nearly four hundred years ago—still appeals to modern readers and audiences?

1 PREDICTING

Act 1 has introduced the setting, the basic plot premise, and the important characters. Before students read the summary for Act 2, pose the following questions: What plan does Prospero have in mind for Antonio and Alonso? for Ferdinand? How will Ariel and Caliban contribute to or interfere with Prospero's plan? (Responses will vary.)

2 INTERPRETING

How does Gonzalo try to convince Alonso to "be merry"? (He reminds him that their preservation from drowning was a miracle and balances the loss of Ferdinand.) How does Gonzalo's reasoning affect Alonso? (He is irritated rather than comforted since his grief over the loss of his son cannot be so easily dismissed.)

THE TEMPEST
Act 2

1   *As you read the second act, notice how the events that make up the **rising action** complicate the story. How do the plots against Alonso and Prospero and the comic scene with Caliban help to create suspense?*

Summary of Act 2, Scene 1. *Gonzalo, King Alonso's counselor, tries to console the king for the loss of his son Ferdinand. Sebastian and Antonio are sarcastic about Gonzalo's compassion. Alonso regrets having married his daughter to the King of Tunis, because their ship was destroyed returning home from the wedding. An invisible Ariel casts a spell on all of Alonso's party except Antonio and Sebastian. Antonio convinces Sebastian that if they assassinate Alonso, Sebastian will become the King of Naples. As they draw their weapons to murder the king, Ariel awakens Gonzalo. Sebastian and Antonio claim that they drew their weapons to fight off wild beasts who were threatening to attack them. The king's party leaves to continue the search for Ferdinand.*

═══ ACT 2 ═══

Scene 1. *Another part of the island.*

[*Enter* ALONSO, SEBASTIAN, ANTONIO, GONZALO, ADRIAN, FRANCISCO, *and others.*]

Gonzalo.
    Beseech you, sir, be merry. You have cause
    (So have we all) of joy; for our escape
    Is much beyond our loss. Our hint° of woe
    Is common. Every day some sailor's wife,
5   The master of some merchant, and the merchant,°
    Have just our theme of woe; but for the miracle,
    I mean our preservation, few in millions
    Can speak like us. Then wisely, good sir, weigh
    Our sorrow with our comfort.

Alonso.   Prithee peace.

Sebastian.
10   He receives comfort like cold porridge.

Antonio.
    The visitor° will not give him o'er so.

3. **hint:** occasion.

5. **merchant:** merchant ship; **the merchant:** the ship's owner.

11. **visitor:** comforter; consoler (Gonzalo).

ANSWERS TO MARGIN QUESTIONS

Line 19. The incident increases our respect for Gonzalo's intelligence, quick wits, and sensitivity.

Lines 1–26. Alonso's tone is grief-stricken, Gonzalo's philosophical, and Sebastian's and Antonio's mocking.

Sebastian.
Look, he's winding up the watch of his wit;
by-and-by it will strike.

Gonzalo.
Sir—

Sebastian.
15   One. Tell.

Gonzalo.
When every grief is entertained that's offered,
Comes to the entertainer—

Sebastian.
A dollar.

Gonzalo.
Dolor comes to him, indeed. You have spoken
20   truer than you purposed.

Sebastian.
You have taken it wiselier than I meant you
should.

Gonzalo.
Therefore, my lord—

Antonio.
Fie, what a spendthrift is he of his tongue!

Alonso.
I prithee spare.

Gonzalo.
25   Well, I have done. But yet—

Sebastian.
He will be talking.

Antonio.
Which, of he or Adrian, for a good wager, first
begins to crow?

Sebastian.
The old cock.

Antonio.
30   The cock'rel.°

Sebastian.
Done! The wager?

Antonio.
A laughter.°

Sebastian.
A match!

Adrian.
Though this island seem to be desert—

? Notice how Gonzalo will not be intimidated by the cynical Antonio and Sebastian and uses the word *dolor*, which means sorrow, as a pun on *dollar* (line 19). How does this incident affect your perception of Gonzalo?

? The mood in this scene is tense. What do you imagine is the tone of each character's speech? How is Gonzalo's tone different from Sebastian's and Antonio's?

30. **cock'rel:** young rooster.

32. **laughter:** the winner gets a good laugh.

3 LITERARY ELEMENT

Metaphor: What comparison does Sebastian use to make fun of Gonzalo? (He compares his preparing to speak to the winding of a watch.) How does he view the old man? (as dull and slow-witted)

4 GUIDED READING

Clarifying: Make sure students understand that Sebastian and Antonio are mocking the other two characters by betting who will "crow" or speak first—the old cock Gonzalo or the young rooster Adrian.

LITERARY ELEMENT

Theme: In the long, bantering conversation between Sebastian and Antonio in Scene 1, what elements show Shakespeare's comic vision of life? (Possible responses: exchanges of wit; puns; levity in the face of danger) What elements show his tragic vision of life? (Possible response: the cruel insensitivity of Antonio and Sebastian)

ANSWER TO MARGIN QUESTION

Lines 41–42. Both Adrian and Gonzalo are talkative optimists. Like Gonzalo, Adrian is ridiculed by Sebastian and Antonio.

5 LITERARY ELEMENT

Pun: What play on words does Antonio make in lines 41–43? (Adrian says that the island seems of "temperance," meaning "has a mild climate." Antonio takes the word *temperance* and personifies it as a woman.)

6 ANALYZING

What kind of language is Adrian using? (flowery, poetic, romantic language) What figures of speech do Sebastian and Antonio mock in lines 45–47? (They make fun of Adrian's use of personification—"air breathes"—by saying the air has rotten lungs or is perfumed by a fen, or foul-smelling bog.)

7 LITERARY ELEMENT

Characterization: What does Gonzalo mean by "everything advantageous to life" in line 48? (Possible responses: fresh air, water, food, good climate) What does Antonio mean by "means to live"? (Possible responses: money, society, entertainment) What do these comments suggest about their characters? (Possible responses: Gonzalo is innocent, optimistic, satisfied with simple pleasures; Antonio is cynical, worldly, ambitious.)

Zoe Dominic

Antonio.
35 Ha, ha, ha!
Sebastian.
So, you're paid.
Adrian.
Uninhabitable and almost inaccessible—
Sebastian.
Yet—
Adrian.
Yet—
Antonio.
40 He could not miss't.
Adrian.
It must needs be of subtle, tender, and delicate temperance.
Antonio.
Temperance was a delicate wench.
Sebastian.
Ay, and a subtle, as he most learnedly delivered.°
Adrian.
45 The air breathes upon us here most sweetly.
Sebastian.
As if it had lungs, and rotten ones.
Antonio.
Or as 'twere perfumed by a fen.
Gonzalo.
Here is everything advantageous to life.

> ? In what way is Adrian like Gonzalo? How do Sebastian and Antonio treat Adrian?

44. **delivered:** proclaimed; stated.

ANSWER TO MARGIN QUESTION

Lines 49–55. Possible response: Antonio should be played as the more cynical of the two, Sebastian as the more playful.

Antonio.

7 | True; save means to live.

Sebastian.

50 | Of that there's none, or little.

Gonzalo.

How lush and lusty the grass looks! how green!

Antonio.

The ground indeed is tawny.

Sebastian.

With an eye of green in't.

Antonio.

He misses not much.

Sebastian.

55 | No; he doth but mistake the truth totally.

Gonzalo.

But the rarity of it is—which is indeed almost beyond credit—

Sebastian.

As many vouched° rarities are.

Gonzalo.

60 | That our garments, being, as they were, drenched in the sea, hold, notwithstanding, their freshness and gloss, being rather new-dyed than stained with salt water.

Antonio.

If but one of his pockets could speak, would it not say he lies?

Sebastian.

65 | Ay, or very falsely pocket up his report.

Gonzalo.

Methinks our garments are now as fresh as when we put them on first in Afric, at the marriage of the King's fair daughter Claribel to the King of Tunis.

Sebastian.

'Twas a sweet marriage, and we prosper well in our

70 | return.

Adrian.

Tunis was never graced before with such a paragon to their queen.

Gonzalo.

Not since widow Dido's° time.

Antonio.

Widow? A pox o' that! How came that "widow" in?

75 | Widow Dido!

> **?** How would you direct Antonio and Sebastian in this scene? Should they deliver their lines as playful banter or with heavy cynicism?

58. **vouched:** avowed; sworn.

73. **widow Dido's:** In the *Aeneid*, Dido was the widowed queen of Carthage (now Tunis) who fell in love with and was abandoned by Aeneas.

MEETING INDIVIDUAL NEEDS

LEP: For students who are daunted by the protracted witty banter in Scene 1, focus on the physical marvels in the scene: first, that despite being drenched in the sea, the men's clothes seem fresh and new; and second, that the characters' perceptions of the island vary according to their moral character. Also, spend some time discussing the staging of the scene. Students should understand that Gonzalo and Adrian do not hear most of the remarks Sebastian and Antonio exchange. A director might position Sebastian and Antonio to one side of the stage, somewhat separated from the others. ■

8 LITERARY BACKGROUND
The point of the "Dido" banter beginning on line 73 has been largely lost over time but seems to have something to do with the fact that widow-hood is not what we normally associate with the passionate Dido. A number of critics have noted the apparent irrelevance of the Dido allusions and have suggested that Shakespeare intended the excessive, labored wit to underscore Sebastian's and Antonio's shallowness.

Line 97. Possible responses: Sebastian and Antonio repeat "Widow Dido" to hammer home the pun on "Dido" and "died—oh." They may also be laughing giddily at the pointlessness of their own banter.

EVALUATING

Do you find the extended word play and banter among Gonzalo, Adrian, Sebastian, and Antonio amusing or boring? What function might it perform in the development of the play? (Possible response: helps to reveal character and motive)

9 LITERARY ELEMENT

Theme: What point does Gonzalo keep returning to with amazement? (the fact that in spite of the shipwreck, their clothes are like new) This mystery adds to the magical aura of the island.

Sebastian.
  What if he had said "widower Aeneas" too?
  Good Lord, how you take it!

Adrian.
  "Widow Dido," said you? You make me study of that.
  She was of Carthage, not of Tunis.

Gonzalo.
80 This Tunis, sir, was Carthage.

Adrian.
  Carthage?

Gonzalo.
  I assure you, Carthage.

Antonio.
  His word is more than the miraculous harp.°

Sebastian.
  He hath raised the wall, and houses too.

Antonio.
85 What impossible matter will he make easy next?

Sebastian.
  I think he will carry this island home in his pocket
  and give it his son for an apple.

Antonio.
  And, sowing the kernels of it in the sea, bring forth
  more islands.

Gonzalo.
90 Ay!

Antonio.
  Why, in good time!

Gonzalo.
  Sir, we were talking that our garments seem now as
  fresh as when we were at Tunis at the marriage of
  your daughter, who is now Queen.

Antonio.
95 And the rarest that e'er came there.

Sebastian.
  Bate,° I beseech you, widow Dido.

Antonio.
  O, widow Dido? Ay, widow Dido!

Gonzalo.
  Is not, sir, my doublet as fresh as the first day I
  wore it? I mean, in a sort.

Antonio.
100 That "sort" was well fished for.

83. **the miraculous harp:** According to Ovid, Amphion created the walls of Thebes by playing on his harp; Gonzalo has just "recreated" the ancient city of Carthage out of modern Tunis; therefore, his word is more powerful than the "miraculous harp."

96. **Bate:** except.

? Why do Sebastian and Antonio keep repeating "widow Dido"?

ANSWERS TO MARGIN QUESTIONS
Lines 102–109. When the king speaks, banter ends and the mood becomes somber.
Lines 119–123. Possible response: Sebastian's tone is harshly accusatory.

Gonzalo.
When I wore it at your daughter's marriage.

Alonso.
You cram these words into mine ears against
The stomach of my sense. Would I had never
Married my daughter there! for, coming thence,
105   My son is lost; and, in my rate,° she too,
Who is so far from Italy removed
I ne'er again shall see her. O thou mine heir
Of Naples and of Milan, what strange fish
Hath made his meal on thee!

Francisco.   Sir, he may live.
110   I saw him beat the surges under him
And ride upon their backs. He trod the water,
Whose enmity he flung aside, and breasted
The surge most swol'n that met him. His bold head
'Bove the <u>contentious</u> waves he kept, and oared
115   Himself with his good arms in lusty stroke
To the shore, that o'er his wave-worn basis° bowed,
As stooping to relieve him. I not doubt
He came alive to land.

Alonso.   No, no, he's gone.

Sebastian.
Sir, you may thank yourself for this great loss,
120   That would not bless our Europe with your daugh-
          ter,
But rather lose her to an African,
Where she, at least, is banished from your eye
Who hath cause to wet the grief° on't.

Alonso.   Prithee peace.

Sebastian.
You were kneeled to and importuned otherwise
125   By all of us; and the fair soul herself
Weighed, between loathness° and obedience, at
Which end o' the beam should bow. We have lost
          your son,
I fear, forever. Milan and Naples have
Mo° widows in them of this business' making
130   Than we bring men to comfort them.
The fault's your own.

Alonso.   So is the dear'st o' the loss.

Gonzalo.
My Lord Sebastian,
The truth you speak doth lack some gentleness,

105. **rate:** view; opinion.

❓ How does the mood of the scene change when the king speaks in lines 102–109?

116. **his:** the island's; **basis:** beach.

❓ How do you think Sebastian would deliver lines 119–123?

123. **wet the grief:** cry for sadness.

126. **Weighed:** poised; balanced; **loathness:** reluctance.

129. **Mo:** More.

■ contentious (kən·ten'shəs): turbulent

10 LITERARY ELEMENT
Diction: Ask students to list the verbs and adjectives that Francisco uses to describe Ferdinand's swim. (beat, trod, flung aside, breasted, bold, lusty) What impression of Ferdinand do these words evoke? (Possible response: an impression of strength and power)

11 LITERARY ELEMENT
Characterization: What does Alonso's refusal to consider Francisco's conviction that Ferdinand survived suggest about Alonso's character? (Possible response: He is pessimistic and prone to self-pity and self-reproach.)

12 GUIDED READING
Finding the Main Idea: How does Sebastian blame Alonso for their situation in lines 119–123? (He says that Alonso should not have insisted on marrying his daughter to an African because the voyage has resulted in the loss of both his children and in their being shipwrecked.)

13 **LITERARY ELEMENT**

Figure of Speech: Explain the meaning of Gonzalo's metaphor in lines 134–135? (Sebastian is "rubbing the sore"—causing Alonso greater grief—rather that "bringing the plaster"—attempting to heal the wound.) What does this metaphor suggest about Gonzalo's attitude toward Alonso? (Possible response: He feels Alonso should be protected, not accused.)

14 **LITERARY ELEMENT**

Theme: Note the recurring theme of kingship or rightful sovereignty. Who would be king in Gonzalo's ideal state? (No one person would rule.)

13 [135

   And time° to speak it in. You rub the sore
When you should bring the plaster.

Sebastian.   Very well.

Antonio.
   And most chirurgeonly.°

Gonzalo.
   It is foul weather in us all, good sir,
When you are cloudy.

Sebastian.   Foul weather?

Antonio.   Very foul.

Gonzalo.
   Had I plantation° of this isle, my lord—

Antonio.

140
   He'd sow't with nettle seed.

Sebastian.   Or docks, or mallows.

Gonzalo.
   And were the king on't, what would I do?

Sebastian.
   'Scape being drunk, for want of wine.

Gonzalo.
   I' the commonwealth I would by contraries°

14
   Execute all things; for no kind of traffic°
145
   Would I admit; no name of magistrate;
Letters should not be known; riches, poverty,
And use of service,° none; contract, succession,
Bourn, bound of land, tilth,° vineyard, none;
No use of metal,° corn, or wine, or oil;
150
   No occupation; all men idle, all;
And women too, but innocent and pure;
No sovereignty.

Sebastian.   Yet he would be king on't.

Antonio.
   The latter end of his commonwealth forgets the beginning.

Gonzalo.
155
   All things in common nature should produce
Without sweat or endeavor. Treason, felony,
Sword, pike, knife, gun, or need of any engine°
Would I not have; but nature should bring forth,
Of it own kind, all foison,° all abundance,
160
   To feed my innocent people.

Sebastian.
   No marrying 'mong his subjects?

134. **time:** appropriate time.

136. **chirurgeonly:** like an accomplished surgeon.

139. **plantation:** authority to colonize.

143. **by contraries:** contrary to the usual manner.
144. **traffic:** trade.

147. **service:** servants.
148. **Bourn:** boundary; **tilth:** agriculture.
149. **metal:** currency; money.

157. **engine:** destructive weapon.

159. **foison:** plentifulness.

Line 164. Gonzalo's "golden age," adapted by Shakespeare from Michel de Montaigne's essay "Of Cannibals," is an imagined idyllic state without aspects of civilization, such as money, laws, labor, and social inequality. Gonzalo's purpose is to distract Alonso from grief; Shakespeare's purpose is to explore the question of the value of civilization.

Lines 179–184. Possible response: The other characters would show no sign of noticing Ariel among them. (Remind students that Elizabethan actors wore special cloaks to indicate invisibility.)

Antonio.
None, man! All idle—whores and knaves.

Gonzalo.
I would with such perfection govern, sir,
T'excel the golden age.

Sebastian.   Save his Majesty!

Antonio.
165   Long live Gonzalo!

Gonzalo.   And—do you mark me, sir?

Alonso.
Prithee no more. Thou dost talk nothing to me.

Gonzalo.
I do well believe your Highness; and did it to minister
occasion° to these gentlemen, who are of such sensi-
ble° and nimble lungs that they always use to laugh
170   at nothing.

Antonio.
'Twas you we laughed at.

Gonzalo.
Who in this kind of merry fooling am nothing to you.
So you may continue, and laugh at nothing still.

Antonio.
What a blow was there given!

Sebastian.
175   An it had not fall'n flatlong.°

Gonzalo.
You are gentlemen of brave metal. You would lift the
moon out of her sphere if she would continue in it
five weeks without changing.

[*Enter* ARIEL, *invisible, playing solemn music.*]

Sebastian.
We would so, and then go a-batfowling.°

Antonio.
180   Nay, good my lord, be not angry.

Gonzalo.
No, I warrant you. I will not adventure my discretion
so weakly.° Will you laugh me asleep, for I am very
heavy?

Antonio.
Go sleep, and hear us.

[*All sleep except* ALONSO, SEBASTIAN, *and*
ANTONIO.]

? What are the characteristics of Gonzalo's "golden age" (line 164)? What is his purpose in describing it?

167–168. **minister occasion:** provide occasion for laughter.
168–169. **sensible:** responsive.

175. **An:** if; **flatlong:** on the flat rather than the edge of a sword.

179. **a-batfowling:** a technique of hunting birds at night that used a bright light (here, the moon).

181–182. **adventure my discretion so weakly:** risk my reputation as a reasonable man over such a small matter.

? Ariel is supposed to be invisible as he moves among the courtiers, putting them to sleep. How would you convey his invisibility to the audience?

COMPARING LITERATURE
Ask students to reread "The Four Ages" from Ovid's *Metamorphoses* (pp. 425–426) and compare the Golden Age of Greek and Roman mythology with Gonzalo's Golden Age.

15 READER'S RESPONSE
Do you think the utopia, or ideal society, that Gonzalo has described is an appealing one? Do you think it is attainable? (Possible response: Students will probably find the concept of a peaceful, classless society in which no one works or studies, yet in which food is abundant, quite appealing. However, most will recognize that such a society would probably be destroyed ultimately by human greed or ambition.)

16 INTERPRETING
What is Alonso's reaction to Gonzalo's utopian speech? (He is too grief-stricken to pay attention to it.) What is Gonzalo's reaction to the snubs and jeers of Sebastian and Antonio? (He bears their ridicule patiently and tries to turn their scorn to his advantage by cleverly playing with words.)

17 LITERARY ELEMENT
Mood: How does the mood of the scene change after Ariel enters? (It becomes subdued; worldly cares seem less important as sleep overtakes most of the characters.)

18 LITERARY ELEMENT

Plot/Theme: Sleep versus wakefulness is a recurring theme as well as a plot device to keep the action moving. At what earlier point in the play was sleep used to further the plot? (In Act 1, Prospero used magic to induce Miranda to sleep after telling her about his exile.)

19 LITERARY ELEMENT

Rising Action: What is the "occasion" (line 201) to which Antonio refers? (The "occasion" is Sebastian's opportunity to kill his brother Alonso while the king and his companions sleep, thereby making Sebastian king of Naples.)

20 LITERARY ELEMENT

Theme: Note the play on the word *sleep* throughout this exchange. Sebastian thinks he is dreaming Antonio's words of treason, while Antonio accuses Sebastian of letting his good fortune "sleep." How does this punning relate to the theme of illusion and reality? (Possible response: The characters are confused and cannot recognize what is real and what is a dream.)

Alonso.
185　　What, all so soon asleep? I wish mine eyes
　　Would, with themselves, shut up my thoughts. I find
　　They are inclined to do so.
Sebastian.　　　　　　　　　　Please you, sir
　　Do not omit the heavy offer of it.°
　　It seldom visits sorrow; when it doth,
190　　It is a comforter.
Antonio.　　　　　　　We two, my lord,
　　Will guard your person while you take your rest,
　　And watch your safety.
Alonso.　　　　　　　　　　Thank you. Wondrous heavy.

[ALONSO *sleeps.*]　　　　　　　　　　[*Exit* ARIEL.]

18

Sebastian.
　　What a strange drowsiness possesses them!
Antonio.
　　It is the quality o' the climate.
Sebastian.　　　　　　　　　　Why
195　　Doth it not then our eyelids sink? I find not
　　Myself disposed to sleep.
Antonio.　　　　　　　　　Nor I. My spirits are nimble.
　　They fell together all, as by consent.
　　They dropped as by a thunderstroke. What might,
　　Worthy Sebastian—O, what might?—No more!
200　　And yet methinks I see it in thy face,
　　What thou shouldst be. The occasion speaks thee,° and
　　My strong imagination sees a crown
　　Dropping upon thy head.
Sebastian.　　　　　　　　What? Art thou waking?
Antonio.
　　Do you not hear me speak?
Sebastian.　　　　　　　　　　I do; and surely
205　　It is a sleepy language, and thou speakst
　　Out of thy sleep. What is it thou didst say?
　　This is a strange repose, to be asleep
　　With eyes wide open; standing, speaking, moving—
　　And yet so fast asleep.
Antonio.　　　　　　　Noble Sebastian,
210　　Thou letst thy fortune sleep—die, rather; winkst
　　Whiles thou art waking.
Sebastian.　　　　　　　　Thou dost snore distinctly;
　　There's meaning in thy snores.

19

20

188. **omit the heavy offer of it:** miss the opportunity to sleep.

201. **occasion speaks thee:** opportunity names you.

❓ What is Antonio getting at in lines 197–203? What is the tone of the following exchange between Sebastian and Antonio?

Antonio.
    I am more serious than my custom. You
    Must be so too, if heed me; which to do
215   Trebles thee o'er.

Sebastian.   Well, I am standing water.°

Antonio.
    I'll teach you how to flow.°

Sebastian.   Do so. To ebb
    Hereditary sloth instructs me.

Antonio.   O,
    If you but knew how you the purpose cherish
    Whiles thus you mock it! how, in stripping it,
220   You more invest it! Ebbing men indeed
    (Most often) do so near the bottom run
    By their own fear or sloth.

Sebastian.   Prithee say on.
    The setting° of thine eye and cheek proclaim
    A matter° from thee; and a birth, indeed,
225   Which throes° thee much to yield.

215. **Trebles thee o'er:** triples your wealth and power; **standing water:** quiet, in order to listen carefully.
216. **flow:** move forward (toward wealth and power).

223. **setting:** look; expression.
224. **matter:** significant concern.
225. **throes:** pains.

Still from a 1989 production of *The Tempest* by the Roundabout Theater Company.

Martha Swope

Characterization: What does the line "I am more serious than my custom" suggest to you about Antonio? (Possible response: Although in everyday life he is a sarcastic joker, in political matters he can suddenly act ruthlessly.)

ebbing (eb'iŋ): weakening or declining

Figurative Language: Which of the Renaissance "four elements" does the language in lines 215–220 use as a basis for figurative comparisons? (water) What part has water played in the play thus far? (Water, or the sea, has brought the characters to the island and has supposedly drowned Ferdinand, the heir apparent.)

Lines 232–233. No. Antonio's meaning dawns on Sebastian gradually throughout the scene.

Lines 247–248. Possible response: The past prepares the way for the future but does not predetermine it; the future is determined by human actions.

23 LITERARY ELEMENT

Paradox: What is the meaning of Antonio's seemingly contradictory statement? (Out of their conviction that Ferdinand is dead—"no hope"—arises their hope that Sebastian will become king.)

24 GUIDED READING

Finding the Main Idea: According to Antonio, why would Claribel, Alonso's heir, be no threat to Sebastian? (He says that she lives at such a distance from Naples that she would not make the journey back until today's infants are shaving.)

Antonio.   Thus, sir:
Although this lord of weak remembrance,° this
Who shall be of as little memory
When he is earthed, hath here almost persuaded
(For he's a spirit of persuasion, only
230 Professes to persuade) the King his son's alive,
'Tis as impossible that he's undrowned
As he that sleeps here swims.

Sebastian.   I have no hope
That he's undrowned.

Antonio.   O, out of that no hope
What great hope have you! No hope that way is
235 Another way so high a hope that even
Ambition cannot pierce a wink beyond,
But doubts discovery° there. Will you grant with me
That Ferdinand is drowned?

Sebastian.   He's gone.

Antonio.   Then tell me,
Who's the next heir of Naples?

Sebastian.   Claribel.

Antonio.
240 She that is Queen of Tunis; she that dwells
Ten leagues beyond man's life;° she that from Naples
Can have no note, unless the sun were post°—
The man i' the moon's too slow—till newborn chins
Be rough and razorable; she that from whom
245 We all were sea-swallowed, though some cast° again,
And, by that destiny, to perform an act
Whereof what's past is prologue, what to come,
In yours and my discharge.

Sebastian.   What stuff is this? How say you?
'Tis true my brother's daughter's Queen of Tunis;
250 So is she heir of Naples; 'twixt which regions
There is some space.

Antonio.   A space whose ev'ry cubit
Seems to cry out "How shall that Claribel
Measure us° back to Naples? Keep in Tunis,
And let Sebastian wake!" Say this were death
255 That now hath seized them, why, they were no worse
Than now they are. There be that can rule Naples
As well as he that sleeps; lords that can prate
As amply and unnecessarily
As this Gonzalo. I myself could make

226. this lord of weak remembrance: Francisco; Antonio does not believe Francisco's story of Ferdinand swimming to safety.

Does Sebastian in lines 232–233 yet fully comprehend Antonio's meaning?

237. doubts discovery: does not believe what he (Ambition) sees.

241. Ten leagues beyond man's life: i.e., too far away to be of concern.
242. post: messenger.

245. though some cast: were somehow cast upon the shore.

Lines 247–248 are often quoted. What do they mean? Paraphrase them in your own words.

253. Measure us: journey the long distance that the cubits measure. (The cubits are "speaking" here.)

ANSWERS TO MARGIN QUESTIONS

Lines 270–284. Possible response: Antonio is seizing his dagger.

Lines 284–288. Possible response: If Sebastian is still undecided, he should press hesitantly for Antonio to draw first; if Sebastian has decided readily, his tone and gestures should be eager. Answers will vary.

260   A chough of as deep chat.° O, that you bore
The mind that I do! What a sleep were this
For your advancement! Do you understand me?

Sebastian.
Methinks I do.

Antonio.   And how does your content
Tender your own good fortune?

Sebastian.   I remember
265   You did supplant your brother Prospero.

Antonio.   True.
And lock how well my garments sit upon me,
Much feater° than before! My brother's servants
Were then my fellows; now they are my men.

Sebastian.
But, for your conscience—

Antonio.
270   Ay, sir! Where lies that? If 'twere a kibe,°
'Twould put me to° my slipper; but I feel not
This deity in my bosom. Twenty consciences
That stand 'twixt me and Milan, candied be they
And melt, ere they molest!° Here lies your brother,
275   No better than the earth he lies upon
If he were that which now he's like—that's dead;
Whom I with this obedient steel (three inches of it)
Can lay to bed forever; whiles you, doing thus,
To the perpetual wink° for aye might put
280   This ancient morsel, this Sir Prudence, who
Should not upbraid our course. For all the rest,
They'll take suggestion as a cat laps milk;
They'll tell the clock to° any business that
We say befits the hour.

Sebastian.   Thy case, dear friend,
285   Shall be my precedent. As thou gotst Milan,
I'll come by Naples. Draw thy sword. One stroke
Shall free thee from the tribute which thou payest,
And I the King shall love thee.

Antonio.   Draw together;
And when I rear my hand, do you the like,
290   To fall it on Gonzalo.

[*They draw.*]

Sebastian.   O, but one word!

[*They converse apart.*]

[*Enter* ARIEL, *invisible, with music and song.*]

259–260. **make/A chough of as deep chat:** teach a jackdaw to speak as profoundly.

267. **feater:** more neatly or appropriately.

270. **kibe:** a sore or ulcerated spot on the heel.
271. **'Twould put me to:** it would lead me to wear.

274. **melt:** eaten; **molest:** bother me.

? What do you imagine Antonio is doing as he speaks lines 270–284?

279. **wink:** sleep.

283. **tell the clock to:** agree it is time for.

? Sebastian is finally drawn into the conspiracy in lines 284–288. Has he struggled with his conscience, or readily decided to plot against his brother? How would you dramatize either possibility?

supplant (sə·plant′): to take the place of, especially through force

precedent (pres′ə·dənt): a case that may serve as an example for a later one

GUIDED READING
Summarizing: What are some of the arguments Antonio uses to try to persuade Sebastian to act in lines 235–290? (Lines 235–254: Opportunity is ripe, since Ferdinand is dead and Claribel is unlikely to travel back to assume rule. Lines 254–256: Death is no worse than sleeping. Lines 256–260: Anyone can rule. Lines 269–274: Conscience need not bother you. Line 275: The king is no better than the dirt he lies on. Lines 281–284: The others will not object.)

25 DRAMATIC ELEMENT
Staging: How is the audience alerted each time Ariel enters the action? (by music and song) How does this music contribute to the air of enchantment on the island? (Both Ariel and the music seem to cast magic spells.)

26 SPECULATING

Ariel says that Prospero has foreseen the danger to Alonso and sent him back to prevent it. But it was Prospero, through Ariel, who cast the sleeping spell in the first place. Do you think Prospero deliberately tempted Antonio and Sebastian by keeping them awake? (Possible response: Prospero provided an opportunity, but it was Antonio himself who wished to use the opportunity to kill the king.)

27 LITERARY ELEMENT

Theme: What recurring theme do the images in this song reflect? (sleep versus wakefulness)

28 LITERARY ELEMENT

Word Play: What word in line 318 has a double meaning? (Possible response: ''Beasts'' refers to the animals that were supposedly attacking the sleeping king and also to the treacherous plotters, Antonio and Sebastian.)

26

Ariel.
My master through his art foresees the danger
That you, his friend, are in, and sends me forth
(For else his project dies) to keep them living.

[*Sings in* GONZALO's *ear.*]

27

295   While you here do snoring lie,
             Open-eyed conspiracy
                 His time° doth take.   296. **time:** chance; opportunity.
             If of life you keep a care,
             Shake off slumber and beware.
                 Awake, awake!

Antonio.
300   Then let us both be sudden.
Gonzalo.
[*Wakes.*] Now good angels preserve the King!
Alonso.
[*Wakes.*] Why, how now? Ho, awake! Why are you
   drawn?
Wherefore this ghastly looking?
Gonzalo.   What's the matter?
Sebastian.
Whiles we stood here securing your repose,
305   Even now, we heard a hollow burst of bellowing
Like bulls, or rather lions. Did't not wake you?
It struck mine ear most terribly.
Alonso.   I heard nothing.
Antonio.
O, 'twas a din to fright a monster's ear,
To make an earthquake! Sure it was the roar
310   Of a whole herd of lions.
Alonso.   Heard you this, Gonzalo?
Gonzalo.
Upon mine honor, sir, I heard a humming,
And that a strange one too, which did awake me.
I shaked you, sir, and cried. As mine eyes opened,
I saw their weapons drawn. There was a noise;
315   That's verily.° 'Tis best we stand upon our guard,   315. **verily:** true.
Or that we quit this place. Let's draw our weapons.
Alonso.
Lead off this ground, and let's make further search
For my poor son.
Gonzalo.   Heavens keep him from these beasts!

28
For he is sure i' the island.

If you were directing this play, how would you instruct the actor playing Sebastian to deliver lines 304–307?

Lines 319–321. Possible response: The confused Alonso apprehensively urges Gonzalo to exit first; the loyal Gonzalo does so readily. Sebastian and Antonio lurk in the rear while Ariel dances invisibly around them.

Lines 1–14. Possible response: Caliban's anger should be apparent. ". . . I needs must curse" suggests defiance.

Alonso.   Lead away.

Ariel.

320   Prospero my lord shall know what I have done.
       So, King, go safely on to seek thy son.

                    [*Exeunt.*]

> The entire party prepares to leave. How might the exit be handled? How would Sebastian and Antonio act, considering their narrow escape?

29 LITERARY ELEMENT
Imagery: To which of the Renaissance "four elements" does the imagery in Caliban's speech mainly refer? (earth) To what does Caliban compare the spirits that torment him? (apes, hedgehogs, adders)

Summary of Act 2, Scene 2. *On another part of the island, Caliban is gathering wood for Prospero and cursing his master. When Trinculo appears, Caliban, thinking that he might be one of Prospero's spirits sent to plague him, lies down to hide. A storm has just passed and another is about to begin. Trinculo, thinking there is no other shelter, hides under Caliban's cloak, though he is disgusted by the monster's smell and appearance. Stephano, another victim of the shipwreck, enters drunkenly and sees the strange combination of Caliban and Trinculo. In his drunken stupor, he thinks he has discovered a rare monster with two heads and four legs. He gives each of the "heads" some wine. Trinculo and Stephano renew their acquaintance, and Caliban, quite drunk, pledges allegiance to Stephano as his new master. They then go off to explore the island which is to be Stephano's new kingdom, believing that the rest of the ship's party were killed in the storm.*

     Scene 2. *Another part of the island.*

[*Enter* CALIBAN *with a burden of wood. A noise of thunder heard.*]

Caliban.
     All the infections that the sun sucks up
     From bogs, fens, flats, on Prosper fall and make him
     By inchmeal° a disease! His spirits hear me,
     And yet I needs must curse. But they'll nor pinch,
5   Fright me with urchin-shows, pitch me i' the mire,
     Nor lead me, like a firebrand,° in the dark
     Out of my way, unless he bid 'em; but
     For every trifle are they set upon me;
     Sometime like apes that mow° and chatter at me,
10   And after bite me; then like hedgehogs which
     Lie tumbling in my barefoot way and mount
     Their pricks at my footfall; sometime am I
     All wound with adders, who with cloven tongues
     Do hiss me into madness.

[*Enter* TRINCULO.]

3. **By inchmeal:** inch by inch.

6. **firebrand:** will-o'-the-wisp.

9. **mow:** grimace; make faces.

> How would you have Caliban deliver this soliloquy (lines 1–14): coldly and matter-of-factly, or with heated anger?

ANSWERS TO MARGIN QUESTIONS

Lines 24–25. Trinculo inspects—and smells—Caliban.

Lines 37–41. Caliban's garment must be loose enough for Trinculo to drape over himself. The fabric would probably be coarse and dirty. Other details will vary.

Lines 42–49. The general tone of this scene is boisterous.

30 LITERARY ELEMENT

Language/Style: What is the difference between Trinculo's language and that of most of the other characters in the play? (He speaks prose.) Why do you think Shakespeare created this difference? (Trinculo is a member of the lower classes and a clown.) Note that Stephano, too, speaks mainly in prose.

31 GUIDED READING

Identifying Characteristics: Who are Trinculo and Stephano? Encourage students to look back at the Cast of Characters, p. 845, to refresh their memories. (two clownish characters, a jester and a drunken butler, who were on the ship and have washed ashore on a different part of the island from the other groups of castaways)

Lo, now, lo!

15   Here comes a spirit of his, and to torment me
For bringing wood in slowly. I'll fall flat;
Perchance he will not mind° me.

17. **mind:** see.

[*Lies down.*]

Trinculo.
Here's neither bush nor shrub to bear off any weather
at all, and another storm brewing. I hear it sing i' the
20   wind. Yond same black cloud, yond huge one, looks
like a foul bombard° that would shed his liquor. If it
should thunder as it did before, I know not where to
hide my head. Yond same cloud cannot choose but
fall by pailfuls. What have we here? a man or a fish?
25   dead or alive? A fish: he smells like a fish; a very
ancient and fishlike smell; a kind of, not of the newest,
poor John.° A strange fish! Were I in England now, as
once I was, and had but this fish painted,° not a
holiday fool there but would give a piece of silver.
30   There would this monster make a man.° Any strange
beast there makes a man. When they will not give a
doit° to relieve a lame beggar, they will lay out ten to
see a dead Indian. Legged like a man! and his fins like
arms! Warm, o' my troth! I do now let loose my
35   opinion, hold it no longer: this is no fish, but an
islander, that hath lately suffered by a thunderbolt.
[*Thunder.*] Alas, the storm is come again! My best way
is to creep under his gaberdine. There is no other
shelter hereabout. Misery acquaints a man with
40   strange bedfellows. I will here shroud° till the dregs
of the storm be past.

21. **bombard:** a jug made of leather.

❓ What do you imagine Trinculo is doing as he speaks these lines?

27. **poor John:** a type of fish that has been dried and salted.
28. **painted:** painted on a sign for a sideshow.
30. **make a man:** make one a rich man.
32. **doit:** a coin that was worth very little.

40. **shroud:** take cover.

[*Creeps under* CALIBAN's *garment.*]

[*Enter* STEPHANO, *singing; a bottle in his hand.*]
Stephano.
I shall no more to sea, to sea;
Here shall I die ashore.

This is a very scurvy tune to sing at a man's funeral.°
45   Well, here's my comfort.

[*Drinks.*]
The master, the swabber, the boatswain, and I,
The gunner, and his mate,
Loved Mall, Meg, and Marian, and Margery,
But none of us cared for Kate.

❓ What do you imagine Caliban's costume looks like?

44. **scurvy:** low; vile; **funeral:** Stephano thinks Trinculo is dead.

❓ The three characters of Scene 2—Stephano, Trinculo, and Caliban— are now assembled. What is the general tone of this scene?

The Bridgeman Art Library/Art Resource, New York

THE TEMPEST (detail), WILLIAM HOGARTH (1697–1764).

❓ *Does this painting match your image of Caliban? Why or why not?*

William Hogarth is famous for having invented a new art form, the serial story-picture. In his serials, he depicted the fortunes and misfortunes of the main characters in both *The Harlot's Progress* (1732) and *The Rake's Progress* (1735). He thought of his works as dramatic pictures, and wanted them to achieve the same effects as an actor on a stage. ■

32 LITERARY ELEMENT

Irony: What does the audience know that Caliban and Stephano do not that makes their situation humorous? (The audience knows the identity of all the participants and can enjoy their ignorance and fear of one another.)

50   For she had a tongue with a tang,
            Would cry to a sailor "Go hang!"
        She loved not the savor of tar nor of pitch;
        Yet a tailor might scratch her where'er she
                did itch.
            Then to sea, boys, and let her go hang!

55   This is a scurvy tune too; but here's my comfort.

        [*Drinks.*]

        Caliban.
            Do not torment me! O!

32 **Stephano.**
            What's the matter? Have we devils here? Do you put
            tricks upon's with savages and men of Inde,° ha? I
            have not 'scaped drowning to be afeard now of your
60   four legs; for it hath been said, "As proper a man as
            ever went on four legs cannot make him give ground";
            and it shall be said so again, while Stephano breathes
            at nostrils.

        Caliban.
            The spirit torments me. O!

58. **Inde:** India.

How would you stage this scene? Remember, Trinculo is still hidden under Caliban.

Zoe Dominic

ANSWERS TO MARGIN QUESTIONS
Line 71. Caliban thinks that a spirit sent by Prospero is tormenting him.
Lines 73–78. Stephano wants to use liquor to tame Caliban, then take him to Naples and sell him for a high price.

Stephano.

65   This is some monster of the isle, with four legs, who hath got, as I take it, an ague.° Where the devil should he learn our language? I will give him some relief, if it be but for that. If I can recover him, and keep him tame, and get to Naples with him, he's a present for

70   any emperor that ever trod on neat's° leather.

Caliban.

    Do not torment me prithee! I'll bring my wood home faster.

Stephano.

    He's in his fit now and does not talk after the wisest. He shall taste of my bottle. If he have never drunk

75   wine afore, it will go near to remove his fit. If I can recover him and keep him tame, I will not take° too much for him; he shall pay for him that hath him, and that soundly.

Caliban.

    Thou dost me yet but little hurt. Thou wilt anon; I

80   know it by thy° trembling. Now Prosper works upon thee.

Stephano.

    Come on your ways. Open your mouth. Here is that which will give language to you, cat.° Open your mouth. This will shake your shaking, I can tell you,

85   and that soundly. [*Gives* CALIBAN *drink*.] You cannot tell who's your friend. Open your chaps again.

Trinculo.

    I should know that voice. It should be—but he is drowned; and these are devils. O, defend me!

Stephano.

    Four legs and two voices—a most delicate monster!

90   His forward voice now is to speak well of his friend; his backward voice is to utter foul speeches and to detract. If all the wine in my bottle will recover him, I will help his ague. Come!

[*Gives drink.*]

    Amen! I will pour some in thy other mouth.

Trinculo.

95   Stephano!

Stephano.

    Doth thy other mouth call me? Mercy, mercy! This is a devil, and no monster. I will leave him; I have no long spoon.°

66. **ague** (ā′gyo͞o′): a fit of shivering.

70. **neat's:** cow's.

❓ Who or what does Caliban think is tormenting him in line 71?

76. **will not take:** cannot ask.

❓ According to lines 73–78, what is Stephano's scheme?

80. **thy:** Trinculo's, who is under Caliban's cloak.

83. **cat:** a reference to a proverb that says a drink of liquor can make a cat speak.

98. **long spoon:** alludes to an old proverb that says, "He must have a long spoon that eats with the Devil."

33 LITERARY ELEMENT
Irony: What is the discrepancy between what Stephano believes about Caliban and what the audience knows? (Caliban learned to use language from Prospero, and, in fact, uses it far more eloquently than Stephano.)

34 LITERARY ELEMENT
Theme: How does Stephano's ironic comment "You cannot tell who's your friend" reflect the action of the play? (Antonio overthrew his brother and was ready to kill Alonso. The characters in general have trouble seeing beyond appearances to the truth.)

Trinculo.
Stephano! If thou beest Stephano, touch me and speak
100 to me; for I am Trinculo—be not afeard—thy good
friend Trinculo.

Stephano.
35 If thou beest Trinculo, come forth. I'll pull thee by the
lesser legs. If any be Trinculo's legs, these are they.
[*Pulls him out.*] Thou art very Trinculo indeed! How
105 camest thou to be the siege of this mooncalf?° Can he
vent Trinculos?

105. **siege:** excrement; **mooncalf:** monstrous creature.

Trinculo.
I took him to be killed with a thunderstroke. But art
thou not drowned, Stephano? I hope now thou art not
36 drowned. Is the storm overblown? I hid me under the
110 dead mooncalf's gaberdine for fear of the storm. And
art thou living, Stephano? O Stephano, two Neapolitans 'scaped?

❓ What actions do you imagine accompany Trinculo's speech in lines 107–112?

Stephano.
Prithee do not turn me about. My stomach is not
constant.

Caliban (*aside*).
37 115 These be fine things, an if° they be not sprites. That's
a brave god and bears celestial liquor. I will kneel to
him.

115. **an if:** if.

Stephano.
How didst thou 'scape? How camest thou hither?
Swear by this bottle how thou camest hither. I escaped
120 upon a butt of sack° which the sailors heaved o'erboard, by this bottle, which I made of the bark of a
tree with mine own hands since I was cast ashore.

120. **butt of sack:** cask of wine.

Caliban.
I'll swear upon that bottle to be thy true subject, for
the liquor is not earthly.

Stephano.
125 Here! Swear then how thou escapedst.

Trinculo.
Swum ashore, man, like a duck. I can swim like a
duck, I'll be sworn.

Stephano.
Here, kiss the book.° [*Gives him drink.*] Though thou
canst swim like a duck, thou art made like a goose.°

128. **the book:** the bottle.
129. **like a goose:** foolish.

Trinculo.
130 O Stephano, hast any more of this?

ANSWERS TO MARGIN QUESTIONS

Line 149. Stephano's liquor impresses Caliban. He wants Stephano to be his lord and master.

Lines 151–155: Possible response: Both intend to exploit Caliban. However, Stephano relishes Caliban's devoted servility while Trinculo is rather disgusted by Caliban.

Stephano.
The whole butt, man. My cellar is in a rock by the seaside, where my wine is hid. How now, mooncalf? How does thine ague?

Caliban.
Hast thou not dropped from heaven?

Stephano.
135   Out o' the moon, I do assure thee. I was the Man i' the Moon when time was.°

Caliban.
I have seen thee in her, and I do adore thee. My mistress showed me thee, and thy dog, and thy bush.°

Stephano.
Come, swear to that; kiss the book. I will furnish it
140   anon with new contents. Swear.

[CALIBAN *drinks.*]

Trinculo.
By this good light, this is a very shallow monster! I afeard of him? A very weak monster! The Man i' the Moon? A most poor credulous monster! Well drawn,° monster, in good sooth.°

Caliban.
145   I'll show thee every fertile inch o' the island; and I will kiss thy foot. I prithee be my god.

Trinculo.
By this light, a most perfidious and drunken monster! When's god's asleep he'll rob his bottle.

Caliban.
I'll kiss thy foot. I'll swear myself thy subject.

Stephano.
150   Come on then. Down, and swear!

Trinculo.
I shall laugh myself to death at this puppyheaded monster. A most scurvy monster! I could find in my heart to beat him—

Stephano.
Come, kiss.

Trinculo.
155   But that the poor monster's in drink. An <u>abominable</u> monster!

Caliban.
I'll show thee the best springs; I'll pluck thee berries;

136. **when time was:** at one time.

138. **thy dog, and thy bush:** those things that the Man in the Moon was said to have with him.

143. **Well drawn:** drawn from the bottle; Caliban took a long drink.

144. **in good sooth:** to be sure; truly.

(?) What about Stephano impresses Caliban? What does he want from Stephano?

(?) How would you describe Stephano's attitude toward Caliban? How would you describe Trinculo's?

40 SPECULATING

Trinculo mocks Caliban for willingly following someone of low character. In this offhand remark, how may Shakespeare be commenting on typical human behavior? (Possible response: In civilized and uncivilized times, many people have been all too willing to follow unworthy leaders.)

41 LITERARY ELEMENT

Plot: How does this comic subplot reflect the action and themes in the main plot? (Stephano and Trinculo, like Antonio and Sebastian, blindly plan to become rulers.)

Martha Swope

I'll fish for thee, and get thee wood enough.
A plague upon the tyrant that I serve!
160   I'll bear him no more sticks, but follow thee,
Thou wondrous man.

40   **Trinculo.**
A most ridiculous monster, to make a wonder of a poor drunkard!

Caliban.
I prithee let me bring thee where crabs° grow;
165   And I with my long nails will dig thee pignuts,
Show thee a jay's nest, and instruct thee how
To snare the nimble marmoset; I'll bring thee
To clust'ring filberts, and sometimes I'll get thee
Young scamels° from the rock. Wilt thou go with me?

Stephano.
170   I prithee now lead the way without any more talking.
41   Trinculo, the King and all our company else being drowned, we will inherit here. Here, bear my bottle. Fellow Trinculo, we'll fill him by-and-by again.

[CALIBAN *sings drunkenly.*]

? In what tone would you have Caliban deliver his pledge to Stephano (lines 157–161)?

164. **crabs:** crab apples.

169. **scamels:** meaning uncertain; perhaps a type of seabird.

Caliban.
    Farewell, master; farewell, farewell!
Trinculo.
175   A howling monster! a drunken monster!
Caliban.
    No more dams I'll make for fish,
        Nor fetch in firing
        At requiring,
    Nor scrape trenchering,° nor wash dish.
180   'Ban, 'Ban, Ca—Caliban
        Has a new master. Get a new man.

    Freedom, highday! highday, freedom! freedom, high-
    day, freedom!
Stephano.
    O brave monster! lead the way.   [*Exeunt.*]

> ❓ To what master is Caliban bidding farewell in line 174?

179. **trenchering:** A trencher is a wooden platter on which food is served.

> ## First Thoughts
> Do you find Caliban to be a terrifying or a pathetic creature? Why?
>
> ## Identifying Facts
> 1. At the beginning of Act 2, why is Alonso unhappy? What does he regret?
> 2. What do Antonio and Sebastian plan to do to Alonso?
> 3. What does Ariel do before and after the conversation between Sebastian and Antonio?
> 4. What does Stephano think when he finds Trinculo and Caliban together?
> 5. What does Caliban swear to Stephano? What does he hope to achieve?
>
> ## Interpreting Meanings
> 1. What does Gonzalo's speech in Scene 1 reveal about his view of human nature?
> 2. What do we learn about the characters of Sebastian and Antonio from their treatment of Gonzalo?
> 3. Using Ariel, Prospero encourages Sebastian and Antonio to plot against the king but then frustrates their plans.

Why do you think Shakespeare introduced this twist in the plot?
4. How is Stephano's treatment of Caliban similar to Prospero's? How is it different?
5. Note the concrete details in Caliban's speech. How does his language show that he is a creature of "earth," unlike Ariel, who is an "airy spirit"?
6. Act 2 presents the **rising action** of the play. What **complications** are introduced in this act? How do these complications propel the **plot** forward? What do you predict will happen next?

Applying Meanings
Although they need him, Stephano and Trinculo treat Caliban with scorn and contempt. In a similar way, European settlers in North America considered the Native Americans to be "savage," since they did not conform to European values and behavior. Think of your own behavior and feelings when meeting someone exotic, frightening, or just "different." How have you treated that person?

First Thoughts
Answers will vary.

Identifying Facts
1. He thinks his son Ferdinand is dead. going to his daughter's wedding in Tunis
2. to kill him while he sleeps
3. Before, he puts Alonso, Gonzalo, and Adrian to sleep; after, he wakes them.
4. He thinks they are a single four-legged creature.
5. He swears subjection. He thinks Stephano will replenish the bottle and free him from Prospero.

Interpreting Meanings
1. He feels people in their natural state are innocent.
2. They are insensitive and shallow.
3. Possible responses: to build suspense; to reveal the characters of Sebastian and Antonio
4. Both Stephano and Prospero take advantage of Caliban's servility, but Prospero uses magic while Stephano must rely on drink and cleverness. Prospero condemns Caliban, but Stephano pretends to befriend him.
5. Caliban's evocative language is full of references to food, fire, animals, plants, and features of the land.
6. The conspiracy of Antonio and Sebastian against Alonso and the meeting of Caliban and Stephano and Trinculo set the stage for treachery and rebellion. Answers will vary.

Applying Meanings
Answers will vary.

VOCABULARY IN CONTEXT

The words listed below will appear in the side margin at the point of instruction:

1. odious
2. valiant
3. salutations
4. dumb
5. desolate

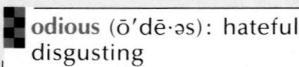 **odious** (ō'dē·əs): hateful; disgusting

1 INTERPRETING

Ferdinand says that "most poor matters/Point to rich ends" (lines 3–4). What does he mean? (Suffering leads to reward.) What "rich end" does Ferdinand hope for? (the love of Miranda)

COMPARING AND CONTRASTING

What other character has been forced to gather wood for Prospero? (Caliban) How are their reactions to their servitude alike and different? (Possible response: Both are angry at Prospero, but Ferdinand undertakes his task more willingly; Caliban performs out of fear alone.)

2 GUIDED READING

Noting Details: Note in the stage directions how much difference a semicolon can make: "Miranda; and Prospero, behind, unseen," indicates that Miranda and Prospero enter separately, and that the girl does not know her father is there. Without this punctuation, readers could conclude that the two characters are acting together to test Ferdinand.

THE TEMPEST
Act 3

 The plot reaches a **climax** *in the third act. As you read the following scenes, identify the* **turning point(s)** *of the plot.*

Summary of Act 3, Scene 1. *Prospero has decided to test Ferdinand's love for Miranda by requiring him to collect wood. Miranda takes pity on Ferdinand and offers to help him. They pledge their love for one another. Prospero, who has been secretly watching, is pleased that his plan is progressing so well.*

ACT 3

Scene 1. *Before* PROSPERO's *cell.*

[*Enter* FERDINAND, *bearing a log.*]
Ferdinand.

1
    There be some sports are painful, and their labor
    Delight in them sets off; some kinds of baseness
    Are nobly undergone, and most poor matters
    Point to rich ends. This my mean task
5   Would be as heavy to me as <u>odious,</u> but
    The mistress which I serve quickens° what's dead
    And makes my labors pleasures. O, she is
    Ten times more gentle than her father's crabbed;
    And he's composed of harshness! I must remove
10   Some thousands of these logs and pile them up,
    Upon a sore injunction.° My sweet mistress
    Weeps when she sees me work, and says such baseness
    Had never like executor. I forget;
    But these sweet thoughts do even refresh my labors.
15   Most busy least when I do it.°

2
[*Enter* MIRANDA; *and* PROSPERO, *behind, unseen.*]
Miranda.   Alas, now pray you
    Work not so hard! I would the lightning had
    Burnt up those logs that you are enjoined to pile!
    Pray set it down and rest you. When this burns,
    'Twill weep° for having wearied you. My father

❓ Consider how Ferdinand delivers lines 1–15 as he alternates between comments about Miranda and her father, Prospero. What changes in tone would you expect?

6. **quickens:** enlivens.

11. **sore injunction:** harsh command.

15. **Most busy least when I do it:** At my busiest moments, thoughts of Miranda make my work seem like nothing.

19. **weep:** The log will drip sap as it burns.

ANSWERS TO MARGIN QUESTIONS
Line 31. Prospero says this line with satisfaction and affection.
Line 37. Possible response: Ferdinand says her name exuberantly; Miranda reacts modestly but with pleasure.

20 Is hard at study; pray now rest yourself;
He's safe for these three hours.

Ferdinand.   O most dear mistress,
The sun will set before I shall discharge
What I must strive to do.

Miranda.   If you'll sit down,
I'll bear your logs the while. Pray give me that.
25 I'll carry it to the pile.

Ferdinand.   No, precious creature.
I had rather crack my sinews, break my back,
Than you should such dishonor undergo
While I sit lazy by.

Miranda.   It would become me
As well as it does you; and I should do it
30 With much more ease; for my good will is to it,
And yours it is against.

Prospero (*aside*).   Poor worm, thou art infected!
This visitation shows it.

Miranda.   You look wearily.

Ferdinand.
No, noble mistress. 'Tis fresh morning with me
When you are by at night. I do beseech you,
35 Chiefly that I might set it in my prayers,
What is your name?

Miranda.   Miranda. O my father,
I have broke your hest° to say so!

Ferdinand.   Admired° Miranda!
Indeed the top of admiration, worth
What's dearest to the world! Full many a lady
40 I have eyed with best regard, and many a time
The harmony of their tongues hath into bondage
Brought my too diligent ear; for several virtues
Have I liked several women; never any
With so full soul but some defect in her
45 Did quarrel with the noblest grace she owed,°
And put it to the foil;° but you, O you,
So perfect and so peerless, are created
Of every creature's best!

Miranda.   I do not know
One of my sex; no woman's face remember,
50 Save, from my glass, mine own; nor have I seen
More that I may call men than you, good friend,
And my dear father. How features are abroad
I am skill-less of;° but, by my modesty

3

4

? Remembering that Prospero has planned for Miranda to fall in love with Ferdinand, how do you imagine Prospero would say line 31?

37. **hest:** injunction; command;
Admired: *Miranda* means "wonderful," "admirable" in Latin.

? How do you think Ferdinand would pronounce the name of his new love in line 37? How should Miranda react to having her name pronounced?

45. **owed:** possessed.
46. **put it to the foil:** ruined or destroyed it.

53. **am skill-less of:** have no knowledge of.

3 LITERARY ELEMENT
Theme: In saying that her work shall be lighter than his because of her willingness to do it, what recurring theme of the play is Miranda evoking? (freedom versus bondage)

4 SPECULATING
Do you think Prospero was sincere in warning Miranda not to tell Ferdinand her name? (Possible response: The warning was given with the expectation that Miranda would disobey it.) How does Miranda's behavior remind you of a typical teenager? (She is torn between obedience to a parent and her desire to act independently and follow her heart.)

5 LITERARY ELEMENT

Theme: Throughout the play, imagination, or fantasy, and reality contend. How does imagination yield to reality in the meeting of Ferdinand and Miranda? (Miranda cannot imagine any man more pleasing than the actual Ferdinand she sees before her.)

5

	(The jewel in my dower), I would not wish
55	Any companion in the world but you;
	Nor can imagination form a shape,
	Besides yourself, to like of.° But I prattle
	Something too wildly, and my father's precepts
	I therein do forget.

Ferdinand.   I am, in my condition,

60   A prince, Miranda; I do think, a king
(I would not so!), and would no more endure
This wooden slavery° than to suffer
The flesh fly blow° my mouth. Hear my soul speak!
The very instant that I saw you, did

65   My heart fly to your service, there resides,

57. **like of:** liken to.

62. **wooden slavery:** enslavement as a wood hauler.
63. **blow:** lay its eggs in.

Why would Ferdinand wish he were not a king?

Martha Swope

ANSWERS TO MARGIN QUESTIONS
Lines 77–86. Responses will vary. Miranda would probably appear to be struggling with herself, but finally her innocent candor would triumph over her inhibitions.
Line 92. Possible response: Lack of surprise, preoccupation with other worries, and sorrow at losing his beloved daughter prevent Prospero from being more glad.

To make me slave to it; and for your sake
Am I this patient log-man.

Miranda.   Do you love me?

Ferdinand.
O heaven, O earth, bear witness to this sound,
And crown what I profess with kind event°
70 If I speak true! if hollowly, invert
What best is boded° me to mischief! I,
Beyond all limit of what else i' the world,
Do love, prize, honor you.

Miranda.   I am a fool
To weep at what I am glad of.

Prospero (*aside*).   Fair encounter
75 Of two most rare affections! Heavens rain grace
On that which breeds between 'em!

Ferdinand.   Wherefore weep you?

Miranda.
At mine unworthiness, that dare not offer
What I desire to give, and much less take
What I shall die to want.° But this is trifling;
80 And all the more it seeks to hide itself,
The bigger bulk it shows. Hence, bashful cunning!
And prompt me plain and holy innocence!
I am your wife, if you will marry me;
If not, I'll die your maid. To be your fellow°
85 You may deny me; but I'll be your servant,
Whether you will or no.

Ferdinand.   My mistress, dearest!
And I thus humble ever.

Miranda.   My husband then?

Ferdinand.
Ay, with a heart as willing
As bondage e'er of freedom. Here's my hand.

Miranda.
90 And mine, with my heart in't; and now farewell
Till half an hour hence.

Ferdinand.   A thousand thousand!°

[*Exeunt* FERDINAND *and* MIRANDA *severally.*°]

Prospero.
So glad of this as they I cannot be,
Who are surprised withal; but my rejoicing
At nothing can be more. I'll to my book;
95 For yet ere suppertime must I perform
Much business appertaining.   [*Exit.*]

69. **kind event:** positive outcome.

71. **boded:** destined.

79. **to want:** for lack of.

84. **fellow:** partner; wife.

? Do you find it surprising that Miranda is the one to propose to Ferdinand? How do you think she would deliver this speech (lines 77–86)? Bashfully? Confidently?

91. **A thousand thousand:** a thousand farewells. **severally:** in different directions.

? Why is Prospero not as "glad of this" (line 92) as Miranda and Ferdinand are?

6 EVALUATING
Do you think Miranda and Ferdinand's love for each other is believable, given that they've just met? (Possible response: Yes, it is believable in that both are young, attractive, and lonely.) Do you think Miranda's direct question in line 67 is in keeping with her character? (Possible response: Yes, she does not have enough experience to be coy.)

7 INTERPRETING
What is Prospero praying for in lines 75–76? (a blessing on Miranda's and Ferdinand's new love) How does this speech contradict Ferdinand's opinion of Prospero's character? (Rather than being opposed to the couple, as Ferdinand thought in line 9, Prospero is actively working to further their union.)

8 LITERARY ELEMENT
Characterization: What does Miranda's speech (lines 77–86) reveal about her character? (Although she is innocent, she experiences desire [lines 77–79]; although she is shy, she can be forceful [lines 81–83]; although she is proud, she is willing to be a servant to the man she loves [lines 84–85].)

9 LITERARY ELEMENT
Climax: How does the romantic plot reach a climax near the end of Scene 1? (Miranda and Ferdinand become engaged.)

Lines 4–6. The joke rests on the word "totters." If the other two on the island are also drunk, then the entire populace is tottering (staggering about) and the "state" is tottering (on the verge of collapse) since no one is able to govern.

Line 16. The pun on "list" gives an additional meaning to "standard," so that Trinculo's line has two meanings: Caliban should be Stephano's lieutenant because he's not a standard-bearer, and, more humorously, Caliban is listing (leaning to one side) and therefore cannot be a standard (one who stands up straight)

Lines 22–23. The irony is that Stephano is a much less worthy master than Prospero, yet Caliban wants to trade the latter for the former.

---

10 LITERARY ELEMENT

Word Play: The slapstick humor on the next three pages involves Stephano's mistaken belief that Trinculo is calling Caliban a liar, when in fact he is saying nothing. What pun on the word "lie" is made in line 18? ("Lie" can be interpreted as "lie down" or "tell a falsehood.")

 valiant (val′yənt): brave

MEETING INDIVIDUAL NEEDS

11 LEP: Make sure students understand that Caliban volunteers to lick Stephano's shoes but refuses to serve Trinculo because "he is not valiant." ■

Summary of Act 3, Scene 2. *Caliban, Trinculo, and Stephano have become quite drunk. Caliban begins to think of Stephano as a "god," and urges him to murder Prospero so that he, Caliban, can be set free, and that Stephano can then rule the island, with Miranda as his queen. Stephano agrees to the plan. Ariel, invisible, has overheard the plot, and with beautiful music diverts them from their plans.*

Scene 2. *Another part of the island.*

[*Enter* CALIBAN, STEPHANO, *and* TRINCULO.]

Stephano.
Tell not me! What the butt is out we will drink water; not a drop before. Therefore bear up and board 'em!° Servant monster, drink to me.

Trinculo.
Servant monster? The folly° of this island! They say
5   there's but five upon this isle. We are three of them. If the other two be brained like us, the state totters.

Stephano.
Drink, servant monster, when I bid thee. Thy eyes are almost set° in thy head.

Trinculo.
Where should they be set else? He were a brave mon-
10   ster indeed if they were set in his tail.

Stephano.
My man-monster hath drowned his tongue in sack. For my part, the sea cannot drown me. I swam, ere I could recover the shore, five-and-thirty leagues off and on, by this light. Thou shalt be my lieutenant, monster,
15   or my standard.°

Trinculo.
Your lieutenant, if you list; he's no standard.°

Stephano.
We'll not run, Monsieur Monster.

Trinculo.
Nor go neither; but you'll lie like dogs, and yet say nothing neither.

Stephano.
20   Mooncalf, speak once in thy life, if thou beest a good mooncalf.

Caliban.
How does thy honor? Let me lick thy shoe. I'll not serve him; he is not <u>valiant</u>.

Trinculo.
Thou liest, most ignorant monster! I am in case° to

2. **bear up and board 'em:** keep drinking!

4. **folly:** fool.

❓ Caliban, Stephano, and Trinculo have been sharing a cask of wine since they met and, by now, they are quite drunk. Explain the joke about the state of the island's affairs (lines 4–6).

8. **set:** glazed over (from drink).

15. **standard:** standard-bearer.

16. **list:** please; **standard:** one who can stand up.

❓ Another, more common, meaning of the word *list* is "to tilt or incline to one side." How does this double meaning give line 16 a comic twist?

❓ What is the irony of Caliban pledging to serve the drunken Stephano in lines 22–23? Do you think Stephano will make a better master for him than Prospero?

24. **in case:** in condition.

ANSWERS TO MARGIN QUESTIONS

Line 34. The irony is that Stephano has no force to back up his authority. He is not Trinculo's and Caliban's superior but their equal.

Lines 40–42: Possible response: Caliban's description of Prospero is fair from Caliban's point of view.

Line 43. Caliban thinks it is Trinculo who has spoken and tries to get Stephano to punish him.

25 justle a constable. Why, thou deboshed fish thou, was
there ever man a coward that hath drunk so much
sack as I today? Wilt thou tell a monstrous lie, being
but half a fish and half a monster?

Caliban.
Lo, how he mocks me! Wilt thou let him, my lord?

Trinculo.
30 "Lord" quoth he? That a monster should be such a
natural!°

31. **natural:** idiot.

Caliban.
Lo, lo, again! Bite him to death I prithee.

Stephano.
Trinculo, keep a good tongue in your head. If you
prove a mutineer—the next tree! The poor monster's
35 my subject, and he shall not suffer indignity.

❓ Stephano, now emboldened by drink and Caliban's attentions, threatens Trinculo with hanging from "the next tree" (line 34). What is ironic about Stephano's treatment of his friend, Trinculo, and of Caliban?

Caliban.
I thank my noble lord. Wilt thou be pleased
To hearken once again to the suit I made to thee?

Stephano.
Marry, will I. Kneel and repeat it; I will stand, and so
shall Trinculo.

[*Enter* ARIEL, *invisible.*]

Caliban.
40 As I told thee before, I am subject to a tyrant,
A sorcerer, that by his cunning hath
Cheated me of the island.

❓ Do you think Caliban's lines 40–42 are a fair description of Prospero?

Ariel.
Thou liest.

Caliban.   Thou liest, thou jesting monkey thou!
I would my valiant master would destroy thee.
45 I do not lie.

❓ Ariel has been carefully watching this exchange under the cover of invisibility. What happens when he speaks out in line 43? Who does Caliban think has spoken?

Stephano.
Trinculo, if you trouble him any more in's tale, by this
hand, I will supplant some of your teeth.

Trinculo.
Why, I said nothing.

Stephano.
Mum then, and no more.—Proceed.

Caliban.
50 I say by sorcery he got this isle;
From me he got it. If thy greatness will
Revenge it on him—for I know thou darest,
But this thing dare not—

12 INFERRING
What does the use of the word "natural" to mean "idiot" suggest about the common view of people who lived close to nature in Shakespeare's time? (Possible response: Many Elizabethans must have thought that civilization and education were necessary to lift "savages" above the brutish level of nature.)

MEETING INDIVIDUAL NEEDS

13 *LEP:* "I will supplant some of your teeth" means "I will knock some of your teeth out." Today "supplant" means "replace," but in Shakespeare's time it could also mean "uproot, cause the downfall of." ∎

Stephano.
That's most certain.

Caliban.
55 Thou shalt be lord of it, and I'll serve thee.

Stephano.
How now shall this be compassed?
Canst thou bring me to the party?

Caliban.
Yea, yea, my lord! I'll yield him thee asleep,
Where thou mayst knock a nail into his head.

Ariel.
60 Thou liest; thou canst not.

Caliban.
What a pied ninny's this! Thou scurvy patch!°
I do beseech thy greatness give him blows
And take his bottle from him. When that's gone,
He shall drink naught but brine, for I'll not show him
65 Where the quick freshes° are.

Stephano.
Trinculo, run into no further danger. Interrupt the monster one word further and, by this hand, I'll turn my mercy out o' doors and make a stockfish° of thee.

Trinculo.
70 Why, what did I? I did nothing. I'll go farther off.

Stephano.
Didst thou not say he lied?

Ariel.
Thou liest.

Stephano.
Do I so? Take thou that!

[*Strikes* TRINCULO.]
As you like this, give me the lie° another time.

Trinculo.
75 I did not give thee the lie. Out o' your wits, and hearing too? A pox o' your bottle! This can sack and drinking do. A murrain° on your monster, and the Devil take your fingers!

Caliban.
Ha, ha, ha!

Stephano.
80 Now forward with your tale.—Prithee stand further off.

What does Caliban think he stands to gain from his new lord (line 55)?

61. **pied:** multicolored (refers to a jester's colorful costume); **patch:** fool; jester.

65. **quick freshes:** fresh-water springs.

68. **stockfish:** dried fish that is beaten to make it more tender.

74. **give me the lie:** call me a liar.

77. **murrain:** disease; plague.

Martha Swope

15 SPECULATING

Why do you think Shakespeare has Caliban express what he would like done to Prospero in such graphically violent terms? (Possible responses: to show that people who are held down against their will often harbor fantasies of revenge; to emphasize Caliban's brutish nature.)

16 INTERPRETING

Caliban warns Stephano to grab Prospero's books of magic. What else, other than magical power, might the books represent? (Possible response: education, civilization)

Caliban.
    Beat him enough. After a little time
    I'll beat him too.

Stephano.   Stand farther.—Come, proceed.

Caliban.
    Why, as I told thee, 'tis a custom with him
85 I' the afternoon to sleep. There thou mayst
        brain him,
    Having first seized his books, or with a log
    Batter his skull, or paunch° him with a stake,
    Or cut his weasand° with thy knife. Remember
    First to possess his books; for without them
90 He's but a sot, as I am, nor hath not

87. **paunch:** stab in the stomach.
88. **weasand:** windpipe.

Line 92. Caliban knows that the books are the source of Prospero's knowledge and power.

Lines 101–102. Possible response: Ariel is standing close to Caliban, listening intently, and reacts with comic outrage.

Lines 103–106. The news that Prospero has an attractive daughter persuades Stephano to act. Possible response: Trinculo, who has been beaten by Stephano and at this point regrets his heavy drinking, is sitting aside and responding unenthusiastically. All he stands to gain is to become Stephano's viceroy.

Lines 118–120. The song expresses violent defiance and freedom.

---

17 COMPARING

How does Caliban's statement about his ignorance of women parallel what Miranda has said about herself? (In lines 48–50 of Act 3, Scene 1, Miranda says she does not know any other women with whom to compare herself.)

MEETING INDIVIDUAL NEEDS

18 *LEP:* "She will become thy bed" (line 101) means that Stephano's bed will look good with Miranda in it and, more crudely, that she will be "good in bed." ∎

19 SPECULATING

How might Shakespeare be playing with his audience in lines 105–107? (When Stephano asks Trinculo, "Dost thou like the plot?" Shakespeare is playfully asking the audience the same question, and he puts his desired answer in Trinculo's mouth.)

20 DRAMATIC ELEMENT

Sound Effects: Suggest that students talented in music compose a tune to fit these lyrics. How might the music differ from that played in Ariel's song in Act 1, Scene 2, lines 378–390? (Possible response: This tune should be raucous while Ariel's should be elegiac.)

One spirit to command. They all do hate him
As rootedly as I. Burn but his books.
He has brave utensils° (for so he calls them)
Which, when he has a house, he'll deck withal.
95 And that most deeply to consider is
The beauty of his daughter. He himself
Calls her a nonpareil.° I never saw a woman
But only Sycorax my dam and she;
But she as far surpasseth Sycorax
100 As great'st does least.

Stephano.   Is it so brave a lass?

Caliban.
Ay, lord. She will become thy bed, I warrant, And bring thee forth brave brood.

Stephano.
Monster, I will kill this man. His daughter and I will
105 be king and queen, save our Graces! and Trinculo and
thyself shall be viceroys. Dost thou like the plot, Trinculo?

Trinculo.
Excellent.

Stephano.
Give me thy hand. I am sorry I beat thee; but while
thou livest, keep a good tongue in thy head.

Caliban.
110 Within this half hour will he be asleep.
Wilt thou destroy him then?

Stephano.   Ay, on mine honor.

Ariel.
This will I tell my master.

Caliban.
Thou makest me merry; I am full of pleasure.
Let us be jocund. Will you troll the catch°
115 You taught me but whilere?°

Stephano.
At thy request, monster, I will do reason,° any reason.
Come on, Trinculo, let us sing.

[*Sings.*]

                    Flout 'em and scout 'em
                    And scout 'em and flout 'em!
120   Thought is free.

Caliban.
That's not the tune.

Why are Prospero's books (line 92) so important to Caliban?

93. **utensils:** furnishings.

97. **nonpareil:** being unparalleled; unequaled.

Where do you think Ariel is during this entire scene? Does he move around much? How do you imagine he reacts to Caliban's plan of action and persuasive speeches?

What finally persuades Stephano to act (lines 103–106)? How do you think Trinculo states his agreement to join Caliban and Stephano? Heartily? Moodily? What does Trinculo stand to gain from this plot?

114. **troll the catch:** sing the round.
115. **whilere:** a short time ago.

116. **do reason:** perform any reasonable request.

Why might the song sung by Stephano and Trinculo (lines 118–120) be a source of pleasure to Caliban?

ANSWERS TO MARGIN QUESTIONS
Lines 122–140. Stephano and Trinculo feel mostly fear at first. Caliban calms their fears, and they all become enchanted by the music.

Lines 132–140. The beauty of Caliban's language, his sensitivity to the heavenly music, and the feelings he expresses show he has human emotions and aspirations.

[ARIEL *plays the tune on a tabor° and pipe.*]

Stephano.

    What is this same?

Trinculo.

    This is the tune of our catch, played by the picture of Nobody.°

Stephano.

125   If thou beest a man, show thyself in thy likeness. If thou beest a devil, take't° as thou list.

Trinculo.

    O, forgive me my sins!

Stephano.

    He that dies pays all debts. I defy thee.
    Mercy upon us!

Caliban.

130   Art thou afeard?

Stephano.

    No, monster, not I.

Caliban.

    Be not afeard. The isle is full of noises,
    Sounds, and sweet airs that give delight and hurt not.

135   Sometimes a thousand twangling instruments
    Will hum about mine ears; and sometime voices
    That, if I then had waked after long sleep,
    Will make me sleep again; and then, in dreaming,
    The clouds methought would open and show riches
    Ready to drop upon me, that, when I waked,

140   I cried to dream again.

Stephano.

    This will prove a brave kingdom to me, where
    I shall have my music for nothing.

Caliban.

    When Prospero is destroyed.

Stephano.

    That shall be by-and-by. I remember the story.

Trinculo.

145   The sound is going away. Let's follow it, and after do our work.

Stephano.

    Lead, monster; we'll follow. I would I could see this taborer! He lays it on.

Trinculo.

    Wilt come? I'll follow Stephano.   [*Exeunt.*]

---

tabor: small drum.

? What is the reaction of the characters to the music? Wonder? Fear? Interest?

123–124. **picture of Nobody:** a traditional picture of a man with head, arms, and legs, but no body. Trinculo means an invisible person.

126. **take 't:** do.

? What does Caliban's description of the island voices (lines 132–140) reveal about his character? Does he seem to be entirely a monster here?

21 READER'S RESPONSE
If you were an actor, would you like to play the role of Caliban? Why or why not? (Possible responses: Yes, because he is a memorable character who speaks many of the play's most beautiful lines and personifies its theme of nature versus civilization; no, because he is a "low" character and the butt of jokes.) How would you play Caliban, in terms of voice, tone, gestures, and appearance, to make your portrayal a successful one? (Answers will vary.)

22 COMPARING AND CONTRASTING

The entrance of Alonso's group follows quickly upon the exit of Caliban's. How does the mood change at this point? (Raucous clowning and deluded pretension are replaced by a mood of dignified weariness and hopelessness.) How are these two groups of characters similar? (Possible responses: Both are mistaken about what is really happening on the island; both are under Prospero's control; both contain characters who believe themselves to be civilized—Stephano and Trinculo in one group, Antonio and Sebastian in the other—but are actually brutish in word and deed.)

23 LITERARY ELEMENT

Theme: As the play progresses, one of its major themes will be reconciliation and forgiveness. How does the interchange between Alonso and Gonzalo at the beginning of Scene 3 foreshadow this theme? (In an earlier scene, Alonso was irritated with Gonzalo for trying to comfort him; now he shows understanding of his feelings.) Alonso explicitly relates forgiveness to weariness. This theme will be taken up later when Prospero, weary of his art, renounces it in favor of general reconciliation.

Summary of Act 3, Scene 3. *Wearied by their efforts to find Ferdinand, the king and his party sit down to rest. As Antonio and Sebastian renew their assassination plot, an unusual spectacle is presented to the party. Ariel, disguised as a harpy (part woman, part bird), presents the illusion of a banquet to the king's party. He chastises them for their wrongdoings, and warns them to repent and change their lives. Alonso, filled with grief, runs from the others and vows to find Ferdinand. The faithful old Gonzalo follows him, afraid that Alonso may do something foolish.*

Scene 3. *Another part of the island.*

22 [*Enter* ALONSO, SEBASTIAN, ANTONIO, GONZALO, ADRIAN, FRANCISCO, *etc.*]

Gonzalo.
By'r Lakin,° I can go no further, sir!
My old bones ache. Here's a maze trod indeed
Through forthrights and meanders. By your patience,
I needs must rest me.

23 **Alonso.** Old lord, I cannot blame thee,
5 Who am myself attached with weariness
To the dulling of my spirits. Sit down and rest.
Even here I will put off my hope, and keep it
No longer for my flatterer. He is drowned
Whom thus we stray to find; and the sea mocks
10 Our frustrate search on land. Well, let him go.

Antonio.
(*aside to* SEBASTIAN) I am right glad that he's so out of hope.
Do not for one repulse forego the purpose
That you resolved t' effect.

Sebastian.
(*aside to* ANTONIO) The next advantage
15 Will we take throughly.

Antonio.
(*aside to* SEBASTIAN) Let it be tonight;
For, now they are oppressed with travel, they
Will not nor cannot use such vigilance
As when they are fresh.

Sebastian.
20 (*aside to* ANTONIO) I say tonight. No more.

[*Solemn and strange music; and* PROSPERO *on the top, invisible.*]

Alonso.
What harmony is this? My good friends, hark!

1. **By'r Lakin:** by our Ladykin (an oath invoking the Virgin Mary).

❓ Of what "advantage" is Sebastian speaking in lines 14–15? How do you feel about these two characters when they speak in whispered asides?

ANSWERS TO MARGIN QUESTIONS

Stage Direction. Students' visualizations of the Shapes will vary. The dialogue of all the characters expresses wonder and curiosity. Sebastian and Antonio's reactions seem to express coarse credulity; Gonzalo and Alonso's responses show aesthetic appreciation.

Lines 37–39. When Prospero says "Honest lord," he is speaking of Gonzalo. The devils are the conspirators. The aside is necessary because Prospero, unlike Ariel, can be heard by the others.

Gonzalo.
Marvelous sweet music!

24 [Enter several strange SHAPES, *bringing in a banquet; and dance about it with gentle actions of salutations; and, inviting the King, etc., to eat, they depart.*]

Alonso.
Give us kind keepers, heavens! What were these?
Sebastian.
25 A living drollery.° Now I will believe
That there are unicorns; that in Arabia
There is one tree, the phoenix' throne, one phoenix
At this hour reigning there.
Antonio.   I'll believe both;
And what does else want credit, come to me,
And I'll be sworn 'tis true. Travelers ne'er did lie,
30 Though fools at home condemn 'em.
Gonzalo.   If in Naples
I should report this now, would they believe me?
If I should say, I saw such islanders
(For certes° these are people of the island),
Who, though they are of monstrous shape, yet, note,
35 Their manners are more gentle, kind, than of
Our human generation you shall find
Many—nay, almost any.
Prospero (*aside*).   Honest lord,
Thou hast said well; for some of you there present
Are worse than devils.
Alonso.   I cannot too much muse°
40 Such shapes, such gesture, and such sound, express-
ing
(Although they want the use of tongue) a kind
Of excellent dumb discourse.
Prospero (*aside*).   Praise in departing.°
Francisco.
They vanished strangely.
Sebastian.   No matter, since
They have left their viands behind; for we have
stomachs.
45 Will't please you taste of what is here?
Alonso.   Not I.
Gonzalo.
Faith, sir, you need not fear. When we were boys,
Who would believe that there were mountaineers

What do you imagine these Shapes look like? Are they ghostly or animal-like? Knowing the characters' personalities as you do, how do you think they will each react to the appearance of the Shapes and the sound of their music?

24. **drollery:** puppet show.

33. **certes:** certainly.

Of whom is Prospero speaking in this aside (lines 37–39)? Why does he need to say this as an aside?
39. **muse:** wonder at.

42. **Praise in departing:** refers to an old proverb that says it is wise to withhold judgment until a matter is concluded.

salutations (sal·yōō·tā'shənz): greetings
dumb (dum): silent

24 VISUALIZING
The banquet scene is one of the most elaborate stage effects in all of Shakespeare. If you were directing a production of *The Tempest*, how would you stage the banquet scene?
Tell students that some stage productions feature Ariel flying down and the food appearing on the table via a removable panel. In most productions, Prospero silently observes or directs the action from aside or above.

25 CULTURAL BACKGROUND
The phoenix in classical mythology was a bird that could burn to death and then arise from the ashes. Sebastian is saying here that he is willing to believe in strange occurrences such as unicorns and phoenixes now that he has seen the Shapes.

26 LITERARY ELEMENT
Theme: Gonzalo's comment about the banquet links the theme of magic transformation to the theme of nature versus civilization. What does the banquet vision lead Gonzalo to understand? (that the beings he sees on the island make the inhabitants of his own civilization seem crude) How does Prospero, in his aside, reinforce the play's comments on civilization? (He says that some of the supposedly civilized characters are worse than devils.)

Lines 56–63. Possible response: Ariel should speak with righteous contempt for the "men of sin"; with a calm, haughty, somewhat playful confidence in his own power; with anger for the injustice against Prospero and Miranda; and with an air that tells the audience he is acting. His costume makes him terrifyingly visible to the men.

Lines 56–85. The purpose of Ariel's speech is to instill terror and guilt in his listeners. Its key words include "sin," "unfit," "mad," "fools," "invulnerable," "requit," "innocent," "foul deed," "incensed," "bereft," "perdition," "wraths," "desolate," "sorrow." The words suggest that the men deserve punishment for their sins.

---

27 LITERARY ELEMENT

Motivation: Why is Alonso at first afraid to taste the banquet? (He is afraid it is poisoned—a common fear of royalty at the time.) Why does he change his mind? (He doesn't mind if it is his last meal since he believes he has lost his son to the tempest.)

28 ANALYZING

Why does Shakespeare have Ariel enter as a harpy? (to frighten the men) What is Prospero's purpose in making the banquet disappear? (Possible responses: It increases the men's fright; it is a dramatic stage effect; it symbolically expresses Prospero's belief that these men do not deserve forgiveness and reconciliation because they are conspirators.)

29 LITERARY ELEMENT

Symbolism: For the second time in the play, a character's sword has been magically rendered harmless. The first occurrence was in Act 1, Scene 2, when Prospero made Ferdinand's sword motionless. What might this action symbolize in terms of the theme of the use of power? (Possible response: Prospero has used his power wisely to prevent violence.)

Dewlapped° like bulls, whose throats had hanging at
'em
Wallets of flesh? or that there were such men
50 Whose heads stood in their breasts?° which now
we find
Each putter-out of five for one° will bring us
Good warrant° of.

Alonso.   I will stand to, and feed;
Although my last, no matter, since I feel
The best is past. Brother, my lord the Duke,
55 Stand to, and do as we.

[*Thunder and lightning. Enter* ARIEL, *like a harpy;*°
claps his wings upon the table; and with a quaint°
device the banquet vanishes.]

Ariel.
You are three men of sin, whom destiny—
That hath to instrument° this lower world
And what is in't—the never-surfeited sea
Hath caused to belch up you, and on this island,
60 Where man doth not inhabit—you 'mongst men
Being most unfit to live. I have made you mad;
And even with suchlike valor men hang and drown
Their proper selves.

[ALONSO, SEBASTIAN, *etc., draw their swords.*]
                    You fools! I and my fellows
Are ministers of Fate. The elements,
65 Of whom your swords are tempered, may as well
Wound the loud winds, or with bemocked-at stabs
Kill the still-closing waters, as diminish
One dowle° that's in my plume. My fellow ministers
Are like invulnerable. If you could hurt,
70 Your swords are now too massy° for your strengths
And will not be uplifted. But remember
(For that's my business to you) that you three
From Milan did supplant good Prospero;
Exposed unto the sea, which hath requit it,°
75 Him and his innocent child; for which foul deed
The powers, delaying (not forgetting), have
Incensed the seas and shores, yea, all the creatures,
Against your peace. Thee of thy son, Alonso,
They have bereft; and do pronounce by me
80 Ling'ring perdition° (worse than any death
Can be at once) shall step by step attend
You and your ways; whose wraths to guard you
from,

---

48. **Dewlapped:** A dewlap is a loose fold of flesh that hangs from the throat.

50. **Whose heads stood in their breasts:** a sight often reported in travel books.

51. **putter-out of five for one:** Before leaving, voyagers would deposit a sum of money with the merchant they worked for, and would receive five times that amount on their return.

52. **Good warrant:** affirmation.

harpy: a hideous creature of mythology with the head and trunk of a woman and the wings and talons of a bird. **quaint:** clever.

57. **hath to instrument:** controls.

How do you think this speech (lines 56–63) should be delivered by Ariel? Forcefully? Arrogantly? Angrily? How do you think his harpy costume will make his speech more effective?

68. **dowle:** small feather.

70. **massy:** massive; heavy.

74. **requit it:** revenged the deed.

What do you think is the purpose of Ariel's speech in lines 56–85? What are some of the key words? What do these words suggest to you?

80. **perdition:** ruin.

ANSWERS TO MARGIN QUESTIONS

Lines 98–105. Alonso heard the thunder say the name of Prospero and disclose Alonso's treachery against the duke. Alonso's intention is to join his supposedly drowned son, Ferdinand, at the bottom of the ocean. Sebastian and Antonio intend to fight the spirits one at a time.

Line 107. Gonzalo and Adrian are not maddened because they are not guilty of any wrongdoing.

Which here, in this most <u>desolate</u> isle, else falls
Upon your heads, is nothing but heart's sorrow
85 And a clear life ensuing.°

[*He vanishes in thunder; then, to soft music, enter the* SHAPES *again, and dance, with mocks and mows,° and carrying out the table.*]

Prospero.
(*aside*) Bravely the figure of this harpy hast thou
Performed, my Ariel; a grace it had, devouring.°
Of my instruction hast thou nothing bated°
In what thou hadst to say. So, with good life°
90 And observation strange, my meaner° ministers
Their several kinds° have done. My high charms
    work,
And these, mine enemies, are all knit up
In their distractions.° They now are in my pow'r;
And in these fits I leave them, while I visit
95 Young Ferdinand, whom they suppose is drowned,
And his and mine loved darling.   [*Exit above.*]

Gonzalo.
I' the name of something holy, sir, why stand you
In this strange stare?

Alonso.   O, it is monstrous, monstrous!
Methought the billows spoke and told me of it;
100 The winds did sing it to me; and the thunder,
That deep and dreadful organ pipe, pronounced
The name of Prosper. It did bass my trespass.°
Therefore my son i' the ooze is bedded; and
I'll seek him deeper than e'er plummet sounded
105 And with him there lie mudded.   [*Exit.*]

Sebastian.   But one fiend at a time,
I'll fight their legions o'er!

Antonio.   I'll be thy second.

                    [*Exeunt* SEBASTIAN *and* ANTONIO.]

Gonzalo.
All three of them are desperate. Their great guilt,
Like poison given to work a great time after,
Now 'gins to bite the spirits. I do beseech you,
110 That are of suppler joints, follow them swiftly
And hinder them from what this ecstasy°
May now provoke them to.

Adrian.   Follow, I pray you.
                    [*Exeunt omnes.*°]

84–85. **nothing but heart's sorrow/And a clear life ensuing:** only sincere repentance and living moral lives (can save you from destruction).
mocks and mows: movements and faces expressing derision and disgust.

87. **a grace it had, devouring:** Ariel, as the harpy, performed gracefully, especially when causing the banquet to vanish.
88. **bated:** omitted.
89. **life:** realism.
90. **observation strange:** remarkable; **meaner:** inferior; of lower rank.
91. **several kinds:** individual assignments.
92–93. **knit up/In their distractions:** ensnared in madness.

102. **bass my trespass:** speak of my sin (in a deep voice).

? What did Alonso hear in the thunder (lines 98–105)? What is his intention as he runs in madness from the stage? Do Sebastian and Antonio rush from the stage with the same intentions?

? Why are Gonzalo and Adrian not affected by the madness of Ariel's spell?

111. **ecstasy:** madness.

omnes: all.

■ **desolate** (des'ə·lit): uninhabited; deserted; forlorn; wretched

30 INFERRING
On the evidence of his long aside at the end of the banquet, how does Prospero feel about the way events are turning out? (He is morally satisfied that the conspirators feel guilt and aesthetically gratified—he commends Ariel's performance as a harpy. At the end of the speech, he expresses tender concern for Ferdinand and Miranda.)

31 LITERARY ELEMENT
Simile: Is Gonzalo's comparison of guilt to poison (lines 107–108) appropriate? Why or why not? (It is appropriate because guilt destroys one's spirit as poison destroys one's body.)

First Thoughts
Answers will vary.

Identifying Facts
1. hauling logs. to test Ferdinand's character and love for Miranda
2. They become engaged.
3. to kill Prospero. Stephano wants to rule the island and marry Miranda.
4. He taunts them by presenting and then withdrawing the banquet. He accuses them of being sinful and unworthy.

Interpreting Meanings
1. Possible answer: Caliban deserves some sympathy because Prospero keeps him a slave and does not see his potential, but his attempted rape of Miranda weighs against him.
2. in his ability to control events on the island
3. The characters are shown as drunken fools whose ambitions are ridiculous and whom Ariel easily manipulates.
4. Both scenes involve characters who plan to kill to become king. The "serious" plotters look stupid as well as evil when they have the same ambitions as the fools.
5. Possible response: The feast represents reconciliation and forgiveness, which the characters must earn through repentance.
6. The lovers are pledged to each other. The buffoons and the aristocratic villains are prevented from gaining their unlawful ends.

Applying Meanings
Answers will vary.

First Thoughts
Did you find either of the conspiracies in this act suspenseful? Why or why not?

Identifying Facts
1. What task does Prospero set for Ferdinand? Why?
2. What happens when Ferdinand and Miranda meet in the forest?
3. What does Caliban convince Stephano to do? Why does Stephano agree to act on Caliban's plan?
4. How does Ariel use a magical banquet to confuse the conspirators? What does he say when the banquet disappears?

Interpreting Meanings
1. Do you think Caliban's complaints about Prospero are justified? Is Caliban a sympathetic character? Explain.
2. In what ways is Prospero a godlike figure?
3. In Act 3, Scene 2, how does Shakespeare keep the comedy from turning serious as the characters discuss murder and abduction?
4. How is Scene 3 parallel to Scene 2? What is the effect of a "serious" scene following a comic scene?
5. How is the magic banquet **symbolic**?
6. *The Tempest* really contains three related plots: one romantic, one comic, and one political. Summarize these three plots in the play thus far. How does each plot reach a **climax**, or **turning point**, in Act 3?

Applying Meanings
Prospero's learning gives him his power and sets him above Caliban and the rest of the characters in the drama. Caliban tells his companions to destroy Prospero's books. Bookburning and censorship have occurred at different times in different societies. Does Caliban have a point in wanting to destroy Prospero's books? Is too much learning a dangerous thing? Or do you think that learning is necessary for society to function well?

VOCABULARY IN CONTEXT
The words listed below will appear in the side margin at the point of instruction:

1. ratify
2. abstemious
3. wanton
4. conspiracy
5. indignation

THE TEMPEST
Act 4

❚❚ *Notice what happens after the climax, during the* **falling action** *of the play. How are the various subplots each approaching a resolution?*

Summary of Act 4, Scene 1. *Prospero, pleased with Ferdinand, promises him Miranda's hand in marriage. Ariel is ordered to prepare a masque, a special kind of entertainment. Spirit figures representing the goddesses Iris, Ceres, and Juno bless the young lovers and promise them a happy marriage. Suddenly, Prospero interrupts the festivities when he remembers Caliban's conspiracy against him. Ariel reports that the three conspirators were last seen dancing by a pond, and he is told to lure them to Prospero's cell with showy garments. Caliban is impatient with Stephano and Trinculo, who are delighted by the finery, and pushes them to go through with the murder of Prospero. Prospero and Ariel call forth spirits and goblins to pursue and torment the conspirators.*

═ **ACT 4** ═══════════════

Scene 1. *Before* PROSPERO's *cell.*

[*Enter* PROSPERO, FERDINAND, *and* MIRANDA.]

Prospero.
    If I have too austerely punished you,
    Your compensation makes amends; for I
    Have given you here a third° of mine own life,
    Or that for which I live; who once again
5   I tender° to thy hand. All thy vexations
    Were but my trials of thy love, and thou
    Hast strangely° stood the test. Here, afore heaven,
    I ratify this my rich gift. O Ferdinand,
    Do not smile at me that I boast her off,°
10   For thou shalt find she will outstrip all praise
    And make it halt behind her.

Ferdinand.   I do believe it
    Against an oracle.°

Prospero.
    Then, as my gift, and thine own acquisition
    Worthily purchased, take my daughter. But

❓ How is the mood now immediately different from that of the preceding scene?

3. **a third:** i.e., his daughter Miranda.

5. **tender:** present.

7. **strangely:** surpassingly.

9. **boast her off:** speak so highly of her.

12. **Against an oracle:** even if an oracle should proclaim against it.

1 GUIDED READING
Identifying the Main Idea: How does Prospero compensate Ferdinand for his hard work? (He gives Ferdinand his daughter, Miranda, in marriage.)

▣ **ratify** (rat′ə·fī): confirm; make valid

2 EVALUATING
Do you think the trials that Prospero gave to Ferdinand were hard ones? (Most students will say no.) What does this tell you about Prospero's intentions? (He intended Ferdinand to pass the test and win Miranda's hand.)

ANSWER TO MARGIN QUESTION

Lines 23–33. Possible response: The tone of the exchange is conciliatory, with Ferdinand clearly the respectful junior and Prospero the respected elder.

3 INTERPRETING

What is Ferdinand promising in his speech beginning, "As I hope/For quiet days."? (to respect Miranda's chastity until their wedding) Why does Shakespeare have Ferdinand refer to the "murkiest den" and "lust" in this speech? (to remind the audience of Caliban's attempted crime against Miranda and to underline his point that Ferdinand's self-control rather than Caliban's animal behavior is rewarded)

MEETING INDIVIDUAL NEEDS

4 LEP: Be sure students understand that "meaner" here means "lesser in rank" not "nastier." Ariel commands a group of spirits, as Prospero commands Ariel. ■

5 LITERARY ELEMENT

Characterization: What is Prospero's motivation for the display of power he is about to present? (He is fulfilling a promise to the young couple; there is also a suggestion that he is—quite properly—proud of his skills.)

6 LITERARY ELEMENT

Verse Form: What is different about Ariel's speech in lines 44–48 compared to Prospero's language, for example? (Every line rhymes with the preceding one.) Why does Ariel use more artful language than the other characters? (Possible response: He is spritely and quick in doing magic and in speaking.)

15
If thou dost break her virgin-knot before
All sanctimonious° ceremonies may
With full and holy rite be minist'red,
No sweet aspersion° shall the heavens let fall
To make this contract grow;° but barren hate,
20
Sour-eyed disdain, and discord shall bestrew
The union of your bed with weeds so loathly
That you shall hate it both. Therefore take heed,
As Hymen's° lamp shall light you!

Ferdinand.   As I hope
For quiet days, fair issue, and long life,
25
With such love as 'tis now, the murkiest den,
The most opportune place, the strong'st suggestion°
Our worser genius can,° shall never melt
Mine honor into lust, to take away
The edge of that day's celebration
30
When I shall think or Phoebus'° steeds are foundered
Or Night kept chained below.

Prospero.   Fairly spoke.
Sit then and talk with her; she is thine own.
What, Ariel! my industrious servant, Ariel!

[*Enter* ARIEL.]

Ariel.
What would my potent master? Here I am.

Prospero.
35
Thou and thy meaner fellows your last service
Did worthily perform; and I must use you
In such another trick. Go bring the rabble,
O'er whom I give thee pow'r, here to this place.
Incite them to quick motion; for I must
40
Bestow upon the eyes of this young couple
Some vanity° of mine art. It is my promise,
And they expect it from me.

Ariel.   Presently?

Prospero.
Ay, with a twink.

Ariel.
Before you can say "Come" and "Go,"
And breathe twice and cry, "So, so,"
45
Each one, tripping on his toe,
Will be here with mop and mow.°
Do you love me master? No?

Prospero.
Dearly, my delicate Ariel. Do not approach

16. **sanctimonious:** blessed; holy.

18. **aspersion:** blessing (literally, a sprinkling).
19. **grow:** be fruitful.

23. **Hymen's:** Hymen, the Greek god of marriage.

26. **suggestion:** temptation.
27. **Our worser genius can:** our evil angel can offer.

30. **or:** either; **Phoebus:** the Greek god who carried the sun across the sky in his horse-drawn chariot.

❓ How would you describe the tone of this exchange between Prospero and Ferdinand (lines 23–33)? Stern? Friendly? Respectful?

41. **vanity:** demonstration.

47. **mop and mow:** gesture and grimace.

ANSWER TO MARGIN QUESTION

Lines 60–138. Possible response: All three goddesses speak in rhymed couplets, unlike most of the other characters. Iris, the humblest, is given pastoral, or landscape, descriptions. Ceres seems largely concerned with Olympian gossip and intrigue. Juno seems the stateliest of the three.

50   Till thou dost hear me call.

Ariel.   Well! I conceive.°   [*Exit.*]

Prospero.
Look thou be true. Do not give dalliance°
Too much the rein. The strongest oaths are straw
To the fire i' the blood. Be more <u>abstemious</u>,
Or else good night your vow!

Ferdinand.   I warrant you, sir.
55   The white cold virgin snow upon my heart
Abates the ardor of my liver.°

Prospero.   Well.
Now come, my Ariel! Bring a corollary°
Rather than want a spirit. Appear, and pertly!
No tongue! All eyes! Be silent.

[*Soft music.*]

[*Enter* IRIS.°]

Iris.
60   Ceres, most bounteous lady, thy rich leas°
Of wheat, rye, barley, fetches, oats, and pease;
Thy turfy mountains, where live nibbling sheep,
And flat meads thatched with stover,° them to keep;
Thy banks with pioned and twilled° brims,
65   Which spongy April at thy hest betrims
To make cold nymphs chaste crowns; and thy
          broom° groves,
Whose shadow the dismissed bachelor loves,
Being lasslorn; thy pole-clipt vineyard;
And thy sea-marge,° sterile and rocky-hard,
70   Where thou thyself dost air—the queen o' the sky,°
Whose wat'ry arch° and messenger am I,
Bids thee leave these, and with her sovereign Grace,

[JUNO *descends.*]

Here on this grass-plot, in this very place,
To come and sport. Her peacocks fly amain;°
75   Approach, rich Ceres, her to entertain.

[*Enter* CERES.]

Ceres.
Hail, many-colored messenger, that ne'er
Dost disobey the wife of Jupiter,
Who, with thy saffron wings, upon my flow'rs
Diffusest honey drops, refreshing show'rs,
80   And with each end of thy blue bow dost crown

---

50. **conceive:** understand.

51. **dalliance:** caressing; fondling.

56. **liver:** thought to be the seat of passion.

57. **corollary:** extra (spirit).

Iris: Greek goddess of the rainbow.

60. **Ceres:** Roman goddess of agriculture; **leas:** fields.

63. **stover:** hay or grass.

64. **pioned and twilled:** undercut banks held in place by branches woven together.

66. **broom:** a shrub bearing yellow flowers.

69. **sea-marge:** seashore.

70. **queen o' the sky:** the Roman goddess Juno, whose husband Jupiter ruled the skies.

71. **wat'ry arch:** rainbow.

74. **amain:** speedily.

 Juno is able to literally descend through a trap door in the floor of the stage, a common device in Elizabethan theater. Her descent would be slow, to suggest both the dignity of her rank and a sense of movement in a rather static scene. What differences do you notice in the language and tone of each goddess' speech?

---

abstemious (ab·stē′mē·əs): moderate; temperate

7 DRAMATIC ELEMENT
Staging: What tone of voice would you have Prospero use in lines 51–54? Why? (Possible response: Prospero would raise his voice in anxiety and with authority, warning Ferdinand of the danger of caressing Miranda too ardently.)

8 LITERARY BACKGROUND
Prospero is about to stage a spectacle, a ceremony in which symbolic goddess figures appear to bless the marriage of Ferdinand and Miranda. The ceremony of the goddesses is a masque, a kind of entertainment that was increasingly popular during the reign of James I. Masques were spectacular, costumed entertainments presented to royal or aristocratic audiences. Dancing, music, costume, and pantomime were at least as important as language. The masque was a prelude to dancing in which the audience joined the performers and all engaged in rampant romantic intrigue.

9 INTERPRETING
Why do you think these particular goddesses were chosen to appear in the masque? (Possible response: Ceres represents the fertility hoped for in the marriage; Juno, wife of Jupiter, represents marriage and female authority; Iris, the rainbow goddess, represents peace after a storm and unbroken promises.)

This work is dominated by a beautiful woman playing a keyboard instrument. Her music has entranced rabbits, dogs, foxes, a monkey, and even a unicorn, drawing them into a magical circle around her.

❓ *Why is this a suitable illustration for the masque scene in the play?* (Possible response: In a masque, music creates a spellbinding mood. In addition, the masque in the play is an enchantment that Prospero creates to dazzle his audience.) ■

Giraudon/Art Resource, New York

French tapestry illustrating the musical arts. *Songs were an important device in Shakespeare's drama, serving both to entertain the audience and to create a particular mood.*

10 [
My bosky acres and my unshrubbed down,°
Rich scarf to my proud earth—why hath thy queen
Summoned me hither to this short-grassed green?

11 [
Iris.
A contract of true love to celebrate
85   And some donation freely to estate
On° the blest lovers.

12 [
Ceres.   Tell me, heavenly bow,
If Venus or her son, as thou dost know,
Do now attend the queen. Since they did plot
The means that dusky Dis° my daughter got,
90   Her and her blind boy's° scandaled company
I have forsworn.

Iris.   Of her society
Be not afraid. I met her Deity
Cutting the clouds towards Paphos,° and her son
Dove-drawn with her. Here thought they to have done
95   Some <u>wanton</u> charm upon this man and maid,
Whose vows are, that no bed-right shall be paid
Till Hymen's torch be lighted; but in vain.
Mars's hot minion° is returned again;
Her waspish-headed° son has broke his arrows,
100   Swears he will shoot no more, but play with sparrows
And be a boy right out.

[*Enter* JUNO.]

Ceres.   Highest queen of state,
Great Juno, comes; I know her by her gait.

Juno.
How does my bounteous sister? Go with me
To bless this twain, that they may prosperous be
105   And honored in their issue.

[*They sing.*]

Juno.
Honor, riches, marriage blessing,
Long continuance, and increasing,
Hourly joys be still° upon you!
Juno sings her blessings on you.

Ceres.
110   Earth's increase, foison° plenty,

81. **bosky:** wooded; **down:** high, open ground.

85–86. **estate/On:** present to.

89. **Dis:** Pluto, god of the underworld, who abducted Ceres' daughter Proserpina.
90. **blind boy's:** Cupid, Venus's son.

93. **Paphos:** in the ancient world, a center of worship for the Roman goddess Venus.

98. **hot minion:** Venus, his beloved.
99. **waspish-headed:** short-tempered.

How would you perform the songs of the goddesses in a way that would keep the audience's attention?
108. **still:** always.

110. **foison:** good harvest.

READER'S RESPONSE

How do you react to reading the masque sequence? Do you think you would enjoy it better in performance? Why or why not? Do you think it could be dropped or cut with little or no loss to the play? (Answers will vary. Students might point out that the masque serves as a celebration of harmony, fertility, and joy in marriage, and also demonstrates once again Prospero's supernatural powers.)

13 LITERARY ELEMENT

Characterization: How has Ferdinand's opinion of Prospero changed since their first meeting? (Awe and respect have replaced his earlier resentment.)

14 INTERPRETING

According to Prospero, what will happen if the audience is not silent? (The spell will be broken and the vision dispersed.) How might this have been an admonition on Shakespeare's part to the audience? (Possible response: He might have been asking the audience to be quiet.)

Barns and garners never empty,
Vines with clust'ring bunches growing,
Plants with goodly burden bowing;
Spring come to you at the farthest

115 In the very end of harvest!°
Scarcity and want shall shun you,
Ceres' blessing so is on you.

Ferdinand.
This is a most majestic vision, and
Harmonious charmingly. May I be bold

120 To think these spirits?

Prospero.   Spirits, which by mine art
I have from their confines called to enact
My present fancies.

Ferdinand.   Let me live here ever!
So rare a wond'red father and a wise
Makes this place Paradise.

[JUNO *and* CERES *whisper, and send* IRIS *on employment.*]

Prospero.   Sweet now, silence!

125 Juno and Ceres whisper seriously.
There's something else to do. Hush and be mute,
Or else our spell is marred.

Iris.
You nymphs, called Naiads, of the wind'ring°
        brooks,
With your sedged crowns and ever-harmless looks,

130 Leave your crisp channels, and on this green land
Answer your summons. Juno does command.
Come, temperate nymphs, and help to celebrate
A contract of true love. Be not too late.

[*Enter certain* NYMPHS.]
You sunburned sicklemen, of August weary,

135 Come hither from the furrow and be merry.
Make holiday. Your rye-straw hats put on,
And these fresh nymphs encounter every one
In country footing.

[*Enter certain* REAPERS, *properly habited.° They join
with the* NYMPHS *in a graceful dance; towards the end
whereof* PROSPERO *starts suddenly and speaks; after
which, to a strange, hollow, and confused noise, they
heavily° vanish.*]

114–115. **Spring come . . . harvest:** May spring come for you immediately after autumn.

❓ How do you think Prospero reacts to Ferdinand's expression of wonder in lines 122–124? Is he flattered? Annoyed? Indifferent?

128. **wind'ring:** winding, or perhaps wandering.

habited: dressed.

heavily: unwillingly.

ANSWERS TO MARGIN QUESTIONS

Lines 139–143. Prospero is upset because he remembers that Caliban's plot to murder him is about to hatch.

Lines 145–146. Possible response: During the masque Miranda has been silent in obedience to her father's command; earlier in the scene she was silent from maidenly modesty.

Prospero.
(*aside*) I had forgot that foul <u>conspiracy</u>
140   Of the beast Caliban and his confederates
Against my life. The minute of their plot
Is almost come.—(*to the* SPIRITS) Well done!
Avoid!° No more!

Ferdinand.
This is strange. Your father's in some passion
145   That works him strongly.

Miranda.   Never till this day
Saw I him touched with anger so distempered.

Prospero.
You do look, my son, in a moved sort,
As if you were dismayed. Be cheerful, sir.
Our revels now are ended. These our actors,

What has made Prospero so upset in lines 139–143?

143. **Avoid:** Away with you.

Lines 145–146 are the first time Miranda has spoken in this scene. Why do you think she has been silent up till now?

conspiracy (kən·spir'ə·sē): a planning together in secrecy to do a foul deed

15 SPECULATING
Why the mighty magician, Prospero, should be so upset about Caliban's ludicrous plan is a much debated question among Shakespeare scholars. Shakespeare may simply have been looking for a way to end the masque and return to the main action. Can you think of a reason why Prospero would be so angry with Caliban? (Possible response: Caliban is Prospero's only failure at transformation, or so Prospero believes.)

MEETING INDIVIDUAL NEEDS

16 ESL: Help students use context to understand the Elizabethan idiom ''in a moved sort'' by pointing out that its meaning is restated in the next line by the word ''dismayed.'' Explain that Ferdinand is upset or dismayed by Prospero's agitation about Caliban's plot. ∎

HUMANITIES CONNECTION

Called Hera by the Greeks, Juno is often depicted as petty, jealous, wrathful, or implacable. In this work, she is offering a queenly benediction to the earth, as two peacocks wing her chariot to heaven.
How does this depiction suit Juno's portrayal in the play? (Possible response: She is stately, powerful, and benevolent.) ∎

Giraudon/Art Resource, New York

JUNO ASCENDING TO HEAVEN IN HER CHARIOT, CHRÉTIEN LEGOUAIS, **fourteenth century.**

The Tempest, Act 4, Scene 1   **911**

ANSWER TO MARGIN QUESTION

Lines 147–164. The speech is full of theater metaphors such as "pageant," "rack," and "globe" (a punning reference to the Globe theater). The speech suggests the transience of art and of life through the words "melted," "vision," "dissolve," "faded," and "dreams." Prospero's statement "Our revels now are ended" (line 149) has been construed as Shakespeare's announcement of his own retirement as a dramatist.

17 COMPARING LITERATURE

Invite students to read aloud Prospero's speech, lines 147–164, to gain a better understanding of its theme.

❓ *How are Prospero's ideas about life different from or similar to those expressed in the* Bhagavad-Gita, *pp. 467–476, or the Taoist anecdote "The Butterfly," p. 548?* (Possible response: All three works emphasize the transitory, illusory nature of life. "The Butterfly" questions whether life is a dream, and the *Gita* states "Creatures are unmanifest in origin, manifest in the midst of life, and unmanifest again in the end.")

18 LITERARY ELEMENT

Tone: How does Prospero's tone in commanding Ariel contrast with his tone toward Ariel at the beginning of the play? (Possible response: It is much gentler. He actually thanks Ariel for coming.)

19 LITERARY ELEMENT

Humor: Although Prospero appears worried by Caliban's conspiracy, Ariel uses imagery that makes the threesome appear ridiculous. Why are their actions absurd? (Possible response: They are so drunk they rebel against the laws of nature.)

17

150 As I foretold you, were all spirits and
Are melted into air, into thin air;
And, like the baseless fabric of this vision,
The cloud-capped towers, the gorgeous palaces,
The solemn temples, the great globe itself,
155 Yea, all which it inherit, shall dissolve,
And, like this insubstantial pageant faded,
Leave not a rack° behind. We are such stuff
As dreams are made on, and our little life
Is rounded with a sleep. Sir, I am vexed.
160 Bear with my weakness. My old brain is troubled.
Be not disturbed with my infirmity.
If you be pleased, retire into my cell
And there repose. A turn or two I'll walk
To still my beating mind.

157. **rack:** cloud.

❓ Some critics consider this speech (lines 147–164) Shakespeare's "farewell to the stage." What in this speech, in terms of tone and language, suggests this interpretation?

165 **Ferdinand.** } We wish your peace.   [*Exeunt.*]
Miranda.

[*Enter* ARIEL.]
Prospero.
Come with a thought! I thank thee, Ariel.
    Come.
Ariel.
Thy thoughts I cleave to. What's thy pleasure?
Prospero.
Spirit, we must prepare to meet with Caliban.
Ariel.
Ay, my commander. When I presented Ceres,
170 I thought to have told thee of it, but I feared
Lest I might anger thee.
Prospero.
Say again, where didst thou leave these varlets?°
Ariel.
I told you, sir, they were redhot with drinking;
So full of valor that they smote the air
175 For breathing in their faces, beat the ground
For kissing of their feet; yet always bending
Towards their project. Then I beat my tabor;
At which like unbacked° colts they pricked their
    ears,
Advanced their eyelids, lifted up their noses
180 As they smelt music. So I charmed their ears
That calf-like they my lowing followed through
Toothed briers, sharp furzes, pricking goss,° and
    thorns,

172. **varlets:** rascals.

178. **unbacked:** unbroken; never ridden.

182. **goss:** gorse, a prickly shrub.

18

19

ANSWER TO MARGIN QUESTION

Lines 196–254. Possible response: The invisible presence of Prospero and Ariel, and the clowns' confusion, wetness, and vulgarity, make the scene comical.

20

185 Which ent'red their frail shins. At last I left them
I' the filthy mantled pool° beyond your cell,
There dancing up to the chins, that the foul lake
O'erstunk their feet.

Prospero.   This was well done, my bird.
Thy shape invisible retain thou still.
The trumpery° in my house, go bring it hither
For stale° to catch these thieves.

Ariel.   I go, I go.   [*Exit.*]

21

Prospero.
190 A devil, a born devil, on whose nature
Nurture° can never stick! on whom my pains,
Humanely taken, all, all lost, quite lost!
And as with age his body uglier grows,
So his mind cankers.° I will plague them all,
195 Even to roaring.

[*Enter* ARIEL, *loaden with glistening apparel, etc.*]
Come, hang them on this line.°

[PROSPERO *and* ARIEL *remain, invisible.*]

[Enter CALIBAN, STEPHANO, *and* TRINCULO, *all wet.*]
Caliban.
Pray you tread softly, that the blind mole may not
Hear a foot fall. We now are near his cell.

Stephano.
Monster, your fairy, which you say is a harmless fairy,
has done little better than played the Jack° with us.

Trinculo.
200 Monster, I do smell all horse-piss, at which my nose
is in great <u>indignation.</u>

Stephano.
So is mine. Do you hear, monster? If I should take a
displeasure against you, look you—

Trinculo.
Thou wert but a lost monster.

Caliban.
205 Good my lord, give me thy favor still.
Be patient, for the prize I'll bring thee to
Shall hoodwink this mischance.° Therefore speak
softly.
All's hushed as midnight yet.

Trinculo.
Ay, but to lose our bottles in the pool—

184. **filthy mantled pool:** scum-covered pond.

188. **trumpery:** showy, yet worthless, things.
189. **stale:** bait.

191. **Nurture:** training; education.

194. **cankers:** becomes infested with hate and ugliness.

195. **line:** linden or lime tree.

❓ A scene leading up to the murder of a king should be one of suspense, but this scene is very comical. What strikes you as comical in this scene?
199. **Jack:** trickster.

207. **hoodwink this mischance:** erase this misfortune.

20 GUIDED READING
Identifying Details: What does Ariel do to Caliban and his friends? (He charms them with music, then leads them to dance in a filthy pond.) What does this show about the relative power of the conspirators and Prospero? (The conspirators are no match for Prospero and, as the coming scene shows, they are not a serious threat to anyone but themselves.)

21 SYNTHESIZING
Who does Prospero call a devil? (Caliban) What reasons does Prospero have for being angry with Caliban? (Aside from the fact that Caliban is conspiring against him, Caliban has lusted after Prospero's daughter and has resisted Prospero's efforts to transform or educate him. Caliban represents Prospero's only failure since coming to the island.)

indignation (in·dig·nā′shən): offense

Lines 210–215. Stephano and Trinculo are soaked, they smell bad, and worst of all, they have lost their bottles of liquor. Their dedication to killing Prospero is faltering.

Line 218. Caliban means that the evil act of murder that will bring about the good result of eliminating Prospero. He and Stephano think they will benefit by assuming control of the island.

Line 221. The allusion to *Macbeth* is ironic because these murderers are ineffectual, whereas Macbeth was deadly.

Line 222. Stephano and Trinculo are distracted by Prospero's deliberate display of fine clothing.

Lines 225–229. Possible response: For comic effect, have the characters try on several garments, preen as they look at themselves in a mirror, and compete for garments and the mirror.

22 ANALYZING

Prompt students to think of the phrase "good mischief" as a recurring motif of the play. What characters have practiced "good mischief"? (Throughout the play, Prospero and Ariel, at his command, have played tricks on Ferdinand, Alonso, and the other castaways, with the intent of doing them good in the end.) What characters have practiced bad mischief? (Antonio and his associates have deprived Prospero of his dukedom.) How does the phrase relate to the theme of the use of power? (Possible response: Sometimes trickery must be used temporarily to achieve higher ends.)

23 LITERARY ELEMENT

Characterization: How does Caliban feel about Stephano and Trinculo now that he sees them distracted by the garments? (Possible response: He is exasperated, disillusioned, and disgusted.)

Stephano.
210   There is not only disgrace and dishonor in that, monster, but an infinite loss.

Trinculo.
That's more to me than my wetting. Yet this is your harmless fairy, monster.

Stephano.
I will fetch off my bottle, though be o'er ears° for my
215   labor.

Caliban.
Prithee, my king, be quiet. Seest thou here?
This is the mouth o' the cell. No noise, and enter.
Do that good mischief which may make this island
Thine own forever, and I, thy Caliban,
220   For aye thy foot-licker.

Stephano.
Give me thy hand. I do begin to have bloody
thoughts.

Trinculo.
O King Stephano! O peer! O worthy Stephano, look
what a wardrobe here is for thee!

Caliban.
Let it alone, thou fool! It is but trash.

Trinculo.
225   O ho, monster! we know what belongs to a frippery.°
O King Stephano!

Stephano.
Put off that gown, Trinculo. By this hand, I'll have that
gown!

Trinculo.
Thy Grace shall have it.

Caliban.
230   The dropsy drown this fool! What do you mean
To dote thus on such luggage? Let't alone,
And do the murder first. If he awake,
From toe to crown he'll fill our skins with pinches,
Make us strange stuff.

Stephano.
235   Be you quiet, monster. Mistress line, is not this my
jerkin? [*Takes it down.*] Now is the jerkin under the
line. Now, jerkin, you are like to lose your hair and
prove a bald jerkin.°

Trinculo.
Do, do! We steal by line and level, an't like your Grace.

Why are Stephano and Trinculo so distressed? What do their complaints suggest about their dedication to murdering Prospero?

214. **fetch off:** get back; **o'er ears:** over my ears (in pond water).

The phrase "good mischief" (line 218) is an example of an oxymoron, or contradiction. What does Caliban mean by "good mischief"? Who will benefit from it?

Line 221 may be an allusion to Shakespeare's tragedy *Macbeth*, in which Macbeth also has bloody thoughts before murdering King Duncan. What is ironic about this allusion here?

Line 222 is where Caliban's plans go wrong. What happens? What distracts Stephano and Trinculo from their goal of killing Prospero?

225. **frippery:** used-clothes shop.

How do you imagine Stephano and Trinculo reacting to the discovery of the "frippery" in lines 225–229? How would you stage their discovery to its full comic effect?

236–238. **jerkin:** jacket; **under the line . . . bald jerkin:** under the linden tree, with a pun; "under the line" also meant "south of the equator." Sailors on such voyages sometimes contracted diseases that resulted in hair loss.

ANSWERS TO MARGIN QUESTIONS
Stage Direction. Answers will vary. The scene should not be too cruel or the comic mood would be utterly lost.

Lines 257–260. Possible response: They deserve to be punished for a while, but not permanently.

Stephano.

240 I thank thee for that jest. Here's a garment for't. Wit shall not go unrewarded while I am king of this country. "Steal by line and level" is an excellent pass of pate.° There's another garment for't.

Trinculo.

Monster, come put some lime° upon your fingers, and
245 away with the rest!

Caliban.

I will have none on't. We shall lose our time
And all be turned to barnacles,° or to apes
With foreheads villainous low.

Stephano.

Monster, lay-to your fingers. Help to bear this away
250 where my hogshead of wine is, or I'll turn you out of my kingdom. Go to, carry this.

Trinculo.

And this.

Stephano.

Ay, and this.

[*A noise of hunters heard. Enter divers* SPIRITS *in shape of dogs and hounds, hunting them about,* PROSPERO *and* ARIEL *setting them on.*]

Prospero.

Hey, Mountain, hey!

Ariel.

255 Silver! there it goes, Silver!

Prospero.

Fury, Fury! There, Tyrant, there! Hark, hark!

[CALIBAN, STEPHANO, *and* TRINCULO *are driven out.*]
Go, charge my goblins that they grind their joints
With dry convulsions, shorten up their sinews
With aged cramps,° and more pinch-spotted make them
260 Than pard or cat o' mountain.°

Ariel.   Hark, they roar.

Prospero.

Let them be hunted soundly. At this hour
Lie at my mercy all mine enemies.
Shortly shall all my labors end, and thou
Shalt have the air at freedom. For a little
265 Follow, and do me service.

[*Exeunt.*]

---

243. **pate:** wit; cleverness.

244. **lime:** a sticky substance, often said to be on thieves' hands.

247. **barnacles:** geese that were believed to grow from the shellfish.

? How do you imagine the staging of the trapping of Caliban, Stephano, and Trinculo? Is it chaotically or skillfully done? How do you imagine the Spirits could be made to appear like dogs?

? Do you think Caliban, Trinculo, and Stephano deserve such pain as punishment (lines 257–260)?

259. **aged cramps:** the pains and discomforts that accompany old age.
260. **pard:** leopard; **cat o' mountain:** wildcat.

---

24 DRAMATIC ELEMENT

Staging: How does Caliban respond to Stephano and Trinculo's repeated commands? (As there is no response, Caliban apparently does not obey.) If you were directing the play, what might you have Caliban do when Stephano and Trinculo command him to help steal the garments? (Possible response: walk away with a disgusted wave of his hands)

25 PREDICTING

Prospero states that his labors will shortly end. What do you think will happen before the play ends? (Possible response: Alonso and Ferdinand will be reunited.)

First Thoughts

Answers will vary.

Identifying Facts

1. a masque featuring three goddesses. Ferdinand and Miranda
2. He remembers Caliban's plot.
3. with bright clothes and trinkets. He sends spirit-dogs to chase them. freedom

Interpreting Meanings

1. Possible responses: Yes, because it does nothing to advance the plot; no, because it consolidates the betrothal of Ferdinand and Miranda and celebrates self-control, harmony, and fertility.
2. Possible responses: magical, lofty, solemnly joyous
3. In Act 4 Caliban is more the leader of the two clowns than the groveling slave. Having seen more of them, he is frustrated with their weakness.
4. He must regain his dukedom and decide the fate of Alonso, Antonio, and the other shipwrecked nobles.
5. Answers will vary. Students should evaluate not just the effect of the masque but the changes in the characters and in the relationships between Ferdinand and Prospero, Prospero and Ariel, and Caliban and his fellow conspirators.

Applying Meanings

Possible responses: musical performances, dancing, parties for weddings and other celebrations

---

> ## First Thoughts

Do you think Prospero has succeeded in revenging himself against all of the conspirators—both those who exiled him and those who planned to kill him and Alonso?

Identifying Facts

1. What entertainment do Ariel and his spirits provide? Who is honored by the entertainment?
2. Why does Prospero stop the festivities?
3. How are Trinculo and Stephano baited by Prospero and Ariel? What does Prospero do at the end of the act? What does he promise to Ariel?

Interpreting Meanings

1. Some critics have said that the masque in Act 4 is merely a transitional device that does little to further the plot. Do you agree? Why or why not?
2. What are the **tone** and **mood** of the masque?
3. Compare Caliban's behavior in Act 4 with his earlier behavior in the presence of Trinculo and Stephano.
4. By the end of Act 4, it is clear that Prospero has succeeded in all of his aims but one. His daughter is betrothed, and the two murder plots have been thwarted. What is there still left for him to do?
5. **Falling action** occurs in the fourth act of a Shakespearean play, after the **turning point**. Some critics refer to "fourth-act fatigue," in which the fourth act is seen mainly as a "catching-up" act which simply explores the effects of the climax on the various characters and marks time while the characters figure out what to do next. Do you think that Act 4 of *The Tempest* simply "marks time"? Why or why not?

Applying Meanings

The masque is presented to honor Ferdinand and Miranda, and to celebrate their betrothal. It also honored King James's daughter and her bridegroom, who witnessed a performance of *The Tempest* in 1613. Can you think of a modern equivalent of the masque, or of a special entertainment meant to celebrate a wedding, engagement, graduation, or other festive occasion?

THE TEMPEST
Act 5

In the final act of the play, the political, comic, and romantic aspects of the plot are resolved as the play reaches its conclusion. Pay attention to the events in the resolution of the play, and note the order in which they occur. Are all loose ends tied up?

1 INTERPRETING
What is the significance of the fact that Prospero is still wearing his magic robes? (He is still controlling the action of the plot and exercising his extraordinary, transformative powers.)

2 LITERARY ELEMENT
Resolution: How do you generally expect comedies to end? (Accept reasonable answers: happily; lovers are united; enemies are reconciled) So far, what elements of the comic vision have been fulfilled in the plot of *The Tempest*? (Miranda and Ferdinand are engaged.)

Summary of Act 5, Scene 1. *Prospero asks Ariel about the king's party, all of whom are still spellbound. Ariel reports that even he, who is not human, is deeply moved, and states that he believes even Prospero would be affected by their pitiable condition. Releasing them from the spell and then casting off his magical powers, Prospero explains everything to Alonso and his followers and forgives them. Prospero reunites Alonso with Ferdinand, and Alonso gives permission for the coming wedding. Next, Caliban and his co-conspirators, Stephano and Trinculo, are forgiven for their plot against Prospero. Prospero assures the others that all will sail in the morning. Ariel is at long last granted his freedom.*

ACT 5

Scene 1. *Before the cell of* PROSPERO.

[*Enter* PROSPERO *in his magic robes, and* ARIEL.]

Prospero.
Now does my project gather to a head.
My charms crack not,° my spirits obey, and Time
Goes upright with his carriage.° How's the day?

Ariel.
On the sixth hour, at which time, my lord
5   You said our work should cease.

Prospero.   I did say so
When first I raised the tempest. Say, my spirit,
How fares the King and 's followers?

Ariel.   Confined together
In the same fashion as you gave in charge,
Just as you left them—all prisoners, sir,
10 In the line grove which weather-fends° your cell.

2. **crack not:** do not fail.

3. **Goes upright with his carriage:** walks upright, despite the load (of events) he carries; i.e., time carries Prospero's plans forward smoothly.

? How do you think Ariel might say line 5? Cautiously? Excitedly? Why is it important?

10. **weather-fends:** defends from weather.

3 LITERARY ELEMENT

Figurative Language: What does Ariel compare Gonzalo's tears to in lines 16–17? (the drops from icicles melting from a roof) Why is this image particularly appropriate? (because Gonzalo and his companions have been "frozen"—rendered immobile—by Prospero's magic spell) Call students' attention to how often Shakespeare has used the images of tears in the play. For example, Miranda, who weeps copiously herself, says of the log Ferdinand is hauling: " . . . when this burns,/'Twill weep for having wearied you" (Act 3, Scene 1, lines 18–19). The imagery of tears connects with the recurring imagery of sea, water, and storm. After they have read the whole play, challenge students to find as many water images as they can.

4 LITERARY ELEMENT

Theme: How does Prospero's statement in lines 26–28 express a crucial theme of the play? (Possible responses: Reason or restraint is superior to ungoverned emotion; forgiveness or reconciliation is the basis of social harmony.)

> ■ **penitent** (pen′i·tent): truly sorry for having done wrong

5 GUIDED READING

Identifying Details: In lines 33–39, what powers does Prospero attribute to fairies? (They leave no footprints on the sand, they make grass sour, and they create mushrooms.)

They cannot budge till your release. The King,
His brother, and yours abide all three distracted,
And the remainder mourning over them,
Brimful of sorrow and dismay; but chiefly

15   Him that you termed, sir, the good old Lord Gonzalo.
      3   His tears run down his beard like winter's drops
      From eaves of reeds.° Your charm so strongly works 'em,
      That if you now beheld them, your affections
      Would become tender.

Prospero.   Dost thou think so, spirit?
Ariel.
20   Mine would, sir, were I human.

Prospero.   And mine shall.
      Hast thou, which art but air, a touch, a feeling
      Of their afflictions, and shall not myself,
      One of their kind, that relish all as sharply
      Passion° as they, be kindlier moved than thou art?

25   Though with their high wrongs I am struck to the quick,
      4   Yet with my nobler reason 'gainst my fury
      Do I take part. The rarer° action is
      In virtue than in vengeance. They being penitent,
      The sole drift of my purpose doth extend

30   Not a frown further. Go, release them, Ariel.
      My charms I'll break, their senses I'll restore,
      And they shall be themselves.
Ariel.   I'll fetch them, sir. [*Exit.*]
Prospero.

[*Makes a magic circle with his staff.*]
      Ye elves of hills, brooks, standing lakes, and groves,
      And ye that on the sands with printless foot
35   Do chase the ebbing Neptune, and do fly him
      5   When he comes back; you demipuppets° that
      By moonshine do the green sour ringlets° make,
      Whereof the ewe not bites; and you, whose pastime
      Is to make midnight mushrumps,° that rejoice
40   To hear the solemn curfew;° by whose aid
      (Weak masters though ye be) I have bedimmed
      The noontide sun, called forth the mutinous winds,
      And 'twixt the green sea and the azured vault
      Set roaring war; to the dread rattling thunder

---

17. **eaves of reeds:** thatched roofs.

> ❓ Of what is Prospero convinced by Ariel in line 20? How does Ariel persuade him?

24. **Passion:** feel strong emotion.

27. **rarer:** nobler; higher.

36. **demipuppets:** small creatures.
37. **green sour ringlets:** bitter grass generally avoided by sheep and thought to grow where a fairy had danced.
39. **mushrumps:** mushrooms; because they grow so quickly, mushrooms were said to be made by fairies.
40. **curfew:** After curfew (approximately 9:00 P.M.), humans stayed indoors and fairies were free to move about.

Lines 33–57. The language is at the same time powerful and restrained, lyrical and solemn. Prospero is as determined in his renunciation of power as he was in his use of it.

Lines 50–57. Possible response: Prospero is willing to give up his powers because they are a "rough magic"—unsubtle and materialistic. Now that he has achieved his limited ends, he will devote himself to higher studies in the knowledge that true freedom and social harmony come from internal rather than external transformation. (Student opinions will vary.)

Stage Direction. Possible response: At first they are all spellbound ("spell-stopped," line 61). As the spell wears off and they understand what is happening, Gonzalo will be glad, Alonso remorseful, Sebastian guilt-ridden and afraid of punishment, and Antonio resentful at the loss of the dukedom.

Lines 71–79. Possible response: The "men of sin" have not earned forgiveness, but forgiveness is necessary for social harmony and the possibility of a better future. Prospero delivers the speech with a certain ambivalence toward Sebastian and Antonio that occasionally breaks into anger—he can't completely forget the wrongs they have done him.

45   Have I given fire and rifted° Jove's stout oak
            With his own bolt; the strong-based promontory
            Have I made shake and by the spurs° plucked up
            The pine and cedar; graves at my command
            Have waked their sleepers, oped, and let 'em forth
50   By my so potent art. But this rough magic
            I here <u>abjure</u>; and when I have required
            Some heavenly music (which even now I do)
            To work mine end upon their senses that
            This airy charm is for, I'll break my staff,
55   Bury it certain fathoms in the earth,
            And deeper than did ever plummet sound
            I'll drown my book.

        [*Solemn music.*]

        [*Here enters* ARIEL *before; then* ALONSO, *with a frantic gesture, attended by* GONZALO; SEBASTIAN *and* ANTONIO *in like manner, attended by* ADRIAN *and* FRANCISCO. *They all enter the circle which* PROSPERO *had made, and there stand charmed; which* PROSPERO *observing, speaks.*]

            A solemn air, and the best comforter
            To an unsettled fancy, cure thy brains,
60   Now useless, boiled within thy skull! There stand,
            For you are spell-stopped.
            Holy Gonzalo, honorable man,
            Mine eyes, ev'n sociable to° the show of thine,
            Fall fellowly drops. The charm dissolves apace;°
65   And as the morning steals upon the night,
            Melting the darkness, so their rising senses
            Begin to chase the ignorant fumes that mantle
            Their clearer reason. O good Gonzalo,
            My true preserver, and a loyal sir
70   To him thou followst! I will pay thy graces
            Home° both in word and deed. Most cruelly
            Didst thou, Alonso, use me and my daughter.
            Thy brother was a furtherer in the act.
            Thou art pinched for't now, Sebastian. Flesh and blood,
75   You, brother mine, that entertained ambition,
            Expelled remorse and nature; who, with Sebastian
            (Whose inward pinches therefore are most strong),
            Would here have killed your king, I do forgive thee,
            Unnatural though thou art. Their understanding
80   Begins to swell, and the approaching tide
            Will shortly fill the reasonable shore,°

---

45. **rifted:** split.

47. **spurs:** roots.

? This speech (lines 33–57) is crucial as Prospero renounces his powers. What is striking to you about the language in this speech?

? Why is Prospero willing to give up his powers? Would you have done the same in his place?

? This is the first time the shipwreck survivors all see Prospero. Considering their personalities and their ties to him, how do you predict they will react to him?

63. **ev'n sociable to:** in sympathetic fellowship with.
64. **apace:** rapidly.

70–71. **pay thy graces/Home:** reward you generously for your loyal services.

? Do you think Alonso, Sebastian, and Antonio deserve or have earned Prospero's forgiveness? How do you imagine Prospero delivers lines 71–79?

81. **the reasonable shore:** i.e., their minds, which are again filling with comprehension.

---

6 EVALUATING

Like Prospero's "revels" speech in Act 4, this one also expresses a magician's renunciation of his powers. Do you think Shakespeare was expressing his own feelings about his work, and a desire to give up the "rough magic" of writing? (Answers will vary.)

> ◼ **abjure** (ab·joor′): to give up; renounce

7 LITERARY ELEMENT

Staging: What might Prospero be doing as he speaks to each of the men in turn? (Accept reasonable responses: He might walk from one to the other in a stately fashion, speaking directly to each and perhaps touching them with his staff.)

8 GUIDED READING

Finding the Main Idea: What kind of life does Ariel hope to lead when he no longer has to serve Prospero? (He wants to live freely and joyously, close to nature.)

9 COMPARING AND CONTRASTING

Who else has Prospero let go of that he will miss? (Miranda) Whom has he not freed? (Caliban) What does this suggest about Shakespeare's view of freedom? (Possible response: Only those who can exercise self-restraint can benefit from freedom.)

10 GUIDED READING

Identifying Details: How does Prospero convince Alonso that he is real and not a ghost? (He embraces Alonso, and Alonso feels his pulse beating.)

That now lies foul and muddy. Not one of them
That yet looks on me or would know me. Ariel,
Fetch me the hat and rapier in my cell.
85 I will discase me,° and myself present
As I was sometime Milan.° Quickly, spirit!
Thou shalt ere long be free.

[*Exit* ARIEL *and returns immediately.*]

[ARIEL *sings and helps to attire him.*]

   Where the bee sucks, there suck I;
   In a cowslip's bell I lie;
90   There I couch when owls do cry.
      On the bat's back I do fly
      After summer merrily.
   Merrily, merrily shall I live now
   Under the blossom that hangs on the bough.

Prospero.
95 Why, that's my dainty Ariel! I shall miss thee,
But yet thou shalt have freedom. So, so, so.
To the King's ship, invisible as thou art!
There shalt thou find the mariners asleep
Under the hatches. The master and the boatswain
100 Being awake, enforce them to this place,
And presently,° I prithee.

Ariel.
I drink the air before me, and return
Or ere your pulse twice beat.   [*Exit.*]

Gonzalo.
All torment, trouble, wonder, and amazement
105 Inhabits here. Some heavenly power guide us
Out of this fearful country!

Prospero.   Behold, sir King,
The wronged Duke of Milan, Prospero.
For more assurance that a living prince
Does now speak to thee, I embrace thy body,
110 And to thee and thy company I bid
A hearty welcome.

Alonso.   Whe'r° thou beest he or no,
Or some enchanted trifle to abuse° me,
As late I have been, I not know. Thy pulse
Beats, as of flesh and blood; and, since I saw thee,
115 The affliction of my mind amends, with which,
I fear, a madness held me. This must crave
(An if this be at all°) a most strange story.

85. **discase me:** take off my magic robe.
86. **As I was sometime Milan:** dressed as I used to be when Duke of Milan.

This is a famous song of Shakespeare's. What is its tone? Of what does Ariel sing?

101. **presently:** immediately.

What is Gonzalo's reaction to seeing Prospero in lines 104–106?

111. **Whe'r:** whether.
112. **abuse:** fool.

117. **An if this be at all:** if this is at all real.

Lines 125–134. In this exchange, Prospero tells Antonio and Sebastian that he knows of, but will not reveal, their plot to kill Alonso. Rather than stir up any more discord, Prospero wants to give them a chance to repent and live in peace with their countrymen.

Lines 140–147. Alonso will benefit from patience in being reunited with his son.

Lines 145–148. Prospero is both consoling Alonso and preparing him for the news of the marriage.

11

Thy dukedom I resign and do entreat
Thou pardon me my wrongs. But how should Prospero
120   Be living and be here?

Prospero.   First, noble friend,
Let me embrace thine age, whose honor cannot
Be measured or confined.

Gonzalo.   Whether this be
Or be not, I'll not swear.

Prospero.   You do yet taste
Some subtleties o' the isle, that will not let you
125   Believe things certain. Welcome, my friends all.
  (*aside to* SEBASTIAN *and* ANTONIO) But you, my
    brace of lords, were I so minded,
I here could pluck his Highness' frown upon you,
And justify you traitors. At this time
I will tell no tales.

12

Sebastian (*aside*).   The Devil speaks in him.

3

Prospero.   No.
130   For you, most wicked sir, whom to call brother
Would even infect my mouth, I do forgive
Thy rankest fault—all of them; and require
My dukedom of thee, which perforce I know
Thou must restore.

Alonso.   If thou beest Prospero,
135   Give us particulars of thy preservation;
How thou hast met us here, who three hours since
Were wracked upon this shore; where I have lost
(How sharp the point of this remembrance is!)
My dear son Ferdinand.

Prospero.   I am woe° for't, sir.

Alonso.
140   Irreparable is the loss, and patience
Says it is past her cure.

Prospero.   I rather think
You have not sought her help, of whose soft grace
For the like loss I have her sovereign aid
And rest myself content.

Alonso.   You the like loss?

Prospero.
145   As great to me as late;° and, supportable
To make the dear loss, have I means much weaker
Than you may call to comfort you; for I
Have lost my daughter.

? What is happening in this exchange between Prospero and Antonio and Sebastian in lines 126–134? Why does Prospero not reveal the plot of Antonio and Sebastian to King Alonso?

139. **woe:** filled with sorrow.

? Patience is personified, or treated like a character, in lines 140–141. How would (or will) Alonso have benefited from having patience?

145. **as late:** just as recent.

? What is Prospero doing in lines 145–148 by telling Alonso of his own loss?

---

11 INTERPRETING
What is Alonso's reaction to seeing Prospero again? (He is amazed, curious, and repentant.) What does he willingly give up? (the dukedom he usurped)

12 INTERPRETING
What do you think Sebastian is feeling most strongly in response to Prospero's aside? (Possible response: fear)

13 EVALUATING
Does Prospero forgive Antonio wholeheartedly? (Possible response: No, he is still angry at him but knows that he has thwarted him completely and need not punish him any further.) What does Antonio's lack of response suggest to you? (Possible response: He sullenly accepts what he cannot change, but will not ask for forgiveness.)

■ **irreparable** (ir·rep'ə·rə·bəl): not able to be repaired

14 LITERARY ELEMENT
Theme: The theme of loss and restoration, which is central to the play, is reflected in the dialogue between Prospero and Alonso. What has each lost and/or regained? (a son and a daughter; a dukedom; their friendship)

ANSWER TO MARGIN QUESTION

Lines 148–152. The dramatic irony of this speech is that the audience knows, but Alonso does not, that the "loss" of Prospero's daughter really refers to her impending marriage to Alonso's son.

15 LITERARY ELEMENT

Resolution: Prospero, as the restorer of order, distinguishes appearance from reality and reassures his visitors that he is in control of events, and all will be made clear to them in time.

16 SPECULATING

At this point, has Prospero given up his power as he said he would in lines 50–57? How do you know? (No, he talks of courts and dukedoms, and promises a wonder to come.) Do you think he will ever resign all his worldly or magical power? (Answers will vary.)

Martha Swope

Alonso.   A daughter?
O heavens, that they were living both in Naples,
150 The King and Queen there! That they were, I wish
Myself were mudded in that oozy bed
Where my son lies. When did you lose your
    daughter?

Prospero.
In this last tempest. I perceive these lords
At this encounter do so much admire°
155 That they devour their reason, and scarce think
Their eyes do offices of truth,° their words
Are natural breath. But, howsoev'r you have
Been justled from your senses, know for certain
That I am Prospero, and that very duke
160 Which was thrust forth of Milan, who most
    strangely
Upon this shore, where you were wracked, was
    landed.
To be the lord on't. No more yet of this;
For 'tis a chronicle of day by day,
Not a relation for a breakfast, nor
165 Befitting this first meeting. Welcome, sir.
This cell's my court. Here have I few attendants,
And subjects none abroad. Pray you look in.
My dukedom since you have given me again,
I will requite° you with as good a thing,
170 At least bring forth a wonder to content ye
As much as me my dukedom.

What is the irony of Alonso's speech (lines 148–152)?

154. **admire:** marvel.

156. **offices of truth:** see correctly.

169. **requite:** repay.

17 [Here PROSPERO *discovers°* FERDINAND *and* MIRANDA *playing at chess.*]

discovers: reveals.

Miranda.
Sweet lord, you play me false.

Ferdinand.   No, my dearest love,
I would not for the world.

Miranda.
Yes, for a score of kingdoms you should wrangle,
175   And I would call it fair play.

Alonso.   If this prove
A vision of the island, one dear son
Shall I twice lose.

Sebastian.   A most high miracle!

Ferdinand.
Though the seas threaten, they are merciful.
I have cursed them without cause.

18

[*Kneels.*]

Alonso.   Now all the blessings
180   Of a glad father compass thee about!
Arise, and say how thou camest here.

Miranda.   O, wonder!
How many goodly creatures are there here!
How beauteous mankind is! O brave new world
That has such people in't!

19

Prospero.   'Tis new to thee.

Alonso.
185   What is this maid with whom thou wast at play?
Your eld'st° acquaintance cannot be three hours.
Is she the goddess that hath severed us
And brought us thus together?

186. **eld'st:** longest possible.

Ferdinand.   Sir, she is mortal;
But by immortal providence she's mine.
190   I chose her when I could not ask my father
For his advice, nor thought I had one. She
Is daughter to this famous Duke of Milan,
Of whom so often I have heard renown
But never saw before; of whom I have
195   Received a second life; and second father
This lady makes him to me.

Alonso.   I am hers.°
But, O, how oddly will it sound that I
Must ask my child° forgiveness!

196. **hers:** her father; Alonso accepts her as a daughter-in-law.

198. **my child:** Miranda.

20

Prospero.   There, sir, stop.

> Remembering that Miranda has seen only two human beings in her life, how do you imagine she reacts when she sees the crowd of shipwreck survivors? How should she deliver lines 183–184?

17 LITERARY ELEMENT
Staging: The scene with Miranda and Ferdinand playing chess is another masque element. How might this scene be staged to convey both a formal and a magical element? (Possible response: A curtain could be dramatically opened to reveal the lovers in a beautiful, but removed, setting, such as a garden, aware of nothing but themselves.)

18 LITERARY ELEMENT
Resolution: What major loss is restored here? (Father and son are reunited after believing each other drowned.) What mood is overtaking the characters and the audience? (Possible responses: joy, relief, hope for the future)

19 COMPARING LITERATURE
British novelist Aldous Huxley used Miranda's words "brave new world" as the title of his novel about society in the future. Have students who have read Huxley's novel report on his vision of the future. Does he view human beings as Miranda does? Do you think Shakespeare's view of humanity was closer to that of Miranda or Huxley? (Most students will see that Shakespeare was far more worldly than Miranda, although perhaps not as cynical as Huxley.)

20 GUIDED READING
Identifying Cause and Effect: Why does Alonso need to seek forgiveness from Miranda? (He sent her off to sea, possibly to her death, with her father, when she was a small child.)

21 GUIDED READING

Identifying Details: To whom does Gonzalo give credit for bringing about the joyful union of Ferdinand and Miranda? (the gods)

■ issue (ish'oo): children; offspring

22 LITERARY ELEMENT

Resolution: What does the arrival of the ship's crew, with their good news, contribute to the play's resolution? (The reunion of the shipwrecked party is now complete; the effects of the storm have been overcome. A second chance is offered to all.)

Let us not burden our remembrance with
A heaviness that's gone.

200

Gonzalo.   I have inly wept,
Or should have spoke ere this. Look down, you gods,
And on this couple drop a blessed crown!
For it is you that have chalked forth the way
Which brought us hither.

Alonso.   I say amen, Gonzalo.

Gonzalo.

205   Was Milan thrust from Milan that his <u>issue</u>
Should become kings of Naples? O, rejoice
Beyond a common joy, and set it down
With gold on lasting pillars: In one voyage
Did Claribel her husband find at Tunis,

210   And Ferdinand her brother found a wife
Where he himself was lost; Prospero his dukedom
In a poor isle; and all of us ourselves
When no man was his own.

Alonso.

(to FERDINAND and MIRANDA) Give me your hands.

215   Let grief and sorrow still° embrace his heart
That doth not wish you joy.

Gonzalo.   Be it so! Amen!

[*Enter* ARIEL, *with the* MASTER *and* BOATSWAIN *amazedly following.*]

O, look, sir; look, sir! Here is more of us!
I prophesied, if a gallows were on land,
This fellow could not drown. Now, blasphemy,°

220   That swearst grace o'erboard,° not an oath on shore?
Hast thou no mouth by land? What is the news?

Boatswain.

The best news is that we have safely found
Our king and company; the next, our ship,
Which, but three glasses° since, we gave out split,

225   Is tight and yare and bravely rigged as when
We first put out to sea.

Ariel.   (*aside to* PROSPERO) Sir, all this service
Have I done since I went.

Prospero.

(*aside to* ARIEL) My tricksy spirit!

Gonzalo points out several examples of people finding or discovering things during the course of the play. What other discoveries were made that he does not mention or know about? What does he mean by the last line of his speech: "and all of us ourselves/ When no man was his own" (lines 212–213)?

215. **still:** always; forever.

219. **blasphemy:** blasphemer.
220. **swearst grace o'erboard:** drive heavenly grace from the ship with your profanity.

224. **glasses:** hours.

Alonso.

230 These are not natural events; they strengthen
From strange to stranger. Say, how came you hither?

Boatswain.

If I did think, sir, I were well awake,
I'ld strive to tell you. We were dead of sleep
And (how we know not) all clapped under hatches,
235 Where, but even now, with strange and several
noises
Of roaring, shrieking, howling, jingling chains,
And mo diversity of sounds, all horrible,
We were awaked; straightway at liberty;
Where we, in all her trim, freshly beheld
240 Our royal, good and gallant ship, our master
Cap'ring to eye her. On a trice, so please you,
Even in a dream, were we divided from them
And were brought moping hither.

Ariel (*aside to* PROSPERO).   Was't well done?

Prospero.

(*aside to* ARIEL) Bravely, my diligence.
245 Thou shalt be free.

Alonso.

This is as strange a maze as e'er men trod,
And there is in this business more than nature
Was ever conduct° of. Some oracle   248. **conduct:** conductor.
Must rectify our° knowledge.   249. **rectify our:** correct our lack of.

Prospero.   Sir, my liege,
250 Do not infest your mind with beating on
The strangeness of this business. At picked leisure,
Which shall be shortly, single I'll resolve° you   252. **resolve:** end your ignorance.
(Which to you shall seem probable) of every
These happened accidents; till when, be cheerful
255 And think of each thing well. (*aside to* ARIEL) Come
hither, spirit.
Set Caliban and his companions free.
Untie the spell. [*Exit* ARIEL.] How fares my
gracious sir?
There are yet missing of your company
Some few odd lads that you remember not.

[*Enter* ARIEL, *driving in* CALIBAN, STEPHANO, *and*
TRINCULO, *in their stol'n apparel.*]

Stephano.

260 Every man shift for all the rest, and let no man take
care for himself; for all is but fortune. Coragio,° bully-   261. **Coragio:** courage.
monster, coragio!

23 LITERARY ELEMENT

Imagery: In lines 232–243,
what specific sensory images
does the boatswain use to create a vivid scene? (sound images such as "roaring, shrieking, howling, jingling chains")
What does the word "moping"
in line 243 imply? (The crew
did not leave its snug ship
eagerly.)

24 SPECULATING

In line 254, Prospero tells the
men to "be cheerful," just as
he advised Ferdinand at the
end of the masque in Act 4. Is
Prospero himself cheerful?
(Accept reasonable responses.
He seems generous but solemn.) Why does he tell others
to be cheerful? (Accept reasonable responses. Perhaps he
is trying to cheer himself up;
he is, after all, about to give
up his wondrous powers, his
daughter, and Ariel's services.)

25 LITERARY ELEMENT

Mood: How does the mood
change with the entrance of
Caliban, Stephano, and Trinculo? (Accept reasonable responses. It changes from benevolent solemnity to farce.)
How do the preceding reconciliation scene and the scene
involving the clowns display
two different aspects of comic
drama? (The first is a comic vision reaffirming universal harmony, and evoking good feelings; the second is the broad
comedy of action generated
by slapstick, wordplay, and
foolishness.)

ANSWERS TO MARGIN QUESTIONS

Lines 265–267. Possible response: Caliban feels fearful of Prospero's power. Line 265 would be spoken sarcastically, as Caliban recognizes the true characters of Stephano and Trinculo.

Lines 267–270. Antonio and Sebastian remain unchanged: They are crude, mocking, and unrepentant.

Line 285. Trinculo is both "in a pickle"—in trouble—and "pickled"—drunk.

READING CHECK

1. Before he was exiled, what was Prospero's position in life? (Duke of Milan)
2. How did he lose that position? (Antonio usurped power and exiled him.)
3. Why are Prospero's books, cloak, and staff significant? (They are the sources of his magic powers.)
4. How did Prospero gain control over Ariel? (He rescued Ariel from captivity in an enchanted tree.)
5. Who came to the aid of Prospero and Miranda when they first landed on the island? (Caliban)
6. What do Ferdinand and Alonso believe has happened to each other on the island? (Each believes the other has drowned.)
7. What does Antonio try to persuade Sebastian to do when the others in their party are asleep? (kill Alonso)

---

26 GUIDED READING

Identifying Details: Who is Setebos? (He is the god of Sycorax, Caliban's mother [see Act 1, Scene 2, lines 375–376].)

27 ANALYZING

Prospero calls Caliban a "thing of darkness" and acknowledges him as his own in lines 279–280. What does this tell you about Prospero's complex feelings for Caliban? (He hates Caliban's base actions and intractability, but nevertheless feels responsible for him. He has served, after all, as Caliban's adoptive father.)

Trinculo.
If these be true spies which I wear in my head, here's
a goodly sight.

26 265 **Caliban.**
O Setebos, these be brave spirits indeed!
How fine my master is! I am afraid
He will chastise me.

Sebastian.   Ha, ha!
What things are these, my Lord Antonio?
Will money buy 'em?

Antonio.   Very like. One of them
270   Is a plain fish and no doubt marketable.

Prospero.
Mark but the badges° of these men, my lords,
Then say if they be true. This misshapen knave,
His mother was a witch, and one so strong
That could control the moon, make flows and ebbs,
275   And deal in her command° without her power.
These three have robbed me, and this demidevil
(For he's a bastard one) had plotted with them
To take my life. Two of these fellows you
Must know and own; this thing of darkness I
27 280   Acknowledge mine.

Caliban.   I shall be pinched to death.

Alonso.
Is not this Stephano, my drunken butler?

Sebastian.
He is drunk now. Where had he wine?

Alonso.
And Trinculo is reeling ripe. Where should they
Find this grand liquor that hath gilded 'em?
285   How camest thou in this pickle?

Trinculo.
I have been in such a pickle, since I saw you last, that
I fear me will never out of my bones. I shall not fear
fly-blowing.°

Sebastian.
Why, how now, Stephano?

Stephano.
290   O, touch me not! I am not Stephano, but a cramp.

Prospero.
You'ld be king o' the isle, sirrah?

Stephano.
I should have been a sore one then.

? How do you think Caliban feels when he says lines 265–267? Fearful? Resigned? Glad?

? What does this joking between Sebastian and Antonio (lines 267–270) at this late point in the play suggest about them? About their repentance?

271. **badges:** emblems worn by servants to indicate who their masters were; Prospero is referring to the stolen clothes Trinculo and Stephano are wearing.

275. **her command:** the moon's duty, controlling the tides.

? Explain the pun in line 285 about Trinculo being in a "pickle."

288. **fly-blowing:** becoming maggot-infested, i.e., Trinculo is so saturated with alcohol that, like pickled meat, he is preserved from spoiling.

8. What does Caliban try to persuade Stephano and Trinculo to do? (kill Prospero)

9. At the end of the play, which character is not reconciled to Prospero? (Antonio)

10. What happens to Ariel at the end of the play? (Prospero frees him.)

RETEACHING

The Tempest is full of bewitching spectacle, colorfully garbed characters, supernatural effects, and exotic scenery. Invite students to draw, paint, or sketch a scene that excited their imaginations. Encourage students to share their illustrations and talk about the details they have chosen to emphasize.

ANSWER TO MARGIN QUESTION

Lines 298–301. Critics debate this point. Possible responses: Caliban does repent, because he has seen Prospero's wisdom in contrast with Stephano's foolishness; he doesn't repent, but, out of self-interest, conceals his hatred for Prospero.

Alonso.
This is as strange a thing as e'er I looked on.
Prospero.
He is as disproportioned in his manners
295 As in his shape. Go, sirrah, to my cell;
Take with you your companions. As you look
To have my pardon, trim° it handsomely.
Caliban.
Ay, that I will! and I'll be wise hereafter,
And seek for grace. What a thrice-double ass
300 Was I to take this drunkard for a god
And worship this dull fool!
Prospero.   Go to! Away!
Alonso.
Hence, and bestow your luggage where you found it.
Sebastian.
Or stole it rather.

[*Exeunt* CALIBAN, STEPHANO, *and* TRINCULO.]
Prospero.
Sir, I invite your Highness and your train
305 To my poor cell, where you shall take your rest
For this one night; which, part of it, I'll waste

297 **trim:** clean.

❓ Do you think Caliban really repents in lines 298–301? Why or why not?

Martha Swope

The Tempest, Act 5, Scene 1   **927**

ANSWERS TO MARGIN QUESTIONS

Lines 320–322. with exuberance

Stage Direction: Everyone is reconciled with the important exception of Antonio and, perhaps, Caliban. Students' opinions of the characters' deservedness will vary.

Epilogue: by responding either positively or negatively to the play. Applause will let the actor leave the stage happily, gratify the author, and let the character go to Naples.

EXTENSION AND ENRICHMENT

Dramatizing a Scene from the Play. The ultimate enrichment activity for a Shakespeare play is to stage it. In conjunction with the Creative Writing Response on page 931, invite interested students to execute their staging plans by performing a scene from *The Tempest*, set in another time and place.

CLOSURE

Critic Robert Langbaum says that the essential message of tragicomedy is that one must lose in order to gain. Looking back at the play, what did characters lose, and what greater good did they gain? Elicit students' responses by asking them whether the play aroused primarily comic or tragic emotions in them. ■

LITERARY ELEMENT

Verse Form: When Shakespeare writes set pieces, such as songs that are set apart from the main action, he usually changes the verse form. What verse form is used here in the Epilogue? (rhymed couplets in a flexible iambic tetrameter)

> ■ **indulgence** (in·dul'jəns): a favor or privilege

With such discourse as, I not doubt, shall make it
Go quick away—the story of my life,
And the particular accidents° gone by
310   Since I came to this isle; and in the morn
I'll bring you to your ship, and so to Naples,
Where I have hope to see the nuptial
Of these our dear-beloved solemnized;
And thence retire me to my Milan, where
315   Every third thought shall be my grave.
Alonso.   I long
To hear the story of your life, which must
Take° the ear strangely.
Prospero.   I'll deliver all;
And promise you calm seas, auspicious gales,
And sail so expeditious that shall catch
320   Your royal fleet far off.—My Ariel, chick,
That is thy charge. Then to the elements
Be free, and fare thou well.—Please you draw near.

[*Exeunt omnes.*]

309. **accidents:** happenings.

317. **Take:** delight.

? How do you imagine Ariel reacts to his new freedom? With exuberance? With disbelief?

EPILOGUE

[*Spoken by* PROSPERO.]
Now my charms are all o'erthrown,
And what strength I have's mine own,
Which is most faint. Now 'tis true
I must be here confined by you,
5   Or sent to Naples. Let me not,
Since I have my dukedom got
And pardoned the deceiver, dwell
In this bare island by your spell;
But release me from my bands
10   With the help of your good hands.°
Gentle breath° of yours my sails
Must fill, or else my project fails,
Which was to please. Now I want°
Spirits to enforce, art to enchant;
15   And my ending is despair
Unless I be relieved by prayer,
Which pierces so that it assaults
Mercy itself and frees all faults.
As you from crimes would pardoned be,
20   Let your indulgence set me free.

[*Exit.*]

? One of the themes of *The Tempest* is harmonious reconciliation. Do you think everyone enjoys reconciliation at the conclusion of the play? Do you think everyone deserves it?

10. **good hands:** applause.

11. **Gentle breath:** good breeze (caused by the applause).

13. **want:** lack.

? How do "you," the audience (or reader) "confine" Prospero? How will your applause and his prayer release him?

A CRITICAL COMMENT

The Tempest *and Shakespeare's Vision of the World*

In *The Tempest,* critics have seen Shakespeare acting out his own career as a playwright and saying farewell to it. The idea is an attractive one. Prospero/Shakespeare, the magician/artist, manipulates his characters through the mazes of terror and joy created by life and their own natures. Finally, he brings them through to reconciliation and bids farewell to his special powers, which could not last forever, in a mixed spirit of regret and satisfaction.

The Tempest is the last of Shakespeare's own plays (he later collaborated on a few plays) and Prospero's final words are too appropriate a valedictory to be denied. Nevertheless, this idea that Prospero represents Shakespeare is at most only one element—and probably the most incidental one—in a play of such richness that all attempts to interpret it allegorically are more or less misleading.

The Tempest is set on an island that is obviously off-course from the route between Naples and Tunis. This island is its own world; Prospero's enchantment has imposed its rule on the island and on the island creatures. By his magic, Prospero brings into this enchanted world a group of people from the world of Naples and Milan, which had formerly been his domain. His purpose is not merely to restore this corrupt world to its former state (Prospero admits that he had been less than perfect as a ruler of Milan) but to bring about the condition of harmony that his magic has achieved on the island. By

bitter experience Prospero has gained knowledge of the world; by study and contemplation he has gained the wisdom to control it. The island has benefited, but he has yet to use his power in the real world.

Prospero has to contend with greed and violence and lust. These vices are manifest in the monstrous figure of Caliban, the "natural" man unimproved by knowledge and discipline. The same vices are embodied more realistically in Alonso and Antonio and Sebastian. Prospero must also contend with the naiveté of Gonzalo and Ferdinand, since innocence is not sturdy enough to prevail in a corrupt world. Tests and ordeals serve to bring both the corrupt and the naive into the light. But there are those who will remain forever in the dark, who, in a harmonious world, must be subjected to rigid control. Caliban is the most notable example, but controls must also be placed on Antonio, who never admits the error of his ways, but recognizes only his failure this time to get what he wanted. Finally we behold Prospero's vision of a restored world, which is presumably Shakespeare's own, when Prospero sets all to rights.

Above all, Prospero brings together Ferdinand and Miranda. Their meeting is the principal purpose of the magic shipwreck at the beginning of the play; their declaration of love is the pivotal scene; and Prospero's revelation of the pair to the rest of the characters is the climactic point of the play. Love; the continuity of life; a wise,

1 EVALUATING
Do you think Prospero ruled his island kingdom perfectly? (No, he was largely insensitive to Caliban's and Ariel's desire for freedom and autonomy.)

2 READER'S RESPONSE
Would you like to have a person like Prospero in a position of authority over you? How do you think people in positions of authority or power should behave toward those in their charge? (Answers will vary.)

3 INTERPRETING
Do you think the fact that Antonio, and perhaps Caliban, are unreformed at the end is a flaw or a loose end in the play? (Possible response: It keeps the play from being entirely comic or romantic, but adds a note of realism, since no society made up of human beings can be totally harmonious.)

ANSWERS

First Thoughts
Answers will vary.

Identifying Facts
1. Prospero reviews their past behavior.
2. Ferdinand alive. Miranda
3. They are sent to clean Prospero's cell and restore his wardrobe.
4. his magic powers; the exclusive company of Miranda; Ariel's service

Interpreting Meanings
1. Ariel sings about living freely in nature. Freedom is preferable to servitude, even to a benevolent master.
2. Alonso is repentant; Antonio shows no remorse. Antonio's reactions leave the reconciliation incomplete.
3. The second interpretation is plausible, for Prospero was Caliban's teacher. Prospero may also be acknowledging that all humans have a darker, baser nature that must be recognized but controlled.
4. Possible response: The Epilogue shows Prospero for the first time allowing someone else to wield power and control the outcome of events.

Applying Meanings
Answers will vary.

THE PLAY AS A WHOLE
Interpreting Meanings
1. Students should mention that Prospero's intellectual interests distracted him from his public duties. Also, Prospero was blind to any potential in

instructed innocence; youth and beauty—these make up the world's harmony.

The Tempest is full of the English Renaissance. Its setting on an "uninhabited island" calls up the excitement associated in the 1500s with discoveries of new lands across remote and dangerous seas. The figure of Caliban reflects contemporary interest in the "savages" which the explorers were telling about. The strange ways of these savages—as reported in accounts that were often highly romanticized—invited critical comparison with European civilization. Some Europeans, like the French essayist Montaigne, tended to view the New World natives as "noble savages" unspoiled by the false values of civilized society. Shakespeare, however, shows Caliban, the "natural man," as a near-brute who needs the restraints and the ideals that reason and the accumulated wisdom of civilization show to human beings.

Like the famous *Utopia* (1516) of Sir Thomas More, *The Tempest* creates in an exotic and untouched land an image of ideal human society. In the play's story

greedy men bring ugliness and unhappiness into a world made for man's sustenance and delight, but forces of love and benevolent authority overcome and reform them. This optimistic estimate of human potentialities is characteristic of the Renaissance, and the inquiry into how the principles of universal order can be used to achieve perfect harmony among men was a concern central to many humanistic philosophers of the Renaissance.

Shakespeare presents these serious ideas in *The Tempest* in the exuberant and colorful manner that we associate with Renaissance "style." The speeches show the soaring lyricism and verbal richness typical of the best Renaissance poetry, and the heroine presents an ideal of beauty and purity such as was imagined by sonnet composers from Petrarch on (see page 806). The earthy comedy of Stephano and Trinculo, the pageantry, and the whole atmosphere of gaiety reflect the popular side of Renaissance vitality in Elizabethan London.

First Thoughts
Do you think that Prospero dealt fairly with all the conspirators? How do you think a modern court would have treated them?

Identifying Facts
1. What does Prospero say to Alonso, Sebastian, Antonio, and Gonzalo when they are brought before him?
2. What does Alonso see that brings him joy? Whom does he meet for the first time?
3. What happens to Caliban and his co-conspirators?

4. What has Prospero lost by the end of the play?

Interpreting Meanings
1. Early in this act, how does Ariel's song illustrate his feeling of release? Why does he prefer freedom to Prospero's benevolent rule?
2. Alonso and Antonio have very different reactions to the disclosures made by Prospero in the final act. What do these reactions reveal about their characters? How do Antonio's reactions affect the **resolution** of the play?

3. At one point in Act 5, Prospero, speaking of Caliban, says: "This thing of darkness I acknowledge mine." Does he mean that Caliban is merely his servant, or do you think that Prospero means something deeper—that he recognizes some flaw within himself? Explain.

4. Discuss the play's **epilogue**. What, if anything, does it contribute to your understanding of Prospero's character?

Applying Meanings

Much has been written about the "forgiveness" theme in many of Shakespeare's plays. Do you think that Prospero was merely practicing self-interest by forgiving those who had plotted against him? Think of a time in your life when you forgave someone for a wrong. Was the forgiveness unconditional, or did you hope to gain something from the person you were forgiving?

The Play as a Whole
Interpreting Meanings

1. What evidence is given in the play that, if Prospero had been a better leader, he might have retained his power in Milan? Are his learning and intellect in some ways detrimental to his being a leader in the "real world," or does he possess some other flaw? In your response, consider Antonio's opinions of Prospero and Prospero's failure to see the obvious problems with Caliban.

2. *The Tempest* is sometimes called a "tragicomedy." Look up the definition of this word—as well as the separate definitions of the words *tragedy* and *comedy*—in a dictionary or a book of literary terms. Using evidence from the play, explain whether or not you believe *The Tempest* should be considered a tragicomedy.

3. Trace the plot lines that involve the three distinct groups of characters in the play: Prospero, Ferdinand, and Miranda; Alonso and his party; and Caliban, Trinculo, and Stephano. In what order are the separate plots presented? How is each plot resolved? What direct connections are there among these plot lines?

4. Michel de Montaigne's (1533–1592) essay "Of Cannibals" was almost certainly one of Shakespeare's sources for *The Tempest*. In this essay, Montaigne presents the idea that primitive societies may actually possess greater justice and harmony than so-called civilized society; they do not need courts, laws, or other confining social institutions. How does Shakespeare explore these ideas in *The Tempest*? Do you think that he agreed with Montaigne's idealized views of "primitive" societies, or was he trying to punch holes in Montaigne's theory?

Creative Writing Response

Writing a Synopsis. Like all of Shakespeare's best works, *The Tempest* can be set in different times and places and still not lose its appeal. Imagine that you are the director of a theater company, and that you have been assigned to create a new version of *The Tempest*, set in a different time and place. Write a synopsis—a brief overview or summary—of how you would change the play and yet keep the basic plot and theme. You could, for example, set the story in a Native American community in the eighteenth century, with Prospero cast as a shaman or medicine man. Be sure to include the major elements of exposition, climax, and resolution in your synopsis.

Critical Writing Response

1. **Contrasting Characters.** Caliban and Ariel are both supernatural beings, but they are very different. In a brief essay, contrast their characters. A chart like

Caliban, insensitive to the detrimental effects of bondage itself, and unable to truly forgive Antonio.

2. Students should consider the hopeful marriage and future stability of the state as the strong comic elements, and the failure to include Antonio and Caliban in the final reconciliation as tragic elements.

3. The shipwrecked party is introduced first, followed by the young lovers and the clownish characters. Students should see that all the plot lines are connected thematically and by interlocking loyalties or betrayals among the characters.

4. Most students will agree that Shakespeare distrusted the purely "natural" society and called for a balance of freedom, self-restraint, and external authority.

Creative Writing Response
Writing a Synopsis. Encourage inventiveness in choice of settings. For example, the exposition in Act 1 might show Alonso's spaceship crashing on a remote planet.

Critical Writing Response
1. Contrasting Characters. Prospero loves Ariel and is repulsed by Caliban; Ariel's appearance is airy, Caliban's earthy; both speak beautiful poetry but Caliban's speech is often venomous; Ariel is often generous, Caliban, selfish; Ariel wants to be free; Caliban, at one point, wants only to find a new master.

➡

2. Editing Shakespeare. Possible revisions: Shorten the scene at the beginning of Act 2 between Gonzalo, Antonio, and Sebastian; give Ferdinand and Miranda more dialogue with other characters; write a monologue for Antonio revealing his feelings after Prospero chastises him. Make sure students give reasons for their changes.

Speaking and Listening
Staging an Episode of the Play. Other possible scenes: in Act 4, when Stephano and Trinculo have been lured into the pond by Ariel, or later when they adorn themselves with Prospero's clothes

Language and Vocabulary
Blank Verse. Example of end-stopped blank verse:

Caliban:
Be not afeard. The isle is full
  of noises,
Sounds, and sweet airs that
  give delight and hurt not.
(Act 3, Scene 2, lines 132–133)

Example of run-on blank verse:

Caliban:
All the infections that the
  sun sucks up
From bogs, fens, flats, on
  Prosper fall and make him
By inchmeal a disease!
(Act 2, Scene 2, lines 1–3) ∎

---

the following may help you organize the material for your essay.

	Caliban	Ariel
Relationship to Prospero		
Appearance		
Speech		
Ambitions		

2. Editing Shakespeare. Imagine that Shakespeare is alive today and that you are his editor. You want to publish *The Tempest*, but you feel that there are certain scenes and characters that don't quite work. You need to write Shakespeare a brief letter in which you outline the changes you want to see him make to *The Tempest*. Perhaps, for example, the masque scene left you cold and you feel it should be removed or shortened. Or perhaps you think that readers will be turned off by the lengthy references to the "widow Dido" in Act 2, Scene 1. Make at least two suggestions for revision in your letter.

Speaking and Listening

Staging an Episode of the Play. Shakespeare is known for his verbal humor, but many of his plays also include scenes that rely on physical comedy. Choose a scene from *The Tempest* that relies on some physical humor. You might, for example, try presenting the episode in Act 2, Scene 2 in which Caliban is mistaken for a fish with four legs. Stage the scene for the class.

Language and Vocabulary

Blank Verse

All of Shakespeare's plays, including *The Tempest*, are written in **blank verse**. Blank verse is unrhymed poetry that is written in

---

iambic pentameter, which means that there are five ("penta") iambs in each line of poetry. An **iamb** is a poetic foot, or group of syllables, that is made up of an unaccented syllable followed by an accented one (⌣ ◞). The words *because* and *Christine* are both iambs, as is the phrase *on time*. Study the following two lines from *The Tempest*, which are written in blank verse:

How many goodly creatures are there here!
How beauteous mankind is! Oh, brave new world,

Much of English is naturally spoken in iambic rhythm. Of course, if the whole play were written in this pattern, it would soon become quite dull. Shakespeare, in order to add variety and emphasis to certain lines, sometimes reversed the pattern of accented and unaccented syllables or used fewer than five feet per line, as in the following example:

Where the bee sucks, there suck I.
In a cowslip's bell I lie,

It is important to follow the punctuation marks at the ends of lines, and not to assume that each line is complete in itself. Lines that end with a punctuation mark, such as a period or a comma, are called **end-stopped** lines. Other lines, which do not end with a punctuation mark, are called **run-on** lines, also known as **enjambment** (see page 812). In order to understand the meaning of these run-on lines, it is necessary to read on to the next line.

Go back through the play and find at least five examples of blank verse—unrhymed iambic pentameter. How many variations of this pattern can you find? Also, look for examples of end-stopped and run-on lines. Why do you think Shakespeare used both of these forms? What do they add to the play?

BEHIND THE SCENES

Shakespeare Around the World

Shakespeare is very much alive today—on the stage, in films, and on television. Continent by continent, Shakespeare draws audiences of eager theatergoers. In India, the celebrated producing-directing team of Ismail Merchant and James Ivory produced a popular comedy entitled *Shakespeare Wallah (Shakespeare Seller),* about a group of touring actors bringing Shakespeare to India's remote provinces. In Japan, the great director Akira Kurosawa created two magnificent films based on Shakespearean masterpieces: *Throne of Blood,* adapted from *Macbeth,* and *Ran,* adapted from *King Lear.*

In North America, Mayan Indians from the Yucatan Peninsula in Mexico presented a colorful production of *Romeo and Juliet* that attained international success. The New York Shakespeare Festival productions have featured some of Hollywood's biggest names—Denzel Washington, Kevin Kline, Meryl Streep, and Tracey Ullman. *Kiss Me Kate*—Cole Porter's musical version of *The Taming of the Shrew*—is always in production somewhere in the U.S., as is *West Side Story*—Leonard Bernstein's musical based loosely on *Romeo and Juliet.* Many people consider the Stratford Festival in Ontario, Canada—which frequently stars Dame Maggie Smith and Christopher Plummer—to be the best Shakespearean company in North America.

In South America, the Teatro do Onitorrinco of Brazil reset *A Midsummer Night's Dream* (in Portuguese, *Sonho de Uma Noite de Verao*) in the Amazon rain forest. The Compania Rajatabla of Venezuela presented *The Tempest* (in Spanish, *La Tempestad*) with Prospero's refuge symbolized by an enormous pre-Columbian idol's head buried in the island's surface.

In England, Stratford-on-Avon is one of the two homes of the Royal Shakespeare Company; the other is at the Barbican Centre in London. Nearby is the home of the Royal National Theatre on the Thames—within walking distance of the site of the former Globe theater. There are also many repertory companies dotted throughout the British Isles. One of these theaters produced the internationally famous rock musical, *Return to the Forbidden Planet,* based on the science fiction film *Forbidden Planet,* which was in turn based on Shakespeare's *The Tempest.*

Shakespeare is very much alive in continental Europe as well. Italian filmmaker Franco Zefferelli has directed productions of *The Taming of the Shrew, Romeo and Juliet,* and *Hamlet.* Denmark's Kronborg Castle, the historic site of *Hamlet,* has been the location of several film productions of the tragedy. Finnish filmmakers have produced an updated version of *Hamlet* with the unlikely title of *Hamlet Goes Business.*

Whether in Texas or Tokyo, Broadway or Brazil, Shakespeare's immortal works are very much a part of the modern world and are likely to remain so for centuries—perhaps millennia—to come.

MORE ABOUT BEHIND THE SCENES

The Tempest has been a magnet for great modern actors. In 1960, Richard Burton played Caliban to Maurice Evans' Prospero in a television production; in 1962, James Earl Jones was Caliban at the New York Shakespeare Festival. Sir John Gielgud played Prospero in five productions spanning sixty years—first at the Old Vic in London in 1930, and last in Peter Greenaway's film adaptation, *Prospero's Books,* in 1991.

Not surprisingly, *The Tempest* has been put to music by several of the world's great composers. In 1690, British composer Henry Purcell composed a score for the *Tempest*-based opera *The Enchanted Island.* French composer Hector Berlioz wrote a symphonic fantasy on the play in 1830, and Russian composer Peter Ilyich Tchaikovsky wrote another in 1873. British composer Ralph Vaughan Williams set Prospero's "revels" speech and Ariel's song "Where the bee sucks" to music in 1951. ■

1. *To become familiar with major literary works of the Enlightenment*
2. *To recognize the rational spirit of the Enlightenment in science, philosophy, and literature*
3. *To understand the role of satire in literature of the Enlightenment*
4. *To interpret and respond to literature of the Enlightenment both orally and in writing.*

1 RESPONDING TO THE QUOTATION

Known as the father of modern philosophy, the French thinker René Descartes (1596–1650) developed a method for seeking the truth in the natural sciences. In this quotation, he expresses the first principle of his method, which was to begin from a position of skepticism. The Cartesian method also involved breaking down a problem into parts and moving systematically and thoroughly from one step to the next before drawing conclusions. Descartes constantly challenged his own perceptions, though he was at least certain that he existed: "I think, therefore I am."

❓ *Why is Descartes an appropriate spokesperson for the Age of Enlightenment?* (He questioned authority and accepted only what he could verify through reason.)

2 HISTORICAL BACKGROUND

Louis XIV: The "Sun King" ruled France for seventy-two years, from 1643 to 1715. To pay for the wasteful wars he waged, and for the magnificence of his court, King Louis placed a heavy burden of taxation on the French people. *How might his rule have paved the way for the French Revolution?* (Possible response: His policies resulted in the majority of people living in poverty while the aristocrats enjoyed extravagant wealth.)

LITERATURE OF THE ENLIGHTENMENT

1

> 66 The first precept was never to accept a thing as true until I knew it as such without a single doubt. 99
>
> —*René Descartes*

During the **Age of Enlightenment**, or, as it is sometimes called, the **Age of Reason**, thinkers continued the Renaissance humanist tradition of challenging authority. Between the seventeenth and eighteenth centuries, people came to believe that human reason was the only reliable authority. Through reason, human beings could probe the secrets of the universe and understand the true relationship between themselves and God.

The Fruits of Discovery

In the seventeenth and eighteenth centuries, Europe and England enjoyed the rewards of exploration. Exotic goods from the East and immense quantities of gold and silver from the Americas enriched the absolute monarchs of Europe—monarchs like France's **Louis XIV**, who dubbed himself the "Sun King" and built the Palace of Versailles.

2

Aristocrats led elegant lives. In every European capital, ladies and gentlemen wearing silks and powdered wigs were carried through the muddy streets in elegant sedan chairs. Fashionable buildings with lavishly decorated interiors were surrounded by vast formal gardens and parks. The wealthy enhanced their reputations by becoming patrons of the arts, particularly of music, which filled their leisure hours. During this period, the great Austrian composers **Wolfgang Amadeus Mozart** and **Joseph Haydn** and the German composer **Johann Sebastian Bach** were favorites of Europe's royal courts. These musicians and others developed the opera, the sonata, and the concerto—all new musical forms.

A Time of Contrasts

In the midst of the affluence enjoyed by a few, many lived in great poverty. The poor flocked to the cities in search of

The best Enlightenment writers, however, tempered their belief in reason with shrewd, open-eyed observation. Point out to students that Voltaire's *Candide* is a work based on the author's keen assessment of the foibles of human nature.

La Fontaine's *Fables* also view the world from a realistic perspective. The wise cock knows what is in the fox's heart. The rats learn that few are willing to sacrifice themselves heroically for others, and that their ingenious plan to hang a bell on the cat will not work if no rat is willing to carry it out.

Both works use the characteristic Enlightenment techniques of satire and wit to show how far short of ideal standards the world falls. In order to make this clear, read aloud a particularly biting section of *Candide*, perhaps the thrashing scene from p. 950. Point out that the purpose of Voltaire's satire is to try to guide people to behave in a more enlightened, reasonable fashion.

Be sure that students also note these similarities and differences between *Candide* and La Fontaine's *Fables*: *Candide*, an episodic narrative, is rich in plot contrivance, exotic settings, and fanciful characters; the *Fables*, by contrast, are tightly controlled, closed forms in which the effect depends on careful phrase-making and precise choice of words.

Virginia Museum of Fine Arts, Richmond. Bequest of Regina V. G. Millhiser

MINERVA SUMMONING LOUIS XIV TO ARMS, late seventeenth-century French tapestry. *Louis XIV's opulent lifestyle typified the monarchies of seventeenth-century Europe.*

work, living in slums and suffering from malnutrition. Inflation was rampant and even basic food was costly. There was no sanitation or safe water supplies, and epidemic illnesses ravaged the cities. In 1665, the plague struck again,

> In the eighteenth century, the contrast between aristocratic affluence and lower-class poverty foreshadowed social upheaval.

killing thousands. The crime rate was high, and the wooden thatch-roofed houses in which common people lived were especially vulnerable to fire. In cities like Paris, the contrast between the rich and the poor was inescapable. The restlessness of the poor during this time foreshadowed social upheavals to come.

You and your students might also enjoy comparing *Candide* with *Don Quixote* (p. 823), a similar quest story featuring a naïve hero. Both Candide and Don Quixote leave home to experience exciting adventures, only to discover that true wisdom can be found just as easily at home.

In its keen observation, its wit, and its criticism of human nature and society, Enlightenment literature exemplifies thoughtful, carefully crafted writing. *Can-* *dide* and the *Fables* are typical products of the period; they reflect the belief expressed by poet Alexander Pope (1688–1744) that "True ease in writing comes from art, not chance / As those move easiest who have learned to dance."

Point out to students that the most direct impact of Enlightenment values on American life is found in our political institutions. Thomas Jefferson, James Madison, Benjamin Franklin, and other founders of our nation were thinkers of the Enlightenment era who believed in the consent of the governed as the legitimizing principle of any state. They constructed a model of government intended to protect the right of the individual to "life, liberty, and the

3 HISTORICAL BACKGROUND

Newton: Sir Isaac Newton (1642–1727) was perhaps the greatest scientist and mathematician of modern times. He laid the foundations of calculus and developed the basic laws of motion that are still taught in physics classes today. From these laws and his observations of the attraction of objects to the earth, Newton postulated the law of gravity. Alexander Pope summed up Newton's influence on the age with this heroic couplet:

Nature and Nature's laws lay hid in night: / God said, "Let Newton be!" and all was light.

4 HISTORICAL BACKGROUND

The Clockwork Universe: The medieval picture of the universe placed the earth at the middle of a closed spherical structure which was believed to be kept in continual motion by God. Galileo's discoveries replaced this earth-centered model with the sun-centered model of Copernicus. Later, Newton explained that the motions of the planets around the sun were governed by the law of gravity. Enlightenment thinkers pictured the universe, therefore, as a giant clock. They needed God only to "wind" the clock; after being wound, the universe ran itself. This "clockwork universe," so different from that of medieval thinkers, was a product of Renaissance humanism and the rise of science.

Science: A Clockwork Universe

The search for knowledge expanded in a climate of inquiry. The Royal Society of London for Improving Natural Knowledge began meeting in 1645 to support scientific research. In France, the Academy of Sciences was created in 1666 to promote mathematics, astronomy, and the physical sciences. The fruits of new scientific research were soon evident in the introduction of the pendulum clock (1656), the steam engine (1705), and the cotton gin (1793).

The most influential scientific developments occurred in mathematics. **René Descartes** believed that human beings, by reason alone, could discover universal truths. **Sir Isaac Newton** developed this idea in *The Mathematical Principles of Natural Philosophy* (1687). This work describes a clockwork universe governed by mechanical laws that can be discovered by reason alone, using the principles of deduction.

3

4

Europe in 1763

pursuit of happiness"—a phrase borrowed almost wholly from the Enlightenment philosopher John Locke. The ideals enshrined in the Declaration of Independence and the United States Constitution have in turn inspired other statemakers, spreading Enlightenment values from eighteenth-century Europe and America to the Asian and African continents.

The other major Enlightenment influence on the modern world can be seen in the development of science and technology. Eighteenth-century faith in reason and progress found concrete expression in the scientific revolution. In order for students to appreciate this fact, ask them to imagine how different the modern world would be without the steam engine, the microscope, or the mercury thermometer. Then suggest that students list a few of the conveniences of modern life made possible by Benjamin Franklin's discovery of electricity.

Two other important innovations from the Enlightenment era greatly affect life today. In 1702 the first daily newspaper was published in England, and in 1709 and 1711 respectively the first literary magazines, *The Tatler* and *The Spectator*, made their debuts. Ask students how Locke's philosophy might have encouraged the publication of inexpensive reading material for the general public. What role do

The Metropolitan Museum of Art, Gift of John Stewart Kennedy, 1910

WOLF AND FOX HUNT, PETER PAUL RUBENS (1577–1640). *The aristocrats of Enlightenment Europe sought out often extravagant leisure time activities to lend excitement and variety to their lives.*

The Rise of Rationalism

The ideas propounded by Descartes, Newton, and others came to be called **rationalism**. Rationalism's influence reached beyond science. It supported the idea that unchanging laws govern politics and morality. In the work of philosophers like **Thomas Hobbes**, rationalism led to the social theory that people choose what is in their best interest. Hobbes argued that people's common interests lead them to make a "social contract." They accept their sovereign's power over them in exchange for protection against their own greedy, evil nature.

Social Theory: The Spark of Revolution

The British philosopher **John Locke** (1632–1704) disagreed with Hobbes and the rationalists. He was an **empiricist**—one who believes that experience, rather than logic, is the only source of knowledge. Locke proposed that at birth, the mind is a blank slate (a *tabula rasa*) on which experience is recorded. His social ideas—that people are born equal and independent—followed from this premise. In Locke's view, revolution was not only a right but often an obligation. His political theories sparked the American Revolution and inspired its leaders—Thomas Paine, Thomas Jefferson, and Benjamin Franklin.

In France, **Jean Jacques Rousseau** (1712–1778) wrote that humanity is naturally good but is corrupted by the

> **❝** Every body continues in its state of rest, or of uniform motion in a right line, unless it is compelled to change that state by forces impressed upon it. **❞**
>
> —*Sir Isaac Newton*, Laws of Motion, I

newspapers and magazines play in spreading ideas?

Finally, remind students that the Age of Reason specialized in satire, the holding up of human folly to the cleansing light of ridicule. The spirit of Swift and Voltaire lives on in the political and social satire of Al Capp, Russell Baker, and Garry Trudeau. Discuss with students why critical laughter—the characteristic Enlightenment response—continues to play a part in contemporary life. After students have finished their reading, encourage them to peruse newspapers and magazines for examples of wit or satire that remind them of Voltaire or La Fontaine.

7 RESPONDING TO THE QUOTATION

❓ *In this quotation, what common human foible is Swift pointing up in his definition of satire?* (our tendency to see others' flaws but never our own)

8 LITERARY BACKGROUND

During the seventeenth century, the English government's exploitation of Ireland, a subject country, resulted in widespread starvation among the Irish poor. In his famous satire "A Modest Proposal," Jonathan Swift exposed the callousness of English behavior by proposing with seeming seriousness that the hungry Irish should eat their own children or sell them like cattle. As this grim example indicates, satire is not always funny or lighthearted.

HUMANITIES CONNECTION

Voltaire was one of a group of French writers of the Enlightenment period known as *philosophes*, who discussed how to improve social and political conditions. This engraving may depict Voltaire and other philosophes meeting in a French coffeehouse or *salon* (drawing room). ∎

7

> ❝Satire is a sort of glass, wherein beholders do generally discover everybody's face but their own. ❞
>
> —*Jonathan Swift, Preface to* The Battle of the Books

The Granger Collection, New York

Table talk with Voltaire and his fellow intellectual friends.
Eighteenth-century engraving.

environment, by education, and by government. He believed that governments must be subject to the will of the people. His writings influenced the architects of the United States Constitution and those of the French government following the French Revolution.

Literature: The Impact of New Ideas

More than in almost any other age, the literature of the seventeenth and eighteenth centuries reflected the enormous impact of new social and scientific ideas. Many writers used **satire** as a weapon against the corrupt social world. **Jean de La Fontaine** (1621–1695) wrote the shrewdly satiric *Fables*. **Molière** (1622–1673) wrote satiric dramas aimed at outmoded social conventions that disguised the worst in human nature. Perhaps the most scathing satire was written by Irish-born writer **Jonathan Swift** (1667–1745). His works, such as *Gulliver's Travels* and "A Modest Proposal," reflect Swift's bitter outrage at the corruption he saw.

8

> The literature of the seventeenth and eighteenth centuries was strongly influenced by new social and scientific ideas. Satire was a popular literary form.

The French philosopher and rational skeptic **Voltaire** (1694–1778) used satire to mock the ideas of his contemporary, Rousseau. Voltaire's ***Candide*** continually challenges Rousseau's assertion that humans are "naturally" good. Voltaire maintained that art should be used to change society, and his satires were directed at people who abused privilege and power.

Government: Revolutions Ignited

The new ideas of the Enlightenment took on concrete form as masses of people, desiring a better life, challenged the power of the monarchies. In England, the civil war that began in 1642 climaxed with the beheading of Charles I.

5. What revolutions did the ideas of the European Enlightenment help to bring about? (the American Revolution of 1775 and the French Revolution of 1789)

FOR FURTHER STUDY
Nonfiction
Peter Gay's *Age of Enlightenment* (Time-Life Books, 1966) presents engaging essays and picture-essays. *The Age of Reason* (Doubleday, 1961) by Harold Nicolson focuses on key personalities. *The Days of the French Revolution* (Morrow, 1981) by Christopher Hibbert tells its story in dramatic detail. ■

The **American Revolution** a century later echoed the same themes in its insistence on the rights of individuals. The **French Revolution** (1789–1799) was also based on the desire for personal freedom. This was somewhat obscured, however, when the lower classes, who had long endured poverty and deprivation, savagely retaliated against the French aristocracy.

9

> The ideas of the Renaissance and the Enlightenment challenged people to free themselves from the oppressions of government.

10

In the short run, the French Revolution failed to establish the ideal government that the philosophers envisioned. The American Revolution, however, succeeded in establishing a stable, representative government with a Constitution and Bill of Rights created by people whose ideas were shaped by the science, the philosophy, and the art of the Age of Enlightenment.

WASHINGTON CROSSING THE DELAWARE, EMANUEL GOTTLIEB LEUTZE (1816–1868). *The American Revolution was a culmination of the political ideas of the Enlightenment.*

The Metropolitan Museum of Art. Gift of John Stewart Kennedy, 1897

9 HISTORICAL BACKGROUND
The Reign of Terror: The French Revolution began in 1789 as a reform movement. As moderates lost control, Louis XIV was executed, and unruly mobs slaughtered aristocrats. In 1793 Robespierre inaugurated a "Reign of Terror" to root out traitors and counter-revolutionaries. Thousands were guillotined before Robespierre himself was overthrown.

10 HISTORICAL BACKGROUND
Napoleon Bonaparte: Despite its aspirations for liberty and equality, the French Revolution ended in dictatorship. Napoleon (1769–1821) took control of faction-ridden France in 1799 and had himself crowned emperor in 1804.

HUMANITIES CONNECTION

George Washington led his troops across the Delaware River on Christmas night 1776 and defeated the British forces at Trenton and Princeton.
❓ *What emotions has the artist attempted to inspire?* (Possible responses: pride, patriotism, admiration for the courage and daring of Washington and his men) ■

WRITING TO LEARN

Social Studies: Work with a partner to write an imaginary dialogue between two Enlightenment social theorists, possibly Rousseau and Hobbes, in which they engage in an argument for and against the innate goodness of human nature. ■

Jean de La Fontaine inherited from his father the post of inspector of forests and waterways in the Champagne region, where Chateau-Thierry is located. La Fontaine held the post from 1652 to 1671. By 1657, however, he was spending a great deal of time in Paris, while his wife (and son, Charles, who was born in 1653) remained at Chateau-Thierry. Though divorce was frowned upon, the couple separated in 1658 and ended their marriage in 1671.

Life in the salons of Paris conferred many benefits on La Fontaine: The patronage of various aristocrats gave him the income and the leisure time that he needed to concentrate on writing, and the opportunity to associate with other writers provided inspiration and encouragement. The list of his Paris friends reads like a roster of the literary greats of seventeenth-century France: playwrights Jean Racine and Jean-Baptiste Poquelin Moliére, poet Nicholas Boileau, novelist Madame de La Fayette, essayist Madame de Sevigne, and the Duke de La Rochefoucauld, who was famous for his maxims.

Yet La Fontaine also made literary use of his early years in Champagne. Many of his fables are set in the countryside and are enlivened by details that reveal his familiarity with the plants and animals of rural France.

Jean de La Fontaine
1621–1695

The Bettmann Archive

Jean de La Fontaine (zhän de la fōn·ten′) was said to be an impractical dreamer who was awkward in social situations. One story illustrates his lack of social graces at a boring dinner party. After making excuses that he needed to leave an hour early for another engagement, his hostess noted that it would only take him twenty minutes to reach his destination. He replied: "But you see, I prefer the longest way."

La Fontaine seems also to have chosen the longest route to a literary career. He was born in 1621 at Château-Thierry (sha′tō′ tē·er′ē) where his father supervised forest areas and water management for the region.

While in school, La Fontaine was first introduced to Greek and Latin, the languages of the classical writers he later came to admire. Rather than pursue classical scholarship, however, La Fontaine entered a seminary in Paris to study theology. But seminary discipline did not suit his dreamy absent-mindedness, and at age twenty-two he returned to Château-Thierry to dabble in legal studies. Four years later, according to his father's wishes, he married Marie Hericart, who was only fourteen years old at the time. La Fontaine had little interest in his marriage, however, and some time later he embarked on his literary career.

When he was thirty-three, La Fontaine published his first work, *The Eunuch*, an adaptation of a comedy by the Roman writer Terence. The play was a failure, but La Fontaine kept writing, and eventually his writing and his charm won him generous sums of money from powerful patrons, including ministers in the king's court. Thanks to this patronage, La Fontaine produced other, more popular works, the most successful being the *Fables*. Based in part on the animal fables of classical writers like Aesop and Phaedrus, the *Fables* appeared in a series of twelve books between the years 1668 and 1694. They were very popular at the time of their publication and continue to be memorized by French students today. They have long been regarded by the French as tiny masterpieces, as models of perfect style.

OBJECTIVES

1. *To recognize La Fontaine's contribution to the literature of the Enlightenment, and to interpret two seventeenth-century French fables*
2. *To identify the characteristics of beast fables*
3. *To write a modern fable based on personal experience*

THEMES IN WORLD LITERATURE

The Wisdom of the World
Parables from the New Testament, pp. 198–203
Anecdotes and Sayings by Saadi, pp. 665–671

The Individual and Society
From *The Pillow Book*, pp. 579–587
The Tempest, pp. 839–932 ∎

VOCABULARY IN CONTEXT

The words listed below will appear in the side margin at the point of instruction:

1. havoc
2. abstain
3. impending
4. fraternal
5. couriers

Reader's Guide

from FABLES

Background

The fables of La Fontaine seem lighthearted at first. They have a playful rhyme scheme and regular rhythm, and their characters are animals that often appear in children's books. But these animals are not those of Disney films—they demonstrate human characteristics in a way that is less than flattering to humans. As a result, La Fontaine's fables reveal a world of deceit and cowardice. One reason beast fables are effective is that particular qualities commonly associated with certain animals (pigs are greedy, donkeys are stubborn, for example) are understandable even to unsophisticated readers.

La Fontaine's fables were not written specifically for children. They contain messages or morals that reflect a harsh reality that only adult readers can fully appreciate. And yet, the didactic, or educational, nature of the fables makes them good teaching tools. In fact, La Fontaine wrote in his preface to the *Fables* about the need for children to learn early the messages of his writings. He believed that children "should not be left in ignorance if we can help it. We should teach them what a lion is, a fox, and so on and why a person is sometimes compared to a fox or a lion."

Writer's Response

As a class, make a list of animals and the human traits we assign to them. For each animal, explain why we associate a certain characteristic with it. Why do you think we enjoy reading about animals who are "like" us?

Literary Focus

The **beast fable** is a brief story in which animals take on the traits of people in order to teach a practical lesson about human life. Animal fables are usually very practical and are often used for satirical purposes—usually to mock corrupt or thoughtless people. The morals or lessons of La Fontaine's fables are expressed in **epigrams**, or clever sayings, that sum up a theme in very compact rhyme like the refrains of songs.

PREREADING FOCUS

Background: Many critics see in La Fontaine's work the beginning of the satirical bent that marks the literature of the Enlightenment. While he was dabbling in various professions, La Fontaine was observing every segment of French society. Enriched by his wit, La Fontaine's fables feature deft characterizations of both the powerful and the powerless in seventeenth-century France. In his hands, tales that had focused on the teaching of moral precepts were transformed into trenchant social commentaries.

The two fables presented here highlight familiar human weaknesses. They also reflect La Fontaine's skill in crafting varying rhythms and humorous rhymes and in juxtaposing several levels of diction to create a comic effect.

Literary Focus: Beast fables are part of the oral literature of many cultures. The tales of Brer Rabbit, told in the American South, are one example of the genre that scholars of Western civilization have traced to the Greek poet Hesiod (eighth century B.C.). The well-known collection attributed to Aesop (Greece, sixth century B.C.) and that of Phaedrus (Rome, first century A.D.) also provided rich material for later writers such as Horace, Plutarch, Chaucer, and Marie de France as well as La Fontaine. George Orwell's *Animal Farm* is a modern adaptation of the beast fable.

havoc (hav′ek): great destruction or ruin

abstain (ab·stān′): do without

impending (im·pend′iŋ) about to happen

LITERARY ELEMENT

Rhyme: Feminine rhyme, in which the last two syllables in each line rhyme, is usually considered more elegant than masculine rhyme, in which only the last syllable of each line rhymes. Where in "The Council Held by the Rats" does feminine rhyme occur? (lines 10–15: revel–devil; eater–meet her; caterwauling–chapter calling) How does the content of those lines evoke images that undercut the elegance of the feminine rhymes and create an ironic effect instead? (A cat that eats rats and then goes out to yowl for its mate is hardly an elegant subject. Also, "meet her" rhymes with "eater" only when slurred, suggesting a colloquial tone and a pedestrian subject.)

1 READER'S RESPONSE

Do you think the rats fail to implement the plan because it is impractical or because they lack the courage to act? Or do you see another reason? (Answers will vary.)

from FABLES
Jean de La Fontaine
translated by
ELIZUR WRIGHT, JR.

"So the fables are a panorama in which we see ourselves," wrote La Fontaine in the preface to his book. As you read these fables, consider how these stories about animals with human characteristics cast light on human behavior.

The Council Held by the Rats

Old Rodilard, a certain cat,
  Such havoc of the rats had made,
'Twas difficult to find a rat
  With nature's debt unpaid.[1]
The few that did remain,
  To leave their holes afraid,
From usual food abstain,
  Not eating half their fill.
  And wonder no one will,
That one who made on rats his revel,
With rats passed not for cat, but devil.
Now, on a day, this dread rat eater,
Who had a wife, went out to meet her;
And while he held his caterwauling,[2]
The unkilled rats, their chapter calling,
Discussed the point, in grave debate,
How they might shun impending fate.
  Their dean, a prudent rat,
Thought best, and better soon than late,
  To bell the fatal cat;
That, when he took his hunting round,
The rats, well cautioned by the sound,

Might hide in safety underground;
  Indeed he knew no other means.
    And all the rest
    At once confessed
  Their minds were with the dean's.
No better plan, they all believed,
Could possibly have been conceived.
No doubt the thing would work right well,
If any one would hang the bell.
  But, one by one, said every rat,
  I'm not so big a fool as that.
The plan, knocked up in this respect,

The council closed without effect.
And many a council I have seen,
Or reverend chapter with its dean,
  That, thus resolving wisely,
  Fell through like this precisely.

    To argue or refute
      Wise counselors abound;
    The man to execute
      Is harder to be found.

---

1. **With nature's debt unpaid:** remaining alive.
2. **caterwauling:** the shrill howl characteristic of cats during mating.

1. In "The Council Held by the Rats," why do the rats hold a council? (to decide what to do about a cat that is killing them off)

2. When do the rats meet to discuss their problem? (when the cat is out serenading a mate)

3. Which rat suggests a solution? (the dean, a "prudent rat")

4. In "The Cock and the Fox," where is the cock when the fox approaches him? (in a tree)

5. What does the fox do when the cock mentions the greyhounds? (hurries off to hide)

RETEACHING

Encourage students to dramatize the tales. In their dramatizations, students may apply the fables to current situations of interest to them. For example, the cat might be a neighborhood bully, and the rats might be kids who are too afraid to thwart him. Alternatively, the fox might be a sports figure trying a ruse, and the cock might be an opposing player who turns the tables on the first competitor.

FOX IN A CHICKEN YARD, JEAN-BAPTISTE HUET (1745–1811).

The Fine Arts Museum of San Francisco. Gift of Mrs. Frank Wilkins in memory of Charles Le Gay.

The Cock and the Fox

Upon a tree there mounted guard
  A veteran cock, adroit and cunning,
  When to the roots a fox up running,
Spoke thus, in tones of kind regard:—
  Our quarrel, brother, is at an end;
  Henceforth I hope to live your friend;
    For peace now reigns
    Throughout the animal domains.
  I bear the news:—come down, I pray,
    And give me the embrace fraternal;
  And please, my brother, don't delay.
    So much the tidings do concern all,
  That I must spread them far today.
  Now you and yours can take your walks
  Without a fear or thought of hawks.
And should you clash with them or others,
  In us you'll find the best of brothers;—
For which you may, this joyful night,
    Your merry bonfires light.
      But, first, let's seal the bliss
      With one fraternal kiss.

"Good friend," the cock replied, "upon my word,
  A better thing I never heard;
    And doubly I rejoice
    To hear it from your voice:
  And really, there must be something in it,
    For yonder come two greyhounds, which, I flatter
    Myself, are couriers on this very matter:
  They come so fast, they'll be here in a minute.
    I'll down, and all of us will seal the blessing
    With general kissing and caressing."
      "Adieu,"[1] said Fox, "my errand's pressing:
      I'll hurry on my way,
        And we'll rejoice some other day."
So off the fellow scampered, quick and light,
To gain the foxholes of a neighboring height—
Less happy in his stratagem than flight.
    The cock laughed sweetly in his sleeve—
    'Tis doubly sweet deceiver to deceive.

1. **Adieu** (ə·dyōō′): French for goodbye.

HUMANITIES CONNECTION

❓ *Does Huet's fox exhibit the craftiness of La Fontaine's animal, or does it seem more realistic? Cite the details on which you base your response.* (Answers will vary.) ■

■ **fraternal** (frə·tʉrn′əl): brotherly

couriers (koor′ē·ərs): messengers

2 CULTURAL DIVERSITY
Because of their speed and agility, greyhounds were traditionally used in France to hunt hares.
❓ *Which of their attributes would make greyhounds a threat to the fox?* (Possible response: A dog fast and agile enough to catch a hare is also fast and agile enough to catch a fox.)

COMPARING AND CONTRASTING
How is the cock like the fox? How are they different? (Both are clever and articulate; both use flattery to deceive. The cock, however, proves itself to be the more "adroit and cunning" of the two when it uses the fox's deceit to catch the cunning creature in its own snare.)

Creating a Board Game. Suggest that students create a board game based on one of the two fables. The object of the game should reflect the theme or the moral of the fable. Artistic students can design the game board, and the entire class can collaborate on deciding the rules and scoring. Encourage students to play the game at home after they have played it in class.

CLOSURE

Point out that La Fontaine's fables have been said to reveal both his wit and his bitterness or cynicism. Ask students to decide which attitude is stronger in each of the two fables. Then ask students to formulate their own definitions of cynicism. Explain that cynicism is common among many Enlightenment writers, and tell students that they will encounter this attitude again in works by Voltaire. ■

ANSWERS

First Thoughts
Answers will vary.

Identifying Facts
1. belling the cat
2. No one dares to do it.
3. The fox announces a truce among all animals and urges the cock to come down and embrace him. He intends to eat the cock.
4. The cock says he sees two dogs coming to "embrace" the fox, and the fox flees.

Interpreting Meanings
1. Possible response: It's especially satisfying to outwit someone who is trying to deceive you.
2. The fox's enemies, the dogs, scare off the fox and in doing so become "friends" of the cock.
3. fox: slyness; rat: sneakiness, cowardice. The fox tries to trick the cock; the rats plan to sneak up and bell the cat but lack courage.
4. first fable: cowardice and inaction; second fable: deceit

Applying Meanings
Answers will vary.

Creative Writing Response
Writing a Fable. Students' fables should be brief anecdotes that feature animal characters. Each fable should illustrate one main point, a moral or a proverb offering advice about life. The moral may come at the beginning or at the end of the fable. ■

First Thoughts
La Fontaine's fables have been criticized for their cynical tone. How would you describe the tone of these two fables?

Identifying Facts
1. What plan does the "dean rat" devise to protect the rats from the cat?
2. Why are the rats unable to put this plan into effect?
3. What does the fox say to trick the cock? What is his real intention?
4. How does the cock get the better of the fox in the end?

Interpreting Meanings
1. In the final **quatrain**, or four lines, of "The Council Held by the Rats," La Fontaine explicitly gives the **moral** of the story in the form of an **epigram**. What is the moral in "The Cock and the Fox"?
2. How could the expression "my enemy's enemy is my friend" apply to the story of the cock and the fox?

3. Consider the characters of the animals in the fables. What qualities do we typically associate with the fox and the rat? How are they apparent in these stories?
4. What human traits are ridiculed in these two **beast fables**?

Applying Meanings
How do you feel about the morals of La Fontaine's fables, and the tone in which they are delivered? Do you think they are too bitter or jaded, or do they confirm any of your own experiences? Explain.

Creative Writing Response
Writing a Fable. Consider a lesson you have learned lately, whether it be the virtue of being on time or the wisdom of not speaking in anger. "Translate" your experience into a fable with its own moral. (You might want to write the moral first.) Your characters should be animals who demonstrate human qualities, like those in the fables of La Fontaine.

Voltaire
1694–1778

Archiv Für Kunst Und Geschichte, Berlin

Voltaire was a writer who believed in writing the truth. He criticized the wastefulness of war, religious intolerance, and the unnecessary poverty and powerlessness of the average citizen. As a result of his frankness, he was twice imprisoned, once exiled from Paris, had his books and pamphlets banned by the French government, and was denied burial by the Parisian clergy when he died. Yet the spirit of his writing prevailed, and thirteen years after his death, the new postrevolutionary government brought Voltaire's remains back to Paris with great ceremony. Thousands of people lined the streets to see the funeral procession.

Voltaire was one of the main founders of modern historical science. He debunked traditional approaches to writing history, preferring to write philosophical treatises on morals. These essays were not abstract, but focused on how people actually lived and worked according to their moral principles. His efforts were not well-received, however, by the people in power. The publication of his most formidable work, *Essay on the Morals and the Spirit of the Nations from Charlemagne to Louis XIII*, caused the book to be banned and Voltaire to be exiled.

Aside from his voluminous correspondence and hundreds of pamphlets on every issue that arose in his time, Voltaire wrote in every literary genre. *La Henriade*, an epic poem about Henry IV, which he wrote during his first imprisonment, was regarded by some of his contemporaries as equal to the works of Homer and Virgil. Between *Oedipe*, written when he was eighteen, and *Irene*, written at age eighty-three, Voltaire wrote numerous plays, most of them great successes. His *Philosophic Dictionary* was perhaps the most widely read nonfiction book of his time. He wrote numerous romances and tales, of which *Candide* has proved to be the most enduring. Voltaire had little patience for purely metaphysical speculation. This emphasis on modest but practical achievement is reflected in the last page of *Candide:* "Let us work without arguing . . . it's the only way to make life endurable."

OBJECTIVES

1. *To recognize Voltaire's place in world literature and to analyze an excerpt from Candide.*
2. *To identify satire and the literary devices used in satire.*
3. *To write an essay explaining an author's purposes, and to write a skit satirizing a public folly*

THEMES IN WORLD LITERATURE

The Individual and Society
  The Book of Ruth, pp. 177–184
  ''The Guest,'' pp. 1244–1257

Satire and the Absurd
  From *Don Quixote*, pp. 821–837 ■

VOCABULARY IN CONTEXT

The words listed below will appear in the side margin at the point of instruction:

1. endowed
2. candor
3. pensive
4. vivacity
5. prodigy
6. clemency
7. ingrates
8. intrigue
9. disconcert
10. obstinate

PREREADING FOCUS

Background: *Candide*, published in 1759, was written when Voltaire was in his early sixties. By then he had become embittered by the death of the woman he loved and by his ill-fated stay in Prussia. Voltaire does not focus on personal issues in *Candide*; instead, he attacks social injustices and the fuzzy thinking that rationalizes them. He takes aim, for example, at the inhumanity of the slave trade in the Americas and at the oppressiveness of the political systems in many of the nation-states of Europe and the New World. As the story gallops along like an action movie, Voltaire satirizes public figures that are especially offensive to him: He lampoons the naiveté of the followers of Leibnitz, his dead lover's favorite philosopher, almost as if he were wishing that she would return to argue with him; and he debunks the myth of Frederick the Great by satirizing the unethical and inhumane practices of the Prussian Army.

Literary Focus: Satirists, Voltaire among them, try to persuade readers to do or believe something by showing the opposite view as absurd.

Reader's Guide

from CANDIDE

Background

Candide is subtitled ''Optimism'' and tells a tale of the woes that befall a naive simpleton who is brought up to believe that this world is the best of all possible worlds. The point of Voltaire's story is to show how Candide's optimism is foolish in a world in which people's lives are shaped for the most part by cruel and incomprehensible forces.

The plot of *Candide* takes the form of a quest: the young man's quest for union with his beloved, Cunegonde. They go through a series of separations and reunions, as Cunegonde is taken as booty by the Bulgarians, held prisoner by the Grand Inquisitor, and forcibly kept as a mistress by the Governor of Buenos Aires—in this, the best of all possible worlds. What happens to Candide himself is no better, but the two lovers somehow survive. The tale is told with great verve and hilarity, and, like all quests of this kind, the journey involves much suffering but ends in wisdom.

Writer's Response

If it were possible for you to live in the ''best of all possible worlds'' right here on earth, what would such a place be like? What kinds of things would you *not* find there? Write a paragraph describing your ideal world.

Literary Focus

Satire is writing that ridicules human weakness, vice, or folly in order to bring about social reform. An expert satirist like Voltaire uses a variety of tools to expose his subject to ridicule—from witty barbs to heavy bludgeons that flatten his opponent's sacred cows. As Voltaire exposes one absurdity after another, readers become convinced that they would be fools not to agree with his point of view. As you read *Candide*, look for Voltaire's outrageous exaggerations and deadpan understatements, for illogic dressed up as common sense, and for situations that are simply silly.

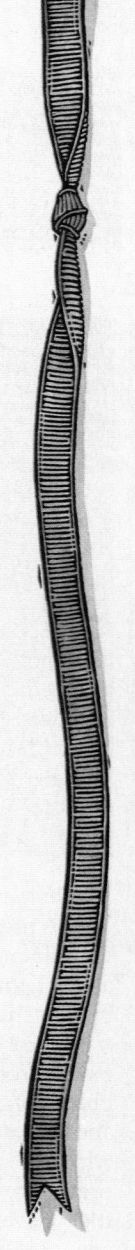

from CANDIDE

François-Marie Arouet de Voltaire

translated by

RICHARD ALDINGTON

Note the first few places where Voltaire's writing makes you chuckle. Then, as you continue reading, think of possible reasons why Voltaire might have wanted to keep you laughing.

Chapter 1

How Candide was brought up in a noble castle, and how he was expelled from the same

In the castle of Baron Thunder-ten-tronckh in Westphalia[1] there lived a youth, <u>endowed</u> by Nature with the most gentle character. His face was the expression of his soul. His judgment was quite honest and he was extremely simple-minded; and this was the reason, I think, that he was named Candide. Old servants in the house suspected that he was the son of the Baron's sister and a decent honest gentleman of the neighborhood, whom this young lady would never marry because he could only prove seventy-one quarterings,[2] and the rest of his genealogical tree was lost, owing to the injuries of time.

The Baron was one of the most powerful lords in Westphalia, for his castle possessed a door and windows. His Great Hall was even decorated with a piece of tapestry. The dogs in his stable yards formed a pack of hounds when necessary; his grooms were his huntsmen; the village curate was his Grand Almoner.[3] They all called him "My Lord," and laughed heartily at his stories.

The Baroness weighed about three hundred and fifty pounds, was therefore greatly respected, and did the honors of the house with a dignity which rendered her still more respectable. Her daughter Cunegonde, aged seventeen, was rosy-cheeked, fresh, plump and tempting. The Baron's son appeared in every respect worthy of his father. The tutor Pangloss was the oracle of the house, and little Candide followed his lessons with all the <u>candor</u> of his age and character.

Pangloss taught metaphysico-theologo-cosmoloonigology.[4] He proved admirably that there is no effect without a cause and that in this best of all possible worlds, My Lord the Baron's castle was the best of castles and his wife the best of all possible Baronesses.

---

1. **Westphalia:** region in western Germany, noted for its hams. Voltaire considered it "vast, sad, sterile, detestable."
2. **quarterings:** divisions on a coat of arms or family tree. Seventy-one quarterings would trace a person's genealogy back over 2,000 years.
3. **Grand Almoner:** member of a noble household responsible for distributing charity to the poor.
4. **metaphysico-theologo-cosmoloonigology:** Voltaire is satirizing the philosopher Leibniz and his followers by embedding the word "loony" in this made-up term.

2 EVALUATING

The assertions that "there is no effect without a cause" and "this is the best of all possible worlds" allude to the doctrine of philosophical optimism developed by the German mathematician Gottfried Wilhelm von Leibnitz (1646–1716). His ideas were popular, and Voltaire devotes most of *Candide* to ridiculing them. *What warped logic does Pangloss use in his "proof" of Leibnitz's assertion that this is the best of all possible worlds?* (faulty reasoning: The idea that because everything has a cause, everything must also have a purpose. Broad generalizations: "Everything is necessarily for the best"; "things cannot be otherwise.")

> **pensive** (pen'siv): thinking deeply and seriously
>
> **vivacity** (vī·vas'ə·tē): liveliness

HUMANITIES CONNECTION

Commissioned by the Baron de Saint-Julien in 1766, this painting depicts the baron's mistress being swung by her husband (the obscure figure at the far left) while the baron lolls on the ground and admires her legs.

❓ *How is Fragonard's painting reminiscent of Cunegonde's witnessing Doctor Pangloss in the bushes with the maid?* (Both scenes are frivolous and lighthearted treatments of illicit sex.) ∎

THE SWING, JEAN-HONORÉ FRAGONARD (1732–1806). *Fragonard was a master of Rococo, the highly ornamental style that dominated eighteenth-century European art.*

Trustees of the Wallace Collection, London

"'Tis demonstrated," said he, "that things cannot be otherwise; for, since everything is made for an end, everything is necessarily for the best end. Observe that noses were made to wear spectacles; and so we have spectacles. Legs were visibly instituted to be breeched, and we have breeches. Stones were formed to be quarried and to build castles; and My Lord has a very noble castle; the greatest Baron in the province should have the best house; and as pigs were made to be eaten, we eat pork all the year round; consequently, those who have asserted that all is well talk nonsense; they ought to have said that all is for the best."

Candide listened attentively and believed innocently; for he thought Miss Cunegonde extremely beautiful, although he was never bold enough to tell her so. He decided that after the happiness of being born Baron of Thunder-ten-tronckh, the second degree of happiness was to be Miss Cunegonde; the third, to see her every day; and the fourth, to listen to Doctor Pangloss, the greatest philosopher of the province and therefore of the whole world.

One day when Cunegonde was walking near the castle, in a little wood which was called The Park, she observed Doctor Pangloss in the bushes, giving a lesson in experimental physics to her mother's waiting-maid, a very pretty and docile brunette. Miss Cunegonde had a great inclination for science and watched breathlessly the reiterated experiments she witnessed; she observed clearly the Doctor's sufficient reason, the effects and the causes, and returned home very much excited, <u>pensive</u>, filled with the desire of learning; reflecting that she might be the sufficient reason of young Candide and that he might be hers.

On her way back to the castle she met Candide and blushed; Candide also blushed. She bade him good-morning in a hesitating voice; Candide replied without knowing what he was saying. Next day, when they left the table after dinner, Cunegonde and Candide found themselves behind a screen; Cunegonde dropped her handkerchief, Candide picked it up; she innocently held his hand; the young man innocently kissed the young lady's hand with remarkable <u>vivacity</u>, tenderness and grace; their lips met, their eyes sparkled, their knees trembled, their hands wandered. Baron Thunder-ten-tronckh passed near the screen, and, observing this cause and effect, expelled Candide from the castle by kicking him in the backside frequently and hard. Cunegonde swooned; when she recovered her senses, the Baroness slapped her in the face; and all was in consternation in the noblest and most agreeable of all possible castles.

Chapter 2

What happened to Candide among the Bulgarians

Candide, expelled from the earthly paradise, wandered for a long time without knowing where he was going, weeping, turning up his eyes to Heaven, gazing back frequently at the noblest of castles which held the most beautiful of young Baronesses; he lay down to sleep supperless between two furrows in the open fields; it snowed heavily in large flakes. The next morning the shivering Candide, penniless, dying of cold and exhaustion, dragged himself towards the neighboring town, which was called Wald-berghoff-trarbk-dikdorff. He halted sadly at the door of an inn. Two men dressed in blue noticed him.

"Comrade," said one, "there's a well-built young man of the right height."

They went up to Candide and very civilly invited him to dinner.

"Gentlemen," said Candide with charming modesty, "you do me a great honor, but I have no money to pay my share."

"Ah, sir," said one of the men in blue, "persons of your figure and merit never pay anything; are you not five feet five tall?"

"Yes, gentlemen," said he, bowing, "that is my height."

"Ah, sir, come to table; we will not only pay your expenses, we will never allow a man like you to be short of money; men were only made to help each other."

"You are in the right," said Candide, "that is what Doctor Pangloss was always telling me, and I see that everything is for the best."

They begged him to accept a few crowns,[5] he took them and wished to give them an I.O.U.; they refused to take it and all sat down to table.

"Do you not love tenderly. . . ."

"Oh, yes," said he. "I love Miss Cunegonde tenderly."

"No," said one of the gentlemen. "We were asking if you do not tenderly love the King of the Bulgarians."[6]

"Not a bit," said he, "for I have never seen him."

"What! He is the most charming of Kings, and you must drink his health."

"Oh, gladly, gentlemen."

And he drank.

"That is sufficient," he was told. "You are now the support, the aid, the defender, the hero of the Bulgarians; your fortune is made and your glory assured."

They immediately put irons on his legs and took him to a regiment. He was made to turn to right and left, to raise the ramrod and return the ramrod, to take aim, to fire, to double up, and he was given thirty strokes with a stick; the next day he drilled not quite so badly, and received only twenty strokes; the day after, he only had ten and was looked on as a prodigy by his comrades.

Candide was completely mystified and could not make out how he was a hero. One fine spring day he thought he would take a walk, going straight ahead, in the belief that to use his legs as he pleased was a privilege of the human species as well as of animals.

---

5. **crowns:** units of money.
6. **King of the Bulgarians:** Voltaire is satirizing the recruiting practices of King Frederick the Great of Prussia, in whose household he once served.

3 GUIDED READING
Sequencing: In which order do the following events occur in the story? (a) Candide sleeps in a snowy field; (b) two men in blue offer Candide dinner; (c) the Baron sees Candide and Cunegonde kissing; (d) Candide treks to a neighboring town; (e) the Baron kicks Candide out. (c, e, a, d, b)

CULTURAL DIVERSITY
Between 1756 and 1763, France, Austria, and Russia battled the combined powers of Prussia and England in the Seven Years' War. Candide is conscripted into the "Bulgarian" (Prussian) Army to fight a war modeled on this war.

 How is Voltaire's bitterness toward Frederick the Great of Prussia reflected in his characterization of the "men in blue," the Prussian Army recruiters? (Possible response: They are characterized as unethical predators, taking any male over five feet tall and using deception to snare recruits.)

prodigy (präd′ə·jē): a person of very great ability

4 LITERARY ELEMENT
Satire: How does Voltaire use exaggeration to satirize inhumane disciplinary practices in the Prussian Army? (For making mistakes in following complex drilling maneuvers, recruits endure harsh beatings; Candide's punishment for desertion is death by exaggerated torture.)

He had not gone two leagues[7] when four other heroes, each six feet tall, fell upon him, bound him and dragged him back to a cell. He was asked by his judges whether he would rather be thrashed thirty-six times by the whole regiment or receive a dozen lead bullets at once in his brain. Although he protested that men's wills are free and that he wanted neither one nor the other, he had to make a choice; by virtue of that gift of God which is called *liberty*, he determined to run the gauntlet[8] thirty-six times and actually did so twice. There were two thousand men in the regiment. That made four thousand strokes which laid bare the muscles and nerves from his neck to his backside. As they were about to proceed to a third turn, Candide, utterly exhausted, begged as a favor that they would be so kind as to smash his head; he obtained this favor; they bound his eyes and he was made to kneel down. At that moment the King of the Bulgarians came by and inquired the victim's crime; and as this King was possessed of a vast genius, he perceived from what he learned about Candide that he was a young metaphysician[9] very ignorant in worldly matters, and therefore pardoned him with a clemency which will be praised in all newspapers and all ages. An honest surgeon healed Candide in three weeks with the ointments recommended by Dioscorides.[10] He had already regained a little skin and could walk when the King of the Bulgarians went to war with the King of the Abares.[11]

After escaping the slaughter of the Seven Years' War, Candide encounters Pangloss in Holland. He informs Candide that his beloved Cunegonde has been disemboweled by the Bulgarians and that the Baron's castle and everyone in it is destroyed. While en route to Portugal, the two survive a shipwreck and arrive in Lisbon just in time for the great earthquake. There the Inquisition arrests them as heretics responsible for the devastation and Candide is publicly flogged; Pangloss, however, is hanged and presumed dead. A "good old woman" then reunites Candide with Cunegonde, who describes how she survived the Bulgarians and came to be held by the Grand Inquisitor. Candide kills the Inquisitor and sails with Cunegonde for South America, where they hope to find the best of all possible worlds and lasting happiness. But Candide loses Cunegonde for the sake of the immediate happiness of the governor of Buenos Aires, and again the sweet-natured youth is forced to run, along with his new footman Cacambo. In their flight, they are nearly skewered and boiled by cannibals, the Oreillons, but Cacambo exhibits his clearheadedness by talking the savages out of their dinner plans.

Chapter 17

Arrival of Candide and his valet in the country of Eldorado and what they saw there

When they reached the frontiers of the Oreillons,[12] Cacambo said to Candide:

---

7. **leagues:** units of distance, each one equal to about three miles.
8. **run the gauntlet:** to run between two rows of soldiers who would strike the victim with clubs or other weapons.
9. **metaphysician:** philosopher who studies the nature of being and reality and the origin and structure of the world.
10. **Dioscorides:** Greek army physician of the first century A.D. who wrote medical treatises. Even in Voltaire's day Dioscorides' works were out of date.

11. **Abares:** that is, the French, who fought against the "Bulgarians," or Prussians, in the Seven Years' War (1756–1763).
12. **Oreillons:** *French,* roughly meaning "Big Ears."

THE STORY OF THE SOLDIER, KAREL DUJARDIN
(1622–1678).

From this story, what can you gather about
Voltaire's attitude toward the military?

"You see this hemisphere is no better than
the other; take my advice, let us go back to
Europe by the shortest road."

"How can we go back," said Candide, "and
where can we go? If I go to my own country,
the Bulgarians and the Abares are murdering
everybody; if I return to Portugal[13] I shall be
burned; if we stay here, we run the risk of
being spitted at any moment. But how can I
make up my mind to leave that part of the
world where Miss Cunegonde is living?"

"Let us go to Cayenne,"[14] said Cacambo,
"we shall find Frenchmen there, for they go
all over the world; they might help us. Perhaps God will have pity on us."

It was not easy to go to Cayenne. They
knew roughly the direction to take, but

mountains, rivers, precipices, brigands and
savages were everywhere terrible obstacles.
Their horses died of fatigue; their provisions
were exhausted; for a whole month they
lived on wild fruits and at last found themselves near a little river fringed with coco-
nut-trees which supported their lives and
their hopes.

Cacambo, who always gave advice as prudent as the old woman's,[15] said to Candide:

"We can go no further, we have walked
far enough; I can see an empty canoe in the
bank, let us fill it with coconuts, get into the
little boat and drift with the current; a river
always leads to some inhabited place. If we
do not find anything pleasant, we shall at
least find something new."

"Come on then," said Candide, "and let us
trust to Providence."

They drifted for some leagues between
banks which were sometimes flowery,
sometimes bare, sometimes flat, sometimes
steep. The river continually became wider;
finally it disappeared under an arch of frightful rocks which towered up to the very sky.
The two travelers were bold enough to trust
themselves to the current under this arch.
The stream, narrowed between walls, carried them with horrible rapidity and noise.
After twenty-four hours they saw daylight
again; but their canoe was wrecked on reefs;
they had to crawl from rock to rock for a
whole league and at last they discovered an
immense horizon, bordered by inaccessible
mountains. The country was cultivated for
pleasure as well as for necessity; everywhere
the useful was agreeable. The roads were

---

13. **Portugal:** Following the earthquake in Lisbon,
Candide had been persecuted by the Inquisition.
He fears being burned as a heretic if he returns.

14. **Cayenne** (kī·en'): seaport in French Guiana in
South America.

15. **the old woman:** The old woman had traveled
with Candide and Cunegonde to the New World.
She knew everything of life, having survived kidnapping by pirates, enslavement in Morocco,
catching the plague in Algiers, and being disfigured by the Turks.

Yale University Art Gallery, Leonard C. Hanna, Jr. Fund

HUMANITIES CONNECTION

Dujardin (dyu·zhar·dan') was a
Dutch painter and etcher
noted for landscapes, portraits,
and genre pictures—realistic
paintings of scenes from
everyday life. Notice how the
listening figures in the painting
focus attention on the storyteller. The viewer is drawn into
the scene by the glance of the
figure on the right.

*What do you imagine the
soldier is saying?* (Answers
will vary.) ■

5 LITERARY ELEMENT

Theme: One of Voltaire's major themes in *Candide* is the
folly of denying or ignoring
evil. Voltaire believed that evil
includes not only harmful acts
but also conditions and events
such as illness and natural disasters that precipitate suffering. He also believed that ignoring evil serves only to
compound it.

*When he is thrown out of
the Baron's castle, Candide
is completely ignorant of the
existence of evil. What might
Voltaire's reasons be for having
Candide experience and witness so much suffering?* (Possible responses: to educate
readers; to arouse complacent
readers; to convince readers
to accept his argument that
this is *not* "the best of all possible worlds.")

6 **LITERARY ELEMENT**

Exaggeration: Andalusia (a region in Spain), Tetuan (the former capital of Spanish Morocco), and Mequinez, or Meknes (another town in Morocco), were all known for their fast and spirited horses. *How does the exaggerated description of Eldorado's sheep contribute to the idea that Eldorado may be "the best of all possible worlds"?* (The sheep of Eldorado are faster than the fastest horses known in Europe.)

7 **LITERARY ELEMENT**

Understatement: What might Candide's understatement that "This country is better than Westphalia" reveal about his intellect? (Like the character played by the comedian Stan Laurel, Candide may be a little slow-witted, but he does notice the obvious.)

COMPARING LITERATURE

The Sumerian hero Gilgamesh, like Candide, arrives at a land beyond seemingly impassable mountains. Compare and contrast what Candide and Cacambo find in Eldorado and what Gilgamesh finds in the Garden of the Gods (pp. 138–151). (Possible response: Both places are filled with gold and jewels. Eldorado, which contains an efficient transportation system, a school, and an effective government, is an idealized version of eighteenth-century Europe. The Garden of the Gods is an idealized Sumerian garden by a sea; even the thistles are made of jewels, and only gods live there.)

SOUTH AMERICAN JUNGLE, from the series *Geographische Charakterbilder* by Adolf Lehmanns, 1911. *Many Europeans of Voltaire's day actually did believe that a utopian land called Eldorado existed in the New World.*

Archiv Für Kunst Und Geschichte, Berlin

covered or rather ornamented with carriages of brilliant material and shape, carrying men and women of singular beauty, who were rapidly drawn along by large red sheep whose swiftness surpassed that of the finest horses of Andalusia, Tetuan and Mequinez.

"This country," said Candide, "is better than Westphalia."

He landed with Cacambo near the first village he came to. Several children of the village, dressed in torn gold brocade, were playing coits[16] outside the village. Our two men from the other world amused themselves by looking on; their coits were large round pieces, yellow, red, and green, which shone with peculiar luster. The travelers were curious enough to pick up some of them; they were of gold, emeralds, and rubies, the least of which would have been the greatest ornament in the Mogul's throne.

"No doubt," said Cacambo, "these children are the sons of the King of this country playing at coits."

At that moment the village schoolmaster appeared to call them into school.

"This," said Candide, "is the tutor of the Royal Family."

The little beggars immediately left their game, abandoning their coits and everything with which they had been playing. Candide picked them up, ran to the tutor, and presented them to him humbly, giving him to

16. **coits:** quoits, a game resembling horseshoes.

understand by signs that their Royal Highnesses had forgotten their gold and their precious stones. The village schoolmaster smiled, threw them on the ground, gazed for a moment at Candide's face with much surprise, and continued on his way.

The travelers did not fail to pick up the gold, the rubies, and the emeralds.

"Where are we?" cried Candide. "The children of the Kings must be well brought up, since they are taught to despise gold and precious stones."

Cacambo was as much surprised as Candide. At last they reached the first house in the village, which was built like a European palace. There were crowds of people round the door and still more inside; very pleasant music could be heard and there was a delicious smell of cooking. Cacambo went up to the door and heard them speaking Peruvian; it was his maternal tongue, for everyone knows that Cacambo was born in a village of Tucuman where nothing else is spoken.

"I will act as your interpreter," he said to Candide, "this is an inn, let us enter."

Immediately two boys and two girls of the inn, dressed in cloth of gold, whose hair was bound up with ribbons, invited them to sit down to the table d'hôte.[17] They served four soups each garnished with two parrots, a boiled condor which weighed two hundred pounds, two roast monkeys of excellent flavor, three hundred colibris[18] in one dish and six hundred hummingbirds in another, exquisite ragouts and delicious pastries, all in dishes of a sort of rock-crystal. The boys and girls brought several sorts of drinks made of sugar-cane. Most of the guests were merchants and coachmen, all extremely polite,

who asked Cacambo a few questions with the most delicate discretion and answered his in a satisfactory manner.

When the meal was over, Cacambo, like Candide, thought he could pay the reckoning by throwing on the table two of the large pieces of gold he had picked up; the host and hostess laughed until they had to hold their sides. At last they recovered themselves.

"Gentlemen," said the host, "we perceive you are strangers; we are not accustomed to seeing them. Forgive us if we began to laugh when you offered us in payment the stones from our highways. No doubt you have none of the money of this country, but you do not need any to dine here. All the hotels established for the utility of commerce are paid for by the government. You have been ill-entertained here because this is a poor village; but everywhere else you will be received as you deserve to be."

Cacambo explained to Candide all that the host had said, and Candide listened in the same admiration and disorder with which his friend Cacambo interpreted.

"What can this country be," they said to each other, "which is unknown to the rest of the world and where all nature is so different from ours? Probably it is the country where everything is for the best; for there must be one country of that sort. And, in spite of what Dr. Pangloss said, I often noticed that everything went very ill in Westphalia."

Chapter 18

What they saw in the land of Eldorado

Cacambo informed the host of his curiosity, and the host said:

"I am a very ignorant man and am all the better for it; but we have here an old man

---

17. **table d'hôte** (tä'bəl dōt'): a complete meal served at a fixed price.
18. **colibris**: hummingbirds with curved bills, once classified as a separate species.

8 **INFERRING**
Candide calls the children "well brought up" because he thinks that they have been "taught to despise gold and precious stones." What does his statement suggest about his attitude toward money? (He considers a desire for wealth coarse or base.) How might you determine whether Voltaire shares this attitude? (by noting what happens to those in the story who desire and value wealth)

9 **LITERARY ELEMENT**
Satire: The inclusion of wildly improbable situations is one hallmark of satire. Which details make the meal in the inn improbable? (parrot garnishes; a boiled condor weighing 200 pounds; diners who can consume a gargantuan meal)

10 **LITERARY ELEMENT**
Characterization: Candide finally realizes and admits that "in spite of what Dr. Pangloss said . . . everything went very ill in Westphalia." What might this statement suggest about Candide? (He is beginning to lose his naiveté.)

11 COMPARING AND CONTRASTING

How is the description of the wise old man's house in Eldorado similar to the description of the Baron's castle in Westphalia? How is it different? (Both descriptions include details such as doors and furnishings; in the description of the Baron's castle, what is actually mediocre is referred to as if it were dazzling; in the description of the old man's house, what is dazzling is referred to as if it were mediocre.)

12 GUIDED READING

Identifying Details: Why do the people of Eldorado not leave the country? (They have willingly taken an oath to remain in Eldorado.)

13 INTERPRETING

According to the old man, how would Eldorado be endangered if the country were discovered by the rest of the world? (The inhabitants would be wiped out, and the country would be sacked for its gold and jewels.) By Voltaire's time, the treasures of Mexico and Peru had been carried off by conquering Europeans. Many Europeans during the Enlightenment approved of the conquerors' expropriations. How would you characterize Voltaire's attitude toward the European conquests of Mexico and Peru? (disapproval)

> **ingrates** (in'grāts): ungrateful people

who has retired from the court and who is the most learned and most communicative man in the kingdom."

And he at once took Cacambo to the old man. Candide now played only the second part and accompanied his valet.

11 They entered a very simple house, for the door was only of silver and the paneling of the apartments in gold, but so tastefully carved that the richest decorations did not surpass it. The antechamber indeed was only encrusted with rubies and emeralds; but the order with which everything was arranged atoned for this extreme simplicity.

The old man received the two strangers on a sofa padded with colibri feathers, and presented them with drinks in diamond cups; after which he satisfied their curiosity in these words:

"I am a hundred and seventy-two years old and I heard from my late father, the King's equerry,[19] the astonishing revolutions of Peru of which he had been an eyewitness. The kingdom where we now are is the ancient country of the Incas, who most imprudently left it to conquer part of the world and were at last destroyed by the Spaniards.

12 "The princes of their family who remained in their native country had more wisdom; with the consent of the nation, they ordered that no inhabitants should ever leave our little kingdom, and this it is that has preserved our innocence and our felicity. The Spaniards had some vague knowledge of this country, which they called Eldorado,[20] and about a hundred years ago an Englishman

named Raleigh[21] came very near to it; but, since we are surrounded by inaccessible rocks and precipices, we have hitherto been exempt from the rapacity[22] of the nations of Europe who have an inconceivable lust for the pebbles and mud of our land and would kill us to the last man to get possession of them." **13**

The conversation was long; it touched upon the form of the government, manners, women, public spectacles, and the arts. Finally Candide, who was always interested in metaphysics, asked through Cacambo whether the country had a religion. The old man blushed a little.

"How can you doubt it?" said he. "Do you think we are ingrates?"

Cacambo humbly asked what was the religion of Eldorado. The old man blushed again.

"Can there be two religions?" said he. "We have, I think, the religion of everyone else; we adore God from evening until morning."

"Do you adore only one god?" said Cacambo, who continued to act as the interpreter of Candide's doubts.

"Manifestly," said the old man, "there are not two or three or four. I must confess that the people of your world ask very extraordinary questions."

Candide continued to press the old man with questions; he wished to know how they prayed to God in Eldorado.

"We do not pray," said the good and respectable sage, "we have nothing to ask from him; he has given us everything necessary and we continually give him thanks."

Candide was curious to see the priests; and asked where they were. The good old man smiled.

---

19. **equerry** (ek'wər·ē): officer in charge of horses.
20. **Eldorado** (el'də·rä'dō): Spanish for "the Golden Man," after the practice of certain Colombian natives of coating their new kings in gold dust. The name eventually came to refer to any legendary place of spectacular riches.
21. **Raleigh:** Sir Walter Raleigh's *Discovery of Guiana* (1595) helped spread the legend of Eldorado.
22. **rapacity:** greed.

"My friends," said he, "we are all priests; the King and all the heads of families solemnly sing praises every morning, accompanied by five or six thousand musicians."

"What! Have you no monks to teach, to dispute, to govern, to intrigue and to burn people who do not agree with them?"

"For that, we should have to become fools," said the old man; "here we are all of the same opinion and do not understand what you mean with your monks."

At all this Candide was in an ecstasy and said to himself:

"This is very different from Westphalia and the castle of His Lordship the Baron; if our friend Pangloss had seen Eldorado, he would not have said that the castle of Thunder-ten-tronckh was the best of all that exists on the earth; certainly, a man should travel."

After this long conversation the good old man ordered a carriage to be harnessed with six sheep and gave the two travelers twelve of his servants to take them to court.

"You will excuse me," he said, "if my age deprives me of the honor of accompanying you. The King will receive you in a manner which will not displease you and doubtless you will pardon the customs of the country if any of them disconcert you."

Candide and Cacambo entered the carriage; the six sheep galloped off and in less than four hours they reached the King's palace, which was situated at one end of the capital. The portal was two hundred and twenty feet high and a hundred feet wide; it is impossible to describe its material. Anyone can see the prodigious superiority it must have over the pebbles and sand we call gold and gems.

Twenty beautiful maidens of the guard received Candide and Cacambo as they alighted from the carriage, conducted them to the baths and dressed them in robes woven from the down of colibris; after which the principal male and female officers of the Crown led them to his Majesty's apartment through two files of a thousand musicians each, according to the usual custom. As they approached the throne room, Cacambo asked one of the chief officers how they should behave in his Majesty's presence; whether they should fall on their knees or flat on their faces, whether they should put their hands on their heads or on their backsides; whether they should lick the dust of the throne room; in a word, what was the ceremony?

"The custom," said the chief officer, "is to embrace the King and to kiss him on either cheek."

Candide and Cacambo threw their arms round his Majesty's neck; he received them with all imaginable favor and politely asked them to supper.

Meanwhile they were carried to see the town, the public buildings rising to the very skies, the marketplaces ornamented with thousands of columns, the fountains of pure water, the fountains of rose-water and of liquors distilled from sugar-cane, which played continually in the public squares paved with precious stones which emitted a perfume like that of cloves and cinnamon.

Candide asked to see the law courts; he was told there were none, and that nobody ever went to law. He asked if there were prisons and was told there were none. He was still more surprised and pleased by the palace of sciences, where he saw a gallery two thousand feet long, filled with instruments of mathematics and physics.

After they had explored all the afternoon about a thousandth part of the town, they were taken back to the King. Candide sat down to table with his Majesty, his valet

intrigue (in·trēg'): plot or scheme secretly

disconcert (dis'kən·surt'): upset, embarrass, or confuse

14 GUIDED READING
Identifying Details: Which details in the narrative show that women in Eldorado are equal in status to men? (They go to school; they work alongside men in the inn; they make up the castle guard and are some of the principal officers of the Crown.)

15 CULTURAL DIVERSITY
In France during the Enlightenment (as now), friends customarily greeted each other by embracing and kissing both cheeks; this greeting would correspond to a hug or a slap on the back in the United States today.

❓ *What might the preferred greeting of the King of Eldorado reveal about his character?* (Possible response: He has no need for pomp and ceremony; he is warm, rather than haughty and authoritarian.)

16 INFERRING
What might the absence of courts and jails in Eldorado, "the land where everything is for the best," suggest about Voltaire's attitude toward the system of criminal justice of his time? (He thought the system was corrupt.)

18 LITERARY ELEMENT

Exaggeration: What unlikely events occur that enable Candide and Cacambo to leave Eldorado? (Three thousand scientists and engineers work for fourteen days and in that process spend twenty million pounds sterling to make a "machine" that hoists Candide, Cacambo, one hundred two red sheep, and a vast load of provisions and riches over a mountain range ten thousand feet high and ten leagues—about thirty miles—broad.)

ANALYZING

What do you think Voltaire's reasons might be for portraying Eldorado as a fantasy land? (Possible response: He thinks that only in an imaginary world could everything be for the best.)

Cacambo and several ladies. Never was better cheer, and never was anyone wittier at supper than his Majesty. Cacambo explained the King's witty remarks to Candide and even when translated they still appeared witty. Among all the things which amazed Candide, this did not amaze him the least.

They enjoyed this hospitality for a month. Candide repeatedly said to Cacambo:

"Once again, my friend, it is quite true that the castle where I was born cannot be compared with this country; but then Miss Cunegonde is not here and you probably have a mistress in Europe. If we remain here, we shall only be like everyone else; but if we return to our own world with only twelve sheep laden with Eldorado pebbles, we shall be richer than all the kings put together; we shall have no more Inquisitors[23] to fear and we can easily regain Miss Cunegonde."

Cacambo agreed with this; it is so pleasant to be on the move, to show off before friends, to make a parade of the things seen on one's travels, that these two happy men resolved to be so no longer and to ask his Majesty's permission to depart.

"You are doing a very silly thing," said the King. "I know my country is small; but when we are comfortable anywhere we should stay there; I certainly have not the right to detain foreigners, that is a tyranny which does not exist either in our manners or our laws; all men are free, leave when you please, but the way out is very difficult. It is impossible to ascend the rapid river by which you miraculously came here and which flows under arches of rock. The mountains which surround the whole of my kingdom are ten thousand feet high and as perpendicular as rocks; they are more than

ten leagues broad and you can only get down from them by way of precipices. However, since you must go, I will give orders to the directors of machinery to make a machine which will carry you comfortably. When you have been taken to the other side of the mountains, nobody can proceed any farther with you; for my subjects have sworn never to pass this boundary and they are too wise to break their oath. Ask anything else of me you wish."

"We ask nothing of your Majesty," said Cacambo, "except a few sheep laden with provisions, pebbles, and the mud of this country."

The King laughed.

"I cannot understand," said he, "the taste you people of Europe have for our yellow mud; but take as much as you wish, and much good may it do you."

He immediately ordered his engineers to make a machine to hoist these two extraordinary men out of his kingdom.

Three thousand learned scientists worked at it; it was ready in a fortnight and only cost about twenty million pounds sterling in the money of that country. Candide and Cacambo were placed on the machine; there were two large red sheep saddled and bridled for them to ride on when they had passed the mountains, twenty sumpter[24] sheep laden with provisions, thirty carrying presents of the most curious productions of the country and fifty laden with gold, precious stones and diamonds. The King embraced the two vagabonds tenderly.

Their departure was a splendid sight and so was the ingenious manner in which they and their sheep were hoisted on to the top of the mountains.

---

23. **Inquisitors:** members of the Roman Catholic tribunal charged with combating heresy.

24. **sumpter:** used for carrying packs and other loads.

The scientists took leave of them after having landed them safely, and Candide's only desire and object was to go and present Miss Cunegonde with his sheep.

"We have sufficient to pay the governor of Buenos Aires," said he, "if Miss Cunegonde can be bought. Let us go to Cayenne, and take ship, and then we will see what kingdom we will buy."

Chapter 19

What happened to them at Surinam, and how Candide made the acquaintance of Martin

Our two travelers' first day was quite pleasant. They were encouraged by the idea of possessing more treasures than all Asia, Europe and Africa could collect. Candide in transport carved the name of Cunegonde on the trees.

On the second day two of the sheep stuck in a marsh and were swallowed up with their loads; two other sheep died of fatigue a few days later; then seven or eight died of hunger in a desert; several days afterwards others fell off precipices. Finally, after they had traveled for a hundred days, they had only two sheep left. Candide said to Cacambo:

"My friend, you see how perishable are the riches of this world; nothing is steadfast but virtue and the happiness of seeing Miss Cunegonde again."

19

The Cleveland Museum of Art, John L. Severance Fund, 71.102

THE KISS OF PEACE AND JUSTICE, LAURENT DE LA HYRE (1606–1656).
❓ *Does justice exist in Voltaire's world?*

The highly lucrative slave trade flourished during the 1700s. The authors of some history books convey the idea that only a few people in the Western world were aware of the slave trade at first and that as soon as more people became aware of it, the slave trade was stopped. How does Candide's encounter with the Negro show that conclusion to be unwarranted? (Voltaire's inclusion of the encounter reveals his perception that his readers were aware of the slave trade. This fact implies that it was not the lack of awareness but apathy and greed that allowed the slave trade to continue.)

20 LITERARY ELEMENT
Plot: Candide's conversation with the Negro is the turning point of the story. What realization does Candide come to after seeing the mutilation of the Negro and listening to his story? (that it is insane to maintain that everything is fine when racism, torture, and so many other evils exist)

■ **HUMANITIES CONNECTION** ■

One of the best portrait painters of his age, Aved moved away from stiff formality in search of a kind of inner truth. Most of his subjects were from the bourgeoisie. Jean-Gabriel de La Porte du Theil was a foreign affairs commissioner who had just played a prominent part in devising a treaty that gave Lorraine to France. ■

"I admit it," said Cacambo, "but we still have two sheep with more treasures than ever the King of Spain will have, and in the distance I see a town I suspect is Surinam,[25] which belongs to the Dutch. We are at the end of our troubles and the beginning of our happiness."

As they drew near the town they met a Negro lying on the ground wearing only half his clothes, that is to say, a pair of blue cotton drawers; this poor man had no left leg and no right hand.

"Good Heavens!" said Candide to him in Dutch, "what are you doing there, my friend, in this horrible state?"

"I am waiting for my master, the famous merchant Mr. Vanderdendur."

"Was it Mr. Vanderdendur," said Candide, "who treated you in this way?"

"Yes, sir," said the Negro, "it is the custom. We are given a pair of cotton drawers twice a year as clothing. When we work in the sugar-mills and the grindstone catches our fingers, they cut off the hand; when we try to run away, they cut off a leg. Both these things happened to me. This is the price paid for the sugar you eat in Europe. But when my mother sold me for ten patagons[26] on the coast of Guinea, she said to me: 'My dear child, give thanks to our fetishes,[27] always worship them, and they will make you happy; you have the honor to be a slave of our lords the white men and thereby you have made the fortune of your father and mother.' Alas! I do not know whether I made their fortune, but they certainly did not make mine. Dogs, monkeys, and parrots are

---

25. **Surinam** (soor'i·näm'): former Dutch colony in South America.
26. **patagons:** units of money used in Patagonia, in southern South America.
27. **fetishes:** sacred objects believed to possess magical powers.

a thousand times less miserable than we are; the Dutch fetishes who converted me tell me every Sunday that we are all of us, whites and blacks, the children of Adam. I am not a genealogist, but if these preachers tell the truth, we are all second cousins. Now, you will admit that no one could treat his relatives in a more horrible way."

"O Pangloss!" cried Candide. "This is an abomination you had not guessed; this is too much, in the end I shall have to renounce optimism."

"What is optimism?" said Cacambo.

"Alas!" said Candide, "it is the mania of maintaining that everything is well when we are wretched."

PORTRAIT OF JEAN-GABRIEL LA PORTE DU THEIL, JACQUES AVED, 1740.

And he shed tears as he looked at his Negro; and he entered Surinam weeping.

The first thing they inquired was whether there was any ship in the port which could be sent to Buenos Aires. The person they addressed happened to be a Spanish captain, who offered to strike an honest bargain with them. He arranged to meet them at an inn. Candide and the faithful Cacambo went and waited for him with their two sheep.

Candide, who blurted everything out, told the Spaniard all his adventures and confessed that he wanted to elope with Miss Cunegonde.

"I shall certainly not take you to Buenos Aires," said the captain. "I should be hanged and you would too. The fair Cunegonde is his Lordship's favorite mistress."

Candide was thunderstruck; he sobbed for a long time; then he took Cacambo aside.

"My dear friend," said he, "this is what you must do. We each have in our pockets five or six million pounds' worth of diamonds; you are more skillful than I am; go to Buenos Aires and get Miss Cunegonde. If the governor makes any difficulties give him a million; if he is still obstinate give him two; you have not killed an Inquisitor, so they will not suspect you. I will fit out another ship, I will go and wait for you at Venice; it is a free country where there is nothing to fear from Bulgarians, Abares, Jews, or Inquisitors."

Cacambo applauded this wise resolution; he was in despair at leaving a good master who had become his intimate friend; but the pleasure of being useful to him overcame the grief of leaving him. They embraced with tears. Candide urged him not to forget the good old woman. Cacambo set off that very same day; he was a very good man, this Cacambo.

Candide remained some time longer at Surinam waiting for another captain to take him to Italy with the two sheep he had left. He engaged servants and bought everything necessary for a long voyage. At last Mr. Vanderdendur, the owner of a large ship, came to see him.

"How much do you want," he asked this man, "to take me straight to Venice with my servants, my baggage, and these two sheep?"

The captain asked for ten thousand piasters.[28] Candide did not hesitate.

"Oh! Ho!" said the prudent Vanderdendur to himself, "this foreigner gives ten thousand piasters immediately! He must be very rich."

He returned a moment afterwards and said he could not sail for less than twenty thousand.

"Very well, you shall have them," said Candide.

"Whew!" said the merchant to himself, "this man gives twenty thousand piasters as easily as ten thousand."

He came back again, and said he could not take him to Venice for less than thirty thousand piasters.

"Then you shall have thirty thousand," replied Candide.

"Oho!" said the Dutch merchant to himself again, "thirty thousand piasters is nothing to this man; obviously the two sheep are laden with immense treasures; I will not insist any further; first let me make him pay the thirty thousand piasters, and then we will see."

Candide sold two little diamonds, the smaller of which was worth more than all the money the captain asked. He paid him in advance. The two sheep were taken on board. Candide followed in a little boat to join the ship which rode at anchor; the captain watched his time, set his sails and weighed anchor; the wind was favorable.

28. **piasters:** units of money.

---

21 SYNTHESIZING
Candide fears the "Bulgarians" and the "Abares" (the Prussians and the French) because of his suffering at the hands of both in the war modeled on the Seven Years' War. Similarly, he fears the agents of the Inquisition because after he discovered that Cunegonde had been sold to the Grand Inquisitor, he killed that high official and fled to South America. *What parallel does Voltaire draw between war and religious or racial persecution?* (Possible response: He points out that both spawn atrocities.)

22 PREDICTING
Vanderdendur raises his price as soon as he sees that Candide is willing to pay an exorbitant amount for the journey. What do you predict Vanderdendur will do next? On what do you base your prediction? (Remembering that Vanderdendur is the one who treated the Negro so abominably, students should predict that he will do something unethical.)

23 GUIDED READING

Finding the Main Idea: Which adjectives would you use to describe the Dutch judge? (Possible responses: self-serving, greedy, unconcerned, dishonest) If you think that this incident shows Voltaire's views of the European legal system of his day, how would you state his views? (He sees it as corrupt and lacking in compassion.)

24 ANALYZING

Why do his encounters with Vanderdendur and the Dutch judge so upset Candide? (Possible response: Both men seem uncaring, as if they had no grudge against Candide personally but were acting out of general misanthropy. The incidents make Candide aware of "the malevolence of men.") Do you think that Voltaire agrees with Candide? Why or why not? (Students should observe that Candide has been bombarded with the malevolence of human beings since he left the Baron's castle.)

HUMANITIES CONNECTION

In the seventeenth century, New World scenes were much in demand in Europe. Peeters painted several other New World scenes, including *The Landing of Columbus in America*, but there is no evidence that he ever crossed the ocean. He seems to have based his work on travelers' reports and sketches by other artists. ∎

DUTCH MEN-OF-WAR IN THE WEST INDIES, BONAVENTURA PEETERS (1614–1652).

Wadsworth Atheneum, Hartford, Ella Gallup Sumner and Mary Catlin Sumner Collection

Candide, bewildered and stupefied, soon lost sight of him.

"Alas!" he cried, "this is a trick worthy of the old world."

He returned to shore, in grief; for he had lost enough to make the fortune of twenty kings.

He went to the Dutch judge; and, as he was rather disturbed, he knocked loudly at the door; he went in, related what had happened and talked a little louder than he ought to have done. The judge began by fining him ten thousand piasters for the noise he had made; he then listened patiently to him, promised to look into his affair as soon as the merchant returned, and charged him another ten thousand piasters for the expenses of the audience.

This behavior reduced Candide to despair; he had indeed endured misfortunes a thousand times more painful; but the calmness of the judge and of the captain who had robbed him, stirred up his bile[29] and plunged him into a black melancholy. The malevolence of men revealed itself to his mind in all its ugliness; he entertained only gloomy ideas. At last a French ship was about to leave for Bordeaux[30] and, since he no longer had any sheep laden with diamonds to put on board, he hired a cabin at a reasonable price and announced throughout the town that he would give the passage, food and

29. **bile:** bodily fluid once believed to cause bitterness of spirit or melancholy.
30. **Bordeaux** (bôr·dō'): a port city in southwest France, located in the region of the same name.

1. Where was Candide raised? (in West-phalia, in the castle of Baron Thunder-ten-tronckh)
2. What was Candide taught by Pangloss? (that everything has a purpose and is for the best)
3. Who is Mademoiselle Cunegonde? (the Baron's daughter, with whom Candide is in love)
4. Why did Candide leave home? (He was caught caressing Cunegonde and was kicked out of the castle.)
5. What do the men in blue offer Candide? (a free dinner and some money)
6. Who is Cacambo? (a footman who attends Candide in South America)
7. How does Candide get to Eldorado? (In a canoe that is swept through a long river tunnel and over rapids; he then crawls several miles.)
8. What color are the sheep of Eldorado? (red)
9. Why does Candide weep as he enters Surinam? (He is saddened by the abominable treatment of the Negro.)
10. What is Candide doing at the end of the story? (cultivating a garden with those whom he loves and respects)

two thousand piasters to an honest man who would make the journey with him, on condition that this man was the most unfortunate and the most disgusted with his condition in the whole province.

Such a crowd of applicants arrived that a fleet would not have contained them. Candide, wishing to choose among the most likely, picked out twenty persons who seemed reasonably sociable and who all claimed to deserve his preference. He collected them in a tavern and gave them supper, on condition that each took an oath to relate truthfully the story of his life, promising that he would choose the man who seemed to him the most deserving of pity and to have the most cause for being discontented with his condition, and that he would give the others a little money.

The sitting lasted until four o'clock in the morning. As Candide listened to their adventures he remembered what the old woman had said on the voyage to Buenos Aires and how she had wagered that there was nobody on the boat who had not experienced very great misfortunes. At each story which was told him, he thought of Pangloss.

"This Pangloss," said he, "would have some difficulty in supporting his system. I wish he were here. Certainly, if everything is well, it is only in Eldorado and not in the rest of the world."

He finally determined in favor of a poor man of letters who had worked ten years for the booksellers at Amsterdam. He judged that there was no occupation in the world which could more disgust a man. | **25**

This man of letters,[31] who was also a good man, had been robbed by his wife, beaten by his son, and abandoned by his daughter, who had eloped with a Portuguese. He had just been deprived of a small post on which he depended and the preachers of Surinam were persecuting him because they thought he was a Socinian.[32]

It must be admitted that the others were at least as unfortunate as he was; but Candide hoped that this learned man would help to pass the time during the voyage. All his other rivals considered that Candide was doing them a great injustice; but he soothed them down by giving each of them a hundred piasters.

With Martin to counsel him, Candide finds his way back to Europe, where little by little he loses the rest of his fortune from Eldorado. Eventually, he is reunited with Cunegonde as well as Cacambo, Pangloss, and the old woman. Candide marries Cunegonde, even though she has by now grown horribly ugly. With their companions, they retire to a little farm, where they learn to work together to cultivate a garden in the hope of making life bearable. | **26**

31. **man of letters:** a term used to refer to a writer or scholar; here, Martin.
32. **Socinian:** a heretic, follower of the sixteenth-century Polish theologian Socinus, whose "rational" Christianity, among other things, denied the divinity of Christ.

25 HISTORICAL BACKGROUND
Voltaire lambastes "the booksellers at Amsterdam" because pirated editions of his books had been published in Holland. He resented this unethical practice because he got no royalties from the sales of those unauthorized editions.

READER'S RESPONSE
Do you think that Voltaire overdoes his criticism of philosophical optimism and exaggerates the prevalence of evil in the world? Or do you think that repetition and exaggeration are necessary to make his points? Explain your response.

26 LITERARY ELEMENT
Theme: How has Candide changed over the course of his quest, and what kinds of lessons has he learned? (He has lost his naiveté; he has learned of the suffering experienced by people throughout the world and of the evil that is harbored in the hearts of human beings.) Formulate one or more of the lessons that Candide has learned into a statement of one of the themes of the selection. (Possible response: There is much that is evil in the world, and people must try to confront it rather than ignore it.) What theme does the last sentence indicate? (Work is the antidote to man's unhappy lot.)

To reteach the excerpt from *Candide*, have students create a travel guide based on Candide's experiences. Under headings such as "Westphalia," "Bulgaria," "Portugal," "Eldorado," and "Surinam," students should list kinds of accommodations, places and people of interest, and cautions for unwary travelers. They should use details from *Candide* to complete each listing. Encourage them to use their sense of humor.

Play for students musical works by Bach, Vivaldi, Mozart, and Haydn. Show slides or illustrations of fine art by Watteau, Boucher, and Canaletto and of rococo architecture and decoration. Then guide students in choosing from these artworks and musical compositions of the period examples that could accompany excerpts from *Candide*.

Ask students to list the forms of injustice and fuzzy thinking that Voltaire assailed (racism and intolerance; oppressive governments and legal systems; violations ranging from torture and slavery to the pirating of published works; general naiveté and apathy). Then ask which have been remedied and which are still serious problems today. Finally, ask students to cite contemporary examples of satire and humor used as devices for reform. ■

ANSWERS

First Thoughts
Answers will vary.

Identifying Facts
1. He kisses and caresses Cunegonde.
2. He was conscripted against his will, beaten, tortured, jailed, and sent to wage war.
3. no injustice, strife, or sorrow. They are seen as mud and stones.
4. He wants to see Cunegonde and to be wealthy.
5. The merchant sails off with Candide's riches. The judge fines Candide, collects a fat fee, and then ignores Candide's grievances.
6. He hopes Martin will be interesting.

Interpreting Meanings
1. Answers will vary.
2. cruelty and natural forces
3. Organized religion is unnecessary, government should serve the people, and a love of wealth corrupts.
4. greed and malevolence
5. "[It] is the mania of maintaining that everything is well when we are wretched." Answers will vary.

Applying Meanings
Answers will vary.

Critical Writing Response
Analyzing an Author's Use of Humor. Each essay should include a statement of purpose and an explanation.

Creative Writing Response
Writing a Satire. Skits should contain clear story lines. ■

▤ First Thoughts
Do you feel sympathy for Candide, or do you think he deserves everything he gets?

Identifying Facts
1. What does Candide do to get himself expelled from the Baron's castle?
2. What happens to Candide among the Bulgarians?
3. Briefly describe the main characteristics of Eldorado. What value do the inhabitants place on gold and gems?
4. What reasons does Candide give for wanting to leave Eldorado and return to his own world?
5. Explain how "the prudent Vanderdendur" and the Dutch judge trick Candide.
6. Why does Candide ultimately select Martin—"a poor man of letters"—to be his traveling companion?

Interpreting Meanings
1. **Satire**, or writing that ridicules human shortcomings in order to improve society, relies on many elements usually associated with comedy—exaggeration, understatement, warped logic, and improbable situations. Using these four elements as headings, list as many examples of each as you can find in the selection.
2. As Chapter 2 illustrates, Candide suffers every time he exercises what he believes to be his free will. What forces does Voltaire suggest get in the way of a person's exercise of free will?
3. From Voltaire's description of Eldorado, what can you infer are his views on organized religion, on the proper role of government, and on wealth?
4. From the contrast he draws between Eldorado and Surinam, what does Voltaire imply are the causes of evil in the world?
5. The character of Candide is used to reflect Voltaire's attitudes both directly and by contrast. Which of Candide's statements do you think most closely expresses Voltaire's personal definition of optimism? Do you agree with Voltaire's view? Explain.

Applying Meanings
Voltaire wrote *Candide* more than 230 years ago. In your opinion, how well has its satire aged? What value, if any, does *Candide* hold for someone growing up in today's world?

Critical Writing Response
Analyzing an Author's Use of Humor. Few readers would deny that Voltaire's writing in *Candide* is savagely witty. But is his humor intended merely to amuse, or does it have a more serious purpose? (Why, for example, do you suppose we find ourselves laughing *at* Voltaire's characters and never *with* them?) Write an essay in which you explain how Voltaire uses humor in *Candide* and how it enables him to fulfill his purpose.

Creative Writing Response
Writing a Satire. Working alone or with a partner, write a short skit in which you satirize a public folly. First, choose a well-known subject and identify the folly that you feel needs to be reformed. Next, devise an improbable situation that will expose the folly. Use exaggeration, understatement, and warped logic to create satiric humor. Remember, your purpose is to promote social reform.

ELEMENTS OF LITERATURE

The Utopia as a Literary Genre

The word *utopia* (yōō·tō′pē·ə) is derived from Greek and means "no place." Sir Thomas More was the first to employ this word for a literary genre when he wrote his famous book *Utopia* (1516), an account of an imaginary republic. He fully intended a pun on the Greek word *eutopia,* which means "place (where all is) well."

The idea of an imaginary earthly paradise goes back to antiquity. Elements of it can be found in the Mesopotamian classic *Gilgamesh* (see page 136), as well as in Homer's descriptions of the Elysian Fields in the *Odyssey.* Plato's *Republic* was the first full-fledged description of a utopia, though of a distinctly Spartan and authoritarian type. Within medieval Christianity itself, and especially after St. Augustine, the attainment of a heavenly city was considered a perfectly reasonable objective.

The main impulse in utopian literature is to imagine a social and political order free of the cruelties and corruptions of the existing order. More's *Utopia,* for example, retains some of Plato's authoritarianism and incorporates the harsh moral codes of More's own time, but its welfare state is socialistic in character, with its abolition of private property and its free universal education, medicine, food, and the like. Voltaire's Eldorado, the city of gold where gold has no monetary value, is essentially in More's tradition.

Countless literary utopias were explored in the seventeenth and eighteenth centuries. Much later, H. G. Wells, the author of *A Modern Utopia,* among many other books of this type, became perhaps the most interesting writer of this genre in the present century. The popularity of utopian literature has produced its opposite as well, the **dystopia,** or anti-utopia, which portrays an imaginary world of pure horror. Aldous Huxley's *Brave New World* and George Orwell's *Animal Farm* and *Nineteen Eighty-four* are examples of this counter-genre. Much of science fiction, we might note, hovers between the utopian and the anti-utopian.

If, as Candide concludes, everything is well "only in Eldorado," why do you suppose he does not try to return there? In other words, what ironic point is Voltaire making by having his hero end up with an ugly wife on a little farm where he does nothing more earth-shattering than cultivate a garden?

COMPARING LITERATURE

Though Eldorado is a form of utopia, the real world described by Voltaire in *Candide* is closer to a *dystopia.* In *The Metamorphosis* (pp. 1155–1195), Franz Kafka creates another near-dystopic world. How is the world in which Gregor Samsa lives similar to the world that Candide lives in? (Both worlds are presided over by unreasonable authorities who are devoid of compassion.)

DISCUSSING THEME

Voltaire thinks that a utopian life is not possible and that the closest that one can come to living a relatively good life is to perform one's work faithfully and to care for one's family and friends. ■

Molière: The playwright Molière was born Jean Baptiste Poquelin in Paris, where his father was an upholsterer for King Louis XIII. Around the age of twenty-five, young Jean Baptiste joined a traveling theater troupe in the tradition of the commedia dell'arte. The troupe's reputation grew, and eventually its members were invited to play before "Sun King" Louis XIV, who granted them his patronage. It was around this time that young Poquelin took the name Molière. He was both an actor and a playwright, and he won increasing acclaim, so that the King eventually gave him a theater of his own. Many of Molière's works were highly controversial. His *Tartuffe, or The Imposter,* for example, offered such scathing portrayals of religious hypocrites that it offended the Church, and the King was forced to ban it.

COMPARING LITERATURE

Students interested in drama might enjoy reading, or viewing a performance of, one of Molière's comedies and reporting on it to the class. They might also compare the humor in Molière's dramas with that in Voltaire's fiction (see *Candide,* pp. 945–962). Both authors employ exaggeration, satire, and *deus ex machina* conclusions (conclusions in which hopeless situations are miraculously sorted out).

BEHIND THE SCENES

Drama in the Enlightenment

Although Renaissance playwrights such as Shakespeare produced a variety of types of plays—comedies, histories, tragedies, and romances—comedy was the form that flourished in the Enlightenment. During this period, writers were concerned with style, wit, and, above all, a rational approach to life. Comedy, by its very nature, tests the rationality of society's norms. Many comic plots dramatize a leading character's temporary departure from such norms, eventually followed by a "return" to society.

In France, the leading comic dramatist was Molière (mōl·yer') (1622–1673). Molière brilliantly succeeded at combining the grace, wit, and elegance of **high comedy**—derived from the ancient Roman tradition of Plautus and Terence—with the slapstick of the commedia dell'arte (kôm·me'dyä del lär'te), a form that was highly popular in seventeenth-century France. After a long period of apprenticeship in the provinces, Molière returned to Paris in 1658 to perform for King Louis XIV, who became his chief patron.

The central characters in Molière's plays suffer from obsessions such as greed in *The Miser,* social status in *The Would-Be Gentleman,* religious hypocrisy in *Tartuffe,* or relentless honesty in *The Misanthrope.* Molière satirizes the extreme natures of these characters, exploiting their comic potential.

Molière and the Comedy of Manners

Because of Molière's keen psychological insight into the manners and mannerisms of his characters, his plays are often said to be the first examples of the **comedy of manners**. The focus of this kind of comedy is on the customs, social class, costume, speech, and gestures of the characters, who are usually drawn from society's middle or upper classes. Comedies of manners usually feature a love plot in which two young people conquer all obstacles to their union—often posed by their curmudgeonly elders—and marry at the end of the play. Some comedies of manners, like Molière's, satirize the behavior of their leading characters, but many rely on the wit and sophistication of their subjects to entertain and amuse the audience.

At about the same time Molière was transforming theater in France, political forces were shaping a new theater in England. In 1642, a civil war between the Puritans, led by Oliver Cromwell, and the supporters of King Charles I rocked England. The Puritans, who eventually defeated the King's forces and beheaded Charles, closed all theaters in England. In 1660, Parliament invited Charles II to return from his exile in France, and the monarchy was restored. The new king, who was especially fond of plays, lost no time in ordering the reopening of the theaters. Thus was born the Restoration Period.

Restoration Drama in England

Several playwrights led the development of **Restoration drama**, which produced mainly witty—and often satirical—comedies of manners. George Etherege (eth'ər·ij) (c. 1635?–1692?) produced only

Molière in the role of Arnolphe in *École des femmes (School for Wives)*. Lithograph by Delpech.

Giraudon/Art Resource, New York

In the eighteenth century, two playwrights, Oliver Goldsmith (1730–1774) and Richard B. Sheridan (1750–1816), had outstanding success in combining elements of the comedy of manners with satire. Goldsmith triumphed with *She Stoops to Conquer* (1773). The best known of Sheridan's plays is probably *The School for Scandal*, which delighted London audiences even as British troops were attempting to stifle the rebellion of the American colonies.

Innovations in Staging

Drama of the Enlightenment developed a number of theatrical innovations that we now take for granted. In Restoration England, for example, plays were performed in enclosed theaters, as opposed to the semi-open-air playhouses of Elizabethan times. This meant that artificial lighting became an important aspect of stage production for the first time. Restoration playhouses also featured the proscenium (prō·sē'nē·əm) arch stage, consisting of a raised platform enclosed above by an arch behind which a curtain could be drawn. Modern departures from the conventional proscenium stage—such as the theater-in-the-round—still tend to be regarded as rather daring, experimental stagings.

Finally, English Restoration drama gave birth to the career of actresses. For the first time, women could play female parts (these had been taken by boys in Shakespeare's era). King Charles II himself, who acquired the nickname of the ''Merry Monarch,'' was pleased by this shift, making no attempt to disguise his fondness for one of the leading actresses of the Restoration theater, Nell Gwyn.

three plays, but these satirical comedies had an important role in setting the tone for drama of the age. Etherege's best play was *The Man of Mode* (1676), which made fun of the affected manners of upper-class courtiers.

William Wycherley (wich'ər·lē) (1640–1716) also satirized phoniness and hypocrisy in comedies such as *The Country Wife* (1675) and *The Plain Dealer* (1676). But it was only in the plays of William Congreve (1670–1729) that the barbed satire of Restoration comedy was tempered by a strain of tolerance and good humor. Critics have often praised Congreve's *The Way of the World* (1700) as the masterpiece of this period.

LITERARY BACKGROUND

Oliver Goldsmith: The writer Oliver Goldsmith was raised in modest circumstances in rural Ireland. During his student days at Trinity College, Dublin, he caroused, gambled, and was a general ne'er-do-well. He started writing to earn money after failed attempts at careers in religion, law, and medicine. Left disfigured by a childhood case of smallpox, Goldsmith has been described as ugly, awkward, stammering, vain, and ridiculous. Yet Goldsmith's comedies, poems, and essays, and his novel *The Vicar of Wakefield* reveal that, as a writer, he had great versatility and grace.

LITERARY BACKGROUND

Richard B. Sheridan: Sheridan was the son of an Irish actor. His career as a playwright was brief—he wrote the first of his four plays at twenty-four and the last at twenty-eight—but impressive, for all his plays were great popular successes and are now considered classics. For years he owned and managed London's Theatre Royal, Drury Lane, while pursuing a successful career in politics. He was ruined financially, however, when the theater burned in 1809. Four years later he lost his seat in Parliament and was arrested for debt. In 1816, as he lay dying, a bailiff representing his creditors stood by his bed.

1 HISTORICAL BACKGROUND

Printing in China: The date of the earliest known printed book is authenticated by an inscription in Chinese characters: "Printed on May 11, 868, by Wang Chieh, for free general distribution, in order in deep reverence to perpetuate the memory of his parents." The first printer to use movable type was Pi Sheng, whose work dates from between A.D. 1041 and 1049, about 400 years before Gutenberg's Bible. His type was made of an amalgam of clay and glue that he hardened by baking.

2 HISTORICAL BACKGROUND

Printing in Europe: The earliest known document printed from movable type is a letter of indulgence issued by Pope Nicholas V, printed by Gutenberg in 1454.

HUMANITIES CONNECTION

Almost 300 copies of the Bible were printed by Gutenberg, of which 45 still exist, most of them owned by various libraries. They are extremely valuable. Some pages have elaborate initial letters and other artwork (known as "illumination") done by hand in the traditional way with colored inks.

? *Why do you suppose Gutenberg made his Bible look as if it had been copied by hand?* (perhaps because he did not want his invention widely known) ■

LANGUAGE
— AND —
CULTURE

THE PRINT REVOLUTION

Who Really *Invented Printing?*

Many people at many different times contributed to the invention of printing. Four thousand years before Christ, the Babylonians stamped soft clay with engraved seals. About 175 B.C., the Chinese engraved stone blocks and made paper copies by rubbing. In A.D. 868, the Chinese produced the oldest existing printed book, made by pressing blank paper to carved wooden blocks. About the same time, Arabic block printing was coming into use in Egypt. In 1405, printing technology in Asia took a giant leap forward in Korea, where artisans cast a bronze movable type. Movable type revolutionized printing. Now, instead of carving a new block for each page of text, printers could rearrange individual characters to create different pages of type.

Europeans got the idea of movable type at the same time, around 1440, but without knowing about the Korean invention. Credit for the invention of movable type in Europe is usually given to Johann Gutenberg, a German. Before Gutenberg's invention, European books were made almost exclusively in monasteries. Many monks, called scribes, would simultaneously hand copy what another monk read aloud. Gutenberg's innovation would make this painstaking process obsolete. Between 1450 and 1455, using a press modeled after a wine press, lead type cast in bronze molds, and traditional pen and ink combined with linseed oil,

Pages from the Gutenberg Bible.

Harry Ransom Humanities Research Center, The University of Texas at Austin

From the Renaissance to the Enlightenment

2 he produced a two-volume Bible. He worked slowly, printing only about twenty impressions an hour. Gutenberg's venture was financed by a **3** wealthy goldsmith named Johann Fust. Unfortunately, Gutenberg could not repay his debt, and Fust seized his equipment.

Printing in the Renaissance

Over the next few decades, many developments occurred in the new printing technology. Since Germans at the time were using Gothic script, which resembles a series of heavy vertical lines, distinguished by dots, dashes, and lighter connecting lines, the first type was cut to look like Gothic handwriting. Unfortunately, Gothic type was almost as much work to read as it was to print. In 1470, Nicholas Jenson designed a much more readable ''roman'' type that is still used today. The first printed newspaper, called the *Gazetta* after the coin paid for one copy, appeared in 1536 in Venice. By the 1570s, printers were able to produce five hundred sheets a day, and apprentice printers in France were complaining that their working days (from 2 A.M. to 8 P.M.) were too long.

One of the first effects of the new technology was increased censorship, for printing threatened the Church's traditional monopoly over knowledge. A printer had to obtain a license from the government authorities for each printed item. But there were many secret presses, and the Reformation kept them humming, producing a constant flow of documents that were not Church-approved. Another change caused by printing was the standardization of European languages. People

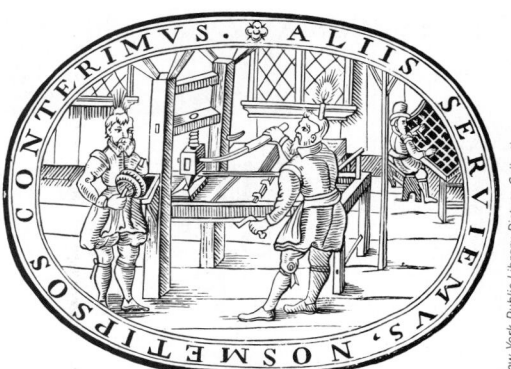

English print office.

New York Public Library Picture Collection

from the same country often used many different words to mean the same thing. In fifteenth-century England, for instance, people could not agree whether to use the word *egg* or *eyren*. Variations like these caused inconsistencies in the printers' texts and slowed the printing process. The need for dictionaries showing standardized spellings became urgent. In 1604, Robert Cawdrey, a schoolmaster, compiled the first English dictionary, *The Table Alphabeticall of Hard Words.*

Perhaps the most important outcome of the new technology was the spread of literacy among ordinary people. During the Middle Ages, books belonged to the privileged few and most people could not read. But during the sixteenth century printed books became cheap and plentiful. More and more people learned to read. Books on such subjects as arithmetic, anatomy, and history were read and discussed, and information that once might have belonged only to a few now was available to anyone who could read. In the few short decades since Gutenberg's invention, printing had transformed Europe.

3 HISTORICAL BACKGROUND
Gutenberg: We have few details about Gutenberg's life. After seizing the presses, Johann Fust printed other books with the help of one of Gutenberg's assistants. Gutenberg himself apparently continued to print elsewhere. He probably died in 1468. No books bearing his name have survived, and there are no authentic portraits of him.

CULTURAL DIVERSITY
Printing in England: Printing was carried on throughout Europe by German printers producing books in Latin. England's first printer, William Caxton (c. 1422–1491), learned his craft in Germany. In 1475 he printed the first book in English, his own translation of a popular medieval romance. He published ninety-six books in all, among them the work of Chaucer and other poets. About one-third of Caxton's output was his translations of famous literary works. For further research, invite students to prepare reports on William Caxton and Wynkyn de Worde, his disciple.

HUMANITIES CONNECTION

The manually operated presses in early printing offices made printing a laborious process. *Compare and contrast early print offices with modern printing plants.* (Possible response: Computer typesetters and four-color printing presses can speedily produce massive volumes of printed material.) ∎

A past participle is a verb form used in conjunction with a *helping verb*, usually a form of *to be* or *to have*. The passive voice uses the past participle with a form of *to be*:

*La Fontaine **was made** a member of the French Academy.*

Both the active voice and the passive voice use *to have* with the past participle to form the perfect tense:

ACTIVE: *People **have called** La Fontaine immoral.*

PASSIVE: *La Fontaine **has been called** immoral.*

With regular verbs, the past participle adds (e)d to the verb stem: *exiled, called.* With irregular verbs, the past participle takes a variety of forms: *brought* (bring), *mistaken* (mistake), *flung* (fling).

ANSWERS TO EXERCISE 1: CHOOSING THE ACTIVE VOICE

1. a) was appointed; b) appointed—active voice
2. a) captured—active; b) was captured
3. a) praises—active; b) is praised
4. a) has read—active; b) have been read
5. a) is mentioned; b) mentions—active
6. a) make—active; b) is made
7. a) advises, happens—active; b) is advised—passive, happens—active
8. a) retells—active; b) are retold
9. a) was painted; b) painted—active
10. a) was established; b) established—active

Language Skills

USING ACTIVE AND PASSIVE VOICES EFFECTIVELY

"English," observes author Roger Garrison, "is a cause-and-effect language." With its noun-verb format, English focuses on who did what. To ensure that your writing is direct and clear, keep verbs in the active voice.

Active and Passive Voices

Voice, like tense, is a characteristic of verbs. Verbs can be in the **active** or the **passive** voice. Verbs in the passive voice can blur the focus. Sentences with verbs in the passive tell what happened, but not who did it. For this reason, overusing the passive makes your writing seem vague or evasive.

PASSIVE VOICE
Voltaire *was exiled* for his writings.

ACTIVE VOICE
The kings of France and Prussia *exiled* Voltaire for his writings.

The passive consists of a form of "to be" and a past participle.

Notice that, in the examples above, the first sentence does not tell who exiled Voltaire. From the Renaissance through modern times, writers have used the passive to conceal responsibility for unpopular actions.

Some sentences using the passive have extra phrases to show who or what performs the action.

PASSIVE
Laura *is admired* from afar by Petrarch.

ACTIVE
Petrarch *admires* Laura from afar.

Though the first sentence does specify who admires Laura, it is unnecessarily wordy and indirect.

Exercise 1: Choosing the Active Voice

Underline the verb in each sentence. Then, for each set, circle the sentence whose verb is in the active voice.

1. a. Petrarch was appointed poet laureate of Italy.
   b. The king of Italy appointed Petrarch poet laureate.
2. a. Barbary pirates captured Cervantes.
   b. Cervantes was captured by Barbary pirates.
3. a. In his sonnets, Shakespeare praises love.
   b. In Shakespeare's sonnets, love is praised.
4. a. Don Quixote has read the medieval epics of the Cid and Roland.
   b. The medieval epics of the Cid and Roland have been read by Don Quixote.
5. a. In *The Tempest*, a "sea change" is mentioned in Ariel's song.

b. Ariel's song in *The Tempest* mentions a "sea change."

6. a. The rats make a decision to bell the cat.
   b. The decision to bell the cat is made by the rats.

7. a. Pangloss advises Candide that everything happens for the best.
   b. Candide is advised that everything happens for the best.

8. a. La Fontaine retells several fables attributed to Aesop.
   b. Several fables attributed to Aesop are retold by La Fontaine.

9. a. The *Mona Lisa* was painted by Leonardo da Vinci.
   b. Leonardo da Vinci painted the *Mona Lisa*.

10. a. Boccaccio's literary reputation was established by the *Decameron*.
    b. The *Decameron* established Boccaccio's literary reputation.

Uses of the Active and Passive Voices

In a few situations, you may use the passive voice. Writers sometimes choose the passive when they do not know who or what performs an action.

PASSIVE   Candide *had been robbed*.
ACTIVE   The captain *had robbed* Candide.

You might write the first sentence if you did not know who had robbed Candide. Writers can also use the passive to create emphasis. In the examples above, the first sentence emphasizes the word *robbed* by placing it last. In most situations, however, choose the active voice. It will keep your writing concise and straightforward.

Exercise 2: Using Active and Passive Voices

Write an original sentence for each situation outlined below. After your sentence, write *A* or *P* to indicate whether you have used the active or the passive voice. Be prepared to give reasons for your choices.

1. You want to summarize Ronsard's message to Hélène: One day, she will be overtaken by old age. She will then be filled with regret for spurning Ronsard.

2. You want to convey the fact that, although Cervantes was plagued by debt throughout his life, his writing was not hindered by his financial difficulties.

3. You want readers to understand that, near the beginning of *The Tempest*, a shipwreck occurs. You do not remember what wrecks the ship.

4. You want to communicate two ideas: 1) that *The Tempest* is filled with fantasy and romance, and 2) that several serious purposes are served by the fantasy and romance.

5. You want to define **satire** and give an example of satire from *Candide*.

Critical Thinking and Writing

RESOLVING A CONTROVERSY

The Renaissance and the Enlightenment were not vastly different from our own time. Breakthroughs in science and thinking had changed the world, just as they have today. As a result, people strove for social and political reforms, just as we do today. Think of modern reforms you and your friends would like to see. In your school, your community, the nation, or the world, which things are most in need of change?

Writing Assignment

Write an informative essay in which you analyze a controversial problem and propose a solution to it. Assume that your audience has not explored the problem in detail. For this assignment, you will examine two sides of an issue, taking both into account to devise a solution.

Background

Sometimes pointing out a problem is the first step toward resolving it. Cervantes' humor exposes the public's shallow tastes. Voltaire and La Fontaine use satire to spotlight hypocrisy and corruption. Reflect on the issues these writers deal with. Then think of modern problems, large or small, that are important to you personally. Choose one that is creating significant controversy.

Prewriting

Defining the Problem. Once you have selected a controversial problem, you need to establish its boundaries. Answering the following questions in depth will help.

1. What is the problem?
2. Why should people care about it? What could happen if it remains unsolved?
3. What is the controversy over the problem? Explain the views and concerns of each side.
4. What is the history of the problem?

Look over your answers, and decide which questions cannot be answered fully without more facts. Conduct a survey, interview experts, or carry out other research to get the facts you need. Then compose a statement summarizing the problem and the controversy that surrounds it.

Developing the Solution. Brainstorm a list of as many solutions as you can come up with. Then go over your list, circling the solutions that represent a compromise in the controversy. Use a chart like the following one to evaluate the solutions you have circled.

Solutions	Merits	Drawbacks
1.		
2.		
3.		
4.		

Choose the solution that best addresses the concerns of both sides in the controversy and that has the fewest drawbacks. Then freewrite to plan in detail how the solution could be implemented.

Writing

Use these guidelines to draft your essay.

1. **Introductory Paragraph.** Begin with either a quote or an anecdote that dramatizes the problem or the controversy. Follow with the statement you composed to summarize the issue. Then supply any brief background information that is basic to an understanding of the issue.

2. **Body Paragraphs.** Though all your body paragraphs should offer more details about the problem you have chosen, each paragraph can also serve a separate purpose. For example, in one paragraph you can show why readers should care about the problem; in another you can explore each side of the controversy; and in yet another you can put forth your solution, noting how it addresses both sides of the issue. You can write an additional paragraph about the way to implement the solution. Use your prewriting notes as sources of facts and details

for each paragraph. Be sure that transitions in each paragraph are appropriate to the paragraph's purpose (see page 56).

3. **Concluding Paragraph.** Summarize both the controversial issue and the solution you have proposed. Then, referring to your chart, evaluate your solution, noting its weaknesses but ending with emphasis on its strengths.

Evaluating and Revising

Use these questions to evaluate and revise your essay.

1. Does your introductory paragraph capture readers' attention and define the problem?

2. Do you provide facts and examples to show why readers should care about the problem?

3. Do you explain the controversy in adequate detail, exploring the history of the issue and specifying the concerns of each side?

4. Have you explained your solution clearly?

5. Does your analysis proceed logically from problem to solution? Have you used appropriate transitions to reveal your line of reasoning?

6. Are your sentences grammatically correct and varied in structure?

Proofreading and Publishing

Proofread to eliminate errors in mechanics, and make a final copy of your essay. Submit it to the editorial department of your local newspaper.

Writing: Point out that the organization of this essay is unusual in that a thesis statement does not appear at the beginning. Rather, the first part of the essay describes the problem or controversy, and subsequent paragraphs present information designed to convince readers that the writer's proposal is the best solution to the problem. A brief summary of both the controversy and the proposed solution appears in the conclusion.

Evaluating and Revising: As students revise, they should watch for verbs in the passive voice. These may indicate that the writer does not know, or does not wish to reveal, who is responsible for a controversial action. "Using Active and Passive Voices Effectively," pp. 968–969, can help students recognize the passive voice and avoid overusing it.

Proofreading and Publishing: Consider cooperating with the social studies department on this assignment and allowing students to earn credit in both subject areas. Students who write about international, national, or state issues might recast their essays as letters to the editor and submit them to such national news magazines as *Time, Newsweek,* or *U.S. News and World Report.* ∎

HUMANITIES CONNECTION

The following annotations are for the artwork surrounding the map, starting in the upper right-hand corner and moving in a counterclockwise direction.

Honoré Daumier: *The Third-Class Carriage,* like many of Daumier's paintings, reveals the unromantic aspects of poverty and the prosaic events of human life. During his time, Daumier (1808–1879) was best known for his satirical cartoons lampooning public figures and human foibles.

German Factory: James Burke entitled this engraving *The Day the Universe Changed,* indicating how deeply the Industrial Revolution affected people's perceptions of the world.

Queen Victoria: Queen of Great Britain and Ireland, and Empress of India, Victoria reigned over the British Empire for most of the nineteenth century—from 1837 to 1901. To many people in this age of change, she was the living symbol of stability, peace, and prosperity.

Romantic View of Nature: Spurred by a thirst for spirituality in this secular and mechanistic era, artists found in nature a manifestation of the deity. As a result, landscape emerged as the single greatest subject in Western European art in the nineteenth century. This bucolic scene typifies the work of German and English landscape painters.

EUROPE IN 1815

- - - - - Boundary of German States, 1815

KINGDOM OF NORWAY AND SWEDEN

SCOTLAND

DENMARK

UNITED KINGDOM OF GREAT BRITAIN AND IRELAND

NETHERLANDS

IRELAND

ENGLAND

London •

• Berlin

PRUSSIA

Rhine River

GERMAN STATES

AUST

Paris •

Seine River

Danube

Riv

SWITZERLAND

FRANCE

ITALIAN STATES

Rome •

N

PORTUGAL

SPAIN

• Madrid

Mediterranean Sea

Si

Atlantic Ocean

NORTH AFRICA

UNIT 10

THE NINETEENTH CENTURY: ROMANTICISM TO REALISM

▼ **Time** ▼
the 1800s

▼ **Place** ▼
Europe

▼ **Literary Significance** ▼

The early nineteenth-century Romantics broke away from the restrained styles and ideas favored by the leaders of the eighteenth-century Enlightenment. The Romantics exalted values that are still important today: a love of nature and the simple life, individual daring, innovation, and the free expression of feelings. Later in the nineteenth century, Realists rebelled against Romanticism. The Realists felt that Romantic emotionalism was no longer an effective tool to describe—or to reform—industrial society. Realistic values, such as the emphasis on factual observation of ordinary people's lives, still exert a powerful influence on today's literature and thought.

Frédéric Chopin: Eugène Delacroix (1798–1863) is regarded by many as the greatest French painter of the first half of the nineteenth century. This portrait of the Polish-born composer Frédéric Chopin typifies the innovations in style and use of color that make Delacroix the forerunner of modern Expressionism. His influence can be seen in the works of Renoir, Monet, Cézanne, Gauguin, Van Gogh, and Picasso.

Shooting of a Group of Citizens: This famous painting by Spanish artist Francisco José de Goya y Lucientes (1746–1828) exposes the brutality of Napoleon's forces during their conquest of Spain. Goya, who was in Madrid when Napoleon's troops occupied the city, may have witnessed an execution of Spanish loyalists on May 3, 1808. Six years later, Goya captured the victims' desperation, fear, and helplessness in the lamplight the soldiers used to illuminate their targets.

Gleaners: Inspired by the social changes brought about by the urbanization and industrialization of France, Jean François Millet (1814–1875) created scenes of laboring peasants, endowing them with strength and dignity. *The Gleaners* provoked controversy during Millet's time, not only for its subject matter, but also for its style and unorthodox technique. Critic Theophile Gautier, for example, claimed that Millet "trowels on top of his dishcloth of a canvas, without oil or turpentine, vast masonries of colored paint so dry that no varnish could quench its thirst." ■

To begin, ask students to identify the dominant European ruler in the early 1800s. (Napoleon, emperor of France and much of continental Europe, 1804–1815) Ask: How does one of the references to Napoleon suggest the interaction of politics and culture? (Beethoven's Third Symphony honored Napoleon.)

Point out that the Romantic literary movement, which glorified nature, developed at the same time as the Industrial Revolution. Ask: Why might people who were entering an industrial age glorify nature? (Possible response: They had moved from working on the land to working indoors in factories and missed natural environments.)

If students are familiar with the works of Dickens or with *Les Misérables*, have them describe the conditions of poverty among the industrial workers in England, France, and other European nations at this time. Also ask volunteers to identify events on the Time Line that foreshadow Communism in Russia. (publication of *The Communist Manifesto*; Russia's freeing of serfs; growth of social unrest; assassination of Czar Alexander II)

Next, have students name authors cited for Realism. (Balzac, Ibsen) Explain that Tolstoy, Dostoevsky, Chekhov, and Maupassant were also Realists, and elicit the fact that Realism dominated literature in the second half of the century.

Finally, ask how the Curies' discovery in 1898 foreshadows twentieth-century events. (Radioactive elements were eventually used to create nuclear weapons.)

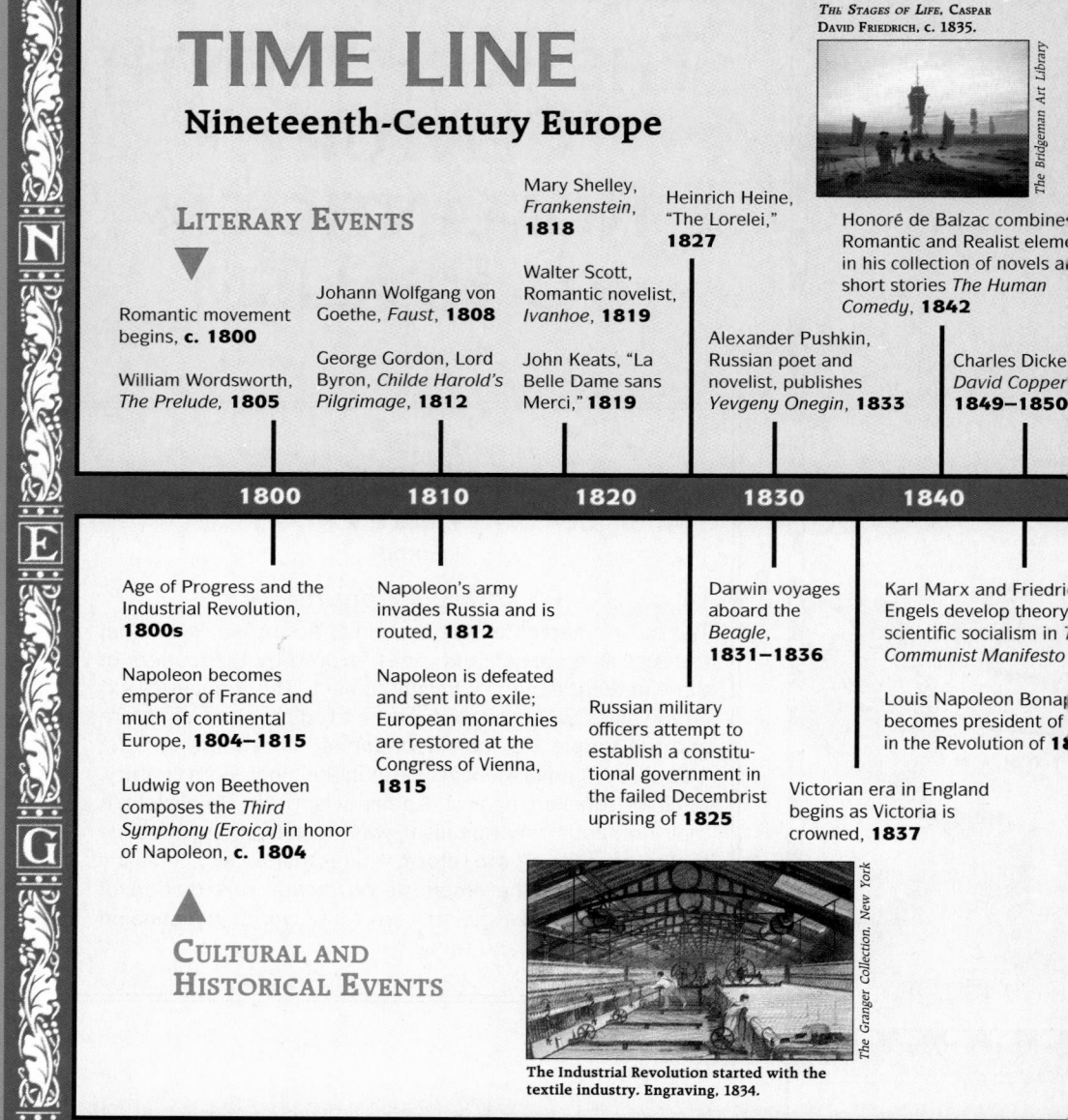

TIME LINE
Nineteenth-Century Europe

THE STAGES OF LIFE, CASPAR DAVID FRIEDRICH, c. 1835.

The Bridgeman Art Library

LITERARY EVENTS ▼

Romantic movement begins, **c. 1800**

William Wordsworth, *The Prelude*, **1805**

Johann Wolfgang von Goethe, *Faust*, **1808**

George Gordon, Lord Byron, *Childe Harold's Pilgrimage*, **1812**

Mary Shelley, *Frankenstein*, **1818**

Walter Scott, Romantic novelist, *Ivanhoe*, **1819**

John Keats, "La Belle Dame sans Merci," **1819**

Heinrich Heine, "The Lorelei," **1827**

Alexander Pushkin, Russian poet and novelist, publishes *Yevgeny Onegin*, **1833**

Honoré de Balzac combine Romantic and Realist eleme in his collection of novels a short stories *The Human Comedy*, **1842**

Charles Dicke *David Copper* **1849–1850**

| 1800 | 1810 | 1820 | 1830 | 1840 |

CULTURAL AND HISTORICAL EVENTS ▲

Age of Progress and the Industrial Revolution, **1800s**

Napoleon becomes emperor of France and much of continental Europe, **1804–1815**

Ludwig von Beethoven composes the *Third Symphony (Eroica)* in honor of Napoleon, **c. 1804**

Napoleon's army invades Russia and is routed, **1812**

Napoleon is defeated and sent into exile; European monarchies are restored at the Congress of Vienna, **1815**

Russian military officers attempt to establish a constitutional government in the failed Decembrist uprising of **1825**

Darwin voyages aboard the *Beagle*, **1831–1836**

Victorian era in England begins as Victoria is crowned, **1837**

Karl Marx and Friedri Engels develop theory scientific socialism in *Communist Manifesto*

Louis Napoleon Bona becomes president of in the Revolution of 18

The Granger Collection, New York

The Industrial Revolution started with the textile industry. Engraving. 1834.

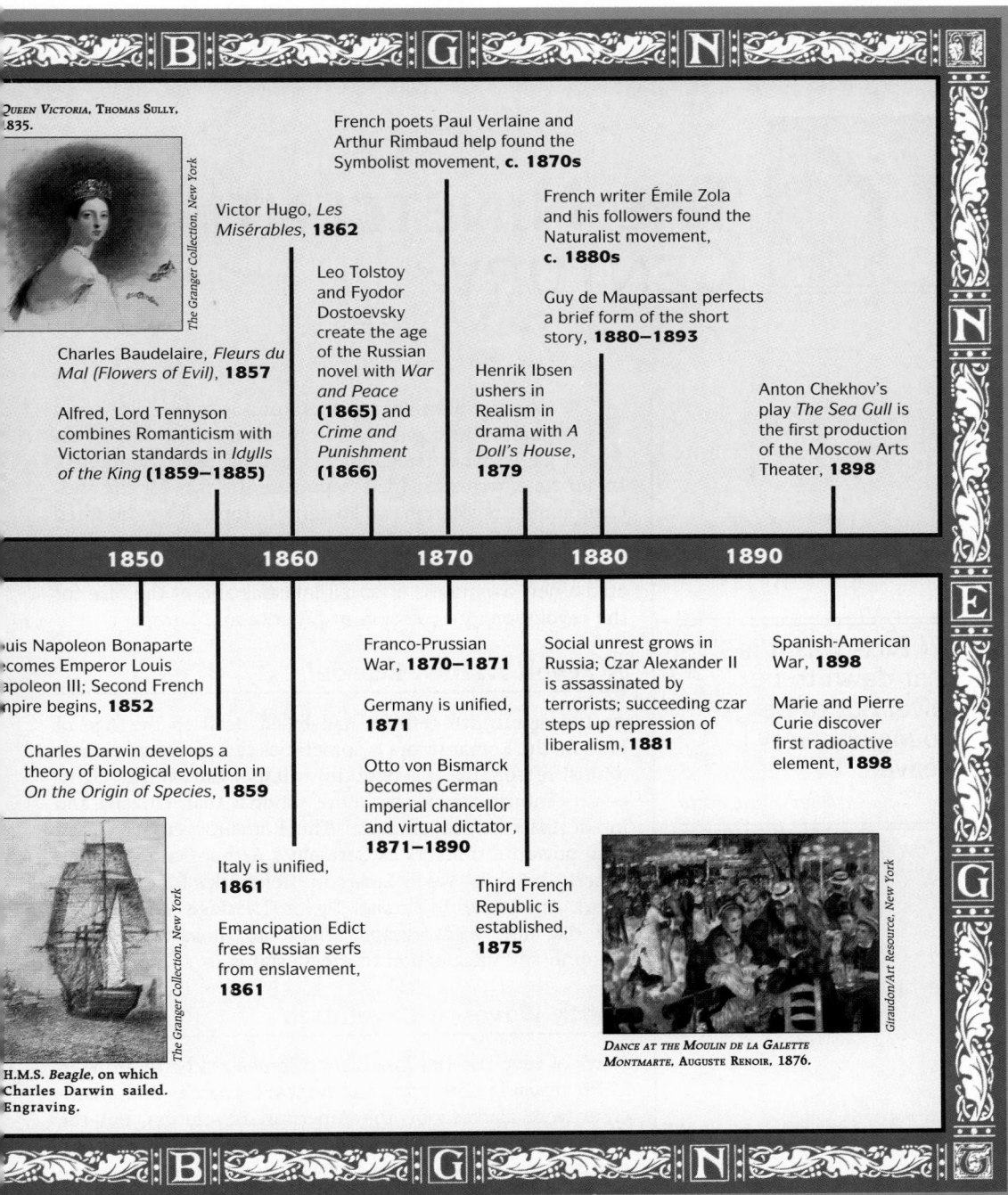

BEGINNINGS ... ENDINGS

Queen Victoria, Thomas Sully, 1835.

The Granger Collection, New York

French poets Paul Verlaine and Arthur Rimbaud help found the Symbolist movement, **c. 1870s**

Victor Hugo, *Les Misérables*, **1862**

French writer Émile Zola and his followers found the Naturalist movement, **c. 1880s**

Leo Tolstoy and Fyodor Dostoevsky create the age of the Russian novel with *War and Peace* **(1865)** and *Crime and Punishment* **(1866)**

Guy de Maupassant perfects a brief form of the short story, **1880–1893**

Charles Baudelaire, *Fleurs du Mal (Flowers of Evil)*, **1857**

Alfred, Lord Tennyson combines Romanticism with Victorian standards in *Idylls of the King* **(1859–1885)**

Henrik Ibsen ushers in Realism in drama with *A Doll's House*, **1879**

Anton Chekhov's play *The Sea Gull* is the first production of the Moscow Arts Theater, **1898**

1850   1860   1870   1880   1890

...uis Napoleon Bonaparte ...comes Emperor Louis ...apoleon III; Second French ...mpire begins, **1852**

Charles Darwin develops a theory of biological evolution in *On the Origin of Species*, **1859**

Franco-Prussian War, **1870–1871**

Germany is unified, **1871**

Otto von Bismarck becomes German imperial chancellor and virtual dictator, **1871–1890**

Italy is unified, **1861**

Emancipation Edict frees Russian serfs from enslavement, **1861**

Social unrest grows in Russia; Czar Alexander II is assassinated by terrorists; succeeding czar steps up repression of liberalism, **1881**

Spanish-American War, **1898**

Marie and Pierre Curie discover first radioactive element, **1898**

Third French Republic is established, **1875**

H.M.S. *Beagle*, on which Charles Darwin sailed. Engraving.

The Granger Collection, New York

Dance at the Moulin de la Galette Montmarte, Auguste Renoir, 1876.

Giraudon/Art Resource, New York

LITERARY BACKGROUND

Frankenstein: Mary Shelley wrote this Romantic work as a ghost story that she intended "to curdle the blood and quicken the beatings of the heart." Ask: What do you know about the title character of *Frankenstein*? (Possible response: He is a scientist who makes a creature from human body parts.) What is the theme of Shelley's novel? (the danger of usurping God's role as creator of life) Invite students to speculate about the reasons for the enduring popularity of *Frankenstein*. (Possible responses: the work's suspense; people's worries that scientific progress will lead to disaster)

CULTURAL BACKGROUND

Darwin: Charles Darwin served as naturalist on the *Beagle* during its five-year voyage around the world. He examined geologic formations, collected fossils, and studied plants and animals. His observations led him to develop his theory of natural selection, which proposed that members of all species compete for survival and that those with a natural advantage have a greater likelihood to survive and pass on their traits to the next generation.

LITERARY BACKGROUND

Tennyson: In *Idylls of the King,* concerning the legendary King Arthur, Tennyson incorporated the Victorian standards of piety, industriousness, and strict moral conduct. The most honored English poet of his day, Tennyson reluctantly accepted a barony and the title *Lord.*

This time line border is derived from the pattern-work of William Morris, the Victorian artist, poet, and designer who criticized the deadening effect of industrialism on nineteenth-century art.   Time Line   **975**

975

OBJECTIVES

1. *To compare and contrast the nineteenth-century movements of Romanticism, Realism, Naturalism, and Symbolism in France, Germany, England, Russia, and Norway*
2. *To analyze the political, social, economic, scientific, and cultural foundations of these movements*
3. *To interpret and respond to nineteenth-century literature orally and in writing*

TEACHER'S RESOURCES: 10

- Unit Introduction Test
- Word Analogies
- Unit Review Test
- Critical Thinking and Writing

1 RESPONDING TO THE QUOTATION

The quotation is from the long autobiographical poem *The Prelude*. The "dawn" referred to is the beginning of the French Revolution. Other writers of the time shared Wordsworth's optimism.

? *Do you think the young are more likely to embrace an era of rapid change? Explain.* (Possible response: Yes; the young are less set in their ways.)

2 CULTURAL BACKGROUND

Enlightenment Philosophers: The ideas of John Locke (1632–1704) are reflected in the Declaration of Independence. Locke argued that governments were established to protect the rights of the people; if a government failed to do so, citizens had a right to rebel. Jean Jacques Rousseau (1712–1778) also criticized oppressive political regimes and argued that governments should derive their authority from the consent of the governed.

3 TEACHING TIP

Assign individual students to research and present to the class the central ideas of one of the theorists of the Romantic movement. Tell them to find that person's views on individuality, free will, and the relationship between humanity and God. After the presentations, ask the class whether each writer's view of life was optimistic or pessimistic.

THE NINETEENTH CENTURY

> 1   " Bliss was it in that dawn to be alive,/but to be young was very heaven. "
>
> —*William Wordsworth*

S ome people think of literature as a quiet, peaceful pursuit. However, literature seems tame only in societies where freedom of speech is taken for granted. In our time, writers helped to prepare the way for the anti-Communist revolution in Eastern Europe. Two hundred years ago, the writings of the philosophers Voltaire and Jean Jacques Rousseau in France and John Locke in England created a new awareness of social injustice and lit the fuse for the revolutionary explosion in America and Europe.

A Revolt Against Reason?

As the eighteenth century had billed itself as the Age of Reason, the Romantic era is sometimes thought of as a revolt against reason. But it is doubtful whether the average eighteenth-century citizen was more rational than citizens and intellectuals before or since. The Romantic era produced such powerful thinkers as Germany's Arthur Schopenhauer, America's Ralph Waldo Emerson, Denmark's Søren Kierkegaard, and England's Samuel Taylor Coleridge. The Romantics did not reject reason. They did, however, elevate emotion and imagination to a new status.

Shock Waves of Revolution

News of revolt in the American colonies reached Europe in 1775, arousing both fears and hopes. Monarchs and aristocrats were alarmed by the American Revolution, but the discontented middle class and peasantry of Europe were inspired by the Americans' struggle for liberty. When the **French Revolution** broke out in 1789, Europe changed overnight. On July 14, 1789, an angry mob stormed the Bastille

As you begin the unit, tell students that the nineteenth century was an era of rapid change in all areas of life and art. It ushered in problems, ideas, and forms of expression that we still think of as "modern." The two main literary trends of the century were Romanticism and Realism. To help students stay focused on the main ideas of this long unit, you might want to structure your teaching as an ongoing debate between students expressing the Romantic and Realist viewpoints.

Start by writing the following list of opposing ideas on the chalkboard:

love of nature vs. concern with social institutions

subjective vs. objective point of view

love of fantasy vs. focus on actual life

emotional expressiveness vs. balanced, reasoned tone

faith in heroic individual effort vs. belief in socially determined fate

vivid, embellished imagery vs. uncluttered, clear expression

Tell students that in literature the word *Romantic* suggests much more than a preoccupation with love. It includes a set of attitudes and interests that can be contrasted with those of Realism. Ask students to study the list of opposing atti-

Archiv Für Kunst Und Geschichte, Berlin

THE STORMING OF THE BASTILLE ON JULY 14, 1789, artist unknown.

4 prison in Paris. That date, now called Bastille Day, which the French celebrate just as Americans celebrate July 4, 1776, marked the beginning of a new era.

Revolutionary fever spread throughout Europe, horrifying most aristocrats and thrilling democratic idealists. During its early years, the French Revolution became a kind of tourist attraction. Intellectuals and artists from across Europe and America visited France to see the new regime firsthand. Thomas Paine, the most powerful propagandist of the American Revolution, emigrated to France to participate in the uprising against the aristocracy. At the beginning of the new century, the French Revolution inspired Simon Bolívar's revolt against the Spanish empire in Latin America.

The Reign of Terror and the Reign of Napoleon

5 **William Wordsworth** (see page 1002) was one of many British liberals who was at first thrilled by the French Revolution. But soon intoxication turned to despair. For in 1793, the revolutionaries executed King Louis XVI, and the French Revolution became the **Reign of Terror**. The guillotines (gil′ə·tēnz′) worked overtime as the extremists of the Revo-

The Granger Collection, New York

Early nineteenth-century British cartoon showing Ned Ludd, the namesake of the Luddites. *Luddites were English laborers who destroyed machinery, which they viewed as a threat to their livelihood. The Luddites' cause captured the imaginations of several Romantic writers. Today, Luddite refers to anyone who opposes technological advances.*

HUMANITIES CONNECTION

In this contemporary painting of the storming of the Bastille, the artist conveys emotions through the postures of the figures, emphasizing their energy and fragility against the looming, inert bulk of the Bastille.

? *What emotions do you think the artist was trying to evoke in viewers?* (Possible responses: sympathy, indignation) ∎

4 CULTURAL DIVERSITY
Social conditions in France had actually been improving for some time before the French Revolution began. The gradual improvements, as well as the influence of French writers such as Voltaire and Rousseau, created rising expectations that led to revolution.

? *What twentieth-century writers have helped inspire social change in their countries?* (Possible responses: *Russia:* Aleksandr Solzhenitsyn; *Czechoslovakia:* Vaclav Havel; *U.S.:* James Baldwin, Ralph Ellison, and other African Americans)

5 HISTORICAL BACKGROUND
The Reign of Terror lasted fifteen months, during which nearly 17,000 people were beheaded and thousands more were allowed to die in disease-ridden prisons.

Introduction

tudes or values on the board and to tell which they think are associated with Romanticism (those on the left) and which are associated with Realism (on the right).

Divide the class into small groups of Realists and Romantics, depending on which set of values and concerns students think are more important in today's world. If there are not enough students to support one side, assign some students to prepare the best case they can for the underrepresented side, despite their personal views. Before students begin reading the selections in the unit, have them debate which set of values are dominant in contemporary American society.

Then tell students to keep these ideas in mind as they read the selections in the unit. When students finish each selection, have them analyze and evaluate its realistic and Romantic elements and decide how well the selection expresses concerns or reflects attitudes of people today. As they read, students may change their minds about which side of the debate they support. Allow them to switch sides at any time or to attempt to reach a consensus between the two sides about the relative importance of Romanticism and Realism today. In broad terms, Goethe's *Faust* and the poetry selections that open the unit reflect Romantic concerns: love of nature, the expression of emotion, the power of

HUMANITIES CONNECTION

❓ *Which elements of this painting might be exaggerations of reality?* (Accept reasonable responses.) *Why might Müller have exaggerated these details?* (to convey the horror felt during the Reign of Terror) ∎

6 READER'S RESPONSE

Why do revolutionaries often become as cruel as the leaders they replace?

7 HISTORICAL BACKGROUND

Between 1800 and 1812, Napoleon's army conquered most of Europe. In France, Napoleon ruled as a dictator, undoing the liberal political policies that were hastily instituted in the early days of the Revolution. However, he did reform and codify French laws to guarantee equal treatment for all.

8 TEACHING TIP

You may want to preview "Russia 1812" by reading the poem aloud (especially the portrait of Napoleon in lines 49–66) and discussing the painting on p. 1018.

9 CULTURAL DIVERSITY

The period of disillusionment in European history that followed the French Revolution might be compared to the era in American history following the Vietnam War and the assassinations of admired leaders.

❓ *Are you and your peers generally idealistic or disillusioned about social and political progress? Why?*

The Snite Museum of Art, University of Notre Dame, Gift of Mrs. Thomas Cusack, 60.42

THE LAST ROLL CALL OF THE VICTIM OF THE TERROR, CHARLES-LOUIS MÜLLER (1815–1892). *The idealism that surrounded the French Revolution exploded with the political chaos and mass executions that followed, known as the Reign of Terror.*

lution beheaded not only their opponents, but also former allies with whom they now disagreed. In 1794 the radical leader of the Reign of Terror, Robespierre, was himself executed. The French Republic was in a state of confusion that did not ease until a young Corsican military officer, **Napoleon Bonaparte** (1769–1821), staged a *coup*, or forceful overthrow, in 1799.

Using aggressive military tactics, Napoleon soon became dictator of continental Europe. The devastation of the Napoleonic Wars is one of the themes of the great Russian novel *War and Peace* by **Leo Tolstoy** (see page 1043). Napoleon's ill-fated invasion and subsequent retreat from Russia are described in Victor Hugo's "Russia 1812" (see page 1017). In 1815, Napoleon was finally defeated by a coalition of English, Prussian, and Russian forces at the Battle of Waterloo and spent the rest of his life in exile.

The writers, artists, and thinkers who reached maturity in the 1790s reacted to these events in different ways. Some, like **Heinrich Heine** in Germany (see page 1011), retained their liberal ideals, while others, like Wordsworth, became increasingly disillusioned and ultimately conservative in

imagination, and the importance of the individual. The prose selections by Maupassant, Tolstoy, and Chekhov in this unit focus on realistic social situations, although students may question whether their authors really maintain an objective point of view. For example, are Chekhov's focus on the individual and his interest in creating a strong mood essentially Romantic?

The unit closes with Ibsen's *A Doll's House*, a play that was considered revolutionary in its day because of its realistic portrayal of social problems in the lives of ordinary people. The play, however, is also full of symbolism, and its main character is ultimately a rebel against societal conventions that restrict her individual development—a true Romantic hero.

Throughout the unit, encourage students to express their personal reactions to the themes and styles of each writer, and to assess how each reflected the concerns of a changing world and influenced the course of twentieth-century literature.

---

their political views. Nevertheless, most of the members of that generation, and the generation that followed it, had enough ideals and views in common to be called by a single label: the **Romantics**.

What Is Romanticism?

Romanticism was a revolt against the restrictions imposed by the classical, aristocratic ideals of the eighteenth century. It was a liberation of the artist's imagination and style. Poets such as Wordsworth declared themselves free to write in the language of everyday speech about everyday people and events. The Romantics idealized nature and the lifestyles of people who lived close to nature, such as farmers and shepherds. This reverence for nature was in part a reaction to the increasingly urban and industrial character of Europe. For some Romantics, disillusionment with nineteenth-century life led to an interest in settings more exotic than the countryside. These writers and artists found inspiration in medieval ballads and courtly tales, as well as in tales of the supernatural.

Another important characteristic of Romanticism is the belief in the importance of the individual. The Romantic individual was daring, rebellious, and free to express previously taboo emotions—to express, in Wordsworth's phrase, "the spontaneous overflow of powerful feelings."

> **Romanticism prizes the free expression of the individual's thoughts and feelings. Love of nature, respect for ordinary people, and an interest in fantasy are typical Romantic values.**

Poets such as **Victor Hugo** (see page 1015), **Paul Verlaine** and **Arthur Rimbaud** (see page 1027), and **Charles Baudelaire** (see page 1021), experimented with rhyme, meter, and subject matter, breaking rules that had been obeyed for generations. In music, the German composer Beethoven turned the highly structured classical sonata into an expansive form for the expression of powerful internal struggles.

> **❝** Classicism is . . . stability within known limits; Romanticism is expansion within limits known and unknown. **❞**
> —*Jacques Barzun*

THE WANDERER, CASPAR DAVID FRIEDRICH (1774–1840). *Friedrich, with his emphasis on the isolation of the individual, was a leader in the German Romantic school of painting.*

Kunsthalle, Hamburg, Germany/Bridgeman Art Library, London/SuperStock, Inc.

10 LITERARY BACKGROUND
Romanticism is derived from the word *romance*. *Romance* originally referred to the Romance languages—French, Spanish, Italian, Portuguese—which developed from Latin. Thus, a "romance" came to mean a literary work written in the vernacular, or popular tongue, rather than in Latin.

11 RESPONDING TO THE QUOTATION
The American historian and critic Jacques Barzun (1907–) has written widely on the Romantic era. The quotation contrasts the comforts of order and stability with the excitement and risks of growth and change. Have students write essays exploring whether classical or Romantic values are more important to them, and why.

HUMANITIES CONNECTION

? *How do you imagine the wanderer feels?* (Accept reasonable responses.) *Which elements of the painting support your opinion?* (Possible responses: interplay between warm and cool colors, posture of the figure, areas of darkness and light) ■

12 TEACHING TIP
Play a recording of the first movement of Beethoven's "Pathétique" piano sonata (No. 8 in C Minor), the "Emperor" Concerto (No. 5 in E Flat), or his Symphony No. 5. Have students discuss what emotions the music evokes in them.

In the Romantic poem "The World Is Too Much with Us" (p. 1004), Wordsworth expresses a nineteenth-century sense of alienation from nature by writing "I'd rather be / A Pagan suckled in a creed outworn; / So might I, standing on this pleasant lea, / Have glimpses that would make me less forlorn." And, indeed, the Romantics' rediscovery of nature as a mystical source of meaning and solace was a return to a theme found in the ancient literature and sacred texts of many cultures.

If this aspect of Romanticism connects it with the past, many elements of Romanticism have continued into the twentieth century as well. For example, the Romantic insistence on the importance of each individual's emotions and subjective attitudes was a view carried into the twentieth century by poets such as Rainer Maria Rilke (p. 1148), whose early works were highly emotional and subjective.

Nowhere did the sense of romantic individualism take stronger hold, however, than in the United States. The Romantic movement began to influence American literature from 1830–1865 in the work of novelists Nathaniel Hawthorne and Herman Melville, poets Walt Whitman and Edgar Allan Poe, and transcendental essayists Ralph Waldo Emerson and Henry David Thoreau, who wrote of the mystical connection between people and nature.

HUMANITIES CONNECTION

Jean-François Millet did much of his best work in the French village of Barbizon, where he could observe the natural scenes and peasant life that he idealized in his paintings.
? *What details does Millet use to make the scene appealing?* (Possible responses: color, perspective, lighting) ■

13 RESPONDING TO THE QUOTATION

Henry James (1843–1916) was an American-born writer who spent much of his life in England and eventually became a British citizen. James was a pioneer of psychological realism, often using the stream of consciousness technique in which the random flow of a character's thoughts are represented. Many of his novels feature encounters between naive Americans and sophisticated Europeans.
? *What characteristics do you look for in a novel to decide if it is true to life?* (Possible responses: believable plots, characters, dialogue, and setting)

14 CULTURAL BACKGROUND

Serfs: Russian serfs were bound to the land they worked on and could only be sold along with it. Serfs lived at their landlord's mercy and could marry only with his permission. The Russian government compensated landowners for giving up land to freed serfs, but the serfs were expected to pay a tax to reimburse the government.

SPRING, JEAN-FRANÇOIS MILLET (1814–1875). *In painting, as in literature, the Romantics presented an idealized view of nature and the peasant life.*

The Granger Collection, New York

13

> **" The only reason for the existence of a novel is that it does attempt to represent life. "**
> —The Art of Criticism, *Henry James*

The New Age Falters

As a new generation of Romantics grew up in the first half of the nineteenth century, it became clear that Europe was in turmoil. In France, the monarchy was restored after Napoleon's downfall. The new monarchy, in turn, was replaced by the Second Republic in 1848. Unsuccessful popular revolts occurred in Italy, Austria, Poland, Hungary, and Belgium.

The most famous of these unsuccessful revolts was the **Decembrist** uprising of 1825 in Russia, in which many intellectuals and writers, including **Alexander Pushkin** (see page 1006), were implicated. The czar executed the military officers who had tried to establish a constitutional government, and a century of botched reforms and revolutions followed. The Russian serfs were freed in 1861, but the nation continued to be plagued by censorship, ignorance, poverty, and tyranny. Russian literature in the nineteenth century became a forum for reformist ideas, in which educated Russians were intensely interested.

1

Progress, Pollution, and Poverty

The political events of the early and mid-nineteenth century—an era often labeled the Age of Progress—went hand

After the Civil War, however, American literature took on a more realistic, even naturalistic, focus. Early Realist writers in the United States include Mark Twain, Sinclair Lewis, and Henry James. The Realist tradition continued into the twentieth century in the works of Willa Cather and Edith Wharton. The grittier Naturalistic school influenced Stephen Crane's *Maggie, A Girl of the Streets*, Theodore Dreiser's *Sister Carrie*, and the works of Jack London.

Twentieth-century British writers who were influenced by the Realist movement include Somerset Maugham and James Joyce (see p. 1207). D. H. Lawrence acknowledged his literary debt to Tolstoy and Dostoevsky, the masters of nineteenth-century Russian fiction.

Soviet writers from the 1930s until the Gorbachev era have had to struggle to write honestly about life in their society, since all writing had to conform to Communist standards. The ironically named official policy of "social realism" demanded that all writers depict revolutionary progress and contented workers, even if the facts contradicted such an optimistic picture. Courageous writers such as Aleksandr Solzhenitsyn (p. 1264) defied Communist dictates to tell the truth about Soviet society as they saw it.

The realistic plays of Henrik Ibsen have

15

in hand with the **Industrial Revolution**. The explosion of scientific knowledge led to many technological achievements, such as the steam engine, the electric dynamo, and the processes for producing aluminum and steel. New inventions—the telegraph, the electric light, and the repeating rifle—were changing the world in exciting, sometimes frightening, ways. Factories were built, and steamboats and railroads, with their attendant noise and smoke, became part of the rural and urban landscape. Farm workers moved to cities to work in factories, but these cities, unprepared for the rapid population growth, offered them only slums to live in. In addition, during this great age of scientific progress and rapid change, **Charles Darwin** (1809–1882) developed a theory of evolution that upset people's ideas about who they were and where they had come from.

16

Many people prospered during the Industrial Revolution. A new middle class of manufacturers, bankers, and lawyers became the most significant force in European society. This dominant class was optimistic that material progress would improve life for all humanity. Few poor people shared this optimism, however. The economic theorist **Karl Marx** (1818–1883), whose ideas influenced Tolstoy and later, in the twentieth century, led to the establishment of Communist systems around the world, was a persuasive critic of the new social order. Most peasants lived in abject poverty. In the cities, people lived in slums, crowding into unsafe and unsanitary buildings. City streets were filthy, and working conditions in factories and mines were inhumane. Children and adults worked twelve-hour days, six days a week,

17

18

KARL MARX, painting c. 1880, artist unknown. *Marx's economic theories, based on his observations of nineteenth-century European society, led to the Communist revolutions that transformed half the world in the twentieth century.*

Archiv Für Kunst Und Geschichte, Berlin

The Industrial Revolution gave rise to a prosperous middle class, but poverty raged amid the growing lower class.

---

with no safety standards or compensation for accidents. British children working in the mines were used as draft animals, pulling carts full of coal. They rarely saw daylight. Furthermore, European nations had escalated their policies of imperialism, increasing their domination of smaller, less powerful countries.

---

15 CULTURAL DIVERSITY

In the nineteenth century, methods of communication, transportation, and production changed more than they had in all of previous history.
? *What new inventions have been developed in your lifetime?* (Possible responses: fax machines, personal computers, VCRs, compact discs)

16 CULTURAL BACKGROUND

Social Darwinism: Darwin theorized that the evolution of species was governed by the indirect working of a principle he called "survival of the fittest." Contrary to Darwin's intention, this idea was often misapplied to social or economic developments. In the late nineteenth century, "survival of the fittest" became a slogan used to justify ruthless economic competition, imperialism, and warfare.

17 HISTORICAL BACKGROUND

Marxism: Marx taught that class warfare was inevitable in all industrialized societies. He said that the struggle between wealthy capitalists and poor workers would cease only with the defeat of the capitalist system and the establishment of a classless society.

18 TEACHING TIP

To help students get a feeling for the desperate conditions many workers faced in the nineteenth century, you may want to play selections from the original cast album of the musical *Les Misérables,* based on the novel by Victor Hugo.

changed the course of modern drama. Among American "problem plays" with which students may be familiar are Arthur Miller's *Death of a Salesman* and Lorraine Hansberry's *A Raisin in the Sun*.

In their avoidance of direct statements of meaning and their preference for using symbols to suggest meaning and mood, the French Symbolist poets of the nineteenth century recall centuries of Chinese and Japanese poetry. Twentieth-century poets who continued in the Symbolist tradition include T. S. Eliot, Ezra Pound, and E. E. Cummings.

---

19 LITERARY BACKGROUND

Literature and Social Reform:

Among those writers who pricked society's conscience by describing the plight of the poor, perhaps none was more popular than English novelist Charles Dickens (1812–1870). Dickens' own father had been thrown into a debtor's prison, forcing young Dickens to work in a factory at the age of twelve. Though sometimes criticized as sentimental, his novels *Oliver Twist, Hard Times, Little Dorrit*, and *A Christmas Carol* vividly portray how the poor, especially children, were abused in nineteenth-century England.

20 RESPONDING TO THE QUOTATION

Guy de Maupassant was a master of the realistic short story. Have students compare Maupassant's view of Realism with that expressed by the French novelist Stendahl: "A novel is a mirror walking along the road."

❓ *Which view of Realism do you prefer? Why?*

HUMANITIES CONNECTION

The works of Edouard Manet (1832–1883) reflect an artistic naturalism.

❓ *What differences in style can you see in Manet's portrait of Zola and in the portrait of Marx on p. 981? (Possible responses: Zola is shown in a more relaxed posture and in a more intimate setting than the formal portrait of Marx.)* ∎

20

> ❝ The Realist, if he is an artist, will try not to show us a commonplace photograph of life, but to give us a more complete view of it, more striking, more convincing than reality itself. ❞
>
> —*Guy de Maupassant*

Many writers were troubled by these conditions. The liberal reforms begun during the revolutions of the late eighteenth century had not brought about an era of justice—in fact, the gap between rich and poor was wider than ever.

19

The Realist Creed

A reaction against Romanticism, which called itself **Realism**, flourished during the last half of the nineteenth century. Like most labels, "Realism" is a bit misleading. The Realists were not the first writers to describe the world as it is. The Romantics were also careful observers of the lives of ordinary people. In fact, some writers, such as Hugo and Pushkin, can be identified with both Romanticism and Realism.

ÉMILE ZOLA, EDOUARD MANET, 1868. *Zola was a leader of the Naturalist movement in literature.*

Archiv Für Kunst Und Geschichte, Berlin

The Nineteenth Century:
Romanticism to Realism

In France, under the leadership of the novelist **Gustave Flaubert**, the Realists tried to make a science of their art by eliminating sentimentality from their tone and excessive decoration from their descriptions. Their aim was to observe and record the daily lives of ordinary people without distorting the truth. Unlike writers who emphasized the noble, uplifting aspects of human life, Realists simply tried to mirror life, whether noble or ignoble, without making judgments. Of course, no artist can ever completely withhold judgment or feeling from his or her work, and good writing does much more than mirror reality. Flaubert's *Madame Bovary* is admired today not so much for its objectivity as for its perfect prose and its satire of the middle class.

> Realism was a reaction against Romanticism in the second half of the nineteenth century. Some Realist writers aimed for scientific objectivity; others inclined toward social satire; and some hoped for social reform.

Naturalism, a radical offshoot of Realism, arose in France in the 1870s. Members of this movement, led by **Émile Zola**, considered free will an illusion, and often showed their characters as helpless victims of heredity, fate, and environment. Writers were no longer to be subjective in their choice of details; in fact, the Naturalists attempted to abolish the boundary between scientist and artist. The most talented Naturalists, however, could not stay within the narrow ideology of their school. French author **Guy de Maupassant** (see page 1032) is sometimes called a Naturalist, but his work is sharpened by irony and an unsurpassed gift for choosing the right detail.

In poetry, **Symbolism** became the major literary movement. Symbolist poets avoided direct statements of meaning and instead used symbols to suggest meaning or mood. Charles Baudelaire is widely acknowledged to be the forerunner of this movement, and Arthur Rimbaud and Paul Verlaine are considered its most prominent poets.

FYODOR DOSTOEVSKY, V. PEROV, 1872. *Russian authors such as Dostoevsky created their own brand of Realist literature in the second half of the nineteenth century.*

Tass/SOVFOTO

READING CHECK

1. The Romantics celebrated nature, emotion, and the individual.   T F (T)
2. Russia was the only country that did not experience revolts and political upheavals in the nineteenth century. T F (F)
3. The Industrial Revolution resulted in prosperity and good working conditions for the laboring classes.   T F (F)
4. The Naturalists believed that people were controlled by fate, environment, and heredity.   T F (T)
5. Both Realism and Romanticism continued to influence writers in the twentieth century.   T F (T)

HUMANITIES CONNECTION

Members of the European lower classes worked long hours, often under dangerous conditions like those shown in this painting of an ironworks. **?** *How might realistic paintings like this one have helped to spark social change?* (by increasing public awareness of conditions and by generating sympathy for the workers) ∎

22 LITERARY BACKGROUND

Psychological Realism: Dostoevsky created tormented heroes who search, largely in vain, for truth and self-fulfillment. His four greatest novels—*Crime and Punishment, The Idiot, The Possessed*, and *The Brothers Karamazov*—anticipated modern psychology by exploring unconscious motives and the power of irrational forces, manifested in dreams and lapses into insanity.

23 CULTURAL DIVERSITY

In their novels, Tolstoy and Dostoevsky asked, "How should people live?" Answers to this question are to some degree culturally determined. To someone born and raised in traditional China, for example, the answer might be, "People should live by honoring their family and their ancestors."

? *How might people from your ethnic or cultural background answer this question?* (Answers will vary.)

IRONWORKS, ADOLPH VON MENZEL, 1875.

Erich Lessing/Archiv Für Kunst Und Geschichte, Berlin

Realism in Russia

Several of the most important Realists emerged from the fringes of Europe: Russia and Norway. When Realism reached Russia, it acquired a softer tone and a grander vision. **Ivan Turgenev**, a Russian writer who had lived in Paris and had been influenced by Flaubert, Zola, and other French writers, examined the lives of serfs and nobles in *A Sportsman's Sketches* (1852), helping to create a clamor for emancipation. He wrote in ornate, lyrical prose brimming with sympathy and warmth. Later Russian novelists, including Leo Tolstoy and **Fyodor Dostoevsky**, learned a great deal from Turgenev. Realism flourished in Russia, fostering a powerful movement that called for the liberation of the serfs and, later, the entire society. Yet the primary aim of the Russian Realists was not social reform, but a desire to answer the ultimate questions of human life. In very different ways, Tolstoy and Dostoevsky repeatedly asked, "How should people live?" and "What are good and evil?"

Both Tolstoy and Dostoevsky wrote gigantic, sprawling novels filled with violence, love, and family crises and peopled with characters from a wide cross section of society. Unlike these two giants, the playwright and short-story

FOR FURTHER STUDY

Nonfiction

Howard Mumford Jones's *Revolution and Romanticism* traces the main themes of Romanticism and the effects of the American and French Revolutions. *Sleeping on the Wing*, by Kenneth Koch and Kate Farrell, includes a good introduction to the works of the French poet Rimbaud. David Thomas's *Henrik Ibsen*, in the Modern Dramatists series, explores Ibsen's influence on modern drama.

Fiction

Charles Dickens's *A Tale of Two Cities*, a dramatic account of the French Revolution, will help students understand the cataclysmic events of the era. His *Oliver Twist* provides a grim portrait of the lives of nineteenth-century London street urchins. The stories of Chekhov, Tolstoy, and Maupassant are all available in paperback editions.

Films

Film versions of *Oliver Twist* and *A Tale of Two Cities* may initiate interest in the Dickens novels. David Lean's beautiful film version of Pasternak's novel *Doctor Zhivago* vividly portrays the effects of nineteenth-century social injustice on early twentieth-century Russia. The film and the novel both chronicle the bitter struggles of the Russian Revolution while telling a moving love story. ▪

writer **Anton Chekhov** (see page 1060) "painted" on a much smaller canvas. He found his subjects and themes in the common illusions and daily sufferings of unremarkable people. Like Tolstoy and Dostoevsky, however, Chekhov dealt with meanings of life and death. His stories and plays are about people's attempts—usually frustrated—to find meaning and purpose in their lives.

Drama: The Stage as Living Room

In the Romantic era, the dominant literary form was poetry. Perhaps this is because poetry seems naturally to lean toward the expression of feelings rather than facts. In the Realist era, the dominant form was prose fiction. Except for some great German Romantic plays (including Goethe's *Faust*, see page 988), Hugo's *Hernani*, and one Russian comedy, Nikolai Gogol's *Inspector General*, drama lagged behind poetry and prose during the nineteenth century. The Realist whose work helped to transform drama was the Norwegian playwright **Henrik Ibsen** (see page 1069).

Nowadays, playgoers are used to seeing plays that reveal the secret scandals, griefs, and pretenses of people who might be their neighbors. We go to a theater and see a living room on the stage, with one of its walls removed so that we can peek in. We eavesdrop upon families in the midst of crisis. But before Ibsen, most plays were not like that. Even Ibsen's early plays were historical tragedies or romantic comedies in verse. In middle age, however, Ibsen began writing about ordinary Norwegians, their families and communities, and the things they didn't want said out loud. He invented the "problem play"—a label that does not do justice to his achievement, because his plays live through their characters rather than their messages about social problems.

The Legacy of the Nineteenth Century

The literary styles of the nineteenth century—from effusive Romantic poetry to terse Realist prose—still influence modern writing. Realistic descriptions of life and powerful expressions of feeling now seem like hallmarks of literary excellence. The great ideas of the nineteenth century—progress, social reform, evolution, psychology—have become the foundations of twentieth-century thought.

> 66 The thing that caused the new social plays of Ibsen to take hold of people with such amazing power was his remarkable ability to translate ethical conflicts into human life, so that we seem always to see people of flesh and blood engaged in breathless struggles about the greatest problems in life. 99
>
> —The Life of Ibsen, *Halvdan Koht*

24

Christie's London/Bridgeman Art Library, London/SuperStock, Inc.

A MASKED BALL IN A THEATER, ALOIS SCHONN (1826–1897).

24 RESPONDING TO THE QUOTATION

The "breathless struggles" that Ibsen embodied in his characters were so effectively dramatized that his work aroused widespread debate and controversy throughout Europe. Critics and audiences were often shocked by his candid treatment of social issues, and many described his work as degrading and sensationalist.
❓ *What social problems might today's playwrights dramatize?* (Possible responses: divorce, drug or child abuse)

25 TEACHING TIP

To reinforce how revolutionary Ibsen's plays were, have students compare the opening pages of *A Doll's House* (p. 1071) with the opening pages of Goethe's *Faust*, Part 1 (p. 988). Help them to see that Ibsen's play is written in conversational dialogue resembling actual speech, rather than in verse, and that Ibsen's stage directions contain detailed descriptions for realistic sets.

26 LITERARY BACKGROUND

One writer who was directly influenced by Ibsen was the Irish dramatist George Bernard Shaw. Unlike Ibsen's works, Shaw's "problem plays" are known for their witty arguments in favor of controversial ideas, rather than for their depth of characterization. However, it was Ibsen's example that gave Shaw the courage to deal with formerly unmentionable social problems and unpopular ideas. ▪

MORE ABOUT THE AUTHOR

Goethe once wrote, "We must not seek to BE anything, but BECOME everything," an aspiration that was central to his characterization of Faust. It is Goethe himself, however, who may well epitomize such a person. His works, numbering 143 volumes, comprise some of the world's most respected poetry and prose. Coming from a man who also led a remarkably active public and private life, Goethe's output is astonishing. In addition to practicing law and serving as a key government official, Goethe directed the Weimar theater for many years. He fell deeply in love time and again, with women from all walks of life.

Through it all Goethe worked, often struggling, on *Faust*, which he called the "chief business" of his literary life. He began writing the drama in 1772 and completed it sixty years later, only months before he died. *Faust* encompasses the main ideas and themes of Goethe's age on the individual, nature, science, God, and society. It is considered one of the first major works on modern man's effort to reconcile individual striving with the welfare of all humanity.

ABOUT THE TRANSLATOR

Louis MacNeice (1907–1963) was born in Belfast, Ireland, and educated at Oxford. He authored several books of poetry, lectured in the classics at the University of London and at Cornell, and wrote and produced radio plays for the BBC.

Johann Wolfgang von Goethe
1749–1832

The Granger Collection, New York

Goethe (gö′tə) is one of the greatest writers in German literature. A versatile and prolific writer, he was also a universal genius who made important contributions to the fields of science, philosophy, and government. In addition, Goethe was a skilled musician, painter, and athlete.

Goethe was born in Frankfurt. After a false start as a law student, Goethe began studying the arts at Strasbourg, where he met Johann Gottfried Herder, a leader of the Sturm und Drang (Storm and Stress) movement that heralded the beginning of German Romanticism. Members of this movement rebelled against the rationalism of the Enlightenment; they emphasized the power of the imagination and spontaneous expression. Goethe's most notable contribution to the Sturm und Drang movement was the novel *The Sorrows of Young Werther* (1774), which made him internationally famous. Werther, the young hero who kills himself out of hopeless love, became a symbol of the Romantic hero.

In 1775, the young duke of Saxe-Weimar, Karl August, invited Goethe to stay at his court, and, within a few years, Weimar blossomed into the cultural center of Germany. During his first ten years at Weimar, Goethe served as chief minister of state, instituting important political reforms; in addition, he studied music, biology, and painting. In 1786, Goethe left to travel in Italy. This trip marked an important shift in his artistic development, as he became influenced by classical art and architecture.

Goethe's life after his return from Italy was especially productive. He wrote several masterpieces during this period: love poems, prose plays, travel books, novels, narrative poems, and several poetic dramas, most notably *Faust* (Part I, 1808; Part II, 1833), generally considered his greatest work.

Goethe did not advertise himself as a mystic, a hermit, or an adventurer, unlike many other Romantic artists. In many ways, he thought of himself as an ordinary man—a public servant, a husband, and a father. But in his old age, Goethe became a living monument, receiving pilgrims who visited him from around the world. No wonder Napoleon, after meeting Goethe, said, *"Voilà un homme!"* ("There is a man!")

OBJECTIVES

1. To recognize the contribution to Romantic literature of Goethe's dramatic poem, Faust
2. To recognize the characteristics of dramatic poetry
3. To write a speech for a character, write a skit, and evaluate a character's actions

THEMES IN WORLD LITERATURE

The Thirst for Knowledge

From the *Epic of Gilgamesh*, pp. 136–152
"The Fall" from *Genesis*, pp. 166–167
Inferno from the *Divine Comedy*, pp. 741–770

The Search for Meaning

"The Grail" from *Perceval*, pp. 720–729
From *Candide*, pp. 945–962 ■

Reader's Guide

from FAUST, PART I

Background

There really was a Dr. Faust. In Germany, in the early sixteenth century, a man named Johannes Faustus gained a wide reputation as a skillful magician. People said that this man, who became a legend in his own time, had sold his soul to the Devil in exchange for knowledge of the magical arts. An English translation of the Faust legend found its way into the hands of Christopher Marlowe (1564–1593), who wrote a popular play called *The Tragical History of Doctor Faustus* (c. 1588).

Goethe's *Faust* follows the traditional plot of the Dr. Faustus legend, but it also expands and enriches the basic elements of the story. In Marlowe's play, Faust, who desires limitless knowledge, makes a pact with the Devil and loses his soul. Goethe's Faust, on the other hand, seeks unlimited experience and at the end of his quest achieves salvation. Later writers and musicians continued to amplify the Faust legend. Most notably, in the German novelist Thomas Mann's *Doktor Faustus* (1947), a modern composer sells his soul in exchange for musical greatness.

Writer's Response

Do you believe that some people are entitled to be "above the law," pushing beyond all limitations, even if in so doing they injure themselves or others? Write a paragraph or two exploring these ideas.

Literary Focus

The **genre** of a literary work is the category or type in which it belongs. Some examples of genre include **drama**, the **epic**, the **novel**, the **short story,** and **lyric poetry.** Goethe's *Faust* is a work that transcends genres. The work includes the dialogue and stage directions common to **drama**, but it is so long, with so many changes of scene, that it is difficult to perform onstage in its entirety. Goethe called it a **tragedy,** but Goethe's version of the story ends with Faust's salvation. In its vast scope, and in the way its hero embodies the values of German society, it resembles an **epic**—but epics are narratives, rather than dramas. Furthermore, the individual scenes in Faust vary in style and verse forms, encompassing virtually all the types of poetry known in Goethe's day.

PREREADING FOCUS

Background: This selection is a small part of Goethe's 8,000-line drama. It introduces the plot's central problem—whether Mephistopheles can win Faust's soul by offering him worldly pleasures and power—and defines the drama's central theme—the nature of Faust's striving. Most of the rest of Part I tells the story of how Faust, aided by the devil's sorcery, seduces and then abandons an innocent maid named Margarete. The story comes full circle at the end of Part II—after a series of often fantastic adventures—when Margarete saves a wretched Faust from damnation by appealing for mercy for his soul. Within this frame, Goethe touches on major themes of nineteenth- and even twentieth-century literature.

Literary Focus: Although Goethe's *Faust* transcends genre, it is above all a drama in verse. Unlike most staged drama, it is primarily a dialogue; rarely do more than two speakers interact at one time. Part I is written primarily in one verse form, now called "Faust verse." Goethe based his verse form on a four-beat iambic meter used in popular German rhyme, a form that he felt suited the folk origins of the Faust legend.

from FAUST, PART I
Johann Wolfgang von Goethe
translated by
LOUIS MACNEICE

 As you read the Prologue, think about how Goethe uses the conversation between the Lord and Mephistopheles to characterize Faust.

Prologue in Heaven

1 [*Enter the* LORD *and the* HEAVENLY HOSTS, *with* MEPHISTOPHELES° *following. The* THREE ARCHANGELS *step forward.*]

Raphael.
The chanting sun, as ever, rivals
The chanting of his brother spheres
And marches round his destined circuit—
A march that thunders in our ears.
5 His aspect cheers the Hosts of Heaven
Though what his essence none can say;
These inconceivable creations
Keep the high state of their first day.°

Gabriel.
And swift, with inconceivable swiftness,
10 The earth's full splendor rolls around,
Celestial radiance alternating
With a dread night too deep to sound;
The sea against the rocks' deep bases
Comes foaming up in far-flung force,
2 15 And rock and sea go whirling onward
In the swift spheres' eternal course.

Michael.
And storms in rivalry are raging
From sea to land, from land to sea,
In frenzy forge the world a girdle
20 From which no inmost part is free.
The blight of lightning flaming yonder

Mephistopheles (mef′ə·stäf′ə·lēz′): the Devil.

8. **the high state of their first day:** Although human beings have fallen from the innocent state in which they were created, the rest of creation—the sun, planets, and other "inconceivable creations"—remains "unfallen."

Marks where the thunderbolt will play;
And yet Thine envoys, Lord, revere
The gentle movement of Thy day.

Choir of Angels.

25 Thine aspect cheers the Hosts of Heaven
Though what Thine essence none can say,
And all Thy loftiest creations
Keep the high state of their first day.

[MEPHISTOPHELES *steps forward.*]

Mephistopheles.
Since you, O Lord, once more approach and ask
30 If business down with us be light or heavy—
And in the past you've usually welcomed me—
That's why you see me also at your levee.°
Excuse me, I can't manage lofty words—
Not though your whole court jeer and find
    me low;
35 My pathos certainly would make you laugh
Had you not left off laughing long ago.
Your suns and worlds mean nothing much to me;
How men torment themselves, that's all I see.
The little god of the world, one can't reshape,
    reshade him;
40 He is as strange today as that first day you
    made him.
His life would be not so bad, not quite,
Had you not granted him a gleam of Heaven's
    light;
He calls it Reason, uses it not the least
Except to be more beastly than any beast.
45 He seems to me—if your Honor does not
    mind—
Like a grasshopper—the long-legged kind—
That's always in flight and leaps as it flies along
And then in the grass strikes up its same old song.
I could only wish he confined himself to the grass!
50 He thrusts his nose into every filth, alas.

Lord.
Mephistopheles, have you no other news?
Do you always come here to accuse?
Is nothing ever right in your eyes on earth?

32. **levee** (lev′ē): a reception.

Archiv Für Kunst Und Geschichte, Berlin

Painting by August von Kreling, 1872, depicting Faust and Mephistopheles.

3 LITERARY ELEMENT
Diction: Impressed with Shakespeare's ability to express human feelings in direct language, Goethe chose to write in a natural and personal voice, using simple language that all readers could understand. How would you describe Mephistopheles' diction in lines 29–36? (Possible response: casual, personal, a rude way to speak to a deity)

4 CULTURAL DIVERSITY
Light is a universal symbol of the divine presence and the knowledge and reason the divine is believed to bestow.
❓ *What qualities does light or fire possess that makes it a metaphor for "Heaven's light" and "Reason," as in lines 42–43?* (Possible response: Light makes the universe visible and fire provides heat, two key elements that enable people to understand life and to survive.)

5 LITERARY ELEMENT
Simile: What does Mephistopheles say about human behavior when he compares man to a grasshopper in lines 45–50? (Possible response: Humans foolishly keep trying and failing to rise above their mortal limits.)

HUMANITIES CONNECTION

❓ *How might the contrast between dark and light in this painting relate to the meeting of Mephistopheles and Faust?* (Possible response: Faust will allow darkness, represented by Mephistopheles, to influence him.) ■

Johann Wolfgang von Goethe   **989**

fervent (fur'vənt): very
warm or intense in feeling

6 CULTURAL BACKGROUND

Elsewhere in Part I, Faust says that he has pursued the study of law, medicine, and theology, as well as philosophy. In other words, he studied all four divisions of the medieval European university. To have earned his doctorate in philosophy alone, Faust would have studied classical texts and languages, the sciences, history, and aesthetics, as well as philosophy. Modern universities have inherited the title Doctor of Philosophy, but in today's world a Ph.D. is earned by mastering one specialized field of study, such as ancient Chinese poetry.

7 INFERRING

Knowing that Faust is a Doctor of Philosophy in medieval Europe, what kind of "ferment in him" would you guess that Mephistopheles is referring to in lines 60–65? (Answers will vary; students should guess that Faust is driven to seek knowledge.)

8 LITERARY ELEMENT

Metaphor: What is the Lord saying about himself and Faust in the elaborate metaphor in lines 68–69? (Possible response: Like a gardener who knows that a sapling that sprouts leaves will flourish and bear fruit, the Lord recognizes that Faust's groping quest will eventually lead him to heaven's light, or the righteous path.)

Mephistopheles.
  No, Lord! I find things there as downright bad
    as ever.
55 I am sorry for men's days of dread and dearth;
  Poor things, *my* wish to plague 'em isn't <u>fervent</u>.

Lord.
  Do you know Faust?

Mephistopheles.
      The Doctor?°

Lord.
          Aye, my servant.

Mephistopheles.
  Indeed! He serves you oddly enough, I think.
  The fool has no earthly habits in meat and
    drink.
60 The ferment in him drives him wide and far,
  That he is mad he too has almost guessed;
  He demands of heaven each fairest star
  And of earth each highest joy and best,
  And all that is new and all that is far
65 Can bring no calm to the deep-sea swell of his
    breast.

Lord.
  Now he may serve me only gropingly,
  Soon I shall lead him into the light.
  The gardener knows when the sapling first
    turns green
  That flowers and fruit will make the future
    bright.

Mephistopheles.
70 What do you wager? You will lose him yet,
  Provided *you* give *me* permission
  To steer him gently the course I set.

Lord.
  So long as he walks the earth alive,
  So long you may try what enters your head;
75 Men make mistakes as long as they strive.

Mephistopheles.
  I thank you for that; as regards the dead,
  The dead have never taken my fancy.
  I favor cheeks that are full and rosy-red;

57. **The Doctor:** doctor of philosophy; Ph.D.

GRETCHEN IN PRISON, JOSEF FAY (1813–1875). Gretchen features prominently later in the poem as the "pure maid" with whom Mephistopheles hopes to tempt Faust.

Archiv Für Kunst Und Geschichte, Berlin

9
80   No corpse is welcome to my house;
     I work as the cat does with the mouse.

Lord.
     Very well; you have my full permission.
     Divert this soul from its primal source
     And carry it, if you can seize it,
     Down with you upon your course—
85   And stand ashamed when you must needs admit:
     A good man with his groping intuitions
     Still knows the path that is true and fit.

Mephistopheles.
     All right—but it won't last for long.
     I'm not afraid my bet will turn out wrong.
90   And, if my aim prove true and strong,
     Allow me to triumph wholeheartedly.
     Dust shall he eat—and greedily—
     Like my cousin the Snake° renowned in tale
         and song.

93. **my cousin the Snake:** In the Garden of Eden, the Devil took on the shape of a serpent and tempted Eve to eat an apple from the Tree of Knowledge.

HUMANITIES CONNECTION

❓ *How do the colors, lighting, and posture of the figures in the illustration of Gretchen in prison reflect a Romantic emphasis on emotion?* (Possible response: The colors are vivid, the lighting and posture dramatic.) *How does Goethe's writing style also stress emotion?* (Possible response: such lines as 60–65 and 82–87 create vivid images and refer to dramatic extremes of emotion) ∎

9 LITERARY ELEMENT

Irony: A statement or situation that is opposite to what is expected is called ironic. What is ironic about Mephistopheles' speech in lines 76–80? (Possible response: The Devil, who traditionally thrives on dead souls, here claims that he is only interested in claiming live ones.)

10 LITERARY ELEMENT

Plot: What turning point in the plot has occurred in lines 81–83 of the "Prologue in Heaven"? (The Lord has agreed to let Mephistopheles try to take Faust's soul.)

WRITING TO LEARN

11 *Science:* Imagine that you are a scientist who has just made a great discovery. Write an essay telling what you have discovered and how you made the discovery. Did it come from logic or intuition? Did you work alone or with a team? ∎

Johann Wolfgang von Goethe   **991**

Lord.
That too you are free to give a trial;
95   I have never hated the likes of you.
Of all the spirits of denial
The joker is the last that I <u>eschew</u>.
Man finds relaxation too attractive—
Too fond too soon of unconditional rest;
100   Which is why I am pleased to give him a companion
Who lures and thrusts and must, as devil, be active.
But ye, true sons of Heaven, it is your duty
To take your joy in the living wealth of beauty.
The changing Essence which ever works and lives
105   Wall you around with love, serene, secure!
And that which floats in flickering appearance
Fix ye it firm in thoughts that must endure.

Choir of Angels.
Thine aspect cheers the Hosts of Heaven
Though what Thine essence none can say,
110   And all Thy loftiest creations
Keep the high state of their first day.

[*Heaven closes.*]

Mephistopheles (*alone*).
I like to see the Old One now and then
And try to keep relations on the level.
It's really decent of so great a person
115   To talk so humanely even to the Devil.

SCENE FROM AUERBACH'S CELLAR, **lithograph, nineteenth century.**

The Granger Collection, New York

Dr. Faust has become disappointed with the extent of human knowledge. Although as a doctor of philosophy he has explored many areas of learning, he still has not learned the meaning of life. He has even dabbled in the art of "white magic," but he has found that it yields him no more knowledge than his own reason. Despairing, Faust considers suicide, but, when he hears the bells ringing in celebration of Easter, he is brought back to the world of simple enjoyment. He goes for a walk in the countryside, thinking that he, like other people, might be satisfied with an acceptance of his limitations. Returning to his study, he struggles with Mephistopheles, who tries to persuade him to try the Devil's way, the way of sensual pleasures, without thought of the whys or the consequences. Faust is in despair again! He cries a curse on love, on hope, on faith, and on patience.

Mephistopheles.
Stop playing with your grief which battens
Like a vulture on your life, your mind!
The worst of company would make you feel
That you are a man among mankind.
5   Not that it's really my proposition
To shove you among the common men;
Though I'm not one of the Upper Ten,°
If you would like a coalition
With me for your career through life,
10   I am quite ready to fit in,
I'm yours before you can say knife.
I am your comrade;
If you so crave,
I am your servant, I am your slave.
Faust.
15   And what have I to undertake in return?
Mephistopheles.
Oh it's early days to discuss what that is.
Faust.
No, no, the devil is an egoist
And ready to do nothing gratis°
Which is to benefit a stranger.
20   Tell me your terms and don't <u>prevaricate</u>!
A servant like you in the house is a danger.
Mephistopheles.
I will bind myself to your service in this world,
To be at your beck and never rest nor slack;
When we meet again on the other side,
25   In the same coin you shall pay me back.

7. **the Upper Ten:** the top level of society; short for "the upper ten thousand."

18. **gratis** (grat'is): for free.

CULTURAL BACKGROUND
In nineteenth-century Europe and the Americas, agricultural life was being replaced by industry, monarchies and feudal communities were breaking down to be replaced with republics governed by ordinary citizens, and great progress was occurring in science and technology. Such changes led philosophers and many writers, including Goethe, to focus on themes concerning the abilities and needs of the individual. The introduction to "The Pact with the Devil" cites two major themes not only in Faust but also in the Romantic period—the search for infinite knowledge and the yearning for a simple existence in harmony with nature.

15 ANALYZING
What strategy does Mephistopheles use in lines 1–14 to gain Faust's sympathy? (Possible response: He appeals to Faust's feelings of despair and pride by empathizing with him and offering help as a humble servant.)

16 LITERARY ELEMENT
Characterization: Faust knows that Mephistopheles would do nothing for free and that he might be a "danger" to him, yet he lends a willing ear to Mephistopheles. Why? (Possible response: His thirst for knowledge is so great that he is willing to go to any length to acquire it.)

■ prevaricate (pri·var'i·kāt): avoid the truth; lie

Johann Wolfgang von Goethe   **993**

Delacroix, known as a powerful colorist and an innovator, was considered the leader of the French Romantic school. *How do the colors in the painting of the meeting between Faust and Mephistopheles reflect the mood, or atmosphere, of their encounter? (Accept reasonable responses.)* ■

17 READER'S RESPONSE

What was your reaction to Faust's feeling about the "other side," in lines 26–30? How would you feel if you were told that you would serve Mephistopheles in an afterlife? (Answers will vary.)

18 CULTURAL DIVERSITY

Faust expresses apathy about a basic tradition of many religions: preparation in this life for an afterlife blessed by God. He is voicing a viewpoint of the Romantic period (called Pantheism): God is part of nature, and God's essence, or truth, should be sought through life experience. Thus Faust's striving to find the meaning of life through experience is also a search for God. *Refer back to your readings in the Bible, the Koran, or the Bhagavad-Gita. How might a follower of an organized faith seek knowledge of God? (Answers will vary; students should note the stress in many faiths on adhering to scriptures.)*

Trustee of the Wallace Collection

MEPHISTOPHELES APPEARS BEFORE FAUST, EUGÈNE DELACROIX (1798–1863).
Why do you think the Faust legend has been a popular theme in literature for centuries? Why do you think it appealed to the Romantics?

Faust.
  The other side gives me little trouble;
  First batter this present world to rubble,
  Then the other may rise—if that's the plan.
  This earth is where my springs of joy have
      started,
30 And this sun shines on me when brokenhearted;
  If I can first from them be parted,
  Then let happen what will and can!
  I wish to hear no more about it—
  Whether there too men hate and love
35 Or whether in those spheres too, in the future,
  There is a Below or an Above.

Mephistopheles.
  With such an outlook you can risk it.
  Sign on the line! In these next days you will get
  Ravishing samples of my arts;
40 I am giving you what never man saw yet.

Faust.

Poor devil, can *you* give anything ever?
Was a human spirit in its high endeavor
Even once understood by one of your breed?
Have you got food which fails to feed?
45 Or red gold which, never at rest,
Like mercury runs away through the hand?
A game at which one never wins?
A girl who, even when on my breast,
Pledges herself to my neighbor with her eyes?
50 The divine and lovely delight of honor
Which falls like a falling star and dies?
Show me the fruits which, before they are
    plucked, decay
And the trees which day after day renew their
    green!

Mephistopheles.

Such a commission doesn't alarm me,
55 I have such treasures to purvey.
But, my good friend, the time draws on when we
Should be glad to feast at our ease on some-
    thing good.

Faust.

If ever I stretch myself on a bed of ease,
Then I am finished! Is that understood?
60 If ever your flatteries can coax me
To be pleased with myself, if ever you cast
A spell of pleasure that can hoax me—
Then let *that* day be my last!
That's my wager!

Mephistopheles.

        Done!

Faust.

            Let's shake!
65 If ever I say to the passing moment
"Linger a while! Thou art so fair!"
Then you may cast me into fetters,
I will gladly perish then and there!
Then you may set the death bell tolling,
70 Then from my service you are free,
The clock may stop, its hand may fall,
And that be the end of time for me!

Johann Wolfgang von Goethe   **995**

---

23 INTERPRETING

Faust is speaking figuratively when he calls himself a slave in line 76. What does he mean? (Possible response: Becoming a servant of the Devil would not make Faust feel any more enslaved than he already does by the limits of his knowledge.)

24 LITERARY BACKGROUND

"The Pact with the Devil" sets the stage for Faust's adventures with Mephistopheles. In line 78, Mephistopheles is referring to the first of these, in which he and Faust will visit the College Banquet, a gathering of students at a tavern.

25 LITERARY ELEMENT

Characterization: What does Faust's speech in lines 83–91 say about his own character? (Possible response: that he believes he is a man of honor, who will keep his word without signing legal contracts)

26 LITERARY ELEMENT

Symbolism: How might signing a contract with a drop of blood be symbolic of the kind of pact Mephistopheles is making with Faust? (Possible response: Unlike a signature, which represents a person's word, blood symbolizes life, which is what Faust is gambling away, body and soul.)

---

pedant (ped''nt): a teacher who emphasizes details or rules instead of genuine learning

hectic (hek'tik): happening in a confused rush

Mephistopheles.
    Think what you're saying, we shall not forget it.
Faust.
    And you are fully within your rights;
75   I have made no mad or outrageous claim.
    If I stay as I am, I am a slave—
    Whether yours or another's, it's all the same.
Mephistopheles.
    I shall this very day at the College Banquet
    Enter your service with no more ado,
80   But just one point—As a life-and-death insurance
    I must trouble you for a line or two.
Faust.
    So you, you pedant, you too like things in writing?
    Have you never known a man? Or a man's word? Never?
    Is it not enough that my word of mouth
85   Puts all my days in bond forever?
    Does not the world rage on in all its streams
    And shall a promise hamper *me?*
    Yet this illusion reigns within our hearts
    And from it who would be gladly free?
90   Happy the man who can inwardly keep his word;
    Whatever the cost, he will not be loath to pay!
    But a parchment, duly inscribed and sealed,
    Is a bogey from which all wince away.
    The word dies on the tip of the pen
95   And wax and leather lord it then.
    What do you, evil spirit, require?
    Bronze, marble, parchment, paper?
    Quill or chisel or pencil of slate?
    You may choose whichever you desire.
Mephistopheles.
100   How can you so exaggerate
    With such a hectic rhetoric?
    Any little snippet is quite good—
    And you sign it with one little drop of blood.
Faust.
    If that is enough and is some use,

A scene from *Faust*, in which Mephistopheles tempts Faust with enchanting visions. *Lithograph by Theodor Hosemann, after Peter Cornelius, 1835.*

27 **LITERARY BACKGROUND**
Goethe got the idea for the Earth Spirit and the more evil spirit of Mephistopheles from medieval European occult literature, which described spirits conjured up through magic. As a young man, Goethe had studied the occult, perhaps because he was dissatisfied with the Enlightenment view that knowledge is acquired only through empirical evidence and reason.

HUMANITIES CONNECTION

Lithography is a method of reproducing art used mainly by printmakers. Invented by Aloys Senefelder in 1796, lithography was not widely used until the 1820s. The artist draws on the smooth surface of limestone with a greasy crayon called a tusche. This grease attracts the printing ink. The stone is then covered with water which sticks to all ungreased surfaces and repels the ink. The stone is inked and printed on paper using a special press. Unlimited reproductions of an artist's work can be printed using this method since there is virtually no wear in printing.

? *Which objects and details in this lithograph suggest the sinister quality of Mephistopheles' offer to Faust? (The skull; the half-animal costume of Mephistopheles)* ∎

105   One may as well pander to your fad.

Mephistopheles.
      Blood is a very special juice.

Faust.
      Only do not fear that I shall break this contract.
      What I promise is nothing more
      Than what all my powers are striving for.
110   I have puffed myself up too much, it is only
      Your sort that really fits my case.
      The great Earth Spirit has despised me
      And Nature shuts the door in my face.
      The thread of thought is snapped asunder,
115   I have long loathed knowledge in all its
         fashions.

In the depths of sensuality
Let us now quench our glowing passions!
And at once make ready every wonder
Of unpenetrated sorcery!
120 Let us cast ourselves into the torrent of time,
Into the whirl of eventfulness,
Where disappointment and success,
Pleasure and pain may chop and change
As chop and change they will and can;
125 It is restless action makes the man.

Mephistopheles.
No limit is fixed for you, no bound;
If you'd like to nibble at everything
Or to seize upon something flying round—
Well, may you have a run for your money!
130 But seize your chance and don't be funny!

Faust.
I've told you, it is no question of happiness.
The most painful joy, enamored hate, enlivening
Disgust—I devote myself to all excess.
My breast, now cured of its appetite for knowledge,
135 From now is open to all and every smart,
And what is allotted to the whole of mankind
That will I sample in my inmost heart,
Grasping the highest and lowest with my spirit,
Piling men's weal and woe upon my neck,
140 To extend myself to embrace all human selves
And to founder in the end, like them, a wreck.

Mephistopheles.
O believe *me*, who have been chewing
These iron rations many a thousand year,
No human being can digest
145 This stuff, from the cradle to the bier.°
This universe—believe a devil—
Was made for no one but a god!
He exists in eternal light
But *us* he has brought into the darkness
150 While *your* sole portion is day and night.

Faust.
I will all the same!

FAUST AND GRETCHEN, ADOLPHE MONTICELLI (1824–1886).

Archiv Für Kunst Und Geschichte, Berlin

145. **bier** (bir): a platform on which a coffin or corpse is placed.

Mephistopheles.

That's very nice.
There's only one thing I find wrong:
Time is short, art is long.
You could do with a little artistic advice.

155 Confederate with one of the poets
And let him flog his imagination
To heap all virtues on your head,
A head with such a reputation:
Lion's bravery,
160 Stag's velocity,
Fire of Italy,
Northern tenacity.
Let *him* find out the secret art
Of combining craft with a noble heart
165 And of being in love like a young man,
Hotly, but working to a plan.
Such a person—*I'd* like to meet him;
"Mr. Microcosm"° is how I'd greet him.

Faust.

What am I then if fate must bar
170 My efforts to reach that crown of humanity
After which all my senses strive?

Mephistopheles.

You are in the end ... what you are.
You can put on full-bottomed wigs with a
million locks,
You can put on stilts instead of your socks,
175 You remain forever what you are.

Faust.

I feel my endeavors have not been worth a pin
When I raked together the treasures of the
human mind,
If at the end I but sit down to find
No new force welling up within.
180 I have not a hair's breadth more of height,
I am no nearer the Infinite.

Mephistopheles.

My very good sir, you look at things
Just in the way that people do;
We must be cleverer than that
185 Or the joys of life will escape from you.

168. **Mr. Microcosm:** i.e., man as the microcosm, or essence, of the world.

31 INTERPRETING
What does Mephistopheles mean by "Time is short, art is long"? (Possible response: Human mortality limits a man's ability to reach perfection or infinite knowledge.)

32 CULTURAL DIVERSITY
In lines 155–168, Mephistopheles is alluding to the Romantic view of the poetic imagination as a superior power that, in the words of English poet Samuel Coleridge, is a "repetition in the finite mind of the eternal act of creation in the infinite I AM." Thus the poet can make plausible the seemingly impossible, such as a heart that is both crafty and noble.

33 ANALYZING
Think about Faust's words in lines 169–171. What does he mean by "crown of humanity"? (Possible response: to reach infinite knowledge) Do you think his ambitions have changed since he made the pact with Mephistopheles? (Answers will vary; students should see that Faust sees experience of the world as a last resort in his quest to know what life means.)

34 SYNTHESIZING
What other speech by Mephistopheles does the passage in lines 172–175 remind you of? Why? (Possible response: his comparison of man to a grasshopper in the "Prologue." In both speeches, Mephistopheles expresses his belief that man cannot transcend his earthly existence.)

Johann Wolfgang von Goethe **999**

READING CHECK

1. What is the "gleam of Heaven's light" the Lord has given people? (reason)
2. What is right on earth in Mephistopheles' eyes? (nothing)
3. What does the Lord say people are too fond of? ("unconditional rest")
4. What kind of knowledge has Faust already sought? (scholarly knowledge)
5. Why is Faust signing a pact with the Devil? (to attain ultimate knowledge)

6. How does Faust sign the pact? (in blood)
7. What does Faust wish to experience and embrace? (all human experience)
8. Who does Mephistopheles believe the universe was made for? (God)
9. What are "the highest gifts that men can prize"? (knowledge and reason)
10. What end does Mephistopheles foresee for Faust? (Faust will be accursed.)

RETEACHING

Have students stage a retelling of these two scenes from *Faust*. Guide students to plot out the sequence of major events in the two scenes and to identify the speakers for each event. Then divide students into three groups, each preparing lines to represent the point of view of the Lord, Mephistopheles, and Faust. Encourage students to be faithful to the characters. Finally, have groups choose speakers and perform their scenes.

35 COMPARING LITERATURE

In "The Search for Everlasting Life" from the *Epic of Gilgamesh* (pp. 136–152), Siduri advises Gilgamesh to accept his mortality and enjoy the earthly life the gods gave him. How is Siduri's advice similar to and different from Mephistopheles' in lines 184–195? (Possible response: Both promote the pleasures of life over restless striving. Siduri suggests wholesome pleasures, whereas Mephistopheles seems to suggest only sensual pleasures.)

36 LITERARY ELEMENT

Imagery: In lines 214–216, to what does Mephistopheles compare himself? (a cruel master taunting his thirsty beast) How does this image contrast with the image of the Lord as the gardener in lines 68–69 of the "Prologue"? (Possible response: Mephistopheles takes delight in Faust's plight; the Lord trusts in the goodness of his creations and tends to them lovingly.)

37 INTERPRETING

Why does Mephistopheles, in lines 216–218 of "The Pact with the Devil," think Faust is "accursed" no matter which path he chooses? (Possible response: If Faust succumbs to the Devil, his soul will be cursed; if he continues to strive, he will be cursed with the impossibility of his goal.)

35

Hell! You have surely hands and feet,
Also a head and you-know-what;
The pleasures I gather on the wing,
Are they less mine? Of course they're not!
190   Suppose I can afford six stallions,
I can add that horsepower to my score
And dash along and be a proper man
As if my legs were twenty-four.
So goodbye to thinking! On your toes!
195   The world's before us. Quick! Here goes!
I tell you, a chap who's intellectual
Is like a beast on a blasted heath
Driven in circles by a demon
While a fine green meadow lies round beneath.

Faust.
200   How do we start?

Mephistopheles.
              We just say go—and skip.
But please get ready for this pleasure trip.

                    [*Exit* FAUST.]

Only look down on knowledge and reason,
The highest gifts that men can prize,
Only allow the spirit of lies
205   To confirm you in magic and illusion,
And then I have you body and soul.
Fate has given this man a spirit
Which is always pressing onwards, beyond control,
And whose mad striving overleaps
210   All joys of the earth between pole and pole.
Him shall I drag through the wilds of life
And through the flats of meaninglessness,
I shall make him flounder and gape and stick
And to tease his insatiableness

36   215   Hang meat and drink in the air before his
          watering lips;

37   In vain he will pray to slake his inner thirst,
And even had he not sold himself to the devil
He would be equally accursed.

1. **Creating a Musical Score.** Have students compile a musical score for the selection using popular and classical music. Students may choose songs to accompany a few key speeches, as well as background music.
2. **Creating Staging Directions.** Explore with students the kinds of sets and costumes they might create for a staging of *Faust* if it were set in the present. Have them write staging directions and draw illustrations for each scene.
3. **Research Project.** Students who are curious about the rest of the play may read Louis MacNeice's translation (Oxford, 1960) or Walter Arndt's version (Norton, 1976). Have students give an oral report summarizing the play and commenting on their reactions to its outcome.

Discuss how little the selection tells about where and when the story takes place and what the characters look like. Ask the class, "What purposes might Goethe have had for leaving these factors to the reader's imagination?" Extend the discussion by noting the importance of visualization to a reader's enjoyment of literature. Elaborate on how authors may use a discrete situation to symbolize every person's experience. ■

First Thoughts

Do you think that Faust is foolish to make a pact with the Devil?

Identifying Facts

1. Why has the Lord asked Mephistopheles to visit Heaven?
2. What does Mephistopheles criticize about the world the Lord has made?
3. What agreement do Mephistopheles and the Lord make about Faust?
4. What agreement does Mephistopheles make with Faust?
5. Faust tells Mephistopheles that he is not seeking happiness. What *does* Faust claim to be seeking?

Interpreting Meanings

1. In the Prologue, Mephistopheles refers to "the little god of the world" and "the Old One." To whom is he referring? What does Mephistopheles' choice of words reveal about his **tone**, or attitude, toward these characters?
2. What is "Romantic" about Goethe's portrayal of the Lord allowing Faust to be tested by Mephistopheles? How is Goethe's Romanticism shown in Faust's unwillingness to rest and be quiet?
3. What is Faust's attitude toward Mephistopheles? What are his reasons for this attitude?
4. Compare and contrast the **characters** of Faust and Mephistopheles. What do their styles of speech reveal about their characters?

Applying Meanings

The world today is very different from the way it was when Goethe wrote *Faust*. Modern scientists, unlocking many of nature's secrets, have gone far beyond what Dr. Faust could have imagined. What are the present dangers of the search for scientific knowledge and the human mastery of nature? How do you think Faust would have responded to the modern world? Do you think he would have been satisfied by the knowledge he could gain in the twentieth century, or would he still want more?

Creative Writing Response

1. **Writing a Speech for a Character.** Choose one of the following characters: Faust, Mephistopheles, the Lord, or one of the Archangels. Write a speech of about ten lines, either in prose or verse, in which the character says something that was on his mind but that he did not say aloud during the sections of *Faust* you have just read.
2. **Writing a Skit.** We sometimes say that a person has sold his or her soul even though that person hasn't actually made a pact with the Devil. For example, a music fan might say, "I'd sell my soul for a ticket to tonight's concert." The expression "I'd sell my soul for . . ." simply means that the speaker is willing to go to great lengths to get what he or she wants. Write a brief skit about a person who wants something so badly that he or she says "I'll sell my soul for . . ." —and is taken literally when the Devil appears. Explore the situation thoroughly in your skit. If possible, perform the skit for the class.

Critical Writing Response

Evaluating a Character's Actions. Refer to the paragraph you wrote in the Writer's Response (see page 987). Have any of your ideas changed since reading *Faust*? Do you think that Faust was justified in pursuing knowledge at the risk of his own soul? Or do you think he should be punished for making such a dangerous bargain with the Devil? What decision would you have made if you were in Faust's shoes? Write a brief essay in which you evaluate Faust's decision.

ANSWERS

First Thoughts
Answers will vary.

Identifying Facts
1. to see if the Devil's business "be light or heavy"
2. The Lord has granted man "Reason," which has turned him "more beastly than any beast."
3. Mephistopheles can try to win Faust's soul.
4. to give Faust worldly knowledge in exchange for his soul
5. infinite knowledge

Interpreting Meanings
1. man and Lord. He is cynical and disrespectful.
2. It is imaginative. The Romantics stressed spontaneity and emotional expression.
3. skeptical and cynical. Faust believes the Devil will take before he gives.
4. Possible response: Faust's formal, lofty speech reveals his idealism and pride. Mephistopheles' casual and direct speech reveals his cynicism.

Applying Meanings
Many students will suggest that Faust's quest for knowledge is an unsatiable one.

Creative Writing Response
1. *Writing a Speech for a Character.* Speeches should match characterizations.
2. *Writing a Skit.* Skits should contain convincing characterization.

Critical Writing Response
Evaluating a Character's Actions. Evaluations should be supported by details. ■

Wordsworth once wrote that his life had been unusually uneventful. The outer details of his long life are indeed easily summarized. He spent all of his feelings of youthful rebellion in the 1790s when he supported the French Revolution and fell in love with Annette Vallon, a Frenchwoman who bore him a daughter. By the end of the decade, disillusioned by the violence of war, he withdrew into the quiet of country life. He spent the remaining fifty years in the Lake District, a region of lakes and gentle hills well-suited to his contemplative character and his love of long country walks. One critic calculated "upon good data" that Wordsworth walked 175,000 to 180,000 miles in his lifetime. Wordsworth traveled, and he saw much of Europe. For traveling companions he usually chose his sister, Dorothy, who shared his household and his love of poetry for most of her life, his wife, Mary, and the poet Samuel Taylor Coleridge, who was by turns his mentor and rival. Wordsworth was spared the worries of "getting and spending" by timely legacies from friends, a repaid debt, and, in 1813, a leisurely government job as the Distributor of Stamps. He died at the age of 80, the most highly regarded English poet of his time.

William Wordsworth
1770–1850

The Granger Collection, New York

Wordsworth was the most influential of the early English Romantic poets. His life paralleled the intellectual and political movements of his time. Rebellious and daring in his youth, he grew increasingly conservative as he got older.

He was born in the Lake District in northwest England, a beautiful area that inspired his poetry all through his life. He lost both of his parents by the time he was thirteen. For many years he was separated from his sister Dorothy, to whom he was very close. Wordsworth consoled himself for these losses by wandering alone in the country, collecting impressions that would inspire some of his greatest poetry.

Wordsworth graduated from Cambridge in 1791, but he had little interest in the careers open to a young man who was educated but without prospects. Then, in 1795, Wordsworth inherited some money from a friend. He set up housekeeping in southwest England with his sister, who became his closest friend and advisor. Like her brother, Dorothy Wordsworth was an accomplished writer. In her diary, she recorded simple, everyday experiences, many of which Wordsworth later transformed into verse by using her notes to jog his memory.

Equally important for Wordsworth's development was his friendship with the poet and critic Samuel Taylor Coleridge. They collaborated on *Lyrical Ballads*, the 1798 volume that ushered in English Romanticism.

Wordsworth's abilities declined as he grew older, although he continued to publish a great deal. Contributing to this decline was a series of tragedies, including the drowning of his beloved brother John in 1805, the deaths of two of his children around the same time, a bitter break with Coleridge that was never healed, and a chronic illness that made Dorothy an invalid.

As he grew older, Wordsworth was regarded as the foremost living English poet. In 1843 he was named Poet Laureate of Great Britain. His masterpiece, *The Prelude*, considered one of the finest long poems in English, appeared immediately after his death in 1850.

OBJECTIVES

1. To recognize Wordsworth's contribution to English Romantic literature
2. To recognize the characteristics of the Petrarchan sonnet in Wordsworth's poem
3. To write an imaginary dialogue with a historical figure
4. To analyze the structure of the sonnet

THEMES IN WORLD LITERATURE

People and Nature
Psalm 104, pp. 188–191
"The Sky Is Just Beyond the Roof,"
pp. 1027–1029

The Stirrings of the Imagination
Haiku Poetry, pp. 572–577
"The Lorelei," pp. 1011–1014
"Invitation to the Voyage,"
pp. 1021–1025 ■

VOCABULARY IN CONTEXT
The words listed below will appear in the side margin at the point of instruction:

1. sordid   4. creed
2. boon   5. forlorn
3. suckled

Reader's Guide

THE WORLD IS TOO MUCH WITH US

Background

Wordsworth marked the beginning of his life as a poet from a moment when he was fourteen years old and marveled at the sight of tree branches silhouetted against the evening sky. From that time on, Wordsworth's poetry expressed an enthusiasm for childhood memories and revealed deep insights about nature and the poetic imagination.

Wordsworth wrote some of the greatest sonnets in the English language. During the eighteenth century, the sonnet had fallen out of favor. Wordsworth and other Romantic poets gave it new life. Wordsworth chose the **Petrarchan sonnet** form (see page 804). Wordsworth uses the sonnet to express political and social themes; in particular, the sonnet becomes a vehicle for statements against tyranny and the urban world of commerce and industry. As in his other poetry, Wordsworth followed the creed set forth in his famous Preface to *Lyrical Ballads:* that poets should use a style of language similar to that spoken by everyday people, rather than the lofty, elevated diction that was currently fashionable. He did not intend, however, to imitate ordinary speech. Rather, he hoped to poetically transform the language that people really spoke.

Wordsworth believed that by developing a close sympathy with nature, human beings could tap their innate and indestructible sense of harmony and joy. "The World Is Too Much with Us" expresses his belief that modern people lack a feeling of identification with nature.

Writer's Response

What does it mean to be "out of tune" with nature? Write a few sentences exploring this issue.

Literary Focus

The **sonnet** is a fourteen-line poem written in **iambic pentameter**. Each line contains ten syllables, five of which are stressed. The **Petrarchan** or **Italian sonnet** has two parts, an **octave** (eight lines) and a **sestet** (six lines). The usual rhyme scheme is *abbaabbacdecde*. In some sonnets the first eight lines raise a question or problem that is answered in the last six lines, or the sestet opposes what is said in the octave. This shift or turn from octave to sestet is often dramatic.

PREREADING FOCUS

Background: Wordsworth's basic themes—the glories of childhood; nature and intuition as sources of wisdom; the importance of moral goodness, gentleness, faith, and simplicity—were in part reactions to the inhumanity of "the dark satanic mills" of industrialization. In Wordsworth's lifetime the city of Manchester, not far from the Lake District, grew tenfold as the rural population migrated to the city to work in its factories.

Like Goethe, Wordsworth also reacted against the logic of the Enlightenment, a school of thought that discouraged the search for meaning in anything but objective observation of the world. Wordsworth believed that the individual could find a more satisfying purpose in life through the creative power of the imagination.

Literary Focus: In his sonnets, Wordsworth used the best words he could come up with, rather than the language or diction of the common people. By its nature and tradition, the sonnet lends itself to more formal diction. Since its introduction in England in the sixteenth century by Sir Thomas Wyatt, nearly every major English poet before Wordsworth had written this specialized form of lyric poetry. The most popular subject for a sonnet was love, courtly in Wyatt's time and more amorous in Shakespeare's. Whatever emotion it expressed, the sonnet has traditionally been lyrical.

Punctuation in Poetry

Note how Wordsworth uses punctuation for dramatic effect in lines 8–10. By setting off two phrases at the beginning of the passage with commas, he emphasizes the more important "we are out of tune." A semicolon, which replaces a conjunction, gives dramatic power to the speaker's belief that "we are out of tune" with nature and yet unmoved. "Great God!" set apart with a dash as well as an exclamation point, expresses the speaker's passion.

1. **Writing and Speaking.** Ask students to rewrite lines 8–10 using as little internal punctuation as possible. Have them read their versions aloud and compare them to Wordsworth's lines.

2. **Writing and Sharing.** Ask students to write two or three lines of verse using semicolons and exclamation marks. Have partners discuss their usage. ■

HUMANITIES CONNECTION

Wordsworth longs to "see" deities embodied in nature. What does Romantic artist Walter Crane see in ocean breakers? (galloping horses) ■

1 LITERARY ELEMENT

Poetic Diction: Here, Wordsworth reverses normal word order ("we lay our powers to waste") to maintain a rhyme scheme required by the sonnet form. Find other examples of reversed word order in the sonnet. ("Little we see," "up-gathered," "it moves us not")

sordid (sôr'did): filthy; lacking decency

boon (bo͞on): blessing; benefit

suckled (suk'ld): brought up

creed (krēd): a statement of religious belief

forlorn (fôr·lôrn'): miserable; hopeless

2 INFERRING

What do you think the speaker is referring to by "creed outworn"? (Greek mythology)

3 LITERARY BACKGROUND

Triton, whose lower body was that of a fish, used a conch shell as a trumpet.

THE WORLD IS TOO MUCH WITH US

William Wordsworth

THE HORSES OF NEPTUNE, WALTER CRANE, 1892.

Archiv Für Kunst Und Geschichte, Berlin

Notice the restless, choppy rhythm of the first several lines of the poem and the reflective and melancholy tone of the last four lines. How do the rhythm and tone affect your mood as you read the poem?

The world is too much with us; late and soon,
Getting and spending, we lay waste our powers:
Little we see in Nature that is ours;
We have given our hearts away, a sordid boon!
5   This Sea that bares her bosom to the moon;
The winds that will be howling at all hours,
And are up-gathered now like sleeping flowers;
For this, for everything, we are out of tune;
It moves us not.—Great God! I'd rather be
10 A Pagan suckled in a creed outworn;
So might I, standing on this pleasant lea,°
Have glimpses that would make me less forlorn;
Have sight of Proteus rising from the sea;
Or hear old Triton° blow his wreathèd horn.

11. **lea** (lē): meadow.

13–14. **Proteus** (prō'tē·əs) . . . **Triton** (trīt''n): in Greek mythology, sons of Neptune, god of the sea.

1. Illustrating the Poem. Ask students to discuss how they would illustrate (1) the "getting and spending" world to which Wordsworth refers in line 2; (2) the natural world described in the poem. Encourage students to use their imaginations. Before they begin drawing, have students brainstorm images for each illustration. Display the finished work.

2. Debating Contrasting Views of Nature. Ask students to consider two opposing ideas: (1) Wordsworth's view; (2) the modern view that nature must be tamed. Form two debate teams, each representing a different viewpoint. Suggest that each group list facts and observations that support its viewpoint. Stage a debate, with students taking turns to make their points and offer rebuttals.

Have students consider Wordsworth's idea of modern man's being "out of tune" with nature. Why is it important to be "in tune" with nature? What is the effect of disharmony with nature on human life? Invite students to explore the theme as it relates to people's lives today. You may wish to have students discuss how and why the same theme recurs in twentieth-century literature. ∎

First Thoughts

Do you agree with Wordsworth that "we lay waste our powers" in the world?

Identifying Facts

1. What does Wordsworth say we have given away?
2. Where is the speaker of the poem standing?
3. What references to ancient Greek mythology does Wordsworth make in this poem?
4. What examples of nature's beauty does Wordsworth describe in the poem?

Interpreting Meanings

1. In your own words, restate the first two lines of the poem.
2. What do you think is the central meaning, or **theme**, of the poem? Does Wordsworth state this theme directly, or is it implied? Explain the dramatic shift in line 9.
3. How does the personification of the sea and the winds contribute to Wordsworth's theme?
4. What is Wordsworth's purpose in alluding to mythology in the last lines of the poem? What do these allusions signify?
5. What advantage does Wordsworth see in being "a Pagan suckled in a creed outworn"? What relationships to nature are represented in the Greek myths?

Applying Meanings

Think about the concerns for saving the environment and for protecting endangered species. Do you see the relevance of Wordsworth's poem to our own time?

Creative Writing Response

Writing a Dialogue. Imagine that you have built a time machine and transported William Wordsworth into the twentieth century. Write a one-page dialogue between Wordsworth and yourself in which Wordsworth expresses his reaction to nature and industry in modern America.

Critical Writing Response

Analyzing the Sonnet Form. Write a brief essay analyzing the **sonnet** form of "The World Is Too Much with Us." Identify the **volta**, or turn, and consider the effect created by the rhyming words before and after the turn. Note the progression of the argument. Finally, explain how an understanding of these elements contributes to your appreciation of the poem. (To review the **Petrarchan sonnet** form, see page 804.)

First Thoughts
Answers will vary.

Identifying Facts
1. our hearts
2. on a lea
3. Proteus and Triton
4. the sea, winds

Interpreting Meanings
1. Possible response: We waste our imaginations on trivial things.
2. Possible responses: Humans do not live in harmony with nature. implied. "Great God!" is an exclamation of frustration that divides the observation in the first part of the poem from the rebellious reaction that follows.
3. Possible response: It suggests that nature is alive.
4. Possible response: to show that a pagan relationship to nature is better than apathy. People in the past had a personal relationship with nature.
5. Possible response: one would be more connected to nature. Greek myth integrates nature into human life by assigning gods with human characteristics to aspects of nature.

Applying Meanings
Answers will vary, but may cite our dependence on nature.

Creative Writing Response
Writing a Dialogue. Wordsworth's speech should reflect views expressed in the poem.

Critical Writing Response
Analyzing the Sonnet Form. Analyses should focus on how structure enhances meaning. ∎

Alexander Pushkin
1799–1837

Tass/SOVFOTO

Alexander Pushkin is considered by many critics to be the father of modern Russian literature. He was born in Moscow to an aristocratic family that had lost most of its fortune. His great-grandfather, of whom he was very proud, was Abram Hannibal, an African who had been brought to the Russian court by Czar Peter the Great. Pushkin's father gave him access to a good library and spurred his interest in literature. Pushkin developed an interest in radical politics and began writing poetry. When he was fifteen, he published his first poem.

Pushkin's early narrative poems made him famous in Russian literary circles. Although the settings and plots of his narrative works were highly Romantic, their portrayals of Russian characters and customs struck a new, realistic note. Later prose works, such as *Tales of the Late I. P. Belkin* (1830), *The Queen of Spades* (1834), and *The Negro of Peter the Great* (1837), showed great mastery of character and style.

Pushkin's highest achievement was in poetry, particularly the historical play *Boris Godunov* (1825) and the long narratives *Eugene Onegin* (1833) and *The Bronze Horseman* (1833). His shorter poems reveal his gift for finding beauty in everyday things. And all his work, like his life, exhibits a high-spirited, dashing casualness that reveals powerful feelings underneath. Peter Ilyich Tchaikovsky, one of several composers who adapted Pushkin's works to music, said that his poems "sang themselves."

In 1831, Pushkin married a flirtatious beauty, Natalya Goncharova. She became involved with a French nobleman at the Russian court, Baron Georges d'Anthes, who pursued her so feverishly that he married her sister in order to be closer to her. Finally Pushkin's patience came to an end and, in January 1837, he provoked d'Anthes into a duel. D'Anthes fired first, and Pushkin was fatally wounded. At his death he was mourned as a national hero. Today he is viewed as a founder of Russian culture, equivalent in stature to Dante in Italy, Shakespeare in England, and Goethe in Germany.

OBJECTIVES
1. *To analyze a lyric poem by a Russian Romantic poet*
2. *To identify setting and recognize how changes in time can create different mini-settings*
3. *To write a poem or paragraph about a place, and to write an essay comparing Pushkin's poem to one by Shelley*

THEMES IN WORLD LITERATURE

The Seasons of a Human Life
"For Wei Pa, In Retirement," p. 528
To Hélène, p. 809

Generations
"Letter to His Two Small Children," pp. 520–521
"A Walk to the Jetty" from *Annie John*, pp. 1320–1328
"Half a Day," pp. 1377–1382 ▪

Reader's Guide

I HAVE VISITED AGAIN

Background

Exile has been a major theme for Russian writers throughout the nineteenth and twentieth centuries, for the simple and painful reason that many Russian writers have been exiled for their political views, Pushkin included. Pushkin's first job, when he was eighteen, was at the foreign office in Russia's capital, St. Petersburg. While there, Pushkin wrote verses that were critical of the czar. Disturbed by the popularity of these politically liberal verses, the government transferred Pushkin to southern Russia. For the rest of his life, Pushkin's every move was observed and reported on by the secret police. He was finally dismissed from the foreign service in 1824 and exiled to his mother's estate. In "I Have Visited Again," a poem written late in his career, Pushkin tells of returning to the estate ten years after his two-year exile there. Notice the several layers of memory in the poem. The speaker remembers his years of exile; but during those years, he remembered other years still further back. He anticipates the future and also imagines that he will be remembered by his descendants.

Writer's Response

Imagine that you have returned to a place—a natural setting, your elementary school, a relative's house, or your childhood home—that you have not visited for several years. Jot down a few sentences describing the mixture of emotions you might feel upon your return.

Literary Focus

The **setting** of a work is the place and time where it occurs. "I Have Visited Again" is a poem about the setting of Pushkin's ancestral estate. It was the scene of some of his most intense memories, both painful and sweet. Pushkin knew every corner of the estate so well, during so many different phases of his life and seasons of the year, that his descriptions of it are quite varied. The estate during his exile, the estate during his return, and the estate as he imagines it in the future are the same location at three different times—in effect they are three different settings.

PREREADING FOCUS

Background: Pushkin wrote "I Have Visited Again" during a difficult time in his life. He was heavily in debt and living in St. Petersburg under the watchful eye of Czar Nicholas. Compelled to live beyond his means by his frivolous wife, Pushkin grew weary of high society. As he had done throughout his life, Pushkin retreated to the country to find peace of mind and to write. Compared to his current life, the time he had spent at his family's country estate a decade earlier seemed idyllic. The nurse who had raised him and fostered his love of the Russian language was then still alive. Her nurturing presence and the soothing countryside had enabled Pushkin to write much of his masterpiece, *Eugene Onegin*, during that visit.

Literary Focus: Knowledge of the time and place in which a literary work is set can help readers gain a deeper appreciation of the work. For example, the shabby country estate in this poem was not uncommon in Russia in the 1830s. Landed gentry with dwindling fortunes, like the Pushkins, were neglecting the plantations that had supported their feudal way of life for centuries. Thus, the poem recalls Pushkin's past, and also chronicles the end of a way of life in Russia.

HUMANITIES CONNECTION

In the poem, trees are a meaningful part of the setting.

❓ *How do the trees in this painting evoke a particular time and place?* (Barren of leaves, the trees suggest the autumn season. As they are growing ungroomed, in a natural state, the trees also suggest a wooded, uncultivated area.) After students have read the poem, have them look at this painting again. Does the mood or atmosphere of the painting match that of the poem? (Answers will vary.) ■

1 LITERARY ELEMENT

Personification: What is personified in lines 6–7, and what kind of relationship does it have to the speaker? (the past; intimate) What is the speaker saying about his own attitudes through this figurative description? (Possible responses: He is happy to be recalling the past; it is still a vital part of him.)

I HAVE VISITED AGAIN
Alexander Pushkin
translated by
D. M. THOMAS

AUTUMN LANDSCAPE, CONSTANTIN KRYZHITSKI.

The Granger Collection, New York

❘❘ *As you read, visualize both the speaker of the poem and the place he is visiting. What kind of person do you imagine the speaker is, and what does this place mean for him?*

. . . I have visited again
That corner of the earth where I spent two
Unnoticed, exiled years. Ten years have passed
Since then, and many things have changed for me,
5   And I have changed too, obedient to life's law—
But now that I am here again, the past
Has flown out eagerly to embrace me, claim me,
And it seems that only yesterday I wandered
Within these groves.

Here is the cottage, sadly
10   Declined now, where I lived with my poor old nurse.
She is no more. No more behind the wall

Do I hear her heavy footsteps as she moved
Slowly, <u>painstakingly</u> about her tasks.

Here are the wooded slopes where often I
15 Sat motionless, and looked down at the lake,
Recalling other shores and other waves . . .
It gleams between golden cornfields and green meadows,
A wide <u>expanse;</u> across its fathomless waters
A fisherman passes, dragging an ancient net.
20 Along the shelving banks, hamlets are scattered
—Behind them the mill, so crooked it can scarcely
Make its sails turn in the wind . . .

On the bounds
Of my <u>ancestral</u> acres, at the spot
Where a road, scarred by many rainfalls, climbs
25 The hill, three pine trees stand—one by itself,
The others close together. When I rode
On horseback past them in the moonlit night,
The friendly rustling murmur of their crowns
Would welcome me. Now, I have ridden out
30 Upon that road, and seen those trees again.

They have remained the same, make the same murmur—
But round their aging roots, where all before
Was <u>barren</u>, naked, a thicket of young pines
Has sprouted; like green children round the shadows
35 Of the two neighboring pines. But in the distance
Their solitary comrade stands, <u>morose,</u>
Like some old bachelor, and round its roots
All is barren as before.

I greet you, young
And unknown tribe of pine trees! I'll not see
40 Your mighty upward thrust of years to come
When you will overtop these friends of mine
And shield their ancient summits from the gaze
Of passers-by. But may my grandson hear
Your welcome murmur when, returning home
45 From lively company, and filled with gay
And pleasant thoughts, he passes you in the night,
And thinks perhaps of me . . .

2 GUIDED READING
Identifying Details: What evidence shows that this "corner
of the earth" has been neglected and is untouched by
progress? (the sadly declined
cottage, the fisherman's ancient net, the crooked mill)

COMPARING LITERATURE
Romantic poets were noted for
their deep feeling for nature.
❓ *Compare Wordsworth's
"The World Is Too Much
with Us" (p. 1004) and Pushkin's poem. How are their
views of people's relationship
to nature similar and different?*
(Possible response: Both see a
deep affinity between people
and nature; Pushkin may view
nature as something only to
visit, whereas Wordsworth
wants people to live in nature.)

WRITING TO LEARN

Social Studies: Research and
write an essay about what life
was like on a country estate in
Russia in the 1830s. ■

3 READER'S RESPONSE
Have you ever felt kinship with
an aspect of nature?

Alexander Pushkin **1009**

Creating an Oral Narrative. Have students collaborate to create a group oral narrative that evokes a particular mood, using the setting of Pushkin's poem. Have volunteers write each of these words from the poem on a flashcard: *years, the past, cottage, nurse, footsteps, slopes, lake, cornfields, fisherman, hamlets, mill, acres, road, pine trees, passers-by, grandson, company.* Deal out the cards to students. Then ask them to decide on a mood they would like to achieve, such as light-hearted, jubilant, or despairing. Each student will then write adjectives on his or her flashcards to describe each noun according to the choice of mood. Finally, invite students to make up a round-robin oral narrative, each in turn inventing a sentence using the words on one of the cards. Students may tape their narrative.

Guide a class discussion of the ways in which change, or "life's law," affects both nature and man in "I Have Visited Again." Does the poet think that the effect of time on people is the same as or different from its effect on nature? In the poet's mind, how is the idea of regeneration in nature related to the idea that an individual might seek immortality through future generations? Can students make the connection also? ■

ANSWERS

First Thoughts
Answers will vary.

Identifying Facts
1. Possible response: a beautiful but neglected country estate, with lake and woods, in Russia in the 1800s
2. in the cottage. his old nurse; she died
3. their murmur. A thicket of young pines has grown up.

Interpreting Meanings
1. Possible response: nostalgic and wistful. Lines 9–13, old nurse and cottage; lines 26–29, speaker on horse, moonlit night, murmur of the pine trees
2. Possible response: the three pine trees. They are aging, but the two that stand together regenerate by producing saplings; likewise, human beings find hope in producing future generations.
3. Possible responses: The cottage has gone into decline, the nurse has died, a thicket of young pines is growing around the old pines.

Applying Meanings
Answers will vary.

Creative Writing Response
Writing a Poem. Students should present specific and realistic changes in themselves and their environment.

Critical Writing Response
Comparing Two Poems. Essays should compare theme, imagery, and mood. ■

First Thoughts
What feelings did the poem arouse in you? How do you think Pushkin feels about the **setting** he describes?

Identifying Facts
1. Describe the **setting** of the poem in your own words.
2. In which building did the speaker live during his exile? With whom did he live, and what happened to that person?
3. What about the speaker's favorite grove of pine trees has remained the same? What has changed?

Interpreting Meanings
1. Briefly describe the **mood**, or atmosphere, of this poem as a whole. Cite the lines and passages that, in your opinion, most strongly express that mood. What elements of the **setting** are described in those passages?
2. **Personification** is a form of figurative language in which an author describes a nonhuman thing or quality in human terms. What objects does Pushkin **personify** in this poem? What comparison does he make between these objects and human beings?
3. In the first stanza, the speaker says that change is "life's law." State two examples from the later stanzas that demonstrate the law of change at work on the speaker's estate.

Applying Meanings
Based on your personal experience and knowledge, do you agree that change often brings its own compensations, and that the new makes up for the loss of the old? Write a paragraph or more explaining your answer.

Creative Writing Response
Writing a Poem. Write either a short poem or a long prose paragraph about returning to an important place—for instance, your home or school—twenty years from now. What do you think will have changed about the place? What do you think will be the same? How do you think *you* will be different? When writing your poem, you might want to choose one object or person to use as a focus of comparison between the past and the present.

Critical Writing Response
Comparing Two Poems. In a brief essay, compare Pushkin's "I Have Visited Again" with the English Romantic poet Percy Bysshe Shelley's "Mutability." Consider what each poet says about the inevitability of change in nature and human lives, and compare the moods evoked by the imagery in both poems.

Mutability
by Percy Bysshe Shelley

1

The flower that smiles today
    Tomorrow dies;
All that we wish to stay
    Tempts and then flies.
5 What is this world's delight?
Lightning that mocks the night,
    Brief even as bright.

2

Virtue, how frail it is!
    Friendship how rare!
10 Love, how it sells poor bliss
    For proud despair!
But we, though soon they fall,
Survive their joy and all
    Which ours we call.

3

15 Whilst skies are blue and bright,
    Whilst flowers are gay,
Whilst eyes that change ere night
    Make glad the day,
Whilst yet the calm hours creep,
20 Dream thou—and from thy sleep
    Then wake to weep.

Heinrich Heine
1797–1856

The Bettmann Archive

Heinrich Heine (hīn′riH hī′nə) was born to German parents in Düsseldorf, which was at that time occupied by France. It later became part of Prussia, the chief state in the German empire. Because they were Jews, the members of Heine's family were subject to severe restrictions. The prejudice he experienced in his youth made Heine a lifelong lover of freedom.

In 1819, Heine, supported by his rich uncle Salomon, enrolled in the University of Bonn, where he studied literature and history, and the next year he transferred to Gottingen to study law. Expelled from school for fighting a duel, Heine moved to Berlin, where he met the great German philosopher Hegel (hā′gəl). He continued his studies until he received his degree in 1825. Meanwhile, he fell in love with and wrote many passionate poems to his uncle's beautiful but vain daughter Amalie, who eventually spurned him and married a wealthier suitor. The rejection provided Heine with fresh inspiration for dozens of beautiful poems, among them "The Lorelei" (lôr′ə·lī) and other *lieder*, or "songs."

In 1831 Heine, weary of being criticized by German authorities for his liberal views, moved to Paris, where he lived for the rest of his life. He quickly made friends with several important French writers, including Victor Hugo (see page 1015). His relationship with his wife—called "Mathilde" in his poetry—was a devoted one even though she was uneducated and, according to Heine, had no idea her husband was a famous poet.

Heine suffered from an incurable disease of the spine. His last eight years were spent in bed—in "my mattress grave," as he called it. Unable to write and in great pain, he dictated poems to a patient young woman he called "La Mouche"—French for "the fly." Some of his greatest poems were written during these years of agony.

For his epitaph, Heine had suggested the modest "Here lies a German poet." Not surprisingly, his last words, gasped out in a coughing fit, were "Paper! Pencil!"

Background: To the German people, the Rhine River is a symbol of Germany and one that often appears in their literature. For example, it is the setting for the German epic saga the *Nibelungenlied*. The epic concerns a great treasure of gold at the bottom of the Rhine (the "Reingold") that is guarded by various creatures, such as dwarfs.

Another classic, the *Odyssey*, might have influenced Heine's characterization of the Lorelei. Like her, the Sirens, who tempt Odysseus and his crew, lure sailors to their deaths with the magical powers of their song. But unlike the boatman, Odysseus evades the lure by having himself tied to the ship's mast and by stopping up the ears of his crew.

Literary Focus: The English novelist George Eliot wrote that Heinrich Heine was essentially a lyric poet. Lyric poetry originated in ancient Greece, where it was sung and accompanied on a lyre. In the Middle Ages, lyric poems were sung by troubadours throughout Europe. Although the form declined in popularity during the Age of Rationalism (1650–1800), it enjoyed a rebirth in the Romantic Age. The Romantic lyric poets abandoned musical accompaniment for their verses, concentrating instead on powerful, evocative imagery. The purpose of such images is to help readers imaginatively re-create the situation the poet is writing about and react to it as they would to the experience itself.

Reader's Guide

THE LORELEI

Background

The Lorelei is the name of a steep, rocky cliff on the Rhine River in Germany. According to legend, the spirit of a woman sits on this rock on full moon nights, combing her hair, singing, and luring boatmen to their deaths. The story of the Lorelei echoes the Greek myth of the Sirens, who tempted Odysseus and his sailors with their sweet singing.

In German, "The Lorelei" has a haunting, melancholy rhythm that cannot be fully captured in an English translation. But in English we can appreciate the visual imagery, the speaker's emotion, and much of the figurative language. The translator also has succeeded in capturing the songlike quality of the poem.

"The Lorelei" first appeared in 1827 in Heine's collection *The Book of Songs*, which has been called the most famous book of poetry in German literature. Composers such as Franz Schubert and Felix Mendelssohn set many of its poems to music. "The Lorelei" became such a beloved song among the German people that when the Nazis banned the works of Jewish writers, including Heine, they kept this lyric in their songbooks with the notation "Author Unknown."

Writer's Response

What classical myth, fairy tale, ghost story, or modern urban legend can you think of that is similar to the myth of the Lorelei? In other words, what story comes to mind that involves a conflict or a relationship between a human being and an alluring but dangerous supernatural being? Briefly sketch the story's basic plot. If you are not familiar with such a tale, feel free to make one up.

Literary Focus

Imagery is language that appeals to the senses of sight, hearing, touch, taste, and smell. "The Lorelei" is brilliant in its use of imagery, especially imagery that appeals to our senses of sight and hearing. Notice the simple language of "The Lorelei" in this translation. The German version is equally straightforward. Yet the pictures Heine creates are surprisingly complex.

THE LORELEI
Heinrich Heine
translated by
LOUIS UNTERMEYER

Have you ever been so captivated by a real event or a fantasy that you became mesmerized, unable to move? As you read, think of yourself as the boatman in the river, spellbound by the beautiful woman combing her hair.

I cannot tell why this imagined
   Despair has fallen on me;
The ghost of an ancient legend
   That will not let me be:

5 The air is cool, and twilight
   Flows down the quiet Rhine;
A mountain alone in the high light
   Still holds the faltering shine.

The last peak rosily gleaming
10   Reveals, enthroned in air,
A maiden, lost in dreaming,
   Who combs her golden hair.

Combing her hair with a golden
   Comb in her rocky bower,°
15 She sings the tune of an olden
   Song that has magical power.

The boatman has heard; it has bound him
   In throes of a strange, wild love;
Blind to the reefs that surround him,
20   He sees but the vision above.

And lo, hungry waters are springing—
   Boat and boatman are gone. . . .
Then silence. And this, with her singing,
   The Lorelei has done.

German picture postcard illustrating lines from "The Lorelei," 1905.

Archiv Für Kunst Und Geschichte, Berlin

14. **bower:** an enclosed place or retreat; a lady's bedroom or private room. It can also refer to any natural enclosure.

1. Creating a Musical Score. Invite students to set "The Lorelei" to music. They can write their own music or use or adapt an existing melody. Students who play instruments can perform the music for the class accompanied by students who enjoy singing. After they have shared their work, you may want to play a recording of Friedrich Schiller's version in the original German.

2. Research Project. Encourage students to read and research the story of the Sirens from Greek mythology. Have them compare that legend to the legend of the Lorelei. What evidence might lead them to conclude that the Lorelei was based on the legend of the Sirens? Point out that many of the towns that border the Rhine were Greek-influenced Roman settlements.

Ask students to reread "The Lorelei" and note the images that suggest the boatman was completely captivated by the Lorelei and was not able to free himself from her spell. Use the poem to spark a discussion of people, ideas, and experiences that can have a mesmerizing, or even a deadly effect, on others. ■

ANSWERS

First Thoughts
Answers will vary.

Interpreting Meanings
1. Possible response: Love can be a mesmerizing, destructive, all-consuming force.
2. Possible response: When we become obsessed with an unattainable goal, we run the risk of losing ourselves.
3. *Sight:* "twilight/Flows down"; "A mountain alone in the high light"; "The last peak rosily gleaming"; *Hearing:* "She sings the tune"; "the quiet Rhine"; "And this, with her singing . . . has done." Possible response: The images that appeal to the sense of sight create a mood of solitude; those that appeal to the sense of hearing create an atmosphere of awe.

Applying Meanings
Possible response: People wish to test themselves in situations fraught with danger. Students' responses may vary.

Creative Writing Response
Writing About a Legend. The episode should be written from the first-person point of view.

Critical Writing Response
Comparing Two Poems. Students' essays should follow block or point-by-point organizational patterns. ■

First Thoughts
What kind of melody do you imagine would accompany the lyrics of "The Lorelei"?

Interpreting Meanings
1. What attitude toward love is reflected in this poem?
2. The lines, "Blind to the reefs that surround him/ He sees but the vision above" refer to the boatman. What broader meaning about human life might they also have?
3. Write down three **images** that appeal to the sense of sight and three images that appeal to the sense of hearing in "The Lorelei." What **mood**, or emotional atmosphere, do these images create?

Applying Meanings
Although the Lorelei is beautiful, she is very dangerous. Why are people sometimes attracted to things that are harmful? Have you ever had this experience? What did you learn from the experience that you wish you had known beforehand?

Creative Writing Response
Writing About a Legend. Refer to the notes you made in the Writer's Response (see page 1012) about a myth, fairy tale, ghost story, or modern legend involving a human being and a supernatural being. Cast yourself as an observer of the scene, and relate an important episode from the tale. You may write your tale in prose or verse. Be sure to use striking **imagery** that appeals to the senses in order to convey the **tone**—cheerful, ironic, gloomy, etc.—that you are striving for.

Critical Writing Response
Comparing Two Poems. The following poem is by Edgar Allan Poe, an American poet who, like Heine, wrote during the Romantic period of the early nineteenth century. In "Eldorado," Poe also wrote about a popular legend—the search for the imaginary land of gold. Write a two- to three-paragraph essay in which you compare "The Lorelei" with "Eldorado." Consider the following elements: **tone,** supernatural agents, **imagery,** the treasure that is sought, and the fates of the boatman and the knight.

Eldorado
by Edgar Allan Poe

> Gaily bedight,°
> A gallant knight,
> In sunshine and in shadow,
> Had journeyed long,
> 5 Singing a song,
> In search of Eldorado.
>
> But he grew old—
> This knight so bold—
> And o'er his heart a shadow
> 10 Fell as he found
> No spot of ground
> That looked like Eldorado.
>
> And, as his strength
> Failed him at length,
> 15 He met a pilgrim shadow—
> "Shadow," said he,
> "Where can it be—
> This land of Eldorado?"
>
> "Over the Mountains
> 20 Of the Moon,
> Down the Valley of the Shadow,
> Ride, boldly ride,"
> The shade replied,—
> "If you seek for Eldorado!"

1. **bedight:** dressed.

Victor Hugo
1802–1885

Topham/The Image Works

Even people who knew nothing of Victor Hugo's work were awed by his physical presence. He was a man of legendary strength, energy, and appetite. He was also a man of enormous vanity, who said at one point that Paris should be renamed "Hugo."

The son of one of Napoleon's officers, Hugo spent his childhood in Madrid, Naples, and Paris. In his schoolwork and in his personal writing, he soon revealed his talent, his perfectionism, and his amazing stamina. Within two years, between the ages of seventeen and nineteen, he wrote 272 articles for a journal he edited with his brother. He published his first collection of poetry in 1822, the year he married his childhood sweetheart, Adèle Foucher. By the time he

was thirty-eight, he had published eight plays, seven volumes of poetry, and the novels *Han d'islande* (1823) and *The Hunchback of Notre Dame* (1831). At forty, as the most popular and respected author in France, Hugo was elected to the French Academy.

In 1843, Hugo's first failure—a play called *Les Burgraves*—led directly to the collapse of Romanticism in the French theater. The same year also brought a personal tragedy. His favorite daughter and her husband were drowned in a boating accident. Hugo's grief, like everything else about him, was colossal. For the next ten years he published nothing. He wrote only for himself, to ease his grief.

As a distraction from his pain during these years, Hugo entered political life. He was formally exiled as a political rebel in 1852, but he was not forgotten. His banishment contributed to his already enormous popularity. In exile, Hugo wrote many of his greatest poems and the protest novel *Les Misérables* (1862). When Napoleon III fell from power in 1870, Hugo returned to France.

Hugo's funeral—attended by more than a million people—was a tremendous spectacle. The funeral parade was miles long, led by entire regiments of cavalry. Behind them followed carriages filled with the greatest dignitaries of Europe. The French people felt they were burying not just a writer, but a national hero.

MORE ABOUT THE AUTHOR

Hugo believed that poets should take on public roles, leading and guiding the people rather than merely reflecting on nature and personal emotions. In keeping with this philosophy, Hugo played an active part in political life. He was elected to the popular assembly in 1848, but fled France in 1851 when Napoleon's nephew proclaimed himself emperor. He lived in exile in the Channel Islands for eighteen years. Upon his return to France, he was treated like a national hero.

As a poet, novelist, and dramatist, Hugo was a Romantic with a humanitarian interest in relieving the sufferings of the common man. Often considered France's greatest lyric poet, Hugo wrote poems characterized by a reflective melancholy.

ABOUT THE TRANSLATOR

Perhaps translator–poet Robert Lowell (1917–1977) was drawn to Victor Hugo's poems because the distinguished Bostonian was himself deeply involved in the public events of his time. A staunch defender of individual liberty, Lowell spoke out against war and injustice. Like Hugo's poetry, Lowell's verse mirrored his private life. As the father of the Confessional school of poetry, Lowell explored his stormy marriages, emotional breakdowns, and religious feelings in his poems.

OBJECTIVES

1. *To analyze an excerpt from a nineteenth-century Romantic poem*
2. *To identify images and determine how they affect the tone of the poem*
3. *To write a newspaper account of the French retreat from Moscow and to compare and contrast Hugo's and Pushkin's views of nature*

THEMES IN WORLD LITERATURE

War and Peace
"The Fall of Troy" from the *Aeneid*, Book 2, pp. 379–406
From *Laments on the War Dead*, pp. 1383–1386
What Is a Hero?
From the *Iliad*, pp. 224–277
"Funeral Speech of Pericles," pp. 284–292
From the *Song of Roland*, pp. 692–702 ■

VOCABULARY IN CONTEXT

The words listed below will appear in the side margin at the point of instruction:

1. vanguard
2. mire
3. obsessed
4. disputing
5. stupefied

PREREADING FOCUS

Background: Before the devastating defeat described in "Russia 1812," Napoleon had extended his empire across much of western Europe. After Czar Alexander I of Russia refused to support Napoleon in his conquests, the French emperor vowed to conquer that country as well. He mounted an impressive force—almost half a million troops—and marched into Russia. Anticipating Napoleon's move, the Czar had prepared for the onslaught. But rather than try to confront the French, the Russians withdrew, stripped the land of its resources, and set fire to the capital. As the French retreated from Moscow, the Russians, under the blinding cover of the constant snowfall, drew them into ever more remote regions devoid of food and shelter.

After his army was defeated on Russian soil, Napoleon's far-flung empire erupted in armed rebellions. Lacking the resources necessary to suppress the uprisings, Napoleon was forced to surrender the lands that he had conquered. Three years after the dissolution of his empire, Napoleon was defeated by the British at Waterloo and confined to the island of St. Helena.

Literary Focus: Hugo often piles image upon image in an effort to make the poem emotionally "real" to the reader. In this poem, Hugo's image clusters help us see, hear, feel, smell, and almost taste the cruel winter of 1812.

Reader's Guide ■

RUSSIA 1812
from The Expiation

Background

"Russia 1812," which shows the influence of both Romanticism and Realism, is excerpted from Hugo's poem *The Expiation* (1852). The subject of this excerpt is Napoleon Bonaparte's retreat from Moscow in 1812. The French army, known also as the Grand Army, had invaded Russia and reached Moscow on September 15 of that year. Expecting to find food and shelter in the city, Napoleon and his soldiers discovered instead that the Russians had evacuated Moscow, set it on fire, and taken all its supplies with them. On October 19, after a brief occupation, Napoleon ordered the Grand Army to retreat. The retreat across the frozen plains of Russia was devastating for the French. It has been said that the Russian winter, not the Russian army, defeated Napoleon. Of the 600,000 men who left for Russia, no more than one third returned.

Oral Response

On a map or globe, find the distance from Moscow to Paris. Then, in an encyclopedia or geographical dictionary, find out as much as you can about the terrain and climate of the territory between Moscow and Paris. With your classmates, discuss the hardships that an army retreating along this route in wintertime might face.

Literary Focus

Imagery is descriptive writing that appeals to our senses of sight, hearing, smell, touch, or taste. "Russia 1812" presents a vivid picture of the retreat from Moscow. As you read, notice the sensory images Hugo uses. Consider how the details in Hugo's poem compare with the details you might find in a nonfiction account of the same event. How does the use of imagery contribute to this realism?

RUSSIA 1812
from The Expiation
Victor Hugo
translated by
ROBERT LOWELL

❚ *As you read, notice what emotions are stirred in you by the*
❚ *imagery of the poem.*

The snow fell, and its power was multiplied.
For the first time the Eagle° bowed its head—
dark days! Slowly the Emperor returned—
behind him Moscow! Its onion domes still burned.
The snow rained down in blizzards—rained and
    froze.
Past each white waste a further white waste rose.
None recognized the captains or the flags.
Yesterday the Grand Army, today its dregs!
No one could tell the <u>vanguard</u> from the flanks.
The snow! The hurt men struggled from the
    ranks,
hid in the bellies of dead horses, in stacks
of shattered caissons.° By the bivouacs,
one saw the picket° dying at his post,
still standing in his saddle, white with frost,
the stone lips frozen to the bugle's mouth!
Bullets and grapeshot° mingled with the snow,
that hailed . . . The Guard, surprised at shivering,
    march
in a dream now; ice rimes° the gray mustache.
The snow falls, always snow! The driving <u>mire</u>
submerges; men, trapped in that white empire,
have no more bread and march on barefoot—
    gaps!
They were no longer living men and troops,
but a dream drifting in a fog, a mystery,
mourners parading under the black sky.

2. **Eagle:** Napoleon's nickname; also the standard for Napoleon's armies.

12. **caissons** (kā'sənz): wagons used for transporting ammunition.
13. **picket:** a soldier stationed to guard a body of troops against a surprise attack.

16. **grapeshot:** a cluster of small iron balls fired from a cannon.

18. **rimes:** frosts.

TEACHER'S RESOURCES
🖝 Vocabulary Activity
    Worksheet
🖝 Vocabulary Test
🖝 Review and Response
    Worksheet

1 LITERARY ELEMENT

Irony: Keeping in mind that this poem is describing a retreating army, what ironic contrast is implied in lines 1–2? (As snow falls, its power to kill living things increases; as soldiers fall, the power of the army diminishes.) Which force, that of nature or that of men, is Hugo portraying as greater? (that of nature)

▦ vanguard (van'gärd'): the leading part of an army

mire (mīr): deep mud or slush

COMPARING LITERATURE

❓ *How is the metrical form of this poem different from that of Baudelaire's "Invitation to the Voyage"?* (Baudelaire used a clear pattern of stanzas and a strict rhyme scheme; Hugo used neither in this poem, although he does use rhyme and half-rhyme in an irregular pattern.)

2 LITERARY ELEMENT

Imagery: What makes the images in lines 10–21 so powerful? (Possible response: The dense images, like the snow, fall relentlessly, evoking the cold and suffering of the soldiers.) Which image is most vivid in your mind? (Answers will vary.)

Meissonier (1815–1891) was known primarily as a painter of military subjects such as this one showing Napoleon and his Grand Army in retreat.

❓ *Which details in the painting echo the realism in Hugo's poem?* (the rutted road, the unimpressive countryside) *Which details seem most dramatic or Romantic?* (Napoleon spotlighted on his white horse, his impeccable dress and that of his officers) ■

3 LITERARY ELEMENT

Metaphor: What is "this kingdom"? (Possible response: the brutal weather and barren land) What similar metaphor occurred earlier? ("white empire," line 20)

■ **obsessed** (əb·sesd′): haunted in mind or preoccupied to an extreme degree

4 ANALYZING

What does Hugo mean in line 31 when he says that "Men slept—and died!"? (Exhausted soldiers fell asleep and soon froze to death.) What effect does this image have on the overall mood of the poem? (Possible responses: It darkens the mood by emphasizing the nearness of death; the exclamation point adds an ironic twist as it makes death seem almost a victory, a release from suffering.)

NAPOLEON'S CAMPAIGN IN FRANCE, ERNEST MEISSONIER, 1864.

Archiv Für Kunst Und Geschichte, Berlin

25 The solitude, vast, terrible to the eye,
    was like a mute avenger everywhere,
    as snowfall, floating through the quiet air,
    buried the huge army in a huge shroud.

3   Could anyone leave this kingdom? A crowd—
30 each man, <u>obsessed</u> with dying, was alone.

4   Men slept—and died! The beaten mob sludged on,
    ditching the guns to burn their carriages.
    Two foes. The North, the Czar.° The North was worse.
    In hollows where the snow was piling up,
35 one saw whole regiments fallen asleep.
    Attila's dawn, Cannaes of Hannibal!°
    The army marching to its funeral!
    Litters, wounded, the dead, deserters—swarms,

33. **Czar** (zär): the ruler of Russia.

36. **Attila's** (at′′l·əz) . . . **Hannibal** (han′ə·b′l): Attila, leader of the barbaric Huns, was finally defeated when he attacked Gaul in A.D. 451. Hannibal, a Carthaginian general, destroyed the Roman army at Cannae, but it was his final victory.

crushing the bridges down to cross a stream.
40 They went to sleep ten thousand, woke up four.
Ney,° bringing up the former army's rear,
hacked his horse loose from three disputing
  Cossacks . . .
All night, the *qui vive?*° The alert! Attacks;
retreats! White ghosts would wrench away our
  guns,
45 or we would see dim, terrible squadrons,
circles of steel, whirlpools of savages,
rush sabering through the camp like dervishes.°
And in this way, whole armies died at night.

The Emperor was there, standing—he saw.
50 This oak already trembling from the axe,
watched his glories drop from him branch by
  branch:
chiefs, soldiers. Each one had his turn and
  chance—
they died! Some lived. These still believed his star,
and kept their watch. They loved the man of war,
55 this small man with his hands behind his back,
whose shadow, moving to and fro, was black
behind the lighted tent. Still believing, they
accused their destiny of *lèse-majesté.*°
His misfortune had mounted on their back.
60 The man of glory shook. Cold stupefied
him, then suddenly he felt terrified.
Being without belief, he turned to God:
"God of armies, is this the end?" he cried.
And then at last the expiation° came,
65 as he heard someone call him by his name,
someone half-lost in shadow, who said, "No,
Napoleon." Napoleon understood,
restless, bareheaded, leaden, as he stood
before his butchered legions in the snow.

41. **Ney** (nā): marshal in charge of the defense of the rear in the French army's retreat from Moscow.
43. *qui vive?* (kē vēv'): a sentry's challenge; literally, "who lives?"

47. **dervishes:** Muslims dedicated to a life of poverty and chastity, who practice a whirling devotional dance.

58. **lèse-majesté** (lez' ma'zhes·tā'): treason; literally, "injured majesty."

64. **expiation:** reparation; atonement.

Victor Hugo   **1019**

1. Creating a Script. Have students work in small groups to write a script for an on-the-spot news broadcast of Napoleon's retreat from Russia during the bitter winter of 1812. Direct them to use the information in the poem as a starting point for their scripts. After each group has finished writing, invite volunteers from each group to perform their group's script for the rest of the class.

2. Research Project. The poem's description of Napoleon's retreat and the harsh Russian winter portrays a grave period in Russian history. Ask students to research the rich diversity of Russian culture and history by selecting one of the following topics: current governmental reorganization; history of Bolshevism; geography, climate, and topography; ethnic minorities; the Russian Orthodox religion.

CLOSURE

Tell students that Baudelaire praised Hugo's verbal gifts and his ability to decipher "the great dictionary of nature." Rimbaud claimed that even Hugo's prose was poetry. Ask students whether they think that Hugo's poetry has withstood the test of time or whether they think that his fame should be attributed to nineteenth-century readers' Romantic taste for grand visions and epics. Have students support their opinions. ■

ANSWERS

First Thoughts
Answers will vary.

Identifying Facts
1. the North, the Czar. the North
2. Possible response: hid in the bellies of dead horses and in stacks of shattered caissons
3. stupefied, then terrified

Interpreting Meanings
1. Possible response: to emphasize how oppressive and inescapable it was. Answers will vary.
2. oak for the Grand Army; branches are dying members of the army.
3. The soldiers still believed in Napoleon and loved him.
4. Possible response: The sentry's challenge is heard only by his own dying men.
5. Possible response: The poet's negative attitude is reflected in "man of war" and "small man," while "man of glory" and "butchered legions" reveal his sense of pity for Napoleon and his men.
6. the awful price of defeat
7. Possible response: Napoleon is atoning for his pride and lust for glory by seeing his army decimated.

Applying Meanings
Answers will vary.

Creative Writing Response
Writing a Newspaper Account. Stories should include specific details.

Critical Writing Response
Comparing Poets' Views. Examples should illuminate Pushkin's and Hugo's views. ■

> ### First Thoughts
Did this poem make you sympathize with the French army? What specific words and phrases helped form your response?

Identifying Facts
1. What two foes of Napoleon does the speaker mention? Which foe was more powerful?
2. What did the French soldiers do to stay alive?
3. Observing the destruction of his army, how did Napoleon feel?

Interpreting Meanings
1. Why do you think Hugo repeats the word *snow* so many times in the opening lines? What effect does this repetition have? What other **imagery** is repeated in the poem?
2. A **metaphor** is a comparison between two unlike things that does not use the words *like* or *as*. In lines 50–52, what metaphor does the poet use in his description of the French army? Explain the comparison in your own words.
3. According to lines 53–58, what was the attitude of the surviving soldiers toward Napoleon?
4. Explain the **irony** of the sentry's question, "*qui vive?*" ("who lives?").
5. Explain how the choice of words reveals the poet's attitude toward Napoleon.
6. Reread lines 67–69. What do you think Napoleon "understood"?
7. Consider the connotations of the word *expiation*. Why do you think Hugo

called the long poem from which "Russia 1812" was taken *The Expiation*? In what sense is the fate of the French army an "expiation"? Of what crime or error have the French been guilty?

Applying Meanings
"Russia 1812" contains many disturbing, graphic images of suffering. Think of a book, magazine article, movie, or television program that contains similar images. What purpose do such graphic portrayals serve today? Do you think people have become insensitive to suffering in literature and the media? Could most people still be affected by the imagery in Hugo's poem? Why or why not?

Creative Writing Response
Writing a Newspaper Account.   Imagine that you are a reporter for either a French or a Russian newspaper in 1812. Write a news story—with a catchy headline—describing the French retreat from Moscow. Include specific details from the poem. Remember to "slant" your story according to your chosen nationality. If you like, accompany your story with an illustration.

Critical Writing Response
Comparing Poets' Views.   Compare and contrast Pushkin's and Hugo's views about nature, providing examples from "I Have Visited Again" and "Russia 1812." What role does nature play in each poem? Does the poet view nature as benevolent or malevolent?

Charles Baudelaire
1821–1867

The Bettmann Archive

One short book, *Flowers of Evil*, made Charles Baudelaire (shȧrl bōd·ler´) the most influential French poet of the nineteenth century. Baudelaire was the first "decadent"—an artist who rejected middle-class society and experienced firsthand the poverty and sordidness of Paris street life. Most of his poems are melancholy and deal with vice, poverty, drunkenness, or something Baudelaire considered worse—boredom.

Baudelaire was born into a well-to-do family, and from the beginning he was a sensitive boy. His father died when he was six, and his mother married someone the boy hated. His stepfather sent him to military school, but Baudelaire rebelled against the school's authorities. When he was eighteen, he moved to Paris, where he lived as a Bohemian in the Paris art community, struggling to write. Disturbed and embarrassed by his decadent lifestyle, his family sent him on a sea voyage to India, but, seasick, he left the ship and spent three weeks on a tropical island.

Back in Paris, young Baudelaire inherited some money from his father's estate; living extravagantly, he managed to squander half of the money in two years. He then launched into an intense period of dissipation, physical illness, and mental disturbance. He lived on the small allowance his mother gave him and devoted himself to art, vowing that writing was the only thing worth doing.

A perfectionist, Baudelaire struggled for many years writing and rewriting the poems in his only published work, *Flowers of Evil*. The title of this collection reflects the quality of its poems, whose morbid, melancholy, and occasionally horrifying images are expressed with delicate skill and exquisite phrases. When the book was published in 1857, the author was fined for offending public morals, and six poems had to be cut out with scissors before the already-printed edition could be offered for sale. This censorship may have contributed to the long downslide that marked Baudelaire's last ten years. During that time he wrote some important prose poems and some fragments, but no poetic masterpieces to match his earlier success. At the age of forty-six, insane and paralyzed, he died in his mother's arms.

OBJECTIVES

1. *To analyze a poem by a poet who bridged the Romantic and Symbolist movements*
2. *To identify the mood created by the poem's refrain*
3. *To describe an imaginary land of bliss and to compare two translations of "Invitation to the Voyage"*

PREREADING FOCUS

Background: Marie Daubrun was twenty-six years old and at the height of her beauty when she met Baudelaire in 1854. She had begun her acting career eight years earlier and had subsequently performed in a number of stage revues. She became famous in the summer of 1847 for her featured performance in a major production. When she returned from touring with the play in 1854, Baudelaire's infatuation with her grew, and he tried to use his influence to get her better acting roles and to convince reviewers to praise her performances. Despite all Baudelaire's efforts, Marie did not return his affection. Nonetheless, Baudelaire began to work on a play, *L'Ivrogne* (Irony), that contained a prominent role for his love. He even offered it to a theater director, but he never completed it.

Literary Focus: The words that Baudelaire uses in the refrain resonate with meaning. Ask students what images or feelings come to mind when they hear the words *grace, measure, richness, quietness,* and *pleasure.* The critic Martin Turnell, in *Baudelaire: A Study of His Poetry*, writes that *grace* refers to everything being in place, *measure* to the supernatural and natural orders, *quietness* to the absence of tension, and *richness* and *pleasure* to material objects.

Reader's Guide

INVITATION TO THE VOYAGE

Background

Like the Romantic poets, Baudelaire wrote subjectively, casting the light of his own moods over his entire world. He was attracted to gloomy subjects and bizarre experiences. Baudelaire, however, saw himself as an anti-Romantic, for he prized precise language and form and considered most Romantic poetry vague and formless. Unlike most Romantics, Baudelaire found inspiration in alleys, sidewalks, and gutters, rather than in hills, brooks, and rainbows. In French literature, Baudelaire's poetry is a bridge between the work of the Romantics and that of the Symbolists, poets who used symbols to suggest, rather than directly state, meaning or mood.

"Invitation to the Voyage" is a rarity among Baudelaire's poems—its tone is mostly light and happy. Much of the poem was inspired by his interrupted sea voyage to India; the final stanza describes Holland as Baudelaire imagined it to be from looking at Dutch landscape paintings. The speaker of the poem invites a woman to accompany him to this imaginary land of bliss. The real-life model for the woman was Marie Daubrun, an actress with whom Baudelaire was infatuated.

The two lines repeated at the end of each stanza—the **refrain**—have been quoted often. The great modern painter Henri Matisse used the second repeated line as the title for a major painting; in French, it is *Luxe, Calme, et Volupté.*

Writer's Response

What is your imaginary land of bliss? In a few sentences, describe what it looks like, what you would do there, and who would accompany you on the voyage.

Literary Focus

A word, phrase, line, or group of lines that is repeated in a literary work is called a **refrain.** Refrains are most often used in songs or in poems that have a songlike quality. "Invitation to the Voyage" has a famous refrain: the two lines that appear as lines 13–14, 27–28, and 41–42. When writers use a refrain, they are usually trying to create some specific emotional effect or **mood.** As you read "Invitation to the Voyage," ask what the refrain contributes to the mood of the poem.

INVITATION TO THE VOYAGE

Charles Baudelaire

translated by
RICHARD WILBUR

SEASCAPE AT SAINT-MARIE (VIEW OF MEDITERRANEAN), VINCENT VAN GOGH (1853–
1890). *Van Gogh is noted for the striking mood of his paintings.*
❓ *What do you feel is the mood of this painting? Is it an appropriate
illustration for the poem? Why or why not?*

◆ *As you read, see if you can visualize the places to which the
poem's speaker would like to journey. Which images are the
most striking?*

My child, my sister,
                    dream
How sweet all things would seem
Were we in that kind land to live together,
And there love slow and long,

TEACHER'S RESOURCES
✔ Review and Response
  Worksheet

HUMANITIES CONNECTION

The Dutch-born artist Van
Gogh, like Baudelaire, struggled with mental illness
throughout his life and created
striking, unusual works.
❓ *How does the intensity of
Van Gogh's vibrating lines
and strong colors mirror Baudelaire's poetic intensity?* (Possible response: Baudelaire also
uses intense sensory images,
including strong colors, as in
lines 7–12 and 35–40.) ■

1 LITERARY ELEMENT

Theme: Based on this verse,
how would you describe the
theme, or main idea, of this
poem? (The theme is the
speaker's desire to escape with
a certain lover to an ideal
place of love, comfort, and
peace.)

COMPARING LITERATURE

The nineteenth-century French
poet Verlaine (see pp. 1027–
1031) wrote "The Sky Is Just
Beyond the Roof" while he
was imprisoned. After students
have read Verlaine's and
Baudelaire's poems, ask the
following question:
❓ *In what sense might the
speaker in "Invitation to
the Voyage" be imprisoned?*
(Possible response: He is
trapped in his environment,
which lacks "grace and measure," and so he yearns for escape to a place where "richness, quietness, and pleasure"
prevail.)

1

2 LITERARY ELEMENT

Imagery/Mood: What mood does the image of "drowned suns that glimmer" convey? (Possible response: The image is ambiguous; it suggests periods of happiness alternating with periods of gloom.)

3 SPECULATING

Do you think that the speaker would be happy if he could somehow be transported to his ideal world and live the life depicted in the poem? (Answers will vary.)

4 LITERARY BACKGROUND

The Industrial Revolution had transformed French society so dramatically that many felt there could be no more poetry. The factories' stench and the cities' poverty would stifle poets' creative impulses. Thus much of the writing of the mid-nineteenth century was escapist, focusing on exotic settings.

5 LITERARY ELEMENT

Alliteration: Why do you think Richard Wilbur used alliteration in "See, sheltered from the swells"? (Possible response: The harmonious sound of the s conveys "quietness" or tranquility.)

6 READER'S RESPONSE

Describe your mood when you finished reading. (Possible responses: peaceful, languishing) What effect did the refrain have on your mood? (Possible response: It made me feel content and drowsy.)

---

5   There love and die among
Those scenes that image you, that sumptuous
     weather.
          Drowned suns that glimmer there
          Through cloud-disheveled air
Move me with such a mystery as appears
10   Within those other skies
          Of your treacherous eyes
When I behold them shining through their tears.

There, there is nothing else but grace and measure,
Richness, quietness, and pleasure.

15   Furniture that wears
          The luster of the years
Softly would glow within our glowing chamber,
          Flowers of rarest bloom
          Proffering their perfume
20 Mixed with the vague fragrances of amber;
          Gold ceilings would there be,
          Mirrors deep as the sea,
The walls all in an Eastern splendor hung—
          Nothing but should address
25   The soul's loneliness,
Speaking her sweet and secret native tongue.

There, there is nothing else but grace and measure,
Richness, quietness, and pleasure.

          See, sheltered from the swells
30   There in the still canals
Those drowsy ships that dream of sailing forth;
          It is to satisfy
          Your least desire, they ply
Hither through all the waters of the earth.
35   The sun at close of day
          Clothes the fields of hay,
Then the canals, at last the town entire
          In hyacinth and gold;
          Slowly the land is rolled
40 Sleepward under a sea of gentle fire.

There, there is nothing else but grace and measure,
Richness, quietness, and pleasure.

1. Creating Travel Folders. Invite students to create travel folders advertising Baudelaire's imaginary land of bliss. Suggest that they first decide on a format, such as a trifold brochure. Also, suggest that they illustrate their folders with drawings, paintings, or collages of their idyllic places. Students should translate Baudelaire's images in their own words.

2. Recasting a Poem. Baudelaire wrote an earlier version of "Invitation to the Voyage" in prose. Have students recast the poem in prose, capturing its original flavor and meaning. Then ask them to compare their prose versions to the poetry and debate the merits of the two forms. Which genre is better suited to depicting the land of bliss? Why?

Invite a volunteer to read the poem aloud. Then ask the class: "Why do you think the speaker wanted to go on this voyage?" Use their responses to spark a discussion of the poem's mood and the elements that contribute to it, especially the refrain. You might also wish to discuss the relationship between the poem's speaker and the poet. How close to the speaker do students place the poet? Are the speaker and the poet the same person? ■

First Thoughts

Would you like to accompany Baudelaire on his voyage? Why or why not?

Interpreting Meanings

1. In line 1, the speaker addresses his lover as "My child, my sister." How does this sentiment contrast with that of "treacherous eyes" in line 11?

2. Find at least two lines or phrases in the poem that hint that the speaker's real life is not happy.

3. What does the first stanza reveal about Baudelaire's concept of love?

4. Lines 13–14 are repeated as a **refrain**. List as many other examples of repetition as you can find in the poem, including repetition of words, sounds, and images. How do these repetitions affect the **mood**, or atmosphere, of the poem?

5. The three stanzas of "Invitation to the Voyage" support the idea presented in the **refrain**. The first stanza represents "pleasure," the second "richness," and the third "quietness." How does the **imagery** of each stanza contribute to this interpretation?

Applying Meanings

"People who lead troubled lives dream of peace; people who lead peaceful lives dream of excitement." Do you agree or disagree with this statement? Apply your opinion to "Invitation to the Voyage."

Creative Writing Response

Describing an Imaginary Land. Drawing on the notes you took for the Writer's Response (see page 1022), describe your imaginary land of bliss. Use **images** that appeal to the senses of sight, hearing, touch, taste, or smell. Feel free to write your description in either poetry or prose. If you use poetry, you might want to experiment with using a refrain.

Critical Writing Response

Comparing Translations. In reading "Invitation to the Voyage," you are not just reading Baudelaire. You are also reading a translation from nineteenth-century French into twentieth-century English. In this case, the translator is one of America's leading poets, Richard Wilbur (b. 1921). Wilbur's book of poems, *Things of This World*, which includes his version of "Invitation to the Voyage," won both the Pulitzer Prize and the National Book Award in 1957.

Here is a different translation of the first stanza and the refrain of Baudelaire's poem, by Francis Duke.

> *from* Invitation to Travel
> by Charles Baudelaire
> translated by
> Francis Duke
>
> My sister, my child,
> How life would have smiled
> At us two, together, down there,
> In love at each breath,
> 5   In love until death,
> In that land whose nature you share!
> Whose suns, in their shrouds
> Of scudding wet clouds
> Arouse in my heart the same cheer,
> 10   The same charmed surprise,
> As your fickle eyes
> When sparkles dart forth through a tear!
>
> There, beauty and harmony dwell
> Where springs of voluptuousness well.

In a two- or three-paragraph essay, compare and contrast Duke's and Wilbur's translations. Consider the meaning and mood of each version; the diction, or word choice; the use of rhythm, rhyme, and other sound effects; and the naturalness of the language. Which title do you prefer? Overall, which version of the poem do you prefer? Why?

First Thoughts
Answers will vary.

Interpreting Meanings
1. The expression of wholesome love and trust contrasts with the evocation of treachery.
2. "Of your treacherous eyes / When I behold them shining through their tears" and "The soul's loneliness. . . ."
3. Possible response: An idyllic setting can nurture love.
4. *Words:* dream (lines 1, 31); love (lines 4, 5); sun[s] (lines 7, 35), gold (lines 21, 38). *Sounds:* s, g, p. *Images:* the setting sun (lines 7, 35); splendor (lines 18–23). These help create the mood of longing for an idyllic life.
5. *First:* "love slow and long" and "sumptuous weather" connote pleasure. *Second:* "luster," "rarest," "gold ceilings," and "Eastern splendor" connote richness. *Third:* "still canals" and "drowsy ships" connote quietness

Applying Meanings
Answers will vary.

Creative Writing Response
Describing an Imaginary Land. Descriptions should include personal images that appeal to the senses.

Critical Writing Response
Comparing Translations. Essays should compare all the elements of the first stanzas and the refrains. ■

SEEING CONNECTIONS

The French Connection: Charles Baudelaire and Edgar Allan Poe

1 In America, Edgar Allan Poe was long regarded as a minor writer, an author of melodramatic poems such as "The Raven" and "Annabel Lee" and thrilling tales of mystery and suspense like "The Fall of the House of Usher" and "The Tell-Tale Heart." However, largely because of the efforts of the French poet Charles Baudelaire, Poe is considered in France to be one of the greatest writers of the nineteenth century.

When Baudelaire was twenty-five, he discovered Poe. Immediately, he felt that he had found his spiritual twin and alter ego. In a letter to a friend, Baudelaire wrote: "The first time I opened a book of his I saw, with horror and delight, not just subjects I had dreamt of, but *sentences* I had thought of, and written by him twenty years before." Baudelaire not only identified with Poe the writer, but also with Poe the man. He saw himself and Poe as tormented artists whose troubled lives drove them to write poems and stories of passion and spiritual and emotional pain. Both men spent most of their professional years in poverty and illness, their work being the driving force of their lives. Identifying with Poe so thoroughly, Baudelaire proceeded to build an elaborate mythology about Poe's life.

2 The French poet became increasingly obsessed with Poe. Some sources claim that Baudelaire even prayed to the spirit of Edgar Allan Poe. He spent much time and energy studying English and asking any American he met to clarify his understanding of a certain line or passage of Poe's. According to one story, Baudelaire once questioned an American tourist who was buying shoes, but he was so disgusted by the man's ignorance of Poe that he insulted the man in anger. Twenty years of Baudelaire's life were devoted to translating Poe's fiction and championing his genius. These translations are today considered some of the finest translations in the world.

3 The publication of Baudelaire's translations and his aggressive promotion of Poe's works and ideas brought Poe a notoriety in France and Europe that he would not experience in America until more than a century after his death. The Symbolist poets, including Valéry, Verlaine, and Mallarmé, were fascinated by Poe and considered him their literary master.

Edgar Allan Poe was either ignored or disparaged by nineteenth-century American critics. He was, however, voraciously read and discussed in France and other European countries. The first and most exhaustive critical work on Poe was published not in America, but in France, in 1933. Poe began to be the subject of literary study in America in the mid-twentieth century, mainly because of the effect of these French critical works. The French, it seems, have taught Americans to appreciate one of their own greatest writers.

Paul Verlaine (1844–1896)
Arthur Rimbaud (1854–1891)

The Granger Collection, New York

The lives of Paul Verlaine (pōl ver·len') and Arthur Rimbaud (àr·tür' ram·bō') were closely linked. These two Symbolist poets shared a turbulent friendship. Both men rebelled against conventional society, sought out experiences of squalor and degradation, died relatively young, and became legendary for their poetry.

Verlaine was one of France's leading poets during the second half of the nineteenth century, though he began his career as an insurance clerk. He hoped that his marriage to sixteen-year-old Mathilde would help cure him of alcoholism, and indeed, he wrote a number of moving poems to her. Soon, however, he discovered Rimbaud and came under his influence. Verlaine abandoned Mathilde for a year-long spree that ended when he shot and wounded Rimbaud in a quarrel and was subsequently sent to prison. When he was released from prison, he found that he had lost his wife and his relationship with Rimbaud forever. From this point on, his life went downhill.

Like Verlaine, Rimbaud was a self-destructive genius. His father abandoned the family when Rimbaud was six, and he was raised in poverty by a strict mother. At the age of fourteen, Rimbaud was already writing first-rate poetry, experimenting with syntax and unusual imagery. In 1871, Rimbaud wrote to Verlaine and sent him a couple of poems, asking for his financial help and patronage. Verlaine responded enthusiastically. Before long Rimbaud began to dominate Verlaine psychologically.

After his stormy relationship with Verlaine, Rimbaud gave up poetry forever and began a career of full-time wandering during which he served with and later deserted the Dutch army, toured with a circus in Scandinavia, and worked in Africa as a gunrunner and possibly a slave trader. Ironically, while he was living in a palm-leaf hut in Africa, Rimbaud became a celebrity in Paris: Verlaine, who thought that his former friend was dead, had published Rimbaud's earlier work, *Illuminations*, with great success, though Rimbaud seemed unaware of it. After a decade of wandering and suffering, Rimbaud returned to France, where he died of cancer.

MORE ABOUT THE AUTHORS

The stormy relationship between the two poets was initiated by Rimbaud, who sent his poems to Verlaine. Verlaine not only invited the teenage poet to visit but also sent him money for the railroad ticket. Verlaine's mother-in-law, with whom the poet and his wife lived, was eager for Rimbaud to visit, for her belief in the stereotype of the "Romantic Poet" led her to expect a witty, elegant, and sensitive young man. Rimbaud was not quite what Madame Mauté de Fleurville had imagined. Verlaine's mother-in-law opened the door to a coarse-looking peasant. Rimbaud was filthy, and his hair was matted. He arrived without luggage. However, his shabby appearance would begin a new trend among aspiring artists.

ABOUT THE TRANSLATOR

Ludwig Lewisohn was seven years old when his German-Jewish family immigrated to South Carolina. He began to question his place in his adopted country only after graduating from Columbia University, when he was unable to secure a teaching position in an American university. Attributing his rejection to anti-Semitism, he may have identified with Rimbaud as an "outsider." Throughout his literary career, Lewisohn championed the cause of maintaining the cultural identity of the Jewish people.

OBJECTIVES

1. To compare a poem by Rimbaud with one by Verlaine that is similar in theme
2. To recognize the use of sensory imagery that appeals to more than one sense simultaneously
3. To write a poem that explores a contrast between setting and feelings and to write an essay analyzing the diction of Verlaine and Rimbaud

THEMES IN WORLD LITERATURE

Freedom and Bondage
The Tempest, pp. 840–932
"Black Cat," p. 1150

War and Peace
From the *Aeneid,* pp. 379–408
From "Russia 1812" from *The Expiation,* pp. 1015–1020

Life and Loss
Poems of Tu Fu, pp. 526–531
"On Her Brother," pp. 630–632 ▪

PREREADING FOCUS

Background: Verlaine's imprisonment for shooting Rimbaud signaled the end of their tempestuous relationship. Verlaine had tried to break with Rimbaud earlier, but then changed his mind and returned. By that time, Rimbaud had decided he wanted to be free. They argued for two nights. On the third day, Verlaine left the hotel, purchased a gun, and shot his friend.

During his eighteen months in prison, Verlaine became a devout Catholic and wrote fine religious poems. In "The Sky Is Just Beyond the Roof," Verlaine explores the theme of remorse for his misspent youth.

After the shooting, Rimbaud traveled around the world and served briefly in the Dutch army. "The Sleeper of the Valley" reflects his attitude toward military service.

Writer's Response: Before students write, remind them that although certain events are supposed to set a certain mood, not everyone who attends those events feels "the right way" inside. Ask students: Did you ever attend a party or family gathering and feel "down" in spite of the laughter, warmth, and festivities around you? Did you ever feel giddy at a "solemn" event? Did you hide your real feelings?

Reader's Guide

THE SKY IS JUST BEYOND THE ROOF
THE SLEEPER OF THE VALLEY

Background

"The Sky Is Just Beyond the Roof" is one of the poems Verlaine wrote while he was in prison for the shooting of Arthur Rimbaud. As you read the poem, imagine that the speaker is looking out the barred window of his cell, over the roof of the prison, at a clear blue sky that represents freedom.

"The Sleeper of the Valley" is one of Rimbaud's more accessible and straightforward poems. Its descriptions present a landscape with one human figure. The poem is built upon a surprising twist.

Writer's Response

People usually associate sunny weather and peaceful landscapes with happiness, but their feelings are often not in tune with their surroundings. In words, briefly sketch a scene—from your own experience, the experience of someone you know, or from your imagination—in which you contrast a person's surroundings with his or her feelings.

Literary Focus

The **Symbolist** poets felt that Romantic poetry was full of overly rich language and **imagery,** and they criticized Romanticism for its sometimes stereotyped imagery and empty wordiness. The Symbolists avoided making direct statements in poetry and instead strove to suggest meaning through the use of precise and evocative images, as well as through the sound of language. In this way, **Symbolism** was akin to music in its ability to suggest an impression or **mood.**

Both Verlaine and Rimbaud were Symbolists who mastered the use of sensory imagery. Their visual images are compact and suggestive, like those of a painter who creates a broad landscape in a few brushstrokes. In addition, both poets have the knack of appealing to more than one sense with a single image or figure of speech. How many distinct images can you find in "The Sky Is Just Beyond the Roof" and "The Sleeper of the Valley"? In what ways are the sounds, imagery, and suggestive language of these poems representative of Symbolism?

THE SKY IS JUST BEYOND THE ROOF

Paul Verlaine
translated by
BERGEN APPLEGATE

❚ *As you read, compare and contrast the views and emotions expressed by Verlaine and Rimbaud. What similarities can you find in the two poets' outlooks on nature and human life? What differences can you find?*

The sky is just beyond the roof
    So blue, so calm;
A treetop just beyond the roof
    Rocks its slow palm.

5 The chime in the sky that I see
    Distantly rings;
A bird on the tree that I see
    Plaintively° sings.

My God, my God, but life is there,
10   Tranquil and sweet;
This peaceful murmur that I hear
    Comes from the street!

What have you done, you who stand here,
    In tears and ruth?°
15 Say, what have you done, you who are here,
    With your lost youth?

THE ROAD TO VERSAILLES, ALFRED SISLEY, 1873.

Archiv Für Kunst Und Geschichte, Berlin

8. **Plaintively:** mournfully.
14. **ruth:** remorse; sorrow.

TEACHER'S RESOURCES
✔ Review and Response
   Worksheet

1 LITERARY ELEMENT
Imagery: How does Verlaine intensify the image in lines 1–6? (by appealing to more than one sense)

2 LITERARY ELEMENT
Symbolism: What might the bird in the second stanza symbolize? (Possible responses: freedom, the poet, moral righteousness or spirituality) How does the bird help to express the poem's theme? (Unlike the speaker, the bird is free, but singing sorrowfully as the poet is. Both seem to mourn his misspent youth.)

3 INTERPRETING
Why does the speaker mourn his lost youth in the final stanza? (Possible response: He has squandered it, and has ended up in a cell from which he can only observe life.)

CULTURAL DIVERSITY
Many of the self-styled "bohemian" poets who lived in Paris in the middle of the nineteenth century rejected Rimbaud's lifestyle of debauchery and filth. Toward the end of the century, however, aspiring artists embraced both dirt and depravity as the emblems of genius. Many young men refused to wash and assumed a dissolute lifestyle in order to appear to have genius they did not necessarily possess.

THE SLEEPER OF THE VALLEY
Arthur Rimbaud
translated by
LUDWIG LEWISOHN

WATERLILIES IN A POND, ISAAC ILYITAH LEVIATAN (1860–1900).

There's a green hollow where a river sings
Silvering the torn grass in its glittering flight,
And where the sun from the proud mountain flings
Fire—and the little valley brims with light.

5   A soldier young, with open mouth, bare head,
Sleeps with his neck in dewy watercress,°
Under the sky and on the grass his bed,
Pale in the deep green and the light's excess.

He sleeps amid the iris and his smile
10 Is like a sick child's slumbering for a while.
Nature, in thy warm lap his chilled limbs hide!

The perfume does not thrill him from his rest.
He sleeps in sunshine, hand upon his breast,
Tranquil—with two red holes in his right side.

6. **watercress:** a white-flowered plant, growing generally in running water.

1. Enacting a Trial. Have the class enact Verlaine's trial as it would be conducted today in an American courtroom. Assign courtroom roles such as judge, bailiff, stenographer, prosecuting and defense attorneys, and members of the jury. Ask students whether they would recommend leniency, parole, or an eighteen-month sentence, based on the feelings expressed in Verlaine's poem.

2. Recreating a Scene. Rimbaud's vivid imagery evokes a memorable scene in "The Sleeper of the Valley." Invite students to re-create the scene through a drawing, a painting, a collage, or a diorama. Students might want to develop descriptions of one or more especially evocative images and write them on index cards to accompany their artwork.

CLOSURE

The critic C. A. Hackett argues that Rimbaud abandoned poetry because he discovered that poetry had no superhuman, earthshaking power. Have students debate this point, focusing on the lives of the two poets and the two poems reproduced in the textbook. ∎

First Thoughts

Which poem did you prefer, and why?

Identifying Facts

1. What is the vantage point of the speaker in "The Sky Is Just Beyond the Roof"? What does he see?
2. Who is the young man in "The Sleeper of the Valley," and what has happened to him?

Interpreting Meanings

1. What emotion does line 9 in "The Sky Is Just Beyond the Roof" express?
2. The first three stanzas of "The Sky Is Just Beyond the Roof" are narrated from the **first-person point of view**. In your opinion, who is the "you" in the fourth stanza? Why is this person in tears?
3. What is the effect of **imagery** that appeals to more than one sense in Rimbaud's "The Sleeper of the Valley"?
4. **Irony** occurs when one thing is said and another thing is meant. Explain how irony is created by the language and imagery of "The Sleeper of the Valley."
5. In what sense do both poems use imagery to suggest the loss of youth?
6. What features of **Symbolism** do you see in these poems? How do these poems differ from the earlier Romantic poetry you have read, such as Wordsworth's "The World Is Too Much with Us" and Pushkin's "I Have Visited Again"?

Applying Meanings

The beautiful imagery of both poems and the irony of "The Sleeper of the Valley" serve to enhance the impact of each situation that the poet is describing. Think of how something you have recently read, seen on television, or seen in a movie dealt with a serious, even depressing, subject, such as imprisonment or the carnage of war. How did the treatment of the subject affect your reaction to it?

Creative Writing Response

Writing a Poem. Refer to the sketch you made in the Writer's Response (see page 1028). Use this sketch as the basis for a poem. In your poem, use imagery to describe the contrast between the person's surroundings and his or her feelings.

Critical Writing Response

Analyzing Diction. In "The Sky Is Just Beyond the Roof" we find words such as *sky, roof, bird,* and *street.* In "The Sleeper of the Valley" we find words and phrases such as *silvering, dewy watercress, iris,* and *chilled limbs.* Write a brief essay comparing and contrasting the **diction**, or word choice, of Verlaine and Rimbaud. Which poet uses simpler, plainer words? Which poet uses more adjectives and adverbs? For each poem, analyze how the poet's diction affects the way we see the objects in the poem and the way we feel about them. Then state why you think each poet might have chosen the kinds of descriptive words he did. Assume that the translations accurately reflect the differences in diction in the original French. You might want to use a chart like the one below to organize your ideas.

	"The Sky Is Just Beyond the Roof"	"The Sleeper of the Valley"
Use of simple, direct language (nouns/verbs)		
Adjectives and adverbs		
Effect of diction		

Paul Verlaine and
Arthur Rimbaud

1031

Maupassant's first published story (discounting those stories published under pseudonyms) made him famous throughout France. The nearly three hundred stories that followed in the next eleven years brought Maupassant great wealth, with which he purchased an estate in his native Normandy and a yacht.

Despite the distractions of fame and the astounding number of stories he wrote, Maupassant never failed to produce tales with minute observations. In *Brief Lives*, the American novelist Wallace Stegner said of Maupassant: "He [Maupassant] saw with great clarity the small characteristic, the tiny episode, the telling relationship, the perverted motive, and he focused on it. . . ." Maupassant expressed his method of observation thus: "Talent is long patience. You must scrutinize whatever you want to express, so long, and so attentively, as to enable you to find some aspect of it which no one has yet seen and expressed."

ABOUT THE TRANSLATOR

Having lived many years in Normandy, Roger Colet now resides in England, where he is writing a biography of Maupassant and translating Maupassant's next-to-last novel, *Bel-Ami*.

Guy de Maupassant
1850–1893

The Granger Collection, New York

Guy de Maupassant (gē də mō·pä·sän′) gave new shape and direction to the short story. His many works have set the standard of excellence for many writers of short fiction.

Maupassant was born into a family of merchants in rural Normandy. Among the friends of his family were many artists and writers, including the great Realist novelist Gustave Flaubert (1821–1880). Maupassant was encouraged to write from an early age, especially by his mother and Flaubert.

After serving in the French army during the Franco-Prussian War, Maupassant studied law and then took a government post in Paris. There he got in touch with Flaubert, who became his mentor. Every week, several great Realist writers met at Flaubert's house to discuss literature. They included Émile

Zola (1840–1902), and the Russian novelist Ivan Turgenev (1818–1883). Flaubert invited the young Maupassant to join the group. At that time, Maupassant was writing poems, historical dramas in verse, and horror stories. Under the influence of his new friends, he turned to realistic prose fiction.

Flaubert's influence was also helpful in getting Maupassant a better job and introductions to literary salons. Later, Maupassant joined a spinoff group of younger Realists, or Naturalists, who met at Zola's house. The Naturalists treated the older Realists with respect, but they were less interested in stylistic beauty and more intent on describing social conditions objectively.

Maupassant's twenties were a period of literary apprenticeship. He did not publish his first Realist story until 1879. But by his thirties, Maupassant had become one of the best-known artists in France, earning enough to quit his government job and support himself as a writer. In 1883 alone, he turned out two novels and seventy short stories. His novels of this time are examples of Realism at its most observant.

Few of his friends suspected that the strong young writer was in constant pain, nearly blind from overwork and disease. Painkilling drugs made his health worse. The end of 1891 brought a complete mental breakdown from which Maupassant never recovered. He died in an asylum before his forty-third birthday.

OBJECTIVES

1. To analyze a nineteenth-century realistic short story
2. To recognize the elements of a tightly constructed plot
3. To write a character sketch and an essay supporting an opinion on theme and resolution

VOCABULARY IN CONTEXT
The words listed below will appear in the side margin at the point of instruction:

1. coddling   4. assuage
2. adorn   5. surreptitiously
3. ravaged

Reader's Guide

THE JEWELS

Background

The realistic short story as a distinct literary form came into its own in the second half of the nineteenth century. Earlier Romantic writers—especially Americans such as Washington Irving, Edgar Allan Poe, and Nathaniel Hawthorne—had created marvelous short tales of fantasy. In contrast, later Realist writers perfected the use of the short story to illuminate the problems of real people. Maupassant is considered to be the most accomplished and influential of these writers. His stories are known for their realistic details, brisk pacing, concentration on essentials, and the unexpected plot twists with which they end. By deftly selecting a detail or two, Maupassant gives individuality to characters who also represent distinct social types.

One of the chief lessons Maupassant learned from the discussion groups at Flaubert's and Zola's homes and from his own writing practice was the importance of being concise. As you read "The Jewels," notice that Maupassant uses only a few sentences to describe major events and characters. The terse style found in this story, as in many others, is partly the result of the fact that Maupassant's stories were originally published in newspapers, which severely restricted the length of his material.

Writer's Response

Imagine that you have inherited a large sum of money, but that it has come from the questionable actions of someone you loved. Would you be ashamed to keep the money, or would you gladly enjoy your good fortune? Write a few sentences on this topic.

Literary Focus

As you read "The Jewels," notice how Maupassant compresses the entire adult lives of the Lantins into a handful of pages. This tightly constructed **plot**, or series of related events, consists of the following elements: **exposition**, or the description of the characters, setting, and conflict; **complications**, which occur when characters attempt to resolve the conflict; the **climax**, when the outcome is determined; and finally, the **resolution**, when all of the story's conflicts are resolved, one way or another.

PREREADING FOCUS

Background: Maupassant's "overnight success" with the story "Ball of Fat" grew out of his experiences with the Médan Group, a set of five young writers who met at Zola's country estate at Médan, near Paris. The group made plans to publish a short-story collection about the Franco-Prussian War, and each of the five fledgling authors (plus Zola himself) wrote a story for the collection. Maupassant's contribution, "Ball of Fat," was "certainly the best of the six," according to Zola. Until that time, none of the Médan Group was aware that Maupassant for several years had been sending samples of his writing to Flaubert for criticism.

Literary Focus: E. M. Forster offers a useful distinction between telling a story and creating a plot: A story is the simple retelling of events as they occurred, one after the other, in time. A plot is an arranging and presenting of events for the purpose of creating a unified artistic effect. For example, in "The Jewels" Maupassant first mentions the party where the Lantins met, next he moves backward in time to describe Madame Lantin's background, then moves forward again to describe the Lantins' marriage in the present of the story.

Style and Tone

Maupassant's prose style is notable for its detachment and conciseness, qualities that contribute to the ironic tone of his work. Tone is the attitude or feeling the author projects toward the subject or audience. An ironic tone is one that emphasizes the contrast between what is expected or appears to be true and what actually happens or is true. For example, here is a sentence from "The Jewels" that appears just after Madame Lantin has returned from the theater "shivering with cold": "The next morning she had a cough, and a week later she died of pneumonia." Maupassant's compression of her illness and death into fifteen words and his cool, seamless transition from the word *cough* to the word *died* are striking illustrations of his ability to pare language for a chilling, ironic effect. Neither the reader nor Monsieur Lantin expect her sudden demise.

1 LITERARY ELEMENT

Plot: In the second paragraph, what information does the author give about the girl's appearance and character? (Her "simple beauty" has "a modest, angelic charm"; she is "decent, quiet and gentle.") What element of plot does this passage illustrate? (exposition)

HUMANITIES CONNECTION

Renoir is famous for his paintings of people, featuring glowing skin tones, naturally relaxed postures, and sensitive facial features.

❓ *What clues does Renoir's painting provide about the character of the woman in the theater box?* (Students should consider socioeconomic level as well as personality, revealed by details of dress, posture, facial expression, and background.) *How might her character resemble that of Madame Lantin?* (Answers will vary.) ∎

coddling (käd'liŋ): treating tenderly

THE JEWELS
Guy de Maupassant
translated by
ROGER COLET

❖ *As you read, pay attention to what is not said as well as what is said. What crucial aspects of the story are implied "between the lines"?*

THE THEATER BOX, PIERRE-AUGUSTE RENOIR (1841–1919). Renoir, an Impressionist painter, moved in the same social circles as Maupassant and fellow Naturalist Émile Zola.

The Granger Collection, New York

Monsieur Lantin had met the girl at a party given one evening by his office superior and love had caught him in its net.

She was the daughter of a country tax collector who had died a few years before. She had come to Paris then with her mother, who struck up acquaintance with a few middle-class families in her district in the hope of marrying her off. They were poor and decent, quiet and gentle. The girl seemed the perfect example of the virtuous woman to whom every sensible young man dreams of entrusting his life. Her simple beauty had a modest, angelic charm and the imperceptible smile which always hovered about her lips seemed to be a reflection of her heart.

Everybody sang her praises and people who knew her never tired of saying: "Happy the man who marries her. Nobody could find a better wife."

Monsieur Lantin, who was then a senior clerk at the Ministry of the Interior with a salary of three thousand five hundred francs[1] a year, proposed to her and married her.

He was incredibly happy with her. She ran his household so skillfully and economically that they gave the impression of living in luxury. She lavished attention on her husband, spoiling and coddling him, and the charm of her person was so great that six

---

1. **francs:** The franc is the basic monetary unit of France.

years after their first meeting he loved her even more than in the early days.

He found fault with only two of her tastes: her love for the theater and her passion for imitation jewelry.

2 Her friends (she knew the wives of a few petty officials) often obtained a box at the theater for her for popular plays, and even for first nights; and she dragged her husband along willy-nilly to these entertainments, which he found terribly tiring after a day's work at the office. He therefore begged her to go to the theater with some lady of her acquaintance who would bring her home afterwards. It was a long time before she gave in, as she thought that this arrangement was not quite respectable. But finally, just to please him, she agreed, and he was terribly grateful to her.

3 Now this love for the theater soon aroused in her a desire to <u>adorn</u> her person. True, her dresses remained very simple, always in good taste, but unpretentious; and her gentle grace, her irresistible, humble, smiling charm seemed to be enhanced by the simplicity of her gowns. But she took to wearing two big rhinestone earrings which sparkled like diamonds, and she also wore necklaces of fake pearls, bracelets of imitation gold, and combs set with colored glass cut to look like real stones.

Her husband, who was rather shocked by this love of show, often used to say: "My dear, when a woman can't afford to buy real jewels, she ought to appear adorned with her beauty and grace alone: those are still the rarest of gems."

But she would smile sweetly and reply: "I can't help it. I like imitation jewelry. It's my only vice. I know you're right, but people can't change their natures. I would have loved to own some real jewels."

Then she would run the pearl necklaces through her fingers and make the cut-glass gems flash in the light, saying: "Look! Aren't they beautifully made? Anyone would swear they were real."

He would smile and say: "You have the taste of a gypsy."

Sometimes, in the evening, when they were sitting together by the fireside, she would place on the tea table the leather box in which she kept her "trash," as Monsieur Lantin called it. Then she would start examining these imitation jewels with passionate attention, as if she were enjoying some deep and secret pleasure; and she would insist on hanging a necklace around her husband's neck, laughing uproariously and crying: "How funny you look!" And then she would throw herself into his arms and kiss him passionately.

4 One night in winter when she had been to the Opera, she came home shivering with cold. The next morning she had a cough, and a week later she died of pneumonia.

Lantin very nearly followed her to the grave. His despair was so terrible that his hair turned white within a month. He wept from morning to night, his heart <u>ravaged</u> by unbearable grief, haunted by the memory, the smile, the voice, the every charm of his dead wife.

Time did nothing to <u>assuage</u> his grief. Often during office hours, when his colleagues came along to chat about the topics of the day, his cheeks would suddenly puff out, his nose wrinkle up, his eyes fill with tears, and with a terrible grimace he would burst out sobbing.

He had left his wife's room untouched, and every day would shut himself in it and think about her. All the furniture and even her clothes remained exactly where they had been on the day she had died.

But life soon became a struggle for him.

2 CULTURAL BACKGROUND
The Parisian theater of the 1870s and 1880s was more accessible to the French middle class than it had been for decades. In part, the *bourgeoisie* enjoyed the theater because the realistic dramas onstage reflected aspects of their own lives: scenery, costumes, properties, acting method, and the dramatic literature itself were intended to mirror real life.

3 LITERARY ELEMENT
Characterization: What might Madame Lantin's love of adornment reveal about her? (Possible response: She is vain and perhaps wants to appear more well off than she is.)

4 LITERARY ELEMENT
Tone: What attitude toward life does Maupassant's detached tone and his compression of events—from Madame Lantin's passionate kisses to her husband's hair turning white—express? (Possible response: The swift movement from passion to death to grief reflects the author's pessimistic view of life as short, cruel, and unpredictable.)

■ **adorn** (ə·dôrn′): decorate
ravaged (rav′ijd): ruined, destroyed
assuage (ə·swāj′): lessen, calm, or ease

His income, which in his wife's hands had covered all their expenses, was now no longer sufficient for him on his own; and he wondered in amazement how she had managed to provide him with excellent wines and rare delicacies which he could no longer afford on his modest salary.

He incurred a few debts and ran after money in the way people do when they are reduced to desperate shifts. Finally, one morning, finding himself without a sou[2] a whole week before the end of the month, he decided to sell something; and immediately the idea occurred to him of disposing of his wife's "trash." He still harbored a sort of secret grudge against those false gems which had irritated him in the past, and indeed the sight of them every day somewhat spoiled the memory of his beloved.

He rummaged for a long time among the heap of gaudy trinkets she had left behind, for she had stubbornly gone on buying jewelry until the last days of her life, bringing home a new piece almost every evening. At last he decided on the large necklace which she had seemed to like best, and which, he thought, might well be worth six or seven francs, for it was beautifully made for a piece of paste.[3]

He put it in his pocket and set off for his Ministry, following the boulevards and looking for a jeweler's shop which inspired confidence.

At last he spotted one and went in, feeling a little ashamed of exposing his poverty in this way, and of trying to sell such a worthless article.

"Monsieur," he said to the jeweler, "I would like to know what you think this piece is worth."

The man took the necklace, examined it, turned it over, weighed it, inspected it with a magnifying glass, called his assistant, made a few remarks to him in an undertone, placed the necklace on the counter and looked at it from a distance to gauge the effect.

Monsieur Lantin, embarrassed by all this ritual, was opening his mouth to say: "Oh, I know perfectly well that it isn't worth anything," when the jeweler said: "Monsieur, this necklace is worth between twelve and fifteen thousand francs; but I couldn't buy it unless you told me where it came from."

The widower opened his eyes wide and stood there gaping, unable to understand what the jeweler had said. Finally he stammered: "What was that you said? . . . Are you sure?"

The other misunderstood his astonishment and said curtly: "You can go somewhere else and see if they'll offer you more. In my opinion it's worth fifteen thousand at the most. Come back and see me if you can't find a better price."

Completely dumbfounded, Monsieur Lantin took back his necklace and left the shop, in obedience to a vague desire to be alone and to think.

Once outside, however, he felt an impulse to laugh, and he thought: "The fool! Oh, the fool! But what if I'd taken him at his word? There's a jeweler who can't tell real diamonds from paste!"

And he went into another jeweler's shop at the beginning of the Rue de la Paix. As soon as he saw the necklace, the jeweler exclaimed: "Why, I know that necklace well: it was bought here."

Monsieur Lantin asked in amazement: "How much is it worth?"

"Monsieur, I sold it for twenty-five thousand. I am prepared to buy it back for

---

2. **sou** (soo): a former French coin.
3. **paste:** fake gem.

The Nelson-Atkins Museum, Kansas City, Missouri

BOULEVARD DES CAPUCINES, CLAUDE MONET (1840–1926).
? *Why have Monsieur Lantin's finances suffered since his wife's death?*

The term *Impressionism* came from the title of a work by Monet—*Impressionism: Sunrise* (1872). Monet and his fellow impressionists Manet, Pissarro, Renoir, and Degas are noted for their casual, natural scenes rather than formal, posed portraits. Their aim was to capture a scene as glimpsed at one fleeting moment. To accomplish this goal, impressionists used vivid colors, expanses of natural light, and the effects of weather and distance on a scene. In this painting Monet used patches of color, rather than sharply defined outlines, to convey the energy of this Paris boulevard scene.

? *What impressions of the boulevard does the painting communicate to you?* (Answers will vary.) ■

eighteen thousand once you have told me, in accordance with the legal requirements, how you came to be in possession of it."

This time Monsieur Lantin was dumbfounded. He sat down and said: "But . . . but . . . examine it carefully, Monsieur. Until now I thought it was paste."

"Will you give me your name, Monsieur?" said the jeweler.

"Certainly. My name's Lantin. I'm an official at the Ministry of the Interior, and I live at No. 16, Rue des Martyrs."

The jeweler opened his books, looked for the entry, and said: "Yes, this necklace was sent to Madame Lantin's address, No. 16, Rue des Martyrs, on the 20th of July 1876."

The two men looked into each other's eyes, the clerk speechless with astonishment, the jeweler scenting a thief. Finally the latter said: "Will you leave the necklace with me for twenty-four hours? I'll give you a receipt."

"Why, certainly," stammered Monsieur Lantin. And he went out folding the piece of paper, which he put in his pocket.

Then he crossed the street, walked up it again, noticed that he was going the wrong way, went back as far as the Tuileries, crossed the Seine, realized that he had gone wrong again, and returned to the Champs-Élysées,[4] his mind a complete blank. He tried to think it out, to understand. His wife couldn't have afforded to buy something so valuable—that was certain. But in that case it was a present! A present! But a present from whom? And why was it given her?

He halted in his tracks and remained standing in the middle of the avenue. A horrible doubt crossed his mind. Her? But in that case all the other jewels were presents,

---

4. **Champs-Élysées** (shänz·ā·lē·zā'): an elegant boulevard in Paris.

too! The earth seemed to be trembling under his feet and a tree in front of him to be falling; he threw up his arms and fell to the ground unconscious.

He came to his senses in a chemist's shop into which the passersby had carried him. He took a cab home and shut himself up.

He wept bitterly until nightfall, biting on a handkerchief so as not to cry out. Then he went to bed worn out with grief and fatigue and slept like a log.

A ray of sunlight awoke him and he slowly got up to go to his Ministry. It was hard to think of working after such a series of shocks. It occurred to him that he could ask to be excused and he wrote a letter to his superior. Then he remembered that he had to go back to the jeweler's and he blushed with shame. He spent a long time thinking it over, but decided that he could not leave the necklace with that man. So he dressed and went out.

It was a fine day and the city seemed to be smiling under the clear blue sky. People were strolling about the streets with their hands in their pockets.

Watching them, Lantin said to himself: "How lucky rich people are! With money you can forget even the deepest of sorrows. You can go where you like, travel, enjoy yourself. Oh, if only I were rich!"

He began to feel hungry, for he had eaten nothing for two days, but his pocket was empty. Then he remembered the necklace. Eighteen thousand francs! Eighteen thousand francs! That was a tidy sum, and no mistake!

When he reached the Rue de la Paix he started walking up and down the pavement opposite the jeweler's shop. Eighteen thousand francs! A score of times he almost went in, but every time shame held him back.

He was hungry, though, very hungry, and

he had no money at all. He quickly made up his mind, ran across the street so as not to have any time to think, and rushed into the shop.

As soon as he saw him the jeweler came forward and offered him a chair with smiling politeness. His assistants came into the shop, too, and glanced surreptitiously at Lantin with laughter in their eyes and on their lips.

"I have made inquiries, Monsieur," said the jeweler, "and if you still wish to sell the necklace, I am prepared to pay you the price I offered you."

"Why, certainly," stammered the clerk.

The jeweler took eighteen large bank notes out of a drawer, counted them and handed them to Lantin, who signed a little receipt and with a trembling hand put the money in his pocket.

Then, as he was about to leave the shop, he turned towards the jeweler, who was still smiling, and lowering his eyes said: "I have . . . I have some other jewels which have come to me from . . . from the same legacy. Would you care to buy them from me, too?"

The jeweler bowed.

"Certainly, Monsieur."

One of the assistants went out, unable to contain his laughter; another blew his nose loudly.

Lantin, red faced and solemn, remained unmoved.

"I will bring them to you," he said.

And he took a cab to go and fetch the jewels.

When he returned to the shop an hour

OUTSIDE THE THEATRE DU VAUDEVILLE, JEAN BERAUD (1849–1936).

Christie's London/Bridgeman Art Library, London/SuperStock, Inc.

MEETING INDIVIDUAL NEEDS

Students who speak French, have French backgrounds, or have visited Paris may be able to furnish information on such textual references as the Tuileries (formal gardens on the site of a former palace), Rue de la Paix and Rue des Martyrs (Peace Street and Martyrs' Street), the river Seine, and the Champs Élysées, as well as the numerous allusions to French currency. ■

11 READER'S RESPONSE

How do you feel toward Lantin as he offers more jewels for sale? (Answers will vary.) How do the jeweler and the assistants feel about him? (They feel contemptuous and superior.)

surreptitiously (sʉr·əp·tish'əs·lē): secretly

HUMANITIES CONNECTION

Beraud, like other French Impressionists, tried to capture not only the surface realities but also the feel of day-to-day city life by painting scenes of city streets.

❓ How does Maupassant achieve the same effect with lines like "the city seemed to be smiling under the clear blue sky. People were strolling about . . . with their hands in their pockets"? (He conveys both realistic detail and underlying impressions.) ■

1. At the beginning of the story, how is Monsieur Lantin employed? (He is senior clerk at the Ministry of the Interior.)
2. What does Lantin's wife agree to do in order to please him? (attend the theater with a woman friend)
3. What occurs a week after Lantin's wife returns from the Opera with a cough? (She dies.)
4. How does Lantin try to pay his debts? (by selling his wife's "trash" necklace)
5. What does Lantin do six months after becoming wealthy? (He remarries.)

12 ANALYZING

The jeweler knows that Madame Lantin did not save money to invest in jewelry. Why does Lantin try to keep up this pretense? (Possible response: to assuage his pride and save face)

13 LITERARY ELEMENT

Resolution: How does the story's final passage resolve Lantin's feelings about his first wife, and his financial concerns, his personal happiness? Are any of these problems left unresolved? (Lantin is financially secure but unhappy. His feelings about his first wife are unclear.)

WRITING TO LEARN

Science: Using specific details about Madame Lantin's gemstones from "The Jewels," write a business letter to a client from the point of view of the jeweler, describing the precious gemstones you are offering for resale. ■

ANSWERS

First Thoughts
Answers will vary.

Identifying Facts
1. The Lantins met at an office party, fell in love, and married. Monsieur Lantin was "incredibly happy," and they lived well on modest means.
2. her love for the theater and for imitation jewelry
3. It declines dramatically.

later he still had had nothing to eat. The jeweler and his assistants began examining the jewels one by one, estimating the value of each piece. Almost all of them had been bought at that shop.

Lantin now began arguing about the valuations, lost his temper, insisted on seeing the sales registers, and spoke more and more loudly as the sum increased.

The large diamond earrings were worth twenty thousand francs, the bracelets thirty-five thousand, the brooches, rings, and lockets sixteen thousand, a set of emeralds and sapphires fourteen thousand, and a solitaire pendant on a gold chain forty thousand—making a total sum of one hundred and ninety-six thousand francs.

12 The jeweler remarked jokingly: "These obviously belonged to a lady who invested all her savings in jewelry."

Lantin replied seriously: "It's as good a way as any of investing one's money."

And he went off after arranging with the jeweler to have a second expert valuation the next day.

Out in the street he looked at the Vendôme column[5] and felt tempted to climb up it as if it were a greasy pole. He felt light

---

5. **Vendôme** (vän·dōm′) **column:** monument to a French marshal in Paris.

---

enough to play leapfrog with the statue of the Emperor perched up there in the sky.

He went to Voisin's for lunch and ordered wine with his meal at twenty francs a bottle.

Then he took a cab and went for a drive in the Bois. He looked at the other carriages with a slightly contemptuous air, longing to call out to the passersby: "I'm a rich man, too! I'm worth two hundred thousand francs!"

Suddenly he remembered his Ministry. He drove there at once, strode into his superior's office, and said: "Monsieur, I have come to resign my post. I have just been left three hundred thousand francs."

He shook hands with his former colleagues and told them some of his plans for the future; then he went off to dine at the Café Anglais.

Finding himself next to a distinguished-looking gentleman, he was unable to refrain from informing him, with a certain coyness, that he had just inherited four hundred thousand francs.

For the first time in his life he was not bored at the theater, and he spent the night with some prostitutes.

13 Six months later he married again. His second wife was a very virtuous woman, but extremely bad-tempered. She made him very unhappy.

1. **Illustrating "The Jewels."** Have students choose scenes (or images) from "The Jewels" to illustrate. Possible topics include Madame Lantin at the theater, Madame Lantin putting a gaudy necklace around her husband's neck and laughing, or Monsieur Lantin's dramatic visits to the jeweler. Encourage students to work in a medium that complements Maupassant's terse prose style.

2. **Research Project.** Some students may have been intrigued by Maupassant's stunning contrasts between "paste" and authentic jewelry. Encourage such students to research some aspect of the history of jewelry. Reports might focus on gems from a particular era (such as the late nineteenth century), a country or fashion center (such as Paris), or a notable artistic style or movement (such as Fabergé).

Ask students to reread the selection in order to locate at least three details that subtly foreshadow the truth about Madame Lantin's jewels—the fact that she received them from an illicit source. ■

First Thoughts

Did you find this story realistic, or unbelievable? Why?

Identifying Facts

1. In two or three sentences, describe the Lantins' married life, including the way they met, their feelings about one another, and their economic circumstances.
2. What two tastes of Madame Lantin's does Monsieur Lantin object to?
3. How does the death of his wife affect Monsieur Lantin's standard of living?

Interpreting Meanings

1. Summarize the **plot** of "The Jewels." Identify the **exposition**, **complications**, **climax**, and **resolution**. How is the story unified by the plot device of Madame Lantin's jewelry?
2. People who know Madame Lantin say, "Happy the man who marries her. Nobody could find a better wife." Evaluate these statements based on what you have learned about Madame Lantin during the course of the story.
3. Monsieur Lantin suffers a **conflict** about whether or not to accept the eighteen thousand francs the jeweler offers for the necklace. Why do you think he hesitates? Why do you think he ultimately decides to take the money?
4. Describe Lantin's behavior at the end of the story, after he has decided to take money for the jewels. Why do you think he resigns his post and brags about his plans for the future? Why does he keep inflating the amount of money he is actually worth?

5. Reread the last paragraph of the story. What is **ironic** about the fact that Monsieur Lantin is unhappy with his second wife? What might this seemingly offhand detail add to the meaning of the story?

Applying Meanings

Would you forgive someone who had disappointed or betrayed you, if you ultimately benefited from his or her behavior?

Creative Writing Response

Writing a Character Sketch. Madame Lantin is the key character in "The Jewels," yet we are told scarcely anything about her—not even her first name. However, from the few details that Maupassant does provide, we are given some clues that help us to understand her personality. Write a brief sketch of Madame Lantin's character as you imagine her. You may create a narrative, a letter, a diary entry, or any other form. Feel free to experiment with **point of view**. For example, you might choose to write from the point of view of Monsieur Lantin or from the perspective of an omniscient narrator.

Critical Writing Response

Supporting an Opinion. Using the notes you made in the Writer's Response (see page 1033), write a brief essay stating and then supporting your opinion about whether or not Monsieur Lantin should have profited from his wife's "legacy." Begin your essay with a thesis statement, in which you concisely state your opinion. Next, cite at least three details from the story or your own experience that support the conclusion you have drawn. Finally, conclude your essay with a restatement of your thesis statement.

Interpreting Meanings

1. *Exposition:* background, marriage; *Complication:* two of her tastes; *Climax:* discovery of her duplicity; *Resolution:* wealth, remarriage, unhappiness. The jewels bring about all the plot developments.
2. Possible response: The statements are ironic; Lantin's happiness is based on a false sense of her goodness.
3. Possible responses: He is ashamed to benefit from her infidelity. He is poor.
4. He enjoys the money when he keeps its source a secret from others, and lying about the amount enhances his enjoyment.
5. Possible responses: She is unpleasant (but true) to him. This suggests that virtue is not what makes Lantin happy.

Applying Meanings
Answers will vary.

Creative Writing Response
Writing a Character Sketch. Sketches should reflect details in the story.

Critical Writing Response
Supporting an Opinion. Thesis statements should be clear and well supported. ■

A CRITICAL COMMENT

The Short Story in the Nineteenth Century

The short story as a distinct genre of literature is a development of the nineteenth century. There are many earlier examples of short prose fiction, but the "tale" was usually a piece of didactic folk literature or a light literary diversion, and it was seldom undertaken by an important writer. When the tale was taken seriously, as, for example, by Boccaccio and Chaucer (see pages 813 and 772), it was usually used for satire or for moralizing. For the most part, short stories before the nineteenth century were told purely for the sake of entertainment.

By the nineteenth century, Guy de Maupassant in France, Anton Chekhov in Russia, and Edgar Allan Poe (1809–1849) in America were turning the story into a more complex literary form. The compactness of the story form gives it a suspenseful intensity and focus of emotional effect that is not found in the novel form. It is significant, in fact, that the first of the modern short stories were suspense tales of mystery and terror, among them Edgar Allan Poe's "Murders in the Rue Morgue," now regarded as the first detective story. Poe and Maupassant developed a technique that for a long time was a hallmark of the short story: the sharp and unexpected twist at the end, which makes a dramatic and usually ironic climax.

In the nineteenth century, the short story, like the novel, was a vehicle for making critical observations about society. As with novelists, and later dramatists such as Ibsen (see page 1069), short story writers were concerned with depicting realistic characters and situations in their works. Yet, writers like Maupassant, Émile Zola, and their followers created a style of writing that moved beyond **Realism**. They called themselves **Naturalists**, a term which they felt was an appropriate way to describe a literature that not only showed the gritty details of everyday life but also exposed various social ills and factors that affected the human condition. The Naturalists used their writings to show how the various factors in a person's life—social class, economic conditions, education, upbringing, environment—all determine or affect his or her behavior and ultimately his or her fate.

The Naturalists were often accused of dwelling on the sordid side of life and ignoring the spiritual qualities of human existence. Despite these criticisms, however, important influences came from the Naturalist movement. Writers ever since have been concerned with facing the truth about the sufferings of people, especially of the poor and exploited, and they have insisted on the freedom to express themselves in realistic language—even if it seems shocking. But the Naturalists did not want merely to shock; they wanted to expose the unpleasant and ugly facts of life with the thought that, by their revelations, something could be done to improve the world in which they lived.

Leo Tolstoy
1828–1910

Tass/SOVFOTO

When Count Leo Nikolayevich Tolstoy (lē'ō nē'kô·lä'ye·vich' tôl'stoi') died in an obscure railroad station at the age of eighty-two, he may have been the most famous man in the world. His death from pneumonia was front-page news in England and America. For, in addition to being the greatest living Russian novelist, Tolstoy was also a social and religious reformer and a symbol of Russia's yearning for freedom.

Tolstoy was born to wealthy aristocratic parents, but he became an orphan when he was nine. He, his three older brothers, and his younger sister were raised by aunts on the family estate. As Tolstoy grew older, he, like many young men of the Russian nobility, led an aimless life.

At nineteen, Tolstoy split his inheritance with his brothers and became the master of his family's estate and its three hundred serfs. Within three years, he managed to gamble away about one fourth of his inher-

itance. Looking for adventure, he joined the Russian army and fought bravely during the Crimean War. The sufferings that he witnessed during the war helped bring out his serious, morally questioning nature.

In 1859, Tolstoy opened a school on his estate for his serfs' children. Soon after, he married Sonya Andreyevna Bers. In addition to bearing him thirteen children, Sonya recopied her husband's illegible manuscripts and took over the management of his estate, enabling Tolstoy to write his greatest works, *War and Peace* and *Anna Karenina.*

After years of moral questioning, Tolstoy underwent a spiritual conversion. During the last thirty years of his life, he condemned ownership, capitalism, the Orthodox Church, and Russia's czarist government. He also repudiated much of his earlier writing—including *Anna Karenina* (1877) and *War and Peace* (1869)—for their "bourgeois" preoccupation with the Russian aristocracy. He became the leader of a utopian movement that championed the poor and was based on principles of community and social justice. His ideas inspired later pacifist reformers such as Mahatma Gandhi and Martin Luther King, Jr.

Although Tolstoy was a pacifist, a Christian, and an aristocrat, the Communist leaders of Russia never dared to ban his books. His rural grave is a major Russian tourist attraction, and his house in Moscow is now the Tolstoy Museum.

MORE ABOUT THE AUTHOR

Several times before his dramatic conversion in 1878, Tolstoy gave up writing to devote himself with a passion to education. At age thirty-one he established a school for his servants' children on his estate of Yasnaya Polyana (Clear Glade), and in his forties he spent five years designing an elementary education program for them. His spiritual conversion at age fifty, however, transformed the final thirty years of his life. The former aristocrat dressed in peasant clothing, became a vegetarian, labored in the fields alongside his former serfs, and refused royalties on his published writings. His declining income led to bitter conflicts between him and his wife— one of which ended in Tolstoy's flight from their home and subsequent death in the Astapovo railroad station.

ABOUT THE TRANSLATORS

Fluent in English, Tolstoy believed that the finest English translations of his works were those done by Aylmer and Louise Maude. Aylmer Maude, an English-born Quaker who became an important biographer of Tolstoy, and his Russian wife, Louise, often visited the count at his estate. The Maudes' translations are still widely deemed the best.

OBJECTIVES

1. *To analyze a short story by a nineteenth-century Russian writer*
2. *To recognize and interpret a parable*
3. *To write an allegory and an essay comparing and contrasting characters from two works*

THEMES IN WORLD LITERATURE

The Uses and Abuses of Power
  From *Candide*, pp. 945–962
  From *Night*, pp. 1232–1242

The Nature of Evil
  "The Fall" from *Genesis*, pp. 166–167
  From *Faust*, Part 1, pp. 988–1001 ■

VOCABULARY IN CONTEXT

The words listed below will appear in the side margin at the point of instruction:

1. disparaged   4. arable
2. aggrieved   5. haggled
3. communal

PREREADING FOCUS

Background: The reign of Czar Alexander II was turbulent. He succeeded his father, Nicholas I, just in time to see Russia defeated in the Crimean War. During the 1860s and 1870s he oversaw the so-called Great Reforms, including the emancipation of the serfs and the establishment of the institution of *zemstvos* (local self-governing councils) and of an independent judiciary. During a wave of terrorism in response to the sweeping changes taking place in Russia, Alexander II was assassinated in 1881.

Literary Focus: In many ways, parables are stylistically similar to anecdotes and anecdotal jokes—terse, simple, and rhythmic. Both parables and jokes commonly establish a central premise or theme and then repeat several variations of it. This repetition creates the familiar rhythm.

For example, Tolstoy presents Pahom in several different circumstances (but for the same basic reason) feeling restless, envious, and dissatisfied with his lot. The author answers the question posed in the title only in the parable's final sentence. This last sentence acts as a sort of punch line.

Reader's Guide

HOW MUCH LAND DOES A MAN NEED?

Background

Until 1861, when they were emancipated by Czar Alexander II, the millions of serfs working on Russian farms were the property of landowners. As property, they were frequently sold, flogged, transferred to other estates, or sent to serve in the army. After 1861, serfs were free to acquire land and money of their own. A few of these serfs, who bought the farms of other peasants or debt-ridden aristocrats, became wealthy. Pahom, the main character of "How Much Land Does a Man Need?" becomes one of these rich, landowning peasants during the course of the story.

As you read, notice how realistically Tolstoy describes several distinct Russian lifestyles. One of these is the lifestyle of the Bashkir (bash·kir') nomads, who live on the steppes, or great, treeless plains. Tolstoy owned a 6,700-acre horse-breeding farm, including a private racetrack at which he held races and wrestling contests with nomads of several tribes.

"How Much Land Does a Man Need?" is one of the best moral tales that Tolstoy wrote after becoming disillusioned with his earlier writings. In this story Tolstoy blends realism and allegory. Written in 1886, the story tells about a peasant who is corrupted and eventually destroyed by the illusion of private ownership.

Writer's Response

If you had the opportunity to become rich, how much land, money, or other possessions would satisfy you? Write a few sentences explaining how much you would need in order to feel completely satisfied.

Literary Focus

Tolstoy's story is often called a **parable**. A parable is a short, simple tale that has a moral lesson. A parable is related to **allegory**, which is a narrative with a double meaning: An allegory can be read at two or more levels. As you follow Pahom's adventures in "How Much Land Does a Man Need?" ask yourself what **theme** Tolstoy is expressing through the actions of his main character. One important clue is the way the character develops in the course of the story. Another clue is the way in which the major **conflict** in the story is resolved.

HOW MUCH LAND DOES A MAN NEED?

Leo Tolstoy

translated by

LOUISE AND AYLMER MAUDE

As you read this story, think about how its ideas might apply not only to nineteenth-century Russian peasants but also to modern Americans. What prices do people sometimes pay for their ambitions?

An elder sister came to visit her younger sister in the country. The elder was married to a shopkeeper in town, the younger to a peasant in the village. As the sisters sat over their tea talking, the elder began to boast of the advantages of town life, saying how comfortably they lived there, how well they dressed, what fine clothes her children wore, what good things they ate and drank, and how she went to the theater, promenades, and entertainments.

The younger sister was piqued, and in turn disparaged the life of a shopkeeper, and stood up for that of a peasant.

"I wouldn't change my way of life for yours," said she. "We may live roughly, but at least we're free from worry. You live in better style than we do, but though you often earn more than you need, you're very likely to lose all you have. You know the proverb, 'Loss and gain are brothers twain.' It often happens that people who're wealthy one day are begging their bread the next. Our way is safer. Though a peasant's life is not a rich one, it's long. We'll never grow rich, but we'll always have enough to eat."

The elder sister said sneeringly:

"Enough? Yes, if you like to share with the pigs and the calves! What do you know of elegance or manners! However much your good man may slave, you'll die as you live—in a dung heap—and your children the same."

"Well, what of that?" replied the younger sister. "Of course our work is rough and hard. But on the other hand, it's sure, and we need not bow to anyone. But you, in your towns, are surrounded by temptations; today all may be right, but tomorrow the Evil One may tempt your husband with cards, wine, or women, and all will go to ruin. Don't such things happen often enough?"

Pahom, the master of the house, was lying on the top of the stove[1] and he listened to the women's chatter.

---

1. **lying on the top of the stove:** lying on a brick or tile oven; the oven's use as a principal item of furniture indicates that the house is both poor and cold.

Compare this painting of a peasant woman in the Russian Impressionistic tradition to Josef Fay's Romantic *Gretchen in Prison*, p. 991.

❓ *What does* The Peasant Woman *reveal about the virtues Malewitsch attributes to peasants?* (The solid shapes and symmetrical design indicate that he sees them as well-balanced, wholesome, solid citizens.) ■

3 LITERARY ELEMENT

Parable: What does the sisters' sudden shift from antagonism to pleasantness indicate about the type of story "How Much Land Does a Man Need?" is? (It is not a realistic story.) What other details indicate the same thing? (the unremarkable presence of the Devil listening and scheming behind the stove)

THE PEASANT WOMAN, KASMIR MALEWITSCH (1878–1935).

Archiv Für Kunst Und Geschichte, Berlin

"It is perfectly true," thought he. "Busy as we are from childhood tilling mother earth, we peasants have no time to let any nonsense settle in our heads. Our only trouble is that we haven't land enough. If I had plenty of land, I shouldn't fear the Devil himself!"

The women finished their tea, chatted a while about dress, and then cleared away the tea things and lay down to sleep.

But the Devil had been sitting behind the stove and had heard all that had been said. He was pleased that the peasant's wife had led her husband into boasting and that he had said that if he had plenty of land he would not fear the Devil himself.

"All right," thought the Devil. "We'll have

a tussle. I'll give you land enough; and by means of the land I'll get you into my power."

2

Close to the village there lived a lady, a small landowner who had an estate of about three hundred acres. She had always lived on good terms with the peasants until she engaged as her manager an old soldier, who took to burdening the people with fines. However careful Pahom tried to be, it happened again and again that now a horse of his got among the lady's oats, now a cow strayed into her garden, now his calves found their way into her meadows—and he always had to pay a fine.

3

Pahom paid up, but grumbled, and, going home in a temper, was rough with his family. All through that summer Pahom had much trouble because of this manager, and he was actually glad when winter came and the cattle had to be stabled. Though he grudged the fodder when they could no longer graze on the pasture land, at least he was free from anxiety about them.

In the winter the news got about that the lady was going to sell her land and that the keeper of the inn on the high road was bargaining for it. When the peasants heard this they were very much alarmed.

"Well," thought they, "if the innkeeper gets the land, he'll worry us with fines worse than the lady's manager. We all depend on that estate."

So the peasants went on behalf of their village council and asked the lady not to sell the land to the innkeeper, offering her a better price for it themselves. The lady agreed to let them have it. Then the peasants tried to arrange for the village council to buy the whole estate, so that it might be held by them all in common. They met twice to discuss it, but could not settle the matter; the Evil One sowed discord among them and they could not agree. So they decided to buy the land individually, each according to his means; and the lady agreed to this plan as she had to the other.

Presently Pahom heard that a neighbor of his was buying fifty acres, and that the lady had consented to accept one half in cash and to wait a year for the other half. Pahom felt envious.

"Look at that," thought he, "the land is all being sold, and I'll get none of it." So he spoke to his wife.

"Other people are buying," said he, "and we must also buy twenty acres or so. Life is becoming impossible. That manager is sim-ply crushing us with his fines."

So they put their heads together and con-sidered how they could manage to buy it. They had one hundred rubles laid by. They sold a colt and one half of their bees, hired out one of their sons as a farm hand and took his wages in advance, borrowed the rest from a brother-in-law, and so scraped together half the purchase money.

Having done this, Pahom chose a farm of forty acres, some of it wooded, and went to the lady to bargain for it. They came to an agreement and he shook hands with her upon it and paid her a deposit in advance. Then they went to town and signed the deeds, he paying half the price down, and undertaking to pay the remainder within two years.

So now Pahom had land of his own. He borrowed seed and sowed it on the land he had bought. The harvest was a good one, and within a year he had managed to pay off his debts both to the lady and to his brother-in-law. So he became a landowner, plowing and sowing his own land, making hay on his own land, cutting his own trees, and feeding his cattle on his own pasture. When he went out to plow his fields, or to look at his growing corn, or at his grass meadows, his heart would fill with joy. The grass that grew and the flowers that bloomed there seemed to him unlike any that grew elsewhere. Formerly, when he had passed by that land, it had appeared the same as any other land, but now it seemed quite different.

3

So Pahom was well contented, and every-thing would have been right if the neigh-boring peasants would only not have trespassed on his wheatfields and meadows. He appealed to them most civilly, but they

Leo Tolstoy **1047**

7 READER'S RESPONSE

Do you think Pahom is wise to forgive his peasant neighbors "again and again"? (Answers will vary.) Do you think his attempts to teach them a lesson is the wisest course of action? (Neither postponing prosecution nor proceeding with it solves the problem; there seems to be no easy and "wise" solution.)

HUMANITIES CONNECTION

Many of Russia's Realists believed that art should reflect national feeling and social consciousness.

? *What is the relationship between the man and the landscape in this painting?* (Possible response: Though the man is in the foreground, the unbroken horizon and the point of view make the land appear vast; the man seems isolated in the landscape.) ■

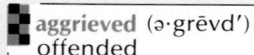
aggrieved (ə·grēvd′): offended

8 ANALYZING

How has Pahom changed since he acquired his forty acres? (Whereas before "his heart would fill with joy" when he worked his own land, now his landowning life seems fraught with dissatisfaction.) In what sense is his relationship with the neighboring peasants a reversal of his relationship with the old soldier earlier in the story? (Before he was a peasant owing money for his stray animals; now he is a landowner fining peasants for their stray animals.)

1048 The Nineteenth Century: Romanticism to Realism

still went on: now the herdsmen would let the village cows stray into his meadows, then horses from the night pasture would get among his corn. Pahom turned them out again and again, and forgave their owners, and for a long time he forbore to prosecute anyone. But at last he lost patience and complained to the District Court. He knew it was the peasants' want of land, and no evil intent on their part, that caused the trouble, but he thought:

"I can't go on overlooking it, or they'll destroy all I have. They must be taught a lesson."

So he had them up, gave them one lesson, and then another, and two or three of the peasants were fined. After a time Pahom's neighbors began to bear him a grudge for this, and would now and then let their cattle onto his land on purpose. One peasant even got into Pahom's wood at night and cut down five young lime trees for their bark. Pahom, passing through the wood one day, noticed something white. He came nearer and saw the stripped trunks lying on the ground, and close by stood the stumps where the trees had been. Pahom was furious.

"If he'd only cut one here and there it would have been bad enough," thought Pahom, "but the rascal has actually cut down a whole clump. If I could only find out who did this, I'd get even with him."

He racked his brains as to who it could be. Finally he decided: "It must be Simon—no one else could have done it." So he went to Simon's homestead to have a look around, but he found nothing and only had an angry scene. However, he now felt more certain than ever that Simon had done it, and he lodged a complaint. Simon was summoned. The case was tried, and retried, and at the end of it all Simon was acquitted, there being no evidence against him. Pahom felt still

MAN IN THE FIELD, WLADIMIR JEGOROWITSCH MAKOWSKI (1846–1920).

Archiv Für Kunst Und Geschichte, Berlin

more aggrieved, and let his anger loose upon the Elders and the Judges.

"You let thieves grease your palms," said he. "If you were honest folk yourselves you wouldn't let a thief go free."

So Pahom quarreled with the judges and with his neighbors. Threats to burn his hut began to be uttered. So though Pahom had more land, his place in the community was much worse than before.

About this time a rumor got about that many people were moving to new parts.

"There's no need for me to leave my land," thought Pahom. "But some of the others may leave our village and then there'd be more room for us. I'd take over their land myself and make my estates somewhat bigger. I could then live more at ease. As it is, I'm still too cramped to be comfortable."

One day Pahom was sitting at home when a peasant, passing through the village, happened to drop in. He was allowed to stay the night, and supper was given him. Pahom had a talk with this peasant and asked him where he came from. The stranger answered that he came from beyond the Volga,[2] where he had been working. One word led to another, and the man went on to say that many people were settling in those parts. He told how some people from his village had settled there. They had joined the community there and had had twenty-five acres per man granted them. The land was so good, he said, that the rye sown on it grew as high as a horse, and so thick that five cuts of a sickle made a sheaf. One peasant, he said, had brought nothing with him but his bare hands, and now he had six horses and two cows of his own.

Pahom's heart kindled with desire.

"Why should I suffer in this narrow hole, if one can live so well elsewhere?" he thought. "I'll sell my land and my homestead here, and with the money I'll start afresh over there and get everything new. In this crowded place one is always having trouble. But I must first go and find out all about it myself."

Toward summer he got ready and started out. He went down the Volga on a steamer to Samara, then walked another three hundred miles on foot, and at last reached the place. It was just as the stranger had said. The peasants had plenty of land: every man had twenty-five acres of communal land given him for his use, and anyone who had

money could buy, besides, at a ruble and a half an acre, as much good freehold land as he wanted.

Having found out all he wished to know, Pahom returned home as autumn came on, and began selling off his belongings. He sold his land at a profit, sold his homestead and all his cattle, and withdrew from membership in the village. He only waited till the spring, and then started with his family for the new settlement.

4

As soon as Pahom and his family reached their new abode, he applied for admission into the council of a large village. He stood treat to the Elders[3] and obtained the necessary documents. Five shares of communal land were given him for his own and his sons' use: that is to say—125 acres (not all together, but in different fields) besides the use of the communal pasture. Pahom put up the buildings he needed and bought cattle. Of the communal land alone he had three times as much as at his former home, and the land was good wheat land. He was ten times better off than he had been. He had plenty of arable land and pasturage, and could keep as many head of cattle as he liked.

At first, in the bustle of building and settling down, Pahom was pleased with it all, but when he got used to it he began to think that even here he hadn't enough land. The first year he sowed wheat on his share of the communal land and had a good crop. He wanted to go on sowing wheat, but had not enough communal land for the purpose, and what he had already used was not available, for in those parts wheat is sown only on

---

2. **the Volga:** the Volga River of western Russia.

3. **stood treat to the Elders:** treated the Elders of the council to food and drink.

Leo Tolstoy   **1049**

9 CULTURAL DIVERSITY
Stretching 2,290 miles from the Valdai Hills between Moscow and St. Petersburg in the north, to the Caspian Sea in the south, the Volga River is Russia's most important (and Europe's longest) river. The Volga makes a hairpin turn—the Samara Bend—where it joins the Samara River. At this junction lies the city of Samara. In the mid–nineteenth century, Samara became an important center for milling flour and trading grains. In recent decades it has been one of Russia's most important producers of agricultural and automotive equipment, as well as watches.
? *What rivers in the United States have historically been most important to the nation's businesses and industries? (Responses might include the Mississippi and the Ohio rivers.)*

communal (kə·myōo′nəl): shared by all

arable (ar′ə·bəl): able to be plowed so as to produce crops

10 GUIDED READING
Identifying Details: In what ways is Pahom "ten times better off"? (He owns much more land, and this land is better for farming and pasturage.)

virgin soil or on fallow land. It is sown for one or two years, and then the land lies fallow till it is again overgrown with steppe grass. There were many who wanted such land, and there was not enough for all, so that people quarreled about it. Those who were better off wanted it for growing wheat, and those who were poor wanted it to let to dealers, so that they might raise money to pay their taxes. Pahom wanted to sow more wheat, so he rented land from a dealer for a year. He sowed much wheat and had a fine crop, but the land was too far from the village—the wheat had to be carted more than ten miles. After a time Pahom noticed that some peasant dealers were living on separate farms and were growing wealthy, and he thought:

11 "If I were to buy some freehold land and have a homestead on it, it would be a different thing altogether. Then it would all be fine and close together."

The question of buying freehold land recurred to him again and again.

He went on in the same way for three years, renting land and sowing wheat. The seasons turned out well and the crops were good, so that he began to lay by money. He might have gone on living contentedly, but he grew tired of having to rent other people's land every year and having to scramble for it. Wherever there was good land to be had, the peasants would rush for it and it was taken up at once, so that unless you were sharp about it, you got none. It happened in the third year that he and a dealer together rented a piece of pasture land from some peasants, and they had already plowed it up, when there was some dispute and the peasants went to law about it, and things fell out so that the labor was all lost.

"If it were my own land," thought Pahom, "I should be independent, and there

wouldn't be all this unpleasantness."

So Pahom began looking out for land which he could buy, and he came across a peasant who had bought thirteen hundred acres, but having got into difficulties was willing to sell again cheap. Pahom bargained and haggled with him, and at last they settled the price at fifteen hundred rubles, part in cash and part to be paid later. They had all but clinched the matter when a passing dealer happened to stop at Pahom's one day to get feed for his horses. He drank tea with Pahom, and they had a talk. The dealer said that he was just returning from the land of the Bashkirs,[4] far away, where he had bought thirteen thousand acres of land, all for a thousand rubles. Pahom questioned him further, and the dealer said:

"All one has to do is to make friends with the chiefs. I gave away about one hundred rubles' worth of silk robes and carpets, besides a case of tea, and I gave wine to those who would drink it; and I got the land for less than three kopecks[5] an acre." And he showed Pahom the title deed, saying:

"The land lies near a river, and the whole steppe is virgin soil."

Pahom plied him with questions, and the dealer said:

"There's more land there than you could cover if you walked a year, and it all belongs to the Bashkirs. They're as simple as sheep, and land can be got almost for nothing."

"There, now," thought Pahom, "with my one thousand rubles, why should I get only thirteen hundred acres, and saddle myself with a debt besides? If I take it out there, I can get more than ten times as much for my money."

---

4. **the Bashkirs** (bash·kirz′): nomads who live on the vast Russian steppes, or plains.
5. **kopecks:** Russian monetary units.

A HOUSE FOR THE NIECES AND NEPHEWS, KONJEW.
Archiv Für Kunst Und Geschichte, Berlin

■ HUMANITIES CONNECTION ■

Like a written character sketch, *A House for the Nieces and Nephews* conveys the subject's personality by showing him at his daily pursuits.

❓ *What attitude toward the peasant does the artist wish to evoke?* (a warm feeling) *Which details in the painting support your opinion?* (Answers will vary.) ■

Leo Tolstoy **1051**

14 INFERRING

What can you infer about Pahom from this series of sentences describing the sights and customs in the land of the Bashkirs? (Possible response: It seems that Pahom has never seen these sights and customs before.)

15 CULTURAL DIVERSITY

Once a nomadic group roaming the great Russian steppe, the Bashkirs are a Muslim people who speak a Turkic language.

In Tolstoy's era the Bashkirs' survival depended on their livestock, from which they received butter, cheese, milk, and meat. They kept horses, and male Bashkirs often dressed in riding pants and tails. Their felt-covered tents, or yurts, were designed for portability since the Bashkirs carried them each time they set out to find new pasture land.

16 SPECULATING

Why do you think the Bashkirs are "much amused" and shouting and laughing? (Possible response: They might be amused that Pahom desires land in exchange for his gifts. Many people, such as Native Americans, found the concept of owning land as ludicrous as the idea of owning the sky.)

Pahom inquired how to get to the place, and as soon as the grain dealer had left him, he prepared to go there himself. He left his wife to look after the homestead, and started on his journey, taking his hired man with him. They stopped at a town on their way and bought a case of tea, some wine, and other presents, as the grain dealer had advised.

On and on they went until they had gone more than three hundred miles, and on the seventh day they came to a place where the Bashkirs had pitched their round tents. It was all just as the dealer had said. The people lived on the steppe, by a river, in felt-covered tents. They neither tilled the ground nor ate bread. Their cattle and horses grazed in herds on the steppe. The colts were tethered behind the tents, and the mares were driven to them twice a day. The mares were milked, and from the milk kumiss[6] was made. It was the women who prepared the kumiss, and they also made cheese. As far as the men were concerned, drinking kumiss and tea, eating mutton, and playing on their pipes was all they cared about. They were all stout and merry, and all the summer long they never thought of doing any work. They were quite ignorant, and knew no Russian, but were good-natured enough.

As soon as they saw Pahom, they came out of their tents and gathered around the visitor. An interpreter was found, and Pahom told them he had come about some land. The Bashkirs seemed very glad; they took Pahom and led him into one of the best tents, where they made him sit on some down cushions placed on a carpet, while they sat around him. They gave him some

tea and kumiss, and had a sheep killed, and gave him mutton to eat. Pahom took presents out of his cart and distributed them among the Bashkirs, and divided the tea amongst them. The Bashkirs were delighted. They talked a great deal among themselves and then told the interpreter what to say.

"They wish to tell you," said the interpreter, "that they like you and that it's our custom to do all we can to please a guest and to repay him for his gifts. You have given us presents, now tell us which of the things we possess please you best, that we may present them to you."

"What pleases me best here," answered Pahom, "is your land. Our land is crowded and the soil is worn out, but you have plenty of land, and it is good land. I never saw the likes of it."

The interpreter told the Bashkirs what Pahom had said. They talked among themselves for a while. Pahom could not understand what they were saying, but saw they were much amused and heard them shout and laugh. Then they were silent and looked at Pahom while the interpreter said:

"They wish me to tell you that in return for your presents they will gladly give you as much land as you want. You have only to point it out with your hand and it is yours."

The Bashkirs talked again for a while and began to dispute. Pahom asked what they were disputing about, and the interpreter told him that some of them thought they ought to ask their chief about the land and not act in his absence, while others thought there was no need to wait for his return.

6

While the Bashkirs were disputing, a man in a large fox-fur cap appeared on the scene. They all became silent and rose to their feet.

---

6. **kumiss** (kōō′mis): a fermented drink made from horse's milk; highly esteemed in Russia as a tonic.

The interpreter said: "This is our chief himself."

Pahom immediately fetched the best dressing gown and five pounds of tea, and offered these to the chief. The chief accepted them and seated himself in the place of honor. The Bashkirs at once began telling him something. The chief listened for a while, then made a sign with his head for them to be silent, and addressing himself to Pahom, said in Russian:

"Well, so be it. Choose whatever piece of land you like; we have plenty of it."

"How can I take as much as I like?" thought Pahom. "I must get a deed to make it secure, or else they may say: 'It is yours,' and afterward may take it away again."

"Thank you for your kind words," he said aloud. "You have much land, and I only want a little. But I should like to be sure which portion is mine. Could it not be measured and made over to me? Life and death are in God's hands. You good people give it to me, but your children might wish to take it back again."

"You are quite right," said the chief. "We will make it over to you."

"I heard that a dealer had been here," continued Pahom, "and that you gave him a little land, too, and signed title deeds to that effect. I should like to have it done in the same way."

The chief understood.

"Yes," replied he, "that can be done quite easily. We have a scribe, and we will go to town with you and have the deed properly sealed."

"And what will be the price?" asked Pahom.

"Our price is always the same: one thousand rubles a day."

Pahom did not understand.

"A day? What measure is that? How many acres would that be?"

"We do not know how to reckon it out," said the chief. "We sell it by the day. As much as you can go around on your feet in a day is yours, and the price is one thousand rubles a day."

Pahom was surprised.

"But in a day you can get around a large tract of land," he said.

The chief laughed.

"It will all be yours!" said he. "But there is one condition: If you don't return on the same day to the spot whence you started, your money is lost."

"But how am I to mark the way that I have gone?"

"Why, we shall go to any spot you like and stay there. You must start from that spot and make your round, taking a spade with you. Wherever you think necessary, make a mark. At every turning, dig a hole and pile up the turf; then afterward we will go around with a plow from hole to hole. You may make as large a circuit as you please, but before the sun sets you must return to the place you started from. All the land you cover will be yours."

Pahom was delighted. It was decided to start early next morning. They talked a while, and after drinking some more kumiss and eating some more mutton, they had tea again, and then the night came on. They gave Pahom a feather bed to sleep on, and the Bashkirs dispersed for the night, promising to assemble the next morning at daybreak and ride out before sunrise to the appointed spot.

7

Pahom lay on the feather bed, but could not sleep. He kept thinking about the land.

"What a large tract I'll mark off!" thought he, "I can easily do thirty-five miles in a day.

18

17

8

19

17 EVALUATING AND PREDICTING
Do you think Pahom's response to the chief's generous offer is appropriate? (Answers will vary.) Do you think it will be effective? (The Bashkirs seem to be fair and agreeable people; Pahom's request probably will be granted.)

18 LITERARY ELEMENT
Dialogue: What literary device does Tolstoy use to communicate information about the Bashkirs' method of selling land? (dialogue) Why do you think Tolstoy chose this method rather than straightforward narrative exposition? (Possible response: Dialogue portrays the characters' personalities more vividly.)

MEETING INDIVIDUAL NEEDS

19 *Advanced Students:* Challenge students to calculate how much land Pahom will acquire—measured in both square miles and in acres—if he manages to walk thirty-five miles. (A thirty-five mile walk would enclose a square of four 8.75–mile sides. The area of such a square is 76.6 square miles or 49,040 acres of land.) ■

If you were Pahom, how would such a dream make you feel? (Answers will vary.)

HUMANITIES CONNECTION

❓ *How does Rodko's idyllic pastoral scene contrast with the way Pahom has come to feel about land?* (Possible response: The painting makes working the land look peaceful and satisfying, but Pahom has grown chronically dissatisfied as he has acquired and worked more land.) ∎

20

The days are long now, and within a circuit of thirty-five miles what a lot of land there will be! I'll sell the poorer land or let it to peasants, but I'll pick out the best and farm it myself. I'll buy two ox teams and hire two more laborers. About a hundred and fifty acres shall be plowland, and I'll pasture cattle on the rest."

Pahom lay awake all night and dozed off only just before dawn. Hardly were his eyes closed when he had a dream. He thought he was lying in that same tent and heard somebody chuckling outside. He wondered who it could be, and rose and went out, and he saw the Bashkir chief sitting in front of the tent holding his sides and rolling about with

laughter. Going nearer to the chief, Pahom asked: "What are you laughing at?" But he saw that it was no longer the chief but the grain dealer who had recently stopped at his house and had told him about the land. Just as Pahom was going to ask: "Have you been here long?" he saw that it was not the dealer, but the peasant who had come up from the Volga long ago, to Pahom's old home. Then he saw that it was not the peasant either, but the Devil himself with hoofs and horns, sitting there and chuckling, and before him lay a man, prostrate on the ground, barefooted, with only trousers and a shirt on. And Pahom dreamed that he looked more attentively to see what sort of man it was

20

HAYING, KONSTANTINE RODKO (b. 1908).

SuperStock, Inc.

lying there, and he saw that the man was dead, and that it was himself. Horror-struck, he awoke.

"What things one dreams about!" thought he.

Looking around he saw through the open door that the dawn was breaking.

"It's time to wake them up," thought he. "We ought to be starting."

He got up, roused his man (who was sleeping in his cart), bade him harness, and went to call the Bashkirs.

"It's time to go to the steppe to measure the land," he said.

The Bashkirs rose and assembled, and the chief came, too. Then they began drinking kumiss again, and offered Pahom some tea, but he would not wait.

"If we are to go, let's go. It's high time," said he.

8

The Bashkirs got ready and they all started; some mounted on horses and some in carts. Pahom drove in his own small cart with his servant and took a spade with him. When they reached the steppe, the red dawn was beginning to kindle. They ascended a hillock (called by the Bashkirs a *shikhan*) and, dismounting from their carts and their horses, gathered in one spot. The chief came up to Pahom and, stretching out his arm toward the plain:

"See," said he, "all this, as far as your eye can reach, is ours. You may have any part of it you like."

Pahom's eyes glistened: it was all virgin soil, as flat as the palm of your hand, as black as the seed of a poppy, and in the hollows different kinds of grasses grew breast-high.

The chief took off his fox-fur cap, placed it on the ground, and said:

"This will be the mark. Start from here, and return here again. All the land you go around shall be yours."

Pahom took out his money and put it on the cap. Then he took off his outer coat, remaining in his sleeveless undercoat. He unfastened his girdle and tied it tight below his stomach, put a little bag of bread into the breast of his coat, and, tying a flask of water to his girdle, he drew up the tops of his boots, took the spade from his man, and stood ready to start. He considered for some moments which way he had better go—it was tempting everywhere.

"No matter," he concluded, "I'll go toward the rising sun."

He turned his face to the east, stretched himself, and waited for the sun to appear above the rim.

"I must lose no time," he thought, "and it's easier walking while it's still cool."

The sun's rays had hardly flashed above the horizon when Pahom, carrying the spade over his shoulder, went down into the steppe.

Pahom started walking neither slowly nor quickly. After having gone a thousand yards he stopped, dug a hole, and placed pieces of turf one on another to make it more visible. Then he went on; and now that he had walked off his stiffness he quickened his pace. After a while he dug another hole.

Pahom looked back. The hillock could be distinctly seen in the sunlight, with the people on it, and the glittering iron rims of the cartwheels. At a rough guess Pahom concluded that he had walked three miles. It was growing warmer; he took off his undercoat, slung it across his shoulder, and went on again. It had grown quite warm now; he looked at the sun—it was time to think of breakfast.

"The first shift is done, but there are four

22

---

21 CULTURAL DIVERSITY
The soil of the steppe in western Russia is known for its depth, blackness, and fertility. The western steppe contains vegetation such as feather grass and fescue, as well as flowers such as tulips, dwarf irises, and adonises.
❓ *What area of the United States is roughly analogous to Russia's steppe?* (the Great Plains)

22 GUIDED READING
Identifying Details: Where are the Bashkirs standing? (on a hillock) Where is Pahom walking? (on the steppe) What is the physical relationship between these two places? (The hillock rises above the steppe to the west; the steppe stretches flatly toward the eastern horizon.)

Characterization: What does Pahom realize about how much of the day has passed? (A quarter of the day is gone.) What does his decision to "go on for another three miles" say about his character? (Pahom is incapable of controlling his greedy impulses. His acquisitiveness is stronger than his good judgment.)

24 ANALYZING

At this point, is it possible for Pahom to circumambulate a square piece of land? (not without superhuman effort. The day is half over, yet he has just begun the second of the square's four sides.)

25 READER'S RESPONSE

What is your opinion of Pahom at this moment? (Answers will vary.) If you were in Pahom's position, would you include the damp hollow or would you turn to the left? (Answers will vary.)

in a day, and it's too soon yet to turn. But I'll just take off my boots," said he to himself.

He sat down, took off his boots, stuck them into his girdle, and went on. It was easy walking now.

"I'll go on for another three miles," thought he, "and then turn to the left. This spot is so fine that it would be a pity to lose it. The further one goes, the better the land seems."

He went straight on for a while, and when he looked around, the hillock was scarcely visible and the people on it looked like black ants, and he could just see something glistening there in the sun.

"Ah," thought Pahom, "I have gone far enough in this direction; it's time to turn. Besides, I'm in a regular sweat, and very thirsty."

He stopped, dug a large hole, and heaped up pieces of turf. Next he untied his flask, had a drink, and then turned sharply to the left. He went on and on; the grass was high, and it was very hot.

Pahom began to grow tired: he looked at the sun and saw that it was noon.

"Well," he thought, "I must have a rest."

He sat down, and ate some bread and drank some water; but he did not lie down, thinking that if he did he might fall asleep. After sitting a little while, he went on again. At first he walked easily; the food had strengthened him; but it had become terribly hot and he felt sleepy. Still he went on, thinking: "An hour to suffer, a lifetime to live."

He went a long way in this direction also, and was about to turn to the left again, when he perceived a damp hollow: "It would be a pity to leave that out," he thought. "Flax would do well there." So he went on past the hollow and dug a hole on the other side of it before he made a sharp turn. Pahom

looked toward the hillock. The heat made the air hazy: it seemed to be quivering, and through the haze the people on the hillock could scarcely be seen.

"Ah," thought Pahom, "I have made the sides too long; I must make this one shorter." And he went along the third side, stepping faster. He looked at the sun: it was nearly halfway to the horizon, and he had not yet done two miles of the third side of the square. He was still ten miles from the goal.

"No," he thought, "though it will make my land lopsided, I must hurry back in a straight line now. I might go too far, and as it is I have a great deal of land."

So Pahom hurriedly dug a hole and turned straight toward the hillock.

9

Pahom went straight toward the hillock, but he now walked with difficulty. He was exhausted from the heat, his bare feet were cut and bruised, and his legs began to fail. He longed to rest, but it was impossible if he meant to get back before sunset. The sun waits for no man, and it was sinking lower and lower.

"Oh, Lord," he thought, "if only I have not blundered trying for too much! What if I am too late?"

He looked toward the hillock and at the sun. He was still far from his goal, and the sun was already near the rim of the sky.

Pahom walked on and on; it was very hard walking, but he went quicker and quicker. He pressed on, but was still far from the place. He began running, threw away his coat, his boots, his flask, and his cap, and kept only the spade which he used as a support.

"What am I to do?" he thought again. I've

THE BIRCH GROVE, A. I. KUIDZHI, 1879.

❓ *Do you see Pahom as a canny businessman, a greedy opportunist, or something in between?*

grasped too much and ruined the whole affair. I can't get there before the sun sets."

And this fear made him still more breathless. Pahom kept on running; his soaking
shirt and trousers stuck to him, and his
mouth was parched. His breast was working
like a blacksmith's bellows, his heart was
beating like a hammer, and his legs were
giving way as if they did not belong to him.
Pahom was seized with terror lest he should
die of the strain.

Though afraid of death, he could not stop.

"After having run all that way they will
call me a fool if I stop now," thought he.

And he ran on and on, and drew near and
heard the Bashkirs yelling and shouting to
him, and their cries inflamed his heart still
more. He gathered his last strength and ran
on.

The sun was close to the rim of the sky
and, cloaked in mist, looked large, and red
as blood. Now, yes, now, it was about to set!

The sun was quite low, but he was also quite
near his goal. Pahom could already see the
people on the hillock waving their arms to
make him hurry. He could see the fox-fur
cap on the ground and the money in it, and
the chief sitting on the ground holding his
sides. And Pahom remembered his dream.

"There's plenty of land," thought he, "but
will God let me live on it? I have lost my
life, I have lost my life! Never will I reach
that spot!"

Pahom looked at the sun, which had
reached the earth: one side of it had already
disappeared. With all his remaining strength
he rushed on, bending his body forward so
that his legs could hardly follow fast enough
to keep him from falling. Just as he reached
the hillock it suddenly grew dark. He looked
up—the sun had already set!

He gave a cry: "All my labor has been in
vain," thought he, and was about to stop,
but he heard the Bashkirs still shouting and

26

27

1. How much land does Pahom acquire in his first purchase? (forty acres)
2. For what crime does Pahom attempt to prosecute a peasant named Simon? (chopping down a clump of five lime trees)
3. Who interrupts Pahom and a peasant (who is getting feed for his horses) just as Pahom is about to purchase thirteen hundred acres of land? (a passing dealer)

4. How much distance does Pahom hope to cover in his bid to acquire land from the Bashkirs? (thirty-five miles)
5. What does Pahom's servant see when he lifts Pahom from the ground on the hillock? (blood running from Pahom's mouth)

28 INTERPRETING

Whom does Pahom recognize in the chief? (the Devil) Why is the chief laughing? (Possible response: He is laughing at his success in assuming power over Pahom, as promised in the story's first section.)

WRITING TO LEARN

Social Studies: Using specific details from "How Much Land Does a Man Need?" write a letter that Pahom might have written to his wife the night before his walk on the Bashkirs' land. ■

ANSWERS

First Thoughts
Answers will vary.

Identifying Facts
1. sells colt and bees, hires out son, borrows from brother-in-law
2. They continually trespass on his land.
3. He tries to get so much that he dies from exhaustion.
4. six feet. It is the length of Pahom's grave.

Interpreting Meanings
1. Unchecked ambition brings a person neither happiness nor health. Pahom's death proves the harm of striving for material gain.
2. The proverb "Loss and gain are brothers twain," and references to death on the land and to the Devil's temptations all foreshadow Pahom's end. Possible response: Pahom's vivid dream
3. The more land Pahom acquires, the more he wants; the

remembered that though to him, from below, the sun seemed to have set, they on the hillock could still see it. He took a long breath and ran up the hillock. It was still light there. He reached the top and saw the cap. Before it sat the chief, laughing and holding his sides. Again Pahom remembered his dream, and he uttered a cry: his legs gave way beneath him, he fell forward and reached the cap with his hands.

"Ah, that's a fine fellow!" exclaimed the

chief. "He has gained much land!"

Pahom's servant came running up and tried to raise him, but he saw that blood was flowing from his mouth. Pahom was dead.

The Bashkirs clicked their tongues to show their pity.

His servant picked up the spade and dug a grave long enough for Pahom to lie in, and buried him in it.

Six feet from his head to his heels was all he needed.

First Thoughts

What do you think about the conclusion of the story? Do you think Pahom met a fitting end? Why or why not?

Identifying Facts

1. Pahom buys his first forty acres of land from an aristocrat. How does he raise the money?
2. After buying his first farm, why does Pahom quarrel with the neighboring peasants?
3. What happens when Pahom attempts to purchase land from the Bashkirs?
4. According to Tolstoy, how much land does a man really need? How is the question in the story's title answered?

Interpreting Meanings

1. What is the central idea, or **theme**, of this story? State it in a sentence or two. How does the **resolution** of the story's **conflict** support the story's theme?

2. Think about the discussion between the two sisters at the beginning of the story. How does their conversation **foreshadow** Pahom's end? What other events foreshadow the ending of the story?

3. Contrast Pahom's attitude toward land with the attitude of the Bashkir chief. What do you think accounts for the difference in their values?

4. A story's **tone** is the attitude the author takes toward its subject or characters. What tone does Tolstoy use when describing Pahom? Cite examples from the story that best reflect the author's attitude toward his main character.

5. How does this story serve as a **parable** that reflects Tolstoy's beliefs about private ownership of property?

Applying Meanings

Have you ever "grasped too much and ruined the whole affair"—that is, lost something because you were too ambi-

1. **Illustrating "How Much Land Does a Man Need?"** Have students choose scenes from "How Much Land Does a Man Need?" to illustrate. Possible scenes include Pahom lying on the stove as his wife and sister-in-law argue (and the Devil hides behind the stove), Pahom discovering the clump of vandalized lime trees, or the "passing dealer" and Pahom having tea.

2. **Research Project.** Some students may be especially interested in the Bashkirs' culture or in the great Russian steppe. Encourage these students to research either topic. Reports might focus on how the Bashkirs (or the steppe) have changed in the century since Tolstoy's story was written.

Ask students to discuss how the desire to have material goods and status in nineteenth-century Russia and in twentieth-century America are comparable. ■

---

tious? Can you think of examples of people from current events, history, or other fictional stories who have failed by being greedy or attempting too much? Describe one such example, applying to it the message of Tolstoy's story.

Creative Writing Response

Writing an Allegory. An **allegory** is a story with characters, settings, and events that symbolize, or stand for, other people or events, or abstract qualities or ideas. As such, an allegory can be read on one level for its literal meaning and on another level for its symbolic meaning. Try writing a brief allegory of your own that illustrates Tolstoy's theme of losing everything by grasping too much. Your allegory may be written as a skit or as a short parable. It should, like Tolstoy's story, blend symbolism and realism.

Critical Writing Response

Comparing and Contrasting Characters in Two Works. Both Goethe's *Faust* (see page 988) and Tolstoy's "How Much Land Does a Man Need?" have characters who are tempted by the Devil. Write an essay in which you compare and contrast the protagonists, Pahom and Faust, and the characters of the Devil as drawn by Goethe and Tolstoy. What do these characters have in common? What characteristics do they *not* share? Consider the motivation, background, and ambition of each character when deciding on your response. You might want to use a chart such as the following to organize your ideas.

	"How Much Land Does a Man Need?"	*Faust*
Devil		
Protagonist		

chief, content with what he has, is willing to share it. Their values may reflect their feudal and nomadic backgrounds.
4. restrained, objective. *Examples:* last paragraph in section 2, in which Pahom is thrilled, but Tolstoy merely reports the scene; description of Pahom's death and the Bashkirs' display of pity.
5. Pahom's bids for ownership fail to bring contentment; the Bashkirs' communal ownership is portrayed as a superior system.

Applying Meanings
Answers will vary but should be roughly analogous to Tolstoy's parable on the evils of ambition.

Creative Writing Response
Writing an Allegory. Students' allegories should treat the theme of losing everything by grasping too much and should have meaning on both realistic and symbolic levels.

Critical Writing Response
Comparing and Contrasting Characters in Two Works. Students' essays should compare and contrast the characteristics of Faust and Pahom and those of the two devils. ■

Anton Chekhov
1860–1904

The Bettmann Archive

Anton Pavlovich Chekhov (än·tōn′ pä·vlô′vich che′kôf′), the grandson of a serf who had bought his own and his family's freedom, was born in the seaport town of Taganrog in the south of Russia. As a child, Anton spent long hours working in his father's grocery store.

When Chekhov was sixteen, his father went bankrupt and fled with his family to Moscow to avoid a prison sentence. Chekhov stayed behind to finish his schooling and supported himself by tutoring. He moved to Moscow after graduation and entered medical school on a scholarship. In order to support himself and his family, who were living in a Moscow slum, Chekhov began writing comic stories for sale to periodicals.

Medicine was good training for his career as a writer. Through his practice as a doctor,

Chekhov came to know hundreds of ordinary people. He continued to write while practicing medicine; eventually, however, he gave up his full-time practice because it took too much of his time away from writing.

Chekhov's fiction was noticed by the influential novelist Dmitri Grigorovich, who advised him to take his writing more seriously. Chekhov also became acquainted with a publisher who supported his efforts as his talent continued to mature. But it was not until the last years of his life that Chekhov achieved some affluence and fame. At this time, he settled with his family on a large country estate. Here he organized famine relief, fought cholera epidemics, and continued to examine poor patients without charge. Although the theme of many of his works is the individual's alienation from others, Chekhov's real-life activities demonstrate that humanity, reason, and generosity were his highest values.

His life was cut short by tuberculosis. Chekhov's finest stories—those of the 1890s—and his four great plays, *The Sea Gull* (1896), *Uncle Vanya* (1897), *The Three Sisters* (1901), and *The Cherry Orchard* (1904), were written while he was fatally ill. In 1901, he married the actress who played the lead role in *The Sea Gull*, but the couple spent their honeymoon in a sanitarium, or health resort. He died in Germany three years later, at the age of forty-four, during the height of his creativity.

OBJECTIVES

1. *To interpret a realistic Russian short story*
2. *To recognize ironic tone*
3. *To write an essay judging the main character and a sketch predicting his future*

VOCABULARY IN CONTEXT

The words listed below will appear in the side margin at the point of instruction:

1. initiated	6. suavely
2. civic	7. stifling
3. benevolent	8. edifying
4. reprehensible	9. petrified
5. dissipated	10. asserted

Reader's Guide

A PROBLEM

Background

What does the term *Chekhovian* mean? It refers to a quiet, wry understanding of the melancholy of everyday life. Chekhov's style is understated, muted, and gloomily comic. His major stories and plays were innovative because they emphasized character and mood rather than plot. The typical Chekhov character is sensitive and intelligent but also idle, foolish, self-deceiving, and alienated—yearning for a fulfillment that never arrives.

Chekhov is famous for communicating **mood**, or atmosphere. Traditional **plot** structure, which relies on action, complications, and a climax, is rarely found in Chekhov's works. His stories and plays—of which "A Problem" is a good example—are primarily concerned with portraying a group of characters and the moods they project. This exploration of mood and the inner world of fictional characters, at the expense of traditional plot structure, has strongly influenced modern fiction writers such as Katherine Mansfield, James Joyce, and Ernest Hemingway.

Writer's Response

Imagine that you are a parent whose son or daughter has been arrested for shoplifting. Would you insist that he or she be brought to justice and punished, or would you pay for the stolen items quietly if possible? What, if anything, do your ideas about family honor have to do with your response? Write a few sentences on these questions.

Literary Focus

Tone is the attitude a writer takes toward a character, a subject, or the reader. In "A Problem," Chekhov's tone is **ironic**—that is, there is a contrast between what is said and what is meant, between what appears to be true and what is really true, and between what is expected and what really happens. In Chekhov's works, characters are often foolish and pathetically touching at the same time. As you read, ask yourself how an ironic tone is used to sketch the various characters of the Uskov family.

PREREADING FOCUS

Background: The Uskov family in "A Problem" belongs to the gentry, the landowning class. They are somewhat snobbish with their talk of "family honor," yet their household is not splendid by aristocratic standards: half their servants can fit in the kitchen. The Uskovs do not have titles such as "Count" or "Prince," as Tolstoy's characters often do.

Encourage students to recognize Chekhov's ironic tone toward his characters. Sometimes it is unmistakably mocking, but the mockery is gentle and affectionate.

The Uskovs were instantly recognizable to nineteenth-century Russian readers, many of whom belonged to the same social class and were all too willing to lament their own weaknesses. Readers who belonged to the aristocracy could look down on the Uskovs patronizingly, while merchants and other self-made entrepreneurs could sneer at the Uskovs' ineffectuality. Yet these hapless gentlefolk are refreshingly emotional compared to their counterparts in British nineteenth-century fiction. They weep, they plead, they get excited. This warmth—some might call it emotional excess—is part of what English-language readers find most "Russian" in Russian literature.

Writer's Response: You might ask pairs of students to role-play the confrontation between the parent and the son or daughter caught shoplifting.

Using the Semicolon

The semicolon is used instead of a comma and a conjunction to indicate a close relationship between independent clauses, as in the following example.

"The official of the Treasury muttered something in reply; after him Ivan Markovitch began talking blandly. . . ."

1. **Writing.** Have students replace the conjunctions in the following with a semicolon and a second subject.

a. "The Colonel got up and paced from corner to corner."

b. "Taking a sledge, Sasha grew calmer, and felt a rush of joy . . . again."

2. **Writing.** Have students replace semicolons with commas and conjunctions in the following passages:

a. "Half of the servants were sent off to the theater or the circus; the other half were sitting in the kitchen . . ."

b. "His face worked; he trembled . . ." ∎

 initiated (i·nish′ē·āt′id): let in on; told about

LITERARY ELEMENT

Exposition: How does Chekhov capture his readers' attention and interest at the very beginning of the story? (He introduces a family with an upsetting secret but does not immediately reveal the secret itself.)

A PROBLEM
Anton Chekhov
translated by
CONSTANCE GARNETT

As you read the story, notice the argument each character makes for or against helping Sasha. Notice, too, how each character's position or argument contributes to our image of his or her personality.

INTERIOR WITH THE ARTIST'S BROTHERS, WILHELM BENDZ, c. 1830.

The Granger Collection, New York

The strictest measures were taken that the Uskovs' family secret might not leak out and become generally known. Half of the servants were sent off to the theater or the circus; the other half were sitting in the kitchen and not allowed to leave it. Orders were given that no one was to be admitted. The wife of the Colonel, her sister, and the governess, though they had been initiated into the secret, kept up a pretense of knowing nothing; they sat in the dining room and did not show themselves in the drawing room or the hall.

Sasha Uskov, the young man of twenty-five who was the cause of all the commotion, had arrived some time before, and by the advice of kind-hearted Ivan Markovitch, his uncle, who was taking his part, he sat meekly in the hall by the door leading to the study, and prepared himself to make an open, candid explanation.

The other side of the door, in the study, a family council was being held. The subject under discussion was an exceedingly disagreeable and delicate one. Sasha Uskov had cashed at one of the banks a false promissory note,[1] and it had become due for payment three days before, and now his two paternal uncles and Ivan Markovitch, the brother of his dead mother, were deciding the question whether they should pay the money and save the family honor, or wash their hands of it and leave the case to go for trial.

To outsiders who have no personal interest in the matter such questions seem simple; for those who are so unfortunate as to have to decide them in earnest they are extremely difficult. The uncles had been talking for a long time, but the problem seemed no nearer decision.

"My friends!" said the uncle who was a colonel, and there was a note of exhaustion and bitterness in his voice. "Who says that family honor is a mere convention? I don't say that at all. I am only warning you against a false view; I am pointing out the possibility of an unpardonable mistake. How can you fail to see it? I am not speaking Chinese; I am speaking Russian!"

"My dear fellow, we do understand," Ivan Markovitch protested mildly.

"How can you understand if you say that I don't believe in family honor? I repeat once more: fa-mil-y ho-nor false-ly un-der-stood is a prejudice! Falsely understood! That's what I say: whatever may be the motives for screening a scoundrel, whoever he may be, and helping him to escape punishment, it is contrary to law and unworthy of a gentleman. It's not saving the family honor; it's civic cowardice! Take the army, for instance. . . . The honor of the army is more precious to us than any other honor, yet we don't screen our guilty members, but condemn them. And does the honor of the army suffer in consequence? Quite the opposite!"

The other paternal uncle, an official in the Treasury, a taciturn,[2] dull-witted, and rheumatic man, sat silent, or spoke only of the fact that the Uskovs' name would get into the newspapers if the case went for trial. His opinion was that the case ought to be hushed up from the first and not become public property; but, apart from publicity in the newspapers, he advanced no other argument in support of this opinion.

The maternal uncle, kind-hearted Ivan Markovitch, spoke smoothly, softly, and with a tremor in his voice. He began with saying that youth has its rights and its peculiar temptations. Which of us has not been young, and who has not been led astray? To say nothing of ordinary mortals, even great men have not escaped errors and mistakes in their youth. Take, for instance, the biography of great writers. Did not every one of them gamble, drink, and draw down upon himself the anger of right-thinking people in his young days? If Sasha's error bordered upon crime, they must remember that Sasha had received practically no education; he had been expelled from the high school in the fifth class; he had lost his parents in early childhood, and so had been left at the tenderest age without guidance and good, benevolent influences. He was nervous,

---

[1]. **promissory note:** a written promise to pay a certain sum of money on demand; an IOU.

[2]. **taciturn** (tas'ə·tʉrn'): silent.

4 GUIDED READING

Summarizing: What arguments does Ivan Markovitch offer in Sasha's defense? (Most youths are temporarily led astray; Sasha was orphaned young and lacked guidance; the anxiety he is experiencing presently is adequate punishment; and it is more worthy of a Christian to help than to punish.)

5 INTERPRETING

Why do you think Ivan Markovitch argues so passionately on behalf of protecting Sasha? (Possible response: He likes to think of himself as an enlightened, compassionate individual and to make grand speeches displaying his kindness and erudition.)

6 LITERARY ELEMENT

Characterization: Lombroso theorized that criminal behavior results from deviant hereditary factors over which the individual has no control. What does the philosophical passage about Lombroso suggest about Ivan Markovitch? (Possible response: He is intellectually pretentious, latching on to the latest fashionable theories.) Chekhov, himself a physician and prison reformer, rejected Lombroso's theories about ''criminal types'' and believed individuals have free will.

7 LITERARY ELEMENT

Point of View: Whose thoughts does the writer reveal in this passage? (Sasha's) What do we learn about him? (He is depressed and indifferent to his fate.)

1064 The Nineteenth Century: Romanticism to Realism

---

4 excitable, had no firm ground under his feet, and, above all, he had been unlucky. Even if he were guilty, anyway he deserved indulgence and the sympathy of all compassionate souls. He ought, of course, to be punished, but he was punished as it was by his conscience and the agonies he was enduring now while awaiting the sentence of his relations. The comparison with the army made by the Colonel was delightful, and did credit to his lofty intelligence; his appeal to their feeling of public duty spoke for the chivalry of his soul, but they must not forget that in each individual the citizen is closely linked with the Christian. . . .

5 "Shall we be false to civic duty," Ivan Markovitch exclaimed passionately, "if instead of punishing an erring boy we hold out to him a helping hand?"

Ivan Markovitch talked further of family honor. He had not the honor to belong to the Uskov family himself, but he knew their distinguished family went back to the thirteenth century; he did not forget for a minute, either, that his precious, beloved sister had been the wife of one of the representatives of that name. In short, the family was dear to him for many reasons, and he refused to admit the idea that, for the sake of a paltry fifteen hundred rubles,[3] a blot should be cast on the escutcheon[4] that was beyond all price. If all the motives he had brought forward were not sufficiently convincing, he, Ivan Markovitch, in conclusion, begged his listeners to ask themselves what was meant by crime? Crime is an immoral act founded upon ill-will. But is the will of man free? Philosophy has not yet given a positive answer to that question. Different

views were held by the learned. The latest school of Lombroso,[5] for instance, denies the freedom of the will, and considers every crime as the product of the purely anatomical peculiarities of the individual. 6

"Ivan Markovitch," said the Colonel, in a voice of entreaty, "we are talking seriously about an important matter, and you bring in Lombroso, you clever fellow. Think a little, what are you saying all this for? Can you imagine that all your thunderings and rhetoric will furnish an answer to the question?"

Sasha Uskov sat at the door and listened. He felt neither terror, shame, nor depression, but only weariness and inward emptiness. It seemed to him that it made absolutely no difference to him whether they forgave him or not; he had come here to hear his sentence and to explain himself 7 simply because kind-hearted Ivan Markovitch had begged him to do so. He was not afraid of the future. It made no difference to him where he was: here in the hall, in prison, or in Siberia.

"If Siberia, then let it be Siberia, damn it all!"

He was sick of life and found it insufferably hard. He was inextricably involved in debt; he had not a farthing[6] in his pocket; his family had become detestable to him; he would have to part from his friends and his women sooner or later, as they had begun to be too contemptuous of his sponging on them. The future looked black.

Sasha was indifferent, and was only disturbed by one circumstance; the other side of the door they were calling him a scoun-

---

3. **rubles:** The ruble is the basic monetary unit of Russia.
4. **escutcheon** (e·skuch'ən): a shield or area on which a coat of arms is displayed.
5. **Lombroso:** Cesare Lombroso (1836–1909) was an Italian physician and criminologist. He believed that a criminal was a distinct human type with specific physical and mental deviations, and that criminals were the result of such factors as heredity.
6. **farthing:** a coin of little value.

COIN DE TABLE (CORNER OF THE TABLE), HENRI FANTIN-LATOUR (1836–1904).

Archiv Für Kunst Und Geschichte, Berlin

8 **EVALUATING**
Do you agree with Sasha's definition of criminal behavior? How would you classify his actions? (Answers will vary. Possible responses: immoral; opportunistic; amoral)

MEETING INDIVIDUAL NEEDS

9 *ESL:* Explain that "IOU" stands for "I Owe You." ■

reprehensible (rep'ri·hen' sə·bəl): deserving of criticism or blame

10 **LITERARY ELEMENT**
Characterization: What does Sasha's opinion of himself and his excuses tell you about his personality? (Possible responses: immature, irresponsible, self-indulgent)

HUMANITIES CONNECTION

In *Corner of the Table*, Fantin-Latour carefully details facial features to portray individual differences.
❓ *In Chekhov's story, how are the personalities of the characters revealed?* (indirectly, through their own thoughts, actions, and words and what others say about them) ■

drel and a criminal. Every minute he was on the point of jumping up, bursting into the study and shouting in answer to the detestable metallic voice of the Colonel:

"You are lying!"

"Criminal" is a dreadful word—that is what murderers, thieves, robbers are; in fact, wicked and morally hopeless people. And Sasha was very far from being all that. . . . It was true he owed a great deal and did not pay his debts. But debt is not a crime, and it is unusual for a man not to be in debt. The Colonel and Ivan Markovitch were both in debt. . . .

"What have I done wrong besides?" Sasha wondered.

He had discounted a forged note. But all the young men he knew did the same. Handrikov and Von Burst always forged IOU's

from their parents or friends when their allowances were not paid at the regular time, and then when they got their money from home they redeemed them before they became due. Sasha had done the same, but had not redeemed the IOU because he had not got the money which Handrikov had promised to lend him. He was not to blame; it was the fault of circumstances. It was true that the use of another person's signature was considered reprehensible; but, still, it was not a crime but a generally accepted dodge, an ugly formality which injured no one and was quite harmless, for in forging the Colonel's signature Sasha had had no intention of causing anybody damage or loss.

"No, it doesn't mean that I am a criminal . . ." thought Sasha. "And it's not in my character to bring myself to commit a crime. I

10

Which of the uncles' arguments do you think is strongest, and why? (Answers will vary.)

■ **dissipated** (dis′ə·pāt′id): spent in harmful indulgence of pleasure, especially gambling

suavely (swäv′lē): smoothly and pleasantly; politely

stifling (stī′fliŋ): suffocating; lacking in fresh air

12 **INTERPRETING**

How does Chekhov describe the quality of each uncle's voice? (the Treasury official "muttered"; Ivan Markovitch talks "blandly and suavely"; the Colonel drowns out others "with his detestable metallic voice.") What do these details suggest about their characters? (Possible response: The Treasury official is weak-willed; Ivan Markovitch, insincere; the Colonel, domineering.)

13 **EVALUATING**

More than once in this story, the characters or the narrator mention frankness, candor, or openness. How important do you think these qualities really are to the characters? (Possible response: They mouth these ideals but do not live up to them.)

---

am soft, emotional.... When I have the money I help the poor...."

Sasha was musing after this fashion while they went on talking the other side of the door.

11 "But, my friends, this is endless," the Colonel declared, getting excited. "Suppose we were to forgive him and pay the money. You know he would not give up leading a <u>dissipated</u> life, squandering money, making debts, going to our tailors and ordering suits in our names! Can you guarantee that this will be his last prank? As far as I am concerned, I have no faith whatever in his reforming!"

12 The official of the Treasury muttered something in reply; after him Ivan Markovitch began talking blandly and <u>suavely</u> again. The Colonel moved his chair impatiently and drowned the other's words with his detestable metallic voice. At last the door opened and Ivan Markovitch came out of the study; there were patches of red on his cleanshaven face.

13 "Come along," he said, taking Sasha by the hand. "Come and speak frankly from your heart. Without pride, my dear boy, humbly and from your heart."

Sasha went into the study. The official of the Treasury was sitting down; the Colonel was standing before the table with one hand in his pocket and one knee on a chair. It was smoky and <u>stifling</u> in the study. Sasha did not look at the official or the Colonel; he felt suddenly ashamed and uncomfortable. He looked uneasily at Ivan Markovitch and muttered:

"I'll pay it ... I'll give it back...."

"What did you expect when you discounted the IOU?" he heard a metallic voice.

"I ... Handrikov promised to lend me the money before now."

Sasha could say no more. He went out of

ROULETTE, WLADIMIR MAJAKOWSKI *(1893–1930)*.

Erich Lessing/Archiv Für Kunst Und Geschichte, Berlin

the study and sat down again on the chair near the door. He would have been glad to go away altogether at once, but he was choking with hatred and he awfully wanted to remain, to tear the Colonel to pieces, to say something rude to him. He sat trying to think of something violent and effective to say to his hated uncle, and at that moment a woman's figure, shrouded in the twilight, appeared at the drawing room door. It was the Colonel's wife. She beckoned Sasha to her, and, wringing her hands, said, weeping:

"*Alexandre*, I know you don't like me, but ... listen to me; listen, I beg you.... But, my dear, how can this have happened? Why, it's awful, awful! For goodness' sake, beg them, defend yourself, entreat them."

Sasha looked at her quivering shoulders, at the big tears that were rolling down her cheeks, heard behind his back the hollow,

READING CHECK

1. What happened to Sasha's parents? (They died when he was young.)
2. Where is Sasha while his fate is being discussed? (sitting in the hall)
3. Which uncle does Sasha most hate? (the Colonel)
4. Which uncle is Sasha's ally? (Ivan Markovitch)
5. What is Ivan Markovitch's relationship to the Uskovs? (His sister married one.)

RETEACHING

Have students write a letter that Sasha might address to Ivan Markovitch justifying or excusing his dishonesty. Encourage students to include examples of unconscious irony in which Sasha reveals something about himself without realizing it.

---

14 nervous voices of worried and exhausted people, and shrugged his shoulders. He had not in the least expected that his aristocratic relations would raise such a tempest over a paltry fifteen hundred rubles! He could not understand her tears nor the quiver of their voices.

An hour later he heard that the Colonel was getting the best of it; the uncles were finally inclining to let the case go for trial.

15 "The matter's settled," said the Colonel, sighing. "Enough."

After this decision all the uncles, even the emphatic Colonel, became noticeably depressed. A silence followed.

"Merciful Heavens!" sighed Ivan Markovitch. "My poor sister!"

And he began saying in a subdued voice that most likely his sister, Sasha's mother, was present unseen in the study at that moment. He felt in his soul how the unhappy, saintly woman was weeping, grieving, and begging for her boy. For the sake of her peace beyond the grave, they ought to spare Sasha.

The sound of a muffled sob was heard. Ivan Markovitch was weeping and muttering something which it was impossible to catch through the door. The Colonel got up and paced from corner to corner. The long conversation began over again.

But then the clock in the drawing room struck two. The family council was over. To avoid seeing the person who had moved him to such wrath, the Colonel went from the study, not into the hall, but into the vestibule.[7] . . . Ivan Markovitch came out into the hall. . . . He was agitated and rubbing his hands joyfully. His tear-stained eyes looked good-humored and his mouth was twisted into a smile.

---

7. **vestibule:** a small entrance hall or room.

"Capital," he said to Sasha. "Thank God! You can go home, my dear, and sleep tranquilly. We have decided to pay the sum, but on condition that you repent and come with me tomorrow into the country and set to work."

16 A minute later Ivan Markovitch and Sasha in their greatcoats and caps were going down the stairs. The uncle was muttering something edifying. Sasha did not listen, but felt as though some uneasy weight were gradually slipping off his shoulders. They had forgiven him; he was free! A gust of joy sprang up within him and sent a sweet chill to his heart. He longed to breathe, to move swiftly, to live! Glancing at the street lamps and the black sky, he remembered that Von Burst was celebrating his name day that evening at the "Bear," and again a rush of joy flooded his soul. . . .

"I am going!" he decided.

But then he remembered he had not a farthing, that the companions he was going to would despise him at once for his empty pockets. He must get hold of some money, come what may!

"Uncle, lend me a hundred rubles," he said to Ivan Markovitch.

His uncle, surprised, looked into his face and backed against a lamppost.

"Give it to me," said Sasha, shifting impatiently from one foot to the other and beginning to pant. "Uncle, I entreat you, give me a hundred rubles."

His face worked; he trembled, and seemed on the point of attacking his uncle. . . .

17 "Won't you?" he kept asking, seeing that his uncle was still amazed and did not understand. "Listen. If you don't, I'll give myself up tomorrow! I won't let you pay the IOU! I'll present another false note tomorrow!"

Petrified, muttering something incoherent in his horror, Ivan Markovitch took a

14 LITERARY ELEMENT
Characterization: What does Sasha's indifference reveal about him? (He is morally and emotionally shallow.)

15 PREDICTING
Do you think the uncles will stick to their decision?

edifying (ed'i·fī'iŋ): morally uplifting
petrified (pe'tri·fīd'): paralyzed with fear

16 LITERARY ELEMENT
Climax: What decision does the family finally make? (They will repay the money as long as Sasha repents.) Why? (Possible response: They are softhearted.) Do you agree with their decision? Explain.

17 COMPARING LITERATURE
How does Sasha's behavior compare or contrast with that of the Prodigal Son (pp. 199–200)? (In contrast to the Prodigal Son, Sasha repeats his misdeed.) How does his family's behavior toward him compare or contrast with the behavior of the Prodigal Son's family? (Possible response: Sasha's family is foolishly generous; the Prodigal's father wisely so.)

WRITING TO LEARN

Social Studies: Chekhov wrote at a time when the rule of the czars and aristocrats in Russia was in decay. Given what you have seen of the Russian gentry in "A Problem," write a paragraph explaining why their society needed reform. ■

Comparing Works. Interested students may wish to read Dostoevsky's short story "An Honest Thief" and write a brief essay comparing and contrasting it with "A Problem." Both Russian stories deal with the moral question of when a misdeed is forgivable. Alternatively, students may wish to read any other short story by Chekhov and write an essay comparing and contrasting it with "A Problem."

2. Writing a Story. Review the term "Chekhovian" on the Reader's Guide page. Invite students to write short stories about contemporary life, including such Chekhovian qualities as concise descriptive style, ironic realism, understanding of social types, and compassionate objectivity. Mention that these qualities have been assimilated into recent short fiction by writers such as Ann Beattie and John Cheever.

Pose the following questions: To what serious moral problem of Sasha's may the title refer? (Sasha's failure to realize the immorality of his actions) What other serious family problem is there? (No family member seems capable of giving Sasha the moral guidance he needs.) What is the least serious problem in the story? (The forged promissory note, which can be paid off.) ■

---

asserted (ə·surt'id): demanded attention

ANSWERS

First Thoughts
Answers will vary.

Identifying Facts
1. Sasha has forged a promissory note. The family can make him stand trial or pay the money for him.
2. They decide to pay the money on condition that Sasha repents.
3. to borrow a hundred rubles

Interpreting Meanings
1. Sasha has been unfortunate and ought to be punished solely by his conscience. Sasha does not have a conscience.
2. Possible response: mocking but compassionate. Examples will vary.
3. His misdeeds are commonplace and he is good-hearted. He realizes he will not or cannot change.
4. **a.** soft-hearted, gullible, foolish, vain
   b. a disciplinarian, rigid, unsympathetic
   c. immature, irresponsible, self-justifying, amoral

Applying Meanings
Answers will vary.

Creative Writing Response
1. Entering the Story. Responses should display a more objective approach to the problem.

2. Imagining a Character's Future. Sketches should show an understanding of Sasha's present character. ■

hundred-ruble note out of his pocketbook and gave it to Sasha. The young man took it and walked rapidly away from him. . . .

Taking a sledge,[8] Sasha grew calmer, and felt a rush of joy within him again. The "rights of youth" of which kind-hearted Ivan

---

8. **sledge:** a horse-drawn sled or sleigh used for transportation over snow or ice.

First Thoughts
Does Sasha remind you of anyone you know or have heard about? Discuss.

Identifying Facts
1. What "problem" does the story's title refer to? What solutions are proposed by the characters in the story?
2. What decision does the family council finally make?
3. What request does Sasha make of Ivan Markovitch at the end of the story?

Interpreting Meanings
1. Ivan Markovitch pleads with the family on Sasha's behalf. What argument does he make? Considering what we learn about Sasha during the course of the story, how is his argument **ironic**?
2. What do you think Chekhov's attitude is toward Sasha? Is his **tone** judgmental, compassionate, or sarcastic? Explain your answer by providing examples from the story.
3. In the first part of "A Problem," how does Sasha manage to justify his behavior, concluding that he is not a criminal? Explain why his opinion of himself changes at the end of the story.
4. Chekhov's description of each character is brief and concise. In a sentence or two, describe each of the following characters in your own words:

Markovitch had spoken at the family council woke up and asserted themselves. Sasha pictured the drinking party before him, and, among the bottles, the women, and his friends, the thought flashed through his mind:

"Now I see that I am a criminal; yes, I am a criminal."

a. Ivan Markovitch; b. the Colonel; c. Sasha.

Applying Meanings
In nineteenth-century Russia, debtors could be thrown into prison for failing to meet their obligations. In twentieth-century America, "having good credit" is generally assumed to be an advantage, and many people carry credit cards—the modern-day promissory note—with pride. Think about how you, your family, and your friends perceive debt. Is it dishonorable to owe money today, or is being in debt a sign of status?

Creative Writing Response
1. **Entering the Story.** Imagine that you are a judge, another relative of Sasha's. Delayed by a court case, you arrive late to the Uskov family council. Your relatives present Sasha's problem to you and say they will abide by whatever decision you make. What is your decision, and why?

2. **Imagining a Character's Future.** What kind of person do you think Sasha will be ten years after the events in the story, when he is thirty-five years old? Do you think he will have changed, or will he still look to his family to bail him out of tight situations? Compose a brief sketch in which members of Sasha's family meet and discuss his character.

Henrik Ibsen
1828–1906

Henrik Ibsen was born in Skien, Norway, the oldest child in a large, well-to-do family. When he was seven, his father suddenly went bankrupt and the family had to move to a farm, where they lived in much-reduced circumstances. A loner, he read avidly and lived mostly in the world of his imagination.

Unable to go to medical school, Ibsen worked for a time as a pharmacist's apprentice. Then, as his interests shifted from science to literature, Ibsen began to read widely and write verse plays until, at twenty-three, with some university theatrical experience behind him, he became stage manager and resident playwright for a new theater at Bergen. There, and later at Christiania (now Oslo), Ibsen became expert in all aspects of stage technique.

Ibsen got married, drifted from job to job, and wrote verse comedies. During this period, Ibsen was extremely poor, and he was discouraged by the negative reception given to most of his plays.

In his late thirties Ibsen finally achieved commercial success with the verse plays *Brand* (1866) and *Peer Gynt* (1867). But, dissatisfied with the quality of his work, Ibsen gave up verse and began to write realistic dramas in prose. Finally, in 1879, came *A Doll's House.* This portrayal of a woman who frees herself from a confining marriage created a scandal throughout northern Europe. Ibsen's next play, *Ghosts* (1881), dealt with the even more controversial subject of syphilis; the play was violently attacked by critics and rejected by all theaters and bookstores. Ibsen's response to his critics was his next masterpiece, *An Enemy of the People* (1882), in which an honest doctor is vilified by his townspeople for speaking the truth about the polluted water of the town.

The great plays that streamed from Ibsen's imagination in his fifties and sixties became the foundation of modern realistic drama. *The Wild Duck* (1884), *Hedda Gabler* (1890), *The Master Builder* (1892), and others were unlike any plays that had been written before. Ibsen's plays are charged with social criticism. The great Realist playwrights who followed Ibsen—George Bernard Shaw, Eugene O'Neill, and Tennessee Williams—continued to develop the techniques that Ibsen had brought to the modern stage.

MORE ABOUT THE AUTHOR

Before Ibsen began writing *A Doll's House*, he jotted down ideas for the play under the heading "Notes for modern tragedy." In the notes he stated the following:

> "There are two kinds of spiritual laws, two kinds of conscience, one in man and a wholly different one in women. They do not understand each other, but woman is judged in practical life according to man's laws, as if she were not a woman, but a man."

In addition to a general awakening of concern for the rights of women in Norway at the time (due in part to the translation of John Stuart Mill's *On the Subjection of Women*), it is likely that Ibsen's stance on women's rights was influenced by Suzanne, his wife, who was a strong feminist. It is also probable that he was affected by the ideas of the novelist Camilla Collett, an outspoken advocate of women's rights, whom Ibsen knew during his stay in Dresden.

ABOUT THE TRANSLATOR

Michael Meyer was born in London in 1921. Called "our greatest living Ibsenite" by the *London Times*, Meyer has translated many of Ibsen's plays and has written a biography of the playwright. Meyer's translations have been used in radio, television, and film, as well as on the stage.

OBJECTIVES

1. *To analyze the realistic techniques used in A Doll's House*
2. *To recognize techniques of characterization*
3. *To write a first-person narrative, a fourth act, and performance notes*
4. *To interpret symbolism, analyze dialogue, and write a theme statement*

THEMES IN WORLD LITERATURE

Conflict of Cultures and Values
The Book of Ruth, pp. 177–184
From the *Apology* of Plato, pp. 293–300
From *Kaffir Boy*, pp. 1365–1376

The Individual and Society
From *The Pillow Book*, pp. 579–587
"The Guest," pp. 1244–1257 ■

PREREADING FOCUS

Background: Ibsen's method of unfolding his plots is called the retrospective technique. Through this technique, Ibsen's characters gradually reveal information about important events that happened prior to the action of the play. In this way, the audience's attention is drawn to the characters' personalities and their motives for acting, rather than to the actions themselves. Through their dialogue, gestures, tones of voice, even their silences, the characters unveil the conflict of the play, and an interesting dramatic tension is created between the events taking place before the audience and the past events to which the characters continue to react.

Literary Focus: In discussing the importance of characterization in his plays, Ibsen said:

"Before I write down one word, I have to have the character in mind through and through. I must penetrate to the last wrinkle of his soul. . . . I have to have his exterior in mind also, down to the last button, how he stands and walks, his behavior, what his voice sounds like."

Ask students to look for the many minute details by which Ibsen reveals Nora's character.

Reader's Guide

A DOLL'S HOUSE

Background

During the nineteenth century, most middle-class European and American women were economically and legally dependent on their husbands. Realistic writers such as Leo Tolstoy, Guy de Maupassant, and Thomas Hardy wrote works sympathizing with defiant, unconventional women, but their rebellious female characters usually came to ruin. In *A Doll's House*, Ibsen creates a modern tragic heroine and allows her to achieve independence.

Upon its publication in 1879, *A Doll's House* was widely translated, read, discussed, attacked, and performed. The portrayal of marital conflict in the play was considered so scandalous that the producers of the German version changed the last act. Ibsen himself, under considerable pressure, wrote an alternate ending. He later regretted this, stating that the entire play was written for the sake of the final scene and its famous "slamming door."

In *A Doll's House*, Ibsen imitates the technique of analysis and retrospection first developed by Sophocles in ancient Greece (see page 301). The major events affecting the characters have already occurred before the curtain is raised; the action of the play serves to expose these events. Ibsen's contemporaries were startled by the detailed set descriptions, the natural dialogue, and the use of real-life situations. In fact, modern drama is often said to date from the appearance of *A Doll's House*.

Writer's Response

How would you define a good marriage? Write a few sentences expressing your views. Do your ideas about marriage come from observing married couples, from television, from books, or elsewhere?

Literary Focus

Characterization is the process by which an author reveals the personality of the characters. In drama, characterization occurs mostly through dialogue, a form of **indirect characterization**. We make up our minds about the characters by listening to the things they say and how they say them, what they look like, and how they act.

A DOLL'S HOUSE

Henrik Ibsen

translated by

MICHAEL MEYER

> *When you read a play, you have the chance to "direct" a performance in your own head. As you read, visualize the set, and imagine the tone of voice and the gestures the actors might use. If you like, "rehearse" several voices for the same line of dialogue until you find the one that best reveals the character.*

IN THE WINTER GARDEN, EDOUARD MANET, 1879.

Archiv Für Kunst Und Geschichte, Berlin

HUMANITIES CONNECTION

In their work, both Manet and Ibsen brought together current social subject matter and unconventional styles. *In the Winter Garden*, painted the year *A Doll's House* was published, shows how the characters in Ibsen's play might have dressed. Compare Manet's painting with Monticelli's *Faust and Gretchen*, p. 998. How does Monticelli show his subjects' feelings? (dramatic gestures, symbolic objects) How does Manet? (subtler expressions and gestures) ∎

CULTURAL DIVERSITY

In *A Doll's House*, Ibsen challenges his society's assumptions and forces his audience to look at the restrictions and expectations with which the women of his day had to cope. *In what ways do you think the lives of women are restricted in the United States today?* (Possible response: They don't earn as much money as men.) *What are some of the expectations placed upon women today?* (They are often expected to take care of families as well as maintain full-time jobs.)

Creating Realistic Dialogue

Since Ibsen wished to explore aspects of his own society, his aim was to create believable characters. To achieve such realism, Ibsen tried to write dialogue that resembled how people actually talk. As a result, his dialogue is marked by sentence fragments, pauses, slang or idiomatic expressions, and the use of gestures or voice inflections to fill in meaning. Here is an example of dialogue using such techniques:

Nora: I? You say *I* know so little of—?
Mrs. Linde: Well, good heavens—those bits of fancywork of yours—well, really! You're a child, Nora.

Speaking and Listening. Ask a pair of students to read this dialogue aloud. Have the class listen and evaluate whether or not the exchange sounds like actual people talking. Then have students analyze the written dialogue and identify the techniques Ibsen used to imitate actual speech. ∎

---

1 LITERARY ELEMENT

Setting: Ibsen gives precise instructions for the play's set in his opening stage directions. How would you characterize the setting? (a comfortable, cozy, nineteenth-century, middle-class home) What effect on his audience do you think Ibsen wished to achieve with such a realistic set? (Possible response: to give the audience the feeling they were witnessing people like themselves)

2 LITERARY ELEMENT

Stage Directions: What kind of information does Ibsen convey directly in the bracketed stage directions? (sound effects, the actions and appearance of the characters) What can this information convey indirectly? (the emotional climate of the setting and characters)

3 SPECULATING

What might Nora's nine-shilling tip suggest about her personality? (Possible response: She is generous, possibly extravagant.)

CHARACTERS

Torvald Helmer, a lawyer
Nora, his wife
Dr. Rank
Mrs. Linde
Nils Krogstad, also a lawyer

The Helmers' Three Small Children
Anne-Marie, their nurse
Helen, the maid
A Porter

The action takes place in the Helmers' apartment.

═ ACT 1 ═

1 *A comfortably and tastefully, but not expensively furnished room. Backstage right a door leads to the hall; backstage left, another door to* HELMER's *study. Between these two doors stands a piano. In the middle of the left-hand wall is a door, with a window downstage of it. Near the window, a round table with armchairs and a small sofa. In the right-hand wall, slightly upstage, is a door; downstage of this, against the same wall, a stove lined with porcelain tiles, with a couple of armchairs and a rocking chair in front of it. Between the stove and the side door is a small table. Engravings on the wall. A what-not with china and other bric-a-brac; a small bookcase with leather-bound books. A carpet on the floor; a fire in the stove. A winter day.*

2 [*A bell rings in the hall outside. After a moment we hear the front door being opened.* NORA *enters the room, humming contentedly to herself. She is wearing outdoor clothes and carrying a lot of parcels, which she puts down on the table right. She leaves the door to the hall open; through it, we can see a* PORTER *carrying a Christmas tree and a basket. He gives these to the* MAID, *who has opened the door for them.*]

Nora. Hide that Christmas tree away, Helen. The children mustn't see it before I've decorated it this evening. (*to the* PORTER, *taking out her purse*) How much?
Porter. A shilling.[1]
Nora. Here's ten shillings. No, keep it.

3 [*The* PORTER *touches his cap and goes.* NORA *closes the door. She continues to laugh happily to herself as she removes her coat, etc. She takes from her pocket a bag containing macaroons and eats a couple. Then she tiptoes across and listens at her husband's door.*]

Nora. Yes, he's here. (*starts humming again as she goes over to the table, right.*)
Helmer (*from his room*). Is that my skylark twittering out there?
Nora (*opening some of the parcels*). It is!
Helmer. Is that my squirrel rustling?
Nora. Yes!
Helmer. When did my squirrel come home?
Nora. Just now. (*pops the bag of macaroons in her pocket and wipes her mouth*) Come out here, Torvald, and see what I've bought.
Helmer. You mustn't disturb me!

[*Short pause; then he opens the door and looks in, his pen in his hand.*]

---

1. **shilling:** a coin of little value.

Helmer. Bought, did you say? All that? Has my little squanderbird been overspending again?

Nora. Oh, Torvald, surely we can let ourselves go a little this year! It's the first Christmas we don't have to scrape.

Helmer. Well, you know, we can't afford to be extravagant.

Nora. Oh yes, Torvald, we can be a little extravagant now. Can't we? Just a tiny bit? You've got a big salary now, and you're going to make lots and lots of money.

Helmer. Next year, yes. But my new salary doesn't start till April.

Nora. Pooh; we can borrow till then.

Helmer. Nora! (*goes over to her and takes her playfully by the ear*) What a little spendthrift² you are! Suppose I were to borrow fifty pounds today, and you spent it all over Christmas, and then on New Year's Eve a tile fell off a roof onto my head—

Nora (*puts her hand over his mouth*). Oh, Torvald! Don't say such dreadful things!

Helmer. Yes, but suppose something like that did happen? What then?

Nora. If anything as frightful as that happened, it wouldn't make much difference whether I was in debt or not.

Helmer. But what about the people I'd borrowed from?

Nora. Them? Who cares about them? They're strangers.

Helmer. Oh, Nora, Nora, how like a woman! No, but seriously, Nora, you know how I feel about this. No debts! Never borrow! A home that is founded on debts and borrowing can never be a place of freedom and beauty. We two have stuck it out bravely up to now; and we shall continue to do so for the few weeks that remain.

Nora (*goes over towards the stove*). Very

well, Torvald. As you say.

Helmer (*follows her*). Now, now! My little songbird mustn't droop her wings. What's this? Is little squirrel sulking? (*takes out his purse*) Nora; guess what I've got here!

Nora (*turns quickly*). Money!

Helmer. Look. (*hands her some bank notes*) I know how these small expenses crop up at Christmas.

Nora (*counts them*). One—two—three—four. Oh, thank you, Torvald, thank you! I should be able to manage with this.

Helmer. You'll have to.

Nora. Yes, yes, of course I will. But come over here, I want to show you everything I've bought. And so cheap! Look, here are new clothes for Ivar—and a sword. And a horse and a trumpet for Bob. And a doll and a cradle for Emmy—they're nothing much, but she'll pull them apart in a few days. And some bits of material and handkerchiefs for the maids. Old Annie-Marie ought to have had something better, really.

Helmer. And what's in that parcel?

Nora (*cries*). No, Torvald, you mustn't see that before this evening!

Helmer. Very well. But now, tell me, my little spendthrift, what do you want for Christmas?

Nora. Me? Oh, pooh, I don't want anything.

Helmer. Oh yes, you do. Now tell me, what within reason would you most like?

Nora. No, I really don't know. Oh, yes—Torvald—!

Helmer. Well?

Nora (*plays with his coat buttons; not looking at him*). If you really want to give me something, you could—you could—

Helmer. Come on, out with it.

Nora (*quickly*). You could give me money, Torvald. Only as much as you feel you can afford; then later I'll buy something with it.

Helmer. But, Nora—

---

2. **spendthrift:** someone who spends money carelessly or wastefully.

4 GUIDED READING

Finding the Main Idea: On what subject do Torvald and Nora disagree in this opening scene? (spending money and borrowing) What are Torvald's views on the subject? (spend sparingly and never borrow) What are Nora's views? (happiness in the present is more important than future debts)

5 LITERARY ELEMENT

Dialogue: What does Torvald's use of pet names and his lecturing tone suggest about his view of Nora? (He sees her as a delightful child in need of guidance.) How does Nora behave toward Torvald? (like a child trying to charm, wheedle, or deceive a parent)

6 SPECULATING

Why do you think Nora is so eager for a gift of money from her husband? (Answers will vary.)

Nora. Oh yes, Torvald dear, please! Please! Then I'll wrap up the notes in pretty gold paper and hang them on the Christmas tree. Wouldn't that be fun?

Helmer. What's the name of that little bird that can never keep any money?

Nora. Yes, yes, squanderbird; I know. But let's do as I say, Torvald; then I'll have time to think about what I need most. Isn't that the best way? Mm?

Helmer (*smiles*). To be sure it would be, if you could keep what I give you and really buy yourself something with it. But you'll spend it on all sorts of useless things for the house, and then I'll have to put my hand in my pocket again.

Nora. Oh, but Torvald—

Helmer. You can't deny it, Nora dear. (*puts his arm around her waist*) The squanderbird's a pretty little creature, but she gets through an awful lot of money. It's incredible what an expensive pet she is for a man to keep.

Nora. For shame! How can you say such a thing? I save every penny I can.

Helmer (*laughs*). That's quite true. Every penny you can. But you can't.

Nora (*hums and smiles, quietly gleeful*). Hm. If you only knew how many expenses we larks and squirrels have, Torvald.

Helmer. You're a funny little creature. Just like your father used to be. Always on the lookout for some way to get money, but as soon as you have any it just runs through your fingers and you never know where it's gone. Well, I suppose I must take you as you are. It's in your blood. Yes, yes, yes, these things are hereditary, Nora.

Nora. Oh, I wish I'd inherited more of Papa's qualities.

Helmer. And I wouldn't wish my darling little songbird to be any different from what she is. By the way, that reminds me. You look awfully—how shall I put it?—

awfully guilty today.

Nora. Do I?

Helmer. Yes, you do. Look me in the eyes.

Nora (*looks at him*). Well?

Helmer (*wags his finger*). Has my little sweet tooth been indulging herself in town today, by any chance?

Nora. No, how can you think such a thing?

Helmer. Not a tiny little digression into a pastry shop?

Nora. No, Torvald, I promise—

Helmer. Not just a wee jam tart?

Nora. Certainly not.

Helmer. Not a little nibble at a macaroon?

Nora. No, Torvald—I promise you, honestly—!

Helmer. There, there. I was only joking.

Nora (*goes over to the table, right*). You know I could never act against your wishes.

Helmer. Of course not. And you've given me your word—(*goes over to her*) Well, my beloved Nora, you keep your little Christmas secrets to yourself. They'll be revealed this evening, I've no doubt, once the Christmas tree has been lit.

Nora. Have you remembered to invite Dr. Rank?

Helmer. No. But there's no need; he knows he'll be dining with us. Anyway, I'll ask him when he comes this morning. I've ordered some good wine. Oh, Nora, you can't imagine how I'm looking forward to this evening.

Nora. So am I. And, Torvald, how the children will love it!

Helmer. Yes, it's a wonderful thing to know that one's position is assured and that one has an ample income. Don't you agree? It's good to know that, isn't it?

Nora. Yes, it's almost like a miracle.

Helmer. Do you remember last Christmas? For three whole weeks you shut yourself away every evening to make flowers for the

Christmas tree, and all those other things you were going to surprise us with. Ugh, it was the most boring time I've ever had in my life.

Nora. I didn't find it boring.

Helmer (*smiles*). But it all came to nothing in the end, didn't it?

Nora. Oh, are you going to bring that up again? How could I help the cat getting in and tearing everything to bits?

Helmer. No, my poor little Nora, of course you couldn't. You simply wanted to make us happy, and that's all that matters. But it's good that those hard times are past.

Nora. Yes, it's wonderful.

Helmer. I don't have to sit by myself and be bored. And you don't have to tire your pretty eyes and your delicate little hands—

Nora (*claps her hands*). No, Torvald, that's true, isn't it? I don't have to any longer! Oh, it's really all just like a miracle. (*takes his arm*) Now I'm going to tell you what I thought we might do, Torvald. As soon as Christmas is over—

[*A bell rings in the hall.*]

Oh, there's the doorbell. (*tidies up one or two things in the room*) Someone's coming. What a bore.

Helmer. I'm not at home to any visitors. Remember!

Maid (*in the doorway*). A lady's called, madam. A stranger.

Nora. Well, ask her to come in.

Maid. And the doctor's here too, sir.

Helmer. Has he gone to my room?

Maid. Yes, sir.

[HELMER *goes into his room. The* MAID *shows in* MRS. LINDE, *who is dressed in traveling clothes; then closes the door.*]

Mrs. Linde (*shyly and a little hesitantly*). Good morning, Nora.

Nora (*uncertainly*). Good morning—

Still from a production of *A Doll's House* by the Midland Community Theatre, Midland, Texas.

Midland Community Theatre at Theatre Midland

Mrs. Linde. I don't suppose you recognize me.

Nora. No, I'm afraid I—Yes, wait a minute—surely—I—(*exclaims*) Why, Christine! Is it really you?

Mrs. Linde. Yes, it's me.

Nora. Christine! And I didn't recognize you! But how could I—? (*more quietly*) How you've changed, Christine!

Mrs. Linde. Yes, I know. It's been nine years—nearly ten—

Nora. Is it so long? Yes, it must be. Oh, these last eight years have been such a happy time for me! So you've come to town? All that way in winter! How brave of you!

Mrs. Linde. I arrived by the steamer this morning.

Nora. Yes, of course, to enjoy yourself over Christmas. Oh, how splendid! We'll have to

10

11

10 GUIDED READING
Identifying Details: What is the miracle to which Nora refers? (Torvald's upcoming promotion with its increased income)

LITERARY ELEMENT
Theme: Alert students to look for additional references to miracles by Nora as the play unfolds. Ask them to consider whether a belief in miracles fits well with other aspects of Nora's personality.

11 INTERPRETING
How does Torvald react to the bell ringing? (He is irritated.) What does this suggest about his life and character? (Possible response: He wants a predictable and circumscribed domestic life with little disturbance from the outside.)

celebrate! But take off your coat. You're not cold, are you? (*helps her off with it*) There! Now let's sit down here by the stove and be comfortable. No, you take the armchair. I'll sit here in the rocking chair. (*clasps* MRS. LINDE's *hands*) Yes, now you look like your old self. Just at first I—you've got a little paler, though, Christine. And perhaps a bit thinner.

Mrs. Linde. And older, Nora. Much, much older.

Nora. Yes, perhaps a little older. Just a tiny bit. Not much (*checks herself suddenly and says earnestly*) Oh, but how thoughtless of me to sit here and chatter away like this! Dear, sweet Christine, can you forgive me?

Mrs. Linde. What do you mean, Nora?

Nora (*quietly*). Poor Christine, you've become a widow.

Mrs. Linde. Yes. Three years ago.

Nora. I know, I know—I read it in the papers. Oh, Christine, I meant to write to you so often, honestly. But I always put it off, and something else always cropped up.

Mrs. Linde. I understand, Nora dear.

Nora. No, Christine, it was beastly of me. Oh, my poor darling, what you've gone through! And he didn't leave you anything?

Mrs. Linde. No.

Nora. No children, either?

Mrs. Linde. No.

Nora. Nothing at all, then?

Mrs. Linde. Not even a feeling of loss or sorrow.

Nora (*looks incredulously at her*). But, Christine, how is that possible?

Mrs. Linde (*smiles sadly and strokes* NORA's *hair*). Oh, these things happen, Nora.

Nora. All alone. How dreadful that must be for you. I've three lovely children. I'm afraid you can't see them now, because they're out with Nanny. But you must tell me everything—

Mrs. Linde. No, no, no. I want to hear about you.

Nora. No, you start. I'm not going to be selfish today, I'm just going to think about you. Oh, but there's one thing I *must* tell you. Have you heard of the wonderful luck we've just had?

Mrs. Linde. No. What?

Nora. Would you believe it—my husband's just been made vice-president of the bank!

Mrs. Linde. Your husband? Oh, how lucky—!

Nora. Yes, isn't it? Being a lawyer is so uncertain, you know, especially if one isn't prepared to touch any case that isn't—well—quite nice. And of course Torvald's been very firm about that—and I'm absolutely with him. Oh, you can imagine how happy we are! He's joining the bank in the new year, and he'll be getting a big salary, and lots of percentages too. From now on we'll be able to live quite differently—we'll be able to do whatever we want. Oh, Christine, it's such a relief! I feel so happy! Well, I mean, it's lovely to have heaps of money and not to have to worry about anything. Don't you think?

Mrs. Linde. It must be lovely to have enough to cover one's needs, anyway.

Nora. Not just our needs! We're going to have heaps and heaps of money!

Mrs. Linde (*smiles*). Nora, Nora, haven't you grown up yet? When we were at school you were a terrible little spendthrift.

Nora (*laughs quietly*). Yes, Torvald still says that. (*wags her finger*) But "Nora, Nora" isn't as silly as you think. Oh, we've been in no position for me to waste money. We've both had to work.

Mrs. Linde. You too?

Nora. Yes, little things—fancywork, crocheting, embroidery and so forth. (*casually*) And other things, too. I suppose you know Torvald left the Ministry when we got married? There were no prospects of promotion in his department, and of course he needed more money. But the first year he overworked himself dreadfully. He had to take on all sorts of extra jobs, and worked day and night. But it was too much for him, and he became frightfully ill. The doctors said he'd have to go to a warmer climate.

Mrs. Linde. Yes, you spent a whole year in Italy, didn't you?

Nora. Yes. It wasn't easy for me to get away, you know. I'd just had Ivar. But, of course, we had to do it. Oh, it was a marvelous trip! And it saved Torvald's life. But it cost an awful lot of money, Christine.

Mrs. Linde. I can imagine.

Nora. Two hundred and fifty pounds. That's a lot of money, you know.

Mrs. Linde. How lucky you had it.

Nora. Well, actually, we got it from my father.

Mrs. Linde. Oh, I see. Didn't he die just about that time?

Nora. Yes, Christine, just about then. Wasn't it dreadful, I couldn't go and look after him. I was expecting little Ivar any day. And then I had my poor Torvald to care for—we really didn't think he'd live. Dear, kind Papa! I never saw him again, Christine. Oh, it's the saddest thing that's happened to me since I got married.

Mrs. Linde. I know you were very fond of him. But you went to Italy—?

Nora. Yes. Well, we had the money, you see, and the doctors said we mustn't delay. So we went the month after Papa died.

Mrs. Linde. And your husband came back completely cured?

Nora. Fit as a fiddle!

Mrs. Linde. But—the doctor?

Nora. How do you mean?

Mrs. Linde. I thought the maid said that the gentleman who arrived with me was the doctor.

Nora. Oh yes, that's Dr. Rank, but he doesn't come because anyone's ill. He's our best friend, and he looks us up at least once every day. No, Torvald hasn't had a moment's illness since we went away. And the children are fit and healthy and so am I. (*jumps up and claps her hands*) Oh, God, oh God, Christine, isn't it a wonderful thing to be alive and happy! Oh, but how beastly of me! I'm only talking about myself. (*sits on a footstool and rests her arms on* MRS. LINDE's *knee*) Oh, please don't be angry with me! Tell me, is it really true you didn't love your husband? Why did you marry him, then?

Mrs. Linde. Well, my mother was still alive; and she was helpless and bedridden. And I had my two little brothers to take care of. I didn't feel I could say no.

Nora. Yes, well, perhaps you're right. He was rich then, was he?

Mrs. Linde. Quite comfortably off, I believe. But his business was unsound, you see, Nora. When he died it went bankrupt and there was nothing left.

Nora. What did you do?

Mrs. Linde. Well, I had to try to make ends meet somehow, so I started a little shop, and a little school, and anything else I could turn my hand to. These last three years have been just one endless slog for me, without a moment's rest. But now it's over, Nora. My poor dead mother doesn't need me any more; she's passed away. And the boys don't need me either; they've got jobs now and can look after themselves.

Nora. How relieved you must feel—

Mrs. Linde. No, Nora. Just unspeakably empty. No one to live for any more. (*gets up restlessly*) That's why I couldn't bear to stay out there any longer, cut off from the world. I thought it'd be easier to find some work here that will exercise and occupy my mind. If only I could get a regular job—office work of some kind—

Nora. Oh but, Christine, that's dreadfully exhausting; and you look practically fin-

17 LITERARY ELEMENT

Exposition: In the dialogue with Mrs. Linde, Nora gives information about events that occurred earlier in her marriage. How does she say the trip to Italy was paid for? (by her father before he died)

18 COMPARING AND CONTRASTING

What is similar about Christine's and Nora's experience of family life and marriage? (Both were expected to and willingly took care of others.) What is different? (Nora seems to have been indulged more with money and attention, and presently has children and a husband with good prospects.)

19 GUIDED READING

Identifying Cause and Effect: Why has Mrs. Linde left home? (Her mother and brothers no longer need her and she thinks it will be easier to find work in the city.) What does she miss most from her past? (having others to live and work for)

A Doll's House, Act 1   **1077**

In art and literature, houses can say a great deal about their inhabitants.

? *In Polenow's painting, what might the house and the grandmother have in common?* (Both show the effects of age; the architecture of the house, like the grandmother's dress, is of another era.) *In titling his play* A Doll's House, *what might Ibsen have been implying about Nora?* (Possible responses: Her life lacks reality. She is more like a doll or a possession than a person.) ■

egocentric (ē′gō·sen′trik): self-centered

20 LITERARY ELEMENT

Characterization: What does Nora's promise to Christine reveal about her motives? (She is genuinely kindhearted and wants to help those she loves.) What does it reveal about her way of dealing with Torvald? (She is indirect and coaxing, rather than straightforward.)

GRANDMOTHER'S HOUSE, WASSILI DMITRIJEWITSCH POLENOW (1844–1927).

Archiv Für Kunst Und Geschichte, Berlin

ished already. It'd be much better for you if you could go away somewhere.

Mrs. Linde (*goes over to the window*). I have no papa to pay for my holidays, Nora.

Nora (*gets up*). Oh, please don't be angry with me.

Mrs. Linde. My dear Nora, it's I who should ask you not to be angry. That's the worst thing about this kind of situation—it makes one so bitter. One has no one to work for; and yet one has to be continually sponging for jobs. One has to live; and so one becomes completely <u>egocentric</u>. When

you told me about this luck you've just had with Torvald's new job—can you imagine?—I was happy not so much on your account, as on my own.

Nora. How do you mean? Oh, I understand. You mean Torvald might be able to do something for you?

Mrs. Linde. Yes, I was thinking that.

Nora. He will too, Christine. Just you leave it to me. I'll lead up to it so delicately, so delicately; I'll get him in the right mood. Oh, Christine, I do so want to help you.

Mrs. Linde. It's sweet of you to bother so much about me, Nora. Especially since you

20

know so little of the worries and hardships of life.

Nora. I? You say *I* know little of—?

Mrs. Linde (*smiles*). Well, good heavens—those bits of fancywork of yours—well, really! You're a child, Nora.

Nora (*tosses her head and walks across the room*). You shouldn't say that so patronizingly.

Mrs. Linde. Oh?

Nora. You're like the rest. You all think I'm incapable of getting down to anything serious—

Mrs. Linde. My dear—

Nora. You think I've never had any worries like the rest of you.

Mrs. Linde. Nora dear, you've just told me about all your difficulties—

Nora. Pooh—that! (*quietly*) I haven't told you about the big thing.

Mrs. Linde. What big thing? What do you mean?

Nora. You patronize me, Christine; but you shouldn't. You're proud that you've worked so long and so hard for your mother.

Mrs. Linde. I don't patronize anyone, Nora. But you're right—I am both proud and happy that I was able to make my mother's last months on earth comparatively easy.

Nora. And you're also proud at what you've done for your brothers.

Mrs. Linde. I think I have a right to be.

Nora. I think so, too. But let me tell you something, Christine. I, too, have done something to be proud and happy about.

Mrs. Linde. I don't doubt it. But—how do you mean?

Nora. Speak quietly! Suppose Torvald should hear! He mustn't, at any price—no one must know, Christine—no one but you.

Mrs. Linde. But what is this?

Nora. Come over here. (*pulls her down onto the sofa beside her*) Yes, Christine—I,

too, have done something to be happy and proud about. It was I who saved Torvald's life.

Mrs. Linde. Saved his—? How did you save it?

Nora. I told you about our trip to Italy. Torvald couldn't have lived if he hadn't managed to get down there—

Mrs. Linde. Yes, well—your father provided the money—

Nora (*smiles*). So Torvald and everyone else thinks. But—

Mrs. Linde. Yes?

Nora. Papa didn't give us a penny. It was I who found the money.

Mrs. Linde. You? All of it?

Nora. Two hundred and fifty pounds. What do you say to that?

Mrs. Linde. But, Nora, how could you? Did you win a lottery or something?

Nora (*scornfully*). Lottery? (*sniffs*) What would there be to be proud of in that?

Mrs. Linde. But where did you get it from, then?

Nora (*hums and smiles secretively*). Hm; tra-la-la-la!

Mrs. Linde. You couldn't have borrowed it.

Nora. Oh? Why not?

Mrs. Linde. Well, a wife can't borrow money without her husband's consent.

Nora (*tosses her head*). Ah, but when a wife has a little business sense, and knows how to be clever—

Mrs. Linde. But Nora, I simply don't understand—

Nora. You don't have to. No one has said I borrowed the money. I could have got it in some other way. (*throws herself back on the sofa*) I could have got it from an admirer. When a girl's as pretty as I am—

Mrs. Linde. Nora, you're crazy!

Nora. You're dying of curiosity now, aren't you, Christine?

21

22

23

21 ANALYZING

What is new and different about Nora's statement and gestures to Mrs. Linde about being patronizing? What do they reveal about Nora for the first time? (They are assertive and reveal that she is aware of how others view her.)

patronize (pā′trən·īz′): treat in a condescending way

22 SPECULATING

How do you think Nora "found" the money for the trip to Italy? (Answers will vary.)

23 INTERPRETING

What has motivated Nora to tell Christine how she financed the Italian trip? (Possible responses: She wants to show that she also has used her wits to benefit her family. She wishes to unburden herself to an old friend.)

READER'S RESPONSE

Have you ever done anything that involved hardship or sacrifice on your part to help someone else? How did you feel afterward?

Identifying Details: What important information has Nora been keeping from her husband? (He was seriously ill and she borrowed money to finance his life-saving trip.)

25 **EVALUATING**

What does Nora think is necessary to the survival of her marriage? (Her husband must be deceived into believing that he owes nothing to her.) Do you agree with her estimation of Helmer's character and values? (Most students will agree.)

CULTURAL DIVERSITY

The view that male identity and pride are rooted in men's role as sole provider for their families was the accepted view in Ibsen's time, and it has been the prevailing view in many societies, past and present. Emotional independence, unfailing strength, and unquestioned authority are other aspects of this view of man as breadwinner.

❓ *Do you think that views of masculine identity have changed in contemporary America?* (Answers will vary.) *Are you familiar with another culture in which men's roles are viewed differently?* (Answers will vary.)

Mrs. Linde. Nora dear, you haven't done anything foolish?

Nora (*sits up again*). Is it foolish to save one's husband's life?

Mrs. Linde. I think it's foolish if without his knowledge you—

Nora. But the whole point was that he mustn't know! Great heavens, don't you see? He hadn't to know how dangerously ill he was. It was me they told that his life was in danger and that only going to a warm climate could save him. Do you suppose I didn't try to think of other ways of getting him down there? I told him how wonderful it would be for me to go abroad like other young wives; I cried and prayed; I asked him to remember my condition, and said he ought to be nice and tender to me; and then I suggested he might quite easily borrow the money. But then he got almost angry with me, Christine. He said I was frivolous, and that it was his duty as a husband not to pander to my moods and caprices—I think that's what he called them. Well, well, I thought, you've got to be saved somehow. And then I thought of a way—

Mrs. Linde. But didn't your husband find out from your father that the money hadn't come from him?

Nora. No, never. Papa died just then. I'd thought of letting him into the plot and asking him not to tell. But since he was so ill—! And as things turned out, it didn't become necessary.

Mrs. Linde. And you've never told your husband about this?

Nora. For heaven's sake, no! What an idea! He's frightfully strict about such matters. And besides—he's so proud of being a man—it'd be so painful and humiliating for him to know that he owed anything to me. It'd completely wreck our relationship. This life we have built together would no longer exist.

Mrs. Linde. Will you never tell him?

Nora (*thoughtfully, half-smiling*). Yes—sometime, perhaps. Years from now, when I'm no longer pretty. You mustn't laugh! I mean, of course, when Torvald no longer loves me as he does now; when it no longer amuses him to see me dance and dress up and play the fool for him. Then it might be useful to have something up my sleeve. (*breaks off*) Stupid, stupid, stupid! That time will never come. Well, what do you think of my big secret, Christine? I'm not completely useless, am I? Mind you, all this has caused me a frightful lot of worry. It hasn't been easy for me to meet my obligations punctually. In case you don't know, in the world of business there are things called quarterly installments and interest, and they're a terrible problem to cope with. So I've had to scrape a little here and save a little there, as best I can. I haven't been able to save much on the housekeeping money, because Torvald likes to live well; and I couldn't let the children go short of clothes—I couldn't take anything out of what he gives me for them. The poor little angels!

Mrs. Linde. So you've had to stint yourself, my poor Nora?

Nora. Of course. Well, after all, it was my problem. Whenever Torvald gave me money to buy myself new clothes, I never used more than half of it; and I always bought what was cheapest and plainest. Thank heaven anything suits me, so that Torvald's never noticed. But it made me a bit sad sometimes, because it's lovely to wear pretty clothes. Don't you think?

Mrs. Linde. Indeed it is.

Nora. And then I've found one or two other sources of income. Last winter I managed to get a lot of copying to do. So I shut myself away and wrote every evening, late into the night. Oh, I often got so tired, so tired. But it was great fun, though, sitting there working and earning money. It was

24

25

almost like being a man.

Mrs. Linde. But how much have you managed to pay off like this?

Nora. Well, I can't say exactly. It's awfully difficult to keep an exact check on these kind of transactions. I only know I've paid everything I've managed to scrape together. Sometimes I really didn't know where to turn. (*smiles*) Then I'd sit here and imagine some rich old gentleman had fallen in love with me—

Mrs. Linde. What! What gentleman?

Nora. Silly! And that now he'd died and when they opened his will it said in big letters: "Everything I possess is to be paid forthwith to my beloved Mrs. Nora Helmer in cash."

Mrs. Linde. But, Nora dear, who was this gentleman?

Nora. Great heavens, don't you understand? There wasn't any old gentleman; he was just something I used to dream up as I sat here evening after evening wondering how on earth I could raise some money. But what does it matter? The old bore can stay imaginary as far as I'm concerned, because now I don't have to worry any longer! (*jumps up*) Oh, Christine, isn't it wonderful? I don't have to worry any more! No more troubles! I can play all day with the children, I can fill the house with pretty things, just the way Torvald likes. And, Christine, it'll soon be spring, and the air'll be fresh and the skies blue—and then perhaps we'll be able to take a little trip somewhere. I shall be able to see the sea again. Oh, yes, yes, it's a wonderful thing to be alive and happy!

[*The bell rings in the hall.*]

Mrs. Linde (*gets up*). You've a visitor. Perhaps I'd better go.

Nora. No, stay. It won't be for me. It's someone for Torvald—

Maid (*in the doorway*). Excuse me, madam,

a gentleman's called who says he wants to speak to the master. But I didn't know—seeing as the doctor's with him—

Nora. Who is this gentleman?

Krogstad (*in the doorway*). It's me, Mrs. Helmer.

[MRS. LINDE *starts, composes herself and turns away to the window.*]

Nora (*takes a step towards him and whispers tensely*). You? What is it? What do you want to talk to my husband about?

Krogstad. Business—you might call it. I hold a minor post in the bank, and I hear your husband is to become our new chief—

Nora. Oh—then it isn't—?

Krogstad. Pure business, Mrs. Helmer. Nothing more.

Nora. Well, you'll find him in his study.

[*Nods indifferently as she closes the hall door behind him. Then she walks across the room and sees to the stove.*]

Mrs. Linde. Nora, who was that man?

Nora. A lawyer called Krogstad.

Mrs. Linde. It was him, then.

Nora. Do you know that man?

Mrs. Linde. I used to know him—some years ago. He was a solicitor's[3] clerk in our town, for a while.

Nora. Yes, of course, so he was.

Mrs. Linde. How he's changed!

Nora. He was very unhappily married, I believe.

Mrs. Linde. Is he a widower now?

Nora. Yes, with a lot of children. Ah, now it's alight.

[*She closes the door of the stove and moves the rocking chair a little to one side.*]

Mrs. Linde. He does—various things now, I hear?

3. **solicitor:** lawyer.

---

26 INFERRING
How does Nora's fantasy of a male benefactor help reveal the economic position of women in her society? (Possible response: Women were completely dependent on male generosity or favor for their survival.)

27 LITERARY ELEMENT
Symbolism: Ibsen's props, costumes, and sound effects often have symbolic as well as functional significance. What does the ringing bell signal on the realistic level? (the arrival of a visitor) What might it signify on a symbolic level? (Possible response: the intrusion of the outside world, or reality, on the illusory happiness of the Helmer household)

28 INTERPRETING
What do Mrs. Linde's movements upon seeing Krogstad suggest about her feelings toward him? (Possible response: She recognizes him but does not wish to be seen or to speak with him. She may be feeling afraid, embarrassed, or vulnerable.)

29 SPECULATING
What do you think Nora imagined or feared Krogstad might want to speak to her husband about? (Some students may guess at this point that Krogstad is the person from whom Nora borrowed money.)

Tone: How would you describe the tone of Dr. Rank's dialogue with Nora and Mrs. Linde? (Possible responses: ironic; knowing; cynical; pessimistic)

31 COMPARING AND CONTRASTING

Mrs. Linde and Dr. Rank have different views on how the physically and spiritually weak should be treated by society. How would you describe their views? (Possible response: He believes the strong should not be pulled down by the weak. She believes the strong should assist the weak.) Can you think of situations in which these points of view are still being argued today? (Possible response: conservative vs. liberal social policy)

Nora. Does he? It's quite possible—I really don't know. But don't let's talk about business. It's so boring.

[DR. RANK *enters from* HELMER's *study.*]

Dr. Rank (*still in the doorway*). No, no, my dear chap, don't see me out. I'll go and have a word with your wife. (*closes the door and notices* MRS. LINDE) Oh, I beg your pardon. I seem to be *de trop*[4] here, too.

Nora. Not in the least. (*introduces them*) Dr. Rank. Mrs. Linde.

Rank. Ah! A name I have often heard in this house. I believe I passed you on the stairs as I came up.

Mrs. Linde. Yes. Stairs tire me. I have to take them slowly.

Rank. Oh, have you hurt yourself?

Mrs. Linde. No, I'm just a little run down.

Rank. Ah, is that all? Then I take it you've come to town to cure yourself by a round of parties?

Mrs. Linde. I have come here to find work.

Rank. Is that an approved remedy for being run down?

Mrs. Linde. One has to live, Doctor.

Rank. Yes, people do seem to regard it as a necessity.

Nora. Oh, really, Dr. Rank. I bet you want to stay alive.

Rank. You bet I do. However wretched I sometimes feel, I still want to go on being tortured for as long as possible. It's the same with all my patients; and with people who are morally sick, too. There's a moral cripple in with Helmer at this very moment—

Mrs. Linde (*softly*). Oh!

Nora. Whom do you mean?

Rank. Oh, a lawyer fellow called Krogstad—you wouldn't know him. He's crippled all

right, morally twisted. But even he started off by announcing, as though it were a matter of enormous importance, that he had to live.

Nora. Oh? What did he want to talk to Torvald about?

Rank. I haven't the faintest idea. All I heard was something about the bank.

Nora. I didn't know that Krog—that this man Krogstad had any connection with the bank.

Rank. Yes, he's got some kind of job down there. (*to* MRS. LINDE) I wonder if in your part of the world you too have a species of creature that spends its time fussing around trying to smell out moral corruption? And when they find a case they give him some nice, comfortable position so that they can keep a good watch on him. The healthy ones just have to lump it.

Mrs. Linde. But surely it's the sick who need care most?

Rank (*shrugs his shoulders*). Well, there we have it. It's that attitude that's turning human society into a hospital.

[NORA, *lost in her own thoughts, laughs half to herself and claps her hands.*]

Rank. Why are you laughing? Do you really know what society is?

Nora. What do I care about society? I think it's a bore. I was laughing at something else—something frightfully funny. Tell me, Dr. Rank—will everyone who works at the bank come under Torvald now?

Rank. Do you find that particularly funny?

Nora (*smiles and hums*). Never you mind! Never you mind! (*walks around the room*) Yes, I find it very amusing to think that we—I mean, Torvald—has obtained so much influence over so many people. (*takes the paper bag from her pocket*) Dr. Rank, would you like a small macaroon?

Rank. Macaroons! I say! I thought they were forbidden here.

---

4. *de trop* (də trō'): French for "in the way."

32

Nora. Yes, well, these are some Christine gave me.

Mrs. Linde. What? I—?

Nora. All right, all right, don't get frightened. You weren't to know Torvald had forbidden them. He's afraid they'll ruin my teeth. But, dash it—for once—! Don't you agree, Dr. Rank? Here! (*pops a macaroon into his mouth*) You, too, Christine. And I'll have one, too. Just a little one. Two at the most. (*begins to walk round again*) Yes, now I feel really, really happy. Now there's just one thing in the world I'd really love to do.

Rank. Oh? And what is that?

Nora. Just something I'd love to say to Torvald.

Rank. Well, why don't you say it?

Nora. No, I daren't. It's too dreadful.

Mrs. Linde. Dreadful?

Rank. Well then, you'd better not. But you can say it to us. What is it you'd so love to say to Torvald?

Nora. I've the most extraordinary longing to say: "Bloody hell!"

Rank. Are you mad?

Mrs. Linde. My dear Nora—!

Midland Community Theatre at Theatre Midland

---

32 LITERARY ELEMENT
Characterization: What aspect of her character does Nora's lie to Dr. Rank about the macaroons confirm? (She routinely deceives and conceals her actions, especially from men, in order to do what she wants.)

33 LITERARY ELEMENT
Characterization: What new aspect of Nora's character is revealed by her secret wish? (Possible response: rebelliousness; anger)

MEETING INDIVIDUAL NEEDS

Auditory Learners: Have three volunteers act out the scene between Dr. Rank, Nora, and Mrs. Linde to convey Nora's growing restlessness and the contrasting cautiousness of the other two characters. ■

34 **ANALYZING**
Have students recall Nora's explanation on page 1078 of how she puts Helmer "in the right mood" before asking him for what she wants. How does she attempt to get him in the mood to give Christine a job? (Possible response: She flatters him by implying that he is "clever" and asks him to grant her a special favor, with the implied promise that she will give favors in return.)

READER'S RESPONSE
How do you feel about Nora's ways of getting what she wants from her husband? What is she winning and what is she losing?

Rank. Say it. Here he is.

Nora (*hiding the bag of macaroons*). Ssh! Ssh!

[HELMER, *with his overcoat on his arm and his hat in his hand, enters from his study.*]

Nora (*goes to meet him*). Well, Torvald dear, did you get rid of him?

Helmer. Yes, he's just gone.

Nora. May I introduce you—? This is Christine. She's just arrived in town.

Helmer. Christine—? Forgive me, but I don't think—

Nora. Mrs. Linde, Torvald dear. Christine Linde.

Helmer. Ah. A childhood friend of my wife's, I presume?

Mrs. Linde. Yes, we knew each other in earlier days.

Nora. And imagine, now she's traveled all this way to talk to you.

Helmer. Oh?

Mrs. Linde. Well, I didn't really—

Nora. You see, Christine's frightfully good at office work, and she's mad to come under some really clever man who can teach her even more than she knows already—

Helmer. Very sensible, madam.

Nora. So when she heard you'd become head of the bank—it was in her local paper—she came here as quickly as she could and—Torvald, you will, won't you? Do a little something to help Christine? For my sake?

Helmer. Well, that shouldn't be impossible. You are a widow, I take it, Mrs. Linde?

Mrs. Linde. Yes.

Helmer. And you have experience of office work?

Mrs. Linde. Yes, quite a bit.

Helmer. Well, then, it's quite likely I may be able to find some job for you—

Nora (*claps her hands*). You see, you see!

34

Helmer. You've come at a lucky moment, Mrs. Linde.

Mrs. Linde. Oh, how can I ever thank you—?

Helmer. There's absolutely no need. (*puts on his overcoat*) But now I'm afraid I must ask you to excuse me—

Rank. Wait. I'll come with you.

[*He gets his fur coat from the hall and warms it at the stove.*]

Nora. Don't be long, Torvald dear.

Helmer. I'll only be an hour.

Nora. Are you going, too, Christine?

Mrs. Linde (*puts on her outdoor clothes*). Yes, I must start to look round for a room.

Helmer. Then perhaps we can walk part of the way together.

Nora (*helps her*). It's such a nuisance we're so cramped here—I'm afraid we can't offer to—

Mrs. Linde. Oh, I wouldn't dream of it. Goodbye, Nora dear, and thanks for everything.

Nora. Au revoir.[5] You'll be coming back this evening, of course. And you too, Dr. Rank. What? If you're well enough? Of course you'll be well enough. Wrap up warmly, though.

[*They go out, talking, into the hall.* CHILDREN's *voices are heard from the stairs.*]

Nora. Here they are! Here they are!

[*She runs out and opens the door. The* NURSE, ANNE-MARIE, *enters with the* CHILDREN.]

Nora. Come in, come in! (*stoops down and kisses them*) Oh, my sweet darlings—! Look at them, Christine! Aren't they beautiful?

Rank. Don't stand here chattering in this draft!

---

5. *Au revoir* (ō' rə·vwär'): French for "goodbye."

Helmer. Come, Mrs. Linde. This is for mothers only.

[DR. RANK, HELMER, *and* MRS. LINDE *go down the stairs. The* NURSE *brings the* CHILDREN *into the room.* NORA *follows, and closes the door to the hall.*]

Nora. How well you look! What red cheeks you've got! Like apples and roses!

[*The* CHILDREN *answer her inaudibly as she talks to them.*]

Nora. Have you had fun? That's splendid. You gave Emmy and Bob a ride on the sledge? What, both together? I say! What a clever boy you are, Ivar! Oh, let me hold her for a moment, Anne-Marie! My sweet little baby doll! (*takes the* SMALLEST CHILD *from the* NURSE *and dances with her*) Yes, yes, mummy will dance with Bob, too. What? Have you been throwing snowballs? Oh, I wish I'd been there! No, don't— I'll undress them myself, Anne-Marie. No, please let me; it's such fun. Go inside and warm yourself; you look frozen. There's some hot coffee on the stove.

[*The* NURSE *goes into the room on the left.* NORA *takes off the* CHILDREN*'s outdoor clothes and throws them anywhere while they all chatter simultaneously.*]

Nora. What? A big dog ran after you? But he didn't bite you? No, dogs don't bite lovely little baby dolls. Leave those parcels alone, Ivar. What's in them? Ah, wouldn't you like to know! No, no; it's nothing nice. Come on, let's play a game. What shall we play? Hide-and-seek? Yes, let's play hide-and-seek. Bob shall hide first. You want me to? All right, let me hide first.

[NORA *and the* CHILDREN *play around the room, and in the* adjacent *room to the right, laughing and shouting. At length* NORA *hides under the table. The* CHILDREN *rush in, look, but cannot find her. Then they hear her half-stifled laughter, run*

to the table, lift up the cloth and see her. Great excitement. She crawls out as though to frighten them. Further excitement. Meanwhile, there has been a knock on the door leading from the hall, but no one has noticed it. Now the door is half opened and* KROGSTAD *enters. He waits for a moment; the game continues.*]

Krogstad. Excuse me, Mrs. Helmer—

Nora (*turns with a stifled cry and half jumps up*). Oh! What do you want?

Krogstad. I beg your pardon—the front door was ajar. Someone must have forgotten to close it.

Nora (*gets up*). My husband is not at home, Mr. Krogstad.

Krogstad. I know.

Nora. Well, what do you want here, then?

Krogstad. A word with you.

Nora. With—? (*to the* CHILDREN, *quietly*) Go inside to Anne-Marie. What? No, the strange gentleman won't do anything to hurt mummy. When he's gone we'll start playing again.

[*She takes the* CHILDREN *into the room on the left and closes the door behind them.*]

Nora (*uneasy, tense*). You want to speak to me?

Krogstad. Yes.

Nora. Today? But it's not the first of the month yet.

Krogstad. No, it is Christmas Eve. Whether or not you have a merry Christmas depends on you.

Nora. What do you want? I can't give you anything today—

Krogstad. We won't talk about that for the present. There's something else. You have a moment to spare?

Nora. Oh, yes. Yes, I suppose so—though—

Krogstad. Good. I was sitting in the café down below and I saw your husband cross the street—

35
36
37

35 INTERPRETING

What do you think Helmer is implying when he says, "This is for mothers only"? (Possible response: Biological mothers have an interest in their children that no man or childless woman could understand or share, or even care to.)

36 ANALYZING

In what ways does Nora's attitude toward her children parallel her husband's attitude toward her? (Possible response: She views them as charming playthings, like dolls, that provide a source of periodic entertainment.)

LITERARY ELEMENT

Theme: In what ways is Nora living in a doll's house? (Possible response: She is treated like a doll and treats her children like dolls, not as serious responsibilities; she and Helmer ignore any real problems and pretend to be completely happy.)

 adjacent (ə·jā'sənt): next to; near

37 LITERARY ELEMENT

Mood: How does the mood change when Krogstad enters the room? (from gaiety to tension)

Nora. Yes.

Krogstad. With a lady.

Nora. Well?

Krogstad. Might I be so bold as to ask; was not that lady a Mrs. Linde?

Nora. Yes.

Krogstad. Recently arrived in town?

Nora. Yes, today.

Krogstad. She is a good friend of yours, is she not?

Nora. Yes, she is. But I don't see—

Krogstad. I used to know her, too, once.

Nora. I know.

Krogstad. Oh? You've discovered that. Yes, I thought you would. Well then, may I ask you a straight question: is Mrs. Linde to be employed at the bank?

Nora. How dare you presume to cross-examine me, Mr. Krogstad? You, one of my husband's employees? But since you ask, you shall have an answer. Yes, Mrs. Linde is to be employed by the bank. And I arranged it, Mr. Krogstad. Now you know.

Krogstad. I guessed right, then.

Nora (*walks up and down the room*). Oh, one has a little influence, you know. Just because one's a woman it doesn't necessarily mean that—When one is in a humble position, Mr. Krogstad, one should think twice before offending someone who—hm—!

Krogstad. —who has influence?

Nora. Precisely.

Krogstad (*changes his tone*). Mrs. Helmer, will you have the kindness to use your influence on my behalf?

Nora. What? What do you mean?

Krogstad. Will you be so good as to see that I keep my humble position at the bank?

Nora. What do you mean? Who is thinking of removing you from your position?

Krogstad. Oh, you don't need to play the innocent with me. I realize it can't be very pleasant for your friend to risk bumping into me. And now I also realize whom I have to thank for being hounded out like this.

Nora. But I assure you—

Krogstad. Look, let's not beat about the bush. There's still time, and I'd advise you to use your influence to stop it.

Nora. But, Mr. Krogstad, I have no influence!

Krogstad. Oh? I thought you just said—

Nora. But I didn't mean it like that! I? How on earth could you imagine that I would have any influence over my husband?

Krogstad. Oh, I've known your husband since we were students together. I imagine he has his weaknesses like other married men.

Nora. If you speak impertinently[6] of my husband, I shall show you the door.

Krogstad. You're a bold woman, Mrs. Helmer.

Nora. I'm not afraid of you any longer. Once the new year is in, I'll soon be rid of you.

Krogstad (*more controlled*). Now listen to me, Mrs. Helmer. If I'm forced to, I shall fight for my little job at the bank as I would fight for my life.

Nora. So it sounds.

Krogstad. It isn't just the money—that's the last thing I care about. There's something else. Well, you might as well know. It's like this, you see. You know of course, as everyone else does, that some years ago I committed an indiscretion.

Nora. I think I did hear something—

Krogstad. It never came into court; but from that day, every opening was barred to me. So I turned my hand to the kind of

---

6. **impertinently:** insolently; without the proper respect or manners.

business you know about. I had to do something; and I don't think I was one of the worst. But now I want to give up all that. My sons are growing up: for their sake, I must try to regain what respectability I can. This job in the bank was the first step on the ladder. And now your husband wants to kick me off that ladder back into the dirt.

Nora. But, my dear Mr. Krogstad, it simply isn't in my power to help you.

Krogstad. You say that because you don't want to help me. But I have the means to make you.

Nora. You don't mean you'd tell my husband that I owe you money?

Krogstad. And if I did?

Nora. That'd be a filthy trick! (*almost in tears*) This secret that is my pride and my joy—that he should hear about it in such a filthy, beastly way—hear about it from you! It'd involve me in the most dreadful unpleasantness—

Krogstad. Only—unpleasantness?

Nora (*vehemently*). All right, do it! You'll be the one who'll suffer. It'll show my husband the kind of man you are, and then you'll never keep your job.

Krogstad. I asked you whether it was merely domestic unpleasantness you were afraid of.

Nora. If my husband hears about it, he will of course immediately pay you whatever is owing. And then we shall have nothing more to do with you.

Krogstad (*takes a step closer*). Listen, Mrs. Helmer. Either you've a bad memory or else you know very little about financial transactions. I had better enlighten you.

Nora. What do you mean?

Krogstad. When your husband was ill, you came to me to borrow two hundred and fifty pounds.

Nora. I didn't know anyone else.

Krogstad. I promised to find that sum for you—

Nora. And you did find it.

Krogstad. I promised to find that sum for you on certain conditions. You were so worried about your husband's illness and so keen to get the money to take him abroad that I don't think you bothered much about the details. So it won't be out of place if I refresh your memory. Well—I promised to get you the money in exchange for an I.O.U., which I drew up.

Nora. Yes, and which I signed.

Krogstad. Exactly. But then I added a few lines naming your father as security for the debt. This paragraph was to be signed by your father.

Nora. Was to be? He did sign it.

Krogstad. I left the date blank for your father to fill in when he signed this paper. You remember, Mrs. Helmer?

Nora. Yes, I think so—

Krogstad. Then I gave you back this I.O.U. for you to post to your father. Is that not correct?

Nora. Yes.

Krogstad. And of course you posted it at once; for within five or six days you brought it along to me with your father's signature on it. Whereupon I handed you the money.

Nora. Yes, well. Haven't I repaid the installments as agreed?

Krogstad. Mm—yes, more or less. But to return to what we are speaking about—that was a difficult time for you just then, wasn't it, Mrs. Helmer?

Nora. Yes, it was.

Krogstad. Your father was very ill, if I am not mistaken.

Nora. He was dying.

Krogstad. He did in fact die shortly afterwards?

40 GUIDED READING
Identifying Details: What has Krogstad revealed about his past that is influencing his present behavior? (He committed some petty crime for which he was not prosecuted, but his reputation was ruined.)

41 LITERARY ELEMENT
Exposition: For the first time Nora's borrowing from Krogstad is directly stated—up until now it has only been hinted at.

42 ANALYZING
What kind of "dreadful unpleasantness" does Nora expect if Helmer finds out her secret? (He would be angry and humiliated by her independent actions on his behalf.)

43 GUIDED READING
Identifying Cause and Effect: What was Nora's motive for borrowing the money? (to pay for her sick husband's trip abroad)

Finding the Main Idea: What does Krogstad force Nora to admit that she has done? (forged her father's signature on the I.O.U.)

CULTURAL DIVERSITY

Krogstad required that a man cosign the I.O.U. because women were not permitted to borrow money on their own at the time.

❓ *How has the economic status of women changed since Ibsen's day?* (Possible response: Many women now earn their own money and can secure credit without a male guarantor.)

COMPARING AND CONTRASTING

How does Nora's view of her forgery differ from Krogstad's? (Nora considers her unselfish motives justification for her action; Krogstad is concerned only with the social and legal consequences of breaking the law.)

READER'S RESPONSE

Do you agree with Nora that the law should take a person's motives into account? Or do you think she is simply naive or self-centered?

Nora. Yes.

Krogstad. Tell me, Mrs. Helmer, do you by any chance remember the date of your father's death? The day of the month, I mean.

Nora. Papa died on the twenty-ninth of September.

Krogstad. Quite correct; I took the trouble to confirm it. And that leaves me with a curious little problem—(*takes out a paper*)—which I simply cannot solve.

Nora. Problem? I don't see—

Krogstad. The problem, Mrs. Helmer, is that your father signed this paper three days after his death.

Nora. What? I don't understand—

Krogstad. Your father died on the twenty-ninth of September. But look at this. Here your father has dated his signature the second of October. Isn't that a curious little problem, Mrs. Helmer?

[NORA *is silent.*]

Krogstad. Can you suggest any explanation?

[*She remains silent.*]

Krogstad. And there's another curious thing. The words "second of October" and the year are written in a hand which is not your father's, but which I seem to know. Well, there's a simple explanation to that. Your father could have forgotten to write in the date when he signed, and someone else could have added it before the news came of his death. There's nothing criminal about that. It's the signature itself I'm wondering about. It *is* genuine, I suppose, Mrs. Helmer? It was your father who wrote his name here?

Nora (*after a short silence, throws back her head and looks defiantly at him*). No, it was not. It was I who wrote Papa's name there.

Krogstad. Look, Mrs. Helmer, do you realize this is a dangerous admission?

Nora. Why? You'll get your money.

Krogstad. May I ask you a question? Why didn't you send this paper to your father?

Nora. I couldn't. Papa was very ill. If I'd asked him to sign this, I'd have had to tell him what the money was for. But I couldn't have told him in his condition that my husband's life was in danger. I couldn't have done that!

Krogstad. Then you would have been wiser to have given up your idea of a holiday.

Nora. But I couldn't! It was to save my husband's life. I couldn't put it off.

Krogstad. But didn't it occur to you that you were being dishonest towards me?

Nora. I couldn't bother about that. I didn't care about you. I hated you because of all the beastly difficulties you'd put in my way when you knew how dangerously ill my husband was.

Krogstad. Mrs. Helmer, you evidently don't appreciate exactly what you have done. But I can assure you that it is no bigger nor worse a crime than the one I once committed and thereby ruined my whole social position.

Nora. You? Do you expect me to believe that you would have taken a risk like that to save your wife's life?

Krogstad. The law does not concern itself with motives.

Nora. Then the law must be very stupid.

Krogstad. Stupid or not, if I show this paper to the police, you will be judged according to it.

Nora. I don't believe that. Hasn't a daughter the right to shield her father from worry and anxiety when he's old and dying? Hasn't a wife the right to save her husband's life? I don't know much about the law, but there must be something somewhere that says that such things are allowed. You ought to know that, you're meant to be a lawyer, aren't you? You can't be a very good lawyer, Mr. Krogstad.

Krogstad. Possibly not. But business, the

44

kind of business we two have been trans-acting—I think you'll admit I understand something about that? Good. Do as you please. But I tell you this. If I get thrown into the gutter for a second time, I shall take you with me.

[*He bows and goes out through the hall.*]

Nora (*stands for a moment in thought, then tosses her head*). What nonsense! He's trying to frighten me! I'm not that stupid. (*busies herself gathering together the children's clothes; then she suddenly stops.*) But—? No, it's impossible. I did it for love, didn't I?

Children (*in the doorway, left*). Mummy, the strange gentleman has gone out into the street.

Nora. Yes, yes, I know. But don't talk to anyone about the strange gentleman. You hear? Not even to Daddy.

Children. No, Mummy. Will you play with us again now?

Nora. No, no. Not now.

Children. Oh but, Mummy, you promised!

Nora. I know, but I can't just now. Go back to the nursery. I've a lot to do. Go away, my darlings, go away.

[*She pushes them gently into the other room, and closes the door behind them. She sits on the sofa, takes up her embroidery, stitches for a few moments, but soon stops.*]

Nora. No! (*throws the embroidery aside, gets up, goes to the door leading to the hall and calls*) Helen! Bring in the Christmas tree! (*She goes to the table on the left and opens the drawer in it; then pauses again.*) No, but it's utterly impossible!

Maid (*enters with the tree*). Where shall I put it, madam?

Nora. There, in the middle of the room.

Maid. Will you be wanting anything else?

Nora. No, thank you. I have everything I need.

[*The* MAID *puts down the tree and goes out.*]

Nora (*busy decorating the tree*). Now—candles here—and flowers here. That loathsome man! Nonsense, nonsense, there's nothing to be frightened about. The Christmas tree must be beautiful. I'll do everything that you like, Torvald. I'll sing for you, dance for you—

[HELMER, *with a bundle of papers under his arm, enters.*]

Nora. Oh—are you back already?

Helmer. Yes. Has anyone been here?

Nora. Here? No.

Helmer. That's strange. I saw Krogstad come out of the front door.

Nora. Did you? Oh yes, that's quite right—Krogstad was here for a few minutes.

Helmer. Nora, I can tell from your face, he has been here and asked you to put in a good word for him.

Nora. Yes.

Helmer. And you were to pretend you were doing it of your own accord? You weren't going to tell me he'd been here? He asked you to do that too, didn't he?

Nora. Yes, Torvald. But—

Helmer. Nora, Nora! And you were ready to enter into such a conspiracy? Talking to a man like that, and making him promises—and then, on top of it all, to tell me an untruth!

Nora. An untruth?

Helmer. Didn't you say no one had been here? (*wags his finger*) My little songbird must never do that again. A songbird must have a clean beak to sing with. Otherwise she'll start twittering out of tune. (*puts his arm around her waist*) Isn't that the way we want things? Yes, of course it is. (*lets go of her*) So let's hear no more about that. (*sits down in front of the stove*) Ah, how cosy and peaceful it is here! (*glances for a few moments at his papers*)

45 COMPARING AND CONTRASTING

How does Nora's scene with her children after Krogstad's visit contrast with the one before his arrival? (Possible response: Too upset and distracted by "real-world" concerns, she cannot play with them.)

46 LITERARY ELEMENT

Symbolism: What might the Christmas tree symbolize? (Possible responses: family happiness, normalcy, tradition) Why might Nora want it in the middle of the room? (Possible response: to dispel the sense of danger and disruption that Krogstad has introduced)

47 LITERARY ELEMENT

Irony: What is ironic about Helmer's use of the word "untruth"? (His choice of this mild circumlocution underscores his ignorance of the web of *lies* that pervades his marriage.)

48 PREDICTING

Do you think Helmer will be able to maintain the cozy and peaceful atmosphere he so desires in his home? What do you think will happen? (Answers will vary.)

The woman who saved her husband's life is not as helpless as she pretends. Why has Nora resumed her helpless female role, or disguise, in the conversation about her costume? (Possible response: She knows this is the role her husband likes her to play, and she is again trying to wheedle a favor out of him.)

Nora (*busy with the tree; after a short silence*). Torvald.

Helmer. Yes.

49 **Nora.** I'm terribly looking forward to that fancy-dress ball at the Stenborgs on Boxing Day.[7]

Helmer. And I'm terribly curious to see what you're going to surprise me with.

Nora. Oh, it's so maddening.

Helmer. What is?

Nora. I can't think of anything to wear. It all seems so stupid and meaningless.

Helmer. So my little Nora has come to that conclusion, has she?

Nora (*behind his chair, resting her arms on its back*). Are you very busy, Torvald?

Helmer. Oh—

Nora. What are those papers?

Helmer. Just something to do with the bank.

Nora. Already?

Helmer. I persuaded the trustees to give me authority to make certain immediate changes in the staff and organization. I want to have everything straight by the new year.

Nora. Then that's why this poor man Krogstad—

Helmer. Hm.

Nora (*still leaning over his chair, slowly strokes the back of his head*). If you hadn't been so busy, I was going to ask you an enormous favor, Torvald.

---

7. **Boxing Day:** the first weekday after Christmas.

Helmer. Well, tell me. What was it to be?

Nora. You know I trust your taste more than anyone's. I'm so anxious to look really beautiful at the fancy-dress ball. Torvald, couldn't you help me to decide what I shall go as, and what kind of costume I ought to wear?

Helmer. Aha! So little Miss Independent's

50

in trouble and needs a man to rescue her, does she?

Nora. Yes, Torvald. I can't get anywhere without your help.

Helmer. Well, well, I'll give the matter thought. We'll find something.

Nora. Oh, how kind of you! (*goes back to the tree; pauses*) How pretty these red flowers look! But, tell me, is it so dreadful, this thing that Krogstad's done?

Helmer. He forged someone else's name. Have you any idea what that means?

Nora. Mightn't he have been forced to do it by some emergency?

Helmer. He probably just didn't think— that's what usually happens. I'm not so heartless as to condemn a man for an isolated action.

Nora. No, Torvald, of course not!

Helmer. Men often succeed in reestablishing themselves if they admit their crime and take their punishment.

Nora. Punishment?

Helmer. But Krogstad didn't do that. He chose to try and trick his way out of it. And that's what has morally destroyed him.

Nora. You think that would—?

Helmer. Just think how a man with that load on his conscience must always be lying and cheating and dissembling—how he must wear a mask even in the presence of those who are dearest to him, even his own wife and children! Yes, the children. That's the worst danger, Nora.

Nora. Why?

Helmer. Because an atmosphere of lies contaminates and poisons every corner of the home. Every breath that the children draw in such a house contains the germs of evil.

Nora (*comes closer behind him*). Do you really believe that?

Helmer. Oh, my dear, I've come across it so often in my work at the bar. Nearly all young criminals are the children of mothers who are constitutional liars.

Nora. Why do you say mothers?

Helmer. It's usually the mother—though of course the father can have the same influence. Every lawyer knows that only too well. And yet this fellow Krogstad has been sitting at home all these years poisoning his children with his lies and pretenses. That's why I say that, morally speaking, he is dead. (*stretches out his hand towards her*) So my pretty little Nora must promise me not to plead his case. Your hand on it. Come, come, what's this? Give me your hand. There. That's settled, now. I assure you it'd be quite impossible for me to work in the same building as him. I literally feel physically ill in the presence of a man like that.

Nora (*draws her hand from his and goes over to the other side of the Christmas tree*). How hot it is in here! And I've so much to do.

Helmer (*gets up and gathers his papers*). Yes, and I must try to get some of this read before dinner. I'll think about your costume, too. And I may even have something up my sleeve to hang in gold paper on the Christmas tree. (*lays his hand on her head*) My precious little songbird!

[*He goes into his study and closes the door.*]

Nora (*softly, after a pause*). It's nonsense. It must be. It's impossible. It *must* be impossible!

Nurse (*in the doorway, left*). The children are asking if they can come in to Mummy.

Nora. No, no, no—don't let them in. You stay with them, Anne-Marie.

Nurse. Very good, madam. (*closes the door*)

Nora (*pale with fear*). Corrupt my little children—! Poison my home! (*short pause; she throws back her head*) It isn't true! It couldn't be true!

51 52

51 **LITERARY ELEMENT**
Irony: What does the audience know, which Helmer does not, that produces the dramatic irony in his speech about wearing masks? (He does not realize that "lying and cheating and dissembling" are exactly what his wife is doing.)

■ contaminates (kən·tam′ə·nātz): corrupts or defiles

52 **SYNTHESIZING**
What view that Helmer expressed earlier in the play is he restating here? (The moral weaknesses of parents are passed on to their children.)

WRITING TO LEARN

Science: Ask students to research what modern science has discovered about hereditary or genetic transmission of traits or qualities that are not physical. For instance, are intelligence, aggressiveness, or the propensity to lie inherited? Ask students to prepare a written report and present an oral summary of their findings to the class. ■

First Thoughts
Answers will vary.

Identifying Facts
1. Torvald has received a big promotion at the bank.
2. an old friend of Nora's who is looking for work. She is the childless widow of a man she never loved and now has to support herself.
3. to pay for a trip to restore Torvald's health. Krogstad. She forged her father's signature
4. to secure his position at the bank. He threatens her by saying he'll expose her forgery.
5. He agrees. He refuses.

Interpreting Meanings
1. Possible responses: He treats her like a child, indulgently and with an air of superiority. Nora accepts her childish role. Their marriage is not a partnership of equals.
2. Possible response: Nora routinely deceives her husband, especially by withholding how she obtained the money for the trip abroad.
3. Possible response: With Torvald she appears only to want to please. With Dr. Rank, she is more open and honest.
4. Possible response: She appears interested in him.

Applying Meanings
Answers will vary.

Creative Writing Response
Adopting a Character's Point of View. First-person narratives should reflect the personality of the character whose point of view is being adopted and that person's dominant feeling about Nora.

First Thoughts
Do you believe that Nora is as happy as she claims to be? Why or why not?

Identifying Facts
1. Why do Nora and Torvald feel Christmas is going to be especially happy this year?
2. Who is Mrs. Linde, and why does she visit Nora? How is her life different from Nora's?
3. Why did Nora borrow money? From whom did she borrow it? What was illegal about the way she borrowed the money?
4. What does Krogstad want Nora to do for him? How does he try to persuade her?
5. How does Torvald respond to Nora's request to help Mrs. Linde? To help Krogstad?

Interpreting Meanings
1. What do Torvald's nicknames for Nora, such as "skylark," "squirrel," and "squanderbird" tell you about their relationship? How does Nora react to these nicknames? How do Torvald's nicknames and Nora's reactions to them help to **characterize** them and reveal the nature of their marriage?
2. On page 1091, Torvald describes Krogstad as a man who "must wear a mask even in the presence of those who are dearest to him." Because of this, Torvald says, "an atmosphere of lies contaminates and poisons" Krogstad's home. How do you know that this statement applies to the Helmers' home as well?
3. Compare and contrast the way Nora interacts with Dr. Rank and with Torvald. What does this behavior tell you about her **character**?
4. Based on what she says about Krogstad and how she reacts to the mention of his name, how do you think Mrs. Linde feels about Krogstad?

Applying Meanings
Do you think the marriage of Nora and Torvald Helmer could be used as the basis of a play about a modern American couple? What aspects of their relationship would you change in order to update it? What aspects of their relationship could be kept unchanged?

Creative Writing Response
Adopting a Character's Point of View. Write a one-page narrative from the point of view of Torvald, Mrs. Linde, Krogstad, or Dr. Rank, in which you discuss Nora's personality and behavior. Your narrative might take the form of a journal entry, a letter, or any other first-person narrative form. In your narrative, have the character whose point of view you have adopted predict what will happen to Nora. Remember that not every character knows everything about Nora at this point in the play.

Midland Community Theatre at Theatre Midland

ACT 2

The same room. In the corner by the piano the Christmas tree stands, stripped and disheveled, its candles burned to their sockets. NORA's outdoor clothes lie on the sofa. She is alone in the room, walking restlessly to-and-fro. At length she stops by the sofa and picks up her coat.

Nora (*drops the coat again*). There's someone coming! (*goes to the door and listens*) No, it's no one. Of course—no one'll come today, it's Christmas Day. Nor tomorrow. But perhaps—! (*opens the door and looks out*) No. Nothing in the letter box. Quite empty. (*walks across the room*) Silly, silly. Of course he won't do anything. It couldn't happen. It isn't possible. Why, I've three small children.

[*The* NURSE, *carrying a large cardboard box, enters from the room on the left.*]

Nurse. I found those fancy dress clothes at last, madam.

Nora. Thank you. Put them on the table.
Nurse (*does so*). They're all rumpled up.
Nora. Oh, I wish I could tear them into a million pieces!
Nurse. Why, madam! They'll be all right. Just a little patience.
Nora. Yes, of course. I'll go and get Mrs. Linde to help me.
Nurse. What, out again? In this dreadful weather? You'll catch a chill, madam.
Nora. Well, that wouldn't be the worst. How are the children?
Nurse. Playing with their Christmas presents, poor little dears. But—
Nora. Are they still asking to see me?
Nurse. They're so used to having their mummy with them.
Nora. Yes, but, Anne-Marie, from now on I shan't be able to spend so much time with them.
Nurse. Well, children get used to anything in time.

◼ **disheveled** (di·shev'əld): untidy; messed up

CULTURAL DIVERSITY
Ibsen's realistic portrayal of ordinary people shocked audiences of his time, who were accustomed to melodramatic entertainment when viewing a play. By addressing issues such as marriage and the role of women in society, *A Doll's House* received an array of negative responses, ranging from vicious reviews to protesters at the theaters. The British novelist Somerset Maugham even used a soft-spoken character in *Of Human Bondage* to condemn the play as "the ruin of the family, the uprooting of morals. . . . I would sooner my daughters were lying dead at my feet than see them listening to the garbage of that shameless fellow."
? *To what subjects might many people today have a similar outraged reaction?*

1 INTERPRETING
To whom and what does Nora refer when she says, "Of course he won't do anything"? (Krogstad and his threat to reveal her borrowing to her husband) What is her emotional state? (very worried and fearful)

Foreshadowing: What might Nora's question to the Nurse hint at her doing in the future? (Possible response: She might leave home or kill herself.)

3 SYNTHESIZING

How does Nora's attitude toward the fancy-dress ball mirror her attitude toward her marriage? (She views her marriage as a performance in which she must maintain an illusion and entertain her husband.) What does the torn dress suggest about the current state of her marriage? (Possible response: Pressures and strains are threatening her smooth performance.)

4 LITERARY ELEMENT

Theme: What does Nora tell Mrs. Linde about Dr. Rank's illness? (He suffers from an infectious disease passed on by his dissolute father—perhaps syphilis.) How does this information relate to the theme of hereditary guilt introduced earlier? (Possible response: Dr. Rank is an example of how the "sins" of a father can actually be passed on to a son without the son sharing the father's "bad" character.)

2

Nora. Do you think so? Do you think they'd forget their mother if she went away from them—forever?

Nurse. Mercy's sake, madam! Forever!

Nora. Tell me, Anne-Marie—I've so often wondered. How could you bear to give your child away—to strangers?

Nurse. But I had to when I came to nurse my little Miss Nora.

Nora. Do you mean you wanted to?

Nurse. When I had the chance of such a good job? A poor girl what's got into trouble can't afford to pick and choose. That good-for-nothing didn't lift a finger.

Nora. But your daughter must have completely forgotten you.

Nurse. Oh no, indeed she hasn't. She's written to me twice, once when she got confirmed and then again when she got married.

Nora (*hugs her*). Dear old Anne-Marie, you were a good mother to me.

Nurse. Poor little Miss Nora, you never had any mother but me.

Nora. And if my little ones had no one else, I know you would—no, silly, silly, silly! (*opens the cardboard box*) Go back to them, Anne-Marie. Now I must—! Tomorrow you'll see how pretty I shall look.

Nurse. Why, there'll be no one at the ball as beautiful as my Miss Nora.

[*She goes into the room, left.*]

Nora (*begins to unpack the clothes from the box, but soon throws them down again*). Oh, if only I dared go out! If I could be sure no one would come and nothing would happen while I was away! Stupid, stupid! No one will come. I just mustn't think about it. Brush this muff. Pretty gloves, pretty gloves! Don't think about it, don't think about it! One, two, three, four, five, six—(*cries*) Ah—they're coming—!

[*She begins to run towards the door, but stops uncertainly.* MRS. LINDE *enters from*

the hall, where she has been taking off her outdoor clothes.]

Nora. Oh, it's you, Christine. There's no one else outside, is there? Oh, I'm so glad you've come.

Mrs. Linde. I hear you were at my room asking for me.

Nora. Yes, I just happened to be passing. I want to ask you to help me with something. Let's sit down here on the sofa. Look at this. There's going to be a fancy-dress ball tomorrow night upstairs at Consul Stenborg's, and Torvald wants me to go as a Neapolitan fisher-girl and dance the tarantella. I learned it in Capri.

Mrs. Linde. I say, are you going to give a performance?

Nora. Yes, Torvald says I should. Look, here's the dress. Torvald had it made for me in Italy—but now it's all so torn, I don't know—

Mrs. Linde. Oh, we'll soon put that right—the stitching's just come away. Needle and thread? Ah, here we are.

Nora. You're being awfully sweet.

Mrs. Linde (*sews*). So you're going to dress up tomorrow, Nora? I must pop over for a moment to see how you look. Oh, but I've completely forgotten to thank you for that nice evening yesterday.

Nora (*gets up and walks across the room*). Oh, I didn't think it was as nice as usual. You ought to have come to town a little earlier, Christine. . . . Yes, Torvald understands how to make a home look attractive.

Mrs. Linde. I'm sure you do, too. You're not your father's daughter for nothing. But, tell me—is Dr. Rank always in such low spirits as he was yesterday?

Nora. No, last night it was very noticeable. But he's got a terrible disease—he's got spinal tuberculosis, poor man. His father was a frightful creature who kept mistresses and so on. As a result Dr. Rank has

3

4

been sickly ever since he was a child—you understand—

Mrs. Linde (*puts down her sewing*). But, my dear Nora, how on earth did you get to know about such things?

Nora (*walks about the room*). Oh, don't be silly, Christine—when one has three children, one comes into contact with women who—well, who know about medical matters, and they tell one a thing or two.

Mrs. Linde (*sews again; a short silence*). Does Dr. Rank visit you every day?

Nora. Yes, every day. He's Torvald's oldest friend, and a good friend to me too. Dr. Rank's almost one of the family.

Mrs. Linde. But, tell me—is he quite sincere? I mean, doesn't he rather say the sort of thing he thinks people want to hear?

Nora. No, quite the contrary. What gave you that idea?

Mrs. Linde. When you introduced me to him yesterday, he said he'd often heard my name mentioned here. But later I noticed your husband had no idea who I was. So how could Dr. Rank—

Nora. Yes, that's quite right, Christine. You see, Torvald's so hopelessly in love with me that he wants to have me all to himself—those were his very words. When we were first married, he got quite jealous if I as much as mentioned any of my old friends back home. So naturally, I stopped talking about them. But I often chat with Dr. Rank about that kind of thing. He enjoys it, you see.

Mrs. Linde. Now listen, Nora. In many ways you're still a child; I'm a bit older than you and have a little more experience of the world. There's something I want to say to you. You ought to give up this business with Dr. Rank.

Nora. What business?

Mrs. Linde. Well, everything. Last night you were speaking about this rich admirer of yours who was going to give you money—

Nora. Yes, and who doesn't exist—unfortunately. But what's that got to do with—?

Mrs. Linde. Is Dr. Rank rich?

Nora. Yes.

Mrs. Linde. And he has no dependants?

Nora. No, no one. But—

Mrs. Linde. And he comes here to see you every day?

Nora. Yes, I've told you.

Mrs. Linde. But how dare a man of his education be so forward?

Nora. What on earth are you talking about?

Mrs. Linde. Oh, stop pretending, Nora. Do you think I haven't guessed who it was who lent you that two hundred pounds?

Nora. Are you out of your mind? How could you imagine such a thing? A friend, someone who comes here every day! Why, that'd be an impossible situation!

Mrs. Linde. Then it really wasn't him?

Nora. No, of course not. I've never for a moment dreamed of—anyway, he hadn't any money to lend then. He didn't come into that till later.

Mrs. Linde. Well, I think that was a lucky thing for you, Nora dear.

Nora. No, I could never have dreamed of asking Dr. Rank— Though I'm sure that if ever I did ask him—

Mrs. Linde. But of course you won't.

Nora. Of course not. I can't imagine that it should ever become necessary. But I'm perfectly sure that if I did speak to Dr. Rank—

Mrs. Linde. Behind your husband's back?

Nora. I've got to get out of this other business—and *that's* been going on behind his back. I've *got* to get out of it.

Mrs. Linde. Yes, well, that's what I told you yesterday. But—

Nora (*walking up and down*). It's much

5 INTERPRETING

If Dr. Rank is not the kind of person who tells others what they want to hear, who is? (Nora, in relation to her husband) What major theme of the play is echoed in this seemingly unimportant dialogue? (truth vs. pleasing illusions)

6 EVALUATING

What do Mrs. Linde's assumptions and questions to Nora reveal about her opinion of Nora's character? (Mrs. Linde thinks Nora is childish, unscrupulous, and naive.) Do you agree with her appraisal? (Possible response: No, Nora is basically loving but afraid to be herself openly.)

7 PREDICTING

Do you think it is possible that Nora may end up asking Dr. Rank for the money? Why or why not? (Possible response: Her growing desperation seems to make the formerly unthinkable possible.)

8 GUIDED READING

Recalling Details: What is Nora keeping from Mrs. Linde at this point? (She forged her father's signature on the I.O.U.)

9 SPECULATING

Do you think Nora means what she says about longing for Helmer's return? Why or why not? (Possible response: Yes, she wants to see if she can charm him into giving her what she wants so she can recapture the former balance and security of their relationship.)

10 GUIDED READING

Identifying Details: After Nora tries and fails to get Torvald to give in to her by promising to do "pretty tricks," what tactic does she use? (She tries to convince him that his self-interest is at stake.)

easier for a man to arrange these things than a woman—

Mrs. Linde. One's own husband, yes.

Nora. Oh, bosh. (*stops walking*) When you've completely repaid a debt, you get your I.O.U. back, don't you?

Mrs. Linde. Yes, of course.

Nora. And you can tear it into a thousand pieces and burn the filthy, beastly thing!

Mrs. Linde (*looks hard at her, puts down her sewing and gets up slowly*). Nora, you're hiding something from me.

Nora. Can you see that?

Mrs. Linde. Something has happened since yesterday morning. Nora, what is it?

Nora (*goes towards her*). Christine! (*listens*) Ssh! There's Torvald. Would you mind going into the nursery for a few minutes? Torvald can't bear to see sewing around. Anne-Marie'll help you.

Mrs. Linde (*gathers some of her things together*). Very well. But I shan't leave this house until we've talked this matter out.

[*She goes into the nursery, left. As she does so,* HELMER *enters from the hall.*]

Nora (*runs to meet him*). Oh, Torvald dear, I've been so longing for you to come back!

Helmer. Was that the dressmaker?

Nora. No, it was Christine. She's helping me mend my costume. I'm going to look rather splendid in that.

Helmer. Yes, that was quite a bright idea of mine, wasn't it?

Nora. Wonderful! But wasn't it nice of me to give in to you?

Helmer (*takes her chin in his hand*). Nice—to give in to your husband? All right, little silly, I know you didn't mean it like that. But I won't disturb you. I expect you'll be wanting to try it on.

Nora. Are you going to work now?

Helmer. Yes. (*shows her a bundle of papers*) Look at these. I've been down to the

bank—(*turns to go into his study*)

Nora. Torvald.

Helmer (*stops*). Yes.

Nora. If little squirrel asked you really prettily to grant her a wish—

Helmer. Well?

Nora. Would you grant it to her?

Helmer. First I should naturally have to know what it was.

Nora. Squirrel would do lots of pretty tricks for you if you granted her wish.

Helmer. Out with it, then.

Nora. Your little skylark would sing in every room—

Helmer. My little skylark does that already.

Nora. I'd turn myself into a little fairy and dance for you in the moonlight, Torvald.

Helmer. Nora, it isn't that business you were talking about this morning?

Nora (*comes closer*). Yes, Torvald—oh, please! I beg of you!

Helmer. Have you really the nerve to bring that up again?

Nora. Yes, Torvald, yes, you must do as I ask! You must let Krogstad keep his place at the bank!

Helmer. My dear Nora, his is the job I'm giving to Mrs. Linde.

Nora. Yes, that's terribly sweet of you. But you can get rid of one of the other clerks instead of Krogstad.

Helmer. Really, you're being incredibly obstinate. Just because you thoughtlessly promised to put in a word for him, you expect me to—

Nora. No, it isn't that, Helmer. It's for your own sake. That man writes for the most beastly newspapers—you said so yourself. He could do you tremendous harm. I'm so dreadfully frightened of him—

Helmer. Oh, I understand. Memories of the past. That's what's frightening you.

Nora. What do you mean?

Helmer. You're thinking of your father, aren't you?

Nora. Yes, yes. Of course. Just think what those dreadful men wrote in the papers about Papa! The most frightful slanders. I really believe it would have lost him his job if the Ministry hadn't sent you down to investigate, and you hadn't been so kind and helpful to him.

Helmer. But, my dear little Nora, there's a considerable difference between your father and me. Your father was not a man of unassailable reputation. But I am. And I hope to remain so all my life.

Nora. But no one knows what spiteful people may not dig up. We could be so peaceful and happy now, Torvald—we could be free from every worry—you and I and the children. Oh, please, Torvald, please—!

Helmer. The very fact of your pleading his cause makes it impossible for me to keep him. Everyone at the bank already knows that I intend to dismiss Krogstad. If the rumor got about that the new vice-president had allowed his wife to persuade him to change his mind—

Nora. Well, what then?

Helmer. Oh, nothing, nothing. As long as my little Miss Obstinate gets her way—! Do you expect me to make a laughingstock of myself before my entire staff—give people the idea that I am open to outside influence? Believe me, I'd soon feel the consequences! Besides—there's something else that makes it impossible for Krogstad to remain in the bank while I am its manager.

Nora. What is that?

Helmer. I might conceivably have allowed myself to ignore his moral obloquies[1]—

Nora. Yes, Torvald, surely?

Helmer. And I hear he's quite efficient at his job. But we—well, we were school

Billy Rose Theatre Collection, New York Public Library for the Performing Arts

friends. It was one of those friendships that one enters into overhastily and so often comes to regret later in life. I might as well confess the truth. We—well, we're on Christian name terms. And the tactless idiot makes no attempt to conceal it when other people are present. On the contrary, he thinks it gives him the right to be familiar with me. He shows off the whole time, with "Torvald this" and "Torvald that." I can tell you, I find it damned annoying. If he stayed, he'd make my position intolerable.

Nora. Torvald, you can't mean this seriously.

Helmer. Oh? And why not?

Nora. But it's so petty. ⌐ 12

Helmer. What did you say? Petty? You think *I* am petty?

Nora. No, Torvald dear, of course you're not. That's just why—

Helmer. Don't quibble! You call my motives petty. Then I must be petty too. Petty!

---

1. **obloquies** (äb'lə·kwēz): verbal abuse; censure.

11

11 SYNTHESIZING
Nora's father is the latest character to be identified as having committed an indiscretion or crime in the past. Who are the other characters with painful secrets? (Nora, Krogstad, Dr. Rank, and Dr. Rank's father)

READER'S RESPONSE
How do Torvald's reasons for not retaining Krogstad make you feel about him?

conceivably (kən·sēv'ə·blē): in a way that could be imagined or believed

quibble (kwib'əl): to evade a central truth by focusing on a small detail

12 ANALYZING
What happens for the first time when Nora says, "But it's so petty"? (She openly criticizes or disagrees with Helmer.)

13 GUIDED READING
Identifying Cause and Effect:
What is the outcome of Nora's attempt to convince Helmer to keep Krogstad employed? (He gets angry and decides to settle the matter immediately.)

> ■ **vindictiveness** (vin·dik′tiv· nəs): a spirit of revenge
> **depraved** (di·prāvd′): morally corrupt; utterly wicked

14 PREDICTING
On the basis of what you already know about Helmer, do you think he will behave with strength or courage in a crisis? (Answers will vary.)

15 LITERARY ELEMENT
Rising Action: In Act 2, tension has been mounting as Nora confronts more and more obstacles to keeping her secret. Do you think she will find any way out, or will her secret be revealed? (Possible response: There seems to be an inevitable momentum toward exposure of the truth.)

I see. Well, I've had enough of this. (*goes to the door and calls into the hall*) Helen!

Nora. What are you going to do?

Helmer (*searching among his papers*). I'm going to settle this matter once and for all.

[*The* MAID *enters.*]

Helmer. Take this letter downstairs at once. Find a messenger and see that he delivers it. Immediately! The address is on the envelope. Here's the money.

Maid. Very good, sir. (*goes out with the letter*)

Helmer (*putting his papers in order*). There now, little Miss Obstinate.

Nora (*tensely*). Torvald—what was in that letter?

Helmer. Krogstad's dismissal.

Nora. Call her back, Torvald! There's still time. Oh, Torvald, call her back! Do it for my sake—for your own sake—for the children! Do you hear me, Torvald? Please do it! You don't realize what this may do to us all!

Helmer. Too late.

Nora. Yes. Too late.

Helmer. My dear Nora, I forgive you this anxiety. Though it is a bit of an insult to me. Oh, but it is! Isn't it an insult to imply that I should be frightened by the vindictiveness of a depraved hack journalist? But I forgive you, because it so charmingly testifies to the love you bear me. (*takes her in his arms*) Which is as it should be, my own dearest Nora. Let what will happen, happen. When the real crisis comes, you will not find me lacking in strength or courage. I am man enough to bear the burden for us both.

Nora (*fearfully*). What do you mean?

Helmer. The whole burden, I say—

Nora (*calmly*). I shall never let you do that.

Helmer. Very well. We shall share it, Nora—as man and wife. And that's as it should be. (*caresses her*) Are you happy now? There, there, there; don't look at me with those frightened little eyes. You're simply imagining things. You go ahead now and do your tarantella, and get some practice on that tambourine. I'll sit in my study and close the door. Then I won't hear anything, and you can make all the noise you want. (*turns in the doorway*) When Dr. Rank comes, tell him where to find me. (*He nods to her, goes into his room with his papers and closes the door.*)

Nora (*desperate with anxiety, stands as though transfixed, and whispers*). He said he'd do it. He will do it. He will do it, and nothing'll stop him. No, never that. I'd rather anything. There must be some escape—Some way out—!

[*The bell rings in the hall.*]

Nora. Dr. Rank—! Anything but that! Anything, I don't care—!

[*She passes her hand across her face, composes herself, walks across and opens the door to the hall.* DR. RANK *is standing there, hanging up his fur coat. During the following scene it begins to grow dark.*]

Nora. Good evening, Dr. Rank. I recognized your ring. But you mustn't go in to Torvald yet. I think he's busy.

Rank. And—you?

Nora (*as he enters the room and she closes the door behind him*). Oh, you know very well I've always time to talk to you.

Rank. Thank you. I shall avail myself of that privilege as long as I can.

Nora. What do you mean by that? As long as you *can*?

Rank. Yes. Does that frighten you?

Nora. Well, it's rather a curious expression. Is something going to happen?

Rank. Something I've been expecting to happen for a long time. But I didn't think it would happen quite so soon.

Nora (*seizes his arm*). What is it? Dr. Rank, you must tell me!

Rank (*sits down by the stove*). I'm on the way out. And there's nothing to be done about it.

Nora (*sighs with relief*). Oh, it's you—?

Rank. Who else? No, it's no good lying to oneself. I am the most wretched of all my patients, Mrs. Helmer. These last few days I've been going through the books of this poor body of mine, and I find I am bankrupt. Within a month I may be rotting up there in the churchyard.

Nora. Ugh, what a nasty way to talk!

Rank. The facts aren't exactly nice. But the worst is that there's so much else that's nasty that's got to come first. I've only one more test to make. When that's done I'll have a pretty accurate idea of when the final disintegration is likely to begin. I want to ask you a favor. Helmer's a sensitive chap, and I know how he hates anything ugly. I don't want him to visit me when I'm in hospital—

Nora. Oh but, Dr. Rank—

Rank. I don't want him there. On any pretext. I shan't have him allowed in. As soon as I know the worst, I'll send you my visiting card with a black cross on it, and then you'll know that the final filthy process has begun.

Nora. Really, you're being quite impossible this evening. And I did hope you'd be in a good mood.

Rank. With death on my hands? And all this to atone for someone else's sin? Is there justice in that? And in every single family, in one way or another, the same merciless law of retribution is at work—

Nora (*holds her hands to her ears*). Nonsense! Cheer up! Laugh!

Rank. Yes, you're right. Laughter's all the damned thing's fit for. My poor innocent spine must pay for the fun my father had as a gay young lieutenant.

Nora (*at the table, left*). You mean he was too fond of asparagus and *foie gras?*[2]

Rank. Yes; and truffles too.

Nora. Yes, of course, truffles, yes. And oysters too, I suppose?

Rank. Yes, oysters, oysters. Of course.

Nora. And all that port and champagne to wash them down. It's too sad that all those lovely things should affect one's spine.

Rank. Especially a poor spine that never got any pleasure out of them.

Nora. Oh yes, that's the saddest thing of all.

Rank (*looks searchingly at her*). Hm—

Nora (*after a moment*). Why did you smile?

Rank. No, it was you who laughed.

Nora. No, it was you who smiled, Dr. Rank!

Rank (*gets up*). You're a worse little rogue than I thought.

Nora. Oh, I'm full of stupid tricks today.

Rank. So it seems.

Nora (*puts both her hands on his shoulders*). Dear, dear Dr. Rank, you mustn't die and leave Torvald and me.

Rank. Oh, you'll soon get over it. Once one is gone, one is soon forgotten.

Nora (*looks at him anxiously*). Do you believe that?

Rank. One finds replacements, and then—

Nora. Who will find a replacement?

Rank. You and Helmer both will, when I am gone. You seem to have made a start already, haven't you? What was this Mrs. Linde doing here yesterday evening?

Nora. Aha! But surely you can't be jealous of poor Christine?

Rank. Indeed I am. She will be my successor in this house. When I have moved on, this lady will—

Nora. Ssh—don't speak so loud! She's in there!

---

2. *foie gras* (fwä grä): a pâté, or spread, made from goose liver.

16 LITERARY ELEMENT
Theme: What relationship to truth does the character of Dr. Rank represent? (He does not lie to himself; he faces unpleasant facts.) Who does Dr. Rank wish to protect from the truth of his condition? (Helmer)

17 READER'S RESPONSE
Do you agree with Dr. Rank (and possibly with Ibsen) that "the same merciless law of retribution is at work" in every family?

18 INTERPRETING
What does the dialogue between Dr. Rank and Nora about her tricks reveal about each of them? (Dr. Rank sees through Nora; Nora is beginning to tire of her recourse to tricks.)

How would you characterize Nora's showing the stockings to Dr. Rank? (Possible responses: flirtatious; playful) Why do you think she is behaving this way? (Possible response: to distract him and herself from their serious problems)

20 LITERARY ELEMENT

Characterization: What does Dr. Rank's sadness about not leaving anything behind reveal about the life he has led? (Possible response: He has been lonely and has had no closer ties than the Helmers.) What other character has expressed similar feelings? (Mrs. Linde)

21 LITERARY ELEMENT

Plot: What secret does Dr. Rank reveal? (He loves Nora.) What secret was Nora about to reveal to him? (her need for money to buy off Krogstad)

ORAL RESPONSE

Ask for two volunteers to enact the "love" scene between Nora and Dr. Rank. Remind students to pay attention to Ibsen's stage directions for clues on how to interpret the dialogue.

Rank. Today again? You see!

Nora. She's only come to mend my dress. Good heavens, how unreasonable you are! (*sits on the sofa*) Be nice now, Dr. Rank. Tomorrow you'll see how beautifully I shall dance; and you must imagine that I'm doing it just for you. And for Torvald, of course; obviously. (*takes some things out of the box*) Dr. Rank, sit down here and I'll show you something.

Rank (*sits*). What's this?

Nora. Look here! Look!

Rank. Silk stockings!

Nora. Flesh-colored. Aren't they beautiful? It's very dark in here now, of course, but tomorrow—! No, no, no; only the soles. Oh well, I suppose you can look a bit higher if you want to.

Rank. Hm—

Nora. Why are you looking so critical? Don't you think they'll fit me?

Rank. I can't really give you a qualified opinion on that.

Nora (*looks at him for a moment*). Shame on you! (*flicks him on the ear with the stockings*) Take that. (*puts them back in the box*)

Rank. What other wonders are to be revealed to me?

Nora. I shan't show you anything else. You're being naughty.

[*She hums a little and looks among the things in the box.*]

Rank (*after a short silence*). When I sit here like this being so intimate with you, I can't think—I cannot imagine what would have become of me if I had never entered this house.

Nora (*smiles*). Yes, I think you enjoy being with us, don't you?

Rank (*more quietly, looking into the middle distance*). And now to have to leave it all—

Nora. Nonsense. You're not leaving us.

Rank (*as before*). And not to be able to leave even the most wretched token of gratitude behind; hardly even a passing sense of loss; only an empty place, to be filled by the next comer.

Nora. Suppose I were to ask you to—? No—

Rank. To do what?

Nora. To give me proof of your friendship—

Rank. Yes, yes?

Nora. No, I mean—to do me a very great service—

Rank. Would you really for once grant me that happiness?

Nora. But you've no idea what it is.

Rank. Very well, tell me, then.

Nora. No, but, Dr. Rank, I can't. It's far too much—I want your help and advice, and I want you to do something for me.

Rank. The more the better. I've no idea what it can be. But tell me. You do trust me, don't you?

Nora. Oh, yes, more than anyone. You're my best and truest friend. Otherwise I couldn't tell you. Well then, Dr. Rank—there's something you must help me to prevent. You know how much Torvald loves me—he'd never hesitate for an instant to lay down his life for me—

Rank (*leans over towards her*). Nora—do you think he is the only one—?

Nora (*with a slight start*). What do you mean?

Rank. Who would gladly lay down his life for you?

Nora (*sadly*). Oh, I see.

Rank. I swore to myself I would let you know that before I go. I shall never have a better opportunity. . . . Well, Nora, now you know that. And now you also know that you can trust me as you can trust nobody else.

Nora (*rises; calmly and quietly*). Let me pass, please.

Rank (*makes room for her but remains seated*). Nora—

Nora (*in the doorway to the hall*). Helen, bring the lamp. (*goes over to the stove*) Oh, dear Dr. Rank, this was really horrid of you.

Rank (*gets up*). That I have loved you as deeply as anyone else has? Was that horrid of me?

Nora. No—but that you should go and tell me. That was quite unnecessary—

Rank. What do you mean? Did you know, then—?

22

[*The* MAID *enters with the lamp, puts it on the table and goes out.*]

Rank. Nora—Mrs. Helmer—I am asking you, did you know this?

Nora. Oh, what do I know, what did I know, what didn't I know—I really can't say. How could you be so stupid, Dr. Rank? Everything was so nice.

Rank. Well, at any rate now you know that I am ready to serve you, body and soul. So—please continue.

Nora (*looks at him*). After this?

Rank. Please tell me what it is.

23

Nora. I can't possibly tell you now.

Rank. Yes, yes! You mustn't punish me like this. Let me be allowed to do what I can for you.

Nora. You can't do anything for me now. Anyway, I don't need any help. It was only my imagination—you'll see. Yes, really. Honestly. (*sits in the rocking chair, looks at him and smiles*) Well, upon my word you *are* a fine gentleman, Dr. Rank. Aren't you ashamed of yourself, now that the lamp's been lit?

Rank. Frankly, no. But perhaps I ought to say—*adieu*?

Nora. Of course not. You will naturally continue to visit us as before. You know quite well how Torvald depends on your company.

Rank. Yes, but you?

Nora. Oh, I always think it's enormous fun having you here.

Rank. That was what misled me. You're a riddle to me, you know. I'd often felt you'd just as soon be with me as with Helmer.

Nora. Well, you see, there are some people whom one loves, and others whom it's almost more fun to be with.

24

Rank. Oh yes, there's some truth in that.

Nora. When I was at home, of course I loved Papa best. But I always used to think it was terribly amusing to go down and talk to the servants; because they never told me what I ought to do; and they were such fun to listen to.

Rank. I see. So I've taken their place?

Nora (*jumps up and runs over to him*). Oh, dear, sweet Dr. Rank, I didn't mean that at all. But I'm sure you understand—I feel the same about Torvald as I did about Papa.

Maid (*enters from the hall*). Excuse me, madam. (*whispers to her and hands her a visiting card*)

Nora (*glances at the card*). Oh! (*puts it quickly in her pocket*)

Rank. Anything wrong?

Nora. No, no, nothing at all. It's just something that—it's my new dress.

Rank. What? But your costume is lying over there.

Nora. Oh—that, yes—but there's another—I ordered it specially—Torvald mustn't know—

Rank. Ah, so that's your big secret?

Nora. Yes, yes. Go in and talk to him—he's in his study—keep him talking for a bit—

Rank. Don't worry. He won't get away from me. (*goes into* HELMER's *study*)

Nora (*to the* MAID). Is he waiting in the kitchen?

Maid. Yes, madam, he came up the back way—

Nora. But didn't you tell him I had a visitor?

25 LITERARY ELEMENT

Suspense: Nora's anxiety has now reached a fever pitch as she struggles more and more desperately to keep her secret from her husband. Do you think Ibsen intended the audience to share Nora's tension and sympathize with her predicament? Why or why not? (Possible response: Ibsen wants the audience to sympathize with Nora since he portrays her as basically kindhearted and Torvald as insensitive and self-centered.)

26 INFERRING

What does Krogstad imply about Torvald's character? (that Torvald is a coward)

27 COMPARING AND CONTRASTING

Who does Krogstad mean when he says, "the three of us"? (Helmer, Nora, and himself) How are all three alike? (Each engages in some form of deception or pretense.)

28 ANALYZING

Why do you think Krogstad has decided not to return the forged document? (so he can maintain power over the Helmers indefinitely)

Maid. Yes, but he wouldn't go.

Nora. Wouldn't go?

Maid. No, madam, not until he'd spoken with you.

Nora. Very well, show him in; but quietly. Helen, you mustn't tell anyone about this. It's a surprise for my husband.

Maid. Very good, madam. I understand. (*goes*)

25 **Nora.** It's happening. It's happening after all. No, no, no, it can't happen, it mustn't happen.

[*She walks across and bolts the door of* HELMER's *study. The* MAID *opens the door from the hall to admit* KROGSTAD, *and closes it behind him. He is wearing an overcoat, heavy boots and a fur cap.*]

Nora (*goes towards him*). Speak quietly. My husband's at home.

Krogstad. Let him hear.

Nora. What do you want from me?

Krogstad. Information.

Nora. Hurry up, then. What is it?

Krogstad. I suppose you know I've been given the sack.

Nora. I couldn't stop it, Mr. Krogstad. I did my best for you, but it didn't help.

Krogstad. Does your husband love you so little? He knows what I can do to you, and yet he dares to—

Nora. Surely you don't imagine I told him?

26 **Krogstad.** No, I didn't really think you had. It wouldn't have been like my old friend Torvald Helmer to show that much courage—

Nora. Mr. Krogstad, I'll trouble you to speak respectfully of my husband.

Krogstad. Don't worry, I'll show him all the respect he deserves. But since you're so anxious to keep this matter hushed up, I presume you're better informed than you were yesterday of the gravity of what you've done?

Nora. I've learned more than you could ever teach me.

Krogstad. Yes, a bad lawyer like me—

Nora. What do you want from me?

Krogstad. I just wanted to see how things were with you, Mrs. Helmer. I've been thinking about you all day. Even duns and hack journalists have hearts, you know.

Nora. Show some heart, then. Think of my little children.

Krogstad. Have you and your husband thought of mine? Well, let's forget that. I just wanted to tell you, you don't need to take this business too seriously. I'm not going to take any action, for the present.

Nora. Oh, no—you won't, will you? I knew it.

27 **Krogstad.** It can all be settled quite amicably. There's no need for it to become public. We'll keep it among the three of us.

Nora. My husband must never know about this.

Krogstad. How can you stop him? Can you pay the balance of what you owe me?

Nora. Not immediately.

Krogstad. Have you any means of raising the money during the next few days?

Nora. None that I would care to use.

28 **Krogstad.** Well, it wouldn't have helped anyway. However much money you offered me now I wouldn't give you back that paper.

Nora. What are you going to do with it?

Krogstad. Just keep it. No one else need ever hear about it. So in case you were thinking of doing anything desperate—

Nora. I am.

Krogstad. Such as running away—

Nora. I am.

Krostad. Or anything more desperate—

Nora. How did you know?

Krogstad. —just give up the idea.

Nora. How did you know?

Isabella Stewart Gardner by John Singer Sargent (1856-1925), The Isabella Stewart Gardner Museum, Boston.

ISABELLA STEWART GARDNER, JOHN SINGER SARGENT (1856–1925).

Krogstad. Most of us think of that at first. I did. But I hadn't the courage—

Nora (*dully*). Neither have I.

Krogstad (*relieved*). It's true, isn't it? You haven't the courage, either?

Nora. No. I haven't. I haven't.

Krogstad. It'd be a stupid thing to do anyway. Once the first little domestic explosion is over . . . I've got a letter in my pocket here addressed to your husband—

Nora. Telling him everything?

Krogstad. As delicately as possible.

Nora (*quickly*). He must never see that letter. Tear it up. I'll find the money somehow—

Krogstad. I'm sorry, Mrs. Helmer. I thought I'd explained—

Nora. Oh, I don't mean the money I owe you. Let me know how much you want from my husband, and I'll find it for you.

Krogstad. I'm not asking your husband for money.

Nora. What do you want, then?

Krogstad. I'll tell you. I want to get on my feet again, Mrs. Helmer. I want to get to the top. And your husband's going to help me. For eighteen months now my record's been clean. I've been in hard straits all that time: I was content to fight my way back inch by inch. Now I've been chucked back into the mud, and I'm not going to be satisfied with just getting back my job. I'm going to get to the top, I tell you. I'm going to get back into the bank, and it's going to be higher up. Your husband's going to create a new job for me—

Nora. He'll never do that!

Krogstad. Oh yes, he will. I know him. He won't dare to risk a scandal. And once I'm in there with him, you'll see! Within a year I'll be his right-hand man. It'll be Nils Krogstad who'll be running that bank, not Torvald Helmer!

Nora. That will never happen.

Krogstad. Are you thinking of—?

Nora. Now I *have* the courage.

Krogstad. Oh, you can't frighten me. A pampered little pretty like you—

Nora. You'll see! You'll see!

30

HUMANITIES CONNECTION

Sargent, an American Impressionist painter, repeats large and small circular patterns in his subject's belt, her necklace, the neckline of her dress, and in the background of this full-length portrait. How does the positioning of the woman's hands relate to these patterns? (Her clasped hands form another circle, reinforcing the circular patterns.) Sargent's subject is Isabella Stewart Gardner, a wealthy patron of the arts, whose Boston home is now an art museum. ∎

29 INFERRING

What action are Krogstad and Nora discussing having the courage to do? (killing oneself) What do both agree on? (They do not have the courage for suicide.)

30 GUIDED READING

Identifying Details: What does Krogstad want even more than money? (high position, power, and the respect of others)

Krogstad. Under the ice? Down in the cold, black water? And then, in the spring, to float up again, ugly, unrecognizable, hairless—?

Nora. You can't frighten me.

Krogstad. And you can't frighten me. People don't do such things, Mrs. Helmer. And anyway, what'd be the use? I've got him in my pocket.

Nora. But afterwards? When I'm no longer—?

31 **Krogstad.** Have you forgotten that then your reputation will be in my hands?

[*She looks at him speechlessly.*]

Krogstad. Well, I've warned you. Don't do anything silly. When Helmer's read my letter, he'll get in touch with me. And remember, it's your husband who has forced me to act like this. And for that I'll never forgive him. Goodbye, Mrs. Helmer. (*He goes out through the hall.*)

32

Nora (*runs to the hall door, opens it a few inches and listens*). He's going. He's not going to give him the letter. Oh, no, no, it couldn't possibly happen. (*opens the door, a little wider*) What's he doing? Standing outside the front door. He's not going downstairs. Is he changing his mind? Yes, he—!

33 [*A letter falls into the letter box. KROGSTAD's footsteps die away down the stairs.*]

Nora (*with a stifled cry, runs across the room towards the table by the sofa; a pause*). In the letter box. (*steals timidly over towards the hall door*) There it is! Oh, Torvald, Torvald! Now we're lost!

Mrs. Linde (*enters from the nursery with NORA's costume*). Well, I've done the best I can. Shall we see how it looks—?

Nora (*whispers hoarsely*). Christine, come here.

Mrs. Linde (*throws the dress on the sofa*). What's wrong with you? You look as though you'd seen a ghost!

Nora. Come here. Do you see that letter? There—look—through the glass of the letter box.

Mrs. Linde. Yes, yes, I see it.

Nora. That letter's from Krogstad—

Mrs. Linde. Nora! It was Krogstad who lent you the money!

Nora. Yes. And now Torvald's going to discover everything.

Mrs. Linde. Oh, believe me, Nora, it'll be best for you both.

34

Nora. You don't know what's happened. I've committed a forgery—

Mrs. Linde. But, for heaven's sake—!

Nora. Christine, all I want is for you to be my witness.

Mrs. Linde. What do you mean? Witness what?

Nora. If I should go out of my mind—and it might easily happen—

Mrs. Linde. Nora!

Nora. Or if anything else should happen to me—so that I wasn't here any longer—

Mrs. Linde. Nora, Nora, you don't know what you're saying!

Nora. If anyone should try to take the blame, and say it was all his fault—you understand—?

Mrs. Linde. Yes, yes—but how can you think—?

Nora. Then you must testify that it isn't true, Christine. I'm not mad—I know exactly what I'm saying—and I'm telling you, no one else knows anything about this. I did it entirely on my own. Remember that.

Mrs. Linde. All right. But I simply don't understand—

Nora. Oh, how could you understand? A—miracle—is about to happen.

Mrs. Linde. Miracle?

Nora. Yes. A miracle. But it's so frightening, Christine. It mustn't happen, not for anything in the world.

35

Mrs. Linde. I'll go over and talk to Krogstad.

Nora. Don't go near him. He'll only do something to hurt you.

Mrs. Linde. Once upon a time he'd have done anything for my sake.

Nora. He?

Mrs. Linde. Where does he live?

Nora. Oh, how should I know—? Oh yes, wait a moment—! (*feels in her pocket*) Here's his card. But the letter, the letter—!

Helmer (*from his study, knocks on the door*). Nora!

Nora (*cries in alarm*). What is it?

Helmer. Now, now, don't get alarmed. We're not coming in—you've closed the door. Are you trying on your costume?

Nora. Yes, yes—I'm trying on my costume. I'm going to look so pretty for you, Torvald.

Mrs. Linde (*who has been reading the card*). Why, he lives just round the corner.

Nora. Yes; but it's no use. There's nothing to be done now. The letter's lying there in the box.

Mrs. Linde. And your husband has the key?

Nora. Yes, he always keeps it.

Mrs. Linde. Krogstad must ask him to send the letter back unread. He must find some excuse—

Nora. But Torvald always opens the box at just about this time—

Mrs. Linde. You must stop him. Go in and keep him talking. I'll be back as quickly as I can.

[*She hurries out through the hall.*]

Nora (*goes over to* HELMER's *door, opens it and peeps in*). Torvald!

Helmer (*offstage*). Well, may a man enter his own drawing room again? Come on, Rank, now we'll see what—(*in the doorway*) But what's this?

Nora. What, Torvald dear?

Helmer. Rank's been preparing me for some great transformation scene.

Rank (*in the doorway*). So I understood. But I seem to have been mistaken.

Nora. Yes, no one's to be allowed to see me before tomorrow night.

Helmer. But, my dear Nora, you look quite worn out. Have you been practicing too hard?

Nora. No, I haven't practiced at all yet.

Helmer. Well, you must.

Nora. Yes, Torvald, I must, I know. But I can't get anywhere without your help. I've completely forgotten everything.

Helmer. Oh, we'll soon put that to rights.

Nora. Yes, help me, Torvald. Promise me you will? Oh, I'm so nervous. All those people—! You must forget everything except me this evening. You mustn't think of business—I won't even let you touch a pen. Promise me, Torvald?

Helmer. I promise. This evening I shall think of nothing but you—my poor, helpless little darling. Oh, there's just one thing I must see to—(*goes towards the hall door*)

Nora. What do you want out there?

Helmer. I'm only going to see if any letters have come.

Nora. No, Torvald, no!

Helmer. Why what's the matter?

Nora. Torvald, I beg you. There's nothing there.

Helmer. Well, I'll just make sure.

[*He moves towards the door.* NORA *runs to the piano and plays the first bars of the Tarantella.*]

Helmer (*at the door, turns*). Aha!

Nora. I can't dance tomorrow if I don't practice with you now.

Helmer (*goes over to her*). Are you really so frightened, Nora dear?

Nora. Yes, terribly frightened. Let me start

36 LITERARY ELEMENT
Theme: What secret has Mrs. Linde revealed about her past relationship with Krogstad? (He once was in love with her.)

37 GUIDED READING
Finding the Main Idea: What is Mrs. Linde's plan to help Nora? (She is going to convince Krogstad to ask Helmer to send the letter back unread.) What must Nora do in the meantime? (keep Helmer from going to the mailbox)

38 LITERARY ELEMENT
Dramatic Irony: How is Helmer's observation about Nora looking "worn out" ironic? (because the audience knows that she is not tired from dancing)

39 CULTURAL BACKGROUND
Tell students that the *Tarantella* is a lively, whirling southern Italian dance, once thought to be a cure for a disease caused by the bite of the tarantula spider. In this sense, it was a dance to ward off death. Nora too is dancing for her life to put off thoughts of suicide and of the death of her relationship with her husband.

What does the speed at which Nora is dancing suggest about her emotional state? (She is in a frenzy of anxiety.)

practicing now, at once—we've still time before dinner. Oh, do sit down and play for me, Torvald dear. Correct me, lead me, the way you always do.

Helmer. Very well, my dear, if you wish it.

[*He sits down at the piano. NORA seizes the tambourine and a long multicolored shawl from the cardboard box, wraps the shawl hastily around her, then takes a quick leap into the center of the room and cries:*]

Nora. Play for me! I want to dance!

[HELMER *plays and* NORA *dances.* DR. RANK *stands behind* HELMER *at the piano and watches her.*]

Helmer (*as he plays*). Slower, slower!

Nora. I can't!

40

Midland Community Theatre at Theatre Midland

Helmer. Not so violently, Nora.

Nora. I must!

Helmer (*stops playing*). No, no, this won't do at all.

Nora (*laughs and swings her tambourine*). Isn't that what I told you?

Rank. Let me play for her.

Helmer (*gets up*). Yes, would you? Then it'll be easier for me to show her.

[RANK *sits down at the piano and plays.* NORA *dances more and more wildly.* HELMER *has stationed himself by the stove and tries repeatedly to correct her, but she seems not to hear him. Her hair works loose and falls over her shoulders; she ignores it and continues to dance.* MRS. LINDE *enters.*]

41

Mrs. Linde (*stands in the doorway as though tongue-tied*). Ah—!

Nora (*as she dances*). Oh, Christine, we're having such fun!

Helmer. But, Nora darling, you're dancing as if your life depended on it.

Nora. It does.

Helmer. Rank, stop it! This is sheer lunacy. Stop it, I say!

[RANK *ceases playing.* NORA *suddenly stops dancing.*]

Helmer (*goes over to her*). I'd never have believed it. You've forgotten everything I taught you.

Nora (*throws away the tambourine*). You see!

Helmer. I'll have to show you every step.

Nora. You see how much I need you! You must show me every step of the way. Right to the end of the dance. Promise me you will, Torvald?

Helmer. Never fear. I will.

Nora. You mustn't think about anything but me—today or tomorrow. Don't open any letters—don't even open the letter box—

Helmer. Aha, you're still worried about that fellow— **42**

Nora. Oh, yes, yes, him too.

Helmer. Nora, I can tell from the way you're behaving, there's a letter from him already lying there.

Nora. I don't know. I think so. But you mustn't read it now. I don't want anything ugly to come between us till it's all over.

Rank (*quietly to* HELMER). Better give her her way.

Helmer (*puts his arm round her*). My child shall have her way. But tomorrow night, when your dance is over—

Nora. Then you will be free. **43**

Maid (*appears in the doorway, right*). Dinner is served, madam.

Nora. Put out some champagne, Helen.

Maid. Very good, madam. (*goes*)

Helmer. I say! What's this, a banquet?

Nora. We'll drink champagne until dawn! (*calls*) And, Helen! Put out some macaroons! Lots of macaroons—for once!

Helmer (*takes her hands in his*). Now, now, now. Don't get so excited. Where's my little songbird, the one I know?

Nora. All right. Go and sit down—and you, too, Dr. Rank. I'll be with you in a minute. Christine, you must help me put my hair up.

Rank (*quietly, as they go*). There's nothing wrong, is there? I mean, she isn't—er—expecting—?

Helmer. Good heavens no, my dear chap. She just gets scared like a child sometimes—I told you before—

[*They go out, right.*]

Nora. Well?

Mrs. Linde. He's left town.

Nora. I saw it from your face.

Mrs. Linde. He'll be back tomorrow evening. I left a note for him. **44**

Nora. You needn't have bothered. You can't

45 PREDICTING

Do you think Nora or anyone else will actually die in Act 3? (Answers will vary.) What may come to an end? (Possible responses: the marriage; Nora's role as entertainer and helpless child)

ANSWERS

First Thoughts
Answers will vary.

Identifying Facts
1. He is in love with her.
2. his position at the bank and respect
3. to speak with Krogstad. Krogstad was once in love with her.

Interpreting Meanings
1. Possible response: Yes, his main concern is appearances.
2. Possible response: Nora's borrowing behind her husband's back and her forgery are threatening the foundations of her marriage.
3. Possible response: Helmer will protect her by taking full responsibility for the loan and forgery.
4. Answers will vary.

Applying Meanings
Have students draw on their personal experiences to support their point of view.

Critical Writing Response
Interpreting Symbolism. Students should use specific references and exact quotes from *A Doll's House* to support their analyses.

stop anything now. Anyway, it's wonderful really, in a way—sitting here and waiting for the miracle to happen.
Mrs. Linde. Waiting for what?
Nora. Oh, you wouldn't understand. Go in and join them. I'll be with you in a moment.

[MRS. LINDE *goes into the dining room.*]
Nora (*stands for a moment as though collecting herself. Then she looks at her*

watch). Five o'clock. Seven hours till midnight. Then another twenty-four hours till midnight tomorrow. And then the tarantella will be finished. Twenty-four and seven? Thirty-one hours to live.

Helmer (*appears in the doorway, right*). What's happened to my little songbird?

Nora (*runs to him with her arms wide*). Your songbird is here!

First Thoughts
How do you think Torvald will respond when he reads the letter from Krogstad?

Identifying Facts
1. What does Nora learn from Dr. Rank that changes her mind about asking him for help?
2. When Krogstad visits Nora, he reveals that he does not want more money. What does he want?
3. What offer does Mrs. Linde make that encourages Nora? What makes Mrs. Linde think she has the power to help?

Interpreting Meanings
1. Do you agree with Nora that Torvald's reasons for firing Krogstad are "petty"? Why or why not?
2. Dr. Rank has inherited a fatal illness from his father. Bitterly, he tells Nora that "in every single family, in one way or another, the same merciless law of retribution is at work." In what way is retribution for past deeds at work in the Helmer family?
3. Near the end of Act 2, Nora believes that a "miracle" will happen. What is the miracle that she hopes for?

4. **Foreshadowing** is the use of clues to hint at what is going to happen later in the plot. What do you anticipate will happen?

Applying Meanings
Nora desperately thinks of ways to postpone the time when her husband will read the letter from Krogstad. Think of a time when you, or someone you know, tried to avoid accepting consequences for something unpleasant. Do you believe that the truth should always come out?

Critical Writing Response
Interpreting Symbolism. Letters and letter boxes play an important part in *A Doll's House*. State three or more ways in which letters or messages help build **suspense** in *A Doll's House*. How does Ibsen use letters as a **symbol**—a physical representation of something abstract—of the fact that Nora and Torvald have not communicated honestly over the years? Think about the way Nora repeatedly tries to keep messages from being sent or received.

Billy Rose Theatre Collection, New York Public Library for the Performing Arts

Act 3 opens with a sense of tension and anticipation.
Do you think Nora's "miracle" will occur? Do you think she will be saved from the consequences of her actions?

ACT 3

The same room. The table which was formerly by the sofa has been moved into the center of the room; the chairs surround it as before. A lamp is burning on the table. The door to the hall stands open. Dance music can be heard from the floor above. MRS. LINDE is seated at the table, absentmindedly glancing through a book. She is trying to read, but seems unable to keep her mind on it. More than once she turns and listens anxiously towards the front door.

Mrs. Linde (*looks at her watch*). Not here yet. There's not much time left. Please God he hasn't—! (*listens again*) Ah, here he is.

[*Goes out into the hall and cautiously opens the front door. Footsteps can be heard softly ascending the stairs.*]

Mrs. Linde (*whispers*). Come in. There's no one here.

Krogstad (*in the doorway*). I found a note from you at my lodgings. What does this mean?

Identifying Cause and Effect:
Krogstad believes that Christine left him because she found a richer man. How does she explain her actions? (She had to marry the richer man in order to support her mother and brothers; it was not her personal wish but a necessity.)

2 **LITERARY ELEMENT**

Figurative Language: What does the image of the shipwrecked man suggest about Krogstad's emotional state? (Possible response: He is lost, lonely, and desperate.)

3 **INTERPRETING**

Why wouldn't it help for Mrs. Linde to give up the promised job at the bank? (Possible response: On the practical level, Helmer would not give the job to Krogstad even if Mrs. Linde gave it up. On the moral level, it would further degrade Krogstad.)

Mrs. Linde. I must speak with you.

Krogstad. Oh? And must our conversation take place in this house?

Mrs. Linde. We couldn't meet at my place; my room has no separate entrance. Come in. We're quite alone. The maid's asleep, and the Helmers are at the dance upstairs.

Krogstad (*comes into the room*). Well, well! So the Helmers are dancing this evening? Are they indeed?

Mrs. Linde. Yes, why not?

Krogstad. True enough. Why not?

Mrs. Linde. Well, Krogstad. You and I must have a talk together.

Krogstad. Have we two anything further to discuss?

Mrs. Linde. We have a great deal to discuss.

Krogstad. I wasn't aware of it.

Mrs. Linde. That's because you've never really understood me.

Krogstad. Was there anything to understand? It's the old story, isn't it—a woman chucking a man because something better turns up?

Mrs. Linde. Do you really think I'm so utterly heartless? You think it was easy for me to give you up?

Krogstad. Wasn't it?

Mrs. Linde. Oh, Nils, did you really believe that?

Krogstad. Then why did you write to me the way you did?

Mrs. Linde. I had to. Since I had to break with you, I thought it my duty to destroy all the feelings you had for me.

Krogstad (*clenches his fists*). So that was it. And you did this for money!

Mrs. Linde. You mustn't forget I had a helpless mother to take care of, and two little brothers. We couldn't wait for you, Nils. It would have been so long before you'd have had enough to support us.

Krogstad. Maybe. But you had no right to cast me off for someone else.

Mrs. Linde. Perhaps not. I've often asked myself that.

Krogstad (*more quietly*). When I lost you, it was just as though all solid ground had been swept from under my feet. Look at me. Now I'm a shipwrecked man, clinging to a spar.[1]

Mrs. Linde. Help may be near at hand.

Krogstad. It was near. But then you came, and stood between it and me.

Mrs. Linde. I didn't know, Nils. No one told me till today that this job I'd found was yours.

Krogstad. I believe you, since you say so. But now you know, won't you give it up?

Mrs. Linde. No—because it wouldn't help you even if I did.

Krogstad. Wouldn't it? I'd do it all the same.

Mrs. Linde. I've learned to look at things practically. Life and poverty have taught me that.

Krogstad. And life has taught me to distrust fine words.

Mrs. Linde. Then it has taught you a useful lesson. But surely you still believe in actions?

Krogstad. What do you mean?

Mrs. Linde. You said you were like a shipwrecked man clinging to a spar.

Krogstad. I have good reason to say it.

Mrs. Linde. I'm in the same position as you. No one to care about, no one to care for.

Krogstad. You made your own choice.

Mrs. Linde. I had no choice—then.

Krogstad. Well?

Mrs. Linde. Nils, suppose we two shipwrecked souls could join hands?

Krogstad. What are you saying?

---

1. **spar:** a pole or mast that supports or extends the sail of a ship.

Mrs. Linde. Castaways have a better chance of survival together than on their own.

Krogstad. Christine!

Mrs. Linde. Why do you suppose I came to this town?

Krogstad. You mean—you came because of me?

Mrs. Linde. I must work if I'm to find life worth living. I've always worked, for as long as I can remember. It's been the greatest joy of my life—my only joy. But now I'm alone in the world, and I feel so dreadfully lost and empty. There's no joy in working just for oneself. Oh, Nils, give me something—someone—to work for.

Krogstad. I don't believe all that. You're just being hysterical and romantic. You want to find an excuse for self-sacrifice.

Mrs. Linde. Have you ever known me to be hysterical?

Krogstad. You mean you really—? Is it possible? Tell me—you know all about my past?

Mrs. Linde. Yes.

Krogstad. And you know what people think of me here?

Mrs. Linde. You said just now that with me you might have become a different person.

Krogstad. I know I could have.

Mrs. Linde. Couldn't it still happen?

Krogstad. Christine—do you really mean this? Yes—you do—I see it in your face. Have you really the courage—?

Mrs. Linde. I need someone to be a mother to; and your children need a mother. And you and I need each other. I believe in you, Nils. I am afraid of nothing—with you.

Krogstad (*clasps her hands*). Thank you, Christine—thank you! Now I shall make the world believe in me as you do! Oh—but I'd forgotten—

Mrs. Linde (*listens*). Ssh! The tarantella! Go quickly, go!

Krogstad. Why? What is it?

Mrs. Linde. You hear that dance? As soon as it's finished, they'll be coming down.

Krogstad. All right, I'll go. It's no good, Christine. I'd forgotten—you don't know what I've just done to the Helmers.

Mrs. Linde. Yes, Nils. I know.

Krogstad. And yet you'd still have the courage to—?

Mrs. Linde. I know what despair can drive a man like you to.

Krogstad. Oh, if only I could undo this!

Mrs. Linde. You can. Your letter is still lying in the box.

Krogstad. Are you sure?

Mrs. Linde. Quite sure. But—

Krogstad (*looks searchingly at her*). Is that why you're doing this? You want to save your friend at any price? Tell me the truth. Is that the reason?

Mrs. Linde. Nils, a woman who has sold herself once for the sake of others doesn't make the same mistake again.

Krogstad. I shall demand my letter back.

Mrs. Linde. No, no.

Krogstad. Of course I shall. I shall stay here till Helmer comes down. I'll tell him he must give me back my letter—I'll say it was only to do with my dismissal, and that I don't want him to read it—

Mrs. Linde. No, Nils, you mustn't ask for that letter back.

Krogstad. But—tell me—wasn't that the real reason you asked me to come here?

Mrs. Linde. Yes—at first, when I was frightened. But a day has passed since then, and in that time I've seen incredible things happen in this house. Helmer must know the truth. This unhappy secret of Nora's must be revealed. They must come to a full understanding. There must be an end of all

4 GUIDED READING
Finding the Main Idea: What is Mrs. Linde's proposed solution to her own and Krogstad's problems? (They should marry and devote themselves to one another.) What image does she use to describe them both? (castaways)

5 READER'S RESPONSE
How do you feel about the proposed marriage of Krogstad and Mrs. Linde? Do you think they are marrying for good reasons? Do you think they will be happy?

6 LITERARY ELEMENT
Turning Point: Mrs. Linde has just changed her mind about two very critical decisions. What are they? (She now considers her first marriage a mistake and has decided not to keep Helmer from seeing the incriminating letter.)

7 INTERPRETING
To what incredible things may Mrs. Linde be referring? (Possible response: Nora's frenzied and desperate dance)

EVALUATING

Do you agree with Mrs.
Linde's decision to allow Helmer to discover the truth? Do
you think she is being a good
friend to Nora or betraying her
trust? (Possible response: It is
Nora's decision, not Mrs.
Linde's, whether or not to tell
Helmer the truth.)

8 LITERARY ELEMENT

Mood: What feelings are generated by the reunion of
Krogstad and Mrs. Linde? (joy;
hopefulness) Why might Ibsen
want to create such a mood
just before the climactic confrontation between Nora and
Helmer? (Possible response: to
increase suspense about the
outcome)

9 INFERRING

Why doesn't Nora want to
leave the party? (She wants to
put off the moment when Helmer will read the letter and
learn the truth.)

10 EVALUATING

How does Nora's beauty give
Helmer pleasure? (His pride is
gratified by other people's admiration of her.)

these shiftings and <u>evasions.</u>

Krogstad. Very well. If you're prepared to
risk it. But one thing I can do—and at
once—

Mrs. Linde (*listens*). Hurry! Go, go! The
dance is over. We aren't safe here another
moment.

Krogstad. I'll wait for you downstairs.

Mrs. Linde. Yes, do. You can see me home.

Krogstad. I've never been so happy in my
life before!

[*He goes out through the front door. The
door leading from the room into the hall
remains open.*]

8   **Mrs. Linde** (*tidies the room a little and gets
her hat and coat*). What a change! Oh, what
a change! Someone to work for—to live for!
A home to bring joy into! I won't let this
chance of happiness slip through my fingers. Oh, why don't they come? (*listens*) Ah,
here they are. I must get my coat on.

[*She takes her hat and coat. HELMER's and
NORA's voices become audible outside. A
key is turned in the lock and HELMER
leads NORA almost forcibly into the hall.
She is dressed in an Italian costume with a
large black shawl. He is in evening dress,
with a black coat.*]

Nora (*still in the doorway, resisting him*).
No, no, no—not in here! I want to go back
upstairs. I don't want to leave so early.

9   **Helmer.** But my dearest Nora—

Nora. Oh, please, Torvald, please! Just
another hour!

Helmer. Not another minute, Nora, my
sweet. You know what we agreed. Come
along, now. Into the drawing room. You'll
catch cold if you stay out here.

[*He leads her, despite her efforts to resist
him, gently into the room.*]

Mrs. Linde. Good evening.

Nora. Christine!

Midland Community Theatre at Theatre Midland

Helmer. Oh, hullo, Mrs. Linde. You still
here?

Mrs. Linde. Please forgive me. I did so
want to see Nora in her costume.

Nora. Have you been sitting here waiting
for me?

Mrs. Linde. Yes. I got here too late, I'm
afraid. You'd already gone up. And I felt I
really couldn't go home without seeing you.

Helmer (*takes off NORA's shawl*). Well,
take a good look at her. She's worth looking at, don't you think? Isn't she beautiful,
Mrs. Linde?

Mrs. Linde. Oh, yes, indeed—

Helmer. Isn't she unbelievably beautiful?
Everyone at the party said so. But dreadfully stubborn she is, bless her pretty little
heart. What's to be done about that? Would
you believe it, I practically had to use force
to get her away!

1

Nora. Oh, Torvald, you're going to regret not letting me stay—just half an hour longer.

Helmer. Hear that, Mrs. Linde? She dances her tarantella—makes a roaring success—and very well deserved—though possibly a trifle too realistic—more so than was aesthetically necessary, strictly speaking. But never mind that. Main thing is—she had a success—roaring success. Was I going to let her stay on after that and spoil the impression? No, thank you! I took my beautiful little Capri signorina—my capricious little Capricienne,[2] what?—under my arm—a swift round of the ballroom, a curtsy to the company, and, as they say in novels, the beautiful apparition disappeared! An exit should always be dramatic, Mrs. Linde. But unfortunately that's just what I can't get Nora to realize. I say, it's hot in here. (*throws his cloak on a chair and opens the door to his study*) What's this? It's dark in here. Ah, yes, of course—excuse me. (*goes in and lights a couple of candles*)

Nora (*whispers softly, breathlessly*). Well?

Mrs. Linde (*quietly*). I've spoken to him.

Nora. Yes?

Mrs. Linde. Nora—you must tell your husband everything.

Nora (*dully*). I knew it.

Mrs. Linde. You have nothing to fear from Krogstad. But you must tell him.

Nora. I shan't tell him anything.

Mrs. Linde. Then the letter will.

Nora. Thank you, Christine. Now I know what I must do. Ssh!

Helmer (*returns*). Well, Mrs. Linde, finished admiring her?

Mrs. Linde. Yes. Now I must say good night.

---

2. **Capri . . . Capricienne:** "Capri signorina" and "Capricienne" both refer to a lady from Capri, a small island off the coat of Italy. Helmer is playing on the similarities in the words *capricious* and *Capricienne.*

Helmer. Oh, already? Does this knitting belong to you?

Mrs. Linde (*takes it*). Thank you, yes. I nearly forgot it.

Helmer. You knit, then?

Mrs. Linde. Why, yes.

Helmer. Know what? You ought to take up embroidery.

Mrs. Linde. Oh? Why?

Helmer. It's much prettier. Watch me, now. You hold the embroidery in your left hand, like this, and then you take the needle in your right hand and go in and out in a slow, easy movement—like this. I am right, aren't I?

Mrs. Linde. Yes, I'm sure—

Helmer. But knitting, now—that's an ugly business—can't help it. Look—arms all huddled up—great clumsy needles going up and down—I say that really was a magnificent champagne they served us.

Mrs. Linde. Well, good night, Nora. And stop being stubborn! Remember!

Helmer. Quite right, Mrs. Linde!

Mrs. Linde. Good night, Mr. Helmer.

Helmer (*accompanies her to the door*). Good night, good night! I hope you'll manage to get home all right? I'd gladly—but you haven't far to go, have you? Good night, good night.

[*She goes. He closes the door behind her and returns.*]

Helmer. Well, we've got rid of her at last. Dreadful bore that woman is!

Nora. Aren't you very tired, Torvald?

Helmer. No, not in the least.

Nora. Aren't you sleepy?

Helmer. Not a bit. On the contrary, I feel extraordinarily exhilarated. But what about you? Yes, you look very sleepy and tired.

Nora. Yes, I am very tired. Soon I shall sleep.

14 Interpreting

If you were playing the part of Nora, how would you read the line, "Oh, you're always right, whatever you do"—with barely suppressed anger, a desire to flatter, or an air of defeat, for example? (Answers will vary.)

> **aloof** (ə·lōōf′): cool and distant

15 Literary Element

Irony: Who is it that Helmer actually thinks about all the time? (himself) Do you think Nora is aware of the irony in her words? (probably, since she is beginning to feel imposed on)

16 Literary Element

Characterization: How do Helmer's words of greeting to Dr. Rank sum up his way of dealing with people? (Possible response: He is insincere and hides his true feelings.)

Helmer. You see, you see! How right I was not to let you stay longer!

14 **Nora.** Oh, you're always right, whatever you do.

Helmer (*kisses her on the forehead*). Now my little songbird's talking just like a real big human being. I say, did you notice how cheerful Rank was this evening?

Nora. Oh? Was he? I didn't have a chance to speak with him.

Helmer. I hardly did. But I haven't seen him in such a jolly mood for ages. (*looks at her for a moment, then comes closer*) I say, it's nice to get back to one's home again, and be all alone with you. Upon my word, you're a distractingly beautiful young woman.

Nora. Don't look at me like that, Torvald!

Helmer. What, not look at my most treasured possession? At all this wonderful beauty that's mine, mine alone, all mine.

Nora (*goes round to the other side of the table*). You mustn't talk to me like that tonight.

Helmer (*follows her*). You've still the tarantella in your blood, I see. And that makes you even more desirable. Listen! Now the other guests are beginning to go. (*more quietly*) Nora—soon the whole house will be absolutely quiet.

Nora. Yes, I hope so.

Helmer. Yes, my beloved Nora, of course you do! You know—when I'm out with you among other people like we were tonight, do you know why I say so little to you, why I keep so aloof from you, and just throw you an occasional glance? Do you know why I do that? It's because I pretend to myself that you're my secret mistress, my clandestine little sweetheart, and that nobody knows there's anything at all between us.

15 **Nora.** Oh, yes, yes, yes—I know you never think of anything but me.

Helmer. And then when we're about to go, and I wrap the shawl round your lovely young shoulders, over this wonderful curve of your neck—then I pretend to myself that you are my young bride, that we've just come from the wedding, that I'm taking you to my house for the first time—that, for the first time, I am alone with you—quite alone with you, as you stand there young and trembling and beautiful. All evening I've had no eyes for anyone but you. When I saw you dance the tarantella, like a huntress, a temptress, my blood grew hot, I couldn't stand it any longer! That was why I seized you and dragged you down here with me—

Nora. Leave me, Torvald! Get away from me! I don't want all this.

Helmer. What? Now, Nora, you're joking with me. Don't want, don't want—? Aren't I your husband?

[*There is a knock on the front door.*]

Nora (*starts*). What was that?

Helmer (*goes towards the hall*). Who is it?

Dr. Rank (*outside*). It's me. May I come in for a moment?

Helmer (*quietly, annoyed*). Oh, what does he want now? (*calls*) Wait a moment. (*walks over and opens the door*) Well! Nice of you not to go by without looking in. 16

Rank. I thought I heard your voice, so I felt I had to say goodbye. (*His eyes travel swiftly around the room.*) Ah, yes—these dear rooms, how well I know them. What a happy, peaceful home you two have.

Helmer. You seemed to be having a pretty happy time yourself upstairs.

Rank. Indeed I did. Why not? Why shouldn't one make the most of this world? As much as one can, and for as long as one can. The wine was excellent—

Helmer. Especially the champagne.

Rank. You noticed that, too? It's almost incredible how much I managed to get down.

Nora. Torvald drank a lot of champagne, too, this evening.

Rank. Oh?

Nora. Yes. It always makes him merry afterwards.

Rank. Well, why shouldn't a man have a merry evening after a well-spent day?

Helmer. Well-spent? Oh, I don't know that I can claim that.

Rank (*slaps him across the back*). I can, though, my dear fellow!

Nora. Yes, of course, Dr. Rank—you've been carrying out a scientific experiment to-day, haven't you?

Rank. Exactly.

Helmer. Scientific experiment! Those are big words for my little Nora to use!

Nora. And may I congratulate you on the finding?

Rank. You may indeed.

Nora. It was good then?

Rank. The best possible finding—both for the doctor and the patient. Certainty.

Nora (*quickly*). Certainty?

Rank. Absolute certainty. So aren't I enti-tled to have a merry evening after that?

Nora. Yes, Dr. Rank. You were quite right to.

Helmer. I agree. Provided you don't have to regret it tomorrow.

Rank. Well, you never get anything in this life without paying for it.

Nora. Dr. Rank—you like masquerades, don't you?

Rank. Yes, if the disguises are sufficiently amusing.

Nora. Tell me. What shall we two wear at the next masquerade?

Helmer. You little gadabout! Are you think-ing about the next one already?

Rank. We two? Yes, I'll tell you. You must go as the Spirit of Happiness—

Helmer. You try to think of a costume that'll convey that.

Rank. Your wife need only appear as her normal, everyday self—

Helmer. Quite right! Well said! But what are you going to be? Have you decided that?

Rank. Yes, my dear friend. I have decided that.

Helmer. Well?

Rank. At the next masquerade, I shall be invisible.

Helmer. Well, that's a funny idea.

Rank. There's a big, black hat—haven't you heard of the invisible hat? Once it's over your head, no one can see you any more.

Helmer (*represses a smile*). Ah yes, of course.

Rank. But I'm forgetting what I came for. Helmer, give me a cigar. One of your black Havanas.

Helmer. With the greatest pleasure. (*offers him the box*)

Rank (*takes one and cuts off the tip*). Thank you.

Nora (*strikes a match*). Let me give you a light.

Rank. Thank you. (*She holds out the match for him. He lights his cigar.*) And now—goodbye.

Helmer. Goodbye, my dear chap, goodbye.

Nora. Sleep well, Dr. Rank.

Rank. Thank you for that kind wish.

Nora. Wish me the same.

Rank. You? Very well—since you ask. Sleep well. And thank you for the light. (*He nods to them both and goes.*)

Helmer (*quietly*). He's been drinking too much.

Nora (*abstractedly*). Perhaps.

[HELMER *takes his bunch of keys from his pocket and goes out into the hall.*]

Nora. Torvald, what do you want out there?

MEETING INDIVIDUAL NEEDS

17 LEP: Help students under-stand that Dr. Rank and Nora are speaking indirectly (almost in a private code) because they share the secret of Dr. Rank's fatal illness. The "certainty" that Rank refers to is the sure knowledge of how much time he has left to live. ∎

18 LITERARY ELEMENT

Theme: How does Dr. Rank's appreciation for Nora differ from Helmer's? (Rank sees and loves Nora as she is; Helmer loves her as she appears in various roles and disguises.)

19 LITERARY ELEMENT

Staging: The appearance of light has had symbolic signifi-cance throughout the play. What might the light of the ci-gar signify? (Possible response: Dr. Rank's understanding and acceptance of his death)

20 ANALYZING

Dr. Rank leaves the Helmers to face his death courageously. What seems to have helped him accept his fate? (telling Nora of his love and simply loving her) What is on Nora's mind as he leaves? (She thinks death is near for her also.)

21 LITERARY ELEMENT

Characterization: What does Helmer's comment about Rank's suffering and loneliness providing a background for his and Nora's happiness reveal about him? (Possible response: He is grossly self-centered, insensitive to others, and deluded about the true nature of his marriage.)

22 PREDICTING

Helmer will soon have an actual opportunity to sacrifice himself to protect Nora from "some terrible danger." Do you think he will behave in accord with his romantic fantasy?

23 LITERARY ELEMENT

Climax: This is the moment that the play has been building up to—Helmer's encounter with reality. What is Nora trying to do? (run away and drown herself) What is she feeling? (terror and attachment to her marriage and children)

Helmer. I must empty the letter box. It's absolutely full. There'll be no room for the newspapers in the morning.

Nora. Are you going to work tonight?

Helmer. You know very well I'm not. Hullo, what's this? Someone's been at the lock.

Nora. At the lock—

Helmer. Yes, I'm sure of it. Who on earth—? Surely not one of the maids? Here's a broken hairpin. Nora, it's yours—

Nora (*quickly*). Then it must have been the children.

Helmer. Well, you'll have to break them of that habit. Hm, hm. Ah, that's done it. (*takes out the contents of the box and calls into the kitchen*) Helen! Helen! Put out the light on the staircase. (*comes back into the drawing room and closes the door to the hall*)

Helmer (*with the letters in his hand*). Look at this! You see how they've piled up? (*glances through them*) What on earth's this?

Nora (*at the window*). The letter! Oh no, Torvald, no!

Helmer. Two visiting cards—from Rank.

Nora. From Dr. Rank?

Helmer (*looks at them*). Peter Rank, M.D. They were on top. He must have dropped them in as he left.

Nora. Has he written anything on them?

Helmer. There's a black cross above his name. Rather gruesome, isn't it? It looks just as though he was announcing his death.

Nora. He is.

Helmer. What? Do you know something? Has he told you anything?

Nora. Yes. When these cards come, it means he's said goodbye to us. He wants to shut himself up in his house and die.

Helmer. Ah, poor fellow. I knew I wouldn't be seeing him for much longer. But so soon—! And now he's going to slink away and hide like a wounded beast.

Nora. When the time comes, it's best to go silently. Don't you think so, Torvald?

Helmer (*walks up and down*). He was so much a part of our life. I can't realize that he's gone. His suffering and loneliness seemed to provide a kind of dark background to the happy sunlight of our marriage. Well, perhaps it's best this way. For him, anyway. (*stops walking*) And perhaps for us too, Nora. Now we have only each other. (*embraces her*) Oh, my beloved wife—I feel as though I could never hold you close enough. Do you know, Nora, often I wish some terrible danger might threaten you, so that I could offer my life and my blood, everything, for your sake.

Nora (*tears herself loose and says in a clear, firm voice*). Read your letters now, Torvald.

Helmer. No, no. Not tonight. Tonight I want to be with you, my darling wife—

Nora. When your friend is about to die—?

Helmer. You're right. This news has upset us both. An ugliness has come between us; thoughts of death and dissolution. We must try to forget them. Until then—you go to your room; I shall go to mine.

Nora (*throws her arms round his neck*). Good night, Torvald! Good night!

Helmer (*kisses her on the forehead*). Good night, my darling little songbird. Sleep well, Nora. I'll go and read my letters.

[*He goes into the study with the letters in his hand, and closes the door.*]

Nora (*wild-eyed, fumbles around, seizes* HELMER's *cloak, throws it round herself and whispers quickly, hoarsely*). Never see him again. Never. Never. Never. (*throws the shawl over her head*) Never see the children again. Them, too. Never. Never. Oh—the icy black water! Oh—that bottomless—that—! Oh, if only it were all over! Now he's got it—he's reading it. Oh no, no! Not yet! Goodbye, Torvald! Goodbye, my darlings!

[*She turns to run into the hall. As she does so,* HELMER *throws open his door and stands there with an open letter in his hand.*]

Helmer. Nora!

Nora (*shrieks*). Ah—!

Helmer. What is this? Do you know what is in this letter?

Nora. Yes, I know. Let me go! Let me go!

Helmer (*holding her back*). Go? Where?

Nora (*tries to tear herself loose*). You mustn't try to save me, Torvald!

Helmer (*staggers back*). Is it true? Is it true, what he writes? Oh, my God! No, no—it's impossible, it can't be true!

The Granger Collection, New York

EDOUARD MANET, HENRI FANTIN-LATOUR (1836–1904).

Nora. It *is* true. I've loved you more than anything else in the world.

Helmer. Oh, don't try to make silly excuses.

Nora (*takes a step towards him*). Torvald—

Helmer. Wretched woman! What have you done?

Nora. Let me go! You're not going to suffer for my sake. I won't let you!

Helmer. Stop being theatrical. (*locks the front door*) You're going to stay here and explain yourself. Do you understand what you've done? Answer me! Do you understand?

Nora (*looks unflinchingly at him and, her expression growing colder, says*). Yes. Now I am beginning to understand.

Helmer (*walking round the room*). Oh, what a dreadful awakening! For eight whole years—she who was my joy and pride—a hypocrite, a liar—worse, worse—a criminal! Oh, the hideousness of it! Shame on you, shame!

[NORA *is silent and stares unblinkingly at him.*]

Helmer (*stops in front of her*). I ought to have guessed that something of this sort would happen. I should have foreseen it. All your father's recklessness and instability—be quiet!—I repeat, all your father's recklessness and instability he has handed on to you! No religion, no morals, no sense of duty! Oh, how I have been punished for closing my eyes to his faults! I did it for your sake. And now you reward me like this.

Nora. Yes. Like this.

Helmer. Now you have destroyed all my happiness. You have ruined my whole future. Oh, it's too dreadful to contemplate! I am in the power of a man who is completely without scruples. He can do what he likes with me, demand what he pleases, order me to do anything—I dare not disobey

24
25
26

24 ANALYZING
What is the cause of confusion in the dialogue in which Nora is trying to run away and Helmer is holding her back? (At first Nora believes that he is going to sacrifice himself to save her, and she wants to prevent this by sacrificing herself first. But he quickly blames her and considers himself the injured party.)

HUMANITIES CONNECTION

The painter Fantin-Latour is known for Impressionistic portraits. In *Edouard Manet,* Fantin-Latour uses strong lighting to emphasize key features—the skillful hands and deep probing eyes—of his friend Edouard Manet, the unconventional and influential French Impressionist.

? *Which of Torvald's characteristics is Ibsen emphasizing as Torvald reacts to Krogstad's letter?* (Possible responses: self-centeredness, authoritarian attitude, insensitivity) ■

25 LITERARY ELEMENT
Irony: What is ironic about Helmer's supposed awakening to the truth about his wife? (Possible response: He still does not understand her or see her clearly.) Who has had a sharper awakening? (Nora)

26 GUIDED READING
Identifying Cause and Effect: To what cause does Helmer attribute Nora's behavior? (her father's weak character, which he believes she has inherited)

27 **INTERPRETING**
What is Helmer's reaction to Nora's statement about being "gone from this world"? (He cares only about his good name and future prospects, not about her possible death.)

28 **LITERARY ELEMENT**
Stage Directions: What do the words "coldly calm" and the fact that Nora says so little while Helmer rants suggest about how Nora is reacting? (Possible response: She is observing him very carefully and growing increasingly angry.)

29 **GUIDED READING**
Identifying Details: What is Helmer's plan for managing the crisis? (He will try to buy off Krogstad; they will keep up the appearance of a happily married couple, but the children will be removed from Nora's care.)

30 **LITERARY ELEMENT**
Irony: What is ironic about Helmer's saying he knows Nora did it all for love after the I.O.U. is returned? (He did not even consider her motives when he thought he was ruined.)

him. I am condemned to humiliation and ruin simply for the weakness of a woman.

Nora. When I am gone from this world, you will be free.

Helmer. Oh, don't be melodramatic. Your father was always ready with that kind of remark. How would it help me if you were "gone from this world," as you put it? It wouldn't assist me in the slightest. He can still make all the facts public; and if he does, I may quite easily be suspected of having been an accomplice in your crime. People may think that I was behind it—that it was I who encouraged you! And for all this I have to thank you, you whom I have carried on my hands through all the years of our marriage! Now do you realize what you've done to me?

Nora (*coldly calm*). Yes.

Helmer. It's so unbelievable I can hardly credit it. But we must try to find some way out. Take off that shawl. Take it off, I say! I must try to buy him off somehow. This thing must be hushed up at any price. As regards our relationship—we must appear to be living together just as before. Only *appear*, of course. You will therefore continue to reside here. That is understood. But the children shall be taken out of your hands. I dare no longer entrust them to you. Oh, to have to say this to the woman I once loved so dearly—and whom I still—! Well, all that must be finished. Henceforth there can be no question of happiness, we must merely strive to save what shreds and tatters—

[*The front door bell rings.* HELMER *starts.*]

Helmer. What can that be? At this hour? Surely not—? He wouldn't—? Hide yourself, Nora. Say you're ill.

[NORA *does not move.* HELMER *goes to the door of the room and opens it. The* MAID *is standing half-dressed in the hall.*]

Maid. A letter for madam.

Helmer. Give it me. (*seizes the letter and shuts the door*) Yes, it's from him. You're not having it. I'll read this myself.

Nora. Read it.

Helmer (*by the lamp*). I hardly dare to. This may mean the end for us both. No. I must know. (*tears open the letter hastily; reads a few lines; looks at a piece of paper which is enclosed with it; utters a cry of joy*) Nora! (*She looks at him questioningly.*) Nora! No—I must read it once more. Yes, yes, it's true! I am saved! Nora, I am saved!

Nora. What about me?

Helmer. You too, of course. We're both saved, you and I. Look! He's returning your I.O.U. He writes that he is sorry for what has happened—a happy accident has changed his life—oh, what does it matter what he writes? We are saved, Nora! No one can harm you now. Oh, Nora, Nora—no, first let me destroy this filthy thing. Let me see—! (*glances at the I.O.U.*) No, I don't want to look at it. I shall merely regard the whole business as a dream. (*He tears the I.O.U. and both letters into pieces, throws them into the stove and watches them burn.*) There. Now they're destroyed. He wrote that ever since Christmas Eve you've been—oh, these must have been three dreadful days for you, Nora.

Nora. Yes. It's been a hard fight.

Helmer. It must have been terrible—seeing no way out except—no, we'll forget the whole sordid business. We'll just be happy and go on telling ourselves over and over again: "It's over! It's over!" Listen to me, Nora. You don't seem to realize. It's over! Why are you looking so pale? Ah, my poor little Nora, I understand. You can't believe that I have forgiven you. But I have, Nora. I swear it to you. I have forgiven you everything. I know that what you did you did for your love of me.

Nora. That is true.

Helmer. You have loved me as a wife

30

Do you think Nora deserves Torvald's forgiveness? How would you describe Torvald's feelings for his wife?

Billy Rose Theatre Collection, New York Public Library for the Performing Arts

should love her husband. It was simply that in your inexperience you chose the wrong means. But do you think I love you any the less because you don't know how to act on your own initiative? No, no. Just lean on me. I shall counsel you. I shall guide you. I would not be a true man if your feminine helplessness did not make you doubly attractive in my eyes. You mustn't mind the hard words I said to you in those first dreadful moments when my whole world

seemed to be tumbling about my ears. I have forgiven you, Nora. I swear it to you; I have forgiven you.

Nora. Thank you for your forgiveness. (*She goes out through the door, right.*) ⌉ 31

Helmer. No, don't go—(*looks in*) What are you doing there?

Nora (*offstage*). Taking off my fancy dress. ⌉ 32

Helmer (*by the open door*). Yes, do that. Try to calm yourself and get your balance again, my frightened little songbird. Don't be afraid. I have broad wings to shield you. (*begins to walk around near the door*) How lovely and peaceful this little home of ours is, Nora. You are safe here; I shall watch over you like a hunted dove which I have snatched unharmed from the claws of the falcon. Your wildly beating little heart shall find peace with me. It will happen, Nora; it will take time; but it will happen, believe me. Tomorrow all this will seem quite different. Soon everything will be as it was before. I shall no longer need to remind you that I have forgiven you; your own heart will tell you that it is true. Do you really think I could ever bring myself to disown you, or even to reproach you? Ah, Nora, you don't understand what goes on in a husband's heart. There is something indescribably wonderful and satisfying for a husband in knowing that he has forgiven his wife—forgiven her unreservedly, from the bottom of his heart. It means that she has become his property in a double sense; he has, as it were, brought her into the world anew; she is now not only his wife but also his child. From now on that is what you shall be to me, my poor, helpless, bewildered little creature. Never be frightened of anything again, Nora. Just open your heart to me. I shall be both your will and your conscience. What's this? Not in bed? Have you changed?

Nora (*in her everyday dress*). Yes, Torvald. I've changed. ⌉ 33

Helmer. But why now—so late—?

Nora. I shall not sleep tonight.

Helmer. But, my dear Nora—

Nora (*looks at her watch*). It isn't that late. Sit down there, Torvald. You and I have a lot to talk about.

[*She sits down on one side of the table.*]

Helmer. Nora, what does this mean? You look quite drawn—

Nora. Sit down. It's going to take a long time. I've a lot to say to you.

Helmer (*sits down on the other side of the table*). You alarm me, Nora. I don't understand you.

Nora. No, that's just it. You don't understand me. And I've never understood you— until this evening. No, don't interrupt me. Just listen to what I have to say. You and I have got to face facts, Torvald.

Helmer. What do you mean by that?

Nora (*after a short silence*). Doesn't anything strike you about the way we're sitting here?

Helmer. What?

Nora. We've been married for eight years. Does it occur to you that this is the first time we two, you and I, man and wife, have ever had a serious talk together?

Helmer. Serious? What do you mean, serious?

Nora. In eight whole years—no, longer— ever since we first met—we have never exchanged a serious word on a serious subject.

Helmer. Did you expect me to drag you into all my worries—worries you couldn't possibly have helped me with?

Nora. I'm not talking about worries. I'm simply saying that we have never sat down seriously to try to get to the bottom of anything.

Helmer. But, my dear Nora, what on earth has that got to do with you?

Nora. That's just the point. You have never understood me. A great wrong has been done to me, Torvald. First by Papa, and then by you.

Helmer. What? But we two have loved you more than anyone in the world!

Nora (*shakes her head*). You have never loved me. You just thought it was fun to be in love with me.

Helmer. Nora, what kind of a way is this to talk?

Nora. It's the truth, Torvald. When I lived with Papa, he used to tell me what he thought about everything, so that I never had any opinions but his. And if I did have any of my own, I kept them quiet, because he wouldn't have liked them. He called me his little doll, and he played with me just the way I played with my dolls. Then I came here to live in your house—

Helmer. What kind of a way is that to describe our marriage?

Nora (*undisturbed*). I mean, then I passed from Papa's hands into yours. You arranged everything the way you wanted it, so that I simply took over your taste in everything— or pretended I did—I don't really know—I think it was a little of both—first one and then the other. Now I look back on it, it's as if I've been living here like a pauper, from hand to mouth. I performed tricks for you, and you gave me food and drink. But that was how you wanted it. You and Papa have done me a great wrong. It's your fault that I have done nothing with my life.

Helmer. Nora, how can you be so unreasonable and ungrateful? Haven't you been happy here?

Nora. No; never. I used to think I was. But I haven't ever been happy.

Helmer. Not—not happy?

Nora. No. I've just had fun. You've always been very kind to me. But our home has never been anything but a playroom. I've been your doll-wife, just as I used to be

Papa's doll-child. And the children have been my dolls. I used to think it was fun when you came in and played with me, just as they think it's fun when I go in and play games with them. That's all our marriage has been, Torvald.

Helmer. There may be a little truth in what you say, though you exaggerate and romanticize. But from now on it'll be different. Playtime is over. Now the time has come for education.

Nora. Whose education? Mine or the children's?

Helmer. Both yours and the children's, my dearest Nora.

Nora. Oh, Torvald, you're not the man to educate me into being the right wife for you.

Helmer. How can you say that?

Nora. And what about me? Am I fit to educate the children?

Helmer. Nora!

Nora. Didn't you say yourself a few minutes ago that you dare not leave them in my charge?

Helmer. In a moment of excitement. Surely you don't think I meant it seriously?

Nora. Yes. You were perfectly right. I'm not fitted to educate them. There's something else I must do first. I must educate myself. And you can't help me with that. It's something I must do by myself. That's why I'm leaving you.

Helmer (*jumps up*). What did you say?

Nora. I must stand on my own feet if I am to find out the truth about myself and about life. So I can't go on living here with you any longer.

Helmer. Nora, Nora!

Nora. I'm leaving you now, at once. Christine will put me up for tonight—

Helmer. You're out of your mind! You can't do this! I forbid you!

Nora. It's no use your trying to forbid me any more. I shall take with me nothing but what is mine. I don't want anything from you, now or ever.

Helmer. What kind of madness is this?

Nora. Tomorrow I shall go home—I mean, to where I was born. It'll be easiest for me to find some kind of a job there.

Helmer. But you're blind! You've no experience of the world—

Nora. I must try to get some, Torvald.

Helmer. But to leave your home, your husband, your children! Have you thought what people will say?

Nora. I can't help that. I only know that I must do this.

Helmer. But this is monstrous! Can you neglect your most sacred duties?

Nora. What do you call my most sacred duties?

Helmer. Do I have to tell you? Your duties towards your husband, and your children.

Nora. I have another duty which is equally sacred.

Helmer. You have not. What on earth could that be?

Nora. My duty towards myself.

Helmer. First and foremost you are a wife and mother.

Nora. I don't believe that any longer. I believe that I am first and foremost a human being, like you—or anyway, that I must try to become one. I know most people think as you do, Torvald, and I know there's something of the sort to be found in books. But I'm no longer prepared to accept what people say and what's written in books. I must think things out for myself, and try to find my own answer.

Helmer. Do you need to ask where your duty lies in your own home? Haven't you an <u>infallible</u> guide in such matters—your religion?

Nora. Oh, Torvald, I don't really know what religion means.

37 INTERPRETING
Does Helmer understand what Nora is saying to him? How do you know? (Possible response: No; he thinks the solution is for him to educate her, which is how he always saw his role.)

38 LITERARY ELEMENT
Resolution: How has Nora decided to solve the problems of her marriage, her children, and herself? (She is leaving to find out the truth about herself and about life.)

39 ANALYZING
What basic conflict of values separates Nora and her husband in their final dialogue? (She believes a person's first duty is to himself or herself. He believes a woman's first duty is to her husband and family.)

 infallible (in·fal′ə·bəl): incapable of error; sure

Helmer. What are you saying?

40 **Nora.** I only know what Pastor Hansen told me when I went to confirmation. He explained that religion meant this and that. When I get away from all this and can think things out on my own, that's one of the questions I want to look into. I want to find out whether what Pastor Hansen said was right—or anyway, whether it is right for me.

Helmer. But it's unheard of for so young a woman to behave like this! If religion cannot guide you, let me at least appeal to your conscience. I presume you have some moral feelings left? Or—perhaps you haven't? Well, answer me.

Nora. Oh, Torvald, that isn't an easy question to answer. I simply don't know. I don't know where I am in these matters. I only know that these things mean something quite different to me from what they do to you. I've learned now that certain laws are different from what I'd imagined them to be; but I can't accept that such laws can be right. Has a woman really not the right to spare her dying father pain, or save her husband's life? I can't believe that.

Helmer. You're talking like a child. You don't understand how society works.

Nora. No, I don't. But now I intend to learn. I must try to satisfy myself which is right, society or I.

Helmer. Nora, you're ill. You're feverish. I almost believe you're out of your mind.

Nora. I've never felt so sane and sure in my life.

Helmer. You feel sure that it is right to leave your husband and your children?

Nora. Yes, I do.

Helmer. Then there is only one possible explanation.

Nora. What?

Helmer. That you don't love me any longer.

Nora. No, that's exactly it.

Helmer. Nora! How can you say this to me?

Nora. Oh, Torvald, it hurts me terribly to have to say it, because you've always been so kind to me. But I can't help it. I don't love you any longer.

Helmer (*controlling his emotions with difficulty*). And you feel quite sure about this, too?

Nora. Yes, absolutely sure. That's why I can't go on living here any longer.

Helmer. Can you also explain why I have lost your love?

Nora. Yes, I can. It happened this evening, when the miracle failed to happen. It was then that I realized you weren't the man I'd thought you to be.

Helmer. Explain more clearly. I don't understand you.

Nora. I've waited so patiently, for eight whole years—well, good heavens, I'm not such a fool as to suppose that miracles occur every day. Then this dreadful thing happened to me, and then I *knew:* "Now the miracle will take place!" When Krogstad's letter was lying out there, it never occurred to me for a moment that you would let that man trample over you. I *knew* that you would say to him: "Publish the facts to the world!" And when he had done this—

Helmer. Yes, what then? When I'd exposed my wife's name to shame and scandal—

Nora. Then I was certain that you would step forward and take all the blame on yourself, and say: "I am the one who is guilty!" **41**

Helmer. Nora!

Nora. You're thinking I wouldn't have accepted such a sacrifice from you? No, of course I wouldn't! But what would my word have counted for against yours? That was the miracle I was hoping for, and dreading. And it was to prevent it happening that I wanted to end my life.

Helmer. Nora, I would gladly work for you

READING CHECK

1. On what day of the year does the play begin? (Christmas Eve)
2. Why does Mrs. Linde visit Nora? (She has recently moved to town and she needs help finding a job.)
3. Why did Nora take out a loan? (to finance a trip to save Helmer's life)
4. Who gave Nora the loan? (Krogstad)
5. What is Krogstad afraid of losing? (his job at the bank)

6. What important secret does Nora keep from Helmer? (the loan)
7. What are Dr. Rank's two secrets? (He is in love with Nora and about to die.)
8. What does Krogstad threaten Nora with? (exposing her crime of forgery)
9. Why does Krogstad return the I.O.U.? (a change of heart due to Mrs. Linde)
10. Why does Nora leave at the end? (to discover the truth about life and herself)

RETEACHING

Have students rotate roles and perform scenes from the play. As students rehearse their parts, encourage them to become the characters they are playing by acquiring the voices, postures, gestures, and attitudes that Ibsen suggests through the dialogue and stage directions in the play. Remind students that Ibsen wanted his characters to be portrayed in a realistic manner.

night and day, and endure sorrow and hardship for your sake. But no man can be expected to sacrifice his honor, even for the person he loves.

Nora. Millions of women have done it.

Helmer. Oh, you think and talk like a stupid child.

Nora. That may be. But you neither think nor talk like the man I could share my life with. Once you'd got over your fright—and you weren't frightened of what might threaten me, but only of what threatened you—once the danger was past, then as far as you were concerned it was exactly as though nothing had happened. I was your little songbird just as before—your doll whom henceforth you would take particular care to protect from the world because she was so weak and fragile. (*gets up*) Torvald, in that moment I realized that for eight years I had been living here with a complete stranger, and had borne him three children—! Oh, I can't bear to think of it! I could tear myself to pieces!

42 LITERARY ELEMENT

Theme: How has the theme of Nora as a child developed in the course of the play? (Helmer still views her as a child, but now she has become a "stupid," wayward child in his eyes rather than a delightful one as before.)

HUMANITIES CONNECTION

Norwegian artist Edvard Munch, an Expressionist, focused not on the external world but on the inner workings of the human mind.

? *What might the woman's posture and surroundings suggest about her mental state?* (She may be depressed or feel imprisoned.) ∎

Ernest Wadsworth Longfellow Fund, Courtesy of Museum of Fine Arts, Boston

SUMMER NIGHT'S DREAM (THE VOICE), EDVARD MUNCH, 1893.

? *Do you think that Nora has succeeded in finding her voice, that is, her independence?*

1. Comparing Different Productions.
Both Claire Bloom and Jane Fonda played Nora in 1973 films of *A Doll's House*. Have students watch a videotape of either or any other filmed version, and compare their interpretations of the characters and themes with the director's and actors' interpretations in the film. What elements invite varying interpretations? What elements are central to the play's meaning?

2. Reacting to a Quote. The scholar and critic Eric Bentley said that Ibsen's characters "typify a civilization and an epoch." Have students write a one-page paper agreeing or disagreeing with Bentley's opinion. Tell them to use quotes from the play and their own experiences to support their views. Ask students to share papers in a small group to get feedback on the strengths and weaknesses of their arguments.

CLOSURE

Ask students to discuss why the title of the play is appropriate. How does the title call attention to the play's theme? How does it highlight the development of the characters in the play? Can you think of another title that would also express the meaning of the play? ■

---

43 READER'S RESPONSE

Do you believe that Helmer has the strength (or the will) to change? Would he be more likely to do so if Nora were to go or stay?

44 COMPARING AND CONTRASTING

In what ways have Nora and Torvald switched roles in their final dialogue? (Torvald is begging her to wait until tomorrow as she once begged him to wait to open Krogstad's letter. In general, she is now making the decisions and educating him on her views of marriage.)

45 SPECULATING

What do you think Nora means by saying about her children, "As I am now, I can be nothing to them"? (Possible response: She knows so little about life or herself that she cannot help them.) How do you think the children might feel about her departure? (Possible response: totally unable to understand why she left them)

46 LITERARY ELEMENT

Sound Effects: Tell students that the final sound of Nora slamming the door is one of the most famous sound effects in theater history. Have them discuss why it is so effective.

Helmer (*sadly*). I see it, I see it. A gulf has indeed opened between us. Oh, but Nora—couldn't it be bridged?

Nora. As I am now, I am no wife for you.

43 **Helmer.** I have the strength to change.

Nora. Perhaps—if your doll is taken from you.

Helmer. But to be parted—to be parted from you! No, no, Nora. I can't conceive of it happening!

Nora (*goes into the room, right*). All the more necessary that it should happen.

[*She comes back with her outdoor things and a small traveling bag, which she puts down on a chair by the table.*]

44 **Helmer.** Nora, Nora, not now! Wait till tomorrow!

Nora (*puts on her coat*). I can't spend the night in a strange man's house.

Helmer. But can't we live here as brother and sister, then—?

Nora (*fastens her hat*). You know quite well it wouldn't last. (*puts on her shawl*) Goodbye, Torvald. I don't want to see the children. I know they're in better hands than mine. As I am now, I can be nothing to them.

45 **Helmer.** But some time, Nora—some time—?

Nora. How can I tell? I've no idea what will happen to me.

Helmer. But you are my wife, both as you are and as you will be.

Nora. Listen, Torvald. When a wife leaves her husband's house, as I'm doing now, I'm told that according to the law he is freed of any obligations towards her. In any case, I release you from any such obligations. You mustn't feel bound to me in any way however small, just as I shall not feel bound to you. We must both be quite free. Here is your ring back. Give me mine.

Helmer. That too?

Nora. That too.

Helmer. Here it is.

Nora. Good. Well, now it's over. I'll leave the keys here. The servants know about everything to do with the house—much better than I do. Tomorrow, when I have left town, Christine will come to pack the things I brought here from home. I'll have them sent on after me.

Helmer. This is the end, then! Nora, will you never think of me any more?

Nora. Yes, of course. I shall often think of you and the children and this house.

Helmer. May I write to you, Nora?

Nora. No. Never. You mustn't do that.

Helmer. But at least you must let me send you—

Nora. Nothing. Nothing.

Helmer. But if you should need help—?

Nora. I tell you, no. I don't accept things from strangers.

Helmer. Nora—can I never be anything but a stranger to you?

Nora (*picks up her bag*). Oh, Torvald! Then the miracle of miracles would have to happen.

Helmer. The miracle of miracles!

Nora. You and I would both have to change so much that—oh, Torvald, I don't believe in miracles any longer.

Helmer. But I want to believe in them. Tell me. We should have to change so much that—!

Nora. That life together between us two could become a marriage. Goodbye.

[*She goes out through the hall.*]

Helmer (*sinks down on a chair by the door and buries his face in his hands*). Nora! Nora! (*looks round and gets up*) Empty! She's gone! (*a hope strikes him*) The miracle of miracles—?

[*The street door is slammed shut downstairs.*] 46

First Thoughts

Do you think that Nora made the right decision? Will a reconciliation between Nora and Torvald be possible in the future?

Identifying Facts

1. What agreement do Mrs. Linde and Krogstad come to that makes them both happy? How does their agreement affect the Helmers?
2. What message does Dr. Rank convey by leaving a calling card with a black cross written on it?
3. What do the first and second letters from Krogstad say? How does Torvald react to each letter?
4. What major action does Nora take at the end of Act 3? What are her plans as the play closes? What violent alternative had she been considering while Torvald was reading the first letter?

Interpreting Meanings

1. Mrs. Linde could stop Krogstad's letter from reaching Torvald, but she decides that Torvald should know the truth about Nora's actions. What is her motive? Do you approve or disapprove of her decision?
2. A **metaphor** is a figure of speech that compares one thing to another without using the words *like* or *as*. When a metaphor is developed over several lines, it is called an **extended metaphor**. Ibsen creates an extended metaphor in Act 3—the "doll's house"—which gives the play its title. What does this metaphor suggest about Nora's relationships with her father, husband, and children?
3. Torvald and Nora have very different ideas about what is moral and just. What do their opinions about the forged note reveal about their attitudes toward law and society?

4. Why does Nora call her husband "a strange man"? Do you think she is justified in using that term? Why or why not?
5. In Act 2, Nora hopes that a "miracle" will take place. Near the end of Act 3, she tells Torvald that in order for their marriage to be restored, "the miracle of miracles" will have to take place. What does Nora mean by "the miracle of miracles"? How does it differ from the miracle she hoped for earlier?
6. Briefly summarize Nora's reasons for leaving Torvald. What has Nora gained that might make up for the loss of her marriage and her children?

Applying Meanings

Act 3 ends with the sound of the front door slamming as Nora leaves her husband. Some critics have said that the echo of that slamming door is still sounding in our world today. Explain the comment, and state whether you agree or disagree, and why.

Creative Writing Response

1. **Writing a Fourth Act.** Write a brief Act 4 for *A Doll's House,* showing what happens to Nora and Torvald after the breakup of their marriage. In order to explain what is happening to Torvald in his household and what is happening to Nora elsewhere, you may need to convey some information through dialogue about absent characters. You may use the same set used for the first three acts, or create an entirely different one. Use any characters from Ibsen's play, or, if you wish, create new characters.
2. **Analyzing a Character.** You are an actress preparing to play the role of Nora. Write a page of notes about her character to help you portray Nora effectively. Consider some or all of the following points: What are Nora's thoughts and

Applying Meanings
Students should support their opinions with concrete examples from their own lives and the world around them.

Creative Writing Response
1. Writing a Fourth Act. Students should dramatize how the two main characters react to their new circumstances by means of dialogue and stage directions.

2. Analyzing a Character. Students' notes should contain careful and detailed analyses of Ibsen's development of Nora's personality.

Critical Writing Response
1. Interpreting a Passage. Students should support their interpretations with quotes from the play and examples from their own experiences and observations.

2. Identifying Theme. Essays should contain clearly stated themes and should use quotes from the play as well as descriptions of specific scenes that develop the themes. Students' opinions should be supported by specific examples from their own lives. ■

feelings at the beginning of the play? How do they change by the end? How are the things she says sometimes different from her inner thoughts and feelings? When other characters are speaking and Nora is onstage, how does she react? Include specific lines of dialogue, and describe what tone of voice, gestures, or bits of stage business you would use in order to bring out the characterization in each passage.

Critical Writing Response
1. Interpreting a Passage. In Act 3, we find the following exchange between Torvald and Nora:

Helmer. Nora, I would gladly work for you night and day, and endure sorrow and hardship for your sake. But no man can be expected to sacrifice his honor, even for the person he loves.

Nora. Millions of women have done it.

In two or more paragraphs, give your interpretation of this passage. Begin by **paraphrasing** it—restating its meaning in your own words. Then, to focus your interpretation, consider some or all of

the following questions: What are Torvald and Nora saying about the differences between men and women? What does Torvald mean by "honor"? What does Nora mean by it? How, in Nora's view, have millions of women sacrificed their honor for love?

To what extent do you agree or disagree with the statements in the passage? What is your view of honor, and of whether people should sacrifice it for love? Do you feel that men and women today have essentially different views of love and honor?

2. Identifying Theme. **Theme** is the central idea or insight in a work of literature. A statement of theme is not a plot summary; nor does it mention specific events or characters. In one sentence, state the theme of *A Doll's House*. In a two- to three-paragraph essay, provide evidence from the play that supports your theme statement. Finally, state whether or not you agree with the theme, and explain the reason for your opinion.

A CRITICAL COMMENT

The Realistic Stage

Although the literature of the nineteenth century held up a mirror to society as it really was, it was not until Ibsen that theater began to reflect the world in a similar way. Before Ibsen, nineteenth-century audiences went to the theater to see spectacle and romance. Theatergoers expected sensational and contrived stories of lost heirs and love affairs, not realistic or truthful depictions of everyday life. Ibsen, and later playwrights such as Anton Chekhov, George Bernard Shaw, and August Strindberg, dramatically altered the theater experience by making the stage an extension of real life. In their plays, these playwrights concentrated on the kinds of conflicts experienced by people in real life.

Ibsen was one of the first playwrights to make an audience forget that what it was watching was imaginary, not real. He treated the stage as if it were a room in which real events were actually taking place. For the audience, it was as though the "fourth wall" of the room had been removed. In order to create a realistic "room," the whole look of the stage changed. Suddenly every detail was important: the set had to look like an actual place, such as a sitting room or a front porch; lighting was used to indicate different times of day both to suggest mood and to create special effects. The way actors moved on stage was intended to look real, not affected or posed.

Finally, the language of the stage had to change to accommodate Realism. A master of dramatic technique, Ibsen developed a style that revealed the inner conflicts of his characters. His dialogue sounds like colloquial speech spoken by real, believable people. Depths of characterization are frequently revealed in an offhand statement or gesture, such as when Torvald pats Nora on the head, calling her his "precious little songbird" at the end of Act 1 of *A Doll's House.* Ibsen was also one of the first playwrights to incorporate elaborate stage directions that would help the actors convey a certain feeling to the audience. He wrote detailed descriptions of the settings and added directions to the script ("a little embarrassed," "laughing," and so on) to indicate how lines should be delivered. Stage directions of this kind were virtually nonexistent in earlier drama, but they have become standard in contemporary Western plays.

LITERARY BACKGROUND

Gothic Elements: The Gothic influence is also apparent in some nineteenth-century Romantic poetry. It can be seen in Coleridge's terrifying medieval poem "Christabel," in Byron's recurrent hero-villain, in the Shelleys' inclinations toward the macabre, and in poems by Edgar Allan Poe, such as "Annabel Lee."

1 HISTORICAL BACKGROUND

Architecture: Horace Walpole (1717–1797) converted his farm at Twickenham into what he called "a little Gothic castle," and for forty years, added architectural detail, armor, and stained glass purchased from European chapels and cathedrals. Because of his influential social position, Walpole's home was the inspiration for many other country houses.

■ HUMANITIES CONNECTION

? *Which elements in* The Vale of Rest *evoke a distant time period?* (the people's clothing and tools) *Which elements create the sinister undertones characteristic of the Gothic style?* (the people's uneasy expressions and the heavy shadows) ■

LANGUAGE
—AND—
CULTURE

THE GOTHIC NOVEL

Imagine a woman in white fleeing from a shadowy castle on the mist-ridden moors on a moonless night. . . . If this image is familiar, you have likely seen or read a popular kind of historical/supernatural novel available in most bookstores. These works belong to a genre called the **Gothic novel**. Though Gothic fiction is very much a part of contemporary literature, its history is a long one. The Gothic novel first became popular during the mid-eighteenth century in England. Unlike people of previous times, members of eighteenth-century English society, especially women, had new-found leisure time and literacy skills to read fiction.

Gothic novels were an unusual literary form because, unlike other novels of this time, their emphasis was on the arousal of terror in both the heroine and the reader—perhaps an unexpectedly lowbrow form of entertainment in a society that considered itself educated and sophisticated. Yet for all their entertainment value, Gothic novels addressed important social concerns, especially those pertaining to women. It is not surprising, then, that Gothic fiction became a special province of women readers and writers.

Nevertheless, the first Gothic novel was written by a man, Horace Walpole, whose *Castle of Otranto* was published in 1764. This work introduced the components that were to become standard in the Gothic genre: a haunted castle; an innocent woman

1

THE VALE OF REST, SIR JOHN EVERETT MILLAIS, 1858–1859. *This painting reflects the Gothic atmosphere that was popular in English art and literature in the nineteenth century.*

The Granger Collection, New York

whose virtue is powerless against a lecherous villain; and a daughter who must rebel against the authority of her father.

Many early Gothic novels, such as Ann Radcliffe's *The Mysteries of Udolpho* (1794), are set in a different historical time, usually in a medieval, southern European, Roman Catholic country. Some critics think that this sense of distance from the writers' own time allowed them to use the novels to make subtle comments on certain social concerns, particularly women's issues. For example, by describing the threats made against a virtuous woman by the villain, writers may have been highlighting the moral, psychological, and legal dependence and vulnerability of women. Also, by representing a woman who acts on her own will in defiance of her father, Gothic writers may have been commenting on the need for women to have a way to voice their concerns.

Gothic novels often employed lurid and sensational plots and narrative styles, and were therefore not always taken seriously by critics and other writers. Even critics who found elements of Gothics praiseworthy easily dismissed the genre in general as light reading. Jane Austen, an important English woman writer of the late eighteenth century, used Gothic devices in her novel *Northanger Abbey* to show the foolishness of interpreting Gothic situations too literally. Yet this did not prevent other important writers from incorporating Gothic images and scenarios into their novels: Mary Shelley's *Frankenstein,* Charlotte Brontë's *Jane Eyre,* and Emily Brontë's *Wuthering Heights* are all examples of the strong influence of the Gothic on the nineteenth-century imagination.

Tate Gallery, London/Art Resource, New York

Illustration by Lady Edna Clark Hall (1879–1979) for *Wuthering Heights*.

By the mid-nineteenth century, the Gothic form had been thoroughly exhausted. Despite this, the legacy of the Gothic novel is discernible in popular entertainment today. For example, elements of Gothic terror, such as the haunted house, have been modified in television programs such as *Dark Shadows* and countless horror films. The Gothic novel also introduced the notion of writing for the sake of arousing terror in the reader. Thus, the Gothic novel is a precursor to modern novels such as Daphne du Maurier's *Rebecca* and *The House on the Strand* and Shirley Jackson's *The Haunting of Hill House,* and to the more graphically violent suspense fiction of Stephen King and horror films such as *Halloween* and *A Nightmare on Elm Street.* Ultimately, the kind of Gothic influences that survive today demonstrate perhaps just how much readers and audiences enjoy entertainments that terrify them.

2 LITERARY BACKGROUND

Women's Concerns: This new genre allowed women to become key players in a literary marketplace previously dominated by men. Not everyone was pleased by this turn of events: in 1855, Nathaniel Hawthorne reacted to this shift in authorship by complaining about that "damned mob of scribbling women." *Do you think novels written by men are different from those written by women? Explain your response.* (Answers will vary.)

3 CULTURAL DIVERSITY

Gothic stories seek to shock and horrify their readers. Such stories were—and still are—very popular in a number of different cultures.

❓ *What function do you think Gothic stories serve for people of all cultures?* (Students might suggest that these stories allow people a harmless and socially acceptable way to participate in frightening events. Such escapist literature also affords people momentary respite from their daily cares.)

HUMANITIES CONNECTION

Emily Brontë's *Wuthering Heights* (1847) has strong Gothic overtones.

❓ *Do you agree with readers who feel that highly imaginative works, like Gothic horror tales, should not be illustrated because they force the reader to imagine characters and events in a specific way? Explain.* ■

You've probably heard someone, after a long argument, say, "But *that's* the whole point!" If you weren't sure exactly what *that* meant, you were experiencing the effects of unclear pronoun reference. Avoiding reference problems helps you to maintain coherence in your writing and your thinking.

Clear Pronoun Reference

Make each pronoun refer unmistakably to its antecedent. A **pronoun**—a word that stands for a noun or another pronoun— can refer to a word, a phrase, or a whole clause. The words referred to are the **antecedents.** Sometimes a pronoun seems to refer to more than one antecedent. To repair this ambiguous reference, reword your sentence.

AMBIGUOUS
Faust sells his soul to the devil in exchange for knowledge of magical arts. *This* is the start of Faust's undoing.

CLEAR
Faust sells his soul to the devil in exchange for knowledge of magical arts. *This exchange* is the start of Faust's undoing.

In the first example, *this* could refer either to Faust's selling of his soul or to the knowledge of magical arts. In the second example, rewording has made the idea clear.

Exercise 1: Correcting Ambiguous Pronoun Reference

Number a paper from 1 to 10 and reword any of the following sentences in which pronoun reference is ambiguous. Mark a *C* by the number of any sentence with no pronoun reference problems.

1. The friendship between Verlaine and Rimbaud caused him trouble for much of his life.
2. Noticing three towering old pine trees and several younger ones, Pushkin realizes that he will not live to see them grow tall.
3. Pushkin knows that his grandson may someday see the pines. Then will he think of him?
4. Because he took him under his wing, Heine's mother was fond of his rich uncle Salomon.
5. The speaker in "The Lorelei" sees an alluring river goddess and falls in love with her. She enchants him and he drowns.
6. Baudelaire had great talents offset by crippling mental problems. He wrote about them beautifully.
7. Ibsen's plays dealt with controversial topics. They are less controversial today.
8. In a short story about jewels, Maupassant demonstrates his mastery of sus-

pense and irony. They bring pleasure but not happiness.

9. Tolstoy was a reformer who embraced pacifist ideas. These later influenced Mahatma Gandhi and Martin Luther King, Jr.

10. In *A Doll's House,* Ibsen explores the effects of possessiveness and immaturity in human relationships. He illustrates them in the interplay between Nora and her husband.

Vague Pronoun Reference

In some sentences, pronouns do not refer clearly to anything. To correct vague pronoun reference in your writing, first clarify your ideas. Then reword your sentences.

VAGUE

Verlaine gazes at a palm against the sky, listens to tranquil sounds coming from outdoors, and laments his lost youth. *This* creates the poem's impact.

CLEAR

Verlaine gazes at a palm against the sky, listens to tranquil sounds coming from outdoors, and laments his lost youth.

The contrast between low-key imagery and devastating regret creates the poem's impact.

In the first example, the italicized pronoun does not refer to anything specific. In the second example, the writer has thought the idea through more completely. The clearer thought permits clearer writing.

Exercise 2: Revising for Clear Pronoun Reference

Reread a composition you have written, underlining each pronoun you have used. Then do the following:

1. Locate the antecedent of each pronoun. Remember that an antecedent can be a word, a phrase, or a clause. Draw an arrow from the pronoun to the antecedent.

2. If you find an ambiguous pronoun reference, decide what the pronoun was meant to refer to. Then reword the sentence for coherence and clarity.

3. If you find a vague pronoun reference, think your ideas through more carefully. Then rewrite the passage, explaining in more detail what you mean.

Background: Lead a discussion in which students identify their favorite and least favorite works from the unit. Encourage a broad range of responses, and elicit reasons for each. As students discuss their reasons for liking or disliking a work, direct their attention to the implied criteria that underlie their reasons. For example, a student who finds a poem "boring" because of "all the silly, overblown ideas" may be expressing a preference for understated diction or for more realistic themes; you might ask which. By supplying more specific terminology, you can help students pinpoint the standards implicit in their responses.

Explain that a literary review includes not only the writer's opinion of a literary work, but also his or her analysis of the various elements that make up the work. Answering the questions in the *Background* and *Prewriting* sections will give students an idea of the range of literary elements. It will also help them to see ways in which the author's treatment of each element can be evaluated.

Prewriting: Be sure students understand that they are to use numbers to rank their own opinions of the action, diction, themes, and so forth in the works they have chosen, with 10 indicating a very high opinion and 1 a very low opinion.

Critical Thinking and Writing

WRITING A LITERARY REVIEW

If the selections in this unit were dramatized on TV, which might you watch? Which would you avoid? On what would you base your decisions? Nineteenth-century European poetry, drama, and prose, so varied in style and rich in scope, call forth a wide range of responses. Your reasons for liking or disliking one of these works can form the basis of an objective judgment.

Writing Assignment

Write a review of one selection from this unit, explaining why you think—or do not think—that the selection is worth reading. Your audience is people your age who share your general interests. In this assignment, you will base your review on a variety of **criteria**, that is, standards or tests by which something can be judged.

Background

To form an evaluation or judgment, you need criteria. Your responses to questions about a given work will reveal what your personal standards, or criteria, for literature are. Choose a work you feel strongly about, and use the questions below to clarify your responses and to pinpoint the elements that evoke them.

1. What **action** takes place in the work? Why does (or doesn't) it interest you?

2. How does the **diction** of the work affect you? Which wording is particularly appealing (or unappealing)?

3. What thoughts and feelings underlie the work, or form its **themes**? How do you respond to them?

4. Which **figurative language** and **images** add to (or detract from) the overall effect?

5. If your work is poetry, which **sound devices**—rhyme, meter, alliteration, assonance—stand out? How do they enhance (or diminish) the appeal of the work? If your work is prose, consider **style**—sentence length and complexity, parallel structure, and repetition.

6. How can you discern the **tone**—the author's attitude? What is your response to it?

Prewriting

Selecting Criteria. To select criteria for your evaluation, review your answers to the questions above. Then make a chart like the following one. Rate each of your criteria from 1 to 10. In the right column, jot down the line or page numbers of the passage on which you based your evaluation of the work.

Criterion	Rating	Examples
Effectiveness of action		
Effectiveness of diction		
Effectiveness of themes		
Effectiveness of figurative language/imagery		
Effectiveness of sound devices/style		
Effectiveness of tone		

If your overall response to the work is positive, focus your review on the elements you rate highest. If your response is negative, focus on the elements you rate lowest.

Examining Background. Freewrite answers to the following questions. If you are unsure of the answers, review the unit introduction as well as the selection introduction.

1. How is the work representative of its time period?
2. How do the events of the author's life contribute to the work?

Writing

Use the following guidelines as you draft your essay.

1. **Introductory Paragraph.** Begin with a clear statement of your opinion of the work's merit. Cite the author and title of the work. Go on to summarize your criteria.

2. **Body Paragraphs.** Devote at least one paragraph to each criterion, using quotes and examples from the work to show the author's treatment of the element in question. Your rating chart will provide a starting point. Include explanations of your own responses. Also, use your freewriting material to speculate on why the author treated each element as he or she did.

3. **Concluding Paragraph.** Here you might reflect on your reasons for choosing your criteria. End with a recommendation to your audience.

Evaluating and Revising

Use these questions to evaluate and revise your draft.

1. Does the introductory paragraph state your opinion and summarize your criteria?
2. Do body paragraphs detail your criteria and show how the work addresses them?
3. Do you include enough examples and quotations?
4. Do you include speculation on why the author wrote as he or she did?
5. Does your conclusion show the worth of your criteria and give a recommendation?
6. Are your sentences varied in structure and grammatically correct?

Proofreading and Publishing

Proofread to eliminate errors, and make a final copy of your review. Submit it to your school magazine or newspaper.

Writing: Before students begin writing, you might want to distribute examples of brief book or film reviews from such magazines as *The New Yorker* or from your local newspaper. Ask students to locate the part of each review that states the reviewer's overall opinion and to identify the specific details with which the reviewer supports his or her opinion. Remind students to illustrate the ideas in their own reviews with specifics from the selections.

Evaluating and Revising: Students with very strong responses to literary works may devote a disproportionately large amount of their review to emphatically stating their opinions, neglecting analysis of literary elements or evaluation of whether or not the author achieved his or her purpose. Encourage students to work with a peer reader to be sure that their evaluations are balanced and supported with adequate literary analysis.

Proofreading and Publishing: Before students begin proofreading, suggest that they focus on clear pronoun reference. The *Language Skills* feature on pp. 1130–1131 can provide guidelines and instructions for correcting problems in this area. ■

The following annotations are for the artwork surrounding the map, starting in the upper right-hand corner and moving in a counterclockwise direction.

Mother Teresa: A nurse and Roman Catholic nun, Mother Teresa spent most of her life helping the poor in India. In 1979, she received the Nobel Peace Prize.

Why do you think Mother Teresa was selected as a subject for this introductory page to the twentieth century? (Possible response: to exemplify the human qualities of compassion and caring)

Hong Kong: Situated on China's subtropical southeast coast, the former British crown colony of Hong Kong is a unique melding of East and West. An important Asian commercial trading center, this cosmopolitan city has a beautiful harbor. In 1898, the British leased Hong Kong from China for 99 years, almost the entire span of the twentieth century. Communist China promised that when the lease expired in 1997 the city would remain capitalist for another fifty years.

Albert Einstein: One of the world's greatest thinkers, Einstein developed theories that revolutionized modern physics. His theory of relativity established the relationship between energy and matter and led to the development of atomic energy.

THE WORLD IN THE TWENTIETH CENTURY

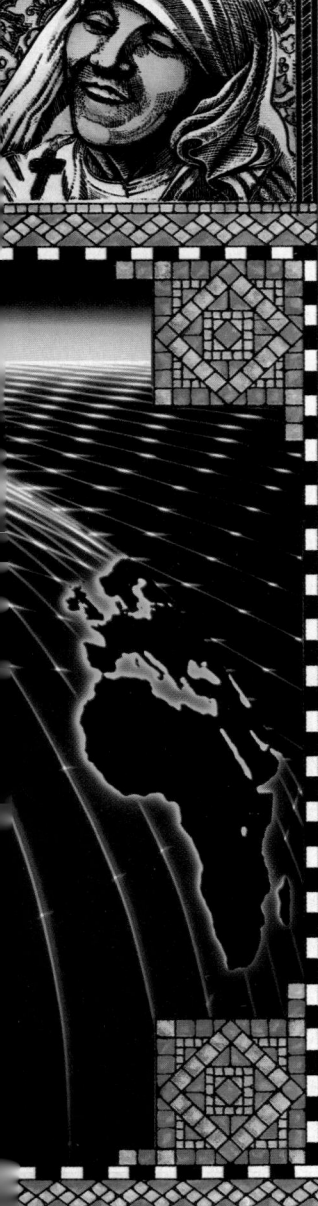

THE TWENTIETH CENTURY

▼ **Time** ▼
1900s

▼ **Place** ▼
The World

▼ **Literary Significance** ▼

In an age of stunning technological advances, widespread warfare, and global communication, humans have gained an increased awareness of the impact they have on their world. Twentieth-century writers have taken on the age-old challenge of finding new ways to express themselves, to understand their places in a constantly—often volatilely—changing world, and to understand the workings of their own minds. The result has been a vibrant array of literary movements ranging from modernism to existentialism, from absurdism to magic realism.

The literature of the twentieth century spans many forms: poetry, fiction, drama, autobiography, and journalism. It has raised new questions and presented new responses to eternal problems such as war, the limitation of personal, political, and intellectual freedoms, and the expression of personal experience. The writings of the twentieth century represent a mosaic of experiences at once bizarre and familiar, at once global and personal.

Rocket Launch: The invention of the multistage rocket has enabled the propulsion of spacecraft into the far reaches of the solar system, satisfying and stimulating age-old human curiosity about outer space.

DNA: Advances in biochemistry and in computer science are represented in this computer model of the double helix, the structure of deoxyribonucleic acid. DNA is the component of living cells that transmits hereditary information. Knowledge of the structure of DNA has led to genetic discoveries that present great promise as well as difficult moral choices for the human race.

Guernica: This detail from Pablo Picasso's famous painting is a reminder of the century's tragic wars. Picasso painted *Guernica* to commemorate the bombing of a village of that name during the Spanish Civil War of the 1930s.

Lenin: This poster depicts Vladimir Ilyich Lenin (1870–1924), the leader of the revolution that brought the Communist party to power in Russia in 1917 and led to the formation of the Soviet Union. ❓ *How have these events played a critical role in shaping this century's history?* (Possible response: They led to the Cold War between the two world powers, the United States and the Soviet Union.) ∎

1135

Point out how historical events, particularly wars, have influenced literary developments in the twentieth century. Ask students why this Time Line is unlike others in the book. (It includes worldwide events.)

Explain that modernism, which dominated the first half of the century, is a literary movement in which nineteenth-century traditions were discarded in favor of experimentation. Modernism flowered at the time of World War I, reflecting the disillusionment of many artists. Joyce, Kafka, and Eliot were leading modernists.

World War I precipitated the fall of czarist Russia and the establishment of the world's first Communist regime, an event that Russian writers like Akhmatova viewed as a mixed blessing. Elsewhere in a devastated Europe, fascism took hold in Italy and the Nazis seized power in Germany. Wiesel coined the term *Holocaust* to describe Nazi Germany's genocide of the Jews before Hitler's defeat in World War II. Existentialism, the postwar philosophy of which Camus was a leading thinker, was in part a response to the horrors of that war.

Camus, Césaire, Senghor, and Rama Rau are among the many twentieth-century writers who were deeply troubled by European colonialism. After World War II and the gradual end of colonialism, strong, distinctive, literary voices emerged from the newly independent nations of Africa, Asia, the West Indies, and Latin America.

TIME LINE
The Twentieth Century

British Prime Minister Winston Churchill (left), American President Franklin Roosevelt (center), and Soviet Marshal Joseph Stalin led the Allies to victory over the Axis Powers in World War II.

The Granger Collection, New York

LITERARY EVENTS

Modernism, **c. 1890–1940**

Selma Lagerlöf is awarded the Nobel Prize, **1909**

James Joyce, *Dubliners*, **1914**

Franz Kafka, *The Metamorphosis*, **1915**

Anna Akhmatova, "Lot's Wife," **early 20s**

T.S. Eliot, *The Waste Land*, **1922**

Isak Dinesen, *Out of Africa*, **1937**

Aimé Césaire coins the term *négritude* and becomes one of the founders of the Negritude movement, **1939**

Gabriela Mistral is awarded the Nobel Prize, **1945**

1900	1910	1920	1930	1940

CULTURAL AND HISTORICAL EVENTS

Great Britain defeats Boers of South Africa in Boer War, **1902**

Wright brothers develop the first aircraft, **1903**

Russo-Japanese War, **1904–1905**

Albert Einstein proposes the theory of relativity, **1905**

Chinese Revolution forces led by Sun Yat-sen overthrow the Manchu dynasty, **1911**

World War I, **1914–1918**

Russian Revolution; V. I. Lenin comes to power in Russia, **1917**

Nineteenth Amendment to U.S. Constitution gives women the vote, **1920**

Rise of Adolf Hitler in Germany and Benito Mussolini in Italy, **1920s**

Josef Stalin replaces Lenin as leader of the USSR, **1924**

Worldwide economic depression begins, **1929**

Adolf Hitler becomes chancellor of Germany, **1933**

Nazis murder over eleven million Jews (the Holocaust), as well as Gypsies and other "undesirables," **1938–1945**

Spanish Civil War, **1936–1939**

Japan invades China, **1937**

World War II begins in Europe; Germany invades Poland, **1939**

Japanese bomb Pearl Harbor, **1941**

U.S. drops atomic bombs on Japan; World War II ends; United Nations founded; Cold War begins, **1945**

European decolonialization, **1945–1970s**

State of Israel is proclaimed, **1948**

People's Republic of China is established, **1949**

The Wright brothers and their aircraft, 1903.

Library of Congress

Chinese students protested for democratic reforms at Tiananmen Square, Beijing, 1989.

Reuters/Bettmann Newsphotos

...handas K. Gandhi.

Wide World Photos

Postmodernism movement; magical realism develops in Latin America, **1960s**

Léopold Sédar Senghor is elected first president of Senegal, **1960**

Barbara Kimenye, *Kalasanda*, **1965**

Yasunari Kawabata is awarded the Nobel Prize, **1968**

...ntha Rama Rau, *Gifts ...Passage*, **1951**

...ert Camus is awarded ...e Nobel Prize, **1957**

...e Wiesel, *Night,* **1958**

Pablo Neruda is awarded the Nobel Prize, **1971**

Yehuda Amichai, *Laments on the War Dead*, **1974**

Gabriel García Márquez is awarded the Nobel Prize, **1982**

Jamaica Kincaid, *Annie John*, **1983**

Wole Soyinka is awarded the Nobel Prize, **1986**

Octavio Paz is awarded the Nobel Prize, **1990**

Naguib Mahfouz, *The Time and the Place*, **1991**

| 1950 | 1960 | 1970 | 1980 | 1990 |

...rean War, **1950–1953**

...viets launch the first ...tellite into outer space, ...57

Berlin Wall is built, **1961**

Cuban missile crisis; U.S. troops go to South Vietnam, **1962**

President John F. Kennedy is assassinated, **1963**

Cultural Revolution in People's Republic of China, **1966–1969**

Six-Day War between Israel and Arab nations, **1967**

Assassination of Martin Luther King, Jr.; USSR invades Czechoslovakia, **1968**

U.S. astronauts land on the moon, **1969**

OPEC oil embargo leads to energy crisis, **1973**

Watergate scandal causes President Nixon to resign, **1974**

Vietnam War ends, **1975**

Shah deposed in Iran; Ayatollah Khomeini comes to power, **1979**

Solidarity trade union is founded in Poland, **1980**

Mikhail Gorbachev becomes premier of USSR and establishes policy of *glasnost* (openness), **1985**

Berlin Wall is dismantled; Communist regimes are replaced by democratic ones in Poland, Czechoslovakia, etc.; Chinese hardliners crack down on prodemocracy students in Tiananmen Square, **1989**

East and West Germany are reunited, **1990**

U.S. and allies wage war against Iraq and liberate Kuwait; USSR dissolves, **1991**

Conflict in Bosnia begins, **1992**

Nelson Mandela is elected president of South Africa, **1994**

American astronaut on a ...acewalk above the earth.

NASA

This time line border contains international symbols and contemporary letter forms from a variety of alphabets worldwide.

LITERARY BACKGROUND

Nobel Prize: Though it has most often been awarded to European males, any writer is eligible to win the Nobel Prize for Literature. In 1909, Selma Lagerlöf became the first woman to win this prize. What other woman won it? (Gabriela Mistral) Nigerian author Soyinka was the first native African to receive the award, and Mahfouz the first author writing in Arabic to do likewise.

CULTURAL BACKGROUND

Women's Rights: Women were granted suffrage as early as 1893 in New Zealand and as late as 1945 in Japan. The many women authors cited on the Time Line—Lagerlöf, Akhmatova, Dinesen, Mistral, Rama Rau, and Kincaid—underscore the century's movement toward social and political equality for women.

CULTURAL BACKGROUND

Négritude: Definitions include "a consciousness of and pride in the cultural and physical aspects of the African heritage"; "an aesthetic and ideological concept affirming the independent validity of Negro culture."

READER'S RESPONSE

With the fall of many of the repressive Communist regimes and the explosion of global communication systems in the late twentieth century, the peoples of the world are perhaps more aware of their differences and their similarities than ever before in history. What do you think will be the outcome of this increased contact? (Possible responses: greater conflict; an era of great creativity)

1. *To gain an overview of twentieth-century literature from Europe, the Americas, Africa and the Middle East, and the rest of Asia*
2. *To recognize and appreciate the many cultures that contribute to modern world literature*
3. *To identify and analyze elements of modern fiction, poetry, and nonfiction*

4. *To interpret and respond to twentieth-century literature both orally and in writing*

1 HISTORICAL BACKGROUND

World War I: One cause of the war was growing nationalism among Eastern European Slavic peoples long dominated by the empires of Ottoman Turkey and Austria-Hungary. When a revolutionary backed by Serbia assassinated an Austrian archduke, Austria-Hungary prepared to crush the Serbs. A system of political alliances then drew other European powers into the war. The issue was not really the fate of Serbia; rather, losses in earlier conflicts and competition for overseas colonies had prompted military buildups and growing belligerence.

The war brought great chaos and devastation. In Russia, revolution toppled the Czar, forcing early withdrawal from the war and the establishment of a Communist regime under Lenin. The monarchies of Austria-Hungary and Turkey collapsed soon after their defeat in the war. Several Eastern European nations gained independence, and Arab lands formerly ruled by Turkey now came under British or French control. Dissatisfaction in Italy over the distribution of lands following World War I led to the rise of Mussolini's Fascists. In a much reduced Germany, the monarchy also toppled, and a weak democracy on the edge of economic ruin set the stage for the rise of Hitler's Nazis. Thus, as students of history often point out, the eventual outcome of World War I was World War II.

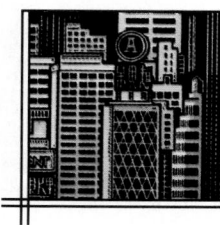

THE TWENTIETH CENTURY

The Bettmann Archive

American troops in France, 1918. *The use of poison gas in World War I added a devastating new dimension to warfare.*

At the beginning of the twentieth century, the colonies of the European empires covered most of the earth. But Europe's long period of exploration, conquest, and colonization was coming to an end. Much of the twentieth century would be marked by periods of widespread warfare with interim periods of uneasy peace. Colonies' demands for independence became increasingly intense, and many European countries that began the century as world powers found their once seemingly limitless resources dwindling. Throughout the world, artists, writers, and poets sought new forms to express the monumental changes they witnessed during this turbulent century.

World War I

Intense competition among the European powers for overseas colonies and markets was a major cause of **World War I** (1914–1918). Germany, Turkey, and Bulgaria joined Austria-Hungary to fight the Allies, who included Great Britain, France, Russia, Italy, and the United States. The conflict was a brutal exercise in trench warfare.

The peace that followed World War I was short-lived. In 1929, an economic downturn known as the **Great Depression** devastated economies throughout the world. The legacy of war and dire economic circumstances was great change and continued aggression in some parts of the world. The **Russian Revolution**, for example, caused the downfall of the monarchy and established Communist rule in Russia. In the Far East, Japan began invading China and other neighboring countries. In Europe, dictators such as Hitler, Mussolini, and Franco came into power, thus planting the seeds for further destruction in World War II.

Twentieth-century world literature is enormously diverse. The selections in the unit come from nearly thirty different nations and were originally written in fifteen different languages. The unit is divided into four geographical regions—Europe, the Americas, Africa and the Middle East, and Asia (i.e., India and the Far East).

To appreciate twentieth-century literature, it is helpful if students have an understanding of certain aspects of modernism, a movement that flourished in the first half of the century and continues to influence writers to this day. Most modernists sought to break with past traditions and experiment with new literary structures and styles. In poetry, this often meant using free verse instead of the metrical or (in Asia) syllabic verse of earlier times; in fiction, it often meant abandoning traditional narrative structure and beginning instead in the middle of the action, jumping around in time, or having "action" take place mainly in characters' minds. The popularity of the short story is itself a product of modernism, for in nineteenth-century Europe and the Americas the novel was paramount, while in most other parts of the world poetry and drama were the most highly regarded literary forms.

Modernist writing, especially poetry,

World War II

World War II began in 1939, when Nazi Germany invaded Poland. The main participants in the war were the **Axis powers**—Germany, Italy, and Japan—and the **Allies**—Great Britain, France, the USSR, China, the United States, and others.

In May 1945, Germany surrendered to the Allies, but it wasn't until after President Harry Truman ordered the atomic bombings of the Japanese cities of Hiroshima and Nagasaki in August that the war finally ended. The jubilation of the victorious Allies was tempered as the world became aware of two horrors: the destructive power of the atomic bomb, and the Nazi attempt to exterminate all European Jews and others they considered "undesirable." In Hiroshima and Nagasaki, over 300,000 people, mostly civil-

2

> 66 The people, and the people alone, are the motive force in the making of world history. 99
>
> —Quotations of Chairman Mao, *Mao Tse Tung*

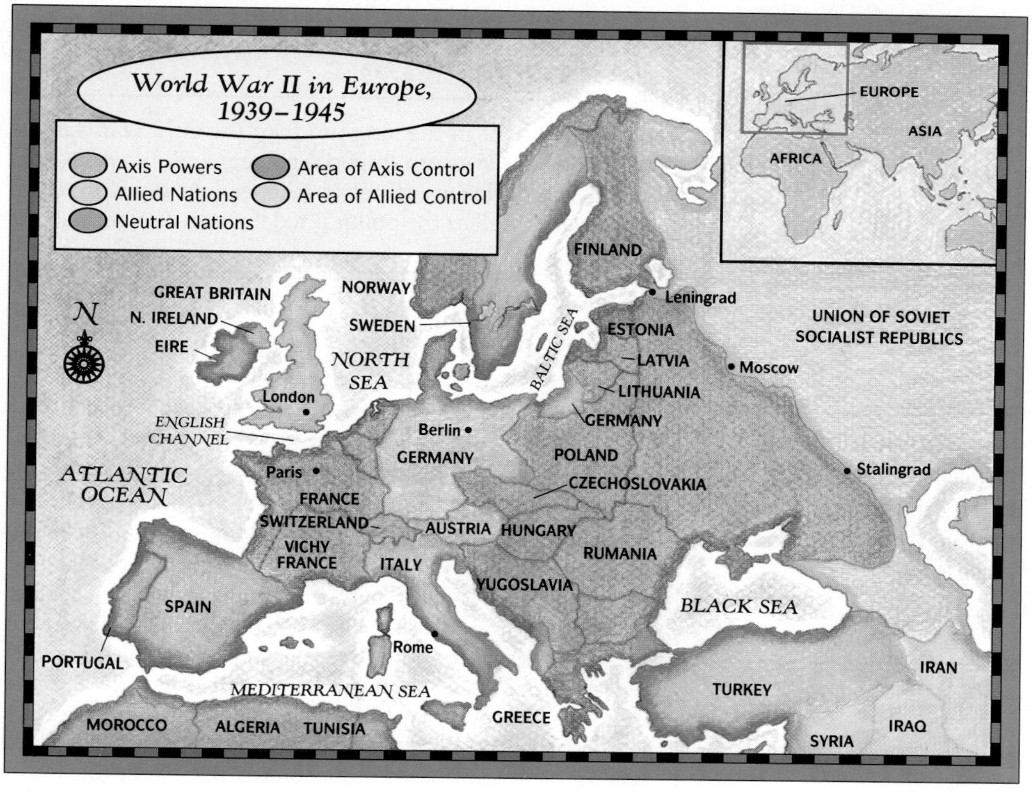

World War II in Europe, 1939–1945

Axis Powers
Allied Nations
Neutral Nations
Area of Axis Control
Area of Allied Control

tends to avoid direct statements of emotion and instead evoke feelings through powerful imagery. The modernist poet Rainer Maria Rilke, in his "thing poems," uses images to capture the essence of a particular animal or object. The free verse of Federico García Lorca exhibits a similar emotional power through images rooted in the soil of his native Spain. One development that had a tremendous impact on modern writing was Sigmund Freud's

(1856–1939) theory of psychoanalysis. Freud believed that people's behavior was determined by unconscious forces arising out of infancy and early childhood experiences. By examining dreams and probing the unconscious through methods such as hypnosis, Freud hoped to unlock the secrets of the human mind. This new psychoanalytical theory prompted many modernist fiction writers to focus on characters' internal conflicts. In "Eveline,"

James Joyce captures the flow of thoughts or "stream of consciousness" in the mind of the main character. Other young female characters face moments of psychological truth in coming-of-age stories by Isak Dinesen, Nadine Gordimer, and Jamaica Kincaid.

Another modernist trend was the tendency to blend realism and fantasy. In reaction to the strict realism that dominated the pre–World War I era, many artists be-

---

3 READER'S RESPONSE

Do you think the end of the Cold War will mean an end to the threat of nuclear warfare? What dangers have been minimized? What dangers still exist?

HISTORICAL BACKGROUND

The End of the Cold War:
During the Cold War era the United States and the Soviet Union often helped escalate civil unrest in less industrialized nations. With the collapse of the U.S.S.R. and the end of the Cold War, these conflicts lost much of their superpower backing. A case in point seems to be the Central American nation of El Salvador. In early 1992, rebel and government forces agreed to a ceasefire, ending twelve years of civil warfare that claimed over 75,000 Salvadoran lives. *Are you hopeful that peace may now come to other troubled spots like the Balkans, the Middle East, and Northern Ireland? Why or why not?* (Students should cite recent news events and offer logical arguments to support their views.)

Library of Congress

Poster for Hitler's National Student Organization during World War II; the caption reads, "The German student fights for leader and people." *Nazi propaganda helped rally the support Hitler needed to carry out his diabolical objectives.*

❝ Nonviolence is the first article of my faith. It is also the last article of my creed. ❞

—*Speech, March 23, 1922, Mohandas K. Gandhi*

---

ians, were burned or irradiated to death by the two bombs. In the German death camps of Auschwitz, Dachau, and elsewhere, the Nazis killed over twelve million people. Altogether, over twelve million soldiers and twenty million civilians were killed during World War II.

The Cold War

The end of World War II marked the beginning of the nuclear age. The United States and the Soviet Union emerged as antagonistic superpowers, and the **Cold War** began. From the end of World War II until the period of *glasnost* ("openness" in Russian) ushered in by Mikhail Gorbachev in the mid-1980s, the U.S. and USSR were involved in a stupendous arms race. At the height of the Cold War, both sides had stockpiled enough nuclear weapons to kill every man, woman, and child on the planet twelve times.

New Nations Emerge

More significant in the long run than the Cold War was the decline of the Western imperial powers and its result—the emergence of dozens of newly independent states in Africa and Asia, as well as the political redefinition of older nations

> The end of World War II ushered in a new era of politics with new players: the U.S. and Soviet superpowers and newly independent nations in Africa, Asia, and Latin America.

there and in Latin America. These nations and others began to assert their own identities and reclaim territories. This process of self-determination, however, was seldom achieved without conflict. For example, war has broken out several times in the Middle East over the establishment of Jewish and Arab states in former British Palestine. Despite much mediation, many Arabs have opposed the creation of a Jewish homeland by the United Nations. Countries like Korea and Vietnam, once freed from foreign rule, were torn apart

came fascinated with the world of dreams and fantasies. Following Freud's interest in the unconscious, painters such as René Magritte and Giorgio de Chirico juxtaposed images in ways that could occur only in dreams.

Point out that Franz Kafka's landmark novella, *The Metamorphosis,* uses this technique to create a surrealistic nightmare world. A similar blend of reality and fantasy exists in Ben Okri's "In the Shadow of War." Argentina's Jorge Luis Borges plays with reality in "Borges and Myself," a short prose piece that experimentally blends fiction and autobiography. Colombia's Gabriel García Márquez combines realism and fantasy in an appealing blend known as magic realism, as illustrated in "The Handsomest Drowned Man in the World." Argentina's Julio Cortázar provides a more disturbing mix in "The Night Face Up." Egypt's Naguib Mahfouz, too, moves into the realm of fantasy to express universal themes about time and change in his story "Half a Day."

Despite the continuing influence of modernism, beginning in the 1930s there was a return to the political and social concerns of nineteenth-century Realism. In Paris during the 1930s, Senegal's Léopold Sédar Senghor joined with fellow students from France's overseas colonies to initiate the *Négritude* movement. The

UPI/Bettmann Newsphotos

Victims of the war in Vietnam, 1965.

by internal factions trying to impose their own rule. Both the Korean and Vietnam wars were, in simplest terms, conflicts between supporters of Communist and democratic governments. South Africa, Northern Ireland, and Central America are some other regions of the globe where violence is a common experience due to the conflicts of race, religion, and political beliefs.

Science and Technology

The twentieth century has seen amazing developments in science and technology—telephones, phonographs, televisions, automobiles, airplanes, computers, space technology, and medical advances such as antibiotics. Particularly important advances have been made in communication and transportation. Not everyone has enjoyed the benefits of these advances, however. The majority of the world's less-industrialized nations still suffers from the effects of poverty and disease. Nor have technological advances in themselves

movement's emphasis on Africa's pre-colonial heritage is powerfully communicated in Senghor's poem "And We Shall Be Steeped." Respect for African traditions is also central to "Life Is Sweet at Kumansenu," a haunting tale by Sierra Leone's Abioseh Nicol. In "Marriage Is a Private Affair," Nigeria's Chinua Achebe examines the clash between modern urban life and more traditional African ways.

The problems of colonialism and racial or ethnic prejudice are treated in "The Train from Rhodesia," "By Any Other Name," and *Kaffir Boy*. Zhang Jie's "Love Must Not Be Forgotten" asks questions about the role of women that provoked a storm of controversy in China when the story first appeared. Chilean Isabel Allende's "And of Clay Are We Created" focuses on the effects of media in contemporary life, while selections by Israel's Yehuda Amichai, Korea's Hwang Sun-won, Vietnam's Nguyen Thi Vinh, and Nigeria's Ben Okri all examine the effects of warfare in each author's homeland.

The horrors of World War II and the Holocaust prompted some postwar writers to search for new ways to find meaning in human existence. Albert Camus was one of several French-language authors who pioneered existentialism, which proposes that each individual defines his or her own existence through the choices he or

5 TEACHING TIP
Encourage students to discuss recent ecological disasters and make suggestions as to how they might be avoided. To prompt discussion, you might mention the problem of tanker oil spills in places such as Alaska. Ask students how we might solve or minimize hazards to the environment.

6 HISTORICAL BACKGROUND
Guernica: During the Spanish Civil War of the 1930s, fascist forces led by General Francisco Franco successfully rebelled against the legally elected government of Spain's democratic monarchy. Those who supported the democratic monarchy—called loyalists—included many famous writers and other artists. Franco's forces, on the other hand, were backed by Hitler's Germany. The Germans bombed the defenseless village of Guernica, in the Basque region of Spain, mainly to test new weaponry and display the might of their air force. Pablo Picasso (1881–1973), born in Spain, was in Paris working on a mural for the Spanish pavilion of the 1937 World's Fair when news of the bombing reached him. A loyalist supporter, he poured his feelings into the mural that became *Guernica*. The painting (pictured on the facing page) is one of the century's most famous. It captures the horror of modern warfare in a nightmare vision that combines the abstract planes of cubism and vivid social protest.

The Bettmann Archive

Mushroom cloud resulting from the atomic bombing of Nagasaki, Japan, by the U.S. in World War II.

❝ He: You saw nothing in Hiroshima. Nothing.
She: I saw everything. Everything. ❞

—Hiroshima, Mon Amour, *Marguerite Duras*

always been a boon to humanity—many of these advances have produced dangerous side effects. For example, technological progress contributed to the massacres in the

> The twentieth century has seen remarkable advances in science and technology. But accompanying these advances have been large-scale disasters.

trenches of World War I, the Holocaust in World War II, nuclear weapons, and ecological disasters such as the nuclear accident at the Chernobyl power plant in the Soviet Union.

Artistic Responses to the Twentieth Century

For many, the nineteenth-century belief that human history was a record of slow but certain progress died in the aftermath of World War I. Traditional values came under attack, and art forms of the past were seen as inadequate to express the experiences of the modern world. By rejecting the old forms, writers, painters, musicians, and other creative artists were free to experiment with new themes and styles.

Film, Art, and Music

Most twentieth-century painters rejected the styles of previous centuries. For example, Pablo Picasso and Georges Braque, who were influenced by African sculpture and by concepts of geometry, developed a style called *cubism*, which reduced objects and figures to their basic geometric forms. In 1937 Picasso painted *Guernica* in reaction to the brutal German bombing of the village of Guernica during the Spanish Civil War. Shortly after he painted this large mural, the German secret police began harassing him at his studio in Nazi-occupied Paris. One officer, noticing a photograph of *Guernica* lying on a table, asked "Did you do that?" "No," Picasso replied, "you did."

After the invention of the motion picture around the turn of the century, films quickly became a new popular art

she makes in life. Once you have explained the existentialist theory, have students freewrite about three personal decisions they consider "defining moments" in their own lives.

While existentialism emphasizes human freedom in philosophical terms, freedom has been a more practical concern to postwar authors living under totalitarian regimes. Ask students if any of them know of the Chinese government's violent crackdown on student dissidents in Tiananmen Square in Beijing on June 3, 1989. How did they react to a government's killing of its young people? Point out to students that such freedoms as the right to assemble and express one's opinions are of vital concern to artists living under restrictive governments. For instance, freedom of expression is a recurrent topic in the prose poems of Russia's Aleksandr Solzhenitsyn. Solzhenitsyn eventually had to emigrate to escape political oppression. The limitations of life lived under a repressive government is also the subject of much of Czeslaw Milosz's poetry.

GUERNICA, PABLO PICASSO (1881–1973).

© 1998 Estate of Pablo Picasso/Artists Rights Society (ARS), New York

form. Most films were escapist—adventures, comedies, or romantic dramas—but others reflected the pessimism of the postwar era. Charlie Chaplin, an early cinematic master, wrote, directed, and acted in many films that took an ironic look at war, industry, and other important issues of the day.

A determination to break new ground was also apparent in popular music. Two of the most innovative popular musical forms of the century were developed by African Americans: jazz and the blues. During the 1950s, rock-and-roll burst on the scene, causing fans to scream and swoon over their new heroes—Buddy Holly, Chuck Berry, Elvis Presley, and Little Richard. Then, in the 1960s, superstar groups such as the Beatles and the Rolling Stones gained adulation. Since then, hard rock, punk rock, new wave, reggae, and rap music have evolved.

Literature in the Twentieth Century

In literature, a broad movement called **modernism** flourished between 1890 and 1940. In general, modernists were concerned with the loss of traditional values brought on by the major advances and disasters of the early twentieth century. Modernist literature usually reflects the fragmentation and uncertainty that writers and poets perceived all around them. Many modernists emphasized psychological exploration over direct social commentary. Some, like **James**

Jazz great Dizzy Gillespie has helped revolutionize the sound of music in the U.S. and abroad.

AP/Wide World Photos

Blues: Music fans often do not realize the enormous impact that the blues, the nonreligious folk music of African Americans, has had on other forms of popular music. Jazz, which evolved from Dixieland, incorporated many blues elements in the 1920s. Larger orchestras, or Big Bands, took jazz into the swing era, but when World War II reduced the size of the big bands, vocalists took center stage, producing music less geared to dancing. Meanwhile, the rural blues of southern blacks had evolved into the more sophisticated urban blues. After the war, small rhythm-and-blues bands, combining urban blues with forties pop, sprung up in black American neighborhoods. Seeking dance music, America's younger generation in the 1950s embraced the speedier version of rhythm and blues that came to be called rock and roll. Early rock stars like Elvis Presley, whose background was in country music, were taught to imitate blues singers by music-industry promoters who rarely gave credit to their sources. As rock and roll evolved, performers drew again and again from the blues, especially in Britain, where black American blues artists often received more recognition than at home.

❓ *What earlier music has influenced the music you like?* (Encourage students to bring in examples of the music to illustrate their points.)

MAKING CONNECTIONS

When García Márquez read Kafka's *The Metamorphosis*, its bizarre fantasy reminded him of Latin American folkore he had learned as a boy. His magic realism is just one of many modern creations that blend the old with the new, the homegrown with the foreign. Most twentieth-century writers display cross-cultural influences and also draw on literature of the past.

Western modernists were much affected by ancient Greek and Asian literatures. Joyce modeled his famous novel *Ulysses* on Homer's *Odyssey*; America's Ezra Pound translated Li Po and studied Noh drama. The cosmopolitan Jorge Luis Borges often alludes to ancient and medieval Arabic, Persian, Far Eastern, and European literatures, all of which he studied avidly. More recently, Octavio Paz, whose poems often include images from ancient Mexican history, employs a simple style much influenced by Japanese verse.

By the same token, Asian modernists were influenced by Western literature. Lu Hsün's readings of European fiction inspired him to become modern China's first great short-story writer. The work of Japan's Yasunari Kawabata was greatly influenced by French Symbolist poetry.

Writers who grew up in what were then European colonies were well versed in the literature of the "mother country," even

LITERARY BACKGROUND

Modernism: This is an umbrella term for an array of literary and artistic movements that developed (some lasting for very short periods) during the first four decades of the twentieth century. All had in common a desire to break with nineteenth-century traditions and move in new directions. Dadaism, Cubism, and Imagism are just three of the many specific movements that fall under the general banner of Modernism.

HUMANITIES CONNECTION

René Magritte (1898–1967) was a Belgian painter whose works moved beyond realism into the realm of surrealism. A graduate of the Brussels Academy of Fine Arts, Magritte worked at a wallpaper factory before becoming a full-time painter. Like Salvador Dali and other twentieth-century modernists, Magritte embraced the bizarre world view of surrealism, often depicting the sea or sky (two childhood loves) from unusual vantage points, such as through keyholes. He also included interesting optical illusions in many of his works.

❓ *What idea might Magritte be exploring in this painting?* (Possible responses: that reality can fall apart like shards of glass from a window) ∎

AKG, London

Sigmund Freud (1856–1939), the founder of modern psychiatry. *Freud's psychoanalytic theories greatly influenced the works of many twentieth-century artists.*

Joyce (see page 1207), turned to experimental techniques such as **stream of consciousness**. In *Ulysses*, Joyce used this technique to describe everything that happens to a man in a single day—including all his thoughts, both conscious and unconscious. Other writers, such as **Franz Kafka** (see page 1154) and the Japanese writer Akutagawa Ryunosuke, used nightmarish settings and situations to express the alienation of the individual in modern society.

Poets such as T. S. Eliot and **Rainer Maria Rilke** (see page 1148) broke with traditional forms to express their own personal visions. In his most famous poem, *The Waste Land*, Eliot describes a world without faith, incapable of restoring its spiritual and moral values. Many other modernist poets abandoned traditional rhyme and meter. In their free-verse poems they experimented with punctuation and the physical appearance of the poem on the page.

LA CLEF DES CHAMPS (*THE KEY OF THE FIELDS*), RENÉ MAGRITTE, 1948. *Gouache. Surrealism is a literary and artistic movement that rejects the division between rational and irrational thought and instead expresses the play of the unconscious mind. The movement had a profound effect on the development of post–World War II artistic movements, such as abstract expressionism in painting and absurdism in literature.*

© 1998 C. Herscovici, Brussels/Artists Rights Society (ARS), New York

when that country's policies outraged them. Rama Rau ironically alludes to Shakespeare in the title of her essay which attacks British ethnocentrism in colonial India. Antigua's Jamaica Kincaid, who says she will never forget that her ancestors came to the New World in chains, still expresses fondness for some British literature.

Almost all modern short-story writers acknowledge a debt to Chekhov and Maupassant; in Zhang's "Love Must Not Be Forgotten," a Chekhov story collection even plays a role in the plot. Modernist poetry was directly influenced by the French Symbolists. Free verse, too, had a nineteenth-century precursor: America's Walt Whitman, who was especially revered by García Lorca and many Latin American poets, including Neruda.

READING CHECK

1. What event set off World War II? (the invasion of Poland by Nazi Germany)
2. What situation arose between the U.S. and the U.S.S.R. after World War II? (the Cold War)
3. Who developed Cubism? (Picasso, Braque)
4. What philosophy did Camus, Sartre, and Beauvoir help develop? (existentialism)
5. What literary movement asserts the value of African traditions? (Négritude)

Responses to War

8 While many modernists wrote elaborate, inward-looking "studies" of human consciousness, other twentieth-century authors turned their pens to direct and blistering accounts of the wars that raged on nearly every continent of the world. Erich Maria Remarque's *All Quiet on the Western Front* and Ernest Hemingway's *A Farewell to Arms* are two novels, written from opposite sides of the battle line, that reveal the tragedy of World War I. **Elie Wiesel** wrote an autobiography of his own imprisonment in a Nazi concentration camp during World War II in *Night* (see page 1232).

In the period of general disenchantment following the world wars, literature increasingly focused on themes of alienation, uncertainty, and despair.

Absurdism and Existentialism

9 To reflect a world in which human existence is seemingly unreasonable and incoherent, playwrights such as Eugène Ionesco, Samuel Beckett, and Harold Pinter created dramas with characters who speak only in banalities and with plots that go nowhere. At the end of Beckett's *Waiting for Godot*, one tramp says, "Well? Shall we go?" and the other responds, "Yes, let's go." The final stage direction, however, is "*They do not move.*"

While the **theater of the absurd** tried to dramatize the "facts" of human existence, some writers began searching for a philosophy that would allow them to understand and accept the apparent senselessness of existence. Simone de Beauvoir, Jean-Paul Sartre, **Albert Camus** (see page 1244), and others developed one such philosophy, which they called **existentialism**. Existentialism takes its name from the idea that a person's physical existence precedes his or her "essence," or meaning. This means that there are no preexisting meanings, values, or guidelines for human beings. But since we want and need clarity and rationality in our lives, the existentialists concluded that each person must create his or her own meaning, or essence, in life. Existentialism had a deep impact on Christian and Jewish thought, and theologians of both faiths developed their own brands of existentialism, which emphasized a reexamination of humanity's relationship with God.

> **❝** I, a stranger and afraid
> In a world I never made. **❞**
> —Last Poems,
> A. E. Housman

AP/Wide World Photos

Simone de Beauvoir and Jean-Paul Sartre, two founders of the literary and philosophical movement existentialism.

8 LITERARY BACKGROUND

Remarque: Born in Osnabrück, Germany, Erich Maria Remarque (1898–1970) fought with the German army during World War I and was wounded several times. His famous novel *All Quiet on the Western Front* (1929) gives a grimly realistic portrait of war and its consequences. When the Nazis came to power in Germany, they publicly burned the book because of its anti-militarist stance and took away Remarque's citizenship. The author, who had already fled to Switzerland, remained there until 1939, when he moved to America.

Hemingway: America's Ernest Hemingway (1899–1961) served the Allies in World War I as an ambulance driver in the Italian army. Later, he covered other conflicts as a war correspondent. A leading modernist, Hemingway is famous for his spare, unemotional prose that suggests the devastating effect of modern warfare on the individual.

9 TEACHING TIP

Interested students might read an absurdist play such as Eugène Ionesco's *Rhinoceros* or Samuel Beckett's *Waiting for Godot* and then write a short skit, using absurdist techniques to illuminate an aspect of their own lives.

Europe

Olga Carlisle's *Poets on Street Corners* provides poems by, and portraits of, Akhmatova and other Soviet poets; Boris Pasternak's novel *Doctor Zhivago* vividly captures the Russian Revolution. The Spanish Civil War is the backdrop of Ernest Hemingway's *For Whom the Bell Tolls*. Nazi persecution of the Jews gains a moving personal perspective in *The Diary of Anne Frank*.

The Americas and Africa

Rita Guibert's *Seven Voices* contains interviews with Neruda, Borges, Paz, and García Márquez. Gerald Moore's *Twelve African Writers* includes portraits of Senghor and Achebe. Langston Hughes's *African Treasury* collects works by Nicol, Soyinka, and others. Camara Laye's *Dark Child* is a charming autobiography. Achebe's novel *Things Fall Apart* captures a changing Africa.

Asia (India and the Far East)

E. M. Forster's novel *A Passage to India* treats the clash of cultures in British India; R. K. Narayan's stories portray everyday Indian life. Two of Akutagawa Ryunosuke's tales were the basis of the acclaimed 1951 film *Rashomon*. Hwang's stories are collected in two recent volumes edited by Martin Holman. Annie Dillard's *Encounters with Chinese Writers* contains a vivid portrait of Zhang. ■

---

10 LITERARY BACKGROUND

Science Fiction: Though the genre had its origins in the nineteenth century, science fiction became especially popular in the twentieth century. In Communist Russia and Eastern Europe, where totalitarian governments practiced censorship and often punished attacks on the state, science fiction became a tool of dissenting writers. By setting a tale in the distant future or in another world and then criticizing or mocking that "alien" society, writers could often veil criticisms of their own societies sufficiently to escape government censorship.

READER'S RESPONSE

Do you think that fiction which makes use of fantasy elements, such as science fiction or Latin American magic realism, is necessarily less serious or "true" than more realistic fiction?

NASA

American astronaut on the moon.

HBJ Photo

Buenos Aires, Argentina, the center of Latin America's literary "Boom."

The Fantastic

Some writers responded to the increasingly hostile and confusing world by creating fantasy or **science fiction** stories. Although the earliest examples of science fiction in literature can be traced back to the 1600s, the genre did not reach its present form until the late 1800s. In the twentieth century, science fiction has developed in two basic directions: an infatuation with technology (Isaac Asimov and others) or an exploration of humanity's precarious place in the universe (H. G. Wells and others). The novels of William Burroughs, Kurt Vonnegut, Jr., and Stanislaw Lem often use the conventions of science fiction to make serious comments about our world.

Cultural Identity and Literature

Twentieth-century writers from less-industrialized nations often address the problems of cultural identity. They have seen their local cultures uprooted by colonialism or foreign influence, and they have had to ask themselves whether they are to celebrate their native traditions, imitate foreign models, or create new modes of expression.

In Latin America, artists have responded in different ways. The Argentinian author **Jorge Luis Borges** (see page 1280), one of the central figures in the Latin American literary "Boom" that followed World War II, devoured nearly everything European libraries had to offer, yet his brand of fiction, which blends fantastic events and philosophical inquiry, is strikingly unique and much imitated today by writers around the world. Chilean poet **Pablo Neruda** (see page 1275) was greatly influenced by the modernist movement, but his epic work, *Las Alturas de Machu Picchu* (*The Heights of Machu Picchu*), reconciles the poet with his country's ancient Indian heritage.

The 1960s saw the development of **magic realism**, which contains elements of both the real world and the world of fantasy. Magic realists such as Colombia's **Gabriel García Márquez** (see page 1289) were influenced by **surrealism**, which encouraged the free association of ideas as a means of exploring the unconscious mind. But magic realists were just as much influenced by the rich folklore traditions of Latin America.

In Africa, there was much controversy over the literary movement known as **Négritude**, which asserted the value of African traditions. Some writers believed that Négritude was a necessary response to years of imperialism, while others, like **Chinua Achebe** (see page 1343) and Wole Soyinka, felt that Négritude tended to idealize Africa's pre-colonial past and that African literature must instead examine that past more critically.

African writers have also debated the question of which language they should write in: that of the colonizers, which in many cases has become the only common language for the descendants of different tribes, or their native tongues. Kenyan author **Ngũgĩ wa Thiong'o** (see page 1429) has taken the latter position, turning to his native language Kikuyu after much success writing in English. Achebe, Soyinka, and others feel that by writing in English they reach a wider audience.

Twentieth-century women writers also struggled to establish a cultural identity, for until the early twentieth century, most women had virtually no political voice and little representation in literature. As the twentieth century unfolded, more and more women writers addressed the plight of their sex in a world controlled by men. In her work *The Second Sex*, Simone de Beauvoir analyzed women's secondary status in society and denounced the male middle class for perceiving women as objects. Colette, Margaret Atwood, and **Jamaica Kincaid** (see page 1320), among many others, have also helped define the politics and culture of the women's movement of the twentieth century.

Diversity of World Literatures

In literature, as in history, many different stories are proceeding at once. As we approach the year 2000, both the end of a century and the end of a millennium, we look back on cataclysmic changes that cannot be easily reduced to some clear shape or significance. Very few people could have predicted the reunification of East and West Germany or the dissolution of the Soviet Union. We know only that challenges to our understanding and imagination remain. "The only certain thing about the future," historian Eric Hobsbawm writes in *The Age of Empire*, "is that it will surprise even those who have seen furthest into it."

11

> **❝** A great writer is, so to speak, a second government in his country. And for that reason no regime has ever loved great writers, only minor ones. **❞**
> —*The First Circle*, Aleksandr Solzhenitsyn

12

Reuters/Bettmann Newsphotos

In November of 1989, the Berlin Wall, which divided Communist East Berlin and democratic West Berlin, came down, heralding the end of Communism in Eastern Europe.

11 LITERARY BACKGROUND

African Literature: Many African writers choose to write in European languages introduced in their countries in colonial times because these languages help them reach a wider audience. Chinua Achebe, for example, has written a few works in his native Ibo, but such works have a relatively small audience unless they are translated. English, on the other hand, is one of the world's most widely spoken languages. By writing in English, Achebe can more readily introduce Ibo and other Nigerian experiences to the rest of the world, thereby fostering his native culture even as he forgoes his native language.

TEACHING TIP

Ask students to discuss the directions they think literature may take in the future. What effects do they think computer technology may ultimately have on world literature? (Students may suggest, among other things, that computer-assisted translations may allow more and more access to the literature of other cultures.)

12 RESPONDING TO THE QUOTATION

? *Can you think of any American writers who acted as a kind of second government? Explain.* (Possible responses: Henry David Thoreau; Harriet Beecher Stowe) ■

Rainer Maria Rilke
1875–1926, Austria/Czechoslovakia

The Granger Collection, New York

The German-language poet Rainer Maria Rilke (rī′nər mä·rē′ä ril′kə) thought that the monotonous routines of everyday life functioned as a husk that prevented new ideas from entering people's minds and souls. To prevent the husk from forming, Rilke spent his life on the road—wandering from nation to nation, stopping briefly wherever admirers provided food and shelter.

Rilke was born to a German-speaking family in Prague, now the capital of Czechoslovakia, when the area was still part of the Austrian empire. During childhood, he was torn between his mother, who dressed him as a girl, and his father, who sent him to military academies. In 1892, Rilke's wealthy uncle came to the rescue by offering to pay for his nephew's studies in philosophy, art, and German literature. Rilke liked these subjects and continued to study them in Munich, Germany. In 1901, Rilke married the German sculptor Clara Westhoff. But he soon discovered that married life did not suit him, and he abandoned his wife and baby daughter so that he could travel and write.

One of the greatest influences on Rilke and his work was the French sculptor Auguste Rodin (rô·dan′), with whom Rilke worked. Rodin showed the young poet that art was hard work, not merely an outpouring of emotion.

After leaving Rodin, Rilke revised much of his earlier verse and composed some of his finest poetry. Soon after this burst of creativity, however, Rilke entered a dry period. Seeking inspiration, he visited northern Africa and then lived in the Italian city of Trieste. Here he began a series of philosophical poems, the *Duino Elegies* (1923). The project was interrupted by World War I, in which he served briefly in the Austrian military. After the war, Rilke settled in Switzerland, completed the *Duino Elegies*, and wrote his complex *Sonnets to Orpheus* (1923). Plagued by ill health since the war, Rilke died of a blood disease when he was only fifty-one. By this time his poems, with their meticulously chiseled images, had already established him as one of the most original poets of the twentieth century.

Reader's Guide

BLACK CAT
THE SWAN

Background

When Rilke was working for Auguste Rodin, he confided to the sculptor that he was suffering from writer's block. Rodin advised him to go to the zoo and look at an animal until he could "see" it, adding that it might take as long as two or three weeks, possibly more. Rilke took this strange advice. He went to the zoo, concentrated on a panther, and then wrote the first of his *Dinggedichte* (ding'gə·dikh't), or "thing poems." What Rilke most admired about Rodin's sculptures was their ability to capture not only the outward appearance of a person, animal, or object, but also its inner vitality and spirit. Each of Rilke's "thing poems," like Rodin's sculptures, seeks to communicate both external reality and the "inward nature of things."

Writer's Response

Choose a person, animal, or thing that you can observe closely. In your journal, write a paragraph describing it in as much detail as you can. Try to also describe what it makes you think of and how it makes you feel. Does it make you feel happy or sad, calm or excited, or something else?

Literary Focus

Figurative language describes one thing in terms of another, usually very different, thing. Figurative language, which includes similes and metaphors, is not meant to be understood on a literal level. A **simile** compares two seemingly unlike things by using a connective word such as *like* or *as* ("My feet are as cold as two chunks of ice"). A **metaphor** compares two seemingly unlike things without the connective ("My feet are chunks of ice"). When the comparison is developed over several lines, it is called an **extended metaphor**. Many writers, for example, have compared life to a journey through a maze: We often make wrong turns or run into dead ends, and we can never know exactly how things will turn out.

MEETING INDIVIDUAL NEEDS

LEP: To help students deal with the syntax in "Black Cat," point out where the three sentences in the poem begin (lines 1, 9, and 12) and end, and help them identify the subjects and predicates. ■

1 LITERARY ELEMENT
Simile: Paraphrase the simile in the first two stanzas. (Your gaze is nullified by the cat, just as a madman's rage is nullified by pounding on walls.) What words, feelings, and images are brought to your mind by the howling madman pounding on the padded walls of his cell? (Answers will vary.) What does the comparison make you think and feel about the cat? (Possible response: She is mysterious, perhaps supernatural.)

2 INTERPRETING
What does Rilke's simile in the third stanza comparing the cat to an audience accomplish? (Possible response: The simile illustrates the cat's intense watchfulness; "menacing and sullen" and "curl to sleep" dramatize the cat's utter mastery of her audience—human beings.)

3 READER'S RESPONSE
How do you react to being compared to a "prehistoric fly"? (Possible response: Most students will say it makes them feel insignificant.)

1150 The Twentieth Century

BLACK CAT
Rainer Maria Rilke
translated by
STEPHEN MITCHELL

In describing the cat, Rilke avoids such clichés as "black as coal" or "black as night." Keep track of the unusual similes and metaphors he uses to describe the cat, and decide which you find the most effective.

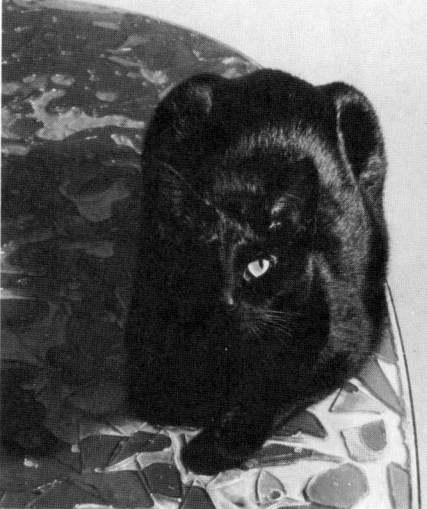
Elaine Tin Nyo

1

A ghost, though invisible, still is like a place
your sight can knock on, echoing; but here
within this thick black pelt, your strongest gaze
will be absorbed and utterly disappear:

5　just as a raving madman, when nothing else
can ease him, charges into his dark night
howling, pounds on the padded wall, and feels
the rage being taken in and pacified.

2

She seems to hide all looks that have ever fallen
10　into her, so that, like an audience,
she can look them over, menacing and sullen,
and curl to sleep with them. But all at once

3

as if awakened, she turns her face to yours;
and with a shock, you see yourself, tiny,
15　inside the golden amber of her eyeballs
suspended, like a prehistoric fly.°

15–16. amber . . . prehistoric fly:
Small, prehistoric creatures such as flies are sometimes perfectly preserved for millions of years in amber, or fossilized tree sap. The color amber takes its name from the translucent yellow or brownish yellow color of this sap.

THE SWAN

Rainer Maria Rilke

translated by

ROBERT BLY

There is an extended comparison in this poem. What things are being compared?

This clumsy living that moves lumbering
as if in ropes through what is not done
reminds us of the awkward way the swan walks.

And to die, which is a letting go
5 of the ground we stand on and cling to every day,
is like the swan when he nervously lets himself down

into the water, which receives him gaily
and which flows joyfully under
and after him, wave after wave,
10 while the swan, unmoving and marvelously calm,
is pleased to be carried, each minute more fully grown,
more like a king, composed, farther and farther on.

J. Azel/Woodfin Camp & Associates

First Thoughts

Which of these poems best expresses the "inward nature" of its subject? Why do you say so?

Identifying Facts

1. According to the first stanza of "Black Cat," why is it easier to "see" a ghost than the black cat?

2. What does the first stanza of "The Swan" compare the swan's walk to? What does the rest of the poem compare the swan's swimming to?

Interpreting Meanings

1. Do you think the **simile** in the second stanza of "Black Cat" is effective? How does it help you to understand the cat's inner nature? Find three other **similes** in the poem, and explain how they contribute to the meaning of the poem.

2. In the last stanza of "Black Cat," the speaker is shocked to see himself reflected in the cat's eyes as if he were a fly suspended in amber. How does this **simile** reveal how the speaker views himself or humanity in general?

1. Comparing Translations. To help students appreciate different translations of the original poem, students might compare Bly's translation of "The Swan" to C. F. MacIntyre's (in *Rainer Maria Rilke, Fifty Selected Poems*, University of California Press, Berkeley, 1947) or Walter Arndt's (in *The Best of Rilke*, University Press of New England, Hanover, 1989). Arndt's book also contains his translation of "Black Cat."

2. Creating a Performance Piece. Robert Bly, a notable reader of poetry, often accompanies his readings with music or simple sound effects. To appreciate the drama of Rilke's poems, invite students to prepare an oral performance of each one, using music and sound effects—plus props, staging, and costumes, if they wish—to express and heighten the mood of each poem.

Students might wish to read their favorite figurative comparisons from these poems to the class and discuss what they find so striking about them. After such a discussion, invite the class to formulate an overall statement about Rilke's animals: How are they similar? How are they different? Which—the similarities or the differences—struck a deeper nerve in students? ▪

Interpreting Meanings

1. Opinions will vary. Possible response: The cat's inner nature seems unknowable; this is disturbing to the speaker. "A ghost is . . . like a place" connects the cat to an eerie realm; "like an audience" gives the cat the power of judgment; "like a prehistoric fly" makes the viewer seem small.

2. Possible response: The mysterious creature seems to transcend its human observers, making humanity seem "prehistoric" by comparison.

3. Land is alien for a swan, just as life is alien to us humans. Death is the realm in which we will find ourselves. The metaphor suggests that death is not a terminus but a passage to a higher serenity.

Applying Meanings
Answers will vary.

Creative Writing Response
1. Writing a "Thing Poem" About an Animal. Students can "leapfrog" to a resonant figurative comparison by using free association to list things that their subject makes them think about.

2. Writing from Another Point of View. For interesting results, students can choose a point of view dramatically different from their own.

Language and Vocabulary
1. d **2.** e **3.** b **4.** c **5.** a ▪

---

3. Explain the **extended metaphor** in "The Swan." How might it refer to a religious or spiritual concept of death and the afterlife?

Applying Meanings
In "The Swan," Rilke says that death is one kind of "letting go / of the ground we stand on and cling to every day." What are other things we "cling to"? Have you ever "let go" of any of these things? Were you nervous at first, like the swan? Think of examples of "letting go" from your own life.

Creative Writing Response
1. Writing a "Thing Poem" About an Animal. Choose an animal that you are familiar with or one that you feel strongly about. You may even choose a mythical animal if you like. Then, like Rilke, try to capture the essential spirit of the creature by describing its outward appearance. Use **imagery** and **figurative language** to describe the animal and to convey your feelings about it. If you wrote about an animal in the Writer's Response (see page 1149), you may use this paragraph as the starting point for your poem.

2. Writing from Another Point of View. Imagine yourself being seen from the **point of view** of another person, or even an animal. Think of a characteristic action that reveals your inner nature. For example, imagine someone (or something) observing you as you perform some task that you do well and enjoy—or a task that you do poorly and hate. How would the onlooker see you?

Write a brief prose passage or poem describing yourself as seen from this other point of view.

Language and Vocabulary
German and English

German, like English, belongs to the **Germanic branch** of the Indo-European family of languages. German and English went their separate ways long ago, but in modern times, English has borrowed many words from German. Some of these words entered English in Europe; others were introduced to American English by German-speaking immigrants in the New World. On a separate piece of paper, match each English word listed in the left-hand column with the right-hand column's information about the word's origin. Check your answers in a dictionary.

1. blitz	**a.** from a German term going back to medieval Latin for "small biscuit with crossed arms"
2. delicatessen	**b.** from the German compound of "bell" + "play"
3. glockenspiel	**c.** from the German words for "garden of children"
4. kindergarten	**d.** shortened from the German word for "lightning war"
5. pretzel	**e.** from the German words for "choice foods"

PRIMARY SOURCES

Rilke's Letters to a Young Poet

Early in the twentieth century, an aspiring young poet named Franz Xaver Kappus wrote to Rilke for advice. The two corresponded for several years. After Rilke died, Kappus published Rilke's letters in Letters to a Young Poet *(1929). The following excerpt is from Rilke's first letter to Kappus.*

You ask whether your verses are any good. You ask me. You have asked others before this. You send them to magazines. You compare them with other poems, and you are upset when certain editors reject your work. Now (since you have said you want my advice) I beg you to stop doing that sort of thing. You are looking outside, and that is what you should most avoid right now. No one can advise or help you— no one. There is only one thing you should do. Go into yourself. Find out the reason that commands you to write; see whether it has spread its roots into the very depths of your heart; confess to yourself whether you would have to die if you were forbidden to write. This most of all: ask yourself in the most silent hour of your night: *must* I write? Dig into yourself for a deep answer. And if this answer rings out in assent, if you meet this solemn question with a strong, simple "*I must,*" then build your life in accordance with this necessity; your whole life, even into its humblest and most indifferent hour, must become a sign and witness to this impulse. Then come close to Nature. Then, as if no one had ever tried before, try to say what you see and feel and love and lose. Don't write love poems; avoid those forms that are too facile and ordinary: they are the hardest to work with, and it takes a great, fully ripened power to create something individual where good, even glorious, traditions exist in abundance. So rescue yourself from these general themes and write about what your everyday life offers you; describe your sorrows and desires, the thoughts that pass through your mind and your belief in some kind of beauty—describe all these with heartfelt, silent, humble sincerity and, when you express yourself, use the Things around you, the images from your dreams, and the objects that you remember. If your everyday life seems poor, don't blame *it*; blame yourself; admit to yourself that you are not enough of a poet to call forth its riches; because for the creator there is no poverty and no poor, indifferent place. And even if you found yourself in some prison, whose walls let in none of the world's sounds— wouldn't you still have your childhood, that jewel beyond all price, that treasure house of memories? Turn your attention to it. Try to raise up the sunken feelings of this enormous past; your personality will grow stronger, your solitude will expand and become a place where you can live in the twilight, where the noise of other people passes by, far in the distance.—And if out of this turning-within, out of this immersion in your own world, *poems* come, then you will not think of asking anyone whether they are good or not.

Franz Kafka
1883–1924, Austria/Czechoslovakia

The Granger Collection, New York

Franz Kafka once wrote that literature should be an axe that smashes through the "frozen sea" inside every person. The "frozen sea" is, in part, the alienation and despair that Kafka and many others felt in the unstable years of the early twentieth century. Kafka's grotesque tales often do strike the reader with the force of an axe. In *The Metamorphosis* (1915), for instance, a man transforms into a giant insect and is treated as a vermin by his family. In *The Trial* (1925), a man is arrested, convicted, tried by a mysterious court, and executed without ever knowing his crime. In *The Castle* (1926), the hero is not allowed to communicate with his employer in a castle.

Like many of his characters, Kafka was lonely and insecure. His insecurities stemmed in part from social frictions in his native Prague, now the capital of Czechoslovakia, which for most of Kafka's life was under Austrian control. Although Kafka was educated in Prague's elite German-language academy and became part of a group of German-speaking Jewish intellectuals known as the Prague Circle, he was keenly aware of his status as an outsider in the Czech population. In fact, as a Czech Jew, Kafka was doubly an outsider: He was distrusted by the Czechs because he spoke German and despised by the Germans because he was a Jew.

Kafka had a distant relationship with his father, a stern man who treated his son with indifference and even contempt. Kafka expressed his feelings of dislike and fear, as well as his continued search for approval, in *Letter to His Father*, a one-hundred-page document that was never actually sent to his father.

Kafka was rarely satisfied with his literary efforts, and before his death from tuberculosis he asked his friend and editor Max Brod (1884–1968) to burn his manuscripts. Fortunately for future readers, Brod ignored the request and published the manuscripts. Kafka's works have had an enormous impact on modern literature. They are so famous that they have given rise to the English word *Kafkaesque*, which is used to describe any situation or setting that is characterized by spiritual anxiety, isolation, surreal distortion, or senselessness.

OBJECTIVES

1. To analyze a short story by Franz Kafka
2. To recognize and interpret symbols
3. To rewrite part of a story from a different point of view, to describe a metamorphosis, to analyze a character, and to respond to a critic
4. To identify the meanings of adjectives formed from people's names
5. To evaluate different translations of the same passages

THEMES IN WORLD LITERATURE

Transformations

From the *Metamorphoses*, pp. 420–427
The Tempest, pp. 844–932

The Search for Meaning

From *Faust, Part 1*, pp. 986–1001
"The Lorelei," pp. 1011–1014 ■

VOCABULARY IN CONTEXT

The words listed below will appear in the side margin at the point of instruction:

1. grueling
2. meticulous
3. premonition
4. profusely
5. protruded
6. deterioration
7. blandishments
8. immaculate
9. substantiate
10. scrutinize

Reader's Guide

THE METAMORPHOSIS

Background

Nearly every culture has myths and folktales about people, animals, or objects that undergo startling transformations. Fairy tales often include such metamorphoses: A frog turns into a prince; a pumpkin turns into Cinderella's coach. One of the world's first story collections, *Metamorphoses* by the Roman poet Ovid (see page 420), retells famous transformation stories from Greek and Roman mythology. While Kafka's story draws on traditions from mythology and folklore, it belongs not to the wonderful, magical world of myth, but to the bizarre world of **surrealism**—art or literature that goes beyond realism to portray the irrational events of dreams or nightmares. *The Metamorphosis* begins with a transformation that plunges us immediately into Kafka's world, where extraordinary events are commonplace.

Although it would be a mistake to reduce Kafka's fiction to its autobiographical elements, tensions in his life can be seen in all of his works, perhaps especially in *The Metamorphosis*. Some scholars have pointed out that *Samsa*, the family name of the characters in the story, is a cryptogram (code version) of *Kafka*. Gregor Samsa, the main character, is like Kafka himself in that he has a boring job, wants to spend more time in artistic pursuits, and has mixed feelings toward his family. Sometimes called a novella, *The Metamorphosis* was the longest work that Kafka published in his lifetime.

Writer's Response

Recall a dream you have had that involved bizarre events that could never happen in real life. In a paragraph or two, describe those events and your reaction to them.

Literary Focus

A **symbol** is a person, place, thing, or event that stands both for itself and something beyond itself. Some symbols are widely recognized: a heart is a symbol for love; a snake is a symbol for evil. Sometimes writers create less obvious symbols. For example, a shark may function as the animal itself while it also stands for something else—cruelty or power or nature. A symbol usually represents an abstract idea or a range of related ideas.

PREREADING FOCUS

Background: Troubled all his life by feelings of self-loathing and worthlessness, Franz Kafka had the recurring terror that he would be abused or destroyed like some annoying pest that people might squash or kick. Kafka was also haunted by the feeling that he was inhabited by some unknown beast that might suddenly reveal itself. These feelings were very much in his mind as he wrote *The Metamorphosis* in November and December of 1912. This story is the only one of his works that Kafka truly wanted published. Still, he did not like to talk about *The Metamorphosis*, pointing out that it was not discreet "to talk about the bugs in one's own family."

Literary Focus: For a number of reasons, the central symbol of the "vermin" is a difficult one to interpret. In the first place, Kafka gives no explicit reason for the metamorphosis, nor does he explain why Gregor continues to lose his human qualities as time passes. Kafka also leaves unclear why Gregor's family has little difficulty recognizing him in his new state. Also surprising is how readily Gregor accepts the change in himself, even trying hard to minimize its enormous impact on him.

1 LITERARY ELEMENT

Plot: Critics have noted that *The Metamorphosis* opens with a climax: the transformation of Gregor Samsa into a "monstrous vermin." The rest of the story is a resolution, showing how Gregor and his family deal with this terrible change. What do you predict this resolution will entail? (Answers will vary.)

THE METAMORPHOSIS

Franz Kafka

translated by

STANLEY CORNGOLD

Some readers view the transformation that occurs at the beginning of this story as a literalization of the hostile expression "You vermin!" which Kafka's father had once used to deride one of Kafka's friends. As you read **The Metamorphosis,** *decide whether the transformation could be a* **symbol.** *If so, what does it symbolize?*

Treat Davidson/Photo Researchers, Inc.

1

When Gregor Samsa woke up one morning from unsettling dreams, he found himself changed in his bed into a monstrous vermin. He was lying on his back as hard as armor plate, and when he lifted his head a little, he saw his vaulted brown belly, sectioned by arch-shaped ribs, to whose dome the cover, about to slide off completely, could barely cling. His many legs, pitifully thin compared with the size of the rest of him, were waving helplessly before his eyes.

"What's happened to me?" he thought. It was no dream. His room, a regular human room, only a little on the small side, lay quiet between the four familiar walls. Over the table, on which an unpacked line of fabric samples was all spread out—Samsa was a traveling salesman—hung the picture which he had recently cut out of a glossy magazine and lodged in a pretty gilt frame. It showed a lady done up in a fur hat and a fur boa,[1] sitting upright and raising up against the viewer a heavy fur muff in which her whole forearm had disappeared.

Gregor's eyes then turned to the window, and the overcast weather—he could hear raindrops hitting against the metal window ledge—completely depressed him. "How about going back to sleep for a few minutes and forgetting all this nonsense," he thought, but that was completely impracticable, since he was used to sleeping on his right side and in his present state could not get into that position. No matter how hard he threw himself onto his right side, he always rocked onto his back again. He must have tried it a hundred times, closing his eyes so as not to have to see his squirming legs, and stopped only when he began to feel a slight, dull pain in his side, which he had never felt before.

"Oh God," he thought, "what a grueling job I've picked! Day in, day out—on the road. The upset of doing business is much worse than the actual business in the home office, and, besides, I've got the torture of traveling, worrying about changing trains, eating miserable food at all hours, constantly seeing new faces, no relationships that last or get more intimate. To the devil with it all!" He felt a slight itching up on top of his belly; shoved himself slowly on his back closer to the bedpost, so as to be able to lift his head

better; found the itchy spot, studded with small white dots which he had no idea what to make of; and wanted to touch the spot with one of his legs but immediately pulled it back, for the contact sent a cold shiver through him.

He slid back again into his original position. "This getting up so early," he thought, "makes anyone a complete idiot. Human beings have to have their sleep. Other traveling salesmen live like harem women.[2] For instance, when I go back to the hotel before lunch to write up the business I've done, these gentlemen are just having breakfast. That's all I'd have to try with my boss; I'd be fired on the spot. Anyway, who knows if that wouldn't be a very good thing for me. If I didn't hold back for my parents' sake, I would have quit long ago, I would have marched up to the boss and spoken my piece from the bottom of my heart. He would have fallen off the desk! It is funny, too, the way he sits on the desk and talks down from the heights to the employees, especially when they have to come right up close on account of the boss's being hard of hearing. Well, I haven't given up hope completely; once I've gotten the money together to pay off my parents' debt to him—that will probably take another five or six years—I'm going to do it without fail. Then I'm going to make the big break. But for the time being I'd better get up, since my train leaves at five."

And he looked over at the alarm clock, which was ticking on the chest of drawers. "God Almighty!" he thought. It was six-thirty, the hands were quietly moving forward, it was actually past the half-hour, it was already nearly a quarter to. Could it be that the alarm hadn't gone off? You could

---

1. **boa** (bō′ə): long scarf worn around the neck.

2. **live like harem women:** that is, lead pampered, leisurely lives.

6 LITERARY ELEMENT

Characterization: Despite the amazing change that has oc- curred, Gregor is concerned only with getting to work. What does this tell you about him? (Possible responses: He feels very responsible for sup- porting his debt-laden family; he is in a psychological state of denial.)

7 LITERARY ELEMENT

Theme: A recurring theme in Kafka's work is that the indi- vidual is alienated, or cut off, from others. Even the name *Samsa* sounds like the Czech word *samsja,* meaning "being alone." How does Gregor's strange chirping voice serve to cut him off from others? (The voice makes communication impossible.)

8 VISUALIZING

Have students visualize this scene in which Gregor's mother, father, and sister all knock on different doors of his room. What does the layout of the rooms suggest about Gre- gor's position in the family? (He plays a central role; the family depends on him for support.)

■ **meticulous** (mə·tik′yōo·ləs): extremely careful

see from the bed that it was set correctly for four o'clock; it certainly had gone off, too. Yes, but was it possible to sleep quietly through a ringing that made the furniture shake? Well, he certainly hadn't slept quietly, but probably all the more soundly for that. But what should he do now? The next train left at seven o'clock; to make it, he would have to hurry like a madman, and the line of samples wasn't packed yet, and he himself didn't feel especially fresh and ready to march around. And even if he did make the train, he could not avoid getting it from the boss, because the messenger boy had been waiting at the five-o'clock train and would have long ago reported his not showing up. He was a tool of the boss, without brains or backbone. What if he were to say he was sick? But that would be extremely embar- rassing and suspicious because during his five years with the firm Gregor had not been sick even once. The boss would be sure to come with the health-insurance doctor, blame his parents for their lazy son, and cut off all excuses by quoting the health- insurance doctor, for whom the world con- sisted of people who were completely healthy but afraid to work. And, besides, in this case would he be so very wrong? In fact, Gregor felt fine, with the exception of his drowsiness, which was really unnecessary after sleeping so late, and he even had a ravenous appetite.

Just as he was thinking all this over at top speed, without being able to decide to get out of bed—the alarm clock had just struck a quarter to seven—he heard a cautious knocking at the door next to the head of his bed. "Gregor," someone called—it was his mother—"it's a quarter to seven. Didn't you want to catch the train?" What a soft voice! Gregor was shocked to hear his own voice answering, unmistakably his own voice, true,

but in which, as if from below, an insistent distressed chirping intruded, which left the clarity of his words intact only for a moment really, before so badly garbling them as they carried that no one could be sure if he had heard right. Gregor had wanted to answer in detail and to explain everything, but, given the circumstances, confined himself to saying, "Yes, yes, thanks, Mother, I'm just getting up." The wooden door must have prevented the change in Gregor's voice from being noticed outside, because his mother was satisfied with this explanation and shuf- fled off. But their little exchange had made the rest of the family aware that, contrary to expectations, Gregor was still in the house, and already his father was knocking on one of the side doors, feebly but with his fist. "Gregor, Gregor," he called, "what's going on?" And after a little while he called again in a deeper, warning voice, "Gregor! Gregor!" At the other side door, however, his sister moaned gently, "Gregor? Is something the matter with you? Do you want anything?" Toward both sides Gregor answered: "I'm all ready," and made an effort, by meticulous pronunciation and by inserting long pauses between individual words, to eliminate everything from his voice that might betray him. His father went back to his breakfast, but his sister whispered, "Gregor, open up, I'm pleading with you." But Gregor had ab- solutely no intention of opening the door and complimented himself instead on the precaution he had adopted from his business trips, of locking all the doors during the night even at home.

First of all he wanted to get up quietly, without any excitement; get dressed; and, the main thing, have breakfast, and only then think about what to do next, for he saw clearly that in bed he would never think things through to a rational conclusion. He remembered how even in the past he had often felt some kind of slight pain, possibly caused by lying in an uncomfortable position, which, when he got up, turned out to be purely imaginary, and he was eager to see how today's fantasy would gradually fade away. That the change in his voice was nothing more than the first sign of a bad cold, an occupational ailment of the traveling salesman, he had no doubt in the least.

It was very easy to throw off the cover; all he had to do was puff himself up a little, and it fell off by itself. But after this, things got difficult, especially since he was so unusually broad. He would have needed hands and arms to lift himself up, but instead of that he had only his numerous little legs, which were in every different kind of perpetual motion and which, besides, he could not control. If he wanted to bend one, the first thing that happened was that it stretched itself out; and if he finally succeeded in getting this leg to do what he wanted, all the others in the meantime, as if set free, began to work in the most intensely painful agitation. "Just don't stay in bed being useless," Gregor said to himself.

First he tried to get out of bed with the lower part of his body, but this lower part—which by the way he had not seen yet and which he could not form a clear picture of—proved too difficult to budge; it was taking so long; and when finally, almost out of his mind, he lunged forward with all his force, without caring, he had picked the wrong direction and slammed himself violently against the lower bedpost, and the searing pain he felt taught him that exactly the lower part of his body was, for the moment anyway, the most sensitive.

He therefore tried to get the upper part of his body out of bed first and warily turned his head toward the edge of the bed. This worked easily, and in spite of its width and weight, the mass of his body finally followed, slowly, the movement of his head. But when at last he stuck his head over the edge of the bed into the air, he got too scared to continue any further, since if he finally let himself fall in this position, it would be a miracle if he didn't injure his head. And just now he had better not for the life of him lose consciousness; he would rather stay in bed.

But when, once again, after the same exertion, he lay in his original position, sighing, and again watched his little legs struggling, if possible more fiercely, with each other and saw no way of bringing peace and order into this mindless motion, he again told himself that it was impossible for him to stay in bed and that the most rational thing was to make any sacrifice for even the smallest hope of freeing himself from the bed. But at the same time he did not forget to remind himself occasionally that thinking things over calmly—indeed, as calmly as possible—was much better than jumping to desperate decisions. At such moments he fixed his eyes as sharply as possible on the window, but unfortunately there was little confidence and cheer to be gotten from the view of the morning fog, which shrouded even the other side of the narrow street. "Seven o'clock already," he said to himself as the alarm clock struck again, "seven o'clock already and still such a fog." And for a little while he lay quietly, breathing shallowly, as if expecting, perhaps, from the complete silence the return of things to the way they really and naturally were.

But then he said to himself, "Before it strikes a quarter past seven, I must be completely out of bed without fail. Anyway, by that time someone from the firm will be here to find out where I am, since the office

---

9 LITERARY ELEMENT
Humor: Although Gregor's story is tragic, it contains a few flashes of black humor. Why is Gregor's attempt to rationalize his condition humorous? (Possible response: The changes in Gregor are so complete, so far-reaching, that it is absurd to think they will disappear once he gets up. Kafka pokes fun at the human tendency to rationalize or minimize very serious problems.)

10 GUIDED READING
Identifying Cause and Effect: Why is Gregor having so much difficulty getting out of bed? (His new insect body is foreign to him, and he cannot coordinate his movements.)

11 READER'S RESPONSE
Have you ever had a dream or nightmare in which you were unable to complete a necessary task? Can you identify with Gregor's predicament here? Explain why or why not. (Responses will vary.)

12 LITERARY ELEMENT
Setting: Outside, everything is shrouded in fog. Why is this element of the setting appropriate? (The fog outside suggests the confusion and lack of clarity caused by Gregor's metamorphosis.)

13 EVALUATING

What conclusions might you draw about Gregor's state of mind when you read that he cannot "repress a smile" at the thought of calling for help? (Possible response: He may be secretly pleased that others will have to help and support him for a change.)

14 CULTURAL DIVERSITY

Kafka, an insurance lawyer who represented sick and injured workers, condemned in his fiction the rigid and inhumane conditions in turn-of-the-century European firms. Although Gregor hasn't missed a day of work in years, his manager comes to check on him the first morning he is late.

? *How does Gregor's office compare with workplaces with which you are familiar?* (Answers will vary.)

15 GUIDED READING

Identifying Cause and Effect: What finally enables Gregor to get out of bed? (His feelings of anger toward his manager and firm seem to propel him out of bed.)

opens before seven." And now he started rocking the complete length of his body out of the bed with a smooth rhythm. If he let himself topple out of bed in this way, his head, which on falling he planned to lift up sharply, would presumably remain unharmed. His back seemed to be hard; nothing was likely to happen to it when it fell onto the carpet. His biggest misgiving came from his concern about the loud crash that was bound to occur and would probably create, if not terror, at least anxiety behind all the doors. But that would have to be risked.

When Gregor's body already projected halfway out of bed—the new method was more of a game than a struggle, he only had to keep on rocking and jerking himself along—he thought how simple everything would be if he could get some help. Two strong persons—he thought of his father and the maid—would have been completely sufficient; they would only have had to shove their arms under his arched back, in this way scoop him off the bed, bend down with their burden, and then just be careful and patient while he managed to swing himself down onto the floor, where his little legs would hopefully acquire some purpose. Well, leaving out the fact that the doors were locked, should he really call for help? In spite of all his miseries, he could not repress a smile at this thought.

He was already so far along that when he rocked more strongly he could hardly keep his balance, and very soon he would have to commit himself, because in five minutes it would be a quarter past seven—when the doorbell rang. "It's someone from the firm," he said to himself and almost froze, while his little legs only danced more quickly. For a moment everything remained quiet. "They're not going to answer," Gregor said to himself, captivated by some senseless

hope. But then, of course, the maid went to the door as usual with her firm stride and opened up. Gregor only had to hear the visitor's first word of greeting to know who it was—the office manager himself. Why was only Gregor condemned to work for a firm where at the slightest omission they immediately suspected the worst? Were all employees louts without exception, wasn't there a single loyal, dedicated worker among them who, when he had not fully utilized a few hours of the morning for the firm, was driven half-mad by pangs of conscience and was actually unable to get out of bed? Really, wouldn't it have been enough to send one of the apprentices to find out—if this prying were absolutely necessary—did the manager himself have to come, and did the whole innocent family have to be shown in this way that the investigation of this suspicious affair could be entrusted only to the intellect of the manager? And more as a result of the excitement produced in Gregor by these thoughts than as a result of any real decision, he swung himself out of bed with all his might. There was a loud thump, but it was not a real crash. The fall was broken a little by the carpet, and Gregor's back was more elastic than he had thought, which explained the not very noticeable muffled sound. Only he had not held his head carefully enough and hit it; he turned it and rubbed it on the carpet in anger and pain.

"Something fell in there," said the manager in the room on the left. Gregor tried to imagine whether something like what had happened to him today could one day happen even to the manager; you really had to grant the possibility. But, as if in rude reply to this question, the manager took a few decisive steps in the next room and made his patent leather boots creak. From the room on the right his sister whispered, to inform Gregor, "Gregor, the manager is here." "I know," Gregor said to himself; but he did not dare raise his voice enough for his sister to hear.

"Gregor," his father now said from the room on the left, "the manager has come and wants to be informed why you didn't catch the early train. We don't know what we should say to him. Besides, he wants to speak to you personally. So please open the door. He will certainly be so kind as to excuse the disorder of the room." "Good morning, Mr. Samsa," the manager called in a friendly voice. "There's something the matter with him," his mother said to the manager while his father was still at the door, talking. "Believe me, sir, there's something the matter with him. Otherwise how would Gregor have missed a train? That boy has nothing on his mind but the business. It's almost begun to rile me that he never goes out nights. He's been back in the city for eight days now, but every night he's been home. He sits there with us at the table, quietly reading the paper or studying timetables. It's already a distraction for him when he's busy working with his fret saw.[3] For instance, in the span of two or three evenings he carved a little frame. You'll be amazed how pretty it is; it's hanging inside his room. You'll see it right away when Gregor opens the door. You know, I'm glad that you've come, sir. We would never have gotten Gregor to open the door by ourselves; he's so stubborn. And there's certainly something wrong with him, even though he said this morning there wasn't." "I'm coming right away," said Gregor slowly and deliberately, not moving in order not to miss a word of the conversation. "I haven't any other explanation myself," said the manager. "I hope it's nothing serious. On the other hand, I must say that we businessmen—fortunately or unfortunately, whichever you prefer—very often simply have to overcome a slight indisposition for business reasons." "So can the manager come in now?" asked his father, impatient, and knocked on the door again. "No," said Gregor. In the room on the left there was an embarrassing silence; in the room on the right his sister began to sob.

Why didn't his sister go in to the others? She had probably just got out of bed and not even started to get dressed. Then what was she crying about? Because he didn't get up and didn't let the manager in, because he was in danger of losing his job, and because then the boss would start hounding his parents about the old debts? For the time being, certainly, her worries were unnecessary. Gregor was still here and hadn't the slightest intention of letting the family down. True, at the moment he was lying on the carpet, and no one knowing his condition could seriously have expected him to let the manager in. But just because of this slight discourtesy, for which an appropriate excuse would easily be found later on, Gregor could not simply be dismissed. And to Gregor it seemed much more sensible to leave him alone now than to bother him with crying and persuasion. But it was just the uncertainty that was tormenting the others and excused their behavior.

"Mr. Samsa," the manager now called, raising his voice, "what's the matter? You barricade yourself in your room, answer only 'yes' and 'no,' cause your parents serious, unnecessary worry, and you neglect—I mention this only in passing—your duties to the firm in a really shocking manner. I am speaking here in the name of your parents and of

---

3. **fret saw:** saw with a long narrow blade and fine teeth, used to cut scrolls and other curved patterns in boards or metal plates.

16 LITERARY ELEMENT

Mood: Which details does Kafka use to create a stifling, claustrophobic mood in these opening pages? (Gregor is trapped inside a strange insect body; he is locked in a room; his family and manager knock on the doors and make demands of him.)

17 EVALUATING

Gregor's whole life is consumed by a job he hates. He is so deadened that when not working, he sits home and studies timetables. What might Kafka be saying about the effects of commerce and materialism on people? (Possible response: The economic imperatives of modern life cut people off from their feelings, creative impulses, and inner selves.)

MEETING INDIVIDUAL NEEDS

18 LEP: Explain that "to overcome a slight indisposition for business reasons" means "to work when feeling sick." Point out that this is a humorous understatement, since Gregor suffers from more than a slight indisposition. Indeed, his metamorphosis means that he can never resume his work. ∎

your employer and ask you in all seriousness for an immediate, clear explanation. I'm amazed, amazed. I thought I knew you to be a quiet, reasonable person, and now you suddenly seem to want to start strutting about, flaunting strange whims. The head of the firm did suggest to me this morning a possible explanation for your tardiness—it concerned the cash payments recently entrusted to you—but really, I practically gave my word of honor that this explanation could not be right. But now, seeing your incomprehensible obstinacy, I am about to lose even the slightest desire to stick up for you in any way at all. And your job is not the most secure. Originally I intended to tell you all this in private, but since you make me waste my time here for nothing, I don't see why your parents shouldn't hear, too. Your performance of late has been very unsatisfactory; I know it is not the best season for doing business, we all recognize that; but a season for not doing any business, there is no such thing. Mr. Samsa, such a thing cannot be tolerated."

"But sir," cried Gregor, beside himself, in his excitement forgetting everything else, "I'm just opening up, in a minute. A slight indisposition, a dizzy spell, prevented me from getting up. I'm still in bed. But I already feel fine again. I'm just getting out of bed. Just be patient for a minute! I'm not as well as I thought yet. But really I'm fine. How something like this could just take a person by surprise! Only last night I was fine, my parents can tell you, or wait, last night I already had a slight premonition. They must have been able to tell by looking at me. Why didn't I report it to the office! But you always think that you'll get over a sickness without staying home. Sir! Spare my parents! There's no basis for any of the accusations that you're making against me now; no one has

ever said a word to me about them. Perhaps you haven't seen the last orders I sent in. Anyway, I'm still going on the road with the eight o'clock train; these few hours of rest have done me good. Don't let me keep you, sir. I'll be at the office myself right away, and be so kind as to tell them this, and give my respects to the head of the firm."

And while Gregor hastily blurted all this out, hardly knowing what he was saying, he had easily approached the chest of drawers, probably as a result of the practice he had already gotten in bed, and now he tried to raise himself up against it. He actually intended to open the door, actually present himself and speak to the manager; he was eager to find out what the others, who were now so anxious to see him, would say at the sight of him. If they were shocked, then Gregor had no further responsibility and could be calm. But if they took everything calmly, then he, too, had no reason to get excited and could, if he hurried, actually be at the station by eight o'clock. At first he slid off the polished chest of drawers a few times, but at last, giving himself a final push, he stood upright; he no longer paid any attention to the pains in his abdomen, no matter how much they were burning. Now he let himself fall against the back of a nearby chair, clinging to its slats with his little legs. But by doing this he had gotten control of himself and fell silent, since he could now listen to what the manager was saying.

"Did you understand a word?" the manager was asking his parents. "He isn't trying to make fools of us, is he?" "My God," cried his mother, already in tears, "maybe he's seriously ill, and here we are, torturing him. Grete![4] Grete!" she then cried. "Mother?" called his sister from the other side. They

---

4. **Grete** (grē′tə)

communicated by way of Gregor's room. "Go to the doctor's immediately. Gregor is sick. Hurry, get the doctor. Did you just hear Gregor talking?" "That was the voice of an animal," said the manager, in a tone conspicuously soft compared with the mother's yelling. "Anna!" "Anna!" the father called through the foyer into the kitchen, clapping his hands, "get a locksmith right away!" And already the two girls were running with rustling skirts through the foyer—how could his sister have gotten dressed so quickly?—and tearing open the door to the apartment. The door could not be heard slamming; they had probably left it open, as is the custom in homes where a great misfortune has occurred.

But Gregor had become much calmer. It was true that they no longer understood his words, though they had seemed clear enough to him, clearer than before, probably because his ear had grown accustomed to them. But still, the others now believed that there was something the matter with him and were ready to help him. The assurance and confidence with which the first measures had been taken did him good. He felt integrated into human society once again and hoped for marvelous, amazing feats from both the doctor and the locksmith, without really distinguishing sharply between them. In order to make his voice as clear as possible for the crucial discussions that were approaching, he cleared his throat a little—taking pains, of course, to do so in a very muffled manner, since this noise, too, might sound different from human coughing, a thing he no longer trusted himself to decide. In the next room, meanwhile, everything had become completely still. Perhaps his parents were sitting at the table with the manager, whispering; perhaps they were all leaning against the door and listening.

Gregor slowly lugged himself toward the door, pushing the chair in front of him, then let go of it, threw himself against the door, held himself upright against it—the pads on the bottom of his little legs exuded a little sticky substance—and for a moment rested there from the exertion. But then he got started turning the key in the lock with his mouth. Unfortunately it seemed that he had no real teeth—what was he supposed to grip the key with?—but in compensation his jaws, of course, were very strong; with their help he actually got the key moving and paid no attention to the fact that he was undoubtedly hurting himself in some way, for a brown liquid came out of his mouth, flowed over the key, and dripped onto the floor. "Listen," said the manager in the next room, "he's turning the key." This was great encouragement to Gregor; but everyone should have cheered him on, his father and mother, too. "Go, Gregor," they should have called, "keep going, at that lock, harder, harder!" And in the delusion that they were all following his efforts with suspense, he clamped his jaws madly on the key with all the strength he could muster. Depending on the progress of the key, he danced around the lock; holding himself upright only by his mouth, he clung to the key, as the situation demanded, or pressed it down again with the whole weight of his body. The clearer click of the lock as it finally snapped back literally woke Gregor up. With a sigh of relief he said to himself, "So I didn't need the locksmith after all," and laid his head down on the handle in order to open wide one wing of the double doors.

Since he had to use this method of opening the door, it was really opened very wide while he himself was still invisible. He first had to edge slowly around the one wing of the door, and do so very carefully if he was not to fall flat on his back just before entering. He was still busy with this difficult maneuver and had no time to pay attention to anything else when he heard the manager burst out with a loud "Oh!"—it sounded like a rush of wind—and now he could see him, standing closest to the door, his hand pressed over his open mouth, slowly backing away, as if repulsed by an invisible, unrelenting force. His mother—in spite of the manager's presence she stood with her hair still unbraided from the night, sticking out in all directions—first looked at his father with her hands clasped, then took two steps toward Gregor, and sank down in the midst of her skirts spreading out around her, her face completely hidden on her breast. With a hostile expression his father clenched his fist, as if to drive Gregor back into his room, then looked uncertainly around the living room, shielded his eyes with his hands, and sobbed with heaves of his powerful chest.

Now Gregor did not enter the room after all but leaned against the inside of the firmly bolted wing of the door, so that only half his body was visible and his head above it, cocked to one side and peeping out at the others. In the meantime it had grown much lighter; across the street one could see clearly a section of the endless, grayish black building opposite—it was a hospital—with its regular windows starkly piercing the façade; the rain was still coming down, but only in large, separately visible drops that were also pelting the ground literally one at a time. The breakfast dishes were laid out lavishly on the table, since for his father breakfast was the most important meal of the day, which he would prolong for hours while reading various newspapers. On the wall directly opposite hung a photograph of Gregor from his army days, in a lieutenant's uniform, his hand on his sword, a carefree smile on his lips, demanding respect for his bearing and his rank. The door to the foyer was open, and since the front door was open, too, it was possible to see out onto the landing and the top of the stairs going down.

"Well," said Gregor—and he was thoroughly aware of being the only one who had kept calm—"I'll get dressed right away, pack up my samples, and go. Will you, will you please let me go? Now, sir, you see, I'm not stubborn and I'm willing to work; traveling is a hardship, but without it I couldn't live. Where are you going, sir? To the office? Yes? Will you give an honest report of everything? A man might find for a moment that he was unable to work, but that's exactly the right time to remember his past accomplishments and to consider that later on, when the obstacle has been removed, he's bound to work all the harder and more efficiently. I'm under so many obligations to the head of the firm, as you know very well. Besides, I also have my parents and my sister to worry about. I'm in a tight spot, but I'll also work my way out again. Don't make things harder for me than they already are. Stick up for me in the office, please. Traveling salesmen aren't well liked there, I know. People think they make a fortune leading the gay life. No one has any particular reason to rectify this prejudice. But you, sir, you have a better perspective on things than the rest of the office, an even better perspective, just between the two of us, than the head of the firm himself, who in his capacity as owner easily lets his judgment be swayed against an employee. And you also know very well that the traveling salesman, who is out of the office practically the whole year round, can so easily become the victim of gossip, coincidences, and unfounded accusations, against which he's completely unable to defend himself,

PAROIS D'OREINES, JEAN DUBUFFET (1901–1985)
❓ What is Gregor's initial reaction to his transformation? Does his reaction surprise you?

since in most cases he knows nothing at all about them except when he returns exhausted from a trip, and back home gets to suffer on his own person the grim consequences, which can no longer be traced back to their causes. Sir, don't go away without a word to tell me you think I'm at least partly right!"

But at Gregor's first words the manager had already turned away and with curled lips looked back at Gregor only over his twitching shoulder. And during Gregor's speech he did not stand still for a minute but, without letting Gregor out of his sight, backed toward the door, yet very gradually, as if there were some secret prohibition against leaving the room. He was already in the foyer, and from the sudden movement with which he took his last step from the living room, one

might have thought he had just burned the sole of his foot. In the foyer, however, he stretched his right hand far out toward the staircase, as if nothing less than an unearthly deliverance were awaiting him there.

Gregor realized that he must on no account let the manager go away in this mood if his position in the firm were not to be jeopardized in the extreme. His parents did not understand this too well; in the course of the years they had formed the conviction that Gregor was set for life in this firm; and furthermore, they were so preoccupied with their immediate troubles that they had lost all consideration for the future. But Gregor had this forethought. The manager must be detained, calmed down, convinced, and finally won over; Gregor's and the family's future depended on it! If only his sister had been there! She was perceptive; she had already begun to cry when Gregor was still lying calmly on his back. And certainly the manager, this ladies' man, would have listened to her; she would have shut the front door and in the foyer talked him out of his scare. But his sister was not there, Gregor had to handle the situation himself. And without stopping to realize that he had no idea what his new faculties of movement were, and without stopping to realize either that his speech had possibly—indeed, probably—not been understood again, he let go of the wing of the door; he shoved himself through the opening, intending to go to the manager, who was already on the landing, ridiculously holding onto the banisters with both hands; but groping for support, Gregor immediately fell down with a little cry onto his numerous little legs. This had hardly happened when for the first time that morning he had a feeling of physical well-being; his little legs were on firm ground; they obeyed him completely, as he noted to his

30

31

HUMANITIES CONNECTION

After his first art show in 1925, French painter Jean Dubuffet withdrew from public life to develop a style of simple, childlike images cut into a heavily-encrusted canvas. When his paintings were shown in Paris in 1944, critics described his style as *l'art brut* ("raw art") because of its crude, often violent quality.
❓ *In what ways does Dubuffet's style reflect Gregor's plight?* (Possible response: The naive, childlike Gregor is set against a cruel, violent world, as the figures in Dubuffet's paintings are set against a harsh background of ash and ground glass.) ■

30 GUIDED READING

Finding the Main Idea: What "mood" is the manager in? (He is frightened, horrified, and disgusted by Gregor's appearance.) Why does Gregor feel his job is in jeopardy? (He assumes that his firm will not want someone who looks like him for an employee.)

31 INTERPRETING

Based on this passage, how does Gregor feel about his sister? (He admires her for her sensitivity and understanding; he believes she could help him get out of his desperate situation.)

Franz Kafka **1165**

Kinesthetic Learners: Suggest that students enact the events on this page—the manager's nervous withdrawal from the apartment, Gregor's desperate attempt to stop the manager, and Mrs. Samsa's frightened reactions to the movements of her son. ■

READER'S RESPONSE

Imagine for a moment that you see a large cockroach or other beetle on the floor of your house. Even though it is harmless, why might you try to crush or kill it? (Answers will vary. Some insects might frighten us because they are ugly or because we associate them with uncleanliness and disease.)

LITERARY ELEMENT

Point of View: Why do you think that readers might have more sympathy for Gregor than his own father has? (Since the third-person narrator describes Gregor's thoughts and feelings in detail, readers tend to feel sympathy for Gregor.)

32 LITERARY ELEMENT

Motivation: After ferociously driving Gregor toward his room, Mr. Samsa directs Gregor's efforts to turn himself around by gesturing with the cane. What feelings motivate the father to act in this way? (He is furious and disgusted by his son's appearance and wants him back in his room as quickly as possible.)

joy; they even strained to carry him away wherever he wanted to go; and he already believed that final recovery from all his sufferings was imminent. But at that very moment, as he lay on the floor rocking with repressed motion, not far from his mother and just opposite her, she, who had seemed so completely self-absorbed, all at once jumped up, her arms stretched wide, her fingers spread, and cried, "Help, for God's sake, help!" held her head bent as if to see Gregor better, but inconsistently darted madly backward instead; had forgotten that the table laden with the breakfast dishes stood behind her; sat down on it hastily, as if her thoughts were elsewhere, when she reached it; and did not seem to notice at all that near her the big coffeepot had been knocked over and coffee was pouring in a steady stream onto the rug.

"Mother, Mother," said Gregor softly and looked up at her. For a minute the manager had completely slipped his mind; on the other hand at the sight of the spilling coffee he could not resist snapping his jaws several times in the air. At this his mother screamed once more, fled from the table, and fell into the arms of his father, who came rushing up to her. But Gregor had no time now for his parents; the manager was already on the stairs; with his chin on the banister, he was taking a last look back. Gregor was off to a running start, to be as sure as possible of catching up with him; the manager must have suspected something like this, for he leaped down several steps and disappeared; but still he shouted "Agh," and the sound carried through the whole staircase. Unfortunately the manager's flight now seemed to confuse his father completely, who had been relatively calm until now, for instead of running after the manager himself, or at least not hindering Gregor in his pursuit, he

seized in his right hand the manager's cane, which had been left behind on a chair with his hat and overcoat, picked up in his left hand a heavy newspaper from the table, and stamping his feet, started brandishing the cane and the newspaper to drive Gregor back into his room. No plea of Gregor's helped, no plea was even understood; however humbly he might turn his head, his father merely stamped his feet more forcefully. Across the room his mother had thrown open a window in spite of the cool weather, and leaning out, she buried her face, far outside the window, in her hands. Between the alley and the staircase a strong draft was created, the window curtains blew in, the newspapers on the table rustled, single sheets fluttered across the floor. Pitilessly his father came on, hissing like a wild man. Now Gregor had not had any practice at all walking in reverse, it was really very slow going. If Gregor had only been allowed to turn around, he could have gotten into his room right away, but he was afraid to make his father impatient by this time-consuming gyration, and at any minute the cane in his father's hand threatened to come down on his back or his head with a deadly blow. Finally, however, Gregor had no choice, for he noticed with horror that in reverse he could not even keep going in one direction; and so, incessantly throwing uneasy side glances at his father, he began to turn around as quickly as possible, in reality turning only very slowly. Perhaps his father realized his good intentions, for he did not interfere with him; instead, he even now and then directed the maneuver from afar with the tip of his cane. If only his father did not keep making this intolerable hissing sound! It made Gregor lose his head completely. He had almost finished the turn when—his mind continually on this hissing—he made a mistake

32

and even started turning back around to his original position. But when he had at last successfully managed to get his head in front of the opened door, it turned out that his body was too broad to get through as it was. Of course in his father's present state of mind it did not even remotely occur to him to open the other wing of the door in order to give Gregor enough room to pass through. He had only the fixed idea that Gregor must return to his room as quickly as possible. He would never have allowed the complicated preliminaries Gregor needed to go through in order to stand up on one end and perhaps in this way fit through the door. Instead, he drove Gregor on, as if there were no obstacle, with exceptional loudness; the voice behind Gregor did not sound like that of only a single father; now this was really no joke anymore, and Gregor forced himself—come what may—into the doorway. One side of his body rose up, he lay lopsided in the opening, one of his flanks was scraped raw, ugly blotches marred the white door, soon he got stuck and could not have budged any more by himself, his little legs on one side dangled tremblingly in midair, those on the other were painfully crushed against the floor—when from behind his father gave him a hard shove, which was truly his salvation, and bleeding profusely, he flew far into his room. The door was slammed shut with the cane, then at last everything was quiet.

2

It was already dusk when Gregor awoke from his deep, comalike sleep. Even if he had not been disturbed, he would certainly not have woken up much later, for he felt that he had rested and slept long enough, but it seemed to him that a hurried step and a cautious shutting of the door leading to the foyer had awakened him. The light of the electric streetlamps lay in pallid streaks on the ceiling and on the upper parts of the furniture, but underneath, where Gregor was, it was dark. Groping clumsily with his antennae, which he was only now beginning to appreciate, he slowly dragged himself toward the door to see what had been happening there. His left side felt like one single long, unpleasantly tautening scar, and he actually had to limp on his two rows of legs. Besides, one little leg had been seriously injured in the course of the morning's events—it was almost a miracle that only one had been injured—and dragged along lifelessly.

Only after he got to the door did he notice what had really attracted him—the smell of something to eat. For there stood a bowl filled with fresh milk, in which small slices of white bread were floating. He could almost have laughed for joy, since he was even hungrier than he had been in the morning, and he immediately dipped his head into the milk, almost to over his eyes. But he soon drew it back again in disappointment; not only because he had difficulty eating on account of the soreness in his left side—and he could eat only if his whole panting body cooperated—but because he didn't like the milk at all, although it used to be his favorite drink, and that was certainly why his sister had put it in the room; in fact, he turned away from the bowl almost with repulsion and crawled back to the middle of the room.

In the living room, as Gregor saw through the crack in the door, the gas had been lit, but while at this hour of the day his father was in the habit of reading the afternoon newspaper in a loud voice to his mother and sometimes to his sister, too, now there wasn't a sound. Well, perhaps this custom

■ profusely (prō·fyo͞os′lē): abundantly

COMPARING LITERATURE
Point out that the story is divided into three parts and that in each part Gregor makes one effort to leave his room and establish human contact with the others. Have students describe what usually happens in traditional tales when a hero makes three attempts to complete a task or reach a goal. (The hero fails in the first two attempts but succeeds in the third.) Have students speculate on whether they think this story will follow that traditional pattern.

33 SYNTHESIZING
What details on this page suggest that Gregor is becoming more insectlike as time passes? (Gregor begins to appreciate his antennae; he rests underneath the furniture; he no longer likes milk, once his favorite drink.)

33

34 GUIDED READING

Finding the Main Idea: Why might the Samsa family's peace and comfort soon come to a "horrible end"? (Without Gregor's job, they will have no income. They might lose their apartment and possessions.)

35 LITERARY ELEMENT

Symbol: Not having eaten all day, Gregor is hungry for food. But Kafka also uses hunger as a symbol for Gregor's unsatisfied need for affection. Ask students to evaluate future story references to food and hunger in this light.

36 COMPARING LITERATURE

In the fairy tale "Beauty and the Beast," the ugly beast needed Beauty to accept his ugliness and love him for his inner qualities.
❓ *In what way is Gregor similar to the beast?* (Gregor, too, needs someone to accept his new form and love him for his inner qualities.)

37 LITERARY ELEMENT

Motivation: What conflicting feelings cause Gregor's sister to enter, leave, and then quickly reenter his room? (She is horrified by her brother's new form but also feels love and a sense of duty toward him.)

of reading aloud, which his sister was always telling him and writing him about, had recently been discontinued altogether. But in all the other rooms, too, it was just as still, although the apartment certainly was not empty. "What a quiet life the family has been leading," Gregor said to himself, and while he stared rigidly in front of him into the darkness, he felt very proud that he had been able to provide such a life in so nice an apartment for his parents and his sister. **But what now if all the peace, the comfort, the contentment, were to come to a horrible end?** In order not to get involved in such thoughts, Gregor decided to keep moving, and he crawled up and down the room.

During the long evening first one of the side doors and then the other was opened a small crack and quickly shut again; someone had probably had the urge to come in and then had had second thoughts. Gregor now settled into position right by the living-room door, determined somehow to get the hesitating visitor to come in, or at least to find out who it might be; but the door was not opened again, and Gregor waited in vain. In the morning, when the doors had been locked, everyone had wanted to come in; now that he had opened one of the doors and the others had evidently been opened during the day, no one came in, and now the keys were even inserted on the outside.

It was late at night when the light finally went out in the living room, and now it was easy for Gregor to tell that his parents and his sister had stayed up so long, since, as he could distinctly hear, all three were now retiring on tiptoe. Certainly no one would come in to Gregor until the morning; and so he had ample time to consider undisturbed how best to rearrange his life. But the empty high-ceilinged room in which he was forced to lie flat on the floor made him nervous,

without his being able to tell why—since it was, after all, the room in which he had lived for the past five years—and turning half unconsciously and not without a slight feeling of shame, he scuttled under the couch where, although his back was a little crushed and he could not raise his head any more, he immediately felt very comfortable and was only sorry that his body was too wide to go completely under the couch.

There he stayed the whole night, which he spent partly in a sleepy trance, from which hunger pangs kept waking him with a start, partly in worries and vague hopes, all of which, however, led to the conclusion that for the time being he would have to lie low and, **by being patient and showing his family every possible consideration, help them bear the inconvenience which he simply had to cause them in his present condition.**

Early in the morning—it was still almost night—Gregor had the opportunity of testing the strength of the resolutions he had just made, for his sister, almost fully dressed, opened the door from the foyer and looked in eagerly. She did not see him right away, **but when she caught sight of him under the couch—God, he had to be somewhere, he couldn't just fly away—she became so frightened that she lost control of herself and slammed the door shut again. But, as if she felt sorry for her behavior, she immediately opened the door again and came in on tiptoe, as if she were visiting someone seriously ill or perhaps even a stranger.** Gregor had pushed his head forward just to the edge of the couch and was watching her. Would she notice that he had left the milk standing, and not because he hadn't been hungry, and would she bring in a dish of something he'd like better? If she were not going to do it of her own free will, he would rather starve than call it to her attention, although, really, he felt an enormous urge to shoot out from under the couch, throw himself at his sister's feet, and beg her for something good to eat. But his sister noticed at once, to her astonishment, that the bowl was still full, only a little milk was spilled around it; she picked it up immediately—not with her bare hands, of course, but with a rag—and carried it out. Gregor was extremely curious to know what she would bring him instead, and he racked his brains on the subject. But he would never have been able to guess what his sister, in the goodness of her heart, actually did. To find out his likes and dislikes, she brought him a wide assortment of things, all spread out on an old newspaper: old, half-rotten vegetables; bones left over from the evening meal, caked with congealed white sauce; some raisins and almonds; a piece of cheese, which two days before Gregor had declared inedible; a plain slice of bread, a slice of bread and butter, and one with butter and salt. In addition to all this she put down some water in the bowl apparently permanently earmarked for Gregor's use. And out of a sense of delicacy, since she knew that Gregor would not eat in front of her, she left hurriedly and even turned the key, just so that Gregor should know that he might make himself as comfortable as he wanted. Gregor's legs began whirring now that he was going to eat. Besides, his bruises must have completely healed, since he no longer felt any handicap, and marveling at this he thought how, over a month ago, he had cut his finger very slightly with a knife and how this wound was still hurting him only the day before yesterday. "Have I become less sensitive?" he thought, already sucking greedily at the cheese, which had immediately and forcibly attracted him ahead of all the other dishes. One right after the other, and with eyes streaming with tears of contentment, he devoured the cheese, the vegetables, and the sauce; the fresh foods, on the other hand, he did not care for; he couldn't even stand their smell and even dragged the things he wanted to eat a bit farther away. He had finished with everything long since and was just lying lazily at the same spot when his sister slowly turned the key as a sign for him to withdraw. That immediately startled him, although he was almost asleep, and he scuttled under the couch again. But it took great self-control for him to stay under the couch even for the short time his sister was in the room, since his body had become a little bloated from the heavy meal, and in his cramped position he could hardly breathe. In between slight attacks of suffocation he watched with bulging eyes as his unsuspecting sister took a broom and swept up, not only his leavings, but even the foods which Gregor had left completely untouched—as if they too were no longer usable—and dumping everything hastily into a pail, which she covered with a wooden lid, she carried everything out. She had hardly turned her back when Gregor came out from under the couch, stretching and puffing himself up.

This, then, was the way Gregor was fed each day, once in the morning, when his parents and the maid were still asleep, and a second time in the afternoon after everyone had had dinner, for then his parents took a short nap again, and the maid could be sent out by his sister on some errand. Certainly they did not want him to starve either, but perhaps they would not have been able to stand knowing any more about his meals than from hearsay, or perhaps his sister wanted to spare them even what was possibly only a minor torment, for really, they were suffering enough as it was.

38 LITERARY ELEMENT
Details: Why do you think Kafka tells us that Grete picks up the bowl with a rag, not her bare hands? (This detail expresses how revolting she finds her brother's new form.)

MEETING INDIVIDUAL NEEDS

39 *LEP:* Explain that *earmarked* means "set aside or reserved for a particular use."

40 EVALUATING
Do you think Gregor may have become less sensitive? Why or why not? (Answers will vary. As Gregor grows more insect-like, he may be losing some human sensibilities, such as sensitivity to pain.)

41 GUIDED READING

Identifying Cause and Effect:
Why do the Samsas assume
Gregor cannot understand
them? (Since they cannot understand him, they assume he
has also lost the ability to understand them.) How might
this assumption affect Gregor?
(He will feel increasingly isolated, since no one will try to
communicate with him.)

42 LITERARY ELEMENT

Foreshadowing: What might
Kafka be hinting at here about
Gregor's fate? (He might starve
to death.) Keeping in mind
that Gregor's hunger symbolizes his need for affection,
what might we expect to occur
between him and his family?
(His sister and parents will
have less and less to do with
Gregor.)

43 CULTURAL DIVERSITY

Gregor's condition, which
makes keeping servants difficult, deals a blow to his family's social standing.
❓ *What types of changes indicate the rise or fall of a
family's status in our society?*

44 INTERPRETING

Mr. Samsa's discussion of the
family's financial situation
comes to Gregor as "pleasant
news." How do you interpret
this? (Gregor thought the family was completely dependent
on him; now it seems that Mr.
Samsa has put away a little
money.) Has Mr. Samsa been
open or fair with Gregor? Explain. (No, he has deliberately
concealed resources and has
done nothing to lighten the
burden on his son.)

41 Gregor could not find out what excuses had been made to get rid of the doctor and the locksmith on that first morning, for since the others could not understand what he said, it did not occur to any of them, not even to his sister, that he could understand what they said, and so he had to be satisfied, when his sister was in the room, with only occasionally hearing her sighs and appeals to the saints. It was only later, when she had begun to get used to everything—there could never, of course, be any question of a complete adjustment—that Gregor some-times caught a remark which was meant to be friendly or could be interpreted as such. "Oh, he liked what he had today," she would **42** say when Gregor had tucked away a good helping, and in the opposite case, which gradually occurred more and more fre-quently, she used to say, almost sadly, "He's left everything again."

But if Gregor could not get any news di-rectly, he overheard a great deal from the neighboring rooms, and as soon as he heard voices, he would immediately run to the door concerned and press his whole body against it. Especially in the early days, there was no conversation that was not somehow about him, if only implicitly. For two whole days there were family consultations at every mealtime about how they should cope; this was also the topic of discussion between meals, for at least two members of the fami-ly were always at home, since no one prob-ably wanted to stay home alone and it was impossible to leave the apartment com-pletely empty. Besides, on the very first day the maid—it was not completely clear what and how much she knew of what had hap-pened—had begged his mother on bended knees to dismiss her immediately; and when **43** she said goodbye a quarter of an hour later, she thanked them in tears for the dismissal, **43** as if for the greatest favor that had ever been done to her in this house, and made a sol-emn vow, without anyone asking her for it, not to give anything away to anyone.

Now his sister, working with her mother, had to do the cooking, too; of course, that did not cause her much trouble, since they hardly ate anything. Gregor was always hear-ing one of them pleading in vain with one of the others to eat and getting no answer except, "Thanks, I've had enough," or some-thing similar. They did not seem to drink anything either. His sister often asked her father if he wanted any beer and gladly of-fered to go out for it herself; and when he did not answer, she said, in order to remove any hesitation on his part, that she could also send the janitor's wife to get it, but then his father finally answered with a definite "No," and that was the end of that.

In the course of the very first day his father explained the family's financial situa-tion and prospects to both the mother and the sister. From time to time he got up from the table to get some kind of receipt or notebook out of the little strongbox he had rescued from the collapse of his business five years before. Gregor heard him open the complicated lock and secure it again after taking out what he had been looking for. These explanations by his father were to **44** some extent the first pleasant news Gregor had heard since his imprisonment. He had always believed that his father had not been able to save a penny from the business, at least his father had never told him anything to the contrary, and Gregor, for his part, had never asked him any questions. In those days Gregor's sole concern had been to do everything in his power to make the family forget as quickly as possible the business disaster which had plunged everyone into a state of total despair. And so he had begun to work with special ardor and had risen almost overnight from stock clerk to traveling salesman, which of course had opened up very different moneymaking possibilities, and in no time his successes on the job were transformed, by means of commissions, into hard cash that could be plunked down on the table at home in front of his astonished and delighted family. Those had been wonderful times, and they had never returned, at least not with the same glory, although later on Gregor earned enough money to meet the expenses of the entire family and actually did so. They had just gotten used to it, the family as well as Gregor, the money was received with thanks and given with pleasure, but no special feeling of warmth went with it any more. Only his sister had remained close to Gregor, and it was his secret plan that she, who, unlike him, loved music and could play the violin movingly, should be sent next year to the Conservatory,[5] regardless of the great expense involved, which could surely be made up for in some other way. Often during Gregor's short stays in the city the Conservatory would come up in his conversations with his sister, but always merely as a beautiful dream which was not supposed to come true, and his parents were not happy to hear even these innocent allusions; but Gregor had very concrete ideas on the subject and he intended solemnly to announce his plan on Christmas Eve.

Thoughts like these, completely useless in his present state, went through his head as he stood glued to the door, listening. Sometimes out of general exhaustion he could not listen any more and let his head bump carelessly against the door, but immediately pulled it back again, for even the slight noise he made by doing this had been heard in the next room and made them all lapse into silence. "What's he carrying on about in there now?" said his father after a while, obviously turning toward the door, and only then would the interrupted conversation gradually be resumed.

Gregor now learned in a thorough way—for his father was in the habit of often repeating himself in his explanations, partly because he himself had not dealt with these matters for a long time, partly, too, because his mother did not understand everything the first time around—that in spite of all their misfortunes, a bit of capital, a very little bit, certainly, was still intact from the old days, which in the meantime had increased a little through the untouched interest. But besides that, the money Gregor had brought home every month—he had kept only a few dollars for himself—had never been completely used up and had accumulated into a tidy principal. Behind his door Gregor nodded emphatically, delighted at this unexpected foresight and thrift. Of course he actually could have paid off more of his father's debt to the boss with this extra money, and the day on which he could have gotten rid of his job would have been much closer, but now things were undoubtedly better the way his father had arranged them.

Now this money was by no means enough to let the family live off the interest; the principal was perhaps enough to support the family for one year, or at the most two, but that was all there was. So it was just a sum that really should not be touched and that had to be put away for a rainy day; but the money to live on would have to be earned. Now his father was still healthy, certainly, but he was an old man who had not worked for the past five years and who in any case

5. **Conservatory:** school of music.

Franz Kafka   **1171**

Employment open to women in Eastern Europe at the turn of the century was quite limited. Gregor feels "shame and grief" because his mother and sister will necessarily have to work at low-status, low-paying jobs.

❓ *Do women and men have equal job opportunities in our society? Explain your answer.* (Answers will vary.)

48 **LITERARY ELEMENT**

Symbol: As Gregor's metamorphosis proceeds, how does his vision change? (He is becoming nearsighted.) What might the shortening of his field of vision symbolize? (Life is falling away from him; he is being confined, even visually, to his own room.)

could not be expected to undertake too much; during these five years, which were the first vacation of his hard-working yet unsuccessful life, he had gained a lot of weight and as a result had become fairly sluggish. And was his old mother now supposed to go out and earn money, when she suffered from asthma, when a walk through the apartment was already an ordeal for her, and when she spent every other day lying on the sofa under the open window, gasping for breath? And was his sister now supposed to work—who for all her seventeen years was still a child and whom it would be such a pity to deprive of the life she had led until now, which had consisted of wearing pretty clothes, sleeping late, helping in the house, enjoying a few modest amusements, and above all, playing the violin? At first, whenever the conversation turned to the necessity of earning money, Gregor would let go **47** of the door and throw himself down on the cool leather sofa which stood beside it, for he felt hot with shame and grief.

Often he lay there the whole long night through, not sleeping a wink and only scrabbling on the leather for hours on end. Or, not balking at the huge effort of pushing an armchair to the window, he would crawl up to the window sill and, propped up in the chair, lean against the window, evidently in some sort of remembrance of the feeling of freedom he used to have from looking out the window. For, in fact, from day to day he saw things even a short distance away less **48** and less distinctly; the hospital opposite, which he used to curse because he saw so much of it, was now completely beyond his range of vision, and if he had not been positive that he was living in Charlotte Street— a quiet but still very much a city street—he might have believed that he was looking out of his window into a desert where the gray

sky and the gray earth were indistinguishably fused. It took his observant sister only twice to notice that his armchair was standing by the window for her to push the chair back to the same place by the window each time she had finished cleaning the room, and from then on she even left the inside casement of the window open.

SPINNING ROUND, JEAN DUBUFFET, 1961.

? How would you describe the tone of Kafka's novella thus far? Comic? Ironic? Tragic? Explain your answer.

© 1998 Artists Rights Society (ARS), New York/ADAGP, Paris

If Gregor had only been able to speak to his sister and thank her for everything she had to do for him, he could have accepted her services more easily; as it was, they caused him pain. Of course his sister tried to ease the embarrassment of the whole situation as much as possible, and as time went on, she naturally managed it better and better, but in time Gregor, too, saw things much more clearly. Even the way she came in was terrible for him. Hardly had she entered the room than she would run straight to the window without taking time to close the door—though she was usually so careful to spare everyone the sight of Gregor's room—then tear open the casements with

49 ESL: Point out that *cowered* means "crouched in fear." Ask students why the sister's movements and the noise of opening the window frighten Gregor so. (Gregor now has the sensibilities of an insect and is frightened by noise, movement, and light.) ∎

50 LITERARY ELEMENT

Conflict: Based on her actions in Gregor's room, what interior conflict does the sister struggle with? (Grete cares about her brother, but is also repulsed by him; she can't bear to look at him or breathe the foul air in his room.)

51 LITERARY ELEMENT

Theme: It is sometimes noted that the title of the story refers not only to Gregor's transformation but also to the changes that his sister and parents undergo. How is Gregor's sister metamorphosing here? (She becomes more purposeful, more mature.)

52 GUIDED READING

Finding the Main Idea: Why does Mrs. Samsa want to see Gregor so much? (He is her only son; she loves him very much; she can't bear being separated from him in this way.) What sort of "reasonable arguments" might Mr. Samsa make to persuade his wife not to see Gregor? (He might say that Gregor will not recognize her or that his appearance will only upset her more.)

eager hands, almost as if she were suffocating, and remain for a little while at the window even in the coldest weather, breathing deeply. With this racing and crashing she frightened Gregor twice a day; the whole time he cowered under the couch, and yet he knew very well that she would certainly have spared him this if only she had found it possible to stand being in a room with him with the window closed.

One time—it must have been a month since Gregor's metamorphosis, and there was certainly no particular reason any more for his sister to be astonished at Gregor's appearance—she came a little earlier than usual and caught Gregor still looking out the window, immobile and so in an excellent position to be terrifying. It would not have surprised Gregor if she had not come in, because his position prevented her from immediately opening the window, but not only did she not come in, she even sprang back and locked the door; a stranger might easily have thought that Gregor had been lying in wait for her, wanting to bite her. Of course Gregor immediately hid under the couch, but he had to wait until noon before his sister came again, and she seemed much more uneasy than usual. He realized from this that the sight of him was still repulsive to her and was bound to remain repulsive to her in the future, and that she probably had to overcome a lot of resistance not to run away at the sight of even the small part of his body that jutted out from under the couch. So, to spare her even this sight, one day he carried the sheet on his back to the couch—the job took four hours—and arranged it in such a way that he was now completely covered up and his sister could not see him even when she stooped. If she had considered this sheet unnecessary, then of course she could have removed it, for it was clear enough that it could not be for his own pleasure that Gregor shut himself off altogether, but she left the sheet the way it was, and Gregor thought that he had even caught a grateful look when one time he cautiously lifted the sheet a little with his head in order to see how his sister was taking the new arrangement.

During the first two weeks, his parents could not bring themselves to come in to him, and often he heard them say how much they appreciated his sister's work, whereas until now they had frequently been annoyed with her because she had struck them as being a little useless. But now both of them, his father and his mother, often waited outside Gregor's room while his sister straightened it up, and as soon as she came out she had to tell them in great detail how the room looked, what Gregor had eaten, how he had behaved this time, and whether he had perhaps shown a little improvement. His mother, incidentally, began relatively soon to want to visit Gregor, but his father and his sister at first held her back with reasonable arguments to which Gregor listened very attentively and of which he wholeheartedly approved. But later she had to be restrained by force, and then when she cried out, "Let me go to Gregor, he is my unfortunate boy! Don't you understand that I have to go to him?" Gregor thought that it might be a good idea after all if his mother did come in, not every day of course, but perhaps once a week; she could still do everything much better than his sister, who, for all her courage, was still only a child and in the final analysis had perhaps taken on such a difficult assignment only out of childish flightiness.

Gregor's desire to see his mother was soon fulfilled. During the day Gregor did not want to show himself at the window, if only out of consideration for his parents, but he couldn't crawl very far on his few square yards of floor space, either; he could hardly put up with just lying still even at night; eating soon stopped giving him the slightest pleasure, so, as a distraction, he adopted the habit of crawling crisscross over the walls and the ceiling. He especially liked hanging from the ceiling; it was completely different from lying on the floor; one could breathe more freely; a faint swinging sensation went through the body; and in the almost happy absent-mindedness which Gregor felt up there, it could happen to his own surprise that he let go and plopped onto the floor. But now, of course, he had much better control of his body than before and did not hurt himself even from such a big drop. His sister immediately noticed the new entertainment Gregor had discovered for himself—after all, he left behind traces of his sticky substance wherever he crawled—and so she got it into her head to make it possible for Gregor to crawl on an altogether wider scale by taking out the furniture which stood in his way— mainly the chest of drawers and the desk. But she was not able to do this by herself; she did not dare ask her father for help; the maid would certainly not have helped her, for although this girl, who was about six- teen, was bravely sticking it out after the previous cook had left, she had asked for the favor of locking herself in the kitchen at all times and of only opening the door on special request. So there was nothing left for his sister to do except to get her mother one day when her father was out. And his mother did come, with exclamations of ex- cited joy, but she grew silent at the door of Gregor's room. First his sister looked to see, of course, that everything in the room was in order; only then did she let her mother come in. Hurrying as fast as he could, Gregor

had pulled the sheet down lower still and pleated it more tightly—it really looked just like a sheet accidently thrown over the couch. This time Gregor also refrained from spying from under the sheet; he renounced seeing his mother for the time being and was simply happy that she had come after all. "Come on, you can't see him," his sister said, evidently leading her mother in by the hand. Now Gregor could hear the two frail women moving the old chest of drawers— heavy for anyone—from its place and his sister insisting on doing the harder part of the job herself, ignoring the warnings of her mother, who was afraid that she would over- exert herself. It went on for a long time. After struggling for a good quarter of an hour, his mother said that they had better leave the chest where it was, because, in the first place, it was too heavy, they would not finish before his father came, and with the chest in the middle of the room, Gregor would be completely barricaded; and, in the second place, it was not at all certain that they were doing Gregor a favor by removing his furniture. To her the opposite seemed to be the case; the sight of the bare wall was heartbreaking; and why shouldn't Gregor also have the same feeling, since he had been used to his furniture for so long and would feel abandoned in the empty room. "And doesn't it look," his mother concluded very softly—in fact she had been almost whis- pering the whole time, as if she wanted to avoid letting Gregor, whose exact where- abouts she did not know, hear even the sound of her voice, for she was convinced that he did not understand the words—"and doesn't it look as if by removing his furniture we were showing him that we have given up all hope of his getting better and are leaving him to his own devices without any consideration? I think the best thing would

53

54

55

56

53 READER'S RESPONSE
If you could change yourself into an insect, what insect would you choose? What activ- ities might you enjoy in your new form? (Answers will vary.)

54 LITERARY ELEMENT
Symbol: What do you think the removal of Gregor's desk and chest of drawers might symbolize? (Only a human would need a desk for paper- work or a chest for clothes. Removing the furniture sym- bolizes the loss of Gregor's humanity.)

55 LITERARY ELEMENT
Theme: By having Gregor hide his shape from his own mother, Kafka suggests that modern life forces us to con- form or cover up our inner selves. Point out that the sheet is reminiscent of a death shroud and that Kafka suggests that the effort to deny or hide one's inner self results in a dying within.

56 LITERARY ELEMENT
Dramatic Irony: As readers, we know something that the Samsas do not: Gregor can understand everything that is said. This dramatic irony adds dark humor to this scene while heightening our sense of Gregor's alienation from his family.

57 LEP: Explain that *addled his brain* means "made him confused." Have students speculate on why not talking to anyone for two months might cause someone to become confused or disoriented. ∎

58 LITERARY ELEMENT

Conflict: At first Gregor goes along with the removal of the furniture. Then he opposes it. What internal conflict does this suggest? (He is caught between functioning on an animal level and trying somehow to salvage his humanity.)

59 ANALYZING

Why do you think Kafka gave Gregor and Grete such similar-sounding names? (He wanted to emphasize their closeness.) Why might Grete want to make Gregor's situation "more terrifying in order that she might do even more for him"? (Responses will vary. Kafka suggests that caring for Gregor has given Grete a purpose in life and has helped her feel important and gain her parents' approval.)

be to try to keep the room exactly the way it was before, so that when Gregor comes back to us again, he'll find everything unchanged and can forget all the more easily what's happened in the meantime."

57 When he heard his mother's words, Gregor realized that the monotony of family life, combined with the fact that not a soul had addressed a word directly to him, must have addled his brain in the course of the past two months, for he could not explain to himself in any other way how in all seriousness he could have been anxious to have his room cleared out. Had he really wanted to have his warm room, comfortably fitted with furniture that had always been in the family, changed into a cave, in which, of course, he would be able to crawl around unhampered in all directions but at the cost of simultaneously, rapidly, and totally forgetting his human past? Even now he had been on the verge of forgetting, and only his mother's voice, which he had not heard for so long, **58** had shaken him up. Nothing should be removed; everything had to stay; he could not do without the beneficial influence of the furniture on his state of mind; and if the furniture prevented him from carrying on this senseless crawling around, then that was no loss but rather a great advantage.

But his sister unfortunately had a different opinion; she had become accustomed, certainly not entirely without justification, to adopt with her parents the role of the particularly well-qualified expert whenever Gregor's affairs were being discussed; and so her mother's advice was now sufficient reason for her to insist, not only on the removal of the chest of drawers and the desk, which was all she had been planning at first, but also on the removal of all the furniture with the exception of the indispensable couch. Of course it was not only childish defiance and

the self-confidence she had recently acquired so unexpectedly and at such a cost that led her to make this demand; she had in fact noticed that Gregor needed plenty of room to crawl around in; and on the other hand, as best she could tell, he never used the furniture at all. Perhaps, however, the romantic enthusiasm of girls her age, which seeks to indulge itself at every opportunity, played a part, by tempting her to make Gregor's situation even more terrifying in order that she might do even more for him. Into **59** a room in which Gregor ruled the bare walls all alone, no human being beside Grete was ever likely to set foot.

And so she did not let herself be swerved from her decision by her mother, who, besides, from the sheer anxiety of being in Gregor's room, seemed unsure of herself, soon grew silent, and helped her daughter as best she could to get the chest of drawers out of the room. Well, in a pinch Gregor could do without the chest, but the desk had to stay. And hardly had the women left the room with the chest, squeezing against it and groaning, than Gregor stuck his head out from under the couch to see how he could feel his way into the situation as considerately as possible. But unfortunately it had to be his mother who came back first, while in the next room Grete was clasping the chest and rocking it back and forth by herself, without of course budging it from the spot. His mother, however, was not used to the sight of Gregor, he could have made her ill, and so Gregor, frightened, scuttled in reverse to the far end of the couch but could not stop the sheet from shifting a little at the front. That was enough to put his mother on the alert. She stopped, stood still for a moment, and then went back to Grete.

Although Gregor told himself over and over again that nothing special was happening, only a few pieces of furniture were being moved, he soon had to admit that this coming and going of the women, their little calls to each other, the scraping of the furniture along the floor had the effect on him of a great turmoil swelling on all sides, and as much as he tucked in his head and his legs and shrank until his belly touched the floor, he was forced to admit that he would not be able to stand it much longer. They were clearing out his room; depriving him of everything that he loved; they had already carried away the chest of drawers, in which he kept the fret saw and other tools; were now budging the desk firmly embedded in the floor, the desk he had done his homework on when he was a student at business college, in high school, yes, even in public school—now he really had no more time to examine the good intentions of the two women, whose existence, besides, he had almost forgotten, for they were so exhausted that they were working in silence, and one could hear only the heavy shuffling of their feet.

And so he broke out—the women were just leaning against the desk in the next room to catch their breath for a minute—changed his course four times, he really didn't know what to salvage first, then he saw hanging conspicuously on the wall, which was otherwise bare already, the picture of the lady all dressed in furs, hurriedly crawled up on it and pressed himself against the glass, which gave a good surface to stick to and soothed his hot belly. At least no one would take away this picture, while Gregor completely covered it up. He turned his head toward the living-room door to watch the women when they returned.

They had not given themselves much of a rest and were already coming back; Grete had put her arm around her mother and was practically carrying her. "So what should we take now?" said Grete and looked around. At that her eyes met Gregor's as he clung to the wall. Probably only because of her mother's presence she kept her self-control, bent her head down to her mother to keep her from looking around, and said, though in a quavering and thoughtless voice: "Come, we'd better go back into the living room for a minute." Grete's intent was clear to Gregor; she wanted to bring his mother into safety and then chase him down from the wall. Well, just let her try! He squatted on his picture and would not give it up. He would rather fly in Grete's face.

But Grete's words had now made her mother really anxious; she stepped to one side, caught sight of the gigantic brown blotch on the flowered wallpaper, and, before it really dawned on her that what she saw was Gregor, cried in a hoarse, bawling voice: "Oh, God, Oh, God!"; and, as if giving up completely, she fell with outstretched arms across the couch and did not stir. "You, Gregor!" cried his sister with raised fist and piercing eyes. These were the first words she had addressed directly to him since his metamorphosis. She ran into the next room to get some kind of spirits to revive her mother; Gregor wanted to help, too—there was time to rescue the picture—but he was stuck to the glass and had to tear himself loose by force; then he, too, ran into the next room, as if he could give his sister some sort of advice, as in the old days; but then had to stand behind her doing nothing while she rummaged among various little bottles; moreover, when she turned around she was startled, a bottle fell on the floor and broke, a splinter of glass wounded Gregor in the face, some kind of corrosive medicine flowed around him; now without waiting any longer, Grete grabbed as many little

60
61
62
63

60 LITERARY ELEMENT
Symbol: Explain that the picture of the woman dressed in furs is not of someone Gregor knows personally. Suggest that the picture symbolizes the poverty of Gregor's emotional life. Deprived of human love and affection, he clings to a romantic fantasy.

61 PREDICTING
After two months of becoming ever more insectlike, Gregor "breaks out" and reveals himself—hoping to reassert his lost humanity and to appeal for understanding and affection. Ask students to predict how he will be received by his family this time.

62 LITERARY ELEMENT
Imagery: What does Kafka suggest with this image of Gregor as a "gigantic brown blotch on the flowered wallpaper?" (Answers will vary. Gregor is reduced to being an ugly stain on the family's otherwise pleasant surroundings.)

MEETING INDIVIDUAL NEEDS

63 LEP: Explain that the spirits that Grete goes for may be ammonia or smelling salts—something to revive Mrs. Samsa, who has fainted. ∎

bottles as she could carry and ran with them inside to her mother; she slammed the door behind her with her foot. Now Gregor was cut off from his mother, who was perhaps near death through his fault; he could not dare open the door if he did not want to chase away his sister, who had to stay with his mother; now there was nothing for him to do except wait; and tormented by self-reproaches and worry, he began to crawl, crawled over everything, walls, furniture and ceiling, and finally in desperation, as the whole room was beginning to spin, fell down onto the middle of the big table.

A short time passed; Gregor lay there prostrate; all around, things were quiet, perhaps that was a good sign. Then the doorbell rang. The maid, of course, was locked up in her kitchen and so Grete had to answer the door. His father had come home. "What's happened?" were his first words; Grete's appearance must have told him everything. Grete answered in a muffled voice, her face was obviously pressed against her father's chest; "Mother fainted, but she's better now. Gregor's broken out." "I knew it," his father said. "I kept telling you, but you women don't want to listen." It was clear to Gregor that his father had put the worst interpretation on Grete's all-too-brief announcement and assumed that Gregor was guilty of some outrage. Therefore, Gregor now had to try to calm his father down, since he had neither the time nor the ability to enlighten him. And so he fled to the door of his room and pressed himself against it for his father to see, as soon as he came into the foyer, that Gregor had the best intentions of returning to his room immediately and that it was not necessary to drive him back; if only the door were opened for him, he would disappear at once.

But his father was in no mood to notice such subtleties; "Ah!" he cried as he entered, in a tone that sounded as if he were at once furious and glad. Gregor turned his head away from the door and lifted it toward his father. He had not really imagined his father looking like this, as he stood in front of him now; admittedly Gregor had been too absorbed recently in his newfangled crawling to bother as much as before about events in the rest of the house and should really have been prepared to find some changes. And yet, and yet—was this still his father? Was this the same man who in the old days used to lie wearily buried in bed when Gregor left on a business trip; who greeted him on his return in the evening, sitting in his bathrobe in the armchair, who actually had difficulty getting to his feet but as a sign of joy only lifted up his arms; and who, on the rare occasions when the whole family went out for a walk, on a few Sundays in June and on the major holidays, used to shuffle along with great effort between Gregor and his mother, who were slow walkers themselves, always a little more slowly than they, wrapped in his old overcoat, always carefully planting down his crutch-handled cane, and, when he wanted to say something, nearly always stood still and assembled his escort around him? Now, however, he was holding himself very erect, dressed in a tight-fitting blue uniform with gold buttons, the kind worn by messengers at banking concerns; above the high stiff collar of the jacket his heavy chin protruded; under his bushy eyebrows his black eyes darted bright, piercing glances; his usually rumpled white hair was combed flat, with a scrupulously exact, gleaming part. He threw his cap—which was adorned with a gold monogram, probably that of a bank—in an arc across the entire room onto the couch, and with the tails of his long uniform jacket slapped back, his hands in his pants pockets, went for Gregor with a sullen look on his face. He probably did not know himself what he had in mind; still he lifted his feet unusually high off the floor, and Gregor staggered at the gigantic size of the soles of his boots. But he did not linger over this, he had known right from the first day of his new life that his father considered only the strictest treatment called for in dealing with him. And so he ran ahead of his father, stopped when his father stood still, and scooted ahead again when his father made even the slightest movement. In this way they made more than one tour of the room, without anything decisive happening; in fact, the whole movement did not even have the appearance of a chase because of its slow tempo. So Gregor kept to the floor for the time being, especially since he was afraid that his father might interpret a flight onto the walls or the ceiling as a piece of particular nastiness. Of course, Gregor had to admit that he would not be able to keep up even this running for long, for whenever his father took one step, Gregor had to execute countless movements. He was already beginning to feel winded, just as in the old days he had not had very reliable lungs. As he now staggered around, hardly keeping his eyes open in order to gather all his strength for the running; in his obtuseness not thinking of any escape other than by running; and having almost forgotten that the walls were at his disposal, though here of course they were blocked up with elaborately carved furniture full of notches and points—at that moment a lightly flung object hit the floor right near him and rolled in front of him. It was an apple; a second one came flying right after it; Gregor stopped dead with fear; further running was useless, for his father was determined to bombard him. He had filled his pockets from the fruit bowl on the buffet and was now pitching one apple after another, for the time being without taking good aim. These little red apples rolled around on the floor as if electrified, clicking into each another. One apple, thrown weakly, grazed Gregor's back and slid off harmlessly. But the very next one that came flying after it literally forced its way into Gregor's back; Gregor tried to drag himself away, as if the startling, unbelievable pain might disappear with a change of place; but he felt nailed to the spot and stretched out his body in a complete confusion of all his senses. With his last glance he saw the door of his room burst open as his mother rushed out ahead of his screaming sister, in her chemise,[6] for his sister had partly undressed her while she was unconscious in order to let her breathe more freely; saw his mother run up to his father and on the way her unfastened petticoats slid to the floor one by one; and saw as, stumbling over the skirts, she forced herself onto his father, and embracing him, in complete union with him—but now Gregor's sight went dim—her hands clasping his father's neck, begged for Gregor's life.

3

Gregor's serious wound, from which he suffered for over a month—the apple remained imbedded in his flesh as a visible souvenir since no one dared to remove it—seemed to have reminded even his father that Gregor was a member of the family, in spite of his present pathetic and repulsive shape, who could not be treated as an enemy; that, on the contrary, it was the commandment of family duty to swallow their disgust and endure him, endure him and nothing more.

6. **chemise** (shə·mēz′): loose, sliplike undergarment.

67 LITERARY ELEMENT
Imagery: How does this image of Mr. Samsa's gigantic soles develop the grotesque and terrifying mood? (The image of a father willing to crush his own son is grotesque and terrifying.)

68 ANALYZING
To escape his father, why doesn't Gregor revert to insectlike behavior and climb the walls? (Possible response: He has just made the decision to assert his humanity; perhaps he has decided to submit to his father's punishment even if it means death.)

69 COMPARING LITERATURE
Have students recall that Satan used a fruit in the Garden of Eden to introduce evil and death into paradise. What do associations with this Biblical story suggest about the present scene? (Possible responses: the devilish nature of Mr. Samsa and the innocence of Gregor; Gregor has been cast out of the family "paradise" and will die)

70 ANALYZING
What does the repetition of the word *endure* suggest about how the Samsas' feelings toward Gregor have changed? (Answers will vary. Any feelings of love, concern, or goodwill that they once felt for Gregor are gone. Now they put up with him out of duty.)

HUMANITIES CONNECTION

World War I left German-born Max Ernst and others filled with revulsion. In the world which he depicts, forms disturb the viewer, like menacing handwriting on the wall of history.

❓ *How is the tone of this picture similar to the tone of The Metamorphosis? (Possible response: Both have an undercurrent of terror, horror, and menace.)* ∎

71 GUIDED READING

Identifying Cause and Effect:
How has Gregor's wound affected him? (He can't get around quickly; he can't climb the walls.) Why do the Samsas open the door and let Gregor watch them at night? (They may feel sad or guilty about his wound; they probably realize he is no longer a threat to them.)

■ deterioration (dë·tir′ē·ə·rā′shən): state of becoming worse

71
And now, although Gregor had lost some of his mobility probably for good because of his wound, and although for the time being he needed long, long minutes to get across his room, like an old war veteran—crawling above ground was out of the question—for this <u>deterioration</u> of his situation he was granted compensation which in his view was entirely satisfactory: every day around dusk the living-room door—which he was in the habit of watching closely for an hour or two beforehand—was opened, so that, lying in the darkness of his room, invisible from the living room, he could see the whole family sitting at the table under the lamp and could listen to their conversation, as it were with general permission; and so it was completely different from before.

Of course, these were no longer the animated conversations of the old days, which Gregor used to remember with a certain nostalgia in small hotel rooms when he'd had

The Bettmann Archive/© 1998 Artists Rights Society (ARS)/ADAGP, Paris

THE BLUE HOUR, MAX ERNST (1891–1976).
❓ *Do you think Gregor might have done anything to deserve—or to make him a likely victim for—his strange transformation; or was it a chance misfortune? Explain your answer.*

to throw himself wearily into the damp bedding. Now things were mostly very quiet. Soon after supper his father would fall asleep in his armchair; his mother and sister would caution each other to be quiet; his mother, bent low under the light, sewed delicate lingerie for a clothing store; his sister, who had taken a job as a salesgirl, was learning shorthand and French in the evenings in order to attain a better position some time in the future. Sometimes his father woke up, and as if he had absolutely no idea that he had been asleep, said to his mother, "Look how long you're sewing again today!" and went right back to sleep, while mother and sister smiled wearily at each other.

72

With a kind of perverse obstinacy his father refused to take off his official uniform even in the house; and while his robe hung uselessly on the clothes hook, his father dozed, completely dressed, in his chair, as if he were always ready for duty and were waiting even here for the voice of his superior. As a result, his uniform, which had not been new to start with, began to get dirty in spite of all the mother's and sister's care, and Gregor would often stare all evening long at this garment, covered with stains and gleaming with its constantly polished gold buttons, in which the old man slept most uncomfortably and yet peacefully.

As soon as the clock struck ten, his mother tried to awaken his father with soft encouraging words and then persuade him to go to bed, for this was no place to sleep properly, and his father badly needed his sleep, since he had to be at work at six o'clock. But with the obstinacy that had possessed him ever since he had become a messenger, he always insisted on staying at the table a little longer, although he invariably fell asleep and then could be persuaded only with the greatest effort to exchange his armchair for bed. However much mother and sister might pounce on him with little admonitions, he would slowly shake his head for a quarter of an hour at a time, keeping his eyes closed, and would not get up. Gregor's mother plucked him by the sleeves, whispered <u>blandishments</u> into his ear, his sister dropped her homework in order to help her mother, but all this was of no use. He only sank deeper into his armchair. Not until the women lifted him up under his arms did he open his eyes, look alternately at mother and sister, and usually say, "What a life. So this is the peace of my old age." And leaning on the two women, he would get up laboriously, as if he were the greatest weight on himself, and let the women lead him to the door, where, shrugging them off, he would proceed independently, while Gregor's mother threw down her sewing and his sister her pen as quickly as possible so as to run after his father and be of further assistance.

Who in this overworked and exhausted family had time to worry about Gregor any more than was absolutely necessary? The household was stinted more and more; now the maid was let go after all; a gigantic bony cleaning woman with white hair fluttering about her head came mornings and evenings to do the heaviest work; his mother took care of everything else, along with all her sewing. It even happened that various pieces of family jewelry, which in the old days his mother and sister had been overjoyed to wear at parties and celebrations, were sold, as Gregor found out one evening from the general discussion of the prices they had fetched. But the biggest complaint was always that they could not give up the apartment, which was much too big for their present needs, since no one could figure out

73

74

72 LITERARY ELEMENT

Symbol: What do you think the uniform that Mr. Samsa refuses to remove might symbolize? (Possible response: Mr. Samsa's judgmental nature, his love of order and authority, and his inability to relate on a personal, humane level)

blandishments (blan'dish·mənts): flattering remarks

73 EVALUATING

Point out that father, mother, and Grete must all work constantly now to pay off the parents' debt and to support themselves. Only Gregor, because of his metamorphosis, is free from the responsibility. Have students discuss whether this situation is more or less equitable than when Gregor was solely responsible for repaying the debt and the support of all of them.

74 CULTURAL DIVERSITY

To some extent, Kafka presents the widespread Marxist view of the early 1900s that families, communities, and other natural human relationships disintegrate in an economic system which allows widespread poverty.

What pressures does poverty place on family life in our society? (Answers will vary.)

75 INTERPRETING
Why do you think the sadness
of his mother and sister causes
the wound on Gregor's back
to "hurt anew"? (Answers will
vary. Gregor received the
wound when he tried but
failed to make contact with his
mother and sister; the wound
is a reminder that he has been
cast out and has no meaningful emotional contact with his
family.)

76 ANALYZING
Think about these memories of
Gregor. Why do you think he
is glad when they fade away?
(These memories remind Gregor that his life as a man was
not happy or meaningful; his
relationships were superficial
and unfulfilling.)

77 LITERARY ELEMENT
Characterization: What do
these details reveal about how
Grete is changing? (She has
become less caring; she has
lost all interest in Gregor; she
is irritable.) How do you explain these changes? (Working
and studying, she has no time
for Gregor; she seems to resent him.)

how Gregor was supposed to be moved. But
Gregor understood easily that it was not
only consideration for him which prevented
their moving, for he could easily have been
transported in a suitable crate with a few air
holes; what mainly prevented the family
from moving was their complete hopelessness and the thought that they had been
struck by a misfortune as none of their relatives and acquaintances had ever been hit.
What the world demands of poor people
they did to the utmost of their ability; his
father brought breakfast for the minor officials at the bank, his mother sacrificed herself to the underwear of strangers, his sister
ran back and forth behind the counter at the
request of the customers; but for anything
more than this they did not have the
75 strength. And the wound in Gregor's back
began to hurt anew when mother and sister,
after getting his father to bed, now came
back, dropped their work, pulled their chairs
close to each other and sat cheek to cheek;
when his mother, pointing to Gregor's room,
said, "Close that door, Grete"; and when Gregor was back in darkness, while in the other
room the women mingled their tears or
stared dry-eyed at the table.

Gregor spent the days and nights almost
entirely without sleep. Sometimes he
thought that the next time the door opened
he would take charge of the family's affairs
again, just as he had done in the old days;
after this long while there again appeared in
his thoughts the boss and the manager, the
salesmen and the trainees, the handyman
76 who was so dense, two or three friends from
other firms, a chambermaid in a provincial
hotel—a happy fleeting memory—a cashier
in a millinery store,[7] whom he had courted

earnestly but too slowly—they all appeared,
intermingled with strangers or people he
had already forgotten; but instead of helping
him and his family, they were all inaccessible, and he was glad when they faded
away. At other times he was in no mood to
worry about his family, he was completely
filled with rage at his miserable treatment,
and although he could not imagine anything
that would pique his appetite, he still made
plans for getting into the pantry to take what
was coming to him, even if he wasn't hungry. No longer considering what she could
do to give Gregor a special treat, his sister,
before running to business every morning
and afternoon, hurriedly shoved any old
food into Gregor's room with her foot; and
in the evening, regardless of whether the
food had only been toyed with or—the most
usual case—had been left completely untouched, she swept it out with a swish of
the broom. The cleaning up of Gregor's
room, which she now always did in the evenings, could not be done more hastily.
Streaks of dirt ran along the walls, fluffs of
dust and filth lay here and there on the floor.
At first, whenever his sister came in, Gregor
would place himself in those corners which
were particularly offending, meaning by his
position in a sense to reproach her. But he
could probably have stayed there for weeks
without his sister's showing any improvement; she must have seen the dirt as clearly
as he did, but she had just decided to leave
it. At the same time she made sure—with
an irritableness that was completely new to
her and which had in fact infected the whole
family—that the cleaning of Gregor's room
remain her province. One time his mother
had submitted Gregor's room to a major
housecleaning, which she managed only after employing a couple of pails of water—
all this dampness, of course, irritated Gregor,

77

---

7. **millinery store:** store that sells women's hats.

too, and he lay prostrate, sour and immobile, on the couch—but his mother's punishment was not long in coming. For hardly had his sister noticed the difference in Gregor's room that evening than, deeply insulted, she ran into the living room and, in spite of her mother's imploringly uplifted hands, burst out in a fit of crying, which his parents—his father had naturally been startled out of his armchair—at first watched in helpless amazement; until they too got going; turning to the right, his father blamed his mother for not letting his sister clean Gregor's room; but turning to the left, he screamed at his sister that she would never again be allowed to clean Gregor's room; while his mother tried to drag his father, who was out of his mind with excitement, into the bedroom; his sister, shaken with sobs, hammered the table with her small fists; and Gregor hissed loudly with rage because it did not occur to any of them to close the door and spare him such a scene and a row.[8]

But even if his sister, exhausted from her work at the store, had gotten fed up with taking care of Gregor as she used to, it was not necessary at all for his mother to take her place and still Gregor did not have to be neglected. For now the cleaning woman was there. This old widow, who thanks to her strong bony frame had probably survived the worst in a long life, was not really repelled by Gregor. Without being in the least inquisitive, she had once accidentally opened the door of Gregor's room, and at the sight of Gregor—who, completely taken by surprise, began to race back and forth although no one was chasing him—she had remained standing, with her hands folded on her stomach, marveling. From that time on she never failed to open the door a crack every morning and every evening and peek in hurriedly at Gregor. In the beginning she also used to call him over to her with words she probably considered friendly, like, "Come over here for a minute, you old dung beetle!" or "Look at that old dung beetle!" To forms of address like these Gregor would not respond but remained immobile where he was, as if the door had not been opened. If only they had given this cleaning woman orders to clean up his room every day, instead of letting her disturb him uselessly whenever the mood took her. Once, early in the morning—heavy rain, perhaps already a sign of approaching spring, was beating on the window panes—Gregor was so exasperated when the cleaning woman started in again with her phrases that he turned on her, of course slowly and decrepitly, as if to attack. But the cleaning woman, instead of getting frightened, simply lifted up high a chair near the door, and as she stood there with her mouth wide open, her intention was clearly to shut her mouth only when the chair in her hand came crashing down on Gregor's back. "So, is that all there is?" she asked when Gregor turned around again, and she quietly put the chair back in the corner.

Gregor now hardly ate anything anymore. Only when he accidentally passed the food laid out for him would he take a bite into his mouth just for fun, hold it in for hours, and then mostly spit it out again. At first he thought that his grief at the state of his room kept him off food, but it was the very changes in his room to which he quickly became adjusted. His family had gotten into the habit of putting in this room things for which they could not find any other place, and now there were plenty of these, since one of the rooms in the apartment had been

8. **row** (rou): quarrel.

78 GUIDED READING
Comparing and Contrasting: How does the cleaning woman's attitude toward Gregor differ from that of the family? (Unlike the Samsas, the cleaning woman does not view Gregor with horror or fear; she treats him like a family pet.)

■ MEETING INDIVIDUAL NEEDS

79 **LEP:** Explain that *dung* is animal manure and that there are several types of dung beetles that feed on and breed in dung. Gregor does not respond to these names because they are so insulting. ■

80 LITERARY ELEMENT
Irony: When Gregor tried to approach his mother and father in a friendly way, they found him menacing and frightening. Now, ironically, when he tries to frighten someone, he can't. Why do you think Gregor wants to frighten the cleaning woman? (He is tired of her insulting names; he wants to regain some respect.)

81 SPECULATING
Why do you think Gregor has all but stopped eating? Keep in mind that his appetite symbolizes his emotional and spiritual hunger. (He probably feels that he has nothing to live for.)

82 Predicting

The three neatness-obsessed boarders don't realize they are living just a few feet away from a huge, wounded "dung beetle." What do you predict might happen if and when they find out? (Answers will vary.)

83 Analyzing

Earlier Gregor's sister wanted him to have an empty den where he could enjoy his insect games. Now his room is a crowded storage area. How has the family's attitude toward Gregor changed? (They see him as a bit of household clutter—too good to be thrown out, perhaps, but of no real use.)

84 Cultural Diversity

The Samsas are embarrassed to have boarders because it represents another decline in their social status. Unaccustomed to the situation and uncomfortable, they begin to act like servants in their own home—bowing, eating in the kitchen, and so on.

? *What are some signs of falling social status in our society?* (Answers will vary.)

85 Guided Reading

Comparing and Contrasting: Contrast the treatment of the three boarders with that given Gregor. (The Samsas bring the boarders platters of fine food and wait on them attentively while their own son lies unattended and starving nearby.)

rented to three boarders. These serious gentlemen—all three had long beards, as Gregor was able to register once through a crack in the door—were obsessed with neatness, not only in their room, but since they had, after all, moved in here, throughout the entire household and especially in the kitchen. They could not stand useless, let alone dirty, junk. Besides, they had brought along most of their own household goods. For this reason many things had become superfluous, and though they certainly weren't salable, on the other hand they could not just be thrown out. All these things migrated into Gregor's room. Likewise the ash can and the garbage can from the kitchen. Whatever was not being used at the moment was just flung into Gregor's room by the cleaning woman, who was always in a big hurry; fortunately, Gregor generally saw only the object involved and the hand that held it. Maybe the cleaning woman intended to reclaim the things as soon as she had a chance or else to throw out everything together in one fell swoop, but, in fact, they would have remained lying wherever they had been thrown in the first place if Gregor had not squeezed through the junk and set it in motion, at first from necessity, because otherwise there would have been no room to crawl in, but later with growing pleasure, although after such excursions, tired to death and sad, he did not budge again for hours.

Since the roomers sometimes also had their supper at home in the common living room, the living-room door remained closed on certain evenings, but Gregor found it very easy to give up the open door, for on many evenings when it was opened he had not taken advantage of it, but instead, without the family's noticing, had lain in the darkest corner of his room. But once the cleaning woman had left the living-room door slightly open, and it also remained opened a little when the roomers came in in the evening and the lamp was lit. They sat down at the head of the table where in the old days his father, his mother, and Gregor had eaten, unfolded their napkins, and picked up their knives and forks. At once his mother appeared in the doorway with a platter of meat, and just behind her came his sister with a platter piled high with potatoes. A thick vapor steamed up from the food. The roomers bent over the platters set in front of them as if to examine them before eating, and, in fact, the one who sat in the middle, and who seemed to be regarded by the other two as an authority, cut into a piece of meat while it was still on the platter, evidently to find out whether it was tender enough or whether it should perhaps be sent back to the kitchen. He was satisfied, and mother and sister, who had been watching anxiously, sighed with relief and began to smile.

The family itself ate in the kitchen. Nevertheless, before going into the kitchen, his father came into this room and, bowing once, cap in hand, made a turn around the table. The roomers rose as one man and mumbled something into their beards. When they were alone again, they ate in almost complete silence. It seemed strange to Gregor that among all the different noises of eating he kept picking up the sound of their chewing teeth, as if this were a sign to Gregor that you needed teeth to eat with and that even with the best make of toothless jaws you couldn't do a thing. "I'm hungry enough," Gregor said to himself, full of grief, "but not for these things. Look how these roomers are gorging themselves, and I'm dying!"

On this same evening—Gregor could not remember having heard the violin during the whole time—the sound of violin playing came from the kitchen. The roomers had already finished their evening meal, the one in the middle had taken out a newspaper, given each of the two others a page, and now, leaning back, they read and smoked. When the violin began to play, they became attentive, got up, and went on tiptoe to the door leading to the foyer, where they stood in a huddle. They must have been heard in the kitchen, for his father called, "Perhaps the playing bothers you, gentlemen? It can be stopped right away." "On the contrary," said the middle roomer. "Wouldn't the young lady like to come in to us and play in here where it's much roomier and more comfortable?" "Oh, certainly," called Gregor's father, as if he were the violinist. The boarders went back into the room and waited. Soon Gregor's father came in with the music stand, his mother with the sheet music, and his sister with the violin. Calmly his sister got everything ready for playing; his parents—who had never rented out rooms before and therefore behaved toward the roomers with excessive politeness—did not even dare sit down on their own chairs; his father leaned against the door, his right hand inserted between two buttons of his uniform coat, which he kept closed; but his mother was offered a chair by one of the roomers, and since she left the chair where the roomer just happened to put it, she sat in a corner to one side.

His sister began to play. Father and mother, from either side, attentively followed the movements of her hands. Attracted by the playing, Gregor had dared to come out a little further and already had his head in the living room. It hardly surprised him that lately he was showing so little consideration for the others; once such consideration had been his greatest pride. And yet he would never have had better reason to keep hidden; for now, because of the dust which lay all over his room and blew around at the slightest movement, he, too, was completely covered with dust; he dragged around with him on his back and along his sides fluff and hairs and scraps of food; his indifference to everything was much too deep for him to have gotten on his back and scrubbed himself clean against the carpet, as once he had done several times a day. And in spite of his state, he was not ashamed to inch out a little farther on the immaculate living-room floor.

Admittedly no one paid any attention to him. The family was completely absorbed by the violin-playing; the roomers, on the other hand, who at first had stationed themselves, hands in pockets, much too close behind his sister's music stand, so that they could all have followed the score, which certainly must have upset his sister, soon withdrew to the window, talking to each other in an undertone, their heads lowered, where they remained, anxiously watched by his father. It now seemed only too obvious that they were disappointed in their expectation of hearing beautiful or entertaining violin-playing, had had enough of the whole performance, and continued to let their peace be disturbed only out of politeness. Especially the way they all blew the cigar smoke out of their nose and mouth toward the ceiling suggested great nervousness. And yet his sister was playing so beautifully. Her face was inclined to one side, sadly and probingly her eyes followed the lines of music. Gregor crawled forward a little farther, holding his head close to the floor, so that it might be possible to catch her eye. Was he an animal, that music could move him so? He felt as if the way to the unknown nourishment he longed for were coming to light. He was

Franz Kafka   **1185**

---

86 SPECULATING

Why do you think Gregor is so attracted by the violin music? (Possible response: It has a soothing or uplifting effect on Gregor's depressed state of mind.)

87 PREDICTING

Ask students to recall that in each chapter of the story Gregor has made one attempt to leave his room. Ask them to predict what will happen in this scene.

■ immaculate (im·mak′yoo· lit): spotlessly clean

88 ANALYZING

Although he has become a filthy insect, Gregor is deeply moved by the music. The boarders, in contrast, are bored. What does this contrast suggest to you? (Gregor's metamorphosis and the suffering resulting from it have made him more sensitive to beauty and other spiritual values.)

89 LITERARY ELEMENT

Theme: Gregor continually hungers for some ''unknown nourishment'' which he never finds. What might this nourishment be? (Some emotional involvement or spiritual belief would give meaning to Gregor's life.)

90 **SPECULATING**
Have students speculate on Gregor's sad fantasy about his sister.

91 **LITERARY ELEMENT**
Characterization: The three boarders—who look identical and act identically—seem almost to be caricatures of real people. What is Kafka suggesting about people who conform? (that people who conform to the established order are lifeless and emotionally shallow. They remind us, in a way, of Gregor before he changed.)

90

determined to force himself on until he reached his sister, to pluck at her skirt, and to let her know in this way that she should bring her violin into his room, for no one here appreciated her playing the way he would appreciate it. He would never again let her out of his room—at least not for as long as he lived; for once, his nightmarish looks would be of use to him; he would be at all the doors of his room at the same time and hiss and spit at the aggressors; his sister, however, should not be forced to stay with him, but would do so of her own free will; she should sit next to him on the couch, bending her ear down to him, and then he would confide to her that he had had the firm intention of sending her to the Conservatory, and that, if the catastrophe had not intervened, he would have announced this to everyone last Christmas—certainly Christmas had come and gone?—without taking notice of any objections. After this declaration his sister would burst into tears of emotion, and Gregor would raise himself up to her shoulder and kiss her on the neck which, ever since she started going out to work, she kept bare, without a ribbon or collar.

"Mr. Samsa!" the middle roomer called to Gregor's father and without wasting another word pointed his index finger at Gregor, who was slowly moving forward. The violin stopped, the middle roomer smiled first at his friends, shaking his head, and then looked at Gregor again. Rather than driving Gregor out, his father seemed to consider it more urgent to start by soothing the roomers although they were not at all upset, and Gregor seemed to be entertaining them more than the violin-playing. He rushed over to them and tried with outstretched arms to drive them into their room and at the same time with his body to block their view of

Gregor. Now they actually did get a little angry—it was not clear whether because of his father's behavior or because of their dawning realization of having had without knowing it such a next-door neighbor as Gregor. They demanded explanations from his father; in their turn they raised their arms, plucked excitedly at their beards, and, dragging their feet, backed off toward their room. In the meantime his sister had overcome the abstracted mood into which she had fallen after her playing had been so suddenly interrupted; and all at once, after holding violin and bow for a while in her slackly hanging hands and continuing to follow the score as if she were still playing, she pulled herself together, laid the instrument on the lap of her mother—who was still sitting in her chair, fighting for breath, her lungs violently heaving—and ran into the next room, which the roomers, under pressure from her father, were nearing more quickly than before. One could see the covers and bolsters on the beds, obeying his sister's practiced hands, fly up and arrange themselves. Before the boarders had reached the room, she had finished turning down the beds and had slipped out. Her father seemed once again to be gripped by his perverse obstinacy to such a degree that he completely forgot any respect still due his tenants. He drove them on and kept on driving until, already at the bedroom door, the middle boarder stamped his foot thunderingly and thus brought him to a standstill. "I herewith declare," he said, raising his hand and casting his eyes around for Gregor's mother and sister, too, "that in view of the disgusting conditions prevailing in this apartment and family"—here he spat curtly and decisively on the floor—"I give notice as of now. Of course, I won't pay a cent for the days I have been living here, either; on the contrary, I shall consider

91

taking some sort of action against you with claims that—believe me—will be easy to substantiate." He stopped and looked straight in front of him, as if he were expecting something. And, in fact, his two friends at once chimed in with the words, "We, too, give notice as of now." Thereupon he grabbed the doorknob and slammed the door with a bang.

Gregor's father, his hands groping, staggered to his armchair and collapsed into it; it looked as if he were stretching himself out for his usual evening nap, but the heavy drooping of his head, as if it had lost all support, showed that he was certainly not asleep. All this time Gregor had lain quietly at the spot where the roomers had surprised him. His disappointment at the failure of his plan—but perhaps also the weakness caused by so much fasting—made it impossible for him to move. He was afraid with some certainty that in the very next moment a general debacle would burst over him, and he waited. He was not even startled by the violin as it slipped from under his mother's trembling fingers and fell off her lap with a reverberating clang.

"My dear parents," said his sister and by way of an introduction pounded her hand on the table, "things can't go on like this. Maybe you don't realize it, but I do. I won't pronounce the name of my brother in front of this monster, and so all I say is: we have to try to get rid of it. We've done everything humanly possible to take care of it and to put up with it; I don't think anyone can blame us in the least."

"She's absolutely right," said his father to himself. His mother, who still could not catch her breath, began to cough dully behind her hand, a wild look in her eyes.

His sister rushed over to his mother and held her forehead. His father seemed to have

been led by Grete's words to more definite thoughts, had sat up, was playing with the cap of his uniform among the plates which were still lying on the table from the roomers' supper, and from time to time looked at Gregor's motionless form.

"We must try to get rid of it," his sister now said exclusively to her father, since her mother was coughing too hard to hear anything. "It will be the death of you two, I can see it coming. People who already have to work as hard as we do can't put up with this constant torture at home, too. I can't stand it anymore either." And she broke out crying so bitterly that her tears poured down onto her mother's face, which she wiped off with mechanical movements of her hand.

"Child," said her father kindly and with unusual understanding, "but what can we do?"

Gregor's sister only shrugged her shoulders as a sign of the bewildered mood that had now gripped her as she cried, in contrast with her earlier confidence.

"If he could understand us," said her father, half questioning; in the midst of her crying Gregor's sister waved her hand violently as a sign that that was out of the question.

"If he could understand us," his father repeated and by closing his eyes, absorbed his daughter's conviction of the impossibility of the idea, "then maybe we could come to an agreement with him. But the way things are——"

"It has to go," cried his sister. "That's the only answer, Father. You just have to try to get rid of the idea that it's Gregor. Believing it for so long, that is our real misfortune. But how can it be Gregor? If it were Gregor, he would have realized long ago that it isn't possible for human beings to live with such a creature, and he would have gone away of his own free will. Then we wouldn't have a

92
93

---

92 EVALUATING
Do you agree that Grete and her parents have done "everything humanly possible" for Gregor? (Answers will vary. Students might suggest that family members have done next to nothing to meet Gregor's emotional needs.)

substantiate (səb·stan'shē·āt'): to prove

93 ANALYZING
Notice that Grete now uses *it*, not *he*, to refer to Gregor. What does this suggest to you? (She has depersonalized Gregor; she wants to break whatever emotional attachment she once felt for him.)

COMPARING LITERATURE
How do Grete's actions and feelings contrast with Beauty's in "Beauty and the Beast"? (Unlike Beauty, Grete rejects the beast; she does not provide the love and understanding that Gregor needs.)

94 EVALUATING

Does Grete characterize Gregor fairly here? (No, she misinterprets and exaggerates Gregor's motivations.) Why do you think she makes these statements? (Gregor's metamorphosis and the changes it has made in Grete's life—going to work, taking in boarders, and so on—have been very stressful; Grete is resentful.)

MEETING INDIVIDUAL NEEDS

95 ESL: Explain that the verb
trek, meaning "travel slowly or laboriously," connotes how difficult movement has become for Gregor. ■

96 PREDICTING

Have students predict an answer to Gregor's question "And now?" What is there left for Gregor? (There is really nothing left for Gregor to do but die.)

97 LITERARY ELEMENT

Characterization: Gregor thinks back on his family with "deep emotion and love." What does this tell you about him? (Answers will vary. In the end, Gregor is noble and loving, able to forgive his family's incapacities.)

94 brother, but we'd be able to go on living and honor his memory. But as things are, this animal persecutes us, drives the roomers away, obviously wants to occupy the whole apartment and for us to sleep in the gutter. Look, Father," she suddenly shrieked, "he's starting in again!" And in a fit of terror that was completely incomprehensible to Gregor, his sister abandoned even her mother, literally shoved herself off from her chair, as if she would rather sacrifice her mother than stay near Gregor, and rushed behind her father, who, upset only by her behavior, also stood up and half-lifted his arms in front of her as if to protect her.

95 But Gregor had absolutely no intention of frightening anyone, let alone his sister. He had only begun to turn around in order to trek back to his room; certainly his movements did look peculiar, since his ailing condition made him help the complicated turning maneuver along with his head, which he lifted up many times and knocked against the floor. He stopped and looked around. His good intention seemed to have been recognized; it had only been a momentary scare. Now they all watched him, silent and sad. His mother lay in her armchair, her legs stretched out and pressed together, her eyes almost closing from exhaustion; his father and his sister sat side by side, his sister had put her arm around her father's neck.

Now maybe they'll let me turn around, Gregor thought and began his labors again. He could not repress his panting from the exertion, and from time to time he had to rest. Otherwise no one harassed him, he was left completely on his own. When he had completed the turn, he immediately began to crawl back in a straight line. He was astonished at the great distance separating him from his room and could not understand at all how, given his weakness, he had covered the same distance a little while ago almost without realizing it. Constantly intent only on rapid crawling, he hardly noticed that not a word, not an exclamation from his family, interrupted him. Only when he was already in the doorway did he turn his head—not completely, for he felt his neck stiffening; nevertheless, he still saw that behind him nothing had changed except that his sister had gotten up. His last glance ranged over his mother, who was now fast asleep.

He was hardly inside his room when the door was hurriedly slammed shut, firmly bolted, and locked. Gregor was so frightened at the sudden noise behind him that his little legs gave way under him. It was his sister who had been in such a hurry. She had been standing up straight, ready and waiting, then she had leaped forward nimbly, Gregor had not even heard her coming, and she cried "Finally!" to her parents as she turned the key in the lock.

96 "And now?" Gregor asked himself, looking around in the darkness. He soon made the discovery that he could no longer move at all. It did not surprise him; rather, it seemed unnatural that until now he had actually been able to propel himself on these thin little legs. Otherwise he felt relatively comfortable. He had pains, of course, throughout his whole body, but it seemed to him that they were gradually getting fainter and fainter and would finally go away altogether. The rotten apple in his back and the inflamed area around it, which were completely covered with fluffy dust, already hardly bothered him. 97 He thought back on his family with deep emotion and love. His conviction that he would have to disappear was, if possible, even firmer than his sister's. He remained in this state of empty and peaceful reflection until the tower clock struck three in the

morning. He still saw that outside the window everything was beginning to grow light. Then, without his consent, his head sank down to the floor, and from his nostrils streamed his last weak breath.

When early in the morning the cleaning woman came—in sheer energy and impatience she would slam all the doors so hard although she had often been asked not to, that once she had arrived, quiet sleep was no longer possible anywhere in the apartment—she did not at first find anything out of the ordinary on paying Gregor her usual short visit. She thought that he was deliberately lying motionless, pretending that his feelings were hurt; she credited him with unlimited intelligence. Because she happened to be holding the long broom, she

Toad (Le Crapaud), Pablo Picasso, 1949.

HUMANITIES CONNECTION

Picasso once wrote, "I keep doing my best not to lose sight of nature. I want to aim at similarity, a profound similarity which is more real than reality, thus becoming surreal."

? *How are Picasso's aims realized in* Toad? (Answers will vary.)

MEETING INDIVIDUAL NEEDS

98 *ESL:* Make sure students understand that the phrase "from his nostrils streamed his last weak breath" describes Gregor's dying. ■

Franz Kafka

1. What metamorphosis does Gregor undergo? (He turns into a giant insect.)
2. Why is Gregor's job so important to the Samsas? (He is paying off his parents' debts and supporting the family.)
3. Who takes responsibility for feeding Gregor in his new form? (Gregor's sister, Grete)
4. Why does Grete remove Gregor's furniture? (She wants him to have room to crawl freely.)
5. What happens when Gregor shows himself to his mother the second time? (Mrs. Samsa faints.)
6. How does Mr. Samsa wound Gregor? (He throws an apple into Gregor's back.)
7. Without Gregor working, how do the Samsas live? (Grete and her parents get jobs.)
8. What draws Gregor from his room the last time? (the sound of Grete's violin-playing)
9. In the end, what happens to Gregor? (He starves to death.)
10. How does Gregor's death affect his family? (It gives them hope for a new life.)

MEETING INDIVIDUAL NEEDS

99 ESL: Explain that *croaked* is slang for "died," and that *dead as a doornail* is a cliché meaning "very dead." Suggest that the cleaning woman's rude slang as well as the way she pokes the body with her broom dehumanizes Gregor's death. ■

100 EVALUATING

What do you think Mrs. Samsa's feeble attempt to stop the cleaning woman from sweeping away the body suggests about her feelings? (Although Mrs. Samsa feels guilty, she wants the body disposed of.) Why do you think Grete comments on Gregor's thinness? (She may feel guilty, since it had been her duty to feed Gregor.)

scrutinize (skrooot''n·iz'): examine very carefully and closely

101 LITERARY ELEMENT

Symbol: Gregor dies in early spring. What symbolic meaning might this have? (The coming of spring signifies new hope and new beginnings. Gregor's death has freed the family to begin anew.)

102 SPECULATING

Why do you think Mr. Samsa can now stand up to the boarders and force them to leave? (Answers will vary. Gregor's death has relieved Mr. Samsa of guilt, embarrassment, and fear; now he has new vitality and wants to reclaim his home.)

tried from the doorway to tickle Gregor with it. When this too produced no results, she became annoyed and jabbed Gregor a little, and only when she had shoved him without any resistance to another spot did she begin to take notice. When she quickly became aware of the true state of things, she opened her eyes wide, whistled softly, but did not dawdle; instead, she tore open the door of the bedroom and shouted at the top of her voice into the darkness: "Come and have a look, it's croaked; it's lying there, dead as a doornail!"

The couple Mr. and Mrs. Samsa sat up in their marriage bed and had a struggle overcoming their shock at the cleaning woman before they could finally grasp her message. But then Mr. and Mrs. Samsa hastily scrambled out of bed, each on his side, Mr. Samsa threw the blanket around his shoulders, Mrs. Samsa came out in nothing but her nightgown; dressed this way, they entered Gregor's room. In the meantime, the door of the living room had also opened, where Grete had been sleeping since the roomers had moved in; she was fully dressed, as if she had not been asleep at all; and her pale face seemed to confirm this. "Dead?" said Mrs. Samsa and looked inquiringly at the cleaning woman, although she could scruti-nize everything for herself and could recognize the truth even without scrutiny. "I'll say," said the cleaning woman, and to prove it she pushed Gregor's corpse with her broom a good distance sideways. Mrs. Samsa made a movement as if to hold the broom back but did not do it. "Well," said Mr. Samsa, "now we can thank God!" He crossed himself, and the three women followed his example. Grete, who never took her eyes off the corpse, said, "Just look how thin he was. Of course he didn't eat anything for such a long time. The food came out again just the

way it went in." As a matter of fact, Gregor's body was completely flat and dry; this was obvious now for the first time, really, since the body was no longer raised up by his little legs and nothing else distracted the eye.

"Come in with us for a little while, Grete," said Mrs. Samsa with a melancholy smile, and Grete, not without looking back at the corpse, followed her parents into their bedroom. The cleaning woman shut the door and opened the window wide. Although it was early in the morning, there was already some mildness mixed in with the fresh air. After all, it was already the end of March.

The three boarders came out of their room and looked around in astonishment for their breakfast; they had been forgotten. "Where's breakfast?" the middle roomer grumpily asked the cleaning woman. But she put her finger to her lips and then hastily and silently beckoned the boarders to follow her into Gregor's room. They came willingly and then stood, their hands in the pockets of their somewhat shabby jackets, in the now already very bright room, surrounding Gregor's corpse.

At that point the bedroom door opened, and Mr. Samsa appeared in his uniform, his wife on one arm, his daughter on the other. They all looked as if they had been crying; from time to time Grete pressed her face against her father's sleeve.

"Leave my house immediately," said Mr. Samsa and pointed to the door, without letting go of the women. "What do you mean by that?" said the middle roomer, somewhat nonplussed, and smiled with a sugary smile. The two others held their hands behind their back and incessantly rubbed them together, as if in joyful anticipation of a big argument, which could only turn out in their favor. "I mean just what I say," answered Mr. Samsa, and with his two companions

RETEACHING

To reteach *The Metamorphosis*, call on groups of students to dramatize these key story scenes:

· Part 1, pp. 1163–1167: Gregor reveals himself to his family and the manager.
· Part 2, pp. 1176–1179: Gregor frightens his mother and is chased and wounded by his father.
· Part 3, pp. 1185–1187: Gregor crawls out to hear the violin and angers the boarders.

Ask students to express the emotions that motivate Gregor and the other characters in each scene.

marched in a straight line toward the roomer. At first the roomer stood still and looked at the floor, as if the thoughts inside his head were fitting themselves together in a new order. "So, we'll go, then," he said and looked up at Mr. Samsa as if, suddenly overcome by a fit of humility, he were asking for further permission even for this decision. Mr. Samsa merely nodded briefly several times, his eyes wide open. Thereupon the roomer actually went immediately into the foyer, taking long strides; his two friends had already been listening for a while, their hands completely still, and now they went hopping right after him, as if afraid that Mr. Samsa might get into the foyer ahead of them and interrupt the contact with their leader. In the foyer all three took their hats from the coat rack, pulled their canes from the umbrella stand, bowed silently, and left the apartment. In a suspicious mood which proved completely unfounded, Mr. Samsa led the two women out onto the landing; leaning over the banister, they watched the three roomers slowly but steadily going down the long flight of stairs, disappearing on each landing at a particular turn of the stairway and a few moments later emerging again; the farther down they got, the more the Samsa family's interest in them wore off, and when a butcher's boy with a carrier on his head came climbing up the stairs with a proud bearing, toward them and then up on past them, Mr. Samsa and the women quickly left the banister and all went back, as if relieved, into their apartment.

They decided to spend this day resting and going for a walk; they not only deserved a break in their work, they absolutely needed one. And so they sat down at the table and wrote three letters of excuse, Mr. Samsa to the management of the bank, Mrs. Samsa to her employer, and Grete to the store owner. While they were writing, the cleaning woman came in to say that she was going, since her morning's work was done. The three letter writers at first simply nodded without looking up, but as the cleaning woman still kept lingering, they looked up, annoyed. "Well?" asked Mr. Samsa. The cleaning woman stood smiling in the doorway, as if she had some great good news to announce to the family but would do so only if she were thoroughly questioned. The little ostrich feather which stood almost upright on her hat and which had irritated Mr. Samsa the whole time she had been with them swayed lightly in all directions. "What do you want?" asked Mrs. Samsa, who inspired the most respect in the cleaning woman. "Well," the cleaning woman answered, and for good-natured laughter could not immediately go on, "look, you don't have to worry about getting rid of the stuff next door. It's already been taken care of." Mrs. Samsa and Grete bent down over their letters, as if to continue writing; Mr. Samsa, who noticed that the cleaning woman was now about to start describing everything in detail, stopped her with a firmly outstretched hand. But since she was not going to be permitted to tell her story, she remembered that she was in a great hurry, cried, obviously insulted, "So long, everyone," whirled around wildly, and left the apartment with a terrible slamming of doors.

"We'll fire her tonight," said Mr. Samsa, but did not get an answer from either his wife or his daughter, for the cleaning woman seemed to have ruined their barely regained peace of mind. They got up, went to the window, and stayed there, holding each other tight. Mr. Samsa turned around in his chair toward them and watched them quietly for a while. Then he called, "Come on now, come over here. Stop brooding over

103 GUIDED READING

Finding the Main Idea: What does the cleaning woman mean by "the stuff next door"? (Gregor's body) What does she mean when she says it has been "taken care of"? (She has disposed of it, probably with the rest of the trash.)

MEETING INDIVIDUAL NEEDS

104 LEP: Make sure students understand that the cleaning woman has ruined Grete's and her mother's peace of mind by causing them to feel sad again. This grieving for Gregor is what Mr. Samsa calls "brooding." Point out that Mr. Samsa continues to deny his son, even after his death, by asking the others not to lament him. ∎

1. Designing a Set and Props. Ask students to imagine a stage version of *The Metamorphosis*. Have them design a simple set—Gregor's room and the living room—that captures the bleak and claustrophobic mood. Have them sketch costumes that accentuate the traits of the characters and discuss how to emphasize the symbolic value of Gregor's desk, the picture of the woman, the bowl of apples, and the violin.

2. Reading and Reporting. One of your students may want to read and report on another of Franz Kafka's well-known short stories. Possibilities include "The Judgment," "A Hunger Artist," "A Country Doctor," and "In the Penal Colony." Ask students to give a brief synopsis of the story and then read aloud selected passages that illustrate the major theme.

Ask students to review the selection in order to answer this question: What do you think is the symbolic meaning of Gregor Samsa's strange metamorphosis? Ask students to cite passages in the text to support their responses. ■

---

105 LITERARY ELEMENT

Mood: What details does Kafka use to develop an optimistic mood? (The weather is warm and sunny; the country is a pleasant change after the claustrophobic apartment; the Samsas' jobs are promising.) What is the purpose of this mood change? (Answers will vary. The change in mood emphasizes that Gregor's death has brought new hope and better prospects to the Samsas.)

EVALUATING

Some critics claim that the story should have ended with Gregor's death. They feel that this epilogue in which the Samsas begin a new, normal life is unnecessary and detracts from the dramatic intensity of the tale. Ask students to discuss whether they agree with this opinion.

ANSWERS

First Thoughts
Answers will vary.

Identifying Facts
1. how he will get out of bed and catch the next train to work
2. He is a traveling salesman. the grueling schedule and lack of meaningful human contact. He must support his family.
3. his sister Grete. At first, Grete is very caring, but she gradually loses interest and comes to hate him.
4. The family gives Gregor no attention or affection. Mr. Samsa hurls an apple at Gregor.
5. The Samsas plan to improve

the past. And have a little consideration for me, too." The women obeyed him at once, hurried over to him, fondled him, and quickly finished their letters.

Then all three of them left the apartment together, something they had not done in months, and took the trolley into the open country on the outskirts of the city. The car, in which they were the only passengers, was completely filled with warm sunshine. Leaning back comfortably in their seats, they discussed their prospects for the time to come, and it seemed on closer examination that these weren't bad at all, for all three positions—about which they had never really asked one another in any detail—were exceedingly advantageous and especially promising for the future. The greatest immediate improvement in their situation would come easily, of course, from a change

in apartments; they would now take a smaller and cheaper apartment, but one better situated and in every way simpler to manage than the old one, which Gregor had picked for them. While they were talking in this vein, it occurred almost simultaneously to Mr. and Mrs. Samsa, as they watched their daughter getting livelier and livelier, that lately, in spite of all the troubles which had turned her cheeks pale, she had blossomed into a good-looking, shapely girl. Growing quieter and communicating almost unconsciously through glances, they thought that it would soon be time, too, to find her a good husband. And it was like a confirmation of their new dreams and good intentions when at the end of the ride their daughter got up first and stretched her young body.

105

First Thoughts
Kafka explicitly forbade his publishers to include any illustration of Gregor as an insect. He felt that any literal representation would be meaningless. Do you agree with his view? Did you form a mental image of the metamorphosed Gregor? Draw your image of Gregor after his transformation, then discuss your drawing with the class.

Identifying Facts
1. After discovering that he has changed into a "monstrous vermin," what is Gregor's chief concern?
2. What does Gregor do for a living? What does he dislike about his job? Explain why he feels he cannot resign.
3. Who is Gregor's primary caretaker? In the course of the story, what change

takes place in this person's attitude toward Gregor?
4. How does the family's treatment of Gregor deteriorate? What does Gregor's father do that permanently injures Gregor?
5. After Gregor dies, what do his parents plan? What is "like a confirmation of their new dreams"?

Interpreting Meanings
1. **Irony** is the difference between what one expects to happen and what actually happens. What is ironic about Gregor's family's reaction to his change in form? Identify another example of irony in the story.
2. Gregor's reaction to Grete's violin playing leads to the **climax** of the novel.

How is his entrance into the living room the "final straw"?

3. In your opinion, what does the "monstrous vermin" **symbolize**? In symbolic terms, what is significant about the kind of creature Gregor transforms into—as opposed, say, to a dog or a cat?

4. The word *samsja* in Czech means "being alone." Do you think it was Gregor's change in form or his inability to communicate that contributed more to his isolation? How might things have been different if he had been able to express himself?

5. As Gregor's condition deteriorates, his family's condition improves. Some critics have said that the title of the novel refers not only to Gregor's metamorphosis, but also to his family's. Do you agree? Explain your response.

Applying Meanings

Although Kafka's story takes place more than seventy years ago, we still read about Gregor with fascination and curiosity. Do you think that this story is relevant to life today? You may not wake up tomorrow and find yourself changed into a bug, but do you ever suffer the same feelings and frustrations as Gregor did? Might there be other ways in which people "transform" because of their problems? Discuss your opinions with the class.

Creative Writing Response

1. **Writing from a Different Point of View.** Except for the last part, after Gregor's death, this novella is told from the **limited third-person point of view**: We are limited to Gregor's view of events. Gregor gives a very matter-of-fact account of his metamorphosis, but we can imagine how the other members of the family are reacting. In a few paragraphs, tell about Gregor's metamorphosis from Grete's point of view. You might start

with, "One morning, as I whispered through the wall to Gregor, I heard strange chirping noises coming out of his room. . . ."

2. **Describing Another Metamorphosis.** Since ancient times, the **motif** of a metamorphosis has been used in stories. Describe a story in which a metamorphosis takes place—it can be from a myth, a book, or a movie. (Think of all those weird shape changes that take place in science fiction movies.) You can make up your own metamorphosis story if you like. Does the metamorphosed form reflect any traits of the original being?

Critical Writing Response

1. **Analyzing a Character.** One of the central conflicts in the story is the relationship between Gregor and his father, which some critics see as reflecting Kafka's view of his relationship with his own father. Write a paragraph in which you analyze Mr. Samsa's character. Before you write, consider the following questions:

    a. How does Mr. Samsa view Gregor's metamorphosis? (Is he sympathetic? indifferent?) How does he treat Gregor?

    b. How does Mr. Samsa change after he gets a job and begins to support the family again?

    c. How do you think Gregor views his father? As a symbol of authority? Or does he think his father is weak? Does Gregor like his father?

2. **Responding to a Critic.** Critic Paul L. Landsburg believes that *The Metamorphosis* is an **allegory**, or a story in which each character and event stands for something else. In an allegory, the writer is trying to teach some moral meaning about life. As you read the

their jobs, move to a new apartment, and make a good marriage for Grete. By stretching her healthy young body, Grete confirms their dreams.

Interpreting Meanings

1. Gregor's family reacts in matter-of-fact ways—as if such a bizarre metamorphosis were not that unusual. Examples will vary.

2. As a result of Gregor's crawling out to hear the music in front of family and boarders, Grete decides that Gregor "must go." Gregor accepts this, retreats to his room, and seems to will his own death.

3. Answers will vary. The "monstrous vermin" symbolizes all that is ugly, frightening, and unacceptable in human experience.

4. Answers will vary. Gregor's previous inability to communicate probably caused the isolation symbolized by the metamorphosis. Had he been able to express himself, he might have found the human affection he craved.

5. Possible response: Yes; Gregor's change stimulates Grete to find a degree of self-assurance and Mr. Samsa to regain his strength and independence.

Applying Meanings

Gregor's metamorphosis, a fantasy occurrence, is still relevant because it speaks symbolically of such modern-day concerns as the isolation of the individual, alienation from work, the failure of family relationships, and the search for meaning in life.

■➞

Creative Writing Response

1. Writing from a Different Point of View. The account should use the first-person point of view consistently. Grete's tone should express her changing feelings for Gregor.

2. Describing Another Metamorphosis. Stories should describe both the "before" and "after" states as well as the cause(s) and effects of the change.

Critical Writing Response

1. Analyzing a Character. The analyses should show that Mr. Samsa reacts angrily and violently to Gregor's change, even though it leads ironically to his greater health, vitality, and self-reliance. Students should note that Gregor basically tries to appease his father, who is distant and threatening.

2. Responding to a Critic. A discussion of the Holocaust might be appropriate here as two of Franz Kafka's sisters died in Nazi concentration camps.

Language and Vocabulary

1. a 2. d 3. a 4. c 5. b ■

quotation below, think about any individuals or groups in society that could suffer the same kind of alienation and treatment that Gregor suffered.

> "To be an exception or in the minority is the original social sin. When in society any group of men characterized by anomalous tastes or racial or social heredity is denounced as 'vermin,' there will always be one group that from then on will see nothing but the other's rottenness, and another fraction within the scorned group that will think and act as if they had truly been transformed into vermin."
> —Paul L. Landsburg

Write two paragraphs in which you discuss how individuals or groups of people can actually begin to act the way they are treated.

Language and Vocabulary

Adjectives from People's Names

The adjective *Kafkaesque* is just one of many English words that come from the names of real people or fictional characters. Such adjectives usually develop when a person's or character's behavior or achievements are so well known that similar behavior or achievements are compared to them.

Choose the correct meaning of each italicized adjective in the phrases below. Check your answers in a dictionary and identify the person or character whose name gave rise to the adjective.

1. a *Herculean* task
   a) arduous   b) tedious
   c) short   d) easy

2. a *Machiavellian* politician
   a) weak   b) idealistic
   c) up-to-date   d) crafty

3. a *platonic* friendship
   a) spiritual or intellectual   b) passionate
   c) deceitful   d) long-standing

4. *quixotic* behavior
   a) mature   b) mysterious
   c) romantic and idealistic   d) fickle

5. *Shakespearean* language
   a) vulgar   b) poetic
   c) redundant   d) puzzling

THE ART OF TRANSLATION

Two Translations of The Metamorphosis

In reading *The Metamorphosis,* you are not simply reading a story by Kafka. You are also reading the work of a skilled translator who has tried to convey the meaning and spirit of Kafka's German in lively, natural English prose.

Whether a translator is faced with a text in French, Russian, Spanish, or Japanese, he or she takes on a difficult task. First of all, a word-for-word translation from the original language into English would probably not make sense. In addition, many foreign words have several possible English equivalents, and some words may have no English equivalents. Furthermore, **idioms**, or expressions specific to a particular language, cannot be translated literally. For example, the idiomatic expression, "He's a wet blanket'' doesn't make much sense when translated to another language, but most languages probably *do* have an equivalent, figurative expression that conveys the same meaning: ''He always manages to bring out the negative aspect of things.'' Translators must find these approximations. Just look at the many ways Gregor's metamorphosed form (*ungeheueres Ungeziefer* in German) has been translated: ''monstrous vermin,'' ''gigantic insect,'' ''enormous bug,'' ''a giant kind of vermin,'' and ''monstrous bug.''

Here are several passages from *The Metamorphosis*. The first passage in each example is from the translation you have just read, by Stanley Corngold. The second passage is from a translation by Willa and Edwin Muir. Read each pair of passages aloud, and discuss how they differ in diction (word choice), naturalness of language, rhythm, and ultimate meaning. Which version do you prefer, and why?

1. **a.** ''Traveling salesmen aren't well liked there, I know. People think they make a fortune leading the gay life. No one has any particular reason to rectify this prejudice.''

   b. ''Travelers are not popular there, I know. People think they earn sacks of money and have a good time. A prejudice there's no particular reason for revising.''

2. **a.** ''In fact, Gregor felt fine, with the exception of his drowsiness, which was really unnecessary after sleeping so late, and he even had a ravenous appetite.''

   b. ''Gregor really felt quite well, apart from a drowsiness that was utterly superfluous after such a long sleep and he was even unusually hungry.''

3. **a.** '' 'That was the voice of an animal,' said the manager, in a tone conspicuously soft compared with the mother's yelling.''

   b. '' 'That was no human voice,' said the chief clerk in a voice noticeably low beside the shrillness of the mother's.''

4. **a.** ''Then, without his consent, his head sank down to the floor, and from his nostrils streamed his last weak breath.''

   b. ''Then his head sank to the floor of its own accord and from his nostrils came the last faint flicker of his breath.''

5. **a.** '' 'Come and have a look, it's croaked; it's lying there, dead as a doornail.' ''

   b. '' 'Just look at this, it's dead; it's lying here dead and done for.' ''

Like the character Edla in "The Rat Trap," Selma Lagerlöf was the daughter of an officer in the Swedish army. Her mother was descended from a family line of clergymen. Lagerlöf's family was of the "lesser gentry," able to maintain good relationships with both the nobility and humble farmers. Most of Lagerlöf's stories vividly evoke peasant life in the beautiful landscape of northern Sweden.

When Lagerlöf was only three, she suffered an attack of infantile paralysis, from which she made a sudden, dramatic recovery, although she continued to walk with a limp for the rest of her life. One critic speculates that her remarkable recovery may have been responsible for her interest in miraculous or near-miraculous transformations in her fiction.

Selma Lagerlöf
1858–1940, Sweden

AP/Wide World Photos

When Selma Lagerlöf (lä′gər·lŭf′) was studying to become a schoolteacher, she attended a lecture that was to change her life. The subject of the lecture was Swedish folk ballads. These narrative songs reminded her of the folklore she had learned as a child in Sweden's Värmland district, and of the happy days in the house that her family was forced to sell when her father died. Lagerlöf's bittersweet memories inspired her to begin writing about the legends and folktales of her childhood. The books she wrote became so popular that she was soon able to repurchase her beloved family home with the money she made.

As a child, Lagerlöf listened to her grandmother tell Swedish folktales, and she never tired of reading books from the family library.

Her first novel, *The Story of Gösta Berling* (1891), was set in her childhood home, Värmland. To her surprise, the novel won first prize in a competition. Success followed success as *Invisible Links* (1894), a collection of Swedish legends and other tales, earned her a Swedish Academy writing scholarship and praise from Sweden's king. By now a household name in her homeland, Lagerlöf retired from her teaching career to devote herself to writing. A trip to the Middle East prompted *Jerusalem* (1901–1902), a two-volume novel about Swedes who immigrated to Jerusalem in quest for spiritual fulfillment. Four years later came the children's book, *The Wonderful Adventures of Nils*, which recounts a young boy's adventures as he travels across Sweden on the back of a goose.

In 1909, Lagerlöf became the first woman writer to win the Nobel Prize for literature. By the time she reached seventy, she was so famous that her birthday was celebrated in Sweden and in several neighboring nations. Although she was a committed pacifist and feminist, her social concerns rarely found their way into her novels. In her final years, however, Lagerlöf was outraged to find herself hailed as a "Nordic princess" in Nazi Germany, and began defiantly arranging for German intellectuals to escape Nazi persecution by coming to Sweden—an activity she continued even after World War II broke out and Sweden declared itself neutral.

OBJECTIVES

1. To analyze a modern Swedish short story
2. To recognize and evaluate the use of the omniscient point of view
3. To write a different conclusion to the story, and to compare and contrast characters from two short stories

THEMES IN WORLD LITERATURE

Choices in Life

"How Siegfried Was Slain" from the *Nibelungenlied*, pp. 732–740
"The Guest," pp. 1244–1257

The Uses and Abuses of Power

Oedipus Rex, pp. 301–371
From the *Ramayana*, pp. 484–494
From *Candide*, pp. 945–962 ■

VOCABULARY IN CONTEXT

The words listed below will appear in the side margin at the point of instruction:

1. incredulous
2. impenetrable
3. deigned

4. forebodings
5. dejectedly

Reader's Guide

THE RAT TRAP

Background

This story takes place in the Värmland area of Sweden where Selma Lagerlöf spent her childhood. Because the region had many iron ore deposits, it became a center of Sweden's iron industry during the second half of the nineteenth century. Iron ore mined in the district was brought to furnaces called ironworks, where it was smelted to remove impurities and then shaped into bars or sheets. The ironmasters who owned the ironworks became very wealthy and bought vast tracts of land, some of which they leased to tenant farmers and retired ironworkers. While the Industrial Revolution brought prosperity to some, it brought poverty to many others. Many farm laborers lost their jobs and became wandering peddlers or beggars. This story includes such a peddler, as well as an ironmaster, his daughter, and an elderly tenant farmer.

Writer's Response

There is a vast difference between the wealthiest and poorest people in our country today. Write a few sentences contrasting the lifestyles of the wealthiest and poorest people in your community.

Literary Focus

Point of view is the vantage point from which a writer tells a story. The traditional vantage point for storytelling is the **omniscient** (or all-knowing) **point of view**. The omniscient narrator is not a character in the story, but a godlike observer who knows everything that is going on in each character's heart and mind. This narrator can also provide us with information that no character knows. ("Thomas was sailing along effortlessly on his roller blades, unaware that the getaway car would soon burst out of the quiet side street.") Selma Lagerlöf uses the omniscient point of view in "The Rat Trap."

PREREADING FOCUS

Background: The evils of the Industrial Revolution and the injustices of the social class system were popular themes for Swedish writers of the late nineteenth century. Writers of the 1880s were inspired by the playwright and novelist August Strindberg, who wrote bitter social satires and tragedies such as *The Red Room* and *Miss Julie*. His followers in the Young Sweden movement wrote realistic works in which they debated the social problems of the day. By the 1890s, reaction against industrialization led to attempts by Swedish writers to preserve the values and traditions of the past. Selma Lagerlöf was among those writers who celebrated the history and culture of various regions of Sweden.

Writer's Response: Before students begin writing, have the class complete a comparison/contrast chart on the subject of lifestyles, listing elements that distinguish one lifestyle from another. Students might mention food, clothing, shelter, entertainment, vacations, and education. Then have them contrast these elements in their writing.

HUMANITIES CONNECTION

The Norwegian painter and printmaker Edvard Munch introduced into European art the demoniac element and visionary psychology that were also making their startling debut in Scandinavian literature. Munch's portraits and landscapes represent a tormented inner state. Recurring themes in his work include fear, desire, isolation, and death.

❓ *What is the mood of this painting?* (Answers will vary.) ∎

1 LITERARY ELEMENT

Tone: What attitude does the narrator seem to take toward the peddler? (Possible response: sympathetic but detached)

2 LITERARY ELEMENT

Metaphor: What metaphor describes the peddler's view of the world? (It is a rat trap.) Explain the elements of the analogy that the peddler develops. (The cheese and pork in the rat trap correspond to the riches and joys in the world. When you try to acquire the "bait," then you are destroyed.)

THE RAT TRAP
Selma Lagerlöf
translated by
FLORENCE AND NABOTH HEDIN

Read the first three paragraphs of "The Rat Trap" and think about the peddler's "rat trap theory" of the world. Does this theory make sense to you? What does the theory reveal about the peddler's view of life?

EVENING IN THE KARL JOHAN STREET, EDVARD MUNCH (1863–1944).

Scala/Art Resource, New York

Once upon a time there was a man who went around selling small rat traps of wire. He made them himself at odd moments, from material he got by begging in the stores or at the big farms. But even so, the business was not especially profitable, so he had to resort to both begging and petty thievery to keep body and soul together. Even so, his clothes were in rags, his cheeks were sunken, and hunger gleamed in his eyes.

No one can imagine how sad and monotonous life can appear to such a vagabond, who plods along the road, left to his own meditations. But one day this man had fallen into a line of thought which really seemed to him entertaining. He had naturally been thinking of his rat traps when suddenly he was struck by the idea that the whole world about him—the whole world with its lands and seas, its cities and villages—was nothing but

1

2

a big rat trap. It had never existed for any other purpose than to set baits for people. It offered riches and joys, shelter and food, heat and clothing, exactly as the rat trap offered cheese and pork, and as soon as anyone let himself be tempted to touch the bait, it closed in on him, and then everything came to an end.

The world had, of course, never been very kind to him, so it gave him unwonted[1] joy to think ill of it in this way. It became a cherished pastime of his, during many dreary ploddings, to think of people he knew who had let themselves be caught in the dangerous snare, and of others who were still circling around the bait.

One dark evening as he was trudging along the road he caught sight of a little gray cottage by the roadside, and he knocked on the door to ask shelter for the night. Nor was he refused. Instead of the sour faces which ordinarily met him, the owner, who was an old man without wife or child, was happy to get someone to talk to in his loneliness. Immediately he put the porridge pot on the fire and gave him supper; then he carved off such a big slice from his tobacco roll that it was enough both for the stranger's pipe and his own. Finally he got out an old pack of cards and played *mjölis*[2] with his guest until bedtime.

The old man was just as generous with his confidences as with his porridge and tobacco. The guest was informed at once that in his days of prosperity his host had been a crofter at Ramsjö Ironworks[3] and had worked on the land. Now that he was no longer able to do day labor, it was his cow which supported him. Yes, that bossy[4] was extraordinary. She could give milk for the creamery every day, and last month he had received all of thirty kronor[5] in payment.

The stranger must have seemed incredulous, for the old man got up and went to the window, took down a leather pouch which hung on a nail in the very window frame, and picked out three wrinkled ten-kronor bills. These he held up before the eyes of his guest, nodding knowingly, and then stuffed them back into the pouch.

The next day both men got up in good season. The crofter was in a hurry to milk his cow, and the other man probably thought he should not stay in bed when the head of the house had gotten up. They left the cottage at the same time. The crofter locked the door and put the key in his pocket. The man with the rat traps said goodbye and thank you, and thereupon each went his own way.

But half an hour later the rat-trap peddler stood again before the door. He did not try to get in, however. He only went up to the window, smashed a pane, stuck in his hand, and got hold of the pouch with the thirty kronor. He took the money and thrust it into his own pocket. Then he hung the leather pouch very carefully back in its place and went away.

As he walked along with the money in his pocket he felt quite pleased with his smartness. He realized, of course, that at first he dared not continue on the public highway, but must turn off the road, into the woods. During the first few hours this caused him no difficulty. Later in the day it

Selma Lagerlöf   **1199**

became worse, for it was a big and confusing forest which he had gotten into. He tried, to be sure, to walk in a definite direction, but the paths twisted back and forth so strangely! He walked and walked, without coming to the end of the wood, and finally he realized that he had only been walking around in the same part of the forest. All at once he recalled his thoughts about the world and the rat trap. Now his own turn had come. He had let himself be fooled by a bait and had been caught. The whole forest, with its trunks and branches, its thickets and fallen logs, closed in upon him like an impenetrable prison from which he could never escape.

It was late in December. Darkness was already descending over the forest. This increased the danger, and increased also his gloom and despair. Finally he saw no way out, and he sank down on the ground, tired to death, thinking that his last moment had come. But just as he laid his head on the ground, he heard a sound—a hard, regular thumping. There was no doubt as to what that was. He raised himself. "Those are the hammer strokes from an iron mill," he thought. "There must be people nearby." He summoned all his strength, got up, and staggered in the direction of the sound.

The Ramsjö Ironworks, which is now closed down, was, not so long ago, a large plant, with smelter,[6] rolling mill,[7] and forge.[8] In the summertime, long lines of heavily-loaded barges and scows slid down the canal which led to a large inland lake, and in the wintertime the roads near the mill were black from all the coal dust which sifted down from the big charcoal crates.

During one of the long dark evenings just before Christmas, the master smith and his helper sat in the dark forge near the furnace waiting for the pig iron, which had been put in the fire, to be ready to put on the anvil.[9] Every now and then one of them got up to stir the glowing mass with a long iron bar, returning in a few moments, dripping with perspiration, though, as was the custom, he wore nothing but a long shirt and a pair of wooden shoes.

All the time there were many sounds to be heard in the forge. The big bellows groaned and the burning coal cracked. The fire boy shoveled charcoal into the maw of the furnace with a great deal of clatter. Outside roared the waterfall, and a sharp north wind whipped the rain against the brick-tiled roof.

It was probably on account of all this noise that the blacksmith did not notice that a man had opened the gate and entered the forge, until he stood close up to the furnace.

Surely it was nothing unusual for poor vagabonds without any better shelter for the night to be attracted to the forge by the glow of light which escaped through the sooty panes, and to come in to warm themselves in front of the fire. The blacksmiths glanced only casually and indifferently at the intruder. He looked the way people of his type usually did, with a long beard, dirty, ragged, and with a bunch of rat traps dangling on his chest.

He asked permission to stay, and the master blacksmith nodded a haughty consent without honoring him with a single word.

The tramp did not say anything, either.

---

6. **smelter:** place where iron ore is fused or melted in order to separate out the impurities.
7. **rolling mill:** machine used to roll out metal bars or sheets.
8. **forge:** here, place where metal is heated in a furnace and then hammered or molded into shape.
9. **anvil:** metal block on which objects are hammered into shape.

THE FOUNDRY, EYRE CROWE (1824–1910).

12 He had not come there to talk but only to warm himself and sleep.

In those days the Ramsjö iron mill was owned by a very prominent ironmaster whose greatest ambition was to ship out good iron to the market. He watched both night and day to see that the work was done as well as possible, and at this very moment he came into the forge on one of his nightly rounds of inspection.

Naturally the first thing he saw was the tall ragamuffin who had eased his way so close to the furnace that steam rose from his wet rags. The ironmaster did not follow the example of the blacksmiths, who had **13** hardly <u>deigned</u> to look at the stranger. He walked close up to him, looked him over very carefully, then tore off his slouch hat[10]

10. **slouch hat:** style of hat with a drooping brim.

to get a better view of his face.

"But of course it is you, Nils Olof!" he said. **13** "How you do look!"

The man with the rat traps had never before seen the ironmaster of Ramsjö and did not even know what his name was. But it occurred to him that if the fine gentleman thought he was an old acquaintance, he might perhaps throw him a couple of kronor. Therefore he did not want to undeceive him all at once.

"Yes, God knows things have gone downhill with me," he said.

"You should not have resigned from the regiment," said the ironmaster. "That was the mistake. If only I had still been in the service at the time, it never would have happened. Well, now, of course, you will come home with me."

To go along up to the manor house and be received by the owner like an old

 deigned (dānd): condescended

14 LITERARY ELEMENT

Characterization: Is the iron-master a generous man? (His offer of hospitality suggests he is.) What other motivations might he have for his offer of hospitality? (Possible responses: a need to ease his loneliness and to reminisce with an old friend)

15 LITERARY ELEMENT

Characterization: What qualities does Edla show by volunteering to go and get the peddler and by the way she approaches him? (Possible responses: generosity, compassion, initiative)

16 GUIDED READING

Identifying Details: Why does Edla say to the peddler "You may be sure, Captain, that you will be allowed to leave us just as freely as you came"? (Because he looks afraid, she suspects he has stolen something and may fear that his crime will be discovered and he will be turned over to the police.)

17 COMPARING AND CONTRASTING

How does the peddler's reaction to Edla's invitation differ from his response to the iron-master's? (While the peddler responds with alarm and defensiveness to the ironmaster's repeated invitations, he is persuaded to accept Edla's invitation by her compassion and friendliness.)

regimental comrade—that, however, did not please the tramp.

"No, I couldn't think of it!" he said, looking quite alarmed.

He thought of the thirty kronor. To go up to the manor house would be like throwing himself voluntarily into the lions' den. He only wanted a chance to sleep here in the forge and then sneak away as inconspicuously as possible.

The ironmaster assumed that he felt embarrassed because of his miserable clothing.

"Please don't think that I have such a fine home that you cannot show yourself there," he said. "Elizabeth is dead, as you may already have heard. My boys are abroad, and there is no one at home except my oldest daughter and myself. We were just saying that it was too bad we didn't have any company for Christmas. Now come along with me and help us make the Christmas food disappear a little faster."

But the stranger said no, and no, and again no, and the ironmaster saw that he must give in.

"It looks as though Captain von Ståhle[11] preferred to stay with you tonight, Stjernström,"[12] he said to the master blacksmith, and turned on his heel.

But he laughed to himself as he went away, and the blacksmith, who knew him, understood very well that he had not said his last word.

It was not more than half an hour before they heard the sound of carriage wheels outside the forge, and a new guest came in, but this time it was not the ironmaster. He had sent his daughter, apparently hoping that she would have better powers of persuasion than he himself.

She entered, followed by a valet,[13] carrying on his arm a big fur coat. She was not at all pretty, but seemed modest and quite shy. In the forge everything was just as it had been earlier in the evening. The master blacksmith and his apprentice still sat on their bench, and iron and charcoal still glowed in the furnace. The stranger had stretched himself out on the floor and lay with a piece of pig iron under his head and his hat pulled down over his eyes. As soon as the young girl caught sight of him she went up and lifted his hat. The man was evidently used to sleeping with one eye open. He jumped up abruptly and seemed to be quite frightened.

"My name is Edla Willmansson," said the young girl. "My father came home and said that you wanted to sleep here in the forge tonight, and then I asked permission to come and bring you home to us. I am so sorry, Captain, that you are having such a hard time."

She looked at him compassionately, with her heavy eyes, and then she noticed that the man was afraid. "Either he has stolen something or else he has escaped from jail," she thought, and added quickly, "You may be sure, Captain, that you will be allowed to leave us just as freely as you came. Only please stay with us over Christmas Eve."

She said this in such a friendly manner that the rat-trap peddler must have felt confidence in her.

"It would never have occurred to me that you would bother with me yourself, miss," he said. "I will come at once."

He accepted the fur coat, which the valet handed him with a deep bow, threw it over his rags, and followed the young lady out to the carriage, without granting the astonished

---

11. **von Ståhle** (fon stô′lə)
12. **Stjernström** (styern′strôm)

13. **valet** (val′it): personal manservant.

blacksmiths so much as a glance.

But while he was riding up to the manor house he had evil <u>forebodings.</u>

"Why the devil did I take that fellow's money?" he thought. "Now I am sitting in the trap and will never get out of it."

The next day was Christmas Eve, and when the ironmaster came into the dining room for breakfast he probably thought with satisfaction of his old regimental comrade whom he had run across so unexpectedly.

"First of all we must see to it that he gets a little flesh on his bones," he said to his daughter, who was busy at the table. "And then we must see that he gets something else to do than to run around the country selling rat traps."

"It is queer that things have gone downhill with him as badly as that," said the daughter. "Last night I did not think there was anything about him to show that he had once been an educated man."

"You must have patience, my little girl," said the father. "As soon as he gets clean and dressed up, you will see something different. Last night he was naturally embarrassed. The tramp manners will fall away from him with the tramp clothes."

Just as he said this the door opened and the stranger entered. Yes, now he was truly clean and well dressed. The valet had bathed him, cut his hair, and shaved him. Moreover, he was dressed in a good-looking suit of clothes which belonged to the ironmaster. He wore a white shirt and a starched collar and whole shoes.

But although his guest was now so well groomed, the ironmaster did not seem pleased. He looked at him with puckered brow, and it was easy enough to understand that when he had seen the strange fellow in the uncertain reflection from the furnace he might have made a mistake, but that now, when he stood there in broad daylight, it was impossible to mistake him for an old acquaintance.

"What does this mean?" he thundered.

The stranger made no attempt to dissimulate. He saw at once that all the splendor had come to an end.

"It is not my fault, sir," he said. "I never pretended to be anything but a poor trader, and I pleaded and begged to be allowed to stay in the forge. But no harm has been done. At worst I can put on my rags again and go away."

"Well," said the ironmaster, hesitating a little, "it was not quite honest, either. You must admit that, and I should not be surprised if the sheriff would like to have something to say in the matter."

The tramp took a step forward and struck the table with his fist.

"Now I am going to tell you, Mr. Ironmaster, how things are," he said. "This whole world is nothing but a big rat trap. All the good things that are offered you are nothing but cheese rinds and bits of pork, set out to drag a poor fellow into trouble. And if the sheriff comes now and locks me up for this, then you, Mr. Ironmaster, must remember that a day may come when you yourself may want to get a big piece of pork, and then you will get caught in the trap."

The ironmaster began to laugh.

"That was not so badly said, my good fellow. Perhaps we should let the sheriff alone on Christmas Eve. But now get out of here as fast as you can."

But just as the man was opening the door, the daughter said, "I think he ought to stay with us today. I don't want him to go." And with that she went and closed the door.

"What in the world are you doing?" said the father.

forebodings (fôr·bod'iŋz): feelings that something, especially evil, is about to take place

18 COMPARING AND CONTRASTING
How do the father's and the daughter's attitudes toward the peddler differ before they discover his identity? (She suspects the peddler is not an educated man; hence, not her father's friend. The father thinks the man's true nature will be revealed when he is cleaned up.)

19 EVALUATING
Do you accept the peddler's argument that the case of mistaken identity is not his fault? (Answers will vary. Some students may point out that he could have told the ironmaster that he was not the old friend; others may say the ironmaster would have attributed such a statement to pride and not believed the man.)

20 READER'S RESPONSE
How do you respond to the peddler's rat trap theory?

21 LITERARY ELEMENT
Turning Point: Why is the daughter's decision to let the peddler stay for Christmas a turning point in the story? (Possible response: Her act of kindness begins the peddler's rehabilitation.)

22 COMPARING LITERATURE
Have students compare and contrast the effect that meeting a poverty-stricken stranger has on Edla in this story and on Lise in "The Ring" (pp. 1214–1222). Do students consider one character's response more realistic than the other's? Or can the differences in the responses be explained as differences in the women's characters?

23 LITERARY ELEMENT
Characterization: How does Edla show that she is capable of great empathy? (She is able to imagine the feelings of a person who is homeless and afraid.)

---

22 The daughter stood there quite embarrassed and hardly knew what to answer. That morning she had felt so happy when she thought how homelike and Christmassy she was going to make things for the poor hungry wretch. She could not get away from the idea all at once, and that was why she had interceded for the vagabond.

23 "I am thinking of this stranger here," said the young girl. "He walks and walks the whole year long, and there is probably not a single place in the whole country where he is welcome and can feel at home. Wherever he turns he is chased away. Always he is afraid of being arrested and cross-examined. I should like to have him enjoy a day of peace with us here—just one in the whole year."

The ironmaster mumbled something in his beard. He could not bring himself to oppose her.

"It was all a mistake, of course," she continued. "But anyway I don't think we ought to chase away a human being whom we have asked to come here, and to whom we have promised Christmas cheer."

"You do preach worse than a parson," said the ironmaster. "I only hope you won't have to regret this."

The young girl took the stranger by the hand and led him up to the table.

"Now sit down and eat," she said, for she could see that her father had given in.

The man with the rat traps said not a word; he only sat down and helped himself to the food. Time after time he looked at **24**

Early landscape by Wassily Kandinsky (1866–1944).
? *Do you think that the rat-trap seller has indeed fallen into a trap? What do you predict will happen to him?*

Roos/Art Resource, New York

READING CHECK

1. To what does the peddler compare the world? (a rat trap)
2. What does the peddler steal from the crofter? (thirty kronor)
3. Who does the ironmaster think the peddler is? (an old army friend)

4. When does he discover his mistake? (the next day when he sees the man groomed)
5. What gift does the peddler leave for Edla? (a rat trap with the stolen thirty kronor and a letter inside)

RETEACHING

To reteach "The Rat Trap," have students imagine that they are casting a movie version of the story. What characteristics would they look for in the actors who would play the three main characters? What famous actors might be suitable for the roles? Have the class vote for the best actor for each role.

24 the young girl who had interceded for him. Why had she done it? What could the crazy idea be?

After that, Christmas Eve at Ramsjö passed just as it always had. The stranger did not cause any trouble because he did nothing but sleep. The whole forenoon he lay on the sofa in one of the guest rooms and slept at one stretch. At noon they woke him up so that he could have his share of the good Christmas fare, but after that he slept again. It seemed as though for many years he had not been able to sleep as quietly and safely as here at Ramsjö.

In the evening, when the Christmas tree was lighted, they woke him up again, and he stood for a while in the drawing room, blinking as though the candlelight hurt him, but after that he disappeared again. Two hours later he was aroused once more. He then had to go down into the dining room and eat the Christmas fish and porridge.

As soon as they got up from the table he went around to each one present and said thank you and good night, but when he came to the young girl she gave him to understand that it was her father's intention that the suit which he wore was to be a Christmas present—he did not have to return it; and if he wanted to spend next Christmas Eve in a place where he could rest in peace, and be sure that no evil would befall him, he would be welcomed back again.

The man with the rat traps did not answer anything to this. He only stared at the young girl in boundless amazement.

The next morning the ironmaster and his daughter got up in good season to go to the early Christmas service. Their guest was still asleep, and they did not disturb him.

When, at about ten o'clock, they drove back from church, the young girl sat and hung her head even more dejectedly than usual. At church she had learned that one of the old crofters of the ironworks had been robbed by a man who went around selling rat traps.

"Yes, that was a fine fellow you let into the house," said her father. "I only wonder how many silver spoons are left in the cupboard by this time." **26**

The wagon had hardly stopped at the front steps when the ironmaster asked the valet whether the stranger was still there. He added that he had heard at church that the man was a thief. The valet answered that the fellow had gone and that he had not taken anything with him at all. On the contrary, he had left behind a little package which Miss Willmansson was to be kind enough to accept as a Christmas present. **27**

The young girl opened the package, which was so badly done up that the contents came into view at once. She gave a little cry of joy. She found a small rat trap, and in it lay three wrinkled ten-kronor notes. But that was not all. In the rat trap lay also a letter written in large, jagged characters:

Honored and noble Miss:

Since you have been so nice to me all day long, as if I was a captain, I want to be nice to you, in return, as if I was a real captain: for I do not want you to be embarrassed at this Christmas season by a thief; but you can give back the money to the old man on the roadside, who has the money pouch hanging on the window frame as a bait for poor wanderers.

The rat trap is a Christmas present from a rat who would have been caught in this world's rat trap if he had not been raised to captain, because in that way he got power to clear himself. **28**

Written with friendship and high regard,

Captain von Ståhle

24 ANALYZING
Why does the peddler find Edla's kindness so difficult to understand? (Possible response: He has not experienced such treatment before; it doesn't fit his rat-trap theory of life.)

25 INFERRING
Why do you think the author so often refers to the peddler as "the man with the rat traps" and never reveals his name? (Possible responses: to make the point that to most people, the peddler is just a nameless vagabond; to emphasize the importance of the rat traps in defining his view of life)

■ **dejectedly** (di·jek′tid·lē): showing low spirits; in a depressed way

26 PREDICTING
What do you think the father and daughter will find when they return home from church? (Answers will vary.)

27 PREDICTING
What do you think the peddler's present to Edla will be? (Answers will vary.)

28 LITERARY ELEMENT
Theme: What message does the author try to communicate by the content of the letter the peddler writes to Edla? (Possible responses: A person responds in kind to the treatment he or she receives; kindness that asks nothing in return has a liberating effect; it enables individuals to escape the traps set by themselves and their society.)

1. Writing a Teleplay. Have students work cooperatively to write a script for a television play, updating "The Rat Trap" to a contemporary setting. Refer them to plays such as *A Doll's House* (pp. 1069–1126) for examples of stage directions. If necessary, review with students the technical elements of a teleplay, such as camera directions to indicate close-ups, long shots, panning, fade-ins, and fade-outs.

2. Comparing Concepts of Generosity. Edla's actions at Christmas are meant to express a Christian ideal of selfless giving. Have students work with partners to choose a religion and research its teachings about generosity and compassion for the less fortunate. After students share their reports with the class, have the entire class decide on the religious teaching that they consider most relevant to American society today.

CLOSURE

One critic has said that the main themes of Selma Lagerlöf's works concern guilt and atonement, the saving qualities of a woman's selfless love, and ways to combine happiness with goodness. Have students discuss how well these themes apply to "The Rat Trap." ∎

ANSWERS

First Thoughts
Answers will vary.

Identifying Facts
1. good things. trap closes
2. to steal money. He can't make a getaway.
3. mistakes him for an old army friend. persuades father to let him stay; even after his identity is revealed, lets him keep suit; invites him to return
4. The peddler robbed the crofter. a rat trap with the stolen money inside and a letter signed "Captain von Ståhle"

Interpreting Meanings
1. She makes the story seem like a fairy tale. omniscient
2. Possible responses: moral confusion, punishment, guilt. It is a dark, confusing place where it is impossible to walk on a straight (moral) path; it closes in upon him.
3. Possible response: It provides a sympathetic but objective view of his predicament.
4. Possible response: because Edla treated him like a social equal. He now feels like the captain they mistook him for.

Applying Meanings
Answers will vary.

Creative Writing Response
Writing a Different Conclusion. Conclusions should use the omniscient point of view.

Critical Writing Response
Comparing and Contrasting Characters. Essays should include similarities and differences and evaluate authors' views based on story details. ∎

⯈ First Thoughts
Did you think the peddler would return the thirty kronor in the end? Did you find his action believable? Why or why not?

Identifying Facts
1. In the rat-trap peddler's theory of the world, what is the bait? What happens after someone takes the bait?
2. Why does the peddler return to the crofter's cottage? Why does he later feel like a rat in a trap?
3. Why does the ironmaster invite the peddler into his home? What kindnesses does Edla show the peddler?
4. What do Edla and her father learn at church on Christmas morning? What do they discover when they return home?

Interpreting Meanings
1. What effect does Lagerlöf achieve with the opening words of the story? What **point of view** is associated with stories that open with these words?
2. After the peddler steals the thirty kronor, he becomes lost in a forest. The forest is clearly real, but it may also be a **symbol**—something that represents a larger idea or concept. What do you think the forest might **symbolize**? Cite details from the story to support your answer.
3. How does Lagerlöf's use of the **omniscient point of view** help us understand the peddler better than if he were telling the story himself?
4. In the peddler's note to Edla, how does he say he managed to avoid "this world's rat trap"? Why do you think the peddler signed his note "Captain von Ståhle"?

Applying Meanings
This story seems to suggest that if someone, even a criminal, is treated with honor and respect, he or she will become honorable and respectable. Do you think this is generally true, or do you think this theory is too simplistic? Discuss your opinion, giving examples from your own experiences.

Creative Writing Response
Writing a Different Conclusion. This story is about a man who was treated honorably and who then acted honorably. If the ironmaster and his daughter had not been kind to the peddler after they discovered he was not who they thought he was, how do you think the peddler would have reacted? How would the story have ended? Write a different ending to the story, beginning with the ironmaster's words on page 1203, "What does this mean?"

Critical Writing Response
Comparing and Contrasting Characters. In a brief essay, compare and contrast Lagerlöf's character of the peddler in "The Rat Trap" with Tolstoy's character Pahom in "How Much Land Does a Man Need?" (see page 1045). Name at least one way in which the characters are alike and at least one way in which they are different. In your final paragraph, state whether you think Lagerlöf or Tolstoy has the more positive view of human nature. You may also state whose view you agree with. Be sure to support general statements with details from the stories. As a prewriting exercise, fill in a chart like the one below.

	Peddler	Pahom
General intelligence		
Effects of poverty		
Effects of greed		

James Joyce
1882–1941, Ireland

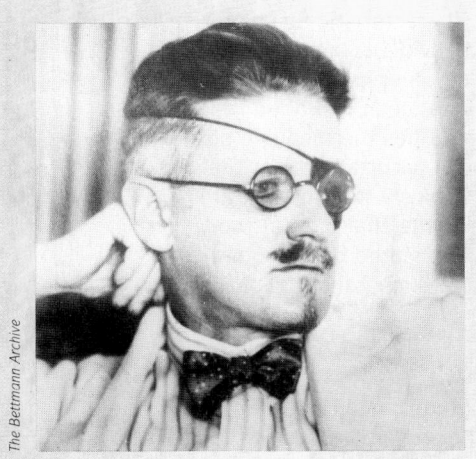

The Bettmann Archive

J ames Joyce was the oldest of ten children born to a poor Roman Catholic family in "dear, dirty Dublin." He was an enthusiastic student and eventually enrolled at Dublin's University College. When he was twenty, however, he left Dublin and repressive Irish Catholic society for the cosmopolitan cities of Paris, Trieste, Rome, and Zurich. At the time of his death he had not set foot in his homeland for nearly thirty years. Yet, ironically, all of his writings deal with his childhood home.

In his first major work, a collection of short stories called *Dubliners* (1914), Joyce provides snapshots of the paralyzing world from which he fled. His simple style here contrasts sharply with his later, more revolutionary, works. Joyce's poetic, autobio-

graphical novel *A Portrait of the Artist as a Young Man* (1916) followed. The novel is full of experimental wordplay and was praised in literary circles on both sides of the Atlantic, though it had met with several rejections before an American company agreed to publish it. Joyce had even greater difficulty publishing his next book, *Ulysses* (1922). This novel vividly illustrates Joyce's blend of realism and symbolism, his groundbreaking use of inventive language, and his ability to capture characters' thoughts with the stream-of-consciousness technique. Loosely paralleling Homer's *Odyssey*, it takes place in Dublin on a single day—June 16, 1904—which, not coincidentally, was the day Joyce fell in love with his future wife, Nora Barnacle.

Joyce's last major work was *Finnegans Wake* (1939). This highly experimental novel is so filled with allusions, foreign expressions, and word coinages that no one can read it without guidance. For example, this passage describes Finnegan's fall off a wall and his subsequent death: "The great fall of the offwall entailed at such short notice the pftjschute of Finnegan, erse solid man, that the humptyhillhead of humself promptly sends an unquiring one well to the west in quest of his tumptytumtoes. . . ."

Although Joyce's books were banned, pirated, and often misunderstood, he is now regarded as one of the greatest literary talents of the twentieth century.

MORE ABOUT THE AUTHOR
James Joyce's rebellion against his upbringing is summarized in the words of Stephen Dedalus, the hero of his autobiographical novel *A Portrait of the Artist as a Young Man:*

> "I will not serve that in which I no longer believe, whether it call itself my home, my fatherland, or my church: and I will try to express myself in some mode of life or art as freely as I can. . . ."

Many of the stories in *Dubliners* are autobiographical to some degree and reflect this theme of rebellion and attempted escape. The first three stories in the collection are told in the first person and are based on Joyce's childhood experiences. Others, which deal with adolescence, maturity, and public life, feature characters based on people Joyce knew in Dublin or represent his visions of who he might have become if he had not left Ireland.

In his rebellion, Joyce longed to think of himself as a European rather than an Irishman. As a student, he had become interested in the literature and culture of the European continent, and Henrik Ibsen (see p. 1069) was a particular hero of his. Joyce made his first trip to Paris in 1902, returned to Dublin several times to see his dying mother, and then left Ireland for good, with Nora Barnacle, in 1904.

OBJECTIVES

1. *To analyze the themes and literary techniques of a modern master of the short story*
2. *To recognize the technique of stream of consciousness and to evaluate its effects*
3. *To freewrite one's own stream of consciousness, and to write a critical essay about the epiphany in "Eveline"*

PREREADING FOCUS

Background: Although Joyce rejected the Catholicism in which he was brought up, his religious background continued to influence his writing. His use of the word *epiphany* suggests his lifelong concern for the spiritual dimension of life and his perception of the artist as a secular priest.

The Christian feast of the Epiphany celebrates the visit of the Magi, or the Three Kings, to the baby Jesus. It is celebrated on January 6, also known as Twelfth Night. Just as Jesus is said to have manifested his essence to the Magi, Joyce hoped to manifest to his readers the essence of human nature, by capturing sudden moments of truth in people's experiences. Joyce described an epiphany as the moment when "the soul of the commonest object . . . seems to us radiant" or when "its soul, its whatness leaps to us from the vestment of its appearance."

Literary Focus: The stream-of-consciousness technique is most often used to present a character's **interior monologue**, an uncensored account of that character's unvoiced point of view. The interior monologue may be a direct report of the character's thoughts, as if the reader were "overhearing" them, or the monologue may be indirect, with the author intruding as guide and commentator on the character's thoughts. Joyce is a master of the direct interior monologue.

Reader's Guide

EVELINE

Background

"Eveline" is the fourth of the fifteen stories in *Dubliners*. Although it is one of the first stories Joyce ever wrote, his characteristic focus on the inner workings of characters' minds is already evident. In all the stories in *Dubliners*, Joyce uses a device he called an **epiphany**. Joyce borrowed the term from theology and used it to mean a sudden remark, symbol, or moment that sums up and clarifies the meaning of a complex experience. Joyce's epiphanies usually occur at or near the end of each story. Sometimes a character achieves a new insight; at other times, only the reader becomes aware of the character's true nature. In either case, the new awareness is not stated directly. Instead, Joyce provides details from which readers must make their own inferences.

Writer's Response

Think of a time when you suddenly changed your opinion, attitude, or behavior. Freewrite about the change and explain what caused it.

Literary Focus

Joyce was one of the first modernists to use **stream of consciousness** as a narrative technique. Early in the century, writers interested in psychology began to recognize that the human mind does not usually operate in a linear fashion; instead, it leaps around from thought to thought and feeling to feeling in what seems to be a random way. For example, eating a cinnamon roll for breakfast may remind a woman of the smell that often filled her grandmother's kitchen. She may then recall a childhood trip to her grandmother's in which the family car broke down, and that may remind her that her own car needs repairs, and so on. Joyce brought stream of consciousness to its highest form in his novels *Ulysses* and *Finnegans Wake,* and we see the beginnings of this technique in "Eveline."

EVELINE

James Joyce

Joyce once wrote that he chose to set his stories in Dublin "because that city seemed to me the center of paralysis." As you read, think about how this famous phrase, "center of paralysis," applies to the character of Eveline.

She sat at the window watching the evening invade the avenue. Her head was leaned against the window curtains and in her nostrils was the odor of dusty cretonne.[1] She was tired.

Few people passed. The man out of the last house passed on his way home; she heard his footsteps clacking along the concrete pavement and afterwards crunching on the cinder path before the new red houses. One time there used to be a field there in which they used to play every evening with other people's children. Then a man from Belfast bought the field and built houses in it—not like their little brown houses but bright brick houses with shining roofs. The children of the avenue used to play together in that field—the Devines, the Waters, the Dunns, little Keogh the cripple, she and her brothers and sisters. Ernest, however, never played: he was too grown up. Her father used often to hunt them in out of the field with his blackthorn stick; but usually little Keogh used to keep *nix*[2] and call out when he saw her father coming. Still they seemed to have been rather happy then. Her father was not so bad then; and besides, her mother was alive. That was a long time ago; she and her brothers and sisters were all grown up; her mother was dead. Tizzie Dunn was dead, too, and the Waters had gone back to England. Everything changes. Now she was going to go away like the others, to leave her home.

Home! She looked round the room, reviewing all its familiar objects which she had dusted once a week for so many years, wondering where on earth all the dust came from. Perhaps she would never see again those familiar objects from which she had never dreamed of being divided. And yet during all those years she had never found out the name of the priest whose yellowing photograph hung on the wall above the broken harmonium[3] beside the colored print of the promises made to Blessed Margaret Mary Alacoque.[4] He had been a school friend of her father. Whenever he showed the photograph to a visitor her father used to pass it with a casual word:

---

1. **cretonne** (krē·tän′): heavy printed cloth used for curtains.
2. **keep *nix***: serve as a lookout.
3. **harmonium**: small organ.
4. **promises . . . Alacoque** (à·là·kôk′): the Lord's promises to Margaret Mary Alacoque (1647–1690), French nun who as a child suffered from self-inflicted paralysis but was miraculously cured when she dedicated herself to a holy life.

5 COMPARING LITERATURE

Have students compare the characters of Eveline in this story and Nora in *A Doll's House* (pp. 1069–1126).

❓ *How are the two women's situations similar? How are they different? Do the characters go through a similar decision-making process about leaving home?* (Both Nora and Eveline think about leaving situations that guarantee them food and shelter, but their reasons for wanting to leave are different. Eveline wants to escape from an abusive father and a life of poverty, while Nora wants to find out who she really is.)

6 GUIDED READING

Identifying Details: What aspect of being married and leaving home does Eveline look forward to? (being treated with respect)

MEETING INDIVIDUAL NEEDS

7 LEP: Students may find confusing the usage of the word *only* in this passage. The father means that only the memory of the mother keeps him from hurting Eveline. He would hurt her if not for that. ∎

The Granger Collection, New York

DUBLIN FROM THE LIFFEY, engraving.
❓ *How does Eveline feel about leaving home?*

"He is in Melbourne now."

5 She had consented to go away, to leave her home. Was that wise? She tried to weigh each side of the question. In her home anyway she had shelter and food; she had those whom she had known all her life about her. Of course she had to work hard both in the house and at business. What would they say of her in the Stores when they found out that she had run away with a fellow? Say she was a fool, perhaps; and her place would be filled up by advertisement. Miss Gavan would be glad. She had always had an edge on her, especially whenever there were people listening.

"Miss Hill, don't you see these ladies are waiting?"

"Look lively, Miss Hill, please."

She would not cry many tears at leaving the Stores.

6 But in her new home, in a distant unknown country, it would not be like that. Then she would be married—she, Eveline. People would treat her with respect then. She would not be treated as her mother had been. Even now, though she was over nineteen, she sometimes felt herself in danger of her father's violence. She knew it was that that had given her the palpitations. When they were growing up he had never gone for her, like he used to go for Harry and Ernest, because she was a girl; but latterly he had **7** begun to threaten her and say what he would do to her only for her dead mother's

7 sake. And now she had nobody to protect her. Ernest was dead and Harry, who was in the church decorating business, was nearly always down somewhere in the country. Besides, the invariable squabble for money on Saturday nights had begun to weary her unspeakably. She always gave her entire wages—seven shillings[5]—and Harry always sent up what he could but the trouble was to get any money from her father. He said she used to squander the money, that she had no head, that he wasn't going to give her his hard-earned money to throw about the streets, and much more, for he was usually fairly bad of a Saturday night. In the end he would give her the money and ask her had she any intention of buying Sunday's dinner.

8 Then she had to rush out as quickly as she could and do her marketing, holding her black leather purse tightly in her hand as she elbowed her way through the crowds and returning home late under her load of provisions. She had hard work to keep the house together and to see that the two young children who had been left to her charge went to school regularly and got their meals regularly.

9 It was hard work—a hard life—but now that she was about to leave it she did not find it a wholly undesirable life.

She was about to explore another life with Frank. Frank was very kind, manly, open-hearted. She was to go away with him by the night boat to be his wife and to live with him in Buenos Aires where he had a home waiting for her. How well she remembered the first time she had seen him; he was lodging in a house on the main road where she used to visit. It seemed a few weeks ago. He was standing at the gate, his peaked cap pushed back on his head and his hair tumbled forward over a face of bronze. Then they had come to know each other. He used to meet her outside the Stores every evening and see her home. He took her to see *The Bohemian Girl* and she felt elated as she sat in an unaccustomed part of the theater with him.

10 He was awfully fond of music and sang a little. People knew that they were courting and, when he sang about the lass that loves a sailor, she always felt pleasantly confused. He used to call her Poppens out of fun. First of all it had been an excitement for her to have a fellow and then she had begun to like him.

11 He had tales of distant countries. He had started as a deck boy at a pound a month on a ship of the Allan Line going out to Canada. He told her the names of the ships he had been on and the names of the different services. He had sailed through the Strait of Magellan and he told her stories of the terrible Patagonians.[6] He had fallen on his feet in Buenos Aires, he said, and had come over to the old country just for a holiday. Of course, her father had found out the affair and had forbidden her to have anything to say to him.

12 "I know these sailor chaps,"[7] he said.

One day he had quarreled with Frank and after that she had to meet her lover secretly.

The evening deepened in the avenue. The white of two letters in her lap grew indistinct. One was to Harry; the other was to her father. Ernest had been her favorite but she liked Harry, too. Her father was becoming old lately, she noticed; he would miss her. Sometimes he could be very nice. Not long before, when she had been laid up for

5. **seven shillings:** A shilling is a former British coin worth five pennies, or one-twentieth of a pound. Seven shillings would have been a low salary.

6. **Patagonians** (pat′ə·gō′nē·ənz): inhabitants of the southern part of Argentina; at the time of the story, Patagonia was still a frontier area, similar to the American West of the last century.

7. **chaps:** fellows.

8 INFERRING
Why doesn't Eveline challenge her father's unfair treatment of her? (She is afraid he will hurt her.)

9 READER'S RESPONSE
Do you think it is easier to cling to familiar situations, even if they are unpleasant, than to face the uncertainties of a probable solution?

10 LITERARY ELEMENT
Irony: The word *bohemian* can refer to a gypsy or a person who lives a free, unconventional life. How does the musical title *The Bohemian Girl* provide an ironic contrast to Eveline's situation? (Eveline is a dutiful daughter who is hemmed in by conventional expectations and is afraid to leave home.)

11 EVALUATING
Judging from his behavior, do you think Frank is a good influence on Eveline? Why or why not? (Answers will vary.)

12 COMPARING AND CONTRASTING
How has Frank's life been different from Eveline's? (He has spent years traveling to distant countries and having adventures. Eveline has never left her hometown.)

READING CHECK

1. As the story opens, what plans does Eveline have? (to leave home and get married in Buenos Aires)
2. How does Eveline's father mistreat her? (He threatens violence, insults her, takes her wages, and then badgers her about meals.)
3. What is the occupation of Eveline's boyfriend, Frank? (sailor)

4. What promise did Eveline make to her dying mother? (to keep the home together as long as she could)
5. Does Eveline go away with Frank? (no) How does her face look at the end of the story? (like that of a helpless animal)

RETEACHING

To reteach "Eveline," write the word *home* on the board and have students complete a semantic map based on Eveline's memories, thoughts, and feelings associated with the word. On completing the map, students can form teams to debate whether Eveline should or should not have left her home to go to Buenos Aires.

13 LITERARY ELEMENT

Stream of Consciousness: What sound does Eveline hear that reminds her of her promise to her dying mother? (the sound of a street organ)

14 GUIDED READING

Cause and Effect: What effect does Eveline's memory of her mother's death have on her decision-making process? (Remembering her mother's sad life motivates Eveline to escape a similar fate by leaving her home.)

15 INTERPRETING

Why might Eveline think that Frank "would drown her"? What is she really afraid of? (Possible responses: the unknown; being overwhelmed by too much life and love.)

16 LITERARY ELEMENT

Simile: In what way is the comparison of Eveline to a helpless animal appropriate? (Possible response: The freedom and happiness of the outside world is beyond her reach; her religion and sense of duty to her family are "the iron railings" that entrap her.)

PREDICTING

When did you know what Eveline's final decision would be? What clues helped you make your prediction? (Most students will select a moment from this final scene. They may mention her distress and nausea, the "mournful" whistle, her fear of "drowning," her prayer to be shown her "duty," her gripping the railing.)

1212 The Twentieth Century

a day, he had read her out a ghost story and made toast for her at the fire. Another day, when their mother was alive, they had all gone for a picnic to the Hill of Howth. She remembered her father putting on her mother's bonnet to make the children laugh.

Her time was running out but she continued to sit by the window, leaning her head against the window curtain, inhaling the odor of dusty cretonne. Down far in the avenue she could hear a street organ playing. She knew the air. Strange that it should come that very night to remind her of the promise to her mother, her promise to keep the home together as long as she could. She remembered the last night of her mother's illness; she was again in the close dark room at the other side of the hall and outside she heard a melancholy air of Italy. The organ player had been ordered to go away and given sixpence. She remembered her father strutting back into the sickroom saying:

"Damned Italians! coming over here!"

As she mused the pitiful vision of her mother's life laid its spell on the very quick of her being—that life of commonplace sacrifices closing in final craziness. She trembled as she heard again her mother's voice saying constantly with foolish insistence:

"Derevaun Seraun![8] Derevaun Seraun!"

She stood up in a sudden impulse of terror. Escape! She must escape! Frank would save her. He would give her life, perhaps love, too. But she wanted to live. Why should she be unhappy? She had a right to happiness. Frank would take her in his arms, fold her in his arms. He would save her.

She stood among the swaying crowd in the station at the North Wall.[9] He held her hand and she knew that he was speaking to her, saying something about the passage over and over again. The station was full of soldiers with brown baggages. Through the wide doors of the sheds she caught a glimpse of the black mass of the boat, lying in beside the quay wall, with illumined portholes. She answered nothing. She felt her cheek pale and cold and, out of a maze of distress, she prayed to God to direct her, to show her what was her duty. The boat blew a long mournful whistle into the mist. If she went, tomorrow she would be on the sea with Frank, steaming towards Buenos Aires. Their passage had been booked. Could she still draw back after all he had done for her? Her distress awoke a nausea in her body and she kept moving her lips in silent fervent prayer.

A bell clanged upon her heart. She felt him seize her hand:

"Come!"

All the seas of the world tumbled about her heart. He was drawing her into them: he would drown her. She gripped with both hands at the iron railing.

"Come!"

No! No! No! It was impossible. Her hands clutched the iron in frenzy. Amid the seas she sent a cry of anguish!

"Eveline! Evvy!"

He rushed beyond the barrier and called to her to follow. He was shouted at to go on but he still called to her. She set her white face to him, passive, like a helpless animal. Her eyes gave him no sign of love or farewell or recognition.

8. **Derevaun Seraun:** Some scholars suggest that the phrase is corrupt Irish Gaelic for "the end of song is raving madness" or "the end of pleasure is pain." Although it does appear to be based on Irish Gaelic, the phrase as it stands is gibberish.

9. **North Wall:** wharf that is part of Dublin Harbor.

1. Reading Another Story from Dubliners. Have students read another story from the collection and compare it to "Eveline" in terms of theme, characters, use of epiphany, and use of stream-of-consciousness narrative technique. Students may be interested in the stories of childhood ("The Sisters," "An Encounter," "Araby") and adolescence ("After the Race," "Two Gallants," "The Boarding House").

2. Writing a Letter from Another Character's Point of View. Have students imagine that Frank writes Eveline from Buenos Aires, trying to persuade her to change her mind about leaving home. What tone would he take in his letter? What kinds of arguments would he use? Invite volunteers to share their letters with the class, and have the class comment on the persuasiveness of each letter.

Have students discuss the various conditions in people's lives that make them spiritually or emotionally paralyzed. Have students also discuss how people like Eveline might be able to overcome their paralysis. ■

First Thoughts

Why do you think Eveline decides to stay in Ireland rather than escape to Buenos Aires with Frank? Do you think she made the right decision?

Identifying Facts

1. What are Eveline's responsibilities in the Hill household?
2. What was Mr. Hill's reaction to the relationship between Frank and his daughter?
3. Summarize the final scene at the quay.

Interpreting Meanings

1. Find an example of loosely associated thoughts or memories that illustrate Joyce's use of the **stream-of-consciousness** narrative technique. What do Eveline's thoughts and memories reveal about her character and the kind of life she led before meeting Frank?
2. Around what **internal conflict** do Eveline's thoughts center? In what way is this also an **external conflict** between her and her society?
3. What finally causes Eveline to refuse to leave with Frank? What events or thoughts earlier in the story **foreshadowed**, or hinted at, this decision?

Applying Meanings

Do you think that the desire to assert our independence must always conflict with our responsibilities to others? Discuss this in relation to a time you felt a conflict between your duties to others and your own need for independence.

Creative Writing Response

Capturing Your Own Stream of Consciousness. In a freewriting exercise, try to capture your own **stream of consciousness**. Remember that stream of consciousness attempts to portray the thinking mind directly, without organizing the thoughts. Start with something you are seeing or thinking or feeling right now. Then jot down the flow of thoughts, emotions, memories, and associations that run through your mind. Don't worry about sentence structure or punctuation or even making sense. Just write down whatever enters your mind. If you wish, you may then edit these jottings and organize them so that you can use them later in a sketch or short story.

Critical Writing Response

Writing About an Epiphany. Write a brief essay about the **epiphany** in "Eveline." In your essay, answer these questions:

1. What is the story's epiphany, or moment of awareness, about Eveline's true nature and desires?
2. What do we learn about Eveline at this point? How does this new awareness differ from our earlier impressions and the impressions she had of herself?
3. Would you say that *she* experiences a new awareness? Or is the awareness merely on the reader's part?

Before writing, you may find it helpful to jot down general answers to these questions and then find details in the story that will help you support and explain your answers.

First Thoughts
Answers will vary.

Identifying Facts
1. to give over her salary, cook, keep house, bring up children
2. He told Eveline she couldn't see him.
3. Eveline meets Frank for their planned elopement but then can't bring herself to go.

Interpreting Meanings
1. Examples will vary. She is dutiful and attached to her home, in spite of oppressive responsibility and ill treatment from her father.
2. *Internal:* whether to stay in her home or leave to find a happier life. *External:* duty to family, which society expects from women, versus desire for fulfillment
3. She is paralyzed by family expectations and her own passivity. Possible responses: attachment to objects in home, history of dutiful behavior, promise to her mother, memory of father's virtues and worry about his age

Applying Meanings
Answers will vary.

Creative Writing Response
Capturing Your Own Stream of Consciousness. To help students freewrite effectively, tell them that their writing will not be formally evaluated.

Critical Writing Response
Writing About an Epiphany. Essays should focus on the final paragraphs of the story. ■

Isak Dinesen was fond of masks and masquerades, and she lived under a series of different names. Born Karen Christentze Dinesen, she became Baroness Karen Blixen after she married. She published works under several pseudonyms, finally settling on her family's last name and the masculine first name Isak, meaning "laughter."

Dinesen saw herself as a modern-day Scheherazade, spinning exotic tales like those in *The Thousand and One Nights* (pp. 638–644). Many of her stories are based on tales she made up to entertain Denys Finch-Hatton on his intermittent visits to her in Africa. Critics have noticed the "Arabian Nights" flavor of her stories and have also heard echoes of the Bible and Icelandic sagas in her work.

Most of Dinesen's major works were written in English, the language she used daily in British East Africa. She felt that writing in a language that was not her native tongue helped free her imagination, as did taking pseudonyms and setting her stories in other time periods.

Dinesen faced despair, disillusionment, and debilitating physical illness in her life, and her works emphasize the importance of facing one's destiny with stoic courage. This theme is strong in *Out of Africa*, the book whose powerful motion-picture version led to a renewed popularity of Dinesen's work in the United States.

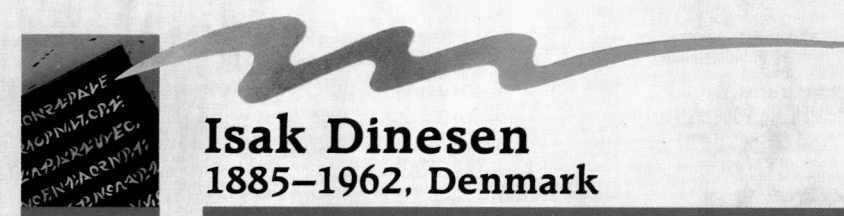

Isak Dinesen
1885–1962, Denmark

The Granger Collection, New York

When the American author Ernest Hemingway accepted the 1954 Nobel Prize for literature, he remarked that the award should instead have gone to Danish writer Isak Dinesen. Hemingway, who loved Africa and set several works there, was especially impressed with Dinesen's *Out of Africa*, an autobiographical account of her years in British East Africa, now Kenya. Although Dinesen is often recognized as the European author who best captured the beauty of the African landscape, she wrote equally well of northern Europe and the Danish upper class.

Born into a family of wealthy aristocrats in coastal Denmark, Dinesen's spirit of adventure was often at odds with her sheltered upbringing. After her father died and the cousin she loved refused to marry her, she defiantly set sail for Africa to marry the cousin's twin brother, Bror Blixen-Finecke. In 1914, the couple established a coffee plantation in what is now Kenya. Blixen's wayward lifestyle, however, left his wife often on her own. After the couple divorced in 1921, Dinesen ran the six-thousand-acre farm by herself for ten years.

Many of Dinesen's stories celebrate the power of women. In *Out of Africa*, Dinesen says that she often visited the Somali women on her property to listen to their stories. "It was a trait common to all these tales," Dinesen wrote, "that the heroine, chaste or not, would get the better of the male characters and come out of the tale triumphant. . . . Within this enclosed women's world . . . I felt the presence . . . of a Millennium when women were to reign supreme in the world."

In 1931, the price of coffee plummeted and Dinesen's plantation went bankrupt. In the same year her lover, the British pilot Denys Finch-Hatton, was killed in a plane crash. These events led Dinesen to return to Denmark and to devote herself to writing. Three years later she published *Seven Gothic Tales*, stories about mysterious events and persecuted heroines in Europe hundreds of years ago. Dinesen's international reputation was cemented with *Out of Africa*, which was published simultaneously in Denmark and Britain in 1937.

OBJECTIVES

1. *To interpret the symbolism used by a twentieth-century Danish writer*
2. *To classify characters in the story as static or dynamic*
3. *To write a dialogue that might have taken place between two characters, and to analyze a dynamic character's personality*
4. *To trace the origins of words derived from place names*

THEMES IN WORLD LITERATURE

The Loss of Innocence

"The Fall" from *Genesis*, pp. 166–168
From *Candide*, pp. 945–962

The Individual and Society

A Doll's House, pp. 1069–1126
"The Guest," pp. 1244–1257 ∎

VOCABULARY IN CONTEXT

The words listed below will appear in the side margin at the point of instruction:

1. gamboling   4. covert
2. glade   5. unconditional
3. rendered

Reader's Guide

THE RING

Background

Denmark, Dinesen's homeland and the setting of "The Ring," is a democratic constitutional monarchy. At the time this story takes place, however, the nation was not democratic. The nobility lived in a grand style, while the rest of the population was very poor and sometimes had to turn to crimes such as poaching—trespassing on a landowner's property to hunt game or catch fish—in order to feed themselves and their families. Such crimes were harshly punished; a livestock thief often faced death if he were caught. Upper-class attitudes toward the plight of the poor varied widely. Some members of the upper class— like Sigismund in "The Ring"—held humanitarian views and advocated social, political, and economic reforms. Many others found such ideas dangerous.

As the story opens, we learn that Lise, the main character, has been determined since childhood to marry Sigismund, a landowner who nevertheless comes from a family of lower rank than hers. Lise's parents have finally agreed to the marriage, and the newlyweds are blissfully happy.

Writer's Response

What kind of person do you think that Lise, a newly married young woman from the upper class, will be? Write your predictions in a few sentences.

Literary Focus

Characters are often classified as static or dynamic. A **static character** is one who changes little or not at all in the course of the story. A **dynamic character**, on the other hand, changes in an important way as a result of the action of the story. The **protagonist**, or main character, of a story is almost always a dynamic character. How the protagonist changes or what he or she learns is usually our best clue as to a story's **theme**, or larger meaning.

PREREADING FOCUS

Background: Denmark was an absolute monarchy until 1849, when a parliament was established. In the late 1800s, small farmers began to gather power by organizing into cooperatives and attending folk high schools inspired by the educator Nikolai Grundtvig. However, the right to vote was not extended to farm workers and women until 1915. Soon afterward, a land reform bill was passed whose purpose was to break up large estates and redistribute the land. Trial by jury was also introduced at this time. Today, Denmark is a modern welfare state much different than the setting of "The Ring," with income assistance for the poor, free hospital care for all, unemployment insurance, and government pension programs.

Literary Focus: Help students distinguish between changes in a character and changes in the reader's understanding of a character. Sometimes a character's basic traits do not change in response to events, but the reader's understanding of those traits is deepened as a result of seeing how the character responds. The protagonist of Joyce's "Eveline" (pp. 1207–1213) is such a character—static but complex, with different facets of her personality revealed by the author in the course of the story.

Using Description to Create a Dramatic Effect

The dramatic effect of Lise's meeting with the thief is achieved by Dinesen's moment-by-moment description of the encounter, which allows readers to visualize the sequence of events and emotions.

1. **Reading/Listening.** Have a volunteer read aloud the description of the encounter on pp. 1219–1221. Have listeners note how precisely the thief's sequence of actions is described by making a numbered list of his movements and Lise's reactions to them.

2. **Writing/Reading/Listening.** Have students write a descriptive scene of their own in which two people communicate without words during a sequence of events. Have students read their scenes aloud to the class and ask for suggestions to make the scenes clearer or more dramatic. ■

---

1 LITERARY ELEMENT

Exposition: What important information does the narrator reveal in the first paragraph of the story? (when and where the story takes place, the ages and family backgrounds of the main characters, their recent long-awaited marriage)

■ **MEETING INDIVIDUAL NEEDS** ■

2 ESL: Explain that the idiom *give in* means "yield" or "surrender." ■

3 LITERARY ELEMENT

Metaphor: To what does the narrator compare the couple's first days of marriage? (paradise)

4 EVALUATING

Are the expectations of the young couple for their marriage realistic? Explain. (Probably not. He thinks he can protect his wife from all danger; she thinks she will never have a secret from her husband.)

5 LITERARY ELEMENT

Characterization: What details suggest that Lise is still quite childish? (It was not too long ago that she was playing with dolls; her wifely responsibilities seem to her like playing house.)

THE RING

Isak Dinesen

> *Read until you come to the paragraph on page 1219 that begins, "This meeting in the wood from beginning to end passed without a word. . . ." Stop and write down what you think will happen during this encounter. When you finish the story, see if your prediction was correct.*

1 On a summer morning a hundred and fifty years ago a young Danish squire and his wife went out for a walk on their land. They had been married a week. It had not been easy for them to get married, for the wife's family was higher in rank and wealthier than the husband's. But the two young people, now twenty-four and nineteen years old, had been set on their purpose for ten years; in **2** the end her haughty parents had had to give in to them.

They were wonderfully happy. The stolen meetings and secret, tearful love letters were now things of the past. To God and man they were one; they could walk arm in arm in broad daylight and drive in the same carriage, and they would walk and drive so till **3** the end of their days. Their distant paradise had descended to earth and had proved, surprisingly, to be filled with the things of everyday life: with jesting and railleries, with breakfasts and suppers, with dogs, haymaking, and sheep. Sigismund, the young husband, had promised himself that from now **4** there should be no stone in his bride's path, nor should any shadow fall across it. Lovisa,[1] the wife, felt that now, every day and for the first time in her young life, she moved and breathed in perfect freedom because she could never have any secret from her husband. **4**

To Lovisa—whom her husband called Lise[2]—the rustic atmosphere of her new life was a matter of wonder and delight. Her husband's fear that the existence he could offer her might not be good enough for her filled her heart with laughter. It was not a long time since she had played with dolls; as now she dressed her own hair, looked over her linen press and arranged her flowers, she again lived through an enchanting and cherished experience: one was doing everything gravely and solicitously, and all the time one knew one was playing. **5**

It was a lovely July morning. Little woolly clouds drifted high up in the sky, the air was full of sweet scents. Lise had on a white muslin frock and a large Italian straw hat. She and her husband took a path through the park; it wound on across the meadows, between small groves and groups of trees, to the sheep field. Sigismund was going to show his wife his sheep. For this reason she

---

1. **Lovisa** (lō·vē′sə)

2. **Lise** (lē′sə)

A Mountain Path at Capel Curig, Wales, Ebenezer Downard, 1860.

HUMANITIES CONNECTION

Ebenezer Downard is known for his landscape paintings and London scenes. This landscape and some others by Downard show the influence of the Pre-Raphaelites, a group who painted directly from nature. The term *Pre-Raphaelite* comes from the group's admiration for art before the High Renaissance. Their paintings were characterized by brilliant lighting and an abundance of detail reminiscent of a photograph. ❓ *What Pre-Raphaelite influences can you see in this landscape?* (Possible responses: detailing in sheep's coat, brilliant sky, nature scene) ∎

6 CULTURAL BACKGROUND

Denmark is a country with poor soil and few natural resources. Its scientists and farmers have had to put forth great effort to figure out how to make farms profitable. England has historically been a major trading partner with Denmark.

7 READER'S RESPONSE

Do you think it is common to have contradictory feelings about the people we love, as Lise has contradictory feelings about Sigismund?

---

had not brought her small white dog, Bijou,[3] with her, for he would yap at the lambs and frighten them, or he would annoy the sheep dogs. Sigismund prided himself on his sheep; he had studied sheep breeding in Mecklenburg[4] and England, and had brought back with him Cotswold rams[5] by which to improve his Danish stock. While they walked he explained to Lise the great possibilities and difficulties of the plan.

She thought: "How clever he is, what a lot of things he knows!" and at the same time: "What an absurd person he is, with his sheep! What a baby he is! I am a hundred years older than he."

But when they arrived at the sheepfold the old sheepmaster Mathias met them with the sad news that one of the English lambs was dead and two were sick. Lise saw that her husband was grieved by the tidings; while he questioned Mathias on the matter she kept silent and only gently pressed his

---

3. **Bijou** (bē′zhoō′): "jewel" (French).
4. **Mecklenburg:** agricultural region in northern Germany.
5. **Cotswold rams:** the males of a kind of sheep originally bred in the Cotswold Hills of southwestern England.

8 LITERARY ELEMENT

Simile: To what is the thief compared here? (a wolf) How is he like a wolf? (Possible response: He is stealthy, predatory.)

■ **MEETING INDIVIDUAL NEEDS** ■

9 ESL: Be sure students understand that "to string up the murderer" means to punish him by hanging. ■

10 LITERARY ELEMENT

Allusion: What children's story is alluded to? ("Little Red Riding Hood") How does the allusion reinforce the characterization of Lise? (Possible response: She responds to a sad, gruesome event as if it were a children's story told for her entertainment.)

11 COMPARING AND CONTRASTING

How does Lise's response to the story of the thief contrast with Sigismund's? (Possible response: He feels sorry for the man; Lise both enjoys the tale and agrees with Mathias that the man should be hanged.)

12 PREDICTING

Do you think Lise will be in any danger setting out alone for home? What do you predict will happen to her? (Possible response: Since she sets out so soon after the story of the missing thief, some students may anticipate the direction the plot will take.)

arm. A couple of boys were sent off to fetch the sick lambs, while the master and servant went into the details of the case. It took some time.

Lise began to gaze about her and to think of other things. Twice her own thoughts made her blush deeply and happily, like a red rose, then slowly her blush died away, and the two men were still talking about sheep. A little while after, their conversation caught her attention. It had turned to a sheep thief.

8 This thief during the last months had broken into the sheepfolds of the neighborhood like a wolf, had killed and dragged away his prey like a wolf, and like a wolf had left no trace after him. Three nights ago the shepherd and his son on an estate ten miles away had caught him in the act. The thief had killed the man and knocked the boy senseless, and had managed to escape. There were men sent out to all sides to catch him, but nobody had seen him.

Lise wanted to hear more about the horrible event, and for her benefit old Mathias went through it once more. There had been a long fight in the sheep house, in many places the earthen floor was soaked with blood. In the fight the thief's left arm was broken; all the same, he had climbed a tall

9 fence with a lamb on his back. Mathias added that he would like to string up the murderer with these two hands of his, and Lise nodded her head at him gravely in approval.

10 She remembered Red Riding Hood's wolf, and felt a pleasant little thrill running down her spine.

Sigismund had his own lambs in his mind, but he was too happy in himself to wish anything in the universe ill. After a minute

11 he said: "Poor devil."

Lise said: "How can you pity such a terrible man? Indeed Grandmamma was right when

11 she said that you were a revolutionary and a danger to society!" The thought of Grandmamma, and of the tears of past days, again turned her mind away from the gruesome tale she had just heard.

The boys brought the sick lambs and the men began to examine them carefully, lifting them up and trying to set them on their legs; they squeezed them here and there and made the little creatures whimper. Lise shrank from the show and her husband noticed her distress.

"You go home, my darling," he said, "this will take some time. But just walk ahead slowly, and I shall catch up with you."

So she was turned away by an impatient husband to whom his sheep meant more than his wife. If any experience could be sweeter than to be dragged out by him to look at those same sheep, it would be this. She dropped her large summer hat with its blue ribbons on the grass and told him to carry it back for her, for she wanted to feel the summer air on her forehead and in her hair. She walked on very slowly, as he had told her to do, for she wished to obey him

12 in everything. As she walked she felt a great new happiness in being altogether alone, even without Bijou. She could not remember that she had ever before in all her life been altogether alone. The landscape around her was still, as if full of promise, and it was hers. Even the swallows cruising in the air were hers, for they belonged to him,[6] and he was hers.

She followed the curving edge of the grove and after a minute or two found that she was out of sight to the men by the sheep

---

6. **him:** that is, Sigismund; in Denmark at the time of the story, birds and other wild animals on an estate were the owner's property, and anyone who hunted or caught them without permission would be prosecuted.

house. What could now, she wondered, be sweeter than to walk along the path in the long flowering meadow grass, slowly, slowly, and to let her husband overtake her there? It would be sweeter still, she reflected, to steal into the grove and to be gone, to have vanished from the surface of the earth from him when, tired of the sheep and longing for her company, he should turn the bend of the path to catch up with her.

An idea struck her; she stood still to think it over.

A few days ago her husband had gone for a ride and she had not wanted to go with him, but had strolled about with Bijou in order to explore her domain. Bijou then, gamboling, had led her straight into the grove. As she had followed him, gently forcing her way into the shrubbery, she had suddenly come upon a glade in the midst of it, a narrow space like a small alcove with hangings of thick green and golden brocade, big enough to hold two or three people in it. She had felt at that moment that she had come into the very heart of her new home.

If today she could find the spot again she would stand perfectly still there, hidden from all the world. Sigismund would look for her in all directions; he would be unable to understand what had become of her and for a minute, for a short minute—or, perhaps, if she was firm and cruel enough, for five—he would realize what a void, what an unendurably sad and horrible place the universe would be when she was no longer in it. She gravely scrutinized the grove to find the right entrance to her hiding place, then went in.

She took great care to make no noise at all, therefore advanced exceedingly slowly. When a twig caught the flounces of her ample skirt she loosened it softly from the muslin, so as not to crack it. Once a branch took hold of one of her long golden curls; she stood still, with her arms lifted, to free it. A little way into the grove the soil became moist; her light steps no longer made any sound upon it. With one hand she held her small handkerchief to her lips, as if to emphasize the secretness of her course. She found the spot she sought and bent down to divide the foliage and make a door to her sylvan closet. At this, the hem of her dress caught her foot and she stopped to loosen it. As she rose she looked into the face of a man who was already in the shelter.

He stood up erect, two steps off. He must have watched her as she made her way straight toward him.

She took him in in one single glance. His face was bruised and scratched, his hands and wrists stained with dark filth. He was dressed in rags, barefooted, with tatters wound round his naked ankles. His arms hung down to his sides, his right hand clasped the hilt of a knife. He was about her own age. The man and the woman looked at each other.

This meeting in the wood from beginning to end passed without a word; what happened could only be rendered by panto-mime. To the two actors in the pantomime it was timeless; according to a clock it lasted four minutes.

She had never in her life been exposed to danger. It did not occur to her to sum up her position, or to work out the length of time it would take to call her husband or Mathias, whom at this moment she could hear shouting to his dogs. She beheld the man before her as she would have beheld a forest ghost: the apparition itself, not the sequels of it, changes the world to the human who faces it.

Although she did not take her eyes off the face before her, she sensed that the alcove

Isak Dinesen   **1219**

18 LITERARY ELEMENT

Climax: At what point in the story does Lise seem most in danger? (when the thief points the knife at her throat) When do you know she is out of danger? (Answers will vary.)

19 INTERPRETING

What is "the horror" that the thief inspires in Lise? (Possible response: The confrontation with the thief forces Lise to abandon her romantic fantasy world and acknowledge all of the horrors of the real world—cruelty, poverty, violence, brutal sexuality, deception, and despair.)

EVALUATING

Would the scene between Lise and the thief have been more effective if the author had used dialogue? (Answers will vary.) What effect does she create by making the encounter a wordless one? (Possible response: The scene is suspenseful and full of unexpressed emotions).

HUMANITIES CONNECTION

The work of the German painter Hans Thoma shows his seriousness of mood and his attention to detail. Although Thoma is generally classified as a Realist painter, his paintings also have a deep poetic intensity.

? *Is this the way you picture Lise? Explain.* ∎

had been turned into a <u>covert</u>. On the ground a couple of sacks formed a couch; there were some gnawed bones by it. A fire must have been made here in the night, for there were cinders strewn on the forest floor.

After a while she realized that he was observing her just as she was observing him. He was no longer just run to earth and crouching for a spring, but he was wondering, trying to know. At that she seemed to see herself with the eyes of the wild animal at bay in his dark hiding place: her silently approaching white figure, which might mean death.

18 He moved his right arm till it hung down straight before him between his legs. Without lifting the hand he bent the wrist and slowly raised the point of the knife till it pointed at her throat. The gesture was mad, unbelievable. He did not smile as he made it, but his nostrils distended, the corners of his mouth quivered a little. Then slowly he put the knife back in the sheath by his belt.

She had no object of value about her, only the wedding ring which her husband had set on her finger in church, a week ago. She drew it off, and in this movement dropped her handkerchief. She reached out her hand with the ring toward him. She did not bargain for her life. She was fearless by nature, **19** and the horror with which he inspired her was not fear of what he might do to her. She commanded him, she besought him to vanish as he had come, to take a dreadful figure out of her life, so that it should never have been there. In the dumb movement her young form had the grave authoritativeness of a priestess conjuring down some monstrous being by a sacred sign.

He slowly reached out his hand to hers, his finger touched hers, and her hand was steady at the touch. But he did not take the

ring. As she let it go it dropped to the ground as her handkerchief had done.

For a second the eyes of both followed it. It rolled a few inches toward him and stopped before his bare foot. In a hardly perceivable movement he kicked it away and again looked into her face. They remained like that, she knew not how long, but she felt that during that time something happened, things were changed.

He bent down and picked up her handkerchief. All the time gazing at her, he again drew his knife and wrapped the tiny bit of cambric round the blade. This was difficult for him to do because his left arm was broken. While he did it his face under the dirt

PORTRAIT OF THE ARTIST'S SISTER, HANS THOMA (1839–1924).
? *Describe Lise's feelings toward her husband: are they wholly loving, or ambivalent?*

READING CHECK

1. How long have Lise and Sigismund been married? (one week)
2. How did a nearby shepherd die? (murdered by an escaping sheep thief)
3. Why does Lise set out for home alone? (Sigismund is busy with sick lambs.)
4. Whom does Lise encounter on her way home? (the sheep thief)
5. What does she lose? (her wedding ring)

RETEACHING

Have pairs of students pantomime the wordless encounter between Lise and the thief. As preparation, have each pair discuss what emotions they want to reveal in their characters and what gestures and facial expressions they can use to convey those emotions.

and suntan slowly grew whiter till it was almost phosphorescent. Fumbling with both hands, he once more stuck the knife into the sheath. Either the sheath was too big and had never fitted the knife, or the blade was much worn—it went in. For two or three more seconds his gaze rested on her face; then he lifted his own face a little, the strange radiance still upon it, and closed his eyes.

The movement was definitive and unconditional. In this one motion he did what she had begged him to do: he vanished and was gone. She was free.

She took a step backward, the immovable, blind face before her, then bent as she had done to enter the hiding place, and glided away as noiselessly as she had come. Once outside the grove she stood still and looked round for the meadow path, found it and began to walk home.

Her husband had not yet rounded the edge of the grove. Now he saw her and helloed to her gaily; he came up quickly and joined her.

The path here was so narrow that he kept half behind her and did not touch her. He began to explain to her what had been the matter with the lambs. She walked a step before him and thought: All is over.

After a while he noticed her silence, came up beside her to look at her face and asked, "What is the matter?"

She searched her mind for something to say, and at last said: "I have lost my ring."

"What ring?" he asked her.

She answered, "My wedding ring."

As she heard her own voice pronounce the words she conceived their meaning.

Her wedding ring. "With this ring"— dropped by one and kicked away by another—"with this ring I thee wed."[7] With this lost ring she had wedded herself to something. To what? To poverty, persecution, total loneliness. To the sorrows and the sinfulness of this earth. "And what therefore God has joined together let man not put asunder."

"I will find you another ring," her husband said. "You and I are the same as we were on our wedding day; it will do as well. We are husband and wife today, too, as much as yesterday, I suppose."

Her face was so still that he did not know if she had heard what he said. It touched him that she should take the loss of his ring so to heart. He took her hand and kissed it. It was cold, not quite the same hand as he had last kissed. He stopped to make her stop with him.

"Do you remember where you had the ring on last?" he asked.

"No," she answered.

"Have you any idea," he asked, "where you may have lost it?"

"No," she answered. "I have no idea at all."

---

7. **With this ring . . . I thee wed:** quotation from the vows exchanged at a wedding ceremony.

unconditional (un·kən·dish'ən·əl): without conditions or reservations

20 INTERPRETING
What is Lise now free of? (Possible response: She is free of the thief's powerful, spellbinding presence.

21 INTERPRETING
Why does Lise think "All is over" after her encounter with the thief? (Possible response: She can no longer take innocent delight in her marriage or her marital "estate" because of her troubling experience in the glade.)

22 PREDICTING
Do you think Lise will tell her husband about the thief?

23 LITERARY ELEMENT
Dramatic Irony: Why is Sigismund's statement "You and I are the same as we were on our wedding day" ironic? (The reader knows that Lise has changed, but her husband does not.)

24 LITERARY ELEMENT
Dynamic Character: How does Lise's final dialogue with Sigismund show that her expectations of marriage have changed? (When the story began, she was convinced she would never have a secret from her husband; now she seems determined to keep her encounter with the thief a secret. In some way, the encounter was a betrayal of her marriage, and she feels ashamed.)

1. Comparing Epiphanies. Have students discuss how the epiphany in "The Ring" compares with the one in Joyce's "Eveline." Help them see that in "Eveline" the epiphany is primarily the reader's, whereas in "The Ring" Lise attains greater self-awareness and personal growth at her moment of truth. Invite students to share with the class other memorable literary epiphanies as well as those in their own lives.

2. Discussing Symbols. In "The Ring," Isak Dinesen associates Sigismund with sheep and the escaped murderer with a wolf. Both animals have long histories of symbolic significance. In Nordic mythology, wolves often represent dark, demonic powers. Sheep, on the other hand, have long been associated with docility and domesticity. Discuss how Dinesen employs the symbols of sheep and wolf.

CLOSURE

Have students discuss what positive and negative effects they think Lise's experience with the thief may have on the rest of her life. Will she cherish the memory, regret it, or forget about it? ■

ANSWERS
First Thoughts
Answers will vary.

Identifying Facts
1. nineteen. her marriage
2. She wants to make her husband miss her. She offers her wedding ring to the thief.
3. "I have no idea at all."

Interpreting Meanings
1. Dishonest behavior can make one feel trapped.
2. She feels a guilty bond.
3. Lise is dynamic, Sigismund is static.
4. her marriage and her sheltered life. her lost innocence
5. She is upset by the loss of something other than the ring.
6. Possible response: Lise and Sigismund live in a "paradise" until Lise loses her innocence.

Applying Meanings
Answers will vary.

Creative Writing Response
Writing a Dialogue. Dialogues should reflect authentic speech patterns.

Critical Writing Response
Analyzing a Dynamic Character. Students may make prewriting charts with "before" and "after" notes.

Language and Vocabulary
1. *Chihuahua*, Mexico 2. serge (cloth) *de Nimes*, France
3. *Joachimsthaler*, St. Joachimstal, Bohemia
4. *Madras*, Coromandel Coast
5. tomb of *Mausolus*, king of Caria, at Halicarnassus
6. *Mecca*, Saudi Arabia 7. *Sardinia*, Italian island 8. *Shanghai*, China 9. *Tangier*, Morocco
10. *Tuxedo Lake*, New York ■

▷ **First Thoughts**
Did you find any character or event in this story confusing or unsettling? If so, describe your thoughts and feelings about it.

Identifying Facts
1. How old is Lise when the story opens? What recent event has made her "wonderfully happy"?
2. What prompts Lise to hide in the clearing in the shrubbery? Summarize the events that take place there.
3. When Sigismund asks if she has any idea where she lost the ring, what does Lise say?

Interpreting Meanings
1. Why do you think Lise says at the beginning of the story that never having secrets from her husband allows her to move and breathe "in perfect freedom"?
2. Why do you think Lise keeps the incident in the glade a secret from her husband?
3. Which of the three main characters are **static**, or unchanging, and which are **dynamic**, or changing? Cite details from the story to support your answer.
4. What might the ring **symbolize**, or represent, in Lise's life? What change in Lise does the loss of the ring represent?
5. What is the **irony** in Sigismund being touched that his wife "should take the loss of his ring so to heart"?
6. Consider the biblical story of the fall of Adam and Eve (see page 166). Explain how "The Ring" could be seen as a modern version of this story.

Applying Meanings
Do you think married people should never have secrets from each other? Or do you think secrets are inevitable? Discuss.

Creative Writing Response
Writing a Dialogue. If Lise and the stranger had spoken, what do you think they would have said to each other? Write the conversation that you imagine taking place between them. Be sure to punctuate their dialogue correctly.

Critical Writing Response
Analyzing a Dynamic Character. Write an essay analyzing Lise, concentrating on the change that occurred when she encountered the man in the glade. In describing her character before and after this incident, remember to consider **(a)** her appearance, **(b)** her actions, **(c)** what she says, **(d)** the response of other characters, and **(e)** the writer's direct comments about her. Include answers to these questions in your essay: Why did Lise decide to enter the glade? Why did she not speak with the man? Why did she offer him her wedding ring? Why did she not tell her husband about the man in the glade?

Language and Vocabulary
Words from Place Names
Many English words come from the names of cities and other places around the world. For example, the strong sheer cotton fabric known as *muslin* was first made in the city of Mosul in northern Iraq, and the fine thin linen known as *cambric* was first made in the northern French town of Cambrai.

All of the following English words also come from the names of places. Use a dictionary to help you explain the origin of each word and the meanings of any unfamiliar words.

1. chihuahua
2. denim
3. dollar
4. madras
5. mausoleum

6. mecca
7. sardine
8. shanghai
9. tangerine
10. tuxedo

Anna Akhmatova
1889–1966, Russia

The Granger Collection, New York

When writers express political views in their writing, they often run into problems with government authorities. Anna Akhmatova (uk·mät′ə·və), however, was persecuted for many years because she did *not* write on political themes. In the years following the Russian Revolution in 1917, only "socially useful" art was tolerated. Akhmatova was viciously attacked and her poems suppressed because they were too "personal."

Akhmatova grew up just outside St. Petersburg in the suburb that had been for centuries the summer palace of the czars. Here she became part of the thriving artistic community of prerevolutionary St. Petersburg. The poetry that Akhmatova began publishing in 1912 illustrates ideas of **acmeism**,

a movement she and her husband, the poet Nikolai Gumilev, helped found. A reaction to French Symbolism (see page 983), which was then fashionable in Russia, acmeism rejected ambiguous symbols and the Symbolists' view of the artist as a mystic. For Akhmatova, the poet was not a visionary but a craftsperson, patiently building poems from words.

Akhmatova's early successes came to an abrupt end with the Russian Revolution in 1917. Five years later, her ex-husband was shot for allegedly plotting against the new Soviet government. Although he and Akhmatova were divorced at this time, she was deemed guilty by association and her poetry suppressed. She was not allowed to publish at all from 1922 to 1940, and in 1946 she was expelled from the Soviet Writers' Union.

In the years of Stalinist terror that followed, Akhmatova watched as friends and colleagues were arrested and sent to prison camps, many never to return. Her own son was imprisoned until Stalin's death in 1953. Akhmatova's long poem "Requiem" captures those dark days in the image of an anonymous woman standing month after month outside a St. Petersburg prison waiting for news of a loved one.

Akhmatova's home became the refuge and meeting place of a younger generation of Russian poets. In her final years, she was recognized officially again and was even allowed to travel to the West.

MORE ABOUT THE AUTHOR
During the years of Communist rule in the former Soviet Union, many of its finest artists were stifled. Some emigrated, some were arrested and silenced, others compromised with the authorities. Akhmatova, who came from the lesser aristocracy, was vulnerable to the charge of writing elitist poetry, though in fact her work had wide popular appeal.

While Joseph Stalin headed the Soviet government (1924–1953), Akhmatova's greatest fear was not for her own safety but for that of her imprisoned son. As a precaution, she memorized her poetry rather than writing it down. Although forbidden to publish, Akhmatova lived in the memories of her fellow Russians. In 1944, when she was permitted to give a reading during one of Stalin's wartime "thaws," three thousand people gave her a standing ovation in Moscow's largest auditorium. Later, when Stalin reportedly asked who had organized the standing ovation, it was clear that the thaw had ended. Once again, Akhmatova was denied publication. Her verse did not appear again in Soviet periodicals until 1959.

ABOUT THE TRANSLATOR
Richard Wilbur. See Unit 10, "Invitation to the Voyage," p. 1021.

OBJECTIVES

1. To analyze a lyric poem by a Russian writer
2. To identify stanza structure and rhyme scheme
3. To write a rhymed stanza

PREREADING FOCUS

Background: In writing ''Lot's Wife,'' Akhmatova may have been remembering a fateful choice she had made in her youth. In 1910 and 1911, when she was a young poet, she and her husband Nikolai Gumilev paid two brief visits to Paris. Akhmatova became friends with the painter Modigliani and many other artists and writers. She was tempted to stay, but returned to Russia instead, and to a lifetime of terror. ''Lot's Wife'' was written in 1922–24, just after Akhmatova was forbidden to publish.

Writer's Response: Invite students who have immigrated to the United States to share their experiences of ''starting anew,'' and their reasons for doing so.

Literary Focus: A stanza is a group of related lines that forms a division in a poem. In a traditional poem, each stanza follows the same pattern. Some of the best-known patterns are the couplet (2 lines), the quatrain (4 lines), the sestet (6 lines), and the octave (8 lines). Ask students to recall the typical stanza divisions in the Petrarchan and Shakespearean sonnets.

Rhyme scheme refers to the pattern of rhyme in a stanza or poem. Rhyme is sometimes ignored in translation, but in ''Lot's Wife,'' Richard Wilbur remains faithful to the rhyme scheme and meter of the original poem.

Reader's Guide ∎

LOT'S WIFE

Background

''Lot's Wife'' is based on the biblical incident recounted in Genesis 19 in which God sends angels to punish the city of Sodom for its wickedness. When the angels arrive disguised as men, only a man named Lot treats them justly. As a result, the angels warn him that God will destroy the city. They tell him to flee with his family and not look back. Lot's wife, however, disobeys the command and glances back. She is immediately turned into a pillar of salt. Akhmatova wrote ''Lot's Wife,'' which was originally published in the *Paris Review*, in the early 1920s, shortly after her former husband was executed, but before the worst years of the Stalin era. At that time, many Russian intellectuals had begun to flee the country, but Akhmatova chose to stay.

Writer's Response

In a paragraph or two, describe how you might feel if you lived in a country that you were compelled to leave because of an intolerable situation—politics, war, or famine. Would you need to ''look back'' on your life there, or would you leave without a backward glance and concentrate on starting anew?

Literary Focus

Akhmatova was a founder of a movement called **acmeism**. Acmeists strove to eliminate ambiguous symbols from their work and instead emphasized the clear communication of ideas through richly textured language. As they saw it, part of the craft of poetry involved organizing thoughts into **stanzas**—line groupings that followed a **rhyme scheme**, or pattern of end-of-line rhymes. In the original Russian, ''Lot's Wife'' is arranged in **quatrains**, or four-line stanzas, in which the first and third lines always rhyme, as do the second and fourth lines. In this English translation by poet Richard Wilbur, the stanza structure and rhyme scheme match those of the original Russian.

Memorizing Poetry

Anna Akhmatova memorized her poems because it would have been dangerous to write them down. For generations, American students memorized poems for a different reason: they were assigned to. If you wish, invite students to memorize "Lot's Wife" or a portion of it. Its strict rhyme and rhythm and simple vocabulary will make it easy to remember.

Depending on your students' abilities, you might ask them to memorize one line apiece, two lines, a stanza, or the entire poem. Alternately, students may wish to commit other favorite poems to memory—perhaps Shakespeare's Sonnet 29 (p. 810). ∎

LOT'S WIFE
Anna Akhmatova
translated by
RICHARD WILBUR

❚❚ *Read to the end of the second stanza. From the images of the city that the speaker recalls, how do you think she feels about leaving?*

THE STORY OF ABRAHAM AND LOT: THE FLIGHT FROM SODOM, RAPHAEL (1483–1520).

Scala/Art Resource, New York

The just man followed then his angel guide
Where he strode on the black highway, hulking
   and bright;
But a wild grief in his wife's bosom cried,
Look back, it is not too late for a last sight

1 ⌐ 5   *Of the red towers of your native Sodom, the square*
Where once you sang, the gardens you shall mourn,

TEACHER'S RESOURCES
✔ Review and Response Worksheet

1 INTERPRETING
In line 5, Akhmatova refers to the "red towers" and "the square" of Sodom. To what other square and city might she be referring? (Red Square in Moscow)

2 LITERARY ELEMENT
Diction: The poet's word choices develop the poem's meaning. In line 9 on p. 1226, *bitter view* implies both the wife's regret and the city's appearance. Why is "welded" (line 10) a better verb than "closed"? (By suggesting heat and strength, it conveys God's anger and firm retribution.) How does the dual meaning of the word *quick* (line 12) enrich the poem? (*Quick* means "alive" as well as "swift"; Lot's wife's feet, rooted, lose both traits.)

HUMANITIES CONNECTION

One of the great artists of the Italian Renaissance, Raphael often painted religious subjects.
❓ *What qualities of the flight from Sodom does the painting capture?* (Possible response: sorrow, intensity, haste) ∎

1. Who are the two major characters in this poem? (a "just man" and his wife)
2. What are the characters doing as the poem opens? (walking on a highway away from their city)
3. What does the wife's grief cause her to do? (look back)

4. What happens to the wife after she looks back? (She is turned into salt.)
5. For what did the wife give up her life? ("a single glance")

RETEACHING
Have volunteers mime the roles of Lot and Lot's wife as students read the poem. Encourage creative decisions on who will read which lines of the poem.

3 LITERARY ELEMENT

Viewpoint: How does the poem's viewpoint change in the last stanza? (The speaker addresses rhetorical questions to the audience instead of narrating.)

First Thoughts
The speaker is sympathetic toward Lot's wife. Students may agree or disagree with the speaker.

Identifying Facts
1. an "angel guide"
2. buildings, gardens, her home. Her eyes are fused shut; her body is turned into salt.
3. in the speaker's heart

Interpreting Meanings
1. It is her home. We should be sympathetic, since her attitude is very human.
2. Stanzas 2 and 3: one thought; stanzas 1 and 4: more than one
3. Encourage students to find parallels between Lot's wife and Akhmatova and between Sodom and the Soviet Union during Akhmatova's adult life.

Applying Meanings
Answers will vary.

Creative Writing Response
Writing a Rhymed Stanza.
Students' verses should follow the *abab* rhyme scheme. ■

And the tall house with empty windows where
You loved your husband and your babes were born.

2   10
She turned, and looking on the bitter view
Her eyes were welded shut by mortal pain;
Into transparent salt her body grew,
And her quick feet were rooted in the plain.

3   15
Who would waste tears upon her? Is she not
The least of our losses, this unhappy wife?
Yet in my heart she will not be forgot
Who, for a single glance, gave up her life.

First Thoughts
How do you think the speaker feels about Lot's wife? Is she seen as foolish and disobedient, or as passionate and courageous? Do you agree with the speaker's views?

Identifying Facts
1. Whom does Lot follow?
2. What particular places in Sodom does Lot's wife want to see one last time? When she looks back and sees Sodom's destruction, what happens to her eyes and body?
3. According to the last stanza, where will Lot's wife not be forgotten?

Interpreting Meanings
1. What, in general, makes Lot's wife care about Sodom, despite its evils? What does the phrase "mortal pain" (line 10) suggest about how we should view her attitude?
2. Often a **stanza** expresses one unit of thought. Which of these stanzas contain one thought? Which express more than one thought?

3. Do you think that Akhmatova is simply retelling a biblical incident in verse? Reread the biography and background sections and explain how the poem might also relate to Akhmatova's life and to the political situation in Russia at the time she wrote the poem.

Applying Meanings
What events in your past do you look back on with affection or nostalgia? Do you think this is usually a negative or a positive thing to do? Explain, providing examples to illustrate your opinion.

Creative Writing Response
Writing a Rhymed Stanza. Write a four-line stanza imitating the *abab* rhyme scheme of Akhmatova's poem. On a separate sheet of paper, you may write two lines to complete the stanza below, or you may write one or more stanzas that are entirely your own.

(a) I came upon a secret place
(b) Where all the world was far away
(a) _____
(b) _____

EXTENSION AND ENRICHMENT

1. Writing a Poem Based on Another Well-Known Story. Have students choose an incident from another story and write a poem based on it. They may follow Akhmatova's rhyme scheme or create another. Encourage them to include their own feelings in their poems.

2. Reacting to a Report. In 1946, Akhmatova was expelled from the Soviet Writers' Union. The Union's report accused Akhmatova of writing poetry that was only for the aristocracy, and unconnected to the people. Ask students to read additional poems by Akhmatova and to write a reply to the charges based on their own impressions of her poems.

CLOSURE

Ask students how they think Akhmatova felt about her homeland. Were her feelings completely negative, or ambivalent? Have students support their opinions with details from Akhmatova's biography and poetry. ■

BEHIND THE SCENES

Pasternak's Tribute to Akhmatova

Russian poet and novelist Boris Pasternak (1890–1960).

Cornell Capa/Magnum Photos, Inc.

One of Anna Akhmatova's friends and colleagues was Boris Pasternak, a famous poet and novelist (his most famous novel is *Doctor Zhivago*). In this tribute poem, Pasternak compares Akhmatova's composition of poetry to the work of a seamstress. What does Pasternak's final line suggest about the value he found in all of Akhmatova's poetry?

To Anna Akhmatova
Boris Pasternak
translated by
Eugene M. Kayden

It seems I'm choosing the essential words
That I can liken to your pristine power.
And if I err, it's all the same to me,

For I shall cling to all my errors still.　　　┐ **1**

I hear the constant patter on wet roofs,
The smothered eclogue[1] of the wooden pave-
　　ments.
A certain city[2] comes clear in every line,
And springs to life in every syllable.

The roads are blocked, despite the tide of
　　spring
All round. Your clients are a stingy, cruel lot.
Bent over piles of work, the sunset burns;
Eyes blear and moist from sewing by a lamp.

You long for the boundless space of Ladoga,[3]
And hasten, weary, to the lake for change
And rest. It's little in the end you gain.
The canals smell rank like musty closet-chests.

And like an empty nut the hot wind frets
Across their waves, across the blinking eyelids
Of stars and branches, posts and lamps, and
　　one
Lone seamstress gazing far above the bridge.

I know that eyes and objects vary greatly
In singleness and sharpness, yet the essence
Of greatest strength, dissolving fear, is the sky
At night beneath the gaze of polar light.

That's how I call to mind your face and glance.　┐
No, not the image of that pillar of salt　　　　　│
Exalts me now, in which five years ago　　　　　├ **2**
You set in rhymes our fear of looking back.　　　┘

But as it springs in all your early work,
Where crumbs of unremitting prose grew
　　strong,
In all affairs, like wires conducting sparks,
Your work throbs high with our remembered
　　past.

---

1. **eclogue:** here, dialogue; used figuratively.
2. **A certain city:** St. Petersburg.
3. **Ladoga** (lä′dô·gä′): a large Russian lake.

LITERARY BACKGROUND

Boris Pasternak (1890–1960) was a celebrated Russian poet and novelist. He established an international literary reputation with *Doctor Zhivago*, a novel set against the background of the Bolshevik Revolution and its violent aftermath. In the novel, Zhivago, a physician, is unable to accept Communist rule. Authorities blocked publication of *Doctor Zhivago* in the Soviet Union, but the novel was issued in several other countries in 1958. It became a best-seller, and Pasternak was awarded the 1958 Nobel Prize for literature. Because *Doctor Zhivago* depicted Communism in a negative light, Pasternak was expelled from the Soviet Writers' Union and threatened with banishment from the Soviet Union. Only after he rejected the Nobel Prize and issued a letter of apology was Pasternak permitted to stay in his native land.

1 INTERPRETING

What does the ironic phrase "I shall cling to all my errors" refer to? (the heroic stubbornness of many Soviet writers who put their art before their personal safety)

2 SYNTHESIZING

In which stanza does Pasternak allude to "Lot's Wife"? (the penultimate stanza) Does Pasternak see "Lot's Wife" as more than a poem about a biblical episode? Explain. ("You set in rhymes our fear of looking back" makes clear that Akhmatova's poem is about, and speaks for, all Russians.) ■

García Lorca was a sickly child. An undiagnosed fever nearly killed him at the age of two months and contributed to his lifelong physical frailness. His emotional vitality, however, overcame this handicap. He was a musician and visual artist as well as a poet and playwright. In 1929 García Lorca, without knowing a word of English, traveled to New York and lived for a time in a dormitory at Columbia University. There he wrote *The Poet in New York*, a Whitmanesque poem that is sometimes called one of the best ever written about New York. Most of García Lorca's poetry, however, was deeply rooted in Spain, and in particular in the Gypsy culture of his native Andalusia.

Federico García Lorca
1898–1936, Spain

Art Resource, New York

On the evening of July 19, 1936, Chilean poet Pablo Neruda (ne·rōō′də) (see page 1275), then living in Spain, went to meet his friend Federico García Lorca (fe′de·rē′kô gärse′ä lôr′kä). Neruda waited and waited, but García Lorca never appeared because he had been kidnapped by Fascist supporters of Spanish dictator Francisco Franco. The kidnappers took García Lorca to a Granada cemetery, forced him to dig his own grave, and then shot him. The murder shocked the world, especially since the thirty-eight-year-old writer had never taken an active role in politics. Viewed as a martyr, he became known as the "Poet of the Blood," and many of his poems about sorrow and death took on additional significance.

Granada, the site of his brutal murder, was also the city near which García Lorca grew up. Born to a well-to-do farm family, García Lorca valued the simple pleasures of rural life and also learned to love music, poetry, and all the arts. In 1919 García Lorca went to Madrid to study at the city's university. Among the talented artists he met there were Juan Ramón Jiménez, already a distinguished poet, and Salvador Dalí, the experimental painter whose surrealism would influence García Lorca's poetry and plays.

His most famous plays are tragedies dealing with thwarted womanhood. *Blood Wedding* (1933) is the story of a bride who runs away with a previous lover and is then murdered by her husband. This play, together with *Yerma* (1934) and *The House of Bernarda Alba* (1936), are considered to be García Lorca's finest dramatic works.

Shortly before his death, García Lorca published *Lament for the Death of a Bullfighter* (1935), considered to be the greatest elegy in modern Spanish poetry and a moving premonition of his own death. García Lorca was at the height of his celebrity when he was murdered by the Fascists. As Pablo Neruda later mourned, "Who could have believed there were monsters on this earth, in his own Granada, capable of such an inconceivable crime?"

OBJECTIVES
1. To analyze a lyric poem by a Spanish poet
2. To recognize free verse
3. To compare translations of a poem

Reader's Guide

THE GUITAR

Background

García Lorca often drew inspiration from the Andalusian (an'də·lōō'zhən) area of southern Spain where he grew up. Here there is a rich tradition of Gypsy folk music that includes *cante jondo* (kän'te hōn'dō), literally "deep song." Highly emotional and rhythmic, *cante jondo* is usually performed by colorfully dressed dancers in the passionate style known as flamenco. Many of García Lorca's poems, including "The Guitar," use modernist images to evoke the passionate feelings associated with *cante jondo*.

The guitar, on which *cante jondo* is traditionally played, is a musical instrument long associated with Spain. It arose, probably in sixteenth-century Spain, from the *vihuela* (ve·wā'la), a guitar-shaped instrument that medieval Spanish minstrels played in place of a lute. Later modifications resulted in what is known as the classical or Spanish guitar, whose reputation as a concert instrument was much enhanced by the great Spanish guitarist Andrés Segovia (sə·gō'vē·ə).

Writer's Response

Different sounds bring different feelings and emotions to mind. Write a few sentences describing your feelings when you hear a guitar (electric or acoustic) or some other musical instrument.

Literary Focus

Free verse is poetry that is free of traditional rules of meter and form. While it does not have a regular **meter** or **rhyme scheme**, free verse does have a conversational rhythm. It also uses poetic devices such as **imagery**, **alliteration**, **repetition**, **assonance** (repeated vowel sounds), and **onomatopoeia**. Because there is no fixed meter to determine where each line should end, the free-verse poet must carefully decide how to break the poem into lines. In making such decisions, he or she considers both the emphasis in meaning and the sound or rhythm that a particular line break helps create. Translators of free-verse poetry must keep the same considerations in mind. "The Guitar," both in the original Spanish and in the English translation, uses free verse.

Line Breaks in Free Verse

Free-verse poets must choose to end their lines in places where the line break will heighten the meaning and enhance the sound of the poem.

1. **Writing and Sharing.** Have a volunteer write "The Guitar" on the board as a prose paragraph. Discuss how the impact of the work has diminished.

2. **Writing and Sharing.** Invite students to invent and share alternative line breaks for "The Guitar." ■

HUMANITIES CONNECTION

In *Guitar*, Picasso stuck used pieces of wallpaper, newspaper, and colored paper to the canvas. Then he painted these over with charcoal and pencil. Thus the guitar, which is composed of fragments from the real world, appears fractured yet at the same time whole.

❓ *How does this technique capture the mood of the age?* (The fractured image mirrors the era's feeling of fragmentation.) ■

1 LITERARY ELEMENT

Diction/Imagery: What words in lines 15–25 suggest pain and death? (Possible responses: "cries," "scalding," "mourns," "arrow," "dead bird," "heart wounded," "swords") What hopeful or life-affirming images appear in the poem? ("crystals of dawn," "white camellias") How are these sets of images related? (Possible response: The music of the guitar is both a celebration of beauty and a lament for sorrow and death.)

READER'S RESPONSE

The poem's imagery becomes more densely packed after line 20, like a flamenco guitar accelerating toward the end of a *cante jondo.* Do you prefer the beginning or the end of the poem?

GUITAR, PABLO PICASSO, 1920.

The Bettmann Archive, © 1998 Estate of Pablo Picasso/Artists Rights Society (ARS), New York

THE GUITAR
Federico García Lorca
translated by
RACHEL BENSON AND ROBERT O'BRIEN

As you read "The Guitar," note the images that convey emotion. What overriding emotion does García Lorca associate with the guitar?

The cry of the guitar
begins.
The crystals of dawn are
breaking.
5 The cry of the guitar
begins.
It's useless to stop it.
It's impossible to
stop it.
10 Its cry monotonous
as the weeping of water,
as the weeping of wind
over the snowfall.
It's impossible to

15 stop it.
It cries for
distant things.
Sand of the scalding South
seeking white camellias.[1]
20 It mourns the arrow without target,
evening without morning, and the first
bird dead upon the branch.
Oh, guitar!
Heart wounded by five swords.

---

1. **camellias** (kə·mēl'yəz): the blooms of an evergreen shrub that grows in mild climates; camellia bushes would not thrive in a hot, sandy place.

1. Analyzing Guitar Music. Students might be interested in comparing "The Guitar" with the Beatles' song "While My Guitar Gently Weeps," which is strikingly similar in theme. Invite a student who can play the guitar to perform the Beatles' song and to put García Lorca's poem to music.

2. Researching Flamenco. Have a group of students research the flamenco music of Andalusian Spain. Be sure they explore the unique rhythm of flamenco music and the poses and movements of traditional flamenco dancers. Encourage students to include photographs and musical recordings in an oral report.

Lead students to understand that the poem expresses the beauty of sorrow and loss by having students point out passages where García Lorca uses beautiful imagery to express painful emotions. The last line of the poem is an example, as are most of the poem's other images. ■

First Thoughts

What is the main emotion you felt while reading the poem? What is the poem's **tone**? Identify the words or phrases that contributed to this tone.

Identifying Facts

1. What word names the sound of the guitar in lines 1 and 5? What is its sound compared to in lines 11–13?
2. According to lines 20–23, what three things does the guitar mourn?
3. What is the guitar compared to in the last line?

Interpreting Meanings

1. In saying that it is "impossible to stop" the guitar, what might García Lorca be suggesting?
2. What aspects of human experience might the **image** in lines 18–19 represent? Explain your answer.
3. What do the **images** in lines 20–23 suggest about the causes of human sorrow?
4. What do you think the "five swords" represent?

Applying Meanings

Music is often used as a symbol for life itself. What instrument or type of music symbolizes life for you? Compare your answer with those of your classmates.

Critical Writing Response

Comparing Translations. In a brief essay, compare the translation by poet Robert Bly (below) with the translation by Benson and O'Brien that you have just read. Focus on differences in **diction**, or word choice, **imagery**, and the way wording in specific lines contributes to the overall sound or **rhythm**. In your topic sentence, state which translation you prefer. In the body of your paper, give examples to explain your preference. Conclude by restating which translation you like better and why.

The Guitar
Federico García Lorca
translated by
Robert Bly

> The crying of the guitar
> starts.
> The goblets
> of the dawn break.
> 5 The crying of the guitar
> starts.
> No use to stop it.
> It is impossible
> to stop it.
> 10 It cries repeating itself
> as the water cries,
> as the wind cries
> over the snow.
> It is impossible
> 15 to stop it.
> It is crying for things
> far off.
> The warm sand of the South
> that asks for white camellias.
> 20 For the arrow with nothing to hit,
> the evening with no dawn coming,
> and the first bird of all dead
> on the branch.
> Guitar!
> 25 Heart wounded, gravely,
> by five swords.

Elie Wiesel
b. 1928, Romania

AP/Wide World Photos

Elie Wiesel (el'ē vē·zel'), a survivor of the Nazi concentration camps, turned to writing as a way to keep alive the memory of the atrocities committed during World War II. Seeking to avert new holocausts, Wiesel has also drawn attention to the plight of Cambodians, Soviet Jews, South African blacks, and other victims of persecution throughout the world.

Wiesel grew up among the devout Hasidic Jews of Sighet, a village in Romania's Carpathian Mountains. News from the outside world rarely filtered into this remote community. When the Nazis arrived in 1944 and rounded up all of the Jews, Wiesel and his family had no idea that they were being sent to Nazi death camps. They ended up in Auschwitz (oush'vits), the most infamous of these camps. Here Elie's mother and youngest sister were among the many Jews who were gassed to death. Meanwhile, Elie and his father were made slave laborers and sent to Buchenwald (boo'k'n·wôld'), another concentration camp, where Elie's father died of starvation and disease.

Finally, on April 11, 1945, the surviving prisoners of Buchenwald were liberated by the United States Third Army. As one of Europe's millions of displaced persons, Wiesel at first settled in France. Always interested in writing, Wiesel began working for a French newspaper while still a student at the Sorbonne in Paris. His friend, the writer François Mauriac, encouraged Wiesel to record for humanity the horrors he had endured. But Wiesel waited ten years before writing about his wartime ordeal. "I was afraid that words might betray it," he later explained. What Wiesel finally wrote was his autobiography *Night* (1958), one of the most significant and powerful accounts of Nazi atrocities ever written.

Since then, Wiesel has written many works about the Holocaust—the term he first used for the Nazi policy of systematic mass murder of European Jews. He has also described prewar Hasidic life and published several collections of Jewish folktales.

around the schoolhouse. "I'm dreaming! I'm dreaming!" he repeated to himself. And he went on sleeping.

When he awoke the sky was clear; the loose window let in a cold, pure air. The Arab was asleep, hunched up under the blankets now, his mouth open, utterly relaxed. But when Daru shook him, he started dreadfully, staring at Daru with wild eyes as if he had never seen him and such a frightened expression that the schoolmaster stepped back. "Don't be afraid. It's me. You must eat." The Arab nodded his head and said yes. Calm had returned to his face, but his expression was vacant and listless.

The coffee was ready. They drank it seated together on the folding bed as they munched their pieces of the cake. Then Daru led the Arab under the shed and showed him the faucet where he washed. He went back into the room, folded the blankets and the bed, made his own bed and put the room in order. Then he went through the classroom and out onto the terrace. The sun was already rising in the blue sky; a soft, bright light was bathing the deserted plateau. On the ridge the snow was melting in spots. The stones were about to reappear. Crouched on the edge of the plateau, the schoolmaster looked at the deserted expanse. He thought of Balducci. He had hurt him, for he had sent him off in a way as if he didn't want to be associated with him. He could still hear the gendarme's farewell and, without knowing why, he felt strangely empty and vulnerable. At that moment, from the other side of the schoolhouse, the prisoner coughed. Daru listened to him almost despite himself and then, furious, threw a pebble that whistled through the air before sinking into the snow. That man's stupid crime revolted him, but to hand him over was contrary to honor. Merely thinking

of it made him smart with humiliation. And he cursed at one and the same time his own people who had sent him this Arab and the Arab, too, who had dared to kill and not managed to get away. Daru got up, walked in a circle on the terrace, waited motionless, and then went back into the schoolhouse.

The Arab, leaning over the cement floor of the shed, was washing his teeth with two fingers. Daru looked at him and said: "Come." He went back into the room ahead of the prisoner. He slipped a hunting jacket on over his sweater and put on walking shoes. Standing, he waited until the Arab had put on his *chèche* and sandals. They went into the classroom and the schoolmaster pointed to the exit, saying: "Go ahead." The fellow didn't budge. "I'm coming," said Daru. The Arab went out. Daru went back into the room and made a package of pieces of rusk,[13] dates, and sugar. In the classroom, before going out, he hesitated a second in front of his desk, then crossed the threshold and locked the door. "That's the way," he said. He started toward the east, followed by the prisoner. But, a short distance from the schoolhouse, he thought he heard a slight sound behind them. He retraced his steps and examined the surroundings of the house; there was no one there. The Arab watched him without seeming to understand. "Come on," said Daru.

They walked for an hour and rested beside a sharp peak of limestone. The snow was melting faster and faster and the sun was drinking up the puddles at once, rapidly cleaning the plateau, which gradually dried and vibrated like the air itself. When they resumed walking, the ground rang under their feet. From time to time a bird rent the

13. **rusk:** dried bread.

19 GUIDED READING

Summarizing: List in order the opportunities Daru gives the Arab to escape. (He leaves him alone in the classroom, does not follow the Arab when he goes outside during the night, and leaves the Arab alone at the shed to wash.)

20 LITERARY ELEMENT

Theme: The Arab has "dared to kill and not managed to get away." How might this apply to all human beings' lives? (Possible response: Everyone is fallible and commits acts that hurt others, and we cannot escape the consequences.)

1. What is Daru's profession? (school-teacher)
2. What is Balducci's profession? (police-man)
3. What crime did the Arab commit? (He killed his cousin.)

4. What unpleasant task does Balducci ask Daru to perform? (take the prisoner to the authorities)
5. How does Daru give the Arab a crucial choice? (He lets him decide whether to walk to prison or walk away.)

RETEACHING
Divide students into pairs to role-play Daru and the Arab at the moment of choice when Daru lets the Arab go. Have students express their character's reasons for the choice, and their character's opinions of the other character's actions.

rapture (rap'chər): a joyous, almost ecstatic condition or feeling

21 INTERPRETING
Why does Daru feel joy and rapture during the walk on the rocky plateau? (There are no people there.) What details about the weather convey Daru's lightened mood? ("the fresh morning light," the "dome of blue sky")

22 LITERARY ELEMENT
Climax: Why is the scene in which Daru gives the Arab food, money, and directions a crucial moment of existential choice for both characters? (Daru has struggled to decide what to do about the prisoner; now the Arab must decide what to do with his freedom.)

23 LITERARY ELEMENT
Falling Action: When Daru gives the Arab control over his own fate, what does he choose? (imprisonment) Why? (Possible responses: He fears the nomads more than prison; he feels remorse for his action; or most likely, he fears the self-imposed responsibility of freedom.)

24 LITERARY ELEMENT
Irony: Why is the scrawled message ironic? (The Arab has chosen to turn himself in.) In what sense is Daru alone? (Daru has now alienated himself from his Arab neighbors and from the French government.) In what sense can he never be alone? (Daru is linked to others by the inescapable consequences of his choices.)

space in front of them with a joyful cry. Daru breathed in deeply the fresh morning light. He felt a sort of rapture before the vast familiar expanse, now almost entirely yellow under its dome of blue sky. They walked an hour more, descending toward the south. They reached a level height made up of crumbly rocks. From there on the plateau sloped down, eastward, toward a low plain where there were a few spindly trees and, to the south, toward outcroppings of rock that gave the landscape a chaotic look.

Daru surveyed the two directions. There was nothing but the sky on the horizon. Not a man could be seen. He turned toward the Arab, who was looking at him blankly. Daru held out the package to him. "Take it," he said. "There are dates, bread, and sugar. You can hold out for two days. Here are a thousand francs,[14] too." The Arab took the package and the money but kept his full hands at chest level as if he didn't know what to do with what was being given him. "Now look," the schoolmaster said as he pointed in the direction of the east, "there's the way to Tinguit. You have a two-hour walk. At Tinguit you'll find the administration and the police. They are expecting you." The Arab looked toward the east, still holding the package and the money against his chest. Daru took his elbow and turned him rather roughly toward the south. At the foot of the height on which they stood could be seen a faint path. "That's the trail across the plateau. In a day's walk from here you'll find pasturelands and the first nomads. They'll take you in and shelter you according to their law." The Arab had now turned toward Daru

and a sort of panic was visible in his expression. "Listen," he said. Daru shook his head: "No, be quiet. Now I'm leaving you." He turned his back on him, took two long steps in the direction of the school, looked hesitantly at the motionless Arab, and started off again. For a few minutes he heard nothing but his own step resounding on the cold ground and did not turn his head. A moment later, however, he turned around. The Arab was still there on the edge of the hill, his arms hanging now, and he was looking at the schoolmaster. Daru felt something rise in his throat. But he swore with impatience, waved vaguely, and started off again. He had already gone some distance when he again stopped and looked. There was no longer anyone on the hill.

Daru hesitated. The sun was now rather high in the sky and was beginning to beat down on his head. The schoolmaster retraced his steps, at first somewhat uncertainly, then with decision. When he reached the little hill, he was bathed in sweat. He climbed it as fast as he could and stopped, out of breath, at the top. The rock fields to the south stood out sharply against the blue sky, but on the plain to the east a steamy heat was already rising. And in that slight haze, Daru, with heavy heart, made out the Arab walking slowly on the road to prison.

A little later, standing before the window of the classroom, the schoolmaster was watching the clear light bathing the whole surface of the plateau, but he hardly saw it. Behind him on the blackboard, among the winding French rivers, sprawled the clumsily chalked-up words he had just read: "You handed over our brother. You will pay for this." Daru looked at the sky, the plateau, and, beyond, the invisible lands stretching all the way to the sea. In this vast landscape he had loved so much, he was alone.

---

14. **a thousand francs:** about eighty dollars at the time of the story; the franc, chief monetary unit of France, was used in Algeria while it was a French colony.

1. Dramatizing a Work. Camus not only wrote fine original plays, but dramatized a classic nineteenth-century realistic novel, Dostoyevsky's *The Possessed,* for the stage. Suggest that interested students rewrite "The Guest" or another work by Camus as a play, and perform or tape it. Point out that the limited setting and cast of characters are well suited to drama.

2. Researching Colonialism. Invite a panel of students to research the history of European colonialism in a specific region of Africa or Asia. Students may then organize a "town meeting" in which each student plays the part of a group affected by colonialism, such as Algerian Arabs or French colonial administrators.

CLOSURE

Ask students whether they agree or disagree with Camus's philosophy that human beings continually face choices out of which they create the meaning in their lives, and that it is impossible to be neutral or uninvolved in important social and moral issues. Use this discussion to link "The Guest" with the horrors of Nazism exposed in Elie Wiesel's *Night.* ■

First Thoughts

"The Guest" has a quiet but troubling ending. Do you think Daru made the right decision? What do you think happens after the end of the story?

Identifying Facts

1. What crime has the Arab committed? What is Daru's attitude toward that crime and toward the colonial government's action in relation to it?

2. What two routes does Daru point out to the Arab? Which route does the Arab take?

3. On returning to his schoolhouse, what message does Daru find on the blackboard?

Interpreting Meanings

1. What does Balducci mean when he says that Daru has "always been a little cracked"? Why does Balducci feel that Daru has insulted him?

2. Why doesn't Daru want to admit the existence of a bond between himself and the Arab? Do Daru's actions acknowledge such a brotherhood? Cite details from the story to support your answer.

3. Why do you think Daru feels "empty and vulnerable"? Do you think his vulnerability is heroic? Do you agree that handing over the Arab is "contrary to honor"? Explain your opinions.

4. Why do you think the Arab chooses the route he does? Based on his choice, in what way is he different from Daru? How do both men's choices reflect Camus's view of **existentialism**?

5. Who wrote the message on Daru's blackboard? What does the appearance of the message suggest about Daru's refusal to take sides in his society's political conflicts?

Applying Meanings

Can freedom be frightening? Do you think it can cause a feeling of isolation? Explain your answers.

Creative Writing Response

Continuing the Story. Imagine what happens between Daru and the Arab after the story ends. Does Daru defend his decision and actions? If so, how? Write the conversation or action that might occur.

Critical Writing Response

Writing About Existentialism. Unlike earlier philosophies that attempted to define objective moral truths and then apply them to the specifics of human existence, **existentialism** suggests that existence comes first and can never be completely defined or understood in objective, scientific terms. Instead, each person gives a *subjective* meaning or purpose to his or her own life through his or her actions and decisions. Existentialism thus places great emphasis on individual freedom. Such freedom, however, can be either liberating or isolating, since each person must journey alone down his or her own moral road.

In a three-paragraph essay, write about how Daru's behavior, attitudes, and experiences reflect Camus's ideas of existentialism. Be sure to address the following three questions. Include a thesis statement at the beginning of your essay.

1. How does Daru's disgust with both the Arab's crime and the colonial government's punishment reflect ideas of existentialism?

2. How does existential thinking help explain Daru's refusal to take the Arab any farther after showing him the two routes?

3. What does the story's outcome suggest about the existentialist's relationship to society?

ANSWERS

First Thoughts
Answers will vary.

Identifying Facts
1. He killed his cousin. disgusted by both
2. to a nomadic region and to prison. prison
3. "You handed over our brother. You will pay for this."

Interpreting Meanings
1. Balducci doesn't understand Daru's personal code of honor. The perceived insult lies in Daru's disgust for Balducci's job.
2. Possible response: He is repulsed by the murder. Yes; he shares food and sets the Arab free.
3. Possible response: he feels that he cannot act without compromising his honor. Opinions will vary.
4. Possible response: he is afraid of the nomads. He cannot handle freedom and solitude. Choices define people's lives.
5. Algerian rebels. Despite his desire to remain neutral, he cannot remain neutral, he cannot remain uninvolved.

Applying Meanings
Answers will vary.

Creative Writing Response
Continuing the Story. Dialogue and action must be consistent with Daru's character.

Critical Writing Response
Writing About Existentialism. You may wish to have students read articles about existentialism before writing. ■

Italo Calvino
1923–1985, Italy

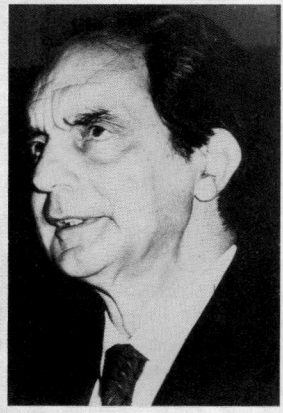

AP/Wide World Photos

When asked whom he considered the greatest Italian writer, Italo Calvino (ē·tal'ō kal·vē'nō) did not choose a poet, playwright, or novelist. Instead he named the Renaissance astronomer, physicist, and philosopher Galileo Galilei. Among Galileo's many accomplishments was the invention of an early telescope. Calvino found Galileo's prose surprisingly poetic and imaginative, especially his descriptions of the moon, which deftly combined objective scientific details with a unique lyrical vision. Calvino's own background in science and in literature led to a similar ability to combine poetic vision and scientific details.

The son of two scientists, Calvino was born in Cuba while his parents were studying tropical plant life there. Soon after Calvino's birth, the family returned to Italy and Calvino's father took a job running a botanical garden in San Remo, on the Italian Riviera. It was here that Calvino fell in love with nature. He intended to study agricultural science at the University of Turin, but World War II interrupted his plans.

Calvino was only nineteen when he joined the Italian Resistance to fight the Germans. After the war Calvino returned to college but decided to study literature rather than science. Upon graduating, he joined the staff of a newly formed publishing house in Turin. He soon published his first book, *The Path to the Nest of Spiders* (1947), a realistic novel based on his experiences as a Resistance fighter. Calvino also began collecting folktales from all over Italy. These were published in *Italian Folktales* (1956).

Calvino's first English anthology, *Adam, One Afternoon* (1957), contains some stories that blend elements of fantasy and realism, and others that are purely realistic. His later works, however, are more fanciful. *Baron in the Trees* (1957) is a story about a boy who moves to the treetops when his family annoys him, and then decides to spend the rest of his life there. The hero of *The Nonexistent Knight* (1962) is an empty suit of armor named Agilulf. The stories are often allegorical, with symbolic meanings that apply to today's world.

OBJECTIVES
1. *To analyze a short story combining realism and fantasy*
2. *To discern atmosphere in fiction*
3. *To re-create in words the atmosphere of a place and to analyze writing style by studying details*

THE ENCHANTED GARDEN
Italo Calvino
t r a n s l a t e d   b y
ARCHIBALD COLQUHOUN AND PEGGY WRIGHT

Reader's Guide

Background Many of the stories in *Adam, One Afternoon* (1957) are set on the Italian Riviera, the fashionable seaside resort where Calvino spent his youth. Like the French Riviera, the Italian Riviera has over the years attracted many wealthy summer residents who built elegant mansions along the coast. Such mansions—or villas, as they are called in Italy—are usually hidden away behind enclosed private gardens like the one described in the following story.

Writer's Response Think of a place that seemed magical or "enchanted" to you—either during your childhood or more recently. In a few sentences, describe the place and how it made you feel.

Literary Focus **Atmosphere** is the emotional effect, the mood or feeling, created by the **setting** of a work of literature. The **atmosphere** may be mild or harsh, gloomy or cheery, beautiful or ugly. It is usually created through evocative imagery and **descriptive details**. The adjective in the title of this story gives us an idea of the atmosphere that Calvino is trying to create.

THE ENCHANTED GARDEN

 In whose eyes is the garden in this story "enchanted"?

Giovannino and Serenella were strolling along the railroad tracks. Below was a scaly sea of somber, clear blue; above, a sky lightly streaked with white clouds. The railroad tracks were shimmering and burning hot. It was fun going along the tracks, there were so many games to play—he balancing on one rail and holding her hand while she walked along on the other, or else both jumping from one sleeper[1] to the next without ever letting their feet touch the stones in between. Giovannino and Serenella had been out looking for crabs, and now they had decided to explore the raiload tracks as far as the tunnel. He liked playing with Serenella, for she did not behave as all the other

1

---
1. **sleeper:** tie or crossbar supporting a railroad track.

PREREADING FOCUS
Literary Focus: Invite students to recall selections they have read that contain a memorable atmosphere, such as Bashō's haiku or Shakespeare's *The Tempest*. Remind them that while atmosphere arises out of setting, setting alone does not dictate atmosphere. The same setting, whether a villa on the Italian Riviera or a riverbank in ancient China, can be made to seem peaceful or violent, pleasant or unpleasant by the writer's choice of details and diction.

TEACHER'S RESOURCES
☞ Review and Response Worksheet
☞ Selection Test

CULTURAL DIVERSITY
Although the story is set in Italy in the 1950s, the most important cultural contrast is between rich and poor, a contrast that exists in virtually all cultures.
❓ *Can you think of a setting within your own culture that would exemplify a similar contrast? (Answers will vary.)*

1 LITERARY ELEMENT
Point of View: What examples of the limited third-person point of view can you find in the first paragraph? (Possible responses: "It was fun going along the tracks"; "He liked playing with Serenella. . . .")

Limited Third-Person Point of View

Remind students that stories whose narrators refer to themselves as "I" are written from the first-person point of view, while works in which narrators stand apart from the other characters and refer to them as "he" or "she" are written from the third-person point of view. If the third-person narrator can enter the minds of all the characters, the narrator is said to be omniscient. If the narrator knows the thoughts of only one character, the point of view is called limited third-person.

Writing and Speaking. Have students re-write paragraphs from "The Enchanted Garden" in the first person. Then have them read their passages aloud and discuss how the moods of the passages have changed. Lead students to see how the author's use of the third person, the point of view of the children, is crucial to establishing the magical atmosphere of the story. ■

2 LITERARY ELEMENT

Characterization: What do the children's actions on the railroad tracks suggest about their characters? (They are curious, adventurous, observant, and eager for experience.)

3 READER'S RESPONSE

Do you think a train is coming, or is it Giovannino's active imagination? (Answers will vary but should take into account the children's characters.)

GARDEN IN MAY, MARIA OAKEY DEWING, 1895.

National Museum of American Art, Washington, D.C./Art Resource, New York

little girls did, forever getting frightened or bursting into tears at every joke. Whenever Giovannino said, "Let's go there," or "Let's do this," Serenella followed without a word.

Ping! They both gave a start and looked up. A telephone wire had snapped off the top of the pole. It sounded like an iron stork shutting its beak in a hurry. They stood with their noses in the air and watched. What a pity not to have seen it! Now it would never happen again.

"There's a train coming," said Giovannino.

Serenella did not move from the rail. "Where from?" she asked.

Giovannino looked around in a knowledgeable way. He pointed at the black hole of the tunnel, which showed clear one moment, then misty the next, through the invisible heat haze rising from the stony track.

"From there," he said. It was as though they already heard a snort from the darkness of the tunnel, and saw the train suddenly appear, belching out fire and smoke, the wheels mercilessly eating up the rails as it hurtled toward them.

"Where shall we go, Giovannino?"

There were big gray aloes down by the sea, surrounded by dense, impenetrable nettles, while up the hillside ran a rambling hedge with thick leaves but no flowers. There was still no sign of the train; perhaps it was coasting, with the engine cut off, and

2

3

would jump out at them all of a sudden. But Giovannino had now found an opening in the hedge. "This way," he called.

The fence under the rambling hedge was an old bent rail. At one point it twisted about on the ground like the corner of a sheet of paper. Giovannino had slipped into the hole and already half vanished.

"Give me a hand, Giovannino."

They found themselves in the corner of a garden, on all fours in a flower bed, with their hair full of dry leaves and moss. Everything was quiet; not a leaf was stirring.

"Come on," said Giovannino, and Serenella nodded in reply.

There were big old flesh-colored eucalyptus trees and winding gravel paths. Giovannino and Serenella tiptoed along the paths, taking care not to crunch the gravel. Suppose the owners appeared now?

Everything was so beautiful: sharp bends in the path and high, curling eucalyptus leaves and patches of sky. But there was always the worrying thought that it was not their garden, and that they might be chased away any moment. Yet not a sound could be heard. A flight of chattering sparrows rose from a clump of arbutus[2] at a turn in the path. Then all was silent again. Perhaps it was an abandoned garden?

But the shade of the big trees came to an end, and they found themselves under the open sky facing flower beds filled with neat rows of petunias and convolvulus,[3] and paths and balustrades and rows of box trees.[4] And up at the end of the garden was a large villa with flashing windowpanes and yellow-and-orange curtains.

And it was all quite deserted. The two children crept forward, treading carefully over the gravel: perhaps the windows would suddenly be flung open, and angry ladies and gentlemen appear on the terraces to unleash great dogs down the paths. Now they found a wheelbarrow standing near a ditch. Giovannino picked it up by the handles and began pushing it along: it creaked like a whistle at every turn. Serenella seated herself in it and they moved slowly forward, Giovannino pushing the barrow with her on top, along the flower beds and fountains.

Every now and then Serenella would point to a flower and say in a low voice, "That one," and Giovannino would put the barrow down, pluck it, and give it to her. Soon she had a lovely bouquet.

Eventually the gravel ended and they reached an open space paved in bricks and mortar. In the middle of this space was a big empty rectangle: a swimming pool. They crept up to the edge; it was lined with blue tiles and filled to the brim with clear water. How lovely it would be to swim in!

"Shall we go for a dip?" Giovannino asked Serenella. The idea must have been quite dangerous if he asked her instead of just saying, "In we go!" But the water was so clear and blue, and Serenella was never afraid. She jumped off the barrow and put her bunch of flowers in it. They were already in bathing suits, since they'd been out for crabs before. Giovannino plunged in—not from the diving board, because the splash would have made too much noise, but from the edge of the pool. Down and down he went with his eyes wide open, seeing only the blue from the tiles and his pink hands like goldfish; it was not the same as under the sea, full of shapeless green-black shadows.

---

2. **arbutus** (är·byōot'əs): flowering shrubs or trailing plants with strawberrylike fruit.
3. **convolvulus** (kən·väl'vyōo·ləs): compact, bushy morning glories.
4. **box trees:** small trees that are often clipped and used as hedges; also called boxwood.

4 LITERARY ELEMENT
Specific Details: Eucalyptus plants have healing properties and are used in a number of medicines. How might they contribute to the special atmosphere of the story? (Possible response: They suggest a sickroom, or a less than wholesome atmosphere.)

SYNTHESIZING
How are the children's experiences given an atmosphere of fairy-tale-like peril? (Possible responses: the telephone wire inexplicably snaps; the train is imagined as belching fire and smoke like a dragon; the silent, abandoned garden seems part of a mysterious, other world.)

5 INTERPRETING
How do you think the children feel as they begin to explore the garden? (Possible responses: wary, somewhat frightened, curious, enthralled, delighted)

6 LITERARY ELEMENT
Imagery: What senses does Calvino appeal to in his description of the dive into the swimming pool? (sight, sound, touch) What is the effect created by the description? (mystery, sensory pleasure, danger)

READING CHECK

1. What are the children doing as the story opens? (playing on the railroad tracks)
2. Which word describes Serenella: fool-hardy, brave, fearful? (brave)
3. Why do the children run into the gar-den? (to get out of the way of an ap-proaching train)

4. What do the children do in the garden? (ride in a wheelbarrow, swim in a pool, eat tea and cake, explore)
5. Where do the children go when they leave the garden? (back to the nearby beach)

RETEACHING

Have students draw or paint the garden they visualize in the story, or their own personal vision of an enchanted environment.

7 GUIDED READING

Finding the Main Idea: Why are the children unable to en-joy the garden completely? (They know they don't belong there and fear being discov-ered and thrown out.)

8 LITERARY ELEMENT

Climax: Whom do the chil-dren discover, and where? (a boy inside the villa) What is unusual about the boy? (He is apparently an invalid, for he is pale and in pajamas on a warm day.)

9 LITERARY ELEMENT

Theme: The children regard the garden as a sort of earthly paradise. What alters their per-ception? (The boy who lives there seems as anxious as they about being turned out of the beautiful garden, perhaps through death.) In the next paragraph, why do the chil-dren's hearts begin to pound? (They sense a lingering injus-tice from long ago.)

10 LITERARY ELEMENT

Symbolism: What symbolic meaning might the butterflies, mentioned three times in the story, have? (The butterflies are beautiful but are "framed on the wall." Like the invalid boy trapped in the room, the butterflies can no longer flit freely.)

A pink form appeared above him: Serenella! He took her hand and they swam up to the surface, a bit anxiously. No, there was no one watching them at all. But it was not so nice as they'd thought it would be; they al-ways had that uncomfortable feeling that they had no right to any of this, and might be chased out at any moment.

They scrambled out of the water, and there beside the swimming pool they found a Ping-Pong table. Instantly Giovannino picked up the paddle and hit the ball, and Serenella, on the other side, was quick to return his shot. And so they went on play-ing, though giving only light taps at the ball, in case someone in the villa heard them. Then Giovannino, in trying to parry a shot that had bounced high, sent the ball sailing away through the air and smack against a gong hanging in a pergola.[5] There was a long, somber boom. The two children crouched down behind a clump of ranunculus.[6] At once two menservants in white coats ap-peared, carrying big trays; when they had put the trays down on a round table under an orange-and-yellow-striped umbrella, off they went.

Giovannino and Serenella crept up to the table. There was tea, milk, and sponge cake. They had only to sit down and help them-selves. They poured out two cups of tea and cut two slices of cake. But somehow they did not feel at all at ease, and sat perched on the edge of their chairs, their knees shak-ing. And they could not really enjoy the tea and cake, for nothing seemed to have any taste. Everything in the garden was like that: lovely but impossible to enjoy properly, with that worrying feeling inside that they were only there through an odd stroke of luck,

---

5. **pergola** (pʉr′gə·lə): arbor; trellis.
6. **ranunculus** (rə·nung′kyo͞o·ləs): buttercups.

and the fear that they'd soon have to give an account of themselves.

Very quietly they tiptoed up to the villa. Between the slits of a Venetian blind they saw a beautiful shady room, with collections of butterflies hanging on the walls. And in the room was a pale little boy. Lucky boy, he must be the owner of this villa and garden. He was stretched out on a chaise longue, turning the pages of a large book filled with figures. He had big white hands and wore pajamas buttoned up to the neck, though it was summer.

As the two children went on peeping through the slits, the pounding of their hearts gradually subsided. Why, the little rich boy seemed to be sitting there and turn-ing the pages and glancing around with more anxiety and worry than their own. Then he got up and tiptoed around, as if he were afraid that at any moment someone would come and turn him out, as if he felt that that book, that chaise longue, and those butter-flies framed on the wall, the garden and games and tea trays, the swimming pool and paths, were only granted to him by some enormous mistake, as if he were incapable of enjoying them and felt the bitterness of the mistake as his own fault.

The pale boy was wandering about his shady room furtively, touching with his white fingers the edges of the cases studded with butterflies; then he stopped to listen. The pounding of Giovannino and Serenella's hearts, which had died down, now got harder than ever. Perhaps it was the fear of a spell that hung over this villa and garden and over all these lovely, comfortable things, the residue of some injustice committed long ago.

Clouds darkened the sun. Very quietly Giovannino and Serenella crept away. They went back along the same paths they had

1. Creative Writing. Have students retell the story from the point of view of another character who is watching the children—perhaps the boy in the story or an unseen adult onlooker. Students may use either the first-person or limited third-person point of view. Invite students to read their versions aloud, and discuss the differences in atmosphere that result from the various points of view.

2. Creating a Soundtrack. Suggest that students create a soundtrack that reflects the action and atmosphere of the story, combining instrumental selections and sound effects suggesting the train, wheelbarrow, pool water, etc. Remind students to keep the garden's enchanted atmosphere in mind when making their selections.

Discuss the following questions: To what extent is "The Enchanted Garden" a realistic story, and to what extent a work of fantasy? Does it have a social message, or is it meant to represent a world apart from the real one? ■

---

come, stepping fast but never at a run. And they went through the hedge again on all fours. Between the aloes they found a path leading down to the small, stony beach, with banks of seaweed along the shore. Then they invented a wonderful new game: a seaweed fight. They threw great handfuls of it in each other's faces till late in the afternoon. And Serenella never once cried.

First Thoughts

What might have made the little rich boy pale, afraid, and unhappy?

Identifying Facts

1. Before entering the garden, what are Giovannino and Serenella doing to amuse themselves?
2. What adjective describes "everything" in the garden?
3. After they leave the garden, what new game do Giovannino and Serenella invent?

Interpreting Meanings

1. How would you describe the **atmosphere** of the garden? Which descriptive details contribute to this atmosphere?
2. Consider the "anxiety and worry" that Giovannino and Serenella feel as they explore the garden and that the boy in pajamas seems to feel later. What may have caused the uneasiness in each case?
3. In what ways is the boy in the villa different from Giovannino and Serenella? What might the contrast suggest about the lives of the rich?
4. What might the garden **symbolize**?

Applying Meanings

Would you say young children are more or less sensitive to their surroundings than adults? Discuss with your classmates.

Creative Writing Response

Creating an Atmosphere. Write a brief descriptive essay in which you re-create the **atmosphere** of a place you found magical or enchanted. You may expand upon the sentences you wrote for the Writer's Response (see page 1259). Use vivid words and **images** to capture the sights, sounds, smells, and textures of the place. Before you write, fill out a chart like the one below to be sure you have enough specific sensory **details**.

Sights	
Sounds	
Smells	
Textures or temperatures	
Tastes	

Critical Writing Response

Writing about Style. In a brief essay, discuss the descriptive style that Calvino employs in this story. Consider his use of vivid **imagery** and precise, scientific **details**, as well as the more mysterious or fantastic details that he uses. As a prewriting activity, list details on a chart like the one below.

Realistic or Precise Details	Mysterious or Fantastic Details

ANSWERS

First Thoughts
Answers will vary.

Identifying Facts
1. looking for crabs and playing on the railroad tracks
2. beautiful
3. a seaweed fight

Interpreting Meanings
1. Possible responses: luxurious and magical but mysterious and forbidding. the silent perfection of the swimming pool, the unattended tea table
2. Possible responses: The protagonists' uneasiness may come from exploring the unknown and forbidden; the invalid boy's from being so close to a beauty he cannot enjoy, or from a "residue of some injustice committed long ago."
3. Possible responses: He is feeble, sheltered. The rich cannot enjoy their wealth.
4. Possible responses: beauty and innocence of childhood, the Garden of Eden, forbidden or ill-gotten pleasures

Applying Meanings
Answers will vary.

Creative Writing Response
Creating an Atmosphere. Remind students that vivid verbs and adjectives and concrete nouns will build atmosphere effectively.

Critical Writing Response
Writing about Style. Students may find that Calvino describes the natural world of flora and fauna in more precise terms than he does the human, social world. ■

Italo Calvino

Craig Line/Wide World Photos

Aleksandr Solzhenitsyn
b. 1918, Russia

Aleksandr Solzhenitsyn (sōl'zhə·nēt'sin) became aware of the shortcomings of the Soviet Union after he had fought bravely for three years in World War II. Then, in a letter to a friend, he referred to premier Josef Stalin as "the boss" in criminals' slang. For this "crime" he was arrested and sent to prisons and labor camps for eight years. He was released after Stalin died in 1953 but still had to spend three years in internal exile in central Asia. There he worked as a teacher and wrote about his experiences.

The result of his efforts was *One Day in the Life of Ivan Denisovich* (1962), a novel about a farmer serving ten years at a Soviet labor camp for a political crime he did not commit. Since Nikita Krushchev, the new Soviet premier, had risen to power by attacking Stalin, books like Solzhenitsyn's were encouraged.

Solzhenitsyn's period of acceptance in his homeland, however, was short-lived. After Krushchev was ousted in 1964, the new, more conservative regime became increasingly uncomfortable with Solzhenitsyn's accounts of Stalinist oppression. The government barred publication of his work and confiscated many of his manuscripts. Solzhenitsyn's relationship with the government deteriorated further after a Paris firm published his famous attack on the Soviet penal system, *The Gulag Archipelago* (1974). Solzhenitsyn was charged with treason, stripped of his Soviet citizenship, and exiled from his homeland. Eventually he settled in the United States, where he became the Soviet Union's best-known writer-in-exile.

When Soviet premier Mikhail Gorbachev (mē'khä·ēl' gôr'bə·chôf') instituted his new policy of *glasnost*, or "openness," in the 1980s, Solzhenitsyn's citizenship was restored and his works were gradually published or reissued in his homeland. In 1990, Solzhenitsyn wrote a long essay entitled "How to Revitalize Russia." More remarkable than his ideas was the fact that he was permitted to express them in Soviet government periodicals that only five years before had denounced him as a traitor.

OBJECTIVES

1. To interpret two prose poems by a contemporary Russian author
2. To recognize the prose poem form
3. To write a prose poem and a paragraph analyzing the theme of a prose poem

Reader's Guide

FREEDOM TO BREATHE
A JOURNEY ALONG THE OKA

Background

Rulers of the Soviet Union, like those of the Russian empire, have generally allowed their people very few freedoms. Under the czars, critics of the government were executed or exiled to remote parts of the empire, such as arctic Siberia, where they often died. A few years after the Russian Revolution of 1917, the new Communist regime began following similar practices. Soviet oppression reached its height under dictator Josef Stalin during the Great Purge of the mid-1930s, when the secret police shot or imprisoned millions of citizens. Matters improved only after Soviet premier Mikhail Gorbachev began instituting reforms in the late 1980s.

As a result of the Russian people's long history of suffering under tyrannical regimes, Russian writers since the time of Pushkin (see page 1006) have often spoken out against government oppression. Solzhenitsyn entered this long tradition when he began publishing in the early 1960s. Most of his works, including the prose poems you are about to read, deal with the lack of human rights and freedom in his homeland.

Writer's Response

People fight in different ways to bring about social and political change—some use guns or bombs while others use pens or videotape. Do you think the "pen is mightier than the sword" in exposing abuses? Write a paragraph expressing your opinion. Try to provide some examples from recent current events to support your opinion.

Literary Focus

Prose poetry is written in prose form, but uses poetic devices such as **rhythm**, **imagery**, and **figurative language** to express a single strong emotion or idea. Solzhenitsyn's prose poems are brief nonfiction pieces that combine the features of prose and poetry.

PREREADING FOCUS

Writer's Response: Ask students to take into consideration the number of people the "pen" can reach, as opposed to the sword, and the potential of each weapon for hurting innocent victims.

Literary Focus: Solzhenitsyn's prose poems differ from most other prose poems as well as from most of the author's own work. The content of Solzhenitsyn's prose poems, unlike that of most others, is primarily political. Solzhenitsyn is not indulging in "art for art's sake," as did the French Symbolist writers of prose poems, such as Baudelaire, Verlaine, and Rimbaud. Instead, Solzhenitsyn is using this form for the same purpose that he used the novel form and the nonfiction form: to awaken his readers to important political issues. These prose poems differ from most of Solzhenitsyn's work in that he is best known for long realistic narratives rather than for the impressionistic beauty of his style.

ABOUT THE TRANSLATOR

Michael Glenny (1927–   ) was born in Bath, England. Twentieth-century Russian classics that he has translated include Solzhenitsyn's *August 1914*, Nabokov's *Mary*, and Bulgakov's *The Master and Margarita* and *Heart of a Dog*. He is a contributor to the London *Times* and other periodicals.

1 LITERARY ELEMENT

Imagery: What images establish mood and setting in the opening paragraphs? ("fine film of rain," "apple tree in blossom," "grass . . . glistens with moisture," "sweet fragrance") How would you characterize the mood of the first two paragraphs? (Possible responses: quiet, calm, peaceful, relaxed)

WRITING TO LEARN

Rewrite one or two of these paragraphs as a free-verse poem. Compare your versions and discuss your reasons for breaking lines after specific words. What word or words are most important thematically to the poem? (freedom, breathing) What image? (the tree) Do your versions emphasize these words? ■

FREEDOM TO BREATHE
Aleksandr Solzhenitsyn

translated by
MICHAEL GLENNY

Stop after you read the first two paragraphs of this prose poem. What kind of a place do you think the speaker is describing? After you finish the poem, see if your impression was correct.

1
A shower fell in the night and now dark clouds drift across the sky, occasionally sprinkling a fine film of rain.

I stand under an apple tree in blossom and I breathe. Not only the apple tree but the grass round it glistens with moisture; words cannot describe the sweet fragrance that pervades the air. I inhale as deeply as I can, and the aroma invades my whole being; I breathe with my eyes open, I breathe with my eyes closed—I cannot say which gives me the greater pleasure.

This, I believe, is the single most precious freedom that prison takes away from us: the freedom to breathe freely, as I now can. No food on earth, no wine, not even a woman's kiss is sweeter to me than this air steeped in the fragrance of flowers, of moisture and freshness.

No matter that this is only a tiny garden, hemmed in by five-story houses like cages in a zoo. I cease to hear the motorcycles backfiring, radios whining, the burble of loudspeakers. As long as there is fresh air to breathe under an apple tree after a shower, we may survive a little longer.

HRW Photo by Russell Dian

Saint Sophia Church in Kiev, in the former Soviet Union.

A JOURNEY ALONG THE OKA

Aleksandr Solzhenitsyn
translated by
MICHAEL GLENNY

Solzhenitsyn uses a description of the Russian countryside to reveal how he feels about an aspect of Soviet life. What are his feelings?

Traveling along country roads in central Russia, you begin to understand why the Russian countryside has such a soothing effect.

It is because of its churches. They rise over ridge and hillside, descending towards wide rivers like red and white princesses, towering above the thatch and wooden huts of everyday life with their slender, carved, and fretted belfries. From far away they greet each other; from distant, unseen villages they rise towards the same sky.

Wherever you may wander, over field or pasture, many miles from any homestead, you are never alone: above the wall of trees, above the hayricks, even above the very curve of the earth itself, the dome of a belfry

2 EVALUATING
Why do you think churches have a soothing effect for Solzhenitsyn? (Possible responses: The churches represent his own Christian faith; a tie to the past; a symbol of defiance against the official atheism of the Communist party.)

3 LITERARY ELEMENT
Personification: What examples of personification do you notice in the second and third paragraphs? (The churches are "like red and white princesses," they "greet each other" and beckon.) How does this personification help the author to express his feelings about churches? (Possible response: It makes the churches seem living, warm, friendly.)

READING CHECK

1. Where is "Freedom to Breathe" set? (in a tiny garden)
2. What does the speaker contrast this setting to? (prison)
3. What feature of the Russian landscape does Solzhenitsyn praise in "A Journey Along the Oka"? (churches)
4. During what era of Russian history were the two poems written? (Soviet, Communist)
5. What does Solzhenitsyn say about the essential nature of people? (always selfish; often evil)

RETEACHING

Tell students that in "Freedom to Breathe" and "A Journey Along the Oka," Solzhenitsyn wasn't just describing a garden and a landscape with churches, he was describing an entire nation and his feelings about its political system. Explain that the tiny garden symbolizes the preciousness of all freedom; the deterioration of churches symbolizes the decay of Russian spirituality.

4 INTERPRETING

Why are the churches "no longer living"? (The former Soviet government discouraged and often suppressed religion.) How has the situation for Russian churches changed since Solzhenitsyn wrote this piece? (More people attend religious services since the government has become more tolerant. Many church buildings have been restored.)

5 CULTURAL BACKGROUND

In the setting of the church, the farm production slogan, which is typical of Communist propaganda, is incongruous. It is used here for ironic effect. The building, once used for spiritual inspiration, is now used for political indoctrination.

6 LITERARY ELEMENT

Tone: Who is Vitka? (He may be the speaker or the speaker's friend.) What effect does the shift in tone in the final paragraph achieve? (Possible responses: It throws an ironic light on the speaker's nostalgia; it points up the fact that the speaker is suppressing his own thoughts, just as the government has.)

WRITING TO LEARN

History: Write a paragraph in which you support or refute Solzhenitsyn's claim that religion "raised man above the level of a beast." Cite details from literature, history, and your own experience. ■

Fred Euphrat

? **What poetic features do Solzhenitsyn's prose poems exhibit?**

is always beckoning to you, from Borki Lovetskie, Lyubichi, or Gavrilovskoe.[1]

But as soon as you enter a village you realize that the churches which welcomed you from afar are no longer living. Their crosses have long since been bent or broken off; the dome with its peeling paint reveals its rusty ribcage; weeds grow on the roofs and in the cracks of the walls; the cemetery is hardly ever cared for, its crosses knocked over and its graves ransacked; the ikons[2] behind the altar have faded from a decade of rain and are scrawled with obscene graffiti.

In the porch there are barrels of salt and a tractor is swinging round towards them, or a lorry is backing up to the vestry door to collect some sacks. In one church, machine tools are humming away; another stands silent, simply locked up. Others have been turned into clubs where propaganda meetings are held ("We Will Achieve High Yields of Milk!") or films shown: _Poem About the Sea, The Great Adventure._

People have always been selfish and often evil. But the Angelus[3] used to toll and its echo would float over village, field, and wood. It reminded man that he must abandon his trivial earthly cares and give up one hour of his thoughts to life eternal. The tolling of the eventide bell, which now survives for us only in a popular song, raised man above the level of a beast.

Our ancestors put their best into these stones and these belfries—all their knowledge and all their faith.

Come on, Vitka,[4] buck up and stop feeling sorry for yourself! The film starts at six, and the dance is at eight. . . .

---

1. **Borki Lovetskie, Lyubichi, Gavrilovskoe:** cities in the former Soviet Union.
2. **ikons** (ī'känz'): religious images or figures, usually of Jesus, Mary, or a saint; also spelled _icons._
3. **Angelus** (an'jə·ləs): the bell rung to announce the time for the Angelus, a prayer said at morning, noon, and evening.
4. **Vitka** (vĕt'kä): a familiar form for Viktor; usually the familiar form would be Vitya. The "ka" ending here shows that the speaker is slightly annoyed at the person being addressed.

1. Reporting on Russia in Transition.
Have a group of students research and present a report on the changes that have occurred in the former Soviet Union in recent years, and on Solzhenitsyn's role in inducing them.

2. Researching Religious Art. The beauty and mysticism of Russian church art have awed the world for centuries. Invite students to find and show photographs of icons, church architecture, and paintings. Suggest that they point out Byzantine influences on the art and architecture.

CLOSURE

Encourage students to discuss their personal responses to the prose poems and to the history they represent. ◾

First Thoughts

Were you surprised by the new information about the speaker's location in the last paragraph in "Freedom to Breathe"? Why do you think Solzhenitsyn provided this information in the last paragraph rather than in the first one?

Identifying Facts

1. What does the speaker in "Freedom to Breathe" say words cannot describe?
2. What does the same speaker say is the single most precious freedom that prison takes away?
3. What does the speaker in "A Journey Along the Oka" find soothing about the Russian countryside?
4. What are the churches used for now?

Interpreting Meanings

1. Solzhenitsyn uses **imagery**—language that appeals to the senses—in both of these **prose poems**. Identify images in "Freedom to Breathe" that relate to at least three different senses.
2. What do the details of **setting** in the last paragraph of "Freedom to Breathe" emphasize about the speaker's view of freedom?
3. Why does the speaker in "A Journey Along the Oka" say the churches are no longer "living"?
4. Prose poems often use **figures of speech**. Find an example of **simile** and **personification** in the second paragraph of "A Journey Along the Oka."

5. The churches in "A Journey Along the Oka" can be taken on both a literal and a symbolic level. What would you say the churches **symbolize**, or represent?

Applying Meanings

Those who have never been in prison probably take the "freedom to breathe" for granted. What are some other freedoms we often take for granted?

Do you think that if we take certain freedoms for granted (the freedom to worship, for example) we risk losing them? Give examples to support your opinion.

Creative Writing Response

Writing a Prose Poem Using Imagery. Think of an experience that is still vivid in your memory. Write a **prose poem** in which you use **images** to communicate what you saw, heard, smelled, tasted, or touched. Try to select images that create the emotions and sensations you associate with the experience: joy, sadness, excitement, peace, or some other feeling.

Critical Writing Response

Analyzing the Poem's Theme. **Theme** is the poem's central idea about life. Write a paragraph about the theme of either "Freedom to Breathe" or "A Journey Along the Oka." Your topic sentence should state what the theme is. Then discuss how Solzhenitsyn gets his theme across, and provide examples from the poem. End your paragraph with a sentence telling how you feel about poetry with social, political, or religious messages.

After World War II, Milosz was offered a post with the Polish Communist government even though he was not a member of the Communist party. In 1949, while working at the Polish embassy in Washington, D.C., Milosz visited Albert Einstein, whom he deeply admired, to ask Einstein whether he should defect to the West. Einstein, who was in exile in America, told Milosz that a poet should not break with his country; Milosz should return to Poland and have faith that the current regime would pass. Milosz recalls driving away "somewhat numbly. All of us yearn for the highest wisdom, but we have to rely on ourselves in the end."

After Milosz defected, he lived in Paris, where he became friends with Albert Camus (p. 1244) and Pablo Neruda (p. 1275). Milosz continued to write, but he supported his family mostly by translating. In addition to Polish and English, he translates from French, Spanish, Yiddish, and Hebrew. Milosz writes his poetry in Polish because, he says, he knows best the language of his childhood. In 1981, Milosz visited Poland for the first time in thirty years.

Milosz's friend, the poet Robert Hass, writes that Milosz's latest poems are "still obsessed with the themes that have haunted him for a lifetime: the mystery of being, the nature of evil, the power and inexpressibility of human experience, and increasingly the astonishments of memory and time."

Czeslaw Milosz
b. 1911, Poland

Bernard Gotfryd/Woodfin Camp & Associates

Czeslaw Milosz (ches'wäf mē'wôsh) was working in Warsaw in 1939 when Soviet Russia and Nazi Germany invaded Poland. In August 1944, during the Nazi occupation, the Poles in Warsaw staged a bloody uprising in which over 150,000 citizens perished. While Milosz was pinned to the ground as German machine guns strafed the street around him, he recalls seeing cobblestones leap upright like porcupine quills. His wife rushed back to their house shortly before it was destroyed by artillery fire and stuffed his writings into a briefcase. Surviving by a miracle each day, said Milosz, "left you with an uncomfortable feeling: 'Why me and not someone else?'"

Milosz first experienced the savagery of war as a small child during World War I. He and his mother traveled through Russia with his father, who was an engineer recruited by the czar's army to build bridges near battle zones. When the family returned home to Lithuania after the war, their town had become part of the new Polish state.

Milosz obtained a law degree in 1934. After the invasion of his homeland in 1939, he remained in Warsaw throughout the six-year Nazi occupation and began to study English. He joined the Polish resistance movement and wrote anti-Nazi poetry that was published by underground presses and read at clandestine poetry readings.

After the war, Milosz accepted a diplomatic post at the Polish embassy in Washington, D.C., where he became increasingly disillusioned with Poland's Communist government. In 1951, while serving as cultural attaché in Paris, Milosz defected, and he spent the next ten years in France. In 1961 he moved to the United States (becoming a U.S. citizen in 1970) and taught Slavic languages and literature at the University of California at Berkeley.

In 1980, Milosz received the Nobel Prize for literature. In his acceptance speech, he expressed his belief that poetry must bear witness to "the demoniac doings of history": "Those who are alive receive a mandate from those who are silent forever. They can fulfill their duties only by trying to reconstruct precisely things as they were and by wresting the past from fictions and legends."

OBJECTIVES

1. To recognize Czeslaw Milosz's place in modern literature and to analyze one of his poems
2. To identify the characteristics of a dramatic monologue
3. To write a dramatic monologue and an essay that considers the role of the poet in wartime

■ THEMES IN WORLD LITERATURE ■

The Search for Meaning
Inferno from the *Divine Comedy*, pp. 741–770
From *Night*, pp. 1232–1242
Life and Loss
From *Faust*, Part I, pp. 986–1001
"Freedom to Breathe," pp. 1265–1266 ■

Reader's Guide

SONG OF A CITIZEN

Background

When he was a university student in the early 1930s, Milosz co-founded a leftist literary group known as Zagary, whose members later became known as the "Catastrophists" because their writings prophesied cosmic devastation. The Nazi occupation of Warsaw, which lasted from 1939 to 1945, fulfilled this dire forecast: The city lay in ashes, and hundreds of thousands of citizens died or were deported to concentration camps.

In addition to the anti-Nazi poems Milosz wrote during the occupation, he composed a poem cycle, "The Voices of Poor People" (1943), which includes "Song of a Citizen." "The Voices of Poor People" takes a bitter look at the destruction of Warsaw and, explains Milosz, presents "a search for a means of how to deal directly with the Nazi occupation." The poem cycle circulated among members of Poland's underground resistance movement but was not published until after the war. Many years later, Milosz heard that a typewritten copy had been found in a suitcase left behind on a train whose passengers had been rounded up and taken away to die at Auschwitz. The suitcase also contained a traveling magician's cape and top hat.

Writer's Response

Write a few sentences about how you might respond if you found yourself facing a cataclysmic disaster—deportation from your homeland, a war, a natural catastrophe, or some other extreme situation. What ideas, feelings, memories, or images do you think would help you to survive and to deal with such devastating losses?

Literary Focus

A **dramatic monologue** is a poem in which a speaker addresses one or more listeners who remain silent. The speaker may be thinking aloud, mulling over a problem, or coming to an important decision. From the speaker's words, the reader can learn the speaker's identity, situation, and character, as well as the setting and the identity of other characters. The speaker may be the poet but more often is an invented character, sometimes disclosing information he or she doesn't consciously intend to reveal.

PREREADING FOCUS

Background: Though the world around him lay in ruins, Milosz wrote poems about spiritual survival and the struggle to comprehend tragic events. Milosz's war poems, including "The Voices of Poor People," were published in 1945 in a volume titled *Rescue*. These include his best-known and most powerful poems. "Song of a Citizen" seems to question the poet's vocation, but elsewhere Milosz has stated that poetry during the Resistance could be a more potent weapon than bullets, providing "an affirmation of faith in survival and in victory over the oppressors."

Literary Focus: The speaker in this dramatic monologue is an invented character, although he is in some ways similar to the poet. Dramatic monologues exist in the literature and folksongs of many cultures. Critics consider the dramatic monologue form to have been perfected by the English writer Robert Browning, especially in his poem "My Last Duchess" (1842). The English writer William Blake uses the technique in his *Songs of Innocence and Experience* (1794), which influenced Milosz when he wrote "The Voices of Poor People." Milosz's contribution to the form is his use of "polyphony," or "many voices," which is based on the idea that everyone has contradictory "voices," or ideas. In "Song of a Citizen," the citizen "speaks" as a stone, a live dog, a poor man, a vodka dealer, a philosopher, and a scientist.

Parallel Structure

Parallel structure, or parallelism, is the repetition of words, phrases, or sentences that have the same grammatical structure or that state a similar idea. Instead of relying on rhyme or meter, Milosz uses parallelism to create a rhythm that helps to emphasize images, unify ideas, and heighten the emotional effect of words. This technique gives his poem the rhythm of an oration or a Biblical psalm.

1. Reading and Listening. Ask students to read the poem aloud and try to identify the parallel elements in lines 5–6, 12–14, 15, 21, 27–28, and 31–42.

2. Writing and Speaking. Ask students to try to imitate Milosz's use of parallelism. Have them copy Milosz's sentences that include parallel elements, but ask them to omit the words and phrases that he uses. They should use his sentences (with blanks) as a "frame" for the sentences they write,

---

TEACHER'S RESOURCES
✔ Review and Response
Worksheet

1 LITERARY ELEMENT

Figurative Language: What kinds of figures of speech does Milosz use in lines 1–4? (metaphor, personification) How do these figures of speech establish the speaker's attitude and mood? (He compares himself to a "stone" and a "poor man" who has witnessed suffering, loss of freedom, and death.)

2 INTERPRETING

In lines 8–16, what do you learn about the speaker's character and situation? (Possible answers: He feels guilty and cowardly to be a survivor. His daily life is a nightmare, from which he escapes by contemplating the universe and envisioning enduring natural phenomena.)

SONG OF A CITIZEN
Czeslaw Milosz

How does this speaker feel about the events he has witnessed, and how does he relate these events to his own life? Whom do you think the speaker is addressing?

A stone from the depths that has witnessed the
    seas drying up
and a million white fish leaping in agony,
I, poor man, see a multitude of white-bellied
    nations
without freedom. I see the crab feeding on their
    flesh.

5   I have seen the fall of States and the perdition of
    tribes,
the flight of kings and emperors, the power of
    tyrants.
I can say now, in this hour,
that I—am, while everything expires,
that it is better to be a live dog than a dead lion,°
10   as the Scripture says.

A poor man, sitting on a cold chair, pressing my
    eyelids,
I sigh and think of a starry sky,
of non-Euclidean space,° of amoebas and their
    pseudopodia,°
of tall mounds of termites.

15 When walking, I am asleep, when sleeping, I
    dream reality,
pursued and covered with sweat, I run.
On city squares lifted up by the glaring dawn,
beneath marble remnants of blasted-down gates,
I deal in vodka and gold.

9. **it . . . lion:** allusion to Ecclesiastes 9:4: "But whoever is joined with all the living has hope, for a living dog is better than a dead lion."

13. **non-Euclidean space:** space that cannot be measured by the simple geometric rules defined by the Greek mathematician Euclid (300 B.C.). **pseudopodia:** footlike projections used for moving and for taking in food.

20 And yet so often I was near,
    I reached into the heart of metal, the soul of
        earth, of fire, of water.
    And the unknown unveiled its face
    as a night reveals itself, serene, mirrored by tide.
    Lustrous copper-leaved gardens greeted me
25 that disappear as soon as you touch them.

    And so near, just outside the window—the
        greenhouse of the worlds
    where a tiny beetle and a spider are equal to
        planets,
    where a wandering atom flares up like Saturn,
    and, close by, harvesters drink from a cold jug
30 in scorching summer.

    This I wanted and nothing more. In my later years
    like old Goethe° to stand before the face of the
        earth,
    and recognize it and reconcile it
    with my work built up, a forest citadel
35 on a river of shifting lights and brief shadows.

    This I wanted and nothing more. So who
    is guilty? Who deprived me
    of my youth and my ripe years, who seasoned
    my best years with horror? Who,
40 who ever is to blame, who, O God?

    And I can think only about the starry sky,
    about the tall mounds of termites.

32. **Goethe** (gö′tə): Johann Wolfgang von Goethe (1749–1832), German writer who sought the meaning of life. See page 986.

Remains of the Warsaw Ghetto, 1943.
❓ *What images of destruction and ruin do you find in the poem?*

AKG London

Czeslaw Milosz   **1273**

Research Project. Have students research post–World War I totalitarian governments in Russia, Italy, Poland, Yugoslavia, Cuba, and, more recently, in southern Asia (Burma and Cambodia), and Africa (Nigeria). You might assign a small group of students to research each country. Ask them to investigate strategies that repressive regimes have used to gain power, suppress free speech, and control cultural life (including the work of artists and writ-

ers). In particular, have them focus on strategies used by dissidents to counteract and undermine repressive governments. Suggest that students consult the Internet, encyclopedias, histories, biographies, magazines, newspapers, and audiovisual sources. Have students present their findings to the class in an oral report or panel discussion.

Underground resistance fighters in Nazi-occupied Warsaw were among the first readers of "Song of a Citizen" in 1943. Ask students to discuss how these freedom fighters may have reacted to the poem: Did the poem offer them comfort, encouragement, and an understanding of their dire condition, or did the poem have some other effect? ■

ANSWERS

First Thoughts
Answers will vary.

Identifying Facts
1. seas drying up, fish leaping, nations without freedom, etc.
2. starry sky, non-Euclidean space, amoebas, the starry sky, termite mounds
3. greenhouse of the worlds
4. to reconcile with the world

Interpreting Meanings
1. cold chair, remnants of gates, city squares
2. See stanzas 2–5. Possible responses: The speaker is selfish, ambitious, angry.
3. See lines 9 and 32. Answers will vary.
4. "poor man," "This I wanted. . . ." Answers will vary.
5. See stanzas 1, 2, 4–5. The laws of nature are enduring.
6. Who is to blame? Answers will vary.

Applying Meanings
Answers will vary.

Creative Writing Response
Writing a Dramatic Monologue. Suggest that small groups collaborate on a monologue.

Critical Writing Response
Responding to a Writer's Questions. Ask students to find other selections that serve a social purpose. ■

▶ **First Thoughts**
Why do you think Milosz titled this poem "Song of a Citizen"? How does this "song" differ from the kind of song you might expect a citizen to sing?

Identifying Facts
1. In the first two stanzas, what things does the speaker say that he sees or has seen?
2. In lines 11–14, what does the speaker think about? What is he thinking about at the end of the poem?
3. What does the speaker say is "just outside the window" (line 26)?
4. What does the speaker say that he wanted in his later years?

Interpreting Meanings
1. What details reveal the **setting** of the poem?
2. Find **images** or details that provide clues to the speaker's character. What kind of person do you think the speaker is? What seems to be the poet's attitude toward him?
3. Identify two **allusions** the speaker makes. What is the meaning of each allusion? Why do you think Milosz used these allusions in his poem?
4. Several phrases or sentences are repeated in the poem. Identify these repetitions, and explain why you think Milosz chose to emphasize them.
5. List **images** from the poem that relate to science and to nature. What point might Milosz be making about the relationship between science, nature, and our perception of the world around us?
6. At the end of the poem, the speaker asks three questions that are really just one question. Phrase this question in your own words. What would you say is the answer to the question?

Applying Meanings
In regard to the horrifying years of the Nazi occupation, Milosz has said that there's "no question of anyone surviving that period in Poland with a clear conscience. There had to be many occasions in which not turning away would have meant heroically choosing to die." What are some examples of situations in the world today that might require such a choice? Do you agree, as the speaker in the poem says, "that it is better to be a live dog than a dead lion," or that personal survival is more important than taking action to help others? Explain.

Creative Writing Response
Writing a Dramatic Monologue. Think of an event that has occurred in your school, community, state, nation, or abroad that has directly affected your life or the life of someone you know. Write a **dramatic monologue** in which a speaker describes or reflects on this event. Remember that in a dramatic monologue the speaker reveals his or her personality, the situation, and the setting by talking about ideas, memories, hopes, fears, and dreams to listeners who do not respond.

Critical Writing Response
Responding to a Writer's Questions. In his *History of Polish Literature,* Milosz questions the poet's role during wartime. He asks, ". . . if the screams of the tortured are audible in the poet's room, is not his activity an offense to human suffering? And if the next hour may bring his death and the destruction of his manuscript, should the poet engage in such a pasttime?" In a brief essay, discuss possible answers to Milosz's questions. What larger purpose can poetry, or art in general, serve "in the midst of an all-pervading savagery"?

Pablo Neruda
1904–1973, Chile

Sergio Larrain/Magnum Photos, Inc.

When the Chilean poet Pablo Neruda (pä′blô ne·rōō′də) was a young boy searching for "creaturely things" behind his house, he saw a child's hand poking through a hole in a fence, offering him a toy sheep made of real wool. Thrilled, Neruda raced home to return with his most treasured possession, a fragrant pine cone, which he dropped through the same hole for the unseen friend on the other side. Neruda often related this incident. He saw poetry as a gift that he shared with the world—a gift that always brought something in return.

Neruda became a poet when he was still a teenager in Temuco, a frontier town in the south of Chile. Neruda's real name was Neftalí Ricardo Reyes Basoalto; he adopted his pen name to avoid upsetting his father, a railroad worker, who frowned on his son's poetic ambitions. A romantic, bohemian figure in black clothing and a black cape, Neruda was only twenty years old when he published *Veinte poemas de amor y una canción desesperada* (1924), a collection of love poems that eventually sold two million copies worldwide. In Latin America, lovers learned these poems by heart.

In the United States, Neruda became known primarily as a political poet. His serious involvement with politics began when he was appointed to the diplomatic service. As consul in Argentina, and later in Spain, Neruda became close friends with the poet Federico García Lorca (see page 1228). When fascist forces murdered García Lorca in the Spanish Civil War (1936–1939), Neruda, like many other idealists of the time, joined the Communist party and wrote letters attacking Chile's repressive, anti-Communist government. In 1946, Neruda was accused of treason and forced to flee his homeland.

Neruda returned to Chile in 1952 and began writing *Elemental Odes* (1954), poems in praise of the simple things in life—from socks to onions. In *Cien sonetos de amor*, or *One Hundred Love Sonnets* (1959), Neruda returned to his earlier themes of love and nature. "Poetry is like bread," Neruda said, "and it must be shared by everyone, the men of letters and the peasants, by everyone in our vast, incredible, extraordinary family of man." Neruda was awarded the Nobel Prize in literature in 1971.

MORE ABOUT THE AUTHOR

Very early in Neruda's life, his family moved from La Frontera, a spectacular forested region in Southern Chile, to the more prosaic flatlands of Temuco. But the landscapes of his birthplace clearly live on in Neruda's poetry.

In Temuco, Neruda's early passion for literature was nourished, in part, by Gabriela Mistral, the Nobel laureate, who was at that time head of a local girl's school; she funneled him Russian novels from the school library. Later in life, Neruda would cite these works, along with those of Rimbaud, Baudelaire, and Walt Whitman, as inspirations as great as the Latin American literature he studied in school. (In fact, the pen name *Neruda* is taken from the nineteenth-century Czech poet Jan Neruda.)

In the late 1940s, Neruda plunged into the political life of his country, serving as a senator and an outspoken critic of the president. In 1969, Neruda himself briefly ran for president, before stepping aside in favor of his friend and fellow Marxist, Salvador Allende. A bloody military coup overthrew the Allende government in 1973. Neruda died two weeks later.

ABOUT THE TRANSLATOR

Stephen Tapscott (1948–   ) is a poet and professor of literature at Massachusetts Institute of Technology.

OBJECTIVES

1. *To recognize the place of Pablo Neruda in modern literature, and to analyze two love sonnets by Pablo Neruda*
2. *To identify the poetic usage of figures of speech, including simile, metaphor, and personification*
3. *To explore symbolic images used to portray feelings of love, and to compare Neruda's sonnets with Renaissance love sonnets*

THEMES IN WORLD LITERATURE

People and Nature
"The White Snake," pp. 46–52
Haiku, pp. 572–577
The Power and Pain of Love
New Kingdom Love Lyrics, p. 81
Renaissance Sonnets, pp. 808–810 ∎

PREREADING FOCUS

Background: Neruda's relationship with Matilde Urrutia clearly influenced all of his later work, channeling his abstract vision into one more earthy and concrete. The poems here are also informed by the house the couple shared at Isla Negra. Together, they transformed the small stone house into a magical environment, full of the simple yet beautiful things that populate Neruda's poems: shells, driftwood, wave-polished stones, ship and church bells, glistening pieces of glass.

Now a museum, the house is also filled with whimsical odds and ends that Neruda picked up on his many trips abroad. All of these sensuous, elemental things, juxtaposed as if the house itself were a poem, no doubt touched Neruda's imagination and became symbols for his life, for his love of Matilde, and for the "strong nest" they tried to build together.

Literary Focus: Figures of speech are most powerful when they reveal what is not usually noticed; this effect is often produced by juxtaposing apparently unrelated things. For example, Neruda compares the dawn to a river and then his beloved's hands to a river. Both the dawn and the river may appear silvery or glistening; a woman's hands at night may appear silvery. But the poet also has in mind the way the dawn, the river, and his beloved's hands shimmer in movement, the way they "tremble" with life.

Reader's Guide

SONNETS 49 AND 71

Background

Neruda's ideas about love changed as he grew older. In his early poems, he presents a speaker who seeks and adores women, yet considers them mainly in terms of what they can do for him: provide a temporary refuge from loneliness. When his lovers leave him, the speaker is in despair. *One Hundred Love Sonnets,* the book in which the following two sonnets first appeared, was written more than thirty-five years after Neruda's first love poems. Most of these sonnets celebrate the simple comfort of a stable, monogamous relationship. They are, in fact, written to Matilde Urrutia, Neruda's third wife. Neruda wrote these sonnets while living with Matilde in a house that overlooked the Pacific at Isla Negra, a small fishing village in central Chile. In the book's dedication, Neruda addresses Matilde:

> My beloved wife, . . . I made these sonnets out of wood; I gave them the sound of that opaque pure substance, and that is how they should reach your ears. Walking in forests or on beaches, along hidden lakes, in latitudes sprinkled with ashes, you and I have picked up pieces of pure bark, pieces of wood subject to the comings and goings of water and the weather. Out of such softened relics . . . I built up these lumber piles of love, and with fourteen boards each I built little houses, so that your eyes, which I adore and sing to, might live in them. Now that I have declared the foundations of my love, I surrender this century to you: wooden sonnets that rise only because you gave them life.

Writer's Response

Freewrite your ideas about what love means to a child, to a mature adult, and to an elderly person. How might one's views of love change with age and experience? What does love mean to you?

Literary Focus

A **figure of speech** is a word or phrase that describes one thing in terms of another, very different thing. A figure of speech is not literally true, but it can help us see the world in an imaginative way. Two of the most common figures of speech are **metaphor** and **personification**.

SONNETS
Pablo Neruda
translated by
STEPHEN TAPSCOTT

❘❘ *Look for images that help you see aspects of Matilde in terms*
❘❘ *of the natural world that Neruda so loved.*

Sonnet 49

It's today: all of yesterday dropped away
among the fingers of the light and the sleeping eyes.
Tomorrow will come on its green footsteps;
no one can stop the river of the dawn.

5 No one can stop the river of your hands,
your eyes and their sleepiness, my dearest.
You are the trembling of time, which passes
between the vertical light and the darkening sky.

The sky folds its wings over you,
10 lifting you, carrying you to my arms
with its punctual, mysterious courtesy.

That's why I sing to the day and to the moon,
to the sea, to time, to all the planets,
to your daily voice, to your nocturnal skin.

Scene from the film *Il Postino* (*The Postman*),
in which the postman Mario and his love
Beatrice, whom Mario has courted by reciting
Neruda's poems, celebrate their wedding.
❓ *Why do you think the connection between
poetry and love is so strong?*

TEACHER'S RESOURCES
✔ Review and Response
  Worksheet

1 LITERARY ELEMENT
Repetition: What effect does
the syntactic repetition in
these lines provide? (Possible
responses: It underscores the
inevitable passage of time; it
yokes nature and the poet's
beloved together.)

2 LITERARY ELEMENT
Figures of Speech: When Neruda writes "The sky folds its
wings over you," he is using
implied metaphor. In contrast,
direct metaphor states that one
thing *is* another: "The sky is a
huge bird with wings to protect you."
❓ *Does Neruda use mostly
   implied metaphor or direct
metaphor? Find one example
of each kind of metaphor.*
(Possible answers: He uses
mostly implied metaphor. Example of direct: "You are the
trembling of time." Indirect:
"the river of your hands.")

HUMANITIES CONNECTION

Neruda's love poems are featured in the 1994 Italian film
The Postman (Il Postino), an
adaptation of a novel by Antonio Skármeta. The fictional
story concerns the friendship
between the cosmopolitan
poet Pablo Neruda and a shy,
inarticulate mailman who uses
Neruda's poems to court a local girl. In the process, the
young man discovers the poet
in himself. ∎

3 INTERPRETING

In Sonnet 71, what do you think the speaker means when he describes the heart as "carnivorous"? What is the image here? (Possible response: The heart eats up the rest of the body, or the other human being. The image suggests a cruel, relentless beast.)

4 LITERARY ELEMENT

Mood/Diction. What word would you use to describe the feeling or atmosphere of each sonnet? Find in each sonnet one descriptive detail that conveys that mood. (Possible responses: Sonnet 49—content, as in "I sing to the day and to the moon," or sleepy, as in "sleeping eyes"; Sonnet 71—angry, as in "lunatic city," or sad/disappointed, as in "grief to grief.")

WRITING TO LEARN

Ask students to write their own love poem in which a person is compared to something in nature. Suggest that they focus on grand or large natural forces instead of the small or delicate imagery conventionally used in love poetry. Alternately, students might use Sonnet 71 as a model, and focus on an unusually startling or unexpected image. ■

Miramax (courtesy of Kobal Collection)

Scene from the film *Il Postino* (*The Postman*). Through an unexpected friendship with Pablo Neruda, a shy postman discovers his own creativity and love of language.

In what ways does everyday reality intrude on the ideal of love in Sonnet 71?

Sonnet 71

Love crosses its islands, from grief to grief,
it sets its roots, watered with tears,
and no one—no one—can escape the heart's progress
as it runs, silent and carnivorous.

3

You and I searched for a wide valley, for another planet   5
where the salt wouldn't touch your hair,
where sorrows couldn't grow because of anything I did,
where bread could live and not grow old.

A planet entwined with vistas and foliage,
a plain, a rock, hard and unoccupied: 10
we wanted to build a strong nest

with our own hands, without hurt or harm or speech,
but love was not like that: love was a lunatic city   4
with crowds of people blanching on their porches.

1. Understanding Surrealism. Surrealism is a movement in art and literature that stresses the bizarre associations of the unconscious. To help students understand, show them a surrealistic painting, such as the Magritte painting on page 1144. Ask students to find surrealist elements in Neruda's sonnets. (The metaphors and images often seem to be disconnected, occurring as they do in dreams.) Ask students to choose one of Neruda's poems from the period of his life most influenced by surrealism, and to read it to the class. (See, especially, poems from *Residence on Earth*.)

2. Reading in Spanish. Ask Spanish-speaking students to find and read the sonnets aloud in Spanish. Compare rhythmical qualities, sound effects, and the almost accidental end-rhymes in the Spanish and English versions.

After students have read and discussed the sonnets, have them close their eyes. Tell them you are going to reread the sonnets aloud, while they listen for the dominant images—the ones that speak most strongly to them. Then suggest they choose one of the images, and work in groups to design a cover for *One Hundred Love Sonnets*. They might think about what images, colors, and type styles are usually used for books of love poems.) ■

First Thoughts

One Hundred Love Sonnets is divided into four parts—morning, afternoon, evening, and night—each corresponding to a different stage in a person's life. To what part of the collection do you think each of the sonnets you have just read belongs?

Identifying Facts

1. What view of love does Sonnet 49 present?
2. In Sonnet 71, what has happened to love? How do you explain the change in the speaker's outlook from Sonnet 49?

Interpreting Meanings

1. Identify at least two examples of **personification** and two examples of **metaphor** in Sonnet 49. In these figures of speech, what recurring **images** of the natural world seem important to Neruda? What do these images reveal about the speaker's feelings?
2. How does the change of tense in line 5 of Sonnet 71 affect the meaning of the poem?
3. These sonnets follow the form of the **Italian**, or **Petrarchan**, **sonnet**, though they don't follow its traditional rhyme scheme. Neruda's nontraditional sonnets do, however, sometimes contain the abrupt turns of thought of the classic sonnet. Identify the change, or turn, in each of the sonnets you have read.
4. What do you think the speaker means in Sonnet 71 when he says that "love was a lunatic city / with crowds of people blanching on their porches"? Does this sonnet present a negative view of love, or is the speaker revealing a side of love that has both positive and negative aspects? Explain.
5. Do you think the views of love presented in the two sonnets contradict each other? Why or why not?

Applying Meanings

The critic Stephen Dobyns noted that by the 1960s, in Chile, Neruda's first collection of love poetry was still being "discussed, wondered over, and dreamt with. Despite having been written in the twenties, it seemed of the moment . . . My wife and her friends felt no doubt about what the poems meant. They had no need for critics. The poems were being spoken directly to them." Discuss whether the two sonnets you have read speak directly to you, a student in the present day. Do they reflect contemporary views of romantic love, or are they dated and irrelevant?

Creative Writing Response

Creating a Love Collage. Cupids, flowers, hearts, and the like are common but clichéd symbols of love. Make a collage of images that signify the uniquely personal meaning of love to you. Look through magazines, postcards, clip-art books, wrapping paper, and other sources for nonstereotypical images that reflect your personal feelings about this subject. Draw or paint images, as well. On a separate sheet of paper, explain the meaning behind each of the images you chose.

Critical Writing Response

Comparing and Contrasting Sonnets. Review one of the Renaissance sonnets you have studied (see pages 804–812), and, in a brief essay, compare and contrast it with one of Neruda's sonnets. In your essay, explore these points: **(a)** the form of each sonnet (Petrarchan or Shakespearean); **(b)** the speaker's intention in each sonnet; **(c)** what you learn about the person to whom the sonnet is addressed; **(d)** the theme of the sonnet; **(e)** the poet's use of figures of speech; **(f)** how the views of love presented in the two sonnets differ from each other.

First Thoughts

Answers will vary. (Neruda himself put Sonnet 49 in the afternoon section, Sonnet 71 in the evening section.)

Identifying Facts

1. Gentle; peaceful; natural
2. It has ended or disappointed the speaker.

Interpreting Meanings

1. Possible answers: metaphor—"the river of the dawn," "the sky folds its wings over you"; personification—"Tomorrow will come on its green footsteps," "the fingers of the light." Images of light, nature, water, flight. His beloved permeates his universe.
2. Possible answers: reveals that the love has changed, died, or become less idealistic
3. Sonnet 49: line 12; Sonnet 71: line 13.
4. Answers will vary; love is confusing and ever changing. positive only in the sense that any "perfect" place is too static for love to grow
5. Answers will vary. Possible responses: Yes—one compares love to nature and one to a "lunatic city." No—both relate love to the passage of time.

Applying Meanings

Answers will vary.

Creative Writing Response

Creating a Love Collage. Look for originality of choices.

Critical Writing Response

Comparing and Contrasting Sonnets. Students should include specific details. ■

Pablo Neruda   **1279**

Borges, who was a quiet suburban librarian during much of his literary career, cared little for politics. When the dictator Juan Perón came to power in Argentina in 1946, however, Borges spoke out to protest Perón's practices. Because Borges already had an international audience, the dictator could not silence him. Instead, Perón attempted to discredit and humiliate Borges by firing him from his library post and making him a poultry inspector. Borges, undaunted, continued to speak for the many who could not voice their opposition to unethical government actions. After the Perón regime was toppled in 1955, the new government honored Borges by making him the director of the National Library of Argentina. During the same year, Borges lost his vision to an eye disease. Nevertheless, he continued to write and teach until his death.

Commenting on *El Hacedor* (*The Maker*), from which "Borges and Myself" is taken, Borges said, "Of all the books I have delivered to the presses, none, I think, is as personal as the straggling collection mustered for this hodgepodge, precisely because it abounds in reflections and interpolations. . . ."

Jorge Luis Borges
1899–1986, Argentina

UPI/Bettmann Newsphotos

When he was six years old, Jorge Luis Borges (hôr′he lōō·ēs′ bôr′hes) announced that he intended to become a writer. He began working at his chosen profession immediately: at the age of nine he translated Oscar Wilde's fairy tale "The Happy Prince" into Spanish. Later in his life, Borges credited his father with inspiring his writing career: He felt that his father had made him aware of poetry—of the idea that words could be powerful and symbolic, not just a means of everyday communication.

Borges learned English at an early age from his English-born grandmother, and he devoured her extensive library. He loved the horror stories of Edgar Allan Poe, the adventures of Robert Louis Stevenson, and the exotic Arabic fairy tales in *The Thousand and One Nights* (see page 638). Ironically, Borges first read the great Spanish classics *El Cid* and *Don Quixote* (see pages 703 and 821) in English translations. Later, when he read *Don Quixote* in its original Spanish, he said it sounded like a bad translation!

The Borges family was traveling in Europe when World War I broke out. They took refuge in neutral Switzerland, where Borges attended school and learned to speak three more languages—French, Latin, and German. After the war, the family moved first to Italy, then to Spain, and finally back to Argentina.

Borges began his career as a poet, and he always considered himself a poet first and foremost. In the 1940s, however, Borges turned to experimental prose, writing stories about transparent tigers, wizards who conjure up visions in a bowl of ink, and encyclopedias that do not record events but cause them. The stories in *The Garden of the Forking Paths* (1941) and *El Aleph* (1945) ignore plot and character and most of the usual elements of fiction. They instead blend fact and fantasy in a world of games and riddles, literary mystery, and philosophical inquiry.

It was also during the 1940s that Borges began using one of his most famous images—that of the labyrinth, or maze. Borges used the labyrinth as a metaphor for our journey through life, with all its surprising twists, turns, and dead ends.

OBJECTIVES
1. To recognize the place of Jorge Luis Borges in modern literature and to analyze a prose work by Borges
2. To identify some of the literary uses of the first-person point of view
3. To write a short diary entry in the first person in order to explore various facets of one's identity

Reader's Guide

BORGES AND MYSELF

Background

Borges was interested in philosophical issues, such as the nature of reality and the interplay between the imagined and the real. He was especially interested in how art affects the way we perceive the world. He believed that reality consists not only of what we have actually seen and done, but also of what we have read and what our reading has led us to imagine.

Borges calls the following story "my personal rendering of the old Jekyll-and-Hyde theme, save that in their case the opposition is between good and evil and in my version the opposites are the spectator and the spectacle."

Writer's Response

Writers and artists often feel that they live two very different lives—an imaginative life and a life as a regular person. Think of a writer or artist you have read or heard about. Describe how that person's public image differs from his or her real personality. (For example, Stephen King writes horror stories but lives a peaceful life in the countryside of New England.)

Literary Focus

Borges writes this story from the **first-person point of view**. The **first-person narrator** is the "I" character who tells the story. Generally, when we read a story with a first-person narrator, we feel as if we are listening to a friend, or as if we are reading someone's letters or diary. In this unusual story, the first-person narrator and the "other man" that he is talking about are different aspects of the same person.

PREREADING FOCUS

Background: Critic Victor Lange says that in "Borges and Myself," we find "the classic formulation of [Borges's] conviction that the self is multifarious, that its countless reflections and projections give it reality as well as iridescence. Borges' self confronts his mirror image, and little by little the living Borges yields to the other. . . ." Thus "Borges and Myself" involves the kind of shift in reality that characterizes both magical realism and good science fiction.

Literary Focus: Besides creating an intimate tone, the first-person point of view limits a writer to portraying only those things that the first-person narrator would reasonably be expected to know or notice. For example, the narrator in "Borges and Myself" can see what "Borges" is doing but does not presume to "know" what he is thinking.

HUMANITIES CONNECTION

M. C. Escher (1898–1972) was a Dutch graphic artist whose work featured striking visual illusions. His prints challenge viewers' perceptions by depicting three-dimensional effects that could not actually exist.

❓ *In what sense do you think Borges and Escher share a fascination with the puzzles and mysteries of life?* (Borges is concerned with the mysteries of human personality and experience; Escher with the puzzles of human perception.) ∎

1 LITERARY ELEMENT
First-Person Point of View:
What personal information does the narrator share with readers? (some of the things he likes) How would you describe the tone that these revelations create? (Possible response: a confiding tone)

2 READER'S RESPONSE
Although the narrator says that he can admit that Borges is a good writer, he refers to Borges's "stubborn habit of falsification and exaggerating." These lines sound humorous when the reader realizes that the author is talking about himself. Do you think that Borges intends this piece as a humorous exercise, or do you think that the realization that he is losing himself to "Borges" really upsets him? (Answers will vary.)

BORGES AND MYSELF

Jorge Luis Borges

translated by

N. T. DI GIOVANNI AND JORGE LUIS BORGES

◆ *As you read, notice how the speaker and Borges are different.*

It's to the other man, to Borges, that things happen. I walk along the streets of Buenos Aires, stopping now and then—perhaps out of habit—to look at the arch of an old entranceway or a grill-work gate; of Borges I get news through the mail and glimpse his name among a committee of professors or in a dictionary of biography. I have a taste for hourglasses, maps, eighteenth-century typography, the roots of words, the smell of coffee, and Stevenson's[1] prose; the other man shares these likes, but in a showy way that turns them into stagy mannerisms. It would be an exaggeration to say that we are on bad terms; I live, I let myself live, so that Borges can weave his tales and poems, and

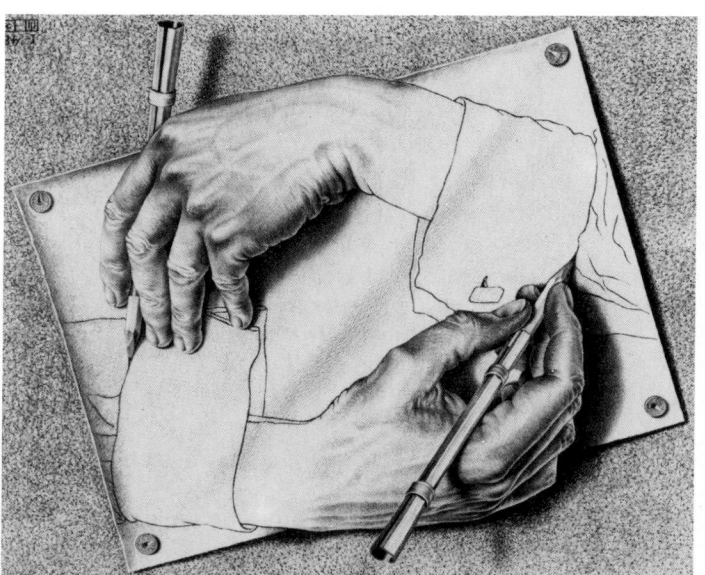

DRAWING HANDS, M. C. ESCHER, 1948.
❓ *Do you think that this drawing aptly reflects Borges's ideas? Why or why not?*

© 1948 M. C. Escher/Cordon Art-Baarn-Holland

those tales and poems are my justification. It is not hard for me to admit that he has managed to write a few worthwhile pages, but these pages cannot save me, perhaps because what is good no longer belongs to anyone—not even the other man—but rather to speech or tradition. In any case, I am

---

1. **Stevenson's:** Robert Louis Stevenson (1850–1894), Scottish writer of adventure novels, poems, and essays.

READING CHECK

1. How does the speaker get news of Borges? (through the mail and in published documents and reference materials)
2. What term does the speaker use to refer to the notion that he and Borges are on bad terms? (an exaggeration)
3. What does the speaker say he can easily admit? (that Borges has written a few worthwhile pages)

4. Where does the speaker recognize more of himself now? (in others' books and in the tuning of a guitar)
5. When, according to the speaker, did he try to rid himself of Borges? (years ago)

RETEACHING

To reteach "Borges and Myself," have students create portraits, either realistic or symbolic, of Borges's two selves. Before they begin, they should choose the facial expressions each self will wear, the activities each self will be engaged in, and the background surroundings that will frame each portrait. Remind students to base their decisions on details, ideas, or themes from the selection.

fated to become lost once and for all, and only some moment of myself will survive in the other man. Little by little, I have been surrendering everything to him, even though I have evidence of his stubborn habit of falsification and exaggerating. Spinoza[2] held that all things try to keep on being themselves; a stone wants to be a stone and the tiger, a tiger. I shall remain in Borges, not in myself (if it is so that I am someone), but I recognize myself less in his books than in those of others or than in the laborious tuning of a guitar. Years ago, I tried ridding myself of him and I went from myths of the outlying slums of the city to games with time and infinity, but those games are now part of Borges and I will have to turn to other things. And so, my life is a running away, and I lose everything and everything is left to oblivion or to the other man.

Which of us is writing this page I don't know.

---

2. **Spinoza:** Baruch Spinoza (1632–1677), Dutch philosopher.

First Thoughts

Who is the speaker in this "story"? How is he different from "Borges"?

Identifying Facts

1. According to the speaker, to whom do "things happen"?
2. According to the speaker, what is the justification for his life?
3. What is the speaker "fated" to become?
4. What does the speaker "have evidence" of?
5. At the end, what is it that the speaker does not know?

Interpreting Meanings

1. What distinction does the speaker make between "Borges" and "myself"? Why would "Borges" seem "showy" or "stagy"?
2. What things does the speaker like? What does he mean when he says that "Borges" turns these things into "stagy mannerisms"?
3. According to the speaker, "Borges's" work does not belong to him, but to "speech or tradition." What do you think this means?

Applying Meanings

Do you think most people can feel like two different people? If so, when and why might someone feel like this?

Creative Writing Response

Letting a "Double" Speak. Think about the different sides of your personality. What part of your personality comes out more strongly at school? at home? when you are alone? Write a short diary entry following the model of "Borges and Myself." The "I" character is your private side that others do not often see. The character with your name is the public part of your personality. You may have the "I" character comment on the daily activities of the other character.

Before you begin writing you may want to fill out a chart like this:

Characteristics I Show in Public	How I Really Am

ANSWERS

First Thoughts
Answers will vary.

Identifying Facts
1. the other man, Borges
2. the things that Borges writes
3. lost
4. Borges's habit of falsification and exaggeration
5. which one is writing the page

Interpreting Meanings
1. Possible response: "Borges" seems showy because he projects the public persona, the famous author. "Myself" is the private self.
2. hourglasses, maps, eighteenth-century typography, etymology, the smell of coffee, and Stevenson's prose. These tastes seem stagy in "Borges" because he displays them publicly.
3. Memorable literary works provoke readers to respond to them, enriching the universe of language and ideas. In this sense, literary works belong to the language or the literary tradition, not to any individual.

Applying Meanings
Answers will vary.

Creative Writing Response
Letting a "Double" Speak.
Diary entries should be written in the first person and should reveal the characteristics of both the public and the private persona. The narrator's point of view should remain consistent throughout the entry. ■

Scripting a Television Drama. Guide students in scripting, as for a television drama, a dialogue between "Borges" and "myself." Have them write brief introductory descriptions of both the characters and the setting. As they think about the characters' lines, remind them that they must include stage directions for the actors and specifications for the camera (*zoom, pan, close up*, and so forth). Encourage the class to brainstorm in order to devise a memorable ending for the dialogue. If a videocamera is available, let them film their enactment of the drama.

CLOSURE

Remind students that one of Borges's trademarks is the image of a maze or labyrinth to represent life. In a labyrinth it is easy to become lost and confused. Although "Borges and Myself" does not contain the labyrinth imagery, ask students to discuss how its theme reflects Borges's concerns. ■

WRITING TO LEARN

Write a poem, a diary entry, or a monologue in which the narrator is a woman in your family or in your circle of acquaintances. The narrator, who was born during the first two or three decades of the twentieth century, will talk about her public and private selves, as de Burgos and Borges do.

Begin by interviewing or recalling details about the narrator. Decide whether she will speak as a child, a teenager, a young adult, a middle-aged adult, or an older person. You may wish to research the history of women's rights in this country in order to learn what the position of women was at various stages of the narrator's life.

When you have finished, share your work with the class. Discuss what you have learned from the assignment. ■

SEEING CONNECTIONS

The Divided Self

Modernism is a twentieth-century literary movement that began in Europe. Influenced by new ideas in psychology, the modernists explored the split between the artist's social and private selves, seeing the artist as a lonely figure struggling in an insensitive world.

The Puerto Rican poet Julia de Burgos (hōōl'ē·ə dā bōōr'gôs) (1914–1953), as both a woman and an artist, was keenly aware of the struggle to remain faithful to her art in the face of society's prejudices and pressures. During her short lifetime, she took part in the fierce controversy over Puerto Rican independence. Because her political views and feminist leanings were not popular, she had difficulty supporting herself through her writing, and she ultimately died in poverty at the age of thirty-nine.

The following poem by de Burgos, like "Borges and Myself," explores the idea that the artist's everyday self is divided from his or her creative self. How is de Burgos's view of this division similar to Borges's? How is it different?

To Julia de Burgos
Julia de Burgos
translated by
Grace Schulman

The people are saying that I am your enemy,
That in poetry I give you to the world.

They lie, Julia de Burgos. They lie, Julia de Burgos.
The voice that rises in my verses is not your voice: it is my voice;
5 For you are the clothing and I am the essence;
Between us lies the deepest abyss.

You are the bloodless doll of social lies
And I the virile spark of human truth;

You are the honey of courtly hypocrisy; not I—
10 I bare my heart in all my poems.

You, like your world, are selfish; not I—
I gamble everything to be what I am.

You are only the serious lady. Señora. Doña[1] Julia.
Not I. I am life. I am strength. I am woman.

15 You belong to your husband, your master. Not I:
I belong to nobody or to all, for to all, to all
I give myself in my pure feelings and thoughts.

You curl your hair and paint your face. Not I:
I am curled by the wind, painted by the sun.

20 You are the lady of the house, resigned, submissive,
Tied to the bigotry of men. Not I:
I am Rocinante,[2] bolting free, wildly
Snuffling the horizons of the justice of God.

---

1. **Doña** (dô'nyä): a Spanish title of respect given to a woman, equivalent to "Lady" or "Madam."
2. **Rocinante** (rō'sē·nän'tä): the horse that carried Don Quixote on his quests (see page 823).

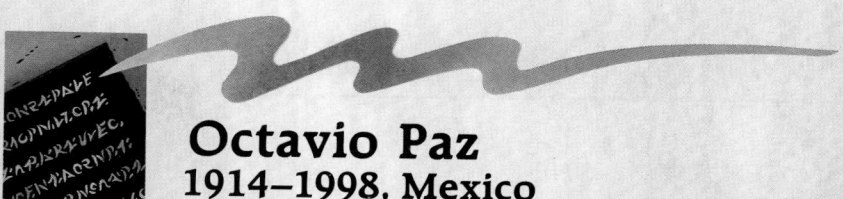

Octavio Paz
1914–1998, Mexico

Octavio Paz and his wife, María José.

Octavio Paz (ôk·tä′vyô päs) was born in Mexico City into a family he called "typically Mexican"—part Spanish, part Indian, and not very wealthy. Paz grew up in his grandfather's home, which he remembered as an old house that was falling apart, but that had a huge, overgrown garden and one large room full of books. Paz read all the books in his grandfather's library and enjoyed his crumbling surroundings.

Paz's poetic talents were recognized when he was very young. His first volume of poetry, *Forest Moon* (1933), was published just after he graduated from the National University of Mexico. By the time his next volume was published in 1937, he was well on his way to literary celebrity. Diplomatic appointments took Paz to Paris, the Far East, and India. An enthusiastic scholar, Paz studied the literature and history of every nation he visited. In form, Paz's poetry often shows the influence of European modernist or Oriental verse, but his subjects and imagery are usually rooted in the sand, stones, and soil of the Mexican landscape. With these simple images, Paz often explores difficult philosophical concepts, such as the nature of truth and reality. For example, the subject of his longest poem, *Sun Stone* (1957), is the carved stone disc that the ancient Aztecs used as their calendar. The poem deals with the complex ideas of circular time and the interrelatedness of all things. Paz is perhaps best known for his literary essays, such as those collected in *The Labyrinth of Solitude*, which deals with the character of the Mexican people.

In accepting the 1990 Nobel Prize for literature, Octavio Paz recalled his early years as a writer. He claimed that he had no idea then why he wrote his poems—he only knew that he felt a deep need to write them. Only later did he come to understand that his poems were his passage to the present, his way of connecting himself to his place and to the modern world. And indeed, as one of the most influential poets and essayists in the world, Octavio Paz truly became a man of his century.

MORE ABOUT THE AUTHOR

Like his grandfather, a novelist and journalist who was an early champion of Indian rights, Octavio Paz spoke out against injustice and oppression. In the late 1960s he ended his diplomatic career in protest over the Mexican government's treatment of student activists; in recent decades he criticized foreign intervention in Central America.

In his book-length essay *The Labyrinth of Solitude* (1950), a famous study of the Mexican psyche, Paz observed that revolutions in Mexico have proved to be counterproductive. The essay also helped to introduce the world to the term *machismo,* an attitude Paz viewed with distaste.

Paz founded several journals in his homeland and held teaching posts at Harvard University and Cambridge University in England. A volume of his *Collected Poems* was published in English in 1987. His essays on modern poetry were collected in *The Other Voice* (1991). Among his many admirers is the Mexican author Carlos Fuentes, who once called Octavio Paz Mexico's greatest living writer.

ABOUT THE TRANSLATOR

A noted poet in his own right, Mark Strand served as the fourth poet laureate of the United States from 1990 to 1991. He has translated poems from Spanish, Italian, and Quechua, the language of the Inca.

OBJECTIVES

1. To interpret a modern Mexican poem
2. To identify personification
3. To write a poem or a paragraph in which an aspect of nature is personified

PREREADING FOCUS

Background: Explain the meaning of the word *cycle* ("a recurring time period or sequence of events"), and discuss examples from nature. Point out that history, too, has its cycles as civilizations rise and fall. In Mexico, for example, the great Olmec civilization (about 1200 to 100 B.C.) was superseded by the highly advanced Mayan civilization (A.D. 250 to 900). In about 900, the Mayan empire fell to the Toltecs, whose empire flourished until about 1200. It then fell to the Aztecs, who were conquered by the Spanish in 1521. About 300 years later, the Mexican people declared their independence from Spain.

Writer's Response: Lead students to see that the cyclical patterns in Mexico's history involve far longer time periods than the cycle of the changing seasons or the life cycle of a human being. Encourage students to identify cycles from nature that involve a long sweep of time. Possibilities include the life cycle of a mountain, a river, a rock, or a species. Some students may choose to describe these longer cycles in their paragraphs.

Literary Focus: Point out that personification is one of the most evocative forms of figurative language. Ask students why they think poets use personification. (Possible response: Readers understand such comparisons because they can identify with the human feelings involved.)

Reader's Guide

WIND AND WATER AND STONE

Background

The cycles of Mexico's social/political history and of its natural history have inspired many of Paz's poems, including the one you are about to read. Much of Mexico is dry, rocky, and sparsely forested. The effects of wind and water are easily visible in this landscape, as certain areas are worn down and other areas are built up. Mexico's great civilizations have followed similar patterns of breaking down and building up. During the Classic period, from about A.D. 250 until the 900s, the Maya civilization (see page 17) thrived. Then came the Toltec empire, which was at its peak from 900 to about 1200. Finally, the great Aztec empire arose. Centered at Tenochtitlán (now Mexico City), which means "stone rising in water," the Aztec empire fell to the Spanish conquerors early in the sixteenth century. Paz singles out the Spaniards' conquest of the Indians as the moment that the true Mexico became isolated and obscured. Mexico remained a colony of Spain until 1821, when a revolution won the new nation its independence.

Writer's Response

Think about some of the cycles in the world—the changing seasons, the water cycle, the human life cycle. Choose a cycle you have observed and write a paragraph describing it. Can you describe it in terms of birth, growth, maturity, decay, death, and rebirth?

Literary Focus

Personification is a figure of speech in which something nonhuman is given human characteristics. For example, if you say "The breeze whispered through the trees," you are personifying the breeze. A breeze can't really whisper; only a human being can. If you say "The night is lonely," you are personifying the night, an inanimate or nonliving thing, by giving it feelings which it really doesn't have. Personification is an important element in the following poem by Paz.

Transitive and Intransitive Verbs

An action verb is transitive if it has a direct object (a noun or a pronoun that receives the verb's action). It is intransitive if it does not have a direct object.

Transitive: I <u>stopped</u> him on Main Street. (*Him* is the direct object.)

Intransitive: I <u>stopped</u> on Main Street.

Reading and Speaking. Have volunteers state whether each action verb in the poem is transitive or intransitive. For each transitive verb, students should identify the direct object. (*hollowed*, trans., *stone; dispersed*, trans., *water; stopped*, trans., *wind; sculpted*, trans., *stone; runs*, intrans.; *sings*, intrans.; *murmurs*, intrans.; *pass*, intrans.; *disappear*, intrans.) ∎

WIND AND WATER AND STONE

Octavio Paz

translated by
MARK STRAND

⫯ *As you read the poem, make a note of the words Paz uses to personify the wind, water, and stone.*

for Roger Caillois[1]

The water hollowed the stone,
the wind dispersed the water,
the stone stopped the wind.
Water and wind and stone.

5   The wind sculpted the stone,
the stone is a cup of water,
the water runs off and is wind.
Stone and wind and water.

The wind sings in its turnings,
10   the water murmurs as it goes,
the motionless stone is quiet.
Wind and water and stone.

One is the other, and is neither:
among their empty names
15   they pass and disappear,
water and stone and wind.

Ruins of the Mayan pyramid "el Castillo," Mexico.

❓ *Does the parallelism of this poem remind you of other poems or stories you have read in this book? Explain.*

1. **Roger Caillois** (rō·zhä' kī·wä'): French writer (1913–1978) who suggested that people were inspired to begin writing when they saw the natural markings on stones.

Robert Frerck/Woodfin Camp & Associates

TEACHER'S RESOURCES

↙ Review and Response Worksheet

LITERARY ELEMENTS

Diction/Theme: What adjective would you use to describe the poem's diction, or word choice? (informal, childlike, simple) What adjective would you use to describe its theme or ideas? (complex, profound)

READER'S RESPONSE

Does this poem remind you of any children's games or rhymes? If so, name one. (Possible responses: the game of paper/scissors/stone; "This Is the House That Jack Built") Would you say that this poem shows Paz's ability to use simple images to explore complex ideas? Explain. (Students should support their opinions by citing details from "Wind and Water and Stone" that support their interpretations of the poem.)

LITERARY ELEMENT

Repetition: Point out to students that each stanza ends with the same words in a different order. How does this repetition reinforce the theme of the poem? (Possible response: Wind, water, and stone are different stages in one natural cycle, and the variation in their order reveals their interconnectedness.)

1. **Illustrating a Science Report.** Encourage students to research and report on one of the three natural processes alluded to in the poem: water erosion, wind erosion, and the evaporation of water. Visual aids such as charts, posters, or even the presentation of simple experiments can be used to enhance students' written and oral reports.

2. **Researching a Symbol.** Students may be interested in researching the significance of stone in ancient Mexican civilizations and in using that information to understand Paz's use of stone imagery in this and other poems. Additional readings should include at least two other short poems by Paz and perhaps portions of his long poem *Sun Stone*.

CLOSURE

Have students attempt to state in one sentence what the poem suggests about time and change. (Possible response: Over time, the forces of nature change everything into something else.) What positive and negative implications might the poem have for humans? (Although human life is transitory, our demise is merely a transformation into something else.) ■

ANSWERS

First Thoughts
Students should support their interpretations by citing details from the poem and by drawing on their knowledge.

Identifying Facts
1. hollows the stone. disperses the water. stops the wind
2. a cup. wind
3. It is quiet. They disappear.

Interpreting Meanings
1. water erosion, wind erosion, and the evaporation of surface water
2. Yes, because the meaning "stone rising in water" is evoked by the poem's imagery. The stone is probably a symbol of Mexican civilization and of all other civilizations as well.
3. The wind sculpts and sings, the water murmurs, and the stone is quiet.
4. They are interrelated. They seem to die or disappear but, in reality, only change their form.
5. The poem suggests that human life and human civilizations are transitory but also cyclical.

Applying Meanings
Students should cite examples to support their opinions.

Creative Writing Response
Personifying Nature. Poems or paragraphs should contain at least three examples of personification. ■

First Thoughts
What deeper meanings can you see in this description of the way wind, water, and stone change and eventually disappear to be transformed into something else?

Identifying Facts
1. What does the water do in stanza 1? What does the wind do? the stone?
2. In stanza 2, what does the stone become when the wind sculpts it? What does the water become after it runs off?
3. In stanza 3, how is the stone different from the wind and water? What eventually happens to the wind and water and stone in stanza 4?

Interpreting Meanings
1. To what three scientific or natural processes do lines 1, 5, and 7 refer?
2. Given what you learned about the ancient meaning of the name *Tenochtitlán* in the Background (see page 1286), do you think the stone in this poem is more than a mere stone? Explain your answer.
3. How are the wind, water, and stone **personified** in stanzas 2 and 3?
4. What does the poem suggest about the relationship of all things in nature? What does the last stanza suggest about the ability of natural things to endure?

5. In what sense might the poem actually be about human beings or human civilizations?

Applying Meanings
Do you see human life and human civilizations as moving in cycles that are constantly repeated? In other words, does everything pass through stages of birth, growth, maturity, decay, death, rebirth, and so on? Discuss your response to Paz's ideas.

Creative Writing Response
Personifying Nature. Write a poem or paragraph in which you **personify** some element of nature, such as a tree, a flower, an animal, or the sun, moon, stars, or sea.

After you have found a subject, fill out a chart like the one below until you are satisfied with your personification. Then use the chart as you write your paragraph or poem.

Subject: Sunset

Detail	Human Quality
Appearance	Dressed in a dusky rose gown
Actions	Lingered like a lover
Feelings	Sadly ducked under the horizon

Gabriel García Márquez
b. 1928, Colombia

AP/Wide World Photos

Gabriel García Márquez (gär·sē'ä mär'kes) recalls that when he was nineteen and reading Franz Kafka's novella *The Metamorphosis* (see page 1154), he suddenly realized that the story's strangeness reminded him of tales his grandmother used to tell him. The surrealistic fiction of Kafka and the imaginative stories told by ordinary Latin Americans were to become major influences on García Márquez's fiction. But it was the second factor, the rich storytelling traditions and the unique imaginative fantasies of Latin America, that he found most valuable.

In his acceptance speech for the Nobel Prize for literature in 1982, García Márquez deplored the way Latin Americans ignore their own heritage and accept the hand-me-downs of European history and culture. He told the audience a story about a statue that stands in the main square of a Central American capital city. The statue is meant to represent the nation's president, but it is in fact a likeness of one of Napoleon's commanders that was purchased from a warehouse of secondhand sculpture in Paris. It is this kind of wholesale borrowing from the traditions of Europe that García Márquez dislikes. He wants Latin Americans to write from their own experience, with its unique blend of rituals and beliefs.

García Márquez spent the first eight years of his life with his grandparents in the small village of Aracataca, just off Colombia's northern Caribbean coast. He re-created this village, calling it Macondo, in his first short novel, *Leaf Storm* (1955), and later in his great novel *One Hundred Years of Solitude* (1967). Although Macondo is little more than a railway station set in a swampy wilderness, it seems that nearly anything that could possibly happen happens there—from the merely strange to the supernatural. With the publication of *One Hundred Years of Solitude* in English in 1970, the technique now called **magic realism** came to international attention. In García Márquez's fiction, as in that of a number of other Latin American authors, the reader is never certain about what is "real" and what is "fantasy."

OBJECTIVES
1. *To analyze the mythic implications of a short story*
2. *To recognize the characteristics of magic realism*
3. *To creatively change a story's premise, and to write an essay analyzing the use of fantastic and realistic elements*

THEMES IN WORLD LITERATURE

Transformations
"Green Willow," pp. 40–45
The Tempest, pp. 839–932
From *The Metamorphosis*, pp. 1154–1194

What Is a Hero?
"Rama and Ravana in Battle" from the *Ramayana*, pp. 484–494
From the *Song of Roland*, pp. 692–702 ■

PREREADING FOCUS

Background: Modern writers often strive to lend a mythic element to their fiction. Such an attempt can be seen in this story in García Márquez's reference to the sirens of the *Odyssey*. Similarities between Esteban and the Aztec god Quetzalcoatl may also be implied. According to myth, Quetzalcoatl, who disappeared into the sea, reappears periodically at times of impending revolutionary change. His statue shows him adorned with snail shells and flowers.

Literary Focus: By infusing real events with magical qualities, García Márquez illuminates the wonder and strangeness in life; and by using a conversational tone, he makes the marvelous credible. In *One Hundred Years of Solitude*, a young man dies. His blood runs through the streets, into his parents' house, and carefully around the rugs, finally stopping at his mother's feet. García Márquez's narration of these fantastic events in a matter-of-fact journalistic style helps readers recognize the mythic potential in events that evoke intense human emotions.

Other important writers of magic realism include Isabel Allende (Chile), Mario Vargas Llosa (Peru), Salman Rushdie (India/Britain), and Jorge Amado (Brazil).

Reader's Guide

THE HANDSOMEST DROWNED MAN IN THE WORLD

Background

"The Handsomest Drowned Man in the World" has many characteristics of **myth**: it features a superhuman character, supernatural events, and includes a marvelous **metamorphosis**, or transformation. This so-called "tale for children" is also enriched by **allusions** that connect it with Homer's *Odyssey*, the epic story of another "superman" who also washes ashore from the sea. Like a mythic hero, Esteban arrives mysteriously and, even though he is dead, soon becomes an important part of the villagers' lives. The story is not about Esteban, however—it is about the villagers, whose imaginations are fired by this bizarre gift from the sea.

Writer's Response

Since the village in which this story is set is on the edge of the sea, drownings would not be unusual. Stop after you finish the first two paragraphs of the story. Then freewrite your responses to the scene. Is there any hint in these opening paragraphs that the story won't be a realistic tale about a drowning?

Literary Focus

Magic realism, a literary style that was born in Latin America and has since been imitated by writers the world over, combines incredible events with realistic details and relates them all in a matter-of-fact tone. The term *magic realism* (*lo real maravilloso*) was coined in 1949 by the Cuban novelist, essayist, and musicologist Alejo Carpentier. He used the term to describe a blurring of the lines that usually separate what seems "real" to the reader from what seems imagined or "unreal" to the same reader. Carpentier believed that by incorporating magic, myth, imagination, and religion into literature, we can expand our rigid concept of "reality."

THE HANDSOMEST DROWNED MAN IN THE WORLD

Gabriel García Márquez

translated by
GREGORY RABASSA

*García Márquez subtitles this story "A Tale for Children," even though it is more complex than an ordinary children's tale. In what sense must the reader become a child to accept and respond to the **magic realism** of the story?*

Pre-Columbian gold mask. *Archaeologists believe this may have been a funerary mask.*

George Holton/Photo Researchers, Inc.

The first children who saw the dark and slinky bulge approaching through the sea let themselves think it was an enemy ship. Then they saw it had no flags or masts and they thought it was a whale. But when it was washed up on the beach, they removed the clumps of seaweed, the jellyfish tentacles, and the remains of fish and flotsam, and only then did they see that it was a drowned man.

They had been playing with him all afternoon, burying him in the sand and digging him up again, when someone chanced to see them and spread the alarm in the village. The men who carried him to the nearest house noticed that he weighed more than any dead man they had ever known, almost as much as a horse, and they said to each other that maybe he'd been floating too long and the water had got into his bones. When they laid him on the floor they said he'd been taller than all other men because there was barely enough room for him in the

1 GUIDED READING

Finding the Main Idea: How do the descriptions show the drowned man as more than an ordinary human being? (He is very large and is encrusted with mud and scales.)

1 COMPARING LITERATURE

Compare the description of the drowned man with the song "Full fathom five" in *The Tempest*, page 863. (In both works, drowned corpses are described as having been transformed.)

2 LITERARY ELEMENT

Magic Realism: The villagers simply have to look at each other to see that they are all there. Is this something that would normally happen? (No; the villagers would know the corpse wasn't one of them by looking at it, not at each other.) This device is typical of magic realism: events usually do not, as in fantasy, defy the laws of nature, but they do seem bizarre or enchanted.

> **haggard** (hag'ərd): gaunt, having a wasted look

■ HUMANITIES CONNECTION

Quilting is often a communal folk art; the women socialize while they work.

❷ *How do the women in the story show the connection between communal work and socializing in traditional cultures?* (They gather to sew for the dead man and to discuss the meaning of his arrival.) ■

house, but they thought that maybe the ability to keep on growing after death was part of the nature of certain drowned men. He had the smell of the sea about him and only his shape gave one to suppose that it was the corpse of a human being, because the skin was covered with a crust of mud and scales.

They did not even have to clean off his face to know that the dead man was a stranger. The village was made up of only twenty-odd wooden houses that had stone courtyards with no flowers and which were spread about on the end of a desertlike cape. There was so little land that mothers always went about with the fear that the wind would carry off their children, and the few dead that the years had caused among them had to be thrown off the cliffs. But the sea was calm and bountiful and all the men fit into seven boats. So when they found the drowned man they simply had to look at one another to see that they were all there.

That night they did not go out to work at sea. While the men went to find out if anyone was missing in neighboring villages, the women stayed behind to care for the drowned man. They took the mud off with grass swabs, they removed the underwater stones entangled in his hair, and they scraped the crust off with tools used for scaling fish. As they were doing that they noticed that the vegetation on him came from faraway oceans and deep water and that his clothes were in tatters, as if he had sailed through labyrinths of coral. They noticed, too, that he bore his death with pride, for he did not have the lonely look of other drowned men who came out of the sea or that <u>haggard</u>, needy look of men who drowned in rivers. But only when they finished cleaning him off did they become aware of the kind of man he was, and it left

Quilt from Cartagena, Colombia.
❷ *Do you find the villagers' reaction to the discovery of the corpse strange? Why or why not?*

Robert Frerck/Woodfin Camp & Associates

them breathless. Not only was he the tallest, strongest, most virile, and best built man they had ever seen, but even though they were looking at him there was no room for him in their imagination.

They could not find a bed in the village large enough to lay him on, nor was there a table solid enough to use for his wake. The tallest men's holiday pants would not fit him, not the fattest ones' Sunday shirts, nor the shoes of the one with the biggest feet. Fascinated by his huge size and his beauty, the women then decided to make him some pants from a large piece of sail and a shirt from some bridal brabant linen[1] so that he could continue through his death with dignity. As they sewed, sitting in a circle and gazing at the corpse between stitches, it seemed to them that the wind had never been so steady nor the sea so restless as on that night, and they supposed that the change had something to do with the dead man. They thought that if that magnificent man had lived in the village, his house would have had the widest doors, the highest ceiling, and the strongest floor, his bedstead would have been made from a midship frame held together by iron bolts, and his wife would have been the happiest woman. They thought that he would have had so much authority that he could have drawn fish out of the sea simply by calling their names and that he would have put so much work into his land that springs would have burst forth from among the rocks so that he would have been able to plant flowers on the cliffs. They secretly compared him to their own men, thinking that for all their lives theirs were incapable of doing what he could do in one night, and they ended up dismissing them deep in their hearts as the weakest, meanest, and most useless creatures on earth. They were wandering through that maze of fantasy when the oldest woman, who as the oldest had looked upon the drowned man with more compassion than passion, sighed:

"He has the face of someone called Esteban."[2]

It was true. Most of them had only to take another look at him to see that he could not have any other name. The more stubborn among them, who were the youngest, still lived for a few hours with the illusion that when they put his clothes on and he lay among the flowers in patent leather shoes his name might be Lautaro.[3] But it was a vain illusion. There had not been enough canvas, the poorly cut and worse sewn pants were too tight, and the hidden strength of his heart popped the buttons on his shirt. After midnight the whistling of the wind died down and the sea fell into its Wednesday drowsiness. The silence put an end to any last doubts: he was Esteban. The women who had dressed him, who had combed his hair, had cut his nails and shaved him, were unable to hold back a shudder of pity when they had to resign themselves to his being dragged along the ground. It was then that they understood how unhappy he must have been with that huge body since it bothered him even after death. They could see him in life, condemned to going through doors sideways, cracking his head on crossbeams, remaining on his feet during visits, not knowing what to do with his soft, pink, sea-lion hands while the lady of the house looked for her most resistant chair and begged him, frightened to death, sit here, Esteban, please, and he, leaning against the wall, smiling, don't bother, ma'am, I'm fine where I am, his heels raw and his back roasted from having done the same thing so

1. **brabant** (brə·bant') **linen:** linen from Brabant, an area in Holland and Belgium known for its fine lace and cloth.

2. **Esteban** (es·te'bän): "Stephen" (Spanish); in Christian tradition, Stephen was the first martyr. He was said to have been stoned to death for his beliefs.

3. **Lautaro** (lou·tär'o)

7 COMPARING AND CONTRASTING

Contrast the way the men feel about Esteban to the way the women feel about him. (The women create romantic fantasies about him and claim him for the village; the men, annoyed, see him as a nuisance.) Why do you think the men are bothered by the women's reactions? (Possible responses: They are jealous; they sense the insult to themselves.)

8 LITERARY ELEMENT

Humor: How does the narrator infuse humor into the description of the funeral procession? (The women scurry around like startled hens, piling protective sea charms on a man who is already dead, while the men grumble.)

9 GUIDED READING

Identifying Details: Who speaks the italicized lines? (the men)

10 CULTURAL BACKGROUND

By mentioning Sir Walter Raleigh, astrolabes, and blunderbusses, García Márquez implies the colonial history of South America.

many times whenever he paid a visit, don't bother, ma'am, I'm fine where I am, just to avoid the embarrassment of breaking up the chair, and never knowing perhaps that the ones who said don't go, Esteban, at least wait till the coffee's ready, were the ones who later on would whisper the big boob finally left, how nice, the handsome fool has gone. That was what the women were thinking beside the body a little before dawn. Later, when they covered his face with a handkerchief so that the light would not bother him, he looked so forever dead, so defenseless, so much like their men that the first furrows of tears opened in their hearts. It was one of the younger ones who began the weeping. The others, coming to, went from sighs to wails, and the more they sobbed the more they felt like weeping, because the drowned man was becoming all the more Esteban for them, and so they wept so much, for he was the most destitute, most peaceful, and most obliging man on earth, poor Esteban. So when the men returned with the news that the drowned man was not from the neighboring villages either, the women felt an opening of jubilation in the midst of their tears.

7 "Praise the Lord," they sighed, "he's ours!"

The men thought the fuss was only womanish frivolity. Fatigued because of the difficult nighttime inquiries, all they wanted was to get rid of the bother of the newcomer once and for all before the sun grew strong on that arid, windless day. They improvised a litter with the remains of foremasts and gaffs,[4] tying it together with rigging so that it would bear the weight of the body until they reached the cliffs. They wanted to tie the anchor from a cargo ship to him so that he would sink easily into the deepest waves,

where fish are blind and divers die of nostalgia, and bad currents would not bring him back to shore, as had happened with other bodies. But the more they hurried, the more the women thought of ways to waste time. **8** They walked about like startled hens, pecking with the sea charms[5] on their breasts, some interfering on one side to put a scapular[6] of the good wind on the drowned man, some on the other side to put a wrist compass on him, and after a great deal of **9** *get away from there, woman, stay out of the way, look, you almost made me fall on top of the dead man,* the men began to feel mistrust in their livers and started grumbling about why so many main-altar decorations for a stranger, because no matter how many nails and holy-water jars he had on him, the sharks would chew him all the same, but the women kept piling on their junk relics, running back and forth, stumbling, while they released in sighs what they did not in tears, so that the men finally exploded with *since when has there ever been such a fuss over a drifting corpse, a drowned nobody, a piece of cold Wednesday meat.*[7] One of the women, mortified by so much lack of care, then removed the handkerchief from the dead man's face and the men were left breathless, too.

He was Esteban. It was not necessary to **10** repeat it for them to recognize him. If they had been told Sir Walter Raleigh, even they might have been impressed with his gringo accent, the macaw on his shoulder, his cannibal-killing blunderbuss, but there could

---

4. **gaffs:** poles supporting a sail.

5. **sea charms:** magic charms that supposedly protect the wearer from dangers at sea.

6. **scapular** (skap′yə·lər): holy images on a string, worn under the clothes as a mark of religious devotion.

7. **Wednesday meat:** meat left over from Sunday dinner.

be only one Esteban in the world and there he was, stretched out like a sperm whale, shoeless, wearing the pants of an undersized child, and with those stony nails that had to be cut with a knife. They only had to take the handkerchief off his face to see that he was ashamed, that it was not his fault that he was so big or so heavy or so handsome, and if he had known that this was going to happen, he would have looked for a more discreet place to drown in, seriously, I even would have tied the anchor off a galleon around my neck and staggered off a cliff like someone who doesn't like things in order not to be upsetting people now with this Wednesday dead body, as you people say, in order not to be bothering anyone with this filthy piece of cold meat that doesn't have anything to do with me. There was so much truth in his manner that even the most mistrustful men, the ones who felt the bitterness of endless nights at sea fearing that their women would tire of dreaming about them and begin to dream of drowned men, even they and others who were harder still shuddered in the marrow of their bones at Esteban's sincerity.

That was how they came to hold the most splendid funeral they could conceive of for an abandoned drowned man. Some women who had gone to get flowers in the neighboring villages returned with other women who could not believe what they had been told, and those women went back for more flowers when they saw the dead man, and they brought more and more until there were so many flowers and so many people that it was hard to walk about. At the final moment it pained them to return him to the waters as an orphan and they chose a father and mother from among the best people, and aunts and uncles and cousins, so that through him all the inhabitants of the village became kinsmen. Some sailors who heard the weeping from a distance went off course, and people heard of one who had himself tied to the mainmast, remembering ancient fables about sirens.[8] While they fought for the privilege of carrying him on their shoulders along the steep escarpment by the cliffs, men and women became aware for the first time of the desolation of their streets, the dryness of their courtyards, the narrowness of their dreams as they faced the splendor and beauty of their drowned man. They let him go without an anchor so that he could come back if he wished and whenever he wished, and they all held their breath for the fraction of centuries the body took to fall into the abyss. They did not need to look at one another to realize that they were no longer all present, that they would never be. But they also knew that everything would be different from then on, that their houses would have wider doors, higher ceilings, and stronger floors so that Esteban's memory could go everywhere without bumping into beams and so that no one in the future would dare whisper the big boob finally died, too bad, the handsome fool has finally died, because they were going to paint their house fronts gay colors to make Esteban's memory eternal and they were going to break their backs digging for springs among the stones and planting flowers on the cliffs so that in future years at dawn the passengers on great liners would awaken, suffocated by the smell

8. **sirens:** in Greek mythology, beautiful but destructive creatures, half-woman and half-bird, whose seductive songs lured sailors to turn their ships onto the rocky coasts; Odysseus, hero of Homer's *Odyssey*, filled his crew's ears with wax so that they could pass the sirens safely. But Odysseus wanted to hear their songs. He had the crew tie him to the ship's mast so that he could listen to the sirens' songs yet not turn the boat onto the rocks.

11 LITERARY ELEMENT
Point of View: Have a student read the sentence beginning, "They only had to take . . ." to highlight the shift in point of view.

12 INTERPRETING
The narrator describes the "truth in [Esteban's] manner" and his "sincerity." Is this an objective description? (No, it is part of the villagers' fantasy.) Why do you think they perceive Esteban in this way? (Possible response: In their desolate circumstances, they need a hero.)

13 GUIDED READING
Finding the Main Idea: What does the beauty of the drowned man make the people realize about their own environment and their own dreams? (The grandeur of Esteban makes them realize the desolation of their environment and the narrowness of their own ambitions.)

14 LITERARY ELEMENT
Theme: What do you think García Márquez is saying about how heroes transform societies, and how heroes are themselves transformed? (Possible response: Heroes transform "ordinary" people by giving them ideals to strive toward. Ironically, in this story ordinary people create a hero out of the longing of their own spirits.)

Gabriel García Márquez   **1295**

1. Who first finds the body on the beach? (children)
2. What was the drowned body encrusted with? (mud and scales)
3. What effect did Esteban's adoption have on the village? (It unified the village.)
4. What do the villagers cover his face with? (a handkerchief)
5. Why don't the villagers tie an anchor to him? (so he can return if he wishes)

RETEACHING

Invite students to imagine that they are one of the children, now grown old, who discovered the drowned man. Ask them to "recall" the event and to tell the story of Esteban and his funeral as if they were speaking to their grandchildren. Students may want to add their own summary of how the village has changed in the decades since Esteban's funeral.

WRITING TO LEARN

Based on your understanding of the story, write a brief essay answering the question, "What is a myth?" In your essay, deal with both the literary elements of myth and the role of myth in society. ■

ANSWERS
First Thoughts
Answers will vary.

Identifying Facts
1. It is set during the age of European colonialism.
2. He is very large and heavy, and has scales. They suppose water is in his bones; they think certain men grow after drowning.
3. Esteban. Possible responses: He is seen as a martyr; the name is considered attractive.
4. The villagers paint their houses, plant flowers, and try to beautify the town to live up to Esteban's memory.

Interpreting Meanings
1. The setting is an isolated village on cliffs overlooking the sea. The place seems insular, cut off from the rest of the world. This isolation lends credibility to the elements of fantasy that García Márquez introduces.

Medialuna Bay, Colombia.

Loren McIntyre/Woodfin Camp & Associates

of gardens on the high seas, and the captain would have to come down from the bridge in his dress uniform, with his astrolabe,[9] his pole star,[10] and his row of war medals, and, pointing to the promontory of roses on the horizon, he would say in fourteen languages, look there, where the wind is so peaceful now that it's gone to sleep beneath the beds, over there, where the sun's so bright that the sunflowers don't know which way to turn, yes, over there, that's Esteban's village.

---

9. **astrolabe:** instrument that can find a star's altitude and help navigators determine their position at sea.
10. **pole star:** Polaris, or the North Star; it is used by navigators in the Northern Hemisphere to determine their location because it remains almost fixed throughout the night.

First Thoughts

What image of the drowned man is strongest in your mind? How did you feel about some of the realistic passages describing Esteban?

Identifying Facts

1. What do details such as the galleon, the blunderbuss, and the astrolabe suggest about the time period of the story?
2. What is unusual about the drowned man? How do the men explain his unusual characteristics?
3. What name do the villagers give the drowned man? Why?
4. How does the village change after the drowned man washes ashore?

Interpreting Meanings

1. **Setting** is a major element in this story, as it is in all of García Márquez's fiction. Briefly describe this story's setting and

1. Differing Points of View. Ask students to describe Esteban, his imagined history, and his effect on them or on the village from the point of view of one of the following imaginary characters, using the prescribed form: children (diary entries); visiting journalist from the city (news report); ship's captain (ship's log); village women (letters); village men (dialogue—work in pairs); Esteban's parents ("Missing" poster).

2. Comparative Literature. Have students find other works in world literature that use techniques of magic realism. The works may be in this book or in outside reading. Have a panel of interested students compare the works, supporting—or attacking—the claims that the works use magic realism and noting resemblances and differences among works.

Ask students: How does this modern literary myth resemble and differ from the ancient myths you read in the first several units of the textbook? What insights did the story give you that you can apply to the ancient myths in retrospect? ■

---

explain how it contributes to the **magic realism** of the story.

2. A strong **theme** is suggested by the fabulous events of this story and the subsequent changes in the village. What does this story reveal about the universal need for heroes and great dreams?

3. This story is told from the **third-person point of view**, but Esteban becomes so real in the minds of the villagers that they imagine him speaking in the **first person**. When Esteban speaks using the pronoun "I" (see pages 1293 and 1294), does he become more real to you?

Applying Meanings

The events of this story make the villagers see "for the first time the desolation of their streets, the dryness of their courtyards," and "the narrowness of their dreams." What experiences in real life might make people look at their lives in a different way and see the shortcomings of how they live?

Creative Writing Response

Changing the Premise. If the man who washed to shore had been alive, do you think the outcome of this story would have been the same? Would the villagers have extended as much love and hospitality toward a live man as they did toward the dead man? Write a story using the same setting, but bring Esteban to life. Be sure to explain who Esteban is and how he happened to wash up on the shore of this village. Feel free to use elements of **magic realism** in your story.

Critical Writing Response

Analyzing Magic Realism. In a brief essay, analyze García Márquez's use of **magic realism** in this story. Before you write, review the story to locate some particularly realistic details. Then locate some of the story's fantastic elements. You might organize your details on a chart like the one below.

Fantastic Events	Realistic Details

At the end of your essay, state your general response to the use of magic realism. Do you like this blurring of fantasy and reality? Or do you prefer either pure fantasy or pure realism?

2. Possible response: People need heroes so much that they will invent them.

3. Students should support their "yes" or "no" answers with reasons.

Applying Meanings

Possible responses: Illness, the death of a loved one, or graduation from school are among the experiences that can make one see life differently.

Creative Writing Response

Changing the Premise. Encourage students to use their imaginations freely in creating a character for Esteban. His history and personality may be quite different from anything in the villagers' fantasies. Point out that most village cultures place great value on hospitality.

Critical Writing Response

Analyzing Magic Realism. Students' essays should include at least two examples of fantasy and of realism, and a clear statement of their reasons for preferring pure fantasy, pure realism, or a blend. ■

Julio Cortázar
1914–1984, Argentina

Bernard Gotfryd/Woodfin Camp & Associates

A visitor to an aquarium is transformed into a salamander; a rich Argentine woman discovers and changes places with her exact double, a beggar in Budapest; a man finds himself vomiting rabbits that gradually destroy his apartment. Welcome to the world of Julio Cortázar.

For Cortázar, the fantastic is not something supernatural, but "something very simple, that can happen in the midst of everyday reality, during this sunny midday, now, between you and I, or on the subway. . . ." Cortázar's views of the fantastic are heavily influenced by French surrealism and the writings of Edgar Allan Poe, whose works Cortázar translated into Spanish.

Born in Belgium to Argentine parents, Julio Cortázar grew up in a suburb of Buenos Aires. Throughout his childhood, Cortázar read voraciously and wrote his own imaginative tales. After high school, Cortázar qualified as a teacher of French literature, but he gave up his university studies in order to take a teaching job to support his family. While he taught, he wrote stories, but he didn't publish his first collection, *Bestiary*, until 1951.

That same year, 1951, was a turning point in another way: Disillusioned by the regime of the Argentine dictator Juan Perón, Cortázar accepted a French government grant to study in Paris. Though he lived in exile most of his life—mainly in France, working as a freelance translator for the United Nations and for various publishers—Cortázar always considered himself a Latin American.

Cortázar once said that a writer's job was "to set fire to language," and the Argentine writer did just that in 1963, when he astounded the publishing world with *Hopscotch*, a long, structurally innovative novel whose chapters can be read in several different sequences.

Cortázar—who was influenced by jazz and classical music, Zen Buddhism, detective novels, and movies—kept the fun-loving, youthful side of his nature alive to the end of his days. "He liberated us all with a new, airy, humorous, and mysterious language, both everyday and mythical," the Mexican novelist Carlos Fuentes said in a tribute to his friend shortly after Cortázar's death from leukemia in 1984.

OBJECTIVES
1. *To interpret a modern short story by a renowned Latin American writer*
2. *To analyze the use of suspense in a story by a magic realist writer*
3. *To write an essay defending a particular interpretation of the story*

VOCABULARY IN CONTEXT
The words listed below will appear in the side margin at the point of instruction:

1. vestibule
2. solace
3. amulet
4. acolytes
5. translucent

Reader's Guide

THE NIGHT FACE UP

Background

The "war of the blossom" cited in Cortázar's editorial footnote at the beginning of this story probably refers to the Aztec holy war called *xochiyaoyotl,* the "flowered war," a ritual held by the Aztecs during relatively peaceful times as a way of keeping up the supply of human prisoners for use in human sacrifice. War and human sacrifice were key elements in the military-dominated Aztec culture, which reached its height in the fifteenth century and was abruptly destroyed by the Spanish conquest of Mexico in the 1520s.

The Aztecs looked upon their practice of human sacrifice as a religious necessity, a sacred duty carried out with one purpose in mind: to feed the sun with human blood so that it would continue to travel in its course across the sky and keep the world alive. The Aztecs called themselves "people of the Sun," and bloodshed played a role in most of their major religious rituals. Every year, on altars at the summits of temple pyramids, hundreds of victims—usually slaves or prisoners of war—met their deaths as a presiding priest cut open their chests and removed their hearts in offerings to the sun god. According to some accounts, at the height of the Aztec Empire, in the late 1400s, as many as twenty thousand prisoners were sacrificed on the temple pyramids in a single year.

Writer's Response

What importance or significance do you think dreams have in human life? At what times, and under what circumstances, are people most likely to have vivid or memorable dreams—or nightmares? Can a dream be so vivid that it seems real? Freewrite your ideas.

Literary Focus

Plot-driven stories always have a certain built-in degree of **suspense**: They generate in us a sense of uncertainty or anxiety about what will happen next in the story. But suspense is not built by elements of plot alone: Atmosphere, vivid details, and pacing can effectively build our mounting anticipation of events. As you read "The Night Face Up," pay attention to the many ways in which Cortázar builds suspense.

PREREADING FOCUS

Background: Like his literary idol Edgar Allan Poe, Cortázar often explored the motif of the double (or doppelgänger), as well as the possibilities of reincarnation. In the collection of stories in which "The Night Face Up" first appeared, Cortázar introduced an idea related to the motif of the doppelgänger: the concept of the figure. According to Cortázar, certain characters and events could be bound together in relationships, or correspondences, called *figures*—uncanny, mysterious relationships between people and events. In Cortázar's works, "figures" are linked by unexpected connections that defy logic and transcend barriers of time and space. In the story that follows, Cortázar explores one of these "figures," leaving the reader with a handful of ambiguities and many intriguing questions.

Literary Focus: The narrative structure of this story is complex. So that students can fully appreciate the suspense Cortázar generates through his deliberate pacing and the bipartite structure of the story, suggest that they keep a log as they read, making note of particularly suspenseful points in the narrative. Visual learners may wish to explore ways to "graph" the rise and fall of action in the two parallel parts of the story as it heads to its surprising conclusion.

Using Prepositional Phrases

A prepositional phrase consists of a preposition (a word, such as *above*, *before*, or *into*, that indicates relationships between nouns or pronouns and other words in a sentence), the noun or pronoun that is its object, and related modifiers. Prepositional phrases can act either as adjectives (modifying nouns or pronouns) or adverbs (modifying verbs, adjectives, or other adverbs). Julio Cortázar frequently uses prepositional phrases to add details to his sentences. Here are some examples from "The Night Face Up":

Modifying a Verb: The sun filtered *through the tall downtown buildings.*

Modifying a Noun: [H]e swung onto the machine, savoring the idea *of the ride.*

1. **Listening and Speaking.** Ask students to locate four other sentences containing prepositional phrases in the first

1 PREDICTING

The epigraph and its accompanying footnote raise questions about what will happen in the story. What do you think will be the connection between the ancient Aztecs and the modern setting? (Possible responses: The man is an archaeologist heading to an Aztec site in Mexico; this will be a time-travel story; the story will deal with a modern-day war of the blossom.)

■ **vestibule** (ves'tə·byool'): entrance hall or lobby

2 SPECULATING

Why do you think Cortázar inserts this information about the man's lack of a name? (Possible responses: to suggest that the man is an Everyman; to suggest that the man may not really know who he is; to give the sense that this is taking place in a dream)

3 GUIDED READING

Recognizing Cause and Effect: What has happened in this passage? (A woman has stepped into the crosswalk while the rider has a green light, so he has had to brake hard and swerve in order to avoid her. There is a collision, and he falls unconscious.)

THE NIGHT FACE UP
Julio Cortázar
translated by
PAUL BLACKBURN

◆ *As you read, identify the points in the narrative where there is a startling shift in setting and situation. How are these transitions handled as the narrative progresses?*

1   *And at certain periods they went out to hunt enemies; they called it the war of the blossom.**

Halfway down the long hotel <u>vestibule</u>, he thought that probably he was going to be late, and hurried on into the street to get out his motorcycle from the corner where the next-door superintendent let him keep it. On the jewelry store at the corner he read that it was ten to nine; he had time to spare. The sun filtered through the tall downtown buildings, and he—because for himself, for just going along thinking, he did not have a name—he swung onto the machine, savoring the idea of the ride. The motor whirred between his legs, and a cool wind whipped his pantslegs.

He let the ministries[1] zip past (the pink, the white), and a series of stores on the main street, their windows flashing. Now he was beginning the most pleasant part of the run, the real ride: a long street bordered with trees, very little traffic, with spacious villas whose gardens rambled all the way down to the sidewalks, which were barely indicated by low hedges. A bit inattentive perhaps, but tooling along on the right side of the street, he allowed himself to be carried away by the freshness, by the weightless contraction of this hardly begun day. This involuntary relaxation, possibly, kept him from preventing the accident. When he saw that the woman standing on the corner had rushed into the crosswalk while he still had the green light, it was already somewhat too late for a simple solution. He braked hard with foot and hand, wrenching himself to the left; he heard the woman scream, and at the collision his vision went. It was like falling asleep all at once.

He came to abruptly. Four or five young men were getting him out from under the cycle. He felt the taste of salt and blood, one knee hurt, and when they hoisted him up he yelped, he couldn't bear the pressure on his right arm. Voices which did not seem to belong to the faces hanging above him encouraged him cheerfully with jokes and as-

---

* The war of the blossom was the name the Aztecs gave to a ritual war in which they took prisoners for sacrifice. It is metaphysics to say that the gods see men as flowers, to be so uprooted, trampled, cut down.—Ed. [Cortázar's note]

---

1. **ministries:** buildings that house the headquarters for government departments.

surances. His single <u>solace</u> was to hear someone else confirm that the lights indeed had been in his favor. He asked about the woman, trying to keep down the nausea which was edging up into his throat. While they carried him face up to a nearby pharmacy, he learned that the cause of the accident had gotten only a few scrapes on the legs. "Nah, you barely got her at all, but when ya hit, the impact made the machine jump and flop on its side . . ." Opinions, recollections of other smashups, take it easy, work him in shoulders first, there, that's fine, and someone in a dustcoat giving him a swallow of something soothing in the shadowy interior of the small local pharmacy.

Within five minutes the police ambulance arrived, and they lifted him onto a cushioned stretcher. It was a relief for him to be able to lie out flat. Completely lucid, but realizing that he was suffering the effects of a terrible shock, he gave his information to the officer riding in the ambulance with him. The arm almost didn't hurt; blood dripped down from a cut over the eyebrow all over his face. He licked his lips once or twice to drink it. He felt pretty good, it had been an accident, tough luck; stay quiet a few weeks, nothing worse. The guard said that the motorcycle didn't seem badly racked up. "Why should it," he replied. "It all landed on top of me." They both laughed, and when they got to the hospital, the guard shook his hand and wished him luck. Now the nausea was coming back little by little; meanwhile they were pushing him on a wheeled stretcher toward a pavilion further back, rolling along under trees full of birds, he shut his eyes and wished he were asleep or chloroformed. But they kept him for a good while in a room with that hospital smell, filling out a form, getting his clothes off, and dressing him in a stiff, grayish smock. They moved his arm carefully, it didn't hurt him. The nurses were constantly making wisecracks, and if it hadn't been for the stomach contractions he would have felt fine, almost happy.

They got him over to X-ray, and twenty minutes later, with the still-damp negative lying on his chest like a black tombstone, they pushed him into surgery. Someone tall and thin in white came over and began to look at the X-rays. A woman's hands were arranging his head, he felt that they were moving him from one stretcher to another. The man in white came over to him again, smiling, something gleamed in his right hand. He patted his cheek and made a sign to someone stationed behind.

It was unusual as a dream because it was full of smells, and he never dreamt smells. First a marshy smell, there to the left of the trail the swamps began already, the quaking bogs from which no one ever returned. But the reek lifted, and instead there came a dark, fresh composite fragrance, like the night under which he moved, in flight from the Aztecs. And it was all so natural, he had to run from the Aztecs who had set out on their manhunt, and his sole chance was to find a place to hide in the deepest part of the forest, taking care not to lose the narrow trail which only they, the Motecas, knew.

What tormented him the most was the odor, as though, notwithstanding the absolute acceptance of the dream, there was something which resisted that which was not habitual, which until that point had not participated in the game. "It smells of war," he thought, his hand going instinctively to the stone knife which was tucked at an angle into his girdle of woven wool. An unexpected sound made him crouch suddenly stock-still and shaking. To be afraid was

9 **LITERARY ELEMENT**

Imagery: What does the image of the "starless night" suggest? (that the man is in utter darkness, with no redeeming light) Throughout the story, be aware of imagery connected with night and darkness. What might be the cumulative effect of such imagery? (a sense of foreboding, fear of the unknown, hopelessness, encroaching evil)

10 **GUIDED READING**

Sequencing: Which phrases in the narrative and the dialogue signal a transition between dreaming and waking? ("leaped forward desperately" in the patient's dream, and "stop bouncing around" spoken by the patient's neighbor)

11 **LITERARY ELEMENT**

Simile: Identify the two similes that the author uses here to describe the feverish state of the man's perceptions. What do these two comparisons have in common? (The patient is compared to someone who sees distant objects or figures through opera glasses in a theater; he is then compared to a man in a movie theater who forces himself to watch a boring film. Both similes involve a person who is watching scenes in a darkened theater; this suggests that the accident victim feels like a spectator beholding images and events over which he has no control.)

9 nothing strange, there was plenty of fear in his dreams. He waited, covered by the branches of a shrub and the starless night. Far off, probably on the other side of the big lake, they'd be lighting the bivouac[2] fires; that part of the sky had a reddish glare. The sound was not repeated. It had been like a broken limb. Maybe an animal that, like himself, was escaping from the smell of war. He stood erect slowly, sniffing the air. Not a sound could be heard, but the fear was still following, as was the smell, that cloying incense of the war of the blossom. He had to press forward, to stay out of the bogs and get to the heart of the forest. Groping uncertainly through the dark, stooping every other moment to touch the packed earth of the trail, he took a few steps. He would have liked to have broken into a run, but the gurgling fens[3] lapped on either side of him. On the path and in darkness, he took his bearings. Then he caught a horrible blast of that foul smell he was most afraid of, and leaped forward desperately.

10 "You're going to fall off the bed," said the patient next to him. "Stop bouncing around, old buddy."

He opened his eyes and it was afternoon, the sun already low in the oversized windows of the long ward. While trying to smile at his neighbor, he detached himself almost physically from the final scene of the nightmare. His arm, in a plaster cast, hung suspended from an apparatus with weights and pulleys. He felt thirsty, as though he'd been running for miles, but they didn't want to give him much water, barely enough to moisten his lips and make a mouthful. The fever was winning slowly and he would have

been able to sleep again, but he was enjoying the pleasure of keeping awake, eyes half-closed, listening to the other patients' conversation, answering a question from time to time. He saw a little white pushcart come up beside the bed, a blond nurse rubbed the front of his thigh with alcohol and stuck him with a fat needle connected to a tube which ran up to a bottle filled with a milky, opalescent liquid. A young intern arrived with some metal and leather apparatus which he adjusted to fit onto the good arm to check something or other. Night fell, and the fever went along dragging him down softly to a state in which things seemed embossed as through opera glasses,[4] they were real and soft and, at the same time, vaguely distasteful; like sitting in a boring movie and thinking that, well, still, it'd be worse out in the street, and staying. 11

A cup of a marvelous golden broth came, smelling of leeks, celery, and parsley. A small hunk of bread, more precious than a whole banquet, found itself crumbling little by little. His arm hardly hurt him at all, and only in the eyebrow where they'd taken stitches a quick, hot pain sizzled occasionally. When the big windows across the way turned to smudges of dark blue, he thought it would not be difficult for him to sleep. Still on his back so a little uncomfortable, running his tongue out over his hot, too-dry lips, he tasted the broth still, and with a sigh of bliss, he let himself drift off.

First there was a confusion, as of one drawing all his sensations, for that moment blunted or muddled, into himself. He realized that he was running in pitch darkness, although, above, the sky crisscrossed with 12

---

2. **bivouac** (biv'wak'): temporary camp for soldiers.
3. **fens:** marshy lowland areas; swamps.

4. **opera glasses:** small binoculars for use in a theater.

Why do you think Aztec religious ceremonies were performed at the summits of large pyramids like this one?

12 LITERARY ELEMENT

Suspense: How does this passage (which continues on page 1304) increase the story's suspense? (The man realizes that losing the trail has exposed him to more danger; the pitch darkness is disorienting; the ominous simile of the scorpion foreshadows evil; the man's ankles sink deeper into the mud, hinting that he is trapped.)

amulet (am′yoo·lit): object worn as a charm or protection to ward off evil or bad luck

treetops was less black than the rest. "The trail," he thought. "I've gotten off the trail." His feet sank into a bed of leaves and mud, and then he couldn't take a step that the branches of shrubs did not whiplash against his ribs and legs. Out of breath, knowing despite the darkness and silence that he was surrounded, he crouched down to listen. Maybe the trail was very near, with the first daylight he would be able to see it again. Nothing now could help him to find it. The hand that had unconsciously gripped the haft of the dagger climbed like a fen scorpion up to his neck where the protecting amulet hung. Barely moving his lips, he mumbled the supplication of the corn which brings about the beneficent moons, and the prayer to Her Very Highness, to the distributor of

12 all Motecan possessions. At the same time he felt his ankles sinking deeper into the mud, and the waiting in the darkness of the obscure grove of live oak grew intolerable

13 to him. The war of the blossom had started at the beginning of the moon and had been going on for three days and three nights now. If he managed to hide in the depths of the forest, getting off the trail further up past the marsh country, perhaps the warriors wouldn't follow his track. He thought of the many prisoners they'd already taken. But the number didn't count, only the consecrated period. The hunt would continue until the priests gave the sign to return. Everything had its number and its limit, and it was within the sacred period, and he on the other side from the hunters.

He heard the cries and leaped up, knife in hand. As if the sky were aflame on the horizon, he saw torches moving among the branches, very near him. The smell of war was unbearable, and when the first enemy jumped him, leaped at his throat, he felt an almost-pleasure in sinking the stone blade flat to the haft into his chest. The lights were already around him, the happy cries. He managed to cut the air once or twice, then a rope snared him from behind.

"It's the fever," the man in the next bed said. "The same thing happened to me when they operated on my duodenum.[5] Take some water, you'll see, you'll sleep all right."

14 Laid next to the night from which he came back, the tepid shadow of the ward seemed delicious to him. A violet lamp kept watch high on the far wall like a guardian eye. You could hear coughing, deep breathing, once in a while a conversation in whis-

pers. Everything was pleasant and secure, without the chase, no . . . But he didn't want to go on thinking about the nightmare. There were lots of things to amuse himself with. He began to look at the cast on his arm, and the pulleys that held it so comfortably in the air. They'd left a bottle of mineral water on the night table beside him. He put the neck of the bottle to his mouth **14** and drank it like a precious liqueur. He could now make out the different shapes in the ward, the thirty beds, the closets with glass doors. He guessed that his fever was down, his face felt cool. The cut over the eyebrow barely hurt at all, like a recollection. He saw himself leaving the hotel again, wheeling out the cycle. Who'd have thought that it would end like this? He tried to fix the moment of the accident exactly, and it got him very angry to notice that there was a void there, an emptiness he could not manage to fill. Between the impact and the moment that they picked him up off the pavement, the passing out or what went on, there was nothing he could see. And at the same time he had the feeling that this void, this nothingness, had lasted an eternity. No, not even time, more as if, in this void, he had passed across something, or had run back immense **15** distances. The shock, the brutal dashing against the pavement. Anyway, he had felt an immense relief in coming out of the black pit while the people were lifting him off the ground. With pain in the broken arm, blood from the split eyebrow, contusion on the knee; with all that, a relief in returning to daylight, to the day, and to feel sustained and attended. That was weird. Someday he'd ask the doctor at the office about that. Now sleep began to take over again, to pull him slowly down. The pillow was so soft, and the coolness of the mineral water in his

---

5. **duodenum** (doo·ād''n·əm): the part of the small intestine that connects with the stomach.

fevered throat. The violet light of the lamp up there was beginning to get dimmer and dimmer.

As he was sleeping on his back, the position in which he came to did not surprise him, but on the other hand the damp smell, the smell of oozing rock, blocked his throat and forced him to understand. Open the eyes and look in all directions, hopeless. He was surrounded by an absolute darkness. Tried to get up and felt ropes pinning his wrists and ankles. He was staked to the ground on a floor of dank, icy stone slabs. The cold bit into his naked back, his legs. Dully, he tried to touch the amulet with his chin and found they had stripped him of it. Now he was lost, no prayer could save him from the final . . . From afar off, as though filtering through the rock of the dungeon, he heard the great kettledrums of the feast. They had carried him to the temple, he was in the underground cells of Teocalli[6] itself, awaiting his turn.

He heard a yell, a hoarse yell that rocked off the walls. Another yell, ending in a moan. It was he who was screaming in the darkness, he was screaming because he was alive, his whole body with that cry fended off what was coming, the inevitable end. He thought of his friends filling up the other dungeons, and of those already walking up the stairs of the sacrifice. He uttered another choked cry, he could barely open his mouth, his jaws were twisted back as if with a rope and a stick, and once in a while they would open slowly with an endless exertion, as if they were made of rubber. The creaking of the wooden latches jolted him like a whip. Rent, writhing, he fought to rid himself of

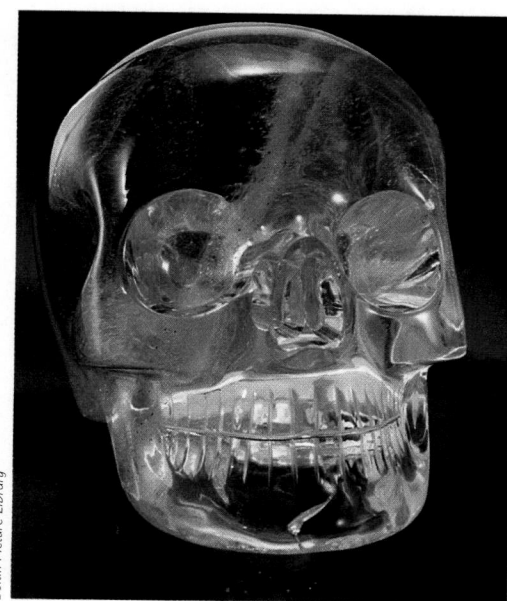

Boltin Picture Library

Crystal skull of the Aztec god of death, Mictlantecuhtli.

❓ *How is death, or the possibility of death, treated in the story? What images create an ominous effect?*

the cords sinking into his flesh. His right arm, the strongest, strained until the pain became unbearable and he had to give up. He watched the double door open, and the smell of the torches reached him before the light did. Barely girdled by the ceremonial loincloths, the priests' <u>acolytes</u> moved in his direction, looking at him with contempt. Lights reflected off the sweaty torsos and off the black hair dressed with feathers. The cords went slack, and in their place the grappling of hot hands, hard as bronze; he felt himself lifted, still face up, and jerked along by the four acolytes who carried him down the passageway. The torchbearers went ahead, indistinctly lighting up the corridor with its dripping walls and a ceiling so low that the acolytes had to duck their heads.

6. **Teocalli** (te′ō·kal′ē): a name for a four-sided pyramid, surmounted by a temple, that was used by the Aztecs for worship and sacrifice.

16
17
18

16 GUIDED READING
Recognizing Cause and Effect: Why is the man now convinced that he will be killed? (Without his protective amulet, he is lost.)

17 READER'S RESPONSE
What dominant feeling is conveyed in this passage? (stark terror) What is the "inevitable end"? (The man believes he is going to be sacrificed.)

■ acolytes (ak′ə·līt′): helpers or assistants, often used in a religious context

18 LITERARY ELEMENT
Imagery: What sensory images does Cortázar use in this description? To what senses do these images appeal? (creaking of the latches—hearing; cords sinking into flesh—touch; double door opening—sight; smell of torches—smell)

HUMANITIES CONNECTION

Mictlantecuhtli, god of the underworld, is one of the most important icons in Aztec culture. He is most often represented by a skull, symbol of both individual death and the continuation of the universe. Because such skulls were a necessary part of the celebrations that marked the end of each fifty-two-year Aztec epoch, many now exist in museums around the world.

❓ *Many Aztec rituals were oriented around death. How would you characterize views of death within your own culture?* ■

Julio Cortázar **1305**

1. After the accident, where is the man in the story taken? (to a hospital)
2. In his nightmares, who pursues and captures the man? (Aztec warriors)
3. How long will the war of the blossom continue? (until the priests give the signal for the warriors to return, evidently after a consecrated period)
4. What does the man wear around his neck? (a protective amulet)

5. At the very end of the story, what does the prisoner's fate seem to be? (The executioner-priest will ritually put him to death.)

To reteach the story, divide the class into two teams. Have the first team make a story map showing all the important events in the hospital patient's waking life. Have the second team chart the sequence of events in the man's nightmares. Then encourage the teams to exchange their story maps and to comment on each other's work.

---

translucent (trans·loo'sənt): allowing light to pass through

19 GUIDED READING
Sequencing: Note that the final transition between waking and dreaming is not marked off by a paragraph break. How does this structural detail affect the pace and tone of the narrative? (It speeds up the narrative toward the climax and makes the story more suspenseful.)

20 INTERPRETING
Whom does the figure of the priest recall? Why is this resemblance ironic? (the surgeon, who had approached the man with a gleaming object in his hand. The similarity is ironic because the doctor wants to save the man's life, while the priest evidently intends to take it.)

21 LITERARY ELEMENT
Extended Simile: The structure of Cortázar's short story suggests the two-part framework of an extended simile: The man lying on his back in a modern hospital bed is *like* an ancient Indian warrior bound hand and foot in an Aztec dungeon, awaiting ritual sacrifice. This simile is explored throughout the narrative and finally pressed to the limit at the end of the story, when Cortázar suggests that the accident victim actually *becomes* the Aztecs' prisoner—and that they were perhaps the same person all along.

Now they were taking him out, taking him out, it was the end. Face up, under a mile of living rock which, for a succession of moments, was lit up by a glimmer of torchlight. When the stars came out up there instead of the roof and the great terraced steps rose before him, on fire with cries and dances, it would be the end. The passage was never going to end, but now it was beginning to end, he would see suddenly the open sky full of stars, but not yet, they trundled him along endlessly in the reddish shadow, hauling him roughly along and he did not want that, but how to stop it if they had torn off the amulet, his real heart, the life-center.

In a single jump he came out into the hospital night, to the high, gentle, bare ceiling, to the soft shadow wrapping him round. He thought he must have cried out, but his neighbors were peacefully snoring. The water in the bottle on the night table was somewhat bubbly, a translucent shape against the dark azure shadow of the windows. He panted, looking for some relief for his lungs, oblivion for those images still glued to his eyelids. Each time he shut his eyes he saw them take shape instantly, and he sat up, completely wrung out, but savoring at the same time the surety that now he was awake, that the night nurse would answer if he rang, that soon it would be daybreak, with the good, deep sleep he usually had at that hour, no images, no nothing . . . It was difficult to keep his eyes open, the drowsiness was more powerful than he. He made one last effort, he sketched a gesture toward the bottle of water with his good hand and did not manage to reach it, his fingers closed again on a black emptiness, and the passageway went on endlessly, rock after rock, with momentary ruddy flares, and

face up he choked out a dull moan because the roof was about to end, it rose, was opening like a mouth of shadow, and the acolytes straightened up, and from on high a waning moon fell on a face whose eyes wanted not to see it, were closing and opening desperately, trying to pass to the other side, to find again the bare, protecting ceiling of the ward. And every time they opened, it was night and the moon, while they climbed the great terraced steps, his head hanging down backward now, and up at the top were the bonfires, red columns of perfumed smoke, and suddenly he saw the red stone, shiny with the blood dripping off it, and the spinning arcs cut by the feet of the victim whom they pulled off to throw him rolling down the north steps. With a last hope he shut his lids tightly, moaning to wake up. For a second he thought he had gotten there, because once more he was immobile in the bed, except that his head was hanging down off it, swinging. But he smelled death, and when he opened his eyes he saw the blood-soaked figure of the executioner-priest coming toward him with the stone knife in his hand. He managed to close his eyelids again, although he knew now he was not going to wake up, that he was awake, that the marvelous dream had been the other, absurd as all dreams are—a dream in which he was going through the strange avenues of an astonishing city, with green and red lights that burned without fire or smoke, on an enormous metal insect that whirred away between his legs. In the infinite lie of the dream, they had also picked him off the ground, someone had approached him also with a knife in his hand, approached him who was lying face up, face up with his eyes closed between the bonfires on the steps.

19

19

20

21

1. **Researching Surrealism.** Julio Cortázar absorbed many of the influences of surrealism. This movement in literature, painting, film, and music inspired such figures as the painters Joan Míro and Salvador Dali, the dramatist Jean Cocteau, and the poet Guillaume Apollinaire. Have students prepare an oral report on one of these figures.

2. **Presenting a Movie Proposal.** Several of Julio Cortázar's short stories were made into films, most notably Michelangelo Antonioni's *Blow-Up* (1966). Have students form teams to write proposals for a film version of "The Night Face Up." Teams should decide on casting, setting (location or studio?), proposed changes to the story line, special effects, and so on. Teams should present their proposals to the class.

CLOSURE

Ask students if they think Cortázar's story is essentially an entertaining tale that presents two levels of consciousness, or if they believe that Cortázar has presented a serious message about human life or behavior in "The Night Face Up." If students believe the writer presents a serious theme, what is it? ∎

First Thoughts

Which aspect of this story puzzles you most? Why?

Identifying Facts

1. How did the motorcycle accident happen, and who was to blame for it?
2. What are the man's injuries? Describe how he feels as he enters the hospital.
3. What are the two principal **settings** for the story? Identify the point at which the first transition between settings occurs. Then identify the final transition.
4. What does the Aztecs' prisoner realize when he finds that his amulet is gone?
5. What happens to the Aztecs' prisoner? to the motorcycle accident victim?

Interpreting Meanings

1. What do you think is Cortázar's purpose in starting with the opening quotation about the war of the blossom, as well as the editorial footnote?
2. How does the author use specific, concrete **details**, such as the lamp and the surgical scalpel, to build **suspense**? In what other ways is suspense built?
3. Find three examples of **similes** in the story. In what sense can the entire story be regarded as a single extended simile—that is, an extended comparison between two different things? Identify as many comparisons in the two parallel parts of the story as you can.
4. Identify several examples of **sensory details** in the story—especially of smells, sounds, and tastes—that seemed particularly realistic to you. Why do you think Cortázar included so many sensory details?
5. Find passages in the story where the words *face up* appear. Now that you have read the story, what do you think the title means?

6. What is the "infinite lie of the dream," as revealed at the end of the story?

Applying Meanings

In describing one of Julio Cortázar's short stories, the critic Paul Zweig commented, "It is as if [the French writer] Proust and Edgar Allan Poe had collaborated to write an episode for *Twilight Zone*." Do you think this story would make an effective episode of a contemporary TV thriller, or do you think the story is too tame, too complicated, too intellectual, or in some other way simply not interesting to today's audiences? Explain your views.

Critical Writing Response

Interpreting the Story. Consider the following possible explanations for the parallel events of the story:

a. A modern motorcycle rider, who subconsciously feels like a sacrificial victim because of his situation in the hospital, dreams that he is an Aztec prisoner.
b. The story has a surprise ending: The modern-day motorcycle rider is actually a dream of the Aztec prisoner, not the other way around.
c. Two different people, occupying the same space but at different times, are thrown into each other's realities by their respective traumatic experiences.
d. The motorcycle rider, near death, is remembering a past life; the Aztecs' prisoner—also near death—is having premonitions of a future life.
e. The story is an exploration of the consciousness of a human mind at the moment of death, when—according to a traditional expression—one's entire life passes before one's eyes in seconds.

Choose one of the explanations above, or develop a convincing explanation of your own, and support it in a well-organized essay, using evidence from the story.

ANSWERS

First Thoughts
Answers will vary.

Identifying Facts
1. The motorcyclist brakes to avoid a pedestrian; the woman is at fault.
2. a broken arm, a split eyebrow, and a contusion on the knee. nauseous and in shock
3. a modern hospital and ancient Mexico; *first transition:* "It was unusual as a dream"; *final transition:* patient reaches for water and finds himself in pyramid passageway.
4. All hope is lost.
5. man is left face up on the pyramid steps as priest approaches.

Interpreting Meanings
1. Answers will vary.
2. Objects, as well as sensations, function as associative links. Pacing, imagery, and atmosphere also contribute.
3. Answers will vary. The story rests on numerous comparisons between the hospital patient and the sacrificial victim.
4. Answers will vary. Sensory images provide transitions and link the two situations.
5. Answers will vary. "Face up" describes the supine position of a sacrificial victim.
6. There is no way to tell the dream from the reality.

Applying Meanings
Answers will vary.

Critical Writing Response
Interpreting the Story. Answers will vary. Students should cite ample evidence from the story. ∎

Isabel Allende
b. 1942, Chile

© Latin Focus

From earliest childhood, Isabel Allende (ä·yen'dā) loved making up her own imaginative tales. By the age of seventeen, she was already making a living with words, working as a journalist in Santiago, the capital of her homeland, Chile. But her storyteller's urge to embellish reality was strong. "I could never be objective," she recalls. "I exaggerated and twisted reality. I would put myself in the middle of every feature."

Allende—who was born in Lima, Peru, where her Chilean diplomat father was stationed—read and traveled widely in her youth. Her parents divorced when she was very young, and much of her childhood was spent with her mother and maternal grandparents in Santiago, Chile.

Growing up, Allende was close to her uncle, Salvador Allende, who would become the president of Chile in 1970. This relationship would be at the center of the biggest crisis of Allende's life: In September 1973, a bloody military coup ended the life of President Salvador Allende and threw Chile into chaos. After more than a year of living under the repressive, violent, new Chilean government, Allende, with her husband, went into exile in Venezuela.

In 1981, Allende learned that her grandfather, who was almost one hundred years old and still living in Chile, was near death. She began to write her recollections of her early family life in Chile, a chronicle that she ultimately transformed into the magic-realist fiction of *The House of the Spirits* (1982), her first novel and an international bestseller.

The need to tell stories is an important theme in all of Allende's works. In her second novel, *Of Love and Shadows* (1984), Allende created a main character who, like herself, is a journalist, a reporter of stories. Her next protagonist, Eva Luna, is also a teller of tales, acting as a kind of modern-day Scheherazade in the novel *Eva Luna* (1988) and the collection *The Stories of Eva Luna* (1991).

Allende now lives in California, where she has taught creative writing at Berkeley. Her most recent success is *Paula* (1995), a critically acclaimed memoir written in honor of her terminally ill daughter.

OBJECTIVES
1. To analyze and interpret a short story from a contemporary Latin American writer
2. To analyze the use of irony to make moral and political statements
3. To write a dramatic scene based on the narrative, and to write an essay analyzing the use of nonfiction as a basis for fiction

THEMES IN WORLD LITERATURE

Life and Loss
Sonnet 64, p. 810
"The Swan," p. 1151
"The Handsomest Drowned Man in the World," pp. 1289–1297

Loss of Innocence
"The Ring," pp. 1214–1222
"Thoughts of Hanoi," pp. 1409–1413. ∎

VOCABULARY IN CONTEXT
The words listed below will appear in the side margin at the point of instruction:
1. subterranean   4. visceral
2. presentiments 5. stratagem
3. quagmire

Reader's Guide

AND OF CLAY ARE WE CREATED

Background

"And of Clay Are We Created" appears in *The Stories of Eva Luna*, which is structured as a frame story in the tradition of *The Thousand and One Nights* (see page 638). A modern counterpart to the medieval Arabic storyteller Scheherazade, Eva Luna tells stories to entertain her lover, Rolf Carlé, a photojournalist and documentary filmmaker. But in this, the volume's final story, Allende turns the tables by making Rolf himself the principal character of Eva Luna's tale.

Although Allende never explicitly identifies the setting of this story, its details are obviously based on one of the most deadly natural disasters of recent times in Latin America: the eruption of the volcano Nevado del Ruiz in Colombia on November 13, 1985. This catastrophe completely destroyed the town of Armero, burying it in a tidal wave of mud. More than 20,000 people were killed. Many of the victims died horrible, slow deaths as they waited in vain for rescuers to reach them. In press coverage of the event, a single image became an emblem of the disaster to millions of people throughout the world: that of thirteen-year-old Omaira Sanchez, trapped up to her neck in mud as rescuers tried to release her.

Writer's Response

Freewrite your ideas about how media coverage influences our perceptions of events. Does media coverage of major events—especially tragic events, such as natural disasters—heighten our awareness and empathy, or does it in some ways desensitize us to harsh realities?

Literary Focus

Irony is a contrast or discrepancy between expectations and reality. Writers often use **situational irony**—which occurs when what actually happens is the opposite of what is expected or appropriate—in obvious, broadly comic ways for humorous or satirical purposes. But writers can also use situational irony in deadly serious, and less obvious, ways. In such cases, irony can be used to make scathing—even bitter—attacks, revealing how absurd or inhumane a situation really is.

PREREADING FOCUS

Background: *The Stories of Eva Luna* (1991) may be regarded as a sequel to Allende's novel *Eva Luna*, which appeared two years previously. In both books, Eva Luna's storytelling voice is paramount. Allende dedicated the novel to her mother, who, she says, gave her a love of stories. Reviewing the novel in an essay entitled "Scheherazade in Chile," critic Alan Ryan commented that the storytelling dimension of Allende's fiction shows that, for Allende, stories literally transform life.

Writer's Response: Before they write, you might ask students to discuss the role of the media in reporting natural disasters and other important current events. Ask them to consider one or more of these questions: Can the media be entirely balanced and objective? (Should it try to be?) Does the media tend to "hype" particular issues or stories? Are certain participants singled out and made into "symbols" of a drama scripted by the media, rather than treated as individual human beings who are entitled to privacy, consideration, and respect?

subterranean (sub′tə·rā′nē·ən): located or happening under the earth

1 READER'S RESPONSE

After reading the first paragraph, pause to consider what you anticipate will happen in the story. How might the title be related to the setting? What might the last sentence of the paragraph foreshadow about Rolf Carlé? (Answers will vary.)

2 HISTORICAL BACKGROUND

The eruption of Mount Ruiz on November 13, 1985, was one of the worst catastrophes in the history of Colombia, killing about 25,000 people. The volcano is located in the Cordillera Central, the highest Andean range in Colombia, containing peaks of over 17,000 feet. In the eruption, snow and ice that covered the volcano melted and mixed with great mudflows that cascaded down the slopes, completely burying the town of Armero. According to accounts, the first mudflows were icy cold; subsequent mudflows were fiery hot.

AND OF CLAY ARE WE CREATED

Isabel Allende

translated by

MARGARET SAYERS PEDEN

Read to page 1312, where Rolf Carlé asks the girl her name. What do you predict will happen to Carlé and the girl in this story? What do you suppose might be the meaning of the story's title?

They discovered the girl's head protruding from the mudpit, eyes wide open, calling soundlessly. She had a First Communion[1] name, Azucena.[2] Lily. In that vast cemetery where the odor of death was already attracting vultures from far away, and where the weeping of orphans and wails of the injured filled the air, the little girl obstinately clinging to life became the symbol of the tragedy. The television cameras transmitted so often the unbearable image of the head budding like a black squash from the clay that there was no one who did not recognize her and know her name. And every time we saw her on the screen, right behind her was Rolf Carlé, who had gone there on assignment, never suspecting that he would find a fragment of his past, lost thirty years before.

First a subterranean sob rocked the cotton fields, curling them like waves of foam. Geologists had set up their seismographs weeks before and knew that the mountain had awakened again. For some time they had predicted that the heat of the eruption could detach the eternal ice from the slopes of the volcano, but no one heeded their warnings; they sounded like the tales of frightened old women. The towns in the valley went about their daily life, deaf to the moaning of the earth, until that fateful Wednesday night in November when a prolonged roar announced the end of the world, and walls of snow broke loose, rolling in an avalanche of clay, stones, and water that descended on the villages and buried them beneath unfathomable meters of telluric[3] vomit. As soon as the survivors emerged from the paralysis of that first awful terror, they could see that houses, plazas, churches, white cotton plantations, dark coffee forests, cattle pastures—all had disappeared. Much later, after soldiers and volunteers had arrived to rescue the living and try to assess the magnitude of the cataclysm, it was cal-

---

1. **First Communion:** occasion on which Roman Catholics receive the sacrament of the Eucharist for the first time.
2. **Azucena** (ä·soo·sä′nä)
3. **telluric:** pertaining to the earth or soil.

culated that beneath the mud lay more than twenty thousand human beings and an indefinite number of animals putrefying in a viscous soup. Forests and rivers had also been swept away, and there was nothing to be seen but an immense desert of mire.

When the station called before dawn, Rolf Carlé and I were together. I crawled out of bed, dazed with sleep, and went to prepare coffee while he hurriedly dressed. He stuffed his gear in the green canvas backpack he always carried, and we said goodbye, as we had so many times before. I had no presentiments. I sat in the kitchen, sipping my coffee and planning the long hours without him, sure that he would be back the next day.

He was one of the first to reach the scene, because while other reporters were fighting their way to the edges of that morass in jeeps, bicycles, or on foot, each getting there however he could, Rolf Carlé had the advantage of the television helicopter, which flew him over the avalanche. We watched on our screens the footage captured by his assistant's camera, in which he was up to his knees in muck, a microphone in his hand, in the midst of a bedlam of lost children, wounded survivors, corpses, and devastation. The story came to us in his calm voice. For years he had been a familiar figure in newscasts, reporting live at the scene of battles and catastrophes with awesome tenac-

3

Vulkan, Dr. Atl, 1945.
? *Is your mental image of the volcanic eruption described in the story anything like the eruption portrayed in this painting? How are the two images alike? How do they differ?*

---

3 LITERARY ELEMENT

Imagery: Allende's graphic images and unusual figures of speech force the reader to focus on the repellent, almost grotesque aspects of the eruption's aftermath. What is the effect of figurative phrases like *telluric vomit, viscous soup,* and *desert of mire*? (to make the situation visceral and disturbing to the reader)

> ■ **presentiments** (prē·zent'ə·mənts): feelings or forewarnings that something is about to happen

---

■ HUMANITIES CONNECTION

Mexican painter, writer, and volcanologist Gerardo Murillo (1875–1964) adopted the pseudonym Dr. Atl ("Doctor Water" in the Aztec language Nahuatl) early in his career. He studied in Europe, but he returned to Mexico when the Revolution broke out and became involved with Diego Rivera's muralist movement. Atl's primary interest was the landscape, which he painted using "atl-colors," or crayons of wax, resins, and pigment that he himself invented. In 1943, Atl began documenting the eruption of the volcano Paricutín. Years later he began to sketch this and other volcanoes from the cockpit of an airplane.
? *How do the colors used in the painting contribute to its effect on the viewer?* (Answers will vary.) ■

Isabel Allende **1311**

ity. Nothing could stop him, and I was always amazed at his equanimity in the face of danger and suffering; it seemed as if nothing could shake his fortitude or deter his curiosity. Fear seemed never to touch him, although he had confessed to me that he was not a courageous man, far from it. I believe that the lens of the camera had a strange effect on him; it was as if it transported him to a different time from which he could watch events without actually participating in them. When I knew him better, I came to realize that this fictive distance seemed to protect him from his own emotions.

Rolf Carlé was in on the story of Azucena from the beginning. He filmed the volunteers who discovered her, and the first persons who tried to reach her; his camera zoomed in on the girl, her dark face, her large desolate eyes, the plastered-down tangle of her hair. The mud was like quicksand around her, and anyone attempting to reach her was in danger of sinking. They threw a rope to her that she made no effort to grasp until they shouted to her to catch it; then she pulled a hand from the mire and tried to move, but immediately sank a little deeper. Rolf threw down his knapsack and the rest of his equipment and waded into the quagmire, commenting for his assistant's microphone that it was cold and that one could begin to smell the stench of corpses.

"What's your name?" he asked the girl, and she told him her flower name. "Don't move, Azucena," Rolf Carlé directed, and kept talking to her, without a thought for what he was saying, just to distract her, while slowly he worked his way forward in mud up to his waist. The air around him seemed as murky as the mud.

It was impossible to reach her from the approach he was attempting, so he retreated and circled around where there seemed to be firmer footing. When finally he was close enough, he took the rope and tied it beneath her arms, so they could pull her out. He smiled at her with that smile that crinkles his eyes and makes him look like a little boy; he told her that everything was fine, that he was here with her now, that soon they would have her out. He signaled the others to pull, but as soon as the cord tensed, the girl screamed. They tried again, and her shoulders and arms appeared, but they could move her no farther; she was trapped. Someone suggested that her legs might be caught in the collapsed walls of her house, but she said it was not just rubble, that she was also held by the bodies of her brothers and sisters clinging to her legs.

"Don't worry, we'll get you out of here," Rolf promised. Despite the quality of the transmission, I could hear his voice break, and I loved him more than ever. Azucena looked at him, but said nothing.

During those first hours Rolf Carlé exhausted all the resources of his ingenuity to rescue her. He struggled with poles and ropes, but every tug was an intolerable torture for the imprisoned girl. It occurred to him to use one of the poles as a lever but got no result and had to abandon the idea. He talked a couple of soldiers into working with him for a while, but they had to leave because so many other victims were calling for help. The girl could not move, she barely could breathe, but she did not seem desperate, as if an ancestral resignation allowed her to accept her fate. The reporter, on the other hand, was determined to snatch her from death. Someone brought him a tire, which he placed beneath her arms like a life buoy, and then laid a plank near the hole to hold his weight and allow him to stay closer to her. As it was impossible to remove the rubble blindly, he tried once or twice to dive toward her feet, but emerged frustrated, covered with mud, and spitting gravel. He concluded that he would have to have a pump to drain the water, and radioed a request for one, but received in return a message that there was no available transport and it could not be sent until the next morning.

8 "We can't wait that long!" Rolf Carlé shouted, but in the pandemonium no one stopped to commiserate. Many more hours would go by before he accepted that time had stagnated and reality had been irreparably distorted.

A military doctor came to examine the girl, and observed that her heart was functioning well and that if she did not get too cold she could survive the night.

"Hang on, Azucena, we'll have the pump tomorrow," Rolf Carlé tried to console her.

"Don't leave me alone," she begged.

"No, of course I won't leave you."

Someone brought him coffee, and he helped the girl drink it, sip by sip. The warm liquid revived her and she began telling him about her small life, about her family and her school, about how things were in that little bit of world before the volcano had erupted. She was thirteen, and she had never been outside her village. Rolf Carlé, buoyed by a premature optimism, was convinced that everything would end well: the pump would arrive, they would drain the water, move the rubble, and Azucena would be transported by helicopter to a hospital where she would recover rapidly and where he could visit her and bring her gifts. He 9 thought, She's already too old for dolls, and I don't know what would please her; maybe a dress. I don't know much about women,

he concluded, amused, reflecting that al-9 though he had known many women in his lifetime, none had taught him these details. To pass the hours he began to tell Azucena about his travels and adventures as a newshound, and when he exhausted his memory, he called upon imagination, inventing things 10 he thought might entertain her. From time to time she dozed, but he kept talking in the darkness, to assure her that he was still there and to overcome the menace of uncertainty.

That was a long night.

Many miles away, I watched Rolf Carlé and the girl on a television screen. I could not bear the wait at home, so I went to National Television, where I often spent entire nights with Rolf editing programs. There, I was near his world, and I could at least get a feeling of what he lived through during those three decisive days. I called all the important people in the city, senators, commanders of the armed forces, the North American ambassador, and the president of National Petroleum, begging them for a 11 pump to remove the silt, but obtained only vague promises. I began to ask for urgent help on radio and television, to see if there wasn't *someone* who could help us. Between calls I would run to the newsroom to monitor the satellite transmissions that periodically brought new details of the catastrophe. While reporters selected scenes with most impact for the news report, I searched for footage that featured Azucena's mudpit. The screen reduced the disaster to a single plane and accentuated the tremendous distance that separated me from Rolf Carlé; nonetheless, I was there with him. The child's every suffering hurt me as it did him; I felt his frustration, his impotence. Faced with the

Isabel Allende 1313

8 LITERARY ELEMENT

Conflict: What is the major conflict in the story at this point? (an external conflict—a struggle against time to free Azucena from the mud) How do Rolf Carlé and Azucena contrast in their attitudes toward the conflict? (Rolf desperately tries every measure to free the girl, while Azucena seems calm and resigned.)

9 LITERARY ELEMENT

Point of View: How does the point of view shift in this passage? (The details about Rolf Carlé's inner thoughts make us realize that he is now a character in Eva Luna's story; she can reveal his thoughts just as an omniscient narrator might.)

10 INFERRING

Why do you think talking and storytelling seem so important to Rolf at this point? (He thinks it's important to reassure Azucena. He is also probably trying to reassure himself.)

11 COMPARING AND CONTRASTING

Rolf has been optimistic about Azucena's chances for survival. How does this passage present a contrast to Rolf's optimism? (Eva Luna is frustrated in her efforts to obtain the pump. The passage acts as a foreshadowing, suggesting that Azucena may not be saved in time, after all.)

Jimmy Dorantes, © Latin Focus

impossibility of communicating with him, the fantastic idea came to me that if I tried, I could reach him by force of mind and in that way give him encouragement. I concentrated until I was dizzy—a frenzied and futile activity. At times I would be overcome with compassion and burst out crying; at other times, I was so drained I felt as if I were staring through a telescope at the light of a star dead for a million years.

I watched that hell on the first morning broadcast, cadavers of people and animals awash in the current of new rivers formed overnight from the melted snow. Above the mud rose the tops of trees and the bell towers of a church where several people had taken refuge and were patiently awaiting rescue teams. Hundreds of soldiers and volunteers from the Civil Defense were clawing through rubble searching for survivors, while long rows of ragged specters awaited their turn for a cup of hot broth. Radio networks announced that their phones were jammed with calls from families offering shelter to orphaned children. Drinking water was in scarce supply, along with gasoline and food. Doctors, resigned to amputating arms and legs without anesthesia, pled that at least they be sent serum and painkillers and antibiotics; most of the roads, however, were impassable, and worse were the bureaucratic obstacles that stood in the way. To top it all, the clay contaminated by decomposing bodies threatened the living with an outbreak of epidemics.

Azucena was shivering inside the tire that held her above the surface. Immobility and tension had greatly weakened her, but she was conscious and could still be heard when a microphone was held out to her. Her tone was humble, as if apologizing for all the fuss. Rolf Carlé had a growth of beard, and dark circles beneath his eyes; he looked near exhaustion. Even from that enormous distance I could sense the quality of his weariness, so different from the fatigue of other adventures. He had completely forgotten the camera; he could not look at the girl through a lens any longer. The pictures we were receiving were not his assistant's but those of other reporters who had appropriated Azucena, bestowing on her the pathetic respon-

15 sibility of embodying the horror of what had happened in that place. With the first light Rolf tried again to dislodge the obstacles that held the girl in her tomb, but he had only his hands to work with; he did not dare use a tool for fear of injuring her. He fed Azucena a cup of the cornmeal mush and bananas the Army was distributing, but she immediately vomited it up. A doctor stated that she had a fever, but added that there was little he could do: antibiotics were being reserved for cases of gangrene. A priest also passed by and blessed her, hanging a medal of the Virgin around her neck. By evening a gentle, persistent drizzle began to fall.

"The sky is weeping," Azucena murmured, and she, too, began to cry.

"Don't be afraid," Rolf begged. "You have to keep your strength up and be calm. Everything will be fine. I'm with you, and I'll get you out somehow."

16 Reporters returned to photograph Azucena and ask her the same questions, which she no longer tried to answer. In the meanwhile, more television and movie teams arrived with spools of cable, tapes, film, videos, precision lenses, recorders, sound consoles, lights, reflecting screens, auxiliary motors, cartons of supplies, electricians, sound technicians, and cameramen: Azucena's face was beamed to millions of screens around the world. And all the while Rolf Carlé kept pleading for a pump. The improved technical facilities bore results, and National Television began receiving sharper pictures and clearer sound; the distance seemed suddenly compressed, and I had the horrible sensation that Azucena and Rolf were by my side, separated from me by impenetrable glass. I was able to follow events hour by hour, I knew everything my love did to wrest the girl from her prison and

help her endure her suffering; I overheard fragments of what they said to one another and could guess the rest; I was present when she taught Rolf to pray, and when he distracted her with the stories I had told him in a thousand and one nights beneath the white mosquito netting of our bed. 17

When darkness came on the second day, Rolf tried to sing Azucena to sleep with old Austrian folk songs he had learned from his mother, but she was far beyond sleep. They spent most of the night talking, each in a stupor of exhaustion and hunger, and shaking with cold. That night, imperceptibly, the unyielding floodgates that had contained Rolf Carlé's past for so many years began to open, and the torrent of all that had lain hidden in the deepest and most secret layers of memory poured out, leveling before it the obstacles that had blocked his consciousness for so long. He could not tell it all to Azucena; she perhaps did not know there was a world beyond the sea or time previous to her own; she was not capable of imagining Europe in the years of the war. So he could not tell her of defeat, nor of the afternoon the Russians had led them to the concentration camp to bury prisoners dead from starvation. Why should he describe to her how the naked bodies piled like a mountain of firewood resembled fragile china? How could he tell this dying child about ovens and gallows? Nor did he mention the night that he had seen his mother naked, shod in stiletto-heeled red boots, sobbing with humiliation. There was much he did not tell, but in those hours he relived for the first time all the things his mind had tried to erase. Azucena had surrendered her fear to him and so, without wishing it, had obliged Rolf to confront his own. There, beside that hellhole of mud, it was impossible for Rolf to flee from 19

18

16 LITERARY ELEMENT
Irony: How does the equipment of the journalists contrast ironically with the supply of medicines in the disaster area? (Possible response: Whereas the journalists have every conceivable technological gadget, essential medicines such as antibiotics are in such short supply that they have to be rationed.)

17 COMPARING LITERATURE
The narrative here explicitly alludes to the classic medieval Arabian collection *The Thousand and One Nights* (pp. 638–645), and Allende also refers to the outer "frame" of *The Stories of Eva Luna*.

18 LITERARY ELEMENT
Metaphor: What is being compared in this metaphor? (Rolf's repressive mechanism is being compared to floodgates that are being forced open by torrents of painful memories.)

19 HISTORICAL BACKGROUND
This passage is probably an allusion to the Holocaust, in which approximately six million Jews perished from Nazi genocide during World War II. Be sure that students understand that Rolf Carlé was born in Europe.

20 GUIDED READING
Comparing and Contrasting: How is Azucena's present situation similar to some of the events that Rolf remembers from his childhood? How are the situations of the two characters different? (Just as Azucena is cruelly imprisoned in the mudpit, Rolf and his sister Katharina were locked in the armoire by their stern, cruel father. Katharina also resembles Azucena in that both girls seem doomed to a wretched destiny. Rolf and Azucena are different, however, in that Rolf's childhood was scarred by family woes and a world war, while Azucena's life is threatened by a natural disaster.)

21 LITERARY ELEMENT
Theme: What does this description of Rolf Carlé's moment of illumination suggest about a central theme of the story? (No matter how hard people try to escape from their deepest emotions or fears, these feelings will always surface in a moment of truth.)

himself any longer, and the visceral terror he had lived as a boy suddenly invaded him. He reverted to the years when he was the age of Azucena, and younger, and, like her, found himself trapped in a pit without escape, buried in life, his head barely above ground; he saw before his eyes the boots and legs of his father, who had removed his belt and was whipping it in the air with the never-forgotten hiss of a viper coiled to strike. Sorrow flooded through him, intact and precise, as if it had lain always in his mind, waiting. He was once again in the armoire[4] where his father locked him to punish him for imagined misbehavior, there where for eternal hours he had crouched with his eyes closed, not to see the darkness, with his hands over his ears, to shut out the beating of his heart, trembling, huddled like a cornered animal. Wandering in the mist of his memories he found his sister Katharina, a sweet, retarded child who spent her life hiding, with the hope that her father would forget the disgrace of her having been born. With Katharina, Rolf crawled beneath the dining room table, and with her hid there under the long white tablecloth, two children forever embraced, alert to footsteps and voices. Katharina's scent melded with his own sweat, with aromas of cooking, garlic, soup, freshly baked bread, and the unexpected odor of putrescent clay. His sister's hand in his, her frightened breathing, her silk hair against his cheek, the candid gaze of her eyes. Katharina . . . Katharina materialized before him, floating on the air like a flag, clothed in the white tablecloth, now a winding sheet, and at last he could weep for her death and for the guilt of having abandoned her. He understood then that

---

4. **armoire** (är·mwär′): a large wardrobe or movable cupboard with doors and shelves.

all his exploits as a reporter, the feats that had won him such recognition and fame, were merely an attempt to keep his most ancient fears at bay, a stratagem for taking refuge behind a lens to test whether reality was more tolerable from that perspective. He took excessive risks as an exercise of courage, training by day to conquer the monsters that tormented him by night. But he had come face to face with the moment of truth; he could not continue to escape his past. He *was* Azucena; he was buried in the clayey mud; his terror was not the distant emotion of an almost forgotten childhood, it was a claw sunk in his throat. In the flush of his tears he saw his mother, dressed in black and clutching her imitation-crocodile pocketbook to her bosom, just as he had last seen her on the dock when she had come to put him on the boat to South America. She had not come to dry his tears, but to tell him to pick up a shovel: the war was over and now they must bury the dead.

"Don't cry. I don't hurt anymore. I'm fine," Azucena said when dawn came.

"I'm not crying for you," Rolf Carlé smiled. "I'm crying for myself. I hurt all over."

The third day in the valley of the cataclysm began with a pale light filtering through storm clouds. The President of the Republic visited the area in his tailored safari jacket to confirm that this was the worst catastrophe of the century; the country was in mourning; sister nations had offered aid; he had ordered a state of siege; the armed forces would be merciless, anyone caught stealing or committing other offenses would be shot on sight. He added that it was impossible to remove all the corpses or count the thousands who had disappeared; the entire valley would be declared holy ground, and bishops would come to celebrate a sol-

22 LITERARY ELEMENT

Irony: What is ironic about the remarks the narrator reports from the President of the Republic? (The President has shown up to appear concerned and involved, but he does absolutely nothing to help, instead simply offering platitudes, clichés, and threats. He seems absolutely unmoved by the plight of Azucena, even though she is right in front of him.)

23 LITERARY ELEMENT

Paradox: What is paradoxical about Eva Luna's conclusion in this passage? (The paradox, or apparent contradiction, resides in the fact that the acceptance of death frees both Azucena and Rolf Carlé from despair.)

WRITING TO LEARN

Science: Write a brief magazine article report about some aspect of volcanoes that this story makes you wonder about: how volcanic eruptions can be predicted; how volcanoes are formed; classifications of volcanic activity; specific information about Nevado del Ruiz. ∎

emn mass for the souls of the victims. He went to the Army field tents to offer relief in the form of vague promises to crowds of the rescued, then to the improvised hospital to offer a word of encouragement to doctors and nurses worn down from so many hours of tribulations. Then he asked to be taken to see Azucena, the little girl the whole world had seen. He waved to her with a limp statesman's hand, and microphones recorded his emotional voice and paternal tone as he told her that her courage had served as an example to the nation. Rolf Carlé interrupted to ask for a pump, and the President assured him that he personally would attend to the matter. I caught a glimpse of Rolf for a few seconds kneeling beside the mudpit. On the evening news broadcast, he was still in the same position; and I, glued to the screen like a fortuneteller to her crystal ball, could tell that something fundamental had changed in him. I knew somehow that during the night his defenses had crumbled and he had given in to grief; finally he was vulnerable. The girl had touched a part of him that he himself had no access to, a part he had never shared with me. Rolf had wanted to console her, but it was Azucena who had given him consolation.

I recognized the precise moment at which Rolf gave up the fight and surrendered to the torture of watching the girl die. I was with them, three days and two nights, spying on them from the other side of life. I was there when she told him that in all her thirteen years no boy had ever loved her and that it was a pity to leave this world without knowing love. Rolf assured her that he loved her more than he could ever love anyone, more than he loved his mother, more than his sister, more than all the women who had slept in his arms, more than he loved me, his life companion, who would have given anything to be trapped in

READING CHECK

1. How many lives were lost in the eruption? (more than 20,000)
2. What does Rolf Carlé need in order to free Azucena? (a pump)
3. Who is Katharina? (Rolf Carlé's sister)
4. What does the President tell Azucena? (that her courage is an example to the nation)

5. After three days and two nights, what does Rolf pray for? (that Azucena will die quickly)

RETEACHING

Have students work in small groups to retell the principal events of the story in the format of a script for a television news report on a *60 Minutes*–style program. As students work on their scripts, encourage them to bear in mind the story's portrayal of journalism and the media.

MEETING INDIVIDUAL NEEDS

24 *LEP:* Help students understand the abrupt shift of pronouns and point of view in the story's final paragraph. Point out that this coda to the story assumes that considerable time has passed. Eva Luna is now addressing Rolf Carlé directly. ■

ANSWERS
First Thoughts
Answers will vary.

Identifying Facts
1. a volcanic eruption. He is sent on assignment and arrives in a helicopter.
2. to pump out the water; he must wait until morning
3. She uses all her contacts and finally procures a pump.
4. They tell each other stories. They learn details of each others' lives.
5. on the night of the second day; horrors of World War II, parental abuse, the death of his sister
6. He sits silently, lost in painful memories.

Interpreting Meanings
1. a. yet there is transport available for media equipment; b. getting in sophisticated equipment occurs with ease, but getting a water pump proves impossible; c. The President does nothing, yet uses Azucena as a symbol of his concern.

---

that well in her place, who would have exchanged her life for Azucena's, and I watched as he leaned down to kiss her poor forehead, consumed by a sweet, sad emotion he could not name. I felt how in that instant both were saved from despair, how they were freed from the clay, how they rose above the vultures and helicopters, how together they flew above the vast swamp of corruption and laments. How, finally, they were able to accept death. Rolf Carlé prayed in silence that she would die quickly, because such pain cannot be borne.

By then I had obtained a pump and was in touch with a general who had agreed to ship it the next morning on a military cargo plane. But on the night of that third day, beneath the unblinking focus of quartz lamps and the lens of a hundred cameras, Azucena gave up, her eyes locked with those of the friend who had sustained her to the

end. Rolf Carlé removed the life buoy, closed her eyelids, held her to his chest for a few moments, and then let her go. She sank slowly, a flower in the mud.

You are back with me, but you are not the same man. I often accompany you to the station and we watch the videos of Azucena again; you study them intently, looking for something you could have done to save her, something you did not think of in time. Or maybe you study them to see yourself as if in a mirror, naked. Your cameras lie forgotten in a closet; you do not write or sing; you sit long hours before the window, staring at the mountains. Beside you, I wait for you to complete the voyage into yourself, for the old wounds to heal. I know that when you return from your nightmares, we shall again walk hand in hand, as before.

24

First Thoughts
Did you predict how this story would end? What feelings were you left with at the end of the story?

Identifying Facts
1. At the beginning of the story, what natural disaster has just occurred? Why does Rolf Carlé end up at the scene of the disaster?
2. Why does Rolf Carlé ask for a pump? What response does he get to his request?
3. What role does Eva Luna play in Carlé's quest for a pump?
4. How do Rolf Carlé and Azucena pass the time as they wait for the pump? What do the two learn about each other?
5. At what point in the story do Carlé's

memories erupt? What are some of his memories about his own childhood?
6. According to Eva Luna at the end of the story, in what ways has Rolf changed?

Interpreting Meanings
1. Explain how each of the following events in the story serves as an example of **situational irony**.
   a. When Rolf Carlé asks for a pump, he is told that no transport is available for one.
   b. Further shipments of state-of-the-art technical equipment arrive, enabling the world to get a better view of the disaster and of Azucena's suffering.
   c. The President of the Republic, in his "tailored safari jacket," waves to Azucena and congratulates her on her courage, but answers vaguely when Rolf Carlé pleads for a pump.

1. **Researching a Historical Event.** Encourage students to explore library news archives for journalists' reporting of the catastrophic eruption of Mount Ruiz in Colombia on November 13, 1985. Students might examine newspaper and magazine reports in both English and Spanish for factual content, objectivity, and tone. Then they might discuss elements of the coverage that they think may have inspired Allende in writing this story.

2. **Discussing Psychological Issues.** Have students get together in small groups to research and report to the class on one of the following psychological topics suggested by the story: the controversy over recovered memories; post-traumatic stress disorder; survivor guilt; the psychological stages in dying.

CLOSURE

Ask students whether they think "And of Clay Are We Created" carries a message for life today in a technological age of information. What is the impact on our lives of being able to have instant access via television to events like wars and natural disasters all over the world? ◼

Identify other examples of irony in the story. What effect does Allende achieve by inserting these ironic details?

2. How does Allende use **irony** to comment on television journalism in this story? What do you think is the most important point she makes about the media?

3. This story is narrated by Eva Luna, who is on the periphery of events. Find places in the story where this **point of view** seems to shift—where we see events from inside the mind of Rolf Carlé. Is this an actual shift in point of view, or is the story consistently told from Eva Luna's perspective? How do you know? Explain how Allende's use of point of view adds to or detracts from the **theme** of the story.

4. In what respects is this a story about storytelling? Identify the main storytellers in this story. Explain what point you think Allende is making about the role of storytelling in our lives.

5. Allende compares the eruption of Rolf Carlé's repressed feelings to the eruption and devastation of the volcano itself. What parallels are there between the volcanic disaster and the mental deluge Rolf experiences? In what sense does Azucena become a **metaphor** for some aspect of Rolf Carlé's inner world?

6. The story's title contains an **allusion** to an idea that dates from biblical times: Human beings are made of clay (or dust), and they return to clay (or dust) in death. This idea appears in Isaiah 45:9 in the Old Testament: "Woe to him who strives with his Maker! . . . Does the clay say to him who fashions it, 'What are you making?' " How does this allusion serve as a clue to the **theme** of the story?

Applying Meanings

At the end of the fourth paragraph, Eva Luna mentions the "fictive distance" that Rolf Carlé has set up "to protect him from his own emotions" in his high-stress profession. In what careers besides journalism do you think people tend to create a protective shell or an emotional barrier so that they can do their jobs objectively? Do you think this tendency is necessary or healthy? Explain your response.

Creative Writing Response

Writing a Scene. Using details from the narrative, write a brief dramatic scene between Azucena and Rolf Carlé for a film version of the story. In your scene, be as faithful as you can to the elements of suspense, characterization, mood, and theme in the story.

Critical Writing Response

Comparing Fact and Fiction. Though this story is a work of fiction, it is based on many of the actual events in the disaster at Armero in 1985: There really was a thirteen-year-old girl trapped up to her neck in mud (though she was being held fast by the body of an aunt, not by siblings); there really was an unanswered request for a water pump; the aftermath of the disaster really was as horrifying as Allende describes it; and the young girl really died. Knowing this, explain, in a brief essay, how you feel about Allende's decision to use this actual event as the basis for a work of fiction. Does the emphasis on the character of Rolf Carlé heighten or detract from the magnitude of the horror of the disaster? Does Allende trivialize and distort a real tale of human anguish by fictionalizing it, or does the act of making a story out of an actual disaster make the event somehow more human and comprehensible?

2. Possible response: The media's extravagant paraphernalia contrasts with the scarcity of medical supplies. Allende hints that the media is self-indulgent, using human tragedy as a means to justify its own existence.

3. Although the point of view seems to alternate between first-person (Eva Luna) and third-person limited (Rolf Carlé), this is not really a shift in point of view because Eva Luna is still telling the story.

4. Possible responses: Both Rolf Carlé and Azucena tell each other stories; the media and the government are telling the world a story. Allende seems to be suggesting that storytelling is a life-sustaining human activity, though it can also promote illusions.

5. Possible responses: Rolf's mental eruption releases buried memories. Azucena may represent the childlike part of Rolf that has been largely buried since his early years.

6. Possible response: Human beings must recognize both the preciousness of life and the inevitability of death.

Applying Meanings
Answers will vary.

Creative Writing Response
Writing a Scene. Allow students to work in pairs or small groups for this activity.

Critical Writing Response
Comparing Fact and Fiction. Students may work in small groups to conduct their research. ◼

Hoping to broaden her horizons, Jamaica Kincaid left Antigua at the age of sixteen to
work as a household servant in
the United States. Eventually
she found employment with a
wealthy New York City couple.
When she left their home to
accept a scholarship at Fran-
conia College in New Hamp-
shire, she still had no plans to
become a writer.

Kincaid's writing career began almost by accident. Her
long association with *The New
Yorker* began when one of her
magazine articles came to the
attention of *New Yorker* col-
umnist George Trow, who was
deeply impressed by her vivid
descriptions of growing up in
Antigua. Trow began to quote
Kincaid in *The New Yorker*'s
"Talk of the Town" column,
and soon she was invited to
write her own *New Yorker* article—about a West Indian Day
parade in Brooklyn. Her success encouraged her to try to
write fiction. The result was
"Girl" and other experimental
stories, which were published
first in *The New Yorker* and
then in *At the Bottom of the
River* (1983). *Annie John* (1985),
Kincaid's semiautobiographical
novel that is set in Antigua,
won kudos from critics
throughout the English-
speaking world. Similar praise
marked the reviews of *Lucy*
(1990), another semiautobiographical novel, which is based
on Kincaid's early experiences
in the United States. In 1996,
she published another novel,
*The Autobiography of My
Mother*.

Jamaica Kincaid
b. 1949, Antigua

Sigrid Estrada

Over the kitchen table in the Vermont
home that Jamaica Kincaid shares with
her American-born husband and children is
a map of the island of Antigua (än·tē′gwə).
It serves as a constant reminder of the tiny
Caribbean island where Kincaid grew up and
where she still sets most of her fiction.

Born Elaine Potter Richardson to an Antiguan couple of African descent, Kincaid
grew up in St. John's, Antigua's largest city.
Antigua was still a British colony during Kincaid's childhood, and she came to hate the
European colonialism that had exploited her
people for so many centuries.

At school Kincaid was a bright but unruly
pupil, often punished for her outspokenness.
Once, her punishment was to copy long passages from John Milton's epic *Paradise Lost*,
a work she can now quote at length.

After attending college in New Hamp-
shire, Kincaid returned to New York City and
began writing for a teenage girls' magazine,
using her pen name for the first time. Soon
Kincaid published her first story, "Girl," in
The New Yorker. The story consists of a
single long sentence of instructions given by
a mother to a daughter who is possibly, from
the mother's point of view, headed for rebellion and trouble.

One of the central subjects of Kincaid's
fiction is the parent-child relationship and
the problems her rebellious heroines have
with their worried mothers. Kincaid also
writes about the anger that West Indians of
African descent feel about their colonial past.
"As I sit here enjoying myself to a degree,"
Kincaid told *New York Times* interviewer
Leslie Garis, "I never give up thinking about
the way I came into the world, how my
ancestors came from Africa to the West Indies as slaves. I just could never forget it."

OBJECTIVES

1. To interpret a selection from a West Indian novel
2. To examine a character's internal conflict
3. To write a description of a significant place and an essay analyzing an internal conflict
4. To read a West Indian poem and to compare and contrast it to the selection

Reader's Guide

A WALK TO THE JETTY
from Annie John

Background

Antigua, the main island of the nation of Antigua and Barbuda, was a British colony for over three hundred years. The British forcibly brought people from Africa to work as slaves on the island's sugar plantations. Today the descendants of these Africans make up most of Antigua's population. Antigua won its independence in 1981, but British influences are still strong on the island. The people speak English and many belong to the Anglican (Episcopalian) Church. The school Jamaica Kincaid attended as a girl was modeled on British schools of the time—boys and girls were educated separately, uniforms were required, and a British curriculum, especially in literature, was stressed.

The selection you are about to read is taken from the last part of the last chapter of Kincaid's coming-of-age novel *Annie John.* In this section of the novel, the young narrator is about to leave Antigua by boat for England.

Writer's Response

When you think back over the years of your childhood, what incidents and images come to your mind? Make a few notes about your strongest memories. Which memories make you happy? Which ones make you sad or angry?

Literary Focus

Much of twentieth-century literature deals with **internal conflicts**, rather than with action-packed **external conflicts**. Annie John, the narrator of this selection, has all kinds of conflicts with other characters throughout the book, but in this excerpt, we see only her internal conflicts.

PREREADING FOCUS

Background: The independent state of Antigua and Barbuda consists of three islands—Antigua, Barbuda, and tiny, uninhabited Redonda. The islands lie in the Caribbean Sea about 400 miles north of Venezuela. St. John's, where Kincaid grew up, is the capital and largest city, although its population is only about 36,000, and was even smaller when Kincaid was a child.

Students unfamiliar with the geography of the region may find it helpful to pinpoint Antigua on a map. Note that all the islands enclosed by the Caribbean Sea are usually known as the West Indies. The larger, more northerly islands of Cuba, Jamaica, Hispaniola (shared by Haiti and the Dominican Republic), and Puerto Rico are sometimes called the Greater Antilles. The smaller islands, including Antigua, that stretch in a crescent southeast of Puerto Rico are usually called the Lesser Antilles. Also part of the West Indies are the Bahama Islands.

Literary Focus: Remind students that *conflict* refers to the struggle on which the events of a plot are centered. Novels usually contain several conflicts. In an *external conflict*, a character struggles with an outside force such as another character, society in general, or an element of nature such as a blizzard or a drought. In an *internal conflict*, the struggle takes place within the character as he or she struggles to reach a decision or to resolve opposing emotions.

Varying Sentence Openings

Note how dull these sentences are: *The day was warm. The old man walked in the park. He enjoyed himself.* Instead of using the subject to open every sentence, good writers vary sentence openings:

Prepositional phrase: The day was warm. *In the park*, the old man walked. He enjoyed himself.

Participial phrase: The day was warm. *Walking in the park*, the old man enjoyed himself.

Adverbial clause: The day was warm. *When the old man walked in the park*, he enjoyed himself.

1. **Reading and Speaking.** Ask students to read the first four sentences of the selection and to note their varied openings. Ask which sentence opens with a subject (the first), a prepositional phrase (the second), and a participial phrase (the fourth).

A WALK TO THE JETTY
from Annie John
Jamaica Kincaid

❚ *As you read, think about why the narrator is leaving her home and how she feels about leaving.*

My mother had arranged with a stevedore[1] to take my trunk to the jetty ahead of me. At ten o'clock on the dot, I was dressed, and we set off for the jetty. An hour after that, I would board a launch that would take me out to sea, where I then would board the ship. Starting out, as if for old time's sake and without giving it a thought, we lined up in the old way: I walking between my mother and my father. I loomed way above my father and could see the top of his head. We must have made a strange sight: a grown girl all dressed up in the middle of a morning, in the middle of the week, walking in step in the middle between her two parents, for people we didn't know stared at us. It was all of half an hour's walk from our house to the jetty, but I was passing through most of the years of my life. We passed by the house where Miss Dulcie, the seamstress that I had been apprenticed to for a time, lived, and just as I was passing by, a wave of bad feeling for her came over me, because I suddenly remembered that the months I spent with her all she had me do was sweep the floor, which was always full of threads and pins and needles, and I never seemed

Antiguan landscape.
❓ *What happens to the narrator as she passes in front of the seamstress's shop? How have her feelings about the seamstress changed?*

---

1. **stevedore** (stē'və·dôr'): a person who loads and unloads cargo on a ship.

to sweep it clean enough to please her. Then she would send me to the store to buy buttons or thread, though I was only allowed to do this if I was given a sample of the button or thread, and then she would find fault even though they were an exact match of the samples she had given me. And all the while she said to me, "A girl like you will never learn to sew properly, you know." At the time, I don't suppose I minded it, because it was customary to treat the first-year apprentice with such scorn, but now I

Jacques Lowe/Woodfin Camp & Associates

placed on the dustheap of my life Miss Dulcie and everything that I had had to do with her.

We were soon on the road that I had taken to school, to church, to Sunday school, to choir practice, to Brownie meetings, to Girl Guide meetings, to meet a friend. I was five years old when I first walked on this road unaccompanied by someone to hold my hand. My mother had placed three pennies in my little basket, which was a duplicate of her bigger basket, and sent me to the chemist's shop[2] to buy a pennyworth of senna leaves, a pennyworth of eucalyptus leaves, and a pennyworth of camphor. She then instructed me on what side of the road to walk, where to make a turn, where to cross, how to look carefully before I crossed, and if I met anyone that I knew to politely pass greetings and keep on my way. I was wearing a freshly ironed yellow dress that had printed on it scenes of acrobats flying through the air and swinging on a trapeze. I had just had a bath, and after it, instead of powdering me with my baby-smelling talcum powder, my mother had, as a special favor, let me use her own talcum powder, which smelled quite perfumy and came in a can that had painted on it people going out to dinner in nineteenth-century London and was called Mazie. How it pleased me to walk out the door and bend my head down to sniff at myself and see that I smelled just like my mother. I went to the chemist's shop, and he had to come from behind the counter and bend down to hear what it was that I wanted to buy, my voice was so little and timid then. I went back just the way I had come, and when I walked into the yard and presented my basket with its three

2. **chemist's shop:** the British term for a pharmacy or drugstore.

Jamaica Kincaid **1323**

5 LITERARY ELEMENT

Hyperbole: Which sentence communicates an intense feeling through hyperbole, or exaggeration? ("If I had just conquered Persia") Why is Annie's mother so proud of her? (Annie has passed a milestone on the road to adulthood.)

6 SPECULATING

Why do you think Annie's mother ended the friendship? (Possible response: She probably considered the girl wayward or wild and her family socially objectionable.) What does this behavior show about the mother? (Possible response: She is loving, strict, interfering, judgmental, and probably class-conscious.)

7 CULTURAL BACKGROUND

When Annie was a child, the currency of Great Britain and its colonies included the *shilling,* a coin worth one twentieth of a *pound,* the chief unit of currency. The *penny* (plural, *pence*) was one twelfth of a shilling; its symbol was *d* (6d = sixpence).

8 GUIDED READING

Cause and Effect: Why did Annie insist that there was something wrong with her eyes? (She had read a story that made wearing glasses seem attractive.)

9 READER'S RESPONSE

Do you find these details about Annie's childhood attitudes believable? (Students should cite personal experiences to support their opinions.)

packages to my mother, her eyes filled with tears and she swooped me up and held me high in the air and said that I was wonderful and good and that there would never be anybody better. If I had just conquered Persia, she couldn't have been more proud of me.

We passed by our church—the church in which I had been christened and received and had sung in the junior choir. We passed by a house in which a girl I used to like and was sure I couldn't live without had lived. Once, when she had mumps, I went to visit her against my mother's wishes, and we sat on her bed and ate the cure of roasted, buttered sweet potatoes that had been placed on her swollen jaws, held there by a piece of white cloth. I don't know how, but my mother found out about it, and I don't know how, but she put an end to our friendship. Shortly after, the girl moved with her family across the sea to somewhere else. We passed the doll store, where I would go with my mother when I was little and point out the doll I wanted that year for Christmas. We passed the store where I bought the much-fought-over shoes I wore to church to be received in. We passed the bank. On my sixth birthday, I was given, among other things, the present of a sixpence. My mother and I then went to this bank, and with the sixpence I opened my own savings account. I was given a little gray book with my name in big letters on it, and in the balance column it said "6d." Every Saturday morning after that, I was given a sixpence—later a shilling, and later a two-and-sixpence piece—and I would take it to the bank for deposit. I had never been allowed to withdraw even a farthing[3] from my bank account until just a

---

3. **farthing:** a former small British coin worth a fourth of a penny.

few weeks before I was to leave; then the whole account was closed out, and I received from the bank the sum of six pounds ten shillings and two and a half pence.

We passed the office of the doctor who told my mother three times that I did not need glasses, that if my eyes were feeling weak a glass of carrot juice a day would make them strong again. This happened when I was eight. And so every day at recess I would run to my school gate and meet my mother, who was waiting for me with a glass of juice from carrots she had just grated and then squeezed, and I would drink it and then run back to meet my chums. I knew there was nothing at all wrong with my eyes, but I had recently read a story in *The Schoolgirl's Own Annual* in which the heroine, a girl a few years older than I was then, cut such a figure to my mind with the way she was always adjusting her small, round, horn-rimmed glasses that I felt I must have a pair exactly like them. When it became clear that I didn't need glasses, I began to complain about the glare of the sun being too much for my eyes, and I walked around with my hands shielding them—especially in my mother's presence. My mother then bought for me a pair of sunglasses with the exact horn-rimmed frames I wanted, and how I enjoyed the gestures of blowing on the lenses, wiping them with the hem of my uniform, adjusting the glasses when they slipped down my nose, and just removing them from their case and putting them on. In three weeks, I grew tired of them and they found a nice resting place in a drawer, along with some other things that at one time or another I couldn't live without.

We passed the store that sold only grooming aids, all imported from England. This store had in it a large porcelain dog—white, with black spots all over and a red ribbon

Sunday at church, Antigua.

of satin tied around its neck. The dog sat in front of a white porcelain bowl that was always filled with fresh water, and it sat in such a way that it looked as if it had just taken a long drink. When I was a small child, I would ask my mother, if ever we were near this store, to please take me to see the dog, and I would stand in front of it, bent over slightly, my hands resting on my knees, and stare at it and stare at it. I thought this dog more beautiful and more real than any actual dog I had ever seen or any actual dog I would ever see. I must have outgrown my interest in the dog, for when it disappeared I never asked what became of it. We passed the library, and if there was anything on this walk that I might have wept over leaving, this most surely would have been the thing. My mother had been a member of the library long before I was born. And since she took me everywhere with her when I was quite little, when she went to the library she

took me along there, too. I would sit in her lap very quietly as she read books that she did not want to take home with her. I could not read the words yet, but just the way they looked on the page was interesting to me. Once, a book she was reading had a large picture of a man in it, and when I asked her who he was she told me that he was Louis Pasteur and that the book was about his life. It stuck in my mind, because she said it was because of him that she boiled my milk to purify it before I was allowed to drink it, that it was his idea, and that that was why the process was called pasteurization. One of the things I had put away in my mother's old trunk in which she kept all my childhood things was my library card. At that moment, I owed sevenpence in overdue fees.

As I passed by all these places, it was as if I were in a dream, for I didn't notice the people coming and going in and out of them, I didn't feel my feet touch ground, I didn't even feel my own body—I just saw these places as if they were hanging in the air, not having top or bottom, and as if I had gone in and out of them all in the same moment. The sun was bright; the sky was blue and just above my head. We then arrived at the jetty.

My heart now beat fast, and no matter how hard I tried, I couldn't keep my mouth from falling open and my nostrils from spreading to the ends of my face. My old fear of slipping between the boards of the jetty and falling into the dark-green water where the dark-green eels lived came over me. When my father's stomach started to go bad, the doctor had recommended a walk every evening right after he ate his dinner. Sometimes he would take me with him. When he took me with him, we usually went

10

10

11

12

10 **INTERPRETING**
What do the details about the library show about Annie's interests? (She loved to read.) Based on earlier details, why did she love reading? (She enjoyed escaping into a different world and found fictional characters romantic and interesting.)

MEETING INDIVIDUAL NEEDS

11 *Advanced Learners:* Students may wish to compile a dictionary of *eponyms*, or words derived from people's names. Entries should include origins and meanings. To get students started, you might mention *boycott, derrick, leotard, maverick, scrooge, silhouette,* and *watt.* ■

12 **READER'S RESPONSE**
Do you think that this description captures Annie's dream-like feelings? Why or why not? (Students should support their opinions by comparing the details cited in the selection to their memories of feelings based on similar experiences.)

13 CULTURAL DIVERSITY

Cricket, a sport played with bats and balls, is popular in Britain and its former colonies. *What sports popular in other countries do you think deserve more attention in America?* (Possible responses: lacrosse, jai alai, Sumo wrestling, rugby, soccer, curling, bocce.)

14 ANALYZING

How are Annie's fears different from the childhood fears she felt on the jetty? (Then her fears were fanciful childhood imaginings of falling into the water; now they are grounded in the reality of leaving home and family.)

15 LITERARY ELEMENT

Internal Conflict: Between what conflicting sets of emotions is Annie torn? (defiance, joy, and excitement vs. fear, sadness, and regret)

16 GUIDED READING

Classifying Details: To what senses do the images appeal? (hearing, sight, smell, and touch)

13 to the jetty, and there he would sit and talk to the night watchman about cricket or some other thing that didn't interest me, because it was not personal; they didn't talk about their wives, or their children, or their parents, or about any of their likes and dislikes. They talked about things in such a strange way, and I didn't see what they found funny, but sometimes they made each other laugh so much that their guffaws would bound out to sea and send back an echo. I was always sorry when we got to the jetty and saw that the night watchman on duty was the one he enjoyed speaking to; it was like being locked up in a book filled with numbers and diagrams and what-ifs. For the thing about not being able to understand and enjoy what they were saying was I had nothing to take my mind off my fear of slipping in between the boards of the jetty.

14 Now, too, I had nothing to take my mind off what was happening to me. My mother and my father—I was leaving them forever. My home on an island—I was leaving it forever. What to make of everything? I felt a familiar hollow space inside. I felt I was being held down against my will. I felt I was burning up from head to toe. I felt that someone was tearing me up into little pieces and soon I would be able to see all the little pieces as they floated out into nothing in the deep blue sea. I didn't know whether to laugh or cry. I could see that it would be better not to think too clearly about any one thing. The launch was being made ready to take me, along with some other passengers, out to the ship that was anchored in the sea. My father paid our fares, and we joined a line of people waiting to board. My mother checked my bag to make sure that I had my passport, the money she had given me, and a sheet of paper placed between some pages in my Bible on which were written the names of the relatives—people I had not known existed—with whom I would live in England. Across from the jetty was a wharf, and some stevedores were loading and unloading barges. I don't know why seeing that struck me so, but suddenly a wave of strong feeling came over me, and my heart swelled with a great gladness as the words "I shall never see this again" spilled out inside me. But then, just as quickly, my heart shriveled up and the words "I shall never see this again" stabbed at me. I don't know what stopped me from falling in a heap at my parents' feet.

When we were all on board, the launch headed out to sea. Away from the jetty, the water became the customary blue, and the launch left a wide path in it that looked like a road. I passed by sounds and smells that were so familiar that I had long ago stopped paying any attention to them. But now here they were, and the ever-present "I shall never see this again" bobbed up and down inside me. There was the sound of the seagull diving down into the water and coming up with something silverish in its mouth. There was the smell of the sea and the sight of small pieces of rubbish floating around in it. There were boats filled with fishermen coming in early. There was the sound of their voices as they shouted greetings to each other. There was the hot sun, there was the blue sea, there was the blue sky. Not very far away, there was the white sand of the shore, with the run-down houses all crowded in next to each other, for in some places only poor people lived near the shore. I was seated in the launch between my parents, and when I realized that I was gripping their hands tightly I glanced quickly to see if they were looking at me with scorn, for I felt sure that they must have known of my never-see-this-again feelings. But instead my

READING CHECK

1. Who is Miss Dulcie? (a seamstress to whom Annie was once apprenticed)
2. What product gave Annie the same scent as her mother? (talcum powder)
3. Who put a stop to Annie's friendship with the girl who had mumps? (Annie's mother)
4. When the family says its goodbyes, who seems the most restrained? (Annie's father)
5. What does Annie wave as she stands on the deck of the ship? (a red handkerchief)

RETEACHING

Ask students to imagine that Annie has arrived in England and is telling her experiences to a relative or a new friend. Have them recount the events detailed in the selection as Annie might recount them in the course of a conversation with someone whom she has not known for a long time.

17

father kissed me on the forehead and my mother kissed me on the mouth, and they both gave over their hands to me, so that I could grip them as much as I wanted. I was on the verge of feeling that it had all been a mistake, but I remembered that I wasn't a child anymore, and that now when I made up my mind about something I had to see it through. At that moment, we came to the ship, and that was that.

18

19

The goodbyes had to be quick, the captain said. My mother introduced herself to him and then introduced me. She told him to keep an eye on me, for I had never gone this far away from home on my own. She gave him a letter to pass on to the captain of the next ship that I would board in Barbados. They walked me to my cabin, a small space that I would share with someone else—a woman I did not know. I had never before slept in a room with someone I did not know. My father kissed me goodbye and told me to be good and to write home often. After he said this, he looked at me, then looked at the floor and swung his left foot, then looked at me again. I could see that he wanted to say something else, something that he had never said to me before, but then he just turned and walked away. My mother said, "Well," and then she threw her

arms around me. Big tears streamed down her face, and it must have been that—for I could not bear to see my mother cry—which started me crying, too. She then tightened her arms around me and held me to her close, so that I felt that I couldn't breathe. With that, my tears dried up and I was suddenly on my guard. "What does she want now?" I said to myself. Still holding me close to her, she said, in a voice that raked across my skin, "It doesn't matter what you do or where you go, I'll always be your mother and this will always be your home."

20

I dragged myself away from her and backed off a little, and then I shook myself, as if to wake myself out of a stupor. We looked at each other for a long time with smiles on our faces, but I know the opposite of that was in my heart. As if responding to some invisible cue, we both said, at the very same moment, "Well." Then my mother turned around and walked out the cabin door. I stood there for I don't know how long, and then I remembered that it was customary to stand on deck and wave to your relatives who were returning to shore. From the deck, I could not see my father, but I could see my mother facing the ship, her eyes searching to pick me out. I removed from my bag a red cotton handkerchief that she had earlier given me for this purpose, and I waved it wildly in the air. Recognizing me immediately, she waved back just as wildly, and we continued to do this until she became just a dot in the matchbox-size launch swallowed up in the big blue sea.

I went back to my cabin and lay down on my berth. Everything trembled as if it had a spring at its very center. I could hear the small waves lap-lapping around the ship. They made an unexpected sound, as if a vessel filled with liquid had been placed on its side and now was slowly emptying out.

17 INTERPRETING

Why is Annie on the verge of feeling that "it had all been a mistake"? (The recognition of her parents' love causes her feelings to shift from defiance to sadness and regret.)

18 GUIDED READING

Finding the Main Idea: Who made the decision for Annie to leave home? (Annie) How does remembering this fact give her strength? (She reminds herself that she is no longer a child and must follow through on her decisions.)

19 SPECULATING

Why do you think that Annie's parents have consented to her decision to emigrate? (Possible response: They may believe that by going abroad Annie can broaden her horizons and fulfill her dreams.)

20 READER'S RESPONSE

How do you react to the passage that describes Annie's last moments with her mother? (Many students will find the passage a true reflection of the love/hate relationship and the lack of understanding that often exist between adolescents and their parents. Annie is trying to assert her independence by escaping the smothering love of her mother and the limitations of Antigua. Her mother's words show she does not understand her daughter's feelings. This is why Annie's smile is empty.)

Chuck Fishman/Woodfin Camp & Associates, Inc.

1. Holding a West Indian Festival.
Groups of students should research an island and then make special presentations on aspects of the island's culture such as music, art, food, dress, language, and tourist attractions. Among the media that students might consider are recordings and videotapes obtained from the library; pamphlets and other publications obtained from government tourist offices; charts, drawings, and clippings from newspapers and magazines; and even prepared foods and live music.

2. Writing a Character's Letters. Ask students to imagine that Annie has arrived in England and is writing to her parents and friends in Antigua. Encourage students to write a series of letters in which Annie describes her trip, her early experiences in England, and her feelings about her homeland.

Ask students to consider what the selection reveals about Annie's attitudes and personality. Then ask how those revelations help explain Annie's decision to go to England. (Romantic and independent, Annie wants to broaden her horizons and seek the kinds of adventures that she has read about.) What kinds of attitudes and feelings prompt Annie to emigrate? (defiant attitudes toward the past and ambitions or dreams about the future) ■

ANSWERS

First Thoughts
Answers will vary.

Identifying Facts
1. *Good*: chemist's, bank, eye doctor, grooming aids store, library; *bad*: seamstress's house, house of friend with mumps
2. the library
3. the fear of falling through the boards

Interpreting Meanings
1. She is romantic, imaginative, and strong-willed. She likes reading and learning.
2. senses are heightened by knowledge that she is leaving
3. eager yet sad. no
4. expressing his feelings vs. behaving with usual restraint. how much he loves and will miss her
5. strict but caring, efficient and intelligent. loves her mother but feels manipulated and smothered by her mother's love
6. The vessel, Annie herself, is being emptied of childhood memories and family ties.

Applying Meanings
Students should cite personal experiences in explaining their responses.

Creative Writing Response
Describing a Place. Descriptions should include several sites and should reflect the narrator's feelings.

Critical Writing Response
Analyzing an Internal Conflict. Essays should state the internal conflict and support it with at least five details. ■

> ### First Thoughts
The narrator has conflicting feelings about her parents and her home. Which of her feelings came through most strongly for you?

Identifying Facts
1. As the narrator walks to the jetty she passes many places that stimulate memories from her childhood. Which places bring back good memories and which evoke bad memories?
2. Which place does the narrator most regret leaving?
3. When the narrator reaches the jetty, what old fear comes over her again?

Interpreting Meanings
1. What does the story about the eyeglasses reveal about the narrator's personality? What do her comments about the library reveal about her own **character**?
2. Why do you think the narrator suddenly notices sounds and smells that she never paid attention to before?
3. What **internal conflict** does the narrator experience about leaving the island? Is it resolved?
4. Reread the passage describing the father's actions after he kisses his daughter goodbye. What **internal conflict** do you think he is feeling? What do you think he wants to say to Annie John?
5. Based on what her daughter tells you, how would you describe the **character** of Annie's mother? What conflicting feelings does Annie seem to have toward this mother who obviously adores her?
6. The last sentence in this selection could be interpreted as a literal description of the ship Annie John is on. But suppose it could also be interpreted **metaphori-cally**—that is, figuratively. What might the writer really be talking about when she describes a vessel "emptying out"?

Applying Meanings
Do the narrator's feelings about her childhood remind you of any of your own feelings? At what point in her narrative did you most identify with her?

Creative Writing Response
Describing a Place. Suppose you are leaving the place where you live and that you know you will not return for a long time. Write a brief description of the spots you will remember and of the experiences and people you associate with them. You might want to imitate the style of this story and describe this place as if you are taking a last walk, perhaps to a bus or train station. Before you write, collect your details in a word cluster or list.

Critical Writing Response
Analyzing an Internal Conflict. Discrepancies, or differences, between a character's thoughts, words, and actions are good indications of an **internal conflict**. In a brief essay, analyze the narrator's internal conflicts. Discuss her personality, her attitudes, and the differences between her thoughts and actions. Support general statements with specific details from the selection. As a first step, you might find it helpful to list details on a chart like the one below to help you see and understand Annie's internal conflicts.

Annie's Remarks	
Annie's Actions	
Annie's Thoughts	
What Discrepancies Reveal	

Additional Reading. Interested students might choose other selections from *Annie John* and several of Derek Walcott's poems about coming of age in the West Indies. They should then write essays comparing and contrasting the two authors' works in terms of themes, settings, tone, speakers' personalities, or internal conflicts. Other students might read and report on V. S. Naipaul's *Miguel Street*, a series of interrelated stories about a boy's coming of age in Trinidad. ■

SEEING CONNECTIONS

Tales of the Islands *by Derek Walcott*

Few people could have predicted that the tiny Caribbean island of St. Lucia, where the predominant language is French creole, would produce a world-famous English-language poet. Yet Jamaica Kincaid's fellow West Indies writer Derek Walcott (born 1930) has achieved international fame for his poetry. His most recent work, *Omeros* (1990), is a book-length narrative poem loosely based on Homer's epic poem the *Odyssey*. (*Omeros* is Greek for "Homer.")

Walcott makes his permanent home in the West Indies, although he has frequently traveled abroad. The islands' exotic beauty and their tragic colonial history (St. Lucia is a former French colony) are central subjects of his work. Many critics suggest that Walcott is torn between cultures: Caribbean and British, black and white. But Walcott sees his own mixed racial heritage as symbolic of the New World.

In the following poem, the final sonnet from a work entitled *Tales of the Islands*, Walcott describes his mixed feelings upon leaving St. Lucia for the first time. The poem's **epigraph**, or opening quotation— "*Adieu foulard*" (ə·dyōō′ fōō·lär′)—comes from a Creole folk song traditionally sung when people leave St. Lucia. The song bids *adieu*, or "farewell," to the *foulard*, or neckerchief, that is part of St. Lucia's national costume. As you read the poem, compare Walcott's tone and mood to that expressed by Jamaica Kincaid in "A Walk to the Jetty." How are these farewells alike and different?

Sunset in St. Lucia.

Timothy O'Keefe/Bruce Coleman, Inc.

Chapter X
"Adieu foulard . . ."
***from* Tales of the Islands**
Derek Walcott

I watched the island narrowing the fine
Writing of foam around the precipices then
The roads as small and casual as twine
Thrown on its mountains; I watched till the
     plane
5 Turned to the final north and turned above
The open channel with the gray sea be-
     tween
The fishermen's islets until all that I love
Folded in cloud; I watched the shallow
     green
That broke in places where there would be
     reef,
10 The silver glinting on the fuselage, each mile
Dividing us and all fidelity strained
Till space would snap it. Then, after a while
I thought of nothing, nothing, I prayed,
     would change;
When we set down at Seawell it had rained.

1 [
2 [

1 INTERPRETING
To what or whom might the *us* in line 11 refer? (the speaker and his homeland or the speaker and the loved ones he leaves behind) What might the speaker not want to change (line 13)? (the people and places he leaves behind) Is it likely that this prayer will be answered? Explain. (No; over time, things usually change.)

LITERARY ELEMENT
Tone: What is the tone of this poem? (sad, regretful) Cite examples of diction, or word choice, that underscore the tone. ("as small and casual as twine," "final north," "gray sea," and "rained")

2 LITERARY ELEMENT
Sonnet: How does the rhyme in the final couplet contribute to the poem's effectiveness? (It has a jarring effect that reinforces the tone and suggests the speaker's painful feelings.)

2 CULTURAL DIVERSITY
Seawell is the international airport at Barbados. The speaker, leaving tiny St. Lucia on a small plane to Barbados, has to change planes at Seawell in order to leave the West Indies. ■

Léopold Sédar Senghor
b. 1906, Senegal

Peter Jordan/Time Magazine

Léopold Sédar Senghor (lā·ȯ·pôld′ sā·dȧr′ sän̄·gôr′) has had a remarkable career as a poet, literary critic, political thinker, four-term president of Senegal, and spokesperson for the **Négritude** movement. He was also the first black African to join the faculty of a French university and the first black member of the prestigious French Academy. Born and educated at a time when the colonizers of French West Africa were encouraging Africans to think of themselves as French, Senghor truly believed that he was a Frenchman who just happened to be black. When he went to Paris to study, however, he realized that the French would never accept him as one of their countrymen. He also realized that he was proud of his own culture and history and afraid that

both would soon disappear in the wake of European colonialism. He shared these thoughts with other black writers in Paris, such as Aimé Césaire and Birago Diop. From their discussions the ideas of Négritude emerged.

Just as many African American leaders urge members of their community to learn about and take pride in their African heritage, so did the proponents of Négritude assert the value and beauty of African culture. The négritude writers drew on African history and art to celebrate black civilizations, and sought to bring African accomplishments before the eyes of the world.

After serving in World War II and helping the French Resistance fight the Nazis, Senghor was one of two West Africans elected to represent his homeland in the French National Assembly. Here he helped draft the new constitutions that gradually brought independence to France's West African possessions. During the 1950s, he was a leading spokesperson for African unity and independence achieved through peaceful means.

In 1960, Senghor became the first president of the new nation of Senegal. Displaying as much skill in politics as he did in poetry, he was elected to the presidency four more times. Today Senegal is recognized as one of Africa's most democratic nations, and Senghor is hailed as a great statesperson, poet, and political and literary theorist.

OBJECTIVES

1. *To read and analyze an African poem that expresses the ideas of Négritude*
2. *To identify sensory images*
3. *To write about the African heritage and the themes of Négritude*

Reader's Guide

AND WE SHALL BE STEEPED

Background

Senghor cofounded the black cultural journal *Presence Africaine*, and stressed an "African presence" in all of his poetry. Although the poems are written in French, their images are drawn from Africa's landscape and history. Their sound—especially when read aloud in the original French—is reminiscent of the powerful, rhythmic chanting of the traditional West African storytellers known as *griots* (grē'ōz). Capturing an "African sound" was so important to Senghor that he specified the traditional African musical instrument that should ideally accompany each poem's recitation. He chose the *khalam* (khä'läm), a four-stringed African guitar, as the instrument to accompany "And We Shall Be Steeped."

Writer's Response

Make a list of reasons why you are proud of your heritage—either as an American or as a member of an ethnic group.

Literary Focus

Imagery is language that appeals to the senses. While most **images** appeal to our sense of sight (*sparkling smile*), some may also appeal to our senses of hearing (*joyous laughter*), smell (*sweaty socks*), touch (*slimy slug*), and taste (*bitter tea*). In the poem you are about to read, Senghor uses a series of vivid images to help "steep" the reader in the "presence of Africa."

PREREADING FOCUS

Background: Before World War II, Senghor helped launch the journal *L'Etudiant noir* ("The Black Student"). His collaborators were Martinique's Aimé Césaire and French Guiana's León Damas, black students in Paris who not only shared Senghor's interest in propagating Négritude but also succeeded in forging influential literary careers.

Other West African instruments that Senghor specifies should be played as accompaniment to his verse include the *balafong* (a kind of xylophone) and the *garong*, the *mbalakh*, the *tabala*, the *talmbatt*, and the *tama* (several kinds of drums). Traditional African music has exerted a great influence on the world of music, affecting such genres as jazz, blues, rock, calypso, reggae, Brazilian music, salsa, zydeco, and rap.

Writer's Response: To prompt students' lists, have them consider several categories of cultural contributions: music, art, food, dress, and family life.

Literary Focus: According to scholar Gerald Moore, Senghor's vivid images make his poetry sing even in translation, which frequently fails to capture the reverberations of his musical rhythms. Translators Reed and Wake point out that Senghor's images are inclusive rather than exclusive, for they embrace all aspects of African life and culture.

Proper Adjectives

A proper adjective is the adjective form of a proper noun. Sometimes a suffix is added to a proper noun to create a proper adjective: *a Senegalese poet*, (Senegal plus -ese). Sometimes no spelling change occurs: *a Senghor poem*. In English, proper adjectives are capitalized.

1. **Reading and Speaking.** Have volunteers identify the two proper adjectives in Senghor's poem and the proper nouns from which they have been formed. (*Sudanese* in line 7, formed from *Sudan*; *African* in line 9, formed from *Africa*)

2. **Writing and Sharing.** Have students write a brief paragraph about their heritage as Americans. Ask them to include at least five proper adjectives. Then, after students have shared their writing, ask them to identify the proper adjectives in their classmates' paragraphs. ∎

TEACHER'S RESOURCES

☞ Review and Response Worksheet

LITERARY ELEMENT

Rhythm: Why do you think so many of the lines open with stressed syllables? (to create the chanting effect that resonates throughout the verse and to simulate the rhythm of the accompanying *khalam*)

HUMANITIES CONNECTION

In some traditional African societies, masks were believed to give their wearers the spiritual power of departed ancestors. ❓ *In what way is the speaker's purpose similar to the purpose of traditional African mask makers?* (Possible response: The speaker is trying to conjure up the spirit of his African heritage by surrounding himself with African things.) ∎

WRITING TO LEARN

Art/Interior Design: You have been asked to decorate a room in the "Négritude style." List the items of Africa's heritage that you might include. (Lists may include the *khalam* as well as the items singled out in the poem.) Sketch the room and its contents, and then present the list and sketch to your client (a classmate) for his or her approval. ∎

AND WE SHALL BE STEEPED

Léopold Sédar Senghor

translated by

JOHN REED AND CLIVE WAKE

As you read this poem, try to re-create in your mind the sights, smells, and sounds of Senghor's imagery.

For Khalam
And we shall be steeped my dear in the presence
    of Africa.
Furniture from Guinea and Congo,[1] heavy and
    polished, somber and serene.
On the walls, pure primordial masks distant and
    yet present.
Stools of honor for hereditary guests, for the
    Princes of the High Lands.[2]
5   Wild perfumes, thick mats of silence
Cushions of shade and leisure, the noise of a
    wellspring of peace.
Classic words. In a distance, antiphonal singing
    like Sudanese[3] cloths
And then, friendly lamp, your kindness to soothe
    this obsessive presence
White black and red, oh red as the African soil.

---

1. **Guinea** (gin'ē) **and Congo:** here, not just the present-day nations of Guinea and Congo, but the entire West African coast from Senegal's Cape Verde peninsula to southern Angola, and the entire river basin of the Congo, West Africa's longest river.
2. **hereditary . . . Lands:** honored ancestors and rulers of great African kingdoms of centuries past.
3. **antiphonal** (an·tif'ə·nəl) **. . . Sudanese:** alternately sung and chanted, like traditional African ritual songs or poems; here, Sudanese refers not to the present-day nation of Sudan but to the western portion of the fertile savanna, or plain, stretching across all of Africa just below the Sahara.

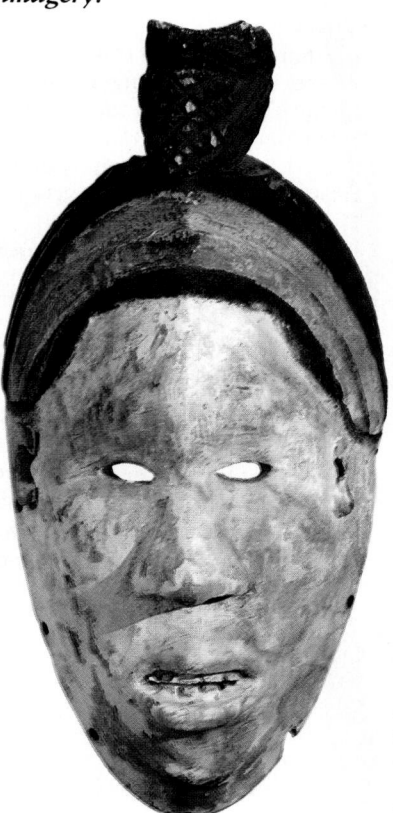

Ceremonial mask from the Ibo people of West Africa.

1. Choral Reading: Have students work in groups to prepare choral readings of the poem. If possible, they should try to obtain recordings of West African music and antiphonal singing to help them achieve an authentic sound. If any students play the guitar or another stringed instrument and are willing to play for the class, their accompaniment should be incorporated into the presentations.

2. Research Project. Interested students might research the names *Guinea* and *Sudan* (briefly explained in the footnotes) and prepare oral reports that elucidate the differences between the historical and the contemporary meanings of the terms. In presenting their oral reports, students should use a map of Africa to pinpoint the regions and the countries under discussion.

Ask students what word they would use to identify the feeling about Africa's heritage that Senghor's poem was meant to inspire in Africans. (Possible response: pride) ■

First Thoughts

Which **image** of the "presence of Africa" could you see, smell, or feel most clearly?

Identifying Facts

1. In the first line, what does the speaker say about "the presence of Africa"? What objects illustrate this presence in later lines?

2. What adjectives describe the African presence in the last line?

Interpreting Meanings

1. In what way are the objects in lines 2, 3, and 4 related to one another? Which **images** in later lines appeal to senses other than sight?

2. The colors in the final line refer to Africa's soils, but they may also refer to the white colonists, the black Africans, and the bloodshed between them. In this context, what earlier **image** does the "red" in the last line contrast with? What does the contrast stress about African history?

3. What overall attitude toward African culture and history does the poem convey?

4. The translators of this poem chose English words that are faithful both to the meaning and musical sounds of the original French. Find examples of **alliteration** and **assonance** that help make the poem musical.

Applying Meanings

What are some of the benefits of taking pride in one's racial or ethnic heritage? Are there also drawbacks? If so, what are they?

Creative Writing Response

Writing About Heritage. Write a poem or a paragraph about your racial or ethnic heritage or your heritage as an American. Include concrete **images** like Senghor does, and choose images that will convey your thoughts and feelings about your heritage.

Critical Writing Response

Writing About Négritude. Senghor's poem is an example of the work inspired by the **Négritude** movement, which encouraged black writers to turn to African culture and history as a source of inspiration and pride. In a brief essay, show how this poem illustrates the ideas of Négritude. Discuss specific **images** and the attitudes toward Africa that they convey. Before you begin writing, you may find it helpful to list the specific images that you plan to discuss and the attitudes that they convey.

First Thoughts
Answers will vary.

Identifying Facts
1. He and his "dear" shall be steeped in the "presence of Africa." Objects include furniture from Guinea and Congo, primordial masks, and traditional stools of honor.
2. white, black, and red

Interpreting Meanings
1. All are household furnishings crafted by Africans from African materials. wild perfumes, thick mats of silence, cushions of shade and leisure, the noise of a wellspring of peace, and antiphonal singing
2. a wellspring of peace. Africa was more peaceful in pre-colonial times.
3. pride and celebration
4. alliteration: *somber / serene, pure / primordial / presence*; assonance: *we / steeped / dear, Congo / polished /somber*

Applying Meanings
Answers will vary.

Creative Writing Response
Writing About Heritage. Students' poems or paragraphs should use at least five images that convey or evoke a particular attitude or emotion.

Critical Writing Response
Writing About Négritude. Students' essays should discuss at least five of the poem's African images and consider how they might inspire modern African or African-American artists and artisans. ■

Léopold Sédar Senghor   **1333**

Scientist, doctor, educator, diplomat, writer—the multi-talented Abioseh Nicol was a true "Renaissance man." Nicol attended school in both Nigeria and Sierra Leone before he won a scholarship to study science and medicine in England. He worked in several English municipal hospitals, became involved in medical research, and taught science and medicine at Cambridge.

Nicol's effectiveness as a public servant and as a school administrator led to his appointment to a number of diplomatic posts throughout West Africa. In carrying out his roles as a diplomat and as a U.N. adviser, he traveled all over the world.

Nicol's best-known nonfiction work, *Africa: A Subjective View* (1965), was derived from a series of essays that he presented at Nigeria's Ibadan University. His poems and stories have appeared in leading English-language magazines and anthologies of African literature; they have also been broadcast on the British Broadcasting Corporation's literature programs and on radio programs throughout West Africa.

Despite Nicol's cosmopolitan background, most of his fiction examines the lives of ordinary rural Africans and the traumatic changes that urbanization has wrought in West Africa.

Abioseh Nicol
1924–1994, Sierra Leone

Courtesy of the United Nations

Like many other African writers, Abioseh Nicol (äb·ē·ō′se nē′kōl) studied abroad. When he returned to his native Sierra Leone after years in Britain, he wrote "Upcountry," a poem contrasting the rural villages to the new cities sprouting up along the Guinea coast. He felt that the heart and spirit of the "real Africa" still survived only in the countryside. This is why he sets most of his stories in small, rural villages. Best known for his 1965 collection, *The Truly Married Woman and Other Stories*, Nicol is regarded as one of Africa's best short-story writers.

Despite active careers in public service, health, science, and education, Nicol always found time to write. In the 1950s, when he was a student in Britain, most books about Africa were written by Europeans. While Nicol recognized the skill of some of these authors, he also saw serious flaws in their portraits of native Africans. It was in part to correct these flaws that he took to writing fiction. He felt that African characters were too often portrayed in disparaging ways, and he sought to correct this slanted view.

In addition to his writing, Nicol excelled in a wide range of fields and made outstanding contributions in all of them. The son of a pharmacist in Freetown, Sierra Leone, Davidson Nicol (Abioseh is a pen name) won a scholarship to study medicine at the University of London. He later became the first black African to receive a fellowship at Cambridge University. In medical circles he won fame for his research into the structure of insulin, the hormone used to treat diabetes. After teaching medicine in England and Nigeria, Nicol returned to his homeland to serve as principal of Fourah Bay College and vice-chancellor of the University of Sierra Leone. He was also his country's ambassador to the United Nations and was affiliated with the Red Cross, the World Health Organization, UNESCO, and just about every important West African conference.

OBJECTIVES
1. To interpret a story set in a village in West Africa in the mid–twentieth century
2. To recognize the use of foreshadowing to build suspense
3. To write an essay analyzing the use of foreshadowing
4. To identify some of the contributions that African languages have made to English

THEMES IN WORLD LITERATURE

Life and Loss
"Letter to His Two Small Children," pp. 518–522
"Lot's Wife," pp. 1223–1226

The Power and Pain of Love
"Song of a Mother to Her Firstborn," pp. 89–93
"Sleep, Darling," pp. 279–283 ■

VOCABULARY IN CONTEXT
The words listed below will appear in the side margin at the point of instruction:
1. crestfallen
2. zenith
3. cajoled
4. complacent
5. intercession

Reader's Guide

LIFE IS SWEET AT KUMANSENU

Background

A small nation on the coast of West Africa, Sierra Leone was a British colony until 1961. Its capital, Freetown, was founded by British abolitionists in 1787 as a haven for freed and runaway slaves. Nicol grew up in Freetown, which is now a large modern city. The rest of his Sierra Leone, however, is largely rural. In the villages, the old tribal religions remain strong, even among villagers who have become Christian or Muslim. Although specific beliefs vary from village to village, most involve faith in spirits and in magic, both good and bad. The story you are about to read focuses on the old West African belief that the spirit of a dead child can creep back into its mother's womb and be born again. To know whether her next child is a manifestation of this restless spirit, the mother marks the body of her dead child and sees if that mark appears on the next child she bears. To break the cycle, the mother must follow special burial customs prescribed by the village spiritual leader.

Writer's Response

One of the **themes** in this story has to do with the clash between an individual and institutional authority. In a few sentences, describe a situation you have witnessed or heard about in which an individual defies the rules or advice of an authority figure. What are the reasons for this challenge to established law or tradition? What are the results of the challenge?

Literary Focus

Foreshadowing is the use of clues to hint at what is going to happen later in a story. Writers use foreshadowing to hook our interest. For example, if a writer mentions (even casually) that a character keeps a gun in her dresser drawer, we instantly wonder why it's there and when she might use it. In "Life Is Sweet at Kumansenu," Nicol drops clues in the very first descriptions of Meji to foreshadow his story's surprise ending.

PREREADING FOCUS

Background: Known as Creoles, the descendants of ex-slaves who founded Freetown in the nineteenth century constitute only a small percentage of Sierra Leone's current population. Most Creoles continue to live in the Freetown area. They come from long-time Christian families and are reasonably well-educated and well-to-do. Outside Freetown, however, Sierra Leone is primarily poor and rural, and traditional religions are still practiced.

The relationship between mother and child, as exemplified in "Life Is Sweet at Kumansenu," has traditionally been strong in West Africa. Mothers carry small children on their backs and devote much time to nurturing them. Such traditions are especially strong in rural communities like Kumansenu in Nicol's story.

Literary Focus: Foreshadowing builds suspense, a feeling of anticipation that makes readers wonder "What is going to happen next?" and "What will happen in the end?" Foreshadowing not only prompts readers to predict events but also to keep reading to find out whether their predictions are correct. Have volunteers give examples of foreshadowing that they have encountered in suspense literature, films, or television programs. How did they respond to particular instances of foreshadowing?

LIFE IS SWEET AT KUMANSENU

Abioseh Nicol

As you read the story, look for a general statement about life that Meji makes and the widow Bola repeats. How would you expand this statement to express the story's theme?

The sea and the wet sand to one side of it; green tropical forest on the other; above it, the slow, tumbling clouds. The clean round blinding disc of sun and the blue sky covered and surrounded the small African village, Kumansenu.

1   A few square mud houses with roofs like helmets were here thatched, and there covered with corrugated zinc, where the prosperity of cocoa or trading had touched the head of the family.

The widow Bola stirred her palm-oil stew[1] and thought of nothing in particular. She chewed a kola nut[2] rhythmically with her strong toothless jaws, and soon unconsciously she was chewing in rhythm with the skipping of Asi, her granddaughter. She looked idly at Asi, as the seven-year-old brought the twisted palmleaf rope smartly over her head and jumped over it, counting in English each time the rope struck the ground and churned up a little red dust. Bola herself did not understand English well, but

The village of Karamasi, Sierra Leone.

Jean Gaumy/Magnum Photos, Inc.

2   she could easily count up to twenty in English, for market purposes. Asi shouted six and then said nine, ten. Bola called out that after six came seven. And I should know, she sighed. Although now she was old and her womb and breasts were withered, there

---

1. **palm-oil stew:** native dish in which various ingredients are cooked in an oil taken from the seeds of palm trees.
2. **kola nut:** fruit of an African tree called the kola; also spelled cola. Kola nuts contain caffeine and are often chewed for their mild stimulating effects.

was a time when she bore children regularly every two years. Six times she had borne a boy child and six times they had died. Some had swollen up and with weak plaintive cries had faded away. Others had shuddered in sudden convulsions, with burning skins, and had rolled up their eyes and died. They had all died; or rather he had died, Bola thought; because she knew it was one child all the time whose spirit had crept up restlessly into her womb to be born and mock her. The sixth time, Musa, the village magician whom time had now transformed into a respectable Muslim, had advised her and her husband to break the bones of the quiet little corpse and mangle it so that it could not come back to torment them alive again. But she had held on to the child and refused to let them mutilate it. Secretly, she had marked it with a sharp pointed stick at the left buttock before it was wrapped in a mat and taken away. When at the seventh time she had borne a son and the purification ceremonies had taken place, she had turned it surreptitiously to see whether the mark was there. It was. She showed it to the old woman who was the midwife and asked her what it was, and she had forced herself to believe that it was an accidental scratch made while the child was being scrubbed with herbs to remove placental blood. But this child had stayed. Meji,[3] he had been called. And he was now thirty years of age and a second-class clerk in government offices in a town ninety miles away. Asi, his daughter, had been left with her to do the things an old woman wanted a small child for: to run and take messages to the neighbors, to fetch a cup of water from the earthenware pot in the kitchen, to sleep with her, and to be fondled.

She threw the washed and squeezed cassava leaves[4] into the red boiling stew, putting in a finger's pinch of salt, and then went indoors, carefully stepping over the threshold to look for the dried red pepper. She found it and then dropped it, leaning against the wall with a little cry. He turned round from the window and looked at her with a twisted half smile of love and sadness. In his short-sleeved, open-necked white shirt and gray gabardine trousers, gold-plated wrist watch and brown suede shoes, he looked like the picture in African magazines of a handsome clerk who would get to the top because he ate the correct food or regularly took the correct laxative, which was being advertised. His skin was grayish brown and he had a large red handkerchief tied round his neck.

"Meji, God be praised," Bola cried. "You gave me quite a turn. My heart is weak and I can no longer take surprises. When did you come? How did you come? By lorry,[5] by fishing boat? And how did you come into the house? The front door was locked. There are so many thieves nowadays. I'm so glad to see you, so glad," she mumbled and wept, leaning against his breast.

Meji's voice was hoarse, and he said, "I'm glad to see you, too, mother," rubbing her back affectionately.

Asi ran in and cried "Papa, Papa," and was rewarded with a lift and a hug.

"Never mind how I came, mother," Meji said, laughing, "I'm here, and that's all that matters."

"We must make a feast, we must have a big feast. I must tell the neighbors at once. Asi, run this very minute to Mr. Addai, the

---

3. **Meji** (mä′jē)

4. **cassava** (kə·sä′və) **leaves:** leaves of a tropical food plant whose roots are something like potatoes.

5. **lorry** (lôr′ē): truck.

Abioseh Nicol   **1337**

6 **SPECULATING**

Why do you think that Meji avoids answering his mother's questions about how he entered her home and insists that no one else in the village be told of his presence? (Possible responses: He may be in some kind of trouble; he may be exhausted or ill and in need of rest; he may dislike being fussed over.)

■ **crestfallen** (krest′fôl′ən): dejected; disheartened

7 **INTERPRETING**

Why does Bola send Asi outside? (Bola thinks Meji is in trouble and wants to question him privately; she does not want Asi to overhear their conversation.)

8 **CULTURAL BACKGROUND**

Since World War II, many young West Africans, particularly males, have left their villages to find jobs in the towns and cities of their homelands.

9 **LITERARY ELEMENT**

Foreshadowing: What might Meji's haggard appearance, his lack of appetite, and his hoarse voice foreshadow? (Possible response: He may be ill or dying.)

■ **zenith** (zē′nith): point in the sky directly overhead

10 **GUIDED READING**

Analyzing Details: What detail may suggest a supernatural aspect to Meji's surprise appearance? (Asi's observation that Meji has no shadow.)

catechist,[6] and tell him your papa is home. Then to Mamie Gbera[7] to ask her for extra provisions, and to Pa Babole[8] for drummers and musicians . . ."

"Stop," said Meji, raising his hand. "This is all quite unnecessary. I don't want to see *anyone*, no one at all. I wish to rest quietly and completely. No one is to know I'm here."

Bola looked very crestfallen. She was so proud of Meji and wanted to show him off. The village would never forgive her for concealing such an important visitor. Meji must have sensed this because he held her shoulder comfortingly and said, "They will know soon enough. Let us enjoy one another, all three of us, this time. Life is too short."

Bola turned to Asi, picked up the packet of pepper and told her to go and drop a little into the boiling pot outside, taking care not to go too near the fire or play with it. After the child had gone, Bola said to her son, "Are you in trouble? Is it the police?"

He shook his head, "No," he said, "it's just that I like returning to you. There will always be this bond of love and affection between us, and I don't wish to share it with others. It is our private affair and that is why I've left my daughter with you." He ended up irrelevantly, "Girls somehow seem to stay with relations longer."

"And don't I know it," said Bola. "But you look pale," she continued, "and you keep scraping your throat. Are you ill?" she laid her hand on his brow. "And you're cold, too."

"It's the cold wet wind," he said, a little harshly. "I'll go and rest now if you can open

and dust my room for me. I'm feeling very tired. Very tired indeed. I've traveled very far today and it has not been an easy journey."

"Of course, my son, of course," Bola replied, bustling away hurriedly but happily.

Meji slept all afternoon till evening, and his mother brought his food to his room and, later, took the empty basins away. Then he slept again till morning.

The next day, Saturday, was a busy one, and after further promising Meji that she would tell no one he was about, Bola went off to market. Meji took Asi for a long walk through a deserted path and up into the hills. She was delighted. They climbed high until they could see the village below in front of them, and the sea in the distance, and the boats with their wide white sails. Soon the sun had passed its zenith and was half way towards the west. Asi had eaten all the food, the dried fish and the flat tapioca pancakes[9] and the oranges. Her father said he wasn't hungry, and this had made the day perfect for Asi, who had chattered, eaten, and then played with her father's fountain pen and other things from his pocket. They soon left for home because he had promised that they would be back before dark; he had carried her down some steep boulders and she had held on to his shoulders because he had said his neck hurt so and she must not touch it. She had said, "Papa, I can see behind you and you haven't got a shadow. Why?"

He had then turned her round facing the sun. Since she was getting drowsy, she had started asking questions and her father had joked with her and humored her. "Papa, why has your watch stopped at twelve o'clock?"

---

6. **Addai** (ə·dī′), **the catechist** (kat′ə·kist′): someone who teaches the catechism to Christians; a catechism is a book that contains all the fundamentals of the religion, usually in question and answer form.

7. **Gbera** (′g·bä′rə)

8. **Babole** (bä·bō′lä)

9. **tapioca** (tap′ē·ō′kə) **pancakes:** pancakes made from a granular substance obtained from the potatolike roots of the cassava plant.

Jacques Brun/Explorer/Photo Researchers, Inc.

A West African village.
❓ *Have you noted anything strange about Meji's behavior?*

"Because the world ends at noon." Asi had chuckled at that. "Papa, why do you wear a scarf always round your neck?" "Because my head will fall off if I don't." She had laughed out loud at that. But soon she had fallen asleep as he bore her homewards.

Just before nightfall, with his mother dressed in her best, they had all three, at her urgent request, gone to his father's grave, taking a secret route and avoiding the main village. It was a small cemetery, not more than twenty years or so old, started when the Rural Health Department had insisted that no more burials were to take place in the backyard of households. Bola took a bottle of wine and a glass and four split halves of kola, each a half sphere, two red and two white. They reached the graveside and she poured some wine into the glass. Then she spoke to her dead husband softly and caressingly. She had brought his son to see him, she said. This son whom God had given success, to the confusion and discomfiture of their enemies. Here he was, a man with a pensionable clerk's job and not a poor farmer, a fisherman, or a simple mechanic.

All the years of their married life, people had said she was a witch because her children had died young. But this boy of theirs had shown that she was a good woman. Let her husband answer her now, to show that he was listening. She threw the four kola nuts up into the air and they fell on to the grave. Three fell with the flat face upwards and one with its flat face downwards. She picked them up again and conversed with him once more and threw the kola nuts up again. But still there was an odd one or sometimes two.

They did not fall with all four faces up, or with all four faces down, to show that he was listening and was pleased. She spoke endearingly, she cajoled, she spoke severely. But all to no avail. She then asked Meji to perform. He crouched by the graveside and whispered. Then he threw the kola nuts and they rolled a little, Bola following them eagerly with her sharp old eyes. They all ended up face downwards. Meji emptied the glass of wine on the grave and then said that he felt nearer his father at that moment than he had ever done before in his life.

Abioseh Nicol

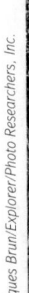

11 LITERARY ELEMENT
Point of View: Whose perspective does the narrator adopt in this passage? (Bola's) Identify remarks that you think most effectively capture Bola's viewpoint or attitudes. (Answers will vary. The passage begins with "Then she spoke to her dead husband . . ." and continues to the top of the second column.)

12 CULTURAL DIVERSITY
Most traditional African religions emphasize the importance of honoring the dead and include the belief that one can communicate with the spirits of loved ones and ancestors.
❓ *With what customs for honoring the dead are you familiar?* (Possible responses: placing headstones, tablets, plants, or flowers on graves; visiting cemeteries, planting trees, making donations or contributions in the name of the dead; naming babies for dead loved ones)

▨ **cajoled** (kə·jōld′): coaxed with flattery and insincere talk

13 LITERARY ELEMENT
Foreshadowing: In addition to showing love or respect for his father, what might Meji's remark signify? (Meji is near death or perhaps has recently become a spirit.)

1339

It was sundown, and they all three went back silently home in the short twilight. That night, going outside the house towards her son's window, she had found, to her sick disappointment, that he had been throwing all the cooked food away out there. She did not mention this when she went to say good night, but she did sniff and say that there was a smell of decay in the room. Meji said that he thought there was a dead rat up in the rafters, and he would clear it away after she had gone to bed.

That night it rained heavily, and sheet lightning turned the darkness into brief silver daylight for one or two seconds at a time. Then the darkness again and the rain. Bola woke soon after midnight and thought she could hear knocking. She went to Meji's room to ask him to open the door, but he wasn't there. She thought he had gone out for a while and had been locked out by mistake. She opened the door quickly, holding an oil lamp upwards. He stood on the veranda, curiously unwet, and refused to come in.

"I have to go away," he said hoarsely, coughing.

Ceremonial mask of the Yoruba people of West Africa.

Sassoonian/Art Resource, New York

"Do come in," she said.

"No," he said, "I have to go, but I wanted to thank you for giving me a chance." **14**

"What nonsense is this?" she said. "Come in out of the rain."

"I did not think I should leave without thanking you."

The rain fell hard, the door creaked, and the wind whistled.

"Life is sweet, mother dear, goodbye, and thank you." **15**

He turned round and started running.

There was a sudden diffuse flash of silent lightning and she saw that the yard was empty. She went back heavily and fell into a restless sleep. Before she slept she said to herself that she must see Mr. Addai next morning, Sunday, or better still, Monday, and tell him about all this, in case Meji was in trouble. She hoped Meji would not be annoyed. He was such a good son.

But it was Mr. Addai who came instead, on Sunday afternoon, quiet and grave, and met Bola sitting on an old stool in the veranda, dressing Asi's hair in tight thin plaits.

Mr. Addai sat down and, looking away, he said, "The Lord giveth and the Lord taketh away." Soon half the village were sitting round the veranda and in the yard.

"But I tell you, he was here on Friday and left Sunday morning," Bola said. "He couldn't have died on Friday." **16**

Bola had just recovered from a fainting fit after being told of her son's death in town. His wife, Asi's mother, had come with the news, bringing some of his property. She said Meji had died instantly at noon on Friday and had been buried on Saturday at sundown. They would have brought him to Kumansenu for burial. He had always wished that. But they could not do so in time as bodies did not last more than a day in the

READING CHECK

1. Where do Asi and Bola live? (in Kumansenu, a small African village)
2. How many boys did Bola bear before Meji was born? (six)
3. Why did Bola mark one infant's dead body? (to recognize its spirit when the mark recurred)
4. What job took Meji away from Kumansenu? (government clerk)

5. What does Meji wear on his neck? (a red handkerchief)
6. What does Asi observe about her father's shadow? (He has none.)
7. Before he leaves, what does Meji say about life? ("Life is sweet.")
8. What causes Bola to faint? (the news that Meji had died before his visit)

9. How did Meji die? (when the sash broke, a window fell and broke his neck)
10. What reason does Bola give Musa for Meji's visit? (to thank her for giving him life)

hot season, and there were no lorries available for hire.

"He was here, he was here," Bola said, rubbing her forehead and weeping.

Asi sat by quietly. Mr. Addai said comfortingly, "Hush, hush, he couldn't have been, because no one in the village saw him."

"He said we were to tell no one," Bola said.

The crowd smiled above Bola's head and shook their heads. "Poor woman," someone said, "she is beside herself with grief."

"He died on Friday," Mrs. Meji repeated, crying. "He was in the office and he pulled up the window to look out and call the messenger. Then the sash broke. The window fell, broke his neck, and the sharp edge almost cut his head off; they say he died at once."

"My papa had a scarf around his neck." Asi shouted suddenly.

"Hush," said the crowd.

Mrs. Meji dipped her hand into her bosom and produced a small gold locket and put it round Asi's neck, to quiet her.

"Your papa had this made last week for your Christmas present. You may as well have it now."

Asi played with it and pulled it this way and that.

"Be careful, child," Mr. Addai said, "it is your father's last gift."

"I was trying to remember how he showed me yesterday to open it," Asi said.

"You have never seen it before," Mrs. Meji said, sharply, trembling with fear mingled with anger.

She took the locket and tried to open it.

"Let me have it," said the village goldsmith, and he tried whispering magic words of incantation. Then he said, defeated, "It must be poor quality gold; it has rusted. I need tools to open it."

"I remember now," Asi said in the flat complacent voice of childhood.

The crowd gathered round quietly and the setting sun glinted on the soft red African gold of the dangling trinket. The goldsmith handed the locket over to Asi and asked in a loud whisper, "How did he open it?"

"Like so," Asi said and pressed a secret catch. It flew open and she spelled out gravely the word inside, "A-S-I."

The silence continued.

"His neck, poor boy," Bola said a little wildly. "This is why he could not eat the lovely meals I cooked for him."

Mr. Addai announced a service of intercession after vespers[10] that evening. The crowd began to leave quietly.

Musa, the magician, was one of the last to leave. He was now very old and bent. In times of grave calamity, it was known that even Mr. Addai did not raise objection to his being consulted.

He bent over further and whispered in Bola's ear. "You should have had his bones broken and mangled thirty-one years ago when he went for the sixth time and then he would not have come back to mock you all these years by pretending to be alive. I told you so. But you women are naughty and stubborn."

Bola stood up, her black face held high, her eyes terrible with maternal rage and pride.

"I am glad I did not," she said, "and that is why he came back specially to thank me before he went for good."

She clutched Asi to her. "I am glad I gave him the opportunity to come back, for life is sweet. I do not expect you to understand why I did so. After all, you are only a man."

18

---

10. **vespers:** evening prayers in a Christian church.

Abioseh Nicol 1341

1. Writing a Newspaper Account. Ask students to imagine that they are local reporters who were present at Bola's house in the final scene of the story. Have each student write a newspaper account of Bola's story. The account should include quotations and speculations or opinions that are based on details in the story.

2. Additional Reading. Have students read part or all of *The Dark Child* (1953), the noted, slightly fictionalized autobiography of Guinean author Camara Laye. Each student should then write a report on a topic dealt with in the book, such as West African buildings and the layout of the village, West African family life, or the role of goldsmiths.

CLOSURE

Remind students of Meji's remark "Life is sweet," which echoes the story's title and is in turn repeated by Bola at the end. Ask students to expand Meji's remark into a statement that captures the story's main theme. (Possible response: Life, no matter how brief, is a unique experience and a valuable gift.) Also, have students state additional themes about maternal love or the clash between an individual and authority that they feel the story expresses. ∎

ANSWERS

First Thoughts
Answers will vary.

Identifying Facts
1. After the sixth baby died, Bola was told to break its bones to prevent the return of the spirit. She refused. The next child lived. Meji's daughter
2. his need to rest. "Life is sweet. . . ."
3. Meji died on the day of his visit. She opens the locket.
4. She should have obeyed him. She is glad she did not.

Interpreting Meanings
1. The lack of a shadow, the handkerchief, and other details heighten suspicions that something is wrong with Meji.
2. Asi would not exist if Meji had never lived. maternal love
3. Answers will vary.
4. Meji's remark echoing title, repeated by Bola. Answers will vary.

Applying Meanings
Answers will vary.

Critical Writing Response
Writing About Foreshadowing. Essays should include at least three examples.

Language and Vocabulary
African Languages and English
1. the instrument, Bantu;
2. type of ape, Bantu; 3. type of antelope, Bushman; 4. okra, Bantu; 5. improvised music, Creole; 6. huge, Gullah; 7. xylophonelike instrument, Mbundu (Bantu); 8. the plant, W. African; 9. journey, Swahili; 10. haul, possibly Congo ∎

> ### First Thoughts
Is this tale merely an entertaining ghost story, or is there more to it than that? Discuss.

Identifying Facts
1. Summarize the background information that the opening paragraphs provide about Bola's seven children. Who is Asi?
2. What reasons does Meji give for wanting no feast or company during his visit home? What are his final words to his mother?
3. What does Mr. Addai tell Bola that Bola at first refuses to believe? How does Asi prove that she *had* seen her father?
4. What does Musa, the village magician, tell Bola at the end? How does Bola respond?

Interpreting Meanings
1. What details in this story **foreshadow** the tale's surprise ending? Reread the story to the end of page 1339. Describe how foreshadowing is used to provide suspense.
2. Bola hugs Asi when Musa says that Bola behaved foolishly years ago. Why is Bola's action significant? What does Bola think that Musa cannot understand because he is a man?
3. Despite its eerie details, would you say this story is life-affirming? Why or why not? How do you feel about the values stressed in the story?
4. The **theme** of a story is sometimes revealed in a single significant passage. In this story, where would you say the theme is stated? What do you think of this theme?

Applying Meanings
In his famous poem "In Memoriam," British poet Alfred, Lord Tennyson (1809–1892) said, " 'Tis better to have loved and lost/ Than never to have loved at all." Do you think that Bola would agree with this sentiment? Do you agree with it? Explain.

Critical Writing Response
Writing About Foreshadowing. In a brief essay, analyze Nicol's use of foreshadowing. Cite all the examples of foreshadowing that you can find and explain what later events they relate to. Before you begin writing, you may find it helpful to list in one column on a separate sheet of paper the examples of foreshadowing that you find. In another column, list the later event each example points to.

Clue	Event It Foreshadows
1. Red handkerchief around Meji's neck	1. His neck was broken.

Language and Vocabulary

African Languages and English

The *kola*, an African tree mentioned several times in the story, takes its English name from a West African word for this tree. From the tree's nutlike seeds comes an extract used to flavor the popular soft drink that we call *cola*. Cola is one of several words that came to English from the native languages of Africa. Some of these words entered English in the Old World; others were brought to the New World by Africans who came here as slaves.

Use a dictionary to find the meanings and origins of these words derived from African languages.

1. banjo
2. chimpanzee
3. gnu
4. gumbo
5. jazz
6. jumbo
7. marimba
8. okra
9. safari
10. tote

Chinua Achebe
b. 1930, Nigeria

AP/Wide World Photos

Chinua Achebe (chin'wä' ä·chä'bä) was born and grew up in the Ibo village of Ogidi when Nigeria was still a British colony. Although Achebe won a scholarship to study medicine, his love of literature and growing involvement with African nationalism changed his career. The nationalist movement after World War II brought with it a new sense of African self-awareness and confidence, and it occurred to Achebe that he and his fellow Africans might have their own stories to tell. Achebe's insight made him question the colonial-era notion that African culture was inferior to the culture

the European colonists had grafted onto Africa, usually by force. As a gesture defining his roots, Achebe dropped his first name, Albert, which his parents had given him in honor of Queen Victoria's husband.

In 1958, while working for the Nigerian Broadcasting Company, Achebe published his first novel, *Things Fall Apart*. The novel tells of an Ibo man whose personal life is ruined as a result of colonial pressures. This was the first of three novels that Achebe wrote to explore the Ibo past and the destructive effects of colonialism on African cultures and on individual Africans.

In 1960, the new nation of Nigeria, with over two hundred ethnic groups, was not a unified country. The four largest ethnic groups, the Ibo, Hausa, Fulani, and Yoruba, were constantly fighting for land and power. Many of the frictions originated in the groups' very different religions, languages, and outlooks on life. Eventually, in 1967, things fell apart. Achebe was one of the many Ibo who unsuccessfully tried to secede from Nigeria and establish a new republic called Biafra. In the worst months of the bloody, three-year civil war, about twelve thousand people, mostly children, starved to death each day. Overall, somewhere between one million and two million people died—many of them from disease and hunger. Several stories in Achebe's story collection *Girls at War* (1973) describe the tragedies and horrors of these years of civil war.

MORE ABOUT THE AUTHOR

One of contemporary Africa's best-known English-language writers, Chinua Achebe spoke the Ibo language before he learned English at the local mission school where his father taught. His father was one of the earliest converts to Christianity in the Achebes' village, a break with tradition that caused social tensions. Many of Achebe's works draw on his childhood experiences and focus on these tensions; others focus on systemic problems of a changing Africa in a changing world.

After winning fame for his novels of Ibo life, Achebe formed a publishing company with the help of Christopher Okigbo, the noted Nigerian poet. Their plans were interrupted by Nigeria's civil war, in which Okigbo died. During the war Achebe traveled throughout the world to win support for the independence of Biafra. When that cause failed, he retired from political life and devoted his time to teaching, writing, and editing.

In addition to publishing five novels, the last in 1987, he has published poetry collections and books of critical essays and has retold many traditional African tales. As the director of Heinemann's publishing offices in Nigeria and the editor of the literary journal *Okike*, Achebe has helped foster the careers of many other African writers. He has also edited *The Heinemann Book of Contemporary African Short Stories* (1992).

OBJECTIVES
1. *To read and interpret a story about ethnic differences and changing times in Africa*
2. *To understand verbal irony*
3. *To write a story sequel and an analysis of a story's conflict*

VOCABULARY IN CONTEXT
The words listed below will appear in the side margin at the point of instruction:
1. cosmopolitan   4. dissuasion
2. disposed   5. theological
3. vehemently

PREREADING FOCUS

Background: The Ibo (also called the Igbo), who constitute about 17 percent of Nigeria's population, are the dominant ethnic group in southeastern Nigeria. Primarily Christian, they formed an educated, prosperous minority in Nigeria at the time of the civil war, when their influence was deeply resented in other parts of the country, particularly in the Hausa and Fulani north. The Ibibio, a smaller group than the Ibo, were traditionally rain-forest farmers in the Cross River section of southeastern Nigeria. Over the years they were influenced by their Ibo neighbors, and many—like Nene in "Marriage Is a Private Affair"— also adopted Christianity.

Writer's Response: To stimulate ideas, you may have students brainstorm definitions for the phrase "generation gap." You may also ask them to summarize the plots of stories, novels, films, or television programs that treat the generation gap in a serious or humorous way.

Literary Focus: Students may be familiar with the term *sarcasm*, which refers to a form of verbal irony that is meant to hurt or taunt. Most irony, however, is less harsh than sarcasm: It reflects the writer's or the speaker's wit and willingness to use restraint.

Reader's Guide

MARRIAGE IS A PRIVATE AFFAIR

Background

Nigeria is a West African nation of great ethnic diversity. Two of the largest ethnic groups in the southeast are the Ibo and the Ibibio. Since the end of World War II, many young Nigerians have left their rural villages to attend universities and settle in large cities such as Lagos, Nigeria's former capital. As a result of this migration, some young people have abandoned their communities' traditions for more westernized ways. Yet many have found it difficult to break away from their roots, and these young people find themselves caught in the clash between the old and the new. "Marriage Is a Private Affair" is about two young people, an Ibo man and an Ibibio woman. They live in Lagos and have broken traditions by marrying each other. In contrast to the young couple is the man's father, a rural villager who rigidly adheres to traditional Ibo ways.

Writer's Response

This story involves a conflict between generations. Do you think that it is inevitable that generations clash? Describe a situation that you have witnessed or heard about that illustrates the problem of conflict between older and younger generations.

Literary Focus

In **verbal irony**, language is used to say one thing but to mean the opposite. For example, a friend is probably being ironic if he tells you, "I just *love* doing five hours of grammar homework every night." As you read "Marriage Is a Private Affair," think about whether Achebe is using verbal irony in the title of his story.

MARRIAGE IS A PRIVATE AFFAIR

Chinua Achebe

> *Read the first five paragraphs, stopping after Nene's question,
> " 'Why shouldn't it?' " Write down at least three questions you
> have about the characters and events of this story. When you
> finish reading the story, see if your questions have been answered.*

"Have you written to your dad yet?" asked Nene[1] one afternoon as she sat with Nnaemeka[2] in her room at 16 Kasanga Street, Lagos.[3]

"No. I've been thinking about it. I think it's better to tell him when I get home on leave!"

"But why? Your leave is such a long way off yet—six whole weeks. He should be let into our happiness now."

Nnaemeka was silent for a while, and then began very slowly as if he groped for his words: "I wish I were sure it would be happiness to him."

"Of course it must," replied Nene, a little surprised. "Why shouldn't it?"

"You have lived in Lagos all your life, and you know very little about people in remote parts of the country."

"That's what you always say. But I don't believe anybody will be so unlike other people that they will be unhappy when their sons are engaged to marry."

"Yes. They are most unhappy if the engagement is not arranged by them. In our case it's worse—you are not even an Ibo."[4]

This was said so seriously and so bluntly that Nene could not find speech immediately. In the cosmopolitan atmosphere of the city it had

Traffic jam on Broad Street in Lagos, Nigeria.

Jackie Phillips/Time Magazine

---

1. **Nene** (nā′nē)
2. **Nnaemeka** ('n·nä·ä·mä′kə)
3. **Lagos** (lä′gäs′): former capital of Nigeria.

4. **Ibo** (ē′bō): member of an African ethnic group living mostly in southeastern Nigeria.

1 CULTURAL DIVERSITY
Lagos, Nigeria's former capital, is a coastal city of more than five million people. It is located in the southwestern corner of the country, far from the rural rain-forest regions of southeastern Nigeria where the Ibo and the Ibibio have traditionally lived.

❓ *Do you think that city dwellers are more open-minded than people who live in rural areas? Explain.* (Students who answer yes may believe that city dwellers are more tolerant of individual differences because they have been exposed to different outlooks and lifestyles. Others may believe that media such as television have negated these differences between city and country.)

cosmopolitan (käz′mə·päl′ə·tən): representative of all or many parts of the world; not bound by local prejudices or habits.

Apostrophes

Apostrophes show where letters have been deleted from contractions: ***don't*** (*do not*); ***it's*** (*it is, it has*). Apostrophes also show possession. A singular noun and a plural noun not ending in *s* use an apostrophe and *s*: *woman's* hat, ***James's*** *toys*, ***women's*** *store*. An apostrophe alone is added to a plural noun that ends in *s*: ***babies'*** *cribs*. Possessive forms of personal pronouns do *not* use apostrophes: *The dog licked its paw.*

Writing and Sharing. Have students use the words below to write ten sentences about the story. Direct them to use contractions for (1) through (4) and possessive forms for (5) through (10): (1) is not, (2) it is, (3) they are, (4) who has; (5) Nene, (6) Lagos, (7) people, (8) it, (9) boys, (10) villagers. ■

HUMANITIES CONNECTION

The Ibos' first contact with Europeans was with slave traders in the fifteenth century. Christian missionaries arrived in the 1850s and began to build churches and establish schools. Many Nigerian leaders were educated at these mission schools. In the twentieth century, the adoption of Western life-styles changed the Ibo way of life.

❓ *How does the carving represent the coming together of two cultures?* (It depicts a biblical scene using African figures.) ■

---

disposed (di·spōzd′): inclined; having a certain tendency

---

2 READER'S RESPONSE

What do you think of marital prohibitions based on ethnicity? (Students who see value in them may believe that common experiences promote understanding and communication. Students who disapprove may consider such restrictions outdated in a multicultural society.)

Carving on a Nigerian church door depicting a scene from the Bible.

Marc & Evelyne Bernheim/Woodfin Camp & Associates

always seemed to her something of a joke that a person's tribe could determine whom he married.

At last she said, "You don't really mean that he will object to your marrying me simply on that account? I had always thought you Ibos were kindly disposed to other people."

"So we are. But when it comes to marriage, well, it's not quite so simple. And this," he added, "is not peculiar to the Ibos. If your father were alive and lived in the heart of Ibibio-land[5] he would be exactly like my father."

"I don't know. But anyway, as your father is so fond of you, I'm sure he will forgive you soon enough. Come on then, be a good boy and send him a nice lovely letter . . ."

"It would not be wise to break the news to him by writing. A letter will bring it upon him with a shock. I'm quite sure about that."

"All right, honey, suit yourself. You know your father."

As Nnaemeka walked home that evening he turned over in his mind different ways of overcoming his father's opposition, especially now that he had gone and found a girl for him. He had thought of showing his letter to Nene but decided on second thoughts not to, at least for the moment. He read it again when he got home, and couldn't help smiling to himself. He remembered Ugoye[6] quite well, an Amazon[7] of a girl who used to beat up all the boys, himself included, on the way to the stream, a complete dunce at school.

I have found a girl who will suit you admirably—Ugoye Nweke,[8] the eldest daughter of our neighbor, Jacob Nweke. She has a proper Christian upbringing. When she stopped schooling some years ago her father (a man of sound judgment) sent her to live in the house of a

---

5. **Ibibio-land** (ib′ə·bē′ō′-): region of southeastern Nigeria that is the traditional homeland of the Ibibio, another African ethnic group.

6. **Ugoye** (ōō·gō′yā)

7. **Amazon:** tall, physically powerful female; from the Amazons, a tribe of strong women warriors in Greek mythology.

8. **Nweke** (′n·wā′kā)

pastor where she has received all the training a wife could need. Her Sunday School teacher has told me that she reads her Bible very fluently. I hope we shall begin negotiations when you come home in December.

On the second evening of his return from Lagos, Nnaemeka sat with his father under a cassia tree. This was the old man's retreat where he went to read his Bible when the parching December sun had set and a fresh, reviving wind blew on the leaves.

"Father," began Nnaemeka suddenly, "I have come to ask for forgiveness."

"Forgiveness? For what, my son?" he asked in amazement.

"It's about this marriage question."

"Which marriage question?"

"I can't—we must—I mean it is impossible for me to marry Nweke's daughter."

"Impossible? Why?" asked his father.

"I don't love her."

"Nobody said you did. Why should you?" he asked.

"Marriage today is different . . ."

"Look here, my son," interrupted his father, "nothing is different. What one looks for in a wife are a good character and a Christian background."

Nnaemeka saw there was no hope along the present line of argument.

"Moreover," he said. "I am engaged to marry another girl who has all of Ugoye's good qualities, and who . . ."

His father did not believe his ears. "What did you say?" he asked slowly and disconcertingly.

"She is a good Christian," his son went on, "and a teacher in a Girls' School in Lagos."

"Teacher, did you say? If you consider that a qualification for a good wife I should like to point out to you, Emeka, that no Christian woman should teach. St. Paul in his letter to the Corinthians[9] says that women should keep silence." He rose slowly from his seat and paced forwards and backwards. This was his pet subject, and he condemned <u>vehemently</u> those church leaders who encouraged women to teach in their schools. After he had spent his emotion on a long homily he at last came back to his son's engagement, in a seemingly milder tone.

"Whose daughter is she, anyway?"

"She is Nene Atang."

"What!" All the mildness was gone again. "Did you say Neneataga, what does that mean?"

"Nene Atang from Calabar. She is the only girl I can marry." This was a very rash reply and Nnaemeka expected the storm to burst. But it did not. His father merely walked away into his room. This was most unexpected and perplexed Nnaemeka. His father's silence was infinitely more menacing than a flood of threatening speech. That night the old man did not eat.

When he sent for Nnaemeka a day later, he applied all possible ways of <u>dissuasion</u>. But the young man's heart was hardened, and his father eventually gave him up as lost.

"I owe it to you, my son, as a duty to show you what is right and what is wrong. Whoever put this idea into your head might as well have cut your throat. It is Satan's work." He waved his son away.

"You will change your mind, Father, when you know Nene."

"I shall never see her," was the reply. From that night the father scarcely spoke to his son. He did not, however, cease hoping that he would realize how serious was the danger he was heading for. Day and night he put him in his prayers.

---

9. **St. Paul . . . Corinthians:** reference to a book in the Bible's New Testament (I Corinthians 14:34).

MEETING INDIVIDUAL NEEDS

3 LEP: Have a volunteer read aloud Nnaemeka's remark in order to capture the hesitation signaled by the use of dashes and caused by his nervousness in approaching the subject of his engagement. ■

4 CULTURAL DIVERSITY
Arranged marriages were common in virtually every culture until fairly recently. Among the upper classes, they were a way of maintaining wealth and position; among the lower classes, the arrangement was necessary, for laborers had little leisure time to find and court potential spouses.
? *What examples of arranged marriages do you know about?* (Possible responses: the mail-order brides of the American West or marriages between immigrants who came to America between 1840 and 1930)

5 INTERPRETING
Why did Nnaemeka's father speak in a "milder tone" before he heard the name? (Possible response: Expecting his son to have chosen an Ibo bride, he was curious to learn who she was and was thinking about the possibility of approving his son's choice.)

▪ **vehemently** (vē′ə·mənt·lē): in a way that displays great passion

dissuasion (di·swā′zhən): turning a person away from a course by persuasion or advice

Chinua Achebe **1347**

Nnaemeka, for his own part, was very deeply affected by his father's grief. But he kept hoping that it would pass away. If it had occurred to him that never in the history of his people had a man married a woman who spoke a different tongue, he might have been less optimistic. "It has never been heard," was the verdict of an old man speaking a few weeks later. In that short sentence he spoke for all of his people. This man had come with others to commiserate with Okeke[10] when news went round about his son's behavior. By that time the son had gone back to Lagos.

"It has never been heard," said the old man again with a sad shake of his head.

"What did Our Lord say?" asked another gentleman. "Sons shall rise against their Fathers; it is there in the Holy Book."

"It is the beginning of the end," said another.

The discussion thus tending to become theological, Madubogwu, a highly practical man, brought it down once more to the ordinary level.

"Have you thought of consulting a native doctor about your son?" he asked Nnaemeka's father.

"He isn't sick," was the reply.

"What is he then? The boy's mind is diseased and only a good herbalist can bring him back to his right senses. The medicine he requires is *Amalile*, the same that women apply with success to recapture their husbands' straying affection."

"Madubogwu is right," said another gentleman. "This thing calls for medicine."

"I shall not call in a native doctor." Nnaemeka's father was known to be obstinately ahead of his more superstitious neighbors in

these matters. "I will not be another Mrs. Ochuba. If my son wants to kill himself, let him do it with his own hands. It is not for me to help him."

"But it was her fault," said Madubogwu. "She ought to have gone to an honest herbalist. She was a clever woman, nevertheless."

"She was a wicked murderess," said Jonathan, who rarely argued with his neighbors because, he often said, they were incapable of reasoning. "The medicine was prepared for her husband, it was his name they called in its preparation and I am sure it would have been perfectly beneficial to him. It was wicked to put it into the herbalist's food, and say you were only trying it out."

Six months later, Nnaemeka was showing his young wife a short letter from his father:

> It amazes me that you could be so unfeeling as to send me your wedding picture. I would have sent it back. But on further thought I decided just to cut off your wife and send it back to you because I have nothing to do with her. How I wish that I had nothing to do with you either.

When Nene read through this letter and looked at the mutilated picture, her eyes filled with tears, and she began to sob.

"Don't cry, my darling," said her husband. "He is essentially good-natured and will one day look more kindly on our marriage." But years passed and that one day did not come.

For eight years, Okeke would have nothing to do with his son, Nnaemeka. Only three times (when Nnaemeka asked to come home and spend his leave) did he write to him.

"I can't have you in my house," he replied on one occasion. "It can be of no interest to me where or how you spend your leave—or your life, for that matter."

---

10. **Okeke** (ō·kā′kā)

READING CHECK

1. Where do Nnaemeka and Nene live? (Lagos, the former capital of Nigeria)
2. What is Okeke's chief objection to his son's marrying Nene? (She is not an Ibo.)
3. What did Okeke do to the wedding picture that Nnaemeka sent him? (He cut off the part showing Nene and kept only the part showing his son.)
4. For how many years does Okeke refuse to see his son? (eight years)
5. What prompts Okeke to consider "making it up" to his son and daughter-in-law? (the news that they have given him two grandsons)

RETEACHING

To reteach the story, have groups of students work together to create a "photograph" album for Nnaemeka. Captions should name the characters, identify their relationships, and describe events in their lives. Students may use their own drawings as the "photographs."

10 The prejudice against Nnaemeka's marriage was not confined to his little village. In Lagos, especially among his people who worked there, it showed itself in a different way. Their women, when they met at their village meeting, were not hostile to Nene. Rather, they paid her such excessive deference as to make her feel she was not one of them. But as time went on, Nene gradually

11 broke through some of this prejudice and even began to make friends among them. Slowly and grudgingly they began to admit that she kept her home much better than most of them.

The story eventually got to the little village in the heart of the Ibo country that Nnaemeka and his young wife were a most happy couple. But his father was one of the few people in the village who knew nothing about this. He always displayed so much temper whenever his son's name was mentioned that everyone avoided it in his presence. By a tremendous effort of will he had succeeded in pushing his son to the back of his mind. The strain had nearly killed him but he had persevered, and won.

Then one day he received a letter from Nene, and in spite of himself he began to glance through it perfunctorily until all of a sudden the expression on his face changed and he began to read more carefully.

. . . Our two sons, from the day they learnt that they have a grandfather, have insisted on being taken to him. I find it impossible to tell them that you will not see them. I implore you to allow Nnaemeka to bring them home for a short time during his leave next month. I shall remain here in Lagos . . .

The old man at once felt the resolution he had built up over so many years falling in. He was telling himself that he must not give in. He tried to steel his heart against all

Marc & Evelyne Bernheim/Woodfin Camp & Associates

Ibo ceremonial mask.
❓ *Does Nene receive the same treatment from Nnaemeka's friends in Lagos as she does from her father-in-law?*

emotional appeals. It was a reenactment of that other struggle. He leaned against a window and looked out. The sky was overcast with heavy black clouds and a high wind began to blow filling the air with dust and dry leaves. It was one of those rare occasions when even Nature takes a hand in a human fight. Very soon it began to rain, the first rain in the year. It came down in large sharp drops and was accompanied by the lightning and thunder which mark a change of season. Okeke was trying hard not to think of his two grandsons. But he knew he was now fighting a losing battle. He tried to hum a favorite hymn but the pattering of large raindrops on the roof broke up the tune. His mind immediately returned to the children. How could he shut his door against them? By a curious mental process he imagined them standing, sad and forsaken, under the harsh angry weather—shut out from his house.

That night he hardly slept, from remorse—and a vague fear that he might die without making it up to them.

Chinua Achebe   **1349**

1. Group Research Project. Using encyclopedias, atlases, and nonfiction books about Africa as sources of information, students should work together to create a large ethnic map of the continent. The map should show the current borders of countries as well as the traditional home regions of Africa's large ethnic groups.

2. Writing Characters' Letters. Have students complete one of the letters mentioned or quoted in the story—one of Nnaemeka's letters asking to visit his father or Nene's letter to Okeke.

CLOSURE

Ask students whether they find believable the change of heart that Okeke seems to experience in the final paragraph of the selection. What does the change suggest about love and family ties? (They can outweigh personal beliefs and attitudes.) ■

ANSWERS

First Thoughts
Answers will vary.

Identifying Facts
1. He is Ibo; she is Ibibio. His father did not arrange the marriage and won't accept a non-Ibo wife for his son.
2. good character and Christian background. He believes it is unsuitable.
3. He refuses to see them. Their disapproval melts as they come to appreciate her.
4. to allow Nnaemeka to bring the two boys to meet their grandfather. It falls away; remorse and fear

Interpreting Meanings
1. He regrets his hardheartedness. As a traditionalist, the birth of grandsons is important to him.
2. It reflects Okeke's turmoil.
3. Yes; public. Everyone gossips about it and talks about what should be done.
4. Though Achebe suggests that Okeke's stubbornness was misguided, his narrative is objective.
5. Possible response: Intransigent views can lead to unhappiness.

Applying Meanings
Answers will vary.

Creative Writing Response
Writing a Sequel. Sequels should include believable dialogue and behavior.

Critical Writing Response
Analyzing a Conflict. Essays should contain logical arguments supporting students' conclusions. ■

First Thoughts
Do you think that Okeke will see his grandsons and make peace with his son and daughter-in-law? Or do you think he will continue to stick by his traditional beliefs and die without seeing his grandsons? What makes you say so?

Identifying Facts
1. What ethnic difference separates Nnaemeka and Nene? In predicting that his father will be unhappy with their marriage, what reasons does Nnaemeka give?
2. What does Okeke, Nnaemeka's father, believe a man must look for in a wife? What is his opinion of Nene's job as a teacher?
3. In a sentence, summarize Okeke's treatment of his son and daughter-in-law for the first eight years of their marriage. In contrast, how do Nnaemeka's Ibo friends in Lagos feel about Nene?
4. What request does Nene make in her letter to her father-in-law? After reading the letter, what happens to the resolution Okeke has "built up over so many years," and what feelings disturb his sleep that night?

Interpreting Meanings
1. Explain in your own words the change of heart that Okeke experiences at the story's end. Why do you think learning about his grandchildren has affected him more than seeing his son's wedding photograph?
2. What role does nature seem to play near the end of the story?
3. Do you think Achebe is using **verbal irony** in the title of this story? Does the story reveal that marriage is a private affair or a public affair? Explain.

4. In the **conflict** between Nnaemeka's ways and his father's, does Achebe seem strongly to favor one side or the other?
5. The **subject** of this story is a marriage that occurs in opposition to a father's wishes. The **theme** is the truth about human nature revealed in the story. In your own words, state what you see as the theme of this story. Remember that a change in a main character and the nature of the conflict's resolution often indicate the theme of a story.

Applying Meanings
In your opinion, should marriage be a "private affair," or should social considerations play an important role? Discuss your views with the class.

Creative Writing Response
Writing a Sequel. Achebe ends his story without resolving the conflict between Okeke and his son. What do you think Okeke will do? Write a brief sequel in which you show Okeke's subsequent behavior. You may incorporate ideas discussed in the First Thoughts question. Be sure your sequel takes into account the characters of Okeke, Nnaemeka, and Nene as Achebe has presented them.

Critical Writing Response
Analyzing a Conflict. The central **conflict** of this story, as in much of Achebe's fiction, is between the old ways and the new. This conflict takes many forms: rural vs. urban lifestyles, arranged marriages vs. love marriages, and housewives vs. career women. Choose one of these conflicts. In a brief essay, describe the conflict and discuss how it is, or is not, resolved by the story's end. At the end of your essay, describe your own response to the issues raised by this conflict.

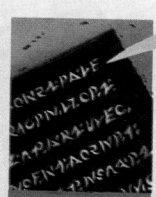

Nadine Gordimer
b. 1923, South Africa

Ulf Andersen/Gamma-Liaison

Now that apartheid is a thing of the past in South Africa, has Nadine Gordimer lost her lifelong subject? Hardly, since she has always maintained that people are her subject and that politics only interests her in terms of its effects on human lives. To the writer Edmund Morris, she once said, "I'm fascinated by observed moments of tension between people; my mind immediately invents causes for this tension. I like to compose alternate lives."

Her own life began in Springs, a small town just outside Johannesburg in the gold-mining area of South Africa. Her parents were Jewish immigrants—her father from Lithuania, her mother from England—and Gordimer received a typical middle-class colonial upbringing. During her childhood, "walled up among the mine dumps," Gordi-

mer turned to reading, which became her passport to a larger world.

Gordimer's first story was published in a Johannesburg weekly when she was just fifteen. In 1949, after a year of study at the University of Witwatersrand, Gordimer moved to Johannesburg and began, in her writing, "to make sense of life." She also began to nourish a growing commitment to a multiracial South Africa, in part through friendships formed with black journalists, musicians, and intellectuals.

Though three of her novels were initially banned at home, Gordimer's fiction has been widely admired abroad for the light she has shed on the corrosive effects of apartheid on the South African people, both white and black. Of her evolution as a writer and a social critic, Gordimer herself has said, "When you're born white in South Africa, you're peeling like an onion. You're sloughing off all the conditioning that you've had since you were a child."

Critics too have seen her work grow and evolve along with the great political and social changes in her country. In the watershed year of 1991, as Nelson Mandela was negotiating with the government to end minority rule, Gordimer was awarded the Nobel Prize in literature. She continues today, in works like *None to Accompany Me* (1994), to make what she sees as "the essential gesture" of all artists—"the hand held out with the best we have to give."

MORE ABOUT THE AUTHOR
Although Nadine Gordimer has always maintained that she is not a political writer, she has been active politically. As she explains it: "I live in a society which is fundamentally out of joint. One can't but be politically concerned." When three of her novels were banned by the all-white government in the 1970s, she published, at her own expense, the government's reasons for banning them. She then organized writers' groups to protest press censorship and founded the Congress of South African Writers, open to people of all races writing in any of South Africa's languages. For a time the nation was so polarized that she was the only white writer in the organization. A long-time member of the African National Congress, which is now the majority party in the democratically elected legislature, Gordimer is heartened by the revival of the black South African oral tradition and is cautiously hopeful for an honest exchange between South Africa's black and white artists.

OBJECTIVES
1. *To interpret a story about racial divisions in South Africa*
2. *To analyze conflict between individuals and groups*
3. *To write an interior monologue from the point of view of one character and to write an essay analyzing details in the story*

THEMES IN WORLD LITERATURE

Conflict of Cultures and Values
A Doll's House, pp. 1071–1126
"By Any Other Name," pp. 1389–1394

The Individual and Society
"The Book of Ruth," pp. 178–184
"The Guest," pp. 1246–1257 ■

VOCABULARY IN CONTEXT

The words listed below will appear in the side margin at the point of instruction.

1. interrogating   4. wryly
2. careered   5. atrophy
3. splaying

PREREADING FOCUS

Background: At the time of this story, the 1950s, the white minority in South Africa (to this day never more than 15 percent of the total population) held a position of immense power and privilege over the native majority. These white South Africans are mostly descendants of Dutch settlers (or Boers), who began colonization in the seventeenth century, and of British settlers, who came in the 1800s. The British wrested control from the Dutch in the Boer War (1899–1902), making South Africa a British colony until 1948 when the Boer-dominated National Party assumed power and made *apartheid* the law of the land.

Writer's Response: It may be helpful for students to brainstorm their thoughts by using a cluster diagram. The incident itself should be the starting point, with branches that include sensory details and speculations about what the incident reveals about the subject.

Literary Response: Remind students that external conflict is different from **internal conflict**, or the struggle of opposing needs, desires, or emotions within a single character. The external conflicts are more obvious in this story, but students may also detect significant internal conflict in some of the characters.

Reader's Guide

THE TRAIN FROM RHODESIA

Background

Until 1991, South Africa was ruled by an all-white minority government that imposed an official policy of complete racial segregation called *apartheid*. The black majority was forced to live in separate neighborhoods and regions; many jobs were assigned on the basis of race; all nonwhites were forced to carry identity cards specifying their race; and blacks and people of mixed race were not allowed to own land, vote, or hold political office. The effect of this policy was to create a huge social, economic, and political gulf between the races. It is this gulf that Gordimer depicts so tangibly in her story of a trainload of white tourists passing through a black village in the 1950s. Rhodesia was the name given by English colonizers to the African country that borders South Africa to the north. After its independence in 1979, this country was renamed Zimbabwe, after the ancient African kingdom of Great Zimbabwe.

Writer's Response

Critics have praised Nadine Gordimer for her ability to capture "the illuminating moment"—the fleeting instant that reveals the complexity of her characters' lives so precisely that the passage "sparkles like a gem." Recall an incident you observed recently or long ago in which you witnessed another person during an "illuminating moment"—that is, doing something that directly revealed an important aspect of his or her character. Write a brief sketch based on the incident, using specific details that would help a reader to deduce the character's inner state.

Literary Focus

Conflict is the clash or struggle between opposing forces. **External conflicts** occur not only between individuals who disagree, but also between groups whose interests cannot be reconciled. Cultural conflicts involving a clash of ideas, values, and traditions often include a fight for political and economic power as well, since a group without at least a share of power can rarely maintain its cultural identity.

THE TRAIN FROM RHODESIA
Nadine Gordimer

This story contains no overt dramatic conflict between the two communities it depicts, yet Gordimer conveys a striking portrait of the great divide that separates them. As you read, look for details that reveal the tensions between the two groups.

The train came out of the red horizon and bore down towards them over the single straight track.

The stationmaster came out of his little brick station with its pointed chalet roof, feeling the creases in his serge uniform in his legs as well. A stir of preparedness rippled through the squatting native venders waiting in the dust; the face of a carved wooden animal, eternally surprised, stuck out of a sack. The stationmaster's barefoot children wandered over. From the grey mud huts with the untidy heads that stood within a decorated mud wall, chickens, and dogs with their skin stretched like parchment over their bones, followed the piccanins[1] down to the track. The flushed and perspiring west cast a reflection, faint, without heat, upon the station, upon the tin shed marked "Goods," upon the walled kraal,[2] upon the grey tin house of the stationmaster and upon the sand, that lapped all around, from sky to sky, cast little rhythmical cups of shadow, so that the sand became the sea, and closed over the children's black feet softly and without imprint.

The stationmaster's wife sat behind the mesh of her veranda. Above her head the hunk of a sheep's carcass moved slightly, dangling in a current of air.

They waited.

The train called out, along the sky; but there was no answer; and the cry hung on: I'm coming . . . I'm coming. . . .

The engine flared out now, big, whisking a dwindling body behind it; the track flared out to let it in.

Creaking, jerking, jostling, gasping, the train filled the station.

Here, let me see that one—the young woman curved her body farther out of the corridor window. Missus? smiled the old man, looking at the creatures he held in his hand. From a piece of string on his grey finger hung a tiny woven basket; he lifted it, questioning. No, no, she urged, leaning down towards him, across the height of the train towards the man in the piece of old rug; that one, that one, her hand commanded. It was a lion, carved out of soft, dry wood that looked like spongecake; heraldic, black and white, with impressionistic detail burnt in.

---

1. **piccanins** (pik'ə·ninz): black children; a highly offensive term in the United States but in wide use among whites in South Africa at the time of this story.
2. **kraal** (kräl): enclosure for domestic animals.

4

The old man held it up to her still smiling, not from the heart, but at the customer.

5

Between its vandyke[3] teeth, in the mouth opened in an endless roar too terrible to be heard, it had a black tongue. Look, said the young husband, if you don't mind! And round the neck of the thing, a piece of fur (rat? rabbit? meerkat?[4]); a real mane, majestic, telling you somehow that the artist had delight in the lion.

6

All up and down the length of the train in the dust the artists sprang, walking bent, like performing animals, the better to exhibit the fantasy held towards the faces on the train. Buck, startled and stiff, staring with round black and white eyes. More lions, standing erect, grappling with strange, thin, elongated warriors who clutched spears and showed no fear in their slits of eyes. How much, they asked from the train, how much?

Give me penny, said the little ones with nothing to sell. The dogs went and sat, quite still, under the dining car, where the train breathed out the smell of meat cooking with onion.

A man passed beneath the arch of reaching arms meeting grey-black and white in the exchange of money for the staring wooden eyes, the stiff wooden legs sticking up in the air; went along under the voices and the bargaining, interrogating the wheels.

7

Past the dogs; glancing up at the dining car where he could stare at the faces, behind glass, drinking beer, two by two, on either side of a uniform railway vase with its pale dead flower. Right to the end, to the guard's van, where the stationmaster's children had just collected their mother's two loaves of bread; to the engine itself, where the stationmaster and the driver stood talking against the steaming complaint of the resting beast.

The man called out to them, something loud and joking. They turned to laugh, in a twirl of steam. The two children careered over the sand, clutching the bread, and burst through the iron gate and up the path through the garden in which nothing grew.

Passengers drew themselves in at the corridor windows and turned into compartments to fetch money, to call someone to look. Those sitting inside looked up: suddenly different, caged faces, boxed in, cut off after the contact of outside. There was an orange a piccanin would like. . . . What about that chocolate? It wasn't very nice. . . .

A girl had collected a handful of the hard kind, that no one liked, out of the chocolate box, and was throwing them to the dogs, over at the dining car. But the hens darted in and swallowed the chocolates, incredibly quick and accurate, before they had even dropped in the dust, and the dogs, a little bewildered, looked up with their brown eyes, not expecting anything.

—No, leave it, said the young woman, don't take it. . . .

Too expensive, too much, she shook her head and raised her voice to the old man, giving up the lion. He held it high where she had handed it to him. No, she said, shaking her head. Three-and-six?[5] insisted her husband, loudly. Yes baas! laughed the old man. *Three-and-six?*—the young man was incredulous. Oh leave it—she said. The young man stopped. Don't you want it? he said, keeping his face closed to the old man. No, never mind, she said, leave it. The old native kept

---

3. **vandyke:** pointed or irregular.
4. **meerkat:** a type of mongoose.

5. **three-and-six:** three shillings and sixpence, a sum of money in the local currency.

Meeting the train in Betchouanaland.
? *What do the details in this photograph suggest about the relationship between those inside the train and those standing along the tracks?*

Archive Photos

his head on one side, looking at them sideways, holding the lion. Three-and-six, he murmured, as old people repeat things to themselves.

The young woman drew her head in. She went into the coupé and sat down. Out of the window, on the other side, there was nothing; sand and bush; and thorn tree. Back through the open doorway, past the figure of her husband in the corridor, there was the station, the voices, wooden animals waving, running feet. Her eye followed the funny little valance of scrolled wood that outlined the chalet roof of the station; she thought of the lion and smiled. That bit of fur round the neck. But the wooden buck, the hippos, the elephants, the baskets that already bulked out of their brown paper under the seat and on the luggage rack! How will they look at home? Where will you put them? What will they mean away from the places you found them? Away from the unreality of the last few weeks? The young man outside. But he is not part of the unreality; he is for good now. Odd . . . somewhere there was an idea that he, that living with him, was part of the holiday, the strange places.

Outside, a bell rang. The stationmaster was leaning against the end of the train, green flag rolled in readiness. A few men who had got down to stretch their legs sprang on to the train, clinging to the observation platforms, or perhaps merely standing on the iron step, holding the rail; but on the train, safe from the one dusty platform, the one tin house, the empty sand.

There was a grunt. The train jerked. Through the glass the beer drinkers looked out, as if they could not see beyond it. Behind the flyscreen, the stationmaster's wife sat facing back at them beneath the darkening hunk of meat.

There was a shout. The flag drooped out. Joints not yet coordinated, the segmented body of the train heaved and bumped back against itself. It began to move; slowly the scrolled chalet moved past it, the yells of the natives, running alongside, jetted up into the air, fell back at different levels. Staring wooden faces waved drunkenly, there, then gone, questioning for the last time at the windows. Here, one-and-six baas!—As one automatically opens a hand to catch a thrown ball, a man fumbled wildly down his

8 INTERPRETING
How does the young woman feel about her trip so far, and what is she concerned about when she gets home? (She is concerned about integrating her experiences with her black neighbors, represented by the purchases she has made, into her familiar life back home.)

9 LITERARY ELEMENT
Diction: What does the use of the word ''safe'' suggest about the feelings of the white travelers toward the black community they have just visited? (They are afraid, alienated, and relieved to be leaving.)

10 CULTURAL DIVERSITY
The older black man addresses the younger white man as ''baas,'' meaning ''master'' or ''boss'' in Afrikaans, a language derived from seventeenth-century Dutch. This mode of address was customary in South Africa at the time of the story and reflects the servility that was forced on blacks by the white minority.
? *Can you think of an example of a mode of address in your culture, past, or present, which shows fear of or respect for another person?* (Possible responses: ''Master,'' ''Sahib'')

READING CHECK

1. Through what type of landscape is the train passing? (desert)
2. What kind of activity are the passengers and the people at the station engaged in? (buying and selling)
3. What feature of the carved lion particularly attracts the young woman? (its fur mane)
4. What transaction takes place between the young man and the woodcarver at

the end of the story? (As the train leaves the station, the old man runs after it, offering to sell for one-and-six; the young man throws the coins down and the carver tosses him the lion.)

5. What becomes of the carved lion in the end? (It is tossed aside and ignored.)

11 READER'S RESPONSE
How do you imagine the old man feels? (Possible responses: relieved to have sold the lion at any price; stripped of his dignity by the young man)

12 MAKING JUDGMENTS
As the train leaves the station, the author refers to its "blind end . . . being pulled helplessly." What do you think these words convey about Gordimer's attitude toward the whites on the train? (Possible response: sees them as deluded and passive, not fully aware of themselves)

13 READER'S RESPONSE
How do you feel toward the young man as he bounds into the compartment "with laughter and triumph"? (Possible responses: anger, pity, or shame at his insensitivity)

- **splaying** (splā´iŋ): flattening, spreading out
- **wryly** (rī´lē): in a twisted manner
- **atrophy** (a´trə·fē): shrink or waste away

14 INFERRING
The woman seems to be suffering from a long-standing unhappiness that goes beyond her personal life. What social conditions revealed in the story may be causing her suffering? (Possible response: She may feel trapped within her social class or guilty about the gulf between the races.)

pocket, brought up the shilling and sixpence and threw them out; the old native, gasping, his skinny toes splaying the sand, flung the lion.

The piccanins were waving, the dogs stood, tails uncertain, watching the train go: past the mud huts, where a woman turned to look up from the smoke of the fire, her hand pausing on her hip.

The stationmaster went slowly in under the chalet.

11 The old native stood, breath blowing out the skin between his ribs, feet tense, balanced in the sand, smiling and shaking his head. In his opened palm, held in the attitude of receiving, was the retrieved shilling and sixpence.

12 The blind end of the train was being pulled helplessly out of the station.

The young man swung in from the corridor, breathless. He was shaking his head with laughter and triumph. Here! he said. And waggled the lion at her. One-and-six!

What? she said.

13 He laughed. I was arguing with him for fun, bargaining—when the train had pulled out already, he came tearing after . . . One-and-six Baas! So there's your lion.

She was holding it away from her, the head with the open jaws, the pointed teeth, the black tongue, the wonderful ruff of fur facing her. She was looking at it with an expression of not seeing, of seeing something different. Her face was drawn up, wryly, like the face of a discomforted child. Her mouth lifted nervously at the corner. Very slowly, cautious, she lifted her finger and touched the mane, where it was joined to the wood.

But how could you, she said. He was shocked by the dismay of her face.

Good Lord, he said, what's the matter?

If you wanted the thing, she said, her voice rising and breaking with the shrill impotence of anger, why didn't you buy it in the first place? If you wanted it, why didn't you pay for it? Why didn't you take it decently, when he offered it? Why did you have to wait for him to run after the train with it, and give him one-and-six? One-and-six!

She was pushing it at him, trying to force him to take the lion. He stood astonished, his hands hanging at his sides.

But you wanted it! You liked it so much?

—It's a beautiful piece of work, she said fiercely, as if to protect it from him.

You liked it so much! You said yourself it was too expensive—

Oh *you*—she said, hopeless and furious. *You* . . . She threw the lion onto the seat.

He stood looking at her.

She sat down again in the corner and, her face slumped in her hands, stared out of the window. Everything was turning round inside her. One-and-six. One-and-six. One-and-six for the wood and the carving and the sinews of the legs and the switch of the tail. The mouth open like that and the teeth. The black tongue, rolling, like a wave. The mane round the neck. To give one-and-six for that. **14** The heat of shame mounted through her legs and body and sounded in her ears like the sound of sand pouring. Pouring, pouring. She sat there, sick. A weariness, a tastelessness, the discovery of a void made her hands slacken their grip, atrophy emptily, as if the hour was not worth their grasp. She was feeling like this again. She had thought it was something to do with singleness, with being alone and belonging too much to oneself.

She sat there not wanting to move or speak, or to look at anything even; so that

1. **Researching the Setting.** Have students find information about the geography, topography, and climate of South Africa, and then deduce which part of the country this story takes place in. Encourage them to draw maps and, if possible, to bring in photographs.
2. **Writing a Sequel.** Ask students to think about what will happen when the young couple returns home to Rhodesia. Will the woman's fears be realized,

or will relations change between the newlyweds when they are back home? Write a brief narrative with dialogue, revealing how the two are getting along.
3. **Examining Conflict.** Brainstorm examples of cultural conflicts or misunderstandings that have affected our society or the lives of individuals you know. What are some ways that such conflicts can be defused? Write a brief essay.

Ask students to summarize the various conflicts between characters and discuss whether or not each is resolved to both characters' satisfaction. Then have them consider whether there is internal conflict within any of the characters. (The young woman, for example, is torn between her attraction to the lion and her realization that there is no place in her everyday life for these feelings.) ■

---

the mood should be associated with nothing, no object, word, or sight that might recur and so recall the feeling again. . . . Smuts blew in grittily, settled on her hands. Her back remained at exactly the same angle, turned against the young man sitting with his hands drooping between his sprawled

legs, and the lion, fallen on its side in the corner.

The train had cast the station like a skin. It called out to the sky, I'm coming, I'm coming; and again, there was no answer.

First Thoughts

Why do you think the young woman on the train is angry when the young man purchases the carved lion for her?

Identifying Facts

1. Who is waiting for the train approaching from the west? What do each of these people do when the train arrives?
2. Who are the people on the train? What do they do when the train pulls into the station?
3. What is the relationship between the young couple? What is the occasion for their trip?
4. What do the old carver and the young man on the train disagree about? How is their conflict resolved?

Interpreting Meanings

1. The story contrasts two **settings**—the interior world of the train and the exterior world of the station outpost. List concrete details that highlight the differences between the two settings.
2. How is the train **personified**—that is, given human or animal qualities? Find examples of words that describe the train as if it were a person or an animal. What do you think Gordimer is trying to say through her use of personification?

3. What does the train seem to represent for the two groups—the people inside and the people outside? How might the train function as a **symbol**?
4. How does the young man see the old man and his carving? How does the woman see them? What does this **conflict** of values suggest about the couple's future?
5. What are the two main **conflicts** ultimately revealed in this story? Is either conflict resolved? Explain.

Creative Writing Response

Writing an Interior Monologue. At the end of the story, we see the young man "sitting with his hands drooping between his sprawled legs." Using this detail as a starting point, what do you imagine the young man is thinking and feeling? Write a paragraph expressing his inner thoughts and feelings.

Critical Writing Response

Analyzing Details. In describing how Gordimer portrays her native land, the critic Paul Gray says, "An overriding injustice must be deduced from small, vividly realized details." Does his analysis apply to this story? In a brief essay, describe the picture of race relations you deduce from small details in the story.

First Thoughts
Answers will vary.

Identifying Facts
1. The stationmaster waves his flag; the vendors sell carved animals; children beg.
2. Some of the white tourists hang out windows to buy from native vendors. A few get off; others ignore the outside.
3. newlyweds; their honeymoon.
4. the price for a carved lion. The carver gives in.

Interpreting Meanings
1. **train:** powerful, comfortable, cut off from nature; **station:** dusty, poor, isolated
2. "resting beast," "cast station like a skin." tourists are interested in self-preservation
3. inside, train is protection, power, comfort, mobility. outside, opportunity, oppression, humiliation. symbol of social and economic barriers
4. He sees carving as a souvenir and the man as an insignificant native. She sees carver's skill and originality. They will be unhappy.
5. between the two cultural groups and between the man and woman. Neither is resolved

Creative Writing Response
Writing an Interior Monologue. Monologue should reflect his surprise and bewilderment.

Critical Writing Response
Analyzing Details. Details may include "her hand commanded," "his opened palm." ■

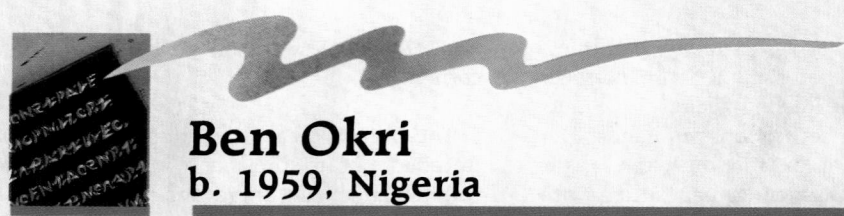

Ben Okri
b. 1959, Nigeria

Touhig Sion/Gamma-Liaison

Ben Okri grew up in Nigeria during a civil war that killed nearly one million people. But he is hesitant to discuss his childhood experiences very deeply; instead, he reserves this pool of memory for use in his fiction, often portraying sensitive young men coming of age in the brutal, nightmarish world that they have inherited.

Okri is a member of the Urhobo people of the delta region in southern Nigeria and the son of a British-trained lawyer. Educated in Nigeria and England, and now residing in London, Okri has both the passionate commitment of an insider and the wise detachment of an observer—a combination that enables him to raise difficult questions about the survival of his homeland. He has no easy answers but has long felt compelled to document the violence, confusion, and corruption that continue to pervade Nigeria nearly forty years after its independence from Britain.

Okri began his literary career with editorials on "vicious landlords, water tanks, and bad roads" written for Lagos daily newspapers. His first novel, *Flowers and Shadows* (1980), published when he was just twenty-one, exposes the dizzying chasm between rich and poor in the teeming city of Lagos. In his second novel, *The Landscapes Within* (1981), Okri turns his gaze inward, questioning the role of the artist in an unjust society.

The stories in *Stars of the New Curfew* (1989) and the novels *The Famished Road* (1991) and *Songs of Enchantment* (1993) give the fullest voice yet to what Okri has called "the tone and the spirit" of Nigeria. These works combine elements of myth and dreams with surrealistic imagery. Yet Okri resists comparisons to magic realists, insisting that he is presenting Nigeria as it is truly experienced by Nigerians. He also insists he is revealing a faith in his country's future:

One has to know about the very hard facts of the world and one has to look at them and know how deadly and powerful they are before one can begin to think or dream oneself into positions out of which hope and then possibilities can come.

And so, alongside the hellish, Okri continues to sketch the noble and idealistic—to reveal "the unbreakable things in us."

OBJECTIVES

1. *To interpret a story about a Nigerian child's experience of civil war*
2. *To infer atmosphere or mood from details of setting and word choice*
3. *To write a sketch from the point of view of a character in the story, and to respond to the opinion of a critic on the writer's work*

THEMES IN WORLD LITERATURE

Coming of Age
"Walk to the Jetty," pp. 1322–1328
From *Kaffir Boy*, pp. 1367–1376
"Cranes," pp. 1404–1408

War and Peace
From *Sundiata*, pp. 105–117
From *Night*, pp. 1234–1241
"Thoughts of Hanoi," pp. 1411–1413 ∎

VOCABULARY IN CONTEXT
The words listed below will appear in the side margin at the point of instruction.

1. stupefying   4. ostentatious
2. oppressive   5. dementedly
3. succumbed

Reader's Guide

IN THE SHADOW OF WAR

Background

It is in the shadow of the Nigerian Civil War (1967–1970) that the events of this story take place. Nigeria gained its independence from Great Britain in 1960, but the task of fashioning a just and stable central government for this country has been a formidable one. There are over two hundred fifty distinct ethnic or tribal groups in Nigeria. Three fifths of the population belong to one of three groups: the Hausa-Fulani in the north; the Yoruba in the southwest; and the Ibo, or Igbo, in the southeast. After independence, each of these groups feared domination by the others. British colonial policy, in fact, favored the advancement of the Ibo people and the development of the southern region at the expense of the north. Fearing the wrath of the Hausa-dominated military government that had come to power in 1966, the Ibo, in 1967, declared their homeland as the independent Republic of Biafra. The central government responded with attempts to cripple and slowly starve the breakaway state. The Biafrans finally surrendered in 1970. Even today, the word *Biafra* still conjures up, in many people's minds, images of starving, swollen-bellied children.

Writer's Response

Should children be protected from the knowledge of certain harsh realities, such as war and urban violence? What might be some of the positive and negative effects of shielding young people from harsh truths? If you were a parent, how would you handle such issues—for example, the devastating effects of war—with your own children? Free-write your ideas.

Literary Focus

The **atmosphere** of a literary work is the mood or feeling that the author creates with words and details. The details of the **setting**, the place where the events unfold, are often important in creating a specific feeling. For example, a story set in a dark cave with a dwindling fire is more likely to create an atmosphere of fear and uncertainty than one of security and confidence. Individual words with their emotional associations also contribute to the atmosphere that pervades a story.

PREREADING FOCUS

Background: The events of the story are told from a third-person-limited point of view, through the eyes of a child. Students should be helped to understand that, because the point of view is limited, the nature of the war going on around the narrator and even the identity of the combatants are not made immediately clear. You might ask students to think about how this point of view adds a universal dimension to a story that also graphically depicts the particular horrors of a specific war.

Literary Focus: Encourage students to use cluster diagrams to explore their personal responses to the words and images that Okri uses to create the atmosphere of Omovo's world. For example, they might put the word "eclipse" in the center of a circle and then surround it with the feelings the term brings up for them.

Examining Word Choice

Ben Okri chooses his words carefully in order to produce strong emotional responses in his readers. He uses specific rather than vague words, such as *glided* instead of *moved*, and words with strong connotations such as *sweat* and *slithered*.

1. **Reading and Speaking.** Have students read the following sentences from "In the Shadow of War" and discuss which words create vivid images and stir strong emotions in them.

a. "He saw them weaving between the eaves of the thatch houses, stumbling through heat-mists."

b. "Her head was bald, and disfigured with a deep corrugation."

c. "Their bodies were tangled with river-weed and their eyes were bloated."

2. **Writing and Sharing.** Ask students to write a paragraph describing an unsettling scene. Urge them to use con-

---

1 LITERARY ELEMENT

Setting: What do the details in the first paragraph reveal about the place where the story is set? (rural village in a tropical climate where soldiers move freely among civilians)

2 GUIDED READING

Interpreting Details: What do the details about the radio reveal? (Possible response: Family has little money, and their country is at war.)

3 LITERARY ELEMENT

Characterization: What kind of man is Omovo's father? (Even with news of an air raid, he calmly carries on with his everyday life; though poor, he has attempted to beautify the home he shares with his son.)

4 LITERARY ELEMENT

Atmosphere: The radio reports there will be an eclipse of the moon that night. How does this detail affect the mood of the story? (Possible response: adds sense of mystery or foreboding)

WRITING TO LEARN

Science: Write an explanation of what occurs during a lunar eclipse and why. Tell how often such phenomena occur; include diagrams. ■

IN THE SHADOW OF WAR
Ben Okri

As you read, look for particular words and images that help you see, hear, and feel what the young boy Omovo is seeing, hearing, and feeling. What words come to mind to describe his experience?

1 That afternoon three soldiers came to the village. They scattered the goats and chickens. They went to the palm-frond bar and ordered a calabash[1] of palm-wine. They drank amidst the flies.

2 Omovo watched them from the window as he waited for his father to go out. They both listened to the radio. His father had bought the old Grundig[2] cheaply from a family that had to escape the city when the war broke out. He had covered the radio with a white cloth and made it look like a household fetish.[3] They listened to the news of bombings and air raids in the interior of the country. His father combed his hair, parted

3 it carefully, and slapped some after-shave on his unshaven face. Then he struggled into the shabby coat that he had long outgrown.

Omovo stared out of the window, irritated with his father. At that hour, for the past seven days, a strange woman with a black veil over her head had been going past the house. She went up the village paths, crossed the Express road, and disappeared into the forest. Omovo waited for her to appear.

4 The main news was over. The radio announcer said an eclipse of the moon was expected that night. Omovo's father wiped the sweat off his face with his palm and said, with some bitterness:

"As if an eclipse will stop this war."

"What is an eclipse?" Omovo asked.

"That's when the world goes dark and strange things happen."

"Like what?"

His father lit a cigarette.

"The dead start to walk about and sing. So don't stay out late, eh."

Omovo nodded.

"Heclipses hate children. They eat them."

Omovo didn't believe him. His father smiled, gave Omovo his ten-kobo[4] allowance, and said:

"Turn off the radio. It's bad for a child to listen to news of war."

Omovo turned it off. His father poured a libation[5] at the doorway and then prayed to his ancestors. When he had finished he picked up his briefcase and strutted out briskly. Omovo watched him as he threaded his way up the path to the bus stop at the

---

1. **calabash** (kal′ə·bash′): cup made from a type of gourd, or hard vegetable casing.
2. **Grundig:** German brand of radio.
3. **fetish** (fet′ish): object believed to have magical or supernatural powers.

4. **kobo** (käb′ō): Nigerian monetary unit.
5. **libation** (lī·bā′shən): liquid poured onto the ground as an offering to the gods.

crete words that create vivid images and strong emotions. Have them read their paragraphs aloud and discuss the effects of their word choice. ∎

5 INTERPRETING
What do you think attracts the children's attention to the passing woman? (Possible responses: the black veil covering her face; her equanimity)

6 DRAWING CONCLUSIONS
What extraordinary, or even supernatural, qualities do the children ascribe to the woman? (has no shadow; feet do not touch ground) Why do you think they do this? (Possible response: to explain what they cannot understand or what frightens them)

John Biggers

Untitled drawing of West African women by John Biggers. From the book *Ananse*.
❓ *From whose point of view do we see the woman in the story?*

■ **stupefying** (stoo′pə·fī′iŋ): dulling the mind and senses; bringing on a drowsy state

oppressive (ə·pres′iv) hard to bear

HUMANITIES CONNECTION

John Biggers (1924–   ) is a widely admired African American artist whose paintings, drawings, and murals often portray the contributions and strength of black women. In 1957, he journeyed to western Africa, a trip which he later documented in *Ananse: The Web of Life in Africa*. The book quickly became important to an entire generation of African American artists as a joyous expression of their links to Africa.
❓ *What is the mood of this drawing? What aspects of the drawing contribute to that mood?* ∎

main road. When a danfo bus[6] came, and his father went with it, Omovo turned the radio back on. He sat on the windowsill and waited for the woman. The last time he saw her she had glided past with agitated flutters of her yellow smock. The children stopped what they were doing and stared at her. They had said that she had no shadow. They had said that her feet never touched the ground. As she went past, the children began to throw things at her. She didn't flinch, didn't quicken her pace, and didn't look back.

The heat was stupefying. Noises dimmed and lost their edges. The villagers stumbled about their various tasks as if they were sleepwalking. The three soldiers drank palm-wine and played draughts[7] beneath the sun's oppressive glare. Omovo noticed that whenever children went past the bar the soldiers called them, talked to them, and gave them some money. Omovo ran down the stairs and slowly walked past the bar. The soldiers stared at him. On his way back one of them called him.

"What's your name" he asked.

Omovo hesitated, smiled mischievously, and said:

"Heclipse."

The soldier laughed, spraying Omovo's

5

6

---

6. **danfo bus:** small bus. In the region surrounding Lagos, Nigeria, *danfo* means "in disrepair."

7. **draughts** (drafts): British game of checkers.

Ben Okri   **1361**

7 **INFERRING**
Why do you think Omovo refuses to take the money from the soldiers? (Possible response: He dislikes the teasing way they treat him.)

8 **LITERARY ELEMENT**
Imagery: Why are the effects of the heat so insistently described in this passage? (Possible response: to contrast the dreamlike lull of the scene with such harsh realities of war as the casualty report)

◼ **succumbed** (sə·kumd′): gave in to; yielded

ostentatious (äs′ten·tā′shəs): showy

9 **LITERARY ELEMENT**
Symbol: What might the forest Omovo enters symbolize? (Possible responses: the unknown, death, evil, endpoint of the journey from innocence to experience)

10 **INFERRING**
What do the details in this passage suggest about the situation in Omovo's country? (Unfinished estates and empty factory suggest economic collapse; empty sheds indicate people have fled in fear for their lives.)

11 **DRAWING CONCLUSIONS**
What does the woman bring the people in the cave? (food) On what evidence do you base your conclusion? (children have swollen bellies)

face with spit. He had a face crowded with veins. His companions seemed uninterested. They swiped flies and concentrated on their game. Their guns were on the table. Omovo noticed that they had numbers on them. The man said:

"Did your father give you that name because you have big lips?"

His companions looked at Omovo and laughed. Omovo nodded.

"You are a good boy," the man said. He paused. Then he asked, in a different voice:

"Have you seen that woman who covers her face with a black cloth?"

"No."

The man gave Omovo ten kobo and said: "She is a spy. She helps our enemies. If you see her come and tell us at once, you hear?"

Omovo refused the money and went back upstairs. He repositioned himself on the windowsill. The soldiers occasionally looked at him. The heat got to him and soon he fell asleep in a sitting position. The cocks, crowing dispiritedly, woke him up. He could feel the afternoon softening into evening. The soldiers dozed in the bar. The hourly news came on. Omovo listened without comprehension to the day's casualties. The announcer succumbed to the stupor, yawned, apologized, and gave further details of the fighting.

Omovo looked up and saw that the woman had already gone past. The men had left the bar. He saw them weaving between the eaves of the thatch houses, stumbling through the heat mists. The woman was further up the path. Omovo ran downstairs and followed the men. One of them had taken off his uniform top. The soldier behind had buttocks so big they had begun to split his pants. Omovo followed them across the Express road. When they got into the forest the men stopped following the woman, and took a different route. They seemed to know what they were doing. Omovo hurried to keep the woman in view.

He followed her through the dense vegetation. She wore faded wrappers and a gray shawl, with the black veil covering her face. She had a red basket on her head. He completely forgot to determine if she had a shadow, or whether her feet touched the ground.

He passed unfinished estates, with their flaking ostentatious signboards and their collapsing fences. He passed an empty cement factory: blocks lay crumbled in heaps and the workers' sheds were deserted. He passed a baobab[8] tree, under which was the intact skeleton of a large animal. A snake dropped from a branch and slithered through the undergrowth. In the distance, over the cliff edge, he heard loud music and people singing war slogans above the noise.

He followed the woman till they came to a rough camp on the plain below. Shadowy figures moved about in the half-light of the cave. The woman went to them. The figures surrounded her and touched her and led her into the cave. He heard their weary voices thanking her. When the woman reappeared she was without the basket. Children with kwashiorkor[9] stomachs and women wearing rags led her halfway up the hill. Then, reluctantly, touching her as if they might not see her again, they went back.

He followed her till they came to a muddied river. She moved as if an invisible force

---

8. **baobab** (bä′ō·bab′): thick-trunked African tree, often called "upside-down tree" because its branches look like roots.

9. **kwashiorkor** (kwä′shē·or′kôr′): severe disease of children, caused by malnutrition; symptoms include stunted growth and a protruding belly.

READING CHECK

1. What repeated occurrence attracts Omovo's attention? (daily passing of a veiled woman carrying a basket)
2. What do the soldiers in the bar want to know from Omovo? (whereabouts of veiled woman)
3. What does the boy hear on the radio that he does not understand? (war news and casualty reports)

4. What does the boy see the soldiers do in the forest? (shoot the veiled woman)
5. Who brings the boy home after he falls and loses consciousness? (the soldiers)

RETEACHING

Ask students to imagine that Omovo has grown up and is telling the events of this story to his own son. Have individual students retell the story aloud, adding information that an adult looking back would understand but that may not have been clear to the child Omovo at the time the events took place.

12 were trying to blow her away. Omovo saw capsized canoes and trailing waterlogged clothes on the dark water. He saw floating **13** items of sacrifice: loaves of bread in polythene[10] wrappings, gourds of food, Coca-Cola cans. When he looked at the ca-**14** noes again they had changed into the shapes of swollen dead animals. He saw outdated currencies on the riverbank. He noticed the terrible smell in the air. Then he heard the sound of heavy breathing from behind him, then someone coughing and spitting. He recognized the voice of one of the soldiers urging the others to move faster. Omovo crouched in the shadow of a tree. The soldiers strode past. Not long afterward he heard a scream. The men had caught up with the woman. They crowded round her.

"Where are the others?" shouted one of them.

The woman was silent.

"You dis witch! You want to die, eh? Where are they?"

She stayed silent. Her head was bowed. One of the soldiers coughed and spat towards the river.

"Talk! Talk!" he said, slapping her.

The fat soldier tore off her veil and threw it to the ground. She bent down to pick it up and stopped in the attitude of kneeling, her head still bowed. Her head was bald, and disfigured with a deep corrugation.[11] There was a livid gash along the side of her face. The bare-chested soldier pushed her. She fell on her face and lay still. The lights changed over the forest and for the first time

Omovo saw that the dead animals on the river were in fact the corpses of grown men. Their bodies were tangled with riverweed and their eyes were bloated. Before he could react, he heard another scream. The woman was getting up, with the veil in her hand. She turned to the fat soldier, drew herself to her fullest height, and spat in his face. Waving the veil in the air, she began to howl dementedly. The two other soldiers backed away. The fat soldier wiped his face and lifted the gun to the level of her stomach. A moment before Omovo heard the shot a violent beating of wings just above him scared him from his hiding place. He ran through the forest screaming. The soldiers tramped after him. He ran through a mist which seemed to have risen from the rocks. As he ran he saw an owl staring at him from a canopy of leaves. He tripped over the roots of a tree and blacked out when his head hit the ground.

15 When he woke up it was very dark. He waved his fingers in front of his face and saw nothing. Mistaking the darkness for blindness he screamed, thrashed around, and ran into a door. When he recovered from his shock he heard voices outside and the radio crackling on about the war. He found his way to the balcony, full of wonder that his sight had returned. But when he got there he was surprised to find his father sitting on the sunken cane chair, drinking palm-wine with the three soldiers. Omovo rushed to his father and pointed frantically at the three men.

"You must thank them," his father said. "They brought you back from the forest."

16 Omovo, overcome with delirium, began to tell his father what he had seen. But his father, smiling apologetically at the soldiers, picked up his son and carried him off to bed.

---

10. **polythene** (päl'i·thēn'): term used in most English-speaking countries, other than the United States, for *polyethylene* (päl'ē·eth'ə·lēn'), a synthetic substance used to make tough, lightweight plastics, films, and the like.

11. **corrugation** (kor'ə·gā'shən): groove or furrow.

12 GUIDED READING
Interpreting Details: What do you conclude occurred at the river? (Possible response: an attack on a camp)

13 INFERRING
What signs of Western industrialization have you seen in the story thus far? (Possible responses: German radio, aftershave, guns, polythene wrappings, cola cans.) Why might Okri have included these details in his story? (Possible response: to show that Africa has been tainted by the detritus of European colonization.)

14 SYNTHESIZING
How do you explain the transformations that Omovo sees? (Possible response: He cannot comprehend this level of violence.)

dementedly (dē·ment'id·lē): madly; wildly

15 LITERARY ELEMENT
Symbol: What might the darkness symbolize? (Possible response: Omovo's newfound awareness of the realities of war, and his unarticulated knowledge of the "darkness" to come.)

16 MAKING JUDGMENTS
How do you evaluate the father "smiling apologetically" at the soldiers? (Possible response: He is in a state of self-protective denial about what his son may have seen the soldiers do.)

Ben Okri   **1363**

1. Comparing and Contrasting War Stories. Ask students to find and analyze other stories and films that deal with young people in the midst of war. Have them chart the similarities and differences among the characters, and make some generalizations about how war can affect young people.

2. Researching the Biafran War. From 1967 until 1970, southeastern Nigeria was horribly scarred by a civil war between the newly independent republic of Biafra and the rest of Nigeria. Report to the class on this war and its aftermath; research news photos and other sources for images of the war that haunted the entire world in the 1960s. Also, bring the class up-to-date on the current status of Nigeria.

CLOSURE

Ask students to imagine a conversation that Omovo and his father will have the next day when they are alone. What questions will Omovo ask about the events of the previous night? How will his father answer his questions? Have them consider how they would answer Omovo if they were in his father's shoes. ∎

ANSWERS

First Thoughts
Answers will vary.

Identifying Facts
1. in a village with his father
2. news of war and an eclipse
3. his father, the soldiers
4. veiled woman
5. bring aid; be killed
6. He falls and blacks out, then awakens at home.

Interpreting Meanings
1. soldiers, heat, flies, "shabby coat." Poor, oppressive
2. He's confused, curious, honest.
3. to keep him inside. death, despair, loss of innocence
4. Woman has no shadow. Canoes turn to corpses. make it seem dreamlike
5. Soldiers are crude and cruel: they taunt and brutalize the woman. embarrassed, angry, betrayed, confused
6. He's masked the real events with less threatening images. a hero, because she's courageous when confronted
7. It brings astonishing news of the larger world. What Omovo sees is much more "real" than what he hears.

Applying Meanings
Answers will vary.

Creative Writing Response
Writing from a Different Point of View. Ask students to interpret specific details.

Critical Writing Response
Evaluating an Opinion. Note Omovo's humane impulses. ∎

First Thoughts
What are some of the possible meanings of the title of this story?

Identifying Facts
1. Where and with whom does Omovo live?
2. What does Omovo hear on the radio?
3. In addition to the radio, what sources of information does the boy have?
4. Whom does Omovo wait to see every day?
5. What does Omovo see the woman do in the forest?
6. What happens to Omovo at the end of the story?

Interpreting Meanings
1. What details help give a picture of where Omovo lives and the circumstances of his family? How would you describe the **atmosphere** created by this **setting**?
2. What do Omovo's words and actions reveal about his **character**?
3. Why do you think Omovo's father tells him about eclipses? In the context of the story, what do you think the eclipse might **symbolize**?
4. Ben Okri is noted for the seamless way he weaves the supernatural or the magical into the natural reality of African life. What seemingly supernatural events take place in this story? What do they add to the story's **atmosphere**?
5. How do you feel about the soldiers in the story? Find details about them that support your opinion. How do you think Omovo feels when his father smiles "apologetically" at the soldiers?
6. Because the story is written from the **point of view** of a child who does not always fully understand what he is experiencing, the story contains many ambiguities. How would you explain what Omovo saw and heard in the forest? Do you think the woman in the veil is a spy, a traitor, a hero, a witch, or something else? Find details from the story to support your opinion.
7. What is the radio's role in the story, and why is it referred to as a "fetish"? What is the difference, to Omovo, between what he hears on the radio and what he sees in the forest?

Applying Meanings
Explain how Okri's story can be viewed as a journey from innocence to experience. Think of some situations that could occur in your own daily life that might prompt a similar journey. Are such psychological journeys inevitable in young people's lives? How can adults help younger people in the passage through such growth experiences?

Creative Writing Response
Writing from a Different Perspective. Write a sketch from the point of view of the mysterious veiled woman. What is she thinking about as she travels through the forest? What has her life been like, and what motivates her to help the people in the cave?

Critical Writing Response
Evaluating an Opinion. In her review of the short story collection that includes "In the Shadow of War," journalist Maria Thomas wrote, "Hopefulness does not grow easily in stories like these. . . . But hope there is because you come from these stories with a sense of an underlying vitality that will not be destroyed." Did you come away from "In the Shadow of War" with a feeling of hope, or with a different feeling? Explain your response in a brief essay, using examples from the story.

Mark Mathabane
b. 1960, South Africa

Fred Jewell/Wide World Photos

Mark Mathabane and members of his family.

If you were to ask Mark Mathabane (mä·tä′bä·nä) who his role models were as he was growing up, he would probably name Arthur Ashe and Joseph Conrad, among others. Ashe, the black American tennis star who in 1973 was finally allowed to play in South Africa, inspired Mathabane to practice the game that eventually won him a scholarship to an American university. Reading Conrad, the Polish-born English novelist, gave Mathabane the courage to try his hand at writing in English even though it was not his native tongue. The result of Mathabane's efforts was *Kaffir Boy* (1986), one of the first accounts of growing up black in twentieth-century South Africa.

In Mathabane's homeland, however, *Kaffir Boy* was banned. This action came as little surprise to Mathabane, who had faced far greater hardships as a result of his country's apartheid laws. These laws kept blacks and whites separate and forced nonwhites into inferior jobs, housing, and schools. Living in a small shack in Alexandra, a black slum just outside Johannesburg, Mathabane's family was extremely poor. There was often no food to eat, and the children slept under the kitchen table.

By law, Mathabane could attend only an all-black "tribal school"—crumbling, under-staffed, overcrowded, and inadequately supplied. The school was not free, and Mathabane's mother had to scrimp and save to pay his tuition. By law, pupils at the tribal schools studied mainly in their native Bantu languages. Mathabane desperately wanted to improve his English—which he saw as his passport to knowledge and freedom.

Although Mathabane won a tennis scholarship to an American university, he soon realized that he would not become a professional tennis player. He then began to devote more time to his studies and to writing his autobiography. When *Kaffir Boy* was published, one of its early admirers was TV talk-show host Oprah Winfrey, who invited Mathabane to appear on her show and arranged a surprise reunion with family members from South Africa. The reunion made headlines nationwide and helped *Kaffir Boy* to become a bestseller around the world.

MORE ABOUT THE AUTHOR

Mark Mathabane describes the Alexandra of his childhood as a black ghetto of one square mile housing more than 150,000 people. Under the apartheid laws, Mathabane's father, though self-trained as a carpenter, was permitted to work only at menial jobs that yielded about ten dollars a week. Under other apartheid laws, he was often arrested for the "crime" of being unemployed.

To distract her children's attention from their hunger pangs, Mathabane's mother—though illiterate—entertained the family by telling stories. Mathabane credits her with firing his imagination and his lifelong love of literature. It was also his mother who insisted on scraping together the funds needed to send Mathabane to school.

Mathabane's interest in tennis eventually led to a meeting with American tennis champion Stan Smith, who was visiting South Africa. Smith helped Mathabane win a tennis scholarship to an American college. However, it was writing, not tennis, that earned Mathabane international fame. The publication of *Kaffir Boy* launched his career as a writer, journalist, and speaker. In 1989 he published a sequel, *Kaffir Boy in America*, and in 1992 he and his wife published *Love in Black and White*, a book about their interracial marriage. Mathabane's most recent book is *African Women: Three Generations* (1994), in which he recounts the lives of his grandmother, mother, and sister.

OBJECTIVES

1. *To interpret a selection from an autobiography about growing up black in South Africa*
2. *To examine and evaluate an autobiography*
3. *To write an autobiographical episode and an essay about the purpose of autobiographies*

THEMES IN WORLD LITERATURE

Conflict of Cultures and Values
The Book of Songs, pp. 512–517
"The Train from Rhodesia," pp. 1351–1357

The Uses and Abuses of Power
"The Burning of Rome" from the *Annals*, pp. 428–435
From *Night*, pp. 1232–1242 ■

VOCABULARY IN CONTEXT
The words listed below will appear in the side margin at the point of instruction:

1. alighted   4. doctrine
2. preoccupied   5. impudently
3. postulated

PREREADING FOCUS

Background: South Africa is the homeland to many native African tribes including the Bushmen, the Zulu, and the Xhosa. White Europeans—mostly Dutch—first settled the southern area around the Cape of Good Hope in the seventeenth century. Britain seized the Cape area in the early 1800s, and many descendants of the Dutch settlers, known as Boers, moved north to found the Transvaal and the Orange Free State. British forces defeated the Boers in the Boer War (1899–1902) and made all of South Africa a British colony. Racial segregation, ardently supported by most Boers and to a somewhat lesser extent by the whites of British descent, became the law of the land when the National Party assumed power in 1948. The laws divided the population into four groups: whites, Asians (mostly people of Indian descent), colored (part black), and black African. Black Africans were restricted from better jobs and from owning land or businesses. During the 1960s, when Mathabane was a boy, government policy insisted on repatriating urban blacks to so-called tribal homelands, even when they did not wish to relocate. Eventually an independent South Africa withdrew from the British Commonwealth and faced years of economic boycott from most nations of the world in protest against the white government's policy of apartheid.

Reader's Guide ■

from KAFFIR BOY

Background

The word *Kaffir* (ka'fər), Arabic for "infidel," was originally applied to certain Bantu-speaking tribes of South Africa. Over the decades it became a derogatory term used by many white South Africans to refer to any black South African. South Africa has long been a nation of great political, economic, and social inequality. This inequality became the law of the land in 1948 when the policy of apartheid (ə·pär'tāt' or -tīt) was instituted. The policy divided the nation along racial lines and protected the interests of the white population (less than a fifth of the population) by ensuring that the nonwhite majority would neither vote nor own valuable land. When Mark Mathabane was growing up—and even when he published *Kaffir Boy* in 1986—South Africa's apartheid laws were very much in place. The South African parliament repealed the most legally binding of these laws in 1991, but political, educational, economic, and social disparities between blacks and whites still divide the nation.

Writer's Response

If you were writing your autobiography, what would you call the book? Choose a title and write it down. Underneath, make a list of the most important events in your life that you would be sure to include in your autobiography.

Literary Focus

An **autobiography** is an account of a person's life as he or she remembers it. The autobiography may be written simply to record an interesting life, or it may have more political or social purposes. Autobiographies are considered **nonfiction**, although some authors are more concerned with accuracy than others. *Kaffir Boy* is viewed as a remarkably honest account, even though Mathabane did change some people's names for their or his own protection.

Hyphenating Compound Adjectives

A compound adjective, or an adjective of more than one part, is generally hyphenated when it precedes the noun that it modifies: *well-polished china*. If the first part of the compound adjective is an adverb that ends in *-ly*, however, the compound adjective is not hyphenated in current American usage: *highly polished china*.

1. **Reading and Speaking.** Have students examine the first three pages of the selection and find ten compound adjectives, including two unhyphenated compound adjectives introduced by *-ly* adverbs, that illustrate these rules.

Ask students to identify the compound adjectives and the nouns that they modify.

2. **Writing and Sharing.** Have students write a description of their classroom or neighborhood. Ask them to include at least seven compound adjectives, some requiring hyphens. ∎

---

from KAFFIR BOY

Mark Mathabane

◆ *As you read this selection, think about the reasons Mathabane wrote his autobiography. What do you think he wanted to prove or achieve? What political changes do you think he wanted to contribute to?*

1 The seven o'clock bus for blacks to Johannesburg was jampacked with men and women on their way to the white world to work. A huge sign above the driver's booth read:

2 AUTHORIZED TO CARRY ONLY 65 SEATED PASSENGERS, AND 15 STANDING.

But there must have been close to a hundred perspiring people squeezed into the stuffy bus. People sat on top of one another; some were sandwiched in the narrow aisle between the rows of seats, and some crowded on the steps. I sat on Granny's lap, in the middle of the bus, by a large smudged window. As the bus droned past Alexandra's boundaries, I glued my eyes to the window, anticipating my first look at the white world. What I saw made me think I had just made a quantum leap into another galaxy. I couldn't stop asking questions.

"What are those?"

"Skyscrapers."

"Why do they reach all the way to the sky?"

"Because many white people live and work in them."

Seconds later. "Wow! look at all those nice houses, Granny! They're so big! Do many white people live and work there, too?"

"No, those are mansions. Each is owned by one family."

"By one family!" I cried in disbelief. Each mansion occupied an area about three times that of the yard I lived in, yet the latter was home for over twenty families.

3 "Yes," Granny said matter-of-factly. "Your grandpa, when he first came to Johannesburg, worked for one such family. The family was so rich they owned an airplane."

"Why are there so many cars in the white people's homes?"

"Because they like to have many cars."

"Those people dressed in white, what game are they playing?"

"The men are playing cricket. Master Smith plays that, too. The women are playing tennis. Mrs. Smith plays it, too, on Tuesday and Thursday."

Suddenly the bus screeched to a halt, and people crashed into each other. I was thrown into the back of the wooden seat in front of me. Smarting, I asked, "Why did the bus suddenly stop? I didn't see any robots."[1]

"Look over there," Granny pointed. "White schoolchildren are crossing the road."

I gazed through the window and for the first time in my life saw white schoolchildren.

---

1. **robots:** traffic lights.

TEACHER'S RESOURCES
✔ Vocabulary Activity Worksheet
✔ Vocabulary Test
✔ Review and Response Worksheet
✔ Language Skills Worksheet
✔ Selection Test

1 CULTURAL DIVERSITY
Under the apartheid laws, public transportation—like virtually every other public service in South Africa—was segregated by race.
❓ *What similar laws once existed in the United States?* (Encourage students to share what they know about the civil rights movement in the United States.)

2 LITERARY ELEMENT
Situational Irony: What is ironic about the situation on the bus? (The sign mandates a maximum of eighty people, but close to a hundred are jammed into the bus.) What situation does the irony underline? (the intolerable living conditions of black South Africans)

3 LITERARY ELEMENT
Autobiography: What does the inclusion of these sharply contrasting details tell you about Mathabane's purposes in writing his autobiography? (to expose to the world the harsh realities of South Africa under apartheid and help effect change)

4 LITERARY ELEMENT
Simile: Why does Mathabane compare the white schoolchildren to "little mannequins"? (Possible response: because their attire is so clean and perfect that it appears brand new and perhaps a little unreal to the black boy)

5 CULTURAL BACKGROUND
Afrikaans is the first language of the descendants of the Boers, the first Dutch settlers in South Africa. Most other white South Africans are of British heritage and speak English as their first language.

4 | I scrutinized them for any differences from black schoolchildren, aside from color. They were like little mannequins. The boys were neatly dressed in snow-white shirts, blazers with badges, preppy caps with badges, ties matching the badges, shiny black and brown shoes, worsted[2] knee-high socks. The girls wore pleated gymdresses with badges, snow-white shirts, caps with badges, blazers with badges, ties matching badges, shining black and brown shoes. A few of the girls had pigtails. On the back of each boy and girl was slung a schoolbag; and each frail, milky-white arm had a wristwatch on it. It suddenly struck me that we didn't even own a clock; we had to rely on cocks for time.[3]

5 | The white schoolchildren were filing out of a large, red-brick building with many large windows, in front of which were beds of multicolored flowers. A tall black man wearing a traffic uniform, a whistle between his thick lips, stood in the middle of the paved road, one hand raised to stop traffic, the other holding a sign that read in English and Afrikaans:

> CHILDREN CROSSING
> STOP
> KINDERS STAP OOR

None of this orderly and safe crossing of the street ever took place at my school; we had to dash across.

The red-brick building stood on a vast tract of land with immaculate lawns, athletic fields, swings, merry-go-rounds, an Olympic-sized swimming pool, tennis courts, and rows of brightly leafed trees. In the driveway leading to the entrance of the building, scores of yellow school buses were parked. Not even the best of tribal schools in Alexandra—in the whole of South Africa—came close to having such magnificent facilities. At our school we didn't even have a school bus.

White schoolboy in Capetown, South Africa.
What are the narrator's feelings toward the white schoolchildren that he sees?

René Burri/Magnum Photos, Inc.

---

2. **worsted** (wŏŏs′tid): made of a smooth, hard-twisted wool.
3. **rely on cocks for time:** that is, rely on roosters crowing to know what time it is.

6 Oh, how I envied the white schoolchildren, how I longed to attend schools like theirs.

Minutes after all the white schoolchildren were safely across, traffic moved. At the next bus stop, we got off, and crossed the street when the robot flashed green. As we walked along the pavement, headed for Granny's workplace, I clutched her long dress, afraid of letting go, lest I be swallowed by the tremendous din of cars zooming up and down and honking in the busy streets. I began feeling dizzy as my eyes darted from one wonder to the next.

There were so many new and fantastic things around me that I walked as if in a dream. As we continued down the road, I became increasingly conscious of the curious looks white people gave us, as if we were a pair of escaped monkeys. Occasionally, Granny and I had to jump off the pavement to make way for *madams* and their poodles and English toy spaniels. By constantly throwing my eyes sideways, I accidentally bumped into a parking meter.

7 ⎡and English toy spaniels. By constantly throwing my eyes sideways, I accidentally bumped into a parking meter.⎦

8 ⎡We went up a side street. "There is Mrs. Smith's house," Granny remarked as she led me up a long driveway of a beautiful villa-type house surrounded by a well-manicured lawn with several beds of colorful, sweet-smelling flowers and rosebushes. We went to a steel gate in the back of the yard, where Granny rang a bell.⎦

"I'm here, madam," she shouted through the gate. Immediately a dog started barking from within; I trembled.

Granny calmed me. A door creaked open, and a high-pitched woman's voice called out, "I'm coming, Ellen. Quiet, Buster, you naughty dog, it's Ellen." The barking ceased. Presently the gate clicked open, and there appeared a short, slender white woman with silver hair and slightly drooping shoulders. She wore white slacks, a white sweater,

white shoes, and a white visor.

"I was just getting ready to leave for tennis," she said to Granny; she had not yet seen me.

"Madam, guess who I have with me today," Granny said with the widest smile.

I appeared like a jack-in-the-box. "Oh, my, you finally brought him with you!" Mrs. Smith exclaimed.

9 ⎡Breaking into a wide smile, revealing gleaming teeth, several of which were made of gold, she continued, "My, what a big lad he is! What small ears!"—touching them playfully—"Is he really your grandson, Ellen?" The warmth in her voice somehow reduced my fears of her; her eyes shone with the same gentleness of the Catholic sisters[4] at the clinic.⎦

"Yes, madam," Granny said proudly; "this is the one I've been telling you about. This is the one who'll some day go to university, like Master Clyde, and take care of me."

"I believe you, Ellen," said Mrs. Smith. "He looks like a very smart pickaninny."[5] Turning to me, she asked, "How old are you?"

"Eleven, madam, eleven," I said, with so wide a smile I thought my jaws would lock.

"He's a year younger than Master Clyde," Granny said, "though the master is much bigger."

"A little chubby, you mean," Mrs. Smith said with a smile. "If you knew how much the little master eats, Ellen; I'm afraid he'll soon turn into a piglet. Sometimes I regret not having had another child. With a sibling, Master Clyde might have turned out differently. As it is, he's so spoiled as an only child."

---

4. **sisters:** here, hospital nurses.
5. **pickaninny:** This term for a small black child, though highly offensive in the United States, is here used more condescendingly than disparagingly.

10 CULTURAL DIVERSITY
Most black South Africans speak one of the group of Bantu languages as their first language and later learn English, Afrikaans, or both.

? *What evidence do you have that Mathabane eventually mastered English?* (the selection itself)

11 READER'S RESPONSE
What is your impression of Mrs. Smith? Why? (Answers will vary.)

Black South African youths. *South African children like these, who did not have documents stating their racial group, did not officially exist according to South African apartheid laws and could not attend public schools. These children were taken off the streets by local residents and taught the basics in a community center.*

Chris Steele-Perkins/Magnum Photos, Inc.

"Pickaninny has one brother and three sisters," Granny said of me, "and the fifth one is on the way."

"My God! What a large family!" Mrs. Smith exclaimed. "What's the pickaninny's name?"

10 Using pidgin English,[6] I proceeded not only to give my name and surname, but also my grade in school, home address, tribal affiliation, name of school, principal and teacher—all in a feverish attempt to justify Granny's label of me as a "smart one."

Mrs. Smith was astounded. "What a clever, clever pickaninny!" She turned to a tall, lean black man with an expressionless face and slightly stooping shoulders, dressed in housekeeper's livery[7] (khaki shirt and pants), who had just emerged from the house and who led a poodle on a leash, and said, "Did you hear that, Absalom? Bantu[8] children are smart. Soon they'll be running the country." Absalom simply tortured out a grin and took the poodle for a walk, after receiving instructions to bring brandy, whisky, wine and gin from the bottle store.[9] Granny remarked that I was a "clever pickaninny" because of all the toys, games and comic books I had received from Master Clyde. Mrs. Smith seemed extremely pleased to hear that. **11**

Before Mrs. Smith left for tennis, she said, "Ellen, your breakfast is near the washing machine in the garage. I'll be back sometime this afternoon. Please see to it that the flowers near the pool are watered, and that the

---

6. **pidgin** (pij'in) **English:** here, a form of simplified English that incorporates Bantu vocabulary and syntax.
7. **livery:** uniform.
8. **Bantu** (ban'tōō): here, black South African, because most black South Africans speak one of the Bantu languages as their first language.
9. **bottle store:** liquor store.

rosebushes near the front of the gate are trimmed."

After a breakfast of coffee and peanut butter-and-jam sandwiches, Granny took out her gardening tools from the shed, and we started working. As the two of us went about the large yard, I raked leaves and watered the flowers; Granny weeded the lawn. Mrs. Smith's neighbor's children kept on casting curious glances over the fence.

12 From the way they looked at me, it seemed they were seeing a black child for the first time in their lives.

At midday, despite a scorching sun, Granny, seemingly indefatigable, went about with impressive skill trimming the rosebushes as we talked about trees and flowers and how to best cultivate them.

13 "Someday I'll build a house as big and beautiful as Mrs. Smith's," I said to Granny. "And a garden just as big and beautiful."

"Then I'll be your gardener," Granny said with a smile.

Toward early afternoon Mrs. Smith returned. She called me to the car to remove several shopping bags from the back seat. She took her tennis rackets, closed the doors, then sighed, "Phew, what a tiring day.

14 Don't ever play tennis," she said to me, "it's a killer."

"What's tennis, madam?" I asked.

"You don't know tennis?" she exclaimed. "What sports do you play?"

"Soccer, madam."

"Ugh, that dangerous sport. Soccer is too rough. You should try tennis someday. It's a gentlemen's sport. Wouldn't you like to be a gentleman?"

"I would like to be a gentleman, madam," I replied, even though I hadn't the faintest idea what constituted a gentleman.

"Do you have tennis courts in Alexandra?"

"Yes, madam." The stadium where I played soccer was adjacent to four ramshackle sand courts, used primarily by kitchen girls and kitchen boys on their day off.

"Then I'll see if I can find an old racket for you," she said.

As we were talking, a busload of white schoolchildren stopped in front of the house, and a young boy, with a mop of rebellious brown hair, alighted and ran up the driveway toward Mrs. Smith. After giving her a kiss, he turned and demanded, "Who is he, Mother?"

"That's Ellen's grandson. The one you've been giving all those comic books and toys to."

"What is he doing here?"

"He's visiting us."

"What for? I don't want him here."

"Why not, Clyde," Mrs. Smith said, "he's a nice pickaninny. Ellen is always nice to you, isn't she?"—the boy nodded with pursed lips—"now be nice to her grandson. Now run along inside and Absalom will show you the things I bought you today."

15 "Did you get my new bicycle and roller skates?"

"Yes, they'll be delivered Saturday. Now run in and change, and have something to eat. Then maybe you can play with pickaninny."

16 "I don't play with Kaffirs,"[10] the white boy declared. "At school they say we shouldn't."

"Watch your filthy mouth, Clyde," Mrs. Smith said, flushing crimson. "I thought I told you a million times to leave all that rubbish about Kaffirs in the classroom. Ellen's people are not Kaffirs, you hear! They're Bantus. Now go in and do as I told you." Turning to Granny, pruning a rosebush

---

10. **Kaffirs:** In South Africa, "Kaffir" is a disparaging term for any black African.

12 Synthesizing
Is it possible that the neighbor's children are seeing a black child for the first time? Explain. (Yes; in the segregated world of South Africa, the only blacks that white children ever saw were adults who worked in the neighborhood.)

Writing to Learn

13 Write a diary entry from the grandmother's point of view. Include details based on her remarks here and in the preceding passages. ■

14 Literary Element
Dramatic Irony: Given what the author and his readers know about his future, why is this remark ironic? (He will play tennis quite well one day and, far from its being a "killer," playing tennis will be his passport to a better life.)

■ **alighted** (ə·līt′id): got down from; descended

15 Interpreting
What do these details reveal about Clyde? (He is self-centered.)

16 Comparing Literature
❓ How do Clyde's comments resemble the attitudes of some of the passengers in "The Train from Rhodesia"? (Possible response: Both reflect condescension and a thoughtlessly cruel racism.)

Mark Mathabane　　**1371**

Though struggling against apartheid seemed like a "losing battle" when Mathabane was young, the South African government—after being subjected to years of pressure exerted by international organizations, state governments, and courageous black and white South Africans—repealed the fundamental law of apartheid in 1991. *What role do you think books like Mathabane's—which was banned in South Africa—might have played in the battle against apartheid?* (Possible response: Such books shocked many governments in the rest of the world into fighting apartheid through economic sanctions and political pressure.)

18 **READER'S RESPONSE**

Does your opinion of Mrs. Smith change here? Why or why not? (Responses will vary, but students who found her condescending before may find her far more sympathetic here.)

---

preoccupied (prē·ä′kyə·pīd′): wholly absorbed with one's thoughts; engrossed

---

17 ⌈ nearby, Mrs. Smith said, in a voice of someone fighting a losing battle, "You know, Ellen, I simply don't understand why those damn uncivilized Boers from Pretoria[11] teach children such things. What future does this country have if this goes on?"

"I agree *makulu*,[12] madam," Granny said, wiping her sweaty brow with her forearm. "All children, black and white, are God's children, madam. The preacher at my church tells us the Bible says so. 'Suffer little children to come unto me, and forbid them not; for of such is the kingdom of heaven,'[13] the Bible says. Is that not so, madam? Do you believe in the words of the Bible, madam?"

18 ⌈ "I'm afraid you're right, Ellen," Mrs. Smith said, somewhat touched. "Yes, I do believe in the Bible. That's why I cannot accept the laws of this country. We white people are hypocrites. We call ourselves Christians, yet our deeds make the Devil look like a saint. I sometimes wish I hadn't left England."

I was struck by the openness of the discussion between Granny and Mrs. Smith.

"You're not like most white people I've worked for, madam," Granny said. "Master and you are kind toward our people. You treat us like human beings."

Mrs. Smith didn't answer; she hurried back indoors. Shortly thereafter, Clyde emerged in a pair of denims and a T-shirt advertising a South African rock group. He called out to me. "Come here, pickaninny. My mother says I should show you around."

---

11. **Boers** (bo͞orz) **from Pretoria** (pri·tôr′ē·ə): white South Africans of mainly Dutch descent whose National Party initiated the apartheid (ə·pär′tāt′) laws when it gained control of South Africa's government in 1948. Pretoria, a city northeast of Johannesburg, is the administrative capital of South Africa.
12. *makulu:* very much; in a big way.
13. 'Suffer . . . heaven': Mark 10:14.

South African youth doing homework.

I went.

I followed him around as he showed me all the things his parents regularly bought him: toys, bicycles, go-carts, pinball machines, Ping-Pong tables, electric trains. I only half-listened; my mind was preoccupied with comparing my situation with his. I couldn't understand why he and his people had to have all the luxuries money can buy, while I and my people lived in abject poverty. Was it because they were whites and we were black? Were they better than we? I could not find the answers; yet I felt there

a student population of over two thousand, did not have half as many books. I was dazed.

Sensing that I was in awe of his magnificent library, Clyde said, "Do you have this many books in your playroom?"

"I don't have a playroom."

"You don't have a playroom," he said bugeyed. "Can you read?" he smiled sinisterly. "Our boy Absalom can't. And he says black children aren't taught much English at school."

"I can read a little English," I said.

"I doubt if you can read any of my books. Here, read," he ordered, pulling one out of the shelves. The book was thick, looked formidable.

I nervously opened a page, toiled through a couple lines, encountering long words I could not pronounce, let alone understand their meaning. Shaking my head in embarrassment, I handed the book back, "I can't read this type of English."

"Then you must be retarded," Clyde laughed. Though he might have meant it in jest, my pride was deeply wounded. "This book is by William Shakespeare," he went on, waving it in my face, "the greatest English writer that ever lived. I could read it from cover to cover when I was half your age. But I don't blame you if you can't. My teachers tell us that Kaffirs can't read, speak, or write English like white people because they have smaller brains, which are already full of tribal things. My teachers say you're not people like us, because you belong to a jungle civilization. That's why you can't live or go to school with us, but can only be our servants."

"Stop saying that rubbish, you naughty boy," Mrs. Smith said angrily as she entered the room just in time to catch the tail end of her son's knowledge of black people's in-

was something wrong about white people having everything, and black people nothing.

We finally came to Clyde's playroom. The room was roughly the size of our house, and was elaborately decorated with posters, pennants of various white soccer and cricket teams, rock stars and photographs of Clyde in various stages of development. But what arrested my attention were the stacks of comic books on the floor, and the shelves and shelves of books. Never had I seen that many books in my life; even our school, with

19

20

21

22

19 LITERARY ELEMENT
Autobiography: Why do you think the author includes Clyde's remarks about the playroom? (to show that many white South Africans were ignorant of the impoverished living conditions of black South Africans)

20 INTERPRETING
What is particularly offensive about Clyde's language here? (A boy himself, he uses the term "boy" in a derogatory manner to refer to a black man.)

21 EVALUATING
Do you think that Clyde could read Shakespeare when he was Mathabane's age, or less than six years old? Explain. (No, Shakespeare's Elizabethan English is probably difficult for him to read even at twelve.) Why does Clyde select a book by Shakespeare to "test" the author's English? (Clyde is a bully who wants to make his unwelcome visitor feel inadequate.)

22 SPECULATING
Under apartheid, South Africa's authoritarian government published or encouraged the publication of fallacious textbooks and other kinds of propaganda that fostered government claims of white supremacy. *Why do you think that censorship and controlling the media are so important to authoritarian regimes?* (Possible response: It is easier to control people's behavior when they are ignorant of the truth.)

Mark Mathabane

1373

postulated (päs′chə·lāt′id): claimed; assumed to be self-evident or true

doctrine (däk′trən): something taught as the principles of a religion, political party, or other group

impudently (im′pyōō·dənt·lē): in a shamelessly bold or disrespectful way

23 GUIDED READING
Finding the Main Idea: What ambition does Clyde's cruelty inspire in the author? (the determination to master English)

24 INFERRING
Do you think that Clyde is sorry about his behavior? Explain. (Probably not; more likely, his mother is sorry and is apologizing for him.)

25 DRAWING CONCLUSIONS
From what book does this quote come? (*Treasure Island*) To what do you think "dead man's chest" refers? (a treasure chest) Why is this sea chantey important to the author? (It represents the world of the imagination available in books.)

22 telligence, as postulated by the doctrine of apartheid. "How many times have I told you that what your teachers say about black people is not true?"

"What do you know, Mama?" Clyde retorted impudently, "you're not a teacher. Besides, there are textbooks where it's so written."

"Still it's not true," insisted Mrs. Smith. "Everything that's in your books is not necessarily true, especially your history books about this country." Changing the subject, she said, "Show him your easy books, and then get your things ready so I can drive you over to your friend's birthday party." Clyde quickly ran down his long list of "easy" books: *The Three Musketeers, Treasure Island, David Copperfield*, the Hardy Boys series, the Sherlock Holmes series, *Tom Sawyer, Robinson Crusoe, The Swiss Family Robinson, The Hunchback of Notre Dame, Black Beauty, A Tale of Two Cities*, and so on. Oh, how I envied Clyde's collection of books. I would have given my life to own just a handful of them.

23 The remark that black people had smaller brains and were thus incapable of reading, speaking, or writing English like white people had so wounded my ego that I vowed that, whatever the cost, I would master English, that I would not rest till I could read, write and speak it just like any white man, if not better. Finally, I had something to aspire to.

Back with Granny, I told her to be on the lookout whenever Mrs. Smith junked any books. At the end of the day, as Granny and I prepared to leave, I was given a small box by Mrs. Smith.

24 "It's from Clyde," she said. "He's sorry that he treated you badly. He's promised not to do it again. I'll see to it he keeps his promise. Come and help Ellen in the garden whenever you can; that way you'll earn some pocket money."

The box contained a couple shirts, pants, and jerseys.[14] Underneath the articles of clothing was a copy of *Treasure Island.*

To learn to express my thoughts and feelings effectively in English became my main goal in life. I saw command of the English language as the crucial key with which to unlock doors leading into that wonderful world of books revealed to me through the reading of Robert Louis Stevenson's gripping tale of buried treasure, mutiny on the high seas, one-legged seamen, and the old sea song that I could recite even in my dreams:

Fifteen men on a dead man's chest
Yo-ho-ho, and a bottle of rum.

25

My heart ached to explore more such worlds, to live them in the imagination in much the same way as I lived the folktales of my mother and grandmother. I reasoned that if I somehow kept improving my English and ingratiated Mrs. Smith by the fact, then possibly she would give me more books like *Treasure Island* each time Granny took me along. Alas, such trips were few and far between. I could not afford to skip school regularly; and besides, each trip did not yield a book. But I clung to my dream.

A million times I wondered why the sparse library at my tribal school did not carry books like *Treasure Island*, why most of the books we read had tribal points of view. I would ask teachers and would be told that under the Bantu Education law black children were supposed to acquire a solid foundation in tribal life, which would prepare them for a productive future in their respective homelands. In this way the dream

---

14. **jerseys:** sweaters.

READING CHECK

1. Through what city is the author traveling at the beginning of the selection? (Johannesburg)
2. What two sports does the author observe white South Africans playing? (cricket and tennis)
3. What primary emotion does the author feel as he sees the white South African schoolchildren and their school? (envy)

4. What is Mrs. Smith's general opinion of apartheid? (She finds it evil and hypocritical.)
5. In the last paragraph, what goal does the author set for himself? (to learn at least two English words a day)

RETEACHING

Ask students to act out an interview between an older Mathabane and a newspaper reporter. The reporter's questions should elicit autobiographical responses based on incidents and details from the selection. You might offer these examples of possible questions: When did you first see a tennis game? What was your home in Alexandra like? What inspired you to learn English so well? What family member was a source of inspiration? Why?

of Dr. Verwoerd,[15] prime minister of South Africa and the architect of Bantu Education, would be realized, for he insisted that "the native child must be taught subjects which will enable him to work with and among his own people; therefore there is no use misleading him by showing him the green pastures of European society, in which he is not allowed to graze. Bantu Education should not be used to create imitation whites."

How I cursed Dr. Verwoerd and his law for prescribing how I should feel and think. I started looking toward the Smiths to provide me with the books about a different reality. Each day Granny came back from work around five in the afternoon, I would be the first to meet her at the gate, always with the same question, "Any books for me today?" Many times there weren't any. Unable to read new English books on a regular basis, I reread the ones I had over and over again, till the pages became dogeared. With each reading each book took on new life, exposed new angles to the story, with the result that I was never bored.

My bleak vocabulary did not diminish my enthusiasm for reading. I constantly borrowed Mr. Brown's[16] pocket-size dictionary to look up meanings of words, and would memorize them like arithmetic tables and write them in a small notebook. Sometimes I would read the dictionary. My pronunciation was appalling, but I had no way of finding out. I was amazed at the number of words in the English language, at the fact that a word could have different shades of meaning, or that certain words looked and sounded alike and yet differed greatly in meaning. Would I ever be able to learn all that?

At the same time I was discovering the richness of the English language I began imitating how white people talked, in the hope of learning proper pronunciation. My efforts were often hilarious, but my determination increased with failure. I set myself the goal of learning at least two new English words a day.

---

15. **Dr. Verwoerd** (fər·voort′): Hendrik Frensch Verwoerd (1901–1966), South African politician and one of the chief architects of apartheid. Verwoerd served as prime minister from 1958 to 1966.

16. **Mr. Brown's:** referring to one of the author's better-educated neighbors, who appears earlier in *Kaffir Boy*.

26 EVALUATING

Do you think Dr. Verwoerd's policies mandated education in tribal ways because he wanted black South Africans to take pride in their heritages? Explain. (No, he wanted black South Africans to remain ignorant of the white world, its opportunities, advantages, and privileges.)

MEETING INDIVIDUAL NEEDS

27 ESL: Students who have similar goals and experiences may want to share them with classmates. ∎

1. Expressing Political Opinions. Have students imagine that Mrs. Smith decided to express her opinions about apartheid by contributing to an anonymous pamphlet to be distributed among South Africans. Ask students to write the passage that she might have written.

2. Creating a Time Line. Have groups of students research different periods of South Africa's history. Depending on the period they are researching, students might consult encyclopedias and nonfiction books or recent newspapers, magazines, and almanacs. Encourage artistic students to put the time line together and to illustrate some of the notable events.

Have students evaluate the effectiveness of Mathabane's autobiography in terms of its political and social purposes. Based on the selection, do they think that the author helped to change the political climate of South Africa? Why or why not? ■

ANSWERS

First Thoughts
Answers will vary.

Identifying Facts
1. Differences include far better schools and housing and far more material possessions.
2. She rebukes him by saying that Mathabane is a Bantu, not a Kaffir. Its racism is illogical, hypocritical, and destructive of the nation's future.
3. a work by Shakespeare; *Treasure Island*
4. "Any books for me today?" He will learn at least two English words a day.

Interpreting Meanings
1. The bus is overcrowded; the houses of whites are spacious. Blacks live in poverty; whites, in luxury. He wants to reveal apartheid's injustices and effect change.
2. ambitious, proud, smart, and respectful. The selection
3. kind, frank, realistic, condescending. He taunts him with a racial slur and mocks his intelligence. At school. Yes; apartheid
4. Although prejudice is deeply rooted, there is hope for change.

Applying Meanings
Answers will vary.

Creative Writing Response
Writing an Autobiographical Episode. Episodes should present an important or interesting event.

Critical Writing Response
Writing About an Author's Purpose. Essays should state and support at least two purposes. ■

First Thoughts
What did you most admire about the narrator? Was there anything you did not admire?

Identifying Facts
1. When Mathabane visits white Johannesburg for the first time, what differences does he notice between white South African life and his own life?
2. Summarize Mrs. Smith's reprimand when her son calls Mathabane a "Kaffir." What does she then say about white South Africa?
3. What does Clyde give Mathabane to test his literacy? What easier book comes in the box with Clyde's hand-me-downs?
4. What question does Mathabane ask each time his grandmother returns from work? What goal does he set at the end of the selection?

Interpreting Meanings
1. Contrast conditions on the bus for blacks with conditions in white Johannesburg. What does the contrast suggest about South Africa? Based on contrasts like these, identify one of the author's purposes in writing his **autobiography**.
2. What adjectives would you use to describe the author as a young boy? What proof do you have that he will master English?
3. What positive and negative qualities does Mrs. Smith display? In what ways is Clyde cruel to the author? Where do you think he learned to behave this way?

Do you think Mathabane uses Clyde's behavior to point to a larger problem in white South African society? If so, what is that problem?

4. What does the different behavior of the people here suggest about South Africa's future?

Applying Meanings
What role does peer pressure play in racial or ethnic prejudice and the way we treat outsiders in general? Why do you think people succumb to peer pressure?

Creative Writing Response
Writing an Autobiographical Episode. Look over the list of life events you wrote down in the Writer's Response: Choose one event and write a few paragraphs about it, presenting it as an episode in the **autobiography** that you may someday write.

Critical Writing Response
Writing About an Author's Purpose. In a brief essay, discuss Mathabane's chief purposes in writing his **autobiography**. Based on this selection, state what those purposes seem to be, and then discuss selection details that help him achieve each purpose. Before writing, you may want to list two or three purposes and supporting details on a chart like the one below.

Purpose	Details That Help Achieve This Purpose

Naguib Mahfouz
b. 1911, Egypt

T. Cambra Pierce/Wide World Photos

As a boy in Cairo's picturesque old quarter, Naguib Mahfouz (nä·jēb' mä'fōoz) encountered many unusual characters who would influence his life and work. Among them was journalist El-Muwaylili, who was experimenting in new forms of fiction. At the time, the novel form was virtually unknown in Arabic literature, where poetry and nonfiction were stressed. El-Muwaylili's efforts inspired Mahfouz to introduce full-fledged novels to Arabic literature. Eventually Mahfouz would become the best-known fiction writer in the Arabic language and the first Arabic author to win the Nobel Prize for literature.

Interested in both philosophy and literature, Mahfouz attended Cairo University, where classes were conducted in English and French. His growing proficiency in these languages allowed him to read many European classics and to familiarize himself with the novel and short-story forms. Still uncertain of his future, Mahfouz submitted a short story to a Cairo magazine. He considers the day it was accepted the most important day of his life.

The course of Mahfouz's writing career seems to recapitulate two centuries of literary movements. His early historical novels, set in the time of the pharaohs, display the idealistic nationalism of Romantic era authors like Johann Wolfgang von Goethe (see page 986). In the chaotic period leading up to World War II, Mahfouz turned to social realism in books like *New Cairo* (1946) and *Midaq Alley* (1947), which vividly evoke his boyhood neighborhood and the effects of war on the average Egyptian. Mahfouz continued in this realistic vein with his masterful Cairo trilogy—*Between the Two Palaces* (1956), *The Palace of Desire* (1957), and *The Sugar Bowl* (1957)—about three generations of a Cairo family who symbolize Egyptian experience in modern times. In the 1960s Mahfouz began to experiment with the stream-of-consciousness technique, as well as the more indirect symbolism associated with modernism. His preoccupation with the individual facing spiritual and emotional crises was prompted in part by the growing Arab-Israeli conflict and Egypt's bitter defeat in the 1967 Six-Day War.

MORE ABOUT THE AUTHOR

It took Naguib Mahfouz almost two decades to win acclaim in his homeland. Even after the Arabic-speaking world, including Egypt, had recognized him as its greatest novelist, the non-Arabic world barely acknowledged his literary gifts. Mahfouz was over seventy when he won the Nobel Prize for literature in 1988, and many of his works are now being translated into English for the first time. Small wonder, then, that among his friends, Mahfouz is known as Al-Sabir, "the patient one."

Despite his interest in world literature, Mahfouz remains the quintessential Egyptian writer: His fiction depicts the experiences of the average Egyptian. Mahfouz's fame as a Nobel laureate has not changed his habits; he still visits downtown Cairo's Ali Baba café every morning at 7:00 A.M. to read his newspaper and catch up on the gossip.

In 1994, a failed attempt was made on Mahfouz's life for what some say are his anti-Islamic works and for his support of Egypt's 1979 peace treaty with Israel.

ABOUT THE TRANSLATOR

Denys Johnson-Davies is one of the foremost English translators of Arabic prose. Acknowledging Johnson-Davies's renown as a translator of short fiction, Doubleday selected him to translate Mahfouz's short stories when they began publishing English-language editions of his work.

OBJECTIVES

1. *To interpret a modern Egyptian story*
2. *To identify theme in a work and to analyze how it is conveyed*
3. *To write a story about a childhood memory and an essay comparing the themes of two selections*
4. *To identify the meanings of words adapted from Arabic and to recognize Arabic's contributions to English*

THEMES IN WORLD LITERATURE

Coming of Age
"A Walk to the Jetty," from *Annie John*, pp. 1320–1328
From *Kaffir Boy*, pp. 1365–1376
"By Any Other Name," pp. 1387–1394

Transformations
From *Metamorphoses*, pp. 420–427
The Metamorphosis, pp. 1154–1195
"Wind and Water and Stone," p. 1288 ∎

VOCABULARY IN CONTEXT
The words listed below will appear in the side margin at the point of instruction:

1. pitiable
2. intricate
3. submission
4. perseverance
5. throngs

PREREADING FOCUS

Background: In his youth Mahfouz lived in Cairo's picturesque Gamaliyya, or Old Quarter. This eastern part of Cairo is famous for its narrow, winding streets and buildings that are hundreds of years old. As the city began to grow, however, Mahfouz's family moved to one of Cairo's modern neighborhoods. Today Cairo is a bustling modern city, the largest in Africa and one of the ten largest in the world.

Literary Focus: Make sure that students understand that the theme is a generalization that can be derived from the specific details of the work. To identify the theme of a work, students should ask themselves the following question: What do the details suggest about life or human nature *in general*? For a work of fiction, students should consider such concepts as characterization, conflict, outcome or resolution, the title of the work, and any symbolism that it may contain. Note that some works may have more than one theme. Though the theme is usually implied, it may be explicit. Ask students to name a genre that usually contains a stated theme. (Possible response: the fable, which usually ends with a moral that states the theme)

Reader's Guide

HALF A DAY

Background

Today, Egypt's chief language is Arabic, and more than ninety percent of all Egyptians are Muslims. Because so much of Egypt is desert, Egyptians have traditionally lived on the fertile banks of the Nile River. Since World War II, more and more people from rural areas along the Nile have moved to Egypt's major cities, also located on the river. The largest of these cities is Cairo (kī'rō), Egypt's capital, where Mahfouz grew up and where the upcoming story is set.

Cairo's population has increased dramatically since Mahfouz was a boy, and many of the city's fields and gardens have given way to tall modern buildings. As in other urban centers all over the world, overcrowding has created many problems, among them noise pollution, inadequate waste removal, and insufficient public transportation. Cairo is also famous for having some of the world's worst traffic jams.

Writer's Response

Write a paragraph supporting or refuting the following statement: "There are too many human beings living on the earth today." Cite details from your everyday life to back up your opinion.

Literary Focus

Theme is the central idea or insight behind a work of literature. Theme moves beyond the specifics of the work to express a general idea or insight about life or human nature. For instance, a story may be about a father watching his son play a baseball game, but the theme may be about fathers' unfulfilled ambitions. The theme of a story usually reveals something about the writer's personal attitudes toward some aspect of life.

Commas in a Series

Commas are used to separate a series of words, phrases, or short clauses:

We visited Egypt, Israel, and Greece.

In Egypt we shopped in Cairo, toured the Nile, and saw the pyramids.

The sightseeing boat arrived, the tourists boarded, and the trip began.

1. **Reading and Speaking.** Copy onto the chalkboard these passages from "Half a Day." Omit the commas. Ask volunteers to add commas as needed.

a. All my clothes were new: the black shoes, the green school uniform, and the red tarboosh.

b. High buildings had taken over, the street surged with children, and disturbing noises shook the air.

2. **Writing.** Have students write a paragraph describing sights and sounds on their way to school. Paragraphs should contain series of words, phrases, or clauses. ∎

HALF A DAY
Naguib Mahfouz
translated by
DENYS JOHNSON-DAVIES

⫾ *Notice specific details that indicate how Mahfouz feels about the modernization of Egypt.*

1 I proceeded alongside my father, clutching his right hand, running to keep up with the long strides he was taking. All my clothes were new: the black shoes, the green school uniform, and the red tarboosh.[1] My delight in my new clothes, however, was not altogether unmarred, for this was no feast day[2] but the day on which I was to be cast into school for the first time.

My mother stood at the window watching our progress, and I would turn toward her from time to time, as though appealing for help. We walked along a street lined with gardens; on both sides were extensive fields planted with crops, prickly pears, henna trees, and a few date palms.

"Why school?" I challenged my father openly. "I shall never do anything to annoy you."

2 "I'm not punishing you," he said, laughing. "School's not a punishment. It's the factory that makes useful men out of boys. Don't you want to be like your father and brothers?"

I was not convinced. I did not believe there was really any good to be had in tearing me away from the intimacy of my home and throwing me into this building that stood at the end of the road like some huge, high-walled fortress, exceedingly stern and grim.

When we arrived at the gate we could see the courtyard, vast and crammed full of boys and girls. "Go in by yourself," said my father, "and join them. Put a smile on your face and be a good example to others."

I hesitated and clung to his hand, but he

The Bettmann Archive

El Azhar Mosque in Cairo, Egypt.
❓ *Does the narrator's reluctance to go to school for the first time strike you as realistic?*

---

1. **tarboosh** (tär·bōōsh'): brimless cloth cap worn by Muslim men.
2. **feast day**: holiday.

TEACHER'S RESOURCES
- ↳ Vocabulary Activity Worksheet
- ↳ Vocabulary Test
- ↳ Review and Response Worksheet
- ↳ Language Skills Worksheet
- ↳ Selection Test

1 GUIDED READING

Finding the Main Idea: In which sentence is the main idea of this paragraph expressed? (the last) What is the effect of this placement? (It stresses the importance of the idea and builds suspense by making us wonder, until the very end, what the narrator's destination will be.)

2 LITERARY ELEMENT

Metaphor: The father's remarks contain a figure of speech. To what does he compare school? (a factory) What kind of figurative language is this comparison? (a metaphor)

3 gently pushed me from him. "Be a man," he said. "Today you truly begin life. You will find me waiting for you when it's time to leave."

I took a few steps, then stopped and looked but saw nothing. Then the faces of boys and girls came into view. I did not know a single one of them, and none of them knew me. I felt I was a stranger who had lost his way. But glances of curiosity were directed toward me, and one boy approached and asked, "Who brought you?"

4 "My father," I whispered.

"My father's dead," he said quite simply.

I did not know what to say. The gate was closed, letting out a <u>pitiable</u> screech. Some of the children burst into tears. The bell rang. A lady came along, followed by a group of men. The men began sorting us into ranks. We were formed into an <u>intricate</u> pattern in the great courtyard surrounded on three sides by high buildings of several floors; from each floor we were overlooked by a long balcony roofed in wood.

"This is your new home," said the woman. "Here, too, there are mothers and fathers. Here there is everything that is enjoyable and beneficial to knowledge and religion. Dry your tears and face life joyfully."

5 We submitted to the facts, and this <u>submission</u> brought a sort of contentment. Living beings were drawn to other living beings, and from the first moments my heart made friends with such boys as were to be my friends and fell in love with such girls as I was to be in love with, so that it seemed my misgivings had had no basis. I had never imagined school would have this rich variety. We played all sorts of different games: swings, the vaulting horse,[3] ball games. In

A busy street in Cairo.

Thomas Nebbia/Woodfin Camp & Associates

the music room we chanted our first songs. We also had our first introduction to language. We saw a globe of the Earth, which revolved and showed the various continents and countries. We started learning the numbers. The story of the Creator of the universe was read to us, we were told of His present world and of His Hereafter, and we heard examples of what He said. We ate delicious food, took a little nap, and woke up to go on with friendship and love, play and learning.

As our path revealed itself to us, however, we did not find it as totally sweet and

---

3. **vaulting horse:** that is, the horse one leaps over in gymnastics.

READING CHECK

1. As the story opens, for what event is the narrator all dressed up? (his first day of school)
2. What promise does the father make before leaving the narrator? (He'll be waiting for him when it is time to leave.)
3. When the narrator tells the other boy that his father brought him, what does the other boy say? ("My father's dead.")

4. What prevents the narrator from crossing the street to reach his home? (heavy traffic)
5. What does the young man from the ironing shop say when he offers to escort the narrator? ("Grandpa, let me take you across.")

RETEACHING

Have students reenact the story in pantomime. The student playing the narrator might change his or her way of walking and perhaps use appropriate props (such as a cane) to indicate the change in age.

unclouded as we had presumed. Dust-laden winds and unexpected accidents came about suddenly, so we had to be watchful, at the ready, and very patient. It was not all a matter of playing and fooling around. Rivalries could bring about pain and hatred or give rise to fighting. And while the lady would sometimes smile, she would often scowl and scold. Even more frequently she would resort to physical punishment.

In addition, the time for changing one's mind was over and gone and there was no question of ever returning to the paradise of home. Nothing lay ahead of us but exertion, struggle, and perseverance. Those who were able took advantage of the opportunities for success and happiness that presented themselves amid the worries.

The bell rang announcing the passing of the day and the end of work. The throngs of children rushed toward the gate, which was opened again. I bade farewell to friends and sweethearts and passed through the gate. I peered around but found no trace of my father, who had promised to be there. I stepped aside to wait. When I had waited for a long time without avail, I decided to return home on my own. After I had taken a few steps, a middle-aged man passed by, and I realized at once that I knew him. He came toward me, smiling, and shook me by the hand, saying, "It's a long time since we last met—how are you?"

With a nod of my head, I agreed with him and in turn asked, "And you, how are you?"

"As you can see, not all that good, the Almighty be praised!"

Again he shook me by the hand and went off. I proceeded a few steps, then came to a startled halt. Good Lord! Where was the street lined with gardens? Where had it disappeared to? When did all these vehicles invade it? And when did all these hordes of humanity come to rest upon its surface? How did these hills of refuse come to cover its sides? And where were the fields that bordered it? High buildings had taken over, the street surged with children, and disturbing noises shook the air. At various points stood conjurers[4] showing off their tricks and making snakes appear from baskets. Then there was a band announcing the opening of a circus, with clowns and weight lifters walking in front. A line of trucks carrying central security troops crawled majestically by. The siren of a fire engine shrieked, and it was not clear how the vehicle would cleave its way to reach the blazing fire. A battle raged between a taxi driver and his passenger, while the passenger's wife called out for help and no one answered. Good God! I was in a daze. My head spun. I almost went crazy. How could all this have happened in half a day, between early morning and sunset? I would find the answer at home with my father. But where was my home? I could see only tall buildings and hordes of people. I hastened on to the crossroads between the gardens and Abu Khoda.[5] I had to cross Abu Khoda to reach my house, but the stream of cars would not let up. The fire engine's siren was shrieking at full pitch as it moved at a snail's pace, and I said to myself, "Let the fire take its pleasure in what it consumes."[6] Extremely irritated, I wondered when I would be able to cross. I stood there a long time, until the young lad employed at the ironing shop on the corner came up to me. He stretched out his arm and said gallantly, "Grandpa, let me take you across."

6 LITERARY ELEMENT
Figurative Language: To what "path" is the narrator referring on p. 1380? (a path in life) What might he mean by "dust-laden winds"? (sudden misfortunes or unpleasantness)

perseverance (pur'sə·vir'əns): continued, patient effort

throngs (thrōngs): great numbers of people gathered together; crowds

7 ANALYZING
What is unusual about the way in which the middle-aged man behaves toward the narrator? (He treats the narrator like an adult.)

8 LITERARY ELEMENT
Foreshadowing: What do the many changes suggest has happened? (Possible response: More time has passed than seemed apparent at first.) What ending might these details foreshadow? (Responses will vary. Encourage students to discuss their ideas with other classmates.)

9 INTERPRETING
What do the young man's remark and actions indicate has happened to the narrator? (He has become an old man.) What does this surprise ending suggest about human life? (It passes very quickly.)

Naguib Mahfouz   **1381**

1. Writing Critical Essays. Over the years Mahfouz has shifted from romantic historical fiction to realistic social commentary to experimental modernist fiction. Have students write essays showing how "Half a Day" blends realism with fantastic elements often associated with modernism. For purposes of comparison, students should cite other modernist works, such as *The Metamorphosis* and "Borges and Myself."

2. Writing Screenplays. Note that many of Mahfouz's novels and short stories have been made into films in Egypt. Then have students work in groups to create screenplays for a short film based on "Half a Day." In adapting the tale into a filmable drama, students should add suitable dialogue, action, characters, and events. After students have completed the screenplays, they may want to act them out.

CLOSURE

Ask students how the title points to the central theme of the story. (It presents the idea that life passes very quickly by suggesting that the years from childhood to old age can seem like only half a day, as they do in the story itself.) ■

ANSWERS

First Thoughts
Answers will vary.

Identifying Facts
1. school. "Be a man."
2. friends, love, games, music; rivalries, scoldings
3. father; greets him
4. questions about changes in setting; offers to help

Interpreting Meanings
1. Narrator is old. Answers will vary.
2. father's absence, man's attitude, changes on street
3. Man recalls first school day so vividly that it seems real.
4. It is fleeting. It stresses that time passes very quickly.
5. Yes. Change is inevitable, time passes quickly as one ages; school changes parent-child relationship.

Applying Meanings
It is a step toward maturity.

Creative Writing Response
Writing About a Childhood Memory. Encourage creativity.

Critical Writing Response
Comparing Themes in Two Stories. Essays should contrast positive and negative themes.

Language and Vocabulary
1. navy commander, Arabic "high leader"; 2. math branch, Ar. "reunion of broken parts"; 3. quality, Ar. "mold"; 4. taxes on shipments, Ar. "information"; 5. purple-red, Ar. "crimson"; 6. zero, Ar. "nothing"; 7. evil person, Ar. "mountain demon"; 8. plant, its red dye, Ar. for same; 9. crocus, its food flavoring, Ar. for same; 10. chief, Ar. "old man" ■

First Thoughts
Were you surprised by the story's ending? Did it add to your enjoyment of the story, or did it confuse you? Explain.

Identifying Facts
1. As the story opens, where is the narrator's father taking him for the first time? What explanations and advice does the father give?
2. Identify four things the narrator likes about his new experience and two things he dislikes.
3. After the bell rings, for whom does the narrator wait in vain? As he walks home alone, what does a middle-aged man on the street do?
4. List three questions the narrator asks himself while walking home. As he waits to cross the busy intersection, what does the "young lad" do and say?

Interpreting Meanings
1. What surprise was revealed at the end of the story? Did you have any idea that the story might end in this way?
2. Reread the story and identify three details that **foreshadow** the surprise ending.
3. Perhaps you have heard the expression, "His life flashed before his eyes." Do you think that Mahfouz, in this story, realistically presents the way an older person's mind might work? Why or why not?
4. What **theme** about time does the ending help convey? How is the title of the story relevant to this theme?
5. Does the story also express **themes** on any of these subjects: change, old age, youth, school, and parent-child relationships? If so, what are they?

Applying Meanings
Why is the first day of school such a memorable event in most children's lives?

Creative Writing Response
Writing About a Childhood Memory.
Write a brief story based on your first day of school or another memorable event in your childhood. Like Mahfouz, you might play tricks with time to make a point about time's passage.

Critical Writing Response
Comparing Themes in Two Stories.
"Half a Day" and Santha Rama Rau's essay "By Any Other Name" (see page 1389) deal with a child's experience of school. Write a statement of **theme** for each selection (both should relate to the effects of school on a child's life). Decide whether the two stories share more similarities or differences and write a brief essay comparing and contrasting their themes.

Language and Vocabulary
Arabic and English

Over the centuries, English has borrowed dozens of words from Arabic. Some came to English directly; others came by way of other European languages such as Spanish, French, Italian, and Latin. Use a dictionary to help you find the origins of these English words. Also, provide the meanings of any unfamiliar words.

1. admiral   6. cipher
2. algebra   7. ghoul
3. caliber   8. henna
4. tariff   9. saffron
5. carmine   10. sheik

Yehuda Amichai
b. 1924, Israel

L ike many Israelis of his generation, Yehuda Amichai (yə·hoō'də ä'mi·khī') has spent much of his life as a soldier. During World War II he served in the Jewish brigade of the British army fighting against German forces in the Middle East. In 1948, after Israel won independence and was attacked by neighboring Arab nations, Amichai fought with the special strike force of the Israeli army. Later, as an army reservist, he was often called upon to fight for his country.

Born to an orthodox Jewish family in southern Germany, Amichai escaped Nazi persecution when he was only twelve. Like many other European Jews lucky enough to escape, Amichai and his family immigrated to the Holy Land, then British-controlled Palestine. There they eventually settled in the city of Jerusalem, where the young Amichai continued his studies of Hebrew literature and the Bible. After serving as a soldier in the 1940s, Amichai completed his studies at Jerusalem's Hebrew University. By then he had already published several Hebrew-language poems in magazines, although his first poetry collection, *Now and in Other Days*, did not appear until 1955.

In addition to writing poems, novels, short stories, and plays, Amichai has taught Hebrew literature both in Israel and abroad. While Hebrew was not his first language, Amichai began learning it during his childhood religious studies in Germany, since ancient Hebrew is the language of Jewish scripture and ritual. Modern spoken Hebrew, however, is very different from ancient Hebrew. Mastering the differences has been a challenge for contemporary Israeli authors, and Amichai is considered one of Israel's first writers to meet that challenge successfully. His style combines the informality of modern spoken Hebrew with the powerful poetic images found in the Old Testament.

At the heart of virtually all of Amichai's poetry is his concern with the effects that frequent warfare and a constant war-ready state have had on the Israeli consciousness.

MORE ABOUT THE AUTHOR

Fluent in German as well as Hebrew, Yehuda Amichai was influenced by the poetry of Rilke (page 1148). Like Rilke, Amichai displays great skill in creating vivid imagery and metaphors. Modern English-language poetry is another source of inspiration to him. The University of California at Berkeley is only one of the American universities at which he has taught as a visiting professor of Hebrew.

In Israel during the 1950s, Amichai was lionized as the leader of a new generation of Hebrew writers who set out "To speak, now, in this tired language / Torn from its sleep in the Bible." As his literary fame grew, he received many literary awards, including the Shlonsky Prize.

In addition to his many volumes of poetry, Amichai has written two novels—*Not of This Time, Not of This Place* (1963) and *O That I Had a Lodging* (1971). His highly regarded short stories include those published in his 1961 collection, *In This Terrible Wind*. Amichai has also written plays for Israel radio and the Israeli stage.

ABOUT THE TRANSLATORS

Warren Bargad and Stanley F. Chyet are among the many translators who have rendered Amichai's verse into English. Others include the British poet Ted Hughes, with whom Amichai collaborated on the 1977 translation of Amichai's volume of poetry titled *Amen*.

OBJECTIVES

1. *To interpret a modern Israeli poem*
2. *To identify and analyze incremental repetition*
3. *To write an elegy and an essay analyzing an extended simile*
4. *To match English words with their Hebrew origins and to recognize Hebrew's contributions to English*

THEMES IN WORLD LITERATURE

War and Peace
From the *Iliad*, pp. 224–277
"Cranes," pp. 1402–1408
"Thoughts of Hanoi," pp. 1409–1413

Life and Loss
From the *Aeneid*, pp. 379–408
"On Her Brother," pp. 630–632

The Search for Meaning
From *Night*, pp. 1232–1242
"Love Must Not Be Forgotten,"
pp. 1414–1427 ■

PREREADING FOCUS

Background: In 1979 Egypt became the first Arab state to recognize Israel and to establish diplomatic relations with the Jewish state. In 1991, after the end of the Cold War, the President of the United States and the last President of the Soviet Union convened a peace conference on the Middle East. Israelis, however, remain divided about the efficacy of negotiating peace with their neighbors. After students have read Amichai's poem, you might ask them to speculate about the poet's feelings on this subject.

Writer's Response: Students should gather information from newspapers and newsmagazines so that they can express informed written opinions. Encourage them to air their views in a class discussion either before or after they record their opinions.

Reader's Guide

from LAMENTS ON THE WAR DEAD

Background

After the ancient Romans conquered the Holy Land, which they called Palestine, the area's Jews revolted unsuccessfully and most were driven into exile. Many of these exiles settled in Europe, where they were severely persecuted over the centuries. In the late 1800s, European Jews formed the Zionist movement, which sought to reestablish in the Holy Land a nation where Jews could live free of oppression. By now Arabs had become Palestine's chief inhabitants, but soon more and more Jews began returning. In 1947, in the wake of world horror at the Holocaust, the United Nations voted to partition Palestine into a Jewish nation and an Arab nation. The Jews accepted the plan, but the Arabs did not. On May 15, 1948, a day after the new Jewish nation of Israel came into being, neighboring Arab countries attacked in the first of several Arab-Israeli wars. With each war, the Israelis emerged as victors, acquiring more land and working to build modern cities and productive farms.

Yehuda Amichai wrote his poetic sequence *Laments on the War Dead* soon after the war of 1973, when Egypt and Syria attacked Israel on the Jewish high holy day of Yom Kippur. Israel won the war, but at great cost, both economically and in terms of human lives.

Writer's Response

Comment on recent events in the Middle East, researching them in current newspapers if necessary. How do you assess the situation? Do you have more sympathy for one group than another?

Literary Focus

Poets often use **repetition** to create rhythm, build suspense, or emphasize a particular word or idea. In **incremental repetition**, a line or section of a poem or song is repeated with some variation in wording. Usually the variation adds significant new information or expresses a significant change in meaning or attitude.

from LAMENTS ON THE WAR DEAD

Yehuda Amichai

t r a n s l a t e d   b y

WARREN BARGAD AND STANLEY F. CHYET

🔖 *Look for the answers the speaker gives to the poem's opening question.*

Modern-day Israel.

J. Leonard Hornstein

6

Is all this sorrow? I don't know.
I stood in the cemetery dressed
in the camouflage clothing of a live man, brown
pants and a shirt yellow as the sun.

5 Graveyards are cheap and unassuming.
Even the wastebaskets are too small to hold
the thin paper that wrapped the store-bought
   flowers.
Graveyards are disciplined, mannered things.
"I'll never forget you," reads
10 a small brick tablet in French.°
I don't know who it is who won't forget,
who's more unknown than the one who's dead.

Is all this sorrow? I think
so. "Be consoled in building the land." How
15 long can we build the land,
to gain in the terrible, three-sided
game of building, consolation, and death?
Yes, all this is sorrow. But
leave a little love always lit,
20 like the nightlight in a sleeping infant's room,
not that he knows what light is
and where it comes from, but it gives him
a bit of security and some silent love.

10. **in French:** Although Hebrew is Israel's chief language, an immigrant from Europe or elsewhere might also continue to use his or her first language, especially on a tombstone.

1. Staging an Interview. Encourage students to role-play an interview between the speaker and a friend, a relative, a religious adviser, or a psychiatric counselor. The interviewer should elicit the experiences, thoughts, and feelings that the speaker expresses in the poem as well as information that serves to elucidate those experiences, thoughts, and feelings.

2. Debate, Panel Discussion, or Letter of Opinion. In a formal debate or panel discussion, volunteers should be encouraged to voice and argue the ideas they expressed in the *Writer's Response*. Other students may wish to express and support their opinions in letters to the editor of a school or local newspaper or a national newsmagazine.

CLOSURE

Ask students to identify the shift in the speaker's tone that occurs in the last lines of the poem. (Before it reflected bewilderment and a lack of hope. Here it reflects a sense of peace and love.) What do the final lines suggest as the remedy for sorrow and loss? (love) ◼

ANSWERS

First Thoughts
Answers will vary.

Identifying Facts
1. "I don't know." "camouflage clothing of a live man"
2. They are cheap and unassuming. They are disciplined, mannered. whose sentiments it reflects
3. "I think so" and "Yes, all this is sorrow." "How long . . . death?"
4. "leave a little love always lit"; a little love and a nightlight in an infant's bedroom

Interpreting Meanings
1. puzzled and dispirited. The cemetery is a symbol of the nation's sorrow.
2. lines 5 and 8, which provide conflicting views. It unifies the poem and creates emphasis appropriate to a lament.
3. a friend, a politician. It is hard to remain hopeful and productive amidst death.
4. other dispirited Israelis. Do not give up hope and love.

Applying Meanings
Possible response: expression of feelings, solidarity of mourners; when too extended or embittered

Creative Writing Response
Writing an Elegy. Elegies should express grief, melancholy, or sadness.

Critical Writing Response
Writing About an Extended Simile. Essays should identify a main theme.

Language and Vocabulary
1. d 2. e 3. a 4. b 5. c ◼

First Thoughts
Would you say the poem ends on a positive or a negative note? Explain your response.

Identifying Facts
1. What is the speaker's first answer to the opening question? What is he wearing as he stands in the cemetery?
2. What two statements does the speaker make about graveyards? What does he not know about the inscription on the small brick tablet?
3. What two answers to the opening question does the speaker give in lines 13–23? What other question does he ask here?
4. In lines 13–23, what does the speaker request? What comparison does he make?

Interpreting Meanings
1. How would you describe the speaker's attitude until line 17? What growing realization on the speaker's part is traced by the **incremental repetition** in lines 1, 13–14, and 18?
2. Identify another example of **incremental repetition** and the contrast it presents. What overall effect does all the repetition have?
3. Who might the speaker be quoting in line 14? What does the question in lines 14–17 reveal about modern Israeli experience?
4. In his request in lines 18–19, whom might the speaker be addressing? What advice might the **extended simile** in lines 18–23 be giving to modern Israelis and other war victims?

Applying Meanings
What positive functions does grieving for the dead provide? When can such grieving become negative?

Creative Writing Response
Writing an Elegy.   An **elegy** is a poem of mourning or lament. Write an elegy in which you honor the memory of the victims of a particular war or another human disaster. Your poem may also address the needs and feelings of survivors, as Amichai's does.

Critical Writing Response
Writing About an Extended Simile.   In a brief essay, explain how the **extended simile** in lines 18–23 helps express the theme of the poem. Include answers to the following questions in your essay: What two dissimilar things are being compared? What qualities do they share? How does the simile bring an abstract concept down to earth?

Language and Vocabulary
Hebrew and English

Over the centuries English has borrowed words from Hebrew. Some came to English directly; many came from other languages, including Yiddish, the Germanic tongue once used by many European Jews. For the exercise below, use a dictionary to help you match the English words in the left-hand column with the information about their origins in the right-hand column. Be sure you know the meanings of all the listed words.

1. amen — a. from the Hebrew for "fitting; right; proper"
2. kibbutz — b. from a Hebrew term meaning "anointed (one)"
3. kosher — c. from the Hebrew for "to rest"
4. messiah — d. from a Hebrew exclamation literally meaning "truly; certainly"
5. sabbath — e. from the modern Hebrew for a collective farm in Israel

Santha Rama Rau
b. 1923, India

Wide World Photo

Santha Rama Rau (sän'thä räm'ä rou) was raised by broad-minded parents who had traveled all over the globe. Still, they were upset when she took her first job. "My family didn't mind my *working*," she explained, "but they were worried about the idea of my *earning money*. It wasn't considered entirely respectable for a girl whose family could afford to support her until she got married to be actually picking up a paycheck." Nevertheless, Rama Rau insisted on a writing career, and finally her parents

relented. After all, their daughter had already published her first book, *Home to India* (1945), and the positive reviews of this autobiographical memoir were strong persuasion indeed.

The daughter of an Indian diplomat, Rama Rau was born when India was still a colony of Britain. When she was eleven, Rama Rau went to Europe to stay with her father, who was serving as India's Deputy High Commissioner in London. She attended London's St. Paul's School for Girls and during the summer often vacationed in France. When she was sixteen, she returned to India and found that she was something of an outsider. In an effort to rediscover her native land, she wrote *Home to India* while she was a student at Wellesley College in Massachusetts.

Living in India after World War II, Rama Rau witnessed firsthand all the excitement surrounding her nation's independence in 1947. In that same year she took a sabbatical, or period of leave, from her editing job at Bombay's *Trend* magazine to accompany her father to his new post as India's first ambassador to Japan. She recounted her experiences in the highly regarded travel book *East of Home*, published in 1950.

Two years later Rama Rau married an American and settled in New York City, where she began contributing articles to American magazines. Her essay "By Any Other Name," reprinted here, was published first in *The New Yorker*.

OBJECTIVES
1. *To interpret an informal essay about the clash of cultures in British India*
2. *To recognize the essay form and the differences between formal and informal (personal) essays*
3. *To write a personal essay and an analysis of the purpose of an author's essay*

THEMES IN WORLD LITERATURE

Conflict of Cultures and Values
The Book of Ruth, pp. 177–184
"The Train from Rhodesia," pp. 1351–1357
From *Kaffir Boy*, pp. 1365–1376

Coming of Age
From *Sundiata: An Epic of Old Mali*, pp. 102–117
"A Walk to the Jetty" from *Annie John*, pp. 1320–1328 ∎

VOCABULARY IN CONTEXT
The words listed below will appear in the side margin at the point of instruction:

1. precarious 4. palpitating
2. provincial 5. tepid
3. insular

PREREADING FOCUS

Background: British India included not only present-day India but also the contemporary countries of Pakistan, Bangladesh, Sri Lanka, and several other nearby nations. Present-day India, independent since 1947, is about 80 percent Hindu.
    Rama Rau, a Hindu of the Brahmin (highest) caste, was grounded in Hindu teachings during the early years of her life. Her instructor was her mother, who educated both Santha and her sister at home until Santha was five and a half years old (when the events of "By Any Other Name" take place). The lesson books that the girls used were written in Hindi, the most widely spoken of India's many languages; however, as the daughter of a distinguished diplomat in British-run India, Santha was quite young when she began to learn English.

Literary Focus: The word *essay* comes from the French *essai*, meaning "attempt." The term was first popularized by the Renaissance writer usually named as the father of the informal essay, Michel de Montaigne (män·tän′) (1533–1592). One of the first great essayists in the English language was Sir Francis Bacon (1561–1626), sometimes named the father of the formal essay. Among the best-known informal essayists in English is Charles Lamb (1775–1834), who published his essays under the pen name Elia.

Reader's Guide

BY ANY OTHER NAME

Background

During the long British presence in India, many British soldiers, settlers, and public officials moved to India to seek their fortunes and aid in governing and controlling the land. These people became known as Anglo-Indians. While the British contributed to the modernization of India, they also often neglected, misinterpreted, or denigrated native Indian customs. In "By Any Other Name," Santha Rama Rau illuminates this clash of cultures by recalling a childhood incident.

Writer's Response

Recall an incident in your own childhood that first introduced you to the traditions of a different ethnic, religious, or national group, either in real life or through a book, movie, or television show. How were these people different from you, and how did you feel about them? Did the incident make you see yourself or your own culture differently?

Literary Focus

An **essay** is a short piece of nonfiction prose that usually examines a single subject. Essays are sometimes classified as formal or informal. A **formal essay** is serious and impersonal in tone. Often it carefully and logically explains a subject or tries to persuade readers to accept a particular way of thinking. An **informal essay**, also called a **personal essay**, generally reveals far more about the personality and feelings of the author. Many informal essays—including Santha Rama Rau's—are autobiographical in nature, recounting an episode or series of related episodes from the author's life.

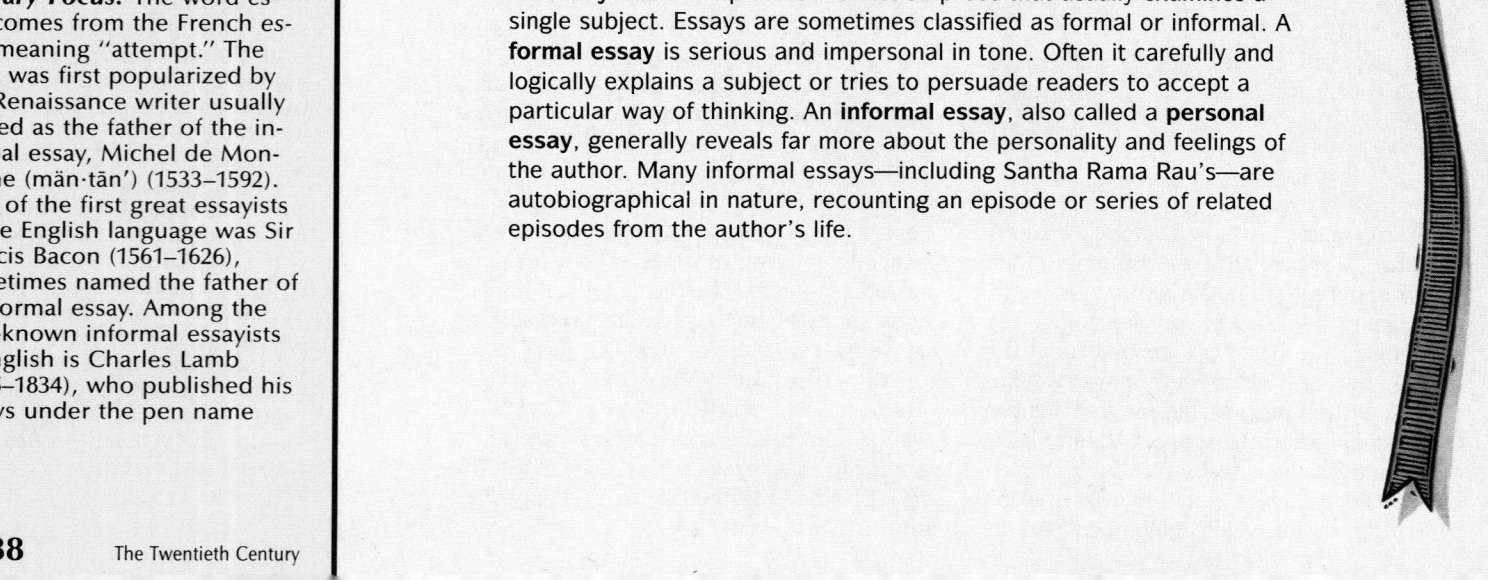

Coordinate Adjectives

By custom, the adjectives before a noun occupy particular positions based on the kinds of information that they convey. For example, we say *big red house*, not *red big house*. We can also use two or more adjectives that occupy the same customary position. These coordinate adjectives are separated with a comma: *costly, elegant house*. You can tell that adjectives are coordinate and thus require a comma if it sounds natural to you to reverse their positions or insert *and* between them.

Reading and Speaking. Using the first two pages of the essay, students should identify examples of coordinate adjectives and the nouns that they modify (*hot, windless morning*; etc.) and examples in which adjectives that precede a noun are not coordinate (*pretty English names*, etc.). ∎

BY ANY OTHER NAME
Santha Rama Rau

The title of this essay comes from Shakespeare's **Romeo and Juliet:**

> *What's in a name? That which we call a rose*
> *By any other name would smell as sweet.*

As you read the essay, think about Rama Rau's reasons for choosing this particular title.

1. At the Anglo-Indian day school in Zorinabad[1] to which my sister and I were sent when she was eight and I was five and a half, they changed our names. On the first day of school, a hot, windless morning of a north Indian September, we stood in the headmistress's study and she said, "Now you're the *new* girls. What are your names?"

My sister answered for us. "I am Premila, and she"—nodding in my direction—"is Santha."

2. The headmistress had been in India, I suppose, fifteen years or so, but she still smiled her helpless inability to cope with Indian names. Her rimless half-glasses glittered, and the <u>precarious</u> bun on the top of her head trembled as she shook her head. "Oh, my dears, those are much too hard for me. Suppose we give you pretty English names. Wouldn't that be more jolly? Let's see, now—Pamela for you, I think." She shrugged in a baffled way at my sister. "That's as close as I can get. And for *you*" she said to me, "how about Cynthia? Isn't that nice?"

My sister was always less easily intimidated than I was, and while she kept a stubborn silence, I said, "Thank you," in a very tiny voice.

We had been sent to that school because my father, among his responsibilities as an officer of the civil service, had a tour of duty to perform in the villages around that steamy little <u>provincial</u> town, where he had his headquarters at that time. He used to make his shorter inspection tours on horseback, and a week before, in the stale heat of a typically postmonsoon[2] day, we had waved goodbye to him and a little procession—an assistant, a secretary, two bearers, and the man to look after the bedding rolls and luggage. They rode away through our large garden, still bright green from the rains, and we turned back into the twilight of the house and the sound of fans whispering in every room.

Up to then, my mother had refused to send Premila to school in the British-run establishments of that time, because, she

---

1. **Zorinabad:** town in northern India.

2. **postmonsoon:** referring to the dry spell that generally follows the rainy season, when ocean winds called monsoons bring rain to India.

TEACHER'S RESOURCES
- ✔ Vocabulary Activity Worksheet
- ✔ Vocabulary Test
- ✔ Review and Response Worksheet
- ✔ Selection Test

1 GUIDED READING
Finding the Main Idea: What is the most important detail in the opening sentence? ("they changed our names") Why do you think the author puts it at the end of the sentence? (for emphasis)

2 EVALUATING
Are *Santha* and *Premila* actually hard for English speakers to pronounce? (no) If not, why do you think the headmistress changes the girls' names? (Possible response: She does not value Indian culture and wants to make Indian students more "English.")

> **precarious** (pri·ker'ē·əs): dependent upon circumstances; uncertain; insecure
>
> **provincial** (prə·vin'shəl): narrow; limited; unsophisticated

3 LITERARY ELEMENT
Theme: Who considered the
examinations and degrees
from the Indian schools invalid? (British authorities) What
does this attitude reveal about
the English? (Possible response: They were ethnocentric and did not respect the
culture of India.)

4 CULTURAL DIVERSITY
Hindi, a modern descendant of
Sanskrit, is the most widely
spoken of the hundreds of languages of India. It has contributed many words to English—
*bandanna, bangle, bungalow,
dungarees, loot, pajamas,
polo, shampoo,* and *thug,* to
name only a few.
❓ *What historical experience
helps to explain the fact
that so many English words
have been borrowed from
Hindi?* (British rule in India
brought together English and
Hindi speakers.)

5 READER'S RESPONSE
Do you find Santha's confusion about her "English name"
surprising? (Responses may
vary, but students should not
find it surprising that a child of
five and a half would have
trouble remembering a foreign
name that was assigned to her
by a stranger.)

---

used to say, "you can bury a dog's tail for
seven years and it still comes out curly, and
you can take a Britisher away from his home
for a lifetime and he still remains insular."
The examinations and degrees from entirely
Indian schools were not, in those days, considered valid. In my case, the question had
never come up, and probably never would
have come up if Mother's extraordinary
good health had not broken down. For the
first time in my life, she was not able to
continue the lessons she had been giving us
every morning. So our Hindi[3] books were
put away, the stories of the Lord Krishna[4]
as a little boy were left in midair, and we
were sent to the Anglo-Indian school.

That first day at school is still, when I
think of it, a remarkable one. At that age, if
one's name is changed, one develops a curious form of dual personality. I remember
having a certain detached and disbelieving
concern in the actions of "Cynthia," but certainly no responsibility. Accordingly, I followed the thin, erect back of the
headmistress down the veranda to my classroom feeling, at most, a passing interest in
what was going to happen to me in this
strange, new atmosphere of School.

The building was Indian in design, with
wide verandas opening onto a central courtyard, but Indian verandas are usually white-
washed, with stone floors. These, in the
tradition of British schools, were painted
dark brown and had matting on the floors.
It gave a feeling of extra intensity to the
heat.

I suppose there were about a dozen Indian
children in the school—which contained
perhaps forty children in all—and four of
them were in my class. They were all sitting
at the back of the room, and I went to join
them. I sat next to a small, solemn girl who
didn't smile at me. She had long, glossy black
braids and wore a cotton dress, but she still
kept on her Indian jewelry—a gold chain
around her neck, thin gold bracelets, and
tiny ruby studs in her ears. Like most Indian
children, she had a rim of black kohl[5] around
her eyes. The cotton dress should have
looked strange, but all I could think of was
that I should ask my mother if I couldn't
wear a dress to school, too, instead of my
Indian clothes.

I can't remember too much about the proceedings in class that day, except for the
beginning. The teacher pointed to me and
asked me to stand up. "Now, dear, tell the
class your name."

I said nothing.

"Come along," she said, frowning slightly.
"What's your name, dear?"

"I don't know," I said, finally.

The English children in the front of the
class—there were about eight or ten of
them—giggled and twisted around in their
chairs to look at me. I sat down quickly and
opened my eyes very wide, hoping in that
way to dry them off. The little girl with the
braids put out her hand and very lightly
touched my arm. She still didn't smile.

Most of that morning I was rather bored.
I looked briefly at the children's drawings
pinned to the wall, and then concentrated
on a lizard clinging to the ledge of the high,
barred window behind the teacher's head.
Occasionally it would shoot out its long yellow tongue for a fly, and then it would rest,
with its eyes closed and its belly palpitating,

---

3. **Hindi** (hin′dē): an Indo-European language that is
now considered the official language of India.
4. **Lord Krishna:** in the Hindu religion, human form
taken by the god Vishnu; many Hindu stories recount episodes in the life of Lord Krishna.

5. **kohl** (kōl): dark powder used as eye makeup.

Schoolgirl in Ahmadabad, India.

as though it were swallowing several times quickly. The lessons were mostly concerned with reading and writing and simple numbers—things that my mother had already taught me—and I paid very little attention. The teacher wrote on the easel blackboard words like "bat" and "cat," which seemed babyish to me; only "apple" was new and incomprehensible.

When it was time for the lunch recess, I followed the girl with braids out onto the veranda. There the children from the other classes were assembled. I saw Premila at once and ran over to her, as she had charge of our lunchbox. The children were all opening packages and sitting down to eat sandwiches. Premila and I were the only ones who had Indian food—thin wheat chapatties,[6] some vegetable curry, and a bottle of buttermilk. Premila thrust half of it into my hand and whispered fiercely that I should go and sit with my class, because that was what the others seemed to be doing.

The enormous black eyes of the little Indian girl from my class looked at my food longingly, so I offered her some. But she only shook her head and plowed her way solemnly through her sandwiches.

I was very sleepy after lunch, because at home we always took a siesta. It was usually a pleasant time of day, with the bedroom darkened against the harsh afternoon sun, the drifting off into sleep with the sound of Mother's voice reading a story in one's mind, and, finally, the shrill, fussy voice of the ayah[7] waking one for tea.

At school, we rested for a short time on low, folding cots on the veranda, and then we were expected to play games. During the hot part of the afternoon we played indoors, and after the shadows had begun to lengthen and the slight breeze of the evening had come up we moved outside to the wide courtyard.

I had never really grasped the system of competitive games. At home, whenever we played tag or guessing games, I was always allowed to "win"—"because," Mother used to tell Premila, "she is the youngest, and we have to allow for that." I had often heard her say it, and it seemed quite reasonable to

6. **chapatties** (chə·pä′tēz): thin unleavened fried bread.

7. **ayah** (ä′yə): nanny in India.

6 SPECULATING
Why do you think *apple*, as common as *cat* in England and the United States, is "new and incomprehensible" to Santha? (Apple trees grow in cool climates, and their fruit was apparently not exported to India at the time of the selection.) What does the teaching of the word *apple* reveal? (British ethnocentricity)

7 CULTURAL BACKGROUND
Curry, meaning "powder made from a blend of spices" or "sauce or stew made with this powder," is an Indian word that has entered the English language. It comes not from Hindi but from Tamil, a language native to southern India. *Which meaning of* curry *is used here?* (the stew)

8 INTERPRETING
Why does Santha's Indian classmate refuse the food she longs for? (School officials have denigrated all aspects of Indian culture, and so the girl will eat only English food at school.)

me, but the result was that I had no clear idea of what "winning" meant.

When we played twos-and-threes[8] that afternoon at school, in accordance with my training, I let one of the small English boys catch me, but was naturally rather puzzled when the other children did not return the courtesy. I ran about for what seemed like hours without ever catching anyone, until it was time for school to close. Much later I learned that my attitude was called "not being a good sport," and I stopped allowing myself to be caught, but it was not for years that I really learned the spirit of the thing.

When I saw our car come up to the school gate, I broke away from my classmates and rushed toward it yelling, "Ayah! Ayah!" It seemed like an eternity since I had seen her that morning—a wizened, affectionate figure **9** in her white cotton sari,[9] giving me dozens of urgent and useless instructions on how to be a good girl at school. Premila followed more sedately, and she told me on the way home never to do that again in front of the other children.

When we got home we went straight to Mother's high, white room to have tea with her, and I immediately climbed onto the bed and bounced gently up and down on the springs. Mother asked how we had liked our first day in school. I was so pleased to be home and to have left that peculiar Cynthia behind that I had nothing whatever to say about school, except to ask what "apple" meant. But Premila told Mother about the classes, and added that in her class they had weekly tests to see if they had learned their lessons well.

I asked, "What's a test?"

Premila said, "You're too small to have them. You won't have them in your class for donkey's years."[10] She had learned the expression that day and was using it for the first time. We all laughed enormously at her **10** wit. She also told Mother, in an aside, that we should take sandwiches to school the next day. Not, she said, that *she* minded. But they would be simpler for me to handle.

That whole lovely evening I didn't think about school at all. I sprinted barefoot across the lawns with my favorite playmate, the cook's son, to the stream at the end of the garden. We quarreled in our usual way, waded in the tepid water under the lime trees, and waited for the night to bring out the smell of the jasmine.[11] I listened with **11** fascination to his stories of ghosts and demons, until I was too frightened to cross the garden alone in the semidarkness. The ayah found me, shouted at the cook's son, scolded me, hurried me in to supper—it was an entirely usual, wonderful evening.

It was a week later, the day of Premila's first test, that our lives changed rather abruptly. I was sitting at the back of my class, in my usual inattentive way, only half listening to the teacher. I had started a rather guarded friendship with the girl with the braids, whose name turned out to be Nalini (Nancy in school). The three other Indian children were already fast friends. Even at that age it was apparent to all of us that friendship with the English or Anglo-Indian **12** children was out of the question. Occasionally, during the class, my new friend and I

---

8. **twos-and-threes:** game similar to tag.
9. **sari** (sä′rē): a long piece of cloth wrapped around the body to form a skirt and mantle; it is the main form of dress worn by Hindu women.
10. **donkey's years:** English expression meaning "a long time."
11. **jasmine** (jaz′min): tropical shrub with fragrant flowers.

READING CHECK
1. How old is Santha at the time of the selection? (five and a half years old)
2. What English name does the headmistress assign to Santha? (Cynthia)
3. How are the sisters' lunches different from those of the other Indian students? (Only they have Indian food.)

4. During the test, why does Premila's teacher stipulate that a vacant desk must separate one Indian student from another? (She believes that all Indians cheat.)
5. What is Premila's reaction to this treatment? (She makes Santha leave school with her.)

RETEACHING
Have students recount significant incidents from the essay from Premila's point of view. Students may choose to write a series of diary entries or oral retellings, beginning with Premila's first day at the school.

would draw pictures and show them to each other secretly.

The door opened sharply and Premila marched in. At first, the teacher smiled at her in a kindly and encouraging way and said, "Now, you're little Cynthia's sister?"

Premila didn't even look at her. She stood with her feet planted firmly apart and her shoulders rigid, and addressed herself directly to me. "Get up," she said. "We're going home."

I didn't know what had happened, but I was aware that it was a crisis of some sort. I rose obediently and started to walk toward my sister.

"Bring your pencils and your notebook," she said.

I went back for them, and together we left the room. The teacher started to say something just as Premila closed the door, but we didn't wait to hear what it was.

In complete silence we left the school grounds and started to walk home. Then I asked Premila what the matter was. All she would say was "We're going home for good."

It was a very tiring walk for a child of five and a half, and I dragged along behind Premila with my pencils growing sticky in my hand. I can still remember looking at the dusty hedges, and the tangles of thorns in the ditches by the side of the road, smelling the faint fragrance from the eucalyptus trees and wondering whether we would ever reach home. Occasionally a horse-drawn tonga[12] passed us, and the women, in their pink or green silks, stared at Premila and me trudging along on the side of the road. A few coolies[13] and a line of women carrying baskets of vegetables on their heads smiled at us. But it was nearing the hottest time of day, and the road was almost deserted. I walked more and more slowly, and shouted to Premila, from time to time, "Wait for me!" with increasing peevishness. She spoke to me only once, and that was to tell me to carry my notebook on my head, because of the sun.

When we got to our house the ayah was just taking a tray of lunch into Mother's room. She immediately started a long, worried questioning about what are you children doing back here at this hour of the day.

Mother looked very startled and very concerned, and asked Premila what had happened.

Premila said, "We had our test today, and she made me and the other Indians sit at the back of the room, with a desk between each one."

Mother said, "Why was that, darling?"

"She said it was because Indians cheat," Premila added. "So I don't think we should go back to that school."

Mother looked very distant, and was silent a long time. At last she said, "Of course not, darling." She sounded displeased.

We all shared the curry she was having for lunch, and afterward I was sent off to the beautifully familiar bedroom for my siesta. I could hear Mother and Premila talking through the open door.

Mother said, "Do you suppose she understood all that?"

Premila said, "I shouldn't think so. She's a baby."

Mother said, "Well, I hope it won't bother her."

Of course, they were both wrong. I understood it perfectly, and I remember it all very clearly. But I put it happily away, because it had all happened to a girl called Cynthia, and I never was really particularly interested in her.

12. **tonga:** two-wheeled carriage.
13. **coolies:** manual laborers.

WRITING TO LEARN

Geography/Earth Science: Based on what you have learned from the essay, write a one-paragraph description of the climate in this part of India. ∎

13 COMPARING LITERATURE
The teacher's overt prejudices are similar to the attitudes and behavior of Clyde in the selection from *Kaffir Boy*.
❓ *In what ways is the teacher's behavior more reprehensible than Clyde's?* (Clyde is a child echoing adult prejudices to another child, whereas the teacher is an adult who is responsible for nurturing children and teaching them the truth, not hurting their feelings and spreading lies about them. Premila's teacher is reminiscent of the school officials whom Clyde echoes and who are to blame for his biased behavior.)

14 EVALUATING
Do you think that the author succeeded in putting it "happily away"? (Possible response: No. At five, she might have been happy merely to stop going to school and to give up her English name, but as she grew older she did not forget the painful prejudices she had encountered; otherwise, she could not have communicated the episode so well in this essay.)

1. Foreign Cuisine. Students interested in the Indian foods mentioned in the essay might obtain Santha Rama Rau's Indian cookbook or perhaps one of Madhur Jaffrey's highly regarded Indian cookbooks, and plan and prepare an Indian meal for their classmates. Other students may want to work together to write individual reviews of the dishes that they sample.

2. Biographical Entries. Interested students should be encouraged to read other autobiographical essays in Rama Rau's *Gifts of Passage* and then write brief paragraphs as they might appear in an encyclopedia, a biographical dictionary, or another reference work.

CLOSURE

Have students discuss what the essay reveals about the conflicts of colonial rule. Why do they think achieving independence has been such an important issue in the twentieth century? ■

ANSWERS

First Thoughts
Answers will vary.

Identifying Facts
1. five and a half and eight. The British were too insular to respect Indian ways.
2. fifteen years. too hard to pronounce
3. She claims not to know her name. They are Indian, not English.

Interpreting Meanings
1. They will lose respect for Indian ways. They are justified.
2. She made no effort to learn Indian ways, and she is insensitive to Indian students' feelings. lack of respect for other cultures
3. During her first test, the teacher isolates the Indian students, claiming that Indians cheat. prejudice and insensitivity
4. The emphasis is on personal experiences and feelings. In her child's mind, names have power, but the title suggests that a change in name is not a change in essence.
5. Possible response: to show that the British do not live up to their noblest ideals

Applying Meanings
Answers will vary.

Creative Writing Response
Writing a Personal Essay. Essays should include thoughts and feelings.

Critical Writing Response
Analyzing an Essay's Purpose. Essays should recognize ethnocentric prejudice as the main concern. ■

First Thoughts
Do you think that because the author was called Cynthia at school, she would have always felt that what happened there was not significant? Why do you think that Premila's name change did not have a similar effect on her?

Identifying Facts
1. How old are the author and her sister at the time of this incident? Why had the girls' mother not sent them to a British-run school before?
2. For about how long has the headmistress lived in India? What reason does she give for changing Santha's and Premila's names?
3. What causes the English children to laugh at the author on her first day of school? How do her clothes and lunch differ from those of the Indian children who have been there longer?

Interpreting Meanings
1. What is Santha's mother afraid might happen if her daughters attend a British-run school? What do the details about the other Indian students show about her fears?
2. What criticisms of the headmistress does the third paragraph imply? What related criticism of the British in India does the eighth paragraph imply?
3. What prompts Premila to leave school? What does the incident reveal about the British attitude toward and treatment of Indians?
4. How do you know that this is an **informal essay**? How does the author's childhood attitude toward names contrast with the idea implied by the title?
5. Why do you think Rama Rau drew her title from a Shakespearean play instead of a classical Indian work?

Applying Meanings
Have you ever felt differently when people called you a different name (Beth or Lizzy instead of Elizabeth, or Chuck instead of Charles)? Explain, providing examples.

Creative Writing Response
Writing a Personal Essay. Write a brief personal essay describing your first day of school or some other school-related experience from your childhood.

Critical Writing Response
Analyzing an Essay's Purpose. In one paragraph, explain what you see as Rama Rau's main purpose in writing this essay. In a second paragraph, describe your response to the essay and tell whether or not you think Rama Rau accomplishes her purpose.

To help you decide what the essay's purpose is, you may find it helpful to list, on a chart like the one below, the selection details that point to the author's purpose. Remember to consider how the title relates to the essay's message.

Detail or Incident	Message It Helps to Convey

Yasunari Kawabata
1899–1972, Japan

Yousof Karsh/Woodfin Camp & Associates

The concern with loneliness and death that pervades the novels and short stories of Yasunari Kawabata (yä·sü′nä·re kä′wä·bä′tä) may be the result of his childhood. His father died when Kawabata was three; the following year, his mother died. Within the next five years, his only sister and his grandmother died. At age fourteen, Kawabata began to record his thoughts and feelings when he saw that his grandfather, who had raised him for about six years, was growing very ill. These writings were published after his grandfather's death as *Diary of a Sixteen-Year-Old* (1925).

Born in Osaka, Japan, Kawabata attended Tokyo Imperial University, where he studied both English literature and Japanese literature. In 1924, he joined with other students to found a literary magazine that became the mouthpiece of a new avant-garde literary movement called Neosensualism, which was influenced, in part, by haiku poetry. Neosensualist writings tried to capture intense, immediate moments in life—images, sensations, and impressions. To achieve this immediacy in his novels, Kawabata placed one psychologically charged scene right after another, with no transitions. This technique gives the effect, one critic wrote, of "a series of brief flashes in a void."

Kawabata's novels include *The Izu Dancer* (1926), *The Snow Country* (1948), *Thousand Cranes* (1952), *The Sound of the Mountain* (1952), and *The House of the Sleeping Beauties* (1961). These novels, which focus on lonely men who try to find comfort in the beauty and goodness of women, are characterized by nostalgia and sadness.

Kawabata died alone in his studio in 1972, about a year and a half after his friend, the novelist Yukio Mishima, had committed ritual suicide for political reasons. Kawabata also took his own life, but he left no explanation of his motives.

In 1968, Kawabata became the first Japanese writer to be awarded the Nobel Prize in literature. In his acceptance speech, he remarked on an aspect of traditional Japanese ink painting that applies, with startling accuracy, to his own work and to his life: "The heart [of it] is in space, abbreviation, what is left undrawn."

ABOUT THE AUTHOR

As a boy, Kawabata wanted to become a painter, an interest that influenced his writing. The journal he helped to found, *Bungei Jidai* ("The Artistic Age"), attempted the literary equivalents of the artistic techniques of expressionism, cubism, dadaism, and surrealism. Kawabata's works contain incongruous imagery, as well as striking visual passages that exhibit a skillful use of color.

By the time Kawabata received the Nobel Prize, he was already an internationally acclaimed writer who had received several French awards, a German award, and every major literary award in Japan. His work is valued in Japan for precisely those qualities that are difficult to capture in translation: exact images (as in a series of linked haiku), an allusive quality, and a poetic sense of nostalgia, melancholy, and impermanence. His characters often experience a tragic sense of loss, usually the loss of beauty, purity, and serenity that they associate with the past. Western readers, who may miss these nuances, sometimes find it hard to understand Kawabata's stories and novels. Readers are not helped by the fact that Kawabata did not worry about novelistic form. More than once, one of his short stories that appeared in a magazine simply grew to novel length through additions in subsequent issues of the same—or even of a different—magazine.

OBJECTIVES

1. *To interpret a modern Japanese short story*
2. *To identify the theme of a short story*
3. *To write a description of a valued object and an essay analyzing a story's themes*
4. *To identify origins and meanings of words from Asian and Pacific languages and recognize these languages' contributions to English*

THEMES IN WORLD LITERATURE

Life and Loss
"Letter to His Two Small Children," pp. 520–521
"Jade Flower Palace," p. 530

Generations
"A Walk to the Jetty," pp. 1320–1328
"Love Must Not Be Forgotten," pp. 1414–1427 ∎

VOCABULARY IN CONTEXT
The words listed below will appear in the side margin at the point of instruction:

1. spurned
2. hexagonal
3. exquisite
4. discrimination
5. antipathy

PREREADING FOCUS

Background: During this period, the typical Japanese household consisted of several generations. This story implies that young women may have contributed all or part of their earnings to the household, receiving in return a small allowance for personal use. Students may notice the absence of men in the story. Because of the war, men worked long hours at their jobs or served in military positions. However, Kawabata emphasizes the wartime setting only in the final scene, so he may have omitted male characters for literary reasons.

Writer's Response: This activity could also be done orally. Have students share anecdotes with the class or with members of small discussion groups.

Literary Focus: Have students consider themes of other short stories they have read. Ask them also to recall how they inferred themes of haiku poems (pp. 572–577). Point out that a work may carry more than one theme and that a reader's own background contributes to the themes a reader perceives. Also point out that clues to the theme of a work can be found in how the main character changes and how conflicts have been resolved. Tell students to be aware that Kawabata often used symbols, as much as plot and characterization, to convey meaning.

Reader's Guide ∎

THE SILVER FIFTY-SEN PIECES

Background

Kawabata is best known for his novels, but he also wrote what he called *tanagokoro no shosetsu,* or "palm-of-the-hand stories." In their deceptive simplicity, these stories resemble haiku poetry (see pages 572–577). Just as a haiku offers brief, vivid images that rival the richness of a longer poem, so these little stories offer images and psychological insights that rival those of longer fiction. Kawabata's palm-of-the-hand stories convey themes that run throughout his work: loneliness, loss, alienation, love, guilt, old age, and death. He produced, some say, as many as 146 of these stories during his career. "Many writers, in their youth, write poetry," he said. "I, instead of poetry, wrote the palm-of-the-hand stories. . . . [T]he poetic spirit of my young days lives on in them."

The protagonist of "The Silver Fifty-Sen Pieces" is a young woman living in Tokyo, Japan, in the years prior to and during Japan's war with China and Manchuria (1937–1945) and just after World War II (1939–1945). Young women living in their parents' household often worked as secretaries or held other low-level jobs for several years before "retiring" to get married by age twenty-five.

Writer's Response

Family members and groups of friends often cherish anecdotes about one another and embellish these stories through repeated telling. These anecdotes usually relate to small events; they are humorous and offer insight into the character of the person they are about. Freewrite some of your recollections of stories your family or friends enjoy telling over and over again about people they know. Aside from the entertainment value of these stories, do you think they might serve a deeper purpose among the members of the group? Explain.

Literary Focus

Theme is the central idea or insight expressed in a work of literature. Theme moves beyond the specific work to express a general idea or insight about life or human nature. Sometimes authors state a theme directly, but more often they imply or suggest it through descriptive details, images, or symbols in the work itself.

THE SILVER FIFTY-SEN PIECES

Yasunari Kawabata
translated by
LANE DUNLOP AND J. MARTIN HOLMAN

◆ *A critic wrote that "Kawabata's prose abounds with tiny flashes of descriptive insight, usually filtering through the consciousness of the main character." Read the story through once. Then, as you read it a second time, try to pinpoint the tiny flashes of insight, or realization, that the main character experiences.*

It was a custom that the two-yen allowance that she received at the start of each month, in silver fifty-sen[1] pieces, be placed in Yoshiko's purse by her mother's own hand.

At that time, the fifty-sen piece had recently been reduced in size. These silver coins, which looked light and felt heavy, seemed to Yoshiko to fill up her small red leather purse with a solid dignity. Often, careful not to waste them, she kept them in her handbag until the end of the month. It was not that Yoshiko <u>spurned</u> such girlish pleasures as going out to a movie theater or a coffee shop with the friends she worked with; she simply saw those diversions as being outside her life. She had never experienced them, and so was never tempted by them.

HRW photo by Sam Dudgeon

Japanese fifty-sen coins, pre–World War II.

Once a week, on her way back from the office, she would stop off at a department store and buy, for ten sen, a loaf of the seasoned French bread she liked so much. Other than that, there was nothing she particularly wanted for herself.

One day, however, at Mitsukoshi's, in the stationery department, a glass paperweight caught her eye. <u>Hexagonal</u>, it had a dog carved on it in relief.[2] Charmed by the dog,

---

1. **two-yen, fifty-sen:** A fifty-sen piece is half of one yen (¥), the basic monetary unit of Japan. (One hundred sen equal one yen.) Exchange rates vary, but one yen has usually been equivalent to an amount much less than one U.S. dollar.

2. **relief:** a sculptured shape raised from a flat background surface.

3 Kinesthetic Learners: Have students handle a palm-sized object with an unusual shape or texture—perhaps a stone with smooth and rough areas. ■

4 INFERRING
What details tell you that buying the paperweight is somehow unusual or significant for Yoshiko? (She returns for ten days to look at it; her heart beats fast when she buys it.)

5 COMPARING AND CONTRASTING
Compare the reaction that Yoshiko's mother and sister have to the paperweight to Yoshiko's reaction. How do these details set up a contrast between Yoshiko and her mother? (Mother thinks the paperweight is a "pretty" toy, whereas Yoshiko sees it as a technically perfect work of art.)

■ **exquisite** (eks′kwi·zit): beautiful, delicate
discrimination (di·scrim′i·na′shən): ability to make fine distinctions

6 DRAWING CONCLUSIONS
What do these lines tell you about how Yoshiko's family members, particularly her mother, feel about Yoshiko? (Possible responses: They feel affectionate amusement, but perhaps Yoshiko's mother sometimes feels that she is too deliberate and serious.)

1398 The Twentieth Century

3 Yoshiko took the paperweight in her hand. Its thrilling coolness, its unexpected weightiness, suddenly gave her pleasure. Yoshiko, who loved this kind of delicately accomplished work, was captivated despite herself. Weighing it in her palm, looking at it from every angle, she quietly and reluctantly put it back in its box. It was forty sen.

4 The next day, she came back. She examined the paperweight again. The day after that, she came back again and examined it anew. After ten days of this, she finally made up her mind.

"I'll take this," she said to the clerk, her heart beating fast.

When she got home, her mother and older sister laughed at her.

"Buying this sort of thing—it's like a toy."

But when each had taken it in her hand and looked at it, they said, "You're right, it *is* rather pretty," and, "It's so ingenious."

5 They tried holding it up against the light. The polished clear glass surface and the misty surface, like frosted glass, of the relief, harmonized curiously. In the hexagonal facets,[3] too, there was an exquisite rightness, like the meter of a poem. To Yoshiko, it was a lovely work of art.

Although Yoshiko hadn't hoped to be complimented on the deliberation with which she had made her purchase, taking ten days to decide that the paperweight was an object worth her possession, she was pleased to receive this recognition of her good taste from her mother and older sister.

Even if she was laughed at for her exaggerated carefulness—taking those ten days to buy something that cost a mere forty sen—Yoshiko would not have been satisfied

---
3. **facets** (fas′its): A facet is one surface of a many-sided solid figure.

unless she had done so. She had never had occasion to regret having bought something on the spur of the moment. It was not that the seventeen-year-old Yoshiko possessed such meticulous discrimination that she spent several days thinking about and looking at something before arriving at a decision. It was just that she had a vague dread of spending carelessly the silver fifty-sen pieces, which had sunk into her mind as an important treasure.

6 Years later, when the story of the paperweight came up and everybody burst out laughing, her mother said seriously, "I thought you were so lovable that time."

To each and every one of Yoshiko's possessions, an amusing anecdote of this sort was attached.

It was a pleasure to do their shopping from the top down, descending regularly from floor to floor, so first they went up to the fifth floor on the elevator. This Sunday, unusually allured by the charm of a shopping trip with her mother, Yoshiko had come to Mitsukoshi's.

Although their shopping for the day was done, when they'd descended to the first floor, her mother, as a matter of course, went on down to the bargain basement.

"But it's so crowded, Mother. I don't like it," grumbled Yoshiko, but her mother didn't hear her. Evidently the atmosphere of the bargain basement, with its competitive jockeying for position, had already absorbed her mother.

7 The bargain basement was a place set up for the sole purpose of making people waste their money, but perhaps her mother would find something. Thinking she'd keep an eye on her, Yoshiko followed her at a distance. It was air-conditioned so it wasn't all that hot.

Women shopping for umbrellas in a Japanese department store in the late 1930s.

How would you describe the relationship between Yoshiko and her mother in the story?

7 LITERARY ELEMENT
Characterization: What do these paragraphs reveal about Yoshiko's mother? (She enjoys competitive shopping but is not pushy; she sometimes buys things impulsively because she is less discriminating than Yoshiko; she shows sensitivity by buying her own stationery; she looks to Yoshiko for approval and permission.)

8 INTERPRETING
Why do you think Yoshiko's mother is so anxious not to leave the store without buying something? (Possible response: Unlike Yoshiko, the enjoyment of buying or of getting a good deal is what matters to her—not the object she buys.)

antipathy (an·tip′ə·thē): strong dislike, aversion

9 LITERARY ELEMENT
Simile: A simile is a figure of speech that compares two unlike things. Why do you think Kawabata uses this simile to describe how Yoshiko is feeling? (Possible response: Yoshiko feels put upon by her mother's vulnerability to the cheap prices but knows she must be patient and understanding.)

First buying three bundles of stationery for twenty-five sen, her mother turned around and looked at Yoshiko. They smiled sweetly at each other. Lately, her mother had been pilfering Yoshiko's stationery, much to the latter's annoyance. Now we can rest easy, their looks seemed to say.

Drawn toward the counters for kitchen utensils and underwear, Yoshiko's mother was not brave enough to thrust her way through the mob of customers. Standing on tiptoe and peering over people's shoulders or putting her hand out through the small spaces between their sleeves, she looked but nevertheless didn't buy anything. At first unconvinced and then making up her mind definitely no, she headed toward the exit.

"Oh, these are just ninety-five sen? My . . ."

Just this side of the exit, her mother picked up one of the umbrellas for sale. Even after they'd burrowed through the whole heaped-up jumble, every single umbrella bore a price tag of ninety-five sen.

Apparently still surprised, her mother said, "They're so cheap, aren't they, Yoshiko? Aren't they cheap?" Her voice was suddenly lively. It was as if her vague, perplexed reluctance to leave without buying something more had found an outlet. "Well? Don't you think they're cheap?"

"They really are." Yoshiko, too, took one of the umbrellas in her hand. Her mother, holding hers alongside it, opened it up.

"Just the ribs alone would be cheap at the price. The fabric—well, it's rayon, but it's so well made, don't you think?"

How was it possible to sell such a respectable item at this price? As the question flashed through Yoshiko's mind, a strange feeling of antipathy welled up in her, as if she'd been shoved by a cripple. Her mother, totally absorbed, opening up one after the other, rummaged through the pile to find an umbrella suitable to her age. Yoshiko waited a while, then said, "Mother, don't you have

1. How old is Yoshiko, and what does she do during the day? (She is seventeen years old, and she works in an office.)
2. What kind of shopper is Yoshiko? (very careful and discriminating)
3. Where do Yoshiko and her mother go shopping? (a bargain basement)
4. What happens to Yoshiko's mother by the end of the story? (She has died in the firebombing of Tokyo.)

5. What object reminds Yoshiko of her life with her mother? (a glass paperweight)

RETEACHING

Ask students to illustrate this story for a magazine. They may actually create the illustrations, or simply list what they would include in each one. Remind them to include symbolic items that show how the different scenes of the story relate to each other.

10 READER'S RESPONSE

When you have shopped or gone elsewhere with your parents or with an older relative or friend, have you experienced feelings similar to or different from Yoshiko's? (Possible responses: *Similar*—my parents sometimes embarrass me. *Different*—I enjoy shopping and going places with my parents.)

11 SPECULATING

Why do you suppose Yoshiko's mother stops her search for an umbrella and decides to leave the store so abruptly? (Possible response: She realizes that she is wasting time and angering her daughter.)

12 SYNTHESIZING

List events and changes between the 1939 setting and the 1946 setting. (Prices have risen; Tokyo has been bombed; the mother died in the bombing; Yoshiko got married; the paperweight is the only possession Yoshiko has from her life in her mother's house.)

13 LITERARY ELEMENT

Theme: How does the paperweight symbolize the theme of the story? (Possible response: A person's possessions can reveal their character, become an embodiment of their past, and indicate how their lives have changed.)

an umbrella at home?"

"Yes, that's so, but . . ." Glancing quickly at Yoshiko, her mother went on, "It's ten years, no, more, I've had it fifteen years. It's worn out and old-fashioned. And, Yoshiko, if I passed this on to somebody, think how happy they would be."

"That's true. It's all right if it's for a gift."

"There's nobody who wouldn't be happy."

Yoshiko smiled. Her mother seemed to be choosing an umbrella with that "somebody" in mind. But it was not anybody close to them. If it were, surely her mother would not have said "somebody."

"What about this one, Yoshiko?"

"That looks good."

Although she gave an unenthusiastic answer, Yoshiko went to her mother's side and began searching for a suitable umbrella.

Other shoppers, wearing thin summer dresses of rayon and saying, "It's cheap, it's cheap," were casually snapping up the umbrellas on their way into and out of the store.

Feeling pity for her mother, who, her face set and slightly flushed, was trying so hard to find the right umbrella, Yoshiko grew angry at her own hesitation.

As if to say, "Why not just buy one, any one, quickly?" Yoshiko turned away from her mother.

"Yoshiko, let's stop this."

"What?"

A weak smile floating at the corners of her mouth, as if to shake something off, her mother put her hand on Yoshiko's shoulder and left the counter. Now, though, it was Yoshiko who felt some indefinable reluctance. But, when she'd taken five or six steps, she felt relieved.

Taking hold of her mother's hand on her shoulder, she squeezed it hard and swung it together with her own. Pressing close to her mother so that they were shoulder to shoulder, she hurried toward the exit.

This had happened seven years ago, in the year 1939.

When the rain pounded against the fire-scorched sheet-metal roof of the shack, Yoshiko, thinking it would have been good if they had bought that umbrella, found herself wanting to make a funny story of it with her mother. Nowadays, the umbrella would have cost a hundred or two hundred yen. But her mother had died in the firebombings of their Tokyo neighborhood of Kanda.[4]

Even if they had bought the umbrella, it probably would have perished in the flames.

By chance, the glass paperweight had survived. When her husband's house in Yokohama[5] had burned down, the paperweight was among those things that she'd frantically stuffed into an emergency bag. It was her one remembrance of life in her mother's house.

From evening on, in the alley, there were the strange-sounding voices of the neighborhood girls. They were talking about how you could make a thousand yen in a single night. Taking up the forty-sen paperweight, which, when she was those girls' age, she had spent ten days thinking about before deciding to buy, Yoshiko studied the charming little dog carved in relief. Suddenly, she realized that there was not a single dog left in the whole burned-out neighborhood. The thought came as a shock to her.

4. **firebombings . . . Kanda:** For three years before the United States dropped atomic bombs on the Japanese cities of Hiroshima and Nagasaki in August 1945, incendiary (fire-making) bombs were used to devastate Tokyo and cripple its industry. The bombs also destroyed many homes and landmarks.
5. **Yokohama** (yō′kə·hä′mə): a port city south of Tokyo on Tokyo Bay.

1. Haiku Poetry. The power of haiku, like the power of Kawabata's palm-of-the-hand stories, arises from the feelings packed into compressed images. Challenge students to reduce the central incidents of this story to a series of haiku-like poems. They should include Yoshiko's purchase of the paperweight, the bargain basement scene, and the final scene in the metal-roofed shack.

2. Comparing Cultures. Encourage students to research, either alone or in a group, similarities and differences between the cultures of Japan and America in the twentieth century. Tell them to use what this story taught them about Japanese culture as a starting point, and ask them to report their findings to the class.

CLOSURE

Have students discuss how Kawabata takes simple objects—silver coins, a paperweight, and cheap umbrellas—and uses them as symbols to help characterize Yoshiko and her mother and to evoke the atmosphere of a neighborhood devastated by war. Also ask students to discuss how material objects might help someone adjust to traumatic changes, such as personal loss or the devastation of one's home during wartime. ■

First Thoughts

What aspect of this story struck you as the most surprising, puzzling, moving, or disturbing? Why?

Identifying Facts

1. How does Yoshiko usually spend her two-yen allowance?
2. Describe the special object that Yoshiko finally buys. How long does she take to make up her mind? How do her mother and sister react to her purchase?
3. What items attract Yoshiko's mother in the bargain basement? Which of these items does she buy?
4. What details at the end of the story identify the time and location in which the story takes place?

Interpreting Meanings

1. Jot down details from the story that **characterize** Yoshiko and her mother. What contrast between their personalities do these details suggest?
2. What conclusions can you draw about the relationship between Yoshiko and her mother from Yoshiko's thoughts and reactions in the final scene?
3. What message or main idea does the author convey in the umbrella episode in the department store?
4. A **symbol** is a person, place, thing, or event that has meaning in itself and that also stands for something more than itself. What do you think the paperweight symbolizes in the story? Why, in the final scene, does it give Yoshiko a shock?
5. Why do you think Kawabata titled this story "The Silver Fifty-Sen Pieces," rather than "The Paperweight" or "Remembrances"?
6. Summarize the **theme** or central insight that this story suggests to you.

Creative Writing Response

Describing a Special Object. Suppose you had to pack and move in such a hurry that you could take only one favorite object with you—a picture, a childhood toy, a gift from a friend, something you yourself made, or some other meaningful object. What object would you choose? Write a paragraph in which you describe the object, tell how it came into your life, and explain what it means to you. Also, explain whether this object has taken on different meanings at different times in your life.

Critical Writing Response

Exploring a Theme. In regard to one of Kawabata's novels, a critic wrote that Kawabata returns again and again to a specific moment in time, creating "circles upon circles of memory, coincidence after coincidence, innocent themes followed by their sinister, scarcely audible overtones and echoes." In a brief essay, use details from the story to explain how this observation applies to "The Silver Fifty-Sen Pieces." Look closely at the final scene. How does the story's conclusion endow the theme with "sinister" echoes?

Language and Vocabulary
East Asian and Pacific Languages

English has borrowed a number of words from Chinese, Japanese, and other Asian and Pacific languages. Use a dictionary to find the origin of each of the following words. Write down the meanings of any unfamiliar words.

1. boomerang
2. karate
3. kiwi
4. taboo
5. yak
6. boondocks
7. ketchup
8. sushi
9. tycoon
10. yo-yo

Hwang Sun-won
b. 1915, Korea

Courtesy of Mercury House Books

Hwang Sun-won has lived through many tragic times in his homeland. Born when Korea was a colony of Japan, Hwang saw the Japanese imprison his father for supporting the unsuccessful Korean rebellion of 1919. He went to Japanese-language schools in Korea and then attended a university in Tokyo. Hwang returned home just as Japanese expansionist policies escalated into World War II. Although he was able to publish his first story collection, *The Marsh*, in 1940, Japanese authorities banned Korean writing soon afterward and Hwang had to continue his work in secret.

With the Japanese surrender in 1945, Korea was free of Japanese oppression, but Hwang and others who lived in the north were now subject to Soviet oppression. As communism spread in the north, Hwang and his family fled to the south, then occupied by American forces. They settled for a time in the capital city of Seoul (sōl), but became refugees again when the Communists invaded Seoul at the beginning of the Korean War. The end of the war in 1953 brought only limited happiness to most Koreans, for their nation remained divided and many people found themselves separated from friends and relatives.

Throughout these turbulent times, Hwang continued to produce fiction, even though its publication was often delayed. "Cranes," reprinted here, and many of Hwang's other works suggest that the political divisions between North Korea and South Korea are arbitrary and cruel.

Hwang has enjoyed widespread acclaim in South Korea since the mid-1950s, when his short novel *Descendents of Cain* (1954) won the Free Literature Prize. Although his work, like that of other Korean writers, has been slow to draw the attention of the West, Hwang recently became one of the first Koreans to have his tales appear in English translations in two full-length volumes, *The Book of Masks* (1989) and *Shadows of a Sound* (1990).

OBJECTIVES

1. To interpret a modern Korean short story
2. To identify and distinguish between internal and external conflicts
3. To write a story or a personal essay about a moment of decision, and a critical essay analyzing a character's internal conflict

Reader's Guide

CRANES

Background

After Japan's defeat in World War II, Korea was liberated by Russian forces in the North and American forces in the South. The two groups then helped establish governments with very different ideologies. The dividing line between North and South Korea became the Thirty-eighth Parallel—a line representing a latitude of 38° North. However, in June of 1950—just a year after the Americans had withdrawn most of their troops—Communist forces from the North crossed that parallel in an invasion that marked the beginning of the Korean War. With the support of the United Nations, American and other Western forces helped the South Koreans defend their territory. In 1953 a truce was finally arranged, although skirmishes at the Thirty-eighth Parallel continued to erupt periodically.

During the Korean War, many villages along the Thirty-eighth Parallel changed hands several times. "Cranes" is set in one such village and the countryside around it.

Writer's Response

A title often provides clues to a story's theme. From Southeast Asia to parts of the Mediterranean, the crane is a symbol of justice, longevity, and goodness. Given this information, what are your expectations of a story that is titled "Cranes"?

Literary Focus

The plots of many stories revolve around a **conflict**, a struggle or clash between opposing characters, forces, or emotions. In an **external conflict**, the struggle is against an outside force, such as another character, society as a whole, or an aspect of nature. In an **internal conflict**, the struggle is between opposing desires, choices, or emotions within a single character. Sometimes a story features an internal conflict that is prompted by an external one. For example, a character who must face a deadly lion may also experience an internal struggle between courage and cowardice.

PREREADING FOCUS

Background: Point out that the Korean War, like all civil wars, sometimes pitted relative against relative and neighbor against neighbor. Have students discuss the emotional and physical turmoil that such a situation might create. Ask students to name other stories they have read that focus on civil warfare.

You might also discuss the problems that writers face in times of war and political repression. Note that Korea has a long literary tradition—in fact, the first book printed with movable metal type was printed in Korea in 1234, predating Gutenberg by two centuries. When the Japanese annexed Korea in 1910, however, they discouraged authors from writing in Korean. By the early 1940s all writing in the Korean language was banned. Writers like Hwang were forced to write in secret, with no hope of immediate publication. The subsequent years of civil war also caused frequent delays in the publication of their works. Have students discuss the effects such turmoil might have had on Korea's writers. Ask: What subject matter is likely to concern writers who have lived through years of civil warfare?

Literary Focus: Have students consider the conflicts of other short stories they have read, classifying those conflicts as external or internal. Have them identify stories in which the characters face internal conflicts that stem from external conflicts.

Capitalization Rules for Direction Words

Direction words such as *north*, *south*, *east*, and *west*, should be capitalized when they name a specific region:

Many jazz musicians were born in the *South*.

Last year we toured the *Northwest*.

Do not capitalize these words when they simply identify or indicate direction or location:

Many birds fly *south* for the winter.

In two miles the road turns to the *northwest*.

1. **Reading and Speaking.** Have students find direction words from the story and explain why each of them is or is not capitalized.

2. **Writing and Sharing.** Have students write five sentences about touring America, each using one of these words: *North, South, East, West,*

---

1 LITERARY ELEMENT

Setting: Where does the story open? (near the Thirty-eighth Parallel, the latitude at which North and South Korea are divided) What political conflict does the setting immediately suggest? (the Korean War or plight of the divided nation)

2 GUIDED READING

Finding the Main Idea: To where has Song-sam returned? (a village of his boyhood) Does it seem to him that the place has changed? (While the village shows few traces of physical destruction, it still seems different to him; people seem to be afraid.)

3 GUIDED READING

Finding the Main Idea: Why is Tok-chae tied up? (Southern forces have taken him prisoner because he was vice-chairman of the local Farmers' Communist League.)

4 INFERRING

For which side is Song-sam fighting? (the South) How do you know? (He is taking charge of the prisoner.)

CRANES

Hwang Sun-won

translated by

PETER H. LEE

As you read this story, pay special attention to the conflicting emotions felt by the main character, Song-sam. How is his **internal conflict** *related to the* **external conflict** *in which he is involved? Can you sympathize with his feelings?*

1 The northern village at the border of the Thirty-eighth Parallel was snugly settled under the high, bright autumn sky.

2 One white gourd lay against another on the dirt floor of an empty farmhouse. The occasional village elders first put out their bamboo pipes before passing by, and the children, too, turned aside some distance off. Their faces were ridden with fear.

The village as a whole showed few traces of destruction from the war, but it did not seem like the same village Song-sam[1] had known as a boy.

At the foot of a chestnut grove on the hill behind the village he stopped and climbed a chestnut tree. Somewhere far back in his mind he heard the old man with a wen[2] shout, "You bad boy, you're climbing up my chestnut tree again!"

The old man must have passed away, for among the few village elders Song-sam had met, the old man was not to be found. Holding the trunk of the tree, Song-sam gazed at the blue sky for a while. Some chestnuts fell to the ground as the dry clusters opened of their own accord.

3 In front of the farmhouse that had been turned into a public peace-police office, a young man stood, tied up. He seemed to be a stranger, so Song-sam approached him to have a close look. He was taken aback; it was none other than his boyhood playmate, Tok-chae.[3]

Song-sam asked the police officer who had come with him from Chontae[4] what it was all about. The prisoner was vice-chairman of the Farmers' Communist League and had just been flushed out of his hideout in his own house, Song-sam learned.

Song-sam sat down on the dirt floor and lit a cigarette.

4 Tok-chae was to be escorted to Chongdan[5] by one of the peace policemen.

After a time, Song-sam lit a new cigarette from the first and stood up.

"I'll take the fellow with me."

---

1. **Song-sam** (sung'säm')
2. **wen:** benign fatty tumor, often on the scalp or face.

3. **Tok-chae** (tuk'chä')
4. **Chontae** (chun'tä')
5. **Chongdan** (chung'dän')

Tok-chae, his face averted, refused to look at Song-sam. They left the village.

Song-sam kept on smoking, but the tobacco had no taste. He just kept drawing in the smoke and blowing it out. Then suddenly he thought that Tok-chae, too, must want a puff. He thought of the days when they used to share dried gourd leaves behind walls, hidden from the adults. But today, how could he offer a cigarette to a fellow like this?

Once, when they were small, he went with Tok-chae to steal some chestnuts from the grandpa[6] with the wen. It was Song-sam's turn to go up the tree. Suddenly there came shouts from the old man. He slipped and fell to the ground. Song-sam got chestnut needles all over his bottom, but he kept on running. It was only when they reached a safe place where the old man could not overtake them that he turned his bottom to Tok-chae. Plucking out those needles hurt so much that he could not keep tears from welling up in his eyes. Tok-chae produced a fistful of chestnuts from his pocket and thrust them into Song-sam's . . . Song-sam threw away the cigarette he had just lit. Then he made up his mind not to light another while he was escorting Tok-chae.

They reached the hill pass, the hill where he and Tok-chae used to cut fodder for the cows until Song-sam had had to move near Chontae, south of the Thirty-eighth Parallel, two years before the liberation.

Song-sam felt a sudden surge of anger in spite of himself and shouted, "So how many have you killed?"

For the first time, Tok-chae cast a quick glance at him and then turned away.

"How many did you kill, you?" he asked again.

Tok-chae turned toward him once again and glared. The glare grew intense and his mouth twitched.

"So you managed to kill many, eh?" Song-sam felt his heart becoming clear from within, as if an obstruction had been removed. "If you were vice-chairman of the Communist League, why didn't you run? You must have been lying low with a secret mission."

Tok-chae did not answer.

"Speak up, what was your mission?"

Tok-chae kept walking. Tok-chae is hiding

Brent Bear/Westlight

Mt. Sorak, Korea.

---

6. **grandpa:** here, not a relative, but a colloquial term for any elderly man.

HUMANITIES CONNECTION

Cranes are often found in Chinese art, where they are used as symbols of long life. Other birds used symbolically include pairs of mandarin ducks, which represent a happy marriage, and peacocks, which stand for dignity.

? *What birds does our culture associate with different human qualities?* (Possible responses: eagle—power; owl—wisdom; loon—craziness, loyalty; bluebird—happiness; dove—peace) ■

8 LITERARY ELEMENT

Theme: What do these and other details suggest about the effects of civil warfare on ordinary people like Tok-chae? (Possible response: It places them in dangerous situations that they cannot cope with and forces them to take sides when often they would prefer not to.)

9 ANALYZING

What two things prevented Tok-chae from evacuating? (his father's refusal to leave the crops that were ready for harvest and his own sense of responsibility as the mainstay of the family) What two traditional values seem to have governed Tok-chae's decision to stay? (loyalty to land and to family)

something, Song-sam thought. He wanted to take a good look at him, but Tok-chae would not turn his averted face.

Fingering the revolver at his side, Song-sam went on: "No excuse is necessary. You are sure to be shot anyway. Why don't you tell the truth, here and now?"

7 "I'm not going to make any excuses. They made me vice-chairman of the league because I was one of the poorest and I was a hard-working farmer. If that constitutes a crime worthy of death, so be it. I am still what I used to be—the only thing I'm good at is digging in the soil." After a short pause, he added, "My old man is bedridden at home. He's been ill almost half a year." Tok-chae's father was a widower, a hard-working poor farmer who lived only for his son. Seven years ago his back had given out and his skin had become diseased.

"You married?"

"Yes," replied Tok-chae after a while.

"To whom?"

"Shorty."

"To Shorty?" How interesting! A woman so small and plump that she knew the earth's vastness but not the sky's altitude. Such a cold fish! He and Tok-chae used to tease her and make her cry. And Tok-chae had married that girl.

"How many kids?"

"The first is arriving this fall, she says."

Song-sam had difficulty swallowing a laugh about to explode in spite of himself. Although he had asked how many kids Tok-chae had, he could not help wanting to burst into laughter at the image of her sitting down, with a large stomach, one span around. But he realized this was no time to laugh or joke over such matters.

"Anyway, it's strange you did not run away."

8 "I tried to escape. They said that once the

Cranes, highly symbolic in all parts of Asia, adorn this Chinese drum stand, 481–221 B.C.

The Cleveland Museum of Art, Purchase from the J. H. Wade Fund, 38.9

South invaded, no man would be spared. So men between seventeen and forty were forcibly taken to the North. I thought of evacuating, even if I had to carry my father on my back. But father said no. How could the farmers leave the land behind when the crops were ready for harvest? He grew old on that farm depending on me as the prop and mainstay of the family. I wanted to be with him in his last moments so that I could close his eyes with my own hand. Besides, where can farmers like us go, who know only living on the land?"

Last June Song-sam had had to take refuge. At night he had broken the news privately to his father. But his father had said

READING CHECK

1. Who is the prisoner that Song-sam comes upon? (Tok-chae, a boyhood friend)
2. Where is Song-sam taking Tok-chae? (to his execution)
3. In their boyhood escapade with the chestnut tree, how did Tok-chae help Song-sam? (by pulling chestnut needles from Song-sam's bottom)
4. How are Song-sam and Tok-chae's fathers similar? (Both are farmers who refuse to leave their land.)
5. What soars at the end of the story? (a couple of Tanjong cranes)

RETEACHING
Have students retell the events of the story in a letter that Song-sam or Tok-chae could have written home to loved ones. Tok-chae's letter might be written from an undisclosed location in the North.

the same thing! Where can a farmer go, leaving all the chores behind? So Song-sam left alone. Roaming about the strange streets and villages in the South, Song-sam had been haunted by thoughts of his old parents and the young children, left with all the chores. Fortunately, his family was safe then, as now.

They crossed the ridge of a hill. This time Song-sam walked with his face averted. The autumn sun was hot on his forehead. This was an ideal day for the harvest, he thought.

When they reached the foot of the hill, Song-sam hesitatingly stopped. In the middle of a field he spied a group of cranes that looked like men in white clothes bending over. This used to be the neutralized zone[7] along the Thirty-eighth Parallel. The cranes were still living here, as before, while the people were all gone.

Once, when Song-sam and Tok-chae were about twelve, they had set a trap here, without the knowledge of the adults, and had caught a crane, a Tanjong crane.[8] They had roped the crane, even its wings, and had paid daily visits, patting its neck and riding on its back. Then one day they overheard the neighbors whispering. Someone had come from Seoul with a permit from the governor-general's office[9] to catch cranes as specimens or something. Then and there the two boys dashed off to the field. That they would be found out and punished was no longer a weighty concern; all they worried about was the fate of their crane. Without a moment's delay, still out of breath from running, they untied the crane's feet and wings. But the bird could hardly walk. It must have been worn out from being bound.

The two held it up in the air. Then, all of a sudden, a shot was fired. The crane fluttered its wings a couple of times and came down again.

It was shot, they thought. But the next moment, as another crane from a nearby bush fluttered its wings, the boys' crane stretched its long neck with a whoop and disappeared into the sky. For a long time the two boys could not take their eyes away from the blue sky into which their crane had soared.

"Hey, why don't we stop here for a crane hunt?" Song-sam spoke up suddenly.

Tok-chae was puzzled, struck dumb.

"I'll make a trap with this rope; you flush[10] a crane over here."

Having untied Tok-chae's hands, Song-sam had already started crawling among the weeds.

Tok-chae's face turned white. "You are sure to be shot anyway"—these words flashed through his mind. Pretty soon a bullet would fly from where Song-sam has gone, he thought.

Some paces away, Song-sam quickly turned toward him.

"Hey, how come you're standing there like you're dumb? Go flush the crane!"

Only then did Tok-chae catch on. He started crawling among the weeds.

A couple of Tanjong cranes soared high into the clear blue autumn sky, fluttering their huge wings.

---

7. **neutralized zone:** demilitarized zone, or strip of no man's land, separating North and South Korea at the Thirty-eighth Parallel.
8. **Tanjong** (tän'jung') **crane:** large, long-legged bird that breeds in North Korea.
9. **governor-general's office:** headquarters of Korea's chief executive appointed by the Japanese government when Korea was a colony of Japan (during Song-sam's boyhood).

---

10. **flush:** to drive a bird from cover.

1. **Exploring Bird Symbols.** Many songs, poems, and works of art use birds as symbols of freedom, thought or imagination, or human spirituality. Ask interested students to gather appropriate examples and share them with classmates, explaining what the bird symbolizes in each. Some students may be interested in exploring specifically the use of the crane motif in Korean brush painting and ceramics.

2. **Research Project.** In barely a generation, South Korea has been transformed from a war-torn country into a thriving nation. Have students form small groups, each to research an aspect of Korean history since the Korean War. Topics may include South Korea's economic expansion; the effect of Western culture on values; the development of democracy; or efforts toward reunification.

CLOSURE

Ask students to state the theme to which, in their opinion, the story's internal conflict and its outcome point. (Possible response: Personal loyalties sometimes take precedence over political ones.) In that context, what might the cranes represent? (the rebirth of the friendship and love that Song-sam and Tok-chae once shared) ■

ANSWERS

First Thoughts
Answers will vary.

Identifying Facts
1. near Korea's Thirty-eighth Parallel. close friends
2. South. He was vice-chairman of the local Farmers' Communist League.
3. His father was too ill to travel and Tok-chae knew nothing but farming.
4. flushing cranes

Interpreting Meanings
1. taking Tok-chae to execution vs. letting him go. The latter course would go against Song-sam's duties as a South Korean soldier.
2. They reveal the friends' closeness and the reasons Song-sam believes Tok-chae's explanations of his past actions.
3. Possible response: civil war involves civilians and divides friends and neighbors. These ties often outweigh political considerations.
4. Possible responses: freedom for Tok-chae, the victory of compassion over violence, hope for Korea

Applying Meanings
Answers will vary.

Creative Writing Response
Writing About a Moment of Decision. Students should explore the interplay between internal and external conflict.

Critical Writing Response
Writing About Conflict. Evaluations should be based on students' beliefs as well as story details. ■

> ### First Thoughts
Do you think Song-sam did the right thing in allowing Tok-chae to go free? Would you have acted similarly if you were in Song-sam's position? Explain.

Identifying Facts
1. Where is the village located? What was Song-sam's relationship with Tok-chae when they were children?
2. For which side in the Korean War is Song-sam fighting? Why is Tok-chae a prisoner?
3. What reasons does Tok-chae give for becoming vice-chairman of the Communist League and for remaining in the village after the Communists abandoned it?
4. When he unties Tok-chae's hands, in what childhood activity does Song-sam suggest the two engage?

Interpreting Meanings
1. In his **internal conflict**, Song-sam must decide between which two courses of action? What is the connection between this conflict and the larger **external conflict** of the story?
2. As Song-sam escorts Tok-chae, he remembers incidents from their childhoods. How do these **flashbacks** contribute to the resolution of the **conflict**?
3. What do the characters' experiences suggest about civil wars in general and the Korean War in particular? What does the story suggest about ties of kinship and friendship?
4. In many Asian cultures, the crane symbolizes long life. Birds often symbolize the soul or spirit, and flight often symbolizes rising to a higher moral plane. Reread the last sentence of the story. What **symbolic** meanings might it have?

Applying Meanings
Do you think individual ties should carry more weight than political or national affiliations? Explain.

Creative Writing Response
Writing About a Moment of Decision. Write a brief personal essay or short story about an important decision in your life. The decision may involve a moral choice, as Song-sam's does. Before you write, ask yourself what events led up to your decision, and how your life, or your outlook on life, has changed since you made the decision.

Critical Writing Response
Writing About Conflict. Write a brief essay about Song-sam's **internal conflict** and the way he eventually resolves it. First, identify the reasons for and against releasing Tok-chae that constitute Song-sam's internal conflict. You may organize your thoughts by listing these factors on a chart like the one below. Conclude your essay by evaluating Song-sam's decision. Explain why you think it was a good or bad resolution to his dilemma.

Taking Tok-chae to Face Execution	Letting Tok-chae Go

Nguyen Thi Vinh
b. 1924, Vietnam

South Vietnamese refugees.

N guyen Thi Vinh (nōō'yin tī vin') bears a family name with a long history. From the sixteenth century to the eighteenth century, the house of Nguyen was one of two ruling families in Vietnam. In 1773 a member of the Nguyen family became Vietnam's emperor, and his descendants ruled the country until its conquest by French forces in the late nineteenth century.

Nguyen Thi Vinh writes about Vietnam's more recent history—especially its decades of warfare during her lifetime. In the early 1950s, she was among the many northerners who fled south to escape the Communists.

She settled in Saigon, capital of the newly created government of South Vietnam, and soon became part of that city's thriving intellectual community.

Best known in Vietnam for her fiction, Nguyen first won fame with *Two Sisters* (1953). She also published a highly regarded book of poetry and served as editor of the South Vietnamese literary journal *New Wind* and the magazine *The East.* Although she was proud of her literary accomplishments, Nguyen did not find peace and contentment in Vietnam. The North-South conflict soon escalated into the Vietnam War, and the violence was underscored by the heartbreaking knowledge that people she had loved in childhood were now fighting as bitter enemies. Those feelings are powerfully expressed in her poem "Thoughts of Hanoi," reprinted here.

After the fall of Saigon to North Vietnamese forces and the subsequent reunification of Vietnam under a Communist government in 1975, Nguyen remained in her homeland as millions of other South Vietnamese fled in fear. She managed to survive those trying times, and in 1983 she emigrated to Norway, where other members of her family had settled.

MORE ABOUT THE AUTHOR

Nguyen (her surname) was born in the Red River delta of what became North Vietnam. After relocating to Saigon (now officially Ho Chi Minh City), she became an active member of the Vietnamese chapter of P.E.N., the well-known international writers' organization. In addition to *Two Sisters*, her most famous works of fiction are *A Poor Hamlet* (1958), *Rising Wave* (1973), and *Birthmark* (1973). A collection of her verse was also published in 1973.

Although Nguyen is best known in her homeland for her short stories, it is her poetry that has appeared most frequently in English translation. "Thoughts of Hanoi" is among her most widely anthologized poems.

ABOUT THE TRANSLATOR

Among today's foremost scholars of Vietnamese literature, Nguyen Ngoc Bich was born in Hanoi in 1937 and later moved to what was then South Vietnam. He came to America to complete his education, doing graduate work in Asian history and comparative literature at Columbia University. His English translations of Vietnamese poetry have appeared in several American journals, and many are collected in *A Thousand Years of Vietnamese Poetry* (1975), his highly regarded compilation.

OBJECTIVES
1. *To interpret a modern Vietnamese poem*
2. *To recognize characteristics of a lyric poem and its speaker*
3. *To write a free-verse poem and an essay comparing two works of literature containing similar conflicts*

PREREADING FOCUS

Background: Have students recall conversations about the Vietnam War that they have had with adults who fought in the war or who lived through the era. What impressions of the war do students have? How did it seem to affect America? Elicit the response that the war sharply divided our nation between those who supported American participation and those who did not. In Vietnam, divisions were of course even more pronounced, and with tragic consequences. For people like Nguyen Thi Vinh, who had fled the Communists in the North and settled in the South, there was the added torment of giving support to forces fighting against relatives, former neighbors, and friends.

Literary Focus: The word *lyric* is from *lyre*, the stringed instrument used in ancient Greece to accompany individual recitation of a short poem that expressed emotion. (Good examples of early Greek lyrics are the poems of Sappho that appear on pp. 279–283.) The Greeks initially used the term *lyric* to distinguish these performances by an individual from those sung by a chorus, called *choric* poems. Later lyric poetry acquired its present definition, distinguishing it from *narrative* poetry, whose chief purpose is to tell a story, and from *dramatic* poetry, which portrays two or more characters in speech or action.

Reader's Guide

THOUGHTS OF HANOI

Background

For centuries, Vietnam has been the site of conflicts between local kingdoms. In the nineteenth century, foreign imperial powers became interested in the region. The French gained control of the country in the late nineteenth century, but they were forced from power by the Japanese, who occupied the area from 1940 to 1945. French attempts to regain control after Japan's defeat in World War II were countered by Communists in the North led by Ho Chi Minh. The two groups fought from 1946 until 1954, when France agreed to withdraw. The country was then temporarily divided into Communist North Vietnam with its capital at Hanoi, and non-Communist South Vietnam with its capital at Saigon. In 1957, Communists in the South began rebelling and Western democracies came to the aid of South Vietnam. The conflict soon escalated into the Vietnam War, in which the United States was a leading player. At a 1973 peace conference, the combatants agreed to a cease-fire and the United States withdrew its troops. Not long afterward, the North Vietnamese government invaded the South and made Vietnam a single nation. The country's decades of warfare sparked massive migrations among the Vietnamese people.

Writer's Response

Write a few sentences about a place you remember fondly. It might be a lake, a neighborhood, a basketball court, or some other place. Include specific details that will make the place come alive to a reader.

Literary Focus

A **lyric poem** is one that expresses personal emotions or thoughts instead of telling a story or portraying characters in action. The voice that talks to us in a lyric poem is called the **speaker**. Sometimes the speaker is the poet, but often the poet assumes a different voice. In "Thoughts of Hanoi," Nguyen Thi Vinh assumes the voice of a Vietnamese male to express her own thoughts and emotions.

THOUGHTS OF HANOI

Nguyen Thi Vinh

translated by

NGUYEN NGOC BICH

As you read the poem, notice how the speaker's childhood memories contrast with his present situation.

The night is deep and chill
as in early autumn. Pitchblack,
it thickens after each lightning flash.
I dream of Hanoi:
1 Co-ngu° Road
ten years of separation
the way back sliced by a frontier of hatred.
I want to bury the past
2 to burn the future
still I yearn
still I fear
those endless nights
waiting for dawn.

Brother,
how is Hang Dao° now?
How is Ngoc Son° temple?
3 Do the trains still run
each day from Hanoi
to the neighboring towns?
To Bac-ninh, Cam-giang, Yen-bai,°
the small villages, islands
4 of brown thatch in a lush green sea?

The girls
bright eyes
ruddy cheeks
four-piece dresses
raven-bill scarves°
sowing harvesting
spinning weaving
all year round,
the boys

5. **Co-ngu** (kō'no͞o')

15. **Hang Dao** (häng' dou')

16. **Ngoc Son** (nōk' sōn')

20. **Bac-ninh** (bäk'nin'), **Cam-giang** (käm'gyäng'), **Yen-bai** (yen'bī'): towns near Hanoi.

27. **raven-bill scarves:** headscarves folded into straight-edged triangular forms, like the bill or beak of a raven.

TEACHER'S RESOURCES

Review and Response Worksheet

1 GUIDED READING

Finding the Main Idea: Hanoi, the capital of Vietnam, was the capital of North Vietnam when the nation was divided. What is the speaker's relationship to Hanoi? (The speaker grew up there.) How long has he been gone? (ten years)

2 INTERPRETING

Why would the speaker want to "bury the past"? (Possible response: to forget attachments to people whom he used to love) What might the speaker mean by wanting to "burn the future"? (Possible response: to destroy the evils of war)

3 SPECULATING

What would you guess are the answers to these questions? (Probably all of these things have been changed or destroyed by the war)

4 LITERARY ELEMENT

Metaphor: To what does the speaker compare the small villages with their thatch-roof huts? (islands in a lush green sea)

5 GUIDED READING

Identifying Details: In lines 23–46 (beginning on p. 1411), what scenes of the past does the speaker "relive"? (girls harvesting and spinning, boys working and flying kites, and children and grandmothers enjoying themselves) What pictures of life before the war does the speaker create? (happy, peaceful)

6 READER'S RESPONSE

If you were the "Brother" the speaker addresses, what would your answer to this question be? Explain your answer.

7 LITERARY ELEMENT

Speaker: Which details here and elsewhere indicate that the speaker is a male? (the details about marching with the army and the remark "we are men," line 66)

8 LITERARY ELEMENT

Paradox: How can a person be a friend and an enemy at the same time? (Possible response: In civil war such contradictions exist. The paradox points up the agonies felt by those forced to take sides against people they love.)

WRITING TO LEARN

Social Studies: Based on the poem's details, write a descriptive paragraph about the city of Hanoi and Vietnamese village life before the war. ∎

1412   The Twentieth Century

5

        plowing
            transplanting
        in the fields
35   in their shops
        running across
            the meadow at evening
        to fly kites
            and sing alternating songs.°

40 Stainless blue sky,
        jubilant voices of children
    stumbling through the alphabet,
        village graybeards strolling to the temple,
    grandmothers basking in twilight sun,
45   chewing betel leaves°
    while the children run—

    Brother,
    how is all that now?
    Or is it obsolete?
50 Are you like me,
    reliving the past,
    imagining the future?

6   Do you count me as a friend
    or am I the enemy in your eyes?
55 Brother, I am afraid
7   that one day I'll be with the March-North Army°
    meeting you on your way to the South.
    I might be the one to shoot you then
    or you me
60 but please
    not with hatred.

    For don't you remember how it was,
    you and I in school together,
    plotting our lives together?
65 Those roots go deep!

    Brother, we are men,
    conscious of more
    than material needs.
    How can this happen to us
8 70 my friend
    my foe?

39. **alternating songs:** songs in which different singers take different parts; rounds.

45. **betel** (bēt′l) **leaves:** leaves of the betel pepper, a plant found in southeastern Asia; the leaves, along with betel palm nuts, are often chewed together like chewing gum.

56. **March-North Army:** that is, the South Vietnamese army marching into North Vietnam.

Larry Downing/Woodfin Camp & Associates

Vietnamese child in Hanoi.

1. Conducting Interviews. Have pairs of students interview people who fought in the Vietnam War or lived through the era, including any Vietnamese immigrants. Interview questions should focus on discovering each person's experiences and feelings about the war as well as the war's more general social effects. Students should tape-record interviews and later transcribe them, pooling some or all in a multimedia class project entitled "The Vietnam War Revisited."

2. Viewing a Documentary on the Vietnam War. Have interested students or the entire class view a videotaped documentary about the Vietnam War and compare their response to it with their response to "Thoughts of Hanoi."

CLOSURE

Have students suggest adjectives to describe the tone of the speaker. Is it sad, nostalgic, or pessimistic? Does the speaker feel total hopelessness, or do you detect a note of hope in his voice? If so, on what does he base his hope? ■

First Thoughts

Did the **paradox**, or apparent contradiction, of the last two lines make sense to you? Think of another circumstance in which someone might be both your friend *and* your foe.

Identifying Facts

1. How many years ago did the speaker leave Hanoi, and by what is the way back now "sliced"?
2. List three specific questions about Hanoi that the speaker asks. What does the speaker ask about the past and future?
3. What kinds of **images** does the speaker describe in lines 23–46?
4. What is the speaker afraid may happen one day? What final question does he ask?

Interpreting Meanings

1. What might "each lightning flash" (line 3) be, and why might the speaker "fear/those endless nights"? What is the "frontier of hatred"?
2. Where does the **speaker** come from, and where is he living now? Which details suggest that the speaker is not the poet?
3. Why do you think the poet wrote so many lines describing the boys and girls of the Hanoi area? What is the "lush green sea"?
4. What is the apparent relationship between the speaker and the person addressed as "Brother"?
5. What overall attitude does this **lyric poem** convey toward warfare, especially civil warfare?

Applying Meanings

The United States was heavily involved in the Vietnam War. What are your feelings about the war, based on your studies and your conversations with older Americans or with Vietnamese refugees in the U.S.?

Creative Writing Response

Writing a Poem. Write a short, free-verse poem called "Thoughts of *X*," in which *X* is some time or place that you miss. You may use the place you wrote about in the Writer's Response (see page 1410) or choose another place or time.

Critical Writing Response

Comparing Viewpoints. Like "Thoughts of Hanoi," Hwang Sun-won's "Cranes" (see page 1404) was written at a time of civil warfare in the author's homeland. In a brief essay, compare and contrast the thoughts, feelings, and actions of the speaker in "Thoughts of Hanoi" and the protagonist in "Cranes." Focus on the physical and emotional effects of warfare in general and civil warfare in particular. Before you begin, you may find it helpful to list your ideas on a chart like the one below.

	"Thoughts of Hanoi"	"Cranes"
Feeling toward the "enemy"		
Thoughts about war		
Actions		
Writer's tone		

ANSWERS

First Thoughts
Answers will vary.

Identifying Facts
1. ten; a frontier of hatred
2. "how is Hang Dao now?" "How is Ngoc Son temple?" "Do the trains . . . towns?" "Are you like me, / reliving the past, / imagining the future?"
3. children playing; peaceful old people
4. He will meet the "Brother" in battle. "How can this happen to us/my friend/my foe?"

Interpreting Meanings
1. Possible response: bombfire or shellfire; night is usually when aerial bombardment occurs and troubling thoughts plague us most. The border created by the bitter civil war
2. Hanoi; South Vietnam. Expecting to march with the army and "we are men"
3. To stress the happiness of a more peaceful era. Acres of rice paddies
4. Possible response: close childhood friends
5. Possible response: War brings horror, suffering, devastation; civil war raises inhuman, unresolvable conflicts.

Applying Meanings
Answers will vary.

Creative Writing Response
Writing a Poem. Poems should establish the speaker's former relationship with the place or time.

Critical Writing Response
Comparing Viewpoints. Essays should include points of comparison listed on the chart. ■

Nguyen Thi Vinh　　**1413**

MORE ABOUT THE AUTHOR

As a youngster, Zhang (her surname) was an avid reader, an activity her mother encouraged. After studying economics at the People's University, Zhang became a statistician in Beijing until the government sent her to Fujian Province to work in an electrical components factory. When she returned to Beijing and embarked on her writing career, her skill won her an appointment as a scriptwriter.

Zhang enjoyed great popularity in her homeland during the late 1970s and early 1980s, when a more moderate Chinese government gave the nation's writers more freedom and prestige than in the previous decades. Works like *Leaden Wings* were nationwide bestsellers. Zhang was even able to pay a visit to the West in 1982. On her return to China, she recorded her impressions in *Notes on a Journey to the U.S.* The impression Zhang made in the U.S. is vividly captured in Annie Dillard's *Encounters with Chinese Writers* (1984).

While Zhang always considered herself a loyal Communist, her frank, probing examinations of Chinese society met with growing disapproval as China's Communist government began returning to its former orthodoxy. After the 1989 crackdown on the student democracy movement in Beijing's Tiananmen Square, Zhang went into voluntary exile, taking a teaching post at Wesleyan University in Connecticut.

Zhang Jie
b. 1937, People's Republic of China

Isolde Ohlbaum

In the early 1980s, the American writer Annie Dillard documented in her book *Encounters with Chinese Writers* a heated exchange between Zhang Jie (jam' jyē') and the American Beat poet Allen Ginsberg. Although Zhang is a small, seemingly fragile woman, and Ginsberg is a large, imposing man, Zhang was not afraid to speak her mind. "Mr. Ginsberg! you should not think only of yourself!" she exclaimed. "You must live and work so as to fulfill your obligations! Have your goals firmly in your mind. You should not take drugs! Think of your responsibility to society!" Such outspokenness and conviction are characteristic of Zhang's novels and short stories, which have caused controversy in China and won praise abroad.

Zhang's concern with social responsibility stems in part from the circumstances of her childhood. Raised in the Chinese capital of Beijing (bā'jing') (formerly Peking), Zhang grew up in dire poverty after her father abandoned the family a few months after her birth. She observed that in China at that time, her father had no binding or legal responsibility to his family.

Feeling that women had more rights under China's new Communist government, Zhang joined the Communist Party as a young woman and supported government policy even when it meant compromising her own desires. She had hoped, for example, to study literature in college. Instead, she studied economics, which the new government felt was of more use to society. Later she was among the many men and women who left their homes to work in factories or on farms in the hopes of improving China's shaky economy.

Speaking of her early life, Zhang recalls that she was "like a darting dragonfly, with no goals in life and no substantial pursuits. Only through literature did I discover myself." Zhang was not able to begin her writing career, however, until the Cultural Revolution ended and more moderate leaders came to power. In 1978 she won a nationwide award for her story "The Music of the Forests." Three years later her novel *Leaden Wings* won China's Mao Dun Literary Prize.

OBJECTIVES
1. *To interpret a modern short story from the People's Republic of China*
2. *To identify and analyze flashbacks*
3. *To write an imaginary diary entry*
4. *To understand transliteration and the different systems by which Chinese words have been transliterated into English*

VOCABULARY IN CONTEXT
The words listed below will appear in the side margin at the point of instruction:
1. prescience
2. scrupulous
3. strictures
4. insuperable
5. allusions

Reader's Guide

LOVE MUST NOT BE FORGOTTEN

Background

In 1949, the Communists established the People's Republic of China under their military hero Mao Zedong (also spelled Mao Tse-tung). The new Communist regime instituted drastic social and economic changes and became increasingly oppressive. During Mao's Cultural Revolution, many moderate political figures were removed from power, imprisoned, and sometimes executed. China's writers were also silenced.

After Mao's death in 1976 China came under more moderate leadership. Encouraged by the new spirit of openness, many writers emerged and began writing of past injustices and the need for future reforms. Zhang Jie won fame for writing of the continued inequality between the sexes despite government claims to the contrary. During the 1980s the government again became more repressive and in 1989 ordered a military crackdown on prodemocracy demonstrators in Beijing's Tiananmen Square. Few writers were allowed to publish within China, and those lucky enough to escape went to live abroad.

Among Chinese readers Zhang Jie enjoys huge popularity, despite much controversy over her 1979 story "Love Must Not Be Forgotten," reprinted here. This story suggests that, for all the changes effected by the Communists, Chinese women still face centuries-old social pressures to marry and subordinate themselves to their husbands and families.

Writer's Response

Although the United States has made progress toward equality between the sexes, do you think that there is still room for improvement? Think of examples that illustrate some of the inequalities that still exist today.

Literary Focus

A **flashback** is a scene in a movie, play, or story that interrupts the present action to show or tell what happened at an earlier time. Writers often use this device to develop a character or to give additional plot information. "Love Must Not Be Forgotten" uses several flashbacks to show the narrator's growing awareness of her mother's true situation and feelings.

PREREADING FOCUS

Background: Despite the easing of government censorship after the death of Mao in 1976, "Love Must Not Be Forgotten" caused a storm of controversy in China in the late 1970s. Until then, the topic of romantic love—especially outside marriage—was strictly taboo in literature. The story's suggestion that antiquated marriage practices still prevailed in China and that such customs kept women in their centuries-old position as second-class citizens disturbed many Communist government officials. Like Anna Akhmatova (pp. 1223–1226), Zhang was attacked for being too "personal." Yet "Love Must Not Be Forgotten" was a huge success, especially among the young, who embraced its daring frankness.

Have students discuss why so many Communist regimes have attacked writers for being too "personal." (Possible responses: A personal view undermines the emphasis on working only for the public good; shows that the regime has not succeeded in making citizens feel fulfilled; and places great value on freedom and the individual, thereby directly or indirectly attacking the ideology.)

Literary Focus: Students might describe films, plays, or television shows that contain memorable flashbacks and discuss how the flashbacks enhanced their understanding of the characters and themes.

LOVE MUST NOT BE FORGOTTEN

Zhang Jie

translated by

GLADYS YANG

In the opening paragraphs of "Love Must Not Be Forgotten," the narrator wonders if she should marry a certain man. As you read the story, decide what advice her mother would probably have given her about her dilemma.

HRW Photo by Darwin Chen

I am thirty, the same age as our People's Republic. For a republic thirty is still young. But a girl of thirty is virtually on the shelf.

Actually, I have a bona fide suitor. Have you seen the Greek sculptor Myron's *Discobolus?*[1] Qiao Lin[2] is the image of that discus thrower. Even the padded clothes he wears in winter fail to hide his fine physique. Bronzed, with clear-cut features, a broad forehead and large eyes, his appearance alone attracts most girls to him.

But I can't make up my mind to marry him. I'm not clear what attracts me to him, or him to me. I know people are gossiping behind my back, "Who does she think she is, to be so choosy?" To them, I'm a nobody playing hard to get. They take offense at such preposterous behavior.

Of course, I shouldn't be captious.[3] In a society where commercial production still exists, marriage, like most other transactions, is still a form of barter.

I have known Qiao Lin for nearly two years, yet still cannot fathom whether he keeps so quiet from aversion to talking or from having nothing to say. When, by way of a small intelligence test, I demand his opinion of this or that, he says "good" or "bad" like a child in kindergarten.

Once I asked, "Qiao Lin, why do you love me?" He thought the question over seriously for what seemed an age. I could see from his normally smooth but now wrinkled forehead that the little gray cells in his handsome head were hard at work cogitating. I felt ashamed to have put him on the spot.

Finally he raised his clear childlike eyes to tell me, "Because you're good!"

---

1. **Myron's** *Discobolus:* famous statue of a handsome athlete by this Greek sculptor of the fifth century B.C.
2. **Qiao Lin** (chyou' lin')
3. **captious** (kap'shəs): fault-finding; critical.

Loneliness flooded my heart. "Thank you, Qiao Lin!" I couldn't help wondering, if we were to marry, whether we could discharge our duties to each other as husband and wife. Maybe, because law and morality would have bound us together. But how tragic simply to comply with law and morality! Was there no stronger bond to link us?

When such thoughts cross my mind I have the strange sensation that instead of being a girl contemplating marriage I am an elderly social scientist.

Perhaps I worry too much. We can live like most married couples, bringing up children together, strictly true to each other according to the law.... Although living in the seventies of the twentieth century, people still consider marriage the way they did millennia ago, as a means of continuing the race, a form of barter or a business transaction in which love and marriage can be separated. Since this is the common practice, why shouldn't we follow suit?

But I still can't make up my mind. As a child, I remember, I often cried all night for no rhyme or reason, unable to sleep and disturbing the whole household. My old nurse, a shrewd though uneducated woman, said an ill wind had blown through my ear. I think this judgment showed prescience, because I still have that old weakness. I upset myself over things which really present no problem, upsetting other people at the same time. One's nature is hard to change.

I think of my mother, too. If she were alive, what would she say about my attitude to Qiao Lin and my uncertainty about marrying him? My thoughts constantly turn to her, not because she was such a strict mother that her ghost is still watching over me since her death. No, she was not just my mother but my closest friend. I loved her so

1 GUIDED READING
Recalling Details: In what year does the opening of the story take place? (1979) How do you know? (According to the Background section on p. 1415, the People's Republic of China was established in 1949. The story opens in the republic's thirtieth year.)

2 ANALYZING
In addition to marriage for the wrong reasons, what is the narrator criticizing here? (production for commercial reasons) What does the criticism reveal about her political ideology? (Possible response: She is an idealistic Communist.)

3 LITERARY ELEMENT
Characterization: What seems to be Qiao Lin's chief flaw in the narrator's eyes? (He is simple.)

4 INTERPRETING
Why would Qiao Lin's simplicity flood the narrator's heart with loneliness? (Possible response: The man she is considering marrying cannot understand her and thus cannot offer any real companionship.)

5 READER'S RESPONSE
How would you respond if you lived in a society where these attitudes regarding marriage prevailed?

prescience (presh'əns): knowledge of something before it happens

Zhang Jie   **1417**

6 LEP: To help students recognize the story's many flashbacks, tell them to pay attention to phrases indicating an earlier time. Here "during her last days" indicates that the incident took place before the story opening. ■

7 LITERARY ELEMENT
Theme: What does the mother consider more important than simply being married? (happiness in the marriage) What might this attitude clarify about the story's title? (Possible response: In contemplating marriage, love must not be forgotten.)

8 LITERARY ELEMENT
Foreshadowing: What does the mention of a secret help build? (suspense) Why? (We keep reading, hoping to learn what the secret is.)

9 READER'S RESPONSE
Do you agree that people often marry because of social pressure? (Answers will vary.)

10 COMPARING AND CONTRASTING
How does this detail about "a handsome fellow" compare with the narrator's own situation? (Possible response: She too is considering marriage to someone whose chief attraction seems to be his good looks, and such a marriage could well prove as mistaken as her mother's.)

much that the thought of her leaving me makes my heart ache.

She never lectured me, just told me quietly in her deep, unwomanly voice about her successes and failures, so that I could learn from her experience. She had evidently not had many successes—her life was full of failures.

6 During her last days she followed me with her fine, expressive eyes, as if wondering how I would manage on my own and as if she had some important advice for me but hesitated to give it. She must have been worried by my naiveté and sloppy ways. She suddenly blurted out, "Shanshan, if you aren't sure what you want, don't rush into marriage—better live on your own!"

Other people might think this strange advice from a mother to her daughter, but to me it embodied her bitter experience. I don't think she underestimated me or my knowledge of life. She loved me and didn't want me to be unhappy.

"I don't want to marry, mother!" I said, not out of bashfulness or a show of coyness. I can't think why a girl should pretend to be coy. She had long since taught me about things not generally mentioned to girls.

"If you meet the right man, then marry him. Only if he's right for you!"

"I'm afraid no such man exists!"

"That's not true. But it's hard. The world is so vast, I'm afraid you may never meet him." Whether married or not was not what concerned her, but the quality of the marriage.

"Haven't you managed fine without a husband?"

"Who says so?"

"I think you've done fine."

"I had no choice...." She broke off, lost in thought, her face wistful. Her wistful lined face reminded me of a withered flower I had pressed in a book.

"Why did you have no choice?"

"You ask too many questions," she parried, not ashamed to confide in me but afraid that I might reach the wrong conclusion. Besides, everyone treasures a secret to carry to the grave. Feeling a bit put out, I demanded bluntly, "Didn't you love my dad?"

"No, I never loved him."

"Did he love you?"

"No, he didn't."

"Then why get married?"

She paused, searching for the right words to explain this mystery, then answered bitterly, "When you're young you don't always know what you're looking for, what you need, and people may talk you into getting married. As you grow older and more experienced you find out your true needs. By then, though, you've done many foolish things for which you could kick yourself. You'd give anything to be able to make a fresh start and live more wisely. Those content with their lot will always be happy, they say, but I shall never enjoy that happiness." She added self-mockingly, "A wretched idealist, that's all I am."

Did I take after her? Did we both have genes which attracted ill winds?

"Why don't you marry again?"

"I'm afraid I'm still not sure what I really want." She was obviously unwilling to tell me the truth.

I cannot remember my father. He and Mother split up when I was very small. I just recall her telling me sheepishly that he was a fine handsome fellow. I could see she was ashamed of having judged by appearances and made a futile choice. She told me, "When I can't sleep at night, I force myself to sober up by recalling all those stupid blunders I made. Of course it's so distasteful that I often hide my face in the sheet for shame,

Chinese woman.
❓ *At what point does the narrative shift from the narrator's story to her mother's story?*

The Bettmann Archive

as if there were eyes watching me in the dark. But distasteful as it is, I take some pleasure in this form of atonement."

I was really sorry that she hadn't remarried. She was such a fascinating character, if she'd married a man she loved, what a happy household ours would surely have been. Though not beautiful, she had the simple charm of an ink landscape. She was a fine writer, too. Another author who knew her well used to say teasingly, "Just reading your

11
12

works is enough to make anyone love you!" ⌐ 12

She would retort, "If he knew that the object of his affection was a white-haired old crone, that would frighten him away." At her age, she must have known what she really wanted, so this was obviously an evasion. I say this because she had quirks which puzzled me.

For instance, whenever she left Beijing on a trip, she always took with her one of the twenty-seven volumes of Chekhov's stories published between 1950 and 1955.[4] She also warned me, "Don't touch these books. If you want to read Chekhov, read that set I bought you." There was no need to caution me. Having a set of my own, why should I touch hers? Besides, she'd told me this over and over again. Still she was on her guard. She seemed bewitched by those books.

So we had two sets of Chekhov's stories at home. Not just because we loved Chekhov, but to parry other people like me who loved Chekhov. Whenever anyone asked to borrow a volume, she would lend one of mine. Once, in her absence, a close friend took a volume from her set. When she found out, she was frantic, and at once took a volume of mine to exchange for it.

Ever since I can remember, those books were on her bookcase. Although I admire Chekhov as a great writer, I was puzzled by the way she never tired of reading him. Why, for over twenty years, had she had to read him every single day? Sometimes, when tired of writing, she poured herself a cup of strong tea and sat down in front of the bookcase, staring raptly at that set of books. If I went into her room then it flustered her, and she either spilt her tea or blushed like

13

---

4. **twenty-seven volumes of Chekhov's . . . 1955:** complete stories of Russian author Anton Chekhov, published in a Chinese edition in the 1950s.

11 CULTURAL DIVERSITY
Traditionally, ink has been a popular medium of Chinese and other Far Eastern art, and landscapes are often depicted in ink.
❓ *What might be the Western equivalent of the phrase "the simple charm of an ink landscape"?* (Possible response: the serenity of a still life)

12 INFERRING
What does the mother do for a living? (She is a writer.)

13 SPECULATING
What do you think may have caused the mother's attitude toward her volumes of Chekhov? (Many students may guess that it was a gift from someone she loved.)

Zhang Jie **1419**

14 GUIDED READING
Recalling Details: Where did we previously encounter the name of the diary? (the story's title)

15 GUIDED READING
Finding the Main Idea: What was the mother's secret? (For over twenty years she loved a man who was "not for her.")

16 LITERARY ELEMENT
Figurative Language: What does the figurative language of the quotation explain about the mother? (Possible response: She never loved anyone else because no one could compare to the wonderful man she loved.)

17 GUIDED READING
Identifying Details: For what reasons did the man marry? (a sense of duty, gratitude, class feeling; love was not a factor)

18 LITERARY ELEMENT
Flashback: Where does a new flashback begin? ("In the spring of 1962 . . .") What apparently prompts the daughter to "flash back" to this incident? (reading the diary)

scrupulous (skrōo'pyə·ləs): characterized by careful attention to what is right or proper

19 LITERARY ELEMENT
Characterization: Based on the narrator's description, what kind of person is the mother's beloved? (a man of distinction, honesty, and sharp intellect)

a girl discovered with her lover.

I wondered: Has she fallen in love with Chekhov? She might have if he'd still been alive.

When her mind was wandering just before her death, her last words to me were: "That set . . ." She hadn't the strength to give it its complete title. But I knew what she meant. "And my diary . . . 'Love Must Not Be Forgotten'. . . . Cremate them with me." **14**

I carried out her last instruction regarding the works of Chekhov, but couldn't bring myself to destroy her diary. I thought, if it could be published, it would surely prove the most moving thing she had written. But naturally publication was out of the question.

At first I imagined the entries were raw material she had jotted down. They read neither like stories, essays, a diary, or letters. But after reading the whole I formed a hazy impression, helped out by my imperfect memory. Thinking it over, I finally realized that this was no lifeless manuscript I was holding, but an anguished, loving heart. For over twenty years one man had occupied her heart, but he was not for her. She used these diaries as a substitute for him, a means of pouring out her feelings to him, day after day, year after year. **15**

No wonder she had never considered any eligible proposals, had turned a deaf ear to idle talk whether well meant or malicious. Her heart was already full, to the exclusion of anybody else. "No lake can compare with the ocean, no cloud with those on Mount Wu."[5] Remembering those lines I often reflected sadly that few people in real life could love like this. No one would love me like this. **16**

I learned that toward the end of the thirties, when this man was doing underground work for the Party in Shanghai,[6] an old worker had given his life to cover him, leaving behind a helpless wife and daughter. Out of a sense of duty, of gratitude to the dead, and deep class feeling, he had unhesitatingly married the daughter. When he saw the endless troubles of couples who had married for "love," he may have thought, "Thank Heaven, though I didn't marry for love, we get on well, able to help each other." For years, as man and wife they lived through hard times. **17**

He must have been my mother's colleague. Had I ever met him? He couldn't have visited our home. Who was he? **18**

In the spring of 1962, Mother took me to a concert. We went on foot, the theater being quite near. On the way a black limousine pulled up silently by the pavement. Out stepped an elderly man with white hair in a black serge tunic suit. What a striking shock of white hair! Strict, scrupulous, distinguished, transparently honest—that was my impression of him. The cold glint of his flashing eyes reminded me of lightning or swordplay. Only ardent love for a woman really deserving his love could fill cold eyes like those with tenderness. **19**

He walked up to Mother and said, "How are you, Comrade Zhong Yu?[7] It's been a long time."

"How are you!" Mother's hand holding mine suddenly turned icy cold and trembled a little.

They stood face to face without looking at each other, each appearing upset, even

---

5. **Mount Wu:** one of a chain of picturesque mountains in eastern China.

6. **Party in Shanghai** (shang'hī'): that is, the Communist Party in the large eastern Chinese city of Shanghai.

7. **Zhong Yu** (jong'yōo')

Exterior gate of the Forbidden City in Beijing, China. *The Forbidden City was the dwelling of the Chinese Imperial family before the era of Communism.*

20 DRAWING CONCLUSIONS
How does Zhang reveal that the man to whom the diary is devoted is the white-haired gentleman? (Both the mother and the distinguished gentleman have cold, trembling hands when they meet.)

21 GUIDED READING
Analyzing: Why does the old gentleman remember this incident in 1953 when the little girl hurt herself? (Possible response: This was probably the day when the mother and the distinguished official first met.)

22 INTERPRETING
In addition to the mother's last story, to what is the man referring? (the situation that exists between him and the mother)

stern. Mother fixed her eyes on the trees by the roadside, not yet in leaf. He looked at me. "Such a big girl already. Good, fine—you take after your mother."

Instead of shaking hands with Mother, he shook hands with me. His hand was as icy as hers and trembling a little. As if transmitting an electric current, I felt a sudden shock. Snatching my hand away I cried, "There's nothing good about that!"

"Why not?" he asked with the surprised expression grown-ups always have when children speak out frankly.

I glanced at Mother's face. I did take after her, to my disappointment. "Because she's not beautiful!"

He laughed, then said teasingly, "Too bad that there should be a child who doesn't find her own mother beautiful. Do you remember in '53, when your mother was transferred to Beijing, she came to our ministry to report for duty? She left you outside on the veranda, but like a monkey you climbed all the stairs, peeped through the cracks in doors, and caught your finger in the door of my office. You sobbed so bitterly that I carried you off to find her."

"I don't remember that." I was annoyed at his harking back to a time when I was still in open-seat pants.

"Ah, we old people have better memories." He turned abruptly and remarked to Mother, "I've read that last story of yours. Frankly speaking, there's something not quite right about it. You shouldn't have condemned the heroine....There's nothing wrong with falling in love, as long as you don't spoil someone else's life.... In fact, the

Zhang Jie   **1421**

MEETING INDIVIDUAL NEEDS

23 Advanced Students: Ask
students familiar with Chekhov
to explain why Zhang Jie selected his works to be a symbol of the story's secret love. ■

HUMANITIES CONNECTION

The events in the flashbacks of
the story occur at the time
when Mao headed the Peo-
ple's Republic of China.
? *What do you think the images on the banner are intended to convey?* (Possible responses: the people of China
living happily under the leadership of Mao; the unity of the
Chinese; the benevolence of
Mao) *What elements of propaganda does the banner display?*
(Possible response: prominent
flags that invoke patriotism;
stereotypical individuals; the
face of a military dictator pictured as benevolent and kind) ■

hero might have loved her, too. Only for the
sake of a third person's happiness, they had
to renounce their love. . . ."

A policeman came over to where the car
was parked and ordered the driver to move
on. When the driver made some excuse, the
old man looked around. After a hasty "Goodbye" he strode back to the car and told the
policeman, "Sorry. It's not his fault, it's
mine. . . ."

I found it amusing watching this old
cadre[8] listening respectfully to the policeman's strictures. When I turned to Mother
with a mischievous smile, she looked as upset as a first-form[9] primary schoolchild
standing forlornly in front of the stern headmistress.[10] Anyone would have thought she
was the one being lectured by the policeman.
The car drove off, leaving a puff of smoke.
Very soon even this smoke vanished with
the wind, as if nothing at all had happened.
But the incident stuck in my mind.

Analyzing it now, I realize he must have
been the man whose strength of character
won Mother's heart. That strength came
from his firm political convictions, his narrow escapes from death in the revolution,
his active brain, his drive at work, his well-
cultivated mind. Besides, strange to say, he
and Mother both liked the oboe. Yes, she
must have worshiped him. She once told me
that unless she worshiped a man, she
couldn't love him even for one day.

But I could not tell whether he loved her
or not. If not, why was there this entry in
her diary?

"This is far too fine a present. But
how did you know that Chekhov's my
favorite writer?"
"You said so."
"I don't remember that."
"I remember. I heard you mention it
when you were chatting with someone."

So he was the one who had given her the
Selected Stories of Chekhov. For her that
was tantamount to a love letter. Maybe this
man, who didn't believe in love, realized by
the time his hair was white that in his heart
was something which could be called love.
By the time he no longer had the right to
love, he made the tragic discovery of this
love for which he would have given his life.
Or did it go deeper even than that?

This is all I remember about him.

Banner showing Chairman Mao, the leader of
China's Communist revolution.

---

8. **old cadre** (ka'drē'): here, former member of a
   cadre, or small unified group; in this case, a
   group of underground rebels.
9. **first-form:** first-grade.
10. **headmistress:** female school principal.

How wretched Mother must have been, deprived of the man to whom she was devoted! To catch a glimpse of his car or the back of his head through its rear window, she carefully figured out which roads he would take to work and back. Whenever he made a speech, she sat at the back of the hall watching his face rendered hazy by cigarette smoke and poor lighting. Her eyes would brim with tears, but she swallowed them back. If a fit of coughing made him break off, she wondered anxiously why no one persuaded him to give up smoking. She was afraid he would get bronchitis again. Why was he so near yet so far?

He, to catch a glimpse of her, looked out of the car window every day straining his eyes to watch the streams of cyclists, afraid that she might have an accident. On the rare evenings on which he had no meetings, he would walk by a roundabout way to our neighborhood, to pass our compound gate. However busy, he would always make time to look in papers and journals for her work. His duty had always been clear to him, even in the most difficult times. But now confronted by this love he became a weakling, quite helpless. At his age it was laughable. Why should life play this trick on him?

Yet when they happened to meet at work, each tried to avoid the other, hurrying off with a nod. Even so, this would make Mother blind and deaf to everything around her. If she met a colleague named Wang[11] she would call him Guo[12] and mutter something unintelligible.

It was a cruel ordeal for her. She wrote:

We agreed to forget each other. But I deceived you, I have never forgotten. I don't think you've forgotten either. We're just deceiving each other, hiding our misery. I haven't deceived you deliberately, though; I did my best to carry out our agreement. I often stay far away from Beijing, hoping time and distance will help me to forget you. But when I return, as the train pulls into the station, my head reels. I stand on the platform looking round intently, as if someone were waiting for me. Of course there is no one. I realize then that I have forgotten nothing. Everything is unchanged. My love is like a tree the roots of which strike deeper year after year—I have no way to uproot it.

At the end of every day, I feel as if I've forgotten something important. I may wake with a start from my dreams wondering what has happened. But nothing has happened. Nothing. Then it comes home to me that you are missing! So everything seems lacking, incomplete, and there is nothing to fill up the blank. We are nearing the ends of our lives, why should we be carried away by emotion like children? Why should life submit people to such ordeals, then unfold before you your lifelong dream? Because I started off blindly, I took the wrong turning, and now there are <u>insuperable</u> obstacles between me and my dream.

Yes, Mother never let me go to the station to meet her when she came back from a trip, preferring to stand alone on the platform and imagine that he had met her. Poor mother with her graying hair was as infatuated as a girl.

Not much space in the diary was devoted to their romance. Most entries dealt with trivia: why one of her articles had not come off; her fear that she had no real talent; the excellent play she missed by mistaking the

---

11. **Wang:** common Chinese family name.
12. **Guo** (gwō): The names "Wang" and "Guo" are written with similar characters; because she is preoccupied, she confuses the two.

26 Literary Element

Allusions: Why does the narrator make a reference to Shakespeare's *Romeo and Juliet* here? (Possible response: Like Juliet, the mother loves someone who society says "is not for her.")

27 Cultural Background

In the Cultural Revolution that began in 1966, Mao gave support to young, militant Red Guards who accused many top Chinese officials of counter-revolutionary practices. In the "purges" that followed, many formerly respected figures were killed.

28 Cultural Background

The radicals in power during the Cultural Revolution frowned on most ancient Chinese traditions, including the ritual of mourning.

? *What are some traditional mourning practices with which you are familiar?* (Possible responses: wearing black or, in some cultures, white; refraining from social activities; and lighting memorial candles)

■ **allusions** (ə·lōō′zhənz): indirect references

Meeting Individual Needs

29 LEP: Make sure students recognize that *you* here refers to the man the mother loved, not the narrator. ■

---

time on the ticket; the drenching she got by going out for a stroll without her umbrella. In spirit they were together day and night, like a devoted married couple. In fact, they spent no more than twenty-four hours together in all. Yet in that time they experienced deeper happiness than some people in a whole lifetime. Shakespeare makes Juliet say, "I cannot sum up half my sum of wealth."[13] And probably that is how Mother felt.

He must have been killed in the Cultural Revolution. Perhaps because of the conditions then, that section of the diary is ambiguous and obscure. Mother had been so fiercely attacked for her writing, it amazed me that she went on keeping a diary. From some veiled <u>allusions</u> I gathered that he had questioned the theories advanced by that "theoretician" then at the height of favor and had told someone, "This is sheer Rightist[14] talk." It was clear from the tear-stained pages of Mother's diary that he had been harshly denounced; but the steadfast old man never knuckled under to the authorities. His last words were, "When I go to meet Marx,[15] I shall go on fighting my case!"

That must have been in the winter of 1969, because that was when Mother's hair turned white overnight, though she was not yet fifty. And she put on a black armband.[16] Her position then was extremely difficult. She was criticized for wearing this old-style

---

13. **Shakespeare . . . wealth:** In *Romeo and Juliet* by William Shakespeare, Juliet makes this remark in describing her love for Romeo.
14. **Rightist:** in politics, conservative or reactionary; Chinese politics during the Cultural Revolution was dominated by Rightist Party members.
15. **Marx:** Karl Marx (1818–1883), German-born economic philosopher and father of modern socialism; a revered figure by Chinese and other Communists.
16. **black armband:** traditional sign of mourning in China and elsewhere.

---

mourning and ordered to say for whom she was in mourning.

"For whom are you wearing that, Mother?" I asked anxiously.

"For my lover." Not to frighten me she explained, "Someone you never knew."

"Shall I put one on too?" She patted my cheeks, as she had when I was a child. It was years since she had shown me such affection. I often felt that as she aged, especially during these last years of persecution, all tenderness had left her, or was concealed in her heart, so that she seemed like a man.

She smiled sadly and said, "No, you needn't wear one." Her eyes were as dry as if she had no more tears to shed. I longed to comfort her or do something to please her. But she said, "Off you go."

I felt an inexplicable dread, as if dear Mother had already half left me. I blurted out, "Mother!"

Quick to sense my desolation, she said gently, "Don't be afraid. Off you go. Leave me alone for a little."

I was right. She wrote:

You have gone. Half my soul seems to have taken flight with you.
I had no means of knowing what had become of you, much less of seeing you for the last time. I had no right to ask either, not being your wife or friend. . . . So we are torn apart. If only I could have borne that inhuman treatment for you, so that you could have lived on! You should have lived to see your name cleared and take up your work again, for the sake of those who loved you. I knew you could not be a counterrevolutionary. You were one of the finest men killed. That's why I love you—I am not afraid now to avow it.
Snow is whirling down. Heavens, even God is such a hypocrite, he is using

HRW Photo by Darwin Chen

this whiteness to cover up your blood and the scandal of your murder.

I have never set store by my life. But now I keep wondering whether anything I say or do would make you contract your shaggy eyebrows in a frown. I must live a worthwhile life like you, and do some honest work for our country. Things can't go on like this—those criminals will get what's coming to them.

I used to walk alone along that small asphalt road, the only place where we once walked together, hearing my footsteps in the silent night. . . . I always paced to and fro and lingered there, but never as wretchedly as now. Then, though you were not beside me, I knew you were still in this world and felt that you were keeping me company. Now I can hardly believe that you have gone.

At the end of the road I would retrace my steps, then walk along it again. Rounding the fence I always looked back, as if you were still standing there waving goodbye. We smiled faintly, like casual acquaintances, to conceal our undying love. That ordinary evening in early spring a chilly wind was blowing as we walked silently away from each other. You were wheezing a little because of your chronic bronchitis. That upset me. I wanted to beg you to slow down, but somehow I couldn't. We both walked very fast, as if some important business were waiting for us. How we prized that single stroll we had together, but we were afraid we might lose control of ourselves and burst out with "I love you"—those three words which had tormented us for years. Probably no one else could believe that we never once even clasped hands!

No, Mother, I believe it. I am the only one able to see into your locked heart.

Ah, that little asphalt road, so haunted by bitter memories. We shouldn't overlook the most insignificant spots on earth. For who knows how much secret grief and joy they may hide. No wonder that when tired of writing, she would pace slowly along that little road behind our window. Sometimes at dawn after a sleepless night, sometimes on a moonless, windy evening. Even in winter during howling gales which hurled sand and pebbles against the window pane. . . . I thought this was one of her eccentricities, not knowing that she had gone to meet him in spirit.

She liked to stand by the window, too, staring at the small asphalt road. Once I thought from her expression that one of our closest friends must be coming to call. I hurried to the window. It was a late autumn evening. The cold wind was stripping dead leaves from the trees and blowing them down the small empty road.

She went on pouring out her heart to him in her diary as she had when he was alive.

30 GUIDED READING
Finding the Main Idea: Why is the mother sadder than before? (When her beloved was alive, she felt his presence; now he is dead.)

31 GUIDED READING
Identifying Pronoun Referents: To what does "it" refer? (the detail that the mother and her beloved never once clasped hands)

32 LITERARY ELEMENT
Imagery: What do the images from nature help capture here? (the mother's desolation)

Zhang Jie **1425**

1. What is the narrator's quandary at the beginning of the story? (She is undecided about marrying a man whom she does not love.)

2. What author's volumes of stories did the mother treasure? (Chekhov's)

3. Why did the mother's beloved marry whom he did? (When a comrade died saving his life, he wed the comrade's daughter to care for her.)

4. In what historical movement was the mother's beloved killed? (the Cultural Revolution)

5. Near the story's end, what does the narrator say will cause a person to suffer for the rest of his or her life? (the chains of an indifferent marriage)

To reteach "Love Must Not Be Forgotten," have students imagine that they work for a Hollywood producer who wants to make a movie about a romance in modern China. Their job is to summarize the story so that the producer can decide whether he or she wants to make it into a film.

---

33 COMPARING LITERATURE

Have students compare and contrast the narrator's feelings about law and morality with those of Nora in *A Doll's House*. How are their situations similar? In what differing ways do they react to the strictures of law and morality?

34 LITERARY ELEMENT

Allusion: Why is an allusion to Hardy, who challenged his era's conventional morality, appropriate here? (Possible response: The mother's and daughter's attitudes challenge accepted ideas about marriage, and the story criticizes the society of its day.)

35 LITERARY ELEMENT

Theme: What does this paragraph's last sentence suggest will be the narrator's decision about marrying Qiao Lin? (She will not.) Why? (Possible response: It would be an "indifferent marriage," since she does not love him.)

36 EVALUATING

Do you agree with the narrator that living singly may be "a sign of a step forward in culture"? Have students support their opinions with logical arguments.

Right up to the day when the pen slipped from her fingers. Her last message was:

I am a materialist, yet I wish there were a Heaven. For then, I know, I would find you there waiting for me. I am going there to join you, to be together for eternity. We need never be parted again or keep at a distance for fear of spoiling someone else's life. Wait for me, dearest, I am coming—

I do not know how, on her deathbed, Mother could still love so ardently with all her heart. To me it seemed not love but a form of madness, a passion stronger than death. If undying love really exists, she reached its extreme. She obviously died happy, because she had known true love. She had no regrets.

33 Now these old people's ashes have mingled with the elements. But I know that no matter what form they may take, they still love each other. Though not bound together by earthly laws or morality, though they never once clasped hands, each possessed the other completely. Nothing could part them. Centuries to come, if one white cloud trails another, two grasses grow side by side, one wave splashes another, a breeze follows another . . . believe me, that will be them.

Each time I read that diary, "Love Must Not Be Forgotten," I cannot hold back my tears. I often weep bitterly, as if I myself experienced their ill-fated love. If not a tragedy it was too laughable. No matter how beautiful or moving I find it, I have no wish to follow suit!

34 Thomas Hardy[17] wrote that "the call seldom produces the comer, the man to love rarely coincides with the hour for loving." I cannot judge them by conventional moral standards. What I deplore is that they did not wait for a "missing counterpart" to call them. If everyone could wait, instead of rushing into marriage, how many tragedies could be averted! **34**

When we reach communism,[18] will there still be cases of marriage without love? Perhaps. . .since the world is so vast, two kindred spirits may never be able to answer each other's call. But how tragic! Could it be that by then we will have devised ways to escape such tragedies? But this is all conjecture.

Maybe after all we are accountable for these tragedies. Who knows? Should we take the responsibility for the old ideas handed down from the past? Because, if you choose not to marry, your behavior is considered a direct challenge to these ideas. You will be called neurotic, accused of having guilty secrets or having made political mistakes. You may be regarded as an eccentric who looks down on ordinary people, not respecting age-old customs—a heretic. In short, they will trump up endless vulgar and futile charges to ruin your reputation. Then you have to succumb to those ideas and marry regardless. But once you put the chains of an indifferent marriage around your neck, you will suffer for it for the rest of your life. **35**

I long to shout: "Mind your own business! Let us wait patiently for our counterparts. Even waiting in vain is better than loveless marriage. To live single is not such a fearful disaster. I believe it may be a sign of a step forward in culture, education, and the quality of life." **36**

---

17. Thomas Hardy: British author (1840–1928) whose fiction often challenged conventional morality and ideas about romantic love; his characters are often destroyed by love.

18. When we reach communism: when we reach a Communist ideal or perfect Communist state, as the teachings of Communism say will one day happen.

1. Research and TV Report. Have students use encyclopedia yearbooks, newspapers, magazines, and other up-to-date sources to research the current attitudes toward love and marriage in China. Students should then work in groups to communicate their findings in a fifteen-minute TV news feature such as those on *60 Minutes*. Different students should take on the roles of interviewers and interviewees.

2. Writing a Dialogue Between Story Characters. Have students work with a partner to write an imaginary dialogue that might take place during a meeting between the narrator and Qiao Lin in which the narrator gives her final decision on the question of their marriage. Invite student pairs to present their dialogues for the class.

CLOSURE

Ask students to consider why this story disturbed so many Communist government officials when it was published in China. Does the story criticize the economic principles of communism? (No.) If not, what are some of the things it does attack? (political repression, stifling of the individual, the myths that China lives up to its principles, that women are liberated, that citizens are fulfilled) ■

First Thoughts

Did you find yourself sympathetic to the narrator's thoughts in the last paragraph? Explain why you agree or disagree with her point of view about marriage.

Identifying Facts

1. How old is the narrator, and why does she say she is virtually "on the shelf"? Who is Qiao Lin?
2. What is "Love Must Not Be Forgotten"? What private information does it reveal?
3. When did the mother's beloved die? What happened afterward?

Interpreting Meanings

1. What do the opening details reveal about the kind of person Qiao Lin is? Do you think the narrator will marry him? Why or why not?
2. What do the **flashbacks** involving the mother's true love reveal about the kind of person he was and the reasons the mother loved him?
3. Some readers feel that this story is very disjointed: It begins with the narrator's feelings about marriage but then veers off into a lengthy **flashback** about the narrator's mother and her love affair. Do you feel that the story is flawed and does not hold together, or do you think that it is a unified piece with a central theme? Explain your response.

Applying Meanings

Do the social pressures that affect the narrator and her mother exist in America today? Discuss.

Creative Writing Response

Writing a Diary Entry. Do you, like the narrator, feel that "If everyone could wait, instead of rushing into marriage, how many tragedies could be averted!"? Write your personal views about marriage, independence, or one of the other related ideas that Zhang Jie deals with in her story, as though you were writing a diary entry.

Language and Vocabulary

Wade-Giles and Pinyin Transliterations

Unlike English and many other **phonetic** languages written in an alphabet where letters represent sounds, Chinese is written in **characters** that represent ideas or meanings. These characters have many pronunciations, depending on the word's context and regional differences. This **ideographic** system has certain advantages: Chinese people who speak very different dialects can still understand each other by using the written characters. But Chinese can be extremely inaccessible to foreigners. For this reason, China's Communist government devised a way to use the Roman alphabet as an alternate way of writing Chinese. The system they developed, called **Pinyin**, came into standard use in the West in 1979 when the Chinese government asked English-language publications to adopt it.

Before 1979, however, the West had been using the **Wade-Giles** system to transliterate—that is, transfer into a different alphabet—Chinese words. Thus, while the names of recent Chinese writers like Zhang Jie (Chang Chieh in the Wade-Giles system) are more familiar under their Pinyin spellings, the names of earlier writers are better known by their Wade-Giles spellings. Except for Zhang Jie, the names of all Chinese writers in this book use Wade-Giles spellings. Consult a recent encyclopedia or another recent reference work to learn the Pinyin spellings of the following writers' names:

1. Li Po
2. Tu Fu
3. Chuang Tzu
4. Lao-tzu

First Thoughts
Students should support opinions with real-life examples and logical arguments.

Identifying Facts
1. thirty; she is not married. the man who wants to marry her
2. the title of the narrator's mother's diary. the great love of the mother's life
3. during the Cultural Revolution. She continued to love him ardently.

Interpreting Meanings
1. Possible response: handsome, conventional, not too bright. Probably not. She does not love him and realizes what a mistake it would be to marry because of social pressure.
2. Possible response: He was distinguished, loyal, faithful, and idealistic.
3. Students should cite story details to support evaluations.

Applying Meanings
Students should support their opinions with real-life examples.

Creative Writing Response
Writing a Diary Entry: Entries should employ the personal style of diaries while stating and supporting opinions.

Language and Vocabulary
1. Li Bo 2. Du Fu 3. Zhuang Zi 4. Laozi ■

LANGUAGE —AND— CULTURE

CONSCIENCE AND CONTROVERSY

At different periods in history, writers the world over have come into conflict with repressive governments. Since the invention of the printing press, when the written word became widely available, down to the present day, there have been governments that have tried to block the writer's pen.

Aleksandr Solzhenitsyn (b. 1918)

Russian author Aleksandr Solzhenitsyn (sōl'zhə·nēt'sin) (see page 1264) moved from obscurity as a high-school teacher to international renown as a writer after the publication of his first novel, *One Day in the Life of Ivan Denisovich* (1962). The novel, based on his own experiences, delivered a scathing condemnation of Soviet prison camps. Solzhenitsyn eventually became a thorn in the side of the Soviet government, which sought to quiet all forms of criticism. In spite of the obvious danger of writing inflammatory fiction under a regime of strict censorship, Solzhenitsyn was committed to his craft and his country. When he won the Nobel Prize for literature in 1970, he did not travel to Stockholm to claim the award, fearing that the Soviet government would not allow him to reenter his country. Solzhenitsyn was finally deported in 1974. He lived in the United States until 1994, when he returned to Russia following the breakup of the Soviet Union.

1

   Solzhenitsyn's writings go beyond the sphere of politics, reaching for what he feels are the higher truths of humanity. In his novel *Cancer Ward,* he wrote ''. . . it is not the task of the writer to defend or criticize one or another mode of distributing the social product, or to defend or criticize one or another form of government organization. The task of the writer is to select more universal and eternal questions, the secrets of the human heart and conscience, the confrontation of life with death, the triumph over spiritual sorrow, the laws of the history of mankind that were born in the depths of time immemorial and that will cease to exist only when the sun ceases to shine.''

Federico García Lorca (1878–1936)

Some writers do not write about politics or governments at all, yet still make enemies of political and military leaders. Nowhere is this point more clearly made than in the life and death of the

Spanish poet and playwright Federico García Lorca (gär·sē′ə lôr′kä (see page 1228). García Lorca is among the best-loved Spanish-language poets of all time. Scholar Edith Helman writes, "Fervent in the love of his people, rooted in the Spanish earth, he inevitably expressed in his poetry . . . all the fears and hatred, frustration and longing of the Spaniards of his time and all times. When he voiced his own passionate love of freedom and impulse to revolt, he gave expression to the feelings of great numbers of inarticulate Spaniards who felt that he was speaking for them." In 1936, García Lorca found himself at the center of one of the great moral struggles of the twentieth century, the Spanish Civil War, which pitted the democratically elected Republic against Fascist forces backed by Hitler and Mussolini. García Lorca was already famous for his work in the theater, which he brought directly to farm workers in small Spanish villages. Early in the war, the Fascists, risking international condemnation, murdered the poet who so eloquently expressed the spirit of the Spanish people. The Fascists, led by Franco, went on to win the war.

Ngũgĩ wa Thiong'o (b. 1938)

Even writers in nominally democratic countries have suffered imprisonment because of their words. By the 1970s, Kenyan author Ngũgĩ ('n·gōō′gē), the head of the Department of Literature at the University of Nairobi (Kenya's capital), had gained international acclaim as an author. But in 1977, Ngũgĩ was arrested. The cause of his arrest was never stated. Government officials—who had already banned a play

that Ngũgĩ coauthored, *Ngaahika Ndeenda (I Will Marry When I Like)*—simply felt that his writings painted the regime in an unflattering light. Although he was never charged with any crime, Ngũgĩ remained in prison for over a year. Finally, mounting pressure by groups such as Amnesty International led to his release. He recorded his experience in his 1981 novel, *Detained*. Ngũgĩ continued to criticize the increasingly repressive Kenyan government. In 1982, hearing that he was soon to be arrested again, the author exiled himself and his family to England, where he lives, writes, and lectures today.

All of these authors hold one thing in common: their writings give a voice to thousands of voiceless people. And nothing worries tyrants more than citizens who, through the words of authors, can articulate their desires.

Schomburg Center for Research in Black Culture/New York Public Library

Kenyan writer Ngũgĩ wa Thiong'o.

WRITING TO LEARN

History: Research and write about the blacklisting of American writers suspected of Communist leanings during the "McCarthy era" in the United States. How do the risks and issues the American writers faced compare with the situations of writers like Solzhenitsyn and Ngũgĩ? ∎

2 CULTURAL BACKGROUND

Spanish Civil War: The Spanish Civil War aroused great fervor outside of Spain as a symbolic showdown between the political right and left—so much so that Americans formed an entire brigade, which fought on the Republican side. Ernest Hemingway chronicled this American participation in his novel *For Whom the Bell Tolls.*

3 LITERARY BACKGROUND

Ngũgĩ's Themes: Ngũgĩ's life and writing were deeply affected by the Mau Mau rebellion of the 1950s, a bloody revolt by black Kenyans against white colonialists, which indirectly led to Kenyan independence in 1963. Ngũgĩ's first published novel, *Weep Not, Child,* recounts the Mau Mau rebellion; his second, *The River Between*, examines the causes of it. *Petals of Blood*, which features a former Mau Mau leader arrested on suspicion of murder, explores corruption in post-colonial Kenya; this last book may have triggered Ngũgĩ's arrest.

Language Skills

VARYING SENTENCES

Although it is possible to construct a seemingly endless variety of sentences in English, there are basically only four main sentence structures. When you can successfully use all four types, you can avoid monotony in your writing, create pleasing rhythms, avoid choppiness, and control the tone and impact of your words.

Simple Sentences

A **simple sentence** consists of one independent clause. An **independent clause** contains a subject and predicate and expresses a complete thought.

SIMPLE SENTENCE
 The British headmistress changes Santha's name to Cynthia.

Compound Sentences

A **compound sentence** contains two or more independent clauses.

COMPOUND SENTENCE
 The British headmistress changes Santha's name to Cynthia, and she changes Premila's name to Pamela.

The independent clauses may be joined with a comma and a coordinating conjunction (*and, but, or, nor*). They may also be joined with a semicolon.

Complex Sentences

A **complex sentence** contains one independent clause and one or more depen-

dent clauses. **Dependent clauses** (also called **subordinate clauses**) begin with words like *although, because, since, when, while, who, what, which,* or *that.* A dependent clause has a subject and predicate but does not express a complete thought.

COMPLEX SENTENCE
 The British headmistress, who is uncomfortable with Indian names, changes Santha's name to Cynthia.

Compound-Complex Sentences

Compound-complex sentences contain one or more independent clauses and one or more dependent clauses.

COMPOUND–COMPLEX SENTENCE
 The British headmistress, who is uncomfortable with Indian names, changes Santha's name to Cynthia, and she changes Premila's name to Pamela.

Note that it is the arrangement of words, not only their meaning, that determines sentence structure.

Exercise 1: Identifying Sentence Structures

Identify which of the four structures each sentence below represents.

1. Truth is like the sun.

2. Zhang Jie wanted to study literature in college, but she chose economics instead.
3. The name of Mahfouz was placed on an Arab boycott list, although the Arab-speaking public continued to read his works.
4. Young Naguib's father urged him to go into school alone; he told him to smile because that would set a good example for the others.
5. Naguib peered around, but he found no trace of his father, who had promised to be there.

Using Complex and Compound-Complex Sentences

Complex and compound-complex sentences increase your ability to express shades of meaning. They also help you to keep your writing concise. To use these sentences effectively, you must subordinate ideas—decide which idea is more important and how the ideas are related.

LOOSE
Zhang Jie once scolded American poet Allen Ginsberg. Her belief was that he was not socially responsible.

SUBORDINATED
Zhang Jie once scolded American poet Allen Ginsberg because she believed he was not socially responsible.

Subordinating the second sentence—making it into a subordinate clause—results in clearer and more concise writing. Subordinate clauses often begin with subordinating conjunctions. The following list provides examples of these conjunctions.

SUBORDINATING CONJUNCTIONS

after	if	unless
although	since	until
as	that	when
because	though	where
before	till	while

Exercise 2: Using Subordinate Clauses

Subordinate the second sentence in each pair, using the subordinating conjunction in parentheses. Combine the sentences to create one complex or compound-complex sentence.

1. The First World War was especially horrible. Each side used poison gas. (because)
2. The Cold War began in 1945. The U.S. and the U.S.S.R. began stockpiling nuclear weapons. (after)
3. Zhang Jie began writing. The Cultural Revolution was over. (when)
4. Rolf Carlé repressed his horrible memories. Azucena reminded him of his past. (until)
5. Two huge cranes fly into the air. The men crawl into the bushes. (as)
6. Raised in North Vietnam, Nguyen Thi Vinh was forced to flee to Hanoi. She endured deep homesickness and anguish over the war. (where)
7. Gregor remained secluded in his room. His family became more unsympathetic over his plight. (while)
8. The villagers' lives have changed. They work to preserve Esteban's memory. (since)
9. The narrator will never be satisfied. He escapes Borges. (until)

Background: In order to complete this assignment, students must be able to summarize a story plot. Use the following activity to give them practice in summarizing.

First, ask students to read the summary of "Pear Tree Dance" by Elizabeth Jolley. Point out that the summary contains only five sentences, and that it mentions only the major events in the story, omitting all details except the pear tree, which is significant because it explains the story's title.

Then choose one short story that students have studied in Unit 11, and have them work in groups of four or five to summarize its plot. Each group's summary should be no more than a paragraph long. Have a member of each group read the summary to the class. Ask group members to discuss how they decided which events should be included and which should be omitted.

Prewriting: To broaden their inferences into general statements of theme, students should reword their inferences so that they can be applied to people in general or to life in general, rather than just to the main characters in the stories.

Critical Thinking and Writing

IDENTIFYING A THEME

Have you ever read a short story and then said, "I don't get it"? To "get it" is to understand the story's theme. Though you probably find the language of modern short stories clear, you may find their themes less so. However, you can learn to identify the theme of—and discover the insights in—any story.

Writing Assignment

In an informative essay, identify the theme of a story you've read in this unit. Your audience is a classmate who has read the work but is having trouble understanding it. In this assignment, you will draw inferences and check them for accuracy.

Background

A **theme** is an underlying truth about life or human nature. Very seldom does an author state a theme directly; rather, the events of the story reveal it. To find the theme of a story, you must make **inferences**, or intelligent guesses. Three steps can help you to identify a theme. In the example below, they are applied to a short story entitled "Pear Tree Dance," by Australian writer Elizabeth Jolley.

1. **Summarize the story's plot.** A toughened old woman, who was raised in a factory town and has always been poor, begins wishing for land in the country. She scrimps and saves but still can't afford the land she wants. Finally, she finds a plot she can afford. To her joy, it includes flowers and a little house. There she plants a pear tree and then dances for the first time in her life.

2. **Infer what the main character learns or how he or she changes.** She learns to dream and then learns that she can attain her dream. In the process she becomes more deeply alive.

3. **Broaden your answer into a statement that could apply to people, or life, in general.** *Daring to dream, and following the dream, enriches people in ways beyond those they can foresee.* This is a statement of theme. Notice that you need at least one complete sentence to express a theme.

Prewriting

Identifying Responses. Freewrite your responses to a favorite short story in this unit. Touch on the following questions.

1. What did you like most about the story?
2. Which parts seemed most intense?
3. How did you feel as you read the story, and what did you think about?

Drawing and Checking Inferences. Summarize the story's plot. Using your summary and your personal responses, infer

FOR FURTHER HELP

Refer students to *Grammar, Usage, and Mechanics: A Reference Guide* at the back of their textbooks for detailed information that will help them write, revise, and proofread their essays.

what the main character has learned and how he or she has changed. To check your inferences, fill out a chart like the one below with supporting facts and events from the story.

Inference	Support from Story
1.	a. _____
	b. _____
	c. _____
2.	a. _____
	b. _____
	c. _____

Then broaden your inferences into a general statement of theme.

Writing

Use the following guidelines as you draft your essay.

1. **Introductory Paragraph.** Begin by noting what originally attracted you to the story, being sure to cite the title, author, and author's country of origin. Explain how your original attraction to the story relates (or doesn't relate) to the story's theme. End the paragraph by stating the theme clearly.

2. **Body Paragraphs.** Use at least one paragraph to explain each inference on which your statement of theme is based. Referring to your prewriting chart, show how facts and details in the story support each inference. Use transitions that keep your logic clear for your readers (see page 56), and arrange paragraphs in a way that makes sense.

3. **Concluding Paragraph.** Quote a line from the story that is especially relevant to the theme. Explain briefly how it relates to the theme, perhaps touching on what the theme means to you. Leave your readers with a clear idea of the theme and the way the story reveals it.

Evaluating and Revising

Use the following checklist as you revise your essay.

1. Does your first paragraph catch the reader's attention, identify the story, and state the theme?
2. Do body paragraphs explain the inferences on which your statement of theme is based?
3. Are your inferences supported with enough facts and details from the story?
4. Are your ideas organized logically and linked with appropriate transitions?
5. Does the concluding paragraph leave the reader with one clear idea about the theme?
6. Are your sentences varied and grammatically correct?

Proofreading and Publishing

Proofread to eliminate errors in mechanics, and make a final copy of your essay. As a class, gather the essays into a booklet that next year's students can use with your literature text.

Writing: One way students can make the logical progression of their essays clear to readers is to include in each sentence a word, phrase, or clause specifying how the sentence relates to the sentence immediately preceding it. These words or phrases may be transitions (see the lists on pp. 56–57) or they may be explanations like the following: *This point is important because . . .; One example of this occurs when . . .;* and so forth. When students evaluate and revise their drafts, they can decide which of these connections and explanations are unnecessary.

Evaluating and Revising: As students revise to ensure sentence variety, they can refer to "Varying Sentences," pp. 1430–1431, and to "Varying Sentence Beginnings and Avoiding Dangling Modifiers," pp. 206–207.

Proofreading and Publishing: Students might want to add other types of material to the class booklet as well. For example, they may choose to include their critical reviews, or any of their creative writing or reading journal entries that were inspired by the selections in the text. ■

WRITING ABOUT LITERATURE

Writing Answers to Essay Questions

The following strategies will help you write answers to the essay questions following each selection in this book. Instructions on the writing process may also be found in the Exercises in Critical Thinking and Writing. A list of these exercises appears in the index on page 1494.

1. Begin by reading the essay question carefully. Make sure you understand exactly what the question is asking you to do, and note how much evidence it asks you to provide.

2. Identify the key verb in the question. It will help you pinpoint your assignment. Look for these key verbs:

▪ **Analyze (Examine).** To *analyze* something is to take it apart and see how it works. You might be asked to analyze one element of a work and explain its effect on other elements or on the work as a whole. For example, you might be asked to analyze Gregor's reaction to finding himself an insect in Franz Kafka's *The Metamorphosis* (see page 1154). Begin by identifying his reaction, and then show how it affects his relationship with his employer, his relationship with his family, and his sense of self. (See **Analyzing Imagery**, page 616, and **Observing and Analyzing a Process**, page 676.)

▪ **Compare/Contrast.** When you *compare*, you point out similarities; when you *contrast*, you point out differences. You might, for example, be asked to compare and contrast two short stories. The best way to organize information for your essay is to use a chart like this one, which shows you similarities and differences at a glance:

	Story A	Story B
Character		
Setting		
Plot		

Vary the chart to suit the particular assignment. If you are asked to compare and contrast two poems, for example, you might use imagery, figures of speech, and tone as your points of discussion. If you are asked to compare and contrast two characters within a play, you might use personality, goals, and change. Once you have decided what points to discuss in your essay, decide on the order in which you will present your ideas. You can discuss all the elements of the first work and then all the elements of the second work (AABB order). Or you can discuss each element in turn (ABAB order), showing how it is similar or different in the two works. (See **Discovering Connections in Literature**, page 58.)

▪ **Describe.** To *describe* means to paint a picture in words. For example, if you were asked to describe the scene at the entrance to Hell in Dante Alighieri's *Inferno* (see page 748), you would try to convey its sights, sounds, and mood so that your readers can experience the scene. If you were asked to describe Eveline in James Joyce's story of the same name (see page 1209), you would discuss what you know about her through direct and indirect characterization—how she looks, acts, speaks, feels, and affects others. (See **Writing a Character Sketch**, page 790.)

▪ **Discuss.** To *discuss* means to comment about something in a general way. For example, if you were asked to discuss the point of one of Jean de La Fontaine's fables (see page 942), you might summarize the fable and comment on its moral.

▪ **Evaluate.** To *evaluate* something is to judge how good or bad—or how effective or ineffective—it is. In thinking about your evaluation, start with your personal reaction to the work. (Did you like it or hate it? Did you find it fascinating or boring?). Next, refine this reaction into a more specific judgment. ("Even though the play was written in the nineteenth century, it still speaks to us today," or "This poem was too rambling to hold my interest.") In the body of your essay, state the reasons for your judgment. For each reason, examine an element of the work and back the reason up with evidence from the work. **Writing a Literary Review** provides hints on selecting criteria (see page 1132).

▪ **Illustrate.** To *illustrate* means to provide examples to support an idea or statement. For example, you might be asked to illustrate the principles of Japanese haiku poetry. You would first define haiku and then show how several haiku poems fit this definition.

▪ **Interpret.** To *interpret* something means to explain its meaning and importance. For example, if you were asked to interpret a Shakespearean sonnet, you might explain each quatrain in turn, then show how the final couplet summarizes or comments on the ideas in the quatrains. If you were asked to interpret a story's meaning, you would first identify the theme and then cite specific details from the work to support your interpretation. (See **Identifying a Theme**, page 1432.)

▪ **Respond.** To *respond* is to give your personal reaction to something. If you were asked to respond to Santha Rama Rau's "By Any Other Name," for example, you would state explicitly whether you liked or disliked it, how it made you feel, and what it made you think about. Be as specific as possible as you explain the reasons for your response. (See **A Personal Response to Literature**, page 122.)

3. Write a thesis statement in which you state the main idea of your essay. Include your thesis statement in the first paragraph, along with any additional sentences that help you catch the reader's attention.

4. Gather evidence to support this thesis statement. If you can use your book, look back over the work for examples and illustrations. For a closed-book essay, make notes on all the supporting details you can remember.

5. Write one paragraph for each main point. Include a topic sentence for each paragraph, and express your ideas as clearly as you can. Don't pad your answer with unrelated details or ideas.

6. End with a concluding paragraph. Summarize or restate your main points, and, if you wish, give your personal response to the work. Try to end your essay with a "clincher" sentence.

Writing and Revising an Essay

You may be asked to choose your own topic for an essay on a specific work.

Prewriting

1. Choose a limited topic that you can cover adequately. If your assignment is an essay of four paragraphs, you can't possibly analyze all the characters in Ibsen's *A Doll's House.* But you do have room to analyze one character or the significance of the title. For ideas on the kinds of topics you might choose, review the list of key verbs on pages 1434–1435.

2. Write a thesis statement. Ask yourself, "What main idea about my topic do I want to discuss?" Then write one or two sentences that state this main idea. If you have trouble expressing your ideas in only one or two sentences, consider narrowing the topic.

3. List two or three main ideas that develop your thesis statement. Jot down the ideas that come to mind when you think about your thesis statement, and choose the strongest two or three. Then go back over the work to find specific points you may have overlooked. Don't rely simply on your memory.

4. Gather and arrange supporting evidence. Your essay should include quotations, specific details, and incidents from **primary sources**, which include the literary work you are writing about, as well as other works, letters, or interviews by the same writer. **Secondary sources**—books, reviews, and critical essays about the work or the writer—may also provide supporting evidence for your ideas.

Before you begin writing, decide which evidence best supports your thesis statement. Then discard any weak or unrelated material. Once you've arranged your main ideas and evidence in the order that seems the most logical, you'll have an informal outline to work from.

Writing

Draft your essay following your outline and notes. Include evidence to support your thesis statement and the main idea of each paragraph. Structure your essay according to this plan:

I. INTRODUCTORY PARAGRAPH
    Catch the reader's interest.
    Tell what the essay will be about.
    Begin or end with the thesis statement.
II. BODY (Paragraphs 2, 3, etc.)
    Develop the thesis statement.
    Include a topic sentence and supporting
      evidence in each paragraph.
III. CONCLUDING PARAGRAPH
    Let the reader know that the essay is
      completed.
    Restate or summarize the thesis statement
      and main ideas.
    Include a personal response (optional).

Evaluating and Revising

Reread your first draft at least twice, checking once for content and once for style.

1. Content. Check to see that you've supported your thesis statement with at least two main ideas and that you've supported each main idea with sufficient evidence. If any part of your evidence appears weak or vague, go back over the work to find more convincing examples.

2. Style. To make your essay read smoothly, you may need to combine related sentences or break up long sentences into shorter ones. Cut unnecessary or repetitive words and phrases.

Proofreading and Publishing

The titles of poems, short stories, and essays should be enclosed in quotation marks; the titles of plays, novels, and other long works (such as epic poems) should be in italics. Sacred works like the Bible and the Koran and the individual books of these works are neither italicized nor placed in quotation marks. In handwriting and typing, italics are indicated by underlining.

Proofreader's Symbols

Symbol	Example	Meaning of Symbol
≡	"An honest thief"	Capitalize a lowercase letter.
/	"Wind And Water And Stone"	Change a capital letter to lowercase.
∧	"Love Must Be Forgotten"	Insert a word.
∧	Lépold Sédar Senghor	Insert or change a letter.
⊙	2000 B.C	Insert a period.
∧	"For Wei Pa In Retirement"	Insert a comma.
∨	Petrarchs sonnets	Insert an apostrophe.
∨ ∨	Half a Day	Insert quotation marks.
underscore	from Kaffir Boy	Set in italics.
∿	Chrétein de Troyes	Change the order of letters.
∼	"Laments on the Dead War"	Change the order of words.
#	Guy deMaupassant	Insert space.
⌒	the nine teenth century	Close up space.
ℓ	Isak Dinesen	Delete.
. . . .	Isak Dinesen	Let it stand (stet).
⌢	Fyodor Dosstoevsky	Delete and close up space.
sp	"The 4 Ages"	Spell it out.
¶	¶In this story, Tolstoy	Indent to begin a new paragraph.

A Model Essay

The following essay is an interpretation of "The Two Brothers," by Leo Tolstoy. The essay shows the writer's revisions for a second draft.

TWO BROTHERS, TWO WAYS TO LIVE

To be content with what one has or to take a risk—what's *is* the best way to live? *Leo* Tolstoy deals with this question in his short parable "The ② Brothers." *Although* He seems to except both ways. *approaches to life* He also seems to favor the risk-taker. In the story, ② brothers come across a stone with writing on it. The *message* stone declares that any one who goes into the forrest, crosses the river, sezes some bear cubs away from their mother and runs up the mountin without looking back will find happiness in a house there. In other words, there will be a great reward *awaits* for one who takes a great risk.

INTRODUCTORY PARAGRAPH
Catches the reader's interest. Presents thesis statement—the story's theme.

BODY
Begins to summarize the story.

The older brother, the cautious one, raises many *reasonable* objections. The message might be a lie or a joke, or the brothers may have misunderstood it. *he says* They might get lost in the forrest or the river might be too wide to swim. The mother bear might kill the brothers. They might not be able to run up the mountain. And *Finally* even if all goes well, the older brother warns, *that* and they reach the house, "the happiness awaiting us there is not at all the sort of happiness we would want." *in brief form* Here are all the reasons why people do not take risks: they can't be sure, *aren't* *what to do* there might be danger, the result might not be worth the effort.

States topic sentence.

Gives details to support topic sentence.

Quotes from story.

Interprets older brother's reaction.

The younger brother gives his reasons for going on. There must be a reason for the message. He does not believe the danger will be great, and if they dont try it, some one else will. He points out that you can't suceed unless you try. Finally, he said, he wouldn't want others to think he was afraid. He is a classic risk-taker. He is confident of the outcome, unconcerned about the danger, and proud of his reputation.

[handwritten edits: adventurous / is willing to take the risks; he believes / feel; also; says; is; casual]

Now they trade old sayings and act on them. "A bird in the hand is worth two in the bush" said the older brother, and settles in. "Beneath a stone no water flows" said the younger brother. He sets out. He follows the instructions on the stone. At the top of the mountain he finds a city. The residents make him their king. After ruling for 5 years, a stronger king defeats him and he is banished and returns to his older brother.

[handwritten edits: the brothers / adages; says; says; ing; whose]

So who made the best decision? Well, both are happy with what has happened to them. The older brother says that he has lived "Quietly and well" but the younger brother, while admitting he has nothing now, believes he has had wonderful experiences. Tolstoy lets both brothers speak, but there is a hint that he favors the younger brother. The younger brother is the one who speaks first, accepting the challenge. And he is the one who speaks last. "I shall always have something to remember, while you have no memories at all," he says, and I can't help

[handwritten edits: brothers / their lives; however; eagerly; of the stone; also]

Margin annotations:

States topic sentence.

Gives details to support topic sentence.

Interprets younger brother's reaction.

States topic sentence.

Supports topic sentence with quotations and details.

CONCLUDING PARAGRAPH

States topic sentence in question form, a cue that essay is drawing to a close.

Explains topic sentence.

Restates thesis statement.

Explains interpretation.

Quotes key passage in story.

Offers personal comment on interpretation.

agreeing with him. A quiet life can be ~~rewarding~~ *satisfying*, but the possi-

bility of a big reward—and the chance for *vivid* memories—tempts

me to aim as high as the younger brother does.

Ends with clincher sentence.

Documenting Sources for a Research Paper

1. Parenthetical citations give brief information in parentheses immediately after a quotation or other reference. More detailed information about each source is given in the bibliography. This method of documenting sources is recommended by the Modern Language Association (MLA).

> **For a quotation from a prose passage by a writer who is identified in the text (page number):**
>
> Joyce ends the chapter with a beautiful image, "the tide . . . flowing in fast to the land with a low whisper of her waves, islanding a few last figures in distant pools" (173).
>
> **For a quotation by a writer whose name is not mentioned in the text (author's last name, page number):**
>
> In *Dubliners,* Joyce's collection of short stories, "[T]he recurrent situation is entrapment" (Levin 5).
>
> **For a quotation from a play (act and scene, and line number if a poetic drama):**
>
> At this point Miranda rejoices, "O brave new world / That has such people in't!" (5.1.213–14).
>
> **For a quotation from a poem (line number):**
>
> In Paul Verlaine's "The Sky Is Just Beyond the Roof," the speaker asks, "Say, what have you done, you who are here, / With your lost youth?" (15–16).

2. Footnotes are placed at the bottom of the page on which the reference appears. A superscript number at the end of the reference within the essay indicates a footnote.[1] Footnotes are generally numbered consecutively within a work.

[1] Harry Levin, ed. *The Portable James Joyce* (New York: Viking, 1965) 5.

[2] Frank O'Connor, *A Short History of Irish Literature* (New York: G. P. Putnam's Sons, 1967) 57.

Check a writing handbook or ask your teacher for the style for footnoting poems, magazine articles, interviews, and books with more than one author.

3. Endnotes are identical to footnotes except that they are listed on a separate page entitled "Notes" at the end of a paper. Endnotes are numbered consecutively.

4. A **Works Cited** section should be included at the end of your essay. This is an alphabetical list of all of the print and nonprint sources you referenced in your essay. The list may include not only books but also magazine articles and videotapes. Entries in your **Works Cited** section are listed alphabetically by the author's last name. Here is a sample **Works Cited** section.

Works Cited

Alazraki, Jaime, ed. *Critical Essays on Jorge Luis Borges.* Boston: G. K. Hall, 1987.

Paz, Octavio. "In Time's Labyrinth." *New Republic* 3 Nov. 1986: 30–35.

A Handbook of Literary Terms

ALLEGORY **A story in which the characters, settings, and events stand for abstract or moral concepts.** An allegory can be read on one level for its literal meaning and on another level for its symbolic, or allegorical, meaning. Leo Tolstoy's "How Much Land Does a Man Need?" (Unit Ten) is an example of an allegory. *See pages* 198, 421, 771, 1044.

ALLITERATION **The repetition of consonant sounds in words that are close to one another.** Alliteration occurs most often at the beginning of words, as in "broken bottle," but consonants within words may also alliterate, as in "always wide awake." The repetition of final consonant sounds in closely grouped words—as in *boasts and jests*—is called **consonance**. Poets may use alliteration and consonance to achieve special rhythmic and musical effects, to emphasize particular images and moods, or to give their poems greater unity. *See pages* 84, 519. *See also* **Assonance.**

ALLUSION **A reference to a statement, person, place, event, or thing that is known from literature, history, religion, myth, politics, or some other field of knowledge.** For example, the title of Anna Akhmatova's poem "Lot's Wife" (Unit Eleven) is an allusion to the Hebrew Bible story of the destruction of Sodom and Gomorrah. Allusions add depth of meaning to a work of literature by inviting comparisons. *See pages* 185, 436, 1290.

ANALOGY **A comparison of two things to show that they are alike in certain respects.** Writers often make analogies to show how something unfamiliar is like something well known or widely experienced. For example, people often draw an analogy between creating a work of art and giving birth. *See pages* 294, 300, 662.

ANECDOTE **A brief and sometimes witty story that focuses on a single interesting incident or event, often in order to make a point or teach a moral lesson.** Sometimes an anecdote reveals the character of a famous person. Taoists, Zen Buddhists, and Sufis, among others, use anecdotes to convey indirectly the teachings of their philosophies. *See pages* 547, 666.

ANTAGONIST *See* **Protagonist.**

ANTITHESIS **A form of parallelism in which contrasting ideas are expressed in a grammatically balanced statement.** The following proverb from the Hebrew Bible balances opposite ideas:

> Faithful are the wounds of a friend; but the kisses of an enemy are deceitful.

See pages 195, 634.

APHORISM **A concise, sometimes witty saying that expresses a principle, truth, or observation about life.** "Don't cry over spilt milk" is a well-known aphorism that points to the uselessness of regretting things that cannot be changed. *See page* 666. *See also* **Epigram, Maxim, Moral, Proverb.**

APOSTROPHE **A figure of speech in which a speaker directly addresses an absent or dead person, a deity, an abstract quality, or something nonhuman as if it were present and capable of responding.** Apostrophe is commonly used in hymns to address a divine being. *See pages* 77, 457.

ARCHETYPE **A pattern or model that serves as the basis for different, but related, versions of a character, plot, image, or theme.** For example, the basic plot of the hero's quest is a recurring pattern in myths and other types of literature from different cultures around the world. *See pages* 8–9, 54–55.

ARGUMENT *See* **Persuasion.**

ASIDE **Private words that a character in a play speaks to another character or to the audience that are not supposed to be overheard by others onstage.** Stage directions usually tell when a speech is an aside. For example, toward the end of Act I in Shakespeare's *The Tempest* (Unit Nine), Prospero makes several asides to Ariel that Miranda and Ferdinand do not hear.

ASSONANCE **The repetition of similar vowel sounds followed by different consonant sounds in words that are close together.** For example, the long *a* sounds in "It's a great day for baseball" create assonance. Certain languages, such as

Japanese, lend themselves to assonance. Like **alliteration**, assonance may be used in poetry to create special rhythmic and musical effects, to emphasize particular images or moods, or to achieve unity. *See pages* 88, 568, 1229. *See also* **Alliteration.**

ATMOSPHERE **The mood or feeling in a literary work.** Atmosphere is usually created through descriptive details and evocative imagery. For example, a story set in a grimy factory town may create a gloomy atmosphere in which characters struggle against despair. *See pages* 729, 1259, 1359. *See also* **Mood.**

AUTOBIOGRAPHY **An account of a person's own life.** *Kaffir Boy* by Mark Mathabane (Unit Eleven) is an autobiography about growing up under apartheid in South Africa. *See pages* 66, 1233, 1366.

BALLAD **A song or songlike poem that tells a story.** Most ballads have a regular pattern of **rhythm** and **rhyme** and use simple language and **refrains** as well as other kinds of **repetition**. Ballads usually tell sensational stories of tragedy, adventure, betrayal, revenge, and jealousy. Arising in the Middle Ages, **folk ballads** were composed by anonymous singers and were passed down orally from generation to generation before they were written down. **Literary ballads**, on the other hand, are composed and written down by known poets, usually in the style of the older folk ballads.

The typical ballad **stanza** is a **quatrain** with the **rhyme scheme** *abcb* (although this is by no means universal). The **meter** is often only loosely **iambic**, with four stresses in the first and third lines and three stresses in the second and fourth lines. The number of unstressed syllables in each line may vary. *See pages* 512, 687.

BIOGRAPHY **An account of a person's life written or told by another person.** For example, Tacitus' historical account of imperial Rome, the *Annals* (Unit Four), includes a biography of the emperor Nero. *See page* 552.

BLANK VERSE **Poetry written in unrhymed iambic pentameter.** *Blank* means that the poetry is unrhymed. *Iambic pentameter* means that each line contains five **iambs**, or metrical feet, each consisting of an unstressed syllable followed by a stressed syllable (˘ ´). Blank verse was the most common metrical form used in English dramatic and epic poetry during the Renaissance. It is the verse form used, for example, in all of Shakespeare's plays, including *The Tempest* (Unit Nine), and in John Milton's epic poem *Paradise Lost*. Because blank verse lends itself easily to slight variations within the basic pattern and can mimic the natural **rhythms** of English speech, it has been used over the centuries by many poets writing in English. Here are the closing lines from *Paradise Lost,* describing Adam and Eve's departure from Paradise:

> The world was all before them, where to choose
> Their place of rest, and Providence their guide;
> They hand in hand, with wand'ring steps and
>   slow,
> Through Eden took their solitary way.

See page 932.

CANTO **A subdivision in a long poem, similar to a chapter in a book.** Dante's *Divine Comedy* (Unit Eight), for example, is divided into one hundred cantos

CHANSON DE GESTE **A kind of epic poem composed in Old French mostly in the eleventh and twelfth centuries, focusing on the heroic deeds of Charlemagne and other feudal lords.** Literally meaning "songs of deeds," *chansons de geste* such as the *Song of Roland* (Unit Eight) share many characteristics with classical **epics**. *See pages* 687, 693.

CHARACTER **An individual in a story, play, or narrative poem.** A character always has human traits, even if the character is an animal, such as the trickster Coyote in American Indian tales, or a god or monster, such as Aphrodite and the giant Sinis in the Greek myth of Theseus (Unit One). Most characters, however, are ordinary human beings, like Nora in Ibsen's *A Doll's House* (Unit Ten).

Characters can be classified as static or dynamic. A **static character** is one who does not change much in the course of a story. A **dynamic character**, on the other hand, changes in some important way as a result of the story's action. Characters can also be classified as flat or round. **Flat characters** have only one or two personality traits. They are one-dimensional—their personalities can be summed up by a single phrase. In contrast, **round characters** have more dimensions to their personalities—they are complex, solid, and multifaceted, like real people. *See pages 599, 785, 1215. See also* **Characterization**.

CHARACTERIZATION   **The process by which the writer reveals the personality of a character.** A writer can reveal a character in the following ways:

1. By telling us directly what the character is like: humble, ambitious, impetuous, easily manipulated, and so on
2. By describing how the character looks and dresses
3. By letting us hear the character speak
4. By revealing the character's private thoughts and feelings
5. By revealing the character's effect on other people—showing how other characters feel or behave toward the character
6. By showing the character's actions

The first method of revealing character is called **direct characterization**. When a writer uses this method, we do not have to figure out what a character's personality is like—the writer tells us directly. The other five methods of revealing a character are known as **indirect characterization**. When a writer uses these methods, we have to exercise our own judgment, putting clues together to figure out what a character is like—just as we do in real life when we are getting to know someone. *See pages 28, 1070. See also* **Character**.

CHORUS   **In classical Greek tragedies, a group of nameless onlookers who comment on and interpret the action of the play.** In most Greek tragedies, the Chorus consists of twelve or fifteen performers who dance as they sing their lines. In Sophocles' *Oedipus Rex* (Unit Four), the Chorus is used as a collective "actor" within the drama itself. *See page 305.*

CLIMAX   **The point of greatest emotional intensity or suspense in a plot.** The climax usually marks the moment toward the end of the plot when the conflict is decided one way or the other. After the climax, the story is usually **resolved**. Long works, such as novels, may have more than one climactic moment, though usually the greatest climax occurs last. *See pages 17, 844, 1033. See also* **Plot, Dramatic Structure.**

COMEDY   **In general, a story that ends happily.** The hero or heroine of a comedy is usually a character who overcomes a series of obstacles and is reconciled with his or her opponents in a way that suggests the renewal of life or the formation of a harmonious society. Shakespeare's *The Tempest* (Unit Nine) contains elements of comedy, as Prospero is ultimately reconciled with Antonio and King Alonso, and the union of the children Miranda and Ferdinand implies that future generations will live in peace. In contrast, the hero or heroine in a **tragedy**, such as *Oedipus Rex*, comes to an unhappy or disastrous end, often due to some **tragic flaw** in his or her personality.

Farce is a type of comedy in which ridiculous and often stereotyped characters are involved in far-fetched, silly situations. The humor in farce is based on crude physical action, slapstick, and clowning. Many of Shakespeare's dramas, including *The Tempest*, contain elements of farce. *See pages 221, 375, 962, 964. See also* **Tragedy**.

CONFLICT   **A struggle or clash between opposing characters, forces, or emotions.** In an **external conflict**, a character struggles against some outside force: another character, society as a whole, or some natural force. An **internal conflict**, on the other hand, is a struggle between opposing needs, desires, or emotions within a single character. Many longer works contain both internal and external conflicts that are often interrelated. *See pages* 40, 382, 732, 1321, 1352, 1403.

CONNOTATIONS   **All the meanings, associations, or emotions that a word suggests.** For example, an expensive restaurant might prefer to advertise its excellent "cuisine" rather than its excellent "cooking." Both words have the same literal meaning, or **denotation**: "prepared food." *Cuisine*, however, has connotations of elegance and sophistication, while *cooking* does not. The same restaurant would certainly not describe its food as "great grub."

Notice the difference between the following pairs of words: young/immature, ambitious/cutthroat, uninhibited/shameless, lenient/lax. In each pair, the second word carries unfavorable connotations that the first word does not. *See page 435.*

CONVENTIONS, EPIC   *See* **Epic**.

COUPLET   **Two consecutive lines of poetry that rhyme.** The Persian epic poem the *Shahname*

(Unit Seven), consists of more than 60,000 couplets. When a couplet forms a complete thought, it is called a **closed couplet**. Shakespeare's **sonnets** (Unit Nine) end in closed couplets. *See pages* 646, 805.

CRISIS *See* **Dramatic Structure**.

DESCRIPTION **Writing that is intended to recreate a person, place, thing, event, or experience.** Description uses **imagery**—language that appeals to the senses to show how something looks, sounds, smells, tastes, or feels to the touch. *See pages* 721, 729.

DICTION **A writer's or speaker's choice of words.** People use different types of words depending on the audience they're addressing, the subject they're discussing, and the effect they're trying to produce. For example, the language a scientist would use in a scholarly article to describe a snowflake would be different from the language used by a poet.

Diction is an essential element of a writer's **style**. It may be, for instance, simple or ornate (big rooms/commodious chambers), general or specific (fish/fantailed goldfish), modern or old-fashioned (men's store/haberdashery). An important aspect of any writer's diction is the **connotation** that the words carry. *See pages* 1031, 1231.

DIDACTIC LITERATURE **A literary work that is meant to instruct, give advice, or convey a philosophy or a moral message.** Much didactic literature, such as the New Testament **parables**, stems from religious teachings. *See pages* 467, 590. *See also* **Fable**.

DILEMMA TALE **A type of moral tale, from the oral tradition, that does not have a resolution but instead ends with a question posed to the audience.** Dilemma tales are particularly popular in Africa, where they are used to uphold community values by inspiring discussions of moral behavior. *See page* 94.

DRAMA **A story that is written to be acted out in front of an audience.** Drama is one of the major **genres**, or forms, of literature. The earliest Western dramas originally had a **sacred** or **ritual** function and were used in religious ceremonies or services. In medieval Japan, a very formal and stylized mode of drama known as **Noh** also developed from religious sources.

In Europe during the Renaissance and Enlightenment, playwrights such as William Shakespeare, Molière, and William Congreve created dramas in several forms—satires, historical plays, comedies, tragedies, and tragicomedies (which combined elements of both comedy and tragedy). In the late nineteenth century, the Norwegian playwright Henrik Ibsen helped influence the direction of much modern drama by creating such **Realist** plays as *A Doll's House* (Unit Ten). *See pages* 302–305, 596–597, 786–787, 840–843, 964–965, 1127.

DRAMATIC MONOLOGUE. **A poem in which a speaker addresses one or more listeners.** The reactions of the listener, who remains silent, must be inferred by the reader. From the speaker's words, the reader learns the speaker's identity, as well as the situation, setting, and the identity of other characters. *See page* 1271.

DRAMATIC STRUCTURE **The method of development of a play's plot.** A typical dramatic structure, especially in the plays of Shakespeare, includes **exposition**, in which relevant background information is presented; **rising action**, which accelerates and adds complications to the plot; the **climax** (sometimes called the **turning point** or **crisis**), which is the moment of greatest emotional intensity or suspense; **falling action**, which unravels the complications; and the **resolution**, which settles the play's conflicts. *See page* 844.

ELEGY **A poem that mourns the death of a person or laments something lost.** Elegies may lament the passing of life and beauty, or they may be meditations on the nature of death. A type of **lyric poetry**, an elegy is usually formal in language and structure, and solemn or even melancholy in **tone**. Modern examples include Yehuda Amichai's "Lament on the War Dead" (Unit Eleven). *See page* 631.

ENJAMBMENT **The running on of a thought from one line of verse to the next.** By cutting down on **end-stopped lines** (lines that conclude a thought with punctuation), enjambment enhances the flow of the poem's language and prevents a strict **rhyme scheme** or **rhythm** from sounding predictable and rigid. *See page* 812.

EPIC **A long narrative poem that relates the great deeds of a larger-than-life hero who embodies the values of a particular society.** Most epics include elements of myth, legend, folklore, and history. Their tone is serious and their language grand. Most **epic heroes** undertake **quests** to achieve something of tremendous value to themselves—like Gilgamesh (Unit Three)—or to their society—like the hero of Virgil's *Aeneid* (Unit Four).

Most ancient epics began as **oral epics**, also known as **primary epics,** which were performed by generations of anonymous storytellers and changed slightly with each retelling. The African epic *Sundiata* (Unit Two), for example, was passed down orally for hundreds of years by storytellers known as **griots** before it was written down in the 1950s. **Literary epics**, on the other hand, are created by individual writers, often from earlier models. Virgil's *Aeneid* is an example of a literary epic modeled after earlier Greek epics—Homer's *Iliad* (Unit Four) and *Odyssey*.

Many epics share standard characteristics and formulas known as **epic conventions**, including

- an **invocation**, or formal plea for aid, to a deity or some other spiritual power to inspire the poet

- action that begins *in medias res* (literally, "in the middle of things") and then **flashes back** to events that take place before the narrative's current time setting

- **epic similes**, or elaborately extended comparisons relating heroic events to simple, everyday events

- a consistently predictable **metrical structure** (originally intended as a memorization aid in oral performances of the epic)

- **stock epithets**, or descriptive adjectives or phrases used repeatedly with—or in place of—a noun or proper name, such as "the wine-dark sea" in Homer's *Odyssey*.
See pages 104, 136–137, 224–227, 458–459, 485, 646–647, 693, 703.

EPIGRAM   A brief, clever, and usually memorable statement that often contains a moral. Fables, such as those in the *Panchatantra* (Unit Five) and by Jean de La Fontaine (Unit Nine), often end with epigrams that summarize the message of the story line. *See pages* 483, 941. *See also* **Aphorism, Maxim, Moral, Proverb**.

EPIPHANY   In a literary work, a moment of sudden insight or revelation that a character experiences. The word *epiphany* comes from the Greek and can be translated as "manifestation" or "showing forth." The term has religious meanings that have been transferred to literature. James Joyce gave the word its literary meaning in an early draft of his novel *A Portrait of the Artist as a Young Man*. In his story "Eveline" (Unit Eleven), for example, the title character's epiphany comes when she realizes she is unable to board the ship with the sailor. *See page* 1208.

EPITHET   An adjective or other descriptive phrase that is regularly used to characterize a person, place, or thing. Phrases such as "Ivan the Terrible" and "Jack the Giant-Killer" are epithets. Homer created so many **stock epithets** in his *Iliad* (Unit Four) and *Odyssey* that his name has been permanently associated with a particular type of epithet. The **Homeric epithet** consists of a compound adjective that is regularly used to modify a particular noun. Famous examples are "the wine-dark sea," "the gray-eyed goddess Athena," and "rosy-fingered dawn." *See pages* 72, 457. *See also* **Epic**.

EPONYM   A real or mythical person from whose name the name of a nation, institution, idea, or term has been derived. For example, Miguel de Cervantes' character Don Quixote (Unit Nine) is the eponym for the word *quixotic*, which describes someone who is like Don Quixote—impractical, romantic, and visionary. *See pages* 436–437.

ESSAY   A short piece of nonfiction prose that examines a single subject from a limited point of view. There are two major types of essays. **Formal essays** are usually serious and impersonal in tone. Because they are written to inform or persuade, they are expected to be factual, logical, and tightly organized. **Informal essays** (also called **personal essays**) generally reveal much about the personalities and feelings of their authors. They tend to be conversational in tone, and many are autobiographical in nature. *See page* 1388.

EXISTENTIALISM   A modern European movement in philosophy, religion, and art that asserts "existence precedes essence," that is, that the universe and everything in it exists but has no meaning, and that people supply meaning through their actions. Some existentialists, such as Albert Camus, emphasize that each person is free to make moral choices that define and give meaning to his or her life. Through their choices and actions, human beings are responsible for what they make of themselves and their lives. *See pages* 1145, 1245, 1257.

FABLE **A very brief story in prose or verse that teaches a moral or a practical lesson about life.** In **beast fables**, the characters are animals that behave and speak like human beings. Some of the most popular fables are those attributed to Aesop, a Greek slave who supposedly lived in the sixth century B.C. Other popular and widely influential fables include those collected in the *Panchatantra* (Unit Five). *See pages* 479, 941. *See also* **Parable**.

FAIRY TALE **A type of folktale that features supernatural elements such as spirits, talking animals, and magic.** Good-hearted, common people who triumph over evil are usually the heroes of fairy tales. Many fairy tales also contain a **moral**—a message about how people ought to behave. *See pages* 46, 52–53.

FALLING ACTION *See* **Dramatic Structure**.

FANTASY **A work that takes place in an unreal world and features incredible characters.** Much **science fiction** is fantasy. *See page* 1146.

FARCE *See* **Comedy**.

FICTION *See* **Nonfiction**.

FIGURE OF SPEECH **A word or phrase that describes one thing in terms of another and is not meant to be understood on a literal level.** Figures of speech (sometimes called **figurative language**) always involve some sort of imaginative comparison between seemingly unlike things. The most common figures of speech are the **simile** (a heart like a comforting fire), the **metaphor** (the dark cloak of night), and **personification** (angry winds shouting through the canyon). *See pages* 89, 370, 1149, 1276. *See also* **Hyperbole, Metaphor, Onomatopoeia, Personification, Simile, Symbol, Understatement**.

FLASHBACK **A scene in a narrative work that interrupts the present action of the plot to "flash backward" and tell what happened at an earlier time.** The flashback is one of the **conventions** of Homer's *Iliad* (Unit Four) and *Odyssey* that became a standard feature of many later epics. *See pages* 225, 228, 1415.

FOIL **A character who is used as a contrast to another character.** The use of a foil emphasizes the differences between two characters,

bringing out the distinctive qualities in each. For example, in the *Nibelungenlied* (Unit Eight), Hagen serves as a foil for Siegfried, thereby emphasizing Siegfried's heroic qualities. *See pages* 740, 837.

FOLKTALE **A story told by the common people.** Folktales belong to the oral tradition. Most folktales are told for entertainment, although they may also teach moral values. Legends, tall tales, fables, ghost stories, and fairy tales are all forms of folktales. *See pages* 1, 7, 26–27.

FORESHADOWING **Clues that hint at what is going to happen later in the plot.** Foreshadowing arouses the reader's curiosity and builds up **suspense**. In "Life Is Sweet at Kumansenu" (Unit Eleven), for example, Abioseh Nicol includes details in his initial description of Meji to foreshadow the story's surprise ending. *See pages* 228, 740, 1335.

FRAME STORY **A story that serves to bind together several different narratives.** Both *The Thousand and One Nights* (Unit Seven) and Boccaccio's *Decameron* (Unit Nine) use frame stories as a device for unifying various shorter stories. *See pages* 478, 638, 814.

FREE VERSE **Poetry that has no regular meter or rhyme scheme.** Free verse usually relies instead on the natural rhythms of ordinary speech. Poets writing in free verse may use **alliteration, internal rhyme, onomatopoeia, repetition**, or other devices to achieve their effects. They may also place great emphasis on **imagery**. *See page* 1229.

GENRE **The category to which a literary work belongs.** Examples of genres include **drama**, the **epic**, the **novel**, the **short story**, and **lyric poetry**. *See pages* 161, 987.

HAIKU **A brief, unrhymed, three-line poem developed in Japan in the 1600s.** In the original language, the first and third lines of a haiku have five syllables each, and the middle line has seven. Haiku generally juxtapose familiar images and present them in a compressed form, forcing the reader to make an imaginative leap to understand the connection between them.

A light-hearted variation on the traditional haiku form is the **senryu**. Senryu are intended to point out the humor and irony of the human condition. *See pages* 563, 572–573, 577, 612–613.

HYMN **A lyric poem or song addressed to a divine being.** Hymns praise the power and wisdom of the deity and often ask for divine help or mercy. *See pages* 66, 72, 455. *See also* **Apostrophe, Psalm.**

HYPERBOLE **A figure of speech that uses exaggeration to express a strong sentiment or create a comic effect.** Also called **overstatement** and **exaggeration**, hyperbole does not express the literal truth; however, it is often used to capture a sense of intensity or to emphasize the essential nature of something. For example, when we say we are "sweating to death" in a stuffy room, we are using a hyperbole to express extreme discomfort. Hyperbole is often used in **satire**, such as Voltaire's *Candide* (Unit Nine), for ridiculing or exposing an opponent's vices or follies. *See pages* 410, 413.

IAMBIC PENTAMETER **A line of poetry made up of five iambs.** An **iamb** is a metrical **foot**, or unit of measure, consisting of an unstressed syllable followed by a stressed syllable (◡ ′). The word *preferred,* for example, is made up of one iamb. Pentameter is derived from the Greek words *penta* ("five") and *meter* ("measure"). **Sonnets** and **blank verse** use iambic pentameter. It is by far the most common verse line in English poetry because of its similarity to the natural rhythms of spoken English. Here, for example, are two lines of iambic pentameter from Shakespeare's *The Tempest:*

> His mother was a witch, and one so strong
> That could control the moon, make flows and ebbs

See pages 805, 932, 1003. *See also* **Meter.**

IMAGERY **Language that appeals to the senses.** Most images are visual—that is, they appeal to the sense of sight. But imagery can also appeal to the reader's senses of hearing, touch, taste, or smell. While imagery is an element in all types of writing that involve **description**, it is especially important in poetry. Writers and poets often use **figures of speech** to create vivid images. *See pages* 280, 575, 1012, 1016, 1028, 1331.

IRONY **A contrast or discrepancy between expectations and reality—between what is said and what is really meant, between what is expected and what really happens, or be-** tween what appears to be true and what is really true. Irony in literature falls into three major categories:

1. Verbal irony occurs when a writer or speaker says one thing but really means the opposite. If you tell a friend who shows up an hour late for an appointment, "I just love being kept waiting in the rain," you are using verbal irony.

2. Situational irony occurs when what actually happens is the opposite of what is expected or appropriate. An example of situational irony takes place in Greek mythology when Zeus falls in love with a mortal woman named Semele. Zeus promises to give Semele anything she wants. To his dismay, she begs to see him in his true form as the Lord of Heaven. Zeus reluctantly agrees, and the brilliant splendor of the god burns her to death.

3. Dramatic irony occurs when the audience or the reader knows something important that a character in a play or story does not know. Dramatic irony can heighten a comic effect or generate **suspense**. In *Oedipus Rex* (Unit Four), for example, when the Corinthian messenger tells Oedipus that the King of Corinth has died of natural causes, Oedipus believes he has been released from the prophecy that says he will murder his father. The audience, however, knows that the truth has yet to come to light. *See pages* 98, 306, 648, 705, 814, 1309, 1344.

LEGEND **A story about extraordinary deeds, based to some extent on fact.** The African epic *Sundiata* (Unit Two), for example, is based on the life of a historical figure, Sundiata Keita, who reestablished the Mandingo Empire of Old Mali in 1235. Through many retellings over time, however, the facts of his life were greatly embellished, and Sundiata Keita became a legendary hero. *See pages* 102–103.

LYRIC POETRY **Songlike poetry that focuses on expressing private emotions or thoughts.** Most lyric poems are short, and they usually imply rather than directly state a single strong emotion. The term *lyric* comes from ancient Greece, where lyric poems, such as those by Sappho (Unit Four), were recited to the accompaniment of a stringed instrument called a lyre. Today, lyric poets still try to make their poems melodious, but they rely only on the musical effects they can create with words (such as **rhyme**, **rhythm**, **alliteration**, and **on-**

omatopoeia). *See pages* 80, 218, 280, 987, 1410.

MAGIC REALISM   **A twentieth-century literary style that combines incredible events with realistic details and relates them all in a matter-of-fact tone.** Magic realism originated in Latin America, where authors such as Gabriel García Márquez and Julio Cortázar (Unit Eleven) drew on elements of **surrealism** and local **folklore** to create a style that is both timeless and innovative. *See pages* 1146, 1290.

MAXIM   **A brief, direct statement that expresses a basic rule of human conduct or a general truth about human behavior.** "It is better to give than to receive" is an example of a well-known maxim. *See pages* 415, 537, 540, 542. *See also* **Epigram, Moral, Proverb.**

METAPHOR   **A figure of speech that makes a comparison between two seemingly unlike things without using the connective words** *like,* *as,* *than,* or *resembles.* A **direct metaphor** states that one thing is another, such as "the stars are icy diamonds." ("Stars like icy diamonds" is a **simile.**) Often metaphors are **implied**: "Against her black formal gown, she wore a constellation of diamonds" implies a comparison between diamonds and stars and between the black gown and a night sky.

- An **extended metaphor** is a metaphor that is developed over several lines of writing or even through an entire poem or paragraph. Marie de France uses an extended metaphor that compares the love of Tristan and Iseult to a honeysuckle in "Chevrefoil" (Unit Eight).
- A type of **cliché**, a **dead metaphor** is a metaphor that has become so common that we no longer even notice that it is a figure of speech. Our everyday language is filled with dead metaphors, such as "the pinnacle of success," "a tower of strength," and "the root of the problem."
- A **mixed metaphor** is the inconsistent mixture of two or more metaphors. Mixed metaphors are usually unintentional and often conjure up ludicrous images. "Those snakes in the grass pulled the rug out from under us." *See pages* 89, 370, 1125.

METER   **A generally regular pattern of stressed and unstressed syllables in poetry.**

Meter is measured in units called feet. A **foot** consists of one stressed syllable and usually one or more unstressed syllables. The standard feet used in English poetry are the **iamb** (as in *convince*), the **trochee** (as in *borrow*), the **anapest** (as in *contradict*), the **dactyl** (as in *accurate*), and the **spondee** (as in *free fall*). In meters such as **iambic pentameter**—which consists of five iambs per line—other feet may be substituted occasionally. Such variations prevent the meter from sounding singsong and monotonous.

When we want to indicate the metrical pattern of a poem, we mark the stressed syllables with the symbol ´ and the unstressed syllables with the symbol ˘. Indicating the metrical pattern of a poem in this way is called **scanning** the poem, or **scansion**. Here, for example, is a passage from *The Tempest* with the scansion marked. Note how Shakespeare varies the basic iambic pentameter by substituting an anapest for one of the feet in the second line and by adding an extra unstressed syllable at the end of the third line.

This blue-eyed hag was hither brought with child
And here was left by the sailors. Thou, my slave,
As thou reportst thyself, wast then her servant

See pages 226, 805, 807, 1229. *See also* **Blank Verse, Iambic Pentameter.**

MIRACLE, MYSTERY, AND MORALITY PLAYS *See* **Drama.**

MODERNISM   **A broad trend in literature and the other arts, from approximately 1890 to 1940, that reflected many artists' concern over society's loss of traditional values.** In general, modernist writers sought new forms to reflect the fragmentation and uncertainty that they felt characterized modern life. Many modernist poets, for example, rejected traditional meter in favor of **free verse.** Novelists such as James Joyce employed a new technique called **stream of consciousness** to record the jagged monologue of their characters' thoughts. *See pages* 1143, 1284.

MOOD   **The overall emotion created by a work of literature.** Mood can usually be described with one or two adjectives, such as eerie, dreamy, jubilant, or angry. All of the elements of literature, from **figures of speech** to to the language's **rhythm**, contribute to the work's mood. *See pages* 527, 916, 1022, 1061. *See also* **Atmosphere**.

MORAL **A lesson about life that a story teaches.** Fables often end with a moral that is clearly stated. *See pages* 46, 203, 483. *See also* **Epigram, Maxim, Proverb**.

MOTIF **In literature, a word, character, object, image, metaphor, or idea that recurs in a work or in several works.** The rose is a motif that has recurred throughout centuries of love poetry. In the *Prose Edda* (Unit Eight), contest is a recurring motif. A literary motif always bears an important relationship to the theme of the work. *See pages* 10, 46, 713, 1193. *See also* **Symbol**.

MOTIVATION **The reasons that compel a character to act as he or she does.** A character's motivations fuel the plot of a story and set it into motion. *See pages* 22, 151.

MYTH **An anonymous, traditional story that explains a belief, a custom, or a mysterious natural phenomenon.** Most myths are related to religion in some way, and almost all of them involve the exploits of gods and heroes. Every culture has its own mythology, including **origin myths**, which explain how things came to be. *See* Unit One.

NARRATIVE **Any work of literature, written or oral, that tells a story.** Narrative literature may be fictional (such as fairy tales and short stories) or nonfictional (such as autobiographies and histories); it may be prose, such as *The Metamorphosis* (Unit Eleven), or poetry, such as the *Iliad* (Unit Four). Narrative is distinguished from drama, which acts out, rather than tells, a story.

NARRATOR **The person or character who tells a story.** *See* **Point of View**.

NATURALISM **A radical offshoot of Realism that arose in France in the 1870s.** Naturalist writers, led by Émile Zola, considered free will an illusion and often showed their characters as helpless victims of heredity, fate, and their environment. *See pages* 983, 1042. *See also* **Realism**.

NEOCLASSICISM **The revival of classical Greek and Roman standards and forms, especially during the late seventeenth and eighteenth centuries.** The neoclassicists valued the classical ideals of order, reason, balance, harmony, clarity, and restraint. In literature, in particular, they studied and tried to emulate the Roman poets Horace and Virgil. *See page* 802.

NOH **A highly stylized form of Japanese drama that originated in the Middle Ages.** Noh dramas, which are still performed in Japan today, incorporate music, dance, and rhyme. *See pages* 596–597. *See also* **Drama**.

NONFICTION **Prose writing that narrates real events.** Nonfiction is distinguished from **fiction**—writing that is basically imaginative rather than factually true. Popular forms of nonfiction are **autobiography**, **biography**, and the **essay**. Other forms of nonfiction include newspaper articles, historical and scientific writing, and even personal diaries and letters.

NOVEL **A long fictional prose narrative, usually of more than fifty thousand words.** In general, the novel uses the same basic literary elements as the short story: **plot**, **character**, **setting**, **theme**, and **point of view**. The novel's length usually permits these elements to be more fully developed than they are in the short story. However, this is not always true of the modern novel. Some are basically character studies, with only the barest plot structures. Others reveal little about their characters and concentrate instead on setting or **tone** or even on language itself.

Although some early prose narratives resemble the novel in form, the novel as a distinct literary genre is widely considered to have emerged in Japan around A.D. 1000 with Lady Murasaki Shikibu's *Tale of Genji* and in Europe with the publication of Miguel de Cervantes' *Don Quixote* in 1605 (Unit Nine). *See page* 588.

ODE **A complex, generally lengthy lyric poem on a serious subject.** The two main types of modern odes are based on classical models. One is highly formal and dignified in style and is generally written for ceremonial or public occasions. This type of ode, called the **Pindaric ode**, derives from the choral odes of the ancient Greek poet Pindar, who wrote them in honor of the victors at the Olympics and other sacred games. The **Horatian ode**, like the lyrics of the Roman poet Horace for whom it is named, tends to be more personal and reflective in style. *See page* 415.

ONOMATOPOEIA **The use of a word whose sound imitates or suggests its meaning.** Many familiar words, such as *clap, squish, snort,* and *whine,* are examples of onomatopoeia. In poetry, onomatopoeia can reinforce meaning while creating evocative and musical effects. *See page* 1229.

OXYMORON **A figure of speech that combines apparently contradictory or opposing ideas.** "Living death," "cruel love," and "deafening silence" are oxymorons. The classic oxymoron "wise fool" is almost a literal translation of the term from the Greek: *Oxys* means "sharp" or "keen," and *moros* means "foolish." *See page* 811.

PARABLE **A short, allegorical story that teaches a moral or religious lesson about life.** The most famous parables in Western literature are those told by Jesus in the Gospels of the New Testament. *See pages* 198, 590, 1044. *See also* **Allegory.**

PARADOX **An apparent contradiction that is actually true.** For example, to say that "she killed him with kindness" is a paradox. The statement challenges us to find an underlying truth that resolves the apparent contradiction. *See pages* 468, 476, 542, 1413. *See also* **Oxymoron.**

PARALLELISM **The repetition of words, phrases, or sentences that have the same grammatical structure or that restate a similar idea.** Also called **parallel structure,** parallelism is used frequently in literature that is meant to be read aloud, such as poetry and speeches, because it helps make the literature memorable. In much biblical writing, such as the Book of Psalms (Unit Three), the rhythm of parallelism helps to unify ideas, emphasize images, and heighten the emotional effect of the words. **Structural parallelism** (repetition of a word or an entire sentence pattern), **restatement** (repetition of an idea using different words), and **antithesis** (the balancing of contrasting ideas) are some of the ways writers achieve the effect of parallelism. *See pages* 186, 195, 476.

PARODY **The imitation of a serious artistic work for amusement or instruction.** Parodies use exaggeration or inappropriate subject matter to make a serious form or particular work of art seem laughable or to highlight its flaws. In *Don Quixote* (Unit Nine), for example, Cervantes parodies the courtly tradition of chivalry and knighthood. *See page* 822.

PASTORAL POETRY **Poetry that depicts rustic life in idealized terms.** The term *pastoral* comes from the Latin word for shepherd, and originally pastorals were about shepherds and nymphs. Today the term has a looser meaning and refers to any poem that portrays an idealized rural setting or that expresses nostalgia for an age or place of lost innocence. *See pages* 67, 379.

PERSONA *See* **Speaker.**

PERSONIFICATION **A kind of metaphor in which a nonhuman thing or quality is talked about as if it were human.** For example, the familiar figure of a blindfolded woman holding a sword and a pair of scales is a personification of justice. The names of many everyday objects, such as the "hands of a clock," and many ordinary expressions, such "an angry sky," involve personification. In poetry, personification invites the reader to view the world as if natural and inanimate objects possess the same feelings, qualities, and souls that people do. Li Ch'ing-chao's "Peonies" (Unit Six) provides a fine example of personification. *See pages* 370, 457, 533, 1286.

PERSUASION **Writing that tries to convince the reader or listener to think or act in a certain way.** Examples of persuasion include political speeches, editorials, and advertisements, as well as many **essays** and longer works of literature. Persuasion may appeal to both the emotions and the intellect. When it appeals primarily to reason rather than to emotion, it is called **argument.** *See page* 285.

PLOT **The series of related events that make up a narrative, such as a story, novel, or epic.** The plot is the underlying structure of a narrative. Most plots are built on these "bare bones": A **basic situation,** or **exposition,** introduces the characters, setting, and, usually, the narrative's major **conflict.** Out of this basic situation, **complications** develop, intensifying the conflict. **Suspense** mounts to a **climax**—the most exciting or tense part of the plot. At the climax, the outcome of the conflict is determined. Finally, all the problems or mysteries of the plot are unraveled in the **resolution,** or **dénouement.** Longer narrative works, such as novels, plays, or epics, often contain **subplots,** or minor plots interwoven with the main plot. *See pages* 17, 639, 1033. *See also* **Dramatic Structure.**

POETRY **A kind of rhythmic, compressed language that uses figures of speech and imagery designed to appeal to our emotions and imaginations.** Most of the world's poetry falls into three major types: **lyric poetry**, the **ballad**, and the **epic**. Some specialized types of poetry, however, such as the **haiku** of Japan, defy these broad categorizations. Though poetry is one of the oldest forms of human expression, it is extremely difficult to define. The English Romantic poet William Wordsworth called it ''the spontaneous overflow of powerful feelings,'' and the Japanese scholar Kamo Mabuchi claimed that it provides ''without explanation the reasons governing order and disorder in the world.'' *See also* **Ballad, Epic, Haiku, Lyric Poetry, Pastoral Poetry, Prose Poetry, Psalm, Rubá'i, Sonnet.**

POINT OF VIEW **The vantage point from which a writer tells a story.** There are three main points of view: **omniscient**, **first-person**, and **limited third-person**.

1. In the **omniscient** (or ''all-knowing'') **point of view**, the person telling the story—the **narrator** —knows everything that's going on in the story. This omniscient narrator is outside the story, a godlike observer who can tell us what all the characters are thinking and feeling, as well as what is happening anywhere in the story. For example, in ''The Rat Trap'' by Selma Lagerlöf (Unit Eleven), the narrator enters into the thoughts and secrets of every character.

2. In the **first-person point of view**, the narrator is a character in the story. Using the pronoun *I*, this narrator tells us his or her own experiences but cannot reveal with certainty any other character's private thoughts. When we read a story in the first person, we hear and see only what the narrator hears and sees. We may have to be skeptical and interpret what this narrator says because a first-person narrator may or may not be objective, honest, or perceptive. The short story ''Borges and Myself'' (Unit Eleven) uses a first-person narrator.

3. In the **limited third-person point of view**, the narrator is outside the story—like an omniscient narrator—but tells the story from the vantage point of only one character. The narrator goes where this chosen character goes and reveals this character's thoughts. The reader learns the events of the narrative through the perceptions of the chosen character. Hwang Sun-won's ''Cranes'' (Unit Eleven) is an example of a story told from the limited third-person point of view. *See pages* 34, 1041, 1197.

PROSE POETRY **Poetry written in prose form, but using poetic devices such as rhythm, imagery, and figurative language to express a single strong emotion or idea.** This form of lyric poetry developed in the nineteenth century in France and was popularized by Charles Baudelaire and Arthur Rimbaud. *See page* 1265.

PROTAGONIST **The main character in a work of fiction, drama, or narrative poetry.** The protagonist is the character whose conflict sets the plot in motion. (The character or force that struggles against or blocks the protagonist is called the **antagonist**.) Most protagonists are **rounded**, **dynamic characters** who change in some important way by the end of the story. Whatever the protagonist's weaknesses, we usually identify with his or her conflict and care about how it is resolved. *See also* **Character**.

PROVERB **A short saying that expresses a common truth or experience, usually about human failings and the ways that people interact with one another.** Proverbs often incorporate such literary elements as **metaphor**, **alliteration**, **parallelism**, and **rhyme**. *See page* 84. *See also* **Aphorism, Epigram, Maxim, Moral.**

PSALM **Any sacred song or hymn.** Psalms were originally sung to the accompaniment of a harp (the word *psalm* comes from a Greek verb meaning ''to pluck''). Today, the term is usually used to refer to any of the 150 poems that make up the Book of Psalms in the Old Testament. These lyric poems greatly influenced the development of **free verse** in the nineteenth and twentieth centuries. *See page* 186. *See also* **Hymn**.

QUATRAIN **A four-line stanza or poem, or a group of four lines unified by a rhyme scheme.** *See pages* 655, 805, 1224. *See also* **Ballad, Rubá'i, Sonnet, Stanza.**

REALISM **In literature and art, the attempt to depict people and things as they are, without idealization.** Although realistic description has long been a tool of writers the world over, Realism as a movement developed during the mid—

nineteenth century as a reaction against Romanticism. Realist writers believed fiction and drama should truthfully depict the harsh, gritty reality of everyday life without beautifying, sentimentalizing, or romanticizing it. Gustave Flaubert, Henrik Ibsen, and Anton Chekhov are considered Realist writers. *See pages 982–985, 1042, 1127. See also* **Naturalism**.

REFRAIN   A repeated word, phrase, line, or group of lines. While refrains are most common in poetry and songs, they are sometimes used in prose, particularly speeches. Refrains are used to create rhythm, build suspense, or emphasize important words or ideas. An example of a refrain occurs in Baudelaire's poem "Invitation to the Voyage" (Unit Ten). *See pages 88, 514, 1022.*

REPETITION   The intentional repeating of a sound, word, phrase, line, or idea in order to create a musical or rhythmic effect, build suspense, add emphasis, or otherwise give unity to language. Many literary elements involve some kind of repetition. For example, **alliteration** repeats consonant sounds, **parallelism** repeats grammatical structures or ideas, **meter** repeats a regular pattern of stressed and unstressed syllables, and **refrains** repeat a line or group of lines. In **incremental repetition**, a line or section of a poem or song is repeated with some variation in wording. Usually, the variation adds significant new information or expresses a significant change in meaning or attitude. Yehuda Amichai's "Laments on the War Dead" (Unit Eleven) uses incremental repetition. *See pages 162, 1384. See also* **Alliteration, Assonance, Consonance, Meter, Parallelism, Refrain, Rhyme.**

RESOLUTION   *See* Plot.

RHYME   The repetition of accented vowel sounds and all sounds following them in words that are close together in a poem. "Lark" and "shark" rhyme, as do "follow" and "hollow." The most common type of rhyme, **end rhyme**, occurs at the ends of lines. **Internal rhymes** occur within lines.

When words sound similar but do not rhyme exactly, they are called **approximate rhymes** (or **half rhymes**, **slant rhymes**, or **imperfect rhymes**). "Lark" and "lurk" are approximate rhymes, as are "follow" and "halo."

The pattern of end rhymes in a poem is called its **rhyme scheme**. A rhyme scheme is indicated by assigning each new end rhyme a different letter of the alphabet. Many traditional forms of poems, such as the **Italian sonnet** and the Persian **rubá'i**, follow strict rhyme schemes. For example, most English translations of the rubá'i follow the rhyme scheme *aaba*, as the following example from Edward FitzGerald's translation of Omar Khayyám's *Rubáiyát* illustrates:

A Book of Verses underneath the Bough,	a
A Jug of Wine, a Loaf of Bread—and Thou	a
Beside me singing in the Wilderness—	b
Oh, Wilderness were Paradise enow!	a

See pages 804–805, 807, 812, 1224, 1229. See also **Consonance, Couplet, Rubá'i, Sonnet.**

RHYTHM   The alternation of stressed and unstressed syllables in language. Rhythm occurs naturally in all forms of spoken and written language. The most obvious kind of rhythm is produced by **meter**, the regular pattern of stressed and unstressed syllables found in some poetry. But writers can also create less structured rhythms by using different kinds of **repetition** (such as **rhyme**, **alliteration**, **assonance**, **parallelism**, and **refrains**), or by balancing long and short words, phrases, or lines. Such rhythms are common in **free verse**. *See pages 88, 804, 932, 1229. See also* **Blank Verse, Free Verse, Meter.**

RISING ACTION   *See* Dramatic Structure.

ROMANCE   Historically, a medieval European verse narrative chronicling the adventures of a brave knight or other hero who must overcome great danger for love of a noble lady or high ideal. The stories of King Arthur and of his chivalrous knights of the Round Table, such as Perceval and Lancelot, are examples of **courtly romances**. Today, the term has come to mean any story that presents a world that is happier, more exciting, or more heroic than the real world. *See pages 688, 822, 838.*

ROMANTICISM   A literary, artistic, and philosophical movement that developed during the late eighteenth and early nineteenth centuries as a reaction against neoclassicism. While neoclassicism (and classicism) emphasize reason, order, harmony, and restraint, Romanticism emphasizes emotion, imagination, intuition, freedom, personal experience, and the beauty of nature. However, many critics feel that the traditional opposition between Romanticism and classicism is all too often forced and exaggerated. The works of the German poet and dramatist Johann Wolfgang von Goethe and the English poet William Wordsworth are closely identified with Romanticism. *See pages* 52, 979.

RUBÁ'I (*plural:* **rubáiyát**) **A Persian word meaning "quatrain," or four-line verse.** The rubá'i is an ancient literary form that Persian poets used to express their thoughts on diverse subjects. In English translation, the most famous example is *The Rubáiyát of Omar Khayyám* (Unit Seven), published by Edward FitzGerald in 1859. Generally faithful to the eleventh-century originals, FitzGerald's translation is widely considered a masterpiece of English poetry in its own right. *See pages* 655, 659.

SATIRE **A kind of writing that ridicules human weakness, vices, or folly in order to bring about social reform.** Satires often try to persuade the reader to do or believe something by showing the opposite view as absurd or—even more forcefully—vicious and inhumane. To achieve their purpose, satirists may use **exaggeration** (such as **hyperbole**), **irony**, **parody**, and **wit**. Voltaire uses all these techniques in his scathing satire of European rationalism, *Candide* (Unit Nine). *See pages* 838, 938, 946, 962.

SCANSION *See* **Meter**.

SCIENCE FICTION **A form of fantasy writing in which scientific facts, assumptions, or hypotheses form the basis of adventures in the future, on other planets, in other dimensions of space or time, or under new variants of scientific laws.** Although science fiction is usually set in the future, writers often use it to comment, in the form of **satire**, on the present. *See page* 1146.

SETTING **The time and place of a story, play, or narrative poem.** Usually, the setting is established early in a narrative through descriptive details and **imagery**. Longer works may have more than one setting. For example, Voltaire's *Candide* (Unit Nine) begins in Europe but moves to South America and other parts of the globe.

Setting is often closely linked to the **mood** of a literary work. For example, the exotic island setting of *The Tempest* (Unit Nine) contributes to the play's mood of isolation, imprisonment, and supernatural mystery. Setting may also reveal **character** by showing whether a character is in harmony with a particular place or in **conflict** with it. In "Life Is Sweet at Kumansenu" (Unit Eleven), for example, the mother Bola accepts and ultimately gains consolation from the traditions of her village. Finally, setting may suggest a story's **theme**. In "Eveline" (Unit Eleven), for example, the main character must make a decision between remaining in the paralyzing setting of Dublin and escaping overseas with a sailor. *See pages* 1007, 1259, 1296–1297. *See also* **Atmosphere, Mood**.

SHORT STORY **A short fictional prose narrative.** Although some ancient prose narratives (such as the Book of Ruth, Unit Three) resemble modern short stories, as a distinct **genre** the short story developed in the nineteenth century. Short stories are more limited than **novels**, usually having only one major **character**, **plot**, **setting**, and **theme**. The short story is usually built on a plot that consists of a **basic situation** or **exposition**, **conflict**, **complications**, **climax**, and **resolution**. However, many modern short stories concentrate less on "what happens" and more on revealing a character or evoking a vivid emotional effect. *See pages* 177, 1042.

SIMILE **A figure of speech that makes a comparison between two seemingly unlike things by using a connective word such as *like, as, than*, or *resembles*.** "A full moon like an accusing face," "hail hard as BB pellets," "an actor's hand opening more gracefully than a blossom," and "clouds resembling stuffed animals" are all examples of similes.

Like an extended metaphor, an **extended simile** is developed over several lines of writing or even through an entire poem or paragraph. An **epic** or **Homeric simile** is an elaborately extended simile that relates heroic events to simple, everyday events. Homer used many such similes in his epic poems, the *Iliad* (Unit Four) and the *Odyssey*. *See page* 370. *See also* **Figure of Speech, Metaphor**.

SONNET **A fourteen-line lyric poem, usually written in iambic pentameter, that has one of several traditional rhyme schemes.** The oldest sonnet form is the **Petrarchan** (or **Italian**) **sonnet,** which was popularized by the fourteenth-century Italian poet Petrarch. This kind of sonnet is divided into two parts: an eight-line **stanza** called the **octave,** having the rhyme scheme *abbaabba*, and a six-line stanza called the **sestet**, having the rhyme scheme *cdecde* or *cdcdcd*. The octave usually presents a problem, poses a question, or expresses an idea that leads up to the **turn** (called the **volta** in Italian), which marks a shift in the poem. The sestet then resolves, answers, or drives home the idea that was developed in the octave.

The other major sonnet form, which was widely used by Shakespeare, is known as the **Shakespearean** (or **English**) **sonnet**. It consists of three stanzas called **quatrains** followed by a concluding stanza called the **couplet**. The three quatrains often express related ideas or examples, while the couplet sums up the poet's conclusion or message. The most common rhyme scheme for the Shakespearean sonnet is *abab cdcd efef gg*. Subsequent generations of poets have developed many variations based on the Petrarchan and Shakespearean forms. *See pages* 804–805, 1003, 1276. *See also* **Couplet, Quatrain, Stanza**.

SPEAKER **In a poem, the voice that addresses us.** The speaker may be the poet or may be a **persona**, a character whose voice and concerns do not necessarily reflect those of the poet. *See pages* 80, 1410.

STANZA **A group of lines in a poem that form a single unit.** A stanza in a poem is something like a paragraph in prose: It often expresses a unit of thought. A stanza may consist of one line or any number of lines beyond that. Stanzas are usually named for the number of lines they contain or for the meter and rhyme scheme that they follow. A **couplet**, for example, consists of two lines, a **tercet** of three lines, and a **quatrain** of four lines. The typical **ballad stanza** is a quatrain with the rhyme scheme *abcb* and an **iambic meter** with four stresses in the first and third lines and three stresses in the second and fourth lines. *See pages* 1224, 1226. *See also* **Rubá'i**.

STREAM OF CONSCIOUSNESS **A modern writing style that tries to depict the random flow of thoughts, emotions, memories, and associations rushing through a character's mind.** Both the Irish novelist James Joyce and the English

novelist Virginia Woolf employ stream-of-consciousness technique in their writings. *See page* 1208.

STYLE **The way a writer expresses his or her thoughts through language.** Style may best be described as *how* an author writes rather than *what* he or she writes. **Diction**, **tone**, **figures of speech**—every choice a writer makes in deciding how to communicate his or her ideas contributes to style. Style is usually viewed separately from content, and it is often what leads critics to classify certain works as "great." *See pages* 429, 435.

SURREALISM **A twentieth-century literary and artistic movement that sought to break down the barriers between rational and irrational thoughts and situations.** Influenced by the theories of Sigmund Freud and using dreamlike imagery, surrealist writers and artists sought to portray the workings of the unconscious mind. Leading figures in the surrealist movement, which flourished in the 1920s and 1930s, include André Breton, Guillaume Apollinaire, and Salvador Dalí. *See page* 1155.

SUSPENSE **The uncertainty or anxiety a reader feels about what will happen next in a story.** Any kind of writing that has an effective plot involves some degree of suspense. *See pages* 51, 494, 1299. *See also* **Plot**.

SYMBOL **A person, place, thing, or event that stands both for itself and for something beyond itself.** Many symbols have become widely recognized: A lion is a symbol of majesty and power; a dove is a symbol of peace. These symbols are sometimes called **public symbols**. But writers often invent new, personal symbols, whose meaning is revealed in a work of poetry or prose. In Maupassant's short story "The Jewels" (Unit Ten), for example, Madame Lantin's jewelry becomes a symbol for the deceptive nature of appearances. *See pages* 746, 1108, 1155. *See also* **Allegory**.

SYMBOLISM **A literary movement that began in France during the late nineteenth century and emphasized the use of highly personal symbols to suggest ideas, emotions, and moods.** The French Symbolists believed that emotions are fleeting, individual, and essentially inexpressible—and that therefore the poet is forced to *suggest* meaning rather than express it. The leading Symbolists, such as Paul Verlaine and

Arthur Rimbaud, were reacting against **Realism** and **Naturalism** and became important influences on the **surrealist** movement of the twentieth century. *See pages* 983, 1028, 1223. *See also* **Naturalism, Realism, Surrealism**.

TANKA **A traditional, five-line form of Japanese poetry.** In the original language, the tanka follows a strict form: The first and third lines contain five syllables each, and the second, fourth, and fifth lines contain seven syllables each. *See pages* 564–565.

TERZA RIMA **An interlocking, three-line stanza form with the rhyme scheme *aba bcb cdc ded,* and so on.** Terza rima is an Italian verse form (Dante used it throughout the *Divine Comedy*) that has also been used by English poets such as Percy Bysshe Shelley. *See pages* 743, 746.

THEME **The central idea or insight of a work of literature.** A theme is not the same as the subject of a work, which can usually be expressed in a word or two: old age, ambition, love. The theme is the idea the writer wishes to convey about the subject—the writer's view of the world or revelation about human nature. In "Life Is Sweet at Kumansenu" (Unit Eleven), for example, Abioseh Nicol's subject is love, but his theme is that love endures despite repeated disappointment and death and ultimately makes life sweet and worth living.

While some stories, poems, and plays have themes that are **directly stated**, most themes are **implied**. It is up to the reader to piece together all the clues the writer has provided about the work's total meaning. Two of the most important clues to consider are how the main character has changed and how the conflict has been resolved. In addition, long works such as novels and plays may have more than one theme. *See pages* 116, 170, 406–407, 460, 1378, 1396, 1432.

TONE **The attitude a writer takes toward the reader, a subject, or a character.** Tone is conveyed through the writer's choice of words and descriptions of **characters** and **setting**. Tone can usually be described with an adjective, such as amused, angry, indifferent, or sarcastic. *See pages* 415, 552, 1061.

TRAGEDY **A play, novel, or other narrative depicting serious and important events, in which the main character comes to an unhappy end.** In the traditional tragedy, the main character is usually dignified, courageous, and often high ranking. The character's downfall may be caused by a **tragic flaw**—an error in judgment or a character weakness—or the downfall may result from forces beyond his or her control. The tragic hero or heroine usually wins some self-knowledge and wisdom, even though he or she suffers defeat, possibly even death.

Tragedy is distinct from **comedy**, in which an ordinary character overcomes obstacles to get what he or she wants. Sophocles' *Oedipus Rex* (Unit Four) is an example of a tragedy. Dramas that contain elements of both tragedy and comedy, such as Shakespeare's *The Tempest* (Unit Nine), are often called **tragicomedies**. *See pages* 302, 305, 371, 844.

TURNING POINT *See* **Dramatic Structure**.

UNDERSTATEMENT **A figure of speech that consists of saying less than what is really meant, or saying something with less force than is appropriate.** Understatement is the opposite of **hyperbole**, or **overstatement**, and is a form of **irony**. To say, "It is a bit wet out there" after coming in from a torrential downpour is to use understatement. Understatement can be used to create a kind of deadpan humor, and it can contribute to an overall satiric tone, as in Cervantes' *Don Quixote* (Unit Nine). *See page* 705.

WIT **A quality of speech or writing that combines verbal cleverness with keen perception, especially of the incongruous.** Wit may be a product of **puns** and wordplay, **hyperbole**, or **verbal irony**. Sei Shōnagon's *The Pillow Book* offers many examples of wit in her **understated** descriptions of humorous situations, as the following example from her chapter entitled "Hateful Things" illustrates:

A man recites his own poems (not especially good ones) and tells one about the praise they have received—most embarrassing.

See page 580.

GRAMMAR, USAGE, AND MECHANICS:
A Reference Guide

Note to Students
As you write and revise formal essays and papers on topics in literature, you may want to review points of grammar, usage, capitalization, punctuation, and spelling. This reference section provides rules and examples that you will find helpful in your writing.

Problems of Agreement

Agreement of Subject and Verb

1. **A verb should agree with its subject in number. Singular subjects take singular verbs. Plural subjects take plural verbs.**

   He watches movies. [The singular verb *watches* agrees with the singular subject *he*.]
   They watch movies. [The plural verb *watch* agrees with the plural subject *they*.]

   Like single-word verbs, verb phrases also agree with their subjects. However, in a verb phrase, only the first auxiliary (helping) verb changes its form to agree with a singular or plural subject.

   The **train was arriving** late.
   Two **trains were arriving** late.

2. **The number of the subject is not changed by a phrase following the subject.**

   This **bag** of marbles **is** full. [*Bag* is the subject, not *marbles*.]
   These **marbles** of glass **are** blue. [*Marbles* is the subject, not *glass*.]

3. **Compound prepositions such as *together with*, *in addition to*, *as well as*, and *along with* following the subject do not affect the number of the subject.**

   Sara, along with Elena, **is going** on the trip. [The subject of the sentence is singular because it names one person, *Sara*. Therefore, the predicate of the sentence uses the singular auxiliary verb form *is*.]

4. **The following indefinite pronouns are singular: *each, either, neither, one, everyone, everybody, no one, nobody, anyone, anybody, someone, somebody*.**

   Each of the dessert chefs **bakes** pastry. [*Each one* bakes.]
   Neither of the pastries **is** an éclair. [*Neither one* is an éclair.]

5. **The following indefinite pronouns are plural: *several, few, both, many*.**

   Several of these trails **are** dangerous for hikers who are inexperienced.

6. **The indefinite pronouns *some, all, most, any,* and *none* may be either singular or plural. These pronouns are singular when they refer to a singular word and plural when they refer to a plural word.**

   Some of the writing **is** scary. [*Some* refers to the singular noun *writing*.]
   Some of the words **are** descriptive. [*Some* refers to the plural noun *words*.]

7. **A compound subject contains two or more nouns or pronouns that are the subject of the same verb. Compound subjects joined by the word *and* are usually plural in form and therefore take a plural verb.**

   Dante, Boccaccio, and **Calvino are** great writers in the Italian language. [Three people *are* writers.]

8. **Compound subjects that name only one person or thing take a singular verb.**

   My **best friend and constant companion is** Kara Kern. [One person is my best friend and constant companion.]

9. **Singular subjects joined by the words *or* or *nor* take a singular verb.**

   Either **Carlos** or **Tony bikes** to school. [*Either* Carlos bikes *or* Tony bikes, not both.]

10. **When a singular subject and a plural subject are joined by *or* or *nor*, the verb agrees with the subject nearer the verb.**

    Neither the producers nor the **director was** present at the screening.
    Neither the director nor the **producers were** present at the screening.

Other Problems in Subject-Verb Agreement

11. **The contractions *don't* and *doesn't* must agree with their subjects.**

    With the singular subjects *I* and *you* and with plural subjects, use the contraction *don't* (*do not*).

    I **don't** speak.   They **don't** tell.
    We **don't** care.   These **don't** work.

    With all other singular subjects, use the singular *doesn't* (*does not*).

    She **doesn't** study.   This **doesn't** move.
    It **doesn't** run well. Donna **doesn't** work here.

12. ***Collective nouns* are singular in form, but they name a group of persons or things. Use a plural verb with a singular collective noun when you are referring to the individual parts or members of the group acting separately. Use a singular verb when you refer to the group acting together as a unit.**

army	club	fleet	jury
assembly	committee	flock	panel
audience	faculty	group	swarm
class	family	herd	team

The family **have** sat down for their dinner. [*Family* is thought of as a group of individuals.]
The family **has** its meals mostly at home. [*Family* is thought of as a single unit.]

Be sure that any pronoun referring to the collective noun agrees with the noun (*their* in the first example above, *its* in the second).

13. **A verb agrees with its subject, not with its predicate nominative, the noun or pronoun complement that refers to the same person or thing as the subject.**

    S   PN
    Cavities are my biggest problem.

    S   PN
    My biggest **problem is** cavities.

14. **Contractions such as *here's*, *where's*, *how's*, and *what's* include the verb *is*. Do not use one of these contractions unless a singular subject follows it.**

    There **are** [not *There's*] **mice** on the counter!

15. **A word or a phrase stating a weight, a measurement, or an amount of money or time is usually considered one item and takes a singular verb.**

    Five dollars is all I can spend.
    One quarter of the grain **was** sold at the market.

Sometimes, however, the amount is thought

of as individual pieces or parts. If so, a plural verb is used.

> **Ten** of the pages **were** missing.
> **Two thirds** of the apples **taste** sour.

16. **The title of a work of art, literature, or music, even when plural in form, takes a singular verb.**

> *Dubliners* contains "Eveline," one of my favorite short stories. [one collection]

17. *Every* or *many a* **before a subject calls for a singular verb.**

> Almost **every** member **was** tired.
> **Many a** student **enjoys** poetry.

18. **A few nouns that look plural in form take singular verbs.**

> The **news is** on at six and ten o'clock.
> **Physics was** Willis's best subject.

Some nouns that end in *-s* take a plural verb even though they refer to a single item.

> The **pliers are** in the toolbox.
> Your **pants are** very stylish.

See also "Maintaining Subject-Verb Agreement" on pages 438–439.

Agreement of Pronoun and Antecedent

1. **A pronoun should agree with its antecedent in number and gender.**

A pronoun usually refers to a noun or another pronoun that comes before it. The word that a pronoun refers to is called its **antecedent**.

A few singular personal pronouns have forms that indicate the gender of the antecedent. *He, him,* and *his* are masculine; *she, her,* and *hers* are feminine; *it* and *its* are neuter.

> **Sei Shōnagon** kept **her** journal in private.
> **Elie Wiesel** wrote **his** memoirs years after the war.

2. **When the antecedent of a personal pronoun is another kind of pronoun, look in a phrase following the antecedent to determine gender.**

> **Each** of the **girls** reads **her** own newspaper.
> **One** of the **boys** cooks **his** own dinner.

3. **When the antecedent may be either masculine or feminine, use both the masculine and the feminine forms.**

> **Every one** of the passengers sat in **his or her** assigned seat.

4. **Use a singular pronoun to refer to *each, either, neither, one, everyone, everybody, no one, nobody, anyone, anybody, someone,* or *somebody.***

> **One** of the boys in the bus forgot **his** book.
> **Each** of the students has **his or her** own locker.

When the meaning of *everyone* and *everybody* is clearly plural, use the plural pronoun.

> **Everyone** talked to **their** [not *his or her*] parents.

5. **Two or more singular antecedents joined by *or* or *nor* should be referred to with a singular pronoun.**

> Neither **Palmira nor Alicia** fixed **herself** any dinner.

6. **Two or more antecedents joined by *and* should be referred to by a plural pronoun.**

> **Tia and Reg** grew **their** own vegetables.

7. **The number of a relative pronoun is determined by the number of its antecedent.**

> **Everyone who** comes to the party will have a good time. [The relative pronoun *who* refers to the singular pronoun *everyone* and thus takes the singular verb form *comes.*]
> **All who** come will have a good time. [*Who* refers to the plural pronoun *all* and thus takes the plural verb form *come.*]

Tips for Writers

Sentences with two or more singular antecedents joined by *or* or *nor* can sound awkward if the antecedents are of different genders. If a sentence sounds awkward, revise it to avoid the problem.

| AWKWARD: | **Nelson** or **Liz** will bring **his** or **her** records. |
| REVISED: | **Nelson** will bring **his** records, or **Liz** will bring **hers.** |

See also "Maintaining Pronoun-Antecedent Agreement" on pages 614–615.

Using Pronouns Correctly

Case

Case is the form of a noun or pronoun that shows its use in a sentence. In English, there are three cases: *nominative*, *objective*, and *possessive*.

Choosing the correct case form for a noun is no problem, because the form remains the same in the nominative and objective cases.

> The **professor** [nominative] carpools with another **professor** [objective].

Only in the possessive case does a noun change its form, usually by adding an apostrophe and *s*.

> My **father's** [possessive] workshop is cluttered with gardening tools and broken appliances.
> **Dad** [nominative] forgot to mail **Sam's** [possessive] application to **school** [objective] yesterday.

The Case Forms of Personal Pronouns

Here are the case forms of personal pronouns. Notice that all personal pronouns except *you* and *it* have different nominative and objective forms.

PERSONAL PRONOUNS

SINGULAR

Nominative Case	Objective Case	Possessive Case
I	me	my, mine
you	you	your, yours
he, she, it	him, her, it	his, her, hers, its

PLURAL

Nominative Case	Objective Case	Possessive Case
we	us	our, ours
you	you	your, yours
they	them	their, theirs

The Nominative Case

1. **The *subject* of a verb is in the nominative case.**

> **He** was excited that **they** had come. [*He* is the subject of *was*; *they* is the subject of *had come*.]

---

2. **A *predicate nominative* is in the nominative case.**

A pronoun used as a predicate nominative always follows a form of the verb *be* or a verb phrase ending in *be* or *been*.

> It is **he**.
> That could be **she**.

The Objective Case

3. **The *direct object* of a verb is in the objective case.**

A *direct object* is a noun or pronoun that receives the action of the verb or shows the result of the action.

> The lesson of La Fontaine's fable impressed **him** and **me**. [*The lesson* is the subject of the verb *impressed*. The lesson impressed *whom*? The answer is *him and me*.]

4. **The *indirect object* of the verb is in the objective case.**

An *indirect object* is a noun or pronoun that tells to whom or for whom something is done. Pronouns used as indirect objects are in the objective case: *me, him, her, us, them*.

> Prospero's magic cloak gave **him** many powers.
> Sei Shōnagon's writing brought **her** much delight.

5. **The *object of a preposition* is in the objective case.**

A prepositional phrase begins with a preposition and ends with a noun or pronoun, which is the *object of the preposition*. A pronoun used as an object of a preposition must be in the objective case.

> Jared sat behind **us**.

Errors often occur when the object of a preposition is compound. You can usually figure out the correct pronouns by trying each one separately in the prepositional phrase.

> Mike raced ahead of him and I. [*Mike raced ahead of him* is correct, but *Mike raced ahead of I* is incorrect. The correct forms of the pronouns are *him* and *me*: Mike raced ahead of **him** and **me**.]

Tips for Writers

Some mistakes in usage are more common than others. In speech, for example, people often incorrectly use the pronoun *me* in a compound subject.

INCORRECT: Faith and **me** built a bookcase.
CORRECT: Faith and **I** built a bookcase.

Many people use incorrect pronoun forms with the preposition *between*. You have probably heard phrases such as *between you and I* and *between you and he*. These phrases are incorrect. The pronouns are objects of a preposition and should be in the objective case. The correct phrases are *between you and me* and *between you and him*.

6. In an infinitive clause, both the subject and object of the infinitive are in the objective case.

> My baby sister wanted **me to carry her**. [*Me* is the subject of *to carry. Her* is the object of *to carry.* The entire infinitive clause is the direct object of *wanted.*]

Special Pronoun Problems

Using Who and Whom Correctly

7. *Who* is used as a subject or predicate nominative, and *whom* is used as an object.

NOMINATIVE	OBJECTIVE
who	whom
whoever	whomever

In spoken English, the use of *whom* is becoming less common. In fact, when you are speaking, you may correctly begin any question with *who*, regardless of the grammar of the sentence. In written English, however, you should make a distinction between *who* and *whom*.

8. The use of *who* or *whom* in a subordinate clause depends on how the pronoun functions in the clause.

When you choose between *who(ever)* and *whom(ever)* in a subordinate clause, follow these steps:

STEP 1:   Find the subordinate clause.
STEP 2:   Decide how the pronoun is used in the clause—as subject, predicate nominative, object of the verb, or object of a preposition.
STEP 3:   Determine the case of the pronoun according to the rules of standard English.
STEP 4:   Select the correct form of the pronoun.

(*Whoever, Whomever*) I choose will lead the group.

STEP 1:   The subordinate clause is *(whoever, whomever) I choose.*
STEP 2:   In this clause, the subject is *I*, the verb is *choose*, and the pronoun is the direct object of the verb *choose; I choose (whoever, whomever).*
STEP 3:   The direct object of a verb is in the objective case.
STEP 4:   The objective form is *whomever.*

ANSWER: **Whomever** I choose will lead the group.

Remember that no words outside the subordinate clause affect the case of the pronoun. In this example, the entire clause is used as the subject of *will lead*, the verb in the main clause. The pronoun *whomever* is used as the direct object (objective case) within its clause.

Frequently, in subordinate clauses *whom* is omitted because it is understood.

> The person [whom] he asked is Joyce.
> The person [whom] she talked to is from the Australian outback.

9. Pronouns used as *appositives* are in the same case as the word to which they refer.

An *appositive* is a noun or pronoun that follows another noun or pronoun to identify or explain it.

The members, **he, she,** and **I,** each read a different part. [Since *members* is the subject of the sentence, the pronouns in apposition with it (*he, she, I*) must be in the nominative case.]

Tips for Writers

To figure out the correct form for a pronoun used with an appositive or as an appositive, read the sentence with only the pronoun.

The teacher asked two students, Emma and (*he, him*), to wash the blackboard. [Omit the direct object, *students:* The teacher asked Emma and him to help.]

(*We, us*) swimmers decided to compete. [Omit the appositive, *swimmers:* We decided to compete.]

---

10. **Use the possessive case of a noun or pronoun before a gerund. Do not confuse the gerund form with the present participle, also an *-ing* form of the verb, which is used as an adjective.**

The panel applauded **my dancing.** [The gerund *dancing* is the object of the verb *applauded.* The possessive form *my* modifies the gerund.]

Can you see **me dancing** a ballet with a professional troupe? [Here the participle *dancing* modifies *me,* the object of *see.*]

The Pronoun in an Incomplete Construction

11. **When *than* and *as* introduce an incomplete construction, use the form of the pronoun that you would use if the construction were completed.**

Notice how pronouns change the meaning of sentences with incomplete constructions.

Vicky likes Paula better than **I.**
Vicky likes Paula better than **me.**

In the first sentence, the nominative case pronoun *I* is the subject of an understood verb: *Vicky likes Paula better than I [like Paula].* In the second sentence, the objective case pronoun *me* is the object of the under-

stood verb: *Vicky likes Paula better than [Vicky likes] me.*

Using Modifiers Correctly

1. **Adjectives and adverbs are modifiers; that is, they state qualities of other parts of speech. Adjectives modify nouns and pronouns. Adverbs modify verbs, adjectives, and other adverbs.**

| **ripe** apple | **juicy** peaches | [adjectives] |
| talk **softly** | jump **well** | [adverbs] |

2. **Use adjectives to compare one noun with another noun that has the same quality.**

That apple is **riper** than this one.
This peach is **juicier** than that one.

3. **Use adverbs to make comparisons between verbs.**

I shoveled the snow slowly, but Phoebe shoveled even **more slowly.**

4. **There are three degrees of comparison: *positive, comparative,* and *superlative.***

POSITIVE	COMPARATIVE	SUPERLATIVE
cool	cooler	coolest
wet	wetter	wettest
tasty	tastier	tastiest
helpful	more helpful	most helpful
slowly	more slowly	most slowly
good	better	best
bad	worse	worst

5. **Avoid double comparisons.**

A **double comparison** is incorrect because it contains both *-er* and *more* or *-est* and *most.*

This is the **dullest** [not *most dullest*] movie I've ever seen.

6. **Be sure your comparisons are clear.**

The snowfall here this year was as much as the Rockies. [This sentence incorrectly compares snowfall to mountains.]

The snowfall here this year was as much as it was in the Rockies. [This sentence correctly compares the snowfall in two different places.]

Tips for Writers

In writing papers about literary topics, you will often need to compare and contrast two or more literary works or specific aspects of them, such as character, plot, or setting. Comparisons, accurately expressed, can help you to make distinct points about works of literature. For example, you may wish to show that the characters in one novel are "more carefully developed" than in another or that the plot of one novel is "less complex" than that of another.

Dangling Modifiers
See pages 206–207.

Misplaced Modifiers

7. A misplaced modifier is a word, phrase, or clause that sounds awkward because it modifies the wrong word(s). Modifying words and phrases should be placed as near as possible to the words they modify.

> MISPLACED: I was awarded a scholarship after four years of study yesterday.
> CORRECTED: Yesterday, I was awarded a scholarship after four years of study.

8. Place an adjective or adverb clause as near as possible to the word it modifies.

> MISPLACED: I carried the box from school, which weighed thirty pounds.
> CORRECTED: From school, I carried the box, **which weighed thirty pounds**.

The Rules for Capitalization

First Words

1. Capitalize the first word in every sentence.

> Each room of the house seemed to have its own color theme. In one room there was a host of blues—pale, slate, and midnight. In another we found only orange and yellow tones.

Traditionally, the first word of a line of poetry is capitalized.

> Water, water, everywhere,
> And all the boards did shrink;

> Water, water, everywhere,
> Nor any drop to drink.
>
> —from "The Rime of the Ancient Mariner," Samuel Taylor Coleridge

Some writers do not follow these practices. When you are quoting, be sure to use capital letters exactly as they are used in the source of the quotation.

Pronoun *I*

2. Capitalize the pronoun *I*.

> Lani and I always walk to school.

Proper Nouns and Proper Adjectives

3. Capitalize proper nouns and proper adjectives.

Common nouns are general names for people, places, or things. A **proper noun** names a particular person, place, or thing. **Proper adjectives** are formed from proper nouns.

Common nouns are not capitalized unless they begin a sentence or a direct quotation or are included in a title (see page 1463). Proper nouns are always capitalized.

> COMMON NOUNS: a philosopher, a country, a ruler
> PROPER NOUNS: Plato, France, Queen Elizabeth
> PROPER ADJECTIVES: Platonic ideas, French bread, Elizabethan drama

Some proper names consist of more than one word. In these names, short prepositions (generally, fewer than five letters) and articles are not capitalized, unless they begin a title or sentence.

> American Federation of Labor
> Alexander the Great

To find out whether a noun should be capitalized, check in a dictionary. The dictionary will tell you if a word should always be capitalized or if it should be capitalized only in certain uses.

Names of People

4. Capitalize the names of people.

> GIVEN NAMES: Len, Beth
> SURNAMES: Andretti, Schwartz

Geographical Names

5. Capitalize geographical names.

TOWNS, CITIES: Los Angeles, Beijing, Madrid
COUNTIES, TOWNSHIPS: Nassau County, Township of Soweto
STATES: Missouri, Nebraska, Connecticut, Oregon
REGIONS: the North, the Northwest, Continental Divide

Words such as *north, west,* and *southeast* are *not* capitalized when they indicate direction, unless they begin a sentence.

west of here, heading northeast

COUNTRIES: the United States, Scotland, Australia
CONTINENTS: North America, Europe, Asia, Antarctica
ISLANDS: Ceylon, Madagascar, Hawaii
MOUNTAINS: the Himalayas, Mount McKinley, the Urals
BODIES OF WATER: Atlantic Ocean, Gulf of Mexico
PARKS: Yellowstone National Park, Hyde Park
ROADS, HIGHWAYS, STREETS: Route 45, Interstate 80, East Eleventh Street

In a hyphenated number, the second word begins with a small letter.

Seventy-seventh Street

Organizations

6. Capitalize names of organizations, businesses, institutions, and government bodies.

ORGANIZATIONS: American Medical Association, National Association for the Advancement of Colored People, United Nations

The word *party* is usually written without a capital letter when it follows a proper adjective: *Republican party, Democratic party, Communist party*

BUSINESSES: General Electric, New York Telephone, Estelle's Dog Grooming
INSTITUTIONS: Sloan-Kettering Hospital, Boston University, Crossroads High School

Do not capitalize words like *hotel, theater,*
college, high school, and *post office* unless they begin a sentence or are part of a proper name.

Reed College · a college course
Trocadero Hotel · a hotel in Miami
Shubert Theater · a theater in New York
Seattle Post Office · a local post office
Suffolk County Courthouse · the courthouse doors

GOVERNMENT BODIES: Atomic Energy Commission, Congress, Department of Agriculture

Historical Events

7. Capitalize the names of historical events and periods, special events, and calendar items.

HISTORICAL EVENTS AND PERIODS: French Revolution, Battle of Gettysburg, Vietnam War, Middle Ages, Great Depression
SPECIAL EVENTS: Special Olympics, the U.S. Open
CALENDAR ITEMS: Thursday, June, Chinese New Year

Nationalities and Races

8. Capitalize the names of nationalities, races, and peoples.

African, Greek, Bantu, Chinese, Comanche, Korean

Brand Names

9. Capitalize the brand names of business products.

Nylon, Skippy, Chrysler, Xerox

Do not capitalize the noun that often follows a brand name: *Skippy peanut butter.*

Tips for Writers
Do not capitalize the names of seasons unless they are personified or are part of the names of special events.

"I saw old Autumn in the misty morn." [personification]

Suzanne was voted Most Likely to Succeed in the annual Spring Election. [special event]

Particular Places, Things, Events

10. Capitalize the names of ships, planets, monuments, awards, and any other particular places, things, or events.

> SHIPS, TRAINS: the **U.S.S.** *Minnow*, the *Titanic*, the *Clipper*
> AIRCRAFT, SPACECRAFT, MISSILES: *Apollo 7*, *Challenger*, *Patriot*
> PLANETS, STARS: **S**aturn, **O**rion **N**ebula

Sun, *moon*, and *earth* are not capitalized unless they begin a sentence or are listed with other heavenly bodies.

> MONUMENTS, MEMORIALS: **G**raceland, the **L**incoln **M**emorial
> BUILDINGS: **M**useum of **M**odern **A**rt, the **E**mpire **S**tate **B**uilding
> AWARDS: **M**edal of **H**onor, **N**obel **P**rize, **P**alm d'**O**r

Specific Courses, Languages

11. Do *not* capitalize names of school subjects, except for languages and for course names followed by a number.

> Chris is taking **E**nglish, **h**istory and **t**yping. I'm taking **F**rench, **d**rama, **T**rigonometry II, and **E**nglish literature.

Do *not* capitalize the name of a class (*freshman, sophomore, junior, senior*) unless it is used as part of a proper noun.

> The sophomore class is going to win the **F**reshman-**S**ophomore game.

Titles of People

12. Capitalize the title of a person when it comes before a name.

> **P**resident **B**ush   **M**r. **C**ovello
> **D**r. **V**aldez   **M**s. **W**elch

Do not capitalize a title used alone or following a person's name, especially if the title is preceded by *a* or *the*.

> Julius Caesar wanted to be **e**mperor of Rome.
> The **g**overnor will present her speech at the groundbreaking ceremony.

13. Capitalize words showing family relationship when used with a person's name but

not when preceded by a possessive or article.

> Ramon's **g**randmother visited us last year.
> For Thanksgiving, we usually go to **A**unt **C**arlene and **U**ncle **M**ax's house.
> Does **C**ousin **E**d like your cat?
> But: My **c**ousin **E**d hates my dog.

Titles of Literary and Other Creative Works

14. Capitalize the first and last words and all important words in titles of books, periodicals, poems, stories, historical documents, movies, television programs, works of art, and musical compositions.

Unimportant words in a title are articles: *a, an, the*
short prepositions (fewer than five letters): *of, to, for, from*
coordinating conjunctions: *and, but, so, nor, or, yet, for*

> BOOKS: *The Tale of Genji*, *Madame Bovary*, *Things Fall Apart*, *The Name of the Rose*
> PERIODICALS: *Time, Life, Newsweek, Field and Stream*
> POEMS: "The World Is Too Much with Us," "The Golden Mean," "Jade Flower Palace"
> STORIES: "The Handsomest Drowned Man in the World," "The Jewels," "Cranes"
> HISTORICAL DOCUMENTS: **C**onstitution, **D**eclaration of **I**ndependence, **M**agna **C**arta
> TELEVISION PROGRAMS: *Murphy Brown, Nova, Murder She Wrote, Saturday Night Live*
> WORKS OF ART: *Odalisque, Waterlilies*
> MUSICAL COMPOSITIONS: *Aida*, "Can't Touch This," Mozart's *Requiem, The Magic Flute*

The words *a, an*, and *the* written before a title are capitalized only when they are the first word of a title or subtitle.

> the *Chicago Sun Times, For Whom the Bell Tolls, The Diary of Anne Frank*, "A Valediction: Forbidding Mourning"

Before the names of magazines and newspapers, *a, an*, and *the* are usually not capitalized.

Religions

15. Capitalize names of religions and their

followers, holy celebrations, holy writings, and specific deities.

RELIGIONS AND FOLLOWERS: **C**atholicism, **Q**uaker, **J**ehovah's **W**itness, **H**indu, **P**rotestant, **J**ewish, **M**uslim, **M**ethodist, **B**uddhist, **A**nglican, **T**aoist, **P**resbyterian
HOLY DAYS AND SEASONS: **E**aster, **Y**om **K**ippur, **K**wanzaa, **P**assover, **C**hristmas, **R**amadan
HOLY WRITINGS: the **B**ible, the **T**almud, the **K**oran, the **V**edas, the **A**cts of the **A**postles
SPECIFIC DEITIES: **A**llah, **G**od, **B**rahma, **J**ehovah, **B**uddha

The word *god* is not capitalized when it refers to the gods of ancient mythology; however, the names of mythological deities are capitalized.

The **g**oddess Athena was thought to be all-wise. The Greek **g**od Hermes was the messenger of the **g**ods; in Roman mythology, he is known as Mercury.

Punctuation

End Marks

End marks—*periods, question marks,* and *exclamation points*—are used to indicate the purpose of a sentence.

1. Use a period to end a statement (*or declarative sentence*).

Your father is here.
The child wanted to know where the toy was.

Notice in the second example that a declarative sentence containing an indirect question is followed by a period.

2. Use a question mark to end a question (*or interrogative sentence*).

Should we buy these?   Is it time yet?

A direct question may have the same word order as a declarative sentence. Since it is a question, however, it is followed by a question mark.

She was a nice person?

3. Use a period or exclamation point to end an imperative sentence.

When an imperative sentence makes a request, it is generally followed by a period.

Please run fast.
Bring me a pen.

Tips for Writers
Be sure to distinguish between a declarative sentence that contains an indirect question and an interrogative sentence, which asks a direct question.

INDIRECT QUESTION: Al asked what road he should take to get to the beach.
DIRECT QUESTION: Al asked, "What road should I take to get to the beach?"

4. Use an exclamation point to end an exclamation.

Excellent! What a great job!
Oops!

Sometimes declarative, interrogative, and imperative sentences show such strong feeling that they are more like exclamations than statements, questions, or requests. If so, an exclamation point should be used instead of a period or question mark.

The house is on fire!   Don't break that!
Won't you leave!

5. Use a period after an abbreviation.

PERSONAL NAMES: D. H. Lawrence, N. K. Sandars
TITLES USED WITH NAMES: Mr., Ms., Mrs., Dr.
STATES: Fla., Mo., Pa., S. Car. (However, the two-letter state abbreviations used with ZIP codes do not take a period.)
TIME OF DAY: A.M., P.M.
YEARS: B.C., A.D.
ADDRESSES: Ave., St., Blvd.
ORGANIZATIONS AND COMPANIES: Co., Inc.
UNITS OF MEASURE: lb., oz., in., ft., yd., mi.

Tips for Writers
If an abbreviation comes at the end of a statement, do not use an additional period as an end mark. However, use a question mark or an exclamation point if one is needed.

Please tell me when it's 2 P.M.
Does she work for Rowe, Inc.?

Abbreviations for government agencies and international organizations and some other frequently used abbreviations are written without periods. Abbreviations for nearly all measurements are also often written without periods, especially in science books.

Commas

1. Use commas to separate two or more adjectives preceding a noun.

> We explored the **hot, damp, smelly attic.**

When the last adjective in a series is thought of as part of the noun, the comma before the adjective is omitted.

> We washed the **small, round glass windows.**

You can use two tests to determine whether two adjectives should be separated by a comma:

TEST 1: Insert the word *and* between the adjectives. If *and* fits sensibly between the adjectives, use a comma. In the first example sentence, *and* can be logically inserted: *hot and damp attic; damp and smelly attic.* In the second sentence, *and* sounds logical between the first two adjectives (*small and round*) but not between the second and third (*round and glass*).

TEST 2: Change the order of the adjectives. If the order can be reversed sensibly, use a comma. *Round, small glass windows* makes sense, but *glass, small round windows* does not.

2. Use commas before *and*, *but*, *or*, *nor*, *for*, *so*, and *yet* when they join independent clauses.

> **Howard stubbed his toe, and he screamed.**
> **María gets up early,** yet **she is always late.**

Do not be misled by compound verbs, which often make a sentence look as though it contains two independent clauses.

> COMPOUND SENTENCE: **Jean cut the vegetables, and Malcolm made the salad.** [two independent clauses]
> COMPOUND VERB: **John Milton outlined** the poem and **wrote** it. [one subject with a compound verb]

In the following correctly punctuated compound sentence, notice that independent clauses appear on both sides of the coordinating conjunction.

> He wrote poetry, and he loved to act.

3. Use commas to set off nonessential clauses and nonessential participial phrases.

A *nonessential* (or *nonrestrictive*) clause or participial phrase adds information that is not necessary to the main idea in the sentence. Omitting such a clause or phrase will not change the basic meaning of the sentence.

> NONESSENTIAL CLAUSE: The letter, **which is not stamped,** cannot be mailed.
> NONESSENTIAL PHRASE: William Blake, **who was an accomplished artist,** illustrated many of his own poems.

When a clause or phrase is necessary to the meaning of a sentence—that is, when it tells *which one or ones*—the clause or phrase is *essential* (or *restrictive*), and commas are *not* used.

Notice how the meaning of each sentence below would change if the essential clause or phrase were omitted.

> ESSENTIAL CLAUSE: Only students **who are taller than five feet eight inches** may try out for the basketball team.
> ESSENTIAL PHRASE: The most famous speech **made by Dr. Martin Luther King, Jr.,** began ''I have a dream. . . .''

An adjective clause or phrase beginning with *that* is usually essential.

> ESSENTIAL CLAUSE: The poster **that I want** has a green border.

4. Use a comma after introductory words such as *well*, *yes*, *no*, and *why* when they begin a sentence.

> **Yes,** my hair is natural.
> **Well,** it's always been this color.

5. Use a comma after an introductory participial phrase.

> **Resting in the shade of the tree,** I felt cooler.
> **Disappointed with the film,** Tia left the theater.

Grammar, Usage, and Mechanics **1465**

6. Use a comma after a series of introductory prepositional phrases.

> **Toward the end of the speech,** we started clapping.
> **By the end of the night,** we were all tired.

A short introductory prepositional phrase does not require a comma unless the comma is necessary to make the meaning clear.

> **With my car** I can get to work faster.
> **With my car,** driving is a pleasure. [The comma is necessary to avoid reading *car driving*.]

7. Use a comma after an introductory adverb clause.

> **When you get home,** give me a call.
> **After you figure it out,** tell me what to do.

8. Use commas to set off elements that interrupt the sentence.

> He is, **in fact,** my best friend.
> My brother, **of course,** scored the winning run.

If an "interrupter" comes at the beginning or at the end of a sentence, only one comma is needed.

> **After all,** he is an expert.
> It happened yesterday, **I think.**

9. Use commas to set off appositives and appositive phrases.

> The Minters, **our neighbors,** were invited to the picnic.

When an appositive has no modifiers and is necessary to the meaning of the sentence, it is called an essential appositive. Such appositives should not be set off by commas.

> The Polish composer **Chopin** is her favorite.
> We **students** took a poll.

10. Use commas to set off words used in direct address.

> **Corey,** you need a new coat.
> I need to ask your advice, **Ms. Kim.**

11. Use commas to set off parenthetical expressions.

> **Strictly speaking,** I don't like it.
> Yesterday, **I believe,** was her birthday.

A contrasting expression introduced by *not* is parenthetical and must be set off by commas.

> I'm sure it was Ferdowsi, **not Saadi,** who wrote the *Shahname*.

12. Use a comma to separate items in dates and addresses.

> My friend traveled to **Paris, France,** on **Sunday, July 14, 1991.**
> I mailed the letter to **29 West Orange Road, Teaneck, NJ 07631,** on **May 19, 1993.**

Notice that no comma separates the month and day (*May 19*) or the house number and street name (*29 West Orange Road*) because each is considered one item. Also, the ZIP code is not separated from the name of the state by a comma: *Teaneck, NJ 07631.*

13. Use a comma after the salutation of a friendly letter and after the closing of any letter.

> Dear Mr. Kilgannon,
> Yours truly,

14. Use a comma after a name followed by an abbreviation such as *Jr., Sr.,* or *M.D.*

> Johnny Chin, **M.D.**
> John F. Kennedy, **Jr.**

Semicolons

1. Use a semicolon between independent clauses in a sentence if they are not joined by *and, but, or, nor, for, so,* or *yet.*

Notice in the following examples that the semicolon replaces the comma and the conjunction joining the independent clauses.

> First I filled the tub, **and** then I took a bath.
> **First I filled the tub;** then I took a bath.

A semicolon can be used between two closely related independent clauses.

> Phoebe baked the bread. Then she set the table.
> **Phoebe baked the bread;** then she set the table.

2. Use a semicolon between independent clauses joined by conjunctive adverbs or transitional expressions.

> Gabe was tired; **however,** he couldn't fall asleep.

I made several dishes; **in addition,** several friends brought appetizers.

When conjunctive adverbs and transitional expressions appear *within* one of the clauses and not *between* clauses, they are usually punctuated as interrupters (set off by commas). The two clauses are still separated by a semicolon.

> We tried to see all the Seurat paintings; the museum, **however,** closed before we could do so.

3. Use a semicolon (rather than a comma) to separate independent clauses joined by a coordinating conjunction when there are commas within the clauses.

> CONFUSING: Broccoli, peppers, and lettuce are vegetables, and nectarines, peaches, and bananas are fruits.
>
> CLEAR: Broccoli, peppers, and lettuce are vegetables; and nectarines, peaches, and bananas are fruits.

4. Use a semicolon between items in a series if the items contain commas.

> He visited **Brussels, Belgium; Naples, Italy; Bombay, India; and Bangkok, Thailand,** on his trip.
>
> Auditions will be held **Tuesday, July 16; Wednesday, July 17; and Thursday, July 18.**

Colons

1. Use a colon before a list of items, especially after expressions like *the following* and *as follows.*

> You will visit **the following cities:** London, Athens, and Cairo.
>
> Other colors are **as follows:** green, yellow, blue, and purple.

If a noun is followed by a list of appositives, then the colon is used to make the meaning of the sentence clear.

> **On the menu there were three choices:** French, Italian, or blue cheese dressing.

Do *not* use a colon before a list that follows a verb or a preposition.

> INCORRECT: Additional games include: table tennis, badminton, croquet, and horseshoes.
>
> CORRECT: Additional games include table tennis, badminton, croquet, and horseshoes.

2. Use a colon before a long, formal statement or quotation.

> Alfred North Whitehead wrote: ''Intelligence is quickness to apprehend as distinct from ability, which is capacity to act wisely on the thing apprehended.''

3. Use a colon between the hour and the minute.

> 4:08 A.M.   9:14 P.M.

4. Use a colon between chapter and verse when referring to passages from the Bible.

> Psalms 110:2   Genesis 2:3

5. Use a colon between volume and issue number or between volume and page number of a periodical.

> *Life* 58:4 [volume and issue number]
> *Life* 58:102 [volume and page number]

6. Use a colon after the salutation of a business letter.

> Dear Dr. Adell: To Whom It May Concern:

Italics

When writing or typing, indicate italics by underlining. If your composition were to be printed, the underlined words would be set in italics. For example, if you type:

> Anton Chekhov wrote <u>The Cherry Orchard</u>.

the sentence would be printed like this:

> Anton Chekhov wrote *The Cherry Orchard.*

If you use a personal computer, you can probably set words in italics yourself.

1. Use italics (underlining) for titles of books, plays, films, newspapers, periodicals, works of art, long musical compositions, long poems, television programs, ships, aircraft, and so on.

> BOOKS: *Love in the Time of Cholera, Divine Comedy*
> PLAYS: *The Misanthrope, Oedipus Rex*

FILMS: *Casablanca, Alien*
PERIODICALS: *Discover,* the *New Statesman*
WORKS OF ART: *Starry Night, Nightwatch*
LONG MUSICAL COMPOSITIONS: *Aida, The 1812 Overture*
TELEVISION SERIES: *The Wonder Years, Masterpiece Theater*
SHIPS: *Titanic, Andrea Doria*
AIRCRAFT, SPACECRAFT: *Luna 7, Saturn 2, Hindenburg*

The words *a, an,* and *the* written before a title are italicized only when they are part of the title.

Holst composed **The Planets**.
I read the **Boston Phoenix** and **People**.

Magazine articles, chapter headings, and titles of short poems, short stories, short musical compositions, and individual episodes of TV shows should be placed in quotation marks, not italicized, when referred to in a composition. See the following section.

2. **Use italics (underlining) for foreign words and for words, letters, and figures referred to as such.**

The word **hullabaloo** comes from Scottish.
The **5** on my test looks like an **8**.

Quotation Marks

1. **Use quotation marks to enclose a direct quotation—a person's exact words.**

Cynthia asked, **"How long is the movie?"**
"It's two hours," I answered.

2. **Begin a direct quotation with a capital letter.**

When he was finished raking the yard, Mack said, **"L**et's cook out."
Amy said, **"A**bout ten minutes." [Although this quotation is not a sentence, it is Amy's complete remark.]

If the direct quotation is a fragment of the original quotation, it may begin with a small letter.

When Shakespeare's Miranda first lays eyes on Ferdinand, she remarks that "**n**othing ill can dwell in such a temple." [The quotation is only a phrase from Miranda's sentence.]

3. **When a quoted sentence is divided into two parts by an interrupting expression, begin the second part with a small letter.**

"Before yesterday," she said, "**t**here were trees here."

If the second part of a quotation is a new sentence, a period (not a comma) follows the interrupting expression, and the second part begins with a capital letter.

"The game already started," May said. "**L**et's go to the movies, instead."

When an interrupting expression is not a part of a quotation, it should not be inside quotation marks.

INCORRECT: "If he doesn't come, he said, we won't have enough people."
CORRECT: **"If he doesn't come,"** he said, **"we won't have enough people."**

When two or more sentences by the same speaker are quoted together, use only one set of quotation marks.

Wanda said, **"Yesterday seemed warmer than today. I wonder what the temperature is?"**

Tips for Writers
Do not use quotation marks for *indirect quotations.*

DIRECT QUOTATIONS: Sasha said, "I've already read that book."
She asked him, "Have you ever been to Memphis?"
INDIRECT QUOTATIONS: Sasha said that he'd already read that book.
She asked him if he'd ever been to Memphis.

4. **Set off a direct quotation from the rest of the sentence by commas or by a question mark or an exclamation point.**

Mr. Rosenfeld said, "Please come back and visit us soon**,"** as he dropped me off at my house.
Grace asked, "Have you been able to locate Suriname**?"** as she opened the oversized atlas on her desk.

5. **Place commas and periods inside closing quotation marks.**

"I haven't read the book," said Janine, "but I saw the movie."

"Mushrooms," a poem by Margaret Atwood, presents vivid images.

6. Place semicolons and colons outside closing quotation marks.

Father's advice was, "Always be polite"; I wonder if his father told him that, too.

Choose one of the following "specials of the day": pot roast, chicken, or pasta salad.

7. If the quotation is a question or an exclamation, place question marks and exclamation points inside the closing quotation marks. Otherwise, place them outside.

"Are we there yet?" I asked, hoping for the best.

What is the meaning of "smart as a whip"?

8. When you write dialogue (a conversation), begin a new paragraph every time the speaker changes.

"I won't go through with it," said Adam softly.

"Well, then," Alice said, "I guess I'll have to do it alone."

"Yes," he said. "You will."

9. When a quoted passage consists of more than one paragraph, put quotation marks at the beginning of each paragraph and at the end of the entire passage. Do not put quotation marks after any paragraph but the last.

"Today," the reporter said, "several buildings were burned to the ground in Waco, Texas.

"Police are ruling the fires accidental and are still searching for the cause of the blaze. Eyewitnesses speculate that it may have been caused by a gas leak."

10. Use single quotation marks to enclose a quotation within a quotation.

Vernon said, "I saw Run DMC live, singing 'Rockbox.' "

Michael asked, "Who said 'Go West, young man'?"

11. Use quotation marks to enclose titles of

articles, short stories, essays, poems, songs, individual episodes of TV shows, chapters, and other parts of books or periodicals.

I'm going to read Flannery O'Connor's short story **"A Good Man Is Hard to Find."**

He likes the song **"My Way."**

Italicize the title of a poem that is long enough to be published in a separate volume. Such poems are usually divided into titled or numbered sections, such as cantos, parts, or books. Long musical compositions include operas, symphonies, ballets, oratorios, and concertos.

When I read *Thurber's Carnival*, I wanted to read "The Scotty Who Knew Too Much," too.

I read "Canto 6" of the *Divine Comedy* by the Italian poet Dante.

See also "Using Quotations Effectively" on pages 120–121.

Apostrophes

With the Possessive Case

1. Add an apostrophe and an *s* to form the possessive case of a singular noun. The *possessive* of a noun or pronoun shows ownership or relationship.

Francine's book   a **fish's** environment

2. Add only an apostrophe to a proper name ending in an *s*-sound if the addition of *'s* would make the name awkward to pronounce.

Ms. Rodriquez's wallet   **Wallace Stevens's**
Mr. Saunders' car   poetry

3. Add only an apostrophe to form the possessive case of a plural noun ending in *s*.

countries' populations   **dentists'** bills

Although most plural nouns end in *s*, some are irregular. To form the possessive case of a plural noun that does not end in *s*, add an apostrophe and an *s*.

children's toys   **women's** careers

Grammar, Usage, and Mechanics   **1469**

Do not use an apostrophe to form the *plural* of a noun. Remember that the apostrophe shows ownership or relationship.

Three **runners** [not **runners'**] wore sneakers.
Three **runners'** [not **runner's**] sneakers were white.

4. **Do not use an apostrophe with a possessive personal pronoun.**

My, your, her, its, our, and *their* are used before a noun. *Mine, yours, hers, ours,* and *theirs,* on the other hand, are never used before a noun; they are used as subjects, complements, or objects in sentences. *His* may be used in either way.

I saw **your** jacket. I saw a jacket of **yours**.
That is **her** baby. That baby is **hers**.

The possessive form of *who* is *whose,* not *who's.* Similarly, the possessive forms for *it* and *they* are *its* and *their,* not *it's* or *they're.*

5. **Add an apostrophe and an *s* to form the possessive case of an indefinite pronoun.**

anyone**'s** guess   neither**'s** book

6. **For possessives of compound words, names of organizations and businesses, and words showing joint possession, make only the last word possessive in form.**

COMPOUND WORDS:
someone else's problem
state legislature's decision
ORGANIZATIONS:
World Wildlife Conservation's plea
Greenpeace's funding
BUSINESS:
Con Edison's workers
JOINT POSSESSION:
Matt and Julie**'s** story had the fewest characters and the most dialogue. [The story belongs to both Matt and Julie.]

When one of the words showing joint possession is a pronoun, both words should be possessive in form.

Eddie's and my surfboards were in desperate need of wax. [not *Eddie and my surfboards*]
Alex's and my relationship has improved since we began to write to each other.

7. **When two or more persons possess something individually, make each of their names possessive in form.**

Mrs. Mackay's and **Mrs. Stone's** husbands both work in the local post office. [the husbands of two different women]
Bill's and **Leon's backpacks** have reflective strips attached to them. [individual, not joint, possession]

With Contractions or Plurals

8. **Use an apostrophe to show where letters or numbers have been omitted in a contraction.**

who is / who's   of the clock / o'clock
1991 / '91   I am / I'm
                      you are / you're

EXCEPTIONS:
will not / won't   shall not / shan't

9. **To prevent confusion, it is best to use an apostrophe and an *s* to form the plurals of lowercase letters, some uppercase letters, numerals, and some words referred to as words.**

My daughter is learning her ABC**'s**.
Good writers dot their *i*'**s** and cross their *t*'**s**.

Hyphens

1. **Use a hyphen in some compound nouns.**

brand-new   great-grandmother   mother-in-law

2. **Use a hyphen to divide a word at the end of a line.**

One of my favorite words is the noun **an-thology**.

Divide an already hyphenated word only at a hyphen.

Yesterday at the fair he went on the **merry-go-round**.

Do not divide a word so that one letter stands alone.

The young couple rented a new **apart-ment** [not a-partment].

A dictionary will indicate the best place to divide a word.

3. **Use a hyphen with compound numbers from _twenty-one_ to _ninety-nine_ and with fractions used as adjectives.**

> twenty-four degrees
> one-third gallon [but _one third_ of the paint]

4. **Use a hyphen with the prefixes _ex-_, _self-_, _all-_, and with the suffix _-elect_, and with all prefixes before a proper noun or proper adjective.**

> **self**-taught, President-**elect**, **mid**-September

Dashes

Use a dash to indicate an abrupt break in thought or speech or an unfinished statement or question.

Many words and phrases are used parenthetically; that is, they break into the main thought of a sentence. Most parenthetical elements are set off by commas or parentheses.

> The general, **I believe,** is a brilliant strategist.
> Radishes, **however,** do not agree with me.

Sometimes these elements demand a stronger emphasis. In such instances, a dash is used.

> She had only one desire—to flee, flee from the dull life she led—but it was too late.
> The real culprit, you see—ah, but that information must remain a secret for the moment.

Parentheses

Use parentheses to enclose material that is added to a sentence but is not considered of major importance.

> During World War I **(from 1914 to 1918)**, the airplane came into prominence in military strategy.

An end mark of punctuation is used inside parentheses only when the parenthetical matter stands alone as a complete sentence. However, an end mark is not placed within parentheses if the mark belongs to the sentence as a whole.

> Mark your answers clearly. (Do not use ink.)
> Senator Tom Harkin (Democrat, Iowa) has made several speeches on that subject.
> The graph shows the changes clearly (see Figure 3).

Spelling

> ## Tips for Writers
> Here are five tips for improving your spelling.
> 1. To learn the spelling of a word, pronounce it, study it, and write it.
> 2. Use a dictionary.
> 3. Spell by syllables.
> 4. Proofread for careless spelling errors.
> 5. Keep a spelling notebook.

Words with _ie_ and _ei_

1. **Write _ie_ when the sound is long _e_, except after _c_.**

achieve	niece	reprieve	ceiling
thief	siege	fiend	conceit

2. **Write _ei_ when the sound is not long _e_.**

neighbor	weigh	freight
reign	heinous	height

> EXCEPTIONS: friend, conscience, financier, seize

Words with _-cede_, _-ceed_, and _-sede_.

3. **Only one English word ends in _-sede_: _supersede_; only three words end in _-ceed_: _exceed_, _proceed_, and _succeed_; most other words with this sound end in _-cede_.**

precede	recede	secede
intercede	concede	accede

Adding Prefixes

4. **When a prefix is added to a word, the spelling of the original word itself remains the same.**

> dis + satisfy = **dis**satisfy
> im + mature = **im**mature

Adding Suffixes

5. **When the suffix _-ness_ or _-ly_ is added to a word, the spelling of the original word remains the same.**

> casual + ly = casual**ly**
> habitual + ly = habitual**ly**

EXCEPTIONS:
1. Words ending in *y* usually change the *y* to *i* before -*ness* and -*ly*: *empty / emptiness; busy / busily*
2. *True, due,* and *whole* drop the final *e* before -*ly*: *truly, duly, wholly*

Most one-syllable adjectives ending in *y* do follow rule 5: *sly / slyness; dry / dryly.*

6. Drop the final silent *e* before adding a suffix that begins with a vowel.

care + ing = caring   sense + ible = sensible

EXCEPTIONS:
1. Keep the final silent *e* in words ending in *ce* or *ge* before a suffix that begins with *a* or *o*: *manageable, courageous*
2. To avoid confusion with other words, keep the final silent *e* in some words:
dye + ing = dyeing [not dying]
singe + ing = singeing [not singing]

7. Keep the final silent *e* before adding a suffix that begins with a consonant.

nine + ty = ninety   definite + ly = definitely

EXCEPTIONS:
true + ly = truly   judge + ment = judgment

8. When a word ends in *y* preceded by a consonant, change the *y* to *i* before any suffix except one beginning with *i*.

accompany + ment = accompaniment
plenty + ful = plentiful

EXCEPTIONS:
1. Some one-syllable words:
shy + ness = shyness
sky + ward = skyward
2. *lady* and *baby* with suffixes:
ladylike   ladyship   babyhood

9. When a word ends in *y* preceded by a vowel, simply add the suffix.

buoy + ant = buoyant   joy + ful = joyful

EXCEPTIONS:
day + ly = daily   pay + ed = paid

Doubling Final Consonants

10. When a word ends in a consonant, double

the final consonant before a suffix that begins with a vowel only if the word: (1) has only one syllable or is accented on the last syllable, and (2) ends in a single consonant preceded by a single vowel.

swim + ing = swimming
repel + ent = repellent

Otherwise, simply add the suffix.

wink + ed = winked
insist + ence = insistence

Plurals of Nouns

11. To form the plurals of most English nouns, add *s*.

violin / violins   night / nights

12. To form the plurals of other nouns, follow these rules.

If the noun ends in *s, x, z, ch,* or *sh,* add *es.*

dress / dresses   fox / foxes   match / matches

If the noun ends in *y* preceded by a consonant, change the *y* to *i* and add *es.*

cry / cries   theory / theories   ruby / rubies

EXCEPTION: The plurals of proper nouns: the *Murphys*, the *Clancys*.

If the noun ends in *y* preceded by a vowel, add *s.*

monkey / monkeys   buoy / buoys

For some nouns ending in *f* or *fe,* change the *f* to *v* and add *s* or *es.*
Noticing how the plural is pronounced will help you remember whether to change the *f* to *v.*

kerchief / kerchiefs   safe / safes   knife / knives

If the noun ends in *o* preceded by a consonant, add *es.*

potato / potatoes   hero / heroes
tomato / tomatoes

If the noun ends in *o* preceded by a vowel, add *s.*

patio / patios   radio / radios   tattoo / tattoos

Nouns for musical terms that end in *o* preceded by a consonant form the plural by adding only *s.*

soprano / soprano**s**   solo / solo**s**
piano / piano**s**

A number of nouns that end in *o* preceded by a consonant have two plural forms.

tornado / tornado**s** *or* tornado**es**
zero / zero**s** *or* zero**es**

The best way to handle plurals of words ending in *o* preceded by a consonant is to check their spelling in a dictionary.
The plurals of some nouns are irregular.

tooth / teeth   man / men   mouse / mice

Some nouns have the same form in both the singular and the plural.

deer   moose   salmon   Swiss

Plurals of Compound Nouns

13. If a compound noun is written as one word, form the plural by adding *s* or *es*.

cupful / cupful**s**   leftover / leftover**s**
eyelash / eyelash**es**

If a compound noun is hyphenated or written as two words, make the main noun plural. The *main noun* is the noun that is modified.

mother-in-law / mother**s**-in-law
notary public / notari**es** public

EXCEPTIONS: drive-in / drive-in**s**
lean-to / lean-to**s**

Plurals of Latin and Greek Loan Words

14. Some nouns borrowed from Latin and Greek form the plural as in the original language.

nucleus / nucl**ei**   crisis / cris**es**   datum / dat**a**

A few Latin and Greek loan words have two plural forms.

vortex / vort**ices** *or* vort**exes**
gymnasium / gymnasi**a** *or* gymnasium**s**

Check a dictionary to find the preferred spelling of such plurals.

Plurals of Numbers, Letters, Symbols, and Words Used as Words

15. To form the plurals of numerals, most capital letters, symbols, and words used as words, add an *s*.

Change the **N**s to **V**s.

To prevent confusion, use an apostrophe and an *s* to form the plurals of lowercase letters, certain capital letters or symbols, and some words used as words.

Your **r's** look like **z's**.

The plurals of decades and centuries may be formed by adding an *s* or an apostrophe and an *s* (*'s*).

During the **1900's** (*or* **1900s**) many new inventions appeared.

Spelling Numbers

16. Always spell out a number that begins a sentence.

Two thousand two hundred cows are kept on this farm.

17. Within a sentence, spell out numbers that can be written in one word or two words; use numerals for other numbers.

Over the weekend we drove **seven hundred miles**.
He has a collection of **325** different butterflies.

18. Spell out numbers used to indicate order.

I placed **third** [not 3rd] in the tournament.

EXCEPTION: Use numerals for dates when you include the name of the month. Always use numerals for years.

School ends on June **3** [not 3rd]. [Writing *the third of June* is also correct.]
In **1945**, Ricardo came from Italy to the United States.

GLOSSARY

The glossary below is an alphabetical list of words found in the selections in this book. Use this glossary just as you use a dictionary—to find out the meanings of unfamiliar words. (A few technical, foreign, or obscure words in this book are not listed here, but instead are defined for you in the footnotes or glosses that accompany each selection.)

Many words in the English language have more than one meaning. This glossary gives the meanings that apply to the words as they are used in the selections of this book. Words closely associated in form and meaning are usually listed together as one entry (for example, *invert* and *inverted*), and the definition is given for the first form.

The following abbreviations are used:

adj., adjective   **n.**, noun   **v.**, verb
adv., adverb   **pl.**, plural form

Unless a word is very simple to pronounce, its pronunciation is given in parentheses. A guide to the pronunciation symbols appears at the bottom of each right-hand glossary page.

For more information about words in this glossary, or about words not listed here, consult a dictionary.

▼ A ▼

abase (ə·bās′) **v.** To humble, humiliate, degrade.

abdicate (ab′di·kāt′) **v.** To formally withdraw from an office or position.

abhor (ab·hôr′) **v.** To draw back in hatred or disgust.

abjure (ab·joor′) **v.** To reject; renounce; give up.

abode (ə·bōd′) **n.** Home; dwelling place.

abominable (ə·bäm′ə·nə·bəl) **adj.** Hateful; repulsive.

abound (ə·bound′) **v.** To be abundant; exist in plentiful amounts.

abstain (ab·stān′) **v.** To do without voluntarily.

abstemious (ab·stē′mē·əs) **adj.** Moderate; temperate.

abyss (ə·bis′) **n. 1.** The void or chaos which existed before the world's creation. **2.** A bottomless pit.

accomplice (ə·käm′plis) **n.** A partner in a criminal act.

accord **v.** To give or bestow upon.

accouterments (ə·koot′ər·mənts) **n. pl.** Equipment issued to a soldier, excluding clothes and weapons.

acolyte (ak′ə·līt′) **n.** An assistant or helper; follower.

acquit (ə·kwit′) **v.** To clear someone of a charge or accusation. —**acquittal n.**

adept (ə·dept′) **adj.** Highly skilled, expert. **n.** (ad′ept′) An expert.

adjacent (ə·jā′sənt) **adj.** Next to; near.

admonition (ad′mə·nish′ən) **n.** A warning or scolding.

adorn (ə·dôrn′) **v.** To decorate.

adversary (ad′vər·ser′ē) **n.** An opponent; enemy.

adverse (ad·vurs′) **adj. 1.** Moving or working in an opposite direction. **2.** Unfavorable; harmful.

advocate (ad′və·kit) **n.** A person who speaks in another's cause.

aesthetic (es·thet′ik) **adj.** Relating to what is tasteful or beautiful in art, nature, and the like. —**aesthetically adv.**

affable (af′ə·bəl) **adj.** Easy to talk to; approachable; good-natured.

afflict (ə·flikt′) **v.** To inflict pain or suffering upon.

afford (ə·fôrd′) **v. 1.** To be able to pay for. **2.** To give.

affront (ə·frunt′) **n.** An open or intentional offense or insult.

aggrieved (ə·grēvd′) **adj.** Offended; wrongly treated; injured in legal rights.

alight v. To dismount; descend.

allay (ə·lā′) **v.** To relieve (fears, for example); pacify; calm.

allot (ə·lät′) **v.** To distribute or apportion by random chance.

allusion (ə·loo′zhən) **n.** An indirect reference; casual mention.

aloof (ə·loof′) **adj.** Cool and distant; reserved.

amiable (ā′mē·ə·bəl) **adj.** Friendly or good-natured.

ample (am′pəl) **adj. 1.** Adequate. **2.** More than enough.

amulet (am′yoo·lit) **n.** Object worn as a charm to ward off evil or bad luck.

anarchy (an′ər·kē) **n. 1.** Political disorder; chaos. **2.** Breakdown of government.

ancestral (an·ses′trəl) **adj.** Coming from an ancestor or forefather.

anguish (ang′gwish) **n.** Great pain and suffering because of loss, worry, or grief.

animated (an′i·māt′id) **adj.** Lively; spirited.

annex (ə·neks′) **v.** To add on or attach, especially to a larger thing.

anticipate (an·tis′ə·pāt′) **v.** To expect.

antipathy (an·tip'ə·thē) *n.* Strong dislike; aversion.

apparition (ap'ə·rish'ən) *n.* A strange figure, like a ghost, that appears suddenly.

appeal *v.* To make an earnest request.

appease (ə·pēz') *v.* To pacify or quiet by giving what is demanded.

apprehension (ap'rē·hen'shən) *n.* A sudden anxious expectation; dread.

approbation (ap'rə·bā'shən) *n.* Official approval.

arable (ar'ə·bəl) *adj.* Able to be plowed so as to produce crops.

ardor (är'dər) *n.* Passion.

arduous (är'jōō·əs) *adj.* That which requires great care or effort.

arid (ar'id) *adj.* Dry; wasted and lifeless.

arrest (ə·rest') *v.* To stop or check the progress or course of.

arrogant (ar'ə·gənt) *adj.* Being unjustifiably proud; haughty.

asinine (as'ə·nīn') *adj.* Like an ass; stupid; silly; stubborn. —**asininely** *adv.*

assail (ə·sāl') *v.* To attack with physical violence; assault.

assent (ə·sent') *v.* To agree.

assert (ə·surt') *v.* To declare. —**assert oneself** *v.* To insist on attention or one's rights.

assiduous (ə·sij'ōō·əs) *adj.* Performed with careful and persistent attention.

assuage (ə·swāj') *v.* To lessen, calm, or ease.

atone (ə·tōn') *v.* To make amends for.

atrophy (a'trə·fē) *v.* To shrink or waste away.

augury (ô'gyōo·rē) *n.* Telling of the future from omens.

auspicious (ôs'pish'əs) *adj.* Of good omen; favorable.

avert (ə·vurt') *v.* **1.** To turn away. **2.** To prevent. —**aversion** *n.*

avid (av'id) *adj.* **1.** Eager; enthusiastic. **2.** Characterized by a very strong desire or craving.

avowal (ə·vou'əl) *n.* An open acknowledgment or admission.

▼ B ▼

babel (bā'bəl) *n.* Tumult; confusion.

baleful (bāl'fəl) *adj.* Of evil or harmful appearance or effect. —**balefully** *adv.*

ballast (bal'əst) *n.* Anything heavy carried in the hold of a ship to improve stability.

barren (ber'ən) *adj.* Sterile; unproductive; empty.

beguile (bē·gīl') *v.* To deceive.

bemuse (bē·myōōz') *v.* To bewilder or confuse.

benevolent (bə·nev'ə·lənt) *adj.* Desiring to do good; kindly.

bereave (bē·rēv') *v.* To deprive of something or someone.

bid *v.* To command.

blandishment (blan'dish·mənt) *n.* A flattering remark, intended to coax or persuade.

blasphemy (blas'fə·mē) *n.* Any act, writing, or speech showing disrespect or irreverence for God or sacred things.

bode *v.* To predict, usually that which is evil.

boon *n.* Blessing; benefit.

boor *n.* A clumsy, ill-mannered person.

bounty *n.* **1.** Reward. **2.** Generosity.

brandish *v.* To wield in an exultant manner.

brood *v.* To contemplate in a troubled way.

▼ C ▼

cajole (kə·jōl') *v.* To coax with insincere flattery.

calamitous (kə·lam'ə·təs) *adj.* Causing an extreme misfortune; disastrous.

caldron (kôl'drən) *n.* A large vat or boiler.

candid (kan'did) *adj.* Honest; straightforward.

candor (kan'dər) *n.* **1.** Honesty and frankness in expression. **2.** A fair and unbiased attitude.

capacity (kə·pas'i·tē) *n.* Ability or talent.

capricious (kə·prish'əs; -prē'shəs) *adj.* Tending to change suddenly and impulsively; flighty.

captivate (kap'tə·vāt') *v.* To fascinate; hold the attention of.

career *v.* To run recklessly or wildly.

censure (sen'shər) *v.* To condemn severely.

chide *v.* To scold mildly.

chivalry (shiv'əl·rē) *n.* The qualities of a knight: courage, honor, and willingness to help the weak and protect women.

chronicle (krän'i·kəl) *n.* A chronologically arranged historical record.

---

fat, āpe, cär; ten, ēven; is, bīte; gō, hôrn, tōol, look; oil, out; up, fur; get; joy; yet; chin; she; thin, then; zh, leisure; ŋ or ng, ring; ə for *a* in *ago*, *e* in *agent*, *i* in *sanity*, *o* in *comply*, *u* in *focus*, ' as in able (ā'b'l).

civic (siv′ik) *adj.* Of or having to do with a city, citizens, or citizenship.

clairvoyant (kler·voi′ənt) *adj.* Able to perceive things that are beyond the range of the senses.

clamber (klam′bər) *v.* To climb clumsily, especially with all fours.

clan *n.* A tribal division; extended family.

clandestine (klan·des′tin) *adj.* Kept hidden or secret because unlawful or evil.

clemency (klem′ən·sē) *n.* Mercy toward an enemy or offender.

coagulate (kō·ag′yoo·lāt′) *v.* To thicken; solidify.

coddle *v.* To treat a weak person tenderly.

cogitate (käj′ə·tāt′) *v.* To ponder carefully or think deeply about.

comely (kum′lē) *adj.* **1.** Pleasing or attractive in appearance. **2.** Seemly; decorous; proper.

commandeer (käm′ən·dir′) *v.* To seize.

commend (kə·mend′) *v.* **1.** To praise. **2.** To recommend. **3.** To entrust.

commiserate (kə·miz′ər·āt′) *v.* To feel pity or sympathy for.

commission (kə·mish′ən) *n.* Money paid to a salesperson or agent, usually a percentage of a sale's proceeds.

communal (kə·myoon′əl) *adj.* Held in common; shared by all.

compatriot (kəm·pā′trē·ət) *n.* A fellow citizen.

compensation (käm′pən·sā′shən) *n.* Anything given in exchange for, especially payment for damage or loss.

complacent (kəm·plā′sənt) *adj.* Overly contented or self-satisfied.

comprise (kəm·prīz′) *v.* To consist of; be composed of.

compunction (kəm·pungk′shən) *n.* Remorse; feeling of guilty uneasiness.

concede (kən·sēd′) *v.* **1.** To grant a privilege. **2.** To admit that something is true.

conceivable (kən·sēv′ə·bəl) *adj.* Able to be imagined or believed. —**conceivably** *adv.*

conciliatory (kən·sil′ē·ə·tôr′ē) *adj.* That which placates or soothes the anger of.

condescend (kän′di·send′) *v.* To deal with a person as if he or she were of inferior status.

conducive (kən·doo′siv) *adj.* That contributes.

confer (kən·fur′) *v.* **1.** To give or bestow. **2.** To consult together.

conflagration (kän′flə·grā′shən) *n.* A large, destructive fire.

conjecture (kən·jek′chər) *n.* A guess.

conjugal (kän′jə·gəl) *adj.* Of or relating to marriage or the marital relation.

consecrate (kän′si·krāt′) *v.* To set apart as holy and sacred.

consign (kən·sīn′) *v.* To assign to an unfavorable, objectionable position or place; relegate.

console (kən·sōl′) *v.* To comfort; ease the grief or sadness of. —**consolation** *n.*

conspicuous (kən·spik′yoo·əs) *adj.* Attracting attention because of an unusual quality or qualities; noticeable. —**conspicuously** *adv.*

conspiracy (kən·spir′ə·sē) *n.* A secret plan to do a foul deed.

consternation (kän′stər·nā′shən) *n.* Strong shock or fear that makes a person feel bewildered or helpless.

constitutional (kän′stə·too′shə·nəl) *adj.* Basic to the makeup of a person or thing.

consume (kən·soom′) *v.* To destroy; burn.

contaminate (kən·tam′ə·nāt′) *v.* To corrupt or defile.

contemplate (kän′təm·plāt′) *v.* **1.** To look at with focused and thoughtful attention. **2.** To ponder deeply. —**contemplation** *n.*

contemptuous (kən·temp′choo·əs) *adj.* Regarding another as mean or unworthy; scornful. —**contemptuously** *adv.*

contentious (kən·ten′shəs) *adj.* Argumentative; quarrelsome.

contrive (kən·trīv′) *v.* To bring about; manage.

converse (kən·vurs′) *v.* To speak with informally.

conviction (kən·vik′shən) *n.* **1.** A deeply held belief. **2.** A judgment of guilt by a court of law.

convulse (kən·vuls′) *v.* To cause to tremble or shake, as with pain or laughter.

corpulent (kôr′pyoo·lənt) *adj.* Obese; excessively fat.

corrosive (kə·rōs′iv) *adj.* Causing to wear away or be eaten away.

cosmopolitan (käz′mə·päl′ə·tən) *adj.* **1.** Common to or representative of all or much of the world. **2.** Worldly or broad-minded in views or habits.

counsel (koun′səl) *n.* Advice.

courier (koor′ē·ər) *n.* A messenger.

courtier (kôrt′ē·ər) *n.* An attendant in a court of royalty.

covenant (kuv′ə·nənt) *n.* A solemn agreement or contract in which two or more parties promise to do or refrain from doing some specific thing.

covert (kuv'ərt, *often, as adj.;* kō'vərt) *n.* A hiding place. *adj.* Covered over; secret; disguised.

cower (kou'ər) *v.* To hunch down or shrink from, as with fear.

credulous (krej'oo·ləs) *adj.* Believing too easily.

creed *n.* **1.** A formal statement or expression of religious faith. **2.** A statement of beliefs or principles on any subject.

crestfallen (krest'fôl'ən) *adj.* Depressed; dejected.

crux *n.* The crucial or critical point.

curate (kyoor'it; -āt) *n.* A member of the clergy.

curt *adj.* Rudely brief.

▼ D ▼

dalliance (dal'yəns) *n.* Flirting.

debacle (di·bä'kəl) *n.* A sudden and complete failure or defeat.

decrepit (dē·krep'it) *adj.* Weak or worn out by old age or long use.

defile (dē·fīl') *v.* To profane; show disrespect and contempt.

deft *adj.* Skillful and quick.

deign (dān) *v.* To perform some action, despite believing it to be beneath one's dignity.

dejected (di·jek'tid) *adj.* Depressed; downcast. —**dejectedly** *adv.*

deluge (del'yōoj') *n.* A great flood.

delusion (di·lōo'zhən) *n.* A false belief; wrong notion.

demented (dē·ment'id) *adj.* Mad; insane; wild.

denounce (di·nouns') *v.* **1.** To inform against. **2.** To publicly censure or condemn.

deploy (dē·ploi') *v.* To position forces systematically over an area.

depraved (dē·prāvd'; di-) *adj.* Morally corrupt; utterly wicked.

desolate (des'ə·lit) *adj.* Uninhabited; forlorn.

despicable (des'pi·kə·bəl; de·spik'ə-) *adj.* Contemptible; vile; low.

destine (des'tin) *v.* To predetermine; ensure or intend by fate.

destitute (des'tə·tōōt') *adj.* **1.** Extremely poor. **2.** (with *of*) Totally lacking.

deteriorate (dē·tir'ē·ə·rāt') *v.* To become or cause to be worse.

detest (dē·test') *v.* To hate. —**detestable** *adj.*

dexterous (deks'tər·əs; -trəs) *adj.* Being skillful in using the body or mind. —**dexterously** *adv.*

dictate (dik'tāt') *n.* A guiding principle; something required by authority.

dictum *n.* A formal pronouncement or statement.

diffuse (di·fyōōs') *adj.* Spread out.

digression (di·gresh'ən) *n.* A temporary turning aside from the main subject.

diligence (dil'ə·jəns) *n.* Careful, hard work.

din *n.* Loud, chaotic noise.

dire *adj.* Dreadful; awful.

discern (di·zurn'; -surn') *v.* To perceive and recognize differences.

discomfiture (dis·kum'fi·chər) *n.* Frustration.

disconcert (dis'kən·surt') *v.* To upset, fluster, or embarrass.

disconsolate (dis·kän'sə·lit) *adj.* Inconsolable; terribly unhappy.

discordant (dis·kôrd''nt) *adj.* Not in agreement; conflicting.

discrimination (di·skrim'i·nā'shən) *n.* The ability to make fine distinctions.

disdain (dis·dān') *n.* Scorn felt for someone considered inferior.

disheveled (di·shev'əld) *adj.* Untidy; in disorder.

disown (dis·ōn') *v.* To refuse to accept as one's own.

disparage (di·spar'ij) *v.* To speak of in a belittling way.

dispel (di·spel') *v.* To scatter; disperse.

dispense (di·spens') *v.* To exempt. —**dispense with** *v.* To eliminate.

disperse (di·spurs') *v.* To break up and scatter; distribute widely.

disposed (di·spōzd') *adj.* Inclined; possessing a certain demeanor or tendency.

dispute (di·spyōot') *v.* To argue; quarrel.

dissimulate (di·sim'yōo·lāt') *v.* To conceal (one's feelings, for example) by pretense.

dissipated (dis'ə·pāt'id) *adj.* Spent or wasted by excessive pleasure-seeking, especially drinking and gambling.

dissolution (dis'ə·lōō'shən) *n.* Death; dissolving.

---

fat, āpe, cär; ten, ēven; is, bīte; gō, hôrn, tōol, look; oil, out; up, fur; get; joy; yet; chin; she; thin, then; zh, leisure; ŋ or ng, ring; ə for *a* in *ago, e* in *agent, i* in *sanity, o* in *comply, u* in *focus,* ' as in able (ā'b'l).

dissuade (di·swād′) *v.* To advise or persuade against an action. —**dissuasion** *n.*

distend (di·stend′) *v.* **1.** To extend or stretch out. **2.** To be or cause to become swollen.

diversified (də·vur′sə·fīd′) *adj.* Varied.

divination (div′ə·nā′shən) *n.* Foretelling the future by means of omens or magic.

divinity (də·vin′ə·tē) *n.* Quality of being like God or a god; a god or deity.

docile (däs′əl) *adj.* Easily managed or controlled; submissive.

doctrine (däk′trin) *n.* The body of beliefs or principles of a religion, political party, and the like.

dominion (də·min′yən) *n.* Sovereignty; power to control or rule.

dumb *adj.* Silent; mute.

duplicity (dōō·plis′ə·tē) *n.* A deception based on hypocritical actions; deceitfulness.

▼ E ▼

ebb *v.* To weaken or decline.

edict (ē′dikt′) *n.* A decree; a publicly proclaimed order.

edify (ed′i·fī′) *v.* To instruct so as to improve morally.

efface (ə·fās′) *v.* To erase.

egocentric (ē′gō·sen′trik) *adj.* Self-centered.

elated *adj.* Very happy.

elude (ē·lōōd′) *v.* To evade or escape from by cleverness or quickness.

eminence (em′i·nəns) *n.* **1.** An elevated thing or place, as a mountain. **2.** Greatness.

emphatic (em·fat′ik) *adj.* Expressed with force or stress. —**emphatically** *adv.*

emulate (em′yōō·lāt′) *v.* To imitate in order to equal or surpass.

endow (en·dou′) *v.* **1.** To give some quality to. **2.** To give money or property which will provide additional income.

engender (en·jen′dər) *v.* To cause to be; produce.

enjoin (en·join′) *v.* To command someone to do or refrain from doing something.

enmity (en′mə·tē) *n.* Hostility.

ensue (en·sōō′) *v.* To follow immediately, as an event.

enterprise (ent′ər·prīz′) *n.* An undertaking.

entreat (en·trēt′) *v.* To ask sincerely and urgently; beg.

equanimity (ek′wə·nim′ə·tē) *n.* The ability to maintain composure and calmness.

eschew (es·chōō′) *v.* To stay away from; avoid.

estrange (e·strānj′) *v.* **1.** To keep apart or separate.

2. To make hostile or unfriendly.

etiquette (et′i·kit) *n.* Established rules of behavior in society or a profession.

evasion (ē·vā′zhən) *n.* The act of evading (a consequence or responsibility, for example) through deception or cleverness.

evoke *v.* To draw forth a mental image or reaction. —**evocation** *n.*

exasperate (eg·zas′pər·āt′) *v.* To annoy; try the patience of.

excel (ek·sel′) *v.* To be better than others.

excursion (eks·kur′zhən) *n.* A short trip taken for pleasure.

execration (ek′si·krā′shən) *n.* The act of cursing or speaking abusively of a person or thing.

executor (ek′si·kyōōt·ər) *n.* A person who carries out some action.

exhilarate (eg·zil′ə·rāt′) *v.* To make lively; stimulate.

exorcise (eks′ôr·sīz′) *v.* To drive out an evil spirit by a religious or magic ritual. —**exorcist** *n.*

expanse (ek·spans′) *n.* A wide, open area.

expedient (ek·spē′dē·ənt) *n.* A thing useful to achieve an end.

exquisite (eks′kwi·zit) *adj.* Very beautiful or delicate.

extirpate (ek′stər·pāt′) *v.* To destroy; exterminate; uproot.

extort (eks·tôrt′) *v.* To get money or goods by threats or violence.

exude (eg·zyōōd′; -zōōd′) *v.* To ooze.

exult (eg·zult′) *v.* To be very happy; to feel joyful and triumphant.

▼ F ▼

faction (fak′shən) *n.* A split within an organization or country; internal conflict.

fallow *adj.* Plowed but not cultivated or planted.

falsification (fôl′sə·fi·kā′shən) *n.* A false or misleading statement.

falter (fôl′tər) *v.* To weaken or waver.

fastidious (fas·tid′ē·əs) *adj.* Overly particular and critical.

fatuous (fach′ōō·əs) *adj.* Contentedly stupid; foolish.

feign (fān) *v.* To pretend.

felicity (fə·lis′i·tē) *n.* Joy; gladness.

fervent (fur′vənt) *adj.* Very warm or intense in feeling.

fervor (fur′vər) *n.* Strong, warm feeling.

filial (fil′ē·əl) *adj.* Of, referring to, or appropriate for one's children.

flaccid (flak′sid; flas′id) *adj.* Flabby; hanging loosely.

flail *v.* To beat with a stick or whip.

flaunt (flônt) *v.* To make a showy, impudent display; show off.

flout *v.* To scoff or jeer at; scorn.

forbear (fôr·ber′) *v.* [past tense, *forbore*] To refrain from; to be patient.

foreboding (fôr·bōd′ing) *n.* A prediction or feeling that something harmful will take place; apprehension.

forestall (fôr·stôl′) *v.* To prevent or delay by taking action ahead of time.

forfeit (fôr′fit) *v.* To lose, give up, or be deprived of because of some crime or failure.

forge *v.* To make a metal object by heating and hammering.

forlorn (fôr·lôrn′) *adj.* Deserted; miserable; hopeless.

formidable (fôr′mə·də·bəl) *adj.* Producing fear or horror.

forswear (fôr·swer′) *v.* To promise abstinence from; pledge to give up.

foster *v.* To bring up or raise with care.

fraternal (frə·tʉrn′əl) *adj.* Brotherly.

frivolity (fri·väl′ə·tē) *n.* Lack of seriousness or sense; silliness.

furtive (fʉr′tiv) *adj.* Secretive; done in a stealthy or sneaky way.

futile (fyōōt′'l) *adj.* Useless; hopeless.

▼ G ▼

gall (gôl) *n.* **1.** Feeling of bitterness. **2.** Irritation; annoyance.

gambol (gam′bəl) *v.* To frolic; to play animatedly.

gaunt (gônt) *adj.* Lean and bony; emaciated; scrawny.

gentility (jen·til′i·tē) *n.* **1.** The quality of being refined and polite. **2.** The condition of being born into the upper classes.

glade *n.* An open area or space, especially in the woods.

glut *n.* Excessive fullness.

goad *v.* To urge on.

grapple (grap′əl) *v.* To struggle in hand-to-hand combat.

grizzled (griz′əld) *adj.* Gray, especially in reference to hair.

grueling (grōō′əl·ing) *adj.* Exhausting; very difficult.

guile (gīl) *n.* Deceitfulness and craftiness; cunning.

guise (gīz) *n.* **1.** Manner or way of dressing. **2.** Deceiving or false appearance.

gyration (jī·rā′shən) *n.* The act of moving in a circular or spiral path around a central axis or point.

▼ H ▼

haggard (hag′ərd) *adj.* Gaunt; having a wasted, wild look.

haggle *v.* To argue about the price of.

hapless (hap′lis) *adj.* Unlucky.

harry *v.* **1.** To disturb or worry; harass. **2.** To force or prod.

havoc (hav′ek) *n.* Vast destruction or ruin.

hectic (hek′tik) *adj.* Happening in a confused or excited rush.

heedless (hēd′lis) *adj.* Paying no attention.

hexagonal (heks·ag′ə·nel) *adj.* Having six angles and six sides.

homage (häm′ij; äm′-) *n.* Something given or done to show respect.

homily (häm′ə·lē) *n.* A sermon, especially on a religious or biblical subject.

hovel (huv′əl) *n.* A small, impoverished dwelling or hut.

hover (huv′ər) *v.* To float or remain suspended in the air; wait close by, especially in an annoying way.

▼ I ▼

icon (ī′kän′) *n.* A picture or image, regarded as sacred, of a religious figure.

ignoble (ig·nō′bəl) *adj.* Not noble; common or low.

immaculate (im·mak′yōō·lit) *adj.* **1.** Spotlessly clean. **2.** Flawless. **3.** Pure; innocent.

imminent (im′ə·nənt) *adj.* Likely to happen very soon.

immutable (im·myōōt′ə·bəl) *adj.* Unchangeable.

impartial (im·pär′shəl) *adj.* Unbiased; not favoring either side in a dispute or contest.

impassive (im·pas′iv) *adj.* Displaying no emotion; calm.

impediment (im·ped′ə·mənt) *n.* Hindrance.

impel (im·pel′) *v.* To propel; drive forward.

impend (im·pend′) *v.* To be about to occur; to loom.

---

fat, āpe, cär; ten, ēven; is, bīte; gō, hôrn, tōōl, look; oil, out; up, fʉr; get; joy; yet; chin; she; thin, then; zh, leisure; ŋ or ng, ring; ə for *a* in *ago*, *e* in *agent*, *i* in *sanity*, *o* in *comply*, *u* in *focus*, ′ as in able (ā′b'l).

impenetrable (im·pen′i·trə·bəl) *adj.* Not capable of being passed through; dense.

imperceptible (im′pər·sep′tə·bəl) *adj.* Not easily sensed. —**imperceptibly** *adv.*

imperial (im·pir′ē·əl) *adj.* **1.** Of or relating to an empire. **2.** Majestic.

imperious (im·pir′ē·əs) *adj.* Bossy; arrogant; domineering.

impervious (im·pʉr′vē·əs) *adj.* Incapable of being attacked.

implacable (im·plā′kə·bəl; -plak′-) *adj.* Not capable of being pacified or quieted.

implore (im·plôr′) *v.* To beg or plead for.

impotent (im′pə·tənt) *adj.* Powerless; ineffective. —**impotently** *adv.*

impregnable (im·preg′nə·bəl) *adj.* Not capable of being penetrated or entered by force.

improvise (im′prə·vīz′) *v.* To make or do with the materials at hand in order to fill a pressing need.

impudent (im′pyo͞o·dənt) *adj.* Disrespectfully bold; brazen. —**impudently** *adv.*

impulsive (im·pul′siv) *adj.* Acting or likely to act without forethought or plan. —**impulsively** *adv.*

incantation (in′kan·tā′shən) *n.* The recitation of magical words to cast a spell or perform magic.

incarnate (in·kär′nit; -nāt) *adj.* Appearing as a recognizable, living example; personified.

incendiary (in·sen′dē·er′ē) *adj.* Related to the deliberate destruction of property by fire.

incense (in·sens′) *v.* To make very angry; enrage.

incessant (in·ses′ənt) *adj.* Unending; continuing or repeating endlessly. —**incessantly** *adv.*

incomprehensible (in′käm′prē·hen′sə·bəl) *adj.* Not understandable.

incongruous (in·kän′gro͞o·əs) *adj.* Inconsistent with expectations; lacking harmony or compatibility.

incredulous (in·krej′o͞o·ləs) *adj.* Disbelieving or unwilling to believe; skeptical.

indefatigable (in′di·fat′i·gə·bəl) *adj.* Untiring.

indiscretion (in′di·skresh′ən) *n.* An unwise or careless act or comment.

indispensable (in′di·spen′sə·bəl) *adj.* Of key importance; necessary.

indisposition (in′dis·pə·zish′ən) *n.* Unwellness or slight sickness.

indulgence (in·dul′jəns) *n.* **1.** The act of giving way to another's or one's own desires. **2.** Something given as a favor.

inert (in·ʉrt′) *adj.* Characterized by mental or physical inactivity or slowness.

inextricable (in·eks′tri·kə·bəl) *adj.* Incapable of being set free or disentangled from.

infallible (in·fal′ə·bəl) *adj.* Incapable of error; reliable.

infamy (in′fə·mē) *n.* Shameful or wicked reputation.

infatuation (in·fach′o͞o·ā′·shən) *n.* An unreasoning or shallow love, affection, or attachment.

infer (in·fʉr′) *v.* To draw a conclusion from evidence or an assumption.

infuse (in·fyo͞oz′) *v.* To put; fill. —**infused** *adj.*

ingenious (in·jēn′yəs) *adj.* Demonstrating creativity or resourcefulness. —**ingenuity** *n.*

ingrate (in′grāt′) *n.* An ungrateful person.

iniquity (i·nik′wi·tē) *n.* Wickedness; sinfulness; wrongdoing.

initiate (i·nish′ē·āt′) *v.* To introduce or instruct.

initiative (i·nish′ə·tiv) *n.* **1.** Responsibility for taking the first step in and following through with a project or plan. **2.** Ability to think or act for oneself, without needing encouragement or urging.

inordinate (in·ôr′də·nit) *adj.* Lacking restraint; excessive.

insensible (in·sen′sə·bəl) *adj.* Lacking sensation or consciousness; unaware.

insignificant (in′sig·nif′i·kənt) *adj.* Unimportant; of no meaning or consequence.

insolent (in′sə·lənt) *adj.* Disrespectful; rude; arrogant.

insouciant (in·so͞o′sē·ənt) *adj.* Calmly indifferent; carefree. —**insouciance** *n.*

instigation (in′stə·gā′shən) *n.* An urging on to some evil act.

insular (in′sə·lər) *adj.* **1.** Isolated. **2.** Narrow-minded.

insuperable (in·so͞o′pər·ə·bəl) *adj.* Incapable of being overcome.

intensive (in·ten′siv) *adj.* Thorough; deep; concentrated. —**intensively** *adv.*

intent (in·tent′) *adj.* Directed or fixed. —**intent on** or **upon** *adj.* Having the attention fixed; strongly directed.

intercede (in′tər·sēd′) *v.* To make an appeal on behalf of another or others. —**intercession** *n.*

interlude (in′tər·lo͞od′) *n.* Entertainment between the acts of a play.

interminable (in·tʉr′mi·nə·bəl) *adj.* That which continues, or seems to continue, without end.

intermittent (in′tər·mit′′nt) *adj.* Ending and beginning again at intervals.

interrogate (in·ter'ə·gāt') **v.** To ask questions of; inspect; examine.

intervene (in'tər·vēn') **v. 1.** To occur between two points in time. **2.** To come between.

intimate (in'tə·mət) **adj. 1.** Innermost or personal. **2.** Closely acquainted; very familiar.

intimation (in'tə·mā'shən) **n.** A hint; subtle implication.

intolerable (in·täl'ər·ə·bəl) **adj.** Unbearable; too painful or severe to be endured.

intrepid (in·trep'id) **adj.** Not afraid; courageous.

intricate (in'tri·kit) **adj.** Elaborately detailed; complex.

intrigue (in·trēg'; *for n., also* in'trēg') **v. 1.** To plot or scheme in a secret manner. **2.** To interest greatly. **n.** A secret plot or scheme.

invariable (in·ver'ē·ə·bəl) **adj.** Never changing; constant.

invert (in·vʉrt') **v.** To place upside down. **—inverted adj.**

inveterate (in·vet'ər·it) **adj.** Long-lasting; long-standing; habitual.

invoke v. To call on God or a god for assistance.

irreparable (ir·rep'ə·rə·bəl) **adj.** Not able to be repaired.

issue (ish'ōō; -yōō) **n.** Children; offspring.

▼ J ▼

jeopardy (jep'ər·dē) **n.** Intense danger or peril.

joust n. A fight between two mounted knights wielding lances.

jubilation (jōō'bə·lā'shən) **n.** Triumphant joyfulness.

judicious (jōō·dish'əs) **adj.** Showing good judgment; wise and cautious.

justification (jus'tə·fi·kā'shən) **n.** A fact or argument that shows that someone is right or has acted reasonably.

juxtapose (juks'tə·pōz') **v.** To place one thing or idea close to or side by side with another.

▼ K ▼

kindred (kin'drid) **n.** Family; kinfolk.

knight-errant (nīt'er'ənt) **n.** A knight looking for adventures that will allow him to correct injustices or show his strength and skill.

knoll (nōl) **n.** Small hill.

▼ L ▼

laborious (lə·bôr'ē·əs) **adj.** Involving intensive work; difficult.

labyrinth (lab'ə·rinth') **n.** A complex network of winding passageways; maze.

lamentation (lam'ən·tā'shən) **n.** An outward show of grief; wailing or crying.

legitimate (lə·jit'ə·mət) **adj. 1.** Born to married parents. **2.** Legal; lawful.

lineage (lin'ē·ij) **n.** Direct descent from an ancestor.

loath (lōth; lō*th*) **adj.** Reluctant.

loin n. [usually plural] The hips or the lower abdomen of the body, regarded as the source of strength and procreative power.

loll v. To lounge about.

lop v. To remove by chopping off.

lout n. An awkward, foolish person; oaf.

lucid (lōō'sid) **adj.** Easily understood.

lumber (lum'bər) **v.** To move about in a clumsy, noisy manner.

▼ M ▼

magnanimous (mag·nan'ə·məs) **adj.** Noble-spirited; generous. **—magnanimity n.**

malice (mal'is) **n.** Active ill will; desire to deliberately harm another; spite. **—malicious adj.**

malignant (mə·lig'nənt) **adj.** Very evil or dangerous.

manifest (man'ə·fest') **v.** To become apparent; show.

manifold (man'ə·fōld') **adj.** Many and diverse.

mannerism (man'ər·iz'əm) **n.** A unique feature of behavior, speech, and so on, that has become habitual.

martyr (märt'ər) **n. 1.** A person who prefers to suffer or die rather than deny his or her principles or beliefs. **2.** A person who undergoes immense pain or suffering for a long time.

materialize (mə·tir'ē·əl·īz') **v.** To appear suddenly, in concrete form.

mean adj. Of little value; inferior.

mediocre (mē'dē·ō'kər) **adj. 1.** Average; ordinary. **2.** Of inferior quality.

meditation (med'ə·tā'shən) **n.** Solemn reflection on spiritual matters.

metaphysics (met'ə·fiz'iks) **n. pl.** A branch of philosophy dealing with the nature of being and reality.

---

fat, āpe, cär; ten, ēven; is, bīte; gō, hôrn, tōol, look; oil, out; up, fʉr; get; joy; yet; chin; she; thin, *th*en; zh, leisure; ŋ or ng, ring; ə for *a* in *ago*, *e* in *agent*, *i* in *sanity*, *o* in *comply*, *u* in *focus*, ' as in able (ā'b'l).

mete *v.* To distribute or dole out; usually with *out*.

meticulous (mə·tik′yoo·ləs) *adj.* Very careful or finicky about details.

minister (min′is·tər) *n.* A person or thing serving as the agent of some higher power.

mire *n.* An area of deep mud or slush.

misalliance (mis·ə·lī′əns) *n.* A bad partnership; a marriage of incompatible partners.

misgiving (mis·giv′ing) *n.* An unsettling feeling of fear or doubt.

monotony (mə·nät′′n·ē) *n.* Boring sameness.

morose (mə·rōs′) *adj.* Gloomy; in a bad or sullen mood.

mortify (môrt′ə·fī′) *v.* To arouse great shame or humiliation.

mundane (mun′dān′) *adj.* Of the world; ordinary, day-to-day.

muster *v.* To gather or bring together.

mutiny (myoot′′n·ē) *n.* A revolt, as by soldiers or sailors, against their officers. —**mutinous** *adj.*

▼ N ▼

nascent (nas′ənt; nā′sənt) *adj.* Coming into existence; in the process of being born.

nativity (nə·tiv′ə·tē) *n.* Birth and, particularly, the circumstances surrounding a birth.

nimble *adj.* Moving about in a quick or light manner. —**nimbly** *adv.*

nocturnal (näk·tur′nəl) *adj.* Of or occurring during the night.

nonplus (nän′plus′) *v.* To puzzle or bewilder into a state of inaction.

novice (näv′is) *n.* A beginner; amateur; newcomer.

nuptial (nup′shəl) *n.* A wedding.

nurture (nur′chər) *v.* To care for, especially by feeding or protecting.

▼ O ▼

obdurate (äb′door·it) *adj.* **1.** Lacking sympathy. **2.** Stubborn. —**obduracy** *n.*

oblation (ə·blā′shən) *n.* **1.** Gift or offering to God or a god. **2.** The bread and wine of the Eucharist.

oblige (ə·blīj′) *v.* **1.** To cause to do something by moral, legal, or physical force. **2.** To perform a favor.

oblivion (ə·bliv′ē·ən) *n.* The state of complete forgetfulness.

obscurity (əb·skyoor′ə·tē) *n.* Inconspicuousness; lack of fame.

obsess (əb·ses′) *v.* To haunt in mind or preoccupy to an extreme degree.

obsolete (äb′sə·lēt′) *adj.* **1.** Outdated. **2.** No longer used.

obstinate (äb′stə·nət) *adj.* Very stubborn.

obtuse (äb·toos′) *adj.* Slow to comprehend; dull-witted. —**obtuseness** *n.*

odious (ō′dē·əs) *adj.* Hateful; disgusting.

ogre (ō′gər) *n.* A monster or giant who eats people.

ominous (äm′ə·nəs) *adj.* Seeming to threaten evil or misfortune; sinister.

omnipotent (äm·nip′ə·tənt) *adj.* All-powerful.

oppressive (ə·pras′iv) *adj.* Hard to bear.

oratory (ôr′ə·tôr′ē) *n.* Public speaking, especially in a traditional manner.

ostentation (äs′tən·tā′shən) *n.* Showiness.

▼ P ▼

pacify (pas′ə·fī′) *v.* To make calm; to appease or make quiet.

painstaking (pānz′tāk′ing) *adj.* Taking great pains or care. —**painstakingly** *adv.*

pallid (pal′id) *adj.* Pale in color or complexion.

palpable (pal′pə·bəl) *adj.* Plainly evident to the senses.

palpitate (pal′pə·tāt′) *v.* To beat more rapidly than normal, usually referring to the heart.

paltry (pôl′trē) *adj.* Trivial; having little or no worth.

pander *v.* To act in a way that helps satisfy the base desires or exploits the weakness of another.

paragon (par′ə·gän′) *n.* Something that is a model or example of perfection.

paternal (pə·tur′nəl) *adj.* Of or referring to the father's side of a family; fatherly.

pathos (pā′thäs′) *n.* The quality in something experienced or observed that moves one to feelings of pity or sorrow.

patriarch (pā′trē·ärk′) *n.* **1.** An elderly and honored man. **2.** A man regarded as the father or founder of a family or institution.

patronize (pā′trən·īz′) *v.* To be helpful to or supportive of someone but treat as an inferior. —**patronizingly** *adv.*

pedant (ped′′nt) *n.* A teacher who places undue emphasis on minor details or rules rather than on genuine learning.

peer *n.* A person who is the equal of another.

peevish (pēv′ish) *adj.* Difficult to please; easily irritated. —**peevishly** *adv.* —**peevishness** *n.*

pelt *n.* The coat or skin of a fur-bearing animal. *v.* To throw things at.

penitent (pen′ə·tent) *adj.* Feeling sorry or regretful for having done wrong.

pensive (pen′siv) *adj.* Thoughtful; considering sad or serious matters.

perfidious (pər·fid′ē·əs) *adj.* Acting in betrayal of trust; treacherous.

peril (per′əl) *n.* Danger.

periphery (pə·rif′ər·ē) *n.* Outer parts or boundary, especially of a rounded object.

perish (per′ish) *v.* **1.** To be destroyed, obliterated, or ruined. **2.** To die suddenly and violently.

perplexed (pər·plekst′) *adj.* Puzzled; confused.

persecution (pur′si·kyo͞o′shən) *n.* The state of being cruelly oppressed or mistreated.

perseverance (pur′sə·vir′əns) *n.* Persistent, patient effort.

pervade (pər·vād′) *v.* To exist widely.

perverse (pər·vurs′) *adj.* Stubbornly persisting in error.

pestilence (pes′tə·ləns) *n.* Any disease, especially one of epidemic proportions, as bubonic plague.

pestilential (pes′tə·len′shəl) *adj.* **1.** Of, causing, or likely to cause infection. **2.** Deadly to a wide population.

petition (pə·tish′ən) *v.* To ask for sincerely or formally.

petrify (pe′tri·fī′) *v.* To paralyze with fear.

phantasm (fan′taz′əm) *n.* A ghost, specter; a vision of something that has no physical reality.

piety (pī′ə·tē) *n.* Loyalty (to God, parents, or country, for example).

pilgrimage (pil′grim·ij) *n.* **1.** A trip undertaken by a pilgrim, especially to a holy place. **2.** A long journey.

pitiable (pit′ē·ə·bəl) *adj.* Arousing or deserving compassion, sometimes mixed with scorn.

plunder (plun′dər) *v.* To steal, especially during a time of war.

ponder (pän′dər) *v.* To consider deeply and carefully.

ponderous (pän′dər·əs) *adj.* Heavy or massive.

portent (pôr′tent′) *n.* Something that foretells or predicts a coming event, often of an unfortunate nature; an omen.

postulate (päs′chə·lāt′) *v.* To assume, as the basis of an argument, the truth of something unproven or unprovable; claim.

practicable (prak′ti·kə·bəl) *adj.* That which can be accomplished or put into practice.

precarious (pri·ker′ē·əs) *adj.* Dependent upon uncertain circumstances or persons.

precedent (pres′ə·dənt) *n.* A case that may serve as an example for a later one.

precept (prē′sept′) *n.* A command or direction for action or behavior.

precinct (prē′siŋkt′) *n.* A district of a city; neighborhood.

precipice (pres′i·pis) *n.* A high, steep cliff.

precipitate (prē·sip′ə·tit) *adj.* Acting or happening very hastily. **—precipitately** *adv.*

precursor (prē·kur′sər) *n.* A person or thing that comes before another; forerunner.

predatory (pred′ə·tôr′ē) *adj.* Living by hunting and feeding on other animals.

preeminent (prē·em′ə·nənt) *adj.* Very fine; surpassing all others.

preliminaries (prē·lim′ə·ner′ēs) *n. pl.* Procedures or steps leading up to main part or action.

premonition (prēm′ə·nish′ən) *n.* A feeling that something unfortunate is going to happen.

preoccupied (prē·äk′yə·pīd′) *adj.* Wholly absorbed with one's thoughts; engrossed. **—preoccupation** *n.*

prescience (presh′əns) *n.* Knowledge of a thing or event before it exists or takes place.

presentiment (prē·zent′ə·mənt) *n.* A feeling or forewarning that something is about to happen.

presumption (prē·zump′shən) *n.* **1.** An overstepping of proper limits. **2.** A supposing.

pretension (prē·ten′shən) *n.* **1.** A claim to nobility or some other distinction. **2.** An extravagant and unjustified outward show; pretentiousness.

prevaricate (pri·var′i·kāt′) *v.* To avoid the truth; lie.

primal (prī′məl) *adj.* **1.** Original. **2.** Of chief importance.

primordial (prī·môr′dē·əl) *adj.* Existing or occurring from the world's beginning.

pristine (pris′tēn′) *adj.* **1.** Original. **2.** Unspoiled.

---

fat, āpe, cär; ten, ēven; is, bīte; gō, hôrn, to͞ol, look; oil, out; up, fur; get; joy; yet; chin; she; thin, then; zh, leisure; ŋ or ng, ring; ə for a in ago, e in agent, i in sanity, o in comply, u in focus, ′ as in able (ā′b'l).

procure (prō·kyoor′) *v.* To obtain or make happen by an effort; secure.

prodigal (präd′i·gəl) *adj.* Carelessly wasteful.

prodigy (präd′ə·jē) *n.* A person of amazing ability. —**prodigious** *adj.*

profound (prō·found′) *adj.* 1. Deeply felt. 2. Having great intellectual depth.

profuse (prō·fyoos′) *adj.* Abundant; pouring out in excess. —**profusely** *adv.*

promontory (präm′ən·tôr′ē) *n.* A high ridge of land that overlooks a body of water.

propaganda (präp′ə·gan′də) *n.* The widespread promotion of the ideas or practices of a particular group or party intended to gain support for one's own cause or to damage another's.

propitiate (prō·pish′ē·āt′) *v.* To appease or pacify.

prostrate (präs′trāt′) *adj.* Lying face down.

protract (prō·trakt′) *v.* To prolong; lengthen.

protrude (prō·trood′) *v.* To jut out.

provincial (prə·vin′shəl) *adj.* 1. Narrow-minded; unsophisticated. 2. From a province, especially a rural one.

prowess (prou′is) *n.* Bravery; courage.

punctual (puŋk′choo·əl) *adj.* Timely; prompt. —**punctually** *adv.*

purge (purj) *v.* To cleanse of impurities; to clear away or out.

▼ Q ▼

quagmire (kwag′mīr) *n.* Area of deep, soft mud; bog.

quarter (kwôrt′ər) *n.* 1. A particular district or neighborhood. 2. Lodgings. 3. Mercy granted to a surrendering enemy.

quibble (kwib′əl) *v.* To evade the truth of a point by focusing on a petty detail.

quicken (kwik′ən) *v.* To become revived.

▼ R ▼

rampart (ram′pärt′; -pərt) *n.* An embankment of earth, usually supporting a wall, that encircles a castle or fort for defense against attack.

rapture (rap′chər) *n.* A joyous, almost ecstatic condition or feeling.

ratify (rat′ə·fī′) *v.* To confirm; make valid or legal.

ravage (rav′ij) *v.* To ruin; destroy.

raze *v.* To lay level with the ground; destroy.

realm (relm) *n.* Kingdom; province; region.

rebuke (ri·byook′) *v.* To reprimand or scold.

reckoning (rek′ən·ing) *n.* 1. The settlement or accounting of rewards or punishments for an action. 2. Counting or calculation.

recompense (rek′əm·pens′) *v.* To pay for; compensate.

reconciliation (rek′ən·sil′ē·ā′shən) *n.* A settling of a quarrel; restoration of harmony.

recriminate (ri·krim′ə·nāt′) *v.* To meet the charges of an accuser by accusing him or her of wrongdoing.

rectify (rek′tə·fī′) *v.* To amend, correct, or make right.

redemption (ri·demp′shən) *n.* A deliverance from sin and its punishments.

redouble (rē·dub′əl) *v.* To double, as in size or degree.

reflect (ri·flekt′) *v.* To contemplate seriously; ponder. —**reflection** *n.*

relent (ri·lent′) *v.* To yield.

relic (rel′ik) *n.* 1. A thing of the past, saved for its historic interest. 2. *pl.* Those fragments surviving from the past.

relinquish (ri·ling′kwish) *v.* To abandon claim to; let go of; yield.

rend *v.* [past tense *rent*] To rip up or tear apart violently.

render *v.* To represent or reproduce in words, pictures, or performance.

renounce (ri·nouns′) *v.* To purposefully give up a claim, right, way of living, and so forth; to repudiate or disown.

renown (ri·noun′) *n.* Illustrious reputation; great fame.

repast (ri·past′) *n.* A meal; feast.

replenish (ri·plen′ish) *v.* To refill or make complete again; to renew the supply.

reprehensible (rep′ri·hen′sə·bəl) *adj.* Deserving of criticism or blame.

repress (ri·pres′) *v.* To hold back, restrain, or curb. —**repression** *n.*

reprimand (rep′rə·mand′) *n.* A severe scolding, especially by someone in authority.

reproach (ri·prōch′) *v.* To scold, reprimand, or censure, especially in a way that produces shame.

reprobation (rep′rə·bā′·shən) *n.* Disapproval; condemnation; rejection.

reprove (ri·proov′) *v.* To scold or censure.

repulse (ri·puls′) *v.* 1. To repel or drive back; reject. 2. To disgust. —**repulsive** *adj.* —**repulsion** *n.*

reputed (ri·pyoot′id) *adj.* Recognized or supposed to be so.

requite (ri·kwīt′) *v.* 1. To repay or reward. 2. [*Archaic*]

To do something in return.

residue (rez′ə·dōō′) *n.* Leftover portion; remainder.

resin (rez′ən) *n.* A semisolid, sticky substance given off by some plants and trees.

resolute (rez′ə·lōōt′) *adj.* Having a decided purpose; determined.

resolve (ri·zälv′) *v.* To determine or decide; settle on.

respite (res′pit) *n.* A temporary period of rest or relief.

resplendent (ri·splen′dənt) *adj.* With much splendor; dazzling; shining brilliantly.

retaliate (ri·tal′ē·āt′) *v.* To do something to get revenge for an injury or evil. **—retaliation** *n.*

retinue (ret′n·yōō′) *n.* A group of assistants and servants who follow an important person.

retort *v.* To reply in a quick, sharp manner.

revel (rev′əl) *v.* To be festive in a noisy manner.

revere (ri·vēr′) *v.* To have great respect and love for.

reverie (rev′ər·ē) *n.* Daydreaming; state of being lost in thought or imagining, especially of pleasant things.

revile (ri·vīl′) *v.* To verbally abuse someone.

rhetoric (ret′ər·ik) *n.* **1.** Language intended to persuade. **2.** Showy, elaborate language that is lacking in clarity and sincerity.

rile *v.* To prod into action by upsetting; irritate.

rout *n.* An utter and overpowering defeat.

ruse (rōōz) *n.* A trick.

▼ S ▼

sacrilege (sak′rə·lij) *n.* The act of taking, using, violating, or treating disrespectfully something which is consecrated to God or religion.

sage *n.* A person greatly respected for wisdom and judgment.

salutation (sal′yōō·tā′shən) *n.* A greeting.

sanctify (saŋk′te·fī′) *v.* To make or set apart as holy.

sanction (saŋk′shən) *n.* Official approval given for an action.

sap *v.* To empty, drain, or exhaust; weaken.

scourge (skurj) *n.* A punishment; a cause of severe trouble or suffering.

scrupulous (skrōō′pyə·ləs) *adj.* Giving careful attention to what is right or proper.

scrutinize (skrōōt′n·īz′) *v.* To examine or inspect carefully and closely.

seduce (si·dōōs′) *v.* To persuade into wrongdoing or disloyalty.

sensuous (sen′shōō·əs) *adj.* Perceived by the senses, especially with pleasure or enjoyment.

sepulcher (sep′əl·kər) *n.* A vault, chamber, or grave for the dead.

sequence (sē′kwəns) *n.* The following of one thing after another in some logical order.

serenity (sə·ren′ə·tē) *n.* Calmness; composure; tranquility.

sever (sev′ər) *v.* **1.** To cut off by force. **2.** To separate; divide.

sheaf *n.* A quantity of cut stalks of grain, and the like, bundled together.

sheer *adj.* Very steep.

shroud *v.* **1.** To wrap a corpse in burial cloth. **2.** To hide or conceal.

siege (sēj) *n.* The besetting of a fortified place by an army to compel surrender.

sinister (sin′is·tər) *adj.* Ominous; indicating lurking evil or harm.

slake *v.* **1.** Satisfy; quench. **2.** To cause a fire to die out.

slough (sluf) *v.* To get rid of or throw off.

sluice (slōōs) *n.* A gate or valve used in opening or closing an artificial passage for water.

sojourn (sō′jurn) *v.* To stop and dwell in a place temporarily.

solace (säl′is) *n.* Comfort in times of trouble.

solder (säd′ər) *v.* To join (metal pieces) with a melted metal compound.

solicitous (sə·lis′ə·təs) *adj.* Showing care or attention; anxiously willing. **—solicitously** *adv.*

somber (säm′bər) *adj.* **1.** Dark and dismal. **2.** Melancholy; depressed.

sonorous (sə·nôr′əs; sän′ər-) *adj.* Quality of sound which is full, deep, and resonant.

sordid (sôr′did) *adj.* **1.** Dirty; squalid. **2.** Dishonorable or ignoble; mean or petty.

sovereignty (säv′rən·tē) *n.* **1.** Supreme political power or authority. **2.** Supremacy in power or position.

spit *n.* A thin, pointed rod used to hold meat over a fire.

---

fat, āpe, cär; ten, ēven; is, bīte; gō, hôrn, tōōl, look; oil, out; up, fur; get; joy; yet; chin; she; thin, then; zh, leisure; ŋ or ng, ring; ə for *a* in *ago*, *e* in *agent*, *i* in *sanity*, *o* in *comply*, *u* in *focus*, ′ as in able (ā′b′l).

splay *v.* To flatten; spread out.

spoils *n. pl.* Goods and land captured in war; booty.

spurn *v.* To reject with contempt.

squander (skwän′dər) *v.* To spend wastefully or extravagantly.

stamina (stam′ə·nə) *n.* Endurance; ability to stand fatigue.

statute (stach′o͞ot) *n.* A law or established rule.

steadfast (sted′fast′) *adj.* Firmly established; unchanging; steady.

stealthy (stel′thē) *adj.* Intentionally secretive or sly. —**stealthily** *adv.*

stifling (stī′fling) *adj.* Suffocating; oppressively lacking in fresh air.

stratagem (strat′ə·jəm) *n.* A trick or plan to fool an enemy.

stricture (strik′chər) *n.* **1.** A condition that limits, restrains, or restricts. **2.** Harsh criticism.

stupefy (sto͞o′pə·fī′) *v.* To dull the mind or deprive of sensibility; stun.

stupendous (sto͞o·pen′dəs) *adj.* Amazing; astonishing in magnitude or scope.

stupor (sto͞o′pər) *n.* Condition in which there is a partial or complete loss of sensibility, as from shock.

suave (swäv) *adj.* Smoothly pleasant and polite. —**suavely** *adv.*

subdue (sub·do͞o′) *v.* **1.** To conquer. **2.** To bring wild land into a cultivated state.

submissive (sub·mis′iv) *adj.* Being obedient and yielding without resistance. —**submission** *n.*

subside (səb·sīd′) *v.* **1.** To descend; move to a lower level. **2.** To become tranquil, less intense.

substantiate (səb·stan′shē·āt′) *v.* To establish the existence or truth of; prove.

subterranean (sub′tə·rā′nē·ən) *adj.* **1.** Located under the earth. **2.** Secret; hidden.

subtle (sut′l) *adj.* **1.** Able to see fine distinctions. **2.** Mentally acute; clever. —**subtly** *adv.*

succumb (sə·kum′) *v.* To give in to; yield.

suckle *v.* **1.** To nurse. **2.** To bring up or rear.

suffice (sə·fīs′) *v.* To meet or satisfy a need; to be sufficient.

sumptuous (sump′cho͞o·əs) *adj.* Expensive; lavish; luxurious.

superfluous (sə·pur′flo͞o·əs) *adj.* **1.** Not necessary or needed. **2.** More than is needed.

supplant (sə·plant′) *v.* To replace, especially through force, trickery, or treachery.

supplication (sup′lə·kā′shən) *n.* A humble prayer or request to a deity or superior.

surety (shoor′ə·tē) *n.* Guarantee.

surpass (sər·pas′) *v.* To excel; outdo all others.

surreptitious (sur′əp·tish′əs) *adj.* Secretive. —**surreptitiously** *adj.*

sway *n.* Influence; clout; dominant control.

syntax (sin′taks′) *n.* The arrangement, organization, and relationship of words in a sentence.

▼ **T** ▼

taciturn (tas′ə·turn′) *adj.* Usually silent; not fond of talking.

tantamount (tant′ə·mount′) *adj.* Equivalent in value, meaning, or effect.

tarry *v.* To stay in a place, especially in expectation; delay; linger.

temper *v.* To bring steel to the required degree of strength and toughness by heating and sudden cooling.

temperate (tem′pər·it) *adj.* Moderate; self-restrained.

tempestuous (tem·pes′cho͞o·əs) *adj.* Like a storm with high winds and heavy rain; violent.

temporal (tem′pə·rəl) *adj.* **1.** Worldly; not eternal. **2.** Of, pertaining to, or limited by, time.

tenet (ten′it) *n.* Any principle or creed held to be true, especially by some organization.

tenuous (ten′yo͞o·əs) *adj.* **1.** Not dense, as the atmosphere at a high altitude. **2.** Insubstantial; fragile; inadequate.

tepid (tep′id) *adj.* Lukewarm.

terminate (tur′mə·nāt′) *v.* To end.

theological (thē′ə·läj′i·kəl) *adj.* Having to do with the study of God.

throng *n.* A multitude of people crowded together.

thwart (thwôrt) *v.* To hinder; block.

timorous (tim′ər·es) *adj.* Fearful; timid. —**timorously** *adv.*

torrid (tôr′id) *adj.* **1.** Very hot, especially with reference to climate. **2.** Extremely passionate.

tortuous (tôr′cho͞o·əs) *adj.* Winding; crooked; not straight.

transact (tran·zakt′) *v.* To carry on or conduct, especially business. —**transaction** *n.*

transgress (trans·gres′) *v.* To go beyond the limits set by laws, commandments, and so forth. —**transgression** *n.*

translucent (trans·lōō′sənt) *adj.* Allowing light to pass through.

tribute (trib′yōōt) *n.* Money paid to one nation's sovereign by another, as a tax, payment for protection, and so on.

tumult (tōō′mult′) *n.* Noisy commotion and uproar; violent disturbance.

turmoil (tur′moil′) *n.* Disturbed activity; violent agitation.

▼ U ▼

unassailable (un′ə·sāl′ə·bəl) *adj.* Unable to be successfully attacked or challenged.

unassuming (un′ə·sōō′ming) *adj.* Modest.

unconditional (un′kən·dish′ən·əl) *adj.* Absolute; without exceptions or reservations.

undermine (un′dər·mīn′) *v.* 1. To wear away the foundations of. 2. To cause to weaken by craft or stealth.

underpin (un′dər·pin′) *v.* To prop up or support from underneath.

undeterred (un·dē·turd′) *adj.* Not kept from action by fear or doubt.

undulate (un′dyōō·lāt′) *v.* To move in a wavelike manner.

unremitting (un′ri·mit′ing) *adj.* Persistent; persevering; not stopping. **—unremittingly *adv.***

unshriven (un·shriv′ən) *adj.* Without forgiveness of sin through confession.

unwonted (un·wän′tid) *adj.* Uncommon; unaccustomed; unusual.

upbraid (up·brād′) *v.* To scold or rebuke strongly.

usurp (yōō·zurp′) *v.* To take power unlawfully.

▼ V ▼

valiant (val′yənt) *adj.* Brave.

valor (val′ər) *n.* Bravery.

vanguard (van′gärd′) *n.* The leading part of an army.

vanquish (vang′kwish) *v.* To conquer.

vehement (vē′ə·mənt) *adj.* With great passion. **—vehemently *adv.***

venerate (ven′ər·āt′) *v.* To look upon with reverence.

vent *v.* To express feelings.

veracious (və·rā′shəs) *adj.* 1. Telling the truth; honest. 2. Characterized by truth and accuracy.

vermin (vur′mən) *n. pl.* Various insects regarded as pests.

versatile (vur′sə·təl) *adj.* Able to do many things.

vestibule (ves′tə·byōōl′) *n.* Entrance hall or lobby.

vex *v.* To irritate; annoy. **—vexation *n.***

vicissitudes (vi·sis′ə·tōōdz′) *n. pl.* Unpredictable and irregular changes in fortune, life, and so on; ups and downs.

vile *adj.* Very bad; evil; wicked; low.

vindictive (vin·dik′tiv) *adj.* Tending to seek revenge; retaliatory. **—vindictiveness *n.***

visceral (vis′ər·əl) *adj.* Felt deep within a person; profound or instinctive.

vivacity (vi·vas′ə·tē) *n.* Liveliness; spiritedness.

void *n.* That which is empty; vacuum. *adj.* Empty; vacant.

vulnerable (vul′nər·ə·bəl) *adj.* Easily attacked, tempted, or damaged.

▼ W ▼

wake *n.* A watch over a dead body before burial.

wane *v.* To grow smaller gradually, said of the moon's face, after it has been fully lighted.

wanton (wän′tən) *adj.* Willfully and intentionally malicious.

wax *v.* To grow larger gradually, said of the lighted portion of the moon's face, until the full moon is visible.

wisp *n.* A slender, filmy fragment or strand.

wrangle (rang′gəl) *v.* To dispute or quarrel angrily and noisily; brawl.

wrathful (rath′fəl) *adj.* Extremely angry.

wrest (rest) *v.* To snatch or wrench forcibly.

writhe (rīth) *v.* To twist and turn in pain.

wryly (rī′lē) *adv.* 1. In a twisted or distorted manner. 2. Ironically.

▼ Z ▼

zenith (zē′nith) *n.* 1. The summit; peak. 2. That point in the sky directly overhead.

---

fat, āpe, cär; ten, ēven; is, bīte; gō, hôrn, tōōl, look; oil, out; up, fur; get; joy; yet; chin; she; thin, then; zh, leisure; ŋ or ng, ring; ə for *a* in *ago, e* in *agent, i* in *sanity, o* in *comply, u* in *focus,* ' as in able (ā′b'l).

INDEX OF SKILLS

Literary Skills

The boldfaced page numbers indicate an extensive treatment of the topic.

Language and Vocabulary Skills

Most of the page numbers listed below refer to discussions that appear in the Language and Vocabulary exercises. The page numbers in italic type refer to subjects covered in the Language Skills exercises found at the end of each unit. Additional page references for some terms may also be found in the Literary Skills index on page 1488.

Writing: A Critical Response

Critical Thinking Skills

The following list refers to the two-page Critical Thinking and Writing exercises that follow each unit. Additional exercises in all of the critical thinking skills, including synthesis, will be found in the Composition Skills index on the preceding pages.

Index of Authors and Titles

Page numbers in italic type refer to the pages on which author biographies appear. Translators of selections are identified by the notation *(trans.).*

INDEX OF AUTHORS AND TITLES

Index of Authors and Titles

Index of Authors and Titles

ACKNOWLEDGMENTS
(Continued from page iv)

Poems by Czeslaw Milosz. Copyright © 1988 by Czeslaw Milosz Royalties, Inc.

Everyman's Library Limited: Quatrain #44 from *A New Selection* from *The Rubáiyát of Omar Khayyám*, translated by Dr. A. J. Arberry. Published by The Unicorn Press, London, 1961.

Faber and Faber Ltd: From "Introduction" from *Voices from Twentieth-Century Africa: Griots and Towncriers*, edited by Chinweizu. Copyright © 1988 by Chinweizu.

Farrar, Straus & Giroux, Inc.: "Russia 1812" by Victor Hugo from *Imitations*, translated by Robert Lowell. Copyright © 1961 by Robert Lowell; copyright renewed © 1986, 1987, 1989 by Caroline Lowell, Harriet Lowell and Sheridan Lowell. "A Walk to the Jetty" from *Annie John* by Jamaica Kincaid. Copyright © 1985 by Jamaica Kincaid. From Appendix to *Cancer Ward* by Alexandr Solzhenitsyn, translated by Nicholas Betthell and David Burg. Copyright © 1968, 1969 by The Bodley Head Ltd. "Freedom to Breathe" and "A Journey Along the Oka" from *Stories and Prose Poems* by Alexandr Solzhenitsyn. Translation copyright © 1971 by Michael Glenny. From "Tales of the Islands" from *Collected Poems 1948–1984* by Derek Walcott. Copyright © 1986 by Derek Walcott.

Estate of Angel Flores: "The Guitar" by Federico García Lorca, translated by Rachel Benson and Robert O'Brien from *An Anthology of Spanish Poetry from Garcilaso to García Lorca in English Translation with Spanish Originals*, edited by Angel Flores. Copyright © 1961 by Angel Flores.

Foreign Languages Press: Quotation by Mao Tse-tung from "On Coalition Government" (April 24, 1945) from *Selected Works*, Vol. III, page 257. Copyright 1945 by Foreign Languages Press.

Grove Press, Inc.: From letter by Ssu-ma Ch'ien to Jen An (Shao-ch'ing), and excerpt from page 118 from *Anthology of Chinese Literature*, edited by Cyril Birch. Copyright © 1965 by Grove Press, Inc. From page 15 from *Hiroshima, Mon Amour* by Marguerite Duras, translated by Richard Seaver. Copyright © 1961 by Grove Press, Inc. "Atsumori" (and excerpts) by Seami Motokiyo, translated by Arthur Waley; "This perfectly still" by Ki no Tomonori (Japanese and English version); "So lonely Am I" by Ono no Komachi; from "Sotoba Komachi" by Kan'ami Kioyotsugu; from "The Tale of the Heike" from "Prose Poem on the Unreal Dwelling" by Matsuo Bashō; and from "Introduction" from *Anthology of Japanese Literature*, edited and translated by Donald Keene. Copyright © 1955 by Grove Press, Inc. Song 103 and Song 130 from *The Book of Songs*, translated by Arthur Waley. Copyright 1937 by Arthur Waley.

Harcourt Brace & Company: "The Enchanted Garden" from *Difficult Loves* by Italo Calvino. Copyright 1949 by Giulio Einaudi editore Torino. Copyright © 1958 by Giulio Einaudi editore s.p.a. English translation copyright © 1984 by Harcourt Brace & Company. Torino. "Oedipus Rex" from *Sophocles: The Oedipus Cycle, an English Version* by Dudley Fitts and Robert Fitzgerald. Copyright 1949 by Harcourt Brace & Company; and copyright renewed © 1977 by Cornelia Fitts and Robert Fitzgerald. CAUTION: All rights, including professional, amateur, motion picture, recitation, lecturing, performance, public reading, radio broadcasting, and television are strictly reserved. Inquiries on all rights should be addressed to Harcourt Brace & Company, Permissions Dept., Orlando, FL 32887-6777. From *Conversations with Czeslaw Milosz* by Ewa Czarnecka & Aleksander Fiut, translated by Richard Lourie. Translation copyright © 1987 by Ewa Czarnecka, Aleksander Fiut, and Czeslaw Milosz. "Sonnet" by Pierre de Ronsard from *Western Literature II: The Middle Ages, Renaissance, Enlightenment* by Robert Hollander and A. Bartlett Giamatti. Copyright © 1971 by Harcourt Brace & Company. "Charles Baudelaire: L'Invitation au Voyage" from *Things of This World* by Richard Wilbur. Copyright © 1956 and renewed © 1984 by Richard Wilbur. "Lot's Wife" from *Walking to Sleep: New Poems and Translations* by Anna Akhmatova, translated by Richard Wilbur from *Paris Review*. Copyright by *Paris Review*. "Parable" from *Ceremony and Other Poems* by Richard Wilbur. Copyright © 1950 and renewed © 1978 by Richard Wilbur.

HarperCollins Publishers, Inc.: "The Swan" from *Selected Poems of Rainer Maria Rilke*, translated by Robert Bly. Copyright © 1981 by Robert Bly. From *The Life of Mahatma Gandhi* by Louis Fischer. Copyright 1950 by Louis Fischer. "How the World Was Made" by Mary Little Bear Inkanish from *American Indian Mythology* by Alice Marriott and Carol K. Rachlin. Copyright © 1968 by Alice Marriott and Carol K. Rachlin. From *The Odyssey of Homer*, translated by Richmond Lattimore. Copyright © 1965, 1967 and renewed © 1993 by Richmond Lattimore. From *An Open Life: Joseph Campbell in Conversation with Michael Toms* by John M. Maher and Dennie Briggs. Copyright © 1989 by the New Dimensions Foundation. "When people see some things as beautiful," "The supreme good is like water," "Do you want to improve the world?", poem by Po Chü-i, and excerpts from *Tao Te Ching*, translated by Stephen Mitchell. Translation copyright © by Stephen Mitchell. "The Handsomest Drowned Man in the World" from *Leaf Storm and Other Stories* by Gabriel García Márquez, translated by Gregory Rabassa. Copyright © 1971 by Gabriel García Márquez. "By Any Other Name" and excerpt from *Gifts of Passage* by Santha Rama Rau. Copyright 1951 and renewed © 1979 by Vasanthi Rama Rau Bowers. "By Any Other Name" originally appeared in *The New Yorker*. From *The First Circle* by Aleksandr Solzhenitsyn, translated by Thomas P. Whit-

REFERENCES:

From *The Sumerians* by Samuel Noah Kramer. Published by The University of Chicago Press, 1963.

From *Hindu Myths, A Sourcebook Translated from the Sanskrit* by Wendy Doniger O'Flaherty. Published by Penguin Books, 1975.

From interview with Carol Sternhell in *Ms.,* July, 1975, September, 1987.

From *Conversaciones con Cortázar* by Ernest González Bermeho. Copyright © 1978.

Illustration Credits